# KEY TO WORLD MAP PAGES

- ▬ **Large scale maps**
  (> 1:3 500 000)
- ▬ **Medium scale maps**
  (1:4 000 000 – 1:9 000 000)
- ▬ **Small scale maps**
  (< 1:10 000 000)

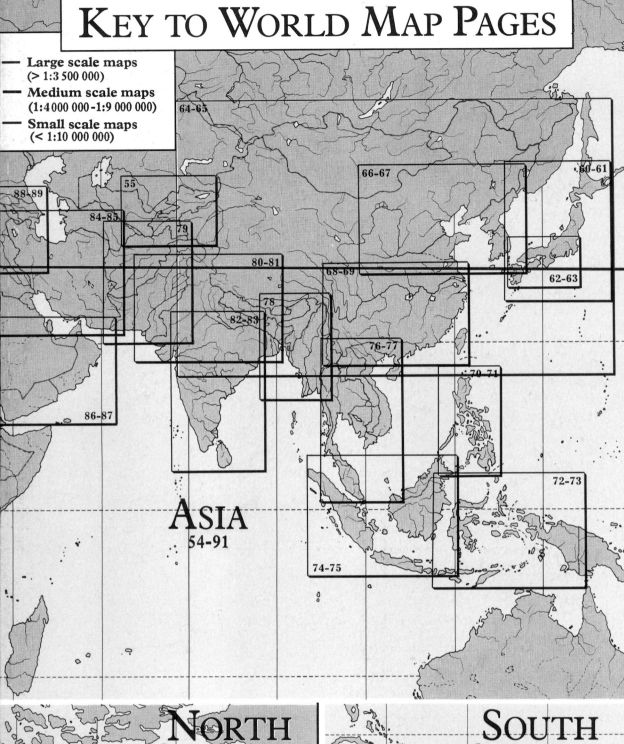

ASIA
54-91

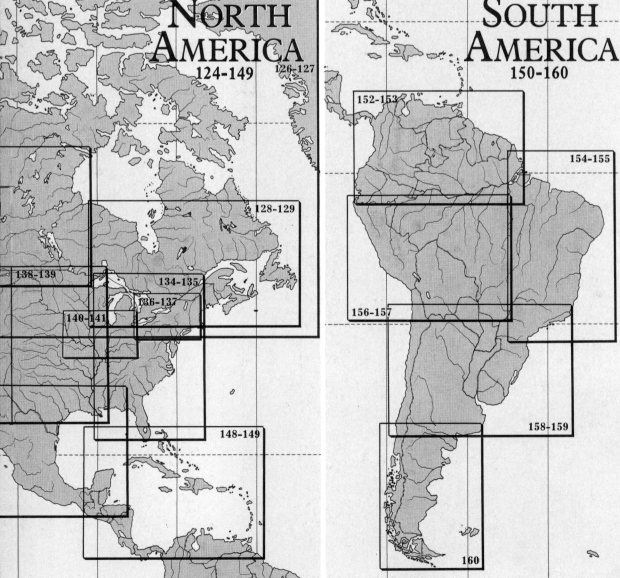

NORTH
AMERICA
124-149    126-127

SOUTH
AMERICA
150-160

# COUNTRY INDEX

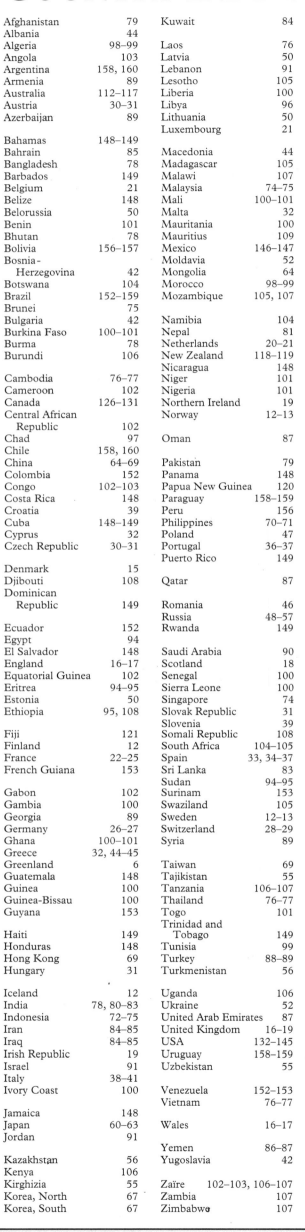

# PHILIP'S

# ATLAS
## OF THE
# WORLD

# PHILIP'S

# ATLAS
## OF THE
# WORLD

Published in Great Britain in 1994
by George Philip Limited,
an imprint of Reed Consumer Books Limited,
Michelin House, 81 Fulham Road, London SW3 6RB,
and Auckland, Melbourne, Singapore and Toronto

Cartography by Philip's

Copyright © 1994 Reed International Books Limited

ISBN 0-540-05831-9

A CIP catalogue record for this book is available from
the British Library

Printed in Spain

# PHILIP'S WORLD MAPS

The reference maps which form the main body of this atlas have been prepared in accordance with the highest standards of international cartography to provide an accurate and detailed representation of the Earth. The scales and projections used have been carefully chosen to give balanced coverage of the world, while emphasizing the most densely populated and economically significant regions. A hallmark of Philip's mapping is the use of hill shading and relief colouring to create a graphic impression of landforms: this makes the maps exceptionally easy to read. However, knowledge of the key features employed in the construction and presentation of the maps will enable the reader to derive the fullest benefit from the atlas.

## Map sequence

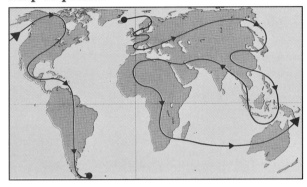

The atlas covers the Earth continent by continent: first Europe; then its land neighbour Asia (mapped north before south, in a clockwise sequence), then Africa, Australia and Oceania, North America and South America. This is the classic arrangement adopted by most cartographers since the 16th century. For each continent, there are maps at a variety of scales. First, physical relief and political maps of the whole continent; then a series of larger-scale maps of the regions within the continent, each followed, where required, by still larger-scale maps of the most important or densely populated areas. The governing principle is that by turning the pages of the atlas, the reader moves steadily from north to south through each continent, with each map overlapping its neighbours. A key map showing this sequence, and the area covered by each map, can be found on the endpapers of the atlas.

## Map presentation

With very few exceptions (e.g. for the Arctic and Antarctic), the maps are drawn with north at the top, regardless of whether they are presented upright or sideways on the page. In the borders will be found the map title; a locator diagram showing the area covered and the page numbers for maps of adjacent areas; the scale; the projection used; the degrees of latitude and longitude; and the letters and figures used in the index for locating place names and geographical features. Physical relief maps also have a height reference panel identifying the colours used for each layer of contouring.

## Map symbols

Each map contains a vast amount of detail which can only be conveyed clearly and accurately by the use of symbols. Points and circles of varying sizes locate and identify the relative importance of towns and cities; different styles of type are employed for administrative, geographical and regional place names. A variety of pictorial symbols denote landscape features such as glaciers, marshes and reefs, and man-made structures including roads, railways, airports, canals and dams. International borders are shown by red lines. Where neighbouring countries are in dispute, for example in the Middle East, the maps show the *de facto* boundary between nations, regardless of the legal or historical situation. The symbols are explained on the first page of the World Maps section of the atlas.

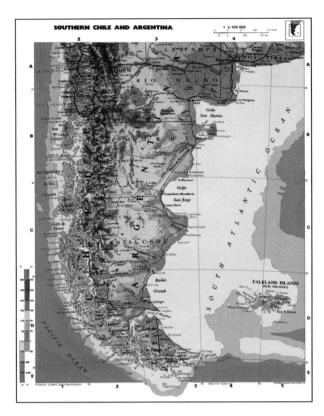

## Map scales

| 1: 16 000 000 |
|---|
| 1 inch = 252 statute miles |

The scale of each map is given in the numerical form known as the 'representative fraction'. The first figure is always one, signifying one unit of distance on the map; the second figure, usually in millions, is the number by which the map unit must be multiplied to give the equivalent distance on the Earth's surface. Calculations can easily be made in centimetres and kilometres, by dividing the Earth units figure by 100 000 (i.e. deleting the last five 0s). Thus 1:1 000 000 means l cm = 10 km. The calculation for inches and miles is more laborious, but 1 000 000 divided by 63 360 (the number of inches in a mile) shows that 1:1 000 000 means approximately 1 inch = 16 miles. The table below provides distance equivalents for scales down to 1:50 000 000.

| LARGE SCALE | | |
|---|---|---|
| 1: 1 000 000 | 1 cm = 10 km | l inch = 16 miles |
| 1: 2 500 000 | 1 cm = 25 km | l inch = 39.5 miles |
| 1: 5 000 000 | 1 cm = 50 km | l inch = 79 miles |
| 1: 6 000 000 | 1 cm = 60 km | l inch = 95 miles |
| 1: 8 000 000 | 1 cm = 80 km | l inch = 126 miles |
| 1: 10 000 000 | 1 cm = 100 km | l inch = 158 miles |
| 1: 15 000 000 | 1 cm = 150 km | l inch = 237 miles |
| 1: 20 000 000 | 1 cm = 200 km | l inch = 316 miles |
| 1: 50 000 000 | 1 cm = 500 km | l inch = 790 miles |
| SMALL SCALE | | |

## Measuring distances

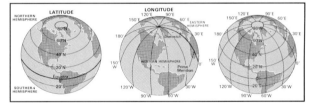

Although each map is accompanied by a scale bar, distances cannot always be measured with confidence because of the distortions involved in portraying the curved surface of the Earth on a flat page. As a general rule, the larger the map scale (i.e. the lower the number of Earth units in the representative fraction), the more accurate and reliable will be the distance measured. On small-scale maps such as those of the world and of entire continents, measurement may only be accurate along the 'standard parallels', or central axes, and should not be attempted without considering the map projection.

## Map projections

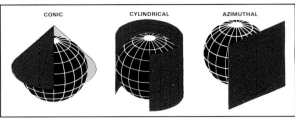

Unlike a globe, no flat map can give a true scale representation of the world in terms of area, shape and position of every region. Each of the numerous systems that have been devised for projecting the curved surface of the Earth on to a flat page involves the sacrifice of accuracy in one or more of these elements. The variations in shape and position of landmasses such as Alaska, Greenland and Australia, for example, can be quite dramatic when different projections are compared.

For this atlas, the guiding principle has been to select projections that involve the least distortion of size and distance. The projection used for each map is noted in the border. Most fall into one of three categories – conic, cylindrical or azimuthal – whose basic concepts are shown above. Each involves plotting the forms of the Earth's surface on a grid of latitude and longitude lines, which may be shown as parallels, curves or radiating spokes.

## Latitude and longitude

Accurate positioning of individual points on the Earth's surface is made possible by reference to the geometrical system of latitude and longitude. Latitude *parallels* are drawn west–east around the Earth and numbered by degrees north and south of the Equator, which is designated 0° of latitude. Longitude *meridians* are drawn north–south and numbered by degrees east and west of the *prime meridian*, 0° of longitude, which passes through Greenwich in England. By referring to these co-ordinates and their subdivisions of minutes (¹⁄₆₀th of a degree) and seconds (¹⁄₆₀th of a minute), any place on Earth can be located to within a few hundred yards. Latitude and longitude are indicated by blue lines on the maps; they are straight or curved according to the projection employed. Reference to these lines is the easiest way of determining the relative positions of places on different maps, and for plotting compass directions.

## Name forms

For ease of reference, both English and local name forms appear in the atlas. Oceans, seas and countries are shown in English throughout the atlas; country names may be abbreviated to their commonly accepted form (e.g. Germany, not The Federal Republic of Germany). Conventional English forms are also used for place names on the smaller-scale maps of the continents. However, local name forms are used on all large-scale and regional maps, with the English form given in brackets only for important cities – the large-scale map of Russia and Central Asia thus shows Moskva (Moscow). For countries which do not use a Roman script, place names have been transcribed according to the systems adopted by the British and US Geographic Names Authorities. For China, the Pin Yin system has been used, with some more widely known forms appearing in brackets, as with Beijing (Peking). Both English and local names appear in the index, the English form being cross-referenced to the local form.

# CONTENTS

NOTE
The titles to the World Maps list the main countries, states and provinces covered by each map. A name given in *italics* indicates that only part of the country is shown on the map.

**Netherlands, Belgium and Luxembourg**
1:1 000 000

**20–21**

**Northern France**
1:2 000 000

**22–23**

**Southern France**
1:2 000 000
Corsica, Monaco

**24–25**

**Germany** 1:2 000 000

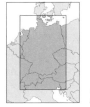

**26–27**

**Switzerland** 1:800 000
Liechtenstein

**28–29**

**Austria, Czech Republic, Slovak Republic and Hungary** 1:2 000 000
*Poland*

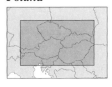

**30–31**

**Malta, Crete, Corfu, Rhodes and Cyprus**
1:800 000 / 1:1 040 000

**32**

**Balearics, Canaries and Madeira** 1:800 000 / 1:1 600 000
Mallorca, Menorca, Ibiza

**33**

**Eastern Spain** 1:2 000 000
Andorra

**34–35**

**Western Spain and Portugal** 1:2 000 000

**36–37**

**Northern Italy, Slovenia and Croatia**
1:2 000 000
San Marino, Slovenia,
*Croatia*

**38–39**

**Southern Italy** 1:2 000 000
Sardinia, Sicily

**40–41**

**The Lower Danube**
1:2 000 000
Bosnia-Herzegovina,
Yugoslavia, Macedonia

**42–43**

**Greece and Albania**
1:2 000 000

**44–45**

**Romania** 1:2 000 000

**46**

**Poland** 1:2 000 000

**47**

**Eastern Europe and Turkey**
1:8 000 000

**48–49**

**Western Russia, Belorussia and the Baltic States** 1:4 000 000
*Russia*, Estonia, Latvia,
Lithuania, Belorussia, *Ukraine*

**50–51**

**Ukraine, Moldavia and the Caucasus** 1:4 000 000
*Russia*, *Ukraine*, Georgia,
*Armenia*, *Azerbaijan*, Moldavia

**52–53**

# ASIA

**Southern Urals** 1:4 000 000
*Russia*

**54**

**Central Asia** 1:4 000 000
*Kazakhstan*, Kirghizia,
Tajikistan, *Uzbekistan*

**55**

**Russia and Central Asia**
1:16 000 000
Russia, Kazakhstan,
Turkmenistan, Uzbekistan

**56–57**

**Asia: Physical**
1:40 000 000

**58**

**Asia: Political**
1:40 000 000

**59**

**Japan** 1:4 000 000
Ryukyu Islands

**60–61**

**Southern Japan** 1:2 000 000

**62–63**

**China** 1:12 000 000
Mongolia

**64–65**

**Northern China and Korea** 1:4 800 000
North Korea, South Korea

**66–67**

**Southern China** 1:4 800 000
Hong Kong, Taiwan, Macau

**68–69**

**Philippines** 1:3 200 000

**70–71**

**Eastern Indonesia**
1:5 600 000

**72–73**

**Western Indonesia**
1:5 600 000
Malaysia, Singapore, Brunei

**74–75**

**Mainland South-East Asia** 1:4 800 000
Thailand, Vietnam, Cambodia,
Laos

**76–77**

**Bangladesh, North-Eastern India and Burma**
1:4 800 000
Bhutan

**78**

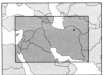

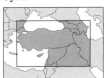

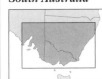

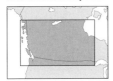

# World Statistics: Countries

This alphabetical list includes all the countries and territories of the world. If a territory is not completely independent, then the country it is associated with is named. The area figures give the total area of land, inland water and ice. Units for areas and populations are thousands. The annual income is the Gross National Product per capita in US dollars. The figures are the latest available, usually 1993.

| Country/Territory | Area km² Thousands | Area miles² Thousands | Population Thousands | Capital | Annual Income US $ |
|---|---|---|---|---|---|
| Adélie Land (Fr.) | 432 | 167 | 0.03 | – | – |
| Afghanistan | 648 | 250 | 19,062 | Kabul | 450 |
| Albania | 28.8 | 11.1 | 3,363 | Tirana | 1,000 |
| Algeria | 2,382 | 920 | 26,346 | Algiers | 1,980 |
| American Samoa (US) | 0.20 | 0.08 | 50 | Pago Pago | 6,000 |
| Amsterdam Is. (Fr.) | 0.05 | 0.02 | 0.03 | – | – |
| Andorra | 0.45 | 0.17 | 58 | Andorra la Vella | – |
| Angola | 1,247 | 481 | 10,609 | Luanda | 620 |
| Anguilla (UK) | 0.09 | 0.04 | 9 | The Valley | – |
| Antigua & Barbuda | 0.44 | 0.17 | 66 | St John's | 4,770 |
| Argentina | 2,767 | 1,068 | 33,101 | Buenos Aires | 2,790 |
| Armenia | 29.8 | 11.5 | 3,677 | Yerevan | 2,150 |
| Aruba (Neths) | 0.19 | 0.07 | 62 | Oranjestad | 6,000 |
| Ascension Is. (UK) | 0.09 | 0.03 | 1.5 | Georgetown | – |
| Australia | 7,687 | 2,968 | 17,529 | Canberra | 17,050 |
| Australian Antarctic Territory | 6,120 | 2,363 | 0 | – | – |
| Austria | 83.9 | 32.4 | 7,884 | Vienna | 20,140 |
| Azerbaijan | 86.6 | 33.4 | 7,398 | Baku | 1,670 |
| Azores (Port.) | 2.2 | 0.87 | 260 | Ponta Delgada | – |
| Bahamas | 13.9 | 5.4 | 262 | Nassau | 11,750 |
| Bahrain | 0.68 | 0.26 | 533 | Manama | 7,130 |
| Bangladesh | 144 | 56 | 119,288 | Dacca | 200 |
| Barbados | 0.43 | 0.17 | 259 | Bridgetown | 6,630 |
| Belau (US) | 0.46 | 0.18 | 16 | Koror | – |
| Belgium | 30.5 | 11.8 | 9,998 | Brussels | 18,950 |
| Belize | 23 | 8.9 | 198 | Belmopan | 2,010 |
| Belorussia | 207.6 | 80.1 | 10,297 | Minsk | 3,110 |
| Benin | 113 | 43 | 4,889 | Porto-Novo | 380 |
| Bermuda (UK) | 0.05 | 0.02 | 62 | Hamilton | 25,000 |
| Bhutan | 47 | 18.1 | 1,612 | Thimphu | 180 |
| Bolivia | 1,099 | 424 | 7,832 | La Paz/Sucre | 650 |
| Bosnia-Herzegovina | 51.2 | 19.8 | 4,366 | Sarajevo | – |
| Botswana | 582 | 225 | 1,373 | Gaborone | 2,590 |
| Bouvet Is. (Nor.) | 0.05 | 0.02 | 0.02 | – | – |
| Brazil | 8,512 | 3,286 | 156,275 | Brasilia | 2,940 |
| British Antarctic Terr. (UK) | 1,709 | 660 | 0.3 | Stanley | – |
| British Indian Ocean Terr. (UK) | 0.08 | 0.03 | 3 | – | – |
| Brunei | 5.8 | 2.2 | 270 | Bandar Seri Begawan | 6,000 |
| Bulgaria | 111 | 43 | 8,963 | Sofia | 1,840 |
| Burkina Faso | 274 | 106 | 9,490 | Ouagadougou | 290 |
| Burma (Myanmar) | 679 | 262 | 43,668 | Rangoon | 500 |
| Burundi | 27.8 | 10.7 | 5,786 | Bujumbura | 210 |
| Cambodia | 181 | 70 | 9,054 | Phnom Penh | 300 |
| Cameroon | 475 | 184 | 12,198 | Yaoundé | 850 |
| Canada | 9,976 | 3,852 | 27,562 | Ottawa | 20,440 |
| Canary Is. (Spain) | 7.3 | 2.8 | 1,700 | Las Palmas/Santa Cruz | – |
| Cape Verde Is. | 4 | 1.6 | 384 | Praia | 750 |
| Cayman Is. (UK) | 0.26 | 0.10 | 29 | Georgetown | – |
| Central African Republic | 623 | 241 | 3,173 | Bangui | 390 |
| Chad | 1,284 | 496 | 5,961 | Ndjamena | 220 |
| Chatham Is. (NZ) | 0.96 | 0.37 | 0.05 | Waitangi | – |
| Chile | 757 | 292 | 13,599 | Santiago | 2,160 |
| China | 9,597 | 3,705 | 1,187,997 | Beijing (Peking) | 370 |
| Christmas Is. (Aus.) | 0.14 | 0.05 | 2.3 | The Settlement | – |
| Cocos (Keeling) Is. (Aus.) | 0.01 | 0.005 | 0.70 | – | – |
| Colombia | 1,139 | 440 | 33,424 | Bogotá | 1,260 |
| Comoros | 2.2 | 0.86 | 585 | Moroni | 500 |
| Congo | 342 | 132 | 2,368 | Brazzaville | 1,120 |
| Cook Is. (NZ) | 0.24 | 0.09 | 17 | Avarua | 900 |
| Costa Rica | 51.1 | 19.7 | 3,099 | San José | 1,850 |
| Croatia | 56.5 | 21.8 | 4,764 | Zagreb | 1,800 |
| Crozet Is. (Fr.) | 0.51 | 0.19 | 35 | – | – |
| Cuba | 111 | 43 | 10,822 | Havana | 3,000 |
| Cyprus | 9.3 | 3.6 | 716 | Nicosia | 8,640 |
| Czech Republic | 78.9 | 30.4 | 10,299 | Prague | 2,370 |
| Denmark | 43.1 | 16.6 | 5,170 | Copenhagen | 23,700 |
| Djibouti | 23.2 | 9 | 467 | Djibouti | 1,000 |
| Dominica | 0.75 | 0.29 | 72 | Roseau | 2,440 |
| Dominican Republic | 48.7 | 18.8 | 7,471 | Santo Domingo | 950 |
| Ecuador | 284 | 109 | 10,741 | Quito | 1,020 |
| Egypt | 1,001 | 387 | 55,163 | Cairo | 620 |
| El Salvador | 21 | 8.1 | 5,396 | San Salvador | 1,070 |
| Equatorial Guinea | 28.1 | 10.8 | 369 | Malabo | 330 |
| Eritrea | 94 | 36 | 3,500 | Asmera | – |
| Estonia | 44.7 | 17.3 | 1,542 | Tallinn | 3,830 |
| Ethiopia | 1,128 | 436 | 55,117 | Addis Ababa | 120 |
| Falkland Is. (UK) | 12.2 | 4.7 | 2 | Stanley | – |
| Faroe Is. (Den.) | 1.4 | 0.54 | 47 | Tórshavn | 23,660 |
| Fiji | 18.3 | 7.1 | 739 | Suva | 1,930 |
| Finland | 338 | 131 | 5,042 | Helsinki | 23,980 |
| France | 552 | 213 | 57,372 | Paris | 20,380 |
| French Guiana (Fr.) | 90 | 34.7 | 104 | Cayenne | 2,500 |
| French Polynesia (Fr.) | 4 | 1.5 | 207 | Papeete | 6,000 |
| Gabon | 268 | 103 | 1,237 | Libreville | 3,780 |
| Gambia, The | 11.3 | 4.4 | 878 | Banjul | 360 |
| Georgia | 69.7 | 26.9 | 5,471 | Tbilisi | 1,640 |
| Germany | 357 | 138 | 80,569 | Berlin | 23,650 |
| Ghana | 239 | 92 | 15,400 | Accra | 400 |
| Gibraltar (UK) | 0.007 | 0.003 | 31 | – | 4,000 |
| Greece | 132 | 51 | 10,300 | Athens | 6,340 |
| Greenland (Den.) | 2,176 | 840 | 57 | Godthåb | 6,000 |
| Grenada | 0.34 | 0.13 | 91 | St George's | 2,180 |
| Guadeloupe (Fr.) | 1.7 | 0.66 | 400 | Basse-Terre | 7,000 |
| Guam (US) | 0.55 | 0.21 | 139 | Agana | 6,000 |
| Guatemala | 109 | 42 | 9,745 | Guatemala City | 930 |
| Guinea | 246 | 95 | 6,116 | Conakry | 450 |
| Guinea-Bissau | 36.1 | 13.9 | 1,006 | Bissau | 190 |
| Guyana | 215 | 83 | 808 | Georgetown | 430 |
| Haiti | 27.8 | 10.7 | 6,764 | Port-au-Prince | 370 |
| Honduras | 112 | 43 | 5,462 | Tegucigalpa | 570 |
| Hong Kong (UK) | 1.1 | 0.40 | 5,801 | – | 13,430 |
| Hungary | 93 | 35.9 | 10,313 | Budapest | 2,720 |
| Iceland | 103 | 40 | 260 | Reykjavik | 23,170 |
| India | 3,288 | 1,269 | 879,548 | Delhi | 330 |
| Indonesia | 1,905 | 735 | 191,170 | Jakarta | 610 |
| Iran | 1,648 | 636 | 56,964 | Tehran | 2,170 |
| Iraq | 438 | 169 | 19,290 | Baghdad | 2,000 |
| Ireland | 70.3 | 27.1 | 3,547 | Dublin | 11,120 |
| Israel | 27 | 10.3 | 4,946 | Jerusalem | 11,950 |
| Italy | 301 | 116 | 57,782 | Rome | 18,580 |
| Ivory Coast | 322 | 125 | 12,910 | Abidjan | 690 |
| Jamaica | 11 | 4.2 | 2,469 | Kingston | 1,480 |
| Jan Mayen Is. (Nor.) | 0.38 | 0.15 | 0.06 | – | – |
| Japan | 378 | 146 | 124,336 | Tokyo | 26,920 |
| Johnston Is. (US) | 0.002 | 0.0009 | 0.30 | – | – |
| Jordan | 89.2 | 34.4 | 4,291 | Amman | 1,060 |
| Kazakhstan | 2,717 | 1,049 | 17,038 | Alma Ata | 7,570 |
| Kenya | 580 | 224 | 26,985 | Nairobi | 340 |
| Kerguelen Is. (Fr.) | 7.2 | 2.8 | 0 | – | – |
| Kermadec Is. (NZ) | 0.03 | 0.01 | 0 | – | – |
| Kirghizia | 198.5 | 76.6 | 4,472 | Bishkek | 4,000 |
| Kiribati | 0.72 | 0.28 | 74 | Tarawa | 750 |
| Korea, North | 121 | 47 | 22,618 | Pyongyang | 900 |
| Korea, South | 99 | 38.2 | 43,663 | Seoul | 6,340 |
| Kuwait | 17.8 | 6.9 | 1,970 | Kuwait City | 16,380 |
| Laos | 237 | 91 | 4,469 | Vientiane | 230 |
| Latvia | 65 | 25 | 2,632 | Riga | 3,410 |
| Lebanon | 10.4 | 4 | 2,838 | Beirut | 2,000 |

| Country/Territory | Area km² Thousands | Area miles² Thousands | Population Thousands | Capital | Annual Income US $ |
|---|---|---|---|---|---|
| Lesotho | 30.4 | 11.7 | 1,836 | Maseru | 580 |
| Liberia | 111 | 43 | 2,580 | Monrovia | 500 |
| Libya | 1,760 | 679 | 4,875 | Tripoli | 5,800 |
| Liechtenstein | 0.16 | 0.06 | 28 | Vaduz | 33,000 |
| Lithuania | 65.2 | 25.2 | 3,759 | Vilnius | 2,710 |
| Luxembourg | 2.6 | 1 | 390 | Luxembourg | 31,780 |
| Macau (Port.) | 0.02 | 0.006 | 374 | – | 2,000 |
| Macedonia | 25.3 | 9.8 | 2,174 | Skopje | – |
| Madagascar | 587 | 227 | 12,827 | Antananarivo | 210 |
| Madeira (Port.) | 0.81 | 0.31 | 280 | Funchal | – |
| Malawi | 118 | 46 | 8,823 | Lilongwe | 230 |
| Malaysia | 330 | 127 | 18,181 | Kuala Lumpur | 2,520 |
| Maldives | 0.30 | 0.12 | 231 | Malé | 460 |
| Mali | 1,240 | 479 | 9,818 | Bamako | 280 |
| Malta | 0.32 | 0.12 | 359 | Valletta | 6,630 |
| Mariana Is. (US) | 0.48 | 0.18 | 22 | Saipan | – |
| Marshall Is. | 0.18 | 0.07 | 49 | Dalap-Uliga-Darrit | – |
| Martinique (Fr.) | 1.1 | 0.42 | 368 | Fort-de-France | 4,000 |
| Mauritania | 1,025 | 396 | 2,143 | Nouakchott | 510 |
| Mauritius | 1.9 | 0.72 | 1,084 | Port Louis | 2,420 |
| Mayotte (Fr.) | 0.37 | 0.14 | 84 | Mamoundzou | – |
| Mexico | 1,958 | 756 | 89,538 | Mexico City | 3,030 |
| Micronesia, Fed. States | 0.70 | 0.27 | 110 | Palikir | – |
| Midway Is. (US) | 0.005 | 0.002 | 0.45 | – | – |
| Moldavia | 33.7 | 13 | 4,458 | Kishinev | 2,170 |
| Monaco | 0.002 | 0.0001 | 30 | – | 20,000 |
| Mongolia | 1,567 | 605 | 2,310 | Ulan Bator | 400 |
| Montserrat (UK) | 0.10 | 0.04 | 11 | Plymouth | – |
| Morocco | 447 | 172 | 26,318 | Rabat | 1,030 |
| Mozambique | 802 | 309 | 14,872 | Maputo | 80 |
| Namibia | 825 | 318 | 1,562 | Windhoek | 1,460 |
| Nauru | 0.02 | 0.008 | 10 | Yaren | – |
| Nepal | 141 | 54 | 20,577 | Katmandu | 180 |
| Netherlands | 41.5 | 16 | 15,178 | Amsterdam | 18,780 |
| Neths Antilles (Neths) | 0.99 | 0.38 | 175 | Willemstad | 6,000 |
| New Caledonia (Fr.) | 19 | 7.3 | 173 | Nouméa | 4,000 |
| New Zealand | 269 | 104 | 3,414 | Wellington | 12,350 |
| Nicaragua | 130 | 50 | 4,130 | Managua | 460 |
| Niger | 1,267 | 489 | 8,252 | Niamey | 300 |
| Nigeria | 924 | 357 | 88,515 | Lagos/Abuja | 340 |
| Niue (NZ) | 0.26 | 0.10 | 2 | Alofi | – |
| Norfolk Is. (Aus.) | 0.03 | 0.01 | 2 | Kingston | – |
| Norway | 324 | 125 | 4,286 | Oslo | 24,220 |
| Oman | 212 | 82 | 1,637 | Muscat | 6,120 |
| Pakistan | 796 | 307 | 115,520 | Islamabad | 400 |
| Panama | 77.1 | 29.8 | 2,515 | Panama City | 2,130 |
| Papua New Guinea | 463 | 179 | 4,056 | Port Moresby | 820 |
| Paraguay | 407 | 157 | 4,519 | Asunción | 1,270 |
| Peru | 1,285 | 496 | 22,454 | Lima | 1,070 |
| Peter 1st Is. (Nor.) | 0.18 | 0.07 | 0 | – | – |
| Philippines | 300 | 116 | 64,259 | Manila | 740 |
| Pitcairn Is. (UK) | 0.03 | 0.01 | 0.06 | Adamstown | – |
| Poland | 313 | 121 | 38,356 | Warsaw | 1,790 |
| Portugal | 92.4 | 35.7 | 9,846 | Lisbon | 5,930 |
| Puerto Rico (US) | 9 | 3.5 | 3,580 | San Juan | 6,470 |
| Qatar | 11 | 4.2 | 453 | Doha | 15,860 |
| Queen Maud Land (Nor.) | 2,800 | 1,081 | 0 | – | – |
| Réunion (Fr.) | 2.5 | 0.97 | 624 | St-Denis | 4,000 |
| Romania | 238 | 92 | 23,185 | Bucharest | 1,390 |
| Ross Dependency (NZ) | 435 | 168 | 0 | – | – |
| Russia | 17,075 | 6,592 | 149,527 | Moscow | 3,220 |
| Rwanda | 26.3 | 10.2 | 7,526 | Kigali | 260 |
| St Christopher & Nevis | 0.36 | 0.14 | 42 | Basseterre | 3,960 |
| St Helena (UK) | 0.12 | 0.05 | 7 | Jamestown | – |
| St Lucia | 0.62 | 0.24 | 137 | Castries | 2,500 |
| St Paul Is. (Fr.) | 0.007 | 0.003 | 0 | – | – |
| St Pierre & Miquelon (Fr.) | 0.24 | 0.09 | 6 | St-Pierre | – |
| St Vincent & Grenadines | 0.39 | 0.15 | 109 | Kingstown | 1,730 |
| San Marino | 0.06 | 0.02 | 23 | San Marino | – |
| São Tomé & Príncipe | 0.96 | 0.37 | 124 | São Tomé | 350 |
| Saudi Arabia | 2,150 | 830 | 15,922 | Riyadh | 7,820 |
| Senegal | 197 | 76 | 7,736 | Dakar | 720 |
| Seychelles | 0.46 | 0.18 | 72 | Victoria | 5,110 |
| Sierra Leone | 71.7 | 27.7 | 4,376 | Freetown | 210 |
| Singapore | 0.62 | 0.24 | 2,812 | Singapore | 14,210 |
| Slovak Republic | 49 | 18.9 | 5,297 | Bratislava | 1,650 |
| Slovenia | 20.3 | 7.8 | 1,996 | Ljubljana | – |
| Solomon Is. | 28.9 | 11.2 | 342 | Honiara | 690 |
| Somalia | 638 | 246 | 9,204 | Mogadishu | 150 |
| South Africa | 1,219 | 471 | 39,790 | Pretoria | 2,560 |
| South Georgia (UK) | 3.8 | 1.4 | 0.05 | – | – |
| South Sandwich Is. (UK) | 0.38 | 0.15 | 0 | – | – |
| Spain | 505 | 195 | 39,085 | Madrid | 12,460 |
| Sri Lanka | 65.6 | 25.3 | 17,405 | Colombo | 500 |
| Sudan | 2,506 | 967 | 26,656 | Khartoum | 310 |
| Surinam | 163 | 63 | 438 | Paramaribo | 3,610 |
| Svalbard (Nor.) | 62.9 | 24.3 | 4 | Longyearbyen | – |
| Swaziland | 17.4 | 6.7 | 792 | Mbabane | 1,060 |
| Sweden | 450 | 174 | 8,678 | Stockholm | 25,110 |
| Switzerland | 41.3 | 15.9 | 6,905 | Bern | 33,610 |
| Syria | 185 | 71 | 12,958 | Damascus | 1,160 |
| Taiwan | 36 | 13.9 | 20,659 | Taipei | 6,600 |
| Tajikistan | 143.1 | 55.2 | 5,465 | Dushanbe | 2,980 |
| Tanzania | 945 | 365 | 27,829 | Dar es Salaam | 100 |
| Thailand | 513 | 198 | 57,760 | Bangkok | 1,580 |
| Togo | 56.8 | 21.9 | 3,763 | Lomé | 410 |
| Tokelau (NZ) | 0.01 | 0.005 | 2 | Nukunonu | – |
| Tonga | 0.75 | 0.29 | 97 | Nuku'alofa | 1,100 |
| Trinidad & Tobago | 5.1 | 2 | 1,265 | Port of Spain | 3,620 |
| Tristan da Cunha (UK) | 0.11 | 0.04 | 0.33 | Edinburgh | – |
| Tunisia | 164 | 63 | 8,410 | Tunis | 1,510 |
| Turkey | 779 | 301 | 58,775 | Ankara | 1,820 |
| Turkmenistan | 488.1 | 188.5 | 3,714 | Ashkhabad | 1,700 |
| Turks & Caicos Is. (UK) | 0.43 | 0.17 | 13 | Grand Turk | – |
| Tuvalu | 0.03 | 0.01 | 12 | Funafuti | 600 |
| Uganda | 236 | 91 | 18,674 | Kampala | 160 |
| Ukraine | 603.7 | 233.1 | 52,200 | Kiev | 2,340 |
| United Arab Emirates | 83.6 | 32.3 | 1,629 | Abu Dhabi | 20,140 |
| United Kingdom | 243.3 | 94 | 57,848 | London | 16,550 |
| United States of America | 9,373 | 3,619 | 255,020 | Washington | 22,240 |
| Uruguay | 177 | 68 | 3,131 | Montevideo | 2,860 |
| Uzbekistan | 447.4 | 172.7 | 21,627 | Tashkent | 1,350 |
| Vanuatu | 12.2 | 4.7 | 157 | Port Vila | 1,120 |
| Vatican City | 0.0004 | 0.0002 | 1 | – | – |
| Venezuela | 912 | 352 | 20,249 | Caracas | 2,730 |
| Vietnam | 332 | 127 | 69,306 | Hanoi | 200 |
| Virgin Is. (UK) | 0.15 | 0.06 | 17 | Road Town | – |
| Virgin Is. (US) | 0.34 | 0.13 | 107 | Charlotte Amalie | 12,000 |
| Wake Is. | 0.008 | 0.003 | 0.30 | – | – |
| Wallis & Futuna Is. (Fr.) | 0.20 | 0.08 | 14 | Mata-Utu | – |
| Western Sahara | 266 | 103 | 250 | El Aaiún | – |
| Western Samoa | 2.8 | 1.1 | 161 | Apia | 960 |
| Yemen | 528 | 204 | 11,282 | Sana | 540 |
| Yugoslavia | 102.3 | 39.5 | 10,469 | Belgrade | 2,940 |
| Zaire | 2,345 | 906 | 39,882 | Kinshasa | 230 |
| Zambia | 753 | 291 | 8,638 | Lusaka | 460 |
| Zimbabwe | 391 | 151 | 10,583 | Harare | 650 |

# WORLD STATISTICS: CITIES

This list shows the principal cities with more than 500,000 inhabitants (for China only cities with more than 1 million are included). The figures are taken from the most recent census or estimate available, and as far as possible are the population of the metropolitan area, e.g. greater New York, Mexico or London. All the figures are in thousands. The top 20 world cities are indicated with their rank in brackets following the name.

**Afghanistan**
Kabul 1,424
**Algeria**
Algiers 1,722
Oran 664
**Angola**
Luanda 1,544
**Argentina**
Buenos Aires [7] 11,256
Córdoba 1,198
Rosario 1,096
Mendoza 775
La Plata 640
San Miguel de
  Tucumán 622
Mar del Plata 520
**Armenia**
Yerevan 1,202
**Australia**
Sydney 3,657
Melbourne 3,081
Brisbane 1,302
Perth 1,193
Adelaide 1,050
**Austria**
Vienna 1,540
**Azerbaijan**
Baku 1,149
**Bangladesh**
Dacca 6,105
Chittagong 2,041
Khulna 877
Rajshahi 517
**Belgium**
Brussels 1,331
Antwerp 668
**Belorussia**
Minsk 1,613
Gomel 506
**Bolivia**
La Paz 1,126
Santa Cruz 696
**Brazil**
São Paulo [11] 9,627
Rio de Janeiro 5,473
Salvador 2,072
Belo Horizonte 2,017
Fortaleza 1,766
Brasília 1,598
Nova Iguaçu 1,512
Curitiba 1,313
Recife 1,297
Pôrto Alegre 1,263
Belém 1,245
Manaus 1,011
Campinas 960
Goiânia 921
Guarulhos 836
São Gonçalo 825
Duque de Caxias 740
São Luís 695
Santo André 691
Osasco 671
São Bernado de
  Campo 655
Maceió 628
Natal 607
Teresina 598
Campo Grande 525
São João de Meriti 508
**Bulgaria**
Sofia 1,141
**Burma (Myanmar)**
Rangoon 2,513
Mandalay 533
**Cambodia**
Phnom Penh 800
**Cameroon**
Douala 884
Yaoundé 750
**Canada**
Toronto 3,893
Montréal 3,127
Vancouver 1,603
Ottawa-Hull 921
Edmonton 840
Calgary 754
Winnipeg 652
Québec 646
Hamilton 600
**Central African Rep.**
Bangui 597
**Chad**
Ndjamena 688
**Chile**
Santiago 5,343

**China**
Shanghai [5] 12,320
Beijing (Peking)[10] 9,750
Tianjin [18] 7,790
Chongqing [20] 6,511
Wenzhou 5,948
Guangzhou 5,669
Hangzhou 5,234
Shenyang 5,055
Dalian 4,619
Jinzhou 4,448
Wuhan 4,273
Qingdao 4,205
Chengdu 4,025
Jilin 3,974
Nanjing 3,682
Jinan 3,376
Xi'an 2,911
Harbin 2,830
Yingkou 2,789
Dandong 2,574
Anshan 2,517
Nanchang 2,471
Zibo 2,460
Lanzhou 2,340
Lupanshui 2,247
Fushun 2,045
Taiyuan 2,177
Changchun 2,110
Kunming 1,976
Tianshui 1,967
Zhengzhou 1,943
Fuxin 1,693
Zigong 1,673
Fuzhou 1,652
Liaoyang 1,612
Zhaozhuang 1,612
Botou 1,593
Hepei 1,541
Guiyang 1,530
Huainan 1,519
Tangshan 1,500
Linyi 1,385
Qiqihar 1,380
Tai'an 1,370
Changsha 1,330
Shijiazhuang 1,320
Huaibei 1,306
Pingxiang 1,305
Xintao 1,272
Yangcheng 1,265
Yulin 1,255
Dongguang 1,230
Chao'an 1,227
Hohhot 1,206
Baotou 1,200
Suining 1,195
Luoyang 1,190
Macheng 1,190
Xintai 1,167
Yichun 1,167
Ürümqi 1,160
Puyang 1,125
Datong 1,110
Handan 1,110
Shaoxing 1,091
Ningbo 1,090
Zhongshan 1,073
Nanning 1,070
Huangshi 1,069
Laiwu 1,054
Leshan 1,039
Heze 1,017
Linhai 1,012
Changshu 1,004
**Colombia**
Bogotá 4,921
Cali 1,624
Medellin 1,581
Barranquilla 1,019
Cartagena 688
**Congo**
Brazzaville 938
Pointe-Noire 576
**Croatia**
Zagreb 1,175
**Cuba**
Havana 2,096
**Czech Republic**
Prague 1,216
**Denmark**
Copenhagen 1,337
**Dominican Rep.**
Santo Domingo 1,601
**Ecuador**
Guayaquil 1,508

Quito 1,101
**Egypt**
Cairo [19] 6,663
Alexandria 3,295
El Gîza 2,096
Shubra el Kheima 812
**El Salvador**
San Salvador 1,522
**Ethiopia**
Addis Ababa 1,913
**Finland**
Helsinki 929
**France**
Paris [12] 9,319
Lyons 1,262
Marseilles 1,087
Lille 959
Bordeaux 696
Toulouse 650
Nice 516
**Gabon**
Libreville 830
**Georgia**
Tbilisi 1,279
**Germany**
Berlin 3,446
Hamburg 1,669
Munich 1,229
Cologne 957
Frankfurt 654
Essen 627
Dortmund 601
Stuttgart 592
Düsseldorf 578
Bremen 553
Duisburg 537
Hanover 517
Leipzig 503
**Ghana**
Accra 965
**Greece**
Athens 3,097
**Guatemala**
Guatemala 2,000
**Guinea**
Conakry 705
**Haiti**
Port-au-Prince 1,144
**Honduras**
Tegucigalpa 679
**Hong Kong**
Kowloon 2,031
Hong Kong 1,251
Tsuen Wan 690
**Hungary**
Budapest 2,016
**India**
Bombay [4] 12,572
Calcutta [8] 10,916
Delhi [14] 8,375
Madras 5,361
Hyderabad 4,280
Bangalore 4,087
Ahmadabad 3,298
Pune 2,485
Kanpur 2,111
Nagpur 1,661
Lucknow 1,642
Surat 1,517
Jaipur 1,514
Kochi 1,140
Coimbatore 1,136
Vadodara 1,115
Indore 1,104
Patna 1,099
Madurai 1,094
Bhopal 1,064
Vishakhapatnam 1,052
Varanasi 1,026
Ludhiana 1,012
Agra 956
Jabalpur 887
Allahabad 858
Meerut 847
Vijayawada 845
Jamshedpur 834
Trivandrum 826
Dhanbad 818
Kozhikode 801
Asansol 764
Nasik 722
Gwalior 720
Tiruchchirappalli 711
Amritsar 709
Durg-Bhilai 689
Mysore 652

Jodhpur 649
Hubli-Dharwad 648
Solapur 621
Faridabad 614
Ranchi 614
Bareilly 608
Srinagar 595
Aurangabad 592
Guwahati 578
Chandigarh 575
Salem 574
Cochin 564
Kota 536
Ghaziabad 520
Jullundur 520
**Indonesia**
Jakarta [16] 7,886
Surabaya 2,224
Medan 1,806
Bandung 1,567
Semarang 1,027
Palembang 787
Ujung Pandang 709
Malang 512
**Iran**
Tehran 6,476
Mashhad 1,759
Esfahan 1,127
Tabriz 1,089
Shiraz 965
Ahvaz 725
Qom 681
Kermanshah 624
Bakhtaran 561
**Iraq**
Baghdad 4,649
Basra 617
Mosul 571
**Ireland**
Dublin 1,024
**Italy**
Rome 2,791
Milan 1,432
Naples 1,206
Turin 992
Palermo 734
Genoa 701
**Ivory Coast**
Abidjan 2,534
**Jamaica**
Kingston 588
**Japan**
Tokyo [6] 11,936
Yokohama 3,220
Osaka 2,624
Nagoya 2,155
Sapporo 1,672
Kobe 1,477
Kyoto 1,461
Fukuoka 1,237
Kawasaki 1,174
Hiroshima 1,086
Kitakyushu 1,026
Sendai 918
Chiba 829
Sakai 808
Okayama 594
Kumamoto 579
Kagoshima 537
Hamamatsu 535
Funabashi 533
Sagamihara 532
Higashiosaka 518
**Jordan**
Amman 1,160
Irbid 680
**Kazakhstan**
Alma-Ata 1,147
Karaganda 613
Astrakhan 510
**Kenya**
Nairobi 1,429
**Kirghizia**
Bishkek 625
**Korea, North**
Pyongyang 2,639
Hamhung 775
Chongjin 754
Chinnamp'o 691
Sinuiju 500
**Korea, South**
Seoul [9] 10,628
Pusan 3,798
Taegu 2,229
Inchon 1,818
Kwangju 1,145

Taejon 1,062
Ulsan 683
Puch'on 668
Suwon 645
Songnam 541
Chonju 517
**Latvia**
Riga 917
**Lebanon**
Beirut 1,500
Tripoli 500
**Libya**
Tripoli 980
Benghazi 650
**Lithuania**
Vilnius 593
**Macedonia**
Skopje 563
**Madagascar**
Antananarivo 802
**Malaysia**
Kuala Lumpur 938
**Mali**
Bamako 646
**Mexico**
Mexico City [3] 13,636
Guadalajara 2,847
Monterrey 2,522
Puebla 1,055
León 872
Ciudad Juárez 798
Tijuana 743
Culiacán Rosales 602
Mexicali 602
Acapulco 592
Mérida 557
Chihuahua 530
San Luis Potosí 526
Aguascalientés 506
**Moldavia**
Kishinev 676
**Mongolia**
Ulan Bator 575
**Morocco**
Casablanca 2,409
Rabat-Salé 893
Fès 562
Marrakesh 549
**Mozambique**
Maputo 1,070
**Netherlands**
Amsterdam 1,091
Rotterdam 1,069
's-Gravenhage 694
The Hague 693
Utrecht 543
**New Zealand**
Auckland 885
**Nicaragua**
Managua 682
**Nigeria**
Lagos 1,097
Ibadan 1,060
Ogbomosho 527
**Norway**
Oslo 683
**Pakistan**
Karachi 5,181
Lahore 2,953
Faisalabad 1,104
Rawalpindi 795
Hyderabad 752
Multan 722
Gujranwala 659
Peshawar 556
**Panama**
Panama City 853
**Paraguay**
Asunción 729
**Peru**
Lima-Callao 6,415
Arequipa 635
Trujillo 532
Callao 515
**Philippines**
Manila [17] 7,832
Quezon City 1,587
Davao 844
Cebu 627
Caloocan 616
**Poland**
Warsaw 1,655
Lódz 852
Kraków 748
Wroclaw 642
Poznaé 585

**Portugal**
Lisbon 1,612
Oporto 1,315
**Puerto Rico**
San Juan 1,816
**Romania**
Bucharest 2,217
**Russia**
Moscow [13] 8,801
St Petersburg 4,467
Nizhniy
  Novgorod 1,443
Novosibirsk 1,443
Yekaterinburg 1,375
Samara 1,258
Omsk 1,159
Chelyabinsk 1,148
Kazan 1,103
Perm 1,094
Ufa 1,094
Rostov 1,025
Volgograd 1,005
Krasnoyarsk 922
Saratov 909
Voronezh 895
Izhevsk 642
Tolyatti 642
Simbirsk 638
Yaroslavl 636
Irkutsk 635
Vladivostok 634
Krasnodar 627
Khabarovsk 608
Barnaul 603
Barnaul 602
Novokuznetsk 601
Orenburg 552
Penza 548
Tula 543
Ryazan 522
Kemerovo 521
Naberezhnyye-
  Chelny 507
Tomsk 506
**Saudi Arabia**
Riyadh 2,000
Jedda 1,400
Mecca 618
Medina 500
**Senegal**
Dakar 1,382
**Singapore**
Singapore 3,003
**Somali Republic**
Mogadishu 1,000
**South Africa**
Cape Town 1,912
Johannesburg 1,726
East Rand 1,038
Durban 982
Pretoria 823
Port Elizabeth 652
West Rand 647
Vereeniging 540
**Spain**
Madrid 3,121
Barcelona 1,707
Valencia 753
Seville 659
Zaragoza 586
Málaga 512
**Sri Lanka**
Colombo 1,863
**Sudan**
Khartoum 561
Omdurman 526
**Sweden**
Stockholm 1,503
Gothenburg 734
**Switzerland**
Zürich 840
**Syria**
Damascus 1,378
Aleppo 1,355
**Taiwan**
Taipei 2,718
Kaohsiung 1,396
Taichung 774
Tainan 690
Panchiao 543
**Tajikistan**
Dushanbe 582
**Tanzania**
Dar es Salaam 1,361
**Thailand**
Bangkok 5,876

**Tunisia**
Tunis 1,395
**Turkey**
Istanbul 6,620
Ankara 2,559
Izmir 1,757
Adana 916
Bursa 835
**Uganda**
Kampala 773
**Ukraine**
Kiev 2,616
Kharkov 1,618
Dnepropetrovsk 1,187
Donetsk 1,117
Odessa 1,106
Zaporozhye 891
Lvov 798
Krivoy Rog 717
Mariupol 520
Nikolayev 508
Lugansk 501
**United Kingdom**
London 6,378
Manchester 1,669
Birmingham 1,400
Liverpool 1,060
Glasgow 730
Newcastle 617
**United States**
New York [1] 18,087
Los Angeles [2] 14,532
Chicago [15] 8,066
San Francisco 6,253
Philadelphia 5,899
Detroit 4,665
Boston 4,172
Washington 3,924
Dallas 3,885
Houston 3,711
Miami 3,193
Atlanta 2,834
Cleveland 2,760
Seattle 2,559
San Diego 2,498
Minneapolis-SP. 2,464
St Louis 2,444
Baltimore 2,382
Pittsburgh 2,243
Phoenix 2,122
Tampa 2,098
Denver 1,848
Cincinnati 1,744
Milwaukee 1,607
Kansas City 1,566
Sacramento 1,481
Portland 1,478
Norfolk 1,396
Columbus 1,377
San Antonio 1,303
Indianapolis 1,250
New Orleans 1,239
Buffalo 1,189
Charlotte 1,162
Providence 1,118
Hartford 1,086
Salt Lake City 1,072
San Jose 782
Jacksonville 672
Memphis 610
**Uruguay**
Montevideo 1,248
**Uzbekistan**
Tashkent 2,094
**Venezuela**
Caracas 3,247
Maracaibo 1,295
Valencia 1,135
Maracay 857
Barquisimeto 718
**Vietnam**
Ho Chi Minh 3,169
Hanoi 2,571
Haiphong 1,279
**Yugoslavia**
Belgrade 1,137
**Zaïre**
Kinshasa 2,796
Lubumbashi 795
**Zambia**
Lusaka 921
**Zimbabwe**
Harare 681
Bulawayo 500

# World Statistics: Distances

The table shows air distances in miles and kilometres between thirty major cities. Known as 'Great Circle' distances, these measure the shortest routes between the cities, which aircraft use where possible. The maps show the world centred on six individual cities, and illustrate, for example, why direct flights from Japan to northern America and Europe are across the Arctic regions, and Singapore is on the direct line route from Europe to Australia. The maps have been constructed on an Azimuthal Equidistant projection, on which all distances measured through the centre point are true to scale. The circular lines are drawn at 5,000, 10,000 and 15,000 km from the central city.

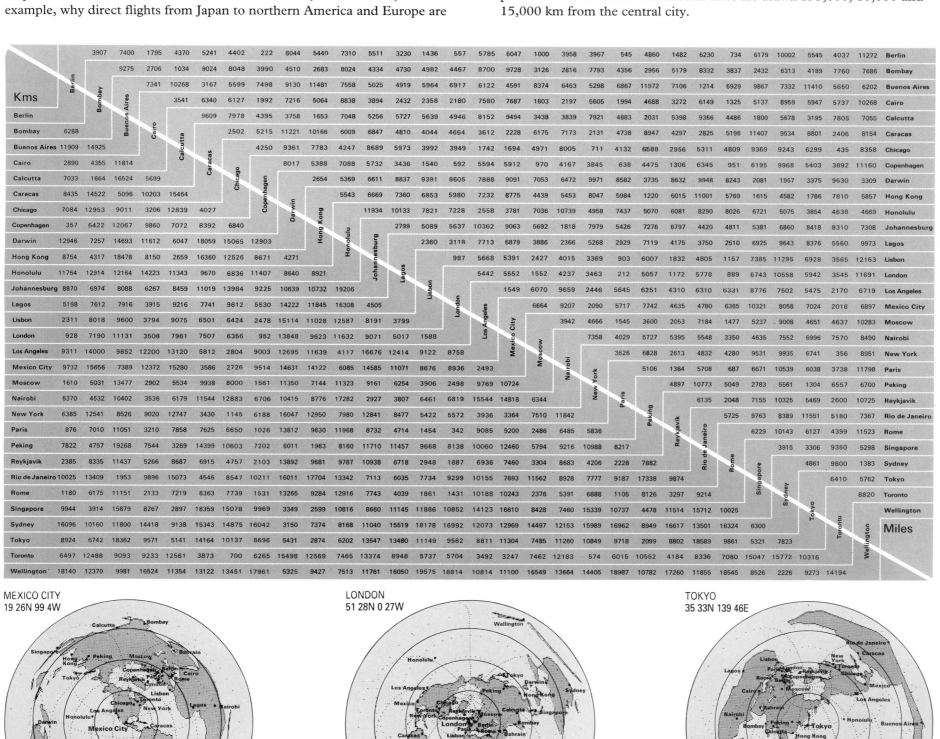

| Kms | Berlin | Bombay | Buenos Aires | Cairo | Calcutta | Caracas | Chicago | Copenhagen | Darwin | Hong Kong | Honolulu | Johannesburg | Lagos | Lisbon | London | Los Angeles | Mexico City | Moscow | Nairobi | New York | Paris | Peking | Reykjavik | Rio de Janeiro | Rome | Singapore | Sydney | Tokyo | Toronto | Wellington |
|---|---|---|---|---|---|---|---|---|---|---|---|---|---|---|---|---|---|---|---|---|---|---|---|---|---|---|---|---|---|---|
| Berlin | Berlin | 3907 | 7400 | 1795 | 4370 | 5241 | 4402 | 222 | 8044 | 5440 | 7310 | 5511 | 3230 | 1436 | 557 | 5785 | 6047 | 1000 | 3958 | 3967 | 545 | 4860 | 1482 | 6230 | 734 | 6179 | 10002 | 5545 | 4037 | 11272 |
| Bombay | 6288 | Bombay | 9275 | 2706 | 1034 | 9024 | 8048 | 3990 | 4510 | 2683 | 8024 | 4334 | 4730 | 4982 | 4467 | 8700 | 9728 | 3126 | 2816 | 7793 | 4356 | 2956 | 5179 | 8332 | 3837 | 2432 | 6313 | 4189 | 7760 | 7686 |
| Buenos Aires | 11909 | 14925 | Buenos Aires | 7341 | 10268 | 3167 | 5599 | 7498 | 9130 | 11481 | 7558 | 5025 | 4919 | 5964 | 6917 | 6122 | 4591 | 8374 | 6463 | 5298 | 6867 | 11972 | 7106 | 1214 | 6929 | 9867 | 7332 | 11410 | 5650 | 6202 |
| Cairo | 2890 | 4355 | 11814 | Cairo | 3541 | 6340 | 6127 | 1992 | 7216 | 5064 | 8838 | 3894 | 2432 | 2358 | 2180 | 7580 | 7687 | 1803 | 2197 | 5605 | 1994 | 4688 | 3272 | 6149 | 1325 | 5137 | 8959 | 5947 | 5737 | 10268 |
| Calcutta | 7033 | 1664 | 16524 | 5699 | Calcutta | 9609 | 7978 | 4395 | 3758 | 1653 | 7048 | 5256 | 5727 | 5639 | 4946 | 8152 | 9494 | 3438 | 3839 | 7921 | 4883 | 2031 | 5398 | 9366 | 4486 | 1800 | 5678 | 3195 | 7805 | 7055 |
| Caracas | 8435 | 14522 | 5096 | 10203 | 15464 | Caracas | 2502 | 5215 | 11221 | 10166 | 6009 | 6847 | 4810 | 4044 | 4664 | 3612 | 2228 | 6175 | 7173 | 2131 | 4738 | 8947 | 4297 | 2825 | 5196 | 11407 | 9534 | 8801 | 2406 | 8154 |
| Chicago | 7084 | 12953 | 9011 | 3206 | 12839 | 4027 | Chicago | 4250 | 9361 | 7783 | 4247 | 8689 | 5973 | 3992 | 3949 | 1742 | 1694 | 4971 | 8005 | 711 | 4132 | 6588 | 2956 | 5311 | 4809 | 9369 | 9243 | 6299 | 435 | 8358 |
| Copenhagen | 357 | 6422 | 12067 | 9860 | 7072 | 8392 | 6840 | Copenhagen | 8017 | 5388 | 7088 | 5732 | 3436 | 1540 | 592 | 5594 | 5912 | 970 | 4167 | 3845 | 638 | 4475 | 1306 | 6345 | 951 | 6195 | 9968 | 5403 | 3892 | 11160 |
| Darwin | 12946 | 7257 | 14693 | 11612 | 6047 | 18059 | 15065 | 12903 | Darwin | 2654 | 5369 | 6611 | 8837 | 9391 | 8605 | 7888 | 9091 | 7053 | 6472 | 9971 | 8582 | 3735 | 8632 | 9948 | 8243 | 2081 | 1957 | 3375 | 9630 | 3309 |
| Hong Kong | 8754 | 4317 | 18478 | 8150 | 2659 | 16360 | 12526 | 8671 | 4271 | Hong Kong | 5543 | 6669 | 7360 | 6853 | 5980 | 7232 | 8775 | 4439 | 5453 | 8047 | 5984 | 1220 | 6015 | 11001 | 5769 | 1615 | 4582 | 1786 | 7810 | 5857 |
| Honolulu | 11764 | 12914 | 12164 | 12223 | 11343 | 9670 | 6836 | 11407 | 8640 | 8921 | Honolulu | 11934 | 10133 | 7821 | 7228 | 2558 | 3781 | 7036 | 10739 | 4958 | 7437 | 5070 | 6081 | 8290 | 8026 | 6721 | 5075 | 3854 | 4638 | 4669 |
| Johannesburg | 8870 | 6974 | 8088 | 6267 | 8459 | 11019 | 13984 | 9225 | 10639 | 10732 | 19206 | Johannesburg | 2799 | 5089 | 5637 | 10362 | 9063 | 5692 | 1818 | 7979 | 5426 | 7276 | 6797 | 4420 | 4811 | 5381 | 6860 | 8418 | 8310 | 7308 |
| Lagos | 5198 | 7612 | 7916 | 3915 | 9216 | 7741 | 9612 | 5530 | 14222 | 11845 | 16308 | 4505 | Lagos | 2360 | 3118 | 7713 | 6879 | 3886 | 2366 | 5268 | 2929 | 7119 | 4175 | 3750 | 2510 | 6925 | 9643 | 8376 | 5560 | 9973 |
| Lisbon | 2311 | 8018 | 9600 | 3794 | 9075 | 6501 | 6424 | 2478 | 15114 | 11028 | 12587 | 8191 | 3799 | Lisbon | 987 | 5668 | 5391 | 2427 | 4015 | 3369 | 903 | 6007 | 1832 | 4805 | 1157 | 7385 | 11295 | 6928 | 3565 | 12163 |
| London | 928 | 7190 | 11131 | 3508 | 7961 | 7507 | 6356 | 952 | 13848 | 9623 | 11632 | 9071 | 5017 | 1588 | London | 5442 | 5552 | 1552 | 4237 | 3463 | 212 | 5057 | 1172 | 5778 | 889 | 6743 | 10558 | 5942 | 3545 | 11691 |
| Los Angeles | 9311 | 14000 | 9852 | 12200 | 13120 | 5812 | 2804 | 9003 | 12695 | 11639 | 4117 | 16676 | 12414 | 9122 | 8758 | Los Angeles | 1549 | 6070 | 9659 | 2446 | 5645 | 6251 | 4310 | 6331 | 8776 | 7502 | 5475 | 2170 | 6719 | |
| Mexico City | 9732 | 15656 | 7389 | 12372 | 15280 | 3586 | 2726 | 9514 | 14631 | 14122 | 6085 | 14585 | 11071 | 8676 | 8936 | 2493 | Mexico City | 6664 | 9207 | 2090 | 5717 | 7742 | 4635 | 4780 | 6365 | 10321 | 8058 | 7024 | 2018 | 6897 |
| Moscow | 1610 | 5031 | 13477 | 2902 | 5534 | 9938 | 8000 | 1561 | 11350 | 7144 | 11323 | 9161 | 6254 | 3906 | 2498 | 9769 | 10724 | Moscow | 3942 | 4666 | 1545 | 3600 | 2053 | 7184 | 1477 | 5237 | 9008 | 4651 | 4637 | 10283 |
| Nairobi | 6370 | 4532 | 10402 | 3536 | 6179 | 11544 | 12883 | 6706 | 10415 | 8776 | 17282 | 2927 | 3807 | 6461 | 6819 | 15544 | 14818 | 6344 | Nairobi | 7358 | 4029 | 5727 | 5395 | 5548 | 3350 | 4635 | 7552 | 6996 | 7570 | 8490 |
| New York | 6385 | 12541 | 8526 | 9020 | 12747 | 3430 | 1145 | 6188 | 16047 | 12950 | 7980 | 12841 | 8477 | 5422 | 5572 | 3936 | 3364 | 7510 | 11842 | New York | 3626 | 6828 | 2613 | 4832 | 4280 | 9531 | 9935 | 6741 | 356 | 8951 |
| Paris | 876 | 7010 | 11051 | 3210 | 7858 | 7625 | 6650 | 1026 | 13812 | 9630 | 11968 | 8732 | 4714 | 1454 | 342 | 9085 | 9200 | 2486 | 6485 | 5836 | Paris | 5106 | 1384 | 5708 | 687 | 6671 | 10539 | 6038 | 3738 | 11798 |
| Peking | 7822 | 4757 | 19268 | 7544 | 3269 | 14399 | 10603 | 7202 | 6011 | 1963 | 8160 | 11710 | 11457 | 9668 | 8138 | 10060 | 12460 | 5794 | 9216 | 10988 | 8217 | Peking | 4897 | 10773 | 5049 | 2783 | 5561 | 1304 | 6557 | 6700 |
| Reykjavik | 2385 | 8335 | 11437 | 5266 | 8687 | 6915 | 4757 | 2103 | 13892 | 9681 | 9787 | 10938 | 6718 | 2948 | 1887 | 6936 | 7460 | 3304 | 8683 | 4206 | 2228 | 7882 | Reykjavik | 6135 | 2048 | 7155 | 10325 | 5469 | 2600 | 10725 |
| Rio de Janeiro | 10025 | 13409 | 1953 | 9896 | 15073 | 4546 | 8547 | 10211 | 16011 | 17704 | 13342 | 7113 | 6035 | 7734 | 9299 | 10155 | 7693 | 11562 | 8928 | 7777 | 9187 | 17338 | 9874 | Rio de Janeiro | 5725 | 9763 | 8389 | 11551 | 5180 | 7367 |
| Rome | 1180 | 6175 | 11151 | 2133 | 7219 | 8363 | 7739 | 1531 | 13265 | 9284 | 12916 | 7743 | 4039 | 1861 | 1431 | 10188 | 10243 | 2376 | 5391 | 6888 | 1105 | 8126 | 3297 | 9214 | Rome | 6229 | 10143 | 6127 | 4399 | 11523 |
| Singapore | 9944 | 3914 | 15879 | 8267 | 2897 | 18359 | 15078 | 9969 | 3349 | 2599 | 10816 | 8660 | 11145 | 11886 | 10852 | 14123 | 16610 | 8428 | 7460 | 15339 | 10737 | 4478 | 11514 | 15712 | 10025 | Singapore | 3915 | 3306 | 9350 | 5298 |
| Sydney | 16096 | 10160 | 11800 | 14418 | 9138 | 15343 | 14875 | 16042 | 3150 | 7374 | 8168 | 11040 | 15519 | 18178 | 16992 | 12073 | 12969 | 14497 | 12153 | 15989 | 16962 | 8949 | 16617 | 13501 | 16324 | 6300 | Sydney | 4861 | 9800 | 1383 |
| Tokyo | 8924 | 6742 | 18362 | 9571 | 5141 | 14164 | 10137 | 8696 | 5431 | 2874 | 6202 | 13547 | 13480 | 11149 | 9562 | 8811 | 11304 | 7485 | 11260 | 10849 | 9718 | 2099 | 8802 | 18589 | 9861 | 5321 | 7823 | Tokyo | 6410 | 5762 |
| Toronto | 6497 | 12488 | 9093 | 9233 | 12561 | 3873 | 700 | 6265 | 15498 | 12569 | 7465 | 13374 | 8948 | 5737 | 5704 | 3492 | 3247 | 7462 | 12183 | 574 | 6015 | 10552 | 4184 | 8336 | 7080 | 15047 | 15772 | 10316 | Toronto | 8820 |
| Wellington | 18140 | 12370 | 9981 | 16524 | 11354 | 13122 | 13451 | 17961 | 5325 | 9427 | 7513 | 11761 | 16050 | 19575 | 18814 | 10814 | 11100 | 16549 | 13664 | 14405 | 18987 | 10782 | 17260 | 11855 | 18545 | 8526 | 2226 | 9273 | 14194 | Miles |

**MEXICO CITY**
19 26N 99 4W

**LONDON**
51 28N 0 27W

**TOKYO**
35 33N 139 46E

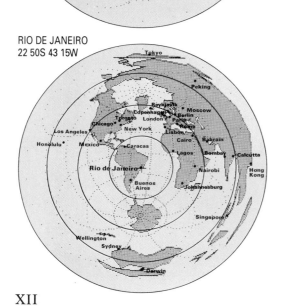

**RIO DE JANEIRO**
22 50S 43 15W

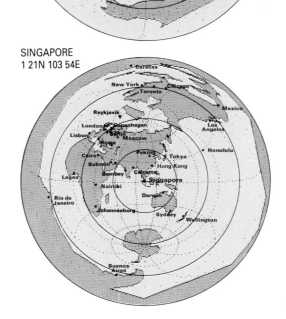

**SINGAPORE**
1 21N 103 54E

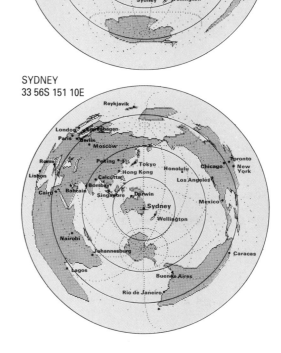

**SYDNEY**
33 56S 151 10E

# World Statistics: Climate

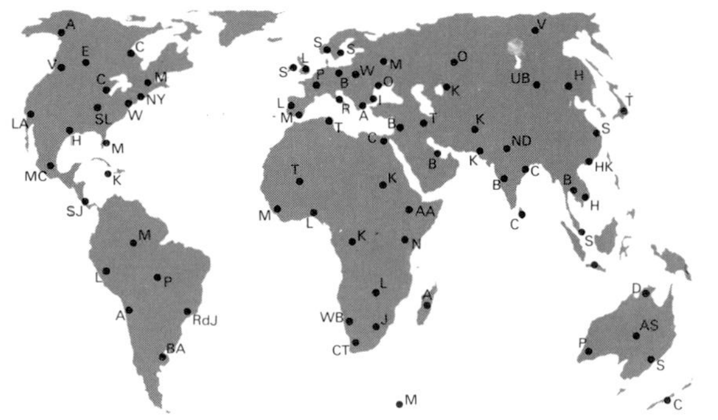

Rainfall and temperature figures are provided for more than 70 cities around the world. As climate is affected by altitude, the height of each city is shown in metres beneath its name. For each month, the figures in red show average temperature in degrees Celsius or centigrade, and in blue the total rainfall or snow in millimetres; the average annual temperature and total annual rainfall are at the end of the rows.

| EUROPE | Jan. | Feb. | Mar. | Apr. | May | June | July | Aug. | Sept. | Oct. | Nov. | Dec. | Year |
|---|---|---|---|---|---|---|---|---|---|---|---|---|---|
| **Athens, Greece** | 62 | 37 | 37 | 23 | 23 | 14 | 6 | 7 | 15 | 51 | 56 | 71 | 402 |
| 107 m | 10 | 10 | 12 | 16 | 20 | 25 | 28 | 28 | 24 | 20 | 15 | 11 | 18 |
| **Berlin, Germany** | 46 | 40 | 33 | 42 | 49 | 65 | 73 | 69 | 48 | 49 | 46 | 43 | 603 |
| 55 m | -1 | 0 | 4 | 9 | 14 | 17 | 19 | 18 | 15 | 9 | 5 | 1 | 9 |
| **Istanbul, Turkey** | 109 | 92 | 72 | 46 | 38 | 34 | 34 | 30 | 58 | 81 | 103 | 119 | 816 |
| 114 m | 5 | 6 | 7 | 11 | 16 | 20 | 23 | 23 | 20 | 16 | 12 | 8 | 14 |
| **Lisbon, Portugal** | 111 | 76 | 109 | 54 | 44 | 16 | 3 | 4 | 33 | 62 | 93 | 103 | 708 |
| 77 m | 11 | 12 | 14 | 16 | 17 | 20 | 22 | 23 | 21 | 18 | 14 | 12 | 17 |
| **London, UK** | 54 | 40 | 37 | 37 | 46 | 45 | 57 | 59 | 49 | 57 | 64 | 48 | 593 |
| 5 m | 4 | 5 | 7 | 9 | 12 | 16 | 18 | 17 | 15 | 11 | 8 | 5 | 11 |
| **Málaga, Spain** | 61 | 51 | 62 | 46 | 26 | 5 | 1 | 3 | 29 | 64 | 64 | 62 | 474 |
| 33 m | 12 | 13 | 16 | 17 | 19 | 29 | 25 | 26 | 23 | 20 | 16 | 13 | 18 |
| **Moscow, Russia** | 39 | 38 | 36 | 37 | 53 | 58 | 88 | 71 | 58 | 45 | 47 | 54 | 624 |
| 156 m | -13 | -10 | -4 | 6 | 13 | 16 | 18 | 17 | 12 | 6 | -1 | -7 | 4 |
| **Odessa, Ukraine** | 57 | 62 | 30 | 21 | 34 | 34 | 42 | 37 | 37 | 13 | 35 | 71 | 473 |
| 64 m | -3 | -1 | 2 | 9 | 15 | 20 | 22 | 22 | 18 | 12 | 9 | 1 | 10 |
| **Paris, France** | 56 | 46 | 35 | 42 | 57 | 54 | 59 | 64 | 55 | 50 | 51 | 50 | 619 |
| 75 m | 3 | 4 | 8 | 11 | 15 | 18 | 20 | 19 | 17 | 12 | 7 | 4 | 12 |
| **Rome, Italy** | 71 | 62 | 57 | 51 | 46 | 37 | 15 | 21 | 63 | 99 | 129 | 93 | 744 |
| 17 m | 8 | 9 | 11 | 14 | 18 | 22 | 25 | 25 | 22 | 17 | 13 | 10 | 16 |
| **Shannon, Irish Republic** | 94 | 67 | 56 | 53 | 61 | 57 | 77 | 79 | 86 | 86 | 96 | 117 | 929 |
| 2 m | 5 | 5 | 7 | 9 | 12 | 14 | 16 | 16 | 14 | 11 | 8 | 6 | 10 |
| **Stockholm, Sweden** | 43 | 30 | 25 | 31 | 34 | 45 | 61 | 76 | 60 | 48 | 53 | 48 | 554 |
| 44 m | -3 | -3 | -1 | 5 | 10 | 15 | 18 | 17 | 12 | 7 | 3 | 0 | 7 |

| ASIA | Jan. | Feb. | Mar. | Apr. | May | June | July | Aug. | Sept. | Oct. | Nov. | Dec. | Year |
|---|---|---|---|---|---|---|---|---|---|---|---|---|---|
| **Bahrain** | 8 | 18 | 13 | 8 | <3 | 0 | 0 | 0 | 0 | 0 | 18 | 18 | 81 |
| 5 m | 17 | 18 | 21 | 25 | 29 | 32 | 33 | 34 | 31 | 28 | 24 | 19 | 26 |
| **Bangkok, Thailand** | 8 | 20 | 36 | 58 | 198 | 160 | 160 | 175 | 305 | 206 | 66 | 5 | 1,397 |
| 2 m | 26 | 28 | 29 | 30 | 29 | 29 | 28 | 28 | 28 | 28 | 26 | 25 | 28 |
| **Beirut, Lebanon** | 191 | 158 | 94 | 53 | 18 | 3 | <3 | <3 | 5 | 51 | 132 | 185 | 892 |
| 34 m | 14 | 14 | 16 | 18 | 22 | 24 | 27 | 28 | 26 | 24 | 19 | 16 | 21 |
| **Bombay, India** | 3 | 3 | 3 | <3 | 18 | 485 | 617 | 340 | 264 | 64 | 13 | 3 | 1,809 |
| 11 m | 24 | 24 | 26 | 28 | 30 | 29 | 27 | 27 | 27 | 28 | 27 | 26 | 27 |
| **Calcutta, India** | 10 | 31 | 36 | 43 | 140 | 297 | 325 | 328 | 252 | 114 | 20 | 5 | 1,600 |
| 6 m | 20 | 22 | 27 | 30 | 30 | 30 | 29 | 29 | 29 | 28 | 23 | 19 | 26 |
| **Colombo, Sri Lanka** | 89 | 69 | 147 | 231 | 371 | 224 | 135 | 109 | 160 | 348 | 315 | 147 | 2,365 |
| 7 m | 26 | 26 | 27 | 28 | 28 | 27 | 27 | 27 | 27 | 27 | 26 | 26 | 27 |
| **Harbin, China** | 6 | 5 | 10 | 23 | 43 | 94 | 112 | 104 | 46 | 33 | 8 | 5 | 488 |
| 160 m | -18 | -15 | -5 | 6 | 13 | 19 | 22 | 21 | 14 | 4 | -6 | -16 | 3 |
| **Ho Chi Minh, Vietnam** | 15 | 3 | 13 | 43 | 221 | 330 | 315 | 269 | 335 | 269 | 114 | 56 | 1,984 |
| 9 m | 26 | 27 | 29 | 30 | 29 | 28 | 28 | 28 | 27 | 27 | 27 | 26 | 28 |
| **Hong Kong** | 33 | 46 | 74 | 137 | 292 | 394 | 381 | 361 | 257 | 114 | 43 | 31 | 2,162 |
| 33 m | 16 | 15 | 18 | 22 | 26 | 28 | 28 | 28 | 27 | 25 | 21 | 18 | 23 |
| **Jakarta, Indonesia** | 300 | 300 | 211 | 147 | 114 | 97 | 64 | 43 | 66 | 112 | 142 | 203 | 1,798 |
| 8 m | 26 | 26 | 27 | 27 | 27 | 27 | 27 | 27 | 27 | 27 | 27 | 26 | 27 |
| **Kabul, Afghanistan** | 31 | 36 | 94 | 102 | 20 | 5 | 3 | 3 | <3 | 15 | 20 | 10 | 338 |
| 1,815 m | -3 | -1 | 6 | 13 | 18 | 22 | 25 | 24 | 20 | 14 | 7 | 3 | 12 |
| **Karachi, Pakistan** | 13 | 10 | 8 | 3 | 3 | 18 | 81 | 41 | 13 | <3 | 3 | 5 | 196 |
| 4 m | 19 | 20 | 24 | 28 | 30 | 31 | 30 | 29 | 28 | 28 | 24 | 20 | 26 |
| **Kazalinsk, Kazakhstan** | 10 | 10 | 13 | 13 | 15 | 5 | 5 | 8 | 8 | 10 | 13 | 15 | 125 |
| 63 m | -12 | -11 | -3 | 6 | 18 | 23 | 25 | 23 | 16 | 8 | -1 | -7 | 7 |
| **New Delhi, India** | 23 | 18 | 13 | 8 | 13 | 74 | 180 | 172 | 117 | 10 | 3 | 10 | 640 |
| 218 m | 14 | 17 | 23 | 28 | 33 | 34 | 31 | 30 | 29 | 26 | 20 | 15 | 25 |
| **Omsk, Russia** | 15 | 8 | 8 | 13 | 31 | 51 | 51 | 51 | 28 | 25 | 18 | 20 | 318 |
| 85 m | -22 | -19 | -12 | -1 | 10 | 16 | 18 | 16 | 10 | 1 | -11 | -18 | -1 |
| **Shanghai, China** | 48 | 58 | 84 | 94 | 94 | 180 | 147 | 142 | 130 | 71 | 51 | 36 | 1,135 |
| 7 m | 4 | 5 | 9 | 14 | 20 | 24 | 28 | 28 | 23 | 19 | 12 | 7 | 16 |
| **Singapore** | 252 | 173 | 193 | 188 | 173 | 173 | 170 | 196 | 178 | 208 | 254 | 257 | 2,413 |
| 10 m | 26 | 27 | 28 | 28 | 28 | 28 | 28 | 27 | 27 | 27 | 27 | 27 | 27 |
| **Tehran, Iran** | 46 | 38 | 46 | 36 | 13 | 3 | 3 | 3 | 3 | 8 | 20 | 31 | 246 |
| 1,220 m | 2 | 5 | 9 | 16 | 21 | 26 | 30 | 29 | 25 | 18 | 12 | 6 | 17 |
| **Tokyo, Japan** | 48 | 74 | 107 | 135 | 147 | 165 | 142 | 152 | 234 | 208 | 97 | 56 | 1,565 |
| 6 m | 3 | 4 | 7 | 13 | 17 | 21 | 25 | 26 | 23 | 17 | 11 | 6 | 14 |
| **Ulan Bator, Mongolia** | <3 | <3 | 3 | 5 | 10 | 28 | 76 | 51 | 23 | 5 | 5 | 3 | 208 |
| 1,325 m | -26 | -21 | -13 | -1 | 6 | 14 | 16 | 14 | 8 | -1 | -13 | -22 | -3 |
| **Verkhoyansk, Russia** | 5 | 5 | 3 | 5 | 8 | 23 | 28 | 25 | 13 | 8 | 8 | 5 | 134 |
| 100 m | -50 | -45 | -32 | -15 | 0 | 12 | 14 | 9 | 2 | -15 | -38 | -48 | -17 |

| AFRICA | Jan. | Feb. | Mar. | Apr. | May | June | July | Aug. | Sept. | Oct. | Nov. | Dec. | Year |
|---|---|---|---|---|---|---|---|---|---|---|---|---|---|
| **Addis Ababa, Ethiopia** | <3 | 3 | 25 | 135 | 213 | 201 | 206 | 239 | 102 | 28 | <3 | 0 | 1,151 |
| 2,450 m | 19 | 20 | 20 | 20 | 19 | 18 | 18 | 19 | 21 | 22 | 21 | 20 | 20 |
| **Antananarivo, Madagas.** | 300 | 279 | 178 | 53 | 18 | 8 | 8 | 10 | 18 | 61 | 135 | 287 | 1,356 |
| 1,372 m | 21 | 21 | 21 | 19 | 18 | 15 | 14 | 15 | 17 | 19 | 21 | 21 | 19 |
| **Cairo, Egypt** | 5 | 5 | 5 | 3 | 3 | <3 | 0 | 0 | <3 | <3 | 3 | 5 | 28 |
| 116 m | 13 | 15 | 18 | 21 | 25 | 28 | 28 | 28 | 26 | 24 | 20 | 15 | 22 |
| **Cape Town, South Africa** | 15 | 8 | 18 | 48 | 79 | 84 | 89 | 66 | 43 | 31 | 18 | 10 | 508 |
| 17 m | 21 | 21 | 20 | 17 | 14 | 13 | 12 | 13 | 14 | 16 | 18 | 19 | 17 |
| **Johannesburg, S. Africa** | 114 | 109 | 89 | 38 | 25 | 8 | 8 | 8 | 23 | 56 | 107 | 125 | 709 |
| 1,665 m | 20 | 20 | 18 | 16 | 13 | 10 | 11 | 13 | 16 | 18 | 19 | 20 | 16 |
| **Khartoum, Sudan** | <3 | <3 | <3 | <3 | 3 | 8 | 53 | 71 | 18 | 5 | <3 | 0 | 158 |
| 390 m | 24 | 25 | 28 | 31 | 33 | 34 | 32 | 31 | 32 | 32 | 28 | 25 | 29 |
| **Kinshasa, Zaïre** | 135 | 145 | 196 | 196 | 158 | 8 | 3 | 3 | 31 | 119 | 221 | 142 | 1,354 |
| 325 m | 26 | 26 | 27 | 27 | 26 | 24 | 23 | 24 | 25 | 26 | 26 | 26 | 25 |
| **Lagos, Nigeria** | 28 | 46 | 102 | 150 | 269 | 460 | 279 | 64 | 140 | 206 | 69 | 25 | 1,836 |
| 3 m | 27 | 28 | 29 | 28 | 28 | 26 | 26 | 25 | 26 | 26 | 28 | 28 | 27 |
| **Lusaka, Zambia** | 231 | 191 | 142 | 18 | 3 | <3 | <3 | 0 | <3 | 10 | 91 | 150 | 836 |
| 1,277 m | 21 | 22 | 21 | 21 | 19 | 16 | 16 | 18 | 22 | 24 | 23 | 22 | 21 |
| **Monrovia, Liberia** | 31 | 56 | 97 | 216 | 516 | 973 | 996 | 373 | 744 | 772 | 236 | 130 | 5,138 |
| 23 m | 26 | 26 | 27 | 27 | 26 | 25 | 24 | 25 | 25 | 25 | 26 | 26 | 26 |
| **Nairobi, Kenya** | 38 | 64 | 125 | 211 | 158 | 46 | 15 | 23 | 31 | 53 | 109 | 86 | 958 |
| 1,820 m | 19 | 19 | 19 | 19 | 18 | 16 | 16 | 16 | 18 | 19 | 18 | 18 | 18 |
| **Timbuktu, Mali** | <3 | <3 | 3 | <3 | 5 | 23 | 79 | 81 | 38 | 3 | <3 | <3 | 231 |
| 301 m | 22 | 24 | 28 | 32 | 34 | 35 | 32 | 30 | 32 | 31 | 28 | 23 | 29 |
| **Tunis, Tunisia** | 64 | 51 | 41 | 36 | 18 | 8 | 3 | 8 | 33 | 51 | 48 | 61 | 419 |
| 66 m | 10 | 11 | 13 | 16 | 19 | 23 | 26 | 27 | 25 | 20 | 16 | 11 | 18 |
| **Walvis Bay, Namibia** | <3 | 5 | 8 | 3 | 3 | <3 | <3 | 3 | <3 | <3 | <3 | <3 | 23 |
| 7 m | 19 | 19 | 19 | 18 | 17 | 16 | 15 | 14 | 14 | 15 | 17 | 18 | 18 |

| AUSTRALIA, NEW ZEALAND AND ANTARCTICA | Jan. | Feb. | Mar. | Apr. | May | June | July | Aug. | Sept. | Oct. | Nov. | Dec. | Year |
|---|---|---|---|---|---|---|---|---|---|---|---|---|---|
| **Alice Springs, Australia** | 43 | 33 | 28 | 10 | 15 | 13 | 8 | 8 | 8 | 18 | 31 | 38 | 252 |
| 579 m | 29 | 28 | 25 | 20 | 15 | 12 | 12 | 14 | 18 | 23 | 26 | 28 | 21 |
| **Christchurch, N. Zealand** | 56 | 43 | 48 | 48 | 66 | 66 | 69 | 48 | 46 | 43 | 48 | 56 | 638 |
| 10 m | 16 | 16 | 14 | 12 | 9 | 6 | 6 | 7 | 9 | 12 | 14 | 16 | 11 |
| **Darwin, Australia** | 386 | 312 | 254 | 97 | 15 | 3 | <3 | 3 | 13 | 51 | 119 | 239 | 1,491 |
| 30 m | 29 | 29 | 29 | 29 | 28 | 26 | 25 | 26 | 28 | 29 | 30 | 29 | 28 |
| **Mawson, Antarctica** | 11 | 30 | 20 | 10 | 44 | 180 | 4 | 40 | 3 | 20 | 0 | 0 | 362 |
| 14 m | 0 | -5 | -10 | -14 | -15 | -16 | -18 | -18 | -19 | -13 | -5 | -1 | -11 |
| **Perth, Australia** | 8 | 10 | 20 | 43 | 130 | 180 | 170 | 149 | 86 | 56 | 20 | 13 | 881 |
| 60 m | 23 | 23 | 22 | 19 | 16 | 14 | 13 | 13 | 15 | 16 | 19 | 22 | 18 |
| **Sydney, Australia** | 89 | 102 | 127 | 135 | 127 | 117 | 117 | 76 | 73 | 71 | 73 | 73 | 1,181 |
| 42 m | 22 | 22 | 21 | 18 | 15 | 13 | 12 | 13 | 15 | 18 | 19 | 21 | 17 |

| NORTH AMERICA | Jan. | Feb. | Mar. | Apr. | May | June | July | Aug. | Sept. | Oct. | Nov. | Dec. | Year |
|---|---|---|---|---|---|---|---|---|---|---|---|---|---|
| **Anchorage, Alaska, USA** | 20 | 18 | 15 | 10 | 13 | 18 | 41 | 66 | 66 | 56 | 25 | 23 | 371 |
| 40 m | -11 | -8 | -5 | 2 | 7 | 12 | 14 | 13 | 9 | 2 | -5 | -11 | 2 |
| **Chicago, Ill., USA** | 51 | 51 | 66 | 71 | 86 | 89 | 84 | 81 | 79 | 66 | 61 | 51 | 836 |
| 251 m | -4 | -3 | 2 | 9 | 14 | 20 | 23 | 22 | 19 | 12 | 5 | -1 | 10 |
| **Churchill, Man., Canada** | 15 | 13 | 18 | 23 | 32 | 44 | 46 | 58 | 51 | 43 | 39 | 21 | 402 |
| 13 m | -28 | -26 | -20 | -10 | -2 | 6 | 12 | 11 | 5 | -2 | -12 | -22 | -7 |
| **Edmonton, Alta., Canada** | 25 | 19 | 19 | 22 | 43 | 77 | 89 | 78 | 39 | 17 | 16 | 25 | 466 |
| 676 m | -15 | -10 | -5 | 4 | 11 | 15 | 17 | 16 | 11 | 6 | -4 | -10 | 3 |
| **Honolulu, Hawaii, USA** | 104 | 66 | 79 | 48 | 25 | 18 | 23 | 28 | 36 | 48 | 64 | 104 | 643 |
| 12 m | 23 | 18 | 19 | 20 | 22 | 24 | 25 | 26 | 26 | 24 | 22 | 19 | 22 |
| **Houston, Tex., USA** | 89 | 76 | 84 | 91 | 119 | 117 | 99 | 99 | 104 | 94 | 89 | 109 | 1,171 |
| 12 m | 12 | 13 | 17 | 21 | 24 | 27 | 28 | 29 | 26 | 22 | 16 | 12 | 21 |
| **Kingston, Jamaica** | 23 | 15 | 23 | 31 | 102 | 89 | 38 | 91 | 99 | 180 | 74 | 36 | 800 |
| 34 m | 25 | 25 | 25 | 26 | 26 | 28 | 28 | 28 | 27 | 27 | 26 | 26 | 26 |
| **Los Angeles, Calif., USA** | 79 | 76 | 71 | 25 | 10 | 3 | <3 | <3 | 5 | 15 | 31 | 66 | 381 |
| 95 m | 13 | 14 | 14 | 16 | 17 | 19 | 21 | 22 | 21 | 18 | 16 | 14 | 17 |
| **Mexico City, Mexico** | 13 | 5 | 10 | 20 | 53 | 119 | 170 | 152 | 130 | 51 | 18 | 8 | 747 |
| 2,309 m | 12 | 13 | 16 | 18 | 19 | 19 | 17 | 18 | 18 | 16 | 14 | 13 | 16 |
| **Miami, Fla., USA** | 71 | 53 | 64 | 81 | 173 | 178 | 155 | 160 | 203 | 234 | 71 | 51 | 1,516 |
| 8 m | 20 | 20 | 22 | 23 | 25 | 27 | 28 | 28 | 27 | 25 | 22 | 21 | 24 |
| **Montréal, Que., Canada** | 72 | 65 | 74 | 74 | 66 | 82 | 90 | 92 | 88 | 76 | 81 | 87 | 946 |
| 57 m | -10 | -9 | -3 | -6 | 13 | 18 | 21 | 20 | 15 | 9 | 2 | -7 | 6 |
| **New York, N.Y., USA** | 94 | 97 | 91 | 81 | 81 | 84 | 107 | 109 | 86 | 89 | 76 | 91 | 1,092 |
| 96 m | -1 | -1 | 3 | 10 | 16 | 20 | 23 | 23 | 21 | 15 | 7 | 2 | 11 |
| **St Louis, Mo., USA** | 58 | 64 | 89 | 97 | 114 | 114 | 89 | 86 | 81 | 74 | 71 | 64 | 1,001 |
| 173 m | 0 | 1 | 7 | 13 | 19 | 24 | 26 | 26 | 22 | 15 | 8 | 2 | 14 |
| **San José, Costa Rica** | 15 | 5 | 20 | 46 | 229 | 241 | 211 | 241 | 305 | 300 | 145 | 41 | 1,798 |
| 1,146 m | 19 | 19 | 21 | 21 | 22 | 21 | 21 | 21 | 21 | 20 | 20 | 19 | 20 |
| **Vancouver, B.C., Canada** | 154 | 115 | 101 | 60 | 52 | 45 | 32 | 41 | 67 | 114 | 150 | 182 | 1,113 |
| 14 m | 3 | 5 | 6 | 9 | 12 | 15 | 17 | 17 | 14 | 10 | 6 | 4 | 10 |
| **Washington, D.C., USA** | 86 | 76 | 91 | 84 | 94 | 99 | 112 | 109 | 94 | 74 | 66 | 79 | 1,064 |
| 22 m | 1 | 2 | 7 | 12 | 18 | 23 | 25 | 24 | 20 | 14 | 8 | 3 | 13 |

| SOUTH AMERICA | Jan. | Feb. | Mar. | Apr. | May | June | July | Aug. | Sept. | Oct. | Nov. | Dec. | Year |
|---|---|---|---|---|---|---|---|---|---|---|---|---|---|
| **Antofagasta, Chile** | 0 | 0 | 0 | <3 | <3 | 3 | 5 | 3 | <3 | 3 | <3 | 0 | 13 |
| 94 m | 21 | 21 | 20 | 18 | 16 | 15 | 14 | 14 | 15 | 16 | 18 | 19 | 17 |
| **Buenos Aires, Argentina** | 79 | 71 | 109 | 89 | 76 | 61 | 56 | 61 | 79 | 86 | 84 | 99 | 950 |
| 27 m | 23 | 23 | 21 | 17 | 13 | 9 | 10 | 11 | 13 | 15 | 19 | 22 | 16 |
| **Lima, Peru** | 3 | <3 | <3 | <3 | 5 | 5 | 8 | 8 | 8 | 3 | 3 | <3 | 41 |
| 120 m | 23 | 24 | 24 | 22 | 19 | 17 | 17 | 16 | 17 | 18 | 19 | 21 | 20 |
| **Manaus, Brazil** | 249 | 231 | 262 | 221 | 170 | 84 | 58 | 38 | 46 | 107 | 142 | 203 | 1,811 |
| 44 m | 28 | 28 | 28 | 27 | 28 | 28 | 28 | 28 | 29 | 29 | 29 | 28 | 28 |
| **Paraná, Brazil** | 287 | 236 | 239 | 102 | 13 | <3 | 3 | 5 | 28 | 127 | 231 | 310 | 1,582 |
| 260 m | 23 | 23 | 23 | 23 | 23 | 21 | 21 | 22 | 24 | 24 | 24 | 23 | 23 |
| **Rio de Janeiro, Brazil** | 125 | 122 | 130 | 107 | 79 | 53 | 41 | 43 | 66 | 79 | 104 | 137 | 1,082 |
| 61 m | 26 | 26 | 25 | 24 | 22 | 21 | 21 | 21 | 21 | 22 | 23 | 25 | 23 |

# WORLD STATISTICS: PHYSICAL DIMENSIONS

Each topic list is divided into continents and within a continent the items are listed in order of size. The order of the continents is as in the atlas, Europe through to South America. Certain lists down to this mark > are complete; below they are selective. The world top ten are shown in square brackets; in the case of mountains this has not been done because the world top 30 are all in Asia. The figures are rounded as appropriate.

## WORLD, CONTINENTS, OCEANS

|  | km² | miles² | % |
|---|---|---|---|
| The World | 509,450,000 | 196,672,000 | – |
| Land | 149,450,000 | 57,688,000 | 29.3 |
| Water | 360,000,000 | 138,984,000 | 70.7 |
| Asia | 44,500,000 | 17,177,000 | 29.8 |
| Africa | 30,302,000 | 11,697,000 | 20.3 |
| North America | 24,241,000 | 9,357,000 | 16.2 |
| South America | 17,793,000 | 6,868,000 | 11.9 |
| Antarctica | 14,100,000 | 5,443,000 | 9.4 |
| Europe | 9,957,000 | 3,843,000 | 6.7 |
| Australia & Oceania | 8,557,000 | 3,303,000 | 5.7 |
| Pacific Ocean | 179,679,000 | 69,356,000 | 49.9 |
| Atlantic Ocean | 92,373,000 | 35,657,000 | 25.7 |
| Indian Ocean | 73,917,000 | 28,532,000 | 20.5 |
| Arctic Ocean | 14,090,000 | 5,439,000 | 3.9 |

## SEAS

**Pacific**

|  | km² | miles² |
|---|---|---|
| South China Sea | 2,974,600 | 1,148,500 |
| Bering Sea | 2,268,000 | 875,000 |
| Sea of Okhotsk | 1,528,000 | 590,000 |
| East China & Yellow | 1,249,000 | 482,000 |
| Sea of Japan | 1,008,000 | 389,000 |
| Gulf of California | 162,000 | 62,500 |
| Bass Strait | 75,000 | 29,000 |

**Atlantic**

|  | km² | miles² |
|---|---|---|
| Caribbean Sea | 2,766,000 | 1,068,000 |
| Mediterranean Sea | 2,516,000 | 971,000 |
| Gulf of Mexico | 1,543,000 | 596,000 |
| Hudson Bay | 1,232,000 | 476,000 |
| North Sea | 575,000 | 223,000 |
| Black Sea | 462,000 | 178,000 |
| Baltic Sea | 422,170 | 163,000 |
| Gulf of St Lawrence | 238,000 | 92,000 |

**Indian**

|  | km² | miles² |
|---|---|---|
| Red Sea | 438,000 | 169,000 |
| The Gulf | 239,000 | 92,000 |

## MOUNTAINS

**Europe**

|  |  | m | ft |
|---|---|---|---|
| Mont Blanc | France/Italy | 4,807 | 15,771 |
| Monte Rosa | Italy/Switzerland | 4,634 | 15,203 |
| Dom | Switzerland | 4,545 | 14,911 |
| Weisshorn | Switzerland | 4,505 | 14,780 |
| Matterhorn/Cervino | Italy/Switzerland | 4,478 | 14,691 |
| Mt Maudit | France/Italy | 4,465 | 14,649 |
| Finsteraarhorn | Switzerland | 4,274 | 14,022 |
| Aletschhorn | Switzerland | 4,182 | 13,720 |
| Jungfrau | Switzerland | 4,158 | 13,642 |
| Barre des Ecrins | France | 4,103 | 13,461 |
| Schreckhorn | Switzerland | 4,078 | 13,380 |
| Gran Paradiso | Italy | 4,061 | 13,323 |
| Piz Bernina | Italy/Switzerland | 4,049 | 13,284 |
| Ortles | Italy | 3,899 | 12,792 |
| Monte Viso | Italy | 3,841 | 12,602 |
| Grossglockner | Austria | 3,797 | 12,457 |
| Wildspitze | Austria | 3,774 | 12,382 |
| Weisskügel | Austria/Italy | 3,736 | 12,257 |
| Balmhorn | Switzerland | 3,709 | 12,169 |
| Dammastock | Switzerland | 3,630 | 11,909 |
| Tödi | Switzerland | 3,620 | 11,877 |
| Presanella | Italy | 3,556 | 11,667 |
| Monte Adamello | Italy | 3,554 | 11,660 |
| Mulhacén | Spain | 3,478 | 11,411 |
| Pico de Aneto | Spain | 3,404 | 11,168 |
| Posets | Spain | 3,375 | 11,073 |
| Marmolada | Italy | 3,342 | 10,964 |
| Etna | Italy | 3,340 | 10,958 |
| Musala | Bulgaria | 2,925 | 9,596 |
| Olympus | Greece | 2,917 | 9,570 |
| Gerlachovka | Slovak Republic | 2,655 | 8,711 |
| Galdhöpiggen | Norway | 2,469 | 8,100 |
| Pietrosul | Romania | 2,305 | 7,562 |
| Hvannadalshnúkur | Iceland | 2,119 | 6,952 |
| Narodnaya | Russia | 1,894 | 6,214 |
| Ben Nevis | UK | 1,343 | 4,406 |

**Asia**

|  |  | m | ft |
|---|---|---|---|
| Everest | China/Nepal | 8,848 | 29,029 |
| Godwin Austen (K2) | China/Kashmir | 8,611 | 28,251 |
| Kanchenjunga | India/Nepal | 8,598 | 28,208 |
| Lhotse | China/Nepal | 8,516 | 27,939 |
| Makalu | China/Nepal | 8,481 | 27,824 |
| Cho Oyu | China/Nepal | 8,201 | 26,906 |
| Dhaulagiri | Nepal | 8,172 | 26,811 |
| Manaslu | Nepal | 8,156 | 26,758 |
| Nanga Parbat | Kashmir | 8,126 | 26,660 |
| Annapurna | Nepal | 8,078 | 26,502 |
| Gasherbrum | China/Kashmir | 8,068 | 26,469 |
| Broad Peak | India | 8,051 | 26,414 |
| Gosainthan | China | 8,012 | 26,286 |
| Disteghil Sar | Kashmir | 7,885 | 25,869 |
| Nuptse | Nepal | 7,879 | 25,849 |
| Masherbrum | Kashmir | 7,821 | 25,659 |
| Nanda Devi | India | 7,817 | 25,646 |
| Rakaposhi | Kashmir | 7,788 | 25,551 |
| Kanjut Sar | India | 7,760 | 25,459 |
| Kamet | India | 7,756 | 25,446 |
| Namcha Barwa | China | 7,756 | 25,446 |
| Gurla Mandhata | China | 7,728 | 25,354 |
| Muztag | China | 7,723 | 25,338 |
| Kongur Shan | China | 7,719 | 25,324 |
| Tirich Mir | Pakistan | 7,690 | 25,229 |
| Saser | Kashmir | 7,672 | 25,170 |
| K'ula Shan | Bhutan/China | 7,543 | 24,747 |
| Pik Kommunizma | Tajikistan | 7,495 | 24,590 |
| Aling Gangri | China | 7,314 | 23,996 |
| Elbrus | Russia | 5,633 | 18,481 |
| Demavend | Iran | 5,604 | 18,386 |
| Ararat | Turkey | 5,165 | 16,945 |
| Gunong Kinabalu | Malaysia (Borneo) | 4,101 | 13,455 |
| Yu Shan | Taiwan | 3,997 | 13,113 |
| Fuji-san | Japan | 3,776 | 12,388 |
| Rinjani | Indonesia | 3,726 | 12,224 |
| Mt Rajang | Philippines | 3,364 | 11,037 |
| Pidurutalagala | Sri Lanka | 2,524 | 8,281 |

**Africa**

|  |  | m | ft |
|---|---|---|---|
| Kilimanjaro | Tanzania | 5,895 | 19,340 |
| Mt Kenya | Kenya | 5,199 | 17,057 |
| Ruwenzori | Uganda/Zaïre | 5,109 | 16,762 |
| Ras Dashan | Ethiopia | 4,620 | 15,157 |
| Meru | Tanzania | 4,565 | 14,977 |
| Karisimbi | Rwanda/Zaïre | 4,507 | 14,787 |
| Mt Elgon | Kenya/Uganda | 4,321 | 14,176 |
| Batu | Ethiopia | 4,307 | 14,130 |
| Guna | Ethiopia | 4,231 | 13,882 |
| Toubkal | Morocco | 4,165 | 13,665 |
| Irhil Mgoun | Morocco | 4,071 | 13,356 |
| Mt Cameroon | Cameroon | 4,070 | 13,353 |
| Amba Ferit | Ethiopia | 3,875 | 13,042 |
| Teide | Spain (Tenerife) | 3,718 | 12,198 |
| Thabana Ntlenyana | Lesotho | 3,482 | 11,424 |
| Emi Kussi | Chad | 3,415 | 11,204 |
| Mt aux Sources | Lesotho/S. Africa | 3,282 | 10,768 |
| Mt Piton | Réunion | 3,069 | 10,069 |

**Oceania**

|  |  | m | ft |
|---|---|---|---|
| Puncak Jaya | Indonesia | 5,029 | 16,499 |
| Puncak Trikora | Indonesia | 4,750 | 15,584 |
| Puncak Mandala | Indonesia | 4,702 | 15,427 |
| Mt Wilhelm | Papua New Guinea | 4,508 | 14,790 |
| Mauna Kea | USA (Hawaii) | 4,205 | 13,796 |
| Mauna Loa | USA (Hawaii) | 4,170 | 13,681 |
| Mt Cook | New Zealand | 3,753 | 12,313 |
| Mt Balbi | Solomon Is. | 2,439 | 8,002 |
| Orohena | Tahiti | 2,241 | 7,352 |
| Mt Kosciusko | Australia | 2,237 | 7,339 |

**North America**

|  |  | m | ft |
|---|---|---|---|
| Mt McKinley | USA (Alaska) | 6,194 | 20,321 |
| Mt Logan | Canada | 5,959 | 19,551 |
| Citlaltepetl | Mexico | 5,700 | 18,701 |
| Mt St Elias | USA/Canada | 5,489 | 18,008 |
| Popocatepetl | Mexico | 5,452 | 17,887 |
| Mt Foraker | USA (Alaska) | 5,304 | 17,401 |
| Ixtaccihuatl | Mexico | 5,286 | 17,342 |
| Lucania | Canada | 5,227 | 17,149 |
| Mt Steele | Canada | 5,073 | 16,644 |
| Mt Bona | USA (Alaska) | 5,005 | 16,420 |
| Mt Blackburn | USA (Alaska) | 4,996 | 16,391 |
| Mt Sanford | USA (Alaska) | 4,940 | 16,207 |
| Mt Wood | Canada | 4,848 | 15,905 |
| Nevado de Toluca | Mexico | 4,670 | 15,321 |
| Mt Fairweather | USA (Alaska) | 4,663 | 15,298 |
| Mt Whitney | USA | 4,418 | 14,495 |
| Mt Elbert | USA | 4,399 | 14,432 |
| Mt Harvard | USA | 4,395 | 14,419 |
| Mt Rainier | USA | 4,392 | 14,409 |
| Blanca Peak | USA | 4,372 | 14,344 |
| Long's Peak | USA | 4,345 | 14,255 |
| Nevado de Colima | Mexico | 4,339 | 14,235 |
| Mt Shasta | USA | 4,317 | 14,163 |
| Tajumulco | Guatemala | 4,220 | 13,845 |
| Gannett Peak | USA | 4,202 | 13,786 |
| Mt Waddington | Canada | 3,994 | 13,104 |
| Mt Robson | Canada | 3,954 | 12,972 |
| Chirripó Grande | Costa Rica | 3,837 | 12,589 |
| Pico Duarte | Dominican Rep. | 3,175 | 10,417 |

**South America**

|  |  | m | ft |
|---|---|---|---|
| Aconcagua | Argentina | 6,960 | 22,834 |
| Illimani | Bolivia | 6,882 | 22,578 |
| Bonete | Argentina | 6,872 | 22,546 |
| Ojos del Salado | Argentina/Chile | 6,863 | 22,516 |
| Tupungato | Argentina/Chile | 6,800 | 22,309 |
| Pissis | Argentina | 6,779 | 22,241 |
| Mercedario | Argentina/Chile | 6,770 | 22,211 |
| Huascaran | Peru | 6,768 | 22,204 |
| Llullaillaco | Argentina/Chile | 6,723 | 22,057 |
| Nudo de Cachi | Argentina | 6,720 | 22,047 |
| Yerupaja | Peru | 6,632 | 21,758 |
| N. de Tres Cruces | Argentina/Chile | 6,620 | 21,719 |
| Incahuasi | Argentina/Chile | 6,600 | 21,654 |
| Ancohuma | Bolivia | 6,550 | 21,489 |
| Sajama | Bolivia | 6,520 | 21,391 |
| Coropuna | Peru | 6,425 | 21,079 |
| Ausangate | Peru | 6,384 | 20,945 |
| Cerro del Toro | Argentina | 6,380 | 20,932 |
| Ampato | Peru | 6,310 | 20,702 |
| Chimborasso | Ecuador | 6,267 | 20,561 |
| Cotopaxi | Ecuador | 5,896 | 19,344 |
| S. Nev. de S. Marta | Colombia | 5,800 | 19,029 |
| Cayambe | Ecuador | 5,796 | 19,016 |
| Pico Bolivar | Venezuela | 5,007 | 16,427 |

**Antarctica**

|  | m | ft |
|---|---|---|
| Vinson Massif | 4,897 | 16,066 |
| Mt Kirkpatrick | 4,528 | 14,855 |
| Mt Markham | 4,349 | 14,268 |

## OCEAN DEPTHS

**Atlantic Ocean**

|  | m | ft |  |
|---|---|---|---|
| Puerto Rico (Milwaukee) Deep | 9,220 | 30,249 | [7] |
| Cayman Trench | 7,680 | 25,197 | [10] |
| Gulf of Mexico | 5,203 | 17,070 | |
| Mediterranean Sea | 5,121 | 16,801 | |
| Black Sea | 2,211 | 7,254 | |
| North Sea | 660 | 2,165 | |
| Baltic Sea | 463 | 1,519 | |
| Hudson Bay | 258 | 846 | |

**Indian Ocean**

|  | m | ft |
|---|---|---|
| Java Trench | 7,450 | 24,442 |
| Red Sea | 2,635 | 8,454 |
| Persian Gulf | 73 | 239 |

**Pacific Ocean**

|  | m | ft |  |
|---|---|---|---|
| Mariana Trench | 11,022 | 36,161 | [1] |
| Tonga Trench | 10,882 | 35,702 | [2] |
| Japan Trench | 10,554 | 34,626 | [3] |
| Kuril Trench | 10,542 | 34,587 | [4] |
| Mindanao Trench | 10,497 | 34,439 | [5] |
| Kermadec Trench | 10,047 | 32,962 | [6] |
| Peru-Chile Trench | 8,050 | 26,410 | [8] |
| Aleutian Trench | 7,822 | 25,662 | [9] |
| Middle American Trench | 6,662 | 21,857 | |

**Arctic Ocean**

|  | m | ft |
|---|---|---|
| Molloy Deep | 5,608 | 18,399 |

## LAND LOWS

|  |  | m | ft |
|---|---|---|---|
| Caspian Sea | Europe | −28 | −92 |
| Dead Sea | Asia | −400 | −1,312 |
| Lake Assal | Africa | −156 | −512 |
| Lake Eyre North | Oceania | −16 | −52 |
| Death Valley | N. America | −86 | −282 |
| Valdés Peninsula | S. America | −40 | −131 |

# RIVERS

### Europe

| | | km | miles |
|---|---|---|---|
| Volga | Caspian Sea | 3,700 | 2,300 |
| Danube | Black Sea | 2,850 | 1,770 |
| Ural | Caspian Sea | 2,535 | 1,574 |
| Dnepr | Volga | 2,285 | 1,420 |
| Kama | Volga | 2,030 | 1,260 |
| Don | Volga | 1,990 | 1,240 |
| Petchora | Arctic Ocean | 1,790 | 1,110 |
| Oka | Volga | 1,480 | 920 |
| Belaya | Kama | 1,420 | 880 |
| Dnestr | Black Sea | 1,400 | 870 |
| Vyatka | Kama | 1,370 | 850 |
| Rhine | North Sea | 1,320 | 820 |
| N. Dvina | Arctic Ocean | 1,290 | 800 |
| Desna | Dnieper | 1,190 | 740 |
| Elbe | North Sea | 1,145 | 710 |
| Vistula | Baltic Sea | 1,090 | 675 |
| Loire | Atlantic Ocean | 1,020 | 635 |
| W. Dvina | Baltic Sea | 1,019 | 633 |

### Asia

| | | km | miles |
|---|---|---|---|
| Yangtze | Pacific Ocean | 6,380 | 3,960 [3] |
| Yenisey-Angara | Arctic Ocean | 5,550 | 3,445 [5] |
| Huang He | Pacific Ocean | 5,464 | 3,395 [6] |
| Ob-Irtysh | Arctic Ocean | 5,410 | 3,360 [7] |
| Mekong | Pacific Ocean | 4,500 | 2,795 [9] |
| Amur | Pacific Ocean | 4,400 | 2,730 [10] |
| Lena | Arctic Ocean | 4,400 | 2,730 |
| Irtysh | Ob | 4,250 | 2,640 |
| Yenisey | Arctic Ocean | 4,090 | 2,540 |
| Ob | Arctic Ocean | 3,680 | 2,285 |
| Indus | Indian Ocean | 3,100 | 1,925 |
| Brahmaputra | Indian Ocean | 2,900 | 1,800 |
| Syr Darya | Aral Sea | 2,860 | 1,775 |
| Salween | Indian Ocean | 2,800 | 1,740 |
| Euphrates | Indian Ocean | 2,700 | 1,675 |
| Vilyuy | Lena | 2,650 | 1,645 |
| Kolyma | Arctic Ocean | 2,600 | 1,615 |
| Amu Darya | Aral Sea | 2,540 | 1,575 |
| Ural | Caspian Sea | 2,535 | 1,575 |
| Ganges | Indian Ocean | 2,510 | 1,560 |
| Si Kiang | Pacific Ocean | 2,100 | 1,305 |
| Irrawaddy | Indian Ocean | 2,010 | 1,250 |
| Tarim-Yarkand | Lop Nor | 2,000 | 1,240 |
| Tigris | Indian Ocean | 1,900 | 1,180 |
| Angara | Yenisey | 1,830 | 1,135 |
| Godavari | Indian Ocean | 1,470 | 915 |
| Sutlej | Indian Ocean | 1,450 | 900 |
| Yamuna | Indian Ocean | 1,400 | 870 |

### Africa

| | | km | miles |
|---|---|---|---|
| Nile | Mediterranean | 6,670 | 4,140 [1] |
| Zaïre/Congo | Atlantic Ocean | 4,670 | 2,900 [8] |
| Niger | Atlantic Ocean | 4,180 | 2,595 |
| Zambezi | Indian Ocean | 3,540 | 2,200 |
| Oubangi/Uele | Zaïre | 2,250 | 1,400 |
| Kasai | Zaïre | 1,950 | 1,210 |
| Shaballe | Indian Ocean | 1,930 | 1,200 |
| Orange | Atlantic Ocean | 1,860 | 1,155 |
| Cubango | Okavango Swamps | 1,800 | 1,120 |
| Limpopo | Indian Ocean | 1,600 | 995 |
| Senegal | Atlantic Ocean | 1,600 | 995 |
| Volta | Atlantic Ocean | 1,500 | 930 |
| Benue | Niger | 1,350 | 840 |

### Australia

| | | km | miles |
|---|---|---|---|
| Murray-Darling | Indian Ocean | 3,750 | 2,330 |
| Darling | Murray | 3,070 | 1,905 |
| Murray | Indian Ocean | 2,575 | 1,600 |
| Murrumbidgee | Murray | 1,690 | 1,050 |

### North America

| | | km | miles |
|---|---|---|---|
| Mississippi-Missouri | Gulf of Mexico | 6,020 | 3,740 [4] |
| Mackenzie | Arctic Ocean | 4,240 | 2,630 |
| Mississippi | Gulf of Mexico | 3,780 | 2,350 |
| Missouri | Mississippi | 3,780 | 2,350 |
| Yukon | Pacific Ocean | 3,185 | 1,980 |
| Rio Grande | Gulf of Mexico | 3,030 | 1,880 |
| Arkansas | Mississippi | 2,340 | 1,450 |
| Colorado | Pacific Ocean | 2,330 | 1,445 |
| Red | Mississippi | 2,040 | 1,270 |
| Columbia | Pacific Ocean | 1,950 | 1,210 |
| Saskatchewan | Lake Winnipeg | 1,940 | 1,205 |
| Snake | Columbia | 1,670 | 1,040 |
| Churchill | Hudson Bay | 1,600 | 990 |
| Ohio | Mississippi | 1,580 | 980 |
| Brazos | Gulf of Mexico | 1,400 | 870 |
| St Lawrence | Atlantic Ocean | 1,170 | 730 |

# South America

| | | km | miles |
|---|---|---|---|
| Amazon | Atlantic Ocean | 6,450 | 4,010 [2] |
| Paraná-Plate | Atlantic Ocean | 4,500 | 2,800 |
| Purus | Amazon | 3,350 | 2,080 |
| Madeira | Amazon | 3,200 | 1,990 |
| São Francisco | Atlantic Ocean | 2,900 | 1,800 |
| Paraná | Plate | 2,800 | 1,740 |
| Tocantins | Atlantic Ocean | 2,750 | 1,710 |
| Paraguay | Paraná | 2,550 | 1,580 |
| Orinoco | Atlantic Ocean | 2,500 | 1,550 |
| Pilcomayo | Paraná | 2,500 | 1,550 |
| Araguaia | Tocantins | 2,250 | 1,400 |
| Juruá | Amazon | 2,000 | 1,240 |
| Xingu | Amazon | 1,980 | 1,230 |
| Ucayali | Amazon | 1,900 | 1,180 |
| Marañón | Amazon | 1,600 | 990 |
| Uruguay | Plate | 1,600 | 990 |
| Magdalena | Caribbean Sea | 1,540 | 960 |

# LAKES

### Europe

| | | km² | miles² |
|---|---|---|---|
| Lake Ladoga | Russia | 17,700 | 6,800 |
| Lake Onega | Russia | 9,700 | 3,700 |
| Saimaa system | Finland | 8,000 | 3,100 |
| Vänern | Sweden | 5,500 | 2,100 |
| Rybinsk Res. | Russia | 4,700 | 1,800 |

### Asia

| | | km² | miles² |
|---|---|---|---|
| Caspian Sea | Asia | 371,800 | 143,550 [1] |
| Aral Sea | Kazakh./Uzbek. | 36,000 | 13,900 [6] |
| Lake Baykal | Russia | 30,500 | 11,780 [9] |
| Tonlé Sap | Cambodia | 20,000 | 7,700 |
| Lake Balkhash | Kazakhstan | 18,500 | 7,100 |
| Dongting Hu | China | 12,000 | 4,600 |
| Issyk Kul | Kirghizia | 6,200 | 2,400 |
| Lake Urmia | Iran | 5,900 | 2,300 |
| Koko Nur | China | 5,700 | 2,200 |
| Poyang Hu | China | 5,000 | 1,900 |
| Lake Khanka | China/Russia | 4,400 | 1,700 |
| Lake Van | Turkey | 3,500 | 1,400 |
| Ubsa Nur | China | 3,400 | 1,300 |

### Africa

| | | km² | miles² |
|---|---|---|---|
| Lake Victoria | E. Africa | 68,000 | 26,000 [3] |
| Lake Tanganyika | C. Africa | 33,000 | 13,000 [7] |
| Lake Malawi/Nyasa | E. Africa | 29,600 | 11,430 [10] |
| Lake Chad | C. Africa | 25,000 | 9,700 |
| Lake Turkana | Ethiopia/Kenya | 8,500 | 3,300 |
| Lake Volta | Ghana | 8,500 | 3,300 |
| Lake Bangweulu | Zambia | 8,000 | 3,100 |
| Lake Rukwa | Tanzania | 7,000 | 2,700 |
| Lake Mai-Ndombe | Zaïre | 6,500 | 2,500 |
| Lake Karíba | Zambia/Zimbabwe | 5,300 | 2,000 |
| Lake Mobutu | Uganda/Zaïre | 5,300 | 2,000 |
| Lake Nasser | Egypt/Sudan | 5,200 | 2,000 |
| Lake Mweru | Zambia/Zaïre | 4,900 | 1,900 |
| Lake Cabora Bassa | South Africa | 4,500 | 1,700 |
| Lake Kyoga | Uganda | 4,400 | 1,700 |
| Lake Tana | Ethiopia | 3,630 | 1,400 |
| Lake Kivu | Rwanda/Zaïre | 2,650 | 1,000 |
| Lake Edward | Uganda/Zaïre | 2,200 | 850 |

### Australia

| | | km² | miles² |
|---|---|---|---|
| Lake Eyre | Australia | 8,900 | 3,400 |
| Lake Torrens | Australia | 5,800 | 2,200 |
| Lake Gairdner | Australia | 4,800 | 1,900 |

### North America

| | | km² | miles² |
|---|---|---|---|
| Lake Superior | Canada/USA | 82,350 | 31,800 [2] |
| Lake Huron | Canada/USA | 59,600 | 23,010 [4] |
| Lake Michigan | USA | 58,000 | 22,400 [5] |
| Great Bear Lake | Canada | 31,800 | 12,280 [8] |
| Great Slave Lake | Canada | 28,500 | 11,000 |
| Lake Erie | Canada/USA | 25,700 | 9,900 |
| Lake Winnipeg | Canada | 24,400 | 9,400 |
| Lake Ontario | Canada/USA | 19,500 | 7,500 |
| Lake Nicaragua | Nicaragua | 8,200 | 3,200 |
| Lake Athabasca | Canada | 8,100 | 3,100 |
| Smallwood Res. | Canada | 6,530 | 2,520 |
| Reindeer Lake | Canada | 6,400 | 2,500 |
| Lake Winnipegosis | Canada | 5,400 | 2,100 |
| Nettilling Lake | Canada | 5,500 | 2,100 |
| Lake Nipigon | Canada | 4,850 | 1,900 |
| Lake Manitoba | Canada | 4,700 | 1,800 |

### South America

| | | km² | miles² |
|---|---|---|---|
| Lake Titicaca | Bolivia/Peru | 8,300 | 3,200 |
| Lake Poopo | Peru | 2,800 | 1,100 |

# ISLANDS

### Europe

| | | km² | miles² |
|---|---|---|---|
| Great Britain | UK | 229,880 | 88,700 [8] |
| Iceland | Atlantic Ocean | 103,000 | 39,800 |
| Ireland | Ireland/UK | 84,400 | 32,600 |
| Novaya Zemlya (N.) | Russia | 48,200 | 18,600 |
| W. Spitzbergen | Norway | 39,000 | 15,100 |
| Novaya Zemlya (S.) | Russia | 33,200 | 12,800 |
| Sicily | Italy | 25,500 | 9,800 |
| Sardinia | Italy | 24,000 | 9,300 |
| N. E. Spitzbergen | Norway | 15,000 | 5,600 |
| Corsica | France | 8,700 | 3,400 |
| Crete | Greece | 8,350 | 3,200 |
| Zealand | Denmark | 6,850 | 2,600 |

### Asia

| | | km² | miles² |
|---|---|---|---|
| Borneo | S. E. Asia | 744,360 | 287,400 [3] |
| Sumatra | Indonesia | 473,600 | 182,860 [6] |
| Honshu | Japan | 230,500 | 88,980 [7] |
| Celebes | Indonesia | 189,000 | 73,000 |
| Java | Indonesia | 126,700 | 48,900 |
| Luzon | Philippines | 104,700 | 40,400 |
| Mindanao | Philippines | 101,500 | 39,200 |
| Hokkaido | Japan | 78,400 | 30,300 |
| Sakhalin | Russia | 74,060 | 28,600 |
| Sri Lanka | Indian Ocean | 65,600 | 25,300 |
| Taiwan | Pacific Ocean | 36,000 | 13,900 |
| Kyushu | Japan | 35,700 | 13,800 |
| Hainan | China | 34,000 | 13,100 |
| Timor | Indonesia | 33,600 | 13,000 |
| Shikoku | Japan | 18,800 | 7,300 |
| Halmahera | Indonesia | 18,000 | 6,900 |
| Ceram | Indonesia | 17,150 | 6,600 |
| Sumbawa | Indonesia | 15,450 | 6,000 |
| Flores | Indonesia | 15,200 | 5,900 |
| Samar | Philippines | 13,100 | 5,100 |
| Negros | Philippines | 12,700 | 4,900 |
| Bangka | Indonesia | 12,000 | 4,600 |
| Palawan | Philippines | 12,000 | 4,600 |
| Panay | Philippines | 11,500 | 4,400 |
| Sumba | Indonesia | 11,100 | 4,300 |
| Mindoro | Philippines | 9,750 | 3,800 |
| Buru | Indonesia | 9,500 | 3,700 |
| Bali | Indonesia | 5,600 | 2,200 |
| Cyprus | Mediterranean | 3,570 | 1,400 |
| Wrangel Is. | Russia | 2,800 | 1,000 |

### Africa

| | | km² | miles² |
|---|---|---|---|
| Madagascar | Indian Ocean | 587,040 | 226,660 [4] |
| Socotra | Indian Ocean | 3,600 | 1,400 |
| Réunion | Indian Ocean | 2,500 | 965 |
| Tenerife | Atlantic Ocean | 2,350 | 900 |
| Mauritius | Indian Ocean | 1,865 | 720 |

### Oceania

| | | km² | miles² |
|---|---|---|---|
| New Guinea | Indon./Pap. NG | 821,030 | 317,000 [2] |
| New Zealand (S.) | New Zealand | 150,500 | 58,100 |
| New Zealand (N.) | New Zealand | 114,700 | 44,300 |
| Tasmania | Australia | 67,800 | 26,200 |
| New Britain | Papua NG | 37,800 | 14,600 |
| New Caledonia | Pacific Ocean | 19,100 | 7,400 |
| Viti Levu | Fiji | 10,500 | 4,100 |
| Hawaii | Pacific Ocean | 10,450 | 4,000 |
| Bougainville | Papua NG | 9,600 | 3,700 |
| Guadalcanal | Solomon Is. | 6,500 | 2,500 |
| Vanua Levu | Fiji | 5,550 | 2,100 |
| New Ireland | Papua NG | 3,200 | 1,200 |

### North America

| | | km² | miles² |
|---|---|---|---|
| Greenland | Greenland | 2,175,600 | 839,800 [1] |
| Baffin Is. | Canada | 508,000 | 196,100 [5] |
| Victoria Is. | Canada | 212,200 | 81,900 [9] |
| Ellesmere Is. | Canada | 212,000 | 81,800 [10] |
| Cuba | Cuba | 110,860 | 42,800 |
| Newfoundland | Canada | 110,680 | 42,700 |
| Hispaniola | Atlantic Ocean | 76,200 | 29,400 |
| Banks Is. | Canada | 67,000 | 25,900 |
| Devon Is. | Canada | 54,500 | 21,000 |
| Melville Is. | Canada | 42,400 | 16,400 |
| Vancouver Is. | Canada | 32,150 | 12,400 |
| Somerset Is. | Canada | 24,300 | 9,400 |
| Jamaica | Caribbean Sea | 11,400 | 4,400 |
| Puerto Rico | Atlantic Ocean | 8,900 | 3,400 |
| Cape Breton Is. | Canada | 4,000 | 1,500 |

### South America

| | | km² | miles² |
|---|---|---|---|
| Tierra del Fuego | Argentina/Chile | 47,000 | 18,100 |
| Falkland Is. (E.) | Atlantic Ocean | 6,800 | 2,600 |
| South Georgia | Atlantic Ocean | 4,200 | 1,600 |
| Galapagos (Isabela) | Pacific Ocean | 2,250 | 870 |

# INTRODUCTION TO WORLD GEOGRAPHY

# THE UNIVERSE

About 15,000 million years ago, time and space began with the most colossal explosion in cosmic history: the 'Big Bang' that initiated the universe. According to current theory, in the first millionth of a second of its existence it expanded from a dimensionless point of infinite mass and density into a fireball about 30,000 million kilometres across; and it has been expanding ever since.

It took almost a million years for the primal fireball to cool enough for atoms to form. They were mostly hydrogen, still the most abundant material in the universe. But the new matter was not evenly distributed around the young universe, and a few 1,000 million years later atoms in relatively dense regions began to cling together under the influence of gravity, forming distinct masses of gas separated by vast expanses of empty space. To begin with, these first proto-galaxies were dark places: the universe had cooled. But gravitational attraction continued, condensing matter into coherent lumps inside the galactic gas clouds. About 3,000 million years later, some of these masses had contracted so much that internal pressure produced the high temperatures necessary to bring about nuclear fusion: the first stars were born.

There were several generations of stars, each feeding on the wreckage of its extinct predecessors as well as the original galactic gas swirls. With each new generation, progressively larger atoms were forged in stellar furnaces and the galaxy's range of elements, once restricted to hydrogen, grew larger. About 10,000 million years after the Big Bang, a star formed on the outskirts of our galaxy with enough matter left over to create a retinue of planets. Nearly 5,000 million years after that, a few planetary atoms had evolved into structures of complex molecules that lived, breathed and eventually pointed telescopes at the sky.

They found that their Sun is just one of more than 100,000 million stars in the home galaxy alone. Our galaxy, in turn, forms part of a local group of 25 or so similar structures, some much larger than our own; there are at least 100 million other galaxies in the universe as a whole. The most distant ever observed, a highly energetic galactic core known only as Quasar PKS 2000–330, lies about 15,000 million light-years away.

## LIFE OF A STAR

For most of its existence, a star produces energy by the nuclear fusion of hydrogen into helium at its core. The duration of this hydrogen-burning period – known as the main sequence – depends on the star's mass; the greater the mass, the higher the core temperatures and the sooner the star's supply of hydrogen is exhausted. Dim, dwarf stars consume their hydrogen slowly, eking it out over 1,000 billion years or more. The Sun, like other stars of its mass, should spend about 10,000 million years on the main sequence; since it was formed less than 5,000 million years ago, it still has half its life left.

Once all a star's core hydrogen has been fused into helium, nuclear activity moves outwards into layers of unconsumed hydrogen. For a time, energy production sharply increases: the star grows hotter and expands enormously, turning into a so-called red giant. Its energy output will increase a thousandfold, and it will swell to a hundred times its present diameter.

After a few hundred million years, helium in the core will become sufficiently compressed to initiate a new cycle of nuclear fusion: from helium to carbon. The star will contract somewhat, before beginning its last expansion, in the Sun's case engulfing the Earth and perhaps Mars. In this bloated condition, the Sun's outer layers will break off into space, leaving a tiny inner core, mainly of carbon, that shrinks progressively under the force of its own gravity: dwarf stars can attain a density more than 10,000 times that of normal matter, with crushing surface gravities to match. Gradually, the nuclear fires will die down, and the Sun will reach its terminal stage: a black dwarf, emitting insignificant amounts of radiation.

However, stars more massive than the Sun may undergo another transformation. The additional mass allows gravitational collapse to continue indefinitely: eventually, all the star's remaining matter shrinks to a point, and its density approaches infinity – a state that will not permit even subatomic structures to survive.

The star has become a black hole: an anomalous 'singularity' in the fabric of space and time. Although vast coruscations of radiation will be emitted by any matter falling into its grasp, the singularity itself has an escape velocity that exceeds the speed of light, and nothing can ever be released from it. Within the boundaries of the black hole, the laws of physics are suspended, but no physicist can ever observe the extraordinary events that may occur.

## THE END OF THE UNIVERSE

The likely fate of the universe is disputed. One theory (top right) dictates that the expansion begun at the time of the Big Bang will continue 'indefinitely', with ageing galaxies moving further and further apart in an immense, dark graveyard. Alternatively, gravity may overcome the expansion (bottom right). Galaxies will fall back together until everything is again concentrated at a single point, followed by a new Big Bang and a new expansion, in an endlessly repeated cycle. The first theory is supported by the amount of visible matter in the universe; the second assumes there is enough dark material to bring about the gravitational collapse.

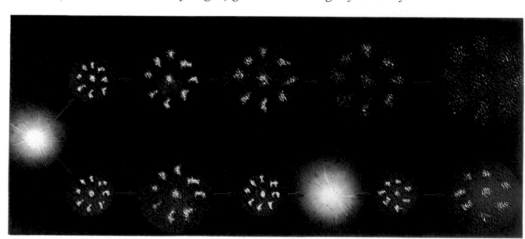

## GALACTIC STRUCTURES

The universe's 100 million galaxies show clear structural patterns, originally classified by the American astronomer Edwin Hubble in 1925. Spiral galaxies like our own (top row) have a central, almost spherical bulge and a surrounding disc composed of spiral arms. Barred spirals (bottom row) have a central bar of stars across the nucleus, with spiral arms trailing from the ends of the bar. Elliptical galaxies (far left) have a uniform appearance, ranging from a flattened disc to a near sphere. So-called SO galaxies (left row, right) have a central bulge, but no spiral arms. A few have no discernible structure at all. Galaxies also vary enormously in size, from dwarfs only 2,000 light-years across to great assemblies of stars 80 or more times larger.

## THE HOME GALAXY

The Sun and its planets are located in one of the spiral arms, a little less than 30,000 light-years from the galactic centre and orbiting around it in a period of more than 200 million years. The centre is invisible from the Earth, masked by vast, light-absorbing clouds of interstellar dust. The galaxy is probably around 12 billion years old and, like other spiral galaxies, has three distinct regions. The central bulge is about 30,000 light-years in diameter. The disc in which the Sun is located is not much more than 1,000 light-years thick but 100,000 light-years from end to end. Around the galaxy is the halo, a spherical zone 150,000 light-years across, studded with globular star-clusters and sprinkled with individual suns.

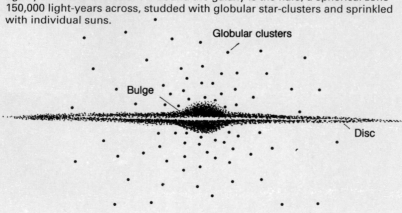

Globular clusters

Bulge

Disc

Solar System

Star charts are drawn as projections of a vast, hollow sphere with the observer in the middle. Each circle below represents one hemisphere, centred on the north and south celestial poles respectively – projections of the Earth's poles in the heavens. At the present era, the north pole is marked by the star Polaris; the south pole has no such convenient reference point. The rectangular map shows the stars immediately above and below the celestial equator.

Astronomical co-ordinates are normally given in terms of 'Right Ascension' for longitude and 'Declination' for latitude or altitude. Since the stars appear to rotate around the Earth once every 24 hours, Right Ascension is measured eastwards – anti-clockwise – in hours and minutes. One hour is equivalent to 15 angular degrees; zero on the scale is the point at which the Sun crosses the celestial equator at the spring equinox, known to astronomers as the First Point in Aries. Unlike the Sun, stars always rise and set at the same point on the horizon. Declination measures (in degrees) a star's angular distance above or below the celestial equator.

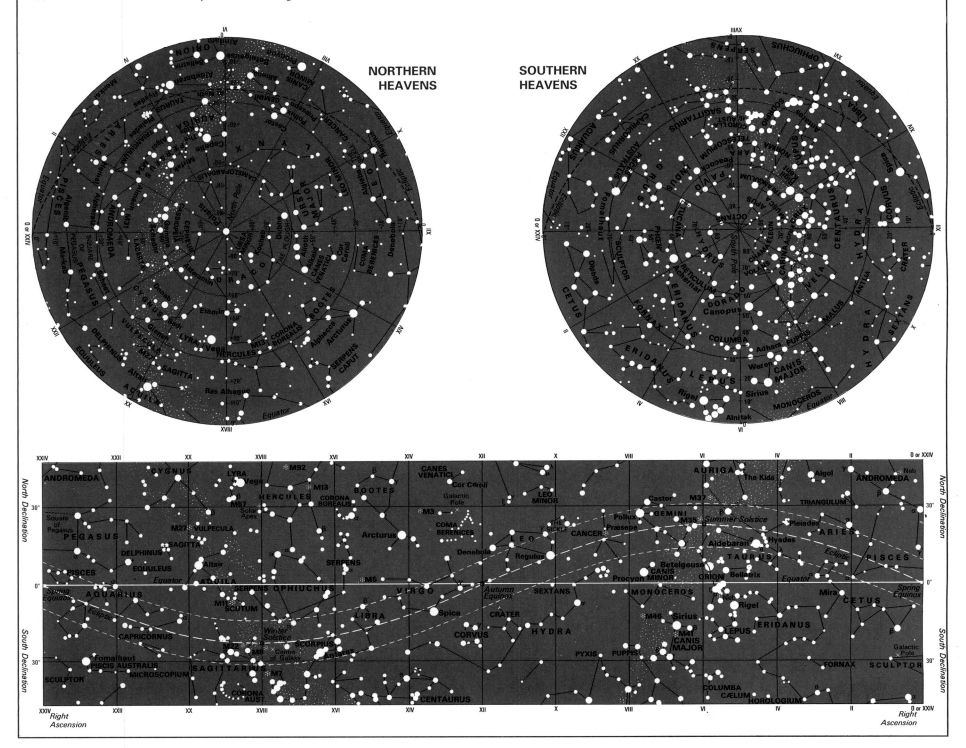

NORTHERN HEAVENS

SOUTHERN HEAVENS

The constellations and their English names

| | | | | | | | |
|---|---|---|---|---|---|---|---|
| Andromeda | Andromeda | Circinus | Compasses | Lacerta | Lizard | Piscis Austrinus | Southern Fish |
| Antila | Air Pump | Columba | Dove | Leo | Lion | Puppis | Ship's Stern |
| Apus | Bird of Paradise | Coma Berenices | Berenice's Hair | Leo Minor | Little Lion | Pyxis | Mariner's Compass |
| Aquarius | Water Carrier | Corona Australis | Southern Crown | Lepus | Hare | Reticulum | Net |
| Aquila | Eagle | Corona Borealis | Northern Crown | Libra | Scales | Sagitta | Arrow |
| Ara | Altar | Corvus | Crow | Lupus | Wolf | Sagittarius | Archer |
| Aries | Ram | Crater | Cup | Lynx | Lynx | Scorpius | Scorpion |
| Auriga | Charioteer | Crux | Southern Cross | Lyra | Harp | Sculptor | Sculptor |
| Boötes | Herdsman | Cygnus | Swan | Mensa | Table | Scutum | Shield |
| Caelum | Chisel | Delphinus | Dolphin | Microscopium | Microscope | Serpens | Serpent |
| Camelopardalis | Giraffe | Dorado | Swordfish | Monoceros | Unicorn | Sextans | Sextant |
| Cancer | Crab | Draco | Dragon | Musca | Fly | Taurus | Bull |
| Canes Venatici | Hunting Dogs | Equuleus | Little House | Norma | Level | Telescopium | Telescope |
| Canis Major | Great Dog | Eridanus | Eridanus | Octans | Octant | Triangulum | Triangle |
| Canis Minor | Little Dog | Fornax | Furnace | Ophiuchus | Serpent Bearer | Triangulum Australe | Southern Triangle |
| Capricornus | Goat | Gemini | Twins | Orion | Orion | Tucana | Toucan |
| Carina | Keel | Grus | Crane | Pavo | Peacock | Ursa Major | Great Bear |
| Cassiopeia | Cassiopeia | Hercules | Hercules | Pegasus | Winged Horse | Ursa Minor | Little Bear |
| Centaurus | Centaur | Horologium | Clock | Perseus | Perseus | Vela | Sails |
| Cepheus | Cepheus | Hydra | Water Snake | Phoenix | Phoenix | Virgo | Virgin |
| Cetus | Whale | Hydrus | Sea Serpent | Pictor | Easel | Volans | Flying Fish |
| Chamaeleon | Chameleon | Indus | Indian | Pisces | Fishes | Vulpecula | Fox |

The 20 nearest stars, excluding the Sun, with their distance from Earth in light-years*

| | |
|---|---|
| Proxima Centauri | 4.3 |
| Alpha Centauri A | 4.3 |
| Alpha Centauri B | 4.3 |
| Barnard's Star | 6.0 |
| Wolf 359 | 8.1 |
| Lal 21185 | 8.2 |
| Sirius A | 8.7 |
| Sirius B | 8.7 |
| UV Ceti A | 9.0 |
| UV Ceti B | 9.0 |
| Ross 154 | 9.3 |
| Ross 248 | 10.3 |
| Epsilon Eridani | 10.8 |
| L 789-6 | 11.1 |
| Ross 128 | 11.1 |
| 61 Cygni A | 11.2 |
| 61 Cygni B | 11.2 |
| Procyon A | 11.3 |
| Procyon B | 11.3 |
| Epsilon Indi | 11.4 |

Many of the nearest stars, like Alpha Centauri A and B, are doubles, orbiting about the common centre of gravity and to all intents and purposes equidistant from Earth. Many of them are dim objects, with no name other than the designation given by the astronomers who investigated them. However, they include Sirius, the brightest star in the sky, and Procyon, the seventh brightest. Both are far larger than the Sun: of the nearest stars, only Epsilon Eridani is similar in size and luminosity.

* A light-year equals approx. 9,500,000,000,000 kilometres

# THE SOLAR SYSTEM

Lying 27,000 light-years from the centre of one of billions of galaxies that comprise the observable universe, our Solar System contains nine planets and their moons, innumerable asteroids and comets, and a miscellany of dust and gas, all tethered by the immense gravitational field of the Sun, the middling-sized star whose thermonuclear furnaces provide them all with heat and light. The Solar System was formed about 4,600 million years ago, when a spinning cloud of gas, mostly hydrogen but seeded with other, heavier elements, condensed enough to ignite a nuclear reaction and create a star. The Sun still accounts for almost 99.9% of the system's total mass; one planet, Jupiter, contains most of the remainder.

By composition as well as distance, the planetary array divides quite neatly in two: an inner system of four small, solid planets, including the Earth, and an outer system, from Jupiter to Neptune, of four huge gas giants. Between the two groups lies a scattering of asteroids, perhaps as many as 40,000; possibly the remains of a planet destroyed by some unexplained catastrophe, they are more likely to be debris left over from the Solar System's formation, prevented by the gravity of massive Jupiter from coalescing into a larger body. The ninth planet, Pluto, seems to be a world of the inner system type: small, rocky and something of an anomaly.

By the 1990s, however, the Solar System also included some newer anomalies: several thousand spacecraft. Most were in orbit around the Earth, but some had probed far and wide around the system. The valuable information beamed back by these robotic investigators has transformed our knowledge of our celestial environment.

Much of the early history of science is the story of people trying to make sense of the errant points of light that were all they knew of the planets. Now, men have themselves stood on the Earth's Moon; probes have landed on Mars and Venus, and orbiting radars have mapped far distant landscapes with astonishing accuracy. In the 1980s, the US *Voyagers* skimmed all four major planets of the outer system, bringing new revelations with each close approach. Only Pluto, inscrutably distant in an orbit that takes it 50 times the Earth's distance from the Sun, remains unvisited by our messengers.

## ORBITS OF THE PLANETS

**The solar planets and their orbits, showing the relative position of each planet at the vernal equinox of 1992.**

Orbits are drawn to exact scale, but with the Sun and planets greatly enlarged for clarity. The Solar System is shown from the viewpoint of an observer a few light-hours distant in the direction of the constellation Hercules. Seen from such a position, above the plane of the ecliptic, all the planets revolve about the Sun in an anti-clockwise direction. The perspective view exaggerates the elliptical form of all the planetary orbits: only Pluto and Mercury follow paths that deviate noticeably from circularity. Near perihelion – its closest approach to the Sun – Pluto actually passes inside the orbit of Neptune, an event that last occurred in 1983. Pluto will not regain its station as the Sun's outermost planet until February 1999.

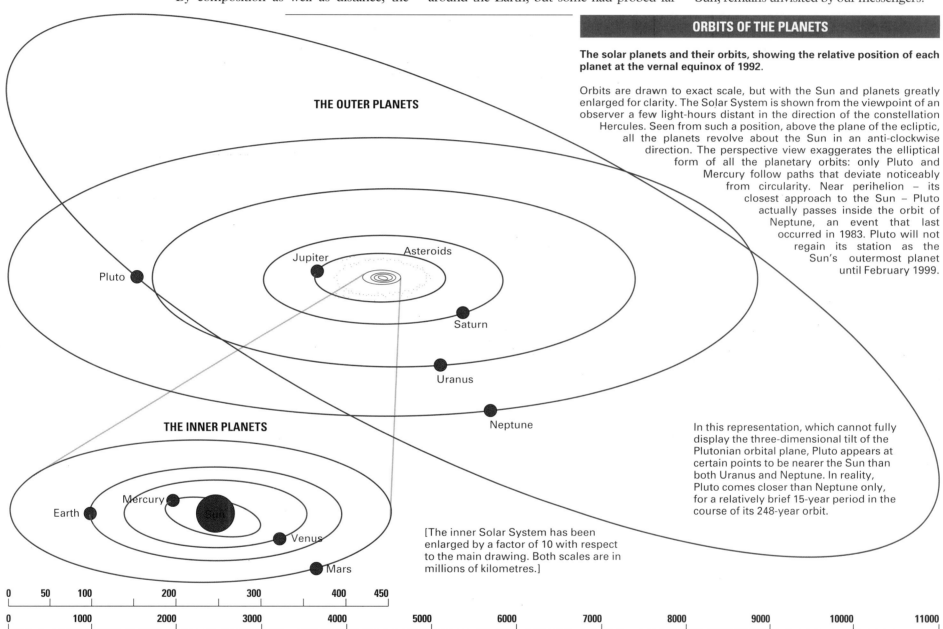

THE OUTER PLANETS

Pluto

Jupiter

Asteroids

Saturn

Uranus

Neptune

THE INNER PLANETS

Earth

Mercury

Sun

Venus

Mars

In this representation, which cannot fully display the three-dimensional tilt of the Plutonian orbital plane, Pluto appears at certain points to be nearer the Sun than both Uranus and Neptune. In reality, Pluto comes closer than Neptune only, for a relatively brief 15-year period in the course of its 248-year orbit.

[The inner Solar System has been enlarged by a factor of 10 with respect to the main drawing. Both scales are in millions of kilometres.]

| 0 | 50 | 100 | | 200 | | 300 | | 400 | 450 |
|---|---|---|---|---|---|---|---|---|---|

| 0 | 1000 | 2000 | 3000 | 4000 | 5000 | 6000 | 7000 | 8000 | 9000 | 10000 | 11000 |
|---|---|---|---|---|---|---|---|---|---|---|---|

## PLANETARY DATA

| | Mean distance from Sun (million km) | Mass (Earth = 1) | Period of orbit (Earth years) | Period of rotation (Earth days) | Equatorial diameter (km) | Average density (water = 1) | Surface gravity (Earth = 1) | Escape velocity (km/sec) | Number of known satellites |
|---|---|---|---|---|---|---|---|---|---|
| *Sun* | – | 332,946 | – | 25.38 | 1,392,000 | 1.41 | 27.9 | 617.5 | – |
| **Mercury** | 58.3 | 0.06 | 0.241 | 58.67 | 4,878 | 5.5 | 0.38 | 4.27 | 0 |
| **Venus** | 107.7 | 0.8 | 0.615 | 243.0 | 12,104 | 5.25 | 0.90 | 10.36 | 0 |
| **Earth** | 149.6 | 1.0 | 1.00 | 0.99 | 12,756 | 5.52 | 1.00 | 11.18 | 1 |
| **Mars** | 227.3 | 0.1 | 1.88 | 1.02 | 6,794 | 3.94 | 0.38 | 5.03 | 2 |
| **Jupiter** | 777.9 | 317.8 | 11.86 | 0.41 | 142,800 | 1.33 | 2.64 | 60.22 | 16 |
| **Saturn** | 1,427.1 | 95.2 | 29.63 | 0.42 | 120,000 | 0.706 | 1.16 | 36.25 | 17 |
| **Uranus** | 2,872.3 | 14.5 | 83.97 | 0.45 | 52,000 | 1.70 | 1.11 | 22.4 | 15 |
| **Neptune** | 4,502.7 | 17.2 | 164.8 | 0.67 | 48,400 | 1.77 | 1.21 | 23.9 | 8 |
| **Pluto** | 5,894.2 | 0.002 | 248.63 | 6.38 | 3,000 | 5.50 | 0.47 | 5.1 | 1 |

Planetary days are given in sidereal time – that is, with respect to the stars rather than the Sun. Most of the information in the table was confirmed by spacecraft and often obtained from photographs and other data transmitted back to the Earth. In the case of Pluto, however, only earthbound observations have been made, and no spacecraft can hope to encounter it until well into the next century. Given the planet's small size and great distance, figures for its diameter and rotation period cannot be definitive.

Since Pluto does not appear to be massive enough to account for the perturbations in the orbits of Uranus and Neptune that led to its 1930 discovery, it is quite possible that a tenth and even more distant planet may exist. Once Pluto's own 248-year orbit has been observed for long enough, further discrepancies may give a clue as to any tenth planet's whereabouts. Even so, distance alone would make it very difficult to locate, especially since telescopes powerful enough to find it are normally engaged in galactic study.

**Mercury** is the closest planet to the Sun and hence the fastest-moving. It has no significant atmosphere and a cratered, wrinkled surface very similar to that of Earth's moon.

**Venus** has much the same physical dimensions as Earth. However, its carbon dioxide atmosphere is 90 times as dense, accounting for a runaway greenhouse effect that makes the Venusian surface, at 475°C, the hottest of all the planets in the Solar System. Radar mapping shows relatively level land with volcanic regions whose sulphurous discharges explain the sulphuric acid rains reported by soft-landing space probes before they succumbed to Venus's fierce climate.

**Earth** seen from space is easily the most beautiful of the inner planets; it is also, and more objectively, the largest, as well as the only home of known life. Living things are the main reason why the Earth is able to retain a substantial proportion of corrosive and highly reactive oxygen in its atmosphere, a state of affairs that contradicts the laws of chemical equilibrium; the oxygen in turn supports the life that constantly regenerates it.

**Mars** was once considered the likeliest of the other planets to share Earth's cargo of life: the seasonal expansion of dark patches strongly suggested vegetation and the planet's apparent ice-caps indicated the vital presence of water. But close inspection by spacecraft brought disappointment: chemical reactions account for the seeming vegetation, the ice-caps are mainly frozen carbon dioxide, and whatever oxygen the planet once possessed is now locked up in the iron-bearing rock that covers its cratered surface and gives it its characteristic red hue.

**Jupiter** masses almost three times as much as all the other planets combined; had it scooped up a little more matter during its formation, it might have evolved into a small companion star for the Sun. The planet is mostly gas, under intense pressure in the lower atmosphere above a core of fiercely compressed hydrogen and helium. The upper layers form strikingly-coloured rotating belts, the outward sign of the intense storms created by Jupiter's rapid diurnal rotation. Close approaches by spacecraft have shown an orbiting ring system and discovered several previously unknown moons: Jupiter has at least 16 moons.

**Saturn** is structurally similar to Jupiter, rotating fast enough to produce an obvious bulge at its equator. Ever since the invention of the telescope, however, Saturn's rings have been the feature that has attracted most observers. *Voyager* probes in 1980 and 1981 sent back detailed pictures that showed them to be composed of thousands of separate ringlets, each in turn made up of tiny icy particles, interacting in a complex dance that may serve as a model for the study of galactic and even larger structures.

**Uranus** was unknown to the ancients. Although it is faintly visible to the naked eye, it was not discovered until 1781. Its composition is broadly similar to Jupiter and Saturn, though its distance from the Sun ensures an even colder surface temperature. Observations in 1977 suggested the presence of a faint ring system, amply confirmed when *Voyager 2* swung past the planet in 1986.

**Neptune** is always more than 4,000 million kilometres from Earth, and despite its diameter of almost 50,000 km, it can only be seen by telescope. Its 1846 discovery was the result of mathematical predictions by astronomers seeking to explain irregularities in the orbit of Uranus, but until *Voyager 2* closed with the planet in 1989, little was known of it. Like Uranus, it has a ring system; *Voyager*'s photographs revealed a total of eight moons.

**Pluto** is the most mysterious of the solar planets, if only because even the most powerful telescopes can scarcely resolve it from a point of light to a disc. It was discovered as recently as 1930, like Neptune as the result of perturbations in the orbits of the two then outermost planets. Its small size, as well as its eccentric and highly tilted orbit, has led to suggestions that it is a former satellite of Neptune, somehow liberated from its primary. In 1978 Pluto was found to have a moon of its own, Charon, apparently half the size of Pluto itself.

# THE EARTH: TIME AND MOTION

The basic unit of time measurement is the day, that is, one rotation of the Earth on its axis. The subdivision of the day into hours, minutes and seconds is arbitrary and simply for our convenience. Our present calendar is based on the solar year of 365.24 days, the time taken by the Earth to orbit the Sun. As the Earth rotates from west to east, the Sun appears to rise in the east and set in the west. When the Sun is setting in Shanghai, on the opposite side of the world New York is just emerging into sunlight. Noon, when the Sun is directly overhead, is coincident at all places on the same meridian, with shadows pointing directly towards the poles.

Calendars based on the movements of the Sun and Moon have been used since ancient times. The Julian Calendar, with its leap year, introduced by Julius Caesar, fixed the average length of the year at 365.25 days, which was about 11 minutes too long (the Earth completes its orbit in 365 days, 5 hours, 48 minutes and 46 seconds of mean solar time). The cumulative error was rectified by the Gregorian Calendar, introduced by Pope Gregory XIII in 1582, when he decreed that the day following 4 October was 15 October, and that century years did not count as leap years unless divisible by 400. England did not adopt the reformed calendar until 1752, when the country found itself 11 days behind the continent.

Britain imposed the Gregorian Calendar on all its possessions, including the American colonies. All dates preceding 2 September were marked 'OS', for 'Old Style'.

## EARTH DATA

Maximum distance from Sun (Aphelion): 152,007,016 km
Minimum distance from Sun (Perihelion): 147,000,830 km
Obliquity of the ecliptic: 23° 27' 08"
Length of year – solar tropical (equinox to equinox): 365.24 days
Length of year – sidereal (fixed star to fixed star): 365.26 days
Length of day – mean solar day: 24h, 03m, 56s
Length of day – mean sidereal day: 23h, 56m, 04s

Superficial area: 510,000,000 sq km
Land surface: 149,000,000 sq km (29.2%)
Water surface: 361,000,000 sq km (70.8%)
Equatorial circumference: 40,077 km.
Polar circumference: 40,009 km.
Equatorial diameter: 12,756.8 km
Polar diameter: 12,713.8 km
Equatorial radius: 6,378.4 km
Polar radius: 6,356.9 km
Volume of the Earth: 1,083,230 x 10⁶ cu km
Mass of the Earth: 5.9 x 10²¹ tonnes

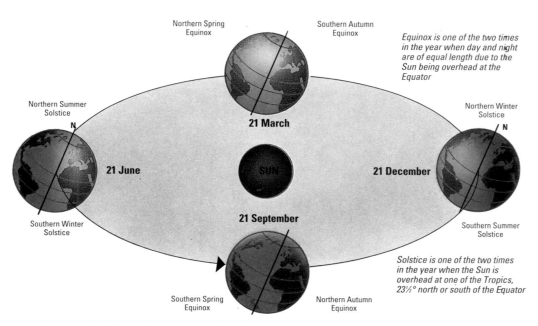

Equinox is one of the two times in the year when day and night are of equal length due to the Sun being overhead at the Equator

Solstice is one of the two times in the year when the Sun is overhead at one of the Tropics, 23½° north or south of the Equator

## THE SEASONS

The Earth revolves around the Sun once a year in an 'anti-clockwise' direction, tilted at a constant angle 66½°. In June, the northern hemisphere is tilted towards the Sun: as a result, it receives more hours of sunshine in a day and therefore has its warmest season, summer. By December, the Earth has rotated halfway round the Sun so that the southern hemisphere is tilted towards the Sun and has its summer; the hemisphere that is tilted away from the Sun has winter. On 21 June the Sun is directly overhead at the Tropic of Cancer (23½° N), and this is midsummer in the northern hemisphere. Midsummer in the southern hemisphere occurs on 21 December, when the Sun is overhead at the Tropic of Capricorn (23½° S).

## DAY AND NIGHT

The Sun appears to rise in the east, reach its highest point at noon, set in the west, to be followed by night. In reality, it is not the Sun that is moving but the Earth revolving from west to east.

At the summer solstice in the northern hemisphere (21 June), the Arctic has total daylight and the Antarctic total darkness. The opposite occurs at the winter solstice (21 December). At the Equator, the length of day and night are almost equal all year.

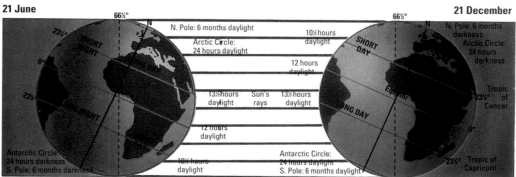

## THE SUN'S PATH

The diagrams on the left illustrate the apparent path of the Sun at (A) the Equator, (B) in mid-latitude (45°), (C) at the Arctic Circle (66½°), and (D) at the North Pole, where there are six months of continuous daylight and six months of continuous night.

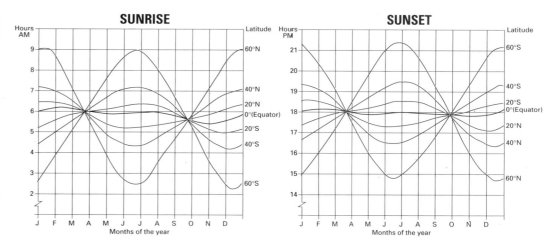

## MEASUREMENTS OF TIME

Astronomers distinguish between solar time and sidereal time. Solar time derives from the period taken by the Earth to rotate on its axis: one rotation defines a solar day. But the speed of the Earth along its orbit around the Sun is not constant. The length of day – or 'apparent solar day', as defined by the apparent successive transits of the Sun – is irregular because the Earth must complete more than one rotation before the Sun returns to the same meridian. The constant sidereal day is defined as the interval between two successive apparent transits of a star, or the first point of Aries, across the same meridian. If the Sun is at the equinox and overhead at a meridian one day, then the next day it will be to the east by approximately 1°. Thus, the Sun will not cross the meridian until four minutes after the sidereal noon.

*From the diagrams on the right it is possible to discover the time of sunrise or sunset on a given date and for latitudes between 60°N and 60°S.*

## THE MOON

## PHASES OF THE MOON

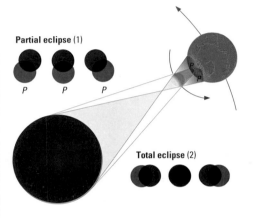

New Moon · Crescent · First quarter · Gibbous · Full Moon · Gibbous · Last quarter · Crescent · New Moon

The Moon rotates more slowly than the Earth, making one complete turn on its axis in just over 27 days. Since this corresponds to its period of revolution around the Earth, the Moon always presents the same hemisphere or face to us, and we never see 'the dark side'. The interval between one Full Moon and the next (and between New Moons) is about 29½ days – a lunar month. The apparent changes in the shape of the Moon are caused by its changing position in relation to the Earth; like the planets, it produces no light of its own and shines only by reflecting the rays of the Sun.

## MOON DATA

**Distance from Earth**
The Moon orbits at a mean distance of 384,199.1 km, at an average speed of 3,683 km/h in relation to the Earth.

**Size and mass**
The average diameter of the Moon is 3,475.1 km. It is 400 times smaller than the Sun but is about 400 times closer to the Earth, so we see them as the same size. The Moon has a mass of $7,348 \times 10^{19}$ tonnes, with a density 3.344 times that of water.

**Visibility**
Only 59% of the Moon's surface is directly visible from Earth. Reflected light takes 1.25 seconds to reach Earth – compared to 8 minutes 27.3 seconds for light to reach us from the Sun.

**Temperature**
With the Sun overhead, the temperature on the lunar equator can reach 117.2°C [243°F]. At night it can sink to –162.7°C [–261°F].

**Partial eclipse (1)**

P  P  P

**Total eclipse (2)**

**Lunar eclipse**

## ECLIPSES

When the Moon passes between the Sun and the Earth, it causes a partial eclipse of the Sun (1) if the Earth passes through the Moon's outer shadow (P), or a total eclipse (2) if the inner cone shadow crosses the Earth's surface. In a lunar eclipse, the Earth's shadow crosses the Moon and, again, provides either a partial or total eclipse. Eclipses of the Sun and the Moon do not occur every month because of the 5° difference between the plane of the Moon's orbit and the plane in which the Earth moves. In the 1990s only 14 lunar eclipses are possible, for example, seven partial and seven total; each is visible only from certain, and variable, parts of the world. The same period witnesses 13 solar eclipses – six partial (or annular) and seven total.

## TIDES

The daily rise and fall of the ocean's tides are the result of the gravitational pull of the Moon and that of the Sun, though the effect of the latter is only 46.6% as strong as that of the Moon. This effect is greatest on the hemisphere facing the Moon and causes a tidal 'bulge'. When lunar and solar forces pull together, with Sun, Earth and Moon in line (near New and Full Moons), higher 'spring tides' (and lower low tides) occur; when lunar and solar forces are least coincidental with the Sun and Moon at an angle (near the Moon's first and third quarters), 'neap tides' occur, which have a small tidal range.

Spring tide · Neap tide · Last quarter · New Moon · Spring tide · Full Moon · Neap tide · Gravitational pull by Sun and Moon · First quarter

---

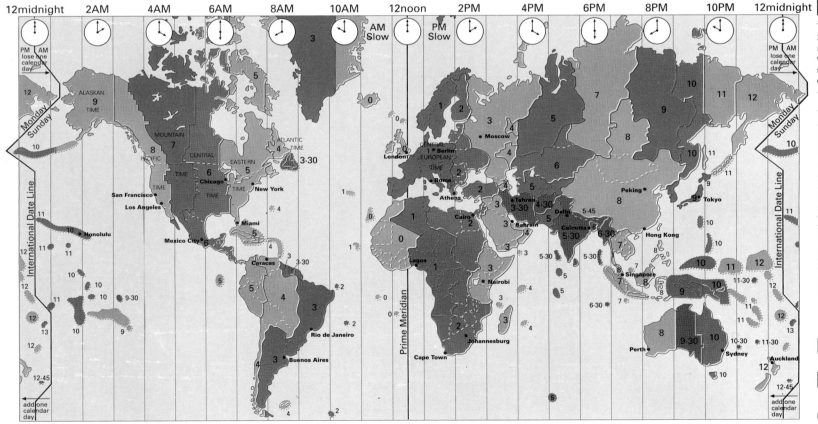

12midnight  2AM  4AM  6AM  8AM  10AM  12noon  2PM  4PM  6PM  8PM  10PM  12midnight

AM Slow  PM Slow

Projection: Mercator

CARTOGRAPHY BY PHILIP'S. COPYRIGHT REED INTERNATIONAL BOOKS LTD

## TIME ZONES

The Earth rotates through 360° in 24 hours, and so moves 15° every hour. The world is divided into 24 standard time zones, each centred on lines of longitude at 15° intervals. The Greenwich meridian lies at the centre of the first zone. All places to the west of Greenwich are one hour behind for every 15° of longitude; places to the east are ahead by one hour for every 15°. When it is 12 noon at the Greenwich meridian, 180° east is midnight of the same day – while 180° west the day is just beginning. To overcome this, the International Date Line was established, approximately following the 180° meridian. Thus, if you travelled eastwards from Japan (140° East) to Samoa (170° West), you would pass from Sunday night into Sunday morning.

 Zones slow or fast of Greenwich Mean Time

 Half-hour zones

 The time when it is 12 noon at Greenwich

# THE EARTH: GEOLOGY

The origin of the Earth is still open to conjecture, although the most widely accepted theory is that it was formed from a solar cloud consisting mainly of hydrogen about 4,600 million years ago. The cloud condensed, forming the planets. The lighter elements floated to the surface of the Earth, where they cooled to form a crust; the inner material remained hot and molten. The first rocks were formed over 3,500 million years ago, but the Earth's surface has since been constantly altered.

The crust consists of a brittle, low-density material, varying from 5 kilometres to 50 kilometres thick beneath the continents, which is predominantly made up of silica and aluminium: hence its name, 'sial'. Below the sial is a basaltic layer known as 'sima', comprising mainly silica and magnesium. The crust accounts for only 1.5% of the Earth's volume.

The mantle lies immediately below the crust, with a distinct change in density and chemical properties. The rock here is rich in iron and magnesium silicates, with temperatures reaching 1,600°C. The rigid upper mantle extends down to a depth of about 1,000 kilometres, below which is a more viscous lower mantle measuring about 1,900 kilometres thick.

The outer core, measuring about 2,310 kilometres thick, consists of molten iron and nickel at temperatures ranging from 2,100°C to 5,000°C, possibly separated from the less dense mantle by an oxidized shell. About 5,000 kilometres below the planetary surface is a liquid transition zone, below which is the solid inner core, a sphere of about 2,700 kilometres diameter, where rock is three times as dense as in the crust. The temperature at the centre of the Earth is probably about 5,000°C.

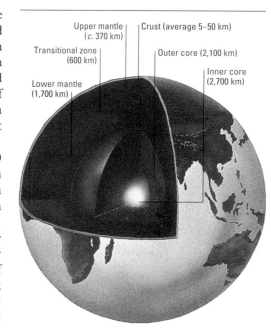

Upper mantle (c. 370 km)  Crust (average 5–50 km)
Transitional zone (600 km)  Outer core (2,100 km)
Lower mantle (1,700 km)  Inner core (2,700 km)

The complementary, almost jigsaw-puzzle fit of the Atlantic coasts led to Alfred Wegener's proposition of continental drift in Germany (1915). His theory suggested that an ancient super-continent, which he called Pangaea, incorporating all the Earth's landmasses, gradually split up to form the continents we know today.

By 180 million years ago, Pangaea had divided into two major groups and the southern part, Gondwanaland, had itself begun to break up with India and Antarctica-Australia becoming isolated.

By 135 million years ago, the widening of the splits in the North Atlantic and Indian Oceans persisted, a South Atlantic gap had appeared, and India continued to move 'north' towards Asia.

By 65 million years ago, South America had completely split from Africa.

To form today's pattern, India 'collided' with Asia (crumpling up sediments to form the Himalayas); South America rotated and moved west to connect with North America; Australia separated from Antarctica and moved north; and the familiar gap developed between Greenland and Europe.

## CONTINENTAL DRIFT

About 200 million years ago the original Pangaea landmass began to split into two continental groups, which further separated over time to produce the present-day configuration.

180 million years ago

135 million years ago

Present day

~~~ Trench
--- Rift
▨ New ocean floor
── Zones of slippage

## PLATE TECTONICS

The original debate about the drift theory of Wegener and others formed a long prelude to a more radical idea: plate tectonics. The discovery that the continents are carried along on the top of slowly-moving crustal plates (which float on heavier liquid material – the lower mantle – much as icebergs do on water) provided the mechanism for the drift theories to work. The plates converge and diverge along margins marked by seismic and volcanic activity. Plates diverge from mid-ocean ridges where molten lava pushes up and forces the plates apart at a rate of up to 40 mm a year; converging plates form either a trench (where the oceanic plates sink below the lighter continental rock) or mountain ranges (where two continents collide).

The debate about plate tectonics is not over, however. In addition to abiding questions such as what force actually moves the plates (massive convection currents in the Earth's interior is the most popular explanation), and why so many volcanoes and earthquakes occur in mid-plate (such as Hawaii and central China), evidence began to emerge in the early 1990s that, with more sophisticated equipment and models, the whole theory might be in doubt.

## VOLCANOES

Of some 850 volcanoes that have produced recorded eruptions, nearly three-quarters lie in the 'Ring of Fire' that surrounds the Pacific Ocean. The 1980s was a bad decade for loss of life here, with three major eruptions – Mount St Helens, USA, in 1980; El Chichon, Mexico, in 1982; and Nevado del Ruiz, Colombia, in 1985 – killing 25,000 people. This is not because the world is becoming less geologically stable: it is simply that populations are growing fast, with over 350 million people now living in areas vulnerable to seismic activity.

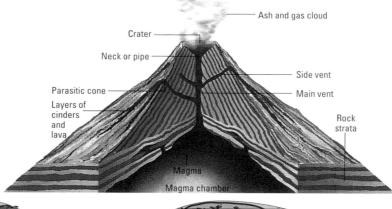

Ash and gas cloud
Crater
Neck or pipe
Side vent
Parasitic cone
Main vent
Layers of cinders and lava
Rock strata
Magma
Magma chamber

### DISTRIBUTION

Land volcanoes active since 1700 ▲

Submarine volcanoes ·

Geysers +

Boundaries of tectonic plates ──

Direction of movement along plate boundaries (cm/year) 7.2 ↗

Volcanoes can suddenly erupt after lying dormant for centuries: in 1991 Mount Pinatubo, Philippines, burst into life after sleeping for more than 600 years.

Shield cone

Hornit cone
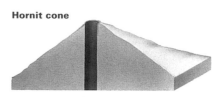

Cinder cone

Caldera

## GEOLOGICAL TIME

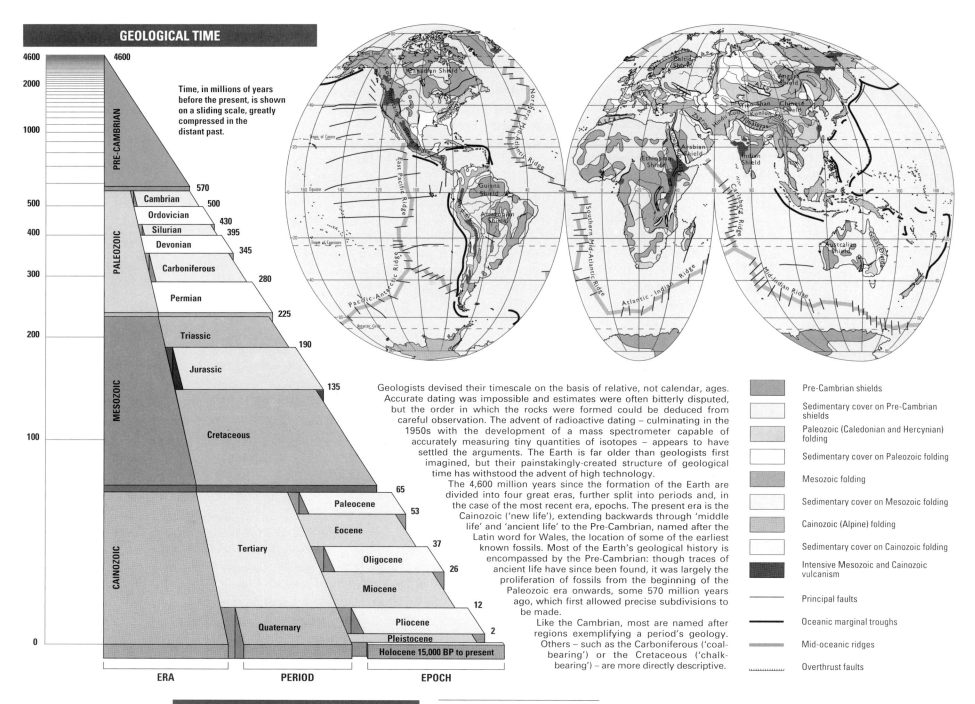

Time, in millions of years before the present, is shown on a sliding scale, greatly compressed in the distant past.

| ERA | PERIOD | EPOCH |
|---|---|---|
| PRE-CAMBRIAN | | |
| PALEOZOIC | Cambrian | |
| | Ordovician | |
| | Silurian | |
| | Devonian | |
| | Carboniferous | |
| | Permian | |
| MESOZOIC | Triassic | |
| | Jurassic | |
| | Cretaceous | |
| CAINOZOIC | Tertiary | Paleocene |
| | | Eocene |
| | | Oligocene |
| | | Miocene |
| | Quaternary | Pliocene |
| | | Pleistocene |
| | | Holocene 15,000 BP to present |

(Scale values: 4600, 2000, 1000, 570, 500, 430, 395, 345, 280, 225, 190, 135, 65, 53, 37, 26, 12, 2)

Geologists devised their timescale on the basis of relative, not calendar, ages. Accurate dating was impossible and estimates were often bitterly disputed, but the order in which the rocks were formed could be deduced from careful observation. The advent of radioactive dating – culminating in the 1950s with the development of a mass spectrometer capable of accurately measuring tiny quantities of isotopes – appears to have settled the arguments. The Earth is far older than geologists first imagined, but their painstakingly-created structure of geological time has withstood the advent of high technology.

The 4,600 million years since the formation of the Earth are divided into four great eras, further split into periods and, in the case of the most recent era, epochs. The present era is the Cainozoic ('new life'), extending backwards through 'middle life' and 'ancient life' to the Pre-Cambrian, named after the Latin word for Wales, the location of some of the earliest known fossils. Most of the Earth's geological history is encompassed by the Pre-Cambrian: though traces of ancient life have since been found, it was largely the proliferation of fossils from the beginning of the Paleozoic era onwards, some 570 million years ago, which first allowed precise subdivisions to be made.

Like the Cambrian, most are named after regions exemplifying a period's geology. Others – such as the Carboniferous ('coal-bearing') or the Cretaceous ('chalk-bearing') – are more directly descriptive.

- Pre-Cambrian shields
- Sedimentary cover on Pre-Cambrian shields
- Paleozoic (Caledonian and Hercynian) folding
- Sedimentary cover on Paleozoic folding
- Mesozoic folding
- Sedimentary cover on Mesozoic folding
- Cainozoic (Alpine) folding
- Sedimentary cover on Cainozoic folding
- Intensive Mesozoic and Cainozoic vulcanism
- Principal faults
- Oceanic marginal troughs
- Mid-oceanic ridges
- Overthrust faults

## EARTHQUAKES

Earthquake magnitude is usually rated according to either the Richter or the Modified Mercalli scale, both devised by seismologists in the 1930s. The Richter scale measures absolute earthquake power with mathematical precision: each step upwards represents a ten-fold increase in shockwave amplitude. Theoretically, there is no upper limit, but the largest earthquakes measured have been rated at between 8.8 and 8.9. The 12-point Mercalli scale, based on observed effects, is often more meaningful, ranging from I (earthquakes noticed only by seismographs) to XII (total destruction); intermediate points include V (people awakened at night; unstable objects overturned), VII (collapse of ordinary buildings; chimneys and monuments fall) and IX (conspicuous cracks in ground; serious damage to reservoirs).

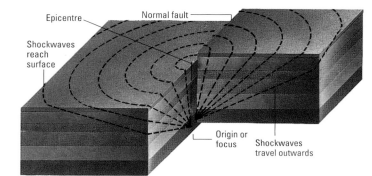

Epicentre — Normal fault — Shockwaves reach surface — Origin or focus — Shockwaves travel outwards

### NOTABLE EARTHQUAKES SINCE 1900

| Year | Location | Mag. | Deaths |
|---|---|---|---|
| 1906 | San Francisco, USA | 8.3 | 503 |
| 1906 | Valparaiso, Chile | 8.6 | 22,000 |
| 1908 | Messina, Italy | 7.5 | 83,000 |
| 1915 | Avezzano, Italy | 7.5 | 30,000 |
| 1920 | Gansu (Kansu), China | 8.6 | 180,000 |
| 1923 | Yokohama, Japan | 8.3 | 143,000 |
| 1927 | Nan Shan, China | 8.3 | 200,000 |
| 1932 | Gansu (Kansu), China | 7.6 | 70,000 |
| 1934 | Bihar, India/Nepal | 8.4 | 10,700 |
| 1935 | Quetta, India* | 7.5 | 60,000 |
| 1939 | Chillan, Chile | 8.3 | 28,000 |
| 1939 | Erzincan, Turkey | 7.9 | 30,000 |
| 1960 | Agadir, Morocco | 5.8 | 12,000 |
| 1962 | Khorasan, Iran | 7.1 | 12,230 |
| 1963 | Skopje, Yugoslavia** | 6.0 | 1,000 |
| 1964 | Anchorage, Alaska | 8.4 | 131 |
| 1968 | N.E. Iran | 7.4 | 12,000 |
| 1970 | N. Peru | 7.7 | 66,794 |
| 1972 | Managua, Nicaragua | 6.2 | 5,000 |
| 1974 | N. Pakistan | 6.3 | 5,200 |
| 1976 | Guatemala | 7.5 | 22,778 |
| 1976 | Tangshan, China | 8.2 | 650,000 |
| 1978 | Tabas, Iran | 7.7 | 25,000 |
| 1980 | El Asnam, Algeria | 7.3 | 20,000 |
| 1980 | S. Italy | 7.2 | 4,800 |
| 1985 | Mexico City, Mexico | 8.1 | 4,200 |
| 1988 | N.W. Armenia | 6.8 | 55,000 |
| 1990 | N. Iran | 7.7 | 36,000 |
| 1993 | Maharashtra, India | 6.4 | 30,000 |
| 1994 | Los Angeles, USA | 6.6 | 51 |

The highest magnitude recorded on the Richter scale is 8.9, in Japan on 2 March 1933 (2,990 deaths). The most devastating quake ever was at Shaanxi (Shensi) province, central China, on 24 January 1566, when an estimated 830,000 people were killed.

\* now Pakistan
\*\* now Macedonia

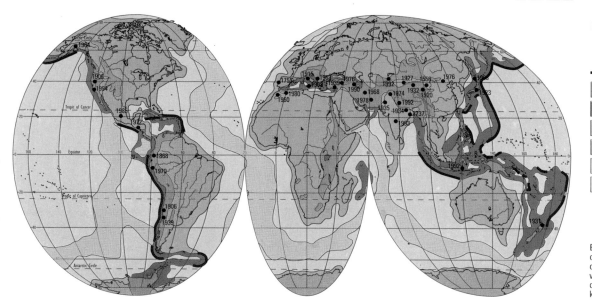

### DISTRIBUTION

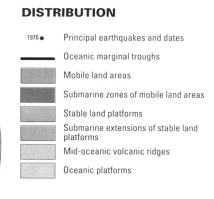

- 1976 ● Principal earthquakes and dates
- Oceanic marginal troughs
- Mobile land areas
- Submarine zones of mobile land areas
- Stable land platforms
- Submarine extensions of stable land platforms
- Mid-oceanic volcanic ridges
- Oceanic platforms

Earthquakes are a series of rapid vibrations originating from the slipping or faulting of parts of the Earth's crust when stresses within build to breaking point, and usually occur at depths between 8 and 30 kilometres.

# THE EARTH: OCEANS

The Earth is a misnamed planet: more than 70% of its total surface area – 361,740,000 square kilometres – is covered by its oceans and seas. This great cloak of liquid water gives the planet its characteristic blue appearance from space, and is one of two obvious differences between the Earth and its near-neighbours in space, Mars and Venus. The other difference is the presence of life, and the two are closely linked.

In a strict geographical sense, the Earth has only three oceans: the Atlantic, Pacific and Indian Oceans. Subdivided vertically instead of horizontally, however, there are many more. The most active is the sunlit upper layer, home of most sea life and the vital interface between air and water. In this surface zone, huge energies are exchanged

between the oceans and the atmosphere above; it is also a kind of membrane through which the ocean breathes, absorbing great quantities of carbon dioxide and partially exchanging them for oxygen, largely through the phytoplankton, tiny plants that photosynthesize solar energy and provide the food base for all other marine life.

As depth increases, so light and colour gradually fade away, the longer wavelengths dying first. At 50 metres, the ocean is a world of green, blue and violet; at 100 metres, only blue remains; by 200 metres, there is only a dim twilight. The temperature falls away with the light, until just before 1,000 metres – the precise depth varies – there occurs a temperature change almost as abrupt as the transition between air and water

far above. Below this thermocline, at a near-stable 3°C, the waters are forever unmoved by the winds of the upper world and are stirred only by the slow action of deep ocean currents. The pressure is crushing, reaching 1,000 atmospheres in the deepest trenches: a force of 1 tonne bearing down on every square centimetre.

Yet even here the oceans support life, and not only the handful of strange, deep-sea creatures that find a living in the near-empty abyss. The deep ocean serves as a gigantic storehouse, both for heat and for assorted atmospheric chemicals, regulating and balancing the proportions of various trace compounds and elements, and ensuring a large measure of stability for both the climate and the ecology that depend on it.

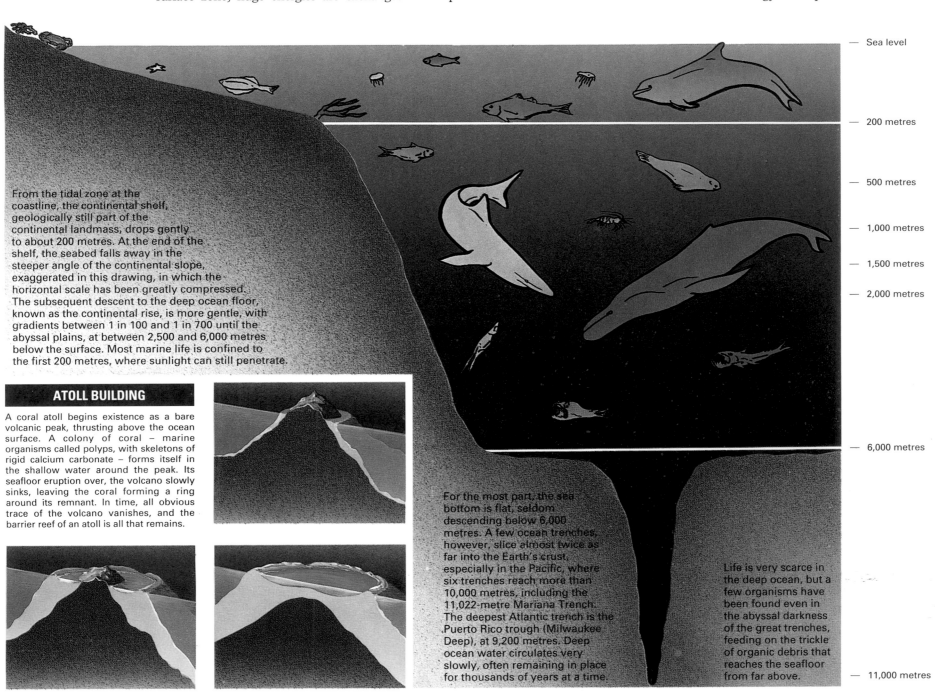

— Sea level

— 200 metres

— 500 metres

— 1,000 metres

— 1,500 metres

— 2,000 metres

— 6,000 metres

— 11,000 metres

From the tidal zone at the coastline, the continental shelf, geologically still part of the continental landmass, drops gently to about 200 metres. At the end of the shelf, the seabed falls away in the steeper angle of the continental slope, exaggerated in this drawing, in which the horizontal scale has been greatly compressed. The subsequent descent to the deep ocean floor, known as the continental rise, is more gentle, with gradients between 1 in 100 and 1 in 700 until the abyssal plains, at between 2,500 and 6,000 metres below the surface. Most marine life is confined to the first 200 metres, where sunlight can still penetrate.

## ATOLL BUILDING

A coral atoll begins existence as a bare volcanic peak, thrusting above the ocean surface. A colony of coral – marine organisms called polyps, with skeletons of rigid calcium carbonate – forms itself in the shallow water around the peak. Its seafloor eruption over, the volcano slowly sinks, leaving the coral forming a ring around its remnant. In time, all obvious trace of the volcano vanishes, and the barrier reef of an atoll is all that remains.

For the most part, the sea bottom is flat, seldom descending below 6,000 metres. A few ocean trenches, however, slice almost twice as far into the Earth's crust, especially in the Pacific, where six trenches reach more than 10,000 metres, including the 11,022-metre Mariana Trench. The deepest Atlantic trench is the Puerto Rico trough (Milwaukee Deep), at 9,200 metres. Deep ocean water circulates very slowly, often remaining in place for thousands of years at a time.

Life is very scarce in the deep ocean, but a few organisms have been found even in the abyssal darkness of the great trenches, feeding on the trickle of organic debris that reaches the seafloor from far above.

## PROFILE OF AN OCEAN

The deep ocean floor is no more uniform than the surface of the continents, although it was not until the development of effective sonar equipment that it was possible to examine submarine contours in detail. The Atlantic (right) and the Pacific show similar patterns. Offshore comes the continental shelf, sliding downwards to the continental slope and the steeper continental rise, after which the seabed rolls onwards into the abyssal plains. In the wide Pacific, these are interrupted by gently-rising abyssal hills; in both oceans, the plains extend all the way to the mid-oceanic ridges, where the upwelling of new crustal material is constantly forcing the oceans wider. Volcanic activity is responsible for the formation of seamounts and tablemounts, or guyots, their flat-topped equivalents. In this cross-section, only the Azores are high enough to break the surface and become islands.

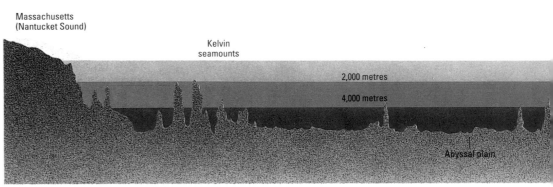

Massachusetts
(Nantucket Sound)

Kelvin
seamounts

2,000 metres

4,000 metres

Abyssal plain

## OCEAN CURRENTS

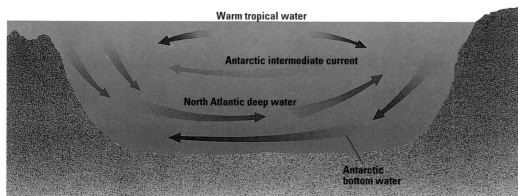

NORTH
Arctic

Atlantic Ocean

SOUTH
Antarctic

**Warm tropical water**

**Antarctic intermediate current**

**North Atlantic deep water**

**Antarctic bottom water**

Moving immense quantities of energy as well as billions of tonnes of water every hour, the ocean currents are a vital part of the great heat engine that drives the Earth's climate. They themselves are produced by a twofold mechanism. At the surface, winds push huge masses of water before them; in the deep ocean, below an abrupt temperature gradient that separates the churning surface waters from the still depths, density variations cause slow vertical movements.

The pattern of circulation of the great surface currents is determined by the displacement known as the Coriolis effect. As the Earth turns beneath a moving object – whether it is a tennis ball or a vast mass of water – it appears to be deflected to one side. The deflection is most obvious near the Equator, where the Earth's surface is spinning eastwards at 1700 km/h; currents moving polewards are curved clockwise in the northern hemisphere and anti-clockwise in the southern.

The result is a system of spinning circles known as gyres. The Coriolis effect piles up water on the left of each gyre, creating a narrow, fast-moving stream that is matched by a slower, broader returning current on the right. North and south of the Equator, the fastest currents are located in the west and in the east respectively. In each case, warm water moves from the Equator and cold water returns to it. Cold currents often bring an upwelling of nutrients with them, supporting the world's most economically important fisheries.

Depending on the prevailing winds, some currents on or near the Equator may reverse their direction in the course of the year – a seasonal variation on which Asian monsoon rains depend, and whose occasional failure can bring disaster to millions of people.

## CURRENTS AND TEMPERATURES

(Northern Hemisphere: winter)

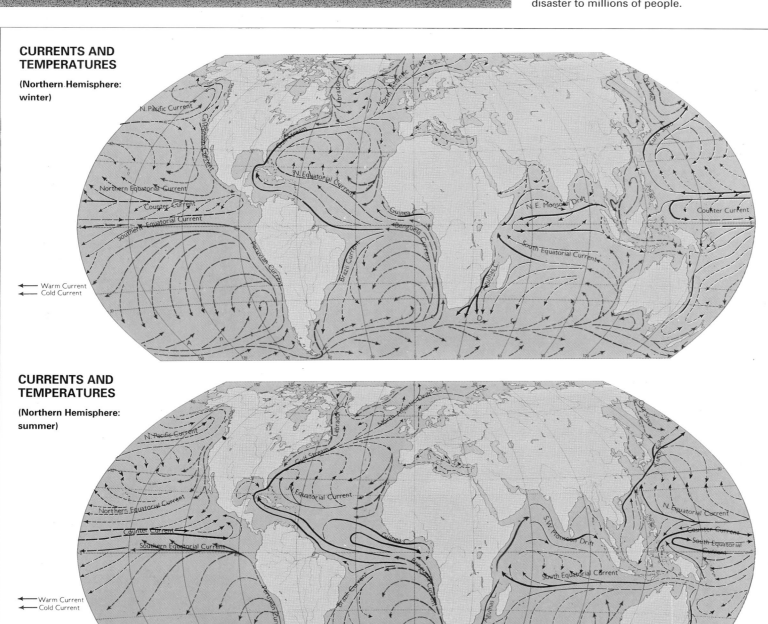

← Warm Current
← Cold Current

## CURRENTS AND TEMPERATURES

(Northern Hemisphere: summer)

← Warm Current
← Cold Current

### SEAWATER

The chemical composition of the sea, in grams per tonne of seawater, excluding the elements of water itself

| | |
|---|---|
| Chlorine | 19,400 |
| Sodium | 10,800 |
| Magnesium | 1,290 |
| Sulphur | 904 |
| Calcium | 411 |
| Potassium | 392 |
| Bromine | 67 |
| Strontium | 8.1 |
| Boron | 4.5 |
| Fluorine | 1.3 |
| Lithium | 0.17 |
| Rubidium | 0.12 |
| Phosphorus | 0.09 |
| Iodine | 0.06 |
| Barium | 0.02 |
| Arsenic | 0.003 |
| Cesium | 0.0003 |

Seawater also contains virtually every other element, although the quantities involved are too small for reliable measurement. In natural conditions, its composition is broadly consistent across the world's seas and oceans; but in coastal areas especially, variations, sometimes substantial, may be caused by the presence of industrial waste and sewage sludge.

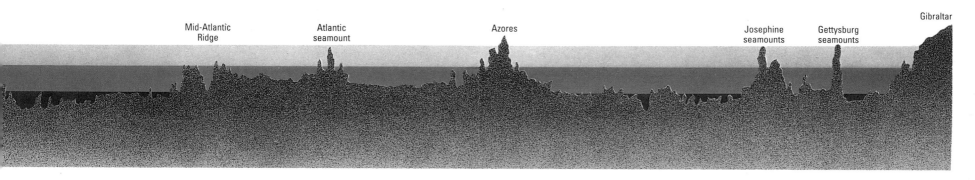

Mid-Atlantic Ridge          Atlantic seamount          Azores          Josephine seamounts     Gettysburg seamounts          Gibraltar

# THE EARTH: ATMOSPHERE

Extending from the surface far into space, the atmosphere is a meteor shield, a radiation deflector, a thermal blanket and a source of chemical energy for the Earth's diverse inhabitants. Five-sixths of its mass is found in the first 15 kilometres, the troposphere, no thicker in relative terms than the skin of an onion. Clouds, cyclonic winds, precipitation and virtually all the phenomena we call weather occur in this narrow layer. Above, a thin layer of ozone blocks ultra-violet radiation. Beyond 100 kilometres, atmospheric density is lower than most laboratory vacuums, yet these tenuous outer reaches, composed largely of hydrogen and helium, trap cosmic debris and incoming high-energy particles alike.

## CIRCULATION OF THE AIR

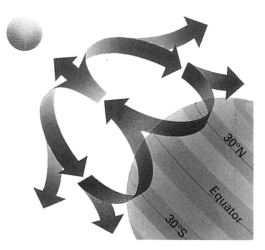

## STRUCTURE OF ATMOSPHERE

## TEMPERATURE

## PRESSURE

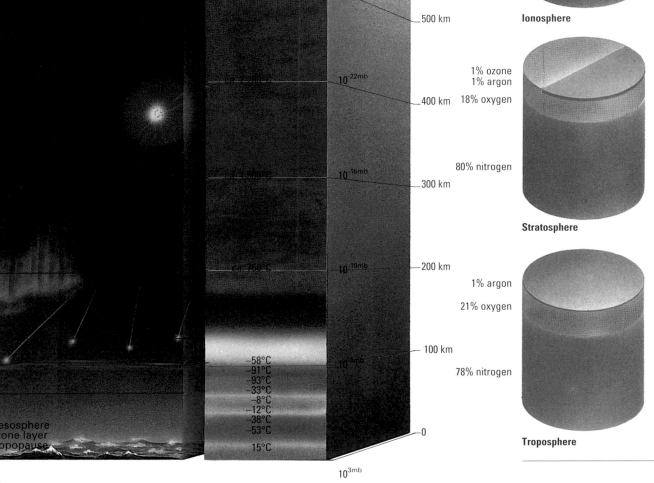

$10^{53}$mb

Inner:
50% helium
50% hydrogen

900 km

$10^{47}$mb

Middle:
25% helium
75% hydrogen

Outer:
100% hydrogen

800 km

$10^{41}$mb

700 km

15% helium

$10^{35}$mb

15% oxygen
and atomic
oxygen

600 km

70% nitrogen

$10^{28}$mb

500 km

$10^{22}$mb

1% ozone
1% argon

400 km   18% oxygen

$10^{16}$mb

80% nitrogen

300 km

$10^{10}$mb

200 km

1% argon

21% oxygen

$10^{3}$mb

100 km

78% nitrogen

−58°C
−91°C
−93°C
−33°C
−8°C
−12°C
−38°C
−53°C

0

Mesosphere
Ozone layer
Tropopause

15°C

$10^{3}$mb

## CHEMICAL STRUCTURE

**Exosphere**

**Ionosphere**

**Stratosphere**

**Troposphere**

### Exosphere
The atmosphere's upper layer has no clear outer boundary, merging imperceptibly with interplanetary space. Its lower boundary, at an altitude of approximately 600 kilometres, is almost equally vague. The exosphere is mainly composed of hydrogen and helium in changing proportions, with a small quantity of atomic oxygen up to 600 kilometres. Helium vanishes with increasing altitude, and above 2,400 kilometres the exosphere is almost entirely composed of hydrogen.

### Ionosphere
Gas molecules in the ionosphere, mainly helium, oxygen and nitrogen, are electrically charged – ionized – by the Sun's radiation. Within the ionosphere's range of 50 to 600 kilometres in altitude, they group themselves into four layers, known conventionally as D, E, F1 and F2, all of which can reflect radio waves of differing frequencies. The high energy of ionospheric gas gives it a notional temperature of more than 2,000°C, although its density is negligible. The auroras – *aurora borealis* and its southern counterpart, *aurora australis* – occur in the ionosphere when charged particles from the Sun interact with the Earth's magnetic fields, at their strongest near the poles.

### Stratosphere
Separated at its upper and lower limits by the distinct thresholds of the stratopause and the tropopause, the stratosphere is a remarkably stable layer between 50 kilometres and about 15 kilometres. Its temperature rises from −55°C at its lower extent to approximately 0°C near the stratopause, where a thin layer of ozone absorbs ultra-violet radiation. 'Mother-of-pearl' or nacreous cloud occurs at about 25 kilometres' altitude. Stratospheric air contains enough ozone to make it poisonous, although it is in any case far too rarified to breathe.

### Troposphere
The narrowest of all the atmospheric layers, the troposphere extends up to 15 kilometres at the Equator but only 8 kilometres at the poles. Since this thin region contains about 85% of the atmosphere's total mass and almost all of its water vapour, it is also the realm of the Earth's weather. Temperatures fall steadily with increasing height by about 1°C for every 100 metres above sea level.

CARTOGRAPHY BY PHILIP'S. COPYRIGHT REED INTERNATIONAL BOOKS LTD

Heated by the relatively high surface temperatures near the Earth's Equator, air expands and rises to create a belt of low pressure. Moving northwards towards the poles, it gradually cools, sinking once more and producing high-pressure belts at about latitudes 30° North and South. Water vapour carried with the air falls as rain, releasing vast quantities of energy as well as liquid water when it condenses.

The high- and low-pressure belts are both areas of comparative calm, but between them, blowing from high-pressure to low-pressure areas, are the prevailing winds. The atmospheric circulatory system is enormously complicated by the Coriolis effect brought about by the spinning Earth: winds are deflected to the right in the northern hemisphere and to the left in the southern, giving rise to the typically cyclonic pattern of swirling clouds carried by the moving masses of air.

Although clouds appear in an almost infinite variety of shapes and sizes, there are recognizable features that form the basis of a classification first put forward by Luke Howard, a London chemist, in 1803 and later modified by the World Meteorological Organization. The system is derived from the altitude of clouds and whether they form hairlike filaments ('cirrus'), heaps or piles ('cumulus'), or layers ('stratus'). Each characteristic carries some kind of message – not always a clear one – to forecasters about the weather to come.

## CLASSIFICATION OF CLOUDS

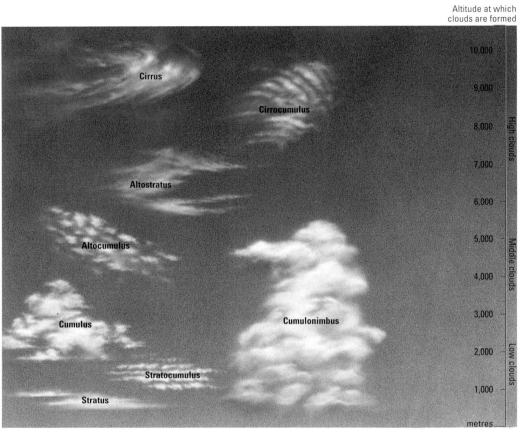

Altitude at which clouds are formed

Clouds form when damp, usually rising, air is cooled. Thus they form when a wind rises to cross hills or mountains; when a mass of air rises over, or is pushed up by, another mass of denser air; or when local heating of the ground causes convection currents.

The types of clouds are classified according to altitude as high, middle or low. The high ones, composed of ice crystals, are cirrus, cirrostratus and cirrocumulus. The middle clouds are altostratus, a grey or bluish striated, fibrous, or uniform sheet producing light drizzle, and altocumulus, a thicker and fluffier version of cirrocumulus.

The low clouds include nimbostratus, a dark grey layer that brings almost continuous rain or snow; cumulus, a detached 'heap' – brilliant white in sunlight but dark and flat at the base; and stratus, which forms dull, overcast skies at low altitudes.

Cumulonimbus, associated with storms and rains, heavy and dense with a flat base and a high, fluffy outline, can be tall enough to occupy middle as well as low altitudes.

## PRESSURE AND WINDS

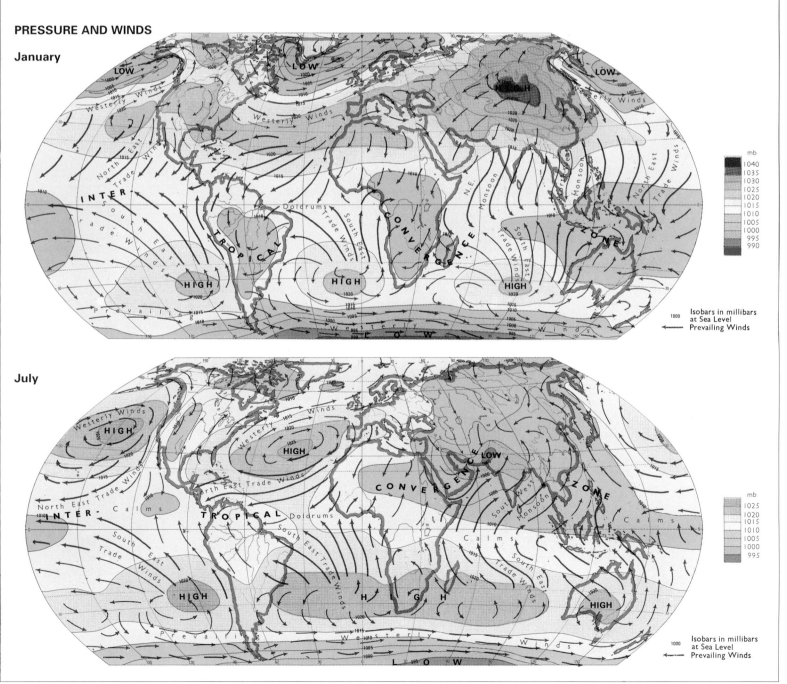

# THE EARTH: CLIMATE

Climate is weather in the long term: the seasonal pattern of hot and cold, wet and dry, averaged over time. At the simplest level, it is caused by the uneven heating of the Earth. Surplus heat at the Equator passes towards the poles, levelling out the energy differential. Its passage is marked by a ceaseless churning of the atmosphere and the oceans, further agitated by the Earth's diurnal spin and the motion it imparts to moving air and water. The heat's means of transport – by winds and ocean currents, by the continual evaporation and recondensation of water molecules – is the weather itself.

There are four basic types of climate, each of which is open to considerable subdivision: tropical, desert, temperate and polar. But although latitude is obviously a critical factor,

it is not the only determinant. The differential heating of land and sea, the funnelling and interruption of winds and ocean currents by landmasses and mountain ranges, and the transpiration of vegetation: all these factors combine to add complexity. New York, Naples and the Gobi Desert share almost the same latitude, for example, but their climates are very different. And although the sheer intricacy of the weather system often defies day-to-day prediction in these or any other places – despite the many satellites and number-crunching supercomputers with which present-day meteorologists are now equipped – their climatic patterns retain a year-on-year stability.

They are not indefinitely stable, however. The planet regularly passes through long,

cool periods lasting about 100,000 years: these are the Ice Ages, probably caused by recurring long-term oscillations in the Earth's orbital path and fluctuations in the Sun's energy output. In the present era, the Earth is nearest to the Sun in the middle of the northern hemisphere's winter; 11,000 years ago, at the end of the last Ice Age, the northern winter fell with the Sun at its most distant.

Left to its own devices, the climate even now should be drifting towards another glacial period. But global warming caused by increasing carbon dioxide levels in the atmosphere, largely the result of 20th-century fuel-burning and deforestation, may well precipitate change far faster than the great, slow cycles of the Solar System.

## Tropical rainy climates
All mean monthly temperatures above 18°C.

| | |
|---|---|
| Af | Rainforest climate |
| Am | Monsoon climate |
| Aw | Savanna climate |

## Dry climates
Low rainfall combined with a wide range of temperatures

| | |
|---|---|
| BS | Steppe climate |
| BW | Desert climate |

## Warm temperate rainy climates
The mean temperature is below 18°C but above –3°C and that of the warmest month is over 10°C.

| | |
|---|---|
| Cw | Dry winter climate |
| Cs | Dry summer climate |
| Cf | Climate with no dry season |

## Cold temperate rainy climates
The mean temperature of the coldest month is below –3°C but that of the warmest month is still over 10°C.

| | |
|---|---|
| Dw | Dry winter climate |
| Df | Climate with no dry season |

## Polar climates
The mean temperature of the warmest month is below 10°C, giving permanently frozen subsoil.

| | |
|---|---|
| ET | Tundra climate |

The mean temperature of the warmest month is below 0°C, giving permanent ice and snow.

| | |
|---|---|
| EF | Polar climate |

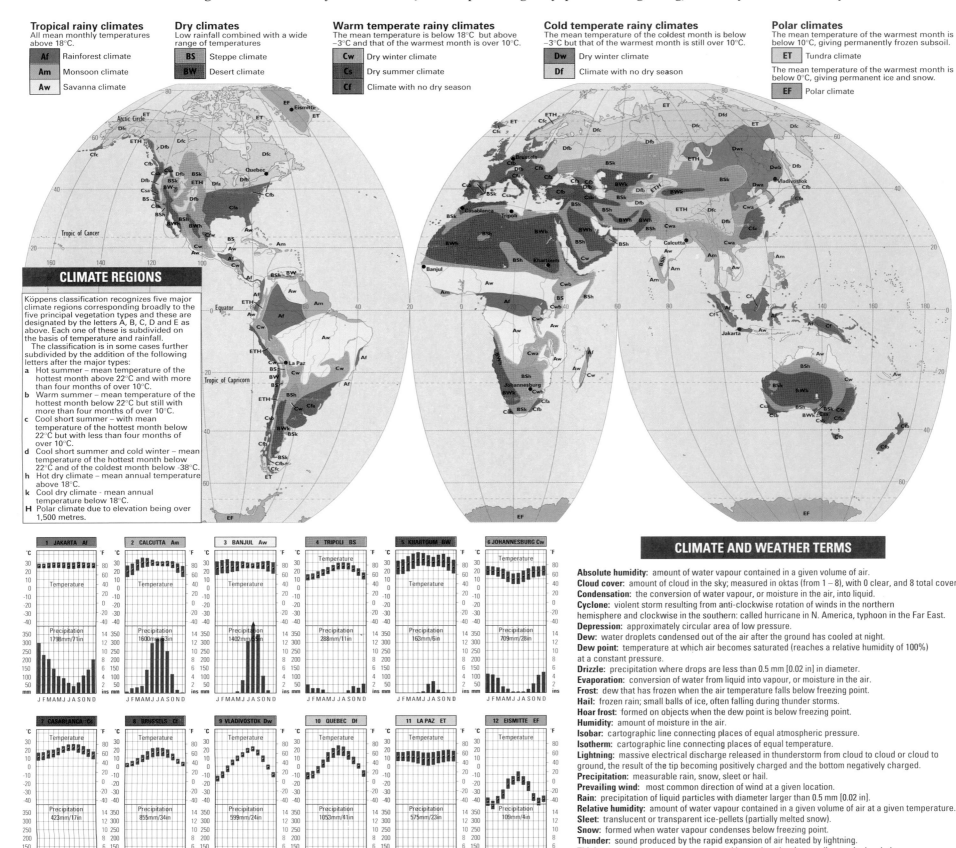

### CLIMATE REGIONS

Köppens classification recognizes five major climate regions corresponding broadly to the five principal vegetation types and these are designated by the letters A, B, C, D and E as above. Each one of these is subdivided on the basis of temperature and rainfall.

The classification is in some cases further subdivided by the addition of the following letters after the major types:
- **a** Hot summer – mean temperature of the hottest month above 22°C and with more than four months of over 10°C.
- **b** Warm summer – mean temperature of the hottest month below 22°C but still with more than four months of over 10°C.
- **c** Cool short summer – with mean temperature of the hottest month below 22°C but with less than four months of over 10°C.
- **d** Cool short summer and cold winter – mean temperature of the hottest month below 22°C and of the coldest month below -38°C.
- **h** Hot dry climate – mean annual temperature above 18°C.
- **k** Cool dry climate - mean annual temperature below 18°C.
- **H** Polar climate due to elevation being over 1,500 metres.

### CLIMATE AND WEATHER TERMS

**Absolute humidity:** amount of water vapour contained in a given volume of air.
**Cloud cover:** amount of cloud in the sky; measured in oktas (from 1 – 8), with 0 clear, and 8 total cover.
**Condensation:** the conversion of water vapour, or moisture in the air, into liquid.
**Cyclone:** violent storm resulting from anti-clockwise rotation of winds in the northern hemisphere and clockwise in the southern: called hurricane in N. America, typhoon in the Far East.
**Depression:** approximately circular area of low pressure.
**Dew:** water droplets condensed out of the air after the ground has cooled at night.
**Dew point:** temperature at which air becomes saturated (reaches a relative humidity of 100%) at a constant pressure.
**Drizzle:** precipitation where drops are less than 0.5 mm [0.02 in] in diameter.
**Evaporation:** conversion of water from liquid into vapour, or moisture in the air.
**Frost:** dew that has frozen when the air temperature falls below freezing point.
**Hail:** frozen rain; small balls of ice, often falling during thunder storms.
**Hoar frost:** formed on objects when the dew point is below freezing point.
**Humidity:** amount of moisture in the air.
**Isobar:** cartographic line connecting places of equal atmospheric pressure.
**Isotherm:** cartographic line connecting places of equal temperature.
**Lightning:** massive electrical discharge released in thunderstorm from cloud to cloud or cloud to ground, the result of the tip becoming positively charged and the bottom negatively charged.
**Precipitation:** measurable rain, snow, sleet or hail.
**Prevailing wind:** most common direction of wind at a given location.
**Rain:** precipitation of liquid particles with diameter larger than 0.5 mm [0.02 in].
**Relative humidity:** amount of water vapour contained in a given volume of air at a given temperature.
**Sleet:** translucent or transparent ice-pellets (partially melted snow).
**Snow:** formed when water vapour condenses below freezing point.
**Thunder:** sound produced by the rapid expansion of air heated by lightning.
**Tidal wave:** giant ocean wave generated by earthquakes (tsunami) or cyclonic winds.
**Tornado:** severe funnel-shaped storm that twists as hot air spins vertically (waterspout at sea).
**Whirlwind:** rapidly rotating column of air, only a few metres across, made visible by dust.

## WINDCHILL FACTOR

In sub-zero weather, even moderate winds significantly reduce effective temperatures. The chart below shows the windchill effect across a range of speeds. Figures in the pink zone are not dangerous to well-clad people; in the blue zone, the risk of serious frostbite is acute.

| | Wind speed (km/h) | | | | |
|---|---|---|---|---|---|
| | 16 | 32 | 48 | 64 | 80 |
| 0°C | -8 | -14 | -17 | -19 | -20 |
| -5°C | -14 | -21 | -25 | -27 | -28 |
| -10°C | -20 | -28 | -33 | -35 | -36 |
| -15°C | -26 | -36 | -40 | -43 | -44 |
| -20°C | -32 | -42 | -48 | -51 | -52 |
| -25°C | -38 | -49 | -56 | -59 | -60 |
| -30°C | -44 | -57 | -63 | -66 | -68 |
| -35°C | -51 | -64 | -72 | -74 | -76 |
| -40°C | -57 | -71 | -78 | -82 | -84 |
| -45°C | -63 | -78 | -86 | -90 | -92 |
| -50°C | -69 | -85 | -94 | -98 | -100 |

## BEAUFORT WIND SCALE

Named for the 19th-century British naval officer who devised it, the Beaufort Scale assesses wind speed according to its effects. It was originally designed as an aid for sailors, but has since been adapted for use on land.

| Scale | Wind speed km/h | mph | Effect |
|---|---|---|---|
| 0 | 0-1 | 0-1 | **Calm** Smoke rises vertically |
| 1 | 1-5 | 1-3 | **Light air** Wind direction shown only by smoke drift |
| 2 | 6-11 | 4-7 | **Light breeze** Wind felt on face; leaves rustle; vanes moved by wind |
| 3 | 12-19 | 8-12 | **Gentle breeze** Leaves and small twigs in constant motion; wind extends small flag. |
| 4 | 20-28 | 13-18 | **Moderate** Raises dust and loose paper; small branches move |
| 5 | 29-38 | 19-24 | **Fresh** Small trees in leaf sway; crested wavelets on inland waters |
| 6 | 39-49 | 25-31 | **Strong** Large branches move; difficult to use umbrellas; overhead wires whistle |
| 7 | 50-61 | 32-38 | **Near gale** Whole trees in motion; difficult to walk against wind |
| 8 | 62-74 | 39-46 | **Gale** Twigs break from trees; walking very difficult |
| 9 | 75-88 | 47-54 | **Strong gale** Slight structural damage |
| 10 | 89-102 | 55-63 | **Storm** Trees uprooted; serious structural damage |
| 11 | 103-117 | 64-72 | **Violent storm** Widespread damage |
| 12 | 118+ | 73+ | **Hurricane** |

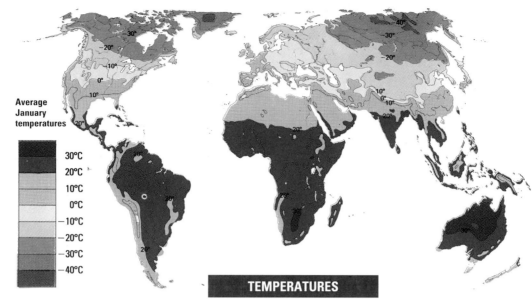

Average January temperatures

30°C
20°C
10°C
0°C
-10°C
-20°C
-30°C
-40°C

**TEMPERATURES**

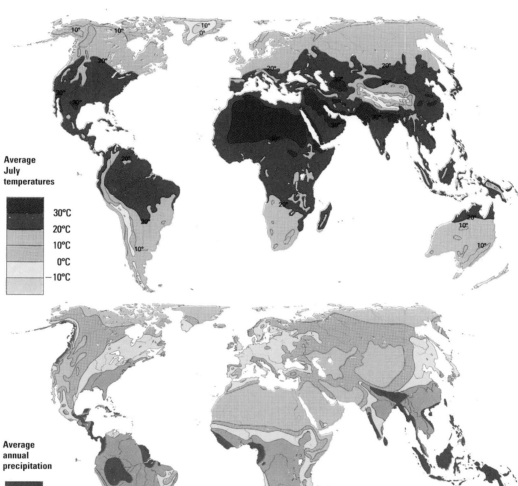

Average July temperatures

30°C
20°C
10°C
0°C
-10°C

Average annual precipitation

3000 mm
2000 mm
1000 mm
500 mm
250 mm

**PRECIPITATION**

## CLIMATE RECORDS

### Temperature

Highest recorded temperature: Al Aziziyah, Libya, 58°C [136.4°F], 13 September 1922.

Highest mean annual temperature: Dallol, Ethiopia, 34.4°C [94°F], 1960–66.

Longest heatwave: Marble Bar, W. Australia, 162 days over 38°C [100°F], 23 October 1923 to 7 April 1924.

Lowest recorded temperature (outside poles): Verkhoyansk, Siberia, –68°C [–90°F], 6 February 1933. Verkhoyansk also registered the greatest annual range of temperature: –70°C to 37°C [–94°F to 98°F].

Lowest mean annual temperature: Polus Nedostupnosti, Pole of Cold, Antarctica, –57.8°C [–72°F].

### Precipitation

Driest place: Arica, N. Chile, 0.8mm [0.03 in] per year (60-year average).

Longest drought: Calama, N. Chile: no recorded rainfall in 400 years to 1971.

Wettest place (average): Tututendo, Colombia: mean annual rainfall 11,770 mm [463.4 in].

Wettest place (12 months): Cherrapunji, Meghalaya, N.E. India, 26,470 mm [1,040 in], August 1860 to August 1861. Cherrapunji also holds the record for rainfall in one month: 930 mm [37 in], July 1861.

Wettest place (24 hours): Cilaos, Réunion, Indian Ocean, 1,870 mm [73.6 in], 15–16 March 1952.

Heaviest hailstones: Gopalganj, Bangladesh, up to 1.02 kg [2.25 lb], 14 April 1986 (killed 92 people).

Heaviest snowfall (continuous): Bessans, Savoie, France, 1,730 mm [68 in] in 19 hours, 5–6 April 1969.

Heaviest snowfall (season/year): Paradise Ranger Station, Mt Rainier, Washington, USA, 31,102 mm [1,224.5 in], 19 February 1971 to 18 February 1972.

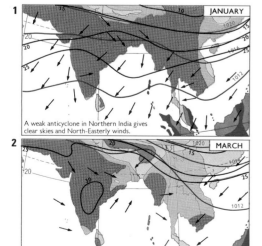

**1** JANUARY
A weak anticyclone in Northern India gives clear skies and North-Easterly winds.

**2** MARCH
Temperatures increase and the anticyclone subsides slightly, sea breezes bringing rain to coastal areas.

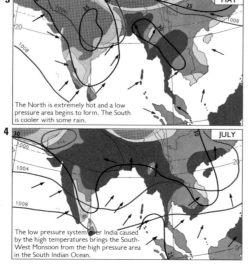

**3** MAY
The North is extremely hot and a low pressure area begins to form. The South is cooler with some rain.

**4** JULY
The low pressure system over India caused by the high temperatures brings the South-West Monsoon from the high pressure area in the South Indian Ocean.

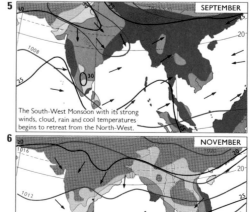

**5** SEPTEMBER
The South-West Monsoon with its strong winds, cloud, rain and cool temperatures begins to retreat from the North-West.

**6** NOVEMBER
The sub-continent is cool and dry but wet in the South-East.

COPYRIGHT. GEORGE PHILIP & SON. LTD.

## THE MONSOON

While it is crucial to the agriculture of South Asia, the monsoon that follows the dry months is unpredictable – in duration as well as intensity. A season of very heavy rainfall, causing disastrous floods, can be succeeded by years of low precipitation, leading to serious drought.

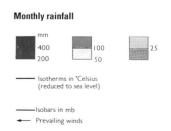

Monthly rainfall

mm
400
200
100
50
25

— Isotherms in °Celsius (reduced to sea level)
— Isobars in mb
→ Prevailing winds

# THE EARTH: WATER AND LAND USE

Fresh water is essential to all terrestrial life, from the humblest bacterium to the most advanced technological society. Yet freshwater resources form a minute fraction of the Earth's 1.41 billion cubic kilometres of water: most human needs must be met from the 2,000 cubic kilometres circulating in rivers at any one time. Agriculture accounts for huge quantities: without large-scale irrigation, most of the world's people would starve. And since fresh water is just as essential for most industrial processes – smelting a tonne of nickel, for example, requires about 4,000 tonnes of water – the growth of population and advancing industry have together put water supplies under strain.

Fortunately, water is seldom used up: the planet's hydrological cycle circulates it with benign efficiency, at least on a global scale. More locally, though, human activity can cause severe shortages: water for industry and agriculture is being withdrawn from many river basins and underground aquifers faster than natural recirculation can replace it.

## THE HYDROLOGICAL CYCLE

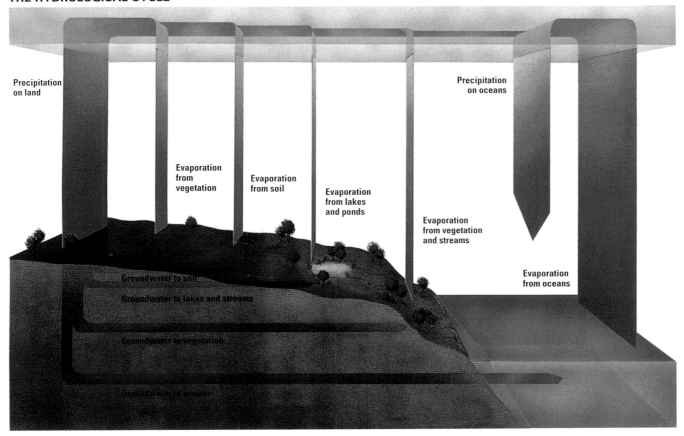

Water vapour is constantly drawn into the air from the Earth's rivers, lakes, seas and plant transpiration. In the atmosphere, it circulates around the planet, transporting energy as well as water itself. When the vapour cools it falls as rain or snow, and returns to the surface to evaporate once more. The whole cycle is driven by the Sun.

## WATER DISTRIBUTION

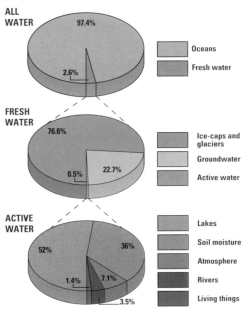

The distribution of planetary water, by percentage. Oceans and ice-caps together account for more than 99% of the total; the breakdown of the remainder is estimated.

Almost all the world's water is 3,000 million years old, and all of it cycles endlessly through the hydrosphere, though at different rates. Water vapour circulates over days, even hours, deep ocean water circulates over millenia, and ice-cap water remains solid for millions of years.

## WATER RUNOFF

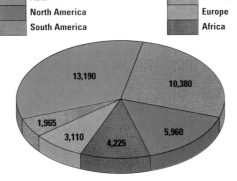

Annual freshwater runoff by continent in cubic kilometres

## WATER UTILIZATION

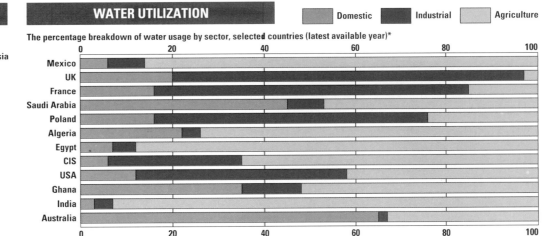

The percentage breakdown of water usage by sector, selected countries (latest available year)*

## WATER SUPPLY

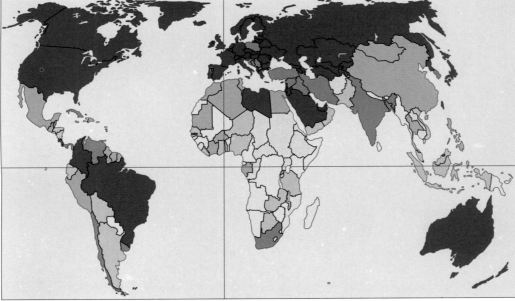

Percentage of total population with access to safe drinking water (latest available year)*

- Over 90% with safe water
- 75 – 90% with safe water
- 60 – 75% with safe water
- 45 – 60% with safe water
- 30 – 45% with safe water
- Under 30% with safe water

### Least well-provided countries

| | |
|---|---|
| Cambodia ............. 3% | Afghanistan ........... 21% |
| Central Africa........12% | Congo..................... 21% |
| Ethiopia................. 19% | Guinea-Bissau ......... 21% |
| Uganda ................. 20% | Sudan..................... 21% |

*Statistics for the new republics of the former USSR, Czechoslovakia and Yugoslavia are not yet available. The map shows the statistics for the entire USSR, Czechoslovakia and Yugoslavia.*

## WATERSHEDS

The world's major rivers; the world's 20 longest are shown in square brackets, led by the Nile and the Amazon.

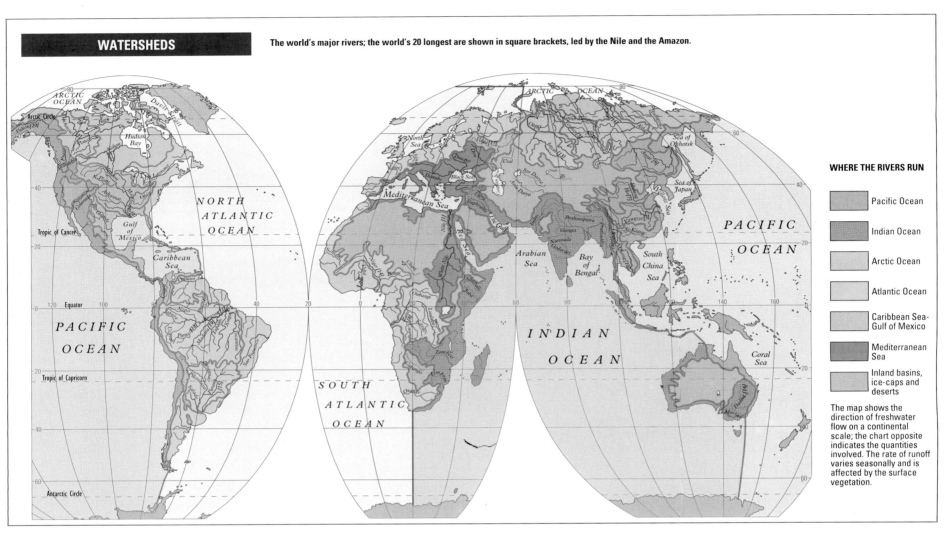

### WHERE THE RIVERS RUN

- Pacific Ocean
- Indian Ocean
- Arctic Ocean
- Atlantic Ocean
- Caribbean Sea-Gulf of Mexico
- Mediterranean Sea
- Inland basins, ice-caps and deserts

The map shows the direction of freshwater flow on a continental scale; the chart opposite indicates the quantities involved. The rate of runoff varies seasonally and is affected by the surface vegetation.

## LAND USE BY CONTINENT

- Forest
- Permanent pasture and rough grazing
- Permanent crops and plantations
- Arable
- Non-productive

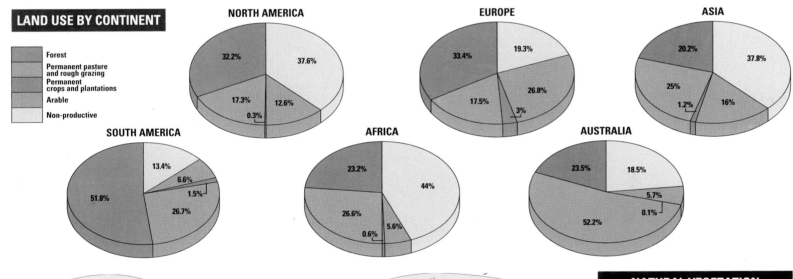

**NORTH AMERICA**
37.6% / 32.2% / 17.3% / 12.6% / 0.3%

**EUROPE**
19.3% / 33.4% / 17.5% / 26.8% / 3%

**ASIA**
37.8% / 20.2% / 25% / 1.2% / 16%

**SOUTH AMERICA**
13.4% / 6.6% / 1.5% / 51.8% / 26.7%

**AFRICA**
23.2% / 44% / 26.6% / 0.6% / 5.6%

**AUSTRALIA**
23.5% / 18.5% / 5.7% / 0.1% / 52.2%

The proportion of productive land has reached its upper limit in Europe, and in Asia more than 80% of potential cropland is already under cultivation. Elsewhere, any increase is often matched by corresponding losses due to desertification and erosion; projections for 2025 show a decline in cropland per capita for all continents, most notably in Africa.

## NATURAL VEGETATION

**Regional variation in vegetation (after Austin Miller)**

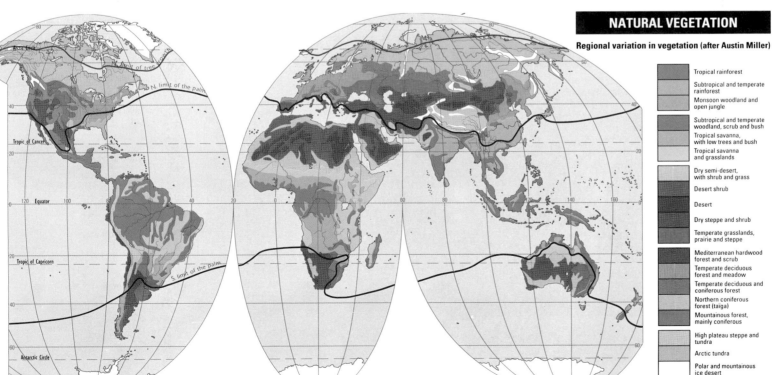

- Tropical rainforest
- Subtropical and temperate rainforest
- Monsoon woodland and open jungle
- Subtropical and temperate woodland, scrub and bush
- Tropical savanna, with low trees and bush
- Tropical savanna and grasslands
- Dry semi-desert, with shrub and grass
- Desert shrub
- Desert
- Dry steppe and shrub
- Temperate grasslands, prairie and steppe
- Mediterranean hardwood forest and scrub
- Temperate deciduous forest and meadow
- Temperate deciduous and coniferous forest
- Northern coniferous forest (taiga)
- Mountainous forest, mainly coniferous
- High plateau steppe and tundra
- Arctic tundra
- Polar and mountainous ice desert

The map illustrates the natural 'climax vegetation' of a region, as dictated by its climate and topography. In most cases, human agricultural activity has drastically altered the vegetation pattern. Western Europe, for example, lost most of its broadleaf forest many centuries ago, while irrigation has turned some natural semi-desert into productive land.

# THE EARTH: LANDSCAPE

Above and below the surface of the oceans, the features of the Earth's crust are constantly changing. The phenomenal forces generated by convection currents in the molten core of our planet carry the vast segments, or 'plates', of the crust across the globe in an endless cycle of creation and destruction. New crust emerges along the central depths of the oceans, where molten magma flows from the margins of neighbouring plates to form the massive mid-ocean ridges. The sea floor spreads, and where ocean plates meet continental plates, they dip back into the Earth's core to melt once again into magma.

Less dense, the continental plates 'float' among the oceans, drifting into and apart from each other at a rate which is almost imperceptibly slow. A continent may travel little more than 25 millimetres each year – in an average lifetime, Europe will move no more than a man's height – yet in the vast span of geological time, this process throws up giant mountain ranges and opens massive rifts in the land's surface.

The world's greatest mountain ranges have been formed in this way: the Himalayas by the collision of the Indo-Australian and Eurasian plates; the Andes by the meeting of the Nazca and South American plates. The Himalayas are a classic example of 'fold mountains', formed by the crumpling of the Earth's surface where two landmasses have been driven together. The coastal range of the Andes, by contrast, was formed by the upsurge of molten volcanic rock created by the friction of the continent 'overriding' the ocean plate.

However, the destruction of the landscape begins as soon as it is formed. Wind, water, ice and sea, the main agents of erosion, mount a constant assault that even the hardest rocks cannot withstand. Mountain peaks may dwindle by as little as a few millimetres each year, but if they are not uplifted by further movements of the crust they will eventually be reduced to rubble. Water is the most powerful destroyer – it has been estimated that 100 billion tonnes of rock is washed into the oceans every year.

When water freezes, its volume increases by about 9%, and no rock is strong enough to resist this pressure. Where water has penetrated tiny fissures or seeped into softer rock, a severe freeze followed by a thaw may result in rockfalls or earthslides, creating major destruction in a few minutes. Over much longer periods, acidity in rainwater breaks down the chemical composition of porous rocks, such as limestone, eating away the rock to form deep caves and tunnels. Chemical decomposition also occurs in riverbeds and glacier valleys, hastening the process of mechanical erosion.

Rivers and glaciers, like the sea itself, generate much of their effect through abrasion – pounding the landscape with the debris they carry with them. But, as well as destroying, they also create new landscapes, many of them spectacular: vast deltas, as seen at the mouth of the Mississippi or the Nile; cliffs, rock arches and stacks, as found along the south coast of Australia; and the fjords cut by long-melted glaciers in British Columbia, Norway and New Zealand.

The vast ridges that divide the Earth's crust beneath each of the world's major oceans mark the boundaries between tectonic plates which are moving very gradually in opposite directions. As the plates shift apart, molten magma rises from the Earth's core to seal the rift and the sea floor slowly spreads towards the continental landmasses. The rate of sea floor spreading has been calculated by magnetic analysis of the rock – at about 40 mm [1.5 in] a year in the North Atlantic. Near the ocean shore, underwater volcanoes mark the line where the continental rise begins. As the plates meet, much of the denser ocean crust dips beneath the continental plate and melts back into the magma.

## THE SPREADING EARTH

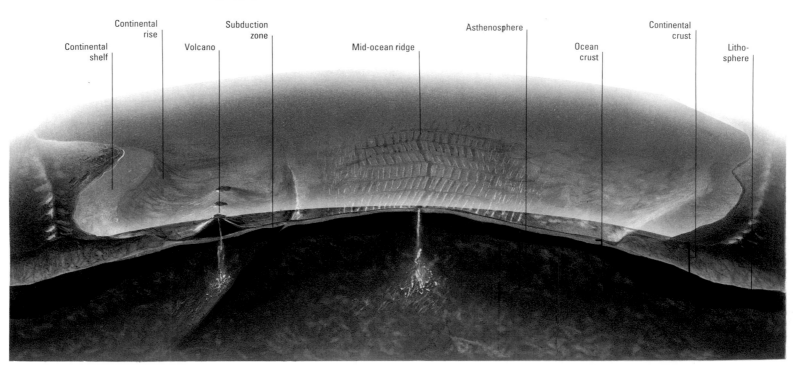

Continental shelf · Continental rise · Volcano · Subduction zone · Mid-ocean ridge · Asthenosphere · Ocean crust · Continental crust · Lithosphere

## TYPES OF ROCK

Rocks are divided into three types, according to the way in which they are formed:

**Igneous rocks,** including granite and basalt, are formed by the cooling of magma from within the Earth's crust.

**Metamorphic rocks,** such as slate, marble and quartzite, are formed below the Earth's surface by the compression or baking of existing rocks.

**Sedimentary rocks,** like sandstone and limestone, are formed on the surface of the Earth from the remains of living organisms and eroded fragments of older rocks.

## MOUNTAIN BUILDING

Mountains are formed when pressures on the Earth's crust caused by continental drift become so intense that the surface buckles or cracks. This happens most dramatically where two tectonic plates collide: the Rockies, Andes, Alps, Urals and Himalayas resulted from such impacts. These are all known as fold mountains, because they were formed by the compression of the rocks, forcing the surface to bend and fold like a crumpled rug.

The other main building process occurs when the crust fractures to create faults, allowing rock to be forced upwards in large blocks; or when the pressure of magma within the crust forces the surface to bulge into a dome, or erupts to form a volcano. Large mountain ranges may reveal a combination of those features; the Alps, for example, have been compressed so violently that the folds are fragmented by numerous faults and intrusions of molten rock.

Over millions of years, even the greatest mountain ranges can be reduced by erosion to a rugged landscape known as a peneplain.

**Types of fold:** Geographers give different names to the degrees of fold that result from continuing pressure on the rock strata. A simple fold may be symmetric, with even slopes on either side, but as the pressure builds up, one slope becomes steeper and the fold becomes asymmetric. Later, the ridge or 'anticline' at the top of the fold may slide over the lower ground or 'syncline' to form a recumbent fold. Eventually, the rock strata may break under the pressure to form an overthrust and finally a nappe fold.

Symmetric · Asymmetric · Recumbent · Overthrust · Nappe

**Types of faults:** Faults are classified by the direction in which the blocks of rock have moved. A normal fault results when a vertical movement causes the surface to break apart; compression causes a reverse fault. Sideways movement causes shearing, known as a strike-slip fault. When the rock breaks in two places, the central block may be pushed up in a horst fault, or sink in a graben fault.

Normal · Reverse · Strike-slip · Horst · Graben

## MOULDING THE LAND

While hidden forces of extraordinary power are moving the continents from below the Earth's crust, the more familiar elements of wind, water, heat and cold combine to sculpt the land surface. Erosion by weathering is seen in desert regions, where rocks degrade into sand through the effects of changing temperatures and strong winds.

The power of water is fiercer still. In severe storms, giant waves pound the shoreline with rocks and boulders, and often destroy concrete coastal defences; but even in quieter conditions, the sea steadily erodes cliffs and headlands and creates new land in the form of sand dunes, spits and salt marshes.

Rivers, too, are incessantly at work shaping the landscape on their way to join the sea. In highland regions, where the flow is rapid, they cut deep gorges and V-shaped valleys. As they reach more gentle slopes, rivers release some of the debris they have carried downstream, broadening out and raising levees along their banks by depositing mud and sand. In the lowland plains, they may drift into meanders, depositing more sediment and even building deltas when they finally approach the sea.

Ice has created some of the world's dramatic landscapes. As glaciers move slowly downhill, they scrape away rock from the mountains and valley sides, creating spectacular features.

## SHAPING FORCES: THE SEA

In areas of hard rock, waves cut steep cliffs and form underwater platforms; debris is deposited as a terrace. Bays are formed when sections of soft rock are carved away between headlands of harder rock; these are then battered until the headlands are reduced to rock arches and stacks.

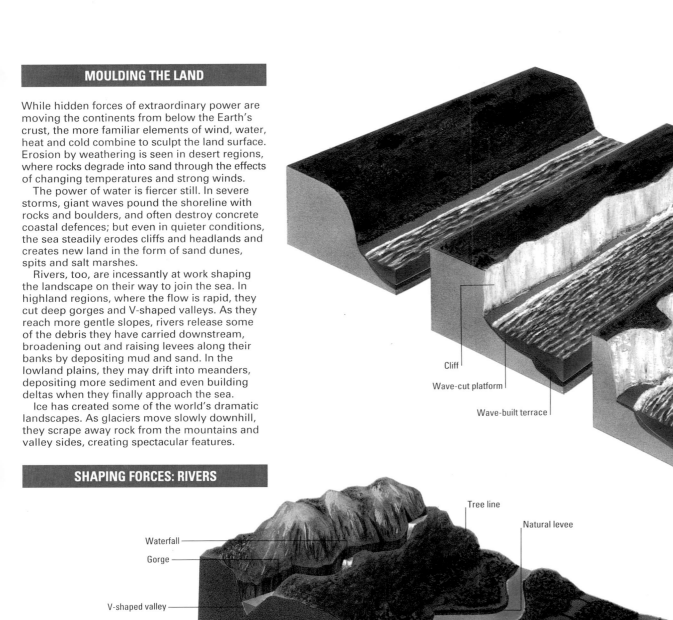

Headland

Cliff

Wave-cut platform

Wave-built terrace

Arch

Stack

Cove

## SHAPING FORCES: RIVERS

Tree line

Natural levee

Waterfall

Gorge

V-shaped valley

Meanders

Floodplain

Rivers shape the landscape according to the speed of their flow. In their youthful, upland stage they erode soft rocks quickly, cutting steep narrow valleys and tumbling in waterfalls over harder rock. As they mature, they deposit some debris and erode outwards to widen the valley. In their old age, where the gradient is minimal, they meander across wide plains, depositing deep layers of sediment.

YOUTH

MATURITY

Sediment

OLD AGE

Man-made levee

## SHAPING FORCES: GLACIERS

Col

Lateral moraine

Arête

Ice-dammed lake

U-shaped valley

Truncated spur

Hanging valley

Crevasse

Medial moraine

Drumlins

Snout

Glaciers are formed from compressed snow accumulating in a valley head or cirque. They move downhill at a rate of a few centimetres to several metres per day, eroding large quantities of rocks, debris or moraine, that are caught up by the glacier and add to the abrasive power of the ice. Glaciers create numerous distinctive landscape features: among the most easily recognized are hanging valleys, cut by tributary glaciers; terminal moraine and drumlins formed by rock debris deposited when a glacier retreats; and the broad U-shape that distinguishes a glacial valley from one cut by a river.

Outwash plain

Terminal moraine

# THE EARTH: ENVIRONMENT

Unique among the planets, the Earth has been the home of living creatures for most of its existence. Precisely how these improbable assemblies of self-replicating chemicals ever began remains a matter of conjecture, but the planet and its passengers have matured together for a very long time. Over 3,000 million years, life has not only adapted to its environment, but it has also slowly changed that environment to suit itself.

The planet and its biosphere – the entirety of its living things – function like a single organism. The British scientist James Lovelock, who first stated this 'Gaia hypothesis' in the 1970s, went further: the planet, he declared, actually was a living organism, equipped on a colossal scale with the same sort of stability-seeking mechanisms

used by lesser lifeforms like bacteria and humans to keep themselves running at optimum efficiency.

Lovelock's theory was inspired by a study of the Earth's atmosphere whose constituents he noted were very far from the state of chemical equilibrium observed elsewhere in the Solar System. The atmosphere has contained a substantial amount of free oxygen for the last 2,000 million years; yet without constant renewal, the oxygen molecules would soon be locked permanently in oxides. The nitrogen, too, would find chemical stability, probably in nitrates (accounting for some of the oxygen). Without living plants and algae to remove it, carbon dioxide would steadily increase from its present-day 0.03%; in a few million years, it

would form a thick blanket similar to the atmosphere of lifeless Venus, where surface temperatures reach 475°C.

It is not enough, however, for the biosphere simply to produce oxygen. While falling concentrations would first be uncomfortable and ultimately prove fatal for most contemporary life, at levels above the current 21% even moist vegetation is highly inflammable, and a massive conflagration becomes almost inevitable – a violent form of negative feedback to set the atmosphere on the path back to sterile equilibrium.

Fortunately, the biosphere has evolved over aeons into a subtle and complex control system, sensing changes and reacting to them quickly but gently, tending always to maintain the balance it has achieved.

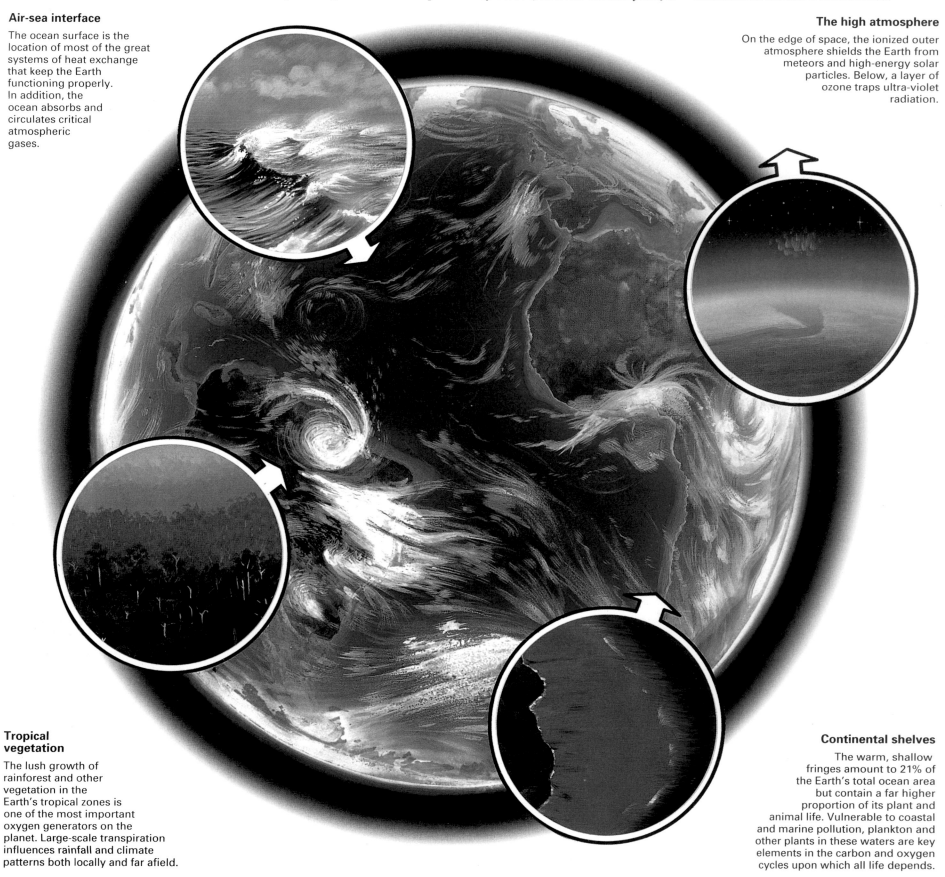

**Air-sea interface**

The ocean surface is the location of most of the great systems of heat exchange that keep the Earth functioning properly. In addition, the ocean absorbs and circulates critical atmospheric gases.

**The high atmosphere**

On the edge of space, the ionized outer atmosphere shields the Earth from meteors and high-energy solar particles. Below, a layer of ozone traps ultra-violet radiation.

**Tropical vegetation**

The lush growth of rainforest and other vegetation in the Earth's tropical zones is one of the most important oxygen generators on the planet. Large-scale transpiration influences rainfall and climate patterns both locally and far afield.

**Continental shelves**

The warm, shallow fringes amount to 21% of the Earth's total ocean area but contain a far higher proportion of its plant and animal life. Vulnerable to coastal and marine pollution, plankton and other plants in these waters are key elements in the carbon and oxygen cycles upon which all life depends.

## THE EARTH'S ENERGY BALANCE

Apart from a modest quantity of internal heat from its molten core, the Earth receives all of its energy from the Sun. If the planet is to remain at a constant temperature, it must reradiate exactly as much energy as it receives. Even a minute surplus would lead to a warmer Earth, a deficit to a cooler one; because the planetary energy budget is constantly audited by the laws of physics, which do not permit juggling, it must balance with absolute precision. The temperature at which thermal equilibrium is reached depends on a multitude of interconnected factors. Two of the most important are the relative brightness of the Earth – its index of reflectivity, called the 'albedo' – and the heat-trapping capacity of the atmosphere – the celebrated 'greenhouse effect'.

Because the Sun is very hot, most of its energy arrives in the form of relatively short-wave radiation: the shorter the waves, the more energy they carry. Some of the incoming energy is reflected straight back into space, exactly as it arrived; some is absorbed by the atmosphere on its way towards the surface; some is absorbed by the Earth itself. Absorbed energy heats the Earth and its atmosphere alike. But since its temperature is very much lower that that of the Sun, outgoing energy is emitted at much longer infra-red wavelengths. Some of the outgoing radiation escapes directly into outer space; some of it is reabsorbed by the atmosphere. Atmospheric energy eventually finds its way back into space, too, after a complex series of interactions. These include the air movements we call the weather and, almost incidentally, the maintenance of life on Earth.

This diagram does not attempt to illustrate the actual mechanisms of heat exchange, but gives a reasonable account (in percentages) of what happens to 100 energy 'units'. Short-wave radiation is shown in yellow, long-wave in red.

## THE CARBON CYCLE

Most of the constituents of the atmosphere are kept in constant balance by complex cycles in which life plays an essential and indeed a dominant part. The control of carbon dioxide, which left to its own devices would be the dominant atmospheric gas, is possibly the most important, although since all the Earth's biological and geophysical cycles interact and interlock, it is hard to separate them even in theory and quite impossible in practice.

The Earth has a huge supply of carbon, only a small quantity of which is in the form of carbon dioxide. Of that, around 98% is dissolved in the sea; the fraction circulating in the air amounts to only 340 parts per million of the atmosphere, where its capacity as a greenhouse gas is the key regulator of the planetary temperature. In turn, life regulates the regulator, keeping carbon dioxide concentrations below danger level.

If all life were to vanish tomorrow from the Earth, the atmosphere would begin the process of change immediately, although it might take several million years to achieve a new, inorganic stability. First, the oxygen content would begin to fall away; with no more assistance than a little solar radiation, a few electrical storms and its own high chemical potential, oxygen would steadily combine with atmospheric nitrogen and volcanic outgassing. In doing so, it would yield sufficient acid to react with carbonaceous rocks such as limestone, releasing carbon dioxide. Once carbon dioxide levels exceeded about 1%, its greenhouse power would increase disproportionately. Rising temperatures – well above the boiling point of water – would speed chemical reactions; in time, the Earth's atmosphere would consist of little more than carbon dioxide and superheated water vapour.

Living things, however, circulate carbon. They do so first by simply existing: after all, the carbon atom is the basic building block of living matter. During life, plants absorb atmospheric carbon dioxide, incorporating the carbon itself into their structure – leaves and trunks in the case of land plants, shells

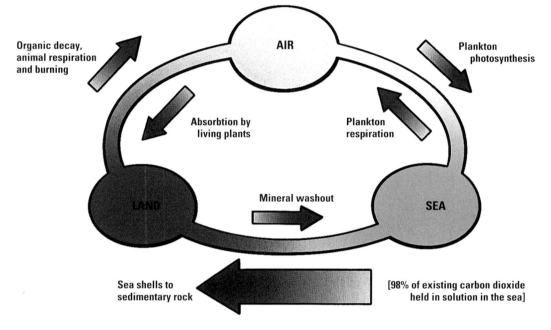

in the case of plankton and the tiny creatures that feed on it. The oxygen thereby freed is added to the atmosphere, at least for a time. Most plant carbon is returned to circulation when the plants die and decay, combining once more with the oxygen released during life. However, a small proportion – about one part in 1,000 – is removed almost permanently, buried beneath mud on land, or at sea sinking as dead matter to the ocean floor. In time, it is slowly compressed into sedimentary rocks such as limestone and chalk.

But in the evolution of the Earth, nothing is quite permanent. On an even longer timescale, the planet's crustal movements force new rock upwards in mid-ocean ridges. Limestone deposits are

moved, and sea levels change; ancient limestone is exposed to weathering, and a little of its carbon is released to be fixed in turn by the current generation of plants.

The carbon cycle has continued quietly for an immensely long time, and without gross disturbance there is no reason why it would not continue almost indefinitely in the future. However, human beings have found a way to release fixed carbon at a rate far faster than existing global systems can recirculate it. Oil and coal deposits represent the work of millions of years of carbon accumulation; but it has taken only a few human generations of high-energy scavenging to endanger the entire complex regulatory cycle.

## THE GREENHOUSE EFFECT

Constituting barely 0.03% of the atmosphere, carbon dioxide has a hugely disproportionate effect on the Earth's climate and even its habitability. Like the glass panes in a greenhouse, it is transparent to most incoming short-wave radiation, which passes freely to heat the planet beneath. But when the warmed Earth retransmits that energy, in the form of longer-wave infra-red radiation, the carbon dioxide functions as an opaque shield, so that the planetary surface (like the interior of a greenhouse) stays relatively hot.

The recent increases in $CO_2$ levels are causing alarm: global warming associated with a runaway greenhouse effect could bring disaster. But a serious reduction would be just as damaging, with surface temperatures falling dramatically; during the last Ice Age, for example, the carbon dioxide concentration was around 180 parts per million, and a total absence of the gas would likely leave the planet a ball of ice, or at best frozen tundra.

The diagram shows incoming sunlight as yellow; high-energy ultra-violet (blue) is trapped by the ozone layer, while outgoing heat from the warmed Earth (red) is partially retained by carbon dioxide.

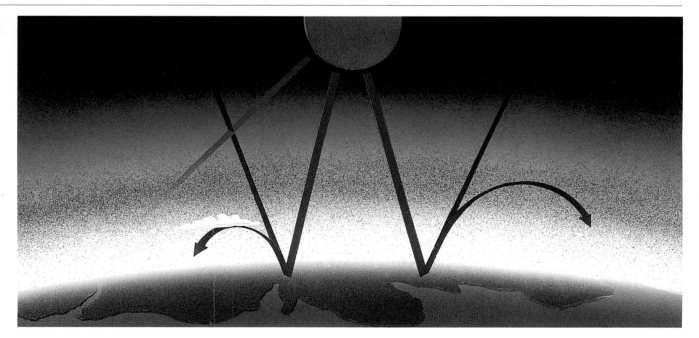

# PEOPLE: DEMOGRAPHY

As the 20th century draws to its close, the Earth's population increases by nearly 10,000 every hour – enough to fill a new major city every week. The growth is almost entirely confined to the developing world, which accounted for 67% of total population in 1950 and is set to reach 84% by 2025. In developed countries, populations are almost static, and in some places, such as Germany, are actually falling. In fact, there is a clear correlation between wealth and low fertility: as incomes rise, reproduction rates drop.

The decline is already apparent. With the exception of Africa, the actual rates of increase are falling nearly everywhere. The population structure, however, ensures that human numbers will continue to rise even as fertility diminishes. Developed nations, like the UK, have an even spread across ages, and usually a growing proportion of elderly people: the over-75s often outnumber the under-5s, and women of child-bearing age form only a small part of the total. Developing nations fall into a pattern somewhere between that of Kenya and Brazil: the great majority of their people are in the younger age groups, about to enter their most fertile years. In time, even Kenya's population profile should resemble the developed model, but the transition will come about only after a few more generations' growth.

It remains to be seen whether the planet will tolerate the population growth that seems inevitable before stability is reached. More people consume more resources, increasing the strain on an already troubled environment. However, more people should mean a greater supply of human ingenuity – the only commodity likely to resolve the crisis.

## LARGEST NATIONS

The world's most populous nations, in millions (1993)

| | | |
|---|---|---|
| 1. | China | 1,187 |
| 2. | India | 879 |
| 3. | USA | 255 |
| 4. | Indonesia | 191 |
| 5. | Brazil | 156 |
| 6. | Russia | 149 |
| 7. | Japan | 124 |
| 8. | Bangladesh | 119 |
| 9. | Pakistan | 115 |
| 10. | Mexico | 89 |
| 11. | Nigeria | 88 |
| 12. | Germany | 80 |
| 13. | Vietnam | 69 |
| 14. | Philippines | 64 |
| 15. | Turkey | 58 |
| 16. | Italy | 57 |
| 17. | UK | 57 |
| 18. | Thailand | 57 |
| 19. | France | 57 |
| 20. | Iran | 56 |
| 21. | Egypt | 55 |
| 22. | Ethiopia | 55 |
| 23. | Ukraine | 52 |
| 24. | S. Korea | 43 |

## CROWDED NATIONS

Population per square kilometre (1993), exc. nations of less than one million.

| | | |
|---|---|---|
| 1. | Hong Kong | 5,273.6 |
| 2. | Singapore | 4,535.5 |
| 3. | Bangladesh | 828.4 |
| 4. | Mauritius | 582.8 |
| 5. | Taiwan | 573.9 |
| 6. | S. Korea | 441.0 |
| 7. | Puerto Rico | 397.8 |
| 8. | Netherlands | 365.7 |
| 9. | Japan | 329.0 |
| 10. | Belgium | 327.8 |
| 11. | Rwanda | 286.2 |
| 12. | Lebanon | 272.9 |
| 13. | India | 267.5 |
| 14. | Sri Lanka | 265.3 |
| 15. | El Salvador | 257.0 |
| 16. | Trinidad & Tobago | 248.0 |
| 17. | UK | 237.8 |
| 18. | Germany | 225.7 |
| 19. | Jamaica | 224.7 |
| 20. | Israel | 183.2 |

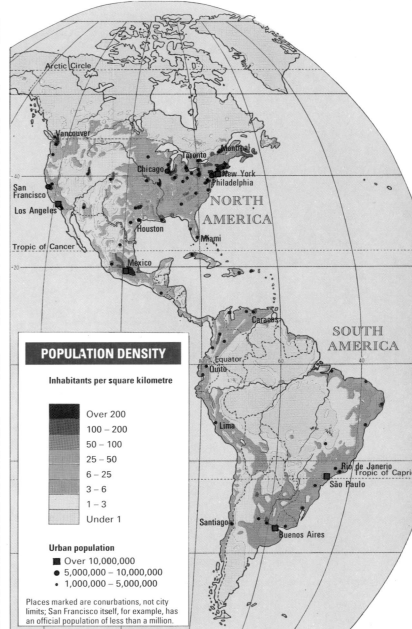

### POPULATION DENSITY

Inhabitants per square kilometre

- Over 200
- 100 – 200
- 50 – 100
- 25 – 50
- 6 – 25
- 3 – 6
- 1 – 3
- Under 1

Urban population
- ■ Over 10,000,000
- ● 5,000,000 – 10,000,000
- • 1,000,000 – 5,000,000

Places marked are conurbations, not city limits; San Francisco itself, for example, has an official population of less than a million.

Projection : Mollweide's Interrupted Homolographic

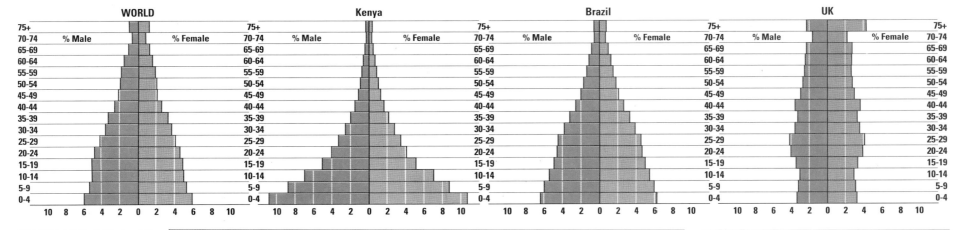

WORLD   Kenya   Brazil   UK

## RATES OF GROWTH

Apparently small rates of population growth lead to dramatic increases over two or three generations. The table below translates annual percentage growth into the number of years required to double a population.

| % change | Doubling time |
|---|---|
| 0.5 | 139.0 |
| 1.0 | 69.7 |
| 1.5 | 46.6 |
| 2.0 | 35.0 |
| 2.5 | 28.1 |
| 3.0 | 23.4 |
| 3.5 | 20.1 |
| 4.0 | 17.7 |

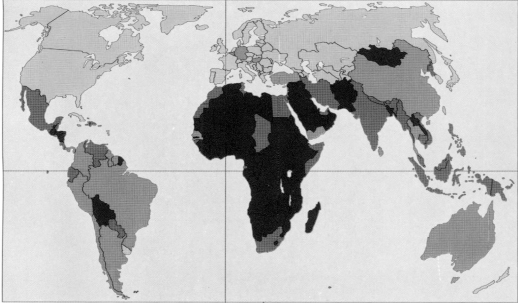

## POPULATION CHANGE

Estimated percentage change in total population, between 1990 and 2000

- Over 40% gain
- 30 – 40% gain
- 20 – 30% gain
- 10 – 20% gain
- 0 – 10% gain
- No change or population loss

| Top 5 countries | | Bottom 5 countries | |
|---|---|---|---|
| Afghanistan | +60% | Hungary | −0.2% |
| Mali | +56% | Singapore | −0.2% |
| Tanzania | +55% | Grenada | −2.4% |
| Ivory Coast | +47% | Tonga | −3.2% |
| Saudi Arabia | +46% | Germany | −3.2% |

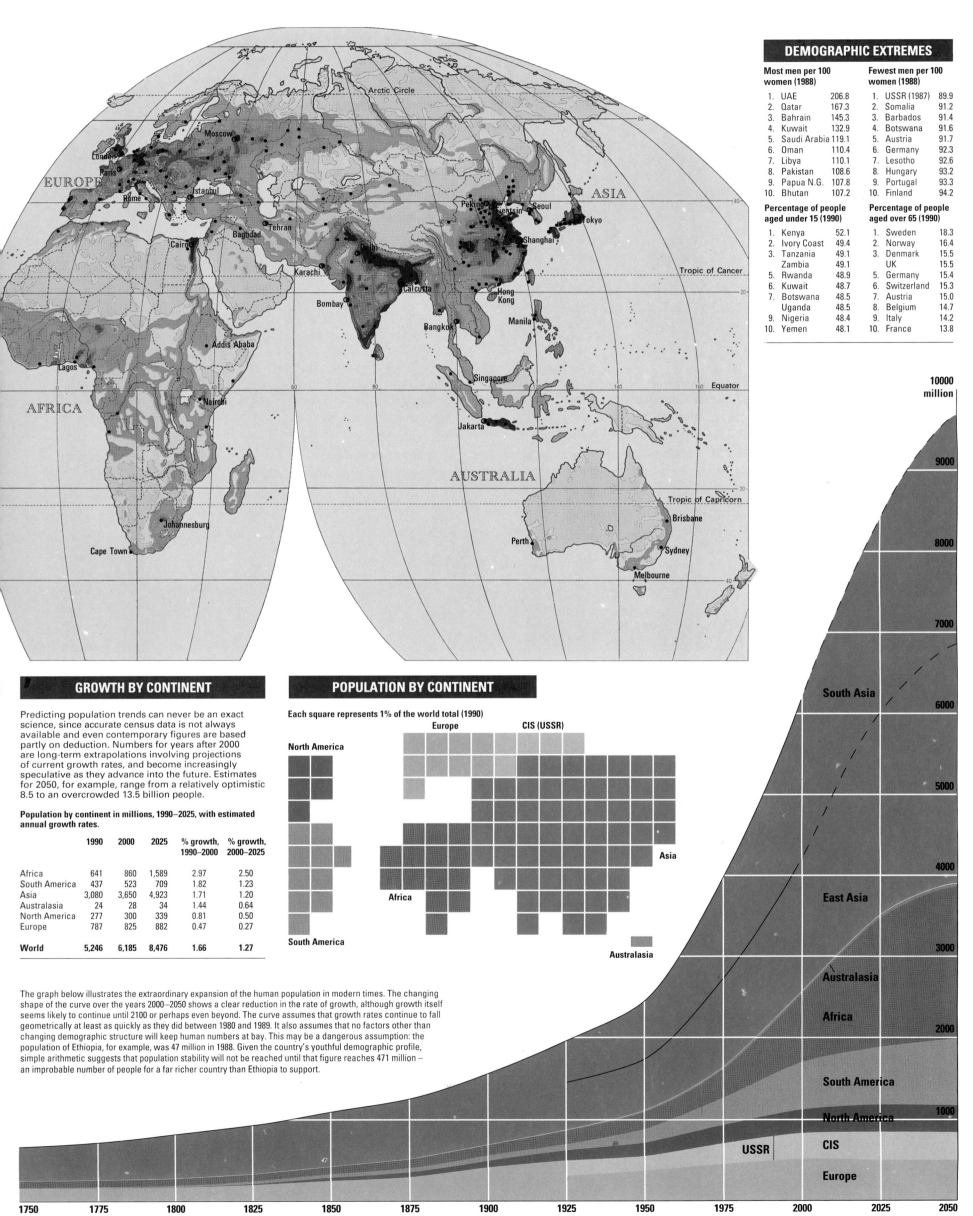

## DEMOGRAPHIC EXTREMES

| Most men per 100 women (1988) | | Fewest men per 100 women (1988) | |
| --- | --- | --- | --- |
| 1. UAE | 206.8 | 1. USSR (1987) | 89.9 |
| 2. Qatar | 167.3 | 2. Somalia | 91.2 |
| 3. Bahrain | 145.3 | 3. Barbados | 91.4 |
| 4. Kuwait | 132.9 | 4. Botswana | 91.6 |
| 5. Saudi Arabia | 119.1 | 5. Austria | 91.7 |
| 6. Oman | 110.4 | 6. Germany | 92.3 |
| 7. Libya | 110.1 | 7. Lesotho | 92.6 |
| 8. Pakistan | 108.6 | 8. Hungary | 93.2 |
| 9. Papua N.G. | 107.8 | 9. Portugal | 93.3 |
| 10. Bhutan | 107.2 | 10. Finland | 94.2 |

| Percentage of people aged under 15 (1990) | | Percentage of people aged over 65 (1990) | |
| --- | --- | --- | --- |
| 1. Kenya | 52.1 | 1. Sweden | 18.3 |
| 2. Ivory Coast | 49.4 | 2. Norway | 16.4 |
| 3. Tanzania | 49.1 | 3. Denmark | 15.5 |
| Zambia | 49.1 | UK | 15.5 |
| 5. Rwanda | 48.9 | 5. Germany | 15.4 |
| 6. Kuwait | 48.7 | 6. Switzerland | 15.3 |
| 7. Botswana | 48.5 | 7. Austria | 15.0 |
| Uganda | 48.5 | 8. Belgium | 14.7 |
| 9. Nigeria | 48.4 | 9. Italy | 14.2 |
| 10. Yemen | 48.1 | 10. France | 13.8 |

## GROWTH BY CONTINENT

Predicting population trends can never be an exact science, since accurate census data is not always available and even contemporary figures are based partly on deduction. Numbers for years after 2000 are long-term extrapolations involving projections of current growth rates, and become increasingly speculative as they advance into the future. Estimates for 2050, for example, range from a relatively optimistic 8.5 to an overcrowded 13.5 billion people.

**Population by continent in millions, 1990–2025, with estimated annual growth rates.**

| | 1990 | 2000 | 2025 | % growth, 1990–2000 | % growth, 2000–2025 |
| --- | --- | --- | --- | --- | --- |
| Africa | 641 | 860 | 1,589 | 2.97 | 2.50 |
| South America | 437 | 523 | 709 | 1.82 | 1.23 |
| Asia | 3,080 | 3,650 | 4,923 | 1.71 | 1.20 |
| Australasia | 24 | 28 | 34 | 1.44 | 0.64 |
| North America | 277 | 300 | 339 | 0.81 | 0.50 |
| Europe | 787 | 825 | 882 | 0.47 | 0.27 |
| World | 5,246 | 6,185 | 8,476 | 1.66 | 1.27 |

## POPULATION BY CONTINENT

**Each square represents 1% of the world total (1990)**

North America
Europe
CIS (USSR)
Asia
Africa
South America
Australasia

The graph below illustrates the extraordinary expansion of the human population in modern times. The changing shape of the curve over the years 2000–2050 shows a clear reduction in the rate of growth, although growth itself seems likely to continue until 2100 or perhaps even beyond. The curve assumes that growth rates continue to fall geometrically at least as quickly as they did between 1980 and 1989. It also assumes that no factors other than changing demographic structure will keep human numbers at bay. This may be a dangerous assumption: the population of Ethiopia, for example, was 47 million in 1988. Given the country's youthful demographic profile, simple arithmetic suggests that population stability will not be reached until that figure reaches 471 million – an improbable number of people for a far richer country than Ethiopia to support.

# PEOPLE: CITIES

In 1750, barely three humans in every hundred lived in a city; by 2000, more than half the world's population will find a home in some kind of urban area. In 1850, only London and Paris had more than a million inhabitants; by 2000, at least 24 cities will each contain over 10 million people. The increase is concentrated in the Third World, if only because levels of urbanization in most developed countries – more than 90% in the UK and Belgium, and almost 75% in the USA, despite that country's great open spaces – have already reached practical limits.

Such large-scale concentration is relatively new to the human race. Although city life has always attracted country dwellers in search of trade, employment or simply human contact, until modern times they paid a high price. Crowding and poor sanitation ensured high death rates, and until about 1850, most cities needed a steady flow of incomers simply to maintain their population levels: for example, there were 600,000 more deaths than births in 18th-century London, and some other large cities showed an even worse imbalance.

With improved public health, cities could grow from their own human resources, and large-scale urban living became commonplace in the developed world. Since about 1950, the pattern has been global. Like their counterparts in 19th-century Europe and the USA, the great new cities are driven into rapid growth by a kind of push-pull mechanism. The push is generated by agricultural overcrowding: only so many people can live from a single plot of land and population pressure drives many into towns. The pull comes from the possibilities of economic improvement – an irresistible lure to the world's rural hopefuls.

Such improvement is not always obvious: the typical Third World city, with millions of people living (often illegally) in shanty towns and many thousands existing homelessly on the ill-made streets, does not present a great image of prosperity. Yet modern shanty towns are healthier than industrializing Pittsburgh or Manchester in the last century, and these human ant-hills teem with industry as well as squalor: throughout the world, above-average rates of urbanization have gone hand-in-hand with above-average rates of economic growth. Surveys demonstrate that Third World city dwellers are generally better off than their rural counterparts, whose poverty is less concentrated but often more desperate. This only serves to increase the attraction of the city for the rural poor.

However, the sheer speed of the urbanization process threatens to overwhelm the limited abilities of city authorities to provide even rudimentary services. The 24 million people expected to live in Mexico City by 2000, for example, would swamp a more efficient local government than Mexico can provide. Improvements are often swallowed up by the relentless rise in urban population: although safe drinking water should reach 75% of Third World city dwellers by the end of the century – a considerable achievement – population growth will add 100 million to the list of those without it.

## THE URBANIZATION OF THE EARTH

City-building, 1850–2000; each white spot represents a city of at least 1 million inhabitants.

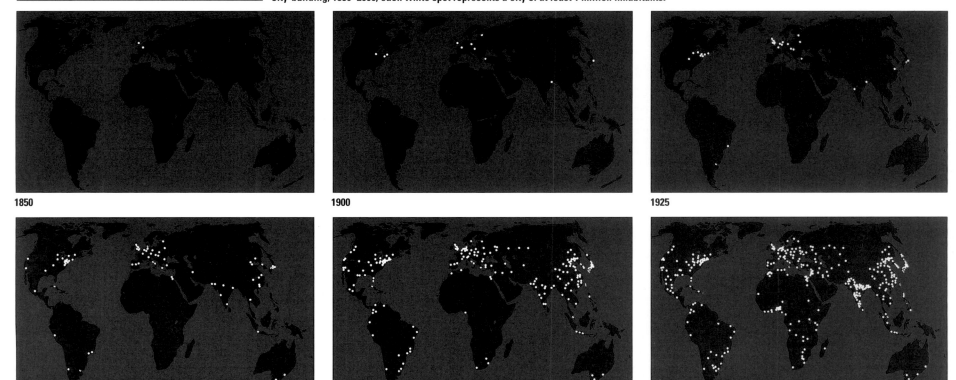

1850

1900

1925

1950

1975

2000

## URBAN POPULATION

Percentage of total population living in towns and cities (1990)

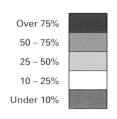

Over 75%

50 – 75%

25 – 50%

10 – 25%

Under 10%

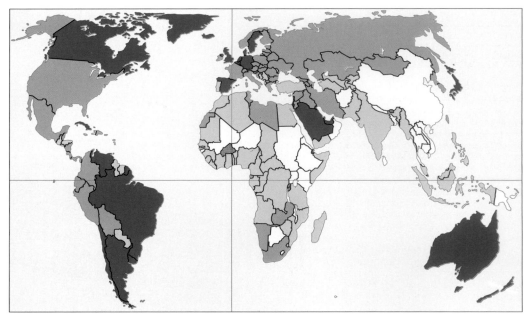

| Most urbanized | | Least urbanized | |
|---|---|---|---|
| Singapore | 100% | Bhutan | 5% |
| Belgium | 97% | Burundi | 7% |
| Kuwait | 96% | Rwanda | 8% |
| Hong Kong | 93% | Burkina Faso | 9% |
| UK | 93% | Nepal | 10% |

## EXPANDING CITIES

The growth of the world's largest cities, 1950–2000. Intermediate rings indicate relative size in 1970 and 1985.

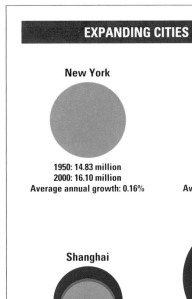

**New York**
1950: 14.83 million
2000: 16.10 million
Average annual growth: 0.16%

**London**
1950: 8.35 million
2000: 10.79 million
Average annual growth: 0.51%

**Tokyo**
1950: 6.25 million
2000: 21.32 million
Average annual growth: 2.5%

**Buenos Aires**
1950: 5.25 million
2000: 13.05 million
Average annual growth: 1.8%

**Calcutta**
1950: 4.45 million
2000: 15.94 million
Average annual growth: 2.6%

**Shanghai**
1950: 4.3 million
2000: 14.69 million
Average annual growth: 2.5%

**Mexico City**
1950: 2.97 million
2000: 24.44 million
Average annual growth: 4.3%

**Rio de Janeiro**
1950: 2.94 million
2000: 13.0 million
Average annual growth: 3.0%

**São Paulo**
1950: 2.28 million
2000: 23.6 million
Average annual growth: 4.8%

**Seoul**
1950: 1.45 million
2000: 12.97 million
Average annual growth: 4.5%

Each set of circles illustrates a city's size in 1950, 1970, 1985 and 2000. In most cases, expansion has been steady and, often, explosive. New York and London, however, went through patches of negative growth during the period. In New York, the world's largest city in 1950, population reached a peak around 1970. London shrank slightly between 1970 and 1985 before resuming a very modest rate of increase. In both cases, the divergence from world trends can be explained in part by counting methods: each is at the centre of a great agglomeration, and definitions of where 'city limits' lie may vary over time. But their relative decline also matches a pattern often seen in mature cities in the developed world, where urbanization, already at a very high level, has reached a plateau.

## CITIES IN DANGER

As the decade of the 1980s advanced, most industrial countries, alarmed by acid rain and urban smog, took significant steps to limit air pollution. These controls, however, are expensive to install and difficult to enforce, and clean air remains a luxury most developed as well as developing cities must live without.

Those taking part in the United Nations' Global Environment Monitoring System (see right) frequently show dangerous levels of pollutants ranging from soot to sulphur dioxide and photochemical smog; air in the majority of cities without such sampling equipment is likely to be at least as bad.

## URBAN AIR POLLUTION

The world's most polluted cities: number of days each year when sulphur dioxide levels exceeded the WHO threshold of 150 micrograms per cubic metre (averaged over 4 to 15 years, 1970s – 1980s)

Sulphur dioxide is the main pollutant associated with industrial cities. According to the World Health Organization, more than seven days in a year above 150 µg per cubic metre bring a serious risk of respiratory disease: at least 600 million people live in urban areas where $SO_2$ concentrations regularly reach damaging levels.

Manila, Philippines
Calcutta, India
Milan, Italy
Zagreb, Croatia
Guangzhou, China
Madrid, Spain
Peking (Beijing), China
Xian, China
Seoul, South Korea
Tehran, Iran
Shenyang, China

120   90   60   30

## LARGEST CITIES

The world's most populous cities, in millions of inhabitants, based on estimates for the year 2000*

| | City | |
|---|---|---|
| 1. | Mexico City | 24.4 |
| 2. | São Paulo | 23.6 |
| 3. | Tokyo-Yokohama | 21.3 |
| 4. | New York | 16.1 |
| 5. | Calcutta | 15.9 |
| 6. | Bombay | 15.4 |
| 7. | Shanghai | 14.7 |
| 8. | Tehran | 13.7 |
| 9. | Jakarta | 13.2 |
| 10. | Buenos Aires | 13.1 |
| 11. | Rio de Janeiro | 13.0 |
| 12. | Seoul | 13.0 |
| 13. | Delhi | 12.8 |
| 14. | Lagos | 12.4 |
| 15. | Cairo-Giza | 11.8 |
| 16. | Karachi | 11.6 |
| 17. | Manila-Quezon | 11.5 |
| 18. | Peking (Beijing) | 11.5 |
| 19. | Dhaka | 11.3 |
| 20. | Osaka-Kobe | 11.2 |
| 21. | Los Angeles | 10.9 |
| 22. | London | 10.8 |
| 23. | Bangkok | 10.3 |
| 24. | Moscow | 10.1 |
| 25. | Tientsin (Tianjin) | 10.0 |
| 26. | Lima-Callao | 8.8 |
| 27. | Paris | 8.8 |
| 28. | Milan | 8.7 |
| 29. | Madras | 7.8 |
| 30. | Baghdad | 7.7 |
| 31. | Chicago | 7.0 |
| 32. | Bogotá | 6.9 |
| 33. | Hong Kong | 6.1 |
| 34. | St Petersburg | 5.8 |
| 35. | Pusan | 5.8 |
| 36. | Santiago | 5.6 |
| 37. | Shenyang | 5.5 |
| 38. | Madrid | 5.4 |
| 39. | Naples | 4.5 |
| 40. | Philadelphia | 4.3 |

[City populations are based on urban agglomerations rather than legal city limits. In some cases, such as Tokyo-Yokohama and Cairo-Giza, where two adjacent cities have merged into one concentration, they have been regarded as a single unit.]

* For list of largest cities in 1993, see page XI

## INFORMAL CITIZENS

Proportion of population living in squatter settlements, selected cities in the developing world (1980s)

Urbanization in most Third World countries has been coming about far faster than local governments can provide services and accommodation for the new city dwellers. Many – in some cities, most – find their homes in improvised squatter settlements, often unconnected to power, water and sanitation networks. Yet despite their ramshackle housing and marginal legality, these communities are often the most dynamic part of a city economy. They are also growing in size; and given the squatters' reluctance to be counted by tax-demanding authorities, the percentages shown here are likely to be underestimates.

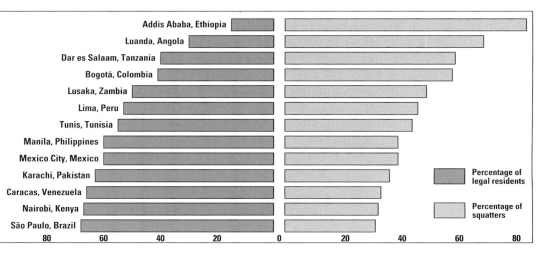

Addis Ababa, Ethiopia
Luanda, Angola
Dar es Salaam, Tanzania
Bogotá, Colombia
Lusaka, Zambia
Lima, Peru
Tunis, Tunisia
Manila, Philippines
Mexico City, Mexico
Karachi, Pakistan
Caracas, Venezuela
Nairobi, Kenya
São Paulo, Brazil

80  60  40  20  0  20  40  60  80

Percentage of legal residents

Percentage of squatters

## URBAN ADVANTAGES

Despite overcrowding and poor housing, living standards in the developing world's cities are almost invariably better than in the surrounding countryside. Resources – financial, material and administrative – are concentrated in the towns, which are usually also the centres of political activity and pressure. Governments – frequently unstable, and rarely established on a solid democratic base – are usually more responsive to urban discontent than rural misery.

In many countries, especially in Africa, food prices are often kept artificially low, appeasing underemployed urban masses at the expense of agricultural development. The imbalance encourages further cityward migration, helping to account for the astonishing rate of post-1950 urbanization and putting great strain on the ability of many nations to provide even modest improvements for their people.

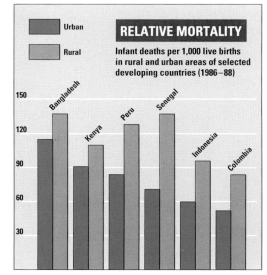

**RELATIVE MORTALITY**

Urban
Rural

Infant deaths per 1,000 live births in rural and urban areas of selected developing countries (1986–88)

150  120  90  60  30

Bangladesh, Kenya, Peru, Senegal, Indonesia, Colombia

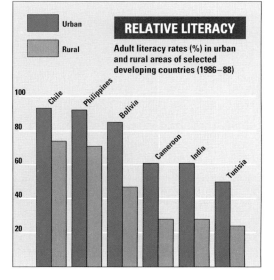

**RELATIVE LITERACY**

Urban
Rural

Adult literacy rates (%) in urban and rural areas of selected developing countries (1986–88)

100  80  60  40  20

Chile, Philippines, Bolivia, Cameroon, India, Tunisia

# PEOPLE: THE HUMAN FAMILY

Strictly speaking, all human beings belong to a single race – *Homo sapiens* has no subspecies. But although all humans are interfertile, anthropologists and geneticists distinguish three main racial types: Caucasoid, Negroid and Mongoloid. Racial differences reflect not so much evolutionary origin as long periods of separation.

Racial affinities are not always obvious. The Caucasoid group stems from Europe, North Africa and India, but still includes Australian aboriginals within its broad type; Mongoloid peoples comprise American Indians and Eskimos as well as most Chinese, central Asians and Malays; Negroids are mostly of African origin, but also include the Papuan peoples of New Guinea.

Migration in modern times has mingled racial groups to an unprecedented extent, and most nations now have some degree of racially mixed population.

Language is almost the definition of a particular human culture; the world has well over 5,000, most of them with only a few hundred thousand speakers. In one important sense, all languages are equal; although different vocabularies and linguistic structures greatly influence patterns of thought, all true human languages can carry virtually unlimited information. But even if, for example, there is no theoretical difference in the communicative power of English and one of the 500 or more tribal languages of Papua New Guinea, an English speaker has access to much more of the global culture than a Papuan who knows no other tongue.

Like language, religion encourages the internal cohesion of a single human group at the expense of creating gulfs of incomprehension between different groups. All religions satisfy a deep-seated human need, assigning men and women to a comprehensible place in what most of them still consider a divinely ordered world. But religion is also a means by which a culture can assert its individuality; the startling rise of Islam in the late 20th century is partly a response by large sections of the developing world to the secular, Western-inspired world order from which many non-Western peoples feel excluded. Like uncounted millions of human beings before them, they find in their religion not only a personal faith but also a powerful group identity.

## WORLD MIGRATION

The greatest voluntary migration was the colonization of North America by 30–35 million European settlers during the 19th century. The greatest forced migration involved 9–11 million Africans taken as slaves to America 1550–1860. The migrations shown on the map are mostly international as population movements within borders are not usually recorded. Many of the statistics are necessarily estimates as so many refugees and migrant workers enter countries illegally and unrecorded. Emigrants may have a variety of motives for leaving, thus making it difficult to distinguish between voluntary and involuntary migrations.

Foreign Born as a % of total population (latest year)
- More than 7.5%
- 3 – 7.5%
- 1.5 – 3%
- Less than 1.5%
- No available data

Migration
- Over 2,000,000 people
- 1 – 2,000,000 people
- 500,000 – 1,000,000 people
- Under 500,000 people

1500 – 1914: Voluntary, Involuntary
Since 1914: Voluntary, Involuntary

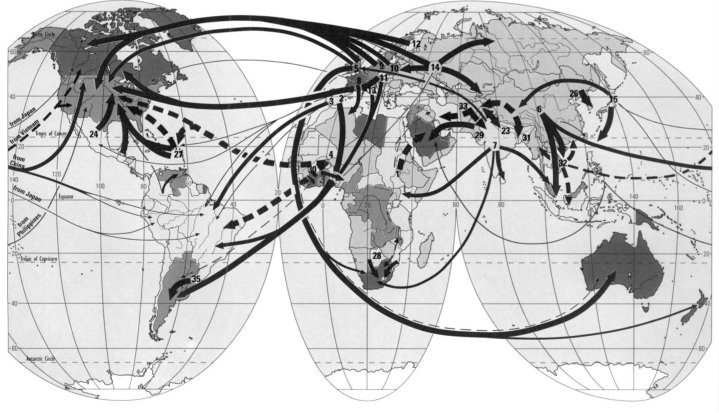

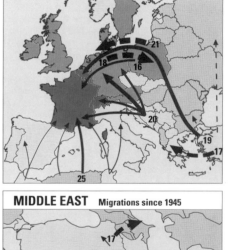

EUROPE   Migrations since 1918

MIDDLE EAST   Migrations since 1945

## BUILDING THE USA

**US Immigration 1820–1990**

'Give me your tired, your poor/Your huddled masses yearning to breathe free....'

So starts Emma Lazarus's poem *The New Colossus*, inscribed on the Statue of Liberty. For decades the USA was the magnet that attracted millions of immigrants, notably from Central and Eastern Europe, the flow peaking in the early years of this century.

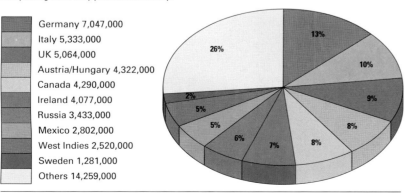

- Germany 7,047,000
- Italy 5,333,000
- UK 5,064,000
- Austria/Hungary 4,322,000
- Canada 4,290,000
- Ireland 4,077,000
- Russia 3,433,000
- Mexico 2,802,000
- West Indies 2,520,000
- Sweden 1,281,000
- Others 14,259,000

**Major world migrations since 1500 (over 1,000,000 people)**

| | | |
|---|---|---|
| 1. | North African and East African slaves to Arabia (4.3m) | 1500–1900 |
| 2. | Spanish to South and Central America (2.3m) | 1530–1914 |
| 3. | Portuguese to Brazil (1.4m) | 1530–1914 |
| 4. | West African slaves to South America (4.6m) | 1550–1860 |
| | to Caribbean (4m) | 1580–1860 |
| | to North and Central America (1m) | 1650–1820 |
| 5. | British and Irish to North America (13.5m) | 1620–1914 |
| | to Australasia and South Africa (3m) | 1790–1914 |
| 6. | Chinese to South-east Asia (22m) | 1820–1914 |
| | to North America (1m) | 1880–1914 |
| 7. | Indian migrant workers (3m) | 1850–1914 |
| 8. | French to North Africa (1.5m) | 1850–1914 |
| 9. | Germans to North America (5m) | 1850–1914 |
| 10. | Poles to North America (3.6m) | 1850–1914 |
| 11. | Austro-Hungarians to North America (3.2m) | 1850–1914 |
| | to Western Europe (3.4m) | 1850–1914 |
| | to South America (1.8m) | 1850–1914 |
| 12. | Scandinavians to North America (2.7m) | 1850–1914 |
| 13. | Italians to North America (5m) | 1860–1914 |
| | to South America (3.7m) | 1860–1914 |
| 14. | Russians to North America (2.2m) | 1880–1914 |
| | to Western Europe (2.2m) | 1880–1914 |
| | to Siberia (6m) | 1880–1914 |
| | to Central Asia (4m) | 1880–1914 |
| 15. | Japanese to Eastern Asia, South-east Asia and America (8m) | 1900–1914 |
| 16. | Poles to Western Europe (1m) | 1920–1940 |
| 17. | Greeks and Armenians from Turkey (1.6m) | 1922–1923 |
| 18. | European Jews to extermination camps (5m) | 1940–1944 |
| 19. | Turks to Western Europe (1.9m) | 1940– |
| 20. | Yugoslavs to Western Europe (2m) | 1940– |
| 21. | Germans to Western Europe (9.8m) | 1945–1947 |
| 22. | Palestinian refugees (2m) | 1947– |
| 23. | Indian and Pakistani refugees (15m) | 1947 |
| 24. | Mexicans to North America (9m) | 1950– |
| 25. | North Africans to Western Europe (1.1m) | 1950– |
| 26. | Korean refugees (5m) | 1950–1954 |
| 27. | Latin Americans and West Indians to North America (4.7m) | 1960– |
| 28. | Migrant workers to South Africa (1.5m) | 1960– |
| 29. | Indians and Pakistanis to The Gulf (2.4m) | 1970– |
| 30. | Migrant workers to Nigeria and Ivory Coast (3m) | 1970– |
| 31. | Bangladeshi and Pakistani refugees (2m) | 1972 |
| 32. | Vietnamese and Cambodian refugees (1.5m) | 1975– |
| 33. | Afghan refugees (6.1m) | 1979– |
| 34. | Egyptians to The Gulf and Libya (2.9m) | 1980– |
| 35. | Migrant workers to Argentina (2m) | 1980– |

## LANGUAGE

**INDO-EUROPEAN FAMILY**
1. Balto-Slavic group (incl. Russian, Ukrainian)
2. Germanic group (incl. English, German)
3. Celtic group
4. Greek
5. Albanian
6. Iranian group
7. Armenian
8. Romance group (incl. Spanish, Portuguese, French, Italian)
9. Indo-Aryan group (incl. Hindi, Bengali, Urdu, Punjabi, Marathi)
10. **CAUCASIAN FAMILY**

**AFRO-ASIATIC FAMILY**
11. Semitic group (incl. Arabic)
12. Kushitic group
13. Berber group
14. **KHOISAN FAMILY**
15. **NIGER-CONGO FAMILY**
16. **NILO-SAHARAN FAMILY**
17. **URALIC FAMILY**

**ALTAIC FAMILY**
18. Turkic group
19. Mongolian group
20. Tungus-Manchu group
21. Japanese and Korean

**SINO-TIBETAN FAMILY**
22. Sinitic (Chinese) languages
23. Tibetic-Burmic languages
24. **TAI FAMILY**

**AUSTRO-ASIATIC FAMILY**
25. Mon-Khmer group
26. Munda group
27. Vietnamese
28. **DRAVIDIAN FAMILY** (incl. Telugu, Tamil)
29. **AUSTRONESIAN FAMILY** (incl. Malay-Indonesian)
30. **OTHER LANGUAGES**

### OFFICIAL LANGUAGES

| Language | Total population | World % |
|---|---|---|
| English | 1,400m | 27.0% |
| Chinese | 1,070m | 19.1% |
| Hindi | 700m | 13.5% |
| Spanish | 280m | 5.4% |
| Russian | 270m | 5.2% |
| French | 220m | 4.2% |
| Arabic | 170m | 3.3% |
| Portuguese | 160m | 3.0% |
| Malay | 160m | 3.0% |
| Bengali | 150m | 2.9% |
| Japanese | 120m | 2.3% |

**Languages** form a kind of tree of development, splitting from a few ancient proto-tongues into branches that have grown apart and further divided with the passage of time. English and Hindi, for example, both belong to the great Indo-European family, although the relationship is only apparent after much analysis and comparison with non-Indo-European languages such as Chinese or Arabic; Hindi is part of the Indo-Aryan subgroup, whereas English is a member of Indo-European's Germanic branch; French, another Indo-European tongue, traces its descent through the Latin, or Romance, branch. A few languages – Basque is one example – have no apparent links with any other, living or dead. Most modern languages, of course, have acquired enormous quantities of vocabulary from each other.

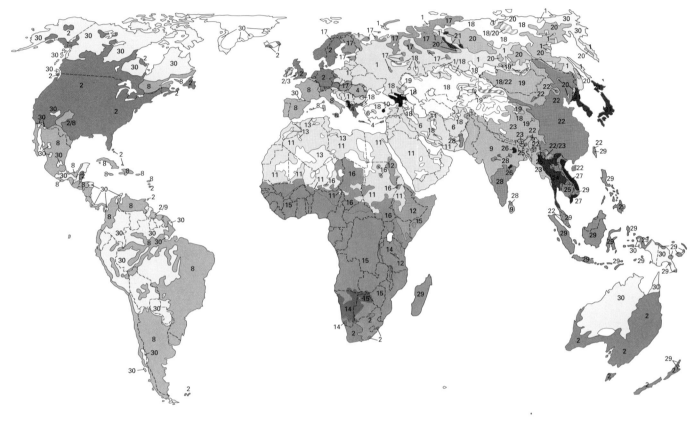

### MOTHER TONGUES

Native speakers of the major languages, in millions (1989)

- Mandarin Chinese 834
- English 443
- Hindi 352
- Spanish 341
- Russian 293
- Arabic 197
- Bengali 184
- Portuguese 173
- Malay 142
- Japanese 125

## RELIGION

- Roman Catholicism
- Orthodox and other Eastern Churches
- Protestantism
- Sunni Islam
- Shia Islam
- Buddhism
- Hinduism
- Confucianism
- Judaism
- Shintoism
- Primitive Religions

**Religions** are not as easily mapped as the physical contours of landscape. Divisions are often blurred and frequently overlapping: most nations include people of many different faiths – or no faith at all. Some religions, like Islam and Christianity, have proselytes worldwide; others, like Hinduism and Confucianism, are restricted to a particular area, though modern migrations have taken some Indians and Chinese very far from their cultural origins. It is also difficult to show the degree to which religion exercises control over daily life: Christian Western Europe, for example, is nowadays far less dominated by its religion than are the Islamic nations of the Middle East. Similarly, figures for the major faiths' adherents make no distinction between nominal believers enrolled at birth and those for whom religion is a vital part of existence.

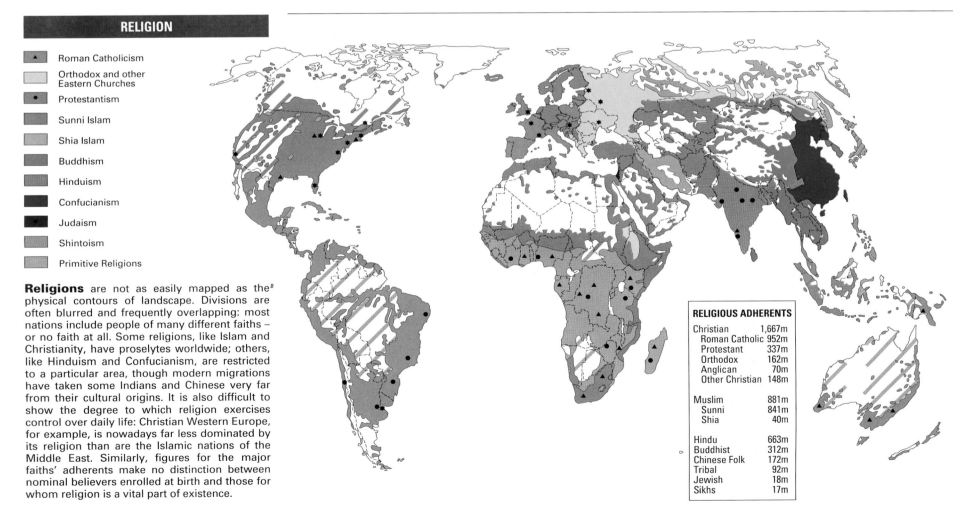

### RELIGIOUS ADHERENTS

| | |
|---|---|
| Christian | 1,667m |
| Roman Catholic | 952m |
| Protestant | 337m |
| Orthodox | 162m |
| Anglican | 70m |
| Other Christian | 148m |
| Muslim | 881m |
| Sunni | 841m |
| Shia | 40m |
| Hindu | 663m |
| Buddhist | 312m |
| Chinese Folk | 172m |
| Tribal | 92m |
| Jewish | 18m |
| Sikhs | 17m |

CARTOGRAPHY BY PHILIP'S. COPYRIGHT REED INTERNATIONAL BOOKS LTD

# PEOPLE: CONFLICT & CO-OPERATION

Humans are social animals, rarely functioning well except in groups. Evolution has made them so: hunter-gatherers in co-operative bands were far more effective than animals that prowled alone. Agriculture, the building of cities and industrialization are all developments that depended on human co-operative ability – and in turn increased the need for it.

Unfortunately, human groups do not always co-operate so well with other human groups, and friction between them sometimes leads to co-operatively organized violence. War is itself a very human activity, with no real equivalent in any other species. Always murderous, it is sometimes purposeful and

may even be very effective. The colonization of the Americas and Australia, for example, was in effect the waging of aggressive war by well-armed Europeans against indigenous peoples incapable of offering a serious defence.

Most often, war achieves little but death and ruin. The great 20th-century wars accomplished nothing for the nations involved in them, although the world paid a price of between 50 and 100 million dead as well as immense material damage. The relative peace in the postwar developed world is at least partly due to the nuclear weapons with which rival powers have armed themselves – weapons so powerful that their

use would leave a scarcely habitable planet with no meaningful distinction between victor and vanquished.

Yet warfare remains endemic: the second half of the 20th century was one of the bloodiest periods in history, and death by organized violence remains unhappily common. The map below attempts to show the serious conflicts that have scarred the Earth since 1945. Most are civil wars in poor countries, rather than international conflicts between rich ones; some of them are still unresolved, while others, like apparently extinct volcanoes, may erupt again at intervals, adding to the world's miserable population of refugees.

## THE WORLD'S REFUGEES

Refugees and their national origin; the host nations and the relative size of their refugee populations (1991)

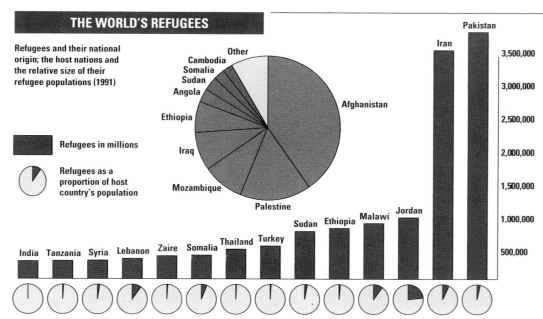

The pie-chart shows the origins of the world's refugees, while the bar-chart shows their destinations. According to the United Nations High Commissioner for Refugees, in 1990 there were almost 15 million refugees, a number that has continued to increase and is almost certain to be amplified during the decade. Some have fled from climatic change, some from economic disaster and others from political persecution; the great majority, however, are the victims of war.

All but a few who make it overseas seek asylum in neighbouring countries, which are often the least equipped to deal with them and where they are rarely welcome. Lacking any rights or power, they frequently become an embarrassment and a burden to their reluctant hosts.

Usually, the best any refugee can hope for is rudimentary food and shelter in temporary camps that all to often become semi-permanent, with little prospect of assimilation by host populations: many Palestinians, for example, have been forced to live in camps since 1948.

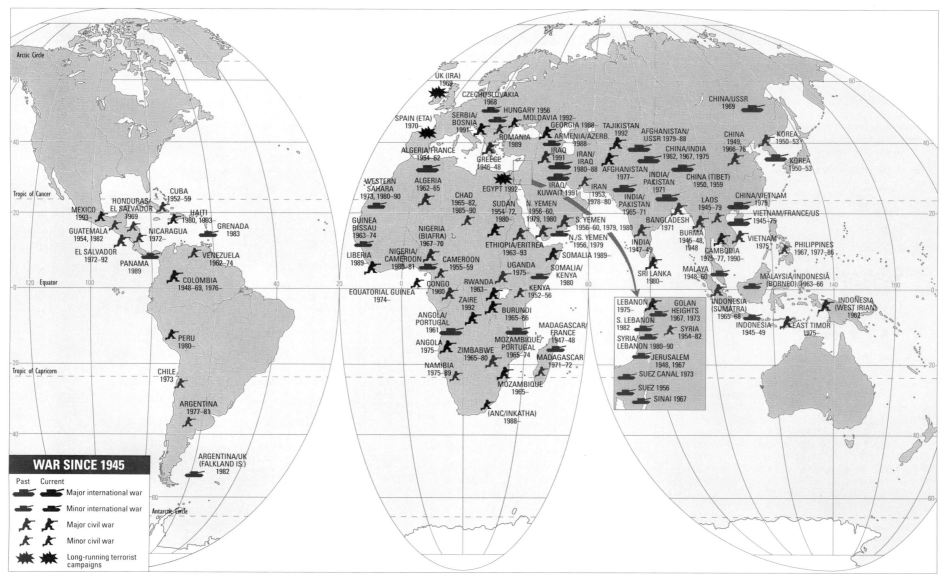

## WAR SINCE 1945

| Past | Current | |
|------|---------|---|
| | | Major international war |
| | | Minor international war |
| | | Major civil war |
| | | Minor civil war |
| | | Long-running terrorist campaigns |

# UNITED NATIONS

The United Nations Organization was born as World War II drew to its conclusion. Six years of strife had strengthened the world's desire for peace, but an effective international organization was needed to help achieve it. That body would replace the League of Nations which, since its inception in 1920, had signally failed to curb the aggression of at least some of its member nations. At the United Nations Conference on International Organization held in San Francisco, the United Nations Charter was drawn up. Ratified by the Security Council and signed by the 51 original members, it came into effect on 24 October 1945.

The Charter set out the aims of the organization: to maintain peace and security, and develop friendly relations between nations; to achieve international co-operation in solving economic, social, cultural and humanitarian problems; to promote respect for human rights and fundamental freedoms; and to harmonize the activities of nations in order to achieve these common goals.

By 1993, the UN had expanded to 183 member countries; it is the largest international political organization, employing 23,000 people worldwide; its headquarters in New York accounts for 7,000 staff and it also has major offices in Rome, Geneva and Vienna.

The United Nations has six principal organs:

## The General Assembly
The forum at which member nations discuss moral and political issues affecting world development, peace and security meets annually in September, under a newly-elected President whose tenure lasts one year. Any member can bring business to the agenda, and each member nation has one vote. Decisions are made by simple majority, save for matters of very great importance, when a two-thirds majority is required.

## The Security Council
A legislative and executive body, the Security Council is the primary instrument for establishing and maintaining international peace by attempting to settle disputes between nations. It has the power to dispatch UN forces to stop aggression, and member nations undertake to make armed forces, assistance and facilities available as required. The Security Council has ten temporary members elected by the General Assembly for two-year terms, and five permanent members – China, France, Russia, UK and USA.

## The Economic and Social Council
By far the largest United Nations executive, the Council operates as a conduit between the General Assembly and the many United Nations agencies it instructs to implement Assembly decisions, and whose work it co-ordinates. The Council also sets up commissions to examine economic conditions, collects data and issues studies and reports, and may make recommendations to the Assembly.

## The Secretariat
This is the staff of the United Nations, and its task is to administer the policies and programmes of the UN and its organs, and assist and advise the Head of the Secretariat, the Secretary-General – a full-time, non-political, appointment made by the General Assembly.

## The Trusteeship Council
The Council administers trust territories with the aim of promoting their advancement. Only one remains – the Trust Territory of the Pacific Is. (Palau), administered by the USA.

## The International Court of Justice (the World Court)
The World Court is the judicial organ of the United Nations. It deals only with United Nations disputes and all members are subject to its jurisdiction. There are 15 judges, elected for nine-year terms by the General Assembly and the Security Council. The Court sits in The Hague.

United Nations agencies and programmes, and intergovernmental agencies co-ordinated by the UN, contribute to harmonious world development. Social and humanitarian operations include:

**United Nations Development Programme (UNDP)** Plans and funds projects to help developing countries make better use of resources.
**United Nations International Childrens' Fund (UNICEF)** Created at the General Assembly's first session in 1945 to help children in the aftermath of World War II, it now provides basic health care and aid worldwide.
**United Nations Fund for Population Activities (UNFPA)** Promotes awareness of population issues and family planning, providing appropriate assistance.
**Food and Agriculture Organization (FAO)** Aims to raise living standards and nutrition levels in rural areas by improving food production and distribution.
**United Nations Educational, Scientific and Cultural Organization (UNESCO)** Promotes international co-operation through broader and better education.
**World Health Organization (WHO)** Promotes and provides for better health care, public and environmental health and medical research.

**Membership** There are seven independent states which are not members of the UN – Kiribati, Nauru, Switzerland, Taiwan, Tonga, Tuvalu and Vatican City. Official languages are Chinese, English, French, Russian, Spanish and Arabic.
**Funding** The UN budget for 1994–95 is US $2.6 billion. Contributions are assessed by the members' ability to pay, with the maximum 25% of the total, the minimum 0.01%. Contributions for 1992–94 were: USA 25%, Japan 12.45%, Germany 8.93%, Russia 6.71%, France 6%, UK 5.02%, Italy 4.29%, Canada 3.11% (others 28.49%).
**Peacekeeping** The UN has been involved in 33 peacekeeping operations worldwide since 1948 and there are currently 17 areas of UN patrol. In July 1993 there were 80,146 'blue berets' from 74 countries.

United Nations agencies are involved in many aspects of international trade, safety and security:

**General Agreement on Tariffs and Trade (GATT)** Sponsors international trade negotiations and advocates a common code of conduct.
**International Maritime Organization (IMO)** Promotes unity amongst merchant shipping, especially in regard to safety, marine pollution and standardization.
**International Labour Organization (ILO)** Seeks to improve labour conditions and promote productive employment to raise living standards.
**World Meteorological Organization (WMO)** Promotes co-operation in weather observation, reporting and forecasting.
**World Intellectual Property Organization (WIPO)** Seeks to protect intellectual property such as artistic copyright, scientific patents and trademarks.
**Disarmament Commission** Considers and makes recommendations to the General Assembly on disarmament issues.
**International Atomic Energy Agency (IAEA)** Fosters development of peaceful uses for nuclear energy, establishes safety standards and monitors the destruction of nuclear material designed for military use.

**The World Bank** comprises three United Nations agencies:

**International Monetary Fund (IMF)** Cultivates international monetary co-operation and expansion of trade.
**International Bank for Reconstruction and Development (IBRD)** Provides funds and technical assistance to developing countries.
**International Finance Corporation (IFC)** Encourages the growth of productive private enterprise in less developed countries.

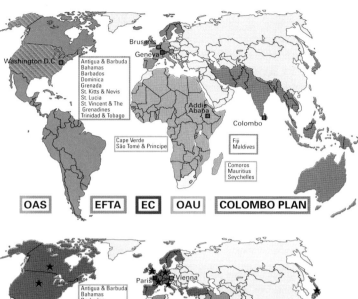

OAS · EFTA · EC · OAU · COLOMBO PLAN

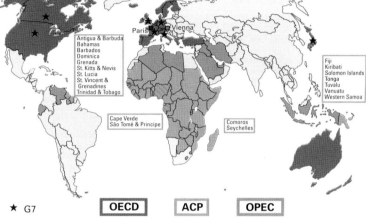

★ G7 · OECD · ACP · OPEC

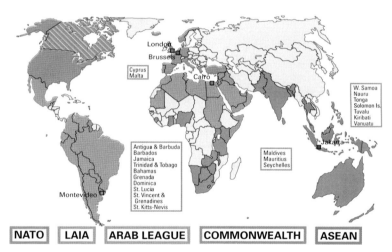

NATO · LAIA · ARAB LEAGUE · COMMONWEALTH · ASEAN

**EC** As from December 1993 the European Union (EU) refers to matters of foreign policy, security and justice. The European Community (EC) refers to all other matters. The 12 members – Belgium, Denmark, France, Germany, Greece, Ireland, Italy, Luxembourg, Netherlands, Portugal, Spain and the UK – aim to integrate economies, co-ordinate social developments and bring about political union. These members of what is now the world's biggest market share agricultural and industrial policies and tariffs on trade.
**EFTA** European Free Trade Association (formed in 1960). Portugal left the 'Seven' in 1989 to join the EC.
**ACP** African-Caribbean-Pacific countries associated with the EC (1963).
**NATO** North Atlantic Treaty Organization (formed in 1949). It continues after 1991 despite the winding up of the Warsaw Pact.
**OAS** Organization of American States (1949). It aims to promote social and economic co-operation between developed countries of North America and developing nations of Latin America.
**ASEAN** Association of South-east Asian Nations (1967).
**OAU** Organization of African Unity (1963). Its 52 members represent over 90% of Africa's population.
**LAIA** Latin American Integration Association (1980).
**OECD** Organization for Economic Co-operation and Development (1961). The 24 major Western free-market economies. 'G7' is its 'inner group' of USA, Canada, Japan, UK, Germany, Italy and France.
**COMMONWEALTH** The Commonwealth of Nations evolved from the British Empire; it comprises 19 nations recognizing the British monarch as head of state and 32 with their own heads of state.
**OPEC** Organization of Petroleum Exporting Countries (1960). It controls about three-quarters of the world's oil supply.
**ARAB LEAGUE** (1945) The League's aim is to promote economic, social, political and military co-operation.
**COLOMBO PLAN** (1951) Its 26 members aim to promote economic and social development in Asia and the Pacific.

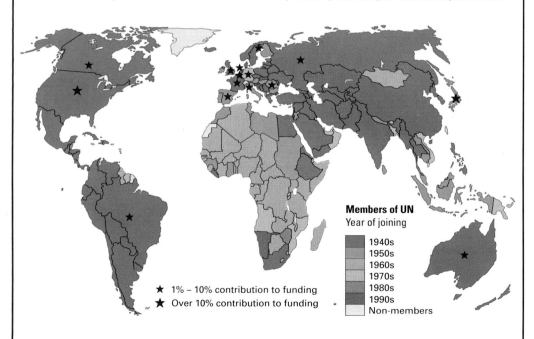

**Members of UN**
Year of joining

- 1940s
- 1950s
- 1960s
- 1970s
- 1980s
- 1990s
- Non-members

★ 1% – 10% contribution to funding
★ Over 10% contribution to funding

# PRODUCTION: AGRICULTURE

The invention of agriculture transformed human existence more than any other development, though it may not have seemed much of an improvement to its first practitioners. Primitive farming required brutally hard work, and it tied men and women to a patch of land, highly vulnerable to local weather patterns and to predators, especially human predators – drawbacks still apparent in much of the world today. It is difficult to imagine early humans being interested in such an existence while there were still animals around to hunt and wild seeds and berries to gather. Probably the spur was population pressure, with consequent overhunting and scarcity.

Despite its difficulties, the new life style had a few overwhelming advantages. It supported far larger populations, eventually including substantial cities, with all the varied cultural and economic activities they allowed. Later still, it furnished the surpluses that allowed industrialization – another enormous step in the course of human development.

Machines relieved many farmers of their burden of endless toil, and made it possible for relatively small numbers to provide food for more than 5,000 million people.

Now, as in the past, the whole business of farming involves the creation of a severely simplified ecology, under the tutelage and for the benefit of the farmer. Natural plant life is divided into crops, to be protected and nurtured, and weeds, the rest, to be destroyed. From the earliest days, crops were selectively bred to increase their food yield, usually at the expense of their ability to survive, which became the farmer's responsibility; 20th-century plant geneticists have carried the technique to highly productive extremes. Due mainly to new varieties of rice and wheat, world grain production has increased by 70% since 1965, more than doubling in the developing countries, although such high yields demand equally high consumption of fertilizers and pesticides to maintain them. Mechanized farmers in North America and Europe

continue to turn out huge surpluses, although not without environmental costs.

Where production is inadequate, the reasons are as likely to be political as agricultural. Africa, the only continent where food production per capita is actually falling, suffers acutely from economic mis-management, as well as from the perennial problems of war and banditry. Dismal harvests in the USSR, despite its excellent farmland, helped bring about the collapse of the Soviet system.

There are other limits to progress too. Increasing population puts relentless pressure on farmers not only to maintain high yields but also to increase them. Most of the world's potential cropland is already under the plough. The overworking of marginal land is one of the prime causes of desertification; new farmlands burned out of former rain-forests are seldom fertile for long. Human numbers may yet outrun the land's ability to feed them, as they did almost 10,000 years ago.

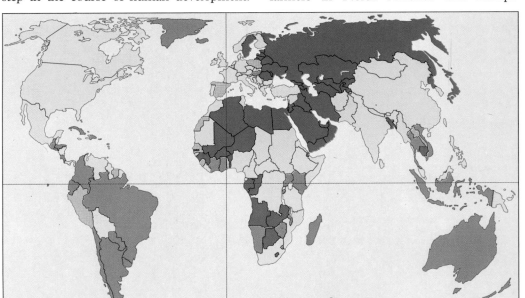

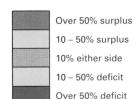

## SELF-SUFFICIENCY IN FOOD

Balance of trade in food products as a percentage of total trade in food products (1988)*

| | |
|---|---|
| | Over 50% surplus |
| | 10 – 50% surplus |
| | 10% either side |
| | 10 – 50% deficit |
| | Over 50% deficit |

| Most self-sufficient | | Least self-sufficient | |
|---|---|---|---|
| Argentina | 95% | Algeria | −98% |
| Zimbabwe | 87% | Djibouti | −97% |
| Honduras | 81% | Yemen | −95% |
| Malawi | 81% | Zambia | −95% |
| Costa Rica | 79% | Japan | −91% |
| Iceland | 78% | Gabon | −90% |
| Chile | 75% | Kuwait | −90% |
| Uruguay | 75% | Brunei | −89% |
| Ecuador | 74% | Burkina Faso | −82% |

## LAND USE

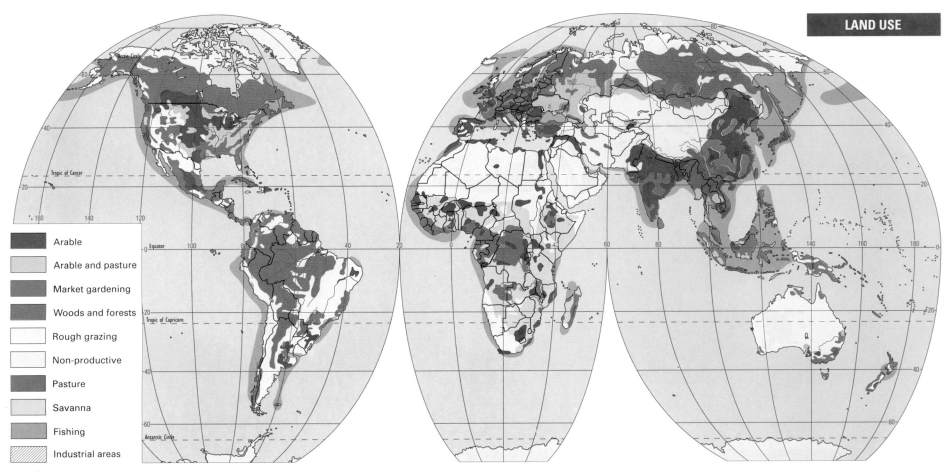

| | |
|---|---|
| | Arable |
| | Arable and pasture |
| | Market gardening |
| | Woods and forests |
| | Rough grazing |
| | Non-productive |
| | Pasture |
| | Savanna |
| | Fishing |
| | Industrial areas |

## STAPLE CROPS

Separate figures for Russia, Ukraine and the other successors of the former USSR are not yet available

**Wheat:** Grown in a range of climates, with most varieties – including the highest-quality bread wheats – requiring temperate conditions. Mainly used in baking, it is also used for pasta and breakfast cereals.

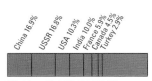

World total (1989): 538,056,000 tonnes

**Rice:** Thrives on the high humidity and temperatures of the Far East, where it is the traditional staple food of half the human race. Usually grown standing in water, rice responds well to continuous cultivation, with three or four crops annually.

World total (1989): 506,291,000 tonnes

**Maize:** Originating in the New World and still an important human food in Africa and Latin America, in the developed world it is processed into breakfast cereals, oil, starches and adhesives. It is also used for animal feed.

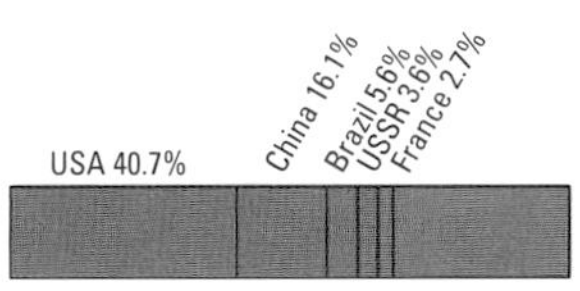

World total (1989): 470,318,000 tonnes

**Barley:** Primarily used as animal feed, but widely eaten by humans in Africa and Asia. Elsewhere, malted barley furnishes beer and spirits. Able to withstand the dry heat of subarid tropics, its growing season is only 80 days.

World total (1989): 168,964,000 tonnes

**Oats:** Most widely used to feed livestock, but eaten by humans as oatmeal or porridge. Oats have a beneficial effect on the cardio-vascular system, and human consumption is likely to increase.

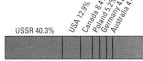

World total (1989): 42,197,000 tonnes

**Rye:** Hardy and tolerant of poor and sandy soils, it is an important foodstuff and animal feed in Central and Eastern Europe. Rye produces a dark, heavy bread as well as alcoholic drinks.

World total (1989): 34,893,000 tonnes

**Millet:** The name covers a number of small grained cereals, members of the grass family with a short growing season. Used to produce flour, meal and animal feed, and fermented to make beer, especially in Africa.

World total (1989): 30,512,000 tonnes

**Potatoes:** The most important of the edible tubers, potatoes grow in well-watered, temperate areas. Weight for weight less nutritious than grain, they are a human staple as well as an important animal feed.

World total (1989): 276,740,000 tonnes

**Cassava:** A tropical shrub that needs high rainfall (over 1000 mm annually) and a 10–30 month growing season to produce its large, edible tubers. Used as flour by humans, as cattle feed and in industrial starches.

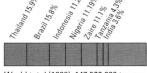

World total (1989): 147,500,000 tonnes

**Soya:** Beans from soya bushes are very high (30–40%) in protein. Most are processed into oil and proprietary protein foods. Consumption since 1950 has tripled, mainly due to the health-conscious developed world.

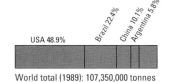

World total (1989): 107,350,000 tonnes

Cereals are grasses with starchy, edible seeds; every important civilization has depended on them as a source of food. The major cereal grains contain about 10% protein and 75% carbohydrate; grain is easy to store, handle and transport, and contributes more than any other group of foods to the energy and protein content of human diet. If all the cereals were consumed directly by man, there would be no shortage of food in the world, but a considerable proportion of the total output is used as animal feed.

Starchy tuber crops or root crops, represented here by potatoes and cassava, are second in importance only to cereals as staple foods; easily cultivated, they provide high yields for little effort and store well – potatoes for up to six months, cassava for up to a year in the ground. Protein content is low (2% or less), starch content high, with some minerals and vitamins present, but populations that rely heavily on these crops may suffer from malnutrition.

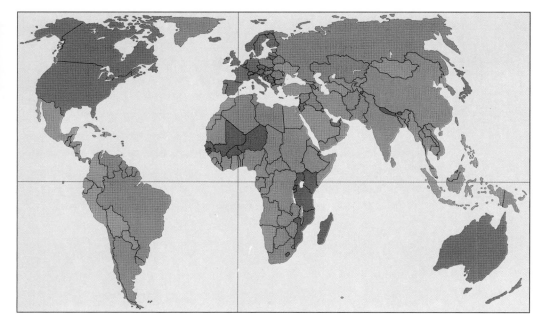

## IMPORTANCE OF AGRICULTURE

**Percentage of the total population dependent on agriculture (1991)**

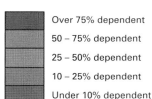

- Over 75% dependent
- 50 – 75% dependent
- 25 – 50% dependent
- 10 – 25% dependent
- Under 10% dependent

| Top 5 countries | | Bottom 5 countries | |
|---|---|---|---|
| Nepal | 92% | Singapore | 0.9% |
| Rwanda | 91% | Hong Kong | 1.2% |
| Burundi | 91% | Bahrain | 1.7% |
| Bhutan | 91% | Belgium | 1.7% |
| Niger | 87% | UK | 1.9% |

## FOOD & POPULATION

Comparison of food production and population by continent (1989). The left column indicates percentage shares of total world food production; the right shows population in proportion.

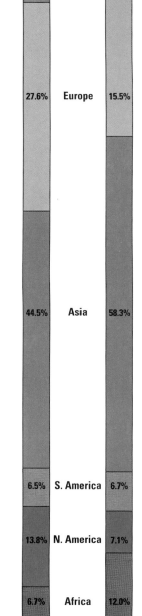

| | FOOD | POPULATION |
|---|---|---|
| Australasia | 1.2% | 0.4% |
| Europe | 27.6% | 15.5% |
| Asia | 44.5% | 58.3% |
| S. America | 6.5% | 6.7% |
| N. America | 13.8% | 7.1% |
| Africa | 6.7% | 12.0% |

## ANIMAL PRODUCTS

Separate figures for Russia, Ukraine and the other successors of the former USSR are not yet available

Traditionally, food animals subsisted on land unsuitable for cultivation, supporting agricultural production with their fertilizing dung. But free-ranging animals grow slowly and yield less meat than those more intensively reared; the demands of urban markets in the developed world have encouraged the growth of factory-like production methods. A large proportion of staple crops, especially cereals, are fed to animals, an inefficient way to produce protein but one likely to continue as long as people value meat and dairy products in their diet.

**Milk:** Many human groups, including most Asians, find raw milk indigestible after infancy, and it is often only the starting point for other dairy products such as butter, cheese and yoghurt. Most world production comes from cows, but sheep's milk and goats' milk are also important.

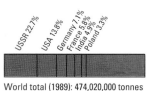

World total (1989): 474,020,000 tonnes

**Cheese:** Least perishable of all dairy products, cheese is milk fermented with selected bacterial strains to produce a foodstuff with a potentially immense range of flavours and textures. The vast majority of cheeses are made from cow's milk, although sheep and goat cheeses are highly prized.

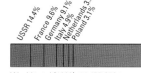

World total (1989): 14,475,276 tonnes

**Butter:** A traditional source of vitamin A as well as calories, butter has lost much popularity in the developed world for health reasons, although it remains a valuable food. Most butter from India, the world's second-largest producer, is clarified into ghee, which has religious as well as nutritional importance.

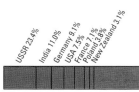

World total (1989): 7,611,826 tonnes

**Lamb and Mutton:** Sheep are the least demanding of domestic animals. Although unsuited to intensive rearing, they can thrive on marginal pastureland incapable of supporting beef cattle on a commercial scale. Sheep are raised as much for their valuable wool as for the meat that they provide, with Australia the world leader.

World total (1989): 6,473,000 tonnes

**Pork:** Although pork is forbidden to many millions, notably Muslims, on religious grounds, more is produced than any other meat in the world, mainly because it is the cheapest. It accounts for about 90% of China's meat output, although per capita meat consumption is relatively low.

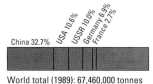

World total (1989): 67,460,000 tonnes

**Beef and Veal:** Most beef and veal is reared for home markets, and the top five producers are also the biggest consumers. The USA produces nearly a quarter of the world's beef and eats even more. Australia, with its small domestic market, is by far the largest exporter.

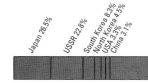

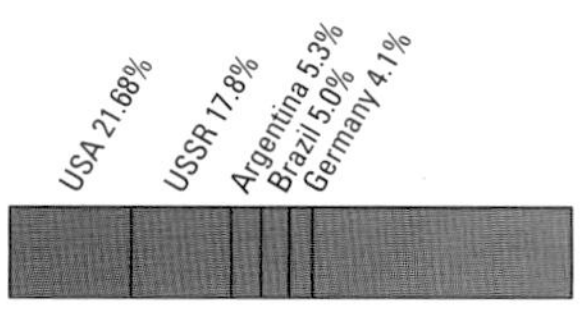

World total (1989): 49,436,000 tonnes

**Fish:** Commercial fishing requires large shoals of fish, often of only one species, within easy reach of markets. Although the great majority are caught wild in the sea, fish-farming of both marine and freshwater species is assuming increasing importance, especially as natural stocks become depleted.

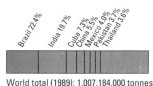

World total (1989): 14,143,923 tonnes

## SUGARS

**Sugar cane:** Confined to tropical regions, cane sugar accounts for the bulk of international trade in the commodity. Most is produced as a foodstuff, but some countries, notably Brazil and South Africa, distil sugar cane and use the resulting ethyl alcohol to make motor fuels.

World total (1989): 1,007,184,000 tonnes

**Sugar beet:** A temperate crop closely related to the humble beetroot, sugar beet's yield after processing is indistinguishable from cane sugar. Sugar beet is steadily replacing sugar cane imports in Europe, to the detriment of the developing countries that rely on it as a major cash crop.

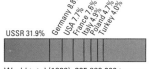

World total (1989): 305,882,000 tonnes

# PRODUCTION: ENERGY

We live in a high-energy civilization. While vast discrepancies exist between rich and poor – a North American consumes 13 times as much energy as a Chinese, for example – even developing nations have more power at their disposal than was imaginable a century ago. Abundant energy supplies keep us warm or cool, fuel our industries and our transport systems, and even feed us: high-intensity agriculture, with its fertilizers, pesticides and machinery, is heavily energy-dependent.

Unfortunately, most of the world's energy comes from fossil fuels: coal, oil and gas deposits laid down over many millions of years. These are the Earth's capital, not its income, and we are consuming that capital at an alarming rate. New discoveries have persistently extended the known reserves: in 1989, the reserves-to-production ratio for oil assured over 45 years' supply, an improvement of almost a decade on the 1970 situation. But despite the effort and ingenuity of prospectors, stocks are clearly limited. They are also very unequally distributed, with the Middle East accounting for most oil reserves, and the CIS, especially Russia, possessing an even higher proportion of the world's natural gas. Coal reserves are more evenly shared, and also more plentiful: coal will outlast oil and gas by a very wide margin.

It is possible to reduce energy demand by improving efficiency: most industrial nations have dramatically increased output since the 1970s without a matching rise in energy consumption. But as fossil stocks continue to diminish, renewable energy sources – solar, wave and wind power, as well as hydro-electricity – must take on greater importance.

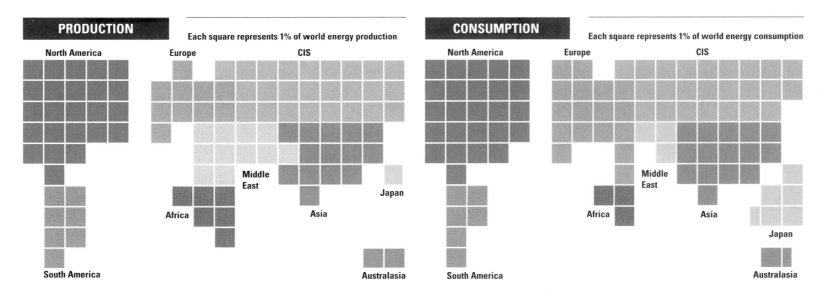

**PRODUCTION** — Each square represents 1% of world energy production

North America · Europe · CIS · Middle East · Africa · Asia · Japan · South America

**CONSUMPTION** — Each square represents 1% of world energy consumption

North America · Europe · CIS · Middle East · Africa · Asia · Japan · South America · Australasia

## CONVERSIONS

For historical reasons, oil is still traded in barrels. The weight and volume equivalents shown below are all based on average density 'Arabian light' crude oil, and should be considered approximate.

The energy equivalents given for a tonne of oil are also somewhat imprecise: oil and coal of different qualities will have varying energy contents, a fact usually reflected in their price on world markets.

**1 barrel:**
   0.136 tonnes
   159 litres
   35 Imperial gallons
   42 US gallons

**1 tonne:**
   7.33 barrels
   1185 litres
   256 Imperial gallons
   261 US gallons

**1 tonne oil:**
   1.5 tonnes hard coal
   3.0 tonnes lignite
   12,000 kWh

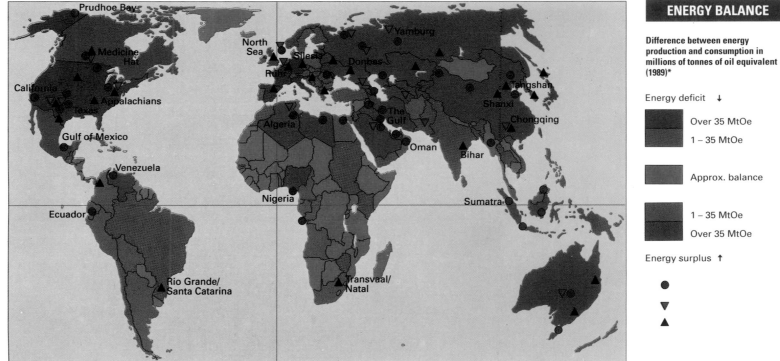

## ENERGY BALANCE

Difference between energy production and consumption in millions of tonnes of oil equivalent (1989)*

Energy deficit ↓
   Over 35 MtOe
   1 – 35 MtOe

   Approx. balance

   1 – 35 MtOe
   Over 35 MtOe

Energy surplus ↑
   ●
   ▽
   ▲

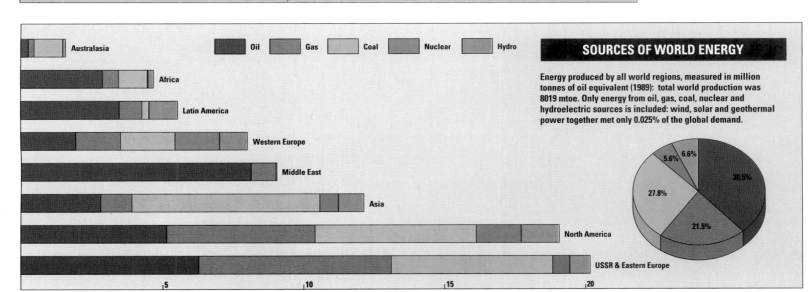

## SOURCES OF WORLD ENERGY

Energy produced by all world regions, measured in million tonnes of oil equivalent (1989): total world production was 8019 mtoe. Only energy from oil, gas, coal, nuclear and hydroelectric sources is included: wind, solar and geothermal power together met only 0.025% of the global demand.

Oil · Gas · Coal · Nuclear · Hydro

Australasia · Africa · Latin America · Western Europe · Middle East · Asia · North America · USSR & Eastern Europe

Pie: 38.5% · 21.5% · 27.8% · 5.6% · 6.6%

*Statistics for the new republics of the former USSR, Czechoslovakia and Yugoslavia are not yet available.
The map shows the statistics for the entire USSR, Czechoslovakia and Yugoslavia.

## FOSSIL FUEL RESERVES

**Known world reserves in years as a multiple of annual production, 1970, 1980 and 1989**

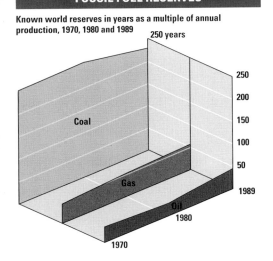

## ENERGY AND OUTPUT

**Tonnes of oil equivalent consumed to produce US $1,000 of GDP, four industrial nations (1973–89)**

Intensity of energy use is a rough indicator of efficiency: the 1973–4 oil crisis caused a dramatic improvement in each of the countries illustrated, although the USA remains relatively profligate. Reliable figures for Russia and the other republics of the former USSR are hard to obtain, but estimates suggest that for equivalent production they use up to four times as much energy as the USA.

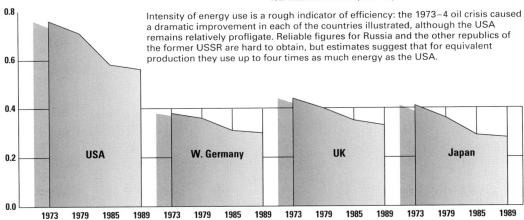

## COAL RESERVES

**World coal reserves by region and country, thousand million tonnes (1988)**

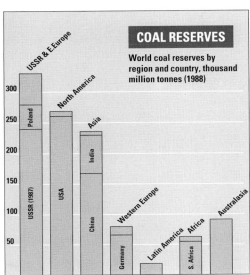

## GAS RESERVES

**World natural gas reserves by region and country, thousand million tonnes (1988)**

Ca: Canada
In: Indonesia
Ma: Malaysia
AD: Abu Dhabi
SA: Saudi Arabia
Qa: Qatar
Iq: Iraq
No: Norway
Ne: Netherlands
Ve: Venezuela
Mx: Mexico
Al: Algeria
Ni: Nigeria

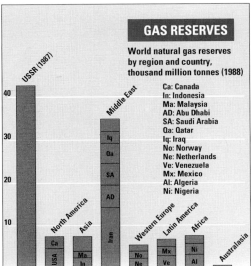

## OIL RESERVES

**World oil reserves by region and country, thousand million tonnes (1988)**

A: Abu Dhabi
V: Venezuela
M: Mexico

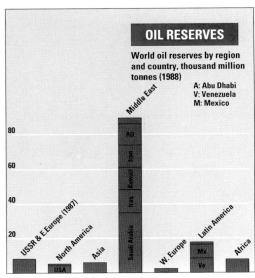

## OIL MOVEMENTS

**Major world movements of oil in millions of tonnes (1989)**

| | |
|---|---|
| Middle East to Western Europe | 195.5 |
| Middle East to Japan | 150.0 |
| Middle East to Asia (exc. Japan and China) | 127.5 |
| Latin America to USA | 126.1 |
| Middle East to USA | 94.1 |
| USSR to Western Europe | 78.1 |
| North Africa to Western Europe | 93.5 |
| West Africa to Western Europe | 39.6 |
| West Africa to USA | 59.8 |
| Canada to USA | 45.0 |
| South-east Asia to Japan | 42.2 |
| Latin America to Western Europe | 28.7 |
| Western Europe to USA | 28.7 |
| Middle East to Latin America | 20.5 |

**Total world movements: 1,577 million tonnes**

Only inter-regional movements in excess of 20 million tonnes are shown. Other Middle Eastern oil shipments throughout the world totalled 47.4 million tonnes; miscellaneous oil exports of the then USSR amounted to 88.8 million tonnes.

## FUEL EXPORTS

**Fuels as a percentage of total value of all exports (1986)***

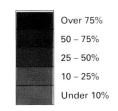

Over 75%
50 – 75%
25 – 50%
10 – 25%
Under 10%

**Direction of trade**

Coal
Oil

Arrows show the major trade direction of selected fuels, and are proportional to export value.

## NUCLEAR POWER

**Percentage of electricity generated by nuclear power stations, leading nations (1988)**

| | | | |
|---|---|---|---|
| 1. | France | 70% | |
| 2. | Belgium | 66% | |
| 3. | Hungary | 49% | |
| 4. | South Korea | 47% | |
| 5. | Sweden | 46% | |
| 6. | Taiwan | 41% | |
| 7. | Switzerland | 37% | |
| 8. | Finland | 36% | |
| 9. | Spain | 36% | |
| 10. | Bulgaria | 36% | |
| 11. | Germany (W) | 34% | |
| 12. | Japan | 28% | |
| 13. | Czechoslovakia | 27% | |
| 14. | UK | 18% | |
| 15. | USA | 17% | |
| 16. | Canada | 16% | |
| 17. | Argentina | 12% | |
| 18. | USSR (1989) | 11% | |
| 19. | Yugoslavia | 6% | |
| 20. | Netherlands | 5% | |

The decade 1980–90 was a bad time for the nuclear power industry. Major projects regularly ran vastly overbudget, and fears of long-term environmental damage were heavily reinforced by the 1986 Soviet disaster at Chernobyl. Although the number of reactors in service continued to increase throughout the period, orders for new plant shrank dramatically, and most countries cut back on their nuclear programmes.

## HYDROELECTRICITY

**Percentage of electricity generated by hydroelectrical power stations, leading nations (1988)**

| | | | |
|---|---|---|---|
| 1. | Paraguay | 99.9% | |
| 2. | Zambia | 99.6% | |
| 3. | Norway | 99.5% | |
| 4. | Congo | 99.1% | |
| 5. | Costa Rica | 98.3% | |
| 6. | Uganda | 98.3% | |
| 7. | Rwanda | 97.7% | |
| 8. | Malawi | 97.6% | |
| 9. | Zaïre | 97.4% | |
| 10. | Cameroon | 97.2% | |
| 11. | Laos | 95.5% | |
| 12. | Nepal | 95.2% | |
| 13. | Iceland | 94.0% | |
| 14. | Uruguay | 93.0% | |
| 15. | Brazil | 91.7% | |
| 16. | Albania | 87.2% | |
| 17. | Fiji | 81.4% | |
| 18. | Ecuador | 80.7% | |
| 19. | C. African Rep. | 80.4% | |
| 20. | Sri Lanka | 80.4% | |

Countries heavily reliant on hydroelectricity are usually small and non-industrial: a high proportion of hydroelectric power more often reflects a modest energy budget than vast hydroelectric resources. The USA, for instance, produces only 8% of power requirements from hydroelectricity; yet that 8% amounts to more than three times the hydro-power generated by all of Africa.

## ALTERNATIVE ENERGY SOURCES

**Solar:** Each year the Sun bestows upon the Earth almost a million times as much energy as is locked up in all the planet's oil reserves, but only an insignificant fraction is trapped and used commercially. In some experimental installations, mirrors focus the Sun's rays on to boilers, whose steam generates electricity by spinning turbines. Solar cells turn the sunlight into electricity directly, and although efficiencies are still low, advancing technology offers some prospect of using the Sun as the main world electricity source by 2100.
**Wind:** Caused by uneven heating of the Earth, winds are themselves a form of solar energy. Windmills have been used for centuries to turn wind power into mechanical work; recent models, often arranged in banks on gust-swept high ground, usually generate electricity.
**Tidal:** The energy from tides is potentially enormous, although only a few installations have been built to exploit it. In theory at least, waves and currents could also provide almost unimaginable power, and the thermal differences in the ocean depths are another huge well of potential energy. But work on extracting it is still in the experimental stage.
**Geothermal:** The Earth's temperature rises by 1°C for every 30 metres' descent, with much steeper temperature gradients in geologically active areas. El Salvador, for example, produces 39% of its electricity from geothermal power stations. More than 130 are operating worldwide.
**Biomass:** The oldest of human fuels ranges from animal dung, still burned in cooking fires in much of North Africa and elsewhere, to sugar cane plantations feeding high-technology distilleries to produce ethanol for motor vehicle engines. In Brazil and South Africa, plant ethanol provides up to 25% of motor fuel. Throughout the developing world, most biomass energy comes from firewood: although accurate figures are impossible to obtain, it may yield as much as 10% of the world's total energy consumption.

*Statistics for the new republics of the former USSR, Czechoslovakia and Yugoslavia are not yet available. The map shows the statistics for the entire USSR, Czechoslovakia and Yugoslavia.*

CARTOGRAPHY BY PHILIP'S. COPYRIGHT REED INTERNATIONAL BOOKS LTD

# PRODUCTION: MINERALS

Even during the Stone Age, when humans often settled near the outcrops of flint on which their technology depended, mineral resources have attracted human exploiters. Their descendants have learned how to make use of almost every known element. These elements can be found, in one form or another, somewhere in the Earth's bountiful crust. Iron remains the most important, but modern industrial civilization has a voracious appetite for virtually all of them.

Mineral deposits once dictated the site of new industries; today, most industrial countries are heavily dependent on imports for many of their key materials. Most mining, and much refining of raw ores, is done in developing countries, where labour is cheap.

The main map below shows the richest sources of the most important minerals at present; some reserves – lead and mercury, for example – are running very low. The map takes no account of undersea deposits, most of which are considered inaccessible. Growing shortages, though, may encourage submarine mining: plans have already been made to recover the nodules of manganese found widely scattered on ocean floors.

## MINERAL EXPORTS

Minerals and metals as a percentage of total exports (1986)

Over 50%
10 – 50%
5 – 10%
Under 5%

Direction of trade

Copper →
Iron →
Bauxite →
(Aluminium)

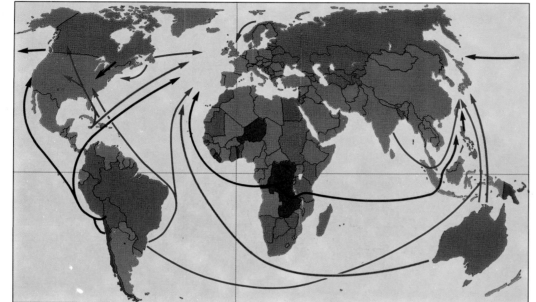

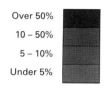

## URANIUM

In its pure state, uranium is an immensely heavy, white metal; but although spent uranium is employed as projectiles in anti-missile cannons, where its mass ensures a lethal punch, its main use is as a fuel in nuclear reactors, and in nuclear weaponry. Uranium is very scarce: the main source is the rare ore pitchblende, which itself contains only 0.2% uranium oxide. Only a minute fraction of that is the radioactive $U^{235}$ isotope, though so-called breeder reactors can transmute the more common $U^{238}$ into highly radioactive plutonium.

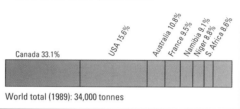

Canada 33.1% | USA 15.6% | Australia 10.8% | France 9.5% | Namibia 9.1% | Niger 8.8% | S. Africa 8.6%

World total (1989): 34,000 tonnes

## METALS

Separate figures for Russia, Ukraine and the other successors of the former USSR are not yet available

* Figures for aluminium are for refined metal; all other figures refer to ore production

**Aluminium:** Produced mainly from its oxide, bauxite, which yields 25% of its weight in aluminium. The cost of refining and production is often too high for producer-countries to bear, so bauxite is largely exported. Lightweight and corrosion resistant, aluminium alloys are widely used in aircraft, vehicles, cans and packaging.

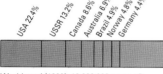

USA 22.4% | USSR 13.2% | Canada 8.6% | Australia 6.9% | Brazil 4.9% | Norway 4.8% | Germany 4.4%

World total (1989): 18,000,000 tonnes *

**Copper:** Derived from low-yielding sulphide ores, copper is an important export for several developing countries. An excellent conductor of heat and electricity, it forms part of most electrical items, and is used in the manufacture of brass and bronze. Major importers include Japan and Germany.

Chile 17.7% | USA 16.5% | USSR 10.4% | Canada 8.1% | Zambia 5.5% | Zaïre 4.6% | Poland 4.4% | China 4.2%

World total (1989): 9,100,000 tonnes *

**Lead:** A soft metal, obtained mainly from galena (lead sulphide), which occurs in veins associated with iron, zinc and silver sulphides. Its use in vehicle batteries accounts for the USA's prime consumer status; lead is also made into sheeting and piping. Its use as an additive to paints and petrol is decreasing.

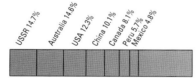

USSR 14.7% | Australia 14.6% | USA 12.3% | China 10.1% | Canada 8.1% | Peru 5.7% | Mexico 4.8%

World total (1989): 3,400,000 tonnes *

**Mercury:** The only metal that is liquid at normal temperatures, most is derived from its sulphide, cinnabar, found only in small quantities in volcanic areas. Apart from its value in thermometers and other instruments, most mercury production is used in anti-fungal and anti-fouling preparations, and to make detonators.

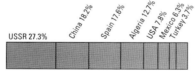

USSR 27.3% | China 18.2% | Spain 17.6% | Algeria 12.7% | Italy 7.8% | Mexico 6.3% | Turkey 3.7%

World total (1989): 5,500,000 kilograms *

**Tin:** Soft, pliable and non-toxic, used to coat 'tin' (tin-plated steel) cans, in the manufacture of foils and in alloys. The principal tin-bearing mineral is cassiterite ($SnO_2$), found in ore formed from molten rock. Producers and refiners were hit by a price collapse in 1991.

Brazil 22.5% | China 14.8% | Malaysia 14.4% | Indonesia 14.2% | Bolivia 7.1% | Thailand 6.6% | USSR 6.3%

World total (1989): 223,000 tonnes *

**Zinc:** Often found in association with lead ores, zinc is highly resistant to corrosion, and about 40% of the refined metal is used to plate sheet steel, particularly vehicle bodies – a process known as galvanizing. Zinc is also used in dry batteries, paints and dyes.

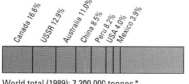

Canada 16.6% | USSR 12.5% | Australia 11.0% | China 8.5% | Peru 8.2% | USA 4.0% | Mexico 3.9%

World total (1989): 7,300,000 tonnes *

## DIAMOND

Most diamond is found in kimberlite, or 'blue ground', a basic peridotite rock; erosion may wash the diamond from its kimberlite matrix and deposit it with sand or gravel on river beds. Only a small proportion of the world's diamond, the most flawless, is cut into gemstones – 'diamonds'; most is used in industry, where the material's remarkable hardness and abrasion resistance finds a use in cutting tools, drills and dies, as well as in styluses. Australia, not among the top 12 producers at the beginning of the 1980s, had by 1986 become world leader and by 1989 was the source of 37.5% of world production. The other main producers were Zaïre (18.9%), Botswana (16.3%), the then USSR (11.8%) and South Africa (9.7%). Between them, these five nations accounted for over 94% of the world total of 96,600,000 carats – at 0.2 grams per carat, almost one tonne.

**Gold:** Regarded for centuries as the most valuable metal in the world and used to make coins, gold is still recognized as the monetary standard. A soft metal, it is alloyed to make jewellery; the electronics industry values its corrosion resistance and conductivity.

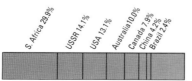

S. Africa 29.9% | USSR 14.1% | USA 13.1% | Australia 10.0% | Canada 7.9% | China 7.9% | Brazil 2.4%

World total (1989): 2,026,000 kilograms *

**Silver:** Most silver comes from ores mined and processed for other metals (including lead and copper). Pure or alloyed with harder metals, it is used for jewellery and ornaments. Industrial use includes dentistry, electronics, photography and as a chemical catalyst.

Mexico 15.5% | USA 13.5% | Peru 12.4% | USSR 10.1% | Canada 8.8% | Australia 7.2% | Poland 6.7%

World total (1989): 14,896,000 kilograms *

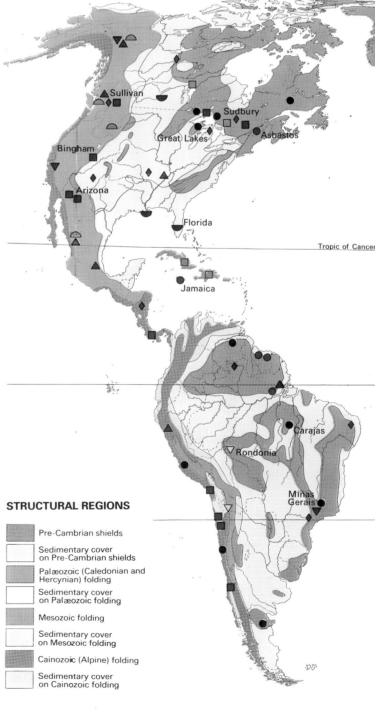

Sullivan
Sudbury
Bingham
Great Lakes
Asbestos
Arizona
Florida
Jamaica
Tropic of Cancer
Carajas
Rondonia
Minas Gerais

## STRUCTURAL REGIONS

Pre-Cambrian shields

Sedimentary cover on Pre-Cambrian shields

Palæozoic (Caledonian and Hercynian) folding

Sedimentary cover on Palæozoic folding

Mesozoic folding

Sedimentary cover on Mesozoic folding

Cainozoic (Alpine) folding

Sedimentary cover on Cainozoic folding

## IRON AND FERRO-ALLOYS

Ever since the art of high-temperature smelting was discovered, some time in the second millennium BC, iron has been by far the most important metal known to man. The earliest iron ploughs transformed primitive agriculture and led to the first human population explosion, while iron weapons – or the lack of them – ensured the rise or fall of entire cultures.

Widely distributed around the world, iron ores usually contain 25–60% iron; blast furnaces process the raw product into pig-iron, which is then alloyed with carbon and other minerals to produce steels of various qualities. From the time of the Industrial Revolution steel has been almost literally the backbone of modern civilization, the prime structural material on which all else is built.

Iron-smelting usually developed close to sources of ore and, later, to the coalfields that fueled the furnaces. Today, most ore comes from a few richly-endowed locations where large-scale mining is possible. Iron and steel plants are generally built at coastal sites so that giant ore carriers, which account for a sizeable proportion of the world's merchant fleet, can easily discharge their cargoes.

**World production of pig-iron and ferro-alloys (1988). All countries with an annual output of more than one million tonnes are shown**

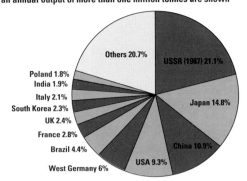

USSR (1987) 21.1%
Japan 14.8%
China 10.9%
USA 9.3%
West Germany 6%
Brazil 4.4%
France 2.8%
UK 2.4%
South Korea 2.3%
Italy 2.1%
India 1.9%
Poland 1.8%
Others 20.7%

Total world production: 545 million tonnes

**Development of world production of pig-iron and ferro-alloys (1945–88) in million tonnes**

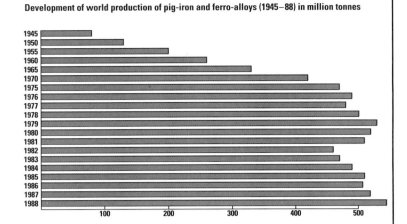

**Chromium:** Most of the world's chromium production is alloyed with iron and other metals to produce steels with various different properties. Combined with iron, nickel, cobalt and tungsten, chromium produces an exceptionally hard steel, resistant to heat; chrome steels are used for many household items where utility must be matched with appearance – cutlery, for example. Chromium is also used in production of refractory bricks, and its salts for tanning and dyeing leather and cloth.

**Manganese:** In its pure state, manganese is a hard, brittle metal. Alloyed with chrome, iron and nickel, it produces abrasion-resistant steels; manganese-aluminium alloys are light but tough. Found in batteries and inks, manganese is also used in glass production. Manganese ores are frequently found in the same location as sedimentary iron ores. Pyrolusite ($MnO_2$) and psilomelane are the main economically-exploitable sources.

**Nickel:** Combined with chrome and iron, nickel produces stainless and high-strength steels; similar alloys go to make magnets and electrical heating elements. Nickel combined with copper is widely used to make coins; cupro-nickel alloy is very resistant to corrosion. Its ores yield only modest quantities of nickel – 0.5 to 3.0% – but also contain copper, iron and small amounts of precious metals. Japan, USA, UK, Germany and France are the principal importers.

USSR 24.4% | China 17.2% | Brazil 15.5% | Australia 10.7% | USA 5.6% | India 5.2% | Canada 4.1% | South Africa 3.0% | Sweden 2.2%

World total production of iron ore (1989): 989,000,000 tonnes

S. Africa 33.7% | USSR 20.9% | India 7.9% | Turkey 6.7% | Albania 5.5% | Finland 3.9%

World total (1989): 12,700,000 tonnes

USSR 36.7% | S. Africa 15.1% | China 11.3% | Gabon 9.7% | Australia 8.9% | India 5.6%

World total (1989): 24,000,000 tonnes

USSR 23.1% | Canada 22.3% | New Caledonia 10.6% | Australia 7.1% | Indonesia 6.6% | Cuba 4.9% | S. Africa 3.7%

World total (1989): 910,000 tonnes

## DISTRIBUTION

**Base metals**
- ■ Copper
- ▲ Lead
- ◖ Mercury
- ▽ Tin
- ◆ Zinc

**Iron and ferro-alloys**
- ● Iron
- ◗ Chrome
- ▨ Nickel
- ▲ Manganese

**Light metals**
- ● Bauxite

**Rare metals**
- ◆ Uranium

**Precious metals**
- ▼ Gold
- ◠ Silver

**Precious stones**
- ◆ Diamonds

**Mineral fertilizers**
- ◗ Phosphates

**Industrial minerals**
- ● Asbestos

Murmansk, Norilsk, Mirnyy, Urals, Nikopol, Krivoy Rog, Almadén, Central Morocco, Kounradskiy, Hebei, Agadez, Yunnan, Bihar, Goa, Philippines, Malaysia, Belitung, Bakwanga, Ok Tedi, Copperbelt, Gove, Weipa, Argyle, Great Dyke, Hamersley Range, Mt. Isa, New Caledonia, Orapa, Witwatersrand, Kimberley, Kalgoorlie, Roxby Downs, Broken Hill

Tropic of Capricorn

# PRODUCTION: MANUFACTURING

In its broadest sense, manufacturing is the application of energy, labour and skill to raw materials in order to transform them into finished goods with a higher value than the various elements used in production.

Since the early days of the Industrial Revolution, manufacturing has implied the use of an organized workforce harnessed to some form of machine. The tendency has consistently been for increasingly expensive human labour to be replaced by increasingly complex machinery, which has evolved over time from water-powered looms to fully-integrated robotic plants.

Obviously, not all the world's industries – or manufacturing countries – have reached the same level. Textiles, for example, the foundation of the early Industrial Revolution in the West, can be mass-produced with fairly modest technology; today, they are usually produced in developing countries, mostly in Asia, where the low labour costs compensate for the large workforce that the relatively simple machinery requires. Nevertheless, the trend towards high-technology production, however uneven, seems inexorable. Gains in efficiency make up for the staggering cost of the equipment itself, and the outcome is that fewer and fewer people are employed to produce more and more goods.

One paradoxical result of the increase in industrial efficiency is a relative decline in the importance of the industrial sector of a nation's economy. The economy has already passed through one transition, generations past, when workers were drawn from the land into factories. The second transition releases labour into what is called the service sector of the economy: a diffuse but vital concept that includes not only such obvious services as transport and administration, but also finance, insurance and activities as diverse as fashion design or the writing of computer software.

The process is far advanced in the mature economies of the West, with Japan not far behind. Almost two-thirds of US wealth, for example, is now generated in the service sector, and less than half of Japan's Gross National Product comes from industry. The shrinkage, though, is only relative: between them, these two industrial giants produce almost twice the amount of manufactured goods as the rest of the world put together. And it is on the solid base of production that their general prosperity is founded.

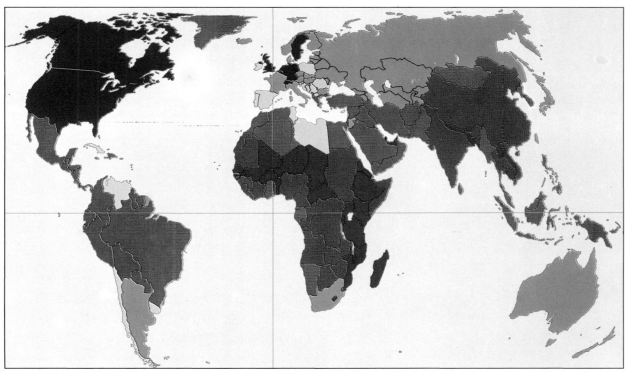

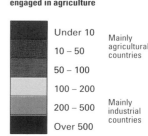

## EMPLOYMENT

The number of workers employed in manufacturing for every 100 workers engaged in agriculture

| | |
|---|---|
| Under 10 | Mainly agricultural countries |
| 10 – 50 | |
| 50 – 100 | |
| 100 – 200 | |
| 200 – 500 | Mainly industrial countries |
| Over 500 | |

**Selected countries (latest available figures, 1986–89)**

| | |
|---|---|
| Singapore | 6,166 |
| Hong Kong | 2,632 |
| UK | 912 |
| Belgium | 751 |
| Germany (W) | 749 |
| USA | 641 |
| Sweden | 615 |
| France | 331 |
| Japan | 320 |
| Czechoslovakia | 286 |

## DIVISION OF EMPLOYMENT

Distribution of workers between agriculture, industry and services, selected countries (late 1980s)

The six countries selected illustrate the usual stages of economic development, from dependence on agriculture through industrial growth to the expansion of the services sector.

- Agriculture
- Industry
- Services

Nepal · Nigeria · Pakistan · Brazil · Hong Kong · USA

## THE WORKFORCE

Percentages of men and women between 15 and 64 in employment, selected countries (late 1980s)

The figures include employees and self-employed, who in developing countries are often subsistence farmers. People in full-time education are excluded. Because of the population age structure in developing countries, the employed population has to support a far larger number of non-workers than its industrial equivalent. For example, more than 52% of Kenya's people are under 15, an age group that makes up less than a tenth of the UK population.

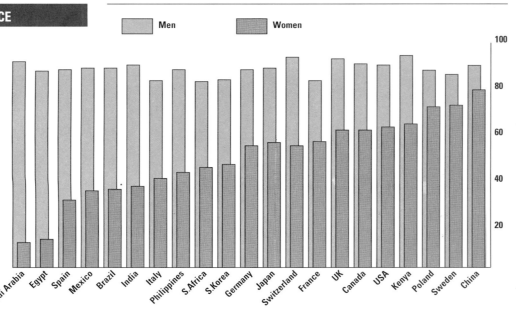

Men · Women

Saudi Arabia · Egypt · Spain · Mexico · Brazil · India · Italy · Philippines · S.Africa · S.Korea · Germany · Japan · Switzerland · France · UK · Canada · USA · Kenya · Poland · Sweden · China

## WEALTH CREATION

The Gross National Product (GNP) of the world's largest economies, US $ billion (1991)

| | | | | | |
|---|---|---:|---|---|---:|
| 1. | USA | 5,686,038 | 21. | Austria | 157,538 |
| 2. | Japan | 3,337,191 | 22. | Iran | 127,366 |
| 3. | Germany | 1,516,785 | 23. | Finland | 121,982 |
| 4. | France | 1,167,749 | 24. | Denmark | 121,695 |
| 5. | Italy | 1,072,198 | 25. | Ukraine | 121,458 |
| 6. | UK | 963,696 | 26. | Indonesia | 111,409 |
| 7. | Canada | 568,765 | 27. | Saudi Arabia | 105,133 |
| 8. | Spain | 486,614 | 28. | Turkey | 103,388 |
| 9. | Russia | 479,546 | 29. | Norway | 102,885 |
| 10. | Brazil | 447,324 | 30. | Argentina | 91,211 |
| 11. | China | 424,012 | 31. | South Africa | 90,953 |
| 12. | Australia | 287,765 | 32. | Thailand | 89,548 |
| 13. | India | 284,668 | 33. | Hong Kong | 77,302 |
| 14. | Netherlands | 278,839 | 34. | Poland | 70,640 |
| 15. | South Korea | 274,464 | 35. | Greece | 65,504 |
| 16. | Mexico | 252,381 | 36. | Israel | 59,128 |
| 17. | Switzerland | 225,890 | 37. | Portugal | 58,451 |
| 18. | Sweden | 218,934 | 38. | Venezuela | 52,775 |
| 19. | Belgium | 192,370 | 39. | Algeria | 52,239 |
| 20. | Taiwan | 161,000 | 40. | Pakistan | 46,725 |

## PATTERNS OF PRODUCTION

Breakdown of industrial output by value, selected countries (1987)

| | Food & agriculture | Textiles & clothing | Machinery & transport | Chemicals | Other |
|---|---|---|---|---|---|
| Algeria | 26% | 20% | 11% | 1% | 41% |
| Argentina | 24% | 10% | 16% | 12% | 37% |
| Australia | 18% | 7% | 21% | 8% | 45% |
| Austria | 17% | 8% | 25% | 6% | 43% |
| Belgium | 19% | 8% | 23% | 13% | 36% |
| Brazil | 15% | 12% | 24% | 9% | 40% |
| Burkina Faso | 62% | 18% | 2% | 1% | 17% |
| Canada | 15% | 7% | 25% | 9% | 44% |
| Denmark | 22% | 6% | 23% | 10% | 39% |
| Egypt | 20% | 27% | 13% | 10% | 31% |
| Finland | 13% | 6% | 24% | 7% | 50% |
| France | 18% | 7% | 33% | 9% | 33% |
| Germany | 12% | 5% | 38% | 10% | 36% |
| Greece | 20% | 22% | 14% | 7% | 38% |
| Hong Kong | 6% | 40% | 20% | 2% | 33% |
| Hungary | 6% | 11% | 37% | 11% | 35% |
| India | 11% | 16% | 26% | 15% | 32% |
| Indonesia | 23% | 11% | 10% | 10% | 47% |
| Iran | 13% | 22% | 22% | 7% | 36% |
| Israel | 13% | 10% | 28% | 8% | 42% |
| Ireland | 28% | 7% | 20% | 15% | 28% |
| Italy | 7% | 13% | 32% | 10% | 38% |
| Japan | 10% | 6% | 38% | 10% | 37% |
| Kenya | 35% | 12% | 14% | 9% | 29% |
| Malaysia | 21% | 5% | 23% | 14% | 37% |
| Mexico | 24% | 12% | 14% | 12% | 39% |
| Netherlands | 19% | 4% | 28% | 11% | 38% |
| New Zealand | 26% | 10% | 16% | 6% | 43% |
| Norway | 21% | 3% | 26% | 7% | 44% |
| Pakistan | 34% | 21% | 8% | 12% | 25% |
| Philippines | 40% | 7% | 7% | 10% | 35% |
| Poland | 15% | 16% | 30% | 6% | 33% |
| Portugal | 17% | 22% | 16% | 8% | 38% |
| Singapore | 6% | 5% | 46% | 8% | 36% |
| South Africa | 14% | 8% | 17% | 11% | 49% |
| South Korea | 15% | 17% | 24% | 9% | 35% |
| Spain | 17% | 9% | 22% | 9% | 43% |
| Sweden | 10% | 2% | 35% | 8% | 44% |
| Thailand | 30% | 17% | 14% | 6% | 33% |
| Turkey | 20% | 14% | 15% | 8% | 43% |
| UK | 14% | 6% | 32% | 11% | 36% |
| USA | 12% | 5% | 35% | 10% | 38% |
| Venezuela | 23% | 8% | 9% | 11% | 49% |

## INDUSTRY AND TRADE

Manufactured goods as a percentage of total exports (1989)

- Over 75%
- 50 – 75%  [USA 69%]
- 25 – 50%  [UK 67%]
- 10 – 25%
- Under 10%

The Far East and South-east Asia (Japan 99.5%, Macau 98.5%, Taiwan 96.8%, Hong Kong 96.1%, South Korea 95.9%) are most dominant, but many countries in Europe (e.g. Austria 98.4%) are also heavily dependent on manufactured goods.

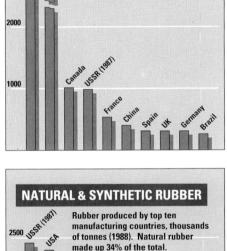

**AUTOMOBILES**
Production of passenger cars in thousands (top ten countries, 1988)

**COMMERCIAL VEHICLES**
Trucks, buses and coaches produced by the top ten manufacturing countries, in thousands (1988)

**TELEVISION SETS**
Production of television receivers in thousands (top ten countries, 1988)

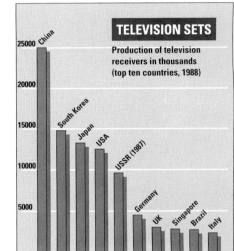

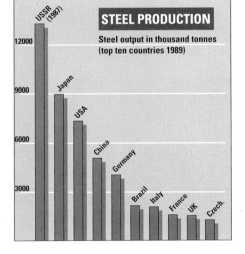

**STEEL PRODUCTION**
Steel output in thousand tonnes (top ten countries 1989)

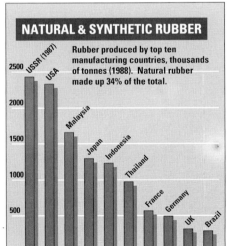

**SHIPBUILDING**
Tonnage produced by top ten shipbuilding countries in thousand tonnes (1989)

**NATURAL & SYNTHETIC RUBBER**
Rubber produced by top ten manufacturing countries, thousands of tonnes (1988). Natural rubber made up 34% of the total.

**WASHING MACHINES**
Production in thousands (top ten countries, 1988)

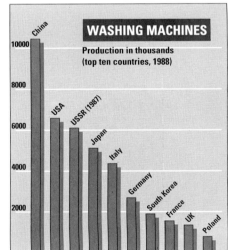

## INDUSTRIAL POWER

Industrial output (mining, manufacturing, construction, energy and water production), top 40 nations, US $ billion (1988)

| | | | | | |
|---|---|---|---|---|---|
| 1. USA | 1,249.54 | | 21. Austria | 50.63 |
| 2. Japan | 1,155.41 | | 22. Belgium | 46.88 |
| 3. W. Germany | 479.69 | | 23. Poland | 39.52 |
| 4. USSR (1987) | 326.54 | | 24. Finland | 35.50 |
| 5. France | 304.95 | | 25. South Africa | 35.46 |
| 6. UK | 295.00 | | 26. Saudi Arabia | 33.36 |
| 7. Italy | 286.00 | | 27. Denmark | 30.79 |
| 8. China | 174.05 | | 28. Iraq | 30.27 |
| 9. Canada | 171.06 | | 29. Czechoslovakia | 30.18 |
| 10. Spain | 126.60 | | 30. Yugoslavia | 29.32 |
| 11. Brazil | 116.13 | | 31. Indonesia | 29.03 |
| 12. Netherlands | 76.48 | | 32. Norway | 28.74 |
| 13. Sweden | 75.17 | | 33. Argentina | 26.27 |
| 14. South Korea | 74.00 | | 34. Turkey | 26.07 |
| 15. India | 72.69 | | 35. Israel | 24.15 |
| 16. Australia | 72.63 | | 36. Algeria | 22.88 |
| 17. E. Germany | 64.66 | | 37. Venezuela | 22.70 |
| 18. Switzerland | 63.37 | | 38. Romania | 22.19 |
| 19. Mexico | 61.57 | | 39. Iran | 19.90 |
| 20. Taiwan | 54.81 | | 40. Thailand | 18.62 |

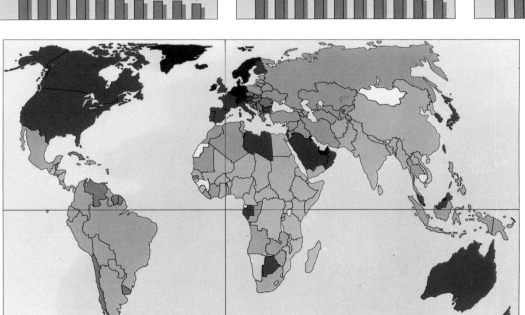

## EXPORTS PER CAPITA

Value of exports in US $, divided by total population (1988)

- Over 10,000
- 5,000 – 10,000
- 1,000 – 5,000  [UK 2,665]
- 500 – 1,000  [USA 1,463]
- 100 – 500
- Under 100
- No data available

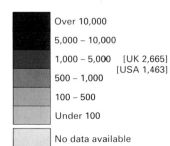

**Highest per capita**

| | |
|---|---|
| Singapore | 16,671 |
| Hong Kong | 12,676 |
| UAE | 10,217 |
| Belgium | 10,200 |
| Bahamas | 8,580 |
| Qatar | 8,431 |

*Statistics for the new republics of the former USSR, Czechoslovakia and Yugoslavia are not yet available. The map shows the statistics for the entire USSR, Czechoslovakia and Yugoslavia.*

CARTOGRAPHY BY PHILIP'S. COPYRIGHT REED INTERNATIONAL BOOKS LTD

# PRODUCTION: TRADE

Thriving international trade is the outward sign of a healthy world economy – the obvious indicator that some countries have goods to sell and others the wherewithal to buy them. Despite local fluctuations, trade throughout the 1980s grew consistently faster than output, increasing in value by almost 50% between 1979–89. It remains dominated by the wealthy, industrialized countries of the Organization for Economic Development:

between them, the 24 OECD members account for almost 75% of world imports and exports in most years. OECD dominance is just as marked in the trade in 'invisibles' – a column in the balance sheet that includes, among other headings, the export of services, interest payments on overseas investments, tourism, and even remittances from migrant workers abroad. In the UK, 'invisibles' account for more than half all trading income.

However, the size of these great trading

economies means that imports and exports usually comprise a fraction of their total wealth: in the case of the export-conscious Japanese, trade in goods and services amounts to less than 18% of GDP. In poorer countries, trade – often in a single commodity – may amount to 50% of GDP or more. And there are oddities: import-export figures for the entrepôt economy of Singapore, the transit point for much Asian trade, are almost double that small nation's total earnings.

## WORLD TRADE

Percentage share of total world exports by value (1990)*

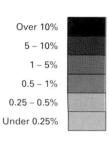

- Over 10%
- 5 – 10%
- 1 – 5%
- 0.5 – 1%
- 0.25 – 0.5%
- Under 0.25%

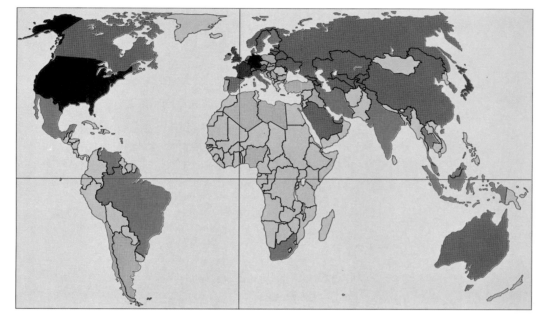

## THE GREAT TRADING NATIONS

The imports and exports of the top ten trading nations as a percentage of world trade (latest available year). Each country's trade in manufactured goods is shown in orange.

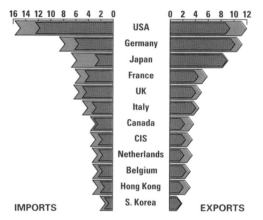

IMPORTS — USA, Germany, Japan, France, UK, Italy, Canada, CIS, Netherlands, Belgium, Hong Kong, S. Korea — EXPORTS

## MAJOR EXPORTS

Leading manufactured items and their exporters, by percentage of world total in US $ (latest available year)

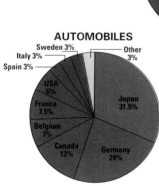

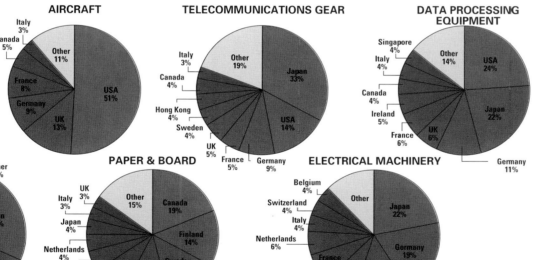

**AIRCRAFT**: USA 51%, UK 13%, Germany 9%, France 8%, Canada 5%, Italy 3%, Other 11%

**TELECOMMUNICATIONS GEAR**: Japan 33%, USA 14%, Germany 9%, France 5%, UK 5%, Sweden 4%, Hong Kong 4%, Canada 4%, Italy 3%, Other 19%

**DATA PROCESSING EQUIPMENT**: USA 24%, Japan 22%, Germany 11%, UK 6%, France 6%, Ireland 5%, Canada 4%, Italy 4%, Singapore 4%, Other 14%

**AUTOMOBILES**: Japan 31.5%, Germany 24%, Canada 12%, Belgium 7%, France 7.5%, USA 6%, Spain 3%, Italy 3%, Sweden 3%, Other 3%

**PAPER & BOARD**: Canada 19%, Finland 14%, Sweden 13%, Germany 12%, USA 8%, France 5%, Netherlands 4%, Japan 4%, Italy 3%, UK 3%, Other 15%

**ELECTRICAL MACHINERY**: Japan 22%, Germany 19%, USA 14%, UK 8%, France 7%, Netherlands 6%, Italy 4%, Switzerland 4%, Belgium 4%, Other

## TRADED PRODUCTS

Top ten manufactures traded, by value in billions of US $ (latest available year)

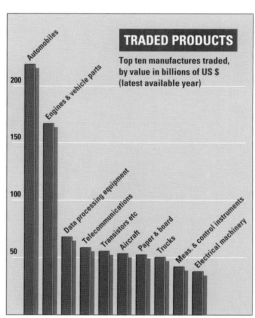

Automobiles; Engines & vehicle parts; Data processing equipment; Telecommunications; Transistors etc; Aircraft; Paper & board; Trucks; Meas & control instruments; Electrical machinery

## DEPENDENCE ON TRADE

Value of exports as a percentage of Gross Domestic Product (1991)

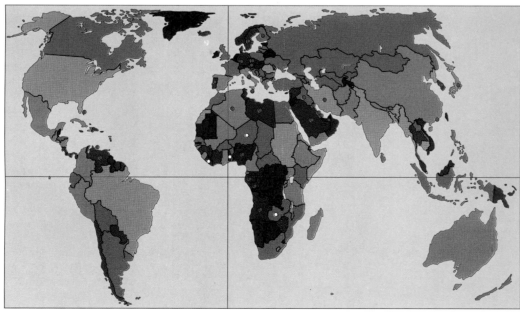

- Over 50% GDP
- 40 – 50% GDP
- 30 – 40% GDP
- 20 – 30% GDP
- 10 – 20% GDP
- Under 10% GDP

- Most dependent on industrial exports (over 75% of total exports)
- Most dependent on fuel exports (over 75% of total exports)
- Most dependent on mineral and metal exports (over 75% of total exports)

*Statistics for the new republics of the former USSR, Czechoslovakia and Yugoslavia are not yet available. The map shows the statistics for the entire USSR, Czechoslovakia and Yugoslavia.

## WORLD SHIPPING

While ocean passenger traffic is nowadays relatively modest, sea transport still carries most of the world's trade. Oil and bulk carriers make up the majority of the world fleet, although the general cargo category was the fastest growing in 1989, a year in which total tonnage increased by 1.5%.

Almost 30% of world shipping sails under a 'flag of convenience', whereby owners take advantage of low taxes by registering their vessels in a foreign country the ships will never see, notably Panama and Liberia.

### MERCHANT FLEETS

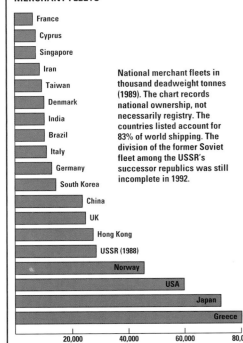

France
Cyprus
Singapore
Iran
Taiwan
Denmark
India
Brazil
Italy
Germany
South Korea
China
UK
Hong Kong
USSR (1988)
Norway
USA
Japan
Greece

20,000  40,000  60,000  80,000

National merchant fleets in thousand deadweight tonnes (1989). The chart records national ownership, not necessarily registry. The countries listed account for 83% of world shipping. The division of the former Soviet fleet among the USSR's successor republics was still incomplete in 1992.

### FREIGHT

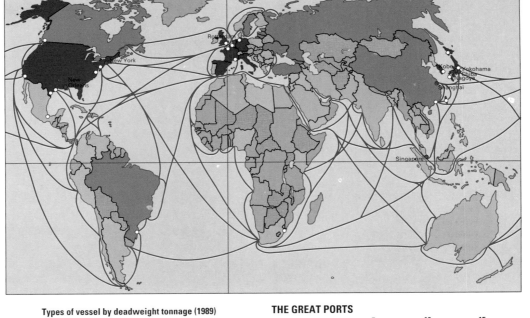

Freight unloaded in millions of tonnes (latest available year)*

Over 100
50 – 100
10 – 50
5 – 10
Under 5
Landlocked countries

**Major seaports**

● Over 100 million tonnes per year
○ 50 – 100 million tonnes per year

### Types of vessel by deadweight tonnage (1989)

Oil tankers 38.4%
Ore & bulk carriers 29.9%
Others 9.7%
General cargo 16.1%
Ferries & passenger ships 0.5%
Liquid gas carriers 1.6%
Container ships 3.8%

### THE GREAT PORTS

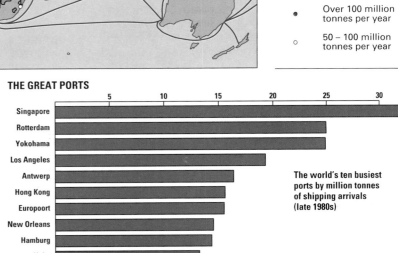

5  10  15  20  25  30

Singapore
Rotterdam
Yokohama
Los Angeles
Antwerp
Hong Kong
Europoort
New Orleans
Hamburg
Kobe

The world's ten busiest ports by million tonnes of shipping arrivals (late 1980s)

## TRADE IN PRIMARY PRODUCTS

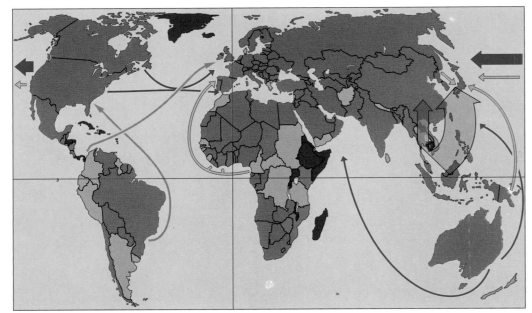

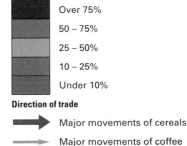

Primary products (excluding fuels, minerals and metals) as a percentage of total export value (latest available year)*

Over 75%
50 – 75%
25 – 50%
10 – 25%
Under 10%

**Direction of trade**

→ Major movements of cereals
→ Major movements of coffee
→ Major movements of hardwoods

Arrows show the major trade directions of selected primary products, and are proportional to export value.

## BALANCE OF TRADE

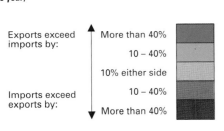

Value of exports in proportion to the value of imports (latest available year)

Exports exceed imports by:
More than 40%
10 – 40%
10% either side
Imports exceed exports by:
10 – 40%
More than 40%

The total world trade balance should amount to zero, since exports must equal imports on a global scale. In practice, at least $100 billion in exports go unrecorded, leaving the world with an apparent deficit and many countries in a better position than public accounting reveals. However, a favourable trade balance is not necessarily a sign of prosperity: many poorer countries must maintain a high surplus in order to service debts, and do so by restricting imports below the levels needed to sustain successful economies.

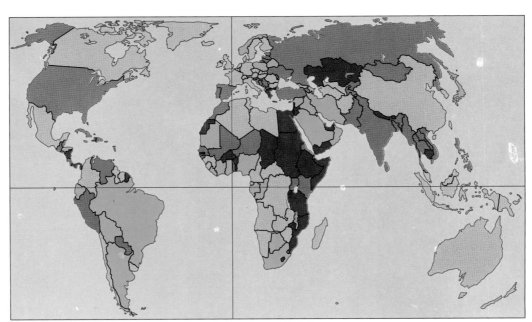

*Statistics for the new republics of the former USSR, Czechoslovakia and Yugoslavia are not yet available. The map shows the statistics for the entire USSR, Czechoslovakia and Yugoslavia.

# QUALITY OF LIFE: WEALTH

Throughout the 1980s, most of the world became at least slightly richer. There were exceptions: in Africa, the poorest of the continents, many incomes actually fell, and the upheavals in Eastern Europe in 1989 left whole populations awash with political freedom but worse off financially in economies still teetering towards capitalism.

Most of the improvements, however, came to those who were already, in world terms, extremely affluent: the gap between rich and poor grew steadily wider. And in those developing countries that showed significant statistical progress, advances were often confined to a few favoured areas, while conditions in other, usually rural, districts went from bad to worse.

The pattern of world poverty varies from region to region. In most of Asia, the process of recognized development is generally under way, with production increases outpacing population growth. By 2000, less than 10% of the Chinese population should be officially rated 'poor': without the means to buy either adequate food or the basic necessities required to take a full part in everyday life. Even India's lower growth rate should be enough to reduce the burden of poverty for at least some of its people. In Latin America, average per capita production is high enough for most countries to be considered 'middle income' in world rankings. But although adequate resources exist, Latin American wealth is distributed with startling inequality. According to a 1990 World Bank report, a tax of only 2% on the richest fifth would raise enough money to pull every one of the continent's 437 million people above the poverty line.

In Africa, solutions will be much harder to find. The bane of high population growth has often been aggravated by incompetent administration, war and a succession of natural disasters. Population is the crux of the problem: numbers are growing anything up to twice as fast as the economies that try to support them. Aid from the developed world is only a partial solution; although Africa receives more aid than any other continent, much has been wasted on overambitious projects or lost in webs of inexperienced or corrupt bureaucracy. Yet without aid, Africa seems doomed to permanent crisis.

The rich countries can afford to increase their spending. The 24 members of the Organisation for Economic Co-operation and Development comprise only 16% of the world's population, yet between them the nations accounted for almost 80% of total world production in 1988, a share that is likely to increase as the year 2000 approaches.

## CURRENCIES

**Currency units of the world's most powerful economies**

1. USA: US Dollar($, US $) = 100 cents
2. Japan: Yen (Y, ¥) = 100 sen
3. Germany: Deutsche Mark (DM) = 100 Pfennige
4. France: French Franc (Fr) = 100 centimes
5. Italy: Italian Lira (L, £, Lit) = 100 centesimi
6. UK: Pound Sterling (£) = 100 pence
7. Canada: Canadian Dollar (C$, Can$) = 100 cents
8. China: Renminbi Yuan (RMBY, $, Y) = 10 jiao = 100 fen
9. Brazil: Cruzado (Cr$) = 100 centavos
10. Spain: Peseta (Pta, Pa) = 100 céntimos
11. India: Indian Rupee (Re, Rs) = 100 paisa
12. Australia: Australian Dollar ($A) = 100 cents
13. Netherlands: Guilder, Florin (Gld, f) = 100 centimes
14. Switzerland: Swiss Franc (SFr, SwF) = 100 centimes
15. South Korea: Won (W) = 100 Chon
16. Sweden: Swedish Krona (SKr) = 100 ore
17. Mexico: Mexican Pesos (Mex$) = 100 centavos
18. Belgium: Belgian Franc (BFr) = 100 centimes
19. Austria: Schilling (S, Sch) = 100 groschen
20. Finland: Markka (FMk) = 100 penni
21. Denmark: Danish Krone (DKr) = 100 ore
22. Norway: Norwegian Krone (NKr) = 100 ore
23. Saudi Arabia: Riyal (SAR, SRI$) = 100 halalah
24. Indonesia: Rupiah (Rp) = 100 sen
25. South Africa: Rand (R) = 100 cents

## CONTINENTAL SHARES

**Shares of population and of wealth (GNP) by continent**

Generalized continental figures show the startling difference between rich and poor, but mask the successes or failures of individual countries. Japan, for example, with less than 4% of Asia's population, produces almost 70% of the continent's output.

**POPULATION**

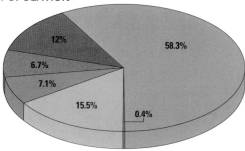

**GNP**

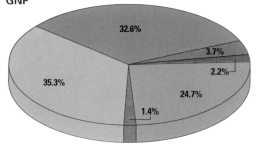

 Europe  Asia  South America
Australia Africa North America

## LEVELS OF INCOME

**Gross National Product per capita: the value of total production divided by the population (1991)**

Over 400% of world average
200 – 400%
100 – 200%
[World average wealth per person US $4,210]
50 – 100%
25 – 50%
10 – 25%
Under 10%

**Richest countries**

| | |
|---|---|
| Switzerland | $33,510 |
| Luxembourg | $31,080 |
| Japan | $26,920 |
| Sweden | $25,490 |

**Poorest countries**

| | |
|---|---|
| Mozambique | $70 |
| Tanzania | $100 |
| Ethiopia | $120 |
| Somalia | $150 |

## INDICATORS

The gap between the world's rich and poor is now so great that it is difficult to illustrate it on a single graph. Car ownership in the USA, for example, is almost 2,000 times as common as it is in Bangladesh. Within each income group, however, comparisons have some meaning: the affluent Japanese on their overcrowded island have far fewer cars than the Americans; the Chinese, perhaps because of propaganda value, have more television sets than people in India, whose per capita income is similar, while Nigerians prefer to spend their money on vehicles.

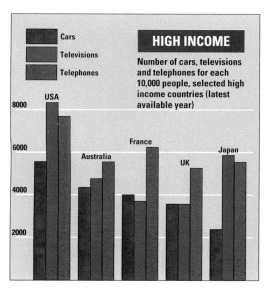

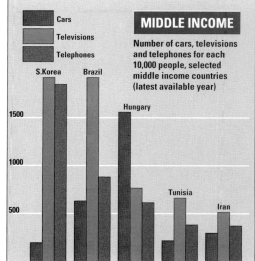

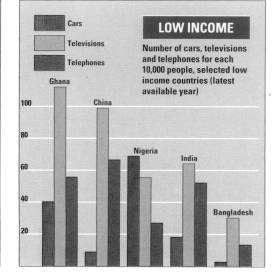

40

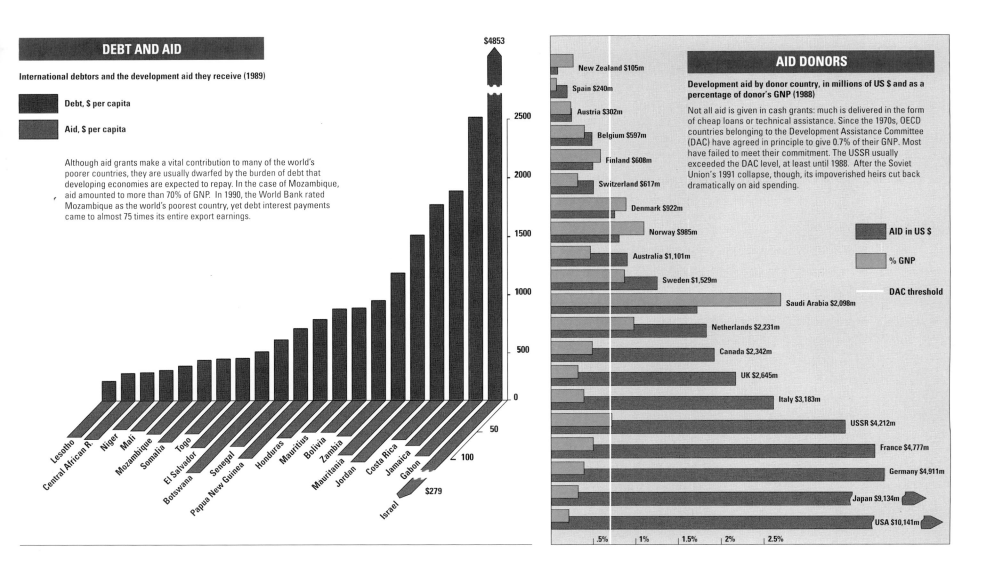

## DEBT AND AID

**International debtors and the development aid they receive (1989)**

■ Debt, $ per capita

■ Aid, $ per capita

Although aid grants make a vital contribution to many of the world's poorer countries, they are usually dwarfed by the burden of debt that developing economies are expected to repay. In the case of Mozambique, aid amounted to more than 70% of GNP. In 1990, the World Bank rated Mozambique as the world's poorest country, yet debt interest payments came to almost 75 times its entire export earnings.

## AID DONORS

**Development aid by donor country, in millions of US $ and as a percentage of donor's GNP (1988)**

Not all aid is given in cash grants: much is delivered in the form of cheap loans or technical assistance. Since the 1970s, OECD countries belonging to the Development Assistance Committee (DAC) have agreed in principle to give 0.7% of their GNP. Most have failed to meet their commitment. The USSR usually exceeded the DAC level, at least until 1988. After the Soviet Union's 1991 collapse, though, its impoverished heirs cut back dramatically on aid spending.

■ AID in US $

■ % GNP

— DAC threshold

---

Inflation (right) is an excellent index of a country's financial stability, and usually its prosperity or at least its prospects. Inflation rates above 20% are generally matched by slow or even negative growth; above 50%, an economy is left reeling. Most advanced countries during the 1980s had to wrestle with inflation that occasionally touched or even exceeded 10%; in Japan, the growth leader, price increases averaged only 1.8% between 1980 and 1988.

Government spending (below right) is more difficult to interpret. Obviously, very low levels indicate a weak state, and high levels a strong one; but in poor countries, the 10–20% absorbed by the government may well amount to most of the liquid cash available, whereas in rich countries most of the 35–50% typically in government hands is returned in services.

GNP per capita figures (below) should also be compared with caution. They do not reveal the vast differences in living costs between different countries: the equivalent of US $100 is worth considerably more in poorer nations than it is in the USA itself.

## INFLATION

**Average annual rate of inflation (1980–91)***

■ Over 50%
■ 20 – 50%
■ 7.5 – 20%
■ 1 – 7.5%
■ Negative inflation
■ No data available

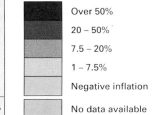

**Highest average inflation**

| | |
|---|---|
| Nicaragua | 584% |
| Argentina | 417% |
| Brazil | 328% |

**Lowest average inflation**

| | |
|---|---|
| Oman | –3.1% |
| Kuwait | –2.7% |
| Saudi Arabia | –2.4% |

## THE WEALTH GAP

**The world's richest and poorest countries, by Gross National Product per capita in US $ (1991)**

| 1. | Switzerland | 33,510 | 1. | Mozambique | 70 |
|---|---|---|---|---|---|
| 2. | Liechtenstein | 33,000 | 2. | Tanzania | 100 |
| 3. | Luxembourg | 31,080 | 3. | Ethiopia | 120 |
| 4. | Japan | 26,920 | 4. | Somalia | 150 |
| 5. | Sweden | 25,490 | 5. | Uganda | 160 |
| 6. | Bermuda | 25,000 | 6. | Bhutan | 180 |
| 7. | Finland | 24,400 | 7. | Nepal | 180 |
| 8. | Norway | 24,160 | 8. | Guinea-Bissau | 190 |
| 9. | Denmark | 23,660 | 9. | Cambodia | 200 |
| 10. | Germany | 23,650 | 10. | Burundi | 210 |
| 11. | Iceland | 22,580 | 11. | Madagascar | 210 |
| 12. | USA | 22,560 | 12. | Sierra Leone | 210 |
| 13. | Canada | 21,260 | 13. | Bangladesh | 220 |
| 14. | France | 20,600 | 14. | Chad | 220 |
| 15. | Austria | 20,380 | 15. | Zaire | 220 |
| 16. | UAE | 19,500 | 16. | Laos | 230 |
| 17. | Belgium | 19,300 | 17. | Malawi | 230 |
| 18. | Italy | 18,580 | 18. | Rwanda | 260 |
| 19. | Netherlands | 18,560 | 19. | Mali | 280 |
| 20. | UK | 16,750 | 20. | Guyana | 290 |

GNP per capita is calculated by dividing a country's Gross National Product by its population.

## STATE SPENDING

**Central government expenditure as a percentage of GNP (latest available year)* [‡ estimate]**

■ Over 45%
■ 35 – 45%
■ 25 – 35%
■ 15 – 25%
■ 0 – 15%
■ No data available

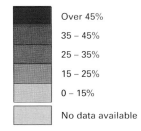

**Top 5 countries**

| | |
|---|---|
| Bulgaria | 77.3% |
| Guinea-Bissau | 63.0% |
| Greece | 60.0% |
| Czechoslovakia | 55.6% |
| Hungary | 54.7% |

*Statistics for the new republics of the former USSR, Czechoslovakia and Yugoslavia are not yet available.*
*The map shows the statistics for the entire USSR, Czechoslovakia and Yugoslavia.*

# QUALITY OF LIFE: STANDARDS

At first sight, most international contrasts are swamped by differences in wealth. The rich not only have more money, they have more of everything, including years of life. Those with only a little money are obliged to spend most of it on food and clothing, the basic maintenance costs of existence; air travel and tourism are unlikely to feature on the lists of their expenditure. However, poverty and wealth are both relative: slum dwellers living on social security payments in an affluent industrial country have far more resources at their disposal than an average African peasant, but feel their own poverty none the less acutely. A middle-class Indian lawyer cannot command a fraction of the earnings of a counterpart in New York, London or Rome; nevertheless, he rightly sees himself as prosperous.

In 1990 the United Nations Development Programme published its first Human Development Index, an attempt to construct a comparative scale by which at least a simplified form of well-being might be measured. The index, running from 1 to 100, combined figures for life expectancy and literacy with a wealth scale that matched incomes against the official poverty lines of a group of industrialized nations. National scores ranged from a startling 98.7 for Sweden to a miserable 11.6 for Niger, reflecting the all-too-familiar gap between rich and poor.

Comparisons between nations with similar incomes are more interesting, showing the effect of government policies. For example, Sri Lanka was awarded 78.9 against 43.9 for its only slightly poorer neighbour, India; Zimbabwe, at 57.6, had more than double the score of Senegal, despite no apparent disparities in average income. Some development indicators may be interpreted in two ways. There is a very clear correlation, for example, between the wealth of a nation and the level of education that its people enjoy. Education helps create wealth, of course; but are rich countries wealthy because they are educated, or well-educated because they are rich? Women's fertility rates appear to fall almost in direct proportion to the amount of secondary education they receive; but high levels of female education are associated with rich countries, where fertility is already low.

Not everything, though, is married to wealth. The countries cited on these pages have been chosen to give a range covering different cultures as well as different economic power, revealing disparities among rich and among poor as well as between the two obvious groups. Income distribution, for example, shows that in Brazil (following the general pattern of Latin America) most national wealth is concentrated in a few hands; Bangladesh is much poorer, but what little wealth there is, is more evenly spread.

Among the developed countries the USA, with its poorest 20% sharing less than 5% of the national cake, has a noticeably less even distribution than Japan where, despite massive industrialization, traditional values act as a brake against poverty. Hungary, still enmeshed in Communism when these statistics were compiled, shows the most even distribution of all, which certainly matches with Socialist theory. However, the inequalities in Communist societies, a contributing factor in the demise of most of them in the late 1980s, are not easily measured in money terms. Communist élites are less often rewarded with cash than with power and privilege, commodities not easily expressed statistically.

There are other limits to statistical analysis. Even without taking account of such imponderables as personal satisfaction, it will always be more difficult to measure a reasonable standard of living than a nation's income or its productivity. Lack of money certainly brings misery, but its presence does not guarantee contentment.

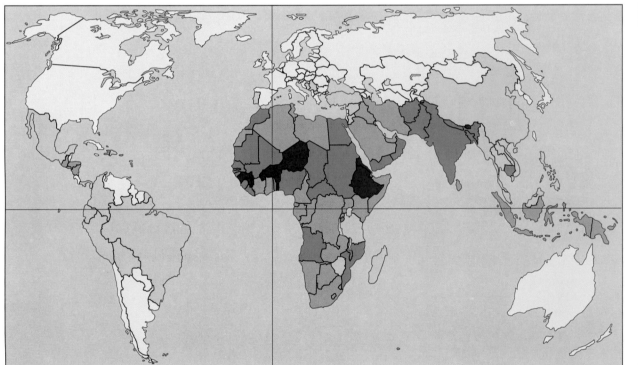

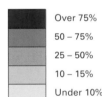

### ILLITERACY

Percentage of the total population unable to read or write (latest available year)*

- Over 75%
- 50 – 75%
- 25 – 50%
- 10 – 15%
- Under 10%

Educational expenditure per person (latest available year)

Top 5 countries

| | |
|---|---|
| Sweden | $997 |
| Qatar | $989 |
| Canada | $983 |
| Norway | $971 |
| Switzerland | $796 |

Bottom 5 countries

| | |
|---|---|
| Chad | $2 |
| Bangladesh | $3 |
| Ethiopia | $3 |
| Nepal | $4 |
| Somalia | $4 |

### EDUCATION

The developing countries made great efforts in the 1970s and 1980s to bring at least a basic education to their people. Primary school enrolments rose above 60% in all but the poorest nations. Figures often include teenagers or young adults, however, and there are still an estimated 300 million children worldwide who receive no schooling at all. Secondary and higher education are expanding far more slowly, and the gap between rich and poor is probably even larger than it appears from the charts here, while the bare statistics provide no real reflection of educational quality.

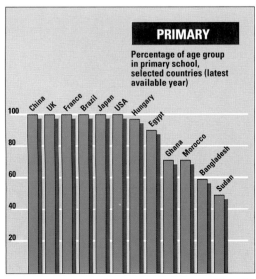

PRIMARY

Percentage of age group in primary school, selected countries (latest available year)

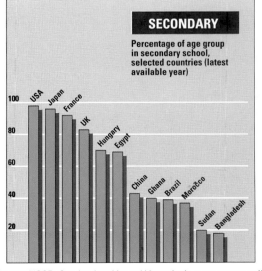

SECONDARY

Percentage of age group in secondary school, selected countries (latest available year)

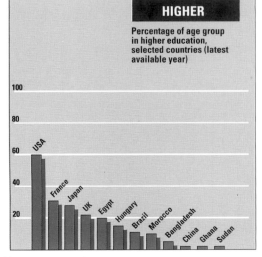

HIGHER

Percentage of age group in higher education, selected countries (latest available year)

*Statistics for the new republics of the former USSR, Czechoslovakia and Yugoslavia are not yet available. The map shows the statistics for the entire USSR, Czechoslovakia and Yugoslavia.*

## DISTRIBUTION OF SPENDING

**Percentage share of household spending (1989)**

- Food
- Clothing
- Energy & Housing
- Medicine & Education
- Transport
- Other

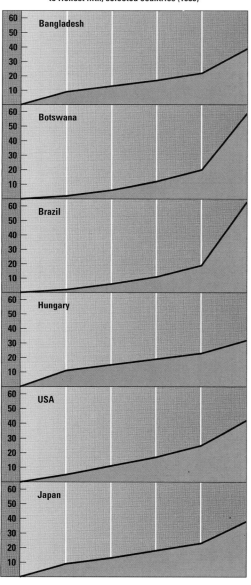

UK    USA    Japan    Hungary    Brazil    Egypt    Nigeria    B'desh

## DISTRIBUTION OF INCOME

**Percentage share of household income from poorest fifth to richest fifth, selected countries (1989)**

- Bangladesh
- Botswana
- Brazil
- Hungary
- USA
- Japan

## FERTILITY AND EDUCATION

**Fertility rates compared with female education, selected countries (latest available year)**

- Fertility rate: average number of children borne per woman
- Percentage of female age group in secondary education

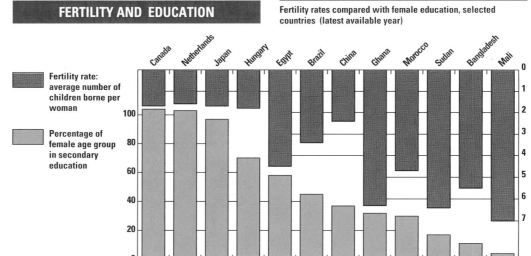

Canada  Netherlands  Japan  Hungary  Egypt  Brazil  China  Ghana  Morocco  Sudan  Bangladesh  Mali

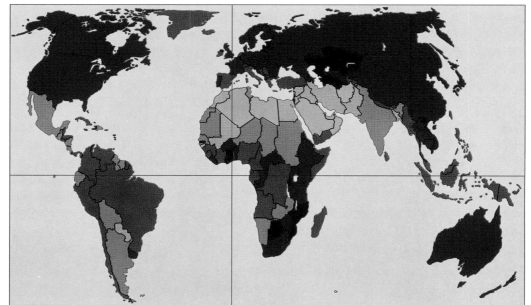

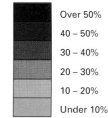

### TOURIST SPENDING

**Nations spending the most on overseas tourism, US $ million (latest available year)**

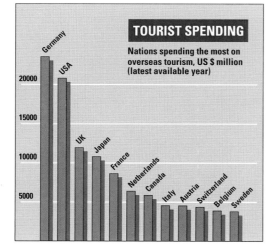

Germany  USA  UK  Japan  France  Netherlands  Canada  Italy  Austria  Switzerland  Belgium  Sweden

### TOURIST EARNING

**Nations receiving the most from overseas tourism, US $ million (latest available year)**

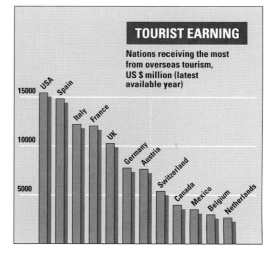

USA  Spain  Italy  France  UK  Germany  Austria  Switzerland  Canada  Mexico  Belgium  Netherlands

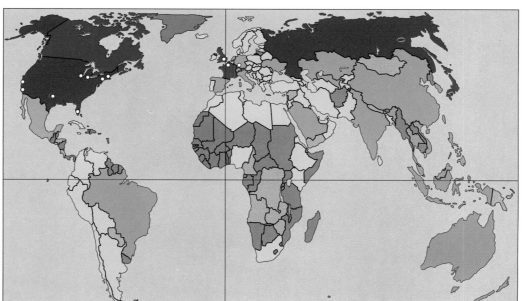

Since the age group for secondary schooling is usually defined as 12–17 years, percentages for countries with a significant number of 11- or 18-year-olds in secondary school may actually exceed 100.
A high proportion of employed women may indicate either an advanced, industrial economy where female opportunities are high, or a poor country where many women's lives are dominated by agricultural toil. The lowest rates are found in Islamic nations, whose religious precepts often exclude women even from fieldwork.

### WOMEN AT WORK

**Women in paid employment as a percentage of the total workforce (latest available year)**

- Over 50%
- 40 – 50%
- 30 – 40%
- 20 – 30%
- 10 – 20%
- Under 10%

**Most women in work**

| | |
|---|---|
| Kazakhstan | 54% |
| Rwanda | 54% |
| Botswana | 53% |

**Fewest women in work**

| | |
|---|---|
| Guinea-Bissau | 3% |
| Oman | 6% |
| Afghanistan | 8% |

Small economies in attractive areas are often completely dominated by tourism: in some West Indian islands, tourist spending provides over 90% of the total income. In cash terms the USA is the world leader: its 1987 earnings exceeded $15 billion, though that sum amounted to only 0.4% of its GDP.

### AIR TRAVEL

**Millions of passenger km [number carried, international/domestic, multiplied by distance flown from airport of origin] (latest year)**

- Over 100,000
- 50,000 – 100,000
- 10,000 – 50,000
- 1,000 – 10,000
- 500 – 1,000
- Under 500
- ○ Major airports (over 20 million passengers in 1991)

The world's busiest airport in terms of total passengers is Chicago's O'Hare; the busiest international airport is Heathrow, the largest of London's airports

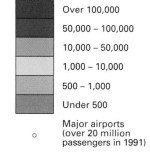

# QUALITY OF LIFE: HEALTH

According to statistics gathered in the late 1980s and early 1990s, a third of the world's population has no access to safe drinking water: malaria is on the increase; cholera, thought vanquished, is reappearing in South America; an epidemic of the AIDS virus is gathering force in Africa; and few developing countries can stretch their health care budgets beyond US $2 per person per year.

Yet human beings, by every statistical index, have never been healthier. In the richest nations, where food is plentiful, the demands of daily work are rarely onerous and medical care is both readily available and highly advanced, the average life expectancy is often more than 75 years – approaching the perceived limits for human longevity. In middle-income nations, such as Brazil and the Philippines, life expectancy usually extends at least to the mid-60s; in China, it has already reached 70 years. Even in poverty-stricken Ethiopia and Chad, lifespans are close to 50 years. Despite economic crisis, drought, famine and even war, every country in the world reported an increase between 1965 and 1990.

It was not always so, even in countries then considered rich. By comparison, in 1880 the life expectancy of an average Berliner was under 30 years and infant mortality in the United Kingdom, then the wealthiest nation, stood at 144 per thousand births – a grim toll exceeded today only by three of the poorest African countries (Mali, Sierra Leone and Guinea). Even by 1910, European death rates were almost twice as high as the world average less than 80 years later; infant mortality in Norway, Europe's healthiest country, was then higher than in present-day Indonesia. In far less than a century, human prospects have improved beyond recognition.

In global terms, the transformation is less the result of high-technology medicine – still too expensive for all but a minority, even in rich countries – than of improvements in agriculture and hence nutrition, matched by the widespread diffusion of the basic concepts of disease and public health. One obvious consequence, as death rates every-where continue to fall, is sustained population growth. Another is the rising expectation of continued improvement felt by both rich and poor nations alike.

In some ways, the task is easier for developing countries, striving with limited resources to attain health levels to which the industrialized world has only recently become accustomed. As the tables below illustrate, infectious disease is rare among the richer nations, while ailments such as cancer, which tend to kill in advanced years, do not seriously impinge on populations with shorter lifespans.

Yet infectious disease is relatively cheap to eliminate, or at least reduce, and it is likely to be easier to raise life expectancy from 60 to 70 years than from 75 to 85 years. The ills of the developed world and its ageing population are more expensive to treat – though most poor countries would be happy to suffer from the problems of the affluent. Western nations regularly spend more money on campaigns to educate their citizens out of overeating and other bad habits than many developing countries can devote to an entire health budget – an irony that marks the dimensions of the rich-poor divide.

Indeed, wealth itself may be the most reliable indicator of longevity. Harmful habits are usually the province of the rich; yet curiously, though the dangerous effects of tobacco have been proved beyond doubt, the affluent Japanese combine very high cigarette consumption with the longest life expectancy of all the major nations. Similarly, heavy alcohol consumption seems to have no effect on longevity: the French, world leaders in 1988 and in most previous surveys, outlive the more moderate British by a year, and the abstemious Indians by almost two decades.

## FOOD CONSUMPTION

**Average daily food intake in calories per person (1989)***

- Over 3,500 cal.
- 3,000 – 3,500 cal.
- 2,500 – 3,000 cal.
- 2,000 – 2,500 cal.
- Under 2,000 cal.
- No available data

**Top 5 countries**
| | |
|---|---|
| Belgium | 3,902 cal. |
| Greece | 3,825 cal. |
| Ireland | 3,778 cal. |
| Bulgaria | 3,707 cal. |
| USA | 3,650 cal. |

**Bottom 5 countries**
| | |
|---|---|
| Ethiopia | 1,666 cal. |
| Mozambique | 1,679 cal. |
| Chad | 1,742 cal. |
| Sierra Leone | 1,799 cal. |
| Angola | 1,806 cal. |

## CAUSES OF DEATH

The rich not only live longer, on average, than the poor; they also die from different causes. Infectious and parasitic diseases, all but eliminated in the developed world, remain a scourge in poorer countries. On the other hand, more than two-thirds of the populations of OECD nations eventually succumb to cancer or circulatory disease; the proportion in Latin America is only about 45%. In addition to the three major diseases shown here, respiratory infection and injury also claim more lives in developing nations, which lack the drugs and medical skills required to treat them.

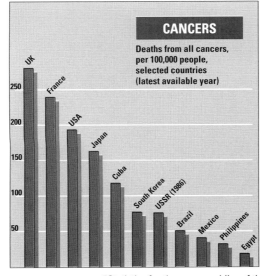

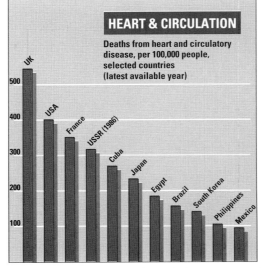

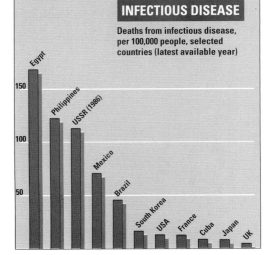

*Statistics for the new republics of the former USSR, Czechoslovakia and Yugoslavia are not yet available. The map shows the statistics for the entire USSR, Czechoslovakia and Yugoslavia.*

CARTOGRAPHY BY PHILIP'S. COPYRIGHT REED INTERNATIONAL BOOKS LTD

## LIFE EXPECTANCY

**Years of life expectancy at birth, selected countries (1988–89)**

The chart shows combined data for both sexes. On average, women live longer than men worldwide, even in developing countries with high maternal mortality rates. Overall, life expectancy is steadily rising, though the difference between rich and poor nations remains dramatic.

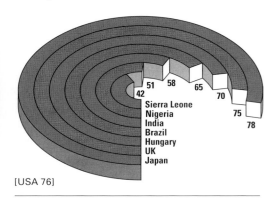

51 58 65 70 75 78
42
Sierra Leone
Nigeria
India
Brazil
Hungary
UK
Japan

[USA 76]

## CHILD MORTALITY

**Number of babies who will die before the age of one year, per 1,000 live births (average 1990–95)***

| | |
|---|---|
| ■ | Over 150 deaths |
| ■ | 100 – 150 deaths |
| ■ | 50 – 100 deaths |
| ■ | 20 – 50 deaths |
| ■ | 10 – 20 deaths |
| □ | Under 10 deaths |

**Highest child mortality**
Afghanistan...................... 162
Mali..................................... 159

**Lowest child mortality**
Iceland ................................. 5
Finland.................................. 5

[USA 9]   [UK 8]

## HOSPITAL CAPACITY

**Hospital beds available for each 1,000 people (latest available year)**

| Highest capacity | | Lowest capacity | |
|---|---|---|---|
| Finland | 14.9 | Bangladesh | 0.2 |
| Sweden | 13.2 | Nepal | 0.2 |
| France | 12.9 | Ethiopia | 0.3 |
| USSR (1986) | 12.8 | Mauritania | 0.4 |
| Netherlands | 12.0 | Mali | 0.5 |
| North Korea | 11.7 | Burkina Faso | 0.6 |
| Switzerland | 11.3 | Pakistan | 0.6 |
| Austria | 10.4 | Niger | 0.7 |
| Czechoslovakia | 10.1 | Haiti | 0.8 |
| Hungary | 9.1 | Chad | 0.8 |

[UK 8] [USA 5.9]

The availability of a bed can mean anything from a private room in a well-equipped Californian teaching hospital to a place in the overcrowded annexe of a rural African clinic. In the Third World especially, quality of treatment can vary enormously from place to place within the same country.

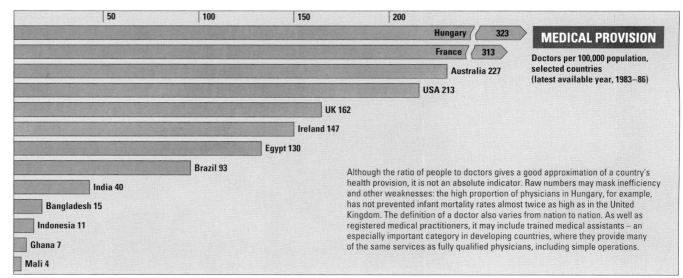

50   100   150   200

Hungary 323
France 313
Australia 227
USA 213
UK 162
Ireland 147
Egypt 130
Brazil 93
India 40
Bangladesh 15
Indonesia 11
Ghana 7
Mali 4

## MEDICAL PROVISION

**Doctors per 100,000 population, selected countries (latest available year, 1983–86)**

Although the ratio of people to doctors gives a good approximation of a country's health provision, it is not an absolute indicator. Raw numbers may mask inefficiency and other weaknesses: the high proportion of physicians in Hungary, for example, has not prevented infant mortality rates almost twice as high as in the United Kingdom. The definition of a doctor also varies from nation to nation. As well as registered medical practitioners, it may include trained medical assistants – an especially important category in developing countries, where they provide many of the same services as fully qualified physicians, including simple operations.

## THE AIDS CRISIS

The Acquired Immune Deficiency Syndrome was first identified in 1981, when American doctors found otherwise healthy young men succumbing to rare infections. By 1984, the cause had been traced to the Human Immunodeficiency Virus (HIV), which can remain dormant for many years and perhaps indefinitely: only half of those known to carry the virus in 1981 had developed AIDS ten years later.

By 1991 the World Health Organization knew of more than 250,000 AIDS cases worldwide and suspected the true number to be at least four times as high. In Western countries in the early 1990s, most AIDS deaths were among male homosexuals or needle-sharing drug-users. However, the disease is spreading fastest among heterosexual men and women, which is its usual vector in the Third World, where most of its victims live. Africa is the most severely hit: a 1992 UN report estimated that 2 million African children will die of AIDS before the year 2000 – and some 10 million will be orphaned.

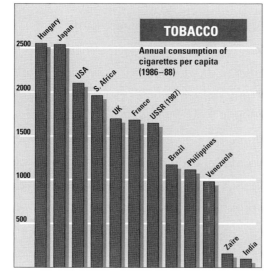

**TOBACCO**

**Annual consumption of cigarettes per capita (1986–88)**

Hungary, Japan, USA, S. Africa, UK, France, USSR (1987), Brazil, Philippines, Venezuela, Zaire, India

2500
2000
1500
1000
500

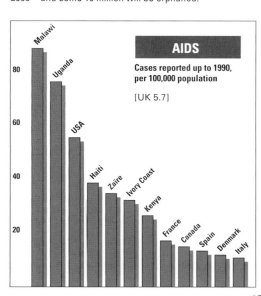

**AIDS**

**Cases reported up to 1990, per 100,000 population**

[UK 5.7]

Malawi, Uganda, USA, Haiti, Zaïre, Ivory Coast, Kenya, France, Canada, Spain, Denmark, Italy

80
60
40
20

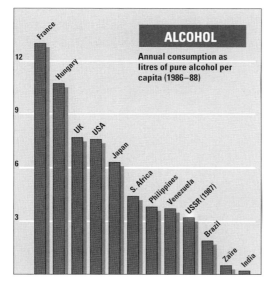

**ALCOHOL**

**Annual consumption as litres of pure alcohol per capita (1986–88)**

France, Hungary, UK, USA, Japan, S. Africa, Philippines, Venezuela, USSR (1987), Brazil, Zaïre, India

12
9
6
3

## CRIME AND PUNISHMENT

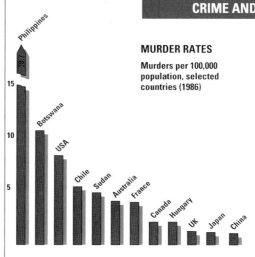

**MURDER RATES**

**Murders per 100,000 population, selected countries (1986)**

Philippines 387

Botswana, USA, Chile, Sudan, Australia, France, Canada, Hungary, UK, Japan, China

15
10
5

Crime rates are difficult to compare internationally. Standards of reporting and detection vary greatly, as do the definitions of many types of crime. Murder is probably the best detected as well as the most heinous, but different legal systems make different distinctions between murder and manslaughter or other forms of culpable homicide. By any reckoning, however, the USA's high murder rate stands out against otherwise similar Western countries, although it is dwarfed by the killings recorded in the very different culture of the Philippines.

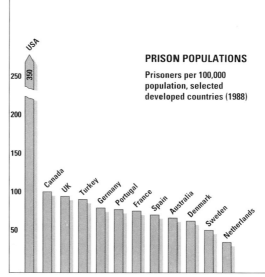

**PRISON POPULATIONS**

**Prisoners per 100,000 population, selected developed countries (1988)**

USA 350

Canada, UK, Turkey, Germany, Portugal, France, Spain, Australia, Denmark, Sweden, Netherlands

250
200
150
100
50

Differences in prison population reflect penal policies as much as the relative honesty or otherwise of different nations, and by no means all governments publish accurate figures. In more than 50 countries, people are still regularly imprisoned without trial, in 60 torture is a normal part of interrogation, and some 130 retain the death penalty, often administered for political crimes and in secret. Over 2,000 executions were recorded in 1990 by the civil rights organization Amnesty International; the real figure, as Amnesty itself maintains, was almost certainly much higher.

*Statistics for the new republics of the former USSR, Czechoslovakia and Yugoslavia are not yet available. The map shows the statistics for the entire USSR, Czechoslovakia and Yugoslavia.*

# QUALITY OF LIFE: ENVIRONMENT

Humans have always had a dramatic effect on their environment, at least since the invention of agriculture almost 10,000 years ago. Generally, the Earth has accepted human interference without any obvious ill effects: the complex systems that regulate the global environment have managed to absorb substantial damage while maintaining a stable and comfortable home for the planet's trillions of lifeforms. But advancing human technology and the rapidly expanding populations it supports are now threatening to overwhelm the Earth's ability to cope.

Industrial wastes, acid rainfall, expanding deserts and large-scale deforestation all combine to create environmental change at a rate far faster than the Earth can easily accommodate. Equipped with chain-saws and flame-throwers, humans can now destroy more forest in a day than their ancestors could in a century, upsetting the balance between plant and animal, carbon dioxide and oxygen, on which all life ultimately depends. The fossil fuels that power industrial civilization have pumped enough carbon dioxide and other greenhouse gases into the atmosphere to make climatic change a near-certainty. Chlorofluorocarbons (CFCs) and other man-made chemicals are rapidly eroding the ozone layer, the planet's screen against ultra-violet radiation.

As a result, the Earth's average temperature has risen by about 0.5°C since the beginning of this century. Further rises seem inevitable, with 1990 marked as the hottest year worldwide since records began. A warmer Earth probably means a wetter Earth, with melting ice-caps raising sea levels and causing severe flooding in some of the world's most densely populated regions. Other climatic models suggest an alternative doom: rising temperatures could increase cloud cover, reflecting more solar energy back into space and causing a new Ice Age.

Either way, the consequences for humans could be disastrous – perhaps the Earth's own way of restoring the ecological balance over the next few thousand years. Fortunately, there is a far faster mechanism available. Humans have provoked the present crisis, but human ingenuity can respond to it. CFC production is already almost at a standstill, and the first faltering steps towards stabilization and the reduction of carbon dioxide have been taken, with Denmark pioneering the way by taxing emissions in 1991.

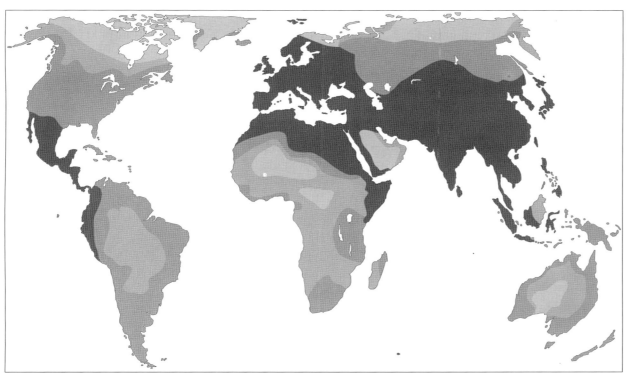

## THE HISTORY OF HUMAN EXPANSION

The growth of ecological control: areas where human activity dominates the environment, from primitive times to the year 2000

By AD 1500

By AD 1900

By AD 2000

Areas not dominated by human activity

## THE RISE IN CARBON DIOXIDE

Emissions of carbon dioxide in millions of tonnes, 1950–91

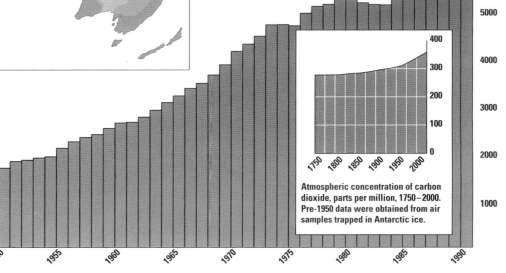

Atmospheric concentration of carbon dioxide, parts per million, 1750–2000. Pre-1950 data were obtained from air samples trapped in Antarctic ice.

Since the beginning of the Industrial Revolution, human activity has pumped steadily more and more carbon dioxide into the atmosphere. Most of it was quietly absorbed by the oceans, whose immense 'sink' capacity meant that 170 years were needed for levels to increase from the pre-industrial 280 parts per million to 300 (inset graph). But the vast increase in fuel-burning since 1950 (main graph) has overwhelmed even the oceanic sink. Atmospheric concentrations are now rising almost as steeply as carbon dioxide emissions themselves.

## GREENHOUSE POWER

Relative contributions to the Greenhouse Effect by the major heat-absorbing gases in the atmosphere

The chart combines greenhouse potency and volume. Carbon dioxide has a greenhouse potential of only 1, but its concentration of 350 parts per million makes it predominant. CFC 12, with 25,000 times the absorption capacity of $CO_2$, is present only as 0.00044 ppm.

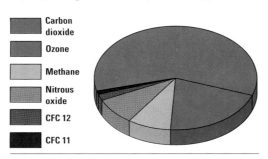

- Carbon dioxide
- Ozone
- Methane
- Nitrous oxide
- CFC 12
- CFC 11

## CARBON DIOXIDE

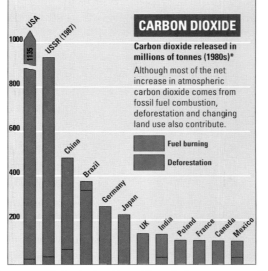

Carbon dioxide released in millions of tonnes (1980s)*

Although most of the net increase in atmospheric carbon dioxide comes from fossil fuel combustion, deforestation and changing land use also contribute.

- Fuel burning
- Deforestation

## GLOBAL WARMING

The rise in average temperatures caused by carbon dioxide and other greenhouse gases (1960–2020)

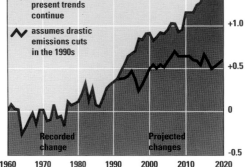

assumes present trends continue

assumes drastic emissions cuts in the 1990s

Recorded change

Projected changes

*Statistics for the new republics of the former USSR, Czechoslovakia and Yugoslavia are not yet available.

CARTOGRAPHY BY PHILIP'S. COPYRIGHT REED INTERNATIONAL BOOKS LTD

## ACID RAIN

**Acid rainfall and sources of acidic emissions (1980s)**

Acid rain is caused when sulphur and nitrogen oxides in the air combine with water vapour to form sulphuric, nitric and other acids.

  Regions where sulphur and nitrogen oxides are released in high concentrations, mainly from fossil fuel combustion

● Major cities with high levels of air pollution (including nitrogen and sulphur emissions)

**Areas of heavy acid deposition**

pH numbers indicate acidity, decreasing from a neutral 7. Normal rain, slightly acid from dissolved carbon dioxide, never exceeds a pH of 5.6.

▓ pH less than 4.0 (most acidic)

▓ pH 4.0 to 4.5

▓ pH 4.5 to 5.0

⌐ ¬ Areas where acid rain is a potential problem

## ANTARCTICA

The vast Antarctic ice-sheet, containing some 70% of the Earth's fresh water, plays a crucial role in the circulation of atmosphere and oceans and hence in determining the planetary climate. The frozen southern continent is also the last remaining wilderness – the largest area to remain free from human colonization.

Ever since Amundsen and Scott raced for the South Pole in 1911, various countries have pressed territorial claims over sections of Antarctica, spurred in recent years by its known and suspected mineral wealth: enough iron ore to supply the world at present levels for 200 years, large oil reserves and, probably, the biggest coal deposits on Earth.

However, the 1961 Antarctic Treaty set aside the area for peaceful uses only, guaranteeing freedom of scientific investigation, banning waste disposal and nuclear testing, and suspending the issue of territorial rights. By 1990, the original 12 signatories had grown to 25, with a further 15 nations granted observer status in subsequent deliberations. However, the Treaty itself was threatened by wrangles between different countries, government agencies and international pressure groups.

Finally, in July, 1991, the belated agreement of the UK and the US assured unanimity on a new accord to ban all mineral exploration for a further 50 years. The ban can only be rescinded if all the present signatories, plus a majority of any future adherents, agree. While the treaty has always lacked a formal mechanism for enforcement, it is firmly underwritten by public concern generated by the efforts of environmental pressure groups such as Greenpeace, which has been foremost in the campaign to have Antarctica declared a 'World Park'.

It now seems likely that the virtually uninhabited continent will remain untouched by tourism, staying nuclear-free and dedicated to peaceful scientific research.

## DESERTIFICATION

Existing deserts

Areas with a high risk of desertification

Areas with a moderate risk of desertification

Former areas of rainforest

Existing rainforest

## DEFORESTATION

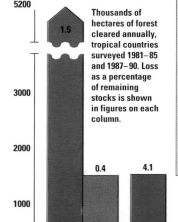

**Thousands of hectares of forest cleared annually, tropical countries surveyed 1981–85 and 1987–90. Loss as a percentage of remaining stocks is shown in figures on each column.**

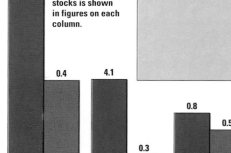
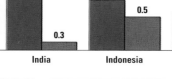

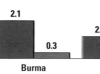
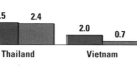

■ 1987–90   ■ 1981–85

Brazil: 1.5 / 0.4
India: 4.1 / 0.3
Indonesia: 0.8 / 0.5
Burma: 2.1 / 0.3
Thailand: 2.5 / 2.4
Vietnam: 2.0 / 0.7
Philippines: 1.5 / 1.0
Costa Rica: 7.6 / 4.0
Cameroon: 0.6 / 0.4

## WATER POLLUTION

  Severely polluted sea areas and lakes

  Less polluted sea areas and lakes

  Areas of frequent oil pollution by shipping

◣ Major oil tanker spills

▲ Major oil rig blow-outs

▼ Offshore dumpsites for industrial and municipal waste

— Severely polluted rivers and estuaries

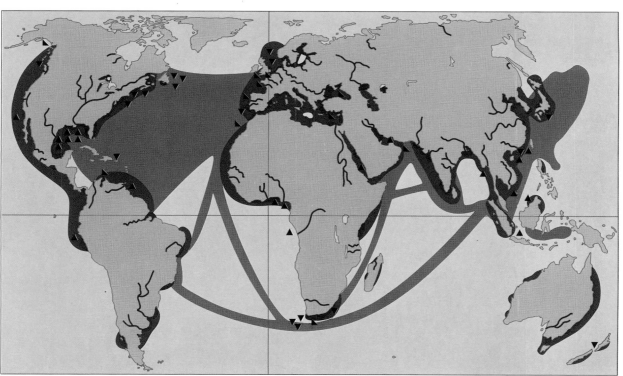

Poisoned rivers, domestic sewage and oil spillage have combined in recent years to reduce the world's oceans to a sorry state of contamination, notably near the crowded coasts of industrialized nations. Shipping routes, too, are constantly affected by tanker discharges. Oil spills of all kinds, however, declined significantly during the 1980s, from a peak of 750,000 tonnes in 1979 to under 50,000 tonnes in 1990. The most notorious tanker spill of that period – when the *Exxon Valdez* (94,999 grt) ran aground in Prince William Sound, Alaska, in March 1989 – released only 267,000 barrels, a relatively small amount compared to the results of blow-outs and war damage. Over 2,500,000 barrels were spilled during the Gulf War of 1991. The worst tanker accident in history occurred in July 1979, when the *Atlantic Empress* and the *Aegean Captain* collided off Trinidad, polluting the Caribbean with 1,890,000 barrels of crude oil.

# CITY MAPS

Oslo, Copenhagen 2, Helsinki, Stockholm 3, London 4, Paris 5, The Ruhr 6, Berlin, Hamburg, Munich 7, Madrid, Barcelona, Lisbon, Athens 8, Turin, Milan, Rome, Naples 9, Prague, Warsaw, Vienna, Budapest 10, Moscow, St Petersburg 11, Osaka, Hong Kong, Seoul 12, Tokyo 13, Peking, Shanghai, Tientsin, Canton 14, Bangkok, Manila, Singapore, Jakarta 15, Delhi, Bombay, Calcutta 16, Istanbul, Tehran, Baghdad, Karachi 17, Lagos, Cairo, Johannesburg 18, Sydney, Melbourne 19, Montréal, Toronto 20, Boston 21, New York 22, Philadelphia 24, Washington, Baltimore 25, Chicago 26, San Francisco 27, Los Angeles 28, Mexico City 29, Havana, Caracas, Lima, Santiago 30, Rio de Janeiro, São Paulo 31, Buenos Aires 32

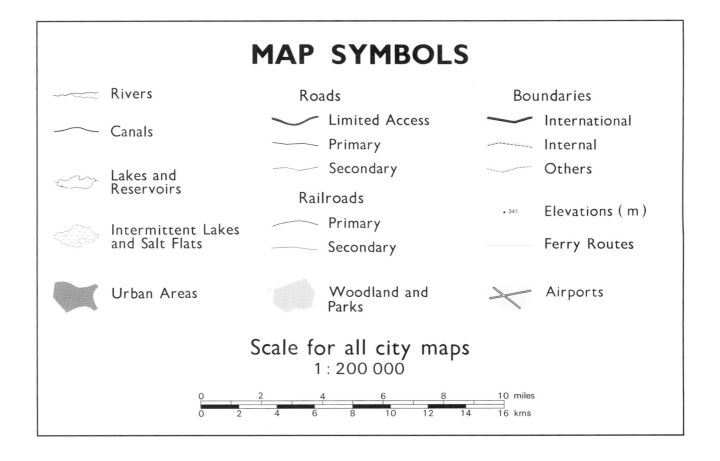

## MAP SYMBOLS

~~~ Rivers

— Canals

Lakes and Reservoirs

Intermittent Lakes and Salt Flats

Urban Areas

**Roads**

Limited Access

Primary

Secondary

**Railroads**

Primary

Secondary

Woodland and Parks

**Boundaries**

International

Internal

Others

• 341  Elevations ( m )

Ferry Routes

✕  Airports

### Scale for all city maps
1 : 200 000

```
0      2      4      6      8      10 miles
0    2    4    6    8   10   12   14   16 kms
```

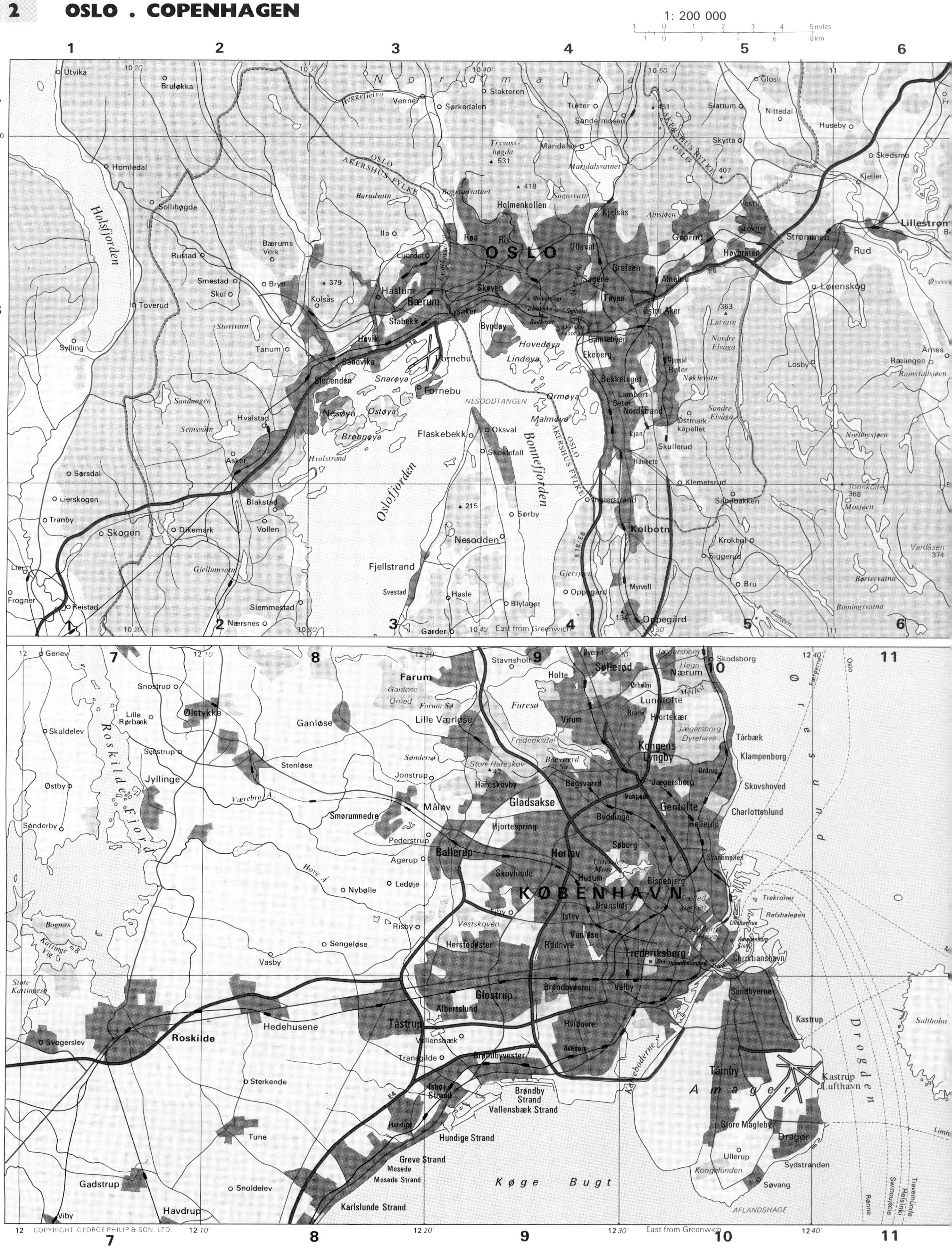

1 : 200 000

miles / km scale bar

### Grid reference numbers
Top: 1 2 3 4 5 6
Rows: A B C (upper map), D E (lower map)
Lower grid: 7 8 9 10 11

### Oslo map (upper)

Utvika, Bruløkka, Glosli, Nittedal, Huseby, Skedsmo, Kjeller, Slattum, Skytta, Nordmarka, Heggelielva, Venner, Sørkedalen, Slakteren, Turter, Søndermøsen, 461, Maridalen, Maridalsvatnet, 407, Homledal, OSLO AKERSHUS FYLKE, Tryvasshøgda 531, Sollihøgda, Burudvatn, 418, Bogstadvatnet, Holmenkollen, Sognsvatn, Kjelsås, Alnsjøen, Vestli, Stovner, Lillestrøm, Rustad, Bærums Verk, Ila, Røa, Ris, OSLO, Ulleval, Grefsen, Grorud, Høybråten, Strømmen, Rud, Smestad, Skui, Bryn, Kolsås, Haslum, Skøyen, Sagene, Tøyen, Alnabru, Østre Aker, 363, Lørenskog, Toverud, Bærum, Lysaker, Universitet, Domkirke, Rådhuset, Lutvatn, Øvere, Sylling, Stabekk, Bygdøy, Hovedøya, Gamlebyen, Nordre Elvåga, Ramstallsjøen, Åmås, Rælingen, Tanum, Høvik, Lindøya, Ekeberg, Oppsal Bøler, Nøklevatn, Sandvika, Forebu, Ormøya, Bekkelaget, Lambert Seter, Nordstrand, Sondre Elvåga, Slependen, Snarøya, Fornebu, Malmøya, Østmark-kapellet, Nordbysjøen, Nesøya, Ostøya, NESODDTANGEN, Flaskebekk, Oksval, Ljan, Skullerud, Brønnøya, Hvalstrand, Skokefall, Hauketo, Sørsdal, Asker, Hvalstad, AKERSHUS FYLKE, Klemetsrud, Tonekollek 368, Lierskogen, Blakstad, OSLOFJORDEN, Sørby, Ingierstrand, Sæterbakken, Mosjøen, Tranby, Vollen, 215, Nesodden, Sørby, Kolbotn, Krokhol, Vardåsen 374, Skogen, Dikemark, Gjellumvatn, Fjellstrand, Gjersjøen, Myrvoll, Siggerud, Bru, Børtervatna, Lier, Svestad, Hasle, Oppgård, Binningsvatna, Frogner, Reistad, Slemmestad, Blylaget, 134, Oppegård, Langen, Nærsnes, Garder, East from Greenwich

### Copenhagen map (lower)

Gerlev, Overød, Jægersborg, Hegn, Skodsborg, Oslo, Nærum, Snostrup, Stavnsholt, Holte, Søllerød, Ørholm, Lundtofte, Skuldelev, Lille Rørbæk, Ølstykke, Farum, Ganløse Orned, Furum Sø, Furesø, Virum, Brede, Hjortekær, Jægersborg Dyrehave, Tårbæk, Svestrup, Ganløse, Lille Værløse, Frederiksdal, Kongens Lyngby, Klampenborg, Jyllinge, Sønderso, Store Hareskov, Bagsværd Sø, Ordrup, Skovshoved, Østby, Jonstrup, Hareskovby, Bagsværd, Jægersborg, Vangede, Roskilde Fjord, Værebro Å, Måløv, Gladsakse, Buddinge, Gentofte, Charlottenlund, Hellerup, Sønderby, Smørumnedre, Hjortespring, Søborg, Svanemøllen, Pederstrup, Herlev, Husum, Utterslev Mose, Agerup, Ballerup, Skovlunde, Bispebjerg, Trekroner, Refshaleøen, Hove Å, Ledøje, KØBENHAVN, Brønshøj, Fælledparken, Nybølle, Islev, Vanløse, Rosenborg Have, Lillebrun, Bognæs, Risby, Vestskoven, Herstedøster, Rødovre, Frederiksberg, Christianshavn, Kattinge Vig, Sengeløse, Valby, Sundbyerne, Store Kartingesk, Vasby, Glostrup, Brøndbyøster, Svogerslev, Albertslund, Hvidovre, Kastrup, Saltholm, Hedehusene, Tåstrup, Vallensbæk, Avedøre, Roskilde, Vallensbæk, Tranegilde, Brøndbyvester, Tårnby, Amager, Kastrup Lufthavn, Drogden, Sterkende, Ishøj Strand, Brøndby Strand, Vallensbæk Strand, Store Magleby, Tune, Hundige, Hundige Strand, Dragør, Ullerup, Sydstranden, Gadstrup, Greve Strand, Mosede, Mosede Strand, Kongelunden, Søvang, Viby, Havdrup, Snoldelev, Karlslunde Strand, KØGE BUGT, AFLANDSHAGE, Rønne, Travemünde Helsinki Świnoujście

East from Greenwich

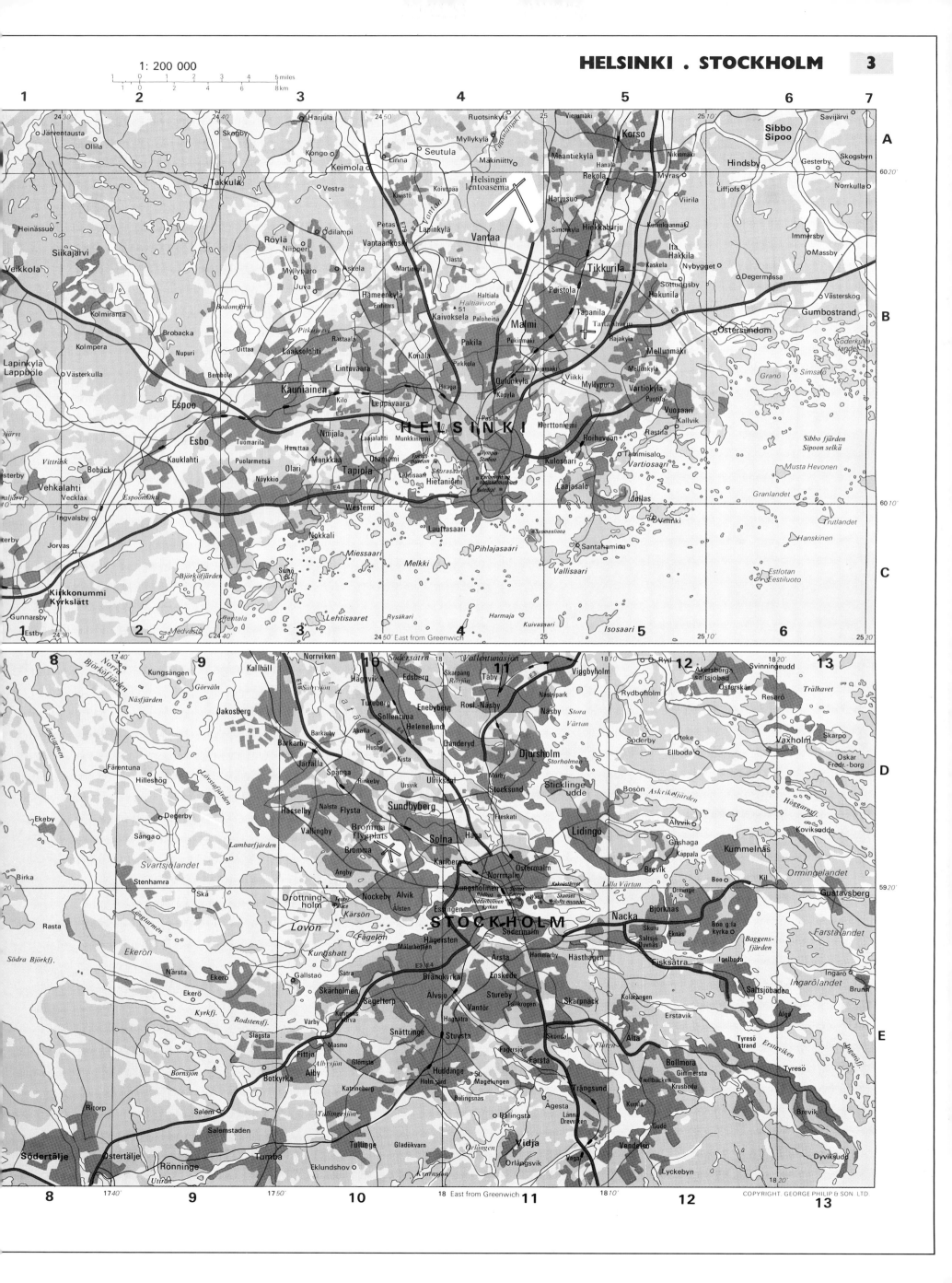

1: 200 000

5 miles
8 km

**A**

24 30 · Järventausta · Ollila · Skogby · Harjula · Ruotsinkylä · Vierumäki · 25 · Savijärvi
Linna · Myllykylä · Maaniekylä · Hanala · Nikinmäki · 25 10 · Sibbo Sipoo
Kongo · Seutula · Mäkiniitty · Korso · Skogsbyn
Keimola · Helsingin lentoasema · Rekola · Myras · Hindsby · Gesterby
Takkula · Vestra · Kivistö · Koivusaari · Simonkylä · Hiekkaharju · Kuninkaanmäki · Immersby · Norrkulla

**B**

60 20' · Heinässuo · Siikajärvi · Röylä · Nipperi · Ödilampi · Lapinkylä · Vantaa · Harusuo · Itä Hakkila · Nybygget · Degermossa · Västerskog
Veikkola · Kolmiranta · Vantaankoski · Ylästö · Maantiekylä · Kaskela · Sottungsby · Hakunila
Brobacka · Myllypuro · Askela · Martinkylä · Haltiala · Tikkurila · Tartanharju · Gumbostrand
Kolmpera · Nupuri · Uittaa · Hämeenkylä · Friherrs · Haltiavuori · 51 · Puistola · Tapanila
Lapinkylä Lappböle · Västerkulla · Bemböle · Pitkäjärvi · Rastaala · Laaksolahti · Kaivoksela · Paloheina · Malmi · Pakila · Pukinmäki · Rajakylä · Mellunmäki · Österslundom · Söderkulla landet · Granö · Simsalo

**HELSINKI**

Espoo · Kauniainen · Kilo · Leppävaara · Lintuvaara · Konala · Pirkkola · Pihlajamäki · Mellunkylä · Vartiokylä · Vuosaari · Kallvik · Sibbo fjärden Sipoon selkä
Esbo · Tuomarila · Hemttaa · Nuijala · Laajalahti · Munkkiniemi · Haaga · Oulunkylä · Kapyla · Viikki · Myllypuro · Puotila
Kauklahti · Puolarmetsä · Olari · Mankkaa · Otaniemi · Herttoniemi · Roihuvuori · Rastila · Musta Hevonen
Vehkalahti · Vecklax · Näykkio · Tapiola · Lehtisaari · Seurasaari · Olympia Stadion · Kulosaari · Vartiosaari · Granlandet
Ingvalsby · Espoonlahti · Westend · Hietaniemi · Laajasalo · Jollas · Trutlandet
Jorvas · Nokkali · Lauttasaari · Suomenlinna · Vuttinki · 60 10'
Björköfjärden · Miessaari · Melkki · Pihlajasaari · Santahamina · Hanskinen

**C**

Kirkkonummi Kyrkslätt · Sumö · Vallisaari · Estlotan Eestiluoto
Gunnarsby · Estby · 24 30 · Medvastö · 24 40 · Lehtisaaret · Rysäkari · Harmaja · Kuivasaari · Isosaari · 25 10' · 25 20'
24 50' East from Greenwich · 25

---

**8** · 17 40' · **9** · **10** · Södersätra · 18 · Vallentunasjön · 18 10 · Ryd · **12** · Åkersberg saltsjobad · **13**
Norra Björköfjärden · Kungsängen · Kallhäll · Norrviken · Edsberg · Skarpäng Rosjön · Täby · Viggbyholm · Rydboholm · Österskär
Görväln · Hägvik · Näsbypark · Svinninge udd · Trälhavet
Näsfjärden · Jakobsberg · Tureberg · Eneby berg · Rosl.-Näsby · Näsby · Resarö · Skarpö

**D**

59 20 · Färentuna · Barkarby · Sollentuna · Akalla · Helenelund · Danderyd · Söderby · Uteke · Vaxholm
Hilleshög · Järfälla · Husby · Kista · Djursholm · Ellboda · Oskar Fredr.-borg
Degerby · Spånga · Rinkeby · Ursvik · Mörby · Storholmen · Askrikefjärden · Hoggarn
Ekeby · Hasselby · Nalsta · Flysta · Sundbyberg · Stocksund · Sticklinge udde · Alvik · Koviksudde
Sänga · Vällingby · Bromma flygplats · Solna · Haga · Bosön · Lidingö · Gåshaga · Kummelnäs · Kappala
Stenhamra · Skå · Bromma · Karlberg · Östermalm · Brevik · Ormingelandet

**STOCKHOLM**

20 · Birka · Svartsjölandet · Angby · Nockeby · Alvik · Kungsholmen · Kaknästornet · Lilla Värtan · Boo · Kil
Rasta · Lambarfjärden · Drottningholm · Alsten · Riddarholmen · Skansen · Orminge · Gustavsberg
Södra Björkfj. · Ekerön · Lovön · Kärsön · Fågelön · Essingen · Södermalm · Nacka · Björknäs · Boo g:fa kyrka · Farstalandet
Närsta · Kungshatt · Hägersten · Årsta · Hammarby · Skuru · Saltsjö Duvnäs · Baggensfjärden · Ingarö
Ekeröv · Gallstao · Sätra · Brännkyrka · Enskede · Hästhagen · Fisksätra · Igelboda · Ingarölandet
Kyrkfj. · Rodstensfj. · Skärholmen · Segeltorp · Alvsjö · Stureby · Skarpnäck · Kolängen · Saltsjöbaden · Brunn

**E**

Slagsta · Varby · Hagsätra · Vantör · Tallkrogen · Erstavik · Älgö
Snättringe · Stuvsta · Älta · Tyresö strand · Erstaviken
Masmo · Glömsta · Skondal · Farsta · Flaten · Bollmora · Gimmersta · Krusboda · Tyresö
Fittja · Albysjön · Alby · Huddinge · St Magelungen · Trångsund · Trollbäcken · Brevik
Botkyrka · Katrineberg · Holmgärd · Balingsnas · Agesta · Kumla · Gudö
Ritorp · Bornsjön · Tullingesjön · Bålingsta · Länna Drevviken
Södertälje · Östertälje · Rönninge · Salem · Salemstaden · Tumba · Gladökvarn · Orlängen · Vidja · Vendelsö · Dyvikudd
Uttran · Eklundshov · Orlångsvik · Vega · Lyckebyn · 18 20'

1: 200 000

COPYRIGHT GEORGE PHILIP AND SON LTD

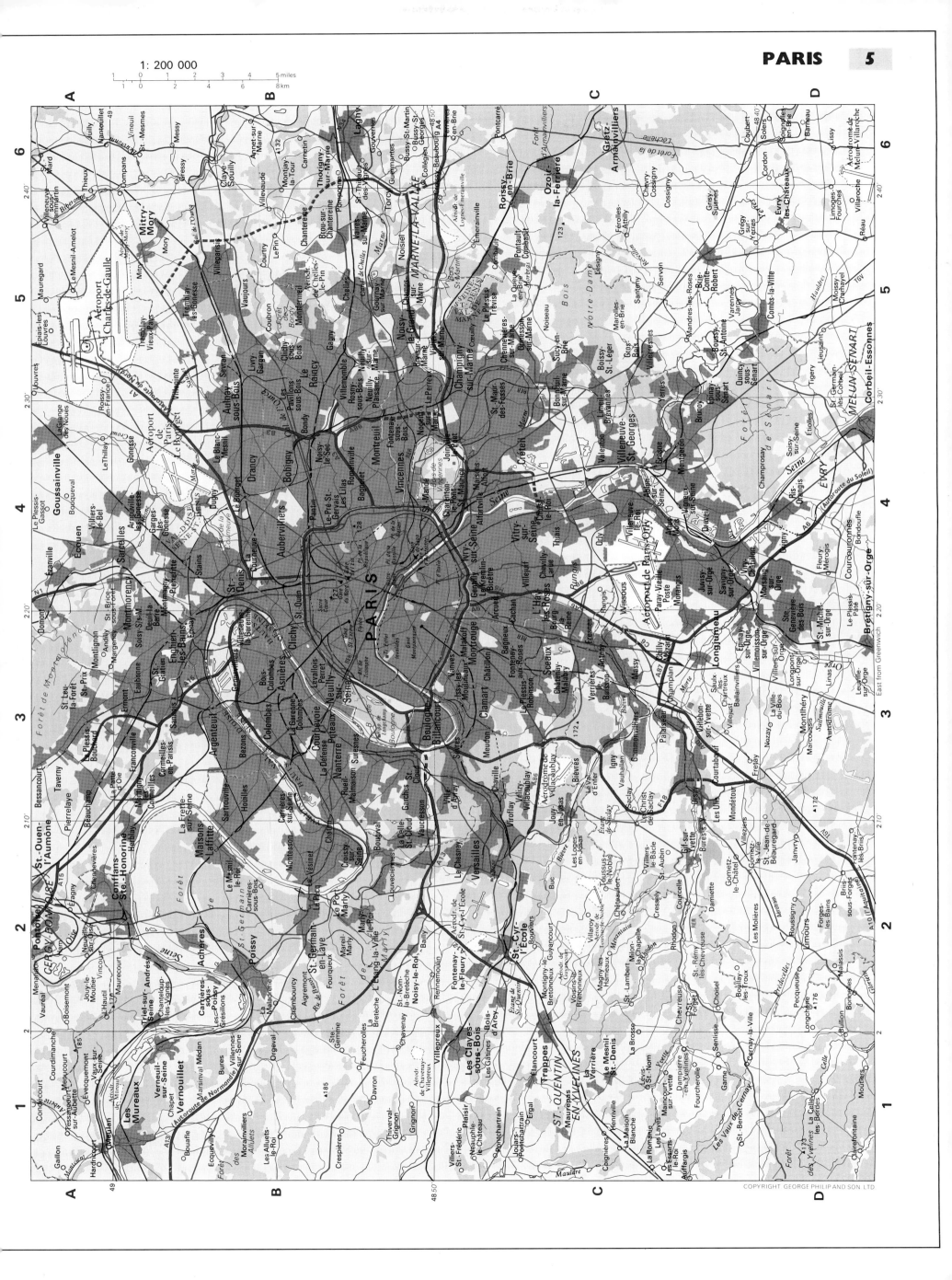

1: 200 000

1 : 200 000

5 miles
8 km

1: 200 000

5 miles
8km

**BERLIN**

**HAMBURG**

**MÜNCHEN**

East from Greenwich

1 : 200 000

5 miles
8 km

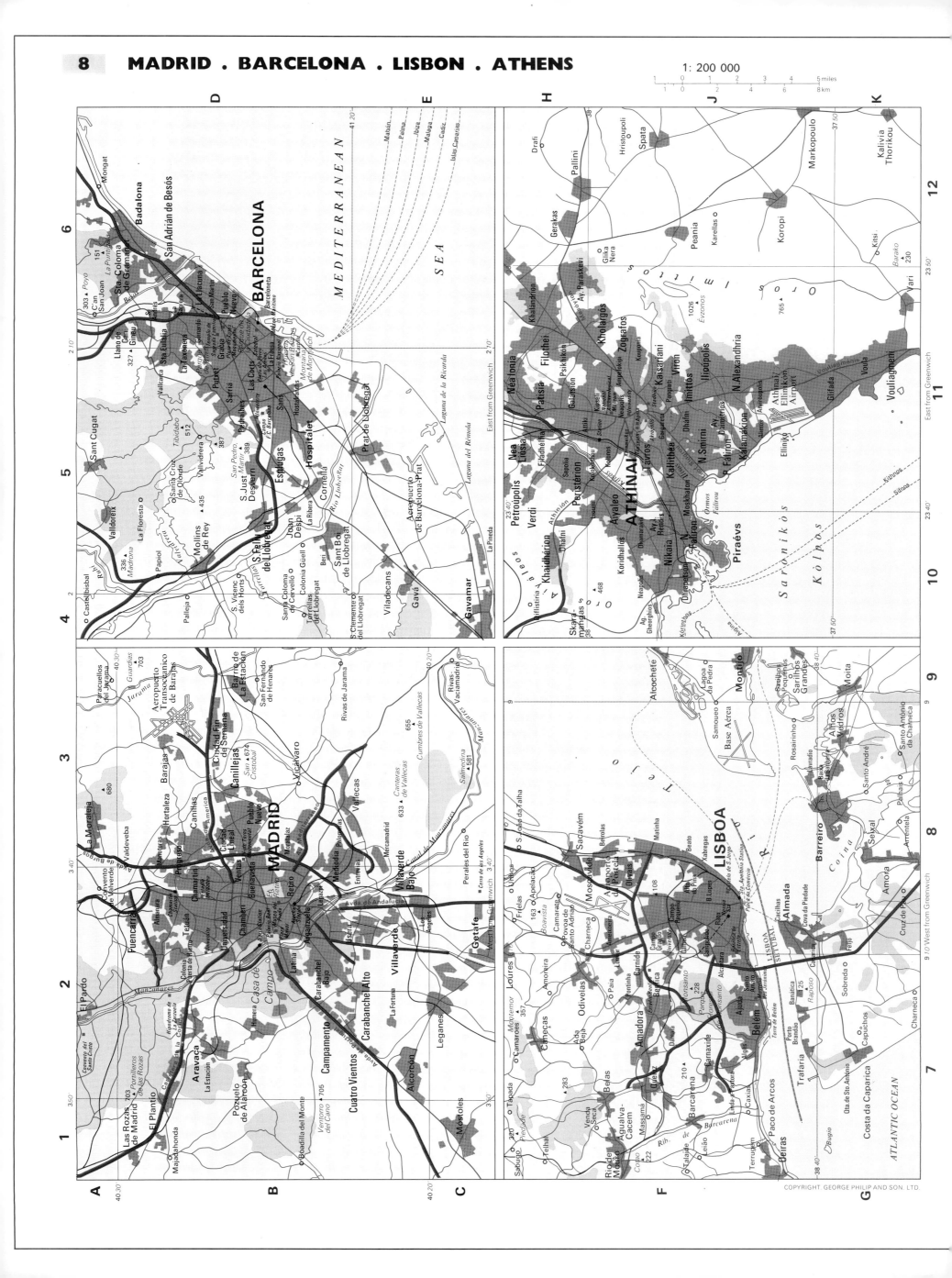

*(Map plates showing Madrid, Barcelona, Lisbon and Athens urban areas.)*

MEDITERRANEAN SEA

BARCELONA

Badalona
San Adrián de Besós
Sta. Coloma de Gramanet

Sant Cugat
Vallcarca
Esplugas
Hospitalet
Cornellá
Prat de Llobregat

Aeropuerto de Barcelona-Prat

Gavá
Gavamar

ATHINAI

Néa Ionia
Kholargós
Zografos
Filothei
Patisia
Psikhikón
Kaisariani
Imittós
Ilioúpolis
N. Alexandría
Voula
Vouliagméni

Piraévs

Saronikós Kólpos

MADRID

El Pardo
Aravaca
Campamento
Cuatro Vientos
Carabanchel Alto
Carabanche Bajo
Alcorcón
Leganes
Getafe
Villaverde
Móstoles

Aeropuerto Transoceánico de Barajas

Barajas
Canillejas
Canillas
Hortaleza
Fuencarral

Vallecas
Vicálvaro

LISBOA

Almada
Barreiro
Montijo
Amadora
Belém
Costa da Caparica

ATLANTIC OCEAN

TEJO

1: 200 000

5 miles
8 km

MILANO

MONZA

TORINO

ROMA

CITTÀ DEL VATICANO

NÁPOLI

Torre del Greco

Torre Annunziata

Vesuvio

Golfo di Napoli

East from Greenwich

1 : 200 000

miles / km scale

## Warsaw (top left)

WARSZAWA

Wołomin, Kobyłka, Marki, Ząbki, Rembertów, Wesoła, Sulejówek, Stara Miłosna, Zielonka, Drewnica, Praga, Wawer, Otwock, Józefów, Falenica, Michelin, Las, Wilanów, Powsin, Natolin, Kabaty, Wolica, Imielin, Kępa, Siekierki, Czerniaków, Sadyba, Siekierki, Mokotów, Wierzbno, Służew, Wyczółki, Pyry, Ursynów, Stegny, Ochota, Wola, Koło, Odolany, Szczęśliwice, Rakowiec, Okęcie, Okęcie Airport, Raków, Włochy, Paluch, Jeziorki, Dawidy, Łady, Janki, Raszyn, Falenty, Sokołów, Michałowice, Ursus, Gołąbki, Komorów, Pruszków, Piastów, Tworki, Nowe Babice, Ożarów-Franciszków, Wieruchów, Lipków, Janów, Stare Babice, Izabelin, Sieraków, Homówek, Klaudyn, Laski, Dąbrowa, Bielany, Wólka Węglowa, Las Bielański, Marymont, Żerań, Tarchomin, Henryków, Marcelin, Bemowo, Górce, Jelonki, Chrzanów, Blizne, Macierzysz, Żoliborz, Muranów, Stare Miasto, Nowe Miasto, Śródmieście, Czyste, Grodzisk, Białołeka Dworska, Brzeziny, Brodno, Pelcowizna, Bródno, Turów, Ossów, Grabicz, Maciołki, Mościska, Piaskowa Góra, Wawrzyszew, Mroczna Park, Lasek Bielański, Wisła (Vistula), Kanał Bródnowski, Drążnia, Targówek, Gocławek, Zbytki, Zabraniec, Zielona, Wiązowna, Miłosna, Międzylesie, Radość, Aleksandrów, Anin, Wawer, Zerzeń, Okrzeszyn, Bartyki, Powsin, Moczydło, Wilanówka, Zawady, Zawadzie, Kępa, Siekierki, Czerniaków

Wisła (Vistula)

## Prague (bottom left)

PRAHA

Stará Boleslav, Brandýs nad Labem, Horní Počernice, Šestajovice, Klánovice, Újezd nad Lesy, Sibřina, Sibřina, Říčany, Kolovraty, Kobylisy, Radonice, Satalice, Čakovice, Kbely, Letňany, Prosek, Kyje, Dolní Počernice, Horní Měcholupy, Petrovice, Uhříněves, Průhonice, Vinoř, Ďáblice, Střížkov, Hrdlořezy, Žižkov, Strašnice, Záběhlice, Michle, Hostivař, Spořilov, Chodov u Prahy, Šeberov, Kunratický les, Háje, Hájek, Libeň, Vysočany, Holešovice, Bubeneč, Dejvice, Střešovice, Malešice, Nové Město, Staré Město, Malá Strana, Smíchov, Vršovice, Nusle, Vinohrady, Krč, Braník, Podolí, Libuš, Písnice, Modřany, Zbraslav, Točná, Cholupice, Radotín, Slivenec, Lochkov, Řeporyje, Zbuzany, Jinočany, Řepy, Ruzyně, Praha-Ruzyně Airport, Liboc, Hlubočepy, Velká Chuchle, Roztoky, Suchdol, Libčice nad Vltavou, Únětice, Horoměřice, Tuchoměřice, Statenice, Nebušice, Klecany, Líbeznice, Měšice, Sluhy, Veleň, Vodochody, Zdiby, Dolní Chabry, Čimice, Troja, Libčice, Velvary, Vltava, Berounka, Zličín, Kopanina, Jenč, Hostivice, Sobín, Chýně, Rudná, Nučice, Loděnice

## Budapest (top right)

BUDAPEST

Újpest, Rákospalota, Pestújhely, Kerepes, Kistarcsa, Nagytarcsa, Csömör, Szilasliget, Sashalom, Mátyásföld, Cinkota, Rákoskeresztúr, Rákoscsaba, Rákoskert, Rákoshegy, Rákosliget, Pécel, Ecser, Maglód, Vecsés, Ferihegy Airport, Gyál, Üllő, Pestszentlőrinc, Pestimre, Soroksár, Pesterzsébet, Csepel, Csepel sziget, Kispest, Kőbánya, Zugló, Angyalföld, Óbuda, Buda, Pest, Ferencváros, Vízváros, Kelenföld, Budafok, Budatétény, Nagytétény, Érd, Diósd, Budaörs, Budakeszi, Máriaremete, Hűvösvölgy, Pesthidegkút, Solymár, Üröm, Békásmegyer, Csillaghegy, Csillebérc, Aquincum, Római Fürdő, Margit-sziget, Szabadság-hegy, Sváb-hegy, Hárs-hegy, Hármashatár-hegy, Szépvölgy, Magyaród, Sikátorpuszta, Csömöri-patak, Szilas-patak, Rákos-patak, Duna (Danube), Soroksári Duna

## Vienna (bottom right)

WIEN

Klosterneuburg, Kritzendorf, Kierling, Weidling, Kahlenbergerdorf, Nussdorf, Grinzing, Sievering, Döbling, Gersthof, Währing, Hernals, Ottakring, Penzing, Hietzing, Hacking, St. Veit, Lainz, Mauer, Kalksburg, Rodaun, Perchtoldsdorf, Liesing, Siebenhirten, Atzgersdorf, Inzersdorf, Rothneusiedl, Oberlaa, Unterlaa, Rannersdorf, Schwechat, Flughafen Wien-Schwechat, Kledering, Simmering, Kaiserebersdorf, Albern, Favoriten, Meidling, Margareten, Wieden, Landstrasse, Leopoldstadt, Brigittenau, Alsergrund, Josefstadt, Neubau, Mariahilf, Donaustadt, Floridsdorf, Stammersdorf, Strebersdorf, Gerasdorf bei Wien, Leopoldau, Kagran, Kaisermühlen, Aspern, Essling, Breitenlee, Süssenbrunn, Deutsch-Wagram, Raasdorf, Parbasdorf, Aderklaa, Helmahof, Neusiedl, Obersdorf, Kapellerfeld, Hirschstetten, Neustift am Walde, Salmannsdorf, Neuwaldegg, Dornbach, Hadersdorf, Weidlingau, Purkersdorf, Mauerbach, Wolfsgraben, Gablitz, Tullnerbach, Pressbaum, Wienerwald, Laab im Walde, Breitenfurt, Kaltenleutgeben, Gaaden, Sittendorf, Sparbach, Gießhübl, St. Andrä-Wördern, Greifenstein, Höflein, Altenberg, Kritzendorf

Donau (Danube), Wienerwald, Lainzer Tiergarten

East from Greenwich

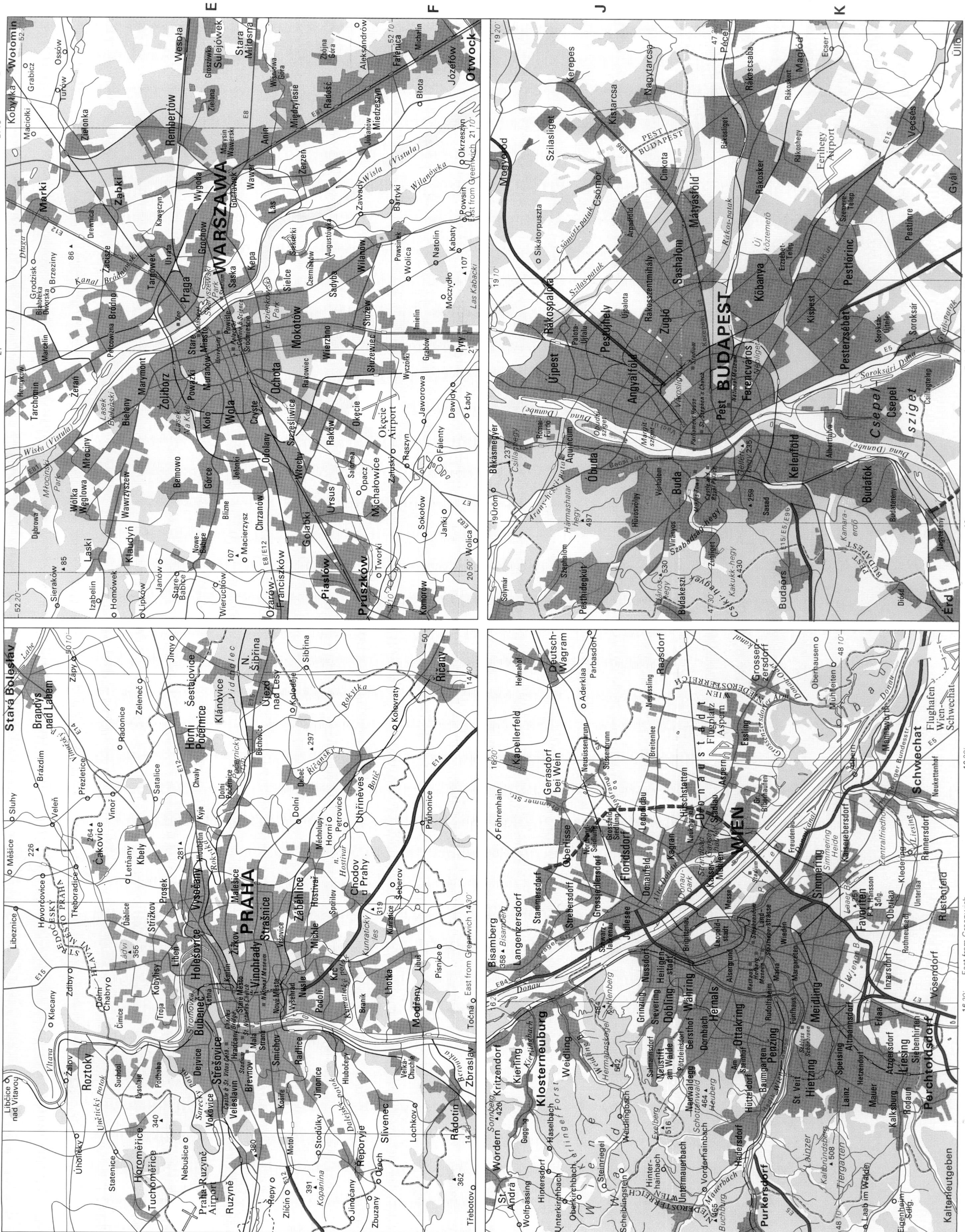

COPYRIGHT GEORGE PHILIP AND SON LTD.

1:200 000

5 miles
8km

## SANKT-PETERBURG

Gulf of Finland

Lisiy Nos
Olgino
Kolomyagi
Novaya Derevnya
Udelnaya
Ruchyi
Vsevolozhsk
Bobylyskaya
Lesnoy
Grazhdanka
Rybatskaya
Berngardovka
Lakhtinskiy
Staraya Derevnya
Ostrova Kirovskiye
Kirov Stadium
Apterkarskiy Ostrov
Petrogradskaya Storona
Vyborgskaya Storona
Polyustrovo
Rzhevka
Noyoye Kovalyova
Krasnaya Gorka
Kalytino
Selytsy
O. Volynyy
O. Dekabristov
Mutnaya-Neva
Finlan Station
Bolshaya-Okhta
Admiralteyskaya Storona
Khirvosti
Koltushi
Pavlovo
Ostrov Vasilyevskiy
Old Admiralty
Hermitage & Winter Palace
Neva
Zanevka
Yanino
Staraya
Oz. Korkinskoye
Tavry
St. Isaac's Cathedral
Moskva Station
Malaya-Okhta
Aleksander Nevsky Abbey
Kudrovo
Novosergiyevka
Razmitelevo
Ozerki
Ostrov Kanonerskiy
Ostrov Gutuyevskiy
Baltic Station
Volynkina Derevnya
Warszawa Station
Vitebsk Station
Fontanka
Obvodyy Kanal
Volodarskoye
Myaglovo
Khaboye
Volkovka
Vesolyy Posolok
Avtovo
Obukhovo
Farforovskaya
Leshozavodskayu
Aleksandrovskoye
Novosaratovka
Strelyna
Posolok Lenina
Uritsk
Ulyanka
Dakhnoye
Airport
Srednaya Rogatka
Novoaleksandrovskoye
Kupchino
Rybatskoye
Ust-Slavyanka
Sosnovaya
Ligovo

East from Greenwich

Leningrad Oblast
Gorod St. Peterburg
Cornaya

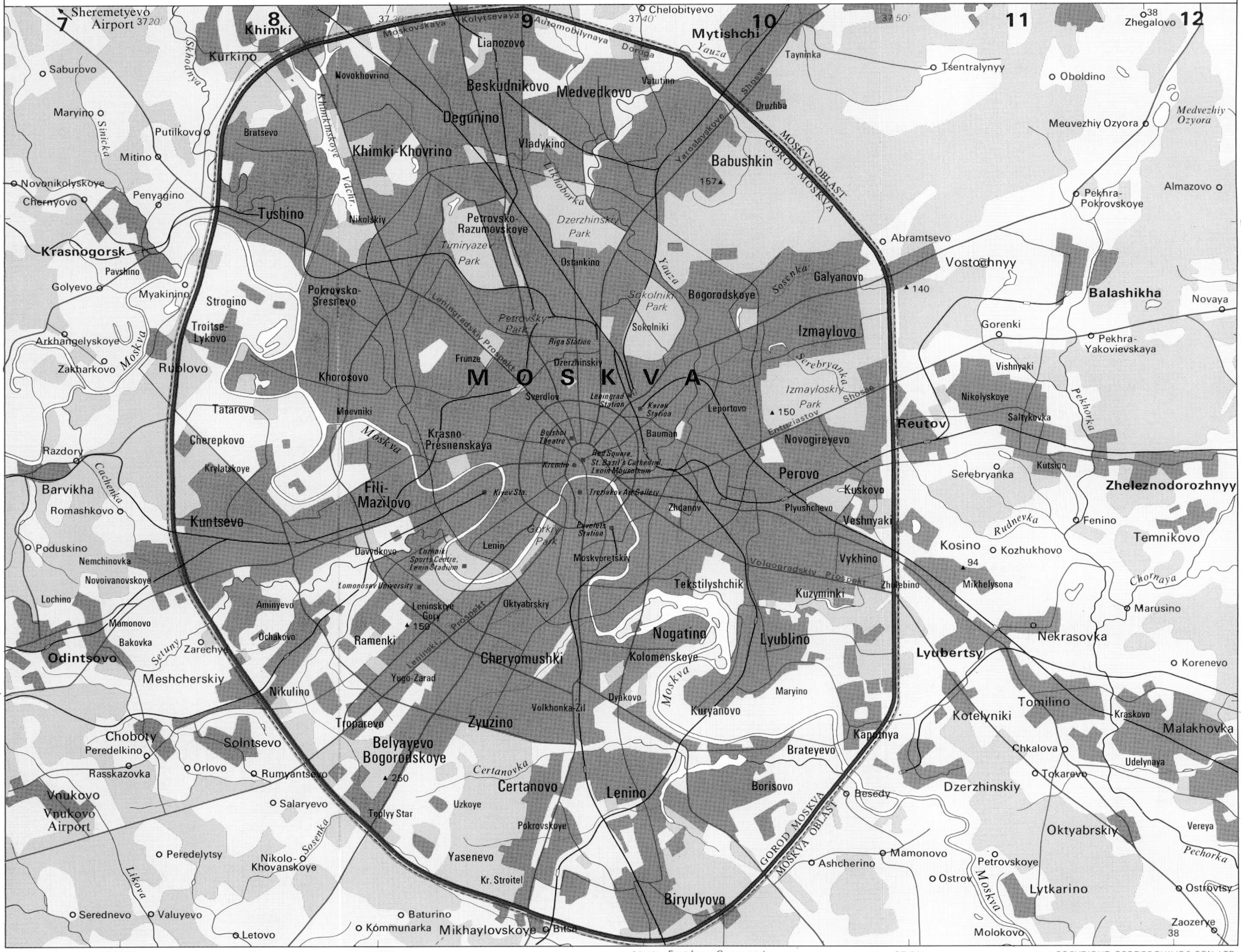

## MOSKVA

Sheremetyevo Airport
Khimki
Kurkino
Saburovo
Lianozovo
Kolytsevaya
Automobilnaya
Mytishchi
Taynka
Tsentralnyy
Zhegalovo
Chelobityevo
Oboldino
Saburovo
Maryino
Novokhovrino
Beskudnikovo
Medvedkovo
Vatutino
Druzhba
Mitino
Putilkovo
Degunino
Khimki-Khovrino
Vladykino
Babushkin
Meuvezhiy Ozyora
Medvezhiy Ozyora
Novonikolskoye
Chernyovo
Penyagino
Bratsevo
Nikolskiy
157
Pekhra-Pokrovskoye
Almazovo
Krasnogorsk
Tushino
Petrovsko-Razumovskoye
Abramtsevo
Vostochnyy
Golyevo
Pavshino
Myakininno
Timiryazev Park
Dzerzhinskiy Park
Ostankino
Yauza
140
Balashikha
Novaya
Strogino
Pokrovsko-Sresnevo
Bogorodskoye
Galyanovp
Gorenki
Pekhra-Yakovievskaya
Arkhangelskoye
Zakharkovo
Troitse-Lykovo
Khorosovo
Frunze
Riga Station
Sokolniki Park
Sokolniki
Izmaylovo
Vishnyaki
Nikolskoye
Rublovo
Serebryanka
Nikolyskoye
Saltykovka
Tatarovo
Moskva
Krasno-Presnenskaya
Sverdlov
Leningrad Station
Kazan Station
Leportovo
Izmayloski Park
Reutov
Razdory
Cherepkovo
Krylatskoye
Bolshoi Theatre
Bauman
150
Novogireyevo
Kutsino
Barvikha
Romashkovo
Fili-Mazilovo
Kremlin
Red Square, St Basil's Cathedral, Lenin Mausoleum
Tretyakov Art Gallery
Perovo
Serebryanka
Zheleznodorozhnyy
Poduskino
Kuntsevo
Davydkovo
Kiyev Sta.
Zhdanov
Plyushchevo
Kuskovo
Veshnyaki
Fenino
Temnikovo
Nemchinovka
Kuzminki
Kosino
Kozhukhovo
Novoivanovskoye
Lochino
Moskvoretskiy
Paveletsk Station
Gorky Park
Vykhino
Zhirebino
Mikhelysona
94
Marusino
Aminyevo
Ochakovo
Central Sports Centre, Lenin Stadium
Lomonosov University
Leninskiye Gory
150
Oktyabrskiy
Tekstilshchik
Kuzyminki
Lyublino
Nekrasovka
Ramenki
Yugo-Zarad
Cheryomushki
Nogatino
Kolomenskoye
Lyubertsy
Koreyevo
Odintsovo
Meshcherskiy
Nikulino
Troparevo
Zyuzino
Volkhonka-Zil
Dyakovo
Maryino
Kuryanovo
Tomilino
Kotelyniki
Kraskovo
Malakhovka
Choboty
Peredelkino
Solntsevo
Belyayevo Bogorodskoye
250
Certanovka
Brateyevo
Kapotnya
Chkalova
Udelnaya
Rasskazovka
Orlovo
Rumyantsevo
Salaryevo
Certanovo
Lenino
Borisovo
Besedy
Dzerzhinskiy
Tokarevo
Vnukovo
Vnukovo Airport
Teplyy Star
Yasenevo
Mamonovo
Petrovskoye
Ostrov
Lytkarino
Pechorka
Ostrovtsy
Peredelytsy
Nikolo-Khovanskoye
Pokrovskoye
Ashcherino
Vereya
Oktyabrskiy
Serednevo
Valuyevo
Letovo
Baturino
Kommunarka
Mikhaylovskoye
Bitsa
Biryulyovo
Kr. Stroitel
Uzkoye
Molokovo
Zaozerye

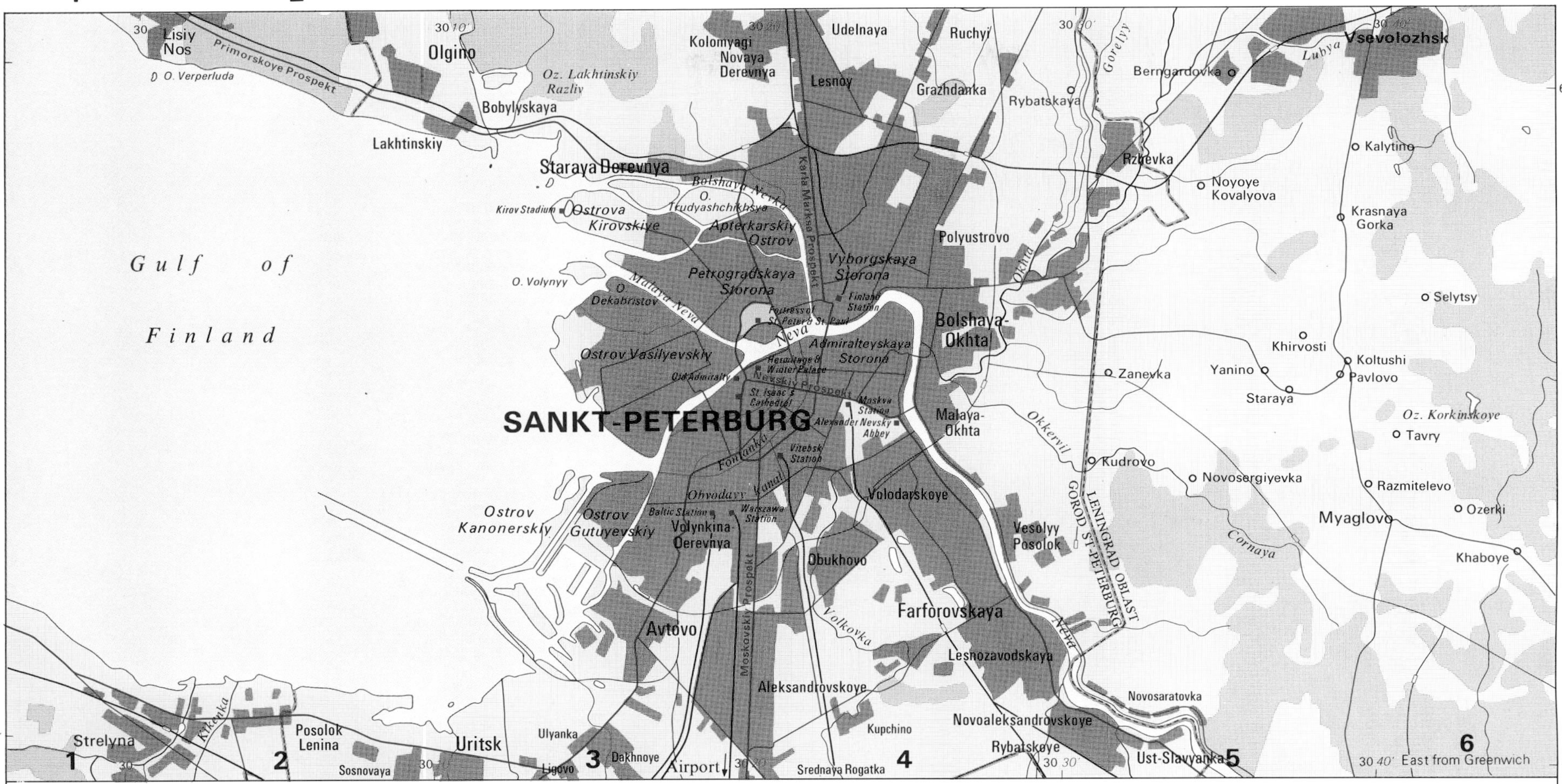

Gorod Moskva
Moskva Oblast
Chornaya
Pechorka
Rudnevka

East from Greenwich

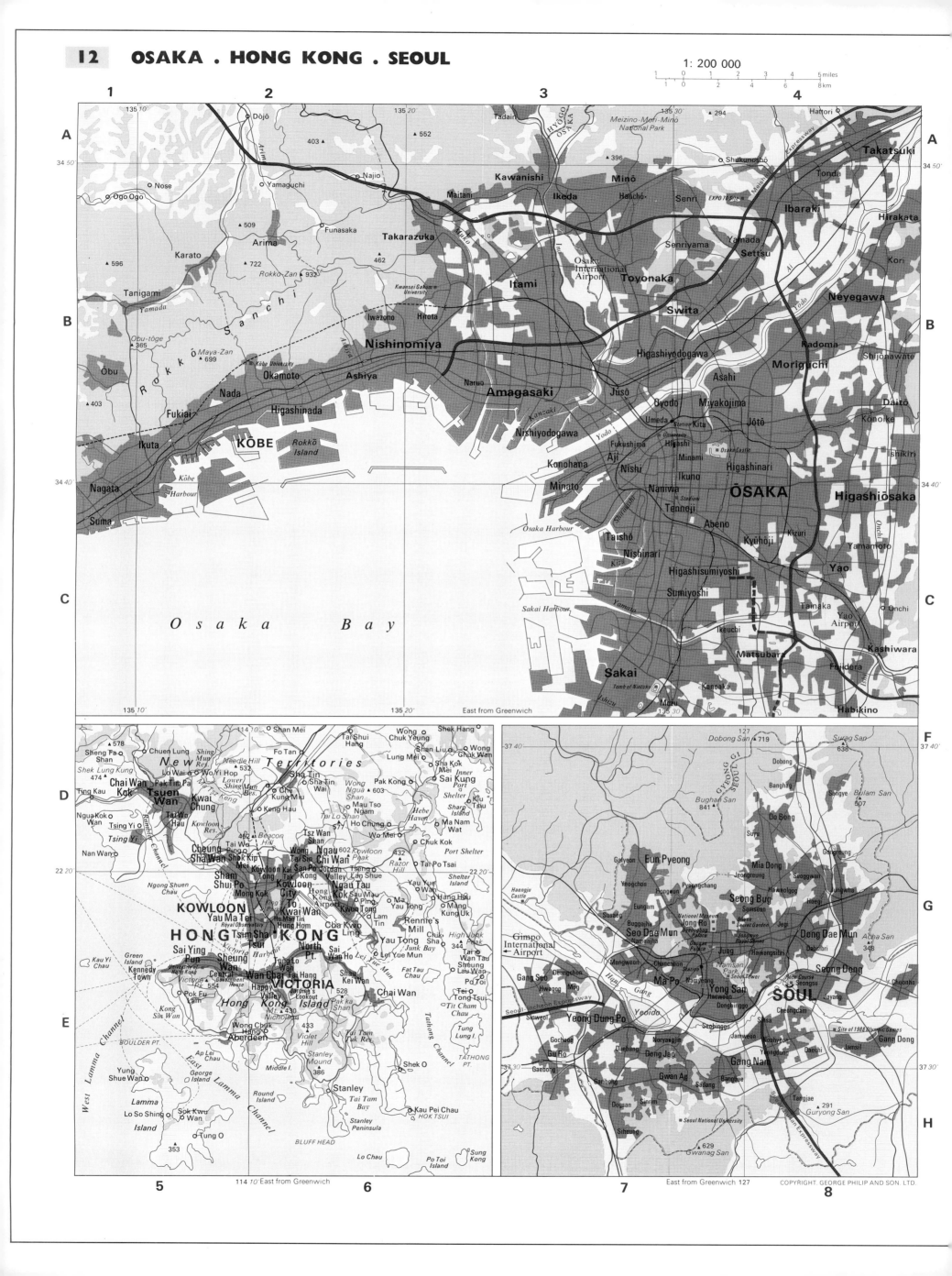

1: 200 000

1 0 1 2 3 4 5 miles
1 0 2 4 6 8 km

**1** | **2** | **3** | **4**

139 30'    139 40'    139 50'

## A

Kujiai
Kawagoe
Kitain Temple
Furuyakami
Onari
Kushiki
Higashimonzen
Kashi-Hazaki
Yamazaki
Matsubushi
Toyofuta

Ofukuro-shinden
Shimo-okudomi
Ōmiya
Yono
Saido
Omagi
Daimon
Angyō
Koshigaya
Yoshikawa
Gamō
Nagareyama
Nazukari
Kashiwa

Fukuoka
Tsuruma
Sunadenshinden
Urawa
Dojo
Tajima
Higashi-kaizuka
Shinoha
Ōhirodo
Yokosuka
Kogane
Haichōbori

Ōi
Fujimi
Mizuho
Harigaya
Numakage
Matsumotoshinden
Toda
Warabi
Hatogaya
Mine
Yanagishima
Misato
Kanegasaku
Mabashi

Shimotomi
Kami-tomi
Sekanoshita
Owada
Chikumazawa
Miyato
Nobidome
Shimo-sasame
Todamachi
Maeda
Yashio
Togasaki
Takegawara
Higurashi

Adachi
Shiro
Niiza
Kiyose
Asaka
Shirako
Yamato
Momote
Shimura
Akabane
Kawaguchi
Adachi-Ku
Ōyada
Mizumoto
Kamishiki

Tokorozawa
Kurume
Kurihara
Nanmasu
Itabashi-Ku
Kami-Itabashi
Ōyama
Jūjō
Takinogawa
Dashinae
Umejima
Gotanno
Kanamachi

## B

Higashimurayama
Ogawa
Nonakashinden
Kodaira
Shimo-shakujii
Suzuki-shinden
Toshimaen
Nerima
Nagasaki
Ikebukuro
Sugamo
Kita-Ku
Tabata
Senju
Kasuga
Hokkin
Honden
Takasago
Katsushika-Ku
Edogawa
Ichikawa
Tōkagi
Nakayama

Kodaira
Tanashi
Hōya
Toshimaen
Toshima-Ku
Mejiro
Komagome
Nippori
Arakawa-Ku
Mukojima
Shirakiwa

Musashino
Koganei
Ōkubo
Numabukuro
Ochiai
Bunkyo
University
National Museum
Asakusa
Taitō-Ku
Sumida
Kameido
Mizue
Hon-ayotoku

## C

Kunitachi
Kokubunji
Yaho
Mitaka
Ogikubo
Asagaya
Shimonakano
Nakano-Ku
Suginami-Ku
Nishishinjuku
Honmachi
Shinjuku-Ku
Ichigaya
Chiyoda-Ku
Nihonbashi
Chūō-Ku
Ryogoku
Funabori
Akita

Fuchū
Takaido
Kamikitazawa
Kitazawa
Yoyogi Park
Aoyama
Akasaka
Kasumigaseki
Ginza
Kōtō-Ku
Fukagawa
Kasai
Urayasu

Shimo-gawara
Kpremasa
Chōfu
Tamaden
Shibuya-Ku
Roppongi
Shiba
Harumi
Tōkyō Disneyland

Inagi
Suge
Komae
Setagaya-Ku
Sangenjaya
Ebisu
Minato-Ku
Shirogane
Tōkyō Harbour

Tama
Hosoyama
Ikuta
Futako-Yamagawaen
Meguro-Ku
Koyamazawa
Gotanda
Shinagawa-Ku
Shinagawa Bay

Okura
Sugo
Maginu
Kodanaka
Ōokayama
Ōsaki
TŌKYŌ

Takaishi
Mampukuji
Mizonokuchi
Kosugi
Ebara
Jiyūgaoka
Ōmachi
Ōmori

## D

Machida
Kanamori
Arima
Kamoshida
Eda
Ōdana
Yamada
Chitose
Ōta-Ku
Ikegami
Ōmori
Tōkyō-Haneda International Airport
HANEDANO-HANA
Hamano

Nagatsuta
Takeshita
Ichgao
Kachida
Hiyoshi
Minami-tsunashima
Saiwai
Kamata
Haneda
Kawasaki
Hamano

Kamitsuruma
Kawawa
Ikebe
Nippa
Ōsone
Kikuna
Kawasaki Harbour
Tōkyō Bay Bridge

Tōkaichiba
Kami-saruyama
Saedo
Kawamukō
Kamoi
Kozukue
Tsurumi-Ku
Nakajima
Sōdegaura

Kawai
Seya
Sōji Temple
Kanagawa-Ku
Sakuragi
Yokohama Harbour
Nakano
Nagara

Shimotsuruma
Yamato
Imajuku
Tsurugamine
Kami-sugata
Kami-hoshikawa
Takayanagi

Fukami
Futatsubashi
Futamatagawa
Hodogaya-Ku
Yokohama
Egawa
Nakasato
Nishiyama

Atsugi N.A.S.
Akuwa
Nishi
Naka-Ku
Honmoku
Nakada
Kisarazu

Ayase
Okazu
Minami-Ku
Isogo-Ku
Kashio
Nagasuga

Shimo-tsuchidana
Izumi
Kōnan
Sasashita
HONMOKU-MISAKI
BANZU-HANA

Totsuka-Ku
Hino
Sugita
Negishi Bay
Obitsu

Fukatani
Harajuku
Kami-nakazato
Tomioka

SAITAMA
CHIBA
Arakawa
Edogawa
Tama
KYŪRYŌ
TOKYO KANAGAWA

*Tokyo Bay*
*Shinagawa Bay*
Land under reclamation

East from Greenwich

1 : 200 000

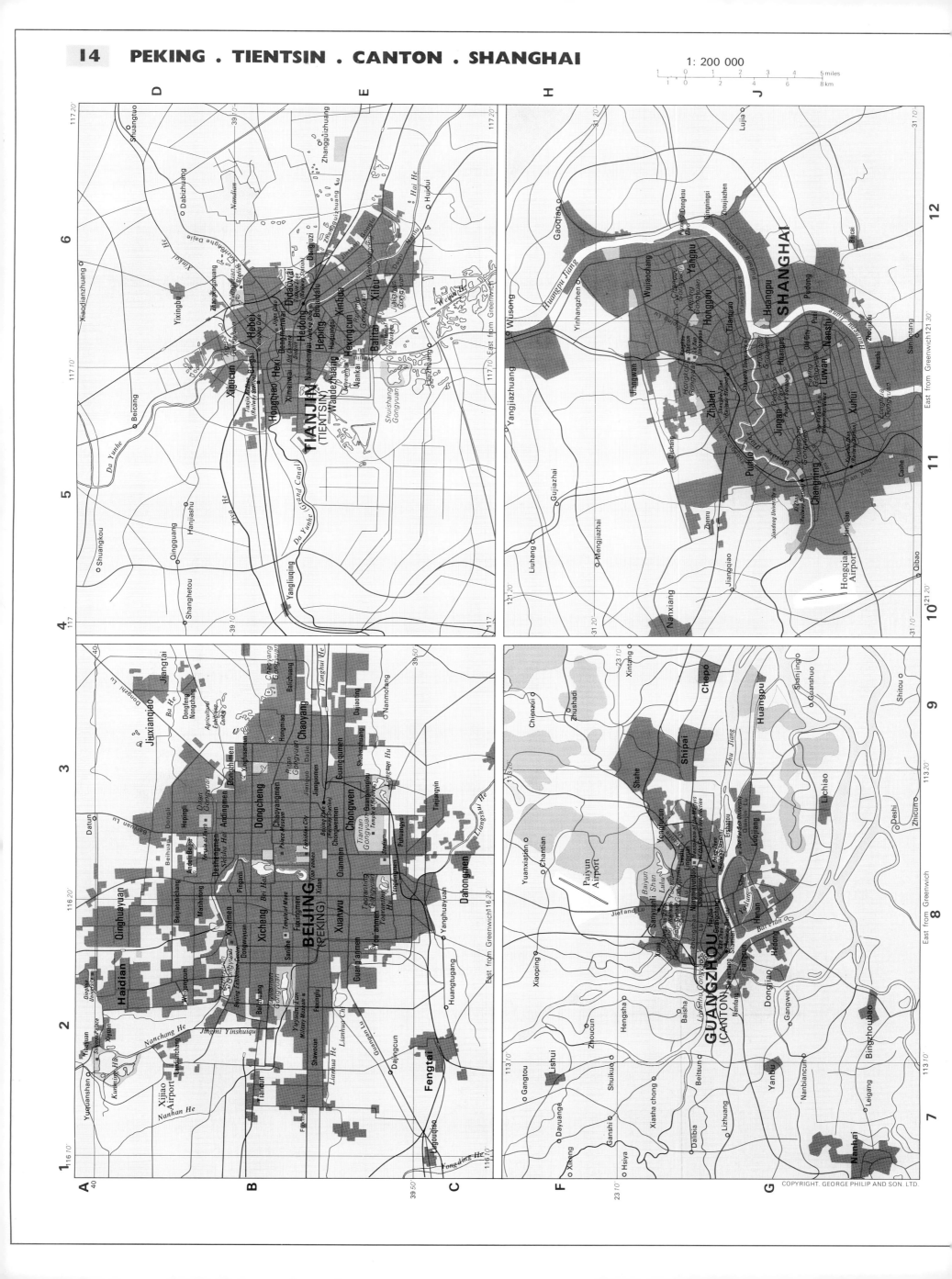

### TIANJIN (TIENTSIN)

Xiaodianzhuang
Shuangtuo
Dabizhuang
Zhangguizhuang
Beicang
Yixingbu
Hebei
Xigucun
Hongqiao Hexi
Hedong
Heping
Hexingcun
Baltai
Xiliou
Xincun
Nankai
Da Yunhe
Beijiashu
Hanjiashu
Da Yunhe (Grand Canal)
Shuishang Gongyuan
Qinguang
Shuangkou
Shanghetou
Yangliuqing
Shanghetou
Hudui
Hai He
Xinkai He

### BEIJING (PEKING)

Jiuxianqiao
Jiangtai
Datun
Qinghuayuan
Haidian
Donei
Hepingli
Beihuan
Anleli Beijie
Deshengmen
Andingmen
Dongcheng
Chaoyangmen
Chaoyang
Balizhuang
Nongchang
Bajiaoting
Hongmiao
Gaomiao
Nanmofang
Baozhimen
Xizhimen
Xicheng
Bei Hai
Jingshan
Dongdan
Dongwuyuan
Maihdrong
Pinganli
Xidan
Xuanwu
Qianmen
Tiantan Gongyuan
Chongwen
Chongwenmen
Guanganmen
Dahongmen
Huangtugang
Yanghuayuan
Yuquanshan
Yihejuan
Yixian
Nanchang He
Jingmi Yinshuiqu
Xijiao Airport
Tiancun
Shaweicun
Dajingcun
Fengtai
Lianhua Chi
Lianhua He
Lugouqiao
Yongding He

### SHANGHAI

Gaoqiao
Wusong
Huangpu Jiang
Yangjiazhuang
Yinhangzhen
Zhangwan
Hongkou
Yangpu
Huangpu
Pudong
Zhabei
Jingan
Luwan
Nanshi
Gujiazhai
Mengjiazhai
Liuhang
Zhenru
Changning
Xuhui
Jiangqiao
Nanxiang
Hongqiao Airport
Qibao

### GUANGZHOU (CANTON)

Xintang
Chepo
Chipazai
Zhushadi
Shipai
Huangpu
Shahe
Lichiao
Shitou
Yuanxiapan
Chantian
Baiyun Shan
Baiyun
Paiyun Airport
Jiefang Lu
Sanyuanli
Lulu
Yantang
Henan
Buretan
Lidojiang
Epianbu
Donghao
Gangwei
Xiaoping
Zhoucun
Hengsha
Baisha
Danghao
Deshi
Zhicun
Lishui
Gangtou
Shuikua
Beitsun
Yanbu
Nanbiancun
Leigang
Bingzhoubao
Xikeng
Hsiya
Dayuangq
Ganshi
Xiasha chong
Dalibia
Lizhuang
Nanhai

East from Greenwich

COPYRIGHT. GEORGE PHILIP AND SON. LTD.

1 : 200 000

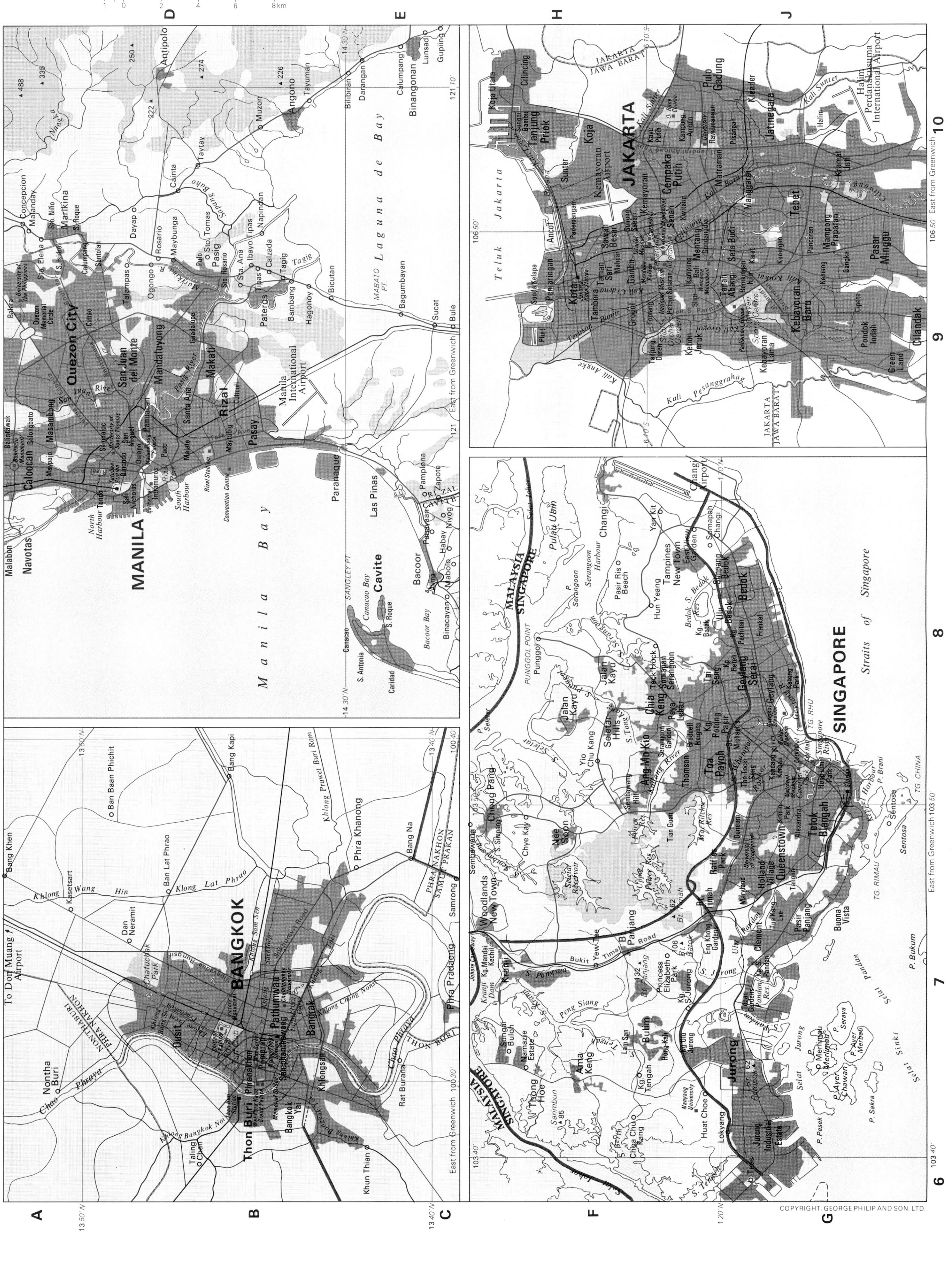

5 miles
8 km

**MANILA**

Quezon City
Caloocan
Navotas
Malabon
San Juan del Monte
Mandaluyong
Makati
Rizal
Pasay
Marikina
Pasig
Taytay
Antipolo
Cainta
Paranaque
Las Pinas
Cavite
Bacoor
Manila International Airport

*Laguna de Bay*

*Manila Bay*

SANGLEY PT.
MABATO PT.

121° East from Greenwich

**BANGKOK**

Thon Buri
Bangkok Yai
Dusit
Pathumwan
Bang Rak
Phra Nakhon
Nontha Buri
Bang Khen
Bang Kapi
Bang Na
Phra Khanong
Phra Pradaeng
Samut Prakan
To Don Muang Airport
Chatuchak Park
Khlong Lat Phrao
Chao Phraya

*PHRA NAKHON SAMUT PRAKAN*
*THON BURI*

100° 30' East from Greenwich

**JAKARTA**

Koja Utara
Cilincing
Tanjung Priok
Pulo Gadung
Klender
Halim Perdanakusuma International Airport
Kemayoran Airport
Kota
Cempaka Putih
Jatinegara
Kramat Jati
Tebet
Pasar Minggu
Kebayoran Baru
Pondok Indah
Cilandak

*Teluk Jakarta*
*JAKARTA JAWA BARAT*

106° 50' East from Greenwich

**SINGAPORE**

Woodlands New Town
Tampines New Town
Changi Airport
Bedok
Serangoon
Ang Mo Kio
Toa Payoh
Seletar Hills
Nee Soon
Queenstown
Telok Blangah
Jurong
Jurong Industrial Estate
Pasir Panjang
Holland Village
Buona Vista

*MALAYSIA*
*SINGAPORE*
*Straits of Singapore*
*Johore Strait*
*Selat Johor*
*Sentosa*
*TG. CHINA*
*TG. RIMAU*

103° 40' East from Greenwich

1: 200 000

0 1 2 3 4 5 miles
0 2 4 6 8 km

CALCUTTA
Haora
Hooghly
Dum Dum
Barakpur
Garden Reach
Behala
Tollygunge
Alipore
Kidderpore
Baranagar
Chandernagore
Chunchura
Bhatpara
Naihati
Shrirampur
Uttarpara
Salt Water Lake
East from Greenwich

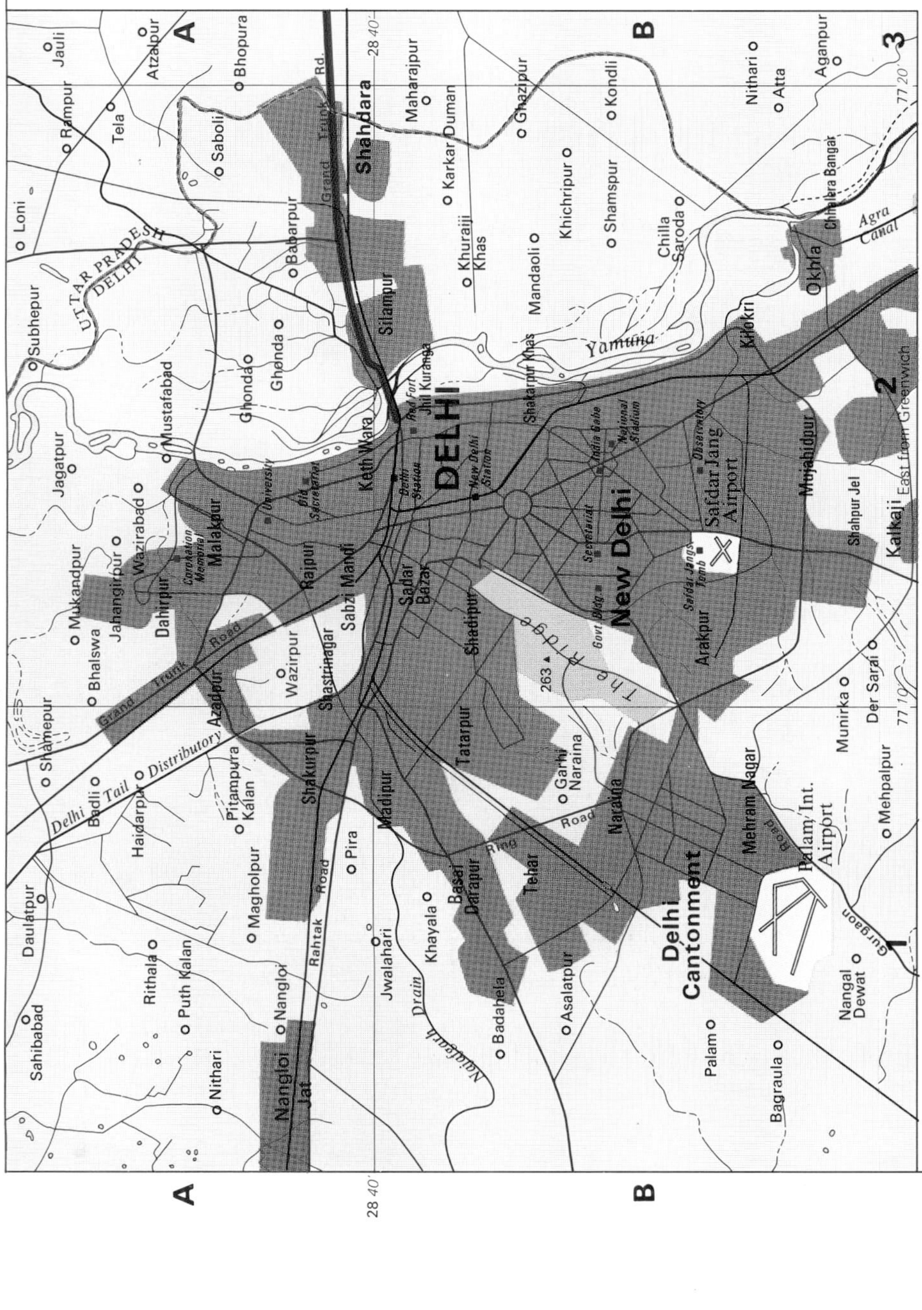

DELHI
New Delhi
Delhi Cantonment
Shahdara
Yamuna
Okhla
Safdar Jang Airport
Palam Int. Airport
UTTAR PRADESH
DELHI
The Ridge
Grand Trunk Road
Agra Canal
East from Greenwich

BOMBAY
Bombay Harbour
ARABIAN SEA
Salsette Island
Thana Creek
Elephanta Island
Bandra
Colaba
Trombay
Santa Cruz Int. Airport
Mahim Bay
Back Bay
Butcher Island
Panvel Creek
Sheva
BANDRA POINT
COLABA POINT
East from Greenwich

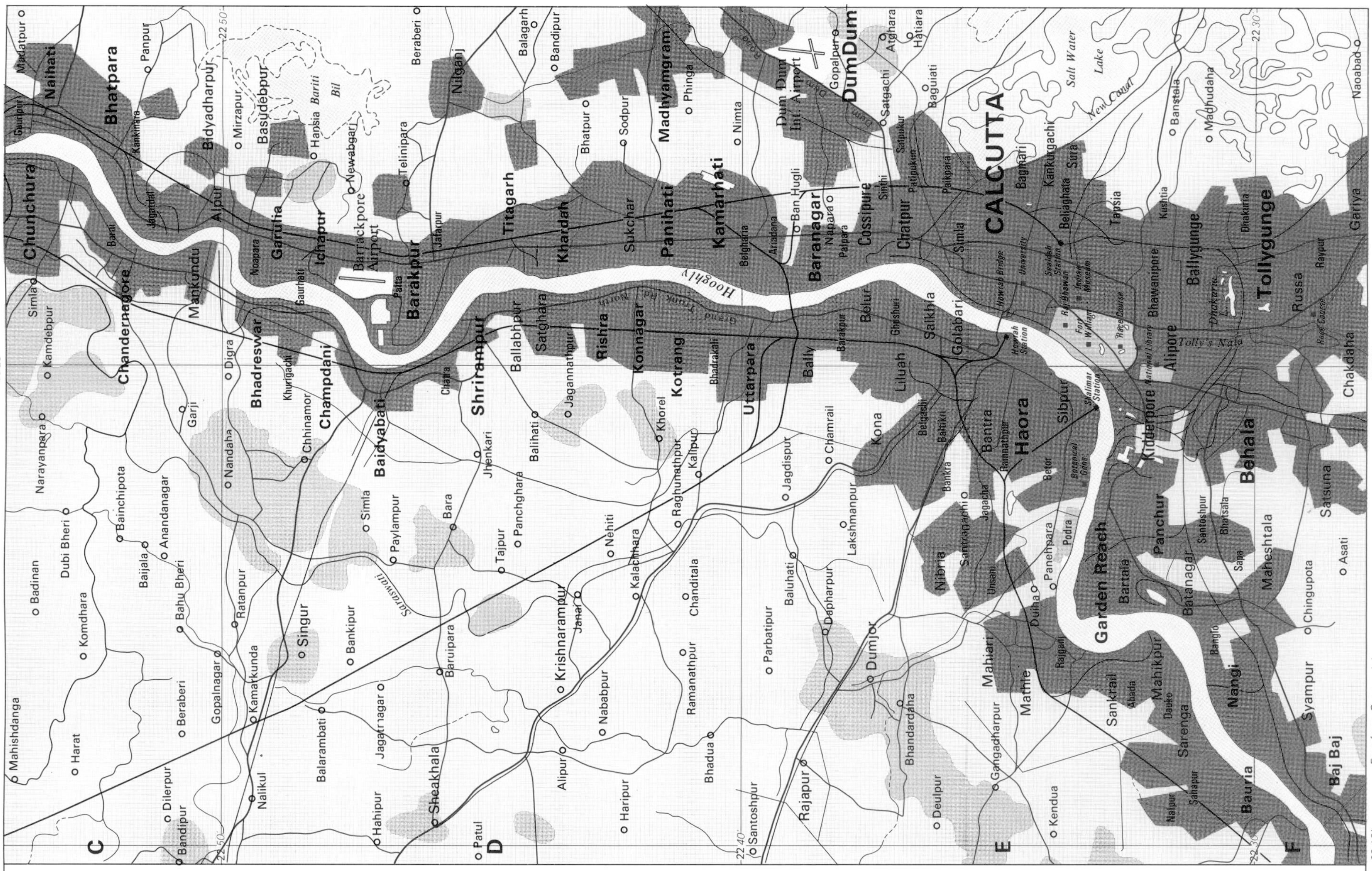

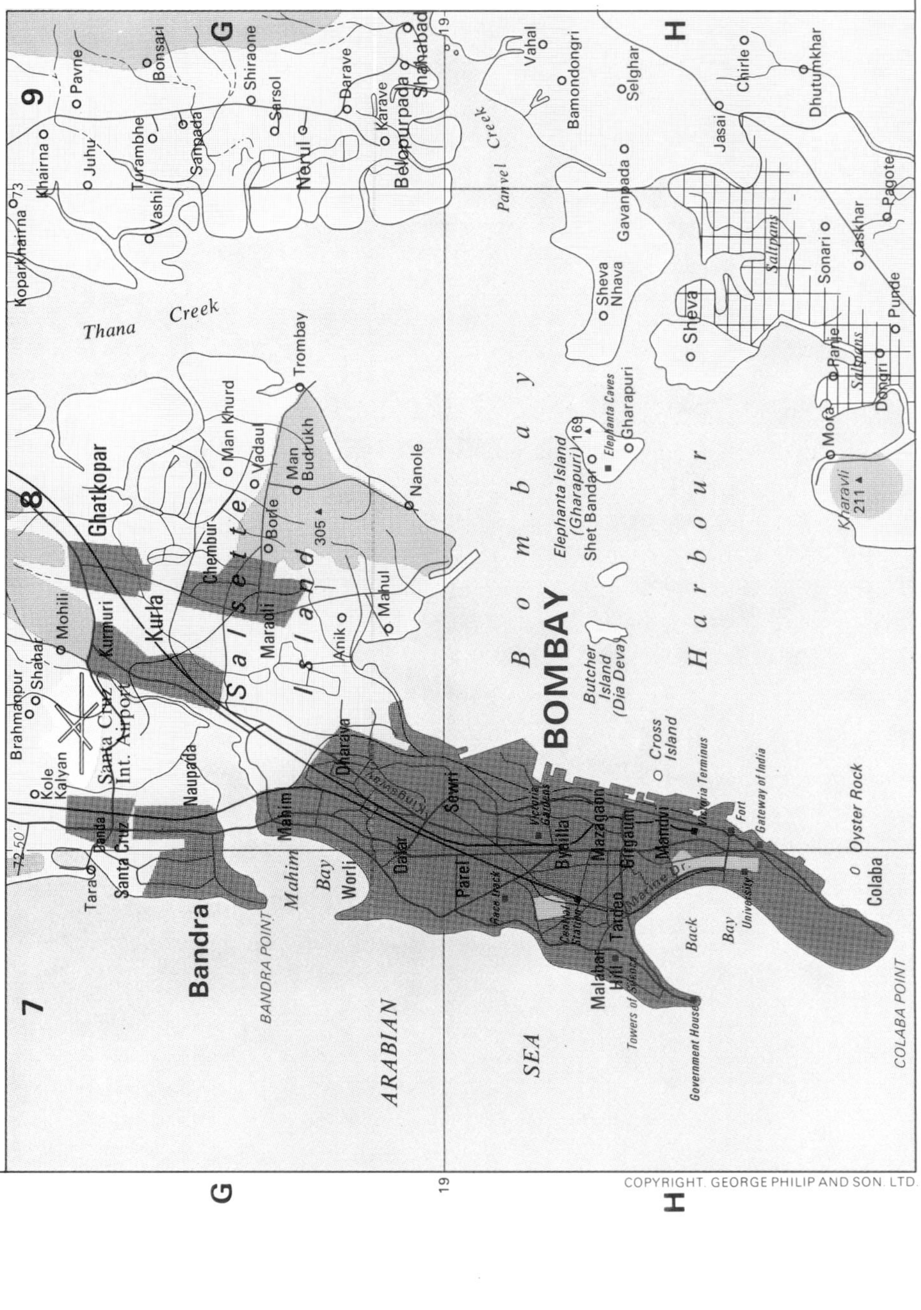

1: 200 000

1 : 200 000

miles / km scale

## ISTANBUL

MARMARA DENIZI

İstinye, Yeniköy, Beykoz, Paşabahçe, Çubuklu, Kanlıca, Anadoluhisarı, Beykoz, Rumelihisarı, Bebek, Boğaziçi (Bosphorus), Beylerbeyi, Çengelköy, Vaniköy, Arnavutköy, Bebek, Balmumcu, Ortaköy, Beşiktaş, Mecidiyeköy, Şişli, Taksim, Beyoğlu, Galata, Haliç (Golden Horn), Eyüp, Kasımpaşa, Hasköy, Kağıthane, Alibeyköy, Rami, Fatih, Eminönü, Topkapı, Yenikapı, Samatya, Yedikule, Bakırköy, Zeytinburnu, Kadıköy, Üsküdar, Kısıklı, Kozyatağı, Fenerbahçe, Erenköy, İçerenköy, Bostancı, Ümraniye
Avazaga, Kağıthane, Küçükköy, Esenler, Atışalan, Mahmutbey, Cebeciköy, Kocasinan, Safraköy, Şenlikköy, Havaalanı, Yeşilköy, İstanbul Hava Alanı

## TEHRAN / TEHRĀN

Niāvarān, Shemirānāt, Ekhtiyārīeh, Tehrān Pars, Narmak, Magidīyeh, Qasemābād, Qasr-e-Fīrūzeh, Mesgarābād, Dūlāb, Farahābād, Doshan Tappeh Airfield, Niru-ye Havā'ī, Eshratābād, Dowlatābād, Shahr-e-Rey, Bāzār, Amīrābād, Akbarābād, Jawādīyeh, Qal'eh-Morgh Airfield, Jamshīdābād, Nematābād, Wastanārd, Yaftabad, Tepe Saif, Mehrābād Airport, Hasanābād, Kan, Fīrūz Bahrām, Guldasteh, Dāvūdīyeh, Dolak, Vanak, Yusofābād, Kūy-e-Gīshā, Park-e-Shāhanshāhī, Ewīn, Bāgh-e-Feiz, Kūy-e-Mekānīr, University, Imperial Palace, Race Course, Sepah Salar Mosque, Majlis, Golistan Palace

## BAGHDAD / BAGHDĀD

AMANAT AL-ASIMA
Saddām City, New Baghdad, Amin, Husaydī, Khalij, Hunaydī, Riyad, Muthana, Khansā, Idris, Nazal, Hikmet Beg, Ishbiliya, Shabib, Nil, Steel Stadium, Shaykh Omar, Mustansirya, Quds, Wahīriya, Wahda, Ammar, Rusafa, Shaikh Omar, Karkh, Salam, Zafra, Fiji, Adawiya, Atifiya, Baghdad Univ, Karadah, Aaffam, Baghdad Unity, Zeblan, Kindī, Iraqi Museum, Um Al Khanazir, Jizā'ir, Jizā'er, Dōra, Dōra Express Way, Tunis, Al Azamiya, Mahrebi, Ramadān, Taiabus, Mutanabi, Al Mansur, Yarmūk, Maarifa, Aqdī Qadisiya, Ta'imim, Khudra, Humra, Ulhud, Firdows, Adel, Abū Ghrib Road, Shaala, Sādūn, Ista'gruh, Saddām Intl. Airport

## KARACHI / KARĀCHI

ARABIAN SEA
Malīr Cantonment, Karachi Intl. Airport, Drigh Road, Phihāi, Korangi, Bhambo Khān, Qarmati, Ghīzri Creek, Pīplāpur, Jāmrīn Road, Liāqatabad, Mahmudabād, Tower of Silence, Sadr, Ghizri, Nazimabad, Goth Goli Mār, Gandhi Gardens, Zoo, Zoological Garden, Goth Sher Shah, Lyāri, Clifton, Chhota Andai, Oyster Rocks, Barra Andai, Masroor, Sind, Bulbai, Liāquatabad, City, Quddi-Azam, Kharī, Kīamāri, West Wharf, Baba I., Bunder, Napier Mole, Manora, Maurīpur, Chauki

East from Greenwich

COPYRIGHT. GEORGE PHILIP AND SON. LTD.

1: 200 000

1 0 1 2 3 4 5 miles
1 0 2 4 6 8 km

## LAGOS

Ikorodu, Ebute-Ikorodu, Gbogbo, Igbopa, Iboju, Ason, Málekete, Ofin, Ogoyo, Alaguntan, Oreta, Osorun, Ogudu, Moba, Ibese, Oworonsoki, Oruba, Onisigun, Erunkan, Agboyi Creek, Ojota, Oke-Ira, University of Lagos, Ikoyi, Fatomo, Fire Cowrie Creek, Shomolu, Igbobi, Yaba, Obalende, Victoria Island, Tarqua Bay, Erukan, Eregun, Oba's Palace, Lagos Island, Lagos State Harbour, Ebute-Metta, Station, Ijora, Lagos, Ibadan, Gbogba, Ejigbo, Idimuu, Arida, Iseri-Osun, Ikotun, Okunola, Cardoso, Osheri-Olofin, Ikeja, Shogunle, Oshodi, Mushin, Idi-Oro, Okota, National Stadium, Iganmu, Iddo, Apapa, Okeogbe, Ikuta, Ogogoro, Porto Novo Creek, Badagri Creek, Lagos Lagoon, Bight of Benin, Bahr el Lubeini

IKORODU, LAGOS MUNICIPALITY

East from Greenwich

Olute, Agboju, Imore, Amuwo, Kiriki, Igbologun, Coker, Ajegunle, Isunba, Ijesa-Tedo, Isolo, Isagatedo, Ewu, Eijgbo, Shoza, Lagos-Ikeja Airport

## EL QÂHIRA

Cairo International Airport, Almaza Airport, Masr el Gedida (Heliopolis), Himiya, El Matariya, Madinet Nasr, El Zeitún, El Qubba, El Wayli el Kubra, El Khenna, El Abbasiya, El Gamáliya, El Muski, Madinet el Muqattam, Gebel el Ahmar, Gebel el Muqattam, Gebel et Tura, EL QÂHIRA, EL BAHR EL AHMAR, EL QÂHIRA, Bahtim, Musturud, Basus, Geziat, Gesirat Muhammad, Warráq el-Hadf, Warráq el Arab, Imbâba, Shubra el Khema, Bulaq, Abdin, Gezirat, El Zamálik, El Duqqi, El Awkaf, El Báhr el Rauda, Masr el Qadima (Old Cairo), El Khalifa, El Basâtin, Tammún, Tura, El Komi el Ahmar, El Baragil, Hakim, El Talibiya, EL GÎZA, University Zoological Gardens, Birsk el Kiyam, Saft el Laban, Tirsa, Abu en Nupras, Shabrámant, El Giza, Minshát el Bekkari, Nahia, Kirdasa, Qasr es Summán, Zâwiyet Abu Musallam, Sphinx, Pyramids, Cheops, Khefren, Mykerinos, Bahr el Lubeini, Nahr el Nil, Qanat el Ismá'iliya, Wâdi el Nahlein, Wâdi el Ahmar, Wâdi Lablába, Wâdi Disla, Burtus, Ausim, Streil, Steil

256▲ 204▲ 193▲ 178▲ 173 83▲

East from Greenwich

## JOHANNESBURG

Daveyton, Petit, Springs, Kwa-Thema, Brakpan, Brenthurst, Delview, Benoni, Benoni South, Boksburg, Boksburg South, Lakefield, Rynfield, Ryfield, New Modder, New Kleinfontein, Modderfontein Deep Levels, Geduld Dam, Van Ryn Dam, Van Dyks Park, Leeupan, Finaalspan, Cinderella, Cinderella Dam, Elsburg, Elspark, Witfield, Isando, Leeupan, Kempton Park, Jan Smuts Airport, Bonaero Park, Rhodesfield, Allengrove, Edleen, Cresslawn, Elandsfontein, Germiston, South Germiston, Simmer and Jack Mines, Rand Airport, Alberton, New Redruth, Alrode, Randhart, Florentia, Dinwiddie, Modderfontein, Eastleigh, Edenvale, Edendale, Dunvegan, Lombardy East, Sandringham, St. Andrews, North Germiston, Klippoortje, Delville, Parkhill, Lambton, Malvern East, Raceview, Kew, Lyndhurst, Linbrojark, Lakeside, Kelvin, Sandton, Sandown, Morningside, Parkmore, Sandhurst, Hurlingham, Bramley, Highlands North, Orange Grove, Norwood, Orchards, Houghton, Observatory, Bedford View, Kensington, Malvern, Cyrildene, Troyeville, Jeppe, South Hills, Rosettenville, Turffontein, Moffat Park, Mondeor, Wemmer Park, Baragwanath, Randburg, Ferndale, Blairgowrie, Bordeaux, Craighall Park, Parkhurst, Greenside, Emmarentia, Parkview, Westcliff, Parktown North, Parktown, JOHANNESBURG, Braamfontein, Fordsburg, Mayfair, Selby, Booysens, Rosettenville, Robertsham, Linden, Franklin Roosevelt Park, Auckland Park, Melville, West Park, Westdene, Crosby, Fontainebleau, Randpark, Robin Hills, Windsor Cresta, Bosmont, Triomf, Newclare, Blackheath, Northcliff, Newlands, Fairland, Welterreden Ext., Weltevreden, Maraisburg, Discovery, Roodepoort, Roodepoort West, Witpoortjie, Florida, Hamberg, Kloofendal, Meadowlands, Orlando East, Orlando West, Mofolo, Dube, Soweto, Jabavu, Molapo, Moroka, Mapetla, Chiawelo, Emndeni, Naledi, Zola, Emdeni, Nancefield, Baragwanath Airfield, Diepkloof, Klipspruit, Krugersdorp, Luipaardsvlei, Silverfields, Kenmare, Lewisham, Cudbembeck, Honeydew, Manufacta, New Canada Dam, Rand Leases Gold Mines, Durban Roodepoort Deep Gold Mines, Alexandra, Orlando Dam, Jukskei River, Klipriviersberg, Bloubosspruit, Elsburgspruit

1818▲

East from Greenwich

1: 200 000

5 miles
8 km

**1** **2** **3** **4**

Doonside
Blacktown
Rooty Hill
Wallgrove
Winston Hills
Severn Hills
Carlingford
Epping
Marsfield
Gordon
Killara
Forestville
Lindfield
Lane Cove National Park
Chatswood
Willoughby
Manly Warringah War Memorial Park
North Manly
Allambie Heights
Dee Why
DEE WHY HEAD
North Manly
Queenscliffe
Manly

Western Freeway
Greystanes
Prospect
Wentworthville
Parramatta North
Parramatta Park
Northmead
Dundas
Rydalmere
Ermington
Eastwood
North Ryde
Ryde
Lane Cove
Middle Cove
Seaforth
Clontarf
Balgowlah Heights
Northbridge
Balgowlah
NORTH POINT

A

Prospect Reservoir
Parramatta
Merrylands
Granville
North Auburn
Rhodes
Gladesville
Baronia Park
Gore Hill
Hunter's Hill
Greenwich
Crows Nest
North Sydney
Mosman
MIDDLE HEAD
NORTH HEAD
SOUTH HEAD

33 50
Horsley Park
Cecil Park
Smithfield
Guildford
Auburn
Villawood
Strathfield
Burwood
Enfield
Drummoyne
Balmain
Sydney Harbour Bridge
Observatory
Kings Cross
SYDNEY
Leichhardt
Camperdown
Univ. of Sydney
Opera House
Government House
Royal Botanic Gardens
Parliament House
Hyde Park
Surry Hills
Paddington
Woollahra
Taronga Zoological Park
Port Jackson
Watsons Bay
Rose Bay
Double Bay
Dover Heights

B
Bossley Park
Fairfield
Regents Park
Bass Hill
Hume Highway
Chullora
Belfield
Ashfield
Marrickville
Newtown
S. Peters
Enmore
Waterloo
Erskineville
Kensington
Centennial Park
Waverley
Bondi

West Hoxton
Hoxton Park Aerodrome
Hoxton Park
Green Valley
Bonnyrigg
Cabramatta
Carramar
Yennora
Warrick Farm Race Track
Georges Hall
Yagoona
Bankstown
Belmore
Lakemba
Campsie
Canterbury
Earlwood
Roseberry
Mascot
Randwick
Univ. of N.S.W.
Kingsford
Coogee
Clovelly

Liverpool
Lurnea
Moorebank
Georges River
Milperra
Punchbowl
Beverley Hills
Arncliffe
Bexley
Barton Park
Pagewood
Maroubra

Bankstown Aerodrome
Revesby
Padstow
Riverwood
Peakhurst
Rockdale
Brighton le Sands
Banksmeadow
Malabar

East Hills
Sydney Airport
Botany
Phillip Bay
Long Bay
Little Bay

Glenfield
Macquarie Fields
Lugarno
Oatley
Blakehurst
Kogarah
Beverly Park
Ramsgate
San Souci
Botany Bay
La Perouse

34
Ingleburn
Military Reserve
Menai
Woronora
Como
Oyster Bay
Jannali
Sylvania
Georges River Bridge
Captain Cook Bridge
Woolooware Bay
Kurnell
Captain Cook Landing Place Park
CAPE BANKS

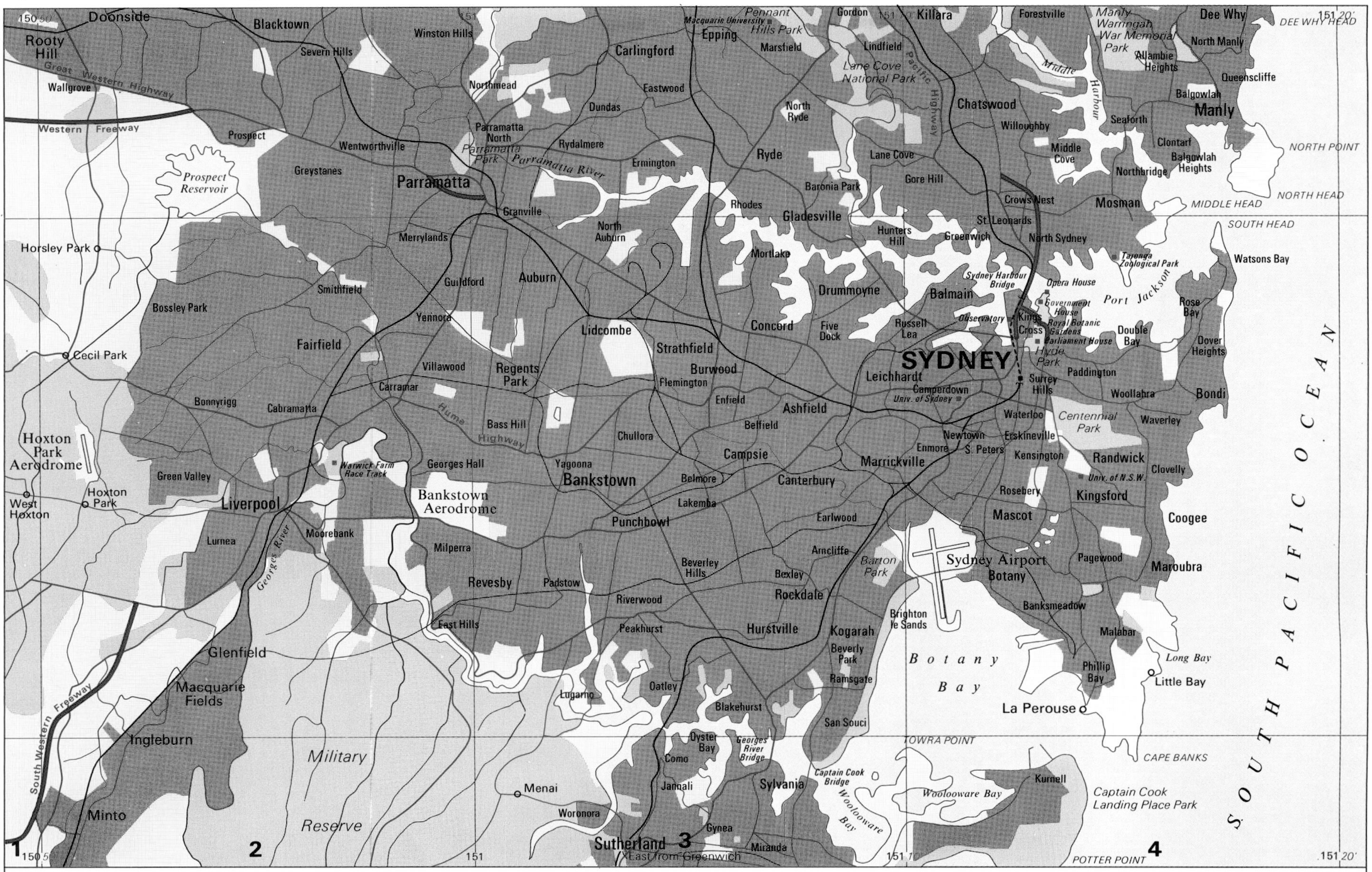

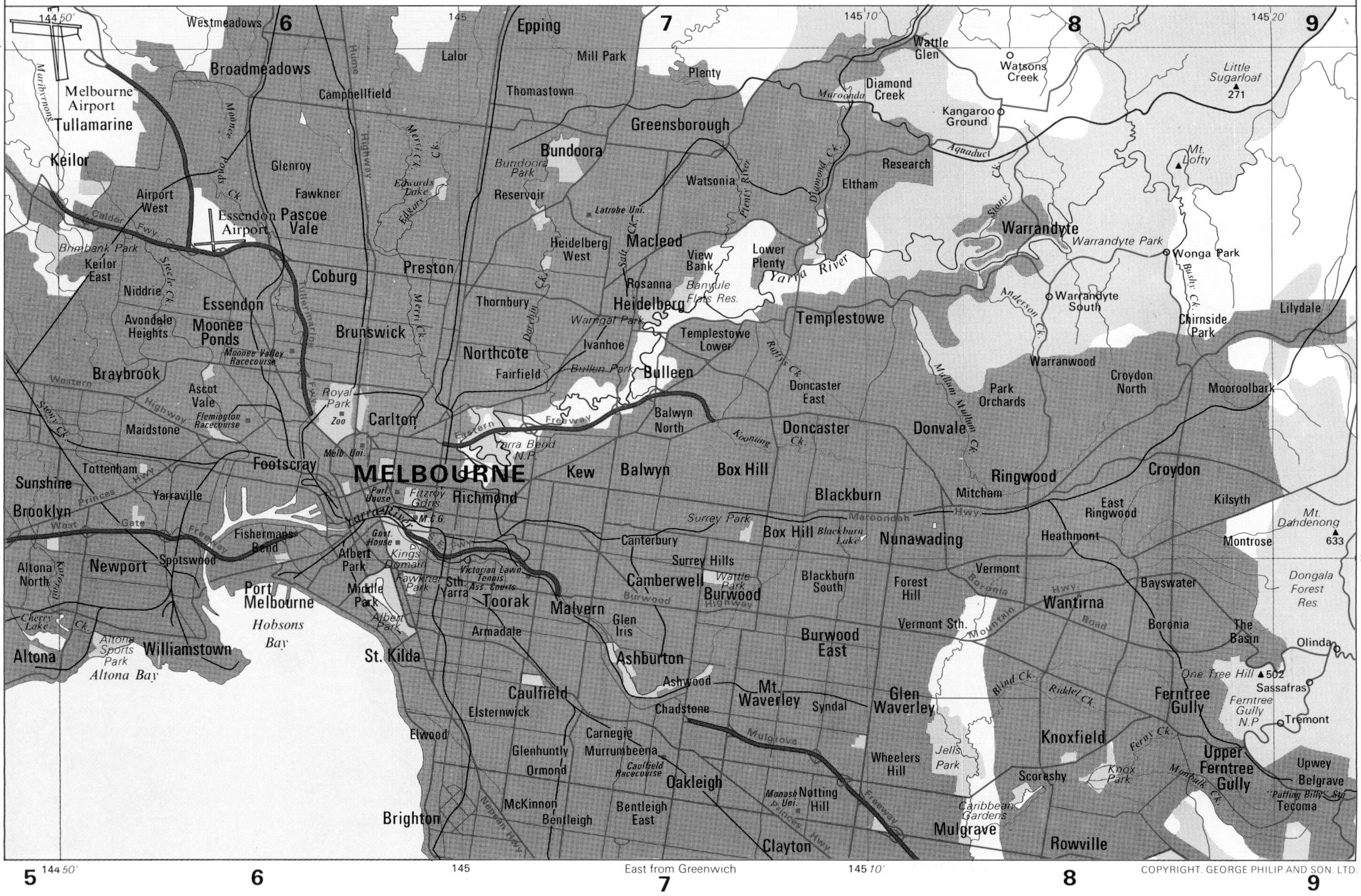

C
Minto
Sutherland
Gymea
Miranda
Potter Point
East from Greenwich
SOUTH PACIFIC OCEAN

150 50    151    151 10    151 20'

**5** **6** **7** **8** **9**

D
37 40'
144 50'
Westmeadows
Epping
Mill Park
Plenty
Wattle Glen
Watsons Creek
Diamond Creek
Kangaroo Ground
Little Sugarloaf 271

Melbourne Airport Tullamarine
Broadmeadows
Campbellfield
Lalor
Thomastown
Greensborough
Maroondah
Mt. Lofty

Keilor
Glenroy
Fawkner
Bundoora Park
Bundoora
Watsonia
Research
Eltham
Warrandyte
Warrandyte Park
Wonga Park

Airport West
Essendon Airport
Pascoe Vale
Reservoir
Edwards Lake
Latrobe Uni.
Macleod
View Bank
Lower Plenty
Yarra River
Warrandyte South
Mt. Lofty

E
Keilor East
Niddrie
Essendon
Moonee Ponds
Coburg
Preston
Heidelberg West
Rosanna
Thornbury
Heidelberg
Banyule Flats Res.
Templestowe
Templestowe Lower
Park Orchards
Warranwood
Croydon North
Lilydale
Chirnside Park

Avondale Heights
Braybrook
Brunswick
Northcote
Fairfield
Ivanhoe
Bulleen
Doncaster East
Donvale
Mooroolbark

Ascot Vale
Moonee Valley Racecourse
Royal Park Zoo
Carlton
Yarra Bend N.P.
Balwyn North
Doncaster
Ringwood
Croydon

Maidstone
Flemington Racecourse
Melb. Uni.
MELBOURNE
Richmond
Kew
Balwyn
Box Hill
Blackburn
Mitcham
East Ringwood
Kilsyth
Mt. Dandenong

Sunshine
Footscray
Yarraville
Park House
Fitzroy Gdns
Surrey Park
Box Hill South
Blackburn Lake
Nunawading
Heathmont
Montrose
633

37 50'
Brooklyn
Spotswood
Fishermans Bend
Albert Park
Kings Domain
Sth. Yarra
Canterbury
Surrey Hills
Camberwell
Blackburn South
Forest Hill
Vermont
Bayswater
Dongala Forest Res.

Altona North
Newport
Port Melbourne
Middle Park
Toorak
Malvern
Glen Iris
Burwood
Burwood East
Vermont Sth.
Wantirna
Boronia
The Basin

Altona
Williamstown
Hobsons Bay
St. Kilda
Armadale
Ashburton
Glen Waverley
One Tree Hill 502
Olinda
Sassafras

Altona Sports Park
Altona Bay
Caulfield
Elsternwick
Chadstone
Mt. Waverley
Syndal
Glen Waverley
Ferntree Gully
Ferntree Gully N.P.
Tremont

F
Elwood
Glenhuntly
Ormond
Carnegie
Murrumbeena
Caulfield Racecourse
Ashwood
Wheelers Hill
Jells Park
Knoxfield
Scoresby
Knox Park
Upwey
Belgrave
Upper Ferntree Gully
Puffing Billy Rly.

Brighton
McKinnon
Bentleigh
Bentleigh East
Oakleigh
Notting Hill
Monash Uni.
Mulgrave
Caribbean Gardens
Rowville
Tecoma

Clayton

144 50'    145    145 10    145 20'

East from Greenwich

1: 200 000

5 miles
8 km

**Montréal (upper map)**

1 2 3 4 5

Lorraine
Ste-Thérèse
Auteuil
Ste-Rose
St-Vincent-de-Paul
Rivière-des-Prairies
Pointe-Aux-Trembles
Montréal-Est
Îles de Boucherville
Boucherville

St-Augustin
St-Thérèse-Ouest
Vimont
Bélanger
Duvernay
Montréal Nord
Anjou
Tetreauville
Longue Point

A

Petit-Brûlé
Chicot
St-Eustache
Fabreville
St-Martin
Ville de Laval
Pont-Viau
St-Léonard
St-Michel
Maisonneuve

La Fresnière
Deux-Montagnes
Laval-Ouest
Chomedey
Laval-des-Rapides
Ahuntsic
Bordeaux
St-Jean-de-dieu
Parc IX Olympique

St-Joseph-du-Lac
Ste-Marthe-sur-le-Lac
Laval-sur-le-Lac
Ste-Dorothée
Pierrefonds
Aéroport de Cartierville
St-Laurent
Outremont
MONTRÉAL
Jacques Cartier
Longueuil
Mackayville

Le Trappe
Pointe-Calumet
Île Bizard
Île-Bizard
Roxboro
Dollard Des Ormeaux
Mont Royal
Parc Mont-Royal
Univ. McGill
St-Lambert
St-Hubert

43.30

Pointe-Calumet
Ste-Geneviève
Pierrefonds
Aéroport de Dorval
Westmount
Hampstead
Côte St-Luc
St-Pierre
Greenfield Park
Notre-Dame

B

Lac des Deux Montagnes
DEUX MONTAGNES
Kirkland
Beaconsfield
Pointe-Claire
Dorval
Lachine
Verdun
Île des Soeurs
Île aux Hérons
Brossard

Île-Cadieux
Baie-d'Urfé
Lasalle
Pont Champlain
La Prairie

Vaudreuil-sur-le-Lac
Senneville
Lac Saint-Louis
Pont Mercier
St. Lawrence
La Praire

Vaudreuil
Terrasse-Vaudreuil
Ste-Anne-de-Bellevue
MONTREAL VAUDREUIL
Caughnawaga
LA PRAIRIE
Canal de la Rive-Sud
St. Jacques

Dorion
Île-Perrot
Notre-Dame-de-L'Île-Perrot
West from Greenwich
Sainte-Catherine
Candiac

73.50    73.40

**Toronto (lower map)**

6 7 8 9 10

Maple
Richvale
Richmond Hill
Buttonville
Cherrywood

C

Kleinburg
Langstaff
Armadale
Dunbarton

43.50

Coleraine
Markham
YORK TORONTO
Milliken
Brown
Fairport

Thornhill
Concord
Newton Brook
Agincourt
Malvern
Rouge Hill
West Rouge
Port Union

Pine Grove
Edgeley
Fisherville
Willowdale
Northmount
MacDonald
Morningside Park
Highland Creek

Woodbridge
G. Ross Lord Park
York University
North York
Lansing
Wobum
West Hill

Black Creek Pioneer Village
Humber Summit
Beaumonte Heights
Armour Heights
York Mills
Bendale

D

Thistletown
Downsview Dells Park
Canada Forces Base
Don Mills
Wexford
Scarborough
Cliffside
Scarborough

Kipling Heights
Lawrence Heights
Wilket Creek Park
Highland Creek

Rexdale
Downsview
Humbergate
Lawrence Heights
Ontario Science Centre
Danforth

Malton
Weston
Black Creek
Leaside
Thorncliffe
Dentonia Park

Cedarvale
Forest Hill
York Mills
East York
Birch Cliff
Kingston Road

Humber Valley Village
Mount Dennis
Don Valley
Key Gardens

Etobicoke
York
Danforth Ave
Riverdale Park

Toronto International Airport (Lester B. Pearson)
Lambton Mills
High Park
University of Toronto
Parliament Buildings
Riverdale
Gardiner Expressway

43.40

Hanlon
Humber Valley Park
Swansea
Bloor Street
CN Tower

Islington
Kingsway
Parkdale
Exhibition Stadium
Toronto Harbour

Markland Wood
Humber Bay
**TORONTO**

E

Burnhamthorpe
Summerville
Ontario Place
Toronto Island
Gibraltar Point

Browns Line
Mimico
Humber Bay
Island Park

New Toronto

Cooksville
Mississauga
Long Branch
Lakeview

Lake Ontario

6 7 8 9 10

79.40    79.30    West from Greenwich    79.20    79.10

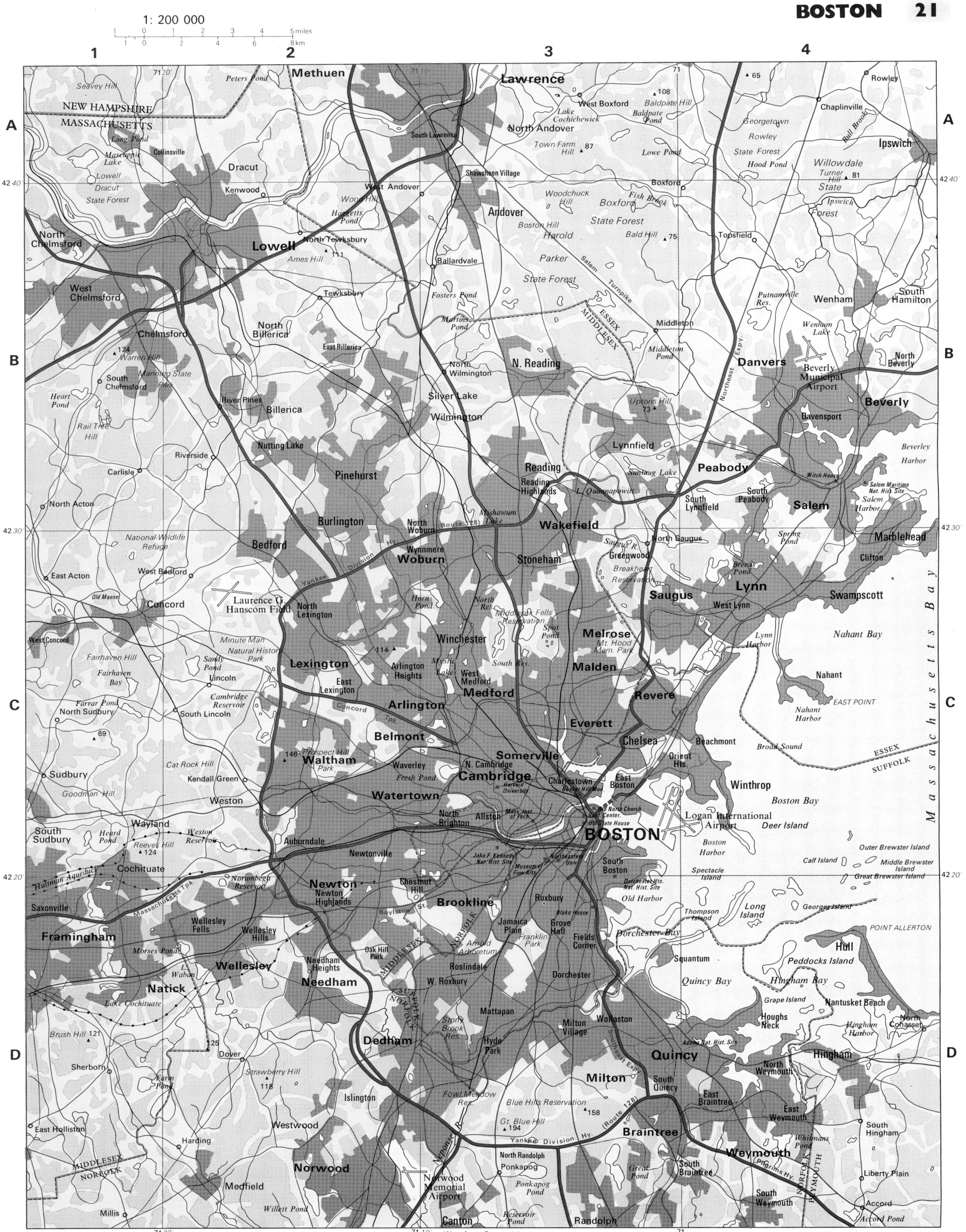

1 : 200 000

5 miles
8 km

1 2 3 4

Methuen
Lawrence
65
Rowley
West Boxford
108
Baldpate Hill
Chaplinville
Georgetown
Rowley
Ipswich

NEW HAMPSHIRE
MASSACHUSETTS
Long Pond
Seavey Hill
Peters Pond
North Andover
Lake Cochichewick
Baldpate Pond
State Forest
Hood Pond
Willowdale
Turner
State
81

A

Musquashi Lake
Collinsville
Dracut
Town Farm Hill
87
Lowe Pond
Putnamville Res.
Wenham
South Hamilton

42 40'
North Chelmsford
Kenwood
West Andover
Shawsheen Village
Woodchuck Hill
Boxford State Forest
Wenham Lake
42 40'

Lowell Dracut State Forest
Wood Hill
Andover
Boston Hill
Harold
Fish Brook
Bald Hill
75
Topsfield

North Chelmsford
Haggetts Pond
Parker State Forest
Salem
Turnpike
Danvers
Beverly Municipal Airport
North Beverly

B
West Chelmsford
Lowell
North Tewksbury
11
Ballardvale
Middleton
Essex
Middlesex
Middleton Pond
Beverly
B

Chelmsford
124
Warren Hill
North Billerica
Tewksbury
Fosters Pond
Uptons Hill
73
Davensport

South Chelmsford
Manning State Park
East Billerica
Martins Pond
N. Reading
Lynnfield
Salem

Heart Pond
Riverside
Billerica
North Wilmington
Silver Lake
Sunlaug Lake
Peabody
South Peabody
Salem Maritime Nat. Hist. Site
Salem Harbor

Rail Tree Hill
Nutting Lake
Wilmington
Reading
South Lynnfield
Witch House
Salem

Carlisle
Pinehurst
Reading Highlands
L. Quannapowitt
North Saugus
Spring Pond
Marblehead

42 30'
North Acton
Burlington
North Woburn (Route 128)
Mishawum Lake
Wakefield
Greenwood
Breakheart Reservation
Clifton
42 30'

National Wildlife Refuge
Bedford
Wynmere Pond
Stoneham
North Saugus
Lynn
Swampscott

East Acton
West Bedford
Woburn
Horn Pond
North Res.
Middlesex Fells Reservation
Saugus
West Lynn

Old Manse
Laurence G. Hanscom Field
North Lexington
Winchester
Spot Pond
Melrose
Mt. Hood Mem. Park
Lynn Harbor
Nahant Bay

42 30'
West Concord
Fairhaven Hill
114
Arlington Heights
Mystic Lakes
South Res.
Malden
Nahant

Concord
Minute Man Natural History Park
Lexington
East Lexington
West Medford
Revere
EAST POINT

C
Farrar Pond
North Sudbury
Sandy Pond
Lincoln
Concord Tpt.
Medford
Everett
Nahant Harbor
C

Goodman Hill
69
Cambridge Reservoir
South Lincoln
Arlington
Chelsea
Broad Sound
ESSEX
SUFFOLK

Sudbury
Cat Rock Hill
146
Prospect Hill
Belmont
Somerville
Charlestown
Beachmont
Orient Hts.
Winthrop

Kendall Green
Waltham Park
Waverley
N. Cambridge
Fresh Pond
Cambridge
Harvard University
East Boston
Boston Bay

Weston
Waltham
Watertown
Mass. Inst. of Tech.
Old North Church
State House
Logan International Airport
Deer Island

South Sudbury
Wayland
Weston Reservoir
Auburndale
North Brighton
Allston
BOSTON
Boston Harbor
Outer Brewster Island

42 20'
Heard Pond
124
Reeves Hill
Cochituate
Norumbega Reservoir
Newtonville
John F. Kennedy Nat. Hist. Site
Northeastern Univ.
South Boston
Spectacle Island
Calf Island
Middle Brewster Island
Great Brewster Island
42 20'

Saxonville
Massachusetts Tpk.
Newton
Newton Highlands
Chestnut Hill
Museum of Fine Arts
Dorchester Hts. Nat. Hist. Site
Thompson Island
Long Island
Georges Island
POINT ALLERTON

Framingham
Wellesley Fells
Wellesley Hills
Boylston St.
Brookline
Roxbury
Blake House
Old Harbor
Squantum
Hull
Peddocks Island

Morses Pond
Wellesley
Jamaica Plain
Grove Hall
Fields Corner
Dorchester Bay
Grape Island
Nantasket Beach

Wahan
Oak Hill Park
Arnold Arboretum
Franklin Park
Quincy Bay
Houghs Neck
Hingham Harbor
North Cohasset

Natick
Lake Cochituate
Needham Heights
Roslindale
Dorchester
Wollaston
Hingham

Brush Hill 121
W. Roxbury
Mattapan
Milton Village
Adams Nat. Hist. Site

D
Sherborn
Karin Pond
25
Dover
Strawberry Hill
118
Needham
Stony Brook Res.
Hyde Park
Milton
Quincy
South Quincy
North Weymouth
Hingham
D

East Holliston
Islington
Fowl Meadow Res.
Blue Hills Reservation
158
East Braintree
East Weymouth

Westwood
Gt. Blue Hill 194
Yankee Division Hwy.
(Route 128)
Braintree
South Braintree
Weymouth
South Hingham

Medfield
Harding
Norwood
North Randolph
Ponkapog
South Braintree
South Weymouth
Liberty Plain

Millis
Willett Pond
Norwood Memorial Airport
Ponkapog Pond
Great Pond
Accord

MIDDLESEX
NORFOLK
Reservoir Pond
Accord Pond

1 2
West from Greenwich
3
71
COPYRIGHT GEORGE PHILIP AND SON LTD
4

Canton
Randolph

Massachusetts Bay

1 : 200 000

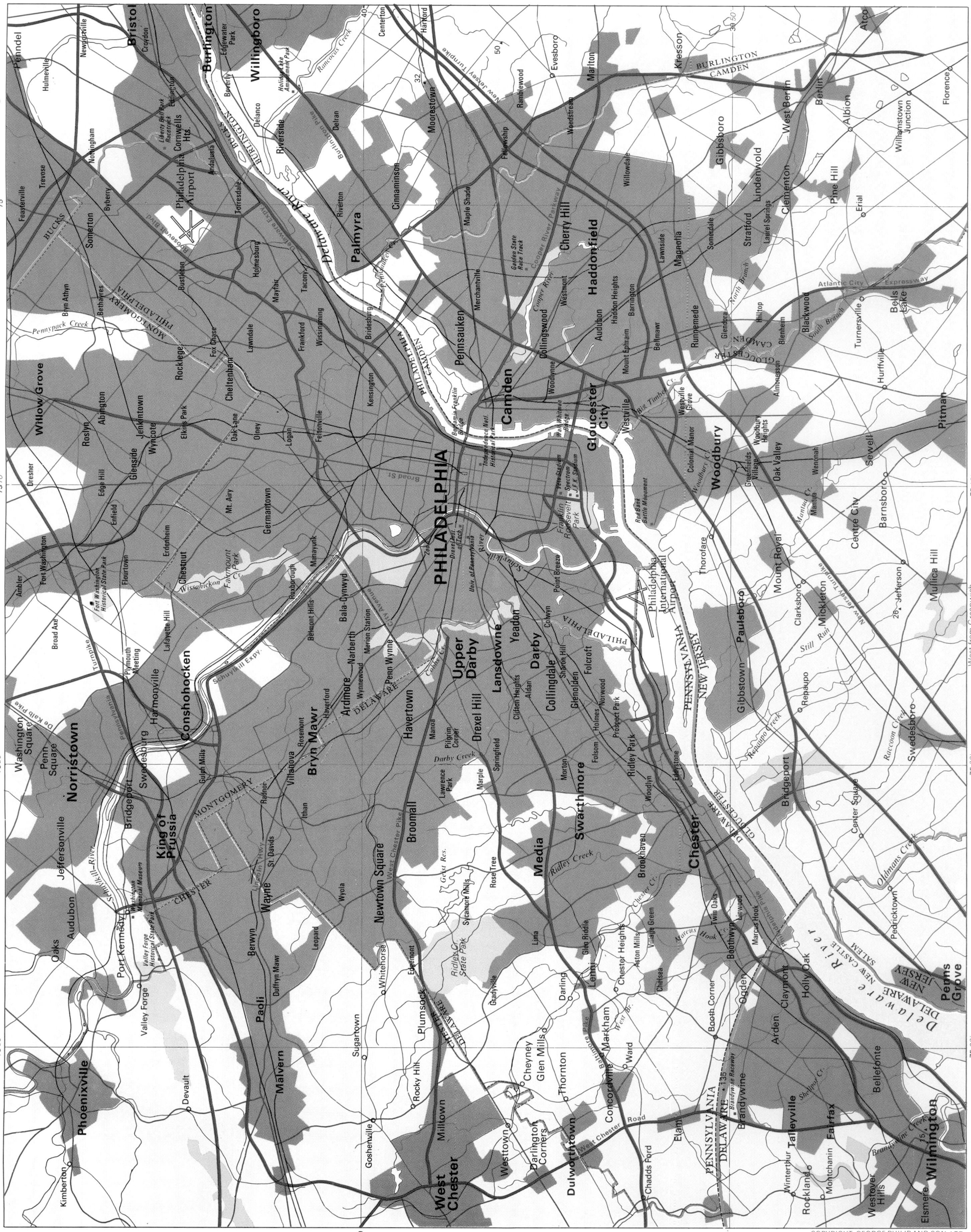

5 miles
8 km

A        B        C

5

Pennsauken
Willingboro
Burlington
Bristol
Penndel
Hulmeville
Newportville
Croydon
Edgewater Park
Beverly
Delanco
Riverside
Delran
Cinnaminson
Moorestown
Maple Shade
Merchantville
Marlton
Evesboro
Evesboro
Kresson
BURLINGTON
CAMDEN
West Berlin
Berlin
Albion
Atco
Florence
Williamstown Junction

Philadelphia Airport
Cornwells Hts.
Torresdale
Andalusia
Riverton
Palmyra
Cherry Hill
Gibbsboro
Lindenwold
Clementon
Pine Hill
Erial

BUCKS
Feasterville
Somerton
Byberry
Holmesburg
Mayfair
Tacony
Frankford
Collingswood
Audubon
Haddon Heights
Barrington
Magnolia
Lawnside
Somerdale
Stratford
Laurel Springs

75

Trevose
Bethayres
Bryn Athyn
Fox Chase
Rockledge
Cheltenham
Wissinoming
Bridesburg
Haddonfield

MONTGOMERY
PHILADELPHIA
Pennypack Creek
Willow Grove
Abington
Roslyn
Jenkintown
Wyncote
Elkins Park
Oak Lane
Logan
Kensington
Camden
Gloucester City
Woodbury
Mount Royal

Dresher
Ambler
Glenside
Edge Hill
Enfield
Mt. Airy
Germantown
Erdenheim
Chestnut Hill
Roxborough
Manayunk
PHILADELPHIA
Gloucester City
Colonial Manor
Oak Valley
Barnsboro
Centre City
Mullica Hill
Pitman

4

Fort Washington
Flourtown
Lafayette Hill
Fort Washington Historical State Park
Wissahickon
Chestnut Hill
Bala-Cynwyd
Bryn Mawr
Ardmore
Narberth
Merion Station
Wynnewood
Philadelphia International Airport
Thorofare
Clarksboro
Paulsboro
Repaupo

3

Broad Axle
Plymouth Meeting
Rosemont
Villanova
Haverford
Penn Wynne
Upper Darby
Lansdowne
Yeadon
Darby
Collingdale
Folcroft
Glenolden
Prospect Park
Woodlyn

Washington Square
Penn Square
Norristown
Conshohocken
Swedesburg
Bridgeport
Harmanville
Gulph Mills
Wynnewood
Havertown
Manoa
Pilgrim Corner
Clifton Heights
Aldan
Springfield
Sharon Hill
Norwood
Ridley Park
Swarthmore

2

King of Prussia
Jeffersonville
Audubon
Oaks
Port Kennedy
Valley Forge Historical State Park
Bridgeport
MONTGOMERY
Radnor
St. Davids
Wayne
Ithan
Broomall
Lawrence Park
Marple
Rose Tree
Media
Brookhaven
Chester
Marcus Hook
Bethayres
Linwood

75 20'

Phoenixville
Kimberton
Devault
Oaks
Malvern
Paoli
Berwyn
Duffryn Mawr
Leopard
Newtown Square
Wyola
Whitehorse
Edgemont
Sycamore Mills
Ridley Creek State Park
Linfia
Silex Riddle
Morton
Twin Oaks
Aston Mills
Chester Heights
Boothwyn
Marcus Hook
Trainer
Ogden

1

West Chester
Sugartown
Plumsock
Milltown
Gosherville
Westtown
Cheyney
Glen Mills
Thornton
Dulworthtown
Darlington Corners
Concordville
Markham
Ward
Chadds Ford
Elam
PENNSYLVANIA
DELAWARE
Talleyville
Fairfax
Arden
Claymont
Holly Oak
Bellefonte
Wilmington
Elsmere
Westover Hills
Rockland
Montchanin
Winterthur
Brandywine
Penns Grove
NEW JERSEY
DELAWARE
Delaware River

PHILADELPHIA

Delaware River
Schuylkill River
Broad St.
Independence Nat. Historical Park
Veterans Stadium
Spectrum
Roosevelt Park
J.F.K. Stadium

DELAWARE
CHESTER
GLOUCESTER
CAMDEN

West from Greenwich

COPYRIGHT GEORGE PHILIP AND SON LTD.

A        B        C

1 : 200 000

1 0 1 2 3 4 5 miles
1 0 2 4 6 8 km

**1**  **2**  **3**  **4**

76 50   76 40   76 30   102

Owings Mills
213   Garrison
Brooklandville   Lutherville-Timonium   Providence
Stevenson   Riderwood   Hampton Nat'l History Site   Graham Mem. Park   Germantown
Scotts Level Br.   Towson   Perry Hall   Loreley
170'   Ruxton   Loch Raven Village   Carney   White Marsh   Joppatowne
Harrisonville   Pikesville   Parkville   Rodgers Forge   67   Putty Hill   Minebank Run   HARFORD / BALTIMORE
Hernwood Hts   Woodmore   Rockdale   BALTIMORE   Mt. Pleasant Park   Linbigh   Fullerton   Whitemarsh   Bird River   Harewood Park
**A**   Randallstown   CITY OF BALTIMORE   Western Run   Overlea   Rossville
Granite   Milford   Pimlico Racetrack   Roland Park   John Hopkins Univ & Art Museum   Elmwood   Middle River
39 20'   Lochearn   Druid Hill Park   Memorial Stadium   Clifton Park   Kenwood   Bowleys Quarters   Martin State Nat'l Airport   39 20'
Woodstock   Hebbville   Lake Ashburton   Druid Lake   North Ave.   Clifton   Rosedale   Carroll Island
Daniels   Woodlawn   Gwynns Falls   Peabody Inst   Civic Center   Chesaco Park   Middleborough   Back River
Patapsco State Park   Leakin Park   Franklin St.   Patterson Park   Essex
Normandy Heights   Catonsville Manor   West Edmondale   BALTIMORE   Eastpoint   North Point   Miller Island
**B**   Valley Mede   Catonsville   Carroll Park   Northwest Branch   Fort McHenry Nat. Mon & Hist. Shrine   Dundalk   Inverness   Edgemere   Hart Island   **B**
Pine Orchard   Della   Bloomsbury   Middle Branch   Turner   Bay Shore Park   Chesapeake Bay
128   Ellicott City   Arbutus   Halethorpe   Lansdowne   Baltimore Highlands   Sparrows Point   Old Road Bay
Oakland Mills   Worthington   Ilchester   112'   Rockburn Branch   Brooklyn   Curtis Bay   Bethlehem Steel Plant   Fort Howard
Columbia   Jonestown   Elkridge   Pumphrey   Arundel Gardens   Arundel Village   Francis Scott Key Bridge   BALTIMORE / ANNE ARUNDEL
Columbia Hills   Linthicum Heights   Shipley   Rippling Ridge   Foremans Corner
**1**   Baltimore Washington Int'l Airport   Ferndale   **3**   **4**

**5**   **6**   **7**   **8**   **9**

Travilah Regional Park   Rockville   Foxhall   Meadowood   Fairland   Calverton   Muirkirk   Montpelier
Travilah   Randolph Hills   Glenmont   Wheaton Regional Park   Beltsville
Watkins Island   Montrose   Wheaton   White Oak   Beltsville Airport
**C**   LOUDOUN / FAIRFAX   The Glen   Kensington   Kemp Mill   Oak View   Greenbelt   **C**
Shady Oak   Cabin John Regional Park   Chevy Chase View   Silver Spring   Adelphi   College Park
99   Great Falls Park   Potomac   Woodmont   Avenel   Langley Park   Berwyn Hts   Lanham
39   Dranesville   Great Falls   Bethesda   Chevy Chase   Takoma Park   Univ of Maryland   Greenbelt Park   Seabrook   39
MARYLAND / VIRGINIA   Cabin John   Glen Echo   Somerset   Chillum   University Park   East Pines   New Carrollton
Belleview   Potomac River   Brookmont   Rock Creek Park   Brightwood   Hyattsville   Riverdale
Reston   Langley   American University   Mt. Rainier   Edmonston   Landover Hills   Glenarden
Dulles Airport Access Rd.   Wolf Trap Farm Park   McLean   WASHINGTON   Bladensburg   Kentland   Palmer Park
**D**   Snakeden Br.   126   Pimmit Hills   Franklin Park   Georgetown   Trinidad Nat'l Arboretum   Cheverly   Fairmount Heights   Kettering   **D**
Hunters Valley   Theodore Roosevelt Memorial   The White House   DISTRICT OF COLUMBIA   Seat Pleasant
Vale   Vienna   Dunn Loring   Arlington   Rosslyn   Lincoln Memorial   The Mall   U.S. Capitol   Capitol Hts   Millwood
Difficult Run   Falls Church   Seven Corners   Hillwood   Arlington Nat'l Cemetery   Library of Congress   Ft du Pont Park   Oakland   Ritchie   District Hts.
Broyhill Park   Annalee Hts.   Pentagon   East Arlington   Washington Nat'l Airport   Coral Hills
**E**   Fairfax   Holmes Acres   L. Barcroft   G. Mason Mem. Br.   East Potomac Park   Anacostia   PRINCE GEORGES   Suitland   Forestville   **E**
416   Kings Park   Baileys Crossroads   Hillcrest Hts.   Morningside
Fairfax Station   Little River Hwy.   Annandale   Parklawn   Glassmanor   Forest Heights   Silver Hill
38 50'   Long Br.   North Springfield   Alexandria   Oxon Hill   Temple Hills Park   Camp Springs   Andrews Air Force Base   38 50'
Butts Corner   Pohick Cr.   West Springfield   Franconia   Rose Hill   Huntington   South Lawn   85   76 50'
Springfield   Groveton   Belle Haven   Fort Foote Village   Oaklawn

**5**   77 20'   **6**   77 10'   West from Greenwich   **7**   77   **8**   **9**

1: 200 000

1   0   1   2   3   4   5 miles
1   0   2   4   6   8 km

**1**          **2**          **3**          **4**

Potawatomi Woods
Wheeling
208 ▲
Chipilly Woods
Chicago Botanic Garden
Northbrook
Glencoe
Techny
Skokie Lagoons
Prospect Heights
Winnetka
**A**
Arlington Heights
Glenview N.A.S.
Northfield
Kenilworth
Mount Prospect
Lake Avenue Woods
Glenview Countryside
Wilmette Harbor
Baha'i Temple
Wilmette
Des Plaines
Beck Lake
Glenview
Glenview Woods
Northwestern University
Niles
Morton Grove
Evanston
Edison Park
Skokie
Park Ridge
Lincolnwood
Rogers Park
42
Rosemont
Norwood Park
Smith Forest Preserve
Chicago-O'Hare International Airport
Lake O'Hare
Jefferson Park
Loyola University
LAKE
Bensenville
Norridge
Schiller Woods
Dunning
Harwood Heights
Irving Park
Uptown
**B**
Schiller Park
Des Plaines
Portage Park
Avondale
Lincoln Park
Lakeview
MICHIGAN
Westdale
Franklin Park
River Grove
Elmwood Park
Belmont Cragin
Belmont Harbor
Northlake
198 ▲
Logan Square
John Kennedy Expwy
Chicago River
Stone Park
Humboldt Park
Old Town
John Hancock Center
Water Tower
Elmhurst
Melrose Park
Frank Lloyd Wright Home
West Town
Lake Shore Drive
Berkeley
Austin
Northwestern Station
Art Institute
Chicago Harbor
Bellwood
River Forest
Garfield Park
Sears Tower
Hillside
Oak Park
La Salle St. Station
The Loop
Grant Park
Maywood
Dwight D. Eisenhower Expwy
Chicago Fire Market
Adler Planetarium
Broadview
Douglas Park
Burnham Park Harbor
Miller Meadow
Forest Park
**CHICAGO**
Westchester
North Riverside
Cicero
Lawndale
41 50
Berwyn
S. Branch
Bridgeport
Bemis Woods
Riverside
Stickney
Michigan Ave
La Grange Park
Chicago Sanitary and Ship Canal
Brighton Park
Dan Ryan Expressway
Brookfield
Forest View
A. E. Stevenson Expwy
Gage Park
Washington Park
Hyde Park
La Grange
Lyons
Chicago Portage National Historical Site
McCook
Clearing
University of Chicago
Museum of Science and Industry
Hinsdale
Western Springs
Summit
Chicago-Midway Airport
Chicago Lawn
Englewood
Jackson Park
Countryside
Bedford Park
**C**
Burr Ridge
La Grange Highlands
Bridgeview
Marquette Park
Ashburn
Hayford
South Shore
Hodgkins
Chatham
Justice
Burbank
Hometown
South Chicago
COOK COUNTY
LAKE COUNTY
Willow Springs
Hickory Hills
Dan Ryan Woods
Calumet Harbor
DU PAGE COUNTY
Des Plaines
Palos Hills
Oak Lawn
Evergreen Park
Beverley
Calumet Park
Roseland
Maple Lake
Longjohn Slough
Calumet
South Deering
Argonne Forest
Saganashkee Slough
Chicago Ridge
Worth
Mount Greenwood
Merrionette Park
Morgan Park
Lake Calumet
Whiting
Sag Bridge
Palos Hills Forest
Palos Park
Calumet Sag Channel
Worth
Tri State Tollway
Alsip
Stony Creek
Blue Island
Calumet Park
Little Calumet River
Robertsdale
Indiana Harbor
41 40
Palos Heights
Calumet Expwy
Burnham
ILLINOIS
INDIANA
Hegewisch
Powderhorn Lake
Tampier Slough
221 ▲
Tinley Creek
Rubio Woods
Crestwood
Robbins
Riverdale
Calumet River
East Chicago
**D**
Orland Lake
Woods
Tinley Creek
Midlothian
Posen
Dolton
Calumet City
180 ▲
Orland Park
Goeselville
Dixmoor
Phoenix
Shabbona Woods
Gary
Oak Forest
Harvey
South Holland
Hammond
Grand Calumet River
Tinley Park
Markham
87 50'          87 40' West from Greenwich          87 30'

**1**          **2**          **3**          **4**

1 : 200 000

5 miles
8 km

**1**     **2**     **3**     **4**

Ross
San Rafael
Kentfield
Green Brae
Kent Woodlands
Larkspur
Corte Madera
San Quentin State Prison
San Quentin
Mill Valley
Homestead Valley
Almonte
Strawberry Point
Alto
Mount Tamalpais State Park
Talmalpais Valley
Muir Beach
Marin City
Coyote Ridge
Tiburon
Belvedere
Richardson Bay
Sausalito
Marin Headlands State Park
Rodeo Cove
Golden Gate National Recr. Area
Point Bonita
Marin Headlands State Park

San Rafael Bay
Marin Islands
POINT SAN PABLO
San Pablo Strait
North Richmond
San Pablo
El Sobrante
Sherwood Forest
Kennedy Grove Regional Rec. Area
Richmond
Red Rock
Richmond–San Rafael Bridge
CONTRA COSTA COUNTY
MARIN COUNTY
POINT RICHMOND
Brooks Island
Richmond Inner Harbour
Golden Gate Fields
El Cerrito
Kensington
Charles Lee Tilden Regional Park
Wildcat Canyon Regional Park
San Pablo Ridge
San Pablo Reservoir
Briones Hills
Briones Reservoir
Briones Regional Park
Pleasant Hill
Concord
Walnut Creek
Walnut Heights
Lafayette
Saranap
Orinda
Orinda Village
Leisure World
Alamo
Rheem Valley
Las Trampas Ridge
Las Trampas Regional Park

Albany
Berkeley
University of California
Lake Temescal
Emeryville
Piedmont
Oakland
Moraga
Redwood Regional Park
Joaquin Miller Park
Anthony Chabot Regional Park
Rocky Ridge
Upper San Leandro Reservoir
CONTRA COSTA COUNTY
ALAMEDA COUNTY

San Francisco Bay
Angel Island State Park
Alcatraz I.
Treasure Island
Yerba Buena I.
Oakland Bay Bridge
Golden Gate Bridge
Ft. Point National Historical Site
San Francisco Maritime State Hist. Park
Fisherman's Wharf
Coit Tower
Chinatown
Western Addition
Presidio of San Francisco
Lincoln Park
POINT LOBOS
Seacliff
Richmond
University of San Francisco
Golden Gate Park
Haight-Ashbury
Buena Vista
Stow L.
Sunset
Mount Davidson
Parkside
West of Twin Peaks
Lake Merced
San Francisco State University
Daly City
Westlake
Broadmoor
Sterling Park
Colma
San Bruno Mountain
Brisbane
Serramonte
Edgemar
Pacific Manor
South San Francisco
Pacifica
San Bruno
Vallemar
Rockaway Beach
Cattle Hill
Tanforan Park
Millbrae

SAN FRANCISCO
South of Market
Mission Dolores
Mission
Bernal Hts.
Potrero
Bayview
Outer Mission
John McLaren Park
Visitacion Valley
Bayshore
China Basin
POTRERO POINT
HUNTERS POINT
Hunters Point
South Basin
Southern Pacific Terminal

Naval Air Station
SAN FRANCISCO COUNTY
ALAMEDA COUNTY
Alameda Memorial State Beach Park
Alameda
L. Merritt
Mills College
Knowland State Arboretum and Park
San Leandro
San Leandro Bay
Bay Farm Island
Metropolitan Oakland International Airport
Mulford Gardens
Fairmont Terrace
Ashland
San Lorenzo
Castro Valley
Cherryland
Hayward
Hayward Municipal Airport
California State University

POINT SAN BRUNO
San Francisco Bay
San Mateo Bridge
San Francisco International Airport
Burlingame
Hillsborough
San Mateo
Hillsdale
Coyote Point
Seal Slough
Brewer Island
Foster City
Bay Meadows Race Track
Marine World
San Francisco Bay National Wildlife Refuge
Redwood Point
Greco Island
Bair Island
Salt Evaporators
RAVENSWOOD POINT
Belmont
San Carlos
San Mateo Bridge
Union City
Alvarado
Salt Evaporators
Coyote Hills Regional Park
Fremont
Newark
Coyote Hills Slough
SAN MATEO COUNTY

San Francisco State Fish and Game Refuge
Sawyer Ridge
Pilarcitos Lake
San Andreas Lake
Crystal Springs
Lower Crystal Springs Reservoir
Upper Crystal Springs Reservoir
Montara Mountain
Pilarcitos Creek
Montara
Moss Beach
Half Moon Bay Airport
El Granada
Miramar
Half Moon Bay
Half Moon Bay Beaches
PILLAR POINT
POINT MONTARA
Kings Mountain
University Heights
Bear Gulch Reservoir
Woodside
Palomar Park
Redwood City
North Fair Oaks
East Palo Alto
Menlo Park
Palo Alto
Stanford University
San Andreas Fault
Bayshore Freeway
DUMBARTON POINT
Dumbarton Bridge
SANTA CLARA CO.
Guadalupe R.
Coyote Cr.

PACIFIC OCEAN

SAN FRANCISCO COUNTY
San Francisco Bay

Golden Gate
Mount Tamalpais State Park
IRON PENINSULA
MARIN PENINSULA
BLUNT POINT
Angel I.
Paradise Cay
Raccoon Str.
Strawberry Point
183
338
796
375
579
593
143
187
281
283
400
323
338
436
582
616
363
305

122°30'   122°20'   West from Greenwich   122°10'

37°50'   37°40'   37°30'

1: 200 000

1 0 1 2 3 4 5 miles
1 0 2 4 6 8 km

A        B        C

Waterman Mountain
Silver Mountain
San Gabriel River
Angeles National Forest
Josephine Pk.
Strawberry Peak 1879
Mount Disappointment
San Gabriel Peak 1877
Mount Markham
Mount Lowe
Mount Harvard
Echo Mountain
Mt. Wilson
Mt. Wilson Observatory
Big Tujunga Canyon
Mount Lukens

Azusa
Irwindale
Duarte
Santa Fe Flood Control Basin
Las Lomas
West Covina
La Puente
Rowland
Fallon
Baldwin Park
Monrovia
Bassett
Puente Hills
Hacienda Hts.
Hilgrove District
Pomona Fwy
Sunshine Acres
LOS ANGELES
ORANGE
La Habra Heights
La Habra
Fuller Park
Buena Park

Sierra Madre
Arcadia
Temple City
El Monte
Whittier
Santa Fe Springs
Colorado Fwy
Norwalk
Artesia

Pasadena
Altadena
La Cañada
Rose Bowl
Flint Peak 575
San Rafael Hills
California Inst. of Tech
South Pasadena
San Marino
San Gabriel
Rosemead
South San Gabriel
Monterey Park
Montebello
Commerce
Pico Rivera
Rio Hondo
San Gabriel River
Los Nietos
San Bernardino Fwy
San Gabriel River Fwy
Bellflower
Artesia Fwy

La Crescenta
Montrose
Tujunga
Highway Highlands
Verdugo Mountains
Eagle Rock
Highland Park
Garvanza
El Sereno
Alhambra
Lincoln Heights
Boyle Heights
East Los Angeles
Maywood
Huntington Park
Bell Gardens
Downey
Clearwater
Hollydale
Hynes
Paramount
North Long Beach

Glendale
Los Angeles River
Los Angeles Fwy
Golden State Fwy
Dodger Stadium
Civic Center
LOS ANGELES
Florence
South Gate
Lynwood
Willowbrook
Compton
Gardena
West from Greenwich

Burbank
Foothill Fwy
Sunland
Stonehurst
Hansen Flood Control Basin
San Fernando Airport
617
Lockheed-Burbank Airport
243
Cahuenga Peak 555
Griffith Park
Universal City
N.B.C.
Hollywood Fwy
Hollywood Bowl
Griffith Park
The Coliseum
Harbour Fwy
Inglewood
The Forum
Hawthorne
Lennox
Lawndale

San Fernando
Pacoima
Panorama City
Sepulveda
Van Nuys
Van Nuys Airport
Sepulveda Flood Control Basin
Studio City
Sun Valley
North Hollywood
Ventura Fwy
West Hollywood
Beverly Hills
Glen Oaks Golf Club
Franklin Reservoir
Stone Canyon Reservoir
Beverly Glen
Bel Air
Westwood Village
Culver City
Twentieth Century Fox
Baldwin Hills Reservoir
Baldwin Hills
Santa Monica Fwy
San Diego Fwy
Los Angeles Intl. Airport
El Segundo
Manhattan Beach

Winneka
Granada Hills
Northridge
Lower Van Norman Lake
Alizo Canyon Wash
Reseda
San Fernando Valley
Tarzana
Encino
216
Sherman Oaks
Tujunga Wash
459
Santa Monica Mts.
648
Encino Reservoir
Brentwood Park
Will Rogers State Historic Park
Santa Ynez Canyon
J. Paul Getty Museum
Pacific Palisades
Santa Monica
Santa Monica Municipal Airport
Venice
Hermosa Beach
Santa Monica Bay

34 10'
118
118 10'
118 20'
118 30'
34 10'
34
34

**1: 200 000**

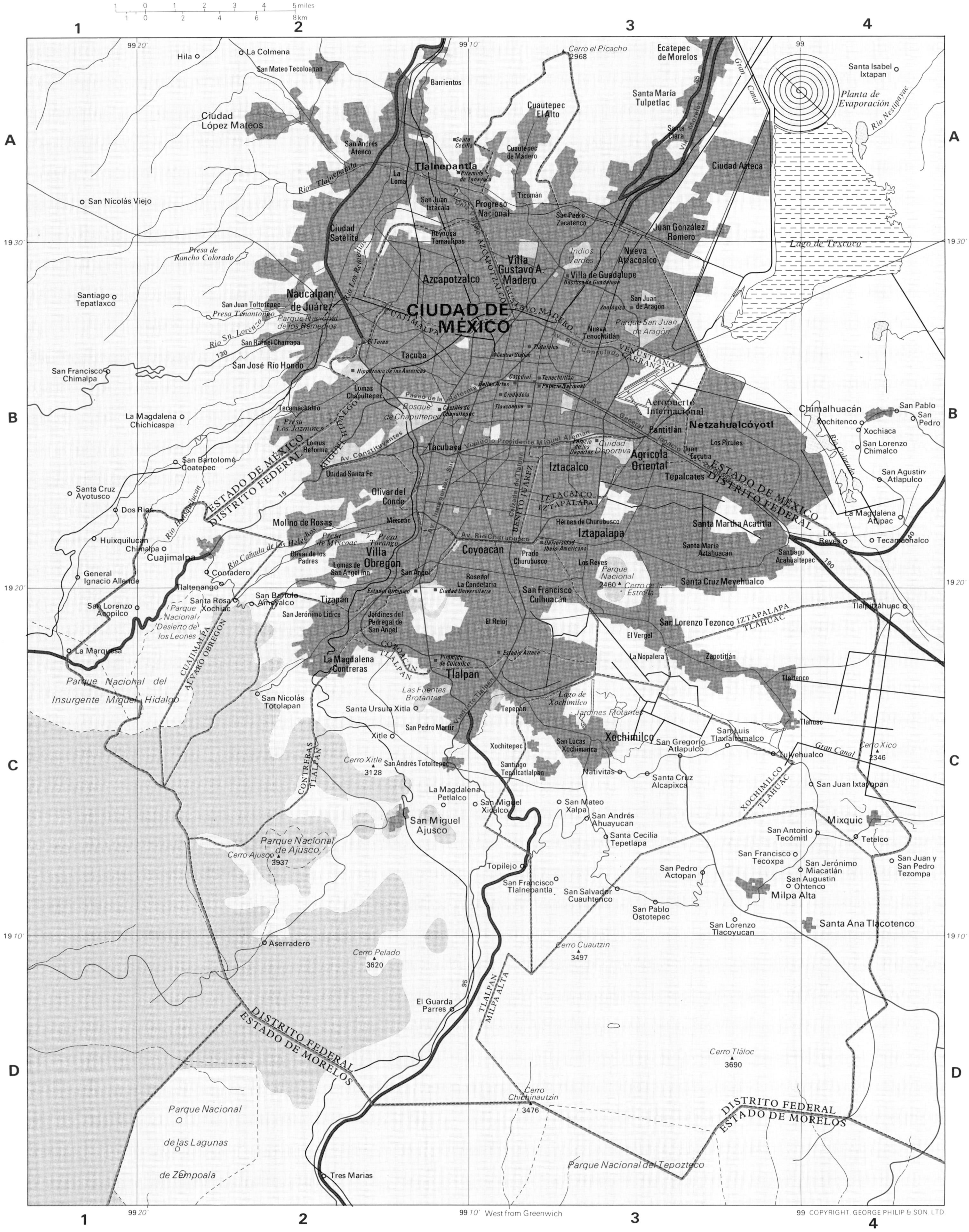

0  1  2  3  4  5 miles
1  0  2  4  6  8 km

99 20'  1  2  99 10'  3  4

## A

Hila
La Colmena
San Mateo Tecoloapan
Cerro el Picacho 2968
Ecatepec de Morelos
Santa Isabel Ixtapan
Planta de Evaporación
Río Nextipayac

Barrientos
Cuautepec El Alto
Santa María Tulpetlac
Santa Cecilia
Cuautepec de Madero
Santa Clara
Ciudad López Mateos
San Andrés Atenco
Tlalnepantla
Pirámide de Tenayuca
Ticomán
Ciudad Azteca

San Nicolás Viejo
La Loma
San Juan Ixtacala
Progreso Nacional
San Pedro Zacatenco
Juan González Romero

19 30'
Presa de Rancho Colorado
Río Tlalnepantla
Ciudad Satélite
Reynosa Tamaulipas
Villa Gustavo A. Madero
Indios Verdes
Nueva Atzacoalco
Lago de Texcoco
19 30'

Santiago Tepatlaxco
Río Los Remedios
Azcapotzalco
Villa de Guadalupe
Basílica de Guadalupe
San Juan de Aragón

Naucalpan de Juárez
San Juan Toltotepec
Presa Tenantongo
Parque Nacional de los Remedios
Río Sn. Lorenzo
**CIUDAD DE MÉXICO**
Zoológica
Parque San Juan de Aragón
San Juan de Aragón
Nueva Tenochtitlán

San Francisco Chimalpa
San Rafael Chamapa
El Toreo
Tacuba
Central Station
Tlatelolco

## B

La Magdalena Chichicaspa
Presa Los Jazmines
Tecamachalco
Lomas Chapultepec
Hipódromo de las Américas
Catedral
Tenochtitlán
Palacio Nacional
Chimalhuacán
San Pablo San Pedro
Xochitenco
Xochiaca

San Bartolomé Coatepec
Lomas Reforma
Bosque de Chapultepec
Castillo de Chapultepec
Bellas Artes
Ciudadela
Tlaxcoaque
San Lorenzo Chimalco

Santa Cruz Ayotusco
Unidad Santa Fe
Av. Constituyentes
Tacubaya
Viaducto Presidente Miguel Alemán
Palacio de los Deportes
Ciudad Deportiva
Pantitlán
Los Piñales
Netzahualcóyotl
San Agustín Atlapulco

Dos Ríos
Olivar del Conde
Iztacalco
Agrícola Oriental
La Magdalena Atliac

Huixquilucan
Chimalpa
Molino de Rosas
Mixcoac
Tepalcates
Tecamachalco

## C

General Ignacio Allende
Contadero
Presa de Mixcoac
Presa Tarango
Coyoacan
Héroes de Churubusco
Iztapalapa
Santa Martha Acatitla
Los Reyes

San Lorenzo Acopilco
Hlatenango
Olivar de los Padres
Villa Obregón
Prado Churubusco
Santa María Aztahuacan
Santiago Acahualtepec

La Marquesa
Santa Rosa Xochiac
San Bartolo Ameyalco
Lomas de San Ángel Inn
San Ángel
Rosedal La Candelaria
Los Reyes
Parque Nacional 2460
Cerro de la Estrella
Santa Cruz Meyehualco
Tlahuac
Tlahuac

Parque Nacional del Insurgente Miguel Hidalgo
San Nicolás Totolapan
Tizapán
Estadio Olímpico
Ciudad Universitaria
San Francisco Culhuacán
San Lorenzo Tezonco
Iztapalapa
Tlahuac

San Jerónimo Lídice
Jardines del Pedregal de San Ángel
El Reloj
El Vergel
Zapotitlán

Santa Úrsula Xitla
La Magdalena Contreras
Pirámide de Cuicuilco
Estadio Azteca
La Nopalera
Tlatenco

Las Fuentes Brotantes
Tlalpan
Lago de Xochimilco
Jardines Flotantes
Tlahuac

Xitle
San Pedro Mártir
Tepepan
Santa Ursula Xitla
Xochitepec
San Gregorio Atlapulco
San Luis Tlaxialtemalco
Tlahuac
Cerro Xico 2346

Cerro Xitle 3128
San Andrés Totoltepec
Santiago Tepalcatlalpan
Nativitas
Santa Cruz Alcapixca
San Juan Ixtayopan

La Magdalena Petlalco
San Miguel Xicalco
San Lucas Xochimanca
Mixquic
Tetelco

San Miguel Ajusco
San Mateo Xalpa
San Andrés Ahuayucan
Santa Cecilia Tepetlapa
San Antonio Tecómitl
San Juan y San Pedro Tezompa

Parque Nacional de Ajusco
Cerro Ajusco 3937
Topilejo
San Pedro Actopan
San Francisco Tecoxpa
San Jerónimo Miacatlán
San Augustín Ohtenco

San Francisco Tlalnepantla
San Salvador Cuauhtenco
Milpa Alta
San Pablo Ostotepec
San Lorenzo Tlacoyucan
Santa Ana Tlacotenco

## D

Aserradero
Cerro Pelado 3620
Cerro Cuautzin 3497
Cerro Tláloc 3690

El Guarda Parres
DISTRITO FEDERAL ESTADO DE MORELOS
Cerro Chichinautzin 3476
DISTRITO FEDERAL ESTADO DE MORELOS

Parque Nacional de las Lagunas de Zempoala
Tres Marias
Parque Nacional del Tepozteco

99 20'  1  2  99 10'  West from Greenwich  3  99  4

1 : 200 000

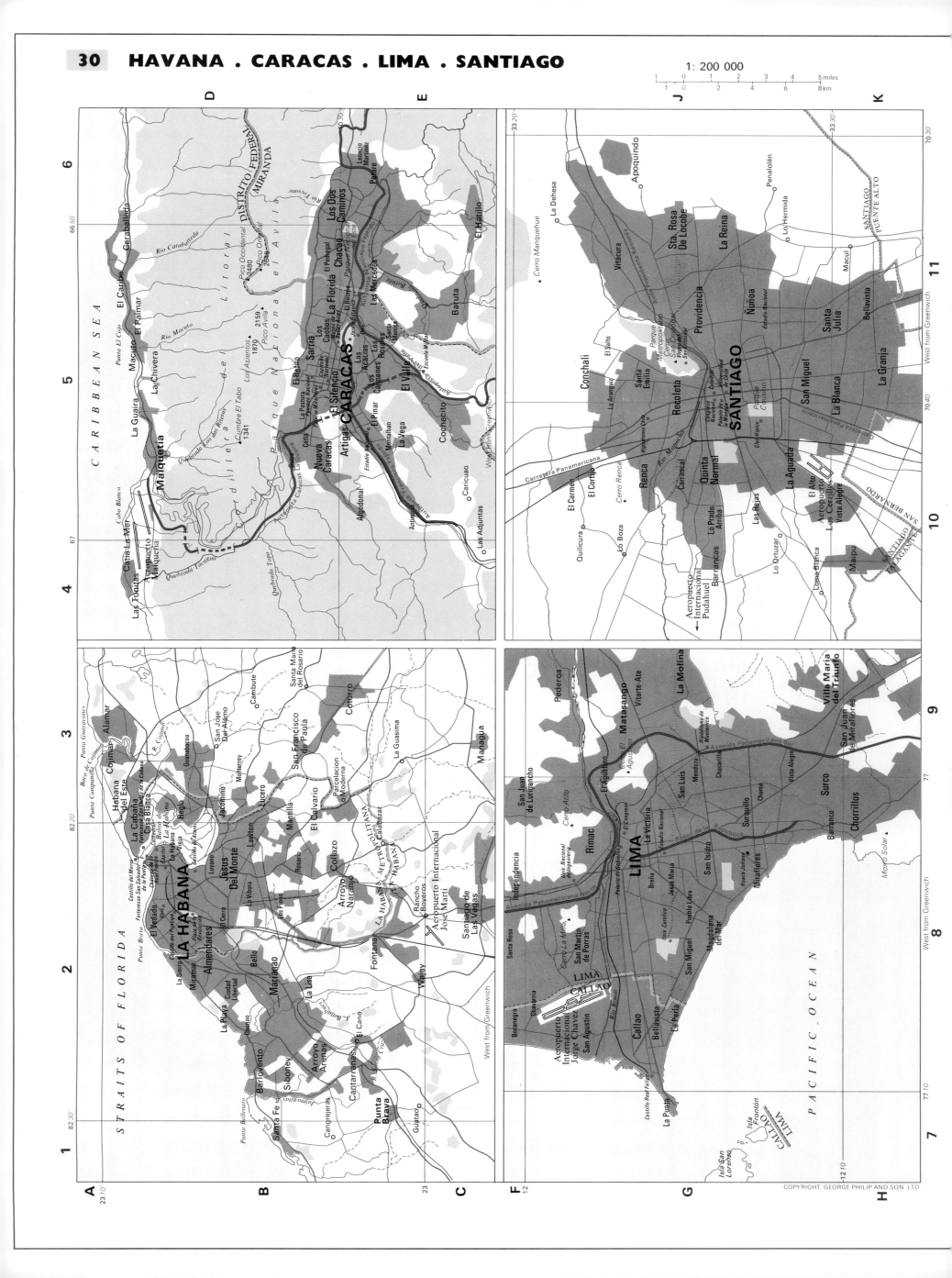

*COPYRIGHT GEORGE PHILIP AND SON LTD*

1: 200 000

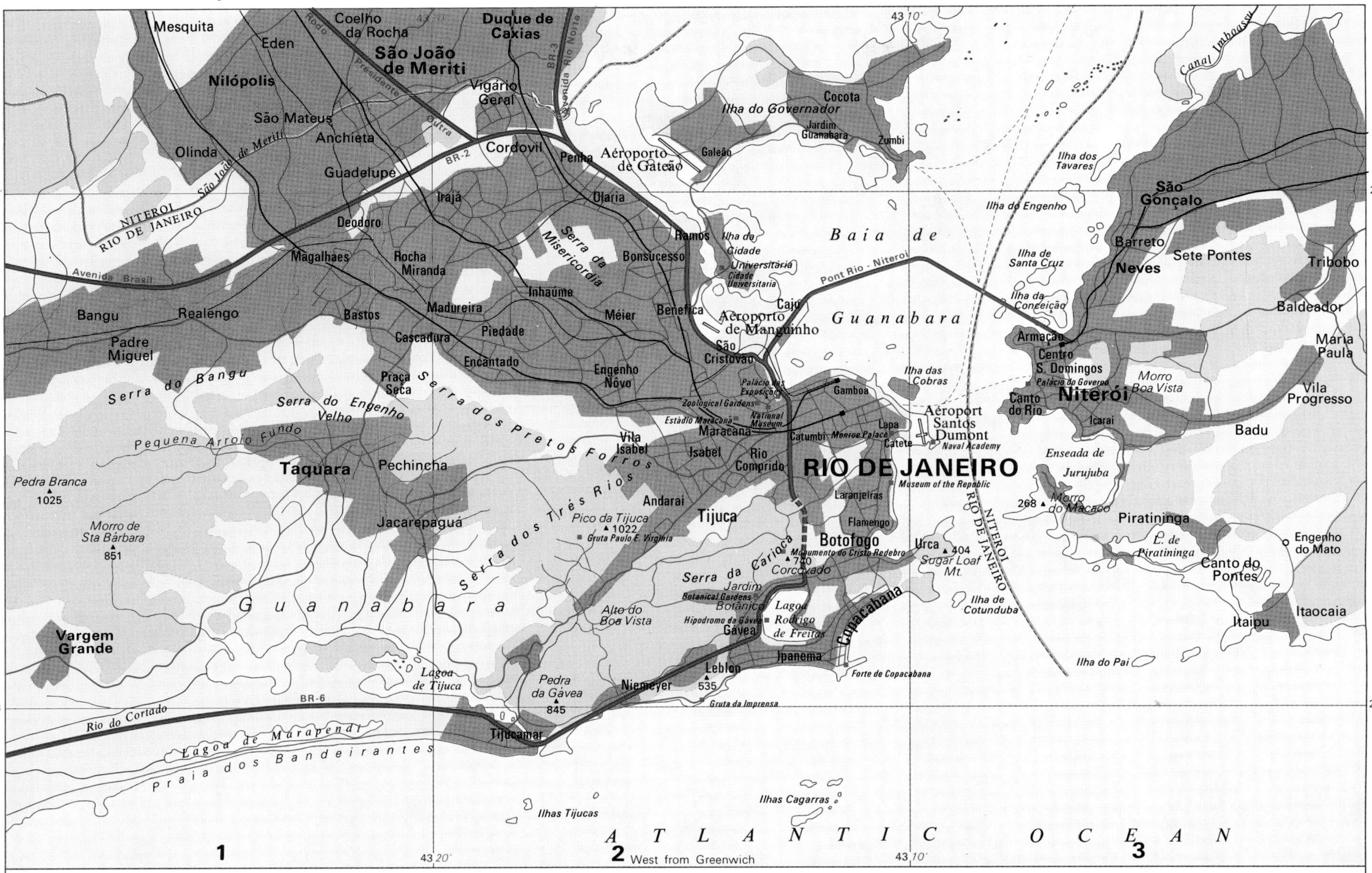

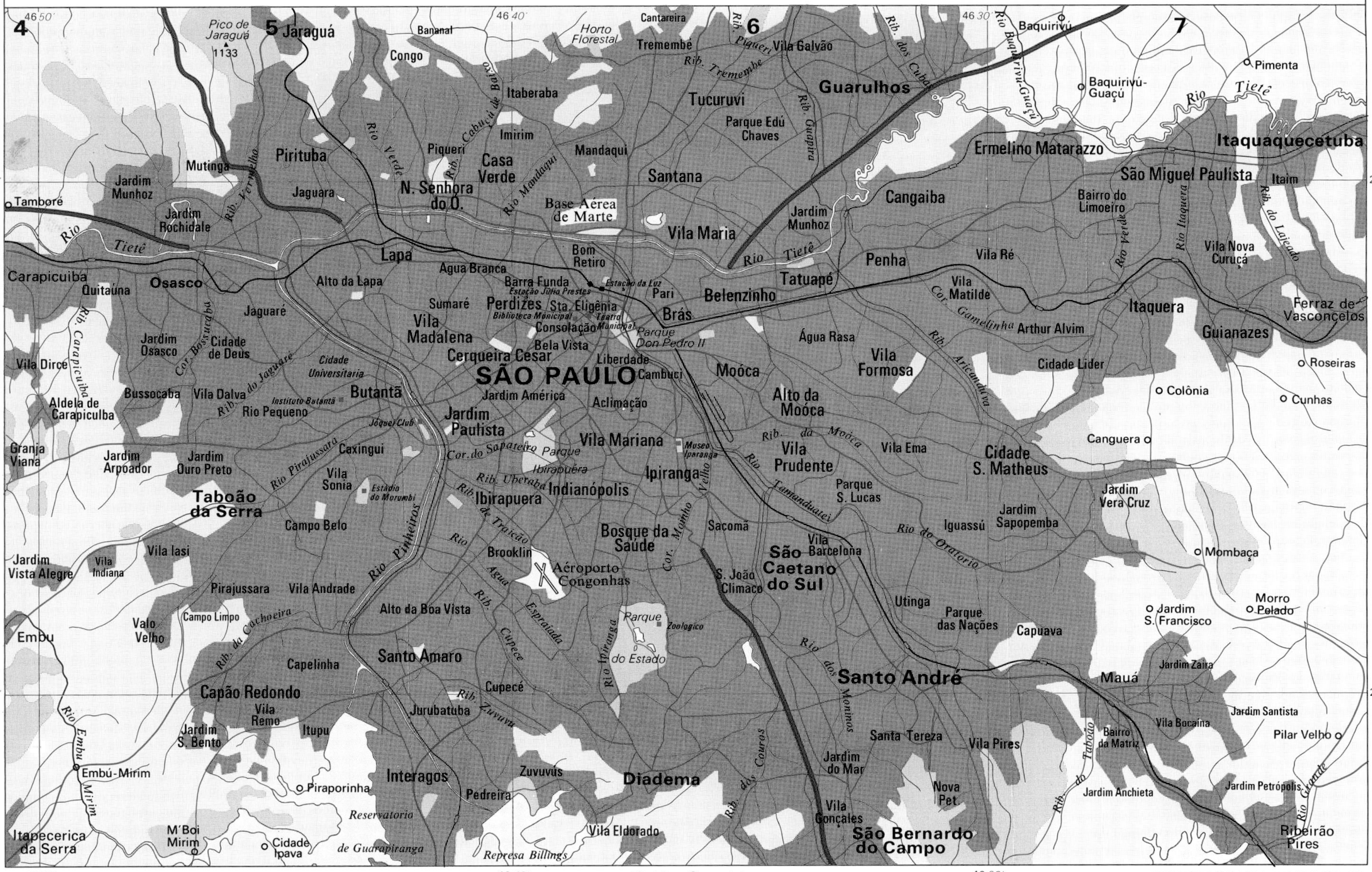

5 miles
8 km

**1    2    3**

## A

Mesquita
Coelho da Rocha
Duque de Caxias
Eden
São João de Meriti
Nilópolis
Vigário Geral
São Mateus
Anchieta
Cordovil
Olinda
Guadelupe
Penha
Aéroporto de Gateão
Ilha do Governador
Cocota
Jardim Guanabara
Zumbi
Galeão
Ilha dos Tavares
São Gonçalo
22 50'
Irajá
Olaria
Ilha de Engenho
NITEROI
RIO DE JANEIRO
Deodoro
Ramos
Ilha de Cidade
Cidade Universitária
B a i a   d e
Barreto
Neves
Sete Pontes
Tribobo
Magalhães
Rocha Miranda
Bonsucesso
Ilha de Santa Cruz
Baldeador
Inhaúme
Méier
Benefica
Aéroporto de Manguinho
Ilha da Conceição
Caju
G u a n a b a r a
Maria Paula
Bangu
Realengo
Madureira
Cascadura
Piedade
São Cristovão
Ilha das Cobras
Armação
Palácio do Governo
Centro
S. Domingos
Niterói
Badu
Padre Miguel
Bastos
Encantado
Engenho Novo
Palácio do Exposição
Gamboa
Canto do Rio
Icarai
Serra do Bangu
Praça Seca
Zoological Gardens
National Museum
Estádio Maracanã
Maracanã
Monroe Palace
Lapa
Catete
Aéroport Santos Dumont
Naval Academy
Morro Boa Vista
Vila Progresso

## B

Pequena Arroio Fundo
Serra da Misericordia
Vila Isabel
Isabel
Catumbi
Rio Comprido
RIO DE JANEIRO
Museum of the Republic
Enseada de Jurujuba
Pedra Branca 1025
Taquara
Pechincha
Serra dos Pretos Forros
Laranjeiras
Morro do Macaco
Piratininga
Morro de Sta Bárbara 851
Jacarepaguá
Andarai
Pico da Tijuca ▲1022
Tijuca
Flamengo
268
P. de Piratininga
Serra dos Três Rios
Gruta Paulo E. Virginia
Botofogo
Urca
404
Sugar Loaf Mt.
Engenho do Mato
Canto do Pontes
G u a n a b a r a
Serra da Carioca
Monumento do Cristo Redentor 720
Corcovado
Botanical Gardens
Jardim Botânico
Alto do Boa Vista
Hipodromo da Gávea
Gávea
Lagoa Rodrigo de Freitas
Ilha de Cotunduba
Itaocaia
Vargem Grande
Lagoa de Tijuca
Leblon
Ipanema
Copacabana
Itaipu
23
BR-6
Rio do Cortado
Pedra da Gávea 845
Niemeyer 535
Forte de Copacabana
Ilha do Pai
23

## C

Lagoa de Marapendi
Tijucamar
Gruta da Imprensa
Praia dos Bandeirantes
Ilhas Tijucas
Ilhas Cagarras
**A T L A N T I C    O C E A N**
43 20'    West from Greenwich    43 10'

**1    2    3**

**4    5    6    7**

46 50'    46 40'    46 30'
Pico de Jaraguá 1133
Jaraguá
Bananal
Cantareira
Horto Florestal
Tremembé
Rib. Piqueri
Vila Galvão
Rib. Baquirivú-Guaçu
Baquirivú
Pimenta
Congo
Rio Tietê

## D

Itaberaba
Piqueri
Imirim
Tucuruvi
Parque Edú Chaves
Guarulhos
Baquirivú-Guaçu
Rio Tietê
Itaquaquecetuba
Mutinga
Jardim Munhoz
Piqueri
Casa Verde
Mandaqui
Santana
Ermelino Matarazzo
São Miguel Paulista
Itaim
Tamboré
Jardim Rochidale
N. Senhora do Ó
Jaguara
Base Aérea de Marte
Jardim Munhoz
Cangaiba
Bairro do Limoeiro
Vila Nova Curuçá
23 30'
Carapicuiba
Quitauna
Osasco
Jaguaré
Lapa
Agua Branca
Vila Maria
Rio Tietê
Penha
Vila Ré
23 30'
Jardim Osasco
Cidade de Deus
Alto da Lapa
Barra Funda
Bom Retiro
Pari
Tatuapé
Vila Matilde
Itaquera
Ferraz de Vasconcelos
Vila Dirce
Bussocaba
Sumaré
Perdizes
Sta. Efigênia
Estação da Luz
Brás
Belenzinho
Arthur Alvim
Guianazes

## E

Aldeia de Carapicuiba
Vila Dalva
Cidade Universitária
Consolação
Bela Vista
Liberdade
Cambuci
Água Rasa
Cidade Líder
Roseiras
Granja Viana
Jardim Arpoador
Butantã
Jardim América
Aclimação
Mooca
Vila Formosa
Colônia
Cunhas
Jardim Ouro Preto
Instituto Botânico
Rio Pequeno
SÃO PAULO
Jardim Paulista
Vila Mariana
Alto da Mooca
Cidade S. Matheus
Cangueira
Jockey Club
Cor. do Sapateiro Parque
Ibirapuera
Museu Ipiranga
Vila Prudente
Vila Ema
Jardim Vera Cruz
Vila Vista Alegre
Jardim Indiana
Coxingui
Ipiranga
Parque S. Lucas
Iguassú
Mombaça

## F

Taboão da Serra
Vila Sonia
Estádio do Morumbi
Indianópolis
Jardim Sapopemba
Campo Belo
Brooklin
Sacomã
São Caetano do Sul
Utinga
Jardim S. Francisco
Morro Pelado
Granja Viana
Pirajussara
Vila Andrade
Bosque da Saúde
Aéroporto Congonhas
S. João Climaco
Parque das Nações
Capuava
Embu
Valo Velho
Campo Limpo
Alto da Boa Vista
Santo Amaro
Parque Zoológico do Estado
Vila Barcelona
Santo André
Jardim Zaíta
Capão Redondo
Capelinha
Cupecé
Mauá
Jardim Vista Alegre
Vila Remo
Jardim S. Bento
Itupu
Jurubatuba
Santa Tereza
Vila Pires
Jardim Santista
23 40'
Embú-Mirim
Interagos
Piraporinha
Zuvuvús
Diadema
Jardim do Mar
Nova Pet.
Pilar Velho
Itapecerica da Serra
M'Boi Mirim
Cidade Ipava
Vila Eldorado
Vila Gonçales
São Bernardo do Campo
Jardim Anchieta
Jardim Petrópolis
Ribeirão Pires
Pedreira
Reservatório
Represa Billings
de Gudrapiranga

West from Greenwich

46 50'    46 40'    46 30'

**4    5    6    7**

1 : 200 000

5 miles
8 km

# BUENOS AIRES

Rio de la Plata

Quilmes
Espeleta
Berazategui
Villa D. Augusta
Villa Sotrel
San Francisco
Villa
Esguia
Ranelagh
Bosques
Don Bosco
Bernal
Gdor. Monteverde
San Francisco Solano
Florencio Varela
Villa Dominico
Wilde
Villa Baxilari
Rafael Calzada
Calypute
Rivadavia
Sarandí
Avellaneda
Villa C. Colón
Gerli
Monte Chingolo
Temperley
José Mármol
Almirante Brown
Burzaco
Ministro Rivadavia
La Boca
San Telmo
Barracas
Villa Alsina
Lanús
Remedios de Escalada
Banfield
Lomas de Zamora
Santa Catalina
Turdera
Llavallol
Villa Hogar Alemán
Monte Grande
Esteban Echeverría
Retiro
Once
Almagro
Diamante
Caraza
Igr. Budge
La Salada
Luis Guillón
Aeroparque de la Ciudad de Buenos Aires
Palermo
Caballito
Flores
Floresta
Nueva Pompeya
Villa Lugano
Villa Madero
Aeropuerto Ezeiza
Ezeiza
Olivos
I. Anchorena
Las Barrancas
Núñez
Belgrano
General Urquiza
La Paternal
Villa Devoto
Versailles
Liniers
Nueva Chicago
DISTRITO FEDERAL
BUENOS AIRES
Ciudad General Belgrano
Laferrere
San Fernando
Martínez
Vicente López
Florida
Saavedra
Villa Ballester
Villa Pueyrredón
General San Martín
San Andrés
Villa Bosch
Lourdes
Saenz Peña
Ciudadela
San Justo
Alto Bonzi
Tablada
Beccar
San Isidro
Boulogne
Villa Adelina
Munro
Carapachay
Santos Lugares
Caseros
Villa D.F. Sarmiento
Ramos Mejía
Villa Luzuriaga
M. J. Haedo
Isidro Casanova
Rafael Castillo
González Catán
Victoria
Acassuso
La Lucila
Lujan
Tigre
Las Conchas
Carupa
General Pacheco
Don Torcuato
El Talar de Pacheco
Los Polvorines
Villa de Mayo
Campo de Mayo
Billinghurst
El Palomar
Hurlingham
Villa Basso
Morón
Ituzaingó
Villa Anza
Castelar
San Antonio de Padua
Libertad
Pontevedra
Benavidez
Grand Bourg
Igr. P. Nogues
José C. Paz
General Sarmiento
San Miguel
Bella Vista
Muniz
Villa Leloir
Villa Reichembach
Villa Leon
Merlo
Villa Rosa
Del Viso
Tortuguitas
Villa Altube
Villa Iglesias
Piñero
Paso del Rey
Moreno
Mariano Acosta
Marcos Paz
Presidente Derqui
Pinazo
Toro
Francisco Alvarez
La Reja
20 de Junio
A. Morales
A. La Horqueta

West from Greenwich

COPYRIGHT. GEORGE PHILIP AND SON. LTD.

# INDEX TO CITY MAPS

Place names in this index are given a letter-figure reference to a map square made from the lines of latitude and longitude that appear on the city maps. The full geographic reference is provided in the border of each map.
The letter-figure reference will take the reader directly to the square, and by using the geographical coordinates the place sought can be pinpointed within that square.

The location given is the city or suburban center, and not necessarily the name. Lakes, airports and other features having a large area are given coordinates for their centers. Rivers that enter the sea, lake or main stream within the map area have the coordinates of that entrance.

If the river flows through the map, then the coordinates are given to the name. The same rule applies to canals. A river carries the symbol → after its name.

As an aid to identification, every place name is followed by the city map name or its abbreviation; for example, Oakland in California will be followed by S.F. Some of the place names so described will be completely independent of the main city.

An explanation of the alphabetical order rules is to be found at the beginning of the World Map Index.

## ABBREVIATIONS USED IN THE INDEX

*Ath.* – Athinai (Athens)
*B.* – Baie, Bahía, Bay, Bucht
*B.A.* – Buenos Aires
*Bagd.* – Baghdad
*Balt.* – Baltimore
*Bangk.* – Bangkok
*Barc.* – Barcelona
*Beij.* – Beijing (Peking)
*Berl.* – Berlin
*Bomb.* – Bombay
*Bost.* – Boston
*Bud.* – Budapest
*C.* – Cabo, Cap, Cape
*Calc.* – Calcutta
*Car.* – Caracas
*Chan.* – Channel
*Chic.* – Chicago
*Cr.* – Creek
*E.* – East
*El Qâ.* – El Qâhira (Cairo)
*G.* – Golfe, Golfo, Gulf, Guba
*Gzh.* – Guangzhou (Canton)
*H.K.* – Hong Kong
*Hbg.* – Hamburg
*Hd.* – Head
*Hels.* – Helsinki
*Hts.* – Heights
*I.(s)* – Île, Ilha, Insel, Isla, Island, Isle
*Ist.* – Istanbul
*J.* – Jabal, Jebel
*Jak.* – Jakarta
*Jobg.* – Johannesburg
*K.* – Kap, Kapp
*Kar.* – Karachi
*Kep.* – Kepulauan
*Købn.* – København (Copenhagen)
*L.* – Lac, Lacul, Lago, Lagoa, Lake
*L.A.* – Los Angeles
*La Hab.* – La Habana (Havana)
*Lisb.* – Lisboa (Lisbon)
*Lon.* – London
*Mdrd.* – Madrid
*Melb.* – Melbourne
*Méx.* – México
*Mil.* – Milano
*Mos.* – Moskva (Moscow)
*Mt. (e)* – Mont, Monte, Monti, Montaña, Mountain
*Mtrl.* – Montréal
*Mün.* – München (Munich)
*N.* – Nord, Norte, North, Northern, Nouveau
*Nápl.* – Nápoli (Naples)
*N.Y.* – New York City
*Os.* – Ostrov
*Oz.* – Ozero
*Pen.* – Peninsula, Peninsule
*Phil.* – Philadelphia
*Pk.* – Park, Peak
*Pra.* – Praha (Prague)
*Pt.* – Point
*Pta.* – Ponta, Punta
*Pte.* – Pointe
*R.* – Rio, River
*Ra. (s)* – Range(s)
*Res.* – Reserve, Reservoir
*Rio J.* – Rio de Janeiro
*S.* – San, South
*S.F.* – San Francisco
*S. Pau.* – São Paulo
*Sa.* – Serra, Sierra
*Sd.* – Sound
*Shang.* – Shanghai
*Sing.* – Singapore
*St.* – Saint, Sankt, Sint
*St-Pet.* – St-Peterburg
*Sta.* – Santa, Station
*Ste.* – Sainte
*Stgo.* – Santiago
*Sto.* – Santo
*Stock.* – Stockholm
*Str.* – Strait, Stretto
*Syd.* – Sydney
*Tehr.* – Tehran
*Tianj.* – Tianjin (Tientsin)
*Tori.* – Torino (Turin)
*Trto.* – Toronto
*W.* – West
*Wash.* – Washington
*Wsaw.* – Warszawa (Warsaw)

## A


Aalām, *Bagd.* 17 F8 33 19N 44 23 E
Abada, *Calc.* 16 E5 22 32N 88 13 E
Abbadia di Stura, *Tori.* 9 B3 45 7N 7 44 E
Abbey Wood, *Lon.* 4 C5 51 29N 0 7 E
Abbots Langley, *Lon.* 4 A2 51 42N 0 25W
Abeno, *Ōsaka* 12 C4 34 38N 135 31 E
Aberdeen, *H.K.* 12 E6 22 14N 114 8 E
Abfanggraben, *Mün.* 7 F11 48 10N 11 41 E
Abington, *Phil.* 24 A4 40 7N 75 7W
Ablon-sur-Seine, *Paris* 5 C4 48 43N 2 25 E
Abord à Plouffe, *Mtrl.* 20 A3 43 32N 73 43W
Abramtsevo, *Mos.* 11 E10 55 49N 37 49 E
Abridge, *Lon.* 4 B5 51 38N 0 7 E
Abû en Numrus, *El Qâ.* 18 D5 29 57N 31 12 E
Acassuso, *B.A.* 32 A3 34 29 S 58 30W
Accord, *Bost.* 21 D4 42 10N 70 52W
Accord Pond, *Bost.* 21 D4 42 10N 70 53W
Accotink Cr. →, *Wash.* 25 D6 38 51N 77 15W
Acerra, *Nápl.* 9 H13 40 56N 14 22 E
Acha San, *Sŏul* 12 G8 37 33N 127 5 E
Acheres, *Paris* 5 B2 48 57N 2 3 E
Acília, *Rome* 9 G9 41 47N 12 21 E
Aclimação, *S. Pau.* 31 E6 23 34 S 46 37W
Acostia →, *Wash.* 25 D8 38 51N 77 1W
Acton, *Lon.* 4 B3 51 30N 0 16W
Açúcar, Pão de, *Rio J.* 31 B3 22 56 S 43 9W
Ada Beja, *Lisb.* 8 F7 38 47N 9 13W
Adabe Cr. →, *S.F.* 27 D4 37 26N 122 6W
Adachi, *Tōkyō* 13 B2 35 49N 139 34 E
Adachi-Ku, *Tōkyō* 13 B3 35 47N 139 47 E
Adams Nat. Hist. Site, *Bost.* 21 D4 42 15N 71 0W
Addington, *Lon.* 4 C4 51 21N 0 1W
Addiscombe, *Lon.* 4 C4 51 22N 0 4W
Adel, *Bagd.* 17 E7 33 20N 44 17 E
Adelphi, *Wash.* 25 C8 39 0N 76 58W
Aderklaa, *Wien* 10 G11 48 17N 16 32 E
Admiralteyskaya Storona, *St-Pet.* 11 B4 59 56N 30 20 E
Áffori, *Mil.* 9 D6 45 31N 9 10 E
Aflandshage, *Købn.* 2 E10 55 33N 12 35 E
Afragola, *Nápl.* 9 H12 40 55N 14 18 E
Aganpur, *Delhi* 16 B3 28 33N 77 20 E
Agboju, *Lagos* 18 B1 6 27N 7 16 E
Agboyi Cr. →, *Lagos* 18 A2 6 33N 7 24 E
Ågerup, *Købn.* 2 D8 55 43N 12 19 E
Ågesta, *Stock.* 3 E11 59 12N 18 6 E
Agincourt, *Trto.* 20 D9 43 47N 79 16W
Agnano Terme, *Nápl.* 9 J12 40 49N 14 10 E
Agora, *Ath.* 8 J11 37 57N 23 43 E
Agra Canal, *Delhi* 16 B2 28 33N 77 17 E
Agricola Oriental, *Méx.* 29 B3 19 23N 99 4W
Agro Romano, *Rome* 9 F8 41 56N 12 17 E
Agua Branca, *S. Pau.* 31 E5 23 31 S 46 40W
Agua Espraiada →, *S. Pau.* 31 E6 23 36 S 46 41W
Água Rasa, *S. Pau.* 31 E6 23 32 S 46 33W
Agualva-Cacem, *Lisb.* 8 F7 38 46N 9 15W
Agustino, Cerro El, *Lima* 30 G8 12 3 S 76 59W
Ahrensfelde, *Berl.* 7 A4 52 34N 13 34 E
Ahuntsic, *Mtrl.* 20 A3 43 32N 73 41W
Ai →, *Ōsaka* 12 B4 34 46N 135 35 E
Aigremont, *Paris* 5 B2 48 54N 2 1 E
Airport West, *Melb.* 19 E6 37 42 S 144 52 E
Aiyaleo, *Ath.* 8 J11 37 59N 23 40 E
Ajegunle, *Lagos* 18 B2 6 26N 7 20 E
Aji, *Ōsaka* 12 B3 34 40N 135 27 E
Ajuda, *Lisb.* 8 F7 38 42N 9 12W
Ajusco, Parque Nacional de, *Méx.* 29 C2 19 12N 99 15W
Akabane, *Tōkyō* 13 B3 35 46N 139 42 E
Akalla, *Stock.* 3 D10 59 24N 17 55 E
Akasaka, *Tōkyō* 13 B3 35 40N 139 43 E
Akbarābād, *Tehr.* 17 C5 35 40N 51 20 E
Åkersberga Saltsjobad, *Stock.* 3 D12 59 26N 18 15 E
Akerselva →, *Oslo* 2 B4 59 54N 10 45 E
Akrópolis, *Ath.* 8 J11 37 57N 23 43 E
Akuwa, *Tōkyō* 13 D2 35 26N 139 30 E
Al 'Azamiyah, *Bagd.* 17 E8 33 22N 44 22 E
Alaguntan, *Lagos* 18 B2 6 25N 7 29 E
Alamar, *La Hab.* 30 B3 23 9N 82 16W
Alameda, *S.F.* 27 B3 37 46N 122 15W
Alameda Memorial State Beach Park, *S.F.* 27 B3 37 45N 122 16W
Alamo, *S.F.* 27 A4 37 51N 122 2W
Albany, *S.F.* 27 A3 37 53N 122 17W
Alberante, *Jobg.* 18 F9 26 16 S 28 7 E
Albern, *Wien* 10 H10 48 9N 16 29 E
Albert Hall, *Lon.* 4 C3 51 29N 0 10W
Albert Park, *Melb.* 19 F6 37 51 S 144 58 E
Albertfalva, *Bud.* 10 K13 47 26N 19 3 E
Alberton, *Jobg.* 18 F9 26 15 S 28 7 E
Albertslund, *Købn.* 2 E9 55 39N 12 21 E
Albertson, *N.Y.* 23 C7 40 46N 73 38W
Albertville, *Jobg.* 18 E8 26 9 S 27 58 E
Albion, *Phil.* 24 C5 39 46N 74 57W
Alby, *Stock.* 3 E10 59 14N 17 51 E
Albysjön, *Stock.* 3 E10 59 14N 17 52 E
Alcantara, *Lisb.* 8 F7 38 43N 9 10W
Alcatraz I., *S.F.* 27 B2 37 49N 122 25W
Alcochete, *Lisb.* 8 F9 38 45N 8 58W
Alcorcón, *Mdrd.* 8 B2 40 20N 3 48W
Aldan, *Phil.* 24 B3 39 55N 75 17W
Aldela de Carapiculba, *S. Pau.* 31 E5 23 34 S 46 49W
Aldene, *N.Y.* 22 D3 40 39N 74 17W
Aldenrade, *Ruhr* 6 A2 51 31N 6 44 E
Alder Planetarium, *Chic.* 26 B3 41 5N 87 36W
Aldershof, *Berl.* 7 B4 52 26N 13 33 E
Aldo Bonzi, *B.A.* 32 C3 34 42 S 58 31W
Aleksandrovskoye, *St-Pet.* 11 B4 59 51N 30 20 E
Aleksandrów, *Wsaw.* 10 E8 52 10N 21 14 E
Alexander Nevsky Abbey, *St-Pet.* 11 B4 59 54N 30 23 E
Alexandra, *Jobg.* 18 E9 26 6 S 28 5 E
Alexandra, *Sing.* 15 G7 1 17N 103 49 E
Alexandria, *Wash.* 25 E7 38 49N 77 5W
Alfortville, *Paris* 5 C4 48 48N 2 24 E
Algés, *Lisb.* 8 F7 38 42N 9 13W
Älgo, *Stock.* 3 E13 59 16N 18 20 E
Algodonal, *Car.* 30 E5 10 29N 66 58W
Alhambra, *L.A.* 28 B4 34 5N 118 7W
Alhos Vedros, *Lisb.* 8 G8 38 39N 9 1W
Alibey →, *Ist.* 17 A2 41 3N 28 56 E
Alibeyköy, *Ist.* 17 A2 41 4N 28 56 E
Alima, *Manila* 15 E3 14 27N 120 55 E
Alimos, *Ath.* 8 J11 37 52N 23 43 E
Aliperti, *Nápl.* 9 H13 40 53N 14 28 E
Alipore, *Calc.* 16 E6 22 31N 88 20 E
Alipur, *Calc.* 16 D5 22 43N 88 12 E
Aliso Canyon Wash →, *L.A.* 28 A1 34 15N 118 31W
Allach, *Mün.* 7 F9 48 11N 11 27 E
Allambie Heights, *Syd.* 19 A4 33 46 S 151 15 E
Allendale, *N.Y.* 22 A4 41 1N 74 9W
Allengrove, *Jobg.* 18 E10 26 5 S 28 14 E
Allentown, *N.Y.* 23 C6 40 47N 73 43W
Allermohe, *Hbg.* 7 E8 53 29N 10 7 E
Allerton, Pt., *Bost.* 21 D4 42 18N 70 52W
Allston, *Bost.* 21 C3 42 21N 71 7W
Alluets, Forêt des, *Paris* 5 B1 48 56N 1 55 E
Almada, *Lisb.* 8 F8 38 41N 9 8W
Almagro, *B.A.* 32 B4 34 38 S 58 24W
Almanara, *Mdrd.* 8 B2 40 28N 3 41W
Almaza Airport, *El Qâ.* 18 C6 30 5N 31 21 E
Almazovo, *Mos.* 11 D12 55 50N 38 3 E
Almendares, *La Hab.* 30 B2 23 6N 82 23W
Almendares →, *La Hab.* 30 B2 23 7N 82 24W
Almirante Brown, *B.A.* 32 C4 34 48 S 58 23W
Almirante G. Brown, Parques, *B.A.* 32 C4 34 40 S 58 28W
Almonesson, *Phil.* 24 C4 39 48N 75 5W
Almonte, *S.F.* 27 A1 37 53N 122 31W
Alnabru, *Oslo* 2 B5 59 55N 10 50 E
Alnsjøen, *Oslo* 2 B5 59 57N 10 51 E
Alperton, *Lon.* 4 B3 51 32N 0 17W
Alpignano, *Tori.* 9 B1 45 6N 7 31 E
Alpine, *N.Y.* 22 B5 40 57N 73 57W
Alpur, *Calc.* 16 C6 22 50N 88 23 E
Alrode, *Jobg.* 18 F9 26 17 S 28 7 E
Alsergrund, *Wien* 10 G10 48 13N 16 21 E
Alsfeld, *Ruhr* 6 A3 51 31N 6 50 E
Alsip, *Chic.* 26 C2 41 40N 87 44W
Alstaden, *Ruhr* 6 B2 51 28N 6 49 E
Ålsten, *Stock.* 3 E10 59 19N 17 57 E
Alster →, *Hbg.* 7 D8 53 38N 10 4 E
Alsterdorf, *Hbg.* 7 D8 53 36N 10 0 E
Älta, *Stock.* 3 E12 59 15N 18 11 E
Altadena, *L.A.* 28 A4 34 11N 118 8W
Alte-Donau →, *Wien* 10 G10 48 14N 16 25 E
Alte Süderelbe, *Hbg.* 7 D7 53 31N 9 52 E
Alten-Essen, *Ruhr* 6 B4 51 29N 7 1 E
Altendorf, *Ruhr* 6 B3 51 27N 6 58 E
Altenhagen, *Ruhr* 6 B6 51 22N 7 27 E
Altenvoerde, *Ruhr* 6 C6 51 18N 7 22 E
Altenwerder, *Hbg.* 7 D7 53 30N 9 55 E
Alter Finkenkrug, *Berl.* 7 A1 52 35N 13 3 E
Altglenicke, *Berl.* 7 B4 52 25N 13 32 E
Altlandsberg Nord, *Berl.* 7 A5 52 34N 13 43 E
Altmannsdorf, *Wien* 10 H9 48 9N 16 18 E
Alto, *S.F.* 27 A1 37 54N 122 30W
Alto da Boa Vista, *S. Pau.* 31 E5 23 38 S 46 42W
Alto da Lapa, *S. Pau.* 31 E5 23 31 S 46 43W
Alto da Moóca, *S. Pau.* 31 E6 23 34 S 46 33W
Alto do Pina, *Lisb.* 8 F8 38 44N 9 7W
Altona, *Hbg.* 7 D7 53 32N 9 56 E
Altona, *Melb.* 19 F5 37 51 S 144 49 E
Altona B., *Melb.* 19 F6 37 52 S 144 51 E
Altona North, *Melb.* 19 F5 37 50 S 144 49 E
Altona Sports Park, *Melb.* 19 F6 37 51 S 144 51 E
Altstadt, *Hbg.* 7 D8 53 32N 10 0 E
Alvarado, *S.F.* 27 C4 37 35N 122 4W
Alvik, *Stock.* 3 E10 59 19N 17 58 E
Älvsjo, *Stock.* 3 E11 59 16N 18 0 E
Älvvik, *Stock.* 3 D12 59 21N 18 15 E
Am Hasenbergl, *Mün.* 7 F10 48 12N 11 33 E
Am Steinhof, *Wien* 10 G9 48 12N 16 17 E
Am Wald, *Mün.* 7 G10 48 3N 11 36 E
Ama Keng, *Sing.* 15 F7 1 23N 103 41 E
Amadora, *Lisb.* 8 F7 38 45N 9 13W
Amagasaki, *Ōsaka* 12 B3 34 42N 135 23 E
Amager, *Købn.* 2 E10 55 36N 12 35 E
Amāl Qādisiya, *Bagd.* 17 F8 33 16N 44 20 E
Amalienborg Slott, *Købn.* 2 D10 55 41N 12 35 E
Amata, *Mil.* 9 D5 45 34N 9 8 E
Ambler, *Phil.* 24 A3 40 9N 75 13W
Ambrose Channel, *N.Y.* 22 D5 40 31N 73 50W
Ameixoeira, *Lisb.* 8 F8 38 46N 9 8W
Ames Hill, *Bost.* 21 B2 42 38N 71 13W
Amin, *Bagd.* 17 F8 33 19N 44 29 E
Aminyevo, *Mos.* 11 E8 55 41N 37 25 E
Amirābād, *Tehr.* 17 C5 35 43N 51 24 E
Amityville, *N.Y.* 23 C8 40 40N 73 23W
Ammersbek →, *Hbg.* 7 C8 53 42N 10 7 E
Amora, *Lisb.* 8 G8 38 37N 9 6W
Amoreira, *Lisb.* 8 F7 38 48N 9 11W
Amorosa, *Jobg.* 18 E8 26 5 S 27 52 E
Ampelokipi, *Ath.* 8 J11 37 58N 23 47 E
Amper →, *Mün.* 7 F9 48 14N 11 25 E
Amselhain, *Berl.* 7 A5 52 38N 13 43 E
Amuwo, *Lagos* 18 B1 6 28N 7 18 E
Anacostia, *Wash.* 25 D8 38 51N 76 59W
Anacostia River Park, *Wash.* 25 D8 38 54N 76 57W
Anadoluhisari, *Ist.* 17 A3 41 4N 29 3 E
Anandanagar, *Calc.* 16 C5 22 51N 88 16 E
Anchieta, *Rio J.* 31 A1 22 48 S 43 21W
Ancol, *Jak.* 15 H9 6 7 S 106 49 E
Andalus, *Bagd.* 17 F7 33 19N 44 18 E
Andalusia, *Phil.* 24 A5 40 4N 74 58W
Andarai, *Rio J.* 31 B2 22 56 S 43 14W
Andeli Beijie, *Beij.* 14 B3 39 57N 116 21 E
Anderson Cr. →, *Melb.* 19 E8 37 44 S 145 12 E
Andilly, *Paris* 5 A3 49 0N 2 17 E
Andingmen, *Beij.* 14 B3 39 55N 116 23 E
Andover, *Bost.* 21 B3 42 39N 71 7W
Andrésy, *Paris* 5 B2 48 58N 2 3 E
Andrews Air Force Base, *Wash.* 25 E8 38 48N 76 52W
Ang Mo Kio, *Sing.* 15 F8 1 22N 103 50 E
Ängby, *Stock.* 3 D10 59 20N 17 53 E
Angel I., *S.F.* 27 A2 37 52N 122 25W
Angel Island State Park, *S.F.* 27 A2 37 52N 122 25W
Angerbruch →, *Ruhr* 6 C3 51 18N 6 59 E
Angerhausen, *Ruhr* 6 B2 51 22N 6 43 E
Angermund, *Ruhr* 6 C2 51 19N 6 46 E
Angke, Kali →, *Jak.* 15 H9 6 6 S 106 46 E
Angono, *Manila* 15 D4 14 31N 121 8 E
Angyalföld, *Bud.* 10 J13 47 32N 19 5 E
Angyō, *Tōkyō* 13 A3 35 50N 139 45 E
Aniene →, *Rome* 9 F10 41 56N 12 35 E
Anik, *Bomb.* 16 G8 19 1N 72 53 E
Anin, *Wsaw.* 10 E7 52 13N 21 9 E
Anjou, *Mtrl.* 20 A4 43 36N 73 33W
Annadale, *N.Y.* 22 D3 40 32N 74 10W
Annalee Heights, *Wash.* 25 D6 38 51N 77 10W
Annandale, *Wash.* 25 D6 38 50N 77 11W
Annen, *Ruhr* 6 B6 51 27N 7 22 E
Annet-sur-Marne, *Paris* 5 B6 48 55N 2 43 E
Anthony Chabot Regional Park, *S.F.* 27 B4 37 46N 122 7W
Antignano, *Nápl.* 9 H12 40 51N 14 13 E
Antimano, *Car.* 30 E5 10 27N 66 59W
Antipolo, *Manila* 15 D5 14 35N 121 10 E
Antony, *Paris* 5 C3 48 44N 2 17 E
Antwerp, *Jobg.* 18 E9 26 5 S 28 9 E
Aoyama, *Tōkyō* 13 C3 35 39N 139 42 E
Ap Lei Chau, *H.K.* 12 E5 22 14N 114 9 E
Apapa, *Lagos* 18 B2 6 26N 7 21 E
Apelacão, *Lisb.* 8 F8 38 48N 9 7W
Apoquindo, *Stgo* 30 J11 33 23 S 70 30W
Apshawa, *N.Y.* 22 A2 41 1N 74 22W
Apterkarskiy Os., *St-Pet.* 11 B4 59 57N 30 20 E
Aquincum, *Bud.* 10 J13 47 33N 19 3 E
Ara →, *Tōkyō* 13 B4 35 41N 139 50 E
Arakawa-Ku, *Tōkyō* 13 B3 35 44N 139 48 E
Arakpur, *Delhi* 16 B2 28 35N 77 11 E
Arany-hegyi-patak →, *Bud.* 10 J13 47 34N 19 4 E
Aravaca, *Mdrd.* 8 B2 40 27N 3 47W
Arbataash, *Bagd.* 17 E7 33 20N 44 19 E
Arbutus, *Balt.* 25 B2 39 15N 76 41W
Arc de Triomphe, *Paris* 5 B3 48 52N 2 17 E
Arcadia, *L.A.* 28 B4 34 7N 118 1W
Arceuil, *Paris* 5 C3 48 48N 2 19 E
Arden, *Phil.* 24 C2 39 48N 75 29W
Ardey Gebirge, *Ruhr* 6 B6 51 24N 7 23 E
Ardmore, *Phil.* 24 A3 40 0N 75 17W
Ardsley, *N.Y.* 23 A5 41 0N 73 50W
Arese, *Mil.* 9 D5 45 32N 9 4 E
Arganzuela, *Mdrd.* 8 B2 40 23N 3 42W
Argenteuil, *Paris* 5 B3 48 56N 2 15 E
Argonne Forest, *Chic.* 26 C1 41 42N 87 53W
Ariadana, *Calc.* 16 E6 22 39N 88 22 E
Aricanduva →, *S. Pau.* 31 E6 23 31 S 46 33W
Arida, *Lagos* 18 A1 6 33N 7 16 E
Arima, *Ōsaka* 12 B2 34 47N 135 15 E
Arima, *Tōkyō* 13 C2 35 33N 139 33 E
Arima →, *Ōsaka* 12 A2 34 50N 135 14 E
Arkhangelyskoye, *Mos.* 11 E7 55 47N 37 17 E
Arkley, *Lon.* 4 B3 51 38N 0 13W
Arlington, *Bost.* 21 C2 42 24N 71 10W
Arlington, *Wash.* 25 D7 38 53N 77 7W
Arlington Heights, *Bost.* 21 C2 42 25N 71 10W
Arlington Heights, *Chic.* 26 A1 42 5N 87 55W
Arlington Nat. Cemetery, *Wash.* 25 D7 38 52N 77 4W
Armação, *Rio J.* 31 B3 22 52 S 43 6W
Armadale, *Melb.* 19 F7 37 51 S 145 0 E
Armadale, *Trto.* 20 C9 43 50N 79 14W
Armainvilliers, Forêt d', *Paris* 5 C6 48 46N 2 42 E
Armour Heights, *Trto.* 20 D8 43 45N 79 25W
Arncliffe, *Syd.* 19 B3 33 56 S 151 8 E
Arnold Arboretum, *Bost.* 21 D3 42 18N 71 8W
Arnouville-les-Gonesse, *Paris* 5 B4 48 59N 2 24 E
Arrentela, *Lisb.* 8 G8 38 37N 9 6W
Arrone →, *Rome* 9 F8 41 55N 12 16 E
Arroyo Arenas, *La Hab.* 30 B2 23 3N 82 27W
Arroyo Cr. →, *S.F.* 26 D2 37 27N 122 25W
Arroyo Naranjo, *La Hab.* 30 B2 23 2N 82 21W
Årsta, *Stock.* 3 E11 59 17N 18 3 E
Artesia, *L.A.* 28 C4 33 51N 118 4W
Arthur Alvim, *S. Pau.* 31 E7 23 32 S 46 28W
Arthur Kill →, *N.Y.* 22 D3 40 32N 74 15W
Artigas, *Car.* 30 E5 10 29N 66 56W
Arundel Gardens, *Balt.* 25 B3 39 12N 76 37W
Arundel Village, *Balt.* 25 B3 39 13N 76 35W
Aryiróupolis, *Ath.* 8 J11 37 52N 23 44 E
Arzano, *Nápl.* 9 H12 40 54N 14 16 E
Asagaya, *Tōkyō* 13 B2 35 41N 139 38 E
Asahi, *Ōsaka* 12 B4 34 43N 135 31 E
Asaka, *Tōkyō* 13 B2 35 47N 139 35 E
Asakusa, *Tōkyō* 13 B3 35 42N 139 47 E
Asalatpur, *Delhi* 16 B1 28 37N 77 4 E
Asati, *Calc.* 16 F5 22 28N 88 15 E
Aschheim, *Mün.* 7 F11 48 10N 11 42 E
Ascot Vale, *Melb.* 19 E6 37 46 S 144 53 E
Aserradero, *Méx.* 29 D2 19 10N 99 16W
Asharoken, *N.Y.* 23 B8 40 55N 73 21W
Ashburn, *Chic.* 26 C2 41 45N 87 43W
Ashburton, *Melb.* 19 F7 37 51 S 145 4 E

36 Chomedey


Chomedey, *Mrtl.* 20 A3 43 32N 73 45W
Chong Nonsi, Khlong →, *Bangk.* 15 B2 13 42N 100 32 E
Chong Pang, *Sing.* 15 F7 1 26N 103 49 E
Chongwen, *Beij.* 14 B3 39 52N 116 23 E
Chongwenmen, *Beij.* 14 B3 39 52N 116 22 E
Chorleywood, *Lon.* 4 B2 51 39N 0 29W
Chornaya →, *Mos.* 11 E12 55 41N 38 0 E
Chorrillos, *Lima* 30 H8 12 10 S 77 1W
Christianshavn, *Købn.* 2 D10 55 40N 12 35 E
Chrome, *N.Y.* 22 D3 40 34N 74 13W
Chrzanów, *Wsaw.* 10 E6 52 13N 20 53 E
Chuen Lung, *H.K.* 12 D5 22 23N 114 6 E
Chuk Kok, *H.K.* 12 D6 22 20N 114 15 E
Chulalongkon Univ., *Bangk.* 15 B2 13 44N 100 31 E
Chullora, *Syd.* 19 B3 33 54 S 151 5 E
Chunchura, *Calc.* 16 C6 22 53N 88 23 E
Chuō-Ku, *Tōkyō* 13 B3 35 40N 139 46 E
Church End, *Lon.* 4 B3 51 35N 0 11W
Chvaly, *Pra.* 10 B3 50 6N 14 35 E
Chye Kay, *Sing.* 15 F7 1 25N 103 49 E
Ciampino, *Rome* 9 G10 41 47N 12 36 E
Ciampino, Aeroporto di, *Rome* 9 G10 41 47N 12 35 E
Cicero, *Chic.* 26 B2 41 51N 87 44W
Cidade, I. da, *Rio J.* 31 B2 22 51 S 43 13W
Cidade de Deus, *S. Pau.* 31 E5 23 33 S 46 45W
Cidade Ipava, *S. Pau.* 31 F5 23 42 S 46 45W
Cidade Lider, *S. Pau.* 31 E7 23 33 S 46 27W
Cidade São Matheus, *S. Pau.* 31 E7 23 35 S 46 29W
Cidena, Kali →, *Jak.* 15 H9 6 9 S 106 48 E
Cilandak, *Jak.* 15 J9 6 17 S 106 47 E
Cilincing, *Jak.* 15 H10 6 6 S 106 54 E
Ciliwung →, *Jak.* 15 J10 6 6 S 106 47 E
Čimice, *Pra.* 10 B2 50 8N 14 25 E
Cinderella, *Jobg.* 18 F10 26 14 S 28 15 E
Cinderella Dam, *Jobg.* 18 F10 26 14 S 28 14 E
Cinecittà, *Rome* 9 F10 41 51N 12 34 E
Cinisello Bálsamo, *Mil.* 9 D6 45 33N 9 13 E
Cinkota, *Bud.* 10 J14 47 31N 19 14 E
Cinnaminson, *Phil.* 24 B5 39 59N 74 59W
Cipete, *Jak.* 15 J9 6 15 S 106 47 E
Cipresso, *Tori.* 9 B3 45 2N 7 48 E
Cisliano, *Mil.* 9 E4 45 26N 8 59 E
Citta degli Studi, *Mil.* 9 E6 45 28N 9 12 E
Città del Vaticano, *Rome* 9 F9 41 54N 12 26 E
City I., *N.Y.* 23 B6 40 50N 73 47W
Ciudad Azteca, *Méx.* 29 A3 19 32N 99 1W
Ciudad Fin de Semana, *Mdrd.* 8 B3 40 26N 3 34W
Ciudad General Belgrano, *B.A.* 32 C3 34 43 S 58 33W
Ciudad Libertad, *La Hab.* 30 B2 23 5N 82 25W
Ciudad Lineál, *Mdrd.* 8 B3 40 26N 3 38W
Ciudad López Mateos, *Méx.* 29 A2 19 33N 99 16W
Ciudad Satélite, *Méx.* 29 A2 19 30N 99 13W
Ciudad Universitaria, *Méx.* 29 C2 19 9N 99 10W
Ciudadela, *B.A.* 32 B3 34 38 S 58 32W
Ciudadela, Parque de la, *Barc.* 8 D6 41 23N 2 11 E
Clairefontaine, *Paris* 5 D1 48 36N 1 54 E
Clamart, *Paris* 5 C3 48 48N 2 15 E
Clapham, *Lon.* 4 C4 51 27N 0 8W
Clapton, *Lon.* 4 B4 51 33N 0 3W
Clark, *N.Y.* 22 D3 40 38N 74 18W
Clarksboro, *Phil.* 24 C3 39 48N 75 13W
Claye-Souilly, *Paris* 5 B6 48 56N 2 41 E
Claygate, *Lon.* 4 C3 51 21N 0 19W
Clayhall, *Lon.* 4 B5 51 35N 0 3 E
Clayhill, *Lon.* 4 A4 51 40N 0 5W
Claymont, *Phil.* 24 C2 39 48N 75 27W
Claypole, *B.A.* 32 C4 34 48 S 58 20W
Clayton, *Melb.* 19 F7 37 55 S 145 7 E
Clearing, *Chic.* 26 C2 41 47N 87 45W
Clearwater, *L.A.* 28 C3 33 52N 118 10W
Clement, *Sing.* 15 G7 1 18N 103 46 E
Clementon, *Phil.* 24 C5 39 48N 74 59W
Clichy, *Paris* 5 B3 48 54N 2 18 E
Clichy-sous-Bois, *Paris* 5 B5 48 54N 2 32 E
Cliffside, *Trto.* 20 D9 43 44N 79 14W
Cliffside Park, *N.Y.* 22 C5 40 49N 73 59W
Clifton, *Bost.* 21 C4 42 29N 70 52W
Clifton, *Kar.* 17 H11 24 48N 67 1 E
Clifton, *N.Y.* 22 D4 40 37N 74 4W
Clifton, *N.Y.* 22 B4 40 51N 74 7W
Clifton, L., *Balt.* 25 B3 39 19N 76 35W
Clifton Heights, *Phil.* 24 B3 39 55N 75 17W
Clifton Park, *Balt.* 25 A3 39 20N 76 35W
Clontarf, *Syd.* 19 A4 33 48 S 151 16 E
Closter, *N.Y.* 22 B5 40 58N 73 57W
Clovelly, *Syd.* 19 B4 33 54 S 151 15 E
Cobbin's Brook →, *Lon.* 4 A5 51 40N 0 0 E
Cobbs Cr. →, *Phil.* 24 B3 39 58N 75 18W
Cobham, *Lon.* 4 D2 51 19N 0 23W
Cobras, I. das, *Rio J.* 31 B3 22 53 S 43 9W
Coburg, *Melb.* 19 E6 37 44 S 144 56 E
Cochecito, *Car.* 30 E5 10 26N 66 55W
Cochichewick, L., *Bost.* 21 A3 42 42N 71 5W
Cochituate, *Bost.* 21 C1 42 20N 71 21W
Cochituate, L., *Bost.* 21 D1 42 16N 71 21W
Cockfosters, *Lon.* 4 B4 51 39N 0 8W
Cocota, *Rio J.* 31 A2 22 48 S 43 11W
Coelho da Rocha, *Rio J.* 31 A1 22 46 S 43 21W
Cœuilly, *Paris* 5 C5 48 48N 2 32 E
Coignières, *Paris* 5 C1 48 44N 1 55 E
Coina, *Lisb.* 8 G8 38 39N 9 5W
Cojimar, *La Hab.* 30 B3 23 9N 82 17W
Cojimar →, *La Hab.* 30 B3 23 9N 82 17W
Cojimar, Boca de, *La Hab.* 30 A3 23 10N 82 17W
Coker, *Lagos* 18 B2 6 28N 7 20 E
Colaba, *Bomb.* 16 H7 18 53N 72 48 E
Colaba Pt., *Bomb.* 16 H7 18 53N 72 48 E
Cold Spring Harbor, *N.Y.* 23 B8 40 52N 73 27W
Cold Spring Terrace, *N.Y.* 23 C8 40 49N 73 25W
Coleraine, *Trto.* 20 D6 43 49N 79 40W
Colindale, *Lon.* 4 B3 51 35N 0 15W
Collazo, *La Hab.* 30 B2 23 2N 82 21W
College Park, *Wash.* 25 D8 38 59N 76 55W
College Point, *N.Y.* 23 C5 40 47N 73 50W
Collégien, *Paris* 5 B6 48 50N 2 41 E
Collegno, *Tori.* 9 B2 45 5N 7 34 E
Collier Row, *Lon.* 4 B5 51 35N 0 9 E
Colliers Wood, *Lon.* 4 C3 51 24N 0 10W
Collingdale, *Phil.* 24 B3 39 54N 75 17W
Collingswood, *Phil.* 24 B4 39 55N 75 5W
Collinsville, *Bost.* 21 A1 42 40N 71 20W
Collinsville, *N.Y.* 22 C2 40 48N 74 26W
Colma, *S.F.* 27 B2 37 40N 122 27W
Colma Cr. →, *S.F.* 27 C2 37 38N 122 23W
Colney Hatch, *Lon.* 4 B4 51 36N 0 9W
Cologno Monzese, *Mil.* 9 D6 45 31N 9 16 E
Colombes, *Paris* 5 B3 48 55N 2 15 E
Colonia, *N.Y.* 22 D3 40 35N 74 18W
Colônia, *S. Pau.* 31 E7 23 33 S 46 27W
Colonia Güell, *Barc.* 8 D5 41 21N 2 2 E
Colonia Puerta de Hierro, *Mdrd.* 8 B2 40 27N 3 43W
Colonial Manor, *Phil.* 24 B4 39 51N 75 9W
Colorado →, *Méx.* 29 B4 19 23N 89 58 E
Colosseo, *Rome* 9 F9 41 53N 12 29 E
Columbia, *Balt.* 25 B1 39 12N 76 50W
Columbia Hills, *Balt.* 25 B1 39 14N 76 51W
Columbia Univ., *N.Y.* 22 C5 40 48N 73 58W
Colwyn, *Phil.* 24 B3 39 54N 75 14W
Combault, *Paris* 5 C5 48 48N 2 37 E
Combs-la-Ville, *Paris* 5 D5 48 39N 2 33 E
Comércio, Praça do, *Lisb.* 8 F8 38 41N 9 9W
Commack, *N.Y.* 23 B9 40 50N 73 19W
Commerce, *L.A.* 28 B4 34 0N 118 9W
Como, *Syd.* 19 C3 34 0 S 151 4 E
Compans, *Paris* 5 B5 48 59N 2 39 E
Compton, *L.A.* 28 C3 33 53N 118 14W
Conceição, I. da, *Rio J.* 31 B3 22 52 S 43 6W
Concepcion, *Manila* 15 D4 14 39N 121 6 E
Conchali, *Stgo* 30 J11 33 22 S 70 39W
Concord, *Bost.* 21 C1 42 27N 71 20W
Concord, *S.F.* 27 A4 37 58N 122 3W
Concord, *Syd.* 19 B3 33 52 S 151 6 E
Concord, *Trto.* 20 D8 43 48N 79 29W
Concordville, *Phil.* 24 B1 39 53N 75 31W
Concorezzo, *Mil.* 9 D6 45 35N 9 19 E
Condécourt, *Paris* 5 A1 49 2N 1 56 E
Coney Island, *N.Y.* 22 D4 40 34N 74 0W
Conflans-Ste.-Honorine, *Paris* 5 B2 48 59N 2 5 E
Congo, *S. Pau.* 31 D5 23 27 S 46 42W
Congonhas, Aéroporto, *S. Pau.* 31 E6 23 38 S 46 39W
Conshohocken, *Phil.* 24 A3 40 4N 75 18W
Contadero, *Méx.* 29 B2 19 20N 99 17W
Convento de Valverde, *Mdrd.* 8 A2 40 30N 3 40W
Coogee, *Syd.* 19 B4 33 55 S 151 16 E
Cooksville, *Trto.* 20 E7 43 35N 79 38W
Cooper →, *Phil.* 24 B4 39 57N 75 6W
Copacabana, *Rio J.* 31 B2 22 58 S 43 11W
Copenhagen = København, *Købn.* 2 D9 55 40N 12 26 E
Copiague, *N.Y.* 23 D8 40 39N 73 23W
Coral Hills, *Wash.* 25 D8 38 51N 76 55W
Corbeil-Essonnes, *Paris* 5 D4 48 36N 2 29 E
Corbets Tey, *Lon.* 4 B6 51 32N 0 15 E
Corbiglia, *Tori.* 9 B1 45 3N 7 29 E
Corcovado, *Rio J.* 31 B2 22 57 S 43 12W
Cordon, *Paris* 5 D6 48 39N 2 41 E
Córdova, *Tori.* 9 B3 45 5N 7 48 E
Cordovil, *Rio J.* 31 A2 22 49 S 43 18W
Cormano, *Mil.* 9 D6 45 32N 9 10 E
Cormeilles-en-Parisis, *Paris* 5 B3 48 58N 2 11 E
Cornaredo, *Mil.* 9 D5 45 30N 9 1 E
Cornaya →, *St-Pet.* 11 B5 59 53N 30 35 E
Cornellá, *Barc.* 8 D5 41 21N 2 4 E
Cornwells Heights, *Phil.* 24 A5 40 4N 74 57W
Coróglio, *Nápl.* 9 J12 40 48N 14 10 E
Coronation Memorial, *Delhi* 16 A2 28 42N 77 12 E
Córsico, *Mil.* 9 E5 45 25N 9 6 E
Corte Madera, *S.F.* 27 A1 37 55N 122 30W
Corte Madera →, *S.F.* 27 A1 37 55N 122 30W
Corviale, *Rome* 9 F9 41 51N 12 25 E
Cos Cob, *N.Y.* 23 A7 41 1N 73 36W
Cossigny, *Paris* 5 C6 48 43N 2 40 E
Cossipure, *Calc.* 16 E6 22 37N 88 22 E
Cotao, *Lisb.* 8 F7 38 45N 9 17W
Côte St.-Luc, *Mtrl.* 20 B4 43 28N 73 39W
Cotorro, *La Hab.* 30 B3 23 2N 82 15W
Cotunduba, I. de, *Rio J.* 31 B3 22 57 S 43 8W
Coubert, *Paris* 5 C6 48 40N 2 41 E
Coubron, *Paris* 5 B5 48 54N 2 34 E
Coulsdon, *Lon.* 4 D4 51 18N 0 7W
Countryside, *Chic.* 26 C1 41 47N 87 52W
Courbevoie, *Paris* 5 B3 48 53N 2 14 E
Courcouronnes, *Paris* 5 D4 48 37N 2 24 E
Courdimanche, *Paris* 5 A1 49 2N 2 0 E
Courellle, *Paris* 5 C2 48 43N 2 7 E
Couros →, *S. Pau.* 31 F6 23 37 S 46 34W
Courtry, *Paris* 5 B5 48 55N 2 35 E
Cousino, Parque, *Stgo* 30 J11 33 27 S 70 40W
Cove Neck, *N.Y.* 23 B8 40 52N 73 29W
Cowley, *Lon.* 4 B2 51 31N 0 28W
Coyoacan, *Méx.* 29 B3 19 21N 99 9W
Coyote Cr. →, *S.F.* 27 D4 37 28N 122 4W
Coyote Hills Regional Park, *S.F.* 27 C4 37 32N 122 7W
Coyote Hills Slough, *S.F.* 27 C4 37 33N 122 7W
Coyote Pt., *S.F.* 27 C3 37 35N 122 18W
Coyote Ridge, *S.F.* 27 A1 37 51N 122 33W
Craighall Park, *Jobg.* 18 E9 26 7 S 28 1 E
Crane →, *Lon.* 4 C2 51 29N 0 29W
Cranford, *Lon.* 4 C2 51 29N 0 25W
Cranford, *N.Y.* 22 D3 40 39N 74 19W
Cranham, *Lon.* 4 B6 51 33N 0 16 E
Cray →, *Lon.* 4 C5 51 28N 0 8 E
Crayford, *Lon.* 4 C6 51 27N 0 11 E
Creekmouth, *Lon.* 4 B5 51 30N 0 6 E
Crerskill, *N.Y.* 22 B5 40 56N 73 57W
Crescenzago, *Mil.* 9 D6 45 30N 9 14 E
Crespières, *Paris* 5 B1 48 52N 1 55 E
Cressely, *Paris* 5 C2 48 44N 2 6 E
Cresslawn, *Jobg.* 18 E10 26 6 S 28 13 E
Crestwood, *Chic.* 26 D2 41 38N 87 43W
Creteil, *Paris* 5 C4 48 47N 2 27 E
Cricklewood, *Lon.* 4 B3 51 33N 0 13W
Crispano, *Nápl.* 9 H12 40 57N 14 17 E
Cristo Redebro, Monumento do, *Rio J.* 31 B2 22 56 S 43 12W
Crockenhill, *Lon.* 4 C5 51 22N 0 9 E
Croissy-Beaubourg, *Paris* 5 C5 48 49N 2 39 E
Croissy-sur-Seine, *Paris* 5 B2 48 52N 2 8 E
Cronenberg, *Ruhr* 6 C4 51 12N 7 9 E
Crosby, *Jobg.* 18 F8 26 11 S 27 59 E
Crosne, *Paris* 5 C4 48 43N 2 27 E
Cross I., *Bomb.* 16 H8 18 56N 72 51 E
Crouch End, *Lon.* 4 B4 51 34N 0 7W
Croud →, *Paris* 5 B4 48 57N 2 24 E
Crown Gardens, *Jobg.* 18 F9 26 15 S 28 0 E
Crown Mines, *Jobg.* 18 F8 26 12 S 27 57 E
Crown Village, *N.Y.* 23 C8 40 40N 73 26W
Crows Nest, *Syd.* 19 A4 33 49 S 151 12 E
Croxley Green, *Lon.* 4 B2 51 38N 0 26W
Croydon, *Lon.* 4 C4 51 22N 0 5W
Croydon, *Melb.* 19 E8 37 48 S 145 17 E
Croydon, *Phil.* 24 A5 40 5N 74 54W
Croydon North, *Melb.* 19 E8 37 46 S 145 16 E
Cruz de Pau, *Lisb.* 8 G8 38 37N 9 7W
Crystal Palace, *Lon.* 4 C4 51 25N 0 4W
Crystal Springs, *S.F.* 27 C2 37 31N 122 20W
Csepel, *Bud.* 10 K13 47 25N 19 4 E
Csepelsziget, *Bud.* 10 K13 47 25N 19 4 E
Csillaghegy, *Bud.* 10 J13 47 35N 19 2 E
Csillagtelep, *Bud.* 10 K13 47 24N 19 5 E
Cski-hegyek, *Bud.* 10 K12 47 30N 18 57 E
Csömör, *Bud.* 10 J14 47 33N 19 14 E
Cuajimalpa, *Méx.* 29 B2 19 21N 99 17W
Cuatro Vientos, *Mdrd.* 8 B2 40 22N 3 47W
Cuautepec de Madero, *Méx.* 29 A3 19 32N 99 8W
Cuautepec El Alto, *Méx.* 29 A3 19 33N 99 7W
Cuautzin, Cerro, *Méx.* 29 D3 19 10N 99 8W
Cubao, *Manila* 15 D4 14 37N 121 3 E
Cubas →, *S. Pau.* 31 D6 23 28 S 46 31W
Cubuklu, *Ist.* 17 A3 41 5N 29 4 E
Cudham, *Lon.* 4 D5 51 19N 0 4 E
Cuffley, *Lon.* 4 A4 51 42N 0 6W
Cuicuilco, Pirámido de, *Méx.* 29 C2 19 17N 99 10W
Culembeeck, *Jobg.* 18 E7 26 9 S 27 49 E
Culiculi, *Manila* 15 D4 14 33N 121 0 E
Cull Creek, *S.F.* 27 B4 37 45N 122 2W
Culver City, *L.A.* 28 B2 34 1N 118 24W
Culverstone Green, *Lon.* 4 C7 51 20N 0 20 E
Cumbre El Tabo, *Car.* 30 D5 10 33N 66 56W
Cumbres de Vallecas, *Mdrd.* 8 B3 40 20N 3 33W
Cunhas, *S. Pau.* 31 E7 23 34 S 46 23W
Cupecé, *S. Pau.* 31 E5 23 39 S 46 40W
Cupece →, *S. Pau.* 31 E6 23 37 S 46 42W
Curtis B., *Balt.* 25 B3 39 13N 76 34W
Curtis Cr. →, *Balt.* 25 B3 39 12N 76 34W
Cusago, *Mil.* 9 E5 45 26N 9 1 E
Cusano Milanese, *Mil.* 9 D6 45 33N 9 11 E
Çuvuşabaşi →, *Ist.* 17 A2 40 58N 28 51 E
Cyrildene, *Jobg.* 18 F9 26 10 S 28 6 E
Czernrakow, *Wsaw.* 10 E7 52 11N 21 3 E
Czyste, *Wsaw.* 10 E6 52 13N 20 57 E


# D


Da Yunhe →, *Tianj.* 14 D5 39 19N 117 10 E
Dabizhuang, *Tianj.* 14 D6 39 11N 117 16 E
Ďablice, *Pra.* 10 B2 50 8N 14 29 E
Dabsibri, *Sŏul* 12 G8 37 33N 127 2 E
Dachang, *Shang.* 14 J11 31 17N 121 24 E
Dachau, *Mün.* 7 F9 48 15N 11 27 E
Dachau-Ost, *Mün.* 7 F9 48 15N 11 27 E
Dachauer Moos, *Mün.* 7 F9 48 13N 11 27 E
Daebang, *Sŏul* 12 G7 37 30N 126 55 E
Daechi, *Sŏul* 12 G8 37 30N 127 2 E
Dagenham, *Lon.* 4 B5 51 32N 0 8 E
Daglfing, *Mün.* 7 G10 48 8N 11 39 E
Dahirpur, *Delhi* 16 A2 28 43N 77 11 E
Dahlem, *Berl.* 7 B2 52 27N 13 16 E
Dahlerau, *Ruhr* 6 C5 51 13N 7 18 E
Dahlwitz-Hoppegarten, *Berl.* 7 A5 52 30N 13 41 E
Dahongmen, *Beij.* 14 C3 39 48N 116 21 E
Daiman, *Tōkyō* 13 A3 35 53N 139 44 E
Daitō, *Ōsaka* 12 B4 34 42N 135 38 E
Dajiaoting, *Beij.* 14 B3 39 51N 116 27 E
Dajingcun, *Beij.* 14 B2 39 50N 116 13 E
Dakhnoye, *St-Pet.* 11 C3 59 49N 30 15 E
Dalar, *Bomb.* 16 G7 19 0N 72 49 E
Dalejsky →, *Pra.* 10 B2 50 2N 14 24 E
Dalibia, *Gzh.* 14 G7 23 2N 113 6 E
Dallgow, *Berl.* 7 A1 52 32N 13 5 E
Dalston, *Lon.* 4 B4 51 32N 0 4W
Dalview, *Jobg.* 18 F11 26 14 S 28 20 E
Daly City, *S.F.* 27 B2 37 42N 122 27W
Damaia, *Lisb.* 8 F7 38 44N 9 12W
Dämeritzsee, *Berl.* 7 B5 52 34N 13 43 E
Damiette, *Paris* 5 C2 48 41N 2 7 E
Dampierre, *Paris* 5 C1 48 42N 1 59 E
Dan Neramit, *Bangk.* 15 B2 13 48N 100 34 E
Dan Ryan Woods, *Chic.* 26 C2 41 44N 87 40W
Dandenong, Mt., *Melb.* 19 E9 37 49 S 145 21 E
Danderyd, *Stock.* 3 D11 59 24N 18 1 E
Danforth, *Trto.* 20 D9 43 43N 79 16W
Daniels, *Balt.* 25 B2 39 19N 76 48W
Danvers, *Bost.* 21 B4 42 34N 70 56W
Dapharpur, *Calc.* 16 E5 22 38N 88 14 E
Darangan, *Manila* 15 E5 14 29N 121 10 E
Darave, *Bomb.* 16 G9 19 1N 73 1 E
Darby, *Phil.* 24 B3 39 55N 75 15W
Darby Cr. →, *Phil.* 24 B3 39 54N 75 15W
Darent →, *Lon.* 4 C6 51 21N 0 12 E
Darling, *Phil.* 24 B2 39 54N 75 28W
Darlington Corners, *Phil.* 24 B1 39 55N 75 34W
Dartford, *Lon.* 4 C6 51 26N 0 13 E
Dashi, *Gzh.* 14 G8 23 1N 113 17 E
Dashimae, *Tōkyō* 13 B3 35 46N 139 46 E
Datteln, *Ruhr* 6 A6 51 39N 7 20 E
Datteln-Hamm Kanal, *Ruhr* 6 A6 51 38N 7 28 E
Datun, *Beij.* 14 A3 40 0N 116 23 E
Dauko, *Calc.* 16 E5 22 31N 88 12 E
Daulatpur, *Delhi* 16 A1 28 44N 77 6 E
Davensport, *Bost.* 21 B4 42 33N 70 54W
Daveyton, *Jobg.* 18 E11 26 9 S 28 24 E
Davidkovo, *Mos.* 11 E8 55 43N 37 29 E
David's I., *N.Y.* 23 B6 40 53N 73 46W
Davidson, Mt., *S.F.* 27 B2 37 44N 122 27W
Davron, *Paris* 5 B1 48 52N 1 56 E
Dāvudiyeh, *Tehr.* 17 C5 35 45N 51 25 E
Dawidy, *Wsaw.* 10 F6 52 8N 20 58 E
Dayap, *Manila* 15 D4 14 35N 121 4 E
Dayuange, *Gzh.* 14 F7 23 11N 113 7 E
Dead Run →, *Balt.* 25 B2 39 18N 76 41W
Dedham, *Bost.* 21 D2 42 15N 71 10W
Dee Why, *Syd.* 19 A4 33 46 S 151 17 E
Deer I., *Bost.* 21 C4 42 21N 70 57W
Deer Park, *N.Y.* 23 C9 40 46N 73 19W
Degerby, *Stock.* 3 D9 59 22N 17 42 E
Degermossa, *Hels.* 3 B6 60 17N 25 12 E
Degunino, *Mos.* 11 D9 55 52N 37 33 E
Deisenhofen, *Mün.* 7 G10 48 0N 11 35 E
Dejvice, *Pra.* 10 B2 50 6N 14 23 E
Dekabristov, Os., *St-Pet.* 11 B3 59 56N 30 15 E
Del Viso, *B.A.* 32 A2 34 27 S 58 47W
Delanco, *Phil.* 24 A5 40 2N 74 57W
Delaware →, *Phil.* 24 A4 40 1N 75 0W
Delbruch, *Ruhr* 6 B4 51 22N 7 8 E
Delhi, *Delhi* 16 B2 28 39N 77 13 E
Delhi Cantonment, *Delhi* 16 B1 28 35N 77 7 E
Delhi Univ., *Delhi* 16 A2 28 41N 77 12 E
Dellwig, *Ruhr* 6 B3 51 29N 6 55 E
Delran, *Phil.* 24 A5 40 0N 74 57W
Delville, *Jobg.* 18 F10 26 11 S 28 13 E
Demarest, *N.Y.* 22 B5 40 57N 73 57W
Denham, *Lon.* 4 B1 51 35N 0 30W
Denham Green, *Lon.* 4 B2 51 34N 0 29W
Denniston Cr. →, *S.F.* 27 C2 37 30N 122 29W
Dentonia Park, *Trto.* 20 D9 43 42N 79 17W
Denville, *N.Y.* 22 B2 40 53N 74 28W
Deodoro, *Rio J.* 31 B1 22 50 S 43 21W
Depgsu Palace, *Sŏul* 12 G7 37 34N 126 58 E
Deptford, *Lon.* 4 C4 51 28N 0 1W
Der Sarai, *Delhi* 16 B2 28 33N 77 10 E
Des Plaines, *Chic.* 26 A1 42 2N 87 54W
Des Plaines →, *Chic.* 26 B1 41 48N 87 49W
Deshengmen, *Beij.* 14 B3 39 56N 116 21 E
Desierto de los Leones, Parque Nacional, *Méx.* 29 C2 19 18N 99 18W
Desio, *Mil.* 9 D6 45 36N 9 12 E
Deuil-la-Barre, *Paris* 5 B3 48 58N 2 19 E
Deulpur, *Calc.* 16 E5 22 36N 88 10 E
Deungchon, *Sŏul* 12 G7 37 33N 126 52 E
Deutsch-Wagram, *Wien* 10 G11 48 17N 16 33 E
Deutsche Oper, *Berl.* 7 A2 52 30N 13 19 E
Deutscher Museum, *Mün.* 7 G10 48 7N 11 35 E
Deux-Montagnes, *Mtrl.* 20 A2 43 32N 73 53W
Deux Montagnes, L. des, *Mtrl.* 20 B2 43 27N 73 59W
Devault, *Phil.* 24 A1 40 4N 75 32W
Dháfni, *Ath.* 8 J11 37 55N 23 44 E
Dhakuria, *Calc.* 16 E6 22 30N 88 22 E
Dhakuria L., *Calc.* 16 E6 22 30N 88 21 E
Dhamarakia, *Ath.* 8 J10 37 58N 23 39 E
Dharava, *Bomb.* 16 G8 19 1N 72 51 E
Dhrapersón, *Ath.* 8 J10 37 56N 23 37 E
Dhutumkhar, *Bomb.* 16 H9 18 54N 73 1 E
Dia Deva, *Bomb.* 16 H8 18 57N 72 53 E
Diadema, *S. Pau.* 31 F6 23 41 S 46 37W
Diamante, *B.A.* 32 C4 34 41 S 58 25W
Diamond Cr. →, *Melb.* 19 E7 37 44 S 145 9 E
Diamond Creek, *Melb.* 19 E8 37 40 S 145 10 E
Didaowai, *Tianj.* 14 E6 39 8N 117 12 E
Diepensiepen, *Ruhr* 6 C3 51 14N 6 58 E
Diepkloof, *Jobg.* 18 F8 26 14 S 27 57 E
Diessem, *Ruhr* 6 C1 51 19N 6 34 E
Difficult Run →, *Wash.* 25 D6 38 55N 77 18W
Digla, W. →, *El Qâ.* 18 D6 29 58N 31 22 E
Digra, *Calc.* 16 D5 22 49N 88 19 E
Dikemark, *Oslo* 2 C2 59 48N 10 22 E
Dilerpur, *Calc.* 16 C5 22 51N 88 10 E
Dinslaken, *Ruhr* 6 A2 51 33N 6 43 E
Dinslakener Bruch, *Ruhr* 6 A2 51 34N 6 44 E
Dinwiddie, *Jobg.* 18 F9 26 16 S 28 9 E
Diósd, *Bud.* 10 K12 47 24N 18 57 E
Dirnismaning, *Mün.* 7 F10 48 13N 11 38 E
Disappointment, Mt., *L.A.* 28 A4 34 15N 118 7W
Discovery, *Jobg.* 18 E8 26 8 S 27 54 E
Disteln, *Ruhr* 6 A4 51 36N 7 9 E
District Heights, *Wash.* 25 D8 38 51N 76 53W
Ditan Gongyuan, *Beij.* 14 B3 39 56N 116 23 E
Dix Hills, *N.Y.* 23 C8 40 48N 73 21W
Dixmoor, *Chic.* 26 D2 41 37N 87 40W
Diyala →, *Bagd.* 17 F9 33 13N 44 30 E
Djakarta = Jakarta, *Jak.* 15 H10 6 9 S 106 52 E
Djursholm, *Stock.* 3 D11 59 24N 18 5 E
Do Bong, *Sŏul* 12 G8 37 37N 127 1 E
Dobbs, *N.Y.* 23 A5 41 1N 73 52W
Döberitz, *Berl.* 7 A1 52 32N 13 3 E
Döbling, *Wien* 10 G10 48 14N 16 20 E
Dobong, *Sŏul* 12 G8 37 39N 127 2 E
Dobong San, *Sŏul* 12 F8 37 40N 127 0 E
Dōbrowa, *Wsaw.* 10 E6 52 19N 20 52 E
Doddinghurst, *Lon.* 4 A6 51 40N 0 18 E
Dodger Stadium, *L.A.* 28 B3 34 4N 118 14W
Dogsan, *Sŏul* 12 H7 37 28N 126 54 E
Doirone, *Tori.* 9 B2 45 3N 7 32 E
Dōjō, *Ōsaka* 12 A2 34 51N 135 14 E
Dōjō, *Tōkyō* 13 A2 35 51N 139 37 E
Dollard-des-Ormeaux, *Mtrl.* 20 B3 43 29N 73 49W
Dollis Hill, *Lon.* 4 B3 51 33N 0 13W
Dolni, *Pra.* 10 B3 50 3N 14 33 E
Dolni Chabry, *Pra.* 10 B2 50 8N 14 26 E
Dolni Počernice, *Pra.* 10 B3 50 5N 14 34 E
Dolton, *Chic.* 26 D3 41 37N 87 35W
Domont, *Paris* 5 A3 49 2N 2 19 E
Don Bosco, *B.A.* 32 C5 34 42 S 58 17W
Don Mills, *Trto.* 20 D8 43 44N 79 21W
Don Pedro II, Parque, *S. Pau.* 31 E6 23 33 S 46 36W
Don Torcuato, *B.A.* 32 A3 34 29 S 58 38W
Donau →, *Bud.* 10 J13 47 33N 19 4 E
Donau-Oder Kanal, *Wien* 10 G11 48 12N 16 32 E
Donaufeld, *Wien* 10 G10 48 15N 16 24 E
Donaukanal, *Wien* 10 G10 48 10N 16 27 E
Donaupark, *Wien* 10 G10 48 14N 16 24 E
Donaustadt, *Wien* 10 G10 48 13N 16 29 E
Doncaster, *Melb.* 19 E7 37 47 S 145 8 E
Doncaster East, *Melb.* 19 E7 37 46 S 145 8 E
Dong Dae Mun, *Sŏul* 12 G8 37 34N 127 2 E
Dong Jag, *Sŏul* 12 G7 37 30N 126 56 E
Dongala Forest Reserve, *Melb.* 19 F9 37 50 S 145 20 E
Dongan Hills, *N.Y.* 22 D4 40 35N 74 5W
Dongbinggo, *Sŏul* 12 G7 37 31N 126 58 E
Dongcheng, *Beij.* 14 B3 39 54N 116 23 E
Dongfeng Nongchang, *Beij.* 14 B3 39 57N 116 28 E
Dongjiao, *Gzh.* 14 G8 23 5N 113 12 E
Dongjuzi, *Tianj.* 14 E6 39 7N 117 14 E
Dongkou, *Shang.* 14 J12 31 17N 121 33 E
Dongmenwai, *Tianj.* 14 E6 39 8N 117 11 E
Dongri, *Bomb.* 16 H8 18 53N 72 57 E
Dongwuyuan, *Beij.* 14 B2 39 55N 116 18 E
Dongzhimen, *Beij.* 14 B3 39 55N 116 24 E
Donvale, *Melb.* 19 E8 37 47 S 145 11 E
Doonside, *Syd.* 19 A2 33 46 S 150 51 E
Doornfontein, *Jobg.* 18 F9 26 11 S 28 3 E
Dōra, *Bagd.* 17 F8 33 15N 44 25 E
Dora Riparia →, *Tori.* 9 B2 45 4N 7 38 E
Dorchester, *Bost.* 21 D3 42 17N 71 4W
Dorchester B., *Bost.* 21 D3 42 18N 71 1W
Dorchester Heights Nat. Hist. Site, *Bost.* 21 D3 42 19N 71 2W
Dorion, *Mtrl.* 20 B1 43 23N 74 1W
Dornach, *Mün.* 7 G11 48 9N 11 41 E
Dornap, *Ruhr* 6 C4 51 15N 7 3 E
Dornbach, *Wien* 10 G9 48 13N 16 18 E
Dorsey Run →, *Balt.* 25 B2 39 11N 76 47W
Dorstfeld, *Ruhr* 6 A6 51 30N 7 24 E
Dortmund, *Ruhr* 6 A6 51 30N 7 28 E
Dorval, *Mtrl.* 20 B3 43 26N 73 45W
Dorval, Aéroport de, *Mtrl.* 20 B3 43 28N 73 44 E
Dos Rios, *Méx.* 29 B1 19 22N 99 20W
Doshan Tappeh Airport, *Tehr.* 17 C5 35 41N 51 28 E
Dotmund-Ems Kanal, *Ruhr* 6 A6 51 35N 7 24 E
Double B., *Syd.* 19 B4 33 52 S 151 15 E
Douglas Park, *Chic.* 26 B2 41 51N 87 42W
Douglaston, *N.Y.* 23 C6 40 46N 73 44W
Dove Elbe →, *Hbg.* 7 E8 53 28N 10 7 E
Dover, *Bost.* 21 D2 42 14N 71 16W
Dover Heights, *Syd.* 19 B4 33 52 S 151 16 E
Dowlatābād, *Tehr.* 17 D5 35 38N 51 27 E
Downe, *Lon.* 4 C5 51 20N 0 3 E
Downey, *L.A.* 28 C4 33 56N 118 9W
Downsview, *Trto.* 20 D7 43 43N 79 30W
Downsview Dells Park, *Trto.* 20 D7 43 44N 79 30W
Dracut, *Bost.* 21 A2 42 40N 71 17W
Dragør, *Købn.* 2 E10 55 35N 12 38 E
Drancy, *Paris* 5 B4 48 55N 2 26 E
Dranesville, *Wash.* 25 C5 39 0N 77 20W
Draveil, *Paris* 5 C4 48 41N 2 23 E
Drayton Green, *Lon.* 4 B3 51 30N 0 19W
Dreilinden, *Berl.* 7 B2 52 24N 13 10 E
Dresher, *Phil.* 24 A4 40 9N 75 9W
Drewnica, *Wsaw.* 10 E7 52 18N 21 6 E
Drexel Hill, *Phil.* 24 B3 39 56N 75 18W
Drexel Inst. of Technology, *Phil.* 24 B3 39 57N 75 11W
Drigh Road, *Kar.* 17 G11 24 52N 67 7 E
Drogden, *Købn.* 2 E11 55 37N 12 42 E
Drottningholm, *Stock.* 3 E10 59 19N 17 53 E
Druento, *Tori.* 9 B2 45 8N 7 34 E
Druid Hill Park, *Balt.* 25 B3 39 19N 76 38W
Druid Lake, *Balt.* 25 B3 39 19N 76 38W
Drummoyne, *Syd.* 19 B3 33 51 S 151 8 E
Druzhba, *Mos.* 11 D10 55 52N 37 44 E
Duarte, *L.A.* 28 B5 34 8N 117 57W
Dubeč, *Pra.* 10 B3 50 3N 14 35 E
Dubi Bheri, *Calc.* 16 C5 22 52N 88 16 E
Duffryn Mawr, *Phil.* 24 A2 40 2N 75 27W
Dugnano, *Mil.* 9 D6 45 33N 9 11 E
Dugny, *Paris* 5 B4 48 57N 2 24 E
Duiha, *Calc.* 16 E5 22 34N 88 15 E
Duisburg, *Ruhr* 6 B2 51 26N 6 45 E
Dulāb, *Tehr.* 17 D5 35 39N 51 27 E
Dulworthtown, *Phil.* 24 B1 39 54N 75 33W
Dum Dum, *Calc.* 16 E6 22 38N 88 25 E
Dum Dum Int. Airport, *Calc.* 16 E6 22 38N 88 26 E
Dumbarton Pt., *S.F.* 27 D4 37 29N 122 6W
Dumjor, *Calc.* 16 E5 22 37N 88 13 E
Dumont, *N.Y.* 22 B5 40 56N 73 59W
Dümpten, *Ruhr* 6 B3 51 27N 6 54 E
Duna →, *Bud.* 10 J13 47 33N 19 4 E
Dunbarton, *Trto.* 20 C10 43 50N 79 6W
Dundalk, *Balt.* 25 B3 39 17N 76 31W
Dundas, *Syd.* 19 A3 33 47 S 151 3 E
Dunearn, *Sing.* 15 G7 1 19N 103 49 E
Dunellen, *N.Y.* 22 D2 40 35N 74 26W
Dunn Loring, *Wash.* 25 D6 38 54N 77 13W
Dunning, *Chic.* 26 B2 41 56N 87 48W
Dunton Green, *Lon.* 4 D6 51 17N 0 11 E
Dunvegan, *Jobg.* 18 E9 26 9 S 28 8 E
Duomo, *Mil.* 9 E6 45 28N 9 11 E
Duomo, *Nápl.* 9 H12 40 51N 14 15 E
Duomo, *Tori.* 9 B3 45 4N 7 45 E
Duque de Caxias, *Rio J.* 31 A2 22 46 S 43 18W
Durban Roodepoort Deep Gold Mines, *Jobg.* 18 F8 26 11 S 27 52 E
Durchholz, *Ruhr* 6 B5 51 23N 7 18 E
Düssel →, *Ruhr* 6 C3 51 13N 6 58 E
Düsseldorf, *Ruhr* 6 C2 51 13N 6 46 E
Düsseldorf-Lohausen, Flughafen, *Ruhr* 6 C2 51 17N 6 45 E
Duvenstedt, *Hbg.* 7 C8 53 42N 10 6 E
Duvenstedter Brook, *Hbg.* 7 C8 53 43N 10 8 E
Duvernay, *Mtrl.* 20 A3 43 35N 73 40W
Dyakovo, *Mos.* 11 E9 55 40N 37 39 E
Dyviksudd, *Stock.* 3 E13 59 11N 18 23 E
Dzerzhinskiy, *Mos.* 11 F11 55 38N 37 51 E
Dzerzhinskiy, *Mos.* 11 E9 55 47N 37 37 E
Dzerzhinskiy Park, *Mos.* 11 E9 55 50N 37 37 E


# E


Eagle Rock, *L.A.* 28 B3 34 8N 118 12 E
Ealing, *Lon.* 4 B3 51 30N 0 18W
Earls Court, *Lon.* 4 C3 51 29N 0 11W
Earlsfield, *Lon.* 4 C3 51 26N 0 10W
Earlwood, *Syd.* 19 B3 33 55 S 151 8 E
East Acton, *Bost.* 21 C1 42 28N 71 24W
East Acton, *Lon.* 4 B3 51 30N 0 14W
East Arlington, *Wash.* 25 D7 38 51N 77 4W
East Atlantic Beach, *N.Y.* 23 D6 40 35N 73 43W
East B., *N.Y.* 23 D7 40 38N 73 32W
East Barnet, *Lon.* 4 B4 51 38N 0 9W
East Bedfont, *Lon.* 4 C2 51 26N 0 28W
East Billerica, *Bost.* 21 B2 42 35N 71 13W
East Boston, *Bost.* 21 C3 42 22N 71 1W
East Braintree, *Bost.* 21 D4 42 13N 70 58W
East Chicago, *Chic.* 26 D4 41 38N 87 26W
East Don →, *Trto.* 20 D8 43 48N 79 25W
East Dulwich, *Lon.* 4 C4 51 26N 0 4W
East Elmhurst, *N.Y.* 23 C5 40 45N 73 52W
East Farmingdale, *N.Y.* 23 C8 40 44N 73 25W
East Finchley, *Lon.* 4 B3 51 35N 0 10W
East Half Hollow Hills, *N.Y.* 23 C9 40 47N 73 19W
East Ham, *Lon.* 4 B5 51 32N 0 3 E
East Hanover, *N.Y.* 22 C2 40 49N 74 21W
East Hills, *N.Y.* 23 C7 40 47N 73 37W
East Hills, *Syd.* 19 B2 33 57 S 150 59 E
East Holliston, *Bost.* 21 D1 42 12N 71 25W
East Horsley, *Lon.* 4 D2 51 16N 0 25W
East Humber →, *Trto.* 20 D7 43 47N 79 35W
East Huntington, *N.Y.* 23 B8 40 52N 73 24W
East Lamma Channel, *H.K.* 12 E5 22 13N 114 9 E
East Lexington, *Bost.* 21 C2 42 25N 71 12W
East Los Angeles, *L.A.* 28 B3 34 1N 118 10 E
East Meadow, *N.Y.* 23 C7 40 42N 73 31W
East Molesey, *Lon.* 4 C2 51 24N 0 21W
East New York, *N.Y.* 23 C5 40 40N 73 53W
East Newark, *N.Y.* 22 C3 40 45N 74 10W
East Northport, *N.Y.* 23 B9 40 52N 73 18W
East Norwich, *N.Y.* 23 B7 40 50N 73 31W
East Orange, *N.Y.* 22 C3 40 46N 74 11W
East Palo Alto, *S.F.* 27 D4 37 28N 122 8W
East Paterson, *N.Y.* 22 B4 40 53N 74 8W
East Pines, *Wash.* 25 D8 38 57N 76 54W
East Point, *Bost.* 21 C4 42 25N 70 54W
East Potomac Park, *Wash.* 25 D7 38 52N 77 1W
East Richmond, *S.F.* 27 A3 37 56N 122 19W
East Ringwood, *Melb.* 19 E8 37 48 S 145 15 E
East River →, *N.Y.* 22 C5 40 44N 73 58W
East Rockaway, *N.Y.* 23 D6 40 38N 73 40W
East Rutherford, *N.Y.* 22 B4 40 50N 74 5W
East Sheen, *Lon.* 4 C3 51 27N 0 16W
East View Garden, *Sing.* 15 F8 1 20N 103 57 E
East Weymouth, *Bost.* 21 D4 42 13N 70 55W
East Wickham, *Lon.* 4 C5 51 28N 0 5 E
East Williston, *N.Y.* 23 C7 40 45N 73 37W
East York, *Trto.* 20 D8 43 40N 79 22W
Eastchester, *N.Y.* 23 B6 40 56N 73 49W
Eastchester B., *N.Y.* 23 B6 40 50N 73 47W
Eastcote, *Lon.* 4 B2 51 34N 0 23W
Eastleigh, *Jobg.* 18 E9 26 7 S 28 9 E
Eastpoint, *Balt.* 25 B3 39 17N 76 34W
Eastwood, *Syd.* 19 A3 33 47 S 151 4 E
Eatons Neck Pt., *N.Y.* 23 B8 40 57N 73 24W
Eaubonne, *Paris* 5 B3 48 59N 2 16 E
Ebara, *Tōkyō* 13 C3 35 35N 139 42 E
Ebisu, *Tōkyō* 13 C3 35 38N 139 42 E
Ebute-Ikorodu, *Lagos* 18 A2 6 35N 7 29 E

Gerthe 37


Ebute-Metta, *Lagos* **18 B2** 6 28N 7 23 E
Ecatepec de Morelos, *Méx.* **29 A3** 19 35N 99 2W
Echo B., *N.Y.* **23 B6** 40 54N 73 45W
Echo Mt., *L.A.* **28 A4** 34 12N 118 8W
Écouen, *Paris* **5 A4** 49 1N 2 22 E
Ecquevilly, *Paris* **5 B1** 48 57N 1 55 E
Ecser, *Bud.* **10 K14** 47 26N 19 19 E
Eda, *Tōkyō* **13 C2** 35 33N 139 33 E
Eddington, *Phil.* **24 A5** 40 5N 74 55W
Eddystone, *Phil.* **24 B2** 39 51N 75 20W
Eden, *Rio J.* **31 A1** 22 47 S 43 23W
Edendale, *Jobg.* **18 E9** 26 8 S 28 9 E
Edenvale, *Jobg.* **18 E9** 26 8 S 28 9 E
Edgars Cr. →, *Melb.* **19 E6** 37 43 S 144 58 E
Edge Hill, *Phil.* **24 A4** 40 7N 75 9W
Edgeley, *Trto.* **20 D7** 43 47N 79 31W
Edgemar, *S.F.* **27 C2** 37 39N 122 29W
Edgemere, *Balt.* **25 B4** 39 14N 76 26W
Edgemont, *Phil.* **24 B2** 39 58N 75 26W
Edgewater Park, *Phil.* **24 A5** 40 3N 74 54W
Edgware, *Lon.* **4 B3** 51 36N 0 15W
Edison, *N.Y.* **22 D2** 40 31N 74 23W
Edison Park, *Chic.* **26 A2** 42 1N 87 48W
Edleen, *Jobg.* **18 E10** 26 5 S 28 12 E
Edmondston, *Wash.* **25 D8** 38 56N 76 54W
Edo →, *Tōkyō* **13 C4** 35 38N 139 52 E
Edogawa, *Tōkyō* **13 B4** 35 43N 139 52 E
Edsberg, *Stock.* **3 D10** 59 26N 17 57 E
Edwards L., *Melb.* **19 E6** 37 42 S 144 59 E
Eestiluoto, *Hels.* **3 C6** 60 7N 25 13 E
Egawa, *Tōkyō* **13 D4** 35 22N 139 54 E
Egenbüttel, *Hbg.* **7 D7** 53 39N 9 51 E
Eggerscheidt, *Ruhr* **6 C3** 51 19N 6 53 E
Egham, *Lon.* **4 C1** 51 25N 0 30W
Eiche, *Berl.* **7 A4** 52 33N 13 35 E
Eiche Sud, *Berl.* **7 A4** 52 33N 13 35 E
Eichlinghofen, *Ruhr* **6 B6** 51 29N 7 24 E
Eichwalde, *Berl.* **7 B4** 52 22N 13 37 E
Eidelstedt, *Hbg.* **7 D7** 53 36N 9 54 E
Eiffel, Tour, *Paris* **5 B3** 48 51N 2 17 E
Eigen, *Ruhr* **6 A3** 51 32N 6 56 E
Eilbek, *Hbg.* **7 D8** 53 34N 10 2 E
Eimsbüttel, *Hbg.* **7 D7** 53 34N 9 57 E
Eissendorf, *Hbg.* **7 E7** 53 27N 9 57 E
Ejby, *Købn.* **2 D9** 55 41N 12 24 E
Ejigbo, *Lagos* **18 A1** 6 33N 7 18 E
Ekeberg, *Oslo* **2 B4** 59 53N 10 46 E
Ekeby, *Stock.* **3 D8** 59 21N 17 35 E
Ekerö, *Stock.* **3 E9** 59 17N 17 46 E
Ekerön, *Stock.* **3 E9** 59 18N 17 41 E
Ekhtiyarieh, *Tehr.* **17 C5** 35 46N 51 28 E
Eklundshov, *Stock.* **3 E10** 59 11N 17 54 E
Eknäs, *Stock.* **3 E12** 59 18N 18 13 E
El 'Abbasiya, *El Qâ.* **18 C5** 30 3N 31 16 E
El Agustino, *Lima* **30 G8** 12 2 S 77 0W
El Alto, *Stgo* **30 J10** 33 29 S 70 42W
El Awkal, *El Qâ.* **18 C5** 30 2N 31 12 E
El Baragil, *El Qâ.* **18 C4** 30 4N 31 9 E
El Basâtîn, *El Qâ.* **18 D5** 29 58N 31 16 E
El Calvario, *La Hab.* **30 B3** 23 3N 82 19W
El Cano, *La Hab.* **30 B2** 23 2N 82 27W
El Caribe, *Car.* **30 D5** 10 36N 66 52W
El Carmen, *Stgo* **30 J10** 33 22 S 70 43W
El Cerrito, *S.F.* **27 A3** 37 54N 122 18W
El Cerro, *La Hab.* **30 B2** 23 6N 82 23W
El Cojo, Pta., *Car.* **30 D5** 10 36N 66 53W
El Cortijo, *Stgo* **30 J10** 33 22 S 70 42W
El Duqqi, *El Qâ.* **18 C5** 30 1N 31 12 E
El Gamâliya, *El Qâ.* **18 C5** 30 2N 31 15 E
El Ghurîya, *El Qâ.* **18 C5** 30 2N 31 15 E
El Giza, *El Qâ.* **18 C5** 30 0N 31 12 E
El Granada, *S.F.* **27 C7** 37 30N 122 27W
El Guarda Parres, *Méx.* **29 D2** 19 9N 99 11W
El Hatillo, *Car.* **30 E6** 10 25N 66 49W
El Khalîfa, *El Qâ.* **18 C5** 30 0N 31 15 E
El Kôm el Ahmar, *El Qâ.* **18 C5** 30 6N 31 10 E
El Ma'âdi, *El Qâ.* **18 D5** 29 57N 31 15 E
El Matarîya, *El Qâ.* **18 C5** 30 7N 31 18 E
El Monte, *L.A.* **28 B4** 34 3N 118 1W
El Muhît Idkû el Gharbi →, *El Qâ.* **18 C4** 30 6N 31 6 E
El Mûskî, *El Qâ.* **18 C5** 30 3N 31 15 E
El Palmar, *Car.* **30 D5** 10 36N 66 53W
El Palomar, *B.A.* **32 B3** 34 36 S 58 37W
El Pardo, *Mdrd.* **8 A2** 40 30N 3 46W
El Pedregal, *Car.* **30 D5** 10 30N 66 51W
El Pinar, *Car.* **30 E5** 10 28N 66 56W
El Plantío, *Mdrd.* **8 B1** 40 28N 3 51W
El Qâhira, *El Qâ.* **18 C5** 30 2N 31 13 E
El Qubba, *El Qâ.* **18 C5** 30 5N 31 16 E
El Recreo, *Car.* **30 E5** 10 29N 66 52W
El Reloj, *Méx.* **29 C3** 19 19N 99 9W
El Retiro, *Car.* **30 D5** 10 31N 66 54W
El Salto, *Stgo* **30 J11** 33 22 S 70 38W
El Segundo, *L.A.* **28 C2** 33 55N 118 24W
El Sereno, *L.A.* **28 B3** 34 6N 118 10 E
El Silencio, *Car.* **30 D5** 10 30N 66 55W
El Sobrante, *S.F.* **27 A3** 37 58N 122 17W
El Talar de Pacheco, *B.A.* **32 A3** 34 27 S 58 38W
El Talibîya, *El Qâ.* **18 D5** 29 59N 31 10 E
El Valle, *Car.* **30 E5** 10 29N 66 54W
El Vedado, *La Hab.* **30 B2** 23 8N 82 23W
El Vergel, *Méx.* **29 C3** 19 18N 99 5W
El Wâyli el Kubra, *El Qâ.* **18 C5** 30 5N 31 17 E
El Zamalik, *El Qâ.* **18 C5** 30 3N 31 12 E
Elam, *Phil.* **24 B1** 39 51N 75 32W
Élancourt, *Paris* **5 C1** 48 47N 1 57 E
Elandsfortein, *Jobg.* **18 E10** 26 9 S 28 13 E
Elbe →, *Hbg.* **7 D6** 53 32N 9 49 E
Elberfeld, *Ruhr* **6 C4** 51 15N 7 9 E
Elephanta Caves, *Bomb.* **16 H8** 18 57N 72 57 E
Elephanta I., *Bomb.* **16 H8** 18 57N 72 56 E
Elisenau, *Berl.* **7 A4** 52 38N 13 37 E
Elizabeth, *N.Y.* **22 D3** 40 39N 74 13W
Elkins Park, *Phil.* **24 A4** 40 4N 75 8W
Elkridge, *Balt.* **25 B2** 39 13N 76 42W
Ellboda, *Stock.* **3 D12** 59 24N 18 15 E
Eller, *Ruhr* **6 C3** 51 12N 6 51 E
Ellerbek, *Hbg.* **7 D7** 53 39N 9 52 E
Ellicott City, *Balt.* **25 B2** 39 15N 76 49W
Ellinghorst, *Ruhr* **6 A3** 51 33N 6 57 E
Ellinikón, *Ath.* **8 J11** 37 50N 23 45 E
Ellis I., *N.Y.* **22 C4** 40 41N 74 2W
Elm Park, *Lon.* **4 B6** 51 32N 0 12 E
Elmers End, *Lon.* **4 C4** 51 23N 0 2W
Elmhurst, *Chic.* **26 B1** 41 53N 87 55W
Elmhurst, *N.Y.* **23 C5** 40 44N 73 53W
Elmont, *N.Y.* **23 C6** 40 42N 73 42W
Elmstead, *Lon.* **4 C5** 51 24N 0 2 E
Elmwood, *Balt.* **25 A3** 39 20N 76 31W
Elmwood, *N.Y.* **23 B8** 40 51N 73 20W
Elmwood Park, *Chic.* **26 B2** 41 55N 87 48W
Elmwood Park, *N.Y.* **22 B4** 40 54N 74 7W
Elsburg, *Jobg.* **18 F10** 26 15 S 28 13 E
Elsburgspruit →, *Jobg.* **18 F10** 26 16 S 28 12 E
Elsmere, *Phil.* **24 C1** 39 44N 75 35W
Elspark, *Jobg.* **18 F10** 26 15 S 28 10 E
Elsternwick, *Melb.* **19 F7** 37 52 S 145 0 E
Eltham, *Lon.* **4 C5** 51 27N 0 3 E
Eltham, *Melb.* **19 E7** 37 42 S 145 9 E
Elthorn Heights, *Lon.* **4 B2** 51 31N 0 20W
Eltingrille, *N.Y.* **22 D4** 40 32N 74 9W
Elwood, *Melb.* **19 F6** 37 53 S 144 59 E
Élysée, *Paris* **5 B3** 48 52N 2 19 E
Embu, *S. Pau.* **31 E4** 23 38 S 46 50W
Embu-Mirim, *S. Pau.* **31 F5** 23 41 S 46 49W
Embu Mirim →, *S. Pau.* **31 F5** 23 43 S 46 47W
Emdeni, *Jobg.* **18 F7** 26 14 S 27 49 E
Émerainville, *Paris* **5 C5** 48 48N 2 37 E
Emerson, *N.Y.* **22 B4** 40 57N 74 2W
Emerson Park, *Lon.* **4 B6** 51 34N 0 13 E
Emeryville, *S.F.* **27 B3** 37 49N 122 17W
Eminonu, *Ist.* **17 A2** 41 0N 28 57 E
Emmarentia, *Jobg.* **18 E9** 26 9 S 28 0 E
Emperor's Palace, *Tōkyō* **13 B3** 35 40N 139 45 E
Empire State Building, *N.Y.* **22 C5** 40 44N 73 59W
Emscher →, *Ruhr* **6 A6** 51 30N 7 26 E
Emscher Bruch, *Ruhr* **6 A4** 51 33N 7 8 E
Emscher Zweigkanal, *Ruhr* **6 A4** 51 33N 7 9 E
Encantado, *Rio J.* **31 B2** 22 53 S 43 18W
Encino, *L.A.* **28 B2** 34 9N 118 28W
Encino Res., *L.A.* **28 B1** 34 8N 118 30W
Enebyberg, *Stock.* **3 D10** 59 25N 17 59 E
Enfield, *Lon.* **4 B4** 51 39N 0 4W
Enfield, *Phil.* **24 A3** 40 6N 75 11W
Enfield, *Syd.* **19 B3** 33 53 S 151 6 E
Enfield Chase, *Lon.* **4 A4** 51 40N 0 8W
Enfield Highway, *Lon.* **4 B4** 51 39N 0 2W
Enfield Lock, *Lon.* **4 A4** 51 40N 0 1W
Enfield Wash, *Lon.* **4 B4** 51 39N 0 2W
Eng Khong Gardens, *Sing.* **15 F7** 1 20N 103 46 E
Engenho, I. do, *Rio J.* **31 B3** 22 50 S 43 6W
Engenho Nôvo, *Rio J.* **31 B2** 22 53 S 43 17W
Engenho Velho, Sa. do, *Rio J.* **31 B1** 22 54 S 43 21W
Engenno do Mato, *Rio J.* **31 B3** 22 56 S 43 2W
Enghein-les-Bains, *Paris* **5 B3** 48 58N 2 18 E
Englewood, *Chic.* **26 C3** 41 46N 87 38W
Englewood, *N.Y.* **22 B5** 40 53N 73 58W
Englewood Cliffs, *N.Y.* **22 B5** 40 53N 73 59W
Englischer Garten, *Mün.* **7 G10** 48 9N 11 35 E
Enmore, *Syd.* **19 B4** 33 54 S 151 10 E
Ennepe →, *Ruhr* **6 C6** 51 17N 7 23 E
Ennepetal, *Ruhr* **6 C6** 51 17N 7 21 E
Ennepetalsp →, *Ruhr* **6 C6** 51 14N 7 24 E
Enskede, *Stock.* **3 E11** 59 17N 18 4 E
Entrevias, *Mdrd.* **8 B2** 40 22N 3 40W
Épiais-les-Louvres, *Paris* **5 A5** 49 1N 2 33 E
Epinay, *Paris* **5 B3** 48 57N 2 19 E
Epinay-sous-Sénart, *Paris* **5 C5** 48 41N 2 30 E
Epinay-sur-Orge, *Paris* **5 C3** 48 40N 2 19 E
Eppende, *Ruhr* **6 B4** 51 28N 7 9 E
Eppenhausen, *Ruhr* **6 B6** 51 22N 7 29 E
Epping, *Lon.* **4 A5** 51 41N 0 6 E
Epping, *Melb.* **19 D7** 37 39 S 145 1 E
Epping, *Syd.* **19 A3** 33 46 S 151 5 E
Epping Forest, *Lon.* **4 B5** 51 39N 0 2 E
Epsom, *Lon.* **4 D3** 51 19N 0 15W
Epsom Racecourse, *Lon.* **4 D3** 51 18N 0 15W
Éragny, *Paris* **5 A2** 49 1N 2 5 E
Ercolano, *Nápl.* **9 J13** 40 48N 14 21 E
Érd, *Bud.* **10 K12** 47 23N 18 56 E
Erdenheim, *Phil.* **24 A3** 40 5N 75 12W
Eregun, *Lagos* **18 A2** 6 35N 7 22 E
Erenköy, *Ist.* **17 B3** 40 58N 29 3 E
Ergal, *Paris* **5 C1** 48 47N 1 55 E
Erial, *Phil.* **24 C4** 39 46N 75 0W
Erith, *Lon.* **4 C6** 51 28N 0 11 E
Erkner, *Berl.* **7 B5** 52 25N 13 44 E
Erkrath, *Ruhr* **6 C3** 51 13N 6 54 E
Erlaa, *Wien* **10 H9** 48 9N 16 19 E
Erle, *Ruhr* **6 A4** 51 33N 7 4 E
Ermelino Matarazzo, *S. Pau.* **31 D7** 23 29 S 46 28W
Ermington, *Syd.* **19 A3** 33 48 S 151 4 E
Ermont, *Paris* **5 B3** 48 59N 2 15 E
Ersébet-Telep, *Bud.* **10 K14** 47 27N 19 10 E
Ershatou, *Gzh.* **14 G8** 23 6N 113 18 E
Erskineville, *Syd.* **19 B4** 33 54 S 151 12 E
Erstavik, *Stock.* **3 E12** 59 16N 18 14 E
Erstaviken, *Stock.* **3 E12** 59 16N 18 20 E
Erunkan, *Lagos* **18 A2** 6 36N 7 23 E
Eschenried, *Mün.* **7 F9** 48 13N 11 24 E
Esenler, *Ist.* **17 A2** 41 1N 28 52 E
Esher, *Lon.* **4 C2** 51 22N 0 20W
Eshratābād, *Tehr.* **17 C5** 35 42N 51 27 E
España, *B.A.* **32 C5** 34 46 S 58 14W
Espeleta, *B.A.* **32 C5** 34 45 S 58 15W
Esplugas, *Barc.* **8 D5** 41 22N 2 5 E
Espoo, *Hels.* **3 B2** 60 13N 24 38 E
Espoonlahti, *Hels.* **3 B2** 60 8N 24 31 E
Esposizione Univ. di Roma (E.U.R.), *Rome* **9 G9** 41 49N 12 28 E
Essen, *Ruhr* **6 B4** 51 27N 7 0 E
Essen-Mülheim, Flughafen, *Ruhr* **6 B3** 51 24N 6 56 E
Essendon, *Melb.* **19 E6** 37 44 S 144 55 E
Essendon Airport, *Melb.* **19 E6** 37 43 S 144 54 E
Essex, *Balt.* **25 B4** 39 18N 76 28W
Essex Falls, *N.Y.* **22 C3** 40 49N 74 16W
Essingen, *Stock.* **3 E10** 59 19N 17 59 E
Essling, *Wien* **10 G11** 48 12N 16 30 E
Est, Gare de l', *Paris* **5 B4** 48 52N 2 21 E
Estado, Parque do, *S. Pau.* **31 E6** 23 38 S 46 38W
Estby, *Hels.* **3 C1** 60 5N 24 27W
Este, Parque Nacional del, *Car.* **30 E5** 10 29N 66 50W
Esteban Echeverria, *B.A.* **32 C4** 34 48 S 58 29W
Estlotan, *Hels.* **3 C6** 60 7N 25 13 E
Estrela, Basilica da, *Lisb.* **8 F8** 38 42N 9 9W
Étiolles, *Paris* **5 D4** 48 38N 2 28 E
Etobicoke, *Trto.* **20 E7** 43 39N 79 34W
Etobicoke Cr. →, *Trto.* **20 E7** 43 35N 79 32W
Etzenhausen, *Mün.* **7 F9** 48 16N 11 27 E
Eun Pyeong, *Sŏul* **12 G7** 37 36N 126 56 E
Eungam, *Sŏul* **12 G7** 37 34N 126 55 E
Evanston, *Chic.* **26 A2** 42 3N 87 40W
Évecquemont, *Paris* **5 A1** 49 0N 1 56 E
Everett, *Bost.* **21 C3** 42 24N 71 3W
Evergreen Park, *Chic.* **26 C2** 41 43N 87 42W
Eversael, *Ruhr* **6 A2** 51 32N 6 39 E
Evesboro, *Phil.* **24 B5** 39 54N 74 55W
Eving, *Ruhr* **6 A6** 51 33N 7 28 E
Evry, *Paris* **5 D4** 48 38N 2 26 E
Évry-les-Châteaux, *Paris* **5 D5** 48 39N 2 39 E
Évzonos, *Ath.* **8 J11** 37 55N 23 49 E
Ewin, *Tehr.* **17 C5** 35 47N 51 23 E
Ewu, *Lagos* **18 A1** 6 33N 7 19 E
Exelberg, *Wien* **10 G9** 48 14N 16 15 E
Eynsford, *Lon.* **4 C6** 51 21N 0 12 E
Eyup, *Ist.* **17 A2** 41 2N 28 55 E
Ez Zeitûn, *El Qâ.* **18 C5** 30 6N 31 18 E
Ézanville, *Paris* **5 A4** 49 1N 2 21 E
Ezeiza, *B.A.* **32 D3** 34 50 S 58 31W
Ezeiza, Aeropuerto, *B.A.* **32 C3** 34 48 S 58 32W


# F


Fabreville, *Mtrl.* **20 A2** 43 33N 73 51W
Fælledparken, *Købn.* **2 D10** 55 42N 12 34 E
Fågelön, *Stock.* **3 E10** 59 18N 17 55 E
Fagersjo, *Stock.* **3 E11** 59 14N 18 4 E
Fagnano, *Mil.* **9 E4** 45 24N 8 59 E
Fahrn, *Ruhr* **6 A2** 51 30N 6 45 E
Faibano, *Nápl.* **9 H13** 40 55N 14 27 E
Fair Lawn, *N.Y.* **22 B4** 40 55N 74 7W
Fairfax, *Phil.* **24 C1** 39 47N 75 33W
Fairfax, *Wash.* **25 D6** 38 50N 77 19W
Fairfax Station, *Wash.* **25 E6** 38 48N 77 19W
Fairfield, *Melb.* **19 E7** 37 46 S 145 2 E
Fairfield, *N.Y.* **22 B3** 40 53N 74 17W
Fairfield, *Syd.* **19 B2** 33 52 S 150 56 E
Fairhaven B., *Bost.* **21 C1** 42 25N 71 21W
Fairhaven Hill, *Bost.* **21 C1** 42 26N 71 21W
Fairland, *Jobg.* **18 E8** 26 8 S 27 57 E
Fairland, *Wash.* **25 C8** 39 4N 76 57W
Fairmont Terrace, *S.F.* **27 B4** 37 42N 122 7W
Fairmount Heights, *Wash.* **25 D8** 38 54N 76 54W
Fairmount Park, *Phil.* **24 A3** 40 0N 75 13W
Fairport, *Trto.* **20 D10** 43 49N 79 4W
Fairview, *N.Y.* **22 C5** 40 48N 73 59W
Fairview, *N.Y.* **23 A6** 41 1N 73 46W
Falenica, *Wsaw.* **10 F8** 52 9N 21 12 E
Falenty, *Wsaw.* **10 F6** 52 8N 20 55 E
Falkenburg, *Berl.* **7 A4** 52 34N 13 32 E
Falkenhagen, *Berl.* **7 A1** 52 34N 13 5 E
Falkensee, *Berl.* **7 A1** 52 34N 13 4 E
Fallon, *L.A.* **28 C5** 33 59N 117 54W
Falls Church, *Wash.* **25 D6** 38 53N 77 12W
Falls Run →, *Balt.* **25 A1** 39 21N 76 52W
Falomo, *Lagos* **18 B2** 6 26N 7 26 E
Fangcun, *Gzh.* **14 G8** 23 6N 113 13 E
Fanwood, *N.Y.* **22 D2** 40 37N 74 23W
Far Rockaway, *N.Y.* **23 D6** 40 36N 73 45W
Farahābād, *Tehr.* **17 C5** 35 41N 51 29 E
Färentuna, *Stock.* **3 D8** 59 23N 17 39 E
Farforovskaya, *St-Pet.* **11 B4** 59 52N 30 27 E
Farm Pond, *Bost.* **21 D2** 42 13N 71 20W
Farmingdale, *N.Y.* **23 C8** 40 43N 73 27W
Farmsen, *Hbg.* **7 D8** 53 36N 10 8 E
Farnborough, *Lon.* **4 C5** 51 21N 0 3 E
Farningham, *Lon.* **4 C6** 51 23N 0 12 E
Farrar Pond, *Bost.* **21 C1** 42 24N 71 21W
Farrarmere, *Jobg.* **18 E10** 26 9 S 28 18 E
Farsta, *Stock.* **3 E11** 59 14N 18 5 E
Farstalandet, *Stock.* **3 E13** 59 18N 18 23 E
Farum, *Købn.* **2 D8** 55 48N 12 21 E
Farum Sø, *Købn.* **2 D9** 55 48N 12 21 E
Fasanerie-Nord, *Mün.* **7 F10** 48 11N 11 32 E
Fasangarten, *Mün.* **7 G10** 48 5N 11 36 E
Fat Tau Chau, *H.K.* **12 E6** 22 16N 114 16 E
Fatih, *Ist.* **17 A2** 41 0N 28 56 E
Favoriten, *Wien* **10 H10** 48 9N 16 23 E
Fawkner, *Melb.* **19 E6** 37 42 S 144 56 E
Fawkner Park, *Melb.* **19 F6** 37 50 S 144 58 E
Feasterville, *Phil.* **24 A4** 40 9N 75 0W
Febrero, Parque de, *B.A.* **32 B4** 34 36 S 58 25W
Feijó, *Lisb.* **8 G8** 38 39N 9 9W
Feldersbruch →, *Ruhr* **6 B5** 51 23N 7 4 E
Feldhausen, *Ruhr* **6 A3** 51 36N 6 58 E
Feldkirchen, *Mün.* **7 G11** 48 8N 11 43 E
Feldmoching, *Mün.* **7 F10** 48 14N 11 32 E
Fellowship, *Phil.* **24 B5** 39 56N 74 57W
Feltham, *Lon.* **4 C2** 51 26N 0 24W
Feltonville, *Phil.* **24 A4** 40 1N 75 8W
Fenerbahce, *Ist.* **17 B3** 40 58N 29 2 E
Fengtai, *Beij.* **14 C2** 39 49N 116 14 E
Fenino, *Mos.* **11 E11** 55 43N 37 56 E
Ferencváros, *Bud.* **10 K13** 47 29N 19 5 E
Ferihegyi Airport, *Bud.* **10 K14** 47 26N 19 14 E
Ferndale, *Balt.* **25 B3** 39 11N 76 38W
Ferndale, *Jobg.* **18 E9** 26 5 S 28 0 E
Ferntree Gully, *Melb.* **19 F8** 37 52 S 145 17 E
Ferntree Gully Nat. Park, *Melb.* **19 F8** 37 52 S 145 19 E
Ferny Cr. →, *Melb.* **19 F8** 37 54 S 145 16 E
Férolles-Attilly, *Paris* **5 C5** 48 44N 2 37 E
Ferraz de Vasconcelos, *S. Pau.* **31 E7** 23 32 S 46 22W
Ferrières-en-Brie, *Paris* **5 C6** 48 49N 2 42 E
Ferry, *N.Y.* **23 A5** 41 0N 73 52W
Fetcham, *Lon.* **4 D2** 51 17N 0 21W
Feucherolles, *Paris* **5 B1** 48 52N 1 58 E
Fichtenau, *Berl.* **7 B5** 52 27N 13 42 E
Fields Corner, *Bost.* **21 D3** 42 18N 71 3W
Fiera Camp, *Mil.* **9 E5** 45 28N 9 9 E
Figino, *Mil.* **9 E5** 45 29N 9 4 E
Fijir, *Bagd.* **17 E8** 33 21N 44 21 E
Filadhélfia, *Ath.* **8 H11** 38 2N 23 43 E
Fili-Masilovo, *Mos.* **11 E8** 55 44N 37 29 E
Filothei, *Ath.* **8 H11** 38 2N 23 46 E
Finaalspan, *Jobg.* **18 F10** 26 16 S 28 16 E
Finchley, *Lon.* **4 B3** 51 36N 0 11W
Finkenkrug, *Berl.* **7 A1** 52 33N 13 3 E
Finkenwerder, *Hbg.* **7 D7** 53 32N 9 51 E
Finsbury, *Lon.* **4 B4** 51 31N 0 6W
Finsbury Park, *Lon.* **4 B4** 51 34N 0 6W
Fiorito, *B.A.* **32 C4** 34 42 S 58 26W
Firdows, *Bagd.* **17 F7** 33 17N 44 17 E
Firōz Bahram, *Tehr.* **17 C4** 35 37N 51 14 E
Fischeln, *Ruhr* **6 C1** 51 18N 6 35 E
Fish Brook →, *Bost.* **21 B3** 42 39N 71 1W
Fishermans Bend, *Melb.* **19 F6** 37 49 S 144 55 E
Fisher's Hill, *Jobg.* **18 F10** 26 10 S 28 10 E
Fisherville, *Trto.* **20 D8** 43 46N 79 28W
Fisksätra, *Stock.* **3 E12** 59 17N 18 15 E
Fittja, *Stock.* **3 E10** 59 14N 17 51 E
Fitzroy Gardens, *Melb.* **19 E6** 37 48 S 144 58 E
Five Cowrie Cr. →, *Lagos* **18 B2** 6 26N 7 25 E
Five Dock, *Syd.* **19 B3** 33 52 S 151 8 E
Fjellstrand, *Oslo* **2 C3** 59 47N 10 36 E
Flachsberg, *Ruhr* **6 C4** 51 11N 7 4 E
Flag →, *Chic.* **26 C1** 41 43N 87 55W
Flamengo, *Rio J.* **31 B2** 22 56 S 43 11W
Flaminio, *Rome* **9 F9** 41 55N 12 28 E
Flaskebekk, *Oslo* **2 B3** 59 51N 10 39 E
Flatbush, *N.Y.* **22 D5** 40 39N 73 56W
Flaten, *Stock.* **3 E11** 59 15N 18 9 E
Flemington, *Syd.* **19 B3** 33 53 S 151 4 E
Flemington Racecourse, *Melb.* **19 E6** 37 47 S 144 54 E
Fleury-Mérogis, *Paris* **5 D4** 48 37N 2 21 E
Flingern, *Ruhr* **6 C2** 51 13N 6 48 E
Flint Pk., *L.A.* **28 B3** 34 9N 118 11 E
Floral Park, *N.Y.* **23 C6** 40 43N 73 42W
Florence, *L.A.* **28 C3** 33 57N 118 13W
Florence, *Phil.* **24 C5** 39 44N 74 55W
Florence Bloom Bird Sanctuary, *Jobg.* **18 E9** 26 7 S 28 0 E
Florencio Varela, *B.A.* **32 C5** 34 49 S 58 18W
Florentia, *Jobg.* **18 F9** 26 16 S 28 8 E
Flores, *B.A.* **32 B4** 34 38 S 58 27W
Floresta, *B.A.* **32 B4** 34 37 S 58 27W
Florham Park, *N.Y.* **22 C2** 40 46N 74 23W
Florida, *B.A.* **32 B4** 34 31 S 58 28W
Florida, *Jobg.* **18 F8** 26 10 S 27 55 E
Florida L., *Jobg.* **18 F8** 26 10 S 27 54 E
Floridsdorf, *Wien* **10 G10** 48 15N 16 26 E
Flourtown, *Phil.* **24 A3** 40 6N 75 13W
Flower Hill, *N.Y.* **23 C6** 40 48N 73 40W
Flushing, *N.Y.* **23 C6** 40 45N 73 49W
Flushing Meadows Corona Park, *N.Y.* **23 C5** 40 44N 73 50W
Flysta, *Stock.* **3 D10** 59 22N 17 54 E
Fo Tan, *H.K.* **12 D6** 22 23N 114 11 E
Föhrenhain, *Wien* **10 G10** 48 19N 16 26 E
Folcroft, *Phil.* **24 B3** 39 53N 75 16W
Folsom, *Phil.* **24 B3** 39 53N 75 19W
Fontainebleau, *Jobg.* **18 E8** 26 6 S 27 57 E
Fontana, *La Hab.* **30 B2** 23 1N 82 24W
Fontanka, *St-Pet.* **11 B3** 59 54N 30 16 E
Fontenay-aux-Roses, *Paris* **5 C3** 48 47N 2 17 E
Fontenay-le-Fleury, *Paris* **5 C2** 48 48N 2 2 E
Fontenay-lès-Briis, *Paris* **5 D2** 48 37N 2 9 E
Fontenay-sous-Bois, *Paris* **5 B4** 48 51N 2 28 E
Foots Cray, *Lon.* **4 C5** 51 24N 0 7 E
Footscray, *Melb.* **19 E6** 37 48 S 144 56 E
Forbidden City, *Beij.* **14 B3** 39 53N 116 21 E
Fordham Univ., *N.Y.* **23 B5** 40 51N 73 51W
Fords, *N.Y.* **22 D3** 40 31N 74 19W
Fordsburg, *Jobg.* **18 F9** 26 12 S 28 2 E
Foremans Corner, *Balt.* **25 B3** 39 11N 76 33W
Forest Gate, *Lon.* **4 B5** 51 32N 0 1 E
Forest Heights, *Wash.* **25 E7** 38 48N 77 0W
Forest Hill, *Lon.* **4 C4** 51 26N 0 2W
Forest Hill, *Melb.* **19 F8** 37 50 S 145 10 E
Forest Hill, *Trto.* **20 D8** 43 41N 79 25W
Forest Hills, *N.Y.* **23 C5** 40 42N 73 51W
Forest Park, *Chic.* **26 B2** 41 51N 87 47W
Forest View, *Chic.* **26 C2** 41 48N 87 47W
Forestville, *Syd.* **19 A4** 33 46 S 151 12 E
Forestville, *Wash.* **25 D8** 38 50N 76 52W
Forges-les-Bains, *Paris* **5 D2** 48 37N 2 5 E
Fornacino, *Tori.* **9 B3** 45 9N 7 44 E
Fornebu, *Oslo* **2 B3** 59 53N 10 36 E
Fornebu Airport, *Oslo* **2 B3** 59 56N 10 37 E
Foro Italico, *Rome* **9 F9** 41 56N 12 26 E
Foro Romano, *Rome* **9 F9** 41 53N 12 29 E
Forst Rantzau, *Hbg.* **7 C6** 53 43N 9 49 E
Forstenried, *Mün.* **7 G9** 48 5N 11 29 E
Forstenrieder Park, *Mün.* **7 G9** 48 3N 11 27 E
Fort du Pont Park, *Wash.* **25 D8** 38 52N 76 56W
Fort Foote Village, *Wash.* **25 E7** 38 46N 77 1W
Fort Howard, *Balt.* **25 B4** 39 11N 76 26W
Fort Lee, *N.Y.* **22 B5** 40 50N 73 58W
Fort McHenry Nat. Mon., *Balt.* **25 B3** 35 15N 76 35W
Fort Washington, *Phil.* **24 A3** 40 8N 75 13W
Fort William, *Calc.* **16 E6** 22 33N 88 20 E
Foster City, *S.F.* **27 C3** 37 33N 122 15W
Fosters Pond, *Bost.* **21 B3** 42 36N 71 8W
Fourcherolle, *Paris* **5 C1** 48 42N 1 58 E
Fourmile Run →, *Wash.* **25 D7** 38 50N 77 2W
Fourqueux, *Paris* **5 B2** 48 53N 2 3 E
Fowl Meadow Res., *Bost.* **21 D3** 42 13N 71 8W
Fox Chase, *Phil.* **24 A4** 40 4N 75 5W
Foxhall, *Wash.* **25 C7** 39 4N 77 3W
Framingham, *Bost.* **21 D1** 42 18N 71 24W
Francisco Alvarez, *B.A.* **32 B1** 34 38 S 58 50W
Francisquito Cr. →, *L.A.* **27 D4** 37 27N 122 9W
Franconia, *Wash.* **25 E7** 38 47N 77 7W
Franconville, *Paris* **5 B3** 48 59N 2 13 E
Francop, *Hbg.* **7 D7** 53 30N 9 51 E
Frankel, *Sing.* **15 G8** 1 18N 103 55 E
Frankford, *Phil.* **24 A4** 40 1N 75 5W
Franklin L., *N.Y.* **22 B3** 40 59N 74 13W
Franklin Lakes, *N.Y.* **22 B3** 40 59N 74 13W
Franklin Park, *Bost.* **21 D3** 42 18N 71 5W
Franklin Park, *Chic.* **26 B1** 41 55N 87 52W
Franklin Park, *Wash.* **25 D7** 38 55N 77 9W
Franklin Res., *L.A.* **28 B2** 34 5N 118 24W
Franklin Roosevelt Park, *Jobg.* **18 E8** 26 8 S 27 59 E
Franklin Roosevelt Park, *Phil.* **24 B3** 39 54N 75 10W
Franklin Square, *N.Y.* **23 C6** 40 42N 73 40W
Frattamaggiore, *Nápl.* **9 H12** 40 56N 14 16 E
Frauenkirche, *Mün.* **7 G10** 48 8N 11 34 E
Frederiksberg, *Købn.* **2 D10** 55 40N 12 33 E
Frederiksdal, *Købn.* **2 D9** 55 46N 12 25 E
Fredersdorf, *Berl.* **7 A5** 52 31N 13 45 E
Fredersdorf Nord, *Berl.* **7 A5** 52 32N 13 45 E
Freeport, *N.Y.* **23 D7** 40 39N 73 35W
Freidrichshain, Volkspark, *Berl.* **7 A3** 52 31N 13 25 E
Freiham, *Mün.* **7 G9** 48 8N 11 25 E
Freimann, *Mün.* **7 F10** 48 11N 11 37 E
Fremont, *S.F.* **27 C4** 37 33N 122 2W
Fresh Meadows, *N.Y.* **23 C6** 40 43N 73 47W
Fresh Pond, *Bost.* **21 C3** 42 22N 71 8W
Freskati, *Stock.* **3 D11** 59 22N 18 3 E
Fresnes, *Paris* **5 C3** 48 45N 2 18 E
Fretay, *Paris* **5 C3** 48 40N 2 12 E
Freudenau, *Wien* **10 G10** 48 11N 16 25 E
Friedenau, *Berl.* **7 B3** 52 28N 13 20 E
Friederikenhof, *Berl.* **7 B3** 52 23N 13 21 E
Friedrichsfeld, *Ruhr* **6 A1** 51 37N 6 39 E
Friedrichsfelde, *Berl.* **7 B4** 52 29N 13 33 E
Friedrichshagen, *Berl.* **7 B4** 52 27N 13 37 E
Friedrichshain, *Berl.* **7 A3** 52 31N 13 25 E
Friedrichshulde, *Hbg.* **7 D7** 53 36N 9 51 E
Friedrichslust, *Berl.* **7 A4** 52 33N 13 43 E
Frielas, *Lisb.* **8 F8** 38 49N 9 6W
Friemersheim, *Ruhr* **6 B2** 51 23N 6 42 E
Friern Barnet, *Lon.* **4 B4** 51 37N 0 9W
Friherrs, *Hels.* **3 B3** 60 16N 24 49 E
Frogner, *Oslo* **2 A6** 60 1N 11 6 E
Frohnau, *Berl.* **7 A2** 52 38N 13 18 E
Frohnhausen, *Ruhr* **6 B3** 51 26N 6 56 E
Frontón, I., *Lima* **30 G7** 12 7 S 77 11W
Frunze, *Mos.* **11 E9** 55 47N 37 33 E
Fuchū, *Tōkyō* **13 B1** 35 40N 139 29 E
Fuencarral, *Mdrd.* **8 B2** 40 29N 3 42W
Fuhlenbrock, *Ruhr* **6 A3** 51 32N 6 54 E
Fuhlsbüttel, *Hbg.* **7 D8** 53 37N 10 1 E
Fujidera, *Ōsaka* **12 C4** 34 34N 135 36 E
Fujikubo, *Tōkyō* **13 B2** 35 50N 139 31 E
Fujimi, *Tōkyō* **13 A2** 35 50N 139 33 E
Fukagawa, *Tōkyō* **13 C3** 35 39N 139 48 E
Fukami, *Tōkyō* **13 D1** 35 28N 139 27 E
Fukiai, *Ōsaka* **12 B2** 34 42N 135 12 E
Fukuoka, *Tōkyō* **13 A2** 35 52N 139 31 E
Fukushima, *Ōsaka* **12 B3** 34 41N 135 28 E
Fulatani, *Tōkyō* **13 D1** 35 22N 139 30 E
Fulham, *Lon.* **4 C3** 51 28N 0 12W
Fuller Park, *L.A.* **28 C5** 33 51N 117 56W
Fullerton, *Balt.* **25 A3** 39 22N 76 30W
Funabori, *Tōkyō* **13 B4** 35 41N 139 52 E
Funasaka, *Ōsaka* **12 B2** 34 48N 135 16 E
Fünfhaus, *Wien* **10 G10** 48 11N 16 20 E
Fünfhausen, *Hbg.* **7 E8** 53 27N 10 2 E
Furesø, *Købn.* **2 D9** 55 47N 12 25 E
Fürstenried, *Mün.* **7 G9** 48 5N 11 28 E
Furth, *Mün.* **7 G10** 48 2N 11 35 E
Furu →, *Tōkyō* **13 A3** 35 54N 139 49 E
Furuyakami, *Tōkyō* **13 A2** 35 54N 139 31 E
Futago-tamagawaen, *Tōkyō* **13 C2** 35 36N 139 39 E
Futamatagawa, *Tōkyō* **13 D2** 35 27N 139 31 E
Futatsubashi, *Tōkyō* **13 D1** 35 28N 139 29 E
Fuxing Dao, *Shang.* **14 J12** 31 16N 121 33 E
Fuxing Gongyuan, *Shang.* **14 J11** 31 13N 121 27 E
Fuxinglu, *Beij.* **14 B2** 39 52N 116 19 E
Fuxingmen, *Beij.* **14 B2** 39 53N 116 19 E


# G


Gadstrup, *Købn.* **2 E7** 55 34N 12 5 E
Gaebong, *Sŏul* **12 H7** 37 29N 126 52 E
Gage Park, *Chic.* **26 C2** 41 47N 87 42W
Gagny, *Paris* **5 B5** 48 53N 2 32 E
Gaillon, *Paris* **5 A1** 49 1N 1 53 E
Galata, *Ist.* **17 A2** 41 1N 28 58 E
Galátsion, *Ath.* **8 H11** 38 1N 23 45 E
Galeâo, *Rio J.* **31 A2** 22 49 S 43 14W
Galéria →, *Rome* **9 F9** 41 57N 12 20 E
Gallows Corner, *Lon.* **4 B6** 51 35N 0 13 E
Gällstaö, *Stock.* **3 E10** 59 17N 17 51 E
Galyanovo, *Mos.* **11 E10** 55 48N 37 47 E
Galyeon, *Sŏul* **12 G7** 37 36N 126 55 E
Gambir, *Jak.* **15 H9** 6 9 S 106 48 E
Gamboa, *Rio J.* **31 B2** 22 53 S 43 11W
Gambolóita, *Mil.* **9 E6** 45 26N 9 13 E
Gamelinha →, *S. Pau.* **31 E6** 23 31 S 46 31W
Gamlebyen, *Oslo* **2 B4** 59 54N 10 46 E
Gamlebyen, *Shang.* **14 J11** 31 13N 121 29 E
Gamō, *Tōkyō* **13 A3** 35 52N 139 48 E
Gang Dong, *Sŏul* **12 G8** 37 30N 127 5 E
Gang Nam, *Sŏul* **12 G7** 37 30N 126 59 E
Gang Sea, *Sŏul* **12 G7** 37 32N 126 51 E
Gangadharpur, *Calc.* **16 E5** 22 35N 88 11 E
Gangtou, *Gzh.* **14 F7** 23 12N 113 8 E
Gangwei, *Gzh.* **14 G8** 23 4N 113 11 E
Ganløse, *Købn.* **2 D8** 55 47N 12 15 E
Ganløse Orned, *Købn.* **2 D8** 55 48N 12 18 E
Ganshi, *Gzh.* **14 F7** 23 10N 113 8 E
Gants Hill, *Lon.* **4 B5** 51 34N 0 4 E
Gaoqiao, *Shang.* **14 H12** 31 21N 121 34 E
Garbagnate Milanese, *Mil.* **9 D5** 45 34N 9 4 E
Garbatella, *Rome* **9 F10** 41 51N 12 30 E
Garches, *Paris* **5 B3** 48 50N 2 11 E
Garching, *Mün.* **7 F11** 48 14N 11 39 E
Garden City, *El Qâ.* **18 C5** 30 2N 31 14 E
Garden City, *N.Y.* **23 C7** 40 43N 73 37W
Garden Reach, *Calc.* **16 E5** 22 33N 88 15 E
Gardena, *L.A.* **28 C3** 33 53N 118 18W
Garder, *Oslo* **2 C3** 59 45N 10 38 E
Garfield, *N.Y.* **22 B4** 40 52N 74 7W
Garfield Park, *Chic.* **26 B2** 41 52N 87 42W
Gargareta, *Ath.* **8 J11** 37 57N 23 43 E
Garges-lès-Gonesse, *Paris* **5 B4** 48 58N 2 25 E
Garhi Naraina, *Delhi* **16 B1** 28 37N 77 8 E
Garibong, *Sŏul* **12 H7** 37 29N 126 54 E
Garin, *B.A.* **32 A2** 34 25 S 58 44W
Gariya, *Calc.* **16 F6** 22 28N 88 23 E
Garji, *Calc.* **16 C5** 22 50N 88 19 E
Garne, *Paris* **5 C1** 48 41N 1 58 E
Garrison, *Balt.* **25 A2** 39 24N 76 45W
Garstedt, *Hbg.* **7 C7** 53 40N 9 59 E
Gartenstadt, *Ruhr* **6 B6** 51 30N 7 30 E
Garulia, *Calc.* **16 D6** 22 48N 88 22 E
Garvanza, *L.A.* **28 B3** 34 6N 118 11 E
Garwood, *N.Y.* **22 D3** 40 38N 74 18W
Gary, *Chic.* **26 D4** 41 35N 87 23W
Gåshaga, *Stock.* **3 D12** 59 21N 18 13 E
Gássino Torinese, *Tori.* **9 B3** 45 7N 7 49 E
Gästerby, *Hels.* **3 C1** 60 8N 24 27 E
Gateão, Aéroporto de, *Rio J.* **31 A2** 22 49 S 43 15W
Gateway of India, *Bomb.* **16 H8** 18 55N 72 50 E
Gatow, *Berl.* **7 B1** 52 29N 13 11 E
Gauhati, *Calc.* **16 D6** 22 48N 88 21 E
Gauripur, *Calc.* **16 C6** 22 53N 88 25 E
Gavà, *Barc.* **8 E5** 41 18N 2 0 E
Gavamar, *Barc.* **8 E4** 41 16N 1 58 E
Gavanpada, *Bomb.* **16 H9** 18 57N 73 0 E
Gávea, *Rio J.* **31 B2** 22 58 S 43 13W
Gávea, Pedra da, *Rio J.* **31 B2** 22 59 S 43 18W
Gbogbo, *Lagos* **18 A3** 6 35N 7 31 E
Gebel el Ahmar, *El Qâ.* **18 C5** 30 2N 31 19 E
Gebel el Muqattam, *El Qâ.* **18 C5** 30 1N 31 17 E
Gebel et Tura, *El Qâ.* **18 D5** 29 56N 31 15 E
Geduld Dam, *Jobg.* **18 F11** 26 12 S 28 24 E
Geiselgasteig, *Mün.* **7 G10** 48 3N 11 33 E
Geist Res., *Phil.* **24 B2** 39 57N 75 24W
Gellért hegy, *Bud.* **10 K13** 47 29N 19 2 E
Gelsenkirchen, *Ruhr* **6 A4** 51 32N 7 2 E
General Ignacio Allende, *Méx.* **29 B1** 19 20N 99 21W
General Pacheco, *B.A.* **32 A3** 34 27 S 58 36W
General San Martín, *B.A.* **32 B3** 34 35 S 58 32W
General Sarmiento, *B.A.* **32 B2** 34 32 S 58 43W
General Urquiza, *B.A.* **32 B4** 34 34 S 58 28W
Gennebreck, *Ruhr* **6 C5** 51 18N 7 12 E
Gennevilliers, *Paris* **5 B3** 48 56N 2 17 E
Gentilly, *Paris* **5 C4** 48 48N 2 21 E
Gentofte, *Købn.* **2 D10** 55 44N 12 32 E
Georges →, *Syd.* **19 B2** 33 56 S 150 55 E
Georges Hall, *Syd.* **19 B2** 33 54 S 150 59 E
Georges I., *Bost.* **21 D4** 42 19N 70 55W
Georges River Bridge, *Syd.* **19 C3** 34 0 S 151 6 E
Georgetown, *Wash.* **25 D7** 38 54N 77 3W
Georgetown Rowley State Forest, *Bost.* **21 A4** 42 41N 70 56W
Georgsweide, *Hbg.* **7 D8** 53 30N 10 1 E
Gerasdorf bei Wein, *Wien* **10 G10** 48 17N 16 28 E
Gerberau, *Mün.* **7 F9** 48 12N 11 27 E
Gèrbido, *Tori.* **9 B2** 45 2N 7 36 E
Gerlev, *Købn.* **2 D7** 55 49N 12 0 E
Gerli, *B.A.* **32 C4** 34 41 S 58 23W
Germantown, *Balt.* **25 A4** 39 24N 76 28W
Germantown, *Phil.* **24 A3** 40 2N 75 11W
Germiston, *Jobg.* **18 F9** 26 13 S 28 10 E
Gerresheim, *Ruhr* **6 C3** 51 14N 6 51 E
Gersthof, *Wien* **10 G9** 48 14N 16 18 E
Gerthe, *Ruhr* **6 A5** 51 31N 7 16 E

38 Gesîrat el Rauda


Gesîrat el Rauda, *El Qâ.* 18 C5 30 1N 31 13 E
Gesîrat Muhammad, *El Qâ.* 18 C5 30 6N 31 11 E
Gesterby, *Hels.* 3 A6 60 20N 25 17 E
Getafe, *Mdrd.* 8 C2 40 18N 3 43W
Gevelsberg, *Ruhr* 6 C6 51 19N 7 21 E
Geylang, *Sing.* 15 G8 1 18N 103 53 E
Geylang →, *Sing.* 15 G8 1 18N 103 52 E
Geylang Serai, *Sing.* 15 G8 1 19N 103 53 E
Gezîrat edn Dhahab, *El Qâ.* 18 D5 29 59N 31 13 E
Gezîrat Warrâq el Hadar, *El Qâ.* 18 C5 30 6N 31 13 E
Gharapuri, *Bomb.* 16 H8 18 57N 72 57 E
Ghatkopar, *Bomb.* 16 G8 19 4N 72 54 E
Ghazipur, *Delhi* 16 B2 28 37N 77 19 E
Ghizri, *Kar.* 17 H11 24 49N 67 2 E
Ghizri Cr. →, *Kar.* 17 H11 24 47N 67 5 E
Ghonda, *Delhi* 16 A2 28 41N 77 16 E
Ghushuri, *Calc.* 16 E6 22 37N 88 21 E
Gianicolense, *Rome* 9 F9 51 53N 12 28 E
Giant, *S.F.* 27 A2 37 58N 122 20W
Gibbsboro, *Phil.* 24 B5 39 50N 74 57W
Gibbstown, *Phil.* 24 C3 39 49N 75 17W
Gibraltar Pt., *Trto.* 20 E8 43 36N 79 23W
Gidea Park, *Lon.* 4 B6 51 35N 0 11 E
Giesing, *Mün.* 7 G10 48 6N 11 35 E
Gif-sur-Yvette, *Paris* 5 C2 48 42N 2 8 E
Gilgo Beach, *N.Y.* 23 D8 40 36N 73 24W
Gilgo I., *N.Y.* 23 D8 40 37N 73 23W
Gillette, *N.Y.* 22 C2 40 40N 74 29W
Gimmersta, *Stock.* 3 E12 59 14N 18 14 E
Ginza, *Tōkyō* 13 C3 35 39N 139 46 E
Girgaum, *Bomb.* 16 H8 18 57N 72 50 E
Giugliano in Campània, *Nápl.* 9 H12 40 55N 14 12 E
Givoletto, *Tori.* 9 B1 45 9N 7 29 E
Gjellumvatn, *Oslo* 2 C2 59 47N 10 26 E
Gjersjøen, *Oslo* 2 C4 59 47N 10 47 E
Glacier Hills, *N.Y.* 22 B2 40 51N 74 28W
Gladbeck, *Ruhr* 6 A3 51 34N 6 58 E
Gladesville, *Syd.* 19 B3 33 50 S 151 8 E
Gladökvarn, *Stock.* 3 E10 59 11N 17 59 E
Gladsakse, *Købn.* 2 D9 55 45N 12 25 E
Glashutte, *Hbg.* 7 C8 53 41N 10 2 E
Glashütte, *Ruhr* 6 C3 51 13N 6 51 E
Glasmoor, *Hbg.* 7 C8 53 42N 10 1 E
Glassmanor, *Wash.* 25 E7 38 49N 77 0W
Glen Cove, *N.Y.* 23 B7 40 52N 73 38W
Glen Echo, *Wash.* 25 D7 38 58N 77 8W
Glen Hd., *N.Y.* 23 C7 40 49N 73 37W
Glen Iris, *Melb.* 19 F7 37 51 S 145 3 E
Glen Mills, *Phil.* 24 B2 39 55N 75 29W
Glen Oaks, *N.Y.* 23 C6 40 45N 73 43W
Glen Riddle, *Phil.* 24 B2 39 53N 75 26W
Glen Ridge, *N.Y.* 22 C3 40 48N 74 12W
Glen Rock, *N.Y.* 22 B4 40 57N 74 7W
Glen Waverley, *Melb.* 19 F8 37 52 S 145 10 E
Glenardon, *Wash.* 25 D8 38 56N 76 51W
Glencoe, *Chic.* 26 A2 42 7N 87 44W
Glendale, *L.A.* 28 B3 34 9N 118 15 E
Glendora, *Phil.* 24 B4 39 50N 75 4W
Glenfield, *Syd.* 19 B2 33 58 S 150 53 E
Glenhazel, *Jobg.* 18 E9 26 8 S 28 6 E
Glenhuntly, *Melb.* 19 F7 37 52 S 145 1 E
Glenmont, *Wash.* 25 C7 39 3N 77 4W
Glenolden, *Phil.* 24 B3 39 54N 75 17W
Glenroy, *Melb.* 19 E6 37 42 S 144 55 E
Glenside, *Phil.* 24 A4 40 6N 75 9W
Glenview, *Chic.* 26 A2 42 3N 87 48W
Glenview Countryside, *Chic.* 26 A2 42 3N 87 49W
Glenview Woods, *Chic.* 26 A2 42 4N 87 46W
Glenville, *N.Y.* 23 A6 41 1N 73 41W
Glenvista, *Jobg.* 18 F9 26 17 S 28 3 E
Glenwood Landing, *N.Y.* 23 C7 40 48N 73 38W
Glienicke, *Berl.* 7 A2 52 38N 13 18 E
Glömsta, *Stock.* 3 E10 59 14N 17 55 E
Glosli, *Oslo* 2 A5 60 1N 10 55 E
Glostrup, *Købn.* 2 E9 55 39N 12 23 E
Gloucester City, *Phil.* 24 B4 39 53N 75 7W
Gocheog, *Sŏul* 12 G7 37 30N 126 52 E
Gocławek, *Wsaw.* 10 E7 52 14N 21 7 E
Goeselville, *Chic.* 26 D2 41 37N 87 46W
Goetjensort, *Hbg.* 7 E8 53 29N 10 2 E
Golabari, *Calc.* 16 E6 22 35N 88 20 E
Golabki, *Wsaw.* 10 E6 52 12N 20 52 E
Golden Gate, *S.F.* 27 B2 37 48N 122 29W
Golden Gate Bridge, *S.F.* 27 B2 37 49N 122 28W
Golden Gate National Recreation Area, *S.F.* 27 B1 37 49N 122 31W
Golden Gate Park, *S.F.* 27 B2 37 46N 122 28W
Golden Horn, *Ist.* 17 A2 41 1N 28 57 E
Golders Green, *Lon.* 4 B3 51 34N 0 11W
Golyevo, *Mos.* 11 E7 55 48N 37 18 E
Gometz-la-Ville, *Paris* 5 C2 48 40N 2 7 E
Gometz-le-Châtel, *Paris* 5 C2 48 40N 2 8 E
Gondangdra, *Jak.* 15 J9 6 11 S 106 49 E
Gonesse, *Paris* 5 B4 48 59N 2 26 E
Gongreung, *Sŏul* 12 G8 37 36N 127 3 E
González Catán, *B.A.* 32 C3 34 46 S 58 38W
Goodman Hill, *Bost.* 21 C1 42 22N 71 23W
Goodmayes, *Lon.* 4 B5 51 33N 0 6 E
Gopalnagar, *Calc.* 16 C5 22 50N 88 13 E
Gopalpur, *Calc.* 16 E6 22 38N 88 26 E
Górce, *Wsaw.* 10 E6 52 15N 20 55 E
Gordon, *Syd.* 19 A3 33 46 S 151 8 E
Gore Hill, *Syd.* 19 A4 33 49 S 151 10 E
Gorelyy →, *St-Pet.* 11 A5 60 1N 30 30 E
Gorenki, *Mos.* 11 E11 55 47N 37 53 E
Gorkiy Park, *Mos.* 11 E9 55 43N 37 36 E
Görväln, *Stock.* 3 D9 59 26N 17 45 E
Gose Elbe →, *Hbg.* 7 E8 53 28N 10 6 E
Gosen, *Berl.* 7 B5 52 23N 13 43 E
Gosener kanal, *Berl.* 7 B5 52 24N 13 42 E
Goshenville, *Phil.* 24 B1 39 59N 75 32W
Gospel Oak, *Lon.* 4 B4 51 32N 0 9W
Gotanda, *Tōkyō* 13 C3 35 37N 139 43 E
Gotanno, *Tōkyō* 13 B3 35 45N 139 49 E
Goth Goli Mār, *Kar.* 17 G11 24 53N 67 1 E
Goth Sher Shāh, *Kar.* 17 G10 24 53N 66 59 E
Gournay-sur-Marne, *Paris* 5 B5 48 51N 2 34 E
Goussainville, *Paris* 5 A4 49 1N 2 27 E
Gouvernes, *Paris* 5 B6 48 51N 2 41 E
Governador, I. do, *Rio J.* 31 A2 22 48 S 43 13W
Governor's I., *N.Y.* 22 C4 40 41N 74 1W
Grabicz, *Wsaw.* 10 E8 52 19N 21 12 E
Grabów, *Wsaw.* 10 F6 52 8N 20 59 E
Gracia, *Barc.* 8 D6 41 24N 2 10 E
Gradyville, *Phil.* 24 B2 39 56N 75 27W
Gräfelfing, *Mün.* 7 G9 48 7N 11 25 E
Grafenwald, *Ruhr* 6 A3 51 34N 6 54 E
Graham Memorial Park, *Balt.* 25 A4 39 25N 76 29W
Gran Canal, *Méx.* 29 A3 19 34N 99 1W
Granada Hills, *L.A.* 28 A1 34 16N 118 30W
Grand Bourg, *B.A.* 32 A2 34 29 S 58 42W
Grand Calumet →, *Chic.* 26 D4 41 37N 87 28W
Grand Union Canal, *Lon.* 4 A2 51 42N 0 26W
Grande →, *S. Pau.* 31 F7 23 43 S 46 24W
Grange, *Tori.* 9 B1 45 7N 7 29 E
Grange Hill, *Lon.* 4 B5 51 36N 0 5 E
Granite, *Balt.* 25 A1 39 20N 76 51W
Graniteville, *N.Y.* 22 D3 40 37N 74 10W
Granja Viana, *S. Pau.* 31 E4 23 35 S 46 50W
Granlandet, *Hels.* 3 B6 60 10N 25 15 E
Granö, *Hels.* 3 B6 60 13N 25 14 E
Grant Park, *Chic.* 26 B3 41 52N 87 37W
Granville, *Syd.* 19 A3 33 49 S 151 1 E
Grape I., *Bost.* 21 D4 42 16N 70 55W
Grass Hassock Channel, *N.Y.* 23 D6 40 36N 73 47W
Grassy B., *N.Y.* 23 D6 40 37N 73 47W
Grassy Sprain Res., *N.Y.* 23 B5 40 58N 73 50W
Gratosóglio, *Mil.* 9 E6 45 24N 9 1 E
Gratzwalde, *Berl.* 7 B5 52 28N 13 42 E
Gravesend, *N.Y.* 22 D5 40 36N 73 56W
Grays, *Lon.* 4 C6 51 28N 0 19 E
Grazhdanka, *St-Pet.* 11 B4 59 59N 30 24 E
Great Blue Hill, *Bost.* 21 D3 42 12N 71 4W
Great Bookham, *Lon.* 4 D2 51 16N 0 21W
Great Brewster I., *Bost.* 21 C4 42 19N 70 53W
Great Captain I., *N.Y.* 23 B7 40 59N 73 37W
Great Falls, *Wash.* 25 D6 38 59N 77 17W
Great Falls Park, *Wash.* 25 D6 38 59N 77 14W
Great Kills, *N.Y.* 22 D4 40 32N 74 9W
Great Kills Harbour, *N.Y.* 22 D4 40 32N 74 8W
Great Neck, *N.Y.* 23 C6 40 48N 73 44W
Great Pond, *Bost.* 21 D3 42 11N 71 2W
Great South B., *N.Y.* 23 D9 40 39N 73 19W
Greco, *Mil.* 9 D6 45 30N 9 12 E
Greco I., *S.F.* 27 C3 37 30N 122 10W
Green Brae, *S.F.* 27 A1 37 57N 122 31W
Green Brook, *N.Y.* 22 D2 40 35N 74 26W
Green I., *H.K.* 12 E5 22 17N 114 6 E
Green Land, *Jak.* 15 J9 6 17 S 106 46 E
Green Pond, *N.Y.* 22 A2 41 1N 74 29W
Green Street, *Lon.* 4 A3 51 40N 0 16W
Green Street Green, *Lon.* 4 C5 51 21N 0 5 E
Green Valley, *Syd.* 19 B2 33 54 S 150 53 E
Green Village, *N.Y.* 22 C2 40 44N 74 27W
Greenbelt, *Wash.* 25 C8 39 0N 76 52W
Greenbelt Park, *Wash.* 25 D8 38 58N 76 53W
Greenfield Park, *Mtrl.* 20 B5 43 29N 73 28W
Greenfields Village, *Phil.* 24 C4 39 49N 75 9W
Greenford, *Lon.* 4 B2 51 31N 0 21W
Greenhithe, *Lon.* 4 C6 51 27N 0 17 E
Greenlawn, *N.Y.* 23 B8 40 52N 73 22W
Greenpoint, *N.Y.* 22 C5 40 43N 73 57W
Greensborough, *Melb.* 19 E7 37 41 S 145 5 E
Greenside, *Jobg.* 18 E9 26 8 S 28 1 E
Greenvale, *N.Y.* 23 C7 40 48N 73 35W
Greenville Chauncey, *N.Y.* 23 B5 40 59N 73 50W
Greenwich, *Lon.* 4 C4 51 28N 0 0 E
Greenwich, *N.Y.* 23 A7 41 1N 73 37W
Greenwich, *Syd.* 19 B4 33 50 S 151 11 E
Greenwich Observatory, *Lon.* 4 C4 51 28N 0 0 E
Greenwich Pt., *N.Y.* 23 A7 41 0N 73 34W
Greenwich Village, *N.Y.* 22 C5 40 44N 73 59W
Greenwood, *Bost.* 21 C3 42 29N 71 2W
Grefsen, *Oslo* 2 B4 59 56N 10 47 E
Grégy-sur-Yerres, *Paris* 5 C5 48 40N 2 37 E
Greiffenburg, *Ruhr* 6 B1 51 20N 6 37 E
Gressy, *Paris* 5 B6 48 58N 2 40 E
Greve Strand, *Købn.* 2 E8 55 34N 12 18 E
Greystanes, *Syd.* 19 A2 33 49 S 150 58 E
Griebnitzsee, *Berl.* 7 B1 52 23N 13 8 E
Griffith Park, *L.A.* 28 B3 34 7N 118 18 E
Grignon, *Paris* 5 B1 48 50N 1 56 E
Grigny, *Paris* 5 D4 48 39N 2 23 E
Grinzing, *Wien* 10 G10 48 15N 16 20 E
Grisy-Suisnes, *Paris* 5 C6 48 41N 2 40 E
Gröbenried, *Mün.* 7 F9 48 13N 11 25 E
Grochów, *Wsaw.* 10 E7 52 15N 21 5 E
Grodzisk, *Wsaw.* 10 E7 52 19N 21 4 E
Grogol, *Jak.* 15 H9 6 9 S 106 47 E
Grogol, Kali →, *Jak.* 15 J9 6 11 S 106 47 E
Gronsdorf, *Mün.* 7 G11 48 7N 11 42 E
Grorud, *Oslo* 2 B5 59 57N 10 52 E
Gross Borstel, *Hbg.* 7 D7 53 36N 9 58 E
Gross Flottbek, *Hbg.* 7 D7 53 33N 9 53 E
Gross Glienicke, *Berl.* 7 B1 52 28N 13 6 E
Gross-Hadern, *Mün.* 7 G9 48 6N 11 29 E
Gross-Lappen, *Mün.* 7 F10 48 11N 11 35 E
Grosse Krampe, *Berl.* 7 B5 52 23N 13 40 E
Grosse Müggelsee, *Berl.* 7 B4 52 26N 13 38 E
Grossenbaum, *Ruhr* 6 B2 51 22N 6 46 E
Grossenzersdorf, *Wien* 10 G11 48 12N 16 33 E
Grossenzersdorfer Arm →, *Wien* 10 G11 48 12N 16 31 E
Grosser Biberhaufen, *Wien* 10 G10 48 12N 16 28 E
Grosser Wannsee, *Berl.* 7 B2 52 25N 13 10 E
Grossfeld-Siedlung, *Wien* 10 G10 48 16N 16 26 E
Grosshesselohe, *Mün.* 7 G10 48 3N 11 32 E
Grossjedlersdorf, *Wien* 10 G10 48 16N 16 23 E
Grossziethen, *Berl.* 7 B3 52 23N 13 26 E
Groszówka, *Wsaw.* 10 E8 52 14N 21 13 E
Grove Hall, *Bost.* 21 D3 42 18N 71 4W
Grove Park, *Lon.* 4 C5 51 25N 0 1 E
Grove Park, *Lon.* 4 C3 51 28N 0 15W
Groveton, *Wash.* 25 E7 38 46N 77 6W
Grugliasco, *Tori.* 9 B1 45 4N 7 34 E
Gruiten, *Ruhr* 6 C4 51 12N 7 0 E
Grumme, *Ruhr* 6 B5 51 30N 7 15 E
Grumo Nevano, *Nápl.* 9 H12 40 56N 14 15 E
Grünau, *Berl.* 7 B4 52 25N 13 34 E
Grunewald, *Berl.* 7 B2 52 28N 13 15 E
Grünwald, *Mün.* 7 G10 48 2N 11 31 E
Grünwalder Forst, *Mün.* 7 G10 48 2N 11 33 E
Grymes Hill, *N.Y.* 22 D4 40 36N 74 6W
Gu Ro, *Sŏul* 12 G7 37 30N 126 51 E
Guadalupe, *Manila* 15 D4 14 34N 121 2 E
Guadalupe →, *S.F.* 27 D4 37 28N 122 4W
Guadalupe, Basilica de, *Méx.* 29 B3 19 29N 99 7W
Guadelupe, *Rio J.* 31 A1 22 49 S 43 20W
Guanabacoa, *La Hab.* 30 B3 23 7N 82 17W
Guanabara, *Rio J.* 31 B1 22 57 S 43 20W
Guanabara, B. de, *Rio J.* 31 B2 22 52 S 43 10W
Guanabara, Jardim, *Rio J.* 31 A2 22 48 S 43 11W
Guang'anmen, *Beij.* 14 B2 39 51N 116 18 E
Guangmingloy, *Beij.* 14 B3 39 51N 116 23 E
Guangqumen, *Beij.* 14 B3 39 52N 116 25 E
Guangzhou, *Gzh.* 14 G8 23 6N 113 13 E
Guanshuo, *Gzh.* 14 G9 23 4N 113 22 E
Guantai, *Nápl.* 9 H12 40 52N 14 11 E
Guapira →, *S. Pau.* 31 D6 23 30 S 46 33W
Guarapiranga, Res. de, *S. Pau.* 31 F5 23 43 S 46 43W
Guardias, *Madr.* 8 B3 40 29N 3 31W
Gurulhos, *S. Pau.* 31 D6 23 28 S 46 32W
Guatao, *La Hab.* 30 B2 23 0N 82 29W
Guayacanes, Pta., *La Hab.* 30 A3 23 10N 82 16W
Gubernador Monteverde, *B.A.* 32 C5 34 47 S 58 16W
Gudö, *Stock.* 3 E12 59 12N 18 12 E
Güell, Parque de, *Barc.* 8 D6 41 24N 2 10 E
Guermantes, *Paris* 5 B6 48 51N 2 42 E
Gugging, *Wien* 10 G9 48 18N 16 15 E
Guianazes, *S. Pau.* 31 E7 23 32 S 46 24W
Guildford, *Syd.* 19 B2 33 51 S 150 59 E
Guinardó, *Barc.* 8 D6 41 24N 2 10 E
Gujiazhai, *Shang.* 14 H11 31 21N 121 23 E
Gulbāi, *Kar.* 17 G10 24 52N 66 58 E
Guldasteh, *Tehr.* 17 D4 35 36N 51 15 E
Gulistan Palace, *Tehr.* 17 C5 35 40N 51 24 E
Gulph Mills, *Phil.* 24 A2 40 4N 75 20W
Gumbostrand, *Hels.* 3 B6 60 15N 25 17 E
Güngören, *Ist.* 17 A2 41 1N 28 52 E
Gunnarsby, *Hels.* 3 C1 60 6N 24 28W
Gunnersbury, *Lon.* 4 C3 51 29N 0 17W
Gunnigfeld, *Ruhr* 6 B4 51 29N 7 8 E
Gunpowder Falls →, *Balt.* 25 A4 39 23N 76 36W
Gunung Sahari, *Jak.* 15 H9 6 9 S 106 49 E
Gupiing, *Manila* 15 E5 14 27N 121 11 E
Guryong San, *Sŏul* 12 H8 37 28N 127 3 E
Gustavsberg, *Stock.* 3 E13 59 19N 18 23 E
Guttenberg, *N.Y.* 22 C4 40 48N 74 0W
Gutuyevskiy, Os., *St-Pet.* 11 B3 59 53N 30 15 E
Guyancourt, *Paris* 5 C2 48 46N 2 4 E
Guyancourt, Aérodrome de, *Paris* 5 C2 48 45N 2 3 E
Gvali-patak →, *Bud.* 10 K13 47 23N 19 7 E
Gwan Ag, *Sŏul* 12 H7 37 29N 126 57 E
Gwang San, *Sŏul* 12 H7 37 27N 126 58 E
Gwynns Falls →, *Balt.* 25 B2 39 19N 76 42W
Gyál, *Bud.* 10 K14 47 23N 19 13 E
Gyeongbong Palace, *Sŏul* 12 G7 37 34N 126 58 E
Gynea, *Syd.* 19 C3 34 1 S 151 5 E


## H


Haaga, *Hels.* 3 B4 60 13N 24 53 E
Haan, *Ruhr* 6 C3 51 11N 6 59 E
Haar, *Mün.* 7 G11 48 6N 11 43 E
Haar, *Ruhr* 6 B5 51 26N 7 13 E
Haarzopf, *Ruhr* 6 B3 51 25N 6 57 E
Habana del Este, *La Hab.* 30 B3 23 9N 82 19W
Habay, *Manila* 15 E3 14 27N 120 56 E
Habikino, *Ōsaka* 12 C4 34 33N 135 36 E
Habinghorst, *Ruhr* 6 A5 51 34N 7 18 E
Hacienda Heights, *L.A.* 28 C5 33 59N 117 59W
Hackbridge, *Lon.* 4 C4 51 23N 0 9W
Hackensack, *N.Y.* 22 B4 40 52N 74 4W
Hackney, *Lon.* 4 B4 51 32N 0 3W
Hackney Wick, *Lon.* 4 B4 51 32N 0 1W
Haddon Heights, *Phil.* 24 B4 39 53N 75 3W
Haddonfield, *Phil.* 24 B4 39 53N 75 3W
Hadersdorf, *Wien* 10 G9 48 12N 16 14 E
Hadley Wood, *Lon.* 4 B3 51 39N 0 10W
Haga, *Stock.* 3 D11 59 21N 18 1 E
Hagem, *Ruhr* 6 A5 51 38N 7 19 E
Hagen, *Ruhr* 6 B6 51 21N 7 27 E
Hägersten, *Stock.* 3 E10 59 18N 17 59 E
Haggetts Pond, *Bost.* 21 B2 42 39N 71 11W
Häggvik, *Stock.* 3 D10 59 26N 17 56 E
Hagonoy, *Manila* 15 D4 14 30N 121 4 E
Hagsätra, *Stock.* 3 E11 59 15N 18 0 E
Hahipur, *Calc.* 16 D5 22 47N 88 10 E
Hahnerberg, *Ruhr* 6 C4 51 12N 7 8 E
Hai He →, *Tianj.* 14 E6 39 4N 117 17 E
Haidarpur, *Delhi* 16 A1 28 43N 77 8 E
Haidhausen, *Mün.* 7 G10 48 7N 11 36 E
Haidian, *Beij.* 14 B2 39 59N 116 16 E
Haight-Ashbury, *S.F.* 27 B2 37 46N 122 26W
Haiguangsi, *Tianj.* 14 E6 39 7N 117 11 E
Hainault, *Lon.* 4 B5 51 36N 0 6 E
Haizhu Guangchang, *Gzh.* 14 G8 23 6N 113 14 E
Hakim, *El Qâ.* 18 C4 30 4N 31 7 E
Hakunila, *Hels.* 3 B5 60 16N 25 6 E
Halchōbori, *Tōkyō* 13 B4 35 48N 139 55 E
Haledon, *N.Y.* 22 B3 40 57N 74 11W
Halesite, *N.Y.* 23 B8 40 53N 73 24W
Halethorpe, *Balt.* 25 B2 39 14N 76 41W
Half Hollow Hills, *N.Y.* 23 C8 40 48N 73 21W
Half Moon B., *S.F.* 26 D2 37 27N 122 25W
Half Moon Bay Airport, *S.F.* 27 C1 37 31N 122 30W
Half Moon Bay Beaches, *S.F.* 26 D2 37 28N 122 28W
Halim, *Jak.* 15 J10 6 15 S 106 53 E
Halim Perdanakusuma Airport, *Jak.* 15 J10 6 16 S 106 53 E
Halstead, *Lon.* 4 D5 51 19N 0 8 E
Halstenbeck, *Hbg.* 7 D7 53 38N 9 50 E
Haltiala, *Hels.* 3 B4 60 16N 24 57 E
Haltiavuori, *Hels.* 3 B4 60 16N 24 56 E
Ham, *Lon.* 4 C3 51 25N 0 18W
Ham, *Paris* 5 A2 49 1N 2 3 E
Hamberg, *Jobg.* 18 E8 26 9 S 27 54 E
Hamborn, *Ruhr* 6 B2 51 29N 6 46 E
Hamburg, *Hbg.* 7 D8 53 33N 10 0 E
Hamburg Flughafen, *Hbg.* 7 D7 53 38N 9 59 E
Hämeenkylä, *Hels.* 3 B3 60 16N 24 48 E
Hamm, *Hbg.* 7 D8 53 33N 10 2 E
Hamm, *Ruhr* 6 C2 51 12N 6 44 E
Hammarby, *Stock.* 3 E11 59 17N 18 5 E
Hamme, *Ruhr* 6 B5 51 29N 7 12 E
Hammel Arverne, *N.Y.* 23 D6 40 35N 73 48W
Hammerbrook, *Hbg.* 7 D8 53 32N 10 1 E
Hammersmith, *Lon.* 4 C3 51 29N 0 14W
Hammond, *Chic.* 26 D4 41 36N 87 29W
Hampstead, *Lon.* 4 B3 51 33N 0 10W
Hampstead, *Mtrl.* 20 B4 43 28N 73 37W
Hampstead Garden Suburb, *Lon.* 4 B3 51 34N 0 11W
Hampstead Heath, *Lon.* 4 B3 51 33N 0 10W
Hampton Court Palace, *Lon.* 4 C2 51 24N 0 20W
Hampton Hill, *Lon.* 4 C2 51 25N 0 21W
Hampton Wick, *Lon.* 4 C3 51 24N 0 18W
Hamrā, *Bagd.* 17 F7 33 18N 44 18 E
Han Gang →, *Sŏul* 12 G7 37 32N 126 55 E
Hanakuri, *Tōkyō* 13 A3 35 50N 139 47 E
Hanala, *Hels.* 3 A5 60 20N 25 2 E
Hancho, *Ōsaka* 12 B4 34 48N 135 28 E
Haneda, *Tōkyō* 13 C3 35 32N 139 44 E
Hang Hau, *H.K.* 12 E6 22 19N 114 16 E
Hanjiashu, *Tianj.* 14 D5 39 11N 117 4 E
Hanlon, *Trto.* 20 E7 43 38N 79 39W
Hansen Flood Control Basin, *L.A.* 28 A2 34 15N 118 23W
Hansia, *Calc.* 16 D6 22 48N 88 25 E
Hanskinen, *Hels.* 3 C6 60 8N 25 15 E
Hanwell, *Lon.* 4 B2 51 30N 0 20W
Hanworth, *Lon.* 4 C2 51 26N 0 23W
Haora, *Calc.* 16 E5 22 34N 88 18 E
Happy Valley, *H.K.* 12 E6 22 16N 114 10 E
Harajuku, *Tōkyō* 13 D2 35 22N 139 30 E
Haraki, *Tōkyō* 13 B4 35 42N 139 56 E
Harat, *Calc.* 16 C5 22 52N 88 11 E
Harbor Hills, *N.Y.* 23 C6 40 46N 73 44W
Harburg, *Hbg.* 7 E7 53 27N 9 59 E
Harding, *Bost.* 21 D2 42 12N 71 19W
Hardricourt, *Paris* 5 A1 49 0N 1 53 E
Harefield, *Lon.* 4 B1 51 36N 0 28W
Hareskovby, *Købn.* 2 D9 55 45N 12 23 E
Harewood Park, *Balt.* 25 A4 39 22N 76 21W
Harigaya, *Tōkyō* 13 B2 35 49N 139 33 E
Haringey, *Lon.* 4 B4 51 34N 0 4W
Haripur, *Calc.* 16 D5 22 42N 88 10 E
Harjula, *Hels.* 3 A3 60 21N 24 45 E
Harjusuo, *Hels.* 3 B5 60 19N 25 0 E
Harkortsee, *Ruhr* 6 B6 51 23N 7 24 E
Harksheide, *Hbg.* 7 C8 53 43N 10 0 E
Harlaching, *Mün.* 7 G10 48 5N 11 33 E
Harlem, *N.Y.* 22 C5 40 48N 73 56W
Harlesden, *Lon.* 4 B3 51 32N 0 14W
Harlington, *Lon.* 4 C2 51 29N 0 25W
Harmaja, *Hels.* 3 C4 60 6N 24 58 E
Harmashatar hegy, *Bud.* 10 J13 47 33N 19 0 E
Harmondsworth, *Lon.* 4 C2 51 29N 0 29W
Harmonville, *Phil.* 24 A3 40 5N 75 18W
Harold Hill, *Lon.* 4 B6 51 35N 0 14 E
Harold Parker State Forest, *Bost.* 21 B3 42 37N 71 4W
Harold Wood, *Lon.* 4 B6 51 35N 0 14 E
Harrington Park, *N.Y.* 22 B5 40 59N 73 59W
Harrison, *N.Y.* 22 C4 40 44N 74 9W
Harrison, *N.Y.* 23 B6 40 57N 73 42W
Harrisonville, *Balt.* 25 A2 39 22N 76 49W
Harrow, *Lon.* 4 B2 51 34N 0 20W
Harrow on the Hill, *Lon.* 4 B2 51 34N 0 21W
Harrow School, *Lon.* 4 B2 51 34N 0 20W
Harrow Weald, *Lon.* 4 B2 51 36N 0 20W
Hart I., *Balt.* 25 B4 39 14N 76 23W
Hart I., *N.Y.* 23 B6 40 51N 73 46W
Hartford, *Phil.* 24 B5 39 58N 74 53W
Hartley, *Lon.* 4 C6 51 22N 0 18 E
Hartsdale, *N.Y.* 23 A6 41 1N 73 48W
Harumi, *Tōkyō* 13 C3 35 38N 139 47 E
Harvard, Mt., *L.A.* 28 A4 34 12N 118 4W
Harvard Univ., *Bost.* 21 C3 42 23N 71 7W
Harvestehude, *Hbg.* 7 D7 53 34N 9 58 E
Harvey, *Chic.* 26 D3 41 36N 87 39W
Harwood Heights, *Chic.* 26 B2 41 57N 87 46W
Hasanābād, *Tehr.* 17 C4 35 44N 51 16 E
Hasbrouck Heights, *N.Y.* 22 B4 40 51N 74 6W
Haselbach, *Wien* 10 G9 48 18N 16 14 E
Haselhorst, *Berl.* 7 A2 52 33N 13 14 E
Hasköy, *Ist.* 17 A2 41 2N 28 57 E
Hasle, *Oslo* 2 C3 59 46N 10 38 E
Hasloh, *Hbg.* 7 C7 53 41N 9 54 E
Haslohfeld, *Hbg.* 7 C7 53 41N 9 56 E
Haslum, *Oslo* 2 B3 59 55N 10 34 E
Haspe, *Ruhr* 6 B6 51 21N 7 25 E
Haspertalsp, *Ruhr* 6 C6 51 17N 7 24 E
Hasselbeck, *Ruhr* 6 C3 51 19N 6 56 E
Hässelby, *Stock.* 3 D10 59 22N 17 50 E
Hasslinghausen, *Ruhr* 6 C5 51 20N 7 16 E
Hasten, *Ruhr* 6 C5 51 11N 7 11 E
Hästhagen, *Stock.* 3 E11 59 18N 18 9 E
Hastings-on-Hudson, *N.Y.* 23 B5 40 59N 73 51W
Hatch End, *Lon.* 4 B2 51 36N 0 22W
Hatiara, *Calc.* 16 E6 22 36N 88 26 E
Hatogaya, *Tōkyō* 13 B3 35 49N 139 44 E
Hattingen, *Ruhr* 6 B5 51 23N 7 11 E
Hatton, *Lon.* 4 C2 51 28N 0 25W
Hattori, *Ōsaka* 12 A4 34 51N 135 36 E
Haukelo, *Oslo* 2 B4 59 50N 10 48 E
Hauldres →, *Paris* 5 D5 48 37N 2 37 E
Hausbruch, *Hbg.* 7 E7 53 28N 9 53 E
Havalimani, *Ist.* 17 B2 40 59N 28 50 E
Havana = La Habana, *La Hab.* 30 B2 23 7N 82 21W
Havdrup, *Købn.* 2 E7 55 33N 12 7 E
Havel →, *Berl.* 7 A2 52 37N 13 11 E
Havelkanal, *Berl.* 7 A2 52 36N 13 10 E
Haverford, *Phil.* 24 A3 40 0N 75 18W
Havering, *Lon.* 4 B6 51 33N 0 12 E
Havering-atte-Bower, *Lon.* 4 B6 51 37N 0 11 E
Havertown, *Phil.* 24 B3 39 58N 75 18W
Hawangsibri, *Sŏul* 12 G8 37 33N 127 1 E
Haweolgog, *Sŏul* 12 G8 37 35N 127 1 E
Haworth, *N.Y.* 22 A5 40 57N 73 59W
Hawthorne, *L.A.* 28 C2 33 54N 118 21W
Hawthorne, *N.Y.* 22 B4 40 57N 74 8W
Hayes, *Lon.* 4 C5 51 22N 0 0 E
Hayes, *Lon.* 4 B2 51 30N 0 25W
Hayes End, *Lon.* 4 B2 51 31N 0 25W
Hayford, *Chic.* 26 C2 41 45N 87 42W
Hayward, *S.F.* 27 B4 37 40N 122 4W
Hayward Fault, *S.F.* 27 B3 37 46N 122 10W
Haywood Municipal Airport, *S.F.* 27 C4 32 39N 122 9W
Headley, *Lon.* 4 D3 51 16N 0 16W
Headstone, *Lon.* 4 B2 51 35N 0 21W
Heard Pond, *Bost.* 21 C1 42 20N 71 23W
Heard Pond, *Bost.* 21 B1 42 33N 71 23W
Heath Park, *Lon.* 4 B6 51 34N 0 12 E
Heathmont, *Melb.* 19 E8 37 49 S 145 14 E
Heathrow Airport, *Lon.* 4 C2 51 28N 0 27W
Hebbville, *Balt.* 25 A2 39 20N 76 45W
Hebe Haven, *H.K.* 12 D6 22 21N 114 15 E
Hebei, *Tianj.* 14 E6 39 9N 117 11 E
Hedehusene, *Købn.* 2 E8 55 39N 12 11 E
Hedong, *Gzh.* 14 G8 23 5N 113 14 E
Hedong, *Tianj.* 14 E6 39 7N 117 11 E
Heerdt, *Ruhr* 6 C2 51 13N 6 42 E
Hegewisch, *Chic.* 26 D3 41 39N 87 32W
Heggelielva →, *Oslo* 2 A3 60 1N 10 36 E
Heide, *Ruhr* 6 C3 51 31N 6 50 E
Heidelberg, *Melb.* 19 E7 37 45 S 145 4 E
Heidelberg West, *Melb.* 19 E7 37 43 S 145 2 E
Heidemühle, *Berl.* 7 B5 52 29N 13 40 E
Heidhausen, *Ruhr* 6 B4 51 22N 7 1 E
Heiligenhaus, *Ruhr* 6 C3 51 19N 6 57 E
Heiligensee, *Berl.* 7 A2 52 36N 13 13 E
Heiligenstadt, *Wien* 10 G10 48 14N 16 21 E
Heimfeld, *Hbg.* 7 E7 53 28N 9 57 E
Heinässuo, *Hels.* 3 B1 60 18N 24 27 E
Heinersdorf, *Berl.* 7 A3 52 34N 13 25 E
Heisingen, *Ruhr* 6 B4 51 24N 7 3 E
Heissen, *Ruhr* 6 B3 51 26N 6 54 E
Helderkruin, *Jobg.* 18 E8 26 7 S 27 51 E
Helenelund, *Stock.* 3 D10 59 24N 17 58 E
Heliopolis, *El Qâ.* 18 C5 30 5N 31 19 E
Hellersdorf, *Berl.* 7 A4 52 32N 13 35 E
Hellerup, *Købn.* 2 D10 55 44N 12 33 E
Helmahof, *Wien* 10 G11 48 18N 16 34 E
Helsingfors = Helsinki, *Hels.* 3 B4 60 10N 24 55 E
Helsinki, *Hels.* 3 B4 60 10N 24 55 E
Helsinki Airport, *Hels.* 3 B4 60 18N 24 58 E
Hempstead, *N.Y.* 23 C7 40 42N 73 37W
Hempstead Harbor, *N.Y.* 23 B7 40 50N 73 39W
Henan, *Gzh.* 14 G8 23 5N 113 14 E
Hendon, *Lon.* 4 B3 51 35N 0 14W
Hengsha, *Gzh.* 14 G8 23 9N 113 12 E
Hengsteysee, *Ruhr* 6 B6 51 24N 7 27 E
Hennigsdorf, *Berl.* 7 A2 52 38N 13 12 E
Henrichenburg, *Ruhr* 6 A5 51 35N 7 19 E
Henriville, *Paris* 5 C1 48 44N 1 56 E
Henrykow, *Wsaw.* 10 E6 52 19N 20 58 E
Henson Cr. →, *Wash.* 25 E8 38 47N 76 58W
Henttaa, *Hels.* 3 B3 60 11N 24 45 E
Heping, *Tianj.* 14 E6 39 7N 117 11 E
Heping Gongyuan, *Shang.* 14 J12 31 16N 121 30 E
Hepingli, *Beij.* 14 B3 39 57N 116 23 E
Herbeck, *Ruhr* 6 C5 51 12N 7 18 E
Herbede, *Ruhr* 6 B5 51 25N 7 16 E
Herblay, *Paris* 5 B2 48 59N 2 9 E
Herdecke, *Ruhr* 6 B6 51 24N 7 25 E
Herlev, *Købn.* 2 D9 55 43N 12 27 E
Hermannskogel, *Wien* 10 G9 48 16N 16 17 E
Hermitage and Winter Palace, *St-Pet.* 11 B3 59 55N 30 19 E
Hermosa Beach, *L.A.* 28 C2 33 51N 118 23W
Hermsdorf, *Berl.* 7 A2 52 37N 13 18 E
Hernals, *Wien* 10 G10 48 13N 16 20 E
Herne, *Ruhr* 6 A5 51 32N 7 13 E
Herne Hill, *Lon.* 4 C4 51 27N 0 6W
Hernwood Heights, *Balt.* 25 A2 39 22N 76 49W
Héroes de Churubusco, *Méx.* 29 B3 19 21N 99 6W
Herongate, *Lon.* 4 B7 51 35N 0 21 E
Herons, Î. aux, *Mtrl.* 20 B4 43 25N 73 34W
Herricks, *N.Y.* 23 C7 40 45N 73 39W
Herring Run →, *Balt.* 25 B3 39 18N 76 30W
Hersham, *Lon.* 4 C2 51 21N 0 22W
Herstedøster, *Købn.* 2 D9 55 40N 12 22 E
Herten, *Ruhr* 6 A4 51 35N 7 8 E
Herttoniemi, *Hels.* 3 B5 60 11N 25 2 E
Hessler, *Ruhr* 6 A4 51 31N 7 3 E
Heston, *Lon.* 4 C2 51 28N 0 22W
Hetterscheidt, *Ruhr* 6 B3 51 20N 6 59 E
Hetzendorf, *Wien* 10 H9 48 9N 16 17 E
Heuberg, *Wien* 10 G9 48 13N 16 16 E
Heven, *Ruhr* 6 B5 51 26N 7 18 E
Hewlett Neck, *N.Y.* 23 D6 40 37N 73 41W
Hexi, *Tianj.* 14 E5 39 8N 117 9 E
Hexingcun, *Tianj.* 14 E6 39 6N 117 10 E
Hextable, *Lon.* 4 C6 51 24N 0 10 E
Heybridge, *Lon.* 4 B7 51 39N 0 22 E
Hibernia, *N.Y.* 22 B2 40 57N 74 29W
Hickory Hills, *Chic.* 26 C2 41 43N 87 49W
Hicksville, *N.Y.* 23 C7 40 46N 73 30W
Hiddinghausen, *Ruhr* 6 B5 51 21N 7 17 E
Hiekkaharju, *Hels.* 3 B5 60 18N 25 2 E
Hiesfeld, *Ruhr* 6 A2 51 33N 6 46 E
Hietaniemi, *Hels.* 3 B4 60 10N 24 54 E
Hietzing, *Wien* 10 G9 48 10N 16 17 E
Higashi, *Ōsaka* 12 B4 34 41N 135 30 E
Higashi-kaizuka, *Tōkyō* 13 A3 35 50N 139 46 E
Higashimonzen, *Tōkyō* 13 A3 35 55N 139 40 E
Higashimurayama, *Tōkyō* 13 B1 35 45N 139 26 E
Higashinada, *Ōsaka* 12 B3 34 42N 135 15 E
Higashinari, *Ōsaka* 12 B4 34 40N 135 32 E
Higashiōsaka, *Ōsaka* 12 C4 34 39N 135 37 E
Higashisumiyoshi, *Ōsaka* 12 C4 34 37N 135 31 E
Higashiyodogawa, *Ōsaka* 12 B3 34 44N 135 28 E
High Beach, *Lon.* 4 B5 51 39N 0 1 E
High Junk Pk., *H.K.* 12 E6 22 17N 114 17 E
High Park, *Trto.* 20 E8 43 38N 79 27W
Higham Hill, *Lon.* 4 B4 51 35N 0 2W
Highbury, *Lon.* 4 B4 51 33N 0 6W
Highgate, *Lon.* 4 B4 51 34N 0 8 E
Highland Cr. →, *Trto.* 20 D9 43 45N 79 13W
Highland Creek, *Trto.* 20 D9 43 46N 79 8W
Highland Park, *L.A.* 28 B3 34 7N 118 13 E
Highland Park, *N.Y.* 22 D2 40 30N 74 25W
Highlands North, *Jobg.* 18 E9 26 8 S 28 5 E
Highway Highlands, *L.A.* 28 A3 34 14N 118 16W
Higurashi, *Tōkyō* 13 B4 35 47N 139 55 E
Hila, *Méx.* 29 A2 19 35N 99 17W
Hillcrest Heights, *Wash.* 25 E8 38 49N 76 57W
Hillerheide, *Ruhr* 6 A5 51 35N 7 12 E
Hilleshög, *Stock.* 3 D9 59 23N 17 42 E
Hillgrove District, *L.A.* 28 B5 34 1N 117 58W
Hillingdon, *Lon.* 4 B2 51 32N 0 27W
Hillingdon Heath, *Lon.* 4 B2 51 31N 0 26W
Hillsborough, *S.F.* 27 C2 37 32N 122 21W
Hillsdale, *N.Y.* 22 A4 41 0N 74 1W
Hillsdale, *S.F.* 27 C3 37 32N 122 18W
Hillsdale Manor, *N.Y.* 22 A4 41 1N 74 3W
Hillside, *Chic.* 26 B1 41 52N 87 55W
Hillside, *N.Y.* 23 C6 40 42N 73 46W
Hillside Manor, *N.Y.* 23 C6 40 44N 73 40W
Hilltop, *Phil.* 24 C4 39 49N 75 4W
Hillwood, *Wash.* 25 D7 38 52N 77 9W
Hilmīya, *El Qâ.* 18 C5 30 6N 31 19 E
Hiltrop, *Ruhr* 6 A5 51 31N 7 15 E
Hindsby, *Hels.* 3 A6 60 20N 25 13 E
Hingham, *Bost.* 21 D4 42 14N 70 54W
Hingham B., *Bost.* 21 D4 42 17N 70 56W
Hingham Harbor, *Bost.* 21 D4 42 15N 70 53W
Hino, *Tōkyō* 13 D2 35 23N 139 35 E
Hinsbeck, *Ruhr* 6 C6 51 22N 7 4 E
Hinschenfelde, *Hbg.* 7 D8 53 35N 10 4 E
Hinsdale, *Chic.* 26 C1 41 47N 87 55W
Hinterhainbach, *Wien* 10 G9 48 14N 16 13 E
Hintersdorf, *Wien* 10 G9 48 18N 16 13 E
Hirakata, *Ōsaka* 12 B4 34 48N 135 38 E
Hirota, *Ōsaka* 12 B3 34 45N 135 20 E
Hirschstetten, *Wien* 10 G10 48 14N 16 27 E
Hither Green, *Lon.* 4 C4 51 26N 0 0 E
Hiyoshi, *Tōkyō* 13 C2 35 32N 139 38 E
Hjortekær, *Købn.* 2 D10 55 47N 12 32 E
Hjortespring, *Købn.* 2 D9 55 44N 12 25 E
Hlubočepy, *Pra.* 10 B2 50 2N 14 23 E
Ho Chung, *H.K.* 12 D6 22 21N 114 14 E
Ho Man Tin, *H.K.* 12 E6 22 18N 114 11 E
Hoboken, *N.Y.* 22 C4 40 44N 74 3W
Hobsons B., *Melb.* 19 F6 37 51 S 144 55 E
Hochbrück, *Mün.* 7 F10 48 14N 11 37 E
Hochdahl, *Ruhr* 6 C3 51 13N 6 55 E
Hochemmerich, *Ruhr* 6 B2 51 24N 6 41 E
Hochfeld, *Ruhr* 6 B2 51 25N 6 45 E
Hochheide, *Ruhr* 6 B2 51 27N 6 40 E
Hochlar, *Ruhr* 6 A5 51 36N 7 11 E
Hochlarmark, *Ruhr* 6 A4 51 34N 7 11 E
Hodgkins, *Chic.* 26 C1 41 46N 87 53W
Hodogaya-Ku, *Tōkyō* 13 D2 35 26N 139 35 E
Hoegi, *Sŏul* 12 G8 37 35N 127 4 E
Hofberg, *Wien* 10 G10 48 12N 16 21 E
Hoffman I., *N.Y.* 22 D4 40 34N 74 3W
Hofstede, *Ruhr* 6 A5 51 30N 7 11 E
Höggarnsfjärden, *Stock.* 3 D13 59 23N 18 22 E
Hohe Mark, Naturpark, *Ruhr* 6 A2 51 35N 6 49 E
Hohe Schaar, *Hbg.* 7 E7 53 29N 9 58 E
Hohenbrunn, *Mün.* 7 G11 48 2N 11 42 E
Hohenfelde, *Hbg.* 7 D8 53 33N 10 1 E
Hohenkirchen, *Mün.* 7 G11 48 1N 11 44 E
Hohenraden, *Hbg.* 7 C6 53 41N 9 49 E
Hohenschönhausen, *Berl.* 7 A4 52 33N 13 30 E
Hohenwisch, *Hbg.* 7 E7 53 29N 9 53 E

Kennedy Grove Regional Rec. Area 39


Hohokus, N.Y. 22 A4 41 0N 74 5W
Hok Tsui, H.K. 12 E6 22 12N 114 15 E
Holborn, Lon. 4 B4 51 31N 0 7W
Holešovice, Pra. 10 B2 50 6N 14 28 E
Holland Village, Sing. 15 G7 1 18N 103 47 E
Hollis, N.Y. 23 C6 40 42N 73 45W
Höllriegelskreuth, Mün. 7 G9 48 2N 11 30 E
Holly Oak, Phil. 24 C2 39 47N 75 27W
Hollydale, L.A. 28 C4 33 55N 118 10W
Hollywood Bowl, L.A. 28 B2 34 6N 118 21W
Hollywood-Burbank Airport, L.A. 28 A2 34 11N 118 21W
Holmenkollen, Oslo 2 B4 59 57N 10 41 E
Holmes, Phil. 24 B3 39 53N 75 18W
Holmes Acres, Wash. 25 D6 38 51N 77 13W
Holmes Run →, Wash. 25 E7 38 48N 77 6W
Holmesburg, Phil. 24 A4 40 2N 75 2W
Holmgård, Stock. 3 E10 59 14N 18 0 E
Holsfjorden, Oslo 2 B1 59 58N 10 17 E
Holsterhausen, Ruhr 6 A5 51 32N 7 11 E
Holte, Købn. 2 D9 55 48N 12 27 E
Holten, Ruhr 6 A2 51 31N 6 47 E
Holthausen, Ruhr 6 B4 51 25N 7 5 E
Holzbüttgen, Ruhr 6 C1 51 13N 6 37 E
Homberg, Ruhr 6 B2 51 27N 6 41 E
Hombruch, Ruhr 6 B6 51 28N 7 27 E
Homerton, Lon. 4 B4 51 32N 0 2W
Homestead Lake, Jobg. 18 F10 26 10 S 28 17 E
Homestead Valley, S.F. 27 A1 37 53N 122 32W
Hometown, Chic. 26 C2 41 44N 87 42W
Homledal, Oslo 2 B1 59 59N 10 18 E
Homówek, Wsaw. 10 E5 52 17N 20 48 E
Hon-gyōtoku, Tōkyō 13 B4 35 41N 139 57 E
Hōnanchō, Tōkyō 13 B2 35 40N 139 39 E
Honcho, Tōkyō 13 B3 35 40N 139 41 E
Honden, Tōkyō 13 B4 35 43N 139 50 E
Honeydew, Jobg. 18 E8 26 4 S 27 55 E
Hong Kah, Sing. 15 F7 1 21N 103 43 E
Hong Kong, H.K. 12 E5 22 17N 114 11 E
Hong Kong, Univ. of, H.K. 12 E5 22 16N 114 8 E
Hong Kong Airport, H.K. 12 E6 22 19N 114 11 E
Hong Kong I., H.K. 12 E6 22 16N 114 11 E
Hong Lim Park, Sing. 15 G8 1 17N 103 50 E
Hongeun, Sŏul 12 G7 37 35N 126 56 E
Honggiao, Shang. 14 J11 31 12N 121 22 E
Honggou, Shang. 14 J11 31 16N 121 29 E
Hongkou Gongyuan, Shang. 14 J11 31 17N 121 28 E
Hongmiao, Beij. 14 B3 39 54N 116 26 E
Hongqiao, Tianj. 14 E5 39 8N 117 9 E
Hongqiao Airport, Shang. 14 J10 31 12N 121 19 E
Honjyo, Tōkyō 13 B3 35 41N 139 48 E
Honmoku, Tōkyō 13 D2 35 24N 139 39 E
Hönow, Berl. 7 A4 52 32N 13 38 E
Höntrop, Ruhr 6 B4 51 27N 7 9 E
Hood Pond, Bost. 21 A4 42 40N 70 57W
Hooghly →, Calc. 16 D6 22 41N 88 21 E
Hook, Lon. 4 C3 51 22N 0 17W
Hopelawn, N.Y. 22 D3 40 31N 74 17W
Hörde, Ruhr 6 B7 51 29N 7 30 E
Horikiri, Tōkyō 13 B4 35 44N 139 50 E
Horn, Hbg. 7 D8 53 33N 10 5 E
Horn Pond, Bost. 21 C2 42 28N 71 9W
Hornchurch, Lon. 4 B6 51 33N 0 14 E
Horneburg, Ruhr 6 A5 51 37N 7 17 E
Horní, Pra. 10 B3 50 2N 14 33 E
Horní Počernice, Pra. 10 B3 50 6N 14 36 E
Hornsey, Lon. 4 B4 51 35N 0 7W
Horoměřice, Pra. 10 B1 50 8N 14 20 E
Horsley Park, Syd. 19 B2 33 50 S 150 51 E
Horst, Ruhr 6 B4 51 26N 7 6 E
Horsthausen, Ruhr 6 A5 51 33N 7 12 E
Hortaleza, Mdrd. 8 B3 40 28N 3 38W
Horto Florestal, S. Pau. 31 D6 23 27 S 46 38W
Horton Kirby, Lon. 4 C6 51 23N 0 14 E
Hösel, Ruhr 6 B3 51 19N 6 54 E
Hosoyama, Tōkyō 13 C2 35 36N 139 31 E
Hospitalet, Barc. 8 D5 41 21N 2 6 E
Hostafranchs, Barc. 8 D5 41 21N 2 8 E
Hoterheide, Ruhr 6 C1 51 16N 6 37 E
Houbetin, Pra. 10 B3 50 6N 14 33 E
Houghs Neck, Bost. 21 D4 42 15N 70 57W
Houghton, Jobg. 18 F9 26 10 S 28 3 E
Houilles, Paris 5 B3 48 56N 2 11 E
Hounslow, Lon. 4 C2 51 28N 0 21W
Houses of Parliament, Lon. 4 C4 51 29N 0 7W
Hove Å →, Købn. 2 D8 55 43N 12 7 E
Hovedøya, Oslo 2 B4 59 53N 10 43 E
Høvik, Oslo 2 B3 59 54N 10 34 E
Hovorčovice, Pra. 10 A3 50 10N 14 31 E
Howard Beach, N.Y. 23 D5 40 39N 73 50W
Hoxton Park, Syd. 19 B2 33 55 S 150 51 E
Hoxton Park Aerodrome, Syd. 19 B2 33 54 S 150 50 E
Hōya, Tōkyō 13 B2 35 44N 139 34 E
Høybråten, Oslo 2 B5 59 56N 10 55 E
Hradčany, Pra. 10 B2 50 5N 14 24 E
Hsiya, Gzh. 14 G7 23 9N 113 6 E
Huangpu, Gzh. 14 G9 23 5N 113 23 E
Huangpu, Shang. 14 J12 31 14N 121 30 E
Huangpu Gongyuan, Shang. 14 J11 31 14N 121 29 E
Huangpu Jiang →, Shang. 14 J11 31 11N 121 29 E
Huangtugang, Beij. 14 C2 39 49N 116 15 E
Huat Choe, Sing. 15 F7 1 20N 103 41 E
Huckarde, Ruhr 6 A6 51 32N 7 24 E
Huckingen, Ruhr 6 B2 51 21N 6 44 E
Huddinge, Stock. 3 E11 59 14N 18 0 E
Hudson →, N.Y. 22 B5 40 43N 73 6W
Huertas de San Beltran, Barc. 8 D5 41 22N 2 9 E
Huguenot, N.Y. 22 D3 40 32N 74 13W
Huguenot Park, N.Y. 22 D3 40 31N 74 12W
Huidui, Tianj. 14 E6 39 4N 117 16 E
Huisquilucan →, Méx. 29 B2 19 24N 99 17W
Huixquilucan, Méx. 29 B1 19 21N 99 21W
Hull, Bost. 21 D4 42 18N 70 54W
Hulman Aqueduct, Bost. 21 C1 42 20N 71 23W
Hulmeville, Phil. 24 A5 40 8N 74 55W
Hulsdonk, Ruhr 6 B1 51 27N 6 36 E
Humaljärvi, Hels. 3 B1 60 10N 24 26 E
Humber →, Trto. 20 D7 43 47N 79 38W
Humber B., Trto. 20 E8 43 37N 79 27W
Humber Bay, Trto. 20 E8 43 38N 79 29W
Humber Summit, Trto. 20 D7 43 45N 79 32W
Humber Valley Park, Trto. 20 E8 43 39N 79 29W
Humber Valley Village, Trto. 20 D7 43 40N 79 31W
Humberlea, Trto. 20 D7 43 43N 79 31W
Humboldt Park, Chic. 26 B2 41 54N 87 42W
Humera, Mdrd. 8 B2 40 25N 3 46W
Hummelsbüttel, Hbg. 7 D8 53 39N 10 4 E
Hun Yeang, Sing. 15 F8 1 21N 103 55 E
Hunaydī, Bagd. 17 F8 33 18N 44 29 E
Hundige, Købn. 2 E8 55 35N 12 18 E
Hundige Strand, Købn. 2 E9 55 35N 12 20 E
Hung Hom, H.K. 12 E6 22 18N 114 11 E
Hunters Hill, Syd. 19 B3 33 50 S 151 9 E
Hunters Pt., S.F. 27 B2 37 43N 122 21W
Hunters Valley, Wash. 25 D6 38 54N 77 17W
Huntington, N.Y. 23 B8 40 51N 73 25W
Huntington, Wash. 25 E7 38 47N 77 4W
Huntington B., N.Y. 23 B8 40 54N 73 24W
Huntington Bay, N.Y. 23 B8 40 56N 73 26W
Huntington Park, L.A. 28 C3 33 58N 118 13W
Huntington Station, N.Y. 23 B8 40 50N 73 23W
Hünxer Wald, Ruhr 6 A2 51 37N 6 49 E
Hurffville, Phil. 24 C4 39 45N 75 6W
Hurīya, Bagd. 17 E7 33 21N 44 19 E
Hurlingham, B.A. 32 B3 34 35 S 58 37W
Hurlingham, Jobg. 18 E9 26 6 S 28 2 E
Hurstville, Syd. 19 B3 33 57 S 151 6 E
Husby, Stock. 3 D10 59 24N 17 56 E
Huseby, Oslo 2 A6 60 0N 11 1 E
Hustivař, Pra. 10 B3 50 3N 14 31 E
Husum, Købn. 2 D9 55 42N 12 27 E
Hütteldorf, Wien 10 G9 48 12N 16 15 E
Huttenheim, Ruhr 6 B2 51 21N 6 43 E
Huttrop, Ruhr 6 B4 51 26N 7 3 E
Hüvösvölgy, Bud. 10 J13 47 32N 19 0 E
Hvalstad, Oslo 2 B2 59 51N 10 27 E
Hvalstrand, Oslo 2 B3 59 50N 10 30 E
Hvidovre, Købn. 2 E9 55 38N 12 27 E
Hwagog, Sŏul 12 G7 37 32N 126 51 E
Hyattsville, Wash. 25 D8 38 57N 76 57W
Hyde Park, Bost. 21 D3 42 15N 71 7W
Hyde Park, Chic. 26 C3 41 47N 87 35W
Hyde Park, Jobg. 18 E9 26 6 S 28 2 E
Hyde Park, Lon. 4 B3 51 30N 0 10W
Hyde Park, Syd. 19 B4 33 52 S 151 12 E
Hynes, L.A. 28 C3 33 52N 118 10W

# I

Ibaraki, Ōsaka 12 B4 34 48N 135 34 E
Ibayo Tipas, Manila 15 D4 14 32N 121 4 E
Ibese, Lagos 18 A2 6 33N 7 28 E
Ibirapuera, S. Pau. 31 E5 23 36 S 46 40W
Ibirapuera, Parque, S. Pau. 31 E6 23 35 S 46 38W
Iboju, Lagos 18 B3 6 25N 7 31 E
Icarai, Rio J. 31 B3 22 54 S 43 6W
Icerenköy, Ist. 17 B3 40 58N 29 6 E
Ichapur, Calc. 16 D6 22 48N 88 22 E
Ichgao, Tōkyō 13 C2 35 32N 139 32 E
Ichigaya, Tōkyō 13 B3 35 41N 139 43 E
Ichikawa, Tōkyō 13 B4 35 43N 139 54 E
Ickenham, Lon. 4 B2 51 33N 0 26W
Ickern, Ruhr 6 A6 51 35N 7 21 E
Iddo, Lagos 18 B2 6 28N 7 22 E
Idi-Oro, Lagos 18 B2 6 31N 7 21 E
Idimu, Lagos 18 A1 6 34N 7 17 E
Idrīs, Bagd. 17 E8 33 22N 44 27 E
Igannmu, Lagos 18 B2 6 28N 7 22 E
Igbobi, Lagos 18 A2 6 31N 7 22 E
Igbologun, Lagos 18 B1 6 24N 7 19 E
Igbopa, Lagos 18 A3 6 32N 7 31 E
Igelboda, Stock. 3 E12 59 17N 18 17 E
Igny, Paris 5 C3 48 44N 2 13 E
Iguassú, S. Pau. 31 E6 23 36 S 46 30W
Ijesa-Tedo, Lagos 18 B1 6 29N 7 19 E
Ijora, Lagos 18 B2 6 27N 7 22 E
Ikebe, Tōkyō 13 C2 35 31N 139 34 E
Ikebukuro, Tōkyō 13 B3 35 43N 139 42 E
Ikeda, Ōsaka 12 B3 34 48N 135 25 E
Ikegami, Tōkyō 13 C3 35 33N 139 42 E
Ikeja, Lagos 18 A2 6 35N 7 20 E
Ikeuchi, Ōsaka 12 C4 34 35N 135 32 E
Ikotun, Lagos 18 A1 6 32N 7 16 E
Ikoyi, Lagos 18 B2 6 27N 7 26 E
Ikuata, Lagos 18 B2 6 24N 7 21 E
Ikuno, Ōsaka 12 B4 34 40N 135 30 E
Ikuta, Ōsaka 12 B2 34 41N 135 10 E
Ikuta, Tōkyō 13 C2 35 36N 139 32 E
Ila, Oslo 2 B3 59 57N 10 35 E
Ilchester, Balt. 25 B2 39 14N 76 46W
Ilford, Lon. 4 B5 51 33N 0 4 E
Ilioúpolis, Ath. 8 J11 37 54N 23 47 E
Illovo, Jobg. 18 E9 26 7 S 28 3 E
Ilsós →, Ath. 8 J11 37 55N 23 41 E
Imajuku, Tōkyō 13 D2 35 28N 139 32 E
Imbāba, El Qâ. 18 C5 30 3N 31 12 E
Imielin, Wsaw. 10 F7 52 9N 21 0 E
Imirim, S. Pau. 31 D6 23 29 S 46 39W
Imittós, Ath. 8 J11 37 55N 23 45 E
Immersby, Hels. 3 B6 60 18N 25 16 E
Imore, Lagos 18 B1 6 25N 7 17 E
Imperial Palace, Tōkyō 13 B3 35 41N 139 45 E
Ina →, Ōsaka 12 B3 34 48N 135 27 E
Inagi, Tōkyō 13 C2 35 38N 139 31 E
Incirano, Mil. 9 D5 45 34N 9 9 E
Independencia, Lima 30 F8 11 59 S 77 3W
Indian Gabe, Delhi 16 B2 28 36N 77 13 E
Indian Museum, Calc. 16 E6 22 33N 88 21 E
Indiana Harbor, Chic. 26 C4 41 40N 87 26W
Indiana Harbor Canal, Chic. 26 D4 41 39N 87 26W
Indianópolis, S. Pau. 31 E6 23 35 S 46 38W
Indios Verdes, Méx. 29 B3 19 29N 99 6W
Ingarö, Stock. 3 E13 59 17N 18 24 E
Ingaröfjärden, Stock. 3 E13 59 14N 18 25 E
Ingarölandet, Stock. 3 E13 59 17N 18 22 E
Ingenieur Budge, B.A. 32 C4 34 43 S 58 27W
Ingierstrand, Oslo 2 C4 59 49N 10 46 E
Ingleburn, Syd. 19 C2 34 0 S 150 52 E
Inglewood, L.A. 28 C3 33 57N 118 19W
Ingrave, Lon. 4 B7 51 35N 0 20 E
Ingvalsby, Hels. 3 C2 60 9N 24 32 E
Inhaúme, Rio J. 31 B2 22 52 S 43 16W
Inner Port Shelter, H.K. 12 D6 22 21N 114 17 E
Interagos, S. Pau. 31 F5 23 41 S 46 42W
Intramuros, Manila 15 D3 14 35N 120 57 E
Invalides, Paris 5 B3 48 51N 2 18 E
Inverness, Balt. 25 B4 39 15N 76 29W
Inwood, N.Y. 23 D6 40 36N 73 45W
Inzersdorf, Wien 10 H10 48 8N 16 20 E
Ipanema, Rio J. 31 B2 22 59 S 43 12W
Ipiranga, S. Pau. 31 E6 23 35 S 46 36W
Ipiranga →, S. Pau. 31 E6 23 37 S 46 37W
Iponri, Lagos 18 B2 6 28N 7 22 E
Ipswich, Bost. 21 A4 42 41N 70 50W
Ipswich →, Bost. 21 A3 42 40N 70 53W
Irajá, Rio J. 31 B2 22 50 S 43 19W
Irving Park, Chic. 26 B2 41 57N 87 42W
Irvington, N.Y. 22 C3 40 43N 74 14W
Irwindale, L.A. 28 B5 34 6N 117 54W
Isabel, Rio J. 31 B2 22 55 S 43 14W
Isagatedo, Lagos 18 A1 6 31N 7 19 E
Isando, Jobg. 18 E10 26 8 S 28 12 E
Isar →, Mün. 7 F11 48 15N 11 41 E
Iselin, N.Y. 22 D3 40 34N 74 19W
Iserbrook, Hbg. 7 D6 53 34N 9 49 E
Iseri-Osun, Lagos 18 A1 6 30N 7 16 E
Ishbīlīya, Bagd. 17 E8 33 21N 44 26 E
Isheri-Olofin, Lagos 18 A1 6 35N 7 16 E
Ishi →, Ōsaka 12 C4 34 34N 135 37 E
Ishikiri, Ōsaka 12 B4 34 40N 135 39 E
Ishizu →, Ōsaka 12 C3 34 33N 135 26 E
Ishøj Strand, Købn. 2 E9 55 36N 12 20 E
Isidro Casanova, B.A. 32 C3 34 42 S 58 36W
Island Channel, N.Y. 23 D5 40 35N 73 52W
Island Park, N.Y. 23 D7 40 36N 73 38W
Island Park, Trto. 20 E8 43 37N 79 22W
Islev, Købn. 2 D9 55 41N 12 27 E
Isleworth, Lon. 4 C3 51 28N 0 19W
Islington, Bost. 21 D2 42 13N 71 13W
Islington, Lon. 4 B4 51 32N 0 6W
Islington, Trto. 20 E7 43 38N 79 30W
Ismaning, Mün. 7 F11 48 13N 11 40 E
Ismayloskiypark, Mos. 11 E10 55 46N 37 46 E
Isogo-Ku, Tōkyō 13 D2 35 23N 139 37 E
Isolo, Lagos 18 A1 6 31N 7 19 E
Isosaari, Hels. 3 C5 60 6N 25 3 E
Issy-les-Moulineaux, Paris 5 C3 48 49N 2 15 E
Istanbul, Ist. 17 B2 41 0N 28 58 E
Istanbul Boğazi, Ist. 17 A3 41 5N 29 3 E
Istanbul Hava Alani, Ist. 17 B2 40 58N 28 50 E
Istead Rise, Lon. 4 C7 51 24N 0 21 E
Istinye, Ist. 17 A3 41 6N 29 3 E
Isunba, Lagos 18 B1 6 25N 7 17 E
Itä Hakkila, Hels. 3 B5 60 17N 25 7 E
Itabashi-Ku, Tōkyō 13 B2 35 46N 139 38 E
Itaberaba, S. Pau. 31 D6 23 28 S 46 39W
Itaewon, Sŏul 12 G7 37 32N 126 58 E
Itaim, S. Pau. 31 D7 23 29 S 46 23W
Itaipu, Rio J. 31 B3 22 58 S 43 2W
Italie, Place d', Paris 5 C4 48 49N 2 22 E
Itami, Ōsaka 12 B3 34 46N 135 24 E
Itaocaia, Rio J. 31 B3 22 58 S 43 2W
Itapecerica da Serra, S. Pau. 31 F5 23 42 S 46 50W
Itaquaquecetuba, S. Pau. 31 D7 23 29 S 46 23W
Itaquera, S. Pau. 31 E7 23 32 S 46 27W
Itaquera →, S. Pau. 31 E7 23 28 S 46 26W
Ithan, Phil. 24 A2 40 1N 75 21W
Itupu, S. Pau. 31 F5 23 40 S 46 43W
Ituzaingo, B.A. 32 B3 34 39 S 58 38W
Ivanhoe, Melb. 19 E7 37 45 S 145 3 E
Iver, Lon. 4 B1 51 32N 0 30W
Ivry-sur-Seine, Paris 5 C4 48 49N 2 22 E
Iwazono, Ōsaka 12 B2 34 45N 135 18 E
Izabelin, Wsaw. 10 E5 52 17N 20 48 E
Izmaylovo, Mos. 11 E10 55 47N 37 47 E
Iztacalco, Méx. 29 B3 19 23N 99 6W
Iztapalapa, Méx. 29 B3 19 21N 99 6W
Izumi, Tōkyō 13 D1 35 25N 139 29 E

# J

J. G. Strijdom Post Office Tower, Jobg. 18 F9 26 11 S 28 2 E
J. Paul Getty Museum, L.A. 28 B1 34 2N 118 33W
Jabavu, Jobg. 18 F8 26 14 S 27 52 E
Jabulani, Jobg. 18 F8 26 14 S 27 51 E
Jacarepaguá, Rio J. 31 B1 22 56 S 43 20W
Jackson Heights, N.Y. 23 C5 40 44N 73 53W
Jackson Park, Chic. 26 C3 41 46N 87 34W
Jacksonville, N.Y. 22 B3 40 57N 74 18W
Jacomino, La Hab. 30 B3 23 6N 82 19W
Jacques Cartier, Mtrl. 20 A5 43 31N 73 27W
Jægersborg, Købn. 2 D10 55 45N 12 31 E
Jægersborg Dyrehave, Købn. 2 D10 55 46N 12 33 E
Jægersborg Hegn, Købn. 2 D10 55 49N 12 33 E
Jafarpur, Calc. 16 D6 22 45N 88 22 E
Jagacha, Calc. 16 E5 22 35N 88 17 E
Jagannathpur, Calc. 16 D5 22 43N 88 18 E
Jagatdal, Calc. 16 C6 22 51N 88 23 E
Jagatmagar, Calc. 16 D5 22 42N 88 17 E
Jagatpur, Delhi 16 A2 28 44N 77 13 E
Jagdispur, Calc. 16 E5 22 39N 88 17 E
Jaguara, S. Pau. 31 E5 23 30 S 46 45W
Jaguaré, S. Pau. 31 E5 23 32 S 46 45W
Jaguaré →, S. Pau. 31 E5 23 32 S 46 45W
Jahangirpur, Delhi 16 A2 28 43N 77 12 E
Jaimanitas →, La Hab. 30 B2 23 5N 82 29W
Jakarta, Jak. 15 H10 6 9 S 106 52 E
Jakarta, Teluk, Jak. 15 H9 6 5 S 106 50 E
Jakobsberg, Stock. 3 D9 59 25N 17 47 E
Jalan Kayu, Sing. 15 F8 1 24N 103 52 E
Jamaica, N.Y. 23 C6 40 42N 73 48W
Jamaica B., N.Y. 23 D6 40 36N 73 49W
Jamaica Plain, Bost. 21 D3 42 18N 71 6W
Jamshīdābād, Tehr. 17 C5 35 42N 51 22 E
Jamsil, Sŏul 12 G8 37 30N 127 4 E
Jamweon, Sŏul 12 G8 37 30N 127 0 E
Jan Smuts Airport, Jobg. 18 E10 26 7 S 28 14 E
Janai, Calc. 16 D5 22 43N 88 15 E
Janā'in, Bagd. 17 F8 33 18N 44 22 E
Janki, Wsaw. 10 F6 52 8N 20 52 E
Jannali, Syd. 19 C3 34 0 S 151 4 E
Jánoshegy, Bud. 10 J12 47 31N 18 57 E
Janów, Wsaw. 10 E6 52 16N 20 50 E
Janvry, Paris 5 D2 48 38N 2 9 E
Jaraguá, S. Pau. 31 D5 23 27 S 46 44W
Jaraguá, Pico de, S. Pau. 31 D5 23 27 S 46 46W
Jarama →, Mdrd. 8 B3 40 29N 3 32W
Jardim América, S. Pau. 31 E6 23 34 S 46 39W
Jardim Anchieta, S. Pau. 31 F7 23 41 S 46 27W
Jardim Arpoador, S. Pau. 31 E5 23 35 S 46 48W
Jardim Munhoz, S. Pau. 31 F6 23 40 S 46 33W
Jardim Osasco, S. Pau. 31 E5 23 33 S 46 47W
Jardim Ouro Preto, S. Pau. 31 E5 23 35 S 46 46W
Jardim Paulista, S. Pau. 31 E5 23 34 S 46 41W
Jardim Petrópolis, S. Pau. 31 E5 23 33 S 46 46W
Jardim Rochidale, S. Pau. 31 E5 23 30 S 46 48W
Jardim Santista, S. Pau. 31 F7 23 40 S 46 24W
Jardim São Bento, S. Pau. 31 F5 23 40 S 46 48W
Jardim São Francisco, S. Pau. 31 E7 23 38 S 46 26W
Jardim Sapopemba, S. Pau. 31 E7 23 35 S 46 29W
Jardim Vera Cruz, S. Pau. 31 E7 23 35 S 46 27W
Jardim Vista Alegre, S. Pau. 31 E5 23 37 S 46 49W
Jardim Zaira, S. Pau. 31 E7 23 38 S 46 25W
Jardines Flotantes, Méx. 29 C3 19 16N 99 6W
Jardines Lookout, H.K. 12 E6 22 16N 114 11 E
Järfälla, Stock. 3 D10 59 23N 17 51 E
Järvafältet, Stock. 3 D10 59 25N 17 51 E
Järventausta, Hels. 3 A1 60 21N 24 28 E
Jasai, Bomb. 16 H9 18 53N 73 0 E
Jaskhar, Bomb. 16 H8 18 54N 72 58 E
Jatinegara, Jak. 15 J10 6 13 S 106 52 E
Jauli, Delhi 16 A3 28 44N 77 20 E
Jawādiyeh, Tehr. 17 D5 35 39N 51 22 E
Jaworowa, Wsaw. 10 F6 52 9N 20 56 E
Jayang, Sŏul 12 G8 37 32N 127 3 E
Jedlesee, Wien 10 G10 48 15N 16 23 E
Jefferson, Phil. 24 C3 39 45N 75 12W
Jefferson Park, Chic. 26 B2 41 58N 87 46W
Jeffersonville, Phil. 24 A2 40 8N 75 23W
Jegi, Sŏul 12 G8 37 34N 127 1 E
Jells Park, Melb. 19 F8 37 53 S 145 11 E
Jelonki, Wsaw. 10 E6 52 14N 20 54 E
Jenfeld, Hbg. 7 D8 53 34N 10 8 E
Jenkintown, Phil. 24 A4 40 6N 75 8W
Jeongreung, Sŏul 12 G8 37 35N 127 0 E
Jericho, N.Y. 23 C7 40 47N 73 32W
Jerónimes, Mosteiro dos, Lisb. 8 F7 38 41N 9 11W
Jersey City, N.Y. 22 C4 40 42N 74 4W
Jésus, Î., Mtrl. 20 A3 43 36N 73 44W
Jesus Del Monte, La Hab. 30 B2 23 6N 82 21W
Jesús Maria, Lima 30 G8 12 4 S 77 3W
Jhenkari, Calc. 16 D5 22 45N 88 18 E
Jhil Kuranga, Delhi 16 B2 28 39N 77 14 E
Jiangqiao, Shang. 14 J11 31 15N 121 20 E
Jiangtai, Beij. 14 B3 39 57N 116 28 E
Jianguomen, Beij. 14 B3 39 53N 116 24 E
Jiangwan, Shang. 14 J11 31 18N 121 28 E
Jianshan Gongyuan, Tianj. 14 E6 39 5N 117 12 E
Jihād, Bagd. 17 F7 33 17N 44 19 E
Jingan, Shang. 14 J11 31 14N 121 25 E
Jinočany, Pra. 10 B1 50 2N 14 16 E
Jinonice, Pra. 10 B2 50 3N 14 22 E
Jirny, Pra. 10 B4 50 7N 14 41 E
Jiuxianqiao, Beij. 14 B3 39 58N 116 28 E
Jiyūgaoka, Tōkyō 13 C3 35 35N 139 40 E
Jizā'er, Bagd. 17 F8 33 15N 44 23 E
Jizīra, Bagd. 17 F8 33 15N 44 25 E
Joan Despi, Barc. 8 D5 41 22N 2 2 E
Joaquin Miller Park, S.F. 27 B3 37 48N 122 11W
Johannesburg, Jobg. 18 F9 26 11 S 28 2 E
Johanneskirchen, Mün. 7 F10 48 10N 11 38 E
Johannesstift, Berl. 7 A2 52 34N 13 12 E
Johannisthal, Berl. 7 B4 52 26N 13 30 E
John F. Kennedy Int. Airport, N.Y. 23 D6 40 39N 73 45W
John F. Kennedy Nat. Hist. Site, Bost. 21 C3 42 20N 71 7W
John Hancock Center, Chic. 26 B3 41 53N 87 37W
John Hopkins Univ., Balt. 25 B3 39 19N 76 37W
John McLaren Park, S.F. 27 B2 37 43N 122 24W
Joinville-le-Pont, Paris 5 C4 48 49N 2 27 E
Jollas, Hels. 3 B5 60 10N 25 5 E
Jones Beach State Park, N.Y. 23 D7 40 35N 73 32W
Jones Falls →, Balt. 25 B3 39 20N 76 36W
Jones Inlet, N.Y. 23 D7 40 34N 73 34W
Jonestown, Balt. 25 B2 39 13N 76 48W
Jong Ro, Sŏul 12 G7 37 34N 126 58 E
Jongmyo Royal Shrine, Sŏul 12 G7 37 34N 126 59 E
Jonstrup, Købn. 2 D9 55 45N 12 20 E
Joppatowne, Balt. 25 A4 39 24N 76 20W
Jordan Valley, H.K. 12 D6 22 20N 114 12 E
Jorge Chavez, Aeropuerto Int., Lima 30 G8 12 2 S 77 8W
Jorvas, Hels. 3 C2 60 8N 24 30 E
José C. Paz, B.A. 32 B2 34 31 S 58 44W
José L. Suárez, B.A. 32 B3 34 32 S 58 34W
José Mármol, B.A. 32 C4 34 47 S 58 22W
Jose Marti, Aeropuerto Int., La Hab. 30 C2 22 59N 82 22W
Josephine Pk., L.A. 28 A4 34 17N 118 7W
Jōsō, Ōsaka 12 B3 34 42N 135 27 E
Jōtō, Ōsaka 12 B4 34 42N 135 33 E
Jouars-Pontchartrain, Paris 5 C1 48 47N 1 53 E
Jouy-en-Josas, Paris 5 C3 48 46N 2 10 E
Jouy-le-Moutier, Paris 5 A2 49 0N 2 2 E
Józefów, Wsaw. 10 F8 52 8N 21 13 E
Juan Escutia, Méx. 29 B3 19 23N 99 3W
Juan González Romero, Méx. 29 A3 19 30N 99 3W
Juhu, Bomb. 16 G9 19 5N 73 0 E
Juilly, Paris 5 A6 49 0N 2 42 E
Jūjā, Tōkyō 13 B3 35 45N 139 43 E
Jukskeirivier →, Jobg. 18 E9 26 5 S 28 5 E
Julianów, Wsaw. 10 E7 52 10N 21 9 E
Jung, Sŏul 12 G7 37 33N 126 59 E
Jungfernheide, Volkspark, Berl. 7 A2 52 32N 13 18 E
Jungfernsee, Berl. 7 B1 52 25N 13 6 E
Jungwha, Sŏul 12 G8 37 35N 127 3 E
Junk B., H.K. 12 E6 22 17N 114 15 E
Jurong, Sing. 15 G7 1 19N 103 40 E
Jurong, Selat, Sing. 15 G7 1 17N 103 42 E
Jurong, Sungei →, Sing. 15 G7 1 17N 103 45 E
Jurubatuba, S. Pau. 31 F5 23 40 S 46 41W
Jurujuba, Enseada de, Rio J. 31 B3 22 54 S 43 6W
Justice, Chic. 26 C2 41 44N 87 49W
Juusjärvi, Hels. 3 B1 60 12N 24 26 E
Juva, Hels. 3 B1 60 16N 24 45 E
Juvisy-sur-Orge, Paris 5 C4 48 41N 2 21 E
Jwalahari, Delhi 16 B1 28 40N 77 6 E
Jyllinge, Købn. 2 D7 55 45N 12 6 E

# K

Kaarst, Ruhr 6 C1 51 13N 6 36 E
Kabaty, Wsaw. 10 F7 52 8N 21 4 E
Kabel, Ruhr 6 B6 51 24N 7 28 E
Kadiköy, Ist. 17 B3 40 59N 29 1 E
Kadoma, Ōsaka 12 B4 34 44N 135 35 E
Kafr es Sammân, El Qâ. 18 D4 29 58N 31 8 E
Kâğithane, Ist. 17 A2 41 4N 28 58 E
Kâğithane →, Ist. 17 A2 41 9N 28 56 E
Kagran, Wien 10 G10 48 14N 16 26 E
Kahlenberg, Wien 10 G9 48 16N 16 19 E
Kai Tak, H.K. 12 D6 22 20N 114 11 E
Kaisariani, Ath. 8 J11 37 57N 23 46 E
Kaiser-Mühlen, Wien 10 G10 48 13N 16 25 E
Kaiserebersdorf, Wien 10 H10 48 9N 16 26 E
Kaiserswerth, Ruhr 6 C2 51 18N 6 44 E
Kaivoksela, Hels. 3 B4 60 15N 24 53 E
Kakukk-hegy, Bud. 10 K12 47 29N 18 57 E
Kalachhara, Calc. 16 D5 22 42N 88 15 E
Kalamákion, Ath. 8 J11 37 52N 23 43 E
Kaldenhausen, Ruhr 6 B2 51 23N 6 39 E
Kalipur, Calc. 16 D5 22 40N 88 17 E
Kalkaji, Delhi 16 B2 28 32N 77 12 E
Kalksburg, Wien 10 H9 48 8N 16 15 E
Kallang →, Sing. 15 F8 1 21N 103 51 E
Kallhäll, Stock. 3 D9 59 26N 17 48 E
Kallithéa, Ath. 8 J11 37 56N 23 43 E
Kallvik, Hels. 3 B5 60 12N 25 8 E
Kaltbründsberg, Wien 10 G9 48 10N 16 13 E
Kaltenleutgeben, Wien 10 H9 48 7N 16 11 E
Kalveboderne, Købn. 2 E10 55 37N 12 31 E
Kalytino, St-Pet. 11 B5 59 59N 30 39 E
Kamaraerdö, Bud. 10 K12 47 26N 18 59 E
Kamarhati, Calc. 16 D6 22 40N 88 23 E
Kamarkunda, Calc. 16 D5 22 49N 88 12 E
Kamata, Tōkyō 13 C3 35 33N 139 43 E
Kamdebpur, Calc. 16 C5 22 53N 88 19 E
Kameari, Tōkyō 13 B4 35 45N 139 50 E
Kameido, Tōkyō 13 B4 35 42N 139 50 E
Kami-hoshikawa, Tōkyō 13 D2 35 27N 139 35 E
Kami-Itabashi, Tōkyō 13 B3 35 45N 139 40 E
Kami-nakazato, Tōkyō 13 D2 35 22N 139 36 E
Kami-saruyama, Tōkyō 13 C2 35 30N 139 31 E
Kami-sugata, Tōkyō 13 D2 35 28N 139 34 E
Kami-tomi, Tōkyō 13 B1 35 48N 139 29 E
Kamikitazawa, Tōkyō 13 C2 35 39N 139 36 E
Kamikiyoto, Tōkyō 13 B2 35 45N 139 30 E
Kamishiki, Tōkyō 13 B4 35 46N 139 57 E
Kamitsuruma, Tōkyō 13 C1 35 30N 139 26 E
Kamiyama, Tōkyō 13 B2 35 46N 139 32 E
Kamoi, Tōkyō 13 D2 35 30N 139 34 E
Kamoshida, Tōkyō 13 C2 35 33N 139 31 E
Kampong Batak, Sing. 15 F8 1 20N 103 54 E
Kampong Mandai Kechil, Sing. 15 F7 1 26N 103 46 E
Kampong Pachitan, Sing. 15 G8 1 19N 103 54 E
Kampong Potong Pasir, Sing. 15 F8 1 20N 103 52 E
Kampong Reteh, Sing. 15 G8 1 19N 103 53 E
Kampong Tengah, Sing. 15 F7 1 22N 103 42 E
Kampong Ulu Jurong, Sing. 15 F7 1 20N 103 42 E
Kampung Ambon, Jak. 15 J10 6 11 S 106 53 E
Kampung Bali, Jak. 15 J9 6 11 S 106 48 E
Kan, Tehr. 17 C4 35 45N 51 16 E
Kanagawa-Ku, Tōkyō 13 D2 35 29N 139 38 E
Kanamachi, Tōkyō 13 B4 35 46N 139 52 E
Kanamori, Tōkyō 13 C1 35 31N 139 27 E
Kanda, Tōkyō 13 B3 35 41N 139 45 E
Kandang Kerbau, Sing. 15 G8 1 18N 103 51 E
Kandilli, Ist. 17 A3 41 4N 29 3 E
Kanegasaku, Tōkyō 13 B4 35 48N 139 56 E
Kangaroo Ground, Melb. 19 E8 37 41 S 145 13 E
Kankinara, Calc. 16 C6 22 51N 88 24 E
Kankurgachi, Calc. 16 E6 22 34N 88 23 E
Kanlica, Ist. 17 A3 41 5N 29 3 E
Kanoaka, Ōsaka 12 C4 34 33N 135 31 E
Kanonerskiy, Os., St-Pet. 11 B3 59 53N 30 13 E
Kanzaki →, Ōsaka 12 B3 34 41N 135 24 E
Kapellerfeld, Wien 10 G10 48 18N 16 29 E
Kapotnya, Mos. 11 F10 55 39N 37 48 E
Käppala, Stock. 3 D12 59 21N 18 13 E
Käpylä, Hels. 3 B4 60 13N 24 57 E
Karachi, Kar. 17 G11 24 50N 67 0 E
Karachi Int. Airport, Kar. 17 G11 24 5N 67 9 E
Karachi Univ., Kar. 17 G11 24 51N 67 0 E
Karagümrük, Ist. 17 A2 41 1N 28 56 E
Karāma, Bagd. 17 E8 33 20N 44 22 E
Karato, Ōsaka 12 B2 34 46N 135 12 E
Karave, Bomb. 16 G9 19 0N 73 0 E
Karet, Jak. 15 J9 6 12 S 106 49 E
Karkar Duman, Delhi 16 B2 28 39N 77 18 E
Karkh, Bagd. 17 E8 33 19N 44 23 E
Karlberg, Stock. 3 D11 59 20N 18 2 E
Karlin, Pra. 10 B2 50 5N 14 26 E
Karlsfeld, Mün. 7 F9 48 13N 11 28 E
Karlshorst, Berl. 7 B4 52 29N 13 31 E
Karlslunde Strand, Købn. 2 E8 55 33N 12 15 E
Karnap, Ruhr 6 A4 51 31N 7 0 E
Karolinenhof, Berl. 7 B4 52 23N 13 38 E
Karow, Berl. 7 A3 52 36N 13 29 E
Karrādah, Bagd. 17 F8 33 17N 44 23 E
Kärsön, Stock. 3 E10 59 19N 17 54 E
Kasai, Tōkyō 13 C4 35 39N 139 52 E
Kasetsart, Bangk. 15 A2 13 50N 100 34 E
Kashi-Hazaki, Tōkyō 13 A3 35 54N 139 42 E
Kashio, Tōkyō 13 D2 35 24N 139 34 E
Kashiwa, Tōkyō 13 A4 35 51N 139 57 E
Kashiwara, Ōsaka 12 C4 34 34N 135 37 E
Kaskela, Hels. 3 B5 60 15N 25 6 E
Kastrup, Købn. 2 E10 55 38N 12 39 E
Kastrup Lufthavn, Købn. 2 E11 55 37N 12 14 E
Kasuga, Tōkyō 13 B2 35 45N 139 38 E
Kasuge, Tōkyō 13 B3 35 45N 139 49 E
Kasumigasek, Tōkyō 13 C3 35 40N 139 46 E
Katabira →, Tōkyō 13 D2 35 27N 139 38 E
Katernberg, Ruhr 6 A4 51 30N 7 4 E
Katong Park, Sing. 15 G8 1 18N 103 53 E
Katrineberg, Stock. 3 E10 59 13N 17 54 E
Katsushika-Ku, Tōkyō 13 B4 35 44N 139 51 E
Kattinge Vig, Købn. 2 D7 55 40N 12 1 E
Kau Pei Chau, H.K. 12 E6 22 12N 114 15 E
Kau Yi Chau, H.K. 12 E5 22 17N 114 4 E
Kauklahti, Hels. 3 B2 60 11N 24 36 E
Kaulsdorf, Berl. 7 B4 52 29N 13 34 E
Kauniainen, Hels. 3 B2 60 13N 24 44 E
Kawagoe, Tōkyō 13 A1 35 54N 139 29 E
Kawaguchi, Tōkyō 13 B3 35 47N 139 43 E
Kawai, Tōkyō 13 D2 35 29N 139 31 E
Kawamukō, Tōkyō 13 C2 35 30N 139 34 E
Kawanishi, Ōsaka 12 B3 34 49N 135 24 E
Kawasaki, Tōkyō 13 C3 35 31N 139 43 E
Kawasaki Harbour, Tōkyō 13 D3 35 30N 139 47 E
Kawawa, Tōkyō 13 C2 35 31N 139 33 E
Kawęczyn, Wsaw. 10 E7 52 16N 21 5 E
Kayu Putih, Jak. 15 J10 6 10 S 106 53 E
Kbely, Pra. 10 B3 50 8N 14 32 E
Kearny, N.Y. 22 C4 40 45N 74 8W
Kebayoran Baru, Jak. 15 J9 6 14 S 106 47 E
Kebayoran Lama, Jak. 15 J9 6 13 S 106 46 E
Kebon Jeruk, Jak. 15 J9 6 11 S 106 46 E
Keferloh, Mün. 7 G11 48 5N 11 43 E
Keilor, Melb. 19 E6 37 42 S 144 50 E
Keilor East, Melb. 19 E6 37 44 S 144 51 E
Keimola, Hels. 3 A3 60 20N 24 49 E
Kelenföld, Bud. 10 K13 47 27N 19 2 E
Kelvedon Hatch, Lon. 4 A6 51 40N 0 16 E
Kelvin, Jobg. 18 E9 26 4 S 28 5 E
Kemang, Jak. 15 J9 6 15 S 106 48 E
Kemayoran, Jak. 15 J10 6 10 S 106 50 E
Kemayoran Airport, Jak. 15 H10 6 8 S 106 50 E
Kemp Mill, Wash. 25 C7 39 0N 77 1W
Kempton Park, Jobg. 18 E10 26 5 S 28 14 E
Kempton Racecourse, Lon. 4 C2 51 24N 0 23W
Kemsing, Lon. 4 D6 51 18N 0 12 E
Kendall Green, Bost. 21 C2 42 22N 71 16W
Kendua, Calc. 16 E5 22 34N 88 10 E
Keng Hau, H.K. 12 D6 22 22N 114 10 E
Kenilworth, Chic. 26 A2 42 5N 87 42W
Kenilworth, N.Y. 22 C3 40 40N 74 16W
Kenley, Lon. 4 D4 51 19N 0 6W
Kenmare, Jobg. 18 E7 26 6 S 27 48 E
Kennedy Grove Regional Rec. Area, S.F. 27 A3 37 56N 122 14W

40 Kennedy Town


Kennedy Town, H.K. 12 E5 22 16N 114 6 E
Kensal Green, Lon. 4 B3 51 32N 0 13W
Kensington, Jobg. 18 F9 26 11 S 28 6 E
Kensington, Lon. 4 C3 51 29N 0 10W
Kensington, N.Y. 22 D5 40 38N 73 57W
Kensington, Phil. 24 B4 39 59N 75 6W
Kensington, S.F. 27 A3 37 54N 122 17W
Kensington, Syd. 19 B4 33 54 S 151 13 E
Kensington, Wash. 25 C7 39 1N 77 4W
Kensington Palace, Lon. 4 B3 51 30N 0 11W
Kent Woodlands, S.F. 27 A1 37 56N 122 34W
Kentfield, S.F. 27 A1 37 57N 122 33W
Kentish Town, Lon. 4 B4 51 32N 0 8W
Kentland, Wash. 25 D8 38 55N 76 53W
Kenton, Lon. 4 B3 51 34N 0 17W
Kenwood, Balt. 25 A4 39 20N 76 30W
Kenwood, Bost. 21 B2 42 40N 71 14W
Kenwood House, Lon. 4 B4 51 34N 0 9W
Kepa, Wsaw. 10 E7 52 13N 21 3 E
Keppel Harbour, Sing. 15 G7 1 15N 103 49 E
Kerameikos, Ath. 8 J11 37 58N 23 42 E
Kerepes, Bud. 10 J14 47 33N 19 17 E
Keston, Lon. 4 C5 51 21N 0 1 E
Keston Mark, Lon. 4 C5 51 21N 0 2 E
Keth Wara, Delhi 16 A2 28 40N 77 13 E
Kettering, Wash. 25 D9 38 53N 76 49W
Kettwig, Ruhr 6 B3 51 22N 6 56 E
Kew, Jobg. 18 E9 26 7 S 28 5 E
Kew, Lon. 4 C3 51 28N 0 17W
Kew, Melb. 19 E7 37 48 S 145 2 E
Kew Gardens, Lon. 4 C3 51 28N 0 17W
Key Gardens, Trto. 20 E9 43 39N 79 18W
Khaboye, St-Pet. 11 B6 59 53N 30 44 E
Khaidhárion, Ath. 8 H10 38 2N 23 38 E
Khairna, Bomb. 16 G9 19 5N 73 0 E
Khalándrion, Ath. 8 H11 38 3N 23 48 E
Khalīj, Bagd. 17 F8 33 18N 44 28 E
Khansā, Bagd. 17 E8 33 21N 44 28 E
Kharavli, Bomb. 16 H8 18 54N 72 55 E
Khardah, Calc. 16 D6 22 43N 88 22 E
Khayala, Delhi 16 B1 28 39N 77 6 E
Khefren, El Qâ. 18 D4 29 58N 31 8 E
Khichripur, Delhi 16 B2 28 37N 77 18 E
Khimki, Mos. 11 D8 55 53N 37 24 E
Khimki-Khovrino, Mos. 11 D9 55 51N 37 31 E
Khimkinskoye Vdkr., Mos. 11 D8 55 51N 37 27 E
Khirvosti, St-Pet. 11 B5 59 56N 30 37 E
Khlongsan, Bangk. 15 B1 13 43N 100 29 E
Kholargós, Ath. 8 J11 37 59N 23 48 E
Khorel, Calc. 16 D5 22 41N 88 18 E
Khorosovo, Mos. 11 E8 55 46N 37 27 E
Khudrā, Bagd. 17 F7 33 19N 44 17 E
Khun Thian, Bangk. 15 B1 13 41N 100 27 E
Khuraiji Khas, Delhi 16 B2 28 38N 77 16 E
Khurigachi, Calc. 16 D5 22 48N 88 21 E
Kiamari, Kar. 17 H10 24 49N 66 58 E
Kidderpore, Calc. 16 E5 22 32N 88 19 E
Kienwerder, Berl. 7 B2 52 22N 13 11 E
Kierling, Wien 10 G9 48 18N 16 16 E
Kierlingbach →, Wien 10 G9 48 18N 16 19 E
Kierlinger Forst, Wien 10 G9 48 17N 16 14 E
Kierst, Ruhr 6 C2 51 18N 6 42 E
Kifisós →, Ath. 8 J11 37 58N 23 42 E
Kikenka →, St-Pet. 11 B2 59 50N 30 3 E
Kikuna, Tōkyō 13 C2 35 30N 139 37 E
Kil, Stock. 3 D12 59 20N 18 19 E
Kilburn, Lon. 4 B3 51 32N 0 11W
Killara, Syd. 19 A4 33 46 S 151 10 E
Kilo, Hels. 3 B3 60 13N 24 47 E
Kilokri, Delhi 16 B2 28 34N 77 15 E
Kilsyth, Melb. 19 E8 37 48 S 145 18 E
Kimberton, Phil. 24 A1 40 7N 75 34W
Kimlin Park, Sing. 15 G7 1 18N 103 49 E
Kindi, Bagd. 17 F8 33 18N 44 22 E
King of Prussia, Phil. 24 A2 40 5N 75 22W
Kings Cross, Syd. 19 B4 33 52 S 151 12 E
Kings Domain, Melb. 19 E6 37 49 S 144 58 E
Kings Mt., S.F. 27 D3 37 27N 122 19W
King's Park, H.K. 12 E6 22 18N 114 10 E
Kings Park, Wash. 25 E6 38 48N 77 17W
King's Point, N.Y. 23 C6 40 48N 73 45W
Kingsbury, Lon. 4 B3 51 34N 0 15W
Kingsford, Syd. 19 B4 33 55 S 151 14 E
Kingston upon Thames, Lon. 4 C3 51 24N 0 17W
Kingston Vale, Lon. 4 C3 51 25N 0 25W
Kingsway, Trto. 20 E7 43 38N 79 32W
Kingswood, Lon. 4 D3 51 17N 0 12W
Kinnelon, N.Y. 22 B2 40 59N 74 23W
Kipling Heights, Trto. 20 D7 43 43N 79 34W
Kipséli, Ath. 8 J11 37 59N 23 45 E
Kirchhellen, Ruhr 6 A3 51 36N 6 56 E
Kirchhörde, Ruhr 6 B6 51 27N 7 27 E
Kirchlinde, Ruhr 6 A6 51 31N 7 22 E
Kirchof, Hbg. 7 E8 53 29N 10 1 E
Kirchsteinbek, Hbg. 7 D8 53 31N 10 7 E
Kirchstockbach, Mün. 7 G11 48 1N 11 40 E
Kirchtrudering, Mün. 7 G11 48 7N 11 40 E
Kirdasa, El Qâ. 18 C4 30 2N 31 6 E
Kirikiri, Lagos 18 B1 6 26N 7 18 E
Kirkkonummi, Hels. 3 C1 60 6N 24 28W
Kirkland, Mtrl. 20 B2 43 26N 73 51W
Kirovskiye, Os., St-Pet. 11 B3 59 57N 30 14 E
Kisarazu, Tōkyō 13 D4 35 21N 139 54 E
Kisikli, Ist. 17 A3 41 1N 29 2 E
Kispest, Bud. 10 K13 47 27N 19 8 E
Kista, Stock. 3 D10 59 24N 17 57 E
Kistarcsa, Bud. 10 J14 47 32N 19 16 E
Kita, Ōsaka 12 B4 34 41N 135 30 E
Kita-Ku, Tōkyō 13 B3 35 44N 139 44 E
Kitain-Temple, Tōkyō 13 A1 35 54N 139 29 E
Kitazawa, Tōkyō 13 C3 35 39N 139 40 E
Kiu Tsiu, H.K. 12 D6 22 22N 114 17 E
Kivistö, Hels. 3 B4 60 18N 24 50 E
Kiyose, Tōkyō 13 B2 35 46N 139 31 E
Kiziltoprak, Ist. 17 B3 40 58N 29 3 E
Kizu →, Ōsaka 12 C3 34 37N 135 27 E
Kizuri, Ōsaka 12 C4 34 38N 135 34 E
Kjeller, Oslo 2 B6 59 58N 11 1 E
Kjelsås, Oslo 2 B4 59 57N 10 47 E
Kladow, Berl. 7 B1 52 27N 13 9 E
Klampenborg, Købn. 2 D10 55 46N 12 35 E
Klánovice, Pra. 10 B3 50 5N 14 40 E
Klaudyń, Wsaw. 10 E6 52 17N 20 50 E
Klecany, Pra. 10 A2 50 10N 14 24 E
Kledering, Wien 10 H10 48 8N 16 26 E
Klein Gleinicke, Berl. 7 B1 52 23N 13 5 E
Klein-Hadern, Mün. 7 G9 48 7N 11 28 E
Klein Jukskei →, Jobg. 18 E8 26 6 S 27 57 E
Kleinburg, Trto. 20 C7 43 51N 79 37W
Kleine Grasbrook, Hbg. 7 D7 53 31N 9 59 E
Kleinmachnow, Berl. 7 B2 52 24N 13 14 E
Kleinschönebeck, Berl. 7 B5 52 29N 13 42 E
Kleinziethen, Berl. 7 B3 52 22N 13 26 E
Klemetsrud, Oslo 2 B5 59 50N 10 51 E
Klender, Jak. 15 J10 6 12 S 106 53 E
Klippoortje, Jobg. 18 F10 26 14 S 28 10 E
Klipriviersberg, Jobg. 18 F9 26 16 S 28 2 E
Klipspruit →, Jobg. 18 F8 26 14 S 27 53 E
Kloofendal, Jobg. 18 E8 26 8 S 27 52 E
Klosterhardt, Ruhr 6 A3 51 32N 6 52 E
Klosterneuburg, Wien 10 G9 48 18N 16 19 E
Knockholt Pound, Lon. 4 D5 51 18N 0 7 E
Knowland State Arboretum and Park, S.F. 27 B4 37 45N 122 7W
Knox Park, Melb. 19 F8 37 54 S 145 15 E
Knoxville, Melb. 19 F8 37 53 S 145 14 E
Köbanya, Bud. 10 K13 47 28N 19 9 E
Kobe, Ōsaka 12 B2 34 41N 135 13 E
Kōbe Harbour, Ōsaka 12 C2 34 39N 135 11 E
København, Købn. 2 D9 55 40N 12 26 E
Kobylisy, Pra. 10 B2 50 7N 14 26 E
Kobyłka, Wsaw. 10 D8 52 20N 21 10 E
Kocasinan, Ist. 17 A2 41 1N 28 50 E
Kočife, Pra. 10 B2 50 3N 14 21 E
Kodaira, Tōkyō 13 B1 35 43N 139 28 E
Kodanaka, Tōkyō 13 C2 35 34N 139 37 E
Kogane, Tōkyō 13 B4 35 49N 139 55 E
Koganei, Tōkyō 13 B2 35 42N 139 31 E
Kogarah, Syd. 19 B3 33 57 S 151 8 E
Køge Bugt, Købn. 2 E9 55 34N 12 24 E
Köhlbrand Rethe, Hbg. 7 D7 53 31N 9 56 E
Köhlfleet, Hbg. 7 D7 53 32N 9 53 E
Koivupää, Hels. 3 B4 60 18N 24 53 E
Koja, Jak. 15 H10 6 8 S 106 52 E
Koja Utara, Jak. 15 H10 6 5 S 106 53 E
Kokobunji, Tōkyō 13 B1 35 42N 139 27 E
Kokobunji-Temple, Tōkyō 13 B4 35 44N 139 55 E
Kol Scholven, Ruhr 6 A3 51 35N 6 59 E
Kolarängen, Stock. 3 E12 59 16N 18 10 E
Kolbotn, Oslo 2 C4 59 48N 10 48 E
Kole Kalyan, Bomb. 16 G8 19 5N 72 50 E
Kolmiranta, Hels. 3 B2 60 15N 24 31 E
Kolmperä, Hels. 3 B2 60 15N 24 32 E
Koło, Wsaw. 10 E6 52 14N 20 56 E
Kolodeje, Pra. 10 B3 50 3N 14 38 E
Kolokinthou, Ath. 8 J11 38 0N 23 42 E
Kolomenskoye, Mos. 11 E10 55 40N 37 40 E
Kolomyagi, St-Pet. 11 A3 60 0N 30 19 E
Kolónos, Ath. 8 J11 37 59N 23 43 E
Kolovraty, Pra. 10 B3 50 0N 14 37 E
Kolsås, Oslo 2 B3 59 55N 10 30 E
Koltushi, St-Pet. 11 B5 59 55N 30 38 E
Komae, Tōkyō 13 C2 35 37N 139 34 E
Komagome, Tōkyō 13 B3 35 43N 139 45 E
Komazawa, Tōkyō 13 C3 35 37N 139 40 E
Komdhara, Calc. 16 C5 22 52N 88 14 E
Kommunarka, Mos. 11 F8 55 35N 37 29 E
Komorów, Wsaw. 10 F5 52 9N 20 48 E
Kona, Calc. 16 E5 22 37N 88 18 E
Konala, Hels. 3 B4 60 14N 24 52 E
Kōnan, Tōkyō 13 D2 35 23N 139 35 E
Kondli, Delhi 16 B2 28 36N 77 19 E
Kong Sin Wan, H.K. 12 E5 22 15N 114 7 E
Kongelunden, Købn. 2 E10 55 34N 12 34 E
Kongens Lyngby, Købn. 2 D10 55 46N 12 30 E
Kongo, Hels. 3 A3 60 20N 24 47 E
Königshardt, Ruhr 6 A3 51 33N 6 51 E
Konnagar, Calc. 16 D6 22 42N 88 21 E
Konohana, Ōsaka 12 B3 34 40N 135 26 E
Kōnoike, Ōsaka 12 B4 34 42N 135 37 E
Konradshöhe, Berl. 7 A2 52 35N 13 13 E
Koonung Cr. →, Melb. 19 E7 37 46 S 145 4 E
Kopanina, Pra. 10 B1 50 3N 14 17 E
Koparkhairna, Bomb. 16 G8 19 6N 72 59 E
Köpenick, Berl. 7 B4 52 26N 13 35 E
Korangi, Kar. 17 H11 24 47N 67 8 E
Koremasa, Tōkyō 13 C1 35 39N 139 29 E
Korenevo, Mos. 11 E12 55 40N 38 0 E
Kori, Ōsaka 12 B4 34 47N 135 38 E
Koridhallós, Ath. 8 J10 37 59N 23 39 E
Korkinskoye, Oz., St-Pet. 11 B6 59 55N 30 42 E
Körne, Ruhr 6 A7 51 30N 7 30 E
Korso, Hels. 3 A5 60 21N 25 5 E
Koshigaya, Tōkyō 13 A3 35 53N 139 47 E
Kosino, Mos. 11 E11 55 43N 37 50 E
Kosugi, Tōkyō 13 C2 35 34N 139 39 E
Kota, Jak. 15 H9 6 7 S 106 48 E
Kotelyniki, Mos. 11 F11 55 39N 37 52 E
Kōtō-Ku, Tōkyō 13 B3 35 40N 139 48 E
Kotrang, Calc. 16 D6 22 41N 88 20 E
Kouponia, Ath. 8 J11 37 57N 23 47 E
Koviksudde, Stock. 3 D13 59 21N 18 21 E
Kowloon, H.K. 12 E5 22 18N 114 10 E
Kowloon City, H.K. 12 E6 22 19N 114 11 E
Kowloon Pk., H.K. 12 D6 22 20N 114 13 E
Kowloon Res., H.K. 12 D5 22 21N 114 9 E
Kowloon Tong, H.K. 12 D6 22 20N 114 10 E
Kozhukhovo, Mos. 11 E11 55 43N 37 53 E
Kozukue, Tōkyō 13 C2 35 30N 139 35 E
Krailling, Mün. 7 G9 48 5N 11 25 E
Kramat Jati, Jak. 15 J10 6 15 S 106 51 E
Krampnitz, Berl. 7 B1 52 27N 13 3 E
Krampnitzsee, Berl. 7 B1 52 27N 13 3 E
Kranji, Sing. 15 F7 1 26N 103 45 E
Kranji, Sungei →, Sing. 15 F7 1 26N 103 44 E
Kranji Dam, Sing. 15 F7 1 26N 103 44 E
Kraskovo, Mos. 11 F11 55 39N 37 58 E
Krasnaya Gorka, St-Pet. 11 B5 59 58N 30 38 E
Krasno-Presnenskaya, Mos. 11 E9 55 45N 37 32 E
Krasnogorsk, Mos. 11 E7 55 49N 37 18 E
Krasnyj Stroitel, Mos. 11 F9 55 36N 37 35 E
Kray, Ruhr 6 B4 51 27N 7 4 E
Krč, Pra. 10 B2 50 2N 14 26 E
Krefeld, Ruhr 6 B1 51 20N 6 33 E
Kremlin, Mos. 11 E9 55 45N 37 38 E
Kresson, Phil. 24 B5 39 51N 74 54W
Kreuzberg, Berl. 7 A3 52 30N 13 24 E
Krishnarampur, Calc. 16 D5 22 43N 88 13 E
Kritzendorf, Wien 10 G9 48 19N 16 18 E
Krokhol, Oslo 2 C5 59 48N 10 55 E
Krugersdorp, Jobg. 18 E7 26 6 S 27 48 E
Krukut, Kali →, Jak. 15 J9 6 13 S 106 48 E
Krumme Lanke, Berl. 7 B2 52 27N 13 14 E
Krummensee, Berl. 7 A5 52 35N 13 41 E
Krupunder, Hbg. 7 D7 53 37N 9 53 E
Krusboda, Stock. 3 E12 59 13N 18 14 E
Krylatskoye, Mos. 11 E8 55 44N 37 23 E
Küçükkoy, Ist. 17 A2 41 3N 28 52 E
Kudrovo, St-Pet. 11 B5 59 54N 30 30 E
Kuivasaari, Hels. 3 C5 60 6N 25 0 E
Kujiai, Tōkyō 13 A1 35 57N 139 26 E
Küllenhahn, Ruhr 6 C4 51 14N 7 8 E
Kulosaari, Hels. 3 B5 60 11N 25 0 E
Kulturpalasset, Wsaw. 10 E7 52 14N 21 0 E
Kumla, Stock. 3 E12 59 13N 18 11 E
Kummelnäs, Stock. 3 D12 59 21N 18 16 E
Kungens kurva, Stock. 3 E10 59 15N 17 53 E
Kungsängen, Stock. 3 D9 59 26N 17 43 E
Kungshatt, Stock. 3 E10 59 17N 17 53 E
Kungsholmen, Stock. 3 D11 59 20N 18 2 E
Kuningan, Jak. 15 J9 6 13 S 106 49 E
Kuninkaanmäki, Hels. 3 B5 60 18N 25 7 E
Kunitachi, Tōkyō 13 B1 35 41N 139 27 E
Kunming Hu, Beij. 14 B2 39 59N 116 13 E
Kunratice, Pra. 10 B2 50 0N 14 28 E
Kunratický →, Pra. 10 B2 50 2N 14 24 E
Kunsthalle, Hbg. 7 D8 53 33N 10 0 E
Kuntsevo, Mos. 11 E8 55 43N 37 23 E
Kupchino, St-Pet. 11 B4 59 50N 30 23 E
Kupferdreh, Ruhr 6 B4 51 23N 7 5 E
Kurbali Dere →, Ist. 17 B3 40 58N 29 1 E
Kurihara, Tōkyō 13 B2 35 45N 139 34 E
Kurkino, Mos. 11 D8 55 53N 37 22 E
Kurla, Bomb. 16 G8 19 4N 72 52 E
Kurmuri, Bomb. 16 G8 19 4N 72 53 E
Kurnell, Syd. 19 C4 34 0 S 151 10 E
Kurume, Tōkyō 13 B2 35 45N 139 31 E
Kuryanovo, Mos. 11 F10 55 39N 37 42 E
Kushihiki, Tōkyō 13 A2 35 54N 139 36 E
Kushtia, Calc. 16 E6 22 31N 88 23 E
Kuskovo, Mos. 11 E10 55 44N 37 48 E
Kutsino, Mos. 11 E11 55 44N 37 55 E
Kuy-e-Gishā, Tehr. 17 C5 35 44N 51 23 E
Kuy-e-Mekānir, Tehr. 17 C5 35 46N 51 22 E
Kuzyminki, Mos. 11 E10 55 42N 37 46 E
Kvarnsjön, Stock. 3 E10 59 11N 17 58 E
Kwa-Thema, Jobg. 18 F11 26 17 S 28 23 E
Kwai Chung, H.K. 12 D5 22 22N 114 7 E
Kwitang, Jak. 15 J10 6 11 S 106 50 E
Kwun Tong, H.K. 12 E6 22 18N 114 13 E
Kyje, Pra. 10 B3 50 6N 14 33 E
Kyōhōji, Ōsaka 12 C4 34 38N 135 33 E
Kyrkfjärden, Stock. 3 E9 59 16N 17 45 E
Kyrkslätt, Hels. 3 C1 60 6N 24 28W


# L


La Aguada, Stgo 30 J10 33 28 S 70 40W
La Blanca, Stgo 30 K11 33 30 S 70 40W
La Boca, B.A. 32 B4 34 38 S 58 22W
La Bottáccia, Rome 9 F8 41 54N 12 18 E
La Bretèche, Paris 5 B2 48 51N 2 1 E
La Brosse, Paris 5 C1 48 43N 1 20 E
La Cabana, La Hab. 30 B3 23 8N 82 20W
La Canada, L.A. 28 A3 34 12N 118 12W
La Cassa, Tori. 9 A2 45 11N 7 30 E
La Celle-les-Bordes, Paris 5 D1 48 38N 1 57 E
La Celle-St.-Cloud, Paris 5 B2 48 50N 2 9 E
La Chivera, Car. 30 D5 10 35N 66 54W
La Colmena, Méx. 29 A2 19 35N 99 16W
La Courneuve, Paris 5 B4 48 55N 2 22 E
La Crescenta, L.A. 28 A3 34 13N 118 14W
La Défense, Paris 5 B3 48 53N 2 12 E
La Dehesa, Stgo 30 J11 33 21 S 70 33W
La Estación, Mdrd. 8 B2 40 27N 3 48W
La Floresta, Barc. 8 D5 41 26N 2 3 E
La Florida, Car. 30 D5 10 30N 66 52W
La Fortuna, Mdrd. 8 B2 40 21N 3 46W
La Fransa, Barc. 8 D5 41 22N 2 9 E
La Fresnière, Mtrl. 20 A2 43 33N 73 58W
La Frette-sur-Seine, Paris 5 B3 48 58N 2 11 E
La Garenne-Colombes, Paris 5 B3 48 54N 2 15 E
La Giustiniana, Rome 9 F9 41 59N 12 24 E
La Grange, Chic. 26 C1 41 48N 87 53W
La Grange des Noues, Paris 5 A4 49 1N 2 28 E
La Grange Highlands, Chic. 26 C1 41 46N 87 53W
La Grange Park, Chic. 26 C1 41 49N 87 51W
La Granja, Stgo 30 K11 33 31 S 70 38W
La Guaira, Car. 30 D5 10 36N 66 55W
La Guardia Airport, N.Y. 23 C5 40 46N 73 52W
La Guasima, La Hab. 30 B3 23 0N 82 17W
La Habana, La Hab. 30 B2 23 7N 82 21W
La habana, B. de, La Hab. 30 B3 23 7N 82 20W
La Habana Vieia, La Hab. 30 B2 23 7N 82 20W
La Habra, L.A. 28 C5 33 56N 117 57W
La Habre Heights, L.A. 28 C5 33 59N 117 56W
La Horqueta →, B.A. 32 C1 34 43 S 58 51W
La Lisa, La Hab. 30 B2 23 3N 82 25W
La Llacuna, Barc. 8 D6 41 24N 2 12 E
La Loma, Méx. 29 A2 19 31N 99 11W
La Lucila, B.A. 32 B4 34 30 S 58 29W
La Magdalena Atlipac, Méx. 29 B4 19 22N 89 56 E
La Magdalena Chichicaspa, Méx. 29 B2 19 24N 99 18W
La Magdalena Contreras, Méx. 29 C2 19 17N 99 13W
La Magdalena Petlalco, Méx. 29 C2 19 13N 99 10W
La Maison Blanche, Paris 5 C1 48 44N 1 54 E
La Maladrerie, Paris 5 B2 48 54N 2 1 E
La Marquesa, Méx. 29 C1 19 18N 99 22W
La Milla, Cerro, Lima 30 G8 12 2 S 77 5W
La Molina, Lima 30 G9 12 4 S 76 56W
La Monachina, Rome 9 F9 41 53N 12 21 E
La Moraleja, Mdrd. 8 A3 40 30N 30 38W
La Nopalera, Méx. 29 C3 19 18N 99 5W
La Pastora, Car. 30 D5 10 31N 66 55W
La Paterna, B.A. 32 B4 34 35 S 58 26W
La Patte-d'Oie, Paris 5 A3 49 0N 2 10 E
La Perla, Lima 30 G8 12 4 S 77 7W
La Perouse, Syd. 19 B4 33 59 S 151 14 E
La Pineda, Barc. 8 E5 41 15N 2 1 E
La Pisana, Rome 9 F9 41 51N 12 23 E
La Playa, La Hab. 30 B2 23 6N 82 26W
La Prairie, Mtrl. 20 B5 43 25N 73 29W
La Puente, L.A. 28 B5 34 1N 117 54W
La Punta, Lima 30 G7 12 4 S 77 10W
La Puntigala, Barc. 8 D6 41 27N 2 13 E
La Queue-en-Brie, Paris 5 C5 48 47N 2 34 E
La Reina, Stgo 30 J11 33 26 S 70 33W
La Reja, B.A. 32 B2 34 38 S 58 48W
La Ribera, Barc. 8 D5 41 21N 2 4 E
La Romanie, Paris 5 C1 48 43N 1 53 E
La Rústica, Rome 9 F10 41 54N 12 36 E
La Sagrera, Barc. 8 D6 41 25N 2 11 E
La Salada, B.A. 32 C4 34 43 S 58 28W
La Scala, Mil. 9 E6 45 28N 9 11 E
La Selce, Rome 9 F9 41 53N 12 20 E
La Sierra, La Hab. 30 B2 23 7N 82 24W
La Taxonera, Barc. 8 D6 41 25N 2 10 E
La Vega, Car. 30 E5 10 28N 66 56W
La Verrière, Paris 5 C1 48 45N 1 57 E
La Vibora, La Hab. 30 B2 23 5N 82 22W
La Victoria, Lima 30 G8 12 3 S 77 2W
La Ville-du-Bois, Paris 5 D3 48 39N 2 16 E
Laab im Walde, Wien 10 H9 48 9N 16 10 E
Laaer Berg, Wien 10 H10 48 9N 16 24 E
Laajalahti, Hels. 3 B3 60 11N 24 48 E
Laajasalo, Hels. 3 B5 60 10N 25 1 E
Laaksolahti, Hels. 3 B3 60 14N 24 45 E
Laar, Ruhr 6 B2 51 27N 6 44 E
Lablâba, W. el →, El Qâ. 18 C5 30 1N 31 19 E
Lachine, Mtrl. 20 B3 43 26N 73 42W
Ládvi, Pra. 10 B2 50 8N 14 27 E
Łady, Wsaw. 10 F6 52 8N 20 57 E
Lafayette, S.F. 27 A4 37 52N 122 6W
Lafayette Hill, Phil. 24 A3 40 5N 75 15W
Lafayette Res., S.F. 27 A4 37 52N 122 8W
Laferrere, B.A. 32 C3 34 45 S 58 35W
Lagny, Paris 5 B6 48 52N 2 42 E
Lagoa da Pedra, Lisb. 8 F9 38 43N 8 58W
Lagos, Lagos 18 B2 6 27N 7 23 E
Lagos Harbour, Lagos 18 B2 6 26N 7 23 E
Lagos-Ikeja Airport, Lagos 18 A1 6 34N 7 19 E
Lagos Island, Lagos 18 B2 6 26N 7 23 E
Lagos Lagoon, Lagos 18 B2 6 30N 7 28 E
Laguna de B., Manila 15 E4 14 29N 121 6 E
Laim, Mün. 7 G10 48 7N 11 30 E
Lainate, Mil. 9 D5 45 34N 9 1 E
Lainz, Wien 10 H9 48 10N 16 16 E
Lainzer Tiergarten, Wien 10 G9 48 10N 16 13 E
Lajeado →, S. Pau. 31 E7 23 28 S 46 24W
Lake Avenue Woods, Chic. 26 A1 42 4N 87 53W
Lake Hiawatha, N.Y. 22 B2 40 52N 74 23W
Lakefield, Jobg. 18 F10 26 11 S 28 17 E
Lakemba, Syd. 19 B3 33 55 S 151 5 E
Lakeside, Jobg. 18 E9 26 5 S 28 8 E
Lakeview, Chic. 26 B3 41 56N 87 38W
Lakeview, Trto. 20 E7 43 35N 79 32W
Lakhtinskiy, St-Pet. 11 B2 59 59N 30 9 E
Lakhtinskiy Razliv, Oz., St-Pet. 11 B3 59 59N 30 12 E
Lakshmanpur, Calc. 16 E5 22 38N 88 16 E
Laleham, Lon. 4 C2 51 24N 0 29W
Lâleli, Ist. 17 A2 41 0N 28 57 E
Lalor, Melb. 19 E6 37 40 S 144 59 E
Lam San, Sing. 15 F7 1 22N 103 43 E
Lam Tin, H.K. 12 E6 22 18N 114 14 E
Lambarfjärden, Stock. 3 D9 59 21N 17 48 E
Lambert, Oslo 2 B4 59 52N 10 48 E
Lambeth, Lon. 4 C4 51 28N 0 6W
Lambrate, Mil. 9 E6 45 28N 9 16 E
Lambro →, Mil. 9 E6 45 24N 9 17 E
Lambro, Parco, Mil. 9 E6 45 29N 9 14 E
Lambton, Jobg. 18 F10 26 14 S 28 10 E
Lambton Hills, Trto. 20 E7 43 39N 79 30W
Lamma I., H.K. 12 E5 22 12N 114 7 E
Lampton, Lon. 4 C2 51 28N 0 21W
Landianchang, Beij. 14 B2 39 57N 116 13 E
Landover Hills, Wash. 25 D8 38 56N 76 54W
Landstrasse, Wien 10 G10 48 12N 16 23 E
Landwehr kanal, Berl. 7 B3 52 29N 13 24 E
Lane Cove, Syd. 19 A3 33 48 S 151 9 E
Lane Cove National Park, Syd. 19 A3 33 47 S 151 8 E
Langen, Oslo 2 C5 59 44N 10 57 E
Langenberg, Ruhr 6 B4 51 20N 7 7 E
Langenbochum, Ruhr 6 A4 51 36N 7 7 E
Langendreer, Ruhr 6 B5 51 28N 7 18 E
Langenhorn, Hbg. 7 D7 53 39N 9 59 E
Langenhorst, Ruhr 6 B4 51 21N 7 1 E
Langenzersdorf, Wien 10 G10 48 18N 16 21 E
Langer See, Berl. 7 B4 52 24N 13 37 E
Langerfeld, Ruhr 6 C5 51 16N 7 14 E
Langley, Wash. 25 D6 38 57N 77 11W
Langley Park, Wash. 25 D8 38 59N 76 58W
Langstaff, Trto. 20 C8 43 50N 79 26W
Längtarmen, Stock. 3 D8 59 24N 17 36 E
Langwald, Mün. 7 F9 48 10N 11 25 E
Lanham, Wash. 25 D8 38 59N 76 51W
Lank-Latum, Ruhr 6 C2 51 18N 6 40 E
Lankwitz, Berl. 7 B3 52 25N 13 21 E
Länna Drevviken, Stock. 3 E11 59 12N 18 8 E
L'Annunziatella, Rome 9 G10 41 49N 12 33 E
Lansdowne, Balt. 25 B3 39 14N 76 38W
Lansdowne, Phil. 24 B3 39 56N 75 16W
Lansing, Trto. 20 D8 43 45N 79 24W
Lanús, B.A. 32 C4 34 42 S 58 23W
Lapa, Rio J. 31 B2 22 54 S 43 10W
Lapa, S. Pau. 31 E5 23 31 S 46 42W
Lapangan Merdeka, Jak. 15 J9 6 10 S 106 49 E
Lapinkylä, Hels. 3 B4 60 18N 24 51 E
Lapinkylä, Hels. 3 B1 60 13N 24 27 E
Lappböle, Hels. 3 B1 60 13N 24 27 E
Laranjeiras, Rio J. 31 B2 22 55 S 43 10W
Larchmont, N.Y. 23 B6 40 55N 73 44W
Larkspur, S.F. 27 A1 37 55N 122 31W
Las, Wsaw. 10 E7 52 13N 21 6 E
Las Acacias, Car. 30 E5 10 29N 66 54W
Las Adjuntas, Car. 30 E4 10 25N 67 0W
Las Barrancas, B.A. 32 A4 34 28 S 58 29W
Las Conchas, B.A. 32 A3 34 25 S 58 34W
Las Corts, Barc. 8 D5 41 23N 2 9 E
Las Fuentes Brotantes, Méx. 29 C2 19 16N 99 11W
Las Kabacki, Wsaw. 10 F7 52 7N 21 2 E
Las Lomas, L.A. 28 B5 34 8N 117 59W
Las Mercedes, Car. 30 E5 10 28N 66 51W
Las Pinas, Manila 15 E3 14 29N 120 58 E
Las Rejas, Stgo 30 J10 33 27 S 70 42W
Las Rozas de Madrid, Mdrd. 8 B1 40 29N 3 52W
Las Trampas Cr. →, S.F. 27 A4 37 53N 122 6W
Las Trampas Regional Park, S.F. 27 B4 37 49N 122 3W
Las Trampas Ridge, S.F. 27 A4 37 50N 122 3W
Las Tunitas, Car. 30 D4 10 36N 67 1W
Lasalle, Mtrl. 20 B4 43 26N 73 37W
Lasek Bielański, Wsaw. 10 E6 52 17N 20 57 E
Lasek Na Kole, Wsaw. 10 E6 52 15N 20 56 E
Laski, Wsaw. 10 E6 52 18N 20 50 E
Latina, Mdrd. 8 B2 40 24N 3 44W
Latrobe Univ., Melb. 19 E7 37 43 S 145 3 E
Lattingtown, N.Y. 23 B7 40 52N 73 34W
Laufzorn, Mün. 7 G10 48 0N 11 33 E
Laurel Hollow, N.Y. 23 B8 40 51N 73 28W
Laurel Springs, Phil. 24 C4 39 49N 75 0W
Laurelton, N.Y. 23 C6 40 40N 73 45W
Laurence Hanscom Field, Bost. 21 C2 42 28N 71 16W
Lausdomini, Nápl. 9 H13 40 55N 14 26 E
Lauttasaari, Hels. 3 C4 60 9N 24 53 E
Lava Nuova, Nápl. 9 J13 40 47N 14 23 E
Laval-des-Rapides, Mtrl. 20 A3 43 33N 73 41W
Laval-Ouest, Mtrl. 20 A2 43 32N 73 52W
Laval-sur-le-Lac, Mtrl. 20 A2 43 31N 73 52W
Lavradio, Lisb. 8 F8 38 40N 9 2W
Lawndale, Chic. 26 B2 41 50N 87 42W
Lawndale, L.A. 28 C2 33 52N 118 22W
Lawndale, Phil. 24 A4 40 3N 75 5W
Lawnside, Phil. 24 B4 39 51N 75 1W
Lawrence, Bost. 21 A3 42 43N 71 7W
Lawrence, N.Y. 23 D6 40 36N 73 43W
Lawrence Heights, Trto. 20 D8 43 43N 79 25W
Lawrence Park, Phil. 24 B2 39 57N 75 20W
Lawton, La Hab. 30 B2 23 5N 82 20W
Layāri, Kar. 17 G11 24 52N 67 0 E
Layāri →, Kar. 17 G10 24 52N 66 58 E
Lazienkowski Park, Wsaw. 10 E7 52 13N 21 1 E
Le Blanc-Mesnil, Paris 5 B4 48 56N 2 27 E
Le Bourget, Paris 5 B4 48 56N 2 25 E
Le Chesnay, Paris 5 C2 48 49N 2 8 E
Le Christ de Saclay, Paris 5 C3 48 43N 1 59 E
Le Kremlin-Bicêtre, Paris 5 C4 48 48N 2 21 E
Le Mesnil-Amelot, Paris 5 A5 49 1N 2 35 E
Le Mesnil-le-Roi, Paris 5 B2 48 56N 2 7 E
Le Mesnil-St.-Denis, Paris 5 C1 48 44N 1 57 E
Le Pecq, Paris 5 B2 48 53N 2 6 E
Le Perreux, Paris 5 B4 48 50N 2 29 E
Le Pin, Paris 5 B5 48 54N 2 37 E
Le Plessis-Bouchard, Paris 5 A3 49 0N 2 14 E
Le Plessis-Gassot, Paris 5 A4 49 2N 2 24 E
Le Plessis-Pâté, Paris 5 D3 48 36N 2 19 E
Le Plessis-Robinson, Paris 5 C3 48 47N 2 15 E
Le Plessis-Trévise, Paris 5 C5 48 48N 2 34 E
Le Port-Marly, Paris 5 B2 48 52N 2 6 E
Le Pré-St.-Gervais, Paris 5 B4 48 53N 2 23 E
Le Raincy, Paris 5 B5 48 53N 2 31 E
Le Thillay, Paris 5 A4 49 0N 2 28 E
Le Trappe, Mtrl. 20 B1 43 30N 74 1W
Le Val d'Enfer, Paris 5 C3 48 45N 2 11 E
Le Vésinet, Paris 5 B2 48 54N 2 8 E
Lea →, Lon. 4 B4 51 30N 0 2W
Lea Bridge, Lon. 4 B4 51 33N 0 2W
Leakin Park, Balt. 25 B2 39 18N 76 41W
Leaside, Trto. 20 D8 43 42N 79 22W
Leatherhead, Lon. 4 D3 51 17N 0 19W
Leaves Green, Lon. 4 D5 51 19N 0 1 E
Leblon, Rio J. 31 B2 22 59 S 43 14W
Léchelle, Forêt de la, Paris 5 C6 48 43N 2 41 E
Ledøje, Købn. 2 D8 55 42N 12 18 E
Lee, Lon. 4 C5 51 27N 0 0 E
Leeupan, Jobg. 18 F10 26 13 S 28 18 E
Leganes, Mdrd. 8 C2 40 19N 3 45W
Legazpi, Mdrd. 8 B2 40 23N 3 41W
Legoa, Kali →, Jak. 15 H10 6 6 S 106 52 E
Lehtisaaret, Hels. 3 C3 60 6N 24 46 E
Lehtisaari, Hels. 3 B4 60 10N 24 51 E
Lei Yue Mun, H.K. 12 E6 22 17N 114 14 E
Leião, Lisb. 8 F7 38 43N 9 17W
Leichhardt, Syd. 19 B3 33 53 S 151 9 E
Leigang, Gzh. 14 G7 23 2N 113 6 E
Léini, Tori. 9 A3 45 11N 7 42 E
Leisure World, S.F. 27 A4 37 51N 122 4W
Lemoyne, Mtrl. 20 B5 43 29N 73 29W
Lemsahl, Hbg. 7 C8 53 41N 10 5 E
Lenin, Mos. 11 E9 55 43N 37 34 E
Leningrad = St. Petersburg, St-Pet. 11 B3 59 55N 30 15 E
Lenino, Mos. 11 F9 55 38N 37 39 E
Leninskiye Gory, Mos. 11 E9 55 41N 37 32 E
Lenne →, Ruhr 6 B7 51 25N 7 30 E
Lennep, Ruhr 6 C5 51 11N 7 15 E
Lenni, Phil. 24 B2 39 53N 75 27W
Lennox, L.A. 28 C2 33 56N 118 20W
Leonardo da Vinci, Aeroporto Int., Rome 9 G8 41 47N 12 15 E
Leoncio Martinez, Car. 30 E6 10 29N 66 48W
Leonia, N.Y. 22 B5 40 51N 73 59W
Leopard, Phil. 24 A2 40 1N 75 26W
Leopardi, Nápl. 9 J13 40 45N 14 24 E
Leopoldau, Wien 10 G10 48 15N 16 26 E
Leopoldstadt, Wien 10 G10 48 13N 16 22 E
Leportovo, Mos. 11 E10 55 46N 37 43 E
Leppävaara, Hels. 3 B3 60 13N 24 49 E
Lera, Mte., Tori. 9 A1 45 10N 7 27 E
L'Éremo, Tori. 9 B3 45 2N 7 44 E
Les Alluets-le-Roi, Paris 5 B1 48 54N 1 55 E
Les Clayes-sous-Bois, Paris 5 C1 48 49N 1 59 E
Les Essarts-le-Roi, Paris 5 C1 48 42N 1 53 E
Les Gâtines, Paris 5 C1 48 48N 1 58 E
Les Grésillons, Paris 5 B2 48 56N 2 1 E
Les Layes, Paris 5 C1 48 43N 1 55 E
Les Lilas, Paris 5 B4 48 52N 2 25 E
Les Loges-en-Josas, Paris 5 C2 48 45N 2 8 E
Les Molières, Paris 5 C2 48 40N 2 4 E
Les Mureaux, Paris 5 B1 48 59N 1 54 E
Les Pavillons-sous-Bois, Paris 5 B5 48 54N 2 30 E
Les Vaux de Cernay →, Paris 5 C1 48 41N 1 59 E
Lésigny, Paris 5 C5 48 44N 2 37 E
Lesnosavodskaya, St-Pet. 11 B4 59 51N 30 29 E
Lesnoy, St-Pet. 11 B4 59 59N 30 22 E
Lester B. Pearson Int. Airport, Trto. 20 D7 43 40N 79 38 E
L'Étang-la-Ville, Paris 5 B2 48 52N 2 4 E
Letná, Pra. 10 B2 50 0 S 14 26 E
Letňany, Pra. 10 B3 50 8N 14 30 E
Letovo, Mos. 11 F8 55 34N 37 24 E
Leuville-sur-Orge, Paris 5 D3 48 36N 2 15 E
Levallois-Perret, Paris 5 B3 48 53N 2 16 E
Lévis St.-Nom, Paris 5 C1 48 43N 1 57 E
Levittown, N.Y. 23 C7 40 43N 73 31W
Lewisdale, Wash. 25 D8 38 58N 76 59W
Lewisham, Jobg. 18 E7 26 7 S 27 49 E
Lewisham, Lon. 4 C4 51 27N 0 1W
Lexington, Bost. 21 C2 42 25N 71 12W
Leyton, Lon. 4 B4 51 33N 0 1W
Leytonstone, Lon. 4 B5 51 34N 0 0 E
L'Hautil, Paris 5 A2 49 0N 2 0 E
L'Hay-les-Roses, Paris 5 C4 48 46N 2 20 E
Lhotka, Pra. 10 B2 50 1N 14 26 E
Liangshui He →, Beij. 14 C3 39 48N 116 23 E
Lianhua Chi, Beij. 14 B2 39 52N 116 16 E
Lianhua He →, Beij. 14 B2 39 52N 116 13 E
Lianozovo, Mos. 11 D9 55 53N 37 34 E
Libčice nad Vitavou, Pra. 10 A2 50 11N 14 22 E
Liben, Pra. 10 B2 50 6N 14 27 E
Liberdade, S. Pau. 31 E6 23 33 S 46 37W
Libertad, B.A. 32 C2 34 41 S 58 41W
Liberty I., N.Y. 22 C4 40 41N 74 2W
Liberty Plain, Bost. 21 D4 42 11N 70 52W
Liberty Res., Balt. 25 A1 39 23N 76 52W
Libeznice, Pra. 10 A2 50 11N 14 29 E
Library of Congress, Wash. 25 D7 38 53N 77 0W
Libuč, Pra. 10 B2 50 0N 14 27 E
Lichiao, Gzh. 14 G8 23 3N 113 18 E
Lichtenbroich, Ruhr 6 C2 51 17N 6 49 E
Lichtenburg, Berl. 7 A4 52 31N 13 30 E
Lichtenplatz, Ruhr 6 C5 51 14N 7 11 E
Lichtenrade, Berl. 7 B3 52 23N 13 24 E
Lichterfelde, Berl. 7 B2 52 25N 13 19 E
Licignano di Nápoli, Nápl. 9 H13 40 54N 14 21 E
Lidcombe, Syd. 19 B3 33 52 S 151 3 E
Lidingö, Stock. 3 D11 59 21N 18 8 E
Lido Beach, N.Y. 23 D7 40 35N 73 37W
Lier, Oslo 2 C1 59 47N 10 13 E
Lierskogen, Oslo 2 C1 59 49N 10 15 E
Lieshi Lingyuan, Gzh. 14 G8 23 7N 113 16 E
Liesing, Wien 10 H9 48 8N 16 17 E
Liesing →, Wien 10 H10 48 8N 16 28 E
Lieusant, Paris 5 D5 48 38N 2 33 E
Liffjofs, Hels. 3 B6 60 19N 25 12 E
Ligovo, St-Pet. 11 C3 59 49N 30 10 E
Lijordet, Oslo 2 B3 59 56N 10 36 E
Likhoborka →, Mos. 11 D9 55 50N 37 37 E
Likova →, Mos. 11 F8 55 36N 37 20 E
Lilla Värtan, Stock. 3 D12 59 20N 18 11 E
Lille Rørbæk, Købn. 2 D7 55 47N 12 6 E

## M

42 Midlothian


Midlothian, Chic. 26 D2 41 37N 87 43W
Miedzeszyn, Wsaw. 10 E8 52 10N 21 11 E
Międzylesie, Wsaw. 10 E8 52 12N 21 10 E
Miessaari, Hels. 3 C3 60 8N 24 47 E
Mikhaylovskoye, Mos. 11 F9 55 35N 37 35 E
Mikhelysona, Mos. 11 E11 55 42N 37 52 E
Milano, Mil. 9 E5 45 28N 9 10 E
Milano Due, Mil. 9 E6 45 29N 9 16 E
Milano San Felice, Mil. 9 E6 45 28N 9 18 E
Milanolago, Mil. 9 E6 45 27N 9 17 E
Milbertshofen, Mün. 7 F10 48 10N 11 34 E
Milburn, N.Y. 22 C3 40 43N 74 19W
Milford, Balt. 25 A2 39 21N 76 43W
Mill Cr. →, S.F. 27 A1 37 53N 122 31W
Mill Hill, Lon. 4 B3 51 37N 0 14W
Mill Neck, N.Y. 23 B7 40 53N 73 33W
Mill Park, Melb. 19 E7 37 40 S 145 3 E
Mill Valley, S.F. 27 A1 37 54N 122 33W
Millbrae, S.F. 27 C2 37 35N 122 22W
Mille-Iles, R. des →, Mtrl. 20 A3 43 39N 73 46W
Miller I., Balt. 25 B4 39 15N 76 21W
Miller Meadow, Chic. 26 B2 41 51N 87 49W
Milliken, Trto. 20 D9 43 49N 79 17W
Millis, Bost. 21 D1 42 10N 71 21W
Mills College, S.F. 27 B3 37 46N 122 10W
Milltown, Phil. 24 B1 39 57N 75 32W
Millwall, Lon. 4 C4 51 29N 0 0 E
Millwood, Wash. 25 D8 38 52N 76 52W
Milon-la-Chapelle, Paris 5 C2 48 43N 2 3 E
Milpa Alta, Méx. 29 C3 19 11N 99 0W
Milperra, Syd. 19 B2 33 56 S 150 59 E
Milspe, Ruhr 6 C5 51 18N 7 19 E
Milton, Bost. 21 D3 42 14N 71 2W
Milton Village, Bost. 21 D3 42 15N 71 4W
Mimico, Trto. 20 E8 43 36N 79 29W
Mimico Cr. →, Trto. 20 E7 43 37N 79 33W
Minami, Ōsaka 12 B4 34 40N 135 30 E
Minami-Ku, Tōkyō 13 D2 35 24N 139 37 E
Minami-tsunashima, Tōkyō 13 C2 35 32N 139 37 E
Minato, Ōsaka 12 C3 34 39N 135 25 E
Minato-Ku, Tōkyō 13 C3 35 39N 139 44 E
Mine, Tōkyō 13 B3 35 49N 139 46 E
Minebank Run →, Balt. 25 A3 39 24N 76 33W
Mineola, N.Y. 23 C7 40 44N 73 38W
Ministro Rivadavia, B.A. 32 D4 34 50 S 58 22W
Minō, Ōsaka 12 B3 34 49N 135 28 E
Minshât el Bekkarî, El Qâ. 18 C4 30 0N 31 8 E
Minto, Syd. 19 C2 34 1 S 150 51 E
Minute Man Nat. Hist. Park, Bost. 21 C2 42 25N 71 16W
Mirafiori, Tori. 9 B2 45 1N 7 36 E
Miraflores, Lima 30 G8 12 7 S 77 2W
Miramar, La Hab. 30 B2 23 7N 82 25W
Miramar, S.F. 27 D2 37 29N 122 27W
Miranda, Syd. 19 C3 34 2 S 151 6 E
Mirzapur, Calc. 16 D6 22 49N 88 24 E
Misato, Tōkyō 13 B4 35 49N 139 51 E
Misericordia, Sa. da, Rio J. 31 B2 22 51 S 43 17W
Mishawum L., Bost. 21 B3 42 30N 71 8W
Mission, S.F. 27 B2 37 44N 122 25W
Mississauga, Trto. 20 E7 43 35N 79 34W
Mitaka, Tōkyō 13 B2 35 41N 139 34 E
Mitcham, Lon. 4 C3 51 23N 0 10W
Mitcham, Melb. 19 E8 37 48 S 145 12 E
Mitcham Common, Lon. 4 C4 51 23N 0 8W
Mitino, Mos. 11 D8 55 51N 37 20 E
Mitry, Paris 5 B5 48 59N 2 36 E
Mitry-Mory, Paris 5 B5 48 59N 2 38 E
Mitry-Mory, Aérodrome de, Paris 5 B5 48 59N 2 37 E
Mitte, Berl. 7 A3 52 32N 13 24 E
Mittel Isarkanal, Mün. 7 F11 48 12N 11 40 E
Mittenheim, Mün. 7 F10 48 15N 11 33 E
Mixcoac, Presa de, Méx. 29 B2 19 21N 99 14W
Mixquic, Méx. 29 C4 19 13N 98 58W
Miyakojima, Ōsaka 12 B4 34 42N 135 31 E
Miyalo, Tōkyō 13 B2 35 49N 139 35 E
Mizonokuchi, Tōkyō 13 C2 35 35N 139 34 E
Mizue, Tōkyō 13 B4 35 41N 139 54 E
Mizuko, Tōkyō 13 A2 35 50N 139 32 E
Mizumoto, Tōkyō 13 B4 35 46N 139 52 E
Mlocinski Park, Wsaw. 10 E6 52 19N 20 57 E
Mlociny, Wsaw. 10 E6 52 18N 20 55 E
Mnevniki, Mos. 11 E8 55 45N 37 28 E
Moba, Lagos 18 B2 6 26N 7 28 E
Moczydło, Wsaw. 10 F7 52 8N 21 2 E
Modderfontein, Jobg. 18 E10 26 5 S 28 10 E
Modderfontein →, Jobg. 18 E9 26 5 S 28 10 E
Modřany, Pra. 10 B2 50 0N 14 24 E
Moers, Ruhr 6 B1 51 26N 6 37 E
Moffat Park, Jobg. 18 F9 26 15 S 28 4 E
Mofolo, Jobg. 18 F8 26 13 S 27 53 E
Mog, Sŏul 12 G7 37 32N 126 52 E
Mogyorod, Bud. 10 J14 47 35N 19 14 E
Mohili, Bomb. 16 G8 19 5N 72 52 E
Moinho Velho →, S. Pau. 31 E6 23 35 S 46 35W
Moissy-Cramayel, Paris 5 D5 48 37N 2 35 E
Moita, Lisb. 8 G9 38 39N 8 59W
Mokotów, Wsaw. 10 E7 52 12N 21 0 E
Molapo, Jobg. 18 F8 26 15 S 27 51 E
Mole →, Lon. 4 D2 51 14N 0 20W
Moletsane, Jobg. 18 F8 26 14 S 27 50 E
Molino de Rosas, Méx. 29 B2 19 21N 99 14W
Mølleå →, Købn. 2 D10 55 48N 12 35 E
Möllen, Ruhr 6 A2 51 35N 6 41 E
Mollins de Rey, Barc. 8 D5 41 24N 2 1 E
Molokovo, Mos. 11 F11 55 35N 37 53 E
Mombaça, S. Pau. 31 E7 23 37 S 46 25W
Mombello, Mil. 9 D5 45 36N 9 7 E
Momote, Tōkyō 13 B2 35 46N 139 32 E
Monash Univ., Melb. 19 F7 37 54 S 145 8 E
Monbulk Cr. →, Melb. 19 F8 37 55 S 145 12 E
Moncalieri, Tori. 9 B3 45 0N 7 41 E
Moncolombone, Tori. 9 A1 45 12N 7 28 E
Mondeor, Jobg. 18 F9 26 16 S 28 0 E
Moneda, Palacio de la, Stgo 30 J11 33 26 S 70 39W
Mong Kok, H.K. 12 E6 22 19N 114 10 E
Mongat, Barc. 8 D6 41 27N 2 16 E
Mongreno, Tori. 9 B3 45 3N 7 45 E
Moninos →, S. Pau. 31 F6 23 40 S 46 33W
Monrovia, L.A. 28 B4 34 9N 118 1W
Monsanto, Lisb. 8 F7 38 44N 9 12W
Monsanto, Parque Florestal de, Lisb. 8 F7 38 43N 9 11W
Mont Royal, Mtrl. 20 A4 43 30N 73 38W
Mont-Royal, Parc, Mtrl. 20 A4 43 30N 73 36W
Montalban, Car. 30 E5 10 28N 66 56W
Montana de Montjuich, Barc. 8 D5 41 21N 2 9 E
Montara, S.F. 27 C2 37 32N 122 30W
Montara, Pt., S.F. 27 C1 37 32N 122 31W
Montara Mt., S.F. 27 C2 37 32N 122 27W
Montchanin, Phil. 24 C1 39 47N 75 35W
Montclair, N.Y. 22 C3 40 49N 74 12W
Monte Chingolo, B.A. 32 C4 34 43 S 58 22W
Monte Grande, B.A. 32 C4 34 48 S 58 27W
Monte Sacro, Rome 9 F10 41 56N 12 32 E
Montebello, L.A. 28 B4 34 1N 118 8W
Montelera, Tori. 9 B1 45 9N 7 26 E
Montemor, Lisb. 8 F7 38 49N 9 12W
Monterey Park, L.A. 28 B4 34 3N 118 7W
Monterrey, La Hab. 30 B3 23 5N 82 18W
Montespaccato, Rome 9 F9 41 54N 12 23 E
Montesson, Paris 5 B2 48 54N 2 8 E
Monteverde Nuovo, Rome 9 F9 41 52N 12 26 E
Montfermeil, Paris 5 B5 48 54N 2 33 E
Montgeron, Paris 5 C4 48 42N 2 27 E
Montigny-le-Bretonneux, Paris 5 C2 48 46N 2 1 E
Montigny-les-Cormeilles, Paris 5 B3 48 59N 2 11 E
Montijo, Lisb. 8 F9 38 42N 8 58W
Montjay-la-Tour, Paris 5 B6 48 54N 2 40 E
Montlhéry, Paris 5 D3 48 38N 2 16 E
Montlignon, Paris 5 A3 49 0N 2 16 E
Montmagny, Paris 5 B4 48 58N 2 21 E
Montmorency, Paris 5 B3 48 59N 2 19 E
Montmorency, Forêt de, Paris 5 A3 49 2N 2 16 E
Montparnasse, Gare, Paris 5 B3 48 50N 2 19 E
Montpelier, Wash. 25 C8 39 3N 76 50W
Montréal, Mtrl. 20 A4 43 30N 73 33W
Montréal, Î. de, Mtrl. 20 A4 43 30N 73 40W
Montréal, Univ. de, Mtrl. 20 B4 43 29N 73 37W
Montréal-Est, Mtrl. 20 A4 43 37N 73 31W
Montréal Nord, Mtrl. 20 A4 43 36N 73 36W
Montreuil, Paris 5 B4 48 51N 2 27 E
Montrose, L.A. 28 A3 34 12N 118 12W
Montrose, Melb. 19 E8 37 49 S 145 19 E
Montrose, Wash. 25 C7 39 2N 77 7W
Montrouge, Paris 5 C3 48 48N 2 18 E
Montvale, N.Y. 22 A4 41 2N 74 1W
Montville, N.Y. 22 B2 40 55N 74 23W
Monza, Mil. 9 D6 45 35N 9 16 E
Monzoro, Mil. 9 E5 45 27N 9 2 E
Moóca, S. Pau. 31 E6 23 33 S 46 35W
Moóca →, S. Pau. 31 E6 23 35 S 46 35W
Moonachie, N.Y. 22 C4 40 50N 74 2W
Moonee Ponds, Melb. 19 E6 37 45 S 144 53 E
Moonee Valley Racecourse, Melb. 19 E6 37 45 S 144 55 E
Moorbek, Hbg. 7 C7 53 41N 9 58 E
Moorburg, Hbg. 7 E7 53 29N 9 55 E
Moorebank, Syd. 19 B2 33 56 S 150 56 E
Moorestown, Phil. 24 B5 39 58N 74 56W
Moorfleet, Hbg. 7 D8 53 30N 10 4 E
Mooroolbark, Melb. 19 E8 37 46 S 145 19 E
Moorwerder, Hbg. 7 E8 53 28N 10 3 E
Moosach, Mün. 7 F10 48 10N 11 30 E
Mora, Bomb. 16 H8 18 54N 72 55 E
Moraga, S.F. 27 B4 37 49N 122 7W
Morainvilliers, Paris 5 B1 48 55N 1 56 E
Morales →, B.A. 32 C2 34 47 S 58 35W
Morangis, Paris 5 C4 48 42N 2 20 E
Moratalaz, Mdrd. 8 B3 40 24N 3 39W
Morbras →, Paris 5 C5 48 46N 2 30 E
Mörby, Stock. 3 D11 59 23N 18 3 E
Morce →, Paris 5 B4 48 57N 2 25 E
Mordon, Lon. 4 C3 51 24N 0 13W
Morehill, Jobg. 18 F11 26 10 S 28 20 E
Moreno, B.A. 32 B2 34 38 S 58 45W
Moreno, Rome 9 G10 41 48N 12 37 E
Morgan Park, Chic. 26 C3 41 41N 87 38W
Moriguchi, Ōsaka 12 B4 34 43N 135 34 E
Morivione, Mil. 9 E6 45 26N 9 12 E
Morningside, Jobg. 18 E9 26 4 S 28 3 E
Morningside, Wash. 25 E8 38 49N 76 53W
Morningside Park, Trto. 20 D9 43 46N 79 12W
Moroka, Jobg. 18 F8 26 15 S 27 52 E
Moron, B.A. 32 B3 34 39 S 58 37W
Morris Plains, N.Y. 22 C2 40 49N 74 29W
Morristown, N.Y. 22 C2 40 47N 74 28W
Morro, Castillo del, La Hab. 30 B2 23 8N 82 21W
Morro Pelado, S. Pau. 31 E7 23 38 S 46 24W
Morro Solar, Lima 30 H8 12 11 S 77 1W
Morsang-sur-Orge, Paris 5 D4 48 39N 2 21 E
Mörsenbroich, Ruhr 6 C2 51 15N 6 48 E
Morses Pond, Bost. 21 D2 42 17N 71 19W
Morte →, Paris 5 C3 48 48N 2 16 E
Mortlake, Lon. 4 C3 51 27N 0 15W
Mortlake, Syd. 19 B3 33 50 S 151 6 E
Morton, Phil. 24 B2 39 54N 75 20W
Morton Grove, Chic. 26 A2 42 2N 87 46W
Mory, Paris 5 B5 48 58N 2 37 E
Moscavide, Lisb. 8 F8 38 47N 9 6W
Moscow = Moskva, Mos. 11 E9 55 45N 37 37 E
Mosede, Købn. 2 E8 55 34N 12 17 E
Mosede Strand, Købn. 2 E8 55 34N 12 17 E
Mosjøen, Oslo 2 C6 50 49N 11 0 E
Moskhaton, Ath. 8 J11 37 55N 23 40 E
Moskva, Mos. 11 E9 55 45N 37 37 E
Moskvoretskiy, Mos. 11 E9 55 42N 37 37 E
Mosman, Syd. 19 A4 33 49 S 151 15 E
Moss Beach, S.F. 27 C2 37 31N 122 30W
Móstoles, Mdrd. 8 C1 40 18N 3 51W
Moto →, Tōkyō 13 A3 35 53N 139 45 E
Motol, Pra. 10 B1 50 3N 14 19 E
Motspur Park, Lon. 4 C3 51 23N 0 14W
Mottingham, Lon. 4 C5 51 26N 0 1 E
Mount Airy, Phil. 24 A3 40 3N 75 10W
Mount Dennis, Trto. 20 D8 43 40N 79 28W
Mount Ephraim, Phil. 24 B4 39 52N 75 5W
Mount Greenwood, Chic. 26 C2 41 42N 87 42W
Mount Hood Memorial Park, Bost. 21 C3 42 26N 71 1W
Mount Pleasant, Lon. 4 B2 51 30N 0 22W
Mount Pleasant Park, Balt. 25 A3 39 22N 76 34W
Mount Prospect, Chic. 26 A1 42 3N 87 54W
Mount Royal, Phil. 24 C3 39 48N 75 12W
Mount Tamalpais State Park, S.F. 27 A1 37 53N 122 34W
Mount Vernon, N.Y. 23 B6 40 54N 73 49W
Mount Waverley, Melb. 19 F7 37 52 S 145 7 E
Mount Wilson Observatory, L.A. 28 A4 34 13N 118 4W
Mountain Lakes, N.Y. 22 B2 40 54N 74 27W
Mountain Spring Ls., N.Y. 22 A2 41 2N 74 21W
Mountain View, N.Y. 22 B3 40 55N 74 15W
Mountainside, N.Y. 22 C2 40 40N 74 21W
Mountnessing, Lon. 4 B7 51 39N 0 21 E
Moûtiers, Paris 5 D1 48 36N 1 58 E
Mozu, Ōsaka 12 C3 34 33N 135 29 E
Müggelberge, Berl. 7 B4 52 25N 13 37 E
Müggelheim, Berl. 7 B4 52 24N 13 40 E
Muggiò, Mil. 9 D6 45 35N 9 13 E
Mugnano di Nápoli, Nápl. 9 H12 40 54N 14 12 E
Mühleiten, Wien 10 G11 48 10N 16 33 E
Mühlenau →, Hbg. 7 C7 53 41N 9 56 E
Mühlenfliess →, Berl. 7 A5 52 32N 13 42 E
Muir Beach, S.F. 27 A1 37 51N 122 34W
Muirkirk, Wash. 25 C8 39 3N 76 53W
Mujahidpur, Delhi 16 B2 28 33N 77 14 E
Mukandpur, Delhi 16 A2 28 44N 77 10 E
Muko →, Ōsaka 12 B3 34 48N 135 22 E
Mukojima, Tōkyō 13 B3 35 43N 139 49 E
Mulbarton, Jobg. 18 F9 26 17 S 28 3 E
Mulford Gardens, S.F. 27 B3 37 42N 122 10W
Mulgrave, Melb. 19 F8 37 55 S 145 12 E
Mülheim, Ruhr 6 B3 51 25N 6 53 E
Mullica Hill, Phil. 24 C3 39 44N 75 13W
Mullum Mullum Cr. →, Melb. 19 E8 37 44 S 145 10 E
Münchehofe, Berl. 7 B5 52 29N 13 40 E
München, Mün. 7 G10 48 8N 11 34 E
Munchen-Riem, Flughafen, Mün. 7 G11 48 7N 11 42 E
Munich = München, Mün. 7 G10 48 8N 11 34 E
Munirka, Delhi 16 B2 28 33N 77 10 E
Muniz, B.A. 32 B2 34 33 S 58 41W
Munkkiniemi, Hels. 3 B4 60 11N 24 52 E
Munro, B.A. 32 B3 34 31 S 58 31W
Munsey Park, N.Y. 23 C6 40 47N 73 40W
Münsterkirche, Ruhr 6 B4 51 27N 7 0 E
Muranów, Wsaw. 10 E6 52 14N 20 58 E
Murayama-chosuichi, Tōkyō 13 B1 35 45N 139 26 E
Murrumbeena, Melb. 19 F7 37 53 S 145 4 E
Musashino, Tōkyō 13 B2 35 42N 139 33 E
Mushin, Lagos 18 A2 6 31N 7 21 E
Musinè, Mte., Tori. 9 B1 45 7N 7 27 E
Musocco, Mil. 9 E5 45 29N 9 8 E
Musta Hevonen, Hels. 3 B6 60 11N 25 14 E
Mustafabad, Delhi 16 A2 28 43N 77 13 E
Mustansiriya, Bagd. 17 E8 33 22N 44 24 E
Musturud, El Qâ. 18 C5 30 8N 31 17 E
Muswell Hill, Lon. 4 B4 51 35N 0 8W
Mutanabi, Bagd. 17 F8 33 19N 44 21 E
Muthana, Bagd. 17 F8 33 19N 44 27 E
Mutinga, S. Pau. 31 D5 23 29 S 46 46W
Muttontown, N.Y. 23 C7 40 49N 73 32W
Muzon, Manila 15 D4 14 32N 121 8 E
Myaglovo, St-Pet. 11 B5 59 53N 30 39 E
Myakinino, Mos. 11 E8 55 48N 37 22 E
Mykerinos, El Qâ. 18 D4 29 28N 31 8 E
Myllykylä, Hels. 3 A4 60 21N 24 57 E
Myllypuro, Hels. 3 B5 60 13N 25 3 E
Myras, Hels. 3 B5 60 19N 25 6 E
Myrvoll, Oslo 2 C4 59 47N 10 48 E
Mystic Lakes, Bost. 21 C3 42 26N 71 8W
Mytishchi, Mos. 11 D10 55 53N 37 44 E


## N


Nababpur, Calc. 16 D5 22 42N 88 12 E
Nações, Parque das, S. Pau. 31 E6 23 38 S 46 30W
Nachstebreck, Ruhr 6 C5 51 17N 7 14 E
Nacka, Stock. 3 E12 59 19N 18 10 E
Nada, Ōsaka 12 B2 34 42N 135 13 E
Nærsnes, Oslo 2 C2 59 45N 10 27 E
Nærum, Købn. 2 D10 55 48N 12 33 E
Nagareyama, Tōkyō 13 A4 35 51N 139 54 E
Nagasaki, Tōkyō 13 B3 35 43N 139 40 E
Nagasuga, Tōkyō 13 D4 35 21N 139 57 E
Nagata, Ōsaka 12 C1 34 39N 135 8 E
Nagatsuta, Tōkyō 13 C2 35 32N 139 31 E
Nagytarcsa, Bud. 10 J14 47 31N 19 17 E
Nagytétény, Bud. 10 K12 47 23N 18 59 E
Nahant, Bost. 21 C4 42 25N 70 54W
Nahant B., Bost. 21 C4 42 26N 70 54W
Nahant Harbor, Bost. 21 C4 42 25N 70 55W
Nahdein, W. el →, El Qâ. 18 C5 30 3N 31 19 E
Nahia, El Qâ. 18 C4 30 2N 31 7 E
Naihati, Calc. 16 C6 22 53N 88 25 E
Najafgarh Drain →, Delhi 16 B1 28 39N 77 4 E
Najio, Ōsaka 12 B2 34 49N 135 18 E
Naka →, Tōkyō 13 B4 35 49N 139 52 E
Naka-Ku, Tōkyō 13 D2 35 25N 139 38 E
Nakada, Tōkyō 13 D2 35 24N 139 30 E
Nakajima, Tōkyō 13 D4 35 25N 139 54 E
Nakano, Tōkyō 13 D4 35 25N 139 56 E
Nakano-Ku, Tōkyō 13 B2 35 42N 139 39 E
Nakasato, Tōkyō 13 B3 35 22N 139 55 E
Nakayama, Tōkyō 13 C2 35 30N 139 32 E
Nalikul, Calc. 16 D5 22 49N 88 10 E
Nalpur, Calc. 16 E5 22 31N 88 10 E
Namazie Estate, Sing. 15 F7 1 25N 103 42 E
Namgajha, Sŏul 12 G7 37 33N 126 55 E
Namsan Park, Sŏul 12 G7 37 32N 126 59 E
Namyeong, Sŏul 12 G7 37 32N 126 57 E
Nan Wan, H.K. 12 D5 22 20N 114 5 E
Nanbiancun, Gzh. 14 G7 23 4N 113 10 E
Nancefield, Jobg. 18 F8 26 17 S 27 54 E
Nanchang He →, Beij. 14 B2 39 58N 116 14 E
Nandaha, Calc. 16 D5 22 49N 88 18 E
Nandang, Gzh. 14 G8 23 6N 113 12 E
Nandian, Tianj. 14 D6 39 10N 117 16 E
Nangal Dewat, Delhi 16 B1 28 33N 77 5 E
Nangi, Calc. 16 E5 22 30N 88 13 E
Nangka →, Manila 15 D4 14 38N 121 8 E
Nangloi, Delhi 16 A1 28 41N 77 3 E
Nangloi Jat, Delhi 16 A1 28 41N 77 3 E
Nanhai, Gzh. 14 G7 23 2N 113 6 E
Nanhan He →, Beij. 14 B2 39 57N 116 11 E
Naniwa, Ōsaka 12 C3 34 39N 135 29 E
Nankai, Tianj. 14 E5 39 7N 117 10 E
Nanmenwai, Tianj. 14 E6 39 8N 117 10 E
Nanole, Bomb. 16 G8 19 1N 72 55 E
Nanshi, Shang. 14 J11 31 12N 121 29 E
Nanterre, Paris 5 B3 48 53N 2 12 E
Nantouillet, Paris 5 A6 49 0N 2 42 E
Nantucket Beach, Bost. 21 D4 42 16N 70 52W
Nanxiang, Shang. 14 J10 31 17N 121 18 E
Naobad, Calc. 16 F6 22 28N 88 26 E
Napara, Calc. 16 E6 22 38N 88 23 E
Napier Mole, Kar. 17 H10 24 49N 66 58 E
Napindan, Manila 15 D4 14 32N 121 5 E
Naples = Nápoli, Nápl. 9 J12 40 50N 14 14 E
Nápoli, Nápl. 9 J12 40 50N 14 14 E
Nápoli, G. di, Nápl. 9 J12 40 46N 14 15 E
Naraina, Delhi 16 B1 28 36N 77 8 E
Narawa, Tōkyō 13 D4 35 25N 139 58 E
Narayanpara, Calc. 16 C5 22 53N 88 18 E
Narberth, Phil. 24 A3 40 0N 75 16W
Narimasu, Tōkyō 13 B3 35 46N 139 35 E
Nārmak, Tehr. 17 C5 35 42N 51 28 E
Närsta, Stock. 3 E9 59 17N 17 43 E
Naruo, Ōsaka 12 B3 34 43N 135 22 E
Näsby, Stock. 3 D11 59 25N 18 5 E
Näsbypark, Stock. 3 D11 59 25N 18 5 E
Näsfjärden, Stock. 3 D9 59 25N 17 41 E
Nassau Shore, N.Y. 23 D8 40 39N 73 26W
Natick, Bost. 21 D2 42 17N 71 21W
Nation, Place de la, Paris 5 B4 48 51N 2 23 E
National Arboretum, Wash. 25 D8 39 54N 76 59W
Nativitas, Méx. 29 C3 19 15N 99 5W
Natolin, Wsaw. 10 F7 52 8N 21 4 E
Naucalpan de Juárez, Méx. 29 B2 19 28N 99 14W
Naupada, Bomb. 16 G8 19 3N 72 50 E
Navíglio di Pavia, Mil. 9 E5 45 24N 9 9 E
Navíglio Grande, Mil. 9 E5 45 25N 9 5 E
Navotas, Manila 15 D3 14 39N 120 56 E
Nazal Hikmat Beg, Bagd. 17 E8 33 23N 44 25 E
Nazimabad, Kar. 17 G11 24 54N 67 1 E
Nazukari, Tōkyō 13 A4 35 50N 139 57 E
Néa Alexandhria, Ath. 8 J11 37 52N 23 46 E
Néa Faliron, Ath. 8 J10 37 55N 23 39 E
Néa Ionía, Ath. 8 H11 38 3N 23 45 E
Néa Liósia, Ath. 8 H11 38 3N 23 43 E
Néa Smírni, Ath. 8 J11 37 54N 23 43 E
Neapolis, Ath. 8 J11 37 58N 23 45 E
Neasden, Lon. 4 B3 51 35N 0 16W
Neauphle-le-Château, Paris 5 C1 48 48N 1 53 E
Nebučice, Pra. 10 B1 50 6N 14 19 E
Nedlitz, Berl. 7 B1 52 25N 13 3 E
Nee Soon, Sing. 15 F7 1 24N 103 49 E
Needham, Bost. 21 D2 42 16N 71 13W
Needham Heights, Bost. 21 D2 42 17N 71 14W
Needle Hill, H.K. 12 D5 22 23N 114 9 E
Negishi B., Tōkyō 13 D2 35 23N 139 38 E
Nehiti, Calc. 16 D5 22 42N 88 16 E
Nekrasovka, Mos. 11 E11 55 41N 37 55 E
Nematābād, Tehr. 17 D5 35 38N 51 21 E
Nemchinovka, Mos. 11 E7 55 42N 37 19 E
Népliget, Bud. 10 K13 47 29N 19 7 E
Neponset →, Bost. 21 D3 42 12N 71 9W
Nerima, Tōkyō 13 B3 35 44N 139 40 E
Nerul, Bomb. 16 G9 19 2N 73 0 E
Nerviano, Mil. 9 D4 45 32N 8 58 E
Nesodden, Oslo 2 C4 59 48N 10 41 E
Nesoddtangen, Oslo 2 B4 59 52N 10 41 E
Nesøya, Oslo 2 B3 59 52N 10 31 E
Nestipayac →, Méx. 29 A4 19 33N 89 57W
Netzahualcóyotl, Méx. 29 B3 19 24N 99 2W
Neu Aubing, Mün. 7 G9 48 8N 11 25 E
Neu Buch, Berl. 7 A4 52 37N 13 31 E
Neu Buchhorst, Berl. 7 B5 52 24N 13 44 E
Neu Fahrland, Berl. 7 B1 52 26N 13 3 E
Neu Lindenberg, Berl. 7 A4 52 36N 13 33 E
Neu Wulmstorf, Hbg. 7 E6 53 27N 9 48 E
Neu Zittau, Berl. 7 B5 52 23N 13 44 E
Neubiberg, Mün. 7 G11 48 4N 11 40 E
Neudorf, Hbg. 7 C8 53 27N 10 4 E
Neudorf, Ruhr 6 B2 51 25N 6 47 E
Neuegenbüttel, Hbg. 7 D7 53 53N 9 54 E
Neuenfelde, Hbg. 7 D6 53 38N 9 48 E
Neuenhagen, Berl. 7 A4 52 32N 13 38 E
Neuenkamp, Ruhr 6 B2 51 26N 6 43 E
Neuessling, Wien 10 G11 48 15N 16 32 E
Neugraben-Fischbek, Hbg. 7 E6 53 28N 9 49 E
Neuhausen, Mün. 7 G10 48 9N 11 32 E
Neuherberg, Mün. 7 F10 48 13N 11 35 E
Neuhönow, Berl. 7 A5 52 34N 13 44 E
Neuilly-Plaisance, Paris 5 B5 48 51N 2 30 E
Neuilly-sur-Marne, Paris 5 B5 48 51N 2 31 E
Neuilly-sur-Seine, Paris 5 B3 48 53N 2 15 E
Neukagran, Wien 10 G10 48 14N 16 27 E
Neukettenhof, Wien 10 H10 48 7N 16 28 E
Neukölln, Berl. 7 B3 52 28N 13 25 E
Neuland, Hbg. 7 E8 53 27N 10 0 E
Neuperlach, Mün. 7 G10 48 6N 11 37 E
Neuried, Mün. 7 G9 48 5N 11 27 E
Neuss, Ruhr 6 C2 51 12N 6 42 E
Neustift am Walde, Wien 10 G9 48 14N 16 17 E
Neusüssenbrunn, Wien 10 G10 48 16N 16 29 E
Neuville-sur-Oise, Paris 5 A2 49 0N 2 3 E
Neuwaldegg, Wien 10 G9 48 14N 16 17 E
Neuwiedenthal, Hbg. 7 E7 53 28N 9 52 E
Neva →, St-Pet. 11 B4 59 56N 30 20 E
Neves, Rio J. 31 B3 22 51 S 43 5W
Neviges, Ruhr 6 C4 51 18N 7 6 E
New Addington, Lon. 4 C4 51 20N 0 0 E
New Ash Green, Lon. 4 C6 51 22N 0 18 E
New Baghdād, Bagd. 17 F8 33 18N 44 28 E
New Barnet, Lon. 4 B3 51 38N 0 10W
New Brighton, N.Y. 22 D4 40 38N 74 5W
New Brunswick, N.Y. 22 D2 40 30N 74 29W
New Canada, Jobg. 18 F8 26 12 S 27 56 E
New Canada Dam, Jobg. 18 F8 26 12 S 27 56 E
New Canal →, Calc. 16 E6 22 33N 88 25 E
New Carrollton, Wash. 25 D8 38 58N 76 52W
New Cassell, N.Y. 23 C7 40 45N 73 32W
New Cross, Lon. 4 C4 51 28N 0 1W
New Delhi, Delhi 16 B2 28 36N 77 11 E
New Dorp, N.Y. 22 D4 40 34N 74 7W
New Dorp Beach, N.Y. 22 D4 40 33N 74 6W
New Hyde Park, N.Y. 23 C7 40 43N 73 39W
New Kleinfontein, Jobg. 18 F11 26 11 S 28 20 E
New Malden, Lon. 4 C3 51 24N 0 15W
New Milford, N.Y. 22 B4 40 56N 74 0W
New Modder, Jobg. 18 F11 26 10 S 28 21 E
New Providence, N.Y. 22 C2 40 42N 74 23W
New Redruth, Jobg. 18 F9 26 15 S 28 7 E
New Rochelle, N.Y. 23 B6 40 55N 73 45W
New South Wales, Univ. of, Syd. 19 B4 33 55 S 151 14 E
New Southgate, Lon. 4 B4 51 37N 0 7W
New Springville, N.Y. 22 D4 40 35N 74 9W
New Territories, H.K. 12 D5 22 23N 114 10 E
New Toronto, Trto. 20 E7 43 35N 79 30W
New Utrecht, N.Y. 22 D5 40 36N 73 59W
New Vernon, N.Y. 22 C2 40 44N 74 30W
New York Aquarium, N.Y. 22 D5 40 33N 73 59W
New York Botanical Gdns., N.Y. 23 B5 40 51N 73 51W
New York Univ., N.Y. 22 C5 40 43N 74 59W
Newabgarj, Calc. 16 D6 22 47N 88 23 E
Newark, N.Y. 22 C3 40 43N 74 10W
Newark, S.F. 27 C4 37 32N 122 2W
Newark B., N.Y. 22 C4 40 40N 74 8W
Newark Int. Airport, N.Y. 22 C3 40 41N 74 10W
Newbury Park, Lon. 4 B5 51 34N 0 5 E
Newclare, Jobg. 18 F8 26 11 S 27 58 E
Newfoundland, N.Y. 22 A2 41 2N 74 25W
Newham, Lon. 4 B5 51 31N 0 1 E
Newlands, Jobg. 18 F8 26 10 S 27 57 E
Newport, Melb. 19 F6 37 50 S 144 51 E
Newportville, Phil. 24 A5 40 7N 74 53W
Newton, Bost. 21 D2 42 19N 71 13W
Newton Brook, Trto. 20 D8 43 47N 79 24W
Newton Highlands, Bost. 21 D2 42 19N 71 13W
Newtonville, Bost. 21 C2 42 20N 71 11W
Newtown, Syd. 19 B4 33 54 S 151 11 E
Newtown Square, Phil. 24 B2 39 59N 75 24W
Neyegawa, Ōsaka 12 B4 34 45N 135 36 E
Ngau Chi Wan, H.K. 12 D6 22 20N 114 12 E
Ngau Tau Kok, H.K. 12 E6 22 19N 114 12 E
Ngong Shuen Chau, H.K. 12 E5 22 19N 114 8 E
Ngua Kok Wan, H.K. 12 D5 22 21N 114 5 E
Nīāvarān, Tehr. 17 C5 35 47N 51 29 E
Nibria, Calc. 16 E5 22 36N 88 15 E
Nichelino, Tori. 9 C2 44 59N 7 38 E
Nichols Run →, Wash. 25 C6 39 2N 77 17W
Nicholson, Mt., H.K. 12 E6 22 15N 114 11 E
Nidāl, Bagd. 17 F8 33 19N 44 25 E
Niddrie, Melb. 19 E6 37 44 S 144 51 E
Nieder Neuendorf, Berl. 7 A2 52 36N 13 12 E
Niederbonsfeld, Ruhr 6 B4 51 22N 7 8 E
Niederdonk, Ruhr 6 C2 51 14N 6 41 E
Niederschöneweide, Berl. 7 B3 52 27N 13 30 E
Niederschönhausen, Berl. 7 A3 52 35N 13 25 E
Niederwenigern, Ruhr 6 B4 51 24N 7 8 E
Niemeyer, Rio J. 31 B2 22 59 S 43 16W
Niendorf, Hbg. 7 D7 53 37N 9 57 E
Nienstedten, Hbg. 7 D7 53 33N 9 51 E
Nierst, Ruhr 6 C2 51 19N 6 43 E
Nihonbashi, Tōkyō 13 B3 35 41N 139 46 E
Niipperi, Hels. 3 B3 60 18N 24 45 E
Niiza, Tōkyō 13 B2 35 48N 139 33 E
Nikaia, Ath. 8 J10 37 57N 23 38 E
Nikinmäki, Hels. 3 A5 60 20N 25 8 E
Nikolassee, Berl. 7 B2 52 25N 13 12 E
Nikolo-Khovanskoye, Mos. 11 F8 55 36N 37 27 E
Nikolskiy, Mos. 11 E8 55 49N 37 29 E
Nikolyskoye, Mos. 11 E11 55 46N 37 53 E
Nikulino, Mos. 11 E8 55 40N 37 25 E
Nil, Bagd. 17 E8 33 21N 44 25 E
Nil, Nahr en →, El Qâ. 18 D5 29 57N 31 14 E
Nile = Nil, Nahr en →, El Qâ. 18 D5 29 57N 31 14 E
Niles, Chic. 26 A2 42 1N 87 48W
Nilganj, Calc. 16 D6 22 45N 88 25 E
Nilópolis, Rio J. 31 A1 22 47 S 43 23W
Nimta, Calc. 16 D6 22 40N 88 24 E
Nincop, Hbg. 7 D6 53 30N 9 48 E
Ningyuan, Tianj. 14 E6 39 9N 117 12 E
Nippa, Tōkyō 13 C2 35 31N 139 36 E
Nippori, Tōkyō 13 B3 35 43N 139 45 E
Niru-ye-Hava'i, Tehr. 17 C5 35 41N 51 26 E
Nishi, Ōsaka 12 B3 34 40N 135 28 E
Nishi, Tōkyō 13 D2 35 26N 139 37 E
Nishi-arai, Tōkyō 13 B3 35 46N 139 48 E
Nishinari, Ōsaka 12 C3 34 37N 135 28 E
Nishinomiya, Ōsaka 12 B2 34 44N 135 18 E
Nishiyama, Tōkyō 13 B2 35 22N 139 57 E
Nishiyodogawa, Ōsaka 12 B3 34 41N 135 26 E
Nisida, I. di, Nápl. 9 J11 40 47N 14 10 E
Niterói, Rio J. 31 B3 22 53 S 43 7W
Nithari, Delhi 16 B3 28 34N 77 20 E
Nittedal, Oslo 2 A5 60 0N 10 57 E
Niyog, Manila 15 E3 14 27N 120 57 E
Noapara, Calc. 16 D6 22 49N 88 22 E
Nobidome, Tōkyō 13 B2 35 48N 139 34 E
Nockeby, Stock. 3 E10 59 19N 17 56 E
Noel Park, Lon. 4 B4 51 35N 0 5W
Nogatino, Mos. 11 E10 55 41N 37 41 E
Nogent-sur-Marne, Paris 5 B4 48 50N 2 28 E
Noiseau, Paris 5 C5 48 46N 2 32 E
Noisiel, Paris 5 B5 48 51N 2 37 E
Noisy-le-Grand, Paris 5 B5 48 50N 2 33 E
Noisy-le-Roi, Paris 5 B2 48 50N 2 3 E
Noisy-le-Sec, Paris 5 B4 48 53N 2 27 E
Nokkala, Hels. 3 C3 60 8N 24 45 E
Nøklevatn, Oslo 2 B5 59 52N 10 52 E
Nolme →, Ruhr 6 B6 51 23N 7 26 E
Nomentano, Rome 9 F10 41 55N 12 30 E
Nonakashinden, Tōkyō 13 B2 35 44N 139 30 E
Nongminyundong Jiangxisuo, Gzh. 14 G8 23 7N 113 15 E
Nonhyeon, Sŏul 12 G8 37 30N 127 1 E
Nontha Buri, Bangk. 15 A1 13 50N 100 29 E
Noordgesig, Jobg. 18 F8 26 13 S 27 56 E
Nord, Gare du, Paris 5 B4 48 52N 2 21 E
Nordbysjøen, Oslo 2 B6 59 51N 11 1 E
Nordereble, Hbg. 7 D7 53 32N 9 59 E
Norderelbe →, Hbg. 7 E8 53 29N 10 3 E
Norderstedt, Hbg. 7 C7 53 42N 9 59 E
Nordmarka, Oslo 2 A4 60 1N 10 38 E
Nordrand-Seidlung, Wien 10 G10 48 16N 16 26 E
Nordre Elvåga, Oslo 2 B5 59 53N 10 54 E
Nordstrand, Oslo 2 B4 59 52N 10 48 E
Normandy Heights, Balt. 25 B2 39 17N 76 48W
Norra Björkföjärden, Stock. 3 D8 59 26N 17 39 E
Norridge, Chic. 26 B2 41 57N 87 49W
Norristown, Phil. 24 A2 40 7N 75 20W
Norrkula, Hels. 3 B6 60 19N 25 20 E
Norrmalm, Stock. 3 D11 59 20N 18 3 E
Norrviken, Stock. 3 D10 59 27N 17 52 E
North Acton, Bost. 21 B1 42 30N 71 23W
North Amityville, N.Y. 23 C8 40 42N 73 25W
North Andover, Bost. 21 A3 42 41N 71 7W
North Arlington, N.Y. 22 C4 40 47N 74 7W
North Auburn, Syd. 19 B3 33 50 S 151 3 E
North Babylon, N.Y. 23 C9 40 43N 73 19W
North Bellmore, N.Y. 23 C7 40 40N 73 32W
North Bergen, N.Y. 22 C4 40 48N 74 0W
North Beverly, Bost. 21 B4 42 34N 70 51W
North Billerica, Bost. 21 B2 42 35N 71 16W
North Branch →, Phil. 24 C4 39 50N 75 5W
North Branch Chicago River →, Chic. 26 B2 41 53N 87 42W
North Brighton, Bost. 21 C3 42 21N 71 8W
North Caldwell, N.Y. 22 B3 40 52N 74 15W
North Cambridge, Bost. 21 C3 42 23N 71 7W
North Cheam, Lon. 4 C3 51 22N 0 11W
North Chelmsford, Bost. 21 B1 42 38N 71 23W
North Cohasset, Bost. 21 D4 42 15N 70 49W
North Cray, Lon. 4 C5 51 25N 0 8 E
North Fair Oaks, S.F. 27 D3 37 28N 122 11W
North Finchley, Lon. 4 B3 51 36N 0 10W
North Germiston, Jobg. 18 F9 26 12 S 28 9 E
North Hackensack, N.Y. 22 B4 40 54N 74 2W
North Haledon, N.Y. 22 B3 40 57N 74 11W
North Harbour, Manila 15 D3 14 37N 120 57 E
North Hd., Syd. 19 A4 33 49 S 151 18 E
North Hills, N.Y. 23 C6 40 46N 73 40W
North Hollywood, L.A. 28 B2 34 9N 118 22W
North Lexington, Bost. 21 C2 42 27N 71 14W
North Lindenhurst, N.Y. 23 C8 40 42N 73 22W
North Long Beach, L.A. 28 C3 33 53N 118 10W
North Manly, Syd. 19 A4 33 46 S 151 17 E
North Massapequa, N.Y. 23 C8 40 42N 73 27W
North Merrick, N.Y. 23 C7 40 41N 73 33W
North New Hyde Park, N.Y. 23 C6 40 44N 73 42W
North Pelham, N.Y. 23 B6 40 54N 73 46W
North Plainfield, N.Y. 22 D2 40 37N 74 27W
North Point, Balt. 25 B4 39 16N 76 29W
North Pt., H.K. 12 E6 22 17N 114 12 E
North Pt., Syd. 19 A4 33 48 S 151 18 E
North Randolph, Bost. 21 D3 42 11N 71 5W
North Reading, Bost. 21 B3 42 34N 71 5W
North Res., Bost. 21 C3 42 28N 71 6W
North Richmond, S.F. 27 A2 37 57N 122 22W
North Riverside, Chic. 26 B2 41 50N 87 48W
North Ryde, Syd. 19 A3 33 47 S 151 7 E
North Saugus, Bost. 21 B3 42 29N 71 1W
North Shore Channel →, Chic. 26 B2 41 58N 87 42W

Pitampura Kalan 43


North Springfield, Wash. 25 E6 38 48N 77 11W
North Stifford, Lon. 4 B6 51 30N 0 18 E
North Sudbury, Bost. 21 C1 42 24N 71 24W
North Sydney, Syd. 19 B4 33 50 S 151 13 E
North Tewksbury, Bost. 21 B2 42 38N 71 14W
North Valley Stream, N.Y. 23 C6 40 41N 73 42W
North Wantagh, N.Y. 23 C7 40 41N 73 30W
North Weymouth, Bost. 21 D4 42 14N 70 56W
North Wilmington, Bost. 21 B3 42 34N 71 9W
North Woburn, Bost. 21 B2 42 30N 71 10W
North Woolwich, Lon. 4 B5 51 30N 0 3 E
North York, Trto. 20 D8 43 45N 79 27W
Northaw, Lon. 4 A4 51 42N 0 8W
Northbridge, Syd. 19 A4 33 49 S 151 15 E
Northbrook, Chic. 26 A1 42 7N 87 50W
Northcliff, Jobg. 18 E8 26 8 S 27 58 E
Northcote, Melb. 19 E7 37 46 S 145 0 E
Northeastern Univ., Bost. 21 C3 42 20N 71 4W
Northfield, Chic. 26 A2 42 5N 87 45W
Northfleet, Lon. 4 C7 51 26N 0 21 E
Northlake, Chic. 26 B1 41 54N 87 53W
Northmead, Jobg. 18 E10 26 9 S 28 19 E
Northmead, Syd. 19 A3 33 47 S 151 0 E
Northmount, Trto. 20 D8 43 46N 79 23W
Northolt, Lon. 4 B2 51 32N 0 22W
Northport, N.Y. 23 B8 40 54N 73 20W
Northport B., N.Y. 23 B8 40 54N 73 22W
Northridge, L.A. 28 A1 34 14N 118 30W
Northumberland Heath, Lon. 4 C6 51 28N 0 10 E
Northvale, N.Y. 22 A5 41 0N 73 59W
Northwest Branch →, Balt. 25 B3 39 16N 76 35W
Northwest Branch →, Wash. 25 C8 39 2N 76 56W
Northwestern Univ., Chic. 26 A2 42 3N 87 40W
Northwood, Lon. 4 B2 51 36N 0 25W
Norumbega Res., Bost. 21 D2 42 19N 71 17W
Norwalk, L.A. 28 C4 33 53N 118 4W
Norwood, Bost. 21 D2 42 11N 71 13W
Norwood, Jobg. 18 E9 26 9 S 28 4 E
Norwood, N.Y. 22 B5 40 59N 73 57W
Norwood, Phil. 24 B3 39 53N 75 17W
Norwood Memorial Airport, Bost. 21 D3 42 11N 71 9W
Norwood Park, Chic. 26 B2 41 59N 87 48W
Noryangjin, Sŏul 12 G7 37 30N 126 56 E
Nose, Ōsaka 12 B2 34 49N 135 10 E
Nossa Senhora do Ó, S. Pau. 31 E5 23 30 S 46 41W
Notre-Dame, Mtrl. 20 B5 43 28N 73 28W
Notre-Dame, Paris 5 B4 48 51N 2 21 E
Notre-Dame, Bois, Paris 5 C5 48 45N 2 34 E
Notre Dame de L'Île Perrot, Mtrl. 20 B2 43 23N 73 53W
Notting Hill, Lon. 4 B3 51 30N 0 12W
Notting Hill, Melb. 19 F7 37 54 S 145 9 E
Nottingham, Phil. 24 A5 40 7N 74 58W
Nova Milanese, Mil. 9 D6 45 35N 9 12 E
Novate Milanese, Mil. 9 D5 45 30N 9 8 E
Novaya Derevnya, St-Pet. 11 A3 60 0N 30 19 E
Nové Mesto, Pra. 10 B2 50 4N 14 25 E
Novoaleksandrovskoye, St-Pet. 11 B4 59 50N 30 31 E
Novogireyevo, Mos. 11 E10 55 45N 37 46 E
Novoivanovskoye, Mos. 11 E7 55 42N 37 21 E
Novokhovrino, Mos. 11 D8 55 53N 37 27 E
Novonikolyskoye, Mos. 11 D7 55 50N 37 14 E
Novosaratovka, St-Pet. 11 B5 59 50N 30 32 E
Novosergiyevka, St-Pet. 11 B5 59 54N 30 34 E
Nowe-Babice, Wsaw. 10 E6 52 15N 20 51 E
Nöykkiö, Hels. 3 B3 60 10N 24 42 E
Noyoye Kovalyova, St-Pet. 11 B5 59 58N 30 34 E
Nozay, Paris 5 D3 48 39N 2 14 E
Nueva Atzacoalco, Méx. 29 B3 19 29N 99 4W
Nueva Caracas, Car. 30 D5 10 30N 66 57W
Nueva Chicago, B.A. 32 B4 34 39 S 58 29W
Nueva Pompeya, B.A. 32 C4 34 40 S 58 25W
Nueva Tenochtitlán, Méx. 29 B3 19 27N 99 5W
Nuijala, Hels. 3 B3 60 12N 24 46 E
Numabukuro, Tōkyō 13 B2 35 43N 139 39 E
Numakage, Tōkyō 13 A2 35 50N 139 37 E
Numata, Tōkyō 13 B3 35 45N 139 46 E
Nunawading, Melb. 19 E8 37 49 S 145 10 E
Nunez, B.A. 32 B4 34 32 S 58 27W
Nunhead, Lon. 4 C4 51 27N 0 3W
Ñuñoa, Stgo 30 J11 33 27 S 70 35W
Nupuri, Hels. 3 B2 60 14N 24 36 E
Nusle, Pra. 10 B2 50 3N 14 26 E
Nussdorf, Wien 10 G10 48 15N 16 21 E
Nuthe →, Berl. 7 B1 52 22N 13 5 E
Nutley, N.Y. 22 C4 40 49N 74 9W
Nutting L., Bost. 21 B2 42 32N 71 16W
Nützenberg, Ruhr 6 C4 51 15N 7 8 E
Nybølle, Købn. 2 D8 55 42N 12 15 E
Nybygget, Hels. 3 B6 60 17N 25 11 E
Nymphenburg, Mün. 7 G10 48 9N 11 30 E
Nymphenburg, Schloss, Mün. 7 G10 48 9N 11 30 E


# O


Oak Beach, N.Y. 23 D9 40 38N 73 19W
Oak Forest, Chic. 26 D2 41 36N 87 44W
Oak Hill Park, Bost. 21 D2 42 17N 71 11W
Oak Lane, Phil. 24 A4 40 3N 75 8W
Oak Lawn, Chic. 26 C2 41 42N 87 45W
Oak Park, Chic. 26 B2 41 52N 87 47W
Oak Ridge, N.Y. 22 A2 41 2N 74 28W
Oak Valley, Phil. 24 C4 39 48N 75 9W
Oak View, Wash. 25 C8 39 1N 76 58W
Oakland, N.Y. 22 A3 41 1N 74 13W
Oakland, S.F. 27 B3 37 48N 122 18W
Oakland, Wash. 25 D8 38 52N 76 54W
Oakland Coliseum, S.F. 27 B3 37 44N 122 11W
Oakland Gardens, N.Y. 23 C6 40 45N 73 46W
Oakland Int. Airport, S.F. 27 B3 37 43N 122 12W
Oakland Mills, Balt. 25 B2 39 13N 76 49W
Oakland Naval Air Station, S.F. 27 B3 37 47N 122 19W
Oaklands, Jobg. 18 E9 26 8 S 28 4 E
Oaklawn, Wash. 25 E8 38 46N 76 56W
Oakleigh, Melb. 19 F7 37 54 S 145 5 E
Oaks, Phil. 24 A2 40 8N 75 26W
Oakwood, N.Y. 22 D4 40 34N 74 7W
Oakwood Beach, N.Y. 22 D4 40 33N 74 7W
Oatley, Syd. 19 B3 33 59 S 151 4 E
Obalende, Lagos 18 B2 6 26N 7 25 E
Oba's Palace, Lagos 18 B2 6 26N 7 22 E
Oberbauer, Ruhr 6 C6 51 17N 7 25 E
Oberföhring, Mün. 7 G10 48 10N 11 37 E
Oberhaching, Mün. 7 G10 48 1N 11 35 E
Oberhausen, Ruhr 6 B3 51 28N 6 54 E
Oberhausen, Wien 10 G11 48 10N 16 34 E
Oberkassel, Ruhr 6 C2 51 14N 6 45 E
Oberkirchbach, Wien 10 G9 48 17N 16 12 E
Oberlaa, Wien 10 H10 48 8N 16 24 E
Oberlisse, Wien 10 G10 48 17N 16 26 E
Obermenzing, Mün. 7 F9 48 10N 11 28 E
Obermoos Schwaige, Mün. 7 F9 48 14N 11 27 E
Oberschleissheim, Mün. 7 F10 48 15N 11 33 E
Oberschöneweide, Berl. 7 B4 52 27N 13 31 E
Oberwengern, Ruhr 6 B6 51 23N 7 22 E
Obitsu →, Tōkyō 13 D4 35 25N 139 56 E
Oboldino, Mos. 11 D11 55 53N 37 56 E
Observatory, Jobg. 18 F9 26 10 S 28 4 E
Ōbu, Ōsaka 12 B1 34 43N 135 8 E
Obu-tōge, Ōsaka 12 B1 34 44N 135 9 E
Óbuda, Bud. 10 J13 47 33N 19 2 E
Obudaisziget, Bud. 10 J13 47 33N 19 3 E
Obukhovo, St-Pet. 11 B4 59 53N 30 22 E
Occidental, Pico, Car. 30 D5 10 32N 66 51W
Oceanside, N.Y. 23 D7 40 38N 73 37W
Ochakovo, Mos. 11 E8 55 41N 37 26 E
Ochiai, Tōkyō 13 B3 35 43N 139 42 E
Ochota, Wsaw. 10 E6 52 13N 20 58 E
Ochsenwerder, Hbg. 7 E8 53 28N 10 4 E
Ochsenzoll, Hbg. 7 C8 53 41N 10 0 E
Odana, Tōkyō 13 C2 35 33N 139 35 E
Oden-Stockach, Mün. 7 G11 48 5N 11 41 E
Odilampi, Hels. 3 B3 60 18N 24 45 E
Odintsovo, Mos. 11 E7 55 40N 37 16 E
Odivelas, Lisb. 8 F7 38 47N 9 10W
Odolany, Wsaw. 10 E6 52 13N 20 55 E
Oeiras, Lisb. 8 F7 38 41N 9 18W
Oella, Balt. 25 B2 39 16N 76 46W
Oer-Erkenschwick, Ruhr 6 A5 51 38N 7 15 E
Oern, Mün. 7 G10 48 10N 11 32 E
Ofin, Lagos 18 A3 6 32N 7 30 E
Ofukuro-shinden, Tōkyō 13 A1 35 53N 139 28 E
Ogawa, Tōkyō 13 B1 35 44N 139 28 E
Ogden, Phil. 24 C2 39 49N 75 27W
Ogikubo, Tōkyō 13 B2 35 42N 139 37 E
Ogo Ogo, Ōsaka 12 B1 34 49N 135 8 E
Ogogoro, Lagos 18 B2 6 25N 7 24 E
Ogongo, Manila 15 D4 14 35N 121 4 E
Ogoyo, Lagos 18 B2 6 25N 7 29 E
Ogudu, Lagos 18 A2 6 34N 7 24 E
O'Hare, L., Chic. 26 B1 41 57N 87 53W
Ōhirodo, Tōkyō 13 A4 35 50N 139 53 E
Ohlsdorf, Hbg. 7 D8 53 37N 10 3 E
Ōi, Tōkyō 13 A2 35 51N 139 31 E
Ōimachi, Tōkyō 13 C3 35 35N 139 43 E
Oise →, Paris 5 A2 49 2N 2 5 E
Oittaa, Hels. 3 B3 60 15N 24 42 E
Ojota, Lagos 18 A2 6 35N 7 23 E
Okamoto, Ōsaka 12 B2 34 43N 135 15 E
Okazu, Tōkyō 13 D2 35 25N 139 31 E
Okęcie, Wsaw. 10 E6 52 11N 20 56 E
Okęcie Airport, Wsaw. 10 E6 52 10N 20 57 E
Okelra, Lagos 18 B2 6 29N 7 22 E
Okeogbe, Lagos 18 B2 6 24N 7 23 E
Okhla, Delhi 16 B2 28 33N 77 16 E
Okhta →, St-Pet. 11 B4 59 56N 30 25 E
Okkervil →, St-Pet. 11 B4 59 56N 30 30 E
Okrzeszyn, Wsaw. 10 F7 52 8N 21 8 E
Oksval, Oslo 2 B4 59 51N 10 40 E
Oktyabrskiy, Mos. 11 F11 55 37N 37 58 E
Oktyabrskiy, Mos. 11 E9 55 41N 37 35 E
Okubo, Tōkyō 13 B3 35 41N 139 42 E
Okunola, Lagos 18 A1 6 35N 7 17 E
Ōkura, Tōkyō 13 C1 35 35N 139 27 E
Olari, Hels. 3 B3 60 10N 24 44 E
Olaria, Rio J. 31 B2 22 50 S 43 16W
Old Brookville, N.Y. 23 C7 40 49N 73 35W
Old Cairo, El Qâ. 18 C5 30 0N 31 14 E
Old Coulsdon, Lon. 4 D4 51 17N 0 6W
Old Forge Village, N.Y. 22 C2 40 48N 74 29W
Old Harbor, Bost. 21 D3 42 19N 71 1W
Old Road B., Balt. 25 B4 39 12N 76 27W
Old Tappan, N.Y. 22 A5 41 0N 73 59W
Old Town, Chic. 26 B3 41 54N 87 37W
Old Westbury, N.Y. 23 C7 40 46N 73 35W
Oldmans Cr. →, Phil. 24 C2 39 47N 75 26W
Olgino, St-Pet. 11 A3 60 0N 30 10 E
Olimpico, Estadio, Méx. 29 C2 19 19N 99 11W
Olinda, Melb. 19 F9 37 51 S 145 21 E
Olinda, Rio J. 31 A1 22 49 S 43 25W
Olivais, Lisb. 8 F8 38 45N 9 7W
Olivar de los Padres, Méx. 29 B2 19 21N 99 14W
Olivar del Conde, Méx. 29 B2 19 22N 99 12W
Olivos, B.A. 32 B4 34 30 S 58 28W
Ollila, Hels. 3 A2 60 20N 24 32 E
Olney, Phil. 24 A4 40 2N 75 8W
Olona →, Mil. 9 E5 45 29N 9 6 E
Ølstykke, Købn. 2 D7 55 47N 12 8 E
Olute, Lagos 18 B1 6 27N 7 17 E
Olympia-Stadion, Hels. 3 B4 60 11N 24 55 E
Olympique Parc, Mtrl. 20 A4 43 33N 73 33W
Ōmagi, Tōkyō 13 A3 35 52N 139 43 E
Ōmiya, Tōkyō 13 A2 35 54N 139 37 E
Ōmori, Tōkyō 13 C3 35 34N 139 43 E
Ōnari, Tōkyō 13 A2 35 55N 139 36 E
Once, B.A. 32 B4 34 37 S 58 24W
Onchi, Ōsaka 12 C4 34 36N 135 38 E
Onchi →, Ōsaka 12 C4 34 38N 135 37 E
One Tree Hill, Melb. 19 F8 37 52 S 145 19 E
Onisigun, Lagos 18 A2 6 35N 7 24 E
Ōokayama, Tōkyō 13 C3 35 36N 139 40 E
Opacz, Wsaw. 10 E6 52 10N 20 53 E
Ophirton, Jobg. 18 F9 26 13 S 28 1 E
Oppegård, Oslo 2 C4 59 45N 10 49 E
Oppsal, Oslo 2 B5 59 53N 10 50 E
Oppum, Ruhr 6 C1 51 19N 6 36 E
Oradell, N.Y. 22 B4 40 57N 74 2W
Oradell Res., N.Y. 22 B4 40 58N 74 0W
Orange, N.Y. 22 C3 40 46N 74 15W
Orange Grove, Jobg. 18 E9 26 9 S 28 5 E
Oratorio →, S. Pau. 31 E6 23 36 S 46 32W
Orbassano, Tori. 9 B2 45 0N 7 31 E
Orchards, Jobg. 18 E9 26 9 S 28 4 E
Ordrup, Købn. 2 D10 55 45N 12 34 E
Orech, Pra. 10 B1 50 1N 14 17 E
Øresund, Købn. 2 D11 55 45N 12 40 E
Oreta, Lagos 18 A3 6 31N 7 31 E
Orge →, Paris 5 D3 48 36N 2 17 E
Orgeval, Paris 5 B1 48 55N 1 58 E
Orhølm, Købn. 2 D10 55 48N 12 30 E
Orient Heights, Bost. 21 C4 42 23N 70 59W
Oriental, Pico, Car. 30 D5 10 32N 66 51W
Origgio, Mil. 9 D5 45 35N 9 1 E
Orinda, S.F. 27 A3 37 52N 122 10W
Orinda Village, S.F. 27 A3 37 53N 122 12W
Orland L., Chic. 26 D1 41 38N 87 52W
Orland Park, Chic. 26 D1 41 37N 87 52W
Orlando Dam, Jobg. 18 F8 26 15 S 27 55 E
Orlando East, Jobg. 18 F8 26 14 S 27 55 E
Orlando West, Jobg. 18 F8 26 13 S 27 54 E
Orlången, Stock. 3 E11 59 11N 18 2 E
Orlångsvik, Stock. 3 E11 59 11N 18 3 E
Orlovo, Mos. 11 F8 55 38N 37 22 E
Orly, Paris 5 C4 48 45N 2 23 E
Ormesson-sur-Marne, Paris 5 C5 48 47N 2 32 E
Orminge, Stock. 3 E12 59 19N 18 14 E
Ormingelandet, Stock. 3 D13 59 20N 18 22 E
Ormond, Melb. 19 F7 37 54 S 145 1 E
Órmos Fálirou, Ath. 8 J11 37 54N 23 40 E
Ormøya, Oslo 2 B4 59 52N 10 45 E
Oros Aiyáleos, Ath. 8 J10 38 0N 23 36 E
Oros Imittoś, Ath. 8 J11 37 53N 23 48 E
Örpadfold, Bud. 10 J14 47 32N 19 12 E
Orpington, Lon. 4 C5 51 22N 0 6 E
Orsay, Paris 5 C3 48 41N 2 11 E
Orsby, Ruhr 6 A2 51 31N 6 41 E
Orsett, Lon. 4 B7 51 30N 0 22 E
Ortaköy, Ist. 17 A3 41 3N 29 1 E
Ortica, Mil. 9 E6 45 28N 9 16 E
Oruba, Lagos 18 A2 6 34N 7 24 E
Ōsaka, Ōsaka 12 C4 34 42N 135 30 E
Ōsaka B., Ōsaka 12 C2 34 35N 135 18 E
Ōsaka Castle, Ōsaka 12 B4 34 41N 135 30 E
Ōsaka Harbour, Ōsaka 12 C3 34 38N 135 25 E
Ōsaka Univ., Ōsaka 12 B3 34 41N 135 29 E
Ōsaki, Tōkyō 13 C3 35 36N 139 42 E
Osasco, S. Pau. 31 E5 23 31 S 46 46W
Osdorf, Berl. 7 B3 52 24N 13 20 E
Osdorf, Hbg. 7 D7 53 34N 9 50 E
Oshodi, Lagos 18 A2 6 33N 7 21 E
Oskar Frederikborg, Stock. 3 D13 59 24N 18 24 E
Oslo, Oslo 2 B4 59 54N 10 43 E
Oslofjorden, Oslo 2 C3 59 40N 10 35 E
Ōsone, Tōkyō 13 C2 35 31N 139 37 E
Osorun, Lagos 18 A2 6 33N 7 29 E
Ospiate, Mil. 9 D5 45 32N 9 6 E
Ossów, Wsaw. 10 E8 52 18N 21 12 E
Ostankino, Mos. 11 E9 55 49N 37 37 E
Østby, Købn. 2 D7 55 45N 12 2 E
Osterath, Ruhr 6 C1 51 16N 6 36 E
Österby, Hels. 3 B1 60 10N 24 25 E
Osterfeld, Ruhr 6 A3 51 30N 6 53 E
Osterley, Lon. 4 C2 51 28N 0 21W
Osterley Park, Lon. 4 C2 51 29N 0 21W
Östermalm, Stock. 3 D11 59 20N 18 4 E
Österskär, Stock. 3 D12 59 26N 18 16 E
Östersundom, Hels. 3 B6 60 15N 25 10 E
Ostertälje, Stock. 3 E8 59 11N 17 39 E
Ostiense, Rome 9 F9 41 51N 12 29 E
Østmarkkapellet, Oslo 2 B5 59 52N 10 51 E
Østøya, Oslo 2 B3 59 52N 10 34 E
Östra Ryd, Stock. 3 D12 59 27N 18 11 E
Østre Aker, Oslo 2 B4 59 54N 10 49 E
Ostrov, Mos. 11 F11 55 36N 37 50 E
Ostrovtsy, Mos. 11 F12 55 36N 38 0 E
Ōta-Ku, Tōkyō 13 C3 35 34N 139 41 E
Otaniemi, Hels. 3 B3 60 11N 24 49 E
Otford, Lon. 4 D6 51 18N 0 11 E
Othmarschen, Hbg. 7 D7 53 33N 9 53 E
Otsuka, Tōkyō 13 B3 35 43N 139 44 E
Ottakring, Wien 10 G9 48 12N 16 18 E
Ottávia, Rome 9 F9 41 57N 12 24 E
Ottaviano, Nápl. 9 H13 40 50N 14 28 E
Ottensen, Hbg. 7 D7 53 33N 9 55 E
Ottobrunn, Mün. 7 G11 48 3N 11 40 E
Ottocalli, Nápl. 9 H12 40 52N 14 17 E
Otwock, Wsaw. 10 F8 52 8N 21 13 E
Ouerenburg, Ruhr 6 B5 51 27N 7 16 E
Ouiapo, Manila 15 D3 14 35N 120 59 E
Oulunkylä, Hels. 3 B4 60 13N 24 58 E
Ourcq, Canal de l', Paris 5 B4 48 54N 2 28 E
Ousit, Bangk. 15 B2 13 47N 100 31 E
Outer Brewster I., Bost. 21 C4 42 20N 70 52W
Outer Mission, S.F. 27 B2 37 43N 122 26W
Outremont, Mtrl. 20 A4 43 31N 73 36W
Overbruch, Ruhr 6 A2 51 32N 6 43 E
Overlea, Balt. 25 A3 39 21N 76 32W
Øverød, Købn. 2 D9 55 48N 12 28 E
Ōwada, Tōkyō 13 B2 35 48N 139 31 E
Owings Mills, Balt. 25 A2 39 25N 76 47W
Oworonsoki, Lagos 18 A2 6 32N 7 24 E
Oxon Hill, Wash. 25 E8 38 48N 76 59W
Oxshott, Lon. 4 D2 51 19N 0 21W
Oyada, Tōkyō 13 B4 35 46N 139 50 E
Ōyama, Tōkyō 13 B3 35 44N 139 42 E
Øyeren, Oslo 2 B6 59 55N 11 6 E
Oyodo, Ōsaka 12 B3 34 42N 135 29 E
Oyster B., N.Y. 23 B7 40 52N 73 31W
Oyster B., Syd. 19 C3 34 0 S 151 5 E
Oyster Bay Cove, N.Y. 23 B8 40 51N 73 29W
Oyster Bay Harbour, N.Y. 23 B7 40 53N 73 32W
Oyster Rock, Bomb. 16 H7 18 54N 72 49 E
Oyster Rocks, Kar. 17 H11 24 48N 66 59 E
Ożarów-Franciszków, Wsaw. 10 E5 52 13N 20 48 E
Ozerki, St-Pet. 11 B6 59 53N 30 42 E
Ozoir-la-Ferrière, Paris 5 C6 48 46N 2 40 E
Ozone Park, N.Y. 23 C5 40 40N 73 50W


# P


Pacific Manor, S.F. 27 C2 37 38N 122 27W
Pacific Palisades, L.A. 28 B1 34 2N 118 32W
Pacifica, S.F. 27 C2 37 37N 122 27W
Packanack L., N.Y. 22 B3 40 56N 74 15W
Paco, Manila 15 D3 14 35N 120 59 E
Paco de Arcos, Lisb. 8 F7 38 41N 9 17W
Paddington, Lon. 4 B3 51 30N 0 10W
Paddington, Syd. 19 B4 33 53 S 151 14 E
Pademangan, Jak. 15 H9 6 7 S 106 49 E
Paderno, Mil. 9 D5 45 33N 9 9 E
Padre Miguel, Rio J. 31 B1 22 52 S 43 25W
Padstow, Syd. 19 B3 33 57 S 151 2 E
Pagewood, Syd. 19 B4 33 56 S 151 14 E
Pagote, Bomb. 16 H8 18 53N 72 59 E
Pai, I. do, Rio J. 31 B3 22 59 S 43 5W
Paia, Lisb. 8 F7 38 46N 9 11W
Paikpara, Calc. 16 E6 22 36N 88 23 E
Paint Br. →, Wash. 25 C8 38 57N 76 55W
Paiyun Airport, Gzh. 14 F8 23 10N 113 15 E
Pak ka Shan, H.K. 12 E6 22 16N 114 13 E
Pak Kong, H.K. 12 D6 22 22N 114 15 E
Pak Tim Pa, H.K. 12 D5 22 22N 114 7 E
Pakila, Hels. 3 B4 60 15N 24 55 E
Palace Museum, Beij. 14 B3 39 54N 116 21 E
Palaión Fáliron, Ath. 8 J11 37 53N 23 42 E
Palaiseau, Paris 5 C3 48 42N 2 14 E
Palam, Delhi 16 B1 28 35N 77 4 E
Palam Int. Airport, Delhi 16 B1 28 32N 77 8 E
Palazzo Reale, Nápl. 9 H12 40 50N 14 15 E
Palazzo Reale, Tori. 9 B3 45 4N 7 40 E
Palazzolo, Mil. 9 D5 45 34N 9 9 E
Palazzuolo, Nápl. 9 H13 40 54N 14 28 E
Palermo, B.A. 32 B4 34 35 S 58 24W
Palhais, Lisb. 8 G8 38 37N 9 2W
Palisades, N.Y. 22 A5 41 1N 73 57W
Palisades Park, N.Y. 22 B4 40 50N 74 1W
Palleja, Barc. 8 D5 41 25N 2 0 E
Palmer Park, Wash. 25 D8 38 55N 76 52W
Palmers Green, Lon. 4 B4 51 36N 0 6W
Palmyra, Phil. 24 A4 40 0N 75 1W
Palo Alto, S.F. 27 D4 37 27N 122 8W
Paloheinä, Hels. 3 B4 60 15N 24 56 E
Palomar Park, S.F. 27 D3 37 29N 122 16W
Palomeras, Mdrd. 8 B3 40 22N 3 39W
Palos Heights, Chic. 26 D2 41 39N 87 47W
Palos Hills, Chic. 26 C2 41 42N 87 49W
Palos Hills Forest, Chic. 26 C1 41 40N 87 52W
Palos Park, Chic. 26 C1 41 40N 87 50W
Palota-Üjfalu, Bud. 10 J13 47 33N 19 7 E
Palpara, Calc. 16 E6 22 38N 88 22 E
Palta, Calc. 16 D6 22 46N 88 23 E
Pamplona, Manila 15 E3 14 27N 120 58 E
Panayaan, Manila 15 E3 14 27N 120 57 E
Panchghara, Calc. 16 D5 22 44N 88 16 E
Panchur, Calc. 16 E5 22 32N 88 16 E
Pancoran, Jak. 15 J9 6 14 S 106 49 E
Pandan, Selat, Sing. 15 G7 1 16N 103 45 E
Pandan, Sungei →, Sing. 15 G7 1 18N 103 43 E
Pandan Res., Sing. 15 G7 1 18N 103 44 E
Panehpara, Calc. 16 E5 22 34N 88 15 E
Pangrati, Ath. 8 J11 37 56N 23 45 E
Pangsua, Sungei →, Sing. 15 F7 1 25N 103 45 E
Panihati, Calc. 16 D6 22 41N 88 22 E
Panjang, Bukit, Sing. 15 F7 1 22N 103 45 E
Panje, Bomb. 16 H8 18 54N 72 57 E
Panke →, Berl. 7 A3 52 31N 13 22 E
Pankow, Berl. 7 A3 52 34N 13 23 E
Panorama City, L.A. 28 A2 34 13N 118 26W
Panpur, Calc. 16 C6 22 51N 88 26 E
Pantheon, Rome 9 F9 41 53N 12 28 E
Pantin, Paris 5 B4 48 53N 2 24 E
Pantitlán, Méx. 29 B3 19 24N 99 4W
Panuacan, Manila 15 D4 14 35N 121 0 E
Panvel Cr. →, Bomb. 16 H9 18 59N 73 0 E
Paoli, Phil. 24 A2 40 2N 75 28W
Papiol, Barc. 8 D5 41 25N 2 0 E
Paracuellos del Jarama, Mdrd. 8 A3 40 30N 3 31W
Paradise Cay, S.F. 27 A2 37 54N 122 28W
Paramount, L.A. 28 C3 33 53N 118 11W
Paramus, N.Y. 22 B4 40 56N 74 2W
Paranaque, Manila 15 D3 14 30N 120 59 E
Paray-Vieille-Poste, Paris 5 C4 48 42N 2 20 E
Parbasdorf, Wien 10 G11 48 16N 16 35 E
Parbatipur, Calc. 16 E5 22 39N 88 13 E
Parcelacion Moderna, La Hab. 30 B3 23 2N 82 19W
Parco Regionale, Mil. 9 D5 45 35N 9 5 E
Parel, Bomb. 16 H7 18 59N 72 49 E
Pari, S. Pau. 31 E6 23 32 S 46 36W
Parioli, Rome 9 F9 41 55N 12 29 E
Paris, Paris 5 B4 48 53N 2 20 E
Paris-Le Bourget, Aéroport de, Paris 5 B4 48 58N 2 26 E
Paris-Orly, Aéroport de, Paris 5 C4 48 43N 2 22 E
Pārk-e-Shahānshāh, Tehr. 17 C5 35 46N 51 24 E
Park Orchards, Melb. 19 E8 37 46 S 145 13 E
Park Ridge, Chic. 26 A1 42 0N 87 50W
Park Ridge, N.Y. 22 A4 41 2N 74 2W
Park Royal, Lon. 4 B3 51 31N 0 16W
Parkchester, N.Y. 23 C5 40 49N 73 50W
Parkdale, Trto. 20 E8 43 38N 79 25W
Parkdene, Jobg. 18 F10 26 11 S 28 15 E
Parkhafen, Hbg. 7 D7 53 32N 9 54 E
Parkhill Gardens, Jobg. 18 F10 26 14 S 28 11 E
Parkhurst, Jobg. 18 E9 26 8 S 28 1 E
Parklawn, Wash. 25 D7 38 50N 77 7W
Parkmore, Jobg. 18 E9 26 5 S 28 2 E
Parkside, S.F. 27 B2 37 44N 122 29W
Parktown, Jobg. 18 F9 26 10 S 28 2 E
Parktown North, Jobg. 18 E9 26 8 S 28 2 E
Parkview, Jobg. 18 E9 26 9 S 28 1 E
Parkville, Balt. 25 A3 39 23N 76 34W
Parkville, N.Y. 22 D5 40 38N 73 57W
Parkwood, Jobg. 18 E9 26 9 S 28 2 E
Parque Edú Chaves, S. Pau. 31 D6 23 29 S 46 34W
Parramatta, Syd. 19 A2 33 49 S 150 59 E
Parramatta →, Syd. 19 A3 33 49 S 151 3 E
Parramatta North, Syd. 19 A3 33 48 S 151 0 E
Parramatta Park, Syd. 19 A3 33 48 S 151 0 E
Parsippany, N.Y. 22 B2 40 51N 74 26W
Paşabahce, Ist. 17 A3 41 6N 29 5 E
Pasadena, L.A. 28 B4 34 9N 118 8W
Pasar Minggu, Jak. 15 J9 6 16 S 106 49 E
Pasay, Manila 15 D3 14 32N 120 59 E
Pascoe Vale, Melb. 19 E6 37 43 S 144 55 E
Pasig, Manila 15 D4 14 33N 121 4 E
Pasig →, Manila 15 D4 14 31N 121 6 E
Pasila, Hels. 3 B4 60 12N 24 56 E
Pasing, Mün. 7 G9 48 8N 11 28 E
Pasir Panjang, Sing. 15 G7 1 17N 103 46 E
Pasir Ris Beach, Sing. 15 F8 1 22N 103 56 E
Paso del Rey, B.A. 32 B2 34 39 S 58 45W
Passaic, N.Y. 22 B4 40 51N 74 9W
Passaic →, N.Y. 22 B3 40 42N 74 10W
Passirana, Mil. 9 D5 45 32N 9 2 E
Patapsco →, Balt. 25 B2 39 19N 76 49W
Patapsco State Park, Balt. 25 B2 39 18N 76 47W
Pateres, Manila 15 D4 14 32N 121 3 E
Paterson, N.Y. 22 B4 40 54N 74 9W
Pathumwan, Bangk. 15 B2 13 44N 100 31 E
Patipukun, Calc. 16 E6 22 36N 88 24 E
Patisia, Ath. 8 H11 38 2N 23 45 E
Patterson Park, Balt. 25 B3 39 17N 76 34W
Patul, Calc. 16 D4 22 45N 88 9 E
Paulo E. Virginia, Gruta, Rio J. 31 B2 22 56 S 43 16W
Paulsboro, Phil. 24 C3 39 49N 75 14W
Paulshof, Berl. 7 A5 52 34N 13 42 E
Pausin, Berl. 7 A1 52 38N 13 2 E
Pavarolo, Tori. 9 B3 45 4N 7 49 E
Pavlovo, St-Pet. 11 B5 59 55N 30 38 E
Pavne, Bomb. 16 G9 19 5N 73 1 E
Pavshino, Mos. 11 E7 55 49N 37 20 E
Paya Lebar, Sing. 15 F8 1 21N 103 52 E
Paylampur, Calc. 16 D5 22 46N 88 15 E
Peabody, Bost. 21 B4 42 32N 70 57W
Peabody Inst., Balt. 25 B3 39 17N 76 37W
Peakhurst, Syd. 19 B3 33 57 S 151 3 E
Pécel, Bud. 10 K14 47 29N 19 20 E
Pecetto Torinese, Tori. 9 B3 45 1N 7 44 E
Pechincha, Rio J. 31 B1 22 55 S 43 20W
Pechorka →, Mos. 11 F12 55 37N 38 2 E
Peckham, Lon. 4 C4 51 28N 0 3W
Pecqueuse, Paris 5 D2 48 38N 2 3 E
Peddocks I., Bost. 21 D4 42 17N 70 56W
Pederstrup, Købn. 2 D9 55 44N 12 20 E
Pedra Branca, Rio J. 31 B1 22 55 S 43 26W
Pedralbes, Barc. 8 D5 41 23N 2 7 E
Pedregal de San Angel, Jardines del, Méx. 29 C2 19 19N 99 12W
Pedreira, S. Pau. 31 F5 23 41 S 46 40W
Pedreros, Lima 30 G8 12 2 S 76 57W
Pedricktown, Phil. 24 C2 39 45N 75 24W
Pedro Cr. →, S.F. 27 C2 37 35N 122 31W
Pedro Valley, S.F. 27 C2 37 35N 122 29W
Peirce Res., Sing. 15 F7 1 22N 103 49 E
Pekhra-Pokrovskoye, Mos. 11 D11 55 50N 37 56 E
Pekhra-Yakovievskaya, Mos. 11 E11 55 47N 37 57 E
Peking = Beijing, Beij. 14 B2 39 53N 116 21 E
Pelado, Cerro, Méx. 29 D2 19 10N 99 14W
Pelcowizna, Wsaw. 10 E7 52 17N 21 0 E
Pelham, N.Y. 23 B6 40 54N 73 46W
Pelham B. Park, N.Y. 23 B6 40 52N 73 48W
Pelham Manor, N.Y. 23 B6 40 53N 73 46W
Penalolén, Stgo 30 J11 33 28 S 70 30W
Peng Siang →, Sing. 15 F7 1 24N 103 43 E
Penge, Lon. 4 C4 51 24N 0 3W
Penha, Rio J. 31 A2 22 49 S 43 17W
Penha, S. Pau. 31 E6 23 31 S 46 32W
Penjaringan, Jak. 15 H9 6 7 S 106 48 E
Penn Square, Phil. 24 A3 40 8N 75 19W
Penn Wynne, Phil. 24 B3 39 59N 75 16W
Pennant Hills Park, Syd. 19 A3 33 46 S 151 6 E
Penndel, Phil. 24 A5 40 9N 74 54W
Penns Grove, Phil. 24 C2 39 44N 75 27W
Pennsauken, Phil. 24 B4 39 57N 75 5W
Pennsauken Cr. →, Phil. 24 B4 39 59N 75 3W
Pennsylvania, Univ. of, Phil. 24 B3 39 51N 75 11W
Pennypack Cr. →, Phil. 24 A4 40 0N 75 3W
Pentala, Hels. 3 C3 60 6N 24 40 E
Penyagino, Mos. 11 D8 55 50N 37 20 E
Penzing, Wien 10 G9 48 11N 16 18 E
Pequannock, N.Y. 22 B3 40 57N 74 17W
Pequena Arroio Fundo →, Rio J. 31 B1 22 58 S 43 21W
Perales del Rio, Mdrd. 8 C3 40 18N 3 38W
Perchtoldsdorf, Wien 10 H9 48 7N 16 17 E
Perdizes, S. Pau. 31 E6 23 32 S 46 39W
Peredelkino, Mos. 11 F8 55 38N 37 20 E
Peredelytsy, Mos. 11 F8 55 36N 37 21 E
Peristérion, Ath. 8 H11 38 1N 23 42 E
Perivale, Lon. 4 B3 51 31N 0 18W
Perlach, Mün. 7 G10 48 5N 11 37 E
Perlacher Forst, Mün. 7 G10 48 4N 11 34 E
Pero, Mil. 9 D5 45 30N 9 5 E
Peropok, Bukit, Sing. 15 G7 1 19N 103 42 E
Perovo, Mos. 11 E10 55 44N 37 45 E
Perrot, Î., Mtrl. 20 B2 43 23N 73 56W
Perry Hall, Balt. 25 A4 39 24N 76 28W
Perth Amboy, N.Y. 22 D3 40 30N 74 16W
Pertusella, Mil. 9 D5 45 35N 9 3 E
Pesanggrahag, Kali →, Jak. 15 J9 6 10 S 106 44 E
Peschiera Borromeo, Mil. 9 E6 45 26N 9 19 E
Pesek, P., Sing. 15 G7 1 17N 103 41 E
Pest, Bud. 10 K13 47 29N 19 4 E
Pesterzsébet, Bud. 10 K13 47 26N 19 6 E
Pesthidegkút, Bud. 10 J12 47 33N 18 57 E
Pestimre, Bud. 10 K14 47 24N 19 11 E
Pestlörinc, Bud. 10 K14 47 26N 19 11 E
Pestujhely, Bud. 10 J13 47 32N 19 7 E
Petare, Car. 30 E6 10 29N 66 48W
Petas, Hels. 3 B4 60 15N 24 50 E
Peters Pond, Bost. 21 A2 42 43N 71 15W
Petit, Jobg. 18 E11 26 6 S 28 22 E
Petit-Brûlé, Mtrl. 20 A1 43 35N 74 2W
Petojo Selatan, Jak. 15 J9 6 10 S 106 48 E
Petrograd = St. Petersburg, St-Pet. 11 B3 59 55N 30 15 E
Petrogradskaya Storona, St-Pet. 11 B4 59 56N 30 20 E
Petroúpolis, Ath. 8 H11 38 3N 23 40 E
Petrovice, Pra. 10 B3 50 2N 14 33 E
Petrovsko-Rasumovskoye, Mos. 11 E9 55 49N 37 34 E
Petrovskoye, Mos. 11 F11 55 36N 37 53 E
Petrovsky Park, Mos. 11 E9 55 47N 37 34 E
Pfaueninsel, Berl. 7 B1 52 26N 13 7 E
Phihāi, Kar. 17 G11 24 50N 67 8 E
Philadelphia, Phil. 24 B3 39 57N 75 11W
Philadelphia Airport, Phil. 24 A5 40 4N 75 0W
Philadelphia Int. Airport, Phil. 24 B3 39 52N 75 16W
Phillip B., Syd. 19 B4 33 58 S 151 14 E
Phinga, Calc. 16 D6 22 41N 88 25 E
Phoenix, Chic. 26 D3 41 36N 87 37W
Phoenixville, Phil. 24 A1 40 7N 75 31W
Phra Khanong, Bangk. 15 B2 13 40N 100 36 E
Phra Pradaeng, Bangk. 15 C2 13 39N 100 33 E
Phranakhon, Bangk. 15 B1 13 44N 100 29 E
Pianezza, Tori. 9 B2 45 6N 7 32 E
Pianura, Nápl. 9 H11 40 51N 14 10 E
Piaslów, Wsaw. 10 E5 52 11N 20 49 E
Pico Rivera, L.A. 28 C4 33 59N 118 5W
Piedade, Lisb. 8 F7 38 49N 9 16W
Piedade, Rio J. 31 B2 22 52 S 43 18W
Piedade, Cova da, Lisb. 8 F8 38 40N 9 8W
Piedmont, S.F. 27 B3 37 49N 122 14W
Pierrefitte, Paris 5 B4 48 58N 2 21 E
Pierrefonds, Mtrl. 20 B2 43 27N 73 52W
Pierrelaye, Paris 5 A2 49 1N 2 8 E
Pietralata, Rome 9 F10 41 55N 12 33 E
Pihlajamäki, Hels. 3 B4 60 14N 24 58 E
Pihlajasaari, Hels. 3 C4 60 8N 24 55 E
Pikesville, Balt. 25 A2 39 22N 76 42W
Pilar Velho, S. Pau. 31 F7 23 40 S 46 22W
Pilarcitos Cr. →, S.F. 27 C2 37 33N 122 24W
Pilarcitos L., S.F. 27 C2 37 33N 122 25W
Pilgrim Corner, Phil. 24 B3 39 57N 75 19W
Pilgrims Hatch, Lon. 4 B6 51 37N 0 17 E
Pillar Pt., S.F. 26 D2 37 29N 122 30W
Pimenta, S. Pau. 31 D7 23 27 S 46 24W
Pimlico, Lon. 4 C4 51 29N 0 8W
Pimmit Hills, Wash. 25 D6 38 54N 77 12W
Pimville, Jobg. 18 F8 26 16 S 27 54 E
Pinazo →, B.A. 32 A2 34 29 S 58 49W
Pine Brook, N.Y. 22 B3 40 51N 74 18W
Pine Grove, Trto. 20 D7 43 47N 79 34W
Pine Hill, Phil. 24 C5 39 47N 74 59W
Pine Orchard, Balt. 25 B1 39 16N 76 52W
Pinehurst, Bost. 21 B2 42 31N 71 12W
Piñero, B.A. 32 B2 34 31 S 58 46W
Pines Lake, N.Y. 22 B3 40 59N 74 15W
Piney Run →, Wash. 25 D6 38 58N 77 14W
Pinganli, Beij. 14 B3 39 56N 116 20 E
Pinheiros →, S. Pau. 31 E5 23 37 S 46 44W
Pinjrāpur, Kar. 17 G11 24 53N 67 4 E
Pinn →, Lon. 4 B2 51 30N 0 28W
Pinnau →, Hbg. 7 C6 53 40N 9 49 E
Pinneberg, Hbg. 7 C6 53 40N 9 48 E
Pinner, Lon. 4 B2 51 35N 0 22W
Pinner Green, Lon. 4 B2 51 35N 0 23W
Pino Torinese, Tori. 9 B3 45 2N 7 46 E
Pinole Cr. →, S.F. 27 A3 37 58N 122 12W
Pioltello, Mil. 9 D6 45 30N 9 19 E
Piossasco, Tori. 9 C1 44 59N 7 27 E
Piqueri, S. Pau. 31 D5 23 29 S 46 41W
Piqueri →, S. Pau. 31 D6 23 27 S 46 34W
Pira, Delhi 16 A1 28 40N 77 7 E
Piraévs, Ath. 8 J10 37 54N 23 39 E
Pirajussara, S. Pau. 31 E5 23 37 S 46 46W
Pirajussara →, S. Pau. 31 E5 23 33 S 46 42W
Piraporinha, S. Pau. 31 F5 23 41 S 46 44W
Piratininga, Rio J. 31 B3 22 56 S 43 4W
Piratininga, L. de, Rio J. 31 B3 22 56 S 43 4W
Pirituba, S. Pau. 31 D5 23 29 S 46 44W
Pirkkola, Hels. 3 B4 60 14N 24 55 E
Pisangan, Jak. 15 J10 6 12 S 106 52 E
Piscataway, N.Y. 22 D2 40 34N 74 27W
Pisnice, Pra. 10 C2 49 59N 14 28 E
Pitampura Kalan, Delhi 16 A1 28 41N 77 7 E

44 Pitkäjärvi


Pitkäjärvi, *Hels.* 3 B3 60 15N 24 45 E
Pitman, *Phil.* 24 C4 39 44N 75 7W
Plainedge, *N.Y.* 23 C8 40 43N 73 27W
Plainfield, *N.Y.* 22 D2 40 36N 74 23W
Plainview, *N.Y.* 23 C8 40 46N 73 27W
Plaisir, *Paris* 5 C1 48 49N 1 56 E
Plandome, *N.Y.* 23 C6 40 48N 73 42W
Plandome Heights, *N.Y.* 23 C6 40 48N 73 42W
Planegg, *Mün.* 7 G9 48 6N 11 25 E
Plazo Mayor, *Mdrd.* 8 B2 40 25N 3 43W
Pleasant Hill, *S.F.* 27 A4 37 56N 122 4W
Plenty, *Melb.* 19 E7 37 40 S 145 5 E
Pluit, *Jak.* 15 H9 6 7 S 106 47 E
Plumsock, *Phil.* 24 B2 39 58N 75 28W
Plumstead, *Lon.* 4 C5 51 29N 0 5 E
Plymouth Meeting, *Phil.* 24 A3 40 6N 75 16W
Plyushchevo, *Mos.* 11 E10 55 44N 37 45 E
Po →, *Tori.* 9 B3 45 7N 7 46 E
Po Toi, *H.K.* 12 E6 22 16N 114 17 E
Po Toi I., *H.K.* 12 E6 22 10N 114 15 E
Podbaba, *Pra.* 10 B2 50 7N 14 22 E
Podoli, *Pra.* 10 B2 50 2N 14 25 E
Podra, *Calc.* 16 E5 22 33N 88 16 E
Poduskino, *Mos.* 11 E7 55 43N 37 15 E
Poggioreale, *Nápl.* 9 H12 40 51N 14 17 E
Pogliano Milanese, *Mil.* 9 D4 45 32N 8 59 E
Pohick Cr. →, *Wash.* 25 E6 38 47N 77 16W
Point Breeze, *Phil.* 24 B3 39 54N 75 13W
Point Lookout, *N.Y.* 23 D7 40 35N 73 34W
Point View Res., *N.Y.* 22 B3 40 58N 74 14W
Pointe-Aux-Trembles, *Mtrl.* 20 A4 43 38N 73 30W
Pointe-Calumet, *Mtrl.* 20 B2 43 29N 73 58W
Pointe-Claire, *Mtrl.* 20 B3 43 27N 73 48W
Poissy, *Paris* 5 B2 48 55N 2 2 E
Pok Fu Lam, *H.K.* 12 E5 22 16N 114 7 E
Pokrovsko-Sresnevo, *Mos.* 11 E8 55 48N 37 27 E
Pokrovskoye, *Mos.* 11 F9 55 37N 37 36 E
Pòllena, *Nápl.* 9 H13 40 51N 14 22 E
Polsum, *Ruhr* 6 A4 51 37N 7 2 E
Polyustrovo, *St-Pet.* 11 B4 59 57N 30 25 E
Pomigliano d'Arco, *Nápl.* 9 H13 40 54N 14 23 E
Pompei, *Nápl.* 9 J13 40 45N 14 29 E
Pomponne, *Paris* 5 B6 48 52N 2 40 E
Pomprap, *Bangk.* 15 B2 13 44N 100 30 E
Pompton →, *N.Y.* 22 B3 40 53N 74 16W
Pompton Lakes, *N.Y.* 22 A3 41 0N 74 15W
Pompton Plains, *N.Y.* 22 B3 40 58N 74 18W
Ponders End, *Lon.* 4 B4 51 38N 0 2W
Pondok Indah, *Jak.* 15 J9 6 16 S 106 46 E
Ponkapog, *Bost.* 21 D3 42 11N 71 4W
Ponkapog Pond, *Bost.* 21 D3 42 11N 71 5W
Pont-Viau, *Mtrl.* 20 A3 43 34N 73 41W
Pontault-Combault, *Paris* 5 C5 48 47N 2 36 E
Pontcarré, *Paris* 5 C6 48 47N 2 42 E
Pontchartrain, *Paris* 5 C1 48 48N 1 54 E
Ponte Galéria, *Rome* 9 G8 41 48N 12 19 E
Pontes, Canto do, *Rio J.* 31 B3 22 56 S 43 3W
Pontevedra, *B.A.* 32 C2 34 44 S 58 41W
Ponticelli, *Nápl.* 9 H12 40 51N 14 19 E
Pontinha, *Lisb.* 8 F7 38 45N 9 11W
Pontoise, *Paris* 5 A2 49 2N 2 4 E
Poortview, *Jobg.* 18 E8 26 5 S 27 51 E
Poplar, *Lon.* 4 B4 51 30N 0 0 E
Poppenbüttel, *Hbg.* 7 D8 53 39N 10 4 E
Port Chester, *N.Y.* 23 A6 41 0N 73 40W
Port Chester Harbour, *N.Y.* 23 B7 40 58N 73 38W
Port Jackson, *Syd.* 19 B4 33 51 S 151 14 E
Port Kennedy, *Phil.* 24 A2 40 6N 75 25W
Port Melbourne, *Melb.* 19 F6 37 50 S 144 54 E
Port Newark, *N.Y.* 22 C4 40 41N 74 9W
Port Reading, *N.Y.* 22 D3 40 34N 74 13W
Port Richmond, *N.Y.* 22 D4 40 38N 74 7W
Port Shelter, *H.K.* 12 D6 22 20N 114 17 E
Port Union, *Trto.* 20 D10 43 47N 79 7W
Port Washington, *N.Y.* 23 C6 40 49N 73 42W
Port Washington North, *N.Y.* 23 B6 40 50N 73 41W
Portage Park, *Chic.* 26 B2 41 56N 87 45W
Portela, Aeroporto da, *Lisb.* 8 F8 38 46N 9 7W
Pórtici, *Nápl.* 9 J12 40 48N 14 19 E
Porto Brandão, *Lisb.* 8 F7 38 40N 9 12W
Porto Novo Cr. →, *Lagos* 18 B2 6 25N 7 22 E
Porto Nuevo, *B.A.* 32 B4 34 35 S 58 22W
Portrero, *S.F.* 27 B3 37 46N 122 25W
Posen, *Chic.* 26 D2 41 38N 87 41W
Posíllipo, *Nápl.* 9 J12 40 49N 14 13 E
Posíllipo, C. di, *Nápl.* 9 J12 40 48N 14 12 E
Posolok Lenina, *St-Pet.* 11 C2 59 50N 30 5 E
Potawatomi Woods, *Chic.* 26 A1 42 8N 87 53W
Potomac, *Wash.* 25 D6 38 59N 77 13W
Potomac →, *Wash.* 25 D7 38 58N 77 9W
Potrero Pt., *S.F.* 27 B2 37 45N 122 22W
Potsdam, *Berl.* 7 B1 52 23N 13 3 E
Potter Pt., *Syd.* 19 C4 34 2 S 151 13 E
Potters Bar, *Lon.* 4 A4 51 41N 0 10W
Potzham, *Mün.* 7 G10 48 1N 11 36 E
Pötzleinsdorf, *Wien* 10 G9 48 14N 16 17 E
Povoa de Santo Adriao, *Lisb.* 8 F8 38 47N 9 9W
Powderhorn L., *Chic.* 26 D3 41 38N 87 31W
Powiĉle, *Wsaw.* 10 E7 52 14N 21 1 E
Powōzki, *Wsaw.* 10 E6 52 15N 20 58 E
Powsin, *Wsaw.* 10 F7 52 8N 21 6 E
Powsinek, *Wsaw.* 10 F7 52 9N 21 6 E
Poyo, *Barc.* 8 D6 41 28N 2 12 E
Pozuelo de Alarcón, *Mdrd.* 8 B2 40 25N 3 48W
Praça Seca, *Rio J.* 31 B1 22 53 S 43 20W
Prado, Museo del, *Mdrd.* 8 B2 40 25N 3 42W
Prado Churubusco, *Méx.* 29 B3 19 20N 99 8W
Praga, *Wsaw.* 10 E7 52 15N 21 2 E
Prague = Praha, *Pra.* 10 B2 50 4N 14 25 E
Praha, *Pra.* 10 B2 50 4N 14 25 E
Praha-Ruzyně Airport, *Pra.* 10 B1 50 6N 14 16 E
Praires, R. des →, *Mtrl.* 20 A4 43 38N 73 36W
Prat de Llobregat, *Barc.* 8 E5 41 19N 2 5 E
Prater, *Wien* 10 G10 48 12N 16 25 E
Pratts Bottom, *Lon.* 4 C5 51 20N 0 7 E
Prawet Buri Rom, Khlong →, *Bangk.* 15 B2 13 43N 100 38 E
Preakness, *N.Y.* 22 B3 40 56N 74 12W
Precotto, *Mil.* 9 D6 45 30N 9 13 E
Prédecelles →, *Paris* 5 D2 48 36N 2 7 E
Pregnana Milanese, *Mil.* 9 D4 45 30N 9 0 E
Prem Prachakan, Khlong →, *Bangk.* 15 B2 13 46N 100 35 E
Prenestino Labicano, *Rome* 9 F10 41 53N 12 33 E
Prenzlauerberg, *Berl.* 7 A3 52 32N 13 24 E
Presidente Derqui, *B.A.* 32 A1 34 29 S 58 50W
Presidente Outra, Rodo, *Rio J.* 31 A1 22 47 S 43 21W
Preston, *Melb.* 19 E6 37 44 S 144 59 E
Pretos Forros, Sa. dos, *Rio J.* 31 B2 22 54 S 43 17W
Préville, *Mtrl.* 20 B5 43 28N 73 29W
Přezletice, *Pra.* 10 B3 50 9N 14 34 E
Primavalle, *Rome* 9 F9 41 55N 12 25 E
Primrose, *Jobg.* 18 F9 26 11 S 28 9 E
Princes B., *N.Y.* 22 D3 40 30N 74 12W
Princess Elizabeth Park, *Sing.* 15 F7 1 21N 103 45 E
Progreso, *Mdrd.* 8 B3 40 27N 3 39W
Progreso Nacional, *Méx.* 29 A3 19 30N 99 9W
Prosek, *Pra.* 10 B3 50 7N 14 30 E
Prospect, *Syd.* 19 A2 33 48 S 150 55 E
Prospect Heights, *Chic.* 26 A1 42 5N 87 55W
Prospect Hill Park, *Bost.* 21 C2 42 23N 71 13W
Prospect Park, *N.Y.* 22 B3 40 55N 74 10W
Prospect Park, *Phil.* 24 B3 39 53N 75 18W
Prospect Pt., *N.Y.* 23 B6 40 52N 73 42W
Prospect Res., *Syd.* 19 A2 33 49 S 150 53 E
Providence, *Balt.* 25 A3 39 25N 76 34W
Providencia, *Stgo* 30 J11 33 25 S 70 36W
Průhonice, *Pra.* 10 C3 50 0N 14 33 E
Pruszków, *Wsaw.* 10 E5 52 10N 20 48 E
Psikhikón, *Ath.* 8 H11 38 1N 23 46 E
Pudong, *Shang.* 14 J12 31 13N 121 30 E
Puduo, *Shang.* 14 J11 31 15N 121 24 E
Pueblo Libre, *Lima* 30 G8 12 5 S 77 4W
Pueblo Nuevo, *Barc.* 8 D6 41 23N 2 11 E
Pueblo Nuevo, *Mdrd.* 8 B3 40 25N 3 37W
Puente Cascallares, *B.A.* 32 C2 34 41 S 58 48W
Puente Hills, *L.A.* 28 C5 33 59N 117 59W
Puffing Billy Station, *Melb.* 19 F9 37 54 S 145 20 E
Puhuangyu, *Beij.* 14 B3 39 50N 116 22 E
Puistola, *Hels.* 3 B5 60 16N 25 2 E
Pukinmäki, *Hels.* 3 B4 60 15N 24 57 E
Pullach, *Mün.* 7 G9 48 3N 11 31 E
Pulo, *Manila* 15 D4 14 34N 121 4 E
Pulo Gadung, *Jak.* 15 J10 6 11 S 106 54 E
Pumphrey, *Balt.* 25 B3 39 13N 76 39W
Punchbowl, *Syd.* 19 B3 33 55 S 151 3 E
Punde, *Bomb.* 16 H8 18 53N 72 57 E
Punggol, *Sing.* 15 F8 1 23N 103 54 E
Punggol, Sungei →, *Sing.* 15 F8 1 24N 103 54 E
Punggol Pt., *Sing.* 15 F8 1 24N 103 54 E
Punta Brava, *La Hab.* 30 B2 23 1N 82 29W
Puolarmetsä, *Hels.* 3 B3 60 11N 24 41 E
Puotila, *Hels.* 3 B5 60 13N 25 6 E
Purchase, *N.Y.* 23 A6 41 2N 73 43W
Purfleet, *Lon.* 4 C6 51 29N 0 14 E
Purkersdorf, *Wien* 10 G9 48 12N 16 11 E
Purley, *Lon.* 4 C4 51 20N 0 6W
Puteaux, *Paris* 5 B3 48 53N 2 14 E
Puth Kalan, *Delhi* 16 A1 28 42N 77 4 E
Putilkovo, *Mos.* 11 D8 55 51N 37 22 E
Putnamville Res., *Bost.* 21 B4 42 36N 70 56W
Putney, *Lon.* 4 C3 51 27N 0 13W
Putty Hill, *Balt.* 25 A3 39 22N 76 30W
Putxet, *Barc.* 8 D5 41 24N 2 8 E
Putzbrunn, *Mün.* 7 G11 48 4N 11 42 E
Pyeongchang, *Sŏul* 12 G7 37 35N 126 57 E
Pyramids, *El Qâ.* 18 D4 29 58N 31 7 E
Pyry, *Wsaw.* 10 F6 52 8N 21 0 E


# Q


Qanât el Ismâilîya, *El Qâ.* 18 C5 30 7N 31 17 E
Qasemābād, *Tehr.* 17 C6 35 4N 51 3 E
Qasr-e-Firōzeh, *Tehr.* 17 D6 35 29N 51 31 E
Qianmen, *Beij.* 14 B3 39 51N 116 21 E
Qibao, *Shang.* 14 K11 31 9N 121 20 E
Qingguang, *Tianj.* 14 D5 39 11N 117 2 E
Qinghua Univ., *Beij.* 14 A2 40 0N 116 17 E
Qinghuayuan, *Beij.* 14 B2 39 59N 116 19 E
Qingningsi, *Shang.* 14 J12 31 16N 121 33 E
Qolhak, *Tehr.* 17 C5 35 45N 51 26 E
Quadraro, *Rome* 9 F10 41 51N 12 33 E
Quaid-i-Azam, *Kar.* 17 G10 24 50N 66 59 E
Qual'eh Murgeh Airport, *Tehr.* 17 D5 35 38N 51 22 E
Qualiano, *Nápl.* 9 H11 40 55N 14 9 E
Quannapowitt, L., *Bost.* 21 B3 42 30N 71 4W
Quartiere Zingone, *Mil.* 9 E5 45 25N 9 3 E
Quarto, *Nápl.* 9 H11 40 52N 14 8 E
Quds, *Bagd.* 17 E8 33 23N 44 24 E
Quebrada Baruta →, *Car.* 30 E5 10 29N 66 53W
Quebrada Tácagua →, *Car.* 30 D4 10 36N 67 1W
Quebrada Topo →, *Car.* 30 D4 10 32N 67 0W
Queen Mary Res., *Lon.* 4 C2 51 24N 0 27W
Queens Village, *N.Y.* 23 C6 40 43N 73 44W
Queensbury, *Lon.* 4 B3 51 35N 0 16W
Queenscliffe, *Syd.* 19 A4 33 47 S 151 17 E
Queenstown, *Sing.* 15 G7 1 18N 103 48 E
Quellerina, *Jobg.* 18 E8 26 9 S 27 56 E
Queluz, *Lisb.* 8 F7 38 45N 9 14W
Quezon City, *Manila* 15 D4 14 37N 121 2 E
Quickborn, *Hbg.* 7 C7 53 43N 9 54 E
Quilicura, *Stgo* 30 J10 33 22 S 70 43W
Quilmes, *B.A.* 32 C5 34 43 S 58 15W
Quincy, *Bost.* 21 D3 42 14N 71 0W
Quincy B., *Bost.* 21 D4 42 16N 70 59W
Quincy-sous-Sénart, *Paris* 5 C5 48 40N 2 32 E
Quinta Normal, *Stgo* 30 J10 33 26 S 70 40W
Quinto Romano, *Mil.* 9 E5 45 28N 9 7 E
Quirinale, *Rome* 9 F9 41 53N 12 29 E
Quitaúna, *S. Pau.* 31 E5 23 31 S 46 48W


# R


Raasdorf, *Wien* 10 G11 48 14N 16 33 E
Raccoon Cr. →, *Phil.* 24 C3 39 48N 75 21W
Raccoon Str., *S.F.* 27 A2 37 52N 122 26W
Radevormwald, *Ruhr* 6 C6 51 12N 7 22 E
Radlett, *Lon.* 4 A3 51 41N 0 19W
Radlice, *Pra.* 10 B2 50 3N 14 23 E
Radnor, *Phil.* 24 A2 40 2N 75 21W
Radonice, *Pra.* 10 B3 50 8N 14 36 E
Radotin, *Pra.* 10 C2 49 59N 14 21 E
Rælingen, *Oslo* 2 B6 59 53N 11 5 E
Rafael Calzada, *B.A.* 32 C4 34 47 S 58 21W
Rafael Castillo, *B.A.* 32 C3 34 42 S 58 36W
Raffles Park, *Sing.* 15 G7 1 19N 103 48 E
Raghunathpur, *Calc.* 16 D5 22 41N 88 16 E
Rahlstedt, *Hbg.* 7 D8 53 35N 10 7 E
Rahm, *Ruhr* 6 B2 51 21N 6 47 E
Rahnsdorf, *Berl.* 7 B5 52 25N 13 41 E
Rahway, *N.Y.* 22 D3 40 36N 74 17W
Rail Tree Hill, *Bost.* 21 B1 42 32N 71 22W
Rainbow Lakes, *N.Y.* 22 B2 40 53N 74 27W
Rainham, *Lon.* 4 B6 51 31N 0 11 E
Rainier, Mt., *Wash.* 25 D8 38 56N 76 57W
Raj Bhawan, *Calc.* 16 E6 22 33N 88 20 E
Rajakylä, *Hels.* 3 B5 60 15N 25 5 E
Rajapur, *Calc.* 16 E5 22 39N 88 11 E
Rajganj, *Calc.* 16 E5 22 34N 88 14 E
Rajpur, *Delhi* 16 A2 28 41N 77 12 E
Rákos-patak →, *Bud.* 10 K14 47 29N 19 12 E
Rákoscsaba, *Bud.* 10 K14 47 28N 19 17 E
Rákoshegy, *Bud.* 10 K14 47 27N 19 14 E
Rákosker, *Bud.* 10 K14 47 28N 19 14 E
Rákoskert, *Bud.* 10 K14 47 27N 19 18 E
Rákosliget, *Bud.* 10 K14 47 29N 19 16 E
Rákospalota, *Bud.* 10 J13 47 34N 19 7 E
Rákosszentmihály, *Bud.* 10 J13 47 31N 19 8 E
Raków, *Wsaw.* 10 E6 52 11N 20 56 E
Rakowiec, *Wsaw.* 10 E6 52 12N 20 58 E
Ramadān, *Bagd.* 17 F8 33 19N 44 20 E
Ramanathpur, *Calc.* 16 D5 22 41N 88 14 E
Rambler Channel, *H.K.* 12 D5 22 21N 114 6 E
Ramblewood, *Phil.* 24 B5 39 55N 74 56W
Ramenki, *Mos.* 11 E8 55 41N 37 28 E
Ramersdorf, *Mün.* 7 G10 48 6N 11 35 E
Ramnathpur, *Calc.* 16 E5 22 35N 88 18 E
Ramos, *Rio J.* 31 B2 22 50 S 43 14W
Ramos Mejia, *B.A.* 32 B3 34 39 S 58 33W
Rampur, *Delhi* 16 A2 28 44N 77 18 E
Ramsgate, *Syd.* 19 B3 33 58 S 151 8 E
Ramstadjøen, *Oslo* 2 B6 59 53N 11 3 E
Rancho Boyeros, *La Hab.* 30 C2 22 59N 82 22W
Rancho Colorado, Presa de, *Méx.* 29 B2 19 29N 99 16W
Rancocas Cr. →, *Phil.* 24 A5 40 2N 74 58W
Rand Afrikaans Univ., *Jobg.* 18 F9 26 11 S 28 0 E
Rand Airport, *Jobg.* 18 F9 26 14 S 28 8 E
Randallstown, *Balt.* 25 A2 39 21N 76 46W
Randburg, *Jobg.* 18 E8 26 5 S 27 57 E
Randhart, *Jobg.* 18 F9 26 16 S 28 7 E
Randolph, *Bost.* 21 D3 42 10N 71 3W
Randolph Hills, *Wash.* 25 C7 39 3N 77 6W
Randpark, *Jobg.* 18 E8 26 6 S 27 58 E
Randwick, *Syd.* 19 B4 33 54 S 151 14 E
Ranelagh, *B.A.* 32 C5 34 47 S 58 14W
Rannersdorf, *Wien* 10 H10 48 7N 16 27 E
Raparkrif, *Jobg.* 18 E8 26 5 S 27 57 E
Raposo, *Lisb.* 8 F7 38 40N 9 11W
Raritan →, *N.Y.* 22 D2 40 30N 74 27W
Raritan B., *N.Y.* 22 E3 40 29N 74 12W
Rasskazovka, *Mos.* 11 F8 55 38N 37 20 E
Rasta, *Stock.* 3 E8 59 18N 17 37 E
Rastaala, *Hels.* 3 B3 60 15N 24 47 E
Rastila, *Hels.* 3 B5 60 12N 25 7 E
Raszyn, *Wsaw.* 10 F6 52 9N 20 54 E
Rat Burana, *Bangk.* 15 B2 13 40N 100 30 E
Ratanpur, *Calc.* 16 D5 22 49N 88 14 E
Rath, *Ruhr* 6 C2 51 16N 6 49 E
Ratingen, *Ruhr* 6 C3 51 18N 6 52 E
Rato, *Lisb.* 8 F8 38 43N 9 8W
Rauxel, *Ruhr* 6 A5 51 34N 7 18 E
Ravenswood Pt., *S.F.* 27 C4 37 30N 122 8W
Rawamangun, *Jak.* 15 J10 6 11 S 106 52 E
Rayners Lane, *Lon.* 4 B2 51 34N 0 23W
Raynes Park, *Lon.* 4 C3 51 24N 0 12W
Raypur, *Calc.* 16 F6 22 28N 88 22 E
Razdory, *Mos.* 11 E7 55 44N 37 17 E
Razmitelevo, *St-Pet.* 11 B5 59 54N 30 39 E
Razor Hill, *H.K.* 12 D6 22 20N 114 15 E
Reading, *Bost.* 21 B3 42 31N 71 5W
Reading Highlands, *Bost.* 21 B3 42 31N 71 5W
Reáglie, *Tori.* 9 B3 45 3N 7 44 E
Real, Palacio, *Mdrd.* 8 B2 40 25N 3 43W
Real Felipe, Castillo, *Lima* 30 G8 12 4 S 77 9W
Real Fuerta, Château de la, *La Hab.* 30 B2 23 8N 82 20W
Realengo, *Rio J.* 31 B1 22 52 S 43 24W
Réau, *Paris* 5 D5 48 36N 2 37 E
Recklinghausen, *Ruhr* 6 A5 51 37N 7 12 E
Recklinghausen-Süd, *Ruhr* 6 A5 51 34N 7 14 E
Recoleta, *Stgo* 30 J11 33 25 S 70 40W
Reconquista →, *B.A.* 32 B3 34 35 S 58 35W
Red Bank Battle Mon., *Phil.* 24 B3 39 52N 75 11W
Red Fort, *Delhi* 16 B2 28 39N 77 14 E
Red Rock, *S.F.* 27 A2 37 55N 122 25W
Red Square, *Mos.* 11 E9 55 45N 37 37 E
Redbridge, *Lon.* 4 B5 51 34N 0 3 E
Redwood City, *S.F.* 27 D3 37 29N 122 14W
Redwood Cr. →, *S.F.* 27 C3 37 31N 122 11W
Redwood Pt., *S.F.* 27 C3 37 32N 122 11W
Redwood Regional Park, *S.F.* 27 B4 37 48N 122 8W
Reeves Hill, *Bost.* 21 C1 42 20N 71 20W
Refshaleøen, *Købn.* 2 D10 55 41N 12 36 E
Regents Park, *Jobg.* 18 F9 26 14 S 28 3 E
Regents Park, *Lon.* 4 B4 51 31N 0 9W
Regents Park, *Syd.* 19 B3 33 52 S 151 1 E
Regi Lagni →, *Nápl.* 9 H13 40 56N 14 23 E
Regina Margherita, *Tori.* 9 B2 45 4N 7 34 E
Regla, *La Hab.* 30 B3 23 7N 82 19W
Rego Park, *N.Y.* 23 C5 40 43N 73 51W
Reiherstieg, *Hbg.* 7 D7 53 30N 9 58 E
Reinickendorf, *Berl.* 7 A3 52 34N 13 22 E
Reinoldikirche, *Ruhr* 6 A6 51 30N 7 28 E
Reistad, *Oslo* 2 C1 59 46N 10 16 E
Reitbrook, *Hbg.* 7 E8 53 28N 10 8 E
Rekola, *Hels.* 3 B5 60 19N 25 4 E
Rellingen, *Hbg.* 7 D7 53 39N 9 50 E
Rembertów, *Wsaw.* 10 E7 52 15N 21 9 E
Remedios de Escalada, *B.A.* 32 C4 34 43 S 58 24W
Rémola, Laguna del, *Barc.* 8 E5 41 16N 2 4 E
Remscheid, *Ruhr* 6 C5 51 11N 7 11 E
Renca, *Stgo* 30 J10 33 24 S 70 42W
Renca, Cerro, *Stgo* 30 J10 33 23 S 70 40W
Rener, *Ist.* 17 A2 41 1N 28 56 E
Renmin Gongyuan, *Tianj.* 14 E6 39 6N 117 12 E
Rennemoulin, *Paris* 5 B2 48 50N 2 2 E
Rennie's Mill, *H.K.* 12 E6 22 18N 114 15 E
Renzel, *Hbg.* 7 C7 53 43N 9 52 E
Repaupo, *Phil.* 24 C3 39 48N 75 18W
Repaupo Cr. →, *Phil.* 24 C3 39 49N 75 20W
Řeporyje, *Pra.* 10 B1 50 1N 14 18 E
République, Place de la, *Paris* 5 B4 48 52N 2 22 E
Repy, *Pra.* 10 B1 50 4N 14 17 E
Resarö, *Stock.* 3 D13 59 25N 18 20 E
Rescaldna, *Mil.* 9 D4 45 36N 8 57 E
Research, *Melb.* 19 E8 37 42 S 145 10 E
Reseda, *L.A.* 28 A1 34 12N 118 31W
Reservoir, *Melb.* 19 E7 37 42 S 145 1 E
Reservoir Pond, *Bost.* 21 D3 42 10N 71 7W
Residenz, *Mün.* 7 G10 48 8N 11 34 E
Resse, *Ruhr* 6 A4 51 34N 7 6 E
Reston, *Wash.* 25 D6 38 57N 77 20W
Retiro, *B.A.* 32 B4 34 35 S 58 23W
Retiro, *Mdrd.* 8 B2 40 24N 3 40W
Reutov, *Mos.* 11 E11 55 45N 37 50 E
Réveillon →, *Paris* 5 C5 48 42N 2 30 E
Revere, *Bost.* 21 C3 42 25N 71 0W
Revesby, *Syd.* 19 B3 33 57 S 151 0 E
Revolucion, Plaza de la, *La Hab.* 30 B2 23 7N 82 23W
Rexdale, *Trto.* 20 D7 43 43N 79 35W
Reynolds Channel, *N.Y.* 23 D6 40 35N 73 41W
Reynosa Tamaulipas, *Méx.* 29 A2 19 30N 99 10W
Rheem Valley, *S.F.* 27 A4 37 50N 122 8W
Rhein-Herne Kanal, *Ruhr* 6 B3 51 29N 6 59 E
Rheinberg, *Ruhr* 6 A1 51 32N 6 37 E
Rheinhausen, *Ruhr* 6 B2 51 24N 6 43 E
Rheinkamp, *Ruhr* 6 B1 51 29N 6 36 E
Rho, *Mil.* 9 D5 45 31N 9 2 E
Rhodes, *Syd.* 19 A3 33 49 S 151 6 E
Rhodesfield, *Jobg.* 18 E10 26 6 S 28 14 E
Rhodon, *Paris* 5 C2 48 42N 2 3 E
Rhodon →, *Paris* 5 C2 48 42N 2 4 E
Rhu, Tg., *Sing.* 15 G8 1 17N 103 51 E
Ribeirão Pires, *S. Pau.* 31 F7 23 42 S 46 23W
Říčanský →, *Pra.* 10 B3 50 5N 14 36 E
Říčany, *Pra.* 10 C3 49 59N 14 39 E
Ricarda, Laguna de la, *Barc.* 8 E5 41 17N 2 6 E
Richardson B., *S.F.* 27 A2 37 52N 122 29W
Richmond, *Lon.* 4 C3 51 27N 0 17W
Richmond, *Melb.* 19 E7 37 48 S 145 0 E
Richmond, *S.F.* 27 B2 37 46N 122 27W
Richmond, *S.F.* 27 A2 37 56N 122 21W
Richmond →, *N.Y.* 22 D3 40 34N 74 11W
Richmond, Pt., *S.F.* 27 A2 37 54N 122 23W
Richmond Hill, *N.Y.* 23 C5 40 41N 73 51W
Richmond Hill, *Trto.* 20 C8 43 51N 79 24W
Richmond Inner Harbour, *S.F.* 27 A2 37 54N 122 20W
Richmond Park, *Lon.* 4 C3 51 26N 0 16W
Richmond Valley, *N.Y.* 22 D3 40 31N 74 13W
Richvale, *Trto.* 20 C8 43 51N 79 26W
Rickers I., *N.Y.* 23 C5 40 47N 73 53W
Rickmansworth, *Lon.* 4 B2 51 38N 0 28W
Riddel Cr. →, *Melb.* 19 F8 37 52 S 145 13 E
Riderwood, *Balt.* 25 A3 39 24N 76 37W
Ridgefield, *N.Y.* 22 C4 40 49N 74 0W
Ridgefield Park, *N.Y.* 22 B4 40 52N 74 1W
Ridgewood, *N.Y.* 23 C5 40 42N 73 53W
Ridley Cr. →, *Phil.* 24 B2 39 51N 75 20W
Ridley Creek State Park, *Phil.* 24 B2 39 57N 75 26W
Ridley Park, *Phil.* 24 B3 39 52N 75 19W
Riedmoos, *Mün.* 7 F10 48 16N 11 32 E
Riem, *Mün.* 7 G11 48 8N 11 41 E
Riemke, *Ruhr* 6 A5 51 30N 7 12 E
Rimac, *Lima* 30 G8 12 2 S 77 2W
Rimau, Tg., *Sing.* 15 G7 1 15N 103 48 E
Ringwood, *Melb.* 19 E8 37 48 S 145 4 E
Rinkeby, *Stock.* 3 D10 59 23N 17 55 E
Rio Comprido, *Rio J.* 31 B2 22 55 S 43 12W
Rio de Janeiro, *Rio J.* 31 B2 22 54 S 43 12W
Rio de Mouro, *Lisb.* 8 F7 38 46N 9 15W
Rio Hondo →, *L.A.* 28 B4 34 2N 118 15W
Rio Pequeno, *S. Pau.* 31 E5 23 34 S 46 44W
Rione Trieste, *Nápl.* 9 H13 40 52N 14 27 E
Ripley, *Lon.* 4 D2 51 17N 0 29W
Rippling Ridge, *Balt.* 25 B3 39 11N 76 37W
Ris, *Oslo* 2 B4 59 56N 10 41 E
Ris-Orangis, *Paris* 5 D4 48 38N 2 24 E
Risby, *Købn.* 2 D8 55 41N 12 19 E
Rishra, *Calc.* 16 D6 22 42N 88 20 E
Ritan Gongyuan, *Beij.* 14 B3 39 53N 116 24 E
Ritchie, *Wash.* 25 D8 38 52N 76 51W
Rithala, *Delhi* 16 A1 28 43N 77 6 E
Ritorp, *Stock.* 3 E8 59 12N 17 38 E
Rivalta di Torino, *Tori.* 9 B1 45 2N 7 31 E
Rivas de Jarama, *Mdrd.* 8 B3 40 22N 3 31W
Rivas-Vaciamadrio, *Mdrd.* 8 C3 40 19N 3 30W
Rivasacco, *Tori.* 9 A1 45 10N 7 29 E
Rive Sud, Canal de la, *Mtrl.* 20 B4 43 24N 73 31W
River Edge, *N.Y.* 22 B4 40 56N 74 1W
River Forest, *Chic.* 26 B2 41 53N 87 49W
River Grove, *Chic.* 26 B1 41 55N 87 50W
River Pines, *Bost.* 21 B2 42 33N 71 17W
River Vale, *N.Y.* 22 B4 40 59N 74 1W
Riverdale, *Chic.* 26 D3 41 38N 87 37W
Riverdale, *N.Y.* 22 B3 40 59N 74 17W
Riverdale, *Trto.* 20 E8 43 39N 79 21W
Riverdale, *Wash.* 25 D8 38 57N 76 54W
Riverdale Park, *Trto.* 20 D8 43 40N 79 21W
Riverhead, *Lon.* 4 D6 51 16N 0 10 E
Riverlea, *Jobg.* 18 F8 26 12 S 27 58 E
Riverside, *Bost.* 21 B2 42 32N 71 18W
Riverside, *Chic.* 26 C2 41 49N 87 49W
Riverside, *N.Y.* 23 B5 40 54N 73 54W
Riverside, *N.Y.* 23 A7 41 1N 73 34W
Riverside, *Phil.* 24 A5 40 2N 74 57W
Riverton, *Phil.* 24 A4 40 0N 75 0W
Riverwood, *Syd.* 19 B3 33 57 S 151 3 E
Rivière-des-Praires, *Mtrl.* 20 A4 43 38N 73 34W
Rivodora, *Tori.* 9 B3 45 5N 7 47 E
Rivoli, *Tori.* 9 B1 45 4N 7 30 E
Riyad, *Bagd.* 17 F8 33 18N 44 27 E
Rizal, *Manila* 15 D4 14 33N 121 0 E
Rizal Park, *Manila* 15 D3 14 35N 120 58 E
Rizel Stadium, *Manila* 15 D3 14 34N 120 59 E
Røa, *Oslo* 2 B3 59 57N 10 39 E
Robassomero, *Tori.* 9 A2 45 11N 7 34 E
Robbins, *Chic.* 26 D2 41 38N 87 42W
Robert E. Lee Memorial Park, *Balt.* 25 A3 39 23N 76 40 E
Robertsdale, *Chic.* 26 C3 41 40N 87 30W
Robertsham, *Jobg.* 18 F9 26 15 S 28 1 E
Robin Hills, *Jobg.* 18 E8 26 6 S 27 58 E
Rocha Miranda, *Rio J.* 31 B1 22 51 S 43 20W
Rochar →, *Sing.* 15 G8 1 18N 103 52 E
Rochelle Park, *N.Y.* 22 B4 40 54N 74 4W
Rock Cr. →, *Wash.* 25 D7 38 54N 77 3W
Rock Creek Park, *Wash.* 25 D7 38 56N 77 2W
Rockaway, *N.Y.* 22 D5 40 32N 73 56W
Rockaway Beach, *S.F.* 27 C2 37 36N 122 29W
Rockaway Islet, *N.Y.* 23 D5 40 34N 73 53W
Rockaway Neck, *N.Y.* 22 B2 40 51N 74 21W
Rockaway Point, *N.Y.* 23 D5 40 33N 73 54W
Rockburn Branch →, *Balt.* 25 B2 39 13N 76 43W
Rockdale, *Balt.* 25 A2 39 21N 76 46W
Rockdale, *Syd.* 19 B3 33 57 S 151 8 E
Rockland, *Phil.* 24 C1 39 47N 75 34W
Rocklege, *Phil.* 24 A4 40 4N 75 5W
Rockleigh, *N.Y.* 22 A5 41 0N 73 55W
Rockville, *Wash.* 25 C6 39 4N 77 10W
Rockville Centre, *N.Y.* 23 D7 40 39N 73 38W
Rocky Hill, *Phil.* 24 B1 39 58N 75 32W
Rocky Ridge, *S.F.* 27 B4 37 47N 122 2W
Rocky Run →, *Wash.* 25 D6 38 58N 77 14W
Rodaon, *Wien* 10 H9 48 8N 16 16 E
Rodeo Cove, *S.F.* 27 B1 37 49N 122 32W
Rodgers Forge, *Balt.* 25 A3 39 22N 76 37W
Roding →, *Lon.* 4 B5 51 30N 0 5 E
Rodość, *Wsaw.* 10 E8 52 11N 21 11 E
Rødovre, *Købn.* 2 D9 55 40N 12 26 E
Rodrigo de Freitas, L., *Rio J.* 31 B2 22 58 S 43 12W
Rodstensfjärden, *Stock.* 3 E9 59 16N 17 48 E
Roehampton, *Lon.* 4 C3 51 27N 0 15W
Rogers Park, *Chic.* 26 A2 42 0N 87 40W
Rohdenhaus, *Ruhr* 6 C4 51 18N 7 0 E
Röhlinghausen, *Ruhr* 6 A4 51 30N 7 9 E
Roihuvuori, *Hels.* 3 B5 60 11N 25 2 E
Roissy, *Paris* 5 C5 48 47N 2 39 E
Roissy-en-France, *Paris* 5 A5 49 0N 2 30 E
Rokkō Sanchi, *Ōsaka* 12 B2 34 44N 135 13 E
Rokko-Zan, *Ōsaka* 12 B2 34 46N 135 16 E
Rokytka →, *Pra.* 10 B3 50 6N 14 27 E
Roland Lake, *Balt.* 25 A3 39 23N 76 38W
Roland Park, *Balt.* 25 A3 39 20N 76 39W
Roma, *Rome* 9 F9 41 54N 12 28 E
Római-Fürdö, *Bud.* 10 J13 47 34N 19 4 E
Romainville, *Paris* 5 B4 48 52N 2 26 E
Romani, *Nápl.* 9 H13 40 52N 14 22 E
Romano Banco, *Mil.* 9 E5 45 25N 9 6 E
Romashkovo, *Mos.* 11 E7 55 43N 37 19 E
Rome = Roma, *Rome* 9 F9 41 54N 12 28 E
Romford, *Lon.* 4 B6 51 34N 0 11 E
Roncáglia, *Tori.* 9 B1 45 2N 7 29 E
Rönninge, *Stock.* 3 E9 59 12N 17 45 E
Ronsdorf, *Ruhr* 6 C5 51 13N 7 11 E
Ronskensiedig, *Ruhr* 6 A2 51 36N 6 41 E
Rontgental, *Berl.* 7 A4 52 38N 13 31 E
Roodekop, *Jobg.* 18 F10 26 17 S 28 11 E
Roodepoort, *Jobg.* 18 E8 26 9 S 27 53 E
Roodepoort-Wes, *Jobg.* 18 E8 26 8 S 27 51 E
Roosevelt, *N.Y.* 23 C7 40 40N 73 35W
Rooty Hill, *Syd.* 19 A2 33 46 S 150 50 E
Roppongi, *Tōkyō* 13 C3 35 39N 139 44 E
Rosairinho, *Lisb.* 8 F8 38 40N 9 0W
Rosanna, *Melb.* 19 E7 37 44 S 145 4 E
Rosario, *La Hab.* 30 B2 23 3N 82 21W
Rosario, *Manila* 15 D4 14 35N 121 4 E
Rose B., *Syd.* 19 B4 33 51 S 151 16 E
Rose Hill, *Wash.* 25 E7 38 47N 77 6W
Rose Tree, *Phil.* 24 B2 39 56N 75 23W
Rosebank, *N.Y.* 22 D4 40 36N 74 4W
Rosebery, *Syd.* 19 B4 33 55 S 151 12 E
Rosedal La Candelaria, *Méx.* 29 B3 19 20N 99 10W
Rosedale, *Balt.* 25 B3 39 19N 76 31W
Rosedale, *N.Y.* 23 D6 40 39N 73 43W
Roseiras, *S. Pau.* 31 E7 23 33 S 46 23W
Roseland, *Chic.* 26 C3 41 42N 87 37W
Roseland, *N.Y.* 22 C3 40 49N 74 17W
Roselle, *N.Y.* 22 D3 40 39N 74 15W
Roselle Park, *N.Y.* 22 D3 40 39N 74 16W
Rosemead, *L.A.* 28 B4 34 4N 118 4W
Rosemere, *Mtrl.* 20 A2 43 34N 73 50W
Rosemont, *Chic.* 26 B1 41 59N 87 52W
Rosemont, *Phil.* 24 A3 40 1N 75 19W
Rosenborg Have, *Købn.* 2 D10 55 41N 12 33 E
Rosengarten, *Hbg.* 7 D6 53 31N 9 49 E
Rosenthal, *Berl.* 7 A3 52 35N 13 22 E
Rosettenville, *Jobg.* 18 F9 26 15 S 28 3 E
Rosherville Dam, *Jobg.* 18 F9 26 13 S 28 6 E
Rósio, *Mil.* 9 E4 45 25N 8 57 E
Rösjön, *Stock.* 3 D11 59 26N 18 0 E
Roskilde, *Købn.* 2 E7 55 38N 12 5 E
Roskilde Fjord, *Købn.* 2 D7 55 45N 12 4 E
Roslags-Näsby, *Stock.* 3 D11 59 25N 18 2 E
Roslindale, *Bost.* 21 D3 42 17N 71 7W
Roslyn, *N.Y.* 23 C7 40 47N 73 38W
Roslyn, *Phil.* 24 A4 40 7N 75 8W
Roslyn Estates, *N.Y.* 23 C6 40 47N 73 40W
Roslyn Harbour, *N.Y.* 23 C7 40 48N 73 38W
Rosne →, *Paris* 5 B4 48 58N 2 25 E
Rosny-sous-Bois, *Paris* 5 B5 48 52N 2 30 E
Ross, *S.F.* 27 A1 37 57N 122 33W
Rosslyn, *Wash.* 25 D7 38 53N 77 4W
Rossville, *Balt.* 25 A4 39 20N 76 28W
Rossville, *N.Y.* 22 D3 40 32N 74 12W
Rosta, *Tori.* 9 B1 45 4N 7 27 E
Rotbach →, *Ruhr* 6 A2 51 34N 6 41 E
Rothenburgsort, *Hbg.* 7 D8 53 32N 10 2 E
Rotherbaum, *Hbg.* 7 D7 53 33N 9 58 E
Rotherhithe, *Lon.* 4 C4 51 29N 0 2W
Rothneusiedl, *Wien* 10 H10 48 8N 16 23 E
Rothschmaige, *Mün.* 7 F9 48 14N 11 27 E
Rouge →, *Trto.* 20 D9 43 47N 79 12W
Rouge Hill, *Trto.* 20 D10 43 48N 79 6W
Round I., *H.K.* 12 E6 22 13N 114 11 E
Roundshaw, *Lon.* 4 C4 51 20N 0 7W
Roussigny, *Paris* 5 D2 48 38N 2 6 E
Rowland, *L.A.* 28 B5 34 0N 117 55W
Rowley, *Bost.* 21 A4 42 43N 70 52W
Rowville, *Melb.* 19 F8 37 55 S 145 14 E
Roxboro, *Mtrl.* 20 A3 43 30N 73 48W
Roxborough, *Phil.* 24 A3 40 1N 75 13W
Roxbury, *Bost.* 21 D3 42 19N 71 5W
Roxbury, *N.Y.* 23 D5 40 33N 73 53W
Roxeth, *Lon.* 4 B2 51 33N 0 20W
Royal Observatory, *H.K.* 12 E6 22 18N 114 10 E
Royal Park, *Melb.* 19 E6 37 46 S 144 57 E
Röylä, *Hels.* 3 B3 60 18N 24 42 E
Royston Park, *Lon.* 4 B2 51 36N 0 22W
Rozas, Portilleros de las, *Mdrd.* 8 B2 40 29N 3 49W
Roztoky, *Pra.* 10 B2 50 9N 14 23 E
Rubbianetta, *Tori.* 9 B2 45 9N 7 34 E
Rubi →, *Barc.* 8 D5 41 26N 2 0 E
Rubio Woods, *Chic.* 26 D2 41 38N 87 45W
Rublovo, *Mos.* 11 E8 55 47N 37 21 E
Ruchyi, *St-Pet.* 11 A4 60 0N 30 25 E
Rud, *Oslo* 2 B6 59 56N 11 0 E
Rüdinghausen, *Ruhr* 6 B6 51 26N 7 22 E
Rudnevka →, *Mos.* 11 E11 55 43N 37 56 E
Rudolfsheim, *Wien* 10 G10 48 12N 16 20 E
Rudolfshöhe, *Berl.* 7 A5 52 37N 13 44 E
Rudow, *Berl.* 7 B3 52 24N 13 29 E
Rueil-Malmaison, *Paris* 5 B3 48 52N 2 11 E
Ruffys Cr. →, *Melb.* 19 E7 37 45 S 145 7 E
Ruggeberg, *Ruhr* 6 C6 51 16N 7 23 E
Ruhlsdorf, *Berl.* 7 B2 52 22N 13 15 E
Ruhr →, *Ruhr* 6 B3 51 27N 6 56 E
Ruhrort, *Ruhr* 6 B2 51 27N 6 44 E
Ruislip, *Lon.* 4 B2 51 34N 0 24W
Rumelihisari, *Ist.* 17 A3 41 4N 29 2 E
Rumeln, *Ruhr* 6 B1 51 24N 6 39 E
Rumyantsevo, *Mos.* 11 F8 55 38N 37 25 E
Rungis, *Paris* 5 C4 48 44N 2 20 E
Runnemede, *Phil.* 24 B4 39 50N 75 4W
Ruotsinkylä, *Hels.* 3 A4 60 21N 24 57 E
Rusāfa, *Bagd.* 17 E8 33 21N 44 23 E
Rush Green, *Lon.* 4 B6 51 33N 0 10 E
Russa, *Calc.* 16 F6 22 29N 88 21 E
Russell Lea, *Syd.* 19 B4 33 52 S 151 10 E
Rustad, *Oslo* 2 B2 59 56N 10 24 E
Rustenfeld, *Wien* 10 H10 48 7N 16 23 E
Rusville, *Jobg.* 18 E10 26 9 S 28 18 E
Rutherford, *N.Y.* 22 C4 40 49N 74 6W
Rüttenscheid, *Ruhr* 6 B3 51 25N 6 58 E
Ruxton, *Balt.* 25 A3 39 23N 76 38W
Ruzyně, *Pra.* 10 B1 50 5N 14 17 E
Rybatskaya, *St-Pet.* 11 B4 59 59N 30 29 E
Rybatskoye, *St-Pet.* 11 B4 59 50N 30 29 E
Rydalmere, *Syd.* 19 A3 33 48 S 151 2 E
Rydboholm, *Stock.* 3 D12 59 26N 18 12 E
Ryde, *Syd.* 19 A3 33 48 S 151 6 E
Rye, *N.Y.* 23 B6 40 58N 73 40W
Rynfield, *Jobg.* 18 E10 26 9 S 28 19 E
Ryogoku, *Tōkyō* 13 B3 35 40N 139 48 E
Rysäkari, *Hels.* 3 C4 60 6N 24 50 E
Rzhevka, *St-Pet.* 11 B5 59 59N 30 31 E

Serangoon Garden 45

# S


Saadōn, Bagd. 17 F8 33 19N 44 25 E
Saarn, Ruhr 6 B3 51 24N 6 51 E
Saavedra, B.A. 32 B4 34 33 S 58 29W
Saboli, Delhi 16 A2 28 42N 77 18 E
Sabugo, Lisb. 8 F7 38 49N 9 17W
Saburovo, Mos. 11 D7 55 53N 37 15 E
Säbysjön, Stock. 3 D10 59 26N 17 52 E
Sabzi Mandi, Delhi 16 A2 28 40N 77 12 E
Sacavém, Lisb. 8 F8 38 47N 9 5W
Saclay, Paris 5 C3 48 43N 2 10 E
Saclay, Étang de, Paris 5 C2 48 44N 2 9 E
Sacoma, S. Pau. 31 E6 23 36 S 46 35W
Sacré-Coeur, Paris 5 B4 48 53N 2 20 E
Sacrow, Berl. 7 B1 52 25N 13 6 E
Sacrower See, Berl. 7 B1 52 26N 13 6 E
Sadang, Sŏul 12 H7 37 29N 126 58 E
Sadar Bazar, Delhi 16 B2 28 39N 77 11 E
Saddām City, Bagd. 17 E8 33 23N 44 27 E
Saddle Brook, N.Y. 22 B4 40 53N 74 5W
Saddle River, N.Y. 22 A4 41 1N 74 6W
Saddle Rock, N.Y. 23 C6 40 47N 73 45W
Sadr, Kar. 17 G11 24 51N 67 2 E
Sadyba, Wsaw. 10 E7 52 11N 21 3 E
Saedo, Tōkyō 13 C2 35 30N 139 33 E
Saensaep, Khlong →, Bangk. 15 B2 13 44N 100 32 E
Sáenz Pena, B.A. 32 B3 34 37 S 58 32W
Safdar Jang Airport, Delhi 16 B2 28 35N 77 12 E
Safdar Jangs Tomb, Delhi 16 B2 28 35N 77 12 E
Safraköy, Ist. 17 A1 41 0N 28 48 E
Saft el Laban, El Qâ. 18 C5 30 1N 31 10 E
Sag Bridge, Chic. 26 C1 41 41N 87 55W
Sagamore Neck, N.Y. 23 B8 40 53N 73 29W
Saganashkee Slough, Chic. 26 C1 41 41N 87 53W
Sagene, Oslo 2 B4 59 55N 10 46 E
Sagrada Família, Temple de, Barc. 8 D6 41 24N 2 10 E
Sahapur, Calc. 16 E5 22 31N 88 11 E
Sahibabad, Delhi 16 A1 28 45N 77 4 E
Sai Kung, H.K. 12 D6 22 22N 114 16 E
Sai Wan Ho, H.K. 12 E6 22 17N 114 12 E
Sai Ying Pun, H.K. 12 E5 22 17N 114 8 E
Saido, Tōkyō 13 A2 35 52N 139 39 E
Sailmouille →, Paris 5 D3 48 37N 2 17 E
St. Albans, N.Y. 23 C6 40 42N 73 44W
St. Andrä, Wien 10 G9 48 19N 16 12 E
St. Andrews, Jobg. 18 E9 26 9 S 28 7 E
St. Aubin, Paris 5 C2 48 44N 2 8 E
St. Augustin, Mtrl. 20 A2 43 37N 73 58W
St. Basil's Cathedral, Mos. 11 E9 55 45N 37 38 E
St.-Benoit, Paris 5 C1 48 40N 1 54 E
St.-Brice-sous-Forêt, Paris 5 A4 49 0N 2 21 E
St.-Cloud, Paris 5 B3 48 50N 2 12 E
St.-Cyr-l'École, Paris 5 C2 48 47N 2 4 E
St.-Cyr-l'École, Aérodrome de, Paris 5 C2 48 48N 2 4 E
St. Davids, Phil. 24 A2 40 2N 75 23W
St.-Denis, Paris 5 B4 48 56N 2 20 E
St. Eustache, Mtrl. 20 A2 43 33N 73 54W
St.-Forget, Paris 5 C2 48 42N 2 0 E
St. Georg, Hbg. 7 D8 53 33N 10 1 E
St.-Germain, Forêt de, Paris 5 B2 48 57N 2 5 E
St. Germain-en-Laye, Paris 5 B2 48 53N 2 4 E
St.-Germain-lès-Corbeil, Paris 5 D4 48 37N 2 29 E
St.-Gratien, Paris 5 B3 48 58N 2 17 E
St. Helier, Lon. 4 C3 51 23N 0 11W
St.-Hubert, Mtrl. 20 B5 43 29N 73 25W
St. Isaac's Cathedral, St-Pet. 11 B3 59 55N 30 19 E
St. Jacques →, Mtrl. 20 B5 43 26N 73 29W
St.-Jean-de-Beauregard, Paris 5 D3 48 39N 2 10 E
St.-Jean-de-dieu, Mtrl. 20 A4 43 34N 73 31W
St. Joseph-du-Lac, Mtrl. 20 A1 43 32N 74 0W
St. Katherine's Dock, Lon. 4 B4 51 30N 0 5W
St. Kilda, Melb. 19 F6 37 51 S 144 58 E
St. Lambert, Mtrl. 20 A5 43 29N 73 29W
St.-Lambert, Paris 5 C2 48 43N 2 1 E
St.-Laurent, Mtrl. 20 A3 43 30N 73 43W
St. Lawrence, Mtrl. 20 A5 43 26N 73 29W
St.-Lazare, Gare, Paris 5 B3 48 52N 2 19 E
St.-Léonard, Mtrl. 20 A4 43 35N 73 34W
St. Leonards, Syd. 19 B4 33 50 S 151 12 E
St. Leu-la-Forêt, Paris 5 A3 49 1N 2 14 E
St.-Louis, L., Mtrl. 20 B3 43 24N 73 48W
St. Magelungen, Stock. 3 E11 59 13N 18 4 E
St.-Mandé, Paris 5 B4 48 50N 2 24 E
St.-Mard, Paris 5 A6 49 2N 2 41 E
St.-Martin, Mtrl. 20 A3 43 33N 73 45W
St.-Martin, Bois, Paris 5 C5 48 48N 2 35 E
St. Mary Cray, Lon. 4 C5 51 23N 0 7 E
St.-Maur-des-Fossés, Paris 5 C4 48 48N 2 29 E
St.-Maurice, Paris 5 C4 48 49N 2 24 E
St.-Mesmes, Paris 5 B6 48 59N 2 41 E
St. Michaeliskirche, Hbg. 7 D7 53 32N 9 59 E
St. Michael's, Sing. 15 G8 1 19N 103 51 E
St.-Michel, Mtrl. 20 A4 43 34N 73 37W
St.-Michel-sur-Orge, Paris 5 D3 48 38N 2 18 E
St. Nikolaus-Kirken, Pra. 10 B2 50 5N 14 23 E
St. Nom-la-Bretêche, Paris 5 B2 48 51N 2 1 E
St.-Ouen, Paris 5 B4 48 56N 2 20 E
St. Ouen-l'Aumône, Paris 5 A2 49 2N 2 6 E
St. Pauli, Hbg. 7 D7 53 33N 9 57 E
St. Pauls Cathedral, Lon. 4 B4 51 30N 0 5W
St. Paul's Cray, Lon. 4 C5 51 23N 0 6 E
St. Petersburg, St-Pet. 11 B3 59 55N 30 15 E
St.-Pierre, Mtrl. 20 B4 43 27N 73 38W
St. Prix, Paris 5 A3 49 0N 2 15 E
St.-Quentin, Étang de, Paris 5 C2 48 47N 2 0 E
St. Quentin-en-Yvelines, Paris 5 C1 48 46N 1 57 E
St.-Rémy-lès-Chevreuse, Paris 5 C2 48 42N 2 4 E
St.-Thibault-des-Vignes, Paris 5 B6 48 52N 2 41 E
St. Veit, Wien 10 G9 48 11N 16 16 E
St.-Vincent-de-Paul, Mtrl. 20 A4 43 36N 73 39W
Ste.-Anne-de-Bellevue, Mtrl. 20 B2 43 24N 73 55W
Ste.-Catherine, Mtrl. 20 B4 43 24N 73 34W
Ste.-Dorothée, Mtrl. 20 A3 43 31N 73 48W
Ste.-Gemme, Paris 5 B1 48 52N 1 59 E
Ste.-Geneviève, Mtrl. 20 B2 43 28N 73 51W
Ste.-Geneviève-des-Bois, Paris 5 D3 48 38N 2 19 E
Ste.-Hélène, Î., Mtrl. 20 A4 43 31N 73 32W
Ste. Marthe-sur-le-Lac, Mtrl. 20 A2 43 31N 73 56W
Ste.-Rose, Mtrl. 20 A3 43 37N 73 46W
Ste. Thérèse, Mtrl. 20 A3 43 38N 73 49W
Ste. Thérèse-Ouest, Mtrl. 20 A2 43 36N 73 50W
Saiwai, Tōkyō 13 C3 35 32N 139 41 E
Sakai, Ōsaka 12 C3 34 34N 135 27 E
Sakai →, Tōkyō 13 D1 35 27N 139 29 E
Sakai Harbour, Ōsaka 12 C3 34 36N 135 26 E
Sakanoshita, Tōkyō 13 B2 35 48N 139 30 E
Sakra, P., Sing. 15 G7 1 15N 103 41 E
Sakuragi, Tōkyō 13 D2 35 28N 139 38 E
Salam, Bagd. 17 E8 33 20N 44 20 E
Salaryevo, Mos. 11 F8 55 37N 37 25 E
Salem, Bost. 21 B4 42 30N 70 54W
Salem, Stock. 3 E9 59 13N 17 46 E
Salem Harbor, Bost. 21 B4 42 30N 70 52W
Salem Maritime Nat. Hist. Site, Bost. 21 B4 42 31N 70 52W
Salemstaden, Stock. 3 E9 59 13N 17 46 E
Salkhia, Calc. 16 E6 22 36N 88 21 E
Salmannsdorf, Wien 10 G9 48 14N 16 14 E
Salmdorf, Mün. 7 G11 48 7N 11 43 E
Salmedina, Mdrd. 8 C3 40 18N 3 35W
Salomea, Wsaw. 10 E6 52 11N 20 55 E
Salsette I., Bomb. 16 G8 19 2N 72 53 E
Salt Cr. →, Chic. 26 C1 41 51N 87 54W
Salt Cr. →, Melb. 19 E7 37 45 S 145 4 E
Salt Water L., Calc. 16 E6 22 33N 88 26 E
Saltholm, Købn. 2 E11 55 38N 12 46 E
Saltsjö-Duvnäs, Stock. 3 E12 59 18N 18 12 E
Saltsjöbaden, Stock. 3 E12 59 16N 18 18 E
Saltykovka, Mos. 11 E11 55 45N 37 54 E
Salvatorkirche, Ruhr 6 B2 51 26N 6 45 E
Sam Sen, Khlong →, Bangk. 15 B2 13 45N 100 33 E
Samatya, Ist. 17 B2 40 59N 28 55 E
Samoueo, Lisb. 8 F8 38 43N 8 59W
Sampaloc, Manila 15 D3 14 36N 120 59 E
Samphanthawong, Bangk. 15 B2 13 44N 100 31 E
Samrong, Bangk. 15 C2 13 39N 100 35 E
Samseon, Sŏul 12 G8 37 34N 127 0 E
San Agustin, Lima 30 G8 12 1 S 77 9W
San Agustin Atlapulco, Méx. 29 B4 19 23N 89 57 E
San Andreas Fault, S.F. 27 D3 37 27N 122 18W
San Andreas L., S.F. 27 C2 37 35N 122 25W
San Andrés, B.A. 32 B3 34 34 S 58 33W
San Andrés, Barc. 8 D6 41 26N 2 11 E
San Andrés Ahuayucan, Méx. 29 C3 19 13N 99 7W
San Andrés Atenco, Méx. 29 A2 19 32N 99 13W
San Andrés Totoltepec, Méx. 29 C2 19 15N 99 10W
San Andrián de Besós, Barc. 8 D6 41 25N 2 13 E
San Angel, Méx. 29 B2 19 20N 99 11W
San Antonia, Manila 15 E3 14 29N 120 53 E
San Antonio de Padua, B.A. 32 C2 34 40 S 58 42W
San Augustin Ohtenco, Méx. 29 C3 19 12N 99 0W
San Bartolo Ameyalco, Méx. 29 C2 19 19N 99 16W
San Bartolomé Coatepec, Méx. 29 B2 19 23N 99 18W
San Basilio, Rome 9 F10 41 56N 12 35 E
San Bóvio, Mil. 9 E6 45 27N 9 18 E
San Bruno, S.F. 27 C2 37 36N 122 24W
San Bruno, Pt., S.F. 27 C2 37 39N 122 22W
San Bruno Mt., S.F. 27 B2 37 41N 122 26W
San Carlos, S.F. 27 C3 37 30N 122 16W
San Carlos de la Cabana, Forteresse, La Hab. 30 B2 23 8N 82 20W
San Clemente del Llobregat, Barc. 8 E4 41 19N 1 59 E
San Cristobal, Mdrd. 8 B3 40 25N 3 35W
San Cristobal, Cerro, Stgo 30 J11 33 25 S 70 38W
San Cristoforo, Mil. 9 E5 45 26N 9 9 E
San Donato Milanese, Mil. 9 E6 45 24N 9 16 E
San Felice, Tori. 9 B3 45 1N 7 46 E
San Feliu de Llobregat, Barc. 8 D5 41 22N 2 2 E
San Fernando, B.A. 32 A3 34 26 S 58 32W
San Fernando, L.A. 28 A2 34 17N 118 26W
San Fernando Airport, L.A. 28 A2 34 17N 118 25W
San Fernando de Henares, Mdrd. 8 B3 40 25N 3 31W
San Fernando Valley, L.A. 28 A1 34 12N 118 31W
San Francisco, S.F. 27 B2 37 46N 122 23W
San Francisco, Univ. of, S.F. 27 B2 37 47N 122 27W
San Francisco B., S.F. 27 C3 37 39N 122 14W
San Francisco Chimalpa, Méx. 29 B1 19 26N 99 20W
San Francisco Culhuacán, Méx. 29 C3 19 19N 99 8W
San Francisco de Paula, La Hab. 30 B3 23 3N 82 17W
San Francisco Int. Airport, S.F. 27 C2 37 37N 122 22W
San Francisco Solano, B.A. 32 C5 34 46 S 58 19W
San Francisco State Univ., S.F. 27 B2 37 43N 122 28W
San Francisco Tecoxpa, Méx. 29 C3 19 12N 99 0W
San Francisco Tlalnepantla, Méx. 29 C3 19 12N 99 8W
San Fruttuoso, Mil. 9 D6 45 34N 9 14 E
San Gabriel, L.A. 28 B4 34 5N 118 5W
San Gabriel →, L.A. 28 C4 33 53N 118 6W
San Gabriel Pk., L.A. 28 A4 34 14N 118 5W
San Giacomo, Tori. 9 A2 45 11N 7 36 E
San Gillio, Tori. 9 B2 45 8N 7 32 E
San Giórgio a Crem, Nápl. 9 J13 40 50N 14 20 E
San Giovanni a Teduccio, Nápl. 9 J12 40 49N 14 18 E
San Giuseppe Vesuviano, Nápl. 9 H13 40 50N 14 29 E
San Gregorio Atlapulco, Méx. 29 C3 19 15N 99 4W
San Isidro, B.A. 32 A3 34 28 S 58 30W
San Isidro, Lima 30 G8 12 5 S 77 2W
San Isidro, Manila 15 D4 14 38N 121 5 E
San Jerónimo Lídice, Méx. 29 C2 19 19N 99 14W
San Jerónimo Miacatlán, Méx. 29 C4 19 12N 98 59W
San Jorge, Castelo de, Lisb. 8 F8 38 42N 9 8W
San Jose Del Alamo, La Hab. 30 B3 23 6N 82 17W
San José Rio Hondo, Méx. 29 B2 19 26N 99 14W
San Juan →, Manila 15 D4 14 35N 121 0 E
San Juan de Aragón, Méx. 29 B3 19 28N 99 4W
San Juan de Aragón, Parque, Méx. 29 B3 19 27N 99 4W
San Juan de Lurigancho, Lima 30 F8 11 59 S 77 0W
San Juan de Miraflores, Lima 30 H9 12 10 S 76 58W
San Juan del Monte, Manila 15 D4 14 36N 121 1 E
San Juan Ixtacala, Méx. 29 A2 19 31N 99 10W
San Juan Ixtayopan, Méx. 29 C4 19 14N 98 59W
San Juan Toltotepec, Méx. 29 B2 19 28N 99 15W
San Juan y San Pedro Tezompa, Méx. 29 C4 19 12N 98 57W
San Just Desvern, Barc. 8 D5 41 22N 2 4 E
San Justo, B.A. 32 C3 34 40 S 58 33W
San Leandro, S.F. 27 B4 37 43N 122 9W
San Leandro B., S.F. 27 B3 37 45N 122 13W
San Leandro Cr. →, S.F. 27 B3 37 44N 122 12W
San Lorenzo, Mil. 9 D4 45 34N 8 57 E
San Lorenzo, S.F. 27 B4 37 41N 122 6W
San Lorenzo →, Méx. 29 B2 19 28N 99 17W
San Lorenzo, I., Lima 30 G7 12 6 S 77 12W
San Lorenzo Acopilco, Méx. 29 C1 19 19N 99 20 E
San Lorenzo Chimalco, Méx. 29 B4 19 24N 89 58 E
San Lorenzo Tezonco, Méx. 29 C3 19 19N 99 3W
San Lorenzo Tlacoyucan, Méx. 29 C3 19 10N 99 2W
San Lucas Xochimanca, Méx. 29 C3 19 15N 99 6W
San Luis, Lima 30 G8 12 4 S 77 0W
San Luis Tlaxialtemalco, Méx. 29 C3 19 16N 99 2W
San Marino, L.A. 28 B4 34 7N 118 5W
San Martin, Barc. 8 D6 41 24N 2 11 E
San Martin de Porras, Lima 30 G8 12 1 S 77 5W
San Martino, Tori. 9 B3 45 6N 7 47 E
San Mateo, S.F. 27 C3 37 33N 122 19W
San Mateo Cr. →, S.F. 27 C2 37 31N 122 22W
San Mateo Tecoloapan, Méx. 29 A2 19 35N 99 14W
San Mateo Xalpa, Méx. 29 C3 19 13N 99 8W
San Máuro Torinese, Tori. 9 B3 45 6N 7 45 E
San Miguel, B.A. 32 B2 34 32 S 58 43W
San Miguel, Lima 30 G8 12 5 S 77 6W
San Miguel, Manila 15 D3 14 36N 120 59 E
San Miguel, Stgo 30 J11 33 29 S 70 39W
San Miguel Ajusco, Méx. 29 C2 19 13N 99 11W
San Miguel Xicalco, Méx. 29 C3 19 13N 99 9W
San Nicholas, Manila 15 D3 14 36N 120 57 E
San Nicola, Rome 9 F9 41 58N 12 21 E
San Nicolás Totolapan, Méx. 29 C2 19 16N 99 16W
San Nicolás Viejo, Méx. 29 A1 19 31N 99 21W
San Onófrio, Rome 9 F9 41 57N 12 25 E
San Pablo, Méx. 29 B4 19 25N 89 56 E
San Pablo, S.F. 27 A2 37 57N 122 20W
San Pablo, Pt., S.F. 27 A2 37 57N 122 25W
San Pablo Cr. →, S.F. 27 A2 37 58N 122 22W
San Pablo Ostotepec, Méx. 29 C3 19 11N 99 5W
San Pablo Res., S.F. 27 A3 37 55N 122 14W
San Pablo Ridge, S.F. 27 A3 37 55N 122 15W
San Pablo Str., S.F. 27 A2 37 58N 122 25W
San Pancrázio, Tori. 9 C2 45 6N 7 32 E
San Pedro, Méx. 29 B4 19 24N 89 56 E
San Pedro, Pt., S.F. 27 C1 37 35N 122 31W
San Pedro Actopan, Méx. 29 C3 19 12N 99 4W
San Pedro Martir, Barc. 8 D5 41 23N 2 6 E
San Pedro Martir, Méx. 29 C2 19 16N 99 10W
San Pedro Zacatenco, Méx. 29 A3 19 30N 99 6W
San Pietro, Rome 9 F9 41 53N 12 27 E
San Pietro, Tori. 9 B3 45 1N 7 45 E
San Pietro a Patierno, Nápl. 9 H12 40 53N 14 17 E
San Pietro all'Olmo, Mil. 9 E5 45 29N 9 0 E
San Po Kong, H.K. 12 D6 22 20N 114 11 E
San Quentin, S.F. 27 A1 37 56N 122 27W
San Rafael, S.F. 27 A1 37 58N 122 30W
San Rafael B., S.F. 27 A2 37 57N 122 28W
San Rafael Chamapa, Méx. 29 B2 19 27N 99 15W
San Rafael Hills, L.A. 28 A3 34 10N 118 12W
San Roque, Manila 15 D4 14 37N 121 5 E
San Salvador Cuauhtenco, Méx. 29 C3 19 11N 99 8W
San Salvador de la Punta, Forteresse, La Hab. 30 B2 23 8N 82 21W
San Sebastiano al Vesúvio, Nápl. 9 H13 40 50N 14 22 E
San Siro, Mil. 9 E5 45 28N 9 7 E
San Souci, Syd. 19 B3 33 59 S 151 8 E
San Telmo, B.A. 32 B4 34 37 S 58 23W
San Vicenc dels Horts, Barc. 8 D5 41 23N 2 0 E
San Vitaliano, Nápl. 9 H13 40 55N 14 28 E
San Vito, Mil. 9 E5 45 24N 9 0 E
San Vito, Nápl. 9 J13 40 49N 14 24 E
San Vito, Tori. 9 B3 45 2N 7 41 E
Sandbakken, Oslo 2 C5 59 49N 10 54 E
Sandermosen, Oslo 2 A4 60 0N 10 48 E
Sanderstead, Lon. 4 D4 51 19N 0 4W
Sandheide, Ruhr 6 C3 51 12N 6 56 E
Sandhurst, Jobg. 18 E9 26 6 S 28 3 E
Sandown, Jobg. 18 E9 26 5 S 28 4 E
Sandown Racecourse, Lon. 4 C2 51 22N 0 21W
Sandringham, Jobg. 18 E9 26 8 S 28 6 E
Sands Point, N.Y. 23 B6 40 50N 73 43W
Sandton, Jobg. 18 E9 26 5 S 28 4 E
Sandungen, Oslo 2 B2 59 52N 10 21 E
Sandvika, Oslo 2 B3 59 53N 10 32 E
Sandy Pond, Bost. 21 C2 42 26N 71 18W
Sånga, Stock. 3 D9 59 21N 17 42 E
Sangano, Tori. 9 B1 45 1N 7 26 E
Sangenjaya, Tōkyō 13 C2 35 37N 139 39 E
Sangley Pt., Manila 15 E3 14 29N 120 54 E
Sangone →, Tori. 9 B2 45 1N 7 32 E
Sangye, Sŏul 12 G7 37 38N 127 3 E
Sankrail, Calc. 16 E5 22 33N 88 13 E
Sanlihe, Beij. 14 B2 39 53N 116 18 E
Sanlintang, Shang. 14 K11 31 9N 121 29 E
Sannois, Paris 5 B3 48 58N 2 15 E
Sanpada, Bomb. 16 G9 19 3N 73 0 E
Sans, Barc. 8 D5 41 22N 2 7 E
Sant Ambrogio, Basilica di, Mil. 9 E6 45 27N 9 10 E
Sant Boi de Llobregat, Barc. 8 D5 41 20N 2 2 E
Sant Cugat, Barc. 8 D5 41 28N 2 5 E
Santa Ana, Manila 15 D4 14 34N 121 0 E
Santa Ana Tlacotenco, Méx. 29 C4 19 11N 98 58W
Santa Bárbara, Morro de, Rio J. 31 B1 22 56 S 43 26W
Santa Catalina, B.A. 32 C4 34 47 S 58 24W
Santa Cecilia Tepetlapa, Méx. 29 C3 19 13N 99 5W
Santa Clara, Méx. 29 A3 19 33N 99 3W
Santa Coloma de Cervelló, Barc. 8 D5 41 21N 2 0 E
Santa Coloma de Gramanet, Barc. 8 D6 41 27N 2 12 E
Santa Cruz, Bomb. 16 G7 19 4N 72 51 E
Santa Cruz →, La Hab. 30 B2 23 4N 82 29W
Santa Cruz, Ilhe de, Rio J. 31 B3 22 51 S 43 7W
Santa Cruz Alcapixca, Méx. 29 C3 19 14N 99 4W
Santa Cruz Ayotusco, Méx. 29 B1 19 22N 99 21W
Santa Cruz de Olorde, Barc. 8 D5 41 25N 2 3 E
Santa Cruz Int. Airport, Bomb. 16 G8 19 5N 72 51 E
Santa Cruz Meyehualco, Méx. 29 B3 19 20N 99 2W
Santa Elena, Manila 15 D4 14 38N 121 5 E
Santa Eligênia Consolação, S. Pau. 31 E6 23 32 S 46 38W
Santa Emilia, Stgo 30 J11 33 23 S 70 39W
Santa Eulalia, Barc. 8 D6 41 25N 2 10 E
Santa Fe, La Hab. 30 B2 23 4N 82 30W
Santa Fe Flood Control Basin, L.A. 28 B5 34 7N 117 57W
Santa Fe Springs, L.A. 28 C4 33 56N 118 3W
Santa Isabel Ixtapan, Méx. 29 A4 19 35N 89 57W
Santa Julia, Stgo 30 K11 33 30 S 70 35W
Santa Lucia, Nápl. 9 J12 40 49N 14 15 E
Santa Margherita, Tori. 9 B3 45 3N 7 43 E
Santa Maria Aztahuacán, Méx. 29 B3 19 21N 99 2W
Santa Maria del Rosario, La Hab. 30 B3 23 3N 82 15W
Santa Maria Tulpetlac, Méx. 29 A3 19 34N 99 3W
Santa Martha Acatitla, Méx. 29 B3 19 21N 99 2W
Santa Monica, Car. 30 E5 10 28N 66 53W
Santa Monica, L.A. 28 B2 34 1N 118 29W
Santa Monica B., L.A. 28 C1 33 58N 118 30W
Santa Monica Mt., L.A. 28 B2 34 6N 118 29W
Santa Rosa, Lima 30 F8 11 59 S 77 5W
Santa Rosa De Locobe, Stgo 30 J11 33 25 S 70 33W
Santa Rosa Xochiac, Méx. 29 C2 19 19N 99 17W
Santa Tereza, S. Pau. 31 F6 23 40 S 46 33W
Santa Ursula Xitla, Méx. 29 C2 19 16N 99 11W
Santa Ynez Canyon →, L.A. 28 B1 34 2N 118 33W
Santahamina, Hels. 3 C5 60 8N 25 2 E
Santana, S. Pau. 31 D6 23 29 S 46 36W
Sant'Anastasia, Nápl. 9 H13 40 51N 14 24 E
Sant'Ántimo, Nápl. 9 H12 40 56N 14 14 E
Santeny, Paris 5 C5 48 43N 2 34 E
Santiago, Stgo 30 J11 33 26 S 70 40W
Santiago Acahualtepec, Méx. 29 B3 19 20N 99 0W
Santiago de Las Vegas, La Hab. 30 C2 22 58N 82 22W
Santiago Tepalcatlalpan, Méx. 29 C3 19 14N 99 8W
Santiago Tepatlaxco, Méx. 29 B1 19 28N 99 20W
Sant'Ilário, Mil. 9 D4 45 34N 8 59 E
Santo Amaro, Lisb. 8 F7 38 42N 9 11W
Santo Amaro, S. Pau. 31 E5 23 39 S 46 42W
Santo Andre, Lisb. 8 G8 38 38N 9 3W
Santo André, S. Pau. 31 E6 23 39 S 46 41W
Santo António, Qta. de, Lisb. 8 G7 38 39N 9 15W
Santo Antônio da Charneca, Lisb. 8 G8 38 37N 9 1W
Santo Niño, Manila 15 D4 14 38N 121 5 E
Santo Rosario, Manila 15 C4 14 33N 121 4 E
Santo Thomas, Univ. of, Manila 15 D3 14 36N 120 59 E
Santo Tomas, Manila 15 D4 14 33N 121 4 E
Santolan, Manila 15 D4 14 36N 121 4 E
Santos Dumont, Aéroport, Rio J. 31 B3 22 54 S 43 9W
Santos Lugares, B.A. 32 B3 34 35 S 58 35W
Santoshpur, Calc. 16 E5 22 31N 88 16 E
Santragachi, Calc. 16 E5 22 35N 88 17 E
Sanyuanli, Gzh. 14 G8 23 8N 113 14 E
São Bernardo do Campo, S. Pau. 31 F6 23 42 S 46 32W
São Caetano do Sul, S. Pau. 31 E6 23 37 S 46 34W
São Cristovão, Rio J. 31 B2 22 53 S 43 13W
São Domingos, Centro, Rio J. 31 B3 22 53 S 43 6W
São Gonçalo, Rio J. 31 B3 22 49 S 43 4W
São João Clímaco, S. Pau. 31 E6 23 37 S 46 35W
São João da Talha, Lisb. 8 F8 38 49N 9 5W
São João de Meriti, Rio J. 31 A1 22 47 S 43 18W
São Lucas, Parque, S. Pau. 31 E6 23 35 S 45 32W
São Mateus, Rio J. 31 A1 22 48 S 43 22W
São Miguel Paulista, S. Pau. 31 D7 23 29 S 46 26W
São Paulo, S. Pau. 31 E6 23 32 S 46 37W
Sapa, Calc. 16 E5 22 30N 88 15 E
Sapang Baho →, Manila 15 D4 14 33N 121 4 E
Sapateiro →, S. Pau. 31 E5 23 35 S 46 41W
Saranap, S.F. 27 A4 37 52N 122 4W
Sarandi, B.A. 32 C4 34 40 S 58 20W
Saraswati →, Calc. 16 D5 22 46N 88 15 E
Sarcelles, Paris 5 B4 48 59N 2 22 E
Sarecky →, Pra. 10 B2 50 7N 14 23 E
Sarenga, Calc. 16 E5 22 32N 88 12 E
Sarilhos Grandes, Lisb. 8 F9 38 40N 8 58W
Sarilhos Pequenos, Lisb. 8 F9 38 40N 8 58W
Sarimbun, Sing. 15 F7 1 24N 103 40 E
Saronikòs Kólpos, Ath. 8 J10 37 52N 23 38 E
Sarriá, Barc. 8 D5 41 22N 2 8 E
Sarria, Car. 30 D5 10 30N 66 53W
Sarsol, Bomb. 16 G9 19 2N 73 0 E
Sartrouville, Paris 5 B3 48 56N 2 11 E
Sasad, Bud. 10 K13 47 28N 19 0 E
Sasashita, Tōkyō 13 D2 35 23N 139 35 E
Sasel, Hbg. 7 D8 53 39N 10 7 E
Sashalom, Bud. 10 J14 47 30N 19 10 E
Saska, Wsaw. 10 E7 52 14N 21 3 E
Sassafras, Melb. 19 F9 37 52 S 145 20 E
Satalice, Pra. 10 B3 50 7N 14 34 E
Satgachi, Calc. 16 E6 22 37N 88 25 E
Satghara, Calc. 16 D6 22 43N 88 21 E
Satpukur, Calc. 16 E6 22 37N 88 24 E
Sätra, Stock. 3 E10 59 17N 17 54 E
Satsuna, Calc. 16 F5 22 28N 88 17 E
Sau Mau Ping, H.K. 12 E6 22 19N 114 13 E
Saugus, Bost. 21 C3 42 28N 71 0W
Saugus →, Bost. 21 C3 42 27N 70 58W
Saulx-les-Chartreux, Paris 5 C3 48 41N 2 16 E
Sausalito, S.F. 27 A2 37 51N 122 28W
Sausset →, Paris 5 B5 48 56N 2 28 E
Savigny-sur-Orge, Paris 5 C4 48 40N 2 21 E
Savijärvi, Hels. 3 A6 60 21N 25 19 E
Savonera, Tori. 9 B2 45 7N 7 36 E
Sawah Besar, Jak. 15 H9 6 8 S 106 49 E
Sawyer Ridge, S.F. 27 C2 37 34N 122 24W
Saxonville, Bost. 21 D1 42 19N 71 24W
Saxonwold, Jobg. 18 E9 26 9 S 28 2 E
Scarborough, Trto. 20 D9 43 44N 79 14W
Scarsdale, N.Y. 23 B6 40 58N 73 47W
Sceaux, Paris 5 C3 48 46N 2 17 E
Schalke, Ruhr 6 A4 51 33N 7 4 E
Schapenrust, Jobg. 18 F11 26 15 S 28 21 E
Scharfenberg, Berl. 7 A2 52 35N 13 15 E
Scheiblingstein, Wien 10 G9 48 16N 16 13 E
Schenefeld, Hbg. 7 D7 53 36N 9 52 E
Scherlebech, Ruhr 6 A4 51 37N 7 8 E
Schildow, Berl. 7 A3 52 38N 13 22 E
Schiller Park, Chic. 26 B1 41 56N 87 52W
Schiller Woods, Chic. 26 B1 41 57N 87 51W
Schlachtensee, Berl. 7 B2 52 26N 13 13 E
Schlossgarten, Berl. 7 A2 52 31N 13 18 E
Schmachtendorf, Ruhr 6 A2 51 32N 6 48 E
Schmargendorf, Berl. 7 B2 52 28N 13 17 E
Schmöckwitz, Berl. 7 B5 52 22N 13 38 E
Schnelsen, Hbg. 7 D7 53 38N 9 54 E
Scholven, Ruhr 6 A4 51 36N 7 0 E
Schönblick, Berl. 7 B5 52 27N 13 43 E
Schönbrunn, Schloss, Wien 10 G9 48 10N 16 19 E
Schöneberg, Berl. 7 B3 52 28N 13 20 E
Schönefeld, Berl. 7 B4 52 23N 13 30 E
Schöneiche, Berl. 7 B5 52 28N 13 41 E
Schönwalde, Berl. 7 A1 52 37N 13 7 E
Schottenwald, Wien 10 G9 48 13N 16 16 E
Schuir, Ruhr 6 B3 51 23N 6 59 E
Schulzendorf, Berl. 7 A2 52 36N 13 16 E
Schuylkill →, Phil. 24 B3 39 53N 75 11W
Schwabing, Mün. 7 G10 48 10N 11 35 E
Schwafheim, Ruhr 6 B1 51 25N 6 36 E
Schwanebeck, Berl. 7 A4 52 37N 13 32 E
Schwanenwerder, Berl. 7 B2 52 26N 13 10 E
Schwarz →, Ruhr 6 C3 51 19N 6 44 E
Schwarzbachtal, Ruhr 6 C3 51 17N 6 51 E
Schwarze, Ruhr 6 A2 51 31N 6 48 E
Schwarze Berge, Hbg. 7 E7 53 27N 9 54 E
Schwarzlackenau, Wien 10 G10 48 16N 16 23 E
Schwechat, Wien 10 H10 48 8N 16 28 E
Schweflinghaüsen, Ruhr 6 C6 51 15N 7 24 E
Schwelm, Ruhr 6 C5 51 16N 7 16 E
Scisciano, Nápl. 9 H13 40 54N 14 28 E
Scoresby, Melb. 19 F8 37 54 S 145 14 E
Scotch Plains, N.Y. 22 D2 40 39N 74 22W
Scotts Level Br. →, Balt. 25 A2 39 23N 76 45W
Sea Cliff, N.Y. 23 B7 40 50N 73 38W
Seabrook, Wash. 25 D9 38 58N 76 49W
Seacliff, S.F. 27 B2 37 47N 122 28W
Seaforth, Syd. 19 A4 33 48 S 151 15 E
Seagate, N.Y. 22 D4 40 34N 74 0W
Seal Slough, S.F. 27 C3 37 34N 122 17W
Sears Tower, Chic. 26 B3 41 52N 87 38W
Seat Pleasant, Wash. 25 D8 38 53N 76 53W
Seavey Hill, Bost. 21 A1 42 42N 71 23W
Šeberov, Pra. 10 B3 50 0N 14 30 E
Secaucus, N.Y. 22 C4 40 47N 74 3W
Secondigliano, Nápl. 9 H12 40 53N 14 15 E
Seddinsee, Berl. 7 B5 52 23N 13 41 E
Sedgefield, N.Y. 22 B2 40 51N 74 26W
Sedriano, Mil. 9 E4 45 29N 8 58 E
Seeberg, Berl. 7 A5 52 33N 13 41 E
Seeburg, Berl. 7 A1 52 30N 13 7 E
Seefeld, Berl. 7 A5 52 37N 13 40 E
Seegefeld, Berl. 7 A1 52 33N 13 5 E
Seehof, Berl. 7 B2 52 24N 13 17 E
Segeltorp, Stock. 3 E10 59 16N 17 56 E
Segrate, Mil. 9 E6 45 29N 9 17 E
Seguro, Mil. 9 E5 45 28N 9 5 E
Seine →, Paris 5 C4 48 48N 2 25 E
Seixal, Lisb. 8 G8 38 38N 9 5W
Selbeck, Ruhr 6 B3 51 22N 6 51 E
Selbecke, Ruhr 6 C6 51 20N 7 28 E
Selby, Jobg. 18 F9 26 12 S 28 2 E
Seletar, P., Sing. 15 F8 1 26N 103 51 E
Seletar, Sungei →, Sing. 15 F8 1 25N 103 51 E
Seletar Hills, Sing. 15 F8 1 23N 103 52 E
Seletar Res., Sing. 15 F7 1 24N 103 48 E
Selghar, Bomb. 16 H9 18 57N 73 1 E
Selhurst, Lon. 4 C4 51 23N 0 5W
Selsdon, Lon. 4 C4 51 20N 0 3W
Selytsy, St-Pet. 11 B6 59 56N 30 42 E
Sembawang, Sing. 15 F7 1 26N 103 48 E
Sembawang, Sungei →, Sing. 15 F7 1 25N 103 48 E
Sembawang Hill, Sing. 15 F7 1 22N 103 49 E
Semsvatn, Oslo 2 B2 59 51N 10 25 E
Senago, Mil. 9 D5 45 34N 9 7 E
Senan, Jak. 15 J10 6 10 S 106 50 E
Sénart, Forêt de, Paris 5 D4 48 40N 2 28 E
Senayan Sports Centre, Jak. 15 J9 6 12 S 106 47 E
Sendling, Mün. 7 G10 48 7N 11 31 E
Sengeløse, Købn. 2 D8 55 40N 12 14 E
Senju, Tōkyō 13 B3 35 44N 139 48 E
Senlikköy, Ist. 17 B1 40 58N 28 47 E
Senlisse, Paris 5 C1 48 41N 1 59 E
Senneville, Mtrl. 20 B2 43 24N 73 57W
Senri, Ōsaka 12 B4 34 49N 135 30 E
Senriyama, Ōsaka 12 B4 34 47N 135 30 E
Sentosa, Sing. 15 G7 1 15N 103 49 E
Sentosa, P., Sing. 15 G7 1 15N 103 49 E
Seo Dae Mun, Sŏul 12 G7 37 34N 126 55 E
Seobinngo, Sŏul 12 G7 37 31N 126 58 E
Seoggwan, Sŏul 12 G8 37 35N 127 2 E
Seong Bug, Sŏul 12 G7 37 35N 127 0 E
Seong Dong, Sŏul 12 G8 37 33N 127 3 E
Seongsu, Sŏul 12 G8 37 32N 127 3 E
Seoul = Sŏul, Sŏul 12 G8 37 34N 127 51 E
Seoul National Univ., Sŏul 12 H7 37 28N 126 57 E
Seoul Tower, Sŏul 12 G7 37 32N 126 59 E
Sepah Salar Mosque, Tehr. 17 C5 35 40N 51 25 E
Sepolia, Ath. 8 H11 38 1N 23 42 E
Sepulveda, L.A. 28 A2 34 13N 118 27W
Sepulveda Flood Control Basin, L.A. 28 A2 34 10N 118 28W
Serangoon, P., Sing. 15 F8 1 23N 103 55 E
Serangoon, Sungei →, Sing. 15 F8 1 23N 103 55 E
Serangoon Garden, Sing. 15 F8 1 21N 103 51 E

46 Serangoon Harbour


| | | | |
|---|---|---|---|
| Serangoon Harbour, *Sing.* | **15 F8** | 1 23N | 103 57 E |
| Seraya, P., *Sing.* | **15 G7** | 1 16N | 103 43 E |
| Serebryanka, *Mos.* | **11 E11** | 55 44N | 37 53 E |
| Serebryanka →, *Mos.* | **11 E10** | 55 47N | 37 44 E |
| Serednevo, *Mos.* | **11 F7** | 55 35N | 37 18 E |
| Serramonte, *S.F.* | **27 C2** | 37 39N | 122 28W |
| Servon, *Paris* | **5 C5** | 48 43N | 2 35 E |
| Šestajovice, *Pra.* | **10 B3** | 50 6N | 14 40 E |
| Sesto San Giovanni, *Mil.* | **9 D6** | 45 31N | 9 13 E |
| Seta Budi, *Jak.* | **15 J9** | 6 12 S | 106 49 E |
| Setagaya-Ku, *Tōkyō* | **13 C2** | 35 37N | 139 36 E |
| Sete Pontes, *Rio J.* | **31 B3** | 22 50 S | 43 4W |
| Seter, *Oslo* | **2 B4** | 59 52N | 10 47 E |
| Séttimo Milanese, *Mil.* | **9 E5** | 45 28N | 9 3 E |
| Séttimo Torinese, *Tori.* | **9 B3** | 45 8N | 7 46 E |
| Settsu, *Ōsaka* | **12 B4** | 34 47N | 135 33 E |
| Setuny →, *Mos.* | **11 E8** | 55 43N | 37 21 E |
| Seurasaari, *Hels.* | **3 B4** | 60 11N | 24 53 E |
| Seutula, *Hels.* | **3 A4** | 60 20N | 24 52 E |
| Seven Corners, *Wash.* | **25 D7** | 38 53N | 77 9W |
| Seven Kings, *Lon.* | **4 B5** | 51 33N | 0 5 E |
| Sevenoaks, *Lon.* | **4 D6** | 51 16N | 0 11 E |
| Severn Hills, *Syd.* | **19 A2** | 33 46 S | 150 57 E |
| Sévesco →, *Mil.* | **9 D5** | 45 35N | 9 9 E |
| Sevran, *Paris* | **5 B5** | 48 56N | 2 31 E |
| Sèvres, *Paris* | **5 C3** | 48 49N | 2 13 E |
| Sewaren, *N.Y.* | **22 D3** | 40 33N | 74 15W |
| Sewell, *Phil.* | **24 C4** | 39 46N | 75 8W |
| Sewri, *Bomb.* | **16 H8** | 18 59N | 72 50 E |
| Seya, *Tōkyō* | **13 D1** | 35 28N | 139 28 E |
| Sforzesso, Castello, *Mil.* | **9 E6** | 45 28N | 9 10 E |
| Sha Kok Mei, *H.K.* | **12 D6** | 22 23N | 114 16 E |
| Sha Tin, *H.K.* | **12 D6** | 22 23N | 114 11 E |
| Sha Tin Wai, *H.K.* | **12 D6** | 22 22N | 114 11 E |
| Shaala, *Bagd.* | **17 E7** | 33 22N | 44 16 E |
| Shabanzhuang, *Beij.* | **14 B3** | 39 51N | 116 25 E |
| Shabbona Woods, *Chic.* | **26 D3** | 41 36N | 87 33W |
| Shabrâmant, *El Qâ.* | **18 D5** | 29 56N | 31 11 E |
| Shadipur, *Delhi* | **16 B2** | 28 38N | 77 11 E |
| Shady Oak, *Wash.* | **25 C6** | 39 1N | 77 17W |
| Shahabad, *Bomb.* | **16 G9** | 19 0N | 73 2 E |
| Shahar, *Bomb.* | **16 G8** | 19 5N | 72 52 E |
| Shahdara, *Delhi* | **16 A2** | 28 40N | 77 18 E |
| Shahe, *Gzh.* | **14 G8** | 23 9N | 113 19 E |
| Shahpur Jel, *Delhi* | **16 B2** | 28 33N | 77 12 E |
| Shahr-e-Rey, *Tehr.* | **17 D5** | 35 36N | 51 25 E |
| Shaikh Aomar, *Bagd.* | **17 E8** | 33 20N | 44 23 E |
| Shakarpor Khas, *Delhi* | **16 B2** | 28 37N | 77 14 E |
| Shakurpur, *Delhi* | **16 A1** | 28 40N | 77 8 E |
| Sham Shui Po, *H.K.* | **12 E5** | 22 19N | 114 9 E |
| Shamepur, *Delhi* | **16 A1** | 28 44N | 77 8 E |
| Shamian, *Gzh.* | **14 G8** | 23 6N | 113 13 E |
| Shamspur, *Delhi* | **16 B2** | 28 36N | 77 17 E |
| Shan Liu, *H.K.* | **12 D6** | 22 23N | 114 16 E |
| Shan Mei, *H.K.* | **12 D6** | 22 24N | 114 10 E |
| Shanghai, *Shang.* | **14 J12** | 31 14N | 121 28 E |
| Shanghetou, *Tianj.* | **14 D5** | 39 11N | 117 0 E |
| Shanjing, *Gzh.* | **14 G9** | 23 4N | 113 23 E |
| Sharea Faisal, *Kar.* | **17 G11** | 24 52N | 67 8 E |
| Sharon Hill, *Phil.* | **24 B3** | 39 54N | 75 16W |
| Sharp I., *H.K.* | **12 D6** | 22 21N | 114 17 E |
| Sharp Park, *S.F.* | **27 C2** | 37 38N | 122 29W |
| Shau Kei Wan, *H.K.* | **12 E6** | 22 16N | 114 13 E |
| Shawocun, *Beij.* | **14 B2** | 39 53N | 116 13 E |
| Shawsheen Village, *Bost.* | **21 A3** | 42 40N | 71 7W |
| Shea Stadium, *N.Y.* | **23 C5** | 40 45N | 73 50W |
| Sheakhala, *Calc.* | **16 D5** | 22 45N | 88 10 E |
| Shebāb, *Bagd.* | **17 E8** | 33 20N | 44 26 E |
| Sheepshead B., *N.Y.* | **22 D5** | 40 35N | 73 55W |
| Shek Hang, *H.K.* | **12 D6** | 22 24N | 114 17 E |
| Shek Kip Mei, *H.K.* | **12 D5** | 22 20N | 114 9 E |
| Shek Lung Kung, *H.K.* | **12 D5** | 22 23N | 114 5 E |
| Shek O, *H.K.* | **12 E6** | 22 13N | 114 15 E |
| Shellpot Cr. →, *Phil.* | **24 C1** | 39 44N | 75 30W |
| Shelter Cove, *S.F.* | **27 C1** | 37 35N | 122 30W |
| Shelter I., *H.K.* | **12 E6** | 22 19N | 114 17 E |
| Shemirānāt, *Tehr.* | **17 C5** | 35 47N | 51 25 E |
| Shenfield, *Lon.* | **4 B6** | 51 37N | 0 19 E |
| Sheng Fa Shan, *H.K.* | **12 D5** | 22 23N | 114 5 E |
| Shenley, *Lon.* | **4 A3** | 51 41N | 0 16W |
| Shepherds Bush, *Lon.* | **4 B3** | 51 30N | 0 13W |
| Shepperton, *Lon.* | **4 C2** | 51 23N | 0 26W |
| Sherborn, *Bost.* | **21 D1** | 42 14N | 71 22W |
| Sherman Oaks, *L.A.* | **28 B2** | 34 8N | 118 29W |
| Sherwood Forest, *S.F.* | **27 A3** | 37 57N | 122 16W |
| Shet Bandar, *Bomb.* | **16 H8** | 18 57N | 72 55 E |
| Sheung Lau Wan, *H.K.* | **12 E6** | 22 16N | 114 16 E |
| Sheung Wan, *H.K.* | **12 E5** | 22 16N | 114 9 E |
| Sheva, *Bomb.* | **16 H8** | 18 56N | 72 57 E |
| Sheva Nhava, *Bomb.* | **16 H8** | 18 57N | 72 57 E |
| Shiba, *Tōkyō* | **13 C3** | 35 38N | 139 45 E |
| Shiba →, *Tōkyō* | **13 A3** | 35 50N | 139 44 E |
| Shibuya-Ku, *Tōkyō* | **13 C3** | 35 39N | 139 41 E |
| Shijōnawate, *Ōsaka* | **12 B4** | 34 44N | 135 37 E |
| Shimo-okudomi, *Tōkyō* | **13 A1** | 35 52N | 139 27 E |
| Shimo-tsuchidana, *Tōkyō* | **13 D1** | 35 24N | 139 27 E |
| Shimogawara, *Tōkyō* | **13 C1** | 35 39N | 139 27 E |
| Shimosalo, *Tōkyō* | **13 B2** | 35 45N | 139 31 E |
| Shimosasame, *Tōkyō* | **13 B2** | 35 48N | 139 37 E |
| Shimoshakujii, *Tōkyō* | **13 B2** | 35 43N | 139 35 E |
| Shimotomi, *Tōkyō* | **13 B1** | 35 49N | 139 27 E |
| Shimotsuruma, *Tōkyō* | **13 D1** | 35 29N | 139 26 E |
| Shimura, *Tōkyō* | **13 B3** | 35 46N | 139 41 E |
| Shinagawa B., *Tōkyō* | **13 C3** | 35 35N | 139 48 E |
| Shinagawa-Ku, *Tōkyō* | **13 C3** | 35 36N | 139 44 E |
| Shing Mun Res., *H.K.* | **12 D5** | 22 23N | 114 8 E |
| Shinjuku-Ku, *Tōkyō* | **13 B3** | 35 41N | 139 42 E |
| Shinkoiwa, *Tōkyō* | **13 B4** | 35 43N | 139 51 E |
| Shinnakano, *Tōkyō* | **13 B3** | 35 41N | 139 40 E |
| Shinoha, *Tōkyō* | **13 A3** | 35 50N | 139 49 E |
| Shipai, *Gzh.* | **14 G9** | 23 8N | 113 20 E |
| Shipley, *Balt.* | **25 B3** | 39 12N | 76 39W |
| Shippan Pt., *N.Y.* | **23 A7** | 41 1N | 73 31W |
| Shirako, *Tōkyō* | **13 B2** | 35 47N | 139 36 E |
| Shiraone, *Bomb.* | **16 G9** | 19 2N | 73 1 E |
| Shirinashi →, *Ōsaka* | **12 C3** | 34 38N | 135 27 E |
| Shirley, *Lon.* | **4 C4** | 51 22N | 0 2W |
| Shiro, *Tōkyō* | **13 B2** | 35 48N | 139 30 E |
| Shirogane, *Tōkyō* | **13 C3** | 35 37N | 139 44 E |
| Shisha Hai, *Beij.* | **14 B3** | 39 55N | 116 21 E |
| Shitou, *Gzh.* | **14 G9** | 23 1N | 113 23 E |
| Shiweitang, *Gzh.* | **14 G8** | 23 6N | 113 12 E |
| Shogunle, *Lagos* | **18 A2** | 6 34N | 7 20 E |
| Shomolu, *Lagos* | **18 A2** | 6 32N | 7 22 E |
| Shooters Hill, *Lon.* | **4 C5** | 51 28N | 0 4 E |
| Shoreditch, *Lon.* | **4 B4** | 51 31N | 0 4W |
| Shoreham, *Lon.* | **4 D6** | 51 19N | 0 10 E |
| Short Hills, *N.Y.* | **22 C2** | 40 44N | 74 21W |
| Shortlands, *Lon.* | **4 C5** | 51 23N | 0 0 E |
| Shrirampur, *Calc.* | **16 D5** | 22 45N | 88 21 E |
| Shuangkou, *Tianj.* | **14 D5** | 39 14N | 117 2 E |
| Shuangtuo, *Tianj.* | **14 D6** | 39 13N | 117 19 E |
| Shubrâ el Kheima, *El Qâ.* | **18 C5** | 30 6N | 31 14 E |
| Shuikuo, *Gzh.* | **14 F8** | 23 10N | 113 10 E |
| Shuishang Gongyuan, *Tianj.* | **14 E5** | 39 5N | 117 9 E |
| Shukunoshō, *Ōsaka* | **12 A4** | 34 50N | 135 31 E |
| Sibbo, *Hels.* | **3 A6** | 60 21N | 25 14 E |
| Sibbo fjärden, *Hels.* | **3 B6** | 60 11N | 25 17 E |
| Siboney, *La Hab.* | **30 B2** | 23 4N | 82 28W |
| Sibpur, *Calc.* | **16 E5** | 22 34N | 88 19 E |
| Sibřina, *Pra.* | **10 B4** | 50 3N | 14 40 E |
| Sidcup, *Lon.* | **4 C5** | 51 25N | 0 6 E |
| Siebenhirten, *Wien* | **10 H9** | 48 8N | 16 17 E |
| Siedlung, *Berl.* | **7 A1** | 52 35N | 13 7 E |
| Siekierki, *Wsaw.* | **10 E7** | 52 12N | 21 4 E |
| Sielce, *Wsaw.* | **10 E7** | 52 12N | 21 2 E |
| Siemensstadt, *Berl.* | **7 A2** | 52 32N | 13 16 E |
| Sieraków, *Wsaw.* | **10 E5** | 52 19N | 20 48 E |
| Sierra Madre, *L.A.* | **28 B4** | 34 9N | 118 3W |
| Sievering, *Wien* | **10 G10** | 48 15N | 16 20 E |
| Siggerud, *Oslo* | **2 C5** | 59 47N | 10 52 E |
| Siheung, *Sŏul* | **12 H7** | 37 28N | 126 54 E |
| Siikajärvi, *Hels.* | **3 B2** | 60 17N | 24 31 E |
| Sikátorpuszta, *Bud.* | **10 J14** | 47 34N | 19 10 E |
| Silampur, *Delhi* | **16 B2** | 28 39N | 77 16 E |
| Silschede, *Ruhr* | **6 B6** | 51 21N | 7 22 E |
| Silver Hill, *Wash.* | **25 E8** | 38 49N | 76 55W |
| Silver L., *Bost.* | **21 B3** | 42 33N | 71 9W |
| Silver Mt., *L.A.* | **28 A5** | 34 12N | 117 55W |
| Silver Spring, *Wash.* | **25 D7** | 38 59N | 77 2W |
| Silverfields, *Jobg.* | **18 E7** | 26 7 S | 27 49 E |
| Silvertown, *Lon.* | **4 C5** | 51 29N | 0 1 E |
| Simla, *Calc.* | **16 E6** | 22 35N | 88 22 E |
| Simmer and Jack Mines, *Jobg.* | **18 F9** | 26 12 S | 28 8 E |
| Simmering, *Wien* | **10 G10** | 48 10N | 16 24 E |
| Simmering Heide, *Wien* | **10 G10** | 48 10N | 16 26 E |
| Simonkylä, *Hels.* | **3 B5** | 60 18N | 25 1 E |
| Simpang Bedok, *Sing.* | **15 G8** | 1 19N | 103 56 E |
| Simsalö, *Hels.* | **3 B6** | 60 14N | 25 17 E |
| Singao, *N.Y.* | **22 B3** | 40 53N | 74 14W |
| Singapore, *Sing.* | **15 G8** | 1 17N | 103 51 E |
| Singapore →, *Sing.* | **15 G8** | 1 17N | 103 51 E |
| Singapore, Univ. of, *Sing.* | **15 G7** | 1 19N | 103 49 E |
| Singapore Airport, *Sing.* | **15 F8** | 1 21N | 103 54 E |
| Singlewell, *Lon.* | **4 C7** | 51 25N | 0 21 E |
| Singur, *Calc.* | **16 D5** | 22 48N | 88 13 E |
| Sinicka →, *Mos.* | **11 D7** | 55 52N | 37 18 E |
| Sinki, Selat, *Sing.* | **15 G7** | 1 15N | 103 42 E |
| Sinrim, *Sŏul* | **12 H7** | 37 28N | 126 56 E |
| Sinsa, *Sŏul* | **12 G8** | 37 31N | 127 0 E |
| Sinthi, *Calc.* | **16 E6** | 22 37N | 88 23 E |
| Sinweol, *Sŏul* | **12 G7** | 37 31N | 126 51 E |
| Sipoo, *Hels.* | **3 A6** | 60 21N | 25 14 E |
| Sipoon selkä, *Hels.* | **3 B6** | 60 11N | 25 17 E |
| Sipson, *Lon.* | **4 C2** | 51 29N | 0 26W |
| Siqeil, *El Qâ.* | **18 C4** | 30 7N | 31 10 E |
| Şişli, *Ist.* | **17 A2** | 41 3N | 28 58 E |
| Skå, *Stock.* | **3 E9** | 59 19N | 17 44 E |
| Skärholmen, *Stock.* | **3 E10** | 59 16N | 17 53 E |
| Skarpäng, *Stock.* | **3 D11** | 59 26N | 18 0 E |
| Skarpnäck, *Stock.* | **3 E11** | 59 16N | 18 7 E |
| Skarpö, *Stock.* | **3 D13** | 59 24N | 18 22 E |
| Skedsmo, *Oslo* | **2 B6** | 59 59N | 11 2 E |
| Skhodnya →, *Mos.* | **11 D8** | 55 53N | 37 23 E |
| Skodsborg, *Købn.* | **2 D10** | 55 49N | 12 34 E |
| Skogby, *Hels.* | **3 A2** | 60 21N | 24 40 E |
| Skogen, *Oslo* | **2 C1** | 59 48N | 10 18 E |
| Skogsbyn, *Hels.* | **3 A6** | 60 20N | 25 18 E |
| Skokie, *Chic.* | **26 A2** | 42 2N | 87 43W |
| Skokie →, *Chic.* | **26 A2** | 42 3N | 87 46W |
| Skokie Lagoons, *Chic.* | **26 A2** | 42 7N | 87 46W |
| Skoklefall, *Oslo* | **2 B4** | 59 50N | 10 40 E |
| Sköndal, *Stock.* | **3 E11** | 59 15N | 18 6 E |
| Skovlunde, *Købn.* | **2 D9** | 55 42N | 12 25 E |
| Skovshoved, *Købn.* | **2 D10** | 55 45N | 12 35 E |
| Skøyen, *Oslo* | **2 B4** | 59 55N | 10 40 E |
| Skui, *Oslo* | **2 B2** | 59 55N | 10 25 E |
| Skuldelev, *Købn.* | **2 D7** | 55 46N | 12 1 E |
| Skullerud, *Oslo* | **2 B5** | 59 51N | 10 50 E |
| Skuru, *Stock.* | **3 E12** | 59 18N | 18 12 E |
| Skytta, *Oslo* | **2 B5** | 59 59N | 10 54 E |
| Slade Green, *Lon.* | **4 C6** | 51 27N | 0 11 E |
| Slagsta, *Stock.* | **3 E9** | 59 15N | 17 48 E |
| Slakteren, *Oslo* | **2 A4** | 60 1N | 10 40 E |
| Slattum, *Oslo* | **2 A5** | 60 0N | 10 55 E |
| Slemmestad, *Oslo* | **2 C2** | 59 46N | 10 29 E |
| Slependen, *Oslo* | **2 B3** | 59 52N | 10 30 E |
| Sligo Cr. →, *Wash.* | **25 C7** | 39 0N | 77 1W |
| Slipi, *Jak.* | **15 J9** | 6 11 S | 106 47 E |
| Slipi Orchard Garden, *Jak.* | **15 J9** | 6 10 S | 106 46 E |
| Slivenec, *Pra.* | **10 B2** | 50 1N | 14 21 E |
| Slone Canyon Res., *L.A.* | **28 B2** | 34 6N | 118 27W |
| Sloop Channel, *N.Y.* | **23 D7** | 40 36N | 73 31W |
| Sluhy, *Pra.* | **10 A3** | 50 11N | 14 33 E |
| Służew, *Wsaw.* | **10 E7** | 52 10N | 21 1 E |
| Służewiec, *Wsaw.* | **10 E7** | 52 10N | 21 0 E |
| Smalleytown, *N.Y.* | **22 D2** | 40 39N | 74 28W |
| Smestad, *Oslo* | **2 B2** | 59 55N | 10 25 E |
| Smichov, *Pra.* | **10 B2** | 50 4N | 14 23 E |
| Smith Forest Preserve, *Chic.* | **26 B2** | 41 59N | 87 45W |
| Smith Mills, *N.Y.* | **22 A2** | 41 0N | 74 23W |
| Smithfield, *Syd.* | **19 B2** | 33 51 S | 150 56 E |
| Smoke Rise, *N.Y.* | **22 A2** | 41 0N | 74 24W |
| Smørumnedre, *Købn.* | **2 D8** | 55 44N | 12 7 E |
| Snakeden Br. →, *Wash.* | **25 D6** | 38 58N | 77 17W |
| Snarøya, *Oslo* | **2 B3** | 59 52N | 10 33 E |
| Snättringe, *Stock.* | **3 E10** | 59 15N | 17 58 E |
| Snoldelev, *Købn.* | **2 E8** | 55 33N | 12 10 E |
| Snostrup, *Købn.* | **2 D7** | 55 48N | 12 7 E |
| Søborg, *Købn.* | **2 D9** | 55 43N | 12 29 E |
| Sobreda, *Lisb.* | **8 G7** | 38 39N | 9 11W |
| Soccavo, *Nápl.* | **9 H12** | 40 50N | 14 11 E |
| Sodegaura, *Tōkyō* | **13 D4** | 35 24N | 139 57 E |
| Söderby, *Stock.* | **3 D12** | 59 24N | 18 12 E |
| Söderkullalandet, *Hels.* | **3 B6** | 60 14N | 25 19 E |
| Södermalm, *Stock.* | **3 E11** | 59 18N | 18 4 E |
| Södersätra, *Stock.* | **3 D10** | 59 27N | 17 56 E |
| Södertälje, *Stock.* | **3 E8** | 59 11N | 17 36 E |
| Sodingen, *Ruhr* | **6 A5** | 51 32N | 7 15 E |
| Sodpur, *Calc.* | **16 D6** | 22 42N | 88 24 E |
| Södra Björkfjärden, *Stock.* | **3 E8** | 59 17N | 17 34 E |
| Soeurs, Î. des, *Mtrl.* | **20 B4** | 43 27N | 73 32W |
| Sognsvatn, *Oslo* | **2 B4** | 59 58N | 10 43 E |
| Soignolles-en-Brie, *Paris* | **5 D6** | 48 39N | 2 43 E |
| Soisy-sous-Montmorency, *Paris* | **5 B3** | 48 59N | 2 17 E |
| Soisy-sur-Seine, *Paris* | **5 D4** | 48 39N | 2 27 E |
| Sojiji Temple, *Tōkyō* | **13 D3** | 35 29N | 139 40 E |
| Sok Kwu Wan, *H.K.* | **12 E5** | 22 12N | 114 7 E |
| Sōka, *Tōkyō* | **13 B3** | 35 49N | 139 48 E |
| Sokolniki, *Mos.* | **11 E10** | 55 47N | 37 40 E |
| Sokolniki Park, *Mos.* | **11 E10** | 55 48N | 37 40 E |
| Sokołów, *Wsaw.* | **10 F6** | 52 9N | 20 51 E |
| Solalinden, *Mün.* | **7 G11** | 48 5N | 11 42 E |
| Solaro, *Mil.* | **9 D5** | 45 36N | 9 6 E |
| Solers, *Paris* | **5 D6** | 48 39N | 2 43 E |
| Solingen, *Ruhr* | **6 C4** | 51 10N | 7 5 E |
| Sollentuna, *Stock.* | **3 D10** | 59 25N | 17 56 E |
| Søllerød, *Købn.* | **2 D9** | 55 48N | 12 29 E |
| Sollihøgda, *Oslo* | **2 B2** | 59 58N | 10 21 E |
| Solln, *Mün.* | **7 G10** | 48 4N | 11 31 E |
| Solna, *Stock.* | **3 D10** | 59 21N | 17 59 E |
| Solntsevo, *Mos.* | **11 F8** | 55 39N | 37 24 E |
| Solymár, *Bud.* | **10 J12** | 47 35N | 18 56 E |
| Somapah Changi, *Sing.* | **15 F8** | 1 20N | 103 57 E |
| Somapan Serangoon, *Sing.* | **15 F8** | 1 21N | 103 53 E |
| Somborn, *Ruhr* | **6 B6** | 51 29N | 7 20 E |
| Somerdale, *Phil.* | **24 B4** | 39 50N | 75 1W |
| Somerset, *Wash.* | **25 D7** | 38 57N | 77 5W |
| Somerton, *Phil.* | **24 A4** | 40 7N | 75 1W |
| Somerville, *Bost.* | **21 C3** | 42 22N | 71 5W |
| Somma, Mte., *Nápl.* | **9 H13** | 40 50N | 14 25 E |
| Somma Vesuviana, *Nápl.* | **9 H13** | 40 52N | 14 26 E |
| Sonari, *Bomb.* | **16 H8** | 18 54N | 72 59 E |
| Sønderby, *Købn.* | **2 D7** | 55 44N | 12 2 E |
| Søndersø, *Købn.* | **2 D9** | 55 46N | 12 21 E |
| Sondre Elvåga, *Oslo* | **2 B5** | 59 51N | 10 54 E |
| Sonnberg, *Wien* | **10 G9** | 48 19N | 16 15 E |
| Sørby, *Oslo* | **2 C4** | 59 49N | 10 41 E |
| Sørkedalen, *Oslo* | **2 A3** | 60 1N | 10 37 E |
| Soroksár, *Bud.* | **10 K13** | 47 24N | 19 7 E |
| Soroksár-Újtelep, *Bud.* | **10 K13** | 47 25N | 19 7 E |
| Soroksari Duna →, *Bud.* | **10 K13** | 47 25N | 19 5 E |
| Sørsdal, *Oslo* | **2 B1** | 59 50N | 10 16 E |
| Sosenka →, *Mos.* | **11 E10** | 55 46N | 37 42 E |
| Sosnovaya, *St-Pet.* | **11 C2** | 59 49N | 30 8 E |
| Sottungsby, *Hels.* | **3 B5** | 60 16N | 25 8 E |
| Sŏul, *Sŏul* | **12 G8** | 37 34N | 127 51 E |
| Soundview, *N.Y.* | **23 C5** | 40 49N | 73 53W |
| South Basin, *S.F.* | **27 B2** | 37 42N | 122 22W |
| South Beach, *N.Y.* | **22 D4** | 40 35N | 74 4W |
| South Boston, *Bost.* | **21 C3** | 42 20N | 71 2W |
| South Braintree, *Bost.* | **21 D4** | 42 11N | 70 59W |
| South Branch →, *Phil.* | **24 C4** | 39 50N | 75 5W |
| South Brooklyn, *N.Y.* | **22 C5** | 40 41N | 73 59W |
| South Chelmsford, *Bost.* | **21 B1** | 42 34N | 71 22W |
| South Chicago, *Chic.* | **26 C3** | 41 44N | 87 32W |
| South Darenth, *Lon.* | **4 C6** | 51 23N | 0 15 E |
| South Deering, *Chic.* | **26 C3** | 41 42N | 87 33W |
| South Floral Park, *N.Y.* | **23 C6** | 40 42N | 73 41W |
| South Gate, *L.A.* | **28 C3** | 33 56N | 118 12W |
| South Germiston, *Jobg.* | **18 F10** | 26 11 S | 28 13 E |
| South Hackensack, *N.Y.* | **22 B4** | 40 51N | 74 2W |
| South Hamilton, *Bost.* | **21 B4** | 42 36N | 70 52W |
| South Harbour, *Manila* | **15 D3** | 14 34N | 120 58 E |
| South Harrow, *Lon.* | **4 B2** | 51 33N | 0 21W |
| South Hd., *Syd.* | **19 B4** | 33 50 S | 151 16 E |
| South Hempstead, *N.Y.* | **23 C7** | 40 40N | 73 37W |
| South Hills, *Jobg.* | **18 F9** | 26 14 S | 28 5 E |
| South Hingham, *Bost.* | **21 D4** | 42 12N | 70 53W |
| South Holland, *Chic.* | **26 D3** | 41 36N | 87 35W |
| South Hornchurch, *Lon.* | **4 B6** | 51 32N | 0 11 E |
| South Huntington, *N.Y.* | **23 C8** | 40 49N | 73 23W |
| South Lawn, *Wash.* | **25 E7** | 38 47N | 77 0W |
| South Lawrence, *Bost.* | **21 A3** | 42 41N | 71 9W |
| South Lincoln, *Bost.* | **21 C2** | 42 24N | 71 19W |
| South Lynnfield, *Bost.* | **21 B4** | 42 30N | 70 59W |
| South Norwood, *Lon.* | **4 C4** | 51 23N | 0 3W |
| South Ockendon, *Lon.* | **4 B6** | 51 30N | 0 16 E |
| South of Market, *S.F.* | **27 B2** | 37 46N | 122 24W |
| South Orange, *N.Y.* | **22 C3** | 40 45N | 74 14W |
| South Oxley, *Lon.* | **4 B2** | 51 37N | 0 23W |
| South Oyster B., *N.Y.* | **23 D8** | 40 38N | 73 27W |
| South Ozone Park, *N.Y.* | **23 C6** | 40 41N | 73 49W |
| South Pasadena, *L.A.* | **28 B4** | 34 7N | 118 8W |
| South Peabody, *Bost.* | **21 B4** | 42 30N | 70 57W |
| South Peters, *Syd.* | **19 B4** | 33 54 S | 151 11 E |
| South Plainfield, *N.Y.* | **22 D2** | 40 35N | 74 24W |
| South Quincy, *Bost.* | **21 D3** | 42 13N | 71 0W |
| South Res., *Bost.* | **21 C3** | 42 26N | 71 6W |
| South San Francisco, *S.F.* | **27 C2** | 37 38N | 122 26W |
| South San Gabriel, *L.A.* | **28 B4** | 34 3N | 118 6W |
| South Shore, *Chic.* | **26 C3** | 41 45N | 87 34W |
| South Sudbury, *Bost.* | **21 C1** | 42 21N | 71 24W |
| South Valley Stream, *N.Y.* | **23 D6** | 40 38N | 73 43W |
| South Westbury, *N.Y.* | **23 C7** | 40 44N | 73 34W |
| South Weymouth, *Bost.* | **21 D4** | 42 10N | 70 56W |
| South Wimbledon, *Lon.* | **4 C3** | 51 24N | 0 11W |
| South Yarra, *Melb.* | **19 F6** | 37 50 S | 144 59 E |
| Southall, *Lon.* | **4 B2** | 51 30N | 0 22W |
| Southborough, *Lon.* | **4 C5** | 51 23N | 0 3 E |
| Southcrest, *Jobg.* | **18 F9** | 26 15 S | 28 5 E |
| Southend, *Lon.* | **4 C4** | 51 25N | 0 0 E |
| Southfields, *Lon.* | **4 C3** | 51 26N | 0 11W |
| Southgate, *Lon.* | **4 B4** | 51 38N | 0 7W |
| Southwark, *Lon.* | **4 C4** | 51 29N | 0 5W |
| Søvang, *Købn.* | **2 E10** | 55 34N | 12 37 E |
| Soweto, *Jobg.* | **18 F8** | 26 14 S | 27 52 E |
| Soya, *Tōkyō* | **13 B4** | 35 44N | 139 55 E |
| Spadenland, *Hbg.* | **7 E8** | 53 28N | 10 3 E |
| Spandau, *Berl.* | **7 A1** | 52 33N | 13 9 E |
| Spånga, *Stock.* | **3 D10** | 59 23N | 17 53 E |
| Sparkhill, *N.Y.* | **22 A5** | 41 1N | 73 55W |
| Sparrows Point, *Balt.* | **25 B4** | 39 13N | 76 29W |
| Spectacle I., *Bost.* | **21 C4** | 42 19N | 70 59W |
| Speicher-See, *Mün.* | **7 F11** | 48 12N | 11 42 E |
| Speising, *Wien* | **10 H9** | 48 10N | 16 17 E |
| Speldorf, *Ruhr* | **6 B2** | 51 26N | 6 49 E |
| Spellen, *Ruhr* | **6 A1** | 51 36N | 6 36 E |
| Sphinx, *El Qâ.* | **18 D4** | 29 58N | 31 8 E |
| Spinaceto, *Rome* | **9 G9** | 41 47N | 12 27 E |
| Splitrock Res., *N.Y.* | **22 B2** | 40 58N | 74 26W |
| Spořilov, *Pra.* | **10 B3** | 50 2N | 14 29 E |
| Spot Pond, *Bost.* | **21 C3** | 42 26N | 71 4W |
| Spotswood, *Melb.* | **19 F6** | 37 50 S | 144 52 E |
| Spree →, *Berl.* | **7 A2** | 52 32N | 13 12 E |
| Spreehafen, *Hbg.* | **7 D7** | 53 31N | 9 59 E |
| Spring Pond, *Bost.* | **21 C4** | 42 29N | 70 56W |
| Springeberg, *Berl.* | **7 B5** | 52 26N | 13 43 E |
| Springfield, *N.Y.* | **22 C3** | 40 42N | 74 18W |
| Springfield, *Phil.* | **24 B3** | 39 56N | 75 19W |
| Springfield, *Wash.* | **25 E6** | 38 46N | 77 10W |
| Springs, *Jobg.* | **18 F11** | 26 15 S | 28 23 E |
| Sprockhövel, *Ruhr* | **6 B5** | 51 22N | 7 14 E |
| Squantum, *Bost.* | **21 D3** | 42 17N | 71 0W |
| Squirrel's Heath, *Lon.* | **4 B6** | 51 34N | 0 12 E |
| Srednaya Rogatka, *St-Pet.* | **11 C4** | 59 49N | 30 22 E |
| Sródmieċcie, *Wsaw.* | **10 E7** | 52 13N | 21 0 E |
| Staaken, *Berl.* | **7 A1** | 52 31N | 13 8 E |
| Staatsoper, *Wien* | **10 G10** | 48 12N | 16 21 E |
| Stabekk, *Oslo* | **2 B3** | 59 54N | 10 36 E |
| Stadlau, *Wien* | **10 G10** | 48 13N | 16 27 E |
| Stahnsdorf, *Berl.* | **7 B2** | 52 23N | 13 12 E |
| Staines, *Lon.* | **4 C2** | 51 26N | 0 29W |
| Stains, *Paris* | **5 B4** | 48 57N | 2 22 E |
| Stamford, *N.Y.* | **23 A7** | 41 2N | 73 32W |
| Stamford Harbor, *N.Y.* | **23 A7** | 41 0N | 73 34W |
| Stamford Hill, *Lon.* | **4 B4** | 51 34N | 0 4W |
| Stammersdorf, *Wien* | **10 G10** | 48 18N | 16 24 E |
| Stanford Univ., *S.F.* | **27 D4** | 37 26N | 122 10W |
| Stanley, *H.K.* | **12 E6** | 22 13N | 114 12 E |
| Stanley Mound, *H.K.* | **12 E6** | 22 13N | 114 12 E |
| Stanley Pen., *H.K.* | **12 E6** | 22 12N | 114 12 E |
| Stanmore, *Lon.* | **4 B3** | 51 37N | 0 18W |
| Stansted, *Lon.* | **4 C6** | 51 20N | 0 18 E |
| Stapleford Abbotts, *Lon.* | **4 B6** | 51 37N | 0 10 E |
| Stapleton, *N.Y.* | **22 D4** | 40 36N | 74 5W |
| Stará Boleslav, *Pra.* | **10 A3** | 50 11N | 14 39 E |
| Stara Milosna, *Wsaw.* | **10 E8** | 52 15N | 21 12 E |
| Staraya, *St-Pet.* | **11 B5** | 59 55N | 30 37 E |
| Staraya Derevnya, *St-Pet.* | **11 B3** | 59 58N | 30 15 E |
| Stare, *Wsaw.* | **10 E7** | 52 15N | 21 0 E |
| Stare Babice, *Wsaw.* | **10 E5** | 52 15N | 20 49 E |
| Staré Mesto, *Pra.* | **10 B2** | 50 5N | 14 25 E |
| State House, *Lagos* | **18 B2** | 6 26N | 7 24 E |
| Staten, *N.Y.* | **22 D4** | 40 34N | 74 7W |
| Staten Island Zoo, *N.Y.* | **22 D4** | 40 38N | 74 6W |
| Statenice, *Pra.* | **10 B1** | 50 9N | 14 19 E |
| Stavnsholt, *Købn.* | **2 D9** | 55 48N | 12 24 E |
| Steele, *Ruhr* | **6 B4** | 51 27N | 7 4 E |
| Steele Creek, *Melb.* | **19 E6** | 37 44 S | 144 52 E |
| Steglitz, *Berl.* | **7 B2** | 52 27N | 13 19 E |
| Stehstücken, *Berl.* | **7 B1** | 52 23N | 13 7 E |
| Steilshoop, *Hbg.* | **7 D8** | 53 36N | 10 2 E |
| Steinberger Slough, *S.F.* | **27 C3** | 37 32N | 122 13W |
| Steinriegel, *Wien* | **10 G9** | 48 16N | 16 12 E |
| Steinstücken, *Berl.* | **7 B1** | 52 21N | 13 7 E |
| Steinwerder, *Hbg.* | **7 D7** | 53 32N | 9 57 E |
| Stellingen, *Hbg.* | **7 D7** | 53 35N | 9 56 E |
| Stenhamra, *Stock.* | **3 D9** | 59 20N | 17 40 E |
| Stenløse, *Købn.* | **2 D8** | 55 46N | 12 11 E |
| Stephansdom, *Wien* | **10 G10** | 48 12N | 16 21 E |
| Stepney, *Lon.* | **4 B4** | 51 30N | 0 3W |
| Sterkende, *Købn.* | **2 E8** | 55 36N | 12 10 E |
| Sterkrade, *Ruhr* | **6 A3** | 51 31N | 6 52 E |
| Sterling Park, *S.F.* | **27 B2** | 37 41N | 122 27W |
| Stevenson, *Balt.* | **25 A2** | 39 24N | 76 42W |
| Stewart Manor, *N.Y.* | **23 C6** | 40 43N | 73 40W |
| Sticklinge udde, *Stock.* | **3 D11** | 59 23N | 18 6 E |
| Stickney, *Chic.* | **26 C2** | 41 49N | 87 46W |
| Stienitzaue, *Berl.* | **7 A5** | 52 38N | 13 44 E |
| Stiepel, *Ruhr* | **6 B5** | 51 25N | 7 14 E |
| Stiftskirche, *Ruhr* | **6 C2** | 51 12N | 6 41 E |
| Still Run →, *Phil.* | **24 C3** | 39 47N | 75 16W |
| Stockholm, *Stock.* | **3 E11** | 59 19N | 18 4 E |
| Stocksund, *Stock.* | **3 D11** | 59 23N | 18 3 E |
| Stockum, *Ruhr* | **6 C2** | 51 16N | 6 44 E |
| Stodůlky, *Pra.* | **10 B1** | 50 3N | 14 19 E |
| Stoke D'Abernon, *Lon.* | **4 D2** | 51 19N | 0 23W |
| Stoke Newington, *Lon.* | **4 B4** | 51 33N | 0 4W |
| Stolpe-Süd, *Berl.* | **7 A2** | 52 37N | 13 14 E |
| Stone, *Lon.* | **4 C6** | 51 26N | 0 16 E |
| Stone Grove, *Lon.* | **4 B3** | 51 37N | 0 16W |
| Stone Park, *Chic.* | **26 B1** | 41 53N | 87 52W |
| Stonebridge, *Lon.* | **4 B3** | 51 32N | 0 16W |
| Stoneham, *Bost.* | **21 C3** | 42 29N | 71 5W |
| Stonehurst, *L.A.* | **28 A2** | 34 15N | 118 21W |
| Stony Brook Res., *Bost.* | **21 D3** | 42 15N | 71 8W |
| Stony Cr. →, *Chic.* | **26 C2** | 41 40N | 87 45W |
| Stony Cr. →, *Melb.* | **19 E6** | 37 49 S | 144 53 E |
| Stora Värtan, *Stock.* | **3 D11** | 59 25N | 18 7 E |
| Store Hareskov, *Købn.* | **2 D9** | 55 46N | 12 23 E |
| Store Kattingesø, *Købn.* | **2 E7** | 55 39N | 12 0 E |
| Store Magleby, *Købn.* | **2 E10** | 55 35N | 12 35 E |
| Storholmen, *Stock.* | **3 D11** | 59 23N | 18 8 E |
| Stovivatn, *Oslo* | **2 B2** | 59 54N | 10 26 E |
| Stovner, *Oslo* | **2 B5** | 59 57N | 10 55 E |
| Stow L., *S.F.* | **27 B2** | 37 46N | 122 28W |
| Stračnice, *Pra.* | **10 B2** | 50 4N | 14 28 E |
| Strandbad Gansehäufe, *Wien* | **10 G10** | 48 13N | 16 26 E |
| Strasslach, *Mün.* | **7 G10** | 48 0N | 11 30 E |
| Strasstrudering, *Mün.* | **7 G11** | 48 6N | 11 41 E |
| Stratford, *Lon.* | **4 B5** | 51 33N | 0 0 E |
| Stratford, *Phil.* | **24 C4** | 39 49N | 75 0W |
| Strathfield, *Syd.* | **19 B3** | 33 52 S | 151 5 E |
| Strawberry Hill, *Bost.* | **21 D2** | 42 14N | 71 15W |
| Strawberry Pk., *L.A.* | **28 A4** | 34 16N | 118 7W |
| Strawberry Pt., *S.F.* | **27 A1** | 37 53N | 122 30W |
| Streatham, *Lon.* | **4 C4** | 51 25N | 0 7W |
| Streatham Vale, *Lon.* | **4 C4** | 51 24N | 0 8W |
| Strebersdorf, *Wien* | **10 G10** | 48 17N | 16 23 E |
| Střečovice, *Pra.* | **10 B2** | 50 5N | 14 23 E |
| Strelyna, *St-Pet.* | **11 C1** | 59 49N | 30 0 E |
| Střížkov, *Pra.* | **10 B2** | 50 7N | 14 28 E |
| Strogino, *Mos.* | **11 E8** | 55 48N | 37 24 E |
| Strømmen, *Oslo* | **2 B5** | 59 56N | 10 59 E |
| Stromovka, *Pra.* | **10 B2** | 50 6N | 14 25 E |
| Strunkede Wasserschloss, *Ruhr* | **6 A5** | 51 33N | 7 12 E |
| Studio City, *L.A.* | **28 B2** | 34 8N | 118 24W |
| Stupinigi, *Tori.* | **9 C2** | 44 59N | 7 36 E |
| Stura di Lanzo →, *Tori.* | **9 A2** | 45 11N | 7 47 E |
| Stureby, *Stock.* | **3 E11** | 59 15N | 18 4 E |
| Stuvsta, *Stock.* | **3 E11** | 59 15N | 18 0 E |
| Styrum, *Ruhr* | **6 B3** | 51 27N | 6 52 E |
| Subhepur, *Delhi* | **16 A2** | 28 44N | 77 15 E |
| Sucat, *Manila* | **15 E4** | 14 27N | 121 2 E |
| Success, L., *N.Y.* | **23 C6** | 40 45N | 73 42W |
| Suchdol, *Pra.* | **10 B2** | 50 8N | 14 22 E |
| Sucre, *Car.* | **30 D5** | 10 31N | 66 57W |
| Sucy-en-Brie, *Paris* | **5 C5** | 48 46N | 2 31 E |
| Sudberg, *Ruhr* | **6 C4** | 51 10N | 7 6 E |
| Sudbury, *Bost.* | **21 C1** | 42 22N | 71 24W |
| Suderelbe →, *Hbg.* | **7 E7** | 53 28N | 9 58 E |
| Suderwich, *Ruhr* | **6 A5** | 51 36N | 7 16 E |
| Sugamo, *Tōkyō* | **13 B3** | 35 44N | 139 43 E |
| Sugar Loaf Mt. = Açúcar, Pão de, *Rio J.* | **31 B3** | 22 56 S | 43 9W |
| Sugartown, *Phil.* | **24 B1** | 39 59N | 75 30W |
| Sugasawa, *Tōkyō* | **13 B2** | 35 46N | 139 32 E |
| Suge, *Tōkyō* | **13 C2** | 35 37N | 139 32 E |
| Suginami-Ku, *Tōkyō* | **13 B2** | 35 41N | 139 37 E |
| Sugita, *Tōkyō* | **13 D2** | 35 22N | 139 37 E |
| Sugō, *Tōkyō* | **13 C2** | 35 34N | 139 33 E |
| Suitland, *Wash.* | **25 D8** | 38 50N | 76 55W |
| Sukchar, *Calc.* | **16 D6** | 22 42N | 88 22 E |
| Sulejówek, *Wsaw.* | **10 E8** | 52 14N | 21 14 E |
| Sulldorf, *Hbg.* | **7 D6** | 53 34N | 9 49 E |
| Sultan Mosque, *Sing.* | **15 G8** | 1 18N | 103 51 E |
| Suma, *Ōsaka* | **12 C1** | 34 38N | 135 8 E |
| Sumaré, *S. Pau.* | **31 E5** | 23 32 S | 46 41W |
| Sumida, *Tōkyō* | **13 B3** | 35 42N | 139 49 E |
| Sumida →, *Tōkyō* | **13 B3** | 35 39N | 139 45 E |
| Sumiyoshi, *Ōsaka* | **12 C4** | 34 36N | 135 30 E |
| Summer Palace, *Beij.* | **14 B2** | 39 59N | 116 13 E |
| Summerville, *Trto.* | **20 E7** | 43 37N | 79 33W |
| Summit, *Chic.* | **26 C2** | 41 47N | 87 47W |
| Summit, *N.Y.* | **22 C2** | 40 43N | 74 22W |
| Sun Valley, *L.A.* | **28 A2** | 34 13N | 118 21W |
| Sunamachi, *Tōkyō* | **13 B4** | 35 40N | 139 50 E |
| Sunashinden, *Tōkyō* | **13 A2** | 35 53N | 139 30 E |
| Sunbury, *Lon.* | **4 C2** | 51 25N | 0 26W |
| Sunda Kelapa, *Jak.* | **15 H9** | 6 6 S | 106 48 E |
| Sundbyberg, *Stock.* | **3 D10** | 59 22N | 17 57 E |
| Sundbyerne, *Købn.* | **2 E10** | 55 39N | 12 36 E |
| Sung Kong, *H.K.* | **12 E6** | 22 11N | 114 17 E |
| Sungai Bambu, *Jak.* | **15 H10** | 6 6 S | 106 53 E |
| Sungai Buloh, *Sing.* | **15 F7** | 1 25N | 103 42 E |
| Sungei Simpang, *Sing.* | **15 F7** | 1 26N | 103 49 E |
| Sunland, *L.A.* | **28 A3** | 34 15N | 118 18W |
| Sunnyridge, *Jobg.* | **18 F10** | 26 10 S | 28 10 E |
| Sunset, *S.F.* | **27 B2** | 37 44N | 122 29W |
| Sunshine, *Melb.* | **19 E5** | 37 48 S | 144 49 E |
| Sunshine Acres, *L.A.* | **28 C5** | 33 56N | 117 59W |
| Suntaug L., *Bost.* | **21 B3** | 42 31N | 71 0W |
| Sunter, *Jak.* | **15 H10** | 6 7 S | 106 51 E |
| Sunter, Kali, *Jak.* | **15 J10** | 6 10 S | 106 53 E |
| Suomenlinna, *Hels.* | **3 C4** | 60 9N | 24 59 E |
| Superga, *Tori.* | **9 B3** | 45 4N | 7 46 E |
| Superga, Basilica di, *Tori.* | **9 B3** | 45 5N | 7 45 E |
| Sura, *Calc.* | **16 E6** | 22 33N | 88 24 E |
| Surag San, *Sŏul* | **12 F8** | 37 40N | 127 4 E |
| Surbiton, *Lon.* | **4 C3** | 51 23N | 0 17W |
| Surco, *Lima* | **30 G8** | 12 9 S | 77 0W |
| Suresnes, *Paris* | **5 B3** | 48 52N | 2 13 E |
| Surquillo, *Lima* | **30 G8** | 12 6 S | 77 1W |
| Surrey Hills, *Melb.* | **19 F7** | 37 50 S | 145 5 E |
| Surrey Hills, *Syd.* | **19 B4** | 33 53 S | 151 13 E |
| Surrey Park, *Melb.* | **19 E7** | 37 49 S | 145 6 E |
| Susaeg, *Sŏul* | **12 G7** | 37 34N | 126 54 E |
| Süssenbrunn, *Wien* | **10 G10** | 48 16N | 16 29 E |
| Sutherland, *Syd.* | **19 C3** | 34 2 S | 151 3 E |
| Sutton, *Lon.* | **4 C3** | 51 21N | 0 11W |
| Sutton at Hone, *Lon.* | **4 C6** | 51 24N | 0 14 E |
| Suyu, *Sŏul* | **12 G8** | 37 37N | 127 0 E |
| Suzukishinden, *Tōkyō* | **13 B2** | 35 43N | 139 31 E |
| Svanemøllen, *Købn.* | **2 D10** | 55 43N | 12 34 E |
| Svartsjölandet, *Stock.* | **3 D9** | 59 20N | 17 43 E |
| Sverdlov, *Mos.* | **11 E9** | 55 46N | 37 36 E |
| Svestad, *Oslo* | **2 C3** | 59 46N | 10 36 E |
| Svestrup, *Købn.* | **2 D7** | 55 46N | 12 8 E |
| Svinningeudd, *Stock.* | **3 D12** | 59 26N | 18 17 E |
| Svinö, *Hels.* | **3 C3** | 60 7N | 24 44 E |
| Svogerslev, *Købn.* | **2 E7** | 55 38N | 12 0 E |
| Swampscott, *Bost.* | **21 C4** | 42 28N | 70 53W |
| Swanley, *Lon.* | **4 C5** | 51 23N | 0 9 E |
| Swanscombe, *Lon.* | **4 C6** | 51 26N | 0 18 E |
| Swansea, *Trto.* | **20 E8** | 43 39N | 79 27W |
| Swarthmore, *Phil.* | **24 B2** | 39 54N | 75 22W |
| Swedesboro, *Phil.* | **24 C3** | 39 45N | 75 17W |
| Swedesburg, *Phil.* | **24 A3** | 40 5N | 75 19W |
| Swinburne I., *N.Y.* | **22 D4** | 40 33N | 74 3W |
| Swita, *Ōsaka* | **12 B4** | 34 45N | 135 30 E |
| Syampur, *Calc.* | **16 F5** | 22 28N | 88 12 E |
| Sycamore Mills, *Phil.* | **24 B2** | 39 57N | 75 25W |
| Sydenham, *Jobg.* | **18 E9** | 26 9 S | 28 5 E |
| Sydney, *Syd.* | **19 B4** | 33 52 S | 151 12 E |
| Sydney, Univ. of, *Syd.* | **19 B4** | 33 54 S | 151 11 E |
| Sydney Airport, *Syd.* | **19 B4** | 33 56 S | 151 10 E |
| Sydney Harbour Bridge, *Syd.* | **19 B4** | 33 51 S | 151 12 E |
| Sydstranden, *Købn.* | **2 E10** | 55 34N | 12 38 E |
| Sylling, *Oslo* | **2 B1** | 59 54N | 10 16 E |
| Sylvania, *Syd.* | **19 C3** | 34 0 S | 151 7 E |
| Syndal, *Melb.* | **19 F7** | 37 52 S | 145 9 E |
| Syon House, *Lon.* | **4 C3** | 51 28N | 0 18W |
| Syosset, *N.Y.* | **23 C7** | 40 49N | 73 30W |
| Szabadság-hegy, *Bud.* | **10 J12** | 47 30N | 18 59 E |
| Szczęsliwice, *Wsaw.* | **10 E6** | 52 12N | 20 57 E |
| Szemere-Telep, *Bud.* | **10 K14** | 47 26N | 19 13 E |
| Széphalom, *Bud.* | **10 J12** | 47 34N | 18 57 E |
| Szilasliget, *Bud.* | **10 J14** | 47 34N | 19 16 E |


# T


| | | | |
|---|---|---|---|
| Tabata, *Tōkyō* | **13 B3** | 35 44N | 139 46 E |
| Tablada, *B.A.* | **32 C3** | 34 41 S | 58 32W |
| Taboão →, *S. Pau.* | **31 F7** | 23 40 S | 46 27W |
| Taboão da Serra, *S. Pau.* | **31 E5** | 23 36 S | 46 45W |
| Tabor, *N.Y.* | **22 B2** | 40 52N | 74 28W |
| Täby, *Stock.* | **3 D11** | 59 26N | 18 2 E |
| Tacony, *Phil.* | **24 A4** | 40 1N | 75 2W |
| Tacuba, *Méx.* | **29 B2** | 19 26N | 99 11W |
| Tacubaya, *Méx.* | **29 B2** | 19 24N | 99 10W |
| Tadain, *Ōsaka* | **12 A3** | 34 51N | 135 24 E |
| Tadworth, *Lon.* | **4 D3** | 51 17N | 0 14W |
| Tagig, *Manila* | **15 D4** | 14 31N | 121 4 E |
| Tagig →, *Manila* | **15 D4** | 14 31N | 121 5 E |
| Tai Hang, *H.K.* | **12 E6** | 22 16N | 114 11 E |
| Tai Lo Shan, *H.K.* | **12 D6** | 22 21N | 114 13 E |
| Tai Po Tsai, *H.K.* | **12 D6** | 22 20N | 114 15 E |
| Tai Seng, *Sing.* | **15 F8** | 1 20N | 103 53 E |
| Tai Shui Hang, *H.K.* | **12 D6** | 22 24N | 114 13 E |
| Tai Tam B., *H.K.* | **12 E6** | 22 12N | 114 13 E |
| Tai Tam Tuk Res., *H.K.* | **12 E6** | 22 14N | 114 13 E |
| Tai Wan Tau, *H.K.* | **12 E6** | 22 17N | 114 17 E |
| Tai Wo Hau, *H.K.* | **12 D5** | 22 21N | 114 7 E |
| Tai Wo Ping, *H.K.* | **12 D5** | 22 20N | 114 9 E |
| Ta'imim, *Bagd.* | **17 F8** | 33 15N | 44 21 E |
| Tainaka, *Ōsaka* | **12 C4** | 34 36N | 135 35 E |
| Taishō, *Ōsaka* | **12 C3** | 34 38N | 135 27 E |
| Taitō-Ku, *Tōkyō* | **13 B3** | 35 43N | 139 47 E |
| Tajima, *Tōkyō* | **13 B2** | 35 48N | 139 36 E |
| Tajpur, *Calc.* | **16 D5** | 22 44N | 88 15 E |
| Takaido, *Tōkyō* | **13 B2** | 35 40N | 139 37 E |
| Takaishi, *Tōkyō* | **13 C2** | 35 36N | 139 31 E |
| Takarazuka, *Ōsaka* | **12 B2** | 34 47N | 135 20 E |
| Takasago, *Tōkyō* | **13 B4** | 35 44N | 139 52 E |
| Takatsuki, *Ōsaka* | **12 A4** | 34 50N | 135 37 E |
| Takayanagi, *Tōkyō* | **13 D4** | 35 23N | 139 57 E |
| Takegahana, *Tōkyō* | **13 B4** | 35 47N | 139 54 E |
| Takenotsuka, *Tōkyō* | **13 B3** | 35 47N | 139 47 E |
| Takeshita, *Tōkyō* | **13 C2** | 35 33N | 139 32 E |
| Takinegawa, *Tōkyō* | **13 B3** | 35 45N | 139 44 E |
| Takkula, *Hels.* | **3 B2** | 60 19N | 24 38 E |
| Takoma Park, *Wash.* | **25 D7** | 38 58N | 77 0W |
| Taksim, *Ist.* | **17 A2** | 41 2N | 28 58 E |
| Talaide, *Lisb.* | **8 F7** | 38 44N | 9 18W |
| Talampas, *Manila* | **15 D4** | 14 36N | 121 4 E |
| Taling Chan, *Bangk.* | **15 B1** | 13 46N | 100 27 E |
| Talleyville, *Phil.* | **24 C1** | 39 48N | 75 32W |
| Tallkrogen, *Stock.* | **3 E11** | 59 16N | 18 4 E |
| Talmapais Valley, *S.F.* | **27 A1** | 37 52N | 122 32W |
| Tama, *Tōkyō* | **13 C1** | 35 38N | 139 26 E |
| Tama →, *Tōkyō* | **13 C2** | 35 32N | 139 39 E |
| Tama Kyźryō, *Tōkyō* | **13 C2** | 35 34N | 139 30 E |
| Tamaden, *Tōkyō* | **13 C2** | 35 39N | 139 38 E |
| Tamagawa-josui →, *Tōkyō* | **13 B1** | 35 41N | 139 47 E |
| Taman Sari, *Jak.* | **15 H9** | 6 8 S | 106 48 E |
| Tamanduatei →, *S. Pau.* | **31 E6** | 23 37 S | 46 38W |
| Tambora, *Jak.* | **15 H9** | 6 8 S | 106 47 E |
| Tamboré, *S. Pau.* | **31 E4** | 23 30 S | 46 50W |
| Tammisalo, *Hels.* | **3 B5** | 60 11N | 25 5 E |
| Tammûh, *El Qâ.* | **18 D5** | 29 55N | 31 15 E |
| Tampier Slough, *Chic.* | **26 D1** | 41 39N | 87 54W |
| Tan Tock Seng, *Sing.* | **15 G8** | 1 19N | 103 50 E |
| Tanah Abang, *Jak.* | **15 J9** | 6 12 S | 106 48 E |
| Tanashi, *Tōkyō* | **13 B2** | 35 43N | 139 32 E |
| Tanforan Park, *S.F.* | **27 C2** | 37 37N | 122 24W |
| Tangjae, *Sŏul* | **12 H8** | 37 29N | 127 2 E |
| Tanglin, *Sing.* | **15 G7** | 1 18N | 103 47 E |
| Tangstedt, *Hbg.* | **7 C7** | 53 40N | 9 51 E |
| Tangstedter Forst, *Hbg.* | **7 C8** | 53 43N | 10 3 E |
| Tanigami, *Ōsaka* | **12 B2** | 34 45N | 135 10 E |
| Tanjung Duren, *Jak.* | **15 J9** | 6 10 S | 106 46 E |
| Tanjung Priok, *Jak.* | **15 H10** | 6 6 S | 106 52 E |
| Tanum, *Oslo* | **2 B2** | 59 53N | 10 28 E |
| Taoranting Gongyuan, *Beij.* | **14 B3** | 39 51N | 116 20 E |
| Taoranting Hu, *Beij.* | **14 B3** | 39 50N | 116 20 E |
| Tapada, *Lisb.* | **8 F7** | 38 49N | 9 16W |
| Tapanila, *Hels.* | **3 B5** | 60 15N | 25 2 E |
| Tapiales, *B.A.* | **32 C3** | 34 42 S | 58 30W |
| Tapiola, *Hels.* | **3 B3** | 60 10N | 24 48 E |
| Tappan, *N.Y.* | **22 A5** | 41 1N | 73 57W |
| Tappan, L., *N.Y.* | **22 A5** | 41 1N | 73 59W |
| Tappeh, *Tehr.* | **17 C5** | 35 41N | 51 29 E |
| Tapsia, *Calc.* | **16 E6** | 22 32N | 88 23 E |
| Taquara, *Rio J.* | **31 B1** | 22 55 S | 43 21W |
| Tara, *Bomb.* | **16 G7** | 19 5N | 72 49 E |
| Tarāblus, *Bagd.* | **17 F8** | 33 19N | 44 21 E |
| Tarango, Presa, *Méx.* | **29 B2** | 19 21N | 99 12W |
| Tårbæk, *Købn.* | **2 D10** | 55 46N | 12 35 E |
| Tarchomin, *Wsaw.* | **10 E6** | 52 19N | 20 58 E |
| Tardeo, *Bomb.* | **16 H7** | 18 57N | 72 48 E |
| Target Rock, *N.Y.* | **23 B8** | 40 55N | 73 24W |
| Targówek, *Wsaw.* | **10 E7** | 52 16N | 21 3 E |
| Tårnby, *Købn.* | **2 E10** | 55 37N | 12 35 E |

Villecresnes 47


Taronga Zoo. Park, Syd. 19 B4 33 50 S 151 14 E
Tarqua B., Lagos 18 B2 6 24N 7 23 E
Tarzana, L.A. 28 A1 34 10N 118 32W
Tåstrup, Købn. 2 E8 55 39N 12 18 E
Tatarovo, Mos. 11 E8 55 45N 37 24 E
Tatarpur, Delhi 16 B1 28 38N 77 9 E
Tatenberg, Hbg. 7 E8 53 29N 10 3 E
Tathong Channel, H.K. 12 E6 22 15N 114 16 E
Tathong Pt., H.K. 12 E6 22 14N 114 17 E
Tatsfield, Lon. 4 D5 51 17N 0 1 E
Tattariharju, Hels. 3 B5 60 15N 25 2 E
Tatuapé, S. Pau. 31 E6 23 31 S 46 33W
Taufkirchen, Mün. 7 G10 48 2N 11 36 E
Tavares, I. dos, Rio J. 31 A3 22 49 S 43 6W
Tavernanova, Nápl. 9 H13 40 54N 14 21 E
Taverny, Paris 5 A3 49 1N 2 13 E
Távros, Ath. 8 J11 37 57N 23 43 E
Tavry, St-Pet. 11 B6 59 54N 30 40 E
Taylortown, N.Y. 22 B2 40 56N 74 23W
Tayninka, Mos. 11 D10 55 53N 37 45 E
Taytay, Manila 15 D4 14 34N 121 7 E
Tayuman, Manila 15 D4 14 31N 121 9 E
Teaneck, N.Y. 22 B4 40 52N 74 1W
Teatro Colón, B.A. 32 B4 34 36 S 58 23 E
Teban Gardens, Sing. 15 G7 1 19N 103 44 E
Tebet, Jak. 15 J10 6 14 S 106 50 E
Tecamachaleo, Méx. 29 B2 19 25N 99 14W
Techny, Chic. 26 A2 42 6N 87 48W
Teck Hock, Sing. 15 F8 1 21N 103 54 E
Tecoma, Melb. 19 F9 37 54 S 145 20 E
Teddington, Lon. 4 C2 51 25N 0 20W
Tegel, Berl. 7 A2 52 34N 13 16 E
Tegel, Flughafen, Berl. 7 A2 52 35N 13 15 E
Tegeler Fliess →, Berl. 7 A3 52 37N 13 21 E
Tegeler See, Berl. 7 A2 52 34N 13 15 E
Tegelort, Berl. 7 A2 52 34N 13 13 E
Tehar, Delhi 16 B1 28 37N 77 7 E
Tehrān, Tehr. 17 C5 35 41N 51 25 E
Tehrān Pars, Tehr. 17 C6 35 44N 51 32 E
Tei Tong Tsui, H.K. 12 E6 22 16N 114 17 E
Tejo →, Lisb. 8 F8 38 45N 9 3W
Tekstilyshchik, Mos. 11 E10 55 42N 37 41 E
Tela, Delhi 16 A2 28 43N 77 19 E
Telhal, Lisb. 8 F7 38 48N 9 18W
Telinipara, Calc. 16 D6 22 46N 88 23 E
Telok Blangah, Sing. 15 G7 1 17N 103 49 E
Teltow, Berl. 7 B2 52 23N 13 17 E
Teltow kanal, Berl. 7 B3 52 26N 13 29 E
Temescal, L., S.F. 27 A3 37 50N 122 13W
Temnikovo, Mos. 11 E12 55 43N 38 1 E
Tempelhof, Berl. 7 B3 52 27N 13 23 E
Tempelhof, Flughafen, Berl. 7 B3 52 28N 13 27 E
Temperley, B.A. 32 C4 34 46 S 58 22W
Temple City, L.A. 28 B4 34 6N 118 3W
Temple Hills Park, Wash. 25 E8 38 48N 76 56W
Templestowe, Melb. 19 E7 37 45 S 145 8 E
Templestowe Lower, Melb. 19 E7 37 45 S 145 6 E
Tenafly, N.Y. 22 B5 40 54N 73 58W
Tenantongo, Presa, Méx. 29 B2 19 28N 99 15W
Tengah →, Sing. 15 F7 1 23N 103 43 E
Tengeh, Sungei →, Sing. 15 F6 1 20N 103 39 E
Tennoji, Ōsaka 12 C4 34 39N 135 30 E
Tenochtitlán, Méx. 29 B3 19 26N 99 7W
Tepalcates, Méx. 29 B3 19 23N 99 3W
Tepe Saif, Tehr. 17 D4 35 36N 51 17 E
Tepepan, Méx. 29 C3 19 16N 99 9W
Teplyy Star, Mos. 11 F9 55 37N 37 30 E
Tepozteco, Parque Nac. del, Méx. 29 D3 19 3N 99 5W
Terrasse Vaudreuil, Mtrl. 20 B2 43 23N 73 59W
Terrazzano, Mil. 9 D5 45 32N 9 4 E
Terrugem, Lisb. 8 F7 38 41N 9 17W
Terusan Banjir, Jak. 15 H9 6 7 S 106 46 E
Terzigno, Nápl. 9 J13 40 48N 14 29 E
Tessancourt-sur-Aubette, Paris 5 A1 49 1N 1 55 E
Testona, Tori. 9 C3 44 59N 7 42 E
Tetelco, Méx. 29 C4 19 12N 98 57W
Tetreauville, Mtrl. 20 A4 43 35N 73 32W
Tetti Neirotti, Tori. 9 B2 45 3N 7 32 E
Tetuán, Mdrd. 8 B2 40 27N 3 42W
Teufelsberg, Berl. 7 B2 52 29N 13 14 E
Tévere →, Rome 9 F9 41 56N 12 27 E
Tewksbury, Bost. 21 B2 42 37N 71 12W
Texcoco, L. de, Méx. 29 B4 19 30N 89 58 E
Thalkirchen, Mün. 7 G10 48 6N 11 32 E
Thames Ditton, Lon. 4 C2 51 23N 0 20W
Thamesmead, Lon. 4 B5 51 30N 0 7 E
Thana Cr. →, Bomb. 16 G8 19 4N 72 54 E
The Basin, Melb. 19 F8 37 51 S 145 19 E
The Glen, Wash. 25 C6 39 2N 77 12W
The Loop, Chic. 26 B3 41 52N 87 37W
The Narrows, N.Y. 22 D4 40 37N 74 3W
The Ridge, Delhi 16 B2 28 37N 77 10 E
The White House, Wash. 25 D7 38 53N 77 1W
The Wilds, Jobg. 18 F9 26 10 S 28 2 E
Theseión, Ath. 8 J11 37 57N 23 43 E
Theydon Bois, Lon. 4 A5 51 40N 0 6 E
Thiais, Paris 5 C4 48 46N 2 23 E
Thieux, Paris 5 A6 49 0N 2 40 E
Thistletown, Trto. 20 D7 43 44N 79 34W
Thiverval-Grignon, Paris 5 B1 48 51N 1 55 E
Thomaston, N.Y. 23 C6 40 47N 73 43W
Thomastown, Melb. 19 E7 37 40 S 145 2 E
Thompson I., Bost. 21 D4 42 19N 70 59W
Thomson, Sing. 15 F8 1 20N 103 50 E
Thon Buri, Bangk. 15 B1 13 45N 100 29 E
Thong Hoe, Sing. 15 F7 1 25N 103 42 E
Thorigny-sur-Marne, Paris 5 B6 48 53N 2 41 E
Thornbury, Melb. 19 E7 37 44 S 145 1 E
Thorncliffe, Trto. 20 D8 43 42N 79 20W
Thornhill, Jobg. 18 E9 26 6 S 28 9 E
Thornhill, Trto. 20 D8 43 48N 79 25W
Thornton, Phil. 24 B1 39 54N 75 31W
Thornton Heath, Lon. 4 C4 51 23N 0 6W
Thorofare, Phil. 24 B3 39 50N 75 11W
Throgs Neck, N.Y. 23 C6 40 48N 73 49W
Tian Guan, Sing. 15 F7 1 21N 103 49 E
Tian'anmen, Beij. 14 B3 39 53N 116 21 E
Tiancun, Beij. 14 B2 39 54N 116 12 E
Tianjin, Tianj. 14 E5 39 7N 117 12 E
Tiantan Gongyuan, Beij. 14 B3 39 51N 116 22 E
Tiateloco, Méx. 29 B3 19 27N 99 8W
Tibidabo, Barc. 8 D5 41 25N 2 6 E
Tiburon, S.F. 27 A2 37 52N 122 27W
Tiburon Pen., S.F. 27 A2 37 53N 122 28W
Tiburtino, Rome 9 F10 41 53N 12 30 E
Ticomán, Méx. 29 A3 19 31N 99 8W
Tiefenbroich, Ruhr 6 C2 51 18N 6 49 E
Tiefersee, Berl. 7 B1 52 24N 13 5 E
Tiejiangyin, Beij. 14 C3 39 49N 116 23 E
Tientsin = Tianjin, Tianj. 14 E5 39 7N 117 12 E
Tiergarten, Berl. 7 A3 52 31N 13 20 E
Tietê →, S. Pau. 31 D7 23 28 S 46 24W
Tigery, Paris 5 D5 48 38N 2 30 E
Tigre, B.A. 32 A3 34 25 S 58 34W
Tigris →, Bagd. 17 F8 33 17N 44 23 E
Tijuca, Rio J. 31 B2 22 56 S 43 13W
Tijuca, L. de, Rio J. 31 B2 22 59 S 43 20W
Tijuca, Pico da, Rio J. 31 B2 22 56 S 43 15W
Tijucamar, Rio J. 31 C2 23 0 S 43 18W
Tijucas, Is., Rio J. 31 C2 23 1 S 43 17W
Tikkurila, Hels. 3 B5 60 17N 25 2 E
Tilanqiao, Shang. 14 J11 31 15N 121 29 E
Tilbury, Lon. 4 C7 51 27N 0 21 E
Timah, Bukit, Sing. 15 F7 1 21N 103 46 E
Timiryazev Park, Mos. 11 E9 55 49N 37 33 E
Ting Kau, H.K. 12 D5 22 22N 114 4 E
Tinley Cr. →, Chic. 26 D2 41 39N 87 45W
Tinley Creek Woods, Chic. 26 D2 41 38N 87 48W
Tinley Park, Chic. 26 D2 41 35N 87 46W
Tipas, Manila 15 D4 14 32N 121 4 E
Tirsa, El Qâ. 18 D5 29 57N 31 12 E
Tishrīyaa, Bagd. 17 F8 33 18N 44 24 E
Tit Cham Chau, H.K. 12 E6 22 15N 114 17 E
Titagarh, Calc. 16 D6 22 44N 88 22 E
Tivoli, Købn. 2 D10 55 40N 12 35 E
Tizapán, Méx. 29 C2 19 19N 99 13W
Tlalnepantla, Méx. 29 A2 19 32N 99 11W
Tlalnepantla →, Méx. 29 A2 19 30N 99 18W
Tláloc, Cerro, Méx. 29 D3 19 7N 99 3W
Tlalpan, Méx. 29 C2 19 17N 99 10W
Tlalpitzáhuac, Méx. 29 C4 19 19N 98 56W
Tlaltenango, Méx. 29 B2 19 20N 99 17W
Tlaltenco, Méx. 29 C3 19 19N 99 0W
Tlaxcoaque, Méx. 29 B3 19 25N 99 8W
To Kwai Wan, H.K. 12 E6 22 18N 114 11 E
Toa Payoh, Sing. 15 F8 1 20N 103 50 E
Tobay Beach, N.Y. 23 D8 40 36N 73 26W
Točná, Pra. 10 C2 49 58N 14 25 E
Tocome →, Car. 30 D6 10 28N 66 49W
Toda, Tōkyō 13 A3 35 50N 139 40 E
Todamachī, Tōkyō 13 B2 35 48N 139 39 E
Todt Hill, N.Y. 22 D4 40 36N 74 6W
Toei, Khlong →, Bangk. 15 B2 13 43N 100 32 E
Togasaki, Tōkyō 13 B4 35 47N 139 51 E
Tōkagi, Tōkyō 13 B4 35 42N 139 55 E
Tōkaichiba, Tōkyō 13 C2 35 31N 139 30 E
Tokarevo, Mos. 11 F11 55 38N 37 54 E
Tokorozawa, Tōkyō 13 B1 35 47N 139 28 E
Tōkyō, Tōkyō 13 C3 35 43N 139 45 E
Tōkyō B., Tōkyō 13 C4 35 33N 139 53 E
Tōkyō-Haneda Int. Airport, Tōkyō 13 C3 35 33N 139 45 E
Tōkyō Harbour, Tōkyō 13 C3 35 38N 139 46 E
Tokyo Univ., Tōkyō 13 B3 35 42N 139 46 E
Tollygunge, Calc. 16 F6 22 29N 88 21 E
Tolly's Nala, Calc. 16 E6 22 33N 88 19 E
Tolworth, Lon. 4 C3 51 22N 0 17W
Tomang, Jak. 15 J9 6 10 S 106 47 E
Tomba di Nerone, Rome 9 F9 41 58N 12 26 E
Tomilino, Mos. 11 F11 55 39N 37 55 E
Tomioka, Tōkyō 13 D2 35 22N 139 37 E
Tonda, Ōsaka 12 B4 34 49N 135 35 E
Tondo, Manila 15 D3 14 36N 120 57 E
Tone-unga →, Tōkyō 13 A4 35 55N 139 56 E
Tonekollen, Oslo 2 C6 50 49N 11 0 E
Tong Kang, Sungei →, Sing. 15 F8 1 23N 103 53 E
Tonghui He →, Beij. 14 B3 39 53N 116 28 E
Tönisheide, Ruhr 6 C4 51 18N 7 3 E
Tonndorf, Hbg. 7 D8 53 35N 10 8 E
Toorak, Melb. 19 F7 37 50 S 145 1 E
Toot Hill, Lon. 4 A6 51 41N 0 11 E
Topilejo, Méx. 29 C3 19 12N 99 9W
Topkapi, Ist. 17 A2 41 1N 28 55 E
Topsfield, Bost. 21 B4 42 38N 70 57W
Tor di Quinto, Rome 9 F9 41 56N 12 27 E
Tor Pignattara, Rome 9 F10 41 52N 12 31 E
Tor Sapienza, Rome 9 F10 41 53N 12 35 E
Torcy, Paris 5 B5 48 51N 2 39 E
Torino, Tori. 9 B2 45 5N 7 39 E
Toro, B.A. 32 B1 34 30 S 58 50W
Toronto, Trto. 20 E9 43 39N 79 13W
Toronto, Univ. of, Trto. 20 E8 43 39N 79 23W
Toronto Harbour, Trto. 20 E8 43 38N 79 21W
Toronto I., Trto. 20 E8 43 37N 79 23W
Toronto Int. Airport, Trto. 20 D7 43 40N 79 38 E
Torre Annunziata, Nápl. 9 J13 40 45N 14 26 E
Torre Cervara, Rome 9 F10 41 55N 12 35 E
Torre del Greco, Nápl. 9 J13 40 47N 14 21 E
Torre Novo, Rome 9 F10 41 51N 12 36 E
Torrellas →, Barc. 8 D5 41 23N 2 1 E
Torrellas del Llobregat, Barc. 8 D4 41 20N 1 59 E
Torresdale, Phil. 24 A5 40 3N 74 59W
Torrevécchia, Rome 9 F9 41 55N 12 25 E
Tortuguitas, B.A. 32 A2 34 28 S 58 44W
Toshima-Ku, Tōkyō 13 B3 35 43N 139 43 E
Toshimaen, Tōkyō 13 B2 35 43N 139 38 E
Totowa, N.Y. 22 B3 40 54N 74 13W
Totsuka-Ku, Tōkyō 13 D2 35 23N 139 32 E
Tottenham, Lon. 4 B4 51 35N 0 4W
Tottenham, Melb. 19 E6 37 48 S 144 51 E
Tottenville, N.Y. 22 D3 40 30N 74 14W
Totteridge, Lon. 4 B3 51 37N 0 11W
Toussus-le-Noble, Paris 5 C2 48 44N 2 6 E
Toussus-le-Noble, Aérodrome de, Paris 5 C2 48 44N 2 6 E
Toverud, Oslo 2 B2 59 55N 10 20 E
Towaco, N.Y. 22 B3 40 55N 74 18W
Tower Hamlets, Lon. 4 B4 51 31N 0 2W
Town Farm Hill, Bost. 21 A3 42 40N 71 3W
Townley, N.Y. 22 C3 40 41N 74 14W
Towra Pt., Syd. 19 C4 34 0 S 151 10 E
Towson, Balt. 25 A3 39 24N 76 36W
Tøyen, Oslo 2 B4 59 55N 10 47 E
Toyofuta, Tōkyō 13 A4 35 54N 139 55 E
Toyonaka, Ōsaka 12 B3 34 46N 135 28 E
Traar, Ruhr 6 B1 51 22N 6 36 E
Trafaria, Lisb. 8 F7 38 40N 9 13W
Tragliata, Rome 9 F8 41 58N 12 14 E
Traicão →, S. Pau. 31 E6 23 35 S 46 41W
Trälhavet, Stock. 3 D13 59 26N 18 22 E
Tranby, Oslo 2 C1 59 49N 10 14 E
Tranegilde, Købn. 2 E9 55 37N 12 20 E
Trångsund, Stock. 3 E11 59 13N 18 8 E
Trappenfelde, Berl. 7 A4 52 34N 13 39 E
Trappes, Paris 5 C1 48 46N 1 59 E
Trastévere, Rome 9 F9 51 53N 12 28 E
Travilah, Wash. 25 C6 39 4N 77 15W
Travilah Regional Park, Wash. 25 C6 39 4N 77 17W
Travis, N.Y. 22 D3 40 35N 74 11W
Treasure I., S.F. 27 B2 37 49N 122 22W
Třeboradice, Pra. 10 B3 50 9N 14 31 E
Třebotov, Pra. 10 C1 49 58N 14 17 E
Trecase, Nápl. 9 J13 40 46N 14 26 E
Trekroner, Købn. 2 D10 55 42N 12 36 E
Tremblay-lès-Gonesse, Paris 5 B5 48 58N 2 30 E
Tremembé, S. Pau. 31 D6 23 27 S 46 36W
Tremembe →, S. Pau. 31 D6 23 27 S 46 34W
Tremont, Melb. 19 F9 37 53 S 145 20 E
Tremont, N.Y. 23 B5 40 50N 73 52W
Trenno, Mil. 9 E5 45 29N 9 6 E
Treptow, Berl. 7 B3 52 29N 13 27 E
Tres Marias, Méx. 29 D2 19 3N 99 15W
Trés Rios, Sa. dos, Rio J. 31 B2 22 56 S 43 17W
Tretiakov Art Gallery, Mos. 11 E9 55 44N 37 38 E
Trevose, Phil. 24 A5 40 8N 74 59W
Trezzano sul Navíglio, Mil. 9 E5 45 24N 9 4 E
Tribobo, Rio J. 31 B3 22 50 S 43 0W
Triel-sur-Seine, Paris 5 B2 48 58N 2 0 E
Trieste, Rome 9 F10 41 55N 12 30 E
Trinidad, Wash. 25 D8 38 54N 76 59W
Triome, Jobg. 18 F8 26 10 S 27 58 E
Trionfale, Rome 9 F9 41 54N 12 26 E
Triulzo, Mil. 9 E6 45 25N 9 16 E
Trócchia, Nápl. 9 H13 40 51N 14 23 E
Troitse-Lykovo, Mos. 11 E8 55 47N 37 23 E
Troja, Pra. 10 B2 50 7N 14 25 E
Trollbäcken, Stock. 3 E12 59 14N 18 12 E
Trombay, Bomb. 16 G8 19 2N 72 56 E
Troparevo, Mos. 11 F8 55 39N 37 29 E
Trottiscliffe, Lon. 4 D7 51 18N 0 21 E
Troy Hills, N.Y. 22 B2 40 50N 74 23W
Troyeville, Jobg. 18 F9 26 11 S 28 4 E
Truc di Miola, Tori. 9 A2 45 11N 7 30 E
Trudyashchikhsya, Os., St-Pet. 11 B3 59 58N 30 18 E
Trutlandet, Hels. 3 C6 60 9N 25 17 E
Tryvasshøgda, Oslo 2 B4 59 59N 10 40 E
Tseng Lan Shue, H.K. 12 D6 22 20N 114 14 E
Tsentralynyy, Mos. 11 D11 55 53N 37 51 E
Tsim Sha Tsui, H.K. 12 E6 22 17N 114 10 E
Tsing Yi, H.K. 12 D5 22 21N 114 6 E
Tsuen Wan, H.K. 12 D5 22 22N 114 7 E
Tsurugamine, Tōkyō 13 D2 35 28N 139 33 E
Tsuruma, Tōkyō 13 A2 35 52N 139 31 E
Tsurumi →, Tōkyō 13 C3 35 32N 139 40 E
Tsurumi-Ku, Tōkyō 13 D3 35 30N 139 41 E
Tsz Wan Shan, H.K. 12 D6 22 20N 114 11 E
Tua Kang Lye, Sing. 15 G7 1 18N 103 46 E
Tuas, Sing. 15 G6 1 19N 103 39 E
Tuchoměřice, Pra. 10 B1 50 7N 14 16 E
Tuckahoe, N.Y. 23 B6 40 56N 73 49W
Tucuruvi, S. Pau. 31 D6 23 28 S 46 35W
Tufello, Rome 9 F10 41 56N 12 32 E
Tufnell Park, Lon. 4 B4 51 33N 0 8W
Tujunga, L.A. 28 A3 34 15N 118 16W
Tujunga Wash →, L.A. 28 A2 34 12N 118 23W
Tullamarine, Melb. 19 E6 37 41 S 144 50 E
Tullinge, Stock. 3 E10 59 12N 17 54 E
Tullingesjön, Stock. 3 E10 59 12N 17 52 E
Tulse Hill, Lon. 4 C4 51 26N 0 6W
Tulyehualco, Méx. 29 C3 19 15N 99 0W
Tumba, Stock. 3 E9 59 12N 17 49 E
Tune, Købn. 2 E8 55 35N 12 10 E
Tung Lo Wan, H.K. 12 E6 22 17N 114 11 E
Tung Lung I., H.K. 12 E6 22 15N 114 17 E
Tung O, H.K. 12 E5 22 11N 114 8 E
Tunis, Bagd. 17 E8 33 23N 44 21 E
Tuomarila, Hels. 3 B3 60 11N 24 41 E
Tura, El Qâ. 18 D5 29 55N 31 16 E
Turambhe, Bomb. 16 G9 19 4N 73 0 E
Turdera, B.A. 32 C4 34 48 S 58 26W
Tureberg, Stock. 3 D10 59 25N 17 55 E
Turffontein, Jobg. 18 F9 26 14 S 28 2 E
Turin = Torino, Tori. 9 B2 45 5N 7 39 E
Turner, Balt. 25 B3 39 14N 76 31W
Turner Hill, Bost. 21 A4 42 40N 70 53W
Turnersville, Phil. 24 C4 39 46N 75 3W
Turnham Green, Lon. 4 C3 51 29N 0 16W
Turów, Wsaw. 10 E8 52 19N 21 11 E
Turter, Oslo 2 A4 60 0N 10 46 E
Tuscolano, Rome 9 F10 41 52N 12 31 E
Tushino, Mos. 11 D8 55 50N 37 24 E
Tuusulanjoki →, Hels. 3 A4 60 20N 24 54 E
Twickenham, Lon. 4 C2 51 26N 0 20W
Twickenham Rugby Ground, Lon. 4 C2 51 27N 0 20W
Twin Oaks, Phil. 24 B2 39 50N 75 25W
Twórki, Wsaw. 10 E5 52 10N 20 49 E
Tyresö, Stock. 3 E13 59 14N 18 20 E
Tyresö strand, Stock. 3 E12 59 15N 18 17 E


# U


Uberaba →, S. Pau. 31 E6 23 35 S 46 41W
Uberruhr, Ruhr 6 B4 51 25N 7 4 E
Ubin, P., Sing. 15 F8 1 24N 103 57 E
Uboldo, Mil. 9 D5 45 36N 9 0 E
Uckendorf, Ruhr 6 B4 51 29N 7 7 E
Udelnaya, St-Pet. 11 A4 60 0N 30 21 E
Udelynaya, Mos. 11 F11 55 38N 37 59 E
Udlding, Mün. 7 F9 48 15N 11 25 E
Uellendahl, Ruhr 6 C5 51 16N 7 10 E
Ueno, Tōkyō 13 B3 35 42N 139 46 E
Uerdingen, Ruhr 6 B1 51 21N 6 38 E
Uhlenhorst, Hbg. 7 D8 53 34N 10 1 E
Üholičky, Pra. 10 B1 50 9N 14 19 E
Uhřiněves, Pra. 10 B3 50 2N 14 35 E
Újezd nad Lesy, Pra. 10 B3 50 4N 14 39 E
Újpalota, Bud. 10 J13 47 32N 19 8 E
Újpest, Bud. 10 J13 47 35N 19 4 E
Ukita, Tōkyō 13 B4 35 40N 139 51 E
Ullerup, Købn. 2 E10 55 34N 12 36 E
Ullevål, Oslo 2 B4 59 56N 10 46 E
Üllo, Bud. 10 K14 47 23N 19 20 E
Ulriksdal, Stock. 3 D10 59 23N 17 59 E
Ulu Bedok, Sing. 15 G8 1 19N 103 55 E
Ulu Pandan →, Sing. 15 G7 1 19N 103 45 E
Ulyanka, St-Pet. 11 B3 59 50N 30 14 E
Um Al-Khanazir, Bagd. 17 F8 33 17N 44 22 E
Umeda, Ōsaka 12 B3 34 41N 135 29 E
Umejima, Tōkyō 13 B3 35 46N 139 48 E
Umraniye, Ist. 17 A3 41 1N 29 4 E
Unětický →, Pra. 10 B2 50 9N 14 24 E
Ungelsheim, Ruhr 6 B2 51 21N 6 43 E
Unhos, Lisb. 8 F8 38 49N 9 7W
Unidad Santa Fe, Méx. 29 B2 19 23N 99 13W
Union, N.Y. 22 C3 40 42N 74 16W
Union City, N.Y. 22 C4 40 45N 74 2W
Union City, S.F. 27 C4 37 36N 122 2W
Union Port, N.Y. 23 C5 40 48N 73 51W
Uniondale, N.Y. 23 C7 40 42N 73 35W
United Nations H.Q., N.Y. 22 C5 40 45N 73 59W
Universal City, L.A. 28 B2 34 8N 118 21W
Universidad de Chila, Stgo 30 J11 33 26 S 70 39W
University Gardens, N.Y. 23 C6 40 46N 73 42W
University Heights, S.F. 27 D3 37 26N 122 13W
University Park, Wash. 25 D8 38 58N 76 56W
Unsani, Calc. 16 E5 22 35N 88 15 E
Unterbach, Ruhr 6 C3 51 12N 6 53 E
Unterbiberg, Mün. 7 G10 48 6N 11 38 E
Unterföhring, Mün. 7 F11 48 11N 11 38 E
Unterhaching, Mün. 7 G10 48 3N 11 37 E
Unterkirchbach, Wien 10 G9 48 17N 16 12 E
Unterlaa, Wien 10 H10 48 8N 16 24 E
Untermauerbach, Wien 10 G9 48 14N 16 11 E
Untermenzing, Mün. 7 F9 48 10N 11 28 E
Unterrath, Ruhr 6 C2 51 16N 6 45 E
Unterschleissheim, Mün. 7 F10 48 16N 11 35 E
Upminster, Lon. 4 B6 51 33N 0 14 E
Upper Brookville, N.Y. 23 B7 40 50N 73 35W
Upper Crystal Springs Res., S.F. 26 D2 37 28N 122 20W
Upper Darby, Phil. 24 B3 39 57N 75 16W
Upper Edmonton, Lon. 4 B4 51 36N 0 3W
Upper Elmers End, Lon. 4 C4 51 23N 0 1W
Upper Fern Tree Gully, Melb. 19 F8 37 53 S 145 18 E
Upper New York B., N.Y. 22 D4 40 39N 74 3W
Upper Norwood, Lon. 4 C4 51 24N 0 6W
Upper Peirce Res., Sing. 15 F7 1 22N 103 47 E
Upper San Leandro Res., S.F. 27 B4 37 46N 122 6W
Upper Sydenham, Lon. 4 C4 51 26N 0 4W
Upper Tooting, Lon. 4 C4 51 25N 0 9W
Upton, Lon. 4 B5 51 32N 0 1 E
Uptons Hill, Bost. 21 B3 42 33N 71 0W
Uptown, Chic. 26 B2 41 58N 87 40W
Upwey, Melb. 19 F9 37 53 S 145 20 E
Urawa, Tōkyō 13 A2 35 51N 139 39 E
Urayasu, Tōkyō 13 C4 35 39N 139 53 E
Urbe, Aeroporto d', Rome 9 F10 41 57N 12 30 E
Urca, Rio J. 31 B3 22 56 S 43 9W
Uritsk, St-Pet. 11 C3 59 49N 30 10 E
Üröm, Bud. 10 J13 47 35N 19 1 E
Ursus, Wsaw. 10 E6 52 11N 20 52 E
Ursvik, Stock. 3 D10 59 23N 17 57 E
Usera, Mdrd. 8 B2 40 22N 3 42W
Ushigome, Tōkyō 13 B3 35 42N 139 44 E
Usküdar, Ist. 17 A3 41 1N 29 0 E
Ust-Slavyanka, St-Pet. 11 C5 59 51N 30 32 E
Uteke, Stock. 3 D12 59 24N 18 15 E
Utfort, Ruhr 6 B1 51 28N 6 37 E
Utinga, S. Pau. 31 E6 23 38 S 46 31W
Utrata, Wsaw. 10 E7 52 15N 21 4 E
Uttarpara, Calc. 16 E5 22 39N 88 21 E
Utterslev Mose, Købn. 2 D9 55 42N 12 29 E
Uttran, Stock. 3 E9 59 12N 17 43 E
Utvika, Oslo 2 A1 60 2N 10 15 E
Uxbridge, Lon. 4 B2 51 32N 0 28W
Uzkoye, Mos. 11 F9 55 37N 37 32 E
Uzunca →, Ist. 17 A1 41 54N 28 50 E


# V


Vadaul, Bomb. 16 G8 19 2N 72 55 E
Værebro Å →, Købn. 2 D8 55 47N 12 7 E
Vahal, Bomb. 16 H9 18 58N 73 2 E
Vaires-sur-Marne, Paris 5 B5 48 52N 2 38 E
Val della Torre, Tori. 9 B1 45 8N 7 27 E
Valby, Købn. 2 E9 55 39N 12 29 E
Valcannuta, Rome 9 F9 41 52N 12 25 E
Valdeveba, Mdrd. 8 B3 40 29N 3 39W
Vale, Wash. 25 D5 38 55N 77 20W
Valentino, Parco del, Tori. 9 B3 45 3N 7 41 E
Valenton, Paris 5 C4 48 44N 2 27 E
Valera, Mil. 9 D5 45 33N 9 3 E
Vallcarca, Barc. 8 D5 41 25N 2 9 E
Valldoreix, Barc. 8 D5 41 27N 2 3 E
Vallecas, Mdrd. 8 B3 40 22N 3 37W
Vallemar, S.F. 27 C2 37 36N 122 28W
Vallensbæk, Købn. 2 E9 55 38N 12 21 E
Vallensbæk Strand, Købn. 2 E9 55 36N 12 23 E
Vallentunasjön, Stock. 3 D11 59 27N 18 1 E
Valleranello, Rome 9 G9 41 46N 12 29 E
Valley Forge, Phil. 24 A2 40 5N 75 27W
Valley Forge Hist. State Park, Phil. 24 A2 40 5N 75 27W
Valley Mede, Balt. 25 B1 39 16N 76 50W
Valley Stream, N.Y. 23 C6 40 40N 73 43W
Vällingby, Stock. 3 D10 59 21N 17 52 E
Vallisaari, Hels. 3 C5 60 7N 25 0 E
Vallvidrera, Barc. 8 D5 41 24N 2 6 E
Valo Velho, S. Pau. 31 E5 23 38 S 46 47W
Valuyevo, Mos. 11 F8 55 30N 37 21 E
Valvidrera →, Barc. 8 D5 41 25N 2 0 E
Van Dyks Park, Jobg. 18 F10 26 15 S 28 18 E
Van Nuys, L.A. 28 A2 34 11N 118 27W
Van Nuys Airport, L.A. 28 A2 34 12N 118 29W
Van Ryn Dam, Jobg. 18 E11 26 8 S 28 21 E
Vanak, Tehr. 17 C5 35 45N 51 23 E
Vangede, Købn. 2 D10 55 45N 12 30 E
Vaniköy, Ist. 17 A3 41 3N 29 3 E
Vanløse, Købn. 2 D9 55 41N 12 28 E
Vantaa, Hels. 3 B4 60 18N 24 56 E
Vantaa →, Hels. 3 B4 60 13N 24 53 E
Vantaankoski, Hels. 3 B4 60 18N 24 50 E
Vantör, Stock. 3 E11 59 16N 18 2 E
Vanves, Paris 5 C3 48 49N 2 17 E
Vanzago, Mil. 9 D4 45 31N 8 59 E
Värby, Stock. 3 E10 59 15N 17 52 E
Vardåsen, Oslo 2 C6 50 48N 11 6 E
Varedo, Mil. 9 D5 45 35N 9 8 E
Varennes-Jarcy, Paris 5 C5 48 40N 2 33 E
Vargem Grande, Rio J. 31 B1 22 58 S 43 27W
Városliget, Bud. 10 J13 47 30N 19 5 E
Vartiokylä, Hels. 3 B5 60 13N 25 6 E
Vartiosaari, Hels. 3 B5 60 11N 25 5 E
Vasby, Købn. 2 D8 55 40N 12 12 E
Vashi, Bomb. 16 G8 19 4N 72 59 E
Vasilyevskiy, Os., St-Pet. 11 B3 59 55N 30 16 E
Västerkulla, Hels. 3 B2 60 16N 24 31 E
Västerskog, Hels. 3 B6 60 16N 25 17 E
Vasto, Nápl. 9 H12 40 51N 14 16 E
Vatutino, Mos. 11 D10 55 52N 37 40 E
Vaucresson, Paris 5 B2 48 50N 2 9 E
Vaudreuil, Mtrl. 20 B1 43 24N 74 1W
Vaudreuil-sur-le Lac, Mtrl. 20 B1 43 25N 74 1W
Vauhallan, Paris 5 C3 48 44N 2 12 E
Vaujours, Paris 5 B5 48 56N 2 34 E
Vauréal, Paris 5 A2 49 2N 2 1 E
Vaux-sur-Seine, Paris 5 A1 49 0N 1 57 E
Vauxhall, Lon. 4 C4 51 29N 0 7W
Vaxholm, Stock. 3 D13 59 24N 18 20 E
Vecklax, Hels. 3 B2 60 10N 24 31 E
Vecsés, Bud. 10 K14 47 24N 19 16 E
Vedano al Lissone, Mil. 9 D6 45 36N 9 16 E
Veddel, Hbg. 7 D8 53 31N 10 2 E
Vega, Stock. 3 E11 59 11N 18 8 E
Vehkalahti, Hels. 3 B2 60 11N 24 30 E
Veikkola, Hels. 3 B1 60 17N 24 26 E
Velbert, Ruhr 6 B4 51 21N 7 1 E
Veleň, Pra. 10 A3 50 10N 14 33 E
Veleslavin, Pra. 10 B2 50 5N 14 21 E
Vélizy-Villacoublay, Paris 5 C3 48 47N 2 11 E
Velka-Chuchle, Pra. 10 B2 50 0N 14 23 E
Venaria, Tori. 9 B2 45 8N 7 37 E
Venda Seca, Lisb. 8 F7 38 46N 9 15W
Vendelsö, Stock. 3 E12 59 12N 18 11 E
Venice, L.A. 28 C2 33 59N 118 27W
Venner, Oslo 2 A3 60 1N 10 36 E
Vennhausen, Ruhr 6 C3 51 13N 6 51 E
Ventas, Mdrd. 8 B2 40 26N 3 40W
Ventorro del Cano, Mdrd. 8 B2 40 23N 3 49W
Verberg, Ruhr 6 B1 51 21N 6 34 E
Verde →, S. Pau. 31 E7 23 29 S 46 27W
Verdi, Ath. 8 H11 38 2N 23 40 E
Verdugo Mt., L.A. 28 A3 34 12N 118 17W
Verdun, Mtrl. 20 B4 43 27N 73 35W
Vereya, Mos. 11 F12 55 37N 38 2 E
Vérhalom, Bud. 10 J13 47 31N 19 1 E
Vermelho →, S. Pau. 31 E5 23 30 S 46 46W
Vermont, Melb. 19 F8 37 50 S 145 12 E
Vermont South, Melb. 19 F8 37 51 S 145 11 E
Verneuil-sur-Seine, Paris 5 B1 48 58N 1 59 E
Vernouillet, Paris 5 B1 48 58N 1 56 E
Verona, N.Y. 22 C3 40 49N 74 15W
Verperluda, Os., St-Pet. 11 B2 59 59N 30 0 E
Verrières-le-Buisson, Paris 5 C3 48 44N 2 16 E
Versailles, B.A. 32 B3 34 38 S 58 31W
Versailles, Paris 5 C2 48 48N 2 7 E
Veshnyaki, Mos. 11 E10 55 43N 37 48 E
Vesolyy Posolok, St-Pet. 11 B4 59 53N 30 28 E
Vestli, Oslo 2 B5 59 58N 10 55 E
Vestra, Hels. 3 B3 60 19N 24 46 E
Vestskoven, Købn. 2 D9 55 41N 12 23 E
Vesuvio, Nápl. 9 J13 40 49N 14 25 E
Vets Stadium, Phil. 24 B3 39 54N 75 10W
Viby, Købn. 2 E7 55 33N 12 1 E
Vicálvaro, Mdrd. 8 B3 40 24N 3 36W
Vicente Lopez, B.A. 32 B4 34 31 S 58 30W
Victoria, B.A. 32 A3 34 27 S 58 32W
Victoria, H.K. 12 E6 22 17N 114 11 E
Victoria, Pont, Mtrl. 20 B4 43 29N 73 32W
Victoria Gardens, Bomb. 16 H8 18 58N 72 50 E
Victoria Harbour, H.K. 12 E5 22 17N 114 10 E
Victoria Island, Lagos 18 B2 6 25N 7 25 E
Victoria L., Jobg. 18 F9 26 13 S 28 9 E
Victoria Lawn Tennis Courts, Melb. 19 F7 37 50 S 145 1 E
Victoria Park, H.K. 12 E5 22 16N 114 8 E
Vidja, Stock. 3 E11 59 12N 18 4 E
Vidrholec, Pra. 10 B3 50 5N 14 39 E
Vienna = Wien, Wien 10 G10 48 12N 16 22 E
Vienna, Wash. 25 D6 38 54N 77 16W
Vieringhausen, Ruhr 6 C4 51 10N 7 9 E
Vierlinden, Ruhr 6 A2 51 32N 6 45 E
Vierumäki, Hels. 3 A5 60 21N 25 2 E
Vierzigstücken, Hbg. 7 D6 53 30N 9 49 E
View Bank, Melb. 19 E7 37 43 S 145 6 E
Vigário Geral, Rio J. 31 A2 22 48 S 43 18W
Vigentino, Mil. 9 E6 45 26N 9 13 E
Viggbyholm, Stock. 3 D11 59 26N 18 7 E
Vighignolo, Mil. 9 E5 45 29N 9 2 E
Vigneux-sur-Seine, Paris 5 C4 48 42N 2 24 E
Viikki, Hels. 3 B5 60 13N 25 1 E
Viirilä, Hels. 3 B5 60 19N 25 8 E
Vila Andrade, S. Pau. 31 E5 23 37 S 46 44W
Vila Barcelona, S. Pau. 31 E6 23 37 S 46 33W
Vila Bocaina, S. Pau. 31 F7 23 40 S 46 26W
Vila Dalva, S. Pau. 31 E5 23 34 S 46 46W
Vila Dirce, S. Pau. 31 E4 23 33 S 46 50W
Vila Eldorado, S. Pau. 31 F6 23 42 S 46 38W
Vila Ema, S. Pau. 31 E6 23 35 S 46 31W
Vila Formosa, S. Pau. 31 E6 23 36 S 46 44W
Vila Galvão, S. Pau. 31 D6 23 27 S 46 34W
Vila Gonçales, S. Pau. 31 F6 23 42 S 46 33W
Vila Iasi, S. Pau. 31 E5 23 37 S 46 47W
Vila Indiana, S. Pau. 31 E5 23 37 S 46 48W
Vila Isabel, Rio J. 31 B2 22 54 S 43 15W
Vila Madalena, S. Pau. 31 E5 23 32 S 46 41W
Vila Maria, S. Pau. 31 E6 23 31 S 46 36W
Vila Mariana, S. Pau. 31 E6 23 34 S 46 36W
Vila Matilde, S. Pau. 31 E6 23 31 S 46 30W
Vila Nova Curuçá, S. Pau. 31 E7 23 31 S 46 25W
Vila Pires, S. Pau. 31 F6 23 41 S 46 30W
Vila Progresso, Rio J. 31 B3 22 53 S 43 1W
Vila Prudente, S. Pau. 31 E6 23 35 S 46 33W
Vila Ré, S. Pau. 31 E7 23 31 S 46 29W
Vila Remo, S. Pau. 31 F5 23 40 S 46 45W
Vila Sonia, S. Pau. 31 E5 23 35 S 46 43W
Viladecans, Barc. 8 E5 41 18N 2 1 E
Villa Ada, Rome 9 F10 41 55N 12 30 E
Villa Adelina, B.A. 32 B3 34 31 S 58 33W
Villa Alianza, B.A. 32 B3 34 37 S 58 33W
Villa Alsina, B.A. 32 C4 34 40 S 58 24W
Villa Altube, B.A. 32 B2 34 31 S 58 45W
Villa Ariza, B.A. 32 B3 34 38 S 58 39W
Villa Augusta, B.A. 32 C5 34 45 S 58 15W
Villa Ballester, B.A. 32 B3 34 33 S 58 33W
Villa Barilari, B.A. 32 C4 34 42 S 58 20W
Villa Basso, B.A. 32 B3 34 38 S 58 36W
Villa Bosch, B.A. 32 B3 34 35 S 58 33W
Villa C. Colon, B.A. 32 C4 34 41 S 58 21W
Villa D. F. Sarmiento, B.A. 32 B3 34 38 S 58 35W
Villa D. Sobral, B.A. 32 C5 34 45 S 58 15W
Villa de Guadalupe, Méx. 29 B3 19 29N 99 6W
Villa de Mayo, B.A. 32 B2 34 30 S 58 40W
Villa Devoto, B.A. 32 B3 34 36 S 58 31W
Villa Dominico, B.A. 32 C5 34 41 S 58 19W
Villa Giambruno, B.A. 32 C5 34 48 S 58 15W
Villa Gustavo A. Madero, Méx. 29 B3 19 29N 99 8W
Villa Hogar Alemán, B.A. 32 C4 34 49 S 58 26W
Villa Iglesias, B.A. 32 B2 34 30 S 58 45W
Villa Leloir, B.A. 32 B2 34 36 S 58 41W
Villa Leon, B.A. 32 B2 34 38 S 58 41W
Villa Lugano, B.A. 32 C4 34 41 S 58 27W
Villa Luzuriago, B.A. 32 C3 34 40 S 58 34W
Villa Lynch, B.A. 32 B3 34 35 S 58 31W
Villa Madero, B.A. 32 C3 34 41 S 58 30W
Villa Maria del Triunfo, Lima 30 G9 12 9 S 76 57W
Villa Obregon, Méx. 29 B2 19 20N 99 12W
Villa Reichembach, B.A. 32 B2 34 39 S 58 40W
Villa Rosa, B.A. 32 A1 34 25 S 58 5W
Villa San Francisco, B.A. 32 C5 34 46 S 58 15W
Villacoublay, Aérodrome de, Paris 5 C3 48 46N 2 12 E
Village Green, Phil. 24 B2 39 52N 75 26W
Villanova, Phil. 24 A2 40 1N 75 20W
Villarbasse, Tori. 9 B1 45 2N 7 27 E
Villaretto, Tori. 9 B3 45 8N 7 41 E
Villaricca, Nápl. 9 H12 40 55N 14 11 E
Villaroche, Paris 5 D5 48 37N 2 39 E
Villaroy, Paris 5 C2 48 46N 2 5 E
Villasanta, Mil. 9 D6 45 36N 9 18 E
Villastanza, Mil. 9 D4 45 32N 8 57 E
Villaverde, Mdrd. 8 B2 40 21N 3 42W
Villaverde Bajo, Mdrd. 8 B2 40 20N 3 40W
Villawood, Syd. 19 B2 33 52 S 150 58 E
Ville-d'Avray, Paris 5 C3 48 49N 2 11 E
Ville de Laval, Mtrl. 20 A3 43 34N 73 43W
Villebon-sur-Yvette, Paris 5 C3 48 41N 2 14 E
Villecresnes, Paris 5 C5 48 43N 2 31 E

48 Villejuif


Villejuif, *Paris* 5 C4 48 47N 2 21 E
Villejust, *Paris* 5 C3 48 41N 2 15 E
Villemoisson-sur-Orge, *Paris* 5 C3 48 40N 2 19 E
Villemomble, *Paris* 5 B5 48 52N 2 30 E
Villeneuve-la-Garenne, *Paris* 5 B3 48 56N 2 19 E
Villeneuve-le-Roi, *Paris* 5 C4 48 43N 2 24 E
Villeneuve-St.-Georges, *Paris* 5 C4 48 43N 2 27 E
Villeneuve-sous-Dammartin, *Paris* 5 A5 49 2N 2 38 E
Villennes-sur-Seine, *Paris* 5 B1 48 56N 2 0 E
Villeparisis, *Paris* 5 B5 48 56N 2 36 E
Villepinte, *Paris* 5 B5 48 57N 2 30 E
Villepreux, *Paris* 5 C1 48 49N 1 59 E
Villevaudé, *Paris* 5 B5 48 55N 2 39 E
Villeziers, *Paris* 5 C3 48 40N 2 10 E
Villiers-le-Bâcle, *Paris* 5 C2 48 44N 2 8 E
Villiers-le-Bel, *Paris* 5 A4 49 0N 2 23 E
Villiers-St. Frédéric, *Paris* 5 C1 48 49N 1 53 E
Villiers-sur-Marne, *Paris* 5 C5 48 49N 2 32 E
Villiers-sur-Orge, *Paris* 5 D3 48 39N 2 18 E
Villinki, *Hels.* 3 C5 60 9N 25 6 E
Villoresi, Canale, *Mil.* 9 D4 45 33N 8 59 E
Vimodrone, *Mil.* 9 D6 45 30N 9 16 E
Vimont, *Mtrl.* 20 A3 43 36N 73 43W
Vincennes, *Paris* 5 B4 48 51N 2 26 E
Vincennes, Bois de, *Paris* 5 C4 48 49N 2 26 E
Vinohrady, *Pra.* 10 B2 50 4N 14 26 E
Vinoř, *Pra.* 10 B3 50 8N 14 34 E
Vinořský →, *Pra.* 10 A3 50 11N 14 39 E
Violet Hill, *H.K.* 12 E6 22 15N 114 11 E
Virányos, *Bud.* 10 J12 47 31N 18 59 E
Virgeo del San Cristóbal, *Stgo* 30 J11 33 25 S 70 38W
Viroflay, *Paris* 5 C3 48 48N 2 10 E
Viron, *Ath.* 8 J11 37 55N 23 46 E
Virreyes, *B.A.* 32 A3 34 27 S 58 33W
Virum, *Købn.* 2 D9 55 47N 12 27 E
Viry-Châtillon, *Paris* 5 C4 48 40N 2 21 E
Vishnyaki, *Mos.* 11 E11 55 46N 37 53 E
Visitacion Valley, *S.F.* 27 B2 37 42N 122 23W
Vista Alegre, *Lima* 30 G9 12 8 S 76 59W
Vista Alegre, *Stgo* 30 K10 33 30 S 70 43W
Vitacura, *Stgo* 30 J11 33 23 S 70 35W
Vitarte-Ate, *Lima* 30 G9 12 3 S 76 57W
Vitinia, *Rome* 9 G9 41 47N 12 24 E
Vitry-sur-Seine, *Paris* 5 C4 48 47N 2 23 E
Vitträsk, *Hels.* 3 B1 60 11N 24 29 E
Vittuone, *Mil.* 9 E4 45 28N 8 57 E
Vladykino, *Mos.* 11 D9 55 51N 37 35 E
Vltava →, *Pra.* 10 A2 50 10N 14 2 E
Vnukovo, *Mos.* 11 F7 55 37N 37 17 E
Voerde, *Ruhr* 6 C6 51 18N 7 23 E
Voerde, *Ruhr* 6 A2 51 35N 6 42 E
Vogelheim, *Ruhr* 6 B3 51 29N 6 59 E
Vohwinkel, *Ruhr* 6 C4 51 13N 7 4 E
Voisins-le-Bretonneux, *Paris* 5 C2 48 45N 2 3 E
Vokovice, *Pra.* 10 B2 50 5N 14 21 E
Volgelsdorf, *Berl.* 7 B5 52 30N 13 44 E
Volkhonka-Zil, *Mos.* 11 F9 55 39N 37 37 E
Volkovka →, *St-Pet.* 11 B4 59 54N 30 25 E
Volksdorf, *Hbg.* 7 D8 53 39N 10 8 E
Volla, *Nápl.* 9 H13 40 52N 14 20 E
Vollen, *Oslo* 2 C2 59 48N 10 27 E
Volmarstein, *Ruhr* 6 B6 51 22N 7 22 E
Volodarskoye, *St-Pet.* 11 B4 59 54N 30 23 E
Volpiano, *Tori.* 9 A3 45 12N 7 46 E
Volynkina-Derevnya, *St-Pet.* 11 B3 59 53N 30 18 E
Volynyy, Os., *St-Pet.* 11 B3 59 57N 30 14 E
Vōmero, *Nápl.* 9 H12 40 50N 14 13 E
Vorderhainbach, *Wien* 10 G9 48 13N 16 12 E
Vorhalle, *Ruhr* 6 B6 51 23N 7 26 E
Vormholz, *Ruhr* 6 B5 51 24N 7 19 E
Vösendorf, *Wien* 10 H10 48 7N 16 20 E
Vostochnyy, *Mos.* 11 E11 55 49N 37 51 E
Vouliagmeni, *Ath.* 8 K11 37 50N 23 46 E
Vrčovice, *Pra.* 10 B2 50 4N 14 28 E
Vsevolozhsk, *St-Pet.* 11 A5 60 0N 30 39 E
Vuosaari, *Hels.* 3 B5 60 13N 25 8 E
Vyborgskaya Storona, *St-Pet.* 11 B4 59 57N 30 22 E
Vyčehrad, *Pra.* 10 B2 50 3N 14 25 E
Vykhino, *Mos.* 11 E10 55 42N 37 48 E
Vysočany, *Pra.* 10 B2 50 6N 14 29 E


# W


Waban, L., *Bost.* 21 D2 42 17N 71 18W
Wachterhof, *Mün.* 7 G11 48 2N 11 42 E
Waddington, *Lon.* 4 D4 51 18N 0 7W
Wadeville, *Jobg.* 18 F10 26 15 S 28 11 E
Wahda, *Bagd.* 17 F8 33 18N 44 26 E
Währing, *Wien* 10 G10 48 14N 16 20 E
Waidmannslust, *Berl.* 7 A3 52 36N 13 20 E
Wajay, *La Hab.* 30 B2 23 0N 82 25W
Wakefield, *Bost.* 21 B3 42 30N 71 5W
Wald, *Ruhr* 6 C4 51 11N 7 3 E
Waldesruh, *Berl.* 7 B4 52 28N 13 37 E
Waldheim, *Berl.* 7 A1 52 34N 13 3 E
Waldperlach, *Mün.* 7 G11 48 4N 11 40 E
Waldtrudering, *Mün.* 7 G11 48 6N 11 42 E
Waldwick, *N.Y.* 22 A4 41 1N 74 5W
Wall Street, *N.Y.* 22 C4 40 42N 74 0W
Wallgrove, *Syd.* 19 A2 33 47 S 150 51 E
Wallington, *Lon.* 4 C4 51 21N 0 8W
Wallington, *N.Y.* 22 B4 40 50N 74 8W
Walnut Cr. →, *S.F.* 27 A4 37 55N 122 3W
Walnut Creek, *S.F.* 27 A4 37 53N 122 3W
Walnut Heights, *S.F.* 27 A4 37 52N 122 2W
Walsum, *Ruhr* 6 A2 51 32N 6 42 E
Walsumer Mark, *Ruhr* 6 A3 51 33N 6 50 E
Walt Whitman Br., *Phil.* 24 B4 39 4N 75 9W
Waltershof, *Hbg.* 7 D7 53 31N 9 54 E
Waltham, *Bost.* 21 C2 42 23N 71 14W
Waltham Abbey, *Lon.* 4 A5 51 41N 0 1 E
Waltham Forest, *Lon.* 4 B4 51 36N 0 0 E
Walthamstow, *Lon.* 4 B4 51 34N 0 1W
Walton on Thames, *Lon.* 4 C2 51 22N 0 23W
Walton on the Hill, *Lon.* 4 D3 51 16N 0 14W
Waltrop, *Ruhr* 6 A6 51 36N 7 25 E
Walworth, *Lon.* 4 C4 51 29N 0 5W
Wambachsee, *Ruhr* 6 B2 51 23N 6 47 E
Wan Chai, *H.K.* 12 E6 22 16N 114 10 E
Wanaque, *N.Y.* 22 A3 41 1N 74 17W
Wandezhuang, *Tianj.* 14 E5 39 6N 117 10 E
Wandle →, *Lon.* 4 C3 51 27N 0 11W
Wandsbek, *Hbg.* 7 D8 53 34N 10 4 E
Wandsworth, *Lon.* 4 C3 51 27N 0 11W
Wang Hin, Khlong →, *Bangk.* 15 A2 13 50N 100 35 E
Wanheim, *Ruhr* 6 B2 51 23N 6 45 E
Wanheimerort, *Ruhr* 6 B2 51 24N 6 45 E
Wanne-Eickel, *Ruhr* 6 A4 51 31N 7 9 E
Wannsee, *Berl.* 7 B1 52 25N 13 9 E
Wansdorf, *Berl.* 7 A1 52 38N 13 5 E
Wanstead, *Lon.* 4 B5 51 34N 0 1 E
Wantagh Seaford, *N.Y.* 23 D8 40 39N 73 28W
Wantirna, *Melb.* 19 F8 37 50 S 145 14 E
Wapping, *Lon.* 4 B4 51 30N 0 3W
Warabi, *Tōkyō* 13 B3 35 49N 139 42 E
Ward, *Phil.* 24 B1 39 52N 75 30W
Warlingham, *Lon.* 4 D4 51 18N 0 2W
Warnberg, *Mün.* 7 G10 48 4N 11 31 E
Warngal Park, *Melb.* 19 E7 37 45 S 145 4 E
Warrandyte, *Melb.* 19 E8 37 43 S 145 13 E
Warrandyte Park, *Melb.* 19 E8 37 44 S 145 14 E
Warrandyte South, *Melb.* 19 E8 37 44 S 145 14 E
Warranwood, *Melb.* 19 E8 37 46 S 145 14 E
Warrâq el 'Arab, *El Qâ.* 18 C5 30 4N 31 11 E
Warrâq el Hadf, *El Qâ.* 18 C5 30 5N 31 12 E
Warren Hill, *Bost.* 21 B1 42 35N 71 21W
Warsaw = Warszawa, *Wsaw.* 10 E7 52 14N 21 0 E
Warszawa, *Wsaw.* 10 E7 52 14N 21 0 E
Wartenberg, *Berl.* 7 A4 52 34N 13 31 E
Warwick Farm Racetrack, *Syd.* 19 B2 33 54 S 150 56 E
Wasa, *Stock.* 3 E11 59 19N 18 5 E
Wasfanārd, *Tehr.* 17 D5 35 38N 51 20 E
Washington, *Wash.* 25 D7 38 53N 77 2W
Washington Heights, *N.Y.* 22 B5 40 51N 73 56W
Washington Memorial Museum, *Phil.* 24 A2 40 5N 75 26W
Washington Nat. Airport, *Wash.* 25 D7 38 51N 77 2W
Washington Park, *Chic.* 26 C3 41 47N 87 36W
Washington Square, *Phil.* 24 A3 40 9N 75 19W
Washington Township, *N.Y.* 22 A4 41 0N 74 3W
Wasserschloss, *Ruhr* 6 A4 51 32N 7 1 E
Watching Mts., *N.Y.* 22 C2 40 43N 74 20W
Watchung, *N.Y.* 22 D2 40 38N 74 29W
Waterloo, *Syd.* 19 B4 33 53 S 151 12 E
Waterman Mt., *L.A.* 28 A5 34 14N 117 56W
Watertown, *Bost.* 21 C2 42 22N 71 10W
Watford, *Lon.* 4 A2 51 40N 0 27W
Watkins Island, *Wash.* 25 C6 39 2N 77 15W
Watsonia, *Melb.* 19 E7 37 43 S 145 6 E
Watsons B., *Syd.* 19 B4 33 50 S 151 18 E
Watsons Creek, *Melb.* 19 E8 37 40 S 145 13 E
Wattenscheid, *Ruhr* 6 B4 51 28N 7 8 E
Wattle Glen, *Melb.* 19 D8 37 39 S 145 11 E
Wattle Park, *Melb.* 19 F7 37 50 S 145 6 E
Watts →, *Wash.* 25 C6 39 2N 77 15W
Waverley, *Bost.* 21 C2 42 23N 71 10W
Waverley, *Jobg.* 18 E9 26 7 S 28 4 E
Waverley, *Syd.* 19 B4 33 53 S 151 15 E
Wawer, *Wsaw.* 10 E7 52 13N 21 8 E
Wawrzyszew, *Wsaw.* 10 E6 52 17N 20 53 E
Wayland, *Bost.* 21 C1 42 21N 71 20W
Wayne, *N.Y.* 22 B3 40 55N 74 15W
Wayne, *Phil.* 24 A2 40 2N 75 24W
Wazirabad, *Delhi* 16 A2 28 43N 77 13 E
Wazīrīya, *Bagd.* 17 E8 33 22N 44 23 E
Wazirpur, *Delhi* 16 A2 28 41N 77 10 E
Weald Park, *Lon.* 4 B6 51 37N 0 16 E
Wedding, *Berl.* 7 A3 52 32N 13 21 E
Weehawken, *N.Y.* 22 C4 40 45N 74 2W
Wegendorf, *Berl.* 7 A5 52 36N 13 45 E
Wehofen, *Ruhr* 6 A2 51 31N 6 46 E
Wehringhausen, *Ruhr* 6 B6 51 21N 7 28 E
Weidling, *Wien* 10 G9 48 17N 16 18 E
Weidling →, *Wien* 10 G9 48 17N 16 19 E
Weidlingbach, *Wien* 10 G9 48 16N 16 15 E
Weigongcum, *Beij.* 14 B2 39 57N 116 16 E
Weijin He →, *Tianj.* 14 E6 39 3N 117 12 E
Weissensee, *Berl.* 7 A3 52 33N 13 27 E
Weitmar, *Ruhr* 6 B5 51 27N 7 11 E
Welcome Monument, *Jak.* 15 J9 6 12N 106 49 E
Weller Creek, *Chic.* 26 A1 42 2N 87 52W
Wellesley, *Bost.* 21 D2 42 17N 71 17W
Wellesley Fells, *Bost.* 21 D2 42 18N 71 18W
Wellesley Hills, *Bost.* 21 D2 42 18N 71 16W
Welling, *Lon.* 4 C5 51 27N 0 6 E
Wellingsbüttel, *Hbg.* 7 D8 53 38N 10 6 E
Weltevreden Park Extension, *Jobg.* 18 E8 26 7 S 27 56 E
Wembley, *Lon.* 4 B3 51 33N 0 17W
Wembley Stadium, *Jobg.* 18 F9 26 13 S 28 1 E
Wembley Stadium, *Lon.* 4 B3 51 33N 0 16W
Wemmer Pan, *Jobg.* 18 F9 26 13 S 28 3 E
Wendenschloss, *Berl.* 7 B4 52 24N 13 35 E
Wengern, *Ruhr* 6 B6 51 24N 7 20 E
Wenham, *Bost.* 21 B4 42 36N 70 53W
Wenham L., *Bost.* 21 B4 42 35N 70 53W
Wenhuagong, *Tianj.* 14 E6 39 5N 117 14 E
Wennington, *Lon.* 4 B6 51 30N 0 12 E
Wenonah, *Phil.* 24 C4 39 47N 75 9W
Wentworthville, *Syd.* 19 A2 33 48 S 150 58 E
Werden, *Ruhr* 6 B4 51 23N 7 1 E
Werne, *Ruhr* 6 B5 51 29N 7 18 E
Werneuchen, *Berl.* 7 A5 52 38N 13 44 E
Wesoła, *Wsaw.* 10 E8 52 15N 21 13 E
West Andover, *Bost.* 21 B2 42 39N 71 10W
West Babylon, *N.Y.* 23 C8 40 43N 73 21W
West Bedford, *Bost.* 21 C2 42 28N 71 18W
West Berlin, *Phil.* 24 C5 39 48N 74 56W
West Boxford, *Bost.* 21 A3 42 42N 71 3W
West Caldwell, *N.Y.* 22 B3 40 51N 74 16W
West Chelmsford, *Bost.* 21 B1 42 36N 71 23W
West Chester, *Phil.* 24 B1 39 57N 75 35W
West Concord, *Bost.* 21 C1 42 27N 71 24W
West Covina, *L.A.* 28 B5 34 4N 117 55W
West Don →, *Trto.* 20 D8 43 44N 79 24W
West Drayton, *Lon.* 4 B2 51 30N 0 28W
West Dulwich, *Lon.* 4 C4 51 26N 0 5W
West Edmondale, *Balt.* 25 B2 39 17N 76 42W
West Ham, *Lon.* 4 B5 51 31N 0 1 E
West Harrow, *Lon.* 4 B2 51 34N 0 21W
West Heath, *Lon.* 4 C5 51 29N 0 7 E
West Hempstead, *N.Y.* 23 C7 40 41N 73 38W
West Hill, *Trto.* 20 D9 43 46N 79 10W
West Hollywood, *L.A.* 28 B2 34 5N 118 21W
West Hoxton, *Syd.* 19 B1 33 55 S 150 49 E
West Islip, *N.Y.* 23 C9 40 41N 73 18W
West Kingsdown, *Lon.* 4 C6 51 20N 0 15 E
West Lamma Channel, *H.K.* 12 E5 22 14N 114 4 E
West Lynn, *Bost.* 21 C4 42 27N 70 58W
West Medford, *Bost.* 21 C3 42 25N 71 7W
West New York, *N.Y.* 22 C4 40 46N 74 1W
West Norwood, *N.Y.* 22 B5 40 59N 73 58W
West of Twin Peaks, *S.F.* 27 B2 37 43N 122 27W
West Orange, *N.Y.* 22 C3 40 46N 74 15W
West Park, *Jobg.* 18 E8 26 9 S 27 59 E
West Paterson, *N.Y.* 22 B3 40 54N 74 11W
West Rouge, *Trto.* 20 D10 43 48N 79 7W
West Roxbury, *Bost.* 21 D3 42 16N 71 9W
West Springfield, *Wash.* 25 E6 38 47N 77 13W
West Thurrock, *Lon.* 4 C6 51 28N 0 16 E
West Town, *Chic.* 26 B2 41 53N 87 42W
West Wharf, *Kar.* 17 H10 24 49N 66 58 E
West Wickham, *Lon.* 4 C4 51 22N 0 0 E
Westbury, *N.Y.* 23 C7 40 45N 73 34W
Westchester, *Chic.* 26 B1 41 51N 87 53W
Westchester, *N.Y.* 23 B5 40 51N 73 51W
Westcliff, *Jobg.* 18 F9 26 10 S 28 1 E
Westdale, *Chic.* 26 B1 41 55N 87 54W
Westdene, *Jobg.* 18 F8 26 10 S 27 59 E
Westend, *Hels.* 3 C3 60 9N 24 48 E
Westerbauer, *Ruhr* 6 B6 51 20N 7 23 E
Westerham, *Lon.* 4 D5 51 16N 0 4 E
Westerham, *Mün.* 7 G10 48 3N 11 36 E
Westerholt, *Ruhr* 6 A4 51 36N 7 5 E
Westerleigh, *N.Y.* 22 D4 40 37N 74 7W
Western Addition, *S.F.* 27 B2 37 47N 122 25W
Western Run →, *Balt.* 25 A2 39 22N 76 39W
Western Springs, *Chic.* 26 C1 41 47N 87 52W
Westfalenhalle, *Ruhr* 6 B6 51 29N 7 27 E
Westfield, *N.Y.* 22 D2 40 39N 74 21W
Westlake, *S.F.* 27 B2 37 42N 122 29W
Westmeadows, *Melb.* 19 D6 37 39 S 144 55 E
Westminster, *Lon.* 4 B4 51 30N 0 7W
Westminster Abbey, *Lon.* 4 C4 51 29N 0 7W
Westmont, *Phil.* 24 B4 39 54N 75 3W
Westmount, *Mtrl.* 20 B4 43 29N 73 35W
Weston, *Bost.* 21 C2 42 22N 71 16W
Weston, *Trto.* 20 D7 43 42N 79 30W
Weston Res., *Bost.* 21 C2 42 20N 71 11W
Westover Hills, *Phil.* 24 C1 39 45N 75 35W
Westtown, *Phil.* 24 B1 39 56N 75 32W
Westville, *Phil.* 24 B4 39 52N 75 7W
Westville Grove, *Phil.* 24 B4 39 51N 75 7W
Westwood, *Bost.* 21 D2 42 12N 71 14W
Westwood, *N.Y.* 22 B4 40 59N 74 3W
Westwood Village, *L.A.* 28 B2 34 3N 118 26W
Wetter, *Ruhr* 6 B6 51 23N 7 23 E
Wexford, *Trto.* 20 D9 43 45N 79 18W
Wey →, *Lon.* 4 D2 51 18N 0 27W
Weybridge, *Lon.* 4 C2 51 22N 0 27W
Weyer, *Ruhr* 6 C4 51 10N 7 1 E
Weymouth, *Bost.* 21 D4 42 12N 70 57W
Whampoa, Sungei →, *Sing.* 15 G8 1 18N 103 52 E
Wheaton, *Wash.* 25 C7 39 2N 77 2W
Wheaton Regional Park, *Wash.* 25 C7 39 3N 77 1W
Wheelers Hill, *Melb.* 19 F8 37 53 S 145 10 E
Wheeling, *Chic.* 26 A1 42 8N 87 54W
Whetstone, *Lon.* 4 B3 51 37N 0 10W
Whippany, *N.Y.* 22 B2 40 49N 74 24W
Whippany →, *N.Y.* 22 B2 40 50N 74 20W
White Marsh, *Balt.* 25 A4 39 23N 76 28W
White Meadow L., *N.Y.* 22 B1 40 55N 74 30W
White Oak, *Wash.* 25 C8 39 2N 76 59W
White Plains, *N.Y.* 23 A6 41 0N 73 46W
Whitechapel, *Lon.* 4 B4 51 31N 0 3W
Whitehorse, *Phil.* 24 B2 39 59N 75 28W
Whiteley Village, *Lon.* 4 C2 51 21N 0 25W
Whitemarsh →, *Balt.* 25 A4 39 22N 76 29W
Whitestone, *N.Y.* 23 C6 40 47N 73 48W
Whiting, *Chic.* 26 C4 41 41N 87 30W
Whitmans Pond, *Bost.* 21 D4 42 12N 70 55W
Whittier, *L.A.* 28 C4 33 58N 118 2W
Whitton, *Lon.* 4 C2 51 27N 0 21W
Whyteleafe, *Lon.* 4 D4 51 18N 0 5W
Wieden, *Wien* 10 G10 48 11N 16 22 E
Wiemelhausen, *Ruhr* 6 B5 51 27N 7 13 E
Wien, *Wien* 10 G10 48 12N 16 22 E
Wien-Schwechat, Flughafen, *Wien* 10 H11 48 6N 16 34 E
Wiener Berg, *Wien* 10 H10 48 9N 16 21 E
Wiener Wald, *Wien* 10 G9 48 16N 16 14 E
Wieruchów, *Wsaw.* 10 E5 52 14N 20 49 E
Wierzbno, *Wsaw.* 10 E7 52 11N 21 1 E
Wilanów, *Wsaw.* 10 E7 52 10N 21 4 E
Wilanówka →, *Wsaw.* 10 F7 52 13N 21 6 E
Wildcat Canyon Regional Park, *S.F.* 27 A3 37 56N 122 17W
Wildcat Cr. →, *S.F.* 27 A3 37 57N 122 15W
Wilde, *B.A.* 32 C5 34 24 S 58 18W
Wilhelmsburg, *Hbg.* 7 E7 53 29N 9 59 E
Wilhelmshagen, *Berl.* 7 B5 52 26N 13 42 E
Wilket Creek Park, *Trto.* 20 D8 43 43N 79 21W
Willesden, *Lon.* 4 B3 51 32N 0 15W
Willesden Green, *Lon.* 4 B3 51 32N 0 13W
Willett Pond, *Bost.* 21 D2 42 10N 71 14W
William Girling Res., *Lon.* 4 B4 51 38N 0 1W
Williams Bridge, *N.Y.* 23 B5 40 52N 73 51W
Williamsburg, *N.Y.* 22 C5 40 42N 73 56W
Williamstown, *Melb.* 19 F6 37 51 S 144 52 E
Williamstown Junction, *Phil.* 24 C5 39 45N 74 56W
Willingboro, *Phil.* 24 A5 40 2N 74 53W
Williston Park, *N.Y.* 23 C7 40 45N 73 38W
Willoughby, *Syd.* 19 A4 33 48 S 151 12 E
Willow Grove, *Phil.* 24 A4 40 8N 75 7W
Willow Springs, *Chic.* 26 C1 41 44N 87 51W
Willowbrook, *L.A.* 28 C3 33 54N 118 13W
Willowbrook, *N.Y.* 22 D4 40 35N 74 8W
Willowdale, *Phil.* 24 B5 39 52N 74 58W
Willowdale, *Trto.* 20 D8 43 46N 79 25W
Willowdale State Forest, *Bost.* 21 B4 42 39N 70 54W
Wilmette, *Chic.* 26 A2 42 4N 87 42W
Wilmette Harbor, *Chic.* 26 A2 42 4N 87 41W
Wilmington, *Bost.* 21 B3 42 33N 71 9W
Wilmington, *Lon.* 4 C6 51 25N 0 12 E
Wilmington, *Phil.* 24 C1 39 44N 75 33W
Wilson, Mt., *L.A.* 28 A4 34 13N 118 4W
Wimbledon, *Lon.* 4 C3 51 25N 0 13W
Wimbledon Common, *Lon.* 4 C3 51 26N 0 14W
Wimbledon Park, *Lon.* 4 C3 51 25N 0 11W
Wimbledon Tennis Ground, *Lon.* 4 C3 51 25N 0 12W
Winchester, *Bost.* 21 C3 42 26N 71 8W
Winchmore Hill, *Lon.* 4 B4 51 38N 0 5W
Windsor Cresta, *Jobg.* 18 E8 26 7 S 27 59 E
Winfield, *N.Y.* 22 D3 40 38N 74 16W
Winnetka, *Chic.* 26 A2 42 6N 87 43W
Winnetka, *L.A.* 28 A1 34 10N 118 32W
Winning, *Mün.* 7 G10 48 2N 11 37 E
Winston Hills, *Syd.* 19 A2 33 46 S 150 57 E
Winterberg, *Ruhr* 6 C5 51 19N 7 12 E
Winterhude, *Hbg.* 7 D8 53 35N 10 0 E
Winterthur, *Phil.* 24 C1 39 48N 75 35W
Winthrop, *Bost.* 21 C4 42 22N 70 58W
Winzeldorf, *Hbg.* 7 C7 53 40N 9 54 E
Wisley Gardens, *Lon.* 4 D2 51 18N 0 28W
Wiśniowa Góra, *Wsaw.* 10 E8 52 13N 21 12 E
Wissahickon Cr. →, *Phil.* 24 A3 40 0N 75 12W
Wissinoming, *Phil.* 24 A4 40 1N 75 4W
Wissous, *Paris* 5 C3 48 44N 2 19 E
Witch House, *Bost.* 21 B4 42 31N 70 54W
Witfield, *Jobg.* 18 F10 26 11 S 28 12 E
Witpoortjie, *Jobg.* 18 E8 26 8 S 27 50 E
Witten, *Ruhr* 6 B6 51 26N 7 20 E
Wittenau, *Berl.* 7 A2 52 35N 13 19 E
Wittlaer, *Ruhr* 6 C2 51 19N 6 44 E
Witwatersrand, Univ. of, *Jobg.* 18 F9 26 11 S 28 1 E
Włochy, *Wsaw.* 10 E6 52 12N 20 54 E
Wo Mei, *H.K.* 12 D6 22 21N 114 15 E
Wo Yi Hop, *H.K.* 12 D5 22 23N 114 8 E
Woburn, *Bost.* 21 C3 42 29N 71 9W
Woburn, *Trto.* 20 D9 43 46N 79 12W
Wohldorf-Ohlstedt, *Hbg.* 7 C8 53 41N 10 7 E
Wola, *Wsaw.* 10 E6 52 14N 20 57 E
Woldingham, *Lon.* 4 D4 51 16N 0 1W
Wolf Lake, *Chic.* 26 D3 41 39N 87 31W
Wolf Trap Farm Park, *Wash.* 25 D6 38 56N 77 17W
Wolfpassing, *Wien* 10 G9 48 18N 16 10 E
Wolica, *Wsaw.* 10 F7 52 9N 21 3 E
Wolica, *Wsaw.* 10 F6 52 7N 20 51 E
Wólka Węglowa, *Wsaw.* 10 E6 52 18N 20 52 E
Wollaston, *Bost.* 21 D3 42 15N 71 2W
Wołomin, *Wsaw.* 10 D8 52 20N 21 12 E
Woltersdorf, *Berl.* 7 B5 52 27N 13 44 E
Wong Chuk Hang, *H.K.* 12 E6 22 15N 114 10 E
Wong Chuk Wan, *H.K.* 12 D6 22 23N 114 17 E
Wong Chuk Yeung, *H.K.* 12 D6 22 24N 114 15 E
Wong Ngua Shan, *H.K.* 12 D6 22 22N 114 14 E
Wong Tai Sin, *H.K.* 12 D6 22 20N 114 11 E
Wonga Park, *Melb.* 19 E8 37 44 S 145 17 E
Wood End, *Lon.* 4 B2 51 33N 0 21W
Wood Green, *Lon.* 4 B4 51 36N 0 6W
Wood Hill, *Bost.* 21 B2 42 39N 71 11W
Woodbridge, *N.Y.* 22 D3 40 33N 74 16W
Woodbridge, *Trto.* 20 D7 43 47N 79 35W
Woodbridge Cr. →, *N.Y.* 22 D3 40 32N 74 15W
Woodbury, *N.Y.* 23 C8 40 49N 73 28W
Woodbury, *Phil.* 24 B4 39 50N 75 9W
Woodbury Cr. →, *Phil.* 24 B4 39 51N 75 11W
Woodbury Heights, *Phil.* 24 C4 39 49N 75 7W
Woodchuck Hill, *Bost.* 21 B3 42 39N 71 4W
Woodcliff Lake, *N.Y.* 22 A4 41 1N 74 2W
Woodford, *Lon.* 4 B5 51 36N 0 1 E
Woodford Bridge, *Lon.* 4 B5 51 36N 0 3 E
Woodford Green, *Lon.* 4 B5 51 36N 0 1 E
Woodford Wells, *Lon.* 4 B5 51 37N 0 1 E
Woodhaven, *N.Y.* 23 C5 40 41N 73 51W
Woodlands, *Sing.* 15 F7 1 26N 103 46 E
Woodlawn, *Balt.* 25 B2 39 19N 76 44W
Woodlyn, *Phil.* 24 B2 39 52N 75 21W
Woodlynne, *Phil.* 24 B4 39 54N 75 6W
Woodmere, *N.Y.* 23 D6 40 38N 73 43W
Woodmont, *Wash.* 25 D7 38 59N 77 5W
Woodmore, *Balt.* 25 A2 39 22N 76 47W
Woodridge, *N.Y.* 22 B4 40 50N 74 4W
Woodrow, *N.Y.* 22 D3 40 32N 74 11W
Woodside, *Lon.* 4 C4 51 23N 0 4W
Woodside, *N.Y.* 23 C5 40 44N 73 54W
Woodside, *S.F.* 27 D3 37 26N 122 16W
Woodstock, *Balt.* 25 B1 39 19N 76 52W
Woodstream, *Phil.* 24 B5 39 54N 74 57W
Woollahra, *Syd.* 19 B4 33 53 S 151 15 E
Woolooware B., *Syd.* 19 C3 34 1 S 151 8 E
Woolwich, *Lon.* 4 C5 51 29N 0 4 E
Wördern, *Wien* 10 G9 48 19N 16 12 E
World Trade Center, *N.Y.* 22 C4 40 42N 74 0W
Worli, *Bomb.* 16 G7 19 1N 72 49 E
Woronora, *Syd.* 19 C3 34 1 S 151 2 E
Worth, *Chic.* 26 C2 41 41N 87 47W
Worthington, *Balt.* 25 B2 39 14N 76 47W
Worthington, *N.Y.* 23 A6 41 2N 73 49W
Wrotham, *Lon.* 4 D6 51 18N 0 18 E
Wrotham Park, *Lon.* 4 A3 51 40N 0 10W
Wuhlgarten, *Berl.* 7 A4 52 31N 13 34 E
Wujiaochang, *Shang.* 14 J12 31 18N 121 31 E
Wülfrath, *Ruhr* 6 C4 51 16N 7 2 E
Wulfsmühle, *Hbg.* 7 C7 53 41N 9 51 E
Wulksfelde, *Hbg.* 7 C8 53 42N 10 6 E
Wupper →, *Ruhr* 6 C5 51 14N 7 18 E
Wuppertal, *Ruhr* 6 C5 51 17N 7 10 E
Würm →, *Mün.* 7 G9 48 8N 11 27 E
Würm-kanal, *Mün.* 7 F9 48 13N 11 29 E
Wusong, *Shang.* 14 H11 31 22N 121 29 E
Wusong Jiang →, *Shang.* 14 J11 31 15N 121 29 E
Wyandanch, *N.Y.* 23 C8 40 44N 73 20W
Wyckoff, *N.Y.* 22 A3 41 0N 74 10W
Wyczółki, *Wsaw.* 10 F6 52 9N 20 59 E
Wygoda, *Wsaw.* 10 E7 52 15N 21 7 E
Wyncote, *Phil.* 24 A4 40 5N 75 8W
Wynnewood, *Phil.* 24 A3 40 0N 75 17W
Wynnmere, *Bost.* 21 C3 42 29N 71 9W
Wyola, *Phil.* 24 A2 40 0N 75 24W


# X


Xabregas, *Lisb.* 8 F8 38 43N 9 6W
Xiaodianzhuang, *Tianj.* 14 D6 39 14N 117 14 E
Xiaoping, *Gzh.* 14 F8 23 12N 113 13 E
Xiasha chong, *Gzh.* 14 G7 23 8N 113 9 E
Xicheng, *Beij.* 14 B2 39 54N 116 19 E
Xico, Cerro, *Méx.* 29 C4 19 15N 98 56W
Xicun, *Gzh.* 14 G8 23 8N 113 13 E
Xidan, *Beij.* 14 B3 39 52N 116 20 E
Xigu Gongyuan, *Tianj.* 14 D6 39 10N 117 10 E
Xigucun, *Tianj.* 14 D5 39 10N 117 9 E
Xijiao Airport, *Beij.* 14 B2 39 57N 116 12 E
Xikeng, *Gzh.* 14 F7 23 11N 113 6 E
Xilou, *Tianj.* 14 E6 39 5N 117 12 E
Ximenwai, *Tianj.* 14 E5 39 8N 117 9 E
Xingfusancun, *Beij.* 14 B3 39 55N 116 25 E
Xinhua, *Tianj.* 14 E6 39 6N 117 12 E
Xinkai He →, *Tianj.* 14 D6 39 12N 117 15 E
Xintang, *Gzh.* 14 G9 23 9N 113 24 E
Xitle, *Méx.* 29 C2 19 15N 99 12W
Xitle, Cerro, *Méx.* 29 C2 19 14N 99 12W
Xiyuan, *Beij.* 14 B2 39 59N 116 14 E
Xizhimen, *Beij.* 14 B2 39 55N 116 19 E
Xochiaca, *Méx.* 29 B4 19 24N 89 58 E
Xochimilco, *Méx.* 29 C3 19 15N 99 5W
Xochimilco, L. de, *Méx.* 29 C3 19 16N 99 7W
Xochitenco, *Méx.* 29 B4 19 24N 89 58 E
Xochitepec, *Méx.* 29 C3 19 15N 99 9W
Xuanwu, *Beij.* 14 B2 39 52N 116 19 E
Xuhui, *Shang.* 14 J11 31 11N 121 26 E


# Y


Yaba, *Lagos* 18 A2 6 30N 7 22 E
Yadun Shui, *Gzh.* 14 G8 23 5N 113 15 E
Yaftābād, *Tehr.* 17 D4 35 37N 51 17 E
Yagoona, *Syd.* 19 B3 33 54 S 151 2 E
Yahara, *Tōkyō* 13 B2 35 44N 139 37 E
Yaho, *Tōkyō* 13 B1 35 40N 139 26 E
Yakire, *Tōkyō* 13 B4 35 45N 139 54 E
Yamada, *Ōsaka* 12 B4 34 47N 135 32 E
Yamada, *Tōkyō* 13 C2 35 33N 139 37 E
Yamada →, *Ōsaka* 12 B2 34 45N 135 10 E
Yamaguchi, *Ōsaka* 12 B2 34 49N 135 14 E
Yamamoto, *Ōsaka* 12 C4 34 38N 135 37 E
Yamato, *Tōkyō* 13 B2 35 46N 139 36 E
Yamato, *Tōkyō* 13 D1 35 29N 139 27 E
Yamato →, *Ōsaka* 12 C3 34 36N 135 26 E
Yamazaki, *Tōkyō* 13 A4 35 55N 139 53 E
Yamuna →, *Delhi* 16 B2 28 37N 77 15 E
Yan Kit, *Sing.* 15 F8 1 21N 103 58 E
Yanagishima, *Tōkyō* 13 B3 35 49N 139 45 E
Yanbu, *Gzh.* 14 G7 23 5N 113 9 E
Yanghuayuan, *Beij.* 14 C2 39 49N 116 18 E
Yangjiazhuang, *Shang.* 14 H11 31 22N 121 25 E
Yangliuqing, *Tianj.* 14 E5 39 8N 117 0 E
Yangpu, *Shang.* 14 J12 31 16N 121 32 E
Yanino, *St-Pet.* 11 B5 59 55N 30 36 E
Yao, *Ōsaka* 12 C4 34 37N 135 36 E
Yao Airport, *Ōsaka* 12 C4 34 35N 135 36 E
Yarmōk, *Bagd.* 17 F7 33 18N 44 19 E
Yarra →, *Melb.* 19 E6 37 51 S 144 53 E
Yarra Bend Nat. Park, *Melb.* 19 E7 37 47 S 145 0 E
Yarraville, *Melb.* 19 E6 37 48 S 144 53 E
Yasenevo, *Mos.* 11 F9 55 36N 37 21 E
Yashio, *Tōkyō* 13 B3 35 48N 139 49 E
Yau Ma Tei, *H.K.* 12 E5 22 18N 114 10 E
Yau Tong, *H.K.* 12 E6 22 17N 114 14 E
Yau Yue Wan, *H.K.* 12 E6 22 19N 114 15 E
Yauza →, *Mos.* 11 D10 55 54N 37 43 E
Yeading, *Lon.* 4 B2 51 31N 0 23W
Yeadon, *Phil.* 24 B3 39 55N 75 15W
Yedikule, *Ist.* 17 B2 40 59N 28 55 E
Yenikapi, *Ist.* 17 A2 41 0N 28 56 E
Yeniköy, *Ist.* 17 A3 41 6N 29 3 E
Yennora, *Syd.* 19 B2 33 51 S 150 58 E
Yeogchon, *Sŏul* 12 G7 37 35N 126 55 E
Yeoido, *Sŏul* 12 G7 37 31N 126 55 E
Yeong Dung Po, *Sŏul* 12 G7 37 31N 126 54 E
Yeongdong, *Sŏul* 12 G8 37 30N 127 1 E
Yerba Buena I., *S.F.* 27 B2 37 48N 122 21W
Yerres, *Paris* 5 C5 48 43N 2 30 E
Yerres →, *Paris* 5 C5 48 43N 2 26 E
Yesilköy, *Ist.* 17 B2 40 57N 28 50 E
Yew Tee, *Sing.* 15 F7 1 23N 103 45 E
Yiewsley, *Lon.* 4 B2 51 31N 0 27W
Yiheyuan, *Beij.* 14 A2 40 0N 116 14 E
Yinhangzhen, *Shang.* 14 H12 31 20N 121 31 E
Yio Chu Kang, *Sing.* 15 F8 1 23N 103 51 E
Yixingbu, *Tianj.* 14 D6 39 11N 117 12 E
Ylästö, *Hels.* 3 B4 60 17N 24 35 E
Yodo →, *Ōsaka* 12 B4 34 45N 135 35 E
Yokohama, *Tōkyō* 13 D3 35 26N 139 41 E
Yokohama Harbour, *Tōkyō* 13 D2 35 27N 139 39 E
Yokosuka, *Tōkyō* 13 A4 35 50N 139 54 E
Yong San, *Sŏul* 12 G7 37 32N 126 58 E
Yongding He →, *Beij.* 14 C1 39 49N 116 10 E
Yongdingmen, *Beij.* 14 B3 39 50N 116 20 E
Yongfucun, *Gzh.* 14 G8 23 8N 113 17 E
Yonkers, *N.Y.* 23 B5 40 56N 73 52W
Yono, *Tōkyō* 13 A2 35 52N 139 37 E
York, *Trto.* 20 D8 43 40N 79 26W
York Mills, *Trto.* 20 D8 43 45N 79 22W
Yoshikawa, *Tōkyō* 13 A4 35 53N 139 50 E
Yotsuga, *Tōkyō* 13 B3 35 40N 139 44 E
You'anmen, *Beij.* 14 B2 39 51N 116 19 E
Yoyogi Park, *Tōkyō* 13 C3 35 40N 139 41 E
Yuanxiatian, *Gzh.* 14 F8 23 12N 113 17 E
Yuexiu Gongyuan, *Gzh.* 14 G8 23 8N 113 16 E
Yugo-Zarad, *Mos.* 11 E9 55 40N 37 30 E
Yung Shue Wan, *H.K.* 12 E5 22 13N 114 6 E
Yuquanshan, *Beij.* 14 A2 40 0N 116 13 E
Yusofābād, *Tehr.* 17 C5 35 43N 51 24 E
Yuyuan Tan, *Beij.* 14 B2 39 53N 116 16 E
Yuyuantan Gongyuan, *Beij.* 14 B2 39 54N 116 16 E
Yvelines, Forêt des, *Paris* 5 D1 48 38N 1 53 E
Yvette →, *Paris* 5 C1 48 43N 1 57 E


# Z


Záběhlice, *Pra.* 10 B2 50 3N 14 29 E
Żacisze, *Wsaw.* 10 E7 52 17N 21 4 E
Zahrā, *Bagd.* 17 E7 33 22N 44 19 E
Zakharkovo, *Mos.* 11 E7 55 46N 37 18 E
Žalov, *Pra.* 10 A2 50 10N 14 22 E
Załuski, *Wsaw.* 10 F6 52 9N 20 55 E
Zamdorf, *Mün.* 7 G10 48 8N 11 35 E
Zanevka, *St-Pet.* 11 B5 59 55N 30 31 E
Zaozerye, *Mos.* 11 F12 55 35N 38 1 E
Zapote, *Manila* 15 E3 14 27N 120 56 E
Zapotitlán, *Méx.* 29 C3 19 18N 99 2W
Zápy, *Pra.* 10 B4 50 9N 14 40 E
Zarechye, *Mos.* 11 E8 55 41N 37 22 E
Zawady, *Wsaw.* 10 E7 52 10N 21 6 E
Zâwiyet Abû Musallam, *El Qâ.* 18 D4 29 56N 31 9 E
Zawrā Park, *Bagd.* 17 F8 33 18N 44 23 E
Zbójna Góra, *Wsaw.* 10 E8 52 11N 21 13 E
Zbraslav, *Pra.* 10 C2 49 58N 14 23 E
Zbuzany, *Pra.* 10 B1 50 1N 14 17 E
Zdiby, *Pra.* 10 B2 50 9N 14 27 E
Zehlendorf, *Berl.* 7 B2 52 26N 13 16 E
Zeleneč, *Pra.* 10 B3 50 8N 14 39 E
Zempoala, Parque Nac. de las Lagunas de, *Méx.* 29 D2 19 5N 99 18W
Zepernick, *Berl.* 7 A4 52 38N 13 33 E
Żerań, *Wsaw.* 10 E6 52 18N 20 58 E
Zerzeń, *Wsaw.* 10 E7 52 12N 21 7 E
Zeytinburnu, *Ist.* 17 B2 40 58N 28 53 E
Zhabei, *Shang.* 14 J11 31 16N 121 26 E
Zhangguizhuang, *Tianj.* 14 E6 39 7N 117 19 E
Zhangxingzhuang, *Tianj.* 14 D6 39 10N 117 12 E
Zhdanov, *Mos.* 11 E10 55 44N 37 41 E
Zhegalovo, *Mos.* 11 D11 55 54N 37 59 E
Zheleznodorozhnyy, *Mos.* 11 E12 55 45N 38 0 E
Zhenru, *Shang.* 14 J11 31 16N 121 22 E
Zhicun, *Gzh.* 14 G8 23 0N 113 18 E
Zhongshan Gongyuan, *Shang.* 14 J11 31 13N 121 24 E
Zhoucun, *Gzh.* 14 F8 23 11N 113 11 E
Zhoujiadu, *Shang.* 14 J11 31 11N 121 29 E
Zhoujiazhen, *Shang.* 14 J12 31 16N 121 33 E
Zhu Jiang →, *Gzh.* 14 G9 23 6N 113 20 E
Zhulebino, *Mos.* 11 E11 55 42N 37 50 E
Zhushadi, *Gzh.* 14 F9 23 11N 113 22 E
Zielona, *Wsaw.* 10 E8 52 14N 21 11 E
Zielonka, *Wsaw.* 10 E7 52 18N 21 9 E
Zitadella, *Berl.* 7 A2 52 31N 13 11 E
Zizhuyuan Gongyuan, *Beij.* 14 B2 39 55N 116 17 E
Žižkov, *Pra.* 10 B2 50 5N 14 28 E
Zličín, *Pra.* 10 B1 50 3N 14 17 E
Zōbki, *Wsaw.* 10 E7 52 17N 21 6 E
Zografos, *Ath.* 8 J11 37 58N 23 47 E
Żoliborz, *Wsaw.* 10 E6 52 16N 20 57 E
Zugliget, *Bud.* 10 K12 47 30N 18 59 E
Zugló, *Bud.* 10 J13 47 31N 19 8 E
Zumbi, *Rio J.* 31 A2 22 49 S 43 10W
Zuvuvu →, *S. Pau.* 31 F5 23 40 S 46 42W
Zuvuvus, *S. Pau.* 31 F6 23 41 S 46 39W
Zweckel, *Ruhr* 6 A3 51 35N 6 57 E
Zyuzino, *Mos.* 11 F9 55 39N 37 34 E

# WORLD MAPS

## MAP SYMBOLS

### SETTLEMENTS

◆ PARIS     ■ Berne     ◉ Livorno     ⊙ Brugge     ⊙ *Algeciras*     ○ *Fréjus*     ○ *Oberammergau*     ○ *Thira*

Settlement symbols and type styles vary according to the scale of each map and indicate the importance of towns on the map rather than specific population figures

∴   Ruins or Archæological Sites       ᵛ   Wells in Desert

### ADMINISTRATION

**Boundaries**

—— International

— — International
(Undefined or Disputed)

·········· Internal

**National Parks**

International boundaries show the *de facto* situation where there are rival claims to territory.

**Country Names**
**NICARAGUA**

**Administrative Areas**

KENT

CALABRIA

### COMMUNICATIONS

**Roads**

—— Primary

⌒ Secondary

·-·-· Trails and Seasonal

**Railroads**

⌒ Primary

⌒ Secondary

······ Under Construction

✧ Airfields

≍ Passes

Ⅎ---Ⅎ Railroad Tunnels

········· Principal Canals

### PHYSICAL FEATURES

〜 Perennial Streams

········ Intermittent Streams

⬭ Perennial Lakes

⬯ Intermittent Lakes

Swamps and Marshes

Permanent Ice and Glaciers

▲ 2259 Elevations (m)

▼ 2604 Sea Depths (m)

*408* Elevation of Lake Surface Above Sea Level (m)

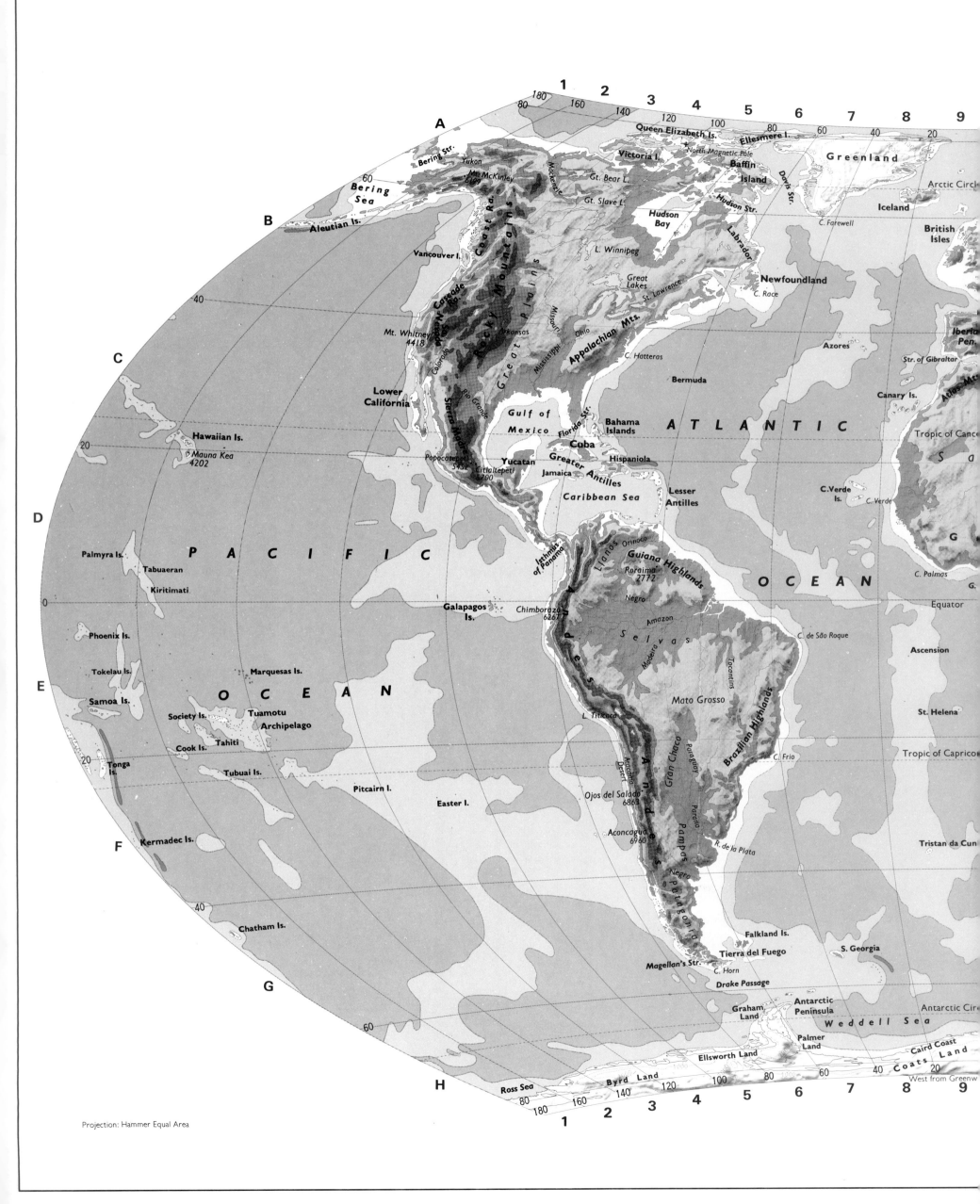

Projection: Hammer Equal Area

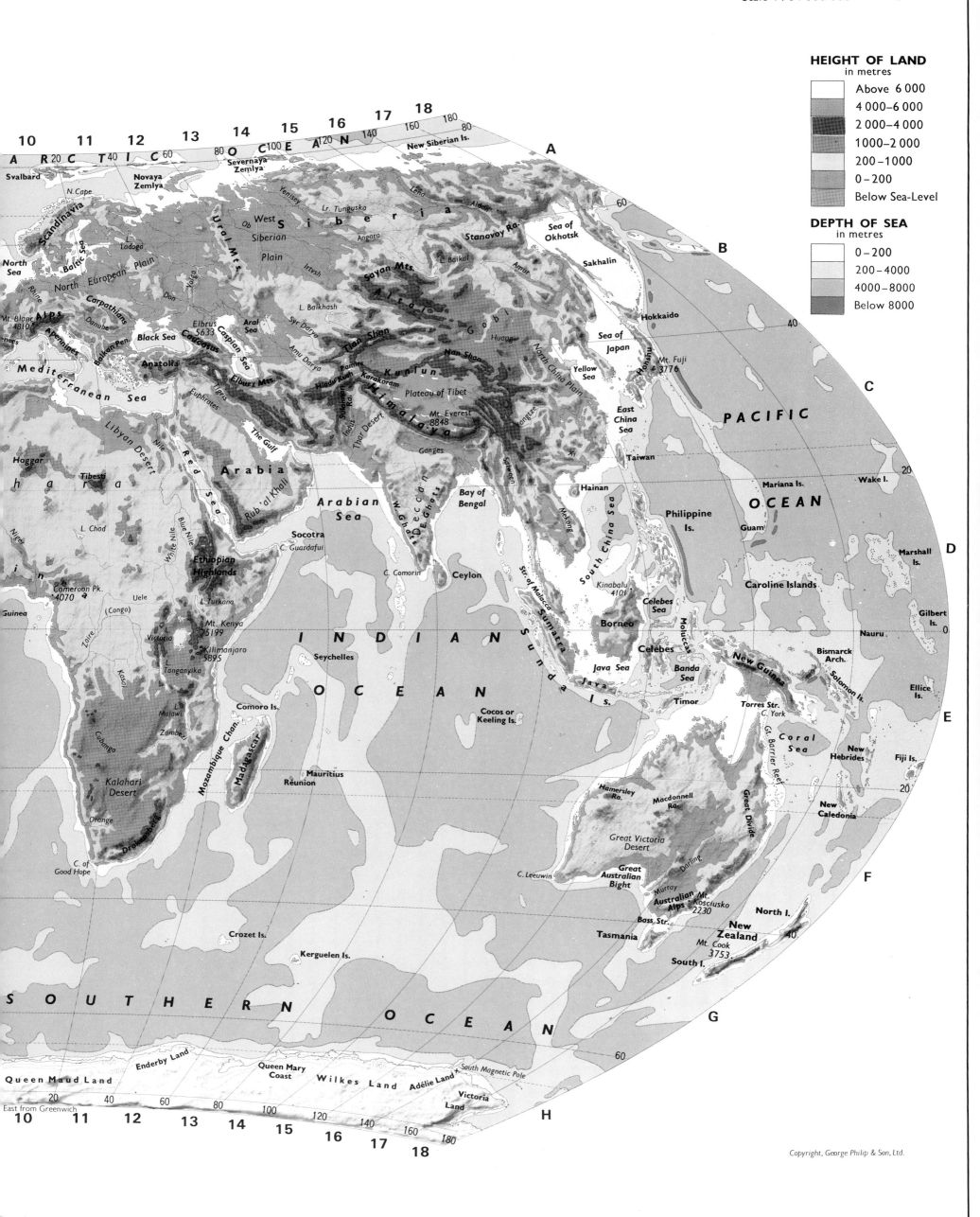

**HEIGHT OF LAND**
in metres

Above 6 000
4 000–6 000
2 000–4 000
1000–2 000
200–1000
0–200
Below Sea-Level

**DEPTH OF SEA**
in metres

0–200
200–4000
4000–8000
Below 8000

ARCTIC OCEAN

Svalbard
N. Cape
Novaya Zemlya
Severnaya Zemlya
New Siberian Is.
Scandinavia
North Sea
Baltic Sea
L. Ladoga
North European Plain
Ural Mts.
Ob
West Siberian Plain
Yenisey
Lr. Tunguska
Lena
Aldan
Siberia
Sea of Okhotsk
Sakhalin
Hokkaido
Sea of Japan
Stanovoy Ra.
Amur
Honshu
Mt. Fuji 3776

Rhine
Alps
Mt. Blanc 4810
Apennines
Carpathians
Danube
Balkan Pen.
Black Sea
Caucasus
Elbrus 5633
Caspian Sea
Aral Sea
Syr Darya
Amu Darya
Irtysh
L. Balkhash
Angara
L. Baikal
Sayan Mts.
Altai
Gobi
Tian Shen
Nan Shan
Huang
North China Plain
Yellow Sea
East China Sea
Taiwan
Mediterranean Sea
Anatolia
Volga
Don
Pamirs
Hindu Kush
Karakoram
Kunlun
Plateau of Tibet
Yangtze
Xi
Salween
Mekong
PACIFIC OCEAN
Hainan
Mariana Is.
Wake I.
Elburz Mts.
Tigris
Euphrates
Indus
Thar Desert
Himalaya
Mt. Everest 8848
Ganges
Bay of Bengal
Libyan Desert
Nile
Red Sea
Arabia
Rub' al Khali
The Gulf
Hoggar
Tibesti
Deccan
W. Ghats
E. Ghats
Arabian Sea
Socotra
C. Guardafui
Philippine Is.
Guam
OCEAN
Marshall Is.
Sahara
Niger
L. Chad
Cameroon Pk. 4070
Guinea
Uele
(Congo)
Ethiopian Highlands
L. Turkana
C. Comorin
Ceylon
Str. of Malacca
Sumatra
South China Sea
Kinabalu 4101
Borneo
Celebes Sea
Celebes
Moluccas
Caroline Islands
Nauru
Gilbert Is.
Zaire
Mt. Kenya 5199
Victoria
Kilimanjaro 5895
L. Tanganyika
Seychelles
INDIAN
Sunda Is.
Java Sea
Java
Banda Sea
Timor
New Guinea
Bismarck Arch.
Solomon Is.
Ellice Is.
Kasai
Cubango
Malawi
Zambezi
Comoro Is.
Mozambique Chan.
Madagascar
OCEAN
Mauritius
Réunion
Cocos or Keeling Is.
Torres Str.
C. York
New Hebrides
Fiji Is.
Kalahari Desert
Orange
Drakensberg
C. of Good Hope
Seychelles
Coral Sea
Gt. Barrier Reef
New Caledonia
Crozet Is.
Kerguelen Is.
Hamersley Ra.
Macdonnell Ra.
Great Victoria Desert
Great Australian Bight
C. Leeuwin
Australian Alps
Mt. Kosciusko 2230
Murray
Darling
Great Divide
North I.
New Zealand
Mt. Cook 3753
South I.
Bass Str.
Tasmania
SOUTHERN OCEAN

Queen Maud Land
Enderby Land
Queen Mary Coast
Wilkes Land
Adélie Land
South Magnetic Pole
Victoria Land

180  160  140  120  100  80  60  40  20
1    2    3    4    5    6    7    8    9

Beaufort Sea

Wrangel I.
Dezhnev C.
Bering Str.
St. Lawrence I. (U.S.)
Pt. Barrow
Banks I.
Parry Is.
Queen Elizabeth Is.
Devon I.
Ellesmere I.
GREENLAND
N. Magnetic Pole
Baffin Bay
Thule
Gt. Coppermine
Victoria I.
Bear I.
Mackenzie
Yukon
ALASKA (U.S.)
Fairbanks
Dawson
Anchorage
Yellowknife
Gt. Slave L.
Baffin I.
Davis Strait
C. Chidley
Godthåb
Denmark Str.
Arctic Circle
ICELAND
Reykjavik
Faroe Is. (Den.)
Norw
Sea
Gulf of Alaska
Juneau
Kodiak Is.
Prince Rupert
Queen Charlotte Is.
Aleutian Islands (U.S.)
Vancouver
Vancouver I.
Seattle
Portland
CANADA
Edmonton
Calgary
Winnipeg
Winnipeg
Nelson
Churchill
Hudson Bay
Schefferville
Newfoundland
St. John's
C. Race
Halifax
Sable I.
UNITED KINGDOM
Glasgow
Dublin
IRELAND
London
FRANC
Missouri
Minneapolis-St.Paul
Milwaukee
Michigan
L. Superior
L. Huron
Montréal
Ottawa
Toronto
Québec
Salt Lake City
Denver
Omaha
Chicago
Detroit
Cleveland
Buffalo
Pittsburgh
Boston
C. Cod
San Francisco
Sacramento
Kansas City
St. Louis
Cincinnati
Ohio
Philadelphia
Baltimore
Washington
New York
C. Finisterre
Bordeaux
PORTUGAL
Madrid
Lisboa
SPAIN
UNITED STATES
Colorado
Oklahoma
Memphis
Atlanta
Norfolk
Azores (Port.)
Gibraltar
Ora
Los Angeles
San Diego
Phoenix
Dallas
El Paso
Birmingham
Bermuda (Br.)
Madeira (Port.)
Tangier
Rabat
Fès
Casablanca
MOROCCO
Marrakech
Ciudad Juárez
Houston
San Antonio
New Orleans
Jacksonville
Canary Is. (Span.)
MEXICO
Rio Grande
Gulf of California
Monterrey
Gulf of Mexico
Miami
La Habana
CUBA
BAHAMAS
ATLANTIC
WESTERN SAHARA
Tropic of Cancer
C. San Lucas
León
MAURITANIA
International Date Line
Midway I.
Guadalajara
Puebla
México
Revilla Gigedo Is. (Mexico)
Hispaniola
HAITI  DOM. REP.
Port-au-Prince
Santo Domingo
San Juan
DOMINICA
Nouakchott
Tombouct
Hawaiian Is. (U.S.)
BELIZE
JAMAICA
Kingston
Leeward Is.
ANTIGUA & BARBUDA
ST. CHRISTOPHER-NEVIS
CAPE VERDE IS.
C. Verde
Dakar
SENEGAL
MAL
Oahu
Honolulu
GUATEMALA
HONDURAS
Guatemala
San Salvador
Tegucigalpa
NICARAGUA
Caribbean Sea
West Indies
ST. LUCIA
Windward Is.
BARBADOS
ST. VINCENT
GAMBIA
GUINEA-BISSAU
Bamako
Hawaii
EL SALVADOR
Managua
GRENADA
TRINIDAD & TOBAGO
Conakry
GUINEA
Clipperton I. (Fr.)
San José
COSTA RICA
Panamá
PANAMA
Barranquilla
Maracaibo
Caracas
Georgetown
Paramaribo
SIERRA LEONE
Freetown
Monrovia
LIBERIA
IVORY COAST
Acc
Palmyra I. (U.S.)
VENEZUELA
Medellín
Bogotá
GUYANA
SURINAM
Cayenne
Fr. Guiana
Abidjan
Kiritimati
PACIFIC
Cali
COLOMBIA
Equator
Baker Is. (U.S.)
Jarvis I. (U.S.)
Quito
ECUADOR
Negro
Japurá
Manaus
Amazon
Belém
São Paulo (Brazil)
Fortaleza
Fernando de Noronha (Brazil)
Gulf of
Abariringa
Galápagos Is. (Ecuador)
Guayaquil
Iquitos
C. de São Roque
Natal
Phoenix Is.
Malden I.
KIRIBATI
Starbuck I.
BRAZIL
Recife
Ascension (Br.)
Tokelau Is.
Penrhyn I.
Marquesas Is. (Fr.)
Madeira
Topajos
Tocantins
Manihiki I.
Flint I.
PERU
São Francisco
Salvador
St. Helena (Br.)
W. SAMOA
AMER. SAMOA
Samoan Is.
Tutuila (U.S.)
FRENCH
OCEAN
Callao
Lima
Marañón
Titicaca
La Paz
Brasília
Cook Is.
Society Is. (Fr.)
Tahiti
Tuamotu
Archipelago (Fr.)
Arequipa
BOLIVIA
Belo Horizonte
TONGA (Friendly Is.)
Niue (N.Z.)
POLYNESIA
Paraná
PARAGUAY
São Paulo
Rio de Janeiro
Tongatapu  Rarotonga
Tubuai Is. (Fr.)
Tropic of Capricorn
Antofagasta
Asunción
Santos
Curitiba
Ducie I. (Br.)
S. Ambrosio (Chile)
Tucumán
Paraguay
Pôrto Alegre
Pitcairn I. (Br.)
Easter I. (Chile)
Sala-y-Gómez
S. Ambrosio
ARGENTINA
Paraná
Río Grande do Sul
Rapa (Fr.)
Córdoba
Uruguay
URUGUAY
CHILE
Valparaíso
Rosario
Arch. de Juan Fernández (Chile)
Santiago
Buenos Aires
Montevideo
Talcahuano
Bahía Blanca
Tristan da Cunha (Br.)
Gough I. (Br.)
International Date Line
Kermadec Is. (N.Z.)
Chiloé
Chatham Is. (N.Z.)
Falkland Is. (Br.)
S. Georgia
Punta Arenas
Tierra del Fuego
Scotia Sea
S. Sandwich Is.
S
C. Horn
FALKLAND IS. DEPENDENCIES
South Orkney Is.
Drake Passage
S. Shetland Is.
Graham Ld.
Antarctic Circle
Antarctic Peninsula
Bellingshausen Sea
Alexander
Palmer Ld.
Weddell Sea
Amundsen Sea
Ellsworth Land
ANTAR
Dronni
Byrd Land

80
60
40
20
West from Greenwich
180  160  140  120  100  80  60  40  20
1    2    3    4    5    6    7    8    9

Projection: Hammer Equal Area

ARCTIC OCEAN

**10** **11** **12** **13** **14** **15** **16** **17** **18** 180

40 60 80 100 120 140 160 80

Svalbard Zemlya Frantsa Iosifa Novaya Zemlya Severnaya Zemlya New Siberian Is. East Siberian Sea **A**
(Norway) Nord Kapp Barents Sea Kara Ust Port Laptev Sea Nizhne-Kolymsk Sea
Narvik Murmansk Sea Tiksi Verkhoyansk Arctic Circle Anadyr

Arkhangelsk Salekhard Yenisey Vilyuysk Lena Yakutsk 60 Bering
Helsinki FINLAND R U S S I A Sea
Oslo St. Peterburg Perm Ob Sea of Kamchatka Sea **B**
Stockholm Yekaterinburg Tomsk Krasnoyarsk Okhotsk Petropavlovsk-
SWEDEN Yaroslavl Novosibirsk Okhotsk C. Lopatka Kamchatskiy
Kobenhavn Moskva Kazan Chelyabinsk Omsk L. Baykal Ulan Sakhalin
DENMARK LATVIA Ufa Novokuznetsk Irtysh Ude Komsomolsk
Hamburg RUSSIA Samara Barnaul Irkutsk Khabarovsk
Amsterdam BELO. Voronezh Orenburg Karaganda Amur Kuril Is.
Berlin POLAND Warszawa Minsk Saratov MONGOLIA Vladivostok Sapporo
GERM. Praha Kiyev Volgograd KAZAKHSTAN Alma Ata Ulaanbaatar N. KOREA Hakodate
Brussel Paris Wien Lvov UKRAINE Rostov Aral L. Balkhash Beijing Harbin Sea of **C**
Budapest Kharkov Astrakhan Sea Changchun Pyongyang Japan
ROMANIA Odessa Caspian Alma Ata Shenyang Soul Kyoto JAPAN
Torino Beograd Bucuresti Black Sea Aral Sea UZBEKISTAN Samarkand KIRGHIZIA Tianjin Dalian KOREA Pusan Tokyo
Milano YUG. BULGARIA Sea GEO. Tbilisi TURKMENISTAN Tashkent Taiyuan Jinan Qingdao Kobe Yokohama
Roma ITALY Sofiya Istanbul Grozny ARM. Baku Dushanbe TA. Lanzhou Xi'an C H I N A Huang He Nagoya
Barcelona Napoli Athinai Ankara AZ. Ashkhabad Mashhad AFGHANISTAN Srinagar Kitakyushu
Sardinia TURKEY Izmir Yerevan Tabriz Kabul Lahore XIZANG Chengdu Wuhan Shanghai
Valencia Sicily Halab SYRIA Tehran Rawalpindi (TIBET) Lhasa Chongqing East China **D**
Mediterranean Sea Crete CYPRUS Dimashq Baghdad IRAN Isfahan Delhi NEPAL Katmandu Changsha Fuzhou Sea
Tunis MALTA Bayrut Jerusalem IRAQ Abadan PAKISTAN Agra Lucknow BHU. Kunming Taibei
Tarabulus TUNISIA Tel Aviv-Yafo Amman Shiraz KUWAIT Kanpur Ganga DESH Guangzhou TAIWAN
ALGERIA El Iskandariya JORDAN BAHRAIN Karachi Ahmadabad I N D I A Calcutta BURMA Hong Kong Tropic of Cancer **E**
Banghazi El Qahira Red QATAR The Gulf Nagpur Hyderabad Bombay DHAKA (MYANMAR) (Br.) Byukyu Is. PACIFIC
Ain Salah EGYPT Makkah SAUDI Ar Riyad U.A.E. Arabian Pune Mandalay Hanoi South Wake I.
LIBYA Aswan Sea ARABIA OMAN Sea Bay of Rangoon VIET. China Sea (U.S.)
NIGER CHAD Omdurman El Khartum YEMEN Aden Gulf of Aden Bangalore Madras Bengal THAILAND Vientiane Hainan NAM OCEAN
Niamey L. Chad SUDAN Asmera ERITREA Socotra Madras Andaman Is. Bangkok CAMBODIA Manila
Kano Ndjamena White Nile DJIBOUTI Lakshadweep Is. (India) Phnom PHILIPPINES NORTHERN
Ibadan NIGERIA Addis Abeba ETHIOPIA Muqdisho Colombo Nicobar Is. Penh Phanh Bho Cebu MARIANAS
Lagos CENTRAL Bangui Blue Nile SOMALI REP. SRI LANKA (India) Ho Chi Minh Yap Guam FEDERATED STATES
QUATORIAL GUINEA AFRICAN Yaounde L. Turkana (CEYLON) Dondra Hd. MALAYSIA (U.S.) MARSHALL IS.
inea Libreville CAMEROON REPUBLIC KENYA MALDIVES Kuala Lumpur BRUNEI SABAH BELAU Caroline Is. Truk OF MICRONESIA **D**
SAO TOME GABON Kisangani UGANDA Kampala Equator PEN. MALAYSIA Kuching Ponape
AND PRINCIPE ZAIRE Congo Kampala Nairobi Medan SINGAPORE Borneo Gilbert Is. **E**
Brazzaville (CONGO) Victoria Mombasa Sumatera Banjarmasin Sulawesi NAURU KIRIBATI
CABINDA Kinshasa Kasai Zanzibar SEYCHELLES Chagos Arch. Palembang INDONESIA Maluku New Ireland
Luanda L. Dar es Salaam Amirante (Br.) Jakarta Ujung Pandang Irian TUVALU
Tanganyika Is. Diego Garcia Bandung Surabaya Jaya PAPUA New
ANGOLA TANZANIA Aldabra (Br.) Jawa Timor NEW Rabaul Britain
Benguela Lubumbashi I N D I A N COMORO Christmas I. Arafura Sea GUINEA SOLOMON Santa Cruz Is. **E**
ZAMBIA Malawi MADAGASCAR (Australia) Timor Port C. York Louisiade IS.
Lusaka Cocos Sea Moresby Arch.
NAMIBIA ZIMBABWE MOZAMBIQUE Antananarivo OCEAN (Keeling Is.) Darwin
Windhoek Harare Rodriguez (Australia) NORTHERN
BOTSWANA Bulawayo MAURITIUS TERRITORY VANUATU
Gaborone Reunion Tropic of Capricorn North West C. Cairns Vanua Levu FIJI
Johannesburg SWA. Maputo (Fr.) WESTERN Alice Townsville Viti Levu Suva New **F**
Pretoria LES. AUSTRALIA Springs QUEENSLAND Caledonia
SOUTH Durban A U S T R A L I A Rockhampton 20
AFRICA Amsterdam SOUTH Brisbane
Cape Town Port Elizabeth (Fr.) AUSTRALIA NEW SOUTH Norfolk I.
C. of Good Hope St. Paul Kalgoorlie- WALES Lord Howe (Australia)
(Fr.) Perth Boulder Newcastle (Australia)
Fremantle Great Sydney North C.
Pr. Edward Is. Crozet Is. C. Leeuwin Australian Adelaide VICTORIA Canberra Auckland
(South Africa) (Fr.) Bight Melbourne Tasman North I.
Kerguelen TASMANIA Sea NEW 40
Bouvet I. (Fr.) Hobart C. Farewell ZEALAND
(Norway) Christchurch Wellington
McDonald I. Heard I. South I.
(Australia) (Australia) Stewart I. Bounty Is. Dunedin
SOUTHERN OCEAN Antipodes Is. (N.Z.) **G**
Macquarie I. Campbell I. Auckland Is. (N.Z.)
(Australia) (N.Z.)
Antarctic Circle
Enderby S Magnetic Pole
Maud Land Land Wilkes Land Balleny Is. **H**
CTICA Ross Sea
East from Greenwich
**10** **11** **12** **13** **14** **15** **16** **17** **18**
20 40 60 80 100 120 140 160 180 80

1 : 28 000 000

```
200 100      200    400      600 miles
400    200    0    200    400   800  1200 km
```

PACIFIC OCEAN

JAPAN

Aleutian Islands

Bering Sea

Sea of Okhotsk

Sakhalin

Komandorskiye Ostrova

Kuriľskiye Ostrova

La Perouse Str.

Hokkaidō

Dutch Harbor
Unimak I.
Pribilof Is.
▼42
St. Matthew (U.S.A.)
Mys Navarin
St. Lawrence I. (U.S.A.)
Nunivak
Nome
Norton Sd.
St. Michael
Kuskokwim
Yukon
Bristol Bay
Kodiak I.
G. of Alaska
Anchorage
Cordova  Mt. McKinley 6194
Mt. St. Elias 5489
Seward
Pr. William Sd.
Fairbanks
ALASKA

Poluostrov Kamchatka
Petropavlovsk-Kamchatskiy
Vlk. Klyuchevskaya 4850
Ostrov Karaginskiy
Mys Olyutorski
Penzhinskaya G.
Gizhiginskaya Guba
Anadyr
Anadyrskiy Zaliv
Mys Chukotskiy
Okhotsko Kolymskoye
Chukotskiy Khrebet
Penzhina
Tauiskaya Guba
Okhotsk
Nikolayevsk
Amur
Khabarovsk
Ulbanskiy Zaliv
Udskaya Guba
Tatarskiy Proliv
Sovetskaya Gavan
Mys Lopatka

Mt. Logan 6050
Whitehorse
Lewes
Skagway
Pr. Rupert
Seena
Rocky Mountains
Dawson Creek
Peace
Ft. Vermilion
Fort Simpson
Fort Norman
Good Hope
Fort McPherson
Herschel I.
Mackenzie Bay
C. Bathurst
Beaufort Sea
Prudhoe Bay
Harrison Bay
Pt. Barrow
C. Halkett
Pt. Hope
C. Lisburne
Chukchi Sea
C. Belcher
Ostrova Vrangelya
Chaunskaya
Nizhne Kolymsk
Kolyma
Srednekolymsk
Alazeya
Indigirka
Zashiversk
Yana
Verkhoyansk
Verkhoyanskiy Khrebet
Yakutsk
Lena
Aldan
Olekma
Vilyuy
Zhigansk
Bulun
Kazache
Kotelnyy
Lyakhovskiye Ostrova
Novosibirskiye Ostrova
O. Bennetta

ARCTIC OCEAN

NORTH AMERICA

Great Bear Lake
Mackenzie
Athabasca
Yellowknife
Gt. Slave Lake
Coppermine
Dolphin & Union Str.
C. Kellett
Banks I.
C. Pr. Alfred
Pr. Patrick
Melville I.
Borden I.
Parry Is.
Prince of Wales I.
Pr. Albert Pen.
Victoria Island
Dubawnt L.
M'Clure Str.
Melville Sd.
Magnetic Pole 1990
Bathurst I.
Ellef Ringnes I.
Sverdrup Is.
Axel Heiberg I.
Nansen Sd.
Eureka
Devon I.
Ellesmere I.
Alert
C. Columbia
Lincoln
Nares Str.
Kane Basin
Smith Sd.
Thule
Humboldt Gletscher
Rasmussen Land
Peary Ld.
Knud Rasmussen Land
Kong Frederik VIII.s Land
Independence Fj.
McKinley Sea
Markham I.
K. Morris Jesup

Canada Basin
Mendeleyev Ridge
3767
3327
Alpha Cordillera
3700
3545
Makarov Basin
3849
Lomonosov Ridge
NORTH POLE
4007
4418
4484
4100
Fram Basin
Nansen Cordillera
3741
Nansen Basin
2104

Laptev Sea
O. Petra
Nordvik
Severnaya Zemlya
Oktyabrskoy Revolyutsii
Ostrov Graham Bell
Zemlya Frantsa Iosifa
O. Ushakova
O. Uedineniya
O. Vise
Anabar
Olenek
Nordvik
Poluostrov Taymyr
Oz. Taymyr
Kheta
Kotuy
Khatanga
Pyasina
Norilsk
Dudinka
Igarka
Yenisey
Taz
Turukhansk
Golchikha
Plato Putorana
SIBERIA
USSR

Hudson Bay
Churchill
Chesterfield
Back
Baker L.
King William I.
Boothia Pen.
Gulf of Boothia
Prince Regent Inlet
Somerset I.
Prince of Wales I.
Barrow Str.
Lancaster Sd.
Baffin I.
Bylot I.
Jones Sd.
Baffin Bay
Southampton I.
Coats I.
Mansel I.
Foxe Channel
Foxe Basin
Pr. Charles I.
Melville Pen.
Fury & Hecla Str.
Wolstenholme
Nettilling L.
Upernavik
C. Dyer
Disko
Umanak
Disko B.
Godhavn
Kong Frederik IX.s Land
Godthåb
Frederikshåb
Julianehåb
Sydprøven
K. Farvel
Hamilton Inlet
C. Charles
Labrador
Ungava B.
C. Chidley
Resolution I.
Hudson Str.
Cumberland Sd.
Davis Str.
GREENLAND (Denmark)
Mont Forel 3360
Kong Christian IX.s Land
Angmagssalik
K. Franz Joseph Fd.
Kong Oscar Fj.
Scoresbysund
K. Brewster
Gunnbjørn Field 3700
Denmark Strait
Iceland Strait Plateau
Breidafjorður
Horn
Fontur
Reykjavik
Hekla 1491
Öraefajökull
ICELAND
3800
Faroe Is.
Shetland Is.
Rockall
4755
Orkney Is.
Hebrides
BRITISH ISLES
SCOTLAND
Glasgow
Edinburgh
Belfast
IRELAND
Dublin
Liverpool
WALES
ENGLAND
London
C. Clear
Cork

Greenland Sea
Jan Mayen
Norwegian Sea
2671
Vestspitsbergen
Svalbard (Norway)
Longyearbyen
Nordaustlandet
Edgeøya
Kvitøya
Nordkapp
Bjørnøya
Barents Sea
Kara Sea
Novaya Zemlya
Ostrov Belyy
Yamal
Baydaratskaya Guba
Poluostrov
Ostrov Kolguyev
Kolskiy Poluostrov
Murmansk
Arkhangelsk
Sev. Dvina
Mezen
Pechora
Vorkuta
Khalmer
Salekhard
Narodnaya 1894
Uralskie Gory
Berezovo
Ob
Surgut
Tobolsk
Urengoy
Nadym
Novy Port
Novaya

Hammerfest
Vadsø
Tromsø
Lofoten
Narvik
Bodø
Trondheim
Oslo
Bergen
NORWAY
SWEDEN
Stockholm
Gulf of Bothnia
Tornio
FINLAND
Helsinki
Ladozhskoye Ozero
Onega
Onezhskoye Ozero
St. Peterburg
Chudskoye Ozero
EST.
Riga
LAT.
Tallinn
LITH.
Kaunas
Vilnius
Kaliningrad
København
DENMARK
North Sea
Skagerrak
Baltic Sea
Gdańsk
Szczecin
Berlin
POLAND
Warszawa
Łódź
Wrocław
GERMANY
Hamburg
Elbe
Köln
Leipzig
Praha
Amsterdam
NETH.
Kiev
UKRAINE
Odessa
Black Sea
Rostov
Volgograd
Saratov
Samara
Moskva
RUSSIA
Volga
EUROPE
Yekaterinburg
Perm
Ufa

Arctic Circle

ATLANTIC OCEAN

Mid-Atlantic Ridge

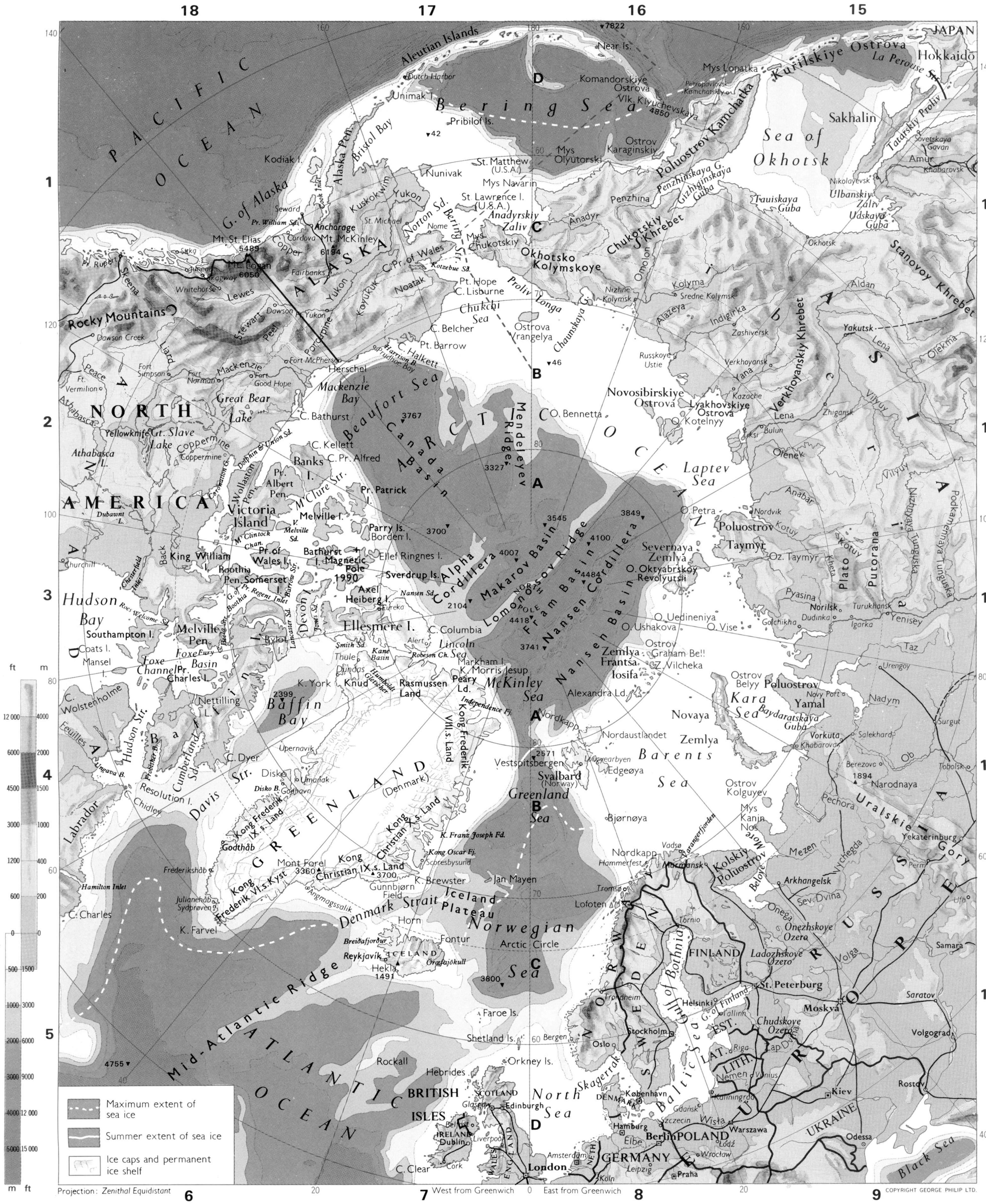

Projection: Zenithal Equidistant

West from Greenwich    East from Greenwich

COPYRIGHT GEORGE PHILIP LTD.

**Legend:**
- Maximum extent of sea ice
- Summer extent of sea ice
- Ice caps and permanent ice shelf

```
ft       m
12 000   4000
6000     2000
4500     1500
3000     1000
1200     400
600      200
0        0
500      1500
1000     3000
2000     6000
3000     9000
4000     12 000
6000     15 000
m        ft
```

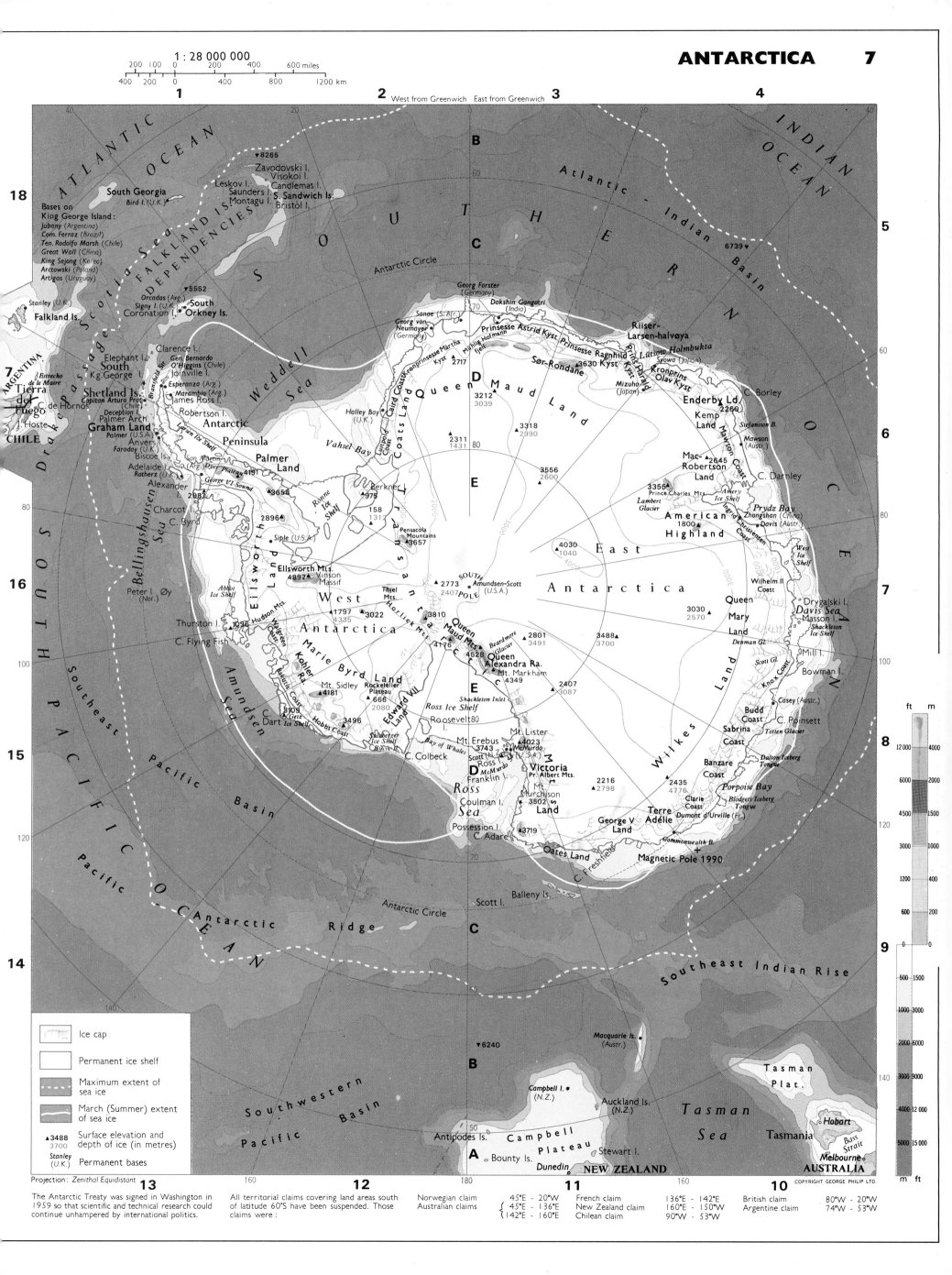

1 : 28 000 000

ft m / m ft

**Ice cap**

**Permanent ice shelf**

**Maximum extent of sea ice**

**March (Summer) extent of sea ice**

▲3488 / 3700   Surface elevation and depth of ice (in metres)

*Stanley (U.K.)*   Permanent bases

Projection: *Zenithal Equidistant*

The Antarctic Treaty was signed in Washington in 1959 so that scientific and technical research could continue unhampered by international politics.

All territorial claims covering land areas south of latitude 60°S have been suspended. Those claims were :

| | |
|---|---|
| Norwegian claim | 45°E – 20°W |
| Australian claims | 45°E – 136°E |
| | 142°E – 160°E |
| French claim | 136°E – 142°E |
| New Zealand claim | 160°E – 150°W |
| Chilean claim | 90°W – 53°W |
| British claim | 80°W – 20°W |
| Argentine claim | 74°W – 53°W |

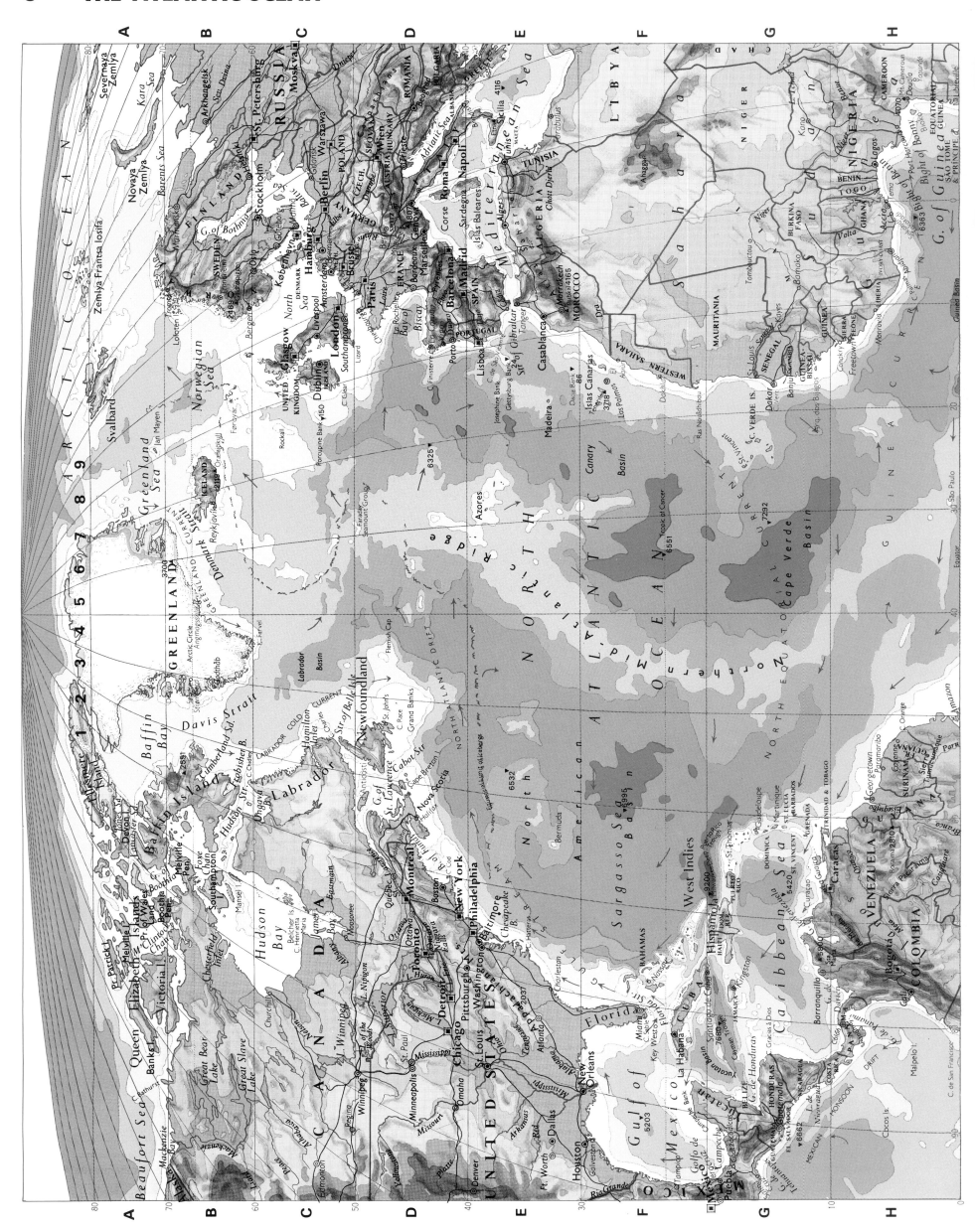

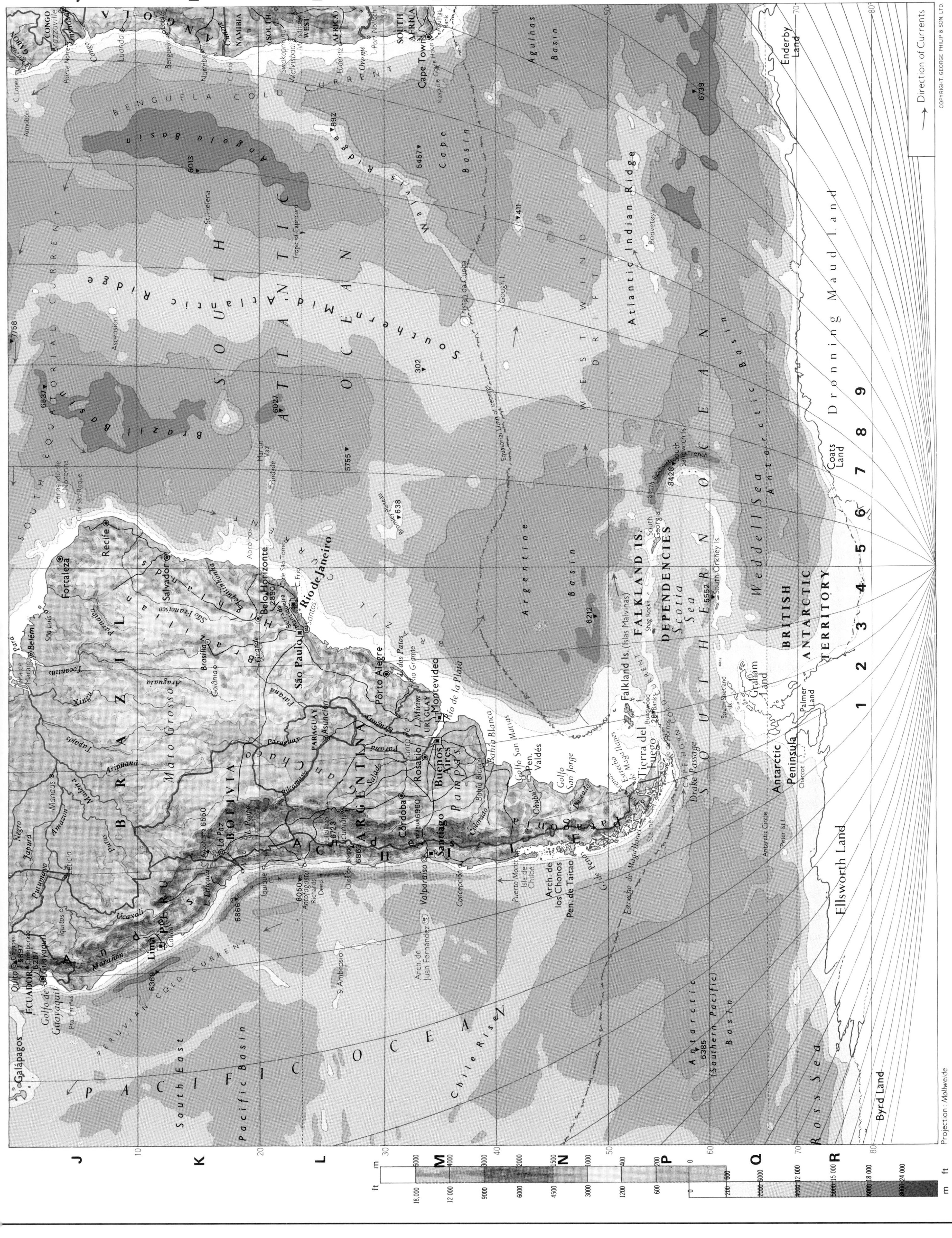

→ Direction of Currents

COPYRIGHT GEORGE PHILIP & SON LTD.

J K L M N P Q R

CONGO
Brazzaville
GABON
Pointe Noire
C. Lopez
Annobón
ANGOLA
Luanda
Benguela
Namibe
C. Frio
NAMIBIA
Swakopmund
Walvisbaai
Lüderitz
SOUTH WEST AFRICA
Orange
SOUTH AFRICA
Cape Town
Kaap die Goeie Hoop
Port Nolloth

BENGUELA COLD CURRENT

Angola Basin
6013

Walvis Ridge
4892

Cape Basin
5457

Agulhas Basin

6739

TROPIC OF CAPRICORN
Tropic of Capricorn

SOUTH ATLANTIC OCEAN

Mid-Atlantic Ridge

Southern

St. Helena
Ascension
7758

Cape Verde

SOUTH EQUATORIAL CURRENT

Brazil Basin
6837

Martin Vaz
Trindade
6027

302

Gough I.
Tristan da Cunha

West Wind

Atlantic Indian Ridge
Bouvetøya

Drift

Enderby Land

Dronning Maud Land

Coats Land

Equatorial Limit of Icebergs

Brazilian Highlands
5755
6638

Recife
Fortaleza
Salvador
Belo Horizonte
2890
Rio de Janeiro
São Paulo
Santos

BRAZIL
São Francisco
Brasília
Goiânia
Mato Grosso
Araguaia
Tocantins
Xingu
Tapajós
Aripuanã
Madeira

Pôrto Alegre
URUGUAY
Montevideo
Rio de la Plata
Buenos Aires
Rosário
Córdoba
PARAGUAY
Asunción
Paraguay
Paraná
Pilcomayo
BOLIVIA
La Paz
6550
6723
8863
6960
ARGENTINA
Santiago
Valparaíso
Concepción
8050
Antofagasta
Richards Deep
6369
6866
PERU
Lima
Marañón
Ucayali
ECUADOR
Quito
6267
Guayaquil
Gulf of Guayaquil
Galápagos
5897

Pampas
Salado
Colorado
Bahía Blanca
Golfo San Matías
Pen. Valdés
Chubut
Golfo San Jorge
Tierra del Fuego
Cape Horn
Drake Passage
Estrecho de Magallanes
Arch. de los Chonos
Pen. de Taitao
Isla de Chiloé
Puerto Montt
Arch. de Juan Fernández
S. Ambrosio
Abrolhos

Argentine Basin
6212

FALKLAND IS.
Falkland Is. (Islas Malvinas)
FALKLAND IS. DEPENDENCIES
South Georgia
Scotia Sea
8428
South Sandwich Is.
South Sandwich Trench
South Orkney Is.
South Shetland Is.

FALKLAND CURRENT

Weddell Sea
6552

Scotia Sea

Antarctic

Weddell Sea Basin

Anterctic

Antarctic Circle
Peter I Øy

Antarctic Peninsula
Graham Land
Palmer Land
Charcot I.

BRITISH ANTARCTIC TERRITORY

Ellsworth Land
Byrd Land
Ross Sea

PACIFIC OCEAN

PERUVIAN COLD CURRENT

South East Pacific Basin

Chile Rise

Antarctic
5385
(Southern Pacific) Basin

SOUTHERN OCEAN

ANDES

Projection: Mollweide

ft m
18 000 5000
12 000 4000
9000 3000
6000 2000
4500 1500
3000 1000
1200 400
600 200
0
200 600
1000
2000 4000
4000 5000
12 000
15 000
18 000 6000
24 000 8000
m ft

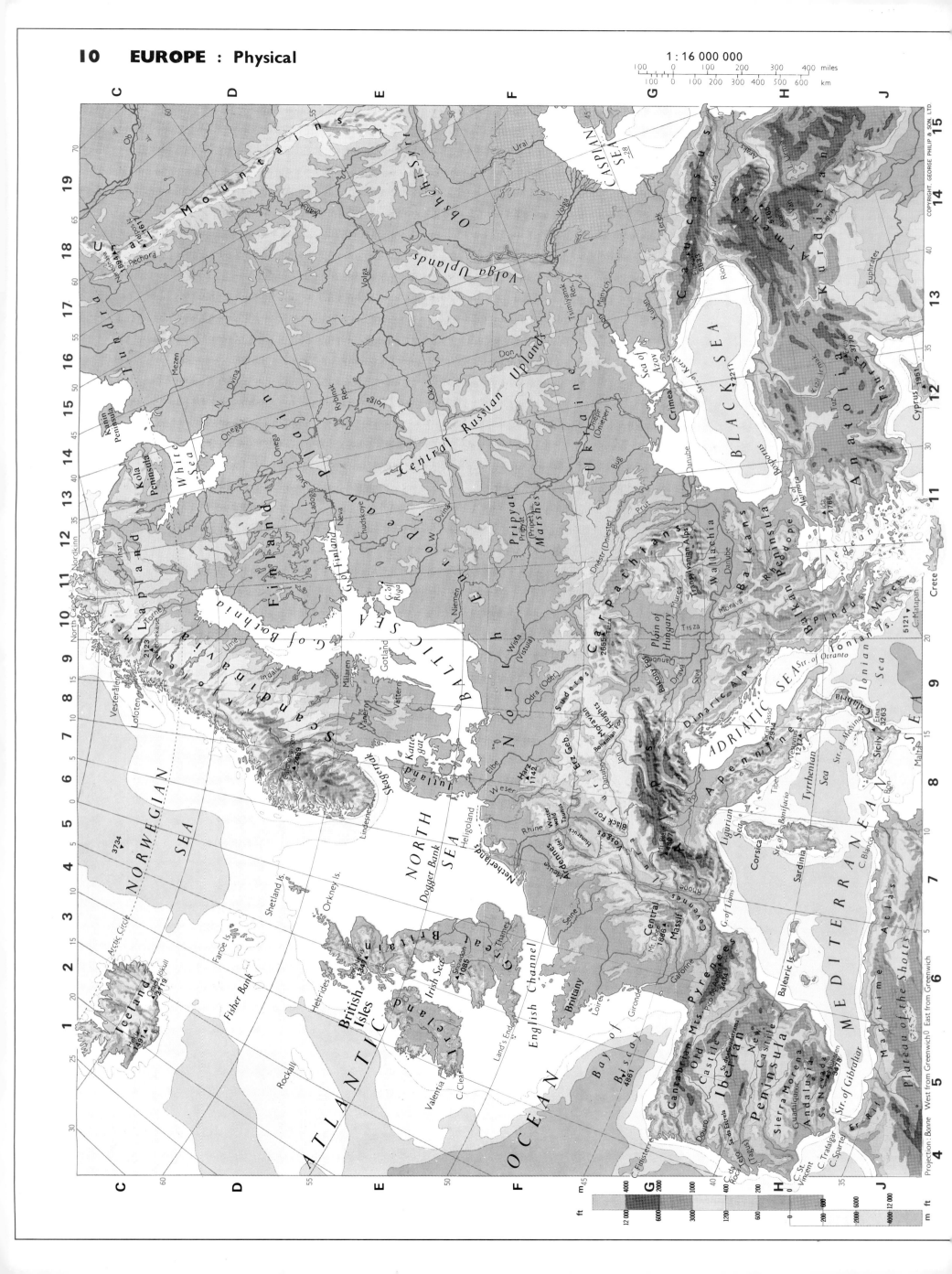

1 : 16 000 000

Projection: Bonne

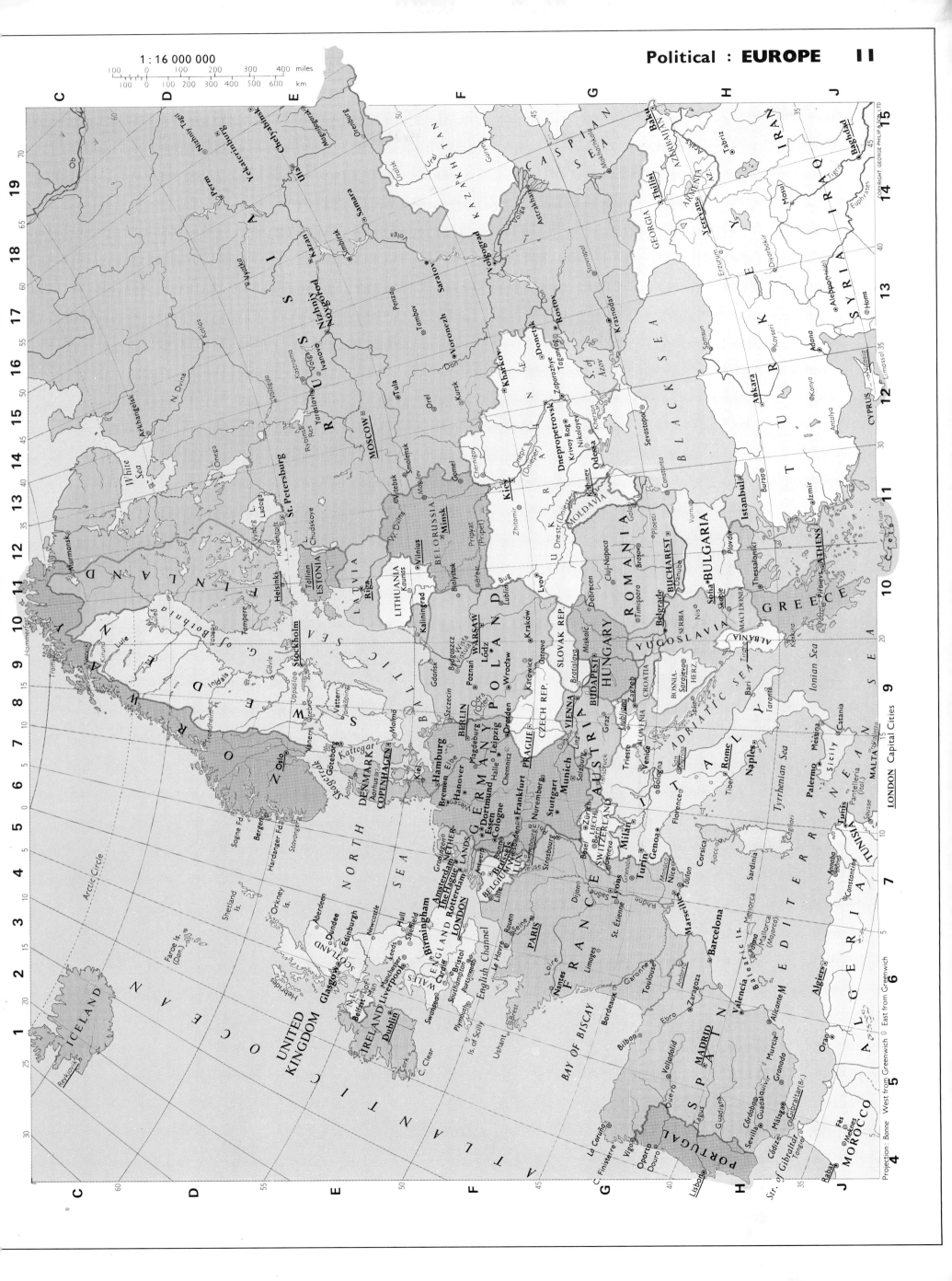

1 : 16 000 000

100    0    100   200   300   400 miles

100   0   100  200  300  400  500  600 km

LONDON Capital Cities

Projection: Bonne     West from Greenwich 0 East from Greenwich

COPYRIGHT GEORGE PHILIP & SON LTD

ICELAND

Reykjavik

ATLANTIC     OCEAN

NORWAY

Hammerfest

Tromsø

Narvik

Kiruna

Bodø

SWEDEN

FINLAND

Murmansk

White Sea

Arkhangelsk

Oslo

Bergen

Stavanger

Stockholm

Helsinki

ESTONIA     Tallinn

LATVIA     Riga

St. Petersburg

Vitebsk

MOSCOW

R  U  S  S  I  A

Nizhniy Novgorod

Kazan

Samara

Yekaterinburg

Perm

Ufa

Chelyabinsk

Nizhniy Tagil

Ob

KAZAKHSTAN

CASPIAN     SEA

Baku

AZERBAIJAN

Tbilisi

GEORGIA

ARMENIA     Yerevan

IRAN

SYRIA

IRAQ     Baghdad

T  U  R  K  E  Y

Ankara

Istanbul

CYPRUS     Nicosia

BLACK     SEA

BULGARIA     Sofia

ROMANIA     BUCHAREST

Belgrade     SERBIA

YUGOSLAVIA

ALBANIA

GREECE

ATHENS

Crete

Thessaloniki

MACEDONIA     Skopje

BOSNIA     Sarajevo     HERZ.

CROATIA

SLOVENIA     Ljubljana

Zagreb

HUNGARY     BUDAPEST

AUSTRIA     VIENNA

SLOVAK REP.     Bratislava

CZECH REP.     PRAGUE

P  O  L  A  N  D     WARSAW

BELORUSSIA     Minsk

LITHUANIA     Vilnius

Kaliningrad

Kiev

Kharkov

Donetsk

Rostov

Dnepropetrovsk

Odessa

MOLDAVIA

UKRAINE

Volgograd

Saratov

Voronezh

Tula

Kursk

Orel

Smolensk

G  E  R  M  A  N  Y     BERLIN

Hamburg

Bremen

Hanover

Cologne

Frankfurt

Munich

Stuttgart

Nuremberg

Dresden

Leipzig

DENMARK     COPENHAGEN

Kiel

NETHER-LANDS     Amsterdam     The Hague     Rotterdam

BELGIUM     Brussels

LUX.

SWITZERLAND     Zürich     Bern

Geneva

Milan

Turin

Genoa

I  T  A  L  Y

Rome

Naples

Palermo

Sicily

Venice

Florence

Bologna

ADRIATIC     SEA

Tyrrhenian Sea

Ionian Sea

MEDITERRANEAN     SEA

MALTA     Valletta

TUNISIA     Tunis

ALGERIA

MOROCCO     Rabat

PORTUGAL     Lisbon     Oporto

S  P  A  I  N     MADRID

Barcelona

Valencia

Málaga

Sevilla

Córdoba

Zaragoza

Bilbao

Balearic Is.

Mallorca

Menorca

BAY OF BISCAY

F  R  A  N  C  E     PARIS

Bordeaux

Toulouse

Marseille

Lyons

Nantes

Nice

Strasbourg

Dijon

UNITED     KINGDOM

LONDON

Birmingham

Manchester

Liverpool

Leeds

Sheffield

Glasgow

Edinburgh

SCOTLAND

ENGLAND

WALES     Cardiff

IRELAND     Dublin

N.I.     Belfast

NORTH     SEA

English Channel

Faroe Is. (Den.)

Shetland

Orkney Is.

Hebrides

Gulf of Bothnia

BALTIC SEA

Arctic Circle

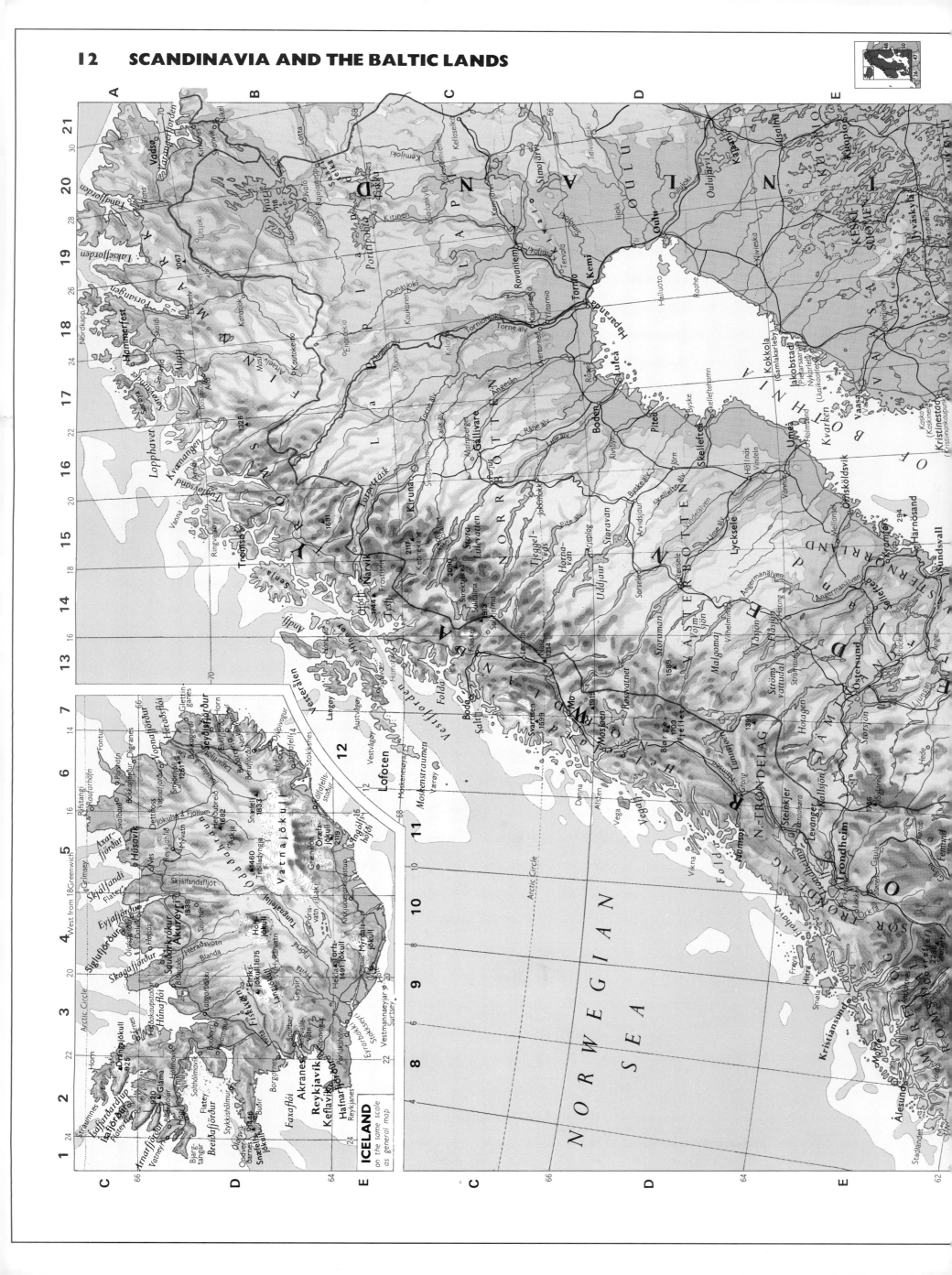

ICELAND
on the same scale
as general map

NORWEGIAN SEA

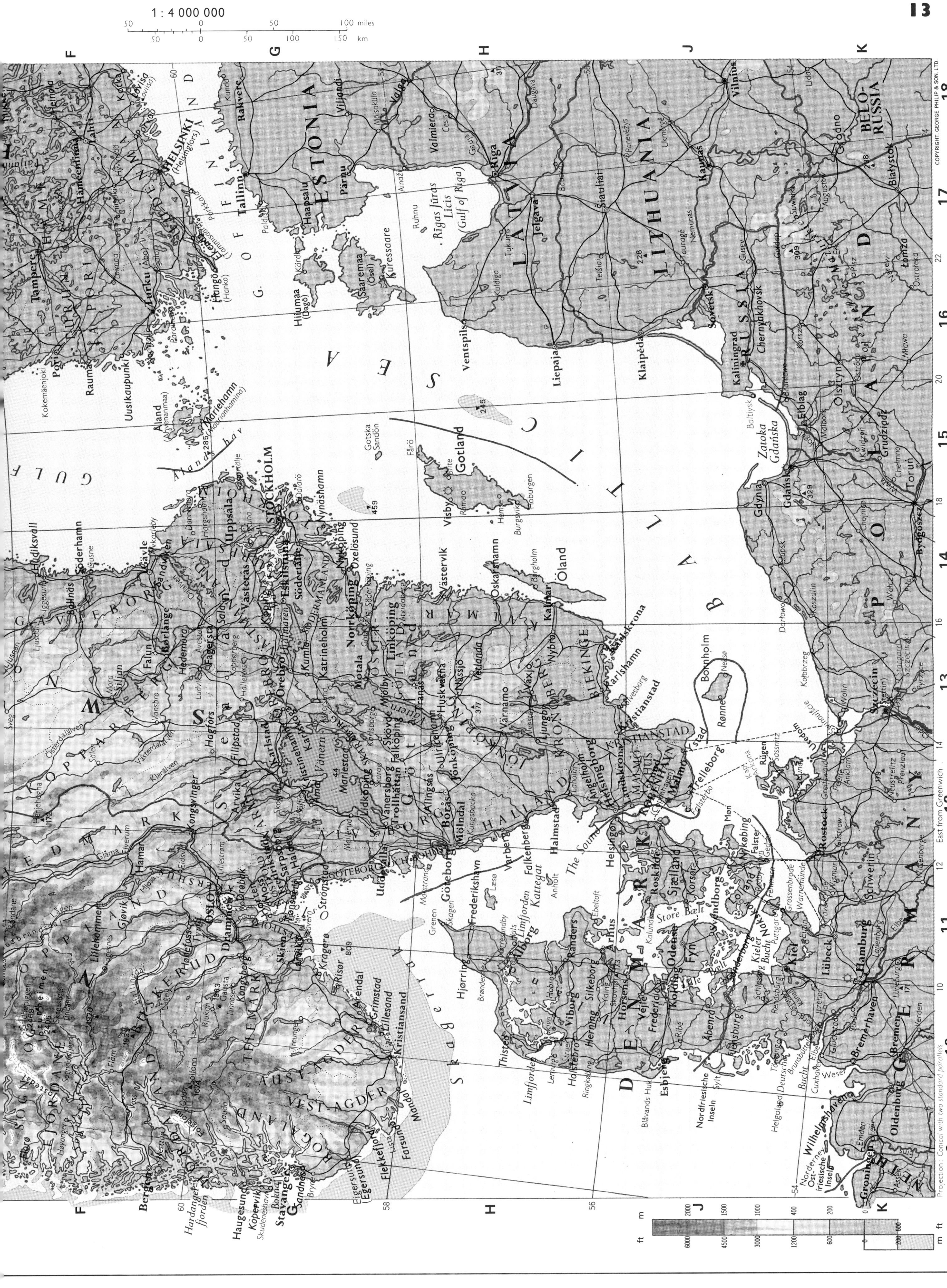

1 : 4 000 000

50    0    50    100 miles
50    0    50    100    150 km

COPYRIGHT. GEORGE PHILIP & SON, LTD.

East from Greenwich

Projection: Conical with two standard parallels

BALTIC SEA

GULF OF BOTHNIA

GULF OF FINLAND

Gulf of Riga (Rīgas Jūras Līcis)

ESTONIA
LATVIA
LITHUANIA
BELO-RUSSIA
POLAND
GERMANY
DENMARK
NORWAY
SWEDEN
FINLAND
RUSSIA

HELSINKI (Helsingfors)
Tampere
Turku (Åbo)
Pori
Rauma
Uusikaupunki
Hangö (Hanko)
Tallinn
Pärnu
Haapsalu
Valga
Valmiera
Rīga
Jelgava
Šiauliai
Liepāja
Ventspils
Klaipėda
Kaunas
Vilnius
Kaliningrad
Chernyakhovsk
Sovetsk
Gdańsk
Gdynia
Elblag
Olsztyn
Grudziądz
Toruń
Bydgoszcz
Szczecin (Stettin)
Rostock
Schwerin
Lübeck
Hamburg
Bremen
Bremerhaven
Oldenburg
Emden
Groningen
Wilhelmshaven

STOCKHOLM
Uppsala
Gävle
Västerås
Eskilstuna
Örebro
Norrköping
Linköping
Nyköping
Oxelösund
Nynäshamn
Motala
Jönköping
Borås
Göteborg
Halmstad
Helsingborg
Malmö
Kristianstad
Karlskrona
Karlshamn
Kalmar
Oskarshamn
Västervik
Visby
Gotland
Öland
Bornholm
Rönne

OSLO
Drammen
Lillehammer
Gjøvik
Hamar
Kongsvinger
Skien
Arendal
Kristiansand
Stavanger
Sandnes
Haugesund
Bergen

København (Copenhagen)
Odense
Ålborg
Århus
Randers
Esbjerg
Kolding
Vejle
Fredericia
Horsens
Viborg
Herning
Roskilde
Helsingør
Næstved

Kiel
Flensburg
Kattegat
Skagerrak
The Sound (Öresund)
Store Bælt

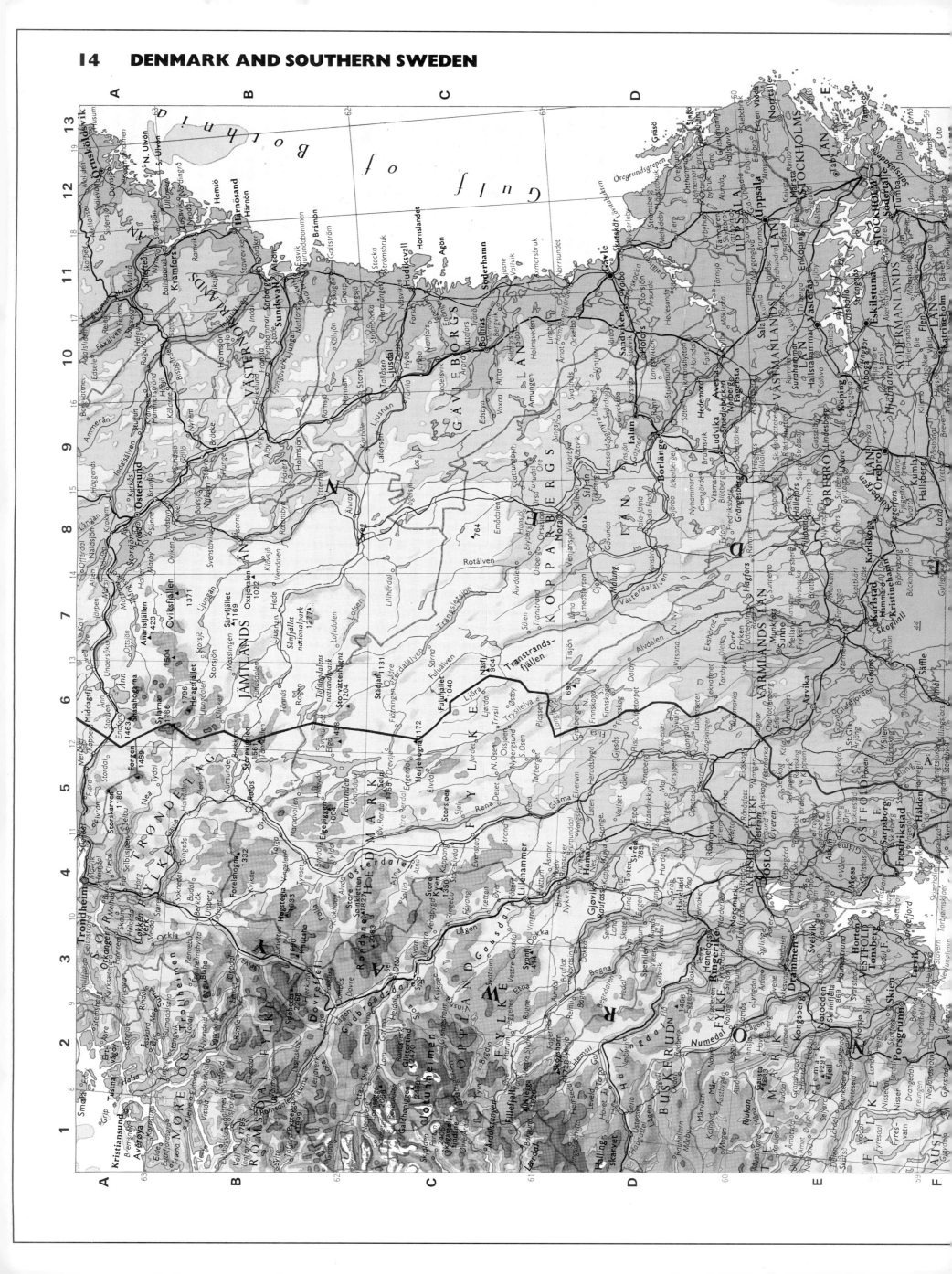

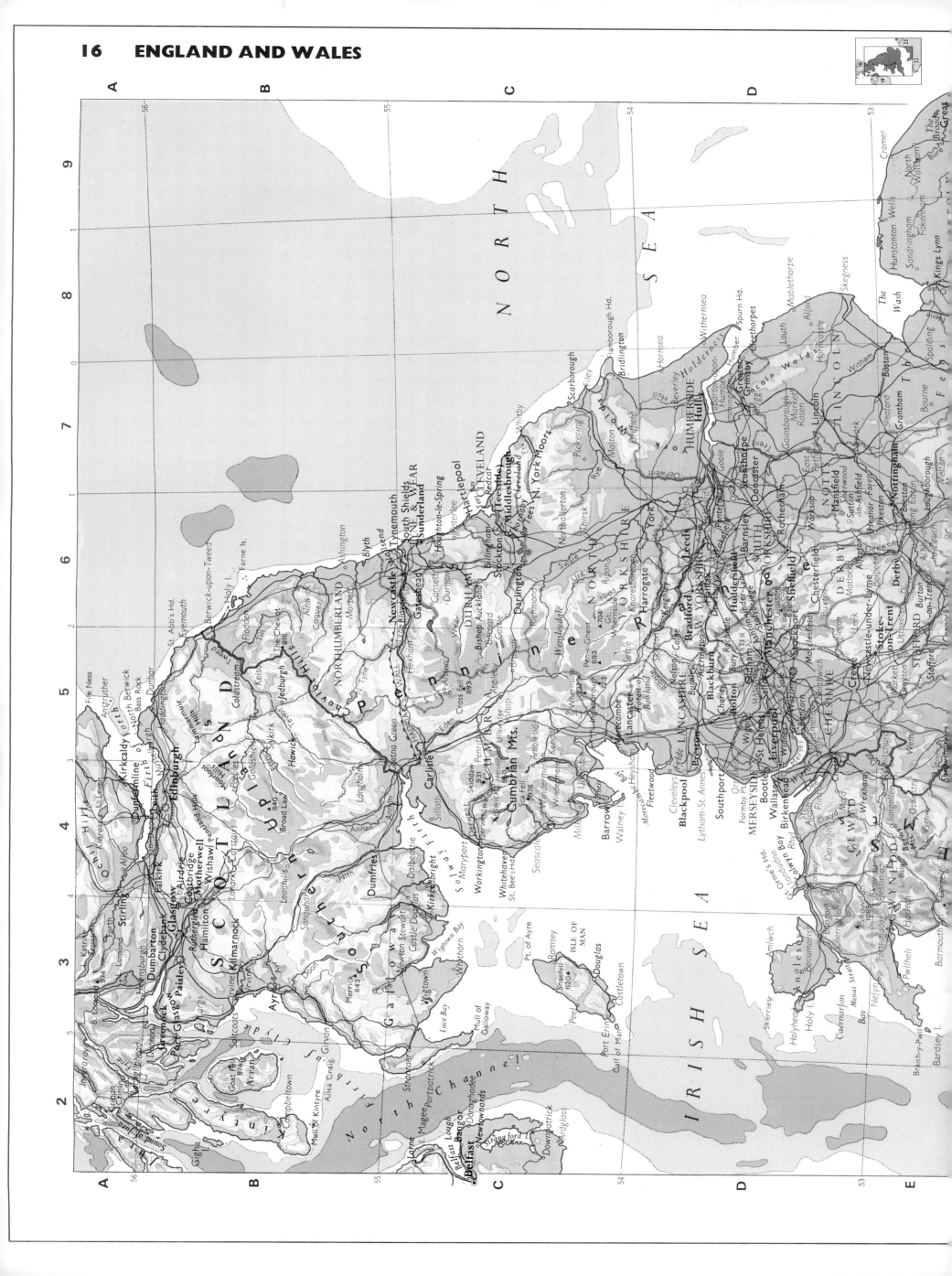

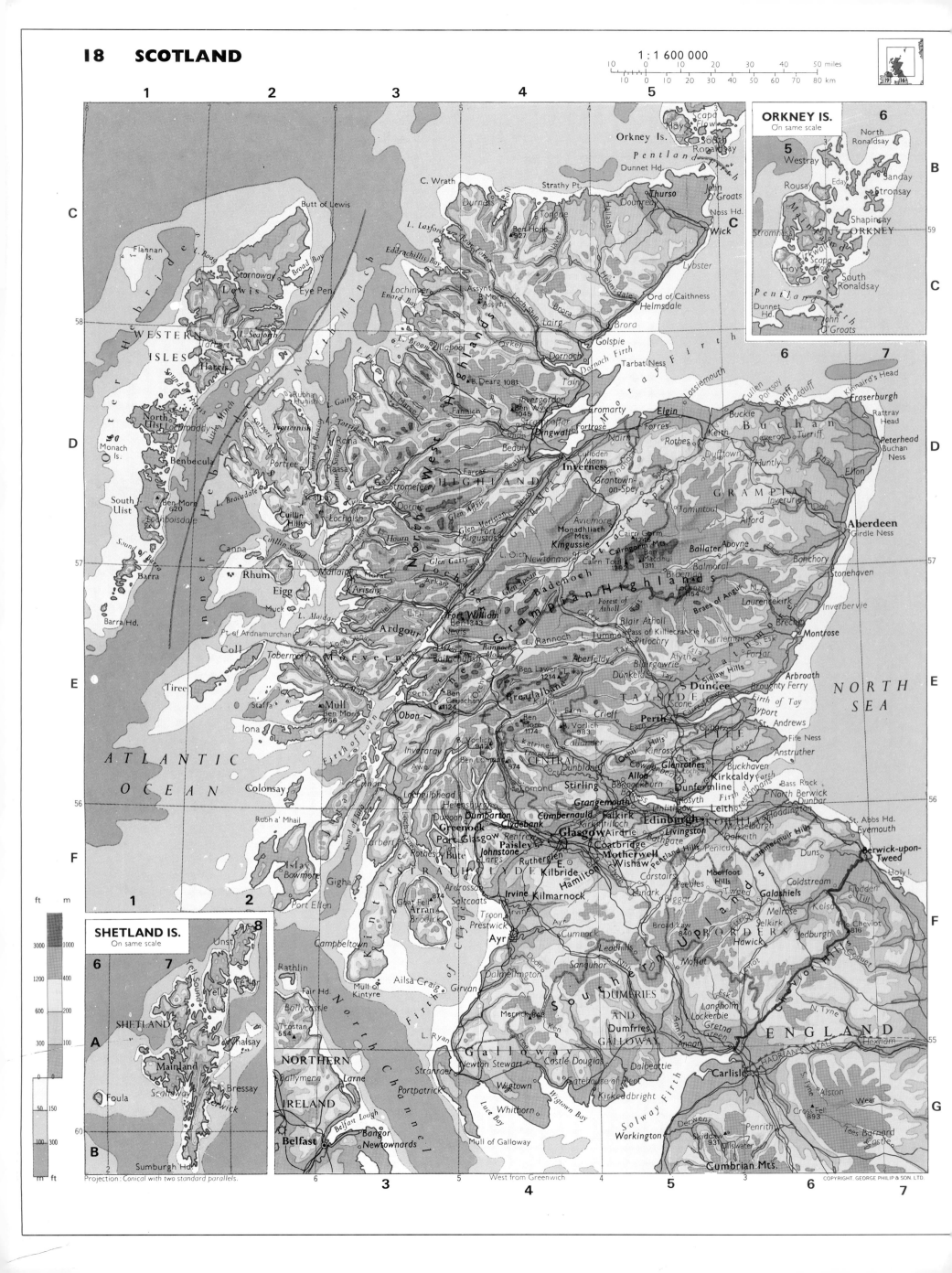

# 18 SCOTLAND

1 : 1 600 000

ORKNEY IS.
On same scale

SHETLAND IS.
On same scale

Projection: Conical with two standard parallels.

West from Greenwich

COPYRIGHT. GEORGE PHILIP & SON, LTD.

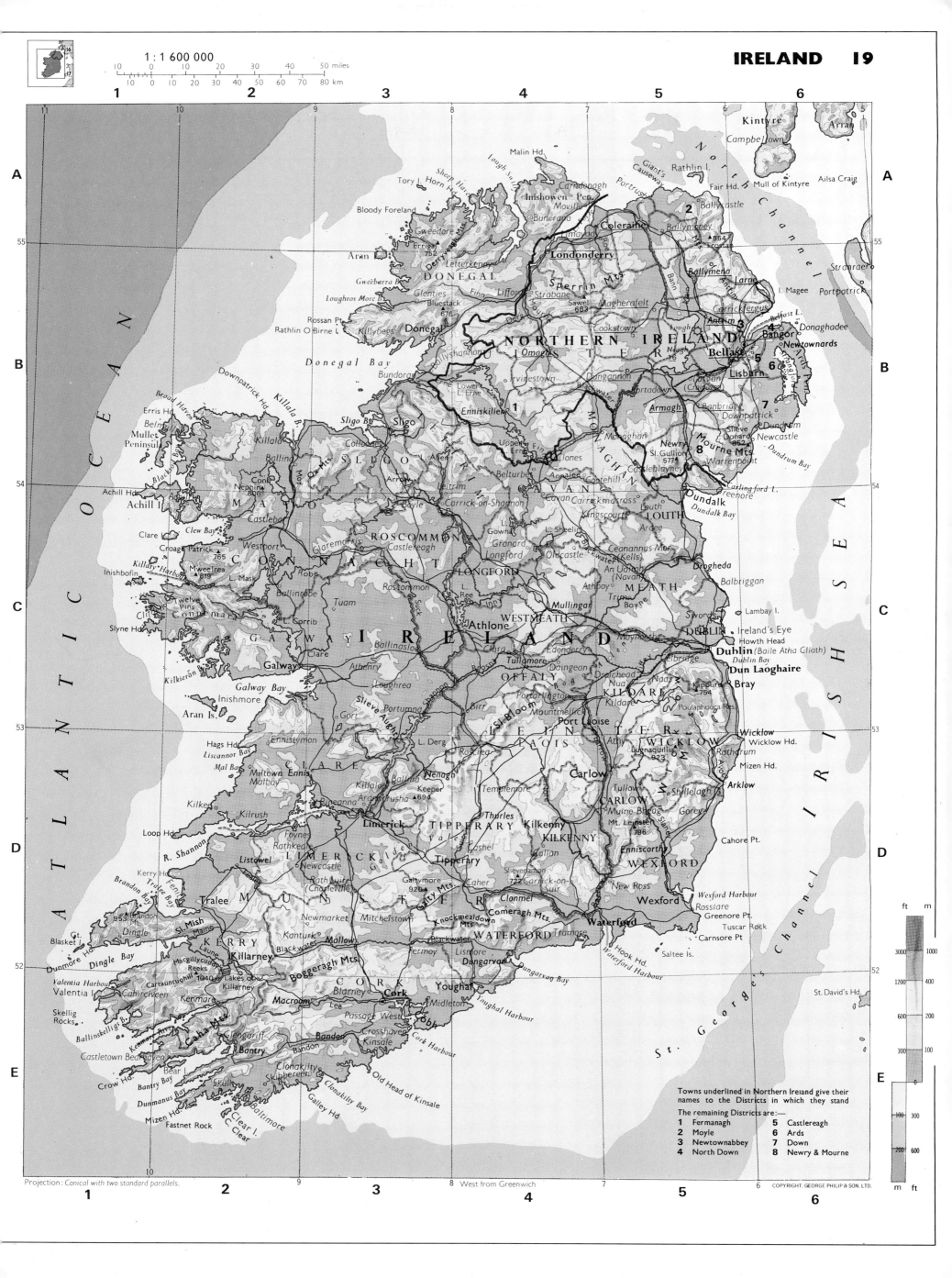

1 : 1 600 000

10  0  10  20  30  40  50 miles

10  0  10  20  30  40  50  60  70  80 km

**ATLANTIC OCEAN**

**NORTH CHANNEL**

**IRISH SEA**

**St. George's Channel**

**DONEGAL**

**NORTHERN IRELAND**

**ULSTER**

**CONNACHT**

**SLIGO**

**MAYO**

**ROSCOMMON**

**LEITRIM**

**CAVAN**

**MONAGHAN**

**LONGFORD**

**WESTMEATH**

**MEATH**

**LOUTH**

**GALWAY**

**IRELAND**

**OFFALY**

**KILDARE**

**DUBLIN**

**CLARE**

**TIPPERARY**

**LAOIS (LEIX)**

**WICKLOW**

**CARLOW**

**KILKENNY**

**LEINSTER**

**WEXFORD**

**LIMERICK**

**MUNSTER**

**KERRY**

**CORK**

**WATERFORD**

Kintyre
Campbeltown
Arran
Ailsa Craig
Mull of Kintyre
Fair Hd.
Ballycastle
Rathlin I.
Giant's Causeway
Portrush
Coleraine
Ballymoney
554
Limavady
Ballymena
Larne
Londonderry
Sperrin Mts.
Sawel 683
Strabane
Magherafelt
Antrim
Carrickfergus
I. Magee
Stranraer
Portpatrick
Malin Hd.
Inishowen Pen.
Moville
Carndonagh
Buncrana
Letterkenny
Belfast L.
Bangor
Donaghadee
Newtownards
Bellast
Lisburn
Cookstown
Dungannon
Portadown
Craigavon
Lurgan
Banbridge
Downpatrick
Dundrum
Newcastle
Armagh
Monaghan
Castleblayney
Newry
Sl. Gullion 577
Slieve Donard 852
Mourne Mts.
Warrenpoint
Carlingford L.
Greenore
Dundrum Bay
Omagh
Enniskillen
Irvinestown
Lough Erne
Upper L. Erne
Clones
Annalee
Cootehill
Belturbet
Carrickmacross
Bundoran
Ballyshannon
Bloody Foreland
Tory I.
Horn Hd.
Sheep Haven
Lough Swilly
Gweedore
Aran
Errigal 752
Derryveagh Mts.
Glenties
Bluestack Mts.
676
Finn
Liffon
Rossan Pt.
Rathlin O Birne I.
Killybegs
Donegal
Loughros More B.
Gweebarra B.
Downpatrick Hd.
Killala
Killala B.
Broad Haven
Erris Hd.
Belmullet
Mullet Peninsula
Achill Hd.
Achill I.
Clare I.
Clew Bay
Croagh Patrick 765
Westport
Mweelrea 819
Killary Harbour
Inishbofin
Inishturk
Twelve Pins
Clifden
Slyne Hd.
Connemara
Ballina
Nephin 806
Conn
L. Conn
Moy
Ox Mts.
Castlebar
L. Mask
Ballinrobe
L. Corrib
Tuam
Robe
Sligo
Sligo Bay
Collooney
Leitrim
L. Allen
Arrow
Boyle
Carrick-on-Shannon
Roscommon
Suck
Lanesborough
Gowna
Granard
L. Sheelin
Longford
L. Ree
Cavan
Kingscourt
Ceanannus Mor (Kells)
An Uaimh (Navan)
Oldcastle
Athboy
Trim
Boyne
Ardee
Dundalk
Dundalk Bay
Drogheda
Balbriggan
Skerries
Swords
Lambay I.
Ireland's Eye
Howth Head
Dublin (Baile Átha Cliath)
Dublin Bay
Dun Laoghaire
Bray
Maynooth
Celbridge
Edenderry
Leixlip
Naas
Kilcock
Kippure 754
Poulaphouca Res.
Kildare
Wicklow
Wicklow Hd.
Rathdrum
Avoca
Mizen Hd.
Lugnaquillia 923
Arklow
Shillelagh
Gorey
Tullow
Mt. Leinster 796
Muine Bheag
Enniscorthy
Cahore Pt.
Wexford
Wexford Harbour
Rosslare
Greenore Pt.
Tuscar Rock
Carnsore Pt.
Saltee Is.
Hook Hd.
Waterford Harbour
New Ross
Waterford
Tramore
Dungarvan
Dungarvan Bay
Youghal
Youghal Harbour
Ballinasloe
Athlone
Mullingar
Athenry
Loughrea
Gort
Portumna
L. Derg
Birr
Tullamore
Daingean
Clara
Mountmellick
Portarlington
Port Laoise
Slieve Bloom
Athy
Carlow
Kilkenny
Callan
Clonmel
Carrick-on-Suir
Clonmel
Comeragh Mts.
Slievenamon 722
Thurles
Templemore
Nenagh
Roscrea
Killaloe
Ballina
Keeper 694
Aughty Mts.
Silvermines
Limerick
Foynes
Rathkeale
Newcastle
Rath Luirc (Charleville)
Galtymore 920
Galty Mts.
Caher
Cahir
Cashel
Tipperary
Knockmealdown Mts.
Mitchelstown
Lismore
Fermoy
Blackwater
Listowel
Abbeyfeale
Newmarket
Kanturk
Mallow
Boggeragh Mts.
Macroom
Blarney
Lee
Cork
Midleton
Cobh
Passage West
Crosshaven
Cork Harbour
Kinsale
Bandon
Clonakilty
Clonakilty Bay
Old Head of Kinsale
Skibbereen
Castletown Bearhaven
Bear I.
Bantry
Bantry Bay
Glengarriff
Kenmare River
Caha Mts.
Dunmanus Bay
Mizen Hd.
Crow Hd.
Skull
Baltimore
Clear I.
C. Clear
Galley Hd.
Fastnet Rock
Cahirciveen
Valentia I.
Valentia Harbour
Skellig Rocks
Ballinskelligs B.
Carrauntoohil 1040
Macgillycuddy's Reeks
Lakes of Killarney
Killarney
Kenmare
Dingle
Dingle Bay
Dunmore Hd.
Brandon Mt. 953
Tralee Bay
Brandon Bay
Blasket
Gt. Blasket
Sl. Mish
Maine
Laune
Sl. Mish
Tralee
Loop Hd.
Kilkee
Kilrush
R. Shannon
Kildysart
Kilkieran
Inishmore
Aran Is.
Ennistymon
Liscannor Bay
Hags Hd.
Mal Bay
Miltown Malbay
Ennis
Shannon
Rineanna
Galway Bay
Galway
Kilronan
Clarinbridge
Clare
Gort
L. Graney
Scariff

Projection : Conical with two standard parallels.

West from Greenwich

COPYRIGHT. GEORGE PHILIP & SON. LTD.

Towns underlined in Northern Ireland give their names to the Districts in which they stand

The remaining Districts are :—

1 Fermanagh     5 Castlereagh
2 Moyle         6 Ards
3 Newtownabbey  7 Down
4 North Down    8 Newry & Mourne

ft  m
3000  1000
1200  400
600  200
300  100
0
m  ft
100  300
200  600

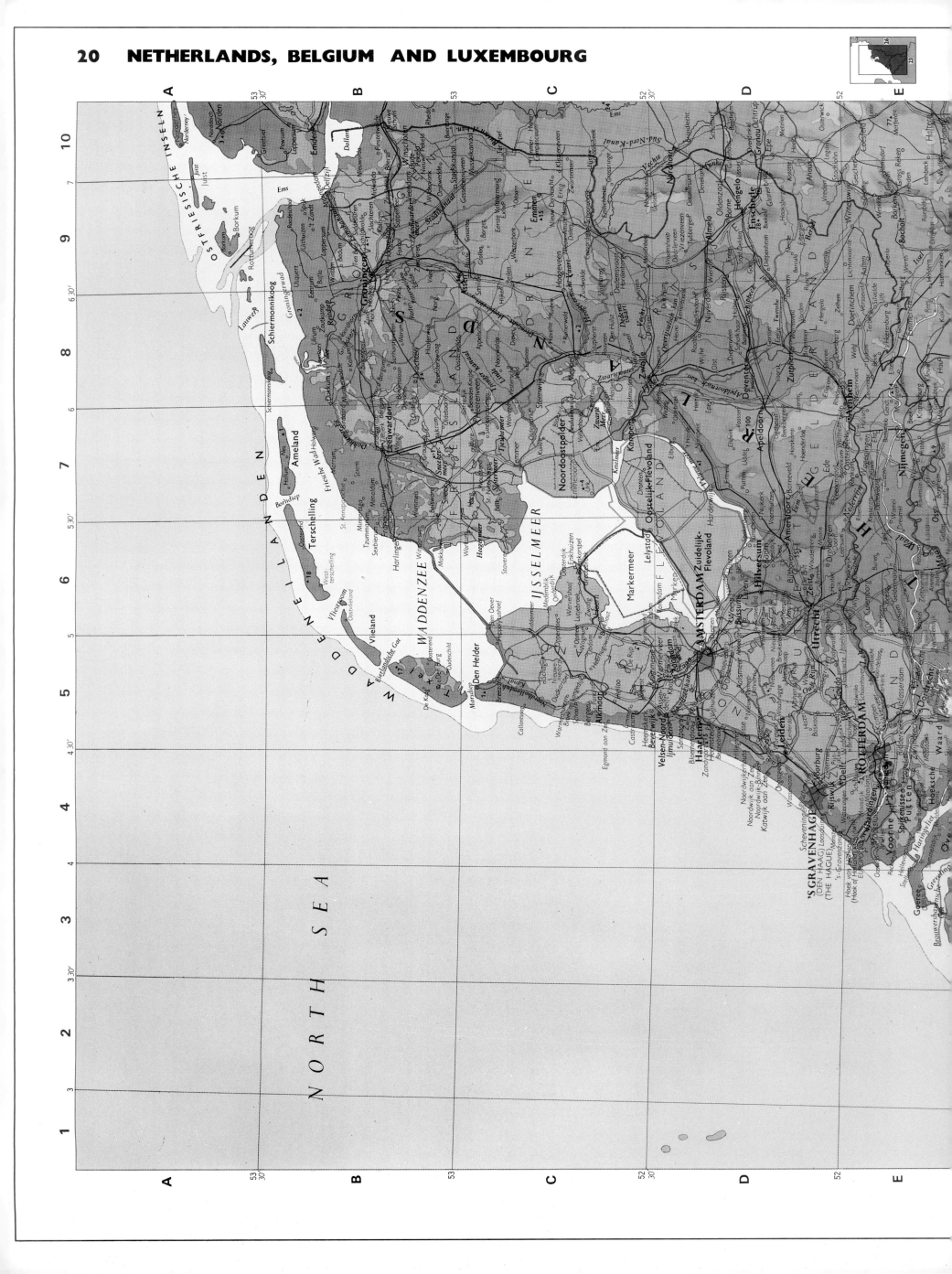

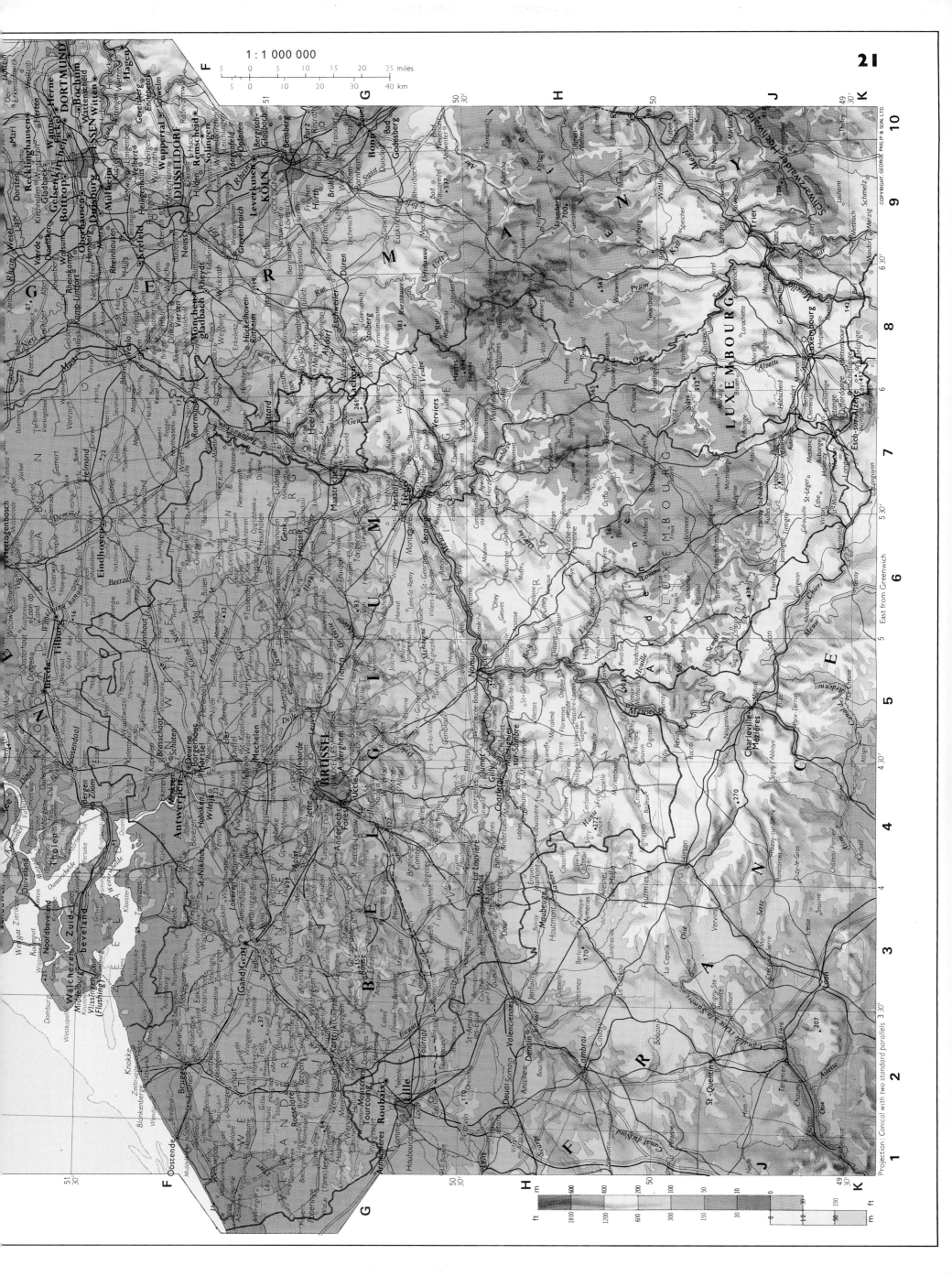

ENGLAND

English Channel

CHANNEL
Guernsey
St. Peter Port
ISLANDS
Jersey
St. Helier
Alderney
St. Anne
Casquets

Baie de la Seine

Cherbourg

Le Havre

Rouen

NORMANDIE

CALVADOS

Caen

Bayeux

Mer d'Iroise

Île d'Ouessant
Brest

Quimper

Douarnenez

Morlaix

St-Brieuc

Golfe de St-Malo

St-Malo
Dinard
Dinan

BRETAGNE

Rennes

Le Mans

MORBIHAN

Lorient

Vannes

Quimperlé

Belle-Île
Presqu'île de Quiberon
Quiberon

St-Nazaire

Nantes

Angers

Tours

Baie de Bourgneuf
Île de Noirmoutier

ANJOU

La Roche-sur-Yon

Île d'Yeu

Les-Sables-d'Olonne

Blois

Poitiers

Châtellerault

DEUX-SÈVRES

Niort

VENDÉE

Pertuis Breton
La Rochelle
Île de Ré

Pertuis d'Antioche
Île d'Oléron

Rochefort

AUNIS

Saintes

Cognac

ANGOUMOIS

CHARENTE

Angoulême

HAUTE-VIENNE

Plymouth

Exeter

Dartmoor

Penzance
Land's End
Lizard Pt.

Falmouth

St. Austell

Newquay

Bodmin

Torquay

Weymouth

Lyme Bay

Portland Bill

Bournemouth
Poole

I. of Wight
Newport

Southampton
Portsmouth

Brighton

Hastings
Eastbourne
Beachy Head

South Downs

Baie de la Somme

Dieppe

Le Tréport

Fécamp
Étretat

Projection: Conical with two standard parallels

West from Greenwich   0   East from Greenwich

ft    m
000   4000
9000  3000
6000  2000
4500  1500
3000  1000
1200   400
600    200
0      0
200    600
2000   6000
m     ft

1 : 2 000 000

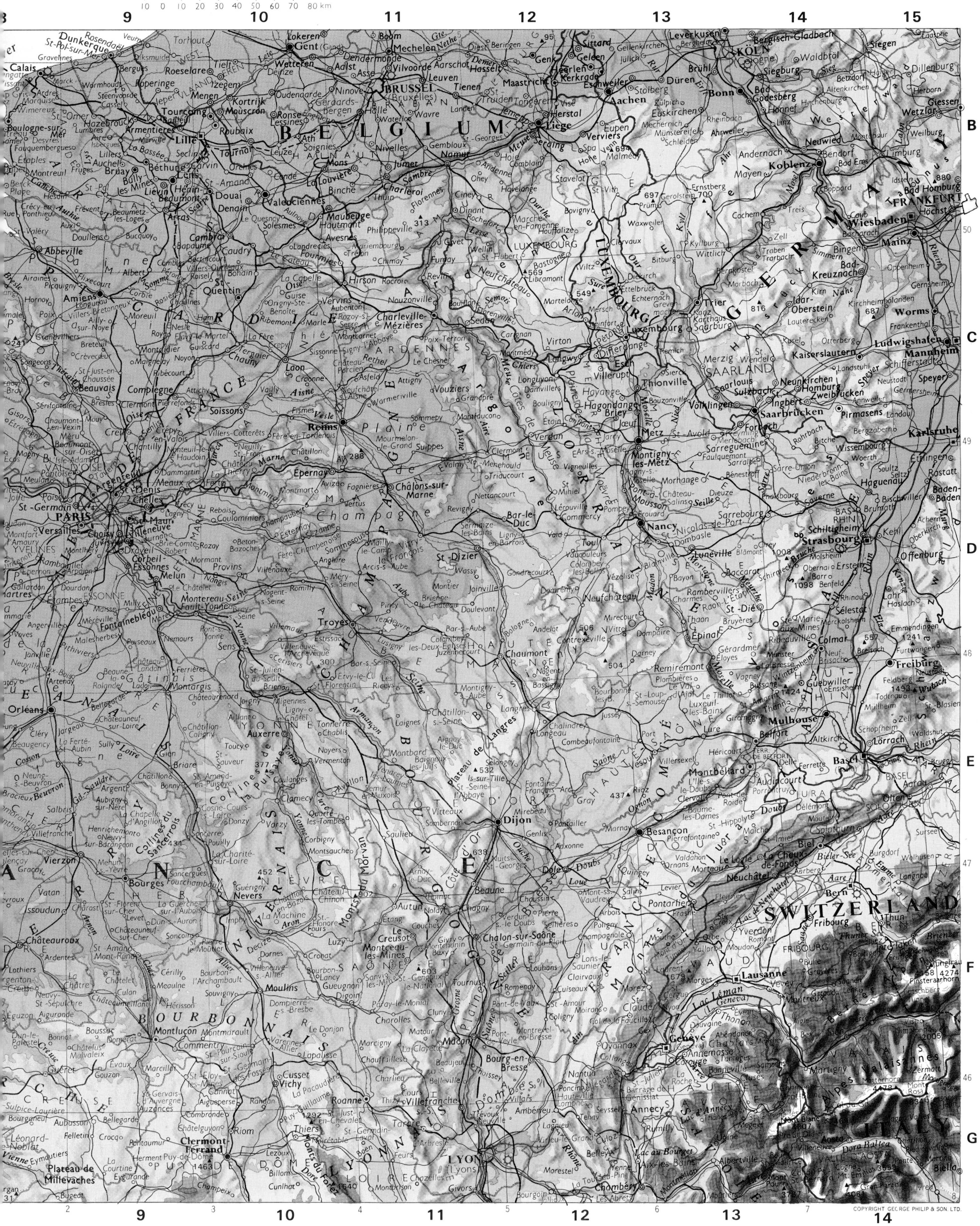

10   0   10   20   30   40   50 miles
10   0   10   20   30   40   50   60   70   80 km

BELGIUM

FRANCE

GERMANY

LUXEMBOURG

SWITZERLAND

Calais · Dunkerque · St-Pol-sur-Mer · Gravelines · Boulogne-sur-Mer · Lille · Roubaix · Tournai · BRUSSEL (Bruxelles) · Gent · Mechelen · Antwerp area · Hasselt · Maastricht · Liège · Verviers · Aachen · KÖLN · Bonn · Bad Godesberg · Siegen · Dillenburg · Giessen · Wetzlar

Amiens · St Quentin · Laon · Soissons · Reims · Charleville-Mézières · Sedan · Luxembourg · Trier · Idar-Oberstein · Worms · Ludwigshafen · Mannheim · Speyer

Paris · Versailles · Melun · Fontainebleau · Épernay · Châlons-sur-Marne · Bar-le-Duc · St Dizier · Verdun · Metz · Nancy · Lunéville · Strasbourg · Baden-Baden · Karlsruhe

Orléans · Auxerre · Troyes · Chaumont · Langres · Épinal · Colmar · Mulhouse · Belfort · Freiburg · Basel

Bourges · Nevers · Dijon · Besançon · Neuchâtel · Bern

Montluçon · Moulins · Mâcon · Bourg-en-Bresse · Genève · Lausanne · Fribourg

Vichy · Roanne · LYON · Clermont-Ferrand · Annecy · Chambéry

Plateau de Millevaches

COPYRIGHT GEORGE PHILIP & SON, LTD.

ATLANTIC OCEAN

Golfe de Gascogne

Île de Noirmoutier
Île d'Yeu
Les Sables-d'Olonne
La Roche-sur-Yon
Challans
Belleville
Cholet
Thouars
Châtellerault
Poitiers
Niort
La Rochelle
Île de Ré
Pertuis Breton
Pertuis d'Antioche
Île d'Oléron
Rochefort
Saintes
Cognac
Angoulême
Royan
Pointe de Grave
Gironde
Étang d'Hourtin et de Carcans
Étang de Lacanau
Bordeaux
Bègles
Cenon
Libourne
Bergerac
Périgueux
Brive-la-Gaillarde
Tulle
Limoges
Châteauroux
Bourges
Nevers
Moulins
Montluçon
Vichy
Clermont-Ferrand
Bassin d'Arcachon
Arcachon
Cap Ferret
La Teste
Étang de Cazaux et de Sanguinet
Étang de Biscarrosse et de Parentis
Marmande
Agen
Villeneuve-sur-Lot
Cahors
Rodez
Montauban
Albi
Toulouse
Castres
Mazamet
Béziers
Narbonne
Carcassonne
Aurillac
Millau
Mende
Dax
Bayonne
Biarritz
St-Jean-de-Luz
San Sebastián
Hendaye
Pau
Tarbes
Lourdes
Bagnères-de-Bigorre
PYRÉNÉES
ANDORRA
Perpignan
ROUSSILLON
Pamplona
Estella
Tudela
Zaragoza (Saragossa)
Huesca
Lérida
Barbastro
Gerona
Figueras
Calahorra
Tarazona

Golfe de Gascogne
ATLANTIC OCEAN

AUNIS
SAINTONGE
ANGOUMOIS
HAUTE-VIENNE
LIMOUSIN
CORRÈZE
CANTAL
DORDOGNE
GIRONDE
LANDES
GASCOGNE
LOT-ET-GARONNE
TARN-ET-GARONNE
LOT
AVEYRON
TARN
HÉRAULT
AUDE
PYRÉNÉES-ATLANTIQUES
HAUTES-PYRÉNÉES
ARIÈGE
BÉARN
NAVARRE
ARAGON
Sierra de la Peña
Sierra de Guara
GERONA
LÉRIDA
BOURBONNAIS
VIENNE
DEUX-SÈVRES
AUVERGNE
PUY-DE-DÔME
CREUSE
CHARENTE
CHARENTE-MARITIME

Projection: Conical with two standard parallels
West from Greenwich  |  East from Greenwich

ft  m
12,000  4000
9000  3000
6000  2000
4500  1500
3000  1000
1200  400
600  200
0  0
600  200
6000  2000
m  ft

1 : 2 000 000

10   0   10   20   30   40   50 miles

10   0   10   20   30   40   50   60   70   80 km

**8**   **9**   **10**   **11**   **12**   **13**   **14**

SWITZERLAND

Bern

FRIBOURG

Lausanne

Genève

LYON

St. Étienne

Grenoble

Valence

Chambéry

Vienne

MARSEILLE

Toulon

Nîmes

Avignon

Arles

Aix-en-Provence

ALPES-DE-HAUTE-PROVENCE

ALPES-MARITIMES

Nice

MONACO

Monte-Carlo

Menton

Cannes

Antibes

Fréjus

St-Raphaël

ILES D'HYÈRES

Golfo di Génova

GÉNOVA

Savona

Albenga

San Remo

Imperia (Maurizio-Oneglia)

La Spezia

Carrara

Massa

Livorno

LIGURIAN SEA

MILANO

TORINO

Novara

Vercelli

Pavia

Asti

Alessandria

Bergamo

Brescia

Cremona

Parma

Piacenza

ITALY

MEDITERRANEAN SEA

du Lion

C. Corse

Capraia

Elba

Bastia

CORSE (CORSICA)

HAUTE-CORSE

Ajaccio

G. d'Ajaccio

CORSE DU SUD

Bonifacio

COPYRIGHT. GEORGE PHILIP & SON. LTD.

**8**   **9**   **10**   **11**   **12**   **13**   **14**

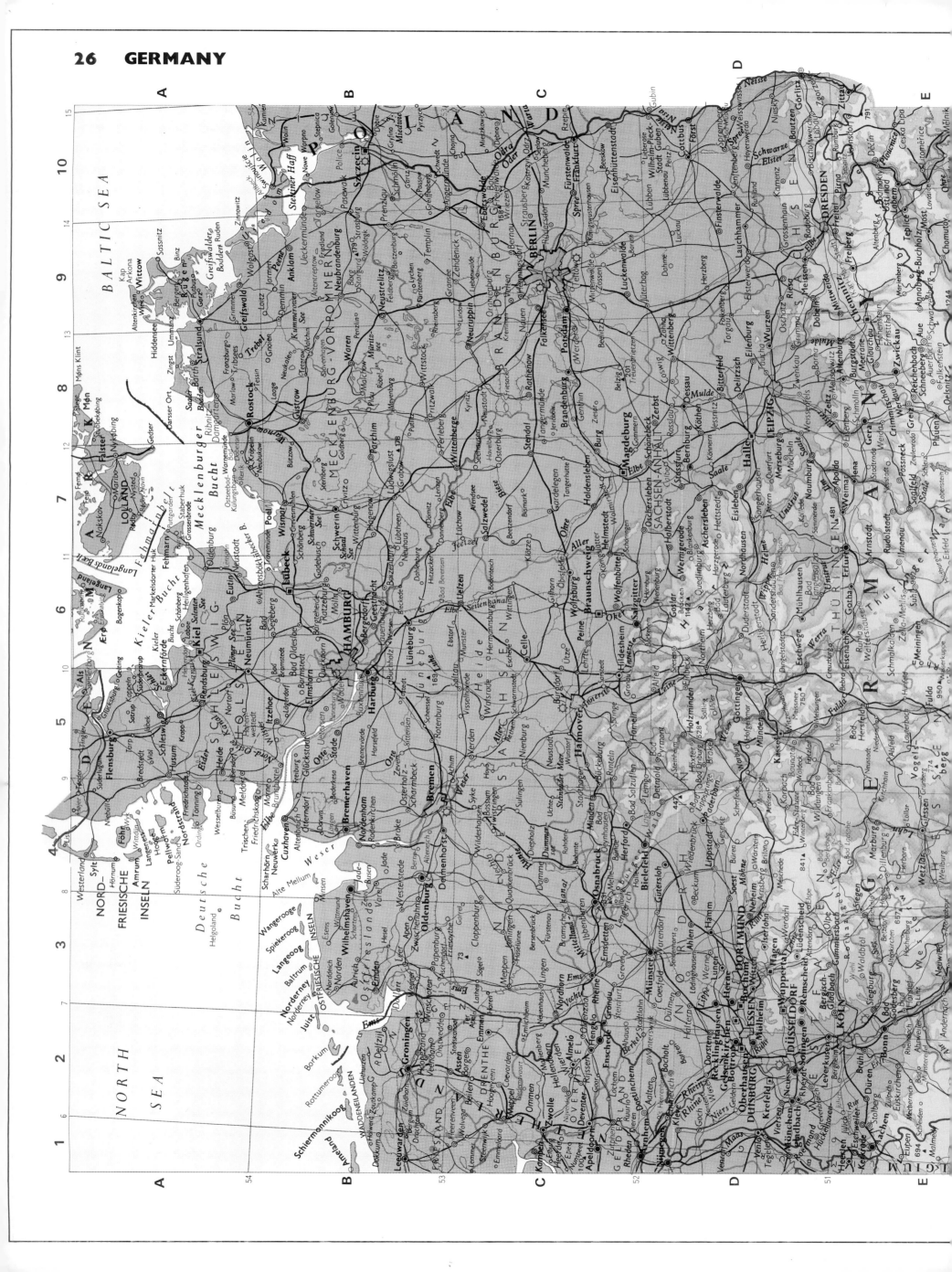

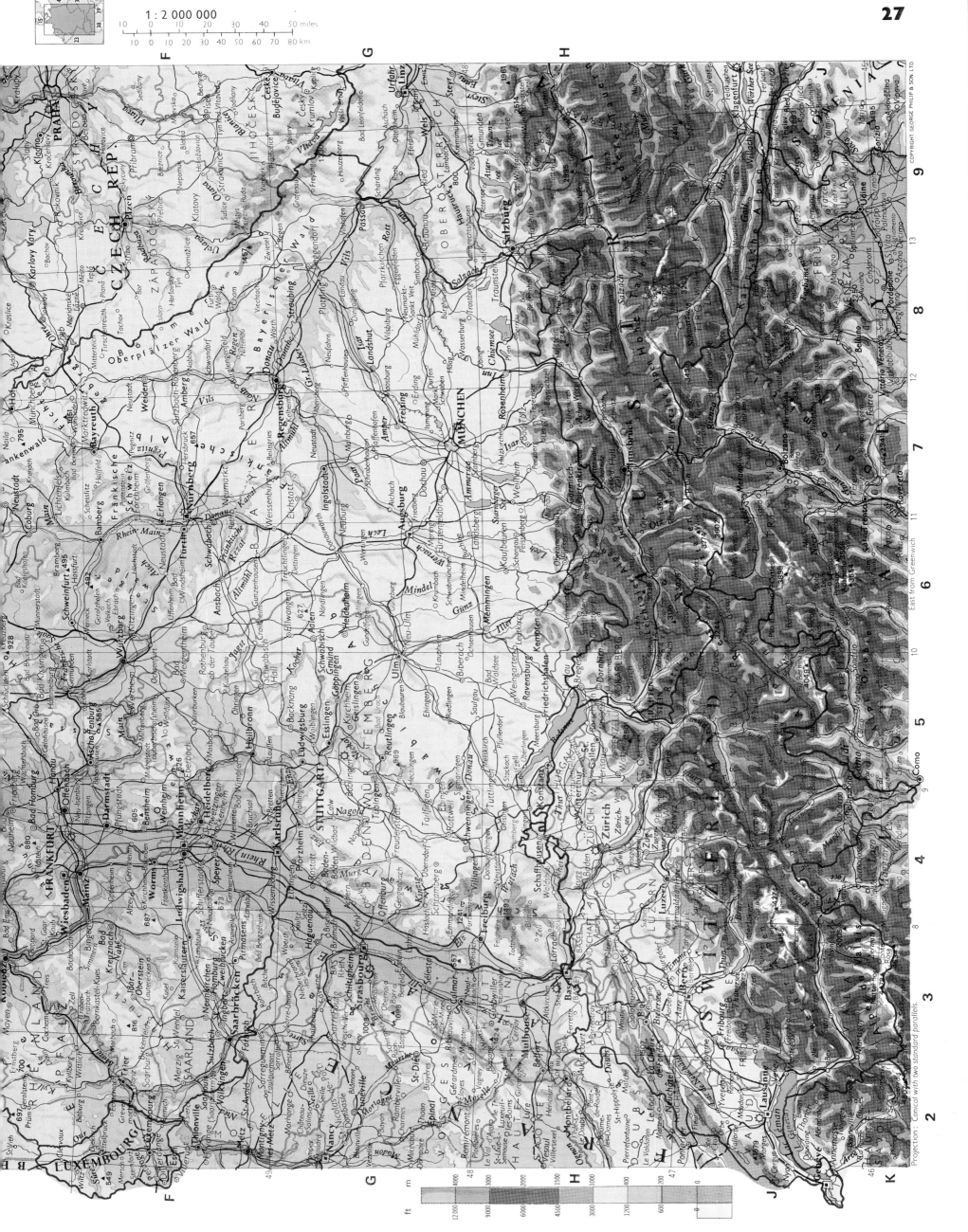

1 : 2 000 000

Projection : Conical with two standard parallels.

East from Greenwich

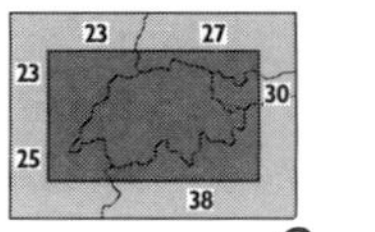

1 2 3 4 5 6

A

HAUTE-SAONE
BELFORT
Belfort
FRANCE
MULHOUSE
HAUT-RHIN
Sundgau
Lörrach
BASEL (BASLE)
Rheinfelden
B. Rheinfelden

47°30'

B

BESANÇON
JURA
Delémont
Moutier
LANDSCHAFT AARGAU
Aarau
Olten
Zofingen
SOLOTHURN
Solothurn
Grenchen
Biel (Bienne)
Langenthal
Burgdorf

DOUBS
La Chaux-de-Fonds
Le Locle
Morteau
Franches Montagnes
St-Imier
Chasseral 1607
Bielersee
Lyss

47°

NEUCHÂTEL
Neuchâtel 429
Peseux
Colombier
Boudry
Ins
BERN (BERNE)
Zollikofen
Köniz
Worb
Münsingen
LUZERN
Langnau i.E.
Entlebuch

C

Pontarlier
Ste-Croix
Chasseron 1607
Grandson
Yverdon
Orbe
Lac de Neuchâtel
Estavayer-le-Lac
Payerne
Avenches
Murten
FRIBOURG (Freibourg)
Marly-le-Grand
FRIBOURG
Gruyère
La Roche
Schwarzenburg
Thun
Steffisburg
Brienzersee
Thunersee
Interlaken
Meiringen

46°30'

Vallorbe
Le Pont
Mt Tendre 1679
Le Brassus
VAUD
Bussigny
LAUSANNE
Morges
Lutry
Vevey
Montreux
Bulle
Gruyères
Châtel-St-Denis 2002
Château d'Oex
Zweisimmen
Frutigen
OBERLAND
Niesen 2362
BERNER ALPEN
Grindelwald
Schreckhorn 4078
Finsteraarhorn 4274

D

St-Claude
Morez
La Côte
Nyon
Rolle
Léman (L. Geneva) 372
Thonon-les-Bains
Evian-les-Bains
St-Gingolph
Villeneuve
Aigle
Monthey
Col des Mosses 1445
Les Diablerets
Bex
St-Maurice
Sierre
Sion
VALAIS
Visp
Brig
Simplon
Dufourspitze

Oyonnax
GENÈVE (GENEVA)
Vernier
Annemasse
HAUTE-SAVOIE
Bellegarde-s.-V.
Genevois
Annecy
Lac d'Annecy
RHÔNE

E

SAVOIE
Aix-les-Bains
Lac du Bourget
Albertville
Ugine
Flumet
Chamonix-Mont-Blanc
Mont Blanc 4807
St-Bernard
Martigny
Orsières
VALLE D'AOSTA
Aosta
Matterhorn (Mt Cervino) 4478
Monte Rosa 4633
Zermatt
Dom 4545
Weisshorn 4505

ft m
9000 3000
6000 2000
4500 1500
3000 1000
1200 500
600 200

Projection: Conical with two standard parallels

1 : 800 000

GERMANY
BAYERN
WÜRTTEMBERG
Ravensburg
Kempten
Konstanz
Friedrichshafen
Lindau
Bregenz
Dornbirn
VORARLBERG
AUSTRIA
TIROL
Schaffhausen
Winterthur
ZÜRICH
St. Gallen
APPENZELL
THURGAU
Feldkirch
Vaduz
LIECHTENSTEIN
Landeck
Luzern
SCHWYZ
Glarus
Chur
Davos
GRAUBÜNDEN
St. Moritz
National-Park
TICINO
Bellinzona
Locarno
Lugano
Chiavenna
Sondrio
Tirano
Domodóssola
Lago Maggiore
Lago di Como
Lecco
Como
Varese
Bergamo
LOMBARDIA
ITALY

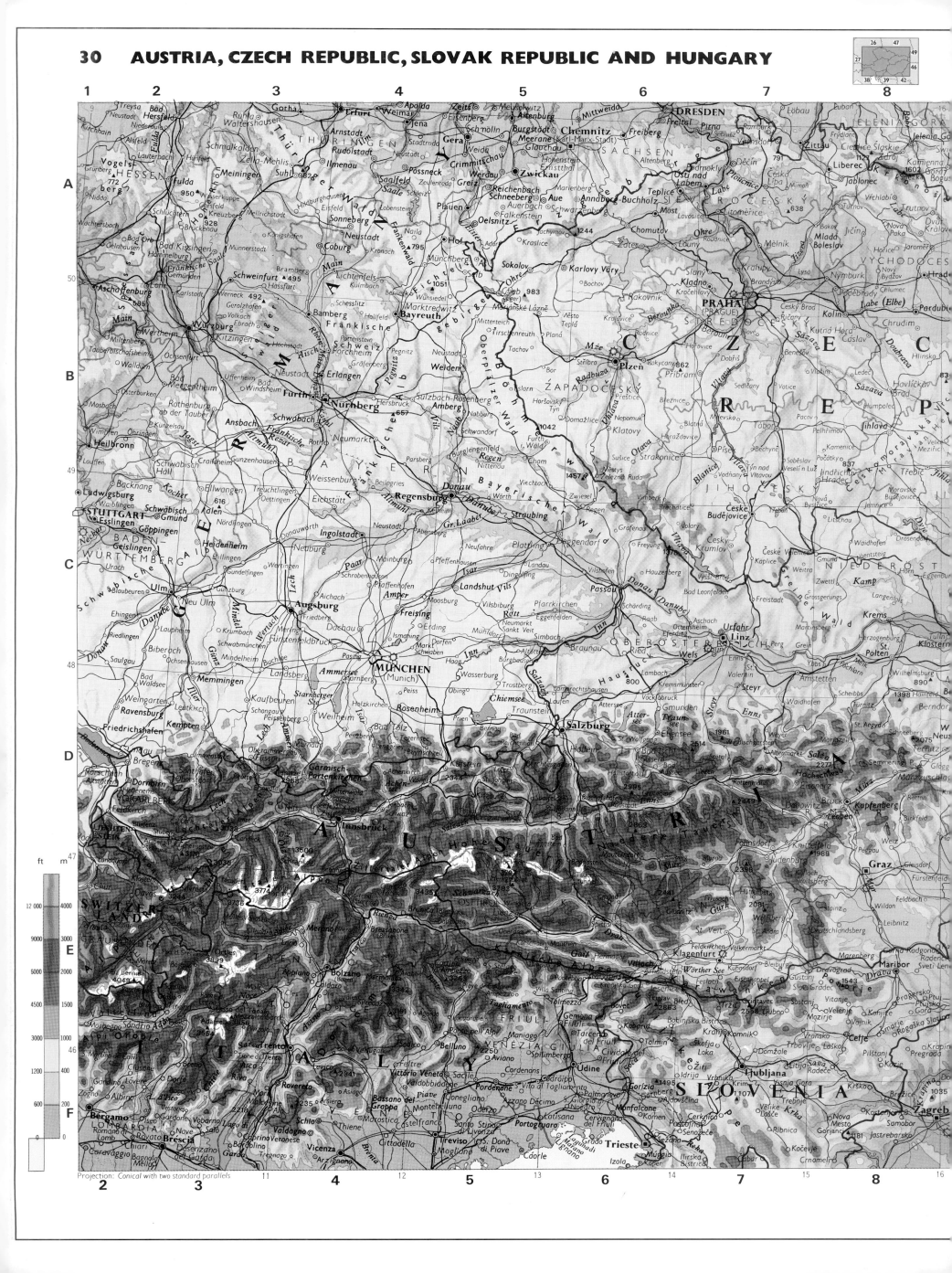

1 : 2 000 000

10  0  10  20  30  40  50 miles
10  0  10  20  30  40  50  60  70  80 km

**POLAND**

**HUNGARY**

**SLOVAK REP.**

**YUGOSLAVIA**

**CROATIA**

WROCŁAW · Wrocław (Breslau) · Namysłów · Wołczyn · Kluczbork · CZĘSTOCHOWA · Częstochowa · Radomsko

Opole · OPOLE · Lubliniec · Herby · Kłobuck

Kielce

WALBRZYCH · Wałbrzych · Dzierżoniów · Kłodzko · Nysa · Prudnik

KATOWICE · Zabrze · Gliwice · Ruda Śląska · Chorzów · Bytom · Sosnowiec · Katowice · Tychy · Rybnik · Radlin · Wodzisław Śl.

KRAKÓW · Kraków · Nowa Huta · Tarnów · TARNÓW · Wieliczka · Bochnia

Rzeszów · RZESZÓW · Łańcut · Jarosław · Przemyśl · PRZEMYŚL

Ostrava · Karvina · Český Těšín · Frýdek-Místek · BIELSKO-BIAŁA · Bielsko-Biała · Żywiec

Olomouc · Přerov · Prostějov · Hranice · Nový Jičín

Brno · Zlín (Gottwaldov) · Uherské Hradiště

NOWY SĄCZ · Nowy Sącz · Nowy Targ · Zakopane · Tatry · Krosno · KROSNO · Sanok · Jasło

BESKYDY · VÝCHODNÉ BESKYDY

Žilina · Martin · Ružomberok · Poprad · Levoča · Kežmarok · Spišská Nová Ves · Prešov · Humenné

Trenčín · Prievidza · Handlová · Banská Bystrica · Zvolen · Brezno

VYCHODOSLOVENSKÝ · Košice · Michalovce · Trebišov · Uzhgorod · ZAKARPAT · Mukachevo

STŘEDOSLOVENSKÝ · Slovenské Rudohorie (Slovak Ore Mts.)

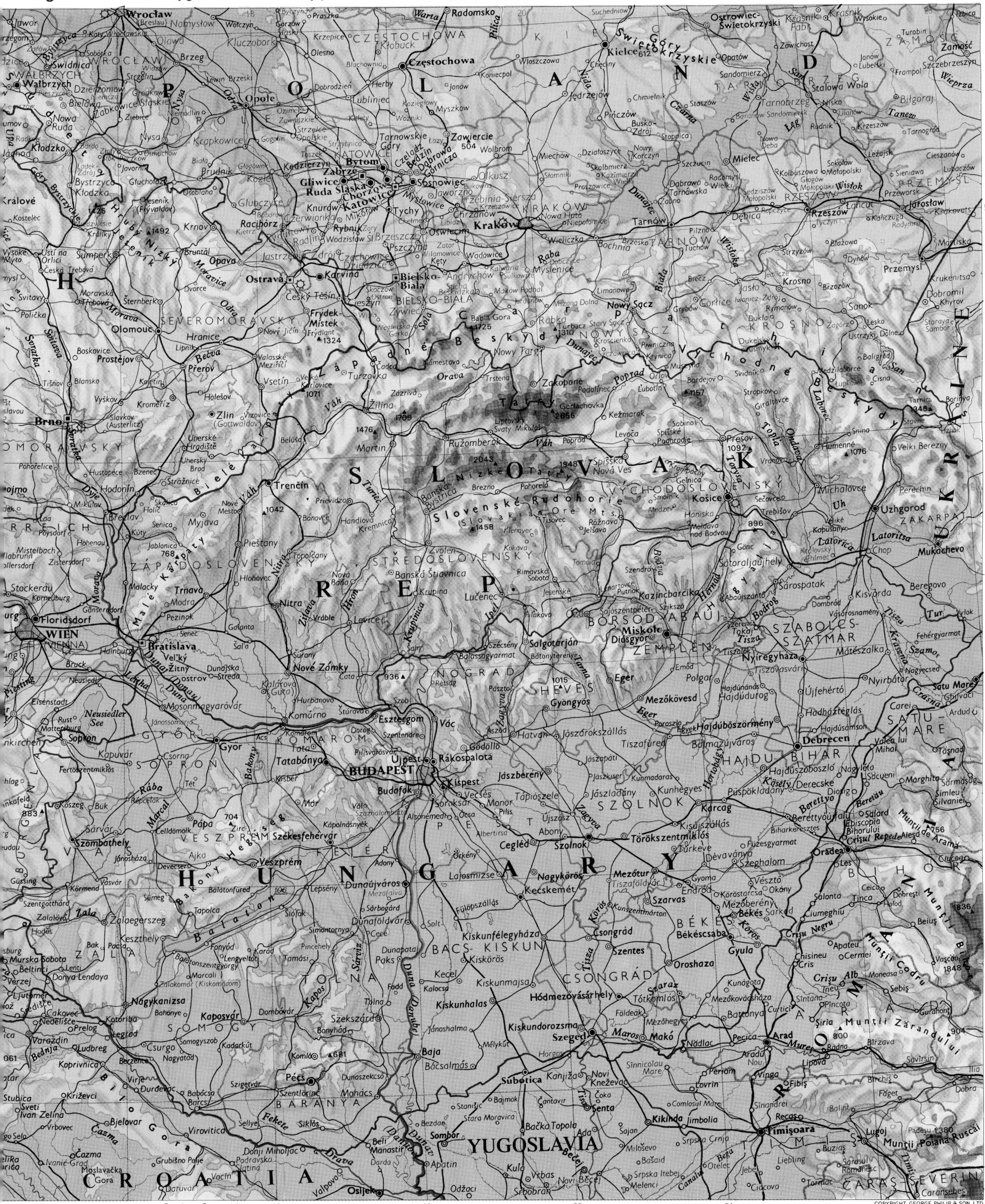

ZÁPADOSLOVENSKÝ · Nitra · Trnava · Piešťany · Topoľčany · Levice · Lučenec · Rimavská Sobota

Bratislava · WIEN (VIENNA) · Floridsdorf · Nové Zámky · Komárno · Štúrovo · Esztergom · Vác

BUDAPEST · Újpest · Kispest · Budafok · Rákospalota · Szentendre

BORSOD-ABAÚJ · ZEMPLÉN · Miskolc · Diósgyőr · Kazincbarcika · Ózd · Eger · Salgótarján

SZABOLCS-SZATMÁR · Nyíregyháza · Mátészalka · Debrecen · Satu Mare · SATU-MARE

NÓGRÁD · HEVES · Gyöngyös · Hatvan · Jászberény · Szolnok · SZOLNOK

HAJDÚ-BIHAR · Hajdúböszörmény · Hajdúnánás · Hajdúszoboszló · Püspökladány · Berettyóújfalu · Oradea

Győr · GYŐR · KOMÁROM · Tatabánya · Tata · Komárom · VESZPRÉM · Veszprém · Székesfehérvár · FEJÉR · Dunaújváros

Sopron · SOPRON · Szombathely · VAS · Pápa · Zirc · Ajka

HUNGARY · BAKONY · Balatonfüred · Siófok · Balaton · Keszthely · ZALA · Zalaegerszeg · Nagykanizsa

SOMOGY · Kaposvár · Dombóvár · TOLNA · Szekszárd · Pécs · BARANYA · Mohács · Bonyhád

BÁCS-KISKUN · Kecskemét · Kiskunfélegyháza · Kiskőrös · Kiskunhalas · Baja · Kalocsa

CSONGRÁD · Szentes · Hódmezővásárhely · Szeged · Makó · Csongrád · Szarvas

BÉKÉS · Békéscsaba · Gyula · Orosháza · Mezőkövesd · Mezőtúr · Túrkeve

Subotica · Kikinda · Timişoara · Arad · Lugoj · CARAŞ-SEVERIN · SEVERIN

Bjelovar · Virovitica · Osijek · Drava · Dunav (Danube)

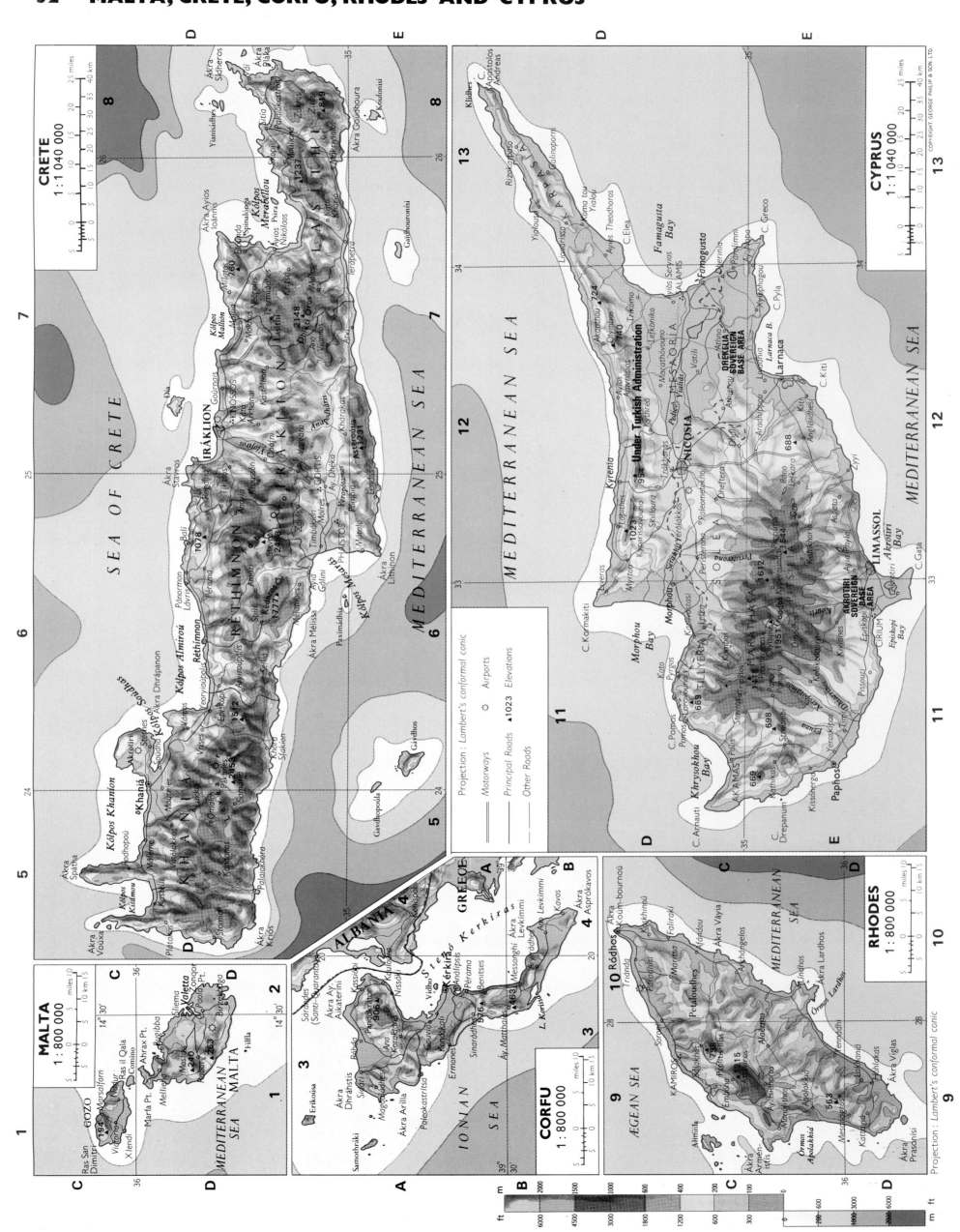

**CRETE**
1:1 040 000

25 miles
40 km

**MALTA**
1:800 000

miles
km

**CORFU**
1:800 000

miles
km

**RHODES**
1:800 000

miles
km

**CYPRUS**
1:1 040 000

25 miles
40 km

COPYRIGHT GEORGE PHILIP & SON LTD.

Projection: Lambert's conformal conic
Motorways
Principal Roads
Other Roads
Airports
Elevations ▲1023

SEA OF CRETE

MEDITERRANEAN SEA

IONIAN SEA

AEGEAN SEA

Projection: Lambert's conformal conic

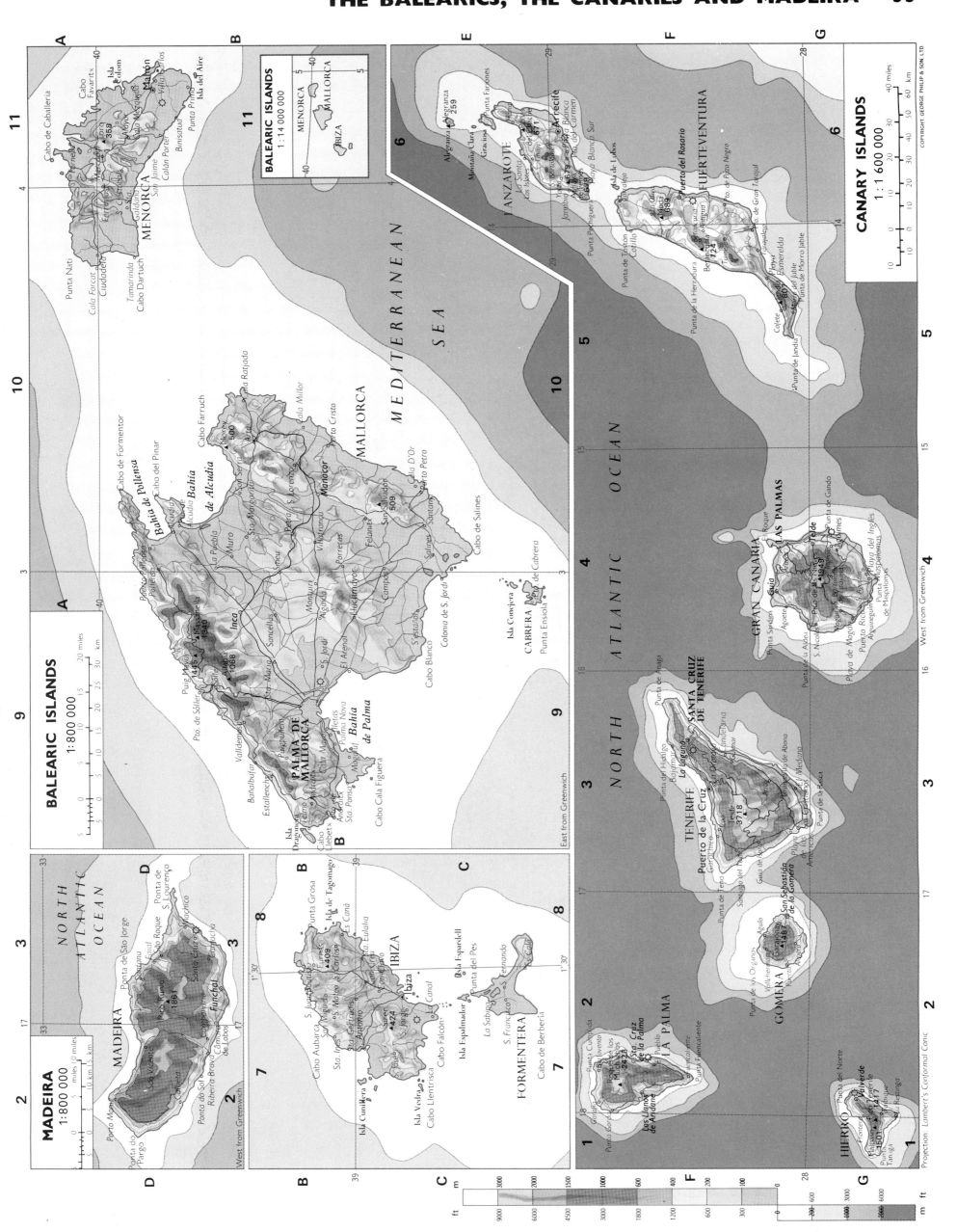

**BALEARIC ISLANDS**
1:14 000 000

**MENORCA**

**MALLORCA**

**IBIZA**

MEDITERRANEAN SEA

**MENORCA**

Cabo de Caballería
Cabo Favaritx
Isla Colom
Mahón
Villa Carlos
Isla del Aire
Punta Prima
Binisafua
Calan Porter
San Juime
Alayor
Mercadal
358
Monte Toro
Fornells
Cala Forcat
Ciudadela
Tamarinda
Cabo Dartuch
Punta Nati

**MALLORCA**

Cabo de Formentor
Cabo del Pinar
Bahía de Pollensa
Pollensa
Puerto de Pollensa
Alcudia
Bahía de Alcudia
Cabo Farruch
Artá
500
Sierra
Capdepera
Cala Ratjada
Cala Millor
Porto Cristo
MALLORCA
Manacor
Sta. Margarita
Petra
S. Lorenzo
Muro
La Puebla
Sineu
Vilafranca
Felanitx
509
San Salvador
Cala D'Or
Porto Petro
Sta. María
Sancellas
Inca
1340
Massanella
1445
1068
Puig Mayor
Pto. de Sóller
Sóller
Estellenchs
Bañalbufar
Valldemosa
Deyá
Andraitx
Santa Ponsa
S. Telmo
Isla Dragonera
Llebetx
Cala Figuera
Cabo Cala Figuera
Palma Nova
Bahía de Palma
PALMA DE MALLORCA
Magaluf
Lluchmayor
El Arenal
Montuiri
Algaida
S. Jordi
Campos
Salines
Santany
S'estaciol
Colonia de S. Jordi
Cabo Salines
Cabo Blanco

CABRERA
Isla Conejera
Pta. de Cabrera
Punta Ensiola

East from Greenwich

**MADEIRA**
1:800 000

NORTH ATLANTIC OCEAN

MADEIRA
Porto Moniz
Ponta do Pargo
Ponta de São Jorge
Santana
Faial
Porto da Cruz
Machico
S. Roque
S. Lourenço
Ponta de S. Lourenço
Seixal
Pico Ruivo
1861
Curral
Funchal
Câmara de Lobos
Ribeira Brava
Ponta do Sol
Calheta
São Vicente

**IBIZA**

IBIZA
Punta Grosa
Isla de Tagomago
S. Juan
Portinatx
Cabo Aubarca
S. Carlos
Sta. Eulalia
Sta. Inés
S. Miguel
San Mateo
S. Antonio
S. Rafael
424
IBIZA
Jesús
Cala Llonga
Salinas
Isla Espardell
Punta del Pes
Cabo Falcón

**FORMENTERA**

Isla Espalmador
S. Francisco
La Sabina
S. Fernando
Cala
FORMENTERA
Cabo Berbería

West from Greenwich

**CANARY ISLANDS**
1:1 600 000

**LANZAROTE**
Alegranza 259
Montaña Clara
Graciosa
Punta Fariones
La Santa
Los Islotes
Haría
619
Arrecife
Tinajo
Tahiche
Tiagua
Playa Blanca Sur
Pto. del Carmen
Yaiza
Isla de Lobos
Rubicón

**FUERTEVENTURA**
Punta de Tostón
Corralejo
Pto. del Rosario
Oliva
689
Betancuria
725
Antigua
Pto. de Gran Tarajal
Gran Tarajal
Punta de la Herradura
Pájara
Cofete
807
Playa de Esmeralda
Punta de Jandía
Punta de Morro Jable

**GRAN CANARIA**
El Roque
Las Palmas
Telde
1949
Gáldar
Guía
Agaete
Pta. Sardina
S. Nicolás
La Aldea
Pto. de Mogán
Puerto Rico
Arguineguín
Maspalomas
Playa del Inglés
Punta de Maspalomas
Punta de Gando

**TENERIFE**
Punta de Anaga
Santa Cruz de Tenerife
La Laguna
Bajamar
Punta del Hidalgo
Pto. de la Cruz
Tacoronte
La Orotava
Candelaria
Güímar
Teide
3718
Icod
Guía
Buenavista
Punta de Teno
Adeje
Los Cristianos
Arona
Granadilla
Valle de Abona
Punta de la Rasca

**GOMERA**
Agulo
Hermigua
Vallehermoso
1481
San Sebastián de la Gomera
Playa de Santiago
Villa de las Rosas
Alajeró

**LA PALMA**
Punta Cumplida
Barlovento
Sta. Cruz de la Palma
2423
Los Sauces
Puntallana
Breña
El Paso
Los Llanos de Aridane
Tazacorte
Punta Gorda
Fuencaliente
Punta Fuencaliente

**HIERRO**
Punta del Norte
Valverde
1501
1047
Frontera
Sabinosa
Pozo de la Salud
Punta Orchilla
Restinga

NORTH ATLANTIC OCEAN

West from Greenwich

Projection: Lambert's Conformal Conic

COPYRIGHT GEORGE PHILIP & SON LTD.

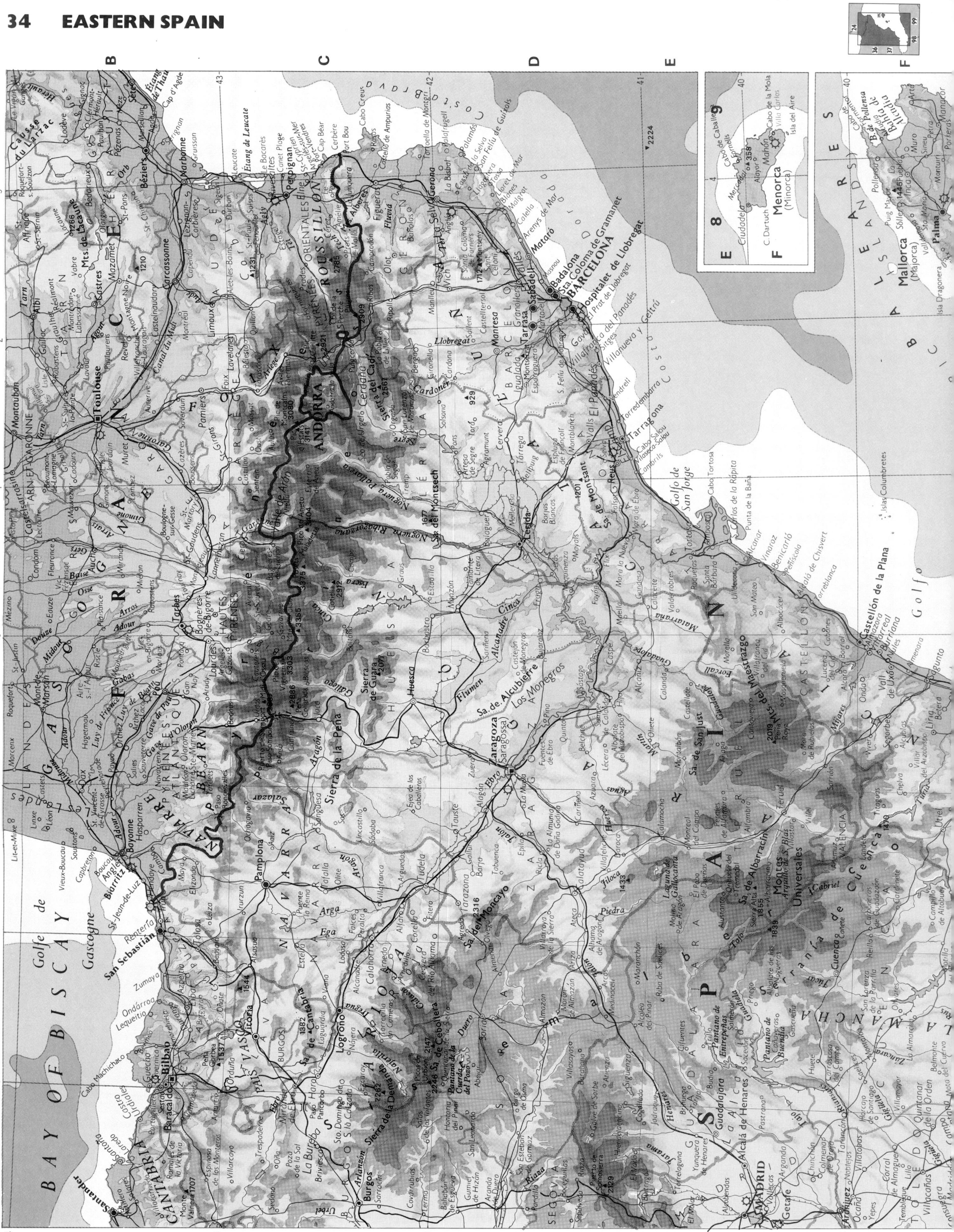

Menorca (Minorch)

Mallorca (Majorca)

BAY OF BISCAY

Golfe de Gascogne

FRANCE

GASCOGNE

NAVARRE

ANDORRA

ROUSSILLON

PYRENEES

HAUTES-PYRENEES

BASSES-PYRENEES

ARIEGE

AUDE

HERAULT

TARN

GERS

Toulouse

Bayonne

Biarritz

San Sebastián

Bilbao

Santander

CANTABRIA

RIOJA

Logroño

Pamplona

Burgos

Zaragoza (Saragossa)

Huesca

Lérida

Barbastro

Tudela

Soria

Guadalajara

Alcalá de Henares

MADRID

Cuenca

VALENCIA

Teruel

Castellón de la Plana

Sagunto

Tarragona

Reus

Tortosa

BARCELONA

Hospitalet de Llobregat

Badalona

Sta Coloma de Gramanet

Sabadell

Tarrasa

Manresa

Granollers

Mataró

Gerona

Figueras

Perpignan

Narbonne

Béziers

Carcassonne

Montauban

Ebro

Duero

Tajo

LA MANCHA

Golfo de San Jorge

Cabo de la Nao

Palma

Mahón

Ciudadela

1 : 2 000 000

10  0  10  20  30  40  50 miles
10  0  10  20  30  40  50  60  70  80 km

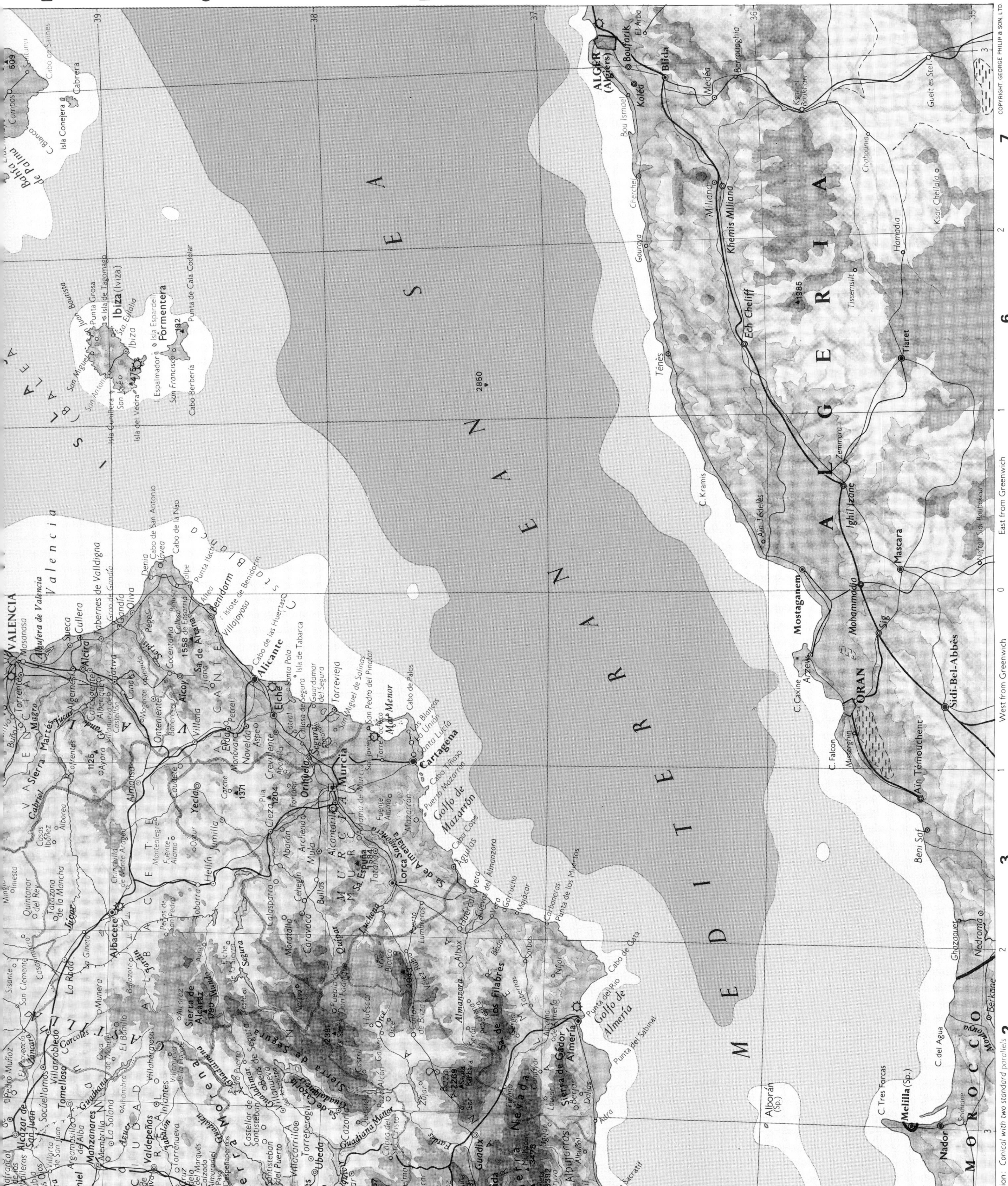

F   G   H   J   K

MEDITERRANEAN SEA

BALEARIC

Campos
509
Cabo de Salinas
Cabrera
Isla Conejera
Bahía de Palma
C. Blanco

Ibiza (Iviza)
San Miguel
San Antonio
Santa Eulalia
Ibiza
Isla de Tagomago
Punta Grosa
San Juan Bautista
Formentera
492
Isla de Espardell
Cabo Berbería
Cabo de Cala Codolar
San Francisco
El Espalmador
Isla del Vedra
Punta de Cala Codolar

2850

VALENCIA
Valencia
Albufera de Valencia
Sueca
Cullera
Tabernes de Valldigna
Gandía
Oliva
Denia
Cabo de San Antonio
Jávea
Cabo de la Nao
Benidorm
Villajoyosa
Alcoy
Alicante
Elche
Santa Pola
Isla de Tabarca
Torrevieja
Guardamar del Segura
San Pedro del Pinatar
Mar Menor
Cabo de Palos
Cartagena
Cabo Tiñoso
Puerto Mazarrón
Golfo de Mazarrón
Cabo Cope
Cabo de Agustas

MURCIA
Murcia
Orihuela
Cieza
Lorca
Águilas
Almería
Golfo de Almería
Cabo de Gata

Sierra Nevada
3478
Granada
Guadix
Motril
Almería

MOROCCO
Melilla (Sp.)
Nador
C. Tres Forcas
Alborán (Sp.)

ALGERIA

ALGER (Algiers)
Koléa
Blida
Boufarik
El Arba
Medéa
Cherchel
Miliana
Khemis Miliana
Ech Cheliff
1985
Ténès
Tiaret
Mostaganem
Mohammadia
Azew
Arzew
ORAN
Sig
Sidi-Bel-Abbès
Mascara
Ighil Izane
Aïn Témouchent
Ben Saf
Ghazaouet
Nedroma

Projection: Conical with two standard parallels

West from Greenwich   East from Greenwich

m   3000   2000   1500   1000   400   200   0
ft  9000   6000   4500   3000   1200   600   0

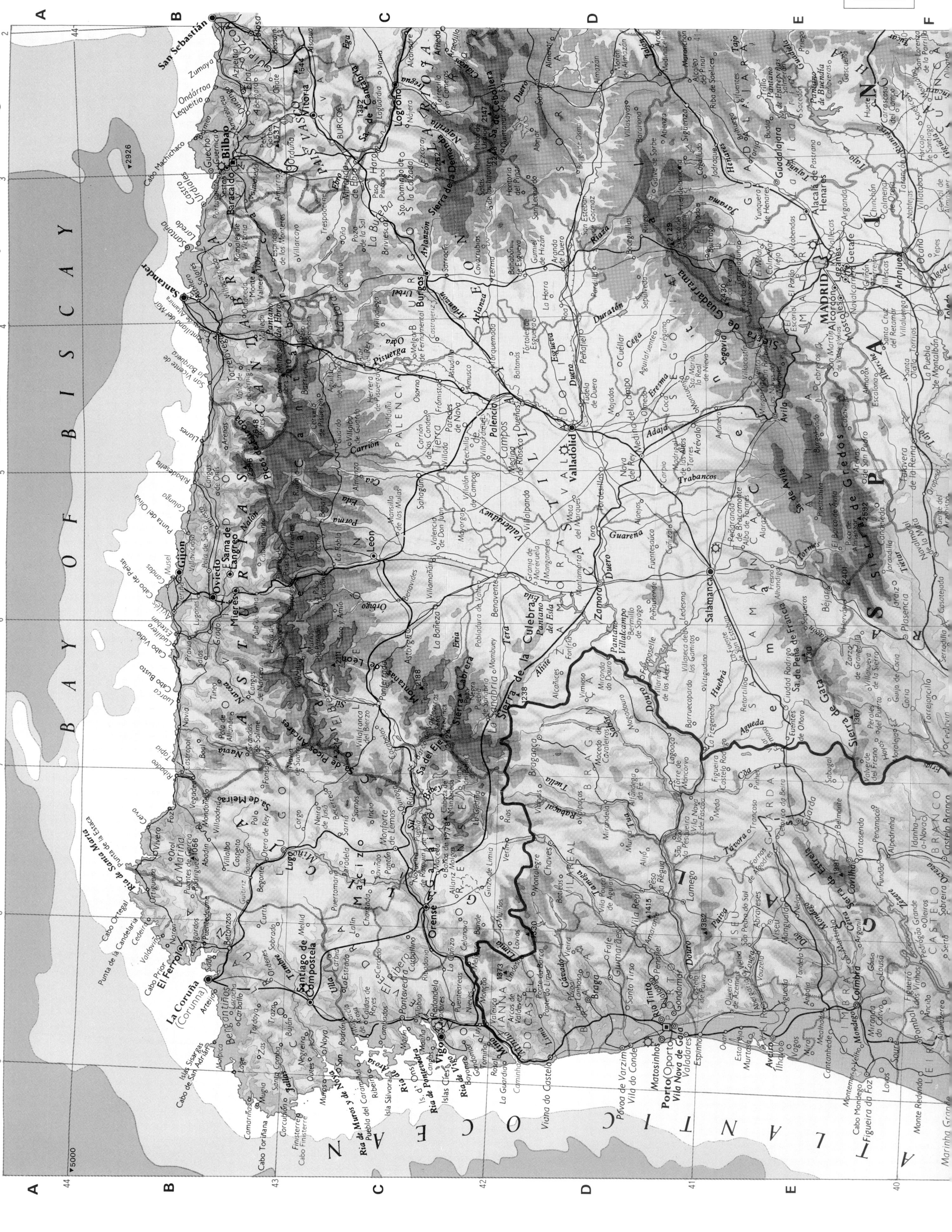

BAY OF BISCAY

ATLANTIC OCEAN

**San Sebastián**

**Bilbao**
Baracaldo

Vitoria

PAIS VASCO

**Santander**

CANTABRIA

GUIPÚZCOA

LA RIOJA

Logroño

Burgos

CASTILLA Y LEÓN

ASTURIAS

**Gijón**
**Oviedo**
Mieres
Sama de Langreo

Picos de Europa

LEÓN

**León**

Palencia
PALENCIA

Carrión

**Valladolid**
VALLADOLID

Duero

Segovia

SEGOVIA

**MADRID**
Alcalá de Henares
Alcorcón
Getafe
Aranjuez

GUADALAJARA
Guadalajara

Ávila
ÁVILA

Sierra de Gredos

Sierra de Guadarrama

**Salamanca**
SALAMANCA

Zamora
ZAMORA

Duero

Sierra de la Culebra

ORENSE
**Orense**

LUGO
**Lugo**

GALICIA

La Coruña
(Coruña)
**La Coruña**

El Ferrol

**Santiago de Compostela**

Pontevedra

**Vigo**

Ría de Vigo

Ría de Pontevedra

Ría de Arosa

Ría de Muros y de Noya

Finisterre
Cabo Finisterre

Cabo Ortegal

BRAGANÇA

VILA REAL

**Porto** (Oporto)
Vila Nova de Gaia
Matosinhos

Aveiro

VISEU

Viseu

GUARDA
Guarda

Coimbra
COIMBRA
Mondego

Douro

CASTELO BRANCO

Castelo Branco

LEIRIA

Serra da Estrela

PORTO

DOURO

MINHO

Braga

Viana do Castelo

Póvoa de Varzim

Rio Tinto

Gondomar

Espinho

Duero

Tajo

CUENCA

TOLEDO

Talavera de la Reina

Tordesillas

Medina del Campo

Aranda de Duero

Sto. Domingo de la Calzada

Haro

Ebro

Pamplona

1 : 2 000 000

10 0 10 20 30 40 50 miles
10 0 10 20 30 40 50 60 70 80 km

MEDITERRANEAN SEA

Golfo de Cádiz

Golfo de Almería

Strait of Gibraltar

West from Greenwich

MOROCCO

LISBOA

Sevilla

Córdoba

Granada

Málaga

Cádiz

Badajoz

Cáceres

Mérida

Huelva

Jaén

Linares

Úbeda

Ciudad Real

Almería

Gibraltar (Br.)

Ceuta (Sp.)

Melilla

Tánger (Tanger)

Tetouan

Larache

Sierra Nevada

Sierra Morena

Guadalquivir

Guadiana

Tejo

ANDALUCÍA

PORTUGAL

ALGARVE

Projection: Conical with two standard parallels

COPYRIGHT GEORGE PHILIP & SON LTD.

SWITZERLAND

LIGURIAN SEA

Golfo di Génova

CORSE
(CORSICA)

ILES D'HYÈRES

MILANO (Milan)
TORINO (Turin)
GENOVA (Genoa)
Lyon (Lyons)
MARSEILLE (Marseilles)
MONACO
Nice
Livorno (Leghorn)

Projection: Conical with two standard parallels

East from Greenwich

ft    m
12 000   4000
9000    3000
6000    2000
4500    1500
3000    1000
1200    400
600    200
0    0
600    200
2000   6000

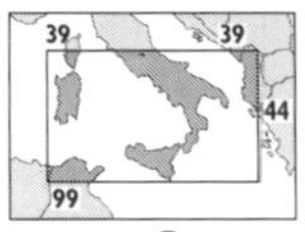

SARDEGNA

SARDINIA

CORSE

CORSICA

CORSE-DU-SUD

TYRRHENIAN SEA

TUNISIA

SICILY

PALERMO

ROMA (Rome)

Golfo dell' Asinara

Golfo di Orosei

Golfo di Oristano

Golfo di Cágliari

Golfo di Gaeta

Golfe de Tunis

Sicilian Channel

MEDITE

Iles de la Galite

Projection: Conical with two standard parallels

East from Greenwich

ft  m
9000  3000
6000  2000
4500  1500
3000  1000
1200  400
600  200
0  0
200  600
2000  6000
4000  12.000
m  ft

1 : 2 000 000

10  0  10  20  30  40  50 miles
10  0  10  20  30  40  50  60  70  80 km

7    8    9    10    11    12

ADRIATIC

SEA

A

B

C

D

E

F

IONIAN

SEA

MEDITERRANEAN SEA

Channel

ABRUZZI
MOLISE
L. di Lésina
Monte Sant'Ángelo
G. di Manfredónia
Manfredónia
Fóggia
Campobasso
Lucera
Cerignola
Canosa
Barletta
Trani
Bisceglie
Molfetta
Giovinazzo
Bari
Andria
Corato
Ruvo di Púglia
Terlizzi
Bitonto
Minervino
Murge
Gravina
Altamura
Matera
Mottola
Massafra
Taranto
Grottáglie
Brindisi
Francavilla Fontana
Mesagne
Manduria
Lecce
Nardò
Galatina
Gallípoli
Otranto
C. d'Otranto
C. Santa Maria di Leuca
Gagliano del Capo
Golfo di Táranto
Potenza
BASILICATA
Avellino
Benevento
Salerno
G. di Salerno
NÁPOLI
Vesuvio
Capri
Sorrento
Amalfi
Eboli
Agrópoli
Castellabate
Punta Licosa
C. Palinuro
G. di Policastro
Maratea
Monte Pollino
Castrovillari
Cassano Iónio
Corigliano
Rossano
Acri
Cosenza
CALABRIA
Paola
Amantea
Crotone
Catanzaro
Golfo di Squillace
Golfo di Sant'Eufémia
Pizzo
Vibo Valéntia
Mileto
G. di Gióia
Gióia Táuro
Palmi
Bagnara
Messina
Str. di Messina
Réggio di Calábria
Palizzi
Mélito di Porto Salvo
Bova Marina
C. Spartivento
Locri
Siderno Marina
Bovalino Marina
Gerace
Isole Eólie o Lípari (Aeolian Is.)
Strómboli
Filicudi
Alicudi
Salina
Lípari
Vulcano
Milazzo
Barcellona
Patti
Sant'Agata di Militello
San Fratello
Mistretta
Troina
Nicosia
Monti Nébrodi
Taormina
Giarre
Riposto
Acireale
Catánia
Golfo di Catánia
Paternò
Adrano
Biancavilla
Centúripe
Enna
Piazza
Caltagirone
Grammichele
Vizzini
Lentini
Carlentini
Augusta
Siracusa
Floridia
Noto
Avola
Pachino
C. Passero
Ispica
Módica
Scicli
Pozzallo
Rágusa
Cómiso
Vittória
Gela
Golfo di Gela
Niscemi
Chiaramonte
Palazzolo
Caltanissetta
Mazzarino
Butera

DRINI
TIRANA
Tiranë (Tirana)
Durrësi (Durazzo)
SHQIPËRIA
ALBANIA
Vlora (Valona)
Berati
Strait of Otranto
Kérkira (Corfu)
Kérkira
Áyios Matthaíos
Levkímmi
Othonoí
Erikoúsa
Karoúsádhes

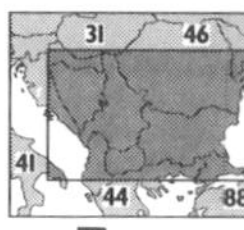

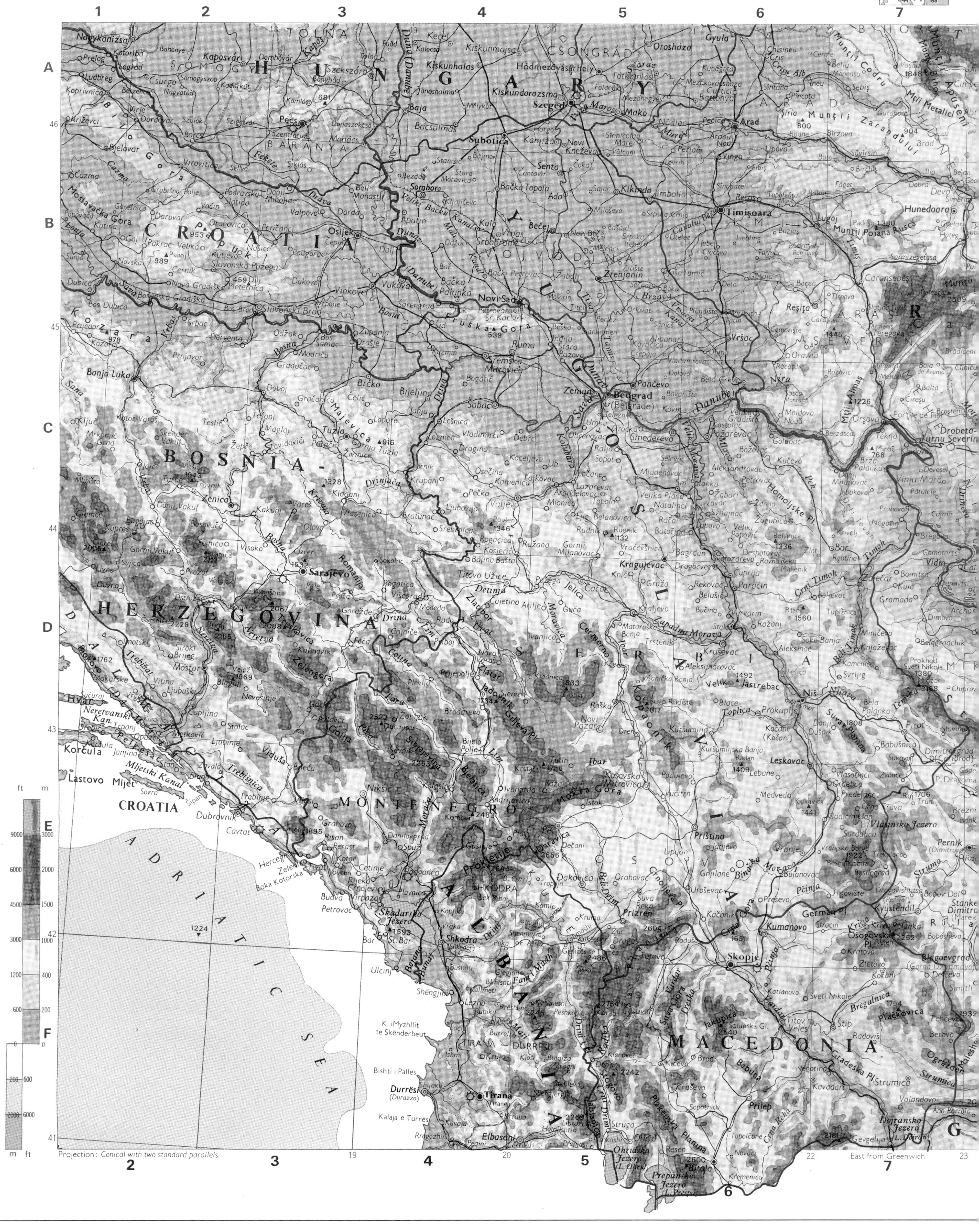

HUNGARY

CROATIA

BOSNIA-HERZEGOVINA

SERBIA

MONTENEGRO

ALBANIA

MACEDONIA

VOJVODINA

KOSOVO

ADRIATIC SEA

Beograd (Belgrade)

Sarajevo

Zagreb

Timişoara

Arad

Skopje

Tirana

Durrësi (Durazzo)

Projection: Conical with two standard parallels

East from Greenwich

ft    m
9000  3000
6000  2000
4500  1500
3000  1000
1200  400
600   200
0

m ft
200  600
2000 6000

1 : 2 000 000

10   0   10   20   30   40   50 miles
10 0 10 20 30 40 50 60 70 80 km

8       9       10       11       12       13       14

**ROMANIA**

TRANSILVANIA · HARGHITA · COVASNA · VRANCEA · PRAHOVA · DIMBOVITA · ARGEŞ · VILCEA · IALOMITA · BRAILA · DOBROGEA · CONSTANTA

Turda · Cimpia Turzii · Ludus · Band · Tirgu-Mureş · Sovata · Bacău · Comăneşti · Crasna · Volintirovka

Aiud · Târnava Mică · Tîrnava Mare · Sighişoara · Odorheiu Secuiesc · Gheorgheni · Nemira 1653 · Tirgu Ocna · Adjud · Birlad · MOLDAVIA · Komrat · Koglinik

Mediaş · Copşa · Dumbrăveni · Agnita · Rupea · Homorod · Baraolt · Covasna 1783 · Focşani · Tecuci · Kagul · UKRAINE · Ozero Kitai · Ozero Sasyk

Sebeş · Alba-Iulia · Sălişte · Sibiu · Fagăraş · Victoria · Braşov · Rîmnicu Sărat · Brăila · Galaţi · Ismail · Kiliya · Vilkovo

**Muntii Făgăraş** 2535 · 2507 · Dunărea (Dunube) · Tulcea · Sulina · Ostrov Sfîntu · Sf. Gheorghe

Rîmnicu Vilcea · Curtea de Argeş · Cîmpulung · Tîrgovişte · Ploieşti · Buzău · Lacul Razelm · Gura Portiţei · Lacul Sinoe

Tirgu Jiu · Piteşti · BUCUREŞTI (Bucharest) · Cernavodă · Constanţa · Siutghiol · Murfatlar

Craiova · Slatina · Alexandria · Giurgiu · Ruse (Ruschuk) · Silistra · Dobrich (Tolbukhin) · Mangalia · Balcic · Kavarna (Cavarna) · Nos Kaliakra

**WALACHIA (VALAHIA)** · Turnu Măgurele · Corabia · Svishtov · Razgrad · VARNA · Şabla (Şabla)

Lom · Kozlovtsi · Pleven · Lovech · Sevlievo · Türgovishte · Devnya · **Varna** · Zlatni Pyassatsi · Drouzhba

**BULGARIA** · Vratsa · Troyan · Gabrovo · Tryavna · Elena · Preslav · Omurtag · Shumen · Provadya · Obzor

Sofiya (Sofia) · Kazanlŭk · Stara Zagora · Sliven · Aytos · Nesebŭr · Pomorie (Ankhialo)

**Stara Planina (Chatal Balkan)** · Sredna Gora · Nova Zagora · Yambol · **Burgas** · Burgaski Zaliv · Sozopol

Plovdiv (Philippopolis) · Chirpan · Dimitrovgrad · Topolovgrad · Primorsko · Michurin (Tsarevo) · Akhtopol

Velingrad · Asenovgrad · Khaskovo · Svilengrad · Malko Tŭrnovo · Rezovo · Ahtastafanos · Igneada

**Rodopi** · Kŭrdzhali · Edirne (Adrianople) · KIRKLARELI · Istranca Dağları · Midye

**GREECE** · Drama · Xanthi · Komotini · **TURKEY** · Lüleburgaz · Çorlu · Çerkesköy · **İSTANBUL** · Üsküdar

Karadeniz Boğazı (Bosporus) · Beykoz

**BLACK SEA**

COPYRIGHT GEORGE PHILIP & SON LTD

8       9       10       11       12       13
24      25      26      27      28

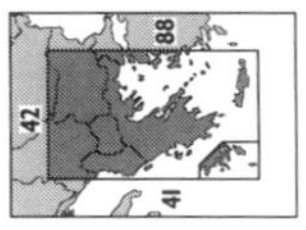

YUGOSLAVIA
MONTENEGRO
MACEDONIA
BULGARIA
ALBANIA
Sofiya
Skopje
Tirana
Thessaloníki
Plovdiv
Pernik
Stara Zagora
Yambol
Sliven
Pleven
Vratsa
Niš
Leskovac
Priština
Prizren
Kumanovo
Prilep
Bitola
Ohrid
Korça
Berati
Durrës
Shkodra
Vlorë
Kérkira
Lárisa
Kateríni
Kaválla
Dráma
Sérrai
Kardhítsa
Tríkkala
Ioánnina
Thásos
Samothráki
Límnos
Gökçeada
Thermaïkós Kólpos
Strimonikós Kólpos
Thrakikón Pélagos
Saros Körfezi
Çanakkale Boğazı
Edirne
Évros
Ayios Evstrátios

1 : 2 000 000

10 0 10 20 30 40 50 miles
10 0 10 20 30 40 50 60 70 80 km

AIYAÍON

Kólpos Kallonís

Plomárion

Kará Burun

Onoússa

Khíos (Chíos)

Psará

Andípsara

Ikaría

Mikonos

Tínos

Ándros

Skíros

Skópelos

Skíathos

(Northern Sporades)

Skántzoúra

STEREÁ ELLAS

ÍLLAS

Khalkís (Chalcis)

ATHÍNAI (ATHENS)

Piraiévs (Piraeus)

Saronikós Kólpos

ATTIKÍ

Aíyina

Méthana

Póros

Ídhra (Hydra)

Spétsai

NÓTIOS

AIYAÍON

KIKLÁDHES (CYCLADES)

Kéa

Kíthnos

Sérifos

Sífnos

Mílos

Kímolos

Síros

Páros

Náxos

Íos

Thíra

Síkinos

Folégandros

Anáfi

Astipálaia

Amorgós

Lévitha

S E A

S E A   O F   C R E T E   (Sea of Candia)

Kíthira (Cerigo)

Andikíthira

Kólpos Kisámou

Khaniá

Khersónisos Akrotíri

Réthimnon

K R Í T I

Iráklion (Candia)

Gávdhos

Gavdhopoúla

PELOPÓNNISOS

Kórinthos

Corinth Canal

Korinthiakós Kólpos

Pátrai

Pírgos

Trípolis

Párnon Óros

Taíyetos Óros

LAKONÍA

MESSINÍA

Kalamai

Kórinthos

Argolikós Kólpos

Náfplion

Árgos

Messiniakós Kólpos

Lakonikós Kólpos

Kiparissiakós Kólpos

Ákra Taínaron

Ákra Maléa

Monemvasía

AITOLÍA

AKARNANÍA

Agrínion

Mesolóngion

Pátraikós Kólpos

DHÍTIKÍ ELLAS

Ithaki (Ithaca)

Levkás (Santa Maura)

Kefallinía (Cephalonia)

Zákinthos (Zante)

Préveza

I O N I A N   S E A

AIYAÍON   P E L A G O S

Kárpathos

Stenón Karpáthos

Stenón Kásos

Kásos

DHEKANISOS (DODECANESE)

Ródhos (Rhodes)

Ródhos

Sími

Tílos (Piscopi)

Nísiros

Kos

Kálimnos

Léros

Pátmos

Sámos

Fournoi

Ikaría

Kuşadasi Körfezi

Ephesus

Samsun Dağı

Menderes

Büyük Menderes

Baba Gölü

Besparmak Dağı

T U R K E Y

M U Ğ L A

Kerme Körfezi

Mandalya Körfezi

Astipálaia

Continuation Eastwards on same scale

East from Greenwich

Projection: Conical with two standard parallels

m   ft
9000   3000
6000   2000
4500   1500
3000   1000
1200   400
600   200
0   0
200   600
2000   6000
m   ft

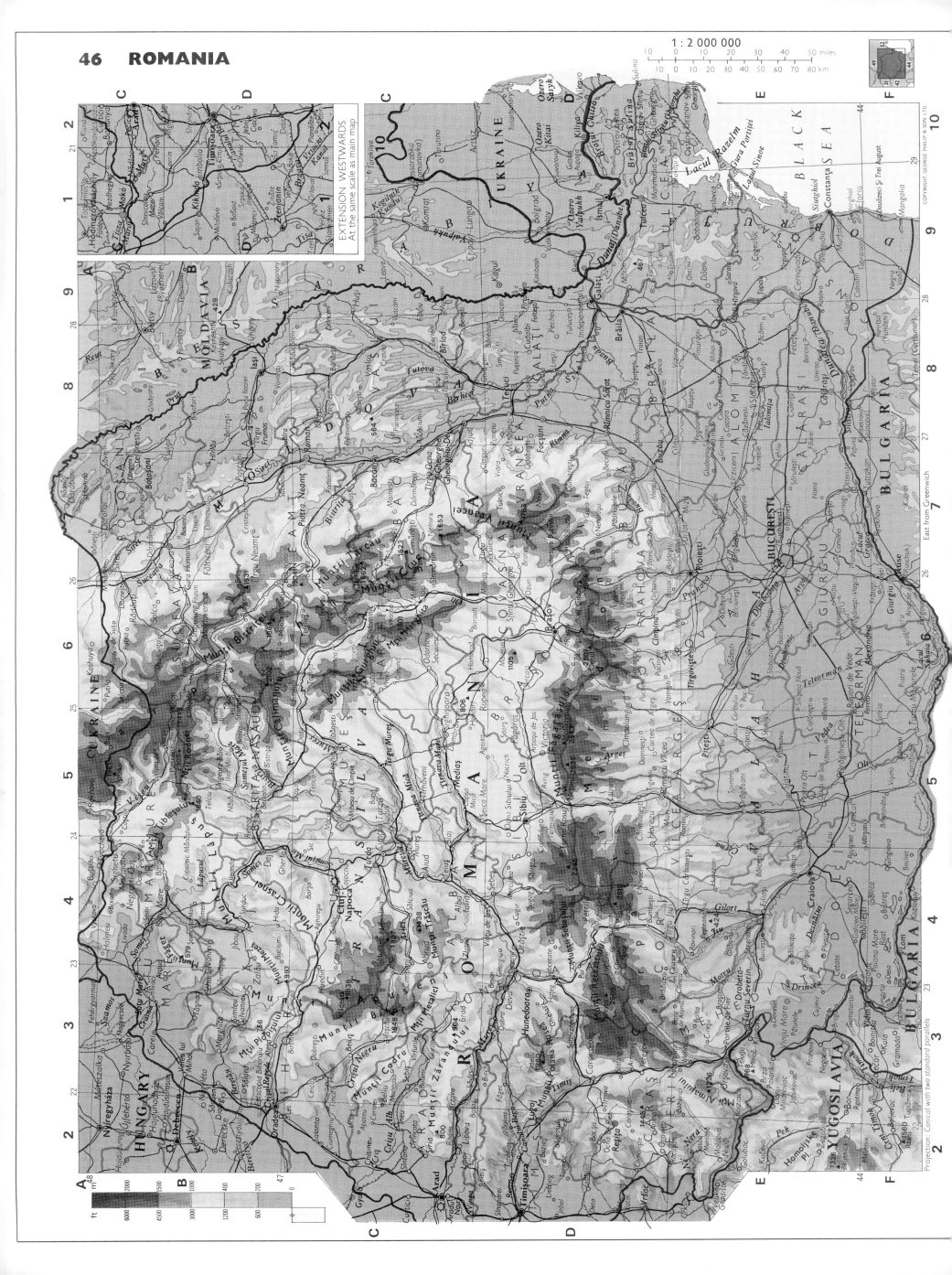

1 : 2 000 000

EXTENSION WESTWARDS
At the same scale as main map

Projection: Conical with two standard parallels

East from Greenwich

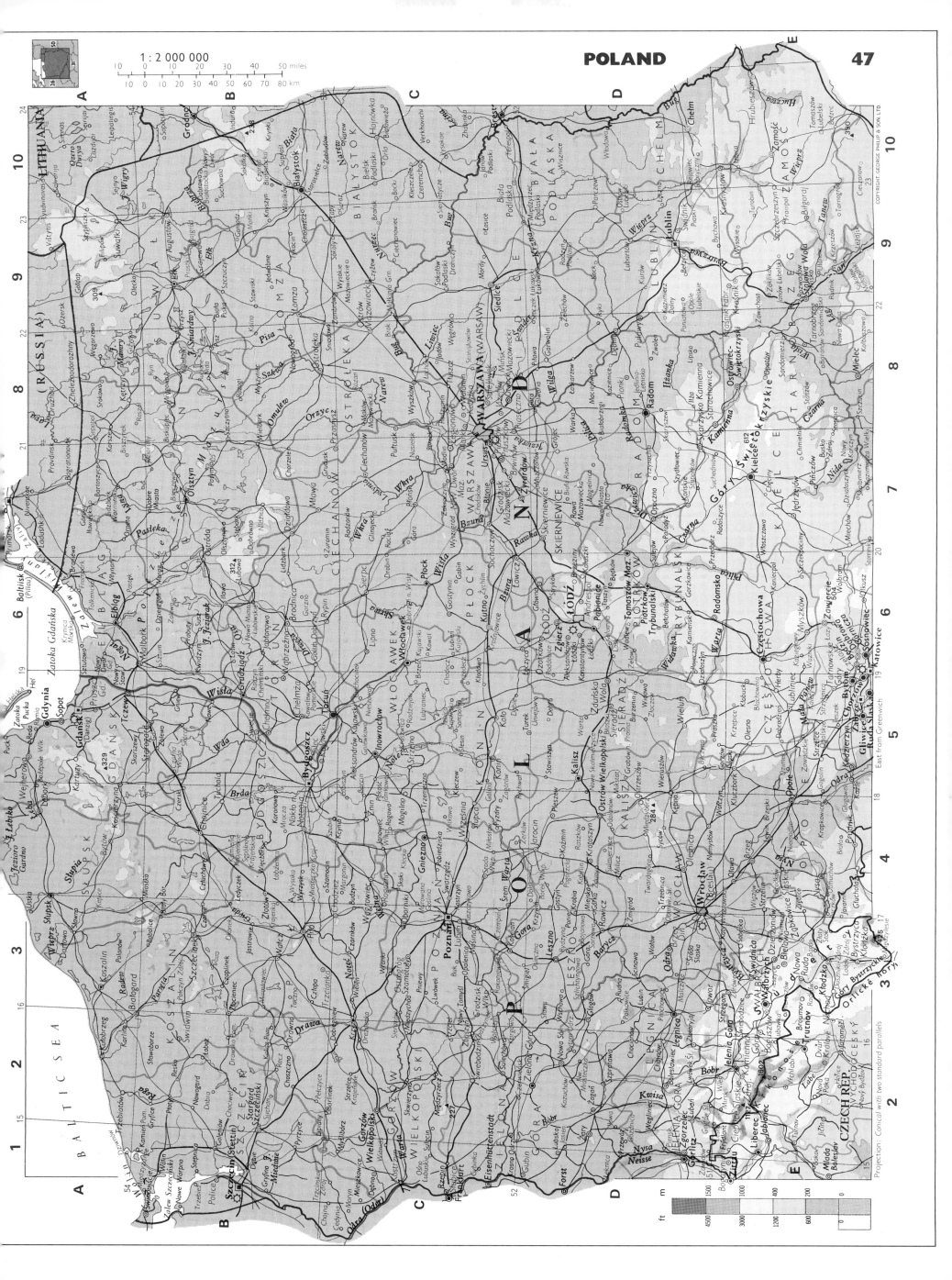

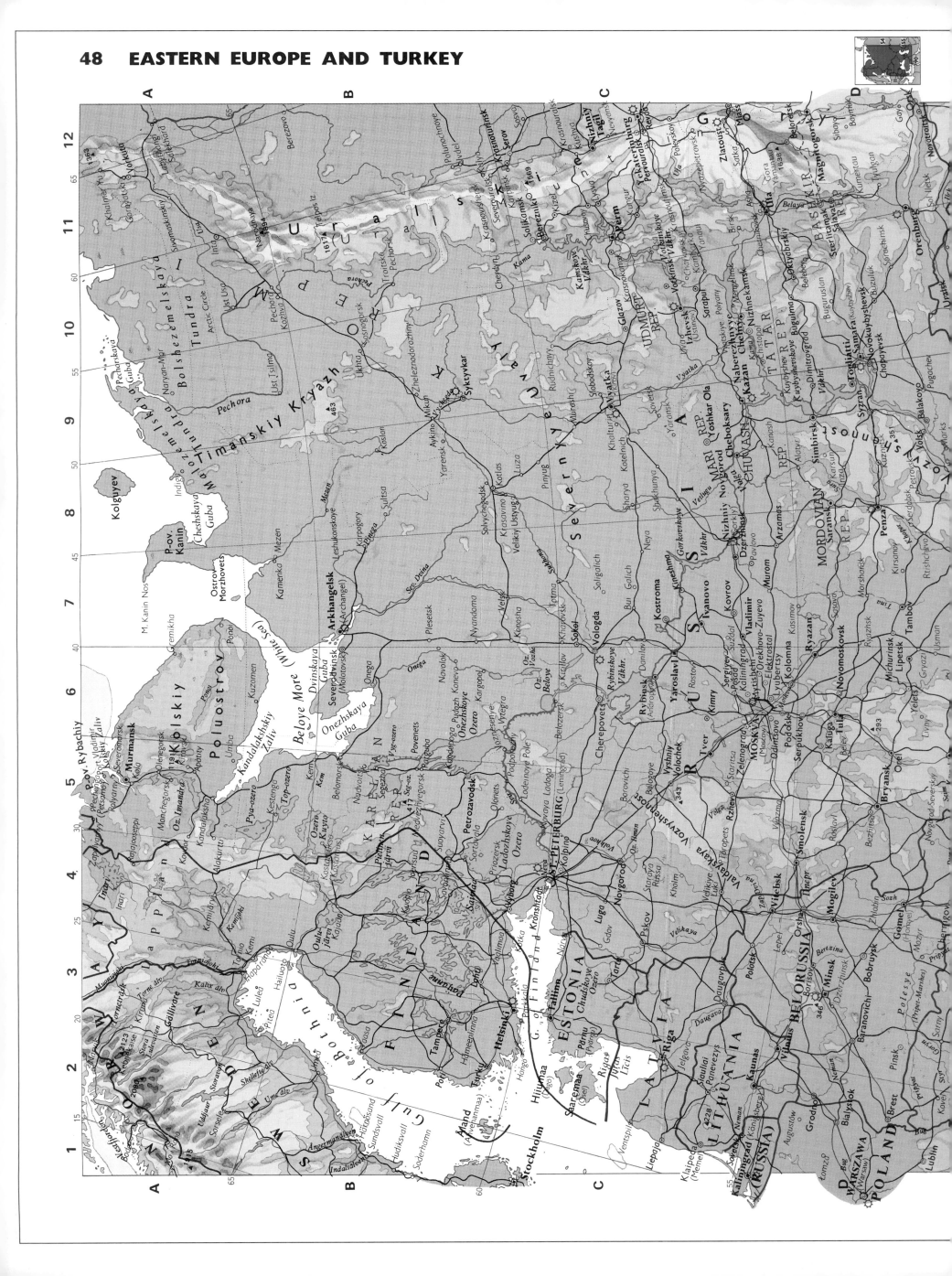

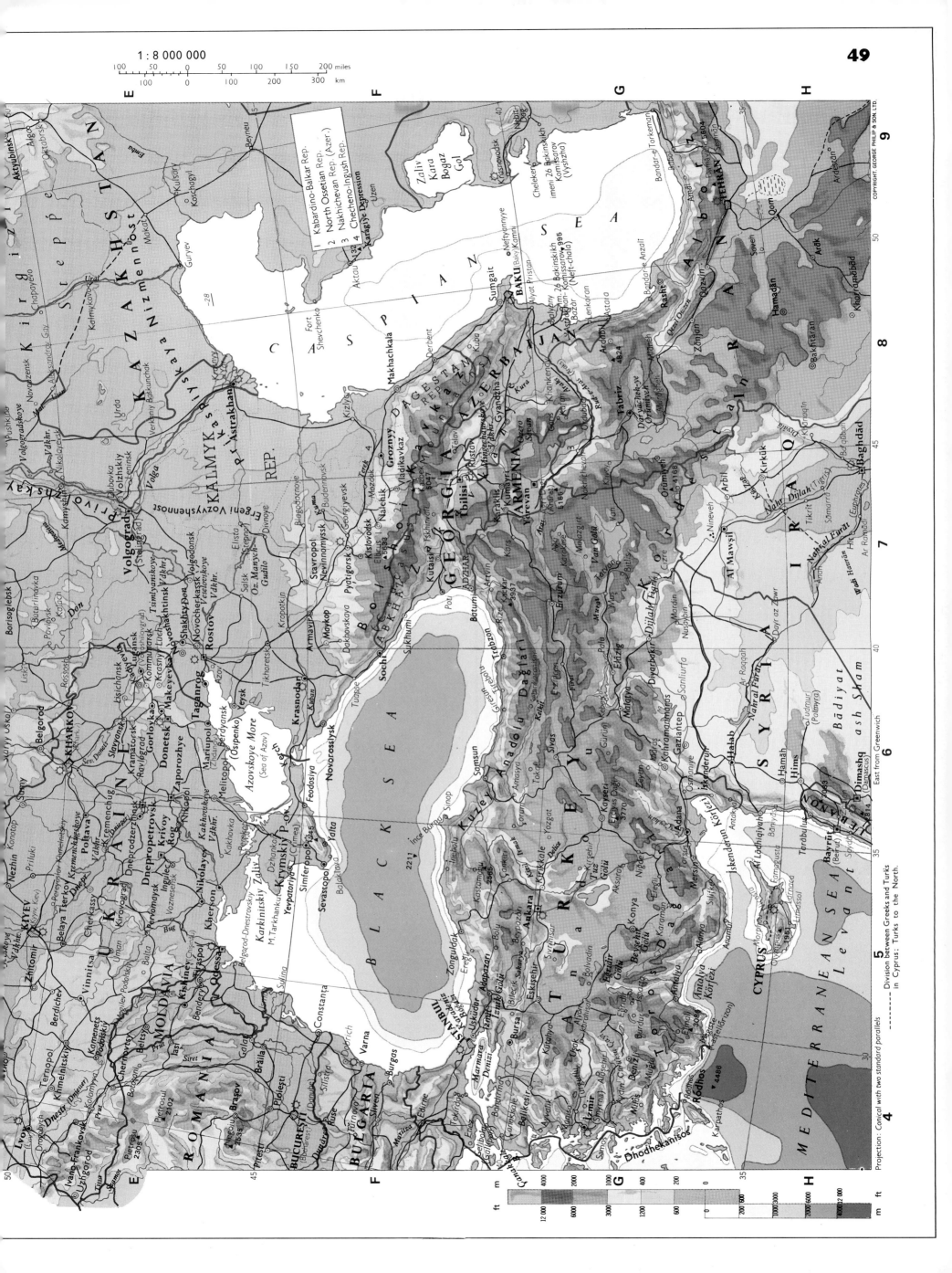

Projection: Conical with two standard parallels

East from Greenwich

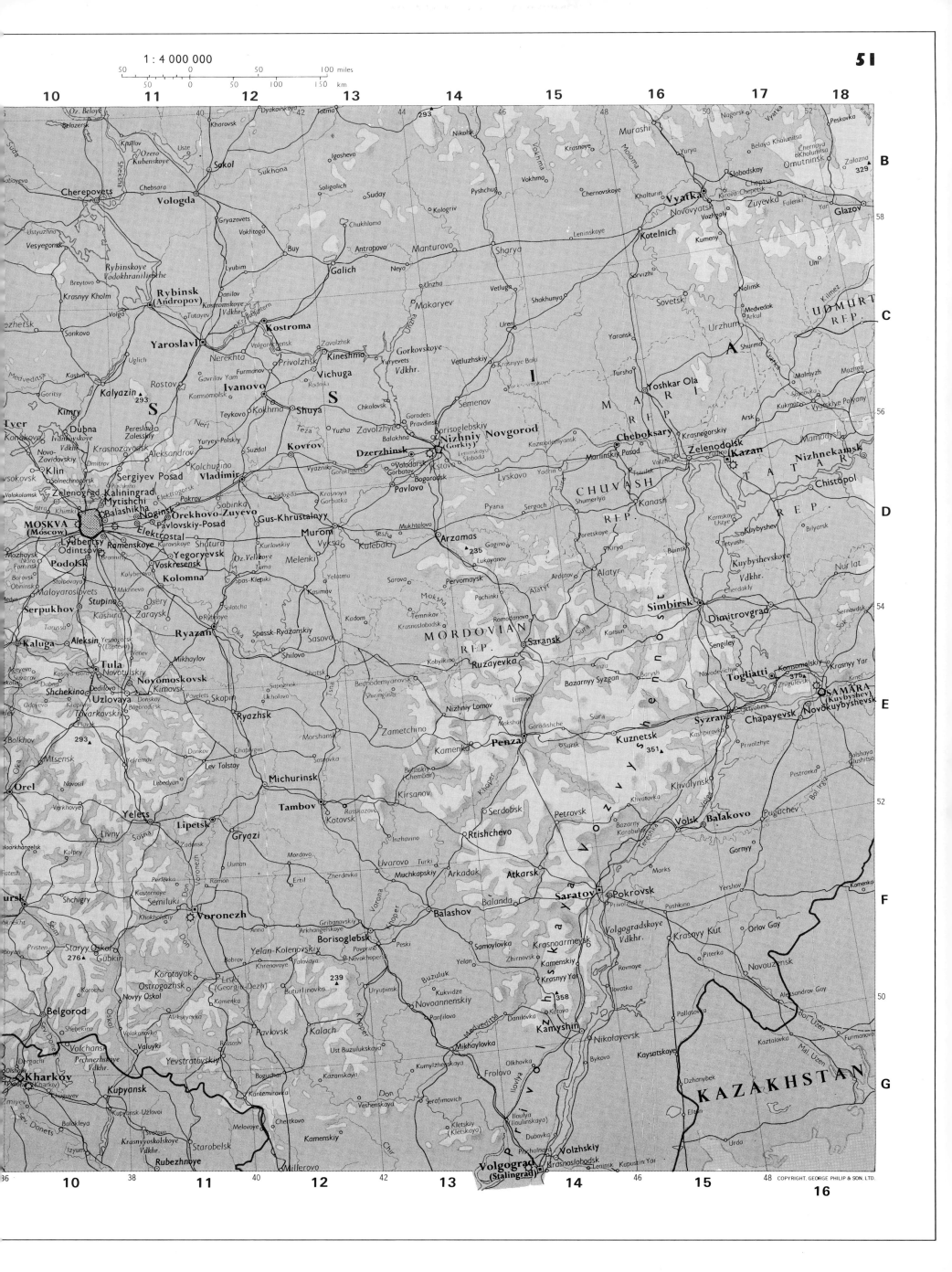

1 : 4 000 000

50    0    50    100 miles
50    0    50    100    150 km

**10** 11 **12** 13 **14** 15 **16** 17 **18**

B
Oz. Beloye
Belozersk
Kirillov
Uste
Ozero
Kubenskoye
Sukhona
Soligalich
Suday
Kologriv
Vokhma
Murashi
Krasnoye
Molona
Belaya Kholunitsa
Chernaya
Kholunitsa
Omutninsk
Zalazna
329

Cherepovets
Chebsara
**Vologda**
Gryazovets
Vokhtoga
Buy
Antropovo
Manturovo
Sharya
Leninskoye
Sovetsk
Kirovo-Chepetsk
**Vyatka**
Novovyatsk
Zuyevka
Falenki
Yar
**Glazov**
58

Ustyuzhna
Vesyegonsk
Rybinskoye
Vodokhranilishche
Breytovo
Krasnyy Kholm
Danilov
Lyubim
Galich
Neya
Vetluga
Shakhunya
Uren
Yaransk
Sorvizhi
Kotelnich
Kumeny
Uni
Malmyzh
Mozhga
UDMURT
REP.
C

ezhsk
Sonkovo
Stolbovo
**Rybinsk
(Andropov)**
Tutayev
Kostromskoye
Vdkhr.
Makaryev
Shakhunya
Yoshkar Ola
Urzhum
Shurma
Arsk
Kukmor
Vyatskiye Polyany
56

Medveditsa
Goritsy
Kalyazin
293
Rostov
Gavrilov Yam
Komsomolsk
Nerekhta
**Kostroma**
Zavolzhsk
**Kineshma**
Privolzhsk
Vichuga
Rodniki
Gorkovskoye
Vdkhr.
Vetluzhskiy
Krasnyye Baki
Tonshayevo
Tursha
**Cheboksary**
Krasnogorskiy
Mariinskiy Posad
Volzhsk
**Zelenodolsk**
Zelenyy Dol
**Kazan**
**Nizhnekamsk**
Mamadysh

**Tver**
Kimry
Kashin
Uglich
Volgorechensk
Furmanov
**Ivanovo**
Teykovo
Shuya
Chkalovsk
Yuryevets
Semenov
Gorodets
Pravdinsk
Borisoglebskiy
Balakhna
Kozmodemyansk
**A**
**M**
**A**
**R**
**I**
REP.
Buinsk
Tetyushi
Bilyarsk
D

**Dubna**
Ivankovskoye
Vdkhr.
Novo-
Zavidovskiy
Pereslavl-
Zalesskiy
Yuryev-Polskiy
Kokhma
Uzha
Zavolzhye
**Nizhniy Novgorod**
(Gorkiy)
Leninskaya
Sloboda
Pyra
Kstovo
Yadrin
**CHUVASH**
Shumerlya
Kanash
Kuybyshevskoye
Vdkhr.
Cherdakly
Nurlat

**Klin**
Solnechnogorsk
Dmitrov
Krasnozavodsk
**Sergiyev Posad**
Kolchugino
**Kovrov**
Vyazniki
Gorokhovets
Bogorodsk
**Dzerzhinsk**
Pavlovo
Lyskovo
Sergach
Pyana
Sergach
REP.
Karsun
Tetyushi
S

Volokolamsk
**Zelenograd**
**Kaliningrad**
Istra
Elektrogorsk
Pokrov
**Vladimir**
Sobinka
Krasnaya
Gorbatka
Sudogda
Murom
Kulebaki
**Arzamas**
235
Gagino
Lukoyanov
Alatyr
**Simbirsk**
Dimitrovgrad
D

**Moskva
(Moscow)**
Mytishchi
Balashikha
Noginsk
**Orekhovo-Zuyevo**
**Elektrostal**
Pavlovskiy-Posad
Gus-Khrustalnyy
Melenki
Vyksa
Sarova
Pervomaysk
Ardatov
Alatyr
Buinsk
Kuybyshevskoye
Sernovsk
54

Mozhaysk
Nara
Lyubertsy
Ramenskoye
Kurovskoye
Shatura
Kurlovskiy
Yelatma
Temnikov
Moksha
Pochinki
Romodanovo
Sura
Sengiley
Novodevichye
**Togliatti**
375
Zhiguli
Komsomolskiy
Krasnyy Yar

Maloyaroslavets
**Podolsk**
Stolbovaya
**Voskresensk**
**Yegoryevsk**
Spas-Klepiki
Tuma
Kasimov
Kadom
Krasnoslobodsk
**MORDOVIAN**
**REP.**
**Saransk**
Bazarnyy Syzgan
Barysh
Sura
Zhigulevsk
**SAMARA**
(Kuybyshev)
**Novokuybyshevsk**
E

Borovsk
Obninsk
**Serpukhov**
Tarusa
Kashira
Zaraysk
Ozery
Rybnoye
Solotcha
Spassk-Ryazanskiy
Sasovo
Kobylkino
**Ruzayevka**
Inza
Novospasskoye
**Syzran**
Kashpirovka
Privolzhye
**Chapayevsk**

**Kaluga**
**Aleksin**
Yesnogorsk
Venev
Mikhaylov
Shilovo
Nizhniy Lomov
Lunino
**Kuznetsk**
351

**Tula**
Novotulskiy
Stupino
Kimovsk
Skopin
Spassk
Sapozhok
Kamenka
**Penza**
Surskoye
Pestravka
Bolshaya
Glushitsa

Shchekino
Dedilovo
**Novomoskovsk**
Povelets
Ukholovo
**Ryazhsk**
Morshansk
Sosnovka
Shingarino
Gorodishche
Kivatovka
Khvalynsk

Uzlovaya
Bogoroditsk
Dankov
Chaplygin
Zametchino
Kamenka
Serdobsk
Privolzhye

Tovarkovskiy
Plavsk
Lev Tolstoy
Lebedyan
Michurinsk
Kirsanov
Khoper
Serdobsk
Petrovsk
Bazarnyy
Karabulak
**Volsk**
**Balakovo**
Pugachev

Bolkhov
293
Mtsensk
Novosil
Yefremov
**Yelets**
**Lipetsk**
Gryazi
**Tambov**
Rasskazovo
Kotovsk
Inzhavino
Uvarovo
**Rtishchevo**
Marks

**Orel**
Livny
Sosna
Zadonsk
Usman
Mordovo
Ertil
Turki
**Arkadak**
**Atkarsk**
Bazarnyy
Karabulak
Gornyy
52

Kolpny
Perlevka
Ramon
Anna
Zherdevka
Muchkapskiy
Balanda
**Saratov**
**Pokrovsk**
Yershov

Kursk
Shchigry
Kastornoye
Semiluki
Khokholskiy
**Voronezh**
Gribanovskiy
Arkhangelskoye
Poyorino
Peski
**Balashov**
Samoylovka
Krasnoarmeysk
Privolzhskiy
Pushkino
Krasnyy Kut
Orlov Gay
F

Arkhangelsk
Pristen
Staryy Oskol
276
Gubkin
Korotoyak
Ostrogozhsk
Yelan-Kolenovskiy
Khrenovoye
Talovaya
239
Uryupinsk
Novokhopersk
Novoanninskiy
Buzuluk
Kukvide
Yelan
Zhirnovsk
Kamenskiy
Krasnyy Yar
Ilovatka
Piterka
Novouzensk

Belgorod
Shebekino
Novyy Oskol
Alekseyevka
Kamenka
Pavlovsk
Buturlinovka
Kalach
Panfilovo
Medveditsa
358
Danilovka
Kotovo
Nikolayevsk
Kaztalovka
Aleksandrov Gay
50

rsk
Drachi
**Kharkov**
Volchansk
Pechenezhskoye
Vdkhr.
Valuyki
Rossosh
Boguchar
Ust Buzulukskaya
Mikhaylovka
Olkhovka
Bykovo
Kaysatskoye
Palassovka
Mal Uzen
Furmanovo

Kupyansk
Staryy Saltov
Kupyansk-Uzlovoi
Svatovo
Melovoye
Chertkovo
Kamenskiy
Kazanskaya
Veshenskaya
Serafimovich
Kletskiy
Dubovka
Frolovo
**Volzhskiy**
Leninsk
Kapustin Yar
Zhdanov
Urda
Elton
**KAZAKHSTAN**
G

iyev
Izyum
Balakleya
Krasnyooskolskoye
Vdkhr.
Starobelsk
Rubezhnoye
Millerovo
Chir
Kalach
Surovikino
Ioulya
(Iloulinskaya)
Krasnoslobodsk
**Volgograd
(Stalingrad)**

**10** 38 **11** 40 **12** 42 **13** 44 **14** 46 **15** 48 **16**

COPYRIGHT. GEORGE PHILIP & SON. LTD.

UKRAINE

MOLDAVIA

ROMANIA

BULGARIA

BLACK SEA

AZOVSKOYE MORE (Sea of Azov)

MARMARA DENIZI (Sea of Marmara)

Karkinitskiy Zaliv

Krymskiy P-ov (Crimea)

Kerchenskiy Proliv

Karadeniz Boğazı (Bosporus)

**Cities and towns:**

Lvov (Lviv), Rovno, Dubno, Korets, Gorodnitsa, Korosten, Nezhin, Sumy, Belgorod, Staryy Oskol, Zhitomir (Zhytomyr), Berdichev, KIYEV (Kyyiv, Kiev), Brovary, Priluki, Romny, Kharkov (Kharkiv), Kupyansk, Ternopol, Khmelnitskiy, Vinnitsa, Belaya Tserkov (Bila Tserkva), Fastov, Pereyaslav, Cherkassy, Poltava, Krasnograd, Chernovtsy, Zhmerinka, Uman, Kirovograd, Znamenka, Kremenchug, Dneprodzerzhinsk, Dnepropetrovsk, Pavlograd, Slavyansk, Kramatorsk, Artemovsk, Gorlovka, Yenakiyevo, Makeyevka, Donetsk (Stalino), Beltsy, Kishinëv (Chişinău), Bender, Tiraspol, Kirovograd, Krivoy Rog (Kryvyy Rih), Nikopol, Zaporozhye, Mariupol (Zhdanov), Iaşi, Bacău, Roman, Bendery, Odessa (Odesa), Nikolayev (Mykolayiv), Kherson, Melitopol, Berdyansk, Yeysk, Galaţi, Brăila, Ismail, Buzău, Ploieşti, Constanţa, BUCUREŞTI (Bucharest), Ruse (Ruščuk), Razgrad, Varna, Burgas, Sliven, Dzhankoy, Yevpatoriya, Simferopol, Sevastopol, Yalta, Feodosiya, Kerch, Novorossiysk, Slavyansk-na-Kubani, Anapa, Gelendzhik, Istanbul, Üsküdar, İzmit, Adapazarı, Bolu, Zonguldak, Ereğli, Karabük, Kastamonu, Sinop, Samsun, Bafra, Ankara, Çorum, Amasya, Tokat, Turhal, Zile, Bursa, Balıkesir, Tekirdağ, Edirne, Kırklareli, Çorlu

**Spot heights:** 471, 384, 2102, 429, 269, 324, 276, 14, 2135, 2211, 2137, 1545, 2543, 2378, 2565, 1261, 1018, 3095, 921

Projection: Conical with two standard parallels

1 : 4 000 000

**53**

50    9    0    50    100 miles
50    0    50    100    150 km

8    9    10    11    12    13    14    15

**A**

50

**B**

**K A Z A K H S T A N**

**RUSSIA**

Orlov Gay

Dzhambeyty

Oz. Chalkar

Chalkar

Povorino    Peski    Krasnyy Kut    Novouzensk    Karsha

Yelan-Kolenovskiy    Buzuluk    Krasnoarmeysk    Zhirnovsk

Novoanninskiy    Krasnyy Yar    Piterka    Alexandrov Gay    Mergeneviy

Kamyshin    Nikolayevsk    Volgogradskoye    Kaztalovka    Mat-Uzen    Furmanovo

Kalach    Panfilovo    Frolovo    Bykovo    Dzhanybek    Urda    Inderborskiy

Volzhskiy    Leninsk    Kapustin Yar    Shungay    Zelënyy    Makhambet

**Volgograd (Stalingrad)**    Krasnoslobodsk    Vladimirovka    Baskunchak    Novobogatinskoye

Tsimlyanskoye Vdkhr.    Kotelnikovo    Akhtubinsk (Petropavlovsk)    Verkhniy    **Guryev**

**C**

48

46

**K A L M Y K    R E P**

**P r i k a s p i y s k a y a    N i z m e n n o s t**

Astrakhan    Krasnyy Yar    Gryushkino

Elista (Stepnoi)    Kirovskiy    Mumra    Liman

Oz. Manych-Gudilo    Krasnoye    Beloye Ozero    Kultay

**C A S P I A N**

Mangyshlakskiy Zaliv

M. Tyub Karagan    Fort Shevchenko    P-ov. Mangyshlak

Kulaly

**D**

44

**Rostov**    Bataysk    Proletarskaya    Salsk    Remontnoye    Divnoye    Kuma    Beloye Ozero

Zernograd    Tikhoretsk    Svetlograd (Petrovskoye)    Blagodarnoye    Budennovsk    Neftekumsk    Staryy Biryuzyak    Tyuleniy    Bryanskoye    O. Chechen    Aktau

**Krasnodar**    Armavir    Stavropol    Nevinnomyssk    Zelenokumsk (Vorontsovo-Aleksandrovskoye)    Aleksandriyskaya    Lopatin

Maykop    Labinsk    Cherkessk    Mineralnyye Vody    Georgiyevsk    Mozdok    Kizlyar

Khadyzhensk    Yessentuki    Pyatigorsk    Prokhladnyy    **CHECHENO-INGUSH REP.**    Kiziyar

Tuapse    Kislovodsk    Karachayevsk    Nalchik    **Groznyy**    Gudermes    **Makhachkala**

**E**

42

**Sochi**    Adler    Gagra    **KABARDINO-BALKAR REP.**    Beslan    **Vladikavkaz (Ordzhonikidze)**    Buynaksk    Kaspiysk

**ABKHAZ REP.**    Sukhumi    **B o l s h o i    K a v k a z**    Kazbek 5047    **G E O R G I A**    Izberbash    Derbent

Ochamchire    Tkvarcheli    Kutaisi    Chiatura    Tskhinvali    Telavi    **AZERBAIJAN**

**F**

40

Poti    Samtredia    Khashuri    Gori    **Tbilisi**    Rustavi    Mingechaurskoye Vdkhr.    Khachmas

Batumi    **ADZHAR REP.**    Akhaltsikhe    Akhalkalaki    Sheki (Nukha)    Baba dag 3629    Siazan

Kobuleti    Ozurgety    Bab Dyuzi 4466    Sumgait

Trabzon    Rize    Kars    **Karakalis**    Dilizhan    **Gyandzha (Kirovabad)**    **AZERBAIJAN**    **BAKU (Baky)**

Kumayri    Aragats 4090    Ozero Sevan    Mir-Bashir    Barda    Kozi Magomed

**ARMENIA**    **Yerevan**    **NAGORNO-KARABAKH**    Imishly    M. Byandovan

**G**

East from Greenwich    40    9    42    10    11    44    12    46    13    48    14

COPYRIGHT. GEORGE PHILIP & SON. LTD.

1 : 4 000 000

50    0    50    100 miles
50    0    50    100    150 km

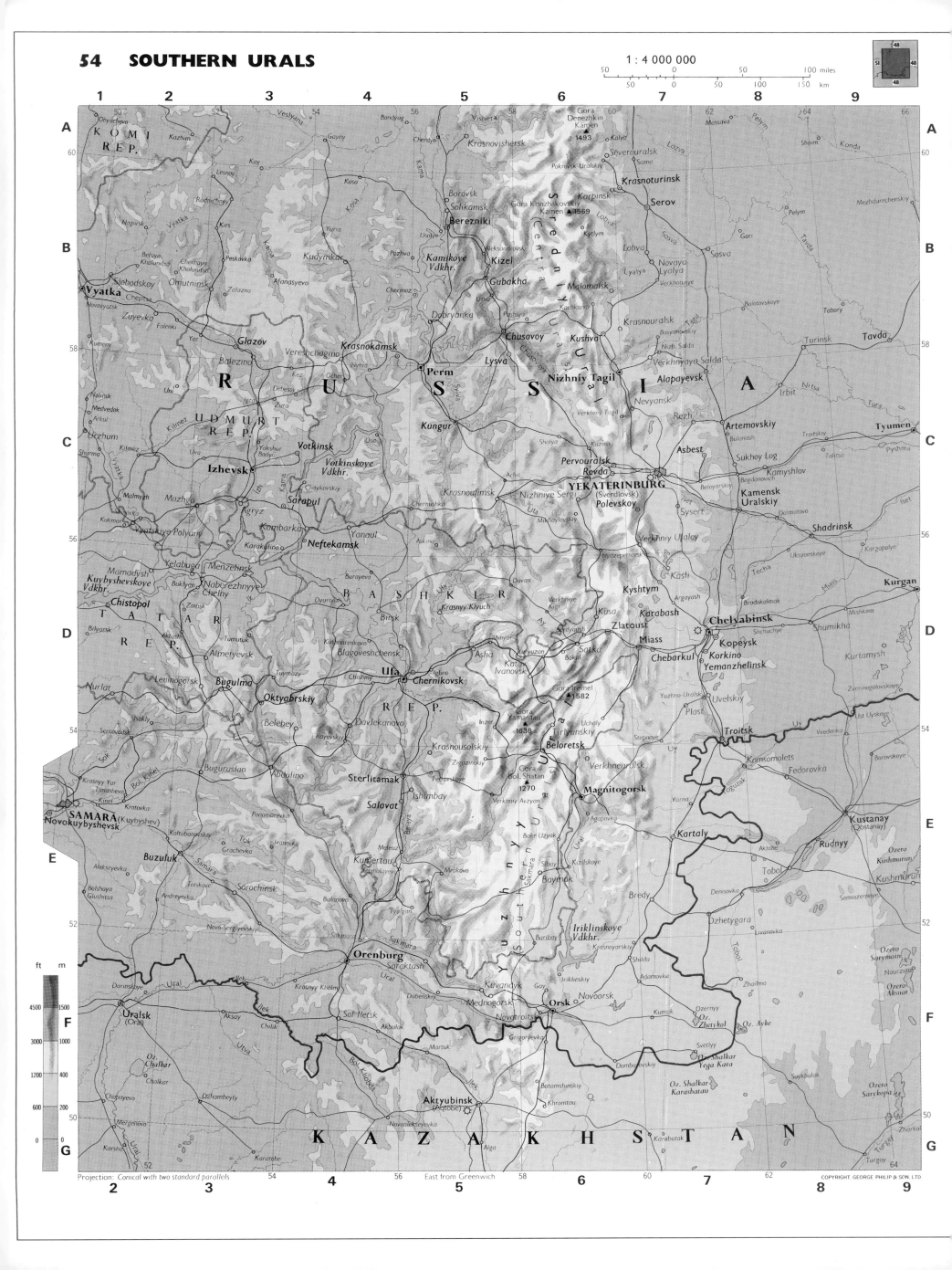

**KOMI REP.**

Obydkevo  Kazhim  Veslyana  Bondyg  Vishera  Gora Denezhkin Kamen ▲1493

Nagorsk  Kay  Gayny  Chendyn  Kalya  Mossava  Pelym  Konda

Belaya Kholunitsa  Chernaya Kholunitsa  Peskovka  Solikamsk  Severouralsk  Lozva  Sosva  Shaim

Vyatka  Slobodskoy  Omutninsk  Kudymkar  Borovsk  Gora Konzhakovskiy Kamen ▲1569  Karpinsk  Severouralsk  Krasnoturinsk  Serov  Mezhdurechenskiy

Glazov  Krasnokamsk  Berezniki  Kizel  Gubakha  Malomalsk  Novaya Lyalya  Verkhoturye  Bolotovskoye  Tabory

**R U S S I A**

Izhevsk  Votkinsk  Perm  Chusovoy  Lysva  Kungur  Nizhniy Tagil  Alapayevsk  Irbit  Tyumen

Sarapul  Votkinskoye Vdkhr.  Kungur  Nizhniye Sergi  YEKATERINBURG (Sverdlovsk)  Artemovskiy  Tyumen

**UDMURT REP.**

Mozhga  Agryz  Kambarka  Neftekamsk  Pervouralsk  Revda  Polevskoy  Kamensk Uralskiy  Shadrinsk

**TATAR REP.**  **BASHKIR REP.**

Chistopol  Naberezhnyye Chelny  Birsk  Kyshtym  Karabash  Kurgan

Bugulma  Ufa  Chernikovsk  Zlatoust  Miass  Chelyabinsk  Kopeysk

Oktyabrskiy  Belebey  Davlekanovo  Asha  Katav Ivanovsk  Satka  Chebarkul  Korkino  Yemanzhelinsk

Beloretsk  Gora Iremel ▲1582  Troitsk

Sterlitamak  Ishimbay  Gora Yamantau 1638  Verkhneuralsk  Magnitogorsk  Kustanay (Qostanay)

**SAMARA (Kuybyshev)**  Novokuybyshevsk  Salavat  Gora Bol. Shatan ▲1270  Kartaly  Rudnyy

Buzuluk  Kumertau  Orenburg  Orsk  Novoorsk

**Uralsk (Oral)**  Sol Iletsk  Mednogorsk  Novotroitsk  Aktyubinsk (Aqtöbe)

**K A Z A K H S T A N**

Projection: Conical with two standard parallels    East from Greenwich    COPYRIGHT GEORGE PHILIP & SON LTD

ft    m
4500  1500
3000  1000
1200  400
600   200
50    50
0     0
F
G

1 : 4 000 000

50        0        50        100 miles
50   0   50   100   150   km

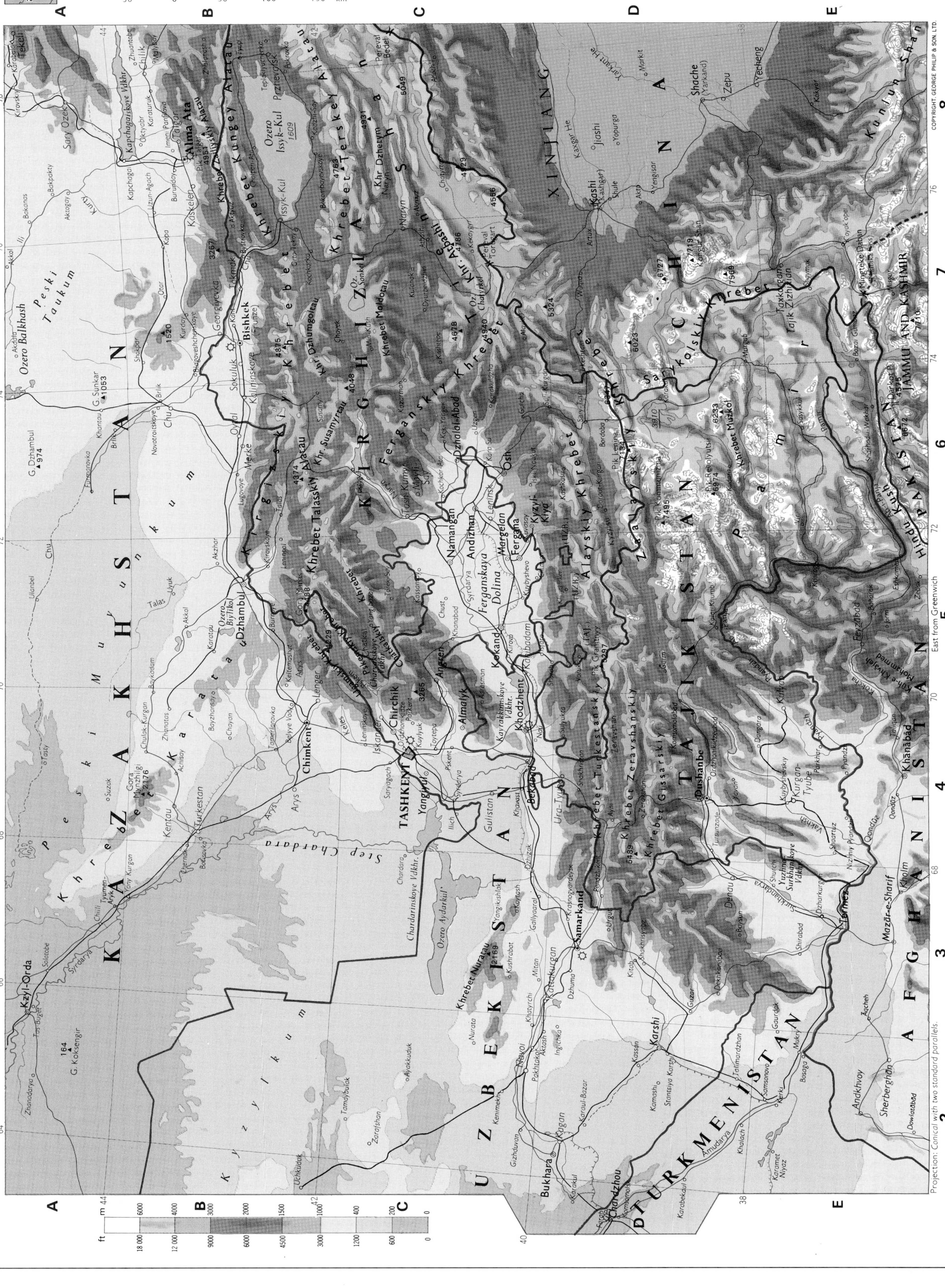

COPYRIGHT GEORGE PHILIP & SON LTD.

East from Greenwich

Projection: Conical with two standard parallels.

KAZAKHSTAN

KIRGHIZIA

UZBEKISTAN

TAJIKISTAN

TURKMENISTAN

AFGHANISTAN

CHINA

XINJIANG

JAMMU AND KASHMIR

PAKISTAN

TASHKENT

Bishkek (Frunze)

Alma-Ata

Samarkand

Dushanbe

Bukhara

Kashi (Kashgar)

Shache (Yarkand)

Yecheng

Zepu

Kzyl-Orda

Chimkent

Chirchik

Andizhan

Namangan

Kokand

Fergana

Margelan

Osh

Khodzhent

Termez

Mazar-e-Sharif

Khanabad

Karshi

Chardzhou

Ozero Balkhash

Ozero Issyk-Kul 1609

Oz. Sonkel

Peski Taukum

Step Chardara

Khrebet Terskey Alatau

Khrebet Kungey Alatau

Khrebet Zailiyskiy Alatau

Khrebet Talasskiy

Ferganskiy Khrebet

Alayskiy Khrebet

Zeravshanskiy Khrebet

Khrebet Turkestanskiy

Khrebet Zeravshanskiy

Khrebet (Gissarskiy)

Khrebet Nuratau

Hindu Kush

Kunlun Shan

Tien Shan

Pamir

Karakum

Kyzylkum

Peski Muyunkum

Syrdarya

Amudarya

Yarkant He

Ferganskaya Dolina

Khrebet Muzkol

6049

4931

4763

4556

4523

4678

4940

4048

5324

6023

6727

7560

7719

8233

6974

5189

3267

3265

1520

4176

974

164

41053

Sary Ozek

Tekeli

Bokonas

Kapal

Akkol

Ili

Aksu

Artux

Kaxgar He

Markit

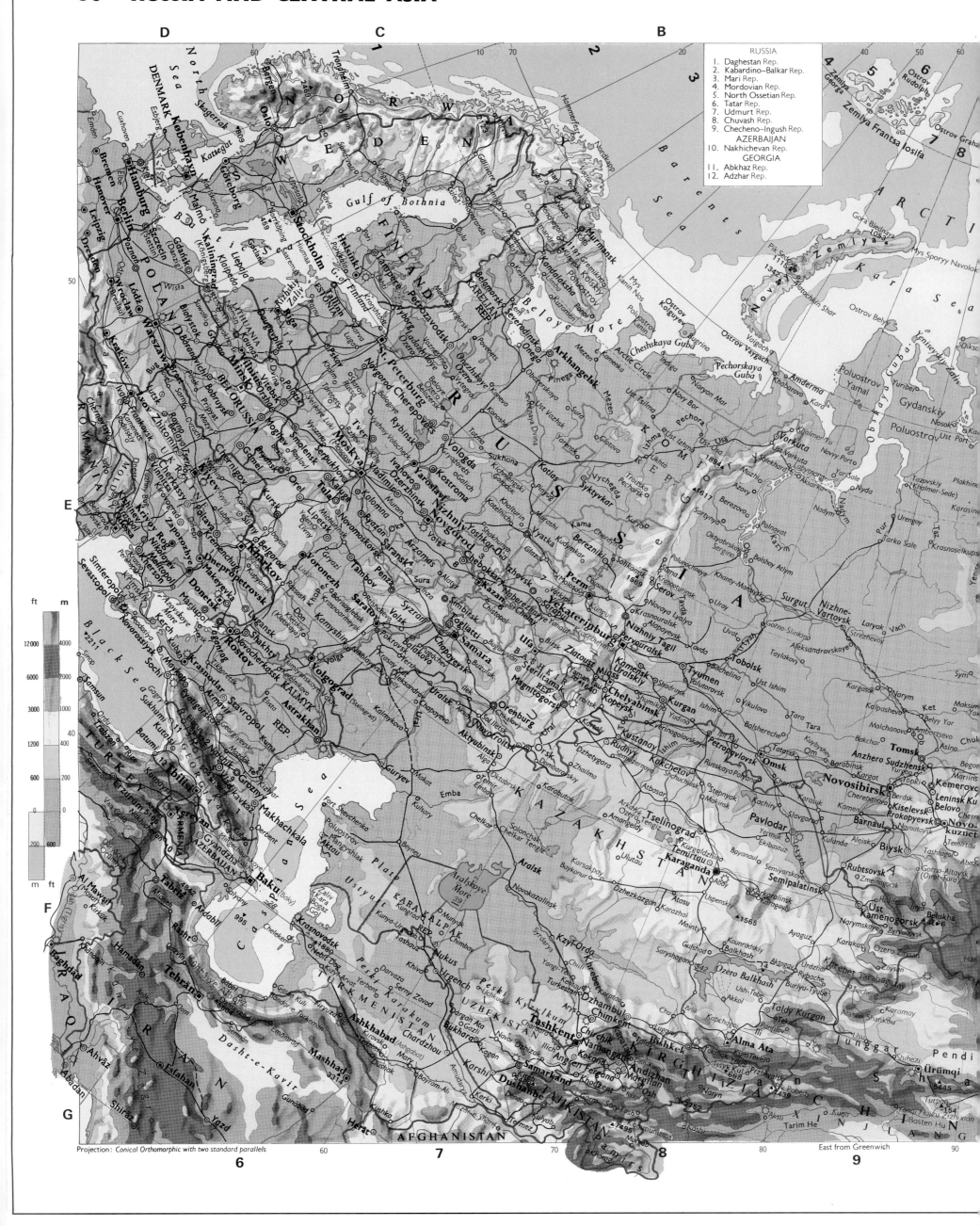

RUSSIA
1. Daghestan Rep.
2. Kabardino–Balkar Rep.
3. Mari Rep.
4. Mordovian Rep.
5. North Ossetian Rep.
6. Tatar Rep.
7. Udmurt Rep.
8. Chuvash Rep.
9. Checheno–Ingush Rep.
AZERBAIJAN
10. Nakhichevan Rep.
GEORGIA
11. Abkhaz Rep.
12. Adzhar Rep.

Projection: Conical Orthomorphic with two standard parallels

East from Greenwich

1 : 16 000 000

100   0   100   200   300   400 miles

100   0   100   200   300   400   500   600 km

A

B

C

D

E

F

10   11   12   13   14

9   10   11   12   13   14   15   16   17   18   19

ARCTIC OCEAN

Severnaya
Zemlya

Laptev Sea

East Siberian Sea

Novosibirskiye Ostrova

Ostrov Vrangelya

Chukotskoye More

Mys Dezhneva
(East C.)

St. Lawrence I.
(U.S.A.)

Poluostrov
Gory
Byrranga
Taymyr

Nordvik

Tiksi

Verkhoyansk

Khrebet Cherskogo

Verkhoyanskiy Khrebet

Srednekolymsk

Okhotsko Kolymskoye

Koryakskiy Khrebet

Sredinnyy
Poluostrov
Kamchatka

Bering
Sea

Norilsk

Arctic Circle

Y A K U T   R E P.

Vilyuysk

Yakutsk

Olekminsk

Magadan

Okhotsk

Sea of
Okhotsk

Petropavlovsk-
Kamchatskiy

R   U   S   S   I   A

Kirensk

Stanovoy Khrebet
Khrebet Dzhugdzhur

Ostrov
Shantar

Sakhalin

Kurilskiye Ostrova

Krasnoyarsk
Kansk
Achinsk

Bratsk

Nizhneudinsk

Komsomolsk

Khabarovsk

Nikolayevsk-
na-Amure

Sovetskaya Gavan

Yuzhno-Sakhalinsk

Irkutsk
Usolye Sibirskoye
Cheremkhovo
Angarsk
Ulan Ude

Chita

Blagoveshchensk

Birobidzhan

Khrebet Sikhote Alin

Sapporo

Hokkaidō

Hakodate

ZAPADNYY   SAYAN
Vostochnyy   Sayan

Abakan
Minusinsk

TUVA REP.
Kyzyl

Ulaanbaatar
(Ulan Bator)

Hangayn Nuruu

Hentiyn
Nuruu

M   O   N   G   O   L   I   A

G   O   B   I

Qiqihar

Harbin

Changchun

Jilin

Fushun
Shenyang
Anshan

Jiamusi

Dongbei
Pingyuan

Da Hinggan Ling

Ussuriysk
Vladivostok
Nakhodka

Chongjin

Sea of JAPAN

Honshū

Niigata

Kanazawa
Toyama

Edrengiyn   Nuruu

C   H   I   N   A

Baotou   Hohhot
Zhangjiakou

Beijing

Yingkou

Dandong
Dalian

NORTH
KOREA

Wŏnsan

Pyŏngyang

Sŏul

Inch'ŏn   SOUTH KOREA

Taejŏn

Taegu

Pusan

Sea of Japan

1 : 40 000 000

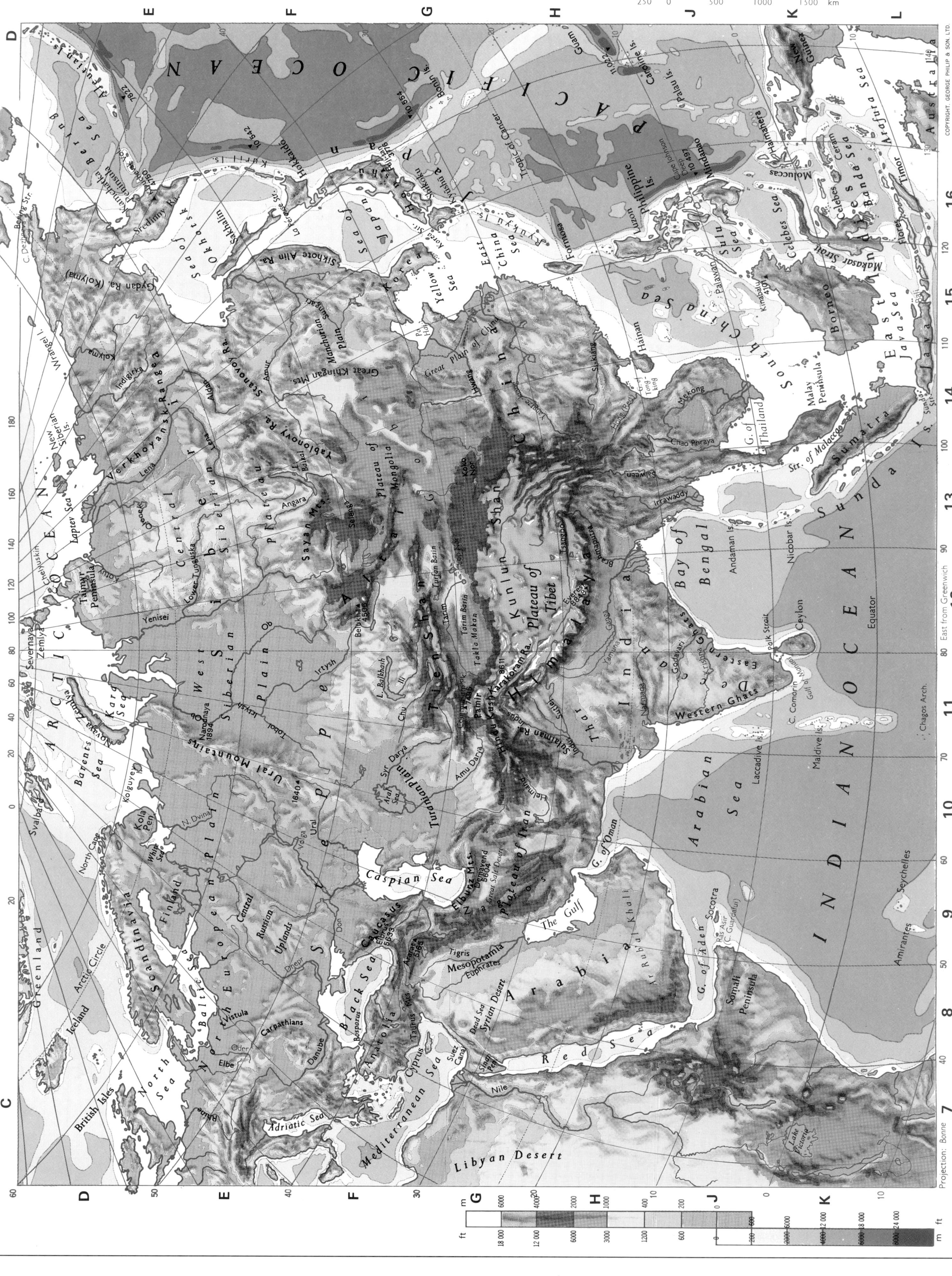

250   0   250   500   750   1000 miles
250   0   500   1000   1500 km

PACIFIC OCEAN

ARCTIC OCEAN

INDIAN OCEAN

Bering Sea
Bering Str.
C. Dezhneva
Kamchatka Peninsula
Sea of Okhotsk
Sredinny Ra.
Gydan Ra. (Kolyma)
Wrangel I.
Kolyma
Indigirka
New Siberian Is.
Verkhoyansk Range
Lena
Aldan
Central Siberian Plateau
Stanovoy Ra.
Sikhote Alin Ra.
Sakhalin
Kuril Is.
Hokkaido   4750
Japan Sea
Honshu   12,467
Sikoku
Kyushu
Korea
Korea Str.
Yellow Sea
East China Sea
Formosa
Ryukyu Is.
Tropic of Cancer
Bonin Is.
Guam
Caroline Is.
Palau Is.
Mindanao   10,497
Philippine Is.
Luzon
Celebes Sea
Sulu Sea
Palawan
Borneo   Kinabalu 13,455
Celebes
Halmahera
Moluccas
Ceram
Banda Sea
Arafura Sea
New Guinea
Australia
Timor
Flores
Java Sea
Java
Sumatra
Sunda Is.
Str. of Malacca
Malay Peninsula
G. of Thailand
Chao Phraya
Mekong
Irrawaddy
Salween
Bay of Bengal
Andaman Is.
Nicobar Is.
Ceylon
Polk Strait
C. Comorin
Gulf of Manaar
Laccadive Is.
Maldive Is.
Chagos Arch.
Eastern Ghats
Western Ghats
Godavari
Kistna
Narbada
Tapti
Deccan
India
Ganges
Jumna
Brahmaputra
Himalaya   Everest
Plateau of Tibet
Kunlun Shan
Tsinling Shan
Great Plain of China
Hwang Ho
Yangtze Kiang
Szechwan
Sikang
Hainan
South China Sea
Manchurian Plain
Great Khingan Mts.
Amur
Sungari
Takla Makan
Tarim
Turfan Basin
Plateau of Mongolia
Gobi
Altai
Sayan Mts.
Bebukha   4506
Angara
Yenisei
Ob
Tobol
Irtysh
Ishim
West Siberian Plain
Ural Mountains   1640
Kara Sea
Novaya Zemlya
Barents Sea
Severnaya Zemlya
Taimyr Peninsula
Khatanga
Laptev Sea
Chelyuskin
Kolguyev
White Sea
Kola Pen.
North Cape
Scandinavia
Finland
Baltic Sea
North Sea
British Isles
Iceland
Greenland
Arctic Circle
North European Plain
Central Russian Uplands
Dnepr
Don
Volga
Ural
W. Dvina
Vistula
Oder
Elbe
Rhine
Danube
Carpathians
Adriatic Sea
Mediterranean Sea
Cyprus
Anatolia
Taurus Mts.
Black Sea
Bosporus
Caucasus   Elbruz 18,493
Ararat   16,946
Caspian Sea
Elburz Mts.   Demavend 18,604
Plateau of Iran
Great Salt Desert
Tigris
Euphrates
Mesopotamia
The Gulf
G. of Oman
Arabian Sea
Zagros
Syrian Desert
Dead Sea
Suez Canal
Sinai Pen.
Nile
Libyan Desert
Red Sea
Arabia
Rub' al Khali
Somali Peninsula
G. of Aden
Ras Asir
C. Guardafui
Socotra
Seychelles
Amirantes
Equator
East from Greenwich
Lake Victoria

Pamir
Hindu Kush
Karakoram Ra.
Tien Shan
Amu Darya
Syr Darya
Aral Sea
Turkestan Plain
Kyzyl Kum
Steppe
Kirghiz Steppe
Ili
Chu
L. Balkhash
Suleiman Ra.
Indus
Thar Desert

ft   m
18 000   6000
12 000   4000
   2000
6000   1000
3000   400
1200   200
600   10
200   0
0
200
6000   2000
12 000   4000
18 000   6000
24 000   8000 m

Projection: Bonne

1 : 40 000 000

250 0 250 500 750 1000 miles
250 0 500 1000 1500 km

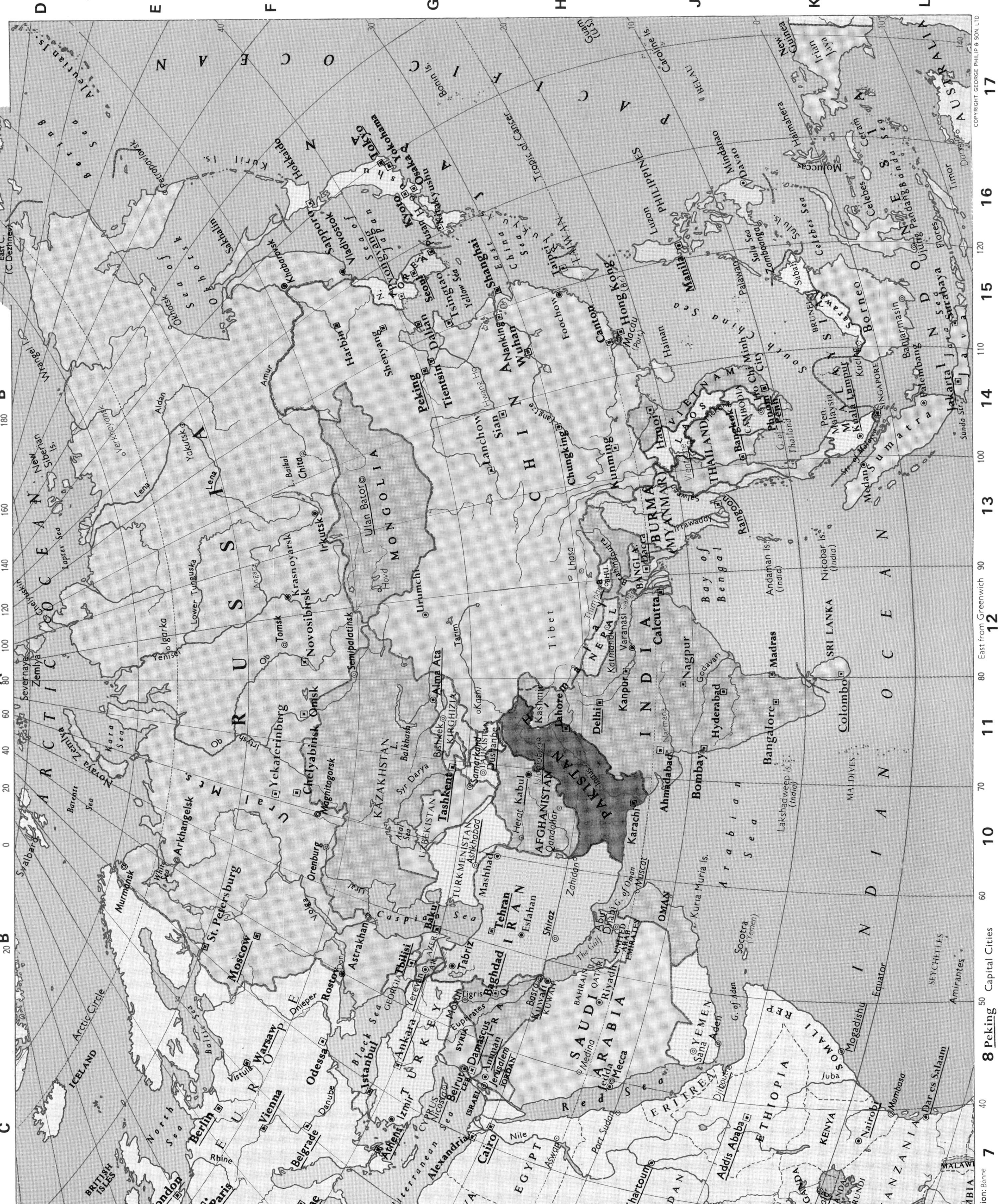

COPYRIGHT GEORGE PHILIP & SON LTD

PACIFIC OCEAN

ARCTIC OCEAN

INDIAN OCEAN

RUSSIA

CHINA

INDIA

MONGOLIA

KAZAKHSTAN

SAUDI ARABIA

IRAN

IRAQ

TURKEY

EGYPT

LIBYA

SUDAN

ETHIOPIA

SOMALI REP

KENYA

TANZANIA

ZAIRE

ZAMBIA

MALAWI

AFRICA

EUROPE

AUSTRALIA

PAKISTAN

AFGHANISTAN

TURKMENISTAN

UZBEKISTAN

TAJIKISTAN

KIRGHIZIA

NEPAL

BHUTAN

BANGLA

BURMA MYANMAR

THAILAND

VIETNAM

LAOS

CAMBODIA

MALAYSIA

INDONESIA

PHILIPPINES

BRUNEI

KOREA

JAPAN

Tibet

Tropic of Cancer

Arctic Circle

Equator

East from Greenwich

Peking
Tientsin
Shanghai
Nanking
Wuhan
Chungking
Sian
Lanchow
Kunming
Canton
Hong Kong (Br.)
Macau (Port.)
Foochow
Shenyang
Harbin
Tsingtao
Dairen
Yellow Sea
East China Sea
South China Sea
Hainan
Taipei
Hwang Ho

Tokyo
Yokohama
Osaka
Kyoto
Nagoya
Kobe
Sapporo
Hokkaido
Kyushu
Shikoku
Honshu
Kitakyushu
Sea of Japan
Pyongyang
Seoul
Pusan

Vladivostok
Khabarovsk
Petropavlovsk
Okhotsk
Sea of Okhotsk
Kuril Is.
Sakhalin
Magadan
Yakutsk
Chita
Irkutsk
L. Baikal
Ulan Bator
Krasnoyarsk
Novosibirsk
Tomsk
Semipalatinsk
Omsk
Chelyabinsk
Yekaterinburg
Magnitogorsk
Orenburg
Novaya Zemlya
Zemlya
Severnaya Zemlya
Svalbard
Murmansk
Arkhangelsk
St. Petersburg
Moscow
Astrakhan
Rostov
Odessa
Warsaw
Berlin
Vienna
Belgrade
Rome
Paris
London
BRITISH ISLES
ICELAND
Tbilisi
Baku
Yerevan
Ankara
Istanbul
Izmir
Athens
CYPRUS
Beirut
Damascus
SYRIA
Amman
JORDAN
ISRAEL
LEBANON
Baghdad
Basra
KUWAIT
BAHRAIN
QATAR
U.A.E.
Abu Dhabi
Dubai
Riyadh
OMAN
Muscat
YEMEN
Sana
Aden
Medina
Mecca
Jedda
Cairo
Alexandria
Khartoum
Port Sudan
Addis Ababa
Mogadishu
Nairobi
Mombasa
Dar es Salaam
Juba
Djibouti
ERITREA

Tehran
Esfahan
Shiraz
Tabriz
Mashhad
Zahidan
Ashkhabad
Kabul
Herat
Kandahar
Quetta
Islamabad
Lahore
Karachi
Delhi
Kanpur
Varanasi
Nagpur
Bombay
Ahmadabad
Hyderabad
Bangalore
Madras
Calcutta
Colombo
SRI LANKA
MALDIVES
Lakshadweep Is. (India)
Andaman Is. (India)
Nicobar Is. (India)
Bay of Bengal
Arabian Sea
Kashmir
Srinagar
Kathmandu
Thimphu
Dacca
Rangoon
Mandalay
Irrawaddy
Bangkok
Hanoi
Hué
Ho Chi Minh City
Phnom Penh
Vientiane
Pen. Malaysia
Kuala Lumpur
SINGAPORE
Medan
Palembang
Jakarta
Bandung
Surabaya
Sumatra
Java
Borneo
Kuching
Sabah
Sarawak
Brunei
Celebes
Celebes Sea
Sulu Sea
Sulu Is.
Zamboanga
Davao
Mindanao
Manila
Luzon
Moluccas
Ceram
Ceram Sea
Halmahera
New Guinea
Irian Jaya
Timor
Flores
Banda Sea
Java Sea
Sunda Str.
Str. of Malacca
Ujung Pandang
Balikpapan
Banjarmasin

Samarkand
Dushanbe
Bishkek
Alma Ata
Tashkent
Balkhash L.
Aral Sea
Syr Darya
Amu Darya
Urumchi
Tarim
Lhasa
Brahmaputra
Ganges
Indus
Godavari
Narmada
Ob
Irtysh
Yenisei
Lena
Aldan
Amur
Ural
Volga
Caspian Sea
Black Sea
Mediterranean Sea
Red Sea
The Gulf
G. of Oman
G. of Aden
Arctic Ocean
Kara Sea
Barents Sea
Laptev Sea
Bering Sea
Aleutian Is.
New Siberian Is.
Wrangel I.
East C. (C. Dezhnev)
North Sea
Baltic Sea
Danube
Rhine
Vistula
Dnieper
Don
Tigris
Euphrates
Nile
Aswan
Socotra (Yemen)
Kuria Muria Is.
SEYCHELLES
Amirantes
Belau
Caroline Is.
Guam (US)
Palawan
Projection: Bonne

8 Peking   Capital Cities

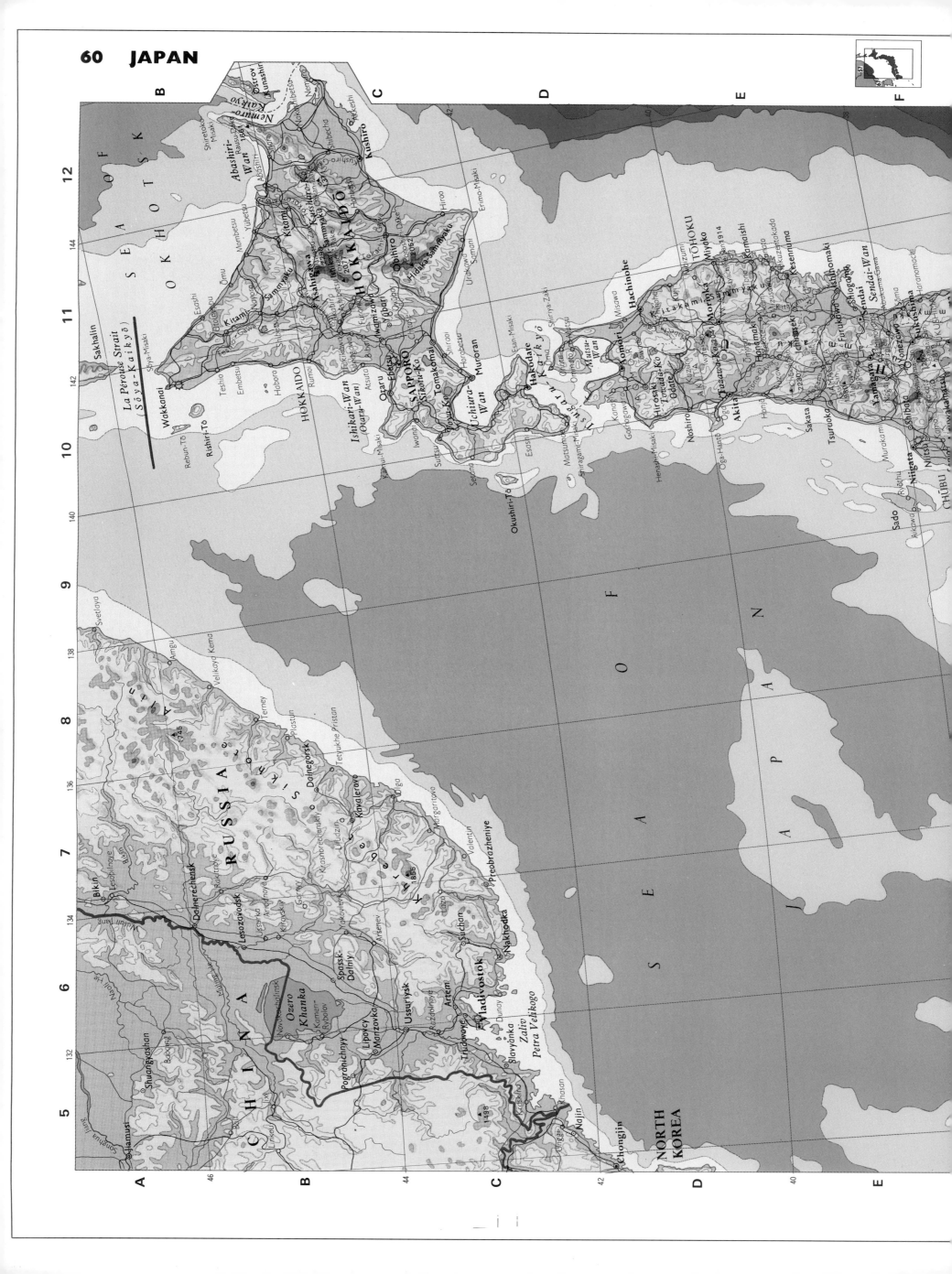

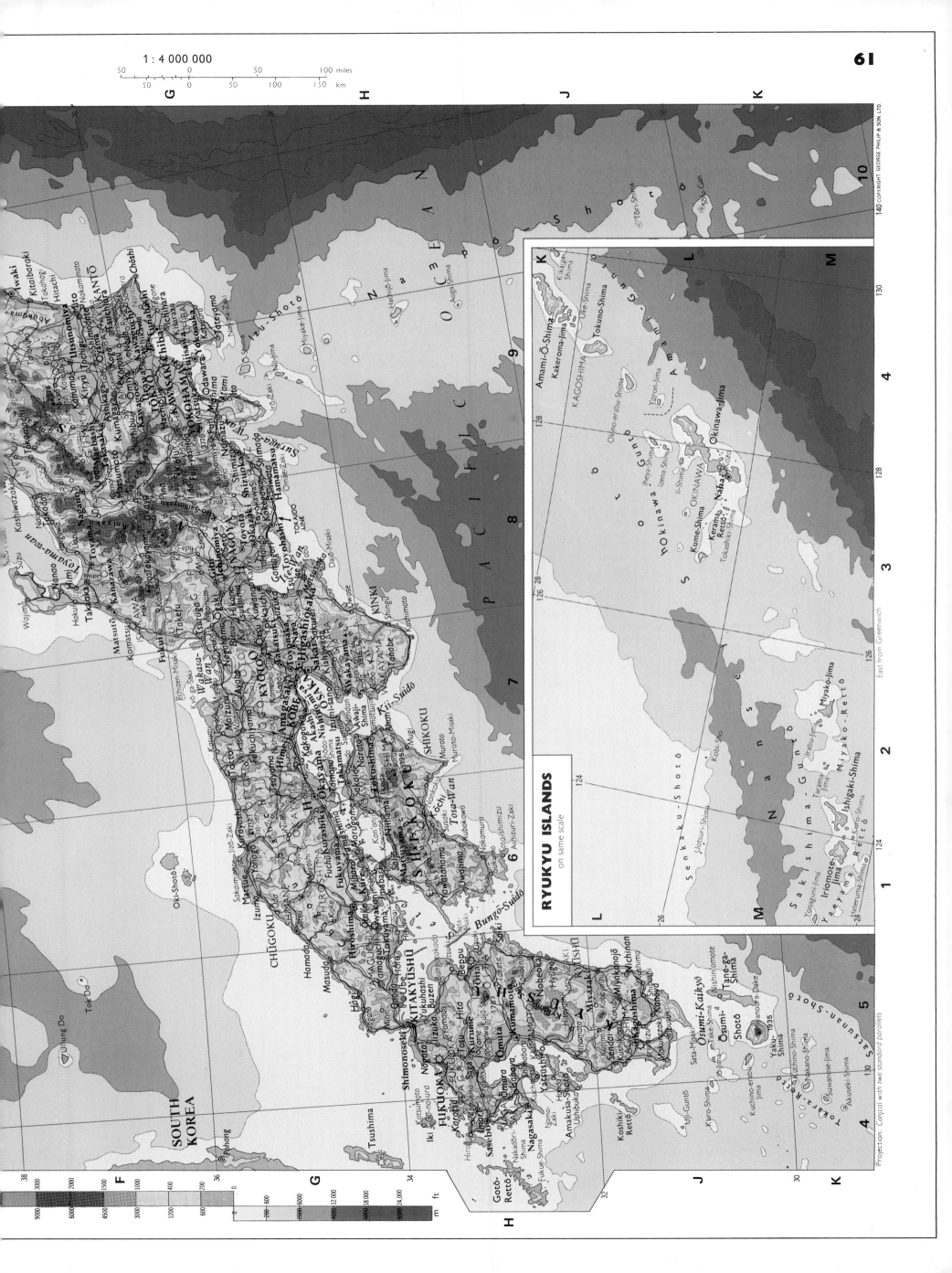

**SEA OF JAPAN**

SOUTH KOREA

CHŪGOKU-DISTRICT

HONS

SHIKOKU
SHIKOKU-DISTRICT

KYŪSHŪ
KYŪSHŪ-DISTRICT

Projection:
Lambert's Conformal
Conic

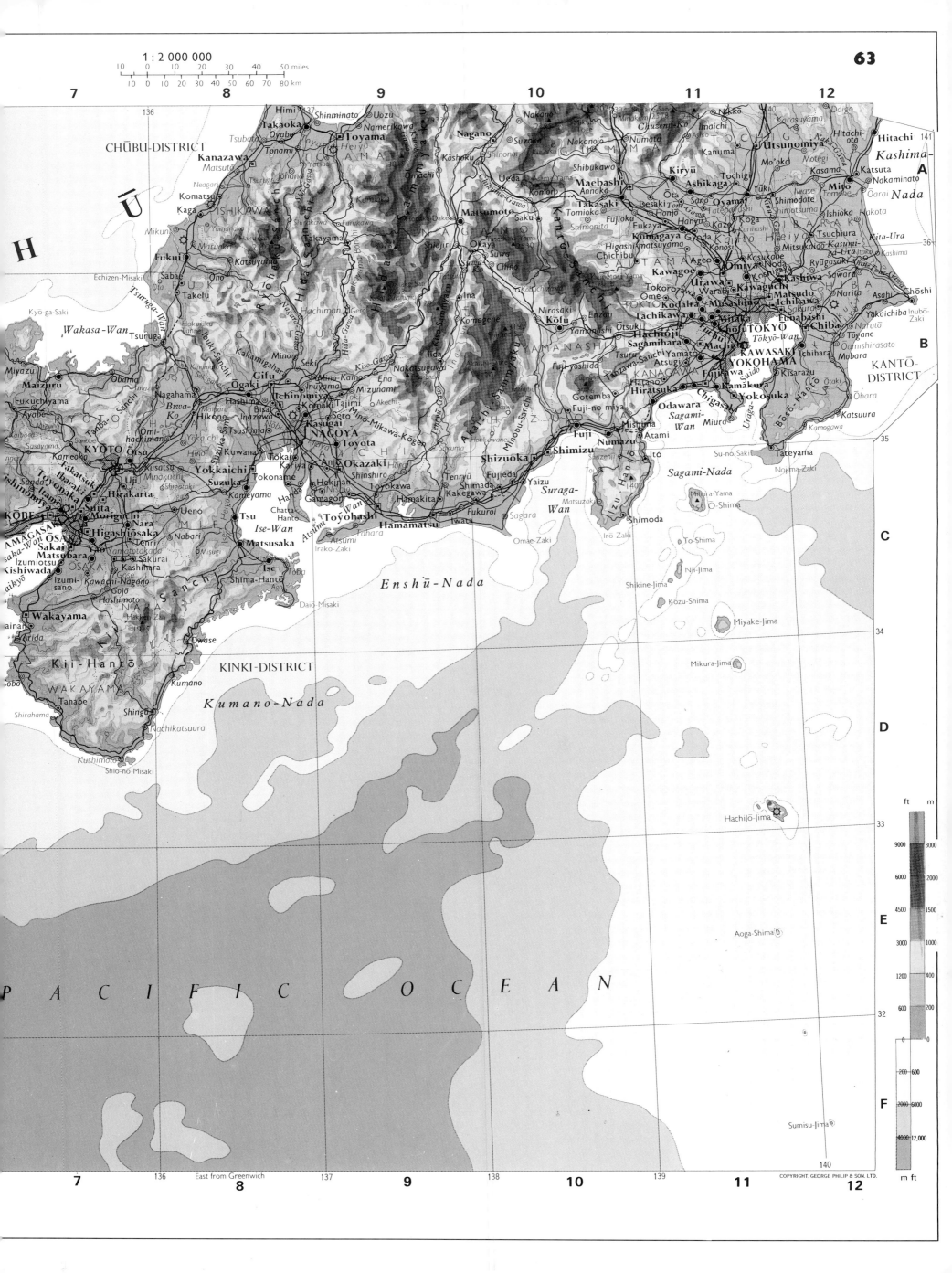

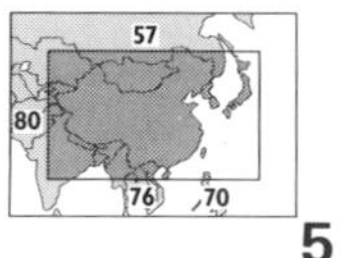

1  2  3  4  5

50

KAZAKHSTAN

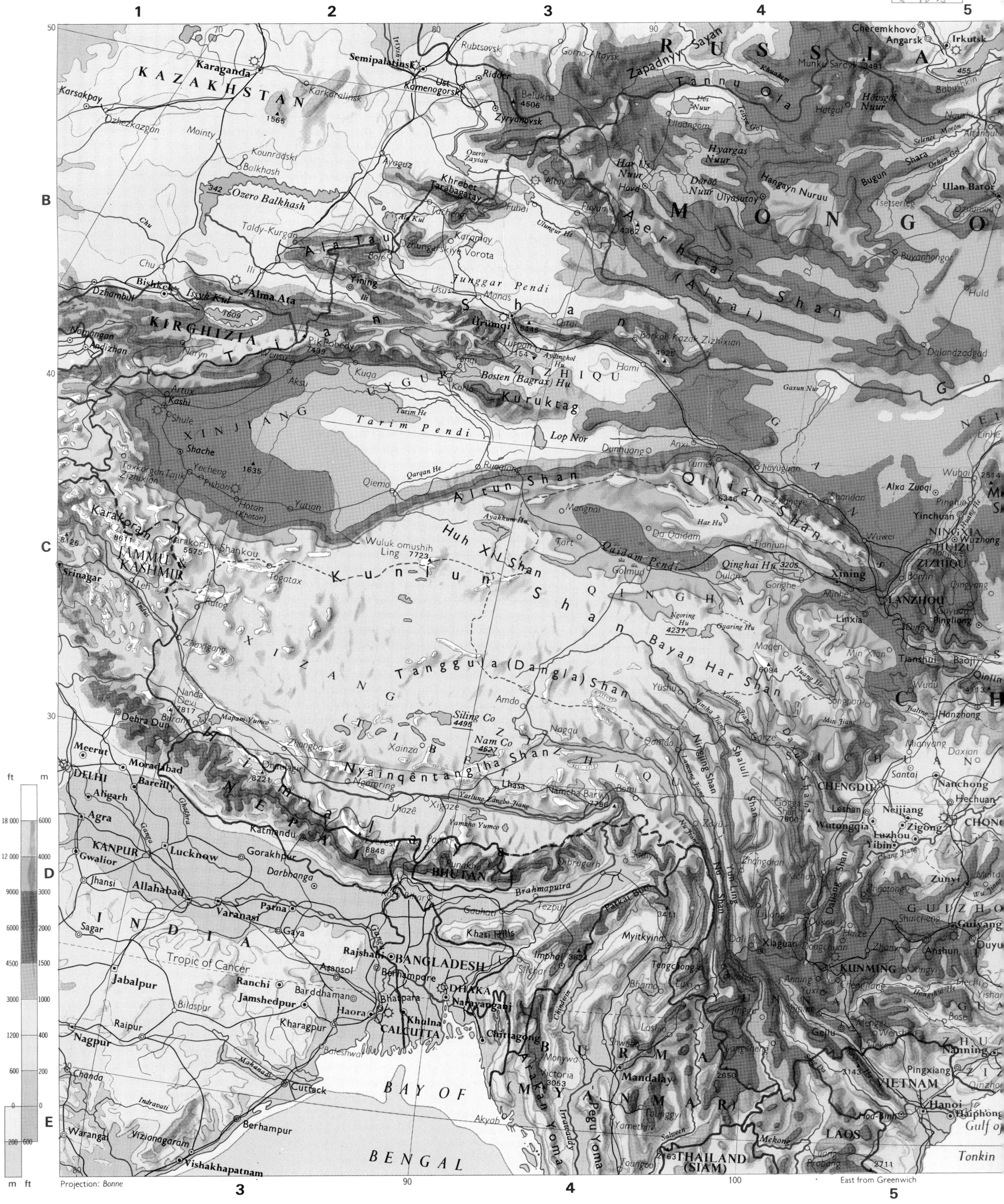

Karaganda
Karsakpay
Dzhezkazgan
Mointy
Kounradski
1565
Balkhash
342  Ozero Balkhash
Taldy-Kurgan
Chu
B
Chu
Bishkek
Dzhambul
Namangan  Andizhan
KIRGHIZIA
Artux  Kashi
Shule

Semipalatinsk
Rubtsovsk
Ust Kamenogorsk
Ridder
Belukha  4506
Zyryanovsk
Ozero Zaysan
Ayaguz
Dzhungarskiye Vorota
Ala Tau
Bole
Yining
Ili
Ala  Tau
4362
Alma Ata
1609
Pik Pobedy  7439
Naryn
Wensu
Aksu
Tarim He
Shache  1635
Yecheng
Pishan
Hotan (Khotan)
Yutian
Qiemo
Qarqan He

Irtysh
Karkaralinsk
80
Gorno-Altaysk
Zapadnyy  Sayan
Altay
Fuyun
Urungu He
Junggar Pendi
Usu
Manas
Ürümqi  8495
Qitai
Turpan  154
Aytingkol
Bosten (Bagrax) Hu
Kuruktag
Altun  Shan
Rb
90
RUSSIA
Tannu  Ola
Tovu  Nuur
Uds  Nuur
Har Us  Nuur
Hovd
MONGO
Aerh-tai  (Altai)  Shan
ZHIQU
4925
Barkol Kazak Zizhixian
Hami
Lop Nor
Dunhuang
Anxi
Ruoqiang

Cheremkhovo
Angarsk
Irkutsk
Munku Sardyk  3491
Hövsgöl  Nuur
Hatgal
455
Hyargas  Nuur
Dara  Nuur  Ulyasutay
Hangayn Nuruu
Bugun  Shara
Orhon Gol
Buyanhongor
Huld
Dalandzadgad
Ulan Bator
Ulaan Bator
GO
NEI

40

Tannu Ola

XINJIANG

Takskorgan Tajik
Zizhixian
C
Karakoram  8611
8126
JAMMU KASHMIR
Srinagar  Leh
Rutog
Zhaxigang

UYGUR
Tarim Pendi
Karakorum Shankou  5575
Togatax
Wuluk omushih
Ling  7723
Huh Xil Shan
Kun-lun
Tart
Ayakkum Hu
Mangnai
Qaidam  Pendi
Golmud
Da Qaidam
Har Hu
8346
Qilian  Shan
Zhangye
Yumen
Jiayuguan
Da
Minhe
Qinghai Hu  3205
Dulan
Gonghe
Xining
ZIZHIXIAN
Wuwei
Sharidan
Pingluo
Yinchuan
Alxa Zuoqi
Yinchuan
NINGXIA
HUIZU
Wuzhong
Qingyang
LANZHOU
Linxia
Pingliang
2514
Mx
C

30

Nanda Devi  7817
Dehra Dun
Mapam Yumco
Meerut
Moradabad
Aligarh
DELHI
Agra
Bareilly
KANPUR  Lucknow
Gwalior
Jhansi
Allahabad
Sagar
INDIA
Jabalpur
Chanda
Indravati
Nagpur
Raipur
Bilaspur
Warangal
Vizianagaram
Vishakhapatnam

Kunlun  Shan
XIZANG
Zhongba
Ghaghra
Zhangmu
Ngamring
NEPAL
8221
Katmandu
Gorakhpur
Darbhanga
Parna
Varanasi
Gaya
Tropic of Cancer
Asansol
Jamshedpur
Ranchi
Barddhaman
Kharagpur
Haora
CALCUTTA
Khulna
Baleshwar
Mahanadi
Cuttack
Berhampur

Qinghai
Tanggula (Dangla) Shan
Amdo
Siling Co  4495
Xainza
Nam Co  4627
Naqu
Nyainqêntanglha Shan
Lhasa
Xigaze
Lhaze
Yarlung Zangbo Jiang
Yamzho Yumco
Namcha Barwa  7756
Bomi
HIMALAYA
8848
BHUTAN
Phuntsholing
Brahmaputra
Tezpur
Gauhati
Dibrugarh
Khasi Hills
Imphal
Silchar
Rajshahi
Berhampore
DHAKA
Bhatpara
Narayanganj
Chittagong
BANGLADESH
Arakan
Akyab
BAY OF
BENGAL

Bayan Har Shan
Yushu
Ngoring Hu
Gyaring Hu  4237
Magen
6094
Yalong Jiang
Garze
Shaluli  Shan
Yangtze
Ningjing Shan
Zado
Qamdo
Min Xian
Songpan
Min Jiang
Dege
Zhongdian
Gongga Shan  7606
Leshan
Wutongqiao
Yibin
Zigong
Luzhou
Mianyang
Santai
CHENGDU
Neijiang
Daxian
SICHUAN
Nanchong
Hechuan
CHONG
Zunyi
Zhaotong
GUIZHOU
Guiyang
Anshun
Duyun
KUNMING
Anning
Chuxiong
Dali
Xiaguan
Dongchuan
YUNNAN
Gejiu
Mengzi
Wenshan
Pingxiang
Nanning

Tianshui
Baoji
Hanzhong
Qinlin
Wudu
Jialing
HUA

Baojji
C

RUSSIA

E

ft  m
18 000  6000
12 000  4000
9000  3000
6000  2000
4500  1500
3000  1000
1200  400
600  200
0  0
200  600
m  ft

D

Projection: Bonne

Nagqu
Nujiang
Salween
BURMA
(MYANMAR)
Myitkyina
Bhamo
Mandalay
Monywa
Victoria  3053
Shwebo
Lashio
Irrawaddy
Pegu Yoma
Arakan Yoma
Yametkin
2650
3143
VIETNAM
Hanoi
Haiphong
Gulf of
LAOS
Mekong
Luang
THAILAND
(SIAM)
8711
Tonkin

30

90  4  100  East from Greenwich  5

Projection: Bonne

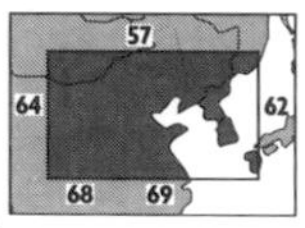

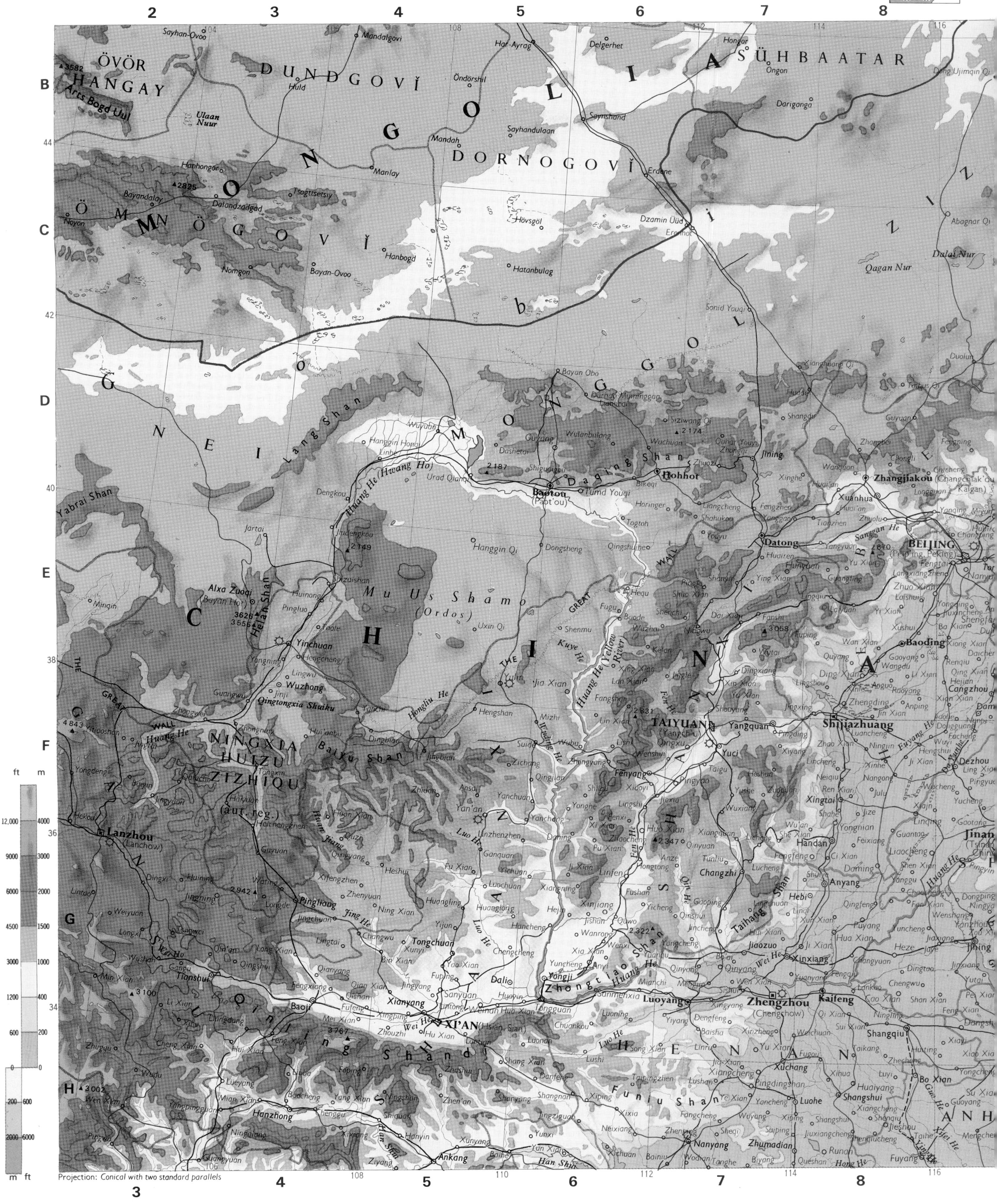

Grid: 2 3 4 5 6 7 8

**ÖVÖR HANGAY**
▲3582 Arts Bogd Uul
DUNDGOVĬ
**MONGOLIA**
SÜHBAATAR
Sayhan-Ovoo
Mandalgovĭ
Har-Ayrag
Delgerhet
Hongor
Öndörshil
Ongon
Ehin Ujimqin Qi
Huld
Ulaan Nuur
Darigonga
44
Hanhongor
Manlay
Sayhandulaan
Saynshand
Erdene
▲2825
Bayandalay
Mandah
**DORNOGOVĬ**
Dzamin Üüd
Ereen
Abagnar Qi
Dalandzadgad
Tsogttsetsiy
Hövsgöl
Ereenhot
**C**
Noyon
Nomgon
Bayan-Ovoo
Hanbogd
Hatanbulag
Sonid Youqi
Qagan Nur
Dalai Nur
**ÖM NÖ GOVĬ**
Duolun
42
**G**
**NEI**
Bayan Obo
Darhan Muminggan Lianheqi
Siziwang Qi
▲2174
Shangdu
Xilinguo Qi
Tianshan Qi
Guyuan
Zhongbei
Feicheng
**D**
Lang Shan
Wuyuan
Hanggin Houqi
Linhe
Dasheto
Guyang
Wulanbulang
Wuchuan
Zhuozi
Jining
Wanggian
Zhuozi
Xinghe
Zhangjiakou (Changchiak'ou) (Kalgan)
**MONGGOL**
Huhe
40
Huang He (Hwang Ho)
Urad Qianqi
▲2187
Shiguaigou
**Daqing Shan**
Hohhot
Xinghe
Huai an
Xuanhua
Yanqing Miyun
Jartai
Baotou (Paot'ou)
Tumd Youqi
Horinger
Shahukou
Tianzhen
Yangyuan
Yanging
**BEIJING (Peiping, Peking)**
Dengkou
Liangcheng
Youyu
Fengzhen
Datong
▲670
Fengtai
Togtoh
Qingshuihe
Huairen
Ying Xian
Guangling
Lanxiangzheng
Zhuozhou
**E**
Itdengkou
▲2149
Hanggin Qi
Dongsheng
Hequ
Shuo Xian
Dai Xian
Fanshi
Laishui
Yi Xian
Nany
Alxa Zuoqi (Bayan Hot)
Izuishan
Mingin
**Mu Us Shamo (Ordos)**
Uxin Qi
Shenmu
Baode
Wuzhai
Fugu
Shenchi
Kelan
Ningwu
▲3058
Fuping
Wan Xian
Quyang
**Baoding**
Xiong Xian
Daicher
▲3628 ▲3556
**Helan Shan**
Pingluo
Taole
Yinchuan
Hengcheng
Yongning
Uxin Qi
Jia Xian
Kuye He
Kelan
Yulin
Hongliu He
**GREAT**
**THE**
Qingxu
Yuci
Xiyang
Wan Xian
Qing Xian
Zhengding
Shijiazhuang
Hejian
Cangzhou
Dam
38
**THE GREAT WALL**
▲4843 Wudoushan
**NINGXIA HUIZU ZIZHIQU (aut. reg.)**
Wuzhong
Qingtongxia Shuiku
Lingwu
Jinji
Hengshan
Mizhi
**TAIYUAN (Yangku)**
▲2831 Yangquan
Pingding
Shouyang
Yuxian
Zhengding
Hengshui
Dezhou
Ling Xian
Pingyuan
Yucheng
**Huang He**
Zhongwei
Guangwu
Baiyu Shan
Dingbian
Zichang
Suide
Wubu
Lin Xian
Benxi
Zhaocheng
▲2347 Qinyuan
Yushe
Wuxiang
Shahe
Shabi
Ren Xian
Nangong
Wuqiang
Xingtai
Jize
Ji Xian
**JIN**
**F**
Hekou
Yongdeng
Jingtai
Haiyuan
Huining
Tongxin
Yanchuan
Yan'an
Yanchang
Yongho
Daning
Xi Xian
Xiangning
Hongtong
Linfen
Changzhi
Lucheng
Dming
Qiu Xian
Feixiang
Handan
Liaocheng
Dongping
Linqing
**SHANXI**
Pingyin
**Lanzhou (Lanchow)**
Dingxi
Longde
Pingliang
▲2942
Zhenyuan
Ning Xian
Zichang
Huangling
Huanglong
Yijun
Fu Xian
Ichuan
Jishan
Hejin
Quwo
▲2324
Yicheng
Fushan
Hongtong
Xinjiang
Anze
Tunliu
Changzhi
Gaoping
Jincheng
Hebi
Anyang
Qingfeng
Fuyang
Juye
Jiaxiang
Heze
Jining
**G**
Weiyuan
Lintao
Qin'an
Longxi
Qingshui
Heshui
Qingyang
Zhenyuan
Pingliang
Jing He
Changwu
Huangling
Luo He
Hancheng
Jishan
Wanrong
Wenxi
Yuanqu
Yuncheng
Jiyuan
Qinyang
Wuzhi
Xinxiang
Yanjin
Fengqiu
Chengwu
Dingtao
Jinxiang
**Tianshui**
▲3100
Li Xian
Gangu
Zhuanglang
Lingtai
Lingtai
Changwu
Yijun
Jingyang
Sanyuan
Fuping
Dali
Linyi
Yongji
Zhongtiao Shan
**Zhongtiao Shan**
Sanmenxia
Mianchi
**Luoyang**
Zhengzhou (Chengchow)
Kaifeng
Cao Xian
Shan Xian
Feng Xian
Dangshan
**QIN LING SHAN**
Qianyang
Baoji
Fufeng
Xingping
Zhouzhi
Weinan
Hua Xian
Tongguan
**XI'AN (Hsian, Sian)**
Wei He
Mei Xian
▲3767
Hu Xian
Lantian
Chuankou
Luonan
Lushi
Song Xian
Yiyang
Dengfeng
Baisha
Xinzheng
**HENAN**
Weichuan
Sui Xian
Shangqiu
**H**
▲3002
Wen Xian
Lueyang
Mian Xian
Yang Xian
Fengxian
Shiquan
Ningshan
Zhen'an
Shangnan
Xichuan
Neixiang
Zhenping
Xixia
Lushan
Pingdingshan
Xiangcheng
Xiangcheng
Luohe
Shangshui
Shangshui
Huaiyang
Bo Xian
**Funiu Shan**
Taipingzhen
Shanyang
**ANH**
Hanzhong
Ningqiang
Hanyin
Ziyang
**Han Shui**
Ankang
Xunyang
Baihe
Yun Xian
Yunxi
**Luo He**
Zhenping
Fangcheng
**Nanyang**
Zhumadian
Jiuxiangcheng
Jieshou
Luohe
Runan
Biyang
Tonghe
Queshan
Hang He
Hai He
Fuyang

**Projection: Conical with two standard parallels**

Elevation scale:
ft / m
12,000 / 4000
9000 / 3000
6000 / 2000
4500 / 1500
3000 / 1000
1200 / 400
600 / 200
0 / 0
200 / 600
2000 / 6000
m / ft

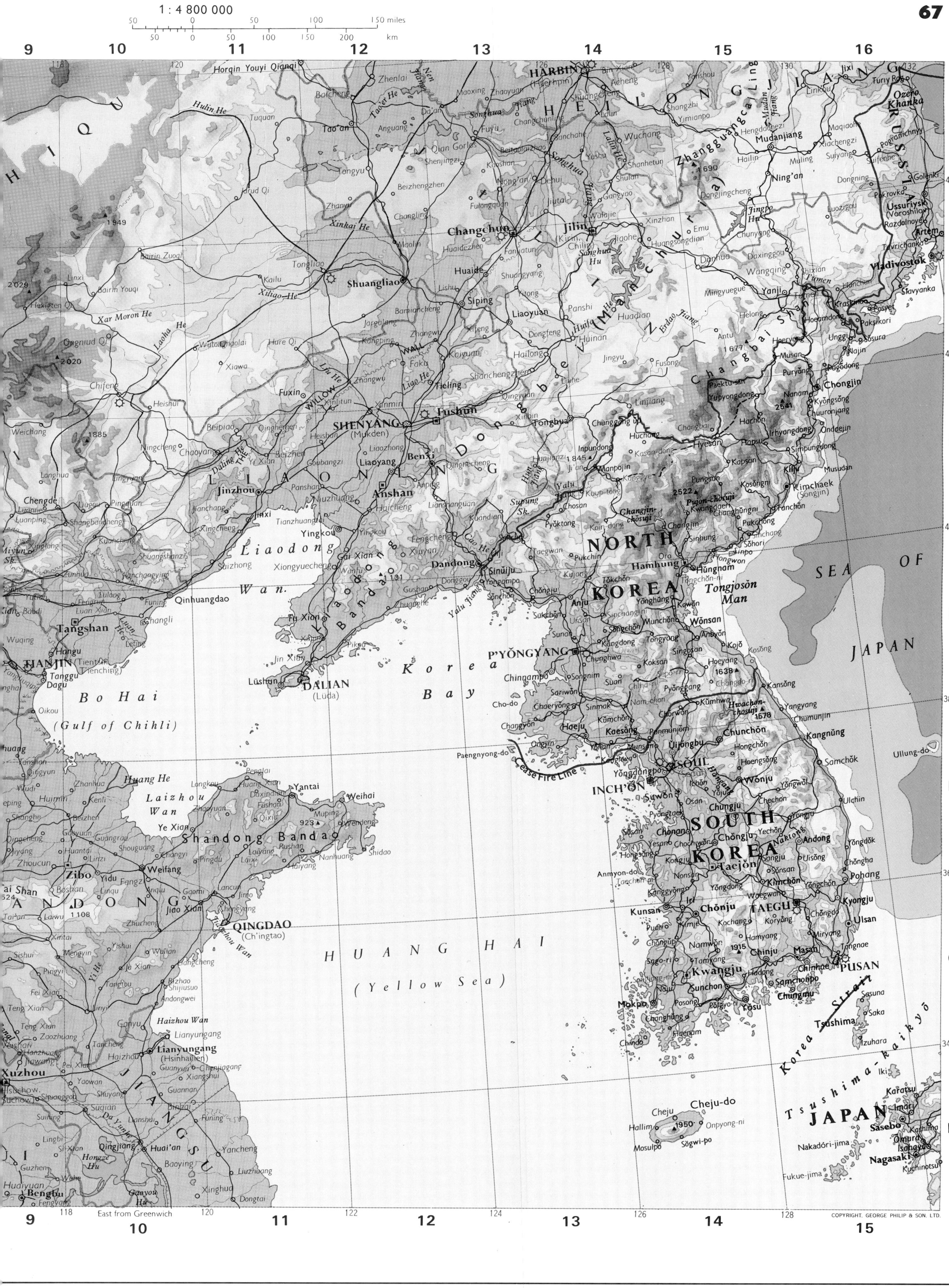

1 : 4 800 000

50  0  50  100  150 miles
50  0  50  100  150  200 km

9  10  11  12  13  14  15  16

Horqin Youyi Qianqi

HEILONGJIANG

HARBIN (Ha'erhpin)

RUSSIA

Ozero Khanka

B

Zhenlai  Nen  Jiang  Da'an  Maoxing  Zhaoyuan  Acheng  Shou  Bin Xian  LinKou  Turiy Rog  Jixi

Hulin He  Songhua  Changchunling  Shangzhi  Yimianpo  Hengdaohezi  Maqiao  Pogranichnyy  Golenki

Tao'an  Anguang  Qian Gorlos  Beidaolangzi  Lalin He  Yushu  Wuchang  Hailin  Mudanjiang  Xiachengzi  Suifenhe  Ussuriysk (Voroshilov)

44

Tongyu  Shenjingzi  Dehui  Nong'an  Jiutai  Shulan  Ning'an  690  Muling  Suiyang  Dongning  Razdolnoye  Artem

Zhanwu  Fuyu  Changchunling  Songhua Hu  Jiaohe  Emu  Chunyang  Wangqing  Dongjingcheng  Luozigou  Pokrovka

Changling  Changchun  Jilin (Kirin)  Fanjiatun  Mingyuegue  Tumen  Kraskino  Slavyanka

C

Huaide  Shuangyang  Dunhua  Daxinggou  Yanji  Hunchun  Tixian  Vladivostok

Shuangliao  Lishu  Yitong  Panshi  Helong  Antu  Paktu-san  Hoeryong  Pogdong  Paksibori

Siping  Liaoyuan  Huinan  Huadian  Jingyu  Changbai Shan  1677  Musan  Najin

42

Xihgo-He  Jargalang  Kaiyuan  Dongfeng  Hailong  Lianjiang  Fusong  Hyesan  Puryong  Chongjin

Kailu  Tongliao  Zhangwu  Xifeng  Shanchengzhen  Jingyu  Chungang  Changbai  Hachon  Irhyongdong  Onddejin

Chifeng  Kangping  Tieling  Qinghemen  Dongfeng  Tonghua  Linjiang  Inpundong  Huchang  2541  Nanam

Xinmin  Faku  Liao He  Kuandian  Tongjiang  Kapsan  Kimchaek (Songjin)

D

Fuxin  Fushun  Qingyuan  Huaishagzi  1845  Manpojin  Kingpye  Pungsan  Kosong-ni  Kilju  Musudan

Beipiao  Heishan  SHENYANG (Mukden)  Liaozhong  Shanchengzhen  Koin-dong  Kuup-tong  2522  Simpungdong

LIAONING  Benxi  Yalu  Supung Sk.  Chosan  Changjin-chosuji  Changjin  Pukchong  Pukchong

Chaoyang  Xinbin  Anshan  Liaoyang  Qingchengzi  Pyoktong  Pujon-chosuji  Kwangdaei  Changhunghni  Tanchon

Jinzhou  Lianshanguan  Yalu Jiang  Taegwan  Sinhung  Sohori

40

Ningcheng  Muzhuang  Panshan  Xiyan  Huanren  Kuandian  Sunjiang  NORTH  Hamhung  Hungnam

Chengde  Jianchang  Jiaxi  Gai Xian  Cao He  Gushan  Sinuiju  Sinbung  Kowon  Tongjoson Man

Liaodong  Tianzhuangtai  Xiongyuecheng  Dandong  Dongqou  Yongampo  Kujang  Sinanju  Wonsan  KOREA

Langhua  Yingkou  Fengcheng  Sonchon  Chongju  Yonghung  Wonju  Anbyon

E

Luanping  Wan.  Fu Xian  Pikou  Huangchi  Sukchon  Songchon  Yangdok  Munchon  Kosong

Qinhuangdao  Changli  Liao Band  Jin Xian  Yalu Jiang  Anju  Singang  Yangdong  Hoeyang  Yangyang

Funing  Jian-chang  Lüshun  Korea Bay  Chunghwa  Koksan  Pyonggang  Hwachon-chosuji  1678  Kansong

TANGSHAN  Hangu  DALIAN (Lüda)  P'YŎNGYANG  Chinnampo  Songnim  Suan  Pyonggang  Chumunjin

Tanggu  Dagu  Cho-do  Sariwon  Sinmak  Ichon  1638  Kangnung

38

TIANJIN (Tientsin, Tienching)  Bo Hai (Gulf of Chihli)  Chaeryong  Kaesong  Panmunjon  Chunchon

Oikou  Changyon  Haeju  Uijongbu  Hongchon  Samchok

Paengnyong-do  Ongjin  Munsan  SŎUL  Hoengsong  Ullung-do

Huang He  Penglai  Longkou  Cease Fire Line  Yongdongpo  Wonju  Yongwol  Ulchin

Zhanhua  Yantai  INCH'ŎN  Suwon  Chechon  F

Wudi  Laizhou Wan  Weihai  Osan  Chungju  Yechon  Andong  Yongdok

Huimin  Ye Xian  923  Muping  Wendeng  SOUTH  Chongju  Yongju  Chonha

Zibo  Weifang  Shandong Banda  Shidao  KOREA  Kongju  Chungju  Naktong  Uisong  Pohang

Yidu  Changyi  Laixi  Nanhuang  Hongsong  Chochiwon  Andong  Kimchon  Kyongju

36

Bozhan  Linqu  Jiao Xian  Anmyon-do  Taedok-ni  Nonsan  Taejŏn  Waegwan  Pohang

Jido Xian  Zhucheng  Taejŏn  Yongdong  TAEGU  Chongdo  Kyongju

Jinan  1 108  QINGDAO (Ch'ingtao)  Kunsan  Iri  Chŏnju  Kimje  Koryong  Miryang  Ulsan

Xintai  Mengyin  Wulian  Kunsan  Chŏngup  Namwon  1915  Chinju  Masan  Tongnae

G

Teng Xian  Je Xian  Tancheng  HUANG HAI (Yellow Sea)  Kwangju  Chungmu  PUSAN

Zoozhuang  Linyi  Kwangju  Suncheon  Chinhae  Samchonpo  Korea Strait  Tsushima

Xuzhou  Lianyungang (Hsinhailien)  Mokpo  Changhung  Yosu  Chindo  Tsushima-kaikyo  Sasuna  Saka  JAPAN

34

JIANGSU  Haizhou Wan  Hwanam  Iki  Karatsu  Imari

Huai'an  Cheju  Cheju-do  Onpyong-ni  Nakadori-jima  Sasebo  Omura  Isahaya

Huaiyuan  Bengbu  Qingjiang  Baoying  Mosulpo  1950  Sŏgwi-po  Fukue-jima  Nagasaki  Kuchinotsu

9  10  11  12  13  14  15

East from Greenwich  COPYRIGHT. GEORGE PHILIP & SON. LTD.

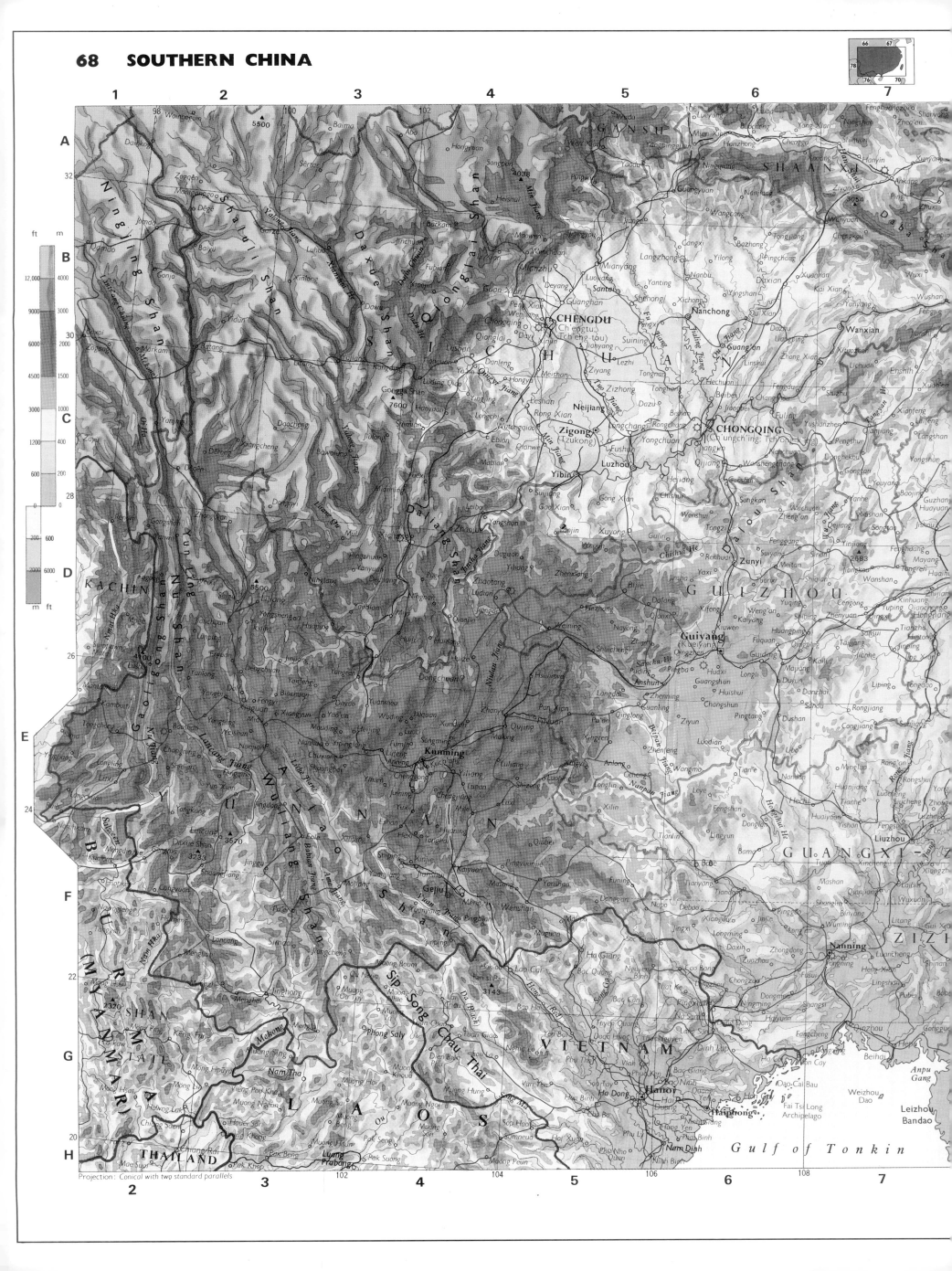

1 : 4 800 000

50  0  50  100  150 miles
50  0  50  100  150  200 km

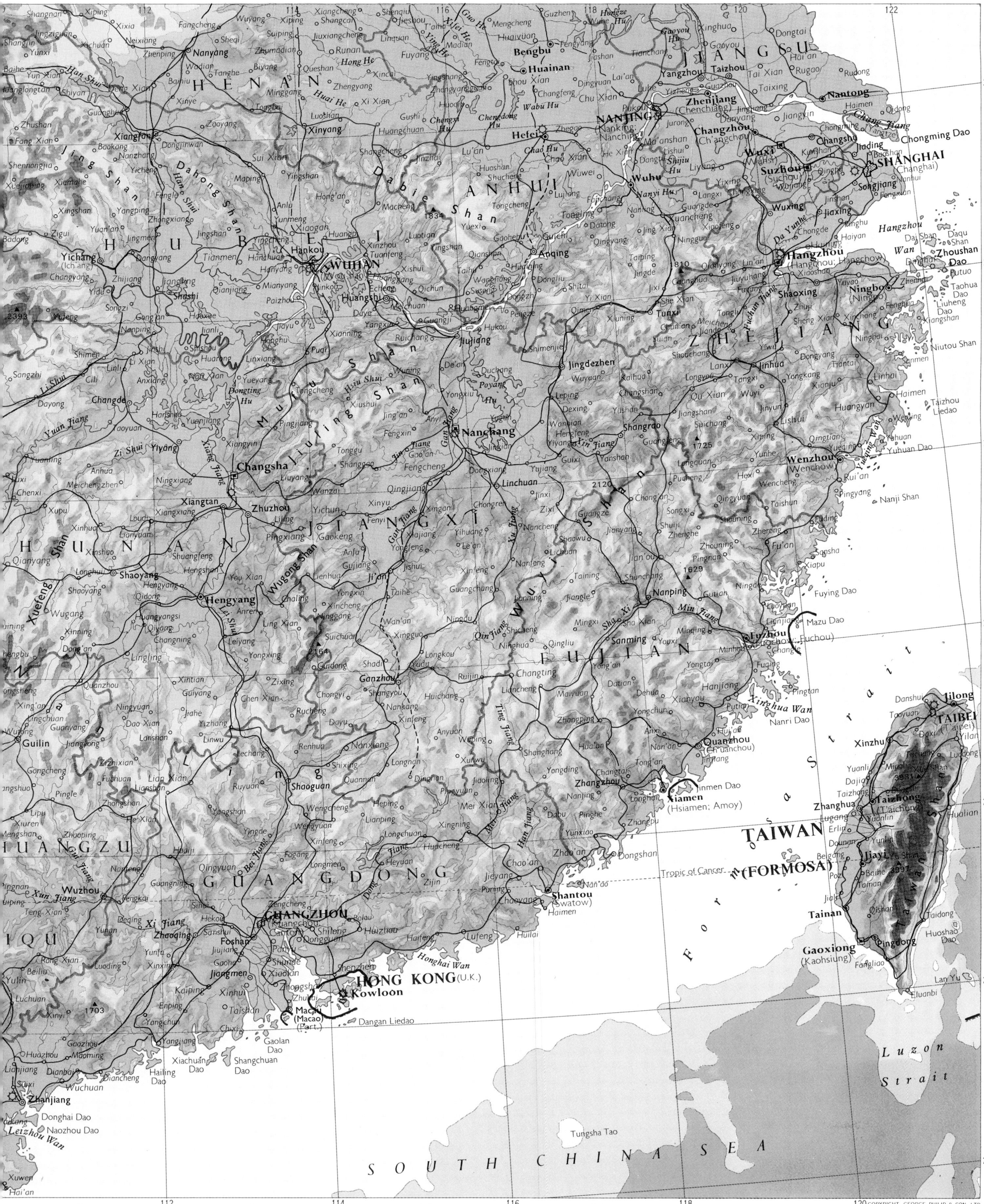

HENAN  ANHUI  JIANGSU  SHANGHAI

HUBEI  WUHAN  Hankou  Hanyang

Nanjing (Nanking)  Hefei  Bengbu  Huainan

ZHEJIANG  Hangzhou (Hangchow)  Ningbo (Ningpo)  Shaoxing

HUNAN  JIANGXI  Nanchang  Changsha  Xiangtan  Zhuzhou

Hengyang  Guilin  Jingdezhen  Wenzhou (Wenchow)

FUJIAN  Fuzhou (Fuchou)  Nanping  Sanming

Quanzhou (Ch'uanchou)  Xiamen (Hsiamen; Amoy)  Zhangzhou

TAIWAN (FORMOSA)  TAIBEI (Taipei)  Jilong  Taizhong (T'aichung)

Taichong  Tainan  Gaoxiong (Kaohsiung)  Pingdong

GUANGDONG  Guangzhou  Foshan  Shantou (Swatow)

HONG KONG (U.K.)  Kowloon  Macau (Macao) (Port.)

GUANGXI  Wuzhou  Zhanjiang

Tropic of Cancer

SOUTH CHINA SEA

Luzon Strait

Formosa Strait

1 : 3 200 000

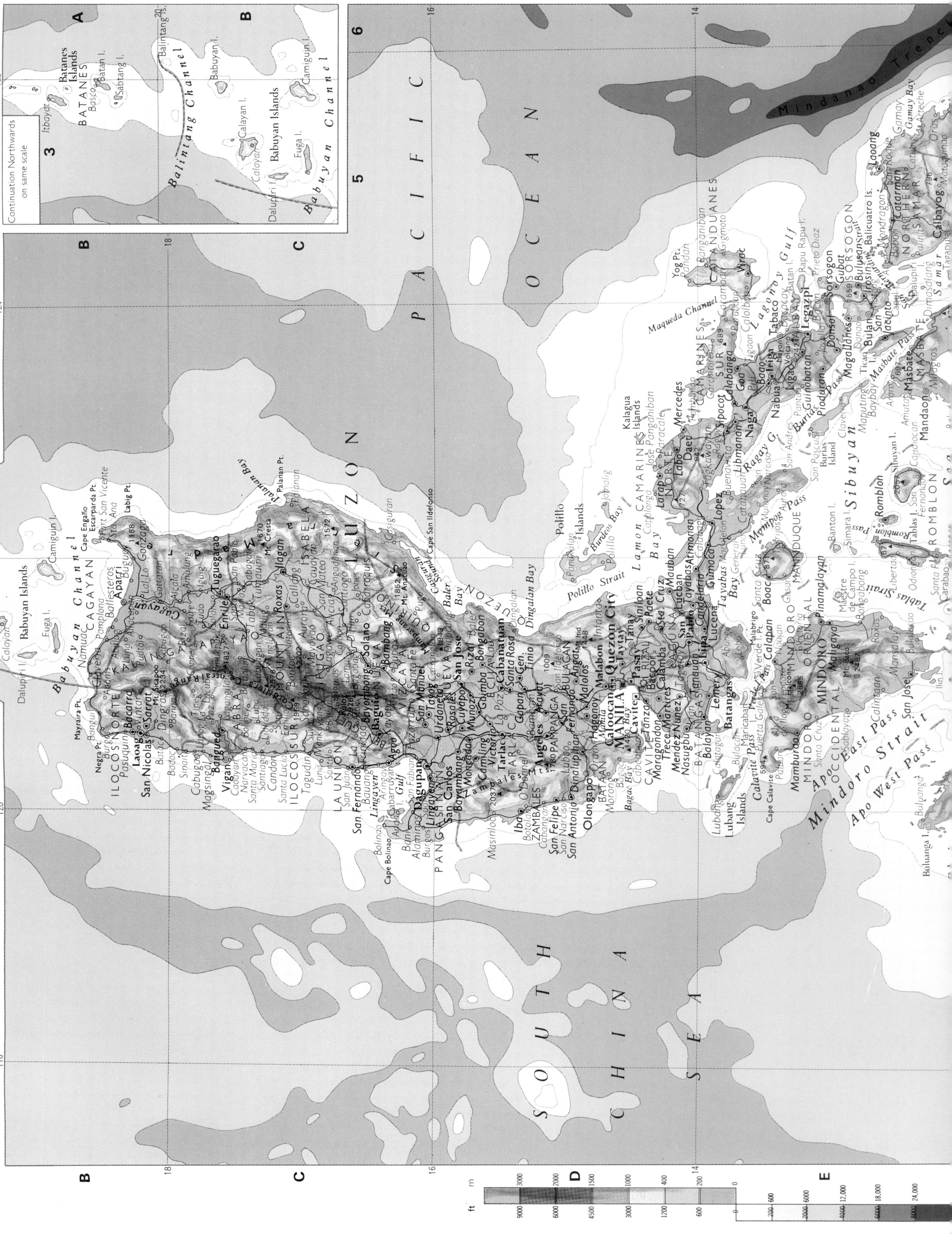

25    0    50    100 miles
25    0    50    100    150 km

**Continuation Northwards on same scale**

BATANES

Batanes Islands
Basco
Batan I.
Sabtang I.
Itbayat

Babuyan Is.
Balintang Channel
Babuyan I.
Camiguin I.
Babuyan Islands
Calayan I.
Fuga I.
Dalupiri I.
Calayan
Babuyan Channel

PACIFIC OCEAN

SOUTH CHINA SEA

Mindanao Trench

LUZON

Babuyan Islands
Calayan I.
Fuga I.
Babuyan Channel
Camiguin I.
Dalupiri I.

ILOCOS NORTE
Laoag
Bacarra
San Nicolas
Sarrat
Cape Engaño
Escarpada Pt.
Cape San Vicente
Port San Vicente
Santa Ana
Palanan Pt.
Palanan Bay

CAGAYAN
Namuac
Aparri
Pamplona
Ballesteros
Buguey

ISABELA
Ilagan
Cauayan

Vigan
ILOCOS SUR
Tagudin
Candon
Narvacan

MOUNTAIN PROVINCE
Baguio
ABRA
Bangued

LA UNION
San Fernando
Lingayen
PANGASINAN
Dagupan
San Carlos

ZAMBALES
San Felipe
San Antonio
San Narciso
Olongapo
BATAAN
Morong

TARLAC
Tarlac
Angeles
PAMPANGA
NUEVA ECIJA
Cabanatuan
San Jose

BULACAN
Malolos
MANILA
Caloocan
Quezon City
Cavite
CAVITE
RIZAL
LAGUNA
Calamba
Batangas
BATANGAS
Lucena
QUEZON
Lucban
Infanta
Baler

Polillo
Polillo Islands
Polillo Strait

Lamon Bay
CAMARINES NORTE
Daet
CAMARINES SUR
Naga
Iriga
Legazpi
ALBAY
Sorsogon
SORSOGON
Gubat

CATANDUANES
Virac

MASBATE
Masbate

SAMAR
Catarman
Calbayog

Sibuyan Sea
Sibuyan I.
ROMBLON
Romblon
Tablas I.

MINDORO
MINDORO ORIENTAL
MINDORO OCCIDENTAL
Calapan
Mamburao

Lubang Islands
Lubang

Apo West Pass
Apo East Pass
Mindoro Strait

Maqueda Channel
Lagonoy Gulf
Ragay Gulf
Ticao I.
Burias I.

ft
24,000
18,000
12,000
6000
2000
600
200
0
600
1200
3000
4500
6000
9000

m
9000
6000
4500
3000
2000
1500
1000
400
200
0

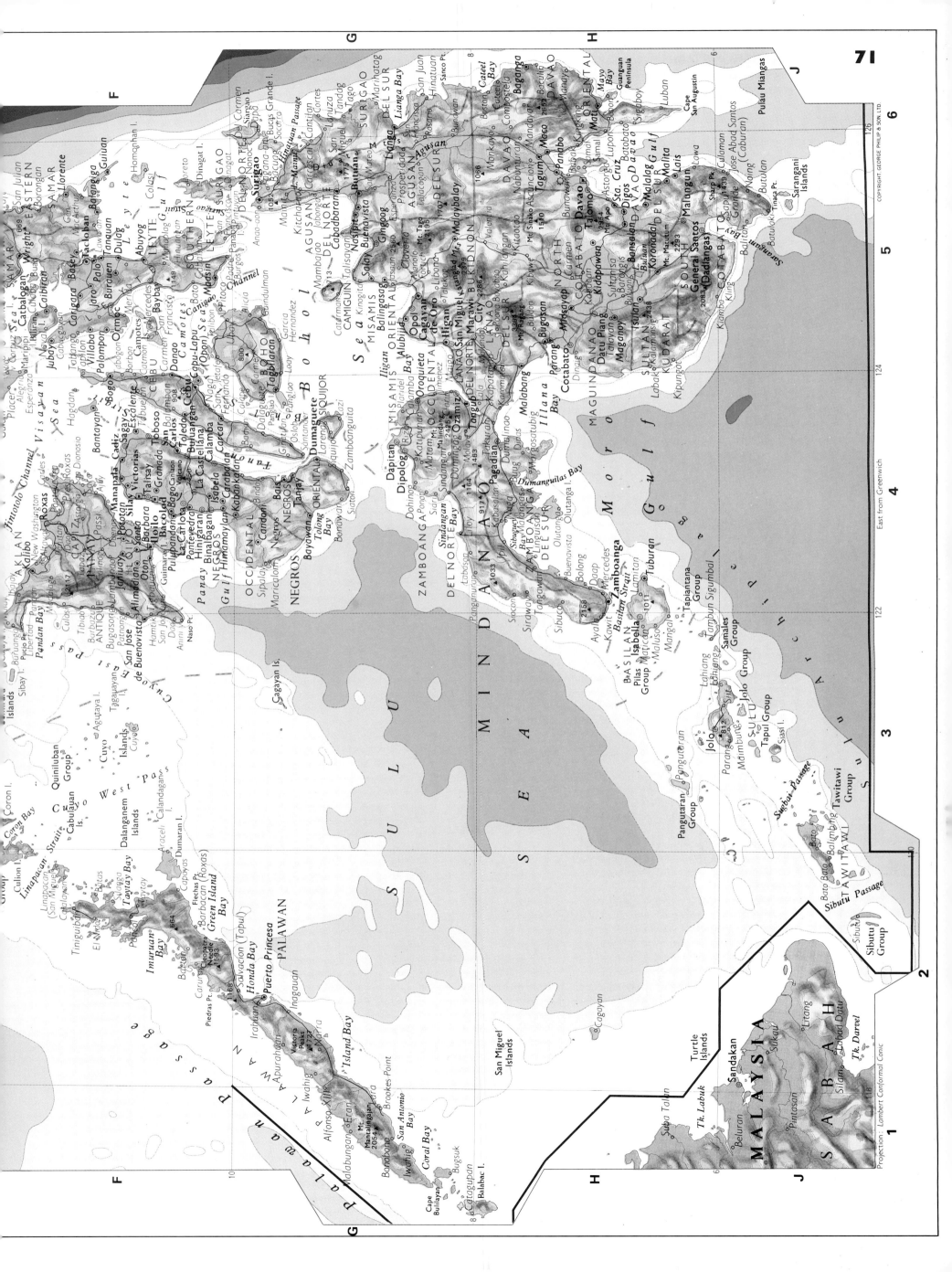

1       2       3

**A**

1346
Tawau
Semporna
120
Teluk Sebuku
Lama

**S U L A W E S I**

**S E A**

Kepulauan Talaud

Bulu
Karakelong
Beo

Tahuna
Kaburuang

Sesayap
Malinau
Bunju
Tarakan

Siau

Sangihe

Kepulauan Sangihe

Biaro

**Morotai**
Sopi

Nomeh
2053
Tanjungselor

Tanjungbatu

Maratua

Rau
Berebere
Wayabula

**BORNEO**

Berau

Tanjungredeb
Dumaring

▼ 5315

Manado 2022
Kema
Tondano

Bangka
Tahulandang

Dol

Mayu
Ibu

Tobelo
Akelamo

**Halmahera**

Tolitoli
Teluk Dondo
Buol
Paleleh
Sumalata
Amurang

2300
Tentolomatinan
Kuandang
Gambuta

Ternate
Spasiu
Tidore

Teluk Buli
Patoni

**TIMUR**

Bontang

Ogomas
2913

2707
Maling

**UTARA**

Tomini

1954
Gorontalo

Tilamuta

Kotamobagu

Makian

Weda
Teluk Weda

0 Equator

Muarakaman

Tenggarong

Muakaman

Samarinda

Songasanga

Sungaitiram

Donggala
Toboli

Parigi

**Teluk Tomini**

Muotong

Kayoa

Wosi

Kepulauan Toglan

Kepulauan Bacan

Lobuha
Gani

Balikpapan

Palu
3724

Poso

Tojo

Toili
Toili

Pati

Maliku

Luwuk

Mandioli

**Bacan**

Lariang

Balease

Toili

Banggai

Obilatu
Obi

Bisa
Sesepe

Tanahgrogot

**Peleng**

Kepulauan Obilatu

Loit
Fluk

**B**

Jangeru

**T E N G A H**

**SULAWESI**

**(CELEBES)**

Kolonodale
Teluk Tolo

Kepulauan Banggai

Taliabu

Mangole

Auponhia
Sanana

**M O L U C C A**

Fluk

Kepulauan Balabalangan
(Paternoster)

Mamuju

Masamba
3016

Tangkelemboke
1782

Kepulauan Sula
Sanana

**S E R A M**

Kotabaru

Masang
3074

Palopo

Manui

Piru

Sebuku

Makale

Ranteкombola
3455

Mekongga
2790

Mondeodo

Kaupalamada
2429
Namlea

**Buru**

Karambu

Majene

Enrekang

Pinrang

**Ambon**
Ambon

Pulau
Laut

**SELATAN**

Teluk Mandar

Polewali

Rappang

Singkang

**TENGGARA**

Kolaka
Kendari

Manui

Monse

Wamsasi

Tifu
Kayeli
Lima

Parepare

Polewali

Watangsoppeng

Sumpangbinangae

Pampanua
Watampone

Wowoni

Leksula
Namrole

Pangkajene

Marek

Buapinang
Roha

**I**   **N**   **D**   **O**   **N**

Ujung Pandang

Maros
Sinjai

Pising

**Muna**

**Butung**

Wangiwangi

5 Sungguminasa

Lompobatang
2871

Cawele

Baubau

Kepulauan

**C**

Kepulauan Masalima

Pattallassang

Bantaeng
Bulukumba

**Kabaena**

Binongko

Tukangbesi

**B**   **A**   **N**   **D**   **A**

Bontosunggu

Batuata
(Watuata I.)

Gunungapi

**Salayar**

Benteng

5888
▼

Damar

Kepulauan
Bone Rate

Tanahjampea

Kalao

Kalaotoa

**Wetar**
Wesiri

Kepulauan
Romang

Bone
Rate

Ilwaki

**F L O R E S   S E A**

**Lesser Sunda Islands**

Selat Wetar
Kisar

Moa
Lakar

**Lombok**

Tambora
2821

Sangeang

Adonara
Pantar
Kalabahi

Atauro

Leti
Kepulauan
Leti

Rinjani
3726
Selong

Mojo
Sumbawa
Besar

Raba

Komodo
Labuhanbajo

Larantuka

**Alor**
Selat Ombai

Bacan
Tutuala

Mataram

Dompu

Sape

Ruteng

**Flores**

Lomblen

Dili
**TIMOR**

Dompu

Parado

Rinca

Aimere
Maumere

Solor

Atapupu

Viqueque

**Sumbawa**

Taliwang

Selat Sumba

Ende

Pante
Macassar

Atambua

**Timor**

Uato-Udo

Memboro

**NUSA TENGGARA TIMUR**

Naikliu
Kefamenanu

**NUSA TENGGARA BARAT**

**Sumba**

Waikabubak

Waingapu

Melolo

**S A W U   S E A**

Pacit
Soe
Nikiniki

**T I M O R   S E A**

**D**

Baing

Semau
Kupang

Raijua
Sawu

Baa
Roti

Dana

Projection: Mercator

120

East from Greenwich

1       2       3

ft   m
12,000   4000
9000   3000
6000   2000
4500   1500
3000   1000
1200   400
600   200
0   0
600   200
6000   2000
12,000   4000
18,000   6000
24,000   8000
m   ft

1 : 5 600 000

50    0    50    100    150    200 miles
50    0    50    100    150    200    250    300 km

4          5          6

130                    135                    140

**PACIFIC**

**OCEAN**

A

Tobi
(Belau)    Helen
Atoll

Kepulauan
Asia

Kepulauan
Mapia

Kepulauan
Ayu

4625

Equator                    0

Gebe
Umera    Kabarai    Waigeo    Wikre
Selpele
Gam    Saonek    Kwoka    Waibeem    Kaironi    Wersa    Kepulauan
3000    Manokwari    Karim    Supriori
Sorong    Jazirah Doberai    Namber    Biak    Bosnik
Batanta    (Vogelkop)    Numfoor    Biak    Kepulauan
Salawati    Klamono    Num    Padaido
Kofiau    Sailolof    Wersar    3100    Ransiki    Selat Yapen
Seget    Wariap    Yapen    Tg. D'Urville    Kepulauan
Adua    Lenmalu    Mogol    Wasian    Serui    Mataboor    Kumamba
Bira    Bonoi    Sarmi
Misool    Bintuni    Nuboai    Ansudu    Sabarania
Tg.    Teluk Berau    Bobo    Wendesi    Teluk    Barapasi    Pegunungan Van Rees
SEA    Fatagar    Saga    Wasior    Cendrawasih    Genyem
Wahai    Kokas    Tariku    Koyabuti    Jayapura
Binaiya    Fakfak    Susunu    Kwatisore    Nabire    Taritatu    (Sentani)    Krau
Masohi    3019    Wefi    Wenut    IRIAN    JAYA
Imahai    Haja    Tum    Ibonma    Kaimana    Enarotali
Seram    Waru    Karufa    Teluk    Wanapiri    Waghete    Puncak    Wamena
(Ceram)    Kamrau    Kamrau    Uta    Jaya    5029    Trikora    Mandala
Geser    Adi    Pegunungan    Puncak    4702
Kepulauan    Manggawitu    Pegunungan Sudirman    Pegunungan Jayawijaya    Maoke
Banda    Gorong    Yapero
Bandanaira    Kepulauan    ESIA    Wanapiri
Kepulauan    Watubela    5
Banda    Teluk Flamingo    Agats    Pulau    Mindiptana
Kepulauan    Har    Teluk    Gumzai    Kola
Kai    Tual    Kai Besar    Dobo    Wokam    Tanahmerah
SEA    7440    Ketil    Bandar    Sewer    Kepulauan    Pirimapun
Eliat    Aru    Kepi    Asike
Daya    Serua    Wangal    Rebi    Kobroor    Kassue    Bade    Myuting
Nila    Markoor    Koba    Gomogomo    Muting
Teun    Molu    Trangan
Tafermaar    Pulau    Kimaan
Larat    Tg. Ngabordamlu    Yos Sudarso    Okaba
Babar    Wuliaru    C
Tepa    Selu    Alusi
Sermata    Masela    Saumlaki    Yamdena    Merauke
Selaru    Adaut    Tg. Vals    Pulau
Eliase    Kepulauan Tanimbar    Komoran

**PAPUA NEW GUINEA**

B

A

**ARAFURA    SEA**

10

D

130                    135                    140

4          5          6

COPYRIGHT GEORGE PHILIP & SON. LTD.

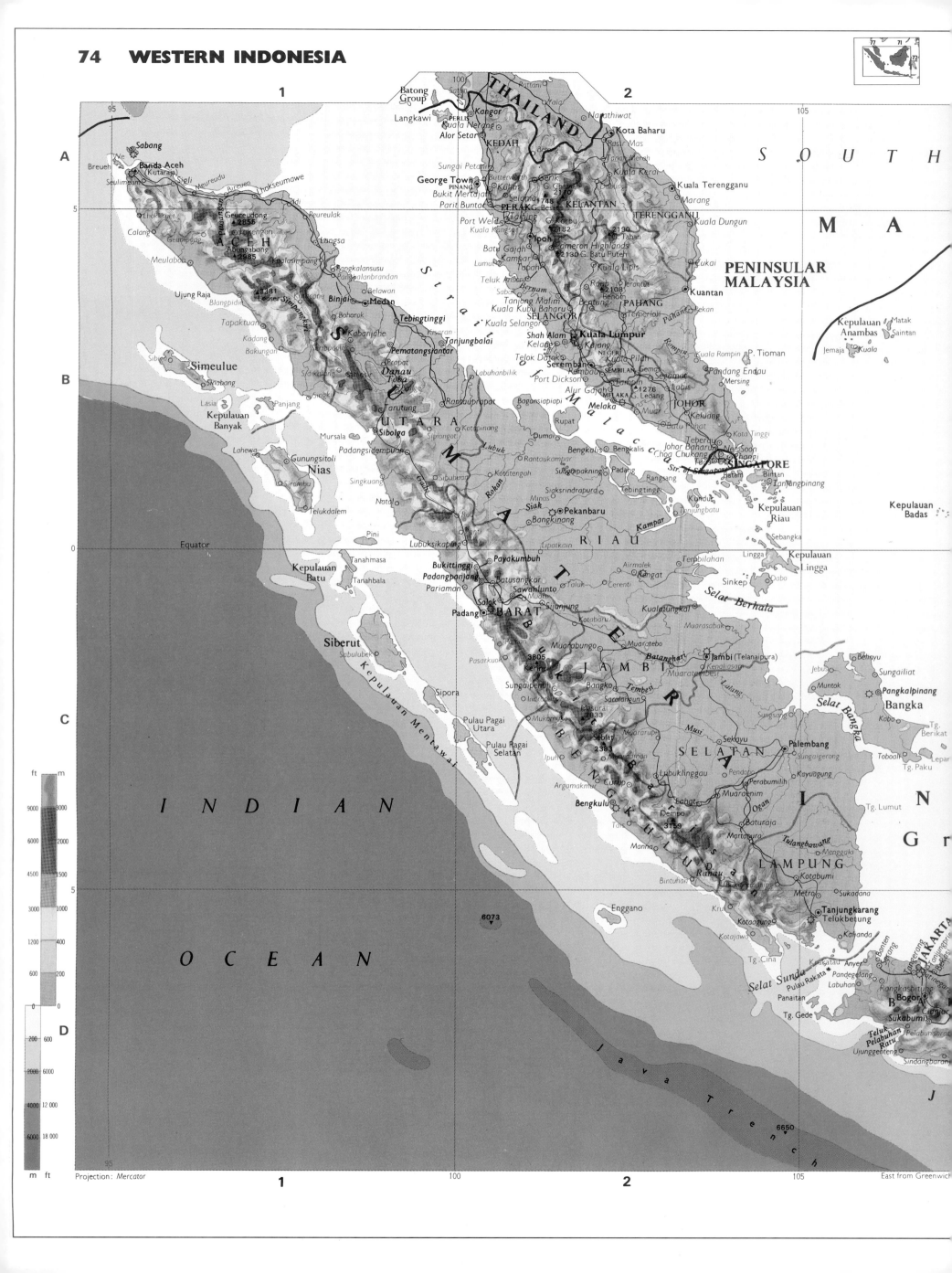

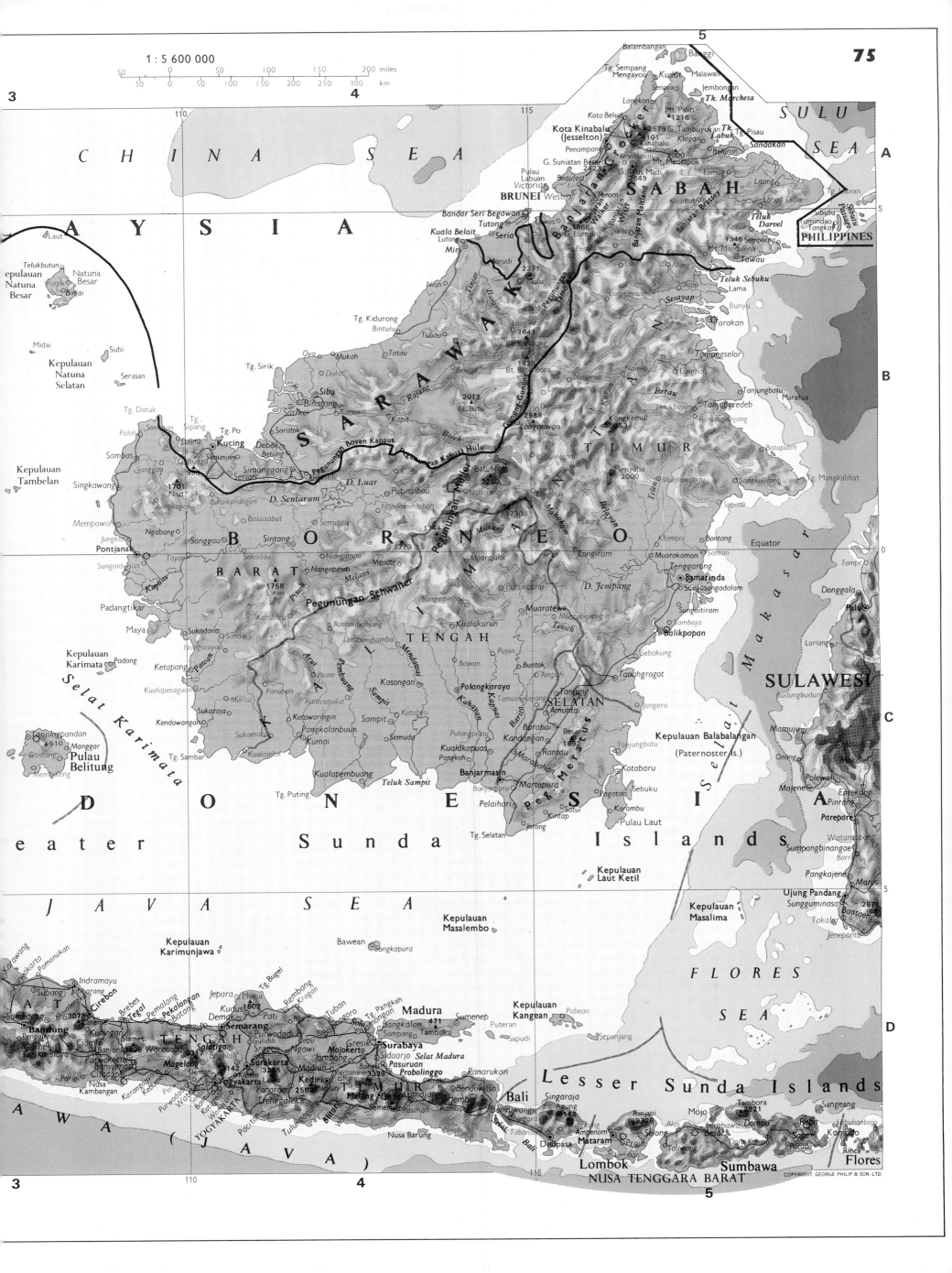

1 : 5 600 000

50   0   50   100   150   200 miles
50  0  50  100  150  200  250  300 km

**C H I N A   S E A**

A

**A Y S I A**

Telukbutun
Kepulauan
Natuna
Besar

Natuna
Besar

Bunguran

Midai

Subi

Serasan

Kepulauan
Natuna
Selatan

Kepulauan
Tambelan

Balambangan
Banggi
Mengayou
Tg. Sampang
Malawali
Kudat
Jembongan
Tk. Marchesa
Senaja
Mt. Palin
1216
Kota Belud
Tambuyukon
Tk.
Labuk
Tg. Pisau
Sandakan
Kota Kinabalu
(Jesselton)
2579
Kinabalu
4101
2000
Klagan
Beluran

**S A B A H**
G. Suniatan Besar
2423
Penampang
G. Trus Madi
2649
Tenom
1866
Lumaku
Keningau
Tg. Labian
Lahad Datu

Pulau
Labuan
Victoria
Western
Lawas
Keningau
2000
Klagan
Sibutu
Umindao
Tangkay
Passage

**BRUNEI**
Bandar Seri Begawan
Tutong
Kuala Belait
Seria
Lutong
Miri
Nieh
Marudi
Baram
2371
G. Mulu
Long Akah
1641
Bt. Batulong
1425
Bt. Batu
Bora
2012
Bt. Batu
2988
Longnawan

Tg. Kidurong
Bintulu
Tubau
Oya
Mukah
Tatau
Dalat
Balui
Beluga
Kanowit
Kapit

**S A R A W A K**
Tg. Sirik
Sibu
Binatang
Sarikei
Rajang
Saratok
Debak
Betung
Boven Kapuas
Pegunungan
Kanus Hulu
Batubroka
2240
Nohabrah
1730

Tg. Datuk
Tg.
Sipang
Tg. Po
Lundu
Sematan
Kucing
Bungo
Simunjon
Serian
Anjungan
Pegunungan Muller
1744
170

Paloh
Sambas
Sanggau
898
1701
Niut
Bengkayang
Singkawang

**B O R N E O**

Mempawah
Ngabang

**B A R A T**
Jungkat
**Pontianak**
Tayan
Sekadau
Nangamau
Nangapinoh
Sintang
Melawi
Sanggau
1758
Saran

Padangtikar
Maya

Kepulauan
Karimata
Padang

Ketapang
Pawan
Nangatayab
Rantaupanjang
Pegunungan Schwaner
Tumbangsamba
Mendawai
Kualakurun

**K A L I M A N T A N**

**T I M U R**
Tg. Mangkalihat

Tg. Redeb
Berau
Kongkemul
2053
Menyapa
2000
Telukbayun
Tanjungbatu
Maratua
Batuputih

Tanjungselor
Nunukan
Tarakan
Lama
Teluk Sebuku
Atap
Bunyu
Sesayap
Berau

Muarawahau

Longiram
Sangkulirang
Bontang

**Equator**
Muarakaman
Santan
Muaramuntai
Sebulu
Samboja
**Samarinda**
Loakulu
D. Jempang
**Balikpapan**
Sungaitiram
Tanjung
Tanahgrogot

Kuningan
Selat Makasar

Tompe

Donggala

**SULAWESI**
Budungbudung
Palu
Mamuju

**K A L I M A N T A N**
**T E N G A H**
Pujon
Bawan
Buntok
Ampah

Sukadana
Sandai
Kotabaru
Rantaupanjang
Tumbangsamba
Kasongan
**Palangkaraya**
Tamianglayang
Tanjung
**SELATAN**
Amuntai

Kendawangan
Kualapesaguan
Marau
Sukaraja
Kotawaringin
Sampit
Kotabesi
Pulangpisau
Kualakapuas
Barabai
Kandangan
1892
Rantau
Onang

Mamuju

Majene

Parepare
Pinrang
Enrekang
Makale

Kuala Sambar
Kuala
Jelai
Kumai
Semuda
Pangkohan
Pangkalanbuun
Teluk Sampit
Tg. Puting
Kualapembuang
**Banjarmasin**
Banjarbaru
Martapura
Pelaihari
Kotabaru
Pulau Laut
Sebuku
Pagatan
Karambu
Kintap
Jorong
Satui
Tg. Selatan

**Peg. Meratus**
Marabahan
Barabai

**D**

**eater   S u n d a   I s l a n d s**

Tanjungpandan
510
Manggar
Gantung
**Pulau
Belitung**
Membulang

**Selat Karimata**

**D O N E S I A**

Kepulauan
Balabalangan
(Paternoster Is.)

Tanjungbatu

**S u n d a**

Kepulauan
Laut Ketil

Watampone
Sumpangbinangae
Barru
Pangkajene
Maros

Ujung Pandang
Sungguminasa
2871
Bantaeng
Takalar
Jeneponto

**J A V A   S E A**

Kepulauan
Masalembo
Bawean
Sangkapura

Kepulauan
Karimunjawa

Kepulauan
Masalima

**F L O R E S**
**S E A**

Kepulauan
Kangean
Pabean
Puteran
Sapudi
Sepanjang

Kalyawang
Pamanukan
Indramayu
Subang
Cirebon
Brebes
Tegal
Pemalang
Pekalongan
Batang
Kudus
1602
Pati
Rembang
Tuban
Jepara
Muria
Demak
Bojonegoro
Tg. Bugel
Tg. Pangkah
Lamongan
Bangkalan
Tambuku
**Madura**
Sumenep

**D**

3075
**Bandung**
Pengalengan
Kuningan
Ciamis
Slamet
3428
Wonosobo
**Semarang**
Purwodadi
Gundih
Cepu
Ngawi
**Surabaya**
Gresik
Sidoarjo
**Surakarta**
3265
Madiun
Kertosono
Jombang
**Mojokerto**
Pasuruan
Probolinggo

**Tengah**
Salatiga
3142
Boyolali
Klaten
**Yogyakarta**
Sragen
**Kediri**
2563
Blitar
3339
**Malang**
Bondowoso
**Bali**
Singaraja
Agung
3142

**T I M U R**
**YOGYAKARTA**
Pacitan
Ponorogo
Trenggalek
Tulungagung
Banyuwangi
Negara
Selat Bali
**Denpasar**
**Mataram**

**A W A   (J A V A)**
Nusa Barung

**Lesser   Sunda   Islands**

Rinjani
**Lombok**
Solong
Praya
Taliwang
**Sumbawa**
**Sumbawa
Besar**
Alas
Mojo
Tambora
2821
Dompu
Raba
Sape
Sangeang
Parado
Rinca
**Flores**
Komodo

**NUSA   TENGGARA   BARAT**

COPYRIGHT GEORGE PHILIP & SON. LTD.

**SULU
SEA**

**PHILIPPINES**

**Makasar**

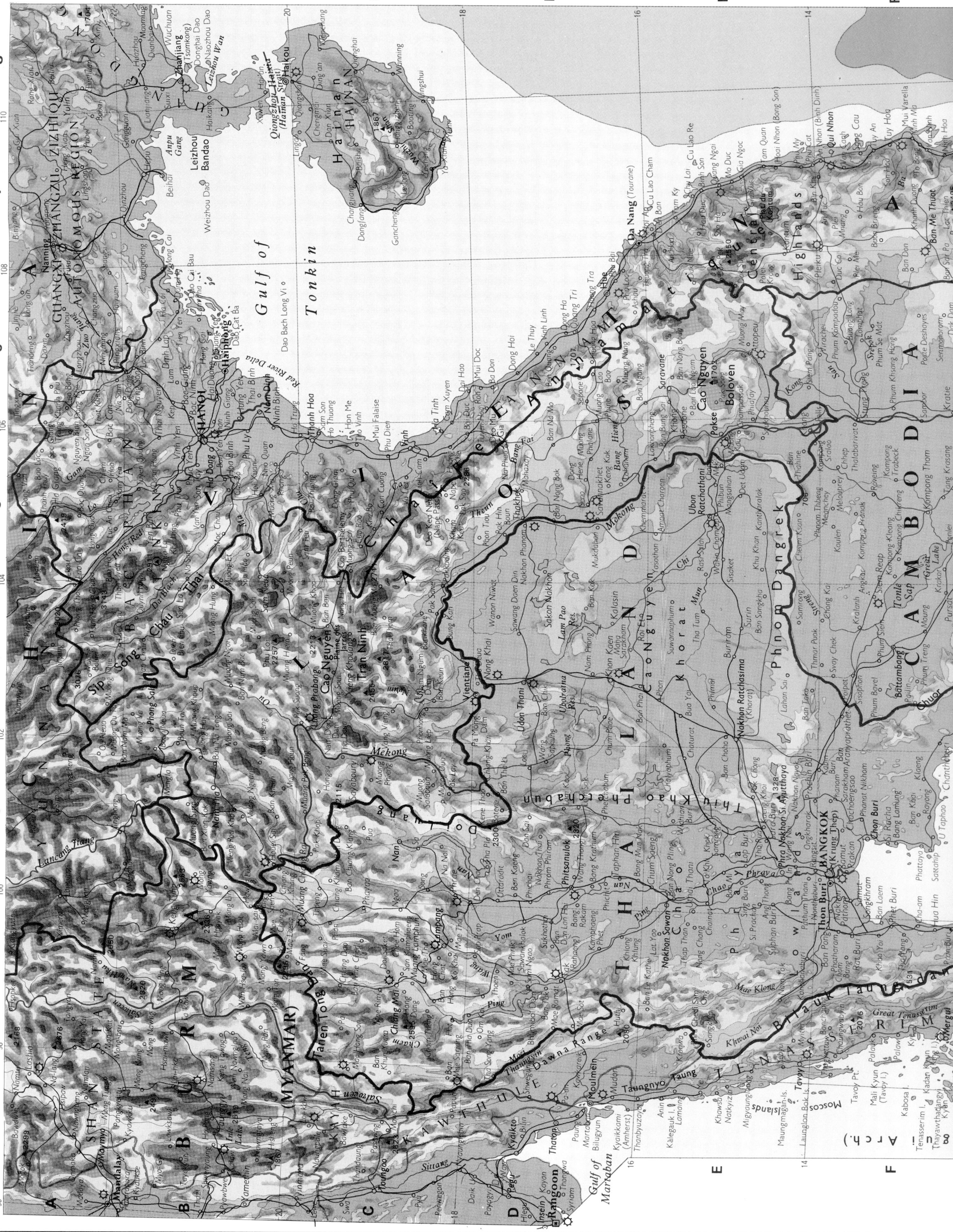

Gulf of Tonkin

HAINAN

Qiongzhou Haixia (Hainan Strait)

Gulf of Martaban

Gulf of Tonkin

GUANGXI ZHUANGZU ZIZHIQU AUTONOMOUS REGION

Nanning

Leizhou Bandao

Haikou

Red River Delta

HANOI

Haiphong

CHINA

YUNNAN

BURMA

MYANMAR

SHAN STATE

KAYAH

KAWTHULE

TENASSERIM

LAOS

THAILAND

CAMBODIA

VIETNAM

Mekong

Lancang Jiang

Luang Prabang

Vientiane

Udon Thani

Nakhon Ratchasima (Khorat)

BANGKOK (Krung Thep)

Thon Buri

Chao Phraya

Phnom Dangrek

Khorat

Battambang

Tonle Sap

Da Nang (Tourane)

Central Highlands

Annam

Pleiku

Qui Nhon (Binh Dinh)

Pakse

Boloven

Ubon Ratchathani

Salween

Mandalay

Rangoon

Pegu

Moulmein

Tavoy

Mergui

Mekong

Nan

Ping

Wang

Yom

Chiang Mai

Phitsanulok

Sukhothai

Thanh Hoa

Vinh

Dong Hoi

Hue

Quang Tri

Great Tenasserim

Tenasserim

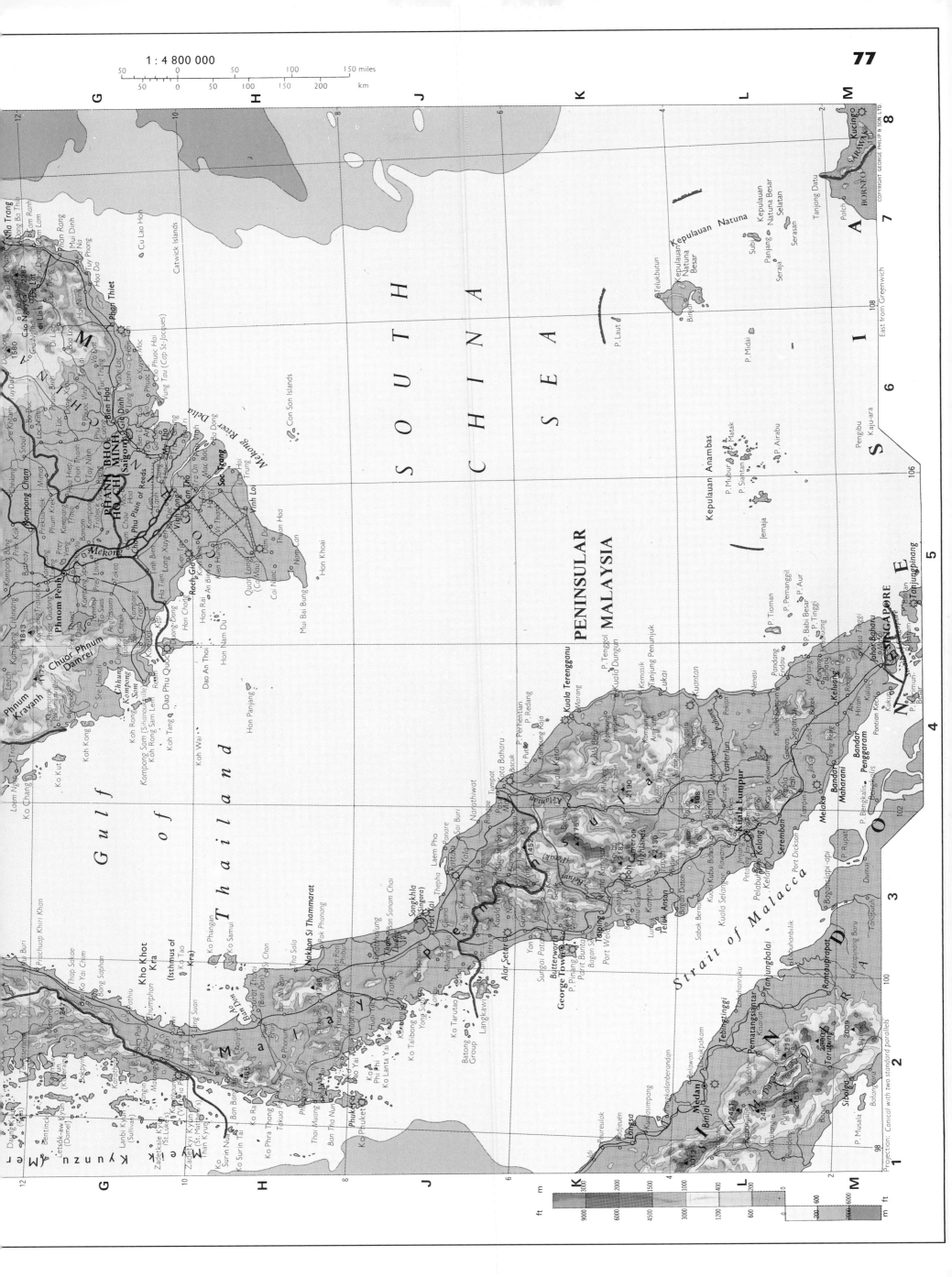

1 : 4 800 000

50      0          50        100              150 miles

50    0    50    100    150    200         km

SOUTH

CHINA

SEA

Gulf

of

Thailand

Strait of Malacca

PENINSULAR
MALAYSIA

SINGAPORE

BORNEO

Kuching

Tanjong Datu

Kepulauan Natuna

Kepulauan
Natuna
Besar

Kepulauan
Natuna
Selatan

Subi

Panjang

Seraja

Serasan

P. Laut

Telukbutun

Birang

Kepulauan Anambas

P. Mubur

Matak

P. Siantan

P. Airabu

P. Midai

Jemaja

Pengibu

Kaju-ara

East from Greenwich

Kuala Terengganu

Morang

P. Tenggol

Kuala Dungun

Kemasik

Tanjung Penunjuk

Cukai

Kuantan

Pekan

Nenasi

Pandang
Fodou

P. Pemanggil

P. Aur

P. Babi Besar

P. Tinggi

P. Tioman

Mersing

P. Perhentian
P. Redang

Kota Baharu
Kota Baharu

Tumpat

Narathiwat

Kelantan

Kuala Krai

Gua Musang

Tanah Merah

Pasir Puteh

Kampung Raja

Taiping

Kuala Lumpur

Kelang

Seremban

Port Dickson

Melaka

Maharani

Bandar
Penggaram

Johor Baharu

Tanjungpinang

Pontian Kecil

Batu Pahat

Kukup

Nho Trang

Phan Thiet

Cu Lao Hon

Catwick Islands

Con Son Islands

Hon Khoai

Mui Bai Bung

Hon Panjang

Quan Long

Cai Nuoc

Nam-Can

Hon Nam Du

Dao An Thoi

Dao Phu Quoc

Rach Gia

Can Tho

Soc Trang

Vinh Loi

Thanh Hoa

MEKONG

Mekong River Delta

PHANH BHO
HO CHI MINH
(Saigon)

Bien Hoa

Phnom Penh

Kompong Cham

Chuor Phnum Damrei

Phnum Kravanh

Koh Kong

Koh Kut

Koh Chang

Kho Khot
Kra

(Isthmus of
Kra)

Ko Samui

Ko Phangan

Ko Tao

Nakhon Si Thammarat

Songkhla
(Singora)

Hat Yai

George Town

Butterworth

Alor Setar

Langkawi

Batong
Group

Ko Tarutao

Ko Talibong

Ko Lanta Yai

Phuket

Ko Phuket

SOUTH   CHINA   SEA

Medan

Binjai

Pematangsiantar

Tebingtinggi

Sibolga

Tanjungbalai

Rantauprapat

INDONESIA

Bandar
Maharani

Projection: Conical with two standard parallels

COPYRIGHT GEORGE PHILIP & SON, LTD.

Mekong River Delta

m
3000
2000
1500
1000
400
200
0

ft
9000
6000
4500
3000
1200
600
0
200
600
6000
m ft

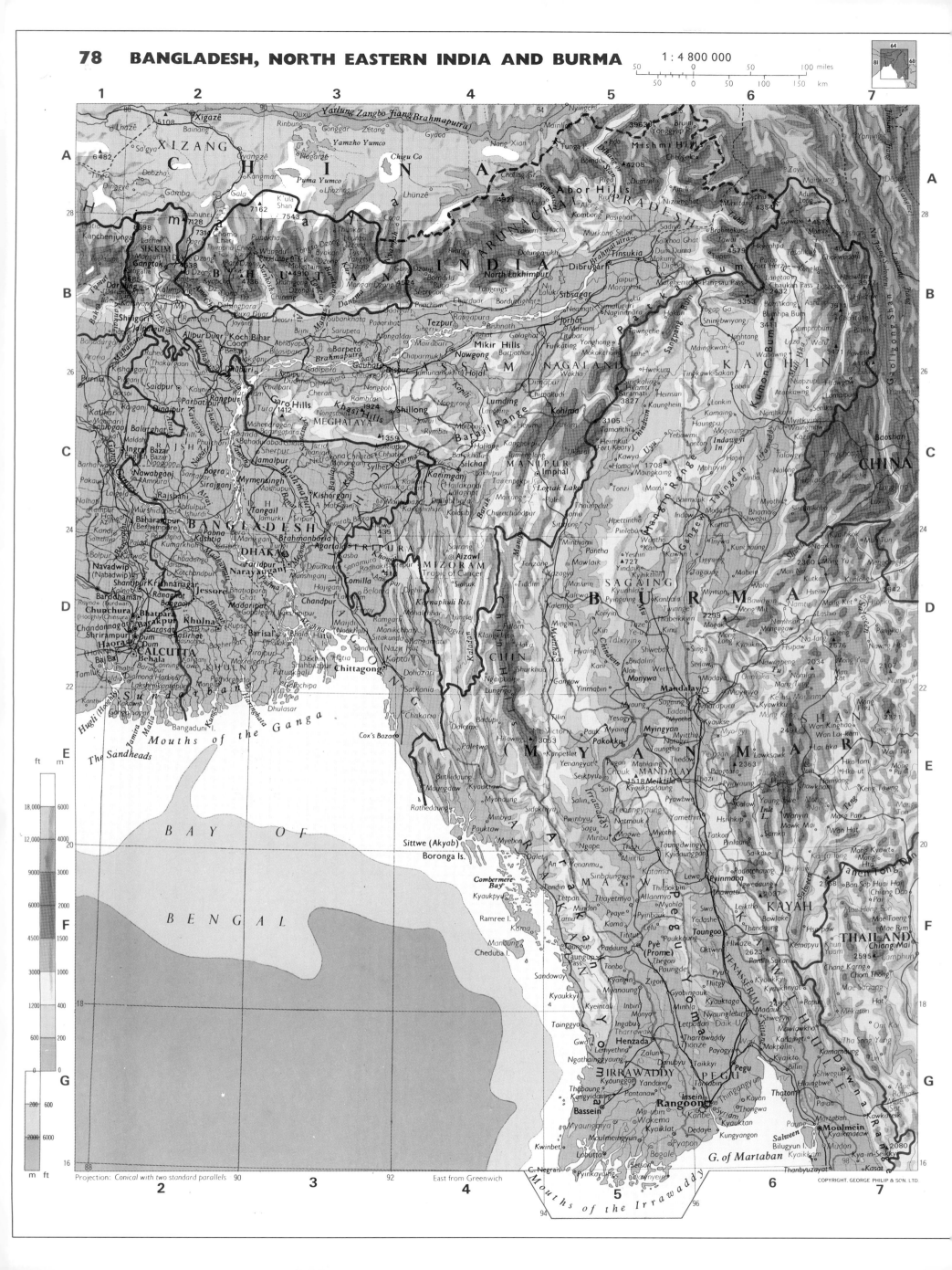

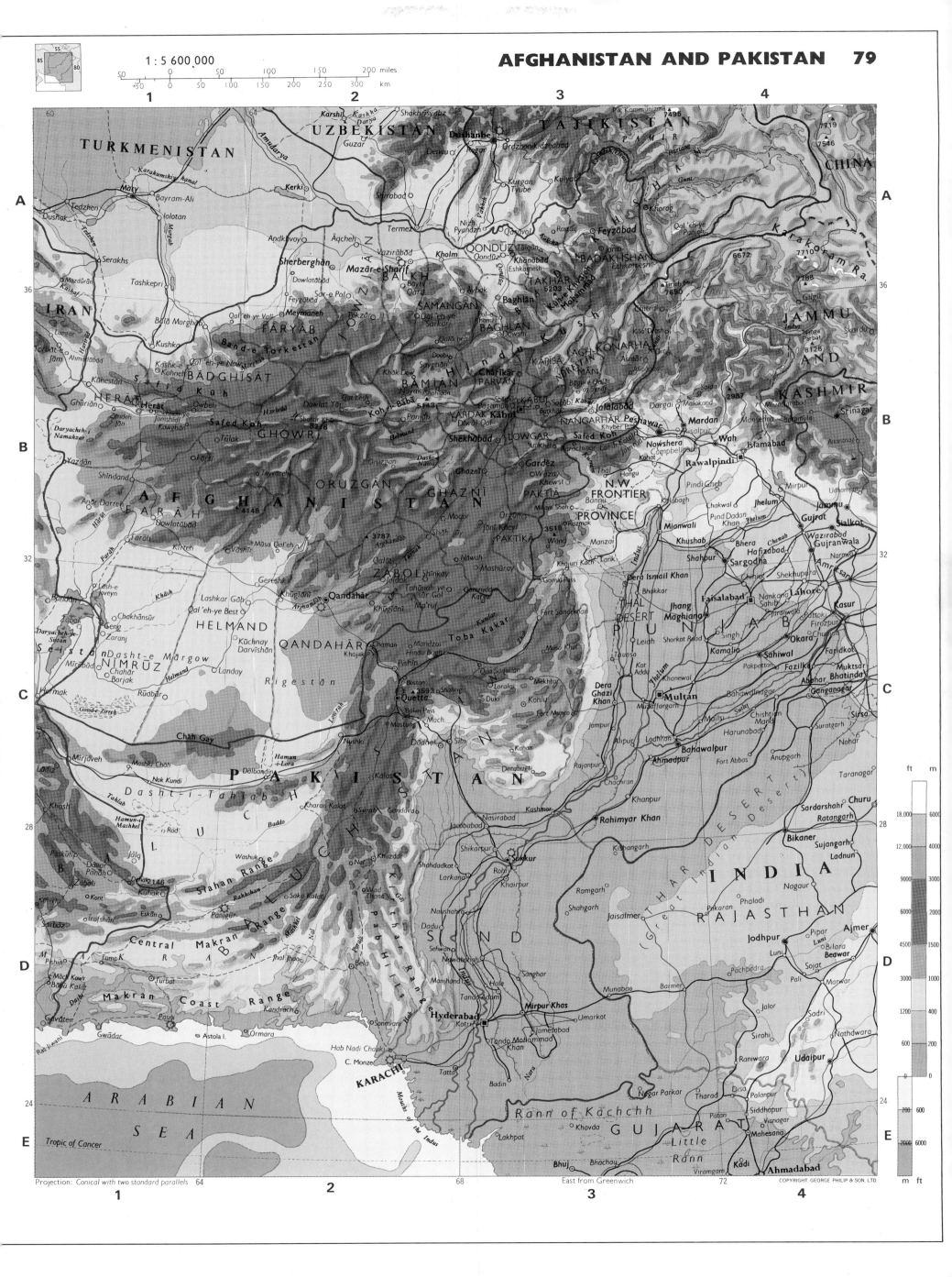

1 : 5 600 000

50  0  50  100  150  200 miles
50  0  50  100  150  200  250  300 km

TURKMENISTAN

UZBEKISTAN

TAJIKISTAN

CHINA

Dushak
Tedzhen
Moty
Bayram-Ali
Iolotan
Kerki
Karshi
Guzar
Shakhrisyabz
Dushanbe
Ordzhonikidzeabad
Regar
Denau
Shirabad
Kulyab
Kurgan-Tyube
Khorog
PAMIR

Serakhs
Mazdūrān
Kalbāt
Tedzhen
Karakumskiy kanal
Amudarya
Karshi
Darya
Termez
Nizh
Pyandzh
Qaravol
Rostaq
Qal'eh-ye
Panjeh
Karakoram Ra.

IRAN

Tashkepri
Andkhvoy
Āqcheh
Vazirabad
Kholm
QONDUZ
Taloqan
Khānābād
Eshkamesh
Feyzābād
BADAKHSHAN
Eshkamesh

Herāt
Bālā Morghāb
Meymaneh
Dowlatābād
Feyzābad
Sor-e Pol
BALKH
Aybak
Baghlān
TAKHAR
Kūhe-Khwāja
Chitrāl
Tarich Mir
7690

FĀRYĀB
SAMANGAN
BAGHLAN
Hindu Kush
NŪRESTĀN
JAMMU

BĀDGHĪSĀT
Band-e Torkestān
Khāk Dow
BĀMIĀN
Chārikār
PARVĀN
KĀPISA
LAGHMAN
KONARHĀ
AND
KASHMIR

Herāt
Owbeh
Dawlat Yār
Koh-i-Bābā
KABUL
Jalālābād
NANGARHĀR
Peshawar
Mardan
Srinagar

GHOWR
Safed Koh
Shekhabad
WARDAK
LOWGAR
Safed Koh
Nowshera
Wah
Islamabad

Tūlak
Chaghcharān
Panjāb
Gardēz
Khyber P.
Rawalpindi

AFGHANISTAN
ORUZGĀN
GHAZNĪ
PAKTIA
N.W.
FRONTIER
Jhelum
Gujrat
Sialkot

FARĀH
4148
Ghaznī
Khewst
PROVINCE
Mianwali
Khushab
Gujranwala

ZĀBOL
3787
Arghandāb
Mogor
3518
PAKTIKA
Wana
Dera Ismail Khan
Bhera
Hafizabad
Sargodha
Amritsar

QANDAHĀR
Qalāt
Nāwah
Mashūray
Tank
THAL
DESERT
PUNJAB
Jhang Maghiana
Faisalabad
Lahore
Kasur

HELMAND
Gereshk
Khūgiāni
Qandahār
Khūgiāni
Ma'ruf
Fort Sandeman
Leiah
Shorkot Road
Singh
Okara
Firozpur

NIMRŪZ
Dasht-e Mārgow
Kūchnay
Darvīshān
Chaman
Pishin
Toba Kakar
Musa Khel
Dera Ghazi Khan
Sahiwal
Fazilka

Zaranj
Landay
Rigestān
Hindu Bagh
Loralai
Kohlu
Multan
Bahawalnagar
Abohar
Bhatinda

Se-istan
Rūdbār
Quetta
3693
Shahrig
Duki
Fort Munro
Muzaffargarh
Chishtian
Ganganagar

Daryacheh-ye Sistan
Bolan Pass
Mach
Sibi
Kahan
Derabugti
Rajanpur
Bahawalpur
Ahmadpur
Fort Abbas
Sirsa

Hīrmak
Mastung
Dādhar
BALUCHISTAN
Khanpur
Rahimyar Khan
Anupgarh
Nohar

Mīrjāveh
Mashkī Chāh
Nok Kundi
Nushki
Kalat
Nasirabad
Kashmor
Sardarshahi
Churu

Lodiz
Dasht-i-Tahlab
Dalbandin
Kharan Kalat
Surab
Gandava
Jacobabad
Ramgarh
Bikaner
Sujangarh
Ratangarh

Khāsh
Hamun-i-Mashkel
Rōd
Baddo
Shikarpur
Sukkur
Kishangarh
INDIA
Ladnu

Pashkūh
Siahan Range
Washuk
Rakhshan
Saru Kalan
Larkana
Rohri
Khairpur
Ramgarh
RAJASTHAN

Dāvar Panāh
Zāboli
2146
Kūhak
Panjgūr
BALUCHISTAN
Kharan
Wad
Thana
Kal Gat
Shahdadkot
Jaisalmer
Shahgarh
Jodhpur
Pipar
Ajmer

Kon
Central Makran Range
Eskān
Kharan Range
Naushahro
Dadu
Sehwan
Nawabshah
Sanghar
Munabao
Barmer
Pali
Beawar

Sarbāz
Makran Coast Range
Tump
Turbat
Bela
Manjhand
Hala
Tando Adam
Mirpur Khas
Umarkot
Jalor
Sadri

Mand
Kandrach
Sonmiani
Hyderabad
Kotri
Jamesabad
Nathdwara

Gwādar
Pasni
Astola I.
Ormara
C. Monze
KARACHI
Tatta
Badin
Tando Mohammad
Nara
Udaipur

ARABIAN
SEA
Hab Nadi Chauki
Mouths of the Indus
Rann of Kachchh
GUJARAT
Little Rann
Mahesana

Tropic of Cancer
Lakhpat
Khavda
Bhuj
Bhachau
Nagar Parkar
Tharad
Disa
Palanpur
Siddhpur
Visnagar
Kādi
Ahmadabad
Viramgam

ft  m
18,000  6000
12,000  4000
9000  3000
6000  2000
4500  1500
3000  1000
1200  400
600  200
0
200  600
2000  6000
m  ft

AFGHANISTAN

PAKISTAN

N.W. FRONTIER PROVINCE

THAL DESERT

PUNJAB

SIND

BALUCHISTAN

RAJASTHAN

THAR DESERT (Great Indian Desert)

HARYANA

HIMACHAL PRADESH

JAMMU AND KASHMIR

GUJARAT

MADHYA

ARABIAN SEA

Mouths of the Indus

Rann of Kachchh

Little Rann

Gulf of Kachchh

Gir Hills

Tropic of Cancer

**Major cities:** Kabul, Peshawar, Rawalpindi, Islamabad, Srinagar, Jammu, Amritsar, Lahore, Multan, Quetta, Qandahar, Hyderabad, KARACHI, Sukkur, Jacobabad, Bikaner, Jaipur, Jodhpur, Jaisalmer, Barmer, Udaipur, Kota, Gwalior, DELHI, Meerut, Ludhiana, Chandigarh, Ambala, Ajmer, AHMADABAD, Vadodara, Rajkot, Bhavnagar, Jamnagar, Porbandar, Bhopal, Indore, Ujjain, Dehra Dun, Simla, Bhuj

Projection: Conical with two standard parallels

ft m
18,000 6000
12,000 4000
9000 3000
6000 2000
4500 1500
3000 1000
1200 400
600 200
0 0
200 600
2000 6000
m ft

1 : 4 800 000

50 0 50 100 miles

50 0 50 100 150 km

JAMMU AND KASHMIR
On same scale as Main Map
CHINA
Kunlun Shan
Karakoram Range
Zaskar Mountains
Deosai Mountains
Ladakh Range
JAMMU AND KASHMIR
N.W. FRONTIER PROVINCE
PUNJAB
HIMACHAL PRADESH
Gilgit
Srinagar
Rawalpindi
Islamabad
Jammu
Sialkot
Leh
Kargil
Nanga Parbat
K2 8611
Masherbrum 7821
Karakoram Pass
SODA PLAINS
Aksai Chin
Bangong Co
Wular L.
Indus
CHINA
Nganglong Kangri
Gangdisê Shan
Mapam Yumco
Kangrinboqê Feng 6714
Nanda Devi 7817
Kamet
Badarinath 7188
XIZANG (TIBET)
Yarlung Zangbo Jiang (Brahmaputra)
Xigazê
Puma Yumco
NEPAL
Mahabharat Lekh
Siwalik Range
Dhaulagiri 8172
Annapurna 8078
Manaslu 8156
Xixabangma Feng 8012
Mt. Everest 8848
Makalu
Kanchenjunga 8598
Katmandu
Lalitpur
Bhaktapur
Biratnagar
BHUTAN
Kula Kangri 7554
Darjeeling
ASSAM
Garo Hills
UTTAR PRADESH
Moradabad
Rampur
Bareilly
Shahjahanpur
Sitapur
Lucknow
KANPUR
Allahabad
Varanasi (Banaras, Benares)
Mirzapur
Gorakhpur
Faizabad
Jhansi
BIHAR
Patna
Gaya
Bhagalpur
Munger
Muzaffarpur
Darbhanga
Rajmahal Hills
Ranchi
Jamshedpur
Dhanbad
Asansol
Durgapur
Kharagpur
WEST BENGAL
CALCUTTA
Haora
Bhatpara
Krishnanagar
BANGLADESH
DHAKA
Rajshahi
Khulna
Jessore
Barisal
Mymensingh
Narayanganj
MADHYA PRADESH
Kaimur Hills
Panna Hills
Maikala Range
Jabalpur
Bilaspur
Raigarh
Sambalpur
Raurkela
Rihand Dam
Hirakud Dam
Mouths of the Ganga
The Sandheads
Baleshwar
Ganga
Damodar
Son
East from Greenwich
COPYRIGHT, GEORGE PHILIP & SON, LTD.

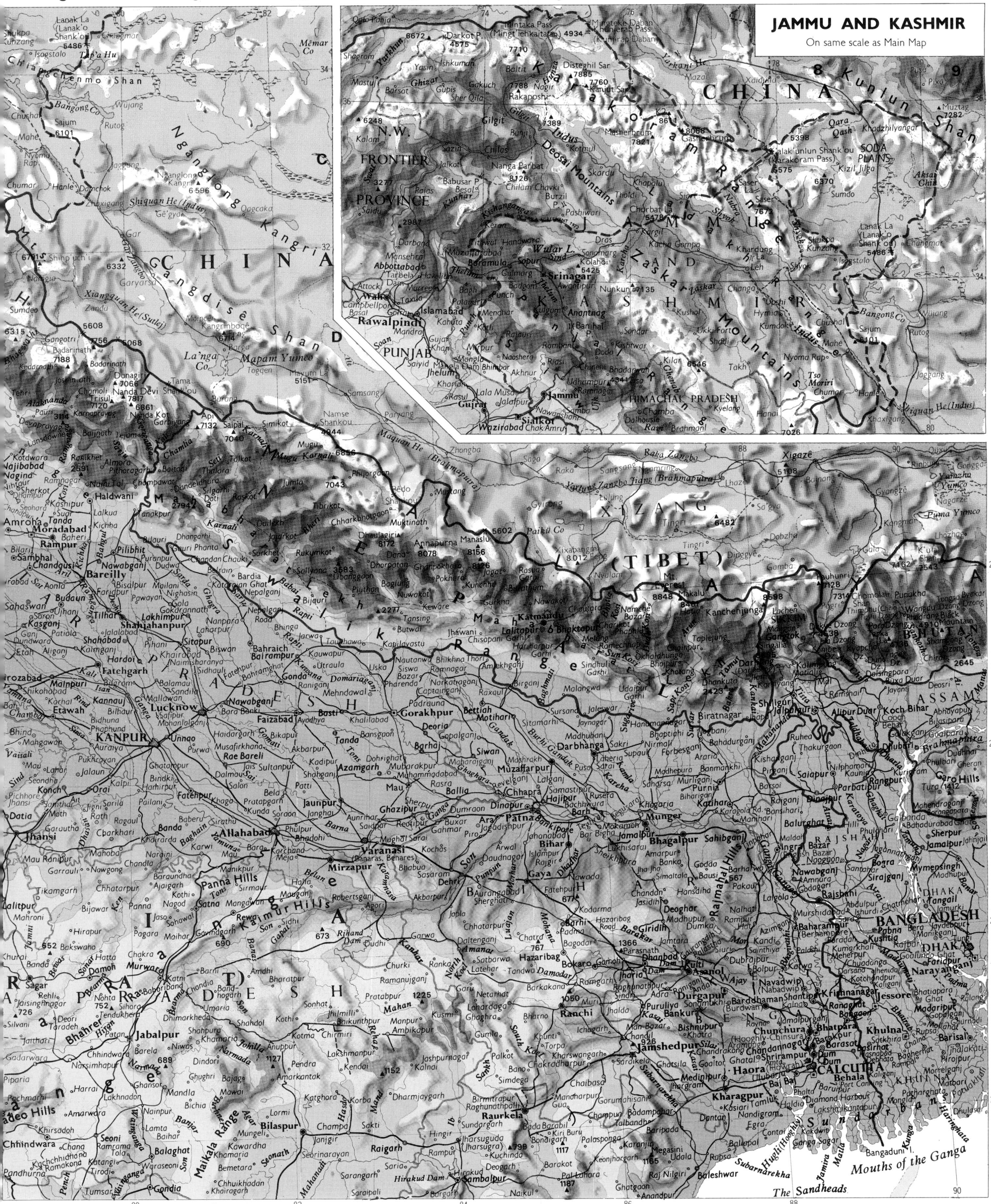

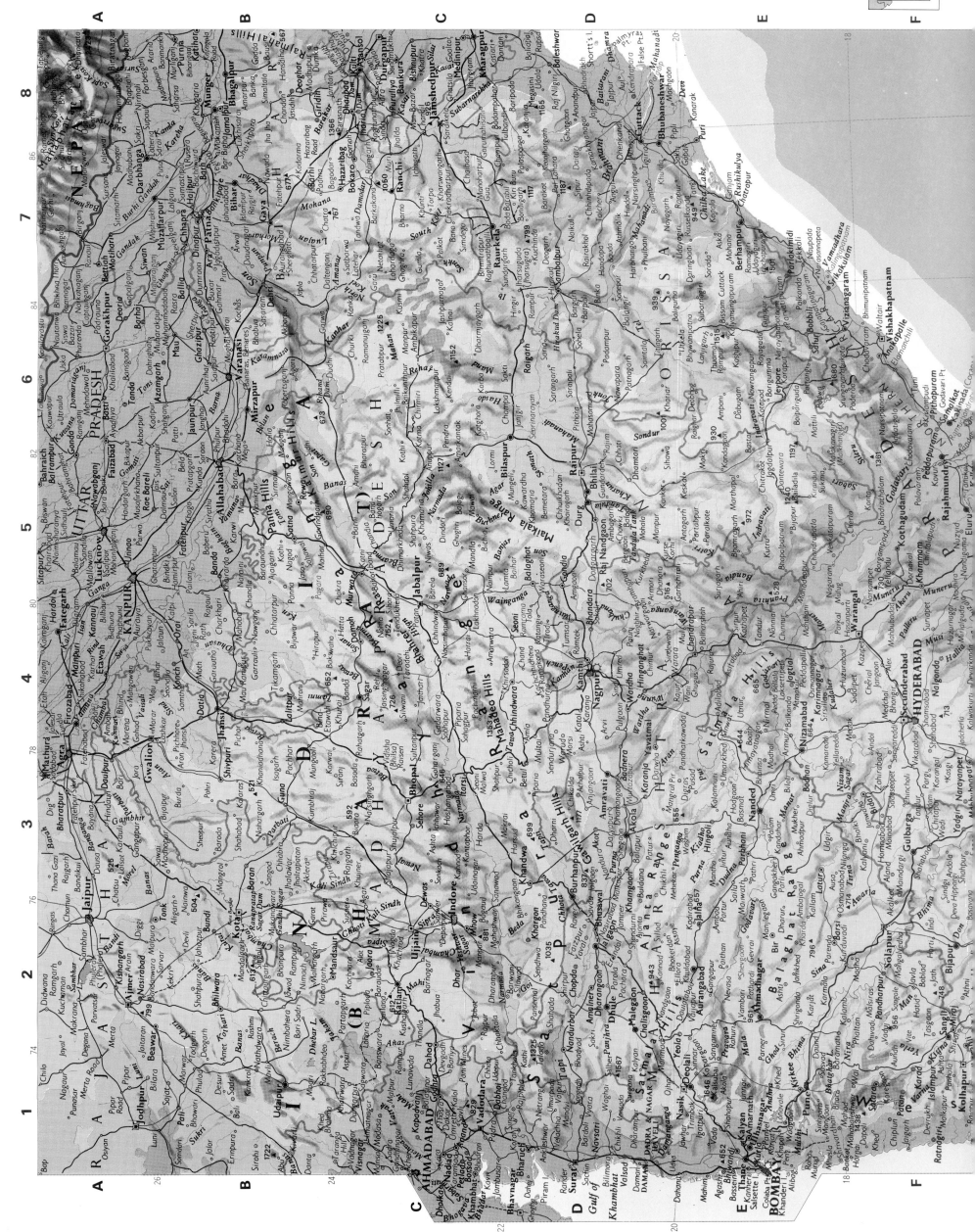

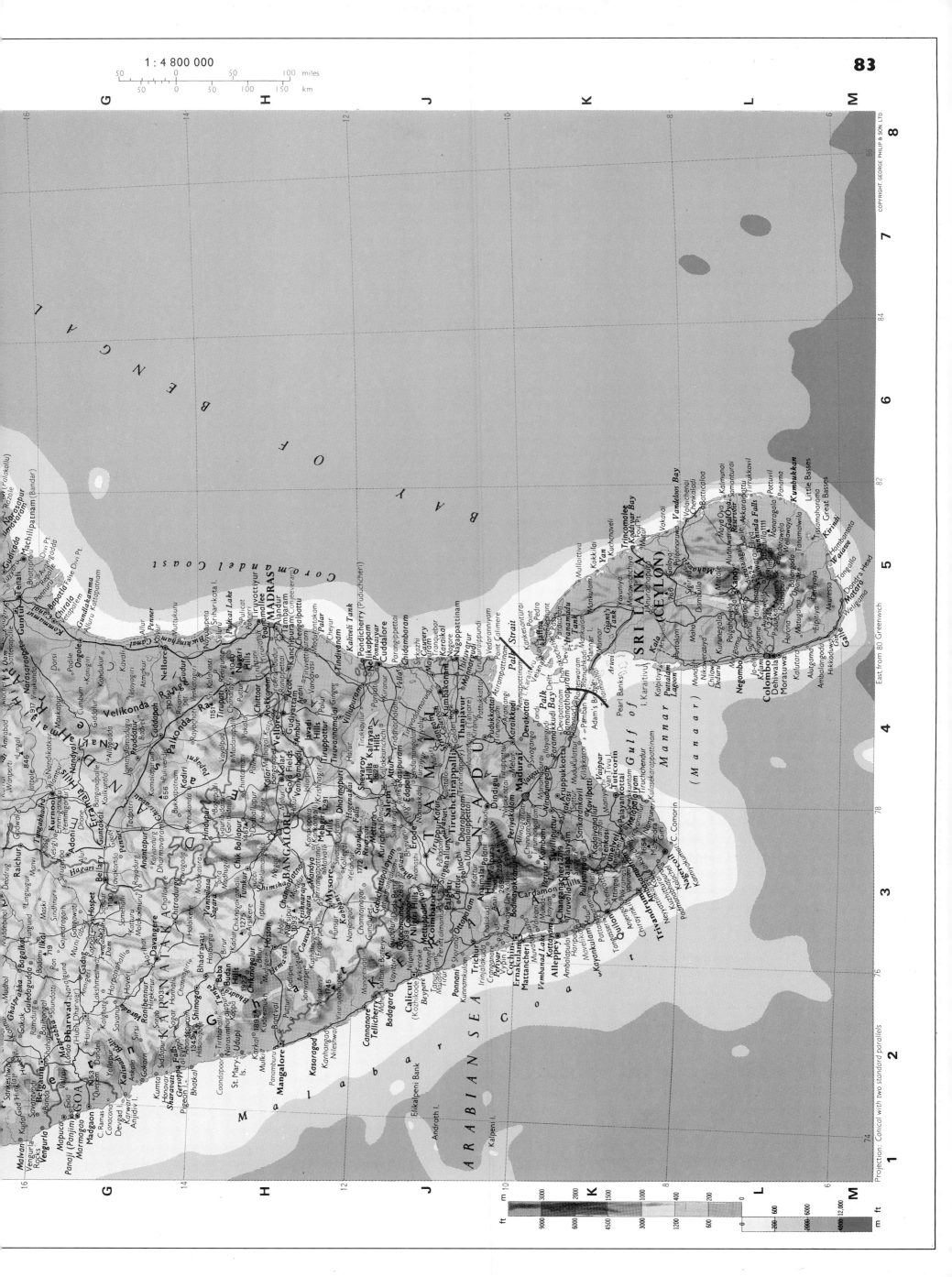

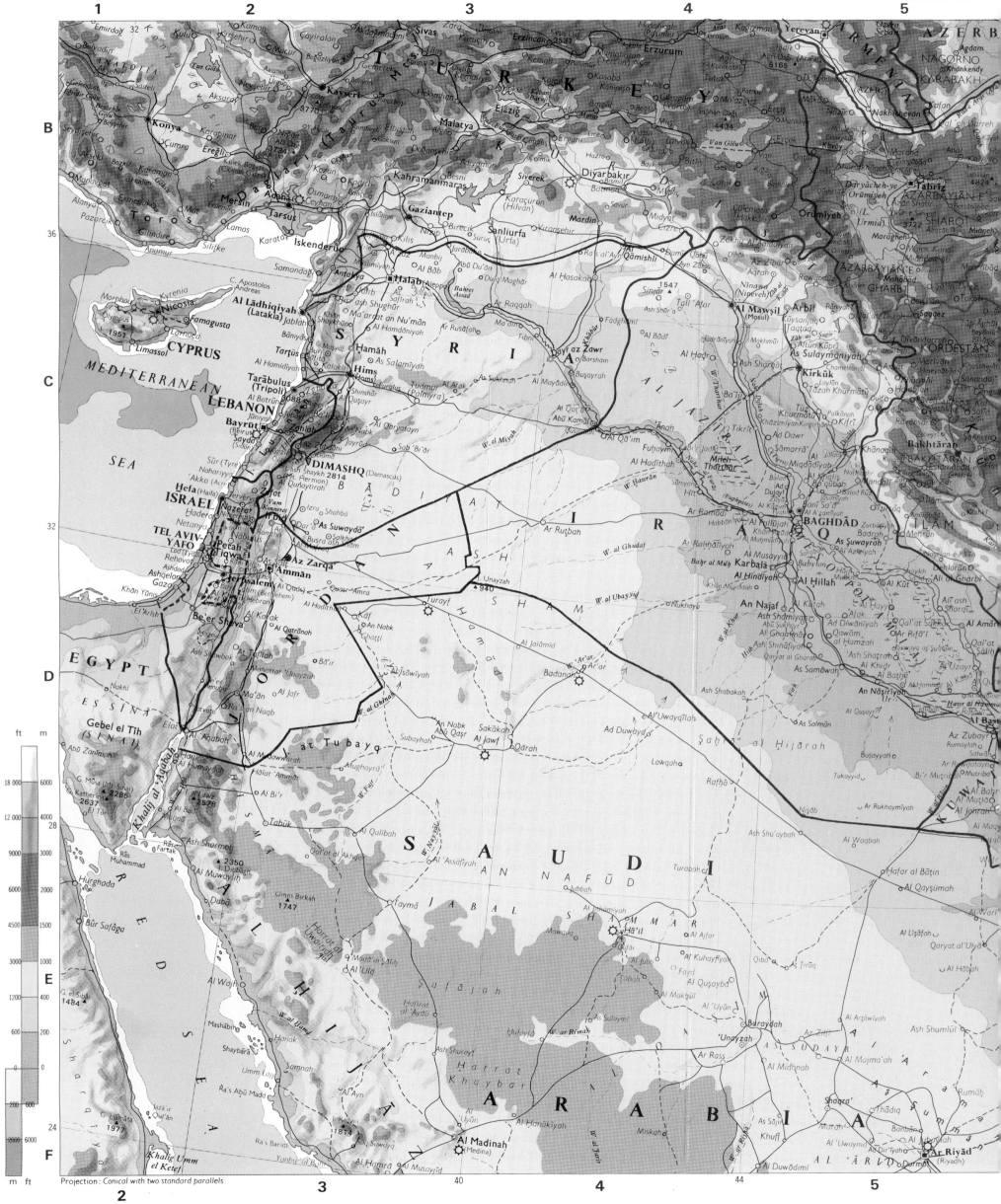

Projection: Conical with two standard parallels

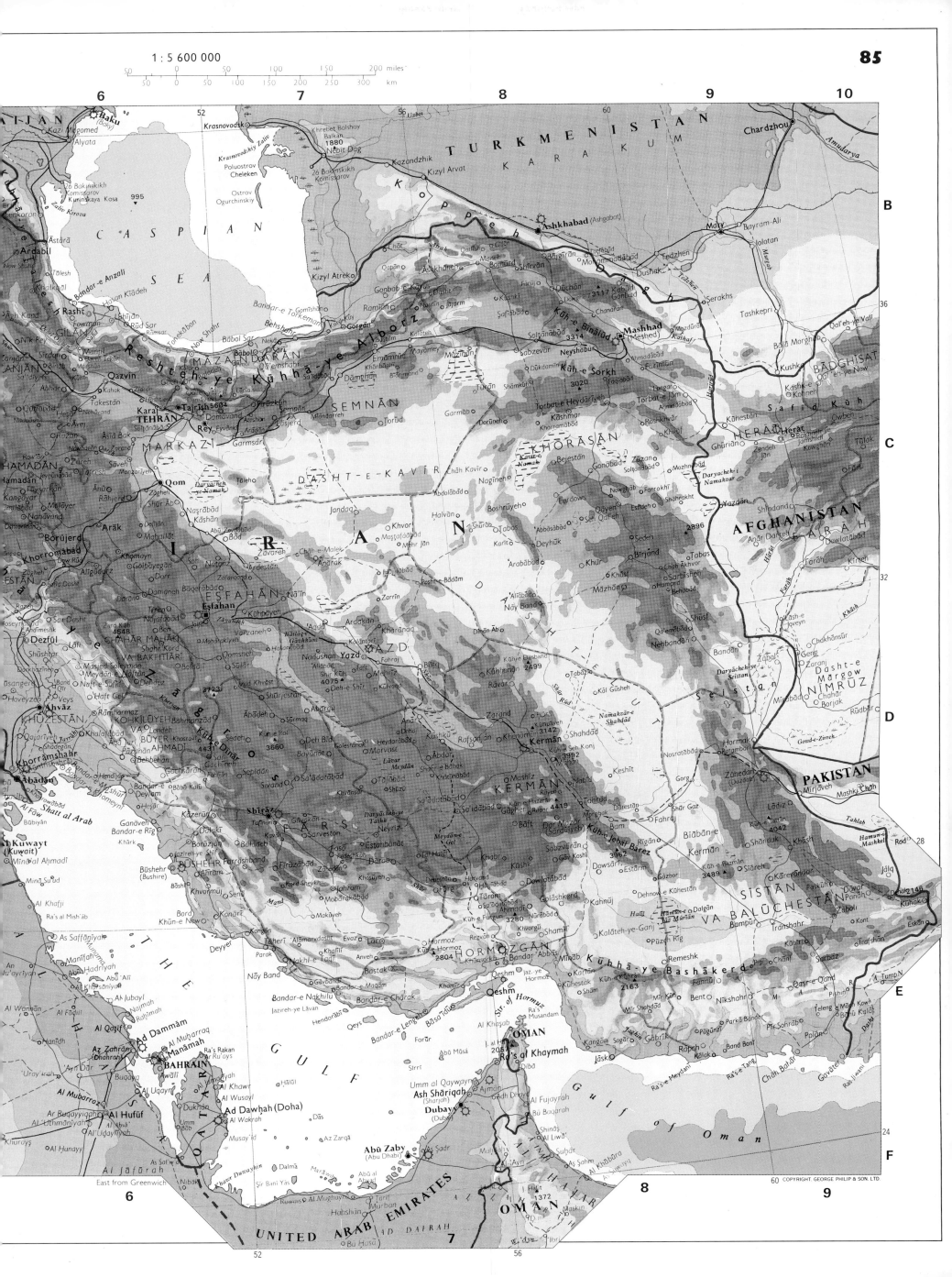

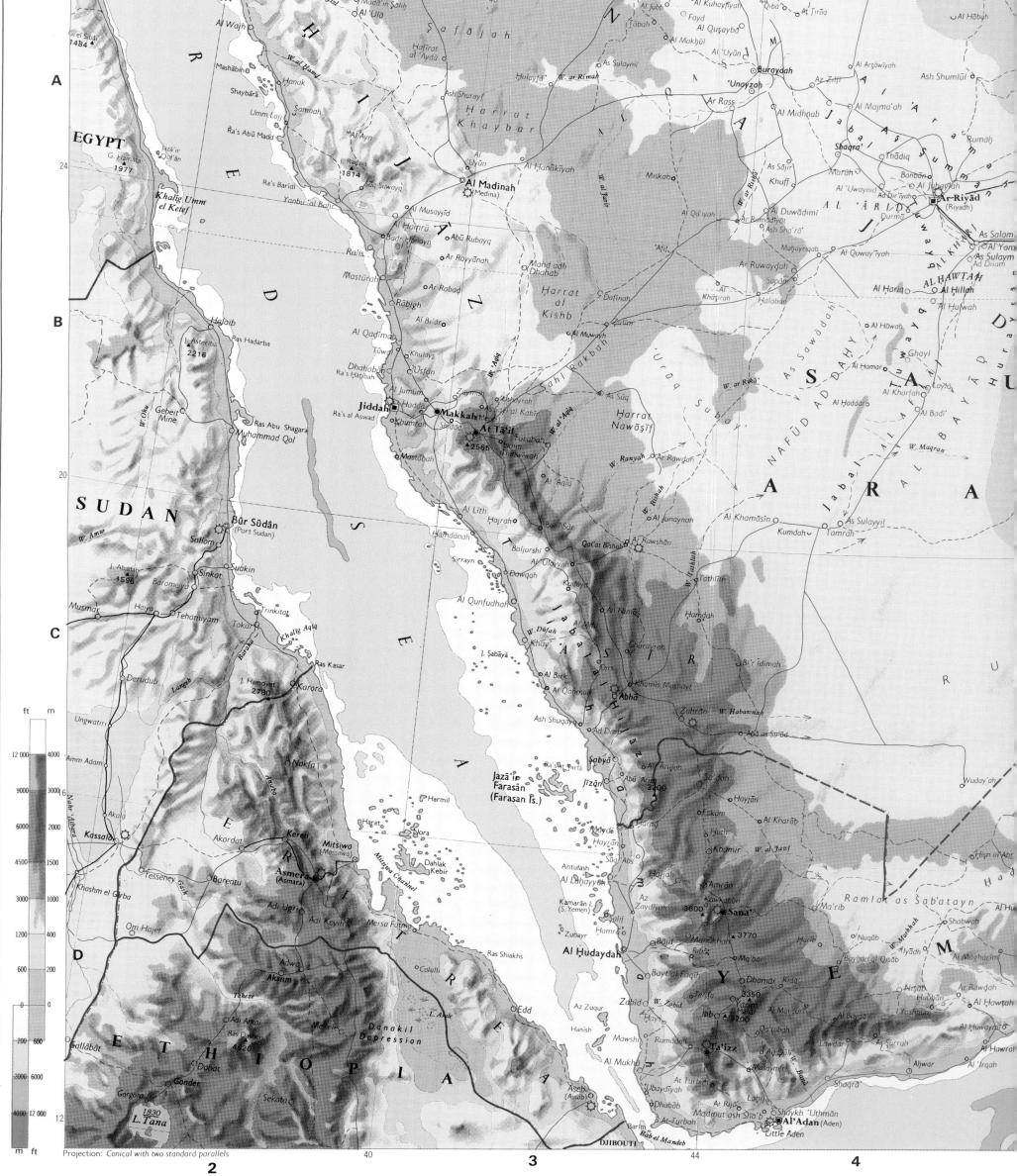

Projection: Conical with two standard parallels

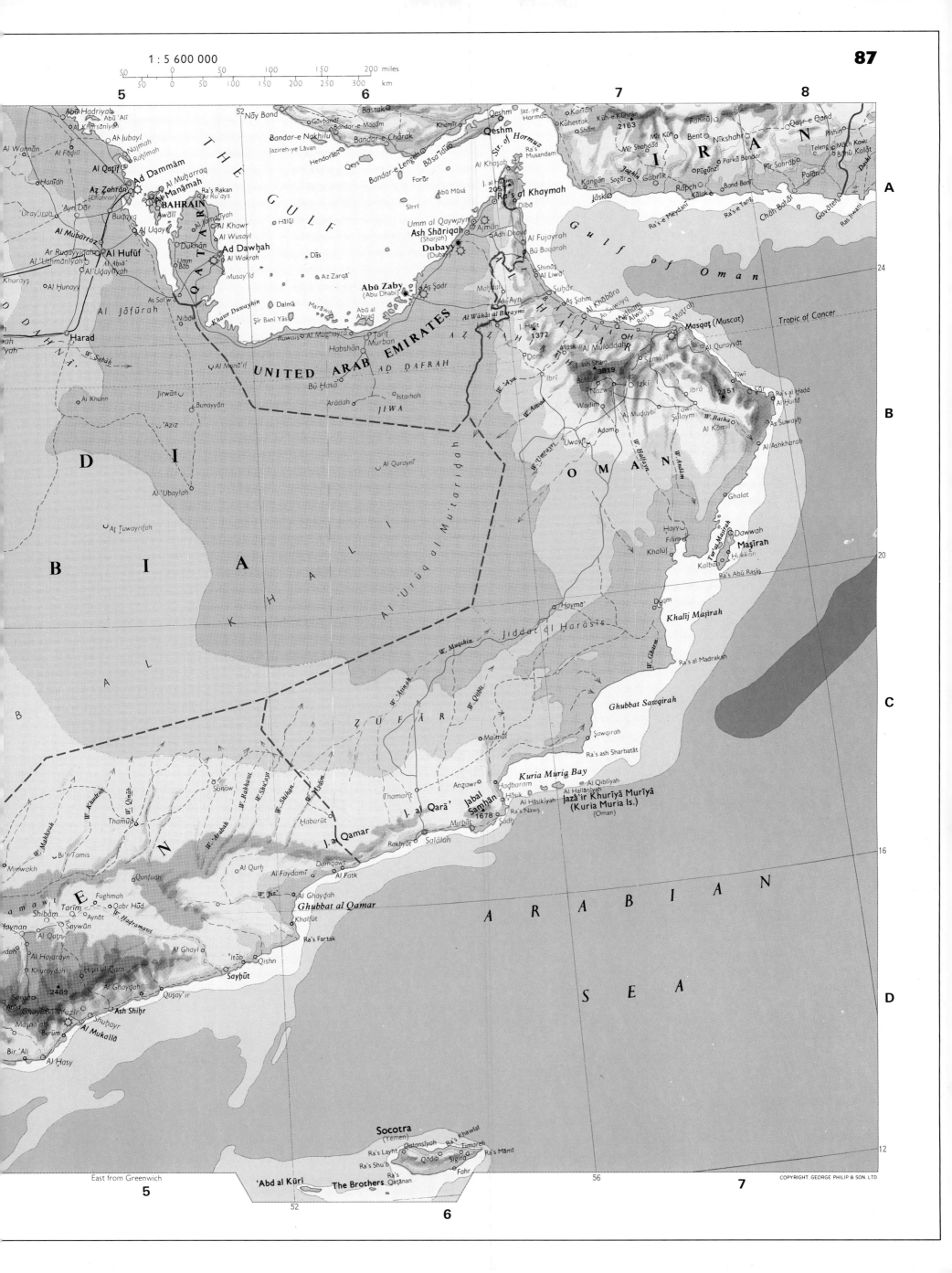

1 : 5 600 000

50    0    50    100    150    200 miles

50    0    50    100   150   200   250   300 km

**5**                              **6**                              **7**                              **8**

Abū Hadriyah
Al Kīm saniyah
Al Jubayl
Najmah
Rahimah
Al Wannān
Al Faqlīt
Al Qaṭīf
Ad Dammām
Hanīdh
Az Zahrān
Al Muharraq
Al Manāmah
Dhahran
Raʾs Rakan
**BAHRAIN**
Ūrayʿirah
ʿAyn Dār
Awālī
Umm
Buqayq
Al Khawr
Al Muḥarraz
Al Uqayl
Al Wusayl
Ar Ruqayyiqah
Dukhān
Al Wakrah
Al Uthmānīyah
Umm
Bāb
Al ʿUdaylīyah
**Ad Dawḥah**
Khurays
Al Hunayy
As Salʿ
**QATAR**
Niban
Nāy Band
Bastak
Qeshm
Jaz.-ye Hormoz
Karīān
Kūh-e Qahd
Bandar-e Magām
Khamīr
Qeshm
Shām
2163
Fannūj
Qaṣr-e Qand
Bandar-e Nakhilu
Bandar-e Chārak
Jazireh-ye Lāvan
Hendorābī
Qeys
Bandar-e Lengeh
Bāsāʾīdu
Str. of Hormuz
Raʾs Musandam
Mīr Shahdād
Mīr Kūh
Nīkshahr
Kūhestak
Shām
**IRAN**
Bent
Teleng
Mach Kowr
Bāhu Kalāt
Daski
Forūr
Abū Mūsā
Al Khaṣab
Kangān
Sogar
Jaghin
Rāpch
Gābrīk
Band Borz
Pārkā Bandar
Pūgūnzi
Raʾs-e Meydānī
Jāsk
Kalāk
Raʾs-e Tang
Chāh Bahār
Gavāter
Raʾs Īrwani

**A**

Stirri
Dās
Az Zarqāʾ
**Abū Zaby**
(Abū Dhabī)
Aṣ Ṣadr
Umm al Qaywayn
Ash Shāriqah
(Sharjah)
Ajmān
Adh Dhayd
**Dubayy**
(Dubai)
Raʾs al Khaymah
Dibā
Al Fujayrah
Bū Baqarah
Shinās
Suḥār
Gulf of Oman
Raʾs-e Meydānī

Gulf
of
Oman

**24**

THE   GULF

Al Jāfūrah
Ḥālūl
Marāwih
Dalmā
Shīr Banī Yās
Musayʾīd
Khawr Dumayḥin
Abū al Abyad
Maḥạ̄t
Al ʿAyn
Al Muladdah
As Sīb
Al Khābūra
As Suwayq
Wudhām
Barkā
Maṭraḥ
**Masqaṭ** (Muscat)
Tropic of Cancer

Al Qurayyat

Nibāk
Al Muḥaydi
Habshān
Ruwais
Al Mughayrā
Tarīf
Murbān
**UNITED   ARAB   EMIRATES**
Al Wāḥat al Buraymī
1372
Danḳ
Maskin
Ibrī
3019
Ibrā
Saygh
Al Manāʾif
AD DAFRAH
Bū Ḥasā
 AZ ZAHIR AL HAJAR
J. al Sham
Bahlā
Nazwā
Izki
Sumāyl
Raʾs al Ḥadd
Al Ḥudd
Al Khunn
Jirwān
Bunayyān
ʿAzīz
Arādah
Istaihah
JIWA
Al Qaraynī
Wadām
Al Muḍaybi
Adam
Sumāyl
Tiwi
2151
Sūr
Raʾs al Ḥadd
Al Ḥudd
Al Ashkharah

**B**

**D**   **I**
**R**   **U**   **B**
**A**
Aṭ Ṭuwayrifah
Al ʿUbaylah
**O**   **M**   **A**   **N**
Uwaybi
W. Tmrayrt
W. Andam
W. Halfayn
W. Baṭḥa
Al Kāmil
Ghalat

Al Khālī
Hayy
Filim
Tūr al Mazārah
Dawwah
**Maṣīrah**
Khalūf
Ḥikman
Kalba
Raʾs Abū Raṣāṣ

**20**

Al ʿUrūq al Muʿtariḍah
Haymāʾ
Duqm
Khalīj Maṣīrah
Raʾs al Madrakah

**C**

Jiddat al Ḥarāsīs
W. Muqshin
W. Aimān
W. Qitbīt
Ghubbat Sawqirah
Şawqirah
Raʾs ash Sharbatāt

ZUFĀR
Maʾmūl
Kuria Muria Bay
Anzawr
Haqbaram
Al Ḥāsik
Al Hallānīyah
Al Qiblīyah
**Jazāʾir Khurīyā Murīyā**
(Kuria Muria Is.)
(Oman)

Şanāw
W. Rakhawt
W. Shkasay
W. Ṭjim
Thamarīt
J. al Qarāʾ
Jabal Samḥān
1678
Raʾs Naws
Sādḥ

Al Khabrāh
W. Qnāb
Ḥasik

**16**

W. Makhbuh
Birr Tamīs
Thamūd
Ḥabarūt
J. al Qamar
Rakhyūt
Salālah
Mirbāṭ
Damqawt

Minwakh
Fughmah
Qunfudh
Al Qurḥ
Al Faydamī
Al Fatk
W. Ġʾa
Al Ghaydah
Ghubbat al Qamar
Khalfūt
Raʾs Fartak

**A   R   A   B   I   A   N**

**D**

Shibām
Tarim
Aynāt
Saywūn
Al Qaṭn
Al Hajarayn
Al Ghayl
ʿItāb
Qishn
Sayhūt
Ghubbat al Qamar

2469
Sargah
Ghayl Bā Wazīr
Hiṣn al Qarn
Khurayḍah
Al Ghaydah
Quṣayʿir
Ash Shiḥr
Maṣnaʿah
Burūm
Al Mukallā
Shuḥayr

**S   E   A**

Bir ʿAlī
Al Ḥasy

East from Greenwich    **5**

**Socotra**
(Yemen)
Raʾs Layḥt
Qatansiyah
Raʾs Khawlaf
Timareh
Qādib
Sigira
Raʾs Mami
Fahr

**12**

ʿAbd al Kūrī
The Brothers
Raʾs Qaṭānan

**52**    **6**    **56**    **7**

Projection: Conical with two standard parallels

Provinces in Turkey are named after the chief towns which are underlined.

Division between Greeks and Turks in Cyprus; Turks to the North.

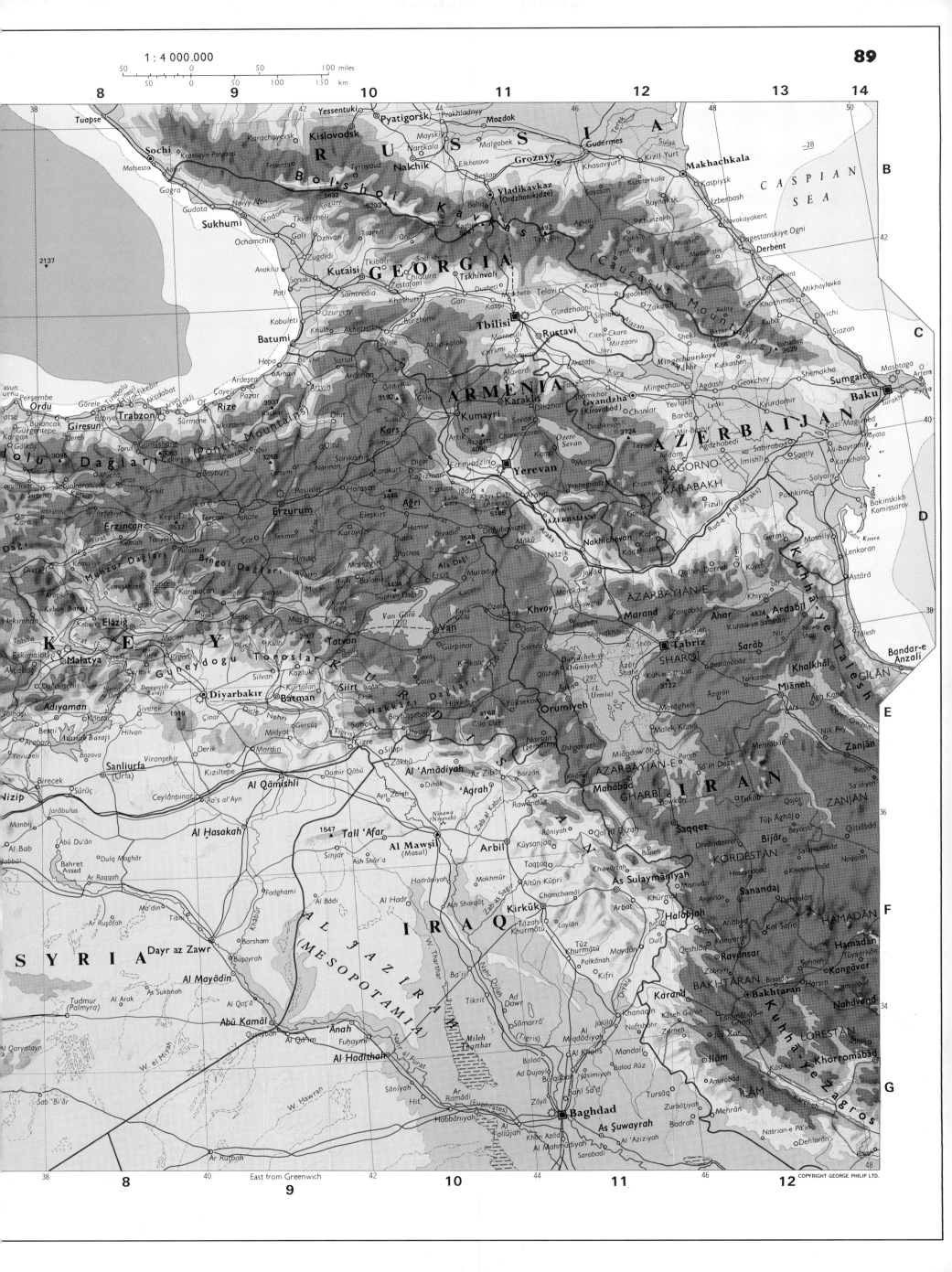

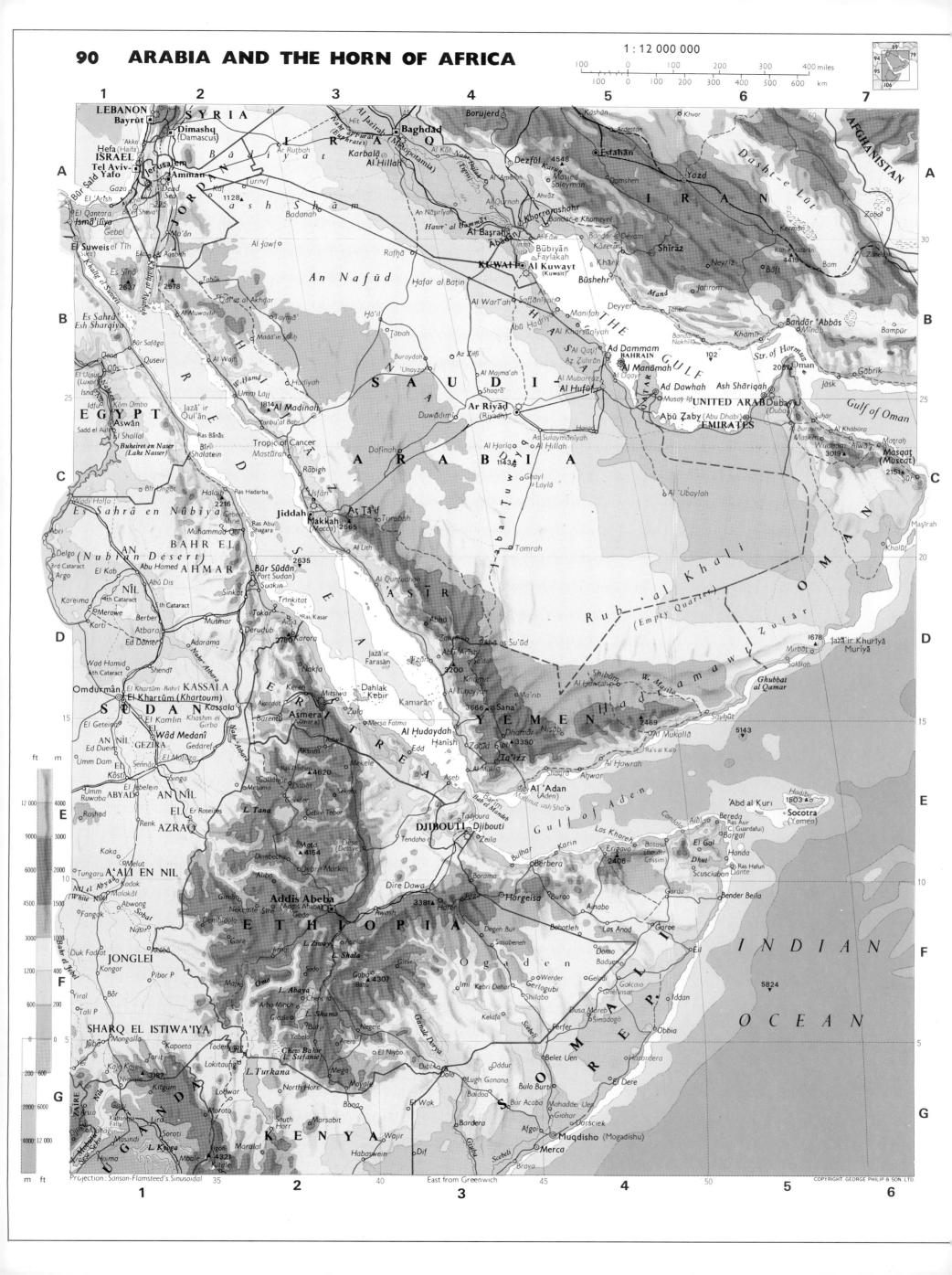

1 : 12 000 000

100      0      100      200      300      400 miles
100    0   100  200   300   400   500   600 km

1 : 2 000 000

10  0  10  20  30  40  50 miles
10  0  10 20 30 40 50 60 70 80 km

**CYPRUS**

Paphos
Episkopi
Episkopi Bay
Limassol
Akrotiri Bay
C. Gata

**M E D I T E R R A N E A N**

**S E A**

Al Hamidiyah
Al Minā'
Tall Kalakh
**Ḥimṣ** (Homs)
Shinshār
Furqlus
-1075

Halbā
Al Qaşayr
Al Buṣayḥ
Al Qaryatayn
Bi'r Ghaddr

ASH SHAMĀL
**Ṭarābulus** (Tripoli)
Zgharta
Qurnat as Sawdā' 3088
Al Batrūn
Dūma
Jubayl
Ibrāhīm
Jūniyah
Bṣharrī Yabrūdo 2616
2464
Al Labwoh
2628
Baʻlabakk
An Nabk

**BAYRŪT** (Beirut)
Ash Shuwayfāt
Zaḥlah
2420
Ash
Jabal
**SYRIA**
J. az Zubaydīyah
1406

Khirbat Qanāfar
al Barūk 1942
Ash Shaykh
**DIMASHQ** (Damascus)
Dūma
Al Qutayfah
Khān Abū Shāmāt

Jazzin
AL
An Nabaţīyah at Taḥta
Mt Hermon 2814
Al Khyān
Al Kiswah
Qaṭanā
Az Zabbānī
Daraytā
A'raj
Al Ḥijānah

Şūr (Tyre)
JANŪB
Qiryat Shemona
1197
Quḥaytirah
As Sanamayn
Burqa
AS ṢAFĀ

Nahariyya
Me'ona
HAZOR
Golan Hts.
Refid
DARʻĀ
W. al Harīr
Shahba
1800
Salah

ʻAkko (Acre)
Zefat
Ḥagalil
Migdal
Izra
AS SUWAYDĀ
Mifraz Hefa
Sakhnīn
Qiryat Yam
Kinneret
Dar'ā
Busrā ash Shām
Salkhad
Jabal Durūz
**Ḥefa** (Haifa)
Qiryat Ata Teverya
Yam
Yarmūk
Tirat Karmel
Nazareth
Kinneret
Al Ramthā
Daʼliyat el Karmel
HEFA
HAZAFON
ʻAfula
ḤEFA
TEL MEGIDDO
Umm el Faḥm
Bet Sheʻan
**Irbid**
Al Mafraq
Umm al Qittayn

**CAESAREA**
Pardes Ḥanna
Bet She'an
Ḥadera
Shōmrōn
Agabat
Al Mafraq
IRBID

**ISRAEL**
Netanya
**NABULUS**
SAMARIA
ʻAjlūn
Umm ad Daraj
1247
Jarash
HAMERKAZ
W. al Farīʻah
Tulkarm
Herzliyya
Under Israeli
Administration
SHILO
AL BALQĀʼ
**Az Zarqāʼ**
Bene Beraq
Azzūn
As Salt
Zarqā
**Tel Aviv-Yafo**
**Petaḥ Tiqwa**
**Ramat Gan**
West Bank
Na'ūr
**AMMĀN**
Bat Yam
Jericho
Rishon le Ziyyon
1016
Rām Allāh
ALQUDS
289
Waqdi as Sīr
N. Soreq
Lod
Ramla
Naʻūr
Ṭ. Ṭunayb
AL ʻĀṢIMAH
Reḥovot
Yavne
Ma'daba
Ashdod
Bet Shemesh
**Jerusalem** (Yerushalayim) (Al Quds)
Qiryat Malʼakhi
Bayt Laḥm (Bethlehem)
Ma'daba
Ashqelon
Qiryat Gat
TEL LAKHISH
Al Khalīl (Hebron)
**Gaza**
N. Shiqma
HAR YEHUDA
Az Zāhirīya
W. al Haydān
AL KHALIL
Dhibān
Gaza Strip
Sederot
Yam Hamelaḥ (Al Baḥr Mayyit)
1065
W. al Mawjib
Khān Yūnis
Rafaḥ
Arad
Al Karak
W. al Ghadaf
W. al Makhrūq
Al Daheir
**Be'er Sheva**
Bor Mashash
AL KARAK
Dimona
1305
Al Mazār
981
W. Bāʼir
Bûr Saʻîd (Port Said)
Rās Burūn
Sabkhet el Bardawîl
El ʻArîsh
Bir el Lahfan
-682
-333
W. al Ḥasa
Bûr Fu'âd
Romāni
Bir el Garārāt
**JORDAN**
Khalîg el Tîna
Bir el Abd
Bir el Gārāf
HADAROM
At Ṭafīlah
Bāʼir
Bir Qatia
Qezi'ot
Bir Kaseiba
-121
J. ash Shawmari
1072
El Qantara
Bir el Jafir
Bir el Duweidar
Muweilih
Bireîn
Mizpe Ramon
Nijil
Mañattat ʻUnayzah
El Quseima
892
Al Jafr
Wābid
Bir Madkūr
Bi'r ad Dabbāghāt
Rum Talat
Al Jamāla
1736
Qa'el Jafr
Ismâ'iliya
Khamsa
El Buheirat el Murrat el Kubra (Gt. Bitter L.)
Bir Hasana
**Hanegev** (Negev Desert)
N. Paran
Bir Beida
Ma'ān
Ra's an Naqb
1435
El SUWEIS
G. Yi'Allaq
1094
W. Qtratya
El 'Agrūd
N. Ḥiyyon
Mañattat ash Shīdīyah
El Suweis (Suez)
875
Bir Taufiq
Bir el Thamāda
W. el Brūk
W. el Mahashm
Bi'r al Māri
MAʻĀN
ʻAin Sudr
W. Sahēira
Nakhl
W. el 'Agaba
Yotvata
Ra's en Naqb
952
Bir Bad
Uyūn Mūsa
W. Varqa
948
G. el Kabrît
W. el Ruâg
W. Giraʼi
'En 'Avrona
Bi'r al Butayyiha
Bi'r al Qattān
**SAUDI**
Ghubbet el Bûs
Ginēfe
Sinî
El Wabeira
ET Thamad
El Kuntilla
El Wabeira
1592
**ARABIA**
Bîr Abu Şandik
Ras Matarma
Gebel el Tîh
Bir Abu Muhammad
SaR
Aqabah
**Sinai Peninsula**
W. Abu Ga'da
1272
W. Abu el Gāini
Al ʻAqabah
Bir el Biarāt
W. an Nuwayb
1165
Bîr Ṭâba
Khatīt el ʻAqaba
Hiql

OANA EL SUWEIS (Suez Canal)

**LEBANON**

JABAL LUBNĀN

Litānī

**E G Y P T**

SINAI

ft    m
9000  3000
6000  2000
4500  1500
3000  1000
1200  400
600   200
0     0
200   600
2000  6000
m     ft

Projection: Polyconic

East from Greenwich

COPYRIGHT, GEORGE PHILIP & SON. LTD.

— — — 1949 Armistice Line, 1967 and 1974 Cease Fire Lines

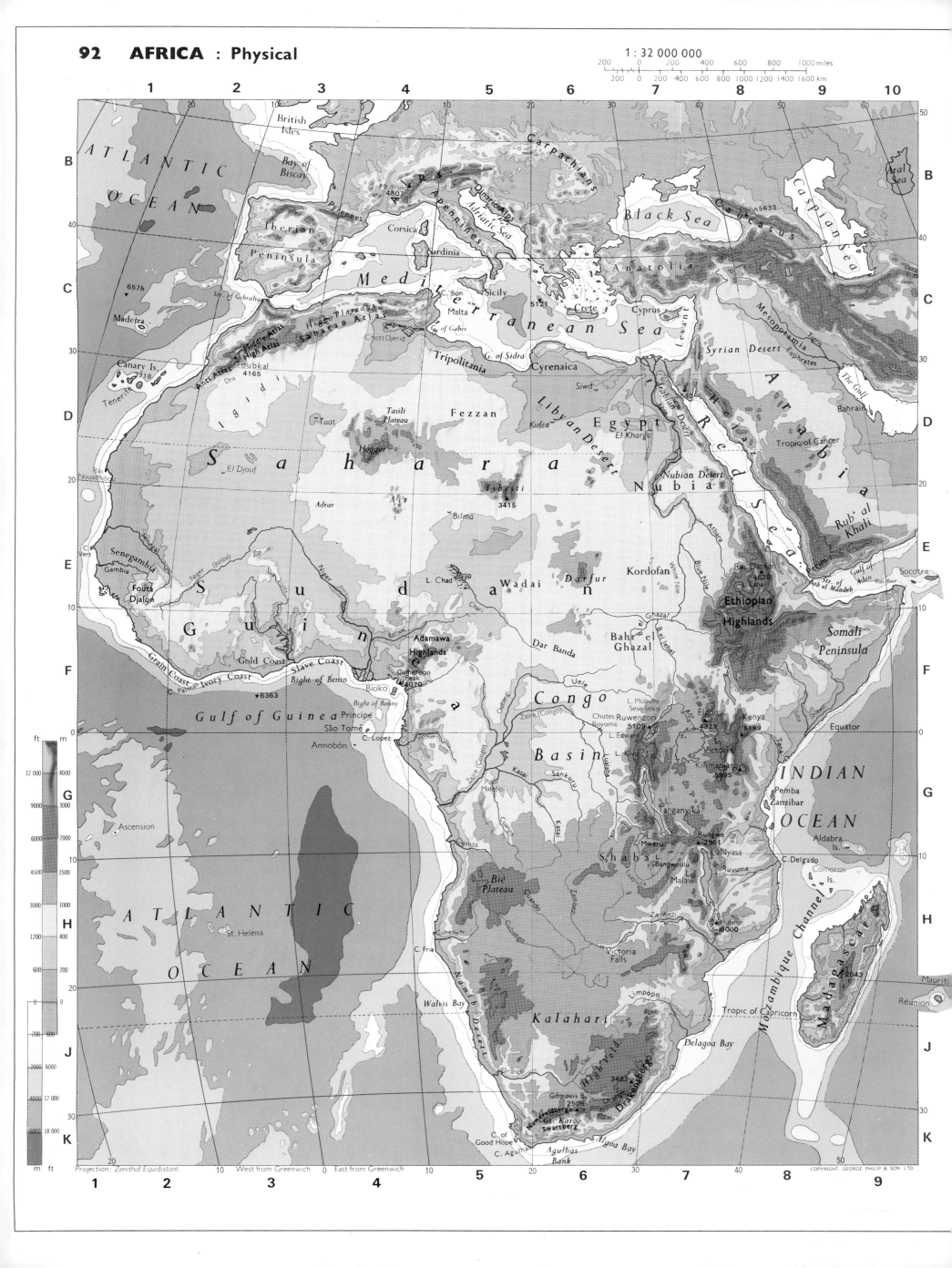

1 : 32 000 000

200    0    200    400    600    800    1000 miles
200    0    200  400  600  800 1000 1200 1400 1600 km

ft     m
12 000   4000
9000    3000
6000    2000
4500    1500
3000    1000
1200    400
600     200
0       0
200     600
2000    6000
4000   12 000
6000   18 000
m      ft

ATLANTIC OCEAN
British Isles
Bay of Biscay
Iberian Peninsula
Pyrenees
Madeira
Str. of Gibraltar
Canary Is.
Tenerife 3718
Ras Nouadhibou
C. Vert
Senegambia
Gambia
Senegal
Fouta Djalon
Grain Coast
Gold Coast
Ivory Coast
C. Palmas
Slave Coast
Bight of Benin
Bioko
Gulf of Guinea
Príncipe
São Tomé
C. Lopez
Annobón
Ascension
St. Helena
ATLANTIC OCEAN
Walvis Bay

Mt. Blanc 4807
Alps
Apennines
Dinaric Alps
Adriatic Sea
Corsica
Sardinia
C. Bon
Sicily
Malta
G. of Gabes
Chott Djerid
Tripolitania
Middle Atlas
High Atlas
Saharan Atlas
High Plateau
Anti Atlas
Toubkal 4165
Dra
Igidi
Tuat
El Djouf
Adrar
Tasili Plateau
Hoggar
Aïr
Bilma
Sahara
Fezzan
Libyan Desert
Kufra
El Kharga
Egypt
Tibesti 3415
L. Chad
Senegal
Niger (Joliba)
Volta
Niger
Benue
Chari
Sudan
Wadai
Darfur
Kordofan
Adamawa Highlands
Cameroon Peak 4079
Dar Banda
Bahr el Ghazal
Guinea
6363
Bight of Bonny

Carpathians
Black Sea
Caucasus
Elbrus 5633
Aral Sea
Caspian Sea
Anatolia
Crete
Cyprus
Mediterranean Sea
Cyrenaica
G. of Sidra
Siwa
Mesopotamia
Tigris
Euphrates
Syrian Desert
Levant
Arabian Desert
Nile
Sinai 2642
The Gulf
Bahrain
Tropic of Cancer
Red Sea
Hejaz
Rub' al Khali
Arabia
Nubian Desert
Nubia
White Nile
Blue Nile
Atbara
Ras Dashan 4620
Lake Tana
Ethiopian Highlands
Str. of Bab el Mandeb
Gulf of Aden
Ras Asir
Socotra
Somali Peninsula
Bahr el Ghazal
Bahr el Jebel
Ghazal
Uele
Ubangi
Congo Basin
Zaire (Congo)
Chutes Boyoma
L. Mobutu Sese Seko
Ruwenzori 5109
L. Edward
L. Kivu
Elgon 4321
Kenya 5199
Victoria
Kilimanjaro 5895
Equator
INDIAN OCEAN
L. Tanganyika
Zaire (Congo)
Kasai
Sankuru
Lulaba
Pool Malebo
Kwango
Kwilu
Cuanza
Shaba
L. Mweru
Bangweulu
Rungwe 2961
Nyasa
L. Malawi
Ruvuma
Luapula
Luangwa
Pemba
Zanzibar
Aldabra Is.
C. Delgado
Comoros Is.
Bié Plateau
Cubango
Cuando
Cuanza
Zambezi
Milanje 3000
Mozambique Channel
Madagascar 2643
Mauriti
Réunion
Kalahari
Okavango
Cubango
Namib Desert
Limpopo
Victoria Falls
C. Fria
Cunene
Tropic of Capricorn
Delagoa Bay
High Veld
Vaal
Orange
Drakensberg 3482
Compass B. 2505
Nuweveldberge
Gt. Karoo Swartberg 2508
C. of Good Hope
C. Agulhas
Agulhas Bank
Algoa Bay

50    40    30    20    10    0    10    20    30    40    50

Projection: Zenithal Equidistant.    West from Greenwich    East from Greenwich
COPYRIGHT GEORGE PHILIP & SON LTD.

1 : 32 000 000

200   0   200   400   600   800   1000 miles
200   0   200   400   600   800   1000   1400   1600 km

1   2   3   4   5   6   7   8   9   10

**A**

ATLANTIC

OCEAN

UNITED KINGDOM   London   NETH.   GERMANY   POLAND   Warsaw

BELG.   Prague   CZECH REP.   Kiev   RUSSIA   Volgograd

Paris   Vienna   SLOVAK REP.   UKRAINE

FRANCE   SWITZ.   AUSTRIA   HUNGARY   KAZAKHSTAN

Bay of Biscay   CROATIA   ROMANIA   Odessa   Aral Sea

BOS. HERZ.   YUG.   BULGARIA   Black Sea   GEORGIA   Caspian Sea

**B**

Corsica   ITALY   Adriatic Sea   Istanbul   ARM.   AZERB.   Baku   TURKMEN.

PORTUGAL   Madrid   SPAIN   Rome   ALB.   MAC.   GREECE   Athens   TURKEY   Ankara

Lisbon   Sardinia   Crete   CYPRUS   Aleppo   Mosul   Tehran

Madeira (Port.)   Tetouan   Algiers   Annaba   Constantine   Sicily   MALTA   SYRIA   Damascus   Baghdad   Esfahan

Casablanca   Rabat   Fès   Oran   TUNISIA   Tunis   Sfax   Tel Aviv-Jaffa   Jerusalem   IRAQ   Basra   IRAN

**C**

Mediterranean Sea   Tripoli   Misratah   Alexandria   Port Said   Suez   ISRAEL   Syrian Desert   JORDAN   KUWAIT

MOROCCO   Marrakesh   Benghazi   CAIRO   El Faiyum   The Gulf

Canary Is. (Sp.)   Djado   Ghadames

Dra   ALGERIA   LIBYA   EGYPT   Asyut   Nile   SAUDI   Riyadh   Bahrain

**D**

WESTERN SAHARA   El Aaiun   In Salah   Marzuq   Al Jawf   Aswan   ARABIA   Medina   Tropic of Cancer

Dakhla   F'Dérik   Wadi Halfa   Mecca   Jedda

Ras Nouadhibou (Cap Blanc)   Sahara   Pt. Sudan   Red Sea

St. Louis   MAURITANIA   Nouakchott   Tombouctou (Timbuktu)   Agades   Atbara   YEMEN

**E**

Dakar   SENEGAL   Senegal   MALI   NIGER   CHAD   Omdurman   Khartoum   Kassala   Mesewa   Asmera   Socotra (Yemen)

GAMBIA   Banjul   Niamey   SUDAN   Wad Medani   ERITREA   Ras Asir (C. Guardafui)

GUINEA-BISSAU   Bamako   BURKINA   Ouagadougou   FASO   Kano   L. Chad   Abéché   El Fasher   El Obeid   DJIBOUTI   Djibouti   G. of Aden   Berbera

Conakry   GUINEA   Bobo-Dioulasso   BENIN   Kaduna   Maiduguri   Ndjamena (Ft. Lamy)   Chari   Blue Nile   L. Tana   Addis Ababa   Hargeisa

**F**

Freetown   SIERRA LEONE   TOGO   NIGERIA   Abuja   Benue   CENTRAL AFRICAN REPUBLIC   Wau   Bel Jebel   ETHIOPIA   Bohot Uen

IVORY COAST   Bouake   GHANA   Ibadan   Enugu   Malakal   White Nile

Monrovia   LIBERIA   Kumasi   Lagos   Porto Novo   Port Harcourt   Oubangui   Bangui   L. Turkana   SOMALI REP.

Abidjan   Yamoussoukro   Accra   CAMEROON   Yaoundé   Zaïre (Congo)   Mogadishu (Mogadiscio)

Sekondi-Takoradi   Bight of Benin   Bioko   Douala   Kisangani   L. Mobutu Sese Seko   UGANDA   Merca

Gulf of Guinea   EQUATORIAL GUINEA   Rio Muni   Kampala   KENYA   Shabelle   Equator

SAO TOMÉ & PRINCIPE   Libreville   Congo   Zaïre (Congo)   Mbandaka   L. Edward   L. Victoria   Kisumu   Nairobi   INDIAN

**0**

C. Lopez   GABON   ZAÏRE   L. Kivu   RWANDA   Kigali   BURUNDI   Bujumbura   Mombasa

Annobon   Lualaba   Kasai   L. Tanganyika   Dodoma   TANZANIA   Zanzibar

**G**

Ascension (Br.)   Brazzaville   Kinshasa   Kananga   Dar-es-Salaam   OCEAN

Pointe Noire   CABINDA   Matadi   Kwango

ATLANTIC   Luanda   L. Mweru   Aldabra Is.

**H**

St. Helena (Br.)   Lobito   ANGOLA   Likasi   Lubumbashi   L. Nyasa   C. Delgado   COMOROS   Antsiranana

Huambo   Ndola   MALAWI   L. Malawi   Ruvuma   Mozambique   Mahajanga   Toamasina

Namibe   ZAMBIA   Lusaka   Lilongwe   Blantyre

Cunene   Cubango   Zambezi   Beira   MADAGASCAR   Antananarivo   MAURITIUS

OCEAN   Livingstone   Harare   MOZAMBIQUE   Réunion (Fr.)

**J**

NAMIBIA   Windhoek   BOTSWANA   ZIMBABWE   Bulawayo   Limpopo   Tropic of Capricorn   Mozambique Channel   Fianarantsoa

Gaborone   Pretoria   Mbabane   SWAZILAND   Maputo

Johannesburg   Vaal   LESOTHO   Maseru

Orange   Kimberley   Bloemfontein   Durban

SOUTH AFRICA   East London

**K**

Cape Town   Port Elizabeth

C. of Good Hope   C. Agulhas

Nairobi   Capital Cities

Projection: Zenithal Equidistant.   West from Greenwich   0   East from Greenwich   COPYRIGHT. GEORGE PHILIP & SON. LTD.

1   2   3   4   5   6   7   8   9

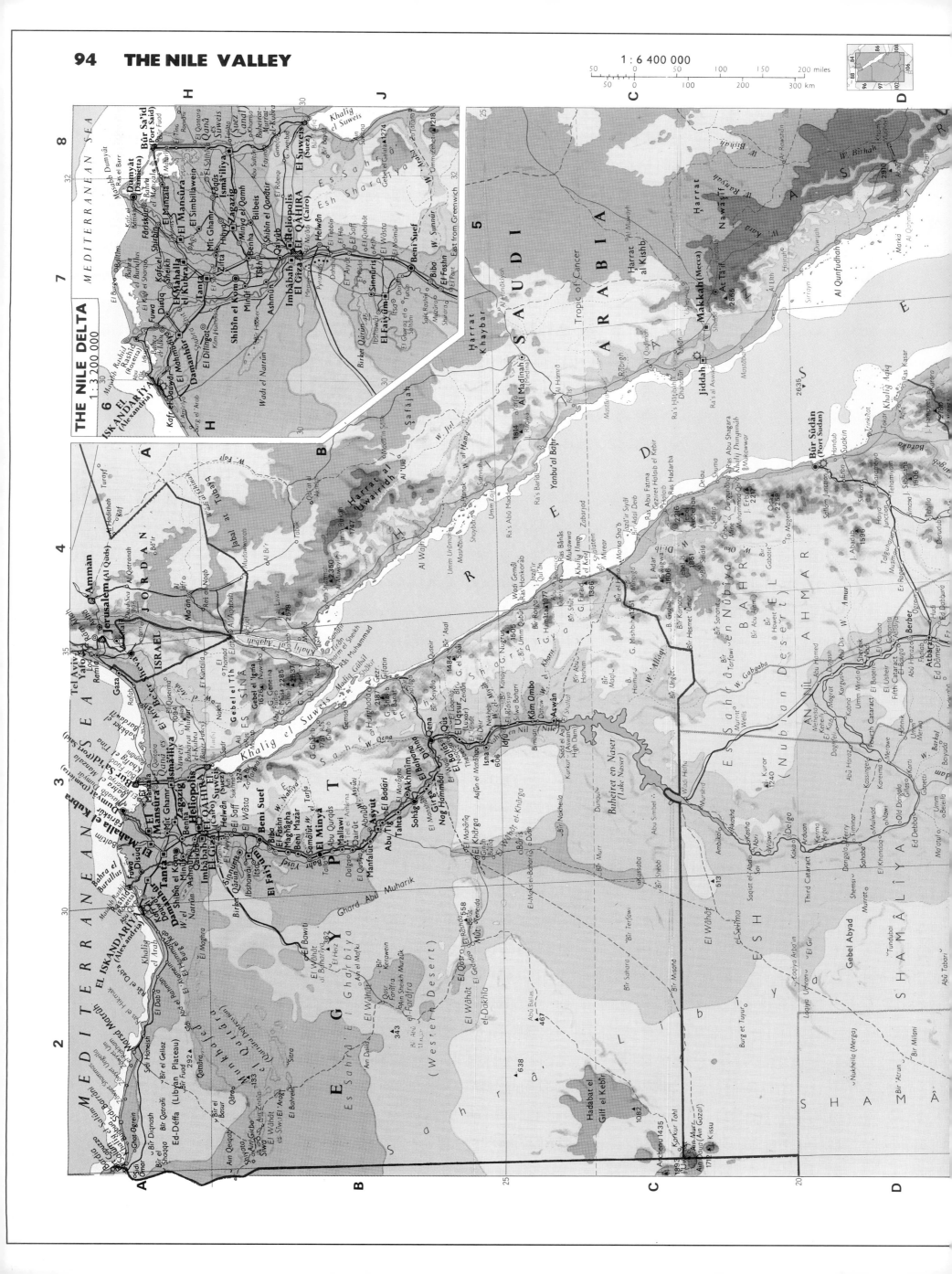

**THE NILE DELTA**
1 : 3 200 000

1 : 6 400 000

MEDITERRANEAN SEA

MEDITERRANEAN SEA

SAUDI ARABIA

EGYPT

JORDAN

ISRAEL

SINA

(Western Desert)

Es Sahrâ el Gharbîya

Es Sahrâ esh Sharqiya

Buheirat en Naser (Lake Nasser)

En Nûbiya

El Bahr el Ahmar

Es Sahrâ

Nubian Desert

Makkah (Mecca)

Jiddah

Bûr Sûdân (Port Sudan)

Bûr Sa'îd (Port Said)

El Iskandarîya (Alexandria)

EL QÂHIRA (Cairo)

Amman (Al Quds)

Jerusalem

Tel Aviv-Yafo

Gaza

Aswân

Atbara

Berber

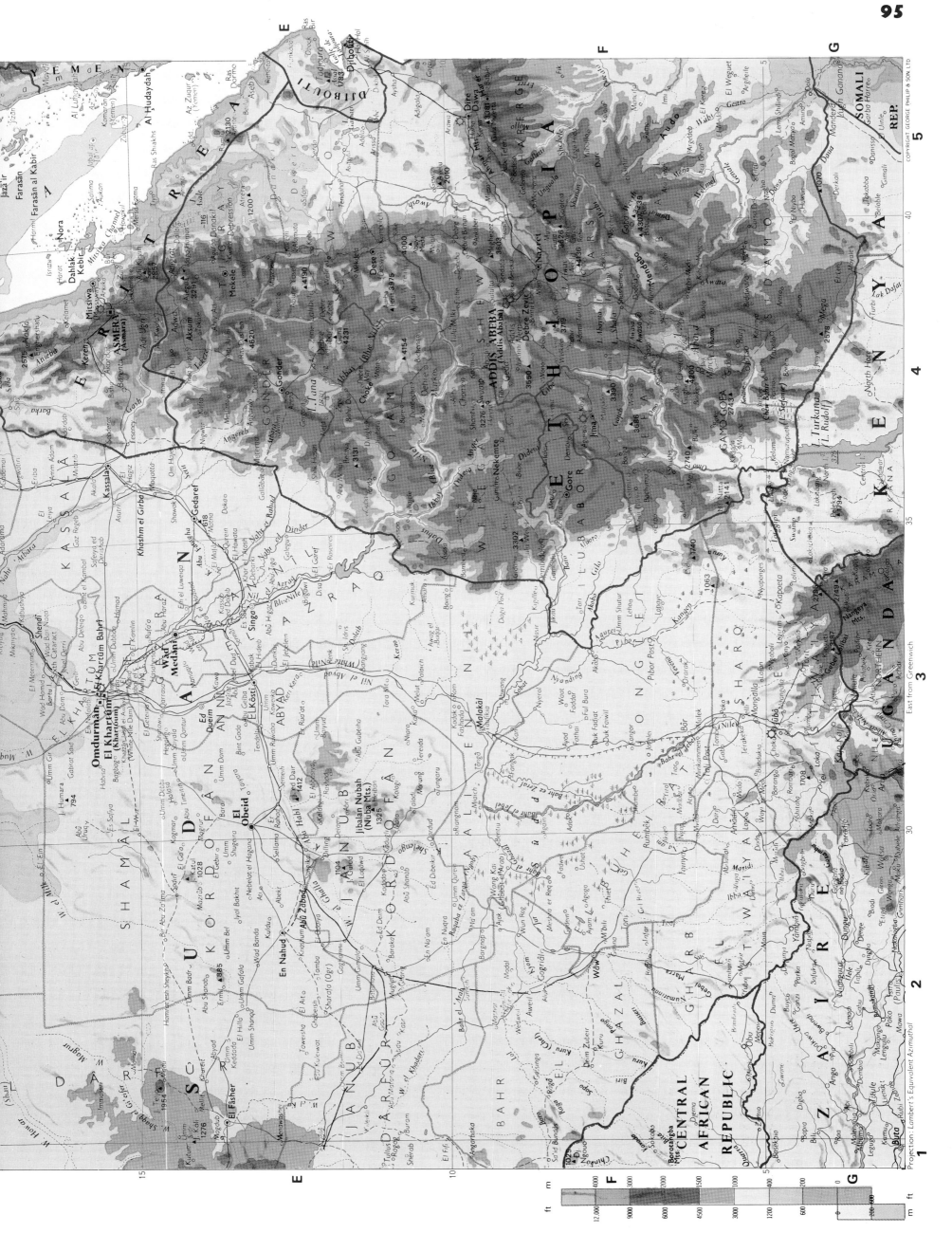

Projection: Lambert's Equivalent Azimuthal

East from Greenwich

YEMEN

Jazā'ir Farasān al Kabīr

Jazā'ir Farasān (Yemen)

Dahlak Kebir

Mitsiwa

ASMERA (Asmara)

ERITREA

DJIBOUTI
Djibouti

ETHIOPIA

HARRAR RANGE
Dire Dawa

Mekele

Aksum

Gonder

L. Tana

GOJJAM

SHEWA

ADDIS ABEBA
(Adis Abeba)

Debre Zeyit

Nazret

AUSSA

OGADEN

SOMALI REP.

Jima

GAMO GOFA

Gore

ITU BABOR

WELEGA

Nekemte

KENYA

L. Turkana (L. Rudolf)

SUDAN

KASSALA

Kassala

Gedaref

Khashm el Girba

Wad Medani

Omdurmān
El Khartūm (Khartoum)
Khartūm Bahrī

EL KHARTŪM

Shendi

EN NIL EL AZRAQ

Blue Nile

El Kosti

Ed Dueim

AN NIL EL ABYAD

Singa

SENNAR

El Obeid

SHAMĀL KORDOFĀN

JANUB KORDOFĀN

Jibalan Nubah (Nuba Mts.)

En Nahud

Abu Zabad

SHAMĀL DĀRFŪR

El Fāsher

JANUB DĀRFŪR

BAHR EL GHAZAL

A'ALI EN NĪL

Malakal

Bōr

Juba

BAHR EL JEBEL

CENTRAL AFRICAN REPUBLIC

ZAIRE

UGANDA
NORTHERN
Nangeya Mts.

m
ft
4000
3000
2000
1500
1000
400
200
0

ft
12,000
9000
6000
4500
3000
1200
600
0

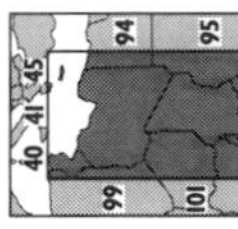

EGYPT

LIBYA

TUNISIA

ALGERIA

SICILIA

MEDITERRANEAN SEA

MALTA

Banghāzī (Benghazi)

Zāwiyat al Bayḍā'

Tarābulus (Tripoli)

Ghudāmis

Sfax

TUNIS

CONSTANTINE

Sousse

Kairouan

Gabès

Sahrā'

SAHARA

Khalīj Surt (Gulf of Sidra)

Tropic of Cancer

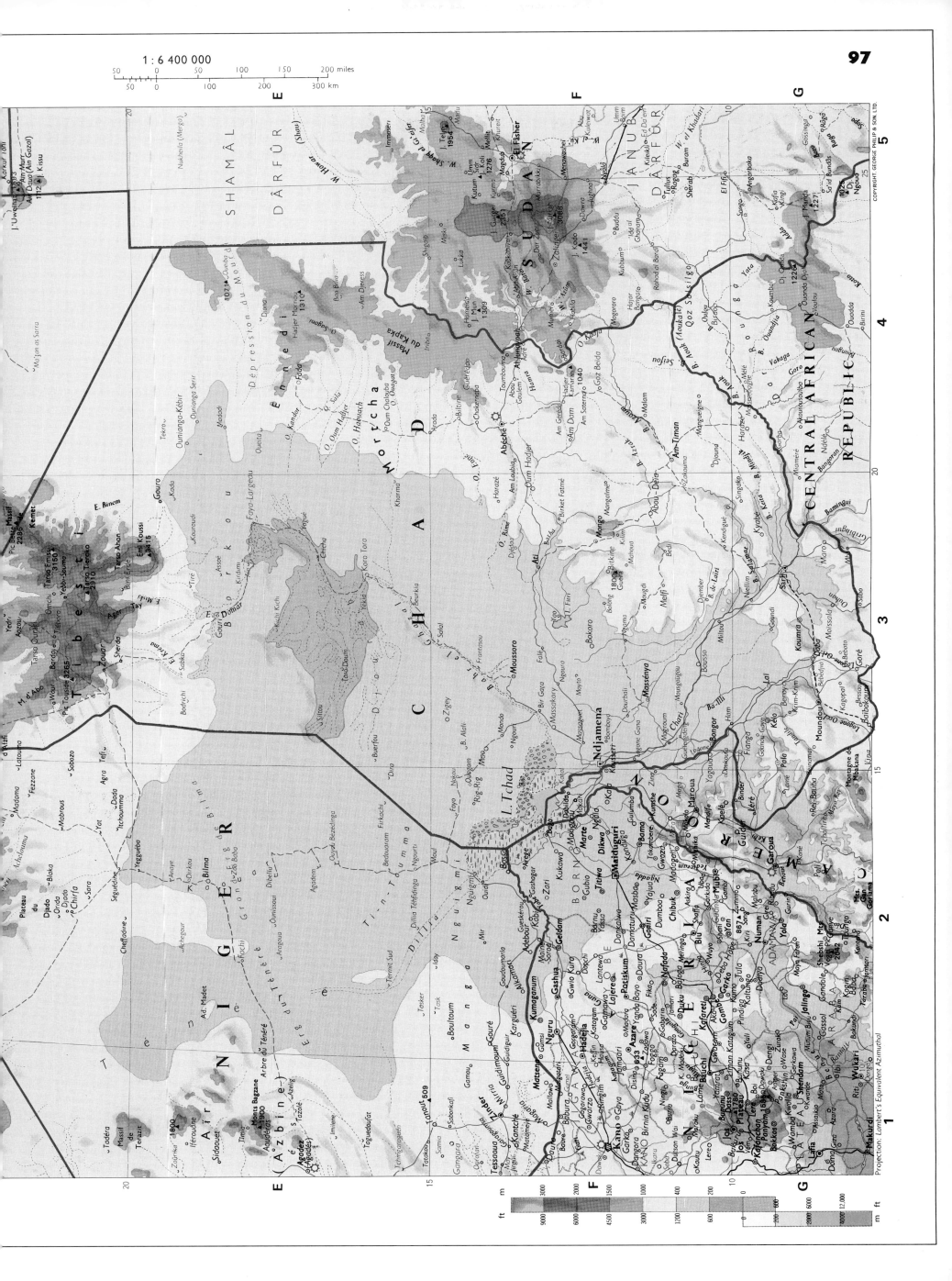

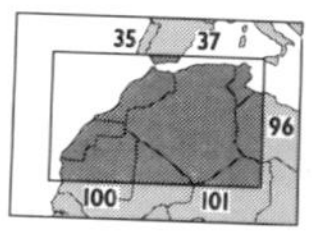

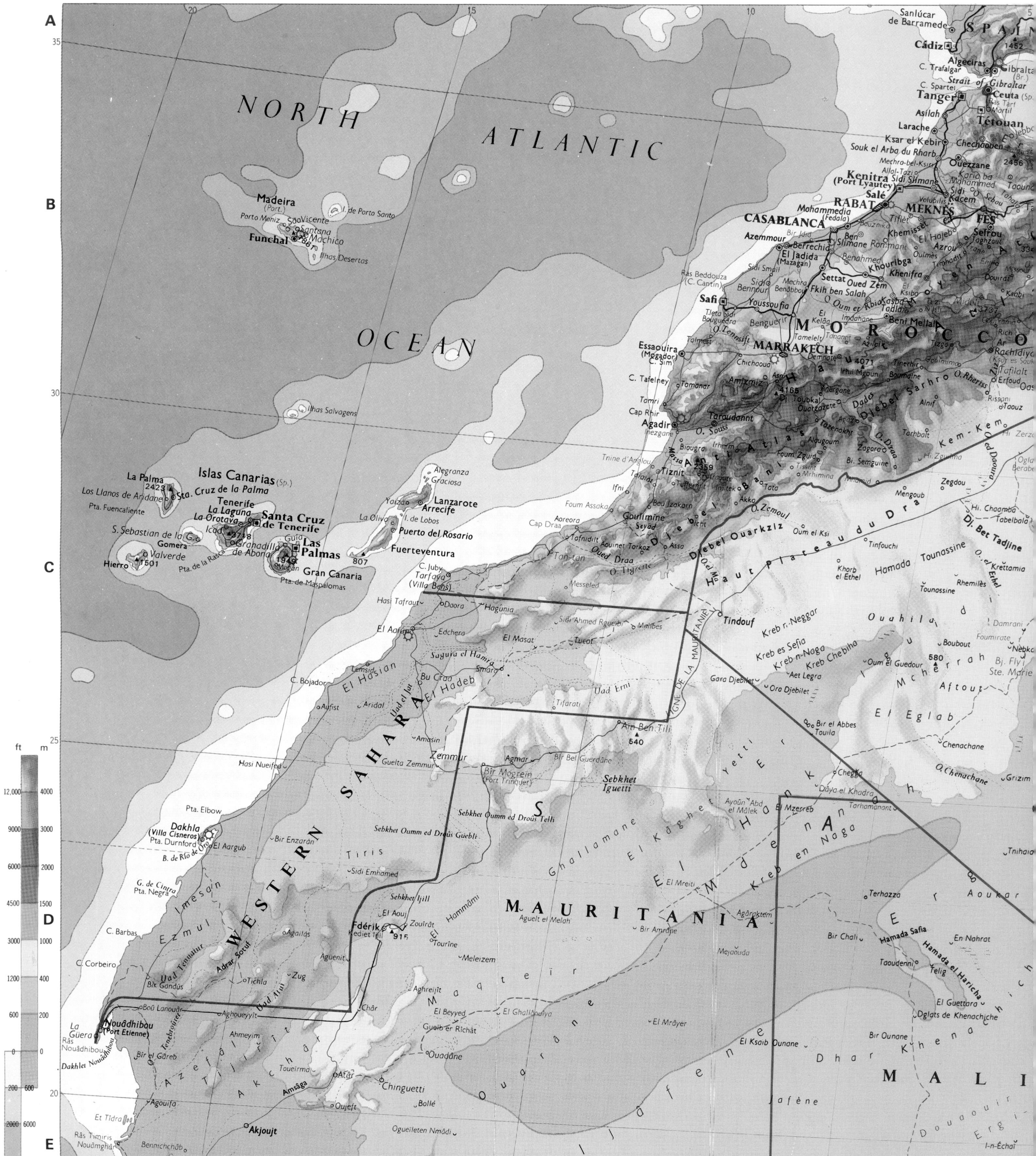

NORTH ATLANTIC OCEAN

**SPAIN**
Sanlúcar de Barramede
Cádiz
Algeciras
Gibraltar
C. Trafalgar
Strait of Gibraltar
Tanger
Ceuta (Sp.)
C. Spartel
Tétouan
Asilah
Larache
Chechaouen
K'sar el Kebir
Ouezzane
Souk el Arba du Rharb
Mechra-bel-Ksiri
Kenitra (Port Lyautey)
Sidi Slimane
Salé
RABAT
MEKNES
FES
Sefrou
CASABLANCA
Mohammedia (Fedala)
Azemmour
Berrechid
Settat
El Jadida (Mazagan)
Khouribga
Khenifra
Oued Zem
Fkih ben Salah
Safi
Youssoufia
Beni Mellal
Essaouira (Mogador)
C. Sim
MARRAKECH
MOROCCO
Demnate
Chichaoua
Cap Tafelney
Tamanar
Taroudannt
Agadir
Inezgane
O. Souss
Tiznit
Ifni
Goulimine
Tan-tan
Djebel Sarhro
Djebel Bani
Haut Plateau du Dra
Oued Draa
Tindouf

**Madeira (Port.)**
São Vicente
I. de Porto Santo
Porto Moniz
Santana
Machico
Funchal
Ilhas Desertas

Ilhas Salvagens

**Islas Canarias (Sp.)**
La Palma
Sta. Cruz de la Palma
Los Llanos de Aridane
Pta. Fuencaliente
Tenerife
La Laguna
La Orotava
Icod
Santa Cruz de Tenerife
S. Sebastian de la G.
Gomera
Valverde
Hierro
Alegranza
Graciosa
Lanzarote
Arrecife
La Oliva
I. de Lobos
Las Palmas
Puerto del Rosario
Gran Canaria
Fuerteventura
Pta. de Maspalomas

C. Juby
Tarfaya (Villa Bens)
El Aaiún
Saguia el Hamra
Smara

**WESTERN SAHARA**
C. Bojador
El Hasian
Bu Craa
El Hadeb
Aridal
Aufist
Amasin
Zemmur
Guelta Zemmur
Hasi Nueifed

Pta. Elbow
C. Barbas
Dakhla (Villa Cisneros)
Pta. Durnford
El Aargub
B. de Río de Oro
Bir Enzarán
Tiris
Sidi Emhamed
Sebkhet Ijill
El Aouj
Zouîrât
Fdérik
915
Tourîne

**MAURITANIA**
Bir el Abbes
Touila
Aïn Ben Tili
540
Chenachane
Sebkhet Iguetti
Sebkhet Oumm ed Drous Telli
Sebkhet Oumm ed Drous Guebli
Bir Moghrein (Fort Trinquet)
Bir Bel Guerdâne
Ayoûn Abd el Mâlek
El Eglab
Mzereb
Ghallamane
El Kaghet
El Kharrob
Hamoûni
Hammâmi
Aguelt el Melah
Bir Amrâne
Meleizem
Mejaouda
Agârektem
Maqteïr
Aguelt
El Beyyed
El Ghallaouiya
Guelb er Richât
Ouadâne
Terhazza
Taoudenni
Hamada Safia
Hamada el Haricha
Telig
En Nahrat
Bir Chali
El Guettara
Dglats de Khenachiche
Dhar Khenachiche
Bir Ounane
El Ksaib Ounane
Adrar
Tichla
Zug
Aguenit
Dad Atui
Chor
Aghreijît
Azefâl
Tijirit
Akchâr
Ahmeyim
Bou Lanouâr
Aghoueyyit
**MALI**
Douaouir

La Güera
Nouâdhibou (Port Étienne)
Râs Nouâdhibou
Nouâdhibou
Bir el Gâreb
Dakhlet Nouâdhibou
Chinguetti
Atar
Toueirma
Amâga
Oujeft
Bollé
Oguileten Nmâdi
Douadir
Akjoujt
Râs Timiris
Noûâmghâr
Bennichâb
Bou Rjeimat
Sebkhet Te-n-Dghâmcha

Projection: Lambert's Equivalent Azimuthal

West from Greenwich

ft  m
12,000  4000
9000  3000
6000  2000
4500  1500
3000  1000
1200  400
600  200
0  0
200  600
2000  6000
4000  12,000
m  ft

1 : 6 400 000

50   0   50   100   150   200 miles
50   0   100   200   300 km

**4**        **5**        **6**        **7**

MEDITERRANEAN SEA

MÁLAGA   Granada   Almería   Motril   Antequera

ORAN (Oahran)   Mostaganem   Arzew   ALGER (Algiers)   El Harrach   Blida   Medea   Bejaia   CONSTANTINE   Annaba   TUNIS   Bizerte (Binzert)   SICILIA   Marsala   Pantelleria (It.)

Melilla (Sp.)   Nador   Sidi-Bel-Abbès   Mascara   Saïda   Tiaret   Sétif   El Eulma   Batna   Guelma   Souk Ahras   El Kef   Kairouan   Sousse   Monastir   Mahdia   Sfax   Îles Kerkenna

Tlemcen   Oujda   Jerada   El Bayadh   Laghouat   Biskra   Khenchela   Tébessa   Gafsa   G. de Gabès   Gabès   Djerba   Zarzis   Médenine   Tatahouine   Tarābulus (Tripoli)

Béchar   Ghardaïa   Ouargla   Touggourt   El Oued   Nefta   Tozeur   Chott Djerid   Chott Melrhir   El Meghaier

GRAND ERG OCCIDENTAL   GRAND ERG ORIENTAL   Ghudāmis   GHARYĀN   Plateau du Tinrhert   Al Hammādah al Ḥamrā'

El Goléa   Timimoun   In Salah   Bordj Omar Driss   In Amenas   Edjeleh   L I B Y A

Plateau du Tademaït   AWBĀRĪ   Tassili n'Ajjer   Ghat   Al Barkāt

H O G G A R   A H A G G A R   Tamanrasset   Mt. Tahat 2918   In Guezzam

Adrar des Iforhas   N I G E R   Massif de Terazit

ALGERIA   TUNISIA

East from Greenwich   **5**        **6**        **7**

COPYRIGHT. GEORGE PHILIP & SON. LTD.

A   35   B   30   C   25   D   20   E

MAURITANIA

SENEGAL

GAMBIA

GUINEA-BISSAU
Arquipélago dos Bijagós

GUINEA

SIERRA
LEONE

LIBERIA

IVORY COAST

BUR
FA

DAKAR

Nouakchott

Tombouctou
(Timbuktu)

Bamako

Ségou

Mopti

Bobo-Dioulasso

Ouag
Koudougo

Freetown

Conakry

Monrovia

Abidjan

Bouaké

Kankan

Kayes

St. Louis

Kuma

Grain Coast

Ivory Coast

GUL

ft    m

12 000   4000
9000   3000
6000   2000
4500   1500
3000   1000
1200   400
600   200
0   0
200   600
2000   6000
4000   12 000
6000   18 000

m   ft

Projection: Lambert's Equivalent Azimuthal

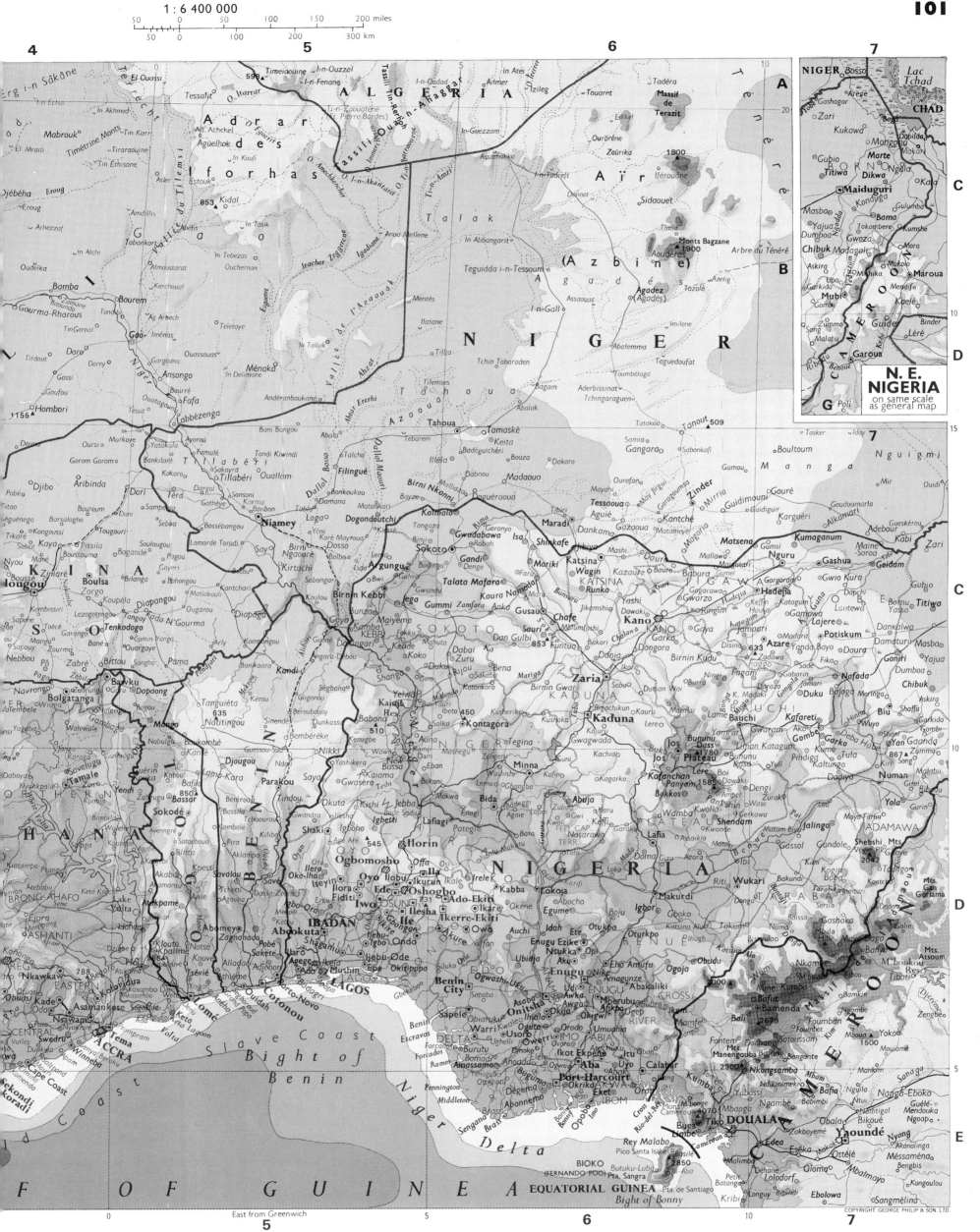

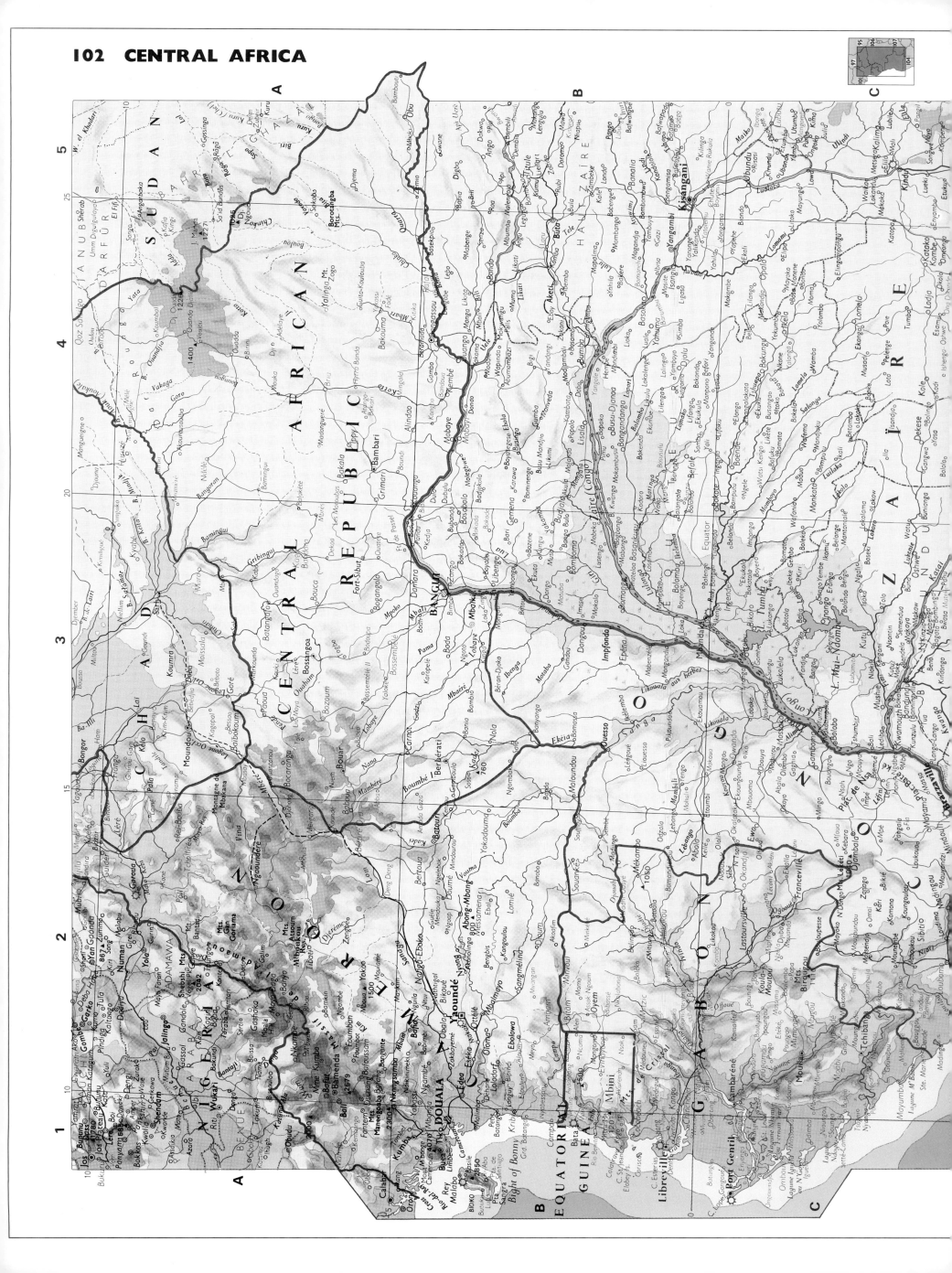

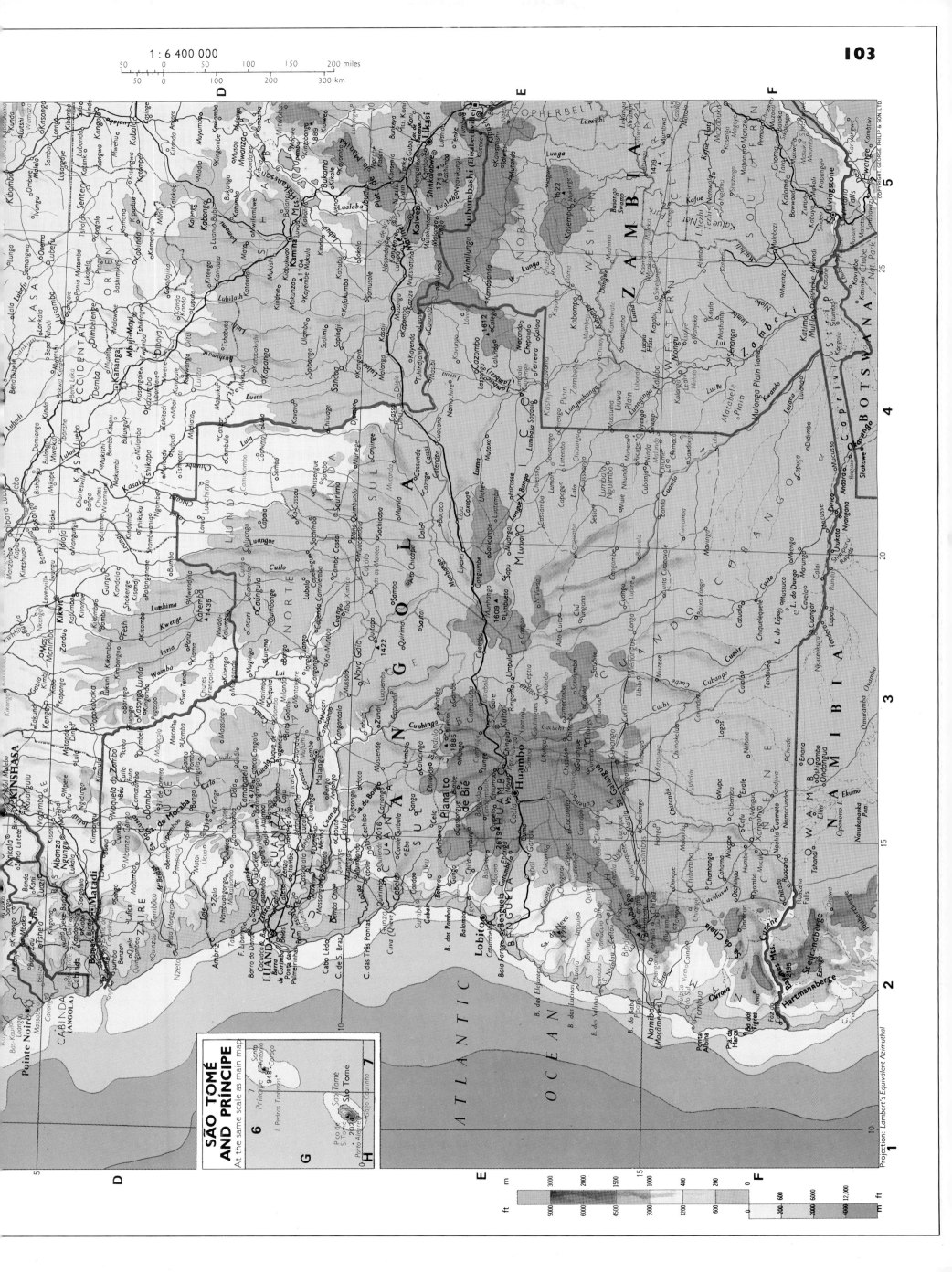

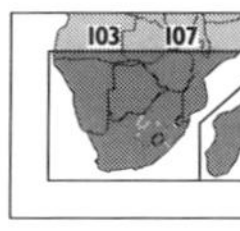

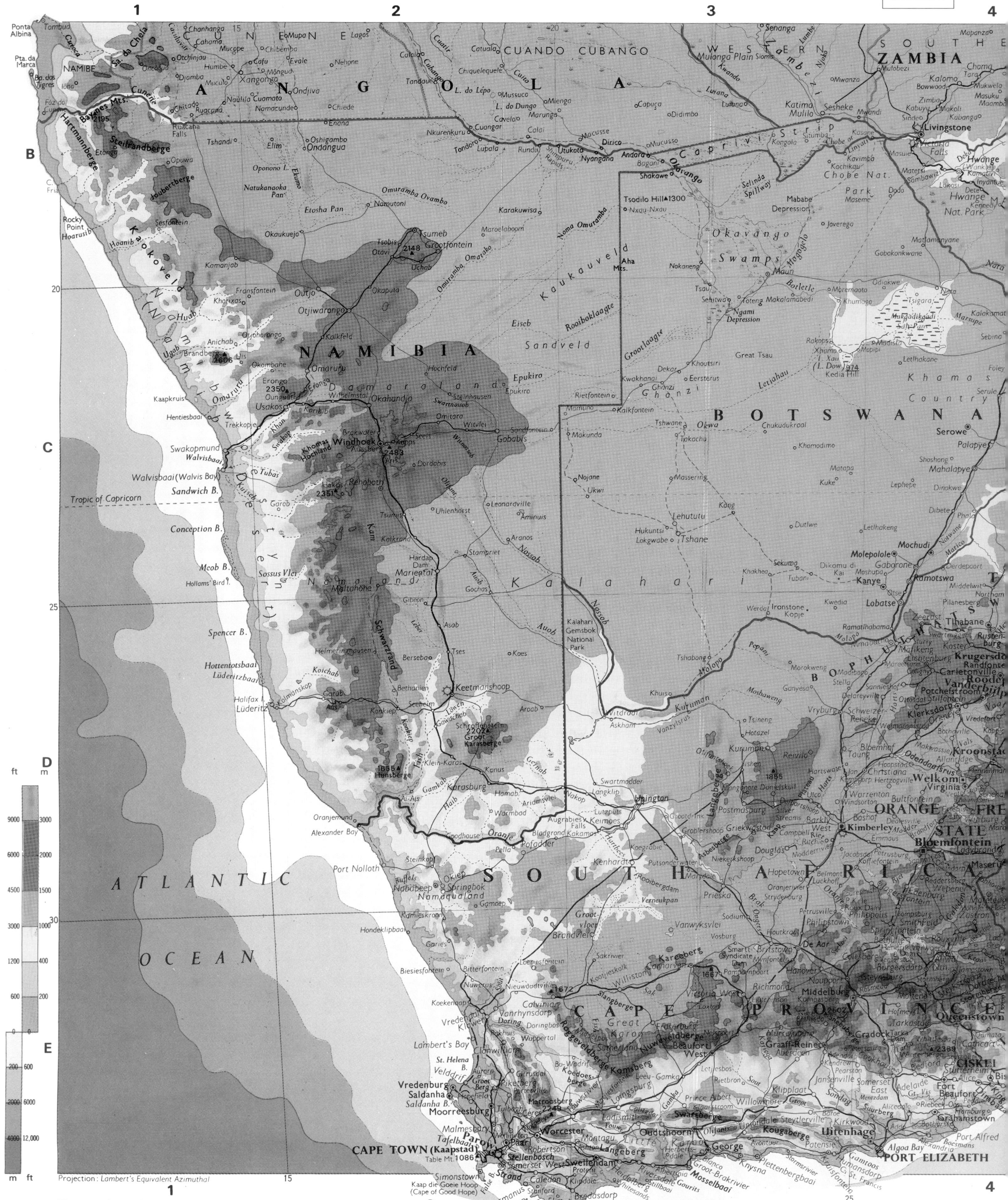

ANGOLA

ZAMBIA

NAMIBIA

BOTSWANA

SOUTH AFRICA

CAPE PROVINCE

ORANGE FREE STATE

ATLANTIC OCEAN

Tropic of Capricorn

CUANDO CUBANGO

Caprivi Strip

Okavango Swamps

Kalahari

Etosha Pan

Windhoek

Walvisbaai (Walvis Bay)

Swakopmund

Lüderitz

Keetmanshoop

CAPE TOWN (Kaapstad)

PORT ELIZABETH

Kimberley

Bloemfontein

Gaborone

Livingstone

Kaap die Goeie Hoop (Cape of Good Hope)

C. Agulhas

ft m

9000 3000
6000 2000
4500 1500
3000 1000
1200 400
600 200
0 0
200 600
2000 6000
4000 12,000
m ft

Projection: Lambert's Equivalent Azimuthal

This map shows the four provinces in South Africa prior to the April
1994 elections. A map at the end of the index shows the proposed
nine new provinces.

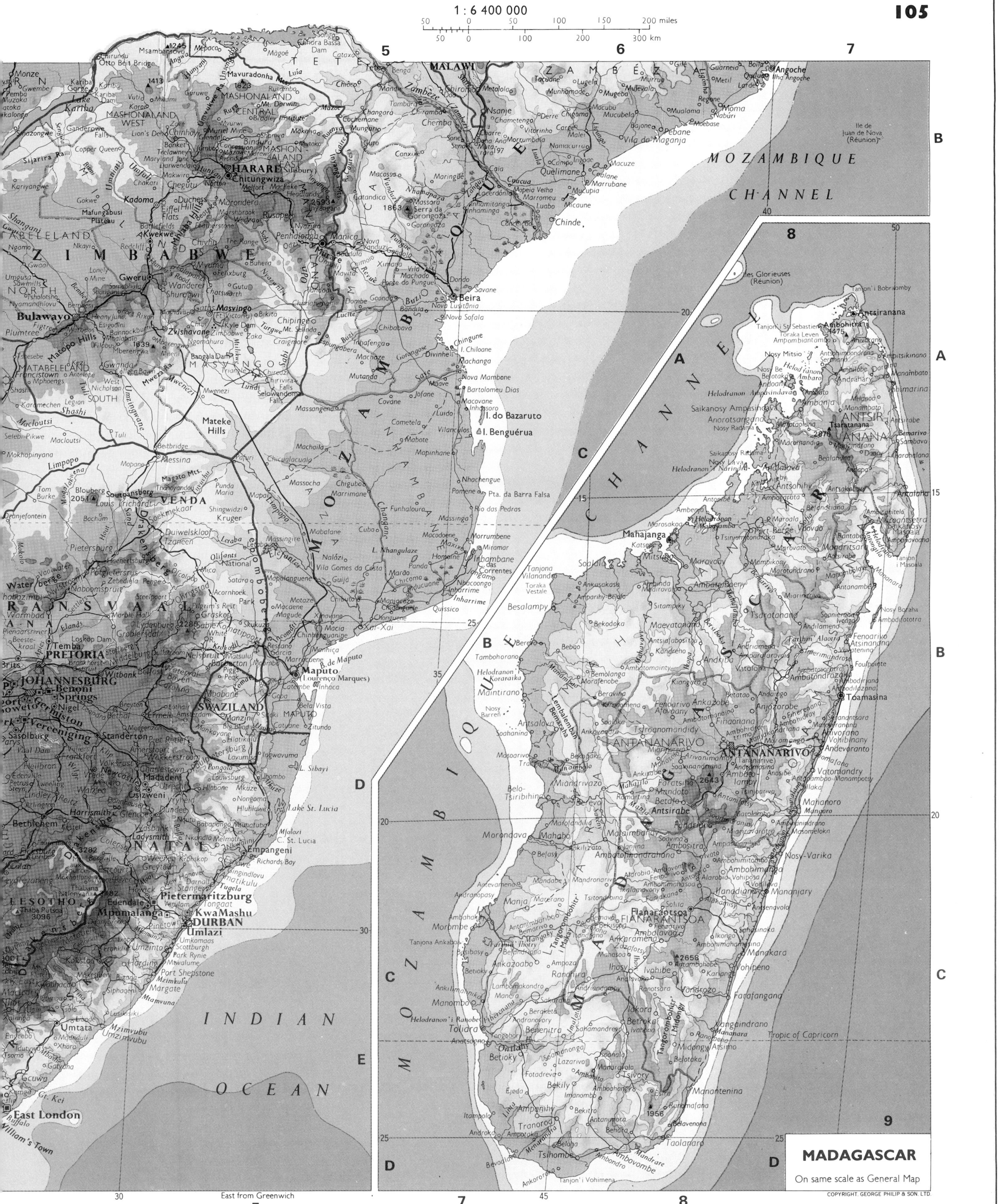

1 : 6 400 000

50    0    50    100    150    200 miles
50    0    100    200    300 km

5          6          7

**MOZAMBIQUE**

MALAWI

ZAMBÉZIA

Ile de Juan de Nova (Réunion)

**MOZAMBIQUE**

**CHANNEL**

ZIMBABWE

HARARE
Chitungwiza

MASHONALAND
MASHONALAND WEST
MASHONALAND CENTRAL

Kadoma
Kwekwe
Gweru

Bulawayo

MATABELELAND
NORTH

Beira
Nova Lusitânia
Nova Sofala

MASVINGO

Masvingo
Zvishavane

I. do Bazaruto
I. Benguérua

SOUTH

VENDA

Kruger
National
Park

Mahajanga

MADAGASCAR

Antsiranana

ANTSIRANANA

Tsaratanana

Antananarivo

ANTANANARIVO

Toamasina

Antsirabe

RANSVAAL

PRETORIA

JOHANNESBURG
Benoni
Springs
Germiston
Nigel
Vereeniging
Soweto
Sasolburg

SWAZILAND
Manzini
MAPUTO

Maputo
(Lourenço Marques)

L. de Maputo

Morondava

Mahabo

Fianarantsoa
FIANARANTSOA

NATAL

LESOTHO

Pietermaritzburg
KwaMashu
DURBAN
Umlazi
Mpumalanga

Toliara

Tropic of Capricorn

INDIAN

Umtata

OCEAN

East London
William's Town

Taolañaro

**MADAGASCAR**

On same scale as General Map

COPYRIGHT. GEORGE PHILIP & SON, LTD.

East from Greenwich

30          5          7          45          8

A   B   C   D   E

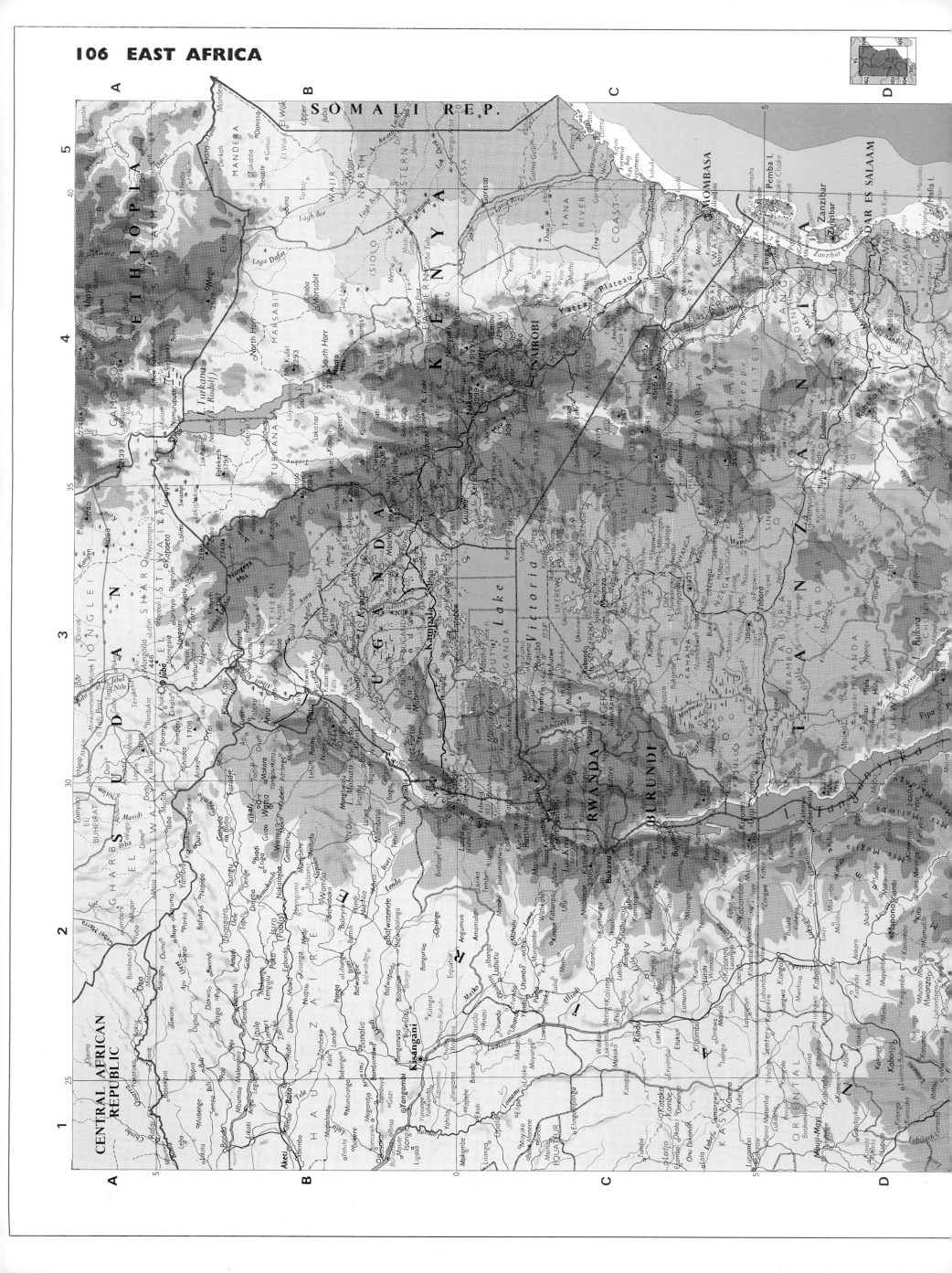

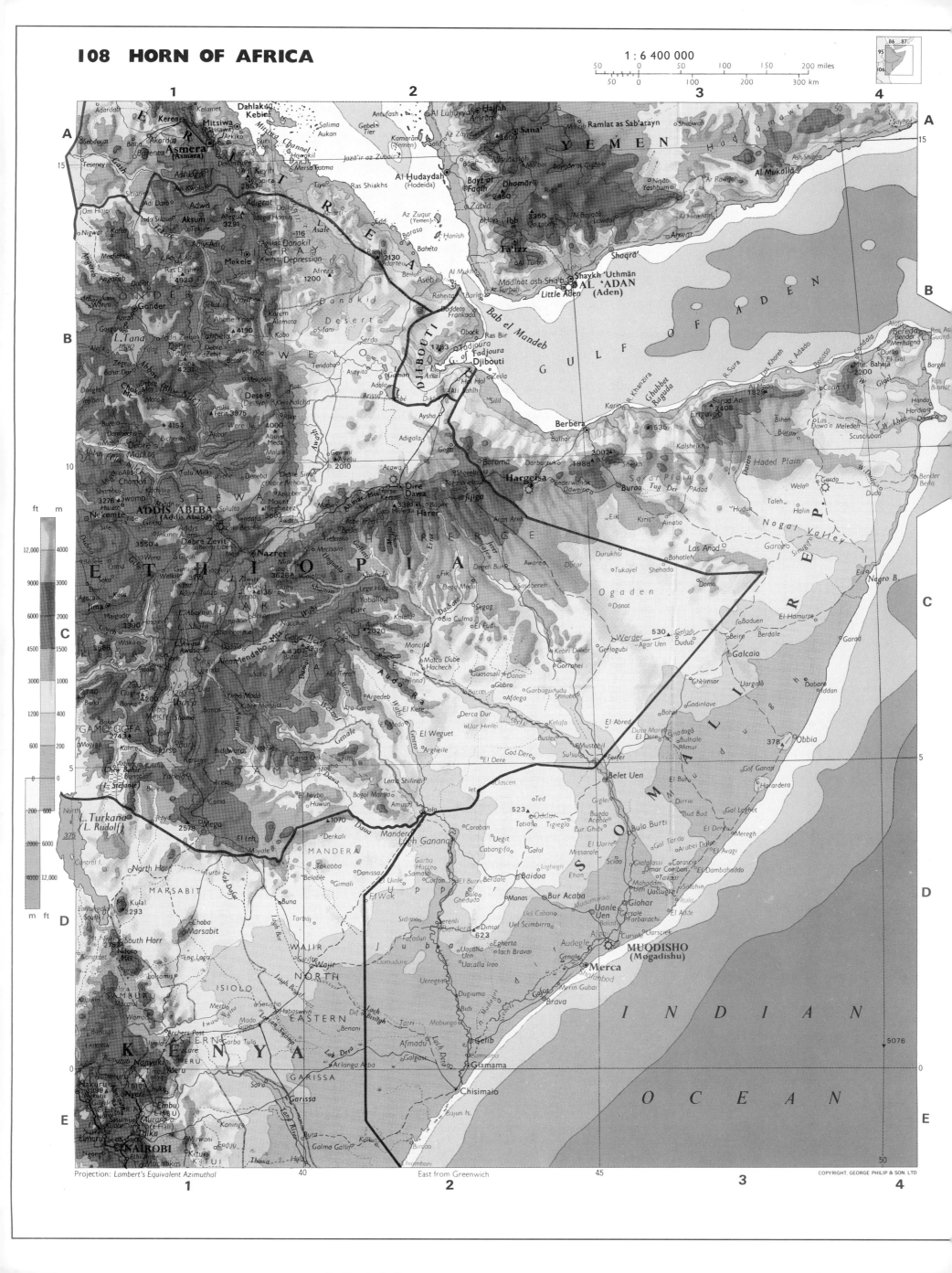

1 : 6 400 000

50    0    50    100    150    200 miles
50    0    100    200    300 km

**YEMEN**

Sana'
Al Hudaydah (Hodeida)
Ta'izz
AL 'ADAN (Aden)
Little Aden

**GULF OF ADEN**

Berbera

**ERITREA**

Asmera (Asmara)
Mitsiwa

**TIGRAY**

Mekele

**DANAKIL DESERT**

**DJIBOUTI**
Djibouti

**SOMALI REP.**

Hargeisa
Burao

Nogal Valley

**ETHIOPIA**

ADDIS ABEBA (Addis Ababa)
Nazret
Harer
Dire Dawa

**Ogaden**

**HARERGE**

Galcaio

Obbia

**SOMALIA**

Belet Uen
Bulo Burti

L. Turkana (L. Rudolf)

**KENYA**

Baidoa
Bur Acaba

MUQDISHO (Mogadishu)
Merca

WAJIR

**MANDERA**

Giohar

**EASTERN**

Brava

Gelib
Giamama
Chisimaio

**INDIAN OCEAN**

NAIROBI

Projection: Lambert's Equivalent Azimuthal

East from Greenwich

COPYRIGHT. GEORGE PHILIP & SON. LTD

ft    m
12,000    4000
9000    3000
6000    2000
4500    1500
3000    1000
1200    400
600    200
200    600
2000    6000
4000    12,000
m    ft

1 2 3 4 5 6 7 8 9 10

Mediterranean Sea
Bayrût SYRIA
Tel Aviv-Yafo Dimashq Baghdad
El Iskandarîya ISRAEL IRAQ IRAN
Bûr Sa'îd Jerusalem Karbala AFGHANISTAN Kabul Rawalpindi CHINA
El Qâhira El Suweis Al Basrah Abadan Qandahar XIZANG Xi'an Wuhan Nanjing Shanghai
Banghazi EGYPT JORDAN Esfahan Quetta Lahore Chengdu Chongqing Hangzhou
LIBYA El Khartûm BAHRAIN QATAR Multan Delhi Mt Everest Kunming Changsha Guiyang Fuzhou
Asyût KUWAIT Ar Riyâd UNITED Agra Katmandu 8848 Wenzhou
SAUDI ARAB Karachi Kanpur Varanasi BURMA Guangzhou
Aswân EMIRATES G. of Oman INDIA Dhaka Mandalay TAIWAN
L. Nasser Tropic of Cancer OMAN Ahmadabad Calcutta Chittagong Hanoi Hong Kong
Dongola Jiddah Narmada Cuttack G. of Hainan
Makkah G. of Kutch Bombay Godavari Rangoon Tonkin
CHAD SUDAN YEMEN Pune Hyderabad Bay of THAILAND South
Omdurmân El Khartûm Al Adan Krishna Bengal Bangkok China
ERITREA Gulf of Aden Socotra Bangalore Madras Andaman Is. Mergui CAMBODIA Ho Chi Minh Sea
Berbera (Yemen) (India) Arch. Phanh Bho Paracel Is.
ETHIOPIA C. Guardafui Arabian Lakshadweep Is. Madurai Nicobar Is. Gulf of
CENTRAL Addis Ababa Ras Asir (India) (India) Thailand SABAH
AFRICA SOMALI REP. Sea Madural Colombo SRI LANKA Isthmus of BRUNEI BORNEO
Wâw Mangalore Arabian (CEYLON) Kra George Town Natuna
ZAIRE Mogadishu Basin Adurutalagala MALAYSIA
Kisangani SOMALI Somali 2524 Nias Kuala Lumpur SARAWAK
L. Mobutu Equator Carlsberg MALDIVES Singapore Kuching
UGANDA Basin Ridge Mentawai Palembang INDONESIA Borneo
KENYA Mt Kenya Is. Sumatera Jakarta Java Sea
RWANDA Nairobi Mid Java Semarang
BURUNDI Victoria 5895 Seychelles Chagos Sunda Strait Surabaya
TANZANIA Kilimanjaro Amirante Is. Mahé Archipelago (Br.) Banda Java Flores
Mombasa Victoria Diego Garcia Cocos or Christmas I. Sea
Dar es Salaam Des Roches Keeling Is. (Austral.) Islands
Aldabra Is. Alphonse Coetivy Is. (Austral.) 7450
St Pierre Providence
ZAMBIA Farquhar Is. Agalega I.
Lusaka COMOROS Tromelin I. 4819 6327
ZIMBABWE Mozambique Carados N. W. Cape
Channel MADAGASCAR Garajos
Harare Toamasina Rodriguez Tropic of Capricorn
BOTSWANA Antananarivo 5322 St Louis MAURITIUS
Bulawayo 2643 Réunion Mascarene AUSTRALIA
NAMIBIA Bloemfontein 6400 Islands Shark Bay WESTERN
Johannesburg Mascarene Basin Geraldton AUSTRALIA
Pretoria 1491 1104 Perth
SOUTH AFRICA Durban Madagascar Geographe Bay Fremantle
Cape Town East London Basin Kalgoorlie
Port Elizabeth 5778 Equatorial Limit of icebergs Albany
Amsterdam I. (Fr.)
Crozet St Paul I. (Fr.)
Agulhas Basin
Basin 2899
Pr. Edward Is. Crozet Is. (Fr.)
(S.A.) Southeast Indian Rise
Marion I. Possession I.
Kerguelen (Fr.)
McDonald Is. Heard I.
5141 5202
(Austral.)
Extreme Limit of Pack Ice
5848
4850 4691
Antarctic Circle Wilkes Land
Queen Maud Land Enderby Land Adélie Land

Projection: Mollweide

ft m
18 000 6000
12 000 4000
6000 2000
3000 1000
1200 400
600 200
0 0
200 600
2000 6000
4000 12 000
6000 18 000
m ft

COPYRIGHT GEORGE PHILIP & SON LTD.

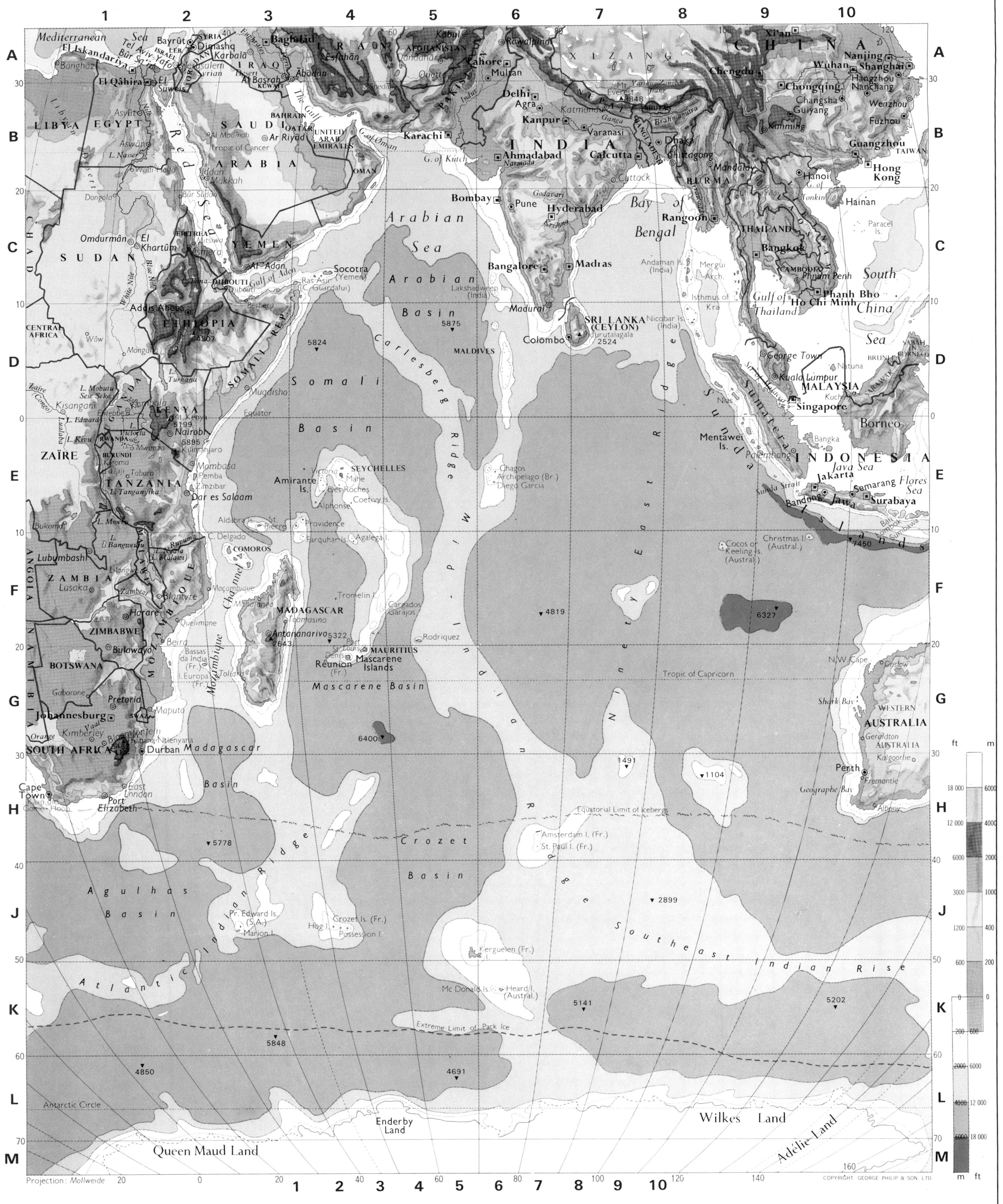

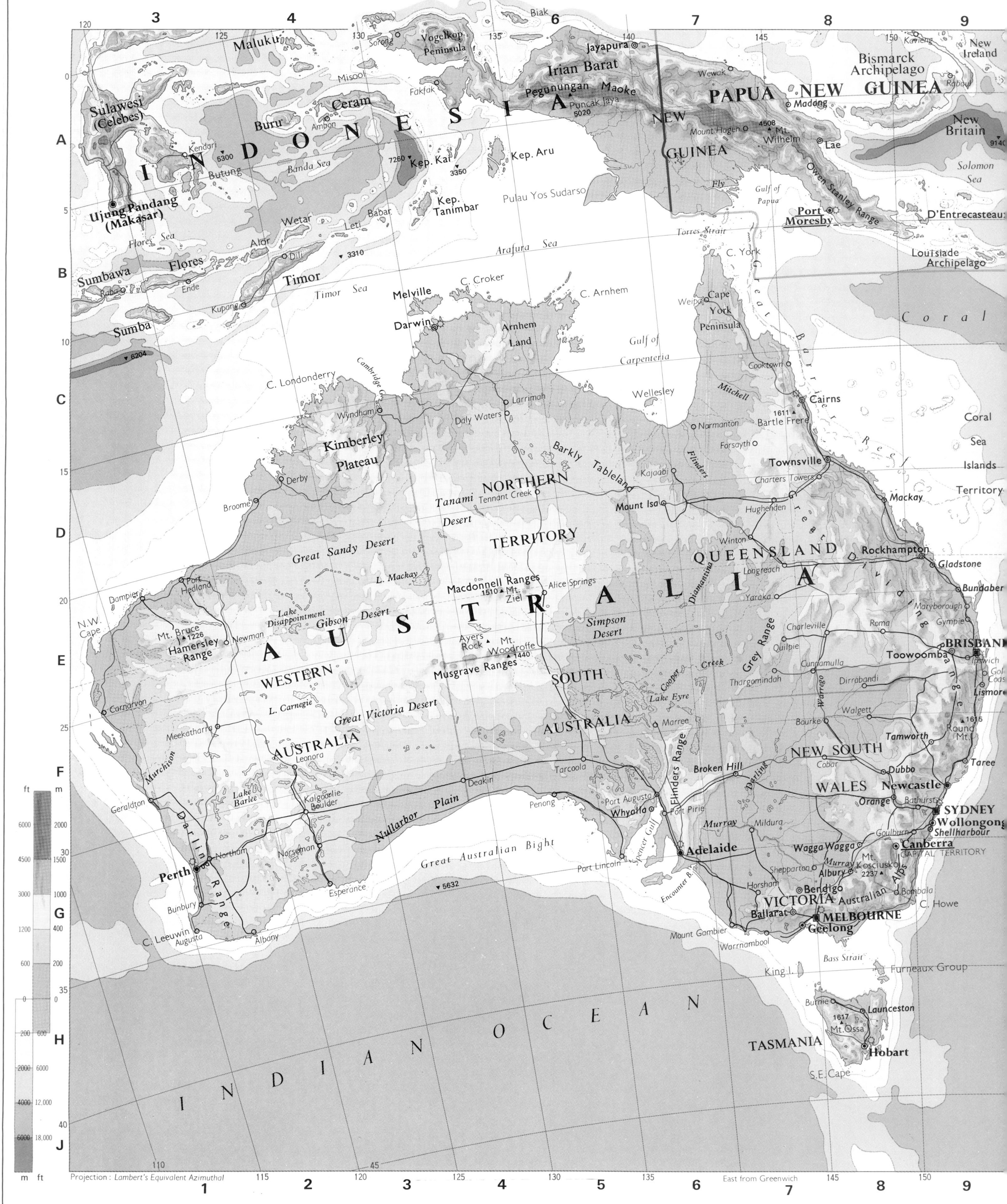

INDONESIA

Sulawesi (Celebes)
Maluku
Buru
Ceram
Butung
Banda Sea
Kendari
Ujung Pandang (Makasar)
Wetar
Flores Sea
Alor
Flores
Ende
Sumba
Sumbawa
Baba
Kupang
Timor
Timor Sea

Sorong
Vogelkop Peninsula
Misool
Fakfak
Kep. Kai
Kep. Aru
Kep. Tanimbar
Pulau Yos Sudarso
Biak
Jayapura
Irian Barat
Pegunungan Maoke
Puncak Jaya 5020
NEW GUINEA
Wewak
Madong
Mount Hagen
Mt. Wilhelm 4508
Lae
Fly
Gulf of Papua
Owen Stanley Range
Port Moresby

PAPUA NEW GUINEA
Bismarck Archipelago
Kavieng
New Ireland
Rabaul
New Britain
Solomon Sea
D'Entrecasteaux
Louisiade Archipelago

Arafura Sea
Torres Strait
C. York
Cape York Peninsula
Weipa

Melville
C. Croker
C. Arnhem
Darwin
Arnhem Land
Gulf of Carpentaria
Wellesley

Coral Sea

C. Londonderry
Cambridge G.
Wyndham
Kimberley Plateau
Derby
Broome

Daly Waters
Larrimah
Barkly Tableland
Mitchell
Cooktown
Cairns
Bartle Frere 1611
Coral Sea Islands

Narmanton
Forsayth
NORTHERN
Townsville
Charters Towers
Flinders
Mackay

Tanami Desert
Tennant Creek
Kajaabi
Mount Isa
Hughenden
TERRITORY
Great Sandy Desert
Winton
QUEENSLAND
Longreach
Rockhampton
Gladstone

Port Hedland
Dampier
N.W. Cape
L. Mackay
Lake Disappointment
Gibson Desert
Macdonnell Ranges 1510
Mt. Ziel
Alice Springs
Yaraka
Diamantina
Bundaber
Maryborough
Gympie

AUSTRALIA
Mt. Bruce 1226
Hamersley Range
Newman
Simpson Desert
Grey Range
Charleville
Roma
BRISBANE
Toowoomba
Ipswich
Gold Coast

WESTERN
Ayers Rock
Mt. Woodroffe 1440
Musgrave Ranges
SOUTH
Cooper Creek
Quilpie
Cunnamulla
Thargomindah
Warrego
Dirrabandi
Lismore

Carnarvon
L. Carnegie
Lake Eyre
AUSTRALIA
Walgett
Round Mt. 1615
Tamworth
Taree

Great Victoria Desert
Marree
Bourke
Cobar
NEW SOUTH
Meekatharra
AUSTRALIA
Marble
Broken Hill
Darling
Dubbo
WALES
Newcastle

Leonora
Tarcoola
Elinders Range
Orange
Bathurst
SYDNEY
Wollongong
Shellharbour

Murchison
Geraldton
L. Barlee
Deakin
Penong
Port Augusta
Whyalla
Port Pirie
Murray
Mildura
Wagga Wagga
Canberra CAPITAL TERRITORY

Kalgoorlie-Boulder
Nullarbor Plain
Spencer Gulf
Albury
Mt. Kosciusko 2237
Bombala

Northam
Norseman
Great Australian Bight
Port Lincoln
Adelaide
Shepparton
Horsham
Bendigo
Australian Alps
C. Howe

Perth
Darling Range
Esperance
5632
Encounter B.
VICTORIA
Ballarat
Geelong
MELBOURNE

Bunbury
Mount Gambier
Warrnambool

C. Leeuwin
Augusta
Albany
Bass Strait
King I.
Furneaux Group

INDIAN OCEAN

Burnie
Launceston
TASMANIA
Mt. Ossa 1617
Hobart
S.E. Cape

ft m
6000 2000
4500 1500
3000 1000
1200 400
600 200
0
200 600
2000 6000
4000 12,000
6000 18,000
m ft

Projection : Lambert's Equivalent Azimuthal
East from Greenwich

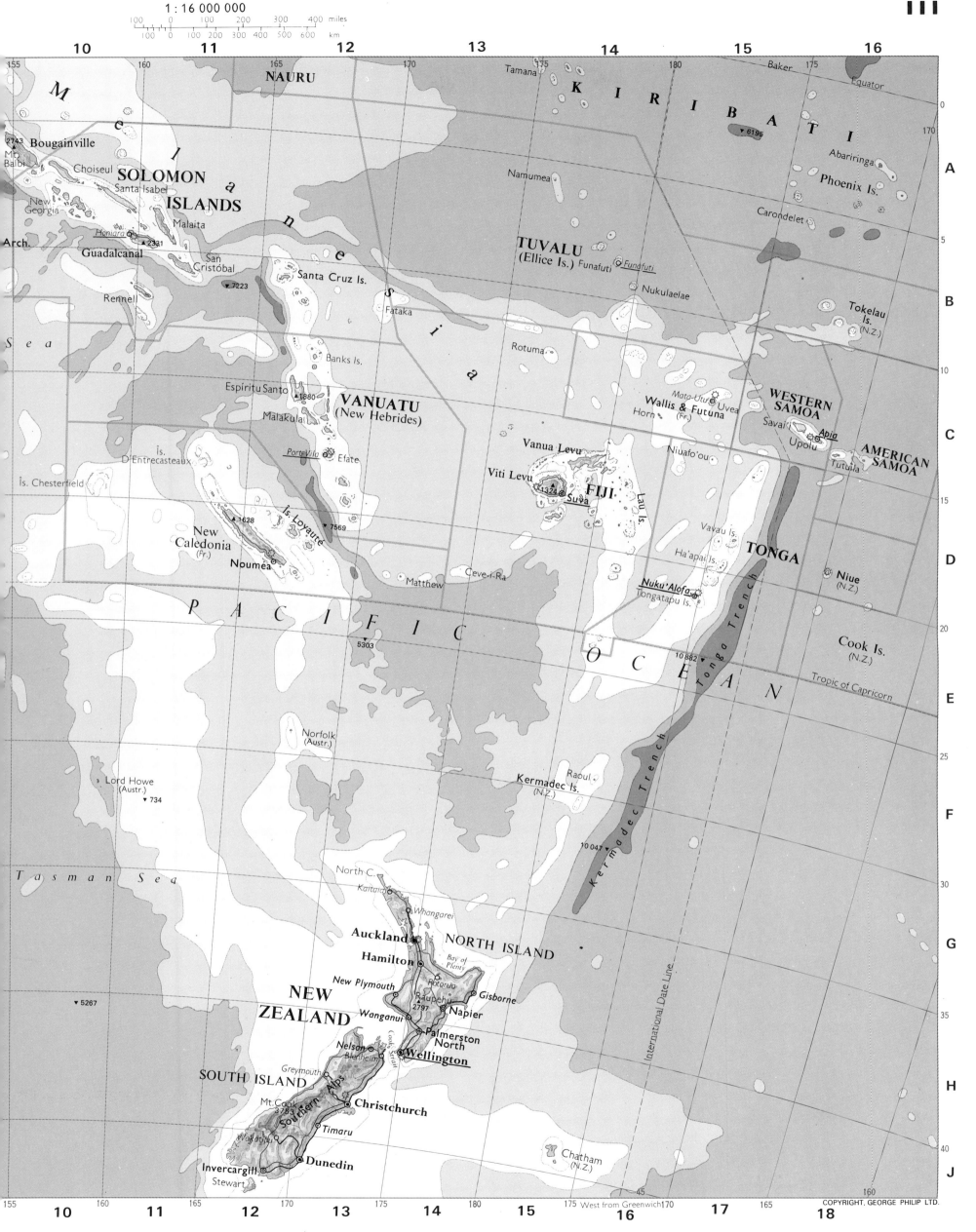

1 : 16 000 000

100   0   100   200   300   400 miles
100   0   100   200   300   400   500   600 km

M e l a n e s i a

NAURU

K I R I B A T I

Equator

Tamana

Baker

▲2743 Bougainville
Mt.
Balbi
Choiseul
New
Georgia
Santa Isabel
SOLOMON
ISLANDS
Malaita
Arch.
Honiara ▲2331
Guadalcanal
San
Cristóbal
Rennell

Abariringa

6195

Phoenix Is.

Carondelet

A

Sea

Santa Cruz Is.
▼7223
Fataka

Namumea

TUVALU
(Ellice Is.) Funafuti
Funafuti
Nukulaelae

Tokelau
Is.
(N.Z.)

B

Banks Is.

Rotuma

5

Espíritu Santo
▲1880
Malakula
VANUATU
(New Hebrides)

Mata-Utu Uvea
Wallis & Futuna
Horn       (Fr.)

WESTERN
SAMOA
Savai'i
Upolu   Apia

C

Îs.
D'Entrecasteaux
Îs. Chesterfield

Port Vila   Efate

Vanua Levu
Viti Levu
▲1324
Suva   FIJI

Niuafo'ou

Tutuila
AMERICAN
SAMOA

▲1628
New
Caledonia
(Fr.)
▼7569
Is. Loyauté
Noumea

Lau Is.

Vavau Is.

TONGA

Niue
(N.Z.)

D

Matthew
Ceve-i-Ra

Ha'apai Is.

15

P    A    C    I    F    I    C

Nuku'Alofa
Tongatapu Is.

Cook Is.
(N.Z.)

▼5303

O    C    E

10 882

Tonga Trench

Tropic of Capricorn

E

20

Norfolk
(Austr.)

A    N

25

Lord Howe
(Austr.)
▼734

Raoul
Kermadec Is.
(N.Z.)

Kermadec Trench

F

10 047

Tasman   Sea

North C.
Kaitaia
Whangarei

International Date Line

30

▼5267

Auckland
Hamilton
New Plymouth
NEW
ZEALAND
Wanganui

NORTH ISLAND
Bay of
Plenty
Rotorua
Ruapehu
2797   Napier
Palmerston
North
Wellington

Gisborne

G

35

Nelson
Blenheim
Cook Strait

SOUTH ISLAND
Greymouth
Mt.Cook
3763
Wanaka
Invercargill
Stewart

Southern   Alps
Christchurch
Timaru

Dunedin

Chatham
(N.Z.)

H

40

J

155       160       165       170       175   West from Greenwich 170       165       160

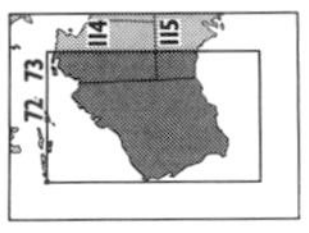

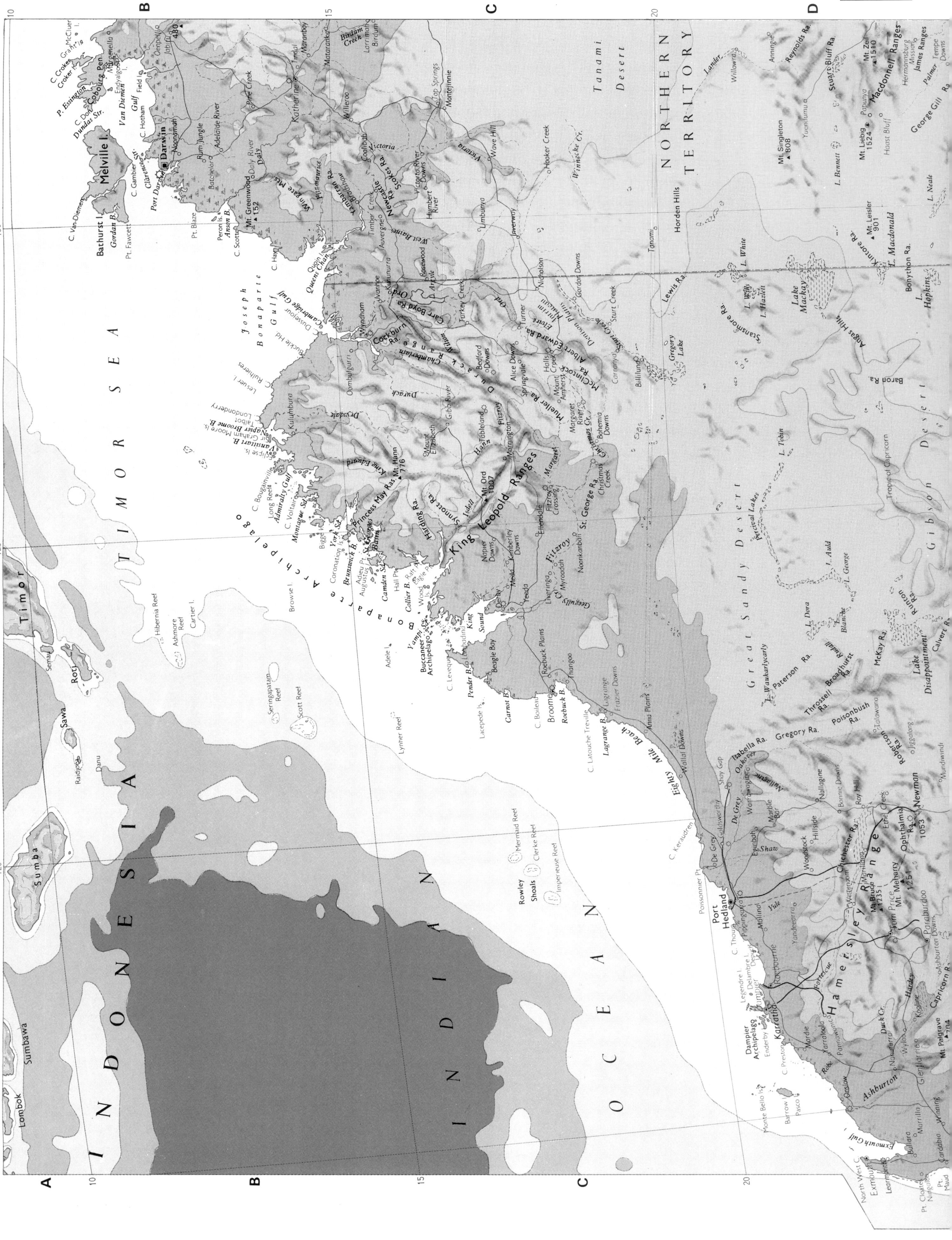

B 15 C 20 D

NORTHERN TERRITORY

Tanami Desert

Gibson Desert

Great Sandy Desert

TIMOR SEA

INDONESIA

INDIAN OCEAN

Timor

Sumba

Sumbawa

Lombok

Roti

Sawu

Savu

Melville I.

Bathurst I.

Darwin

C. Van Diemen

Cobourg Pen.

P. Essington

Dundas Str.

Van Diemen Gulf

C. Crocker

C. McCluer

Croker I.

Goulburn Is.

Field I.

Daly River

Adelaide River

Rum Jungle

Pine Creek

Katherine

Mataranka

Birdum Creek

Larrimah

Daly Waters

Top Springs

Hooker Creek

Wave Hill

Victoria River Downs

Humbert River

Timber Creek

Wyndham

Kununurra

Ord

Carr Boyd Ra.

Cockburn Ra.

Durack Ra.

Chamberlain

King Edward R.

Prince Regent R.

Admiralty Gulf

Cambridge Gulf

Joseph Bonaparte Gulf

Bonaparte Archipelago

Buccaneer Archipelago

King Leopold Ranges

Mt. Ord 1007

Fitzroy Crossing

Derby

Broome

Roebuck Bay

Eighty Mile Beach

De Grey

Port Hedland

Marble Bar

Nullagine

Newman

Dampier Archipelago

Karratha

Hamersley Range

Lake Mackay

Lake Disappointment

Lake Dora

Lake Blanche

Lake Auld

Lake George

L. White

L. Hazlett

Reynolds Ra.

Macdonnell Ranges

Mt. Zeil 1510

Mt. Liebig 1524

Hermannsburg

James Ranges

George Gill Ra.

L. Neale

L. Hopkins

Mt. Singleton 808

Tropic of Capricorn

Ashburton

Exmouth Gulf

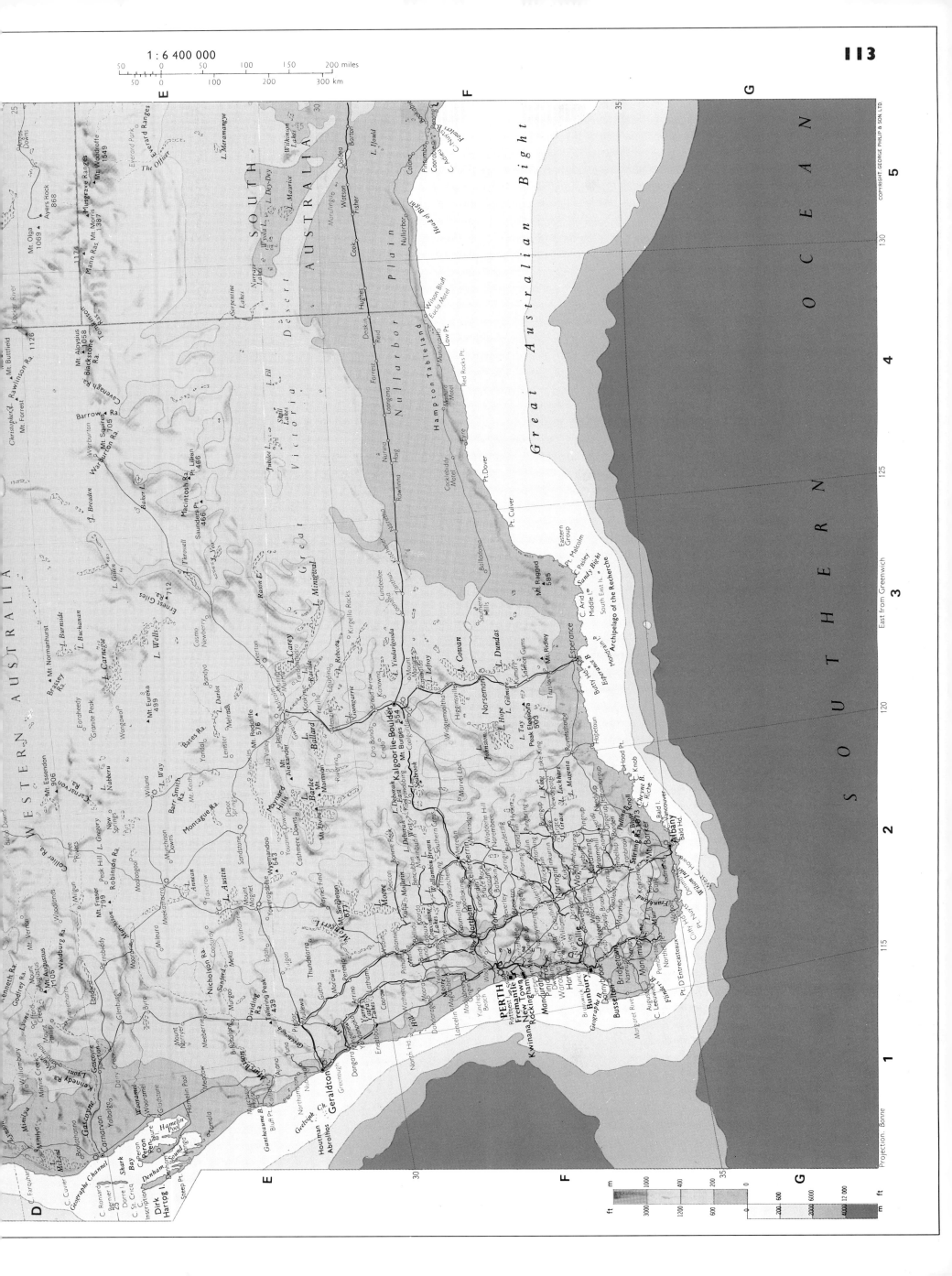

1 : 6 400 000

50    0    50    100    150    200 miles

50   0   100   200        300 km

E                    F                    G

5

W E S T E R N   A U S T R A L I A

S O U T H   A U S T R A L I A

Great Victoria Desert

Gibson Desert

Nullarbor Plain

Hampton Tableland

Nullarbor

Great   Australian   Bight

S O U T H E R N

O C E A N

PERTH
Fremantle
New Town
Kwinana
Rockingham

Bunbury
Busselton
Bridgetown
Manjimup

Albany

Kalgoorlie-Boulder

Norseman

Esperance
Archipelago of the Recherche

Geraldton

Houtman
Abrolhos

Carnarvon

Shark
Bay

Dirk
Hartog I.

Hamelin
Pool

D

E

F

G

1        2        3        4        5

Projection. Bonne                    East from Greenwich                    COPYRIGHT GEORGE PHILIP & SON LTD.

m
ft
3000
1200
600
0
600
1200

m
1000
400
200
0
200
2000
4000

ft
12 000
6000
0

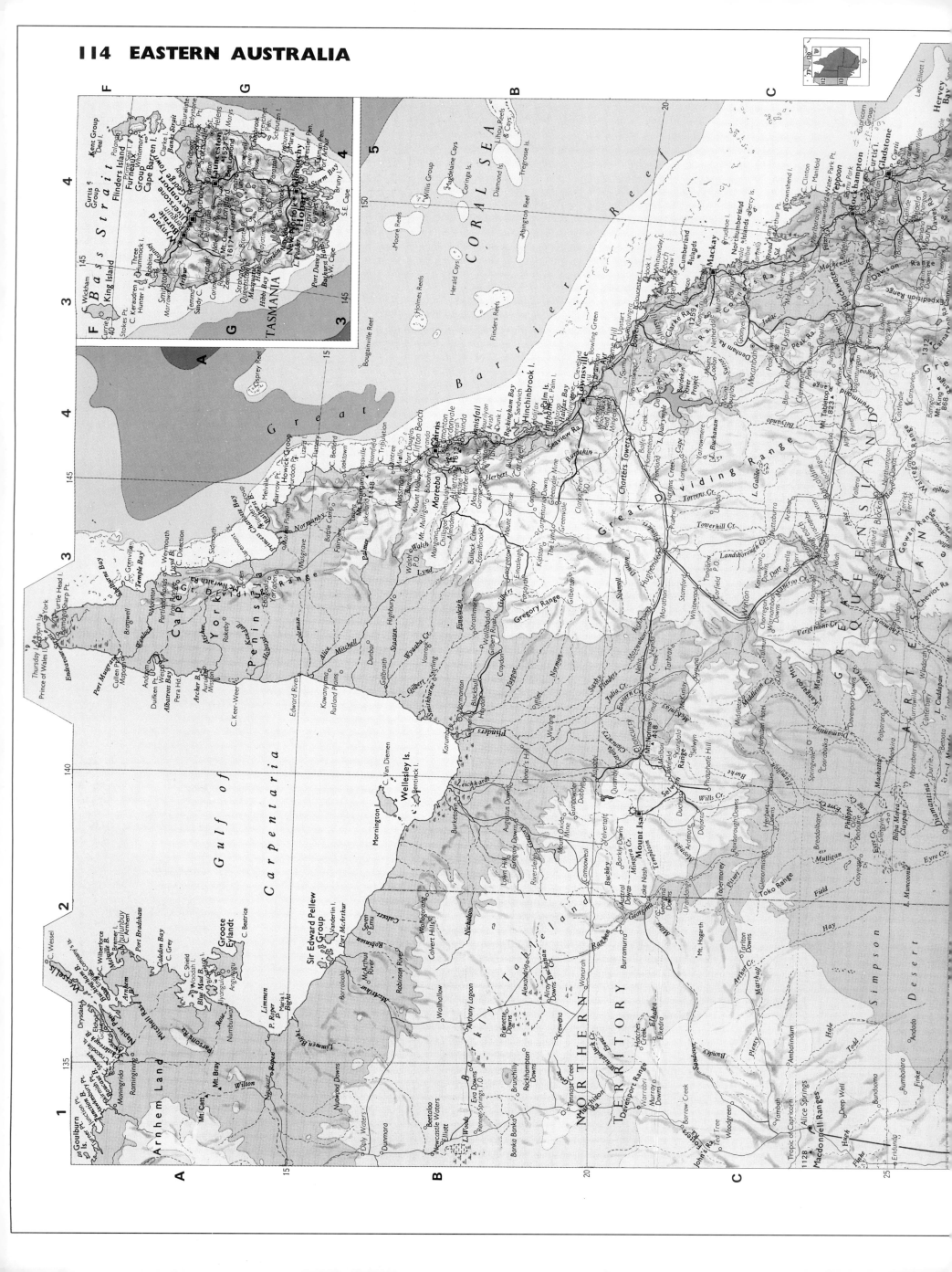

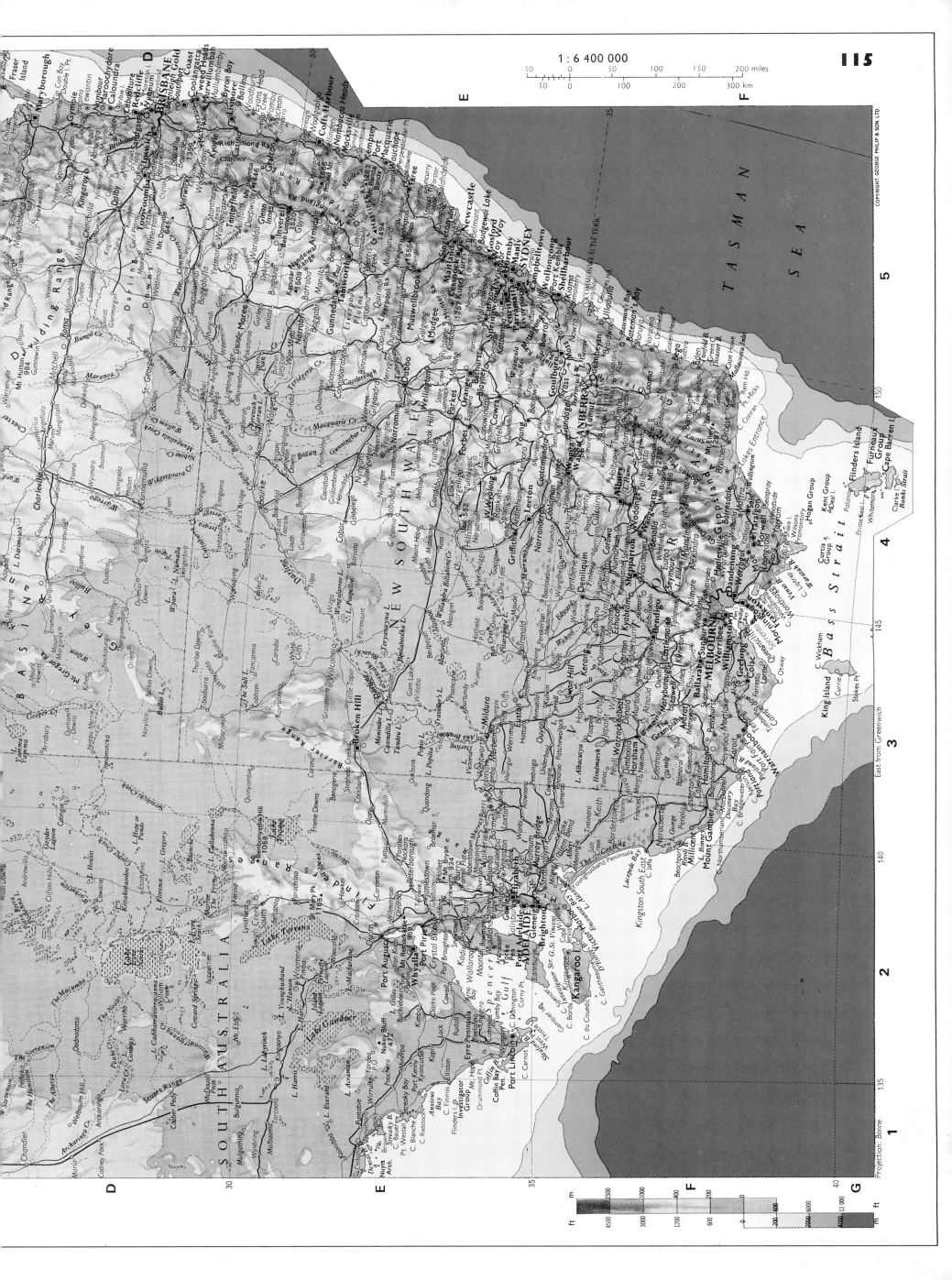

Projection: Alber's Equal area with two standard parallels

**Grid columns:** 2 3 4 5

**Grid rows:** A B C D E

Parakylia · Leigh Creek South · Telford · Benbonyathe 1058 · Caraduc · Peri Lake

L. Younghusband · Mt. Deception 685 · Beltana · Mt. Hack 1083 · Lake Frome · Packsaddle

L. Hanson · Nilpena · Broughams Gate · White Cliffs · Momba · Tilpa

L. Hart · Arcoona · Woomera · Parachilna · Frome Downs · McDougalls Well · Koonawarra · Glen Gowrie · Kalkaroo

Wirraminna · Pimba · Benagerie · Mulga Valley · Sturts Meadows · Grassmere · Menamurtee · Wilcannia

Island Lagoon · St. Mary Pk. 1165 · Wilpena · Wilpena Cr. · Mooleulooloo · Wilangee · Langidoon · Cawkers Well · Wongalar · L. Poopelloe

Lake Gairdner · Pernatty Lagoon · Cotabena · Hawker · Mount Victor · Silverton · Stephens Creek · Wahratta · Volo · Goonalga

Mt. Ive · L. Macfarlane · Woocalla · Gordon · Hesso · Glenorchy · Boolcoomata · Broken Hill · Baden Park

Lake Gilles · Mt. Brown 965 · Quorn · Carrieton · Mannahill · Mutooroo · Menindee L. · Menindee · Leonora Downs · Teryaweyna L. · Mount Manara

Buckleboo · Port Augusta West · Port Augusta · Eurelia · Olary · Cawndilla L. · Tandou L. · Boolaboolka L. · Gypsum Pal

Kimba · Siam · Nectar Brook · Wilmington · Orroroo · Black Rock · Nackara · Yunta · Netley Gap · Kimberley · Gum Lake · Darnick · Beilpajah · Ivan

Iron Knob · Mt. Remarkable 969 · Booleroo Centre · Peterborough · Quondong · Oakbank · L. Popilta · Popio L. · Tartna Point

Darke Peak · Iron Baron · Whyalla · Port Pirie · Napperby · Jamestown · Terowie · Braemar · Morgan Vale · Belmore · Bulpunga · Arumpo · Manfred · Mossgiel

Pondooma · Laura · Gladstone · Hallett · Canopus · Gluepot · Burtundy · Hatfield P.O. · Culpataro · Clare

Crystal Brook · Gulnare · Spalding · Mt. Bryan 934 · Magenta

Cowell · Gawler Ranges · Gulf · Snowtown · Blyth · Clare · Burra · L. Victoria · Murray · Wentworth · Bidura · Oxley · Willara

Rudall · Port Broughton · Brinkworth · Farrell Flat · Robertstown · Renmark · Merbein · Mildura · Dalrymple · Lethero

Wallaroo · Bute · Balaklava · Owen · Point Pass · Morgan · Waikerie · Berri · Yamba · Meringur · Red Cliffs · Pitarpunga L. · Maude

Arno Bay · Kadina · Willamulka · Hoyleton · Riverton · Barmera · Loxton · Werrimull · Nangiloc · Benanee · Lachlan

Ungarra · Moonta · Bowmans · Eudunda · Holder · Maggea · Taplan · Nowingi · Robinvale · Murrumbidgee · Perekerten

Tumby Bay · Maitland · Port Wakefield · Nuriootpa · Angaston · Sedan · Swan Reach · Mantung · Meribah · Hattah · Balranald · Moulamein

Koppio · Ardrossan · Mallala · Tanunda · Truro · Kunlara · Alawoona · Walpeup · Kulwin · Natya · Edward

Koonibie · Port Victoria · Salisbury · Elizabeth · Sanderston · Wanbi · Veitch · Cowangie · Ouyen · Piangil · Niemur · Wak

Port Lincoln · Minlaton · Gawler · Port Adelaide · Opeville · Kalyan · Sandalwood · Peebinga · Tutye · Underbool · Pier Millan · Swan Hill

Thistle I. · Corny Pt. · ADELAIDE · Woodside · Mannum · Karoonda · Marama · Pinnaroo · Patchewollock · Speed · Tyrrell · Waitchie · Wak

Gambier Is. · Glenelg · St. Vincent · Mt. Barker · Murray Bridge · Tailem Bend · Peake · Geranium · Lameroo · Yarto · Ultima · Meatian · Kerang

West Pt. · Marion Bay · Brighton · McLaren Vale · Strathalbyn · Cooke Plains · Tintinara · Hopetoun · Berriwillock · Culgoa · Mincha

C. Spencer · Investigator Strait · Yorke Peninsula · Vincent · Finniss · Milang · L. Alexandrina · Coonalpyn · L. Albacutya · Rainbow · Jeparit · Brim · Quambatook · Tragowel

Normanville · Victor Harbor · L. Albert · L. Yumali · Meningie · Culburra · Yaapeet · Birchip · Wycheproof · Koondrook · Cohuna

Western River · Kingscote · Nepean Bay · Cape Jervis · Encounter Bay · Younghusband Peninsula · Salt Creek · Keith · Lake Hindmarsh · Warracknabeal · Charlton

C. Borda · Penneshaw · Backstairs Passage · Bordertown · Diapur · Nhill · Antwerp · Litchfield · Korong Vale · Roches

KANGAROO I. · D'Estrees Bay · Wolseley · Kaniva · Dimboola · Minyip · Donald · Wedderburn · Cope Cope · Mitiamo · Lockington

Vivonne · The Coorong · Lacepede Bay · Frances · Goroke · Natimuk · Murtoa · Wimmera · St. Arnaud · Inglewood · Bridgewater · Elmore

C. du Couedic · Vivonne Bay · Kingston S.E. · Morea · Noradjuha (Carpolac) · Horsham · Bolangum · Emu · Dunolly · Maldon

C. Jaffa · Reedy Creek · Kybybolite · Glenorchy · Wimmera · Deep Lead · St. Arnaud · Maryborough · Castlemaine

Naracoorte · Toolondo · Glenelg · The Grampians · Stawell · Avoca · Talbot · Clunes · Kyneton · Wooden

C. Northumberland · George · Glenroy · Balmoral · Mt. William 1167 · Ararat · Maryborough · Beaufort · Daylesford · Creswick · BALLARAT

Kalangadoo · Penola · Englefield · Cavendish · Willaura · Minera · Bacch · Mars

Beachport · Rivoli B. · Millicent · Casterton · Coleraine · Skipton · Scarsdale · Elaine

L. Bonney · Nangwarry · Dunkeld · Penshurst · Derrinallum · Cressy · Inverleigh · Werribee · Lara

MOUNT GAMBIER · Dartmoor · Branxholme · Condah · Macarthur · Mortlake · Camperdown · GEELONG · Willia

C. Bridgewater · Heywood · Koroit · Terang · Alvie · Winchelsea · Queenscliff · Torqu

Discovery Bay · Portland · Portland Bay · Port Fairy · Cobden · Colac · Aireys Inlet · Lorne

C. Nelson · WARRNAMBOOL · Allansford · Timboon · Forrest · Apollo Bay

Port Campbell · Lavers Hill · C. Otway

SOUTH AUSTRALIA · N E · NE · VIC · Wimmera

Spencer Gulf · Lake Torrens · Flinders Ranges · Barrier Range · Darling · Mt. Lofty Range

**Elevation scale (left):**

| ft | m |
|---|---|
| 6000 | 2000 |
| 4500 | 1500 |
| 3000 | 1000 |
| 1200 | 400 |
| 600 | 200 |
| 0 | 0 |
| 200 | 600 |
| 2000 | 6000 |
| 4000 | 12 000 |

m · ft

**Longitude markers:** 136 · 138 · 140 · 142 · 144

**Latitude markers:** 32 · 34 · 36 · 38

1 : 3 200 000

20    0    20    40    60 miles
20  0  20  40  60  80
km

**6**    **7**    **8**    **9**    **10**

Louth   146   Carinda   148   Barraba   Black Mountain   Coffs Harbour
Currawerea   Byrock   Gwabegar   Turrawan   1684   Chandlers Pk.   Dorrigo   Bellingen
urranyalpa   Wilgaroon   Glenariff   Coonabarabran   Kingstown   Armidale   Nambucca Heads
Burnamwood   Colossal   Coolabah   Pine Ridge   Boggabri   Namoi   Manilla   Uralla   Macksville
Everdale   Cobar   Canbelego   Hermidale   Haddon Rig   Armatree   Gunnedah   Tamworth   Limbri   Walcha   Macleay   Smithtown **A**

**SOUTH**   **WALES**

**T A S M A N**

**S E A**

1 : 2 800 000

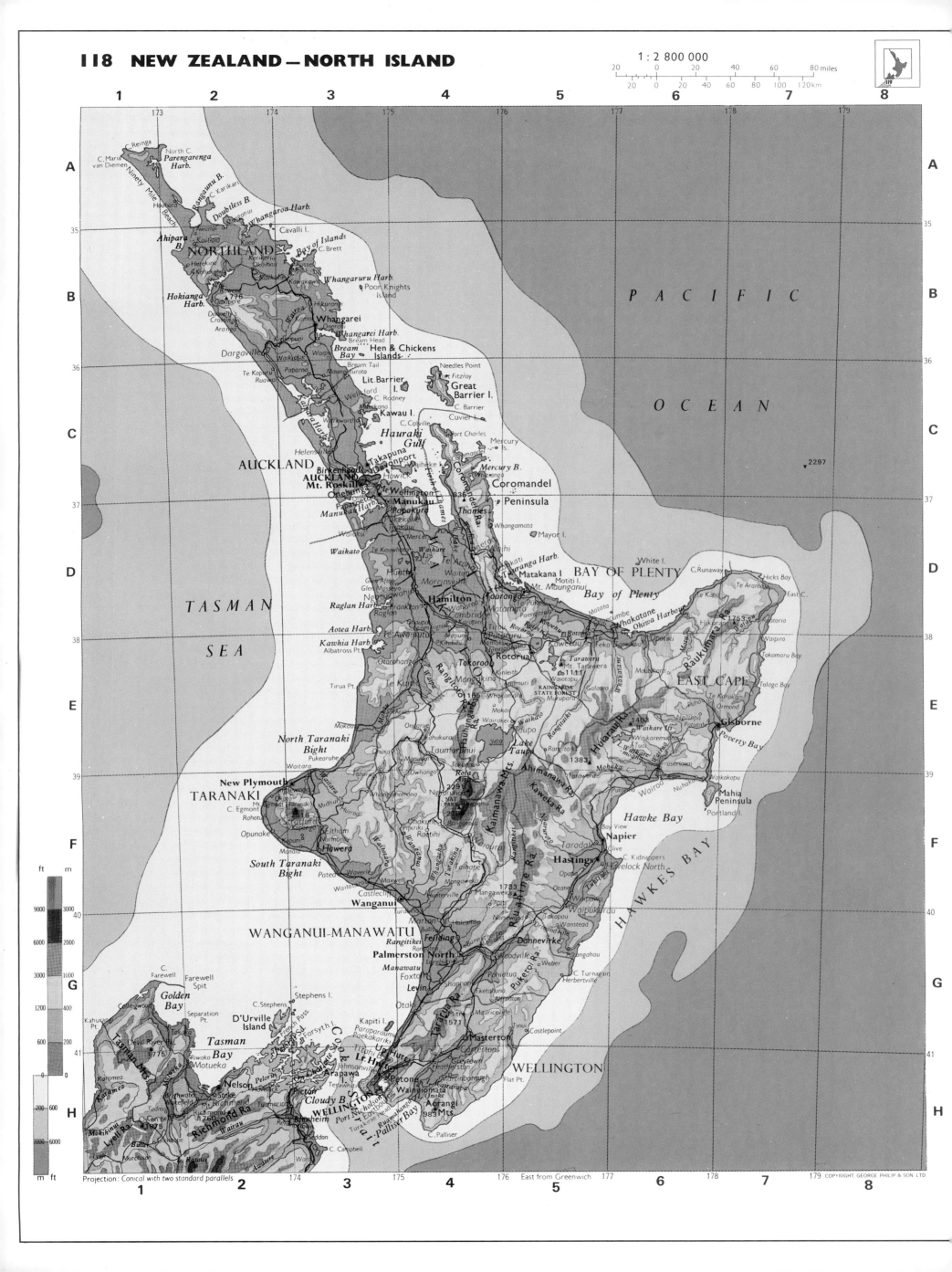

**PACIFIC**

**OCEAN**

*NORTHLAND*

AUCKLAND
**AUCKLAND**
**Mt. Roskill**
**Manukau**
**Papakura**

*Hauraki Gulf*

**Coromandel**
*Peninsula*

**Hamilton**

*Cambridge*

**BAY OF PLENTY**
*Bay of Plenty*

**Whakatane**

**EAST CAPE**

**Gisborne**
*Poverty Bay*

*TASMAN*

*SEA*

*North Taranaki Bight*

**Rotorua**

*Lake Taupo*

**New Plymouth**
**TARANAKI**

*South Taranaki Bight*

*Hawke Bay*

**Napier**

**Hastings**
*Havelock North*

*HAWKES BAY*

**Wanganui**

**WANGANUI-MANAWATU**

**Feilding**

**Palmerston North**

**Dannevirke**

**Levin**

*Golden Bay*

*Farewell Spit*

*D'Urville Island*

*Tasman Bay*

**Nelson**

*Richmond Ra.*

**Masterton**

**WELLINGTON**

**WELLINGTON**

*Cook Strait*

*Palliser Bay*

Projection: Conical with two standard parallels

East from Greenwich

COPYRIGHT GEORGE PHILIP & SON LTD

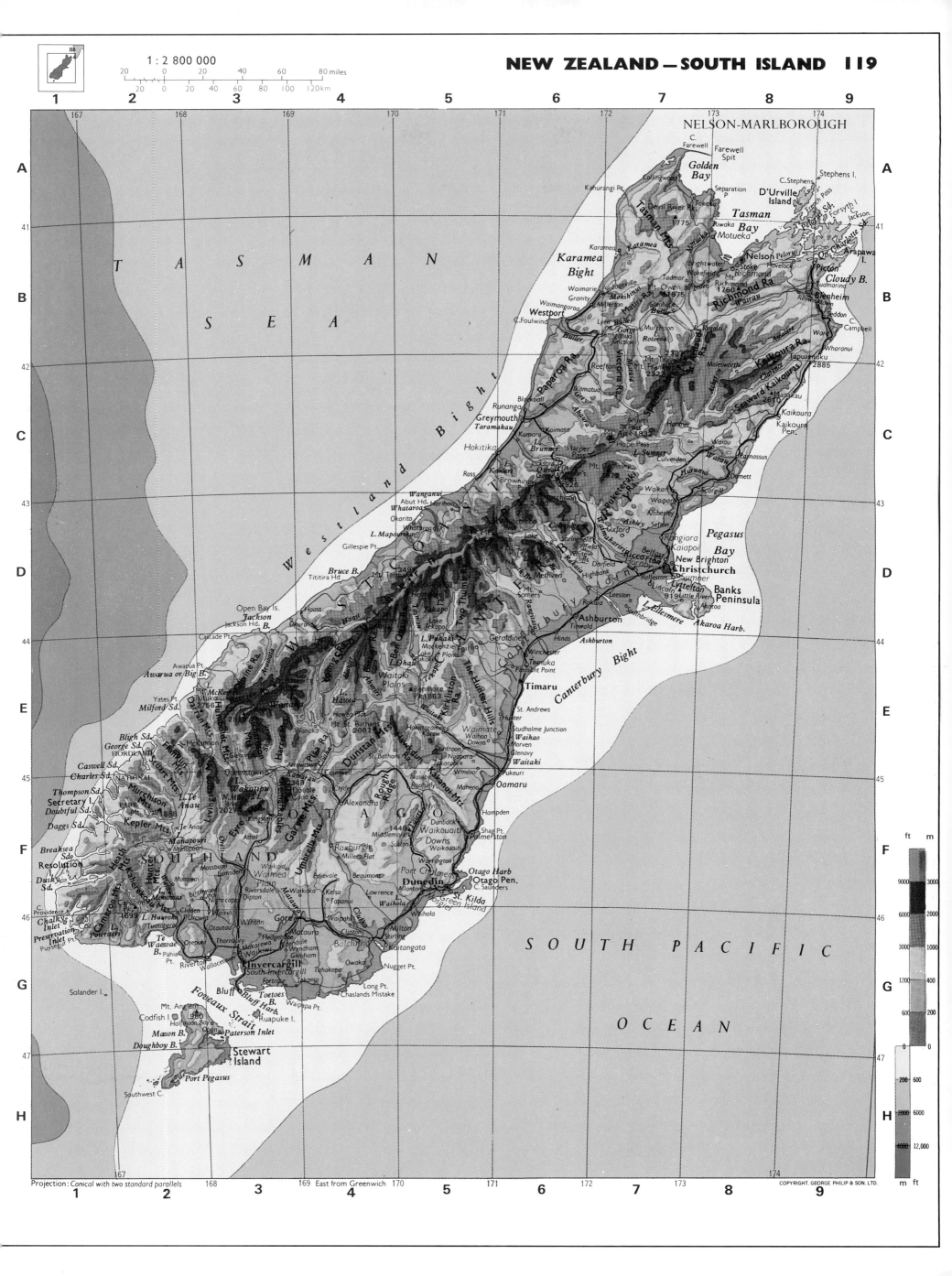

1 : 2 800 000

20    0    20    40    60    80 miles
20  0  20  40  80  100  120km

NELSON-MARLBOROUGH

C. Farewell
Farewell Spit
C. Stephens    Stephens I.
Golden Bay
Separation P.    D'Urville Island
Collingwood
Kahurangi Pt.    Takaka    French Pass    Forsyth I.
Tasman Bay    Queen Charlotte Sd.    Jackson
Devil River Pt.    Riwaka    C.    Port Pelorus Sd.    Arapawa I.
Tasman Mts.    1775    Motueka    Pelorus    Picton
Karamea    Nelson    Cloudy B.
Karamea Bight    Brightwater    Wairau    Blenheim
Mt. Owen    Richmond Ra.    Seddon
Waimarie    Seddonville    1875    Belgrove    Renwick    C. Campbell
Granity    Millerton    Mt. Owen    Wakefield    Richmond
Waimangaroa    1760    Richmond Ra.    Wharanui
Westport    Lyell    Murchison    Maruia    2337    Molesworth
C. Foulwind    Buller    Gorge    Rotoroa    Seaward Kaikouras    Tapuaenuku
Inangahua    Mt. Franklin    2885
Junction    Victoria Ra.    2322    Kaikoura Ra.    2610
Reefton    Mt. Una    Clarence    Kaikoura
Runanga    Blackball    Grey    Inangahua    Hanmer    Kaikoura Pen.
Greymouth    Ikamatua    Lewis    Hope Pass    Waiau
Taramakau    Kumara    Kaimata    L. Sumner    Culverden
Hokitika    L. Brunner    Harper Pass    Hurunui    Waipara
Ross    Jacksons    Otira    Hope Pass    Amberley    Scargill
Kaniere    Browning    1926    Waikari    Domett
Wanganui    Arthurs Pass    Sheffield    Pegasus
Abut Hd. Harihari    Mt. Murchison    Oxford    Bay
Whataroa    2400    Ashley    Rangiora    Kaiapoi
Okarito    Springfield    Sefton    Belfast    New Brighton
L. Mapourika    Lake    Darfield    Rolleston    Riccarton    Christchurch
Gillespie Pt.    Whataroa    White-    Hornby    Sumner
Bruce B.    Mt. Tasman    cliffs    Lincoln    Lyttelton
Tititira Hd.    3497    Methven    Rakaia    Leeston    Banks Peninsula
Mt. Cook    Highbank    Rolleston    Little River
Open Bay Is.    Mt. Somers    Rakaia    919    Akaroa
Jackson    Haast    Okuru    Rangitata    L. Ellesmere    Akaroa Harb.
Jackson Hd.    B.    Timaru    Leeston    L. Ellesmere
Cascade Pt.    Winchester    Ashburton    Akaroa Harb.
Awarua Pt.    Hinds
Awarua or Big B.    Mt. McKinnon    Takapo    Geraldine    Ashburton
Yates Pt.    Mt. Cook    Tekapo    Fairlie    Canterbury Bight
Milford Sd.    2756    L. Pukaki    Mackenzie    Pleasant Point
Bligh Sd.    3497    L. Tekapo    Plains    St. Andrews
George Sd.    FIORDLAND    L. Ohau    Benmore    Huter
Caswell Sd.    Mt. Earnslaw    Pk. 1863    Waimate    Studholme Junction
Charles Sd.    NATIONAL    Mt. St. Bathans    Korow    Waihao
Thompson Sd.    PARK    2087    Waihao    Waihao Downs
Secretary I.    Mt. Lyall 1858    St. Bathans    Ngapara    Morven
Doubtful Sd.    Queenstown    Naseby    Tokarahi    Glenavy
Daggs Sd.    Kepler Mts.    Cromwell    Hyde    Oamaru    Waitaki
Breaksea    Arrowtown    1449    Dunback    Hampden
Sde.    Manapouri    Alexandra    Middlemarch    Waikouaiti
Resolution    L. Te Anau    Roxburgh    Sutton    Waikouaiti Downs
Dusky Sd.    Te Anau    Millers Flat    Hyde    Palmerston
Providence    SOUTH    Clyde    Port Chalmers
Chalky    Inlet    Lumsden    Waikaia    Beaumont    Otago Harb.
Preservation Inlet    Mt. Lyall    Mossburn    Lowrence    Dunedin    Otago Pen.
Puysegur Pt.    1699    L. Hauroko    Gore    Waipahi    St. Kilda
Te Waewae B.    Dipton    Clinton    Waihola    Green Island
Pahia Pt.    Winton    Mataura    Milton
Riverton    Otautau    Wyndham    Stirling
Wallacetown    Edendale    Glenham    Kaitangata
Invercargill    Mokoreta    Owaka
South Invercargill    Takanui    Long Pt.    Nugget Pt.
Bluff    Toetoes    Waipapa Pt.    Chaslands Mistake
Bluff Harb.    Toetoes B.
Solander I.    Foveaux Strait
Mt. Anglem    Bluff    SOUTH PACIFIC
Codfish I.    980    Ruapuke I.
Halfmoon Bay    Oban
Mason B.    Paterson Inlet    OCEAN
Doughboy B.    Stewart Island
Port Pegasus
Southwest C.

TASMAN SEA

Westland Bight

CANTERBURY

OTAGO

SOUTHLAND

Projection : Conical with two standard parallels    East from Greenwich

COPYRIGHT. GEORGE PHILIP & SON. LTD.

ft    m
9000    3000
6000    2000
3000    1000
1200    400
600    200
0    0
200    600
2000    6000
4000    12,000
m    ft

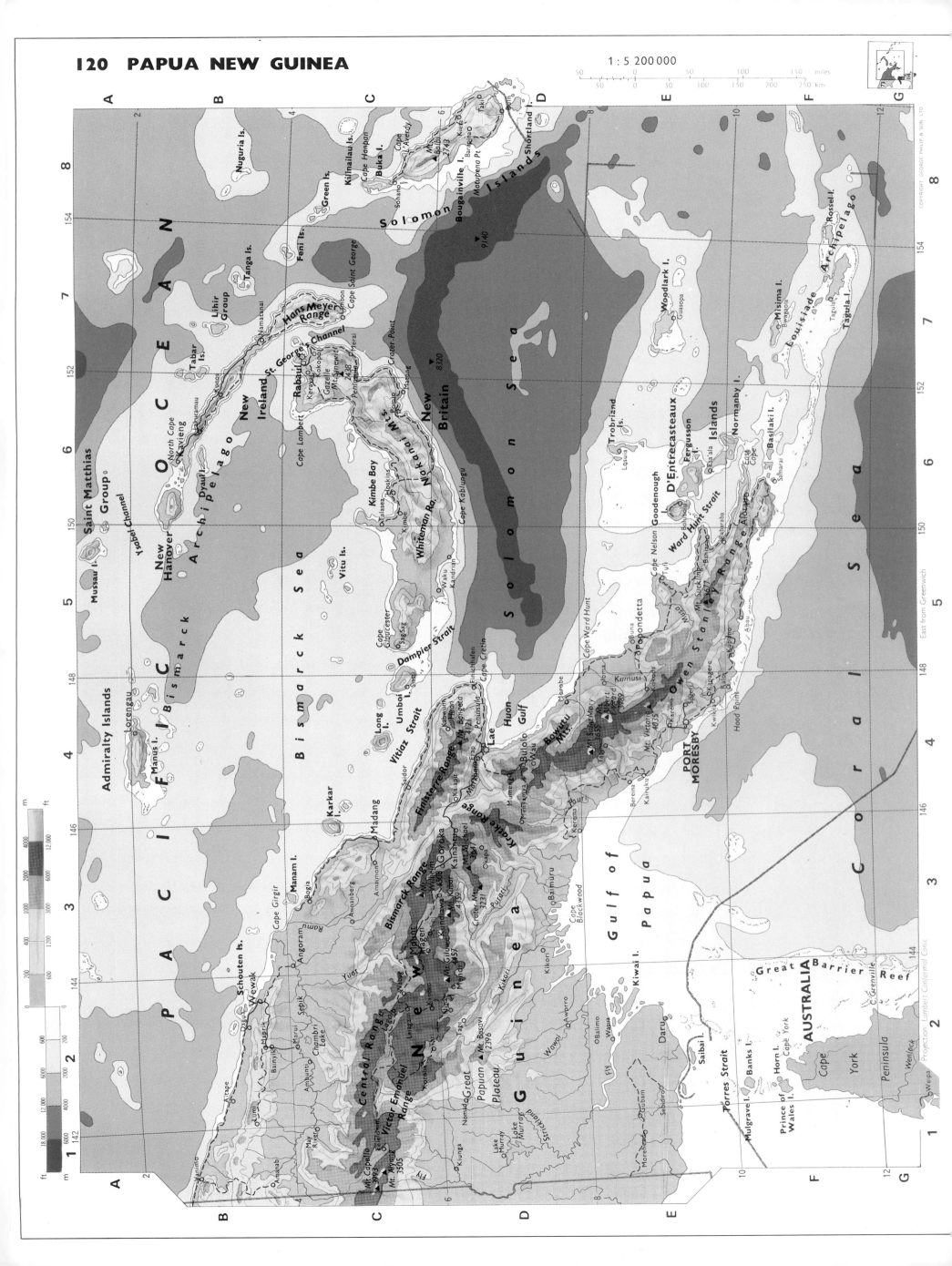

1 : 5 200 000

COPYRIGHT GEORGE PHILIP & SON, LTD.

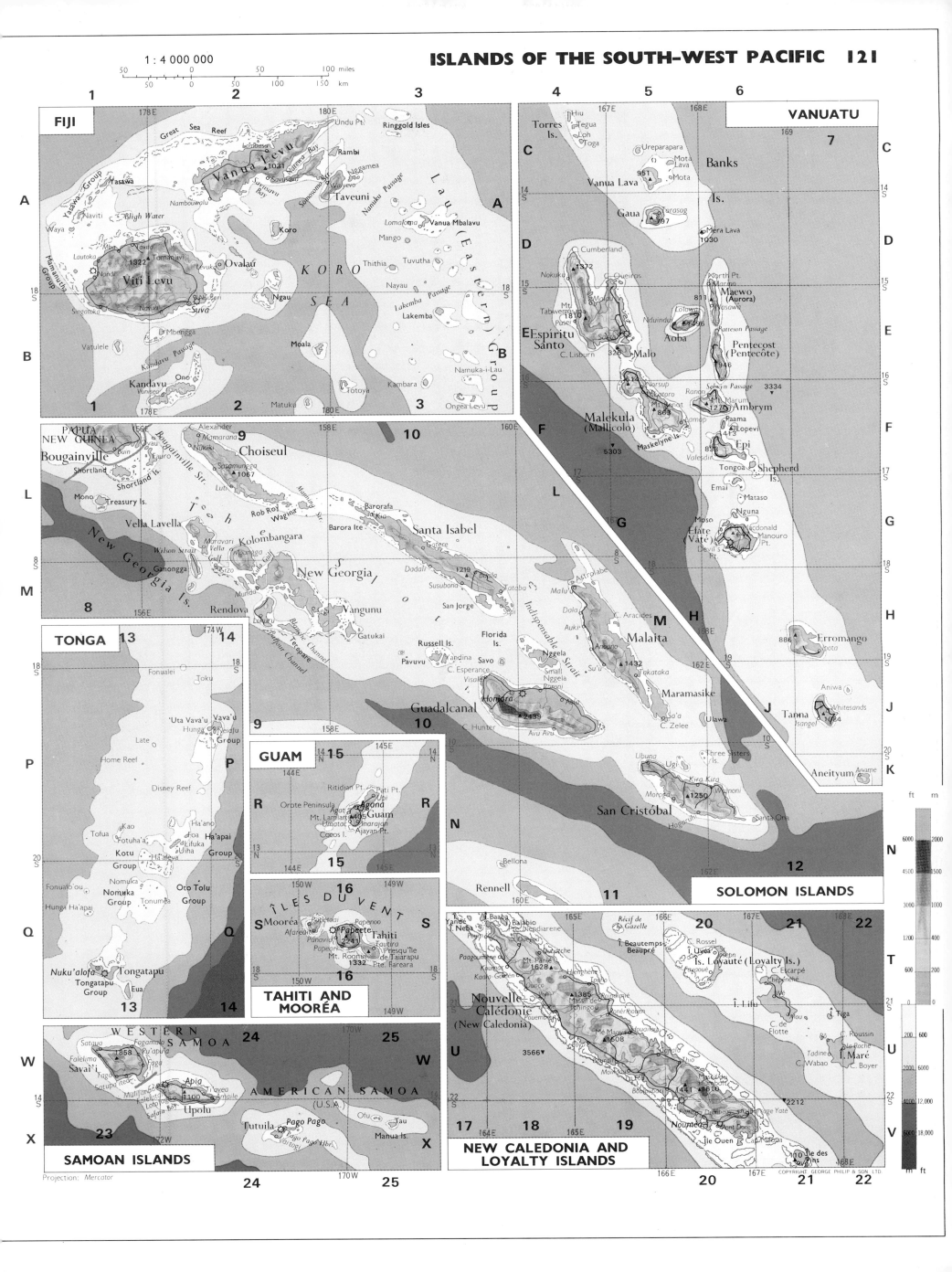

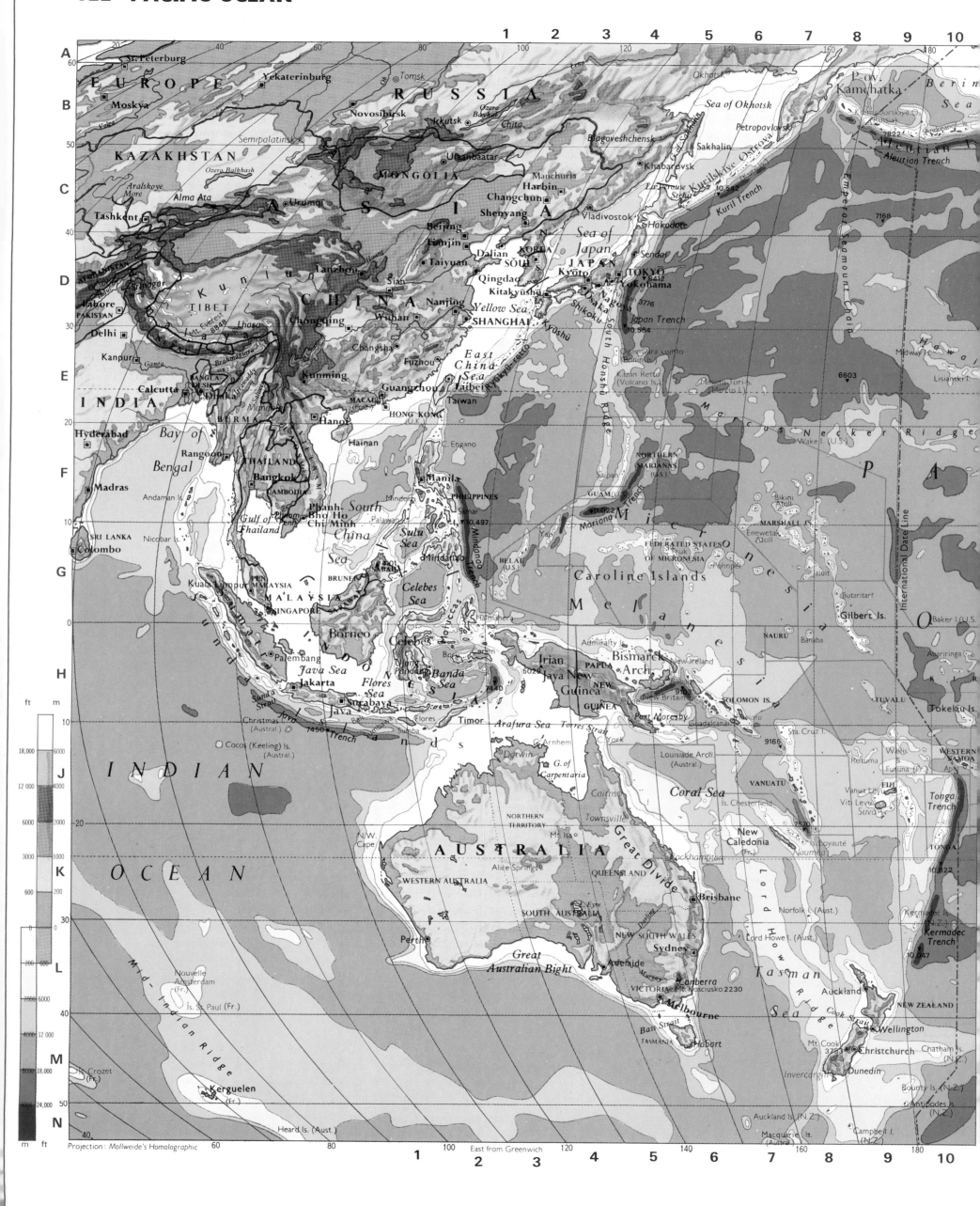

Projection: Mollweide's Homolographic

East from Greenwich

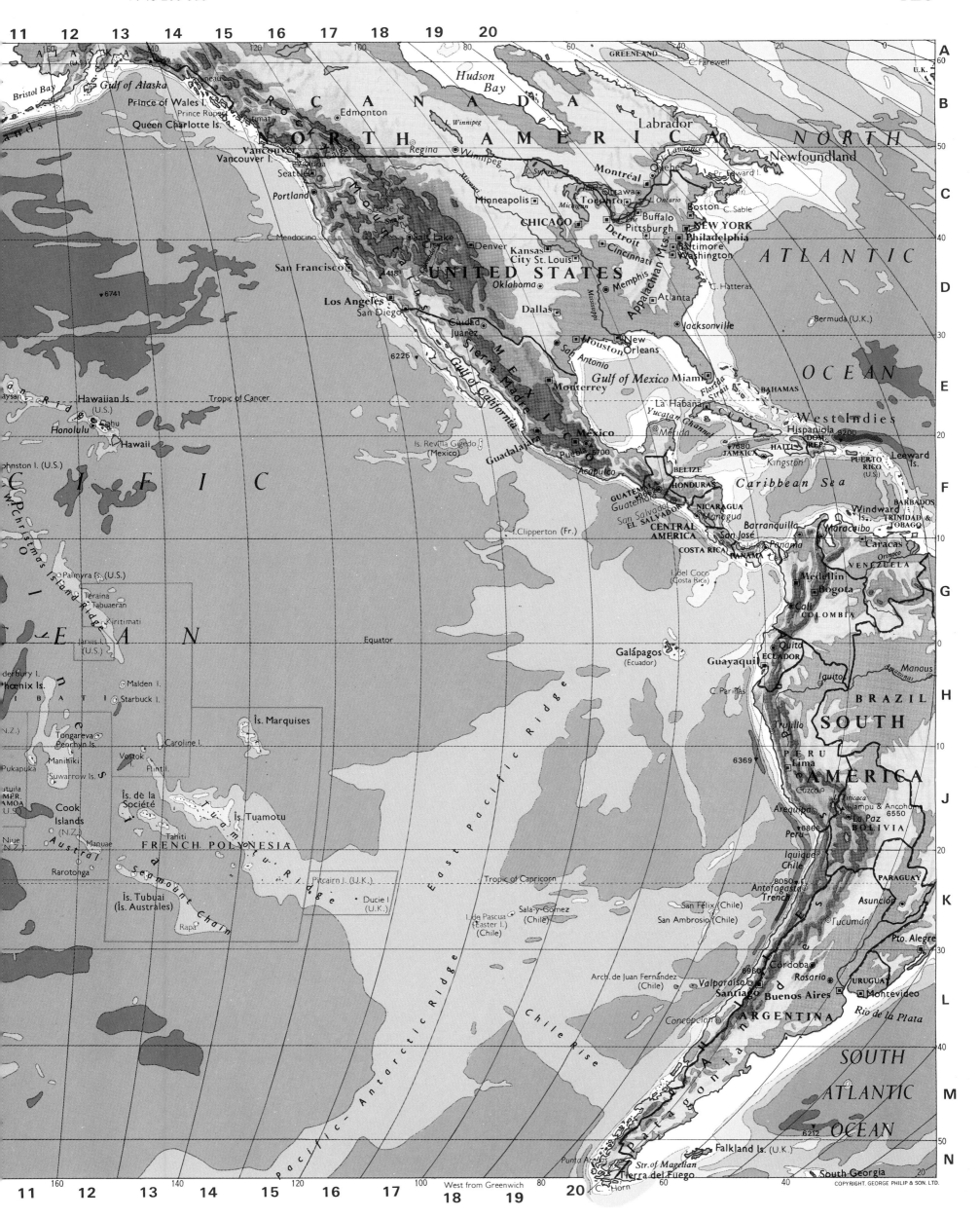

1 : 43 200 000

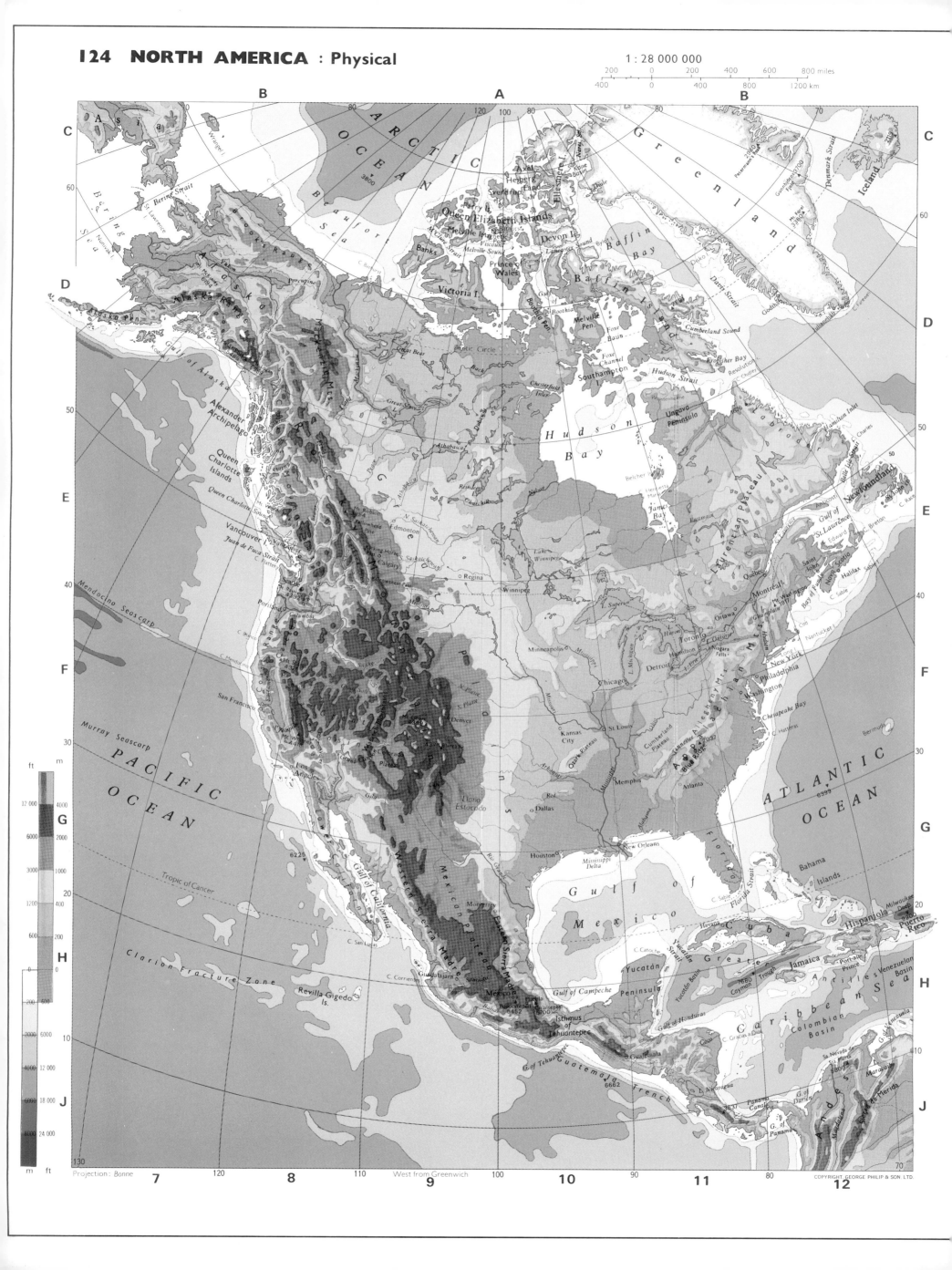

1 : 28 000 000

Projection: Bonne

West from Greenwich

1 : 28 000 000

200   0   200   400   600   800 miles
400   0   400   800   1200 km

ARCTIC OCEAN

GREENLAND (Denmark)

Queen Elizabeth Is.

Ellesmere I.

Denmark Strait

Reykjavik

ICELAND

Bering Strait
Bering Sea

Beaufort Sea

ALASKA
Fairbanks
Anchorage
Arctic Circle

Victoria I.

Baffin Bay

Godthåb

NUVIK

KITIKMEOT

NORTHWEST TERRITORIES

Buffin I.

Davis Strait

YUKON TERRITORY
Whitehorse

Mackenzie
Great Bear L.
Yellowknife
Great Slave L.
FORT SMITH

KEEWATIN

Hudson Strait

NEWFOUNDLAND

Gulf of Alaska
Juneau

BRITISH COLUMBIA
Skeena
Finlay
Peace
Athabasca
L. Athabasca
N. Saskatchewan

CANADA

Churchill
Nelson

Hudson Bay

Eastmain

Labrador

St. Lawrence

SPM

Fraser

ALBERTA
Edmonton
SASKATCHEWAN
S. Saskatchewan
Calgary
Regina

MANITOBA
L. Winnipeg
Winnipeg

ONTARIO

QUEBEC

Québec

NEW BRUNS WICK
Fredericton
P.R. EDWARD
Charlottetown
NOVA SCOTIA
Halifax

St. John's

Victoria
Vancouver
WASHINGTON
Seattle
Olympia
Portland
Columbia
Salem
OREGON

MONTANA
Helena

NORTH DAKOTA
Bismarck

L. Superior

MINNESOTA
St. Paul
Minneapolis
WISCONSIN
Madison
Milwaukee

L. Michigan
L. Huron
MICHIGAN
Lansing

Toronto
Detroit
L. Ontario
Ottawa
Montréal
Montpelier
MAINE
Augusta
Concord
Boston
MASS.
Providence
Hartford

IDAHO
Boise
Snake

Missouri
SOUTH DAKOTA
Pierre

WYOMING
Cheyenne

N. Platte
NEBRASKA
Lincoln

IOWA
Des Moines

Chicago
ILLINOIS
INDIANA
Indianapolis
Springfield

Toledo
Cleveland
OHIO
Columbus
Pittsburgh
PENNSYLVANIA
Harrisburg

Buffalo
NEW YORK
Albany
NEW YORK
Trenton
Philadelphia
N.J.
Dover

Sacramento
San Francisco
San Jose
CALIFORNIA
Carson City
NEVADA

Salt Lake City
UTAH

COLORADO
Denver

KANSAS
Topeka

Kansas City
MISSOURI
Jefferson City
St. Louis

KENTUCKY
Frankfort

Cincinnati
WEST VIRGINIA
VIRGINIA
Richmond
Washington D.C.
MD.
Annapolis

LOS ANGELES
San Diego

ARIZONA
Phoenix
Tucson
Gila
Colorado

Las Vegas

Santa Fe
NEW MEXICO
Albuquerque

OKLAHOMA
Oklahoma City

Red River

ARKANSAS
Little Rock

TENNESSEE
Nashville
Memphis

NORTH CAROLINA
Raleigh
Columbia
SOUTH CAROLINA

El Paso

TEXAS
Dallas
Austin

LOUISIANA
Baton Rouge
Jackson
MISSISSIPPI
ALABAMA
Montgomery

Birmingham
GEORGIA
Atlanta

Jacksonville

PACIFIC OCEAN

Rio Grande

Houston
New Orleans

FLORIDA
Tallahassee
Tampa
Miami

ATLANTIC OCEAN

Bermuda (Br.)

Tropic of Cancer

Monterrey

MEXICO

Gulf of Mexico

Havana
CUBA

C. Sable
Str. of Florida

BAHAMAS
Nassau

Turks & Caicos (Br.)

DOMINICAN REP.
HAITI
San Juan
PUERTO RICO

Revilla Gigedo Is. (Mexico)

Guadalajara
MEXICO

Cayman Is. (Br.)
JAMAICA
Port-au-Prince
Kingston
Santo Domingo

Caribbean Sea

Belmopan
BELIZE
GUATEMALA
HONDURAS
Guatemala
San Salvador
EL SALVADOR
Tegucigalpa
NICARAGUA
Managua
L. Nicaragua

Maracaibo
VENEZUELA
Barranquilla

Panama
PANAMA
COSTA RICA
San José

Medellín
COLOMBIA
Bogotá

SOUTH AMERICA

West from Greenwich

**7** Capital Cities
Washington
U.S. State Capitals and Canadian Provincial Capitals

| | | | |
|---|---|---|---|
| C. | CONNECTICUT | N.H. | NEW HAMPSHIRE |
| D. | DELAWARE | N.J. | NEW JERSEY |
| D.C. | DISTRICT OF COLUMBIA | R.I. | RHODE ISLAND |
| M. | MARYLAND | VER. | VERMONT |
| MASS. | MASSACHUSETTS | SPM | ST. PIERRE ET MIQUELON |

Projection: Bonne

COPYRIGHT. GEORGE PHILIP & SON. LTD.

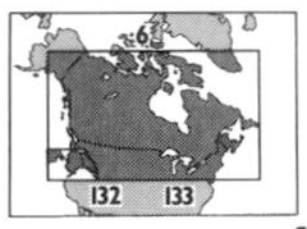

PACIFIC OCEAN

ALASKA

YUKON TERRITORY

BRITISH COLUMBIA

ALBERTA

SASKATCHEWAN

MANITOBA

NORTHWEST TERRITORIES

KEEWATIN

KITIKMEOT

NUNAVUT

Amundsen Gulf

Victoria Island

Banks Island

Prince Albert Pen.

Somerset Island

Prince of Wales Island

Queen Maud Gulf

Coronation Gulf

Great Bear Lake

Great Slave Lake

Lake Athabasca

Reindeer Lake

Edmonton

Vancouver

Victoria

Calgary

Lethbridge

Medicine Hat

Saskatoon

Regina

Moose Jaw

Prince Albert

Winnipeg

St. Boniface

Seattle

Tacoma

Spokane

WASHINGTON

MONTANA

WYOMING

NORTH DAKOTA

SOUTH DAKOTA

MINNESOTA

NEBRASKA

WISCONSIN

IOWA

UNITED STATES

Duluth

Minneapolis

St. Paul

Omaha

Sioux City

Fargo

Bismarck

Rapid City

Lake of the Woods

Projection: Bonne

**ALASKA**
1 : 24 000 000

100   0   100   200   300 miles
100   0   200   400 km

BERING SEA

Brooks Range

Seward Pen.

Nome

Fairbanks

Anchorage

Kodiak

Aleutian Is.

Bristol Bay

Kuskokwim Bay

GULF OF ALASKA

PACIFIC OCEAN

West from Greenwich

ft   m
9000   3000
6000   2000
4500   1500
3000   1000
1200   400
600   200
0   0
200   600
2000   6000
m   ft

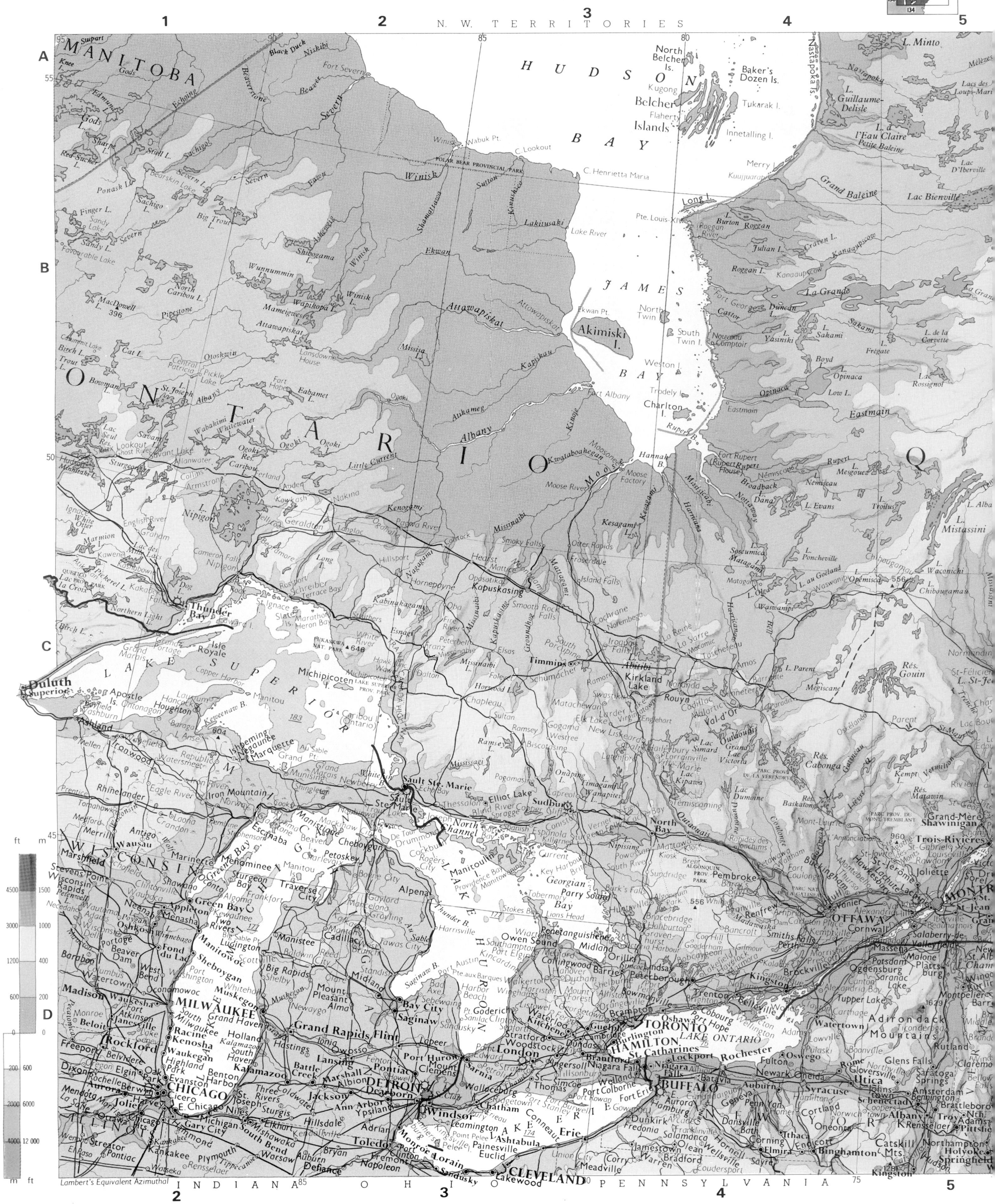

N.W. TERRITORIES

**MANITOBA**

**ONTARIO**

HUDSON BAY

North Belcher Is.
Baker's Dozen Is.
Kugong
Belcher Islands
Tukarak I.
Innetalling I.

JAMES BAY

Akimiski I.
North Twin
South Twin I.
Weston I.
Charlton I.
Trodely I.

Polar Bear Provincial Park

L. Minto

l. Guillaume-Delisle
l. à l'Eau Claire
Petite Baleine
Grand Baleine
Lac Bienville

LAKE SUPERIOR
Thunder Bay
Isle Royale
Duluth
Superior
Ashland

Timmins
Kirkland Lake
Kapuskasing
Cochrane
Rouyn
Val-d'Or

Sault Ste. Marie
Sudbury
Elliot Lake
North Bay

LAKE HURON
Georgian Bay
Manitoulin I.
Parry Sound

LAKE MICHIGAN

WISCONSIN
Wausau
Marshfield
Green Bay
Appleton
Oshkosh
Manitowoc
Sheboygan
MILWAUKEE
Madison
Beloit
Rockford
Freeport
CHICAGO
Joliet

Escanaba
Marquette
Iron Mountain
Traverse City
Cadillac
Muskegon
Grand Rapids
Lansing
Flint
DETROIT
Dearborn
Ann Arbor
Jackson
Kalamazoo
Battle Creek
Port Huron
Windsor

Bay City
Saginaw

INDIANA
South Bend
Toledo

OHIO
CLEVELAND
Lakewood
Sandusky

PENNSYLVANIA

LAKE ONTARIO
TORONTO
Hamilton
St. Catharines
London
Kitchener
Guelph
Brantford
Barrie
Peterborough
Kingston
OTTAWA
Cornwall

LAKE ERIE
BUFFALO
Niagara Falls
Rochester
Syracuse
Utica
Albany
Binghamton

Adirondack Mountains

Trois-Rivières
Shawinigan
Grand-Mère
Joliette
MONTREAL

Québec

L. Nipigon
L. Mistassini
Rés. Gouin

1 : 5 600 000

50 0 50 100 150 200 miles
50 0 50 100 150 200 250 300 km

6 7 8 9

A 55

COAST OF LABRADOR

NEWFOUNDLAND

QUEBEC

Kaniapiskau Lake

Smallwood Res.

Churchill Falls

Labrador City

L. Melville

Happy Valley-Goose Bay

Meaty Mts.

Long Range Mts.

Str. of Belle Isle

Belle I.

Battle Harbour

Corner Brook

GROS MORNE NAT. PARK

Bay of Islands

GULF OF ST. LAWRENCE

Î. d'Anticosti

Sept-Îles

Rimouski

Rivière-du-Loup

Mts. Chic-Chocs

Pén. de Gaspé

Chaleur Bay

Îs. de la Madeleine (Quebec)

Bathurst

NEW BRUNSWICK

Chatham

Newcastle

PRINCE EDWARD ISLAND

Summerside

Charlottetown

Cape Breton Island

Sydney Mines

New Waterford

Glace Bay

Cabot Strait

MIQUELON

SAINT-PIERRE ET MIQUELON (Fr.)

Fredericton

Moncton

Amherst

NOVA SCOTIA

New Glasgow

Stellarton

Truro

Saint John

Bay of Fundy

Dartmouth

Halifax

MAINE

Sherbrooke

Bangor

Augusta

Auburn

Lewiston

Portland

BOSTON

Sable I. (Nova Scotia)

Yarmouth

Liverpool

ATLANTIC

OCEAN

6 7 8

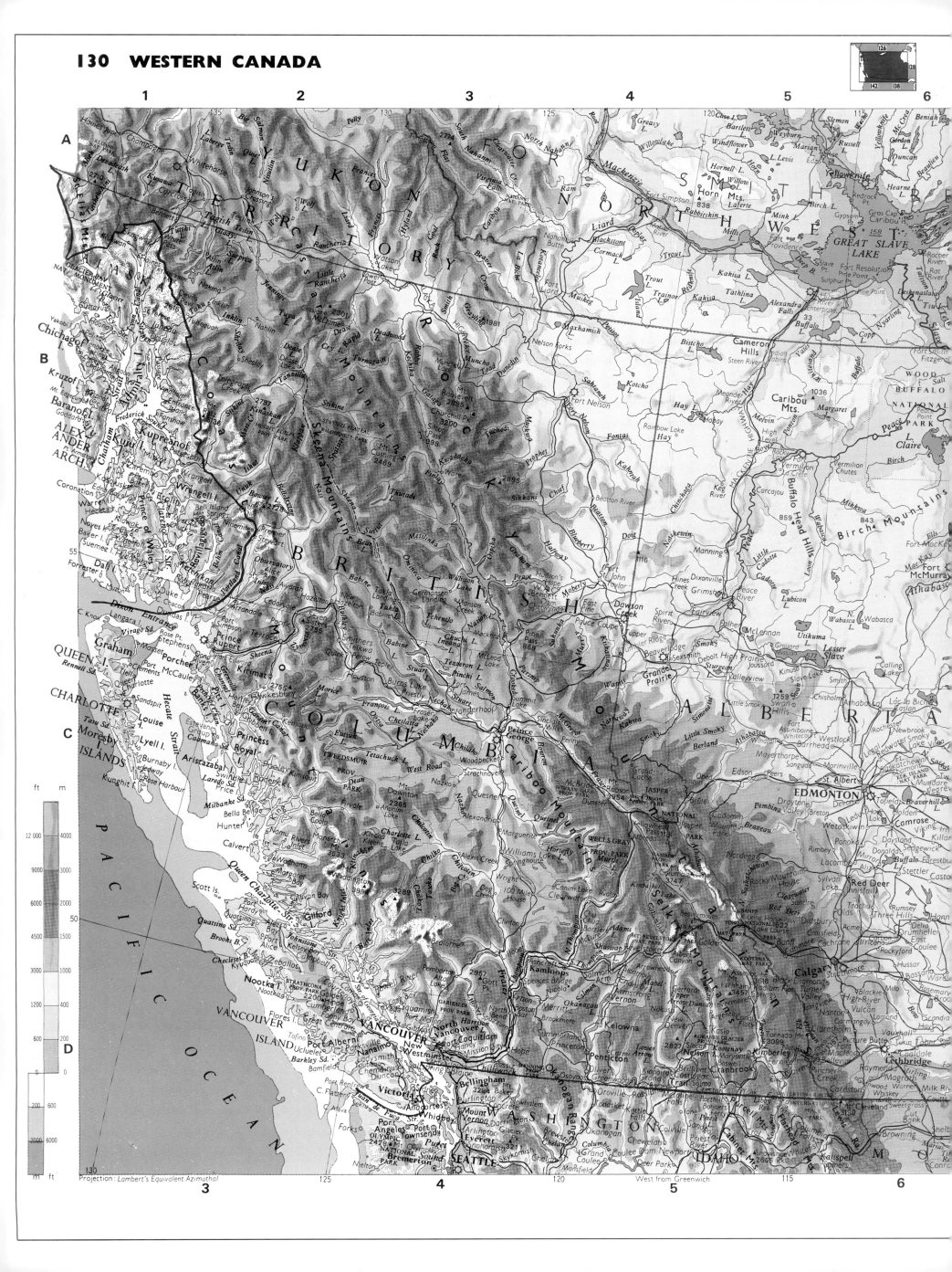

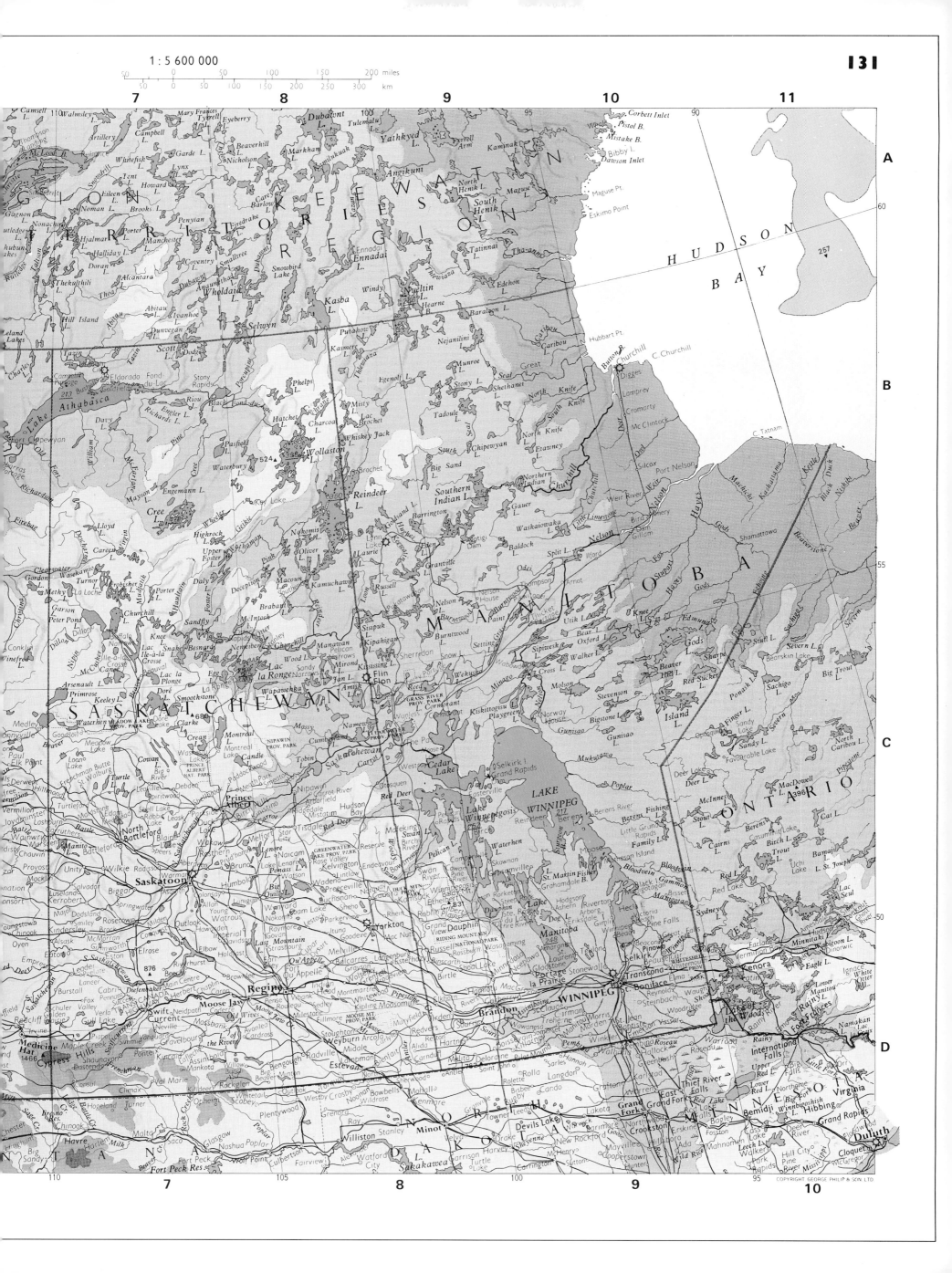

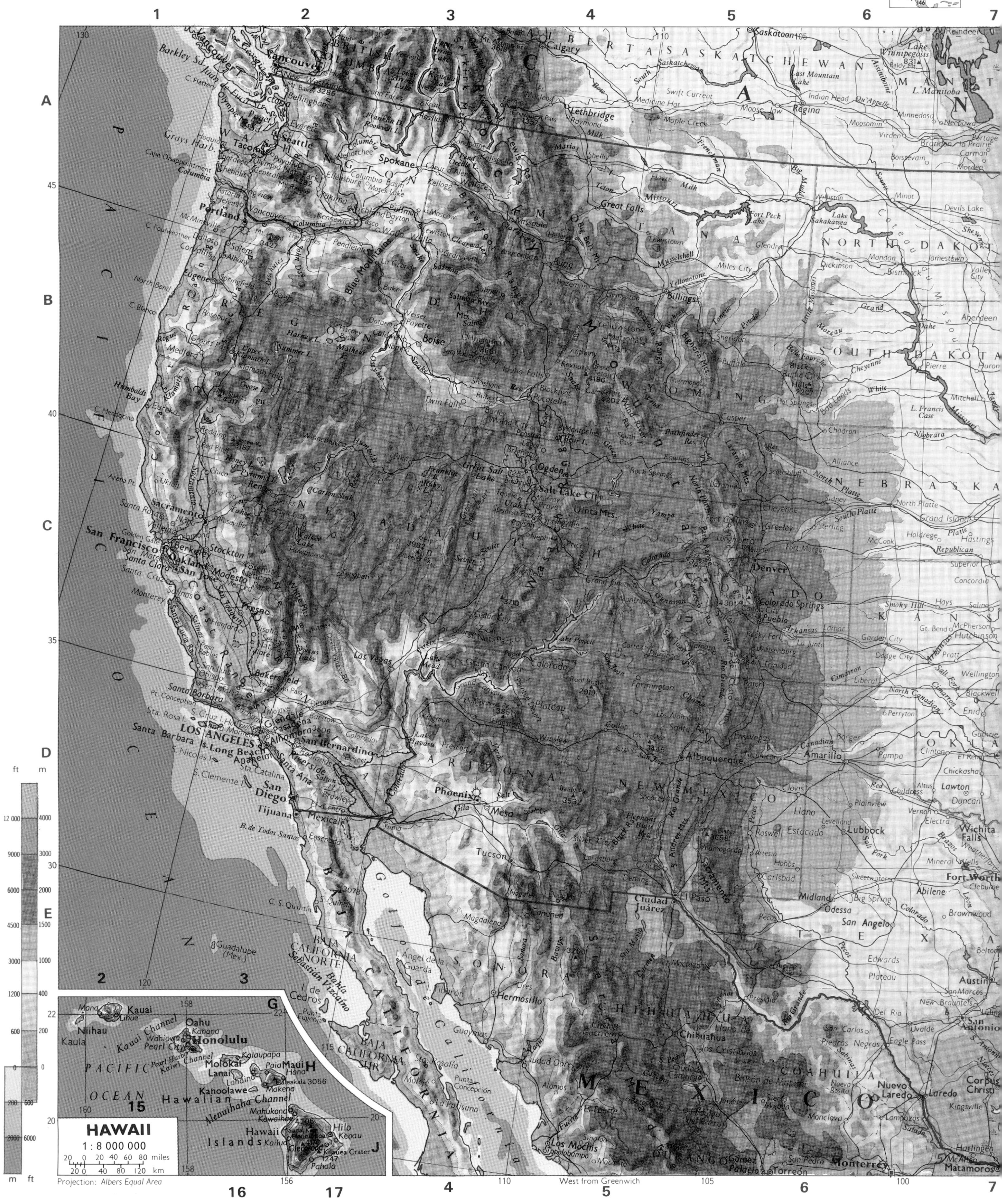

BRITISH COLUMBIA

WASHINGTON
OREGON
IDAHO
MONTANA
NORTH DAKOTA
SOUTH DAKOTA
WYOMING
NEBRASKA
NEVADA
UTAH
COLORADO
KANSAS
CALIFORNIA
ARIZONA
NEW MEXICO
OKLAHOMA
TEXAS

ALBERTA  SASKATCHEWAN  MANITOBA

Vancouver
Seattle
Tacoma
Spokane
Portland
Salem
Boise
Great Falls
Billings
Calgary
Lethbridge
Regina
Sacramento
San Francisco
Oakland
San Jose
Fresno
Bakersfield
LOS ANGELES
Long Beach
San Diego
Tijuana
Mexicali
Phoenix
Mesa
Tucson
Las Vegas
Salt Lake City
Ogden
Denver
Colorado Springs
Pueblo
Albuquerque
Santa Fe
El Paso
Ciudad Juárez
Amarillo
Lubbock
Fort Worth
Abilene
Midland
Odessa
San Angelo
Austin
San Antonio
Laredo
Nuevo Laredo
Monterrey
Chihuahua
Hermosillo
Ciudad Obregón
Los Mochis
Torreón
Durango

MEXICO
BAJA CALIFORNIA NORTE
BAJA CALIFORNIA SUR
SONORA
CHIHUAHUA
COAHUILA
DURANGO

PACIFIC OCEAN

Golfo de California

West from Greenwich

Projection: Albers Equal Area

**HAWAII**
1 : 8 000 000
20  0  20  40  60  80 miles
20  0  40  80  120 km

Hawaiian Islands
Kauai
Niihau
Oahu
Honolulu
Pearl City
Molokai
Lanai
Maui
Kahoolawe
Hawaii
Hilo
Haleakala 3056
Kilauea Crater
PACIFIC OCEAN

ft  m
12 000  4000
9000  3000
6000  2000
4500  1500
3000  1000
1200  400
600  200
0
600  200
6000  2000
m  ft

1 : 9 600 000

50 0 50 100 150 200 250 300 miles
50 0 50 100 150 200 250 300 350 400 450 km

8    9    10    11    12    13

**Major labels and place names:**

GULF OF MEXICO · ATLANTIC OCEAN · BAHAMAS

CANADA · Lake Winnipeg · Lake of the Wood · Winnipeg · Lake Superior · Lake Michigan · Lake Huron · Lake Erie · Lake Ontario · Thunder Bay · Duluth · Sault Ste. Marie · MONTREAL · Ottawa · Quebec · TORONTO · Hamilton · Buffalo · MAINE · VERMONT · N. HAMPSHIRE · MASS · Boston · NEW BRUNSWICK

MINNESOTA · Minneapolis · St. Paul · WISCONSIN · Madison · Milwaukee · IOWA · Des Moines · Sioux City · Omaha · Council Bluffs · Lincoln · Kansas City · Topeka · Wichita · MISSOURI · St. Louis · ILLINOIS · CHICAGO · Peoria · Springfield · INDIANA · Indianapolis · OHIO · Columbus · Cincinnati · Dayton · Cleveland · Toledo · Akron · Youngstown · DETROIT · Grand Rapids · Lansing · Flint · Pittsburgh · PENNSYLVANIA · Philadelphia · Baltimore · Washington D.C. · NEW YORK · Jersey City · Newark · Allentown · Scranton · Harrisburg · Wilmington · Camden · Atlantic City · Delaware Bay · Chesapeake Bay

WEST VIRGINIA · Charleston · Wheeling · KENTUCKY · Louisville · Lexington · Frankfort · Evansville · TENNESSEE · Nashville · Memphis · Chattanooga · Knoxville · NORTH CAROLINA · Raleigh · Charlotte · Winston Salem · Greensboro · Durham · Asheville · Wilmington · SOUTH CAROLINA · Columbia · Charleston · Richmond · Norfolk · Virginia Beach · Roanoke · Lynchburg · Newport News · Portsmouth · Cape Hatteras

GEORGIA · Atlanta · Columbus · Macon · Savannah · Augusta · ALABAMA · Birmingham · Montgomery · Mobile · MISSISSIPPI · Jackson · Vicksburg · Meridian · LOUISIANA · New Orleans · Baton Rouge · Shreveport · Lake Charles · ARKANSAS · Little Rock · Fort Smith · OKLAHOMA · Oklahoma City · Tulsa · Dallas · Fort Worth · Houston · Galveston · Beaumont · Port Arthur · Waco · Austin · Rio Grande · Laguna Madre · Brownsville

FLORIDA · Jacksonville · Tampa · St. Petersburg · Orlando · Miami · West Palm Beach · Fort Lauderdale · Key West · Tallahassee · Pensacola · Daytona Beach · Lake Okeechobee · C. Canaveral · C. Sable · Florida Keys · Delta of the Mississippi · Grand Bahama I. · Gt. Abaco · Little Abaco · New Providence · Eleuthera I. · Andros · Long I. · N.W. Providence Channel · N.E. Providence Chan. · Exuma Sound

COPYRIGHT. GEORGE PHILIP & SON. LTD

95    90    85    80

8    9    10    11    12

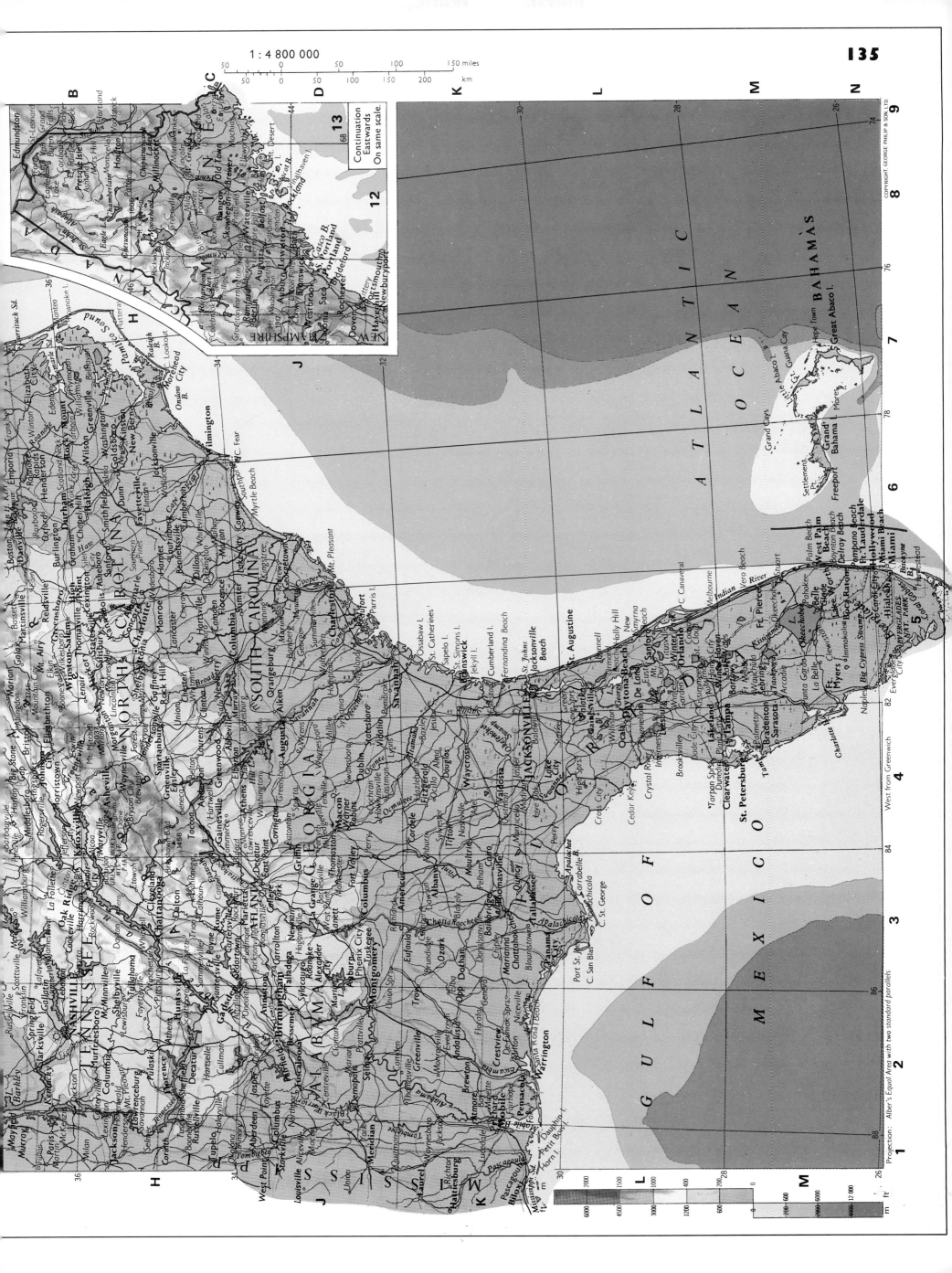

1 : 4 800 000

50        0        50        100        150 miles

50    0    50    100    150    200
km

Continuation
Eastwards
On same scale.

NEW HAMPSHIRE

MAINE

QUEBEC

ATLANTIC

OCEAN

BAHAMAS

Great Abaco I.

Little Abaco I.
Gt. Guana Cay

Grand Cays

Grand'
Bahama I.

Freeport

West Palm Beach
Palm Beach
Pompano Beach
Ft. Lauderdale
Hollywood
Miami
Miami Beach
Biscayne B.

EVERGLADES
NAT. PARK

ATLANTIC OCEAN

VIRGINIA

NORTH CAROLINA

SOUTH CAROLINA

GEORGIA

FLORIDA

TENNESSEE

ALABAMA

MISSISSIPPI

GULF OF MEXICO

West from Greenwich

Projection: Alber's Equal Area with two standard parallels

COPYRIGHT. GEORGE PHILIP & SON, LTD.

ft. m
6000
4500  3000
3000
1200
600
0
0        200
600        2000
6000        12 000

Column indices (top): 1 2 3 4 5 6 7
Row indices (left): A B C D E F G

**Bodies of water and regions:**
Georgian Bay
LAKE HURON
LAKE ONTARIO
LAKE ERIE
Lake St. Clair
Bruce Peninsula
Nottawasaga Bay
Long Point Bay

**States / Provinces:**
MICHIGAN
ONTARIO
CANADA
NEW YORK
OHIO
PENNSYLVANIA
W.VA.

**Major cities:**
TORONTO
Mississauga
Hamilton
Burlington
Kitchener
Waterloo
London
Sarnia
St. Catharines
Niagara Falls
BUFFALO
Lackawanna
Rochester
Irondequoit
DETROIT
Windsor
CLEVELAND
Lakewood
Parma
Euclid
Shaker Hts.
Akron
Canton
Youngstown
Warren
Mansfield
PITTSBURGH
Steubenville
McKeesport
Altoona
Johnstown
State College
Williamsport
Elmira
Erie
Jamestown

Projection: Bonne

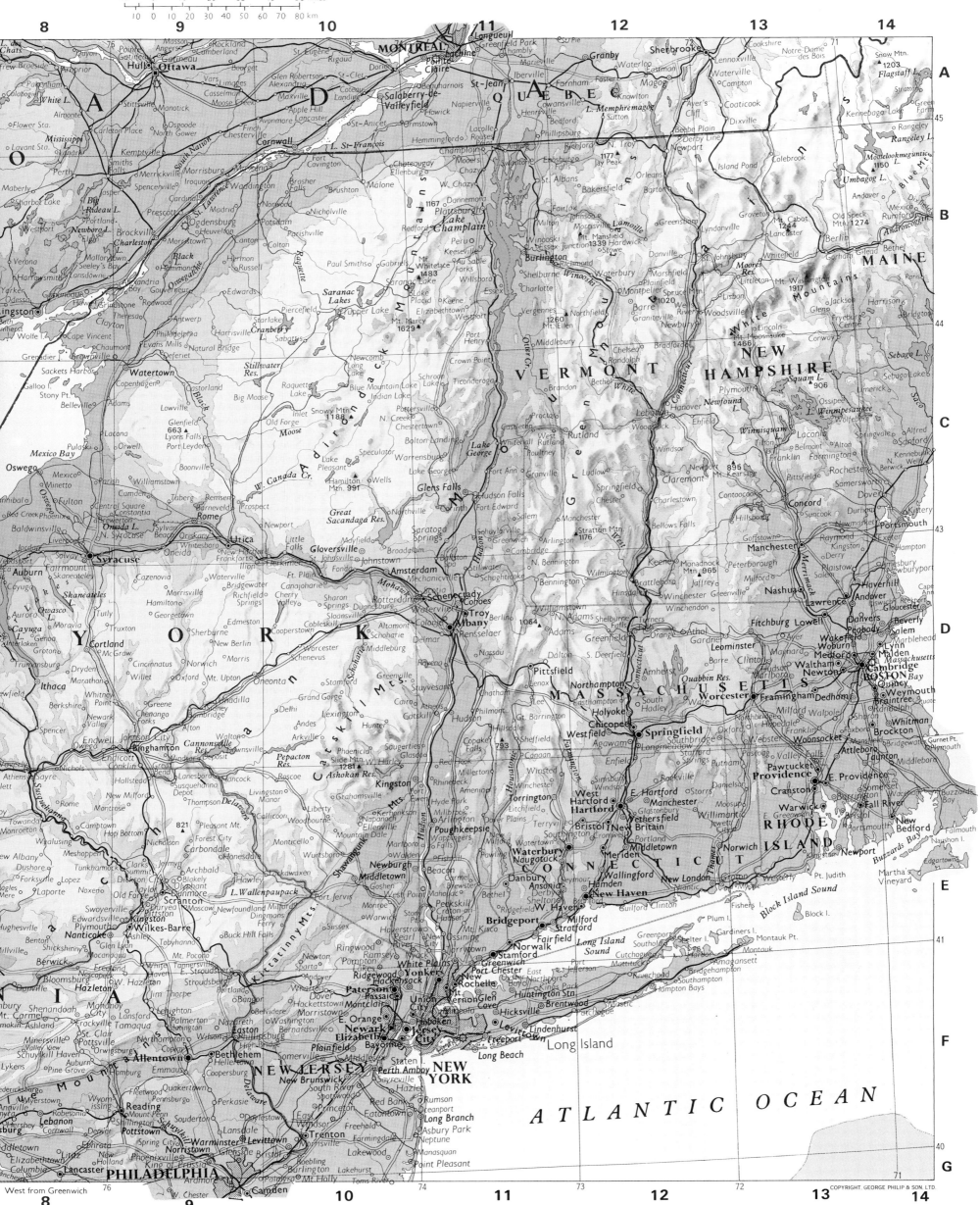

1 : 2 000 000

10    0    10    20    30    40    50 miles
10    0    10   20   30   40   50   60   70   80 km

ATLANTIC OCEAN

West from Greenwich

COPYRIGHT. GEORGE PHILIP & SON. LTD

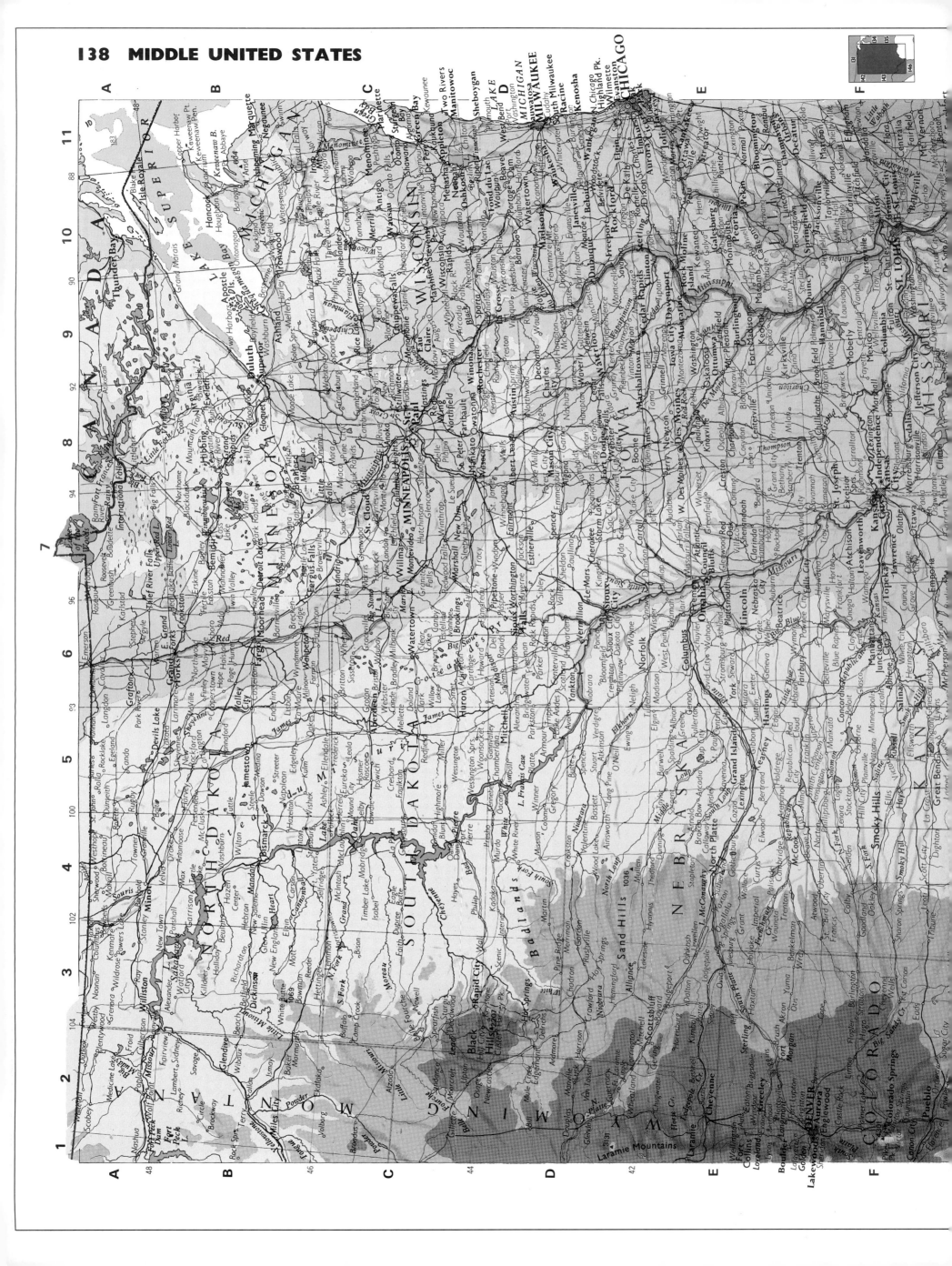

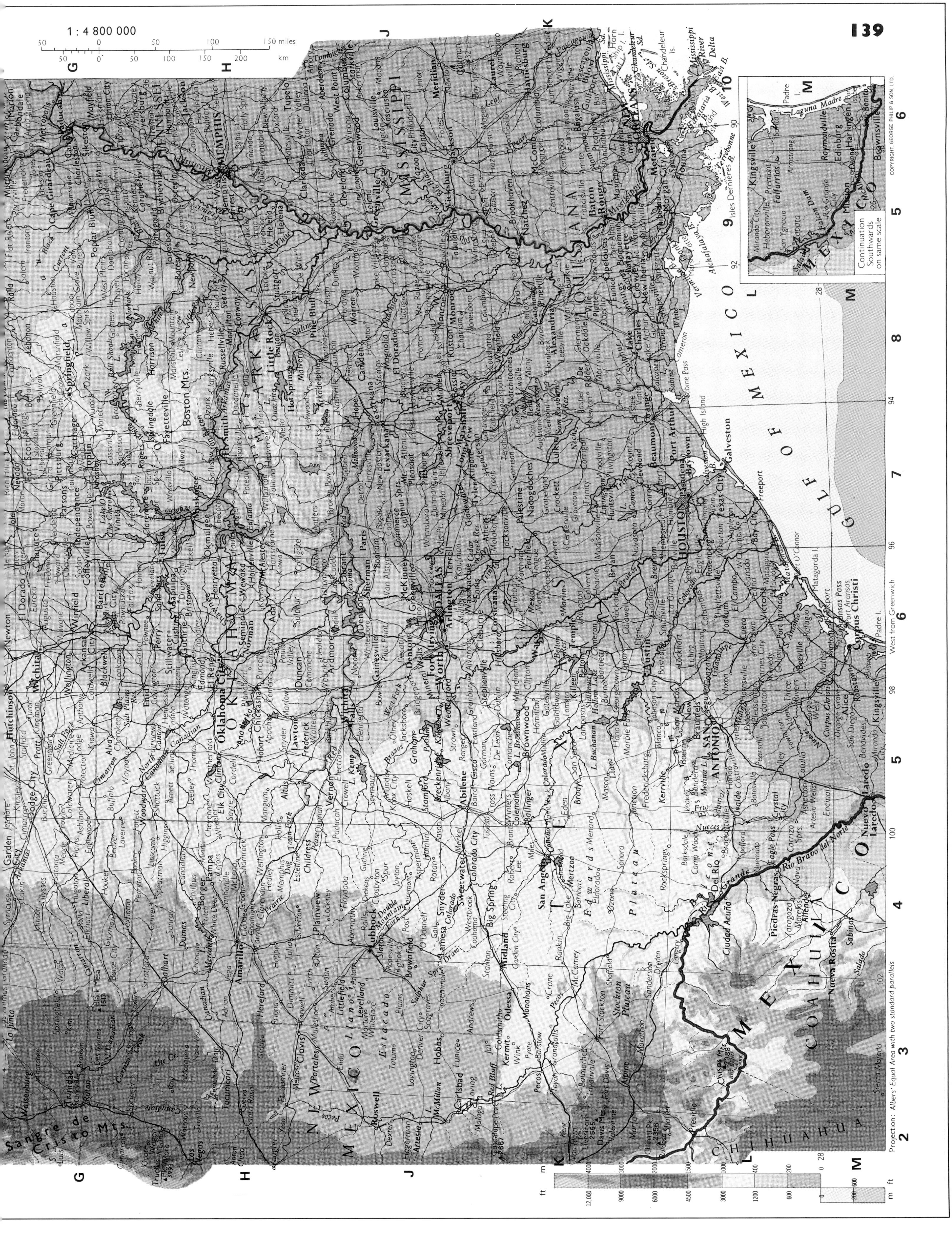

1 : 4 800 000

50    0    50    100    150 miles

50    0    50   100   150   200
km

TENNESSEE

MISSISSIPPI

ARKANSAS

LOUISIANA

OKLAHOMA

TEXAS

NEW MEXICO

COAHUILA

CHIHUAHUA

MEXICO

GULF OF MEXICO

MEMPHIS

Little Rock

Baton Rouge

NEW ORLEANS

HOUSTON

Galveston

DALLAS

Fort Worth

Arlington

Oklahoma City

Tulsa

Wichita Falls

Austin

SAN ANTONIO

Corpus Christi

Laredo

Nuevo Laredo

Amarillo

Lubbock

Midland

Odessa

Roswell

Carlsbad

Shreveport

Texarkana

Boston Mts.

Ouachita Mts.

Edwards Plateau

Llano Estacado

Stockton Plateau

Rio Grande

Rio Bravo del Norte

Sangre de Cristo Mts.

West from Greenwich

Projection: Albers' Equal Area with two standard parallels

Continuation Southwards on same scale

Laguna Madre

Brownsville

Kingsville

Mississippi River Delta

ft
12,000
9000
6000
4500
3000
1500
600
200
0

m
ft
600
200
0

Grid columns: 1 2 3 4 5 6 7

Rows: A B C D E F G

Latitude markers: 43, 42, 41, 40, 39, 38

Longitude markers: 95, 94, 93, 92, 91, 90, 89

**States:** WISCONSIN, IOWA, ILLINOIS, MISSOURI, KANSAS

**Major cities and towns:**

Madison, Mason City, Clear Lake, Britt, Algona, Emmetsburg, Whittemore, Calmar, Wisconsin, Eastman, Sauk City, De Forest, Mazomanie, Middleton, Verona, Monona, Spring Green, Muscoda, Highland, Mt. Horeb, Oregon

Marathon, Pocahontas, Rolfe, Kanawha, Garner, Nora Springs, Rockford, Charles City, Greene, Nashua, New Hampton, Postville, Prairie du Chien, Boscobel, Dodgeville, Mineral Point, New Glarus, Stoughton, Edgerton, Evansville

Fort Dodge, Webster City, Iowa Falls, Ackley, Parkersburg, Cedar Falls, Waterloo, Denver, Oelwein, Strawberry Point, Colesburg, Dubuque, E. Dubuque, Platteville, Dickeyville, Darlington, South Wayne, Monroe, Brodhead, Beloit, Janesville

Sac City, Rockwell City, Lake City, Lohrville, Gowrie, Stanhope, Jewell, Story City, Grundy Center, Reinbeck, La Porte City, Jesup, Independence, Manchester, Dyersville, Cascade, Bellevue, Elizabeth, Galena, Stockton, Warren, Orangeville, Durand, Freeport, Cedarville, Winnebago, Pecatonica, Byron, Rockford

Carroll, Scranton, Jefferson, Boone, Ames, Nevada, State Center, Marshalltown, Toledo, Tama, Vinton, Shellsburg, Center Point, Monticello, Anamosa, Wyoming, Maquoketa, Preston, Sabula, Mt. Carroll, Milledgeville, Thomson, Polo, Oregon, Rochelle

Perry, Madrid, Cambridge, Melbourne, Belle Plaine, Marengo, Marion, Cedar Rapids, Mechanicsville, Lowden, De Witt, Clinton, Fulton, Sterling, Dixon, Rock Falls, Amboy

Urbandale, Adel, Altoona, Des Moines, Newton, Grinnell, Brooklyn, Oxford, Coralville, Iowa City, West Liberty, Tipton, Durant, Davenport, Rock Island, Bettendorf, E. Moline, Moline, Geneseo, Atkinson, Princeton, Walnut

Stuart, Anita, Van Meter, Winterset, Martensdale, Monroe, Sully, Montezuma, Deep River, North English, Kalona, Washington, Muscatine, Milan, Aledo, Viola, Alpha, Cambridge, Sheffield, Kewanee, Hennepin, Granville, La Salle, Peru

Cumberland, Greenfield, Indianola, Pleasantville, Pella, New Sharon, Sigourney, Keota, Columbus Junction, Reynolds, Orion, Galva, Toulon, Oneida, Wyoming, Wenona, Varna

Orient, Lorimor, Knoxville, Oskaloosa, Hedrick, Richland, Crawfordville, Wapello, Keithsburg, Alexis, Princeville, Spring Valley

New Virginia, Lacona, Melcher, Lovilia, Eddyville, Brighton, Winfield, Mt. Pleasant, New London, Oquawka, Roseville, Abingdon, Monmouth, Gladstone, Little York, Victoria, Chillicothe, Upper Peoria L., Minonk, Washburn

Creston, Corning, Murray, Chariton, Melrose, Albia, Blakesburg, Eldon, Ottumwa, Fairfield, Birmingham, Hillsboro, Burlington, Mediapolis, Stronghurst, Roseville, Farmington, Elmwood, Brimfield, Peoria Heights, Eureka, El Paso

Villisca, Lenox, Diagonal, Grand River, Humeston, Moravia, Moulton, Bloomfield, Milton, Keosauqua, West Point, Ft. Madison, La Harpe, London Mills, Canton, St. David, Peoria, East Peoria, Washington, Metamora

Clearfield, Mount Ayr, Leon, Seymour, Centerville, Corydon, Mystic, Cincinnati, Bedford, Blockton, Lamoni, Lineville, Cantril, Keokuk, Hamilton, Warsaw, Plymouth, Augusta, Rushville, Table Grove, Lewistown, Astoria, Bartonville, Creve Coeur, Pekin, Morton, Mackinaw, Normal, Bloomington

Hopkins, Sheridan, Grant City, Princeton, Mercer, Unionville, Downing, Memphis, Kahoka, Alexandria, Canton, Monticello, La Harpe, Blandinsville, Bushnell, Macomb, Avon, Delavan, Minier, Congerville

Maryville, Eagleville, Newtown, Lancaster, Queen City, La Belle, Golden, Industry, La Moine, Vermont, San Jose, Mason City, Manito, Oakford, McLean, Heyworth

Ravenwood, Albany, Bethany, Princeton, Spickard, Green City, Novinger, Kirksville, Edina, Gorin, N. Fabius, La Grange, Loraine, Versailles, Mt. Sterling, Astoria, Lincoln, Clinton, Atlanta

Rosendale, King City, Gilman City, Galt, Milan, Trenton, Browning, La Plata, Atlanta, Baring, Ewing, Quincy, Camp Point, Clayton, Beardstown, Virginia, Petersburg, Mt. Pulaski

Saint Joseph, Union Star, Stanberry, Jamesport, Chula, Linneus, Brookfield, Shelbyville, Palmyra, Hull, Barry, Chapin, Ashland, Williamsburg, Illiopolis, Warrensburg

Savannah, Maysville, Gallatin, Chillicothe, Meadville, Bucklin, Macon, North Fork, Clarence, Hannibal, Louisiana, Jacksonville, New Berlin, Pawnee, Springfield, Riverton, Decatur, Blue Mound, Mt. Zion

Dearborn, Cameron, Hamilton, Breckenridge, Marceline, Salt River, Monroe City, Paris, Perry, Louisiana, Winchester, Bluffs, Meredosia, Franklin, Murrayville, Waverly, Auburn, Chatham, Edinburg, Stonington, Moweaqua

Plattsburg, Kingston, Polo, Braymer, Bosworth, Keytesville, Huntsville, Moberly, Madison, Frankford, Pleasant Hill, Roodhouse, White Hall, Palmyra, Girard, Virden, Kincaid, Taylorville, Assumption

Smithville, Lawson, Lathrop, Richmond, Carrollton, Brunswick, Salisbury, Higbee, Centralia, Mexico, Clarksville, Bowling Green, Kampsville, Carrollton, Greenfield, Carlinville, Morrisonville, Nokomis, Paha

Kansas City, Gladstone, Excelsior Springs, Norborne, Glasgow, Fayette, Columbia, Sturgeon, Laddonia, Vandalia, Elsberry, Hardin, Jerseyville, Gillespie, Litchfield, Hillsboro, Raymond, Ramsey

Independence, Liberty, Lexington, Waverly, Marshall, Slater, Boonville, New Franklin, Fulton, Mexico, Wellsville, Bellflower, Troy, Moscow Mills, Winfield, Brighton, Bunker Hill, Mt. Olive, Staunton, Sorento

Raytown, Blue Springs, Wellington, Concordia, Sedalia, Sweet Springs, Tipton, California, Jamestown, Montgomery City, Auxvasse, Hawk Point, Cuivre, Alton, Godfrey, Bethalto, Wood River, Worden, Mulberry Grove, Greenville, Vandalia

Shawnee, Leawood, Grandview, Belton, Pleasant Hill, Warrensburg, Holden, Whiteman, La Monte, Otterville, Jefferson City, Chamois, Gasconade, Hermann, Washington, Pacific, St. Charles, Florissant, Overland, University City, Granite City, Collinsville, Highland, Kaysport, Salem

Louisburg, Freeman, Harrisonville, Garden City, South Grand, Windsor, Cole Camp, Versailles, Linn, Freeburg, Gerald, Union, New Haven, St. Louis, Kirkwood, Affton, East St. Louis, Belleville, Columbia, Waterloo, Lebanon, Mascoutah, Carlyle, Aviston, Centralia

Adrian, Montrose, Clinton, Harry S. Truman Res., Warsaw, Bagnell Dam, Tuscumbia, Lake of the Ozarks, Iberia, Camdenton, Eldon, Belle, Owensville, Bourbeuse, Hermann, Sullivan, Hillsboro, Festus, Crystal City, De Soto, Red Bud, New Athens, Nashville, Okawville, Carlyle, Sandoval

Amoret, Hume, Butler, Appleton City, Deepwater, Lowry City, Cross Timbers, Osceola, Roscoe, Hermitage, Dixon, Saint James, Cuba, Steelville, Potosi, Bonne Terre, Flat River, Sainte Genevieve, Sparta, Tamaroa, Coulterville

Nevada, Bronaugh, Sheldon, Jerico Springs, Eldorado Springs, Stockton, Collins, Weaubleau, Urbana, Pomme de Terre L., Humansville, Buffalo, Lebanon, Crocker, Fort Leonard Wood, Richland, Newburg, Rolla, Waynesville, Dillard, Caledonia, St. Marys, Perryville, Chester, Ava, Murphysboro, Carbondale, Du Quoin, Pinckneyville, Percy, Evansville, Christopher, Zeigler, Herrin, Centerville

**Rivers and features:** Des Moines, Iowa, Cedar, Mississippi, Wapsipinicon, Turkey, Skunk, Chariton, Grand, Thompson, Platte, Missouri, Osage, Gasconade, Meramec, Illinois, Sangamon, Mark Twain L., Thomas Hill Res., L. Red Rock, Rathbun L., Coralville L., Lake of the Ozarks, Harry S. Truman Res.

Elevation scale: ft / m — 1200/400, 600/200, 0/0

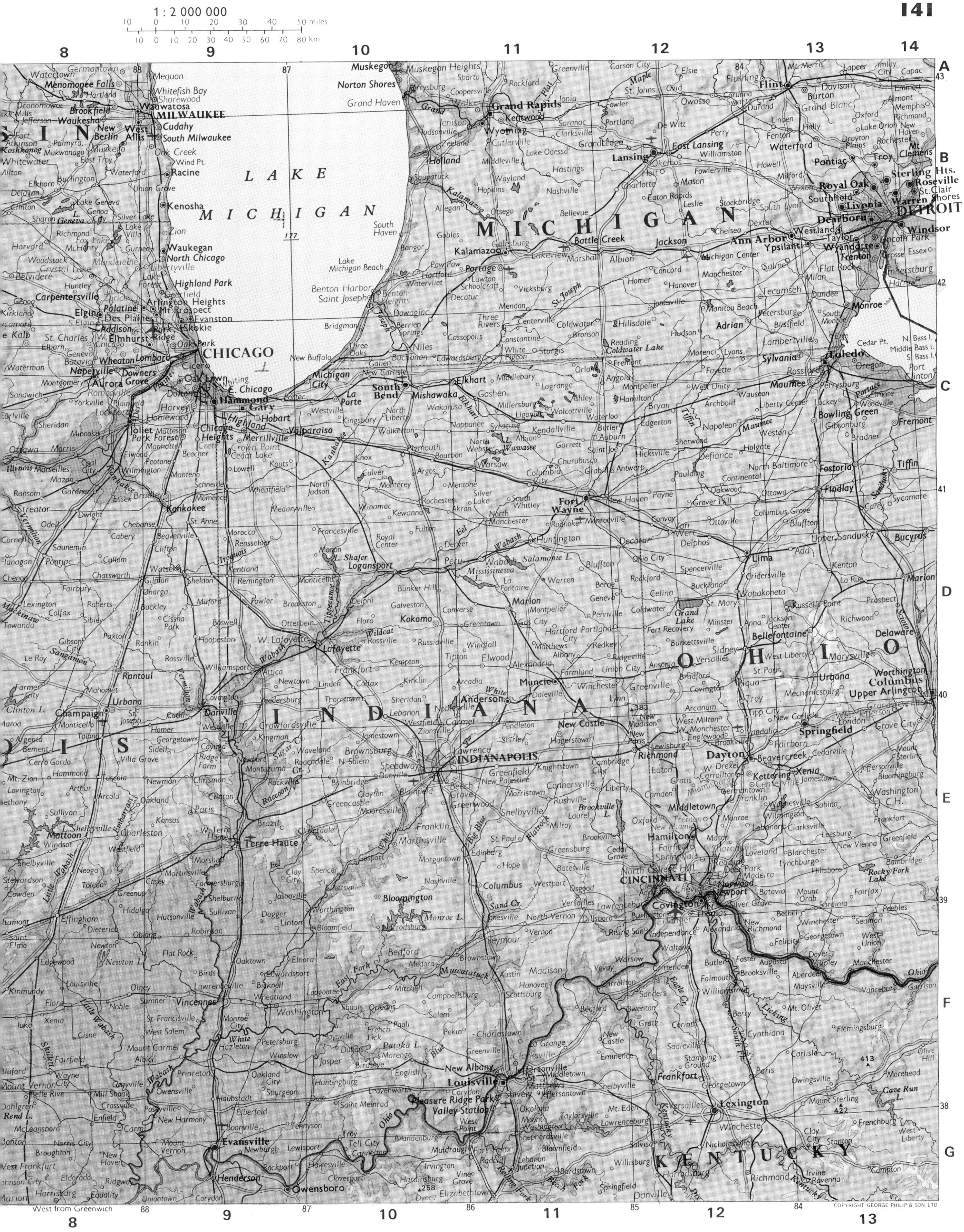

1 : 2 000 000

10   0   10   20   30   40   50 miles
10   0   10   20   30   40   50   60   70   80 km

8        9        10        11        12        13        14

LAKE MICHIGAN

WISCONSIN

MICHIGAN

INDIANA

OHIO

ILLINOIS

KENTUCKY

MILWAUKEE

CHICAGO

DETROIT

Windsor

Grand Rapids

Lansing

Flint

Toledo

Fort Wayne

Lafayette

INDIANAPOLIS

CINCINNATI

Dayton

Columbus

Louisville

Evansville

Lexington

Frankfort

Owensboro

West from Greenwich

8        9        10        11        12        13

COPYRIGHT GEORGE PHILIP & SON LTD

A
B
C
D
E
F
G

1 : 4 800 000

Projection: Albers' Equal Area with two standard parallels

West from Greenwich

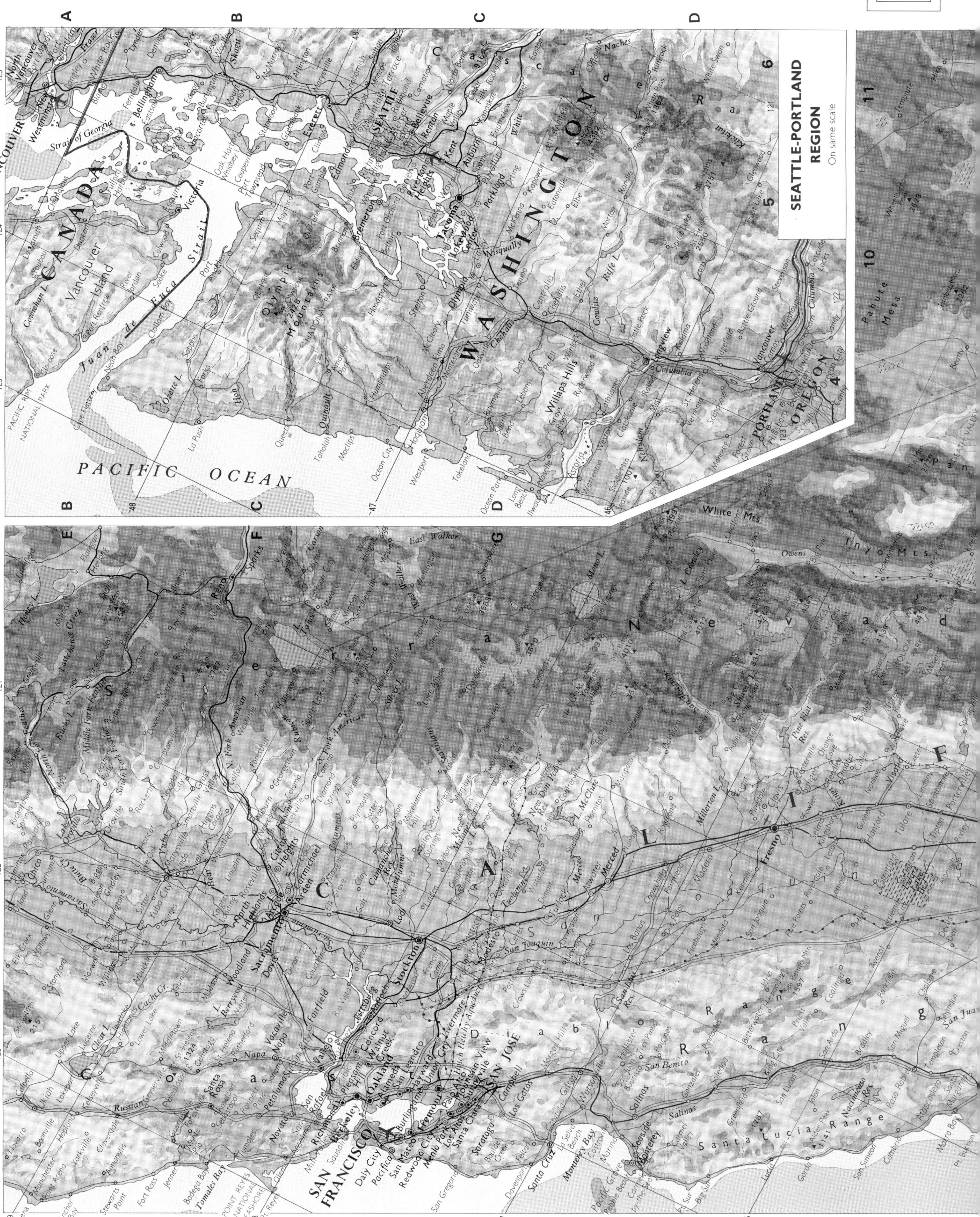

SEATTLE-PORTLAND REGION
On same scale

PACIFIC OCEAN

CANADA

VANCOUVER

Vancouver Island

Strait of Georgia

Juan de Fuca Strait

Olympic Mountains

WASHINGTON

OREGON

SEATTLE

Tacoma

PORTLAND

Willapa Hills

Columbia

Vancouver

PACIFIC RIM NATIONAL PARK

White Mts.

Inyo Mts.

Owens

Sierra Nevada

Reno

Sparks

CALIFORNIA

Sacramento

San Francisco

Oakland

Berkeley

SAN JOSE

Fresno

Stockton

Modesto

Merced

Salinas

Monterey

Napa

Santa Rosa

Santa Lucia Range

Diablo Range

Coast Range

San Joaquin

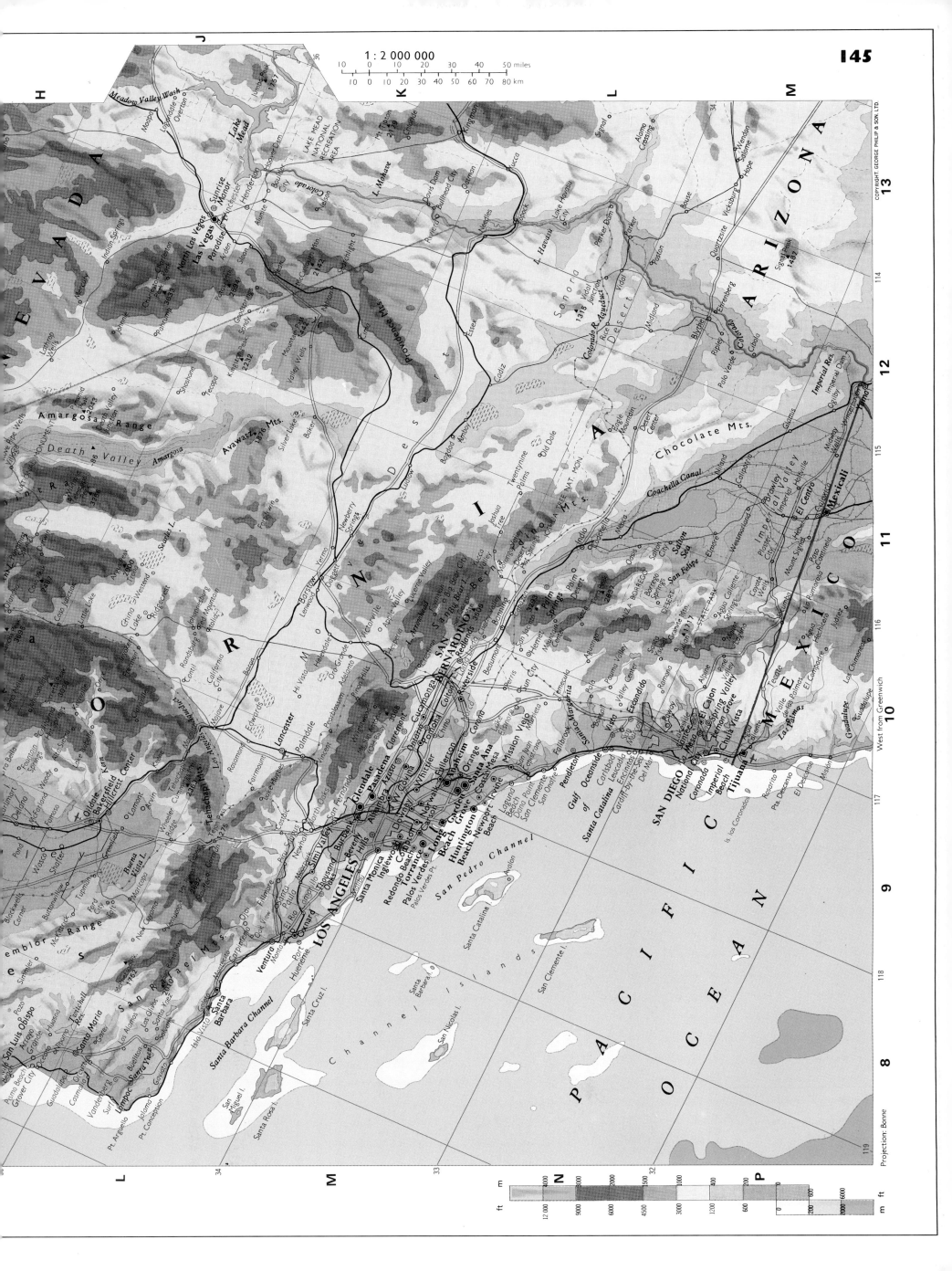

1 : 2 000 000

10   0   10   20   30   40   50 miles
10   0   10   20   30   40   50   60   70   80 km

West from Greenwich

Projection: Bonne

**NEVADA**

**ARIZONA**

**CALIFORNIA**

**MEXICO**

**PACIFIC OCEAN**

Lake Mead

LAKE MEAD NATIONAL RECREATION AREA

Death Valley

Amargosa Range

Mojave Desert

San Bernardino Mts.

Chocolate Mts.

Colorado R. Aqueduct

Coachella Canal

Salton Sea

Imperial Valley

LOS ANGELES

SAN DIEGO

SAN BERNARDINO

Las Vegas

North Las Vegas

Paradise

Henderson

Pasadena

Glendale

Burbank

Long Beach

Santa Monica

Inglewood

Torrance

Huntington Beach

Newport Beach

Santa Ana

Anaheim

Fullerton

Orange

Riverside

Redlands

Colton

Ontario

Pomona

Lancaster

Palmdale

Bakersfield

Barstow

Needles

Kingman

Mexicali

Tijuana

El Centro

Brawley

Oceanside

Carlsbad

Escondido

Santa Barbara

Ventura

Oxnard

Palm Springs

Indio

Twentynine Palms

Joshua Tree

Santa Catalina I.

San Clemente I.

Santa Cruz I.

Santa Rosa I.

San Miguel I.

San Nicolas I.

Channel Islands

Santa Barbara Channel

San Pedro Channel

Palos Verdes Pt.

Pt. Conception

Pt. Arguello

San Pedro Channel

Gulf of Santa Catalina

Colorado R.

Imperial Dam

Imperial Res.

Yuma

Quartzsite

Parker

Parker Dam

Blythe

Hoover Dam

Davis Dam

L. Mohave

Bullhead City

Lake Havasu City

Mt. Tipton 2189

Sonoran Desert

ft    m
12 000  4000
9000  3000
6000  2000
4500  1500
3000  1000
1200  400
600   200
0     0
200   600
2000  6000
4000  12000
m    ft

REFERENCE TO NUMBERS
1 Federal District      5 México
2 Aguascalientes       6 Morelos
3 Guanajuato           7 Querétaro
4 Hidalgo              8 Tlaxcala

Projection: Bi-polar oblique Conical Orthomorphic      West from Greenwich

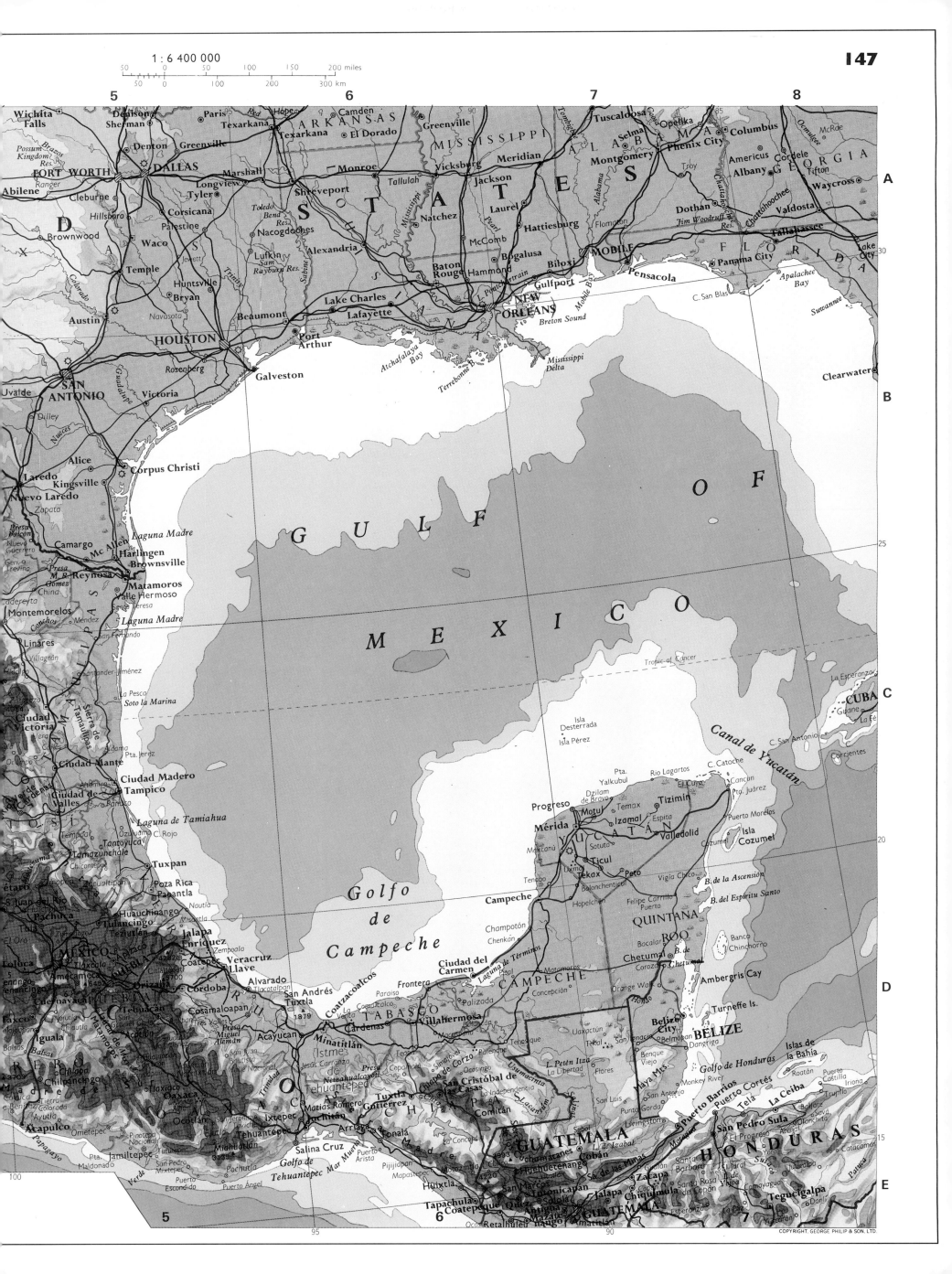

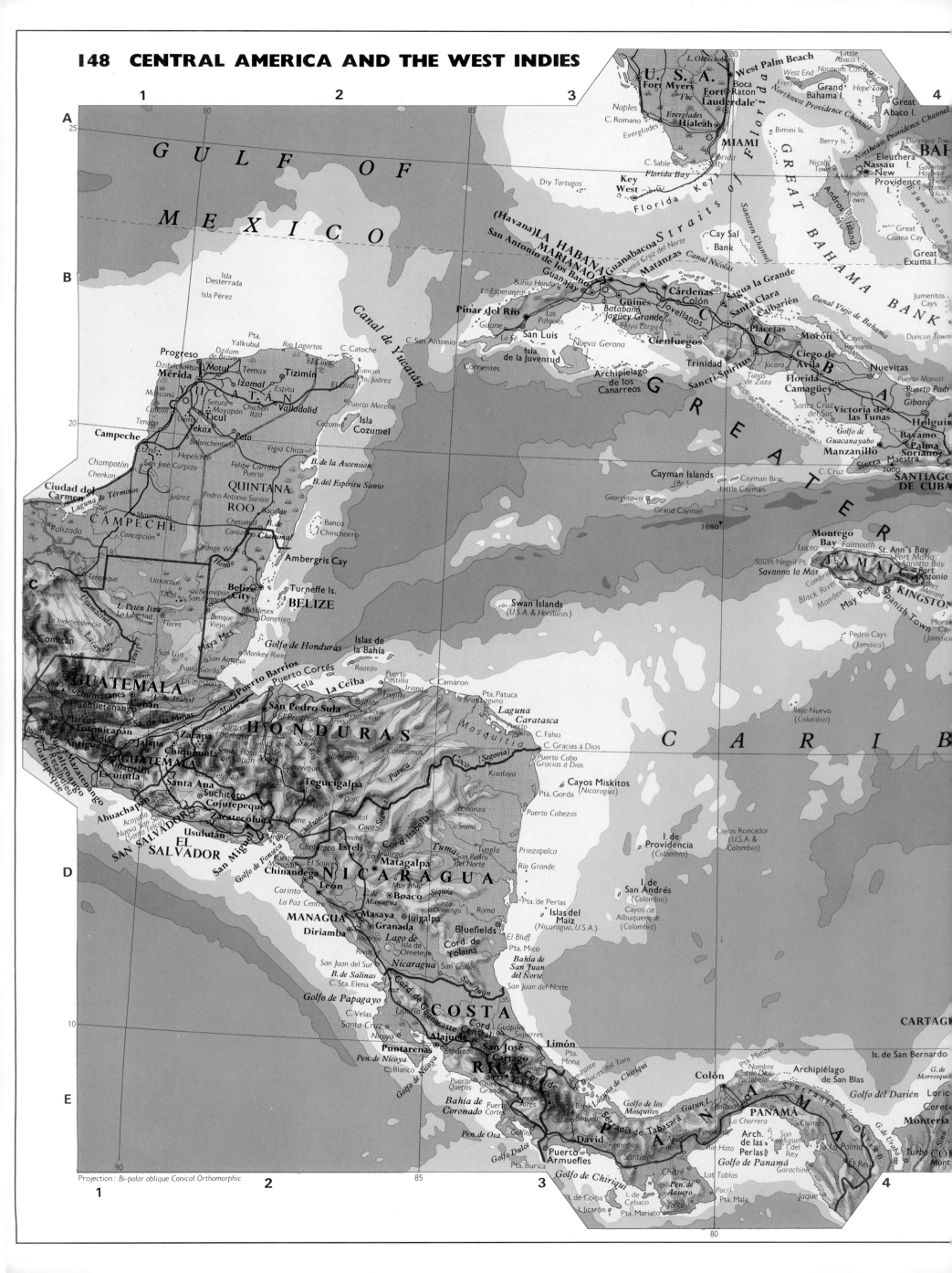

GULF OF MEXICO

U.S.A.
West Palm Beach
Fort Myers
Fort Lauderdale
Boca Raton
Naples
Everglades
Hialeah
MIAMI
Key West
Dry Tortugas
Florida Bay

Grand Bahama I.
Great Abaco I.
Little Abaco I.
Bimini Is.
Berry Is.
Nassau
New Providence
Eleuthera
BAH
Great Exuma I.

(Havana) LA HABANA
MARIANAO
San Antonio de los Baños
Guanajay
Pinar del Río
San Luis
Isla de la Juventud
Nueva Gerona
Matanzas
Cárdenas
Güines
Jovellanos
Colón
Santa Clara
Caibarién
Placetas
Cienfuegos
Trinidad
Sancti Spíritus
Ciego de Ávila
Morón
Camagüey
Nuevitas
CUBA
GREATER
Victoria de las Tunas
Holguín
Bayamo
Manzanillo
Palma Soriano
SANTIAGO DE CUBA
Sierra Maestra

Cayman Islands (Br.)
Georgetown
Grand Cayman
Cayman Brac
Little Cayman

Montego Bay
Lucea
Savanna la Mar
Black River
JAMAICA
Spanish Town
KINGSTON

YUCATÁN
Progreso
Mérida
Motul
Izamal
Tizimín
Valladolid
Campeche
Ciudad del Carmen
CAMPECHE
QUINTANA ROO
Chetumal
Ambergris Cay
Belize City
BELIZE
Turneffe Is.

Swan Islands (U.S.A. & Honduras)

GUATEMALA
Huehuetenango
Cobán
GUATEMALA
Antigua
Escuintla
Santa Ana
SAN SALVADOR
EL SALVADOR
San Miguel

HONDURAS
San Pedro Sula
La Ceiba
Tegucigalpa
Islas de la Bahía
Puerto Barrios
Puerto Cortés
Tela

Cayos Miskitos (Nicaragua)
Puerto Cabezas
CARIB

NICARAGUA
Chinandega
León
MANAGUA
Masaya
Granada
Bluefields
Lago de Nicaragua

I. de Providencia (Colombia)
I. de San Andrés (Colombia)
Cayos de Albuquerque (Colombia)
Islas del Maíz (Nicaragua, U.S.A.)

COSTA RICA
Puntarenas
Alajuela
San José
Cartago
Limón
David
Puerto Armuelles

PANAMÁ
Colón
Archipiélago de San Blas
Golfo del Darién
Golfo de Panamá
Arch. de las Perlas
Golfo de Chiriquí

CARTAGE

1 : 6 400 000

50   0   50   100   150   200 miles
50   0   100   200   300 km

5        6        7        8

ft   m

12,000   4000

9000   3000

6000   2000

3000   1000

1200   400

600   200

0   0

200   600

2000   6000

4000   12,000

6000   18,000

8000   24,000

m   ft

A T L A N T I C

O C E A N

Tropic of Cancer

AMAS

Arthur's Town
The Bight
Cat I.
San Salvador
(Watling I., Guanahani)
Conception I.
Rum Cay
Long I.
Clarence Town
andy
Crooked I. Passage
Richmond
Albert Town
Snug Corner
Acklins I.
Cay Verde
Mira por vos Cay
Hogsty Reef
Cay Santa
Domingo
Little Inagua I.
Lake Rosa
Great
Inagua I.
Matthew
Town
Crooked I.
Plana Cays
Mayaguana I.
Caicos Passage
Caicos
Islands
(Br.)
Turks I. Passage
Turks Islands
(Br.)
Puerto Rico Trench

Banes
antilla
Moa
Mayarí
Baracoa
GUANTÁNAMO
Guantánamo
Paso de los Vientos
(Windward Passage)
Pta. de
Maisí
Cap-à-Foux
Cap-Haïtien
Port-de-Paix
Fort-Liberté
Î. de la Tortue
Jean-Rabel
Cap. St.-
Nicolas
Monte Cristi
La Isabela
Puerto Plata
Santiago de
los Cabelleros
Vega
C. Frances Viejo
San Francisco de Macoris
Nagua
Sanchez
Sabana de la Mar
Milwaukee
Deep
9200
Bayamón
SAN JUAN
Carolina
Virgin Gorda
Tortola
(Br.)
St. Thomas
Road Town
Virgin Is.
(Br.)
Anegada
Anegada Passage
Sombrero (Anguilla)
Anguilla (Br.)

Golfe de
la Gonâve
Gonaïves
St.-Marc
Hinche
Cordillera
Central
3175
DOMINICAN
REP.
Hato Mayor
C. Engano
Higüey
Aguadilla
Arecibo
Ponce
1388
Caguas
Fajardo
Virgin Is.
(U.S.A.)
St. Croix
Christiansted
Frederiksted
St.-Martin (Guad.)
St. Maarten
(Neth.)
Saba (Neth.)
St. Eustatius
(Neth.)
St.-Barthélemy (Fr.)
Barbuda
ST.
CHRISTOPHER-
NEVIS
Basseterre
Nevis
ANTIGUA
& BARBUDA
St. Johns
Antigua

Jérémie
Damé
Marie
Î. de la Gonâve
Carcasse
PORT-
AU-PRINCE
H A I T I
Massif de la Hotte
2280
Aquin
Les Cayes
Pointe-à-Gravois
Î.-a-Vache
Jacmel
Étang Saumâtre
San Juan
2280
Pedernales
Bani
Azua de
Compostela
San Cristóbal
SANTO DOMINGO
San Pedro
de Macoris
La Romana
B. de
Yuma
I. Saona
I. Mona
(U.S.A.)
Mayagüez
Isla
Mona
PUERTO
RICO
(U.S.A.)
Guayama
Charlotte Amalie
Redonda
Montserrat
Guadeloupe Passage
Ste-Rose
GUADELOUPE
(Fr.)
Basse-Terre
Moule
Pointe-à-Pitre
Desirade
Marie-Galante (Fr.)
Grand-Bourg
I. des Saintes
(Guad.)
Dominica Passage
Portsmouth
DOMINICA
Roseau

H I S P A N I O L A
A N T I L L E S
Barahona
C. Beata
I. Beata

B E A N
S E A
L E S S E R
A N T I L L E S
L E E W A R D   I S L A N D S
I. de Aves (Bird I.)
(Venezuela)
Mt. Pelée
1397
Ste-Marie
François
Rivière-Pilo
FORT-DE-FRANCE
MARTINIQUE
St. Lucia Channel (Fr.)
Castries
Soufrière
ST. LUCIA

W I N D W A R D   I S L A N D S
L E S S E R   A N T I L L E S
St. Vincent Passage
Soufrière 1234
ST. VINCENT
Kingstown
Speightstown
Bridgetown
& THE
BARBADOS
60

L E S S E R   A N T I L L E S
Aruba
(Neth.)
Curaçao
Bonaire
Willemstad
NETH.
ANTILLES
Is. de Aves
(Ven.)
Is. Los Roques
(Ven.)
I. Orchila
(Ven.)
I. Blanquilla (Ven.)
I. Los Hermanos
(Ven.)
Is. Los Testigos
(Ven.)
Hillsborough
The Grenadines
GRENADINES
St. George's
GRENADA
Tobago
Scarborough

Pta. Gallinas
C. San Román
Pen. de la
Guajira
Pta.
Espada
Pen. de
Paraguaná
Punto Fijo
C. San
Antonio
Ríohacha
Uribia
GUAJIRA
Golfo de
Venezuela
Punta
Cardón
Coro
La Vela de Coro
FALCÓN
Puerto
Cumarebo
Galera
Pt.
Tobago
Port of
Spain
Trinidad
TRINIDAD
& TOBAGO
San Fernando
Serpent's Mouth

BARRAN-
QUILLA
Baranoa
Santa
Marta
Cienaga
Soledad
Sabanalarga
Calamar
Fundación
Plato
Zambrano
Sierra Nevada de Santa Marta 5800
San
Rafael
MARACAIBO
La
Concepción
Santa Rita
Cabimas
Altagracia
Mene de Mauroa
Baragua
San Felipe
LARA
BARQUISIMETO
Carora
Puerto
Cabello
Maiquetía
La Guaira
CARACAS
Maracay
DISTRITO FEDERAL
I. La Tortuga
(Ven.)
MIRANDA
Higuerote
Codera
Río Chico
La Cruz
Puerto
NUEVA
ESPARTA
I. Margarita
La Asunción
Porlamar
Pen. de Paria
Carúpano
Río
Caribe
Güiria
Golfo de Paria
Río Claro
10
Cumaná
SUCRE
Caripito
Maturín
MONAGAS
Caicara
Anaco
DELTA
Tucupita
AMACUR
E

C E S A R
ZULIA
Machiques
Lago de
Maracaibo
La Ceiba
Betijoque
Valera
Trujillo
TRUJILLO
Carache
PORTUGUESA
Guanare
BARINAS
Barinas
Acarigua
San Carlos
COJEDES
El Baúl
Calabozo
G U A R I C O
San Juan de los Morros
S. Juan de
los Morros
Villa
de Cura
Valle de la
Pascua
Aragua de
Barcelona
Barcelona
ANZOÁTEGUI
El Tigre
Pariaguán
Soledad
Ciudad Guayana
Upata
Sierra Imataca
Guasipati
El Callao
Tumeremo

MÉRIDA
Mérida
Ciudad
Bolivia
San Fernando de
Apure
Apure
O r i n o c o
Ciudad
Bolívar
V E N E Z U E L A
Caicara
Emb. de Guri
Tumeremo

West from Greenwich
COPYRIGHT. GEORGE PHILIP & SON. LTD.

A
B
C
D
E

25
20
15
10

# 150 SOUTH AMERICA : Physical

1 : 24 000 000

100  0  100  200  300  400  500 miles
100  0    200   400   600   800 km

Projection: Lambert's Equivalent Azimuthal

COPYRIGHT. GEORGE PHILIP & SON, LTD.

West from Greenwich

1 : 24 000 000

100  0  100  200  300  400  500 miles
100  0  200  400  600  800 km

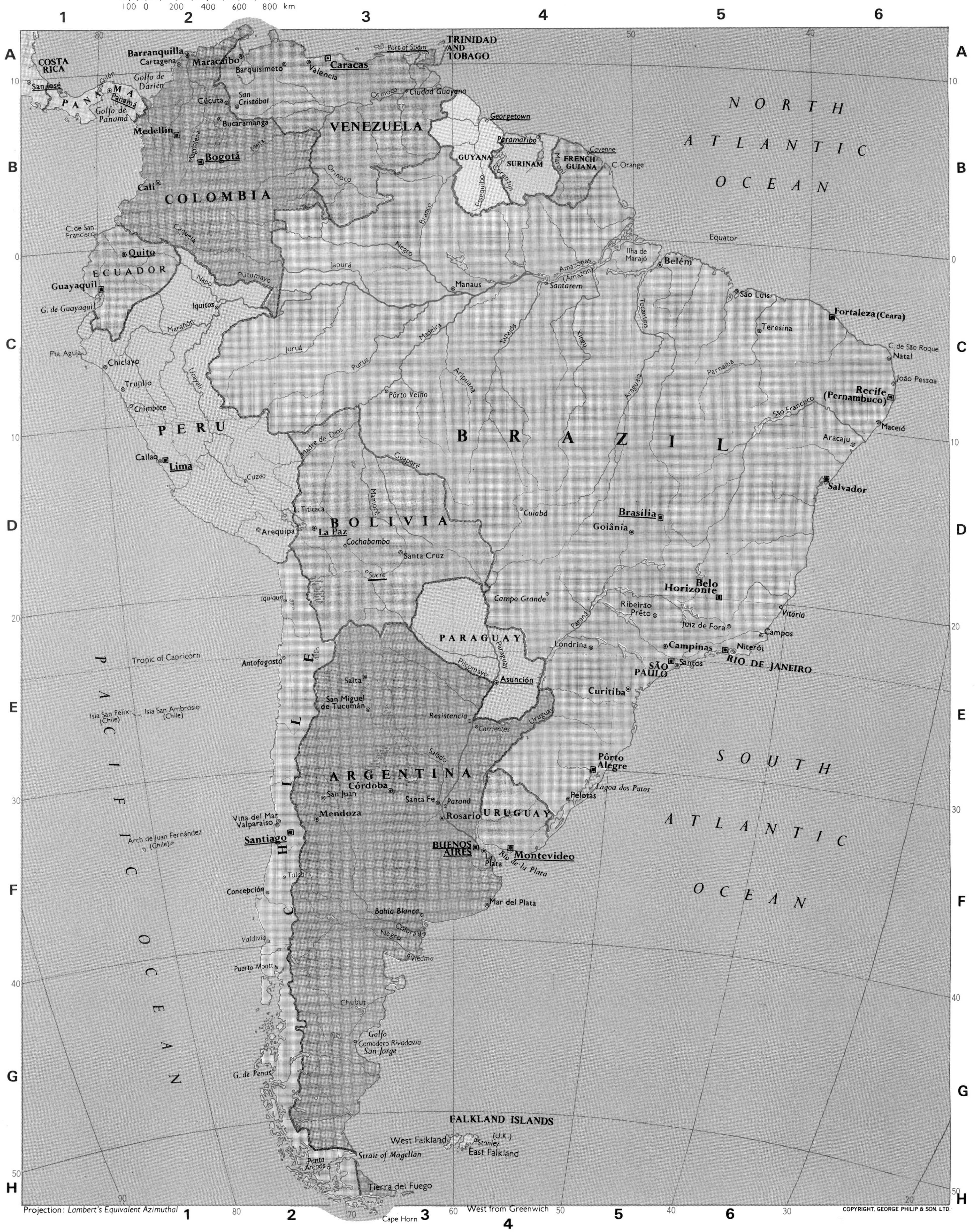

**1** **2** **3** **4** **5** **6**

A

COSTA RICA
San José
PANAMA
Golfo de Panamá
Golfo de Darién
Panamá
Colón
Barranquilla
Cartagena
Maracaibo
Cúcuta
Barquisimeto
Valencia
**Caracas**
Port of Spain
**TRINIDAD AND TOBAGO**

B

Medellín
**Bogotá**
Bucaramanga
San Cristóbal
Magdalena
Meta
**VENEZUELA**
Orinoco
Ciudad Guayana
Georgetown
Paramaribo
**GUYANA**
Essequibo
Corentijn
**SURINAM**
Maroni
**FRENCH GUIANA**
Cayenne
C. Orange

NORTH
ATLANTIC
OCEAN

Cali
**COLOMBIA**
Caquetá
Orinoco

C. de San Francisco
**Quito**
**ECUADOR**
Guayaquil
G. de Guayaquil
Iquitos
Napo
Putumayo
Japurá
Negro
Branco
Manaus
Santarem
Amazonas
Amazon
Equator
Ilha de Marajó
Belém
São Luís
Teresina
**Fortaleza (Ceara)**
C. de São Roque
Natal

C

Pta. Aguja
Chiclayo
Trujillo
Chimbote
Marañón
Ucayali
Juruá
Purus
Madeira
Madre de Dios
Pôrto Velho
Tapajós
Xingu
Araguaia
Tocantins
Parnaíba
São Francisco
João Pessoa
**Recife (Pernambuco)**

**PERU**
Cuzco
Callao
**Lima**
Guaporé
Aripuana
Mamoré
**BRAZIL**
Maceió
Aracaju

D

Arequipa
L. Titicaca
**La Paz**
Cochabamba
**BOLIVIA**
Santa Cruz
**Sucre**
Cuiabá
**Brasília**
Goiânia
Salvador

Iquique
Campo Grande
**Belo Horizonte**
Ribeirão Prêto
Juiz de Fora
Vitória
Campos

Tropic of Capricorn
Antofagasta
**PARAGUAY**
Paraná
Londrina
Campinas
Niterói
**RIO DE JANEIRO**
**SÃO PAULO**
Santos

E

Salta
San Miguel de Tucumán
Pilcomayo
Paraguay
**Asunción**
Curitiba
Isla San Félix (Chile)
Isla San Ambrosio (Chile)
Resistencia
Corrientes
Uruguay
Salado

SOUTH
ATLANTIC
OCEAN

PACIFIC OCEAN

**ARGENTINA**
**Córdoba**
San Juan
Mendoza
Santa Fe
Paraná
**Rosario**
**URUGUAY**
Pôrto Alegre
Pelotas
Lagoa dos Patos

F

CHILE
Viña del Mar
Valparaíso
**Santiago**
Arch de Juan Fernández (Chile)
Talca
**BUENOS AIRES**
La Plata
Río de la Plata
**Montevideo**
Mar del Plata

Concepción
Bahía Blanca
Colorado
Valdivia
Negro
Viedma
Puerto Montt

G

Chubut
Golfo San Jorge
Comodoro Rivadavia
G. de Penas

H

**FALKLAND ISLANDS**
West Falkland
Stanley (U.K.)
East Falkland
Strait of Magellan
Punta Arenas
Tierra del Fuego
Cape Horn
West from Greenwich

Projection: Lambert's Equivalent Azimuthal

1 : 6 400 000

50   0   50   100   150   200 miles
50   0   100   200   300 km

**5**　　　　　**6**　　　　　**7**

ATLANTIC

OCEAN

La Blanquilla (Ven.)
Los Hermanos (Ven.)
St. Georges GRENADA
Is. Los Testigos (Ven.)
Tobago
NUEVA ESPARTA
Margarita
La Asunción
I. La Tortuga (Ven.)
Porlamar
Pta. Arenas
I. Coche
Scarborough
Cumaná
Carúpano
Pen. de Paria
Pta. Peñas
TRINIDAD
Puerto La Cruz
Barcelona
SUCRE
Golfo de San Fernando
AND TOBAGO
Guanta
2596
Caicara
Trinidad
Galeota Point
Anaco
MONAGAS
Maturín
Cantaura
DELTA
A
El Tigre
ANZOATEGUI
Tucupita
10
Orinoco
AMACURO
Morawhanna
Ciudad Guayana
Boca Grande
I. Corocoro
Ciudad Bolívar
Guri Dam
Mabaruma
Upata
BARIMA WAINI
B
El Dorado
Matthew's Ridge
POMEROON-SUPERNAAM
Kokerite
Charity
Anna Regina
Suddie
ESSEQUIBO ISLANDS-WEST DEMERARA
Parika
Georgetown
CUYUNI
Cuyuni
Bartica
DEMERARA-MAHAICA
GUYANA
Mazaruni
MAHAICA-BERBICE
MAZARUNI
Issano
New Amsterdam
Angel Falls 2560
Linden (Mackenzie)
Nieuw Nickerie
Paramaribo
UPPER-ITUNI
Tumatumari
Nieuw Amsterdam
Cayenne
La Gran Sabana
Roraima 2772
Kaieteur Falls
POTARO-SIPARUNI
DEMERARA
BERBICE
SURINAM
5
Wilhelmina Geb.
FRENCH
Iles du Salut
Pakaraima
Orinduik
MAROWIJNE
GUIANA
Boa Vista
EAST BERBICE
CORENTYNE
RORAIMA
UPPER TAKUTU-UPPER ESSEQUIBO
Serra Tumucumaque
AMAPÁ
690
734
Macapá
BRAZIL
MANAUS
Represa de Balbina
Santarém
Amazonas
Ilha de Marajó
50
PARÁ
D
AMAZONAS

West from Greenwich
COPYRIGHT. GEORGE PHILIP & SON. LTD.

ATLANTIC OCEAN

FORTALEZA (Ceará)

NATAL
RIO GRANDE DO NORTE
João Pessoa (Paraíba)
RECIFE (Pernambuco)
Olinda
MACEIÓ

CEARÁ
PERNAMBUCO
PIAUÍ
MARANHÃO
PARÁ
TOCANTINS
AMAPÁ

SÃO LUÍS
BELÉM
Macapá
Sobral
Parnaíba
Teresina
Caxias
Imperatriz
Tocantinópolis
Juazeiro do Norte
Crato
Mossoró
Campina Grande
Caruaru
Ilha de Marajó
Baía de Marajó

São Francisco
Tocantins
Xingu

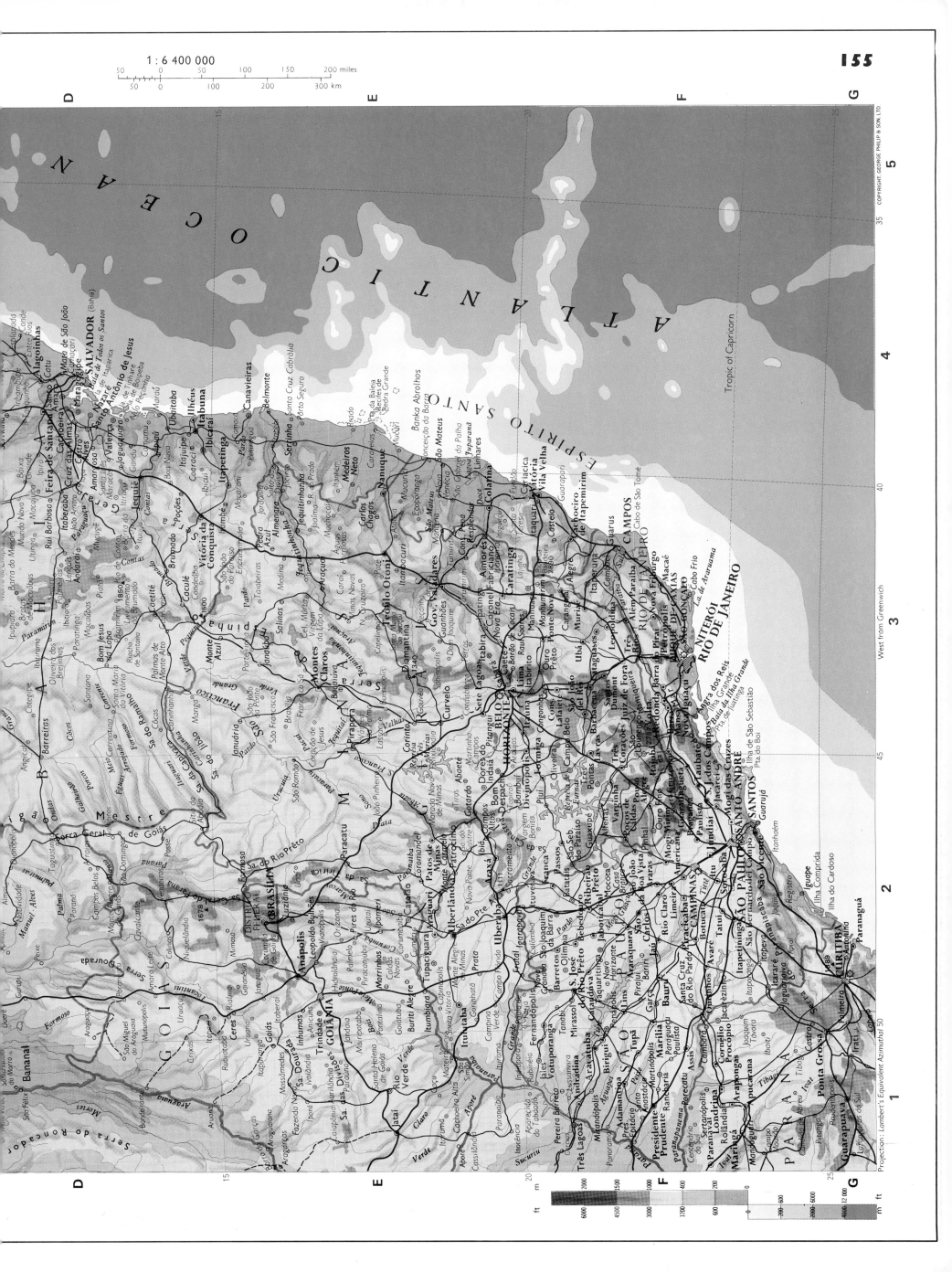

PACIFIC OCEAN

P E R U

PACIFIC OCEAN

Projection: Lambert's Equivalent Azimuthal

1 : 6 400 000

50   0   50   100   150   200 miles
50   0   100   200   300 km

**5**     **6**     **7**

A

5

L. de Coari
Coari
Itanhauá
Purus
Madeira
Prêto do Igapó-Açu
Novo Aripuaná
Abacaxis
Maués
Tapajós
Itaituba
Pôrto Alegre
Bacajá
Iriri
Itaboca
Aruma
Itapinima
Capoeira
Canumã
Tucunaré
Entre Rios
Borba
Munducurus
Sai-Cinza
Jaburu
Itatuba
Manicoré
Santa Maria dos Marmelas
Canumã
Canoas
Miriti
Crepori
Caruá
Nazaré
São Félis
Purus
Axioma
Três Casas
Prainha
Canudos
Juruena
Teles Pires
Tapajós
Xingu
Riosinho

Z O N A S
B R A Z I L
P A R Á
Z

B

Pinhuã
Canutama
Caranopatuba
Taquauã
Madeira
Aripuanã
Recreio
Serra do Cachimbo
Cachimbo
Alto Iriri
Xingu
Irirí-Novo

Purus
Lábrea
Majuria
Humaitá
Calama
Madeira
Jamari
Jiparaná
Aripuanã
Barracão do Barreta
S. Benedito

Itui
Abuná
Pôrto Velho
Jamari
Caritianas
Serra dos Apiacás
Peixoto de Azevedo
Cachimbo

404
Bom Comércio
Manoa
Abuná
Jaciparaná
Ariquemes
Nova Vida
Serra do Norte
Arinos
Pôrto Cajueiro
Manitsauá-Missu
Campo de Diauarum

Villa Bella Esperanza
Guajará-Mirim
Guayaramerin
Sa. dos Pacaás Novos
Jaru
Rondônia
Serra do Norte
Pouso Alegre
Serra dos Caiabis
Serra Formosa
Liberdade
Suiá Missu

10

Riberalta
Principe da Beira
Presidente Hermes
Pimenta Bueno
Barão de Melgaço
Camararé
Serra do Tombador
Teles Pires
Pôrto dos Meinacos
Serra do Roncador

R O N D Ô N I A

Puerto Siles
San Joaquim
Versalles
Mategua
Pedras Negras
663 Vilhena
Nhambiquara
Jurena
Verde
Romero
Coliseu
Chavantina

Lago Rogoaguado
Exaltación
Magdalena
Guaporé
Nhecolândia
Juruena
Utiariti
Aruanã

Puerto Villazón
Serrania de Huanchaca
Saturnina
Serra Azul

San Ramón
Baures
San Martin
Paraguá
Sangue

B E N I
Llanos de Mojos
San Javier
Trinidad
El Carmen
Loreto
Perseverancia
Paraguá
669
Nortelândia
Diamantino
Cuiabá
Alto Paraguai
915
Chapada dos Guimarães
Mortes
Araguaia

M A T O   G R O S S O
Planalto do Mato Grosso

San Francisco
San Lorenzo
Sécure
Negro
Mato Grosso
Guaporé
Tapirapuã
Rosário Oeste
Serra Azul
Barra do Bugres
Acorizal
Várzea Grande
Cuiabá
Coronel Ponce
Poxoreu
Tesouro
Rio das Garças
Aruanã
Araguaiana
Barro do Garças
Araguaya

15

B O L I V I A
Concepción
San Ignacio
San Javier
Santa Ana
Cáceres
Poconé
Barão de Melgaço
Jaciara
Guiratinga
Ponte Branca
Baliza
Iporã
Ivolândia

Cochabamba
Santa Rosa de la Roca
Portachuelo
Montero
El Cerro
San Miguel
San José
Cuiabá
São Lourenço
Rondonópolis
Itiquira
Alto Garças
Santa Rita do Araguaia
Caiapônia
Sa. das Divisões

S A N T A   C R U Z
Warnes
Buena Vista
San Carlos
Laguna Concepción
San José
Pôrto Jofre
Pantanal do São Lourenço
Itiquira
Correntes
Alto Garças
Serra do Caiapó
Mineiros
Rio Verde

Santa Cruz
Cotoca
El Palmar
Llanos de Chiquitos
1425 Serr de Santiago
Santo Corazón
La Cal
Lagoa Uberaba
Lagoa Mandioré
Taquari
Baús
Jataí

D

Villegrande
Bañados de Izozog
Roboré
Santa Ana
Puerto Suárez
Corumbá
Ladário
Pantanal do Rio Negro
Coxim
Rio Verde de Mato Grosso
Paraíso
Itarumã
Aporé
Cachoeira Alta
Apore

Sucre
Grande
Parapeti
Gutiérrez
Fortin General Pando
M A T O   G R O S S O   D O   S U L
Alto Sucuriú
Paranaíba

Lagunillas
Charagua
Fortin Ingavi
Coimbra
Albuquerque
Pôrto Esperança
Negro
Torquinho
Rochedo
Verde
Sucuriú
Inocência
Paranaíba

Camiri
Carandaiti
Bahia Negra
Miranda
Aquidauana
Terenos
Ribas do Rio Pardo
Aparecida do Taboado

C H A C O
Fortin Coronel Eugenio Garay
Fortin Madrejon
Puerto Olimpo
Sa. da Bodoquena
Aquidauana
Jango
Água Clara
Pereira Barreto

20

CHUQUISACA
Camargo
5614
Carandaiti
N U E V A   B O R E A L
Chaco
Puerto Guaraní
A L T O
Puerto Murtinho
Bonito
Nioaque
Nidrolândia
Três Lagoas
Andradina

Tarija
T A R I J A
Villa Montes
Fortin Garrapatal
P A R A G U A Y
A S U N C I Ó N
P A R A G U A Y
Jardim
Guia Lopes da Laguna
Xavantina
Mirandópolis
Aguapei

Yacuiba
BOQUERON
La Esmeralda
Anhandui
Panorama

Tartagal
**5**

S A L T A

West from Greenwich

**6**     **7**

E

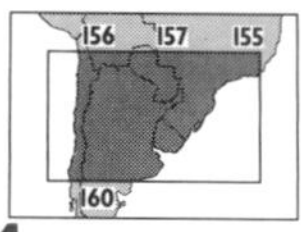

BOLIVIA

PARAGUAY

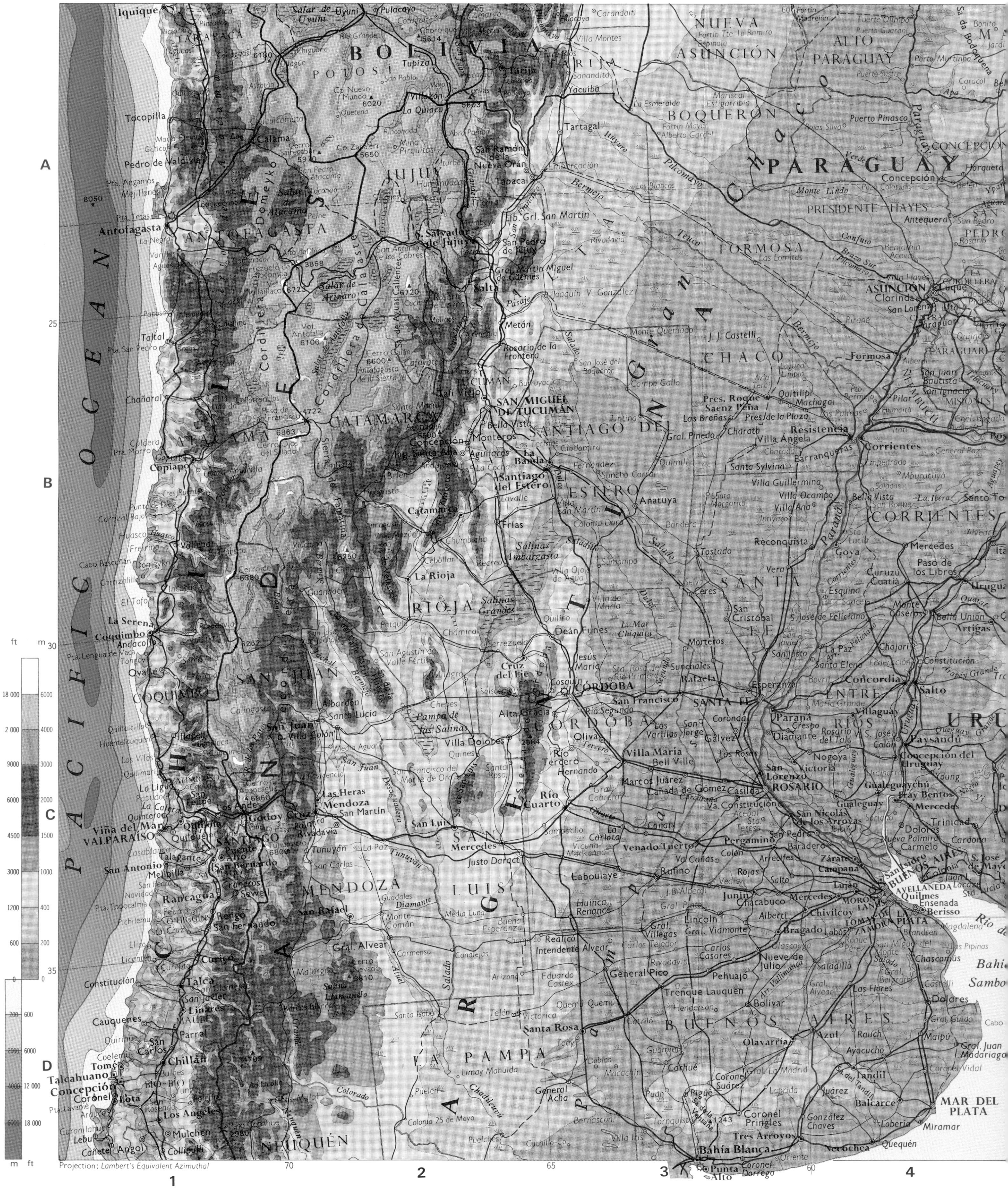

ASUNCIÓN

ALTO PARAGUAY

BOQUERÓN

PRESIDENTE HAYES

FORMOSA

CHACO

CORRIENTES

SANTA FE

CÓRDOBA

ENTRE RÍOS

URUGUAY

LA RIOJA

SAN JUAN

COQUIMBO

MENDOZA

SAN LUIS

BUENOS AIRES

LA PAMPA

NEUQUÉN

CATAMARCA

SANTIAGO DEL ESTERO

TUCUMÁN

JUJUY

POTOSÍ

TARAPACÁ

ANTOFAGASTA

PACIFIC OCEAN

CORDILLERA DE LOS ANDES

GRAN CHACO

Iquique, Tocopilla, Antofagasta, Taltal, Chañaral, Copiapó, Caldera, Huasco, Vallenar, La Serena, Coquimbo, Ovalle, Illapel, Los Vilos, La Ligua, Valparaíso, Viña del Mar, Santiago, San Antonio, Rancagua, San Fernando, Curicó, Talca, Linares, Constitución, Chillán, Concepción, Talcahuano, Coronel, Los Angeles

San Miguel de Tucumán, Salta, S. Salvador de Jujuy, La Quiaca, Catamarca, La Rioja, San Juan, Mendoza, San Luis, Córdoba, Rosario, Santa Fe, Paraná, Santiago del Estero, Resistencia, Corrientes, Formosa, Asunción, Concepción, Bahía Blanca, Mar del Plata, Buenos Aires, Avellaneda, Quilmes

Projection: Lambert's Equivalent Azimuthal

ft — m

18 000 — 6000
— 4000
— 3000
9000 — 2000
6000 — 1500
4500 — 1000
3000 — 400
1200 — 200
600 — 0
0 — 600
— 6000
12 000 — 
18 000 — 6000

m — ft

1 : 6 400 000

50 0 50 100 150 200 miles
50 0 100 200 300 km

**5** 6 7

BELO HORIZONTE
Lima
Itabirito
Congonhas
Cons. Lafaiete
Ouro Prêto
Ponte Nova
Vitória
Itaquari
Vila Velha
Guarapari

TO GROSSO
DO SUL
Três Lagoas
Andradina
Mirassol
S. José do Rio Prêto
Olímpia
Passos
Oliveira
Campo Belo
São João del Rei
Carangola
Castelo
Cachoeiro de Itapemirim

Nioaque
Maracaju
Xavantina
Araçatuba
Birigui
Catanduva
Bebedouro
Batatais
S. Seb. do Paraíso
Represa de Furnas
Três Pontas
Ubá
Muriaé
Alegre

Dourados
Pres. Epitácio
Panorama
Adamantina
Tupã
Lins
Jaboticabal
Ribeirão Prêto
Mococa
Guaxupé
Alfenas
Lavras
Barbacena
Cataguases
Leopoldina
Campos

Ponta Porã
Pedro Juan Caballero
Presidente Prudente
Martinópolis
Marília
Garça
Jaú
São Carlos
Araraquara
São João da Boa Vista
Poços de Caldas
Varginha
Três Corações
Juiz de Fora
Santos Dumont
Rio de Janeiro

Paranavaí
Nova Esperança
Ranharia
Paraguaçu Paulista
Assis
Bauru
Rio Claro
Limeira
Americana
Mogi-Mirim
Pouso Alegre
São Lourenço
Volta Redonda
Barra do Piraí
Campos

Umuarama
Cianorte
Maringá
Apucarana
Londrina
Arapongas
Rolândia
Cornélio Procópio
Jacarèzinho
Piracicaba
CAMPINAS
Botucatu
Jundiaí
Bragança
Guaratinguetá
Resende
Nova Iguaçu
DUQUE DE CAXIAS
SÃO GONÇALO
NITERÓI

Cruzeiro do Oeste
Guaíra
Goio Erê
PARANÁ
Mandaguari
Campo Mourão
Avaré
Tatuí
Sorocaba
ITAPETININGA
SÃO PAULO
São José dos Campos
Jacareí
Mogi das Cruzes
Serra dos Órgãos
RIO DE JANEIRO
Tropic of Capricorn

BRAZIL
Foz do Iguaçu
Guarapuava
Ponta Grossa
Castro
Itararé
Itapeva
São Bernardo do Campo
SANTO ANDRÉ
São Vicente
SANTOS
Guarujá
Ilha de São Sebastião

Iguaçu Falls
União da Vitória
Palmeira
Lapa
CURITIBA
Antonina
Paranaguá
Guaratuba
Itanhaém
Iguape
Ilha Comprida
Ilha do Cardoso

MISIONES
Pto. Mendes
Chopim
Rio Negro
Mafra
São Francisco do Sul
Joinvile

Encarnación
Obera
SANTA CATARINA
Caçador
Blumenau
Itajaí
Brusque
Ilha de Santa Catarina
Florianópolis

Santa Rosa
Erechim
Campos Novos
Rio do Sul
Lajes
Tubarão
Laguna
Cabo Santa Marta Grande

Caràzinho
Passo Fundo
Vacaria
Criciúma
Araranguá

Santo Angelo
Cruz Alta
Bento Gonçalves
Caxias do Sul

São Luís Gonzaga
RIO GRANDE
Santa Maria
Santa Cruz do Sul
Montenegro
Nôvo Hamburgo
Taquara

Santiago
São Borja
Cachoeira do Sul
Canoas
São Leopoldo
Osorio
Viamão
PORTO ALEGRE

Alegrete
DO SUL
São Gabriel
Dom Pedrito
Camaquã
Lagoa dos Patos

Rosário do Sul
Santana do Livramento
Rivera
Bagé
Pelotas
Mostardas

Tacuarembó
Melo
Rio Grande
Lagoa Mangueira

URUGUAY
Jaguarão
Santa Vitória do Palmar
Treinta y Tres

ATLANTIC

MONTEVIDEO
Maldonado
Rocha

OCEAN

5304

West from Greenwich

55 50 45 40

COPYRIGHT. GEORGE PHILIP & SON. LTD

A
B
C
D

1 : 6 400 000

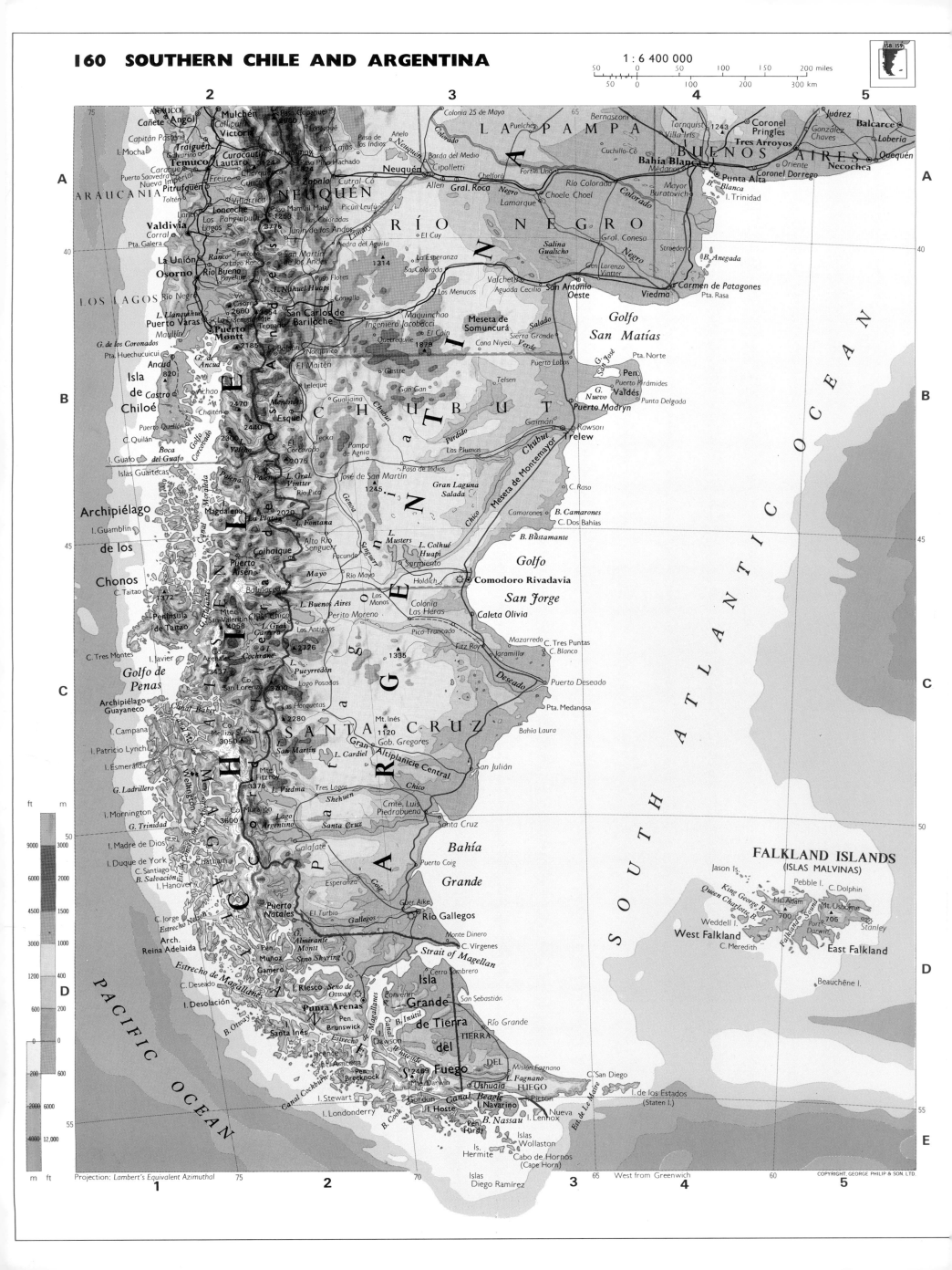

Projection: Lambert's Equivalent Azimuthal

COPYRIGHT. GEORGE PHILIP & SON. LTD.

# INDEX

The index contains the names of all the principal places and features shown on the World Maps. Each name is followed by an additional entry in italics giving the country or region within which it is located. The alphabetical order of names composed of two or more words is governed primarily by the first word and then by the second. This is an example of the rule:

| | | | |
|---|---|---|---|
| Mīr Kūh, *Iran* . . . . . . . . . | **85 E8** | 26 22 N | 58 55 E |
| Mīr Shahdād, *Iran* . . . . . . . | **85 E8** | 26 15 N | 58 29 E |
| Miraj, *India* . . . . . . . . . . | **82 F2** | 16 50 N | 74 45 E |
| Miram Shah, *Pakistan* . . . . . | **79 B3** | 33 0 N | 70 2 E |
| Miramar, *Mozam.* . . . . . . . . | **105 C6** | 23 50 S | 35 35 E |

Physical features composed of a proper name (Erie) and a description (Lake) are positioned alphabetically by the proper name. The description is positioned after the proper name and is usually abbreviated:

| | | | |
|---|---|---|---|
| Erie, L., *N. Amer.* . . . . . . . . | **136 D3** | 42 15 N | 81 0 W |

Where a description forms part of a settlement or administrative name however, it is always written in full and put in its true alphabetic position:

| | | | |
|---|---|---|---|
| Mount Morris, *U.S.A.* . . . . . . | **136 D7** | 42 44 N | 77 52 W |

Names beginning with M' and Mc are indexed as if they were spelt Mac. Names beginning St. are alphabetised under Saint, but Sankt, Sint, Sant', Santa and San are all spelt in full and are alphabetised accordingly. If the same place name occurs two or more times in the index and all are in the same country, each is followed by the name of the administrative subdivision in which it is located. The names are placed in the alphabetical order of the subdivisions. For example:

| | | | |
|---|---|---|---|
| Jackson, *Ky., U.S.A.* . . . . . . | **134 G4** | 37 33 N | 83 23 W |
| Jackson, *Mich., U.S.A.* . . . . . | **141 B12** | 42 15 N | 84 24 W |
| Jackson, *Minn., U.S.A.* . . . . . | **138 D7** | 43 37 N | 95 1 W |

The number in bold type which follows each name in the index refers to the number of the map page where that feature or place will be found. This is usually the largest scale at which the place or feature appears.

The letter and figure which are in bold type immediately after the page number give the grid square on the map page, within which the feature is situated. The letter represents the latitude and the figure the longitude.

In some cases the feature itself may fall within the specified square, while the name is outside. This is usually the case only with features which are larger than a grid square.

For a more precise location the geographical coordinates which follow the letter/figure references give the latitude and the longitude of each place. The first set of figures represent the latitude which is the distance north or south of the Equator measured as an angle at the centre of the earth. The Equator is latitude 0°, the North Pole is 90°N, and the South Pole 90°S.

The second set of figures represent the longitude, which is the distance East or West of the prime meridian, which runs through Greenwich, England. Longitude is also measured as an angle at the centre of the earth and is given East or West of the prime meridian, from 0° to 180° in either direction.

The unit of measurement for latitude and longitude is the degree, which is subdivided into 60 minutes. Each index entry states the position of a place in degrees and minutes, a space being left between the degrees and the minutes.

The latitude is followed by N(orth) or S(outh) and the longitude by E(ast) or W(est).

Rivers are indexed to their mouths or confluences, and carry the symbol ↠ after their names. A solid square ■ follows the name of a country while, an open square □ refers to a first order administrative area.

## ABBREVIATIONS USED IN THE INDEX

*A.C.T.* — Australian Capital Territory
*Afghan.* — Afghanistan
*Ala.* — Alabama
*Alta.* — Alberta
*Amer.* — America(n)
*Arch.* — Archipelago
*Ariz.* — Arizona
*Ark.* — Arkansas
*Atl. Oc.* — Atlantic Ocean
*B.* — Baie, Bahía, Bay, Bucht, Bugt
*B.C.* — British Columbia
*Bangla.* — Bangladesh
*Barr.* — Barrage
*Bos.-H.* — Bosnia-Herzegovina
*C.* — Cabo, Cap, Cape, Coast
*C.A.R.* — Central African Republic
*C. Prov.* — Cape Province
*Calif.* — California
*Cent.* — Central
*Chan.* — Channel
*Colo.* — Colorado
*Conn.* — Connecticut
*Cord.* — Cordillera
*Cr.* — Creek
*Czech.* — Czech Republic
*D.C.* — District of Columbia
*Del.* — Delaware
*Dep.* — Dependency
*Des.* — Desert
*Dist.* — District
*Dj.* — Djebel
*Domin.* — Dominica
*Dom. Rep.* — Dominican Republic
*E.* — East
*El Salv.* — El Salvador

*Eq. Guin.* — Equatorial Guinea
*Fla.* — Florida
*Falk. Is.* — Falkland Is.
*G.* — Golfe, Golfo, Gulf, Guba, Gebel
*Ga.* — Georgia
*Gt.* — Great, Greater
*Guinea-Biss.* — Guinea-Bissau
*H.K.* — Hong Kong
*H.P.* — Himachal Pradesh
*Hants.* — Hampshire
*Harb.* — Harbor, Harbour
*Hd.* — Head
*Hts.* — Heights
*I.(s).* — Île, Ilha, Insel, Isla, Island, Isle
*Ill.* — Illinois
*Ind.* — Indiana
*Ind. Oc.* — Indian Ocean
*Ivory C.* — Ivory Coast
*J.* — Jabal, Jebel, Jazira
*Junc.* — Junction
*K.* — Kap, Kapp
*Kans.* — Kansas
*Kep.* — Kepulauan
*Ky.* — Kentucky
*L.* — Lac, Lacul, Lago, Lagoa, Lake, Limni, Loch, Lough
*La.* — Louisiana
*Liech.* — Liechtenstein
*Lux.* — Luxembourg
*Mad. P.* — Madhya Pradesh
*Madag.* — Madagascar
*Man.* — Manitoba
*Mass.* — Massachusetts
*Md.* — Maryland

*Me.* — Maine
*Medit. S.* — Mediterranean Sea
*Mich.* — Michigan
*Minn.* — Minnesota
*Miss.* — Mississippi
*Mo.* — Missouri
*Mont.* — Montana
*Mozam.* — Mozambique
*Mt.(e).* — Mont, Monte, Monti, Montaña, Mountain
*N.* — Nord, Norte, North, Northern, Nouveau
*N.B.* — New Brunswick
*N.C.* — North Carolina
*N. Cal.* — New Caledonia
*N. Dak.* — North Dakota
*N.H.* — New Hampshire
*N.I.* — North Island
*N.J.* — New Jersey
*N. Mex.* — New Mexico
*N.S.* — Nova Scotia
*N.S.W.* — New South Wales
*N.W.T.* — North West Territory
*N.Y.* — New York
*N.Z.* — New Zealand
*Nebr.* — Nebraska
*Neths.* — Netherlands
*Nev.* — Nevada
*Nfld.* — Newfoundland
*Nic.* — Nicaragua
*O.* — Oued, Ouadi
*Occ.* — Occidentale
*O.F.S.* — Orange Free State
*Okla.* — Oklahoma
*Ont.* — Ontario
*Or.* — Orientale

*Oreg.* — Oregon
*Os.* — Ostrov
*Oz.* — Ozero
*P.* — Pass, Passo, Pasul, Pulau
*P.E.I.* — Prince Edward Island
*Pa.* — Pennsylvania
*Pac. Oc.* — Pacific Ocean
*Papua N.G.* — Papua New Guinea
*Pass.* — Passage
*Pen.* — Peninsula, Péninsule
*Phil.* — Philippines
*Pk.* — Park, Peak
*Plat.* — Plateau
*P-ov.* — Poluostrov
*Prov.* — Province, Provincial
*Pt.* — Point
*Pta.* — Ponta, Punta
*Pte.* — Pointe
*Qué.* — Québec
*Queens.* — Queensland
*R.* — Rio, River
*R.I.* — Rhode Island
*Ra.(s).* — Range(s)
*Raj.* — Rajasthan
*Reg.* — Region
*Rep.* — Republic
*Res.* — Reserve, Reservoir
*S.* — San, South, Sea
*Si. Arabia* — Saudi Arabia
*S.C.* — South Carolina
*S. Dak.* — South Dakota
*S.I.* — South Island
*S. Leone* — Sierra Leone
*Sa.* — Serra, Sierra
*Sask.* — Saskatchewan
*Scot.* — Scotland

*Sd.* — Sound
*Sev.* — Severnaya
*Sib.* — Siberia
*Sprs.* — Springs
*St.* — Saint, Sankt, Sint
*Sta.* — Santa, Station
*Ste.* — Sainte
*Sto.* — Santo
*Str.* — Strait, Stretto
*Switz.* — Switzerland
*Tas.* — Tasmania
*Tenn.* — Tennessee
*Tex.* — Texas
*Tg.* — Tanjung
*Trin. & Tob.* — Trinidad & Tobago
*U.A.E.* — United Arab Emirates
*U.K.* — United Kingdom
*U.S.A.* — United States of America
*Ut. P.* — Uttar Pradesh
*Va.* — Virginia
*Vdkhr.* — Vodokhranilishche
*Vf.* — Vîrful
*Vic.* — Victoria
*Vol.* — Volcano
*Vt.* — Vermont
*W.* — Wadi, West
*W. Va.* — West Virginia
*Wash.* — Washington
*Wis.* — Wisconsin
*Wlkp.* — Wielkopolski
*Wyo.* — Wyoming
*Yorks.* — Yorkshire
*Yug.* — Yugoslavia

162 A Coruña

# A


A Coruña = La Coruña, *Spain* **36 B2** 43 20N 8 25W
Aachen, *Germany* **26 E2** 50 47N 6 4 E
Aadorf, *Switz.* **29 B7** 47 30N 8 55 E
Aalborg = Ålborg, *Denmark* **15 G3** 57 2N 9 54 E
Aalen, *Germany* **27 G6** 48 49N 10 6 E
A'âli en Nîl □, *Sudan* **95 F3** 9 30N 31 30 E
Aalsmeer, *Neths.* **20 D5** 52 17N 4 43 E
Aalst, *Belgium* **21 G4** 50 56N 4 2 E
Aalst, *Neths.* **21 F6** 51 23N 5 29 E
Aalten, *Neths.* **20 E9** 51 56N 6 35 E
Aalter, *Belgium* **21 F2** 51 5N 3 28 E
Aarau, *Switz.* **28 B6** 47 23N 8 4 E
Aarberg, *Switz.* **28 B4** 47 2N 7 16 E
Aardenburg, *Belgium* **21 F2** 51 16N 3 28 E
Aare →, *Switz.* **28 A6** 47 33N 8 14 E
Aargau □, *Switz.* **28 B6** 47 26N 8 10 E
Aarhus = Århus, *Denmark* **15 H4** 56 8N 10 11 E
Aarle, *Neths.* **21 E7** 51 30N 5 38 E
Aarschot, *Belgium* **21 G5** 50 59N 4 49 E
Aarsele, *Belgium* **21 G2** 51 0N 3 26 E
Aartrijke, *Belgium* **21 F2** 51 7N 3 6 E
Aarwangen, *Switz.* **28 B5** 47 15N 7 46 E
Aba, *China* **68 A3** 32 59N 101 42 E
Aba, *Nigeria* **101 D6** 5 10N 7 19 E
Aba, *Zaïre* **106 B3** 3 58N 30 17 E
Âbâ, Jazîrat, *Sudan* **95 E3** 13 30N 32 31 E
Abacaxis →, *Brazil* **153 D6** 3 54 S 58 47W
Ābādān, *Iran* **85 D6** 30 22N 48 20 E
Abade, *Ethiopia* **95 F4** 9 22N 38 3 E
Ābādeh, *Iran* **85 D7** 31 8N 52 40 E
Abadin, *Spain* **36 B3** 43 21N 7 29W
Abadla, *Algeria* **99 B4** 31 2N 2 45W
Abaeté, *Brazil* **155 E2** 19 9 S 45 27W
Abaeté →, *Brazil* **155 E2** 18 2 S 45 12W
Abaetetuba, *Brazil* **154 B2** 1 40 S 48 50W
Abagnar Qi, *China* **66 C9** 43 52N 116 2 E
Abai, *Paraguay* **159 B4** 25 58 S 55 54W
Abak, *Nigeria* **101 E6** 4 58N 7 50 E
Abakaliki, *Nigeria* **101 D6** 6 22N 8 2 E
Abakan, *Russia* **57 D10** 53 40N 91 10 E
Abalemma, *Niger* **101 B6** 16 12N 7 50 E
Abana, *Turkey* **88 C6** 41 59N 34 1 E
Abancay, *Peru* **156 C3** 13 35 S 72 55W
Abanilla, *Spain* **35 G3** 38 12N 1 3W
Abano Terme, *Italy* **39 C8** 45 22N 11 46 E
Abapó, *Bolivia* **157 D5** 18 48 S 63 25W
Abarán, *Spain* **35 G3** 38 12N 1 23W
Abariringa, *Kiribati* **122 H10** 2 50 S 171 40W
Abarqū, *Iran* **85 D7** 31 10N 53 20 E
Abashiri, *Japan* **60 B12** 44 0N 144 15 E
Abashiri-Wan, *Japan* **60 B12** 44 0N 144 30 E
Abau, *Papua N. G.* **120 F5** 10 11 S 148 46 E
Abaújszántó, *Hungary* **31 C14** 48 16N 21 12 E
Abay, *Kazakhstan* **56 E8** 49 38N 72 53 E
Abaya, L., *Ethiopia* **95 F4** 6 30N 37 50 E
Abaza, *Russia* **56 D10** 52 39N 90 6 E
Abbadia San Salvatore, *Italy* **39 F8** 42 53N 11 40 E
'Abbāsābād, *Iran* **85 C8** 33 34N 58 23 E
Abbay = Nîl el Azraq →, *Sudan* **95 D3** 15 38N 32 31 E
Abbaye, Pt., *U.S.A.* **134 B1** 46 58N 88 8W
Abbé, L., *Ethiopia* **95 E5** 11 8N 41 47 E
Abbeville, *France* **23 B8** 50 6N 1 49 E
Abbeville, *La., U.S.A.* **139 K8** 29 58N 92 8W
Abbeville, *S.C., U.S.A.* **135 H4** 34 11N 82 23W
Abbiategrasso, *Italy* **38 C5** 45 23N 8 55 E
Abbieglassie, *Australia* **115 D4** 27 15 S 147 28 E
Abbot Ice Shelf, *Antarctica* **7 D16** 73 0 S 92 0W
Abbotsford, *Canada* **130 D4** 49 5N 122 20W
Abbotsford, *U.S.A.* **138 C9** 44 57N 90 19W
Abbottabad, *Pakistan* **80 B5** 34 10N 73 15 E
Abcoude, *Neths.* **20 D5** 52 17N 4 59 E
Abd al Kūrī, *Ind. Oc.* **87 D6** 12 5N 52 20 E
Ābdar, *Iran* **85 D7** 30 16N 55 19 E
'Abdolābād, *Iran* **85 C8** 34 12N 56 30 E
Abdulino, *Russia* **54 E3** 53 42N 53 40 E
Abéché, *Chad* **97 F4** 13 50N 20 35 E
Abejar, *Spain* **34 D2** 41 48N 2 47W
Abekr, *Sudan* **95 E2** 12 45N 28 50 E
Abêlessa, *Algeria* **99 D5** 22 58N 4 47 E
Abengourou, *Ivory C.* **100 D4** 6 42N 3 27W
Åbenrå, *Denmark* **15 J3** 55 3N 9 25 E
Abensberg, *Germany* **27 G7** 48 49N 11 51 E
Abeokuta, *Nigeria* **101 D5** 7 3N 3 19 E
Aber, *Uganda* **106 B3** 2 12N 32 25 E
Aberaeron, *U.K.* **17 E3** 52 15N 4 16W
Aberayron = Aberaeron, *U.K.* **17 E3** 52 15N 4 16W
Abercorn = Mbala, *Zambia* **107 D3** 8 46 S 31 24 E
Abercorn, *Australia* **115 D5** 25 12 S 151 5 E
Aberdare, *U.K.* **17 F4** 51 43N 3 27W
Aberdare Ra., *Kenya* **106 C4** 0 15 S 36 50 E
Aberdeen, *Australia* **117 B9** 32 9 S 150 56 E
Aberdeen, *Canada* **131 C7** 52 20N 106 8W
Aberdeen, *S. Africa* **104 E3** 32 28 S 24 2 E
Aberdeen, *U.K.* **18 D6** 57 9N 2 6W
Aberdeen, *Ala., U.S.A.* **135 J1** 33 49N 88 33W
Aberdeen, *Idaho, U.S.A.* **142 E7** 42 57N 112 50W
Aberdeen, *Ohio, U.S.A.* **141 F13** 38 39N 83 46W
Aberdeen, *S. Dak., U.S.A.* **138 C5** 45 28N 98 29W
Aberdeen, *Wash., U.S.A.* **144 D3** 46 59N 123 50W
Aberdovey = Aberdyfi, *U.K.* **17 E3** 52 33N 4 3W
Aberdyfi, *U.K.* **17 E3** 52 33N 4 3W
Aberfeldy, *Australia* **117 D7** 37 42 S 146 22 E
Aberfeldy, *U.K.* **18 E5** 56 37N 3 50W
Abergaria-a-Velha, *Portugal* **36 E2** 40 41N 8 32W
Abergavenny, *U.K.* **17 F4** 51 49N 3 1W
Abernathy, *U.S.A.* **139 J4** 33 50N 101 51W
Abert, L., *U.S.A.* **142 E3** 42 38N 120 14W
Aberystwyth, *U.K.* **17 E3** 52 25N 4 6W
Abha, *Si. Arabia* **94 D5** 18 0N 42 34 E
Abhar, *Iran* **85 B6** 36 9N 49 13 E
Abhayapuri, *India* **78 B3** 26 24N 90 38 E
Abia □, *Nigeria* **101 D6** 5 30N 7 35 E
Abidiya, *Sudan* **94 D3** 18 18N 34 3 E
Abidjan, *Ivory C.* **100 D4** 5 26N 3 58W
Abilene, *Kans., U.S.A.* **138 F6** 38 55N 97 13W
Abilene, *Tex., U.S.A.* **139 J5** 32 28N 99 43W
Abingdon, *U.K.* **17 F6** 51 40N 1 17W
Abingdon, *Ill., U.S.A.* **140 D6** 40 48N 90 24W
Abingdon, *Va., U.S.A.* **135 G5** 36 43N 81 59W
Abington Reef, *Australia* **114 B4** 18 0 S 149 35 E
Abitau →, *Canada* **131 B7** 59 53N 109 3W
Abitau L., *Canada* **131 A7** 60 27N 107 15W
Abitibi L., *Canada* **128 C4** 48 40N 79 40W
Abiy Adi, *Ethiopia* **95 E4** 13 39N 39 3 E
Abkhaz Republic □, *Georgia* **53 E9** 43 0N 41 0 E
Abkit, *Russia* **57 C16** 64 10N 157 10 E
Abminga, *Australia* **115 D1** 26 8 S 134 51 E
Abnûb, *Egypt* **94 B3** 27 18N 31 4 E
Abo, Massif d', *Chad* **97 D3** 21 41N 16 8 E
Abocho, *Nigeria* **101 D6** 7 35N 6 56 E
Abohar, *India* **80 D6** 30 10N 74 10 E
Aboisso, *Ivory C.* **100 D4** 5 30N 3 5W
Abolo, *Congo* **102 B2** 0 8N 14 16 E
Abomey, *Benin* **101 D5** 7 10N 2 5 E
Abondance, *France* **25 B10** 46 18N 6 43 E
Abong-Mbang, *Cameroon* **102 B2** 4 0N 13 8 E
Abongabong, *Indonesia* **74 B1** 4 15N 96 48 E
Abonnema, *Nigeria* **101 E6** 4 41N 6 49 E
Abony, *Hungary* **31 D13** 47 12N 20 3 E
Aboso, *Ghana* **100 D4** 5 23N 1 57W
Abou-Deïa, *Chad* **97 F3** 11 20N 19 20 E
Abou Goulem, *Chad* **97 F4** 13 37N 21 38 E
Aboyne, *U.K.* **18 D6** 57 4N 2 48W
Abra □, *Phil.* **70 C3** 17 35N 120 45 E
Abra de Ilog, *Phil.* **70 E3** 13 27N 120 44 E
Abra Pampa, *Argentina* **158 A2** 22 43 S 65 42W
Abrantes, *Portugal* **37 F2** 39 24N 8 7W
Abraveses, *Portugal* **36 E3** 40 41N 7 55W
Abreojos, Pta., *Mexico* **146 B2** 26 50N 113 40W
Abreschviller, *France* **23 D14** 48 39N 7 6 E
Abri, *Esh Shamâliya, Sudan* **94 C3** 20 50N 30 27 E
Abri, *Janub Kordofân, Sudan* **95 E3** 11 40N 30 21 E
Abrolhos, Banka, *Brazil* **155 E4** 18 0 S 38 0W
Abrud, *Romania* **46 C4** 46 19N 23 5 E
Abruzzi □, *Italy* **39 F10** 42 15N 14 0 E
Absaroka Range, *U.S.A.* **142 D9** 44 45N 109 50W
Abū al Khaṣīb, *Iraq* **85 D6** 30 25N 48 0 E
Abū 'Alī, *Si. Arabia* **85 E6** 27 20N 49 27 E
Abū 'Alī →, *Lebanon* **91 A4** 34 25N 35 50 E
Abu 'Arīsh, *Si. Arabia* **86 C3** 16 53N 42 48 E
Abû Ballas, *Egypt* **94 C2** 24 26N 27 36 E
Abu Deleiq, *Sudan* **95 D3** 15 57N 33 48 E
Abu Dhabi = Abū Ẓāby, *U.A.E.* **85 E7** 24 28N 54 22 E
Abû Dis, *Sudan* **94 D3** 19 12N 33 38 E
Abû Dom, *Sudan* **95 D3** 16 18N 32 25 E
Abū Du'ān, *Syria* **84 B3** 36 25N 38 15 E
Abu el Gairi, W. →, *Egypt* **91 F2** 29 35N 33 30 E
Abû Gabra, *Sudan* **95 E2** 11 2N 26 50 E
Abu Ga'da, W. →, *Egypt* **91 F1** 29 15N 32 53 E
Abû Gubeiha, *Sudan* **95 E3** 11 30N 31 15 E
Abu Habl, Khawr →, *Sudan* **95 E3** 12 37N 31 0 E
Abū Ḥadrīyah, *Si. Arabia* **85 E6** 27 20N 48 58 E
Abu Hamed, *Sudan* **94 D3** 19 32N 33 13 E
Abu Haraz, *An Nîl el Azraq, Sudan* **95 E3** 14 35N 33 30 E
Abû Haraz, *Esh Shamâliya, Sudan* **94 D3** 19 8N 32 18 E
Abû Higar, *Sudan* **95 E3** 12 50N 33 59 E
Abū Kamāl, *Syria* **84 C4** 34 30N 41 0 E
Abū Madd, Ra's, *Si. Arabia* **84 E3** 24 50N 37 7 E
Abu Matariq, *Sudan* **95 E2** 10 59N 26 9 E
Abu Qir, *Egypt* **94 H7** 31 18N 30 0 E
Abu Qireiya, *Egypt* **94 C4** 24 5N 35 28 E
Abu Qurqâs, *Egypt* **94 J7** 28 1N 30 44 E
Abū Raṣāṣ, Ra's, *Oman* **87 B7** 20 10N 58 38 E
Abū Rubayq, *Si. Arabia* **86 B2** 23 44N 39 42 E
Abû Ṣafāt, W. →, *Jordan* **91 E5** 30 24N 36 7 E
Abû Simbel, *Egypt* **94 C3** 22 18N 31 40 E
Abū Şukhayr, *Iraq* **84 D5** 31 54N 44 30 E
Abu Tig, *Egypt* **94 B3** 27 4N 31 15 E
Abu Tiga, *Sudan* **95 E3** 12 47N 34 12 E
Abû Zabad, *Sudan* **95 E2** 12 25N 29 10 E
Abū Ẓāby, *U.A.E.* **85 E7** 24 28N 54 22 E
Abū Zeydābād, *Iran* **85 C6** 33 54N 51 45 E
Abufari, *Brazil* **157 B5** 5 25 S 62 59W
Abuja, *Nigeria* **101 D6** 9 16N 7 2 E
Abukuma-Gawa →, *Japan* **60 E10** 38 6N 140 52 E
Abukuma-Sammyaku, *Japan* **60 F10** 37 30N 140 45 E
Abulug, *Phil.* **70 B3** 18 27N 121 27 E
Abumombazi, *Zaïre* **102 B4** 3 42N 22 10 E
Abunã, *Brazil* **157 B4** 9 40 S 65 20W
Abunã →, *Brazil* **157 B4** 9 41 S 65 20W
Abung, *Phil.* **70 E3** 13 46N 121 26 E
Aburatsu, *Japan* **62 F3** 31 34N 131 24 E
Aburo, *Zaïre* **106 B3** 2 4N 30 53 E
Abut Hd., *N.Z.* **119 D5** 43 7 S 170 15 E
Abwong, *Sudan* **95 F3** 9 2N 32 14 E
Åby, *Sweden* **15 F10** 58 40N 16 10 E
Aby, Lagune, *Ivory C.* **100 D4** 5 15N 3 14W
Acacías, *Colombia* **152 C3** 3 59N 73 46W
Acajutla, *El Salv.* **148 D2** 13 36N 89 50W
Açallândia, *Brazil* **154 C2** 5 0 S 47 30W
Acámbaro, *Mexico* **146 C4** 20 0N 100 40W
Acanthus, *Greece* **44 D5** 40 27N 23 47 E
Acaponeta, *Mexico* **146 C3** 22 30N 105 20W
Acapulco, *Mexico* **147 D5** 16 51N 99 56W
Acarai, Serra, *Brazil* **153 C6** 1 50N 57 50W
Acaraú, *Brazil* **154 B3** 2 53 S 40 7W
Acari, *Brazil* **154 C4** 6 31 S 36 38W
Acarí, *Peru* **156 D3** 15 25 S 74 36W
Acarigua, *Venezuela* **152 B4** 9 33N 69 12W
Acatlán, *Mexico* **147 D5** 18 10N 98 3W
Acayucan, *Mexico* **147 D6** 17 59N 94 58W
Accéglio, *Italy* **38 D3** 44 28N 6 59 E
Accomac, *U.S.A.* **134 G8** 37 43N 75 40W
Accous, *France* **24 E3** 43 0N 0 36W
Accra, *Ghana* **101 D4** 5 35N 0 6W
Accrington, *U.K.* **16 D5** 53 46N 2 22W
Acebal, *Argentina* **158 C3** 33 20 S 60 50W
Acerenza, *Italy* **41 B8** 40 50N 15 58 E
Acerra, *Italy* **41 B7** 40 57N 14 22 E
Aceuchal, *Spain* **37 G4** 38 39N 6 30W
Achacachi, *Bolivia* **156 D4** 16 3 S 68 43W
Achaguas, *Venezuela* **152 B4** 7 46N 68 14W
Achalpur, *India* **82 D3** 21 22N 77 32 E
Achao, *Chile* **160 B2** 42 28 S 73 30W
Achel, *Belgium* **21 F6** 51 15N 5 29 E
Acheng, *China* **67 B14** 45 30N 126 58 E
Achenkirch, *Austria* **30 D4** 47 32N 11 45 E
Achensee, *Austria* **30 D4** 47 26N 11 45 E
Acher, *India* **80 H5** 23 10N 72 32 E
Achern, *Germany* **27 G4** 48 37N 8 5 E
Acheron →, *N.Z.* **119 C8** 42 16 S 173 4 E
Achill, *Ireland* **19 C2** 53 56N 9 55W
Achill Hd., *Ireland* **19 C1** 53 59N 10 15W
Achill I., *Ireland* **19 C1** 53 58N 10 5W
Achill Sd., *Ireland* **19 C2** 53 53N 9 55W
Achim, *Germany* **26 B5** 53 1N 9 2 E
Achinsk, *Russia* **57 D10** 56 20N 90 20 E
Achisay, *Kazakhstan* **55 B4** 43 35N 68 53 E
Achit, *Russia* **54 C5** 56 48N 57 54 E
Achol, *Sudan* **95 F3** 6 35N 31 32 E
Acıgöl, *Turkey* **88 E3** 37 50N 29 50 E
Acireale, *Italy* **41 E8** 37 37N 15 9 E
Ackerman, *U.S.A.* **139 J10** 33 19N 89 11W
Ackley, *U.S.A.* **140 B3** 42 33N 93 3W
Acklins I., *Bahamas* **149 B5** 22 30N 74 0W
Acme, *Canada* **130 C6** 51 33N 113 30W
Acobamba, *Peru* **156 C3** 12 52 S 74 35W
Acomayo, *Peru* **156 C3** 13 55 S 71 38W
Aconcagua □, *Chile* **158 C1** 32 15 S 70 30W
Aconcagua, Cerro, *Argentina* **158 C2** 32 39 S 70 0W
Aconquija, Mt., *Argentina* **158 B2** 27 0 S 66 0W
Acopiara, *Brazil* **154 C4** 6 6 S 39 27W
Açores, Is. dos = Azores, *Atl. Oc.* **8 E6** 38 44N 29 0W
Acorizal, *Brazil* **157 D6** 15 12 S 56 22W
Acquapendente, *Italy* **39 F8** 42 45N 11 50 E
Acquasanta, *Italy* **39 F10** 42 46N 13 24 E
Acquaviva delle Fonti, *Italy* **41 B9** 40 53N 16 50 E
Acqui, *Italy* **38 D5** 44 40N 8 28 E
Acraman, L., *Australia* **115 E2** 32 2 S 135 23 E
Acre = 'Akko, *Israel* **91 C4** 32 55N 35 4 E
Acre □, *Brazil* **156 B3** 9 1 S 71 0W
Acre →, *Brazil* **156 B4** 8 45 S 67 22W
Acri, *Italy* **41 C9** 39 29N 16 23 E
Acs, *Hungary* **31 D11** 47 42N 18 2 E
Actium, *Greece* **45 F2** 38 57N 20 45 E
Acton, *Canada* **136 C4** 43 38N 80 3W
Açu, *Brazil* **154 C4** 5 34 S 36 54W
Ad Dahnā, *Si. Arabia* **87 A5** 24 30N 48 10 E
Aḑ Ḑāli', *Yemen* **86 D4** 13 42N 44 44 E
Ad Dammām, *Si. Arabia* **85 E6** 26 20N 50 5 E
Ad Darb, *Si. Arabia* **86 C3** 18 2N 43 7 E
Ad Dawhah, *Qatar* **85 E6** 25 15N 51 35 E
Ad Dawr, *Iraq* **84 C4** 34 27N 43 47 E
Aḑ Ḑiffah, *Libya* **96 B4** 30 30N 24 30 E
Ad Dilam, *Si. Arabia* **86 B4** 23 55N 47 10 E
Ad Dir'iyah, *Si. Arabia* **84 E5** 24 44N 46 35 E
Ad Dīwānīyah, *Iraq* **84 D5** 32 0N 45 0 E
Ad Dujayl, *Iraq* **84 C5** 33 51N 44 14 E
Ad Durūz, J., *Jordan* **91 C5** 32 35N 36 40 E
Ada, *Ghana* **101 D5** 5 44N 0 40 E
Ada, *Serbia* **42 B5** 45 49N 20 9 E
Ada, *Minn., U.S.A.* **138 B6** 47 18N 96 31W
Ada, *Ohio, U.S.A.* **141 D13** 40 46N 83 49W
Ada, *Okla., U.S.A.* **139 H6** 34 46N 96 41W
Adad, *Somali Rep.* **108 C3** 9 27N 46 49 E
Adaja →, *Spain* **36 D6** 41 32N 4 52W
Ådalslinden, *Sweden* **14 A10** 63 27N 16 55 E
Adam, *Oman* **87 B7** 22 15N 57 28 E
Adam, Mt., *Falk. Is.* **160 D4** 51 34 S 60 4W
Adamantina, *Brazil* **155 F1** 21 42 S 51 4W
Adamaoua, Massif de l', *Cameroon* **101 D7** 7 20N 12 20 E
Adamawa □, *Nigeria* **101 D7** 9 20N 12 30 E
Adamawa Highlands = Adamaoua, Massif de l', *Cameroon* **101 D7** 7 20N 12 20 E
Adamello, Mt., *Italy* **38 B7** 46 10N 10 34 E
Adami Tulu, *Ethiopia* **95 F4** 7 53N 38 41 E
Adaminaby, *Australia* **117 D8** 36 0 S 148 45 E
Adamovka, *Russia* **54 F6** 51 32N 59 56 E
Adams, *Phil.* **70 B3** 18 28N 120 54 E
Adams, *Mass., U.S.A.* **137 D11** 42 38N 73 7W
Adams, *N.Y., U.S.A.* **137 C8** 43 49N 76 1W
Adams, *Wis., U.S.A.* **138 D10** 43 57N 89 49W
Adam's Bridge, *Sri Lanka* **83 K4** 9 15N 79 40 E
Adams L., *Canada* **130 C5** 51 10N 119 40W
Adams Mt., *U.S.A.* **144 D5** 46 12N 121 30W
Adam's Peak, *Sri Lanka* **83 L5** 6 48N 80 30 E
Adamuz, *Spain* **37 G6** 38 2N 4 32W
Adana, *Turkey* **88 E6** 37 0N 35 16 E
Adana □, *Turkey* **88 E6** 37 0N 35 30 E
Adanero, *Spain* **36 E6** 40 56N 4 36W
Adapazarı, *Turkey* **88 C4** 40 48N 30 25 E
Adarama, *Sudan* **95 D3** 17 10N 34 52 E
Adare, C., *Antarctica* **7 D11** 71 0 S 171 0 E
Adaut, *Indonesia* **73 C4** 8 8 S 131 7 E
Adavale, *Australia* **115 D3** 25 52 S 144 32 E
Adda →, *Italy* **38 C6** 45 8N 9 53 E
Addis Ababa = Addis Abeba, *Ethiopia* **95 F4** 9 2N 38 42 E
Addis Abeba, *Ethiopia* **95 F4** 9 2N 38 42 E
Addis Alem, *Ethiopia* **95 F4** 9 0N 38 17 E
Addison, *Ill., U.S.A.* **141 C8** 41 55N 88 0W
Addison, *N.Y., U.S.A.* **136 D7** 42 1N 77 14W
Addo, *S. Africa* **104 E4** 33 32 S 25 45 E
Addyston, *U.S.A.* **141 E12** 39 8N 84 43W
Adebour, *Niger* **97 F2** 13 17N 11 50 E
Ādeh, *Iran* **84 B5** 37 42N 45 11 E
Adel, *Ga., U.S.A.* **135 K4** 31 8N 83 25W
Adel, *Iowa, U.S.A.* **140 C2** 41 37N 94 1W
Adelaide, *Australia* **116 C3** 34 52 S 138 30 E
Adelaide, *Bahamas* **148 A4** 25 4N 77 31W
Adelaide, *S. Africa* **104 E4** 32 42 S 26 20 E
Adelaide I., *Antarctica* **7 C17** 67 15 S 68 30W
Adelaide Pen., *Canada* **126 B10** 68 15N 97 30W
Adelaide River, *Australia* **112 B5** 13 15 S 131 7 E
Adelanto, *U.S.A.* **145 L9** 34 35N 117 22W
Adelboden, *Switz.* **28 D5** 46 29N 7 33 E
Adele I., *Australia* **112 C3** 15 32 S 123 9 E
Adélie, Terre, *Antarctica* **7 C10** 68 0 S 140 0 E
Adélie Land = Adélie, Terre, *Antarctica* **7 C10** 68 0 S 140 0 E
Ademuz, *Spain* **34 E3** 40 5N 1 13W
Aden = Al 'Adan, *Yemen* **86 D4** 12 45N 45 0 E
Aden, G. of, *Asia* **90 E4** 12 30N 47 30 E
Adendorp, *S. Africa* **104 E3** 32 15 S 24 30 E
Adh Dhayd, *U.A.E.* **85 E7** 25 17N 55 53 E
Adhoi, *India* **80 H4** 23 26N 70 32 E
Adi, *Indonesia* **73 B4** 4 15 S 133 30 E
Adi Daro, *Ethiopia* **95 E4** 14 20N 38 14 E
Adi Keyih, *Eritrea* **95 E4** 14 51N 39 22 E
Adi Kwala, *Eritrea* **95 E4** 14 38N 38 48 E
Adi Ugri, *Eritrea* **95 E4** 14 58N 38 48 E
Adieu, C., *Australia* **113 F5** 32 0 S 132 10 E
Adieu Pt., *Australia* **112 C3** 15 14 S 124 35 E
Adigala, *Ethiopia* **95 E5** 10 24N 42 15 E
Adige →, *Italy* **39 C9** 45 9N 12 20 E
Adigrat, *Ethiopia* **95 E4** 14 20N 39 26 E
Adilabad, *India* **82 E4** 19 33N 78 20 E
Adin, *U.S.A.* **142 F3** 41 12N 120 57W
Adinkerke, *Belgium* **21 F1** 51 5N 2 36 E
Adirondack Mts., *U.S.A.* **137 C10** 44 0N 74 0W
Adıyaman, *Turkey* **89 E8** 37 45N 38 16 E
Adıyaman □, *Turkey* **89 E8** 37 30N 38 10 E
Adjim, *Tunisia* **96 B2** 33 47N 10 50 E
Adjohon, *Benin* **101 D5** 6 41N 2 32 E
Adjud, *Romania* **46 C8** 46 7N 27 10 E
Adjumani, *Uganda* **106 B3** 3 20N 31 50 E
Adlavik Is., *Canada* **129 B8** 55 2N 57 45W
Adler, *Russia* **53 E8** 43 28N 39 52 E
Adliswil, *Switz.* **29 B7** 47 19N 8 32 E
Admer, *Algeria* **99 D6** 20 21N 5 27 E
Admer, Erg d', *Algeria* **99 D6** 24 0N 9 5 E
Admiralty G., *Australia* **112 B4** 14 20 S 125 55 E
Admiralty I., *U.S.A.* **126 C6** 57 30N 134 30W
Admiralty Inlet, *U.S.A.* **142 C2** 48 8N 122 58W
Admiralty Is., *Papua N. G.* **120 B4** 2 0 S 147 0 E
Ado, *Nigeria* **101 D5** 6 36N 2 56 E
Ado Ekiti, *Nigeria* **101 D6** 7 38N 5 12 E
Adok, *Sudan* **95 F3** 8 10N 30 20 E
Adola, *Ethiopia* **95 E5** 11 14N 41 44 E
Adonara, *Indonesia* **72 C2** 8 15 S 123 5 E
Adoni, *India* **83 G3** 15 33N 77 18 E
Adony, *Hungary* **31 D11** 47 6N 18 52 E
Adour →, *France* **24 E2** 43 32N 1 32W
Adra, *India* **81 H12** 23 30N 86 42 E
Adra, *Spain* **35 J1** 36 43N 3 3W
Adrano, *Italy* **41 E7** 37 40N 14 49 E
Adrar, *Algeria* **99 C4** 27 51N 0 11W
Adrasman, *Tajikistan* **55 C4** 40 38N 69 58 E
Adré, *Chad* **97 F4** 13 40N 22 20 E
Adrī, *Libya* **96 C2** 27 32N 13 2 E
Ádria, *Italy* **39 C9** 45 4N 12 3 E
Adrian, *Mich., U.S.A.* **141 C12** 41 54N 84 2W
Adrian, *Mo., U.S.A.* **140 F2** 38 24N 94 21W
Adrian, *Tex., U.S.A.* **139 H3** 35 16N 102 40W
Adriatic Sea, *Europe* **10 G9** 43 0N 16 0 E
Adua, *Indonesia* **73 B3** 1 45 S 129 50 E
Adula, *Switz.* **29 D8** 46 30N 9 3 E
Adung Long, *Burma* **78 A6** 28 7N 97 42 E
Adur, *India* **83 K3** 9 8N 76 40 E
Adwa, *Ethiopia* **95 E4** 14 15N 38 52 E
Adzhar Republic □, *Georgia* **53 F10** 41 30N 42 0 E
Adzopé, *Ivory C.* **100 D4** 6 7N 3 49W
Ægean Sea, *Europe* **45 F7** 38 30N 25 0 E
Æolian Is. = Eólie, Is., *Italy* **41 D7** 38 30N 14 50 E
Aerhtai Shan, *Mongolia* **64 B4** 46 40N 92 45 E
Ærø, *Denmark* **15 K4** 54 52N 10 25 E
Ærøskøbing, *Denmark* **15 K4** 54 53N 10 24 E
Aesch, *Switz.* **28 B5** 47 28N 7 36 E
Aëtós, *Greece* **45 G3** 37 15N 21 50 E
Afafi, Massif d', *Niger* **97 D3** 22 11N 15 10 E
'Afak, *Iraq* **84 C5** 32 4N 45 15 E
Afanasyevo, *Russia* **54 B3** 58 52N 53 15 E
Afándou, *Greece* **32 C10** 36 18N 28 12 E
Afarag, Erg, *Algeria* **99 D5** 23 50N 2 47 E
Afars & Issas, Terr. of = Djibouti ■, *Africa* **90 E3** 12 0N 43 0 E
Afdega, *Ethiopia* **108 C2** 6 4N 43 30 E
Affreville = Khemis Miliana, *Algeria* **99 A5** 36 11N 2 14 E
Affton, *U.S.A.* **140 F6** 38 33N 90 20W
Afghanistan ■, *Asia* **79 B2** 33 0N 65 0 E
Afgoi, *Somali Rep.* **90 G3** 2 7N 44 59 E
'Afīf, *Si. Arabia* **86 B3** 23 53N 42 56 E
Afikpo, *Nigeria* **101 D6** 5 53N 7 54 E
Aflou, *Algeria* **99 B5** 34 7N 2 3 E
Afmadu, *Somali Rep.* **108 D2** 0 31N 42 4 E
Afogados da Ingàzeira, *Brazil* **154 C4** 7 45 S 37 39W
Afognak I., *U.S.A.* **126 C4** 58 15N 152 30W
Afragola, *Italy* **41 B7** 40 54N 14 15 E
Afrera, *Ethiopia* **95 E5** 13 16N 41 5 E
Africa **92 E6** 10 0N 20 0 E
'Afrīn, *Syria* **84 B3** 36 32N 36 50 E
Afşin, *Turkey* **88 D7** 38 14N 36 55 E
Afton, *U.S.A.* **137 D9** 42 14N 75 32W
Aftout, *Algeria* **98 C4** 26 50N 3 45W
Afuá, *Brazil* **153 D7** 0 15 S 50 20W
Afula, *Israel* **91 C4** 32 37N 35 17 E
Afyonkarahisar, *Turkey* **88 D4** 38 45N 30 33 E
Afyonkarahisar □, *Turkey* **88 D4** 38 45N 30 30 E
Aga, *Egypt* **94 H7** 30 55N 31 10 E
Agadès = Agadez, *Niger* **97 E1** 16 58N 7 59 E
Agadez, *Niger* **97 E1** 16 58N 7 59 E
Agadir, *Morocco* **98 B3** 30 28N 9 55W
Agaete, *Canary Is.* **33 F4** 28 6N 15 43W
Agailás, *Mauritania* **98 D2** 22 37N 14 22W
Agana, *Guam* **121 R15** 13 28N 144 45 E
Agapa, *Russia* **57 B9** 71 27N 89 15 E
Agapovka, *Russia* **54 E6** 53 18N 59 8 E
Agar, *India* **80 H7** 23 40N 76 2 E
Agaro, *Ethiopia* **95 F4** 7 50N 36 38 E
Agartala, *India* **78 D3** 23 50N 91 23 E
Agăş, *Romania* **46 C7** 46 28N 26 15 E
Agassiz, *Canada* **130 D4** 49 14N 121 46W
Agats, *Indonesia* **73 C5** 5 33 S 138 0 E
Agbélouvé, *Togo* **101 D5** 6 35N 1 14 E
Agboville, *Ivory C.* **100 D4** 5 55N 4 15W

**Ampasindava, Helodranon' 165**


Aliquippa, *U.S.A.* **136 F4** 40 37N 80 15W
Aliste →, *Spain* **36 D5** 41 34N 5 58W
Alitus, *Lithuania* **50 D4** 54 24N 24 3 E
Alivérion, *Greece* **45 F6** 38 24N 24 2 E
Aliwal North, *S. Africa* **104 E4** 30 45 S 26 45 E
Alix, *Canada* **130 C6** 52 24N 113 11W
Aljezur, *Portugal* **37 H2** 37 18N 8 49W
Aljustrel, *Portugal* **37 H2** 37 55N 8 10W
Alkamari, *Niger* **97 F2** 13 27N 11 10 E
Alken, *Belgium* **21 G6** 50 53N 5 18 E
Alkmaar, *Neths.* **20 C5** 52 37N 4 45 E
All American Canal, *U.S.A.* **143 K6** 32 45N 115 15W
Allacapan, *Phil.* **70 B3** 18 15N 121 35 E
Allada, *Benin* **101 D5** 6 41N 2 9 E
Allah Dad, *Pakistan* **80 G2** 25 38N 67 34 E
Allahabad, *India* **81 G9** 25 25N 81 58 E
Allakh-Yun, *Russia* **57 C14** 60 50N 137 5 E
Allal Tazi, *Morocco* **98 B3** 34 30N 6 20W
Allan, *Canada* **131 C7** 51 53N 106 4W
Allanche, *France* **24 C6** 45 14N 2 57 E
Allanmyo, *Burma* **78 F5** 19 30N 95 17 E
Allanridge, *S. Africa* **104 D4** 27 45 S 26 40 E
Allansford, *Australia* **116 E5** 38 26 S 142 39 E
Allanton, *N.Z.* **119 F5** 45 55 S 170 15 E
Allanwater, *Canada* **128 B1** 50 14N 90 10W
Allaqi, Wadi →, *Egypt* **94 C3** 23 7N 32 47 E
Allariz, *Spain* **36 C3** 42 11N 7 50W
Allassac, *France* **24 C5** 45 15N 1 29 E
Alle, *Belgium* **21 J5** 49 51N 4 58 E
Allegan, *U.S.A.* **141 B11** 42 32N 85 51W
Allegany, *U.S.A.* **136 D6** 42 6N 78 30W
Allegheny →, *U.S.A.* **136 F5** 40 27N 80 1W
Allegheny Plateau, *U.S.A.* **134 G6** 38 0N 80 0W
Allegheny Reservoir, *U.S.A.* **136 E6** 41 50N 79 0W
Allègre, *France* **24 C7** 45 12N 3 41 E
Allen, *Argentina* **160 A3** 38 58 S 67 50W
Allen, *Phil.* **70 E5** 12 30N 124 17 E
Allen, Bog of, *Ireland* **19 C4** 53 15N 7 0W
Allen, L., *Ireland* **19 B3** 54 12N 8 5W
Allende, *Mexico* **146 B4** 28 20N 100 50W
Allentown, *U.S.A.* **137 F9** 40 37N 75 29W
Allentsteig, *Austria* **30 C8** 48 41N 15 20 E
Alleppey, *India* **83 K3** 9 30N 76 28 E
Aller →, *Germany* **26 C5** 52 57N 9 10 E
Alleur, *Belgium* **21 G7** 50 39N 5 31 E
Allevard, *France* **25 C10** 45 24N 6 5 E
Alliance, *Surinam* **153 B7** 5 50N 54 50W
Alliance, *Nebr., U.S.A.* **138 D3** 42 6N 102 52W
Alliance, *Ohio, U.S.A.* **136 F3** 40 55N 81 6W
Allier □, *France* **24 B6** 46 25N 2 40 E
Allier →, *France* **23 F10** 46 57N 3 4 E
Allingåbro, *Denmark* **15 H4** 56 28N 10 20 E
Allison, *U.S.A.* **140 B4** 42 45N 92 48W
Alliston, *Canada* **128 D4** 44 9N 79 52W
Alloa, *U.K.* **18 E5** 56 7N 3 49W
Allora, *Australia* **115 D5** 28 2 S 152 0 E
Allos, *France* **25 D10** 44 15N 6 38 E
Alluitsup Paa = Sydprøven, *Greenland* **6 C5** 60 30N 45 35W
Alma, *Canada* **129 C5** 48 35N 71 40W
Alma, *Ga., U.S.A.* **135 K4** 31 33N 82 28W
Alma, *Kans., U.S.A.* **138 F6** 39 1N 96 17W
Alma, *Mich., U.S.A.* **134 D3** 43 23N 84 39W
Alma, *Nebr., U.S.A.* **138 E5** 40 6N 99 22W
Alma, *Wis., U.S.A.* **138 C9** 44 20N 91 55W
Alma Ata, *Kazakhstan* **55 B8** 43 15N 76 57 E
Almada, *Portugal* **37 G1** 38 40N 9 9W
Almaden, *Australia* **114 B3** 17 22 S 144 40 E
Almadén, *Spain* **37 G6** 38 49N 4 52W
Almagro, *Spain* **37 G7** 38 50N 3 45W
Almagro I., *Phil.* **71 F5** 11 56N 124 18 E
Almalyk, *Uzbekistan* **55 C4** 40 50N 69 35 E
Almanor, L., *U.S.A.* **142 F3** 40 14N 121 9W
Almansa, *Spain* **35 G3** 38 51N 1 5W
Almanza, *Spain* **36 C5** 42 39N 5 3W
Almanzor, Pico de, *Spain* **36 E5** 40 15N 5 18W
Almanzora →, *Spain* **35 H3** 37 14N 1 46W
Almas, *Brazil* **155 D2** 11 33 S 47 9W
Almaş, Mţii., *Romania* **46 E3** 44 49N 22 12 E
Almaty = Alma Ata, *Kazakhstan* **55 B8** 43 15N 76 57 E
Almazán, *Spain* **34 D2** 41 30N 2 30W
Almazora, *Spain* **34 F4** 39 57N 0 3W
Almeirim, *Brazil* **153 D7** 1 30 S 52 34W
Almeirim, *Portugal* **37 F2** 39 12N 8 37W
Almelo, *Neths.* **20 D9** 52 22N 6 42 E
Almenar, *Spain* **34 D2** 41 43N 2 12W
Almenara, *Brazil* **155 E3** 16 11 S 40 42W
Almenara, *Spain* **34 F4** 39 46N 0 14W
Almenara, Sierra de, *Spain* **35 H3** 37 34N 1 32W
Almendralejo, *Spain* **37 G4** 38 41N 6 26W
Almería, *Spain* **35 J2** 36 52N 2 27W
Almería □, *Spain* **35 H2** 37 20N 2 20W
Almería, G. de, *Spain* **35 J2** 36 41N 2 28W
Almetyevsk, *Russia* **54 D3** 54 53N 52 20 E
Almirante, *Panama* **148 E3** 9 10N 82 30W
Almirante Montt, G., *Chile* **160 D2** 51 52 S 72 50W
Almiropótamos, *Greece* **45 F6** 38 16N 24 11 E
Almirós, *Greece* **45 E4** 39 11N 22 45 E
Almiroú, Kólpos, *Greece* **32 D6** 35 23N 24 20 E
Almodôvar, *Portugal* **37 H2** 37 31N 8 2W
Almodóvar del Campo, *Spain* **37 G6** 38 43N 4 10W
Almogia, *Spain* **37 J6** 36 50N 4 32W
Almonaster la Real, *Spain* **37 H4** 37 52N 6 48W
Almont, *U.S.A.* **136 D1** 42 55N 83 3W
Almonte, *Canada* **137 A8** 45 14N 76 12W
Almonte →, *Spain* **37 F4** 39 41N 6 28W
Almora, *India* **81 E8** 29 38N 79 40 E
Almoradi, *Spain* **35 G4** 38 7N 0 46W
Almorox, *Spain* **36 E6** 40 14N 4 24W
Almoustarat, *Mali* **101 B5** 17 35N 0 8 E
Almuñécar, *Spain* **37 J7** 36 43N 3 41W
Alnif, *Morocco* **98 B3** 31 10N 5 8W
Alnwick, *U.K.* **16 B6** 55 25N 1 42W
Aloi, *Uganda* **106 B3** 2 16N 33 10 E
Alon, *Burma* **78 D5** 22 12N 95 5 E
Alor, *Indonesia* **72 C2** 8 15 S 124 30 E
Alor Setar, *Malaysia* **77 J3** 6 7N 100 22 E
Alora, *Spain* **37 J6** 36 49N 4 46W
Alosno, *Spain* **37 H3** 37 33N 7 7W
Alotau, *Papua N. G.* **120 F6** 10 16 S 150 30 E
Alougoum, *Morocco* **98 B3** 30 17N 6 56W
Aloysius, Mt., *Australia* **113 E4** 26 0 S 128 38 E
Alpaugh, *U.S.A.* **144 K7** 35 53N 119 29W
Alpedrinha, *Portugal* **36 E3** 40 6N 7 27W
Alpena, *U.S.A.* **134 C4** 45 4N 83 27W
Alpercatas →, *Brazil* **154 C3** 6 2 S 44 19W
Alpes-de-Haute-Provence □, *France* **25 D10** 44 8N 6 10 E
Alpes-Maritimes □, *France* **25 E11** 43 55N 7 10 E
Alpha, *Australia* **114 C4** 23 39 S 146 37 E
Alpha, *U.S.A.* **140 C6** 41 12N 90 23W
Alphen, *Neths.* **21 F5** 51 29N 4 58 E
Alphen aan den Rijn, *Neths.* **20 D5** 52 7N 4 40 E
Alphonse, *Seychelles* **109 E4** 7 0 S 52 45 E
Alpiarça, *Portugal* **37 F2** 39 15N 8 35W
Alpine, *Ariz., U.S.A.* **143 K9** 33 51N 109 9W
Alpine, *Calif., U.S.A.* **145 N10** 32 50N 116 46W
Alpine, *Tex., U.S.A.* **139 K3** 30 22N 103 40W
Alpnach, *Switz.* **29 C6** 46 57N 8 17 E
Alps, *Europe* **10 F7** 46 30N 9 30 E
Alpu, *Turkey* **88 D4** 39 46N 30 58 E
Alrø, *Denmark* **15 J4** 55 52N 10 5 E
Alroy Downs, *Australia* **114 B2** 19 20 S 136 5 E
Alsace, *France* **23 D14** 48 15N 7 25 E
Alsask, *Canada* **131 C7** 51 21N 109 59W
Alsásua, *Spain* **34 C2** 42 54N 2 10W
Alsen, *Sweden* **14 A7** 63 23N 13 56 E
Alsfeld, *Germany* **26 E5** 50 44N 9 19 E
Alsónémedi, *Hungary* **31 D12** 47 20N 19 15 E
Alsten, *Norway* **12 D12** 65 58N 12 40 E
Alta, *Norway* **12 B17** 69 57N 23 10 E
Alta, Sierra, *Spain* **34 E3** 40 31N 1 30W
Alta Gracia, *Argentina* **158 C3** 31 40 S 64 30W
Alta Lake, *Canada* **130 C4** 50 10N 123 0W
Alta Sierra, *U.S.A.* **145 K8** 35 42N 118 33W
Altaelva →, *Norway* **12 B17** 69 46N 23 45 E
Altafjorden, *Norway* **12 A17** 70 5N 23 5 E
Altagracia, *Venezuela* **152 A3** 10 45N 71 30W
Altagracia de Orituco, *Venezuela* **152 B4** 9 52N 66 23W
Altai = Aerhtai Shan, *Mongolia* **64 B4** 46 40N 92 45 E
Altamachi →, *Bolivia* **156 D4** 16 8 S 66 50W
Altamaha →, *U.S.A.* **135 K5** 31 20N 81 20W
Altamira, *Brazil* **153 D7** 3 12 S 52 10W
Altamira, *Chile* **158 B2** 25 47 S 69 51W
Altamira, *Colombia* **152 C2** 2 3N 75 47W
Altamira, *Mexico* **147 C5** 22 24N 97 55W
Altamira, Cuevas de, *Spain* **36 B6** 43 20N 4 5W
Altamont, *Ill., U.S.A.* **141 E8** 39 4N 88 45W
Altamont, *N.Y., U.S.A.* **137 D10** 42 43N 74 3W
Altamura, *Italy* **41 B9** 40 50N 16 33 E
Altanbulag, *Mongolia* **64 A5** 50 16N 106 30 E
Altar, *Mexico* **146 A2** 30 40N 111 50W
Altata, *Mexico* **146 C3** 24 30N 108 0W
Altavas, *Phil.* **71 F4** 11 32N 122 29 E
Altavista, *U.S.A.* **134 G6** 37 6N 79 17W
Altay, *China* **64 B3** 47 48N 88 10 E
Altdorf, *Switz.* **29 C7** 46 52N 8 36 E
Alte Mellum, *Germany* **26 B4** 53 45N 8 6 E
Altea, *Spain* **35 G4** 38 38N 0 2W
Altenberg, *Germany* **26 E9** 50 46N 13 47 E
Altenbruch, *Germany* **26 B4** 53 48N 8 44 E
Altenburg, *Germany* **26 E8** 50 59N 12 28 E
Altenkirchen, *Mecklenburg-Vorpommern, Germany* **26 A9** 54 38N 13 20 E
Altenkirchen, *Rhld-Pfz., Germany* **26 E3** 50 41N 7 38 E
Altenmarkt, *Austria* **30 D7** 47 43N 14 39 E
Altenteptow, *Germany* **26 B9** 53 42N 13 15 E
Alter do Chão, *Portugal* **37 F3** 39 12N 7 40W
Altıntaş, *Turkey* **88 D4** 39 4N 30 10 E
Altiplano, *Bolivia* **156 D4** 17 0 S 68 0W
Altkirch, *France* **23 E14** 47 37N 7 15 E
Altmühl →, *Germany* **27 G7** 48 54N 11 54 E
Alto Adige = Trentino-Alto Adige □, *Italy* **38 B8** 46 30N 11 0 E
Alto Araguaia, *Brazil* **157 D7** 17 15 S 53 20W
Alto Cuchumatanes = Cuchumatanes, Sierra de los, *Guatemala* **148 C1** 15 35N 91 25W
Alto Cuito, *Angola* **103 E3** 13 27 S 18 49 E
Alto del Inca, *Chile* **158 A2** 24 10 S 68 10W
Alto Garças, *Brazil* **157 D7** 16 56 S 53 32W
Alto Iriri →, *Brazil* **157 B7** 8 50 S 53 25W
Alto Ligonha, *Mozam.* **107 F4** 15 30 S 38 11 E
Alto Molocue, *Mozam.* **107 F4** 15 50 S 37 35 E
Alto Paraguai, *Brazil* **157 C6** 14 30 S 56 31W
Alto Paraguay □, *Paraguay* **158 A4** 21 0 S 58 30W
Alto Paraná □, *Paraguay* **159 B5** 25 30 S 54 50W
Alto Parnaíba, *Brazil* **154 C2** 9 6 S 45 57W
Alto Purús →, *Peru* **156 B3** 9 12 S 70 28W
Alto Río Senguerr, *Argentina* **160 C2** 45 2 S 70 50W
Alto Santo, *Brazil* **154 C4** 5 31 S 38 15W
Alto Sucuriú, *Brazil* **157 D7** 19 19 S 52 47W
Alto Turi, *Brazil* **154 B2** 2 54 S 45 38W
Alton, *Canada* **136 C4** 43 54N 80 5W
Alton, *U.S.A.* **140 F6** 38 53N 90 11W
Alton Downs, *Australia* **115 D2** 26 7 S 138 57 E
Altoona, *Iowa, U.S.A.* **140 C3** 41 39N 93 28W
Altoona, *Pa., U.S.A.* **136 F6** 40 31N 78 24W
Altopáscio, *Italy* **38 E7** 43 50N 10 40 E
Altos, *Brazil* **154 C3** 5 3 S 42 28W
Altötting, *Germany* **27 G8** 48 14N 12 41 E
Altstätten, *Switz.* **29 B9** 47 22N 9 33 E
Altūn Kūprī, *Iraq* **84 C5** 35 45N 44 9 E
Altun Shan, *China* **64 C3** 38 30N 88 0 E
Alturas, *U.S.A.* **142 F3** 41 29N 120 32W
Altus, *U.S.A.* **139 H5** 34 38N 99 20W
Alubijid, *Phil.* **71 G5** 8 35N 124 29 E
Alucra, *Turkey* **53 F8** 40 22N 38 47 E
Alūksne, *Latvia* **50 C5** 57 24N 27 3 E
Alùla, *Somali Rep.* **90 E5** 11 50N 50 45 E
Alunite, *U.S.A.* **145 K12** 35 59N 114 55W
Alupka, *Ukraine* **52 D6** 44 23N 34 2 E
Alur Gajah, *Malaysia* **74 B2** 2 23N 102 13 E
Alushta, *Ukraine* **52 D6** 44 40N 34 25 E
Alusi, *Indonesia* **73 C4** 7 35 S 131 40 E
Alustante, *Spain* **34 E3** 40 36N 1 40W
Al'Uzayr, *Iraq* **84 D5** 31 19N 47 25 E
Alva, *U.S.A.* **139 G5** 36 48N 98 40W
Alvaiázere, *Portugal* **36 F2** 39 49N 8 23W
Älvängen, *Sweden* **15 G6** 57 58N 12 8 E
Alvarado, *Mexico* **147 D5** 18 40N 95 50W
Alvarado, *U.S.A.* **139 J6** 32 24N 97 13W
Alvarães, *Brazil* **153 D5** 3 12 S 64 50W
Alvaro Obregón, Presa, *Mexico* **146 B3** 27 55N 109 52W
Alvdal, *Norway* **14 B4** 62 6N 10 37 E
Alvear, *Argentina* **158 B4** 29 5 S 56 30W
Alverca, *Portugal* **37 G1** 38 56N 9 1W
Alveringen, *Belgium* **21 F1** 51 1N 2 43 E
Alvesta, *Sweden* **13 H13** 56 54N 14 35 E
Alvie, *Australia* **116 E5** 38 14 S 143 30 E
Alvin, *U.S.A.* **139 L7** 29 26N 95 15W
Alvinston, *Canada* **136 D3** 42 49N 81 52W
Alvito, *Portugal* **37 G3** 38 15N 8 0W
Älvkarleby, *Sweden* **13 F14** 60 34N 17 26 E
Älvros, *Sweden* **14 B8** 62 3N 14 38 E
Älvsborgs län □, *Sweden* **15 F6** 58 30N 12 30 E
Älvsbyn, *Sweden* **12 D16** 65 40N 21 0 E
Älvsered, *Sweden* **15 G6** 57 14N 12 51 E
Alwar, *India* **80 F7** 27 38N 76 34 E
Alwaye, *India* **83 J3** 10 8N 76 24 E
Alxa Zuoqi, *China* **66 E3** 38 50N 105 40 E
Alyaskitovyy, *Russia* **57 C15** 64 45N 141 30 E
Alyata, *Azerbaijan* **53 G13** 39 58N 49 25 E
Alyth, *U.K.* **18 E5** 56 38N 3 15W
Alzada, *U.S.A.* **138 C2** 45 2N 104 25W
Alzano Lombardo, *Italy* **38 C6** 45 44N 9 43 E
Alzette →, *Lux.* **21 J8** 49 45N 6 6 E
Alzey, *Germany* **27 F4** 49 48N 8 4 E
Am Dam, *Chad* **97 F4** 12 40N 20 35 E
Am Géréda, *Chad* **97 F4** 12 53N 21 14 E
Am-Timan, *Chad* **97 F4** 11 0N 20 10 E
Amacuro □, *Venezuela* **153 B5** 8 50N 61 5W
Amadeus, L., *Australia* **113 D5** 24 54 S 131 0 E
Amâdi, *Sudan* **95 F3** 5 29N 30 25 E
Amadi, *Zaïre* **106 B2** 3 40N 26 40 E
Amadjuak, *Canada* **127 B12** 64 0N 72 39W
Amadjuak L., *Canada* **127 B12** 65 0N 71 8W
Amadora, *Portugal* **37 G1** 38 45N 9 13W
Amagasaki, *Japan* **63 C7** 34 42N 135 20 E
Amager, *Denmark* **15 J6** 55 37N 12 35 E
Amagi, *Japan* **62 D2** 33 25N 130 39 E
Amahai, *Indonesia* **73 B3** 3 20 S 128 55 E
Amaimon, *Papua N. G.* **120 C3** 5 12 S 145 30 E
Amakusa-Nada, *Japan* **62 E2** 32 35N 130 5 E
Amakusa-Shotō, *Japan* **62 E2** 32 15N 130 10 E
Amalapuram, *India* **83 F5** 16 35N 81 55 E
Amalfi, *Colombia* **152 B2** 6 55N 75 4W
Amalfi, *Italy* **41 B7** 40 39N 14 34 E
Amaliás, *Greece* **45 G3** 37 47N 21 22 E
Amalner, *India* **82 D2** 21 5N 75 5 E
Amambaí, *Brazil* **159 A4** 23 5 S 55 13W
Amambaí →, *Brazil* **159 A5** 23 22 S 53 56W
Amambay □, *Paraguay* **159 A4** 23 0 S 56 0W
Amambay, Cordillera de, *S. Amer.* **159 A4** 23 0 S 55 45W
Amami-Guntō, *Japan* **61 L4** 27 16N 129 21 E
Amami-Ō-Shima, *Japan* **61 L4** 28 0N 129 0 E
Amana →, *Venezuela* **153 B5** 9 45N 62 39W
Amanã, L., *Brazil* **153 D5** 2 35 S 64 40W
Amanab, *Papua N. G.* **120 B1** 3 40 S 141 14 E
Amanda Park, *U.S.A.* **144 C3** 47 28N 123 55W
Amándola, *Italy* **39 F10** 42 59N 13 21 E
Amangeldy, *Kazakhstan* **56 D7** 50 10N 65 10 E
Amantea, *Italy* **41 C9** 39 8N 16 3 E
Amapá, *Brazil* **153 C7** 2 5N 50 50W
Amapá □, *Brazil* **153 C7** 1 40N 52 0W
Amapari, *Brazil* **153 C7** 0 37N 51 39W
Amara, *Sudan* **95 E3** 10 25N 34 10 E
Amarante, *Brazil* **154 C3** 6 14 S 42 50W
Amarante, *Portugal* **36 D2** 41 16N 8 5W
Amarante do Maranhão, *Brazil* **154 C2** 5 36 S 46 45W
Amaranth, *Canada* **131 C9** 50 36N 98 43W
Amarapura, *Burma* **78 E6** 21 54N 96 3 E
Amaravati →, *India* **83 J4** 11 0N 78 15 E
Amareleja, *Portugal* **37 G3** 38 12N 7 13W
Amargosa, *Brazil* **155 D4** 13 2 S 39 36W
Amargosa →, *U.S.A.* **145 J10** 36 14N 116 51W
Amargosa Range, *U.S.A.* **145 J10** 36 20N 116 45W
Amâri, *Greece* **32 D6** 35 13N 24 40 E
Amarillo, *U.S.A.* **139 H4** 35 13N 101 50W
Amarnath, *India* **82 E1** 19 12N 73 22 E
Amaro, Mt., *Italy* **39 F11** 42 5N 14 6 E
Amaro Leite, *Brazil* **155 D2** 13 58 S 49 9W
Amarpur, *India* **81 G12** 25 5N 87 0 E
Amasra, *Turkey* **88 C5** 41 45N 32 23 E
Amassama, *Nigeria* **101 D6** 5 1N 6 2 E
Amasya, *Turkey* **88 C6** 40 40N 35 50 E
Amasya □, *Turkey* **88 C6** 40 40N 35 50 E
Amataurá, *Brazil* **152 D4** 3 29 S 68 6W
Amatikulu, *S. Africa* **105 D5** 29 3 S 31 33 E
Amatitlán, *Guatemala* **148 D1** 14 29N 90 38W
Amatrice, *Italy* **39 F10** 42 38N 13 16 E
Amay, *Belgium* **21 G6** 50 33N 5 19 E
Amazon = Amazonas →, *S. Amer.* **153 D7** 0 5 S 50 0W
Amazonas □, *Brazil* **157 B5** 5 0 S 65 0W
Amazonas □, *Peru* **156 B2** 5 0 S 78 0W
Amazonas □, *Venezuela* **152 C4** 3 30N 66 0W
Amazonas →, *S. Amer.* **153 D7** 0 5 S 50 0W
Ambad, *India* **82 E2** 19 38N 75 50 E
Ambahakily, *Madag.* **105 C7** 21 36 S 43 41 E
Ambala, *India* **80 D7** 30 23N 76 56 E
Ambalangoda, *Sri Lanka* **83 L5** 6 15N 80 5 E
Ambalapulai, *India* **83 K3** 9 25N 76 25 E
Ambalavao, *Madag.* **105 C8** 21 50 S 46 56 E
Ambalindum, *Australia* **114 C2** 23 23 S 135 0 E
Ambam, *Cameroon* **102 B2** 2 20N 11 15 E
Ambanja, *Madag.* **105 A8** 13 40 S 48 27 E
Ambarchik, *Russia* **57 C17** 69 40N 162 20 E
Ambarijeby, *Madag.* **105 A8** 14 56 S 47 41 E
Ambaro, Helodranon', *Madag.* **105 A8** 13 23 S 48 38 E
Ambartsevo, *Russia* **56 D9** 57 30N 83 52 E
Ambasamudram, *India* **83 K3** 8 43N 77 25 E
Ambato, *Ecuador* **152 D2** 1 5 S 78 42W
Ambato, Sierra de, *Argentina* **158 B2** 28 25 S 66 10W
Ambato Boeny, *Madag.* **105 B8** 16 28 S 46 43 E
Ambatofinandrahana, *Madag.* **105 C8** 20 33 S 46 48 E
Ambatolampy, *Madag.* **105 B8** 19 20 S 47 35 E
Ambatondrazaka, *Madag.* **105 B8** 17 55 S 48 28 E
Ambatosoratra, *Madag.* **105 B8** 17 37 S 48 31 E
Ambenja, *Madag.* **105 B8** 15 17 S 46 58 E
Amberg, *Germany* **27 F7** 49 25N 11 52 E
Ambergris Cay, *Belize* **147 D7** 18 0N 88 0W
Ambérieu-en-Bugey, *France* **25 C9** 45 57N 5 20 E
Amberley, *N.Z.* **119 D7** 43 9 S 172 44 E
Ambert, *France* **24 C7** 45 33N 3 44 E
Ambidédi, *Mali* **100 C2** 14 35N 11 47W
Ambikapur, *India* **81 H10** 23 15N 83 15 E
Ambikol, *Sudan* **94 C3** 21 20N 30 50 E
Ambilobé, *Madag.* **105 A8** 13 10 S 49 3 E
Ambinanindrano, *Madag.* **105 C8** 20 5 S 48 23 E
Ambjörnarp, *Sweden* **15 G7** 57 25N 13 17 E
Ambleside, *U.K.* **16 C5** 54 26N 2 58W
Amblève, *Belgium* **21 H8** 50 21N 6 10 E
Amblève →, *Belgium* **21 H7** 50 25N 5 45 E
Ambo, *Ethiopia* **95 E4** 12 20N 37 30 E
Ambo, *Peru* **156 C2** 10 5 S 76 10W
Ambodifototra, *Madag.* **105 B8** 16 59 S 49 52 E
Ambodilazana, *Madag.* **105 B8** 18 6 S 49 10 E
Ambohimahasoa, *Madag.* **105 C8** 21 7 S 47 13 E
Ambohimanga, *Madag.* **105 C8** 20 52 S 47 36 E
Ambohitra, *Madag.* **105 A8** 12 30 S 49 10 E
Ambon, *Indonesia* **72 B3** 3 43 S 128 12 E
Ambon, *Indonesia* **72 B3** 3 35 S 128 20 E
Amboseli L., *Kenya* **106 C4** 2 40 S 37 10 E
Ambositra, *Madag.* **105 C8** 20 31 S 47 25 E
Ambovombé, *Madag.* **105 D8** 25 11 S 46 5 E
Amboy, *Calif., U.S.A.* **145 L11** 34 33N 115 45W
Amboy, *Ill., U.S.A.* **140 C7** 41 44N 89 20W
Ambridge, *U.S.A.* **136 F4** 40 36N 80 14W
Ambriz, *Angola* **103 D2** 7 48 S 13 8 E
Ambrym, *Vanuatu* **121 F6** 16 15 S 168 10 E
Ambunti, *Papua N. G.* **120 C2** 4 13 S 142 52 E
Ambur, *India* **83 H4** 12 48N 78 43 E
Amby, *Australia* **115 D4** 26 30 S 148 11 E
Amchitka I., *U.S.A.* **126 C1** 51 32N 179 0 E
Amderma, *Russia* **56 C7** 69 45N 61 30 E
Ameca, *Mexico* **146 C4** 20 30N 104 0W
Ameca →, *Mexico* **146 C3** 20 40N 105 15W
Amecameca, *Mexico* **147 D5** 19 7N 98 46W
Ameland, *Neths.* **20 B7** 53 27N 5 45 E
Amélia, *Italy* **39 F9** 42 34N 12 25 E
Amélie-les-Bains-Palalda, *France* **24 F6** 42 29N 2 41 E
Amen, *Russia* **57 C18** 68 45N 180 0 E
Amendolaro, *Italy* **41 C9** 39 58N 16 34 E
America, *Neths.* **21 F7** 51 27N 5 59 E
American Falls, *U.S.A.* **142 E7** 42 47N 112 51W
American Falls Reservoir, *U.S.A.* **142 E7** 42 47N 112 52W
American Highland, *Antarctica* **7 D6** 73 0 S 75 0 E
American Samoa ■, *Pac. Oc.* **121 X24** 14 20 S 170 40W
Americana, *Brazil* **159 A6** 22 45 S 47 20W
Americus, *U.S.A.* **135 J3** 32 4N 84 14W
Amersfoort, *Neths.* **20 D6** 52 9N 5 23 E
Amersfoort, *S. Africa* **105 D4** 26 59 S 29 53 E
Amery, *Australia* **113 F2** 31 9 S 117 5 E
Amery, *Canada* **131 B10** 56 34N 94 3W
Amery Ice Shelf, *Antarctica* **7 C6** 69 30 S 72 0 E
Ames, *U.S.A.* **140 B3** 42 2N 93 37W
Amesbury, *U.S.A.* **137 D14** 42 51N 70 56W
Amfíklia, *Greece* **45 F4** 38 38N 22 35 E
Amfilokhía, *Greece* **45 F3** 38 52N 21 9 E
Amfípolis, *Greece* **44 D5** 40 48N 23 52 E
Ámfissa, *Greece* **45 F4** 38 32N 22 22 E
Amga, *Russia* **57 C14** 60 50N 132 0 E
Amga →, *Russia* **57 C14** 62 38N 134 32 E
Amgu, *Russia* **57 E14** 45 45N 137 15 E
Amgun →, *Russia* **57 D14** 52 56N 139 38 E
Amherst, *Canada* **129 C7** 45 48N 64 8W
Amherst, *Mass., U.S.A.* **137 D12** 42 23N 72 31W
Amherst, *N.Y., U.S.A.* **136 D6** 42 59N 78 48W
Amherst, *Ohio, U.S.A.* **136 E2** 41 24N 82 14W
Amherst, *Tex., U.S.A.* **139 H3** 34 1N 102 25W
Amherst I., *Canada* **137 B8** 44 8N 76 43W
Amherstburg, *Canada* **128 D3** 42 6N 83 6W
Amiata, Mte., *Italy* **39 F8** 42 54N 11 40 E
Amiens, *France* **23 C9** 49 54N 2 16 E
Amigdhalokefáli, *Greece* **45 J5** 35 23N 23 30 E
Amili, *India* **78 A5** 28 25N 95 52 E
Amindaion, *Greece* **44 D3** 40 42N 21 42 E
Amīrābād, *Iran* **84 C5** 33 20N 46 16 E
Amirante Is., *Seychelles* **109 E4** 6 0 S 53 0 E
Amisk L., *Canada* **131 C8** 54 35N 102 15W
Amistad, Presa de la, *Mexico* **146 B4** 29 24N 101 0W
Amite, *U.S.A.* **139 K9** 30 44N 90 30W
Amizmiz, *Morocco* **98 B3** 31 12N 8 15W
Åmli, *Norway* **15 F2** 58 45N 8 32 E
Amlwch, *U.K.* **16 D3** 53 24N 4 21W
Amm Adam, *Sudan* **95 D4** 16 20N 36 1 E
'Ammān, *Jordan* **91 D4** 31 57N 35 52 E
Ammanford, *U.K.* **17 F3** 51 48N 4 4W
Ammassalik = Angmagssalik, *Greenland* **6 C6** 65 40N 37 20W
Ammerån, *Sweden* **14 A10** 63 9N 16 13 E
Ammerån →, *Sweden* **14 A10** 63 9N 16 13 E
Ammersee, *Germany* **27 G7** 48 0N 11 7 E
Ammerzoden, *Neths.* **20 E6** 51 45N 5 13 E
Amnat Charoen, *Thailand* **76 E5** 15 51N 104 38 E
Amo Jiang →, *China* **68 F3** 23 0N 101 50 E
Āmol, *Iran* **85 B7** 36 23N 52 20 E
Amorebieta, *Spain* **34 B2** 43 13N 2 44W
Amoret, *U.S.A.* **140 F2** 38 15N 94 35W
Amorgós, *Greece* **45 H7** 36 50N 25 57 E
Amory, *U.S.A.* **135 J1** 33 59N 88 29W
Amos, *Canada* **128 C4** 48 35N 78 5W
Åmot, *Buskerud, Norway* **14 E3** 59 54N 9 54 E
Åmot, *Telemark, Norway* **14 E2** 59 34N 8 0 E
Åmotsdal, *Norway* **14 E2** 59 37N 8 26 E
Amour, Djebel, *Algeria* **99 B5** 33 42N 1 37 E
Amoy = Xiamen, *China* **69 E12** 24 25N 118 4 E
Ampang, *Malaysia* **77 L3** 3 8N 101 45 E
Ampanihy, *Madag.* **105 C7** 24 40 S 44 45 E
Ampasindava, Helodranon', *Madag.* **105 A8** 13 40 S 48 15 E

166 Ampasindava, Saikanosy

Ampasindava, Saikanosy, *Madag.* **105 A8** 13 42 S 47 55 E
Ampato, Nevado, *Peru* **156 D3** 15 40 S 71 56W
Ampenan, *Indonesia* **75 D5** 8 35 S 116 13 E
Amper, *Nigeria* **101 D6** 9 25N 9 40 E
Amper ~▸, *Germany* **27 G7** 48 30N 11 57 E
Ampère, *Algeria* **99 A6** 35 44N 5 27 E
Ampezzo, *Italy* **39 B9** 46 25N 12 48 E
Amposta, *Spain* **34 E5** 40 43N 0 34 E
Ampotaka, *Madag.* **105 D7** 25 3 S 44 41 E
Ampoza, *Madag.* **105 C7** 22 20 S 44 44 E
Amqui, *Canada* **129 C6** 48 28N 67 27W
'Amrān, *Yemen* **86 D3** 15 41N 43 55 E
Amravati, *India* **82 D3** 20 55N 77 45 E
Amreli, *India* **80 J4** 21 35N 71 17 E
Amrenene el Kasba, *Algeria* **99 D5** 22 10N 0 30 E
Amriswil, *Switz.* **29 A8** 47 33N 9 18 E
Amritsar, *India* **80 D6** 31 35N 74 57 E
Amroha, *India* **81 E8** 28 53N 78 30 E
Amrum, *Germany* **26 A4** 54 37N 8 21 E
Amsel, *Algeria* **99 D6** 22 47N 5 29 E
Amsterdam, *Neths.* **20 D5** 52 23N 4 54 E
Amsterdam, *U.S.A.* **137 D10** 42 56N 74 11W
Amsterdam, I., *Ind. Oc.* **109 H6** 38 30 S 77 30 E
Amstetten, *Austria* **30 C7** 48 7N 14 51 E
Amudarya ~▸, *Uzbekistan* **56 E6** 43 40N 59 0 E
Amulung, *Phil.* **70 C3** 17 50N 121 43 E
Amundsen Gulf, *Canada* **126 A7** 71 0N 124 0W
Amundsen Sea, *Antarctica* **7 D15** 72 0 S 115 0W
Amuntai, *Indonesia* **75 C5** 2 28 S 115 25 E
Amur, *Somali Rep.* **108 C3** 5 16N 46 30 E
Amur ~▸, *Russia* **57 D15** 52 56N 141 10 E
Amurang, *Indonesia* **72 A2** 1 5N 124 40 E
Amuri Pass, *N.Z.* **119 C7** 42 31 S 172 11 E
Amurrio, *Spain* **34 B1** 43 3N 3 0W
Amursk, *Russia* **57 D14** 50 14N 136 54 E
Amurzet, *Russia* **57 E14** 47 50N 131 5 E
Amusco, *Spain* **36 C6** 42 10N 4 28W
Amutag, *Phil.* **70 E4** 12 23N 123 16 E
Amvrakikós Kólpos, *Greece* **45 F2** 39 0N 20 55 E
Amvrosiyevka, *Ukraine* **53 C8** 47 43N 38 30 E
Amyderya = Amudarya ~▸, *Uzbekistan* **56 E6** 43 40N 59 0 E
Amzeglouf, *Algeria* **99 C5** 26 50N 0 1 E
An, *Burma* **78 F5** 19 48N 94 0 E
An Bien, *Vietnam* **77 H5** 9 45N 105 0 E
An Hoa, *Vietnam* **76 E7** 15 40N 108 5 E
An Khe, *Vietnam* **76 F7** 13 57N 108 39 E
An Nabatīyah at Tahta, *Lebanon* **91 B4** 33 23N 35 27 E
An Nabk, *Si. Arabia* **84 D3** 31 20N 37 20 E
An Nabk, *Syria* **91 A5** 34 2N 36 44 E
An Nabk Abū Qaşr, *Si. Arabia* **84 D3** 30 21N 38 34 E
An Nafūd, *Si. Arabia* **84 D4** 28 15N 41 0 E
An Najaf, *Iraq* **84 C5** 32 3N 44 15 E
An Nāşirīyah, *Iraq* **84 D5** 31 0N 46 15 E
An Nawfaliyah, *Libya* **96 B3** 30 54N 17 58 E
An Nhon, *Vietnam* **76 F7** 13 55N 109 7 E
An Nīl □, *Sudan* **94 D3** 19 30N 33 0 E
An Nīl el Abyad □, *Sudan* **95 E3** 14 0N 32 15 E
An Nīl el Azraq □, *Sudan* **95 E3** 12 30N 34 30 E
An Nimāş, *Si. Arabia* **86 C3** 19 7N 42 8 E
An Nu'ayrīyah, *Si. Arabia* **85 E6** 27 30N 48 30 E
An Nuwaybʻī, W. ~▸, *Si. Arabia* **91 F3** 29 18N 34 57 E
An Thoi, Dao, *Vietnam* **77 H4** 9 58N 104 0 E
An Uaimh, *Ireland* **19 C5** 53 39N 6 40W
Anabar ~▸, *Russia* **57 B12** 73 8N 113 36 E
'Anabtā, *Jordan* **91 C4** 32 19N 35 7 E
Anabuki, *Japan* **62 C6** 34 2N 134 11 E
Anaco, *Venezuela* **153 B5** 9 27N 64 28W
Anaconda, *U.S.A.* **142 C7** 46 8N 112 57W
Anacortes, *U.S.A.* **144 B4** 48 30N 122 37W
Anacuao, Mt., *Phil.* **70 C3** 16 16N 121 53 E
Anadarko, *U.S.A.* **139 H5** 35 4N 98 15W
Anadia, *Brazil* **154 C4** 9 42 S 36 18W
Anadia, *Portugal* **36 E2** 40 26N 8 27W
Anadolu, *Turkey* **88 D4** 39 0N 30 0 E
Anadyr, *Russia* **57 C18** 64 35N 177 20 E
Anadyr ~▸, *Russia* **57 C18** 64 55N 176 5 E
Anadyrskiy Zaliv, *Russia* **57 C19** 64 0N 180 0 E
Anáfi, *Greece* **45 H7** 36 22N 25 48 E
Anafópoulo, *Greece* **45 H7** 36 17N 25 50 E
Anaga, Pta. de, *Canary Is.* **33 F3** 28 34N 16 9W
Anagni, *Italy* **40 A6** 41 44N 13 8 E
'Ānah, *Iraq* **84 C4** 34 25N 42 0 E
Anaheim, *U.S.A.* **145 M9** 33 50N 117 55W
Anahim Lake, *Canada* **130 C3** 52 28N 125 18W
Anáhuac, *Mexico* **146 B4** 27 14N 100 9W
Anai Mudi, Mt., *India* **83 J3** 10 12N 77 4 E
Anaimalai Hills, *India* **83 J3** 10 20N 76 40 E
Anajás, *Brazil* **154 B2** 0 59 S 49 57W
Anajatuba, *Brazil* **154 B3** 3 16 S 44 37W
Anakapalle, *India* **82 F6** 17 42N 83 6 E
Anakie, *Australia* **114 C4** 23 32 S 147 45 E
Anaklia, *Georgia* **53 E9** 42 22N 41 35 E
Analalava, *Madag.* **105 A8** 14 35 S 48 0 E
Análipsis, *Greece* **32 A3** 39 36N 19 55 E
Anamã, *Brazil* **153 D5** 3 35 S 61 22W
Anambar ~▸, *Pakistan* **80 D3** 30 15N 68 50 E
Anambas, Kepulauan, *Indonesia* **74 B3** 3 20N 106 30 E
Anambas Is. = Anambas, Kepulauan, *Indonesia* **74 B3** 3 20N 106 30 E
Anambra □, *Nigeria* **101 D6** 6 20N 7 0 E
Aname, *Vanuatu* **121 K7** 20 8 S 169 47 E
Anamoose, *U.S.A.* **138 B4** 47 53N 100 15W
Anamosa, *U.S.A.* **140 B5** 42 7N 91 17W
Anamur, *Turkey* **88 E5** 36 8N 32 58 E
Anamur Burnu, *Turkey* **88 E5** 36 2N 32 47 E
Anan, *Japan* **62 D6** 33 54N 134 40 E
Anand, *India* **80 H5** 22 32N 72 59 E
Anandpur, *India* **82 D8** 21 16N 86 13 E
Anánes, *Greece* **45 H6** 36 33N 24 9 E
Anantapur, *India* **83 G3** 14 39N 77 42 E
Anantnag, *India* **81 C6** 33 45N 75 10 E
Ananyev, *Ukraine* **52 C3** 47 44N 29 47 E
Anao-aon, *Phil.* **71 G5** 9 47N 125 25 E
Anapa, *Russia* **52 D7** 44 55N 37 25 E
Anapodháris ~▸, *Greece* **32 E7** 34 59N 25 20 E
Anápolis, *Brazil* **155 E2** 16 15 S 48 50W
Anapu ~▸, *Brazil* **153 D7** 1 53 S 50 53W
Anār, *Iran* **85 D7** 30 55N 55 13 E
Anār Darreh, *Afghan.* **79 B1** 32 46N 61 39 E
Anārak, *Iran* **85 C7** 33 25N 53 40 E
Anatolia = Anadolu, *Turkey* **88 D4** 39 0N 30 0 E
Anatone, *U.S.A.* **142 C5** 46 8N 117 8W
Anatsogno, *Madag.* **105 C7** 23 33 S 43 46 E
Añatuya, *Argentina* **158 B3** 28 20 S 62 50W
Anauá ~▸, *Brazil* **153 C5** 0 58N 61 21W
Anaunethad L., *Canada* **131 A8** 60 55N 104 25W
Anavilhanas, Arquipélago das, *Brazil* **153 D5** 2 42 S 60 45W
Anaye, *Niger* **97 E2** 19 15N 12 50 E
Anbyŏn, *N. Korea* **67 E14** 39 1N 127 35 E
Ancash □, *Peru* **156 B2** 9 30 S 77 45W
Ancenis, *France* **22 E5** 47 21N 1 10W
Ancho, Canal, *Chile* **160 D2** 50 0 S 74 20W
Anchor Bay, *U.S.A.* **144 G3** 38 48N 123 34W
Anchorage, *U.S.A.* **126 B5** 61 13N 149 54W
Anci, *China* **66 E9** 39 20N 116 40 E
Ancohuma, Nevada, *Bolivia* **156 D4** 16 0 S 68 50W
Ancón, *Peru* **156 C2** 11 50 S 77 10W
Ancona, *Italy* **39 E10** 43 37N 13 30 E
Ancud, *Chile* **160 B2** 42 0 S 73 50W
Ancud, G. de, *Chile* **160 B2** 42 0 S 73 0W
Anda, *China* **65 B7** 46 24N 125 19 E
Anda, *Phil.* **70 C2** 16 17N 119 57 E
Andacollo, *Argentina* **158 D1** 37 10 S 70 42W
Andacollo, *Chile* **158 C1** 30 5 S 71 10W
Andado, *Australia* **114 D2** 25 25 S 135 15 E
Andahuaylas, *Peru* **156 C3** 13 40 S 73 25W
Andalgalá, *Argentina* **158 B2** 27 40 S 66 30W
Åndalsnes, *Norway* **14 B1** 62 35N 7 43 E
Andalucía □, *Spain* **37 H6** 37 35N 5 0W
Andalusia, *U.S.A.* **135 K2** 31 18N 86 29W
Andalusia □ = Andalucía □, *Spain* **37 H6** 37 35N 5 0W
Andaman Is., *Ind. Oc.* **58 H13** 12 30N 92 30 E
Andara, *Namibia* **104 B3** 18 2 S 21 9 E
Andaraí, *Brazil* **155 D3** 12 48 S 41 20W
Andeer, *Switz.* **29 C8** 46 36N 9 26 E
Andelfingen, *Switz.* **29 A7** 47 36N 8 41 E
Andelot, *France* **23 D12** 48 15N 5 18 E
Andenne, *Belgium* **21 H6** 50 28N 5 5 E
Andéranboukane, *Mali* **101 B5** 15 26N 3 2 E
Anderlecht, *Belgium* **21 G4** 50 50N 4 19 E
Anderlues, *Belgium* **21 H4** 50 25N 4 16 E
Andermatt, *Switz.* **29 C7** 46 38N 8 35 E
Andernach, *Germany* **26 E3** 50 24N 7 25 E
Andernos-les-Bains, *France* **24 D2** 44 44N 1 6W
Anderslöv, *Sweden* **15 J7** 55 26N 13 19 E
Anderson, *Calif., U.S.A.* **142 F2** 40 27N 122 18W
Anderson, *Ind., U.S.A.* **141 D11** 40 10N 85 41W
Anderson, *Mo., U.S.A.* **139 G7** 36 39N 94 27W
Anderson, *S.C., U.S.A.* **135 H4** 34 31N 82 39W
Anderson ~▸, *Canada* **126 B7** 69 42N 129 0W
Anderson, Mt., *S. Africa* **105 D5** 25 5 S 30 42 E
Andes = Andes, Cord. de los, *S. Amer.* **156 C3** 20 0 S 68 0W
Andes, *S. Amer.* **156 C2** 10 0 S 75 53W
Andes, Cord. de los, *S. Amer.* **156 C3** 20 0 S 68 0W
Andfjorden, *Norway* **12 B14** 69 10N 16 20 E
Andhra, L., *India* **82 E1** 18 54N 73 32 E
Andhra Pradesh □, *India* **83 F4** 18 0N 79 0 E
Andijon = Andizhan, *Uzbekistan* **55 C6** 41 10N 72 15 E
Andikíthira, *Greece* **45 J5** 35 52N 23 15 E
Andīmeshk, *Iran* **85 C6** 32 27N 48 21 E
Andímilos, *Greece* **45 H6** 36 47N 24 12 E
Andíparos, *Greece* **45 H7** 37 0N 25 3 E
Andípaxoi, *Greece* **45 E2** 39 9N 20 13 E
Andípsara, *Greece* **45 F7** 38 30N 25 29 E
Andírrion, *Greece* **45 F3** 38 24N 21 46 E
Andizhan, *Uzbekistan* **55 C6** 41 10N 72 15 E
Andkhvoy, *Afghan.* **79 A2** 36 52N 65 8 E
Andoany, *Madag.* **105 A8** 13 25 S 48 16 E
Andoas, *Peru* **152 D2** 2 55 S 76 25W
Andol, *India* **82 F4** 17 51N 78 4 E
Andong, *S. Korea* **67 F15** 36 40N 128 43 E
Andongwei, *China* **67 G10** 35 6N 119 20 E
Andorra ■, *Europe* **34 C6** 42 30N 1 30 E
Andorra La Vella, *Andorra* **34 C6** 42 31N 1 32 E
Andover, *U.K.* **17 F6** 51 13N 1 29W
Andover, *Mass., U.S.A.* **137 D13** 42 40N 71 8W
Andover, *N.Y., U.S.A.* **136 D7** 42 10N 77 48W
Andover, *Ohio, U.S.A.* **136 E4** 41 36N 80 34W
Andradina, *Brazil* **155 F1** 20 54 S 51 23W
Andrahary, Mt., *Madag.* **105 A8** 13 37 S 49 17 E
Andraitx, *Spain* **33 B9** 39 39N 2 25 E
Andramasina, *Madag.* **105 B8** 19 11 S 47 35 E
Andranopasy, *Madag.* **105 C7** 21 17 S 43 44 E
Andreanof Is., *U.S.A.* **126 C2** 52 0N 178 0W
Andreapol, *Russia* **50 C8** 56 40N 32 17 E
Andrespol, *Poland* **47 D6** 51 45N 19 34 E
Andrewilla, *Australia* **115 D2** 26 31 S 139 17 E
Andrews, *S.C., U.S.A.* **135 J6** 33 27N 79 34W
Andrews, *Tex., U.S.A.* **139 J3** 32 19N 102 33W
Andreyevka, *Russia* **54 E2** 52 19N 51 55 E
Ándria, *Italy* **41 A9** 41 13N 16 17 E
Andriba, *Madag.* **105 B8** 17 30 S 46 58 E
Andrijevica, *Montenegro* **42 E4** 42 45N 19 48 E
Andrítsaina, *Greece* **45 G3** 37 29N 21 52 E
Androka, *Madag.* **105 C7** 24 58 S 44 2 E
Andropov = Rybinsk, *Russia* **51 B11** 58 5N 38 50 E
Ándros, *Greece* **45 G6** 37 50N 24 57 E
Andros I., *Bahamas* **148 B4** 24 30N 78 0W
Andros Town, *Bahamas* **148 B4** 24 43N 77 47W
Andrychów, *Poland* **31 B12** 49 51N 19 18 E
Andújar, *Spain* **37 G6** 38 3N 4 5W
Andulo, *Angola* **103 E3** 11 25 S 16 45 E
Anegada, B., *Argentina* **160 B4** 40 20 S 62 20W
Anegada I., *Virgin Is.* **149 C7** 18 45N 64 20W
Anegada Passage, *W. Indies* **149 C7** 18 15N 63 45W
Aného, *Togo* **101 D5** 6 12N 1 34 E
Aneityum, *Vanuatu* **121 K7** 20 12 S 169 45 E
Añelo, *Argentina* **160 A3** 38 20 S 68 45W
Anergane, *Morocco* **98 B3** 31 4N 7 14W
Aneto, Pico de, *Spain* **34 C5** 42 37N 0 40 E
Añez, *Bolivia* **157 D5** 15 40 S 63 10W
Anfu, *China* **69 D10** 27 21N 114 40 E
Ang Thong, *Thailand* **76 E3** 14 35N 100 31 E
Angadanan, *Phil.* **70 C3** 16 45N 121 45 E
Angamos, Punta, *Chile* **158 A1** 23 1 S 70 32W
Angara ~▸, *Russia* **57 D10** 58 5N 94 20 E
Angarab, *Ethiopia* **95 E4** 13 11N 37 7 E
Angarsk, *Russia* **57 D11** 52 30N 104 0 E
Angas Downs, *Australia* **113 E5** 25 2 S 132 14 E
Angas Hills, *Australia* **112 D4** 23 0 S 127 50 E
Angaston, *Australia* **116 C3** 34 30 S 139 8 E
Angat, *Phil.* **70 D3** 14 56N 121 2 E
Ånge, *Sweden* **14 B9** 62 31N 15 35 E
Ángel de la Guarda, I., *Mexico* **146 B2** 29 30N 113 30W
Angel Falls, *Venezuela* **153 B5** 5 57N 62 30W
Angeles, *Phil.* **70 D3** 15 9N 120 33 E
Ängelholm, *Sweden* **15 H6** 56 15N 12 58 E
Angellala, *Australia* **115 D4** 26 24 S 146 54 E
Angels Camp, *U.S.A.* **144 G6** 38 4N 120 32W
Anger ~▸, *Ethiopia* **95 F4** 9 37N 36 6 E
Angereb ~▸, *Ethiopia* **95 E4** 13 45N 36 40 E
Ångermanälven ~▸, *Sweden* **14 B12** 62 40N 18 0 E
Angermünde, *Germany* **26 B10** 53 1N 14 0 E
Angers, *Canada* **137 A9** 45 31N 75 29W
Angers, *France* **22 E6** 47 30N 0 35W
Angerville, *France* **23 D8** 48 19N 2 0 E
Ängesån ~▸, *Sweden* **12 C17** 66 50N 22 15 E
Anghiari, *Italy* **39 E9** 43 32N 12 3 E
Angical, *Brazil* **155 D3** 12 0 S 44 42W
Angikuni L., *Canada* **131 A9** 62 0N 100 0W
Angkor, *Cambodia* **76 F4** 13 22N 103 50 E
Anglem Mt., *N.Z.* **119 G2** 46 45 S 167 53 E
Anglés, *Spain* **34 D7** 41 57N 2 38 E
Anglesey, *U.K.* **16 D3** 53 17N 4 20W
Anglet, *France* **24 E2** 43 29N 1 31W
Angleton, *U.S.A.* **139 L7** 29 10N 95 26W
Angleur, *Belgium* **21 G7** 50 36N 5 35 E
Anglin ~▸, *France* **24 B4** 46 42N 0 52 E
Anglisidhes, *Cyprus* **32 E12** 34 51N 33 27 E
Anglure, *France* **23 D10** 48 35N 3 50 E
Angmagssalik, *Greenland* **6 C6** 65 40N 37 20W
Ango, *Zaïre* **106 B2** 4 10N 26 5 E
Angoche, *Mozam.* **107 F4** 16 8 S 39 55 E
Angoche, I., *Mozam.* **107 F4** 16 20 S 39 50 E
Angol, *Chile* **158 D1** 37 56 S 72 45W
Angola, *Ind., U.S.A.* **141 C12** 41 38N 85 0W
Angola, *N.Y., U.S.A.* **136 D5** 42 38N 79 2W
Angola ■, *Africa* **103 E3** 12 0 S 18 0 E
Angoon, *U.S.A.* **130 B2** 57 30N 134 35W
Angoram, *Papua N. G.* **120 C3** 4 4 S 144 4 E
Angoulême, *France* **24 C4** 45 39N 0 10 E
Angoumois, *France* **24 C4** 45 50N 0 25 E
Angra dos Reis, *Brazil* **159 A7** 23 0 S 44 10W
Angren, *Uzbekistan* **55 C5** 41 1N 70 12 E
Angtassom, *Cambodia* **77 G5** 11 1N 104 41 E
Angu, *Zaïre* **106 B1** 3 25N 24 28 E
Anguang, *China* **67 B12** 45 15N 123 45 E
Anguilla ■, *W. Indies* **149 C7** 18 14N 63 5W
Anguo, *China* **66 E8** 38 28N 115 15 E
Angurugu, *Australia* **114 A2** 14 0 S 136 25 E
Angus, Braes of, *U.K.* **18 E5** 56 51N 3 10W
Anhanduí ~▸, *Brazil* **159 A5** 21 46 S 52 9W
Anhée, *Belgium* **21 H5** 50 18N 4 53 E
Anholt, *Denmark* **15 H5** 56 42N 11 33 E
Anhua, *China* **69 C8** 28 23N 111 12 E
Anhui □, *China* **69 B11** 32 0N 117 0 E
Anhwei □ = Anhui □, *China* **69 B11** 32 0N 117 0 E
Anichab, *Namibia* **104 C1** 21 0 S 14 46 E
Anicuns, *Brazil* **155 E2** 16 28 S 49 58W
Ánidhros, *Greece* **45 H7** 36 38N 25 43 E
Anie, *Togo* **101 D5** 7 42N 1 8 E
Animas, *U.S.A.* **143 L9** 31 57N 108 48W
Ånimskog, *Sweden* **15 F6** 58 53N 12 35 E
Anina, *Romania* **42 B6** 45 6N 21 51 E
Anini-y, *Phil.* **71 F3** 10 25N 121 55 E
Anita, *U.S.A.* **140 C2** 41 27N 94 46W
Anivorano, *Madag.* **105 B8** 18 44 S 48 58 E
Aniwa, *Vanuatu* **121 J7** 19 17 S 169 35 E
Anjangaon, *India* **82 D3** 21 10N 77 20 E
Anjar, *India* **80 H4** 23 6N 70 10 E
Anjidiv I., *India* **83 G2** 14 40N 74 10 E
Anjō, *Japan* **63 C9** 34 57N 137 5 E
Anjou, *France* **22 E6** 47 20N 0 15W
Anjozorobe, *Madag.* **105 B8** 18 22 S 47 52 E
Anju, *N. Korea* **67 E13** 39 36N 125 40 E
Anka, *Nigeria* **101 C6** 12 13N 5 58 E
Ankaboa, Tanjona, *Madag.* **105 C7** 21 58 S 43 20 E
Ankang, *China* **66 H5** 32 40N 109 1 E
Ankara, *Turkey* **88 D5** 39 57N 32 54 E
Ankara □, *Turkey* **88 D5** 39 55N 32 50 E
Ankaramena, *Madag.* **105 C8** 21 57 S 46 39 E
Ankazoabo, *Madag.* **105 C7** 22 18 S 44 31 E
Ankazobe, *Madag.* **105 B8** 18 20 S 47 10 E
Ankeny, *U.S.A.* **140 C3** 41 44N 93 36W
Ankisabe, *Madag.* **105 B8** 19 17 S 46 29 E
Anklam, *Germany* **26 B9** 53 48N 13 40 E
Ankleshwar, *India* **82 D1** 21 38N 73 3 E
Ankober, *Ethiopia* **95 F4** 9 35N 39 40 E
Ankoro, *Zaïre* **106 D2** 6 45 S 26 55 E
Anlong, *China* **68 E5** 25 2N 105 27 E
Anlu, *China* **69 B9** 31 15N 113 45 E
Anmyŏn-do, *S. Korea* **67 F14** 36 25N 126 25 E
Ånn, *Sweden* **14 A6** 63 19N 12 34 E
Ann, C., *U.S.A.* **137 D14** 42 38N 70 35W
Ann Arbor, *U.S.A.* **141 B13** 42 17N 83 45W
Anna, *Russia* **51 F12** 51 28N 40 23 E
Anna, *Ill., U.S.A.* **139 G10** 37 28N 89 15W
Anna, *Ohio, U.S.A.* **141 D12** 40 24N 84 11W
Anna Plains, *Australia* **112 C3** 19 17 S 121 37 E
Anna Regina, *Guyana* **153 B6** 7 10N 58 30W
Annaba, *Algeria* **99 A6** 36 50N 7 46 E
Annaberg-Buchholz, *Germany* **26 E8** 50 34N 12 58 E
Annaka, *Japan* **63 A10** 36 19N 138 54 E
Annalee ~▸, *Ireland* **19 B4** 54 3N 7 15W
Annam = Trung-Phan, *Vietnam* **76 E7** 16 0N 108 0 E
Annamitique, Chaîne, *Asia* **76 D6** 17 0N 106 0 E
Annan, *U.K.* **18 G5** 54 57N 3 17W
Annan ~▸, *U.K.* **18 G5** 54 58N 3 18W
Annanberg, *Papua N. G.* **120 C3** 4 52 S 144 42 E
Annapolis, *U.S.A.* **134 F7** 38 59N 76 30W
Annapolis Royal, *Canada* **129 D6** 44 44N 65 32W
Annapurna, *Nepal* **81 E10** 28 34N 83 50 E
Annean, L., *Australia* **113 E2** 26 54 S 118 14 E
Anneberg, *Sweden* **15 G6** 57 32N 12 6 E
Annecy, *France* **25 C10** 45 55N 6 8 E
Annecy, L. d', *France* **25 C10** 45 52N 6 10 E
Annemasse, *France* **25 B10** 46 12N 6 16 E
Anning, *China* **68 E4** 24 55N 102 26 E
Anningie, *Australia* **112 D5** 21 50 S 133 7 E
Anniston, *U.S.A.* **135 J3** 33 39N 85 50W
Annobón, *Atl. Oc.* **93 G4** 1 25 S 5 36 E
Annonay, *France* **25 C8** 45 15N 4 40 E
Annot, *France* **25 E10** 43 58N 6 38 E
Annotto Bay, *Jamaica* **148 C4** 18 17N 76 45W
Annuello, *Australia* **116 C5** 34 53 S 142 55 E
Annville, *U.S.A.* **137 F8** 40 20N 76 31W
Annweiler, *Germany* **27 F3** 49 12N 7 58 E
Áno Arkhánai, *Greece* **45 J7** 35 16N 25 11 E
Áno Porróia, *Greece* **44 C5** 41 17N 23 2 E
Áno Viánnos, *Greece* **32 D7** 35 2N 25 21 E
Anoano, *Solomon Is.* **121 M11** 8 59 S 160 46 E
Anoka, *U.S.A.* **138 C8** 45 12N 93 23W
Anorotsangana, *Madag.* **105 A8** 13 56 S 47 55 E
Anóyia, *Greece* **32 D6** 35 16N 24 52 E
Anping, *Hebei, China* **66 E8** 38 15N 115 30 E
Anping, *Liaoning, China* **67 D12** 41 5N 123 30 E
Anpu Gang, *China* **68 G7** 21 25N 109 50 E
Anqing, *China* **69 B11** 30 30N 117 3 E
Anqiu, *China* **67 F10** 36 25N 119 10 E
Anren, *China* **69 D9** 26 43N 113 18 E
Ans, *Belgium* **21 G7** 50 39N 5 32 E
Ansai, *China* **66 F5** 36 50N 109 20 E
Ansbach, *Germany* **27 F6** 49 17N 10 34 E
Anseba ~▸, *Eritrea* **95 D4** 16 0N 38 30 E
Anserma, *Colombia* **152 B2** 5 13N 75 48W
Anseroeul, *Belgium* **21 G3** 50 43N 3 32 E
Anshan, *China* **65 B7** 41 3N 122 58 E
Anshan, *Liaoning, China* **67 D12** 41 5N 122 58 E
Anshun, *China* **68 D5** 26 18N 105 57 E
Ansião, *Portugal* **36 F2** 39 56N 8 27W
Ansirabe, *Madag.* **105 B8** 19 55 S 47 2 E
Ansley, *U.S.A.* **138 E5** 41 18N 99 23W
Ansó, *Spain* **34 C4** 42 51N 0 48W
Anson, *U.S.A.* **139 J5** 32 45N 99 54W
Anson B., *Australia* **112 B5** 13 20 S 130 6 E
Ansongo, *Mali* **101 B5** 15 25N 0 35 E
Ansonia, *Conn., U.S.A.* **137 E11** 41 21N 73 5W
Ansonia, *Ohio, U.S.A.* **141 D12** 40 13N 84 38W
Anstruther, *U.K.* **18 E6** 56 14N 2 40W
Ansudu, *Indonesia* **73 B5** 2 11 S 139 22 E
Antabamba, *Peru* **156 C3** 14 40 S 73 0W
Antakya, *Turkey* **88 E7** 36 14N 36 10 E
Antalaha, *Madag.* **105 A9** 14 57 S 50 20 E
Antalya, *Turkey* **88 E4** 36 52N 30 45 E
Antalya □, *Turkey* **88 E4** 36 55N 30 45 E
Antalya Körfezi, *Turkey* **88 E4** 36 15N 31 30 E
Antananarivo, *Madag.* **105 B8** 18 55 S 47 31 E
Antananarivo □, *Madag.* **105 B8** 19 0 S 47 0 E
Antanimbaribe, *Madag.* **105 C7** 21 30 S 44 48 E
Antarctic Pen., *Antarctica* **7 C18** 67 0 S 60 0W
Antarctica **7 E3** 90 0 S 0 0 E
Antelope, *Zimbabwe* **107 G2** 21 2 S 28 31 E
Antenor Navarro, *Brazil* **154 C4** 6 44 S 38 27W
Antequera, *Paraguay* **158 A4** 24 8 S 57 7W
Antequera, *Spain* **37 H6** 37 5N 4 33W
Antero, Mt., *U.S.A.* **143 G10** 38 41N 106 15W
Anthemoús, *Greece* **44 D5** 40 31N 23 15 E
Anthony, *Kans., U.S.A.* **139 G5** 37 9N 98 2W
Anthony, *N. Mex., U.S.A.* **143 K10** 32 0N 106 36W
Anthony Lagoon, *Australia* **114 B2** 18 0 S 135 30 E
Anti Atlas, *Morocco* **98 C2** 30 0N 8 30W
Anti-Lebanon = Ash Sharqi, Al Jabal, *Lebanon* **91 B5** 33 40N 36 10 E
Antibes, *France* **25 E11** 43 34N 7 6 E
Antibes, C. d', *France* **25 E11** 43 31N 7 7 E
Anticosti, I. d', *Canada* **129 C7** 49 30N 63 0W
Antifer, C. d', *France* **22 C7** 49 41N 0 10 E
Antigo, *U.S.A.* **138 C10** 45 9N 89 9W
Antigonish, *Canada* **129 C7** 45 38N 61 58W
Antigua, *Canary Is.* **33 F5** 28 24N 14 1W
Antigua, *Guatemala* **148 D1** 14 34N 90 41W
Antigua, *W. Indies* **149 C7** 17 0N 61 50W
Antigua & Barbuda ■, *W. Indies* **149 C7** 17 20N 61 48W
Antilla, *Cuba* **148 B4** 20 40N 75 50W
Antimony, *U.S.A.* **143 G8** 38 7N 112 0W
Antioch, *U.S.A.* **144 G5** 38 1N 121 48W
Antioche, Pertuis d', *France* **24 B2** 46 6N 1 20W
Antioquia, *Colombia* **152 B2** 6 40N 75 55W
Antioquia □, *Colombia* **152 B2** 7 0N 75 30W
Antipodes Is., *Pac. Oc.* **122 M9** 49 45 S 178 40 E
Antique □, *Phil.* **71 F4** 11 10N 122 5 E
Antler, *U.S.A.* **138 A4** 48 59N 101 17W
Antler ~▸, *Canada* **131 D8** 49 8N 101 0W
Antlers, *U.S.A.* **139 H7** 34 14N 95 37W
Antofagasta, *Chile* **158 A1** 23 50 S 70 30W
Antofagasta □, *Chile* **158 A2** 24 0 S 69 0W
Antofagasta de la Sierra, *Argentina* **158 B2** 26 5 S 67 20W
Antofalla, *Argentina* **158 B2** 25 30 S 68 5W
Antofalla, Salar de, *Argentina* **158 B2** 25 40 S 67 45W
Antoing, *Belgium* **21 G2** 50 34N 3 27 E
Anton, *U.S.A.* **139 J3** 33 49N 102 10W
Anton Chico, *U.S.A.* **143 J11** 35 12N 105 9W
Antongila, Helodrano, *Madag.* **105 B8** 15 30 S 49 50 E
Antonibé, *Madag.* **105 B8** 15 7 S 47 24 E
Antonibé, Presqu'île d', *Madag.* **105 A8** 14 55 S 47 20 E
Antonina, *Brazil* **159 B6** 25 26 S 48 42W
Antonito, *U.S.A.* **143 H10** 37 5N 106 0W
Antonovo, *Kazakhstan* **53 B14** 49 25N 51 42 E
Antrain, *France* **22 D5** 48 28N 1 30W
Antrim, *U.K.* **19 B5** 54 43N 6 13W
Antrim □, *U.K.* **19 B5** 54 55N 6 20W
Antrim, Mts. of, *U.K.* **19 B5** 54 57N 6 8W
Antrim Plateau, *Australia* **112 C4** 18 8 S 128 20 E
Antrodoco, *Italy* **39 F10** 42 25N 13 4 E
Antropovo, *Russia* **51 B13** 58 26N 42 51 E

Azärbayjan 169


Asyût, *Egypt* **94 B3** 27 11N 31 4 E
Asyûti, Wadi ➝, *Egypt* **94 B3** 27 11N 31 16 E
Aszód, *Hungary* **31 D12** 47 39N 19 28 E
At Ṭafīlah, *Jordan* **91 E4** 30 45N 35 30 E
At Ta'if, *Si. Arabia* **86 B3** 21 5N 40 27 E
At Tāj, *Libya* **96 D4** 24 13N 23 18 E
At Tamīmī, *Libya* **96 B4** 32 20N 23 4 E
Aṭ Ṭirāq, *Si. Arabia* **84 E5** 27 19N 44 33 E
At Turbah, *Yemen* **86 D4** 13 13N 44 7 E
At Turbah, *Yemen* **86 D3** 12 40N 43 30 E
Aṭ Ṭuwayrifah, *Si. Arabia* **87 B5** 21 30N 49 35 E
Atacama □, *Chile* **158 B2** 27 30 S 70 0W
Atacama, Desierto de, *Chile* **158 A2** 24 0 S 69 20W
Atacama, Salar de, *Chile* **158 A2** 23 30 S 68 20W
Ataco, *Colombia* **152 C2** 3 35N 75 23W
Atakor, *Algeria* **99 D6** 23 27N 5 31 E
Atakpamé, *Togo* **101 D5** 7 31N 1 13 E
Atalándi, *Greece* **45 F4** 38 39N 22 58 E
Atalaya, *Peru* **156 C3** 10 45 S 73 50W
Atalaya de Femes, *Canary Is.* **33 F6** 28 56N 13 47W
Ataléia, *Brazil* **155 E3** 18 3 S 41 6W
Atambua, *Indonesia* **72 C2** 9 7 S 124 54 E
Atami, *Japan* **63 B11** 35 5N 139 4 E
Atankawng, *Burma* **78 C6** 25 50N 97 47 E
Atapupu, *Indonesia* **72 C2** 9 0 S 124 51 E
Atâr, *Mauritania* **98 D2** 20 30N 13 5W
Atara, *Russia* **57 C13** 63 10N 129 10 E
Ataram, Erg n-, *Algeria* **99 D5** 23 57N 2 0 E
Atarfe, *Spain* **37 H7** 37 13N 3 40W
Atascadero, *Calif., U.S.A.* **143 J3** 35 32N 120 44W
Atascadero, *Calif., U.S.A.* **144 K6** 35 29N 120 40W
Atasu, *Kazakhstan* **56 E8** 48 30N 71 0 E
Atauro, *Indonesia* **72 C3** 8 10 S 125 30 E
Atbara, *Sudan* **94 D3** 17 42N 33 59 E
'Atbara ➝, *Sudan* **94 D3** 17 40N 33 56 E
Atbasar, *Kazakhstan* **56 D7** 51 48N 68 20 E
Atbashi, *Kirghizia* **55 C7** 41 10N 75 48 E
Atbashi, Khrebet, *Kirghizia* **55 C7** 40 50N 75 30 E
Atchafalaya B., *U.S.A.* **139 L9** 29 25N 91 25W
Atchison, *U.S.A.* **138 F7** 39 34N 95 7W
Atebubu, *Ghana* **101 D4** 7 47N 1 0W
Ateca, *Spain* **34 D3** 41 20N 1 49W
Aterno ➝, *Italy* **39 F10** 42 11N 13 51 E
Atesine, Alpi, *Italy* **38 B8** 46 55N 11 30 E
Atessa, *Italy* **39 F11** 42 5N 14 27 E
Ath, *Belgium* **21 G3** 50 38N 3 47 E
Athabasca, *Canada* **130 C6** 54 45N 113 20W
Athabasca ➝, *Canada* **131 B6** 58 40N 110 50W
Athabasca, L., *Canada* **131 B7** 59 15N 109 15W
Athboy, *Ireland* **19 C5** 53 37N 6 55W
Athenry, *Ireland* **19 C3** 53 18N 8 45W
Athens = Athínai, *Greece* **45 G5** 37 58N 23 46 E
Athens, *Ala., U.S.A.* **135 H2** 34 48N 86 58W
Athens, *Ga., U.S.A.* **135 J4** 33 57N 83 23W
Athens, *N.Y., U.S.A.* **137 D11** 42 16N 73 49W
Athens, *Ohio, U.S.A.* **134 F4** 39 20N 82 6W
Athens, *Pa., U.S.A.* **137 E8** 41 57N 76 31W
Athens, *Tenn., U.S.A.* **135 H3** 35 27N 84 36W
Athens, *Tex., U.S.A.* **139 J7** 32 12N 95 51W
Atherley, *Canada* **136 B5** 44 37N 79 20W
Atherton, *Australia* **114 B4** 17 17 S 145 30 E
Athiéme, *Benin* **101 D5** 6 37N 1 40 E
Athienou, *Cyprus* **32 D12** 35 3N 33 32 E
Athínai, *Greece* **45 G5** 37 58N 23 46 E
Athlone, *Ireland* **19 C4** 53 26N 7 57W
Athna, *Cyprus* **32 D12** 35 3N 33 47 E
Athni, *India* **82 F2** 16 44N 75 6 E
Athol, *N.Z.* **119 F3** 45 30 S 168 35 E
Atholl, Forest of, *U.K.* **18 E5** 56 51N 3 50W
Atholville, *Canada* **129 C6** 47 59N 66 43W
Áthos, *Greece* **44 D6** 40 9N 24 22 E
Athus, *Belgium* **21 J7** 49 34N 5 50 E
Athy, *Ireland* **19 D5** 53 0N 7 0W
Ati, *Chad* **97 F3** 13 13N 18 20 E
Ati, *Sudan* **95 E2** 13 5N 29 2 E
Atiak, *Uganda* **106 B3** 3 12N 32 2 E
Atiamuri, *N.Z.* **118 E5** 38 24 S 176 5 E
Atico, *Peru* **156 D3** 16 14 S 73 40W
Atienza, *Spain* **34 D2** 41 12N 2 52W
Atikokan, *Canada* **128 C1** 48 45N 91 37W
Atikonak L., *Canada* **129 B7** 52 40N 64 32W
Atimonan, *Phil.* **70 D3** 14 0N 121 55 E
'Ātinah, W. ➝, *Oman* **87 C6** 18 23N 53 28 E
Atirampattinam, *India* **83 J4** 10 28N 79 20 E
Atka, *Russia* **57 C16** 60 50N 151 48 E
Atkarsk, *Russia* **51 F14** 51 55N 45 2 E
Atkinson, *Ill., U.S.A.* **140 C6** 41 25N 90 1W
Atkinson, *Nebr., U.S.A.* **138 D5** 42 32N 98 59W
Atlanta, *Ga., U.S.A.* **135 J3** 33 45N 84 23W
Atlanta, *Ill., U.S.A.* **140 D7** 40 16N 89 14W
Atlanta, *Mo., U.S.A.* **140 E4** 39 54N 92 29W
Atlanta, *Tex., U.S.A.* **139 J7** 33 7N 94 10W
Atlantic, *U.S.A.* **138 E7** 41 24N 95 1W
Atlantic City, *U.S.A.* **134 F8** 39 21N 74 27W
Atlantic Ocean **8 H7** 0 0 20 0W
Atlántico □, *Colombia* **152 A2** 10 45N 75 0W
Atlas Mts. = Haut Atlas, *Morocco* **98 B3** 32 30N 5 0W
Atlin, *Canada* **130 B2** 59 31N 133 41W
Atlin, L., *Canada* **130 B2** 59 26N 133 45W
Atmakur, *India* **83 G4** 14 37N 79 40 E
Atmore, *U.S.A.* **135 K2** 31 2N 87 29W
Atō, *Japan* **62 C3** 34 25N 131 40 E
Atok, *Phil.* **70 C3** 16 35N 120 41 E
Atoka, *U.S.A.* **139 H6** 34 23N 96 8W
Átokos, *Greece* **45 F2** 38 28N 20 49 E
Atolia, *U.S.A.* **145 K9** 35 19N 117 37W
Atouguia, *Portugal* **37 F1** 39 20N 9 20W
Atoyac ➝, *Mexico* **147 D5** 16 30N 97 31W
Atrak ➝, *Iran* **85 B8** 37 50N 57 0 E
Ätran, *Sweden* **15 G6** 57 7N 12 57 E
Atrato ➝, *Colombia* **152 B2** 8 17N 76 58W
Atrauli, *India* **80 E8** 28 2N 78 20 E
Atri, *Italy* **39 F10** 42 35N 14 0 E
Atsbi, *Ethiopia* **95 E4** 13 52N 39 50 E
Atsoum, Mts., *Cameroon* **101 D7** 6 41N 12 57 E
Atsugi, *Japan* **63 B11** 35 25N 139 21 E
Atsumi, *Japan* **63 C9** 34 35N 137 4 E
Atsumi-Wan, *Japan* **63 C9** 34 44N 137 13 E
Atsuta, *Japan* **60 C10** 43 24N 141 26 E
Attalla, *U.S.A.* **135 H2** 34 1N 86 6W
Attáviros, *Greece* **32 C9** 36 12N 27 50 E
Attawapiskat, *Canada* **128 B3** 52 56N 82 24W
Attawapiskat ➝, *Canada* **128 B3** 52 57N 82 18W
Attawapiskat, L., *Canada* **128 B2** 52 18N 87 54W
Attendorn, *Germany* **26 D3** 51 8N 7 54 E
Attersee, *Austria* **30 D6** 47 55N 13 32 E
Attert, *Belgium* **21 J7** 49 45N 5 47 E
Attica, *U.S.A.* **141 D9** 40 18N 87 15W
Attichy, *France* **23 C10** 49 25N 3 3 E
Attigny, *France* **23 C11** 49 28N 4 35 E
Attikamagen L., *Canada* **129 A6** 55 0N 66 30W
Attikí □, *Greece* **45 F5** 38 10N 23 40 E
Attleboro, *U.S.A.* **137 E13** 41 57N 71 17W
Attock, *Pakistan* **80 C5** 33 52N 72 20 E
Attopeu, *Laos* **76 E6** 14 48N 106 50 E
Attunga, *Australia* **117 A9** 30 55 S 150 50 E
Attur, *India* **83 J4** 11 35N 78 30 E
'Atūd, *Yemen* **87 D5** 14 53N 48 10 E
Atuel ➝, *Argentina* **158 D2** 36 17 S 66 50W
Atvacık, *Turkey* **88 D2** 39 36N 26 24 E
Åtvidaberg, *Sweden* **15 F10** 58 12N 16 0 E
Atwater, *U.S.A.* **144 H6** 37 21N 120 37W
Atwood, *Canada* **136 C3** 43 40N 81 1W
Atwood, *U.S.A.* **138 F4** 39 48N 101 3W
Atyrau, *Kazakhstan* **53 C14** 47 5N 52 0 E
Au Sable ➝, *U.S.A.* **134 C4** 44 25N 83 20W
Au Sable Pt., *U.S.A.* **128 C2** 46 40N 86 10W
Aubagne, *France* **25 E9** 43 17N 5 37 E
Aubange, *Belgium* **21 J7** 49 34N 5 48 E
Aubarca, C., *Spain* **33 B7** 39 4N 1 22 E
Aube □, *France* **23 D11** 48 15N 4 10 E
Aube ➝, *France* **23 D10** 48 34N 3 43 E
Aubel, *Belgium* **21 G7** 50 42N 5 51 E
Aubenas, *France* **25 D8** 44 37N 4 24 E
Aubenton, *France* **23 C11** 49 50N 4 12 E
Auberry, *U.S.A.* **144 H7** 37 7N 119 29W
Aubigny-sur-Nère, *France* **23 E9** 47 30N 2 24 E
Aubin, *France* **24 D6** 44 33N 2 15 E
Aubrac, Mts. d', *France* **24 D7** 44 40N 3 2 E
Auburn, *Ala., U.S.A.* **135 J3** 32 36N 85 29W
Auburn, *Calif., U.S.A.* **144 G5** 38 54N 121 4W
Auburn, *Ill., U.S.A.* **140 E7** 39 36N 89 45W
Auburn, *Ind., U.S.A.* **141 C11** 41 22N 85 4W
Auburn, *N.Y., U.S.A.* **137 D8** 42 56N 76 34W
Auburn, *Nebr., U.S.A.* **138 E7** 40 23N 95 51W
Auburn, *Wash., U.S.A.* **144 C4** 47 18N 122 14W
Auburn Ra., *Australia* **115 D5** 25 15 S 150 30 E
Auburndale, *U.S.A.* **135 L5** 28 4N 81 48W
Aubusson, *France* **24 C6** 45 57N 2 11 E
Auch, *France* **24 E4** 43 39N 0 36 E
Auchel, *France* **23 B9** 50 30N 2 29 E
Auchi, *Nigeria* **101 D6** 7 6N 6 13 E
Auckland, *N.Z.* **118 C3** 36 52 S 174 46 E
Auckland □, *N.Z.* **118 E6** 36 50 S 175 0 E
Auckland Is., *Pac. Oc.* **122 N8** 50 40 S 166 5 E
Aude □, *France* **24 E6** 43 8N 2 28 E
Aude ➝, *France* **24 E7** 43 13N 3 14 E
Audegle, *Somali Rep.* **108 D2** 1 59N 44 50 E
Auden, *Canada* **128 B2** 50 14N 87 53W
Auderghem, *Belgium* **21 G4** 50 49N 4 26 E
Auderville, *France* **22 C5** 49 43N 1 57W
Audierne, *France* **22 D2** 48 1N 4 34W
Audincourt, *France* **23 E13** 47 30N 6 50 E
Audo, *Ethiopia* **95 F5** 6 20N 41 50 E
Audubon, *U.S.A.* **140 C2** 41 43N 94 56W
Aue, *Germany* **26 E8** 50 34N 12 43 E
Auerbach, *Germany* **26 E8** 50 30N 12 25 E
Aueti Paraná ➝, *Brazil* **152 D4** 1 51 S 65 37W
Aufist, *W. Sahara* **98 C2** 25 44N 14 39W
Augathella, *Australia* **115 D4** 25 48 S 146 35 E
Augrabies Falls, *S. Africa* **104 D3** 28 35 S 20 20 E
Augsburg, *Germany* **27 G6** 48 22N 10 54 E
Augusta, *Italy* **41 E8** 37 14N 15 12 E
Augusta, *Ark., U.S.A.* **139 H9** 35 17N 91 22W
Augusta, *Ga., U.S.A.* **135 J5** 33 28N 81 58W
Augusta, *Ill., U.S.A.* **140 D6** 40 14N 90 57W
Augusta, *Kans., U.S.A.* **139 G6** 37 41N 96 59W
Augusta, *Ky., U.S.A.* **141 F12** 38 47N 84 0W
Augusta, *Maine, U.S.A.* **129 D6** 44 19N 69 47W
Augusta, *Mont., U.S.A.* **142 C7** 47 30N 112 24W
Augusta, *Wis., U.S.A.* **138 C9** 44 41N 91 7W
Augustenborg, *Denmark* **15 K3** 54 57N 9 53 E
Augustów, *Poland* **47 B9** 53 51N 23 0 E
Augustus, Mt., *Australia* **112 D2** 24 20 S 116 50 E
Augustus Downs, *Australia* **114 B2** 18 35 S 139 55 E
Augustus I., *Australia* **112 C3** 15 20 S 124 30 E
Aukan, *Eritrea* **95 D5** 15 29N 40 50 E
Auki, *Solomon Is.* **121 M11** 8 45 S 160 42 E
Aukum, *U.S.A.* **144 G6** 38 34N 120 43W
Auld, L., *Australia* **112 D3** 22 25 S 123 50 E
Aulla, *Italy* **38 D6** 44 12N 10 0 E
Aulnay, *France* **24 B3** 46 2N 0 22W
Aulne ➝, *France* **22 D2** 48 17N 4 16W
Aulnoye-Aymeries, *France* **23 B10** 50 12N 3 50 E
Ault, *France* **22 B8** 50 8N 1 26 E
Ault, *U.S.A.* **138 E2** 40 35N 104 44W
Aulus-les-Bains, *France* **24 F5** 42 49N 1 19 E
Aumale, *France* **23 C8** 49 46N 1 46 E
Aumont-Aubrac, *France* **24 D7** 44 43N 3 17 E
Auna, *Nigeria* **101 C5** 10 9N 4 42 E
Aundh, *India* **82 F2** 17 33N 74 23 E
Aunis, *France* **24 B3** 46 5N 0 50W
Auponhia, *Indonesia* **72 B3** 1 58 S 125 27 E
Aups, *France* **25 E10** 43 37N 6 15 E
Aur, P., *Malaysia* **77 L5** 2 35N 104 10 E
Aura, *Burma* **78 B6** 26 59N 97 57 E
Auraiya, *India* **81 F8** 26 28N 79 33 E
Aurangabad, *Bihar, India* **81 G11** 24 45N 84 18 E
Aurangabad, *Maharashtra, India* **82 E2** 19 50N 75 23 E
Auray, *France* **22 E4** 47 40N 2 59W
Aurès, *Algeria* **99 A6** 35 8N 6 30 E
Aurich, *Germany* **26 B3** 53 28N 7 30 E
Aurilândia, *Brazil* **155 E1** 16 44 S 50 28W
Aurillac, *France* **24 D6** 44 55N 2 26 E
Auronza, *Italy* **39 B9** 46 33N 12 27 E
Aurora = Maewo, *Vanuatu* **121 E6** 15 10 S 168 10 E
Aurora, *Canada* **136 C5** 44 0N 79 28W
Aurora, *Isabela, Phil.* **70 C3** 16 59N 121 38 E
Aurora, *Quezon, Phil.* **70 E4** 13 21N 122 31 E
Aurora, *S. Africa* **104 E2** 32 40 S 18 29 E
Aurora, *Colo., U.S.A.* **138 F2** 39 44N 104 52W
Aurora, *Ill., U.S.A.* **141 C8** 41 45N 88 19W
Aurora, *Mo., U.S.A.* **139 G8** 36 58N 93 43W
Aurora, *Nebr., U.S.A.* **138 E6** 40 52N 98 0W
Aurora, *Ohio, U.S.A.* **136 E3** 41 21N 81 20W
Aursmoen, *Norway* **14 E5** 59 55N 11 26 E
Aurukun Mission, *Australia* **114 A3** 13 20 S 141 45 E
Aus, *Namibia* **104 D2** 26 35 S 16 12 E
Auschwitz = Oświecim, *Poland* **31 A12** 50 2N 19 11 E
Aust-Agder fylke □, *Norway* **13 G9** 58 55N 7 40 E
Austerlitz = Slavkov, *Czech.* **31 B9** 49 10N 16 52 E
Austin, *Ind., U.S.A.* **141 F11** 38 45N 85 49W
Austin, *Minn., U.S.A.* **138 D8** 43 40N 92 58W
Austin, *Nev., U.S.A.* **142 G5** 39 30N 117 4W
Austin, *Pa., U.S.A.* **136 E6** 41 38N 78 6W
Austin, *Tex., U.S.A.* **139 K6** 30 17N 97 45W
Austin, L., *Australia* **113 E2** 27 40 S 118 0 E
Austral Downs, *Australia* **114 C2** 20 30 S 137 45 E
Austral Is. = Tubuai Is., *Pac. Oc.* **123 K12** 25 0 S 150 0W
Austral Seamount Chain, *Pac. Oc.* **123 K13** 24 0 S 150 0W
Australia ■, *Oceania* **122 K5** 23 0 S 135 0 E
Australian Alps, *Australia* **117 D8** 36 30 S 148 30 E
Australian Capital Territory □, *Australia* **115 F4** 35 30 S 149 0 E
Austria ■, *Europe* **30 E7** 47 0N 14 0 E
Austvågøy, *Norway* **12 B13** 68 20N 14 40 E
Autazes, *Brazil* **153 D6** 3 35 S 59 8W
Autelbas, *Belgium* **21 J7** 49 39N 5 52 E
Auterive, *France* **24 E5** 43 21N 1 29 E
Authie ➝, *France* **23 B8** 50 22N 1 38 E
Authon-du-Perche, *France* **22 D7** 48 12N 0 54 E
Autlán, *Mexico* **146 D4** 19 40N 104 30W
Autun, *France* **23 F11** 46 58N 4 17 E
Auvelais, *Belgium* **21 H5** 50 27N 4 38 E
Auvergne, *Australia* **112 C5** 15 39 S 130 1 E
Auvergne, *France* **24 C7** 45 20N 3 15 E
Auvergne, Mts. d', *France* **24 C6** 45 20N 2 55 E
Auvézère ➝, *France* **24 C4** 45 12N 0 50 E
Auxerre, *France* **23 E10** 47 48N 3 32 E
Auxi-le-Château, *France* **23 B9** 50 15N 2 8 E
Auxonne, *France* **23 E12** 47 10N 5 20 E
Auxvasse, *U.S.A.* **140 E5** 39 1N 91 54W
Auzances, *France* **24 B6** 46 2N 2 30 E
Auzat-sur-Allier, *France* **24 C7** 45 27N 3 19 E
Ava, *U.S.A.* **140 G7** 37 53N 89 30W
Avallon, *France* **23 E10** 47 30N 3 53 E
Avalon, *U.S.A.* **145 M8** 33 21N 118 20W
Avalon Pen., *Canada* **129 C9** 47 30N 53 20W
Avanigadda, *India* **83 G5** 16 0N 80 56 E
Avaré, *Brazil* **159 A6** 23 4 S 48 58W
Ávas, *Greece* **44 D7** 40 57N 25 56 E
Avawatz Mts., *U.S.A.* **145 K10** 35 40N 116 30W
Aveiro, *Brazil* **153 D6** 3 10 S 55 5W
Aveiro, *Portugal* **36 E2** 40 37N 8 38W
Aveiro □, *Portugal* **36 E2** 40 40N 8 35W
Āvej, *Iran* **85 C6** 35 40N 49 15 E
Avelgem, *Belgium* **21 G2** 50 47N 3 27 E
Avellaneda, *Argentina* **158 C4** 34 50 S 58 10W
Avellino, *Italy* **41 B7** 40 54N 14 46 E
Avenal, *U.S.A.* **144 K6** 36 0N 120 8W
Avenches, *Switz.* **28 C4** 46 53N 7 2 E
Averøya, *Norway* **14 A1** 63 5N 7 35 E
Aversa, *Italy* **41 B7** 40 58N 14 11 E
Avery, *U.S.A.* **142 C6** 47 15N 115 49W
Aves, I. de, *W. Indies* **149 C7** 15 45N 63 55W
Aves, Is. de, *Venezuela* **149 D6** 12 0N 67 30W
Avesnes-sur-Helpe, *France* **23 B10** 50 8N 3 55 E
Avesta, *Sweden* **13 F14** 60 9N 16 10 E
Aveyron □, *France* **24 D6** 44 22N 2 45 E
Aveyron ➝, *France* **24 D5** 44 5N 1 16 E
Avezzano, *Italy* **39 F10** 42 2N 13 24 E
Avgó, *Greece* **45 J7** 35 33N 25 37 E
Aviá Terai, *Argentina* **158 B3** 26 45 S 60 50W
Aviano, *Italy* **39 B9** 46 3N 12 35 E
Avigliana, *Italy* **38 C4** 45 7N 7 13 E
Avigliano, *Italy* **41 B8** 40 44N 15 41 E
Avignon, *France* **25 E8** 43 57N 4 50 E
Ávila, *Spain* **36 E6** 40 39N 4 43W
Ávila □, *Spain* **36 E6** 40 30N 5 0W
Ávila, Sierra de, *Spain* **36 E5** 40 40N 5 15W
Avila Beach, *U.S.A.* **145 K6** 35 11N 120 44W
Avilés, *Spain* **36 B5** 43 35N 5 57W
Avionárion, *Greece* **45 F6** 38 31N 24 8 E
Avisio ➝, *Italy* **39 B8** 46 7N 11 5 E
Aviston, *U.S.A.* **140 F7** 38 36N 89 36W
Aviz, *Portugal* **37 F3** 39 4N 7 53W
Avize, *France* **23 D11** 48 59N 4 1 E
Avoca, *Ireland* **19 D5** 52 52N 6 13W
Avoca, *U.S.A.* **136 D7** 42 25N 77 25W
Avoca ➝, *Australia* **116 C5** 35 40 S 143 43 E
Avola, *Canada* **130 C5** 51 45N 119 19W
Avola, *Italy* **41 F8** 36 56N 15 7 E
Avon, *Ill., U.S.A.* **140 D6** 40 40N 90 26W
Avon, *N.Y., U.S.A.* **136 D7** 42 55N 77 45W
Avon, *S. Dak., U.S.A.* **138 D5** 43 0N 98 4W
Avon □, *U.K.* **17 F5** 51 30N 2 40W
Avon ➝, *Australia* **113 F2** 31 40 S 116 7 E
Avon ➝, *Avon, U.K.* **17 F5** 51 30N 2 43W
Avon ➝, *Hants., U.K.* **17 G6** 50 44N 1 45W
Avon ➝, *Warks., U.K.* **17 F5** 51 57N 2 9W
Avondale, *Zimbabwe* **107 F3** 17 43 S 30 58 E
Avonlea, *Canada* **131 D7** 50 0N 105 0W
Avonmore, *Canada* **137 A10** 45 10N 74 58W
Avonmouth, *U.K.* **17 F5** 51 30N 2 42W
Avramov, *Bulgaria* **43 E11** 42 45N 26 38 E
Avranches, *France* **22 D5** 48 40N 1 20W
Avre ➝, *France* **22 D8** 48 47N 1 22 E
Avrig, *Romania* **46 D5** 45 43N 24 21 E
Avtovac, *Bos.-H.* **42 D3** 43 9N 18 35 E
Avu Avu, *Solomon Is.* **121 M11** 9 50 S 160 22 E
Awag el Baqar, *Sudan* **95 E3** 10 10N 33 10 E
A'waj ➝, *Syria* **91 B5** 33 23N 36 20 E
Awaji, *Japan* **63 C7** 34 32N 135 1 E
Awaji-Shima, *Japan* **62 C6** 34 30N 134 50 E
'Awālī, *Bahrain* **85 E6** 26 0N 50 30 E
Awantipur, *India* **81 C6** 33 55N 75 3 E
Awanui, *N.Z.* **118 B2** 35 4 S 173 17 E
Awarja ➝, *India* **82 F3** 17 5N 76 15 E
Awarua B., *N.Z.* **119 E3** 44 28 S 168 4 E
Awarua Pt., *N.Z.* **119 E3** 44 15 S 168 5 E
Awasa, L., *Ethiopia* **95 F4** 7 0N 38 30 E
Awash, *Ethiopia* **90 F3** 9 1N 40 10 E
Awash ➝, *Ethiopia* **95 E5** 11 45N 41 5 E
Awaso, *Ghana* **100 D4** 6 15N 2 22W
Awatere ➝, *N.Z.* **119 B9** 41 37 S 174 10 E
Awbārī, *Libya* **96 C2** 26 46N 12 57 E
Awbārī □, *Libya* **96 C2** 26 35N 12 46 E
Awe, L., *U.K.* **18 E3** 56 15N 5 15W
Aweil, *Sudan* **95 F2** 8 42N 27 20 E
Awgu, *Nigeria* **101 D6** 6 4N 7 24 E
Awjilah, *Libya* **96 C4** 29 8N 21 7 E
Aworro, *Papua N. G.* **120 D2** 7 43 S 143 11 E
Ax-les-Thermes, *France* **24 F5** 42 44N 1 50 E
Axarfjörður, *Iceland* **12 C5** 66 15N 16 45W
Axel, *Neths.* **21 F3** 51 16N 3 55 E
Axel Heiberg I., *Canada* **6 B3** 80 0N 90 0W
Axim, *Ghana* **100 E4** 4 51N 2 15W
Axinim, *Brazil* **153 D6** 4 2 S 59 22W
Axintele, *Romania* **46 E7** 44 37N 26 47 E
Axioma, *Brazil* **157 B5** 6 45 S 64 31W
Axiós ➝, *Greece* **44 D4** 40 57N 22 35 E
Axminster, *U.K.* **17 G4** 50 47N 3 1W
Axvall, *Sweden* **15 F7** 58 23N 13 34 E
Aÿ, *France* **23 C11** 49 3N 4 1 E
Ay ➝, *Russia* **54 C5** 56 8N 57 40 E
Ayaantang, *Eq. Guin.* **102 B2** 1 58N 10 24 E
Ayabaca, *Peru* **156 A2** 4 40 S 79 53W
Ayabe, *Japan* **63 B7** 35 20N 135 20 E
Ayacucho, *Argentina* **158 D4** 37 5 S 58 20W
Ayacucho, *Peru* **156 C3** 13 0 S 74 0W
Ayaguz, *Kazakhstan* **56 E9** 48 10N 80 10 E
Ayakkuduk, *Uzbekistan* **55 C2** 41 12N 65 12 E
Ayakudi, *India* **83 J3** 10 28N 77 56 E
Ayala, *Phil.* **71 H3** 6 57N 121 57 E
Ayamonte, *Spain* **37 H3** 37 12N 7 24W
Ayan, *Russia* **57 D14** 56 30N 138 16 E
Ayancık, *Turkey* **52 F6** 41 57N 34 35 E
Ayapel, *Colombia* **152 B2** 8 19N 75 9W
Ayas, *Turkey* **52 F5** 40 2N 32 21 E
Ayaviri, *Peru* **156 C3** 14 50 S 70 35W
Aybak, *Afghan.* **79 A3** 36 15N 68 5 E
Aybastı, *Turkey* **88 C7** 40 41N 37 23 E
Aydim, W. ➝, *Oman* **87 C6** 18 8N 53 8 E
Aydın, *Turkey* **88 E2** 37 51N 27 51 E
Aydin □, *Turkey* **88 E2** 37 50N 28 0 E
Aye, *Belgium* **21 H6** 50 14N 5 18 E
Ayenngré, *Togo* **101 D5** 8 40N 1 1 E
Ayer's Cliff, *Canada* **137 A12** 45 10N 72 3W
Ayers Rock, *Australia* **113 E5** 25 23 S 131 5 E
Ayiá, *Greece* **44 E4** 39 43N 22 45 E
Ayía Aikateríni, Ákra, *Greece* **32 A3** 39 50N 19 50 E
Ayía Ánna, *Greece* **45 F5** 38 52N 23 24 E
Ayía Dhéka, *Greece* **32 D6** 35 3N 24 58 E
Ayía Gálini, *Greece* **32 D6** 35 6N 24 41 E
Ayía Marína, *Kásos, Greece* **45 J8** 35 27N 26 53 E
Ayía Marína, *Leros, Greece* **45 G8** 37 11N 26 48 E
Ayia Napa, *Cyprus* **32 E13** 34 59N 34 0 E
Ayía Paraskeví, *Greece* **44 E8** 39 14N 26 16 E
Ayia Phyla, *Cyprus* **32 E12** 34 43N 33 1 E
Ayía Rouméli, *Greece* **45 J5** 35 14N 23 58 E
Ayia Varvára, *Greece* **32 D7** 35 8N 25 1 E
Ayiássos, *Greece* **45 E8** 39 5N 26 23 E
Ayion Óros, *Greece* **44 D6** 40 25N 24 6 E
Áyios Amvrósios, *Cyprus* **32 D12** 35 20N 33 35 E
Áyios Andréas, *Greece* **45 G4** 37 21N 22 45 E
Áyios Evstrátios, *Greece* **44 E6** 39 34N 24 58 E
Áyios Ioánnis, Ákra, *Greece* **32 D7** 35 20N 25 40 E
Áyios Isidhoros, *Greece* **32 C9** 36 9N 27 51 E
Áyios Kiríkos, *Greece* **45 G8** 37 34N 26 17 E
Áyios Matthaíos, *Greece* **32 B3** 39 30N 19 47 E
Áyios Mírono, *Greece* **45 J7** 35 15N 25 1 E
Áyios Nikólaos, *Greece* **32 D7** 35 11N 25 41 E
Áyios Pétros, *Greece* **45 F2** 38 38N 20 33 E
Áyios Seryios, *Cyprus* **32 D12** 35 12N 33 53 E
Áyios Theodhoros, *Cyprus* **32 D13** 35 22N 34 1 E
Áyios Yeóryios, *Greece* **45 G5** 37 28N 23 57 E
Aykathonisi, *Greece* **45 G8** 37 28N 27 0 E
Ayke, Ozero, *Kazakhstan* **54 F7** 50 57N 61 36 E
Aykin, *Russia* **48 B8** 62 15N 49 56 E
Aylesbury, *U.K.* **17 F7** 51 48N 0 49W
Aylmer, *Canada* **136 D4** 42 46N 80 59W
Aylmer, L., *Canada* **126 B8** 64 0N 110 8W
'Ayn al Ghazālah, *Libya* **96 B4** 32 10N 23 20 E
'Ayn Zaqqūt, *Libya* **96 C3** 29 0N 19 30 E
Ayna, *Spain* **35 G2** 38 34N 2 3W
Aynāt, *Yemen* **87 C5** 16 4N 49 9 E
Ayni, *Tajikistan* **55 D4** 39 23N 68 32 E
Ayolas, *Paraguay* **158 B4** 27 10 S 56 59W
Ayom, *Sudan* **95 F2** 7 49N 28 23 E
Ayon, Ostrov, *Russia* **57 C17** 69 50N 169 0 E
Ayora, *Spain* **35 F3** 39 3N 1 3W
Ayr, *Australia* **114 B4** 19 35 S 147 25 E
Ayr, *U.K.* **18 F4** 55 28N 4 37W
Ayr ➝, *U.K.* **18 F4** 55 29N 4 40W
Ayrancı, *Turkey* **88 E5** 37 21N 33 41 E
Ayre, Pt. of, *U.K.* **16 C3** 54 27N 4 21W
Aysha, *Ethiopia* **95 E5** 10 50N 42 23 E
Aytos, *Bulgaria* **43 E12** 42 42N 27 16 E
Aytoska Planina, *Bulgaria* **43 E12** 42 45N 27 30 E
Ayu, Kepulauan, *Indonesia* **73 A4** 0 35N 131 5 E
Ayutla, *Guatemala* **148 D1** 14 40N 92 10W
Ayutla, *Mexico* **147 D5** 16 58N 99 17W
Ayvacık, *Turkey* **88 C7** 40 59N 36 38 E
Ayvalık, *Turkey* **88 D2** 39 20N 26 46 E
Aywaille, *Belgium* **21 H7** 50 28N 5 40 E
Az Zabdānī, *Syria* **91 B5** 33 43N 36 5 E
Aẓ Ẓāhirīyah, *Jordan* **91 D3** 31 25N 34 58 E
Aẓ Ẓahrān, *Si. Arabia* **85 E6** 26 10N 50 7 E
Az Zarqā, *Jordan* **91 C5** 32 5N 36 4 E
Az Zāwiyah, *Libya* **96 B2** 32 52N 12 56 E
Az Zaydīyah, *Yemen* **86 D3** 15 20N 43 1 E
Az Zībār, *Iraq* **84 B5** 36 52N 44 4 E
Az-Zilfī, *Si. Arabia* **84 E5** 26 12N 44 52 E
Az Zubayr, *Iraq* **84 D5** 30 20N 47 50 E
Az Zuqur, *Yemen* **86 D3** 14 0N 42 45 E
Azambuja, *Portugal* **37 F2** 39 4N 8 51W
Azamgarh, *India* **81 F10** 26 5N 83 13 E
Azangaro, *Peru* **156 C3** 14 55 S 70 13W
Azaouak, Vallée de l', *Mali* **101 B5** 15 50N 3 20 E
Āzār Shahr, *Iran* **84 B5** 37 45N 45 59 E
Azärbayjan = Azerbaijan ■, *Asia* **53 F12** 40 20N 48 0 E

**Baran 171**

Balaguer, *Spain* **34 D5** 41 50N 0 50 E
Balakété, *C.A.R.* **102 A3** 6 56N 19 54 E
Balakhna, *Russia* **51 C13** 56 25N 43 32 E
Balaklava, *Australia* **116 C3** 34 7 S 138 22 E
Balaklava, *Ukraine* **52 D5** 44 30N 33 30 E
Balakleya, *Ukraine* **52 B7** 49 28N 36 55 E
Balakovo, *Russia* **51 E15** 52 4N 47 55 E
Balamban, *Phil.* **71 F4** 10 30N 123 43 E
Balambangan, *Malaysia* **75 A5** 7 17N 116 55 E
Balancán, *Mexico* **147 D6** 17 48N 91 32W
Balanda, *Russia* **51 F14** 51 30N 44 40 E
Balangiga, *Phil.* **71 F5** 11 7N 125 23 E
Balangir, *India* **82 D6** 20 43N 83 35 E
Balapur, *India* **82 D3** 20 40N 76 45 E
Balashikha, *Russia* **51 D10** 55 49N 37 59 E
Balashov, *Russia* **51 F13** 51 30N 43 10 E
Balasinor, *India* **80 H5** 22 57N 73 23 E
Balasore = Baleshwar, *India* **82 D8** 21 35N 87 3 E
Balassagyarmat, *Hungary* **31 C12** 48 4N 19 15 E
Balât, *Egypt* **94 B2** 25 36N 29 19 E
Balaton, *Hungary* **31 E10** 46 50N 17 40 E
Balatonfüred, *Hungary* **31 E10** 46 58N 17 54 E
Balatonszentgyörgy, *Hungary* **31 E10** 46 41N 17 19 E
Balayan, *Phil.* **70 E3** 13 57N 120 44 E
Balazote, *Spain* **35 G2** 38 54N 2 9W
Balbalan, *Phil.* **70 C3** 17 27N 121 12 E
Balbi, Mt., *Papua N. G.* **120 C8** 5 55 S 154 58 E
Balboa, *Panama* **148 E4** 8 57N 79 34W
Balbriggan, *Ireland* **19 C5** 53 35N 6 10W
Balcarce, *Argentina* **158 D4** 38 0 S 58 10W
Balcarres, *Canada* **131 C8** 50 50N 103 35W
Balchik, *Bulgaria* **43 D13** 43 28N 28 11 E
Balclutha, *N.Z.* **119 G4** 46 15 S 169 45 E
Bald Hd., *Australia* **113 G2** 35 6 S 118 1 E
Bald I., *Australia* **113 F2** 34 57 S 118 27 E
Bald Knob, *U.S.A.* **139 H9** 35 19N 91 34W
Baldock L., *Canada* **131 B9** 56 33N 97 57W
Baldwin, *Fla., U.S.A.* **135 K4** 30 18N 81 59W
Baldwin, *Mich., U.S.A.* **134 D3** 43 54N 85 51W
Baldwinsville, *U.S.A.* **137 C8** 43 10N 76 20W
Baldy Peak, *U.S.A.* **143 K9** 33 54N 109 34W
Bale, *Croatia* **39 C10** 45 4N 13 46 E
Bale □, *Ethiopia* **95 F5** 6 20N 41 30 E
Baleares □, *Spain* **34 F7** 39 30N 3 0 E
Baleares, Is., *Spain* **33 B10** 39 30N 3 0 E
Balearic Is. = Baleares, Is., *Spain* **33 B10** 39 30N 3 0 E
Baleia, Pta. da, *Brazil* **155 E4** 17 40 S 39 7W
Balen, *Belgium* **21 F6** 51 10N 5 10 E
Băleni, *Romania* **46 D8** 45 48N 27 51 E
Baler, *Phil.* **70 D3** 15 46N 121 34 E
Baler Bay, *Phil.* **70 D3** 15 50N 121 35 E
Balerna, *Switz.* **29 E8** 45 52N 9 0 E
Baleshwar, *India* **82 D8** 21 35N 87 3 E
Balezino, *Russia* **54 B3** 58 2N 53 6 E
Balfate, *Honduras* **148 C2** 15 48N 86 25W
Balfe's Creek, *Australia* **114 C4** 20 12 S 145 55 E
Balfour, *S. Africa* **105 D4** 26 38 S 28 35 E
Balfour Channel, *Solomon Is.* **121 M9** 8 43 S 157 27 E
Balharshah, *India* **82 E4** 19 50N 79 23 E
Bali, *Cameroon* **101 D6** 5 54N 10 0 E
Balí, *Greece* **32 D6** 35 25N 24 47 E
Bali, *Indonesia* **75 D4** 8 20 S 115 0 E
Bali □, *Indonesia* **75 D4** 8 20 S 115 0 E
Bali, Selat, *Indonesia* **75 D4** 8 18 S 114 25 E
Balicuatro Is., *Phil.* **70 E5** 12 39N 124 24 E
Baligród, *Poland* **31 B15** 49 20N 22 17 E
Balık Gölü, *Turkey* **89 D10** 39 46N 43 34 E
Balikeşir, *Turkey* **88 D2** 39 35N 27 58 E
Balikeşir □, *Turkey* **88 D2** 39 45N 28 0 E
Balikpapan, *Indonesia* **75 C5** 1 10 S 116 55 E
Balimbing, *Phil.* **71 J2** 5 5N 119 58 E
Balimo, *Papua N. G.* **120 E2** 8 6 S 142 57 E
Baling, *Malaysia* **77 K3** 5 41N 100 55 E
Balintang Channel, *Phil.* **70 B3** 19 49N 121 40 E
Balintang Is., *Phil.* **70 B4** 19 58N 122 9 E
Baliton, *Phil.* **71 J5** 5 44N 125 14 E
Baliza, *Brazil* **157 D7** 16 0 S 52 20W
Baljurshi, *Si. Arabia* **86 C3** 19 51N 41 33 E
Balk, *Neths.* **20 C7** 52 54N 5 35 E
Balkan Mts. = Stara Planina, *Bulgaria* **43 D8** 43 15N 23 0 E
Balkan Peninsula, *Europe* **10 G10** 42 0N 23 0 E
Balkh □, *Afghan.* **79 A2** 36 50N 67 0 E
Balkhash, *Kazakhstan* **56 E8** 46 50N 74 50 E
Balkhash, Ozero, *Kazakhstan* **56 E8** 46 0N 74 50 E
Ballachulish, *U.K.* **18 E3** 56 40N 5 10W
Balladonia, *Australia* **113 F3** 32 27 S 123 51 E
Ballara, *Australia* **116 B4** 32 19 S 140 45 E
Ballarat, *Australia* **115 F3** 37 33 S 143 50 E
Ballard, L., *Australia* **113 E3** 29 20 S 120 40 E
Ballater, *U.K.* **18 D5** 57 2N 3 2W
Balldale, *Australia* **117 C7** 35 50 S 146 33 E
Ballenas, Canal de, *Mexico* **146 B2** 29 10N 113 45W
Balleny Is., *Antarctica* **7 C11** 66 30 S 163 0 E
Ballesteros, *Phil.* **70 B3** 18 25N 121 31 E
Ballia, *India* **81 G11** 25 46N 84 12 E
Ballidu, *Australia* **113 F2** 30 35 S 116 45 E
Ballina, *Australia* **115 D5** 28 50 S 153 31 E
Ballina, *Mayo, Ireland* **19 B2** 54 7N 9 10W
Ballina, *Tipp., Ireland* **19 D3** 52 49N 8 27W
Ballinasloe, *Ireland* **19 C3** 53 20N 8 12W
Ballinger, *U.S.A.* **139 K5** 31 45N 99 57W
Ballinrobe, *Ireland* **19 C2** 53 36N 9 13W
Ballinskelligs B., *Ireland* **19 E1** 51 46N 10 11W
Ballon, *France* **22 D7** 48 10N 0 14 E
Ballycastle, *U.K.* **19 A5** 55 12N 6 15W
Ballymena, *U.K.* **19 B5** 54 53N 6 18W
Ballymena □, *U.K.* **19 B5** 54 53N 6 18W
Ballymoney, *U.K.* **19 A5** 55 5N 6 30W
Ballymoney □, *U.K.* **19 A5** 55 5N 6 23W
Ballyshannon, *Ireland* **19 B3** 54 30N 8 10W
Balmaceda, *Chile* **160 C2** 46 0 S 71 50W
Balmazújváros, *Hungary* **31 D14** 47 37N 21 21 E
Balmhorn, *Switz.* **28 D5** 46 26N 7 42 E
Balmoral, *Australia* **116 D4** 37 15 S 141 48 E
Balmoral, *U.K.* **18 D5** 57 3N 3 13W
Balmorhea, *U.S.A.* **139 K3** 30 59N 103 45W
Balombo, *Angola* **103 E2** 12 21 S 14 46 E
Balonne →, *Australia* **115 D4** 28 47 S 147 56 E
Balqash Kol = Balkhash, Ozero, *Kazakhstan* **56 E8** 46 0N 74 50 E
Balrampur, *India* **81 F10** 27 30N 82 20 E
Balranald, *Australia* **116 C5** 34 38 S 143 33 E
Balş, *Romania* **46 E5** 44 22N 24 5 E
Balsapuerto, *Peru* **156 B2** 5 48 S 76 33W
Balsas, *Mexico* **147 D5** 18 0N 99 40W
Balsas →, *Goiás, Brazil* **154 C2** 9 58 S 47 52W
Balsas →, *Maranhão, Brazil* **154 C3** 7 15 S 44 35W
Balsas →, *Mexico* **146 D4** 17 55N 102 10W
Bålsta, *Sweden* **14 E11** 59 35N 17 30 E
Balsthal, *Switz.* **28 B5** 47 19N 7 41 E
Balston Spa, *U.S.A.* **137 D11** 43 0N 73 52W
Balta, *Romania* **46 E3** 44 54N 22 38 E
Balta, *Russia* **53 E11** 42 58N 44 32 E
Balta, *Ukraine* **52 B3** 48 2N 29 45 E
Balta, *U.S.A.* **138 A4** 48 10N 100 2W
Baltanás, *Spain* **36 D6** 41 56N 4 15W
Bălţi = Beltsy, *Moldavia* **52 C3** 47 48N 28 0 E
Baltic Sea, *Europe* **13 H15** 57 0N 19 0 E
Baltîm, *Egypt* **94 H7** 31 35N 31 10 E
Baltimore, *Ireland* **19 E2** 51 29N 9 22W
Baltimore, *U.S.A.* **134 F7** 39 17N 76 37W
Baltit, *Pakistan* **81 A6** 36 15N 74 40 E
Baltrum, *Germany* **26 B3** 53 43N 7 25 E
Baluchistan □, *Pakistan* **79 D2** 27 30N 65 0 E
Balud, *Phil.* **70 E4** 12 2N 123 12 E
Balurghat, *India* **81 G13** 25 15N 88 44 E
Balya, *Turkey* **88 D2** 39 44N 27 35 E
Balygychan, *Russia* **57 C16** 63 56N 154 12 E
Balzar, *Ecuador* **152 D2** 2 2 S 79 54W
Bam, *Iran* **85 D8** 29 7N 58 14 E
Bama, *China* **68 E6** 24 8N 107 12 E
Bama, *Nigeria* **101 C7** 11 33N 13 41 E
Bamako, *Mali* **100 C3** 12 34N 7 55W
Bamba, *Mali* **101 B4** 17 5N 1 24W
Bamba, *Zaïre* **103 D3** 5 45 S 18 23 E
Bambam, *Phil.* **70 D3** 15 40N 120 20 E
Bambamarca, *Peru* **156 B2** 6 36 S 78 32W
Bambang, *Phil.* **70 C3** 16 23N 121 6 E
Bambari, *C.A.R.* **102 A4** 5 40N 20 35 E
Bambaroo, *Australia* **114 B4** 18 50 S 146 10 E
Bamberg, *Germany* **27 F6** 49 54N 10 53 E
Bamberg, *U.S.A.* **135 J5** 33 18N 81 2W
Bambesi, *Ethiopia* **95 F3** 9 45N 34 40 E
Bambey, *Senegal* **100 C1** 14 42N 16 28W
Bambili, *Zaïre* **106 B2** 3 40N 26 0 E
Bambuí, *Brazil* **155 F2** 20 1 S 45 58W
Bamenda, *Cameroon* **101 D7** 5 57N 10 11 E
Bamfield, *Canada* **130 D3** 48 45N 125 10W
Bāmīān □, *Afghan.* **79 B2** 35 0N 67 0 E
Bamiancheng, *China* **67 C13** 43 15N 124 2 E
Bamingui, *C.A.R.* **102 A4** 7 34N 20 11 E
Bamkin, *Cameroon* **101 D7** 6 3N 11 27 E
Bampūr, *Iran* **85 E9** 27 15N 60 21 E
Ban Aranyaprathet, *Thailand* **76 F4** 13 41N 102 30 E
Ban Ban, *Laos* **76 C4** 19 31N 103 30 E
Ban Bang Hin, *Thailand* **77 H2** 9 32N 98 35 E
Ban Chiang Klang, *Thailand* **76 C3** 19 25N 100 55 E
Ban Chik, *Laos* **76 D4** 17 15N 102 22 E
Ban Choho, *Thailand* **76 E4** 15 2N 102 9 E
Ban Dan Lan Hoi, *Thailand* **76 D2** 17 0N 99 35 E
Ban Don = Surat Thani, *Thailand* **77 H2** 9 6N 99 20 E
Ban Don, *Vietnam* **76 F6** 12 53N 107 48 E
Ban Don, Ao, *Thailand* **77 H2** 9 20N 99 25 E
Ban Dong, *Thailand* **76 C3** 19 30N 100 59 E
Ban Hong, *Thailand* **76 C2** 18 18N 98 50 E
Ban Kaeng, *Thailand* **76 D3** 17 29N 100 7 E
Ban Keun, *Laos* **76 C4** 18 22N 102 35 E
Ban Khai, *Thailand* **76 F3** 12 46N 101 18 E
Ban Kheun, *Laos* **76 B3** 20 13N 101 7 E
Ban Khlong Kua, *Thailand* **77 J3** 6 57N 100 8 E
Ban Khuan Mao, *Thailand* **77 J2** 7 50N 99 37 E
Ban Khun Yuam, *Thailand* **76 C1** 18 49N 97 57 E
Ban Ko Yai Chim, *Thailand* **77 G2** 11 17N 99 26 E
Ban Kok, *Thailand* **76 D4** 16 40N 103 40 E
Ban Laem, *Thailand* **76 F2** 13 13N 99 59 E
Ban Lao Ngam, *Laos* **76 E6** 15 28N 106 10 E
Ban Le Kathe, *Thailand* **76 E2** 15 49N 98 53 E
Ban Mae Chedi, *Thailand* **76 C2** 19 11N 99 31 E
Ban Mae Laeng, *Thailand* **76 B2** 20 1N 99 17 E
Ban Mae Sariang, *Thailand* **76 C1** 18 10N 97 56 E
Ban Mê Thuôt = Buon Me Thuot, *Vietnam* **76 F7** 12 40N 108 3 E
Ban Mi, *Thailand* **76 E3** 15 3N 100 32 E
Ban Muong Mo, *Laos* **76 C4** 19 4N 103 58 E
Ban Na Mo, *Laos* **76 D5** 17 7N 105 40 E
Ban Na San, *Thailand* **77 H2** 8 53N 99 52 E
Ban Na Tong, *Laos* **76 B3** 20 56N 101 47 E
Ban Nam Bac, *Laos* **76 B4** 20 38N 102 20 E
Ban Nam Ma, *Laos* **76 A3** 22 2N 101 37 E
Ban Ngang, *Laos* **76 E6** 15 59N 106 11 E
Ban Nong Bok, *Laos* **76 D5** 17 5N 104 48 E
Ban Nong Boua, *Laos* **76 E6** 15 40N 106 33 E
Ban Nong Pling, *Thailand* **76 E3** 15 40N 100 10 E
Ban Pak Chan, *Thailand* **77 G2** 10 32N 98 51 E
Ban Phai, *Thailand* **76 D4** 16 4N 102 44 E
Ban Pong, *Thailand* **76 F2** 13 50N 99 55 E
Ban Ron Phibun, *Thailand* **77 H2** 8 9N 99 51 E
Ban Sanam Chai, *Thailand* **77 J3** 7 33N 100 25 E
Ban Sangkha, *Thailand* **76 E4** 14 37N 103 52 E
Ban Tak, *Thailand* **76 D2** 17 2N 99 4 E
Ban Tako, *Thailand* **76 E4** 14 5N 102 40 E
Ban Tha Dua, *Thailand* **76 D2** 17 59N 98 39 E
Ban Tha Li, *Thailand* **76 D3** 17 37N 101 25 E
Ban Tha Nun, *Thailand* **77 H2** 8 12N 98 18 E
Ban Thahine, *Laos* **76 E5** 14 12N 105 33 E
Ban Xien Kok, *Laos* **76 B3** 20 54N 100 39 E
Ban Yen Nhan, *Vietnam* **76 B6** 20 57N 106 2 E
Baña, Punta de la, *Spain* **34 E5** 40 33N 0 40 E
Banā, W. →, *Yemen* **86 D4** 13 3N 45 24 E
Banaba, *Kiribati* **122 H8** 0 45 S 169 50 E
Bañalbufar, *Spain* **33 B9** 39 42N 2 31 E
Banalia, *Zaïre* **106 B2** 1 32N 25 5 E
Banam, *Cambodia* **77 G5** 11 20N 105 17 E
Banamba, *Mali* **100 C3** 13 29N 7 22W
Banana, *Australia* **114 C5** 24 28 S 150 8 E
Bananal, I. do, *Brazil* **155 D1** 11 30 S 50 30W
Banaras = Varanasi, *India* **81 G10** 25 22N 83 0 E
Banas →, *Gujarat, India* **80 H4** 23 45N 71 25 E
Banas →, *Mad. P., India* **81 G9** 24 15N 81 30 E
Bânâs, Ras, *Egypt* **94 C4** 23 57N 35 50 E
Banaz, *Turkey* **88 D3** 38 44N 29 46 E
Banbān, *Si. Arabia* **84 E5** 25 1N 46 35 E
Banbridge, *U.K.* **19 B5** 54 21N 6 17W
Banbridge □, *U.K.* **19 B5** 54 21N 6 16W
Banbury, *U.K.* **17 E6** 52 4N 1 21W
Banchory, *U.K.* **18 D6** 57 3N 2 30W
Bancroft, *Canada* **128 C4** 45 3N 77 51W
Band, *Romania* **46 C5** 46 30N 24 25 E
Band Bonī, *Iran* **85 E8** 25 30N 59 33 E
Band-e Torkestān, *Afghan.* **79 B2** 35 30N 64 0 E
Band Qīr, *Iran* **85 D6** 31 39N 48 53 E
Banda, *Cameroon* **102 B2** 3 58N 14 32 E
Banda, *India* **81 G9** 25 30N 80 26 E
Banda, Kepulauan, *Indonesia* **73 B3** 4 37 S 129 50 E
Banda Aceh, *Indonesia* **74 A1** 5 35N 95 20 E
Banda Banda, Mt., *Australia* **117 A10** 31 10 S 152 28 E
Banda Elat, *Indonesia* **73 C4** 5 40 S 133 5 E
Banda Is. = Banda, Kepulauan, *Indonesia* **73 B3** 4 37 S 129 50 E
Banda Sea, *Indonesia* **72 C3** 6 0 S 130 0 E
Bandai-San, *Japan* **60 F10** 37 36N 140 4 E
Bandama →, *Ivory C.* **100 D3** 6 32N 5 30W
Bandān, *Iran* **85 D9** 31 23N 60 44 E
Bandanaira, *Indonesia* **73 B3** 4 32 S 129 54 E
Bandanwara, *India* **80 F6** 26 9N 74 38 E
Bandar = Machilipatnam, *India* **83 F5** 16 12N 81 8 E
Bandār 'Abbās, *Iran* **85 E8** 27 15N 56 15 E
Bandar-e Anzalī, *Iran* **85 B6** 37 30N 49 30 E
Bandar-e Chārak, *Iran* **85 E7** 26 45N 54 20 E
Bandar-e Deylam, *Iran* **85 D6** 30 5N 50 10 E
Bandar-e Khomeyni, *Iran* **85 D6** 30 30N 49 5 E
Bandar-e Lengeh, *Iran* **85 E7** 26 35N 54 58 E
Bandar-e Maqām, *Iran* **85 E7** 26 56N 53 29 E
Bandar-e Ma'shur, *Iran* **85 D6** 30 35N 49 10 E
Bandar-e Nakhīlū, *Iran* **85 E7** 26 58N 53 30 E
Bandar-e Rīg, *Iran* **85 D6** 29 29N 50 38 E
Bandar-e Torkeman, *Iran* **85 B7** 37 0N 54 10 E
Bandar Maharani = Muar, *Malaysia* **77 L4** 2 3N 102 34 E
Bandar Penggaram = Batu Pahat, *Malaysia* **77 M4** 1 50N 102 56 E
Bandar Seri Begawan, *Brunei* **75 B4** 4 52N 115 0 E
Bandawe, *Malawi* **107 E3** 11 58 S 34 5 E
Bande, *Belgium* **21 H6** 50 10N 5 25 E
Bande, *Spain* **36 C3** 42 3N 7 58W
Bandeira, Pico da, *Brazil* **155 F3** 20 26 S 41 47W
Bandeirante, *Brazil* **155 D1** 13 41 S 50 48W
Bandera, *Argentina* **158 B3** 28 55 S 62 20W
Bandera, *U.S.A.* **139 L5** 29 44N 99 5W
Banderas, B. de, *Mexico* **146 C3** 20 40N 105 30W
Bandia →, *India* **82 E5** 19 2N 80 28 E
Bandiagara, *Mali* **100 C4** 14 12N 3 29W
Bandırma, *Turkey* **88 C3** 40 20N 28 0 E
Bandon, *Ireland* **19 E3** 51 44N 8 45W
Bandon →, *Ireland* **19 E3** 51 40N 8 41W
Bandoua, *C.A.R.* **102 B4** 4 39N 21 42 E
Bandula, *Mozam.* **107 F3** 19 0 S 33 7 E
Bandundu, *Zaïre* **102 C3** 3 15 S 17 22 E
Bandung, *Indonesia* **75 D3** 6 54 S 107 36 E
Bandya, *Australia* **113 E3** 27 40 S 122 5 E
Băneasa, *Romania* **46 D8** 45 56N 27 55 E
Bāneh, *Iran* **84 C5** 35 59N 45 53 E
Bañeres, *Spain* **35 G4** 38 44N 0 38W
Banes, *Cuba* **149 B4** 21 0N 75 42W
Banff, *Canada* **130 C5** 51 10N 115 34W
Banff, *U.K.* **18 D6** 57 40N 2 32W
Banff Nat. Park, *Canada* **130 C5** 51 30N 116 15W
Banfora, *Burkina Faso* **100 C4** 10 40N 4 40W
Bang Fai →, *Laos* **76 D5** 16 57N 104 45 E
Bang Hieng →, *Laos* **76 D5** 16 10N 105 10 E
Bang Krathum, *Thailand* **76 D3** 16 34N 100 18 E
Bang Lamung, *Thailand* **76 F3** 13 3N 100 56 E
Bang Mun Nak, *Thailand* **76 D3** 16 2N 100 23 E
Bang Pa In, *Thailand* **76 E3** 14 14N 100 35 E
Bang Rakam, *Thailand* **76 D3** 16 45N 100 7 E
Bang Saphan, *Thailand* **77 G2** 11 14N 99 28 E
Bangala Dam, *Zimbabwe* **107 G3** 21 7 S 31 25 E
Bangalore, *India* **83 H3** 12 59N 77 40 E
Bangante, *Cameroon* **101 D7** 5 8N 10 32 E
Bangaon, *India* **81 H13** 23 0N 88 47 E
Bangassou, *C.A.R.* **102 B4** 4 55N 23 7 E
Bangeta, Mt., *Papua N. G.* **120 D4** 6 21 S 147 3 E
Banggai, Kepulauan, *Indonesia* **72 B2** 1 40 S 123 30 E
Banggai Arch., *Indonesia* **72 B2** 2 0 S 123 15 E
Banggi, P., *Malaysia* **75 A5** 7 17N 117 12 E
Banghāzī, *Libya* **96 B4** 32 11N 20 3 E
Banghāzī □, *Libya* **96 B4** 32 7N 20 4 E
Bangil, *Indonesia* **75 D4** 7 36 S 112 50 E
Bangjang, *Sudan* **95 E3** 11 23N 32 41 E
Bangka, P., *Sulawesi, Indonesia* **72 A3** 1 50N 125 5 E
Bangka, P., *Sumatera, Indonesia* **74 C3** 2 0 S 105 50 E
Bangka, Selat, *Indonesia* **74 C3** 2 30 S 105 30 E
Bangkalan, *Indonesia* **75 D4** 7 2 S 112 46 E
Bangkinang, *Indonesia* **74 B2** 0 18N 101 5 E
Bangko, *Indonesia* **74 C2** 2 5 S 102 9 E
Bangkok, *Thailand* **76 F3** 13 45N 100 35 E
Bangladesh ■, *Asia* **78 C3** 24 0N 90 0 E
Bangolo, *Ivory C.* **100 D3** 7 1N 7 29W
Bangong Co, *India* **81 B8** 35 50N 79 20 E
Bangor, *Down, U.K.* **19 B6** 54 40N 5 40W
Bangor, *Gwynedd, U.K.* **16 D3** 53 13N 4 9W
Bangor, *Maine, U.S.A.* **129 D6** 44 48N 68 46W
Bangor, *Mich., U.S.A.* **141 B10** 42 18N 86 7W
Bangor, *Pa., U.S.A.* **137 F9** 40 52N 75 13W
Bangu, *Zaïre* **103 D4** 9 3 S 19 12 E
Bangued, *Phil.* **70 C3** 17 40N 120 37 E
Bangui, *C.A.R.* **102 B3** 4 23N 18 35 E
Bangui, *Phil.* **70 B3** 18 32N 120 46 E
Banguru, *Zaïre* **106 B2** 0 30N 27 10 E
Bangweulu, L., *Zambia* **107 E3** 11 0 S 30 0 E
Bangweulu Swamp, *Zambia* **107 E3** 11 20 S 30 15 E
Bani, *Dom. Rep.* **149 C5** 18 16N 70 22W
Bani, *Phil.* **70 C2** 16 11N 119 52 E
Bani →, *Mali* **100 C4** 14 30N 4 12W
Bani, Djebel, *Morocco* **98 C3** 29 16N 8 0W
Bani Bangou, *Niger* **101 B5** 15 3N 2 42 E
Banī Sa'd, *Iraq* **84 C5** 33 34N 44 32 E
Banī Sār, *Si. Arabia* **86 B3** 20 6N 41 27 E
Banī Walīd, *Libya* **96 B2** 31 36N 13 53 E
Bania, *Ivory C.* **100 D4** 9 4N 3 6W
Baniara, *Papua N. G.* **120 E5** 9 44 S 149 54 E
Banihal Pass, *India* **81 C6** 33 30N 75 12 E
Banīnah, *Libya* **96 B4** 32 0N 20 12 E
Bāniyās, *Syria* **84 C3** 35 10N 36 0 E
Banja Luka, *Bos.-H.* **42 C2** 44 49N 17 11 E
Banjar, *Indonesia* **75 D3** 7 24 S 108 30 E
Banjarmasin, *Indonesia* **75 C4** 3 20 S 114 35 E
Banjarnegara, *Indonesia* **75 D3** 7 24 S 109 42 E
Banjul, *Gambia* **100 C1** 13 28N 16 40W
Banka Banka, *Australia* **114 B1** 18 50 S 134 0 E
Banket, *Zimbabwe* **107 F3** 17 27 S 30 19 E
Bankilaré, *Niger* **101 C5** 14 35N 0 44 E
Bankipore, *India* **81 G11** 25 35N 85 10 E
Banks, Is., *Vanuatu* **121 C5** 13 50 S 167 30 E
Banks I., *B.C., Canada* **130 C3** 53 20N 130 0W
Banks I., *N.W.T., Canada* **126 A7** 73 15N 121 30W
Banks I., *Papua N. G.* **120 F2** 10 10 S 142 15 E
Banks Pen., *N.Z.* **119 D8** 43 45 S 173 15 E
Banks Str., *Australia* **114 G4** 40 40 S 148 10 E
Bankura, *India* **81 H12** 23 11N 87 18 E
Bankya, *Bulgaria* **42 E8** 42 43N 23 8 E
Bann →, *Down, U.K.* **19 B5** 54 30N 6 31W
Bann →, *L'derry., U.K.* **19 A5** 55 10N 6 34W
Banna, *Phil.* **70 C3** 17 59N 120 39 E
Bannalec, *France* **22 E3** 47 57N 3 42W
Bannang Sata, *Thailand* **77 J3** 6 16N 101 16 E
Bannerton, *Australia* **116 C5** 34 42 S 142 47 E
Banning, *U.S.A.* **145 M10** 33 56N 116 53W
Banningville = Bandundu, *Zaïre* **102 C3** 3 15 S 17 22 E
Bannockburn, *Canada* **136 B7** 44 39N 77 33W
Bannockburn, *U.K.* **18 E5** 56 5N 3 55W
Bannockburn, *Zimbabwe* **107 G2** 20 17 S 29 48 E
Bannu, *Pakistan* **79 B3** 33 0N 70 18 E
Bañolas, *Spain* **34 C7** 42 16N 2 44 E
Banon, *France* **25 D9** 44 2N 5 38 E
Baños de la Encina, *Spain* **37 G7** 38 10N 3 46W
Baños de Molgas, *Spain* **36 C3** 42 15N 7 40W
Bánovce, *Slovak Rep.* **31 C11** 48 44N 18 16 E
Bansilan □, *Phil.* **71 H3** 6 40N 121 40 E
Banská Bystrica, *Slovak Rep.* **31 C12** 48 46N 19 14 E
Banská Štiavnica, *Slovak Rep.* **31 C11** 48 25N 18 55 E
Bansko, *Bulgaria* **43 F8** 41 52N 23 28 E
Banswara, *India* **80 H6** 23 32N 74 24 E
Bantayan, *Phil.* **71 F4** 11 10N 123 43 E
Bantayan I., *Phil.* **71 F4** 11 13N 123 44 E
Banten, *Indonesia* **74 D3** 6 5 S 106 8 E
Banton I., *Phil.* **70 E4** 12 56N 122 4 E
Bantry, *Ireland* **19 E2** 51 40N 9 28W
Bantry B., *Ireland* **19 E2** 51 35N 9 50W
Bantul, *Indonesia* **75 D4** 7 55 S 110 19 E
Bantva, *India* **80 J4** 21 29N 70 12 E
Bantval, *India* **83 H2** 12 55N 75 0 E
Banya, *Bulgaria* **43 E9** 42 33N 24 50 E
Banyak, Kepulauan, *Indonesia* **74 B1** 2 10N 97 10 E
Banyo, *Cameroon* **101 D7** 6 52N 11 45 E
Banyuls-sur-Mer, *France* **24 F7** 42 28N 3 8 E
Banyumas, *Indonesia* **75 D3** 7 32 S 109 18 E
Banyuwangi, *Indonesia* **75 D4** 8 13 S 114 21 E
Banzare Coast, *Antarctica* **7 C9** 68 0 S 125 0 E
Banzyville = Mobayi, *Zaïre* **102 B4** 4 15N 21 8 E
Bao Ha, *Vietnam* **76 A5** 22 11N 104 21 E
Bao Lac, *Vietnam* **76 A5** 22 57N 105 40 E
Bao Loc, *Vietnam* **77 G6** 11 32N 107 48 E
Bao'an, *China* **69 F10** 22 27N 114 10 E
Baocheng, *China* **66 H4** 33 12N 106 56 E
Baode, *China* **66 E6** 39 1N 111 5 E
Baodi, *China* **67 E9** 39 38N 117 20 E
Baoding, *China* **66 E8** 38 50N 115 28 E
Baoji, *China* **66 G4** 34 20N 107 5 E
Baojing, *China* **68 C7** 28 45N 109 41 E
Baokang, *China* **69 B8** 31 54N 111 12 E
Baoro, *C.A.R.* **102 A3** 5 40N 15 58 E
Baoshan, *Shanghai, China* **69 B13** 31 27N 121 26 E
Baoshan, *Yunnan, China* **68 E2** 25 10N 99 5 E
Baotou, *China* **66 D6** 40 32N 110 2 E
Baoying, *China* **67 H10** 33 17N 119 20 E
Bap, *India* **80 F5** 27 23N 72 18 E
Bapatla, *India* **83 G5** 15 55N 80 30 E
Bapaume, *France* **23 B9** 50 7N 2 50 E
Bāqerābād, *Iran* **85 C6** 33 2N 51 58 E
Ba'qūbah, *Iraq* **84 C5** 33 45N 44 50 E
Baquedano, *Chile* **158 A2** 23 20 S 69 52W
Bar, *Montenegro* **42 E4** 42 8N 19 8 E
Bar, *Ukraine* **52 B2** 49 4N 27 40 E
Bar Bigha, *India* **81 G11** 25 21N 85 47 E
Bar Harbor, *U.S.A.* **129 D6** 44 23N 68 13W
Bar-le-Duc, *France* **23 D12** 48 47N 5 10 E
Bar-sur-Aube, *France* **23 D11** 48 14N 4 40 E
Bar-sur-Seine, *France* **23 D11** 48 7N 4 20 E
Barabai, *Indonesia* **75 C5** 2 32 S 115 34 E
Barabinsk, *Russia* **56 D8** 55 20N 78 20 E
Baraboo, *U.S.A.* **138 D10** 43 28N 89 45W
Baracaldo, *Spain* **34 B2** 43 18N 2 59W
Baracoa, *Cuba* **149 B5** 20 20N 74 30W
Baradero, *Argentina* **158 C4** 33 52 S 59 29W
Baradine, *Australia* **117 A8** 30 56 S 149 4 E
Baraga, *U.S.A.* **138 B10** 46 47N 88 30W
Barahona, *Dom. Rep.* **149 C5** 18 13N 71 7W
Barahona, *Spain* **34 D2** 41 17N 2 39W
Baraka →, *Sudan* **94 D4** 18 13N 37 35 E
Barakot, *India* **81 J11** 21 33N 84 59 E
Barakpur, *India* **81 H13** 22 44N 88 30 E
Barakula, *Australia* **115 D5** 26 30 S 150 33 E
Baralaba, *Australia* **114 C4** 24 13 S 149 50 E
Baralzon L., *Canada* **131 B9** 60 0N 98 3W
Baram →, *Malaysia* **75 B4** 4 35N 113 58 E
Baramati, *India* **82 E2** 18 11N 74 33 E
Baramba, *India* **82 D7** 20 25N 85 23 E
Barameiya, *Sudan* **94 D4** 18 32N 36 38 E
Baramula, *India* **81 B6** 34 15N 74 20 E
Baran, *India* **80 G7** 25 9N 76 40 E

172 Baranavichy


Baranavichy =
Baranovichi, *Belorussia* **50 E5** 53 10N 26 0 E
Baranoa, *Colombia* **152 A3** 10 48N 74 55W
Baranof I., *U.S.A.* **130 B1** 57 0N 135 0W
Baranovichi, *Belorussia* .. **50 E5** 53 10N 26 0 E
Baranów Sandomierski,
*Poland* **47 E8** 50 29N 21 30 E
Baranya □, *Hungary* **31 F11** 46 0N 18 15 E
Barão de Cocais, *Brazil* . **155 E3** 19 56 S 43 28W
Barão de Grajaú, *Brazil* . **154 C3** 6 45 S 43 1W
Barão de Melgaço,
*Mato Grosso, Brazil* ... **157 D6** 16 14 S 55 52W
Barão de Melgaço,
*Rondônia, Brazil* **157 C5** 11 50 S 60 45W
Baraolt, *Romania* **46 C6** 46 5N 25 34 E
Barapasi, *Indonesia* **73 B5** 2 15 S 137 5 E
Barapina, *Papua N. G.* .. **120 D8** 6 21 S 155 25 E
Barasat, *India* **81 H13** 22 46N 88 31 E
Barat Daya, Kepulauan,
*Indonesia* **72 C3** 7 30 S 128 0 E
Barataria B., *U.S.A.* **139 L10** 29 20N 89 55W
Baraut, *India* **80 E7** 29 13N 77 7 E
Baraya, *Colombia* **152 C2** 3 10N 75 4W
Barbacan, *Phil.* **71 F2** 10 20N 119 21 E
Barbacena, *Brazil* **155 F3** 21 15 S 43 56W
Barbacoas, *Colombia* **152 C2** 1 45N 78 0W
Barbacoas, *Venezuela* ... **152 B4** 9 29N 66 58W
Barbados ■, *W. Indies* .. **149 D8** 13 10N 59 30W
Barbalha, *Brazil* **154 C4** 7 19 S 39 17W
Barban, *Croatia* **39 C11** 45 5N 14 4 E
Barbastro, *Spain* **34 C5** 42 2N 0 5 E
Barbate, *Spain* **37 J5** 36 13N 5 56W
Barbaza, *Phil.* **71 F4** 11 12N 122 2 E
Barberino di Mugello,
*Italy* **39 D8** 44 1N 11 15 E
Barberton, *S. Africa* **105 D5** 25 42 S 31 2 E
Barberton, *U.S.A.* **136 E3** 41 0N 81 39W
Barbezieux, *France* **24 C3** 45 28N 0 9W
Barbosa, *Colombia* **152 B3** 5 57N 73 37W
Barbourville, *U.S.A.* **135 G4** 36 52N 83 53W
Barbuda, *W. Indies* **149 C7** 17 30N 61 40W
Barcaldine, *Australia* **114 C4** 23 43 S 145 6 E
Barcarrota, *Spain* **37 G4** 38 31N 6 51W
Barcellona Pozzo di
Gotto, *Italy* **41 D8** 38 8N 15 15 E
Barcelona, *Spain* **34 D7** 41 21N 2 10 E
Barcelona, *Venezuela* **153 A5** 10 10N 64 40W
Barcelona □, *Spain* **34 D7** 41 30N 2 0 E
Barcelonette, *France* **25 D10** 44 23N 6 40 E
Barcelos, *Brazil* **153 D5** 1 0 S 63 0W
Barcin, *Poland* **47 C4** 52 52N 17 55 E
Barcoo →, *Australia* **114 D3** 25 30 S 142 50 E
Barcs, *Hungary* **31 F10** 45 58N 17 28 E
Barczewo, *Poland* **47 B7** 53 50N 20 42 E
Barda, *Azerbaijan* **53 F12** 40 25N 47 10 E
Barda del Medio,
*Argentina* **160 A3** 38 45 S 68 11W
Bardai, *Chad* **97 D3** 21 25N 17 0 E
Bardas Blancas, *Argentina* **158 D2** 35 49 S 69 45W
Barddhaman, *India* **81 H12** 23 14N 87 39 E
Bardejov, *Slovak Rep.* **31 B14** 49 18N 21 15 E
Bardera, *Somali Rep.* **90 G3** 2 20N 42 27 E
Bardi, *Italy* **38 D6** 44 38N 9 43 E
Bardia, *Libya* **96 B5** 31 45N 25 5 E
Bardo, *Poland* **47 E3** 50 31N 16 42 E
Bardoli, *India* **82 D1** 21 12N 73 5 E
Bardolino, *Italy* **38 C7** 45 33N 10 43 E
Bardsey I., *U.K.* **16 E3** 52 46N 4 47W
Bardstown, *U.S.A.* **141 G11** 37 49N 85 28W
Bareilly, *India* **81 E8** 28 22N 79 27 E
Barellan, *Australia* **117 C7** 34 16 S 146 24 E
Barentin, *France* **22 C7** 49 33N 0 58 E
Barenton, *France* **22 D6** 48 38N 0 50W
Barents Sea, *Arctic* **6 B9** 73 0N 39 0 E
Barentu, *Eritrea* **95 D4** 15 2N 37 35 E
Barfleur, *France* **22 C5** 49 40N 1 17W
Barfleur, Pte. de, *France* **22 C5** 49 42N 1 16W
Barga, *Italy* **38 D7** 44 5N 10 30 E
Bargal, *Somali Rep.* **90 E5** 11 25N 51 0 E
Bargara, *Australia* **114 C5** 24 50 S 152 25 E
Barge, *Italy* **38 D4** 44 43N 7 19 E
Bargnop, *Sudan* **95 F2** 9 32N 28 25 E
Bargo, *Australia* **117 C9** 34 18 S 150 35 E
Bargteheide, *Germany* **26 B6** 53 42N 10 13 E
Barguzin, *Russia* **57 D11** 53 37N 109 37 E
Barh, *India* **81 G11** 25 29N 85 46 E
Barhaj, *India* **81 F10** 26 18N 83 44 E
Barhi, *India* **81 G11** 24 15N 85 25 E
Bari, *India* **80 F7** 26 39N 77 39 E
Bari, *Italy* **41 A9** 41 6N 16 52 E
Bari Doab, *Pakistan* **80 D5** 30 20N 73 0 E
Bariadi □, *Tanzania* **106 C3** 2 45 S 34 40 E
Barīm, *Yemen* **86 D3** 12 39N 43 25 E
Barima →, *Guyana* **153 B5** 8 33N 60 25W
Barinas, *Venezuela* **152 B3** 8 36N 70 15W
Barinas □, *Venezuela* .. **152 B4** 8 10N 69 50W
Baring, *U.S.A.* **140 D4** 40 15N 92 12W
Baring, C., *Canada* **126 B8** 70 0N 117 30W
Baringa, *Zaïre* **102 B4** 0 45N 20 52 E
Baringo, *Kenya* **106 B4** 0 47N 36 16 E
Baringo □, *Kenya* **106 B4** 0 55N 36 0 E
Baringo, L., *Kenya* **106 B4** 0 47N 36 16 E
Barinitas, *Venezuela* **152 B3** 8 45N 70 25W
Baripada, *India* **82 D8** 21 57N 86 45 E
Bariri, *Brazil* **155 F2** 22 4 S 48 44W
Bârîs, *Egypt* **94 C3** 24 42N 30 31 E
Barisal, *Bangla.* **78 D3** 22 45N 90 20 E
Barito →, *Indonesia* **75 C4** 4 0 S 114 50 E
Barjac, *France* **25 D8** 44 20N 4 22 E
Barjols, *France* **25 E10** 43 34N 6 2 E
Barjūj, Wadi →, *Libya* . **96 C2** 25 26N 12 12 E
Bark L., *Canada* **136 A7** 45 27N 77 51W
Barka = Baraka →,
*Sudan* **94 D4** 18 13N 37 35 E
Barkam, *China* **68 B4** 31 51N 102 28 E
Barker, *U.S.A.* **136 C6** 43 20N 78 33W
Barkley Sound, *Canada* .. **130 D3** 48 50N 125 10W
Barkly Downs, *Australia* . **114 C2** 20 30 S 138 30 E
Barkly East, *S. Africa* ... **104 E4** 30 58 S 27 33 E
Barkly Tableland,
*Australia* **114 B2** 17 50 S 136 40 E
Barkly West, *S. Africa* .. **104 D3** 28 5 S 24 31 E
Barkol, *China* **64 B4** 43 37N 93 2 E
Barkol, Wadi →, *Sudan* **94 D3** 17 40N 32 0 E
Barksdale, *U.S.A.* **139 L4** 29 44N 100 2W
Barlee, L., *Australia* **113 E2** 29 15 S 119 30 E
Barlee, Mt., *Australia* ... **113 D4** 24 38 S 128 13 E
Barletta, *Italy* **41 A9** 41 20N 16 17 E
Barlinek, *Poland* **47 C2** 53 0N 15 15 E
Barlovento, *Canary Is.* .. **33 F2** 28 48N 17 48W
Barlow L., *Canada* **131 A8** 62 0N 103 0W
Barmedman, *Australia* ... **117 C7** 34 9 S 147 21 E
Barmer, *India* **80 G4** 25 45N 71 20 E
Barmera, *Australia* **116 C4** 34 15 S 140 28 E
Barmouth, *U.K.* **16 E3** 52 44N 4 3W
Barmstedt, *Germany* **26 B5** 53 47N 9 46 E
Barnagar, *India* **80 H6** 23 7N 75 19 E
Barnard Castle, *U.K.* **16 C6** 54 33N 1 55W
Barnato, *Australia* **117 A6** 31 38 S 145 0 E
Barnaul, *Russia* **56 D9** 53 20N 83 40 E
Barnesville, *U.S.A.* **135 J3** 33 3N 84 9W
Barnet, *U.K.* **17 F7** 51 37N 0 15W
Barneveld, *Neths.* **20 D7** 52 7N 5 36 E
Barneveld, *U.S.A.* **137 C9** 43 16N 75 14W
Barneville-Cartevert,
*France* **22 C5** 49 23N 1 46W
Barngo, *Australia* **114 D4** 25 3 S 147 20 E
Barnhart, *U.S.A.* **139 K4** 31 8N 101 10W
Barnsley, *U.K.* **16 D6** 53 33N 1 29W
Barnstaple, *U.K.* **17 F3** 51 5N 4 3W
Barnsville, *U.S.A.* **138 B6** 46 43N 96 28W
Baro, *Nigeria* **101 D6** 8 35N 6 18 E
Baro →, *Ethiopia* **95 F3** 8 26N 33 13 E
Baroda = Vadodara, *India* **80 H5** 22 20N 73 10 E
Baroda, *India* **80 G7** 25 29N 76 35 E
Baroe, *S. Africa* **104 E3** 33 13 S 24 33 E
Baron Ra., *Australia* **112 D4** 23 30 S 127 45 E
Barora Ite, *Solomon Is.* . **121 L10** 7 36 S 158 24 E
Barorafa, *Solomon Is.* ... **121 L10** 7 30 S 158 20 E
Barpali, *India* **82 D6** 21 11N 83 35 E
Barpathar, *India* **78 B4** 26 17N 93 53 E
Barpeta, *India* **78 B3** 26 20N 91 10 E
Barqin, *Libya* **96 C2** 27 33N 13 34 E
Barques, Pt. Aux, *U.S.A.* **134 C4** 44 4N 82 58W
Barquinha, *Portugal* **37 F2** 39 28N 8 25W
Barquísimeto, *Venezuela* . **152 A4** 10 4N 69 19W
Barr, *France* **23 D14** 48 25N 7 28 E
Barra, *Brazil* **154 D3** 11 5 S 43 10W
Barra, *U.K.* **18 E1** 57 0N 7 30W
Barra, Sd. of, *U.K.* **18 D1** 57 4N 7 25W
Barra da Estiva, *Brazil* .. **155 D3** 13 38 S 41 19W
Barra de Navidad, *Mexico* **146 D4** 19 12N 104 41W
Barra do Corda, *Brazil* .. **154 C2** 5 30 S 45 10W
Barra do Dande, *Angola* . **103 D2** 8 28 S 13 22 E
Barra do Mendes, *Brazil* . **155 D3** 11 43 S 42 4W
Barra do Piraí, *Brazil* ... **155 F3** 22 30 S 43 50W
Barra Falsa, Pta. da,
*Mozam.* **105 C6** 22 58 S 35 37 E
Barra Hd., *U.K.* **18 E1** 56 47N 7 40W
Barra Mansa, *Brazil* **155 F3** 22 35 S 44 12W
Barraba, *Australia* **117 A9** 30 21 S 150 35 E
Barracão do Barreto,
*Brazil* **157 B6** 8 48 S 58 24W
Barrackpur = Barakpur,
*India* **81 H13** 22 44N 88 30 E
Barrafranca, *Italy* **41 E7** 37 22N 14 10 E
Barranca, *Lima, Peru* ... **156 C2** 10 45 S 77 50W
Barranca, *Loreto, Peru* .. **152 D2** 4 50 S 76 50W
Barrancabermeja,
*Colombia* **152 B3** 7 0N 73 50W
Barrancas, *Colombia* **152 A3** 10 57N 72 50W
Barrancas, *Venezuela* **153 B5** 8 55N 62 5W
Barrancos, *Portugal* **37 G4** 38 10N 6 58W
Barranqueras, *Argentina* . **158 B4** 27 30 S 59 0W
Barranquilla, *Colombia* .. **152 A3** 11 0N 74 50W
Barras, *Brazil* **154 B3** 4 15 S 42 18W
Barras, *Colombia* **152 D3** 1 45 S 73 13W
Barraute, *Canada* **128 C4** 48 26N 77 38W
Barre, *Mass., U.S.A.* **137 D12** 42 25N 72 6W
Barre, *Vt., U.S.A.* **137 B12** 44 12N 72 30W
Barre do Bugres, *Brazil* . **157 C6** 15 0 S 57 11W
Barreal, *Argentina* **158 C2** 31 33 S 69 28W
Barrei, *Ethiopia* **108 C2** 6 10N 42 49 E
Barreiras, *Brazil* **155 D3** 12 8 S 45 0W
Barreirinha, *Brazil* **153 D6** 2 47 S 57 3W
Barreirinhas, *Brazil* **154 B3** 2 30 S 42 50W
Barreiro, *Portugal* **37 G1** 38 40N 9 6W
Barreiros, *Brazil* **154 C4** 8 49 S 35 12W
Barrême, *France* **25 E10** 43 57N 6 23 E
Barren, Nosy, *Madag.* ... **105 B7** 18 25 S 43 40 E
Barretos, *Brazil* **155 F2** 20 30 S 48 35W
Barrhead, *Canada* **130 C6** 54 10N 114 24W
Barrie, *Canada* **128 D4** 44 24N 79 40W
Barrier, C., *N.Z.* **118 C4** 36 25 S 175 32 E
Barrier Ra., *Australia* ... **116 A4** 31 0 S 141 30 E
Barrier Ra., *Otago, N.Z.* **119 E4** 44 15 S 169 32 E
Barrier Ra., *W. Coast,*
*N.Z.* **119 E3** 44 30 S 168 30 E
Barrière, *Canada* **130 C4** 51 12N 120 7W
Barrington, *U.S.A.* **137 E13** 41 44N 71 18W
Barrington L., *Canada* .. **131 B8** 56 55N 100 15W
Barrington Tops, *Australia* **117 B9** 32 6 S 151 28 E
Barringun, *Australia* **115 D4** 29 1 S 145 41 E
Barro do Garças, *Brazil* . **157 D7** 15 54 S 52 16W
Barrow, *U.S.A.* **126 A4** 71 18N 156 47W
Barrow →, *Ireland* **19 D4** 52 10N 6 57W
Barrow, C., *U.S.A.* **124 B4** 71 10N 156 20W
Barrow Creek, *Australia* . **114 C1** 21 30 S 133 55 E
Barrow I., *Australia* **112 D2** 20 45 S 115 20 E
Barrow-in-Furness, *U.K.* . **16 C4** 54 8N 3 15W
Barrow Pt., *Australia* **114 A3** 14 20 S 144 40 E
Barrow Ra., *Australia* ... **113 E4** 26 0 S 127 40 E
Barrow Str., *Canada* **6 B3** 74 20N 95 0W
Barruecopardo, *Spain* ... **36 D4** 41 4N 6 40W
Barruelo, *Spain* **36 C6** 42 54N 4 17W
Barry, *U.K.* **17 F4** 51 23N 3 19W
Barry, *U.S.A.* **140 E5** 39 42N 91 2W
Barry's Bay, *Canada* **128 C4** 45 29N 77 41W
Barsalogho, *Burkina Faso* **101 C4** 13 25N 1 3W
Barsat, *Pakistan* **81 A5** 36 10N 72 45 E
Barsham, *Syria* **84 C4** 35 21N 40 33 E
Barsi, *India* **82 E2** 18 10N 75 50 E
Barsø, *Denmark* **15 J3** 55 7N 9 33 E
Barstow, *Calif., U.S.A.* .. **145 L9** 34 54N 117 1W
Barstow, *Tex., U.S.A.* ... **139 K3** 31 28N 103 24W
Barth, *Germany* **26 A8** 54 20N 12 36 E
Barthélemy, Col, *Vietnam* **76 C5** 19 26N 104 6 E
Bartica, *Guyana* **153 B6** 6 25N 58 40W
Bartin, *Turkey* **88 C5** 41 38N 32 21 E
Bartle Frere, *Australia* ... **110 D8** 17 27 S 145 50 E
Bartlesville, *U.S.A.* **139 G7** 36 45N 95 59W
Bartlett, *Calif., U.S.A.* .. **144 J8** 36 29N 118 2W
Bartlett, *Tex., U.S.A.* ... **139 K6** 30 48N 97 26W
Bartlett, L., *Canada* **130 A5** 63 5N 118 20W
Bartolomeu Dias, *Mozam.* **107 G4** 21 10 S 35 8 E
Barton, *Australia* **113 F5** 30 31 S 132 39 E
Barton, *Phil.* **71 F2** 10 24N 119 8 E
Barton upon Humber,
*U.K.* **16 D7** 53 41N 0 27W
Bartonville, *U.S.A.* **140 D7** 40 39N 89 39W
Bartoszyce, *Poland* **47 A7** 54 15N 20 55 E
Bartow, *U.S.A.* **135 M5** 27 54N 81 50W
Barú, I. de, *Colombia* ... **152 A2** 10 15N 75 35W
Barú, Volcan, *Panama* .. **148 E3** 8 55N 82 35W
Barumba, *Zaïre* **106 B1** 1 3N 23 37 E
Baruth, *Germany* **26 C9** 52 3N 13 31 E
Barvaux, *Belgium* **21 H6** 50 21N 5 29 E
Barvenkovo, *Ukraine* **52 B7** 48 57N 37 0 E
Barwani, *India* **80 H6** 22 2N 74 57 E
Barycz →, *Poland* **47 D3** 51 42N 16 15 E
Barysaw = Borisov,
*Belorussia* **50 D6** 54 17N 28 28 E
Barysh, *Russia* **51 E15** 53 39N 47 8 E
Barzān, *Iraq* **84 B5** 36 55N 44 3 E
Bas-Rhin □, *France* **23 D14** 48 40N 7 30 E
Bašaid, *Serbia* **42 B5** 45 38N 20 25 E
Bāsa'idū, *Iran* **85 E7** 26 35N 55 20 E
Basal, *Pakistan* **80 C5** 33 33N 72 13 E
Basankusa, *Zaïre* **102 B3** 1 5N 19 50 E
Basawa, *Afghan.* **80 B4** 34 15N 70 50 E
Bascharage, *Lux.* **21 J7** 49 34N 5 55 E
Basco, *Phil.* **70 A3** 20 27N 121 58 E
Bascuñán, C., *Chile* **158 B1** 28 52 S 71 35W
Basècles, *Belgium* **21 G3** 50 32N 3 39 E
Basel, *Switz.* **28 A5** 47 35N 7 35 E
Basel-Stadt □, *Switz.* ... **28 A5** 47 35N 7 35 E
Baselland □, *Switz.* **28 B5** 47 26N 7 45 E
Basento →, *Italy* **41 B9** 40 21N 16 50 E
Basey, *Phil.* **71 F5** 11 17N 125 4 E
Bāshī, *Iran* **85 D6** 28 41N 51 4 E
Bashkir Republic □,
*Russia* **54 D5** 54 0N 57 0 E
Bashkortostan = Bashkir
Republic □, *Russia* ... **54 D5** 54 0N 57 0 E
Basilaki I., *Papua N. G.* . **120 F6** 10 35 S 151 0 E
Basilan, *Phil.* **71 H4** 6 35N 122 0 E
Basilan □, *Phil.* **71 H4** 6 33N 122 4 E
Basilan Str., *Phil.* **71 H4** 6 50N 122 0 E
Basildon, *U.K.* **17 F8** 51 34N 0 29 E
Basilicata □, *Italy* **41 B9** 40 30N 16 0 E
Basim = Washim, *India* . **82 D3** 20 3N 77 0 E
Basin, *U.S.A.* **142 D9** 44 23N 108 2W
Basingstoke, *U.K.* **17 F6** 51 15N 1 5W
Basirhat, *Bangla.* **78 D2** 22 40N 88 54 E
Baška, *Croatia* **39 D11** 44 58N 14 45 E
Başkale, *Turkey* **89 D10** 38 2N 43 59 E
Baskatong, Rés., *Canada* **128 C4** 46 46N 75 50W
Basle = Basel, *Switz.* ... **28 A5** 47 35N 7 35 E
Basmat, *India* **82 E3** 19 15N 77 12 E
Basoda, *India* **80 H7** 23 52N 77 54 E
Basodino, *Switz.* **29 D6** 46 25N 8 28 E
Basoka, *Zaïre* **106 B1** 1 16N 23 40 E
Basongo, *Zaïre* **103 C4** 4 15 S 20 20 E
Basque, Pays, *France* ... **24 E2** 43 15N 1 20W
Basque Provinces = País
Vasco □, *Spain* **34 C2** 42 50N 2 45W
Basra = Al Başrah, *Iraq* . **84 D5** 30 30N 47 50 E
Bass Rock, *U.K.* **18 E6** 56 5N 2 40W
Bass Str., *Australia* **114 F4** 39 15 S 146 30 E
Bassano, *Canada* **130 C6** 50 48N 112 20W
Bassano del Grappa, *Italy* **39 C8** 45 45N 11 45 E
Bassar, *Togo* **101 D5** 9 19N 0 57 E
Basse Santa-Su, *Gambia* . **100 C2** 13 13N 14 15W
Basse-Terre, *Guadeloupe* **149 C7** 16 0N 61 44W
Bassecourt, *Switz.* **28 B4** 47 20N 7 15 E
Bassein, *Burma* **78 G5** 16 45N 94 30 E
Bassein, *India* **82 E1** 19 26N 72 48 E
Basseterre,
*St. Christopher-Nevis* .. **149 C7** 17 17N 62 43W
Bassett, *Nebr., U.S.A.* .. **138 D5** 42 35N 99 32W
Bassett, *Va., U.S.A.* **135 G6** 36 46N 79 59W
Bassevelde, *Belgium* **21 F3** 51 15N 3 41 E
Bassi, *India* **80 D7** 30 44N 76 21 E
Bassigny, *France* **23 E12** 48 0N 5 30 E
Bassikounou, *Mauritania* . **100 B3** 15 55N 6 1W
Bassilly, *Belgium* **21 G3** 50 40N 3 56 E
Bassum, *Germany* **26 C4** 52 50N 8 42 E
Båstad, *Sweden* **15 H6** 56 25N 12 51 E
Bastak, *Iran* **85 E7** 27 15N 54 25 E
Baştām, *Iran* **85 B7** 36 29N 55 4 E
Bastar, *India* **82 E5** 19 15N 81 40 E
Bastelica, *France* **25 F13** 42 1N 9 3 E
Basti, *India* **81 F10** 26 52N 82 55 E
Bastia, *France* **25 F13** 42 40N 9 30 E
Bastia Umbra, *Italy* **39 E9** 43 4N 12 34 E
Bastogne, *Belgium* **21 H7** 50 1N 5 43 E
Bastrop, *U.S.A.* **139 K6** 30 7N 97 19W
Basyanovskiy, *Russia* **54 B7** 58 19N 60 44 E
Bat Yam, *Israel* **91 C3** 32 2N 34 44 E
Bata, *Eq. Guin.* **102 B1** 1 57N 9 50 E
Bata, *Romania* **46 C3** 46 1N 22 4 E
Bataan, *Phil.* **70 D3** 14 40N 120 25 E
Batabanó, *Cuba* **148 B3** 22 40N 82 20W
Batabanó, G. de, *Cuba* .. **148 B3** 22 30N 82 30W
Batac, *Phil.* **70 B3** 18 3N 120 34 E
Batagoy, *Russia* **57 C14** 67 38N 134 38 E
Batak, *Bulgaria* **43 F9** 41 57N 24 12 E
Batalha, *Portugal* **37 F2** 39 40N 8 50W
Batam, *Indonesia* **74 B2** 1 5N 104 3 E
Batama, *Zaïre* **106 B2** 0 58N 26 33 E
Batamay, *Russia* **57 C13** 63 30N 129 15 E
Batamshinskiy,
*Kazakhstan* **54 F6** 50 36N 58 16 E
Batan I., *Phil.* **70 A3** 20 30N 121 50 E
Batanes □, *Phil.* **70 A3** 20 40N 121 55 E
Batanes Is., *Phil.* **70 A3** 20 30N 121 50 E
Batang, *China* **68 B2** 30 1N 99 0 E
Batang, *Indonesia* **75 D3** 6 55 S 109 45 E
Batangafo, *C.A.R.* **102 A3** 7 25N 18 20 E
Batangas, *Phil.* **70 E3** 13 35N 121 10 E
Batangas □, *Phil.* **70 E3** 13 15N 121 5 E
Batanghari, *Indonesia* ... **74 C2** 1 36 S 103 37 E
Batanta, *Indonesia* **73 B4** 0 55 S 130 40 E
Batas, *Phil.* **71 F2** 11 10N 119 37 E
Batas I., *Phil.* **71 F2** 11 10N 119 36 E
Batatais, *Brazil* **159 A6** 20 54 S 47 37W
Batavia, *Ill., U.S.A.* **141 C8** 41 51N 88 19W
Batavia, *N.Y., U.S.A.* ... **136 D6** 43 0N 78 11W
Batavia, *Ohio, U.S.A.* ... **141 E12** 39 5N 84 11W
Bataysk, *Russia* **53 C8** 47 3N 39 45 E
Batchelor, *Australia* **112 B5** 13 4 S 131 1 E
Batéké, Plateau, *Congo* . **102 C3** 3 30 S 15 45 E
Bateman's B., *Australia* . **117 C9** 35 40 S 150 12 E
Batemans Bay, *Australia* . **117 C9** 35 44 S 150 11 E
Bates Ra., *Australia* **113 E3** 27 27 S 121 5 E
Batesburg, *U.S.A.* **135 J5** 33 54N 81 33W
Batesville, *Ark., U.S.A.* . **139 H9** 35 46N 91 39W
Batesville, *Ind., U.S.A.* . **141 E11** 39 18N 85 13W
Batesville, *Miss., U.S.A.* . **139 H10** 34 19N 89 57W
Batesville, *Tex., U.S.A.* . **139 L5** 28 58N 99 37W
Bath, *U.K.* **17 F5** 51 22N 2 22W
Bath, *Maine, U.S.A.* **129 D6** 43 55N 69 49W
Bath, *N.Y., U.S.A.* **136 D7** 42 20N 77 19W
Batheay, *Cambodia* **77 G5** 11 59N 104 57 E
Bathgate, *U.K.* **18 F5** 55 54N 3 38W
Bathmen, *Neths.* **20 D8** 52 15N 6 29 E
Bathurst = Banjul,
*Gambia* **100 C1** 13 28N 16 40W
Bathurst, *Australia* **117 B8** 33 25 S 149 31 E
Bathurst, *Canada* **129 C6** 47 37N 65 43W
Bathurst, *S. Africa* **104 E4** 33 30 S 26 50 E
Bathurst, C., *Canada* **126 A7** 70 34N 128 0W
Bathurst B., *Australia* ... **114 A3** 14 16 S 144 25 E
Bathurst Harb., *Australia* **114 G4** 43 15 S 146 10 E
Bathurst I., *Australia* ... **112 B5** 11 30 S 130 10 E
Bathurst I., *Canada* **6 B2** 76 0N 100 30W
Bathurst Inlet, *Canada* .. **126 B9** 66 50N 108 1W
Batie, *Burkina Faso* **100 D4** 9 53N 2 53W
Batlow, *Australia* **117 C8** 35 31 S 148 9 E
Batman, *Turkey* **89 E9** 37 55N 41 5 E
Batna, *Algeria* **99 A6** 35 34N 6 15 E
Bato, *Leyte, Phil.* **71 F5** 10 13N 124 48 E
Bato, *Sulu, Phil.* **71 J3** 5 15N 120 3 E
Bato Bato, *Phil.* **71 J2** 5 6N 119 49 E
Batoala, *Gabon* **102 B2** 0 48N 13 27 E
Batobato, *Phil.* **71 H6** 6 50N 126 5 E
Batočina, *Serbia* **42 C6** 44 7N 21 5 E
Batoka, *Zambia* **107 F2** 16 45 S 27 15 E
Baton Rouge, *U.S.A.* **139 K9** 30 27N 91 11W
Batong, Ko, *Thailand* ... **77 J2** 6 32N 99 12 E
Bátonyterenye, *Hungary* . **31 C12** 48 3N 19 50 E
Batopilas, *Mexico* **146 B3** 27 0N 107 45W
Batouri, *Cameroon* **102 B2** 4 30N 14 25 E
Battambang, *Cambodia* .. **76 F4** 13 7N 103 12 E
Batticaloa, *Sri Lanka* **83 L5** 7 43N 81 45 E
Battice, *Belgium* **21 G7** 50 39N 5 50 E
Battipáglia, *Italy* **41 B7** 40 38N 15 0 E
Battle, *U.K.* **17 G8** 50 55N 0 30 E
Battle →, *Canada* **131 C7** 52 43N 108 15W
Battle Camp, *Australia* .. **114 B3** 15 20 S 144 40 E
Battle Creek, *U.S.A.* **141 B11** 42 19N 85 11W
Battle Ground, *U.S.A.* .. **144 E4** 45 47N 122 32W
Battle Harbour, *Canada* . **129 B8** 52 16N 55 35W
Battle Lake, *U.S.A.* **138 B7** 46 17N 95 43W
Battle Mountain, *U.S.A.* . **142 F5** 40 38N 116 56W
Battlefields, *Zimbabwe* .. **107 F2** 18 37 S 29 47 E
Battleford, *Canada* **131 C7** 52 45N 108 15W
Battonya, *Hungary* **31 E14** 46 16N 21 3 E
Batu, *Ethiopia* **90 F2** 6 55N 39 45 E
Batu, Bukit, *Malaysia* ... **75 B4** 2 16N 113 43 E
Batu, Kepulauan,
*Indonesia* **74 C1** 0 30 S 98 25 E
Batu Bora, Bukit,
*Malaysia* **75 B4** 2 43N 114 43 E
Batu Caves, *Malaysia* ... **77 L3** 3 15N 101 40 E
Batu Gajah, *Malaysia* ... **77 K3** 4 28N 101 3 E
Batu Is. = Batu,
Kepulauan, *Indonesia* . **74 C1** 0 30 S 98 25 E
Batu Pahat, *Malaysia* ... **77 M4** 1 50N 102 56 E
Batu Puteh, Gunong,
*Malaysia* **74 B2** 4 15N 101 31 E
Batuata, *Indonesia* **72 C2** 6 12 S 122 42 E
Batulaki, *Phil.* **71 J5** 5 34N 125 19 E
Batumi, *Georgia* **53 F9** 41 30N 41 30 E
Baturaja, *Indonesia* **74 C2** 4 11 S 104 15 E
Baturité, *Brazil* **154 B4** 4 28 S 38 45W
Batusangkar, *Indonesia* . **74 C2** 0 27 S 100 35 E
Bau, *Malaysia* **75 B4** 1 25N 110 9 E
Bauang, *Phil.* **70 C3** 16 31N 120 20 E
Baubau, *Indonesia* **72 C2** 5 25 S 122 38 E
Bauchi, *Nigeria* **101 C6** 10 22N 9 48 E
Bauchi □, *Nigeria* **101 C6** 10 30N 10 0 E
Baud, *France* **22 E3** 47 52N 3 1W
Baudette, *U.S.A.* **138 A7** 48 43N 94 36W
Baudour, *Belgium* **21 H3** 50 29N 3 50 E
Bauer, C., *Australia* **115 E1** 32 44 S 134 4 E
Baugé, *France* **22 E6** 47 31N 0 8W
Bauhinia Downs, *Australia* **114 C4** 24 35 S 149 18 E
Bauma, *Switz.* **29 B7** 47 23N 8 53 E
Baume-les-Dames, *France* **23 E13** 47 22N 6 22 E
Baunatal, *Germany* **26 D5** 51 13N 9 25 E
Baunei, *Italy* **40 B2** 40 2N 9 41 E
Baures, *Bolivia* **157 C5** 13 35 S 63 35W
Bauru, *Brazil* **159 A6** 22 10 S 49 0W
Baús, *Brazil* **157 D7** 18 22 S 52 47W
Bauska, *Latvia* **50 C4** 56 24N 24 15 E
Bautzen, *Germany* **26 D10** 51 11N 14 25 E
Bavānāt, *Iran* **85 D7** 30 28N 53 27 E
Bavanište, *Serbia* **42 C5** 44 49N 20 53 E
Bavaria = Bayern □,
*Germany* **27 F7** 49 7N 11 30 E
Båven, *Sweden* **14 F10** 59 0N 16 56 E
Bavi Sadri, *India* **80 G6** 24 28N 74 30 E
Bavispe →, *Mexico* **146 B3** 29 30N 109 11W
Bawdwin, *Burma* **78 D6** 23 5N 97 20 E
Bawean, *Indonesia* **75 D4** 5 46 S 112 35 E
Bawku, *Ghana* **101 C4** 11 3N 0 19W
Bawlake, *Burma* **78 F6** 19 11N 97 21 E
Bawolung, *China* **68 C3** 28 50N 101 16 E
Baxley, *U.S.A.* **135 K4** 31 47N 82 21W
Baxoi, *China* **68 B1** 30 1N 96 50 E
Baxter, *U.S.A.* **140 C3** 41 49N 93 9W
Baxter Springs, *U.S.A.* .. **139 G7** 37 2N 94 44W
Bay Bulls, *Canada* **129 C9** 47 19N 52 50W
Bay City, *Mich., U.S.A.* . **134 D4** 43 36N 83 54W
Bay City, *Oreg., U.S.A.* . **142 D2** 45 31N 123 53W
Bay City, *Tex., U.S.A.* .. **139 L7** 28 59N 95 58W
Bay de Verde, *Canada* ... **129 C9** 48 5N 52 54W
Bay Minette, *U.S.A.* **135 K2** 30 53N 87 46W
Bay St. Louis, *U.S.A.* ... **139 K10** 30 19N 89 20W

Bradford 177


Bon Sar Pa, Vietnam 76 F6 12 24N 107 35 E
Bonaduz, Switz. 29 C8 46 49N 9 25 E
Bonaire, Neth. Ant. 149 D6 12 10N 68 15W
Bonang, Australia 117 D8 37 11 S 148 41 E
Bonanza, Nic. 148 D3 13 54N 84 35W
Bonaparte Arch., Australia 112 B3 14 0 S 124 30 E
Boñar, Spain 36 C5 42 52N 5 19W
Bonaventure, Canada 129 C6 48 5N 65 32W
Bonavista, Canada 129 C9 48 40N 53 5W
Bonavista, C., Canada 129 C9 48 42N 53 5W
Bonawan, Phil. 71 G4 9 8N 122 55 E
Bondeno, Italy 39 D8 44 53N 11 22 E
Bondo, Zaïre 102 B4 3 55N 23 53 E
Bondoukou, Ivory C. 100 D4 8 2N 2 47W
Bondowoso, Indonesia 75 D4 7 55 S 113 49 E
Bondyug, Russia 54 A4 60 29N 55 56 E
Bone, Teluk, Indonesia 72 B2 4 10 S 120 50 E
Bone Rate, Indonesia 72 C2 7 25 S 121 5 E
Bone Rate, Kepulauan, Indonesia 72 C2 6 30 S 121 10 E
Bonefro, Italy 41 A7 41 42N 14 55 E
Bo'ness, U.K. 18 E5 56 0N 3 38W
Bong Son = Hoai Nhon, Vietnam 76 E7 14 28N 109 1 E
Bongabon, Phil. 70 D3 15 38N 121 8 E
Bongabong, Phil. 70 E3 12 45N 121 29 E
Bongandanga, Zaïre 102 B4 1 24N 21 3 E
Bongo, Zaïre 102 C3 1 47 S 17 41 E
Bongor, Chad 97 F3 10 35N 15 20 E
Bongouanou, Ivory C. 100 D4 6 42N 4 15W
Bonham, U.S.A. 139 J6 33 35N 96 11W
Bonheiden, Belgium 21 F5 51 1N 4 32 E
Bonifacio, France 25 G13 41 24N 9 10 E
Bonifacio, Bouches de, Medit. S. 40 A2 41 12N 9 15 E
Bonin Is. = Ogasawara Gunto, Pac. Oc. 122 E6 27 0N 142 0 E
Bonke, Ethiopia 95 F4 6 5N 37 16 E
Bonn, Germany 26 E3 50 43N 7 6 E
Bonnat, France 24 B5 46 20N 1 54 E
Bonne Terre, U.S.A. 139 G9 37 55N 90 33W
Bonners Ferry, U.S.A. 142 B5 48 42N 116 19W
Bonnétable, France 22 D7 48 11N 0 25 E
Bonneuil-Matours, France 22 F7 46 41N 0 34 E
Bonneval, France 22 D8 48 11N 1 24 E
Bonneville, France 25 B10 46 4N 6 24 E
Bonney, L., Australia 116 D4 37 50 S 140 20 E
Bonnie Doon, Australia 117 D6 37 2 S 145 53 E
Bonnie Downs, Australia 114 C3 22 7 S 143 50 E
Bonnie Rock, Australia 113 F2 30 29 S 118 22 E
Bonny, Nigeria 101 E6 4 25N 7 13 E
Bonny →, Nigeria 101 E6 4 20N 7 10 E
Bonny, Bight of, Africa 101 E6 3 30N 9 20 E
Bonny-sur-Loire, France 23 E9 47 33N 2 50 E
Bonnyville, Canada 131 C6 54 20N 110 45W
Bonobono, Phil. 71 G1 8 40N 117 36 E
Bonoi, Indonesia 73 B5 1 45 S 137 41 E
Bonorva, Italy 40 B1 40 25N 8 47 E
Bonsall, U.S.A. 145 M9 33 16N 117 14W
Bontang, Indonesia 75 B5 0 10N 117 30 E
Bonthain, Indonesia 72 C1 5 34 S 119 56 E
Bonthe, S. Leone 100 D2 7 30N 12 33W
Bontoc, Phil. 70 C3 17 7N 120 58 E
Bonyeri, Ghana 100 D4 5 1N 2 46W
Bonyhád, Hungary 31 E11 46 18N 18 32 E
Bonython Ra., Australia 112 D4 23 40 S 128 45 E
Bookabie, Australia 113 F5 31 50 S 132 41 E
Booker, U.S.A. 139 G4 36 27N 100 32W
Boolaboolka L., Australia 116 B5 32 38 S 143 10 E
Boolarra, Australia 117 E7 38 20 S 146 20 E
Boolcoomata, Australia 116 A4 31 57 S 140 33 E
Booleroo Centre, Australia 116 B3 32 53 S 138 21 E
Booligal, Australia 117 B6 33 58 S 144 53 E
Boom, Belgium 21 F4 51 6N 4 20 E
Boonah, Australia 115 D5 27 58 S 152 41 E
Boone, Iowa, U.S.A. 140 B3 42 4N 93 53W
Boone, N.C., U.S.A. 135 G5 36 13N 81 41W
Booneville, Ark., U.S.A. 139 H8 35 8N 93 55W
Booneville, Miss., U.S.A. 135 H1 34 39N 88 34W
Boonville, Calif., U.S.A. 144 F3 39 1N 123 22W
Boonville, Ind., U.S.A. 141 F9 38 3N 87 16W
Boonville, Mo., U.S.A. 140 F4 38 58N 92 44W
Boonville, N.Y., U.S.A. 137 C9 43 29N 75 20W
Booral, Australia 117 B9 32 30 S 151 56 E
Boorindal, Australia 115 E4 30 22 S 146 11 E
Booroomugga, Australia 117 A7 31 17 S 146 27 E
Boorowa, Australia 117 C8 34 28 S 148 44 E
Boothia, Gulf of, Canada 127 A11 71 0N 90 0W
Boothia Pen., Canada 126 A10 71 0N 94 0W
Bootle, Cumb., U.K. 16 C4 54 17N 3 24W
Bootle, Mersey., U.K. 16 D4 53 28N 3 1W
Booué, Gabon 102 C2 0 5 S 11 55 E
Bophuthatswana □, S. Africa 104 D4 25 49 S 25 30 E
Boppard, Germany 27 E3 50 13N 7 36 E
Boquerón □, Paraguay 157 E5 23 0 S 60 0W
Boquete, Panama 148 E3 8 46N 82 27W
Boquilla, Presa de la, Mexico 146 B3 27 40N 105 30W
Boquillas del Carmen, Mexico 146 B4 29 17N 102 53W
Bor, Czech. 30 B5 49 41N 12 45 E
Bor, Serbia 42 C7 44 5N 22 7 E
Bôr, Sudan 95 F3 6 10N 31 40 E
Bor, Turkey 88 E6 37 54N 34 32 E
Bor Mashash, Israel 91 D3 31 7N 34 50 E
Boradā →, Syria 91 B5 33 33N 36 34 E
Borah Peak, U.S.A. 142 D7 44 8N 113 47W
Borama, Somali Rep. 90 F3 9 55N 43 7 E
Borang, Sudan 95 G3 4 50N 30 59 E
Borangapara, India 78 C3 25 14N 90 14 E
Borås, Sweden 15 G6 57 43N 12 56 E
Borāzjān, Iran 85 D6 29 22N 51 10 E
Borba, Brazil 153 D6 4 12 S 59 34W
Borba, Portugal 37 G3 38 50N 7 26W
Borbon, Phil. 71 F5 10 50N 124 2 E
Borborema, Planalto da, Brazil 154 C4 7 0 S 37 0W
Borçka, Turkey 53 F9 41 25N 41 41 E
Borculo, Neths. 20 D9 52 7N 6 31 E
Bord Khūn-e Now, Iran 85 D6 28 3N 51 28 E
Borda, C., Australia 116 C2 35 45 S 136 34 E
Bordeaux, France 24 D3 44 50N 0 36W
Borden, Australia 113 F2 34 3 S 118 12 E
Borden, Canada 129 C7 46 18N 63 47W
Borden I., Canada 6 B2 78 30N 111 30W
Borders □, U.K. 18 F6 55 35N 2 50W
Bordertown, Australia 116 D4 36 19 S 140 45 E
Borðeyri, Iceland 12 D3 65 12N 21 6W
Bordighera, Italy 38 E4 43 47N 7 40 E
Bordj bou Arreridj, Algeria 99 A5 36 4N 4 45 E
Bordj Bourguiba, Tunisia 96 B2 32 12N 10 2 E
Bordj el Hobra, Algeria 99 B5 32 9N 4 51 E
Bordj Fly Ste. Marie, Algeria 98 C4 27 19N 2 32W
Bordj-in-Eker, Algeria 99 D6 24 9N 5 3 E
Bordj Menaiel, Algeria 99 A5 36 46N 3 43 E
Bordj Messouda, Algeria 99 B6 30 12N 9 25 E
Bordj Nili, Algeria 99 B5 33 28N 3 2 E
Bordj Omar Driss, Algeria 99 C6 28 10N 6 40 E
Bordj-Tarat, Algeria 99 C6 25 55N 9 3 E
Bordj Zelfana, Algeria 99 B5 32 27N 4 15 E
Bordoba, Kirghizia 55 D6 39 31N 73 16 E
Borea Creek, Australia 117 C7 35 5 S 146 35 E
Borek Wielkopolski, Poland 47 D4 51 54N 17 11 E
Boremore, Australia 117 B8 33 15 S 149 0 E
Boren Kapuas, Pegunungan, Malaysia 75 B4 1 25N 113 15 E
Borensberg, Sweden 15 F9 58 34N 15 17 E
Borgå, Finland 13 F18 60 24N 25 40 E
Borgarnes, Iceland 12 D3 64 32N 21 55W
Børgefjellet, Norway 12 D12 65 20N 13 45 E
Borger, Neths. 20 C9 52 54N 6 44 E
Borger, U.S.A. 139 H4 35 39N 101 24W
Borgerhout, Belgium 21 F4 51 12N 4 28 E
Borghamn, Sweden 15 F8 58 23N 14 41 E
Borgholm, Sweden 13 H14 56 52N 16 39 E
Bórgia, Italy 41 D9 38 50N 16 30 E
Borgloon, Belgium 21 G6 50 48N 5 21 E
Borgo San Dalmazzo, Italy 38 D4 44 19N 7 29 E
Borgo San Lorenzo, Italy 39 E8 43 57N 11 21 E
Borgo Valsugano, Italy 39 B8 46 3N 11 27 E
Borgomanero, Italy 38 C5 45 41N 8 28 E
Borgonovo Val Tidone, Italy 38 C6 45 1N 9 28 E
Borgorose, Italy 39 F10 42 12N 13 14 E
Borgosésia, Italy 38 C5 45 43N 8 17 E
Borgvattnet, Sweden 14 A9 63 26N 15 48 E
Borikhane, Laos 76 C4 18 33N 103 43 E
Borislav, Ukraine 50 G3 49 18N 23 28 E
Borisoglebsk, Russia 51 F13 51 27N 42 5 E
Borisoglebskiy, Russia 51 C13 56 28N 43 59 E
Borisov, Belorussia 50 D6 54 17N 28 28 E
Borisovka, Kazakhstan 55 B4 43 15N 68 10 E
Borispol, Ukraine 50 F7 50 21N 30 59 E
Borja, Peru 152 D2 4 20 S 77 40W
Borja, Spain 34 D3 41 48N 1 34W
Borjas Blancas, Spain 34 D5 41 31N 0 52 E
Borken, Germany 26 D2 51 51N 6 52 E
Borkou, Chad 97 E3 18 15N 18 50 E
Borkum, Germany 26 B2 53 36N 6 42 E
Borlänge, Sweden 13 F13 60 29N 15 26 E
Borley, C., Antarctica 7 C5 66 15 S 52 30 E
Bormida →, Italy 38 D5 44 23N 8 13 E
Bórmio, Italy 38 B7 46 28N 10 22 E
Born, Neths. 21 F7 51 2N 5 49 E
Borna, Germany 26 D8 51 8N 12 31 E
Borndiep, Neths. 20 B7 53 27N 5 35 E
Borne, Neths. 20 D9 52 18N 6 46 E
Bornem, Belgium 21 F4 51 6N 4 14 E
Borneo, E. Indies 75 B4 1 0N 115 0 E
Bornholm, Denmark 13 J13 55 10N 15 0 E
Borno □, Nigeria 101 C7 11 30N 13 0 E
Bornos, Spain 37 J5 36 48N 5 42W
Bornu Yassa, Nigeria 101 C7 12 14N 12 25 E
Borobudur, Indonesia 75 D4 7 36 S 110 13 E
Borodino, Russia 50 D9 55 31N 35 40 E
Borogontsy, Russia 57 C14 62 42N 131 8 E
Boromo, Burkina Faso 100 C4 11 45N 2 58W
Boron, U.S.A. 145 L9 35 0N 117 39W
Borong Is., Burma 78 F4 19 58N 93 6 E
Borongan, Phil. 71 F5 11 37N 125 26 E
Bororen, Australia 114 C5 24 13 S 151 33 E
Borotangba Mts., C.A.R. 95 F1 6 30N 25 0 E
Borovan, Bulgaria 43 D8 43 27N 23 45 E
Borovichi, Russia 50 B8 58 25N 33 55 E
Borovsk, Russia 51 D10 55 12N 36 24 E
Borovsk, Russia 54 B5 59 43N 56 40 E
Borovskoye, Kazakhstan 54 E9 53 48N 64 12 E
Borrego Springs, U.S.A. 145 M10 33 15N 116 23W
Borriol, Spain 34 E4 40 4N 0 4W
Borroloola, Australia 114 B2 16 4 S 136 17 E
Borşa, Romania 46 B5 47 41N 24 50 E
Borsod-Abaúj-Zemplén □, Hungary 31 C13 48 20N 21 0 E
Borssele, Neths. 21 F3 51 26N 3 45 E
Bort-les-Orgues, France 24 C6 45 24N 2 29 E
Borth, U.K. 17 E3 52 29N 4 3W
Borujerd, Iran 85 C6 33 55N 48 50 E
Borzhomi, Georgia 53 F10 41 48N 43 28 E
Borzna, Ukraine 50 F8 51 18N 32 26 E
Borzya, Russia 57 D12 50 24N 116 31 E
Bosa, Italy 40 B1 40 17N 8 32 E
Bosaga, Turkmenistan 55 E2 37 33N 65 41 E
Bosanska Brod, Bos.-H. 42 B3 45 10N 18 0 E
Bosanska Dubica, Bos.-H. 39 C13 45 10N 16 50 E
Bosanska Gradiška, Bos.-H. 42 B2 45 10N 17 15 E
Bosanska Kostajnica, Bos.-H. 39 C13 45 11N 16 33 E
Bosanska Krupa, Bos.-H. 39 D13 44 53N 16 10 E
Bosanski Novi, Bos.-H. 39 C13 45 2N 16 22 E
Bosanski Šamac, Bos.-H. 42 B3 45 3N 18 29 E
Bosansko Grahovo, Bos.-H. 39 D13 44 12N 16 26 E
Bosansko Petrovac, Bos.-H. 39 D13 44 35N 16 21 E
Bosaso, Somali Rep. 90 E4 11 12N 49 18 E
Bosavi, Mt., Papua N. G. 120 D2 6 30 S 142 49 E
Boscastle, U.K. 17 G3 50 42N 4 42W
Boscobel, U.S.A. 140 A6 43 8N 90 42W
Boscotrecase, Italy 41 B7 40 46N 14 28 E
Bose, China 68 F6 23 53N 106 35 E
Boshan, China 67 F9 36 28N 117 49 E
Boshoek, S. Africa 104 D4 25 30 S 27 9 E
Boshof, S. Africa 104 D4 28 31 S 25 13 E
Boshrūyeh, Iran 85 C8 33 50N 57 30 E
Bosilegrad, Serbia 42 E7 42 30N 22 27 E
Boskoop, Neths. 20 D5 52 4N 4 40 E
Boskovice, Czech. 31 B9 49 29N 16 40 E
Bosna →, Bos.-H. 42 B3 45 4N 18 29 E
Bosna i Hercegovina = Bosnia-Herzegovina ■, Europe 42 D2 44 0N 17 0 E
Bosnia-Herzegovina ■, Europe 42 D2 44 0N 17 0 E
Bosnik, Indonesia 73 B5 1 5 S 136 10 E
Bōsō-Hantō, Japan 63 B12 35 20N 140 20 E
Bosobolo, Zaïre 102 B3 4 15N 19 50 E
Bosporus = Karadeniz Boğazı, Turkey 88 C3 41 10N 29 10 E
Bossangoa, C.A.R. 102 A3 6 35N 17 30 E
Bossekop, Norway 12 B17 69 57N 23 15 E
Bossembélé, C.A.R. 102 A3 5 25N 17 40 E
Bossembélé II, C.A.R. 102 A3 5 41N 16 38 E
Bossier City, U.S.A. 139 J8 32 31N 93 44W
Bosso, Niger 97 F2 13 43N 13 19 E
Bostānābād, Iran 84 B5 37 50N 46 50 E
Bosten Hu, China 64 B3 41 55N 87 40 E
Boston, Phil. 71 H6 7 52N 126 22 E
Boston, U.K. 16 E7 52 59N 0 2W
Boston, U.S.A. 137 D13 42 22N 71 4W
Boston Bar, Canada 130 D4 49 52N 121 30W
Bosusulu, Zaïre 102 B4 0 50N 20 45 E
Bosut →, Croatia 42 B3 45 20N 18 45 E
Boswell, Canada 130 D5 49 28N 116 45W
Boswell, Ind., U.S.A. 141 D9 40 31N 87 23W
Boswell, Okla., U.S.A. 139 H7 34 2N 95 52W
Boswell, Pa., U.S.A. 136 F5 40 10N 79 2W
Bosworth, U.S.A. 140 E3 39 28N 93 20W
Botad, India 80 H4 22 15N 71 40 E
Botan →, Turkey 89 E9 37 44N 41 47 E
Botany B., Australia 115 E5 34 0 S 151 14 E
Botene, Laos 76 D3 17 35N 101 12 E
Botevgrad, Bulgaria 43 E8 42 55N 23 47 E
Bothaville, S. Africa 104 D4 27 23 S 26 34 E
Bothnia, G. of, Europe 12 E16 63 0N 20 15 E
Bothwell, Australia 114 G4 42 20 S 147 1 E
Bothwell, Canada 136 D3 42 38N 81 52W
Boticas, Portugal 36 D3 41 41N 7 40W
Botletle →, Botswana 104 C3 20 10 S 23 15 E
Botolan, Phil. 70 D3 15 17N 120 1 E
Botoroaga, Romania 46 E6 44 8N 25 32 E
Botoşani, Romania 46 B7 47 42N 26 41 E
Botoşani □, Romania 46 B7 47 50N 26 50 E
Botro, Ivory C. 100 D3 7 51N 5 19W
Botswana ■, Africa 104 C3 22 0 S 24 0 E
Bottineau, U.S.A. 138 A4 48 50N 100 27W
Bottrop, Germany 21 E9 51 34N 6 59 E
Botucatu, Brazil 159 A6 22 55 S 48 30W
Botwood, Canada 129 C8 49 6N 55 23W
Bou Alam, Algeria 99 B5 33 50N 1 26 E
Bou Ali, Algeria 99 C4 27 11N 0 4W
Bou Djébéha, Mali 100 B4 18 25N 2 45W
Bou Guema, Algeria 99 C5 28 49N 0 19 E
Bou Ismael, Algeria 99 A5 36 38N 2 42 E
Bou Izakarn, Morocco 98 C3 29 12N 9 46W
Boû Lanouâr, Mauritania 98 D1 21 12N 16 34W
Bou Saâda, Algeria 99 A5 35 11N 4 9 E
Bou Salem, Tunisia 96 A1 36 45N 9 2 E
Bouaké, Ivory C. 100 D3 7 40N 5 2W
Bouanga, Congo 102 C3 2 7 S 16 8 E
Bouar, C.A.R. 102 A3 6 0N 15 40 E
Bouârfa, Morocco 99 B4 32 32N 1 58W
Bouca, C.A.R. 102 A3 6 45N 18 25 E
Boucau, France 24 E2 43 32N 1 29W
Boucaut B., Australia 114 A1 12 0 S 134 25 E
Bouches-du-Rhône □, France 25 E9 43 37N 5 2 E
Bouda, Algeria 99 C4 27 50N 0 27W
Boudenib, Morocco 98 B4 31 59N 3 31W
Boudry, Switz. 28 C3 46 57N 6 50 E
Boufarik, Algeria 99 A5 36 34N 2 58 E
Bougainville, C., Australia 112 B4 13 57 S 126 4 E
Bougainville I., Solomon Is. 121 L8 6 0 S 155 0 E
Bougainville Reef, Australia 114 B4 15 30 S 147 5 E
Bougainville Str., Solomon Is. 121 L9 6 40 S 156 10 E
Bougaroun, C., Algeria 99 A6 37 6N 6 30 E
Bougie = Bejaia, Algeria 99 A6 36 42N 5 2 E
Bougouni, Mali 100 C3 11 30N 7 20W
Bouillon, Belgium 21 J6 49 44N 5 3 E
Bouïra, Algeria 99 A5 36 20N 3 59 E
Boulder, Colo., U.S.A. 138 E2 40 1N 105 17W
Boulder, Mont., U.S.A. 142 C7 46 14N 112 7W
Boulder City, U.S.A. 145 K12 35 59N 114 50W
Boulder Creek, U.S.A. 144 H4 37 7N 122 7W
Boulder Dam = Hoover Dam, U.S.A. 145 K12 36 1N 114 44W
Boulembo, Gabon 102 C2 1 26 S 12 0 E
Bouli, Mauritania 100 B2 15 17N 12 18W
Boulia, Australia 114 C2 22 52 S 139 51 E
Bouligny, France 23 C12 49 17N 5 45 E
Boulogne →, France 22 E5 47 12N 1 47W
Boulogne-sur-Gesse, France 24 E4 43 18N 0 38 E
Boulogne-sur-Mer, France 23 B8 50 42N 1 36 E
Bouloire, France 22 E7 47 59N 0 45 E
Bouloupari, N. Cal. 121 U20 21 52 S 166 4 E
Boulsa, Burkina Faso 101 C4 12 39N 0 34W
Boultoum, Niger 97 F2 14 45N 10 25 E
Boumalne, Morocco 98 B3 31 25N 6 0W
Boun Neua, Laos 76 B3 21 38N 101 54 E
Boun Tai, Laos 76 B3 21 23N 101 58 E
Bouna, Ivory C. 100 D4 9 10N 3 0W
Boundary Peak, U.S.A. 144 H8 37 51N 118 21W
Boundiali, Ivory C. 100 D3 9 30N 6 20W
Bountiful, U.S.A. 142 F8 40 53N 111 53W
Bounty Is., Pac. Oc. 122 M9 48 0 S 178 30 E
Bourail, N. Cal. 121 U19 21 34 S 165 30 E
Bourbeuse →, U.S.A. 140 F6 38 24N 90 53W
Bourbon, U.S.A. 141 C10 41 18N 86 7W
Bourbon-Lancy, France 24 B7 46 37N 3 45 E
Bourbon-l'Archambault, France 24 B7 46 36N 3 4 E
Bourbonnais, France 24 B7 46 28N 3 0 E
Bourbonne-les-Bains, France 23 E12 47 54N 5 45 E
Bourem, Mali 101 B4 17 0N 0 24W
Bourg, France 24 C3 45 3N 0 34W
Bourg-Argental, France 25 C8 45 18N 4 32 E
Bourg-de-Péage, France 25 C9 45 2N 5 3 E
Bourg-en-Bresse, France 25 B9 46 13N 5 12 E
Bourg-St.-Andéol, France 25 D8 44 23N 4 39 E
Bourg-St.-Maurice, France 25 C10 45 35N 6 46 E
Bourg-St.-Pierre, Switz. 28 E4 45 57N 7 12 E
Bourganeuf, France 24 C5 45 57N 1 45 E
Bourges, France 23 E9 47 9N 2 25 E
Bourget, Canada 137 A9 45 26N 75 9W
Bourget, L. du, France 25 C9 45 44N 5 52 E
Bourgneuf, B. de, France 22 E4 47 3N 2 10W
Bourgneuf-en-Retz, France 22 E5 47 2N 1 58W
Bourgogne, France 23 F11 47 0N 4 50 E
Bourgoin-Jallieu, France 25 C9 45 36N 5 17 E
Bourgueil, France 22 E7 47 17N 0 10 E
Bourke, Australia 115 E4 30 8 S 145 55 E
Bournemouth, U.K. 17 G6 50 43N 1 53W
Bourriot-Bergonce, France 24 D3 44 7N 0 14W
Bouse, U.S.A. 145 M13 33 56N 114 0W
Boussac, France 24 B6 46 22N 2 13 E
Boussens, France 24 E4 43 12N 0 58 E
Bousso, Chad 97 F3 10 34N 16 52 E
Boussu, Belgium 21 H3 50 26N 3 48 E
Boutilimit, Mauritania 100 B2 17 45N 14 40W
Bouvet I. = Bouvetøya, Antarctica 9 P9 54 26 S 3 24 E
Bouvetøya, Antarctica 9 P9 54 26 S 3 24 E
Bouznika, Morocco 98 B3 33 46N 7 6W
Bouzonville, France 23 C13 49 17N 6 32 E
Bova Marina, Italy 41 E8 37 59N 15 56 E
Bovalino Marina, Italy 41 D9 38 9N 16 10 E
Bovec, Slovenia 39 B10 46 20N 13 33 E
Bovenkarspel, Neths. 20 C6 52 41N 5 14 E
Bovigny, Belgium 21 H7 50 12N 5 55 E
Bovill, U.S.A. 142 C5 46 51N 116 24W
Bovino, Italy 41 A8 41 15N 15 20 E
Bow Island, Canada 130 D6 49 50N 111 23W
Bowbells, U.S.A. 138 A3 48 48N 102 15W
Bowdle, U.S.A. 138 C5 45 27N 99 39W
Bowelling, Australia 113 F2 33 25 S 116 30 E
Bowen, Australia 114 C4 20 0 S 148 16 E
Bowen Mts., Australia 117 D7 37 0 S 147 50 E
Bowie, Ariz., U.S.A. 143 K9 32 19N 109 29W
Bowie, Tex., U.S.A. 139 J6 33 34N 97 51W
Bowkān, Iran 84 B5 36 31N 46 12 E
Bowland, Forest of, U.K. 16 D5 54 0N 2 30W
Bowling Green, Ky., U.S.A. 134 G2 36 59N 86 27W
Bowling Green, Mo., U.S.A. 140 E5 39 21N 91 12W
Bowling Green, Ohio, U.S.A. 141 C13 41 23N 83 39W
Bowling Green, C., Australia 114 B4 19 19 S 147 25 E
Bowman, U.S.A. 138 B3 46 11N 103 24W
Bowman I., Antarctica 7 C8 65 0 S 104 0 E
Bowmans, Australia 116 C3 34 10 S 138 17 E
Bowmanville, Canada 128 D4 43 55N 78 41W
Bowmore, U.K. 18 F2 55 45N 6 18W
Bowral, Australia 117 C9 34 26 S 150 27 E
Bowraville, Australia 115 E5 30 37 S 152 52 E
Bowron →, Canada 130 C4 54 3N 121 50W
Bowser L., Canada 130 B3 56 30N 129 30W
Bowsman, Canada 131 C8 52 14N 101 12W
Bowutu Mts., Papua N. G. 120 D4 7 45 S 147 10 E
Bowwood, Zambia 107 F2 17 5 S 26 20 E
Boxholm, Sweden 15 F9 58 12N 15 3 E
Boxmeer, Neths. 21 E7 51 38N 5 56 E
Boxtel, Neths. 21 E6 51 36N 5 20 E
Boyabat, Turkey 52 F6 41 28N 34 42 E
Boyabo, Zaïre 102 B3 3 43N 18 46 E
Boyaca = Casanare □, Colombia 152 B3 6 0N 73 0W
Boyce, U.S.A. 139 K8 31 23N 92 40W
Boyer →, Canada 130 B5 58 27N 115 57W
Boyer, C., N. Cal. 121 U22 21 37 S 168 6 E
Boyle, Ireland 19 C3 53 58N 8 19W
Boyne →, Ireland 19 C5 53 43N 6 15W
Boyne City, U.S.A. 134 C3 45 13N 85 1W
Boyni Qara, Afghan. 79 A2 36 20N 67 0 E
Boynton Beach, U.S.A. 135 M5 26 32N 80 4W
Boyolali, Indonesia 75 D4 7 32 S 110 35 E
Boyoma, Chutes, Zaïre 102 B5 0 35N 25 23 E
Boyup Brook, Australia 113 F2 33 50 S 116 23 E
Boz Dağ, Turkey 88 E3 37 18N 29 11 E
Boz Dağları, Turkey 88 D3 38 20N 28 0 E
Bozburun, Turkey 45 H10 36 43N 28 8 E
Bozcaada, Turkey 44 E8 39 49N 26 3 E
Bozdoğan, Turkey 88 E3 37 40N 28 17 E
Bozeman, U.S.A. 142 D8 45 41N 111 2W
Bozen = Bolzano, Italy 39 B8 46 30N 11 20 E
Bozene, Zaïre 102 B3 2 56N 19 12 E
Bożepole Wielkopolski, Poland 47 A4 54 33N 17 56 E
Boževac, Serbia 42 C6 44 32N 21 24 E
Bozkır, Turkey 88 E5 37 11N 32 14 E
Bozouls, France 24 D6 44 28N 2 43 E
Bozoum, C.A.R. 102 A3 6 25N 16 35 E
Bozova, Turkey 89 E8 37 21N 38 32 E
Bozovici, Romania 46 E3 44 56N 22 1 E
Bozüyük, Turkey 88 D4 39 54N 30 3 E
Bra, Italy 38 D4 44 41N 7 50 E
Brabant □, Belgium 21 G5 50 46N 4 30 E
Brabant L., Canada 131 B8 55 58N 103 43W
Brabrand, Denmark 15 H4 56 9N 10 7 E
Brač, Croatia 39 E13 43 20N 16 40 E
Bracadale, L., U.K. 18 D2 57 20N 6 30W
Bracciano, Italy 39 F9 42 6N 12 10 E
Bracciano, L. di, Italy 39 F9 42 8N 12 11 E
Bracebridge, Canada 128 C4 45 2N 79 19W
Brach, Libya 96 C2 27 31N 14 20 E
Bracieux, France 23 E8 47 30N 1 30 E
Bräcke, Sweden 14 B9 62 45N 15 26 E
Brackettville, U.S.A. 139 L4 29 19N 100 25W
Bracki Kanal, Croatia 39 E13 43 24N 16 40 E
Brad, Romania 46 C3 46 10N 22 50 E
Brádano →, Italy 41 B9 40 23N 16 51 E
Bradenton, U.S.A. 135 M4 27 30N 82 34W
Bradford, Canada 136 B5 44 7N 79 34W
Bradford, U.K. 16 D6 53 47N 1 45W
Bradford, Ill., U.S.A. 140 C7 41 11N 89 39W
Bradford, Ohio, U.S.A. 141 D12 40 8N 84 27W
Bradford, Pa., U.S.A. 136 E6 41 58N 78 38W
Bradford, Vt., U.S.A. 137 C12 43 59N 72 9W

Burullus, Bahra el 179


Brunna, *Sweden* **14 E11** 59 52N 17 25 E
Brunnen, *Switz.* **29 C7** 46 59N 8 37 E
Brunner, L., *N.Z.* **119 C6** 42 37 S 171 27 E
Bruno, *Canada* **131 C7** 52 20N 105 30W
Brunsbüttel, *Germany* **26 B5** 53 52N 9 13 E
Brunssum, *Neths.* **21 G7** 50 57N 5 59 E
Brunswick = Braunschweig, *Germany* **26 C6** 52 17N 10 28 E
Brunswick, *Ga., U.S.A.* **135 K5** 31 10N 81 30W
Brunswick, *Maine, U.S.A.* **129 D6** 43 55N 69 58W
Brunswick, *Md., U.S.A.* **134 F7** 39 19N 77 38W
Brunswick, *Mo., U.S.A.* **140 E3** 39 26N 93 8W
Brunswick, *Ohio, U.S.A.* **136 E3** 41 14N 81 51W
Brunswick, Pen. de, *Chile* **160 D2** 53 30 S 71 30W
Brunswick B., *Australia* **112 C3** 15 15 S 124 50 E
Brunswick Junction, *Australia* **113 F2** 33 15 S 115 50 E
Bruntál, *Czech.* **31 B10** 50 0N 17 27 E
Bruny I., *Australia* **114 G4** 43 20 S 147 15 E
Brus Laguna, *Honduras* **148 C3** 15 47N 84 35W
Brusartsi, *Bulgaria* **42 D8** 43 40N 23 5 E
Brush, *U.S.A.* **138 E3** 40 15N 103 37W
Brushton, *U.S.A.* **137 B10** 44 50N 74 31W
Brusio, *Switz.* **29 D10** 46 14N 10 8 E
Brusque, *Brazil* **159 B6** 27 5 S 49 0W
Brussel, *Belgium* **21 G4** 50 51N 4 21 E
Brussels = Brussel, *Belgium* **21 G4** 50 51N 4 21 E
Brussels, *Canada* **136 C3** 43 44N 81 15W
Brustem, *Belgium* **21 G6** 50 48N 5 14 E
Bruthen, *Australia* **117 D7** 37 42 S 147 50 E
Bruxelles = Brussel, *Belgium* **21 G4** 50 51N 4 21 E
Bruyères, *France* **23 D13** 48 10N 6 40 E
Brwinów, *Poland* **47 C7** 52 9N 20 40 E
Bryagovo, *Bulgaria* **43 F10** 41 58N 25 8 E
Bryan, *Ohio, U.S.A.* **141 C12** 41 28N 84 33W
Bryan, *Tex., U.S.A.* **139 K6** 30 40N 96 22W
Bryan, Mt., *Australia* **116 B3** 33 30 S 139 0 E
Bryanka, *Ukraine* **53 B8** 48 32N 38 45 E
Bryansk, *Russia* **50 E9** 53 13N 34 25 E
Bryanskoye, *Russia* **53 D12** 44 20N 47 10 E
Bryant, *U.S.A.* **138 C6** 44 35N 97 28W
Bryne, *Norway* **13 G8** 58 44N 5 38 E
Bryson City, *U.S.A.* **135 H4** 35 26N 83 27W
Brza Palanka, *Serbia* **42 C7** 44 28N 22 27 E
Brzava →, *Serbia* **42 B5** 45 21N 20 45 E
Brzeg, *Poland* **47 E4** 50 52N 17 30 E
Brzeg Din, *Poland* **47 D3** 51 16N 16 41 E
Brześć Kujawski, *Poland* **47 C5** 52 36N 18 55 E
Brzesko, *Poland* **31 B13** 49 59N 20 34 E
Brzeszcze, *Poland* **31 B12** 49 59N 19 10 E
Brzeziny, *Poland* **47 D6** 51 49N 19 42 E
Brzozów, *Poland* **31 B15** 49 41N 22 3 E
Bsharri, *Lebanon* **91 A5** 34 15N 36 0 E
Bū Athlah, *Libya* **96 B3** 30 9N 15 39 E
Bū Baqarah, *U.A.E.* **85 E8** 25 35N 56 25 E
Bu Craa, *W. Sahara* **98 C2** 26 45N 12 50W
Bū Ḩasā, *U.A.E.* **85 F7** 23 30N 53 20 E
Bua Yai, *Thailand* **76 E4** 15 33N 102 26 E
Buad I., *Phil.* **71 F5** 11 40N 124 51 E
Buala, *Solomon Is.* **121 M10** 8 10 S 159 35 E
Buapinang, *Indonesia* **72 B2** 4 40 S 121 30 E
Buba, *Guinea-Biss.* **100 C2** 11 40N 14 59W
Bubanda, *Zaïre* **102 B3** 4 14N 19 38 E
Bubanza, *Burundi* **106 C2** 3 6 S 29 23 E
Būbiyān, *Kuwait* **85 D6** 29 45N 48 15 E
Bucak, *Turkey* **88 E4** 37 28N 30 36 E
Bucaramanga, *Colombia* **152 B3** 7 0N 73 0W
Bucas Grande I., *Phil.* **71 G5** 9 40N 125 57 E
Buccaneer Arch., *Australia* **112 C3** 16 7 S 123 20 E
Bucchiánico, *Italy* **39 F11** 42 20N 14 10 E
Bucecea, *Romania* **46 B7** 47 47N 26 28 E
Buchach, *Ukraine* **50 G4** 49 5N 25 25 E
Buchan, *Australia* **117 D8** 37 30 S 148 12 E
Buchan, *U.K.* **18 D6** 57 32N 2 8W
Buchan Ness, *U.K.* **18 D7** 57 29N 1 48W
Buchanan, *Canada* **131 C8** 51 40N 102 45W
Buchanan, *Liberia* **100 D2** 5 57N 10 2W
Buchanan, *U.S.A.* **141 C10** 41 50N 86 22W
Buchanan, L., *Queens., Australia* **114 C4** 21 35 S 145 52 E
Buchanan, L., *W. Austral., Australia* **113 E3** 25 33 S 123 2 E
Buchanan, L., *U.S.A.* **139 K5** 30 45N 98 25W
Buchanan Cr. →, *Australia* **114 B2** 19 13 S 136 33 E
Buchans, *Canada* **129 C8** 48 50N 56 52W
Bucharest = Bucureşti, *Romania* **46 E7** 44 27N 26 10 E
Buchholz, *Germany* **26 B5** 53 19N 9 51 E
Buchloe, *Germany* **27 G6** 48 3N 10 45 E
Buchon, Pt., *U.S.A.* **144 K6** 35 15N 120 54W
Buchs, *Switz.* **29 B8** 47 10N 9 28 E
Bückeburg, *Germany* **26 C5** 52 16N 9 2 E
Buckeye, *U.S.A.* **143 K7** 33 22N 112 35W
Buckhannon, *U.S.A.* **134 F5** 39 0N 80 8W
Buckhaven, *U.K.* **18 E5** 56 10N 3 2W
Buckie, *U.K.* **18 D6** 57 40N 2 58W
Buckingham, *Canada* **128 C4** 45 37N 75 24W
Buckingham, *U.K.* **17 F7** 52 0N 0 59W
Buckingham B., *Australia* **114 A2** 12 10 S 135 40 E
Buckingham Canal, *India* **83 G5** 14 0N 80 5 E
Buckinghamshire □, *U.K.* **17 F7** 51 50N 0 55W
Buckland, *U.S.A.* **141 D12** 40 37N 84 16W
Buckle Hd., *Australia* **112 B4** 14 26 S 127 52 E
Buckleboo, *Australia* **116 B2** 32 54 S 136 12 E
Buckley, *Ill., U.S.A.* **141 D8** 40 36N 88 2W
Buckley, *Wash., U.S.A.* **142 C2** 47 10N 122 2W
Buckley →, *Australia* **114 C2** 20 10 S 138 49 E
Bucklin, *Kans., U.S.A.* **139 G5** 37 33N 99 38W
Bucklin, *Mo., U.S.A.* **140 E4** 39 47N 92 53W
Bucks L., *U.S.A.* **144 F5** 39 54N 121 12W
Buco Zau, *Angola* **103 C2** 4 46 S 12 33 E
Bucquoy, *France* **23 B9** 50 9N 2 43 E
Buctouche, *Canada* **129 C7** 46 30N 64 45W
Bucureşti, *Romania* **46 E7** 44 27N 26 10 E
Bucyrus, *U.S.A.* **141 D14** 40 48N 82 59W
Budafok, *Hungary* **31 D12** 47 26N 19 2 E
Budalin, *Burma* **78 D5** 22 20N 95 10 E
Budapest, *Hungary* **31 D12** 47 29N 19 5 E
Budaun, *India* **81 E8** 28 5N 79 10 E
Budd Coast, *Antarctica* **7 C8** 68 0 S 112 0 E
Buddabadah, *Australia* **117 A7** 31 56 S 147 14 E
Buddusò, *Italy* **40 B2** 40 35N 9 18 E
Bude, *U.K.* **17 G3** 50 49N 4 33W
Budel, *Neths.* **21 F7** 51 17N 5 34 E
Budennovsk, *Russia* **53 D11** 44 50N 44 10 E
Budeşti, *Romania* **46 E7** 44 13N 26 30 E
Budge Budge = Baj Baj, *India* **81 H13** 22 30N 88 5 E
Budgewoi, *Australia* **117 B9** 33 13 S 151 34 E
Búðareyri, *Iceland* **12 D6** 65 2N 14 13W
Búðir, *Iceland* **12 D2** 64 49N 23 23W
Budia, *Spain* **34 E2** 40 38N 2 46W
Budjala, *Zaïre* **102 B3** 2 50N 19 40 E
Búdrio, *Italy* **39 D8** 44 31N 11 31 E
Budva, *Montenegro* **42 E3** 42 17N 18 50 E
Budzyń, *Poland* **47 C3** 52 54N 16 59 E
Buea, *Cameroon* **101 E6** 4 10N 9 9 E
Buellton, *U.S.A.* **145 L6** 34 37N 120 12W
Buena Vista, *Bolivia* **157 D5** 17 27 S 63 40W
Buena Vista, *Colo., U.S.A.* **143 G10** 38 51N 106 8W
Buena Vista, *Va., U.S.A.* **134 G6** 37 44N 79 21W
Buena Vista L., *U.S.A.* **145 K7** 35 12N 119 18W
Buenaventura, *Colombia* **152 C2** 3 53N 77 4W
Buenaventura, *Mexico* **146 B3** 29 50N 107 30W
Buenaventura, B. de, *Colombia* **152 C2** 3 48N 77 17W
Buenavista, *Luzon, Phil.* **70 E4** 13 35N 122 34 E
Buenavista, *Mindanao, Phil.* **71 G5** 8 59N 125 24 E
Buenavista, *Zamboanga del S., Phil.* **71 H4** 7 15N 122 16 E
Buendía, Pantano de, *Spain* **34 E2** 40 25N 2 43W
Buenópolis, *Brazil* **155 E3** 17 54 S 44 11W
Buenos Aires, *Argentina* **158 C4** 34 30 S 58 20W
Buenos Aires, *Colombia* **152 C3** 1 36N 73 18W
Buenos Aires, *Costa Rica* **148 E3** 9 10N 83 20W
Buenos Aires □, *Argentina* **158 D4** 36 30 S 60 0W
Buenos Aires, L., *Chile* **160 C2** 46 35 S 72 30W
Buesaco, *Colombia* **152 C2** 1 23N 77 9W
Buffalo, *Mo., U.S.A.* **139 G8** 37 39N 93 6W
Buffalo, *N.Y., U.S.A.* **136 D6** 42 53N 78 53W
Buffalo, *Okla., U.S.A.* **139 G5** 36 50N 99 38W
Buffalo, *S. Dak., U.S.A.* **138 C3** 45 35N 103 33W
Buffalo, *Wyo., U.S.A.* **142 D10** 44 21N 106 42W
Buffalo →, *Canada* **130 A5** 60 5N 115 5W
Buffalo Head Hills, *Canada* **130 B5** 57 25N 115 55W
Buffalo L., *Canada* **130 C6** 52 27N 112 54W
Buffalo Narrows, *Canada* **131 B7** 55 51N 108 29W
Buffels →, *S. Africa* **104 D2** 29 36 S 17 3 E
Buford, *U.S.A.* **135 H4** 34 10N 84 0W
Bug →, *Poland* **47 C8** 52 31N 21 5 E
Bug →, *Ukraine* **52 C4** 46 59N 31 58 E
Buga, *Colombia* **152 C2** 4 0N 76 15W
Buganda, *Uganda* **106 C3** 0 0 31 30 E
Buganga, *Uganda* **106 C3** 0 3 S 32 0 E
Bugasan, *Phil.* **71 H5** 7 27N 124 14 E
Bugasong, *Phil.* **71 F4** 11 3N 122 4 E
Bugeat, *France* **24 C5** 45 36N 1 55 E
Bugel, Tanjung, *Indonesia* **75 D4** 6 26 S 111 3 E
Buggenhout, *Belgium* **21 F4** 51 1N 4 12 E
Bugibba, *Malta* **32 D1** 35 57N 14 25 E
Bugojno, *Bos.-H.* **42 C2** 44 2N 17 25 E
Bugsuk, *Phil.* **71 G1** 8 15N 117 15 E
Buguey, *Phil.* **70 B3** 18 17N 121 50 E
Bugulma, *Russia* **54 D3** 54 33N 52 48 E
Buguma, *Nigeria* **101 E6** 4 42N 6 55 E
Bugun Shara, *Mongolia* **64 B5** 49 0N 104 0 E
Bugun Shara, *Mongolia* **64 B5** 49 0N 104 0 E
Buguruslan, *Russia* **54 E3** 53 39N 52 26 E
Buhăeşti, *Romania* **46 C8** 46 47N 27 32 E
Buheirat-Murrat-el-Kubra, *Egypt* **94 H8** 30 15N 32 40 E
Buhl, *Idaho, U.S.A.* **142 E6** 42 36N 114 46W
Buhl, *Minn., U.S.A.* **138 B8** 47 30N 92 46W
Buhuşi, *Romania* **46 C7** 46 41N 26 45 E
Buick, *U.S.A.* **139 G9** 37 38N 91 2W
Builth Wells, *U.K.* **17 E4** 52 10N 3 26W
Buin, *Papua N. G.* **121 L8** 6 48 S 155 42 E
Buinsk, *Russia* **51 D16** 55 0N 48 18 E
Buíque, *Brazil* **154 C4** 8 37 S 37 9W
Buir Nur, *Mongolia* **65 B6** 47 50N 117 42 E
Buis-les-Baronnies, *France* **25 D9** 44 17N 5 16 E
Buitenpost, *Neths.* **20 B8** 53 15N 6 9 E
Buitrago, *Spain* **36 E7** 40 58N 3 38W
Bujalance, *Spain* **37 H6** 37 54N 4 23W
Buján, *Spain* **36 C2** 42 59N 8 36W
Bujanovac, *Serbia* **42 E6** 42 28N 21 44 E
Bujaraloz, *Spain* **34 D4** 41 29N 0 10W
Buje, *Croatia* **39 C10** 45 24N 13 39 E
Bujumbura, *Burundi* **106 C2** 3 16 S 29 18 E
Bük, *Hungary* **31 D9** 47 22N 16 45 E
Buk, *Poland* **47 C3** 52 21N 16 30 E
Buka I., *Papua N. G.* **120 C8** 5 10 S 154 35 E
Bukachacha, *Russia* **57 D12** 52 55N 116 50 E
Bukama, *Zaïre* **107 D2** 9 10 S 25 50 E
Bukavu, *Zaïre* **106 C2** 2 20 S 28 52 E
Bukene, *Tanzania* **106 C3** 4 15 S 32 48 E
Bukhara, *Uzbekistan* **55 D2** 39 48N 64 25 E
Bukhoro = Bukhara, *Uzbekistan* **55 D2** 39 48N 64 25 E
Bukidnon □, *Phil.* **71 G5** 8 0N 125 0 E
Bukima, *Tanzania* **106 C3** 1 50 S 33 25 E
Bukit Mertajam, *Malaysia* **77 K3** 5 22N 100 28 E
Bukittinggi, *Indonesia* **74 C2** 0 20 S 100 20 E
Bukkapatnam, *India* **83 G3** 14 14N 77 46 E
Buklyan, *Russia* **54 D3** 55 42N 52 10 E
Bukoba, *Tanzania* **106 C3** 1 20 S 31 49 E
Bukoba □, *Tanzania* **106 C3** 1 30 S 32 0 E
Bukowno, *Poland* **31 A12** 50 17N 19 35 E
Bukuru, *Nigeria* **101 D6** 9 42N 8 48 E
Bukuya, *Uganda* **106 B3** 0 40N 31 52 E
Bula, *Guinea-Biss.* **100 C1** 12 7N 15 43W
Bula, *Indonesia* **73 B4** 3 6 S 130 30 E
Bulacan, *Phil.* **70 E3** 13 40N 120 21 E
Bulacan □, *Phil.* **70 D3** 15 0N 121 5 E
Bülach, *Switz.* **29 A7** 47 31N 8 32 E
Bulahdelah, *Australia* **117 B10** 32 23 S 152 13 E
Bulalacao, *Phil.* **70 E3** 12 31N 121 26 E
Bulan, *Phil.* **70 E4** 12 40N 123 52 E
Bulanash, *Russia* **54 C8** 57 16N 62 0 E
Bulancak, *Turkey* **89 C8** 40 56N 38 14 E
Bulandshahr, *India* **80 E7** 28 28N 77 51 E
Bulanık, *Turkey* **89 D10** 39 4N 42 14 E
Bulanovo, *Russia* **54 E4** 52 27N 55 10 E
Bûlâq, *Egypt* **94 B3** 25 10N 30 38 E
Bulawayo, *Zimbabwe* **107 G2** 20 7 S 28 32 E
Buldan, *Turkey* **88 D3** 38 2N 28 50 E
Buldana, *India* **82 D3** 20 30N 76 18 E
Buldon, *Phil.* **71 H5** 7 33N 124 25 E
Bulgaria ■, *Europe* **43 E10** 42 35N 25 30 E
Bulgroo, *Australia* **115 D3** 25 47 S 143 58 E
Bulgunnia, *Australia* **115 E1** 30 10 S 134 53 E
Bulhale, *Somali Rep.* **108 C3** 5 20N 46 29 E
Bulhar, *Somali Rep.* **90 E3** 10 25N 44 30 E
Buli, Teluk, *Indonesia* **72 A3** 1 5N 128 25 E
Buliluyan, C., *Phil.* **71 G1** 8 20N 117 15 E
Bulki, *Ethiopia* **95 F4** 6 11N 36 31 E
Bulkley →, *Canada* **130 B3** 55 15N 127 40W
Bull Shoals L., *U.S.A.* **139 G8** 36 22N 92 35W
Bullange, *Belgium* **21 H8** 50 24N 6 15 E
Bullaque →, *Spain* **37 G6** 38 59N 4 17W
Bullara, *Australia* **112 D1** 22 40 S 114 3 E
Bullaring, *Australia* **113 F2** 32 30 S 117 45 E
Bullas, *Spain* **35 G3** 38 2N 1 40W
Bulle, *Switz.* **28 C4** 46 37N 7 3 E
Buller →, *N.Z.* **119 B6** 41 44 S 171 36 E
Buller, Mt., *Australia* **117 D7** 37 10 S 146 28 E
Buller Gorge, *N.Z.* **119 B7** 41 40 S 172 10 E
Bulli, *Australia* **117 C9** 34 15 S 150 57 E
Bullock Creek, *Australia* **114 B3** 17 43 S 144 31 E
Bulloo →, *Australia* **115 D3** 28 43 S 142 30 E
Bulloo Downs, *Queens., Australia* **115 D3** 28 31 S 142 57 E
Bulloo Downs, *W. Austral., Australia* **112 D2** 24 0 S 119 32 E
Bulloo L., *Australia* **115 D3** 28 43 S 142 25 E
Bulls, *N.Z.* **118 G4** 40 10 S 175 24 E
Bully-les-Mines, *France* **23 B9** 50 27N 2 44 E
Bulnes, *Chile* **158 D1** 36 42 S 72 19W
Bulo Burti, *Somali Rep.* **90 G4** 3 50N 45 33 E
Bulo Ghedudo, *Somali Rep.* **108 D2** 2 52N 43 1 E
Bulolo, *Papua N. G.* **120 D4** 7 10 S 146 40 E
Bulongo, *Zaïre* **103 C4** 4 45 S 21 30 E
Bulpunga, *Australia* **116 B4** 33 47 S 141 45 E
Bulqiza, *Albania* **44 C2** 41 30N 20 21 E
Bulsar = Valsad, *India* **82 D1** 20 40N 72 58 E
Bultfontein, *S. Africa* **104 D4** 28 18 S 26 10 E
Buluan, L., *Phil.* **71 H5** 6 40N 124 49 E
Buluangan, *Phil.* **71 F4** 10 24N 123 20 E
Bulukumba, *Indonesia* **72 C2** 5 33 S 120 11 E
Bulun, *Russia* **57 B13** 70 37N 127 30 E
Bulungu, *Zaïre* **103 D4** 6 4 S 21 54 E
Bulusan, *Phil.* **70 E5** 12 45N 124 8 E
Bumba, *Zaïre* **102 B4** 2 13N 22 30 E
Bumbiri I., *Tanzania* **106 C3** 1 40 S 31 55 E
Bumhkang, *Burma* **78 B6** 26 51N 97 40 E
Bumhpa Bum, *Burma* **78 B6** 26 51N 97 14 E
Bumi →, *Zimbabwe* **107 F2** 17 0 S 28 20 E
Bumtang →, *Bhutan* **78 B3** 26 56N 90 53 E
Buna, *Kenya* **106 B4** 2 58N 39 30 E
Buna, *Papua N. G.* **120 E5** 8 42 S 148 27 E
Bunawan, *Agusan del S., Phil.* **71 G5** 8 12N 125 57 E
Bunawan, *Davao del S., Phil.* **71 H5** 7 14N 125 38 E
Bunazi, *Tanzania* **106 C3** 1 3 S 31 23 E
Bunbah, Khalīj, *Libya* **96 B4** 32 20N 23 15 E
Bunbury, *Australia* **113 F2** 33 20 S 115 35 E
Buncrana, *Ireland* **19 A4** 55 8N 7 28W
Bundaberg, *Australia* **115 C5** 24 54 S 152 22 E
Bünde, *Germany* **26 C4** 52 11N 8 33 E
Bundey →, *Australia* **114 C2** 21 46 S 135 37 E
Bundi, *India* **80 G6** 25 30N 75 35 E
Bundooma, *Australia* **114 C1** 24 54 S 134 16 E
Bundoran, *Ireland* **19 B3** 54 24N 8 17W
Bundukia, *Sudan* **95 F3** 5 14N 30 55 E
Bundure, *Australia* **117 C7** 35 10 S 146 1 E
Bung Kan, *Thailand* **76 C4** 18 23N 103 37 E
Bungatakada, *Japan* **62 D3** 33 35N 131 25 E
Bungendore, *Australia* **117 C8** 35 14 S 149 30 E
Bungil Cr. →, *Australia* **114 D4** 27 5 S 149 5 E
Bungo, Gunong, *Malaysia* **75 B4** 1 16N 110 9 E
Bungo-Suidō, *Japan* **62 E4** 33 0N 132 15 E
Bungoma, *Kenya* **106 B3** 0 34N 34 34 E
Bungu, *Tanzania* **106 D4** 7 35 S 39 0 E
Bunia, *Zaïre* **106 B3** 1 35N 30 20 E
Bunji, *Pakistan* **81 B6** 35 45N 74 40 E
Bunker Hill, *Ill., U.S.A.* **140 E7** 39 3N 89 57W
Bunker Hill, *Ind., U.S.A.* **141 D10** 40 40N 86 6W
Bunkie, *U.S.A.* **139 K8** 30 57N 92 11W
Bunnell, *U.S.A.* **135 L5** 29 28N 81 16W
Bunnik, *Neths.* **20 D6** 52 4N 5 12 E
Bunnythorpe, *N.Z.* **118 G4** 40 16 S 175 39 E
Buñol, *Spain* **35 F4** 39 25N 0 47W
Bunsbeek, *Belgium* **21 G5** 50 50N 4 56 E
Bunschoten, *Neths.* **20 D6** 52 14N 5 22 E
Buntok, *Indonesia* **75 C4** 1 40 S 114 58 E
Bununu, *Nigeria* **101 D6** 9 51N 9 32 E
Bununu Dass, *Nigeria* **101 C6** 10 5N 9 31 E
Bünyan, *Turkey* **88 D6** 38 51N 35 51 E
Bunyu, *Indonesia* **75 B5** 3 35N 117 50 E
Bunza, *Nigeria* **101 C5** 12 8N 4 0 E
Buol, *Indonesia* **72 A2** 1 15N 121 32 E
Buon Brieng, *Vietnam* **76 F7** 13 9N 108 12 E
Buon Me Thuot, *Vietnam* **76 F7** 12 40N 108 3 E
Buong Long, *Cambodia* **76 F6** 13 44N 106 59 E
Buorkhaya, Mys, *Russia* **57 B14** 71 50N 132 40 E
Buqayq, *Si. Arabia* **85 E6** 26 0N 49 45 E
Buqbua, *Egypt* **94 A2** 31 29N 25 29 E
Bur Acaba, *Somali Rep.* **90 G3** 3 12N 44 20 E
Bûr Fuad, *Egypt* **94 H8** 31 15N 32 20 E
Bur Ghibi, *Somali Rep.* **108 D3** 3 56N 45 7 E
Bûr Safâga, *Egypt* **94 B3** 26 43N 33 57 E
Bûr Sa'îd, *Egypt* **94 H8** 31 16N 32 18 E
Bûr Sûdân, *Sudan* **94 D4** 19 32N 37 9 E
Bûr Taufiq, *Egypt* **94 J8** 29 54N 32 32 E
Bura, *Kenya* **106 C4** 1 4 S 39 58 E
Buran, *Somali Rep.* **108 B3** 10 14N 48 44 E
Burao, *Somali Rep.* **90 F4** 9 32N 45 32 E
Burāq, *Syria* **91 B5** 33 11N 36 29 E
Buras, *U.S.A.* **139 L10** 29 22N 89 32W
Burauen, *Phil.* **71 F5** 10 58N 124 53 E
Buraydah, *Si. Arabia* **84 E5** 26 20N 44 8 E
Burayevo, *Russia* **54 D4** 55 50N 55 24 E
Burbank, *U.S.A.* **145 L8** 34 11N 118 19W
Burcher, *Australia* **117 B7** 33 30 S 147 16 E
Burdekin →, *Australia* **114 B4** 19 38 S 147 25 E
Burdeos Bay, *Phil.* **70 D4** 14 44N 122 6 E
Burdett, *Canada* **130 D6** 49 50N 111 32W
Burdur, *Turkey* **88 E4** 37 45N 30 17 E
Burdur □, *Turkey* **88 E4** 37 45N 30 15 E
Burdur Gölü, *Turkey* **88 E4** 37 44N 30 10 E
Burdwan = Barddhaman, *India* **81 H12** 23 14N 87 39 E
Bure, *Ethiopia* **95 E4** 10 40N 37 4 E
Bure →, *U.K.* **16 E9** 52 38N 1 45 E
Büren, *Germany* **26 D4** 51 33N 8 34 E
Buren, *Neths.* **20 E6** 51 55N 5 20 E
Bureya →, *Russia* **57 E13** 49 27N 129 30 E
Burford, *Canada* **136 C4** 43 7N 80 27W
Burg, *Sachsen-Anhalt, Germany* **26 C7** 52 16N 11 50 E
Burg, *Schleswig-Holstein, Germany* **26 A7** 54 25N 11 10 E
Burg el Arab, *Egypt* **94 H6** 30 54N 29 32 E
Burg et Tuyur, *Sudan* **94 C2** 20 55N 27 56 E
Burg Stargard, *Germany* **26 B9** 53 29N 13 19 E
Burgas, *Bulgaria* **43 E12** 42 33N 27 29 E
Burgaski Zaliv, *Bulgaria* **43 E12** 42 30N 27 39 E
Burgdorf, *Germany* **26 C5** 52 27N 10 0 E
Burgdorf, *Switz.* **28 B5** 47 3N 7 37 E
Burgenland □, *Austria* **31 D9** 47 20N 16 20 E
Burgeo, *Canada* **129 C8** 47 37N 57 38W
Burgersdorp, *S. Africa* **104 E4** 31 0 S 26 20 E
Burges, Mt., *Australia* **113 F3** 30 50 S 121 5 E
Burghausen, *Germany* **27 G8** 48 10N 12 50 E
Búrgio, *Italy* **40 E6** 37 35N 13 18 E
Bürglen, *Switz.* **29 C7** 46 53N 8 40 E
Burglengenfeld, *Germany* **27 F8** 49 11N 12 2 E
Burgo de Osma, *Spain* **34 D1** 41 35N 3 4W
Burgohondo, *Spain* **36 E6** 40 26N 4 47W
Burgos, *Ilocos N., Phil.* **70 B3** 18 31N 120 39 E
Burgos, *Pangasinan, Phil.* **70 C2** 16 4N 119 52 E
Burgos, *Spain* **34 C1** 42 21N 3 41W
Burgos □, *Spain* **34 C1** 42 21N 3 42W
Burgstädt, *Germany* **26 E8** 50 55N 12 49 E
Burgsvik, *Sweden* **13 H15** 57 3N 18 19 E
Burguillos del Cerro, *Spain* **37 G4** 38 23N 6 35W
Burgundy = Bourgogne, *France* **23 F11** 47 0N 4 50 E
Burhanpur, *India* **82 D3** 21 18N 76 14 E
Burhou, *U.K.* **22 C4** 49 45N 2 15W
Buri Pen., *Eritrea* **95 D4** 15 25N 39 55 E
Burias, *Phil.* **70 E4** 12 55N 123 5 E
Burias Pass, *Phil.* **70 E4** 13 0N 123 15 E
Buribay, *Russia* **54 F6** 51 57N 58 10 E
Burica, Pta., *Costa Rica* **148 E3** 8 3N 82 51W
Burigi, L., *Tanzania* **106 C3** 2 2 S 31 22 E
Burin, *Canada* **129 C8** 47 1N 55 14W
Buriram, *Thailand* **76 E4** 15 0N 103 0 E
Buriti Alegre, *Brazil* **155 E2** 18 9 S 49 3W
Buriti Bravo, *Brazil* **154 C3** 5 50 S 43 50W
Buriti dos Lopes, *Brazil* **154 B3** 3 10 S 41 52W
Burj Sāfitā, *Syria* **84 C3** 34 48N 36 7 E
Burji, *Ethiopia* **95 F4** 5 29N 37 51 E
Burkburnett, *U.S.A.* **139 H5** 34 6N 98 34W
Burke, *U.S.A.* **142 C6** 47 31N 115 49W
Burke →, *Australia* **114 C2** 23 12 S 139 33 E
Burketown, *Australia* **114 B2** 17 45 S 139 33 E
Burkettsville, *U.S.A.* **141 D12** 40 21N 84 39W
Burkina Faso ■, *Africa* **100 C4** 12 0N 1 0W
Burk's Falls, *Canada* **128 C4** 45 37N 79 24W
Burley, *U.S.A.* **142 E7** 42 32N 113 48W
Burlingame, *U.S.A.* **144 H4** 37 35N 122 21W
Burlington, *Canada* **136 C5** 43 18N 79 45W
Burlington, *Colo., U.S.A.* **138 F3** 39 18N 102 16W
Burlington, *Ill., U.S.A.* **141 B8** 42 3N 88 33W
Burlington, *Iowa, U.S.A.* **140 D5** 40 49N 91 14W
Burlington, *Kans., U.S.A.* **138 F7** 38 12N 95 45W
Burlington, *Ky., U.S.A.* **141 E12** 39 2N 84 43W
Burlington, *N.C., U.S.A.* **135 G6** 36 6N 79 26W
Burlington, *N.J., U.S.A.* **137 F10** 40 4N 74 51W
Burlington, *Vt., U.S.A.* **137 B11** 44 29N 73 12W
Burlington, *Wash., U.S.A.* **144 B4** 48 28N 122 20W
Burlington, *Wis., U.S.A.* **134 D1** 42 41N 88 17W
Burlyu-Tyube, *Kazakhstan* **56 E8** 46 30N 79 10 E
Burma ■, *Asia* **78 E6** 21 0N 96 30 E
Burnaby I., *Canada* **130 C2** 52 25N 131 19W
Burnamwood, *Australia* **117 A6** 31 7 S 144 53 E
Burnet, *U.S.A.* **139 K5** 30 45N 98 14W
Burney, *U.S.A.* **142 F3** 40 53N 121 40W
Burngup, *Australia* **113 F2** 33 2 S 118 42 E
Burnham, *U.S.A.* **136 F7** 40 38N 77 34W
Burnie, *Australia* **114 G4** 41 4 S 145 56 E
Burnley, *U.K.* **16 D5** 53 47N 2 15W
Burnoye, *Kazakhstan* **55 B5** 42 36N 70 47 E
Burns, *Oreg., U.S.A.* **142 E4** 43 35N 119 3W
Burns, *Wyo., U.S.A.* **138 E2** 41 12N 104 21W
Burns Lake, *Canada* **130 C3** 54 20N 125 45W
Burnside →, *Canada* **126 B9** 66 51N 108 4W
Burnside, L., *Australia* **113 E3** 25 22 S 123 0 E
Burnt River, *Canada* **136 B6** 44 41N 78 42W
Burntwood →, *Canada* **131 B9** 56 8N 96 34W
Burntwood L., *Canada* **131 B8** 55 22N 100 26W
Burqān, *Kuwait* **84 D5** 29 0N 47 57 E
Burra, *Australia* **116 B3** 33 40 S 138 55 E
Burragorang, L., *Australia* **117 B9** 33 52 S 150 37 E
Burramurra, *Australia* **114 C2** 20 25 S 137 15 E
Burreli, *Albania* **44 C2** 41 36N 20 1 E
Burren Junction, *Australia* **115 E4** 30 7 S 148 59 E
Burrendong, L., *Australia* **117 B8** 32 45 S 149 10 E
Burrendong Dam, *Australia* **115 E4** 32 39 S 149 6 E
Burriana, *Spain* **34 F4** 39 50N 0 4W
Burrinjuck Res., *Australia* **117 C8** 35 0 S 148 36 E
Burro, Serranías del, *Mexico* **146 B4** 29 0N 102 0W
Burruyacú, *Argentina* **158 B3** 26 30 S 64 40W
Burry Port, *U.K.* **17 F3** 51 41N 4 17W
Bursa, *Turkey* **88 C3** 40 15N 29 5 E
Bursa □, *Turkey* **88 C3** 40 10N 30 0 E
Burseryd, *Sweden* **15 G7** 57 12N 13 17 E
Burstall, *Canada* **131 C7** 50 39N 109 54W
Burton, *U.S.A.* **141 B13** 43 0N 83 40W
Burton L., *Canada* **128 B4** 54 45N 78 20W
Burton upon Trent, *U.K.* **16 E6** 52 48N 1 39W
Burtundy, *Australia* **116 B5** 33 45 S 142 15 E
Buru, *Indonesia* **72 B3** 3 30 S 126 30 E
Buruanga, *Phil.* **71 F3** 11 51N 121 53 E
Burullus, Bahra el, *Egypt* **94 H7** 31 25N 31 0 E

180 Burūm


Burūm, *Yemen* **87 D5** 14 22N 48 59 E
Burûn, Râs, *Egypt* **91 D2** 31 14N 33 7 E
Burunday, *Kazakhstan* **55 B8** 43 20N 76 51 E
Burundi ■, *Africa* **106 C3** 3 15 S 30 0 E
Bururi, *Burundi* **106 C2** 3 57 S 29 37 E
Burutu, *Nigeria* **101 D6** 5 20N 5 29 E
Burwell, *U.S.A.* **138 E5** 41 47N 99 8W
Bury, *U.K.* **16 D5** 53 36N 2 19W
Bury St. Edmunds, *U.K.* **17 E8** 52 15N 0 42 E
Buryat Republic □, *Russia* **57 D11** 53 0N 110 0 E
Buryn, *Ukraine* **50 F8** 51 13N 33 50 E
Burzenin, *Poland* **47 D5** 51 28N 18 47 E
Busalla, *Italy* **38 D5** 44 34N 8 58 E
Busango Swamp, *Zambia* **107 E2** 14 15 S 25 45 E
Buşayrah, *Syria* **84 C4** 35 9N 40 26 E
Buşayyah, *Iraq* **84 D5** 30 0N 46 10 E
Busca, *Italy* **38 D4** 44 31N 7 29 E
Bushati, *Albania* **44 C1** 41 58N 19 34 E
Būshehr, *Iran* **85 D6** 28 55N 50 55 E
Būshehr □, *Iran* **85 D6** 28 20N 51 45 E
Bushell, *Canada* **131 B7** 59 31N 108 45W
Bushenyi, *Uganda* **106 C3** 0 35 S 30 10 E
Bushire = Būshehr, *Iran* **85 D6** 28 55N 50 55 E
Bushnell, *Ill., U.S.A.* **138 E9** 40 33N 90 31W
Bushnell, *Nebr., U.S.A.* **138 E3** 41 14N 103 54W
Busia □, *Kenya* **106 B3** 0 25N 34 6 E
Busie, *Ghana* **100 C4** 10 29N 2 22W
Businga, *Zaïre* **102 B4** 3 16N 20 59 E
Buskerud fylke □, *Norway* **14 D3** 60 13N 9 0 E
Busko Zdrój, *Poland* **47 E7** 50 28N 20 42 E
Buslei, *Ethiopia* **108 C2** 5 28N 44 25 E
Busoga □, *Uganda* **106 B3** 0 5N 33 30 E
Busovača, *Bos.-H.* **42 C2** 44 6N 17 53 E
Busra ash Shām, *Syria* **91 C5** 32 30N 36 25 E
Bussang, *France* **23 E13** 47 50N 6 50 E
Busselton, *Australia* **113 F2** 33 42 S 115 15 E
Busseto, *Italy* **38 D7** 44 59N 10 2 E
Bussigny, *Switz.* **28 C3** 46 33N 6 33 E
Bussum, *Neths.* **20 D6** 52 16N 5 10 E
Bustamante, B., *Argentina* **160 C3** 45 5 S 66 18W
Busto, C., *Spain* **36 B4** 43 34N 6 28W
Busto Arsizio, *Italy* **38 C5** 45 40N 8 50 E
Busu-Djanoa, *Zaïre* **102 B4** 1 43N 21 23 E
Busuanga, *Phil.* **70 E2** 12 10N 120 0 E
Busuanga, *Phil.* **70 E2** 12 14N 119 52 E
Büsum, *Germany* **26 A4** 54 7N 8 50 E
Buta, *Zaïre* **106 B1** 2 50N 24 53 E
Butare, *Rwanda* **106 C2** 2 31 S 29 52 E
Butaritari, *Kiribati* **122 G9** 3 30N 174 0 E
Bute, *Australia* **116 B3** 33 51 S 138 2 E
Bute, *U.K.* **18 F3** 55 48N 5 2W
Bute Inlet, *Canada* **130 C4** 50 40N 124 53W
Butemba, *Uganda* **106 B3** 1 9N 31 37 E
Butembo, *Zaïre* **106 B2** 0 9N 29 18 E
Butera, *Italy* **41 E7** 37 10N 14 10 E
Bütgenbach, *Belgium* **21 H8** 50 26N 6 12 E
Butha Qi, *China* **65 B7** 48 0N 122 32 E
Buthidaung, *Burma* **78 E4** 20 52N 92 32 E
Butiaba, *Uganda* **106 B3** 1 50N 31 20 E
Butkhāk, *Afghan.* **79 B3** 34 30N 69 22 E
Butler, *Ind., U.S.A.* **141 C12** 41 26N 84 52W
Butler, *Ky., U.S.A.* **141 F12** 38 47N 84 22W
Butler, *Mo., U.S.A.* **140 F2** 38 16N 94 20W
Butler, *Pa., U.S.A.* **136 F5** 40 52N 79 54W
Butom Odrzánski, *Poland* **47 D2** 51 44N 15 48 E
Bütschwil, *Switz.* **29 B8** 47 23N 9 5 E
Butte, *Mont., U.S.A.* **142 C7** 46 0N 112 32W
Butte, *Nebr., U.S.A.* **138 D5** 42 58N 98 51W
Butte Creek →, *U.S.A.* **144 F5** 39 12N 121 56W
Butterworth = Gcuwa, *S. Africa* **105 E4** 32 20 S 28 11 E
Butterworth, *Malaysia* **77 K3** 5 24N 100 23 E
Buttfield, Mt., *Australia* **113 D4** 24 45 S 128 9 E
Button B., *Canada* **131 B10** 58 45N 94 23W
Buttonwillow, *U.S.A.* **145 K7** 35 24N 119 28W
Butty Hd., *Australia* **113 F3** 33 54 S 121 39 E
Butuan, *Phil.* **71 G5** 8 57N 125 33 E
Butuku-Luba, *Eq. Guin.* **101 E6** 3 29N 8 33 E
Butulan, *Phil.* **71 J5** 5 38N 125 26 E
Butung, *Indonesia* **72 C2** 5 0 S 122 45 E
Buturlinovka, *Russia* **51 F12** 50 50N 40 35 E
Butzbach, *Germany* **26 E4** 50 24N 8 40 E
Bützow, *Germany* **26 B7** 53 51N 11 59 E
Buug, *Phil.* **71 H4** 7 40N 123 2 E
Buxar, *India* **81 G10** 25 34N 83 58 E
Buxton, *Guyana* **153 B6** 6 48N 58 2W
Buxton, *S. Africa* **104 D3** 27 38 S 24 42 E
Buxton, *U.K.* **16 D6** 53 16N 1 54W
Buxy, *France* **23 F11** 46 44N 4 40 E
Buy, *Russia* **51 B12** 58 28N 41 28 E
Buyaga, *Russia* **57 D13** 59 50N 127 0 E
Buynaksk, *Russia* **53 E12** 42 48N 47 7 E
Büyük Kemikli Burun, *Turkey* **44 D8** 40 20N 26 15 E
Büyük Menderes →, *Turkey* **88 E2** 37 28N 27 11 E
Büyükçekmece, *Turkey* **43 F13** 41 2N 28 35 E
Buzançais, *France* **22 F8** 46 54N 1 25 E
Buzău, *Romania* **46 D7** 45 10N 26 50 E
Buzău □, *Romania* **46 D7** 45 20N 26 30 E
Buzău →, *Romania* **46 D8** 45 26N 27 44 E
Buzău, Pasul, *Romania* **46 D7** 45 35N 26 12 E
Buzen, *Japan* **62 D3** 33 35N 131 5 E
Buzet, *Croatia* **39 C10** 45 24N 13 58 E
Buzi →, *Mozam.* **107 F3** 19 50 S 34 43 E
Buziaş, *Romania* **46 D2** 45 38N 21 36 E
Buzuluk, *Russia* **54 E3** 52 48N 52 12 E
Buzuluk →, *Russia* **51 F13** 50 15N 42 7 E
Buzzards Bay, *U.S.A.* **137 E14** 41 45N 70 37W
Bwagaoia, *Papua N. G.* **120 F7** 10 40 S 152 52 E
Bwana Mkubwe, *Zaïre* **107 E2** 13 8 S 28 38 E
Byala, *Ruse, Bulgaria* **43 D10** 43 28N 25 44 E
Byala, *Varna, Bulgaria* **43 E12** 42 53N 27 55 E
Byala Slatina, *Bulgaria* **43 D8** 43 26N 23 55 E
Byandovan, Mys, *Azerbaijan* **53 G13** 39 45N 49 28 E
Bychawa, *Poland* **47 D9** 51 1N 22 36 E
Byczyna, *Poland* **47 D5** 51 7N 18 12 E
Bydgoszcz, *Poland* **47 B5** 53 10N 18 0 E
Bydgoszcz □, *Poland* **47 B4** 53 16N 17 33 E
Byelarus = Belorussia ■, *Europe* **50 E5** 53 30N 27 0 E
Byelorussia = Belorussia ■, *Europe* **50 E5** 53 30N 27 0 E
Byers, *U.S.A.* **138 F2** 39 43N 104 14W
Byesville, *U.S.A.* **136 G3** 39 58N 81 32W
Byhalia, *U.S.A.* **139 H10** 34 52N 89 41W
Bykhov, *Belorussia* **50 E7** 53 31N 30 14 E
Bykovo, *Russia* **53 B11** 49 50N 45 25 E
Bylas, *U.S.A.* **143 K8** 33 8N 110 7W
Bylderup, *Denmark* **15 K3** 54 57N 9 6 E
Bylot I., *Canada* **127 A12** 73 13N 78 34W
Byrd, C., *Antarctica* **7 C17** 69 38 S 76 7W
Byro, *Australia* **113 E2** 26 5 S 116 11 E
Byrock, *Australia* **117 A7** 30 40 S 146 27 E
Byron, *U.S.A.* **140 B7** 42 8N 89 15W
Byron Bay, *Australia* **115 D5** 28 43 S 153 37 E
Byrranga, Gory, *Russia* **57 B11** 75 0N 100 0 E
Byrranga Mts. = Byrranga, Gory, *Russia* **57 B11** 75 0N 100 0 E
Byrum, *Denmark* **15 G5** 57 16N 11 0 E
Byske, *Sweden* **12 D16** 64 57N 21 11 E
Byske älv →, *Sweden* **12 D16** 64 57N 21 13 E
Bystrovka, *Kirghizia* **55 B7** 42 47N 75 42 E
Bystrzyca →, *Lublin, Poland* **47 D9** 51 21N 22 46 E
Bystrzyca →, *Wrocław, Poland* **47 D3** 51 12N 16 55 E
Bystrzyca Kłodzka, *Poland* **47 E3** 50 19N 16 39 E
Byten, *Belorussia* **50 E4** 52 50N 25 27 E
Bytom, *Poland* **47 E5** 50 25N 18 54 E
Bytów, *Poland* **47 A4** 54 10N 17 30 E
Byumba, *Rwanda* **106 C3** 1 35 S 30 4 E
Bzenec, *Czech.* **31 C10** 48 58N 17 18 E
Bzura →, *Poland* **47 C7** 52 25N 20 15 E


## C


C.I.S. = Commonwealth of Independent States ■, *Eurasia* **57 D11** 60 0N 100 0 E
Ca →, *Vietnam* **76 C5** 18 45N 105 45 E
Ca Mau = Quan Long, *Vietnam* **77 H5** 9 7N 105 8 E
Ca Mau, Mui = Bai Bung, Mui, *Vietnam* **77 H5** 8 38N 104 44 E
Ca Na, *Vietnam* **77 G7** 11 20N 108 54 E
Caacupé, *Paraguay* **158 B4** 25 23 S 57 5W
Caála, *Angola* **103 E3** 12 46 S 15 30 E
Caamano Sd., *Canada* **130 C3** 52 55N 129 25W
Caapiranga, *Brazil* **153 D5** 3 18 S 61 13W
Caazapá, *Paraguay* **158 B4** 26 8 S 56 19W
Caazapá □, *Paraguay* **159 B4** 26 10 S 56 0W
Cabadbaran, *Phil.* **71 G5** 9 10N 125 38 E
Cabagan, *Phil.* **70 C3** 17 26N 121 46 E
Cabalian, *Phil.* **71 F5** 10 16N 125 10 E
Caballeria, C. de, *Spain* **33 A11** 40 5N 4 5 E
Cabana, *Peru* **156 B2** 8 25 S 78 5W
Cabanaconde, *Peru* **156 D3** 15 38 S 71 58W
Cabañaquinta, *Spain* **36 B5** 43 10N 5 38W
Cabanatuan, *Phil.* **70 D3** 15 30N 120 58 E
Cabanes, *Spain* **34 E5** 40 9N 0 2 E
Cabangon, *Phil.* **70 D3** 15 10N 120 3 E
Cabanillas, *Peru* **156 D3** 15 36 S 70 28W
Cabano, *Canada* **129 C6** 47 40N 68 56W
Čabar, *Croatia* **39 C11** 45 36N 14 39 E
Cabarroquis, *Phil.* **70 C3** 16 50N 121 30 E
Cabarruyan I., *Phil.* **70 C2** 16 18N 119 59 E
Cabazon, *U.S.A.* **145 M10** 33 55N 116 47W
Cabcaben, *Phil.* **70 D3** 14 27N 120 35 E
Cabedelo, *Brazil* **154 C5** 7 0 S 34 50W
Cabery, *U.S.A.* **141 D8** 41 0N 88 12W
Cabeza del Buey, *Spain* **37 G5** 38 44N 5 13W
Cabildo, *Chile* **158 C1** 32 30 S 71 5W
Cabimas, *Venezuela* **152 A3** 10 23N 71 25W
Cabinda, *Angola* **103 D2** 5 33 S 12 11 E
Cabinda □, *Angola* **103 D2** 5 0 S 12 30 E
Cabinet Mts., *U.S.A.* **142 C6** 48 0N 115 30W
Cabiri, *Angola* **103 D2** 8 52 S 13 39 E
Cabo Blanco, *Argentina* **160 C3** 47 15 S 65 47W
Cabo Frio, *Brazil* **155 F3** 22 51 S 42 3W
Cabo Pantoja, *Peru* **152 D2** 1 0 S 75 10W
Cabo Raso, *Argentina* **160 B3** 44 20 S 65 15W
Cabonga, Réservoir, *Canada* **128 C4** 47 20N 76 40W
Cabool, *U.S.A.* **139 G8** 37 7N 92 6W
Caboolture, *Australia* **115 D5** 27 5 S 152 58 E
Cabora Bassa Dam = Cahora Bassa Dam, *Mozam.* **107 F3** 15 20 S 32 50 E
Caborca, *Mexico* **146 A2** 30 40N 112 10W
Cabot, Mt., *U.S.A.* **137 B13** 44 30N 71 25W
Cabot Str., *Canada* **129 C8** 47 15N 59 40W
Cabra, *Spain* **37 H6** 37 30N 4 28W
Cabra del Santo Cristo, *Spain* **35 H1** 37 42N 3 16W
Cábras, *Italy* **40 C1** 39 57N 8 30 E
Cabrera, I., *Spain* **33 B9** 39 8N 2 57 E
Cabrera, Sierra, *Spain* **36 C4** 42 12N 6 40W
Cabri, *Canada* **131 C7** 50 35N 108 25W
Cabriel →, *Spain* **35 F3** 39 14N 1 3W
Cabruta, *Venezuela* **152 B4** 7 50N 66 10W
Cabugcayan, *Phil.* **71 F5** 11 29N 124 34 E
Cabugao, *Phil.* **70 C3** 17 48N 120 27 E
Cabulauan Is., *Phil.* **71 F3** 11 25N 120 8 E
Caburan = Jose Abad Santos, *Phil.* **71 J5** 5 55N 125 39 E
Cabuyaro, *Colombia* **152 C3** 4 18N 72 49W
Cacabelos, *Spain* **36 C4** 42 36N 6 44W
Čačak, *Serbia* **42 D5** 43 54N 20 20 E
Cacao, *Fr. Guiana* **153 C7** 4 33N 52 26W
Cáceres, *Brazil* **157 D6** 16 5 S 57 40W
Cáceres, *Colombia* **152 B2** 7 35N 75 20W
Cáceres, *Spain* **37 F4** 39 26N 6 23W
Cáceres □, *Spain* **37 F4** 39 45N 6 0W
Cache Bay, *Canada* **128 C4** 46 22N 80 0W
Cache Cr. →, *U.S.A.* **144 G5** 38 42N 121 42W
Cachepo, *Portugal* **37 H3** 37 20N 7 49W
Cachéu, *Guinea-Biss.* **100 C1** 12 14N 16 8W
Cachi, *Argentina* **158 B2** 25 5 S 66 10W
Cachimbo, *Brazil* **157 B7** 8 57 S 54 54W
Cachimbo, Serra do, *Brazil* **157 B6** 9 30 S 55 30W
Cachingues, *Angola* **103 E3** 13 5 S 16 43 E
Cachoeira, *Brazil* **155 D4** 12 30 S 39 0W
Cachoeira Alta, *Brazil* **155 E1** 18 48 S 50 58W
Cachoeira de Itapemirim, *Brazil* **155 F3** 20 51 S 41 7W
Cachoeira do Sul, *Brazil* **159 C5** 30 3 S 52 53W
Cachoeiro do Arari, *Brazil* **154 B2** 1 1 S 48 58W
Cachopo, *Portugal* **37 H3** 37 20N 7 49W
Cachuela Esperanza, *Bolivia* **157 C4** 10 32 S 65 38W
Cacólo, *Angola* **103 E3** 10 9 S 19 21 E
Caconda, *Angola* **103 E3** 13 48 S 15 8 E
Cacongo, *Angola* **103 D2** 5 11 S 12 5 E
Caçu, *Brazil* **155 E1** 18 37 S 51 4W
Cacula, *Angola* **103 E2** 14 29 S 14 10 E
Caculé, *Brazil* **155 D3** 14 30 S 42 13W
Cacuso, *Angola* **103 D3** 9 25 S 15 45 E
Çadarache, *France* **25 E9** 43 41N 5 43 E
Čadca, *Slovak Rep.* **31 B11** 49 26N 18 45 E
Caddo, *U.S.A.* **139 H6** 34 7N 96 16W
Cadell Cr. →, *Australia* **114 C3** 22 35 S 141 51 E
Cadenazzo, *Switz.* **29 D7** 46 9N 8 57 E
Cader Idris, *U.K.* **16 E4** 52 43N 3 56W
Cadí, Sierra del, *Spain* **34 C6** 42 17N 1 42 E
Cadibarrawirracanna, L., *Australia* **115 D2** 28 52 S 135 27 E
Cadillac, *Canada* **128 C4** 48 14N 78 23W
Cadillac, *France* **24 D3** 44 38N 0 20W
Cadillac, *U.S.A.* **134 C3** 44 15N 85 24W
Cadiz, *Phil.* **71 F4** 10 57N 123 15 E
Cádiz, *Spain* **37 J4** 36 30N 6 20W
Cadiz, *U.S.A.* **136 F4** 40 22N 81 0W
Cádiz □, *Spain* **37 J5** 36 36N 5 45W
Cádiz, G. de, *Spain* **37 J4** 36 40N 7 0W
Cadney Park, *Australia* **115 D1** 27 55 S 134 3 E
Cadomin, *Canada* **130 C5** 53 2N 117 20W
Cadotte →, *Canada* **130 B5** 56 43N 117 10W
Cadours, *France* **24 E5** 43 44N 1 2 E
Cadoux, *Australia* **113 F2** 30 46 S 117 7 E
Caen, *France* **22 C6** 49 10N 0 22W
Caernarfon, *U.K.* **16 D3** 53 8N 4 17W
Caernarfon B., *U.K.* **16 D3** 53 4N 4 40W
Caernarvon = Caernarfon, *U.K.* **16 D3** 53 8N 4 17W
Caerphilly, *U.K.* **17 F4** 51 34N 3 13W
Caesarea, *Israel* **91 C3** 32 30N 34 53 E
Caeté, *Brazil* **155 E3** 19 55 S 43 40W
Caetité, *Brazil* **155 D3** 13 50 S 42 32W
Cafayate, *Argentina* **158 B2** 26 2 S 66 0W
Cafifi, *Colombia* **152 B3** 5 13N 71 4W
Cafu, *Angola* **103 F3** 16 30 S 15 8 E
Cagayan □, *Phil.* **70 B3** 18 0N 121 50 E
Cagayan →, *Phil.* **70 B3** 18 25N 121 42 E
Cagayan de Oro, *Phil.* **71 G5** 8 30N 124 40 E
Cagayan Is., *Phil.* **71 G3** 9 40N 121 16 E
Cagayan Sulu I., *Phil.* **71 H2** 7 1N 118 30 E
Cagli, *Italy* **39 E9** 43 32N 12 38 E
Cágliari, *Italy* **40 C2** 39 15N 9 6 E
Cágliari, G. di, *Italy* **40 C2** 39 8N 9 10 E
Cagnano Varano, *Italy* **41 A8** 41 49N 15 47 E
Cagnes-sur-Mer, *France* **25 E11** 43 40N 7 9 E
Caguán →, *Colombia* **152 D3** 0 8 S 74 18W
Caguas, *Puerto Rico* **149 C6** 18 14N 66 2W
Caha Mts., *Ireland* **19 E2** 51 45N 9 40W
Cahama, *Angola* **103 F2** 16 17 S 14 19 E
Caher, *Ireland* **19 D4** 52 23N 7 56W
Cahersiveen, *Ireland* **19 E1** 51 57N 10 13W
Cahora Bassa Dam, *Mozam.* **107 F3** 15 20 S 32 50 E
Cahore Pt., *Ireland* **19 D5** 52 34N 6 11W
Cahors, *France* **24 D5** 44 27N 1 27 E
Cahuapanas, *Peru* **156 B2** 5 15 S 77 0W
Cahuinari →, *Colombia* **152 D3** 1 21 S 70 44W
Cai Bau, Dao, *Vietnam* **76 B6** 21 10N 107 27 E
Cai Nuoc, *Vietnam* **77 H5** 8 56N 105 1 E
Caia, *Mozam.* **107 F4** 17 51 S 35 24 E
Caiabis, Serra dos, *Brazil* **157 C6** 11 30 S 56 30W
Caianda, *Angola* **103 E4** 11 2 S 23 31 E
Caiapó, Serra do, *Brazil* **157 D7** 17 0 S 52 0W
Caiapônia, *Brazil* **157 D7** 16 57 S 51 49W
Caibarién, *Cuba* **148 B4** 22 30N 79 30W
Caibiran, *Phil.* **71 F5** 11 34N 124 35 E
Caicara, *Bolívar, Venezuela* **152 B4** 7 38N 66 10W
Caicara, *Monagas, Venezuela* **153 B5** 9 52N 63 38W
Caicó, *Brazil* **154 C4** 6 20 S 37 0W
Caicos Is., *W. Indies* **149 B5** 21 40N 71 40W
Caicos Passage, *W. Indies* **149 B5** 22 45N 72 45W
Cailloma, *Peru* **156 D3** 15 9 S 71 45W
Caine →, *Bolivia* **157 D4** 18 23 S 65 21W
Caird Coast, *Antarctica* **7 D1** 75 0 S 25 0W
Cairn Gorm, *U.K.* **18 D5** 57 7N 3 40W
Cairn Toul, *U.K.* **18 D5** 57 3N 3 44W
Cairngorm Mts., *U.K.* **18 D5** 57 6N 3 42W
Cairns, *Australia* **114 B4** 16 57 S 145 45 E
Cairo = El Qâhira, *Egypt* **94 H7** 30 1N 31 14 E
Cairo, *Ga., U.S.A.* **135 K3** 30 52N 84 13W
Cairo, *Ill., U.S.A.* **139 G10** 37 0N 89 11W
Cairo Montenotte, *Italy* **38 D5** 44 23N 8 16 E
Caithness, Ord of, *U.K.* **18 C5** 58 9N 3 37W
Caiundo, *Angola* **103 F3** 15 50 S 17 28 E
Caiza, *Bolivia* **157 E4** 20 2 S 65 40W
Cajabamba, *Peru* **156 B2** 7 38 S 78 4W
Cajamarca, *Peru* **156 B2** 7 5 S 78 28W
Cajamarca □, *Peru* **156 B2** 6 15 S 78 50W
Cajapió, *Brazil* **154 B3** 2 58 S 44 48W
Cajarc, *France* **24 D5** 44 29N 1 50 E
Cajatambo, *Peru* **156 C2** 10 30 S 77 2W
Cajàzeiras, *Brazil* **154 C4** 6 52 S 38 30W
Ćajetina, *Serbia* **42 D4** 43 47N 19 42 E
Cajidiocan, *Phil.* **70 E4** 12 22N 122 41 E
Čajniče, *Bos.-H.* **42 D4** 43 34N 19 5 E
Çakirgol, *Turkey* **53 F8** 40 33N 39 40 E
Čakovec, *Croatia* **39 B13** 46 23N 16 26 E
Çal, *Turkey* **88 D3** 38 4N 29 23 E
Cala, *Spain* **37 H4** 37 59N 6 21W
Cala →, *Spain* **37 H4** 37 38N 6 5W
Cala Cadolar, Punta de, *Spain* **35 G6** 38 38N 1 35 E
Cala d'Or, *Spain* **33 B10** 39 23N 3 14 E
Cala Figuera, C., *Spain* **33 B9** 39 27N 2 31 E
Cala Forcat, *Spain* **33 A10** 40 0N 3 47 E
Cala Mayor, *Spain* **33 B9** 39 33N 2 37 E
Cala Mezquida, *Spain* **33 B11** 39 55N 4 16 E
Cala Millor, *Spain* **33 B10** 39 35N 3 22 E
Cala Ratjada, *Spain* **33 B10** 39 43N 3 27 E
Calabanga, *Phil.* **70 E4** 13 42N 123 17 E
Calabar, *Nigeria* **101 E6** 4 57N 8 20 E
Calabozo, *Venezuela* **152 B4** 9 0N 67 28W
Calábria □, *Italy* **41 C9** 39 24N 16 30 E
Calaburras, Pta. de, *Spain* **37 J6** 36 30N 4 38W
Calaceite, *Spain* **34 D5** 41 1N 0 11 E
Calacota, *Bolivia* **156 D4** 17 16 S 68 38W
Calafat, *Romania* **46 F3** 43 58N 22 59 E
Calafate, *Argentina* **160 D2** 50 19 S 72 15W
Calahorra, *Spain* **34 C3** 42 18N 1 59W
Calais, *France* **23 B8** 50 57N 1 56 E
Calais, *U.S.A.* **129 C6** 45 11N 67 17W
Calais, Pas de, *France* **23 B8** 50 30N 1 20 E
Calalaste, Cord. de, *Argentina* **158 B2** 25 0 S 67 0W
Calalayan, *Phil.* **71 F2** 11 30N 119 38 E
Calama, *Brazil* **157 B5** 8 0 S 62 50W
Calama, *Chile* **158 A2** 22 30 S 68 55W
Calamar, *Bolívar, Colombia* **152 A3** 10 15N 74 55W
Calamar, *Vaupés, Colombia* **152 C3** 1 58N 72 32W
Calamarca, *Bolivia* **156 D4** 16 55 S 68 9W
Calamba, *Cavite, Phil.* **71 G4** 8 35N 123 39 E
Calamba, *Misamis, Phil.* **71 F4** 10 11N 123 17 E
Calamba, *Negros, Phil.* **70 D3** 14 13N 121 10 E
Calamian Group, *Phil.* **71 F2** 11 50N 119 55 E
Calamocha, *Spain* **34 E3** 40 50N 1 17W
Calán Porter, *Spain* **33 B11** 39 52N 4 8 E
Calañas, *Spain* **37 H4** 37 40N 6 53W
Calanda, *Spain* **34 E4** 40 56N 0 15W
Calandagan I., *Phil.* **71 F3** 10 39N 120 15 E
Calandula, *Angola* **103 D3** 9 6 S 15 57 E
Calang, *Indonesia* **74 B1** 4 37N 95 37 E
Calangiánus, *Italy* **40 B2** 40 56N 9 12 E
Calanscio, Sarīr, *Libya* **96 C4** 27 0N 21 30 E
Calapan, *Phil.* **70 E3** 13 25N 121 7 E
Calape, *Phil.* **71 G4** 9 54N 123 52 E
Călăraşi, *Romania* **46 E8** 44 12N 27 20 E
Călăraşi □, *Romania* **46 E8** 44 10N 27 0 E
Calasparra, *Spain* **35 G3** 38 14N 1 41W
Calatafimi, *Italy* **40 E5** 37 56N 12 50 E
Calatagan, *Phil.* **70 E3** 13 50N 120 38 E
Calatayud, *Spain* **34 D3** 41 20N 1 40W
Calato = Kálathos, *Greece* **45 H10** 36 9N 28 8 E
Calauag, *Phil.* **70 E4** 13 55N 122 15 E
Calavà, C., *Italy* **41 D7** 38 11N 14 55 E
Calavite, C., *Phil.* **70 E3** 13 26N 120 20 E
Calavite Pass, *Phil.* **70 E3** 13 36N 120 25 E
Calayan, *Phil.* **70 B3** 19 16N 121 28 E
Calayan I., *Phil.* **70 B3** 19 20N 121 27 E
Calbayog, *Phil.* **70 E5** 12 4N 124 38 E
Calbe, *Germany* **26 D7** 51 57N 11 47 E
Calca, *Peru* **156 C3** 13 22 S 72 0W
Calcasieu L., *U.S.A.* **139 L8** 29 55N 93 18W
Calci, *Italy* **38 E7** 43 44N 10 31 E
Calcutta, *India* **81 H13** 22 36N 88 24 E
Caldaro, *Italy* **39 B8** 46 23N 11 15 E
Caldas □, *Colombia* **152 B2** 5 15N 75 30W
Caldas da Rainha, *Portugal* **37 F1** 39 24N 9 8W
Caldas de Reyes, *Spain* **36 C2** 42 36N 8 39W
Caldas Novas, *Brazil* **155 E2** 17 45 S 48 38W
Calder →, *U.K.* **16 D6** 53 44N 1 21W
Caldera, *Chile* **158 B1** 27 5 S 70 55W
Caldwell, *Idaho, U.S.A.* **142 E5** 43 40N 116 41W
Caldwell, *Kans., U.S.A.* **139 G6** 37 2N 97 37W
Caldwell, *Tex., U.S.A.* **139 K6** 30 32N 96 42W
Caledon, *S. Africa* **104 E2** 34 14 S 19 26 E
Caledon →, *S. Africa* **104 E4** 30 31 S 26 5 E
Caledon B., *Australia* **114 A2** 12 45 S 137 0 E
Caledonia, *Canada* **136 C5** 43 7N 79 58W
Caledonia, *Mo., U.S.A.* **140 G6** 37 45N 90 46W
Caledonia, *N.Y., U.S.A.* **136 D7** 42 58N 77 51W
Calella, *Spain* **34 D7** 41 37N 2 40 E
Calemba, *Angola* **104 B2** 16 0 S 15 44 E
Calenzana, *France* **25 F12** 42 31N 8 51 E
Caleta Olivia, *Argentina* **160 C3** 46 25 S 67 25W
Calexico, *U.S.A.* **145 N11** 32 40N 115 30W
Calf of Man, *U.K.* **16 C3** 54 3N 4 49W
Calgary, *Canada* **130 C6** 51 0N 114 10W
Calheta, *Madeira* **33 D2** 32 44N 17 11W
Calhoun, *U.S.A.* **135 H3** 34 30N 84 57W
Cali, *Colombia* **152 C2** 3 25N 76 35W
Calicut, *India* **83 J2** 11 15N 75 43 E
Caliente, *U.S.A.* **143 H6** 37 37N 114 31W
California, *Mo., U.S.A.* **140 F4** 38 38N 92 34W
California, *Pa., U.S.A.* **136 F5** 40 4N 79 54W
California □, *U.S.A.* **143 H4** 37 30N 119 30W
California, Baja, *Mexico* **146 A1** 32 10N 115 12W
California, Baja, T.N. □, *Mexico* **146 B2** 30 0N 115 0W
California, Baja, T.S. □, *Mexico* **146 B2** 25 50N 111 50W
California, G. de, *Mexico* **146 B2** 27 0N 111 0W
California City, *U.S.A.* **145 K9** 35 10N 117 55W
California Hot Springs, *U.S.A.* **145 K8** 35 51N 118 41W
Călimăneşti, *Romania* **46 D5** 45 14N 24 20 E
Călimani, Munţii, *Romania* **46 B5** 47 12N 25 0 E
Călineşti, *Romania* **46 D5** 45 21N 24 18 E
Calingasta, *Argentina* **158 C2** 31 15 S 69 30W
Calinog, *Phil.* **71 F4** 11 7N 122 32 E
Calintaan, *Phil.* **70 E3** 12 35N 120 57 E
Calipatria, *U.S.A.* **145 M11** 33 8N 115 31W
Calistoga, *U.S.A.* **144 G4** 38 35N 122 35W
Calitri, *Italy* **41 B8** 40 54N 15 25 E
Calitzdorp, *S. Africa* **104 E3** 33 33 S 21 42 E
Callabonna, L., *Australia* **115 D3** 29 40 S 140 5 E
Callac, *France* **22 D3** 48 25N 3 27W
Callan, *Ireland* **19 D4** 52 33N 7 25W
Callander, *U.K.* **18 E4** 56 15N 4 14W
Callang, *Phil.* **70 C3** 17 2N 121 38 E
Callantsoog, *Neths.* **20 C5** 52 50N 4 42 E
Callao, *Peru* **156 C2** 12 0 S 77 0W
Callaway, *U.S.A.* **138 E5** 41 18N 99 56W
Callender, *U.S.A.* **140 B2** 42 22N 94 17W
Calles, *Mexico* **147 C5** 23 2N 98 42W
Callide, *Australia* **114 C5** 24 18 S 150 28 E
Calling Lake, *Canada* **130 B6** 55 15N 113 12W
Calliope, *Australia* **114 C5** 24 0 S 151 16 E
Callosa de Ensarriá, *Spain* **35 G4** 38 40N 0 8W
Callosa de Segura, *Spain* **35 G4** 38 1N 0 53W
Calmar, *U.S.A.* **140 A5** 43 11N 91 52W
Calola, *Angola* **103 F3** 16 25 S 17 48 E
Calolbon, *Phil.* **70 E5** 13 36N 124 6 E
Caloocan, *Phil.* **70 D3** 14 39N 120 58 E

182 Capu-Lapu


Capu-Lapu, Phil. 71 F4 10 20N 123 55 E
Cápua, Italy 41 A7 41 7N 14 15 E
Capul I., Phil. 70 E5 12 26N 124 10 E
Caquetá □, Colombia 152 C3 1 0N 74 0W
Caquetá →, Colombia 152 D4 1 15 S 69 15W
Carabalan, Phil. 71 F4 10 6N 122 57 E
Carabao I., Phil. 70 E3 12 4N 121 56 E
Carabobo, Venezuela 152 A4 10 2N 68 5W
Carabobo □, Venezuela 152 A4 10 10N 68 5W
Caracal, Romania 46 E5 44 8N 24 22 E
Caracaraí, Brazil 153 C5 1 50N 61 8W
Caracas, Venezuela 152 A4 10 30N 66 55W
Caracol, Brazil 154 C3 9 15 S 43 22W
Caracollo, Bolivia 156 D4 17 39 S 67 10W
Caradoc, Australia 116 A5 30 35 S 143 5 E
Caragabal, Australia 117 B7 33 49 S 147 45 E
Caráglio, Italy 38 D4 44 25N 7 25 E
Carahue, Chile 160 A2 38 43 S 73 12W
Caraí, Brazil 155 E3 17 12 S 41 42W
Carajás, Serra dos, Brazil 154 C1 6 0 S 51 30W
Caramoan, Phil. 70 E4 13 46N 123 52 E
Caranapatuba, Brazil 157 B5 6 38 S 62 34W
Carandaiti, Bolivia 157 E5 20 45 S 63 4W
Carangola, Brazil 155 F3 20 44 S 42 5W
Carani, Australia 113 F2 30 57 S 116 28 E
Caransebeş, Romania 46 D3 45 28N 22 18 E
Carantec, France 22 D3 48 40N 3 55W
Caraparaná →, Colombia 152 D3 1 45 S 73 13W
Carapelle →, Italy 41 A8 41 3N 15 55 E
Caras, Peru 156 B2 9 3 S 77 47W
Caraş Severin □, Romania 42 B7 45 10N 22 10 E
Caraşova, Romania 42 B6 45 11N 21 51 E
Caratasca, L., Honduras 148 C3 15 20N 83 40W
Caratinga, Brazil 155 E3 19 50 S 42 10W
Caraúbas, Brazil 154 C4 5 43 S 37 33W
Caravaca, Spain 35 G3 38 8N 1 52W
Caravággio, Italy 38 C6 45 30N 9 39 E
Caravelas, Brazil 155 E4 17 45 S 39 15W
Caraveli, Peru 156 D3 15 45 S 73 25W
Caràzinho, Brazil 159 B5 28 16 S 52 46W
Carballino, Spain 36 C2 42 26N 8 5W
Carballo, Spain 36 B2 43 13N 8 41W
Carberry, Canada 131 D9 49 50N 99 25W
Carbia, Spain 36 C2 42 48N 8 14W
Carbó, Mexico 146 B2 29 42N 110 58W
Carbon, Canada 130 C6 51 30N 113 9W
Carbonara, C., Italy 40 C2 39 8N 9 30 E
Carbondale, Colo., U.S.A. 142 G10 39 24N 107 13W
Carbondale, Ill., U.S.A. 139 G10 37 44N 89 13W
Carbondale, Pa., U.S.A. 137 E9 41 35N 75 30W
Carbonear, Canada 129 C9 47 42N 53 13W
Carboneras, Spain 35 J3 37 0N 1 53W
Carboneras de Guadazaón, Spain 34 F3 39 54N 1 50W
Carbonia, Italy 40 C1 39 10N 8 30 E
Carcabuey, Spain 37 H6 37 27N 4 17W
Carcagente, Spain 35 F4 39 8N 0 28W
Carcajou, Canada 130 B5 57 47N 117 6W
Carcar, Phil. 71 F4 10 6N 123 38 E
Carcasse, C., Haiti 149 C5 18 30N 74 28W
Carcassonne, France 24 E6 43 13N 2 20 E
Carche, Spain 35 G3 38 26N 1 9W
Carchi □, Ecuador 152 C2 0 45N 78 0W
Carcoar, Australia 117 B8 33 36 S 149 8 E
Carcross, Canada 126 B6 60 13N 134 45W
Cardabia, Australia 112 D1 23 2 S 113 48 E
Çardak, Turkey 88 E3 37 49N 29 39 E
Cardamon Hills, India 83 K3 9 30N 77 15 E
Cárdenas, Cuba 148 B3 23 0N 81 30W
Cárdenas, San Luis Potosí, Mexico 147 C5 22 0N 99 41W
Cárdenas, Tabasco, Mexico 147 D6 17 59N 93 21W
Cardenete, Spain 34 F3 39 46N 1 41W
Cardiel, L., Argentina 160 C2 48 55 S 71 10W
Cardiff, U.K. 17 F4 51 28N 3 11W
Cardiff-by-the-Sea, U.S.A. 145 M9 33 1N 117 17W
Cardigan, U.K. 17 E3 52 6N 4 41W
Cardigan B., U.K. 17 E3 52 30N 4 30W
Cardinal, Canada 137 B9 44 47N 75 23W
Cardón, Punta, Venezuela 152 A3 11 37N 70 14W
Cardona, Spain 34 D6 41 56N 1 40 E
Cardona, Uruguay 158 C4 33 53 S 57 18W
Cardoner →, Spain 34 D6 41 41N 1 51 E
Cardross, Canada 131 D7 49 50N 105 40W
Cardston, Canada 130 D6 49 15N 113 20W
Cardwell, Australia 114 B4 18 14 S 146 2 E
Careen L., Canada 131 B7 57 0N 108 11W
Carei, Romania 46 B3 47 40N 22 29 E
Careiro, Brazil 153 D6 3 12 S 59 45W
Careme, Indonesia 75 D3 6 55 S 108 27 E
Carentan, France 22 C5 49 19N 1 15W
Carey, Idaho, U.S.A. 142 E7 43 19N 113 57W
Carey, Ohio, U.S.A. 141 D13 40 57N 83 23W
Carey, L., Australia 113 E3 29 0 S 122 15 E
Carey L., Canada 131 A8 62 12N 102 55W
Careysburg, Liberia 100 D2 6 34N 10 30W
Cargados Garajos, Ind. Oc. 109 F4 17 0 S 59 0 E
Cargèse, France 25 F12 42 7N 8 35 E
Carhaix-Plouguer, France 22 D3 48 18N 3 36W
Carhuamayo, Peru 156 C2 10 51 S 76 4W
Carhuas, Peru 156 B2 9 15 S 77 39W
Carhué, Argentina 158 D3 37 10 S 62 50W
Caria, Turkey 88 E3 37 20N 28 10 E
Cariacica, Brazil 155 F3 20 16 S 40 25W
Cariango, Angola 103 E3 10 37 S 15 20 E
Caribbean Sea, W. Indies 149 C5 15 0N 75 0W
Cariboo Mts., Canada 130 C4 53 0N 121 0W
Caribou, U.S.A. 129 C6 46 52N 68 1W
Caribou →, Man., Canada 131 B10 59 20N 94 44W
Caribou →, N.W.T., Canada 130 A3 61 27N 125 45W
Caribou I., Canada 128 C2 47 22N 85 49W
Caribou Is., Canada 130 A6 61 55N 113 15W
Caribou L., Man., Canada 131 B9 59 21N 96 10W
Caribou L., Ont., Canada 128 B2 50 25N 89 5W
Caribou Mts., Canada 130 B5 59 12N 115 40W
Carichic, Mexico 146 B3 27 56N 107 3W
Carigara, Phil. 71 F5 11 18N 124 41 E
Carignan, France 23 C12 49 38N 5 10 E
Carignano, Italy 38 D4 44 55N 7 40 E
Carillo, Mexico 146 B4 26 50N 103 55W
Carin, Somali Rep. 108 B3 10 59N 49 13 E
Carinda, Australia 117 A7 30 28 S 147 41 E
Cariñena, Spain 34 D3 41 20N 1 13W
Carinhanha, Brazil 155 D3 14 15 S 44 46W
Carinhanha →, Brazil 155 D3 14 20 S 43 47W
Carini, Italy 40 D6 38 9N 13 10 E
Carinola, Italy 40 A6 41 11N 13 58 E
Carinthia □ = Kärnten □, Austria 30 E6 46 52N 13 30 E
Caripito, Venezuela 153 A5 10 8N 63 6W
Caritianas, Brazil 157 B5 9 20 S 63 6W
Carlbrod = Dimitrovgrad, Serbia 42 D7 43 2N 22 48 E
Carlentini, Italy 41 E8 37 15N 15 2 E
Carles, Phil. 71 F4 11 34N 123 8 E
Carleton Place, Canada 128 C4 45 8N 76 9W
Carletonville, S. Africa 104 D4 26 23 S 27 22 E
Carlin, U.S.A. 142 F5 40 43N 116 7W
Carlingford, L., Ireland 19 B5 54 2N 6 5W
Carlinville, U.S.A. 140 E7 39 17N 89 53W
Carlisle, U.K. 16 C5 54 54N 2 55W
Carlisle, Ky., U.S.A. 141 F12 38 19N 84 1W
Carlisle, Pa., U.S.A. 136 F7 40 12N 77 12W
Carlit, Pic, France 24 F5 42 35N 1 55 E
Carloforte, Italy 40 C1 39 10N 8 18 E
Carlos Casares, Argentina 158 D3 35 32 S 61 20W
Carlos Chagas, Brazil 155 E3 17 43 S 40 45W
Carlos Tejedor, Argentina 158 D3 35 25 S 62 25W
Carlow, Ireland 19 D5 52 50N 6 58W
Carlow □, Ireland 19 D5 52 43N 6 50W
Carlsbad, Calif., U.S.A. 145 M9 33 10N 117 21W
Carlsbad, N. Mex., U.S.A. 139 J2 32 25N 104 14W
Carlyle, Canada 131 D8 49 40N 102 20W
Carlyle, U.S.A. 138 F10 38 37N 89 22W
Carlyle Res., U.S.A. 140 F7 38 37N 89 21W
Carmacks, Canada 126 B6 62 5N 136 16W
Carmagnola, Italy 38 D4 44 50N 7 42 E
Carman, Canada 131 D9 49 30N 98 0W
Carmangay, Canada 130 C6 50 10N 113 10W
Carmanville, Canada 129 C9 49 23N 54 19W
Carmarthen, U.K. 17 F3 51 52N 4 20W
Carmarthen B., U.K. 17 F3 51 40N 4 30W
Carmaux, France 24 D6 44 3N 2 10 E
Carmel, Ind., U.S.A. 141 E10 39 59N 86 8W
Carmel, N.Y., U.S.A. 137 E11 41 26N 73 41W
Carmel-by-the-Sea, U.S.A. 144 J5 36 33N 121 55W
Carmel Valley, U.S.A. 144 J5 36 29N 121 43W
Carmelo, Uruguay 158 C4 34 0 S 58 20W
Carmen, Bolivia 156 C4 11 40 S 67 51W
Carmen, Colombia 152 B2 9 43N 75 8W
Carmen, Paraguay 159 B4 27 13 S 56 12W
Carmen, Bohol, Phil. 71 G5 9 50N 124 12 E
Carmen, Cebu, Phil. 71 F5 10 35N 124 1 E
Carmen, Mindanao, Phil. 71 H5 7 13N 124 45 E
Carmen →, Mexico 146 A3 30 42N 106 29W
Carmen, I., Mexico 146 B2 26 0N 111 20W
Carmen de Patagones, Argentina 160 B4 40 50 S 63 0W
Cármenes, Spain 36 C5 42 58N 5 34W
Carmensa, Argentina 158 D2 35 15 S 67 40W
Carmi, U.S.A. 141 F8 38 5N 88 10W
Carmichael, U.S.A. 144 G5 38 38N 121 19W
Carmila, Australia 114 C4 21 55 S 149 24 E
Carmona, Spain 37 H5 37 28N 5 42W
Carnarvon, Queens., Australia 114 C4 24 48 S 147 45 E
Carnarvon, W. Austral., Australia 113 D1 24 51 S 113 42 E
Carnarvon, S. Africa 104 E3 30 56 S 22 8 E
Carnarvon Ra., Queens., Australia 114 D4 25 15 S 148 30 E
Carnarvon Ra., W. Austral., Australia 113 E3 25 20 S 120 45 E
Carnation, U.S.A. 144 C5 47 39N 121 55W
Carnaxide, Portugal 37 G1 38 43N 9 14W
Carndonagh, Ireland 19 A4 55 15N 7 16W
Carnduff, Canada 131 D8 49 10N 101 50W
Carnegie, U.S.A. 136 F4 40 24N 80 5W
Carnegie, L., Australia 113 E3 26 5 S 122 30 E
Carnic Alps = Karnische Alpen, Europe 30 E6 46 36N 13 0 E
Carniche Alpi = Karnische Alpen, Europe 30 E6 46 36N 13 0 E
Carnot, C.A.R. 102 B3 4 59N 15 56 E
Carnot, C., Australia 115 E2 34 57 S 135 38 E
Carnot B., Australia 112 C3 17 20 S 122 15 E
Carnsore Pt., Ireland 19 D5 52 10N 6 20W
Caro, U.S.A. 134 D4 43 29N 83 24W
Carol City, U.S.A. 135 N5 25 56N 80 16W
Carolina, Brazil 154 C2 7 10 S 47 30W
Carolina, Puerto Rico 149 C6 18 23N 65 58W
Carolina, S. Africa 105 D5 26 5 S 30 6 E
Caroline I., Kiribati 123 H12 9 15 S 150 3W
Caroline Is., Pac. Oc. 122 G6 8 0N 150 0 E
Caroline Pk., N.Z. 119 F2 45 57 S 167 15 E
Caron, Canada 131 C7 50 30N 105 50W
Caroni →, Venezuela 153 B5 8 21N 62 43W
Caroona, Australia 115 E5 31 24 S 150 26 E
Carora, Venezuela 152 A3 10 11N 70 5W
Carovigno, Italy 41 B10 40 42N 17 40 E
Carpathians, Europe 10 F10 49 30N 21 0 E
Carpaţii Meridionali, Romania 46 D5 45 30N 25 0 E
Carpenédolo, Italy 38 C7 45 22N 10 25 E
Carpentaria, G. of, Australia 114 A2 14 0 S 139 0 E
Carpentaria Downs, Australia 114 B3 18 44 S 144 20 E
Carpentersville, U.S.A. 141 B8 42 6N 88 17W
Carpentras, France 25 D9 44 3N 5 2 E
Carpi, Italy 38 D7 44 47N 10 52 E
Carpina, Brazil 154 C4 7 51 S 35 15W
Carpino, Italy 41 A8 41 50N 15 51 E
Carpinteria, U.S.A. 145 L7 34 24N 119 31W
Carpio, Spain 36 D5 41 13N 5 7W
Carpolac = Morea, Australia 116 D4 36 45 S 141 18 E
Carr Boyd Ra., Australia 112 C4 16 15 S 128 35 E
Carrabelle, U.S.A. 135 L3 29 51N 84 40W
Carranglan, Phil. 70 D3 15 58N 121 4 E
Carranya, Australia 112 C4 19 14 S 127 46 E
Carrara, Italy 38 D7 44 5N 10 7 E
Carrascal, Phil. 71 G5 9 22N 125 56 E
Carrascosa del Campo, Spain 34 E2 40 2N 2 45W
Carrauntoohill, Ireland 19 E2 52 0N 9 49W
Carretas, Punta, Peru 156 C2 14 12 S 76 17W
Carrick-on-Shannon, Ireland 19 C3 53 57N 8 7W
Carrick-on-Suir, Ireland 19 D4 52 22N 7 30W
Carrickfergus, U.K. 19 B6 54 43N 5 50W
Carrickfergus □, U.K. 19 B6 54 43N 5 49W
Carrickmacross, Ireland 19 C5 53 58N 6 43W
Carrieton, Australia 116 B3 32 25 S 138 31 E
Carrington, U.S.A. 138 B5 47 27N 99 8W
Carrión →, Spain 36 D6 41 53N 4 32W
Carrión de los Condes, Spain 36 C6 42 20N 4 37W
Carrizal Bajo, Chile 158 B1 28 5 S 71 20W
Carrizalillo, Chile 158 B1 29 5 S 71 30W
Carrizo Cr. →, U.S.A. 139 G3 36 55N 103 55W
Carrizo Springs, U.S.A. 139 L5 28 31N 99 52W
Carrizozo, U.S.A. 143 K11 33 38N 105 53W
Carroll, U.S.A. 140 B2 42 4N 94 52W
Carrollton, Ga., U.S.A. 135 J3 33 35N 85 5W
Carrollton, Ill., U.S.A. 138 F9 39 18N 90 24W
Carrollton, Ky., U.S.A. 141 F11 38 41N 85 11W
Carrollton, Mo., U.S.A. 140 E3 39 22N 93 30W
Carrollton, Ohio, U.S.A. 136 F3 40 34N 81 5W
Carron →, U.K. 18 D3 57 30N 5 30W
Carron, L., U.K. 18 D3 57 22N 5 35W
Carrot →, Canada 131 C8 53 50N 101 17W
Carrot River, Canada 131 C8 53 17N 103 35W
Carrouges, France 22 D6 48 34N 0 10W
Carruthers, Canada 131 C7 52 52N 109 16W
Çarşamba, Turkey 88 C7 41 11N 36 44 E
Carse of Gowrie, U.K. 18 E5 56 30N 3 10W
Carsoli, Italy 39 F10 42 7N 13 3 E
Carson, Calif., U.S.A. 145 M8 33 48N 118 17W
Carson, N. Dak., U.S.A. 138 B4 46 25N 101 34W
Carson →, U.S.A. 144 F8 39 45N 118 40W
Carson City, Mich., U.S.A. 141 A12 43 11N 84 51W
Carson City, Nev., U.S.A. 144 F7 39 10N 119 46W
Carson Sink, U.S.A. 142 G4 39 50N 118 25W
Carstairs, U.K. 18 F5 55 42N 3 41W
Cartagena, Colombia 152 A2 10 25N 75 33W
Cartagena, Spain 35 H4 37 38N 0 59W
Cartago, Colombia 152 C2 4 45N 75 55W
Cartago, Costa Rica 148 E3 9 50N 83 55W
Cartaxo, Portugal 37 F2 39 10N 8 47W
Cartaya, Spain 37 H3 37 16N 7 9W
Carteret, France 22 C5 49 23N 1 47W
Cartersville, U.S.A. 135 H3 34 10N 84 48W
Carterton, N.Z. 118 H4 41 2 S 175 31 E
Carterville, U.S.A. 140 G7 37 46N 89 5W
Carthage, Ark., U.S.A. 139 H8 34 4N 92 33W
Carthage, Ill., U.S.A. 140 D5 40 25N 91 8W
Carthage, Mo., U.S.A. 139 G7 37 11N 94 19W
Carthage, S. Dak., U.S.A. 138 C6 44 10N 97 43W
Carthage, Tex., U.S.A. 139 J7 32 9N 94 20W
Cartier I., Australia 112 B3 12 31 S 123 29 E
Cartwright, Canada 129 B8 53 41N 56 58W
Caruaru, Brazil 154 C4 8 15 S 35 55W
Carubig, Phil. 70 E5 12 24N 125 3 E
Carúpano, Venezuela 153 A5 10 39N 63 15W
Caruray, Phil. 71 F2 10 20N 119 0 E
Carutapera, Brazil 154 B2 1 13 S 46 1W
Caruthersville, U.S.A. 139 G10 36 11N 89 39W
Carvalho, Brazil 153 D7 2 16 S 51 29W
Carvin, France 23 B9 50 30N 2 57 E
Carvoeiro, Brazil 153 D5 1 30 S 61 59W
Carvoeiro, C., Portugal 37 F1 39 21N 9 24W
Casa Branca, Brazil 155 F2 21 46 S 47 4W
Casa Branca, Portugal 37 G2 38 29N 8 12W
Casa Grande, U.S.A. 143 K8 32 53N 111 45W
Casablanca, Chile 158 C1 33 20 S 71 25W
Casablanca, Morocco 98 B3 33 36N 7 36W
Casacalenda, Italy 41 A7 41 45N 14 50 E
Casal di Principe, Italy 41 B7 41 0N 14 8 E
Casalbordino, Italy 39 F11 42 10N 14 34 E
Casale Monferrato, Italy 38 C5 45 8N 8 28 E
Casalmaggiore, Italy 38 D7 44 59N 10 25 E
Casalpusterlengo, Italy 38 C6 45 10N 9 40 E
Casamance →, Senegal 100 C1 12 33N 16 46W
Casamássima, Italy 41 B9 40 58N 16 55 E
Casanare □, Colombia 152 B3 5 30N 72 0W
Casanare □, Colombia 152 B3 6 0N 73 0W
Casanare →, Colombia 152 B4 6 2N 69 51W
Casarano, Italy 41 B11 40 0N 18 10 E
Casares, Spain 37 J5 36 27N 5 16W
Casas Grandes, Mexico 146 A3 30 22N 108 0W
Casas Ibañez, Spain 35 F3 39 17N 1 30W
Casasimarro, Spain 35 F2 39 22N 2 3W
Casatejada, Spain 36 F5 39 54N 5 40W
Casavieja, Spain 36 E6 40 17N 4 46W
Cascade, Idaho, U.S.A. 142 D5 44 31N 116 2W
Cascade, Iowa, U.S.A. 140 B6 42 18N 91 1W
Cascade, Mont., U.S.A. 142 C8 47 16N 111 42W
Cascade Locks, U.S.A. 144 E5 45 40N 121 54W
Cascade Pt., N.Z. 119 E3 44 1 S 168 20 E
Cascade Ra., U.S.A. 124 E7 47 0N 121 30W
Cascais, Portugal 37 G1 38 41N 9 25W
Cascavel, Brazil 159 A5 24 57 S 53 28W
Cáscina, Italy 38 E7 43 40N 10 32 E
Caselle Torinese, Italy 38 C4 45 12N 7 39 E
Caserta, Italy 41 A7 41 5N 14 20 E
Cashel, Ireland 19 D4 52 31N 7 53W
Cashmere, U.S.A. 142 C3 47 31N 120 28W
Cashmere Downs, Australia 113 E2 28 57 S 119 35 E
Casibare →, Colombia 152 C3 3 48N 72 18W
Casiguran, Phil. 70 C4 16 22N 122 7 E
Casiguran Sound, Phil. 70 C3 16 6N 121 58 E
Casilda, Argentina 158 C3 33 10 S 61 10W
Casimcea, Romania 46 E9 44 45N 28 23 E
Casino, Australia 115 D5 28 52 S 153 3 E
Casiquiare →, Venezuela 152 C4 2 1N 67 7W
Casitas, Peru 156 A1 3 54 S 80 39W
Caslan, Canada 130 C6 54 38N 112 31W
Čáslav, Czech. 30 B8 49 54N 15 22 E
Casma, Peru 156 B2 9 30 S 78 20W
Casmalia, U.S.A. 145 L6 34 50N 120 32W
Casola Valsenio, Italy 39 D8 44 12N 11 40 E
Cásoli, Italy 39 F11 42 7N 14 18 E
Caspe, Spain 34 D4 41 14N 0 1W
Casper, U.S.A. 142 E10 42 51N 106 19W
Caspian Sea, Asia 49 F9 43 0N 50 0 E
Casquets, Chan. Is. 22 C4 49 46N 2 15W
Cass City, U.S.A. 134 D4 43 36N 83 11W
Cass Lake, U.S.A. 138 B7 47 23N 94 37W
Cassà de la Selva, Spain 34 D7 41 53N 2 52 E
Cassai, Angola 103 E4 10 33 S 21 59 E
Cassamba, Angola 103 E4 13 6 S 20 18 E
Cassano Iónio, Italy 41 C9 39 47N 16 20 E
Cassel, France 23 B9 50 48N 2 30 E
Casselman, Canada 137 A9 45 19N 75 5W
Casselton, U.S.A. 138 B6 46 54N 97 13W
Cassiar, Canada 130 B3 59 16N 129 40W
Cassiar Mts., Canada 130 B2 59 30N 130 30W
Cassilândia, Brazil 157 D7 19 9 S 51 45W
Cassinga, Angola 103 F3 15 5 S 16 4 E
Cassino, Italy 40 A6 41 30N 13 50 E
Cassis, France 25 E9 43 14N 5 32 E
Cassoalala, Angola 103 D2 9 30 S 14 22 E
Cassoango, Angola 103 E4 13 42 S 20 56 E
Cassopolis, U.S.A. 141 C10 41 55N 86 1W
Cassunda, Angola 103 E4 10 57 S 21 3 E
Cassville, Mo., U.S.A. 139 G8 36 41N 93 52W
Cassville, Wis., U.S.A. 140 B6 42 43N 90 59W
Cástagneto Carducci, Italy 38 E7 43 9N 10 36 E
Castaic, U.S.A. 145 L8 34 30N 118 38W
Castanhal, Brazil 154 B2 1 18 S 47 55W
Casteau, Belgium 21 G4 50 32N 4 2 E
Castéggio, Italy 38 C6 45 1N 9 8 E
Castejón de Monegros, Spain 34 D4 41 37N 0 15W
Castel di Sangro, Italy 39 G11 41 47N 14 6 E
Castel San Giovanni, Italy 38 C6 45 4N 9 25 E
Castel San Pietro, Italy 39 D8 44 23N 11 30 E
Castelbuono, Italy 41 E7 37 56N 14 4 E
Casteldelfino, Italy 38 D4 44 35N 7 4 E
Castelfiorentino, Italy 38 E7 43 36N 10 58 E
Castelfranco Emília, Italy 38 D8 44 37N 11 2 E
Castelfranco Véneto, Italy 39 C8 45 40N 11 56 E
Casteljaloux, France 24 D4 44 19N 0 6 E
Castellabate, Italy 41 B7 40 18N 14 55 E
Castellammare, G. di, Italy 40 D5 38 5N 12 55 E
Castellammare del Golfo, Italy 40 D5 38 2N 12 53 E
Castellammare di Stábia, Italy 41 B7 40 47N 14 29 E
Castellamonte, Italy 38 C4 45 23N 7 42 E
Castellana Grotte, Italy 41 B10 40 53N 17 10 E
Castellane, France 25 E10 43 50N 6 31 E
Castellaneta, Italy 41 B9 40 40N 16 57 E
Castellar de Santisteban, Spain 35 G1 38 16N 3 8W
Castelleone, Italy 38 C6 45 19N 9 47 E
Castelli, Argentina 158 D4 36 7 S 57 47W
Castelló de Ampurias, Spain 34 C8 42 15N 3 4 E
Castellón □, Spain 34 E4 40 15N 0 5W
Castellón de la Plana, Spain 34 F4 39 58N 0 3W
Castellote, Spain 34 E4 40 48N 0 15W
Castelltersol, Spain 34 D7 41 45N 2 8 E
Castelmáuro, Italy 41 A7 41 50N 14 40 E
Castelnau-de-Médoc, France 24 C3 45 2N 0 48W
Castelnaudary, France 24 E5 43 20N 1 58 E
Castelnovo ne' Monti, Italy 38 D7 44 27N 10 26 E
Castelnuovo di Val di Cécina, Italy 38 E7 43 12N 10 54 E
Castelo, Brazil 155 F3 20 33 S 41 14W
Castelo Branco, Portugal 36 F3 39 50N 7 31W
Castelo Branco □, Portugal 36 F3 39 52N 7 45W
Castelo de Paiva, Portugal 36 D2 41 2N 8 16W
Castelo de Vide, Portugal 37 F3 39 25N 7 27W
Castelo do Piauí, Brazil 154 C3 5 20 S 41 33W
Castelsarrasin, France 24 D5 44 2N 1 7 E
Casteltérmini, Italy 40 E6 37 32N 13 38 E
Castelvetrano, Italy 40 E5 37 40N 12 46 E
Castendo, Angola 103 D2 8 39 S 14 10 E
Casterton, Australia 116 D4 37 30 S 141 30 E
Castets, France 24 E2 43 52N 1 6W
Castiglione del Lago, Italy 39 E9 43 7N 12 3 E
Castiglione della Pescáia, Italy 38 F7 42 46N 10 53 E
Castiglione della Stiviere, Italy 38 C7 45 23N 10 30 E
Castiglione Fiorentino, Italy 39 E8 43 20N 11 55 E
Castilblanco, Spain 37 F5 39 17N 5 5W
Castilla, Peru 156 B1 5 12 S 80 38W
Castilla, Playa de, Spain 37 H4 37 0N 6 33W
Castilla La Mancha □, Spain 37 F7 39 30N 3 30W
Castilla La Nueva = Castilla La Mancha □, Spain 37 F7 39 30N 3 30W
Castilla La Vieja = Castilla y Leon □, Spain 36 D6 42 0N 5 0W
Castilla y Leon □, Spain 36 D6 42 0N 5 0W
Castillon, Barr. de, France 25 E10 43 53N 6 33 E
Castillon-en-Couserans, France 24 F5 42 56N 1 1 E
Castillon-la-Bataille, France 24 D3 44 51N 0 2W
Castillonès, France 24 D4 44 39N 0 37 E
Castillos, Uruguay 159 C5 34 12 S 53 52W
Castle Dale, U.S.A. 142 G8 39 13N 111 1W
Castle Douglas, U.K. 18 G5 54 57N 3 57W
Castle Point, N.Z. 118 G5 40 54 S 176 15 E
Castle Rock, Colo., U.S.A. 138 F2 39 22N 104 51W
Castle Rock, Wash., U.S.A. 144 D4 46 17N 122 54W
Castlebar, Ireland 19 C2 53 52N 9 17W
Castleblaney, Ireland 19 B5 54 7N 6 44W
Castlecliff, N.Z. 118 F3 39 57 S 174 59 E
Castlegar, Canada 130 D5 49 20N 117 40W
Castlemaine, Australia 116 D6 37 2 S 144 12 E
Castlereagh, Ireland 19 C3 53 47N 8 30W
Castlereagh □, U.K. 19 B6 54 33N 5 53W
Castlereagh →, Australia 117 A7 30 12 S 147 32 E
Castlereagh B., Australia 114 A2 12 10 S 135 10 E
Castletown, I. of Man 16 C3 54 4N 4 40W
Castletown Bearhaven, Ireland 19 E2 51 40N 9 54W
Castlevale, Australia 114 C4 24 30 S 146 48 E
Castor, Canada 130 C6 52 15N 111 50W

Champagne, Plaine de 183


Castres, France 24 E6 43 37N 2 13 E
Castricum, Neths. 20 C5 52 33N 4 40 E
Castries, St. Lucia 149 D7 14 2N 60 58W
Castril, Spain 35 H2 37 48N 2 46W
Castro, Brazil 159 A5 24 45 S 50 0W
Castro, Chile 160 B2 42 30 S 73 50W
Castro Alves, Brazil 155 D4 12 46 S 39 33W
Castro del Río, Spain 37 H6 37 41N 4 29W
Castro Marim, Portugal 37 H3 37 13N 7 26W
Castro Urdiales, Spain 34 B1 43 23N 3 11W
Castro Verde, Portugal 37 H2 37 41N 8 4W
Castrojeriz, Spain 36 C6 42 17N 4 9W
Castropol, Spain 36 B3 43 32N 7 0W
Castroreale, Italy 41 D8 38 5N 15 15 E
Castrovillari, Italy 41 C9 39 49N 16 11 E
Castroville, Calif., U.S.A. 144 J5 36 46N 121 45W
Castroville, Tex., U.S.A. 139 L5 29 21N 98 53W
Castrovirreyna, Peru 156 C2 13 20 S 75 18W
Castuera, Spain 37 G5 38 43N 5 37W
Casummit Lake, Canada 128 B1 51 29N 92 22W
Caswell Sound, N.Z. 119 E2 44 59 S 167 8 E
Çat, Turkey 89 D9 39 40N 41 3 E
Cat Ba, Dao, Vietnam 76 B6 20 50N 107 0 E
Cat I., Bahamas 149 B4 24 30N 75 30W
Cat I., U.S.A. 139 K10 30 14N 89 6W
Cat L., Canada 128 B1 51 40N 91 50W
Čata, Slovak Rep. 31 D11 47 58N 18 38 E
Catabola, Angola 103 E3 12 9 S 17 16 E
Catacamas, Honduras 148 D2 14 54N 85 56W
Catacáos, Peru 156 B1 5 20 S 80 45W
Cataguases, Brazil 155 F3 21 23 S 42 39W
Catagupan, Phil. 71 G1 8 1N 116 58 E
Catahoula L., U.S.A. 139 K8 31 31N 92 7W
Çatak, Turkey 89 D10 38 1N 43 8 E
Catalão, Brazil 155 E2 18 10 S 47 57W
Çatalca, Turkey 88 C3 41 8N 28 27 E
Catalina, Canada 129 C9 48 31N 53 4W
Catalonia = Cataluña □, Spain 34 D6 41 40N 1 15 E
Cataluña □, Spain 34 D6 41 40N 1 15 E
Çatalzeytin, Turkey 88 C6 41 57N 34 12 E
Catamarca, Argentina 158 B2 28 30 S 65 50W
Catamarca □, Argentina 158 B2 27 0 S 65 50W
Catanauan, Phil. 70 E4 13 36N 122 19 E
Catanduanes, Phil. 70 E5 13 50N 124 20 E
Catanduva, Brazil 159 A6 21 5 S 48 58W
Catánia, Italy 41 E8 37 31N 15 4 E
Catánia, G. di, Italy 41 E8 37 25N 15 8 E
Catanzaro, Italy 41 D9 38 54N 16 38 E
Cataonia, Turkey 88 E6 37 30N 36 0 E
Catarman, Camiguin, Phil. 71 G5 9 8N 124 40 E
Catarman, N. Samar, Phil. 70 E5 12 28N 124 35 E
Catbalogan, Phil. 71 F5 11 46N 124 53 E
Cateel, Phil. 71 H6 7 47N 126 24 E
Cateel Bay, Phil. 71 H6 7 54N 126 25 E
Catende, Angola 103 E4 11 14 S 21 30 E
Catende, Brazil 154 C4 8 40 S 35 43W
Catete, Angola 103 D2 9 6 S 13 43 E
Cathcart, Australia 117 D8 36 52 S 149 24 E
Cathcart, S. Africa 104 E4 32 18 S 27 10 E
Cathlamet, U.S.A. 144 D3 46 12N 123 23W
Catio, Guinea-Biss. 100 C1 11 17N 15 15W
Catismiña, Venezuela 153 C5 4 5N 63 40W
Catita, Brazil 154 C3 9 31 S 43 1W
Catlettsburg, U.S.A. 134 F4 38 25N 82 36W
Catlin, U.S.A. 141 D9 40 4N 87 42W
Catmon, Phil. 71 F5 10 43N 124 1 E
Catoche, C., Mexico 147 C7 21 40N 87 8W
Catolé do Rocha, Brazil 154 C4 6 21 S 37 45W
Catral, Spain 35 G4 38 10N 0 47W
Catria, Mt., Italy 39 E9 43 28N 12 42 E
Catrimani, Brazil 153 C5 0 27N 61 41W
Catrimani →, Brazil 153 C5 0 28N 61 44W
Catskill, U.S.A. 137 D11 42 14N 73 52W
Catskill Mts., U.S.A. 137 D10 42 10N 74 25W
Catt, Mt., Australia 114 A1 13 49 S 134 23 E
Cattaraugus, U.S.A. 136 D6 42 22N 78 52W
Cattólica, Italy 39 E9 43 58N 12 43 E
Cattólica Eraclea, Italy 40 E6 37 27N 13 24 E
Catu, Brazil 155 D4 12 21 S 38 23W
Catuala, Angola 103 F3 16 25 S 19 2 E
Catumbela, Angola 103 E2 12 25 S 13 34 E
Catur, Mozam. 107 E4 13 45 S 35 30 E
Catwick Is., Vietnam 77 G7 10 0N 109 0 E
Cauayan, Phil. 70 C3 16 56N 121 46 E
Cauca □, Colombia 152 C2 2 30N 76 50W
Cauca →, Colombia 152 B3 8 54N 74 28W
Caucaia, Brazil 154 B4 3 40 S 38 35W
Caucasia, Colombia 152 B2 8 0N 75 12W
Caucasus = Bolshoi Kavkas, Asia 53 E11 42 50N 44 0 E
Caudebec-en-Caux, France 22 C7 49 30N 0 42 E
Caudete, Spain 35 G3 38 42N 1 2W
Caudry, France 23 B10 50 7N 3 22 E
Caulnes, France 22 D4 48 18N 2 10W
Caulónia, Italy 41 D9 38 23N 16 25 E
Caúngula, Angola 103 D3 8 26 S 18 38 E
Cauquenes, Chile 158 D1 36 0 S 72 22W
Caura →, Venezuela 153 B5 7 38N 64 53W
Caurés →, Brazil 153 D5 1 21 S 62 20W
Cauresi →, Mozam. 107 F3 17 8 S 33 0 E
Causapscal, Canada 129 C6 48 19N 67 12W
Caussade, France 24 D5 44 10N 1 33 E
Causse-Méjean, France 24 D7 44 18N 3 42 E
Cauterets, France 24 F3 42 52N 0 8W
Cautín □, Chile 160 A2 39 0 S 72 30W
Caux, Pays de, France 22 C7 49 38N 0 35 E
Cava dei Tirreni, Italy 41 B7 40 42N 14 42 E
Cávado →, Portugal 36 D2 41 32N 8 48W
Cavaillon, France 25 E9 43 50N 5 2 E
Cavalaire-sur-Mer, France 25 E10 43 10N 6 33 E
Cavalcante, Brazil 155 D2 13 48 S 47 30W
Cavalese, Italy 39 B8 46 17N 11 29 E
Cavalier, U.S.A. 138 A6 48 48N 97 37W
Cavalla = Cavally →, Africa 100 E3 4 22N 7 32W
Cavalli Is., N.Z. 118 B2 35 0 S 173 58 E
Cavallo, I. de, France 25 G13 41 22N 9 16 E
Cavally →, Africa 100 E3 4 22N 7 32W
Cavan, Ireland 19 C4 54 0N 7 22W
Cavan □, Ireland 19 C4 53 58N 7 10W
Cavárzere, Italy 39 C9 45 8N 12 6 E
Cave City, U.S.A. 134 G3 37 8N 85 58W
Cavenagh Ra., Australia 113 E4 26 12 S 127 55 E
Cavendish, Australia 116 D5 37 31 S 142 2 E
Caviana, I., Brazil 153 C7 0 10N 50 10W
Cavite, Phil. 70 D3 14 29N 120 55 E
Cavite □, Phil. 70 D3 14 15N 120 50 E
Cavour, Italy 38 D4 44 47N 7 22 E
Cavtat, Croatia 42 E3 42 35N 18 13 E
Cavuşcu Gölü, Turkey 88 D4 38 22N 31 53 E
Cawkers Well, Australia 116 A5 31 41 S 142 57 E
Cawndilla L., Australia 116 B5 32 30 S 142 15 E
Cawnpore = Kanpur, India 81 F9 26 28N 80 20 E
Caxias, Brazil 154 B3 4 55 S 43 20W
Caxias do Sul, Brazil 159 B5 29 10 S 51 10W
Caxine, C., Algeria 99 A4 35 56N 0 27W
Caxito, Angola 103 D2 8 30 S 13 30 E
Caxopa, Angola 103 E4 11 52 S 20 52 E
Çay, Turkey 88 D4 38 35N 31 1 E
Cay Sal Bank, Bahamas 148 B3 23 45N 80 0W
Cayambe, Ecuador 152 C2 0 2N 77 59W
Cayambe, Ecuador 152 C2 0 3N 78 8W
Çaycuma, Turkey 88 C5 41 25N 32 4 E
Çayeli, Turkey 89 C9 41 5N 40 45 E
Cayenne, Fr. Guiana 153 B7 5 5N 52 18W
Cayenne □, Fr. Guiana 153 C7 5 0N 53 0W
Cayeux-sur-Mer, France 23 B8 50 10N 1 30 E
Cayiralan, Turkey 88 D6 39 17N 35 38 E
Caylus, France 24 D5 44 15N 1 47 E
Cayman Brac, Cayman Is. 148 C4 19 43N 79 49W
Cayman Is. ■, W. Indies 148 C3 19 40N 80 30W
Cayo Romano, Cuba 149 B4 22 0N 78 0W
Cayuga, Canada 136 D5 42 59N 79 50W
Cayuga, Ind., U.S.A. 141 E9 39 57N 87 28W
Cayuga, N.Y., U.S.A. 137 D8 42 54N 76 44W
Cayuga L., U.S.A. 137 D8 42 41N 76 41W
Cazaje, Angola 103 E4 11 2 S 20 45 E
Cazalla de la Sierra, Spain 37 H5 37 56N 5 45W
Căzăneşti, Romania 46 E8 44 36N 27 3 E
Cazaux et de Sanguinet, Étang de, France 24 D2 44 29N 1 10W
Cazères, France 24 E5 43 13N 1 5 E
Cazin, Bos.-H. 39 D12 44 57N 15 57 E
Čazma, Croatia 39 C13 45 45N 16 39 E
Čazma →, Croatia 39 C13 45 35N 16 29 E
Cazombo, Angola 103 E4 11 54 S 22 56 E
Cazorla, Spain 35 H1 37 55N 3 2W
Cazorla, Venezuela 152 B4 8 1N 67 0W
Cazorla, Sierra de, Spain 35 G2 38 5N 2 55W
Cea →, Spain 36 C5 42 0N 5 36W
Ceamurlia de Jos, Romania 46 E9 44 43N 28 47 E
Ceanannus Mor, Ireland 19 C5 53 42N 6 53W
Ceará = Fortaleza, Brazil 154 B4 3 45 S 38 35W
Ceará □, Brazil 154 C4 5 0 S 40 0W
Ceará Mirim, Brazil 154 C4 5 38 S 35 25W
Ceauru, L., Romania 46 E4 44 58N 23 11 E
Cebaco, I. de, Panama 148 E3 7 33N 81 9W
Cebollar, Argentina 158 B2 29 10 S 66 35W
Cebollera, Sierra de, Spain 34 D2 42 0N 2 30W
Cebreros, Spain 36 E6 40 27N 4 28W
Cebu, Phil. 71 F4 10 18N 123 54 E
Ceccano, Italy 40 A6 41 34N 13 18 E
Cece, Hungary 31 E11 46 46N 18 39 E
Cechi, Ivory C. 100 D4 6 15N 4 25W
Čechy, Czech. 30 B6 49 58N 13 30 E
Cecil Plains, Australia 115 D5 27 30 S 151 11 E
Cécina, Italy 38 E7 43 19N 10 33 E
Cécina →, Italy 38 E7 43 19N 10 29 E
Ceclavin, Spain 36 F4 39 50N 6 45W
Cedar →, U.S.A. 140 C5 41 17N 91 21W
Cedar City, U.S.A. 143 H7 37 41N 113 4W
Cedar Creek Reservoir, U.S.A. 139 J6 32 11N 96 4W
Cedar Falls, Iowa, U.S.A. 140 B4 42 32N 92 27W
Cedar Falls, Wash., U.S.A. 144 C5 47 25N 121 45W
Cedar Grove, U.S.A. 141 E12 39 22N 84 56W
Cedar Key, U.S.A. 135 L4 29 8N 83 2W
Cedar L., Canada 131 C8 53 10N 100 0W
Cedar Lake, U.S.A. 141 C9 41 22N 87 26W
Cedar Point, U.S.A. 141 C13 41 44N 83 21W
Cedar Rapids, U.S.A. 140 C5 41 59N 91 40W
Cedartown, U.S.A. 135 H3 34 1N 85 15W
Cedarvale, Canada 130 B3 55 1N 128 22W
Cedarville, S. Africa 105 E4 30 23 S 29 3 E
Cedarville, Calif., U.S.A. 142 F3 41 32N 120 10W
Cedarville, Ill., U.S.A. 140 B7 42 23N 89 38W
Cedarville, Ohio, U.S.A. 141 E13 39 44N 83 49W
Cedeira, Spain 36 B2 43 39N 8 2W
Cedral, Mexico 146 C4 23 50N 100 42W
Cedrino →, Italy 40 B2 40 23N 9 44 E
Cedro, Brazil 154 C4 6 34 S 39 3W
Cedros, I. de, Mexico 146 B1 28 10N 115 20W
Ceduna, Australia 115 E1 32 7 S 133 46 E
Cedynia, Poland 47 C1 52 53N 14 12 E
Cefalù, Italy 41 D7 38 3N 14 1 E
Cega →, Spain 36 D6 41 33N 4 46W
Cegléd, Hungary 31 D12 47 11N 19 47 E
Céglie Messápico, Italy 41 B10 40 39N 17 31 E
Cehegín, Spain 35 G3 38 6N 1 48W
Ceheng, China 68 E5 24 58N 105 48 E
Cehu-Silvaniei, Romania 46 B4 47 24N 23 9 E
Ceica, Romania 46 C3 46 53N 22 10 E
Ceira →, Portugal 36 E2 40 13N 8 16W
Cekhira, Tunisia 96 B2 34 20N 10 5 E
Cela, Angola 103 E3 11 25 S 15 7 E
Celano, Italy 39 F10 42 6N 13 30 E
Celanova, Spain 36 C3 42 9N 7 58W
Celaya, Mexico 146 C4 20 31N 100 37W
Celbridge, Ireland 19 C5 53 20N 6 33W
Celebes = Sulawesi □, Indonesia 72 B2 2 0 S 120 0 E
Celebes Sea = Sulawesi Sea, Indonesia 72 A2 3 0N 123 0 E
Celendín, Peru 156 B2 6 52 S 78 10W
Čelić, Bos.-H. 42 C3 44 43N 18 47 E
Celica, Ecuador 152 D2 4 7 S 79 59W
Celina, U.S.A. 141 D12 40 33N 84 35W
Celje, Slovenia 39 B12 46 16N 15 18 E
Celldömölk, Hungary 31 D10 47 16N 17 10 E
Celle, Germany 26 C6 52 37N 10 4 E
Celles, Belgium 21 G2 50 42N 3 28 E
Celorico da Beira, Portugal 36 E3 40 38N 7 24W
Cement, U.S.A. 139 H5 34 56N 98 8W
Çemişgezek, Turkey 89 D8 39 3N 38 56 E
Cenepa →, Peru 152 D2 4 40 S 78 10W
Cengong, China 68 D7 27 13N 108 44 E
Ceno →, Italy 38 D7 44 4N 10 5 E
Centallo, Italy 38 D4 44 30N 7 35 E
Centenário do Sul, Brazil 155 F1 22 48 S 51 36W
Center, N. Dak., U.S.A. 138 B4 47 7N 101 18W
Center, Tex., U.S.A. 139 K7 31 48N 94 11W
Center Point, U.S.A. 140 B5 42 12N 91 46W
Centerfield, U.S.A. 143 G8 39 8N 111 49W
Centerville, Calif., U.S.A. 144 J7 36 44N 119 30W
Centerville, Iowa, U.S.A. 140 D4 40 44N 92 52W
Centerville, Mich., U.S.A. 141 C11 41 55N 85 32W
Centerville, Pa., U.S.A. 136 F5 40 3N 79 59W
Centerville, S. Dak., U.S.A. 138 D6 43 7N 96 58W
Centerville, Tenn., U.S.A. 135 H2 35 47N 87 28W
Centerville, Tex., U.S.A. 139 K7 31 16N 95 59W
Cento, Italy 39 D8 44 43N 11 16 E
Central, Brazil 154 D3 11 8 S 42 8W
Central, U.S.A. 143 K9 32 47N 108 9W
Central □, Kenya 106 C4 0 30 S 37 30 E
Central □, Malawi 107 E3 13 30 S 33 30 E
Central □, U.K. 18 E4 56 10N 4 30W
Central □, Zambia 107 E2 14 25 S 28 50 E
Central, Cordillera, Bolivia 157 D5 18 30 S 64 55W
Central, Cordillera, Colombia 152 C2 5 0N 75 0W
Central, Cordillera, Costa Rica 148 D3 10 10N 84 5W
Central, Cordillera, Dom. Rep. 149 C5 19 15N 71 0W
Central, Cordillera, Peru 156 B2 7 0 S 77 30W
Central, Cordillera, Phil. 70 C3 17 20N 120 57 E
Central, Sistema, Spain 36 E5 40 40N 5 55W
Central African Rep. ■, Africa 102 A4 7 0N 20 0 E
Central City, Ky., U.S.A. 134 G2 37 18N 87 7W
Central City, Nebr., U.S.A. 138 E5 41 7N 98 0W
Central I., Kenya 106 B4 3 30N 36 0 E
Central Makran Range, Pakistan 79 D2 26 30N 64 15 E
Central Patricia, Canada 128 B1 51 30N 90 9W
Central Ra., Papua N. G. 120 C2 5 0 S 143 0 E
Central Russian Uplands, Europe 10 E13 54 0N 36 0 E
Central Siberian Plateau, Russia 58 C14 65 0N 105 0 E
Centralia, Ill., U.S.A. 140 F7 38 32N 89 8W
Centralia, Mo., U.S.A. 140 E4 39 13N 92 8W
Centralia, Wash., U.S.A. 144 D4 46 43N 122 58W
Centreville, Ala., U.S.A. 135 J2 32 57N 87 8W
Centreville, Miss., U.S.A. 139 K9 31 5N 91 4W
Centúripe, Italy 41 E7 37 37N 14 41 E
Cephalonia = Kefallinía, Greece 45 F2 38 20N 20 30 E
Čepin, Croatia 42 B3 45 32N 18 34 E
Ceprano, Italy 40 A6 41 33N 13 30 E
Ceptura, Romania 46 D7 45 1N 26 21 E
Cepu, Indonesia 75 D4 7 9 S 111 35 E
Ceram = Seram, Indonesia 73 B3 3 10 S 129 0 E
Ceram Sea = Seram Sea, Indonesia 72 B3 2 30 S 128 30 E
Cerbère, France 24 F7 42 26N 3 10 E
Cerbicales, Is., France 25 G13 41 33N 9 22 E
Cerbu, Romania 46 E5 44 46N 24 46 E
Cercal, Portugal 37 H2 37 48N 8 40W
Cercemaggiore, Italy 41 A7 41 27N 14 43 E
Cerdaña, Spain 34 C6 42 22N 1 35 E
Cerdedo, Spain 36 C2 42 33N 8 23W
Cère →, France 24 D5 44 55N 1 49 E
Cerea, Italy 39 C8 45 12N 11 13 E
Ceres, Argentina 158 B3 29 55 S 61 55W
Ceres, Brazil 155 E2 15 17 S 49 35W
Ceres, Italy 38 C4 45 19N 7 22 E
Ceres, S. Africa 104 E2 33 21 S 19 18 E
Ceres, U.S.A. 144 H6 37 35N 120 57W
Céret, France 24 F6 42 30N 2 42 E
Cereté, Colombia 152 B2 8 53N 75 48W
Cerfontaine, Belgium 21 H4 50 11N 4 26 E
Cerignola, Italy 41 A8 41 17N 15 53 E
Cerigo = Kíthira, Greece 45 H6 36 9N 23 12 E
Cérilly, France 24 B6 46 37N 2 50 E
Cerisiers, France 23 D10 48 8N 3 30 E
Cerizay, France 22 F6 46 50N 0 40W
Çerkeş, Turkey 88 C5 40 49N 32 52 E
Çerkezköy, Turkey 88 C2 41 17N 27 59 E
Cerknica, Slovenia 39 C11 45 48N 14 21 E
Cermerno, Serbia 42 D5 43 35N 20 25 E
Çermik, Turkey 89 D8 38 8N 39 26 E
Cerna, Romania 46 D9 45 4N 28 17 E
Cerna →, Romania 46 E5 44 15N 24 25 E
Cernavodă, Romania 46 E9 44 22N 28 3 E
Cernay, France 23 E14 47 44N 7 10 E
Cernik, Croatia 42 B2 45 17N 17 22 E
Cerralvo, I., Mexico 146 C3 24 20N 109 45W
Cerreto Sannita, Italy 41 A7 41 17N 14 34 E
Cerritos, Mexico 146 C4 22 27N 100 20W
Cerro Gordo, U.S.A. 141 E8 39 53N 88 44W
Cerro Sombrero, Chile 160 D3 52 45 S 69 15W
Certaldo, Italy 38 E8 43 32N 11 2 E
Cervaro →, Italy 41 A8 41 30N 15 52 E
Cervera, Spain 34 D6 41 40N 1 16 E
Cervera de Pisuerga, Spain 36 C6 42 51N 4 30W
Cervera del Río Alhama, Spain 34 C3 42 2N 1 58W
Cérvia, Italy 39 D9 44 15N 12 20 E
Cervignano del Friuli, Italy 39 C10 45 49N 13 20 E
Cervinara, Italy 41 A7 41 2N 14 36 E
Cervione, France 25 F13 42 20N 9 29 E
Cervo, Spain 36 B3 43 40N 7 24W
César □, Colombia 152 B3 9 0N 73 30W
Cesaro, Italy 41 E7 37 50N 14 38 E
Cesena, Italy 39 D9 44 9N 12 14 E
Cesenático, Italy 39 D9 44 12N 12 22 E
Cēsis, Latvia 50 C4 57 17N 25 28 E
Česká Lípa, Czech. 30 A7 50 45N 14 30 E
Česka Republika □, Czech. 30 B7 49 30N 14 40 E
Česká Třebová, Czech. 31 B9 49 54N 16 27 E
České Budějovice, Czech. 30 C7 48 55N 14 25 E
České Velenice, Czech. 30 C8 48 45N 15 1 E
Ceskomoravská Vrchovina, Czech. 30 B8 49 30N 15 40 E
Český Brod, Czech. 30 A7 50 4N 14 52 E
Český Krumlov, Czech. 30 C7 48 43N 14 21 E
Český Těšin, Czech. 31 B11 49 45N 18 39 E
Çeşme, Turkey 45 F8 38 20N 26 23 E
Cessnock, Australia 117 B9 32 50 S 151 21 E
Cestos →, Liberia 100 D3 5 40N 9 10W
Cetate, Romania 46 E4 44 7N 23 2 E
Cétin Grad, Croatia 39 C12 45 9N 15 45 E
Cetina →, Croatia 39 E13 43 26N 16 42 E
Cetinje, Montenegro 42 E3 42 23N 18 59 E
Cetraro, Italy 41 C8 39 30N 15 56 E
Ceuta, Morocco 98 A3 35 52N 5 18W
Ceva, Italy 38 D5 44 23N 8 3 E
Cévennes, France 24 D7 44 10N 3 50 E
Ceyhan, Turkey 88 E6 37 4N 35 47 E
Ceyhan →, Turkey 88 E6 36 38N 35 40 E
Ceylânpınar, Turkey 89 E9 36 50N 40 2 E
Ceylon = Sri Lanka ■, Asia 83 L5 7 30N 80 50 E
Cèze →, France 25 D8 44 6N 4 43 E
Cha-am, Thailand 76 F2 12 48N 99 58 E
Chá Pungana, Angola 103 E3 13 44 S 18 39 E
Chaam, Neths. 21 E5 51 30N 4 52 E
Chabeuil, France 25 D9 44 54N 5 3 E
Chablais, France 25 B10 46 20N 6 36 E
Chablis, France 23 E10 47 47N 3 48 E
Chabounia, Algeria 99 A5 35 30N 2 38 E
Chacabuco, Argentina 158 C3 34 40 S 60 27W
Chachapoyas, Peru 156 B2 6 15 S 77 50W
Chachasp, Peru 156 D3 15 30 S 72 15W
Chachoengsao, Thailand 76 F3 13 42N 101 5 E
Chachro, Pakistan 80 G4 25 5N 70 15 E
Chaco □, Argentina 158 B3 26 30 S 61 0W
Chaco □, Paraguay 158 B3 26 0 S 60 0W
Chad ■, Africa 97 F3 15 0N 17 15 E
Chad, L. = Tchad, L., Chad 97 F2 13 30N 14 30 E
Chadan, Russia 57 D10 51 17N 91 35 E
Chadileuvú →, Argentina 158 D2 37 46 S 66 0W
Chadiza, Zambia 107 E3 14 45 S 32 27 E
Chadron, U.S.A. 138 D3 42 50N 103 0W
Chadyr-Lunga, Moldavia 52 C3 46 3N 28 51 E
Chae Hom, Thailand 76 C2 18 43N 99 35 E
Chaem →, Thailand 76 C2 18 11N 98 38 E
Chaeryŏng, N. Korea 67 E13 38 24N 125 36 E
Chagda, Russia 57 D14 58 45N 130 38 E
Chagny, France 23 F11 46 57N 4 45 E
Chagoda, Russia 50 B9 59 10N 35 15 E
Chagos Arch., Ind. Oc. 58 K11 6 0 S 72 0 E
Chāh Ākhvor, Iran 85 C8 32 41N 59 40 E
Chāh Bahār, Iran 85 E9 25 20N 60 40 E
Chāh-e-Malek, Iran 85 D8 28 35N 59 7 E
Chāh Gay Hills, Afghan. 79 C1 29 30N 64 0 E
Chāh Kavīr, Iran 85 D7 31 45N 54 52 E
Chahār Borjak, Afghan. 79 C1 30 17N 62 3 E
Chahtung, Burma 78 B7 26 41N 98 10 E
Chaillé-les-Marais, France 24 B2 46 25N 1 2W
Chainat, Thailand 76 E3 15 11N 100 8 E
Chaitén, Chile 160 B2 42 55 S 72 43W
Chaiya, Thailand 77 H2 9 23N 99 14 E
Chaj Doab, Pakistan 80 C5 32 15N 73 0 E
Chajari, Argentina 158 C4 30 42 S 58 0W
Chakaria, Bangla. 78 E4 21 45N 92 5 E
Chake Chake, Tanzania 106 D4 5 15 S 39 45 E
Chakhānsūr, Afghan. 79 C1 31 10N 62 0 E
Chakonipau, L., Canada 129 A6 56 18N 68 30W
Chakradharpur, India 81 H11 22 45N 85 40 E
Chakwadam, Burma 78 B7 27 29N 98 31 E
Chakwal, Pakistan 79 B4 32 56N 72 53 E
Chala, Peru 156 D3 15 48 S 74 20W
Chalais, France 24 C4 45 16N 0 3 E
Chalakudi, India 83 J3 10 18N 76 20 E
Chalchihuites, Mexico 146 C4 23 29N 103 53W
Chalcis = Khalkís, Greece 45 F5 38 27N 23 42 E
Chaleur B., Canada 129 C6 47 55N 65 30W
Chalfant, U.S.A. 144 H8 37 32N 118 21W
Chalhuanca, Peru 156 C3 14 15 S 73 15W
Chalindrey, France 23 E12 47 43N 5 26 E
Chaling, China 69 D9 26 58N 113 30 E
Chalisgaon, India 82 D2 20 30N 75 10 E
Chalkar, Kazakhstan 53 A14 50 40N 51 53 E
Chalkar, Ozero, Kazakhstan 53 A14 50 50N 51 50 E
Chalky Inlet, N.Z. 119 G1 46 3 S 166 31 E
Challans, France 22 F5 46 50N 1 52W
Challapata, Bolivia 156 D4 18 53 S 66 50W
Challis, U.S.A. 142 D6 44 30N 114 14W
Chalna, India 81 H13 22 36N 89 35 E
Chalon-sur-Saône, France 23 F11 46 48N 4 50 E
Chalonnes-sur-Loire, France 22 E6 47 20N 0 45W
Châlons-sur-Marne, France 23 D11 48 58N 4 20 E
Châlus, France 24 C4 45 39N 0 58 E
Chalyaphum, Thailand 76 E4 15 48N 102 2 E
Cham, Germany 27 F8 49 12N 12 40 E
Cham, Switz. 29 B6 47 11N 8 28 E
Cham, Cu Lao, Vietnam 76 E7 15 57N 108 30 E
Chama, U.S.A. 143 H10 36 54N 106 35W
Chamah, Gunong, Malaysia 74 A2 5 13N 101 35 E
Chaman, Pakistan 79 C2 30 58N 66 25 E
Chamba, India 80 C7 32 35N 76 10 E
Chamba, Tanzania 107 E4 11 37 S 37 0 E
Chambal →, India 81 F8 26 29N 79 15 E
Chamberlain, U.S.A. 138 D5 43 49N 99 20W
Chamberlain →, Australia 112 C4 15 30 S 127 54 E
Chambers, U.S.A. 143 J9 35 11N 109 26W
Chambersburg, U.S.A. 134 F7 39 56N 77 40W
Chambéry, France 25 C9 45 34N 5 55 E
Chambly, Canada 137 A11 45 27N 73 17W
Chambord, Canada 129 C5 48 25N 72 6W
Chambri L., Papua N. G. 120 C2 4 15 S 143 10 E
Chamchamal, Iraq 84 C5 35 32N 44 50 E
Chamela, Mexico 146 D3 19 32N 105 5W
Chamical, Argentina 158 C2 30 22 S 66 27W
Chamkar Luong, Cambodia 77 G4 11 0N 103 45 E
Chamois, U.S.A. 140 F5 38 41N 91 46W
Chamonix-Mont-Blanc, France 25 C10 45 55N 6 51 E
Champa, India 81 H10 22 2N 82 43 E
Champagne, Canada 130 A1 60 49N 136 30W
Champagne, France 23 D11 48 40N 4 20 E
Champagne, Plaine de, France 23 D11 49 0N 4 30 E

Chunya 185


Cheshire □, U.K. 16 D5 53 14N 2 30W
Cheshskaya Guba, Russia 48 A8 67 20N 47 0 E
Cheslatta L., Canada 130 C3 53 49N 125 20W
Chesley, Canada 136 B3 44 17N 81 5W
Cheste, Spain 35 F4 39 30N 0 41W
Chester, U.K. 16 D5 53 12N 2 53W
Chester, Calif., U.S.A. 142 F3 40 19N 121 14W
Chester, Ill., U.S.A. 139 G10 37 55N 89 49W
Chester, Mont., U.S.A. 142 B8 48 31N 110 58W
Chester, Pa., U.S.A. 134 F8 39 51N 75 22W
Chester, S.C., U.S.A. 135 H5 34 43N 81 12W
Chesterfield, U.K. 16 D6 53 14N 1 26W
Chesterfield, Is., N. Cal. 122 J7 19 52 S 158 15 E
Chesterfield Inlet, Canada 126 B10 63 30N 90 45W
Chesterton Ra., Australia 115 D4 25 30 S 147 27 E
Chesterville, Canada 137 A9 45 6N 75 14W
Chesuncook L., U.S.A. 129 C6 46 0N 69 21W
Chetaibi, Algeria 99 A6 37 1N 7 20 E
Chéticamp, Canada 129 C7 46 37N 60 59W
Chetumal, B. de, Mexico 147 D7 18 40N 88 10W
Chetwynd, Canada 130 B4 55 45N 121 36W
Chevanceaux, France 24 C3 45 18N 0 14W
Cheviot, U.S.A. 141 E12 39 10N 84 37W
Cheviot, The, U.K. 16 B5 55 29N 2 8W
Cheviot Hills, U.K. 16 B5 55 20N 2 30W
Cheviot Ra., Australia 114 D3 25 20 S 143 45 E
Chew Bahir, Ethiopia 95 G4 4 40N 36 50 E
Chewelah, U.S.A. 142 B5 48 17N 117 43W
Cheyenne, Okla., U.S.A. 139 H5 35 37N 99 40W
Cheyenne, Wyo., U.S.A. 138 E2 41 8N 104 49W
Cheyenne →, U.S.A. 138 C4 44 41N 101 18W
Cheyenne Wells, U.S.A. 138 F3 38 49N 102 21W
Cheyne B., Australia 113 F2 34 35 S 118 50 E
Chhabra, India 80 G7 24 40N 76 54 E
Chhapra, India 81 G11 25 48N 84 44 E
Chhata, India 80 F7 27 42N 77 30 E
Chhatak, Bangla. 78 C3 25 5N 91 37 E
Chhatarpur, India 81 G8 24 55N 79 35 E
Chhep, Cambodia 76 F5 13 45N 105 24 E
Chhindwara, India 81 H8 22 2N 78 59 E
Chhlong, Cambodia 77 F5 12 15N 105 58 E
Chhuk, Cambodia 77 G5 10 46N 104 28 E
Chi →, Thailand 76 E5 15 11N 104 43 E
Chiai, Taiwan 65 D7 23 29N 120 25 E
Chiamussu = Jiamusi, China 65 B8 46 40N 130 26 E
Chiang Dao, Thailand 76 C2 19 22N 98 58 E
Chiang Kham, Thailand 76 C3 19 32N 100 18 E
Chiang Khan, Thailand 76 D3 17 52N 101 36 E
Chiang Khong, Thailand 76 B3 20 17N 100 24 E
Chiang Mai, Thailand 76 C2 18 47N 98 59 E
Chiang Saen, Thailand 76 B3 20 16N 100 5 E
Chiange, Angola 103 F2 15 35 S 13 40 E
Chiapa →, Mexico 147 D6 16 42N 93 0W
Chiapa de Corzo, Mexico 147 D6 16 42N 93 0W
Chiapas □, Mexico 147 D6 17 0N 92 45W
Chiaramonte Gulfi, Italy 41 E7 37 1N 14 41 E
Chiaravalle, Italy 39 E10 43 38N 13 17 E
Chiaravalle Centrale, Italy 41 D9 38 41N 16 25 E
Chiari, Italy 38 C6 45 31N 9 55 E
Chiasso, Switz. 29 E8 45 50N 9 2 E
Chiatura, Georgia 53 E10 42 15N 43 17 E
Chiautla, Mexico 147 D5 18 18N 98 34W
Chiávari, Italy 38 D6 44 20N 9 20 E
Chiavenna, Italy 38 B6 46 18N 9 23 E
Chiba, Japan 63 B12 35 30N 140 7 E
Chiba □, Japan 63 B12 35 30N 140 20 E
Chibabava, Mozam. 105 C5 20 17 S 33 35 E
Chibemba, Cunene, Angola 103 F2 15 48 S 14 8 E
Chibemba, Huila, Angola 103 F3 16 20 S 15 20 E
Chibia, Angola 103 F2 15 10 S 13 42 E
Chibougamau, Canada 128 C5 49 56N 74 24W
Chibougamau L., Canada 128 C5 49 50N 74 20W
Chibuk, Nigeria 101 C7 10 52N 12 50 E
Chic-Chocs, Mts., Canada 129 C6 48 55N 66 0W
Chicacole = Srikakulam, India 82 E6 18 14N 83 58 E
Chicago, U.S.A. 141 C9 41 53N 87 38W
Chicago Heights, U.S.A. 141 C9 41 30N 87 38W
Chichagof I., U.S.A. 130 B1 57 30N 135 30W
Chichaoua, Morocco 98 B3 31 32N 8 44W
Chicheng, China 66 D8 40 55N 115 55 E
Chichester, U.K. 17 G7 50 50N 0 47W
Chichibu, Japan 63 A11 36 5N 139 10 E
Ch'ich'ihaerh = Qiqihar, China 57 E13 47 26N 124 0 E
Chickasha, U.S.A. 139 H5 35 3N 97 58W
Chiclana de la Frontera, Spain 37 J4 36 26N 6 9W
Chiclayo, Peru 156 B2 6 42 S 79 50W
Chico, U.S.A. 144 F5 39 44N 121 50W
Chico →, Chubut, Argentina 160 B3 44 0 S 67 0W
Chico →, Santa Cruz, Argentina 160 C3 50 0 S 68 30W
Chicomo, Mozam. 105 C5 24 31 S 34 6 E
Chicontepec, Mexico 147 C5 20 58N 98 10W
Chicopee, U.S.A. 137 D12 42 9N 72 37W
Chicoutimi, Canada 129 C5 48 28N 71 5W
Chicualacuala, Mozam. 105 C5 22 6 S 31 42 E
Chidambaram, India 83 J4 11 20N 79 45 E
Chidenguele, Mozam. 105 C5 24 55 S 34 11 E
Chidley, C., Canada 127 B13 60 23N 64 26W
Chiede, Angola 103 F3 17 15 S 16 22 E
Chiefs Pt., Canada 136 B3 44 41N 81 18W
Chiem Hoa, Vietnam 76 A5 22 12N 105 17 E
Chiemsee, Germany 27 H8 47 53N 12 27 E
Chiengi, Zambia 107 D2 8 45 S 29 10 E
Chiengmai = Chiang Mai, Thailand 76 C2 18 47N 98 59 E
Chiengo, Angola 103 E4 13 20 S 21 55 E
Chienti →, Italy 39 E10 43 18N 13 45 E
Chieri, Italy 38 D4 45 0N 7 50 E
Chiers →, France 23 C11 49 39N 4 59 E
Chiese →, Italy 38 C7 45 8N 10 25 E
Chieti, Italy 39 F11 42 22N 14 10 E
Chièvres, Belgium 21 G3 50 35N 3 48 E
Chifeng, China 67 C10 42 18N 118 58 E
Chigasaki, Japan 63 B11 35 19N 139 24 E
Chigirin, Ukraine 52 B5 49 4N 32 38 E
Chignecto B., Canada 129 C7 45 30N 64 40W
Chigorodó, Colombia 152 B2 7 41N 76 42W
Chiguana, Bolivia 158 A2 21 0 S 67 58W
Chiha-ri, N. Korea 67 E14 38 40N 126 30 E
Chihli, G. of = Bo Hai, China 67 E10 39 0N 119 0 E
Chihuahua, Mexico 146 B3 28 40N 106 3W
Chihuahua □, Mexico 146 B3 28 40N 106 3W
Chiili, Kazakhstan 55 A3 44 20N 66 15 E
Chik Bollapur, India 83 H3 13 25N 77 45 E
Chikhli, India 82 D3 20 20N 76 18 E
Chikmagalur, India 83 H2 13 15N 75 45 E
Chikodi, India 83 F2 16 26N 74 38 E
Chikugo, Japan 62 D2 33 14N 130 28 E
Chikuma-Gawa →, Japan 63 A10 36 59N 138 35 E
Chikwawa, Malawi 107 F3 16 2 S 34 50 E
Chilac, Mexico 147 D5 18 20N 97 24W
Chilako →, Canada 130 C4 53 53N 122 57W
Chilam Chavki, Pakistan 81 B6 35 5N 75 5 E
Chilanga, Zambia 107 F2 15 33 S 28 16 E
Chilapa, Mexico 147 D5 17 40N 99 11W
Chilas, Pakistan 81 B6 35 25N 74 5 E
Chilcotin →, Canada 130 C4 51 44N 122 23W
Childers, Australia 115 D5 25 15 S 152 17 E
Childress, U.S.A. 139 H4 34 25N 100 13W
Chile ■, S. Amer. 160 B2 35 0 S 72 0W
Chile Chico, Chile 160 C2 46 33 S 71 44W
Chile Rise, Pac. Oc. 123 L18 38 0 S 92 0W
Chilecito, Argentina 158 B2 29 10 S 67 30W
Chilete, Peru 156 B2 7 10 S 78 50W
Chilhowee, U.S.A. 140 F3 38 36N 93 51W
Chilia, Braţul →, Romania 46 D10 45 25N 29 20 E
Chilik, Kazakhstan 54 F3 51 7N 53 55 E
Chilik, Kazakhstan 55 B9 43 33N 78 17 E
Chililabombwe, Zambia 107 E2 12 18 S 27 43 E
Chilin = Jilin, China 67 C14 43 44N 126 30 E
Chilka L., India 82 E7 19 40N 85 25 E
Chilko →, Canada 130 C4 52 0N 123 40W
Chilko, L., Canada 130 C4 51 20N 124 10W
Chillagoe, Australia 114 B3 17 7 S 144 33 E
Chillán, Chile 158 D1 36 40 S 72 10W
Chillicothe, Ill., U.S.A. 140 D7 40 55N 89 29W
Chillicothe, Mo., U.S.A. 140 E3 39 48N 93 33W
Chillicothe, Ohio, U.S.A. 134 F4 39 20N 82 59W
Chilliwack, Canada 130 D4 49 10N 121 54W
Chilo, India 80 F5 27 25N 73 32 E
Chiloane, I., Mozam. 105 C5 20 40 S 34 55 E
Chiloé □, Chile 160 B2 43 0 S 73 0W
Chiloé, I. de, Chile 160 B2 42 30 S 73 50W
Chilonda, Angola 103 E3 11 19 S 16 12 E
Chilpancingo, Mexico 147 D5 17 30N 99 30W
Chiltern, Australia 117 D7 36 10 S 146 36 E
Chiltern Hills, U.K. 17 F7 51 44N 0 42W
Chilton, U.S.A. 134 C1 44 2N 88 10W
Chiluage, Angola 103 D4 9 30 S 21 50 E
Chilubi, Zambia 107 E2 11 5 S 29 58 E
Chilubula, Zambia 107 E3 10 14 S 30 51 E
Chilumba, Malawi 107 E3 10 28 S 34 12 E
Chilung, Taiwan 65 D7 25 3N 121 45 E
Chilwa, L., Malawi 107 F4 15 15 S 35 40 E
Chimaltitán, Mexico 146 C4 21 46N 103 50W
Chimán, Panama 148 E4 8 45N 78 40W
Chimay, Belgium 21 H4 50 3N 4 20 E
Chimbay, Uzbekistan 56 E6 42 57N 59 47 E
Chimborazo, Ecuador 152 D2 1 29 S 78 55W
Chimborazo □, Ecuador 152 D2 1 0 S 78 40W
Chimbote, Peru 156 B2 9 0 S 78 35W
Chimion, Uzbekistan 55 C5 40 15N 71 32 E
Chimishliya, Moldavia 46 C9 46 34N 28 44 E
Chimkent, Kazakhstan 55 B4 42 18N 69 36 E
Chimoio, Mozam. 107 F3 19 4 S 33 30 E
Chimpembe, Zambia 107 D2 9 31 S 29 33 E
Chin □, Burma 78 D4 22 0N 93 0 E
Chin Hills, Burma 78 D4 22 30N 93 30 E
Chin Ling Shan = Qinling Shandi, China 66 H5 33 50N 108 10 E
China, Mexico 147 B5 25 40N 99 20W
China ■, Asia 66 E3 30 0N 110 0 E
China Lake, U.S.A. 145 K9 35 44N 117 37W
Chinacota, Colombia 152 B3 7 37N 72 36W
Chinan = Jinan, China 66 F9 36 38N 117 1 E
Chinandega, Nic. 148 D2 12 35N 87 12W
Chinati Peak, U.S.A. 139 K2 29 57N 104 29W
Chincha Alta, Peru 156 C2 13 25 S 76 7W
Chinchilla, Australia 115 D5 26 45 S 150 38 E
Chinchilla de Monte Aragón, Spain 35 G3 38 53N 1 40W
Chinchón, Spain 34 E1 40 9N 3 26W
Chinchorro, Banco, Mexico 147 D7 18 35N 87 20W
Chinchou = Jinzhou, China 67 D11 41 5N 121 3 E
Chinchoua, Gabon 102 B1 0 1N 9 48 E
Chincoteague, U.S.A. 134 G8 37 56N 75 23W
Chinde, Mozam. 107 F4 18 35 S 36 30 E
Chindo, S. Korea 67 G14 34 28N 126 15 E
Chindwin →, Burma 78 E5 21 26N 95 15 E
Chineni, India 81 C6 33 2N 75 15 E
Chinga, Mozam. 107 F4 15 13 S 38 35 E
Chingola, Zambia 107 E2 12 31 S 27 53 E
Chingole, Malawi 107 E3 13 4 S 34 17 E
Chingoroi, Angola 103 E2 13 37 S 14 1 E
Ch'ingtao = Qingdao, China 67 F11 36 5N 120 20 E
Chinguar, Angola 103 E3 12 25 S 16 45 E
Chinguetti, Mauritania 98 D2 20 25N 12 24W
Chingune, Mozam. 105 C5 20 33 S 34 58 E
Chinhae, S. Korea 67 G15 35 9N 128 47 E
Chinhanguanine, Mozam. 105 D5 25 21 S 32 30 E
Chinhoyi, Zimbabwe 107 F3 17 20 S 30 8 E
Chiniot, Pakistan 79 C4 31 45N 73 0 E
Chínipas, Mexico 146 B3 27 22N 108 32W
Chinju, S. Korea 67 G15 35 12N 128 2 E
Chinle, U.S.A. 143 H9 36 9N 109 33W
Chinnamanur, India 83 K3 9 50N 77 24 E
Chinnampo, N. Korea 67 E13 38 52N 125 10 E
Chinnur, India 82 E4 18 57N 79 49 E
Chino, Japan 63 B10 35 59N 138 9 E
Chino, U.S.A. 145 L9 34 1N 117 41W
Chino Valley, U.S.A. 143 J7 34 45N 112 27W
Chinon, France 22 E7 47 10N 0 15 E
Chinook, Canada 131 C6 51 28N 110 59W
Chinook, U.S.A. 142 B9 48 35N 109 14W
Chinsali, Zambia 107 E3 10 30 S 32 2 E
Chintamani, India 83 H4 13 26N 78 3 E
Chióggia, Italy 39 C9 45 13N 12 15 E
Chíos = Khíos, Greece 45 F8 38 27N 26 9 E
Chipata, Zambia 107 E3 13 38 S 32 28 E
Chipewyan L., Canada 131 B9 58 0N 98 27W
Chipinge, Zimbabwe 107 G3 20 13 S 32 28 E
Chipiona, Spain 37 J4 36 44N 6 26W
Chipley, U.S.A. 135 K3 30 47N 85 32W
Chiplun, India 82 F1 17 31N 73 34 E
Chipman, Canada 129 C6 46 6N 65 53W
Chipoka, Malawi 107 E3 13 57 S 34 28 E
Chippenham, U.K. 17 F5 51 27N 2 7W
Chippewa →, U.S.A. 138 C8 44 25N 92 5W
Chippewa Falls, U.S.A. 138 C9 44 56N 91 24W
Chiprovtsi, Bulgaria 42 D7 43 24N 22 52 E
Chiquián, Peru 156 C2 10 10 S 77 0W
Chiquimula, Guatemala 148 D2 14 51N 89 37W
Chiquinquira, Colombia 152 B3 5 37N 73 50W
Chiquitos, Llanos de, Bolivia 157 D5 18 0 S 61 30W
Chir →, Russia 53 B10 48 30N 43 0 E
Chirala, India 83 G5 15 50N 80 26 E
Chiramba, Mozam. 107 F3 16 55 S 34 39 E
Chiran, Japan 62 F2 31 22N 130 27 E
Chirawa, India 80 E6 28 14N 75 42 E
Chirayinkil, India 83 K3 8 41N 76 49 E
Chirchik, Uzbekistan 55 C4 41 29N 69 35 E
Chirfa, Niger 97 D2 20 55N 12 22 E
Chirgua →, Venezuela 152 B4 8 54N 67 58W
Chiricahua Peak, U.S.A. 143 L9 31 51N 109 18W
Chiriquí, G. de, Panama 148 E3 8 0N 82 10W
Chiriquí, L. de, Panama 148 E3 9 10N 82 0W
Chirivira Falls, Zimbabwe 107 G3 21 10 S 32 12 E
Chirnogi, Romania 46 E7 44 7N 26 32 E
Chirpan, Bulgaria 43 E10 42 10N 25 19 E
Chirripó Grande, Cerro, Costa Rica 148 E3 9 29N 83 29W
Chisamba, Zambia 107 E2 14 55 S 28 20 E
Chishmy, Russia 54 D4 54 35N 55 23 E
Chisholm, Canada 130 C6 54 55N 114 10W
Chishtian Mandi, Pakistan 80 E5 29 50N 72 55 E
Chishui, China 68 C5 28 30N 105 42 E
Chishui He →, China 68 C5 28 49N 105 50 E
Chisimaio, Somali Rep. 108 E2 0 22 S 42 32 E
Chisimba Falls, Zambia 107 E3 10 12 S 30 56 E
Chişinău = Kishinev, Moldavia 52 C3 47 0N 28 50 E
Chisineu Criş, Romania 46 C2 46 32N 21 37 E
Chisone →, Italy 38 D4 44 49N 7 25 E
Chisos Mts., U.S.A. 139 L3 29 5N 103 15W
Chistopol, Russia 51 D17 55 25N 50 38 E
Chita, Colombia 152 B3 6 11N 72 28W
Chita, Russia 57 D12 52 0N 113 35 E
Chitado, Angola 103 F2 17 10 S 14 8 E
Chitapur, India 83 F3 17 10N 77 5 E
Chitembo, Angola 103 E3 13 30 S 16 50 E
Chitipa, Malawi 107 D3 9 41 S 33 19 E
Chitose, Japan 60 C10 42 49N 141 39 E
Chitrakot, India 82 E5 19 10N 81 40 E
Chitral, Pakistan 79 B3 35 50N 71 56 E
Chitravati →, India 83 G4 14 45N 78 15 E
Chitré, Panama 148 E3 7 59N 80 27W
Chittagong, Bangla. 78 D3 22 19N 91 48 E
Chittagong □, Bangla. 78 C3 24 5N 91 0 E
Chittaurgarh, India 80 G6 24 52N 74 38 E
Chittoor, India 83 H4 13 15N 79 5 E
Chittur, India 83 J3 10 40N 76 45 E
Chitungwiza, Zimbabwe 107 F3 18 0 S 31 6 E
Chiumba, Angola 103 E3 12 29 S 16 8 E
Chiume, Angola 103 F4 15 3 S 21 14 E
Chiusa, Italy 39 B8 46 38N 11 34 E
Chiusi, Italy 39 E8 43 1N 11 58 E
Chiva, Spain 35 F4 39 27N 0 41W
Chivacoa, Venezuela 152 A4 10 10N 68 54W
Chivasso, Italy 38 C4 45 10N 7 52 E
Chivay, Peru 156 D3 15 40 S 71 35W
Chivhu, Zimbabwe 107 F3 19 2 S 30 52 E
Chivilcoy, Argentina 158 C4 34 55 S 60 0W
Chiwanda, Tanzania 107 E3 11 23 S 34 55 E
Chixi, China 69 G9 22 0N 112 58 E
Chizera, Zambia 107 E1 13 10 S 25 0 E
Chkalov = Orenburg, Russia 54 F4 51 45N 55 6 E
Chkolovsk, Russia 51 C13 56 50N 43 10 E
Chloride, U.S.A. 145 K12 35 25N 114 12W
Chlumec, Czech. 30 A8 50 9N 15 29 E
Chmielnik, Poland 47 E7 50 37N 20 43 E
Cho Bo, Vietnam 76 B5 20 46N 105 10 E
Cho-do, N. Korea 67 E13 38 30N 124 40 E
Cho Phuoc Hai, Vietnam 77 G6 10 26N 107 18 E
Choa Chukang, Malaysia 74 B2 1 22N 103 41 E
Choba, Kenya 106 B4 2 30N 38 5 E
Chobe National Park, Botswana 104 B3 18 0 S 25 0 E
Chochiwŏn, S. Korea 67 F14 36 37N 127 18 E
Chocianów, Poland 47 D2 51 27N 15 55 E
Chociwel, Poland 47 B2 53 29N 15 21 E
Chocó □, Colombia 152 B2 6 0N 77 0W
Chocontá, Colombia 152 B3 5 9N 73 41W
Choctawhatchee B., U.S.A. 133 D9 30 20N 86 20W
Chodaków, Poland 47 C7 52 16N 20 18 E
Chodavaram, India 82 F6 17 50N 82 57 E
Chodecz, Poland 47 C6 52 24N 19 2 E
Chodziez, Poland 47 C3 52 58N 16 58 E
Choele Choel, Argentina 160 A3 39 11 S 65 40W
Chōfu, Japan 63 B11 35 39N 139 33 E
Choiseul, Solomon Is. 121 L9 7 0 S 156 40 E
Choisy-le-Roi, France 23 D9 48 45N 2 24 E
Choix, Mexico 146 B3 26 40N 108 23W
Chojna, Poland 47 C1 52 58N 14 25 E
Chojnice, Poland 47 B4 53 42N 17 32 E
Chojnów, Poland 47 D2 51 18N 15 58 E
Chōkai-San, Japan 60 E10 39 6N 140 3 E
Choke, Ethiopia 95 E4 11 18N 37 15 E
Chokurdakh, Russia 57 B15 70 38N 147 55 E
Cholame, U.S.A. 144 K6 35 44N 120 18W
Cholet, France 22 E6 47 4N 0 52W
Cholpon-Ata, Kirghizia 55 B8 42 40N 77 6 E
Choluteca, Honduras 148 D2 13 20N 87 14W
Choluteca →, Honduras 148 D2 13 0N 87 20W
Chom Bung, Thailand 76 F2 13 37N 99 36 E
Chom Thong, Thailand 76 C2 18 25N 98 41 E
Choma, Zambia 107 F2 16 48 S 26 59 E
Chomen Swamp, Ethiopia 95 F4 9 20N 37 10 E
Chomun, India 80 F6 27 15N 75 40 E
Chomutov, Czech. 30 A6 50 28N 13 23 E
Chon Buri, Thailand 76 F3 13 21N 101 1 E
Chon Thanh, Vietnam 77 G6 11 24N 106 36 E
Chonan, S. Korea 67 F14 36 48N 127 9 E
Chone, Ecuador 152 D2 0 40 S 80 0W
Chong Kai, Cambodia 76 F4 13 57N 103 35 E
Chong Mek, Thailand 76 E5 15 10N 105 27 E
Chong'an, China 69 D12 27 45N 118 0 E
Chongde, China 69 B13 30 32N 120 26 E
Chŏngdo, S. Korea 67 G15 35 38N 128 42 E
Chŏngha, S. Korea 67 F15 36 12N 129 21 E
Chongjin, N. Korea 67 D15 41 47N 129 50 E
Chŏngju, N. Korea 67 E13 39 40N 125 5 E
Chŏngju, S. Korea 67 F14 36 39N 127 27 E
Chongli, China 66 D8 40 58N 115 15 E
Chongming, China 69 B13 31 38N 121 23 E
Chongming Dao, China 69 B13 31 40N 121 30 E
Chongoyape, Peru 156 B2 6 35 S 79 25W
Chongqing, Sichuan, China 68 C6 29 35N 106 25 E
Chongqing, Sichuan, China 68 B4 30 38N 103 40 E
Chongren, China 69 D11 27 46N 116 3 E
Chŏngŭp, S. Korea 67 G14 35 35N 126 50 E
Chongzuo, China 68 F6 22 23N 107 20 E
Chŏnju, S. Korea 67 G14 35 50N 127 4 E
Chonos, Arch. de los, Chile 160 C2 45 0 S 75 0W
Chopda, India 82 D2 21 20N 75 15 E
Chopim →, Brazil 159 B5 25 35 S 53 5W
Chorbat La, India 81 B7 34 42N 76 37 E
Chorley, U.K. 16 D5 53 39N 2 39W
Chornobyl = Chernobyl, Ukraine 50 F7 51 20N 30 15 E
Chorolque, Cerro, Bolivia 158 A2 20 59 S 66 5W
Choroszcz, Poland 47 B9 53 10N 22 59 E
Chorregon, Australia 114 C3 22 40 S 143 32 E
Chortkov, Ukraine 50 G4 49 2N 25 46 E
Chŏrwŏn, S. Korea 67 E14 38 15N 127 10 E
Chorzele, Poland 47 B7 53 15N 20 55 E
Chorzów, Poland 47 E5 50 18N 18 57 E
Chos-Malal, Argentina 158 D1 37 20 S 70 15W
Chosan, N. Korea 67 D13 40 50N 125 47 E
Chōshi, Japan 63 B12 35 45N 140 51 E
Choszczno, Poland 47 B2 53 7N 15 25 E
Chota, Peru 156 B2 6 33 S 78 39W
Choteau, U.S.A. 142 C7 47 49N 112 11W
Chotila, India 80 H4 22 23N 71 15 E
Chowchilla, U.S.A. 144 H6 37 7N 120 16W
Chowkham, Burma 78 E6 20 52N 97 28 E
Choybalsan, Mongolia 65 B6 48 4N 114 30 E
Chrisman, U.S.A. 141 E9 39 48N 87 41W
Christchurch, N.Z. 119 D7 43 33 S 172 47 E
Christchurch, U.K. 17 G6 50 44N 1 45W
Christian I., Canada 136 B4 44 50N 80 12W
Christiana, S. Africa 104 D4 27 52 S 25 8 E
Christiansfeld, Denmark 15 J3 55 21N 9 29 E
Christiansted, Virgin Is. 149 C7 17 45N 64 42W
Christie B., Canada 131 A6 62 32N 111 10W
Christina →, Canada 131 B6 56 40N 111 3W
Christmas Cr. →, Australia 112 C4 18 29 S 125 23 E
Christmas Creek, Australia 112 C4 18 29 S 125 23 E
Christmas I. = Kiritimati, Kiribati 123 G12 1 58N 157 27W
Christmas I., Ind. Oc. 109 F9 10 30 S 105 40 E
Christopher L., Australia 113 D4 24 49 S 127 42 E
Chrudim, Czech. 30 B8 49 58N 15 43 E
Chrzanów, Poland 31 A12 50 10N 19 21 E
Chtimba, Malawi 107 E3 10 35 S 34 13 E
Chu, Kazakhstan 55 B6 43 36N 73 42 E
Chu →, Kazakhstan 55 A3 45 0N 67 44 E
Chu →, Vietnam 76 C5 19 53N 105 45 E
Chu Chua, Canada 130 C4 51 22N 120 10W
Chu Lai, Vietnam 76 E7 15 28N 108 45 E
Chu Xian, China 69 A12 32 19N 118 20 E
Chuadanga, Bangla. 78 D2 23 38N 88 51 E
Ch'uanchou = Quanzhou, China 69 E12 24 55N 118 34 E
Chuankou, China 66 G6 34 20N 110 59 E
Chūbu □, Japan 63 A9 36 45N 137 30 E
Chubut □, Argentina 160 B3 43 30 S 69 0W
Chubut →, Argentina 160 B3 43 20 S 65 5W
Chuchi L., Canada 130 B4 55 12N 124 30W
Chudovo, Russia 50 B7 59 10N 31 41 E
Chudskoye, Oz., Estonia 50 B5 58 13N 27 30 E
Chūgoku □, Japan 62 C4 35 0N 133 0 E
Chūgoku-Sanchi, Japan 62 C4 35 0N 133 0 E
Chuguyev, Ukraine 52 B7 49 55N 36 45 E
Chugwater, U.S.A. 138 E2 41 46N 104 50W
Chukhloma, Russia 51 B13 58 45N 42 40 E
Chukotskiy Khrebet, Russia 57 C18 68 0N 175 0 E
Chukotskoye More, Russia 57 C19 68 0N 175 0W
Chula, U.S.A. 140 E3 39 55N 93 29W
Chula Vista, U.S.A. 145 N9 32 39N 117 5W
Chulak-Kurgan, Kazakhstan 55 B4 43 46N 69 9 E
Chulman, Russia 57 D13 56 52N 124 52 E
Chulucanas, Peru 156 B1 5 8 S 80 10W
Chulumani, Bolivia 156 D4 16 24 S 67 31W
Chulym →, Russia 56 D9 57 43N 83 51 E
Chum Phae, Thailand 76 D4 16 40N 102 6 E
Chum Saeng, Thailand 76 E3 15 55N 100 15 E
Chuma, Bolivia 156 D4 15 24 S 68 56W
Chumar, India 81 C8 32 40N 78 35 E
Chumbicha, Argentina 158 B2 29 0 S 66 10W
Chumerna, Bulgaria 43 E10 42 45N 25 55 E
Chumikan, Russia 57 D14 54 40N 135 10 E
Chumphon, Thailand 77 G2 10 35N 99 14 E
Chumpi, Peru 156 D3 15 4 S 73 46W
Chumuare, Mozam. 107 E3 14 31 S 31 50 E
Chumunjin, S. Korea 67 F15 37 55N 128 54 E
Chuna →, Russia 57 D10 57 47N 94 37 E
Chun'an, China 69 C12 29 35N 119 3 E
Chunchŏn, S. Korea 67 F14 37 58N 127 44 E
Chunchura, India 81 H13 22 53N 88 27 E
Chunga, Zambia 107 F2 15 0 S 26 2 E
Chunggang-ŭp, N. Korea 67 D14 41 48N 126 48 E
Chunghwa, N. Korea 67 E13 38 52N 125 47 E
Chungju, S. Korea 67 F14 36 58N 127 58 E
Chungking = Chongqing, China 68 C6 29 35N 106 25 E
Chungmu, S. Korea 67 G15 34 50N 128 20 E
Chungt'iaoshan = Zhongtiao Shan, China 66 G6 35 0N 111 10 E
Chunian, Pakistan 80 D6 30 57N 74 0 E
Chunya, Tanzania 107 D3 8 30 S 33 27 E

# 186 Chunya



Chunya □, *Tanzania* **106 D3** 7 48 S 33 0 E
Chunyang, *China* **67 C15** 43 38N 129 23 E
Chuquibamba, *Peru* **156 D3** 15 47 S 72 44W
Chuquibambilla, *Peru* **156 C3** 14 7 S 72 41W
Chuquicamata, *Chile* **158 A2** 22 15 S 69 0W
Chuquisaca □, *Bolivia* **157 E5** 20 30 S 63 30W
Chur, *Switz.* **29 C9** 46 52N 9 32 E
Churachandpur, *India* **78 C4** 24 20N 93 40 E
Churchill, *Canada* **131 B10** 58 47N 94 11W
Churchill →, *Man., Canada* **131 B10** 58 47N 94 12W
Churchill →, *Nfld., Canada* **129 B7** 53 19N 60 10W
Churchill, C., *Canada* **131 B10** 58 46N 93 12W
Churchill Falls, *Canada* **129 B7** 53 36N 64 19W
Churchill L., *Canada* **131 B7** 55 55N 108 20W
Churchill Pk., *Canada* **130 B3** 58 10N 125 10W
Churdan, *U.S.A.* **140 B2** 42 9N 94 29W
Churfisten, *Switz.* **29 B8** 47 8N 9 17 E
Churu, *India* **80 E6** 28 20N 74 50 E
Churubusco, *U.S.A.* **141 C11** 41 14N 85 19W
Churwalden, *Switz.* **29 C9** 46 47N 9 33 E
Chushal, *India* **81 C8** 33 40N 78 40 E
Chusovaya →, *Russia* **54 B5** 58 18N 56 22 E
Chusovoy, *Russia* **54 B5** 58 15N 57 40 E
Chust, *Uzbekistan* **55 C5** 41 0N 71 13 E
Chuuronjang, *N. Korea* **67 D15** 41 35N 129 40 E
Chuvash Republic □, *Russia* **51 D15** 55 30N 47 0 E
Chuwārtah, *Iraq* **84 C5** 35 43N 45 34 E
Chuxiong, *China* **68 E3** 25 2N 101 28 E
Ci Xian, *China* **66 F8** 36 20N 114 25 E
Ciacova, *Romania* **46 D2** 45 35N 21 10 E
Ciamis, *Indonesia* **75 D3** 7 20 S 108 21 E
Cianjur, *Indonesia* **74 D3** 6 49 S 107 8 E
Cibola, *U.S.A.* **145 M12** 33 17N 114 42W
Cicero, *U.S.A.* **134 E2** 41 48N 87 48W
Cicero, *Ill., U.S.A.* **141 C9** 41 51N 87 45W
Cícero Dantas, *Brazil* **154 D4** 10 36 S 38 23W
Cidacos →, *Spain* **34 C3** 42 21N 1 38W
Cide, *Turkey* **52 F5** 41 53N 33 1 E
Ciechanów, *Poland* **47 C7** 52 52N 20 38 E
Ciechanów □, *Poland* **47 B7** 53 0N 20 30 E
Ciechanowiec, *Poland* **47 C9** 52 40N 22 31 E
Ciechocinek, *Poland* **47 C5** 52 53N 18 45 E
Ciego de Avila, *Cuba* **148 B4** 21 50N 78 50W
Ciénaga, *Colombia* **152 A3** 11 1N 74 15W
Ciénaga de Oro, *Colombia* **152 B2** 8 53N 75 37W
Cienfuegos, *Cuba* **148 B3** 22 10N 80 30W
Cieplice Śląskie Zdrój, *Poland* **47 E2** 50 50N 15 40 E
Cierp, *France* **24 F4** 42 55N 0 40 E
Cíes, Is., *Spain* **36 C2** 42 12N 8 55W
Cieszanów, *Poland* **47 E10** 50 14N 23 8 E
Cieszyn, *Poland* **31 B11** 49 45N 18 35 E
Cieza, *Spain* **35 G3** 38 17N 1 23W
Çifteler, *Turkey* **88 D4** 39 22N 31 2 E
Cifuentes, *Spain* **34 E2** 40 47N 2 37W
Cihanbeyli, *Turkey* **88 D5** 38 40N 32 55 E
Cihuatlán, *Mexico* **146 D4** 19 14N 104 35W
Cijara, Pantano de, *Spain* **37 F6** 39 18N 4 52W
Cilacap, *Indonesia* **75 D3** 7 43 S 109 0 E
Çıldır, *Turkey* **53 F10** 41 7N 43 8 E
Çıldır Gölü, *Turkey* **89 C10** 41 5N 43 15 E
Cili, *China* **69 C8** 29 30N 111 8 E
Cilicia, *Turkey* **88 E5** 36 30N 33 40 E
Cîlnicu, *Romania* **46 E4** 44 54N 23 4 E
Cilo Dağı, *Turkey* **89 E10** 37 28N 43 55 E
Cima, *U.S.A.* **145 K11** 35 14N 115 30W
Cimarron, *Kans., U.S.A.* **139 G4** 37 48N 100 21W
Cimarron, *N. Mex., U.S.A.* **139 G2** 36 31N 104 55W
Cimarron →, *U.S.A.* **139 G6** 36 10N 96 17W
Cimone, Mte., *Italy* **38 D7** 44 10N 10 40 E
Cîmpic Turzii, *Romania* **46 C4** 46 34N 23 53 E
Cîmpina, *Romania* **46 D6** 45 10N 25 45 E
Cîmpulung, *Argeş, Romania* **46 D6** 45 17N 25 3 E
Cîmpulung, *Suceava, Romania* **46 B6** 47 32N 25 30 E
Cîmpuri, *Romania* **46 C7** 46 0N 26 50 E
Çınar, *Turkey* **89 E9** 37 46N 40 19 E
Cinca →, *Spain* **34 D5** 41 26N 0 21 E
Cincer, *Bos.-H.* **42 D2** 43 55N 17 5 E
Cincinnati, *Iowa, U.S.A.* **140 D4** 40 38N 92 56W
Cincinnati, *Ohio, U.S.A.* **141 E12** 39 6N 84 31W
Cîndeşti, *Romania* **46 D7** 45 15N 26 42 E
Çine, *Turkey* **88 E3** 37 37N 28 2 E
Ciney, *Belgium* **21 H6** 50 18N 5 5 E
Cíngoli, *Italy* **39 E10** 43 23N 13 10 E
Cinigiano, *Italy* **39 F8** 42 53N 11 23 E
Cinto, Mte., *France* **25 F12** 42 24N 8 54 E
Ciorani, *Romania* **46 E7** 44 45N 26 25 E
Čiovo, *Croatia* **39 E13** 43 30N 16 17 E
Cipó, *Brazil* **154 D4** 11 6 S 38 31W
Circeo, Monte, *Italy* **40 A6** 41 14N 13 3 E
Çirçir, *Turkey* **88 C7** 40 5N 36 47 E
Circle, *Alaska, U.S.A.* **126 B5** 65 50N 144 4W
Circle, *Mont., U.S.A.* **138 B2** 47 25N 105 35W
Circleville, *Ohio, U.S.A.* **134 F4** 39 36N 82 57W
Circleville, *Utah, U.S.A.* **143 G7** 38 10N 112 16W
Cirebon, *Indonesia* **75 D3** 6 45 S 108 32 E
Cirencester, *U.K.* **17 F6** 51 43N 1 59W
Cireşu, *Romania* **46 E3** 44 47N 22 31 E
Cirey-sur-Vezouze, *France* **23 D13** 48 35N 6 57 E
Ciriè, *Italy* **38 C4** 45 14N 7 35 E
Cirium, *Cyprus* **32 E11** 34 40N 32 53 E
Cirò, *Italy* **41 C10** 39 23N 17 3 E
Ciron →, *France* **24 D3** 44 36N 0 18W
Cisco, *U.S.A.* **139 J5** 32 23N 98 59W
Ciskei □, *S. Africa* **105 E4** 33 0 S 27 0 E
Cislău, *Romania* **46 D7** 45 14N 26 20 E
Cisna, *Poland* **31 B15** 49 12N 22 20 E
Cisnădie, *Romania* **46 D5** 45 42N 24 9 E
Cisne, *U.S.A.* **141 F8** 38 31N 88 26W
Cisneros, *Colombia* **152 B2** 6 33N 75 4W
Cissna Park, *U.S.A.* **141 D9** 40 34N 87 54W
Cisterna di Latina, *Italy* **40 A5** 41 35N 12 50 E
Cisternino, *Italy* **41 B10** 40 45N 17 26 E
Citaré →, *Brazil* **153 C7** 1 11N 54 35W
Citeli-Ckaro, *Georgia* **53 F12** 41 33N 46 0 E
Citlaltépetl, *Mexico* **147 D5** 19 0N 97 20W
Citrus Heights, *U.S.A.* **144 G5** 38 42N 121 17W
Citrusdal, *S. Africa* **104 E2** 32 35 S 19 0 E
Città della Pieve, *Italy* **39 F9** 42 57N 12 0 E
Città di Castello, *Italy* **39 E9** 43 27N 12 14 E
Città Sant' Angelo, *Italy* **39 F11** 42 32N 14 5 E
Cittadella, *Italy* **39 C8** 45 39N 11 48 E
Cittaducale, *Italy* **39 F9** 42 24N 12 58 E
Cittanova, *Italy* **41 D9** 38 22N 16 5 E
Ciuc, Munţii, *Romania* **46 C7** 46 25N 26 5 E
Ciucaş, *Romania* **46 D6** 45 31N 25 56 E
Ciudad Altamirano, *Mexico* **146 D4** 18 20N 100 40W
Ciudad Bolívar, *Venezuela* **153 B5** 8 5N 63 36W
Ciudad Camargo, *Mexico* **146 B3** 27 41N 105 10W
Ciudad Chetumal, *Mexico* **147 D7** 18 30N 88 20W
Ciudad de Valles, *Mexico* **147 C5** 22 0N 99 0W
Ciudad del Carmen, *Mexico* **147 D6** 18 38N 91 50W
Ciudad Delicias = Delicias, *Mexico* **146 B3** 28 10N 105 30W
Ciudad Guayana, *Venezuela* **153 B5** 8 0N 62 30W
Ciudad Guerrero, *Mexico* **146 B3** 28 33N 107 28W
Ciudad Guzmán, *Mexico* **146 D4** 19 40N 103 30W
Ciudad Juárez, *Mexico* **146 A3** 31 40N 106 28W
Ciudad Madero, *Mexico* **147 C5** 22 19N 97 50W
Ciudad Mante, *Mexico* **147 C5** 22 50N 99 0W
Ciudad Obregón, *Mexico* **146 B3** 27 28N 109 59W
Ciudad Ojeda, *Venezuela* **152 A3** 10 12N 71 19W
Ciudad Real, *Spain* **37 G7** 38 59N 3 55W
Ciudad Real □, *Spain* **37 G7** 38 50N 4 0W
Ciudad Rodrigo, *Spain* **36 E4** 40 35N 6 32W
Ciudad Trujillo = Santo Domingo, *Dom. Rep.* **149 C6** 18 30N 69 59W
Ciudad Victoria, *Mexico* **147 C5** 23 41N 99 9W
Ciudadela, *Spain* **33 B10** 40 0N 3 50 E
Ciulniţa, *Romania* **46 E8** 44 26N 27 22 E
Civa Burnu, *Turkey* **88 C7** 41 21N 36 38 E
Cividale del Friuli, *Italy* **39 B10** 46 6N 13 25 E
Cívita Castellana, *Italy* **39 F9** 42 18N 12 24 E
Civitanova Marche, *Italy* **39 E10** 43 18N 13 41 E
Civitavécchia, *Italy* **39 F8** 42 6N 11 46 E
Civitella del Tronto, *Italy* **39 F10** 42 48N 13 40 E
Civray, *France* **24 B4** 46 10N 0 17 E
Çivril, *Turkey* **88 D3** 38 20N 29 43 E
Cixerri →, *Italy* **40 C1** 39 20N 8 40 E
Cizre, *Turkey* **89 E10** 37 19N 42 10 E
Clacton-on-Sea, *U.K.* **17 F9** 51 47N 1 10 E
Clain →, *France* **22 F7** 46 47N 0 33 E
Claire, L., *Canada* **130 B6** 58 35N 112 5W
Clairemont, *U.S.A.* **139 J4** 33 9N 100 44W
Clairton, *U.S.A.* **136 F5** 40 18N 79 53W
Clairvaux-les-Lacs, *France* **25 B9** 46 35N 5 45 E
Clallam Bay, *U.S.A.* **144 B2** 48 15N 124 16W
Clamecy, *France* **23 E10** 47 28N 3 30 E
Clanton, *U.S.A.* **135 J2** 32 51N 86 38W
Clanwilliam, *S. Africa* **104 E2** 32 11 S 18 52 E
Clara, *Ireland* **19 C4** 53 20N 7 38W
Clara →, *Australia* **114 B3** 19 8 S 142 30 E
Claraville, *U.S.A.* **145 K8** 35 24N 118 20W
Clare, *Australia* **116 B3** 33 50 S 138 37 E
Clare, *U.S.A.* **134 D3** 43 49N 84 46W
Clare □, *Ireland* **19 D3** 52 45N 9 0W
Clare →, *Ireland* **19 C2** 53 22N 9 5W
Clare I., *Ireland* **19 C2** 53 48N 10 0W
Claremont, *Calif., U.S.A.* **145 L9** 34 6N 117 43W
Claremont, *N.H., U.S.A.* **137 C12** 43 23N 72 20W
Claremont Pt., *Australia* **114 A3** 14 1 S 143 41 E
Claremore, *U.S.A.* **139 G7** 36 19N 95 36W
Claremorris, *Ireland* **19 C3** 53 45N 9 0W
Clarence, *U.S.A.* **140 E4** 39 45N 92 16W
Clarence →, *Australia* **115 D5** 29 25 S 153 22 E
Clarence →, *N.Z.* **119 C8** 42 10 S 173 56 E
Clarence, I., *Chile* **160 D2** 54 0 S 72 0W
Clarence I., *Antarctica* **7 C18** 61 10 S 54 0W
Clarence Str., *Australia* **112 B5** 12 0 S 131 0 E
Clarence Str., *U.S.A.* **130 B2** 55 40N 132 10W
Clarence Town, *Bahamas* **149 B5** 23 6N 74 59W
Clarendon, *Ark., U.S.A.* **139 H9** 34 42N 91 19W
Clarendon, *Tex., U.S.A.* **139 H4** 34 56N 100 53W
Clarenville, *Canada* **129 C9** 48 10N 54 1W
Claresholm, *Canada* **130 C6** 50 0N 113 33W
Clarie Coast, *Antarctica* **7 C9** 68 0 S 135 0 E
Clarin, *Phil.* **71 G4** 8 12N 123 52 E
Clarinda, *U.S.A.* **138 E7** 40 44N 95 2W
Clarion, *Iowa, U.S.A.* **140 B3** 42 44N 93 44W
Clarion, *Pa., U.S.A.* **136 E5** 41 13N 79 23W
Clarion →, *U.S.A.* **136 E5** 41 7N 79 41W
Clark, *U.S.A.* **138 C6** 44 53N 97 44W
Clark, Pt., *Canada* **136 B3** 44 4N 81 45W
Clark Fork, *U.S.A.* **142 B5** 48 9N 116 11W
Clark Fork →, *U.S.A.* **142 B5** 48 9N 116 15W
Clark Hill Res., *U.S.A.* **135 J4** 33 45N 82 20W
Clarkdale, *U.S.A.* **143 J7** 34 46N 112 3W
Clarke City, *Canada* **129 B6** 50 12N 66 38W
Clarke I., *Australia* **114 G4** 40 32 S 148 10 E
Clarke L., *Canada* **131 C7** 54 24N 106 54W
Clarke Ra., *Australia* **114 C4** 20 40 S 148 30 E
Clark's Fork →, *U.S.A.* **142 D9** 45 39N 108 43W
Clark's Harbour, *Canada* **129 D6** 43 25N 65 38W
Clarks Summit, *U.S.A.* **137 E9** 41 30N 75 42W
Clarksburg, *U.S.A.* **134 F5** 39 17N 80 30W
Clarksdale, *U.S.A.* **139 H9** 34 12N 90 35W
Clarkston, *U.S.A.* **142 C5** 46 25N 117 3W
Clarksville, *Ark., U.S.A.* **139 H8** 35 28N 93 28W
Clarksville, *Iowa, U.S.A.* **140 B4** 42 47N 92 40W
Clarksville, *Mich., U.S.A.* **141 B11** 42 50N 85 15W
Clarksville, *Ohio, U.S.A.* **141 E13** 39 24N 83 59W
Clarksville, *Tenn., U.S.A.* **135 G2** 36 32N 87 21W
Clarksville, *Tex., U.S.A.* **139 J7** 33 37N 95 3W
Claro →, *Brazil* **155 E1** 19 8 S 50 40W
Clatskanie, *U.S.A.* **144 D3** 46 6N 123 12W
Claude, *U.S.A.* **139 H4** 35 7N 101 22W
Claveria, *Cagayan, Phil.* **70 E4** 12 54N 123 15 E
Claveria, *Masbate, Phil.* **71 G5** 8 38N 124 55 E
Claveria, *Mindanao, Phil.* **70 B3** 18 37N 121 4 E
Clay, *U.S.A.* **144 G5** 38 17N 121 10W
Clay Center, *U.S.A.* **138 F6** 39 23N 97 8W
Clay City, *Ind., U.S.A.* **141 E9** 39 17N 87 7W
Clay City, *Ky., U.S.A.* **141 G13** 37 52N 83 55W
Claypool, *U.S.A.* **143 K8** 33 25N 110 51W
Claysville, *U.S.A.* **136 F4** 40 7N 80 25W
Clayton, *Idaho, U.S.A.* **142 D6** 44 16N 114 24W
Clayton, *Ind., U.S.A.* **141 E10** 39 41N 86 31W
Clayton, *N. Mex., U.S.A.* **139 G3** 36 27N 103 11W
Cle Elum, *U.S.A.* **142 C3** 47 12N 120 56W
Clear, C., *Ireland* **19 E2** 51 26N 9 30W
Clear I., *Ireland* **19 E2** 51 26N 9 30W
Clear L., *U.S.A.* **144 F4** 39 2N 122 47W
Clear Lake, *Iowa, U.S.A.* **140 A3** 43 8N 93 23W
Clear Lake, *S. Dak., U.S.A.* **138 C6** 44 45N 96 41W
Clear Lake, *Wash., U.S.A.* **142 B2** 48 27N 122 15W
Clear Lake Reservoir, *U.S.A.* **142 F3** 41 56N 121 5W
Clearfield, *Iowa, U.S.A.* **140 D2** 40 48N 94 29W
Clearfield, *Pa., U.S.A.* **134 E6** 41 2N 78 27W
Clearfield, *Utah, U.S.A.* **142 F7** 41 7N 112 2W
Clearlake Highlands, *U.S.A.* **144 G4** 38 57N 122 38W
Clearmont, *U.S.A.* **142 D10** 44 38N 106 23W
Clearwater, *Canada* **130 C4** 51 38N 120 2W
Clearwater, *U.S.A.* **135 M4** 27 58N 82 48W
Clearwater →, *Alta., Canada* **130 C6** 52 22N 114 57W
Clearwater →, *Alta., Canada* **131 B6** 56 44N 111 23W
Clearwater Cr. →, *Canada* **130 A3** 61 36N 125 30W
Clearwater Mts., *U.S.A.* **142 C6** 46 5N 115 20W
Clearwater Prov. Park, *Canada* **131 C8** 54 0N 101 0W
Cleburne, *U.S.A.* **139 J6** 32 21N 97 23W
Cleethorpes, *U.K.* **16 D7** 53 33N 0 2W
Cleeve Hill, *U.K.* **17 F6** 51 54N 2 0W
Clelles, *France* **25 D9** 44 50N 5 38 E
Clemency, *Lux.* **21 J7** 49 35N 5 53 E
Cleopatra Needle, *Phil.* **71 F2** 10 7N 118 58 E
Clerke Reef, *Australia* **112 C2** 17 22 S 119 20 E
Clermont, *Australia* **114 C4** 22 49 S 147 39 E
Clermont, *France* **23 C9** 49 23N 2 24 E
Clermont-en-Argonne, *France* **23 C12** 49 5N 5 4 E
Clermont-Ferrand, *France* **24 C7** 45 46N 3 4 E
Clermont-l'Hérault, *France* **24 E7** 43 38N 3 26 E
Clerval, *France* **23 E13** 47 25N 6 30 E
Clervaux, *Lux.* **21 H8** 50 4N 6 2 E
Cléry-St.-André, *France* **23 E8** 47 50N 1 46 E
Cles, *Italy* **38 B8** 46 21N 11 4 E
Cleveland, *Australia* **115 D5** 27 30 S 153 15 E
Cleveland, *Miss., U.S.A.* **139 J9** 33 45N 90 43W
Cleveland, *Ohio, U.S.A.* **136 E3** 41 30N 81 42W
Cleveland, *Okla., U.S.A.* **139 G6** 36 19N 96 28W
Cleveland, *Tenn., U.S.A.* **135 H3** 35 10N 84 53W
Cleveland, *Tex., U.S.A.* **139 K7** 30 21N 95 5W
Cleveland □, *U.K.* **16 C9** 54 35N 1 8 E
Cleveland, C., *Australia* **114 B4** 19 11 S 147 1 E
Cleveland Heights, *U.S.A.* **136 E3** 41 30N 81 34W
Clevelândia, *Brazil* **159 B5** 26 24 S 52 23W
Clevelândia do Norte, *Brazil* **153 C7** 3 49N 51 52W
Cleves, *U.S.A.* **141 E12** 39 10N 84 45W
Clew B., *Ireland* **19 C2** 53 54N 9 50W
Clewiston, *U.S.A.* **135 M5** 26 45N 80 56W
Clifden, *Ireland* **19 C1** 53 30N 10 2W
Clifden, *N.Z.* **119 G2** 46 1 S 167 42 E
Cliffdell, *U.S.A.* **144 D5** 46 56N 121 5W
Clifton, *Australia* **115 D5** 27 59 S 151 53 E
Clifton, *Ariz., U.S.A.* **143 K9** 33 3N 109 18W
Clifton, *Ill., U.S.A.* **141 D9** 40 56N 87 56W
Clifton, *Tex., U.S.A.* **139 K6** 31 47N 97 35W
Clifton Beach, *Australia* **114 B4** 16 46 S 145 39 E
Clifton Forge, *U.S.A.* **134 G6** 37 49N 79 50W
Clifton Hills, *Australia* **115 D2** 27 1 S 138 54 E
Climax, *Canada* **131 D7** 49 10N 108 20W
Clinch →, *U.S.A.* **135 H3** 35 53N 84 29W
Clingmans Dome, *U.S.A.* **135 H4** 35 34N 83 30W
Clint, *U.S.A.* **143 L10** 31 35N 106 14W
Clinton, *B.C., Canada* **130 C4** 51 6N 121 35W
Clinton, *Ont., Canada* **128 D3** 43 37N 81 32W
Clinton, *N.Z.* **119 G4** 46 12 S 169 23 E
Clinton, *Ark., U.S.A.* **139 H8** 35 36N 92 28W
Clinton, *Ill., U.S.A.* **138 E10** 40 9N 88 57W
Clinton, *Ind., U.S.A.* **141 E9** 39 40N 87 24W
Clinton, *Iowa, U.S.A.* **140 C6** 41 51N 90 12W
Clinton, *Mass., U.S.A.* **137 D13** 42 25N 71 41W
Clinton, *Mo., U.S.A.* **140 F3** 38 22N 93 46W
Clinton, *N.C., U.S.A.* **135 H6** 35 0N 78 22W
Clinton, *Okla., U.S.A.* **139 H5** 35 31N 98 58W
Clinton, *S.C., U.S.A.* **135 H5** 34 29N 81 53W
Clinton, *Tenn., U.S.A.* **135 G3** 36 6N 84 8W
Clinton, *Wash., U.S.A.* **144 C4** 47 59N 122 21W
Clinton, *Wis., U.S.A.* **141 B8** 42 34N 88 52W
Clinton C., *Australia* **114 C5** 22 30 S 150 45 E
Clinton Colden L., *Canada* **126 B9** 63 58N 107 27W
Clintonville, *U.S.A.* **138 C10** 44 37N 88 46W
Clipperton, I., *Pac. Oc.* **123 F17** 10 18N 109 13W
Clisson, *France* **22 E5** 47 5N 1 16W
Clive, *N.Z.* **118 F5** 39 36 S 176 58 E
Clive L., *Canada* **130 A5** 63 13N 118 54W
Cliza, *Bolivia* **157 D4** 17 36 S 65 56W
Cloates, Pt., *Australia* **112 D1** 22 43 S 113 40 E
Clocolan, *S. Africa* **105 D4** 28 55 S 27 34 E
Clodomira, *Argentina* **158 B3** 27 35 S 64 14W
Clonakilty, *Ireland* **19 E3** 51 37N 8 53W
Clonakilty B., *Ireland* **19 E3** 51 33N 8 50W
Cloncurry, *Australia* **114 C3** 20 40 S 140 28 E
Cloncurry →, *Australia* **114 B3** 18 37 S 140 40 E
Clones, *Ireland* **19 B4** 54 10N 7 13W
Clonmel, *Ireland* **19 D4** 52 22N 7 42W
Cloppenburg, *Germany* **26 C4** 52 50N 8 3 E
Cloquet, *U.S.A.* **138 B8** 46 43N 92 28W
Clorinda, *Argentina* **158 B4** 25 16 S 57 45W
Cloud Peak, *U.S.A.* **142 D10** 44 23N 107 11W
Cloudcroft, *U.S.A.* **143 K11** 32 58N 105 45W
Cloudy B., *N.Z.* **119 B9** 41 25 S 174 10 E
Cloverdale, *Calif., U.S.A.* **144 G4** 38 48N 123 1W
Cloverdale, *Ind., U.S.A.* **141 E10** 39 31N 86 48W
Cloverport, *U.S.A.* **141 G10** 37 50N 86 38W
Clovis, *Calif., U.S.A.* **144 J7** 36 49N 119 42W
Clovis, *N. Mex., U.S.A.* **139 H3** 34 24N 103 12W
Cloyes-sur-le-Loir, *France* **22 E8** 48 0N 1 14 E
Club Terrace, *Australia* **117 D8** 37 35 S 148 58 E
Cluj □, *Romania* **46 C4** 46 45N 23 30 E
Cluj-Napoca, *Romania* **46 C4** 46 47N 23 38 E
Clunes, *Australia* **116 D5** 37 20 S 143 45 E
Cluny, *France* **25 B8** 46 26N 4 38 E
Cluses, *France* **25 B10** 46 5N 6 35 E
Clusone, *Italy* **38 C6** 45 54N 9 58 E
Clutha →, *N.Z.* **119 G4** 46 20 S 169 49 E
Clwyd □, *U.K.* **16 D4** 53 5N 3 20W
Clwyd →, *U.K.* **16 D4** 53 20N 3 30W
Clyde, *N.Z.* **119 F4** 45 12 S 169 20 E
Clyde, *U.S.A.* **136 C8** 43 5N 76 52W
Clyde →, *U.K.* **18 F4** 55 56N 4 29W
Clyde, Firth of, *U.K.* **18 F4** 55 20N 5 0W
Clyde River, *Canada* **127 A13** 70 30N 68 30W
Clydebank, *U.K.* **18 F4** 55 54N 4 25W
Clymer, *U.S.A.* **136 D5** 40 40N 79 1W
Côa →, *Portugal* **36 D3** 41 5N 7 6W
Coachella, *U.S.A.* **145 M10** 33 41N 116 10W
Coachella Canal, *U.S.A.* **145 N12** 32 43N 114 57W
Coahoma, *U.S.A.* **139 J4** 32 18N 101 18W
Coahuayana →, *Mexico* **146 D4** 18 41N 103 45W
Coahuayutla, *Mexico* **146 D4** 18 19N 101 42W
Coahuila □, *Mexico* **146 B4** 27 0N 103 0W
Coal →, *Canada* **130 B3** 59 39N 126 57W
Coal City, *U.S.A.* **141 C8** 41 17N 88 17W
Coal I., *N.Z.* **119 G1** 46 8 S 166 40 E
Coalane, *Mozam.* **107 F4** 17 48 S 37 2 E
Coalcomán, *Mexico* **146 D4** 18 40N 103 10W
Coaldale, *Canada* **130 D6** 49 45N 112 35W
Coalgate, *U.S.A.* **139 H6** 34 32N 96 13W
Coalinga, *U.S.A.* **144 J6** 36 9N 120 21W
Coalville, *U.K.* **16 E6** 52 43N 1 21W
Coalville, *U.S.A.* **142 F8** 40 55N 111 24W
Coaraci, *Brazil* **155 D4** 14 38 S 39 32W
Coari, *Brazil* **153 D5** 4 8 S 63 7W
Coari →, *Brazil* **153 D5** 4 30 S 63 33W
Coari, L. de, *Brazil* **153 D5** 4 15 S 63 22W
Coast □, *Kenya* **106 C4** 2 40 S 39 45 E
Coast Mts., *Canada* **130 C3** 55 0N 129 20W
Coast Ranges, *U.S.A.* **124 E7** 39 0N 123 0W
Coatbridge, *U.K.* **18 F4** 55 52N 4 2W
Coatepec, *Mexico* **147 D5** 19 27N 96 58W
Coatepeque, *Guatemala* **148 D1** 14 46N 91 55W
Coatesville, *U.S.A.* **134 F8** 39 59N 75 50W
Coaticook, *Canada* **129 C5** 45 10N 71 46W
Coats I., *Canada* **127 B11** 62 30N 83 0W
Coats Land, *Antarctica* **7 D1** 77 0 S 25 0W
Coatzacoalcos, *Mexico* **147 D6** 18 7N 94 25W
Cobadin, *Romania* **46 E9** 44 5N 28 13 E
Cobalt, *Canada* **128 C4** 47 25N 79 42W
Cobán, *Guatemala* **148 C1** 15 30N 90 21W
Cobar, *Australia* **117 A6** 31 27 S 145 48 E
Cobberas, Mt., *Australia* **117 D8** 36 53 S 148 12 E
Cobden, *Australia* **116 E5** 38 20 S 143 3 E
Cóbh, *Ireland* **19 E3** 51 50N 8 18W
Cobham, *Australia* **115 E3** 30 18 S 142 7 E
Cobija, *Bolivia* **156 C4** 11 0 S 68 50W
Cobleskill, *U.S.A.* **137 D10** 42 41N 74 29W
Coboconk, *Canada* **136 B6** 44 39N 78 48W
Cobourg, *Canada* **128 D4** 43 58N 78 10W
Cobourg Pen., *Australia* **112 B5** 11 20 S 132 15 E
Cobram, *Australia* **117 C6** 35 54 S 145 40 E
Cobre, *U.S.A.* **142 F6** 41 7N 114 24W
Cóbué, *Mozam.* **107 E3** 12 0 S 34 58 E
Coburg, *Germany* **27 E6** 50 15N 10 58 E
Coca, *Spain* **36 D6** 41 13N 4 32W
Coca →, *Ecuador* **152 D2** 0 29 S 76 58W
Cocachacra, *Peru* **156 D3** 17 5 S 71 45W
Cocal, *Brazil* **154 B3** 3 28 S 41 34W
Cocanada = Kakinada, *India* **82 F6** 16 57N 82 11 E
Cocentaina, *Spain* **35 G4** 38 45N 0 27W
Cochabamba, *Bolivia* **157 D4** 17 26 S 66 10W
Coche, I., *Venezuela* **153 A5** 10 47N 63 56W
Cochem, *Germany* **27 E3** 50 8N 7 7 E
Cochemane, *Mozam.* **107 F3** 17 0 S 32 54 E
Cochin, *India* **83 K3** 9 59N 76 22 E
Cochin China = Nam-Phan, *Vietnam* **77 G6** 10 30N 106 0 E
Cochise, *U.S.A.* **143 K9** 32 7N 109 55W
Cochran, *U.S.A.* **135 J4** 32 23N 83 21W
Cochrane, *Alta., Canada* **130 C6** 51 11N 114 30W
Cochrane, *Ont., Canada* **128 C3** 49 0N 81 0W
Cochrane →, *Canada* **131 B8** 59 0N 103 40W
Cochrane, L., *Chile* **160 C2** 47 10 S 72 0W
Cockburn, *Australia* **116 B4** 32 5 S 141 0 E
Cockburn, Canal, *Chile* **160 D2** 54 30 S 72 0W
Cockburn I., *Canada* **128 C3** 45 55N 83 22W
Cockburn Ra., *Australia* **112 C4** 15 46 S 128 0 E
Cocklebiddy Motel, *Australia* **113 F4** 32 0 S 126 3 E
Coco →, *Cent. Amer.* **148 D3** 15 0N 83 8W
Coco, Pta., *Colombia* **152 C2** 2 58N 77 43W
Cocoa, *U.S.A.* **135 L5** 28 21N 80 44W
Cocobeach, *Gabon* **102 B1** 0 59N 9 34 E
Cocora, *Romania* **46 E8** 44 45N 27 3 E
Côcos, *Brazil* **155 D3** 14 10 S 44 33W
Côcos →, *Brazil* **155 D3** 12 44 S 44 48W
Cocos, I. del, *Pac. Oc.* **123 G19** 5 25N 87 55W
Cocos I., *Guam* **121 R15** 13 14N 144 39 E
Cocos Is., *Ind. Oc.* **109 F8** 12 10 S 96 55 E
Cod, C., *U.S.A.* **133 B13** 42 5N 70 10W
Codajás, *Brazil* **153 D5** 3 55 S 62 0W
Codera, C., *Venezuela* **152 A4** 10 35N 66 4W
Coderre, *Canada* **131 C7** 50 11N 106 31W
Codfish I., *N.Z.* **119 G2** 46 47 S 167 38 E
Codigoro, *Italy* **39 D9** 44 50N 12 5 E
Codó, *Brazil* **154 B3** 4 30 S 43 55W
Codogno, *Italy* **38 C6** 45 10N 9 42 E
Codpa, *Chile* **156 D4** 18 50 S 69 44W
Codróipo, *Italy* **39 C10** 45 57N 13 0 E
Codru, Munţii, *Romania* **46 C3** 46 30N 22 15 E
Cody, *U.S.A.* **142 D9** 44 32N 109 3W
Coe Hill, *Canada* **128 D4** 44 52N 77 50W
Coelemu, *Chile* **158 D1** 36 30 S 72 48W
Coelho Neto, *Brazil* **154 B3** 4 15 S 43 0W
Coen, *Australia* **114 A3** 13 52 S 143 12 E
Coeroeni →, *Surinam* **153 C6** 3 21N 57 31W
Coesfeld, *Germany* **26 D3** 51 56N 7 10 E
Coetivy Is., *Seychelles* **109 E4** 7 8 S 56 16 E
Cœur d'Alene, *U.S.A.* **142 C5** 47 45N 116 51W
Cœur d'Alene L., *U.S.A.* **142 C5** 47 32N 116 48W
Coevorden, *Neths.* **20 C9** 52 40N 6 44 E
Cofete, *Canary Is.* **33 F5** 28 6N 14 23W
Coffeyville, *U.S.A.* **139 G7** 37 2N 95 37W
Coffin B., *Australia* **115 E2** 34 38 S 135 28 E
Coffin Bay Peninsula, *Australia* **115 E2** 34 32 S 135 15 E
Coffs Harbour, *Australia* **117 A10** 30 16 S 153 5 E
Cofrentes, *Spain* **35 F3** 39 13N 1 5W
Cogealac, *Romania* **46 E9** 44 36N 28 36 E
Coghinas →, *Italy* **40 B1** 40 55N 8 48 E
Coghinas, L. di, *Italy* **40 B2** 40 46N 9 3 E

Copperopolis 187

Cognac, France 24 C3 45 41N 0 20W
Cogne, Italy 38 C4 45 37N 7 21 E
Cogolludo, Spain 34 E1 40 59N 3 10W
Cohagen, U.S.A. 142 C10 47 3N 106 37W
Cohoes, U.S.A. 137 D11 42 46N 73 42W
Cohuna, Australia 116 C6 35 45 S 144 15 E
Coiba, I., Panama 148 E3 7 30N 81 40W
Coig →, Argentina 160 D3 51 0 S 69 10W
Coihaique, Chile 160 C2 45 30 S 71 45W
Coimbatore, India 83 J3 11 2N 76 59 E
Coimbra, Brazil 157 D6 19 55 S 57 48W
Coimbra, Portugal 36 E2 40 15N 8 27W
Coimbra □, Portugal 36 E2 40 12N 8 25W
Coín, Spain 37 J6 36 40N 4 48W
Coipasa, L. de, Bolivia 156 D4 19 12 S 68 7W
Coipasa, Salar de, Bolivia 156 D4 19 26 S 68 9W
Cojata, Peru 156 D4 15 2 S 69 25W
Cojedes □, Venezuela 152 B4 9 20N 68 20W
Cojedes →, Venezuela 152 B4 8 34N 68 5W
Cojimies, Ecuador 152 C1 0 20N 80 0W
Cojocna, Romania 46 C4 46 45N 23 50 E
Cojutepequé, El Salv. 148 D2 13 41N 88 54W
Čoka, Serbia 42 B5 45 57N 20 12 E
Cokeville, U.S.A. 142 E8 42 5N 110 57W
Colaba Pt., India 82 E1 18 54N 72 47 E
Colac, Australia 116 E5 38 21 S 143 35 E
Colachel = Kolachel, India 83 K3 8 10N 77 15 E
Colares, Portugal 37 G1 38 48N 9 30W
Colasi, Phil. 71 F5 10 43N 125 44 E
Colatina, Brazil 155 E3 19 32 S 40 37W
Colbeck, C., Antarctica 7 D13 77 6 S 157 48W
Colbinabbin, Australia 117 D6 36 38 S 144 48 E
Colborne, Canada 136 B7 44 0N 77 53W
Colby, U.S.A. 138 F4 39 24N 101 3W
Colchagua □, Chile 158 C1 34 30 S 71 0W
Colchester, U.K. 17 F8 51 54N 0 55 E
Coldstream, U.K. 18 F6 55 39N 2 14W
Coldwater, Canada 136 B5 44 42N 79 40W
Coldwater, Kans., U.S.A. 139 G5 37 16N 99 20W
Coldwater, Mich., U.S.A. 141 C11 41 57N 85 0W
Coldwater, Ohio, U.S.A. 141 D12 40 29N 84 38W
Coldwater, L., U.S.A. 141 C12 41 48N 84 59W
Cole Camp, U.S.A. 140 F3 38 28N 93 12W
Colebrook, Australia 114 G4 42 31 S 147 21 E
Colebrook, U.S.A. 137 B13 44 54N 71 30W
Coleman, Canada 130 D6 49 40N 114 30W
Coleman, U.S.A. 139 K5 31 50N 99 26W
Coleman →, Australia 114 B3 15 6 S 141 38 E
Colenso, S. Africa 105 D4 28 44 S 29 50 E
Coleraine, Australia 116 D4 37 36 S 141 40 E
Coleraine, U.K. 19 A5 55 8N 6 40W
Coleraine □, U.K. 19 A5 55 8N 6 40W
Coleridge, L., N.Z. 119 D6 43 17 S 171 30 E
Coleroon →, India 83 J4 11 25N 79 50 E
Colesberg, S. Africa 104 E4 30 45 S 25 5 E
Colesburg, U.S.A. 140 B5 42 38N 91 12W
Coleville, U.S.A. 144 G7 38 34N 119 30W
Colfax, Calif., U.S.A. 144 F6 39 6N 120 57W
Colfax, Ill., U.S.A. 141 D8 40 34N 88 37W
Colfax, Ind., U.S.A. 141 D10 40 12N 86 40W
Colfax, La., U.S.A. 139 K8 31 31N 92 42W
Colfax, Wash., U.S.A. 142 C5 46 53N 117 22W
Colhué Huapi, L., Argentina 160 C3 45 30 S 69 0W
Cólico, Italy 38 B6 46 8N 9 22 E
Coligny, France 25 B9 46 23N 5 21 E
Coligny, S. Africa 105 D4 26 17 S 26 15 E
Colima, Mexico 146 D4 19 10N 103 40W
Colima □, Mexico 146 D4 19 10N 103 40W
Colima, Nevado de, Mexico 146 D4 19 35N 103 45W
Colina, Chile 158 C1 33 13 S 70 45W
Colina do Norte, Guinea-Biss. 100 C2 12 28N 15 0W
Colinas, Goiás, Brazil 155 D2 14 15 S 48 2W
Colinas, Maranhão, Brazil 154 C3 6 0 S 44 10W
Colinton, Australia 117 C8 35 50 S 149 10 E
Coll, U.K. 18 E2 56 40N 6 35W
Collaguasi, Chile 158 A2 21 5 S 68 45W
Collarada, Peña, Spain 34 C4 42 43N 0 29W
Collarenebri, Australia 115 D4 29 33 S 148 34 E
Collbran, U.S.A. 143 G10 39 14N 107 58W
Colle di Val d'Elsa, Italy 39 E8 43 25N 11 7 E
Colle Salvetti, Italy 38 E7 43 34N 10 27 E
Colle Sannita, Italy 41 A7 41 22N 14 48 E
Collécchio, Italy 38 D7 44 45N 10 10 E
Colleen Bawn, Zimbabwe 107 G2 21 0 S 29 12 E
College Park, U.S.A. 135 J3 33 40N 84 27W
Collette, Canada 129 C6 46 40N 65 30W
Collie, N.S.W., Australia 117 A8 31 41 S 148 18 E
Collie, W. Austral., Australia 113 F2 33 22 S 116 8 E
Collier B., Australia 112 C3 16 10 S 124 15 E
Collier Ra., Australia 112 D2 24 45 S 119 10 E
Colline Metallifere, Italy 38 E7 43 10N 11 0 E
Collingwood, Canada 128 D3 44 29N 80 13W
Collingwood, N.Z. 119 A7 40 41 S 172 40 E
Collins, Canada 128 B2 50 17N 89 27W
Collins, U.S.A. 140 G3 37 54N 93 37W
Collinsville, Australia 114 C4 20 30 S 147 56 E
Collinsville, U.S.A. 140 F7 38 40N 89 59W
Collipulli, Chile 158 D1 37 55 S 72 30W
Collo, Algeria 99 A6 36 58N 6 37 E
Collonges, France 25 B9 46 9N 5 52 E
Collooney, Ireland 19 B3 54 11N 8 28W
Colmar, France 23 D14 48 5N 7 20 E
Colmars, France 25 D10 44 11N 6 39 E
Colmenar, Spain 37 J6 36 54N 4 20W
Colmenar de Oreja, Spain 34 E1 40 6N 3 25W
Colmenar Viejo, Spain 36 E7 40 39N 3 47W
Colne, U.K. 16 D5 53 51N 2 11W
Colo →, Australia 117 B9 33 25 S 150 52 E
Cologna Véneta, Italy 39 C8 45 19N 11 21 E
Cologne = Köln, Germany 26 E2 50 56N 6 58 E
Colom, I., Spain 33 B11 39 58N 4 16 E
Coloma, U.S.A. 144 G6 38 48N 120 53W
Colomb-Béchar = Béchar, Algeria 99 B4 31 38N 2 18W
Colombey-les-Belles, France 23 D12 48 32N 5 54 E
Colombey-les-Deux-Églises, France 23 D11 48 13N 4 50 E
Colômbia, Brazil 155 F2 20 10 S 48 40W
Colombia ■, S. Amer. 152 C3 3 45N 73 0W
Colombier, Switz. 28 C3 46 58N 6 53 E
Colombo, Sri Lanka 83 L4 6 56N 79 58 E
Colome, U.S.A. 138 D5 43 16N 99 43W
Colón, Argentina 158 C4 32 12 S 58 10W
Colón, Cuba 148 B3 22 42N 80 54W
Colón, Panama 148 E4 9 20N 79 54W
Colón, Peru 156 A1 5 0 S 81 0W
Colona, Australia 113 F5 31 38 S 132 4 E
Colonella, Italy 39 F10 42 52N 13 50 E
Colonia, Uruguay 158 C4 34 25 S 57 50W
Colonia de San Jordi, Spain 33 B9 39 19N 2 59 E
Colonia Dora, Argentina 158 B3 28 34 S 62 59W
Colonial Heights, U.S.A. 134 G7 37 15N 77 25W
Colonne, C. delle, Italy 41 C10 39 2N 17 11 E
Colonsay, Canada 131 C7 51 59N 105 52W
Colonsay, U.K. 18 E2 56 4N 6 12W
Colorado □, U.S.A. 143 G10 39 30N 105 30W
Colorado →, Argentina 160 A4 39 50 S 62 8W
Colorado →, N. Amer. 143 L6 31 45N 114 40W
Colorado →, U.S.A. 139 L7 28 36N 95 59W
Colorado City, U.S.A. 139 J4 32 24N 100 52W
Colorado Desert, U.S.A. 132 D3 34 20N 116 0W
Colorado Plateau, U.S.A. 143 H8 37 0N 111 0W
Colorado River Aqueduct, U.S.A. 145 L12 34 17N 114 10W
Colorado Springs, U.S.A. 138 F2 38 50N 104 49W
Colorno, Italy 38 D7 44 55N 10 21 E
Colotlán, Mexico 146 C4 22 6N 103 16W
Colquechaca, Bolivia 157 D4 18 40 S 66 1W
Colton, Calif., U.S.A. 145 L9 34 4N 117 20W
Colton, N.Y., U.S.A. 137 B10 44 33N 74 56W
Colton, Wash., U.S.A. 142 C5 46 34N 117 8W
Columbia, Ill., U.S.A. 140 F6 38 27N 90 12W
Columbia, La., U.S.A. 139 J8 32 6N 92 5W
Columbia, Miss., U.S.A. 139 K10 31 15N 89 50W
Columbia, Mo., U.S.A. 140 F4 38 57N 92 20W
Columbia, Pa., U.S.A. 137 F8 40 2N 76 30W
Columbia, S.C., U.S.A. 135 H5 34 0N 81 2W
Columbia, Tenn., U.S.A. 135 H2 35 37N 87 2W
Columbia →, U.S.A. 142 C1 46 15N 124 5W
Columbia, C., Canada 6 A4 83 0N 70 0W
Columbia, District of □, U.S.A. 134 F7 38 55N 77 0W
Columbia, Mt., Canada 130 C5 52 8N 117 20W
Columbia Basin, U.S.A. 142 C4 46 45N 119 5W
Columbia Falls, U.S.A. 142 B6 48 23N 114 11W
Columbia Heights, U.S.A. 138 C8 45 3N 93 15W
Columbiana, U.S.A. 136 F4 40 53N 80 42W
Columbretes, Is., Spain 34 F5 39 50N 0 50 E
Columbus, Ga., U.S.A. 135 J3 32 28N 84 59W
Columbus, Ind., U.S.A. 141 E11 39 13N 85 55W
Columbus, Kans., U.S.A. 139 G7 37 10N 94 50W
Columbus, Miss., U.S.A. 135 J1 33 30N 88 25W
Columbus, Mont., U.S.A. 142 D9 45 38N 109 15W
Columbus, N. Dak., U.S.A. 138 A3 48 54N 102 47W
Columbus, N. Mex., U.S.A. 143 L10 31 50N 107 38W
Columbus, Nebr., U.S.A. 138 E6 41 26N 97 22W
Columbus, Ohio, U.S.A. 141 E13 39 58N 83 0W
Columbus, Tex., U.S.A. 139 L6 29 42N 96 33W
Columbus, Wis., U.S.A. 138 D10 43 21N 89 1W
Columbus Grove, U.S.A. 141 D12 40 55N 84 4W
Columbus Junction, U.S.A. 140 C5 41 17N 91 22W
Colunga, Spain 36 B5 43 29N 5 16W
Colusa, U.S.A. 144 F4 39 13N 122 1W
Colville, U.S.A. 142 B5 48 33N 117 54W
Colville →, U.S.A. 126 A4 70 25N 150 30W
Colville, C., N.Z. 118 C4 36 29 S 175 21 E
Colwyn Bay, U.K. 16 D4 53 17N 3 44W
Coma, Ethiopia 95 F4 8 29N 36 53 E
Comácchio, Italy 39 D9 44 41N 12 10 E
Comalcalco, Mexico 147 D6 18 16N 93 13W
Comallo, Argentina 160 B2 41 0 S 70 5W
Comana, Romania 46 E7 44 10N 26 10 E
Comanche, Okla., U.S.A. 139 H6 34 22N 97 58W
Comanche, Tex., U.S.A. 139 K5 31 54N 98 36W
Comandante Luis Piedrabuena, Argentina 160 C3 49 59 S 68 54W
Comănești, Romania 46 C7 46 25N 26 26 E
Comarapa, Bolivia 157 D5 17 54 S 64 29W
Comayagua, Honduras 148 D2 14 25N 87 37W
Combahee →, U.S.A. 135 J5 32 30N 80 31W
Combara, Australia 117 A8 31 10 S 148 22 E
Combeaufontaine, France 23 E12 47 38N 5 54 E
Comber, Canada 136 D2 42 14N 82 33W
Combermere Bay, Burma 78 F4 19 37N 93 34 E
Comblain-au-Pont, Belgium 21 H7 50 29N 5 35 E
Combles, France 23 B9 50 2N 2 50 E
Combourg, France 22 D5 48 25N 1 46W
Comboyne, Australia 117 A10 31 34 S 152 27 E
Combronde, France 24 C7 45 58N 3 5 E
Comeragh Mts., Ireland 19 D4 52 17N 7 35W
Comet, Australia 114 C4 23 36 S 148 38 E
Comilla, Bangla. 78 D3 23 28N 91 10 E
Comines, Belgium 21 G1 50 46N 3 0 E
Comino, Malta 32 C1 36 2N 14 20 E
Comino, C., Italy 40 B2 40 28N 9 47 E
Cómiso, Italy 41 F7 36 57N 14 35 E
Comitán, Mexico 147 D6 16 18N 92 9W
Commentry, France 24 B6 46 20N 2 46 E
Commerce, Ga., U.S.A. 135 H4 34 12N 83 28W
Commerce, Tex., U.S.A. 139 J7 33 15N 95 54W
Commercy, France 23 D12 48 43N 5 34 E
Commewijne □, Surinam 153 B7 5 25N 54 45W
Committee B., Canada 127 B11 68 30N 86 30W
Commonwealth B., Antarctica 7 C10 67 0 S 144 0 E
Commonwealth of Independent States ■, Eurasia 57 D11 60 0N 100 0 E
Commoron Cr. →, Australia 115 D5 28 22 S 150 8 E
Communism Pk. = Kommunizma, Pik, Tajikistan 55 D6 39 0N 72 2 E
Como, Italy 38 C6 45 48N 9 5 E
Como, L. di, Italy 38 B6 46 5N 9 17 E
Comodoro Rivadavia, Argentina 160 C3 45 50 S 67 40W
Comorin, C., India 83 K3 8 3N 77 40 E
Comoriște, Romania 46 D2 45 10N 21 35 E
Comoro Is. = Comoros ■, Ind. Oc. 93 H8 12 10 S 44 15 E
Comoros ■, Ind. Oc. 93 H8 12 10 S 44 15 E
Comox, Canada 130 D4 49 42N 124 55W
Compiègne, France 23 C9 49 24N 2 50 E
Comporta, Portugal 37 G2 38 22N 8 46W
Compostela, Mexico 146 C4 21 15N 104 53W
Compostela, Phil. 71 H6 7 40N 126 2 E
Comprida, I., Brazil 159 A6 24 50 S 47 42W
Compton, U.S.A. 145 M8 33 54N 118 13W
Compton Downs, Australia 115 E4 30 28 S 146 30 E
Con Cuong, Vietnam 76 C5 19 2N 104 54 E
Con Son, Is., Vietnam 77 H6 8 41N 106 37 E
Cona Niyeu, Argentina 160 B3 41 58 S 67 0W
Conakry, Guinea 100 D2 9 29N 13 49W
Conara Junction, Australia 114 G4 41 50 S 147 26 E
Conargo, Australia 117 C6 35 16 S 145 10 E
Concarneau, France 22 E3 47 52N 3 56W
Conceição, Brazil 154 C4 7 33 S 38 31W
Conceição, Mozam. 107 F4 18 47 S 36 7 E
Conceição da Barra, Brazil 155 E4 18 35 S 39 45W
Conceição do Araguaia, Brazil 154 C2 8 0 S 49 2W
Conceição do Canindé, Brazil 154 C3 7 54 S 41 34W
Concepción, Argentina 158 B2 27 20 S 65 35W
Concepción, Bolivia 157 D5 16 15 S 62 8W
Concepción, Chile 158 D1 36 50 S 73 0W
Concepción, Mexico 147 D6 18 15N 90 5W
Concepción, Paraguay 158 A4 23 22 S 57 26W
Concepción, Peru 156 C2 11 54 S 75 19W
Concepción □, Chile 158 D1 37 0 S 72 30W
Concepción →, Mexico 146 A2 30 32N 113 2W
Concepción, Est. de, Chile 160 D2 50 30 S 74 55W
Concepción, L., Bolivia 157 D5 17 20 S 61 20W
Concepción, Punta, Mexico 146 B2 26 55N 111 59W
Concepción del Oro, Mexico 146 C4 24 40N 101 30W
Concepción del Uruguay, Argentina 158 C4 32 35 S 58 20W
Conception, Pt., U.S.A. 145 L6 34 27N 120 28W
Conception B., Namibia 104 C1 23 55 S 14 22 E
Conception I., Bahamas 149 B4 23 52N 75 9W
Concession, Zimbabwe 107 F3 17 27 S 30 56 E
Conchas Dam, U.S.A. 139 H2 35 22N 104 11W
Conche, Canada 129 B8 50 55N 55 58W
Concho, U.S.A. 143 J9 34 28N 109 36W
Concho →, U.S.A. 139 K5 31 34N 99 43W
Conchos →, Chihuahua, Mexico 146 B4 29 32N 105 0W
Conchos →, Tamaulipas, Mexico 147 B5 25 9N 98 35W
Concord, Calif., U.S.A. 144 H4 37 59N 122 2W
Concord, Mich., U.S.A. 141 B12 42 11N 84 38W
Concord, N.C., U.S.A. 135 H5 35 25N 80 35W
Concord, N.H., U.S.A. 137 C13 43 12N 71 32W
Concordia, Argentina 158 C4 31 20 S 58 2W
Concórdia, Brazil 152 D4 4 36 S 66 36W
Concordia, Mexico 146 C3 23 18N 106 2W
Concordia, Kans., U.S.A. 138 F6 39 34N 97 40W
Concordia, Mo., U.S.A. 140 F3 38 59N 93 34W
Concots, France 24 D5 44 26N 1 40 E
Concrete, U.S.A. 142 B3 48 32N 121 45W
Condah, Australia 116 D4 37 57 S 141 44 E
Condamine, Australia 115 D5 26 56 S 150 9 E
Condat, France 24 C6 45 21N 2 46 E
Condé, Angola 103 E2 10 50 S 14 37 E
Conde, Brazil 155 D4 11 49 S 37 37W
Conde, U.S.A. 138 C5 45 9N 98 6W
Condé-sur-l'Escaut, France 23 B10 50 26N 3 34 E
Condé-sur-Noireau, France 22 D6 48 51N 0 33W
Condeúba, Brazil 155 D3 14 52 S 42 0W
Condobolin, Australia 115 E4 33 4 S 147 6 E
Condom, France 24 E4 43 57N 0 22 E
Condon, U.S.A. 142 D3 45 14N 120 11W
Condove, Italy 38 C4 45 8N 7 19 E
Conegliano, Italy 39 C9 45 53N 12 18 E
Conejera, I., Spain 33 B9 39 11N 2 58 E
Conejos, Mexico 146 B4 26 14N 103 53W
Conflans-en-Jarnisy, France 23 C12 49 10N 5 52 E
Confolens, France 24 B4 46 2N 0 40 E
Confuso →, Paraguay 158 B4 25 9 S 57 34W
Congjiang, China 68 E7 25 43N 108 52 E
Congleton, U.K. 16 D5 53 10N 2 12W
Congo = Zaïre →, Africa 103 D2 6 4 S 12 24 E
Congo, Brazil 154 C4 7 48 S 36 40W
Congo (Kinshasa) = Zaïre ■, Africa 103 C4 3 0 S 23 0 E
Congo ■, Africa 102 C3 1 0 S 16 0 E
Congo Basin, Africa 92 G6 0 10 S 24 30 E
Congonhas, Brazil 155 F3 20 30 S 43 52W
Congress, U.S.A. 143 J7 34 9N 112 51W
Conil, Spain 37 J4 36 17N 6 10W
Coniston, Canada 128 C3 46 29N 80 51W
Conjeeveram = Kanchipuram, India 83 H4 12 52N 79 45 E
Conjuboy, Australia 114 B3 18 35 S 144 35 E
Conklin, Canada 131 B6 55 38N 111 5W
Conlea, Australia 115 E3 30 7 S 144 35 E
Conn, L., Ireland 19 B2 54 3N 9 15W
Connacht, Ireland 19 C3 53 23N 8 40W
Conneaut, U.S.A. 136 E4 41 57N 80 34W
Connecticut □, U.S.A. 137 E12 41 30N 72 45W
Connecticut →, U.S.A. 137 E12 41 16N 72 20W
Connell, U.S.A. 142 C4 46 40N 118 52W
Connellsville, U.S.A. 136 F5 40 1N 79 35W
Connemara, Ireland 19 C2 53 29N 9 45W
Connemaugh →, U.S.A. 136 F5 40 28N 79 19W
Conner, Phil. 70 C3 17 48N 121 19 E
Connerré, France 22 D7 48 3N 0 30 E
Connersville, U.S.A. 141 E11 39 39N 85 8W
Connors Ra., Australia 114 C4 21 40 S 149 10 E
Conoble, Australia 117 B6 32 55 S 144 33 E
Cononaco →, Ecuador 152 D2 1 32 S 75 35W
Cononbridge, U.K. 18 D4 57 32N 4 30W
Conquest, Canada 131 C7 51 32N 107 14W
Conrad, Iowa, U.S.A. 140 B4 42 14N 92 52W
Conrad, Mont., U.S.A. 142 B8 48 10N 111 57W
Conran, C., Australia 117 D8 37 49 S 148 44 E
Conroe, U.S.A. 139 K7 30 19N 95 27W
Conselheiro Lafaiete, Brazil 155 F3 20 40 S 43 48W
Conselheiro Pena, Brazil 155 E3 19 10 S 41 30W
Consort, Canada 131 C6 52 1N 110 46W
Constance = Konstanz, Germany 27 H5 47 39N 9 10 E
Constance, L. = Bodensee, Europe 29 A8 47 35N 9 25 E
Constanța, Romania 46 E9 44 14N 28 38 E
Constanța □, Romania 46 E9 44 15N 28 15 E
Constantina, Spain 37 H5 37 51N 5 40W
Constantine, Algeria 99 A6 36 25N 6 42 E
Constantine, U.S.A. 141 C11 41 50N 85 40W
Constitución, Chile 158 D1 35 20 S 72 30W
Constitución, Uruguay 158 C4 31 0 S 57 50W
Consuegra, Spain 37 F7 39 28N 3 36W
Consul, Canada 131 D7 49 20N 109 30W
Contact, U.S.A. 142 F6 41 46N 114 45W
Contai, India 81 J12 21 54N 87 46 E
Contamana, Peru 156 B3 7 19 S 74 55W
Contarina, Italy 39 C9 45 2N 12 13 E
Contas →, Brazil 155 D4 14 17 S 39 1W
Contes, France 25 E11 43 49N 7 19 E
Conthey, Switz. 28 D4 46 14N 7 18 E
Continental, U.S.A. 141 C12 41 6N 84 16W
Contoocook, U.S.A. 137 C13 43 13N 71 45W
Contra Costa, Mozam. 105 D5 25 9 S 33 30 E
Contres, France 22 E8 47 24N 1 26 E
Contrexéville, France 23 D12 48 10N 5 53 E
Contumaza, Peru 156 B2 7 23 S 78 57W
Convención, Colombia 152 B3 8 28N 73 21W
Conversano, Italy 41 B10 40 57N 17 8 E
Converse, U.S.A. 141 D11 40 35N 85 52W
Convoy, U.S.A. 141 D12 40 55N 84 43W
Conway = Conwy, U.K. 16 D4 53 17N 3 50W
Conway = Conwy →, U.K. 16 D4 53 18N 3 50W
Conway, Ark., U.S.A. 139 H8 35 5N 92 26W
Conway, N.H., U.S.A. 137 C13 43 59N 71 7W
Conway, S.C., U.S.A. 135 J6 33 51N 79 3W
Conway, L., Australia 115 D2 28 17 S 135 35 E
Conwy, U.K. 16 D4 53 17N 3 50W
Conwy →, U.K. 16 D4 53 18N 3 50W
Coober Pedy, Australia 115 D1 29 1 S 134 43 E
Cooch Behar = Koch Bihar, India 78 B2 26 22N 89 29 E
Coodardy, Australia 113 E2 27 15 S 117 39 E
Cook, Australia 113 F5 30 37 S 130 25 E
Cook, U.S.A. 138 B8 47 49N 92 39W
Cook, B., Chile 160 E2 55 10 S 70 0W
Cook, Mt., N.Z. 119 D5 43 36 S 170 9 E
Cook Inlet, U.S.A. 126 C4 60 0N 152 0W
Cook Is., Pac. Oc. 123 J11 17 0 S 160 0W
Cook Strait, N.Z. 118 H3 41 15 S 174 29 E
Cooke Plains, Australia 116 C3 35 23 S 139 34 E
Cookeville, U.S.A. 135 G3 36 10N 85 30W
Cookhouse, S. Africa 104 E4 32 44 S 25 47 E
Cookshire, Canada 137 A13 45 25N 71 38W
Cookstown, U.K. 19 B5 54 40N 6 43W
Cookstown □, U.K. 19 B5 54 40N 6 43W
Cooksville, Canada 136 C5 43 36N 79 35W
Cooktown, Australia 114 B4 15 30 S 145 16 E
Coolabah, Australia 117 A7 31 1 S 146 43 E
Cooladdi, Australia 115 D4 26 37 S 145 23 E
Coolah, Australia 117 A8 31 48 S 149 41 E
Coolamon, Australia 115 E4 34 46 S 147 8 E
Coolangatta, Australia 115 D5 28 11 S 153 29 E
Coolgardie, Australia 113 F3 30 55 S 121 8 E
Coolibah, Australia 112 C5 15 33 S 130 56 E
Coolidge, U.S.A. 143 K8 32 59N 111 31W
Coolidge Dam, U.S.A. 143 K8 33 0N 110 20W
Cooma, Australia 117 D8 36 12 S 149 8 E
Coon Rapids, U.S.A. 140 C2 41 53N 94 41W
Coonabarabran, Australia 117 A8 31 14 S 149 18 E
Coonalpyn, Australia 116 C3 35 43 S 139 52 E
Coonamble, Australia 117 A8 30 56 S 148 27 E
Coonana, Australia 113 F3 31 0 S 123 0 E
Coondapoor, India 83 H2 13 42N 74 40 E
Coongie, Australia 115 D3 27 9 S 140 8 E
Coongoola, Australia 115 D4 27 43 S 145 51 E
Cooninie, L., Australia 115 D2 26 4 S 139 59 E
Coonoor, India 83 J3 11 21N 76 45 E
Cooper, U.S.A. 139 J7 33 23N 95 42W
Cooper →, U.S.A. 135 J6 32 50N 79 56W
Cooper Cr. →, N. Terr., Australia 110 C5 12 7 S 132 41 E
Cooper Cr. →, S. Austral., Australia 115 D2 28 29 S 137 46 E
Cooperstown, N. Dak., U.S.A. 138 B5 47 27N 98 8W
Cooperstown, N.Y., U.S.A. 137 D10 42 42N 74 56W
Coopersville, U.S.A. 141 A11 43 4N 85 57W
Coorabie, Australia 113 F5 31 54 S 132 18 E
Coorabulka, Australia 114 C3 23 41 S 140 20 E
Coorow, Australia 113 E2 29 53 S 116 2 E
Cooroy, Australia 115 D5 26 22 S 152 54 E
Coos Bay, U.S.A. 142 E1 43 22N 124 13W
Cootamundra, Australia 117 C8 34 36 S 148 1 E
Cootehill, Ireland 19 B4 54 5N 7 5W
Cooyar, Australia 115 D5 26 59 S 151 51 E
Cooyeana, Australia 114 C2 24 29 S 138 45 E
Copahue Paso, Argentina 158 D1 37 49 S 71 8W
Copainalá, Mexico 147 D6 17 8N 93 11W
Copán, Honduras 148 D2 14 50N 89 9W
Copatana, Brazil 152 D4 2 48 S 67 4W
Cope, U.S.A. 138 F3 39 40N 102 51W
Cope, C., Spain 35 H3 37 26N 1 28W
Cope Cope, Australia 116 D5 36 27 S 143 5 E
Copenhagen = København, Denmark 15 J6 55 41N 12 34 E
Copertino, Italy 41 B11 40 17N 18 2 E
Copeville, Australia 116 C3 34 47 S 139 51 E
Copiapó, Chile 158 B1 27 30 S 70 20W
Copiapó →, Chile 158 B1 27 19 S 70 56W
Copley, Australia 116 A3 30 36 S 138 26 E
Copp L., Canada 130 A6 60 14N 114 40W
Copparo, Italy 39 D8 44 52N 11 49 E
Coppename →, Surinam 153 B6 5 48N 55 55W
Copper Center, U.S.A. 126 B5 61 58N 145 18W
Copper Cliff, Canada 128 C3 46 28N 81 4W
Copper Harbor, U.S.A. 134 B2 47 28N 87 53W
Copper Queen, Zimbabwe 107 F2 17 29 S 29 18 E
Copperbelt □, Zambia 107 E2 13 15 S 27 30 E
Coppermine, Canada 126 B8 67 50N 115 5W
Coppermine →, Canada 126 B8 67 49N 116 4W
Copperopolis, U.S.A. 144 H6 37 58N 120 38W

188 Coquet


Coquet →, U.K. 16 B6 55 18N 1 45W
Coquilhatville = Mbandaka, Zaïre 102 B3 0 1N 18 18 E
Coquille, U.S.A. 142 E1 43 11N 124 11W
Coquimbo, Chile 158 B1 30 0S 71 20W
Coquimbo □, Chile 158 C1 31 0S 71 0W
Corabia, Romania 46 F5 43 48N 24 30 E
Coração de Jesus, Brazil 155 E3 16 43 S 44 22W
Coracora, Peru 156 D3 15 5 S 73 45W
Coradi, Is., Italy 41 B10 40 27N 17 10 E
Coral Bay, Phil. 71 G1 8 25N 117 20 E
Coral Gables, U.S.A. 135 N5 25 45N 80 16W
Coral Harbour, Canada 127 B11 64 8N 83 10W
Coral Sea, Pac. Oc. 122 J7 15 0S 150 0 E
Coralville, U.S.A. 140 C5 41 40N 91 35W
Coralville Res., U.S.A. 140 C5 41 50N 91 40W
Corantijn →, Surinam 153 B6 5 50N 57 8W
Coraopolis, U.S.A. 136 F4 40 31N 80 10W
Corato, Italy 41 A9 41 12N 16 22 E
Corbeil-Essonnes, France 23 D9 48 36N 2 26 E
Corbie, France 23 C9 49 54N 2 30 E
Corbières, France 24 F6 42 55N 2 35 E
Corbigny, France 23 E10 47 16N 3 40 E
Corbin, U.S.A. 134 G3 36 57N 84 6W
Corbion, Belgium 21 J6 49 48N 5 0 E
Corbones →, Spain 37 H5 37 36N 5 39W
Corby, U.K. 17 E7 52 29N 0 41W
Corby Glen, U.K. 17 E7 52 49N 0 31W
Corcoles →, Spain 35 F1 39 12N 3 18W
Corcoran, U.S.A. 144 J7 36 6N 119 33W
Corcubión, Spain 36 C1 42 56N 9 12W
Cordele, U.S.A. 135 K4 31 58N 83 47W
Cordell, U.S.A. 139 H5 35 17N 98 59W
Cordenons, Italy 39 C9 45 59N 12 42 E
Cordes, France 24 D5 44 5N 1 57 E
Cordisburgo, Brazil 155 E3 19 7 S 44 21W
Córdoba, Argentina 158 C3 31 20 S 64 10W
Córdoba, Mexico 147 D5 18 50N 97 0W
Córdoba, Spain 37 H6 37 50N 4 50W
Córdoba □, Argentina 158 C3 31 22 S 64 15W
Córdoba □, Colombia 152 B2 8 20N 75 40W
Córdoba □, Spain 37 G6 38 5N 5 0W
Córdoba, Sierra de, Argentina 158 C3 31 10 S 64 25W
Cordon, Phil. 70 C3 16 42N 121 32 E
Cordova, Ala., U.S.A. 135 J2 33 46N 87 11W
Cordova, Alaska, U.S.A. 126 B5 60 33N 145 45W
Cordova, Ill., U.S.A. 140 C6 41 41N 90 19W
Corella, Spain 34 C3 42 7N 1 48W
Corella →, Australia 114 B3 19 34 S 140 47 E
Coremas, Brazil 154 C4 7 1 S 37 58W
Corentyne →, Guyana 153 B6 5 50N 57 8W
Corfield, Australia 114 C3 21 40 S 143 21 E
Corfu = Kérkira, Greece 32 A3 39 38N 19 50 E
Corfu, Str of, Greece 32 A4 39 34N 20 0 E
Corgo, Spain 36 C3 42 56N 7 25W
Corguinho, Brazil 157 D7 19 53 S 54 52W
Cori, Italy 40 A5 41 39N 12 53 E
Coria, Spain 36 F4 39 58N 6 33W
Coricudgy, Australia 117 B9 32 51 S 150 24 E
Corigliano Cálabro, Italy 41 C9 39 36N 16 31 E
Coringa Is., Australia 114 B4 16 58 S 149 58 E
Corinna, Australia 114 G4 41 35 S 145 10 E
Corinth = Kórinthos, Greece 45 G4 37 56N 22 55 E
Corinth, Ky., U.S.A. 141 F12 38 30N 84 34W
Corinth, Miss., U.S.A. 135 H1 34 56N 88 31W
Corinth, N.Y., U.S.A. 137 C11 43 15N 73 49W
Corinth, G. of = Korinthiakós Kólpos, Greece 45 F4 38 16N 22 30 E
Corinth Canal, Greece 45 G4 37 58N 23 0 E
Corinto, Brazil 155 E3 18 20 S 44 30W
Corinto, Nic. 148 D2 12 30N 87 10W
Corj □, Romania 46 D4 45 5N 23 25 E
Cork, Ireland 19 E3 51 54N 8 30W
Cork □, Ireland 19 E3 51 50N 8 50W
Cork Harbour, Ireland 19 E3 51 46N 8 16W
Corlay, France 22 D3 48 20N 3 5W
Corleone, Italy 40 E6 37 48N 13 16 E
Corleto Perticara, Italy 41 B9 40 23N 16 2 E
Çorlu, Turkey 43 F12 41 11N 27 49 E
Cormack L., Canada 130 A4 60 56N 121 37W
Cormóns, Italy 39 C10 45 58N 13 29 E
Cormorant, Canada 131 C8 54 14N 100 35W
Cormorant L., Canada 131 C8 54 15N 100 50W
Corn Is. = Maiz, Is. del, Nic. 148 D3 12 15N 83 4W
Cornélio Procópio, Brazil 159 A5 23 7 S 50 40W
Cornell, Ill., U.S.A. 141 D8 41 0N 88 44W
Cornell, Wis., U.S.A. 138 C9 45 10N 91 9W
Corner Brook, Canada 129 C8 48 57N 57 58W
Corníglio, Italy 38 D7 44 29N 10 5 E
Corning, Ark., U.S.A. 139 G9 36 25N 90 35W
Corning, Calif., U.S.A. 142 G2 39 56N 122 11W
Corning, Iowa, U.S.A. 140 D2 40 59N 94 44W
Corning, N.Y., U.S.A. 136 D7 42 9N 77 3W
Corno, Monte, Italy 39 F10 42 28N 13 34 E
Cornwall, Canada 128 C5 45 2N 74 44W
Cornwall □, U.K. 17 G3 50 26N 4 40W
Corny Pt., Australia 116 C2 34 55 S 137 0 E
Coro, Venezuela 152 A4 11 25N 69 41W
Coroaci, Brazil 155 E3 18 35 S 42 17W
Coroatá, Brazil 154 B3 4 8 S 44 0W
Coroban, Somali Rep. 108 D2 3 58N 42 44 E
Corocoro, Bolivia 156 D4 17 15 S 68 28W
Corocoro, I., Venezuela 153 B5 8 30N 60 10W
Coroico, Bolivia 156 D4 16 0S 67 50W
Coromandel, Brazil 155 E2 18 28 S 47 13W
Coromandel, N.Z. 118 C4 36 45 S 175 31 E
Coromandel Coast, India 83 H5 12 30N 81 0 E
Coromandel Pen., N.Z. 118 C4 37 0S 175 45 E
Coromandel Ra., N.Z. 118 C4 37 0S 175 40 E
Coron, Phil. 70 E3 12 1N 120 12 E
Coron Bay, Phil. 71 F3 11 54N 120 8 E
Coron I., Phil. 71 F3 11 55N 120 14 E
Corona, Australia 115 E3 31 16 S 141 24 E
Corona, Calif., U.S.A. 145 M9 33 53N 117 34W
Corona, N. Mex., U.S.A. 143 J11 34 15N 105 36W
Coronado, U.S.A. 145 N9 32 41N 117 11W
Coronado, B. de, Costa Rica 148 E3 9 0N 83 40W
Coronados, G. de los, Chile 160 B2 41 40 S 74 0W
Coronados, Is. los, U.S.A. 145 N9 32 25N 117 15W
Coronation, Canada 130 C6 52 5N 111 27W
Coronation Gulf, Canada 126 B8 68 25N 110 0W
Coronation I., Antarctica 7 C18 60 45 S 46 0W
Coronation I., U.S.A. 130 B2 55 52N 134 20W
Coronation Is., Australia 112 B3 14 57 S 124 55 E
Coronda, Argentina 158 C3 31 58 S 60 56W
Coronel, Chile 158 D1 37 0S 73 10W
Coronel Bogado, Paraguay 158 B4 27 11 S 56 18W
Coronel Dorrego, Argentina 158 D3 38 40 S 61 10W
Coronel Fabriciano, Brazil 155 E3 19 31 S 42 38W
Coronel Murta, Brazil 155 E3 16 37 S 42 11W
Coronel Oviedo, Paraguay 158 B4 25 24 S 56 30W
Coronel Ponce, Brazil 157 D6 15 34 S 55 1W
Coronel Pringles, Argentina 158 D3 38 0S 61 30W
Coronel Suárez, Argentina 158 D3 37 30 S 61 52W
Coronel Vidal, Argentina 158 D4 37 28 S 57 45W
Corongo, Peru 156 B2 8 30 S 77 53W
Coronie □, Surinam 153 B6 5 55N 56 20W
Coropuna, Nevado, Peru 156 D3 15 30 S 72 41W
Çorovoda, Albania 44 D2 40 31N 20 14 E
Corowa, Australia 117 C7 35 58 S 146 21 E
Corozal, Belize 147 D7 18 23N 88 23W
Corozal, Colombia 152 B2 9 19N 75 18W
Corps, France 25 D9 44 50N 5 56 E
Corpus, Argentina 159 B4 27 10 S 55 30W
Corpus Christi, U.S.A. 139 M6 27 47N 97 24W
Corpus Christi, L., U.S.A. 139 L6 28 2N 97 52W
Corque, Bolivia 156 D4 18 20 S 67 41W
Corral, Chile 160 A2 39 52 S 73 26W
Corral de Almaguer, Spain 34 F1 39 45N 3 10W
Corralejo, Canary Is. 33 F6 28 43N 13 53W
Corréggio, Italy 38 D7 44 46N 10 47 E
Corrente, Brazil 154 D2 10 27 S 45 10W
Corrente →, Brazil 155 D3 13 8 S 43 28W
Correntes →, Brazil 157 D6 17 38 S 55 8W
Correntes, C. das, Mozam. 105 C6 24 6 S 35 34 E
Correntina, Brazil 155 D3 13 20 S 44 39W
Corrèze □, France 24 C5 45 20N 1 45 E
Corrèze →, France 24 C5 45 10N 1 28 E
Corrib, L., Ireland 19 C2 53 5N 9 10W
Corrientes, Argentina 158 B4 27 30 S 58 45W
Corrientes □, Argentina 158 B4 28 0S 57 0W
Corrientes →, Argentina 158 C4 30 42 S 59 38W
Corrientes →, Peru 152 D3 3 43 S 74 35W
Corrientes, C., Colombia 152 B2 5 30N 77 34W
Corrientes, C., Cuba 148 B3 21 43N 84 30W
Corrientes, C., Mexico 146 C3 20 25N 105 42W
Corrigan, U.S.A. 139 K7 31 0N 94 52W
Corrigin, Australia 113 F2 32 20 S 117 53 E
Corrowidgie, Australia 117 D8 36 56 S 148 50 E
Corry, U.S.A. 136 E5 41 55N 79 39W
Corryong, Australia 117 D7 36 12 S 147 53 E
Corse, France 25 F13 42 0N 9 0 E
Corse, C., France 25 E13 43 1N 9 25 E
Corse-du-Sud □, France 25 G13 41 45N 9 0 E
Corsica = Corse, France 25 F13 42 0N 9 0 E
Corsicana, U.S.A. 139 J6 32 6N 96 28W
Corte, France 25 F13 42 19N 9 11 E
Corte do Pinto, Portugal 37 H3 37 42N 7 29W
Cortegana, Spain 37 H4 37 52N 6 49W
Cortes, Phil. 71 G6 9 17N 126 11 E
Cortez, U.S.A. 143 H9 37 21N 108 35W
Cortina d'Ampezzo, Italy 39 B9 46 32N 12 9 E
Cortland, U.S.A. 137 D8 42 36N 76 11W
Cortona, Italy 39 E8 43 16N 12 0 E
Coruche, Portugal 37 G2 38 57N 8 30W
Çoruh →, Turkey 89 C9 41 38N 41 38 E
Çorum, Turkey 88 C6 40 30N 34 57 E
Çorum □, Turkey 88 C6 40 40N 35 0 E
Corumbá, Brazil 157 D6 19 0S 57 30W
Corumbá →, Brazil 155 E2 18 19 S 48 55W
Corumbá de Goiás, Brazil 155 E2 16 0S 48 50W
Corumbaíba, Brazil 155 E2 18 9 S 48 34W
Corund, Romania 46 C6 46 30N 25 13 E
Corunna = La Coruña, Spain 36 B2 43 20N 8 25W
Corunna, U.S.A. 141 B12 42 59N 84 7W
Corvallis, U.S.A. 142 D2 44 34N 123 16W
Corvette, L. de la, Canada 128 B5 53 25N 74 3W
Corydon, Ind., U.S.A. 141 F10 38 13N 86 7W
Corydon, Iowa, U.S.A. 140 D3 40 46N 93 19W
Corydon, Ky., U.S.A. 141 G9 37 44N 87 43W
Cosalá, Mexico 146 C3 24 28N 106 40W
Cosamaloapan, Mexico 147 D5 18 23N 95 50W
Cosenza, Italy 41 C9 39 17N 16 14 E
Coşereni, Romania 46 E7 44 38N 26 35 E
Coshocton, U.S.A. 136 F3 40 16N 81 51W
Cosmo Newberry, Australia 113 E3 28 0S 122 54 E
Cosne-sur-Loire, France 23 E9 47 24N 2 54 E
Coso Junction, U.S.A. 145 J9 36 3N 117 57W
Coso Pk., U.S.A. 145 J9 36 13N 117 44W
Cospeito, Spain 36 B3 43 12N 7 34W
Cosquín, Argentina 158 C3 31 15 S 64 30W
Cossato, Italy 38 C5 45 34N 8 10 E
Cossé-le-Vivien, France 22 E6 47 57N 0 54W
Cosson →, France 22 E8 47 30N 1 15 E
Costa Blanca, Spain 35 G4 38 25N 0 10W
Costa Brava, Spain 34 D8 41 30N 3 0 E
Costa del Sol, Spain 37 J6 36 30N 4 30W
Costa Dorada, Spain 34 E6 40 45N 1 15 E
Costa Mesa, U.S.A. 145 M9 33 38N 117 55W
Costa Rica ■, Cent. Amer. 148 D3 10 0N 84 0W
Costa Smeralda, Italy 40 A2 41 5N 9 35 E
Costigliole d'Asti, Italy 38 D5 44 48N 8 11 E
Costilla, U.S.A. 143 H11 36 59N 105 32W
Coştiui, Romania 46 B5 47 53N 24 2 E
Cosumnes →, U.S.A. 144 G5 38 16N 121 26W
Coswig, Germany 26 D8 51 52N 12 31 E
Cotabato, Phil. 71 H5 7 14N 124 15 E
Cotabena, Australia 116 A3 31 42 S 138 11 E
Cotacajes →, Bolivia 156 D4 16 0S 67 1W
Cotagaita, Bolivia 158 A2 20 45 S 65 40W
Cotahuasi, Peru 156 D3 15 12 S 72 50W
Côte d'Azur, France 25 E11 43 25N 7 10 E
Côte-d'Ivoire ■ = Ivory Coast ■, Africa 100 D3 7 30N 5 0W
Côte d'Or, France 23 E11 47 10N 4 50 E
Côte-d'Or □, France 23 E11 47 30N 4 50 E
Coteau des Prairies, U.S.A. 138 C6 45 20N 97 50W
Coteau du Missouri, U.S.A. 138 B4 47 0N 100 0W
Coteau Landing, Canada 137 A10 45 15N 74 13W
Cotegipe, Brazil 155 D3 12 2 S 44 15W
Cotentin, France 22 C5 49 15N 1 30W
Côtes-d'Armor □, France 22 D4 48 25N 2 40W
Côtes de Meuse, France 23 C12 49 15N 5 22 E
Côtes-du-Nord = Côtes-d'Armor □, France 22 D4 48 25N 2 40W
Cotiella, Spain 34 C5 42 31N 0 19 E
Cotillo, Canary Is. 33 F5 28 41N 14 1W
Cotina →, Bos.-H. 42 D3 43 36N 18 50 E
Cotoca, Bolivia 157 D5 17 49 S 63 3W
Cotonou, Benin 101 D5 6 20N 2 25 E
Cotopaxi, Ecuador 152 D2 0 40 S 78 30W
Cotopaxi □, Ecuador 152 D2 0 5 S 78 55W
Cotronei, Italy 41 C9 39 9N 16 45 E
Cotswold Hills, U.K. 17 F5 51 42N 2 10W
Cottage Grove, U.S.A. 142 E2 43 48N 123 3W
Cottbus, Germany 26 D10 51 44N 14 20 E
Cottingham, U.K. 16 C5 53 47N 0 23W
Cottonwood, U.S.A. 143 J7 34 45N 112 1W
Cotulla, U.S.A. 139 L5 28 26N 99 14W
Coubre, Pte. de la, France 24 C2 45 42N 1 15W
Couches, France 23 F11 46 53N 4 30 E
Couço, Portugal 37 G2 38 59N 8 17W
Coudersport, U.S.A. 136 E6 41 46N 78 1W
Couedic, C. du, Australia 116 D2 36 5 S 136 40 E
Couëron, France 22 E5 47 13N 1 44W
Couesnon →, France 22 D5 48 38N 1 32W
Couhé, France 24 B4 46 17N 0 11 E
Coulanges-sur-Yonne, France 23 E10 47 31N 3 33 E
Coulee City, U.S.A. 142 C4 47 37N 119 17W
Coulman I., Antarctica 7 D11 73 35 S 170 0 E
Coulommiers, France 23 D10 48 50N 3 3 E
Coulonge →, Canada 128 C4 45 52N 76 46W
Coulonges-sur-l'Autize, France 24 B3 46 29N 0 36W
Coulterville, Calif., U.S.A. 144 H6 37 43N 120 12W
Coulterville, Ill., U.S.A. 140 F7 38 11N 89 36W
Council, Alaska, U.S.A. 126 B3 64 55N 163 45W
Council, Idaho, U.S.A. 142 D5 44 44N 116 26W
Council Bluffs, U.S.A. 138 E7 41 16N 95 52W
Council Grove, U.S.A. 138 F6 38 40N 96 29W
Coupeville, U.S.A. 144 B4 48 13N 122 41W
Courantyne →, S. Amer. 153 B6 5 55N 57 5W
Courcelles, Belgium 21 H4 50 28N 4 22 E
Courçon, France 24 B3 46 15N 0 50W
Couronne, C., France 25 E9 43 19N 5 3 E
Cours-la-Ville, France 25 B8 46 7N 4 19 E
Coursan, France 24 E7 43 14N 3 4 E
Courseulles-sur-Mer, France 22 C6 49 20N 0 29W
Court-St.-Etienne, Belgium 21 G5 50 38N 4 34 E
Courtenay, Canada 130 D3 49 45N 125 0W
Courtland, U.S.A. 144 G5 38 20N 121 34W
Courtrai = Kortrijk, Belgium 21 G2 50 50N 3 17 E
Courtright, Canada 136 D2 42 49N 82 28W
Courville-sur-Eure, France 22 D8 48 28N 1 15 E
Coushatta, U.S.A. 139 J8 32 1N 93 21W
Coutances, France 22 C5 49 3N 1 28W
Couterne, France 22 D6 48 30N 0 25W
Coutras, France 24 C3 45 3N 0 8W
Coutts, Canada 130 D6 49 0N 111 57W
Couvet, Switz. 28 C3 46 57N 6 38 E
Couvin, Belgium 21 H4 50 3N 4 29 E
Covarrubias, Spain 34 C1 42 4N 3 31W
Covasna, Romania 46 D7 45 50N 26 10 E
Covasna □, Romania 46 D7 45 50N 26 0 E
Coveñas, Colombia 152 B2 9 24N 75 44W
Coventry, U.K. 17 E6 52 25N 1 31W
Coventry L., Canada 131 A7 61 15N 106 15W
Covilhã, Portugal 36 E3 40 17N 7 31W
Covington, Ga., U.S.A. 135 J4 33 36N 83 51W
Covington, Ind., U.S.A. 141 D9 40 9N 87 24W
Covington, Ky., U.S.A. 141 E12 39 5N 84 31W
Covington, Ohio, U.S.A. 141 D12 40 7N 84 21W
Covington, Okla., U.S.A. 139 G6 36 18N 97 35W
Covington, Tenn., U.S.A. 139 H10 35 34N 89 39W
Cowal, L., Australia 117 B7 33 40 S 147 25 E
Cowan, Canada 131 C8 52 5N 100 45W
Cowan, L., Australia 113 F3 31 45 S 121 45 E
Cowan L., Canada 131 C7 54 0N 107 15W
Cowangie, Australia 116 C4 35 12 S 141 26 E
Cowansville, Canada 137 A12 45 14N 72 46W
Cowarie, Australia 115 D2 27 45 S 138 15 E
Cowcowing Lakes, Australia 113 F2 30 55 S 117 20 E
Cowden, U.S.A. 141 E8 39 15N 88 52W
Cowdenbeath, U.K. 18 E5 56 7N 3 20W
Cowell, Australia 116 B2 33 39 S 136 56 E
Cowes, U.K. 17 G6 50 45N 1 18W
Cowl Cowl, Australia 117 B6 33 36 S 145 18 E
Cowlitz →, U.S.A. 144 D4 46 6N 122 55W
Cowra, Australia 117 B8 33 49 S 148 42 E
Coxilha Grande, Brazil 159 B5 28 18 S 51 30W
Coxim, Brazil 157 D7 18 30 S 54 55W
Coxim →, Brazil 157 D7 18 34 S 54 46W
Cox's Bazar, Bangla. 78 E3 21 26N 91 59 E
Cox's Cove, Canada 129 C8 49 7N 58 5W
Coyame, Mexico 146 B3 29 28N 105 6W
Coyote Wells, U.S.A. 145 N11 32 44N 115 58W
Coyuca de Benítez, Mexico 147 D4 17 1N 100 8W
Coyuca de Catalan, Mexico 146 D4 18 18N 100 41W
Cozad, U.S.A. 138 E5 40 52N 99 59W
Cozumel, Mexico 147 C7 20 31N 86 55W
Cozumel, I. de, Mexico 147 C7 20 30N 86 40W
Craboon, Australia 117 B8 32 3 S 149 30 E
Cracow = Kraków, Poland 31 A12 50 4N 19 57 E
Cracow, Australia 115 D5 25 17 S 150 17 E
Cradock, S. Africa 104 E4 32 8 S 25 36 E
Craig, Alaska, U.S.A. 130 B2 55 29N 133 9W
Craig, Colo., U.S.A. 142 F10 40 31N 107 33W
Craigavon = Lurgan, U.K. 19 B5 54 28N 6 20W
Craigmore, Zimbabwe 107 G3 20 28 S 32 50 E
Crailsheim, Germany 27 F6 49 7N 10 5 E
Craiova, Romania 46 E4 44 21N 23 48 E
Cramsie, Australia 114 C3 23 20 S 144 15 E
Cranberry Portage, Canada 131 C8 54 35N 101 23W
Cranbrook, Tas., Australia 114 G4 42 0S 148 5 E
Cranbrook, W. Austral., Australia 113 F2 34 18 S 117 33 E
Cranbrook, Canada 130 D5 49 30N 115 46W
Crandon, U.S.A. 138 C10 45 34N 88 54W
Crane, Oreg., U.S.A. 142 E4 43 25N 118 35W
Crane, Tex., U.S.A. 139 K3 31 24N 102 21W
Cranston, U.S.A. 137 E13 41 47N 71 26W
Craon, France 22 E6 47 50N 0 58W
Craonne, France 23 C10 49 27N 3 46 E
Craponne-sur-Arzon, France 24 C7 45 19N 3 51 E
Crasna, Romania 46 C8 46 32N 27 51 E
Crasna →, Romania 46 B3 47 44N 22 35 E
Crasnei, Munţii, Romania 46 C4 47 0N 23 20 E
Crater L., U.S.A. 142 E2 42 56N 122 6W
Crater Mt., Papua N. G. 120 D3 6 37 S 145 7 E
Crater Pt., Papua N. G. 120 C7 5 25 S 152 9 E
Crateús, Brazil 154 C3 5 10 S 40 39W
Crati →, Italy 41 C9 39 41N 16 30 E
Crato, Brazil 154 C4 7 10 S 39 25W
Crato, Portugal 37 F3 39 16N 7 39W
Cravo Norte, Colombia 152 B3 6 18N 70 12W
Cravo Norte →, Colombia 152 B3 6 18N 70 12W
Crawford, U.S.A. 138 D3 42 41N 103 25W
Crawfordsville, U.S.A. 141 D10 40 2N 86 54W
Crawley, U.K. 17 F7 51 7N 0 10W
Crazy Mts., U.S.A. 142 C8 46 12N 110 20W
Crean L., Canada 131 C7 54 5N 106 9W
Crécy-en-Brie, France 23 D9 48 50N 2 53 E
Crécy-en-Ponthieu, France 23 B8 50 15N 1 53 E
Crediton, Canada 136 C3 43 17N 81 33W
Credo, Australia 113 F3 30 28 S 120 45 E
Cree →, Canada 131 B7 58 57N 105 47W
Cree →, U.K. 18 G4 54 51N 4 24W
Cree L., Canada 131 B7 57 30N 106 30W
Creede, U.S.A. 143 H10 37 51N 106 56W
Creel, Mexico 146 B3 27 45N 107 38W
Creighton, U.S.A. 138 D6 42 28N 97 54W
Creil, France 23 C9 49 15N 2 29 E
Crema, Italy 38 C6 45 21N 9 40 E
Cremona, Italy 38 C7 45 8N 10 2 E
Crepaja, Serbia 42 B5 45 1N 20 38 E
Crepori →, Brazil 157 B6 5 42 S 57 8W
Crépy, France 23 C10 49 35N 3 32 E
Crépy-en-Valois, France 23 C9 49 14N 2 54 E
Cres, Croatia 39 D11 44 58N 14 25 E
Cresbard, U.S.A. 138 C5 45 10N 98 57W
Crescent, Okla., U.S.A. 139 H6 35 57N 97 36W
Crescent, Oreg., U.S.A. 142 E3 43 28N 121 42W
Crescent City, U.S.A. 142 F1 41 45N 124 12W
Crescentino, Italy 38 C5 45 11N 8 7 E
Crespino, Italy 39 D8 44 59N 11 51 E
Crespo, Argentina 158 C3 32 2 S 60 19W
Cressy, Australia 116 E5 38 2 S 143 40 E
Crest, France 25 D9 44 44N 5 2 E
Cresta, Mt., Phil. 70 C4 17 17N 122 6 E
Crested Butte, U.S.A. 143 G10 38 52N 106 59W
Crestline, Calif., U.S.A. 145 L9 34 14N 117 18W
Crestline, Ohio, U.S.A. 136 F2 40 47N 82 44W
Creston, Canada 130 D5 49 10N 116 31W
Creston, Calif., U.S.A. 144 K6 35 32N 120 33W
Creston, Iowa, U.S.A. 140 C2 41 4N 94 22W
Creston, Wash., U.S.A. 142 C4 47 46N 118 31W
Crestview, Calif., U.S.A. 144 H8 37 46N 118 58W
Crestview, Fla., U.S.A. 135 K2 30 46N 86 34W
Creswick, Australia 116 D5 37 25 S 143 58 E
Crete = Kríti, Greece 32 D7 35 15N 25 0 E
Crete, U.S.A. 138 E6 40 38N 96 58W
Crete, Sea of, Greece 45 H6 36 0N 25 0 E
Cretin, C., Papua N. G. 120 D4 6 40 S 147 53 E
Creus, C., Spain 34 C8 42 20N 3 19 E
Creuse □, France 24 B6 46 10N 2 0 E
Creuse →, France 24 B4 47 0N 0 34 E
Creuzburg, Germany 26 D6 51 3N 10 15 E
Crevalcore, Italy 39 D8 44 41N 11 10 E
Crèvecœur-le-Grand, France 23 C9 49 37N 2 5 E
Crevillente, Spain 35 G4 38 12N 0 48W
Crewe, U.K. 16 D5 53 6N 2 28W
Criciúma, Brazil 159 B6 28 40 S 49 23W
Cridersville, U.S.A. 141 D12 40 39N 84 9W
Crieff, U.K. 18 E5 56 22N 3 50W
Crikvenica, Croatia 39 C11 45 11N 14 40 E
Crimea = Krymskiy Poluostrov, Ukraine 52 D5 45 0N 34 0 E
Crimmitschau, Germany 26 E8 50 48N 12 23 E
Cristal, Mts. de, Gabon 102 B2 0 30N 10 30 E
Cristalândia, Brazil 154 D2 10 36 S 49 11W
Cristeşti, Romania 46 B7 47 15N 26 33 E
Cristino Castro, Brazil 154 C3 8 49 S 44 13W
Crişul Alb →, Romania 42 A6 46 42N 21 17 E
Crişul Negru →, Romania 46 C2 46 42N 21 16 E
Crişul Repede →, Romania 46 C1 46 55N 20 59 E
Crittenden, U.S.A. 141 F12 38 47N 84 36W
Crivitz, Germany 26 B7 53 35N 11 39 E
Crixás, Brazil 155 D2 14 27 S 49 58W
Crna Gora = Montenegro □, Montenegro 42 E4 42 40N 19 20 E
Crna Gora, Serbia 42 E6 42 10N 21 30 E
Crna Reka →, Macedonia 42 F6 41 33N 21 59 E
Crna Trava, Serbia 42 E7 42 49N 22 19 E
Crni Drim →, Macedonia 42 F5 41 17N 20 40 E
Crni Timok →, Serbia 42 D7 43 53N 22 15 E
Crnoljeva Planina, Serbia 42 E6 42 20N 21 0 E
Črnomelj, Slovenia 39 C12 45 33N 15 10 E
Croaghpatrick, Ireland 19 C2 53 46N 9 40W
Croatia ■, Europe 39 C13 45 20N 16 0 E
Crocker, U.S.A. 140 G4 37 57N 92 16W
Crocker, Banjaran, Malaysia 75 A5 5 40N 116 30 E
Crockett, U.S.A. 139 K7 31 19N 95 27W
Crocodile = Krokodil →, Mozam. 105 D5 25 14 S 32 18 E
Crocodile Is., Australia 114 A1 12 3 S 134 58 E
Crocq, France 24 C6 45 52N 2 21 E
Croisette, C., France 25 E9 43 14N 5 22 E
Croisic, Pte. du, France 22 E4 47 19N 2 31W
Croix, L. La, Canada 128 C1 48 20N 92 15W
Croker, C., Australia 112 B5 10 58 S 132 35 E
Croker I., Australia 112 B5 11 12 S 132 32 E
Cromarty, Canada 131 B10 58 3N 94 9W

Dalgān 189


Cromarty, *U.K.* ........ **18 D4** 57 40N 4 2W
Cromer, *U.K.* .......... **16 E9** 52 56N 1 18 E
Cromwell, *N.Z.* ........ **119 F4** 45 3 S 169 14 E
Cronat, *France* ........ **23 F10** 46 43N 3 40 E
Cronulla, *Australia* ...... **117 C9** 34 3 S 151 8 E
Crooked →, *Canada* .... **130 C4** 54 50N 122 54W
Crooked →, *U.S.A.* .... **142 D3** 44 32N 121 16W
Crooked I., *Bahamas* .... **149 B5** 22 50N 74 10W
Crooked Island Passage, *Bahamas* ........... **149 B5** 23 0N 74 30W
Crookston, *Minn., U.S.A.* **138 B6** 47 47N 96 37W
Crookston, *Nebr., U.S.A.* **138 D4** 42 56N 100 45W
Crooksville, *U.S.A.* ..... **134 F4** 39 46N 82 6W
Crookwell, *Australia* .... **117 C8** 34 28 S 149 24 E
Crosby, *Minn., U.S.A.* .. **138 B8** 46 29N 93 58W
Crosby, *N. Dak., U.S.A.* **131 D8** 48 55N 103 18W
Crosby, *Pa., U.S.A.* ..... **136 E6** 41 45N 78 23W
Crosbyton, *U.S.A.* ...... **139 J4** 33 40N 101 14W
Cross →, *Nigeria* ....... **101 E6** 4 42N 8 21 E
Cross City, *U.S.A.* ...... **135 L4** 29 38N 83 7W
Cross Fell, *U.K.* ......... **16 C5** 54 44N 2 29W
Cross L., *Canada* ....... **131 C9** 54 45N 97 30W
Cross Plains, *U.S.A.* .... **139 J5** 32 8N 99 11W
Cross River □, *Nigeria* .. **101 D6** 6 0N 8 0 E
Cross Sound, *U.S.A.* .... **126 C6** 58 0N 135 0W
Cross Timbers, *U.S.A.* .. **140 F3** 38 1N 93 14W
Crossett, *U.S.A.* ........ **139 J9** 33 8N 91 58W
Crossfield, *Canada* ...... **130 C6** 51 25N 114 0W
Crosshaven, *Ireland* ..... **19 E3** 51 48N 8 19W
Crossley, Mt., *N.Z.* ..... **119 C7** 42 50 S 172 5 E
Crossville, *U.S.A.* ....... **141 F8** 38 10N 88 4W
Croton-on-Hudson, *U.S.A.* ............. **137 E11** 41 12N 73 55W
Crotone, *Italy* ........... **41 C10** 39 5N 17 6 E
Crow →, *Canada* ....... **130 B4** 59 41N 124 20W
Crow Agency, *U.S.A.* ... **142 D10** 45 36N 107 28W
Crow Hd., *Ireland* ...... **19 E1** 51 34N 10 9W
Crowell, *U.S.A.* ......... **139 J5** 33 59N 99 43W
Crowl Creek, *Australia* .. **117 B6** 32 0 S 145 30 E
Crowley, *U.S.A.* ........ **139 K8** 30 13N 92 22W
Crowley, L., *U.S.A.* .... **144 H8** 37 35N 118 42W
Crown Point, *U.S.A.* .... **141 C9** 41 25N 87 22W
Crows Landing, *U.S.A.* .. **144 H5** 37 23N 121 6W
Crows Nest, *Australia* ... **115 D5** 27 16 S 152 4 E
Crowsnest Pass, *Canada* . **130 D6** 49 40N 114 40W
Croydon, *Australia* ...... **114 B3** 18 13 S 142 14 E
Croydon, *U.K.* .......... **17 F7** 51 18N 0 5W
Crozet Is., *Ind. Oc.* ..... **109 J4** 46 27 S 52 0 E
Crozon, *France* ......... **22 D2** 48 15N 4 30W
Cruz, C., *Cuba* ......... **148 C4** 19 50N 77 50W
Cruz Alta, *Brazil* ....... **159 B5** 28 45 S 53 40W
Cruz das Almas, *Brazil* .. **155 D4** 12 0 S 39 6W
Cruz de Malta, *Brazil* ... **154 C3** 8 15 S 40 20W
Cruz del Eje, *Argentina* .. **158 C3** 30 45 S 64 50W
Cruzeiro, *Brazil* ........ **155 F2** 22 33 S 45 0W
Cruzeiro do Oeste, *Brazil* **159 A5** 23 46 S 53 4W
Cruzeiro do Sul, *Brazil* .. **156 B3** 7 35 S 72 35W
Cry L., *Canada* ......... **130 B3** 58 45N 129 0W
Crystal Bay, *U.S.A.* ..... **144 F7** 39 15N 120 0W
Crystal Brook, *Australia* . **116 B3** 33 21 S 138 12 E
Crystal City, *Mo., U.S.A.* **140 F6** 38 13N 90 23W
Crystal City, *Tex., U.S.A.* **139 L5** 28 41N 99 50W
Crystal Falls, *U.S.A.* .... **134 B1** 46 5N 88 20W
Crystal Lake, *U.S.A.* .... **141 B8** 42 14N 88 19W
Crystal River, *U.S.A.* ... **135 L4** 28 54N 82 35W
Crystal Springs, *U.S.A.* .. **139 K9** 31 59N 90 21W
Csongrád, *Hungary* ..... **31 E13** 46 43N 20 12 E
Csongrád □, *Hungary* ... **31 E13** 46 32N 20 15 E
Csorna, *Hungary* ....... **31 D10** 47 38N 17 18 E
Csurgo, *Hungary* ....... **31 E10** 46 16N 17 9 E
Cu Lao Hon, *Vietnam* ... **77 G7** 10 54N 108 18 E
Cua Rao, *Vietnam* ...... **76 C5** 19 16N 104 27 E
Cuácua →, *Mozam.* ..... **107 F4** 17 54 S 37 0 E
Cuamato, *Angola* ....... **103 F3** 17 2 S 15 7 E
Cuamba, *Mozam.* ....... **107 E4** 14 45 S 36 22 E
Cuando →, *Angola* ..... **103 F4** 17 30 S 23 15 E
Cuando Cubango □, *Angola* ............. **103 F3** 16 25 S 20 0 E
Cuangar, *Angola* ........ **103 F3** 17 36 S 18 39 E
Cuango, *Angola* ......... **103 D3** 6 15 S 16 42 E
Cuanza →, *Angola* ...... **92 G5** 9 2 S 13 30 E
Cuanza Norte □, *Angola* **103 D2** 8 50 S 14 30 E
Cuanza Sul □, *Angola* ... **103 E2** 10 50 S 14 50 E
Cuarto →, *Argentina* .... **158 C3** 33 25 S 63 2W
Cuatrociénegas, *Mexico* .. **146 B4** 26 59N 102 5W
Cuauhtémoc, *Mexico* .... **146 B3** 28 25N 106 52W
Cuba, *Portugal* ......... **37 G3** 38 10N 7 54W
Cuba, *Mo., U.S.A.* ...... **140 F5** 38 4N 91 24W
Cuba, *N. Mex., U.S.A.* .. **143 J10** 36 1N 107 4W
Cuba, *N.Y., U.S.A.* ..... **136 D6** 42 13N 78 17W
Cuba ■, *W. Indies* ...... **148 B4** 22 0N 79 0W
Cuba City, *U.S.A.* ...... **140 B6** 42 36N 90 26W
Cubal, *Angola* .......... **103 E2** 12 26 S 14 3 E
Cuballing, *Australia* ..... **113 F2** 32 50 S 117 10 E
Cubango →, *Africa* ..... **103 F4** 18 50 S 22 25 E
Cubanja, *Angola* ........ **103 E4** 14 49 S 21 20 E
Cubia, *Angola* .......... **103 F4** 15 58 S 21 42 E
Çubuk, *Turkey* ......... **88 C5** 40 14N 33 3 E
Cucamonga, *U.S.A.* ..... **145 L9** 34 10N 117 30W
Cuchi, *Angola* .......... **103 E3** 14 37 S 16 58 E
Cuchillo-Có, *Argentina* .. **160 A4** 38 20 S 64 37W
Cuchivero →, *Venezuela* **152 B4** 7 40N 65 57W
Cuchumatanes, Sierra de los, *Guatemala* ....... **148 C1** 15 35N 91 25W
Cucuí, *Brazil* ........... **152 C4** 1 12N 66 50W
Cucurpe, *Mexico* ........ **146 A2** 30 20N 110 43W
Cucurrupí, *Colombia* .... **152 C2** 4 23N 76 56W
Cúcuta, *Colombia* ....... **152 B3** 7 54N 72 31W
Cudahy, *U.S.A.* ......... **141 B9** 42 58N 87 52W
Cudalbi, *Romania* ....... **46 D8** 45 46N 27 41 E
Cuddalore, *India* ........ **83 J4** 11 46N 79 45 E
Cuddapah, *India* ........ **83 G4** 14 30N 78 47 E
Cuddapan, L., *Australia* . **114 D3** 25 45 S 141 26 E
Cudgewa, *Australia* ..... **117 D7** 36 10 S 147 42 E
Cudillero, *Spain* ........ **36 B4** 43 33N 6 9W
Cue, *Australia* .......... **113 E2** 27 25 S 117 54 E
Cuéllar, *Spain* .......... **36 D6** 41 23N 4 21W
Cuemba, *Angola* ........ **103 E3** 11 50 S 17 42 E
Cuenca, *Ecuador* ....... **152 D2** 2 50 S 79 9W
Cuenca, *Spain* .......... **34 E2** 40 5N 2 10W
Cuenca □, *Spain* ....... **34 F2** 40 0N 2 0W
Cuenca, Serranía de, *Spain* .............. **34 F3** 39 55N 1 50W
Cuerdo del Pozo, Pantano de la, *Spain* ......... **34 D2** 41 51N 2 44W
Cuernavaca, *Mexico* ..... **147 D5** 18 50N 99 20W
Cuero, *U.S.A.* .......... **139 L6** 29 6N 97 17W
Cuers, *France* .......... **25 E10** 43 14N 6 5 E
Cuervo, *U.S.A.* ......... **139 H2** 35 2N 104 25W
Cuesmes, *Belgium* ...... **21 H3** 50 26N 3 56 E
Cuevas, Cerro, *Bolivia* .. **157 E4** 22 0 S 65 12W
Cuevas del Almanzora, *Spain* ............... **35 H3** 37 18N 1 58W
Cuevo, *Bolivia* ......... **157 E5** 20 15 S 63 30W
Cugir, *Romania* ......... **46 D4** 45 48N 23 25 E
Cuiabá, *Brazil* .......... **157 D6** 15 30 S 56 0W
Cuiabá →, *Brazil* ...... **157 D6** 17 5 S 56 36W
Cuilco, *Guatemala* ...... **148 C1** 15 24N 91 58W
Cuillin Hills, *U.K.* ...... **18 D2** 57 14N 6 15W
Cuillin Sd., *U.K.* ....... **18 D2** 57 4N 6 20W
Cuima, *Angola* ......... **103 E3** 13 25 S 15 45 E
Cuiseaux, *France* ....... **25 B9** 46 30N 5 22 E
Cuité, *Brazil* ........... **154 C4** 6 29 S 36 9W
Cuito →, *Angola* ....... **103 F4** 18 1 S 20 48 E
Cuito Cuanavale, *Angola* **103 F3** 15 10 S 19 10 E
Cuitzeo, L. de, *Mexico* .. **146 D4** 19 55N 101 5W
Cuiuni →, *Brazil* ...... **153 D5** 0 45 S 63 7W
Cuivre →, *U.S.A.* ..... **140 F6** 38 55N 90 44W
Cuivre, West Fork →, *U.S.A.* ............. **140 E6** 39 2N 90 58W
Cujmir, *Romania* ....... **46 E3** 44 13N 22 57 E
Cukai, *Malaysia* ........ **77 K4** 4 13N 103 25 E
Culaba, *Phil.* ........... **71 F5** 11 40N 124 32 E
Culan, *France* .......... **24 B6** 46 34N 2 20 E
Culasi, *Phil.* ........... **71 F4** 11 26N 122 3 E
Culauan, *Phil.* .......... **71 J5** 5 58N 125 40 E
Culbertson, *U.S.A.* ..... **138 A2** 48 9N 104 31W
Culburra, *Australia* ..... **116 C3** 35 50 S 139 58 E
Culcairn, *Australia* ..... **115 F4** 35 41 S 147 3 E
Culebra, Sierra de la, *Spain* ............... **36 D4** 41 55N 6 20W
Culemborg, *Neths.* ...... **20 E6** 51 58N 5 14 E
Culgoa, *Australia* ....... **116 C5** 35 44 S 143 6 E
Culgoa →, *Australia* ... **115 D4** 29 56 S 146 20 E
Culiacán, *Mexico* ....... **146 C3** 24 50N 107 23W
Culiacán →, *Mexico* .... **146 C3** 24 30N 107 42W
Culion, *Phil.* ........... **71 F3** 11 54N 120 1 E
Culiseu →, *Brazil* ...... **157 C7** 12 14 S 53 17W
Cúllar de Baza, *Spain* ... **35 H2** 37 35N 2 34W
Cullarin Ra., *Australia* .. **117 C8** 34 30 S 149 30 E
Cullen, *U.K.* ........... **18 D6** 57 45N 2 50W
Cullen Pt., *Australia* .... **114 A3** 11 57 S 141 54 E
Cullera, *Spain* .......... **35 F4** 39 9N 0 17W
Cullman, *U.S.A.* ........ **135 H2** 34 11N 86 51W
Culloden Moor, *U.K.* .... **18 D4** 57 29N 4 7W
Cullom, *U.S.A.* ......... **141 D8** 40 53N 88 16W
Culoz, *France* .......... **25 C9** 45 47N 5 46 E
Culpataro, *Australia* ..... **116 B6** 33 40 S 144 22 E
Culpeper, *U.S.A.* ....... **134 F7** 38 30N 78 0W
Culuene →, *Brazil* ..... **157 C7** 12 56 S 52 51W
Culver, *U.S.A.* ......... **141 C10** 41 13N 86 25W
Culver, Pt., *Australia* ... **113 F3** 32 54 S 124 43 E
Culverden, *N.Z.* ........ **119 C7** 42 47 S 172 49 E
Cuma, *Angola* .......... **103 E3** 12 52 S 15 5 E
Cumali, *Turkey* ......... **45 H9** 36 42N 27 28 E
Cumaná, *Venezuela* ..... **153 A5** 10 30N 64 5W
Cumare, *Colombia* ...... **152 C3** 0 49N 72 32W
Cumari, *Brazil* ......... **155 E2** 18 16 S 48 11W
Cumberland, *Canada* .... **130 D3** 49 40N 125 0W
Cumberland, *Iowa, U.S.A.* **140 C2** 41 16N 94 52W
Cumberland, *Md., U.S.A.* **134 F6** 39 39N 78 46W
Cumberland, *Wis., U.S.A.* **138 C8** 45 32N 92 1W
Cumberland →, *U.S.A.* . **135 G2** 36 15N 87 0W
Cumberland, C., *Vanuatu* **121 D4** 14 39 S 166 37 E
Cumberland I., *U.S.A.* ... **135 K5** 30 50N 81 25W
Cumberland Is., *Australia* **114 C4** 20 35 S 149 10 E
Cumberland L., *Canada* . **131 C8** 54 3N 102 18W
Cumberland Pen., *Canada* **127 B13** 67 0N 64 0W
Cumberland Plateau, *U.S.A.* ............. **135 H3** 36 0N 85 0W
Cumberland Sd., *Canada* **127 B13** 65 30N 66 0W
Cumborah, *Australia* .... **115 D4** 29 40 S 147 45 E
Cumbres Mayores, *Spain* **37 G4** 38 4N 6 39W
Cumbria □, *U.K.* ....... **16 C5** 54 35N 2 55W
Cumbrian Mts., *U.K.* .... **16 C4** 54 30N 3 0W
Cumbum, *India* ......... **83 G4** 15 40N 79 10 E
Cuminá →, *Brazil* ...... **153 D6** 1 30 S 56 0W
Cuminapanema →, *Brazil* **153 D7** 1 9 S 54 54W
Cummings Mt., *U.S.A.* .. **145 K8** 35 2N 118 34W
Cummins, *Australia* ..... **115 E2** 34 16 S 135 43 E
Cumnock, *Australia* ..... **117 B8** 32 59 S 148 46 E
Cumnock, *U.K.* ......... **18 F4** 55 27N 4 18W
Cumpas, *Mexico* ........ **146 A3** 30 0N 109 48W
Cumplida, Pta., *Canary Is.* **33 F2** 28 50N 17 48W
Çumra, *Turkey* ......... **88 E5** 37 34N 32 45 E
Cuncumén, *Chile* ....... **158 C1** 31 53 S 70 38W
Cundeelee, *Australia* .... **113 F3** 30 43 S 123 26 E
Cunderdin, *Australia* .... **113 F2** 31 37 S 117 12 E
Cundinamarca □, *Colombia* ............. **152 C3** 5 0N 74 0W
Cunene □, *Angola* ...... **103 F3** 16 30 S 15 0 E
Cunene →, *Angola* ..... **103 F2** 17 20 S 11 50 E
Cúneo, *Italy* ........... **38 D4** 44 23N 7 31 E
Cunhinga, *Angola* ....... **103 E3** 12 11 S 16 47 E
Cunillera, I., *Spain* ..... **33 C7** 38 59N 1 13 E
Cunjamba, *Angola* ...... **103 F4** 15 27 S 20 10 E
Cunlhat, *France* ........ **24 C7** 45 38N 3 32 E
Cunnamulla, *Australia* ... **115 D4** 28 2 S 145 38 E
Cuorgnè, *Italy* .......... **38 C4** 45 23N 7 39 E
Cupar, *Canada* ......... **131 C8** 50 57N 104 10W
Cupar, *U.K.* ........... **18 E5** 56 20N 3 3W
Cupica, G. de, *Colombia* **152 B2** 6 25N 77 30W
Ćuprija, *Serbia* ......... **42 D6** 43 57N 21 26 E
Curaçá, *Brazil* .......... **154 C4** 8 59 S 39 54W
Curaçao, *Neth. Ant.* ..... **149 D6** 12 10N 69 0W
Curacautín, *Chile* ....... **160 A2** 38 26 S 71 53W
Curahuara de Carangas, *Bolivia* ............. **156 D4** 17 52 S 68 26W
Curanilahue, *Chile* ...... **158 D1** 37 29 S 73 28W
Curaray →, *Peru* ....... **152 D3** 2 20 S 74 5W
Curatabaca, *Venezuela* .. **153 B5** 6 19N 62 51W
Cure →, *France* ........ **23 E10** 47 40N 3 41 E
Curepto, *Chile* ......... **158 D1** 35 8 S 72 1W
Curiapo, *Venezuela* ..... **153 B5** 8 33N 61 5W
Curicó, *Chile* .......... **158 C1** 34 55 S 71 20W
Curicó □, *Chile* ........ **158 C1** 34 50 S 71 15W
Curicuriari →, *Brazil* ... **152 D4** 0 14 S 66 48W
Curimatá, *Brazil* ........ **154 D3** 10 2 S 44 17W
Curiplaya, *Colombia* ..... **152 C3** 0 16N 74 52W
Curitiba, *Brazil* ......... **159 B6** 25 20 S 49 10W
Currabubula, *Australia* .. **117 A9** 31 16 S 150 44 E
Currais Novos, *Brazil* ... **154 C4** 6 13 S 36 30W
Curralinho, *Brazil* ...... **154 B2** 1 45 S 49 46W
Currant, *U.S.A.* ........ **142 G6** 38 51N 115 32W
Curranyalpa, *Australia* ... **117 A6** 30 53 S 144 39 E
Curraweena, *Australia* ... **117 A6** 30 47 S 145 54 E
Currawilla, *Australia* .... **114 D3** 25 10 S 141 20 E
Current →, *U.S.A.* ..... **139 G9** 36 15N 90 55W
Currie, *Australia* ........ **114 F3** 39 56 S 143 53 E
Currie, *U.S.A.* ......... **142 F6** 40 16N 114 45W
Currie, Mt., *S. Africa* ... **105 E4** 30 29 S 29 21 E
Currituck Sd., *U.S.A.* ... **135 G8** 36 20N 75 52W
Cursole, *Somali Rep.* .... **108 D3** 2 14N 45 25 E
Curtea de Argeş, *Romania* **46 D5** 45 12N 24 42 E
Curtis, *Spain* ........... **36 B2** 43 7N 8 4W
Curtis, *U.S.A.* ......... **138 E4** 40 38N 100 31W
Curtis Group, *Australia* .. **114 F4** 39 30 S 146 37 E
Curtis I., *Australia* ...... **114 C5** 23 35 S 151 10 E
Curuá →, *Pará, Brazil* .. **153 D7** 2 24 S 54 5W
Curuá →, *Pará, Brazil* .. **157 B7** 5 23 S 54 22W
Curuá, I., *Brazil* ........ **154 A1** 0 48N 50 10W
Curuaés →, *Brazil* ...... **157 B7** 7 30 S 54 45W
Curuápanema →, *Brazil* **153 D6** 2 25 S 55 2W
Curuçá, *Brazil* .......... **154 B2** 0 43 S 47 50W
Curuguaty, *Paraguay* .... **159 A4** 24 31 S 55 42W
Çürüksu Çayi →, *Turkey* **49 G4** 37 27N 27 11 E
Curup, *Indonesia* ....... **74 C2** 4 26 S 102 13 E
Curupira, Serra, *S. Amer.* **153 C5** 1 25N 64 30W
Cururu →, *Brazil* ...... **157 B6** 7 12 S 58 3W
Cururupu, *Brazil* ....... **154 B3** 1 50 S 44 50W
Curuzú Cuatiá, *Argentina* **158 B4** 29 50 S 58 5W
Curvelo, *Brazil* ......... **155 E3** 18 45 S 44 27W
Curyo, *Australia* ........ **116 C5** 35 50 S 142 47 E
Cushing, *U.S.A.* ........ **139 H6** 35 59N 96 46W
Cushing, Mt., *Canada* ... **130 B3** 57 35N 126 57W
Cusihuiriáchic, *Mexico* .. **146 B3** 28 10N 106 50W
Cusna, Monte, *Italy* ..... **38 D7** 44 13N 10 25 E
Cusset, *France* ......... **24 B7** 46 8N 3 28 E
Custer, *U.S.A.* ......... **138 D3** 43 46N 103 36W
Cut Bank, *U.S.A.* ....... **142 B7** 48 38N 112 20W
Cutervo, *Peru* .......... **156 B2** 6 25 S 78 55W
Cuthbert, *U.S.A.* ....... **135 K3** 31 46N 84 48W
Cutler, *U.S.A.* ......... **144 J7** 36 31N 119 17W
Cutral-Có, *Argentina* .... **160 A3** 38 58 S 69 15W
Cutro, *Italy* ............ **41 C9** 39 1N 16 58 E
Cuttaburra →, *Australia* **115 D3** 29 43 S 144 22 E
Cuttack, *India* .......... **82 D7** 20 25N 85 57 E
Cuvelai, *Angola* ........ **103 F3** 15 44 S 15 48 E
Cuvier, C., *Australia* .... **113 D1** 23 14 S 113 22 E
Cuvier I., *N.Z.* ......... **118 C4** 36 27 S 175 50 E
Cuxhaven, *Germany* ..... **26 B4** 53 51N 8 41 E
Cuyabeno, *Ecuador* ..... **152 D2** 0 16 S 75 53W
Cuyahoga Falls, *U.S.A.* .. **136 E3** 41 8N 81 29W
Cuyapo, *Phil.* .......... **70 D3** 15 46N 120 40 E
Cuyo, *Phil.* ............ **71 F3** 10 50N 121 5 E
Cuyo East Pass, *Phil.* ... **71 F3** 11 0N 121 28 E
Cuyo I., *Phil.* .......... **71 F3** 10 51N 121 2 E
Cuyo West Pass, *Phil.* ... **71 F3** 11 0N 120 30 E
Cuyuni →, *Guyana* ..... **153 B6** 6 23N 58 41W
Cuzco, *Bolivia* ......... **156 E4** 20 0 S 66 50W
Cuzco, *Peru* ........... **156 C3** 13 32 S 72 0W
Cuzco □, *Peru* ......... **156 C3** 13 31 S 71 59W
Čvrsnica, *Bos.-H.* ...... **42 D2** 43 36N 17 35 E
Cwmbran, *U.K.* ........ **17 F4** 51 39N 3 3W
Cyangugu, *Rwanda* ..... **106 C2** 2 29 S 28 54 E
Cybinka, *Poland* ........ **47 C1** 52 12N 14 46 E
Cyclades = Kikládhes, *Greece* .............. **45 G6** 37 20N 24 30 E
Cygnet, *Australia* ...... **114 G4** 43 8 S 147 1 E
Cynthiana, *U.S.A.* ..... **141 F12** 38 23N 84 18W
Cypress Hills, *Canada* ... **131 D7** 49 40N 109 30W
Cyprus ■, *Asia* ........ **32 E12** 35 0N 33 0 E
Cyrenaica, *Libya* ....... **92 C6** 27 0N 23 0 E
Cyrene = Shaḥḥāt, *Libya* **96 B4** 32 48N 21 54 E
Czaplinek, *Poland* ...... **47 B3** 53 34N 16 14 E
Czar, *Canada* .......... **131 C6** 52 27N 110 50W
Czarna →, Piotrkow Trybunalski, *Poland* ............. **47 D6** 51 18N 19 55 E
Czarna →, *Tarnobrzeg, Poland* .............. **47 E8** 50 3N 21 21 E
Czarna Woda, *Poland* ... **47 B5** 53 51N 18 6 E
Czarne, *Poland* ........ **47 B3** 53 42N 16 58 E
Czarnków, *Poland* ...... **47 C3** 52 55N 16 38 E
Czech Rep. ■, *Europe* .. **30 B7** 50 0N 15 0 E
Czechowice-Dziedzice, *Poland* ............. **31 B11** 49 54N 18 59 E
Czeladz, *Poland* ........ **47 E6** 50 16N 19 2 E
Czempiń, *Poland* ....... **47 C3** 52 9N 16 33 E
Czeremcha, *Poland* ..... **47 C10** 52 31N 23 21 E
Czersk, *Poland* ......... **47 B4** 53 46N 17 58 E
Czerwieńsk, *Poland* ..... **47 C2** 52 1N 15 13 E
Czerwionka, *Poland* ..... **31 A11** 50 7N 18 37 E
Częstochowa, *Poland* .... **47 E6** 50 49N 19 7 E
Częstochowa □, *Poland* . **47 E6** 50 45N 19 0 E
Człopa, *Poland* ......... **47 B3** 53 6N 16 6 E
Człuchów, *Poland* ...... **47 B4** 53 41N 17 22 E
Czyzew, *Poland* ........ **47 C9** 52 48N 22 19 E


# D


Da →, *Vietnam* ........ **76 B5** 21 15N 105 20 E
Da Hinggan Ling, *China* . **65 B7** 48 0N 121 0 E
Da Lat, *Vietnam* ........ **77 G7** 11 56N 108 25 E
Da Nang, *Vietnam* ...... **76 D7** 16 4N 108 13 E
Da Qaidam, *China* ...... **64 C4** 37 50N 95 15 E
Da Yunhe →, *China* .... **67 G11** 34 25N 120 5 E
Da'an, *China* .......... **67 B13** 45 30N 124 7 E
Daap, *Phil.* ............ **71 H4** 7 4N 122 12 E
Daarlerveen, *Neths.* ..... **20 D9** 52 26N 6 34 E
Dab'a, Râs el, *Egypt* .... **94 H6** 31 3N 28 31 E
Daba Shan, *China* ...... **68 B7** 32 0N 109 0 E
Dabai, *Nigeria* ......... **101 C6** 11 25N 5 15 E
Dabajuro, *Venezuela* .... **152 A3** 11 2N 70 40W
Dabakala, *Ivory C.* ..... **100 D4** 8 15N 4 20W
Dabaro, *Somali Rep.* .... **108 C3** 6 21N 48 43 E
Dabeiba, *Colombia* ..... **152 B2** 7 1N 76 16W
Dabhoi, *India* .......... **80 H5** 22 10N 73 20 E
Dąbie, *Konin, Poland* ... **47 C5** 52 5N 18 50 E
Dąbie, *Szczecin, Poland* . **47 B1** 53 27N 14 45 E
Dabie Shan, *China* ..... **69 B10** 31 20N 115 20 E
Dabo, *Indonesia* ........ **74 C2** 0 30 S 104 33 E
Dabola, *Guinea* ........ **100 C2** 10 50N 11 5W
Dabou, *Ivory C.* ....... **100 D4** 5 20N 4 23W
Daboya, *Ghana* ........ **101 D4** 9 30N 1 20W
Dabrowa Górnicza, *Poland* .............. **47 E6** 50 15N 19 10 E
Dabrowa Tarnówska, *Poland* .............. **31 A13** 50 10N 20 59 E
Dąbrówno, *Poland* ..... **47 B7** 53 27N 20 2 E
Dabu, *China* .......... **69 E11** 24 22N 116 41 E
Dabung, *Malaysia* ...... **77 K4** 5 23N 102 1 E
Dabus →, *Ethiopia* .... **95 E4** 10 48N 35 10 E
Dacato →, *Ethiopia* .... **95 F5** 7 25N 42 40 E
Dacca = Dhaka, *Bangla.* **78 D3** 23 43N 90 26 E
Dacca = Dhaka □, *Bangla.* ............. **78 C3** 24 25N 90 25 E
Dachau, *Germany* ...... **27 G7** 48 16N 11 27 E
Dadale, *Solomon Is.* .... **121 M10** 8 7 S 159 6 E
Dadanawa, *Guyana* ..... **153 C6** 2 50N 59 30W
Daday, *Turkey* ......... **52 F5** 41 28N 33 27 E
Dade City, *U.S.A.* ...... **135 L4** 28 22N 82 11W
Dades, Oued →, *Morocco* ............ **98 B3** 30 58N 6 44W
Dadiya, *Nigeria* ........ **101 D7** 9 35N 11 24 E
Dadra and Nagar Haveli □, *India* ...... **82 D1** 20 5N 73 0 E
Dadri = Charkhi Dadri, *India* ............... **80 E7** 28 37N 76 17 E
Dadu, *Pakistan* ........ **79 D2** 26 45N 67 45 E
Dadu He →, *China* .... **68 C4** 29 31N 103 46 E
Dăeni, *Romania* ........ **46 E9** 44 51N 28 10 E
Daet, *Phil.* ............ **70 D4** 14 2N 122 55 E
Dafang, *China* ......... **68 D5** 27 9N 105 39 E
Dagana, *Senegal* ....... **100 B1** 16 30N 15 35W
Dagash, *Sudan* ........ **94 D3** 19 19N 33 25 E
Dagestanskiye Ogni, *Russia* ............... **53 E13** 42 6N 48 12 E
Dagg Sd., *N.Z.* ........ **119 F1** 45 23 S 166 45 E
Daggett, *U.S.A.* ....... **145 L10** 34 52N 116 52W
Daghestan Republic □, *Russia* ............... **53 E12** 42 30N 47 0 E
Daghfeli, *Sudan* ....... **94 D3** 19 18N 32 40 E
Dagö = Hiiumaa, *Estonia* **50 B3** 58 50N 22 45 E
Dagu, *China* .......... **67 E9** 38 59N 117 40 E
Dagua, *Papua N. G.* .... **120 B2** 3 27 S 143 20 E
Daguan, *China* ........ **68 D4** 27 43N 103 56 E
Dagupan, *Phil.* ........ **70 C3** 16 3N 120 20 E
Dahab, *Egypt* ......... **94 B3** 28 31N 34 31 E
Dahlak Kebir, *Eritrea* ... **90 D3** 15 50N 40 10 E
Dahlenburg, *Germany* ... **26 B6** 53 11N 10 43 E
Dahlgren, *U.S.A.* ...... **141 F8** 38 12N 88 41W
Dahlonega, *U.S.A.* ..... **135 H4** 34 32N 83 59W
Dahme, *Germany* ...... **26 D9** 51 51N 13 25 E
Dahod, *India* .......... **80 H6** 22 50N 74 15 E
Dahomey = Benin ■, *Africa* .............. **101 D5** 10 0N 2 0 E
Dahong Shan, *China* .... **69 B9** 31 25N 113 0 E
Dahra, *Senegal* ........ **100 B1** 15 22N 15 30W
Dahra, Massif de, *Algeria* **99 A5** 36 7N 1 21 E
Daḥy, Nafūd ad, *Si. Arabia* ........... **86 B4** 22 0N 45 25 E
Dai Hao, *Vietnam* ...... **76 C6** 18 1N 106 25 E
Dai-Sen, *Japan* ........ **62 B5** 35 22N 133 32 E
Dai Shan, *China* ....... **69 B14** 30 25N 122 10 E
Dai Xian, *China* ....... **66 E7** 39 4N 112 58 E
Daicheng, *China* ....... **66 E9** 38 42N 116 38 E
Daigo, *Japan* .......... **63 A12** 36 46N 140 21 E
Daimanji-San, *Japan* .... **62 A5** 36 14N 133 20 E
Daimiel, *Spain* ........ **35 F1** 39 5N 3 35W
Daingean, *Ireland* ...... **19 C4** 53 18N 7 15W
Dainkog, *China* ........ **68 A1** 32 30N 97 58 E
Daintree, *Australia* ..... **114 B4** 16 20 S 145 20 E
Daiō-Misaki, *Japan* .... **63 C8** 34 15N 136 45 E
Dairût, *Egypt* ......... **94 B3** 27 34N 30 43 E
Daisetsu-Zan, *Japan* .... **60 C11** 43 30N 142 57 E
Daitari, *India* ......... **82 D7** 21 10N 85 46 E
Daito, *Japan* .......... **62 B4** 35 19N 132 58 E
Dajarra, *Australia* ..... **114 C2** 21 42 S 139 30 E
Dajia, *Taiwan* ......... **69 E13** 24 22N 120 37 E
Dajin Chuan →, *China* . **68 B3** 31 16N 101 59 E
Dak Dam, *Cambodia* .... **76 F6** 12 20N 107 21 E
Dak Nhe, *Vietnam* ..... **76 E6** 15 28N 107 48 E
Dak Pek, *Vietnam* ...... **76 E6** 15 4N 107 44 E
Dak Song, *Vietnam* ..... **77 F6** 12 19N 107 35 E
Dak Sui, *Vietnam* ...... **76 E6** 14 55N 107 43 E
Dakar, *Senegal* ........ **100 C1** 14 34N 17 29W
Dakhla, *W. Sahara* ..... **98 D1** 23 50N 15 53W
Dakhla, El Wâhât el-, *Egypt* ............... **94 B2** 25 30N 28 50 E
Dakhovskaya, *Russia* ... **53 D9** 44 13N 40 13 E
Dakingari, *Nigeria* ...... **101 C5** 11 37N 4 1 E
Dakor, *India* .......... **80 H5** 22 45N 73 11 E
Dakoro, *Niger* ......... **101 C6** 14 31N 6 46 E
Dakota City, *Iowa, U.S.A.* **140 B2** 42 43N 94 12W
Dakota City, *Nebr., U.S.A.* .............. **138 D6** 42 25N 96 25W
Đakovica, *Serbia* ....... **42 E5** 42 22N 20 26 E
Đakovo, *Croatia* ....... **42 B3** 45 19N 18 24 E
Dala, *Angola* .......... **103 E4** 11 3 S 20 17 E
Dala, *Solomon Is.* ...... **121 M11** 8 30 S 160 41 E
Dalaba, *Guinea* ........ **100 C2** 10 42N 12 15W
Dalachi, *China* ........ **66 F3** 36 48N 105 0 E
Dalaguete, *Phil.* ....... **71 G4** 9 46N 123 32 E
Dalai Nur, *China* ...... **66 C9** 43 20N 116 45 E
Dālakī, *Iran* .......... **85 D6** 29 26N 51 17 E
Dalälven, *Sweden* ...... **13 F14** 60 12N 16 43 E
Dalaman, *Turkey* ...... **88 E3** 36 48N 28 47 E
Dalaman →, *Turkey* .... **88 E3** 36 41N 28 43 E
Dalandzadgad, *Mongolia* **66 C3** 43 27N 104 30 E
Dalanganem Is., *Phil.* ... **71 F3** 10 40N 120 17 E
Dalarö, *Sweden* ........ **13 G15** 59 8N 18 24 E
Dalat, *Malaysia* ........ **75 B4** 2 44N 111 56 E
Dālbandīn, *Pakistan* .... **79 C2** 29 0N 64 23 E
Dalbeattie, *U.K.* ....... **18 G5** 54 55N 3 50W
Dalbosjön, *Sweden* ..... **15 F6** 58 40N 12 45 E
Dalby, *Australia* ....... **115 D5** 27 10 S 151 17 E
Dalby, *Sweden* ........ **15 J7** 55 40N 13 22 E
Dale, *U.S.A.* .......... **141 F10** 38 10N 86 59W
Dalen, *Neths.* ......... **20 C9** 52 42N 6 46 E
Dalen, *Norway* ........ **14 E2** 59 26N 8 0 E
Dalet, *Burma* ......... **78 F4** 19 59N 93 51 E
Daletme, *Burma* ....... **78 E4** 21 36N 92 46 E
Daleville, *U.S.A.* ...... **141 D11** 40 7N 85 33W
Dalfsen, *Neths.* ........ **20 C8** 52 31N 6 16 E
Dalga, *Egypt* .......... **94 B3** 27 39N 30 41 E
Dalgān, *Iran* .......... **85 E8** 27 31N 59 19 E

190 Dalhart


Dalhart, *U.S.A.* 139 G3 36 4N 102 31W
Dalhousie, *Canada* 129 C6 48 5N 66 26W
Dalhousie, *India* 80 C6 32 38N 75 58 E
Dali, *Shaanxi, China* 66 G5 34 48N 109 58 E
Dali, *Yunnan, China* 68 E3 25 40N 100 10 E
Dalian, *China* 67 E11 38 50N 121 40 E
Daliang Shan, *China* 68 D4 28 0N 102 45 E
Dalias, *Spain* 35 J2 36 49N 2 52W
Daling He →, *China* 67 D11 40 55N 121 40 E
Dāliyat el Karmel, *Israel* 91 C4 32 43N 35 2 E
Dalj, *Croatia* 42 B3 45 29N 18 59 E
Dalkeith, *U.K.* 18 F5 55 54N 3 5W
Dall I., *U.S.A.* 130 C2 54 59N 133 25W
Dallarnil, *Australia* 115 D5 25 19 S 152 2 E
Dallas, *Oreg., U.S.A.* 142 D2 44 55N 123 19W
Dallas, *Tex., U.S.A.* 139 J6 32 47N 96 49W
Dallas Center, *U.S.A.* 140 C3 41 41N 93 58W
Dallas City, *U.S.A.* 140 D5 40 38N 91 10W
Dallol, *Ethiopia* 95 E5 14 14N 40 17 E
Dalmacija = Dalmatia □, *Croatia* 42 D2 43 20N 17 0 E
Dalmatia □, *Croatia* 42 D2 43 20N 17 0 E
Dalmatovo, *Russia* 54 C8 56 16N 62 56 E
Dalmellington, *U.K.* 18 F4 55 20N 4 25W
Dalnegorsk, *Russia* 57 E14 44 32N 135 33 E
Dalnerechensk, *Russia* 57 E14 45 50N 133 40 E
Daloa, *Ivory C.* 100 D3 7 0N 6 30W
Dalou Shan, *China* 68 C6 28 15N 107 0 E
Dalsjöfors, *Sweden* 15 G7 57 46N 13 5 E
Dalskog, *Sweden* 15 F6 58 44N 12 18 E
Daltenganj, *India* 81 G11 24 0N 84 4 E
Dalton, *Canada* 128 C3 48 11N 84 1W
Dalton, *Ga., U.S.A.* 135 H3 34 46N 84 58W
Dalton, *Mass., U.S.A.* 137 D11 42 28N 73 11W
Dalton, *Nebr., U.S.A.* 138 E3 41 25N 102 58W
Dalton Iceberg Tongue, *Antarctica* 7 C9 66 15 S 121 30 E
Dalupiri I., *Cagayan, Phil.* 70 B3 19 5N 121 12 E
Dalupiri I., *N. Samar, Phil.* 70 E5 12 25N 124 16 E
Dalvík, *Iceland* 12 D4 65 58N 18 32W
Daly →, *Australia* 112 B5 13 35 S 130 19 E
Daly City, *U.S.A.* 144 H4 37 42N 122 28W
Daly L., *Canada* 131 B7 56 32N 105 39W
Daly Waters, *Australia* 114 B1 16 15 S 133 24 E
Dam Doi, *Vietnam* 77 H5 8 50N 105 12 E
Dam Ha, *Vietnam* 76 B6 21 21N 107 36 E
Daman, *India* 82 D1 20 25N 72 57 E
Daman □, *India* 82 D1 20 25N 72 58 E
Dāmaneh, *Iran* 85 C6 33 1N 50 29 E
Damanhûr, *Egypt* 94 H7 31 0N 30 30 E
Damanzhuang, *China* 66 E9 38 5N 116 35 E
Damar, *Indonesia* 72 C3 7 7 S 128 40 E
Damara, *C.A.R.* 102 B3 4 58N 18 42 E
Damaraland, *Namibia* 104 C2 21 0 S 17 0 E
Damascus = Dimashq, *Syria* 91 B5 33 30N 36 18 E
Damaturu, *Nigeria* 101 C7 11 45N 11 55 E
Damāvand, *Iran* 85 C7 35 47N 52 0 E
Damāvand, Qolleh-ye, *Iran* 85 C7 35 56N 52 10 E
Damba, *Angola* 103 D3 6 44 S 15 20 E
Dame Marie, *Haiti* 149 C5 18 36N 74 26W
Dāmghān, *Iran* 85 B7 36 10N 54 17 E
Dămienesti, *Romania* 46 C8 46 44N 27 1 E
Damietta = Dumyât, *Egypt* 94 H7 31 24N 31 48 E
Daming, *China* 66 F8 36 15N 115 6 E
Damīr Qābū, *Syria* 84 B4 36 58N 41 51 E
Dammam = Ad Dammām, *Si. Arabia* 85 E6 26 20N 50 5 E
Dammarie, *France* 22 D8 48 20N 1 30 E
Dammartin-en-Goële, *France* 23 C9 49 3N 2 41 E
Dammastock, *Switz.* 29 C6 46 38N 8 24 E
Damme, *Germany* 26 C4 52 32N 8 12 E
Damodar →, *India* 81 H12 23 17N 87 35 E
Damoh, *India* 81 H8 23 50N 79 28 E
Damous, *Algeria* 99 A5 36 31N 1 42 E
Dampier, *Australia* 112 D2 20 41 S 116 42 E
Dampier, Selat, *Indonesia* 73 B4 0 40 S 131 0 E
Dampier Arch., *Australia* 112 D2 20 38 S 116 32 E
Dampier Str., *Papua N. G.* 120 C5 5 50 S 148 0 E
Damqawt, *Yemen* 87 C6 16 34N 52 50 E
Damrei, Chuor Phnum, *Cambodia* 77 G4 11 30N 103 0 E
Damville, *France* 22 D8 48 51N 1 5 E
Damvillers, *France* 23 C12 49 20N 5 21 E
Dan-Gulbi, *Nigeria* 101 C6 11 40N 6 15 E
Dana, *Indonesia* 72 D2 11 0 S 122 52 E
Dana, L., *Canada* 128 B4 50 53N 77 20W
Dana, Mt., *U.S.A.* 144 H7 37 54N 119 12W
Danakil Depression, *Ethiopia* 95 E5 12 45N 41 0 E
Danao, *Cebu, Phil.* 71 F5 10 31N 124 1 E
Danao, *Sorsogon, Phil.* 70 E4 12 44N 123 51 E
Danbury, *U.S.A.* 137 E11 41 24N 73 28W
Danby L., *U.S.A.* 143 J6 34 13N 115 5W
Dand, *Afghan.* 80 D1 31 28N 65 32 E
Dandaragan, *Australia* 113 F2 30 40 S 115 40 E
Dandeldhura, *Nepal* 81 E9 29 20N 80 35 E
Dandenong, *Australia* 117 E6 38 0 S 145 15 E
Dandong, *China* 67 D13 40 10N 124 20 E
Danfeng, *China* 66 H6 33 45N 110 25 E
Danforth, *U.S.A.* 129 C6 45 40N 67 52W
Dangan Liedao, *China* 69 F10 22 2N 114 8 E
Dangara, *Tajikistan* 55 D4 38 6N 69 22 E
Danger Is. = Pukapuka, *Cook Is.* 123 J11 10 53 S 165 49W
Danger Pt., *S. Africa* 104 E2 34 40 S 19 17 E
Dangla, *Ethiopia* 95 E4 11 18N 36 56 E
Dangora, *Nigeria* 101 C6 11 30N 8 7 E
Dangrek, Phnom, *Thailand* 76 E5 14 15N 105 0 E
Dangriga, *Belize* 147 D7 17 0N 88 13W
Dangshan, *China* 66 G9 34 27N 116 22 E
Dangtu, *China* 69 B12 31 32N 118 25 E
Dangyang, *China* 69 B8 30 52N 111 44 E
Daniel, *U.S.A.* 142 E8 42 52N 110 4W
Daniel's Harbour, *Canada* 129 B8 50 13N 57 35W
Danielskuil, *S. Africa* 104 D3 28 11 S 23 33 E
Danielson, *U.S.A.* 137 E13 41 48N 71 53W
Danilov, *Russia* 51 B12 58 16N 40 13 E
Danilovgrad, *Montenegro* 42 E4 42 38N 19 9 E
Danilovka, *Russia* 51 F14 50 25N 44 12 E
Daning, *China* 66 F6 36 28N 110 45 E
Danissa, *Kenya* 106 B5 3 15N 40 58 E
Danja, *Nigeria* 101 C6 11 21N 7 30 E
Danje-ia-Menha, *Angola* 103 D2 9 32 S 14 39 E
Dank, *Oman* 87 B7 23 33N 56 16 E
Dankalwa, *Nigeria* 101 C7 11 52N 12 12 E
Dankama, *Nigeria* 101 C6 13 20N 7 44 E
Dankov, *Russia* 51 E11 53 20N 39 5 E
Danleng, *China* 68 B4 30 1N 103 31 E
Danlí, *Honduras* 148 D2 14 4N 86 35W
Dannemora, *Sweden* 13 F14 60 12N 17 51 E
Dannemora, *U.S.A.* 137 B11 44 43N 73 44W
Dannenberg, *Germany* 26 B7 53 7N 11 4 E
Dannevirke, *N.Z.* 118 G5 40 12 S 176 8 E
Dannhauser, *S. Africa* 105 D5 28 0 S 30 3 E
Danot, *Ethiopia* 108 C3 7 33N 45 17 E
Danshui, *Taiwan* 69 E13 25 12N 121 25 E
Dansville, *U.S.A.* 136 D7 42 34N 77 42W
Dantan, *India* 81 J12 21 57N 87 20 E
Dante, *Somali Rep.* 90 E5 10 25N 51 16 E
Danube →, *Europe* 46 D10 45 20N 29 40 E
Danubyu, *Burma* 78 G5 17 15N 95 35 E
Danukandi, *Bangla.* 78 D3 23 32N 90 43 E
Danvers, *U.S.A.* 137 D14 42 34N 70 56W
Danville, *Ill., U.S.A.* 141 D9 40 8N 87 37W
Danville, *Ind., U.S.A.* 141 E10 39 46N 86 32W
Danville, *Ky., U.S.A.* 141 G12 37 39N 84 46W
Danville, *Va., U.S.A.* 135 G6 36 36N 79 23W
Danyang, *China* 69 B12 32 0N 119 31 E
Danzhai, *China* 68 D6 26 11N 107 48 E
Danzig = Gdańsk, *Poland* 47 A5 54 22N 18 40 E
Dao, *Antique, Phil.* 71 F3 10 30N 121 57 E
Dao, *Capiz, Phil.* 71 F4 11 24N 122 41 E
Dão →, *Portugal* 36 E2 40 20N 8 11W
Dao Xian, *China* 69 E8 25 36N 111 31 E
Daocheng, *China* 68 C3 29 0N 100 10 E
Daora, *W. Sahara* 98 C2 27 5N 12 59W
Daoud = Aïn Beïda, *Algeria* 99 A6 35 50N 7 29 E
Daoulas, *France* 22 D2 48 22N 4 17W
Dapa, *Phil.* 71 G6 9 46N 126 3 E
Dapitan, *Phil.* 71 G4 8 39N 123 25 E
Dapong, *Togo* 101 C5 10 55N 0 16 E
Daqing Shan, *China* 66 D6 40 40N 111 0 E
Daqu Shan, *China* 69 B14 30 25N 122 20 E
Dar es Salaam, *Tanzania* 106 D4 6 50 S 39 12 E
Dar Mazār, *Iran* 85 D8 29 14N 57 20 E
Dar'ā, *Syria* 91 C5 32 36N 36 7 E
Dar'ā □, *Syria* 91 C5 32 55N 36 10 E
Dārāb, *Iran* 85 D7 28 50N 54 30 E
Darabani, *Romania* 46 A7 48 10N 26 39 E
Daraj, *Libya* 96 B2 30 10N 10 28 E
Dārān, *Iran* 85 C6 32 59N 50 24 E
Daraut Kurgan, *Kirghizia* 55 D6 39 33N 72 11 E
Daravica, *Serbia* 42 E5 42 32N 20 8 E
Daraw, *Egypt* 94 C3 24 22N 32 51 E
Dārayyā, *Syria* 91 B5 33 28N 36 15 E
Darazo, *Nigeria* 101 C7 11 1N 10 24 E
Darband, *Pakistan* 80 B5 34 20N 72 50 E
Darband, Kūh-e, *Iran* 85 D8 31 34N 57 8 E
Darbhanga, *India* 81 F11 26 15N 85 55 E
Darburruk, *Somali Rep.* 108 C2 9 44N 44 31 E
Darby, *U.S.A.* 142 C6 46 1N 114 11W
Darda, *Croatia* 42 B3 45 40N 18 41 E
Dardanelle, *Ark., U.S.A.* 139 H8 35 13N 93 9W
Dardanelle, *Calif., U.S.A.* 144 G7 38 20N 119 50W
Dardanelles = Çanakkale Boğazı, *Turkey* 44 D8 40 17N 26 32 E
Darende, *Turkey* 88 D7 38 31N 37 30 E
Dārestān, *Iran* 85 D8 29 9N 58 42 E
Darfield, *N.Z.* 119 D7 43 29 S 172 7 E
Darfo, *Italy* 38 C7 45 52N 10 11 E
Dârfûr, *Sudan* 92 E6 13 40N 24 0 E
Dargai, *Pakistan* 79 B3 34 25N 71 55 E
Dargan Ata, *Uzbekistan* 56 E7 40 29N 62 10 E
Dargaville, *N.Z.* 118 B2 35 57 S 173 52 E
Darhan Muminggan Lianheqi, *China* 66 D6 41 40N 110 28 E
Dari, *Sudan* 95 F3 5 48N 30 26 E
Darién, G. del, *Colombia* 152 B2 9 0N 77 0W
Darién, Serranía del, *Colombia* 152 B2 8 30N 77 30W
Dariganga, *Mongolia* 66 B7 45 21N 113 45 E
Darinskoye, *Kazakhstan* 54 F2 51 20N 51 44 E
Darjeeling = Darjiling, *India* 81 F13 27 3N 88 18 E
Darjiling, *India* 81 F13 27 3N 88 18 E
Dark Cove, *Canada* 129 C9 48 47N 54 13W
Darkan, *Australia* 113 F2 33 20 S 116 43 E
Darke Peak, *Australia* 116 B2 33 27 S 136 12 E
Darkhazīneh, *Iran* 85 D6 31 54N 48 39 E
Darkot Pass, *Pakistan* 81 A5 36 45N 73 26 E
Darling →, *Australia* 116 C4 34 4 S 141 54 E
Darling Downs, *Australia* 115 D5 27 30 S 150 30 E
Darling Ra., *Australia* 113 F2 32 30 S 116 0 E
Darlington, *U.K.* 16 C6 54 33N 1 33W
Darlington, *S.C., U.S.A.* 135 H6 34 18N 79 52W
Darlington, *Wis., U.S.A.* 140 B6 42 41N 90 7W
Darlot, L., *Australia* 113 E3 27 48 S 121 35 E
Darłowo, *Poland* 47 A3 54 25N 16 25 E
Dărmănești, *Romania* 46 C7 46 21N 26 33 E
Darmstadt, *Germany* 27 F4 49 51N 8 40 E
Darnah, *Libya* 96 B4 32 40N 22 35 E
Darnah □, *Libya* 96 B4 31 0N 23 40 E
Darnall, *S. Africa* 105 D5 29 23 S 31 18 E
Darnétal, *France* 22 C8 49 25N 1 10 E
Darney, *France* 23 D13 48 5N 6 2 E
Darnick, *Australia* 116 B5 32 48 S 143 38 E
Darnley, C., *Antarctica* 7 C6 68 0 S 69 0 E
Darnley B., *Canada* 126 B7 69 30N 123 30W
Daroca, *Spain* 34 D3 41 9N 1 25W
Darr, *Australia* 114 C3 23 13 S 144 7 E
Darr →, *Australia* 114 C3 23 39 S 143 50 E
Darran Mts., *N.Z.* 119 E2 44 37 S 167 59 E
Darrington, *U.S.A.* 142 B3 48 15N 121 36W
Darsana, *Bangla.* 78 D2 23 35N 88 48 E
Darsi, *India* 83 G4 15 46N 79 44 E
Darsser Ort, *Germany* 26 A8 54 29N 12 31 E
Dart →, *U.K.* 17 G4 50 24N 3 36W
Dart, C., *Antarctica* 7 D14 73 6 S 126 20W
Dartmoor, *Australia* 116 D4 37 56 S 141 19 E
Dartmoor, *U.K.* 17 G4 50 36N 4 0W
Dartmouth, *Australia* 114 C3 23 31 S 144 44 E
Dartmouth, *Canada* 129 D7 44 40N 63 30W
Dartmouth, *U.K.* 17 G4 50 21N 3 35W
Dartmouth, L., *Australia* 115 D4 26 4 S 145 18 E
Dartuch, C., *Spain* 33 B10 39 55N 3 49 E
Daru, *Papua N. G.* 120 E2 9 3 S 143 13 E
Daruvar, *Croatia* 42 B2 45 35N 17 14 E
Darvaza, *Turkmenistan* 56 E6 40 11N 58 24 E
Darvel, Teluk, *Malaysia* 75 B5 4 50N 118 20 E
Darwha, *India* 82 D3 20 15N 77 45 E
Darwin, *Australia* 112 B5 12 25 S 130 51 E
Darwin, *U.S.A.* 145 J9 36 15N 117 35W
Darwin, Mt., *Chile* 160 D3 54 47 S 69 55W
Darwin River, *Australia* 112 B5 12 50 S 130 58 E
Daryapur, *India* 82 D3 20 55N 77 20 E
Daryoi Amu = Amudarya →, *Uzbekistan* 56 E6 43 40N 59 0 E
Dās, *U.A.E.* 85 E7 25 20N 53 30 E
Dashetai, *China* 66 D5 41 0N 109 5 E
Dashkesan, *Azerbaijan* 53 F12 40 25N 46 0 E
Dasht, *Iran* 85 B8 37 17N 56 7 E
Dasht →, *Pakistan* 79 D1 25 10N 61 40 E
Dasht-i-Nawar, *Afghan.* 80 C3 33 52N 68 0 E
Daska, *Pakistan* 80 C6 32 20N 74 20 E
Dassa-Zoume, *Benin* 101 D5 7 46N 2 14 E
Dasseneiland, *S. Africa* 104 E2 33 25 S 18 3 E
Datça, *Turkey* 45 H9 36 46N 27 40 E
Datia, *India* 81 G8 25 39N 78 27 E
Datian, *China* 69 E11 25 40N 117 50 E
Datong, *Anhui, China* 69 B11 30 48N 117 44 E
Datong, *Shanxi, China* 66 D7 40 6N 113 18 E
Dattapur = Dhamangaon, *India* 82 D4 20 45N 78 15 E
Datu, Tanjung, *Indonesia* 75 B3 2 5N 109 39 E
Datu Piang, *Phil.* 71 H5 7 2N 124 30 E
Datuk, Tanjong, *Malaysia* 75 B3 2 5N 109 39 E
Daugava →, *Latvia* 50 C4 57 4N 24 3 E
Daugavpils, *Latvia* 50 D5 55 53N 26 32 E
Daulatabad, *India* 82 E2 19 57N 75 15 E
Daule, *Ecuador* 152 D2 1 56 S 79 56W
Daule →, *Ecuador* 152 D2 2 10 S 79 52W
Daulpur, *India* 80 F7 26 45N 77 59 E
Daun, *Germany* 27 E2 50 10N 6 53 E
Daund, *India* 82 E2 18 26N 74 40 E
Dauphin, *Canada* 131 C8 51 9N 100 5W
Dauphin I., *U.S.A.* 135 K1 30 15N 88 11W
Dauphin L., *Canada* 131 C9 51 20N 99 45W
Dauphiné, *France* 25 C9 45 15N 5 25 E
Daura, *Borno, Nigeria* 101 C7 11 31N 11 24 E
Daura, *Kaduna, Nigeria* 101 C6 13 2N 8 21 E
Dausa, *India* 80 F7 26 52N 76 20 E
Davangere, *India* 83 G2 14 25N 75 55 E
Davao, *Phil.* 71 H5 7 0N 125 40 E
Davao □, *Phil.* 71 H5 7 0N 125 55 E
Davao, G. of, *Phil.* 71 H5 6 30N 125 48 E
Davao del Sur □, *Phil.* 71 H5 6 30N 125 25 E
Davao Oriental □, *Phil.* 71 H6 7 10N 126 30 E
Dāvar Panāh, *Iran* 85 E9 27 25N 62 15 E
Davenport, *Calif., U.S.A.* 144 H4 37 1N 122 12W
Davenport, *Iowa, U.S.A.* 140 C6 41 32N 90 35W
Davenport, *Wash., U.S.A.* 142 C4 47 39N 118 9W
Davenport Downs, *Australia* 114 C3 24 8 S 141 7 E
Davenport Ra., *Australia* 114 C1 20 28 S 134 0 E
David, *Panama* 148 E3 8 30N 82 30W
David City, *U.S.A.* 138 E6 41 15N 97 8W
David Gorodok, *Belorussia* 50 E5 52 4N 27 8 E
Davidson, *Canada* 131 C7 51 16N 105 59W
Davis, *U.S.A.* 144 G5 38 33N 121 44W
Davis Dam, *U.S.A.* 145 K12 35 11N 114 34W
Davis Inlet, *Canada* 129 A7 55 50N 60 59W
Davis Mts., *U.S.A.* 139 K2 30 50N 103 55W
Davis Sea, *Antarctica* 7 C7 66 0 S 92 0 E
Davis Str., *N. Amer.* 127 B14 65 0N 58 0W
Davlekanovo, *Russia* 54 D4 54 13N 55 3 E
Davos, *Switz.* 29 C9 46 48N 9 49 E
Davy L., *Canada* 131 B7 58 53N 108 18W
Dawa →, *Ethiopia* 95 G5 4 11N 42 6 E
Dawaki, *Bauchi, Nigeria* 101 D6 9 25N 9 33 E
Dawaki, *Kano, Nigeria* 101 C6 12 5N 8 23 E
Dawes Ra., *Australia* 114 C5 24 40 S 150 40 E
Dawna Range, *Burma* 78 G7 16 30N 98 30 E
Dawnyein, *Burma* 78 G5 15 54N 95 36 E
Dawqah, *Si. Arabia* 86 C3 19 36N 40 54 E
Dawson, *Canada* 126 B6 64 10N 139 30W
Dawson, *Ga., U.S.A.* 135 K3 31 46N 84 27W
Dawson, *N. Dak., U.S.A.* 138 B5 46 52N 99 45W
Dawson, I., *Chile* 160 D2 53 50 S 70 50W
Dawson Creek, *Canada* 130 B4 55 45N 120 15W
Dawson Inlet, *Canada* 131 A10 61 50N 93 25W
Dawson Ra., *Australia* 114 C4 24 30 S 149 48 E
Dawu, *China* 68 B3 30 55N 101 10 E
Dawwah, *Oman* 87 B7 20 33N 58 48 E
Dax, *France* 24 E2 43 44N 1 3W
Daxi, *Taiwan* 69 E13 24 52N 121 20 E
Daxian, *China* 68 B6 31 15N 107 23 E
Daxin, *China* 68 F6 22 50N 107 11 E
Daxindian, *China* 67 F11 37 30N 120 50 E
Daxinggou, *China* 67 C15 43 25N 129 40 E
Daxue Shan, *Sichuan, China* 68 B3 30 30N 101 30 E
Daxue Shan, *Yunnan, China* 68 F2 23 42N 99 48 E
Dayao, *China* 68 E3 25 43N 101 20 E
Daye, *China* 69 B10 30 6N 114 58 E
Dayi, *China* 68 B4 30 41N 103 29 E
Daylesford, *Australia* 116 D6 37 21 S 144 9 E
Dayong, *China* 69 C8 29 11N 110 30 E
Dayr az Zawr, *Syria* 84 C4 35 20N 40 5 E
Daysland, *Canada* 130 C6 52 50N 112 20W
Dayton, *Iowa, U.S.A.* 140 B2 42 14N 94 6W
Dayton, *Ky., U.S.A.* 141 E12 39 47N 84 28W
Dayton, *Nev., U.S.A.* 144 F7 39 14N 119 36W
Dayton, *Ohio, U.S.A.* 134 F3 39 45N 84 12W
Dayton, *Pa., U.S.A.* 136 F5 40 53N 79 15W
Dayton, *Tenn., U.S.A.* 135 H3 35 30N 85 1W
Dayton, *Wash., U.S.A.* 142 C4 46 19N 117 59W
Daytona Beach, *U.S.A.* 135 L5 29 13N 81 1W
Dayu, *China* 69 E10 25 24N 114 22 E
Dayville, *U.S.A.* 142 D4 44 28N 119 32W
Dazhu, *China* 68 B6 30 41N 107 15 E
Dazu, *China* 68 C5 29 40N 105 42 E
De Aar, *S. Africa* 104 E3 30 39 S 24 0 E
De Bilt, *Neths.* 20 D6 52 6N 5 11 E
De Forest, *U.S.A.* 140 A7 43 15N 89 20W
De Funiak Springs, *U.S.A.* 135 K2 30 43N 86 7W
De Grey, *Australia* 112 D2 20 12 S 119 12 E
De Grey →, *Australia* 112 D2 20 12 S 119 13 E
De Kalb, *U.S.A.* 138 E10 41 56N 88 46W
De Koog, *Neths.* 20 B5 53 6N 4 46 E
De Land, *U.S.A.* 135 L5 29 2N 81 18W
De Leon, *U.S.A.* 139 J5 32 7N 98 32W
De Panne, *Belgium* 21 F1 51 6N 2 34 E
De Pere, *U.S.A.* 134 C1 44 27N 88 4W
De Queen, *U.S.A.* 139 H7 34 2N 94 21W
De Quincy, *U.S.A.* 139 K8 30 27N 93 26W
De Ridder, *U.S.A.* 139 K8 30 51N 93 17W
De Rijp, *Neths.* 20 C5 52 33N 4 51 E
De Smet, *U.S.A.* 138 C6 44 23N 97 33W
De Soto, *U.S.A.* 140 F6 38 8N 90 34W
De Tour Village, *U.S.A.* 134 C4 46 0N 83 56W
De Witt, *Ark., U.S.A.* 139 H9 34 18N 91 20W
De Witt, *Iowa, U.S.A.* 140 C6 41 49N 90 33W
De Witt, *Mich., U.S.A.* 141 B12 42 51N 84 34W
Dead Sea, *Asia* 91 D4 31 30N 35 30 E
Deadwood, *U.S.A.* 138 C3 44 23N 103 44W
Deadwood L., *Canada* 130 B3 59 10N 128 30W
Deakin, *Australia* 113 F4 30 46 S 128 58 E
Deal, *U.K.* 17 F9 51 13N 1 25 E
Deal I., *Australia* 114 F4 39 30 S 147 20 E
Dealesville, *S. Africa* 104 D4 28 41 S 25 44 E
De'an, *China* 69 C10 29 21N 115 46 E
Dean, Forest of, *U.K.* 17 F5 51 50N 2 35W
Deán Funes, *Argentina* 158 C3 30 20 S 64 20W
Dearborn, *Mich., U.S.A.* 128 D3 42 19N 83 11W
Dearborn, *Mo., U.S.A.* 140 E2 39 32N 94 46W
Dease →, *Canada* 130 B3 59 56N 128 32W
Dease L., *Canada* 130 B2 58 40N 130 5W
Dease Lake, *Canada* 130 B2 58 25N 130 6W
Death Valley, *U.S.A.* 145 J10 36 15N 116 50W
Death Valley Junction, *U.S.A.* 145 J10 36 20N 116 25W
Death Valley National Monument, *U.S.A.* 145 J10 36 45N 117 15W
Deauville, *France* 22 C7 49 23N 0 2 E
Deba Habe, *Nigeria* 101 C7 10 14N 11 20 E
Debak, *Malaysia* 75 B4 1 34N 111 25 E
Debaltsevo, *Ukraine* 52 B8 48 22N 38 26 E
Debao, *China* 68 F6 23 21N 106 46 E
Debar, *Macedonia* 42 F5 41 31N 20 30 E
Debden, *Canada* 131 C7 53 30N 106 50W
Debdou, *Morocco* 99 B4 33 59N 3 0W
Debessy, *Russia* 54 C3 57 39N 53 49 E
Dębica, *Poland* 31 A14 50 2N 21 25 E
Dęblin, *Poland* 47 D8 51 34N 21 50 E
Debno, *Poland* 47 C1 52 44N 14 41 E
Débo, L., *Mali* 100 B4 15 14N 4 15W
Debolt, *Canada* 130 B5 55 12N 118 1W
Deborah East, L., *Australia* 113 F2 30 45 S 119 0 E
Deborah West, L., *Australia* 113 F2 30 45 S 118 50 E
Debrc, *Serbia* 42 C4 44 38N 19 53 E
Debre Birhan, *Ethiopia* 95 F4 9 41N 39 31 E
Debre Markos, *Ethiopia* 95 E4 10 20N 37 40 E
Debre May, *Ethiopia* 95 E4 11 20N 37 25 E
Debre Sina, *Ethiopia* 95 F4 9 51N 39 50 E
Debre Tabor, *Ethiopia* 95 E4 11 50N 38 26 E
Debre Zebit, *Ethiopia* 95 E4 11 48N 38 30 E
Debrecen, *Hungary* 31 D14 47 33N 21 42 E
Dečani, *Serbia* 42 E5 42 30N 20 10 E
Decatur, *Ala., U.S.A.* 135 H2 34 36N 86 59W
Decatur, *Ga., U.S.A.* 135 J3 33 47N 84 18W
Decatur, *Ill., U.S.A.* 140 E8 39 51N 88 57W
Decatur, *Ind., U.S.A.* 141 D12 40 50N 84 56W
Decatur, *Mich., U.S.A.* 141 B11 42 7N 85 58W
Decatur, *Tex., U.S.A.* 139 J6 33 14N 97 35W
Decazeville, *France* 24 D6 44 34N 2 15 E
Deccan, *India* 82 F4 18 0N 79 0 E
Deception, Mt., *Australia* 116 A3 30 42 S 138 16 E
Deception L., *Canada* 131 B8 56 33N 104 13W
Dechang, *China* 68 D4 27 25N 102 11 E
Děčín, *Czech.* 30 A7 50 47N 14 12 E
Decize, *France* 23 F10 46 50N 3 28 E
Deckerville, *U.S.A.* 136 C2 43 32N 82 44W
Decollatura, *Italy* 41 C9 39 2N 16 21 E
Decorah, *U.S.A.* 138 D9 43 18N 91 48W
Deda, *Romania* 46 C5 46 56N 24 50 E
Dedaye, *Burma* 78 G5 16 24N 95 53 E
Dedéagach = Alexandroúpolis, *Greece* 44 D7 40 50N 25 54 E
Dedegöl Dağları, *Turkey* 88 E4 37 15N 31 18 E
Dedemsvaart, *Neths.* 20 C8 52 36N 6 28 E
Dedham, *U.S.A.* 137 D13 42 15N 71 10W
Dedilovo, *Russia* 51 E10 53 59N 37 50 E
Dédougou, *Burkina Faso* 100 C4 12 30N 3 25W
Deduru Oya, *Sri Lanka* 83 L4 7 32N 79 50 E
Dedza, *Malawi* 107 E3 14 20 S 34 20 E
Dee →, *Clwyd, U.K.* 16 D4 53 15N 3 7W
Dee →, *Gramp., U.K.* 18 D6 57 4N 2 7W
Deep B., *Canada* 130 A5 61 15N 116 35W
Deep Lead, *Australia* 116 D5 37 0 S 142 43 E
Deep River, *U.S.A.* 140 C4 41 35N 92 22W
Deep Well, *Australia* 114 C1 24 20 S 134 0 E
Deepwater, *Australia* 115 D5 29 25 S 151 51 E
Deepwater, *U.S.A.* 140 F3 38 16N 93 47W
Deer →, *Canada* 131 B10 58 23N 94 13W
Deer Lake, *Nfld., Canada* 129 C8 49 11N 57 27W
Deer Lake, *Ont., Canada* 131 C10 52 36N 94 20W
Deer Lodge, *U.S.A.* 142 C7 46 24N 112 44W
Deer Park, *Ohio, U.S.A.* 141 E12 39 13N 84 23W
Deer Park, *Wash., U.S.A.* 142 C5 47 57N 117 28W
Deer River, *U.S.A.* 138 B8 47 20N 93 48W
Deeral, *Australia* 114 B4 17 14 S 145 55 E
Deerdepoort, *S. Africa* 104 C4 24 37 S 26 27 E
Deerlijk, *Belgium* 21 G2 50 51N 3 22 E
Deferiet, *U.S.A.* 137 B9 44 2N 75 41W
Defiance, *U.S.A.* 141 C12 41 17N 84 22W
Dêgê, *China* 68 B2 31 44N 98 39 E
Degebe →, *Portugal* 37 G3 38 13N 7 29W
Degeh Bur, *Ethiopia* 90 F3 8 11N 43 31 E
Degema, *Nigeria* 101 E6 4 50N 6 48 E
Degersheim, *Switz.* 29 B8 47 23N 9 12 E
Deggendorf, *Germany* 27 G8 48 49N 12 59 E
Deh Bīd, *Iran* 85 D7 30 39N 53 11 E
Deh-e Shīr, *Iran* 85 D7 31 29N 53 45 E
Dehaj, *Iran* 85 D7 30 42N 54 53 E
Dehak, *Iran* 79 D1 27 11N 62 37 E
Dehdez, *Iran* 85 D6 31 43N 50 17 E
Dehestān, *Iran* 85 D7 28 30N 55 35 E

**Dvinsk 193**

Dorum, *Germany* **26 B4** 53 40N 8 33 E
Doruma, *Zaïre* **106 B2** 4 42N 27 33 E
Dorūneh, *Iran* **85 C8** 35 10N 57 18 E
Dos Bahías, C., *Argentina* **160 B3** 44 58 S 65 32W
Dos Hermanas, *Spain* **37 H5** 37 16N 5 55W
Dos Palos, *U.S.A.* **144 J6** 36 59N 120 37W
Dosso, *Niger* **101 C5** 13 0N 3 13 E
Dothan, *U.S.A.* **135 K3** 31 13N 85 24W
Dottignies, *Belgium* **21 G2** 50 44N 3 19 E
Doty, *U.S.A.* **144 D3** 46 38N 123 17W
Douai, *France* **23 B10** 50 21N 3 4 E
Douala, *Cameroon* **101 E6** 4 0N 9 45 E
Douarnenez, *France* **22 D2** 48 6N 4 21W
Douăzeci Şi Trei August, *Romania* **46 F9** 43 55N 28 40 E
Double Island Pt., *Australia* **115 D5** 25 56 S 153 11 E
Doubrava →, *Czech.* **30 B8** 49 40N 15 30 E
Doubs □, *France* **23 E13** 47 10N 6 20 E
Doubs →, *France* **23 F12** 46 53N 5 1 E
Doubtful Sd., *N.Z.* **119 F1** 45 20 S 166 49 E
Doubtless B., *N.Z.* **118 A2** 34 55 S 173 26 E
Doudeville, *France* **22 C7** 49 43N 0 47 E
Doué-la-Fontaine, *France* **22 E6** 47 11N 0 16W
Douentza, *Mali* **100 C4** 14 58N 2 48W
Doughboy B., *N.Z.* **119 H2** 47 2 S 167 40 E
Douglas, *S. Africa* **104 D3** 29 4 S 23 46 E
Douglas, *U.K.* **16 C3** 54 9N 4 29W
Douglas, *Alaska, U.S.A.* **130 B2** 58 17N 134 24W
Douglas, *Ariz., U.S.A.* **143 L9** 31 21N 109 33W
Douglas, *Ga., U.S.A.* **135 K4** 31 31N 82 51W
Douglas, *Wyo., U.S.A.* **138 D2** 42 45N 105 24W
Douglastown, *Canada* **129 C7** 48 46N 64 24W
Douglasville, *U.S.A.* **135 J3** 33 45N 84 45W
Douirat, *Morocco* **98 B4** 33 2N 4 11W
Doukáton, Ákra, *Greece* **45 F2** 38 34N 20 30 E
Doulevant-le-Château, *France* **23 D11** 48 23N 4 55 E
Doullens, *France* **23 B9** 50 10N 2 20 E
Doumé, *Cameroon* **102 B2** 4 15N 13 25 E
Douna, *Mali* **100 C3** 13 13N 6 0W
Dounan, *Taiwan* **69 F13** 23 41N 120 26 E
Dounguila, *Congo* **102 C2** 2 53 S 11 58 E
Dounreay, *U.K.* **18 C5** 58 34N 3 44W
Dour, *Belgium* **21 H3** 50 24N 3 46 E
Dourada, Serra, *Brazil* **155 D2** 13 10 S 48 45W
Dourados, *Brazil* **159 A5** 22 9 S 54 50W
Dourados →, *Brazil* **159 A5** 21 58 S 54 18W
Dourdan, *France* **23 D9** 48 30N 2 1 E
Douro →, *Europe* **36 D2** 41 8N 8 40W
Douvaine, *France* **25 B10** 46 19N 6 16 E
Douz, *Tunisia* **96 B1** 33 25N 9 0 E
Douze →, *France* **24 E3** 43 54N 0 30W
Dove →, *U.K.* **16 E6** 52 51N 1 36W
Dove Creek, *U.S.A.* **143 H9** 37 46N 108 54W
Dover, *Australia* **114 G4** 43 18 S 147 2 E
Dover, *U.K.* **17 F9** 51 7N 1 19 E
Dover, *Del., U.S.A.* **134 F8** 39 10N 75 32W
Dover, *Ky., U.S.A.* **141 F13** 38 43N 83 52W
Dover, *N.H., U.S.A.* **137 C14** 43 12N 70 56W
Dover, *N.J., U.S.A.* **137 F10** 40 53N 74 34W
Dover, *Ohio, U.S.A.* **136 F3** 40 32N 81 29W
Dover, Pt., *Australia* **113 F4** 32 32 S 125 32 E
Dover, Str. of, *Europe* **22 B8** 51 0N 1 30 E
Dover-Foxcroft, *U.S.A.* **129 C6** 45 11N 69 13W
Dover Plains, *U.S.A.* **137 E11** 41 43N 73 35W
Dovey = Dyfi →, *U.K.* **17 E4** 52 32N 4 0W
Dovrefjell, *Norway* **14 B3** 62 15N 9 33 E
Dow Rūd, *Iran* **85 C6** 33 28N 49 4 E
Dowa, *Malawi* **107 E3** 13 38 S 33 58 E
Dowagiac, *U.S.A.* **141 C10** 41 59N 86 6W
Dowgha'i, *Iran* **85 B8** 36 54N 58 32 E
Dowlat Yār, *Afghan.* **79 B2** 34 30N 65 45 E
Dowlatābād, *Farāh, Afghan.* **79 B1** 32 47N 62 40 E
Dowlatābād, *Fāryāb, Afghan.* **79 A2** 36 26N 64 55 E
Dowlatābād, *Iran* **85 D8** 28 20N 56 40 E
Down □, *U.K.* **19 B6** 54 20N 5 47W
Downers Grove, *U.S.A.* **141 C8** 41 48N 88 1W
Downey, *Calif., U.S.A.* **145 M8** 33 56N 118 7W
Downey, *Idaho, U.S.A.* **142 E7** 42 26N 112 7W
Downham Market, *U.K.* **17 E8** 52 36N 0 22 E
Downieville, *U.S.A.* **144 F6** 39 34N 120 50W
Downing, *U.S.A.* **140 D4** 40 29N 92 22W
Downpatrick, *U.K.* **19 B6** 54 20N 5 43W
Downpatrick Hd., *Ireland* **19 B2** 54 20N 9 21W
Dowsārī, *Iran* **85 D8** 28 25N 57 59 E
Dowshī, *Afghan.* **79 B3** 35 35N 68 43 E
Doyle, *U.S.A.* **144 E6** 40 2N 120 6W
Doylestown, *U.S.A.* **137 F9** 40 21N 75 10W
Draa, C., *Morocco* **98 C2** 28 47N 11 0W
Draa, Oued →, *Morocco* **98 C2** 28 40N 11 10W
Drac →, *France* **25 C9** 45 12N 5 42 E
Drachten, *Neths.* **20 B8** 53 7N 6 5 E
Drăgăneşti, *Romania* **46 E5** 44 9N 24 32 E
Drăgăneşti-Viaşca, *Romania* **46 E6** 44 5N 25 33 E
Dragaš, *Serbia* **42 E5** 42 5N 20 35 E
Drăgăşani, *Romania* **46 E5** 44 39N 24 17 E
Dragina, *Serbia* **42 C4** 44 30N 19 25 E
Dragocvet, *Serbia* **42 D6** 43 58N 21 15 E
Dragoman, Prokhod, *Bulgaria* **42 E7** 42 58N 22 53 E
Dragonera, I., *Spain* **33 B9** 39 35N 2 19 E
Dragovishtitsa, *Bulgaria* **42 E7** 42 22N 22 39 E
Draguignan, *France* **25 E10** 43 32N 6 27 E
Drain, *U.S.A.* **142 E2** 43 40N 123 19W
Drake, *Australia* **115 D5** 28 55 S 152 25 E
Drake, *U.S.A.* **138 B4** 47 55N 100 23W
Drake Passage, *S. Ocean* **7 B17** 58 0 S 68 0W
Drakensberg, *S. Africa* **105 E4** 31 0 S 28 0 E
Dráma, *Greece* **44 C6** 41 9N 24 10 E
Dráma □, *Greece* **44 C6** 41 20N 24 0 E
Drammen, *Norway* **14 E4** 59 42N 10 12 E
Drangajökull, *Iceland* **12 C2** 66 9N 22 15W
Drangedal, *Norway* **14 E3** 59 6N 9 3 E
Dranov, Ostrov, *Romania* **46 E10** 44 55N 29 30 E
Dras, *India* **81 B6** 34 25N 75 48 E
Drau = Drava →, *Croatia* **31 F11** 45 33N 18 55 E
Drava →, *Croatia* **31 F11** 45 33N 18 55 E
Draveil, *France* **23 D9** 48 41N 2 25 E
Dravograd, *Slovenia* **39 B12** 46 36N 15 5 E
Drawa →, *Poland* **47 C2** 52 52N 15 59 E
Drawno, *Poland* **47 B2** 53 13N 15 46 E
Drawsko Pomorskie, *Poland* **47 B2** 53 35N 15 50 E
Drayton Plains, *U.S.A.* **141 B13** 42 42N 83 23W
Drayton Valley, *Canada* **130 C6** 53 12N 114 58W
Dreibergen, *Neths.* **20 D6** 52 3N 5 17 E
Dren, *Serbia* **42 D5** 43 8N 20 44 E
Drenthe □, *Neths.* **20 C9** 52 52N 6 40 E
Drentsche Hoofdvaart, *Neths.* **20 C8** 52 39N 6 4 E
Drepanum, C., *Cyprus* **32 E11** 34 54N 32 19 E
Dresden, *Canada* **136 D2** 42 35N 82 11W
Dresden, *Germany* **26 D9** 51 2N 13 45 E
Dreux, *France* **22 D8** 48 44N 1 23 E
Drexel, *U.S.A.* **141 E12** 39 45N 84 18W
Drezdenko, *Poland* **47 C2** 52 50N 15 49 E
Driel, *Neths.* **20 E7** 51 57N 5 49 E
Driffield = Great Driffield, *U.K.* **16 C7** 54 0N 0 25W
Driftwood, *U.S.A.* **136 E6** 41 20N 78 8W
Driggs, *U.S.A.* **142 E8** 43 44N 111 6W
Drin i zi →, *Albania* **44 C2** 41 37N 20 28 E
Drina →, *Bos.-H.* **42 C4** 44 53N 19 21 E
Drincea →, *Romania* **46 E3** 44 20N 22 55 E
Drînceni, *Romania* **46 C9** 46 49N 28 10 E
Drini →, *Albania* **44 B2** 42 20N 20 0 E
Drinjača →, *Bos.-H.* **42 C4** 44 15N 19 8 E
Drissa = Verkhnedvinsk, *Belorussia* **50 D5** 55 45N 27 58 E
Drivstua, *Norway* **14 B3** 62 26N 9 47 E
Drniš, *Croatia* **39 E13** 43 51N 16 10 E
Drøbak, *Norway* **14 E4** 59 39N 10 39 E
Drobin, *Poland* **47 C6** 52 42N 19 58 E
Drogheda, *Ireland* **19 C5** 53 45N 6 20W
Drogichin, *Belorussia* **50 E4** 52 15N 25 8 E
Drogobych, *Ukraine* **50 G3** 49 20N 23 30 E
Drohiczyn, *Poland* **47 C9** 52 24N 22 39 E
Drohobych = Drogobych, *Ukraine* **50 G3** 49 20N 23 30 E
Droichead Nua, *Ireland* **19 C5** 53 11N 6 50W
Droitwich, *U.K.* **17 E5** 52 16N 2 10W
Drôme □, *France* **25 D9** 44 38N 5 15 E
Drôme →, *France* **25 D8** 44 46N 4 46 E
Dromedary, C., *Australia* **117 D9** 36 17 S 150 10 E
Dronero, *Italy* **38 D4** 44 29N 7 22 E
Dronfield, *Australia* **114 C3** 21 12 S 140 3 E
Dronne →, *France* **24 C3** 45 2N 0 9W
Dronninglund, *Denmark* **15 G4** 57 10N 10 19 E
Dronrijp, *Neths.* **20 B7** 53 11N 5 39 E
Dropt →, *France* **24 D3** 44 35N 0 6W
Drosendorf, *Austria* **30 C8** 48 52N 15 37 E
Drouin, *Australia* **117 E6** 38 10 S 145 53 E
Drouzhba, *Bulgaria* **43 D13** 43 15N 28 0 E
Drumbo, *Canada* **136 C4** 43 16N 80 35W
Drumheller, *Canada* **130 C6** 51 25N 112 40W
Drummond, *U.S.A.* **142 C7** 46 40N 113 9W
Drummond I., *U.S.A.* **128 C3** 46 1N 83 39W
Drummond Pt., *Australia* **115 E2** 34 9 S 135 16 E
Drummond Ra., *Australia* **114 C4** 23 45 S 147 10 E
Drummondville, *Canada* **128 C5** 45 55N 72 25W
Drumright, *U.S.A.* **139 H6** 35 59N 96 36W
Drunen, *Neths.* **21 E6** 51 41N 5 8 E
Druskininkai, *Lithuania* **50 D3** 54 3N 23 58 E
Drut →, *Belorussia* **50 E7** 53 8N 30 5 E
Druten, *Neths.* **20 E7** 51 53N 5 36 E
Druya, *Latvia* **50 D5** 55 45N 27 28 E
Druzhina, *Russia* **57 C15** 68 14N 145 18 E
Drvar, *Bos.-H.* **39 D13** 44 21N 16 23 E
Drvenik, *Croatia* **39 E13** 43 27N 16 3 E
Drwęca →, *Poland* **47 C5** 53 0N 18 42 E
Dry Tortugas, *U.S.A.* **148 B3** 24 38N 82 55W
Dryanovo, *Bulgaria* **43 E10** 42 59N 25 28 E
Dryden, *Canada* **131 D10** 49 47N 92 50W
Dryden, *U.S.A.* **139 K3** 30 3N 102 7W
Drygalski I., *Antarctica* **7 C7** 66 0 S 92 0 E
Drysdale →, *Australia* **112 B4** 13 59 S 126 51 E
Drysdale I., *Australia* **114 A2** 11 41 S 136 0 E
Drzewiczka →, *Poland* **47 D7** 51 36N 20 36 E
Dschang, *Cameroon* **101 D7** 5 32N 10 3 E
Du Bois, *U.S.A.* **136 E6** 41 8N 78 46W
Du Quoin, *U.S.A.* **140 F7** 38 1N 89 14W
Duanesburg, *U.S.A.* **137 D10** 42 45N 74 11W
Duaringa, *Australia* **114 C4** 23 42 S 149 42 E
Ḍubā, *Si. Arabia* **84 E2** 27 10N 35 40 E
Dubai = Dubayy, *U.A.E.* **85 E7** 25 18N 55 20 E
Dubawnt →, *Canada* **131 A8** 64 33N 100 6W
Dubawnt, L., *Canada* **131 A8** 63 4N 101 42W
Dubayy, *U.A.E.* **85 E7** 25 18N 55 20 E
Dubbeldam, *Neths.* **20 E5** 51 47N 4 43 E
Dubbo, *Australia* **117 B8** 32 11 S 148 35 E
Dubele, *Zaïre* **106 B2** 2 56N 29 35 E
Dübendorf, *Switz.* **29 B7** 47 24N 8 37 E
Dubenskiy, *Russia* **54 F5** 51 27N 56 38 E
Dubica, *Croatia* **39 C13** 45 11N 16 48 E
Dublin, *Ireland* **19 C5** 53 20N 6 18W
Dublin, *Ga., U.S.A.* **135 J4** 32 32N 82 54W
Dublin, *Tex., U.S.A.* **139 J5** 32 5N 98 21W
Dublin □, *Ireland* **19 C5** 53 24N 6 20W
Dublin B., *Ireland* **19 C5** 53 18N 6 5W
Dubna, *Russia* **51 C10** 56 44N 37 10 E
Dubna, *Russia* **51 D10** 54 8N 36 59 E
Dubno, *Ukraine* **50 F4** 50 25N 25 45 E
Dubois, *Idaho, U.S.A.* **142 D7** 44 10N 112 14W
Dubois, *Ind., U.S.A.* **141 F10** 38 27N 86 48W
Dubossary, *Moldavia* **52 C3** 47 15N 29 10 E
Dubossary Vdkhr., *Moldavia* **52 C3** 47 30N 29 0 E
Dubovka, *Russia* **53 B11** 49 5N 44 50 E
Dubovskoye, *Russia* **53 C10** 47 28N 42 46 E
Dubrajpur, *India* **81 H12** 23 48N 87 25 E
Dubréka, *Guinea* **100 D2** 9 46N 13 31W
Dubrovitsa, *Ukraine* **50 F5** 51 31N 26 35 E
Dubrovnik, *Croatia* **42 E3** 42 39N 18 6 E
Dubrovskoye, *Russia* **57 D12** 58 55N 111 10 E
Dubulu, *Zaïre* **102 B4** 4 18N 20 16 E
Dubuque, *U.S.A.* **140 B6** 42 30N 90 41W
Duchang, *China* **69 C11** 29 18N 116 12 E
Duchesne, *U.S.A.* **142 F8** 40 10N 110 24W
Duchess, *Australia* **114 C2** 21 20 S 139 50 E
Ducie I., *Pac. Oc.* **123 K15** 24 40 S 124 48W
Duck Cr. →, *Australia* **112 D2** 22 37 S 116 53 E
Duck Lake, *Canada* **131 C7** 52 50N 106 16W
Duck Mountain Prov. Park, *Canada* **131 C8** 51 45N 101 0W
Duckwall, Mt., *U.S.A.* **144 H6** 37 58N 120 7W
Düdelange, *Lux.* **21 K8** 49 29N 6 5 E
Duderstadt, *Germany* **26 D6** 51 30N 10 15 E
Dudhnai, *India* **78 C3** 25 59N 90 47 E
Düdingen, *Switz.* **28 C4** 46 52N 7 12 E
Dudinka, *Russia* **57 C9** 69 30N 86 13 E
Dudley, *U.K.* **17 E5** 52 30N 2 5W
Dudna →, *India* **82 E3** 19 17N 76 54 E
Dudo, *Somali Rep.* **108 C4** 9 20N 50 12 E
Dudub, *Ethiopia* **108 C3** 6 55N 46 43 E
Duenas, *Phil.* **71 F4** 11 4N 122 37 E
Dueñas, *Spain* **36 D6** 41 52N 4 33W
Dueré, *Brazil* **155 D2** 11 20 S 49 17W
Duero = Douro →, *Europe* **36 D2** 41 8N 8 40W
Dūfah, W. →, *Si. Arabia* **86 C3** 18 45N 41 49 E
Duffel, *Belgium* **21 F5** 51 6N 4 30 E
Dufftown, *U.K.* **18 D5** 57 26N 3 9W
Dufourspitz, *Switz.* **28 E5** 45 56N 7 52 E
Dugger, *U.S.A.* **141 E9** 39 4N 87 18W
Dugi Otok, *Croatia* **39 E12** 44 0N 15 3 E
Dugiuma, *Somali Rep.* **108 D2** 1 15N 42 34 E
Dugo Selo, *Croatia* **39 C13** 45 51N 16 18 E
Duifken Pt., *Australia* **114 A3** 12 33 S 141 38 E
Duisburg, *Germany* **26 D2** 51 27N 6 42 E
Duitama, *Colombia* **152 B3** 5 50N 73 2W
Duiveland, *Neths.* **21 E4** 51 38N 4 0 E
Duiwelskloof, *S. Africa* **105 C5** 23 42 S 30 10 E
Dukati, *Albania* **44 D1** 40 16N 19 32 E
Dūkdamīn, *Iran* **85 C8** 35 59N 57 43 E
Duke I., *U.S.A.* **130 C2** 54 50N 131 20W
Dukelský průsmyk, *Slovak Rep.* **31 B14** 49 25N 21 42 E
Dukhān, *Qatar* **85 E6** 25 25N 50 50 E
Dukhovshchina, *Russia* **50 D8** 55 15N 32 27 E
Duki, *Pakistan* **79 C3** 30 14N 68 25 E
Dukla, *Poland* **31 B14** 49 30N 21 35 E
Duku, *Bauchi, Nigeria* **101 C7** 10 43N 10 43 E
Duku, *Sokoto, Nigeria* **101 C5** 11 11N 4 55 E
Dulag, *Phil.* **71 F5** 10 57N 125 2 E
Dulce →, *Argentina* **158 C3** 30 32 S 62 33W
Dulce, G., *Costa Rica* **148 E3** 8 40N 83 20W
Dulf, *Iraq* **84 C5** 35 7N 45 51 E
Dŭlgopol, *Bulgaria* **43 D12** 43 3N 27 22 E
Duliu, *China* **66 E9** 39 2N 116 55 E
Dullewala, *Pakistan* **80 D4** 31 50N 71 25 E
Dülmen, *Germany* **26 D3** 51 49N 7 18 E
Dulovo, *Bulgaria* **43 D12** 43 48N 27 9 E
Dulq Maghār, *Syria* **84 B3** 36 22N 38 39 E
Dululu, *Australia* **114 C5** 23 48 S 150 15 E
Duluth, *U.S.A.* **138 B8** 46 47N 92 6W
Dum Dum, *India* **81 H13** 22 39N 88 33 E
Dum Hadjer, *Chad* **97 F3** 13 18N 19 41 E
Dūmā, *Lebanon* **91 A4** 34 12N 35 50 E
Dūmā, *Syria* **91 B5** 33 34N 36 24 E
Dumaguete, *Phil.* **71 G4** 9 17N 123 15 E
Dumai, *Indonesia* **74 B2** 1 35N 101 28 E
Dumalinao, *Phil.* **71 H4** 7 49N 123 23 E
Dumanguilas Bay, *Phil.* **71 H4** 7 34N 123 4 E
Dumaran, *Phil.* **71 F2** 10 33N 119 50 E
Dumas, *Ark., U.S.A.* **139 J9** 33 53N 91 29W
Dumas, *Tex., U.S.A.* **139 H4** 35 52N 101 58W
Dumbarton, *U.K.* **18 F4** 55 58N 4 35W
Dumbea, *N. Cal.* **121 V20** 22 10 S 166 27 E
Dumbleyung, *Australia* **113 F2** 33 17 S 117 42 E
Dumbo, *Angola* **103 E3** 14 6 S 17 24 E
Dumbrăveni, *Romania* **46 C5** 46 14N 24 34 E
Dumfries, *U.K.* **18 F5** 55 4N 3 37W
Dumfries & Galloway □, *U.K.* **18 F5** 55 5N 4 0W
Dumingag, *Phil.* **71 G4** 8 20N 123 20 E
Dumka, *India* **81 G12** 24 12N 87 15 E
Dümmersee, *Germany* **26 C4** 52 30N 8 21 E
Dumoine →, *Canada* **128 C4** 46 13N 77 51W
Dumoine L., *Canada* **128 C4** 46 55N 77 55W
Dumraon, *India* **81 G11** 25 33N 84 8 E
Dumyât, *Egypt* **94 H7** 31 24N 31 48 E
Dumyât, Masabb, *Egypt* **94 H7** 31 28N 31 51 E
Dun Laoghaire, *Ireland* **19 C5** 53 17N 6 9W
Dun-le-Palestel, *France* **24 B5** 46 18N 1 39 E
Dun-sur-Auron, *France* **23 F9** 46 53N 2 33 E
Duna →, *Hungary* **31 F11** 45 51N 18 48 E
Dunaföldvár, *Hungary* **31 E11** 46 50N 18 57 E
Dunaj →, *Slovak Rep.* **31 D11** 47 50N 18 50 E
Dunajec →, *Poland* **31 A13** 50 15N 20 44 E
Dunajská Streda, *Slovak Rep.* **31 D10** 48 0N 17 37 E
Dunapatai, *Hungary* **31 E12** 46 39N 19 4 E
Dunărea →, *Romania* **46 D10** 45 20N 29 40 E
Dunaszekcsö, *Hungary* **31 E11** 46 6N 18 45 E
Dunaújváros, *Hungary* **31 E11** 47 0N 18 57 E
Dunav →, *Serbia* **42 C6** 44 47N 21 20 E
Dunavtsi, *Bulgaria* **42 D7** 43 57N 22 53 E
Dunay, *Russia* **60 C6** 42 52N 132 22 E
Dunback, *N.Z.* **119 F5** 45 23 S 170 36 E
Dunbar, *Australia* **114 B3** 16 0 S 142 22 E
Dunbar, *U.K.* **18 E6** 56 0N 2 32W
Dunblane, *U.K.* **18 E5** 56 10N 3 58W
Duncan, *Canada* **130 D4** 48 45N 123 40W
Duncan, *Ariz., U.S.A.* **143 K9** 32 43N 109 6W
Duncan, *Okla., U.S.A.* **139 H6** 34 30N 97 57W
Duncan, L., *Canada* **128 B4** 53 29N 77 58W
Duncan L., *Canada* **130 A6** 62 51N 113 58W
Duncan Town, *Bahamas* **148 B4** 22 15N 75 45W
Duncannon, *U.S.A.* **136 F7** 40 23N 77 2W
Dundalk, *Canada* **136 B4** 44 10N 80 24W
Dundalk, *Ireland* **19 B5** 54 1N 6 25W
Dundalk Bay, *Ireland* **19 C5** 53 55N 6 15W
Dundas, *Canada* **128 D4** 43 17N 79 59W
Dundas, L., *Australia* **113 F3** 32 35 S 121 50 E
Dundas I., *Canada* **130 C2** 54 30N 130 50W
Dundas Str., *Australia* **112 B5** 11 15 S 131 35 E
Dundee, *S. Africa* **105 D5** 28 11 S 30 15 E
Dundee, *U.K.* **18 E6** 56 29N 3 0W
Dundee, *U.S.A.* **141 C13** 41 57N 83 40W
Dundgovĭ □, *Mongolia* **66 B4** 45 10N 106 0 E
Dundoo, *Australia* **115 D3** 27 40 S 144 37 E
Dundrum, *U.K.* **19 B6** 54 17N 5 50W
Dundrum B., *U.K.* **19 B6** 54 12N 5 40W
Dundwara, *India* **81 F8** 27 48N 79 9 E
Dunedin, *N.Z.* **119 F5** 45 50 S 170 33 E
Dunedin, *U.S.A.* **135 L4** 28 1N 82 47W
Dunedin →, *Canada* **130 B4** 59 30N 124 5W
Dunfermline, *U.K.* **18 E5** 56 5N 3 28W
Dungannon, *Canada* **136 C3** 43 51N 81 36W
Dungannon, *U.K.* **19 B5** 54 30N 6 47W
Dungannon □, *U.K.* **19 B5** 54 30N 6 55W
Dungarpur, *India* **80 H5** 23 52N 73 45 E
Dungarvan, *Ireland* **19 D4** 52 6N 7 40W
Dungarvan Bay, *Ireland* **19 D4** 52 5N 7 35W
Dungeness, *U.K.* **17 G8** 50 54N 0 59 E
Dungo, L. do, *Angola* **103 F3** 17 15 S 19 0 E
Dungog, *Australia* **117 B9** 32 22 S 151 46 E
Dungu, *Zaïre* **106 B2** 3 40N 28 32 E
Dungunâb, *Sudan* **94 C4** 21 10N 37 9 E
Dungunâb, Khalij, *Sudan* **94 C4** 21 5N 37 12 E
Dunhinda Falls, *Sri Lanka* **83 L5** 7 5N 81 6 E
Dunhua, *China* **67 C15** 43 20N 128 14 E
Dunhuang, *China* **64 B4** 40 8N 94 36 E
Dunières, *France* **25 C8** 45 13N 4 20 E
Dunk I., *Australia* **114 B4** 17 59 S 146 29 E
Dunkeld, *Australia* **116 D5** 37 40 S 142 22 E
Dunkeld, *U.K.* **18 E5** 56 34N 3 36W
Dunkerque, *France* **23 A9** 51 2N 2 20 E
Dunkery Beacon, *U.K.* **17 F4** 51 15N 3 37W
Dunkirk = Dunkerque, *France* **23 A9** 51 2N 2 20 E
Dunkirk, *U.S.A.* **136 D5** 42 29N 79 20W
Dunkuj, *Sudan* **95 E3** 12 50N 32 49 E
Dunkwa, *Central, Ghana* **100 D4** 6 0N 1 47W
Dunkwa, *Central, Ghana* **101 D4** 5 30N 1 0W
Dunlap, *U.S.A.* **138 E7** 41 51N 95 36W
Dúnleary = Dun Laoghaire, *Ireland* **19 C5** 53 17N 6 9W
Dunmanus B., *Ireland* **19 E2** 51 31N 9 50W
Dunmara, *Australia* **114 B1** 16 42 S 133 25 E
Dunmore, *U.S.A.* **137 E9** 41 25N 75 38W
Dunmore Hd., *Ireland* **19 D1** 52 10N 10 35W
Dunmore Town, *Bahamas* **148 A4** 25 30N 76 39W
Dunn, *U.S.A.* **135 H6** 35 19N 78 37W
Dunnellon, *U.S.A.* **135 L4** 29 3N 82 28W
Dunnet Hd., *U.K.* **18 C5** 58 38N 3 22W
Dunning, *U.S.A.* **138 E4** 41 50N 100 6W
Dunnville, *Canada* **136 D5** 42 54N 79 36W
Dunolly, *Australia* **116 D5** 36 51 S 143 44 E
Dunoon, *U.K.* **18 F4** 55 57N 4 56W
Dunqul, *Egypt* **94 C3** 23 26N 31 37 E
Duns, *U.K.* **18 F6** 55 47N 2 20W
Dunseith, *U.S.A.* **138 A4** 48 50N 100 3W
Dunsmuir, *U.S.A.* **142 F2** 41 13N 122 16W
Dunstable, *U.K.* **17 F7** 51 53N 0 31W
Dunstan Mts., *N.Z.* **119 E4** 44 53 S 169 35 E
Dunster, *Canada* **130 C5** 53 8N 119 50W
Duntroon, *N.Z.* **119 E5** 44 51 S 170 40 E
Dunvegan L., *Canada* **131 A7** 60 8N 107 10W
Duolun, *China* **66 C9** 42 12N 116 28 E
Duong Dong, *Vietnam* **77 G4** 10 13N 103 58 E
Dupax, *Phil.* **70 C3** 16 17N 121 5 E
Dupree, *U.S.A.* **138 C4** 45 4N 101 35W
Dupuyer, *U.S.A.* **142 B7** 48 13N 112 30W
Duqm, *Oman* **87 C7** 19 39N 57 42 E
Duque de Caxias, *Brazil* **155 F3** 22 45 S 43 19W
Duque de York, I., *Chile* **160 D1** 50 37 S 75 25W
Durack →, *Australia* **112 C4** 15 33 S 127 52 E
Durack Ra., *Australia* **112 C4** 16 50 S 127 40 E
Durağan, *Turkey* **88 C6** 41 25N 35 3 E
Durance →, *France* **25 E8** 43 55N 4 45 E
Durand, *Ill., U.S.A.* **140 B7** 42 26N 89 20W
Durand, *Mich., U.S.A.* **141 B13** 42 55N 83 59W
Durango = Victoria de Durango, *Mexico* **146 C4** 24 3N 104 39W
Durango, *Spain* **34 B2** 43 13N 2 40W
Durango, *U.S.A.* **143 H10** 37 16N 107 53W
Durango □, *Mexico* **146 C4** 25 0N 105 0W
Duranillin, *Australia* **113 F2** 33 30 S 116 45 E
Durant, *Iowa, U.S.A.* **140 C6** 41 36N 90 54W
Durant, *Okla., U.S.A.* **139 J6** 33 59N 96 25W
Duratón →, *Spain* **36 D6** 41 37N 4 7W
Durazno, *Uruguay* **158 C4** 33 25 S 56 31W
Durazzo = Durrësi, *Albania* **44 C1** 41 19N 19 28 E
Durban, *France* **24 F6** 42 59N 2 49 E
Durban, *S. Africa* **105 D5** 29 49 S 31 1 E
Durbo, *Somali Rep.* **108 B4** 11 37N 50 20 E
Dúrcal, *Spain* **37 J7** 37 0N 3 34W
Đurđevac, *Croatia* **42 A2** 46 2N 17 3 E
Düren, *Germany* **26 E2** 50 48N 6 30 E
Durg, *India* **82 D5** 21 15N 81 22 E
Durgapur, *India* **81 H12** 23 30N 87 20 E
Durham, *Canada* **128 D3** 44 10N 80 49W
Durham, *U.K.* **16 C6** 54 47N 1 34W
Durham, *Calif., U.S.A.* **144 F5** 39 39N 121 48W
Durham, *N.C., U.S.A.* **135 G6** 35 59N 78 54W
Durham □, *U.K.* **16 C6** 54 42N 1 45W
Durham Downs, *Australia* **115 D4** 26 6 S 149 5 E
Ḍurmā, *Si. Arabia* **86 A4** 24 37N 46 8 E
Durness, *U.K.* **18 C4** 58 34N 4 45W
Durrësi, *Albania* **44 C1** 41 19N 19 28 E
Durrie, *Australia* **114 D3** 25 40 S 140 15 E
Dursunbey, *Turkey* **88 D3** 39 35N 28 37 E
Durtal, *France* **22 E6** 47 40N 0 18W
Duru, *Zaïre* **106 B2** 4 14N 28 50 E
D'Urville, Tanjung, *Indonesia* **73 B5** 1 28 S 137 54 E
D'Urville I., *N.Z.* **119 A8** 40 50 S 173 55 E
Duryea, *U.S.A.* **137 E9** 41 20N 75 45W
Dusa Mareb, *Somali Rep.* **90 F4** 5 30N 46 15 E
Dûsh, *Egypt* **94 C3** 24 35N 30 41 E
Dushak, *Turkmenistan* **56 F7** 37 13N 60 1 E
Dushan, *China* **68 E6** 25 48N 107 30 E
Dushanbe, *Tajikistan* **55 D4** 38 33N 68 48 E
Dusheti, *Georgia* **53 E11** 42 10N 44 42 E
Dusky Sd., *N.Z.* **119 F1** 45 47 S 166 30 E
Dussejour, C., *Australia* **112 B4** 14 45 S 128 13 E
Düsseldorf, *Germany* **26 D2** 51 15N 6 46 E
Dussen, *Neths.* **20 E5** 51 44N 4 59 E
Duszniki-Zdrój, *Poland* **47 E3** 50 24N 16 24 E
Dutch Harbor, *U.S.A.* **126 C3** 53 53N 166 32W
Dutlwe, *Botswana* **104 C3** 23 58 S 23 46 E
Dutsan Wai, *Nigeria* **101 C6** 10 50N 8 10 E
Dutton, *Canada* **136 D3** 42 39N 81 30W
Dutton →, *Australia* **114 C3** 20 44 S 143 10 E
Duvan, *Russia* **54 D5** 55 42N 57 54 E
Duved, *Sweden* **14 A6** 63 24N 12 55 E
Duvno, *Bos.-H.* **42 D2** 43 42N 17 13 E
Duyun, *China* **68 D6** 26 18N 107 29 E
Düzce, *Turkey* **88 C4** 40 50N 31 10 E
Duzdab = Zāhedān, *Iran* **85 D9** 29 30N 60 50 E
Dve Mogili, *Bulgaria* **43 D10** 43 35N 25 55 E
Dvina, Sev. →, *Russia* **48 B7** 64 32N 40 30 E
Dvinsk = Daugavpils, *Latvia* **50 D5** 55 53N 26 32 E

Fergana 197


Eveleth, *U.S.A.* **138 B8** 47 28N 92 32W
Evensk, *Russia* **57 C16** 62 12N 159 30 E
Evenstad, *Norway* **14 C5** 61 25N 11 7 E
Everard, L., *Australia* **115 E1** 31 30 S 135 0 E
Everard Park, *Australia* **113 E5** 27 1 S 132 43 E
Everard Ras., *Australia* **113 E5** 27 5 S 132 28 E
Everdale, *Australia* **117 A6** 31 52 S 144 46 E
Evere, *Belgium* **21 G4** 50 52N 4 25 E
Everest, Mt., *Nepal* **81 E12** 28 5N 86 58 E
Everett, *Pa., U.S.A.* **136 F6** 40 1N 78 23W
Everett, *Wash., U.S.A.* **144 C4** 47 59N 122 12W
Evergem, *Belgium* **21 F3** 51 7N 3 43 E
Everglades, The, *U.S.A.* **135 N5** 25 50N 81 0W
Everglades City, *U.S.A.* **135 N5** 25 52N 81 23W
Everglades National Park, *U.S.A.* **135 N5** 25 30N 81 0W
Evergreen, *U.S.A.* **135 K2** 31 26N 86 57W
Everson, *U.S.A.* **142 B2** 48 57N 122 22W
Everton, *Australia* **117 D7** 36 25 S 146 33 E
Evesham, *U.K.* **17 E6** 52 6N 1 57W
Évian-les-Bains, *France* **25 B10** 46 24N 6 35 E
Evinayong, *Eq. Guin.* **102 B2** 1 26N 10 35 E
Évinos →, *Greece* **45 F3** 38 27N 21 40 E
Évisa, *France* **25 F12** 42 15N 8 48 E
Évora, *Portugal* **37 G3** 38 33N 7 57W
Évora □, *Portugal* **37 G3** 38 33N 7 50W
Evowghlī, *Iran* **84 B5** 38 43N 45 13 E
Évreux, *France* **22 C8** 49 3N 1 8 E
Evritanía □, *Greece* **45 E3** 39 5N 21 30 E
Évron, *France* **22 D6** 48 10N 0 24W
Évros □, *Greece* **44 C8** 41 10N 26 0 E
Evrótas →, *Greece* **45 H4** 36 50N 22 40 E
Évvoia, *Greece* **45 F5** 38 30N 24 0 E
Évvoia □, *Greece* **45 F5** 38 40N 23 40 E
Ewe, L., *U.K.* **18 D3** 57 49N 5 38W
Ewing, *Mo., U.S.A.* **140 E5** 40 6N 91 43W
Ewing, *Nebr., U.S.A.* **138 D5** 42 16N 98 21W
Ewo, *Congo* **102 C2** 0 48 S 14 45 E
Exaltación, *Bolivia* **157 C4** 13 10 S 65 20W
Excelsior Springs, *U.S.A.* **140 E2** 39 20N 94 13W
Excideuil, *France* **24 C5** 45 20N 1 4 E
Exe →, *U.K.* **17 G4** 50 38N 3 27W
Exeter, *Canada* **136 C3** 43 21N 81 29W
Exeter, *U.K.* **17 G4** 50 43N 3 31W
Exeter, *Calif., U.S.A.* **144 J7** 36 18N 119 9W
Exeter, *N.H., U.S.A.* **137 D14** 42 59N 70 57W
Exeter, *Nebr., U.S.A.* **138 E6** 40 39N 97 27W
Exira, *U.S.A.* **140 C2** 41 35N 94 52W
Exloo, *Neths.* **20 C9** 52 53N 6 52 E
Exmes, *France* **22 D7** 48 45N 0 10 E
Exmoor, *U.K.* **17 F4** 51 10N 3 59W
Exmouth, *Australia* **112 D1** 21 54 S 114 10 E
Exmouth, *U.K.* **17 G4** 50 37N 3 26W
Exmouth G., *Australia* **112 D1** 22 15 S 114 15 E
Expedition Ra., *Australia* **114 C4** 24 30 S 149 12 E
Extremadura □, *Spain* **37 F4** 39 30N 6 5W
Exuma Sound, *Bahamas* **148 B4** 24 30N 76 20W
Eyasi, L., *Tanzania* **106 C4** 3 30 S 35 0 E
Eyeberry L., *Canada* **131 A8** 63 8N 104 43W
Eyemouth, *U.K.* **18 F6** 55 53N 2 5W
Eygurande, *France* **24 C6** 45 40N 2 26 E
Eyjafjörður, *Iceland* **12 C4** 66 15N 18 30W
Eymet, *France* **24 D4** 44 40N 0 25 E
Eymoutiers, *France* **24 C5** 45 40N 1 45 E
Eynesil, *Turkey* **89 C8** 41 4N 39 9 E
Eyrarbakki, *Iceland* **12 E3** 63 52N 21 9W
Eyre, *Australia* **113 F4** 32 15 S 126 18 E
Eyre (North), L., *Australia* **115 D2** 28 30 S 137 20 E
Eyre (South), L., *Australia* **115 D2** 29 18 S 137 25 E
Eyre, L., *Australia* **110 F6** 29 30 S 137 26 E
Eyre Cr. →, *Australia* **115 D2** 26 40 S 139 0 E
Eyre Mts., *N.Z.* **119 F3** 45 25 S 168 25 E
Eyre Pen., *Australia* **115 E2** 33 30 S 136 17 E
Eyvānkī, *Iran* **85 C6** 35 24N 51 56 E
Ez Zeidab, *Sudan* **94 D3** 17 25N 33 55 E
Ezcaray, *Spain* **34 C2** 42 19N 3 0W
Ezine, *Turkey* **44 E8** 39 48N 26 20 E
Ezmul, *Mauritania* **98 D1** 22 15N 15 40W
Ezouza →, *Cyprus* **32 E11** 34 44N 32 27 E

# F

Fabens, *U.S.A.* **143 L10** 31 30N 106 10W
Fåborg, *Denmark* **15 J4** 55 6N 10 15 E
Fabriano, *Italy* **39 E9** 43 20N 12 52 E
Făcăeni, *Romania* **46 E8** 44 32N 27 53 E
Facatativá, *Colombia* **152 C3** 4 49N 74 22W
Fachi, *Niger* **97 E2** 18 6N 11 34 E
Facture, *France* **24 D3** 44 39N 0 58W
Fada, *Chad* **97 E4** 17 13N 21 34 E
Fada-n-Gourma, *Burkina Faso* **101 C5** 12 10N 0 30 E
Fadd, *Hungary* **31 E11** 46 28N 18 49 E
Faddeyevskiy, Ostrov, *Russia* **57 B15** 76 0N 144 0 E
Fadghāmī, *Syria* **84 C4** 35 53N 40 52 E
Fadlab, *Sudan* **94 D3** 17 42N 34 2 E
Faenza, *Italy* **39 D8** 44 17N 11 53 E
Fafa, *Mali* **101 B5** 15 22N 0 48 E
Fafe, *Portugal* **36 D2** 41 27N 8 11W
Faga, *W. Samoa* **121 W23** 13 39 S 172 8W
Fagam, *Nigeria* **101 C7** 11 1N 10 1 E
Fagamalo, *W. Samoa* **121 W23** 13 25 S 172 21W
Făgăras, *Romania* **46 D5** 45 48N 24 58 E
Făgăras, Munţii, *Romania* **46 D5** 45 40N 24 40 E
Fågelsjö, *Sweden* **14 C8** 61 50N 14 35 E
Fagernes, *Norway* **13 F10** 60 59N 9 14 E
Fagersta, *Sweden* **13 F13** 60 1N 15 46 E
Făget, *Romania* **46 D3** 45 52N 22 10 E
Făget, Munţii, *Romania* **46 B4** 47 40N 23 10 E
Fagnano, L., *Argentina* **160 D3** 54 30 S 68 0W
Fagnano Castello, *Italy* **41 C9** 39 31N 16 4 E
Fagnières, *France* **23 D11** 48 58N 4 20 E
Fahlīān, *Iran* **85 D6** 30 11N 51 28 E
Fahr, *Yemen* **87 D6** 12 26N 54 8 E
Fahraj, *Kermān, Iran* **85 D8** 29 0N 59 0 E
Fahraj, *Yazd, Iran* **85 D7** 31 46N 54 36 E
Faial, *Madeira* **33 D3** 32 47N 16 53W
Faido, *Switz.* **29 D7** 46 29N 8 48 E
Fair Hd., *U.K.* **19 A5** 55 14N 6 10W
Fair Oaks, *U.S.A.* **144 G5** 38 39N 121 16W
Fairbank, *U.S.A.* **143 L8** 31 43N 110 11W
Fairbanks, *U.S.A.* **126 B5** 64 51N 147 43W
Fairborn, *U.S.A.* **141 E12** 39 49N 84 2W
Fairbury, *Ill., U.S.A.* **141 D8** 40 45N 88 31W
Fairbury, *Nebr., U.S.A.* **138 E6** 40 8N 97 11W
Faire, *Phil.* **70 C3** 17 53N 121 34 E
Fairfax, *Ohio, U.S.A.* **141 E13** 39 5N 83 37W
Fairfax, *Okla., U.S.A.* **139 G6** 36 34N 96 42W
Fairfield, *Australia* **117 B9** 33 53 S 150 57 E
Fairfield, *Ala., U.S.A.* **135 J2** 33 29N 86 55W
Fairfield, *Calif., U.S.A.* **144 G4** 38 15N 122 3W
Fairfield, *Conn., U.S.A.* **137 E11** 41 9N 73 16W
Fairfield, *Idaho, U.S.A.* **142 E6** 43 21N 114 44W
Fairfield, *Ill., U.S.A.* **141 F8** 38 23N 88 22W
Fairfield, *Iowa, U.S.A.* **140 C5** 40 56N 91 57W
Fairfield, *Mont., U.S.A.* **142 C8** 47 37N 111 59W
Fairfield, *Ohio, U.S.A.* **141 E12** 39 21N 84 34W
Fairfield, *Tex., U.S.A.* **139 K7** 31 44N 96 10W
Fairford, *Canada* **131 C9** 51 37N 98 38W
Fairhope, *U.S.A.* **135 K2** 30 31N 87 54W
Fairlie, *N.Z.* **119 E5** 44 5 S 170 49 E
Fairmead, *U.S.A.* **144 H6** 37 5N 120 10W
Fairmont, *Minn., U.S.A.* **138 D7** 43 39N 94 28W
Fairmont, *W. Va., U.S.A.* **134 F5** 39 29N 80 9W
Fairmount, *U.S.A.* **145 L8** 34 45N 118 26W
Fairplay, *U.S.A.* **143 G11** 39 15N 106 2W
Fairport, *U.S.A.* **136 C7** 43 6N 77 27W
Fairport Harbor, *U.S.A.* **136 E3** 41 45N 81 17W
Fairview, *Australia* **114 B3** 15 31 S 144 17 E
Fairview, *Canada* **130 B5** 56 5N 118 25W
Fairview, *Mont., U.S.A.* **138 B2** 47 51N 104 3W
Fairview, *Okla., U.S.A.* **139 G5** 36 16N 98 29W
Fairview, *Utah, U.S.A.* **142 G8** 39 50N 111 0W
Fairweather, Mt., *U.S.A.* **126 C6** 58 55N 137 32W
Faisalabad, *Pakistan* **79 C4** 31 30N 73 5 E
Faith, *U.S.A.* **138 C3** 45 2N 102 2W
Faizabad, *India* **81 F10** 26 45N 82 10 E
Faizpur, *India* **82 D2** 21 14N 75 49 E
Fajardo, *Puerto Rico* **149 C6** 18 20N 65 39W
Fakam, *Yemen* **86 C3** 16 38N 43 49 E
Fakfak, *Indonesia* **73 B4** 3 0 S 132 15 E
Fakiya, *Bulgaria* **43 E12** 42 10N 27 6 E
Fakobli, *Ivory C.* **100 D3** 7 23N 7 23W
Fakse, *Denmark* **15 J6** 55 15N 12 8 E
Fakse B., *Denmark* **15 J6** 55 11N 12 15 E
Fakse Ladeplads, *Denmark* **15 J6** 55 11N 12 9 E
Faku, *China* **67 C12** 42 32N 123 21 E
Falaise, *France* **22 D6** 48 54N 0 12W
Falaise, Mui, *Vietnam* **76 C5** 19 6N 105 45 E
Falakrón Óros, *Greece* **44 C5** 41 15N 23 58 E
Falam, *Burma* **78 D4** 23 0N 93 45 E
Falces, *Spain* **34 C3** 42 24N 1 48W
Fălciu, *Romania* **46 C9** 46 17N 28 7 E
Falcón □, *Venezuela* **152 A4** 11 0N 69 50W
Falcón, C., *Spain* **33 C7** 38 50N 1 23 E
Falcon, C., *Algeria* **99 A4** 35 50N 0 50W
Falcon Dam, *U.S.A.* **139 M5** 26 50N 99 20W
Falconara Marittima, *Italy* **39 E10** 43 37N 13 23 E
Falconer, *U.S.A.* **136 D5** 42 7N 79 13W
Faléa, *Mali* **100 C2** 12 16N 11 17W
Falelatai, *W. Samoa* **121 W24** 13 55 S 171 59W
Falelima, *W. Samoa* **121 W23** 13 32 S 172 41W
Falenki, *Russia* **54 B2** 58 22N 51 35 E
Faleshty, *Moldavia* **52 C2** 47 32N 27 44 E
Falfurrias, *U.S.A.* **139 M5** 27 14N 98 9W
Falher, *Canada* **130 B5** 55 44N 117 15W
Falirakí, *Greece* **32 C10** 36 22N 28 12 E
Falkenberg, *Germany* **26 D9** 51 34N 13 13 E
Falkenberg, *Sweden* **15 H6** 56 54N 12 30 E
Falkensee, *Germany* **26 C9** 52 35N 13 6 E
Falkenstein, *Germany* **26 E8** 50 27N 12 24 E
Falkirk, *U.K.* **18 F5** 56 0N 3 47W
Falkland, East, I., *Falk. Is.* **160 D5** 51 40 S 58 30W
Falkland, West, I., *Falk. Is.* **160 D4** 51 40 S 60 0W
Falkland Is. ■, *Atl. Oc.* **160 D5** 51 30 S 59 0W
Falkland Is. Dependency □, *Atl. Oc.* **7 B1** 57 0 S 40 0W
Falkland Sd., *Falk. Is.* **160 D5** 52 0 S 60 0W
Falkonéra, *Greece* **45 H5** 36 50N 23 52 E
Falköping, *Sweden* **15 F7** 58 12N 13 33 E
Fall River, *U.S.A.* **137 E13** 41 43N 71 10W
Fall River Mills, *U.S.A.* **142 F3** 41 3N 121 26W
Fallbrook, *U.S.A.* **143 K5** 33 25N 117 12W
Fallbrook, *Calif., U.S.A.* **145 M9** 33 23N 117 15W
Fallon, *Mont., U.S.A.* **138 B2** 46 50N 105 8W
Fallon, *Nev., U.S.A.* **142 G4** 39 28N 118 47W
Falls City, *Nebr., U.S.A.* **138 E7** 40 3N 95 36W
Falls City, *Oreg., U.S.A.* **142 D2** 44 52N 123 26W
Falls Creek, *U.S.A.* **136 E6** 41 9N 78 48W
Falmouth, *Jamaica* **148 C4** 18 30N 77 40W
Falmouth, *U.K.* **17 G2** 50 9N 5 5W
Falmouth, *U.S.A.* **141 F12** 38 41N 84 20W
False B., *S. Africa* **104 E2** 34 15 S 18 40 E
False Divi Pt., *India* **83 G5** 15 43N 80 50 E
Falset, *Spain* **34 D5** 41 7N 0 50 E
Falso, C., *Honduras* **148 C3** 15 12N 83 21W
Falster, *Denmark* **15 K5** 54 45N 11 55 E
Falsterbo, *Sweden* **15 J6** 55 23N 12 50 E
Fălticeni, *Romania* **46 B7** 47 21N 26 20 E
Falun, *Sweden* **13 F13** 60 37N 15 37 E
Famagusta, *Cyprus* **32 D12** 35 8N 33 55 E
Famagusta Bay, *Cyprus* **32 D13** 35 15N 34 0 E
Famatina, Sierra de, *Argentina* **158 B2** 27 30 S 68 0W
Family L., *Canada* **131 C9** 51 54N 95 27W
Famoso, *U.S.A.* **145 K7** 35 37N 119 12W
Fan Xian, *China* **66 G8** 35 55N 115 38 E
Fana, *Mali* **100 C3** 13 0N 6 56W
Fanárion, *Greece* **44 E3** 39 24N 21 47 E
Fandriana, *Madag.* **105 C8** 20 14 S 47 21 E
Fang, *Thailand* **76 C2** 19 55N 99 13 E
Fang Xian, *China* **69 A8** 32 3N 110 40 E
Fangchang, *China* **69 B12** 31 5N 118 4 E
Fangcheng, *Guangxi Zhuangzu, China* **68 G7** 21 42N 108 21 E
Fangcheng, *Henan, China* **66 H7** 33 18N 112 59 E
Fangliao, *Taiwan* **69 F13** 22 22N 120 38 E
Fangshan, *China* **66 E6** 38 3N 111 25 E
Fangzi, *China* **67 F10** 36 33N 119 10 E
Fani i Madh →, *Albania* **44 C2** 41 56N 20 16 E
Fanjiatun, *China* **67 C13** 43 40N 125 15 E
Fannich, L., *U.K.* **18 D4** 57 40N 5 0W
Fannūj, *Iran* **85 E8** 26 35N 59 38 E
Fanny Bay, *Canada* **130 D4** 49 37N 124 48W
Fanø, *Denmark* **15 J2** 55 25N 8 25 E
Fano, *Italy* **39 E10** 43 50N 13 0 E
Fanshaw, *U.S.A.* **130 B2** 57 11N 133 30W
Fanshi, *China* **66 E7** 39 12N 113 20 E
Fao = Al Fāw, *Iraq* **85 D6** 30 0N 48 30 E
Faqirwali, *Pakistan* **80 E5** 29 27N 73 0 E
Fara in Sabina, *Italy* **39 F9** 42 13N 12 44 E
Farab, *Turkmenistan* **55 D1** 39 9N 63 36 E
Faradje, *Zaïre* **106 B2** 3 50N 29 45 E
Farafangana, *Madag.* **105 C8** 22 49 S 47 50 E
Farâfra, El Wâhât el-, *Egypt* **94 B2** 27 15N 28 20 E
Farāh, *Afghan.* **79 B1** 32 20N 62 7 E
Farāh □, *Afghan.* **79 B1** 32 25N 62 10 E
Farahalana, *Madag.* **105 A9** 14 26 S 50 10 E
Faraid, Gebel, *Egypt* **94 C4** 23 33N 35 19 E
Faramana, *Burkina Faso* **100 C4** 11 56N 4 45W
Faranah, *Guinea* **100 C2** 10 3N 10 45W
Farasān, Jazā'ir, *Si. Arabia* **86 C3** 16 45N 41 55 E
Farasan Is. = Farasān, Jazā'ir, *Si. Arabia* **86 C3** 16 45N 41 55 E
Faratsiho, *Madag.* **105 B8** 19 24 S 46 57 E
Farbarachi, *Somali Rep.* **108 D3** 2 30N 45 30 E
Fardes →, *Spain* **35 H1** 37 35N 3 0W
Fareham, *U.K.* **17 G6** 50 52N 1 11W
Farewell, C., *N.Z.* **119 A7** 40 29 S 172 43 E
Farewell C. = Farvel, Kap, *Greenland* **124 D15** 59 48N 43 55W
Farewell Spit, *N.Z.* **119 A8** 40 35 S 173 0 E
Farghona = Fergana, *Uzbekistan* **55 C5** 40 23N 71 19 E
Fargo, *U.S.A.* **138 B6** 46 53N 96 48W
Fari'a →, *Jordan* **91 C4** 32 12N 35 27 E
Faribault, *U.S.A.* **138 C8** 44 18N 93 16W
Faridkot, *India* **80 D6** 30 44N 74 45 E
Faridpur, *Bangla.* **78 D2** 23 15N 89 55 E
Färila, *Sweden* **14 C9** 61 48N 15 50 E
Farim, *Guinea-Biss.* **100 C1** 12 27N 15 9W
Farīmān, *Iran* **85 C8** 35 40N 59 49 E
Farina, *Australia* **115 E2** 30 3 S 138 15 E
Farinha →, *Brazil* **154 C2** 6 51 S 47 30W
Fariones, Pta., *Canary Is.* **33 E6** 29 13N 13 28W
Fâriskûr, *Egypt* **94 H7** 31 20N 31 43 E
Farmakonisi, *Greece* **45 G9** 37 17N 27 8 E
Farmer City, *U.S.A.* **141 D8** 40 15N 88 39W
Farmersburg, *U.S.A.* **141 E9** 39 15N 87 23W
Farmerville, *U.S.A.* **139 J8** 32 47N 92 24W
Farmington, *Calif., U.S.A.* **144 H6** 37 55N 120 59W
Farmington, *Ill., U.S.A.* **140 D6** 40 42N 90 0W
Farmington, *Iowa, U.S.A.* **140 D5** 40 38N 91 44W
Farmington, *Mo., U.S.A.* **140 G6** 37 47N 90 25W
Farmington, *N.H., U.S.A.* **137 C13** 43 24N 71 4W
Farmington, *N. Mex., U.S.A.* **143 H9** 36 44N 108 12W
Farmington, *Utah, U.S.A.* **142 F8** 41 0N 111 12W
Farmington →, *U.S.A.* **137 E12** 41 51N 72 38W
Farmland, *U.S.A.* **141 D11** 40 15N 85 5W
Farmville, *U.S.A.* **134 G6** 37 18N 78 24W
Farnborough, *U.K.* **17 F7** 51 17N 0 46W
Farne Is., *U.K.* **16 B6** 55 38N 1 37W
Farnham, *Canada* **137 A12** 45 17N 72 59W
Faro, *Brazil* **153 D6** 2 10 S 56 39W
Faro, *Portugal* **37 H3** 37 2N 7 55W
Fårö, *Sweden* **13 H15** 57 55N 19 5 E
Faro □, *Portugal* **37 H2** 37 12N 8 10W
Faroe Is. = Føroyar, *Atl. Oc.* **8 B8** 62 0N 7 0W
Farquhar, C., *Australia* **113 D1** 23 50 S 113 36 E
Farquhar Is., *Seychelles* **109 F4** 11 0 S 52 0 E
Farrars Cr. →, *Australia* **114 D3** 25 35 S 140 43 E
Farrāshband, *Iran* **85 D7** 28 57N 52 5 E
Farrell, *U.S.A.* **136 E4** 41 13N 80 30W
Farrell Flat, *Australia* **116 B3** 33 48 S 138 48 E
Farrokhī, *Iran* **85 C8** 33 50N 59 31 E
Farruch, C., *Spain* **33 B10** 39 47N 3 21 E
Farrukhabad-cum-Fatehgarh, *India* **81 F8** 27 30N 79 32 E
Fārs □, *Iran* **85 D7** 29 30N 55 0 E
Fársala, *Greece* **44 E4** 39 17N 22 23 E
Farsī, *Afghan.* **79 B1** 33 47N 63 15 E
Farsø, *Denmark* **15 H3** 56 46N 9 19 E
Farsund, *Norway* **13 G9** 58 5N 6 55 E
Fartak, Râs, *Si. Arabia* **84 D2** 28 5N 34 34 E
Fartak, Ra's, *Yemen* **87 D6** 15 38N 52 15 E
Fartura, Serra da, *Brazil* **159 B5** 26 21 S 52 52W
Faru, *Nigeria* **101 C6** 12 48N 6 12 E
Fārūj, *Iran* **85 B8** 37 14N 58 14 E
Farum, *Denmark* **15 J6** 55 49N 12 21 E
Farvel, Kap, *Greenland* **124 D15** 59 48N 43 55W
Farwell, *U.S.A.* **139 H3** 34 23N 103 2W
Fāryāb □, *Afghan.* **79 B2** 36 0N 65 0 E
Fasā, *Iran* **85 D7** 29 0N 53 39 E
Fasano, *Italy* **41 B10** 40 50N 17 20 E
Fashoda, *Sudan* **95 F3** 9 50N 32 2 E
Fastnet Rock, *Ireland* **19 E2** 51 22N 9 37W
Fastov, *Ukraine* **50 F6** 50 7N 29 57 E
Fatagar, Tanjung, *Indonesia* **73 B4** 2 46 S 131 57 E
Fatehgarh, *India* **81 F8** 27 25N 79 35 E
Fatehpur, *Raj., India* **80 F6** 28 0N 74 40 E
Fatehpur, *Ut. P., India* **81 G9** 25 56N 81 13 E
Fatesh, *Russia* **51 E9** 52 8N 35 57 E
Fatick, *Senegal* **100 C1** 14 19N 16 27W
Fatima, *Canada* **129 C7** 47 24N 61 53W
Fátima, *Portugal* **37 F2** 39 37N 8 39W
Fatoya, *Guinea* **100 C3** 11 37N 9 10W
Faucille, Col de la, *France* **25 B10** 46 22N 6 2 E
Faulkton, *U.S.A.* **138 C5** 45 2N 99 8W
Faulquemont, *France* **23 C13** 49 3N 6 36 E
Fauquembergues, *France* **23 B9** 50 36N 2 5 E
Faure I., *Australia* **113 E1** 25 52 S 113 50 E
Făurei, *Romania* **46 D8** 45 6N 27 19 E
Fauresmith, *S. Africa* **104 D4** 29 44 S 25 17 E
Fauro, *Solomon Is.* **121 L9** 6 55 S 156 7 E
Fauske, *Norway* **12 C13** 67 17N 15 25 E
Fauvillers, *Belgium* **21 J7** 49 51N 5 40 E
Favara, *Italy* **40 E6** 37 19N 13 39 E
Favaritx, C., *Spain* **33 A11** 40 0N 4 15 E
Favignana, *Italy* **40 E5** 37 56N 12 18 E
Favignana, I., *Italy* **40 E5** 37 56N 12 18 E
Favourable Lake, *Canada* **128 B1** 52 50N 93 39W
Fawn →, *Canada* **128 A2** 55 20N 87 35W
Fawnskin, *U.S.A.* **145 L10** 34 16N 116 56W
Faxaflói, *Iceland* **12 D2** 64 29N 23 0W
Faya-Largeau, *Chad* **97 E3** 17 58N 19 6 E
Fayaoué, *Vanuatu* **121 K4** 20 38 S 166 33 E
Fayd, *Si. Arabia* **84 E4** 27 1N 42 52 E
Fayence, *France* **25 E10** 43 38N 6 42 E
Fayette, *Ala., U.S.A.* **135 J2** 33 41N 87 50W
Fayette, *Iowa, U.S.A.* **140 B5** 42 51N 91 48W
Fayette, *Mo., U.S.A.* **140 E4** 39 9N 92 41W
Fayette, *Ohio, U.S.A.* **141 C12** 41 40N 84 20W
Fayetteville, *Ark., U.S.A.* **139 G7** 36 4N 94 10W
Fayetteville, *N.C., U.S.A.* **135 H6** 35 3N 78 53W
Fayetteville, *Tenn., U.S.A.* **135 H2** 35 9N 86 34W
Fayón, *Spain* **34 D5** 41 15N 0 20 E
Fazenda Libongo, *Angola* **103 D2** 8 24 S 13 24 E
Fazenda Nova, *Brazil* **155 E1** 16 11 S 50 48W
Fazilka, *India* **80 D6** 30 27N 74 2 E
Fazilpur, *Pakistan* **80 E4** 29 18N 70 29 E
Fdérik, *Mauritania* **98 D2** 22 40N 12 45W
Feale →, *Ireland* **19 D2** 52 26N 9 40W
Fear, C., *U.S.A.* **135 J7** 33 50N 77 58W
Feather →, *U.S.A.* **142 G3** 38 47N 121 36W
Feather Falls, *U.S.A.* **144 F5** 39 36N 121 16W
Featherston, *N.Z.* **118 H4** 41 6 S 175 20 E
Featherstone, *Zimbabwe* **107 F3** 18 42 S 30 55 E
Fécamp, *France* **22 C7** 49 45N 0 22 E
Fedala = Mohammedia, *Morocco* **98 B3** 33 44N 7 21W
Federación, *Argentina* **158 C4** 31 0 S 57 55W
Fedeshkūh, *Iran* **85 D7** 28 49N 53 50 E
Fedjadj, Chott el, *Tunisia* **96 B1** 33 52N 9 14 E
Fedorovka, *Kazakhstan* **54 E8** 53 38N 62 42 E
Fehérgyarmat, *Hungary* **31 D15** 48 0N 22 30 E
Fehmarn, *Germany* **26 A7** 54 26N 11 10 E
Fehmarn Bælt, *Denmark* **26 A7** 54 35N 11 20 E
Fei Xian, *China* **67 G9** 35 18N 117 59 E
Feijó, *Brazil* **156 B3** 8 9 S 70 21W
Feilding, *N.Z.* **118 G4** 40 13 S 175 35 E
Feira de Santana, *Brazil* **155 D4** 12 15 S 38 57W
Feixiang, *China* **66 F8** 36 30N 114 45 E
Fejér □, *Hungary* **31 D11** 47 9N 18 30 E
Fejø, *Denmark* **15 K5** 54 55N 11 30 E
Feke, *Turkey* **88 E6** 37 48N 35 56 E
Fekete →, *Hungary* **31 F11** 45 47N 18 15 E
Felanitx, *Spain* **33 B10** 39 28N 3 9 E
Feldbach, *Austria* **30 E8** 46 57N 15 52 E
Feldberg, *Baden-W., Germany* **27 H3** 47 51N 7 58 E
Feldberg, *Mecklenburg-Vorpommern, Germany* **26 B9** 53 20N 13 26 E
Feldkirch, *Austria* **30 D2** 47 15N 9 37 E
Feldkirchen, *Austria* **30 E7** 46 44N 14 6 E
Felicity, *U.S.A.* **141 F12** 38 51N 84 6W
Felipe Carrillo Puerto, *Mexico* **147 D7** 19 38N 88 3W
Felixlândia, *Brazil* **155 E3** 18 47 S 44 55W
Felixstowe, *U.K.* **17 F9** 51 58N 1 22 E
Felletin, *France* **24 C6** 45 53N 2 11 E
Felton, *U.K.* **16 B6** 55 18N 1 42W
Felton, *U.S.A.* **144 H4** 37 3N 122 4W
Feltre, *Italy* **39 B8** 46 1N 11 55 E
Femø, *Denmark* **15 K5** 54 58N 11 53 E
Femunden, *Norway* **14 B5** 62 10N 11 53 E
Fen He →, *China* **66 G6** 35 36N 110 42 E
Fenelon Falls, *Canada* **136 B6** 44 32N 78 45W
Feneroa, *Ethiopia* **95 E4** 13 5N 39 3 E
Feng Xian, *Jiangsu, China* **66 G9** 34 43N 116 35 E
Feng Xian, *Shaanxi, China* **66 H4** 33 54N 106 40 E
Fengári, *Greece* **44 D7** 40 25N 25 32 E
Fengcheng, *Jiangxi, China* **69 C10** 28 12N 115 48 E
Fengcheng, *Liaoning, China* **67 D13** 40 28N 124 5 E
Fengdu, *China* **68 C6** 29 55N 107 41 E
Fengfeng, *China* **66 F8** 36 28N 114 8 E
Fenggang, *China* **68 D6** 27 57N 107 47 E
Fenghua, *China* **69 C13** 29 40N 121 25 E
Fenghuang, *China* **68 D7** 27 57N 109 29 E
Fenghuangzui, *China* **68 A7** 33 30N 109 23 E
Fengjie, *China* **68 B7** 31 5N 109 36 E
Fengkai, *China* **69 F8** 23 24N 111 30 E
Fengle, *China* **69 B9** 31 29N 112 29 E
Fengning, *China* **66 D9** 41 10N 116 33 E
Fengqing, *China* **68 E2** 24 38N 99 55 E
Fengqiu, *China* **66 G8** 35 2N 114 25 E
Fengrun, *China* **67 E10** 39 48N 118 8 E
Fengshan, *Guangxi Zhuangzu, China* **68 E7** 24 39N 109 15 E
Fengshan, *Guangxi Zhuangzu, China* **68 E6** 24 31N 107 3 E
Fengtai, *Anhui, China* **69 A11** 32 50N 116 40 E
Fengtai, *Beijing, China* **66 E9** 39 50N 116 18 E
Fengxian, *China* **69 B13** 30 55N 121 26 E
Fengxiang, *China* **66 G4** 34 29N 107 25 E
Fengxin, *China* **69 C10** 28 41N 115 18 E
Fengyang, *China* **67 H9** 32 51N 117 29 E
Fengyi, *China* **68 E3** 25 37N 100 20 E
Fengzhen, *China* **66 D7** 40 25N 113 2 E
Feni Is., *Papua N. G.* **120 C7** 4 0 S 153 40 E
Fenit, *Ireland* **19 D2** 52 17N 9 51W
Fennimore, *U.S.A.* **140 B6** 42 59N 90 39W
Fenny, *Bangla.* **78 D3** 22 55N 91 32 E
Feno, C. de, *France* **25 G12** 41 58N 8 33 E
Fenoarivo Afovoany, *Madag.* **105 B8** 18 26 S 46 34 E
Fenoarivo Atsinanana, *Madag.* **105 B8** 17 22 S 49 25 E
Fens, The, *U.K.* **16 E8** 52 45N 0 2 E
Fenton, *U.S.A.* **141 B13** 42 48N 83 42W
Fenxi, *China* **66 F6** 36 40N 111 31 E
Fenyang, *China* **65 C6** 37 19N 111 46 E
Fenyang, *Shanxi, China* **66 F6** 37 18N 111 48 E
Fenyi, *China* **69 D10** 27 45N 114 47 E
Feodosiya, *Ukraine* **52 D6** 45 2N 35 16 E
Fer, C. de, *Algeria* **99 A6** 37 3N 7 10 E
Ferdows, *Iran* **85 C8** 33 58N 58 2 E
Fère-Champenoise, *France* **23 D10** 48 45N 3 59 E
Fère-en-Tardenois, *France* **23 C10** 49 10N 3 30 E
Ferentino, *Italy* **40 A6** 41 42N 13 14 E
Ferfer, *Somali Rep.* **90 F4** 5 4N 45 9 E
Fergana, *Uzbekistan* **55 C5** 40 23N 71 19 E

Fukue-Shima 199


Fort Klamath, *U.S.A.* ... **142 E3** 42 42N 122 0W
Fort Knox, *U.S.A.* ...... **141 G11** 37 54N 85 57W
Fort Lallemand, *Algeria* . **99 B6** 31 13N 6 17 E
Fort-Lamy = Ndjamena, *Chad* ............... **97 F2** 12 10N 14 59 E
Fort Laramie, *U.S.A.* ... **138 D2** 42 13N 104 31W
Fort Lauderdale, *U.S.A.* . **135 M5** 26 7N 80 8W
Fort Leonard Wood, *U.S.A.* ............. **140 G4** 37 46N 92 11W
Fort Liard, *Canada* ..... **130 A4** 60 14N 123 30W
Fort Liberté, *Haiti* ..... **149 C5** 19 42N 71 51W
Fort Lupton, *U.S.A.* .... **138 E2** 40 5N 104 49W
Fort Mackay, *Canada* ... **130 B6** 57 12N 111 41W
Fort McKenzie, *Canada* . **129 A6** 57 20N 69 0W
Fort Macleod, *Canada* ... **130 D6** 49 45N 113 30W
Fort MacMahon, *Algeria* . **99 C5** 29 43N 1 45 E
Fort McMurray, *Canada* . **130 B6** 56 44N 111 7W
Fort McPherson, *Canada* **126 B6** 67 30N 134 55W
Fort Madison, *U.S.A.* .... **140 D5** 40 38N 91 27W
Fort Meade, *U.S.A.* ..... **135 M5** 27 45N 81 48W
Fort Miribel, *Algeria* .... **99 C5** 29 25N 2 55 E
Fort Morgan, *U.S.A.* .... **138 E3** 40 15N 103 48W
Fort Myers, *U.S.A.* ..... **135 M5** 26 39N 81 52W
Fort Nelson, *Canada* .... **130 B4** 58 50N 122 44W
Fort Nelson →, *Canada* . **130 B4** 59 32N 124 0W
Fort Norman, *Canada* ... **126 B7** 64 57N 125 30W
Fort Payne, *U.S.A.* ..... **135 H3** 34 26N 85 43W
Fort Peck, *U.S.A.* ...... **142 B10** 48 1N 106 27W
Fort Peck Dam, *U.S.A.* . **142 C10** 48 0N 106 26W
Fort Peck L., *U.S.A.* .... **142 C10** 48 0N 106 26W
Fort Pierce, *U.S.A.* ..... **135 M5** 27 27N 80 20W
Fort Pierre, *U.S.A.* ..... **138 C4** 44 21N 100 22W
Fort Pierre Bordes = Ti-n-Zaouatène, *Algeria* .... **99 E5** 19 55N 2 55 E
Fort Plain, *U.S.A.* ...... **137 D10** 42 56N 74 37W
Fort Portal, *Uganda* ..... **106 B3** 0 40N 30 20 E
Fort Providence, *Canada* **130 A5** 61 3N 117 40W
Fort Qu'Appelle, *Canada* **131 C8** 50 45N 103 50W
Fort Recovery, *U.S.A.* .. **141 D12** 40 25N 84 47W
Fort Resolution, *Canada* . **130 A6** 61 10N 113 40W
Fort Rixon, *Zimbabwe* .. **107 G2** 20 2 S 29 17 E
Fort Rosebery = Mansa, *Zambia* ............. **107 E2** 11 13 S 28 55 E
Fort Ross, *U.S.A.* ...... **144 G3** 38 32N 123 13W
Fort Rousset = Owando, *Congo* .............. **102 C3** 0 29 S 15 55 E
Fort Rupert, *Canada* .... **128 B4** 51 30N 78 40W
Fort Saint, *Tunisia* ...... **96 B1** 30 19N 9 31 E
Fort St. James, *Canada* .. **130 C4** 54 30N 124 10W
Fort St. John, *Canada* ... **130 B4** 56 15N 120 50W
Fort Sandeman, *Pakistan* **79 C3** 31 20N 69 31 E
Fort Saskatchewan, *Canada* ............. **130 C6** 53 40N 113 15W
Fort Scott, *U.S.A.* ...... **139 G7** 37 50N 94 42W
Fort Severn, *Canada* .... **128 A2** 56 0N 87 40W
Fort Shevchenko, *Kazakhstan* .......... **53 E14** 43 40N 51 20 E
Fort-Sibut, *C.A.R.* ...... **102 A3** 5 46N 19 10 E
Fort Simpson, *Canada* ... **130 A4** 61 45N 121 15W
Fort Smith, *Canada* ..... **130 B6** 60 0N 111 51W
Fort Smith, *U.S.A.* ..... **139 H7** 35 23N 94 25W
Fort Stanton, *U.S.A.* ... **143 K11** 33 30N 105 31W
Fort Stockton, *U.S.A.* ... **139 K3** 30 53N 102 53W
Fort Sumner, *U.S.A.* .... **139 H2** 34 28N 104 15W
Fort Thomas, *U.S.A.* .... **141 E12** 39 5N 84 27W
Fort Trinquet = Bir Mogrein, *Mauritania* .. **98 C2** 25 10N 11 25W
Fort Valley, *U.S.A.* ..... **135 J4** 32 33N 83 53W
Fort Vermilion, *Canada* . **130 B5** 58 24N 116 0W
Fort Walton Beach, *U.S.A.* ............. **135 K2** 30 25N 86 36W
Fort Wayne, *U.S.A.* ..... **141 C11** 41 4N 85 9W
Fort William, *U.K.* ...... **18 E3** 56 48N 5 8W
Fort Worth, *U.S.A.* ..... **139 J6** 32 45N 97 18W
Fort Yates, *U.S.A.* ...... **138 B4** 46 5N 100 38W
Fort Yukon, *U.S.A.* ..... **126 B5** 66 34N 145 16W
Fortaleza, *Bolivia* ...... **156 C4** 12 6 S 66 49W
Fortaleza, *Brazil* ....... **154 B4** 3 45 S 38 35W
Forteau, *Canada* ........ **129 B8** 51 28N 56 58W
Forth →, *U.K.* ......... **18 E5** 56 9N 3 50W
Forth, Firth of, *U.K.* .... **18 E6** 56 5N 2 55W
Forthassa Rharbia, *Algeria* **99 B4** 32 52N 1 18W
Fortín Coronel Eugenio Garay, *Paraguay* ...... **157 E5** 20 31 S 62 8W
Fortín Garrapatal, *Paraguay* ........... **157 E5** 21 27 S 61 30W
Fortín General Pando, *Paraguay* ........... **157 D6** 19 45 S 59 47W
Fortín Madrejón, *Paraguay* ........... **157 E6** 20 45 S 59 52W
Fortín Uno, *Argentina* ... **160 A3** 38 50 S 65 18W
Fortore →, *Italy* ....... **39 G12** 41 55N 15 17 E
Fortrose, *N.Z.* .......... **119 G3** 46 38 S 168 45 E
Fortrose, *U.K.* .......... **18 D4** 57 35N 4 10W
Fortuna, *Spain* ......... **35 G3** 38 11N 1 7W
Fortuna, *Calif., U.S.A.* .. **142 F1** 40 36N 124 9W
Fortuna, *N. Dak., U.S.A.* **138 A3** 48 55N 103 47W
Fortune B., *Canada* ..... **129 C8** 47 30N 55 22W
Fos-sur-Mer, *France* ..... **25 E8** 43 26N 4 56 E
Foshan, *China* .......... **69 F9** 23 4N 113 5 E
Fossacesia, *Italy* ........ **39 F11** 42 15N 14 30 E
Fossano, *Italy* .......... **38 D4** 44 33N 7 40 E
Fosses-la-Ville, *Belgium* . **21 H5** 50 24N 4 41 E
Fossil, *U.S.A.* .......... **142 D3** 45 0N 120 9W
Fossilbrook, *Australia* ... **114 B3** 17 47 S 144 29 E
Fossombrone, *Italy* ...... **39 E9** 43 41N 12 49 E
Fosston, *U.S.A.* ........ **138 B7** 47 35N 95 45W
Foster, *Canada* ......... **137 A12** 45 17N 72 30W
Foster, *U.S.A.* .......... **141 F12** 38 48N 84 13W
Foster →, *Canada* ...... **131 B7** 55 47N 105 49W
Fosters Ra., *Australia* ... **114 C1** 21 35 S 133 48 E
Fostoria, *U.S.A.* ........ **141 C13** 41 10N 83 25W
Fotuha'a, *Tonga* ........ **121 P13** 19 49 S 174 44W
Fougamou, *Gabon* ....... **102 C2** 1 16 S 10 30 E
Fougères, *France* ....... **22 D5** 48 21N 1 14W
Foul Pt., *Sri Lanka* ..... **83 K5** 8 35N 81 18 E
Foula, *U.K.* ............ **18 A6** 60 10N 2 5W
Foulness I., *U.K.* ....... **17 F8** 51 36N 0 55 E
Foulpointe, *Madag.* ..... **105 B8** 17 41 S 49 31 E
Foulwind, C., *N.Z.* ..... **119 B6** 41 45 S 171 28 E
Foum Assaka, *Morocco* . **98 C2** 29 8N 10 24W
Foum Zguid, *Morocco* ... **98 B3** 30 2N 6 59W
Foumban, *Cameroon* .... **101 D7** 5 45N 10 50 E
Foundiougne, *Senegal* ... **100 C1** 14 5N 16 32W
Fountain, *Colo., U.S.A.* . **138 F2** 38 41N 104 42W
Fountain, *Utah, U.S.A.* .. **142 G8** 39 41N 111 37W
Fountain Springs, *U.S.A.* **145 K8** 35 54N 118 51W
Fourchambault, *France* .. **23 E10** 47 2N 3 3 E
Fourchu, *Canada* ....... **129 C7** 45 43N 60 17W
Fouriesburg, *S. Africa* ... **104 D4** 28 38 S 28 14 E
Fourmies, *France* ....... **23 B11** 50 1N 4 2 E
Fournás, *Greece* ........ **45 E3** 39 3N 21 52 E
Foúrnoi, *Greece* ........ **45 G8** 37 36N 26 32 E
Fours, *France* .......... **23 F10** 46 50N 3 42 E
Fouta Djalon, *Guinea* ... **100 C2** 11 20N 12 10W
Foux, Cap-à-, *Haiti* .... **149 C5** 19 43N 73 27W
Foveaux Str., *N.Z.* ...... **119 G3** 46 42 S 168 10 E
Fowey, *U.K.* ........... **17 G3** 50 20N 4 39W
Fowler, *Calif., U.S.A.* ... **144 J7** 36 38N 119 41W
Fowler, *Colo., U.S.A.* ... **138 F2** 38 8N 104 2W
Fowler, *Ind., U.S.A.* .... **141 D9** 40 37N 87 19W
Fowler, *Kans., U.S.A.* ... **139 G4** 37 23N 100 12W
Fowler, *Mich., U.S.A.* ... **141 B12** 43 0N 84 45W
Fowlers B., *Australia* .... **113 F5** 31 59 S 132 34 E
Fowlerton, *U.S.A.* ...... **139 L5** 28 28N 98 48W
Fowlerville, *U.S.A.* ..... **141 B12** 42 40N 84 4W
Fox →, *Canada* ........ **131 B10** 56 3N 93 18W
Fox Valley, *Canada* ..... **131 C7** 50 30N 109 25W
Foxe Basin, *Canada* ..... **127 B12** 66 0N 77 0W
Foxe Chan., *Canada* ..... **127 B11** 65 0N 80 0W
Foxe Pen., *Canada* ...... **127 B12** 65 0N 76 0W
Foxhol, *Neths.* .......... **20 B9** 53 10N 6 43 E
Foxpark, *U.S.A.* ........ **142 F10** 41 5N 106 9W
Foxton, *N.Z.* ........... **118 G4** 40 29 S 175 18 E
Foyle, Lough, *U.K.* ..... **19 A4** 55 6N 7 8W
Foynes, *Ireland* ......... **19 D2** 52 37N 9 5W
Foz, *Spain* ............. **36 B3** 43 33N 7 20W
Fóz do Cunene, *Angola* . **103 F2** 17 15 S 11 48 E
Foz do Gregório, *Brazil* . **156 B3** 6 47 S 70 44W
Foz do Iguaçu, *Brazil* ... **159 B5** 25 30 S 54 30W
Foz do Riosinho, *Brazil* . **156 B3** 7 11 S 71 50W
Frackville, *U.S.A.* ...... **137 F8** 40 47N 76 14W
Fraga, *Spain* ........... **34 D5** 41 32N 0 21 E
Fraire, *Belgium* ......... **21 H5** 50 16N 4 31 E
Frameries, *Belgium* ..... **21 H3** 50 24N 3 54 E
Framingham, *U.S.A.* .... **137 D13** 42 17N 71 25W
Frampol, *Poland* ........ **47 E9** 50 41N 22 40 E
Franca, *Brazil* .......... **155 F2** 20 33 S 47 30W
Francavilla al Mare, *Italy* **39 F11** 42 25N 14 16 E
Francavilla Fontana, *Italy* **41 B10** 40 32N 17 35 E
France ■, *Europe* ....... **11 F6** 47 0N 3 0 E
Frances, *Australia* ...... **116 D4** 36 41 S 140 55 E
Frances →, *Canada* .... **130 A3** 60 16N 129 10W
Frances L., *Canada* ..... **130 A3** 61 23N 129 30W
Francés Viejo, C., *Dom. Rep.* ........... **149 C6** 19 40N 69 55W
Francesville, *U.S.A.* .... **141 D10** 40 59N 86 53W
Franceville, *Gabon* ...... **102 C2** 1 40 S 13 32 E
Franche-Comté, *France* .. **23 F12** 46 50N 5 55 E
Franches Montagnes, *Switz.* ............ **28 B4** 47 10N 7 0 E
Francisco de Orellana, *Ecuador* ............ **152 D2** 0 28 S 76 58W
Francisco I. Madero, *Coahuila, Mexico* ..... **146 B4** 25 48N 103 18W
Francisco I. Madero, *Durango, Mexico* ..... **146 C4** 24 32N 104 22W
Francisco Sá, *Brazil* ..... **155 E3** 16 28 S 43 30W
Francistown, *Botswana* .. **105 C4** 21 7 S 27 33 E
Francofonte, *Italy* ....... **41 E7** 37 13N 14 50 E
François, *Canada* ....... **129 C8** 47 35N 56 45W
François L., *Canada* ..... **130 C3** 54 0N 125 30W
Francorchamps, *Belgium* . **21 H7** 50 27N 5 57 E
Franeker, *Neths.* ........ **20 B7** 53 12N 5 33 E
Frankado, *Djibouti* ...... **95 E5** 12 30N 43 12 E
Frankenberg, *Germany* .. **26 D4** 51 3N 8 47 E
Frankenthal, *Germany* .. **27 F4** 49 32N 8 21 E
Frankenwald, *Germany* .. **27 E7** 50 18N 11 36 E
Frankford, *U.S.A.* ...... **140 E5** 39 29N 91 19W
Frankfort, *S. Africa* ..... **105 D4** 27 17 S 28 30 E
Frankfort, *Ind., U.S.A.* .. **141 D10** 40 17N 86 31W
Frankfort, *Kans., U.S.A.* . **138 F6** 39 42N 96 25W
Frankfort, *Ky., U.S.A.* ... **141 F12** 38 12N 84 52W
Frankfort, *Mich., U.S.A.* . **134 C2** 44 38N 86 14W
Frankfort, *Ohio, U.S.A.* . **141 E13** 39 24N 83 11W
Frankfurt am Main, *Germany* ............ **27 E4** 50 7N 8 40 E
Frankfurt an der Oder, *Germany* ............ **26 C10** 52 20N 14 31 E
Fränkische Alb, *Germany* **27 F7** 49 20N 11 30 E
Fränkische Rezal →, *Germany* ............ **27 F7** 49 11N 11 1 E
Fränkische Saale →, *Germany* ............ **27 E5** 50 30N 9 42 E
Fränkische Schweiz, *Germany* ............ **27 F7** 49 45N 11 10 E
Frankland →, *Australia* . **113 G2** 35 0 S 116 48 E
Franklin, *Ill., U.S.A.* .... **140 E6** 39 37N 90 3W
Franklin, *Ind., U.S.A.* ... **141 E10** 39 29N 86 3W
Franklin, *Ky., U.S.A.* ... **135 G2** 36 43N 86 35W
Franklin, *La., U.S.A.* ... **139 L9** 29 48N 91 30W
Franklin, *Mass., U.S.A.* . **137 D13** 42 5N 71 24W
Franklin, *N.H., U.S.A.* .. **137 C13** 43 27N 71 39W
Franklin, *Nebr., U.S.A.* . **138 E5** 40 6N 98 57W
Franklin, *Ohio, U.S.A.* .. **141 E12** 39 34N 84 18W
Franklin, *Pa., U.S.A.* ... **136 E5** 41 24N 79 50W
Franklin, *Tenn., U.S.A.* . **135 H2** 35 55N 86 52W
Franklin, *Va., U.S.A.* ... **135 G7** 36 41N 76 56W
Franklin, *W. Va., U.S.A.* **134 F6** 38 39N 79 20W
Franklin B., *Canada* .... **126 B7** 69 45N 126 0W
Franklin D. Roosevelt L., *U.S.A.* ............. **142 B4** 48 18N 118 9W
Franklin I., *Antarctica* ... **7 D11** 76 10 S 168 30 E
Franklin L., *U.S.A.* ..... **142 F6** 40 25N 115 22W
Franklin Mts., *Canada* .. **126 B7** 65 0N 125 0W
Franklin Mts., *N.Z.* .... **119 E2** 44 55 S 167 45 E
Franklin Str., *Canada* .. **126 A10** 72 0N 96 0W
Franklinton, *U.S.A.* .... **139 K9** 30 51N 90 9W
Franklinville, *U.S.A.* ... **136 D6** 42 20N 78 27W
Franklyn Mt., *N.Z.* ..... **119 C7** 42 4 S 172 42 E
Franks Pk., *U.S.A.* ..... **142 E9** 43 58N 109 18W
Frankston, *Australia* .... **117 E6** 38 8 S 145 8 E
Frankton Junc., *N.Z.* ... **118 D4** 37 47 S 175 16 E
Fränsta, *Sweden* ........ **14 B10** 62 30N 16 11 E
Frantsa Iosifa, Zemlya, *Russia* ............. **56 A6** 82 0N 55 0 E
Franz, *Canada* .......... **128 C3** 48 25N 84 30W
Franz Josef Land = Frantsa Iosifa, Zemlya, *Russia* ............. **56 A6** 82 0N 55 0 E
Franzburg, *Germany* .... **26 A8** 54 9N 12 52 E
Frascati, *Italy* .......... **40 A5** 41 48N 12 41 E
Fraser →, *B.C., Canada* **130 D4** 49 7N 123 11W
Fraser →, *Nfld., Canada* **129 A7** 56 39N 62 10W
Fraser, Mt., *Australia* ... **113 E2** 25 35 S 118 20 E
Fraser I., *Australia* ..... **115 D5** 25 15 S 153 10 E
Fraser Lake, *Canada* .... **130 C4** 54 0N 124 50W
Fraserburg, *S. Africa* ... **104 E3** 31 55 S 21 30 E
Fraserburgh, *U.K.* ...... **18 D6** 57 41N 2 3W
Fraserdale, *Canada* ..... **128 C3** 49 55N 81 37W
Frasertown, *N.Z.* ....... **118 E6** 38 58 S 177 28 E
Frashëri, *Albania* ....... **44 D2** 40 23N 20 26 E
Frasne, *France* ......... **23 F13** 46 50N 6 10 E
Frauenfeld, *Switz.* ...... **29 A7** 47 34N 8 54 E
Fray Bentos, *Uruguay* ... **158 C4** 33 10 S 58 15W
Frazier Downs, *Australia* **112 C3** 18 48 S 121 42 E
Frechilla, *Spain* ........ **36 C6** 42 8N 4 50W
Fredericia, *Denmark* .... **15 J3** 55 34N 9 45 E
Frederick, *Md., U.S.A.* .. **134 F7** 39 25N 77 25W
Frederick, *Okla., U.S.A.* **139 H5** 34 23N 99 1W
Frederick, *S. Dak., U.S.A.* ............. **138 C5** 45 50N 98 31W
Frederick Sd., *U.S.A.* ... **130 B2** 57 10N 134 0W
Fredericksburg, *Tex., U.S.A.* ............. **139 K5** 30 16N 98 52W
Fredericksburg, *Va., U.S.A.* ............. **134 F7** 38 18N 77 28W
Fredericktown, *U.S.A.* .. **139 G9** 37 34N 90 18W
Frederico I. Madero, Presa, *Mexico* ........ **146 B3** 28 7N 105 40W
Fredericton, *Canada* .... **129 C6** 45 57N 66 40W
Fredericton Junc., *Canada* **129 C6** 45 41N 66 40W
Frederikshåb, *Greenland* . **6 C5** 62 0N 49 43W
Frederikshavn, *Denmark* . **15 G4** 57 28N 10 31 E
Frederikssund, *Denmark* . **15 J6** 55 50N 12 3 E
Frederiksted, *Virgin Is.* .. **149 C7** 17 43N 64 53W
Fredonia, *Ariz., U.S.A.* . **143 H7** 36 57N 112 32W
Fredonia, *Kans., U.S.A.* . **139 G7** 37 32N 95 49W
Fredonia, *N.Y., U.S.A.* .. **136 D5** 42 26N 79 20W
Fredrikstad, *Norway* .... **14 E4** 59 13N 10 57 E
Freeburg, *U.S.A.* ....... **140 F5** 38 19N 91 56W
Freehold, *U.S.A.* ....... **137 F10** 40 16N 74 17W
Freel Peak, *U.S.A.* ..... **144 G7** 38 52N 119 54W
Freeland, *U.S.A.* ....... **137 E9** 41 1N 75 54W
Freels, C., *Canada* ...... **129 C9** 49 15N 53 30W
Freeman, *Calif., U.S.A.* . **145 K9** 35 35N 117 53W
Freeman, *Mo., U.S.A.* .. **140 F2** 38 37N 94 30W
Freeman, *S. Dak., U.S.A.* **138 D6** 43 21N 97 26W
Freeport, *Bahamas* ..... **148 A4** 26 30N 78 47W
Freeport, *Canada* ....... **129 D6** 44 15N 66 20W
Freeport, *Ill., U.S.A.* .... **140 B7** 42 17N 89 36W
Freeport, *N.Y., U.S.A.* .. **137 F11** 40 39N 73 35W
Freeport, *Tex., U.S.A.* .. **139 L7** 28 57N 95 21W
Freetown, *S. Leone* ..... **100 D2** 8 30N 13 17W
Frégate, L., *Canada* ..... **128 B5** 53 15N 74 45W
Fregenal de la Sierra, *Spain* ................ **37 G4** 38 10N 6 39W
Fregene, *Italy* .......... **40 A5** 41 50N 12 12 E
Fréhel, C., *France* ...... **22 D4** 48 40N 2 20W
Freiberg, *Germany* ..... **26 E9** 50 55N 13 20 E
Freibourg = Fribourg, *Switz.* ............... **28 C4** 46 49N 7 9 E
Freiburg, *Baden-W., Germany* ............ **27 H3** 48 0N 7 52 E
Freiburg, *Niedersachsen, Germany* ............ **26 B5** 53 49N 9 17 E
Freiburger Alpen, *Switz.* . **28 C4** 46 37N 7 10 E
Freire, *Chile* ........... **160 A2** 38 54 S 72 38W
Freirina, *Chile* ......... **158 B1** 28 30 S 71 10W
Freising, *Germany* ...... **27 G7** 48 24N 11 47 E
Freistadt, *Austria* ....... **30 C7** 48 30N 14 30 E
Freital, *Germany* ....... **26 E9** 51 0N 13 40 E
Fréjus, *France* ......... **25 E10** 43 25N 6 44 E
Fremantle, *Australia* .... **113 F2** 32 7 S 115 47 E
Fremont, *Calif., U.S.A.* .. **144 H4** 37 32N 121 57W
Fremont, *Ind., U.S.A.* ... **141 C12** 41 44N 84 56W
Fremont, *Mich., U.S.A.* . **134 D3** 43 28N 85 57W
Fremont, *Nebr., U.S.A.* . **138 E6** 41 26N 96 30W
Fremont, *Ohio, U.S.A.* .. **141 C13** 41 21N 83 7W
Fremont →, *U.S.A.* .... **143 G8** 38 24N 110 42W
Fremont L., *U.S.A.* ..... **142 E9** 42 57N 109 48W
French Camp, *U.S.A.* ... **144 H5** 37 53N 121 16W
French Creek →, *U.S.A.* **136 E5** 41 24N 79 50W
French Guiana ■, *S. Amer.* ............. **153 C7** 4 0N 53 0W
French I., *Australia* ..... **117 E6** 38 20 S 145 22 E
French Lick, *U.S.A.* .... **141 F10** 38 33N 86 37W
French Pass, *N.Z.* ...... **119 A8** 40 55 S 173 55 E
French Polynesia ■, *Pac. Oc.* ............. **123 J13** 20 0 S 145 0W
French Terr. of Afars & Issas = Djibouti ■, *Africa* ............... **90 E3** 12 0N 43 0 E
Frenchburg, *U.S.A.* .... **141 G13** 37 57N 83 38W
Frenchglen, *U.S.A.* ..... **142 E4** 42 50N 118 55W
Frenchman Butte, *Canada* **131 C7** 53 35N 109 38W
Frenchman Cr. →, *Mont., U.S.A.* ....... **142 B10** 48 31N 107 10W
Frenchman Cr. →, *Nebr., U.S.A.* ............. **138 E4** 40 14N 100 50W
Frenda, *Algeria* ........ **99 A5** 35 2N 1 1 E
Fresco →, *Brazil* ....... **157 B7** 7 15 S 51 30W
Freshfield, C., *Antarctica* **7 C10** 68 25 S 151 10 E
Fresnay-sur-Sarthe, *France* **22 D7** 48 17N 0 1 E
Fresnillo, *Mexico* ....... **146 C4** 23 10N 103 0W
Fresno, *U.S.A.* ......... **144 J7** 36 44N 119 47W
Fresno Alhandiga, *Spain* . **36 E5** 40 42N 5 37W
Fresno Reservoir, *U.S.A.* **142 B9** 48 36N 109 57W
Freudenstadt, *Germany* .. **27 G4** 48 27N 8 25 E
Freux, *Belgium* ......... **21 J6** 49 59N 5 27 E
Frévent, *France* ......... **23 B9** 50 15N 2 17 E
Frew →, *Australia* ..... **114 C2** 20 0 S 135 38 E
Frewena, *Australia* ...... **114 B2** 19 25 S 135 25 E
Freycinet Pen., *Australia* **114 G4** 42 10 S 148 25 E
Freyming-Merlebach, *France* .............. **23 C13** 49 8N 6 48 E
Freyung, *Germany* ...... **27 G9** 48 48N 13 33 E
Fria, *Guinea* ........... **100 C2** 10 27N 13 38W
Fria, C., *Namibia* ....... **104 B1** 18 0 S 12 0 E
Friant, *U.S.A.* ......... **144 J7** 36 59N 119 43W
Frías, *Argentina* ........ **158 B2** 28 40 S 65 5W
Fribourg, *Switz.* ........ **28 C4** 46 49N 7 9 E
Fribourg □, *Switz.* ...... **28 C4** 46 40N 7 0 E
Frick, *Switz.* ........... **28 A6** 47 31N 8 1 E
Friday Harbor, *U.S.A.* .. **144 B3** 48 32N 123 1W
Friedberg, *Bayern, Germany* ............ **27 G6** 48 21N 10 59 E
Friedberg, *Hessen, Germany* ............ **27 E4** 50 21N 8 46 E
Friedland, *Germany* ..... **26 B9** 53 40N 13 33 E
Friedrichshafen, *Germany* **27 H5** 47 39N 9 29 E
Friedrichskoog, *Germany* **26 A4** 54 1N 8 52 E
Friedrichstadt, *Germany* . **26 A5** 54 23N 9 6 E
Friendly Is. = Tonga ■, *Pac. Oc.* ............. **121 P13** 19 50 S 174 30W
Friesach, *Austria* ....... **30 E7** 46 57N 14 24 E
Friesack, *Germany* ...... **26 C8** 52 43N 12 35 E
Friesche Wad, *Neths.* .... **20 B7** 53 22N 5 44 E
Friesland □, *Neths.* ..... **20 B7** 53 5N 5 50 E
Friesoythe, *Germany* .... **26 B3** 53 1N 7 51 E
Frillesås, *Sweden* ....... **15 G6** 57 20N 12 12 E
Frio →, *U.S.A.* ........ **139 L5** 28 26N 98 11W
Friona, *U.S.A.* ......... **139 H3** 34 38N 102 43W
Frisian Is., *Europe* ...... **26 B2** 53 30N 6 0 E
Fristad, *Sweden* ........ **15 G7** 57 50N 13 0 E
Fritch, *U.S.A.* ......... **139 H4** 35 38N 101 36W
Fritsla, *Sweden* ........ **15 G6** 57 33N 12 47 E
Fritzlar, *Germany* ...... **26 D5** 51 8N 9 19 E
Friuli-Venezia Giulia □, *Italy* ................ **39 B10** 46 0N 13 0 E
Frobisher B., *Canada* ... **127 B13** 62 30N 66 0W
Frobisher Bay = Iqaluit, *Canada* ............. **127 B13** 63 44N 68 31W
Frobisher L., *Canada* ... **131 B7** 56 20N 108 15W
Frogmore, *Australia* .... **117 C8** 34 15 S 148 52 E
Frohavet, *Norway* ...... **12 E10** 63 50N 9 35 E
Froid, *U.S.A.* .......... **138 A2** 48 20N 104 30W
Froid-Chapelle, *Belgium* . **21 H4** 50 9N 4 19 E
Frolovo, *Russia* ........ **53 B10** 49 45N 43 40 E
Fromberg, *U.S.A.* ...... **142 D9** 45 24N 108 54W
Frombork, *Poland* ...... **47 A6** 54 21N 19 41 E
Frome, *U.K.* ........... **17 F5** 51 16N 2 17W
Frome, L., *Australia* .... **116 A3** 30 45 S 139 45 E
Frome Downs, *Australia* . **116 A3** 31 13 S 139 45 E
Frómista, *Spain* ........ **36 C6** 42 16N 4 25W
Front Range, *U.S.A.* .... **142 G11** 40 25N 105 45W
Front Royal, *U.S.A.* .... **134 F6** 38 55N 78 12W
Fronteira, *Portugal* ..... **37 F3** 39 3N 7 39W
Fronteiras, *Brazil* ....... **154 C3** 7 5 S 40 37W
Frontera, *Canary Is.* .... **33 G2** 27 47N 17 59W
Frontera, *Mexico* ....... **147 D6** 18 30N 92 40W
Frontignan, *France* ...... **24 E7** 43 27N 3 45 E
Frosinone, *Italy* ........ **40 A6** 41 38N 13 20 E
Frosolone, *Italy* ........ **41 A7** 41 34N 14 27 E
Frostburg, *U.S.A.* ...... **134 F6** 39 39N 78 56W
Frostisen, *Norway* ...... **12 B14** 68 14N 17 10 E
Frouard, *France* ........ **23 D13** 48 47N 6 8 E
Frøya, *Norway* ......... **12 E10** 63 43N 8 40 E
Fruges, *France* ......... **23 B9** 50 30N 2 8 E
Frumoasa, *Romania* ..... **46 C6** 46 28N 25 48 E
Frunze = Bishkek, *Kirghizia* ............ **55 B7** 42 54N 74 46 E
Fruška Gora, *Serbia* ..... **42 B4** 45 7N 19 30 E
Frutal, *Brazil* .......... **155 F2** 20 0 S 49 0W
Frutigen, *Switz.* ........ **28 C5** 46 35N 7 38 E
Frýdek-Místek, *Czech.* .. **31 B11** 49 40N 18 20 E
Frýdlant, *Severočeský, Czech.* ................ **30 A8** 50 56N 15 9 E
Frýdlant, *Severomoravský, Czech.* ............... **31 B11** 49 35N 18 20 E
Fryvaldov = Jeseník, *Czech.* ................ **31 B10** 50 0N 17 8 E
Fthiótis □, *Greece* ...... **45 F4** 38 50N 22 25 E
Fu Jiang →, *China* ..... **68 C6** 30 0N 106 16 E
Fu Xian, *Liaoning, China* **67 E11** 39 38N 121 58 E
Fu Xian, *Shaanxi, China* . **66 F5** 36 0N 109 20 E
Fu'an, *China* ........... **69 D12** 27 11N 119 36 E
Fubian, *China* .......... **68 B4** 31 17N 102 22 E
Fucécchio, *Italy* ........ **38 E7** 43 44N 10 51 E
Fucheng, *China* ........ **66 F9** 37 50N 116 10 E
Fuchou = Fuzhou, *China* **69 D12** 26 5N 119 16 E
Fuchū, *Hiroshima, Japan* **62 C5** 34 34N 133 14 E
Fūchū, *Tōkyō, Japan* .... **63 B11** 35 40N 139 29 E
Fuchuan, *China* ........ **69 E8** 24 50N 111 5 E
Fuchun Jiang →, *China* . **69 B13** 30 5N 120 5 E
Fúcino, Conca del, *Italy* . **39 F10** 42 1N 13 31 E
Fuding, *China* ......... **69 D13** 27 20N 120 12 E
Fuencaliente, *Canary Is.* . **33 F2** 28 28N 17 50W
Fuencaliente, *Spain* ..... **37 G6** 38 25N 4 18W
Fuencaliente, Pta., *Canary Is.* ........... **33 F2** 28 27N 17 51W
Fuengirola, *Spain* ....... **37 J6** 36 32N 4 41W
Fuente Alamo, *Albacete, Spain* ................ **35 G3** 38 44N 1 24W
Fuente Álamo, *Murcia, Spain* ................ **35 H3** 37 42N 1 6W
Fuente de Cantos, *Spain* . **37 G4** 38 15N 6 18W
Fuente del Maestre, *Spain* **37 G4** 38 31N 6 28W
Fuente el Fresno, *Spain* . **37 F7** 39 14N 3 46W
Fuente Ovejuna, *Spain* .. **37 G5** 38 15N 5 25W
Fuentes de Andalucía, *Spain* ................ **37 H5** 37 28N 5 20W
Fuentes de Ebro, *Spain* .. **34 D4** 41 31N 0 38W
Fuentes de León, *Spain* .. **37 G4** 38 5N 6 32W
Fuentes de Oñoro, *Spain* **36 E4** 40 33N 6 52W
Fuentesaúco, *Spain* ..... **36 D5** 41 15N 5 30W
Fuerte →, *Mexico* ...... **146 B3** 25 50N 109 25W
Fuerte Olimpo, *Paraguay* **158 A4** 21 0 S 57 51W
Fuerteventura, *Canary Is.* **33 F6** 28 30N 14 0W
Fufeng, *China* ......... **66 G4** 34 22N 108 0 E
Fuga I., *Phil.* .......... **70 B3** 18 52N 121 20 E
Fughmah, *Yemen* ....... **87 C5** 16 9N 49 26 E
Fugløysund, *Norway* .... **12 A16** 70 15N 20 20 E
Fugong, *China* ......... **68 D2** 27 5N 98 47 E
Fugou, *China* .......... **66 G8** 34 3N 114 25 E
Fugu, *China* ........... **66 E6** 39 2N 111 3 E
Fuhai, *China* .......... **64 B3** 47 2N 87 25 E
Fuḩaymī, *Iraq* ......... **84 C4** 34 16N 42 10 E
Fuji, *Japan* ............ **63 B10** 35 9N 138 39 E
Fuji-San, *Japan* ........ **63 B10** 35 22N 138 44 E
Fuji-yoshida, *Japan* ..... **63 B10** 35 30N 138 46 E
Fujian □, *China* ........ **69 E12** 26 0N 118 0 E
Fujieda, *Japan* ......... **63 C10** 34 52N 138 16 E
Fujinomiya, *Japan* ...... **63 B10** 35 10N 138 40 E
Fujioka, *Japan* ......... **63 A11** 36 15N 139 3 E
Fujisawa, *Japan* ........ **63 B11** 35 22N 139 29 E
Fukaya, *Japan* ......... **63 A11** 36 12N 139 12 E
Fukien = Fujian □, *China* **69 E12** 26 0N 118 0 E
Fukuchiyama, *Japan* .... **63 B7** 35 19N 135 9 E
Fukue-Shima, *Japan* .... **61 H4** 32 40N 128 45 E

200 Fukui


Fukui, *Japan* **63 A8** 36 5N 136 10 E
Fukui □, *Japan* **63 B8** 36 0N 136 12 E
Fukuma, *Japan* **62 D2** 33 46N 130 28 E
Fukuoka, *Japan* **62 D2** 33 39N 130 21 E
Fukuoka □, *Japan* **62 D2** 33 30N 131 0 E
Fukuroi, *Japan* **63 C9** 34 45N 137 55 E
Fukushima, *Japan* **60 F10** 37 44N 140 28 E
Fukushima □, *Japan* **60 F10** 37 30N 140 15 E
Fukuyama, *Japan* **62 C5** 34 35N 133 20 E
Fulda, *Germany* **26 E5** 50 32N 9 41 E
Fulda →, *Germany* **26 D5** 51 27N 9 40 E
Fuling, *China* **68 C6** 29 40N 107 20 E
Fullerton, *Calif., U.S.A.* **145 M9** 33 53N 117 56W
Fullerton, *Nebr., U.S.A.* **138 E5** 41 22N 97 58W
Fulongquan, *China* **67 B13** 44 20N 124 42 E
Fulton, *Ill., U.S.A.* **140 C6** 41 52N 90 11W
Fulton, *Ind., U.S.A.* **141 D10** 40 57N 86 16W
Fulton, *Mo., U.S.A.* **140 F5** 38 52N 91 57W
Fulton, *N.Y., U.S.A.* **137 C8** 43 19N 76 25W
Fulton, *Tenn., U.S.A.* **135 G1** 36 31N 88 53W
Fuluälven →, *Sweden* **14 C7** 61 18N 13 4 E
Fulufjället, *Sweden* **14 C6** 61 32N 12 41 E
Fumay, *France* **23 C11** 49 58N 4 40 E
Fumel, *France* **24 D4** 44 30N 0 58 E
Fumin, *China* **68 E4** 25 10N 102 20 E
Funabashi, *Japan* **63 B12** 35 45N 140 0 E
Funafuti, *Pac. Oc.* **111 B14** 8 30 S 179 0 E
Funchal, *Madeira* **33 D3** 32 38N 16 54W
Fundación, *Colombia* **152 A3** 10 31N 74 11W
Fundão, *Brazil* **155 E3** 19 55 S 40 24W
Fundão, *Portugal* **36 E3** 40 8N 7 30W
Fundy, B. of, *Canada* **129 D6** 45 0N 66 0W
Funing, *Hebei, China* **67 E10** 39 53N 119 12 E
Funing, *Jiangsu, China* **67 H10** 33 45N 119 50 E
Funing, *Yunnan, China* **68 F5** 23 35N 105 45 E
Funiu Shan, *China* **66 H7** 33 30N 112 20 E
Funsi, *Ghana* **100 C4** 10 21N 1 54W
Funtua, *Nigeria* **101 C6** 11 30N 7 18 E
Fuping, *Hebei, China* **66 E8** 38 48N 114 12 E
Fuping, *Shaanxi, China* **66 G5** 34 42N 109 10 E
Fuqing, *China* **69 E12** 25 41N 119 21 E
Fuquan, *China* **68 D6** 26 40N 107 27 E
Fur, *Denmark* **15 H3** 56 50N 9 0 E
Furano, *Japan* **60 C11** 43 21N 142 23 E
Furāt, Nahr al →, *Asia* **84 D5** 31 0N 47 25 E
Fūrg, *Iran* **85 D7** 28 18N 55 13 E
Furkapass, *Switz.* **29 C7** 46 34N 8 35 E
Furmanov, *Russia* **51 C12** 57 10N 41 9 E
Furmanovka, *Kazakhstan* **55 A6** 44 17N 72 57 E
Furmanovo, *Kazakhstan* **53 B13** 49 42N 49 25 E
Furnás, *Spain* **33 B8** 39 3N 1 32 E
Furnas, Reprêsa de, *Brazil* **155 F2** 20 50 S 45 30W
Furneaux Group, *Australia* **114 G4** 40 10 S 147 50 E
Furness, *U.K.* **16 C4** 54 14N 3 8W
Furqlus, *Syria* **91 A6** 34 36N 37 8 E
Fürstenau, *Germany* **26 C3** 52 32N 7 40 E
Fürstenberg, *Germany* **26 B9** 53 11N 13 9 E
Fürstenfeld, *Austria* **30 D9** 47 3N 16 3 E
Fürstenfeldbruck, *Germany* **27 G7** 48 10N 11 15 E
Fürstenwalde, *Germany* **26 C10** 52 20N 14 3 E
Fürth, *Germany* **27 F6** 49 29N 11 0 E
Furth im Wald, *Germany* **27 F8** 49 19N 12 51 E
Furtwangen, *Germany* **27 G4** 48 3N 8 14 E
Furukawa, *Japan* **60 E10** 38 34N 140 58 E
Furusund, *Sweden* **14 E12** 59 40N 18 55 E
Fury and Hecla Str., *Canada* **127 B11** 69 56N 84 0W
Fusagasuga, *Colombia* **152 C3** 4 21N 74 22W
Fuscaldo, *Italy* **41 C9** 39 25N 16 1 E
Fushan, *Shandong, China* **67 F11** 37 30N 121 15 E
Fushan, *Shanxi, China* **66 G6** 35 58N 111 51 E
Fushë Arrëzi, *Albania* **44 B2** 42 4N 20 2 E
Fushun, *Liaoning, China* **67 D12** 41 50N 123 56 E
Fushun, *Sichuan, China* **68 C5** 29 13N 104 52 E
Fusio, *Switz.* **29 D7** 46 27N 8 40 E
Fusong, *China* **67 C14** 42 20N 127 15 E
Füssen, *Germany* **27 H6** 47 35N 10 43 E
Fusui, *China* **68 F6** 22 40N 107 56 E
Futago-Yama, *Japan* **62 D3** 33 35N 131 36 E
Futrono, *Chile* **160 B2** 40 8 S 72 24W
Futuna, *Wall. & F. Is.* **122 J9** 14 25 S 178 20 E
Fuwa, *Egypt* **94 H7** 31 12N 30 33 E
Fuxin, *China* **67 C11** 42 5N 121 48 E
Fuyang, *Anhui, China* **66 H8** 33 0N 115 48 E
Fuyang, *Zhejiang, China* **69 B12** 30 5N 119 57 E
Fuyang He →, *China* **66 E9** 38 12N 117 0 E
Fuying Dao, *China* **69 D13** 26 34N 120 9 E
Fuyu, *China* **67 B13** 45 12N 124 43 E
Fuyuan, *China* **68 E5** 25 40N 104 16 E
Füzesgyarmat, *Hungary* **31 D14** 47 6N 21 14 E
Fuzhou, *China* **69 D12** 26 5N 119 16 E
Fylde, *U.K.* **16 D5** 53 50N 2 58W
Fyn, *Denmark* **15 J4** 55 20N 10 30 E
Fyne, L., *U.K.* **18 F3** 56 0N 5 20W
Fyns Amtskommune □, *Denmark* **15 J4** 55 15N 10 30 E
Fyresvatn, *Norway* **14 E2** 59 6N 8 10 E


## G


Gaanda, *Nigeria* **101 C7** 10 10N 12 27 E
Gabarin, *Nigeria* **101 C7** 11 8N 10 27 E
Gabas →, *France* **24 E3** 43 46N 0 42W
Gabela, *Angola* **103 E2** 11 0 S 14 24 E
Gabès, *Tunisia* **96 B2** 33 53N 10 2 E
Gabès, G. de, *Tunisia* **96 B2** 34 0N 10 30 E
Gabgaba, W. →, *Egypt* **94 C3** 22 10N 33 5 E
Gabin, *Poland* **47 C6** 52 23N 19 41 E
Gabon ■, *Africa* **102 C2** 0 10 S 10 0 E
Gaborone, *Botswana* **104 C4** 24 45 S 25 57 E
Gabriels, *U.S.A.* **137 B10** 44 26N 74 12W
Gābrīk, *Iran* **85 E8** 25 44N 58 28 E
Gabro, *Ethiopia* **108 C2** 6 18N 43 16 E
Gabrovo, *Bulgaria* **43 E10** 42 52N 25 19 E
Gacé, *France* **22 D7** 48 49N 0 20 E
Gāch Sār, *Iran* **85 B6** 36 7N 51 19 E
Gachsārān, *Iran* **85 D6** 30 15N 50 45 E
Gacko, *Bos.-H.* **42 D3** 43 10N 18 33 E
Gadag, *India* **83 G2** 15 30N 75 45 E
Gadamai, *Sudan* **95 D4** 17 11N 36 10 E
Gadap, *Pakistan* **80 G2** 25 5N 67 28 E
Gadarwara, *India* **81 H8** 22 50N 78 50 E
Gadebusch, *Germany* **26 B7** 53 41N 11 6 E
Gadein, *Sudan* **95 F2** 8 10N 28 45 E
Gadhada, *India* **80 J4** 22 0N 71 35 E
Gadmen, *Switz.* **29 C6** 46 45N 8 16 E
Gádor, Sierra de, *Spain* **35 J2** 36 57N 2 45W
Gadsden, *Ala., U.S.A.* **135 H2** 34 1N 86 1W
Gadsden, *Ariz., U.S.A.* **143 K6** 32 33N 114 47W
Gadwal, *India* **83 F3** 16 10N 77 50 E
Gadyach, *Ukraine* **50 F9** 50 21N 34 0 E
Gadzi, *C.A.R.* **102 B3** 4 47N 16 42 E
Găeşti, *Romania* **46 E6** 44 48N 25 19 E
Gaeta, *Italy* **40 A6** 41 12N 13 35 E
Gaeta, G. di, *Italy* **40 A6** 41 0N 13 25 E
Gaffney, *U.S.A.* **135 H5** 35 5N 81 39W
Gafsa, *Tunisia* **96 B1** 34 24N 8 43 E
Gagarin = Gzhatsk, *Russia* **50 D9** 55 38N 35 0 E
Gagetown, *Canada* **129 C6** 45 46N 66 10W
Gagino, *Russia* **51 D14** 55 15N 45 1 E
Gagliano del Capo, *Italy* **41 C11** 39 50N 18 23 E
Gagnoa, *Ivory C.* **100 D3** 6 56N 5 16W
Gagnon, *Canada* **129 B6** 51 50N 68 5W
Gagnon, L., *Canada* **131 A6** 62 3N 110 27W
Gagra, *Georgia* **53 E9** 43 20N 40 10 E
Gahini, *Rwanda* **106 C3** 1 50 S 30 30 E
Gahmar, *India* **81 G10** 25 27N 83 49 E
Gai Xian, *China* **67 D12** 40 22N 122 20 E
Gaibanda, *Bangla.* **78 C2** 25 20N 89 36 E
Gaïdhouronísi, *Greece* **32 E7** 34 53N 25 41 E
Gail, *U.S.A.* **139 J4** 32 46N 101 27W
Gail →, *Austria* **30 E6** 46 36N 13 53 E
Gaillac, *France* **24 E5** 43 54N 1 54 E
Gaillon, *France* **22 C8** 49 10N 1 20 E
Gaimán, *Argentina* **160 B3** 43 10 S 65 25W
Gaines, *U.S.A.* **136 E7** 41 46N 77 35W
Gainesville, *Fla., U.S.A.* **135 L4** 29 40N 82 20W
Gainesville, *Ga., U.S.A.* **135 H4** 34 18N 83 50W
Gainesville, *Mo., U.S.A.* **139 G8** 36 36N 92 26W
Gainesville, *Tex., U.S.A.* **139 J6** 33 38N 97 8W
Gainsborough, *U.K.* **16 D7** 53 23N 0 46W
Gairdner, L., *Australia* **116 A2** 31 30 S 136 0 E
Gairloch, L., *U.K.* **18 D3** 57 43N 5 45W
Gais, *Switz.* **29 B8** 47 22N 9 27 E
Gaj, *Croatia* **42 B2** 45 28N 17 3 E
Gakuch, *Pakistan* **81 A5** 36 7N 73 45 E
Gal Laghet, *Somali Rep.* **108 D3** 4 9N 47 10 E
Gal Oya Res., *Sri Lanka* **83 L5** 7 5N 81 30 E
Gal Tardo, *Somali Rep.* **108 D3** 3 34N 45 58 E
Galachipa, *Bangla.* **78 D3** 22 8N 90 26 E
Galán, Cerro, *Argentina* **158 B2** 25 55 S 66 52W
Galana →, *Kenya* **106 C5** 3 9 S 40 8 E
Galangue, *Angola* **103 E3** 13 42 S 16 9 E
Galangue, Serra, *Angola* **103 E3** 14 18 S 15 52 E
Galanta, *Slovak Rep.* **31 C10** 48 11N 17 45 E
Galápagos, *Pac. Oc.* **123 H18** 0 0 91 0W
Galashiels, *U.K.* **18 F6** 55 37N 2 50W
Galatás, *Greece* **45 G5** 37 30N 23 26 E
Galatea, *N.Z.* **118 E5** 38 24 S 176 45 E
Galaţi, *Romania* **46 D9** 45 27N 28 2 E
Galaţi □, *Romania* **46 D8** 45 45N 27 30 E
Galatia, *Turkey* **88 D5** 39 30N 33 0 E
Galatina, *Italy* **41 B11** 40 10N 18 10 E
Galátone, *Italy* **41 B11** 40 8N 18 3 E
Galax, *U.S.A.* **135 G5** 36 40N 80 56W
Galaxídhion, *Greece* **45 F4** 38 22N 22 23 E
Galbraith, *Australia* **114 B3** 16 25 S 141 30 E
Galcaio, *Somali Rep.* **90 F4** 6 30N 47 30 E
Galdhøpiggen, *Norway* **14 C2** 61 38N 8 18 E
Galeana, *Mexico* **146 C4** 24 50N 100 4W
Galela, *Indonesia* **73 A3** 1 50N 127 49 E
Galena, *U.S.A.* **140 B6** 42 25N 90 26W
Galera, *Spain* **35 H2** 37 45N 2 33W
Galera, Pta., *Chile* **160 A2** 39 59 S 73 43W
Galera Point, *Trin. & Tob.* **149 D7** 10 8N 61 0W
Galesburg, *Ill., U.S.A.* **140 D6** 40 57N 90 22W
Galesburg, *Mich., U.S.A.* **141 B11** 42 17N 85 26W
Galeton, *U.S.A.* **136 E7** 41 44N 77 39W
Galgasc, *Somali Rep.* **108 D2** 0 11N 41 38 E
Galheirão →, *Brazil* **155 D2** 12 23 S 45 5W
Galheiros, *Brazil* **155 D2** 13 18 S 46 25W
Gali, *Georgia* **53 E9** 42 37N 41 46 E
Galicea Mare, *Romania* **46 E4** 44 4N 23 19 E
Galich, *Russia* **51 B13** 58 23N 42 12 E
Galiche, *Bulgaria* **43 D8** 43 34N 23 50 E
Galicia □, *Spain* **36 C3** 42 43N 7 45W
Galien, *U.S.A.* **141 C10** 41 48N 86 30W
Galilee = Hagalil, *Israel* **91 C4** 32 53N 35 18 E
Galilee, L., *Australia* **114 C4** 22 20 S 145 50 E
Galilee, Sea of = Yam Kinneret, *Israel* **91 C4** 32 45N 35 35 E
Galinoporni, *Cyprus* **32 D13** 35 31N 34 18 E
Galion, *U.S.A.* **136 F2** 40 44N 82 47W
Galite, Is. de la, *Tunisia* **99 A6** 37 30N 8 59 E
Galiuro Mts., *U.S.A.* **143 K8** 32 30N 110 20W
Gallabat, *Sudan* **95 E4** 12 58N 36 11 E
Gallardon, *France* **23 D8** 48 32N 1 42 E
Gallarte, *Italy* **38 C5** 45 40N 8 48 E
Gallatin, *Mo., U.S.A.* **140 E3** 39 55N 93 58W
Gallatin, *Tenn., U.S.A.* **135 G2** 36 24N 86 27W
Galle, *Sri Lanka* **83 L5** 6 5N 80 10 E
Gállego →, *Spain* **34 D4** 41 39N 0 51W
Gallegos →, *Argentina* **160 D3** 51 35 S 69 0W
Galley Hd., *Ireland* **19 E3** 51 32N 8 56W
Galliate, *Italy* **38 C5** 45 27N 8 44 E
Gallinas, Pta., *Colombia* **152 A3** 12 28N 71 40W
Gallipoli = Gelibolu, *Turkey* **44 D8** 40 28N 26 43 E
Gallípoli, *Italy* **41 B11** 40 8N 18 0 E
Gallipolis, *U.S.A.* **134 F4** 38 49N 82 12W
Gällivare, *Sweden* **12 C16** 67 9N 20 40 E
Gallo, C., *Italy* **40 D6** 38 13N 13 19 E
Gallocanta, L. de, *Spain* **34 E3** 40 58N 1 30W
Galloway, *U.K.* **18 G4** 55 0N 4 25W
Galloway, Mull of, *U.K.* **18 G4** 54 38N 4 50W
Gallup, *U.S.A.* **143 J9** 35 32N 108 45W
Gallur, *Spain* **34 D3** 41 52N 1 19W
Gallyaaral, *Uzbekistan* **55 C3** 40 2N 67 35 E
Galong, *Australia* **117 C8** 34 37 S 148 34 E
Galt, *Calif., U.S.A.* **144 G5** 38 15N 121 18W
Galt, *Mo., U.S.A.* **140 D3** 40 8N 93 23W
Galtström, *Sweden* **14 B11** 62 10N 17 30 E
Galtür, *Austria* **30 E3** 46 58N 10 11 E
Galty Mts., *Ireland* **19 D3** 52 22N 8 10W
Galtymore, *Ireland* **19 D3** 52 22N 8 12W
Galva, *U.S.A.* **140 C6** 41 10N 90 3W
Galvarino, *Chile* **160 A2** 38 24 S 72 47W
Galve de Sorbe, *Spain* **34 D1** 41 13N 3 10W
Galveston, *Ind., U.S.A.* **141 D10** 40 35N 86 11W
Galveston, *Tex., U.S.A.* **139 L7** 29 18N 94 48W
Galveston B., *U.S.A.* **139 L7** 29 36N 94 50W
Gálvez, *Argentina* **158 C3** 32 0 S 61 14W
Gálvez, *Spain* **37 F6** 39 42N 4 16W
Galway, *Ireland* **19 C2** 53 16N 9 4W
Galway □, *Ireland* **19 C2** 53 16N 9 3W
Galway B., *Ireland* **19 C2** 53 10N 9 20W
Gam, *Indonesia* **73 B4** 0 27 S 130 36 E
Gam →, *Vietnam* **76 B5** 21 55N 105 12 E
Gamagori, *Japan* **63 C9** 34 50N 137 14 E
Gamari, L., *Ethiopia* **95 E5** 11 32N 41 40 E
Gamawa, *Nigeria* **101 C7** 12 10N 10 31 E
Gamay, *Phil.* **70 E5** 12 23N 125 18 E
Gamay Bay, *Phil.* **70 E5** 12 21N 125 21 E
Gamba, *Angola* **103 E3** 11 42 S 17 14 E
Gambaga, *Ghana* **101 C4** 10 30N 0 28W
Gambat, *Pakistan* **80 F3** 27 17N 68 26 E
Gambela, *Ethiopia* **95 F3** 8 14N 34 38 E
Gambia ■, *W. Afr.* **100 C1** 13 25N 16 0W
Gambia →, *W. Afr.* **100 C1** 13 28N 16 34W
Gambier, C., *Australia* **112 B5** 11 56 S 130 57 E
Gambier Is., *Australia* **116 C2** 35 3 S 136 30 E
Gambo, *C.A.R.* **102 B4** 4 39N 22 16 E
Gamboli, *Pakistan* **80 E3** 29 53N 68 24 E
Gamboma, *Congo* **102 C3** 1 55 S 15 52 E
Gamboula, *C.A.R.* **102 B3** 4 8N 15 9 E
Gambuta, *Indonesia* **72 A2** 0 30N 123 20 E
Gamerco, *U.S.A.* **143 J9** 35 34N 108 46W
Gamlakarleby = Kokkola, *Finland* **12 E17** 63 50N 23 8 E
Gammon →, *Canada* **131 C9** 51 24N 95 44W
Gammouda, *Tunisia* **96 A1** 35 3N 9 39 E
Gamoda-Saki, *Japan* **62 D6** 33 50N 134 45 E
Gamu-Gofa □, *Ethiopia* **95 F4** 5 40N 36 40 E
Gan, *France* **24 E3** 43 12N 0 27W
Gan Gan, *Argentina* **160 B3** 42 30 S 68 10W
Gan Goriama, Mts., *Cameroon* **101 D7** 7 44N 12 45 E
Gan Jiang →, *China* **69 C10** 29 15N 116 0 E
Ganado, *Ariz., U.S.A.* **143 J9** 35 43N 109 33W
Ganado, *Tex., U.S.A.* **139 L6** 29 2N 96 31W
Gananoque, *Canada* **128 D4** 44 20N 76 10W
Ganaveh, *Iran* **85 D6** 29 35N 50 35 E
Gäncä = Gyandzha, *Azerbaijan* **53 F12** 40 45N 46 20 E
Gand = Gent, *Belgium* **21 F3** 51 2N 3 42 E
Ganda, *Angola* **103 E2** 13 3 S 14 35 E
Gandak →, *India* **81 G11** 25 39N 85 13 E
Gandara, *Phil.* **70 E5** 12 1N 124 49 E
Gandava, *Pakistan* **79 C2** 28 32N 67 32 E
Gander, *Canada* **129 C9** 48 58N 54 35W
Gander L., *Canada* **129 C9** 48 58N 54 35W
Ganderowe Falls, *Zimbabwe* **107 F2** 17 20 S 29 10 E
Gandesa, *Spain* **34 D5** 41 3N 0 26 E
Gandhi Sagar, *India* **80 G6** 24 40N 75 40 E
Gandi, *Nigeria* **101 C6** 12 55N 5 49 E
Gandía, *Spain* **35 G4** 38 58N 0 9W
Gandino, *Italy* **38 C6** 45 50N 9 52 E
Gando, Pta., *Canary Is.* **33 G4** 27 55N 15 22W
Gandole, *Nigeria* **101 D7** 8 28N 11 35 E
Gandu, *Brazil* **155 D4** 13 45 S 39 30W
Ganedidalem = Gani, *Indonesia* **72 B3** 0 48 S 128 14 E
Ganetti, *Sudan* **94 D3** 18 0N 31 10 E
Ganga →, *India* **81 H14** 23 20N 90 30 E
Ganga, Mouths of the, *India* **81 J13** 21 30N 90 0 E
Ganganagar, *India* **80 E5** 29 56N 73 56 E
Gangapur, *India* **80 F7** 26 32N 76 49 E
Gangara, *Niger* **97 F1** 14 35N 8 29 E
Gangaw, *Burma* **78 D5** 22 5N 94 5 E
Gangawati, *India* **83 G3** 15 30N 76 36 E
Ganges = Ganga →, *India* **81 H14** 23 20N 90 30 E
Ganges, *France* **24 E7** 43 56N 3 42 E
Gangoh, *India* **80 E7** 29 46N 77 18 E
Gangtok, *India* **78 B2** 27 20N 88 37 E
Gangu, *China* **66 G3** 34 40N 105 15 E
Gangyao, *China* **67 B14** 44 12N 126 37 E
Gani, *Indonesia* **72 B3** 0 48 S 128 14 E
Ganj, *India* **81 F8** 27 45N 78 57 E
Gannat, *France* **24 B7** 46 7N 3 11 E
Gannett Peak, *U.S.A.* **142 E9** 43 11N 109 39W
Gannvalley, *U.S.A.* **138 C5** 44 2N 98 59W
Ganongga, *Solomon Is.* **121 M9** 8 5 S 156 35 E
Ganquan, *China* **66 F5** 36 20N 109 20 E
Gänserdorf, *Austria* **31 C9** 48 20N 16 43 E
Ganshui, *China* **68 C6** 28 40N 106 40 E
Gansu □, *China* **66 G3** 36 0N 104 0 E
Ganta, *Liberia* **100 D3** 7 15N 8 59W
Gantheaume, C., *Australia* **116 D2** 36 4 S 137 32 E
Gantheaume B., *Australia* **113 E1** 27 40 S 114 10 E
Gantsevichi, *Belorussia* **50 E5** 52 49N 26 30 E
Ganyem, *Indonesia* **73 B6** 2 46 S 140 12 E
Ganyu, *China* **67 G10** 34 50N 119 8 E
Ganyushkino, *Kazakhstan* **53 C13** 46 35N 49 20 E
Ganzhou, *China* **69 E10** 25 51N 114 56 E
Gao, *Mali* **101 B5** 18 0N 1 0 E
Gao Xian, *China* **68 C5** 28 21N 104 32 E
Gao'an, *China* **69 C10** 28 26N 115 17 E
Gaohe, *China* **69 F9** 22 46N 112 57 E
Gaohebu, *China* **69 B11** 30 43N 116 49 E
Gaokeng, *China* **69 D9** 27 40N 113 58 E
Gaolan Dao, *China* **69 G9** 21 55N 113 10 E
Gaoligong Shan, *China* **68 E2** 24 45N 98 45 E
Gaomi, *China* **67 F10** 36 20N 119 42 E
Gaoping, *China* **66 G7** 35 45N 112 55 E
Gaotang, *China* **66 F9** 36 50N 116 15 E
Gaoua, *Burkina Faso* **100 C4** 10 20N 3 8W
Gaoual, *Guinea* **100 C2** 11 45N 13 25W
Gaoxiong, *Taiwan* **69 F13** 22 38N 120 18 E
Gaoyang, *China* **66 E8** 38 40N 115 45 E
Gaoyou, *China* **69 A12** 32 47N 119 26 E
Gaoyou Hu, *China* **67 H10** 32 45N 119 20 E
Gaoyuan, *China* **67 F9** 37 8N 117 58 E
Gaozhou, *China* **69 G8** 21 58N 110 50 E
Gap, *France* **25 D10** 44 33N 6 5 E
Gapan, *Phil.* **70 D3** 15 19N 120 57 E
Gar, *China* **64 C2** 32 10N 79 58 E
Garabogazkol Aylagy = Kara Bogaz Gol, Zaliv, *Turkmenistan* **49 F9** 41 0N 53 30 E
Garachico, *Canary Is.* **33 F3** 28 22N 16 46W
Garachiné, *Panama* **148 E4** 8 0N 78 12W
Garad, *Somali Rep.* **108 C3** 6 57N 49 24 E
Garafia, *Canary Is.* **33 F2** 28 48N 17 57W
Garajonay, *Canary Is.* **33 F2** 28 7N 17 14W
Garanhuns, *Brazil* **154 C4** 8 50 S 36 30W
Garawe, *Liberia* **100 E3** 4 35N 8 0W
Garba Harre, *Somali Rep.* **108 D2** 3 19N 42 13 E
Garba Tula, *Kenya* **106 B4** 0 30N 38 32 E
Garbagududu, *Ethiopia* **108 C2** 6 12N 43 50 E
Garber, *U.S.A.* **139 G6** 36 26N 97 35W
Garberville, *U.S.A.* **142 F2** 40 6N 123 48W
Garça, *Brazil* **155 F2** 22 14 S 49 37W
Garças →, *Mato Grosso, Brazil* **157 D7** 15 54 S 52 16W
Garças →, *Pernambuco, Brazil* **154 C4** 8 43 S 39 41W
Garchitorena, *Phil.* **70 E4** 13 52N 123 40 E
Garcia Hernandez, *Phil.* **71 G5** 9 37N 124 18 E
Garcias, *Brazil* **157 E7** 20 34 S 52 13W
Gard, *Somali Rep.* **90 F4** 9 30N 49 6 E
Gard □, *France* **25 D8** 44 2N 4 10 E
Gard →, *France* **25 E8** 43 51N 4 37 E
Garda, L. di, *Italy* **38 C7** 45 40N 10 40 E
Gardanne, *France* **25 E9** 43 27N 5 27 E
Garde L., *Canada* **131 A7** 62 50N 106 13W
Gardelegen, *Germany* **26 C7** 52 32N 11 21 E
Garden City, *Kans., U.S.A.* **139 G4** 37 58N 100 53W
Garden City, *Mo., U.S.A.* **140 F2** 38 34N 94 12W
Garden City, *Tex., U.S.A.* **139 K4** 31 52N 101 29W
Garden Grove, *U.S.A.* **145 M9** 33 47N 117 55W
Gardēz, *Afghan.* **79 B3** 33 37N 69 9 E
Gardhíki, *Greece* **45 F3** 38 50N 21 55 E
Gardiner, *U.S.A.* **142 D8** 45 2N 110 22W
Gardiners I., *U.S.A.* **137 E12** 41 6N 72 6W
Gardner, *Ill., U.S.A.* **141 C8** 41 12N 88 17W
Gardner, *Mass., U.S.A.* **137 D13** 42 34N 71 59W
Gardner Canal, *Canada* **130 C3** 53 27N 128 8W
Gardnerville, *U.S.A.* **144 G7** 38 56N 119 45W
Gardno, Jezioro, *Poland* **47 A4** 54 40N 17 7 E
Gardo, *Somali Rep.* **108 C3** 9 30N 49 6 E
Gare Tigre, *Fr. Guiana* **153 C7** 4 58N 53 9W
Garešnica, *Croatia* **42 B1** 45 36N 16 56 E
Garéssio, *Italy* **38 D5** 44 12N 8 1 E
Garey, *U.S.A.* **145 L6** 34 53N 120 19W
Garfield, *U.S.A.* **142 C5** 47 1N 117 9W
Gargaliánoi, *Greece* **45 G3** 37 4N 21 38 E
Gargan, Mt., *France* **24 C5** 45 37N 1 39 E
Gargano, Mte., *Italy* **41 A8** 41 43N 15 43 E
Gargouna, *Mali* **101 B5** 15 56N 0 13 E
Garhshankar, *India* **80 D7** 31 13N 76 11 E
Gari, *Russia* **54 B8** 59 26N 62 21 E
Garibaldi Prov. Park, *Canada* **130 D4** 49 50N 122 40W
Garies, *S. Africa* **104 E2** 30 32 S 17 59 E
Garigliano →, *Italy* **40 A6** 41 13N 13 44 E
Garissa, *Kenya* **106 C4** 0 25 S 39 40 E
Garissa □, *Kenya* **106 C5** 0 20 S 40 0 E
Garkida, *Nigeria* **101 C7** 10 27N 12 36 E
Garko, *Nigeria* **101 C6** 11 45N 8 53 E
Garland, *U.S.A.* **142 F7** 41 47N 112 10W
Garlasco, *Italy* **38 C5** 45 11N 8 55 E
Garm, *Tajikistan* **55 D5** 39 0N 70 20 E
Garmāb, *Iran* **85 C8** 35 25N 56 45 E
Garmisch-Partenkirchen, *Germany* **27 H7** 47 30N 11 5 E
Garmsār, *Iran* **85 C7** 35 20N 52 25 E
Garner, *U.S.A.* **140 A3** 43 6N 93 36W
Garnett, *U.S.A.* **138 F7** 38 17N 95 14W
Garo Hills, *India* **81 G14** 25 30N 90 30 E
Garoe, *Somali Rep.* **90 F4** 8 25N 48 33 E
Garonne →, *France* **24 C3** 45 2N 0 36W
Garonne, Canal Latéral à la →, *France* **24 D4** 44 15N 0 18 E
Garoua, *Cameroon* **101 D7** 9 19N 13 21 E
Garrel, *Germany* **26 C3** 52 58N 7 59 E
Garrett, *U.S.A.* **141 C11** 41 21N 85 8W
Garrigue, *France* **24 E7** 43 40N 3 55 E
Garrison, *Ky., U.S.A.* **141 F13** 38 36N 83 10W
Garrison, *Mont., U.S.A.* **142 C7** 46 31N 112 49W
Garrison, *N. Dak., U.S.A.* **138 B4** 47 40N 101 25W
Garrison, *Tex., U.S.A.* **139 K7** 31 49N 94 30W
Garrison Res. = Sakakawea, L., *U.S.A.* **138 B3** 47 30N 101 25W
Garrovillas, *Spain* **37 F4** 39 40N 6 33W
Garrucha, *Spain* **35 H3** 37 11N 1 49W
Garry →, *U.K.* **18 E5** 56 47N 3 47W
Garry, L., *Canada* **126 B9** 65 58N 100 18W
Garsen, *Kenya* **106 C5** 2 20 S 40 5 E
Garson L., *Canada* **131 B6** 56 19N 110 2W
Gartempe →, *France* **24 B4** 46 47N 0 49 E
Gartz, *Germany* **26 B10** 53 12N 14 23 E
Garu, *Ghana* **101 C4** 10 55N 0 11W
Garub, *Namibia* **104 D2** 26 37 S 16 0 E
Garut, *Indonesia* **75 D3** 7 14 S 107 53 E
Garvão, *Portugal* **37 H2** 37 42N 8 21W
Garvie Mts., *N.Z.* **119 F3** 45 30 S 168 50 E
Garwa = Garoua, *Cameroon* **101 D7** 9 19N 13 21 E
Garwa, *India* **81 G10** 24 11N 83 47 E
Garwolin, *Poland* **47 D8** 51 55N 21 38 E
Gary, *U.S.A.* **141 C9** 41 36N 87 20W
Garz, *Germany* **26 A9** 54 17N 13 21 E
Garzê, *China* **68 B3** 31 38N 100 1 E
Garzón, *Colombia* **152 C2** 2 10N 75 40W
Gas City, *U.S.A.* **141 D11** 40 29N 85 37W
Gas-San, *Japan* **60 E10** 38 32N 140 1 E
Gasan, *Phil.* **70 E3** 13 19N 121 51 E
Gasan Kuli, *Turkmenistan* **56 F6** 37 40N 54 20 E
Gascogne, *France* **24 E4** 43 45N 0 20 E
Gascogne, G. de, *Europe* **34 B2** 44 0N 2 0W
Gasconade, *U.S.A.* **140 F5** 38 40N 91 34W
Gasconade →, *U.S.A.* **140 F5** 38 41N 91 33W
Gascony = Gascogne, *France* **24 E4** 43 45N 0 20 E
Gascoyne →, *Australia* **113 D1** 24 52 S 113 37 E
Gascoyne Junc. T.O., *Australia* **113 E2** 25 2 S 115 17 E
Gascueña, *Spain* **34 E2** 40 18N 2 31W
Gash, Wadi →, *Ethiopia* **95 D4** 16 48N 35 51 E
Gashaka, *Nigeria* **101 D7** 7 20N 11 29 E
Gasherbrum, *Pakistan* **81 B7** 35 40N 76 40 E

**Gigen 201**



Gashua, *Nigeria* . . . . . . . . **101 C7** 12 54N 11 0 E
Gaspé, *Canada* . . . . . . . . . **129 C7** 48 52N 64 30W
Gaspé, C. de, *Canada* . . . **129 C7** 48 48N 64 7W
Gaspé, Pén. de, *Canada* . **129 C6** 48 45N 65 40W
Gaspésie, Parc Prov. de la, *Canada* . . . . . . . . . . **129 C6** 48 55N 65 50W
Gassaway, *U.S.A.* . . . . . . **134 F5** 38 41N 80 47W
Gasselte, *Neths.* . . . . . . . . **20 C9** 52 58N 6 48 E
Gasselternijveen, *Neths.* . **20 C9** 52 59N 6 51 E
Gássino Torinese, *Italy* . . **38 C4** 45 8N 7 50 E
Gassol, *Nigeria* . . . . . . . . **101 D7** 8 34N 10 25 E
Gasteiz = Vitoria, *Spain* . **34 C2** 42 50N 2 41W
Gastonia, *U.S.A.* . . . . . . . **135 H5** 35 16N 81 11W
Gastoúni, *Greece* . . . . . . . **45 G3** 37 51N 21 15 E
Gastoúri, *Greece* . . . . . . . **44 E1** 39 34N 19 54 E
Gastre, *Argentina* . . . . . . **160 B3** 42 20 S 69 15W
Gata, C., *Cyprus* . . . . . . . **32 E12** 34 34N 33 2 E
Gata, C. de, *Spain* . . . . . . **35 J2** 36 41N 2 13W
Gata, Sierra de, *Spain* . . . **36 E4** 40 20N 6 45W
Gataga →, *Canada* . . . . . **130 B3** 58 35N 126 59W
Gătaia, *Romania* . . . . . . . **46 D2** 45 26N 21 30 E
Gatchina, *Russia* . . . . . . . **50 B7** 59 35N 30 9 E
Gates, *U.S.A.* . . . . . . . . . . **136 C7** 43 9N 77 42W
Gateshead, *U.K.* . . . . . . . . **16 C6** 54 57N 1 37W
Gatesville, *U.S.A.* . . . . . . **139 K6** 31 26N 97 45W
Gaths, *Zimbabwe* . . . . . . . **107 G3** 20 2 S 30 32 E
Gatico, *Chile* . . . . . . . . . . **158 A1** 22 29 S 70 20W
Gâtinais, *France* . . . . . . . **23 D9** 48 5N 2 40 E
Gâtine, Hauteurs de, *France* . . . . . . . . . . . . . . **24 B3** 46 35N 0 45W
Gatineau →, *Canada* . . . **128 C4** 45 27N 75 42W
Gatineau, Parc de la, *Canada* . . . . . . . . . . . . . **128 C4** 45 40N 76 0W
Gattaran, *Phil.* . . . . . . . . . **70 B3** 18 4N 121 38 E
Gattinara, *Italy* . . . . . . . . **38 C5** 45 37N 8 22 E
Gatukai, *Solomon Is.* . . . . **121 M10** 8 45 S 158 15 E
Gatun, L., *Panama* . . . . . **148 E4** 9 7N 79 56W
Gatyana, *S. Africa* . . . . . . **105 E4** 32 16 S 28 31 E
Gau, *Fiji* . . . . . . . . . . . . . . **121 B2** 18 2 S 179 18 E
Gaua, *Vanuatu* . . . . . . . . . **121 D5** 14 15 S 167 30 E
Gaucín, *Spain* . . . . . . . . . **37 J5** 36 31N 5 19W
Gauer L., *Canada* . . . . . . **131 B9** 57 0N 97 50W
Gauhati, *India* . . . . . . . . . **81 F14** 26 10N 91 45 E
Gauja →, *Latvia* . . . . . . . **50 C4** 57 10N 24 16 E
Gaula →, *Norway* . . . . . . **12 E11** 63 21N 10 14 E
Gaurain-Ramecroix, *Belgium* . . . . . . . . . . . . . **21 G3** 50 36N 3 30 E
Gaurdak, *Turkmenistan* . . **55 E3** 37 50N 66 4 E
Gausta, *Norway* . . . . . . . . **14 E2** 59 50N 8 37 E
Gāv Koshī, *Iran* . . . . . . . . **85 D8** 28 38N 57 12 E
Gavá, *Spain* . . . . . . . . . . . **34 D6** 41 18N 2 0 E
Gāvakān, *Iran* . . . . . . . . . **85 D7** 29 37N 53 10 E
Gavarnie, *France* . . . . . . . **24 F3** 42 44N 0 1W
Gavāter, *Iran* . . . . . . . . . . **85 E9** 25 10N 61 31 E
Gāvbandī, *Iran* . . . . . . . . . **85 E7** 27 12N 53 4 E
Gavdhopoúla, *Greece* . . . **32 E6** 34 56N 24 0 E
Gávdhos, *Greece* . . . . . . . **32 E6** 34 50N 24 5 E
Gavere, *Belgium* . . . . . . . . **21 G3** 50 55N 3 40 E
Gavião, *Portugal* . . . . . . . **37 F3** 39 28N 7 56W
Gaviota, *U.S.A.* . . . . . . . . **145 L6** 34 29N 120 13W
Gävleborgs län □, *Sweden* **14 C10** 61 30N 16 15 E
Gavorrano, *Italy* . . . . . . . . **38 F7** 42 55N 10 49 E
Gavray, *France* . . . . . . . . . **22 D5** 48 55N 1 20W
Gavrilov Yam, *Russia* . . . **51 C11** 57 18N 39 49 E
Gávrion, *Greece* . . . . . . . . **45 G6** 37 54N 24 44 E
Gawachab, *Namibia* . . . . . **104 D2** 27 4 S 17 55 E
Gawai, *Burma* . . . . . . . . . . **78 B6** 27 56N 97 30 E
Gawilgarh Hills, *India* . . . **82 D3** 21 15N 76 45 E
Gawler, *Australia* . . . . . . **116 C3** 34 30 S 138 42 E
Gaxun Nur, *China* . . . . . . **64 B5** 42 22N 100 30 E
Gay, *Russia* . . . . . . . . . . . **54 F6** 51 27N 58 27 E
Gaya, *India* . . . . . . . . . . . . **81 G11** 24 47N 85 4 E
Gaya, *Niger* . . . . . . . . . . . **101 C5** 11 52N 3 28 E
Gaya, *Nigeria* . . . . . . . . . . **101 C6** 11 57N 9 0 E
Gaylord, *U.S.A.* . . . . . . . . **134 C3** 45 2N 84 41W
Gayndah, *Australia* . . . . . **115 D5** 25 35 S 151 32 E
Gayny, *Russia* . . . . . . . . . . **54 A4** 60 18N 54 19 E
Gaysin, *Ukraine* . . . . . . . . **52 B3** 48 57N 29 25 E
Gayvoron, *Ukraine* . . . . . . **52 B3** 48 22N 29 52 E
Gaza, *Egypt* . . . . . . . . . . . **91 D3** 31 30N 34 28 E
Gaza □, *Mozam.* . . . . . . . **105 C5** 23 10 S 32 45 E
Gaza Strip, *Egypt* . . . . . . **91 D3** 31 29N 34 25 E
Gazaoua, *Niger* . . . . . . . . **97 F1** 13 32N 7 55 E
Gāzbor, *Iran* . . . . . . . . . . . **85 D8** 28 5N 58 51 E
Gazelle Pen., *Papua N. G.* **120 C6** 4 40 S 152 0 E
Gazi, *Zaïre* . . . . . . . . . . . . **106 B1** 1 3N 24 30 E
Gaziantep, *Turkey* . . . . . . **88 E7** 37 6N 37 23 E
Gaziantep □, *Turkey* . . . . **88 E7** 37 0N 37 0 E
Gazipaşa, *Turkey* . . . . . . . **88 E5** 36 16N 32 18 E
Gazli, *Uzbekistan* . . . . . . **56 E7** 40 14N 63 24 E
Gbarnga, *Liberia* . . . . . . . **100 D3** 7 19N 9 13W
Gbekebo, *Nigeria* . . . . . . . **101 D5** 6 20N 4 56 E
Gboko, *Nigeria* . . . . . . . . . **101 D6** 7 17N 9 4 E
Gbongan, *Nigeria* . . . . . . . **101 D5** 7 28N 4 20 E
Gcuwa, *S. Africa* . . . . . . . **105 E4** 32 20 S 28 11 E
Gdańsk, *Poland* . . . . . . . . **47 A5** 54 22N 18 40 E
Gdańsk □, *Poland* . . . . . . **47 A5** 54 10N 18 30 E
Gdańska, Zatoka, *Poland* **47 A6** 54 30N 19 20 E
Gdov, *Russia* . . . . . . . . . . **50 B5** 58 48N 27 55 E
Gdynia, *Poland* . . . . . . . . . **47 A5** 54 35N 18 33 E
Gebe, *Indonesia* . . . . . . . . **73 A3** 0 5N 129 25 E
Gebeit Mine, *Sudan* . . . . . **94 C4** 21 3N 36 29 E
Gebel Mûsa, *Egypt* . . . . . **94 J8** 28 32N 33 59 E
Gebze, *Turkey* . . . . . . . . . . **88 C3** 40 47N 29 25 E
Gecha, *Ethiopia* . . . . . . . . **95 F4** 7 30N 35 18 E
Gedaref, *Sudan* . . . . . . . . **95 E4** 14 2N 35 28 E
Gede, Tanjung, *Indonesia* **74 D3** 6 46 S 105 12 E
Gedinne, *Belgium* . . . . . . . **21 J5** 49 59N 4 56 E
Gediz, *Turkey* . . . . . . . . . . **88 D3** 39 1N 29 24 E
Gediz →, *Turkey* . . . . . . . **88 D2** 38 35N 26 48 E
Gedo, *Ethiopia* . . . . . . . . . **95 F4** 9 2N 37 25 E
Gèdre, *France* . . . . . . . . . . **24 F4** 42 47N 0 2 E
Gedser, *Denmark* . . . . . . . **15 K5** 54 35N 11 55 E
Gedser Odde, *Denmark* . . **15 K5** 54 30N 11 58 E
Geegully Cr. →, *Australia* **112 C3** 18 32 S 123 41 E
Geel, *Belgium* . . . . . . . . . . **21 F5** 51 10N 4 59 E
Geelong, *Australia* . . . . . . **116 E6** 38 10 S 144 22 E
Geelvink Chan., *Australia* **113 E1** 28 30 S 114 0 E
Geer →, *Belgium* . . . . . . . **21 G7** 50 51N 5 42 E
Geesthacht, *Germany* . . . **26 B6** 53 25N 10 20 E
Geffen, *Neths.* . . . . . . . . . . **20 E6** 51 44N 5 28 E
Geidam, *Nigeria* . . . . . . . . **101 C7** 12 57N 11 57 E
Geikie →, *Canada* . . . . . . **131 B8** 57 45N 103 52W
Geili, *Sudan* . . . . . . . . . . . **95 D3** 16 1N 32 37 E
Geilo, *Norway* . . . . . . . . . . **14 D2** 60 32N 8 14 E
Geinica, *Slovak Rep.* . . . . **31 C13** 48 51N 20 55 E
Geisingen, *Germany* . . . . **27 H4** 47 55N 8 37 E
Geislingen, *Germany* . . . . **27 G5** 48 37N 9 51 E
Geita, *Tanzania* . . . . . . . . **106 C3** 2 48 S 32 12 E
Geita □, *Tanzania* . . . . . . **106 C3** 2 50 S 32 10 E
Gejiu, *China* . . . . . . . . . . . **68 F4** 23 20N 103 10 E
Gel →, *Sudan* . . . . . . . . . . **95 F2** 7 5N 29 10 E
Gel River, *Sudan* . . . . . . . **95 F2** 7 5N 29 10 E
Gela, *Italy* . . . . . . . . . . . . . **41 E7** 37 6N 14 18 E
Gela, G. di, *Italy* . . . . . . . **41 F7** 37 0N 14 8 E
Geladi, *Ethiopia* . . . . . . . . **90 F4** 6 59N 46 30 E
Gelderland □, *Neths.* . . . . **20 D8** 52 5N 6 10 E
Geldermalsen, *Neths.* . . . . **20 E6** 51 53N 5 17 E
Geldern, *Germany* . . . . . . **26 D2** 51 32N 6 18 E
Geldrop, *Neths.* . . . . . . . . **21 F7** 51 25N 5 32 E
Geleen, *Neths.* . . . . . . . . . **21 G7** 50 57N 5 49 E
Gelehun, *S. Leone* . . . . . . **100 D2** 8 20N 11 40W
Gelendost, *Turkey* . . . . . . **88 D4** 38 7N 31 1 E
Gelendzhik, *Russia* . . . . . . **52 D8** 44 33N 38 10 E
Gelib, *Somali Rep.* . . . . . . **108 D2** 0 29N 42 46 E
Gelibolu, *Turkey* . . . . . . . **44 D8** 40 28N 26 43 E
Gelidonya Burnu, *Turkey* **88 E4** 36 12N 30 24 E
Gelnhausen, *Germany* . . . **27 E5** 50 12N 9 12 E
Gelsenkirchen, *Germany* . **26 D3** 51 30N 7 5 E
Gelting, *Germany* . . . . . . . **26 A5** 54 43N 9 53 E
Gemas, *Malaysia* . . . . . . . **77 L4** 2 37N 102 36 E
Gembloux, *Belgium* . . . . . **21 G5** 50 34N 4 43 E
Gemena, *Zaïre* . . . . . . . . . **102 B3** 3 13N 19 48 E
Gemerek, *Turkey* . . . . . . . **88 D7** 39 15N 36 10 E
Gemert, *Neths.* . . . . . . . . . **21 E7** 51 33N 5 41 E
Gemlik, *Turkey* . . . . . . . . . **88 C3** 40 26N 29 9 E
Gemona del Friuli, *Italy* . **39 B10** 46 16N 13 7 E
Gemsa, *Egypt* . . . . . . . . . . **94 B3** 27 39N 33 35 E
Gemünden, *Germany* . . . . **27 E5** 50 3N 9 43 E
Genale, *Ethiopia* . . . . . . . **95 F4** 6 0N 39 30 E
Genale, *Somali Rep.* . . . . **108 D2** 1 48N 44 42 E
Genappe, *Belgium* . . . . . . **21 G4** 50 37N 4 30 E
Genç, *Turkey* . . . . . . . . . . **89 D9** 38 44N 40 34 E
Gençay, *France* . . . . . . . . . **24 B4** 46 23N 0 23 E
Gendringen, *Neths.* . . . . . **20 E8** 51 52N 6 21 E
Gendt, *Neths.* . . . . . . . . . . **20 E7** 51 53N 5 59 E
Geneina, Gebel, *Egypt* . . **94 J8** 29 2N 33 55 E
Genemuiden, *Neths.* . . . . **20 C8** 52 38N 6 2 E
General Acha, *Argentina* **158 D3** 37 20 S 64 38W
General Alvear, *Buenos Aires, Argentina* **158 D3** 36 0 S 60 0W
General Alvear, *Mendoza, Argentina* . . . . . . . . . . . **158 D2** 35 0 S 67 40W
General Artigas, *Paraguay* **158 B4** 26 52 S 56 16W
General Belgrano, *Argentina* . . . . . . . . . . . **158 D4** 36 35 S 58 47W
General Cabrera, *Argentina* . . . . . . . . . . . **158 C3** 32 53 S 63 52W
General Carrera, L., *Chile* **160 C2** 46 35 S 72 0W
General Cepeda, *Mexico* . **146 B4** 25 23N 101 27W
General Conesa, *Argentina* **160 B4** 40 6 S 64 25W
General Guido, *Argentina* **158 D4** 36 40 S 57 50W
General Juan Madariaga, *Argentina* . . . . . . . . . . . **158 D4** 37 0 S 57 0W
General La Madrid, *Argentina* . . . . . . . . . . . **158 D3** 37 17 S 61 20W
General Lorenzo Vintter, *Argentina* . . . . . . . . . . . **160 B4** 40 45 S 64 26W
General Luna, *Phil.* . . . . . . **70 E4** 13 41N 122 10 E
General MacArthur, *Phil.* **71 F5** 11 18N 125 28 E
General Martin Miguel de Güemes, *Argentina* . . . . **158 A3** 24 50 S 65 0W
General Paz, *Argentina* . . **158 B4** 27 45 S 57 36W
General Pico, *Argentina* . **158 D3** 35 45 S 63 50W
General Pinedo, *Argentina* **158 B3** 27 15 S 61 20W
General Pinto, *Argentina* **158 C3** 34 45 S 61 50W
General Sampaio, *Brazil* . **154 B4** 4 2 S 39 29W
General Santos, *Phil.* . . . . **71 H5** 6 5N 125 14 E
General Tinio, *Phil.* . . . . . **70 D3** 15 39N 121 10 E
General Toshevo, *Bulgaria* **43 D13** 43 42N 28 6 E
General Trevino, *Mexico* **147 B5** 26 14N 99 29W
General Trías, *Mexico* . . . **146 B3** 28 21N 106 22W
General Viamonte, *Argentina* . . . . . . . . . . . **158 D3** 35 1 S 61 3W
General Villegas, *Argentina* . . . . . . . . . . . **158 D3** 35 5 S 63 0W
General Vintter, L., *Argentina* . . . . . . . . . . . **160 B2** 43 55 S 71 40W
Generoso, Mte., *Switz.* . . **29 E8** 45 56N 9 2 E
Genesee, *Idaho, U.S.A.* . . **142 C5** 46 33N 116 56W
Genesee, *Pa., U.S.A.* . . . . **136 E7** 41 59N 77 54W
Genesee →, *U.S.A.* . . . . . **136 C7** 43 16N 77 36W
Geneseo, *Ill., U.S.A.* . . . . **140 C6** 41 27N 90 9W
Geneseo, *Kans., U.S.A.* . . **138 F5** 38 31N 98 10W
Geneseo, *N.Y., U.S.A.* . . . **136 D7** 42 48N 77 49W
Geneva = Genève, *Switz.* **28 D2** 46 12N 6 9 E
Geneva, *Ala., U.S.A.* . . . . **135 K3** 31 2N 85 52W
Geneva, *Ill., U.S.A.* . . . . . **141 C8** 41 53N 88 18W
Geneva, *Ind., U.S.A.* . . . . **141 D12** 40 36N 84 58W
Geneva, *N.Y., U.S.A.* . . . . **136 D7** 42 52N 76 59W
Geneva, *Nebr., U.S.A.* . . . **138 E6** 40 32N 97 36W
Geneva, *Ohio, U.S.A.* . . . **136 E4** 41 48N 80 57W
Geneva, L. = Léman, Lac, *Switz.* . . . . . . . . . . . **28 D3** 46 26N 6 30 E
Geneva, L., *U.S.A.* . . . . . . **141 B8** 42 38N 88 30W
Genève, *Switz.* . . . . . . . . . **28 D2** 46 12N 6 9 E
Genève □, *Switz.* . . . . . . . **28 D2** 46 10N 6 10 E
Geng, *Afghan.* . . . . . . . . . . **79 C1** 31 22N 61 28 E
Gengenbach, *Germany* . . . **27 G4** 48 25N 8 2 E
Genggang, *China* . . . . . . . **68 F2** 23 32N 99 20 E
Genichesk, *Ukraine* . . . . . **52 C6** 46 12N 34 50 E
Genil →, *Spain* . . . . . . . . **37 H5** 37 42N 5 19W
Génissiat, Barr. de, *France* **25 B9** 46 1N 5 48 E
Genk, *Belgium* . . . . . . . . . . **21 G7** 50 58N 5 32 E
Genkai-Nada, *Japan* . . . . . **62 D2** 34 0N 130 0 E
Genlis, *France* . . . . . . . . . **23 E12** 47 11N 5 12 E
Gennargentu, Mti. del, *Italy* . . . . . . . . . . . . . . . **40 C2** 40 0N 9 10 E
Gennep, *Neths.* . . . . . . . . . **21 E7** 51 41N 5 59 E
Gennes, *France* . . . . . . . . . **22 E6** 47 20N 0 17W
Genoa = Génova, *Italy* . . **38 D5** 44 24N 8 56 E
Genoa, *Australia* . . . . . . . **117 D8** 37 29 S 149 35 E
Genoa, *Ill., U.S.A.* . . . . . . **141 B8** 42 6N 88 42W
Genoa, *N.Y., U.S.A.* . . . . . **137 D8** 42 40N 76 32W
Genoa, *Nebr., U.S.A.* . . . . **138 E6** 41 27N 97 44W
Genoa, *Nev., U.S.A.* . . . . . **144 F7** 39 2N 119 50W
Genoa →, *Argentina* . . . . **160 B2** 44 55 S 70 5W
Genoa City, *U.S.A.* . . . . . **141 B8** 42 30N 88 20W
Génova, *Italy* . . . . . . . . . . **38 D5** 44 24N 8 56 E
Génova, G. di, *Italy* . . . . . **38 E6** 44 0N 9 0 E
Gent, *Belgium* . . . . . . . . . . **21 F3** 51 2N 3 42 E
Gentbrugge, *Belgium* . . . . **21 F3** 51 3N 3 47 E
Genthin, *Germany* . . . . . . **26 C8** 52 24N 12 10 E
Gentio do Ouro, *Brazil* . . **154 D3** 11 25 S 42 30W
Geographe B., *Australia* . **113 F2** 33 30 S 115 15 E
Geographe Chan., *Australia* . . . . . . . . . . . . **113 D1** 24 30 S 113 0 E
Geokchay, *Azerbaijan* . . . **53 F12** 40 42N 47 43 E
Georga, Zemlya, *Russia* . **56 A5** 80 30N 49 0 E
George, *S. Africa* . . . . . . . **104 E3** 33 58 S 22 29 E
George →, *Canada* . . . . . **129 A6** 58 49N 66 10W
George, L., *N.S.W., Australia* . . . . . . . . . . . . **117 C8** 35 10 S 149 25 E
George, L., *S. Austral., Australia* . . . . . . . . . . . . **116 D4** 37 25 S 140 0 E
George, L., *W. Austral., Australia* . . . . . . . . . . . . **112 D3** 22 45 S 123 40 E
George, L., *Uganda* . . . . . **106 B3** 0 5N 30 10 E
George, L., *Fla., U.S.A.* . . **135 L5** 29 17N 81 36W
George, L., *N.Y., U.S.A.* . **137 C11** 43 37N 73 33W
George Gill Ra., *Australia* **112 D5** 24 22 S 131 45 E
George River = Port Nouveau-Québec, *Canada* . . . . . . . . . . . . . **127 C13** 58 30N 65 59W
George Sound, *N.Z.* . . . . **119 E2** 44 52 S 167 25 E
George Town, *Bahamas* . **148 B4** 23 33N 75 47W
George Town, *Malaysia* . **77 K3** 5 25N 100 15 E
George V Land, *Antarctica* . . . . . . . . . . . **7 C10** 69 0 S 148 0 E
George VI Sound, *Antarctica* . . . . . . . . . . . **7 D17** 71 0 S 68 0W
George West, *U.S.A.* . . . **139 L5** 28 20N 98 7W
Georgetown, *Australia* . . . **114 B3** 18 17 S 143 33 E
Georgetown, *Ont., Canada* . . . . . . . . . . . . . **128 D4** 43 40N 79 56W
Georgetown, *P.E.I., Canada* . . . . . . . . . . . . . **129 C7** 46 13N 62 24W
Georgetown, *Cayman Is.* **148 C3** 19 20N 81 24W
Georgetown, *Gambia* . . . **100 C2** 13 30N 14 47W
Georgetown, *Guyana* . . . **153 B6** 6 50N 58 12W
Georgetown, *Calif., U.S.A.* . . . . . . . . . . . . . **144 G6** 38 54N 120 50W
Georgetown, *Colo., U.S.A.* . . . . . . . . . . . . . **142 G11** 39 42N 105 42W
Georgetown, *Ill., U.S.A.* . **141 E9** 39 59N 87 38W
Georgetown, *Ky., U.S.A.* . **134 F3** 38 13N 84 33W
Georgetown, *Ohio, U.S.A.* . . . . . . . . . . . . . **141 F13** 38 52N 83 54W
Georgetown, *S.C., U.S.A.* **135 J6** 33 23N 79 17W
Georgetown, *Tex., U.S.A.* **139 K6** 30 38N 97 41W
Georgi Dimitrov, *Bulgaria* **43 E8** 42 15N 23 54 E
Georgi Dimitrov, Yazovir, *Bulgaria* . . . . . . . . . . . . **43 E10** 42 37N 25 18 E
Georgia □, *U.S.A.* . . . . . **135 J4** 32 50N 83 15W
Georgia ■, *Asia* . . . . . . . . **53 E10** 42 0N 43 0 E
Georgia, Str. of, *Canada* . **130 D4** 49 25N 124 0W
Georgian B., *Canada* . . . . **128 C3** 45 15N 81 0W
Georgievsk, *Russia* . . . . . **53 D10** 44 12N 43 28 E
Georgina →, *Australia* . . **114 C2** 23 30 S 139 47 E
Georgina Downs, *Australia* . . . . . . . . . . . . **114 C2** 21 10 S 137 40 E
Georgiu-Dezh = Liski, *Russia* . . . . . . . . . . . . . . **51 F11** 51 3N 39 30 E
Georgiyevka, *Kazakhstan* **55 B7** 43 3N 74 43 E
Gera, *Germany* . . . . . . . . . **26 E8** 50 53N 12 11 E
Geraardsbergen, *Belgium* **21 G3** 50 45N 3 53 E
Geral, Serra, *Bahia, Brazil* **155 D3** 14 0 S 41 0W
Geral, Serra, *Goiás, Brazil* **154 D2** 11 15 S 46 30W
Geral, Serra, *Sta. Catarina, Brazil* . . . **159 B6** 26 25 S 50 0W
Geral de Goiás, Serra, *Brazil* . . . . . . . . . . . . . . . **155 D2** 12 0 S 46 0W
Geral do Paranã Serra, *Brazil* . . . . . . . . . . . . . . . **155 E2** 15 0 S 47 30W
Gerald, *U.S.A.* . . . . . . . . . **140 F5** 38 24N 91 20W
Geraldine, *N.Z.* . . . . . . . . **119 E6** 44 5 S 171 15 E
Geraldine, *U.S.A.* . . . . . . **142 C8** 47 36N 110 16W
Geraldton, *Australia* . . . . **113 E1** 28 48 S 114 32 E
Geraldton, *Canada* . . . . . **128 C2** 49 44N 86 59W
Geranium, *Australia* . . . . . **116 C4** 35 23 S 140 11 E
Gérardmer, *France* . . . . . . **23 D13** 48 3N 6 50 E
Gercüş, *Turkey* . . . . . . . . . **89 E9** 37 34N 41 23 E
Gerede, *Turkey* . . . . . . . . . **52 F5** 40 45N 32 10 E
Gereshk, *Afghan.* . . . . . . . **79 C2** 31 47N 64 35 E
Gérgal, *Spain* . . . . . . . . . . **35 H2** 37 7N 2 31W
Gerik, *Malaysia* . . . . . . . . **77 K3** 5 50N 101 15 E
Gering, *U.S.A.* . . . . . . . . . **138 E3** 41 50N 103 40W
Gerlach, *U.S.A.* . . . . . . . . **142 F4** 40 39N 119 21W
Gerlachovka, *Slovak Rep.* **31 B13** 49 11N 20 7 E
Gerlogubi, *Ethiopia* . . . . . **90 F4** 6 53N 45 3 E
German Planina, *Macedonia* . . . . . . . . . . . . **42 E7** 42 20N 22 0 E
Germansen Landing, *Canada* . . . . . . . . . . . . . **130 B4** 55 43N 124 40W
Germantown, *U.S.A.* . . . . **141 E12** 39 38N 84 22W
Germany ■, *Europe* . . . . **26 E6** 51 0N 10 0 E
Germersheim, *Germany* . . **27 F4** 49 13N 8 20 E
Germiston, *S. Africa* . . . . **105 D4** 26 15 S 28 10 E
Gernsheim, *Germany* . . . . **27 F4** 49 44N 8 29 E
Gero, *Japan* . . . . . . . . . . . **63 B9** 35 48N 137 14 E
Gerolstein, *Germany* . . . . **27 E2** 50 12N 6 40 E
Gerolzhofen, *Germany* . . . **27 F6** 49 54N 10 21 E
Gerona, *Spain* . . . . . . . . . . **34 D7** 41 58N 2 46 E
Gerona □, *Spain* . . . . . . . **34 C7** 42 11N 2 30 E
Gérouville, *Belgium* . . . . . **21 J6** 49 37N 5 26 E
Gerrard, *Canada* . . . . . . . **130 C5** 50 30N 117 17W
Gerringong, *Australia* . . . **117 C9** 34 46 S 150 47 E
Gers □, *France* . . . . . . . . . **24 E4** 43 35N 0 30 E
Gers →, *France* . . . . . . . . **24 D4** 44 9N 0 39 E
Gersfeld, *Germany* . . . . . . **26 E5** 50 27N 9 57 E
Gersoppa Falls, *India* . . . **83 G2** 14 12N 74 46 E
Gerze, *Turkey* . . . . . . . . . . **88 C6** 41 48N 35 12 E
Geseke, *Germany* . . . . . . . **26 D4** 51 38N 8 29 E
Geser, *Indonesia* . . . . . . . **73 B4** 3 50 S 130 54 E
Gesso →, *Italy* . . . . . . . . . **38 D4** 44 24N 7 33 E
Gestro, Wabi →, *Ethiopia* . . . . . . . . . . . . . **95 G5** 4 12N 42 2 E
Gesves, *Belgium* . . . . . . . . **21 H6** 50 24N 5 4 E
Getafe, *Spain* . . . . . . . . . . **36 E7** 40 18N 3 44W
Gethsémani, *Canada* . . . . **129 B7** 50 13N 60 40W
Gettysburg, *Pa., U.S.A.* . . **134 F7** 39 50N 77 14W
Gettysburg, *S. Dak., U.S.A.* . . . . . . . . . . . . . **138 C5** 45 1N 99 57W
Getz Ice Shelf, *Antarctica* **7 D14** 75 0 S 130 0W
Geul →, *Neths.* . . . . . . . . **21 G7** 50 53N 5 43 E
Geureudong, Mt., *Indonesia* . . . . . . . . . . . **74 B1** 4 13N 96 42 E
Geurie, *Australia* . . . . . . . **117 B8** 32 22 S 148 50 E
Gevaş, *Turkey* . . . . . . . . . . **89 D10** 38 15N 43 6 E
Gévaudan, *France* . . . . . . **24 D7** 44 40N 3 40 E
Gevgelija, *Macedonia* . . . **42 F7** 41 9N 22 30 E
Gévora →, *Spain* . . . . . . . **37 G4** 38 53N 6 57W
Gex, *France* . . . . . . . . . . . **25 B10** 46 21N 6 3 E
Geyikli, *Turkey* . . . . . . . . . **44 E8** 39 50N 26 12 E
Geyser, *U.S.A.* . . . . . . . . . **142 C8** 47 16N 110 30W
Geyserville, *U.S.A.* . . . . . **144 G4** 38 42N 122 54W
Geysir, *Iceland* . . . . . . . . . **12 D3** 64 19N 20 18W
Geyve, *Turkey* . . . . . . . . . . **88 C4** 40 30N 30 18 E
Ghâbat el Arab = Wang Kai, *Sudan* . . . . . . . . . . . **95 F2** 9 3N 29 23 E
Ghaghara →, *India* . . . . . **81 G11** 25 45N 84 40 E
Ghalat, *Oman* . . . . . . . . . . **87 B7** 21 6N 58 53 E
Ghalla, Wadi el →, *Sudan* . . . . . . . . . . . . . . **95 E2** 10 25N 27 32 E
Ghallamane, *Mauritania* . **98 D3** 23 15N 10 0W
Ghana ■, *W. Afr.* . . . . . . **101 D4** 8 0N 1 0W
Ghansor, *India* . . . . . . . . . **81 H9** 22 39N 80 1 E
Ghanzi, *Botswana* . . . . . . **104 C3** 21 50 S 21 34 E
Ghanzi □, *Botswana* . . . . **104 C3** 21 50 S 21 45 E
Gharb el Istiwa'iya □, *Sudan* . . . . . . . . . . . . . . **95 F2** 5 0N 30 0 E
Gharbîya, Es Sahrâ el, *Egypt* . . . . . . . . . . . . . . **94 B2** 27 40N 26 30 E
Ghard Abû Muharik, *Egypt* . . . . . . . . . . . . . . **94 B2** 26 50N 30 0 E
Ghardaïa, *Algeria* . . . . . . **99 B5** 32 20N 3 37 E
Ghârib, G., *Egypt* . . . . . . **94 J8** 28 6N 32 54 E
Ghârib, Râs, *Egypt* . . . . . **94 J8** 28 6N 33 18 E
Gharm, W. →, *Oman* . . . **87 C7** 19 57N 57 38 E
Gharyān, *Libya* . . . . . . . . . **96 B2** 32 10N 13 0 E
Gharyān □, *Libya* . . . . . . **96 B2** 30 35N 12 0 E
Ghat, *Libya* . . . . . . . . . . . . **96 D2** 24 59N 10 11 E
Ghatal, *India* . . . . . . . . . . **81 H12** 22 40N 87 46 E
Ghatampur, *India* . . . . . . . **81 F9** 26 8N 80 13 E
Ghatere, *Solomon Is.* . . . **121 L10** 7 55 S 159 0 E
Ghatprabha →, *India* . . . **83 F2** 16 15N 75 20 E
Ghaţţi, *Si. Arabia* . . . . . . **84 D3** 31 16N 37 31 E
Ghawdex = Gozo, *Malta* **32 C1** 36 3N 14 13 E
Ghayl, *Si. Arabia* . . . . . . **86 B4** 21 40N 46 20 E
Ghayl Bā Wazīr, *Yemen* . **87 D5** 14 47N 49 22 E
Ghazal, Bahr el →, *Chad* **97 F3** 13 0N 15 47 E
Ghazâl, Bahr el →, *Sudan* . . . . . . . . . . . . . . **95 F3** 9 31N 30 25 E
Ghazaouet, *Algeria* . . . . . **99 A4** 35 8N 1 50W
Ghaziabad, *India* . . . . . . . **80 E7** 28 42N 77 26 E
Ghazipur, *India* . . . . . . . . **81 G10** 25 38N 83 35 E
Ghaznī, *Afghan.* . . . . . . . . **79 B3** 33 30N 68 28 E
Ghaznī □, *Afghan.* . . . . . . **79 B3** 32 10N 68 20 E
Ghedi, *Italy* . . . . . . . . . . . . **38 C7** 45 24N 10 16 E
Ghelari, *Romania* . . . . . . . **46 D3** 45 38N 22 45 E
Ghèlinsor, *Somali Rep.* . . **90 F4** 6 28N 46 39 E
Ghent = Gent, *Belgium* . **21 F3** 51 2N 3 42 E
Gheorghe Gheorghiu-Dej, *Romania* . . . . . . . . . . . . **46 C7** 46 17N 26 47 E
Gheorgheni, *Romania* . . . **46 C6** 46 43N 25 41 E
Ghergani, *Romania* . . . . . **46 E6** 44 37N 25 37 E
Gherla, *Romania* . . . . . . . **46 B4** 47 2N 23 57 E
Ghilarza, *Italy* . . . . . . . . . **40 B1** 40 8N 8 50 E
Ghisonaccia, *France* . . . . **25 F13** 42 1N 9 26 E
Ghisoni, *France* . . . . . . . . **25 F13** 42 7N 9 12 E
Ghizao, *Afghan.* . . . . . . . . **80 C1** 33 20N 65 44 E
Ghizar →, *Pakistan* . . . . **81 A5** 36 15N 73 43 E
Ghod →, *India* . . . . . . . . . **82 E2** 18 30N 74 35 E
Ghogha, *India* . . . . . . . . . . **80 J5** 21 40N 72 20 E
Ghot Ogrein, *Egypt* . . . . . **94 A2** 31 10N 25 20 E
Ghotaru, *India* . . . . . . . . . **80 F4** 27 20N 70 1 E
Ghotki, *Pakistan* . . . . . . . **80 E3** 28 5N 69 21 E
Ghowr □, *Afghan.* . . . . . . **79 B2** 34 0N 64 20 E
Ghudaf, W. al →, *Iraq* . . **84 C4** 32 56N 43 30 E
Ghudāmis, *Libya* . . . . . . . **96 B1** 30 11N 9 29 E
Ghughri, *India* . . . . . . . . . **81 H9** 22 39N 80 41 E
Ghugus, *India* . . . . . . . . . . **82 E4** 19 58N 79 12 E
Ghulam Mohammad Barrage, *Pakistan* . . . . . **80 G3** 25 30N 68 20 E
Ghurayrah, *Si. Arabia* . . . **86 C3** 18 37N 42 41 E
Ghūrīān, *Afghan.* . . . . . . . **79 B1** 34 17N 61 25 E
Gia Dinh, *Vietnam* . . . . . . **77 G6** 10 49N 106 42 E
Gia Lai = Pleiku, *Vietnam* **76 F7** 13 57N 108 0 E
Gia Nghia, *Vietnam* . . . . . **77 G6** 11 58N 107 42 E
Gia Ngoc, *Vietnam* . . . . . **76 E7** 14 50N 108 58 E
Gia Vuc, *Vietnam* . . . . . . . **76 E7** 14 42N 108 34 E
Giamama, *Somali Rep.* . . . **108 D2** 0 4N 42 44 E
Giannutri, *Italy* . . . . . . . . **38 F8** 42 16N 11 5 E
Giant Forest, *U.S.A.* . . . . **144 J8** 36 36N 118 43W
Giant Mts. = Krkonoše, *Czech.* . . . . . . . . . . . . . . **30 A8** 50 50N 15 35 E
Giants Causeway, *U.K.* . . **19 A5** 55 15N 6 30W
Giarabub = Al Jaghbūb, *Libya* . . . . . . . . . . . . . . **96 C4** 29 42N 24 38 E
Giarre, *Italy* . . . . . . . . . . . **41 E8** 37 44N 15 10 E
Giaveno, *Italy* . . . . . . . . . **38 C4** 45 3N 7 20 E
Gibara, *Cuba* . . . . . . . . . . **148 B4** 21 9N 76 11W
Gibb River, *Australia* . . . **112 C4** 16 26 S 126 26 E
Gibbon, *U.S.A.* . . . . . . . . . **138 E5** 40 45N 98 51W
Gibe →, *Ethiopia* . . . . . . **95 F4** 7 20N 37 36 E
Gibellina, *Italy* . . . . . . . . . **40 E6** 37 48N 13 0 E
Gibraléon, *Spain* . . . . . . . **37 H4** 37 23N 6 58W
Gibraltar ■, *Europe* . . . . **37 J5** 36 7N 5 22W
Gibraltar, Str. of, *Medit. S.* . . . . . . . . . . . . . **37 K5** 35 55N 5 40W
Gibson City, *U.S.A.* . . . . . **141 D8** 40 28N 88 22W
Gibson Desert, *Australia* . **112 D4** 24 0 S 126 0 E
Gibsonburg, *U.S.A.* . . . . . **141 C13** 41 23N 83 19W
Gibsons, *Canada* . . . . . . . **130 D4** 49 24N 123 32W
Gibsonville, *U.S.A.* . . . . . **144 F6** 39 46N 120 54W
Giddalur, *India* . . . . . . . . . **83 G4** 15 20N 78 57 E
Giddings, *U.S.A.* . . . . . . . **139 K6** 30 11N 96 56W
Gidole, *Ethiopia* . . . . . . . . **95 F4** 5 40N 37 25 E
Gien, *France* . . . . . . . . . . . **23 E9** 47 40N 2 36 E
Giessen, *Germany* . . . . . . . **26 E4** 50 34N 8 40 E
Gieten, *Neths.* . . . . . . . . . . **20 B9** 53 1N 6 46 E
Gīfān, *Iran* . . . . . . . . . . . . **85 B8** 37 54N 57 28 E
Gifatin, Geziret, *Egypt* . . **94 B3** 27 10N 33 50 E
Gifford Creek, *Australia* . **112 D2** 24 3 S 116 16 E
Gifhorn, *Germany* . . . . . . . **26 C6** 52 29N 10 32 E
Gifu, *Japan* . . . . . . . . . . . . **63 B8** 35 30N 136 45 E
Gifu □, *Japan* . . . . . . . . . . **63 B8** 35 40N 137 0 E
Gigant, *Russia* . . . . . . . . . **53 C9** 46 28N 41 20 E
Giganta, Sa. de la, *Mexico* **146 B2** 25 30N 111 30W
Gigen, *Bulgaria* . . . . . . . . **43 D9** 43 40N 24 28 E

Great Belt 203


Goodenough I., Papua N. G. 120 E6 9 20 S 150 15 E
Gooderham, Canada 128 D4 44 54N 78 21W
Goodeve, Canada 131 C8 51 4N 103 10W
Gooding, U.S.A. 142 E6 42 56N 114 43W
Goodland, U.S.A. 138 F4 39 21N 101 43W
Goodnight, U.S.A. 139 H4 35 2N 101 11W
Goodooga, Australia 115 D4 29 3 S 147 28 E
Goodsoil, Canada 131 C7 54 24N 109 13W
Goodsprings, U.S.A. 143 J6 35 50N 115 26W
Goole, U.K. 16 D7 53 42N 0 52W
Goolgowi, Australia 117 B6 33 58 S 145 41 E
Goolwa, Australia 116 C3 35 30 S 138 47 E
Goomalling, Australia 113 F2 31 15 S 116 49 E
Goombalie, Australia 115 D4 29 59 S 145 26 E
Goonalga, Australia 116 A5 31 45 S 143 37 E
Goonda, Mozam. 107 F3 19 48 S 33 57 E
Goondiwindi, Australia 115 D5 28 30 S 150 21 E
Goongarrie, L., Australia 113 F3 30 3 S 121 9 E
Goonumbla, Australia 117 B8 32 59 S 148 11 E
Goonyella, Australia 114 C4 21 47 S 147 58 E
Goor, Neths. 20 D9 52 13N 6 33 E
Gooray, Australia 115 D5 28 25 S 150 2 E
Goose →, Canada 129 B7 53 20N 60 35W
Goose L., U.S.A. 142 F3 41 56N 120 26W
Gooty, India 83 G3 15 7N 77 41 E
Gopalganj, Bangla. 78 D2 23 1N 89 50 E
Gopalganj, India 81 F11 26 28N 84 30 E
Goppenstein, Switz. 28 D5 46 23N 7 46 E
Göppingen, Germany 27 G5 48 42N 9 40 E
Gor, Spain 35 H2 37 23N 2 58W
Góra, Leszno, Poland 47 D3 51 40N 16 31 E
Góra, Płock, Poland 47 C7 52 39N 20 6 E
Góra Kalwaria, Poland 47 D8 51 59N 21 14 E
Gorakhpur, India 81 F10 26 47N 83 23 E
Goražde, Bos.-H. 42 D3 43 38N 18 58 E
Gorbatov, Russia 51 C13 56 12N 43 2 E
Gorbea, Peña, Spain 34 B2 43 1N 2 50W
Gorda, U.S.A. 144 K5 35 53N 121 26W
Gorda, Pta., Nic. 148 D3 14 20N 83 10W
Gorda, Pta., Canary Is. 33 F2 28 45N 18 0W
Gordan B., Australia 112 B5 11 35 S 130 10 E
Gordon, U.S.A. 138 D3 42 48N 102 12W
Gordon →, Australia 114 G4 42 27 S 145 30 E
Gordon, I., Chile 160 D3 54 55 S 69 30W
Gordon Downs, Australia 112 C4 18 48 S 128 33 E
Gordon L., Alta., Canada 131 B6 56 30N 110 25W
Gordon L., N.W.T., Canada 130 A6 63 5N 113 11W
Gordonia, S. Africa 104 D3 28 13 S 21 10 E
Gordonvale, Australia 114 B4 17 5 S 145 50 E
Gore, Australia 115 D5 28 17 S 151 30 E
Goré, Chad 97 G3 7 59N 16 31 E
Gore, Ethiopia 95 F4 8 12N 35 32 E
Gore, N.Z. 119 G3 46 5 S 168 58 E
Gore Bay, Canada 128 C3 45 57N 82 28W
Görele, Turkey 89 C8 41 2N 39 0 E
Gorey, Ireland 19 D5 52 41N 6 18W
Gorg, Iran 85 D8 29 29N 59 43 E
Gorgān, Iran 85 B7 36 50N 54 29 E
Gorgona, Italy 38 E6 43 27N 9 52 E
Gorgora, Ethiopia 95 E4 12 15N 37 17 E
Gorham, U.S.A. 137 B13 44 23N 71 10W
Gori, Georgia 53 E11 42 0N 44 7 E
Gorin, U.S.A. 140 D4 40 22N 92 1W
Gorinchem, Neths. 20 E5 51 50N 4 59 E
Gorinhatã, Brazil 155 E2 19 15 S 49 45W
Goritsy, Russia 51 C10 57 4N 36 43 E
Gorízia, Italy 39 C10 45 56N 13 37 E
Górka, Poland 47 D3 51 39N 16 58 E
Gorki = Nizhniy Novgorod, Russia 51 C14 56 20N 44 0 E
Gorki, Belorussia 50 D7 54 17N 30 59 E
Gorkiy = Nizhniy Novgorod, Russia 51 C14 56 20N 44 0 E
Gorkovskoye Vdkhr., Russia 51 C13 57 2N 43 4 E
Gørlev, Denmark 15 J5 55 30N 11 15 E
Gorlice, Poland 31 B14 49 35N 21 11 E
Görlitz, Germany 26 D10 51 10N 14 59 E
Gorlovka, Ukraine 52 B8 48 19N 38 5 E
Gorman, Calif., U.S.A. 145 L8 34 47N 118 51W
Gorman, Tex., U.S.A. 139 J5 32 12N 98 41W
Gorna Dzhumayo = Blagoevgrad, Bulgaria 42 E8 42 2N 23 5 E
Gorna Oryakhovitsa, Bulgaria 43 D10 43 7N 25 40 E
Gornja Radgona, Slovenia 39 B13 46 40N 16 2 E
Gornja Tuzla, Bos.-H. 42 C3 44 35N 18 46 E
Gornji Grad, Slovenia 39 B11 46 20N 14 52 E
Gornji Milanovac, Serbia 42 C5 44 0N 20 29 E
Gornji Vakuf, Bos.-H. 42 D2 43 57N 17 34 E
Gorno Ablanovo, Bulgaria 43 D10 43 37N 25 43 E
Gorno-Altaysk, Russia 56 D9 51 50N 86 5 E
Gorno Slinkino, Russia 56 C8 60 5N 70 0 E
Gornyatski, Russia 48 A11 67 32N 64 3 E
Gornyi, Russia 60 B6 44 57N 133 59 E
Gornyy, Russia 51 F16 51 50N 48 30 E
Gorodenka, Ukraine 52 B1 48 41N 25 29 E
Gorodets, Russia 51 C13 56 38N 43 28 E
Gorodishche, Russia 51 E14 53 13N 45 40 E
Gorodishche, Ukraine 52 B4 49 17N 31 27 E
Gorodnitsa, Ukraine 50 F5 50 46N 27 19 E
Gorodnya, Ukraine 50 F7 51 55N 31 33 E
Gorodok, Belorussia 50 D7 55 30N 30 3 E
Gorodok, Ukraine 50 G3 49 46N 23 32 E
Goroka, Papua N. G. 120 D3 6 7 S 145 25 E
Goroke, Australia 116 D4 36 43 S 141 29 E
Gorokhov, Ukraine 50 F4 50 30N 24 45 E
Gorokhovets, Russia 51 C13 56 13N 42 39 E
Gorom Gorom, Burkina Faso 101 C4 14 26N 0 14W
Goromonzi, Zimbabwe 107 F3 17 52 S 31 22 E
Gorongose →, Mozam. 105 C5 20 30 S 34 40 E
Gorongoza, Mozam. 107 F3 18 44 S 34 2 E
Gorongoza, Sa. da, Mozam. 107 F3 18 27 S 34 2 E
Gorontalo, Indonesia 72 A2 0 35N 123 5 E
Goronyo, Nigeria 101 C6 13 29N 5 39 E
Górowo Iławeckie, Poland 47 A7 54 17N 20 30 E
Gorredijk, Neths. 20 C8 53 0N 6 3 E
Gorron, France 22 D6 48 25N 0 50W
Gorssel, Neths. 20 D8 52 12N 6 12 E
Gort, Ireland 19 C3 53 4N 8 50W
Gortis, Greece 32 D6 35 4N 24 58 E
Gorumahisani, India 82 C8 22 20N 86 24 E
Gorzkowice, Poland 47 D6 51 13N 19 36 E
Gorzno, Poland 47 B6 53 12N 19 38 E
Gorzów Śląski, Poland 47 D5 51 3N 18 22 E
Gorzów Wielkopolski, Poland 47 C2 52 43N 15 15 E
Gorzów Wielkopolski □, Poland 47 C2 52 45N 15 30 E
Göschenen, Switz. 29 C7 46 40N 8 36 E
Gose, Japan 63 C7 34 27N 135 44 E
Gosford, Australia 117 B9 33 23 S 151 18 E
Goshen, Calif., U.S.A. 144 J7 36 21N 119 25W
Goshen, Ind., U.S.A. 141 C11 41 35N 85 50W
Goshen, N.Y., U.S.A. 137 E10 41 24N 74 20W
Goshogawara, Japan 60 D10 40 48N 140 27 E
Goslar, Germany 26 D6 51 55N 10 23 E
Gospič, Croatia 39 D12 44 35N 15 23 E
Gosport, U.K. 17 G6 50 48N 1 8W
Gosport, U.S.A. 141 E10 39 21N 86 40W
Gossau, Switz. 29 B8 47 25N 9 15 E
Gosse →, Australia 114 B1 19 32 S 134 37 E
Gostivar, Macedonia 42 F5 41 48N 20 57 E
Gostyń, Poland 47 D4 51 50N 17 3 E
Gostynin, Poland 47 C6 52 26N 19 29 E
Göta älv →, Sweden 15 G5 57 42N 11 54 E
Göta kanal, Sweden 13 G12 58 30N 15 58 E
Göteborg, Sweden 15 G5 57 43N 11 59 E
Göteborgs och Bohus län □, Sweden 13 G11 58 30N 11 30 E
Gotemba, Japan 63 B10 35 18N 138 56 E
Götene, Sweden 15 F7 58 32N 13 30 E
Gotha, Germany 26 E6 50 56N 10 42 E
Gothenburg, U.S.A. 138 E4 40 56N 100 10W
Gotland, Sweden 13 H15 57 30N 18 33 E
Gotse Delchev, Bulgaria 43 F8 41 43N 23 46 E
Gotska Sandön, Sweden 13 G15 58 24N 19 15 E
Gōtsu, Japan 62 B4 35 0N 132 14 E
Göttingen, Germany 26 D5 51 31N 9 55 E
Gottwald = Zmiyev, Ukraine 52 B7 49 39N 36 27 E
Gottwaldov = Zlin, Czech. 31 B10 49 14N 17 40 E
Goubangzi, China 67 D11 41 20N 121 52 E
Gouda, Neths. 20 D5 52 1N 4 42 E
Goúdhoura, Ákra, Greece 32 E8 34 59N 26 6 E
Goudiry, Senegal 100 C2 14 15N 12 45W
Gough I., Atl. Oc. 9 N8 40 10 S 9 45W
Gouin, Rés., Canada 128 C5 48 35N 74 40W
Gouitafla, Ivory C. 100 D3 7 30N 5 53W
Goulburn, Australia 117 C8 34 44 S 149 44 E
Goulburn Is., Australia 114 A1 11 40 S 133 20 E
Goulia, Ivory C. 100 C3 10 1N 7 11W
Goulimine, Morocco 98 C3 28 56N 10 0W
Goulmina, Morocco 98 B4 31 41N 4 57W
Gouménissa, Greece 44 D4 40 56N 22 37 E
Gounou-Gaya, Chad 97 G3 9 38N 15 31 E
Goúra, Greece 45 G4 37 56N 22 20 E
Gouraya, Algeria 99 A5 36 31N 1 56 E
Gourdon, France 24 D5 44 44N 1 23 E
Gouré, Niger 97 F2 14 0N 10 10 E
Gouri, Chad 97 E3 19 36N 19 36 E
Gourits →, S. Africa 104 E3 34 21 S 21 52 E
Gourma Rharous, Mali 101 B4 16 55N 1 50W
Goúrnais, Greece 32 D7 35 19N 25 16 E
Gournay-en-Bray, France 23 C8 49 29N 1 44 E
Gourock Ra., Australia 117 C8 36 0 S 149 25 E
Goursi, Burkina Faso 100 C4 12 42N 2 37W
Gouvêa, Brazil 155 E3 18 27 S 43 44W
Gouverneur, U.S.A. 137 B9 44 20N 75 28W
Gouviá, Greece 32 A3 39 39N 19 50 E
Gouzon, France 24 B6 46 12N 2 14 E
Govan, Canada 131 C8 51 20N 105 0W
Governador Valadares, Brazil 155 E3 18 15 S 41 57W
Governor's Harbour, Bahamas 148 A4 25 10N 76 14W
Gowan Ra., Australia 114 C4 25 0 S 145 0 E
Gowanda, U.S.A. 136 D6 42 28N 78 56W
Gower, U.K. 17 F3 51 35N 4 10W
Gowna, L., Ireland 19 C4 53 52N 7 35W
Gowrie, U.S.A. 140 B2 42 17N 94 17W
Goya, Argentina 158 B4 29 10 S 59 10W
Goyder Lagoon, Australia 115 D2 27 3 S 138 58 E
Goyllarisquisga, Peru 156 C2 10 31 S 76 24W
Göynük, Turkey 88 C4 40 24N 30 48 E
Goz Beïda, Chad 97 F4 12 10N 21 20 E
Goz Regeb, Sudan 95 D4 16 3N 35 33 E
Gozdnica, Poland 47 D2 51 28N 15 4 E
Gozo, Malta 32 C1 36 3N 14 13 E
Graaff-Reinet, S. Africa 104 E3 32 13 S 24 32 E
Grabill, U.S.A. 141 C12 41 13N 84 57W
Grabow, Germany 26 B7 53 17N 11 31 E
Grabów, Poland 47 D5 51 31N 18 7 E
Grabs, Switz. 29 B8 47 11N 9 27 E
Gračac, Croatia 39 D12 44 18N 15 57 E
Gračanica, Bos.-H. 42 C3 44 43N 18 18 E
Graçay, France 23 E8 47 10N 1 50 E
Grace, U.S.A. 142 E8 42 35N 111 44W
Graceville, U.S.A. 138 C6 45 34N 96 26W
Grachevka, Russia 54 E3 52 55N 52 52 E
Gracias a Dios, C., Honduras 148 C3 15 0N 83 10W
Graciosa, I., Canary Is. 33 E6 29 15N 13 32W
Gradačac, Bos.-H. 42 C3 44 52N 18 26 E
Gradaús, Brazil 154 C1 7 43 S 51 11W
Gradaús, Serra dos, Brazil 154 C1 8 0 S 50 45W
Gradeška Planina, Macedonia 42 F7 41 30N 22 15 E
Gradets, Bulgaria 43 E11 42 46N 26 30 E
Grado, Italy 39 C10 45 40N 13 20 E
Grado, Spain 36 B4 43 23N 6 4W
Gradule, Australia 115 D4 28 32 S 149 15 E
Grady, U.S.A. 139 H3 34 49N 103 19W
Graeca, Lacul, Romania 46 E7 44 5N 26 10 E
Graénalon, L., Iceland 12 D5 64 10N 17 20W
Grafenau, Germany 27 G9 48 51N 13 24 E
Gräfenberg, Germany 27 F7 49 39N 11 15 E
Grafton, Australia 115 D5 29 38 S 152 58 E
Grafton, Ill., U.S.A. 140 F6 38 58N 90 26W
Grafton, N. Dak., U.S.A. 138 A6 48 25N 97 25W
Gragnano, Italy 41 B7 40 42N 14 30 E
Graham, Canada 128 C1 49 20N 90 30W
Graham, N.C., U.S.A. 135 G6 36 5N 79 25W
Graham, Tex., U.S.A. 139 J5 33 6N 98 35W
Graham →, Canada 130 B4 56 31N 122 17W
Graham, Mt., U.S.A. 143 K9 32 42N 109 52W
Graham Bell, Os., Russia 56 A7 81 0N 62 0 E
Graham I., Canada 130 C2 53 40N 132 30W
Graham Land, Antarctica 7 C17 65 0 S 64 0W
Grahamdale, Canada 131 C9 51 23N 98 30W
Grahamstown, S. Africa 104 E4 33 19 S 26 31 E
Grahovo, Montenegro 42 E3 42 40N 18 40 E
Graïba, Tunisia 96 B2 34 30N 10 13 E
Graide, Belgium 21 J6 49 58N 5 4 E
Graie, Alpi, Europe 38 C4 45 30N 7 10 E
Grain Coast, W. Afr. 100 E3 4 20N 10 0W
Grajaú, Brazil 154 C2 5 50 S 46 4W
Grajaú →, Brazil 154 B3 3 41 S 44 48W
Grajewo, Poland 47 B9 53 39N 22 30 E
Gramada, Bulgaria 42 D7 43 49N 22 39 E
Gramat, France 24 D5 44 48N 1 43 E
Grammichele, Italy 41 E7 37 12N 14 37 E
Grámmos, Óros, Greece 44 D2 40 18N 20 47 E
Grampian □, U.K. 18 D6 57 20N 3 0W
Grampian Highlands = Grampian Mts., U.K. 18 E5 56 50N 4 0W
Grampian Mts., U.K. 18 E5 56 50N 4 0W
Gran →, Surinam 153 C6 4 1N 55 30W
Gran Altiplanicie Central, Argentina 160 C3 49 0 S 69 30W
Gran Canaria, Canary Is. 33 G4 27 55N 15 35W
Gran Chaco, S. Amer. 158 B3 25 0 S 61 0W
Gran Paradiso, Italy 38 C4 45 33N 7 17 E
Gran Sasso d'Italia, Italy 39 F10 42 25N 13 30 E
Granada, Nic. 148 D2 11 58N 86 0W
Granada, Phil. 71 F4 10 40N 123 2 E
Granada, Spain 35 H1 37 10N 3 35W
Granada, U.S.A. 139 F3 38 4N 102 19W
Granada □, Spain 37 H7 37 18N 3 0W
Granadilla de Abona, Canary Is. 33 F3 28 7N 16 33W
Granard, Ireland 19 C4 53 47N 7 30W
Granbury, U.S.A. 139 J6 32 27N 97 47W
Granby, Canada 128 C5 45 25N 72 45W
Grand →, Mich., U.S.A. 141 A10 43 4N 86 15W
Grand →, Mo., U.S.A. 140 E3 39 23N 93 7W
Grand →, S. Dak., U.S.A. 138 C4 45 40N 100 45W
Grand Bahama, Bahamas 148 A4 26 40N 78 30W
Grand Bank, Canada 129 C8 47 6N 55 48W
Grand Bassam, Ivory C. 100 D4 5 10N 3 49W
Grand Béréby, Ivory C. 100 E3 4 38N 6 55W
Grand Blanc, U.S.A. 141 B13 42 56N 83 38W
Grand-Bourg, Guadeloupe 149 C7 15 53N 61 19W
Grand Canal = Yun Ho →, China 67 E9 39 10N 117 10 E
Grand Canyon, U.S.A. 143 H7 36 3N 112 9W
Grand Canyon National Park, U.S.A. 143 H7 36 15N 112 30W
Grand Cayman, Cayman Is. 148 C3 19 20N 81 20W
Grand Cess, Liberia 100 E3 4 40N 8 12W
Grand Coulee, U.S.A. 142 C4 47 57N 119 0W
Grand Coulee Dam, U.S.A. 142 C4 47 57N 118 59W
Grand Erg de Bilma, Niger 97 E2 18 30N 14 0 E
Grand Erg Occidental, Algeria 99 B5 30 20N 1 0 E
Grand Erg Oriental, Algeria 99 C6 30 0N 6 30 E
Grand Falls, Canada 129 C8 48 56N 55 40W
Grand Forks, Canada 130 D5 49 0N 118 30W
Grand Forks, U.S.A. 138 B6 47 55N 97 3W
Grand-Fougeray, France 22 E5 47 44N 1 43W
Grand Haven, U.S.A. 141 A10 43 4N 86 13W
Grand I., U.S.A. 134 B2 46 31N 86 40W
Grand Island, U.S.A. 138 E5 40 55N 98 21W
Grand Isle, U.S.A. 139 L10 29 14N 90 0W
Grand Junction, Colo., U.S.A. 143 G9 39 4N 108 33W
Grand Junction, Iowa, U.S.A. 140 B2 42 2N 94 14W
Grand L., La., U.S.A. 139 L8 29 55N 92 47W
Grand L., Ohio, U.S.A. 141 D12 40 32N 84 25W
Grand Lac Victoria, Canada 128 C4 47 35N 77 35W
Grand Lahou, Ivory C. 100 D3 5 10N 5 5W
Grand L., N.B., Canada 129 C6 45 57N 66 7W
Grand L., Nfld., Canada 129 C8 49 0N 57 30W
Grand L., Nfld., Canada 129 B7 53 40N 60 30W
Grand Lake, U.S.A. 142 F11 40 15N 105 49W
Grand Ledge, U.S.A. 141 B12 42 45N 84 45W
Grand-Leez, Belgium 21 G5 50 35N 4 45 E
Grand-Lieu, L. de, France 22 E5 47 6N 1 40W
Grand Manan I., Canada 129 D6 44 45N 66 52W
Grand Marais, Canada 138 B9 47 45N 90 25W
Grand Marais, U.S.A. 134 B3 46 40N 85 59W
Grand-Mère, Canada 128 C5 46 36N 72 40W
Grand Popo, Benin 101 D5 6 15N 1 57 E
Grand Portage, U.S.A. 128 C2 47 58N 89 41W
Grand Rapids, Canada 131 C9 53 12N 99 19W
Grand Rapids, Mich., U.S.A. 141 B10 42 58N 85 40W
Grand Rapids, Minn., U.S.A. 138 B8 47 14N 93 31W
Grand River, U.S.A. 140 D3 40 49N 93 58W
Grand St-Bernard, Col du, Switz. 28 E4 45 50N 7 10 E
Grand Santi, Fr. Guiana 153 C7 4 20N 54 24W
Grand Teton, U.S.A. 142 E8 43 54N 111 50W
Grand Valley, U.S.A. 142 G9 39 27N 108 3W
Grand View, Canada 131 C8 51 10N 100 42W
Grandas de Salime, Spain 36 B4 43 13N 6 53W
Grande →, Jujuy, Argentina 158 A2 24 20 S 65 2W
Grande →, Mendoza, Argentina 158 D2 36 52 S 69 45W
Grande →, Bolivia 157 D5 15 51 S 64 39W
Grande →, Bahia, Brazil 154 D3 11 30 S 44 30W
Grande →, Minas Gerais, Brazil 155 F1 20 6 S 51 4W
Grande →, Spain 35 F4 39 6N 0 48W
Grande →, Venezuela 153 B5 8 36N 61 39W
Grande, B., Argentina 160 D3 50 30 S 68 20W
Grande, I., Brazil 155 F3 23 9 S 44 14W
Grande, Rio →, U.S.A. 139 N6 25 58N 97 9W
Grande, Serra, Goiás, Brazil 154 D2 11 15 S 46 30W
Grande, Serra, Piauí, Brazil 154 C2 8 0 S 45 10W
Grande Baie, Canada 129 C5 48 19N 70 52W
Grande Baleine, R. de la →, Canada 128 A4 55 16N 77 47W
Grande Cache, Canada 130 C5 53 53N 119 8W
Grande de Santiago →, Mexico 146 C3 21 20N 105 50W
Grande Dixence, Barr. de la, Switz. 28 D4 46 5N 7 23 E
Grande-Entrée, Canada 129 C7 47 30N 61 40W
Grande Prairie, Canada 130 B5 55 10N 118 50W
Grande-Rivière, Canada 129 C7 48 26N 64 30W
Grande Sauldre →, France 23 E9 47 27N 2 5 E
Grande-Vallée, Canada 129 C6 49 14N 65 8W
Grandes-Bergeronnes, Canada 129 C6 48 16N 69 35W
Grandfalls, U.S.A. 139 K3 31 20N 102 51W
Grandoe Mines, Canada 130 B3 56 29N 129 54W
Grândola, Portugal 37 G2 38 12N 8 35W
Grandpré, France 23 C11 49 20N 4 50 E
Grandson, Switz. 28 C3 46 49N 6 39 E
Grandview, Mo., U.S.A. 140 F2 38 53N 94 32W
Grandview, Wash., U.S.A. 142 C4 46 15N 119 54W
Grandview Heights, U.S.A. 141 E13 39 58N 83 2W
Grandvilliers, France 23 C8 49 40N 1 57 E
Graneros, Chile 158 C1 34 5 S 70 45W
Grangemouth, U.K. 18 E5 56 1N 3 43W
Granger, Wash., U.S.A. 142 C3 46 21N 120 11W
Granger, Wyo., U.S.A. 142 F9 41 35N 109 58W
Grangeville, U.S.A. 142 D5 45 56N 116 7W
Granite City, U.S.A. 140 F6 38 42N 90 9W
Granite Falls, U.S.A. 138 C7 44 49N 95 33W
Granite Mt., U.S.A. 145 M10 33 5N 116 28W
Granite Peak, Australia 113 E3 25 40 S 121 20 E
Granite Peak, U.S.A. 142 D9 45 10N 109 48W
Granitnyy, Pik, Kirghizia 55 D5 39 32N 70 20 E
Granity, N.Z. 119 B6 41 39 S 171 51 E
Granja, Brazil 154 B3 3 7 S 40 50W
Granja de Moreruela, Spain 36 D5 41 48N 5 44W
Granja de Torrehermosa, Spain 37 G5 38 19N 5 35W
Granollers, Spain 34 D7 41 39N 2 18 E
Gransee, Germany 26 B9 53 0N 13 10 E
Grant, U.S.A. 138 E4 40 53N 101 42W
Grant, Mt., U.S.A. 142 G4 38 34N 118 48W
Grant City, U.S.A. 140 D2 40 29N 94 25W
Grant I., Australia 112 B5 11 10 S 132 52 E
Grant Range, U.S.A. 143 G6 38 30N 115 25W
Grantham, U.K. 16 E7 52 55N 0 39W
Grantown-on-Spey, U.K. 18 D5 57 19N 3 36W
Grants, U.S.A. 143 J10 35 9N 107 52W
Grants Pass, U.S.A. 142 E2 42 26N 123 19W
Grantsburg, U.S.A. 138 C8 45 47N 92 41W
Grantsville, U.S.A. 142 F7 40 36N 112 28W
Granville, France 22 D5 48 50N 1 35W
Granville, Ill., U.S.A. 140 C7 41 16N 89 14W
Granville, N. Dak., U.S.A. 138 A4 48 16N 100 47W
Granville, N.Y., U.S.A. 134 D9 43 24N 73 16W
Granville L., Canada 131 B8 56 18N 100 30W
Grao de Gandía, Spain 35 F4 39 0N 0 7W
Grapeland, U.S.A. 139 K7 31 30N 95 29W
Gras, L. de, Canada 126 B8 64 30N 110 30W
Graskop, S. Africa 105 C5 24 56 S 30 49 E
Grass →, Canada 131 B9 56 3N 96 33W
Grass Range, U.S.A. 142 C9 47 0N 109 0W
Grass River Prov. Park, Canada 131 C8 54 40N 100 50W
Grass Valley, Calif., U.S.A. 144 F6 39 13N 121 4W
Grass Valley, Oreg., U.S.A. 142 D3 45 22N 120 47W
Grassano, Italy 41 B9 40 38N 16 17 E
Grasse, France 25 E10 43 38N 6 56 E
Grassmere, Australia 116 A5 31 24 S 142 38 E
Gratis, U.S.A. 141 E12 39 38N 84 32W
Gratz, U.S.A. 141 F12 38 28N 84 57W
Graubünden □, Switz. 29 C9 46 45N 9 30 E
Graulhet, France 24 E5 43 45N 1 59 E
Graus, Spain 34 C5 42 11N 0 20 E
Gravatá, Brazil 154 C4 8 10 S 35 29W
Grave, Neths. 20 E7 51 46N 5 44 E
Grave, Pte. de, France 24 C2 45 34N 1 4W
's-Graveland, Neths. 20 D6 52 15N 5 7 E
Gravelbourg, Canada 131 D7 49 50N 106 35W
Gravelines, France 23 B9 50 59N 2 10 E
's-Gravendeel, Neths. 20 E5 51 47N 4 37 E
's-Gravenhage, Neths. 20 D4 52 7N 4 17 E
Gravenhurst, Canada 136 B5 44 52N 79 20W
's-Gravenpolder, Neths. 21 F3 51 28N 3 54 E
's-Gravensande, Neths. 20 D4 52 0N 4 9 E
Gravesend, Australia 115 D5 29 35 S 150 20 E
Gravesend, U.K. 17 F8 51 25N 0 22 E
Gravina di Púglia, Italy 41 B9 40 48N 16 25 E
Gravois, Pointe-à-, Haiti 149 C5 18 15N 73 56W
Gravone →, France 25 G12 41 58N 8 45 E
Gray, France 23 E12 47 22N 5 35 E
Grayling, U.S.A. 134 C3 44 40N 84 43W
Grayling →, Canada 130 B3 59 21N 125 0W
Grays Harbor, U.S.A. 142 C1 46 59N 124 1W
Grays L., U.S.A. 142 E8 43 4N 111 26W
Grays River, U.S.A. 144 D3 46 21N 123 37W
Grayson, Canada 131 C8 50 45N 102 40W
Grayville, U.S.A. 141 F9 38 16N 88 0W
Graz, Austria 30 D8 47 4N 15 27 E
Grazalema, Spain 37 J5 36 46N 5 23W
Grdelica, Serbia 42 E7 42 55N 22 3 E
Greasy L., Canada 130 A4 62 55N 122 12W
Great Abaco I., Bahamas 148 A4 26 25N 77 10W
Great Artesian Basin, Australia 114 C3 23 0 S 144 0 E
Great Australian Bight, Australia 113 F5 33 30 S 130 0 E
Great Bahama Bank, Bahamas 148 B4 23 15N 78 0W
Great Barrier I., N.Z. 118 C4 36 11 S 175 25 E
Great Barrier Reef, Australia 114 B4 18 0 S 146 50 E
Great Barrington, U.S.A. 137 D11 42 12N 73 22W
Great Basin, U.S.A. 124 F8 40 0N 117 0W
Great Bear →, Canada 126 B7 65 0N 124 0W
Great Bear L., Canada 126 B7 65 30N 120 0W
Great Belt = Store Bælt, Denmark 15 J5 55 20N 11 0 E

206 Halin


Halin, Somali Rep. 108 C3 9 6N 48 37 E
Hall, Austria 30 D4 47 17N 11 30 E
Hall Beach, Canada 127 B11 68 46N 81 12W
Hall Pt., Australia 112 C3 15 40 S 124 23 E
Hallands län □, Sweden 15 H6 56 50N 12 50 E
Hallands Väderö, Sweden 15 H6 56 27N 12 34 E
Hallandsås, Sweden 15 H7 56 22N 13 0 E
Halle, Belgium 21 G4 50 44N 4 13 E
Halle, Nordrhein-Westfalen, Germany 26 C4 52 4N 8 20 E
Halle, Sachsen-Anhalt, Germany 26 D7 51 29N 12 0 E
Hällefors, Sweden 13 G13 59 47N 14 31 E
Hallein, Austria 30 D6 47 40N 13 5 E
Hällekis, Sweden 15 F7 58 38N 13 27 E
Hallett, Australia 116 B3 33 25 S 138 55 E
Hallettsville, U.S.A. 139 L6 29 27N 96 57W
Hällevadsholm, Sweden 15 F5 58 35N 11 33 E
Hallia →, India 82 F4 16 55N 79 20 E
Halliday, U.S.A. 138 B3 47 21N 102 20W
Halliday L., Canada 131 A7 61 21N 108 56W
Hallim, S. Korea 67 H14 33 24N 126 15 E
Hallingdal →, Norway 13 F10 60 34N 9 12 E
Hällnäs, Sweden 12 D15 64 19N 19 36 E
Hallock, U.S.A. 131 D9 48 47N 96 57W
Halls Creek, Australia 112 C4 18 16 S 127 38 E
Hallstahammar, Sweden 14 E10 59 38N 16 15 E
Hallstatt, Austria 30 D6 47 33N 13 38 E
Hallstead, U.S.A. 137 E9 41 58N 75 45W
Halmahera, Indonesia 72 A3 0 40N 128 0 E
Halmeu, Romania 46 B4 47 57N 23 2 E
Halmstad, Sweden 15 H6 56 41N 12 52 E
Halq el Oued, Tunisia 96 A2 36 53N 10 18 E
Hals, Denmark 15 H4 56 59N 10 18 E
Halsafjorden, Norway 14 A2 63 5N 8 10 E
Hälsingborg = Helsingborg, Sweden 15 H6 56 3N 12 42 E
Halstad, U.S.A. 138 B6 47 21N 96 50W
Haltdalen, Norway 14 B5 62 56N 11 8 E
Haltern, Germany 26 D3 51 44N 7 10 E
Halul, Qatar 85 E7 25 40N 52 40 E
Ḩalvān, Iran 85 C8 33 57N 56 15 E
Ham, France 23 C10 49 45N 3 4 E
Ham Tan, Vietnam 77 G6 10 40N 107 45 E
Ham Yen, Vietnam 76 A5 22 4N 105 3 E
Hamab, Namibia 104 D2 28 7 S 19 16 E
Hamad, Sudan 95 D3 15 20N 33 32 E
Hamada, Japan 62 C4 34 56N 132 4 E
Hamadān, Iran 85 C6 34 52N 48 32 E
Hamadān □, Iran 85 C6 35 0N 49 0 E
Hamadia, Algeria 99 A5 35 28N 1 57 E
Hamāh, Syria 84 C3 35 5N 36 40 E
Hamakita, Japan 63 C9 34 45N 137 47 E
Hamamatsu, Japan 63 C9 34 45N 137 45 E
Hamar, Norway 14 D5 60 48N 11 7 E
Hamarøy, Norway 12 B13 68 5N 15 38 E
Hamâta, Gebel, Egypt 94 C3 24 17N 35 0 E
Hamber Prov. Park, Canada 130 C5 52 20N 118 0W
Hamburg, Germany 26 B5 53 32N 9 59 E
Hamburg, Ark., U.S.A. 139 J9 33 14N 91 48W
Hamburg, Iowa, U.S.A. 138 E7 40 36N 95 39W
Hamburg, N.Y., U.S.A. 136 D6 42 43N 78 50W
Hamburg, Pa., U.S.A. 137 F9 40 33N 75 59W
Hamburg □, Germany 26 B6 53 30N 10 0 E
Ḩamḑ, W. al →, Si. Arabia 84 E3 24 55N 36 20 E
Ḩamḑah, Si. Arabia 86 C3 19 2N 43 36 E
Ḩamḑānah, Si. Arabia 86 C3 19 59N 40 34 E
Hamden, U.S.A. 137 E12 41 23N 72 54W
Hame □ = Hämeen lääni □, Finland 13 F18 61 30N 24 0 E
Hämeen lääni □, Finland 13 F18 61 30N 24 0 E
Hämeenlinna, Finland 13 F18 61 0N 24 28 E
Hamélé, Ghana 100 C4 10 56N 2 45W
Hamelin Pool, Australia 113 E1 26 22 S 114 20 E
Hameln, Germany 26 C5 52 7N 9 24 E
Hamer Koke, Ethiopia 95 F4 5 15N 36 45 E
Hamerkaz □, Israel 91 C3 32 15N 34 55 E
Hamersley Ra., Australia 112 D2 22 0 S 117 45 E
Hamhung, N. Korea 67 E14 39 54N 127 30 E
Hami, China 64 B4 42 55N 93 25 E
Hamilton, Australia 116 D5 37 45 S 142 2 E
Hamilton, Canada 128 D4 43 15N 79 50W
Hamilton, N.Z. 118 D4 37 47 S 175 19 E
Hamilton, U.K. 18 F4 55 47N 4 2W
Hamilton, Ill., U.S.A. 140 D5 40 24N 91 21W
Hamilton, Ind., U.S.A. 141 C12 41 33N 84 56W
Hamilton, Mo., U.S.A. 138 F8 39 45N 93 59W
Hamilton, Mo., U.S.A. 140 E3 39 45N 94 0W
Hamilton, Mont., U.S.A. 142 C6 46 15N 114 10W
Hamilton, N.Y., U.S.A. 137 D9 42 50N 75 33W
Hamilton, Ohio, U.S.A. 141 E12 39 24N 84 34W
Hamilton, Tex., U.S.A. 139 K5 31 42N 98 7W
Hamilton →, Australia 114 C2 23 30 S 139 47 E
Hamilton City, U.S.A. 144 F4 39 45N 122 1W
Hamilton Hotel, Australia 114 C3 22 45 S 140 40 E
Hamilton Inlet, Canada 129 B8 54 0N 57 30W
Hamiota, Canada 131 C8 50 11N 100 38W
Hamlet, U.S.A. 135 H6 34 53N 79 42W
Hamley Bridge, Australia 116 C3 34 17 S 138 35 E
Hamlin = Hameln, Germany 26 C5 52 7N 9 24 E
Hamlin, N.Y., U.S.A. 136 C7 43 17N 77 55W
Hamlin, Tex., U.S.A. 139 J4 32 53N 100 8W
Hamm, Germany 26 D3 51 40N 7 49 E
Hammam Bouhadjar, Algeria 99 A4 35 23N 0 58W
Hammamet, Tunisia 96 A2 36 24N 10 38 E
Hammamet, G. de, Tunisia 96 A2 36 10N 10 48 E
Hammarstrand, Sweden 14 A10 63 7N 16 20 E
Hamme, Belgium 21 F4 51 6N 4 8 E
Hamme-Mille, Belgium 21 G5 50 47N 4 43 E
Hammel, Denmark 15 H3 56 16N 9 52 E
Hammelburg, Germany 27 E5 50 7N 9 54 E
Hammerfest, Norway 12 A17 70 39N 23 41 E
Hammond, Ill., U.S.A. 141 E8 39 48N 88 36W
Hammond, Ind., U.S.A. 141 C9 41 38N 87 30W
Hammond, La., U.S.A. 139 K9 30 30N 90 28W
Hammonton, U.S.A. 134 F8 39 39N 74 48W
Hamoir, Belgium 21 H7 50 25N 5 32 E
Hamont, Belgium 21 F7 51 15N 5 32 E
Hamoyet, Jebel, Sudan 94 D4 17 33N 38 2 E
Hampden, N.Z. 119 F5 45 18 S 170 50 E
Hampshire □, U.K. 17 F6 51 3N 1 20W
Hampshire Downs, U.K. 17 F6 51 10N 1 10W
Hampton, Ark., U.S.A. 139 J8 33 32N 92 28W
Hampton, Iowa, U.S.A. 140 B3 42 45N 93 13W
Hampton, N.H., U.S.A. 137 D14 42 57N 70 50W
Hampton, S.C., U.S.A. 135 J5 32 52N 81 7W
Hampton, Va., U.S.A. 134 G7 37 2N 76 21W
Hampton Tableland, Australia 113 F4 32 0 S 127 0 E
Ḩamrā', Yemen 86 D3 15 3N 43 0 E
Hamrat esh Sheykh, Sudan 95 E2 14 38N 27 55 E
Hamtik, Phil. 71 F3 10 42N 121 59 E
Hamur, Turkey 89 D10 39 59N 42 36 E
Hamyang, S. Korea 67 G14 35 32N 127 42 E
Han Jiang →, China 69 F11 23 25N 116 40 E
Han Shui →, China 69 B10 30 35N 114 18 E
Hana, U.S.A. 132 H17 20 45N 155 59W
Hanak, Si. Arabia 84 E3 25 32N 37 0 E
Hanamaki, Japan 60 E10 39 23N 141 7 E
Hanang, Tanzania 106 C4 4 30 S 35 25 E
Hanau, Germany 27 E4 50 8N 8 56 E
Hanbogd, Mongolia 66 C4 43 11N 107 10 E
Hancheng, China 66 G6 35 31N 110 25 E
Hanchuan, China 69 B9 30 40N 113 50 E
Hancock, Mich., U.S.A. 138 B10 47 8N 88 35W
Hancock, Minn., U.S.A. 138 C7 45 30N 95 48W
Hancock, N.Y., U.S.A. 137 E9 41 57N 75 17W
Handa, Japan 63 C8 34 53N 136 55 E
Handa, Somali Rep. 90 E5 10 37N 51 2 E
Handan, China 66 F8 36 35N 114 28 E
Handen, Sweden 14 E12 59 12N 18 12 E
Handeni, Tanzania 106 D4 5 25 S 38 2 E
Handeni □, Tanzania 106 D4 5 30 S 38 0 E
Handlová, Slovak Rep. 31 C11 48 45N 18 35 E
Handub, Sudan 94 D4 19 15N 37 16 E
Handwara, India 81 B6 34 21N 74 20 E
Handzame, Belgium 21 F2 51 2N 3 0 E
Hanegev, Israel 91 E3 30 50N 35 0 E
Haney, Canada 130 D4 49 12N 122 40W
Hanford, U.S.A. 144 J7 36 20N 119 39W
Hang Chat, Thailand 76 C2 18 20N 99 21 E
Hang Dong, Thailand 76 C2 18 41N 98 55 E
Hangang →, S. Korea 67 F14 37 50N 126 30 E
Hangayn Nuruu, Mongolia 64 B4 47 30N 99 0 E
Hangchou = Hangzhou, China 69 B13 30 18N 120 11 E
Hanggin Houqi, China 66 D4 40 58N 107 4 E
Hanggin Qi, China 66 E5 39 52N 108 50 E
Hangö, Finland 13 G17 59 50N 22 57 E
Hangu, China 67 E9 39 18N 117 53 E
Hangu, Pakistan 79 B3 33 30N 71 10 E
Hangzhou, China 69 B13 30 18N 120 11 E
Hangzhou Wan, China 69 B13 30 15N 120 45 E
Hanhongor, Mongolia 66 C3 43 55N 104 28 E
Ḩanīdh, Si. Arabia 85 E6 26 35N 48 38 E
Ḩanīsh, Yemen 86 D3 13 45N 42 46 E
Haniska, Slovak Rep. 31 C14 48 37N 21 15 E
Hanjiang, China 69 E12 25 26N 119 6 E
Hankinson, U.S.A. 138 B6 46 4N 96 54W
Hanko = Hangö, Finland 13 G17 59 50N 22 57 E
Hanko, Finland 13 G17 59 50N 22 57 E
Hankou, China 69 B10 30 35N 114 30 E
Hanksville, U.S.A. 143 G8 38 22N 110 43W
Hanle, India 81 C8 32 42N 79 4 E
Hanmer Springs, N.Z. 119 C7 42 32 S 172 50 E
Hann →, Australia 112 C4 17 26 S 126 17 E
Hann, Mt., Australia 112 C4 15 45 S 126 0 E
Hanna, Canada 130 C6 51 40N 111 54W
Hannaford, U.S.A. 138 B5 47 19N 98 11W
Hannah, U.S.A. 138 A5 48 58N 98 42W
Hannah B., Canada 128 B4 51 40N 80 0W
Hannahs Bridge, Australia 117 A8 31 55 S 149 41 E
Hannibal, U.S.A. 140 E5 39 42N 91 22W
Hannik, Sudan 94 D3 18 12N 32 20 E
Hannover, Germany 26 C5 52 23N 9 43 E
Hannut, Belgium 21 G6 50 40N 5 4 E
Hanoi, Vietnam 64 D5 21 5N 105 55 E
Hanover = Hannover, Germany 26 C5 52 23N 9 43 E
Hanover, Canada 136 B3 44 9N 81 2W
Hanover, S. Africa 104 E3 31 4 S 24 29 E
Hanover, Ind., U.S.A. 141 F11 38 43N 85 28W
Hanover, N.H., U.S.A. 137 C12 43 42N 72 17W
Hanover, Ohio, U.S.A. 136 F2 40 4N 82 16W
Hanover, Pa., U.S.A. 134 F7 39 48N 76 59W
Hanover, I., Chile 160 D2 51 0 S 74 50W
Hanpan, C., Papua N. G. 120 C8 5 0 S 154 35 E
Hans Meyer Ra., Papua N. G. 120 C7 4 20 S 152 55 E
Hanshou, China 69 C8 28 56N 111 50 E
Hansi, India 80 E6 29 10N 75 57 E
Hanson, L., Australia 116 A2 31 0 S 136 15 E
Hanyang, China 69 B10 30 35N 114 2 E
Hanyin, China 68 A7 32 54N 108 28 E
Hanyū, Japan 63 A11 36 10N 139 32 E
Hanyuan, China 68 C4 29 21N 102 40 E
Hanzhong, China 66 H4 33 10N 107 1 E
Hanzhuang, China 67 G9 34 33N 117 23 E
Haora, India 81 H13 22 37N 88 20 E
Haoxue, China 69 B9 30 3N 112 24 E
Haparanda, Sweden 12 D18 65 52N 24 8 E
Hapert, Neths. 21 F6 51 22N 5 15 E
Happy, U.S.A. 139 H4 34 45N 101 52W
Happy Camp, U.S.A. 142 F2 41 48N 123 23W
Happy Valley-Goose Bay, Canada 129 B7 53 15N 60 20W
Hapsu, N. Korea 67 D15 41 13N 128 51 E
Hapur, India 80 E7 28 45N 77 45 E
Ḩaql, Si. Arabia 91 F3 29 10N 34 58 E
Haquira, Peru 156 C3 14 14 S 72 12W
Har, Indonesia 73 C4 5 16 S 133 14 E
Har-Ayrag, Mongolia 66 B5 45 47N 109 16 E
Har Hu, China 64 C4 38 20N 97 38 E
Har Us Nuur, Mongolia 64 B4 48 0N 92 0 E
Har Yehuda, Israel 91 D3 31 35N 34 57 E
Ḩaraḑ, Si. Arabia 87 A5 24 22N 49 0 E
Ḩaraḑ, Yemen 86 C3 16 26N 43 5 E
Haranomachi, Japan 60 F10 37 38N 140 58 E
Harardera, Somali Rep. 90 G4 4 33N 47 38 E
Harare, Zimbabwe 107 F3 17 43 S 31 2 E
Ḩarāsīs, Jiddat al, Oman 87 C7 19 30N 56 0 E
Harat, Eritrea 95 D4 16 5N 39 26 E
Harazé, Chad 97 G4 9 57N 20 48 E
Harazé, Chad 97 F3 14 20N 19 12 E
Harbin, China 67 B14 45 48N 126 40 E
Harbiye, Turkey 88 E7 36 10N 36 8 E
Harboør, Denmark 15 H2 56 38N 8 10 E
Harbor Beach, U.S.A. 134 D4 43 51N 82 39W
Harbor Springs, U.S.A. 134 C3 45 26N 85 0W
Harbour Breton, Canada 129 C8 47 29N 55 50W
Harbour Grace, Canada 129 C9 47 40N 53 22W
Harburg, Germany 26 B5 53 27N 9 58 E
Hårby, Denmark 15 J4 55 13N 10 7 E
Harda, India 80 H7 22 27N 77 5 E
Hardangerfjorden, Norway 13 F8 60 15N 6 0 E
Hardap Dam, Namibia 104 C2 24 32 S 17 50 E
Hardegarijp, Neths. 20 B7 53 13N 5 57 E
Harden, Australia 117 C8 34 32 S 148 24 E
Hardenberg, Neths. 20 C9 52 34N 6 37 E
Harderwijk, Neths. 20 D7 52 21N 5 38 E
Hardey →, Australia 112 D2 22 45 S 116 8 E
Hardin, Ill., U.S.A. 140 E6 39 10N 90 37W
Hardin, Mont., U.S.A. 142 D10 45 44N 107 37W
Harding, S. Africa 105 E4 30 35 S 29 55 E
Harding Ra., Australia 112 C3 16 17 S 124 55 E
Hardinsburg, U.S.A. 141 G10 37 47N 86 28W
Hardisty, Canada 130 C6 52 40N 111 18W
Hardman, U.S.A. 142 D4 45 10N 119 41W
Hardoi, India 81 F9 27 26N 80 6 E
Hardwar = Haridwar, India 80 E8 29 58N 78 9 E
Hardwick, U.S.A. 137 B12 44 30N 72 22W
Hardy, U.S.A. 139 G9 36 19N 91 29W
Hardy, Pen., Chile 160 E3 55 30 S 68 20W
Hare B., Canada 129 B8 51 15N 55 45W
Harelbeke, Belgium 21 G2 50 52N 3 20 E
Haren, Germany 26 C3 52 47N 7 18 E
Haren, Neths. 20 B9 53 11N 6 36 E
Harer, Ethiopia 90 F3 9 20N 42 8 E
Harerge □, Ethiopia 95 F5 7 12N 42 0 E
Hareto, Ethiopia 95 F4 9 23N 37 6 E
Harfleur, France 22 C7 49 30N 0 10 E
Hargeisa, Somali Rep. 90 F3 9 30N 44 2 E
Harghita □, Romania 46 C6 46 30N 25 30 E
Harghita, Mţii., Romania 46 C6 46 25N 25 35 E
Hargshamn, Sweden 13 F15 60 12N 18 30 E
Hari →, Indonesia 74 C2 1 16 S 104 5 E
Haria, Canary Is. 33 E6 29 8N 13 32W
Ḩarīb, Yemen 86 D4 14 56N 45 30 E
Haricha, Hamada el, Mali 98 D4 22 40N 3 15W
Haridwar, India 80 E8 29 58N 78 9 E
Harihar, India 83 G2 14 32N 75 44 E
Harihari, N.Z. 119 D5 43 9 S 170 33 E
Harima-Nada, Japan 62 C6 34 30N 134 35 E
Haringhata →, Bangla. 78 E2 22 0N 89 58 E
Haringvliet, Neths. 20 E4 51 48N 4 10 E
Haripad, India 83 K3 9 14N 76 28 E
Harīrūd →, Asia 85 B9 37 24N 60 38 E
Harlan, Iowa, U.S.A. 138 E7 41 39N 95 19W
Harlan, Ky., U.S.A. 135 G4 36 51N 83 19W
Harlech, U.K. 16 E3 52 52N 4 7W
Harlem, U.S.A. 142 B9 48 32N 108 47W
Harlingen, Neths. 20 B6 53 11N 5 25 E
Harlingen, U.S.A. 139 M6 26 12N 97 42W
Harlowton, U.S.A. 142 C9 46 26N 109 50W
Harmånger, Sweden 14 C11 61 55N 17 20 E
Harmil, Eritrea 95 D5 16 30N 40 10 E
Harney Basin, U.S.A. 142 E4 43 30N 119 0W
Harney L., U.S.A. 142 E4 43 14N 119 8W
Harney Peak, U.S.A. 138 D3 43 52N 103 32W
Härnön, Sweden 14 B12 62 36N 18 0 E
Härnösand, Sweden 14 B11 62 38N 17 55 E
Haro, Spain 34 C2 42 35N 2 55W
Harp L., Canada 129 A7 55 5N 61 50W
Harpanahalli, India 83 G3 14 47N 76 2 E
Harper, Liberia 100 E3 4 25N 7 43W
Harper Pass, N.Z. 119 C6 42 42 S 171 55 E
Harplinge, Sweden 15 H6 56 45N 12 45 E
Harrand, Pakistan 80 E4 29 28N 70 3 E
Harriman, U.S.A. 135 H3 35 56N 84 33W
Harrington Harbour, Canada 129 B8 50 31N 59 30W
Harris, U.K. 18 D2 57 50N 6 55W
Harris, Sd. of, U.K. 18 D1 57 44N 7 6W
Harris L., Australia 115 E2 31 10 S 135 10 E
Harris Mts., N.Z. 119 E3 44 49 S 168 49 E
Harrisburg, Ill., U.S.A. 139 G10 37 44N 88 32W
Harrisburg, Nebr., U.S.A. 138 E3 41 33N 103 44W
Harrisburg, Oreg., U.S.A. 142 D2 44 16N 123 10W
Harrisburg, Pa., U.S.A. 136 F8 40 16N 76 53W
Harrismith, S. Africa 105 D4 28 15 S 29 8 E
Harrison, Ark., U.S.A. 139 G8 36 14N 93 7W
Harrison, Idaho, U.S.A. 142 C5 47 27N 116 47W
Harrison, Nebr., U.S.A. 138 D3 42 41N 103 53W
Harrison, C., Canada 129 B8 54 55N 57 55W
Harrison Bay, U.S.A. 126 A4 70 40N 151 0W
Harrison L., Canada 130 D4 49 33N 121 50W
Harrisonburg, U.S.A. 134 F6 38 27N 78 52W
Harrisonville, U.S.A. 140 F2 38 39N 94 21W
Harriston, Canada 128 D3 43 57N 80 53W
Harrisville, U.S.A. 136 B1 44 39N 83 17W
Harrodsburg, Ind., U.S.A. 141 E10 39 1N 86 33W
Harrodsburg, Ky., U.S.A. 141 G12 37 46N 84 51W
Harrogate, U.K. 16 D6 53 59N 1 32W
Harrow, U.K. 17 F7 51 35N 0 15W
Harry S. Truman Reservoir, U.S.A. 140 F3 38 16N 93 24W
Harsefeld, Germany 26 B5 53 26N 9 31 E
Harsīn, Iran 84 C5 35 12N 46 34 E
Harskamp, Neths. 20 D7 52 8N 5 46 E
Harstad, Norway 12 B14 68 48N 16 30 E
Hart, U.S.A. 134 D2 43 42N 86 22W
Hart, L., Australia 116 A2 31 10 S 136 25 E
Hartbees →, S. Africa 104 D3 28 45 S 20 32 E
Hartberg, Austria 30 D8 47 17N 15 58 E
Hartford, Conn., U.S.A. 137 E12 41 46N 72 41W
Hartford, Ky., U.S.A. 134 G2 37 27N 86 55W
Hartford, Mich., U.S.A. 141 B10 42 13N 86 10W
Hartford, S. Dak., U.S.A. 138 D6 43 38N 96 57W
Hartford, Wis., U.S.A. 138 D10 43 19N 88 22W
Hartford City, U.S.A. 141 D11 40 27N 85 22W
Hartland, Canada 129 C6 46 20N 67 32W
Hartland, U.S.A. 141 A8 43 6N 88 21W
Hartland Pt., U.K. 17 F3 51 2N 4 32W
Hartlepool, U.K. 16 C6 54 42N 1 11W
Hartley Bay, Canada 130 C3 53 25N 129 15W
Hartmannberge, Namibia 104 B1 17 0 S 13 0 E
Hartney, Canada 131 D8 49 30N 100 35W
Harts →, S. Africa 104 D3 28 24 S 24 17 E
Hartselle, U.S.A. 135 H2 34 27N 86 56W
Hartshorne, U.S.A. 139 H7 34 51N 95 34W
Hartsville, U.S.A. 135 H5 34 23N 80 4W
Hartwell, U.S.A. 135 H4 34 21N 82 56W
Harunabad, Pakistan 80 E5 29 35N 73 8 E
Harur, India 83 H4 12 3N 78 29 E
Harvand, Iran 85 D7 28 25N 55 43 E
Harvard, U.S.A. 141 B8 42 25N 88 37W
Harvey, Australia 113 F2 33 5 S 115 54 E
Harvey, Ill., U.S.A. 141 C9 41 36N 87 50W
Harvey, N. Dak., U.S.A. 138 B5 47 47N 99 56W
Harwich, U.K. 17 F9 51 56N 1 18 E
Haryana □, India 80 E7 29 0N 76 10 E
Harz, Germany 26 D6 51 40N 10 40 E
Harzé, Belgium 21 H7 50 27N 5 40 E
Harzgerode, Germany 26 D7 51 38N 11 8 E
Hasaheisa, Sudan 95 E3 14 44N 33 20 E
Hasan Kīādeh, Iran 85 B6 37 24N 49 58 E
Ḩasanābād, Iran 85 C7 32 8N 52 44 E
Hasanpur, India 80 E8 28 43N 78 17 E
Haselünne, Germany 26 C3 52 40N 7 30 E
Hashima, Japan 63 B8 35 20N 136 40 E
Hashimoto, Japan 63 C7 34 19N 135 37 E
Hashtjerd, Iran 85 C6 35 52N 50 40 E
Ḩāsik, Oman 87 C6 17 22N 55 17 E
Håsjö, Sweden 14 A10 63 1N 16 5 E
Haskell, Okla., U.S.A. 139 H7 35 50N 95 40W
Haskell, Tex., U.S.A. 139 J5 33 10N 99 44W
Haslach, Germany 27 G4 48 16N 8 7 E
Haslev, Denmark 15 J5 55 18N 11 57 E
Hasparren, France 24 E2 43 24N 1 18W
Hassa, Turkey 88 E7 36 48N 36 29 E
Hasselt, Belgium 21 G6 50 56N 5 21 E
Hasselt, Neths. 20 C8 52 36N 6 6 E
Hassene, Adrar, Algeria 99 D5 21 0N 4 0 E
Hassfurt, Germany 27 E6 50 2N 10 30 E
Hassi Berrekrem, Algeria 99 B6 33 45N 5 16 E
Hassi bou Khelala, Algeria 99 B4 30 17N 0 18W
Hassi Daoula, Algeria 99 B6 33 4N 5 38 E
Hassi Djafou, Algeria 99 B5 30 55N 3 35 E
Hassi el Abiod, Algeria 99 B5 31 47N 3 37 E
Hassi el Biod, Algeria 99 C6 28 30N 6 0 E
Hassi el Gassi, Algeria 99 B6 30 52N 6 5 E
Hassi el Hadjar, Algeria 99 B5 31 28N 4 45 E
Hassi er Rmel, Algeria 99 B5 32 56N 3 17 E
Hassi Imoulaye, Algeria 99 C6 29 54N 9 10 E
Hassi Inifel, Algeria 99 C5 29 50N 3 41 E
Hassi Messaoud, Algeria 99 B6 31 43N 6 8 E
Hassi Rhénami, Algeria 99 B6 31 50N 5 58 E
Hassi Tartrat, Algeria 99 B6 30 5N 6 28 E
Hassi Zerzour, Morocco 98 B4 30 51N 3 56W
Hastière-Lavaux, Belgium 21 H5 50 13N 4 49 E
Hastings, Australia 117 E6 38 18 S 145 12 E
Hastings, N.Z. 118 F5 39 39 S 176 52 E
Hastings, U.K. 17 G8 50 51N 0 36 E
Hastings, Mich., U.S.A. 141 B11 42 39N 85 17W
Hastings, Minn., U.S.A. 138 C8 44 44N 92 51W
Hastings, Nebr., U.S.A. 138 E5 40 35N 98 23W
Hastings Ra., Australia 117 A10 31 15 S 152 14 E
Hat Yai, Thailand 77 J3 7 1N 100 27 E
Hatanbulag, Mongolia 66 C5 43 8N 109 5 E
Hatano, Japan 63 B11 35 22N 139 14 E
Hatay = Antalya, Turkey 88 E4 36 52N 30 45 E
Hatay □, Turkey 88 E7 36 25N 36 15 E
Hatch, U.S.A. 143 K10 32 40N 107 9W
Hatches Creek, Australia 114 C2 20 56 S 135 12 E
Hatchet L., Canada 131 B8 58 36N 103 40W
Haţeg, Romania 46 D3 45 36N 22 55 E
Haţeg, Mţii., Romania 46 D4 45 25N 23 0 E
Hatert, Neths. 20 E7 51 49N 5 50 E
Hateruma-Shima, Japan 61 M1 24 3N 123 47 E
Hatfield P.O., Australia 116 B5 33 54 S 143 49 E
Hatgal, Mongolia 64 A5 50 26N 100 9 E
Hathras, India 80 F8 27 36N 78 6 E
Hato de Corozal, Colombia 152 B3 6 11N 71 45W
Hato Mayor, Dom. Rep. 149 C6 18 46N 69 15W
Hattah, Australia 116 C5 34 48 S 142 17 E
Hattem, Neths. 20 D8 52 28N 6 4 E
Hatteras, C., U.S.A. 135 H8 35 14N 75 32W
Hattiesburg, U.S.A. 139 K10 31 20N 89 17W
Hatvan, Hungary 31 D12 47 40N 19 45 E
Hau Bon = Cheo Reo, Vietnam 76 F7 13 25N 108 28 E
Hau Duc, Vietnam 76 E7 15 20N 108 13 E
Haubstadt, U.S.A. 141 F9 38 12N 87 34W
Haug, Norway 14 D4 60 23N 10 26 E
Haugastøl, Norway 14 D1 60 30N 7 50 E
Haugesund, Norway 13 G8 59 23N 5 13 E
Hauhungaroa Ra., N.Z. 118 E4 38 42 S 175 40 E
Haulerwijk, Neths. 20 B8 53 4N 6 20 E
Haultain →, Canada 131 B7 55 51N 106 46W
Haungpa, Burma 78 C6 25 29N 96 7 E
Hauraki G., N.Z. 118 C4 36 35 S 175 5 E
Hausruck, Austria 30 C6 48 6N 13 30 E
Haut Atlas, Morocco 98 B3 32 30N 5 0W
Haut-Rhin □, France 23 E14 48 0N 7 15 E
Haut Zaïre □, Zaïre 106 B2 2 20N 26 0 E
Haute-Corse □, France 25 F13 42 30N 9 30 E
Haute-Garonne □, France 24 E5 43 30N 1 30 E
Haute-Loire □, France 24 C7 45 5N 3 50 E
Haute-Marne □, France 23 D12 48 10N 5 20 E
Haute-Saône □, France 23 E13 47 45N 6 10 E
Haute-Savoie □, France 25 C10 46 0N 6 20 E
Haute-Vienne □, France 24 C5 45 50N 1 10 E
Hauterive, Canada 129 C6 49 10N 68 16W
Hautes-Alpes □, France 25 D10 44 42N 6 20 E
Hautes Fagnes = Hohe Venn, Belgium 21 H8 50 30N 6 5 E
Hautes Fagnes, Belgium 21 G8 50 34N 6 6 E
Hautes-Pyrénées □, France 24 F4 43 0N 0 10 E
Hauteville-Lompnès, France 25 C9 45 58N 5 36 E
Hautmont, France 23 B10 50 15N 3 55 E
Hautrage, Belgium 21 H3 50 29N 3 46 E
Hauts-de-Seine □, France 23 D9 48 52N 2 15 E
Hauts Plateaux, Algeria 99 B4 35 0N 1 0 E
Hauzenberg, Germany 27 G9 48 39N 13 38 E
Havana = La Habana, Cuba 148 B3 23 8N 82 22W
Havana, U.S.A. 140 D6 40 18N 90 4W
Havant, U.K. 17 G7 50 51N 0 59W
Havasu, L., U.S.A. 145 L12 34 18N 114 28W

Havel →, *Germany* 26 C8 52 40N 12 1 E
Havelange, *Belgium* 21 H6 50 23N 5 15 E
Havelian, *Pakistan* 80 B5 34 2N 73 10 E
Havelock, *N.B., Canada* 129 C6 46 2N 65 24W
Havelock, *Ont., Canada* 128 D4 44 26N 77 53W
Havelock, *N.Z.* 119 B8 41 17 S 173 48 E
Havelock North, *N.Z.* 118 F5 39 40 S 176 53 E
Havelte, *Neths.* 20 C8 52 46N 6 14 E
Haverfordwest, *U.K.* 17 F3 51 48N 4 59W
Haverhill, *U.S.A.* 137 D13 42 47N 71 5W
Haveri, *India* 83 G2 14 53N 75 24 E
Havering, *U.K.* 17 F8 51 33N 0 20 E
Haverstraw, *U.S.A.* 137 E11 41 12N 73 58W
Håverud, *Sweden* 15 F6 58 50N 12 28 E
Havîrna, *Romania* 46 A7 48 4N 26 43 E
Havlíčkův Brod, *Czech.* 30 B8 49 36N 15 33 E
Havneby, *Denmark* 15 J2 55 5N 8 34 E
Havre, *U.S.A.* 142 B9 48 33N 109 41W
Havre-Aubert, *Canada* 129 C7 47 12N 61 56W
Havre-St.-Pierre, *Canada* 129 B7 50 18N 63 33W
Havza, *Turkey* 88 C6 41 0N 35 35 E
Haw →, *U.S.A.* 135 H6 35 36N 79 3W
Hawaii □, *U.S.A.* 132 H16 19 30N 156 30W
Hawaii I., *Pac. Oc.* 132 J17 20 0N 155 0W
Hawaiian Is., *Pac. Oc.* 132 H17 20 30N 156 0W
Hawaiian Ridge, *Pac. Oc.* 123 E11 24 0N 165 0W
Hawarden, *Canada* 131 C7 51 25N 106 36W
Hawarden, *U.S.A.* 138 D6 43 0N 96 29W
Hawea, L., *N.Z.* 119 E4 44 28 S 169 19 E
Hawea Flat, *N.Z.* 119 E4 44 40 S 169 19 E
Hawera, *N.Z.* 118 F3 39 35 S 174 19 E
Hawesville, *U.S.A.* 141 G10 37 54N 86 45W
Hawick, *U.K.* 18 F6 55 25N 2 48W
Hawk Junction, *Canada* 128 C3 48 5N 84 38W
Hawk Point, *U.S.A.* 140 F5 38 58N 91 8W
Hawkdun Ra., *N.Z.* 119 E5 44 53 S 170 5 E
Hawke B., *N.Z.* 118 F6 39 25 S 177 20 E
Hawker, *Australia* 116 A3 31 59 S 138 22 E
Hawke's Bay □, *N.Z.* 118 F5 39 45 S 176 35 E
Hawkesbury, *Canada* 128 C5 45 37N 74 37W
Hawkesbury I., *Canada* 130 C3 53 37N 129 3W
Hawkesbury Pt., *Australia* 114 A1 11 55 S 134 5 E
Hawkinsville, *U.S.A.* 135 J4 32 17N 83 28W
Hawkwood, *Australia* 115 D5 25 45 S 150 50 E
Hawley, *U.S.A.* 138 B6 46 53N 96 19W
Hawrān, *Syria* 91 C5 32 45N 36 15 E
Hawsh Mūssá, *Lebanon* 91 B4 33 45N 35 55 E
Hawthorne, *U.S.A.* 142 G4 38 32N 118 38W
Hawzen, *Ethiopia* 95 E4 13 58N 39 28 E
Haxtun, *U.S.A.* 138 E3 40 39N 102 38W
Hay, *Australia* 117 C6 34 30 S 144 51 E
Hay →, *Australia* 114 C2 24 50 S 138 0 E
Hay →, *Canada* 130 A5 60 50N 116 26W
Hay, C., *Australia* 112 B4 14 5 S 129 29 E
Hay L., *Canada* 130 B5 58 50N 118 50W
Hay Lakes, *Canada* 130 C6 53 12N 113 2W
Hay-on-Wye, *U.K.* 17 E4 52 4N 3 9W
Hay River, *Canada* 130 A5 60 51N 115 44W
Hay Springs, *U.S.A.* 138 D3 42 41N 102 41W
Hayachine-San, *Japan* 60 E10 39 34N 141 29 E
Hayange, *France* 23 C13 49 20N 6 2 E
Hayato, *Japan* 62 F2 31 40N 130 43 E
Hayden, *Ariz., U.S.A.* 143 K8 33 0N 110 47W
Hayden, *Colo., U.S.A.* 142 F10 40 30N 107 16W
Haydon, *Australia* 114 B3 18 0 S 141 30 E
Hayes, *U.S.A.* 138 C4 44 23N 101 1W
Hayes →, *Canada* 131 B10 57 3N 92 12W
Hayjān, *Yemen* 86 C4 16 40N 44 5 E
Haymā', *Oman* 87 C7 19 56N 56 19 E
Haymana, *Turkey* 88 D5 39 26N 32 31 E
Haynan, *Yemen* 87 D5 15 50N 48 18 E
Haynesville, *U.S.A.* 139 J8 32 58N 93 8W
Hayrabolu, *Turkey* 88 C2 41 12N 27 5 E
Ḥayrān, *Yemen* 86 C3 16 8N 43 5 E
Hays, *Canada* 130 C6 50 6N 111 48W
Hays, *U.S.A.* 138 F5 38 53N 99 20W
Ḥays, *Yemen* 86 D3 13 56N 43 29 E
Haysville, *U.S.A.* 141 F10 38 28N 86 55W
Hayward, *Calif., U.S.A.* 144 H4 37 40N 122 5W
Hayward, *Wis., U.S.A.* 138 B9 46 1N 91 29W
Haywards Heath, *U.K.* 17 F7 51 1N 0 6W
Ḥayy, *Oman* 87 B7 20 46N 58 18 E
Hazafon □, *Israel* 91 C4 32 40N 35 20 E
Hazar Gölü, *Turkey* 89 D8 38 29N 39 25 E
Hazarām, Kūh-e, *Iran* 85 D8 29 30N 57 18 E
Hazard, *U.S.A.* 134 G4 37 15N 83 12W
Hazaribag, *India* 81 H11 23 58N 85 26 E
Hazaribag Road, *India* 81 G11 24 12N 85 57 E
Hazebrouck, *France* 23 B9 50 42N 2 31 E
Hazelton, *Canada* 130 B3 55 20N 127 42W
Hazelton, *U.S.A.* 138 B4 46 29N 100 17W
Hazen, *N. Dak., U.S.A.* 138 B4 47 18N 101 38W
Hazen, *Nev., U.S.A.* 142 G4 39 34N 119 3W
Hazerswoude, *Neths.* 20 D5 52 5N 4 36 E
Hazlehurst, *Ga., U.S.A.* 135 K4 31 52N 82 36W
Hazlehurst, *Miss., U.S.A.* 139 K9 31 52N 90 24W
Hazleton, *Ind., U.S.A.* 141 F9 38 29N 87 33W
Hazleton, *Pa., U.S.A.* 137 F9 40 57N 75 59W
Hazlett, L., *Australia* 112 D4 21 30 S 128 48 E
Ḥazor, *Israel* 91 B4 33 2N 35 32 E
He Xian, *Anhui, China* 69 B12 31 45N 118 20 E
He Xian, *Guangxi Zhuangzu, China* 69 E8 24 27N 111 30 E
Head of Bight, *Australia* 113 F5 31 30 S 131 25 E
Headlands, *Zimbabwe* 107 F3 18 15 S 32 2 E
Healdsburg, *U.S.A.* 144 G4 38 37N 122 52W
Healdton, *U.S.A.* 139 H6 34 14N 97 29W
Healesville, *Australia* 117 D6 37 35 S 145 30 E
Heanor, *U.K.* 16 D6 53 1N 1 20W
Heard I., *Ind. Oc.* 109 K6 53 0 S 74 0 E
Hearne, *U.S.A.* 139 K6 30 53N 96 36W
Hearne B., *Canada* 131 A9 60 10N 99 10W
Hearne L., *Canada* 130 A6 62 20N 113 10W
Hearst, *Canada* 128 C3 49 40N 83 41W
Heart →, *U.S.A.* 138 B4 46 46N 100 50W
Heart's Content, *Canada* 129 C9 47 54N 53 27W
Heath →, *Bolivia* 156 C4 12 31 S 68 38W
Heath Mts., *N.Z.* 119 F2 45 39 S 167 9 E
Heath Pt., *Canada* 129 C7 49 8N 61 40W
Heath Steele, *Canada* 129 C6 47 17N 66 5W
Heathcote, *Australia* 117 D6 36 56 S 144 45 E
Heavener, *U.S.A.* 139 H7 34 53N 94 36W
Hebbronville, *U.S.A.* 139 M5 27 18N 98 41W
Hebei □, *China* 66 E9 39 0N 116 0 E
Hebel, *Australia* 115 D4 28 58 S 147 47 E
Heber, *U.S.A.* 145 N11 32 44N 115 32W
Heber Springs, *U.S.A.* 139 H9 35 30N 92 2W
Hebert, *Canada* 131 C7 50 30N 107 10W
Hebgen L., *U.S.A.* 142 D8 44 52N 111 20W
Hebi, *China* 66 G8 35 57N 114 7 E
Hebrides, *U.K.* 18 D1 57 30N 7 0W
Hebron = Al Khalīl, *Jordan* 91 D4 31 32N 35 6 E
Hebron, *Canada* 127 C13 58 5N 62 30W
Hebron, *N. Dak., U.S.A.* 138 B3 46 54N 102 3W
Hebron, *Nebr., U.S.A.* 138 E6 40 10N 97 35W
Hecate Str., *Canada* 130 C2 53 10N 130 30W
Hechi, *China* 68 E7 24 40N 108 2 E
Hechingen, *Germany* 27 G4 48 20N 8 58 E
Hechtel, *Belgium* 21 F6 51 8N 5 22 E
Hechuan, *China* 68 B6 30 2N 106 12 E
Hecla, *U.S.A.* 138 C5 45 53N 98 9W
Hecla I., *Canada* 131 C9 51 10N 96 43W
Heddal, *Norway* 14 E3 59 36N 9 9 E
Hédé, *France* 22 D5 48 18N 1 49W
Hede, *Sweden* 14 B7 62 23N 13 30 E
Hedemora, *Sweden* 13 F13 60 18N 15 58 E
Hedgehope, *N.Z.* 119 G3 46 12 S 168 34 E
Hedley, *U.S.A.* 139 H4 34 52N 100 39W
Hedmark fylke □, *Norway* 14 C5 61 17N 11 40 E
Hedrick, *U.S.A.* 140 C4 41 11N 92 19W
Hedrum, *Norway* 14 E4 59 7N 10 5 E
Heeg, *Neths.* 20 C7 52 58N 5 37 E
Heegermeer, *Neths.* 20 C7 52 56N 5 32 E
Heemskerk, *Neths.* 20 C5 52 31N 4 40 E
Heemstede, *Neths.* 20 D5 52 22N 4 37 E
Heer, *Neths.* 21 G7 50 50N 5 43 E
Heerde, *Neths.* 20 D8 52 24N 6 2 E
's Heerenburg, *Neths.* 20 E8 51 53N 6 16 E
Heerenveen, *Neths.* 20 C7 52 57N 5 55 E
Heerhugowaard, *Neths.* 20 C5 52 40N 4 51 E
Heerlen, *Neths.* 21 G7 50 55N 5 58 E
Heers, *Belgium* 21 G6 50 45N 5 18 E
Heesch, *Neths.* 20 E7 51 44N 5 32 E
Heestert, *Belgium* 21 G2 50 47N 3 25 E
Heeze, *Neths.* 21 F7 51 23N 5 35 E
Ḥefa, *Israel* 91 C3 32 46N 35 0 E
Ḥefa □, *Israel* 91 C4 32 40N 35 0 E
Hefei, *China* 69 B11 31 52N 117 18 E
Hegang, *China* 65 B8 47 20N 130 19 E
Hegyalja, *Hungary* 31 C14 48 25N 21 25 E
Heichengzhen, *China* 66 F4 36 24N 106 3 E
Heide, *Germany* 26 A5 54 10N 9 7 E
Heidelberg, *Germany* 27 F4 49 23N 8 41 E
Heidelberg, *C. Prov., S. Africa* 104 E3 34 6 S 20 59 E
Heidelberg, *Trans., S. Africa* 105 D4 26 30 S 28 23 E
Heidenheim, *Germany* 27 G6 48 40N 10 10 E
Heigun-To, *Japan* 62 D4 33 47N 132 14 E
Heijing, *China* 68 E3 25 22N 101 44 E
Heilbron, *S. Africa* 105 D4 27 16 S 27 59 E
Heilbronn, *Germany* 27 F5 49 8N 9 13 E
Heiligenblut, *Austria* 30 D5 47 2N 12 51 E
Heiligenhafen, *Germany* 26 A6 54 21N 10 58 E
Heiligenstadt, *Germany* 26 D6 51 22N 10 9 E
Heilongjiang □, *China* 67 B14 48 0N 126 0 E
Heilunkiang = Heilongjiang □, *China* 67 B14 48 0N 126 0 E
Heino, *Neths.* 20 D8 52 26N 6 14 E
Heinola, *Finland* 13 F19 61 13N 26 2 E
Heinsch, *Belgium* 21 J7 49 42N 5 44 E
Heinsun, *Burma* 78 C5 25 52N 95 35 E
Heirnkut, *Burma* 78 C5 25 14N 94 44 E
Heishan, *China* 67 D12 41 40N 122 5 E
Heishui, *Liaoning, China* 67 C10 42 8N 119 30 E
Heishui, *Sichuan, China* 68 A4 32 4N 103 2 E
Heist, *Belgium* 21 F2 51 20N 3 15 E
Heist-op-den-Berg, *Belgium* 21 F5 51 5N 4 44 E
Hejaz = Al Ḥijāz, *Si. Arabia* 86 A2 26 0N 37 30 E
Hejian, *China* 66 E9 38 25N 116 5 E
Hejiang, *China* 68 C5 28 43N 105 46 E
Hejin, *China* 66 G6 35 35N 110 42 E
Hekelgem, *Belgium* 21 G4 50 55N 4 7 E
Hekımhan, *Turkey* 89 D7 38 50N 37 55 E
Hekinan, *Japan* 63 C9 34 52N 137 0 E
Hekla, *Iceland* 12 E4 63 56N 19 35W
Hekou, *Gansu, China* 66 F2 36 10N 103 28 E
Hekou, *Guangdong, China* 69 F9 23 13N 112 45 E
Hekou, *Yunnan, China* 64 D5 22 30N 103 59 E
Hel, *Poland* 47 A5 54 37N 18 47 E
Helagsfjället, *Sweden* 14 B6 62 54N 12 25 E
Helan Shan, *China* 66 E3 38 30N 105 55 E
Helchteren, *Belgium* 21 F6 51 4N 5 22 E
Helden, *Neths.* 21 F7 51 19N 6 0 E
Helechosa, *Spain* 37 F6 39 22N 4 53W
Helena, *Ark., U.S.A.* 139 H9 34 32N 90 36W
Helena, *Mont., U.S.A.* 142 C7 46 36N 112 2W
Helendale, *U.S.A.* 145 L9 34 44N 117 19W
Helensburgh, *Australia* 117 C9 34 11 S 151 1 E
Helensburgh, *U.K.* 18 E4 56 0N 4 44W
Helensville, *N.Z.* 118 C3 36 41 S 174 29 E
Helgeroa, *Norway* 14 F3 59 0N 9 45 E
Helgoland, *Germany* 26 A3 54 10N 7 51 E
Heligoland = Helgoland, *Germany* 26 A3 54 10N 7 51 E
Heligoland B. = Deutsche Bucht, *Germany* 26 A4 54 15N 8 0 E
Heliopolis, *Egypt* 94 H7 30 6N 31 17 E
Hellebæk, *Denmark* 15 H6 56 4N 12 32 E
Hellendoorn, *Neths.* 20 D8 52 24N 6 27 E
Hellevoetsluis, *Neths.* 20 E4 51 50N 4 8 E
Hellín, *Spain* 35 G3 38 31N 1 40W
Helmand □, *Afghan.* 79 C2 31 20N 64 0 E
Helmand →, *Afghan.* 79 C1 31 12N 61 34 E
Helme →, *Germany* 26 D7 51 40N 11 20 E
Helmond, *Neths.* 21 F7 51 29N 5 41 E
Helmsdale, *U.K.* 18 C5 58 7N 3 40W
Helmstedt, *Germany* 26 C7 52 16N 11 0 E
Helnæs, *Denmark* 15 J4 55 9N 10 0 E
Helong, *China* 67 C15 42 40N 129 0 E
Helper, *U.S.A.* 142 G8 39 41N 110 51W
Helsingborg, *Sweden* 15 H6 56 3N 12 42 E
Helsinge, *Denmark* 15 H6 56 2N 12 12 E
Helsingfors, *Finland* 13 F18 60 15N 25 3 E
Helsingør, *Denmark* 15 H6 56 2N 12 35 E
Helsinki, *Finland* 13 F18 60 15N 25 3 E
Helska, Mierzeja, *Poland* 47 A5 54 45N 18 40 E
Helston, *U.K.* 17 G2 50 7N 5 17W
Helvellyn, *U.K.* 16 C4 54 31N 3 1W
Helvoirt, *Neths.* 21 E6 51 38N 5 14 E
Helwân, *Egypt* 94 J7 29 50N 31 20 E
Hemavati →, *India* 83 H3 12 30N 76 20 E
Hemet, *U.S.A.* 145 M10 33 45N 116 58W
Hemingford, *U.S.A.* 138 D3 42 19N 103 4W
Hemphill, *U.S.A.* 139 K8 31 20N 93 51W
Hempstead, *U.S.A.* 139 K6 30 6N 96 5W
Hemse, *Sweden* 13 H15 57 15N 18 22 E
Hemsö, *Sweden* 14 B12 62 43N 18 5 E
Hen & Chickens Is., *N.Z.* 118 B3 35 58 S 174 45 E
Henan □, *China* 66 G8 34 0N 114 0 E
Henares →, *Spain* 34 E1 40 24N 3 30W
Henashi-Misaki, *Japan* 60 D9 40 37N 139 51 E
Hendaye, *France* 24 E2 43 23N 1 47W
Hendek, *Turkey* 88 C4 40 48N 30 44 E
Henderson, *Argentina* 158 D3 36 18 S 61 43W
Henderson, *Ky., U.S.A.* 141 G9 37 50N 87 35W
Henderson, *N.C., U.S.A.* 135 G6 36 20N 78 25W
Henderson, *Nev., U.S.A.* 145 J12 36 2N 114 59W
Henderson, *Tenn., U.S.A.* 135 H1 35 26N 88 38W
Henderson, *Tex., U.S.A.* 139 J7 32 9N 94 48W
Hendersonville, *U.S.A.* 135 H4 35 19N 82 28W
Hendījān, *Iran* 85 D6 30 14N 49 43 E
Hendon, *Australia* 115 D5 28 5 S 151 50 E
Hendorf, *Romania* 46 C5 46 4N 24 55 E
Heng Xian, *China* 68 F7 22 40N 109 17 E
Hengcheng, *China* 66 E4 38 18N 106 28 E
Hengdaohezi, *China* 67 B15 44 52N 129 0 E
Hengelo, *Gelderland, Neths.* 20 D8 52 3N 6 19 E
Hengelo, *Overijssel, Neths.* 20 D9 52 16N 6 48 E
Hengfeng, *China* 69 C10 28 12N 115 48 E
Hengshan, *Hunan, China* 69 D9 27 16N 112 45 E
Hengshan, *Shaanxi, China* 66 F5 37 58N 109 5 E
Hengshui, *China* 66 F8 37 41N 115 40 E
Hengyang, *Hunan, China* 69 D9 26 52N 112 33 E
Hengyang, *Hunan, China* 69 D9 26 51N 112 30 E
Hénin-Beaumont, *France* 23 B9 50 25N 2 58 E
Henlopen, C., *U.S.A.* 134 F8 38 48N 75 6W
Hennan, *Sweden* 14 B9 62 3N 15 46 E
Hennebont, *France* 22 E3 47 49N 3 19W
Hennenman, *S. Africa* 104 D4 27 59 S 27 1 E
Hennepin, *U.S.A.* 140 C7 41 15N 89 21W
Hennessey, *U.S.A.* 139 G6 36 6N 97 54W
Hennigsdorf, *Germany* 26 C9 52 38N 13 13 E
Henrichemont, *France* 23 E9 47 20N 2 30 E
Henrietta, *U.S.A.* 139 J5 33 49N 98 12W
Henrietta, Ostrov, *Russia* 57 B16 77 6N 156 30 E
Henrietta Maria C., *Canada* 128 A3 55 9N 82 20W
Henry, *U.S.A.* 140 C7 41 7N 89 22W
Henryetta, *U.S.A.* 139 H6 35 27N 95 59W
Hensall, *Canada* 136 C3 43 26N 81 30W
Hentiyn Nuruu, *Mongolia* 65 B5 48 30N 108 30 E
Henty, *Australia* 115 F4 35 30 S 147 0 E
Henzada, *Burma* 78 G5 17 38N 95 26 E
Hephaestia, *Greece* 44 E7 39 55N 25 14 E
Heping, *China* 69 E10 24 29N 115 0 E
Heppner, *U.S.A.* 142 D4 45 21N 119 33W
Hepu, *China* 68 G7 21 40N 109 12 E
Hepworth, *Canada* 136 B3 44 37N 81 9W
Heqing, *China* 68 D3 26 37N 100 11 E
Hequ, *China* 66 E6 39 20N 111 15 E
Héraðsflói, *Iceland* 12 D6 65 42N 14 12W
Héraðsvötn →, *Iceland* 12 D4 65 45N 19 25W
Herald Cays, *Australia* 114 B4 16 58 S 149 9 E
Herāt, *Afghan.* 79 B1 34 20N 62 7 E
Herāt □, *Afghan.* 79 B1 35 0N 62 0 E
Hérault □, *France* 24 E7 43 34N 3 15 E
Hérault →, *France* 24 E7 43 17N 3 26 E
Herbault, *France* 22 E8 47 36N 1 8 E
Herbert →, *Australia* 114 B4 18 31 S 146 17 E
Herbert Downs, *Australia* 114 C2 23 7 S 139 9 E
Herberton, *Australia* 114 B4 17 20 S 145 25 E
Herbertville, *N.Z.* 118 G5 40 30 S 176 33 E
Herbignac, *France* 22 E4 47 27N 2 18W
Herborn, *Germany* 26 E4 50 40N 8 19 E
Herby, *Poland* 47 E5 50 45N 18 50 E
Hercegnovi, *Montenegro* 42 E3 42 30N 18 33 E
Herculaneum, *U.S.A.* 140 F6 38 16N 90 23W
Herðubreið, *Iceland* 12 D5 65 11N 16 21W
Hereford, *U.K.* 17 E5 52 4N 2 42W
Hereford, *U.S.A.* 139 H3 34 49N 102 24W
Hereford and Worcester □, *U.K.* 17 E5 52 10N 2 30W
Herefoss, *Norway* 15 F2 58 32N 8 23 E
Herekino, *N.Z.* 118 B2 35 18 S 173 11 E
Herent, *Belgium* 21 G5 50 54N 4 40 E
Herentals, *Belgium* 21 F5 51 12N 4 51 E
Herenthout, *Belgium* 21 F5 51 8N 4 45 E
Herfølge, *Denmark* 15 J6 55 26N 12 9 E
Herford, *Germany* 26 C4 52 7N 8 40 E
Héricourt, *France* 23 E13 47 32N 6 45 E
Herington, *U.S.A.* 138 F6 38 40N 96 57W
Herisau, *Switz.* 29 B8 47 22N 9 17 E
Hérisson, *France* 24 B6 46 32N 2 42 E
Herjehogna, *Norway* 13 F12 61 43N 12 7 E
Herk →, *Belgium* 21 G6 50 56N 5 12 E
Herkenbosch, *Neths.* 21 F8 51 9N 6 4 E
Herkimer, *U.S.A.* 137 D10 43 0N 74 59W
Herlong, *U.S.A.* 144 E6 40 8N 120 8W
Herm, *Chan. Is.* 22 C4 49 30N 2 28W
Hermagor-Pressegger See, *Austria* 30 E6 46 38N 13 23 E
Herman, *U.S.A.* 138 C6 45 49N 96 9W
Hermann, *U.S.A.* 138 F9 38 42N 91 27W
Hermannsburg, *Germany* 26 C6 52 49N 10 6 E
Hermannsburg Mission, *Australia* 112 D5 23 57 S 132 45 E
Hermanus, *S. Africa* 104 E2 34 27 S 19 12 E
Herment, *France* 24 C6 45 45N 2 24 E
Hermidale, *Australia* 117 A7 31 30 S 146 42 E
Hermiston, *U.S.A.* 142 D4 45 51N 119 17W
Hermitage, *N.Z.* 119 D5 43 44 S 170 5 E
Hermitage, *U.S.A.* 140 G3 37 56N 93 19W
Hermite, I., *Chile* 160 E3 55 50 S 68 0W
Hermon, Mt. = Ash Shaykh, J., *Lebanon* 91 B4 33 25N 35 50 E
Hermosillo, *Mexico* 146 B2 29 10N 111 0W
Hernád →, *Hungary* 31 D14 47 56N 21 8 E
Hernandarias, *Paraguay* 159 B5 25 20 S 54 40W
Hernandez, *U.S.A.* 144 J6 36 24N 120 46W
Hernando, *Argentina* 158 C3 32 28 S 63 40W
Hernando, *U.S.A.* 139 H10 34 50N 90 0W
Herne, *Belgium* 21 G4 50 44N 4 2 E
Herne, *Germany* 21 E10 51 33N 7 12 E
Herne Bay, *U.K.* 17 F9 51 22N 1 8 E
Herning, *Denmark* 15 H2 56 8N 8 58 E
Heroica = Caborca, *Mexico* 146 A2 30 40N 112 10W
Heroica Nogales = Nogales, *Mexico* 146 A2 31 20N 110 56W
Heron Bay, *Canada* 128 C2 48 40N 86 25W
Herradura, Pta. de la, *Canary Is.* 33 F5 28 26N 14 8W
Herreid, *U.S.A.* 138 C4 45 50N 100 4W
Herrera, *Spain* 37 H6 37 26N 4 55W
Herrera de Alcántar, *Spain* 37 F3 39 39N 7 25W
Herrera de Pisuerga, *Spain* 36 C6 42 35N 4 20W
Herrera del Duque, *Spain* 37 F5 39 10N 5 3W
Herrick, *Australia* 114 G4 41 5 S 147 55 E
Herrin, *U.S.A.* 139 G10 37 48N 89 2W
Herrljunga, *Sweden* 15 F7 58 5N 13 1 E
Hersbruck, *Germany* 27 F7 49 30N 11 25 E
Herseaux, *Belgium* 21 G2 50 43N 3 15 E
Herselt, *Belgium* 21 F5 51 3N 4 53 E
Hersonissos, *Greece* 32 D7 35 18N 25 22 E
Herstal, *Belgium* 21 G7 50 40N 5 38 E
Hertford, *U.K.* 17 F7 51 47N 0 4W
Hertfordshire □, *U.K.* 17 F7 51 51N 0 5W
's-Hertogenbosch, *Neths.* 21 E6 51 42N 5 17 E
Hertzogville, *S. Africa* 104 D4 28 9 S 25 30 E
Hervás, *Spain* 36 E5 40 16N 5 52W
Herve, *Belgium* 21 G7 50 38N 5 48 E
Herwijnen, *Neths.* 20 E6 51 50N 5 7 E
Herzberg, *Brandenburg, Germany* 26 D9 51 40N 13 13 E
Herzberg, *Niedersachsen, Germany* 26 D6 51 38N 10 20 E
Herzele, *Belgium* 21 G3 50 53N 3 53 E
Herzliyya, *Israel* 91 C3 32 10N 34 50 E
Herzogenbuchsee, *Switz.* 28 B5 47 11N 7 42 E
Herzogenburg, *Austria* 30 C8 48 17N 15 41 E
Ḥeṣār, *Fārs, Iran* 85 D6 29 52N 50 16 E
Ḥeṣār, *Markazī, Iran* 85 C6 35 49N 49 24 E
Hesdin, *France* 23 B9 50 21N 2 2 E
Hesel, *Germany* 26 B3 53 18N 7 36 E
Heshui, *China* 66 G5 36 0N 108 0 E
Heshun, *China* 66 F7 37 22N 113 32 E
Hesperange, *Lux.* 21 J8 49 35N 6 10 E
Hesperia, *U.S.A.* 145 L9 34 25N 117 18W
Hesse = Hessen □, *Germany* 26 E5 50 40N 9 20 E
Hessen □, *Germany* 26 E5 50 40N 9 20 E
Hetch Hetchy Aqueduct, *U.S.A.* 144 H5 37 29N 122 19W
Hettinger, *U.S.A.* 138 C3 46 0N 102 42W
Hettstedt, *Germany* 26 D7 51 39N 11 30 E
Heugem, *Neths.* 21 G7 50 49N 5 42 E
Heule, *Belgium* 21 G2 50 51N 3 15 E
Heusden, *Belgium* 21 F6 51 2N 5 17 E
Heusden, *Neths.* 20 E6 51 44N 5 8 E
Hève, C. de la, *France* 22 C7 49 30N 0 5 E
Heverlee, *Belgium* 21 G5 50 52N 4 42 E
Heves □, *Hungary* 31 D13 47 50N 20 0 E
Hewett, C., *Canada* 127 A13 70 16N 67 45W
Hexham, *U.K.* 16 C5 54 58N 2 7W
Hexi, *Yunnan, China* 68 E4 24 9N 102 38 E
Hexi, *Zhejiang, China* 69 D12 27 58N 119 38 E
Hexigten Qi, *China* 67 C9 43 18N 117 30 E
Hexrivier, *S. Africa* 104 E2 33 30 S 19 35 E
Ḥeydarābād, *Iran* 85 D7 30 33N 55 38 E
Heyfield, *Australia* 117 D7 37 59 S 146 47 E
Heysham, *U.K.* 16 C5 54 5N 2 53W
Heythuysen, *Neths.* 21 F7 51 15N 5 55 E
Heyuan, *China* 69 F10 23 39N 114 40 E
Heywood, *Australia* 116 E4 38 8 S 141 37 E
Heze, *China* 66 G8 35 14N 115 20 E
Hezhang, *China* 68 D5 27 8N 104 41 E
Hi-no-Misaki, *Japan* 62 B4 35 26N 132 38 E
Hi Vista, *U.S.A.* 145 L9 34 45N 117 46W
Hialeah, *U.S.A.* 135 N5 25 50N 80 17W
Hiawatha, *Kans., U.S.A.* 138 F7 39 51N 95 32W
Hiawatha, *Utah, U.S.A.* 142 G8 39 29N 111 1W
Hibbing, *U.S.A.* 138 B8 47 25N 92 56W
Hibbs B., *Australia* 114 G4 42 35 S 145 15 E
Hibernia Reef, *Australia* 112 B3 12 0 S 123 23 E
Hibiki-Nada, *Japan* 62 C2 34 0N 130 0 E
Hickory, *U.S.A.* 135 H5 35 44N 81 21W
Hicks, Pt., *Australia* 117 D8 37 49 S 149 17 E
Hicks Bay, *N.Z.* 118 D7 37 34 S 178 21 E
Hicksville, *N.Y., U.S.A.* 137 F11 40 46N 73 32W
Hicksville, *Ohio, U.S.A.* 141 C12 41 18N 84 46W
Hida, *Romania* 46 B4 47 10N 23 19 E
Hida-Gawa →, *Japan* 63 B9 35 26N 137 3 E
Hida-Sammyaku, *Japan* 63 A9 36 30N 137 40 E
Hida-Sanchi, *Japan* 63 A9 36 10N 137 0 E
Hidaka, *Japan* 62 B6 35 30N 134 44 E
Hidaka-Sammyaku, *Japan* 60 C11 42 35N 142 45 E
Hidalgo, *Mexico* 147 C5 24 15N 99 26W
Hidalgo, *U.S.A.* 141 E8 39 9N 88 9W
Hidalgo □, *Mexico* 147 C5 20 30N 99 10W
Hidalgo, Presa M., *Mexico* 146 B3 26 30N 108 35W
Hidalgo, Pta. del, *Canary Is.* 33 F3 28 33N 16 19W
Hidalgo del Parral, *Mexico* 146 B3 26 58N 105 40W
Hiddensee, *Germany* 26 A9 54 30N 13 6 E
Hidrolândia, *Brazil* 155 E2 17 0 S 49 15W
Hieflau, *Austria* 30 D7 47 36N 14 46 E
Hiendelaencina, *Spain* 34 D1 41 5N 3 0W
Hienghène, *N. Cal.* 121 T18 20 41 S 164 56 E
Hierapolis, *Turkey* 88 E3 37 57N 28 50 E
Hierro, *Canary Is.* 33 G1 27 44N 18 0W
Higashi-matsuyama, *Japan* 63 A11 36 2N 139 25 E
Higashiajima-San, *Japan* 60 F10 37 40N 140 10 E
Higashiōsaka, *Japan* 63 C7 34 40N 135 37 E
Higasi-Suidō, *Japan* 62 D1 34 0N 129 30 E
Higbee, *U.S.A.* 140 E4 39 19N 92 31W
Higgins, *U.S.A.* 139 G4 36 7N 100 2W
Higgins Corner, *U.S.A.* 144 F5 39 2N 121 5W
Higginsville, *Australia* 113 F3 31 42 S 121 38 E
Higginsville, *U.S.A.* 140 E3 39 4N 93 43W
High Atlas = Haut Atlas, *Morocco* 98 B3 32 30N 5 0W
High I., *Canada* 129 A7 56 40N 61 10W
High Island, *U.S.A.* 139 L7 29 34N 94 24W

Hyargas Nuur 209


Hornell L., *Canada* **130 A5** 62 20N 119 25W
Hornepayne, *Canada* **128 C3** 49 14N 84 48W
Hornitos, *U.S.A.* **144 H6** 37 30N 120 14W
Hornos, C. de, *Chile* **160 E3** 55 50 S 67 30W
Hornoy, *France* **23 C8** 49 50N 1 54 E
Hornsby, *Australia* **117 B9** 33 42 S 151 2 E
Hornsea, *U.K.* **16 D7** 53 55N 0 10W
Hornslandet, *Sweden* **14 C11** 61 35N 17 37 E
Hornslet, *Denmark* **15 H4** 56 18N 10 19 E
Hornu, *Belgium* **21 H3** 50 26N 3 50 E
Hörnum, *Germany* **26 A4** 54 44N 8 18 E
Horobetsu, *Japan* **60 C10** 42 24N 141 6 E
Horovice, *Czech.* **30 B6** 49 48N 13 53 E
Horqin Youyi Qianqi, *China* **67 A12** 46 5N 122 3 E
Horqueta, *Paraguay* **158 A4** 23 15 S 56 55W
Horred, *Sweden* **15 G6** 57 22N 12 28 E
Horse Creek, *U.S.A.* **138 E3** 41 57N 105 10W
Horse Is., *Canada* **129 B8** 50 15N 55 50W
Horsefly L., *Canada* **130 C4** 52 25N 121 0W
Horsens, *Denmark* **15 J3** 55 52N 9 51 E
Horsens Fjord, *Denmark* **15 J4** 55 50N 10 0 E
Horsham, *Australia* **116 D5** 36 44 S 142 13 E
Horsham, *U.K.* **17 F7** 51 4N 0 20W
Horšovský Týn, *Czech.* **30 B5** 49 31N 12 58 E
Horst, *Neths.* **21 F8** 51 27N 6 3 E
Horten, *Norway* **14 E4** 59 25N 10 32 E
Hortobágy →, *Hungary* **31 D14** 47 30N 21 6 E
Horton, *U.S.A.* **138 F7** 39 40N 95 32W
Horton →, *Canada* **126 B7** 69 56N 126 52W
Horw, *Switz.* **29 B6** 47 1N 8 19 E
Horwood, L., *Canada* **128 C3** 48 5N 82 20W
Hosaina, *Ethiopia* **95 F4** 7 30N 37 47 E
Hosdurga, *India* **83 H3** 13 49N 76 17 E
Ḥoseynābād, *Khuzestān, Iran* **85 C6** 32 45N 48 20 E
Ḥoseynābād, *Kordestān, Iran* **84 C5** 35 33N 47 8 E
Hoshangabad, *India* **80 H7** 22 45N 77 45 E
Hoshiarpur, *India* **80 D6** 31 30N 75 58 E
Hosingen, *Lux.* **21 H8** 50 1N 6 6 E
Hoskins, *Papua N. G.* **120 C6** 5 29 S 150 27 E
Hosmer, *U.S.A.* **138 C5** 45 34N 99 28W
Hososhima, *Japan* **62 E3** 32 26N 131 40 E
Hospental, *Switz.* **29 C7** 46 37N 8 34 E
Hospet, *India* **83 G3** 15 15N 76 20 E
Hospitalet de Llobregat, *Spain* **34 D7** 41 21N 2 6 E
Hoste, I., *Chile* **160 E3** 55 0 S 69 0W
Hostens, *France* **24 D3** 44 30N 0 40W
Hot, *Thailand* **76 C2** 18 8N 98 29 E
Hot Creek Range, *U.S.A.* **142 G5** 38 40N 116 20W
Hot Springs, *Ark., U.S.A.* **139 H8** 34 31N 93 3W
Hot Springs, *S. Dak., U.S.A.* **138 D3** 43 26N 103 29W
Hotagen, *Sweden* **12 E13** 63 50N 14 30 E
Hotan, *China* **64 C2** 37 25N 79 55 E
Hotazel, *S. Africa* **104 D3** 27 17 S 22 58 E
Hotchkiss, *U.S.A.* **143 G10** 38 48N 107 43W
Hotham, C., *Australia* **112 B5** 12 2 S 131 18 E
Hoting, *Sweden* **12 D14** 64 8N 16 15 E
Hotolishti, *Albania* **44 C2** 41 10N 20 25 E
Hotte, Massif de la, *Haiti* **149 C5** 18 30N 73 45W
Hottentotsbaai, *Namibia* **104 D1** 26 8 S 14 59 E
Hotton, *Belgium* **21 H6** 50 16N 5 26 E
Houailou, *N. Cal.* **121 U19** 21 17 S 165 38 E
Houat, I. de, *France* **22 E4** 47 24N 2 58W
Houck, *U.S.A.* **143 J9** 35 20N 109 10W
Houdan, *France* **23 D8** 48 48N 1 35 E
Houdeng-Goegnies, *Belgium* **21 H4** 50 29N 4 10 E
Houei Sai, *Laos* **76 B3** 20 18N 100 26 E
Houffalize, *Belgium* **21 H7** 50 8N 5 48 E
Houghton, *U.S.A.* **138 B10** 47 7N 88 34W
Houghton L., *U.S.A.* **134 C3** 44 21N 84 44W
Houghton-le-Spring, *U.K.* **16 C6** 54 51N 1 28W
Houhora Heads, *N.Z.* **118 A2** 34 49 S 173 9 E
Houille →, *Belgium* **21 H5** 50 8N 4 50 E
Houlton, *U.S.A.* **129 C6** 46 8N 67 51W
Houma, *U.S.A.* **139 L9** 29 36N 90 43W
Houndé, *Burkina Faso* **100 C4** 11 34N 3 31W
Hourtin, *France* **24 C2** 45 11N 1 4W
Hourtin-Carcans, Étang d', *France* **24 C2** 45 10N 1 6W
Houston, *Canada* **130 C3** 54 25N 126 39W
Houston, *Mo., U.S.A.* **139 G9** 37 22N 91 58W
Houston, *Tex., U.S.A.* **139 L7** 29 46N 95 22W
Houten, *Neths.* **20 D6** 52 2N 5 10 E
Houthalen, *Belgium* **21 F6** 51 2N 5 23 E
Houthem, *Belgium* **21 G1** 50 48N 2 57 E
Houthulst, *Belgium* **21 G2** 50 59N 3 20 E
Houtman Abrolhos, *Australia* **113 E1** 28 43 S 113 48 E
Houyet, *Belgium* **21 H6** 50 11N 5 1 E
Hov, *Denmark* **15 J4** 55 55N 10 15 E
Hova, *Sweden* **15 F8** 58 53N 14 14 E
Høvåg, *Norway* **15 F2** 58 10N 8 16 E
Hovd, *Mongolia* **64 B4** 48 2N 91 37 E
Hove, *U.K.* **17 G7** 50 50N 0 10W
Hoveyzeh, *Iran* **85 D6** 31 27N 48 4 E
Hövsgöl, *Mongolia* **66 C5** 43 37N 109 39 E
Hövsgöl Nuur, *Mongolia* **64 A5** 51 0N 100 30 E
Howakil, *Eritrea* **95 D5** 15 10N 40 16 E
Howar, Wadi →, *Sudan* **95 D2** 17 30N 27 8 E
Howard, *Australia* **115 D5** 25 16 S 152 32 E
Howard, *Kans., U.S.A.* **139 G6** 37 28N 96 16W
Howard, *Pa., U.S.A.* **136 E7** 41 1N 77 40W
Howard, *S. Dak., U.S.A.* **138 C6** 44 1N 97 32W
Howard I., *Australia* **114 A2** 12 10 S 135 24 E
Howard L., *Canada* **131 A7** 62 15N 105 57W
Howe, *U.S.A.* **142 E7** 43 48N 113 0W
Howe, C., *Australia* **117 D9** 37 30 S 150 0 E
Howell, *U.S.A.* **141 B13** 42 36N 83 56W
Howick, *Canada* **137 A11** 45 11N 73 51W
Howick, *N.Z.* **118 C3** 36 54 S 174 56 E
Howick, *S. Africa* **105 D5** 29 28 S 30 14 E
Howick Group, *Australia* **114 A4** 14 20 S 145 30 E
Howitt, L., *Australia* **115 D2** 27 40 S 138 40 E
Howley, *Canada* **129 C8** 49 12N 57 2W
Howrah = Haora, *India* **81 H13** 22 37N 88 20 E
Howth Hd., *Ireland* **19 C5** 53 21N 6 3W
Höxter, *Germany* **26 D5** 51 45N 9 26 E
Hoy, *U.K.* **18 C5** 58 50N 3 15W
Hoya, *Germany* **26 C5** 52 47N 9 10 E
Høyanger, *Norway* **13 F9** 61 13N 6 4 E
Hoyerswerda, *Germany* **26 D10** 51 26N 14 14 E
Hoyleton, *Australia* **116 C3** 34 2 S 138 34 E
Hoyos, *Spain* **36 E4** 40 9N 6 45W
Hpawlum, *Burma* **78 B7** 27 12N 98 12 E
Hpettintha, *Burma* **78 C5** 24 14N 95 23 E
Hpizow, *Burma* **78 B7** 26 57N 98 24 E
Hradec Králové, *Czech.* **30 A8** 50 15N 15 50 E
Hrádek, *Czech.* **31 C9** 48 46N 16 16 E
Hranice, *Czech.* **31 B10** 49 34N 17 45 E
Hrodna = Grodno, *Belorussia* **50 E3** 53 42N 23 52 E
Hron →, *Slovak Rep.* **31 D11** 47 49N 18 45 E
Hrubieszów, *Poland* **47 E10** 50 49N 23 51 E
Hrubý Nízký Jeseník, *Czech.* **31 A10** 50 7N 17 10 E
Hrvatska = Croatia ■, *Europe* **39 C13** 45 20N 16 0 E
Hsenwi, *Burma* **78 D6** 23 22N 97 55 E
Hsiamen = Xiamen, *China* **69 E12** 24 25N 118 4 E
Hsian = Xi'an, *China* **66 G5** 34 15N 109 0 E
Hsinhailien = Lianyungang, *China* **67 G10** 34 40N 119 11 E
Hsipaw, *Burma* **78 D6** 22 37N 97 18 E
Hsüchou = Xuzhou, *China* **67 G9** 34 18N 117 10 E
Htawgaw, *Burma* **78 C7** 25 57N 98 23 E
Hu Xian, *China* **66 G5** 34 8N 108 42 E
Hua Hin, *Thailand* **76 F2** 12 34N 99 58 E
Hua Xian, *Henan, China* **66 G8** 35 30N 114 30 E
Hua Xian, *Shaanxi, China* **66 G5** 34 30N 109 48 E
Hua'an, *China* **69 E11** 25 1N 117 32 E
Huacaya, *Bolivia* **157 E5** 20 45 S 63 43W
Huacheng, *China* **69 E10** 24 4N 115 37 E
Huachinera, *Mexico* **146 A3** 30 9N 108 55W
Huacho, *Peru* **156 C2** 11 10 S 77 35W
Huachón, *Peru* **156 C2** 10 35 S 76 0W
Huade, *China* **66 D7** 41 55N 113 59 E
Huadian, *China* **67 C14** 43 0N 126 40 E
Huai He →, *China* **69 A12** 33 0N 118 30 E
Huai Yot, *Thailand* **77 J2** 7 45N 99 37 E
Huai'an, *Hebei, China* **66 D8** 40 30N 114 20 E
Huai'an, *Jiangsu, China* **67 H10** 33 30N 119 10 E
Huaide, *China* **67 C13** 43 30N 124 40 E
Huaidezhen, *China* **67 C13** 43 48N 124 50 E
Huaihua, *China* **68 D7** 27 32N 109 57 E
Huaiji, *China* **69 F9** 23 55N 112 12 E
Huainan, *China* **69 A11** 32 38N 116 58 E
Huaining, *China* **69 B11** 30 24N 116 40 E
Huairen, *China* **66 E7** 39 48N 113 20 E
Huairou, *China* **66 D9** 40 20N 116 35 E
Huaiyang, *China* **66 H8** 33 40N 114 52 E
Huaiyuan, *Anhui, China* **67 H9** 32 55N 117 10 E
Huaiyuan, *Guangxi Zhuangzu, China* **68 E7** 24 31N 108 22 E
Huajianzi, *China* **67 D13** 41 23N 125 20 E
Huajuapan de Leon, *Mexico* **147 D5** 17 50N 97 48W
Hualapai Peak, *U.S.A.* **143 J7** 35 5N 113 54W
Hualian, *Taiwan* **69 F13** 23 59N 121 37 E
Huallaga →, *Peru* **156 B2** 5 15 S 75 30W
Huallanca, *Peru* **156 B2** 8 50 S 77 56W
Huamachuco, *Peru* **156 B2** 7 50 S 78 5W
Huambo, *Angola* **103 E3** 12 42 S 15 54 E
Huambo □, *Angola* **103 E3** 13 0 S 16 0 E
Huan Jiang →, *China* **66 G5** 34 28N 109 0 E
Huan Xian, *China* **66 F4** 36 33N 107 7 E
Huancabamba, *Peru* **156 B2** 5 10 S 79 15W
Huancane, *Peru* **156 D4** 15 10 S 69 44W
Huancapi, *Peru* **156 C3** 13 40 S 74 0W
Huancavelica, *Peru* **156 C2** 12 50 S 75 5W
Huancavelica □, *Peru* **156 C3** 13 0 S 75 0W
Huancayo, *Peru* **156 C2** 12 5 S 75 12W
Huanchaca, *Bolivia* **156 E4** 20 15 S 66 40W
Huanchaca, Serranía de, *Bolivia* **157 C5** 14 30 S 60 39W
Huang Hai = Yellow Sea, *China* **67 G12** 35 0N 123 0 E
Huang He →, *China* **67 F10** 37 55N 118 50 E
Huang Xian, *China* **67 F11** 37 38N 120 30 E
Huangchuan, *China* **69 A10** 32 15N 115 10 E
Huanggang, *China* **69 B10** 30 29N 114 52 E
Huangling, *China* **66 G5** 35 34N 109 15 E
Huanglong, *China* **66 G5** 35 30N 109 59 E
Huanglongtan, *China* **69 A8** 32 40N 110 33 E
Huangmei, *China* **69 B10** 30 5N 115 56 E
Huangpi, *China* **69 B10** 30 50N 114 22 E
Huangping, *China* **68 D6** 26 52N 107 54 E
Huangshi, *China* **69 B10** 30 10N 115 3 E
Huangsongdian, *China* **67 C14** 43 45N 127 25 E
Huangyan, *China* **69 C13** 28 38N 121 19 E
Huangyangsi, *China* **69 D8** 26 33N 111 39 E
Huaning, *China* **68 E4** 24 17N 102 56 E
Huanjiang, *China* **68 E7** 24 50N 108 18 E
Huanta, *Peru* **156 C3** 12 55 S 74 20W
Huantai, *China* **67 F9** 36 58N 117 56 E
Huánuco, *Peru* **156 B2** 9 55 S 76 15W
Huánuco □, *Peru* **156 B2** 9 55 S 76 14W
Huanuni, *Bolivia* **156 D4** 18 16 S 66 51W
Huanzo, Cordillera de, *Peru* **156 C3** 14 35 S 73 20W
Huaping, *China* **68 D3** 26 46N 101 25 E
Huaral, *Peru* **156 C2** 11 32 S 77 13W
Huaraz, *Peru* **156 B2** 9 30 S 77 32W
Huari, *Peru* **156 B2** 9 14 S 77 14W
Huarmey, *Peru* **156 C2** 10 5 S 78 5W
Huarochiri, *Peru* **156 C2** 12 9 S 76 15W
Huarocondo, *Peru* **156 C3** 13 26 S 72 14W
Huarong, *China* **69 C9** 29 29N 112 30 E
Huascarán, *Peru* **156 B2** 9 8 S 77 36W
Huascarán, Nevado, *Peru* **156 B2** 9 7 S 77 37W
Huasco, *Chile* **158 B1** 28 30 S 71 15W
Huasco →, *Chile* **158 B1** 28 27 S 71 13W
Huasna, *U.S.A.* **145 K6** 35 6N 120 24W
Huatabampo, *Mexico* **146 B3** 26 50N 109 50W
Huauchinango, *Mexico* **147 C5** 20 11N 98 3W
Huautla de Jiménez, *Mexico* **147 D5** 18 8N 96 51W
Huaxi, *China* **68 D6** 26 25N 106 40 E
Huay Namota, *Mexico* **146 C4** 21 56N 104 30W
Huayin, *China* **66 G6** 34 35N 110 5 E
Huayllay, *Peru* **156 C2** 11 3 S 76 21W
Huayuan, *China* **68 C7** 28 37N 109 29 E
Huazhou, *China* **69 G8** 21 33N 110 33 E
Hubbard, *Iowa, U.S.A.* **140 B3** 42 18N 93 18W
Hubbard, *Tex., U.S.A.* **139 K6** 31 51N 96 48W
Hubbart Pt., *Canada* **131 B10** 59 21N 94 41W
Hubei □, *China* **69 B9** 31 0N 112 0 E
Hubli-Dharwad = Dharwad, *India* **83 G2** 15 22N 75 15 E
Huchang, *N. Korea* **67 D14** 41 25N 127 2 E
Hückelhoven, *Germany* **26 D2** 51 6N 6 13 E
Huczwa →, *Poland* **47 E10** 50 49N 23 58 E
Huddersfield, *U.K.* **16 D6** 53 38N 1 49W
Hudi, *Sudan* **94 D3** 17 43N 34 18 E
Hudiksvall, *Sweden* **14 C11** 61 43N 17 10 E
Hudson, *Canada* **131 C10** 50 6N 92 9W
Hudson, *Mass., U.S.A.* **137 D13** 42 23N 71 34W
Hudson, *Mich., U.S.A.* **141 C12** 41 51N 84 21W
Hudson, *N.Y., U.S.A.* **137 D11** 42 15N 73 46W
Hudson, *Wis., U.S.A.* **138 C8** 44 58N 92 45W
Hudson, *Wyo., U.S.A.* **142 E9** 42 54N 108 35W
Hudson →, *U.S.A.* **137 F10** 40 42N 74 2W
Hudson Bay, *N.W.T., Canada* **127 C11** 60 0N 86 0W
Hudson Bay, *Sask., Canada* **131 C8** 52 51N 102 23W
Hudson Falls, *U.S.A.* **137 C11** 43 18N 73 35W
Hudson Mts., *Antarctica* **7 D16** 74 32 S 99 20W
Hudson Str., *Canada* **127 B13** 62 0N 70 0W
Hudson's Hope, *Canada* **130 B4** 56 0N 121 54W
Hudsonville, *U.S.A.* **141 B11** 42 52N 85 52W
Hue, *Vietnam* **76 D6** 16 30N 107 35 E
Huebra →, *Spain* **36 D4** 41 2N 6 48W
Huechucuicui, Pta., *Chile* **160 B2** 41 48 S 74 2W
Huedin, *Romania* **46 C4** 46 52N 23 2 E
Huehuetenango, *Guatemala* **148 C1** 15 20N 91 28W
Huejúcar, *Mexico* **146 C4** 22 21N 103 13W
Huelgoat, *France* **22 D3** 48 22N 3 46W
Huelma, *Spain* **35 H1** 37 39N 3 28W
Huelva, *Spain* **37 H4** 37 18N 6 57W
Huelva □, *Spain* **37 H4** 37 40N 7 0W
Huelva →, *Spain* **37 H5** 37 27N 6 0W
Huentelauquén, *Chile* **158 C1** 31 38 S 71 33W
Huércal Overa, *Spain* **35 H3** 37 23N 1 57W
Huerta, Sa. de la, *Argentina* **158 C2** 31 10 S 67 30W
Huertas, C. de las, *Spain* **35 G4** 38 21N 0 24W
Huerva →, *Spain* **34 D4** 41 39N 0 52W
Huesca, *Spain* **34 C4** 42 8N 0 25W
Huesca □, *Spain* **34 C5** 42 20N 0 1 E
Huéscar, *Spain* **35 H2** 37 44N 2 35W
Huetamo, *Mexico* **146 D4** 18 36N 100 54W
Huete, *Spain* **34 E2** 40 10N 2 43W
Hugh →, *Australia* **114 D1** 25 1 S 134 1 E
Hughenden, *Australia* **114 C3** 20 52 S 144 10 E
Hughes, *Australia* **113 F4** 30 42 S 129 31 E
Hughli →, *India* **81 J13** 21 56N 88 4 E
Hugo, *U.S.A.* **138 F3** 39 8N 103 28W
Hugoton, *U.S.A.* **139 G4** 37 11N 101 21W
Hui Xian, *Gansu, China* **66 H4** 33 50N 106 4 E
Hui Xian, *Henan, China* **66 G7** 35 27N 113 12 E
Hui'an, *China* **69 E12** 25 1N 118 43 E
Hui'anbu, *China* **66 F4** 37 28N 106 38 E
Huiarau Ra., *N.Z.* **118 E5** 38 45 S 176 55 E
Huichang, *China* **69 E10** 25 32N 115 45 E
Huichapán, *Mexico* **147 C5** 20 24N 99 40W
Huidong, *China* **68 D4** 26 34N 102 35 E
Huifa He →, *China* **67 C14** 43 0N 127 50 E
Huíla, *Angola* **103 F2** 15 4 S 13 32 E
Huila □, *Colombia* **152 C2** 2 30N 75 45W
Huila, Nevado del, *Colombia* **152 C2** 3 0N 76 0W
Huilai, *China* **69 F11** 23 0N 116 18 E
Huili, *China* **68 D4** 26 35N 102 17 E
Huimin, *China* **67 F9** 37 27N 117 28 E
Huinan, *China* **67 C14** 42 40N 126 2 E
Huinca Renancó, *Argentina* **158 C3** 34 51 S 64 22W
Huining, *China* **66 G3** 35 38N 105 0 E
Huinong, *China* **66 E4** 39 5N 106 35 E
Huiroa, *N.Z.* **118 F3** 39 15 S 174 30 E
Huise, *Belgium* **21 G3** 50 54N 3 36 E
Huishui, *China* **68 D6** 26 7N 106 38 E
Huisne →, *France* **22 E7** 47 59N 0 11 E
Huissen, *Neths.* **20 E7** 51 57N 5 57 E
Huiting, *China* **66 G9** 34 5N 116 5 E
Huitong, *China* **68 D7** 26 51N 109 45 E
Huixtla, *Mexico* **147 D6** 15 9N 92 28W
Huize, *China* **68 D4** 26 24N 103 15 E
Huizen, *Neths.* **20 D6** 52 18N 5 14 E
Huizhou, *China* **69 F10** 23 0N 114 23 E
Hukou, *China* **69 C11** 29 45N 116 21 E
Hukuntsi, *Botswana* **104 C3** 23 58 S 21 45 E
Hula, *Ethiopia* **95 F4** 6 33N 38 30 E
Ḥulayfā', *Si. Arabia* **84 E4** 25 58N 40 45 E
Huld, *Mongolia* **66 B3** 45 5N 105 30 E
Hulin He →, *China* **67 B12** 45 0N 122 10 E
Hull = Kingston upon Hull, *U.K.* **16 D7** 53 45N 0 20W
Hull, *Canada* **128 C4** 45 25N 75 44W
Hull, *U.S.A.* **140 E5** 39 43N 91 13W
Hull →, *U.K.* **16 D7** 53 43N 0 25W
Hulst, *Neths.* **21 F4** 51 17N 4 2 E
Hulun Nur, *China* **65 B6** 49 0N 117 30 E
Humahuaca, *Argentina* **158 A2** 23 10 S 65 25W
Humaitá, *Brazil* **157 B5** 7 35 S 63 1W
Humaitá, *Paraguay* **158 B4** 27 2 S 58 31W
Humansdorp, *S. Africa* **104 E3** 34 2 S 24 46 E
Humansville, *U.S.A.* **140 G3** 37 48N 93 35W
Humbe, *Angola* **103 F2** 16 40 S 14 55 E
Humber →, *U.K.* **16 D7** 53 40N 0 10W
Humberside □, *U.K.* **16 D7** 53 50N 0 30W
Humbert River, *Australia* **112 C5** 16 30 S 130 45 E
Humble, *U.S.A.* **139 L8** 29 59N 93 18W
Humboldt, *Canada* **131 C7** 52 15N 105 9W
Humboldt, *Iowa, U.S.A.* **140 B2** 42 44N 94 13W
Humboldt, *Tenn., U.S.A.* **139 H10** 35 50N 88 55W
Humboldt →, *U.S.A.* **142 F4** 39 59N 118 36W
Humboldt Gletscher, *Greenland* **6 B4** 79 30N 62 0W
Humboldt Mts., *N.Z.* **119 E3** 44 30 S 168 15 E
Humboldt, Massif du, *N. Cal.* **121 U20** 21 53 S 166 25 E
Hume, *Calif., U.S.A.* **144 J8** 36 48N 118 54W
Hume, *Mo., U.S.A.* **140 F2** 38 6N 94 34W
Hume, L., *Australia* **117 D7** 36 0 S 147 5 E
Humenné, *Slovak Rep.* **31 C14** 48 55N 21 50 E
Humeston, *U.S.A.* **140 D3** 40 52N 93 30W
Humpata, *Angola* **103 F2** 15 2 S 13 24 E
Humphreys, Mt., *U.S.A.* **144 H8** 37 17N 118 40W
Humphreys Peak, *U.S.A.* **143 J8** 35 21N 111 41W
Humpolec, *Czech.* **30 B8** 49 31N 15 20 E
Humptulips, *U.S.A.* **144 C3** 47 14N 123 57W
Humula, *Australia* **117 C7** 35 30 S 147 46 E
Hūn, *Libya* **96 C3** 29 2N 16 0 E
Hun Jiang →, *China* **67 D13** 40 50N 125 38 E
Húnaflói, *Iceland* **12 D3** 65 50N 20 50W
Hunan □, *China* **69 D9** 27 30N 112 0 E
Hunchun, *China* **67 C16** 42 52N 130 28 E
Hundested, *Denmark* **15 J5** 55 58N 11 52 E
Hundred Mile House, *Canada* **130 C4** 51 38N 121 18W
Hunedoara, *Romania* **46 D3** 45 40N 22 50 E
Hunedoara □, *Romania* **46 D3** 45 50N 22 54 E
Hünfeld, *Germany* **26 E5** 50 40N 9 47 E
Hung Yen, *Vietnam* **76 B6** 20 39N 106 4 E
Hunga, *Tonga* **121 P13** 18 41 S 174 7W
Hunga Ha'api, *Tonga* **121 Q13** 20 41 S 175 7W
Hungary ■, *Europe* **31 D12** 47 20N 19 20 E
Hungary, Plain of, *Europe* **10 F9** 47 0N 20 0 E
Hungerford, *Australia* **115 D3** 28 58 S 144 24 E
Hŭngnam, *N. Korea* **67 E14** 39 49N 127 45 E
Huni Valley, *Ghana* **100 D4** 5 33N 1 56W
Hunsberge, *Namibia* **104 D2** 27 45 S 17 12 E
Hunsrück, *Germany* **27 F3** 49 30N 7 0 E
Hunstanton, *U.K.* **16 E8** 52 57N 0 30 E
Hunsur, *India* **83 H3** 12 16N 76 16 E
Hunte →, *Germany* **26 C4** 52 30N 8 19 E
Hunter, *N.Z.* **119 E6** 44 36 S 171 2 E
Hunter, *N. Dak., U.S.A.* **138 B6** 47 12N 97 13W
Hunter, *N.Y., U.S.A.* **137 D10** 42 13N 74 13W
Hunter →, *N.Z.* **119 E4** 44 21 S 169 27 E
Hunter, C., *Solomon Is.* **121 M10** 9 48 S 159 50 E
Hunter I., *Australia* **114 G3** 40 30 S 144 45 E
Hunter I., *Canada* **130 C3** 51 55N 128 0W
Hunter Mts., *N.Z.* **119 F2** 45 43 S 167 25 E
Hunter Ra., *Australia* **117 B9** 32 45 S 150 15 E
Hunters Road, *Zimbabwe* **107 F2** 19 9 S 29 49 E
Hunterville, *N.Z.* **118 F4** 39 56 S 175 35 E
Huntingburg, *U.S.A.* **141 F10** 38 18N 86 57W
Huntingdon, *Canada* **128 C5** 45 6N 74 10W
Huntingdon, *U.K.* **17 E7** 52 20N 0 11W
Huntingdon, *U.S.A.* **136 F6** 40 30N 78 1W
Huntington, *Ind., U.S.A.* **141 D11** 40 53N 85 30W
Huntington, *N.Y., U.S.A.* **137 F11** 40 52N 73 26W
Huntington, *Oreg., U.S.A.* **142 D5** 44 21N 117 16W
Huntington, *Utah, U.S.A.* **142 G8** 39 20N 110 58W
Huntington, *W. Va., U.S.A.* **134 F4** 38 25N 82 27W
Huntington Beach, *U.S.A.* **145 M8** 33 40N 118 5W
Huntington Park, *U.S.A.* **143 K4** 33 58N 118 15W
Huntley, *U.S.A.* **141 B8** 42 10N 88 26W
Huntly, *N.Z.* **118 D4** 37 34 S 175 11 E
Huntly, *U.K.* **18 D6** 57 27N 2 48W
Huntsville, *Canada* **128 C4** 45 20N 79 14W
Huntsville, *Ala., U.S.A.* **135 H2** 34 44N 86 35W
Huntsville, *Mo., U.S.A.* **140 E4** 39 26N 92 33W
Huntsville, *Tex., U.S.A.* **139 K7** 30 43N 95 33W
Hunyani →, *Zimbabwe* **107 F3** 15 57 S 30 39 E
Hunyuan, *China* **66 E7** 39 42N 113 42 E
Hunza →, *India* **81 B6** 35 54N 74 20 E
Huo Xian, *China* **66 F6** 36 36N 111 42 E
Huon G., *Papua N. G.* **120 D4** 7 0 S 147 30 E
Huon Pen., *Papua N. G.* **120 D4** 6 20 S 147 30 E
Huong Hoa, *Vietnam* **76 D6** 16 37N 106 45 E
Huong Khe, *Vietnam* **76 C5** 18 13N 105 41 E
Huonville, *Australia* **114 G4** 43 0 S 147 5 E
Huoqiu, *China* **69 A11** 32 20N 116 12 E
Huoshan, *Anhui, China* **69 A12** 32 28N 118 30 E
Huoshan, *Anhui, China* **69 B11** 31 25N 116 20 E
Huoshao Dao, *Taiwan* **69 F13** 22 40N 121 30 E
Hupeh = Hubei □, *China* **69 B9** 31 0N 112 0 E
Ḥūr, *Iran* **85 D8** 30 50N 57 7 E
Hurbanovo, *Slovak Rep.* **31 D11** 47 51N 18 11 E
Hure Qi, *China* **67 C11** 42 45N 121 45 E
Hurezani, *Romania* **46 E4** 44 49N 23 40 E
Hurghada, *Egypt* **94 B3** 27 15N 33 50 E
Hurley, *N. Mex., U.S.A.* **143 K9** 32 42N 108 8W
Hurley, *Wis., U.S.A.* **138 B9** 46 27N 90 11W
Huron, *Calif., U.S.A.* **144 J6** 36 12N 120 6W
Huron, *Ohio, U.S.A.* **136 E2** 41 24N 82 33W
Huron, *S. Dak., U.S.A.* **138 C5** 44 22N 98 13W
Huron, L., *U.S.A.* **136 B2** 44 30N 82 40W
Hurricane, *U.S.A.* **143 H7** 37 11N 113 17W
Hurso, *Ethiopia* **95 F5** 9 35N 41 33 E
Hurum, *Norway* **14 C2** 61 9N 8 46 E
Hurunui →, *N.Z.* **119 C8** 42 54 S 173 18 E
Hurup, *Denmark* **15 H2** 56 46N 8 25 E
Húsavík, *Iceland* **12 C5** 66 3N 17 21W
Huşi, *Romania* **46 C9** 46 41N 28 7 E
Huskvarna, *Sweden* **13 H13** 57 47N 14 15 E
Hussar, *Canada* **130 C6** 51 3N 112 41W
Hustopéce, *Czech.* **31 C9** 48 57N 16 43 E
Husum, *Germany* **26 A5** 54 27N 9 3 E
Husum, *Sweden* **14 A13** 63 21N 19 12 E
Hutchinson, *Kans., U.S.A.* **139 F6** 38 5N 97 56W
Hutchinson, *Minn., U.S.A.* **138 C7** 44 54N 94 22W
Ḥūth, *Yemen* **86 C3** 16 14N 43 58 E
Hutsonville, *U.S.A.* **141 E9** 39 7N 87 40W
Huttenberg, *Austria* **30 E7** 46 56N 14 33 E
Huttig, *U.S.A.* **139 J8** 33 2N 92 11W
Hutton, Mt., *Australia* **115 D4** 25 51 S 148 20 E
Huttwil, *Switz.* **28 B5** 47 7N 7 50 E
Huwun, *Ethiopia* **95 G5** 4 23N 40 6 E
Huy, *Belgium* **21 G6** 50 31N 5 15 E
Hvammur, *Iceland* **12 D3** 65 13N 21 49W
Hvar, *Croatia* **39 E13** 43 11N 16 28 E
Hvarski Kanal, *Croatia* **39 E13** 43 15N 16 35 E
Hvítá, *Iceland* **12 D3** 64 40N 21 5W
Hvítá →, *Iceland* **12 D3** 64 30N 21 58W
Hvítárvatn, *Iceland* **12 D4** 64 37N 19 50W
Hwachon-chosuji, *S. Korea* **67 E14** 38 5N 127 50 E
Hwang Ho = Huang He →, *China* **67 F10** 37 55N 118 50 E
Hwange, *Zimbabwe* **107 F2** 18 18 S 26 30 E
Hwange Nat. Park, *Zimbabwe* **104 B4** 19 0 S 26 30 E
Hwekum, *Burma* **78 B5** 26 7N 95 22 E
Hyannis, *U.S.A.* **138 E4** 42 0N 101 46W
Hyargas Nuur, *Mongolia* **64 B4** 49 0N 93 0 E

**Itumbiara 211**


Inglewood, *Vic., Australia* **116 D5** 36 29 S 143 53 E
Inglewood, *N.Z.* **118 F3** 39 9 S 174 14 E
Inglewood, *U.S.A.* **145 M8** 33 58N 118 21W
Ingólfshöfði, *Iceland* **12 E5** 63 48N 16 39W
Ingolstadt, *Germany* **27 G7** 48 45N 11 26 E
Ingomar, *U.S.A.* **142 C10** 46 35N 107 23W
Ingonish, *Canada* **129 C7** 46 42N 60 18W
Ingore, *Guinea-Biss.* **100 C1** 12 24N 15 48W
Ingraj Bazar, *India* **81 G13** 24 58N 88 10 E
Ingrid Christensen Coast, *Antarctica* **7 C6** 69 30 S 76 0 E
Ingul →, *Ukraine* **52 C5** 46 50N 32 0 E
Ingulec, *Ukraine* **52 C5** 47 42N 33 14 E
Ingulets →, *Ukraine* **52 C5** 46 35N 32 48 E
Inguri →, *Georgia* **53 E9** 42 38N 41 35 E
Ingwavuma, *S. Africa* **105 D5** 27 9 S 31 59 E
Inhaca, I., *Mozam.* **105 D5** 26 1 S 32 57 E
Inhafenga, *Mozam.* **105 C5** 20 36 S 33 53 E
Inhambane, *Mozam.* **105 C6** 23 54 S 35 30 E
Inhambane □, *Mozam.* **105 C5** 22 30 S 34 20 E
Inhambupe, *Brazil* **155 D4** 11 47 S 38 21W
Inhaminga, *Mozam.* **107 F4** 18 26 S 35 0 E
Inharrime, *Mozam.* **105 C6** 24 30 S 35 0 E
Inharrime →, *Mozam.* **105 C6** 24 30 S 35 0 E
Inhuma, *Brazil* **154 C3** 6 40 S 41 42W
Inhumas, *Brazil* **155 E2** 16 22 S 49 30W
Iniesta, *Spain* **35 F3** 39 27N 1 45W
Ining = Yining, *China* **56 E9** 43 58N 81 10 E
Inini □, *Fr. Guiana* **153 C7** 4 0N 53 0W
Inírida →, *Colombia* **152 C4** 3 55N 67 52W
Inishbofin, *Ireland* **19 C1** 53 35N 10 12W
Inishmore, *Ireland* **19 C2** 53 8N 9 45W
Inishowen, *Ireland* **19 A4** 55 14N 7 15W
Injune, *Australia* **115 D4** 25 53 S 148 32 E
Inklin, *Canada* **130 B2** 58 56N 133 5W
Inklin →, *Canada* **130 B2** 58 50N 133 10W
Inkom, *U.S.A.* **142 E7** 42 48N 112 15W
Inle L., *Burma* **78 E6** 20 30N 96 58 E
Inn →, *Austria* **27 G9** 48 35N 13 28 E
Innamincka, *Australia* **115 D3** 27 44 S 140 46 E
Inner Hebrides, *U.K.* **18 D2** 57 0N 6 30W
Inner Mongolia = Nei Monggol Zizhiqu □, *China* **66 C6** 42 0N 112 0 E
Inner Sound, *U.K.* **18 D3** 57 30N 5 55W
Innerkip, *Canada* **136 C4** 43 13N 80 42W
Innerkirchen, *Switz.* **28 C6** 46 43N 8 14 E
Innerste →, *Germany* **26 C5** 52 45N 9 40 E
Innetalling I., *Canada* **128 A4** 56 0N 79 0W
Innisfail, *Australia* **114 B4** 17 33 S 146 5 E
Innisfail, *Canada* **130 C6** 52 0N 113 57W
In'no-shima, *Japan* **62 C5** 34 19N 133 10 E
Innsbruck, *Austria* **30 D4** 47 16N 11 23 E
Inny →, *Ireland* **19 C4** 53 30N 7 50W
Ino, *Japan* **62 D5** 33 33N 133 26 E
Inocência, *Brazil* **155 E1** 19 47 S 51 48W
Inongo, *Zaïre* **102 C3** 1 55 S 18 30 E
Inoni, *Congo* **102 C3** 3 4 S 15 39 E
Inoucdjouac, *Canada* **127 C12** 58 25N 78 15W
Inowrocław, *Poland* **47 C5** 52 50N 18 12 E
Inpundong, *N. Korea* **67 D14** 41 25N 126 34 E
Inquisivi, *Bolivia* **156 D4** 16 50 S 67 10W
Ins, *Switz.* **28 B4** 47 1N 7 7 E
Inscription, C., *Australia* **113 E1** 25 29 S 112 59 E
Insein, *Burma* **78 G6** 16 50N 96 5 E
Însurăţei, *Romania* **46 E8** 44 50N 27 40 E
Inta, *Russia* **48 A11** 66 5N 60 8 E
Intendente Alvear, *Argentina* **158 D3** 35 12 S 63 32W
Interior, *U.S.A.* **138 D4** 43 44N 101 59W
Interlaken, *Switz.* **23 F14** 46 41N 7 50 E
International Falls, *U.S.A.* **138 A8** 48 36N 93 25W
Intiyaco, *Argentina* **158 B3** 28 43 S 60 5W
Intragna, *Switz.* **29 D7** 46 11N 8 42 E
Intutu, *Peru* **152 D3** 3 32 S 74 48W
Inubō-Zaki, *Japan* **63 B12** 35 42N 140 52 E
Inútil, B., *Chile* **160 D2** 53 30 S 70 15W
Inuvik, *Canada* **126 B6** 68 16N 133 40W
Inuyama, *Japan* **63 B8** 35 23N 136 56 E
Inveraray, *U.K.* **18 E3** 56 13N 5 5W
Inverbervie, *U.K.* **18 E6** 56 50N 2 17W
Invercargill, *N.Z.* **119 G3** 46 24 S 168 24 E
Inverell, *Australia* **115 D5** 29 45 S 151 8 E
Invergordon, *U.K.* **18 D4** 57 41N 4 10W
Inverleigh, *Australia* **116 E6** 38 6 S 144 3 E
Invermere, *Canada* **130 C5** 50 30N 116 2W
Inverness, *Canada* **129 C7** 46 15N 61 19W
Inverness, *U.K.* **18 D4** 57 29N 4 12W
Inverness, *U.S.A.* **135 L4** 28 50N 82 20W
Inverurie, *U.K.* **18 D6** 57 15N 2 21W
Inverway, *Australia* **112 C4** 17 50 S 129 38 E
Investigator Group, *Australia* **115 E1** 34 45 S 134 20 E
Investigator Str., *Australia* **116 C2** 35 30 S 137 0 E
Inya, *Russia* **56 D9** 50 28N 86 37 E
Inyanga, *Zimbabwe* **107 F3** 18 12 S 32 40 E
Inyangani, *Zimbabwe* **107 F3** 18 5 S 32 50 E
Inyantue, *Zimbabwe* **107 F2** 18 30 S 26 40 E
Inyo Mts., *U.S.A.* **143 H5** 36 40N 118 0W
Inyokern, *U.S.A.* **145 K9** 35 39N 117 49W
Inywa, *Burma* **78 D6** 23 56N 96 17 E
Inza, *Russia* **51 E15** 53 55N 46 25 E
Inzer, *Russia* **54 D5** 54 14N 57 34 E
Inzhavino, *Russia* **51 E13** 52 22N 42 30 E
Iō-Jima, *Japan* **61 J5** 30 48N 130 18 E
Ioánnina, *Greece* **44 E2** 39 42N 20 47 E
Ioánnina □, *Greece* **44 E2** 39 39N 20 57 E
Iola, *U.S.A.* **139 G7** 37 55N 95 24W
Ioma, *Papua N. G.* **120 E4** 8 19 S 147 52 E
Ion Corvin, *Romania* **46 E8** 44 7N 27 50 E
Iona, *U.K.* **18 E2** 56 20N 6 25W
Ione, *Calif., U.S.A.* **144 G6** 38 21N 120 56W
Ione, *Wash., U.S.A.* **142 B5** 48 45N 117 25W
Ionia, *U.S.A.* **141 B11** 42 59N 85 4W
Ionian Is. = Iónioi Nísoi, *Greece* **45 F2** 38 40N 20 0 E
Ionian Sea, *Europe* **10 H9** 37 30N 17 30 E
Iónioi Nísoi, *Greece* **45 F2** 38 40N 20 0 E
Iori →, *Azerbaijan* **53 F12** 41 3N 46 17 E
Íos, *Greece* **45 H7** 36 41N 25 20 E
Iowa □, *U.S.A.* **138 D8** 42 18N 93 30W
Iowa →, *U.S.A.* **140 C5** 41 10N 91 1W
Iowa City, *U.S.A.* **140 C5** 41 40N 91 32W
Iowa Falls, *U.S.A.* **140 B3** 42 31N 93 16W
Ipala, *Tanzania* **106 C3** 4 30 S 32 52 E
Ipameri, *Brazil* **155 E2** 17 44 S 48 9W
Iparía, *Peru* **156 B3** 9 17 S 74 29W
Ipáti, *Greece* **45 F4** 38 52N 22 14 E
Ipatinga, *Brazil* **155 E3** 19 32 S 42 30W
Ipatovo, *Russia* **53 D10** 45 45N 42 50 E
Ipel →, *Europe* **31 C12** 48 10N 19 35 E
Ipiales, *Colombia* **152 C2** 0 50N 77 37W
Ipiaú, *Brazil* **155 D4** 14 8 S 39 44W
Ipil, *Phil.* **71 H4** 7 47N 122 35 E
Ipin = Yibin, *China* **68 C5** 28 45N 104 32 E
Ipirá, *Brazil* **155 D4** 12 10 S 39 44W
Ipiranga, *Brazil* **152 D4** 3 13 S 65 57W
Ípiros □, *Greece* **44 E2** 39 30N 20 30 E
Ipixuna, *Brazil* **156 B3** 7 0 S 71 40W
Ipixuna →, *Amazonas, Brazil* **156 B3** 7 11 S 71 51W
Ipixuna →, *Amazonas, Brazil* **157 B5** 5 45 S 63 2W
Ipoh, *Malaysia* **77 K3** 4 35N 101 5 E
Iporá, *Brazil* **155 D1** 11 23 S 50 40W
Ippy, *C.A.R.* **102 A4** 6 5N 21 7 E
İpsala, *Turkey* **44 D8** 40 55N 26 23 E
Ipsárion Óros, *Greece* **44 D6** 40 40N 24 40 E
Ipswich, *Australia* **115 D5** 27 35 S 152 40 E
Ipswich, *U.K.* **17 E9** 52 4N 1 9 E
Ipswich, *Mass., U.S.A.* **137 D14** 42 41N 70 50W
Ipswich, *S. Dak., U.S.A.* **138 C5** 45 27N 99 2W
Ipu, *Brazil* **154 B3** 4 23 S 40 44W
Ipueiras, *Brazil* **154 B3** 4 33 S 40 43W
Ipupiara, *Brazil* **155 D3** 11 49 S 42 37W
Iput →, *Belorussia* **50 E7** 52 26N 31 2 E
Iqaluit, *Canada* **127 B13** 63 44N 68 31W
Iquique, *Chile* **156 E3** 20 19 S 70 5W
Iquitos, *Peru* **152 D3** 3 45 S 73 10W
Irabu-Jima, *Japan* **61 M2** 24 50N 125 10 E
Iracoubo, *Fr. Guiana* **153 B7** 5 30N 53 10W
Īrafshān, *Iran* **85 E9** 26 42N 61 56 E
Irahuan, *Phil.* **71 G2** 9 48N 118 41 E
Iráklia, *Greece* **45 H7** 36 50N 25 28 E
Iráklion, *Greece* **32 D7** 35 20N 25 12 E
Iráklion □, *Greece* **32 D7** 35 10N 25 10 E
Irako-Zaki, *Japan* **63 C9** 34 35N 137 1 E
Irala, *Paraguay* **159 B5** 25 55 S 54 35W
Iramba □, *Tanzania* **106 C3** 4 30 S 34 30 E
Iran ■, *Asia* **85 C7** 33 0N 53 0 E
Iran, Gunung-Gunung, *Malaysia* **75 B4** 2 20N 114 50 E
Iran Ra. = Iran, Gunung-Gunung, *Malaysia* **75 B4** 2 20N 114 50 E
Iranamadu Tank, *Sri Lanka* **83 K5** 9 23N 80 29 E
Īrānshahr, *Iran* **85 E9** 27 15N 60 40 E
Irapa, *Venezuela* **153 A5** 10 34N 62 35W
Irapuato, *Mexico* **146 C4** 20 40N 101 30W
Iraq ■, *Asia* **84 C5** 33 0N 44 0 E
Irarrar, O. →, *Mali* **99 D5** 20 0N 1 30 E
Irati, *Brazil* **159 B5** 25 25 S 50 38W
Irbid, *Jordan* **91 C4** 32 35N 35 48 E
Irbid □, *Jordan* **91 C5** 32 15N 36 35 E
Irbit, *Russia* **54 C8** 57 41N 63 3 E
Irebu, *Zaïre* **102 C3** 0 40 S 17 46 E
Irecê, *Brazil* **154 D3** 11 18 S 41 52W
Iregua →, *Spain* **34 C7** 42 27N 2 24 E
Ireland ■, *Europe* **19 D4** 53 0N 8 0W
Ireland's Eye, *Ireland* **19 C5** 53 25N 6 4W
Irele, *Nigeria* **101 D6** 7 40N 5 40 E
Iremel, Gora, *Russia* **54 D6** 54 33N 58 50 E
Ireng →, *Brazil* **153 C6** 3 33N 59 51W
Iret, *Russia* **57 C16** 60 3N 154 20 E
Irgiz, Bolshaya →, *Russia* **51 E16** 52 10N 49 10 E
Irhârharene, *Algeria* **99 C6** 27 37N 7 30 E
Irharrhar, O. →, *Algeria* **99 C6** 28 3N 6 15 E
Irherm, *Morocco* **98 B3** 30 7N 8 18W
Irhil Mgoun, *Morocco* **98 B3** 31 30N 6 28W
Irhyangdong, *N. Korea* **67 D15** 41 15N 129 30 E
Iri, *S. Korea* **67 G14** 35 59N 127 0 E
Irian Jaya □, *Indonesia* **73 B5** 4 0 S 137 0 E
Iriba, *Chad* **97 E4** 15 7N 22 15 E
Irid, Mt., *Phil.* **70 D3** 14 47N 121 19 E
Irié, *Guinea* **100 D3** 8 15N 9 10W
Iriga, *Phil.* **70 E4** 13 25N 123 25 E
Iriklinskiy, *Russia* **54 F6** 51 39N 58 38 E
Iriklinskoye Vdkhr., *Russia* **54 E6** 52 0N 59 0 E
Iringa, *Tanzania* **106 D4** 7 48 S 35 43 E
Iringa □, *Tanzania* **106 D4** 7 48 S 35 43 E
Irinjalakuda, *India* **83 J3** 10 21N 76 14 E
Iriomote-Jima, *Japan* **61 M1** 24 19N 123 48 E
Iriona, *Honduras* **148 C2** 15 57N 85 11W
Iriri →, *Brazil* **153 D7** 3 52 S 52 37W
Iriri Novo →, *Brazil* **157 B7** 8 46 S 53 22W
Irish Republic ■, *Europe* **19 D4** 53 0N 8 0W
Irish Sea, *Europe* **16 D3** 54 0N 5 0W
Irkeshtam, *Kirghizia* **55 D6** 39 41N 73 55 E
Irkineyeva, *Russia* **57 D10** 58 30N 96 49 E
Irkutsk, *Russia* **57 D11** 52 18N 104 20 E
Irma, *Canada* **131 C6** 52 55N 111 14W
Irō-Zaki, *Japan* **63 C10** 34 36N 138 51 E
Iroise, Mer d', *France* **22 D2** 48 15N 4 45W
Iron Baron, *Australia* **116 B2** 32 58 S 137 11 E
Iron Gate = Portile de Fier, *Europe* **46 E3** 44 42N 22 30 E
Iron Knob, *Australia* **116 B2** 32 46 S 137 8 E
Iron Mountain, *U.S.A.* **134 C1** 45 49N 88 4W
Iron Ra., *Australia* **114 A3** 12 46 S 143 16 E
Iron River, *U.S.A.* **138 B10** 46 6N 88 39W
Ironbridge, *U.K.* **17 E5** 52 38N 2 29W
Irondequoit, *U.S.A.* **136 C7** 43 13N 77 35W
Ironstone Kopje, *Botswana* **104 D3** 25 17 S 24 5 E
Ironton, *Mo., U.S.A.* **139 G9** 37 36N 90 38W
Ironton, *Ohio, U.S.A.* **134 F4** 38 32N 82 41W
Ironwood, *U.S.A.* **138 B9** 46 27N 90 9W
Iroquois →, *U.S.A.* **141 C9** 41 5N 87 49W
Iroquois Falls, *Canada* **128 C3** 48 46N 80 41W
Irosin, *Phil.* **70 E5** 12 42N 124 2 E
Irpen, *Ukraine* **50 F7** 50 30N 30 15 E
Irrara Cr. →, *Australia* **115 D4** 29 35 S 145 31 E
Irrawaddy □, *Burma* **78 G5** 17 0N 95 0 E
Irrawaddy →, *Burma* **78 G5** 15 50N 95 6 E
Irsina, *Italy* **41 B9** 40 45N 16 15 E
Irtysh →, *Russia* **56 C7** 61 4N 68 52 E
Irumu, *Zaïre* **106 B2** 1 32N 29 53 E
Irún, *Spain* **34 B3** 43 20N 1 52W
Irunea = Pamplona, *Spain* **34 C3** 42 48N 1 38W
Irurzun, *Spain* **34 C3** 42 55N 1 50W
Irvine, *Canada* **131 D6** 49 57N 110 16W
Irvine, *U.K.* **18 F4** 55 37N 4 40W
Irvine, *Calif., U.S.A.* **145 M9** 33 41N 117 46W
Irvine, *Ky., U.S.A.* **141 G13** 37 42N 83 58W
Irvinestown, *U.K.* **19 B4** 54 28N 7 38W
Irving, *U.S.A.* **139 J6** 32 49N 96 56W
Irvington, *U.S.A.* **141 G10** 37 53N 86 17W
Irvona, *U.S.A.* **136 F6** 40 46N 78 33W
Irwin →, *Australia* **113 E1** 29 15 S 114 54 E
Irymple, *Australia* **116 C5** 34 14 S 142 8 E
Is-sur-Tille, *France* **23 E12** 47 30N 5 8 E
Isa, *Nigeria* **101 C6** 13 14N 6 24 E
Isaac →, *Australia* **114 C4** 22 55 S 149 20 E
Isabel, *U.S.A.* **138 C4** 45 24N 101 26W
Isabela, *Phil.* **71 F4** 10 12N 122 59 E
Isabela □, *Phil.* **70 C4** 17 0N 122 0 E
Isabela, I., *Mexico* **146 C3** 21 51N 105 55W
Isabella, *Phil.* **71 H4** 6 40N 122 10 E
Isabella, Cord., *Nic.* **148 D2** 13 30N 85 25W
Isabella Ra., *Australia* **112 D3** 21 0 S 121 4 E
Ísafjarðardjúp, *Iceland* **12 C2** 66 10N 23 0W
Ísafjörður, *Iceland* **12 C2** 66 5N 23 9W
Isagarh, *India* **80 G7** 24 48N 77 51 E
Isahaya, *Japan* **62 E2** 32 52N 130 2 E
Isaka, *Tanzania* **106 C3** 3 56 S 32 59 E
Isakly, *Russia* **54 D2** 54 8N 51 32 E
Isana = Içana →, *Brazil* **152 C4** 0 26N 67 19W
Isangi, *Zaïre* **102 B4** 0 52N 24 10 E
Isar →, *Germany* **27 G8** 48 49N 12 58 E
Isarco →, *Italy* **39 B8** 46 57N 11 18 E
Ísari, *Greece* **45 G3** 37 22N 22 0 E
Isbergues, *France* **23 B9** 50 36N 2 28 E
Isbiceni, *Romania* **46 F5** 43 45N 24 40 E
Iscayachi, *Bolivia* **157 E4** 21 31 S 65 3W
Íschia, *Italy* **40 B6** 40 45N 13 51 E
Iscuandé, *Colombia* **152 C2** 2 28N 77 59W
Isdell →, *Australia* **112 C3** 16 27 S 124 51 E
Ise, *Japan* **63 C8** 34 25N 136 45 E
Ise-Heiya, *Japan* **63 C8** 34 40N 136 30 E
Ise-Wan, *Japan* **63 C8** 34 43N 136 43 E
Isefjord, *Denmark* **15 J5** 55 53N 11 50 E
Iseltwald, *Switz.* **28 C5** 46 43N 7 58 E
Isenthal, *Switz.* **29 C7** 46 55N 8 34 E
Iseo, *Italy* **38 C7** 45 40N 10 3 E
Iseo, L. d', *Italy* **38 C7** 45 45N 10 3 E
Iseramagazi, *Tanzania* **106 C3** 4 37 S 32 10 E
Isère □, *France* **25 C9** 45 15N 5 40 E
Isère →, *France* **25 D8** 44 59N 4 51 E
Iserlohn, *Germany* **26 D3** 51 22N 7 40 E
Isérnia, *Italy* **41 A7** 41 35N 14 12 E
Isesaki, *Japan* **63 A11** 36 19N 139 12 E
Iseyin, *Nigeria* **101 D5** 8 0N 3 36 E
Isfara, *Tajikistan* **55 C5** 40 7N 70 38 E
Isherton, *Guyana* **153 C6** 2 20N 59 25W
Ishigaki-Shima, *Japan* **61 M2** 24 20N 124 10 E
Ishikari-Gawa →, *Japan* **60 C10** 43 15N 141 23 E
Ishikari-Sammyaku, *Japan* **60 C11** 43 30N 143 0 E
Ishikari-Wan, *Japan* **60 C10** 43 25N 141 1 E
Ishikawa □, *Japan* **63 A8** 36 30N 136 30 E
Ishim, *Russia* **56 D7** 56 10N 69 30 E
Ishim →, *Russia* **56 D8** 57 45N 71 10 E
Ishimbay, *Russia* **54 E5** 53 28N 56 2 E
Ishinomaki, *Japan* **60 E10** 38 32N 141 20 E
Ishioka, *Japan* **63 A12** 36 11N 140 16 E
Ishizuchi-Yama, *Japan* **62 D5** 33 45N 133 6 E
Ishkashim = Eshkamish, *Tajikistan* **55 E5** 36 44N 71 37 E
Ishkuman, *Pakistan* **81 A5** 36 30N 73 50 E
Ishmi, *Albania* **44 C1** 41 33N 19 34 E
Ishpeming, *U.S.A.* **134 B2** 46 29N 87 40W
Ishurdi, *Bangla.* **78 C2** 24 9N 89 3 E
Isigny-sur-Mer, *France* **22 C5** 49 19N 1 6W
Isil Kul, *Russia* **56 D8** 54 55N 71 16 E
Isiolo, *Kenya* **106 B4** 0 24N 37 33 E
Isiolo □, *Kenya* **106 B4** 2 30N 37 30 E
Isipingo Beach, *S. Africa* **105 E5** 30 0 S 30 57 E
Isiro, *Zaïre* **106 B2** 2 53N 27 40 E
Isisford, *Australia* **114 C3** 24 15 S 144 21 E
Iskander, *Uzbekistan* **55 C4** 41 36N 69 41 E
İskederun, *Turkey* **88 E7** 36 9N 36 35 E
İskenderun, *Turkey* **88 E7** 36 32N 36 10 E
İskenderun Körfezi, *Turkey* **88 E6** 36 40N 35 50 E
Iski-Naukat, *Kirghizia* **55 C6** 40 16N 72 36 E
İskilip, *Turkey* **52 F6** 40 45N 34 29 E
Iskŭr →, *Bulgaria* **43 D9** 43 45N 24 25 E
Iskŭr, Yazovir, *Bulgaria* **43 E8** 42 23N 23 30 E
Iskut →, *Canada* **130 B2** 56 45N 131 49W
Isla →, *U.K.* **18 E5** 56 32N 3 20W
Isla Cristina, *Spain* **37 H3** 37 13N 7 17W
Isla Vista, *U.S.A.* **145 L7** 34 25N 119 53W
İslâhiye, *Turkey* **88 E7** 37 0N 36 35 E
Islamabad, *Pakistan* **79 B4** 33 40N 73 10 E
Islamkot, *Pakistan* **80 G4** 24 42N 70 13 E
Islampur, *India* **82 F2** 17 2N 74 20 E
Island →, *Canada* **130 A4** 60 25N 121 12W
Island Bay, *Phil.* **71 G2** 9 6N 118 10 E
Island Falls, *Canada* **128 C3** 49 35N 81 20W
Island Falls, *U.S.A.* **129 C6** 46 1N 68 16W
Island L., *Canada* **131 C10** 53 47N 94 25W
Island Lagoon, *Australia* **116 A2** 31 30 S 136 40 E
Island Pond, *U.S.A.* **137 B13** 44 49N 71 53W
Islands, B. of, *Canada* **129 C8** 49 11N 58 15W
Islands, B. of, *N.Z.* **118 B3** 35 15 S 174 6 E
Islay, *U.K.* **18 F2** 55 46N 6 10W
Isle →, *France* **24 D3** 44 55N 0 15W
Isle aux Morts, *Canada* **129 C8** 47 35N 59 0W
Isle of Wight □, *U.K.* **17 G6** 50 40N 1 20W
Isle Royale, *U.S.A.* **138 A10** 48 0N 88 54W
Isleta, *U.S.A.* **143 J10** 34 55N 106 42W
Isleton, *U.S.A.* **144 G5** 38 10N 121 37W
Ismail, *Ukraine* **52 D3** 45 22N 28 46 E
Ismâ'ilîya, *Egypt* **94 H8** 30 37N 32 18 E
Ismaning, *Germany* **27 G7** 48 14N 11 41 E
Ismay, *U.S.A.* **138 B2** 46 30N 104 48W
Isna, *Egypt* **94 B3** 25 17N 32 30 E
Isogstalo, *India* **81 B8** 34 15N 78 46 E
Isola del Gran Sasso d'Italia, *Italy* **39 F10** 42 30N 13 40 E
Ísola del Liri, *Italy* **40 A6** 41 39N 13 32 E
Ísola della Scala, *Italy* **38 C8** 45 16N 11 0 E
Ísola di Capo Rizzuto, *Italy* **41 D10** 38 56N 17 5 E
İsparta, *Turkey* **88 E4** 37 47N 30 30 E
İsparta □, *Turkey* **88 E4** 38 0N 31 0 E
Isperikh, *Bulgaria* **43 D11** 43 43N 26 50 E
Íspica, *Italy* **41 F7** 36 47N 14 53 E
İspir, *Turkey* **53 F9** 40 28N 41 1 E
Israel ■, *Asia* **91 D3** 32 0N 34 50 E
Issano, *Guyana* **153 B6** 5 49N 59 26W
Issia, *Ivory C.* **100 D3** 6 33N 6 33W
Issoire, *France* **24 C7** 45 32N 3 15 E
Issoudun, *France* **23 F8** 46 57N 2 0 E
Issyk-Kul, *Kirghizia* **55 B8** 42 26N 76 12 E
Issyk-Kul, Ozero, *Kirghizia* **55 B8** 42 25N 77 15 E
Ist, *Croatia* **39 D11** 44 17N 14 47 E
Istaihah, *U.A.E.* **85 F7** 23 19N 54 4 E
İstanbul, *Turkey* **88 C3** 41 0N 29 0 E
İstanbul □, *Turkey* **88 C3** 41 0N 29 0 E
Istiaía, *Greece* **45 F5** 38 57N 23 9 E
Istmina, *Colombia* **152 B2** 5 10N 76 39W
Istok, *Serbia* **42 E5** 42 45N 20 24 E
Istokpoga, L., *U.S.A.* **135 M5** 27 23N 81 17W
Istra, *Croatia* **39 C11** 45 10N 14 0 E
Istra, *Russia* **51 D10** 55 55N 36 50 E
İstranca Dağları, *Turkey* **43 F12** 41 48N 27 36 E
Istres, *France* **25 E8** 43 31N 4 59 E
Istria = Istra, *Croatia* **39 C11** 45 10N 14 0 E
Isulan, *Phil.* **71 H5** 6 30N 124 29 E
Itá, *Paraguay* **158 B4** 25 29 S 57 21W
'Itāb, *Yemen* **87 D5** 15 20N 51 29 E
Itabaiana, *Paraíba, Brazil* **154 C4** 7 18 S 35 19W
Itabaiana, *Sergipe, Brazil* **154 D4** 10 41 S 37 37W
Itabaianinha, *Brazil* **154 D4** 11 16 S 37 47W
Itaberaba, *Brazil* **155 D3** 12 32 S 40 18W
Itaberaí, *Brazil* **155 E2** 16 2 S 49 48W
Itabira, *Brazil* **155 E3** 19 37 S 43 13W
Itabirito, *Brazil* **155 F3** 20 15 S 43 48W
Itaboca, *Brazil* **153 D5** 4 50 S 62 40W
Itabuna, *Brazil* **155 D4** 14 48 S 39 16W
Itacajá, *Brazil* **154 C2** 8 19 S 47 46W
Itacaunas →, *Brazil* **154 C2** 5 21 S 49 8W
Itacoatiara, *Brazil* **153 D6** 3 8 S 58 25W
Itacuaí →, *Brazil* **156 A3** 4 20 S 70 12W
Itaguaçu, *Brazil* **155 E3** 19 48 S 40 51W
Itaguari →, *Brazil* **155 D3** 14 11 S 44 40W
Itaguatins, *Brazil* **154 C2** 5 47 S 47 29W
Itaim →, *Brazil* **154 C3** 7 2 S 42 2W
Itainópolis, *Brazil* **154 C3** 7 24 S 41 31W
Itaipu Dam, *Brazil* **159 B5** 25 30 S 54 30W
Itaituba, *Brazil* **153 D6** 4 10 S 55 50W
Itajaí, *Brazil* **159 B6** 27 50 S 48 39W
Itajubá, *Brazil* **155 F2** 22 24 S 45 30W
Itajuípe, *Brazil* **155 D4** 14 41 S 39 22W
Itaka, *Tanzania* **107 D3** 8 50 S 32 49 E
Itako, *Japan* **63 B12** 35 56N 140 33 E
Italy ■, *Europe* **11 G8** 42 0N 13 0 E
Itamataré, *Brazil* **154 B2** 2 16 S 46 24W
Itambacuri, *Brazil* **155 E3** 18 1 S 41 42W
Itambé, *Brazil* **155 E3** 15 15 S 40 37W
Itampolo, *Madag.* **105 C7** 24 41 S 43 57 E
Itanhauã →, *Brazil* **153 D5** 4 45 S 63 48W
Itanhém, *Brazil* **155 E3** 17 9 S 40 20W
Itano, *Japan* **62 C6** 34 7N 134 28 E
Itapaci, *Brazil* **155 D2** 14 57 S 49 34W
Itapagé, *Brazil* **154 B4** 3 41 S 39 34W
Itaparica, I. de, *Brazil* **155 D4** 12 54 S 38 42W
Itapebi, *Brazil* **155 E4** 15 56 S 39 32W
Itapecuru-Mirim, *Brazil* **154 B3** 3 24 S 44 20W
Itaperuna, *Brazil* **155 F3** 21 10 S 41 54W
Itapetinga, *Brazil* **155 E3** 15 15 S 40 15W
Itapetininga, *Brazil* **159 A6** 23 36 S 48 7W
Itapeva, *Brazil* **159 A6** 23 59 S 48 59W
Itapicuru →, *Bahia, Brazil* **154 D4** 11 47 S 37 32W
Itapicuru →, *Maranhão, Brazil* **154 B3** 2 52 S 44 12W
Itapinima, *Brazil* **157 B5** 5 25 S 60 44W
Itapipoca, *Brazil* **154 B4** 3 30 S 39 35W
Itapiranga, *Brazil* **153 D6** 2 45 S 58 1W
Itapiúna, *Brazil* **154 B4** 4 33 S 38 57W
Itaporanga, *Brazil* **154 C4** 7 18 S 38 0W
Itapuá □, *Paraguay* **159 B4** 26 40 S 55 40W
Itapuranga, *Brazil* **155 E2** 15 40 S 49 59W
Itaquari, *Brazil* **155 F3** 20 20 S 40 25W
Itaquatiara, *Brazil* **153 D6** 2 58 S 58 30W
Itaquí, *Brazil* **158 B4** 29 8 S 56 30W
Itararé, *Brazil* **159 A6** 24 6 S 49 23W
Itarsi, *India* **80 H7** 22 36N 77 51 E
Itarumã, *Brazil* **155 E1** 18 42 S 51 25W
Itatí, *Argentina* **158 B4** 27 16 S 58 15W
Itatira, *Brazil* **154 B4** 4 30 S 39 37W
Itatuba, *Brazil* **157 B5** 5 46 S 63 20W
Itatupa, *Brazil* **153 D7** 0 37 S 51 12W
Itaueira, *Brazil* **154 C3** 7 36 S 43 2W
Itaueira →, *Brazil* **154 C3** 6 41 S 42 55W
Itaúna, *Brazil* **155 F3** 20 4 S 44 34W
Itbayat, *Phil.* **70 A3** 20 47N 121 51 E
Itbayat I., *Phil.* **70 A3** 20 46N 121 50 E
Itchen →, *U.K.* **17 G6** 50 57N 1 20W
Ite, *Peru* **156 D3** 17 55 S 70 57W
Itéa, *Greece* **45 F4** 38 25N 22 25 E
Itezhi Tezhi, L., *Zambia* **107 F2** 15 30 S 25 30 E
Ithaca = Itháki, *Greece* **45 F2** 38 25N 20 40 E
Ithaca, *U.S.A.* **137 D8** 42 27N 76 30W
Itháki, *Greece* **45 F2** 38 25N 20 40 E
Itinga, *Brazil* **155 E3** 16 36 S 41 47W
Itiquira, *Brazil* **157 D7** 17 12 S 54 7W
Itiquira →, *Brazil* **157 D6** 17 18 S 56 44W
Itiruçu, *Brazil* **155 D3** 13 31 S 40 9W
Itiúba, *Brazil* **154 D4** 10 43 S 39 51W
Ito, *Japan* **63 C11** 34 58N 139 5 E
Itoigawa, *Japan* **61 F8** 37 2N 137 51 E
Iton →, *France* **22 C8** 49 9N 1 12 E
Itonamas →, *Bolivia* **157 C5** 12 28 S 64 24W
Itsa, *Egypt* **94 J7** 29 15N 30 47 E
Itsukaichi, *Japan* **62 C4** 34 22N 132 22 E
Itsuki, *Japan* **62 E2** 32 24N 130 50 E
Íttiri, *Italy* **40 B1** 40 38N 8 32 E
Ittoqqortoormiit = Scoresbysund, *Greenland* **6 B6** 70 20N 23 0W
Itu, *Brazil* **159 A6** 23 17 S 47 15W
Itu, *Nigeria* **101 D6** 5 10N 7 58 E
Ituaçu, *Brazil* **155 D3** 13 50 S 41 18W
Ituango, *Colombia* **152 B2** 7 4N 75 45W
Ituiutaba, *Brazil* **155 E2** 19 0 S 49 25W
Itumbiara, *Brazil* **155 E2** 18 20 S 49 10W

Junín de los Andes 213

Jelgava, Latvia 13 H17 56 41N 23 49 E
Jelica, Serbia 42 D5 43 50N 20 17 E
Jelli, Sudan 95 F3 5 25N 31 45 E
Jellicoe, Canada 128 C2 49 40N 87 30W
Jelšava, Slovak Rep. 31 C13 48 37N 20 15 E
Jemaja, Indonesia 74 B3 3 5N 105 45 E
Jemaluang, Malaysia 77 L4 2 16N 103 52 E
Jemappes, Belgium 21 H3 50 27N 3 54 E
Jember, Indonesia 75 D4 8 11 S 113 41 E
Jemeppe, Belgium 21 G7 50 37N 5 30 E
Jemnice, Czech. 30 B8 49 1N 15 34 E
Jena, Germany 26 E7 50 56N 11 33 E
Jena, U.S.A. 139 K8 31 41N 92 8W
Jenbach, Austria 30 D4 47 24N 11 47 E
Jendouba, Tunisia 96 A1 36 29N 8 47 E
Jeneponto, Indonesia 72 C1 5 41 S 119 42 E
Jenkins, U.S.A. 134 G4 37 10N 82 38W
Jenner, U.S.A. 144 G3 38 27N 123 7W
Jennings, La., U.S.A. 139 K8 30 13N 92 40W
Jennings, Mo., U.S.A. 140 F6 38 43N 90 16W
Jennings →, Canada 130 B2 59 38N 132 5W
Jepara, Indonesia 75 D3 7 40 S 109 14 E
Jeparit, Australia 116 D5 36 8 S 142 1 E
Jequié, Brazil 155 D3 13 51 S 40 5W
Jequitaí →, Brazil 155 E3 17 4 S 44 50W
Jequitinhonha, Brazil 155 E3 16 30 S 41 0W
Jequitinhonha →, Brazil 155 E4 15 51 S 38 53W
Jerada, Morocco 99 B4 34 17N 2 10W
Jerantut, Malaysia 77 L4 3 56N 102 22 E
Jérémie, Haiti 149 C5 18 40N 74 10W
Jeremoabo, Brazil 154 D4 10 4 S 38 21W
Jerez, Punta, Mexico 147 C5 22 58N 97 40W
Jerez de García Salinas, Mexico 146 C4 22 39N 103 0W
Jerez de la Frontera, Spain 37 J4 36 41N 6 7W
Jerez de los Caballeros, Spain 37 G4 38 20N 6 45W
Jericho = Arīḥā, Syria 84 C3 35 49N 36 35 E
Jericho = El Arīḥā, Jordan 91 D4 31 52N 35 27 E
Jericho, Australia 114 C4 23 38 S 146 6 E
Jerichow, Germany 26 C8 52 30N 12 2 E
Jerico Springs, U.S.A. 140 G2 37 37N 94 1W
Jerilderie, Australia 117 C6 35 20 S 145 41 E
Jermyn, U.S.A. 137 E9 41 31N 75 31W
Jerome, U.S.A. 143 J8 34 45N 112 7W
Jersey, Chan. Is. 17 H5 49 13N 2 7W
Jersey City, U.S.A. 137 F10 40 44N 74 4W
Jersey Shore, U.S.A. 136 E7 41 12N 77 15W
Jerseyville, U.S.A. 140 E6 39 7N 90 20W
Jerusalem, Israel 91 D4 31 47N 35 10 E
Jervis B., Australia 117 C9 35 8 S 150 46 E
Jesenice, Slovenia 39 B11 46 28N 14 3 E
Jeseník, Czech. 31 B10 50 0N 17 8 E
Jesenké, Slovak Rep. 31 C13 48 20N 20 10 E
Jesselton = Kota Kinabalu, Malaysia 75 A5 6 0N 116 4 E
Jessnitz, Germany 26 D8 51 42N 12 19 E
Jessore, Bangla. 78 D2 23 10N 89 10 E
Jesup, Ga., U.S.A. 135 K5 31 36N 81 53W
Jesup, Iowa, U.S.A. 140 B4 42 29N 92 4W
Jesús, Peru 156 B2 7 15 S 78 25W
Jesús Carranza, Mexico 147 D5 17 28N 95 1W
Jesús María, Argentina 158 C3 30 59 S 64 5W
Jetafe, Phil. 71 F5 10 9N 124 9 E
Jetmore, U.S.A. 139 F5 38 4N 99 54W
Jetpur, India 80 J4 21 45N 70 10 E
Jette, Belgium 21 G4 50 53N 4 20 E
Jevnaker, Norway 14 D4 60 15N 10 26 E
Jewell, U.S.A. 140 B3 42 20N 93 39W
Jewett, Ohio, U.S.A. 136 F3 40 22N 81 2W
Jewett, Tex., U.S.A. 139 K6 31 22N 96 9W
Jewett City, U.S.A. 137 E13 41 36N 72 0W
Jeyḥūnābād, Iran 85 C6 34 58N 48 59 E
Jeypore, India 82 E6 18 50N 82 38 E
Jeziorak, Jezioro, Poland 47 B6 53 40N 19 35 E
Jeziorany, Poland 47 B7 53 58N 20 46 E
Jeziorka →, Poland 47 D7 51 59N 20 57 E
Jhajjar, India 80 E7 28 37N 76 42 E
Jhal Jhao, Pakistan 79 D2 26 20N 65 35 E
Jhalakati, Bangla. 78 D3 22 39N 90 12 E
Jhalawar, India 80 G7 24 40N 76 10 E
Jhang Maghiana, Pakistan 79 C4 31 15N 72 22 E
Jhansi, India 81 G8 25 30N 78 36 E
Jharia, India 81 H12 23 45N 86 26 E
Jharsuguda, India 82 D7 21 56N 84 5 E
Jhelum, Pakistan 79 B4 33 0N 73 45 E
Jhelum →, Pakistan 80 D5 31 20N 72 10 E
Jhunjhunu, India 80 E6 28 10N 75 30 E
Ji Xian, Hebei, China 66 F8 37 35N 115 30 E
Ji Xian, Henan, China 66 G8 35 22N 114 5 E
Ji Xian, Shanxi, China 66 F6 36 7N 110 40 E
Jia Xian, Henan, China 66 H7 33 59N 113 12 E
Jia Xian, Shaanxi, China 66 E6 38 12N 110 28 E
Jiading, China 69 B13 31 22N 121 15 E
Jiahe, China 69 E9 25 38N 112 19 E
Jiali, Taiwan 69 F13 23 12N 120 10 E
Jialing Jiang →, China 68 C6 29 30N 106 20 E
Jiamusi, China 65 B8 46 40N 130 26 E
Ji'an, Jiangxi, China 69 D10 27 6N 114 59 E
Ji'an, Jilin, China 67 D14 41 5N 126 10 E
Jianchang, China 67 D11 40 55N 120 35 E
Jianchangying, China 67 D10 40 10N 118 50 E
Jianchuan, China 68 D2 26 38N 99 55 E
Jiande, China 69 C12 29 23N 119 15 E
Jiangbei, China 68 C6 29 40N 106 34 E
Jiangcheng, China 68 F3 22 36N 101 52 E
Jiangdi, China 68 D4 26 57N 103 37 E
Jiange, China 68 A5 32 4N 105 32 E
Jiangjin, China 68 C6 29 14N 106 14 E
Jiangkou, China 68 D7 27 40N 108 49 E
Jiangle, China 69 D11 26 42N 117 23 E
Jiangling, China 69 B9 30 25N 112 12 E
Jiangmen, China 69 F9 22 32N 113 0 E
Jiangshan, China 69 C12 28 40N 118 37 E
Jiangsu □, China 67 H10 33 0N 120 0 E
Jiangxi □, China 69 D10 27 30N 116 0 E
Jiangyin, China 69 B13 31 54N 120 17 E
Jiangyong, China 69 E8 25 20N 111 22 E
Jiangyou, China 68 B5 31 44N 104 43 E
Jianhe, China 68 D7 26 37N 108 31 E
Jianli, China 69 C9 29 46N 112 56 E
Jianning, China 69 D11 26 50N 116 50 E
Jian'ou, China 69 D12 27 3N 118 17 E
Jianshi, China 68 B7 30 37N 109 38 E
Jianshui, China 68 F4 23 36N 102 43 E
Jianyang, Fujian, China 69 D12 27 20N 118 5 E
Jianyang, Sichuan, China 68 B5 30 24N 104 33 E
Jiao Xian, China 67 F11 36 18N 120 1 E
Jiaohe, Hebei, China 66 E9 38 2N 116 20 E
Jiaohe, Jilin, China 67 C14 43 40N 127 22 E
Jiaoling, China 69 E11 24 41N 116 12 E
Jiaozhou Wan, China 67 F11 36 5N 120 10 E
Jiaozuo, China 66 G7 35 16N 113 12 E
Jiashan, China 69 A11 32 46N 117 59 E
Jiawang, China 67 G9 34 28N 117 26 E
Jiaxiang, China 66 G9 35 25N 116 20 E
Jiaxing, China 69 B13 30 49N 120 45 E
Jiayi, Taiwan 69 F13 23 30N 120 24 E
Jiayu, China 69 C9 29 55N 113 55 E
Jibão, Serra do, Brazil 155 D3 14 48 S 45 0W
Jibiya, Nigeria 101 C6 13 5N 7 12 E
Jibou, Romania 46 B4 47 15N 23 17 E
Jibuti = Djibouti ■, Africa 90 E3 12 0N 43 0 E
Jicarón, I., Panama 148 E3 7 10N 81 50W
Jičín, Czech. 30 A8 50 25N 15 28 E
Jiddah, Si. Arabia 86 B2 21 29N 39 10 E
Jieshou, China 66 H8 33 18N 115 22 E
Jiexiu, China 66 F6 37 2N 111 55 E
Jieyang, China 69 F11 23 35N 116 21 E
Jigawa □, Nigeria 101 C6 12 0N 9 45 E
Jiggalong, Australia 112 D3 23 21 S 120 47 E
Jihlava, Czech. 30 B8 49 28N 15 35 E
Jihlava →, Czech. 30 C9 48 55N 16 36 E
Jihočeský □, Czech. 30 B7 49 8N 14 35 E
Jihomoravský □, Czech. 31 B9 49 5N 16 30 E
Jijel, Algeria 99 A6 36 52N 5 50 E
Jijiga, Ethiopia 90 F3 9 20N 42 50 E
Jijona, Spain 35 G4 38 34N 0 30W
Jikamshi, Nigeria 101 C6 12 12N 7 45 E
Jilin, China 67 C14 43 44N 126 30 E
Jilin □, China 67 C13 44 0N 127 0 E
Jiloca →, Spain 34 D3 41 21N 1 39W
Jilong, Taiwan 69 E13 25 8N 121 42 E
Jílové, Czech. 30 B7 49 52N 14 29 E
Jima, Ethiopia 95 F4 7 40N 36 47 E
Jimbolia, Romania 46 D1 45 47N 20 43 E
Jimena de la Frontera, Spain 37 J5 36 27N 5 24W
Jimenbuen, Australia 117 D8 36 42 S 148 53 E
Jiménez, Mexico 146 B4 27 10N 104 54W
Jimenez, Phil. 71 G4 8 20N 123 50 E
Jimo, China 67 F11 36 23N 120 30 E
Jin Jiang →, China 69 C10 28 24N 115 48 E
Jin Xian, Hebei, China 66 E8 38 2N 115 2 E
Jin Xian, Liaoning, China 67 E11 38 55N 121 42 E
Jinan, China 66 F9 36 38N 117 1 E
Jincheng, China 66 G7 35 29N 112 50 E
Jinchuan, China 68 B4 31 30N 102 3 E
Jind, India 80 E7 29 19N 76 22 E
Jindabyne, Australia 117 D8 36 25 S 148 35 E
Jindrichuv Hradeç, Czech. 30 B8 49 10N 15 2 E
Jing He →, China 66 G5 34 27N 109 4 E
Jing Shan, China 69 B8 31 20N 111 35 E
Jing Xian, Anhui, China 69 B12 30 38N 118 25 E
Jing Xian, Hunan, China 68 D7 26 33N 109 40 E
Jing'an, China 69 C10 28 50N 115 17 E
Jingbian, China 66 F5 37 20N 108 30 E
Jingchuan, China 66 G4 35 20N 107 20 E
Jingde, China 69 B12 30 15N 118 27 E
Jingdezhen, China 69 C11 29 20N 117 11 E
Jingdong, China 68 E3 24 23N 100 47 E
Jinggu, China 68 F3 23 35N 100 41 E
Jinghai, China 66 E9 38 55N 116 55 E
Jinghong, China 68 F3 22 0N 100 45 E
Jingjiang, China 69 A13 32 2N 120 16 E
Jingle, China 66 E6 38 20N 111 55 E
Jingmen, China 69 B9 31 0N 112 10 E
Jingning, China 66 G3 35 30N 105 43 E
Jingpo Hu, China 67 C15 43 55N 128 55 E
Jingshan, China 69 B9 31 1N 113 7 E
Jingtai, China 66 F3 37 10N 104 6 E
Jingxi, China 68 F6 23 8N 106 27 E
Jingxing, China 66 E8 38 2N 114 8 E
Jingyang, China 66 G5 34 30N 108 50 E
Jingyu, China 67 C14 42 25N 126 45 E
Jingyuan, China 66 F3 36 30N 104 40 E
Jingziguan, China 66 H6 33 15N 111 0 E
Jinhua, China 69 C12 29 8N 119 38 E
Jining, Nei Mongol Zizhiqu, China 66 D7 41 5N 113 0 E
Jining, Shandong, China 66 G9 35 22N 116 34 E
Jinja, Uganda 106 B3 0 25N 33 12 E
Jinjang, Malaysia 77 L3 3 13N 101 39 E
Jinji, China 66 F4 37 58N 106 8 E
Jinjiang, Fujian, China 69 E12 24 43N 118 33 E
Jinjiang, Yunnan, China 68 D3 26 14N 100 34 E
Jinjie, China 68 F6 23 15N 107 18 E
Jinjini, Ghana 100 D4 7 26N 3 42W
Jinkou, China 69 B10 30 20N 114 8 E
Jinmen Dao, China 69 E12 24 25N 118 25 E
Jinning, China 68 E4 24 38N 102 38 E
Jinotega, Nic. 148 D2 13 6N 85 59W
Jinotepe, Nic. 148 D2 11 50N 86 10W
Jinping, Guizhou, China 68 D7 26 41N 109 10 E
Jinping, Yunnan, China 68 F4 22 45N 103 18 E
Jinsha, China 68 D6 27 29N 106 12 E
Jinsha Jiang →, China 68 C5 28 50N 104 36 E
Jinshan, China 69 B13 30 54N 121 10 E
Jinshi, China 69 C8 29 40N 111 50 E
Jintan, China 69 B12 31 42N 119 36 E
Jintotolo Channel, Phil. 71 F4 11 48N 123 5 E
Jinxi, Jiangxi, China 69 D11 27 56N 116 45 E
Jinxi, Liaoning, China 67 D11 40 52N 120 50 E
Jinxian, China 69 C11 28 26N 116 17 E
Jinxiang, China 66 G9 35 5N 116 22 E
Jinyun, China 69 C13 28 35N 120 5 E
Jinzhai, China 69 B10 31 40N 115 53 E
Jinzhou, China 67 D11 41 5N 121 3 E
Jiparaná →, Brazil 157 B5 8 3 S 62 52W
Jipijapa, Ecuador 152 D1 1 0 S 80 40W
Jiquilpan, Mexico 146 D4 19 57N 102 42W
Jirwān, Si. Arabia 87 B5 23 27N 50 53 E
Jishan, China 66 G6 35 34N 110 58 E
Jishou, China 68 C7 28 21N 109 43 E
Jishui, China 69 D10 27 12N 115 8 E
Jisr ash Shughūr, Syria 84 C3 35 49N 36 18 E
Jitarning, Australia 113 F2 32 48 S 117 57 E
Jitra, Malaysia 77 J3 6 16N 100 25 E
Jiu →, Romania 46 F4 43 47N 23 48 E
Jiudengkou, China 66 E4 39 56N 106 40 E
Jiujiang, Guangdong, China 69 F9 22 50N 113 0 E
Jiujiang, Jiangxi, China 69 C10 29 42N 115 58 E
Jiuling Shan, China 69 C10 28 40N 114 40 E
Jiulong, China 68 C3 28 57N 101 31 E
Jiutai, China 67 B13 44 10N 125 50 E
Jiuxiangcheng, China 66 H8 33 12N 114 50 E
Jiuxincheng, China 66 E8 39 17N 115 59 E
Jiuyuhang, China 69 B12 30 18N 119 56 E
Jixi, Anhui, China 69 B12 30 5N 118 34 E
Jixi, Heilongjiang, China 67 B16 45 20N 130 50 E
Jiyang, China 67 F9 37 0N 117 12 E
Jīz', W. →, Yemen 87 C6 16 12N 52 14 E
Jīzān, Si. Arabia 86 C3 17 0N 42 20 E
Jize, China 66 F8 36 54N 114 56 E
Jizera →, Czech. 30 A7 50 10N 14 43 E
Jizō-Zaki, Japan 62 B5 35 34N 133 20 E
Joaçaba, Brazil 159 B5 27 5 S 51 31W
Joaíma, Brazil 155 E3 16 39 S 41 2W
João, Brazil 154 B1 2 46 S 50 59W
João Amaro, Brazil 155 D3 12 46 S 40 22W
João Câmara, Brazil 154 C4 5 32 S 35 48W
João Pessoa, Brazil 154 C5 7 10 S 34 52W
João Pinheiro, Brazil 155 E2 17 45 S 46 10W
Joaquim Távora, Brazil 155 F2 23 30 S 49 58W
Joaquín V. González, Argentina 158 B3 25 10 S 64 0W
Jobourg, Nez de, France 22 C5 49 41N 1 57W
Jódar, Spain 35 H1 37 50N 3 21W
Jodhpur, India 80 F5 26 23N 73 8 E
Joensuu, Finland 48 B4 62 37N 29 49 E
Jœuf, France 23 C13 49 12N 6 0 E
Jofane, Mozam. 105 C5 21 15 S 34 18 E
Joggins, Canada 129 C7 45 42N 64 27W
Jogjakarta = Yogyakarta, Indonesia 75 D4 7 49 S 110 22 E
Jōhana, Japan 63 A8 36 30N 136 57 E
Johannesburg, S. Africa 105 D4 26 10 S 28 2 E
Johannesburg, U.S.A. 145 K9 35 22N 117 38W
Jōhen, Japan 62 E4 32 58N 132 32 E
John Day, U.S.A. 142 D4 44 25N 118 57W
John Day →, U.S.A. 142 D3 45 44N 120 39W
John H. Kerr Reservoir, U.S.A. 135 G6 36 36N 78 18W
John o' Groats, U.K. 18 C5 58 39N 3 3W
Johnnie, U.S.A. 145 J10 36 25N 116 5W
John's Ra., Australia 114 C1 21 55 S 133 23 E
Johnson, U.S.A. 139 G4 37 34N 101 45W
Johnson City, Ill., U.S.A. 140 G8 37 49N 88 56W
Johnson City, N.Y., U.S.A. 137 D9 42 7N 75 58W
Johnson City, Tenn., U.S.A. 135 G4 36 19N 82 21W
Johnson City, Tex., U.S.A. 139 K5 30 17N 98 25W
Johnsonburg, U.S.A. 136 E6 41 29N 78 41W
Johnsondale, U.S.A. 145 K8 35 58N 118 32W
Johnson's Crossing, Canada 130 A2 60 29N 133 18W
Johnsonville, N.Z. 118 H3 41 13 S 174 48 E
Johnston, L., Australia 113 F3 32 25 S 120 30 E
Johnston Falls = Mambilima Falls, Zambia 107 E2 10 31 S 28 45 E
Johnston I., Pac. Oc. 123 F11 17 10N 169 8W
Johnstone Str., Canada 130 C3 50 28N 126 0W
Johnstown, N.Y., U.S.A. 137 C10 43 0N 74 22W
Johnstown, Pa., U.S.A. 136 F6 40 20N 78 55W
Johor □, Malaysia 74 B2 2 0N 103 30 E
Johor Baharu, Malaysia 77 M4 1 28N 103 46 E
Joigny, France 23 E10 47 58N 3 20 E
Joinvile, Brazil 159 B6 26 15 S 48 55W
Joinville, France 23 D12 48 27N 5 10 E
Joinville I., Antarctica 7 C18 65 0 S 55 30W
Jojutla, Mexico 147 D5 18 37N 99 11W
Jokkmokk, Sweden 12 C15 66 35N 19 50 E
Jökulsá á Bru →, Iceland 12 D6 65 40N 14 16W
Jökulsá á Fjöllum →, Iceland 12 C5 66 10N 16 30W
Jolfā, Āzarbājān-e Sharqī, Iran 84 B5 38 57N 45 38 E
Jolfā, Eşfahan, Iran 85 C6 32 58N 51 37 E
Joliet, U.S.A. 141 C8 41 32N 88 5W
Joliette, Canada 128 C5 46 3N 73 24W
Jolo, Phil. 71 H3 6 0N 121 0 E
Jolo Group, Phil. 71 J3 6 0N 121 9 E
Jolon, U.S.A. 144 K5 35 58N 121 9W
Jomalig, Phil. 70 D4 14 42N 122 22 E
Jombang, Indonesia 75 D4 7 33 S 112 14 E
Jomda, China 68 B2 31 28N 98 12 E
Jome, Indonesia 72 B3 1 16 S 127 30 E
Jomfruland, Norway 15 F3 58 52N 9 36 E
Jönåker, Sweden 15 F10 58 44N 16 40 E
Jonava, Lithuania 50 D4 55 8N 24 12 E
Jones, Phil. 70 C3 16 33N 121 42 E
Jones Sound, Canada 6 B3 76 0N 85 0W
Jonesboro, Ark., U.S.A. 139 H9 35 50N 90 42W
Jonesboro, Ill., U.S.A. 139 G10 37 27N 89 16W
Jonesboro, La., U.S.A. 139 J8 32 15N 92 43W
Jonesburg, U.S.A. 140 F5 38 51N 91 18W
Jonesport, U.S.A. 129 D6 44 32N 67 37W
Jonesville, Ind., U.S.A. 141 E11 39 5N 85 54W
Jonesville, Mich., U.S.A. 141 C12 41 59N 84 40W
Jonglei, Sudan 95 F3 6 25N 30 50 E
Jonglei □, Sudan 95 F3 7 30N 32 30 E
Joniškis, Lithuania 50 C3 56 13N 23 35 E
Jönköping, Sweden 13 H13 57 45N 14 10 E
Jönköpings län □, Sweden 13 H13 57 30N 14 30 E
Jonquière, Canada 129 C5 48 27N 71 14W
Jonsberg, Sweden 15 F10 58 30N 16 48 E
Jonsered, Sweden 15 G6 57 45N 12 10 E
Jonzac, France 24 C3 45 27N 0 28W
Joplin, U.S.A. 139 G7 37 6N 94 31W
Jordan, U.S.A. 142 C10 47 19N 106 55W
Jordan ■, Asia 91 E5 31 0N 36 0 E
Jordan →, Asia 91 D4 31 48N 35 32 E
Jordan Valley, U.S.A. 142 E5 42 59N 117 3W
Jordânia, Brazil 155 E3 15 55 S 40 11W
Jordanów, Poland 31 B12 49 41N 19 49 E
Jorge, C., Chile 160 D1 51 40 S 75 35W
Jorhat, India 78 B5 26 45N 94 12 E
Jorm, Afghan. 79 A3 36 50N 70 52 E
Jörn, Sweden 12 D16 65 4N 20 1 E
Jorong, Indonesia 75 C4 3 58 S 114 56 E
Jorquera →, Chile 158 B2 28 3 S 69 58W
Jos, Nigeria 101 D6 9 53N 8 51 E
Jošanička Banja, Serbia 42 D5 43 24N 20 47 E
Jose Abad Santos, Phil. 71 J5 5 55N 125 39 E
José Batlle y Ordóñez, Uruguay 159 C4 33 20 S 55 10W
José de San Martín, Argentina 160 B2 44 4 S 70 26W
Jose Panganiban, Phil. 70 D4 14 17N 122 41 E
Joseni, Romania 46 C6 46 42N 25 29 E
Joseph, U.S.A. 142 D5 45 21N 117 14W
Joseph, L., Nfld., Canada 129 B6 52 45N 65 18W
Joseph, L., Ont., Canada 136 A5 45 10N 79 44W
Joseph Bonaparte G., Australia 112 B4 14 35 S 128 50 E
Joseph City, U.S.A. 143 J8 34 57N 110 20W
Joshua Tree, U.S.A. 145 L10 34 8N 116 19W
Joshua Tree National Monument, U.S.A. 145 M10 33 55N 116 0W
Josselin, France 22 E4 47 57N 2 33W
Jostedal, Norway 13 F9 61 35N 7 15 E
Jotunheimen, Norway 14 C2 61 35N 8 25 E
Jourdanton, U.S.A. 139 L5 28 55N 98 33W
Joure, Neths. 20 C7 52 58N 5 48 E
Joussard, Canada 130 B5 55 22N 115 50W
Jovellanos, Cuba 148 B3 22 40N 81 10W
Jovellar, Phil. 70 E4 13 4N 123 36 E
Jowai, India 78 C4 25 26N 92 12 E
Jowzjān □, Afghan. 79 A2 36 10N 66 0 E
Joyeuse, France 25 D8 44 29N 4 16 E
Józefów, Poland 47 C8 52 10N 21 11 E
Ju Xian, China 67 F10 36 35N 118 20 E
Juan Aldama, Mexico 146 C4 24 20N 103 23W
Juan Bautista Alberdi, Argentina 158 C3 34 26 S 61 48W
Juan de Fuca Str., Canada 144 B2 48 15N 124 0W
Juan de Nova, Ind. Oc. 105 B7 17 3 S 43 45 E
Juan Fernández, Arch. de, Pac. Oc. 123 L20 33 50 S 80 0W
Juan José Castelli, Argentina 158 B3 25 27 S 60 57W
Juan L. Lacaze, Uruguay 158 C4 34 26 S 57 25W
Juanjuí, Peru 156 B2 7 10 S 76 45W
Juárez, Argentina 158 D4 37 40 S 59 43W
Juárez, Mexico 145 N11 32 20N 115 57W
Juárez, Sierra de, Mexico 146 A1 32 0N 116 0W
Juatinga, Ponta de, Brazil 155 F3 23 17 S 44 30W
Juàzeiro, Brazil 154 C3 9 30 S 40 30W
Juàzeiro do Norte, Brazil 154 C4 7 10 S 39 18W
Jubay, Phil. 71 F5 11 33N 124 18 E
Jubayl, Lebanon 91 A4 34 5N 35 39 E
Jubbah, Si. Arabia 84 D4 28 2N 40 56 E
Jubbulpore = Jabalpur, India 81 H8 23 9N 79 58 E
Jübek, Germany 26 A5 54 31N 9 24 E
Jubga, Russia 53 D8 44 19N 38 48 E
Jubilee L., Australia 113 E4 29 0 S 126 50 E
Júcar →, Spain 35 F4 39 5N 0 10W
Júcaro, Cuba 148 B4 21 37N 78 51W
Juchitán, Mexico 147 D5 16 27N 95 5W
Judaea = Har Yehuda, Israel 91 D3 31 35N 34 57 E
Judenburg, Austria 30 D7 47 12N 14 38 E
Judith →, U.S.A. 142 C9 47 44N 109 39W
Judith, Pt., U.S.A. 137 E13 41 22N 71 29W
Judith Gap, U.S.A. 142 C9 46 41N 109 45W
Jufari →, Brazil 153 D5 1 13 S 62 0W
Jugoslavia = Yugoslavia ■, Europe 42 D5 44 0N 20 0 E
Juigalpa, Nic. 148 D2 12 6N 85 26W
Juillac, France 24 C5 45 20N 1 19 E
Juist, Germany 26 B2 53 40N 7 0 E
Juiz de Fora, Brazil 155 F3 21 43 S 43 19W
Jujuy □, Argentina 158 A2 23 20 S 65 40W
Julesburg, U.S.A. 138 E3 40 59N 102 16W
Juli, Peru 156 D4 16 10 S 69 25W
Julia Cr. →, Australia 114 C3 20 0 S 141 11 E
Julia Creek, Australia 114 C3 20 39 S 141 44 E
Juliaca, Peru 156 D3 15 25 S 70 10W
Julian, U.S.A. 145 M10 33 4N 116 38W
Julian Alps = Julijske Alpe, Slovenia 39 B11 46 15N 14 1 E
Julianakanaal, Neths. 21 F7 51 6N 5 52 E
Julianatop, Surinam 153 C6 3 40N 56 30W
Julianehåb, Greenland 6 C5 60 43N 46 0W
Jülich, Germany 26 E2 50 55N 6 20 E
Julierpass, Switz. 29 D9 46 28N 9 32 E
Julijske Alpe, Slovenia 39 B11 46 15N 14 1 E
Julimes, Mexico 146 B3 28 25N 105 27W
Jullundur, India 80 D6 31 20N 75 40 E
Julu, China 66 F8 37 15N 115 2 E
Jumbo, Zimbabwe 107 F3 17 30 S 30 58 E
Jumbo Pk., U.S.A. 145 J12 36 12N 114 11W
Jumentos Cays, Bahamas 149 B4 23 0N 75 40W
Jumet, Belgium 21 H4 50 27N 4 25 E
Jumilla, Spain 35 G3 38 28N 1 19W
Jumla, Nepal 81 E10 29 15N 82 13 E
Jumna = Yamuna →, India 81 G9 25 30N 81 53 E
Junagadh, India 80 J4 21 30N 70 30 E
Junaynah, Si. Arabia 86 B4 22 33N 46 18 E
Junction, Tex., U.S.A. 139 K5 30 29N 99 46W
Junction, Utah, U.S.A. 143 G7 38 14N 112 13W
Junction B., Australia 114 A1 11 52 S 133 55 E
Junction City, Kans., U.S.A. 138 F6 39 2N 96 50W
Junction City, Oreg., U.S.A. 142 D2 44 13N 123 12W
Junction Pt., Australia 114 A1 11 45 S 133 50 E
Jundah, Australia 114 C3 24 46 S 143 2 E
Jundiaí, Brazil 159 A6 24 30 S 47 0W
Juneau, U.S.A. 126 C6 58 18N 134 25W
Junee, Australia 117 C7 34 53 S 147 35 E
Jungfrau, Switz. 28 C5 46 32N 7 58 E
Junggar Pendi, China 64 B3 44 30N 86 0 E
Junglinster, Lux. 21 J8 49 43N 6 15 E
Jungshahi, Pakistan 80 G2 24 52N 67 44 E
Juniata →, U.S.A. 136 F7 40 30N 77 40W
Junín, Argentina 158 C3 34 33 S 60 57W
Junín, Peru 156 C2 11 12 S 76 0W
Junín □, Peru 156 C3 11 30 S 75 0W
Junín de los Andes, Argentina 160 A2 39 45 S 71 0W

214 Jūniyah


Jūniyah, *Lebanon* **91 B4** 33 59N 35 38 E
Junnar, *India* **82 E1** 19 12N 73 58 E
Juntura, *U.S.A.* **142 E4** 43 45N 118 5W
Juparanã, L., *Brazil* **155 E3** 19 16 S 40 8W
Jupiter →, *Canada* **129 C7** 49 29N 63 37W
Juquiá, *Brazil* **155 F2** 24 19 S 47 38W
Jur, Nahr el →, *Sudan* **95 F2** 8 45N 29 15 E
Jura = Jura, Mts. du, *Europe* **25 B10** 46 40N 6 5 E
Jura = Schwäbische Alb, *Germany* **27 G5** 48 30N 9 30 E
Jura, *Europe* **23 F13** 46 35N 6 5 E
Jura, *U.K.* **18 F3** 56 0N 5 50W
Jura □, *France* **23 F12** 46 47N 5 45 E
Jura, Mts. du, *Europe* **25 B10** 46 40N 6 5 E
Jura, Sd. of, *U.K.* **18 F3** 55 57N 5 45W
Jura Suisse, *Switz.* **28 B3** 47 10N 7 0 E
Jurado, *Colombia* **152 B2** 7 7N 77 46W
Jurilovca, *Romania* **46 E9** 44 46N 28 52 E
Jurong, *China* **69 B12** 31 57N 119 9 E
Juruá →, *Brazil* **152 D4** 2 37 S 65 44W
Juruena, *Brazil* **157 C6** 13 0 S 58 10W
Juruena →, *Brazil* **157 B6** 7 20 S 58 3W
Juruti, *Brazil* **153 D6** 2 9 S 56 4W
Jussey, *France* **23 E12** 47 50N 5 55 E
Justo Daract, *Argentina* **158 C2** 33 52 S 65 12W
Jutaí, *Brazil* **156 B4** 5 11 S 68 54W
Jutaí →, *Brazil* **152 D4** 2 43 S 66 57W
Jüterbog, *Germany* **26 D9** 52 0N 13 6 E
Juticalpa, *Honduras* **148 D2** 14 40N 86 12W
Jutland = Jylland, *Denmark* **15 H3** 56 25N 9 30 E
Jutphaas, *Neths.* **20 D6** 52 2N 5 6 E
Juventud, I. de la, *Cuba* **148 B3** 21 40N 82 40W
Juvigny-sous-Andaine, *France* **22 D6** 48 32N 0 30W
Juvisy-sur-Orge, *France* **23 D9** 48 42N 2 22 E
Jūy Zar, *Iran* **84 C5** 33 50N 46 18 E
Juye, *China* **66 G9** 35 22N 116 5 E
Juzennecourt, *France* **23 D11** 48 10N 4 58 E
Jylland, *Denmark* **15 H3** 56 25N 9 30 E
Jyväskylä, *Finland* **12 E18** 62 14N 25 50 E


# K


K2, Mt., *Pakistan* **81 B7** 35 58N 76 32 E
Kaala-Gomén, *N. Cal.* **121 T18** 20 40 S 164 25 E
Kaap Plateau, *S. Africa* **104 D3** 28 30 S 24 0 E
Kaapkruis, *Namibia* **104 C1** 21 55 S 13 57 E
Kaapstad = Cape Town, *S. Africa* **104 E2** 33 55 S 18 22 E
Kaatsheuvel, *Neths.* **21 E6** 51 39N 5 2 E
Kabacan, *Phil.* **71 H5** 7 8N 124 49 E
Kabaena, *Indonesia* **72 C2** 5 15 S 122 0 E
Kabala, *S. Leone* **100 D2** 9 38N 11 37W
Kabale, *Uganda* **106 C3** 1 15 S 30 0 E
Kabalo, *Zaïre* **103 D5** 6 0 S 27 0 E
Kabambare, *Zaïre* **106 C2** 4 41 S 27 39 E
Kabango, *Zaïre* **107 D2** 8 35 S 28 30 E
Kabanjahe, *Indonesia* **74 B1** 3 6N 98 30 E
Kabankalan, *Phil.* **71 G4** 9 59N 122 49 E
Kabara, *Mali* **100 B4** 16 40N 2 50W
Kabardinka, *Russia* **52 D7** 44 40N 37 57 E
Kabardino-Balkar Republic □, *Russia* **53 E10** 43 30N 43 30 E
Kabare, *Indonesia* **73 B4** 0 4 S 130 58 E
Kabarega Falls, *Uganda* **106 B3** 2 15N 31 30 E
Kabasalan, *Phil.* **71 H4** 7 47N 122 44 E
Kabba, *Nigeria* **101 D6** 7 50N 6 3 E
Kabe, *Japan* **62 C4** 34 31N 132 31 E
Kabi, *Niger* **97 F2** 13 30N 12 35 E
Kabin Buri, *Thailand* **76 F3** 13 57N 101 43 E
Kabinakagami L., *Canada* **128 C3** 48 54N 84 25W
Kabīr, Zab al →, *Iraq* **84 C4** 36 0N 43 0 E
Kabkabīyah, *Sudan* **97 F4** 13 50N 24 0 E
Kablungu, C., *Papua N. G.* **120 D6** 6 20 S 150 1 E
Kabna, *Sudan* **94 D3** 19 6N 32 40 E
Kabo, *C.A.R.* **102 A3** 7 35N 18 38 E
Kabompo, *Zambia* **107 E1** 13 36 S 24 14 E
Kabondo, *Zaïre* **103 D5** 8 58 S 25 40 E
Kabongo, *Zaïre* **103 D5** 7 22 S 25 33 E
Kabou, *Togo* **101 D5** 9 28N 0 55 E
Kaboudia, Rass, *Tunisia* **96 A2** 35 13N 11 10 E
Kabra, *Australia* **114 C5** 23 25 S 150 25 E
Kabūd Gonbad, *Iran* **85 B8** 37 5N 59 45 E
Kabugao, *Phil.* **70 B3** 18 2N 121 11 E
Kābul, *Afghan.* **79 B3** 34 28N 69 11 E
Kābul □, *Afghan.* **79 B3** 34 30N 69 0 E
Kabul →, *Pakistan* **79 B4** 33 55N 72 14 E
Kabunga, *Zaïre* **106 C2** 1 38 S 28 3 E
Kaburuang, *Indonesia* **72 A3** 3 50N 126 30 E
Kabushiya, *Sudan* **95 D3** 16 54N 33 41 E
Kabwe, *Zambia* **107 E2** 14 30 S 28 29 E
Kabwum, *Papua N. G.* **120 D4** 6 11 S 147 15 E
Kačanik, *Serbia* **42 E6** 42 13N 21 12 E
Kachanovo, *Russia* **50 C5** 57 25N 27 38 E
Kachchh, Gulf of, *India* **80 H3** 22 50N 69 15 E
Kachchh, Rann of, *India* **80 G4** 24 0N 70 0 E
Kachebera, *Zambia* **107 E3** 13 50 S 32 50 E
Kachin □, *Burma* **78 B6** 26 0N 97 30 E
Kachira, L., *Uganda* **106 C3** 0 40 S 31 7 E
Kachiry, *Kazakhstan* **56 D8** 53 10N 75 50 E
Kachisi, *Ethiopia* **95 F4** 9 40N 37 50 E
Kachkanar, *Russia* **54 B6** 58 42N 59 33 E
Kachot, *Cambodia* **77 G4** 11 30N 103 3 E
Kackar, *Turkey* **53 F9** 40 45N 41 10 E
Kadaingti, *Burma* **78 G6** 17 37N 97 32 E
Kadaiyanallur, *India* **83 K3** 9 3N 77 22 E
Kadanai →, *Afghan.* **80 D1** 31 22N 65 45 E
Kadarkút, *Hungary* **31 E10** 46 13N 17 39 E
Kade, *Ghana* **101 D4** 6 7N 0 56W
Kadi, *India* **80 H5** 23 18N 72 23 E
Kadina, *Australia* **116 B2** 33 55 S 137 43 E
Kadınhanı, *Turkey* **88 D5** 38 14N 32 13 E
Kadiri, *India* **83 G4** 14 12N 78 13 E
Kadirli, *Turkey* **88 E7** 37 23N 36 5 E
Kadiyevka, *Ukraine* **53 B8** 48 35N 38 40 E
Kadoka, *U.S.A.* **138 D4** 43 50N 101 31W
Kadom, *Russia* **51 D13** 54 37N 42 30 E
Kadoma, *Zimbabwe* **107 F2** 18 20 S 29 52 E
Kâdugli, *Sudan* **95 E2** 11 0N 29 45 E
Kaduna, *Nigeria* **101 C6** 10 30N 7 21 E
Kaduna □, *Nigeria* **101 C6** 11 0N 7 30 E
Kadzhi-Say, *Kirghizia* **55 B8** 42 8N 77 10 E
Kaédi, *Mauritania* **100 B2** 16 9N 13 28W
Kaelé, *Cameroon* **101 C7** 10 7N 14 27 E
Kaeng Khoï, *Thailand* **76 E3** 14 35N 101 0 E
Kaeo, *N.Z.* **118 B2** 35 6 S 173 49 E
Kaesŏng, *N. Korea* **67 F14** 37 58N 126 35 E
Kāf, *Si. Arabia* **84 D3** 31 25N 37 29 E
Kafakumba, *Zaïre* **103 D4** 9 38 S 23 46 E
Kafan, *Armenia* **89 D12** 39 18N 46 15 E
Kafanchan, *Nigeria* **101 D6** 9 40N 8 20 E
Kafareti, *Nigeria* **101 C7** 10 25N 11 12 E
Kaffrine, *Senegal* **100 C1** 14 8N 15 36W
Kafia Kingi, *Sudan* **102 A4** 9 20N 24 25 E
Kafinda, *Zambia* **107 E3** 12 32 S 30 20 E
Kafirévs, Ákra, *Greece* **45 F6** 38 9N 24 38 E
Kafr el Dauwâr, *Egypt* **94 H7** 31 8N 30 8 E
Kafr el Sheikh, *Egypt* **94 H7** 31 15N 30 50 E
Kafue, *Zambia* **107 F2** 15 46 S 28 9 E
Kafue Flats, *Zambia* **107 F2** 15 40 S 27 25 E
Kafue Nat. Park, *Zambia* **107 F2** 15 0 S 25 30 E
Kafulwe, *Zambia* **107 D2** 9 0 S 29 1 E
Kaga, *Afghan.* **80 B4** 34 14N 70 10 E
Kaga, *Japan* **63 A8** 36 16N 136 15 E
Kaga Bandoro, *C.A.R.* **102 A3** 7 0N 19 10 E
Kagan, *Uzbekistan* **55 D2** 39 43N 64 33 E
Kagawa □, *Japan* **62 C6** 34 15N 134 0 E
Kagera □, *Tanzania* **106 C3** 2 0 S 31 30 E
Kagera →, *Uganda* **106 C3** 0 57 S 31 47 E
Kağizman, *Turkey* **89 C10** 40 5N 43 10 E
Kagoshima, *Japan* **62 F2** 31 35N 130 33 E
Kagoshima □, *Japan* **62 F2** 31 30N 130 30 E
Kagoshima-Wan, *Japan* **62 F2** 31 25N 130 40 E
Kagul, *Moldavia* **52 D3** 45 50N 28 15 E
Kahak, *Iran* **85 B6** 36 6N 49 46 E
Kahama, *Tanzania* **106 C3** 4 8 S 32 30 E
Kahama □, *Tanzania* **106 C3** 3 50 S 32 0 E
Kahang, *Malaysia* **77 L4** 2 12N 103 32 E
Kahayan →, *Indonesia* **75 C4** 3 40 S 114 0 E
Kahe, *Tanzania* **106 C4** 3 30 S 37 25 E
Kahemba, *Zaïre* **103 D3** 7 18 S 18 55 E
Kaherekoau Mts., *N.Z.* **119 F2** 45 45 S 167 15 E
Kahil, Djebel bou, *Algeria* **99 B5** 34 26N 4 0 E
Kahilangan, *Phil.* **71 H5** 7 48N 124 48 E
Kahniah →, *Canada* **130 B4** 58 15N 120 55W
Kahnūj, *Iran* **85 E8** 27 55N 57 40 E
Kahoka, *U.S.A.* **140 D5** 40 25N 91 44W
Kahoolawe, *U.S.A.* **132 H16** 20 33N 156 37W
Kahramanmaraş, *Turkey* **88 E7** 37 37N 36 53 E
Kahramanmaraş □, *Turkey* **88 E7** 37 35N 36 33 E
Kâhta, *Turkey* **89 E8** 37 46N 38 36 E
Kahurangi, Pt., *N.Z.* **119 A7** 40 50 S 172 10 E
Kahuta, *Pakistan* **80 C5** 33 35N 73 24 E
Kai, Kepulauan, *Indonesia* **73 C4** 5 55 S 132 45 E
Kai Besar, *Indonesia* **73 C4** 5 35 S 133 0 E
Kai Is. = Kai, Kepulauan, *Indonesia* **73 C4** 5 55 S 132 45 E
Kai-Ketil, *Indonesia* **73 C4** 5 45 S 132 40 E
Kai Xian, *China* **68 B7** 31 11N 108 21 E
Kaiama, *Nigeria* **101 D5** 9 36N 4 1 E
Kaiapit, *Papua N. G.* **120 D4** 6 18 S 146 18 E
Kaiapoi, *N.Z.* **119 D7** 43 24 S 172 40 E
Kaibara, *Japan* **63 B7** 35 8N 135 5 E
Kaieteur Falls, *Guyana* **153 B6** 5 1N 59 10W
Kaifeng, *China* **66 G8** 34 48N 114 21 E
Kaihua, *China* **69 C12** 29 12N 118 20 E
Kaikohe, *N.Z.* **118 B2** 35 25 S 173 49 E
Kaikoura, *N.Z.* **119 C8** 42 25 S 173 43 E
Kaikoura Pen., *N.Z.* **119 C8** 42 25 S 173 43 E
Kaikoura Ra., *N.Z.* **119 B8** 41 59 S 173 41 E
Kailahun, *S. Leone* **100 D2** 8 18N 10 39W
Kailashahar, *India* **78 C4** 24 19N 92 0 E
Kaili, *China* **68 D6** 26 33N 107 59 E
Kailu, *China* **67 C11** 43 38N 121 18 E
Kailua Kona, *U.S.A.* **132 J17** 19 39N 155 59W
Kaimana, *Indonesia* **73 B4** 3 39 S 133 45 E
Kaimanawa Mts., *N.Z.* **118 F4** 39 15 S 175 56 E
Kaimata, *N.Z.* **119 C6** 42 34 S 171 28 E
Kaimganj, *India* **81 F8** 27 33N 79 24 E
Kaimon-Dake, *Japan* **62 F2** 31 11N 130 32 E
Kaimur Hills, *India* **81 G9** 24 30N 82 0 E
Kainan, *Japan* **63 C7** 34 9N 135 12 E
Kainantu, *Papua N. G.* **120 D3** 6 18 S 145 52 E
Kaingaroa Forest, *N.Z.* **118 E5** 38 24 S 176 30 E
Kainji Res., *Nigeria* **101 C5** 10 1N 4 40 E
Kaipara Harbour, *N.Z.* **118 C3** 36 25 S 174 14 E
Kaiping, *China* **69 F9** 22 23N 112 42 E
Kaipokok B., *Canada* **129 B8** 54 54N 59 47W
Kairana, *India* **80 E7** 29 24N 77 15 E
Kaironi, *Indonesia* **73 B4** 0 47 S 133 40 E
Kairouan, *Tunisia* **96 A2** 35 45N 10 5 E
Kairuku, *Papua N. G.* **120 E4** 8 51 S 146 35 E
Kaiserslautern, *Germany* **27 F3** 49 30N 7 43 E
Kaitaia, *N.Z.* **118 B2** 35 8 S 173 17 E
Kaitangata, *N.Z.* **119 G4** 46 17 S 169 51 E
Kaithal, *India* **80 E7** 29 48N 76 26 E
Kaitu →, *Pakistan* **80 C4** 33 10N 70 30 E
Kaiwi Channel, *U.S.A.* **132 H16** 21 15N 157 30W
Kaiyang, *China* **68 D6** 27 4N 106 59 E
Kaiyuan, *Liaoning, China* **67 C13** 42 28N 124 1 E
Kaiyuan, *Yunnan, China* **68 F4** 23 40N 103 12 E
Kajaani, *Finland* **12 D19** 64 17N 27 46 E
Kajabbi, *Australia* **114 B3** 20 0 S 140 1 E
Kajana = Kajaani, *Finland* **12 D19** 64 17N 27 46 E
Kajang, *Malaysia* **77 L3** 2 59N 101 48 E
Kajiado, *Kenya* **106 C4** 1 53 S 36 48 E
Kajiado □, *Kenya* **106 C4** 2 0 S 36 30 E
Kajiki, *Japan* **62 F2** 31 44N 130 40 E
Kajo Kaji, *Sudan* **95 G3** 3 58N 31 40 E
Kaka, *Sudan* **95 E3** 10 38N 32 10 E
Kakabeka Falls, *Canada* **128 C2** 48 24N 89 37W
Kakamas, *S. Africa* **104 D3** 28 45 S 20 33 E
Kakamega, *Kenya* **106 B3** 0 20N 34 46 E
Kakamega □, *Kenya* **106 B3** 0 20N 34 46 E
Kakamigahara, *Japan* **63 B8** 35 28N 136 48 E
Kakanj, *Bos.-H.* **42 C3** 44 9N 18 7 E
Kakanui Mts., *N.Z.* **119 F5** 45 10 S 170 30 E
Kake, *Japan* **62 C4** 34 36N 132 19 E
Kakegawa, *Japan* **63 C10** 34 45N 138 1 E
Kakeroma-Jima, *Japan* **61 K4** 28 8N 129 14 E
Kakhib, *Russia* **53 E12** 42 28N 46 34 E
Kakhovka, *Ukraine* **52 C5** 46 40N 33 15 E
Kakhovskoye Vdkhr., *Ukraine* **52 C6** 47 5N 34 0 E
Kakinada, *India* **82 F6** 16 57N 82 11 E
Kakisa →, *Canada* **130 A5** 61 3N 118 10W
Kakisa L., *Canada* **130 A5** 60 56N 117 43W
Kakogawa, *Japan* **62 C6** 34 46N 134 51 E
Kakwa →, *Canada* **130 C5** 54 37N 118 28W
Kāl Gūsheh, *Iran* **85 D8** 30 59N 58 12 E
Kal Safīd, *Iran* **84 C5** 34 52N 47 23 E
Kala, *Nigeria* **101 C7** 12 2N 14 40 E
Kala Oya →, *Sri Lanka* **83 K4** 8 20N 79 45 E
Kalaa-Kebira, *Tunisia* **96 A2** 35 59N 10 32 E
Kalabagh, *Pakistan* **79 B3** 33 0N 71 28 E
Kalabahi, *Indonesia* **72 C2** 8 13 S 124 31 E
Kalabáka, *Greece* **44 E3** 39 42N 21 39 E
Kalabakan, *Malaysia* **75 B5** 4 25N 117 29 E
Kalabo, *Zambia* **103 E4** 14 58 S 22 40 E
Kalach, *Russia* **51 F12** 50 22N 41 0 E
Kalach na Donu, *Russia* **53 B10** 48 43N 43 32 E
Kaladar, *Canada* **136 B7** 44 37N 77 5W
Kalagua Is., *Phil.* **70 D4** 14 30N 122 55 E
Kalahari, *Africa* **104 C3** 24 0 S 21 30 E
Kalahari Gemsbok Nat. Park, *S. Africa* **104 D3** 25 30 S 20 30 E
Kalai-Khumb, *Tajikistan* **55 D5** 38 28N 70 46 E
Kālak, *Iran* **85 E8** 25 29N 59 22 E
Kalakamati, *Botswana* **105 C4** 20 40 S 27 25 E
Kalakan, *Russia* **57 D12** 55 15N 116 45 E
Kalakh, *Syria* **84 C3** 34 55N 36 10 E
K'alak'unlun Shank'ou, *Pakistan* **81 B7** 35 33N 77 46 E
Kalam, *Pakistan* **81 B5** 35 34N 72 30 E
Kalama, *U.S.A.* **144 E4** 46 1N 122 51W
Kalama, *Zaïre* **106 C2** 2 52 S 28 35 E
Kalamansig, *Phil.* **71 H5** 6 33N 124 3 E
Kalamariá, *Greece* **44 D4** 40 33N 22 55 E
Kalamata, *Greece* **45 G4** 37 3N 22 10 E
Kalamazoo, *U.S.A.* **141 B11** 42 17N 85 35W
Kalamazoo →, *U.S.A.* **141 B10** 42 40N 86 10W
Kalamb, *India* **82 E2** 18 3N 74 48 E
Kalambo Falls, *Tanzania* **107 D3** 8 37 S 31 35 E
Kálamos, *Attikí, Greece* **45 F5** 38 17N 23 52 E
Kálamos, *Ionioi Nísoi, Greece* **45 F2** 38 37N 20 55 E
Kalamoti, *Greece* **45 F8** 38 15N 26 4 E
Kalangadoo, *Australia* **116 D4** 37 34 S 140 41 E
Kalannie, *Australia* **113 F2** 30 22 S 117 5 E
Kalāntarī, *Iran* **85 C7** 32 10N 54 8 E
Kalao, *Indonesia* **72 C2** 7 21 S 121 0 E
Kalaotoa, *Indonesia* **72 C2** 7 20 S 121 50 E
Kalārne, *Sweden* **14 B10** 62 59N 16 8 E
Kalárovo, *Slovak Rep.* **31 D11** 47 54N 18 0 E
Kalasin, *Thailand* **76 D4** 16 26N 103 30 E
Kalat, *Pakistan* **79 C2** 29 8N 66 31 E
Kalāteh, *Iran* **85 B7** 36 33N 55 41 E
Kalāteh-ye-Ganj, *Iran* **85 E8** 27 31N 57 55 E
Kálathos, *Greece* **45 H10** 36 9N 28 8 E
Kalaus →, *Russia* **53 D11** 45 40N 44 7 E
Kalávrita, *Greece* **45 F4** 38 3N 22 8 E
Kalaw, *Burma* **78 E6** 20 38N 96 34 E
Kalbān, *Oman* **87 B7** 20 18N 58 38 E
Kalbarri, *Australia* **113 E1** 27 40 S 114 10 E
Kale, *Turkey* **88 E3** 37 27N 28 49 E
Kalecik, *Turkey* **52 F5** 40 4N 33 26 E
Kalehe, *Zaïre* **106 C2** 2 6 S 28 50 E
Kalema, *Tanzania* **106 C3** 1 12 S 31 55 E
Kalemie, *Zaïre* **106 D2** 5 55 S 29 9 E
Kalemyo, *Burma* **78 D5** 23 11N 94 4 E
Kalety, *Poland* **47 E5** 50 35N 18 52 E
Kalewa, *Burma* **78 D5** 23 10N 94 15 E
Kálfafellsstaður, *Iceland* **12 D6** 64 11N 15 53W
Kalgan = Zhangjiakou, *China* **66 D8** 40 48N 114 55 E
Kalgoorlie-Boulder, *Australia* **113 F3** 30 40 S 121 22 E
Kaliakra, Nos, *Bulgaria* **43 D13** 43 21N 28 30 E
Kalianda, *Indonesia* **74 D3** 5 50 S 105 45 E
Kalibo, *Phil.* **71 F4** 11 43N 122 22 E
Kaliganj, *Bangla.* **81 H13** 22 25N 89 8 E
Kalima, *Zaïre* **106 C2** 2 33 S 26 32 E
Kalimantan, *Indonesia* **75 C4** 0 0 114 0 E
Kalimantan Barat □, *Indonesia* **75 C4** 0 0 110 30 E
Kalimantan Selatan □, *Indonesia* **75 C5** 2 30 S 115 30 E
Kalimantan Tengah □, *Indonesia* **75 C4** 2 0 S 113 30 E
Kalimantan Timur □, *Indonesia* **75 B5** 1 30N 116 30 E
Kálimnos, *Greece* **45 H8** 37 0N 27 0 E
Kalimpong, *India* **81 F13** 27 4N 88 35 E
Kalinadi →, *India* **83 G2** 14 50N 74 7 E
Kalinga □, *Phil.* **70 C3** 17 30N 121 20 E
Kalinin = Tver, *Russia* **51 C9** 56 55N 35 55 E
Kaliningrad, *Russia* **48 C6** 55 58N 37 54 E
Kaliningrad, *Russia* **50 D2** 54 42N 20 32 E
Kalininskoye, *Kirghizia* **55 B6** 42 50N 73 49 E
Kalinkavichy = Kalinkovichi, *Belorussia* **50 E6** 52 12N 29 20 E
Kalinkovichi, *Belorussia* **50 E6** 52 12N 29 20 E
Kalinovik, *Bos.-H.* **42 D3** 43 31N 18 29 E
Kalipetrovo, *Bulgaria* **43 C12** 44 5N 27 14 E
Kaliro, *Uganda* **106 B3** 0 56N 33 30 E
Kalirrákhi, *Greece* **44 D6** 40 40N 24 35 E
Kalispell, *U.S.A.* **142 B6** 48 12N 114 19W
Kalisz, *Poland* **47 D5** 51 45N 18 8 E
Kalisz □, *Poland* **47 D4** 51 30N 18 0 E
Kalisz Pomorski, *Poland* **47 B2** 53 17N 15 55 E
Kaliua, *Tanzania* **106 D3** 5 5 S 31 48 E
Kaliveli Tank, *India* **83 H4** 12 5N 79 50 E
Kalix →, *Sweden* **12 D17** 65 50N 23 11 E
Kalka, *India* **80 D7** 30 46N 76 57 E
Kalkan, *Turkey* **88 E3** 36 15N 29 23 E
Kalkaroo, *Australia* **116 A5** 31 12 S 143 54 E
Kalkaska, *U.S.A.* **134 C3** 44 44N 85 11W
Kalkfeld, *Namibia* **104 C2** 20 57 S 16 14 E
Kalkfontein, *Botswana* **104 C3** 22 4 S 20 57 E
Kalkrand, *Namibia* **104 C2** 24 1 S 17 35 E
Kallakkurichi, *India* **83 J4** 11 44N 79 1 E
Kållandsö, *Sweden* **15 F7** 58 40N 13 5 E
Kallidaikurichi, *India* **83 K3** 8 38N 77 31 E
Kallithéa, *Greece* **45 G5** 37 55N 23 41 E
Kallmeti, *Albania* **44 C1** 41 51N 19 41 E
Kallonís, Kólpos, *Greece* **45 E8** 39 10N 26 10 E
Kallsjön, *Sweden* **12 E12** 63 38N 13 0 E
Kalmalo, *Nigeria* **101 C6** 13 40N 5 20 E
Kalmar, *Sweden* **13 H14** 56 40N 16 20 E
Kalmthout, *Belgium* **21 F4** 51 23N 4 29 E
Kalmyk Republic □, *Russia* **53 C12** 46 5N 46 1 E
Kalmykovo, *Kazakhstan* **53 B14** 49 0N 51 47 E
Kalna, *India* **81 H13** 23 13N 88 25 E
Kalo, *Papua N. G.* **120 F4** 10 1 S 147 48 E
Kalocsa, *Hungary* **31 E12** 46 32N 19 0 E
Kalofer, *Bulgaria* **43 E9** 42 37N 24 59 E
Kalokhorio, *Cyprus* **32 E12** 34 51N 33 2 E
Kaloko, *Zaïre* **103 D5** 6 47 S 25 48 E
Kalol, *Gujarat, India* **80 H5** 22 37N 73 31 E
Kalol, *Gujarat, India* **80 H5** 23 15N 72 33 E
Kalolímnos, *Greece* **45 G9** 37 4N 27 8 E
Kalomo, *Zambia* **107 F2** 17 0 S 26 30 E
Kalona, *U.S.A.* **140 C5** 41 29N 91 43W
Kalonerón, *Greece* **45 G3** 37 20N 21 38 E
Kalpi, *India* **81 F8** 26 8N 79 47 E
Kalrayan Hills, *India* **83 J4** 11 45N 78 40 E
Kalsubai, *India* **82 E1** 19 35N 73 45 E
Kaltbrunn, *Switz.* **29 B8** 47 13N 9 2 E
Kaltungo, *Nigeria* **101 D7** 9 48N 11 19 E
Kalu, *Pakistan* **80 G2** 25 5N 67 39 E
Kaluga, *Russia* **51 D10** 54 35N 36 10 E
Kalulong, Bukit, *Malaysia* **75 B4** 3 14N 114 39 E
Kalulushi, *Zambia* **107 E2** 12 50 S 28 3 E
Kalundborg, *Denmark* **15 J5** 55 41N 11 5 E
Kalush, *Ukraine* **50 G4** 49 3N 24 23 E
Kałuszyn, *Poland* **47 C8** 52 13N 21 52 E
Kalutara, *Sri Lanka* **83 L4** 6 35N 80 0 E
Kalwaria, *Poland* **31 B12** 49 53N 19 41 E
Kalya, *Russia* **54 A6** 60 15N 59 59 E
Kalyan, *Australia* **116 C3** 34 55 S 139 49 E
Kalyan, *India* **82 D2** 20 30N 74 3 E
Kalyazin, *Russia* **51 C10** 57 15N 37 55 E
Kama, *Burma* **78 F5** 19 1N 95 4 E
Kama, *Zaïre* **106 C2** 3 30 S 27 5 E
Kama →, *Russia* **54 D3** 55 45N 52 0 E
Kamachumu, *Tanzania* **106 C3** 1 37 S 31 37 E
Kamae, *Japan* **62 E3** 32 48N 131 56 E
Kamaing, *Burma* **78 C6** 25 26N 96 35 E
Kamaishi, *Japan* **60 E10** 39 16N 141 53 E
Kamakura, *Japan* **63 B11** 35 19N 139 33 E
Kamalia, *Pakistan* **80 D5** 30 44N 72 42 E
Kamamaung, *Burma* **78 G6** 17 21N 97 40 E
Kamapanda, *Zambia* **107 E1** 12 5 S 24 0 E
Kamaran, *Yemen* **86 D3** 15 21N 42 35 E
Kamashi, *Uzbekistan* **55 D2** 38 51N 65 23 E
Kamativi, *Zimbabwe* **107 F2** 18 15 S 27 27 E
Kamba, *Nigeria* **101 C5** 11 50N 3 45 E
Kambalda, *Australia* **113 F3** 31 10 S 121 37 E
Kambam, *India* **83 K3** 9 45N 77 16 E
Kambar, *Pakistan* **80 F3** 27 37N 68 1 E
Kambarka, *Russia* **54 C4** 56 15N 54 11 E
Kambia, *S. Leone* **100 D2** 9 3N 12 53W
Kambolé, *Zambia* **107 D3** 8 47 S 30 48 E
Kambos, *Cyprus* **32 D11** 35 2N 32 44 E
Kambove, *Zaïre* **107 E2** 10 51 S 26 33 E
Kambuie, *Zaïre* **103 D4** 6 59 S 22 19 E
Kamchatka, P-ov., *Russia* **57 D16** 57 0N 160 0 E
Kamchatka Pen. = Kamchatka, P-ov., *Russia* **57 D16** 57 0N 160 0 E
Kamen, *Russia* **56 D9** 53 50N 81 30 E
Kamen Kashirskiy, *Ukraine* **50 F4** 51 39N 24 56 E
Kamen-Rybolov, *Russia* **60 B6** 44 46N 132 2 E
Kamenets-Podolskiy, *Ukraine* **52 B2** 48 45N 26 40 E
Kamenica, *Serbia* **42 D7** 43 27N 22 27 E
Kamenica, *Serbia* **42 C4** 44 25N 19 40 E
Kamenice, *Czech.* **30 B8** 49 18N 15 2 E
Kamenjak, Rt., *Croatia* **39 D10** 44 47N 13 55 E
Kamenka, *Russia* **48 A7** 65 58N 44 0 E
Kamenka, *Russia* **51 E14** 53 10N 44 5 E
Kamenka, *Russia* **51 F11** 50 47N 39 20 E
Kamenka, *Ukraine* **52 B5** 49 3N 32 6 E
Kamenka Bugskaya, *Ukraine* **50 F4** 50 8N 24 16 E
Kamenka Dneprovskaya, *Ukraine* **52 C6** 47 29N 34 14 E
Kameno, *Bulgaria* **43 E12** 42 34N 27 18 E
Kamenolomini, *Russia* **53 C9** 47 40N 40 14 E
Kamensk-Shakhtinskiy, *Russia* **53 B9** 48 23N 40 20 E
Kamensk Uralskiy, *Russia* **54 C8** 56 25N 62 2 E
Kamenskiy, *Russia* **51 F14** 50 48N 45 25 E
Kamenskiy, *Russia* **53 B9** 49 20N 41 15 E
Kamenskoye, *Russia* **57 C17** 62 45N 165 30 E
Kamenyak, *Bulgaria* **43 D11** 43 24N 26 57 E
Kamenz, *Germany* **26 D10** 51 17N 14 7 E
Kameoka, *Japan* **63 B7** 35 0N 135 35 E
Kameyama, *Japan* **63 C8** 34 51N 136 27 E
Kami, *Albania* **44 B2** 42 17N 20 18 E
Kami-Jima, *Japan* **62 E2** 32 27N 130 20 E
Kami-koshiki-Jima, *Japan* **62 F1** 31 50N 129 52 E
Kamiah, *U.S.A.* **142 C5** 46 14N 116 2W
Kamień Krajeński, *Poland* **47 B4** 53 32N 17 32 E
Kamień Pomorski, *Poland* **47 B1** 53 57N 14 43 E
Kamienna →, *Poland* **47 D8** 51 6N 21 47 E
Kamienna Góra, *Poland* **47 E3** 50 47N 16 2 E
Kamieńsk, *Poland* **47 D6** 51 12N 19 29 E
Kamieskroon, *S. Africa* **104 E2** 30 9 S 17 56 E
Kamiita, *Japan* **62 C6** 34 6N 134 22 E
Kamilukuak, L., *Canada* **131 A8** 62 22N 101 40W
Kamina, *Zaïre* **103 D5** 8 45 S 25 0 E
Kaminak L., *Canada* **131 A9** 62 10N 95 0W
Kaminoyama, *Japan* **60 E10** 38 9N 140 17 E
Kamioka, *Japan* **63 A9** 36 25N 137 15 E
Kamiros, *Greece* **32 C9** 36 20N 27 56 E
Kamituga, *Zaïre* **106 C2** 3 2 S 28 10 E
Kamloops, *Canada* **130 C4** 50 40N 120 20W
Kamnik, *Slovenia* **39 B11** 46 14N 14 37 E
Kamo, *Armenia* **53 F11** 40 21N 45 7 E
Kamo, *Japan* **60 F9** 37 39N 139 3 E
Kamo, *N.Z.* **118 B3** 35 42 S 174 20 E
Kamoa Mts., *Guyana* **153 C6** 1 30N 59 0W
Kamogawa, *Japan* **63 B12** 35 5N 140 5 E
Kamoke, *Pakistan* **80 C6** 32 4N 74 4 E
Kamp →, *Austria* **30 C8** 48 23N 15 42 E
Kampala, *Uganda* **106 B3** 0 20N 32 30 E
Kampar, *Malaysia* **77 K3** 4 18N 101 9 E
Kampar →, *Indonesia* **74 B2** 0 30N 103 8 E
Kampen, *Neths.* **20 C7** 52 33N 5 53 E
Kamperland, *Neths.* **21 E3** 51 34N 3 43 E
Kamphaeng Phet, *Thailand* **76 D2** 16 28N 99 30 E

Kaspiyskiy 215


Kampolombo, L., Zambia 107 E2 11 37 S 29 42 E
Kampong To, Thailand 77 J3 6 3N 101 13 E
Kampot, Cambodia 77 G5 10 36N 104 10 E
Kampsville, U.S.A. 140 E6 39 18N 90 37W
Kamptee, India 82 D4 21 9N 79 19 E
Kampti, Burkina Faso 100 C4 10 7N 3 25W
Kampuchea = Cambodia ■, Asia 76 F5 12 15N 105 0 E
Kampung →, Indonesia 73 C5 5 44 S 138 24 E
Kampung Air Putih, Malaysia 77 K4 4 15N 103 10 E
Kampung Jerangau, Malaysia 77 K4 4 50N 103 10 E
Kampung Raja, Malaysia 77 K4 5 45N 102 35 E
Kampungbaru = Tolitoli, Indonesia 72 A2 1 5N 120 50 E
Kamrau, Teluk, Indonesia 73 B4 3 30 S 133 36 E
Kamsack, Canada 131 C8 51 34N 101 54W
Kamskoye Ustye, Russia 51 D16 55 10N 49 20 E
Kamskoye Vdkhr., Russia 54 B5 58 0N 56 0 E
Kamuchawie L., Canada 131 B8 56 18N 101 59W
Kamui-Misaki, Japan 60 C10 43 20N 140 21 E
Kamyanets-Podilskyy = Kamenets-Podolskiy, Ukraine 52 B2 48 45N 26 40 E
Kāmyārān, Iran 84 C5 34 47N 46 56 E
Kamyshin, Russia 51 F14 50 10N 45 24 E
Kamyshlov, Russia 54 C8 56 50N 62 43 E
Kamyzyak, Russia 53 C13 46 4N 48 10 E
Kan, Burma 78 D5 22 25N 94 5 E
Kanaaupscow, Canada 128 B4 54 2N 76 30W
Kanab, U.S.A. 143 H7 37 3N 112 32W
Kanab →, U.S.A. 143 H7 36 24N 112 38W
Kanagawa □, Japan 63 B11 35 20N 139 20 E
Kanagi, Japan 60 D10 40 54N 140 27 E
Kanairiktok →, Canada 129 A7 55 2N 60 18W
Kanakapura, India 83 H3 12 33N 77 28 E
Kanália, Greece 44 E4 39 30N 22 53 E
Kananga, Zaïre 103 D4 5 55 S 22 18 E
Kanarraville, U.S.A. 143 H7 37 32N 113 11W
Kanash, Russia 51 D15 55 30N 47 32 E
Kanaskat, U.S.A. 144 C5 47 19N 121 54W
Kanastraíon, Ákra, Greece 44 E5 39 57N 23 45 E
Kanawha →, U.S.A. 134 F4 38 50N 82 9W
Kanazawa, Japan 63 A8 36 30N 136 38 E
Kanbalu, Burma 78 D5 23 12N 95 31 E
Kanchanaburi, Thailand 76 E2 14 2N 99 31 E
Kanchenjunga, Nepal 81 F13 27 50N 88 10 E
Kanchipuram, India 83 H4 12 52N 79 45 E
Kańczuga, Poland 31 B15 49 59N 22 25 E
Kanda Kanda, Zaïre 103 D4 6 52 S 23 48 E
Kandahar = Qandahār, Afghan. 79 C2 31 32N 65 30 E
Kandalaksha, Russia 48 A5 67 9N 32 30 E
Kandalakshkiy Zaliv, Russia 48 A5 66 0N 35 0 E
Kandangan, Indonesia 75 C5 2 50 S 115 20 E
Kandanos, Greece 45 J5 35 19N 23 44 E
Kandanos, Kríti, Greece 32 D5 35 20N 23 45 E
Kandavu, Fiji 121 B2 19 0 S 178 15 E
Kandavu Passage, Fiji 121 B2 18 45 S 178 0 E
Kandep, Papua N. G. 120 C2 5 54 S 143 32 E
Kander →, Switz. 28 C5 46 33N 7 38 E
Kandersteg, Switz. 28 D5 46 28N 7 40 E
Kandhíla, Greece 45 G4 37 46N 22 22 E
Kandhkot, Pakistan 80 E3 28 16N 69 8 E
Kandhla, India 80 E7 29 18N 77 19 E
Kandi, Benin 101 C5 11 7N 2 55 E
Kandi, India 81 H13 23 58N 88 5 E
Kandıra, Turkey 88 C4 41 4N 30 9 E
Kandla, India 80 H4 23 0N 70 10 E
Kandos, Australia 117 B8 32 45 S 149 58 E
Kandrian, Papua N. G. 120 D5 6 14 S 149 37 E
Kandy, Sri Lanka 83 L5 7 18N 80 43 E
Kane, U.S.A. 136 E6 41 40N 78 49W
Kane Basin, Greenland 6 B4 79 1N 70 0W
Kanevskaya, Russia 53 C8 46 3N 39 3 E
Kanfanar, Croatia 39 C10 45 7N 13 50 E
Kangaba, Mali 100 C3 11 56N 8 25W
Kangal, Turkey 88 D7 39 14N 37 23 E
Kangān, Fārs, Iran 85 E7 27 50N 52 3 E
Kangān, Hormozgān, Iran 85 E8 25 48N 57 28 E
Kangar, Malaysia 77 J3 6 27N 100 12 E
Kangaroo I., Australia 116 C2 35 45 S 137 0 E
Kangavar, Iran 85 C6 34 40N 48 0 E
Kangding, China 68 B3 30 2N 101 57 E
Kāngdong, N. Korea 67 E14 39 9N 126 5 E
Kangean, Kepulauan, Indonesia 75 D5 6 55 S 115 23 E
Kangean Is. = Kangean, Kepulauan, Indonesia 75 D5 6 55 S 115 23 E
Kanggye, N. Korea 67 D14 41 0N 126 35 E
Kanggyŏng, S. Korea 67 F14 36 10N 127 0 E
Kanghwa, S. Korea 67 F14 37 45N 126 30 E
Kangnŭng, S. Korea 67 F15 37 45N 128 54 E
Kango, Gabon 102 B2 0 11N 10 5 E
Kangoya, Zaïre 103 D4 9 55 S 22 48 E
Kangping, China 67 C12 42 43N 123 18 E
Kangpokpi, India 78 C4 25 8N 93 58 E
Kangyidaung, Burma 78 G5 16 56N 94 54 E
Kanhangad, India 83 H2 12 21N 74 58 E
Kanheri, India 82 E1 19 13N 72 50 E
Kani, Ivory C. 100 D3 8 29N 6 36W
Kaniama, Zaïre 103 D4 7 30 S 24 12 E
Kaniapiskau →, Canada 129 A6 56 40N 69 30W
Kaniapiskau L., Canada 129 B6 54 10N 69 55W
Kanibadam, Tajikistan 55 C5 40 17N 70 25 E
Kaniere, L., N.Z. 119 C6 42 50 S 171 10 E
Kanin, P-ov., Russia 48 A8 68 0N 45 0 E
Kanin Nos, Mys, Russia 48 A7 68 45N 43 20 E
Kanin Pen. = Kanin, P-ov., Russia 48 A8 68 0N 45 0 E
Kanina, Albania 44 D1 40 23N 19 30 E
Kaniva, Australia 116 D4 36 22 S 141 18 E
Kanjiža, Serbia 42 A5 46 3N 20 4 E
Kanjut Sar, Pakistan 81 A6 36 7N 75 25 E
Kankakee, U.S.A. 141 C9 41 7N 87 52W
Kankakee →, U.S.A. 141 C8 41 23N 88 15W
Kankan, Guinea 100 C3 10 23N 9 15W
Kanker, India 82 D5 20 10N 81 40 E
Kankunskiy, Russia 57 D13 57 37N 126 8 E
Kanmuri-Yama, Japan 62 C4 34 30N 132 4 E
Kannabe, Japan 62 C5 34 32N 133 23 E
Kannapolis, U.S.A. 135 H5 35 30N 80 37W
Kannauj, India 81 F8 27 3N 79 56 E
Kano, Nigeria 101 C6 12 2N 8 30 E
Kano □, Nigeria 101 C6 11 30N 8 30 E
Kan'onji, Japan 62 C5 34 7N 133 39 E
Kanoroba, Ivory C. 100 D3 9 7N 6 8W
Kanowha, U.S.A. 140 B3 42 57N 93 47W
Kanowit, Malaysia 75 B4 2 14N 112 20 E
Kanowna, Australia 113 F3 30 32 S 121 31 E
Kanoya, Japan 62 F2 31 25N 130 50 E
Kanpetlet, Burma 78 E4 21 10N 93 59 E
Kanpur, India 81 F9 26 28N 80 20 E
Kansas, U.S.A. 141 E9 39 33N 87 56W
Kansas □, U.S.A. 138 F6 38 30N 99 0W
Kansas →, U.S.A. 138 F7 39 7N 94 37W
Kansas City, Kans., U.S.A. 140 E2 39 7N 94 38W
Kansas City, Mo., U.S.A. 140 E2 39 6N 94 35W
Kansenia, Zaïre 107 E2 10 20 S 26 0 E
Kansk, Russia 57 D10 56 20N 95 37 E
Kansŏng, S. Korea 67 E15 38 24N 128 30 E
Kansu = Gansu □, China 66 G3 36 0N 104 0 E
Kant, Kirghizia 55 B7 42 53N 74 51 E
Kantang, Thailand 77 J2 7 25N 99 31 E
Kantché, Niger 97 F1 13 31N 8 30 E
Kanté, Togo 101 D5 9 57N 1 3 E
Kantemirovka, Russia 53 B8 49 43N 39 55 E
Kantharalak, Thailand 76 E5 14 39N 104 39 E
Kantō □, Japan 63 A11 36 15N 139 30 E
Kantō-Heiya, Japan 63 A11 36 0N 139 30 E
Kantō-Sanchi, Japan 63 B10 35 59N 138 50 E
Kantu-long, Burma 78 F6 19 57N 97 36 E
Kanturk, Ireland 19 D3 52 10N 8 55W
Kanuma, Japan 63 A11 36 34N 139 42 E
Kanus, Namibia 104 D2 27 50 S 18 39 E
Kanye, Botswana 104 C4 24 55 S 25 28 E
Kanzenze, Zaïre 103 E5 10 30 S 25 12 E
Kanzi, Ras, Tanzania 106 D4 7 1 S 39 33 E
Kao, Fiji 121 P13 19 40 S 175 1W
Kaohsiung = Gaoxiong, Taiwan 69 F13 22 38N 120 18 E
Kaohsiung, Taiwan 65 D7 22 35N 120 16 E
Kaokoveld, Namibia 104 B1 19 15 S 14 30 E
Kaolack, Senegal 100 C1 14 5N 16 8W
Kaoshan, China 67 B13 44 38N 124 50 E
Kaouar, Niger 97 E2 19 5N 12 52 E
Kapadvanj, India 80 H5 23 5N 73 0 E
Kapagere, Papua N. G. 120 E4 9 46 S 147 42 E
Kapanga, Zaïre 103 D4 8 30 S 22 40 E
Kapatagan, Phil. 71 H4 7 52N 123 44 E
Kapchagai, Kazakhstan 55 B8 43 51N 77 14 E
Kapchagaiskoye Vdkhr., Kazakhstan 55 B8 43 45N 77 50 E
Kapellen, Belgium 21 F4 51 19N 4 25 E
Kapéllo, Ákra, Greece 45 H5 36 9N 23 3 E
Kapema, Zaïre 107 E2 10 45 S 28 22 E
Kapfenberg, Austria 30 D8 47 26N 15 18 E
Kapia, Zaïre 103 C3 4 17 S 19 46 E
Kapiri Mposhi, Zambia 107 E2 13 59 S 28 43 E
Kāpīsā □, Afghan. 79 B3 35 0N 69 20 E
Kapiskau →, Canada 128 B3 52 47N 81 55W
Kapit, Malaysia 75 B4 2 0N 112 55 E
Kapiti I., N.Z. 118 G3 40 50 S 174 56 E
Kapka, Massif du, Chad 97 E4 15 7N 21 45 E
Kaplice, Czech. 30 C7 48 42N 14 30 E
Kapoe, Thailand 77 H2 9 34N 98 32 E
Kapoeta, Sudan 95 G3 4 50N 33 35 E
Kápolnásnyék, Hungary 31 D11 47 16N 18 41 E
Kaponga, N.Z. 118 F3 39 29 S 174 9 E
Kapos →, Hungary 31 E11 46 44N 18 30 E
Kaposvár, Hungary 31 E10 46 25N 17 47 E
Kapowsin, U.S.A. 144 D4 46 59N 122 13W
Kappeln, Germany 26 A5 54 37N 9 56 E
Kapps, Namibia 104 C2 22 32 S 17 18 E
Kaprije, Croatia 39 E12 43 42N 15 43 E
Kaprijke, Belgium 21 F3 51 13N 3 38 E
Kapsan, N. Korea 67 D15 41 4N 128 19 E
Kapsukas = Mariyampol, Lithuania 50 D3 54 33N 23 19 E
Kapuas, Indonesia 75 C4 3 10 S 114 5 E
Kapuas →, Indonesia 75 C3 0 25 S 109 20 E
Kapuas Hulu, Pegunungan, Malaysia 75 B4 1 30N 113 30 E
Kapuas Hulu Ra. = Kapuas Hulu, Pegunungan, Malaysia 75 B4 1 30N 113 30 E
Kapulo, Zaïre 107 D2 8 18 S 29 15 E
Kapunda, Australia 116 C3 34 20 S 138 56 E
Kapuni, N.Z. 118 F3 39 29 S 174 8 E
Kapurthala, India 80 D6 31 23N 75 25 E
Kapuskasing, Canada 128 C3 49 25N 82 30W
Kapuskasing →, Canada 128 C3 49 49N 82 0W
Kapustin Yar, Russia 53 B11 48 37N 45 40 E
Kaputar, Australia 115 E5 30 15 S 150 10 E
Kaputir, Kenya 106 B4 2 5N 35 28 E
Kapuvár, Hungary 31 D10 47 36N 17 1 E
Kara, Russia 56 C7 69 10N 65 0 E
Kara, Turkey 45 H9 36 58N 27 30 E
Kara Bogaz Gol, Zaliv, Turkmenistan 49 F9 41 0N 53 30 E
Kara Kalpak Republic □, Uzbekistan 56 E6 43 0N 58 0 E
Kara Kum = Karakum, Peski, Turkmenistan 56 F6 39 30N 60 0 E
Kara-Saki, Japan 62 C1 34 41N 129 30 E
Kara Sea, Russia 56 B7 75 0N 70 0 E
Kara Su, Kirghizia 55 C6 40 44N 72 53 E
Karabash, Russia 54 D7 55 29N 60 14 E
Karabekaul, Turkmenistan 55 D2 38 30N 64 8 E
Karabük, Turkey 52 F5 41 12N 32 37 E
Karabulak, Kazakhstan 55 A9 44 54N 78 30 E
Karaburun, Turkey 45 F8 38 41N 26 28 E
Karaburuni, Albania 44 D1 40 25N 19 20 E
Karabutak, Kazakhstan 54 G7 49 59N 60 14 E
Karacabey, Turkey 88 C3 40 12N 28 21 E
Karacasu, Turkey 88 E3 37 43N 28 35 E
Karachala, Azerbaijan 53 G13 39 45N 48 53 E
Karachayevsk, Russia 53 E9 43 50N 41 55 E
Karachev, Russia 50 E9 53 10N 35 5 E
Karachi, Pakistan 79 D2 24 53N 67 0 E
Karád, Hungary 31 E10 46 41N 17 51 E
Karad, India 82 F2 17 15N 74 10 E
Karadeniz Boğazı, Turkey 88 C3 41 10N 29 10 E
Karaga, Ghana 101 D4 9 58N 0 28W
Karaganda, Kazakhstan 56 E8 49 50N 73 10 E
Karagayly, Kazakhstan 56 E8 49 26N 76 0 E
Karaginskiy, Ostrov, Russia 57 D17 58 45N 164 0 E
Karagiye Depression, Kazakhstan 49 F9 43 27N 51 45 E
Karagüney Dağları, Turkey 88 C6 40 30N 34 40 E
Karagwe □, Tanzania 106 C3 2 0 S 31 0 E
Karaikal, India 83 J4 10 59N 79 50 E
Karaikkudi, India 83 J4 10 5N 78 45 E
Karaisali, Turkey 88 E6 37 16N 35 2 E
Karaitivu I., Sri Lanka 83 K4 9 45N 79 52 E
Karaj, Iran 85 C6 35 48N 51 0 E
Karak, Malaysia 77 L4 3 25N 102 2 E
Karakas, Kazakhstan 56 E9 48 20N 83 30 E
Karakitang, Indonesia 72 A3 3 14N 125 28 E
Karaklis, Armenia 53 F11 40 48N 44 30 E
Karakoçan, Turkey 89 D9 38 57N 40 2 E
Karakoram Pass, Pakistan 81 B7 35 33N 77 50 E
Karakoram Ra., Pakistan 81 B7 35 30N 77 0 E
Karakul, Tajikistan 55 D6 39 2N 73 33 E
Karakul, Uzbekistan 55 D1 39 22N 63 50 E
Karakuldzha, Kirghizia 55 C6 40 39N 73 26 E
Karakulino, Russia 54 C3 56 1N 53 43 E
Karakum, Peski, Turkmenistan 56 F6 39 30N 60 0 E
Karakurt, Turkey 89 C10 40 10N 42 37 E
Karal, Chad 97 F2 12 50N 14 46 E
Karalon, Russia 57 D12 57 5N 115 50 E
Karaman, Turkey 88 E5 37 14N 33 13 E
Karamay, China 64 B3 45 30N 84 58 E
Karambu, Indonesia 75 C5 3 53 S 116 6 E
Karamea, N.Z. 119 B7 41 14 S 172 6 E
Karamea →, N.Z. 119 B7 41 13 S 172 26 E
Karamea Bight, N.Z. 119 B6 41 22 S 171 40 E
Karamet Niyaz, Turkmenistan 55 E2 37 45N 64 34 E
Karamoja □, Uganda 106 B3 3 0N 34 15 E
Karamsad, India 80 H5 22 35N 72 50 E
Karand, Iran 84 C5 34 16N 46 15 E
Karanganyar, Indonesia 75 D3 7 38 S 109 37 E
Karanja, India 82 D3 20 29N 77 31 E
Karapınar, Turkey 88 E5 37 43N 33 32 E
Karapiro, N.Z. 118 D4 37 53 S 175 32 E
Karasburg, Namibia 104 D2 28 0 S 18 44 E
Karasino, Russia 56 C9 66 50N 86 50 E
Karasjok, Norway 12 B18 69 27N 25 30 E
Karasu, Turkey 88 C4 41 4N 30 46 E
Karasu →, Turkey 89 D8 39 42N 39 25 E
Karasuk, Russia 56 D8 53 44N 78 2 E
Karasuyama, Japan 63 A12 36 39N 140 9 E
Karataş Burnu, Turkey 88 E6 36 32N 35 1 E
Karatau, Kazakhstan 55 B5 43 10N 70 28 E
Karatau, Khrebet, Kazakhstan 55 B4 43 30N 69 30 E
Karatepe, Turkey 88 E7 37 22N 36 16 E
Karativu, Sri Lanka 83 K4 8 22N 79 47 E
Karatobe, Kazakhstan 54 G3 49 44N 53 30 E
Karatoya →, India 78 C2 24 7N 89 36 E
Karaturuk, Kazakhstan 55 B8 43 35N 77 50 E
Karaul-Bazar, Uzbekistan 55 D2 39 30N 64 48 E
Karauli, India 80 F7 26 30N 77 4 E
Karávi, Greece 45 H5 36 49N 23 37 E
Karavostasi, Cyprus 32 D11 35 8N 32 50 E
Karawa, Zaïre 102 B4 3 18N 20 17 E
Karawang, Indonesia 75 D3 6 30 S 107 15 E
Karawanken, Europe 30 E7 46 30N 14 40 E
Karayazı, Turkey 89 D10 39 41N 42 9 E
Karazhal, Kazakhstan 56 E8 48 2N 70 49 E
Karbalā, Iraq 84 C5 32 36N 44 3 E
Kårböle, Sweden 14 C9 61 59N 15 22 E
Karcag, Hungary 31 D13 47 19N 20 57 E
Karcha →, Pakistan 81 B7 34 45N 76 10 E
Karda, Russia 57 D11 55 0N 103 16 E
Kardeljovo, Croatia 42 D2 43 4N 17 26 E
Kardhámila, Greece 45 F8 38 35N 26 5 E
Kardhítsa, Greece 44 E3 39 23N 21 54 E
Kardhítsa □, Greece 44 E3 39 15N 21 50 E
Kärdla, Estonia 50 B3 58 50N 22 40 E
Kareeberge, S. Africa 104 E3 30 59 S 21 50 E
Kareima, Sudan 94 D3 18 30N 31 49 E
Karelian Republic □, Russia 48 A5 65 30N 32 30 E
Karema, Papua N. G. 120 E4 9 12 S 147 18 E
Karevāndar, Iran 85 E9 27 53N 60 44 E
Kargapolye, Russia 54 D9 55 57N 64 24 E
Kargasok, Russia 56 D9 59 3N 80 53 E
Kargat, Russia 56 D9 55 10N 80 15 E
Kargı, Turkey 52 F6 41 11N 34 30 E
Kargil, India 81 B7 34 32N 76 12 E
Kargopol, Russia 48 B6 61 30N 38 58 E
Kargowa, Poland 47 C2 52 5N 15 51 E
Karguéri, Niger 97 F2 13 27N 10 30 E
Karia ba Mohammed, Morocco 98 B3 34 22N 5 12W
Kariaí, Greece 44 D6 40 14N 24 19 E
Karīān, Iran 85 E8 26 57N 57 14 E
Kariba, Zimbabwe 107 F2 16 28 S 28 50 E
Kariba, L., Zimbabwe 107 F2 16 40 S 28 25 E
Kariba Dam, Zimbabwe 107 F2 16 30 S 28 35 E
Kariba Gorge, Zambia 107 F2 16 30 S 28 50 E
Karibib, Namibia 104 C2 22 0 S 15 56 E
Karikari, C., N.Z. 118 A2 34 46 S 173 24 E
Karimata, Kepulauan, Indonesia 75 C3 1 25 S 109 0 E
Karimata, Selat, Indonesia 75 C3 2 0 S 108 40 E
Karimata Is. = Karimata, Kepulauan, Indonesia 75 C3 1 25 S 109 0 E
Karimnagar, India 82 E4 18 26N 79 10 E
Karimunjawa, Kepulauan, Indonesia 75 D4 5 50 S 110 30 E
Karin, Somali Rep. 90 E4 10 50N 45 52 E
Káristos, Greece 45 F6 38 1N 24 29 E
Karīt, Iran 85 C8 33 29N 56 55 E
Kariya, Japan 63 C9 34 58N 137 1 E
Karkal, India 83 H2 13 15N 74 56 E
Karkar I., Papua N. G. 120 C4 4 40 S 146 0 E
Karkaralinsk, Kazakhstan 56 E8 49 26N 75 30 E
Karkinitskiy Zaliv, Ukraine 52 D5 45 56N 33 0 E
Karkur Tohl, Egypt 94 C2 22 5N 25 5 E
Karl Libknekht, Russia 50 F9 51 40N 35 35 E
Karl-Marx-Stadt = Chemnitz, Germany 26 E8 50 50N 12 55 E
Karla, L. = Voiviïs Límni, Greece 44 E4 39 30N 22 45 E
Karlino, Poland 47 A2 54 3N 15 53 E
Karlobag, Croatia 39 D12 44 32N 15 5 E
Karlovac, Croatia 39 C12 45 31N 15 36 E
Karlovka, Ukraine 52 B6 49 29N 35 8 E
Karlovy Vary, Czech. 30 A5 50 13N 12 51 E
Karlsbad = Karlovy Vary, Czech. 30 A5 50 13N 12 51 E
Karlsborg, Sweden 15 F8 58 33N 14 33 E
Karlshamn, Sweden 13 H13 56 10N 14 51 E
Karlskoga, Sweden 13 G13 59 22N 14 33 E
Karlskrona, Sweden 13 H13 56 10N 15 35 E
Karlsruhe, Germany 27 F4 49 3N 8 23 E
Karlstad, Sweden 13 G12 59 23N 13 30 E
Karlstad, U.S.A. 138 A6 48 35N 96 31W
Karlstadt, Germany 27 F5 49 57N 9 46 E
Karnal, India 80 E7 29 42N 77 2 E
Karnali →, Nepal 81 E9 28 45N 81 16 E
Karnaphuli Res., Bangla. 78 D4 22 40N 92 20 E
Karnataka □, India 83 H3 13 15N 77 0 E
Karnes City, U.S.A. 139 L6 28 53N 97 54W
Karnische Alpen, Europe 30 E6 46 36N 13 0 E
Kärnten □, Austria 30 E6 46 52N 13 30 E
Karo, Mali 100 C4 12 16N 3 18W
Karoi, Zimbabwe 107 F2 16 48 S 29 45 E
Karomatan, Phil. 71 H4 7 55N 123 44 E
Karonga, Malawi 107 D3 9 57 S 33 55 E
Karoonda, Australia 116 C3 35 1 S 139 59 E
Karora, Sudan 94 D4 17 44N 38 15 E
Káros, Greece 45 H7 36 54N 25 40 E
Karousádhes, Greece 44 E1 39 47N 19 45 E
Karpasia □, Cyprus 32 D13 35 32N 34 15 E
Kárpathos, Greece 45 J9 35 37N 27 10 E
Kárpathos, Stenón, Greece 45 J9 36 0N 27 30 E
Karpinsk, Russia 54 B7 59 45N 60 1 E
Karpogory, Russia 48 B7 63 59N 44 27 E
Karrebæk, Denmark 15 J5 55 12N 11 39 E
Kars, Turkey 53 F10 40 40N 43 5 E
Kars □, Turkey 89 C10 40 40N 43 0 E
Karsakpay, Kazakhstan 56 E7 47 55N 66 40 E
Karsha, Kazakhstan 53 B14 49 45N 51 35 E
Karshi, Uzbekistan 55 D2 38 53N 65 48 E
Karsiyang, India 81 F13 26 56N 88 18 E
Karst, Croatia 39 C11 45 35N 14 0 E
Karsun, Russia 51 D15 54 14N 46 57 E
Kartál Óros, Greece 44 C7 41 15N 25 13 E
Kartaly, Russia 54 E7 53 3N 60 40 E
Kartapur, India 80 D6 31 27N 75 32 E
Karthaus, U.S.A. 136 E6 41 8N 78 9W
Kartuzy, Poland 47 A5 54 22N 18 10 E
Karuah, Australia 117 B9 32 37 S 151 56 E
Karufa, Indonesia 73 B4 3 50 S 133 20 E
Karumba, Australia 114 B3 17 31 S 140 50 E
Karumo, Tanzania 106 C3 2 25 S 32 50 E
Karumwa, Tanzania 106 C3 3 12 S 32 38 E
Karungu, Kenya 106 C3 0 50 S 34 10 E
Karup, Denmark 15 H3 56 19N 9 10 E
Karur, India 83 J4 10 59N 78 2 E
Karviná, Czech. 31 B11 49 53N 18 25 E
Karwi, India 81 G9 25 12N 80 57 E
Kaş, Turkey 88 E3 36 11N 29 37 E
Kasache, Malawi 107 E3 13 25 S 34 20 E
Kasai, Japan 62 C6 34 55N 134 52 E
Kasai →, Zaïre 103 C3 3 30 S 16 10 E
Kasai Occidental □, Zaïre 103 D4 6 0 S 22 0 E
Kasai Oriental □, Zaïre 103 D4 5 0 S 24 30 E
Kasaji, Zaïre 103 E4 10 25 S 23 27 E
Kasama, Japan 63 A12 36 23N 140 16 E
Kasama, Zambia 107 E3 10 16 S 31 9 E
Kasan-dong, N. Korea 67 D14 41 18N 126 55 E
Kasane, Namibia 104 B3 17 34 S 24 50 E
Kasanga, Tanzania 107 D3 8 30 S 31 10 E
Kasangulu, Zaïre 103 C3 4 33 S 15 15 E
Kasaoka, Japan 62 C5 34 30N 133 30 E
Kasaragod, India 83 H2 12 30N 74 58 E
Kasat, Burma 78 G7 15 56N 98 13 E
Kasba, Bangla. 78 D3 23 45N 91 2 E
Kasba L., Canada 131 A8 60 20N 102 10W
Kasba Tadla, Morocco 98 B3 32 36N 6 17W
Kaseda, Japan 62 F2 31 25N 130 19 E
Kāseh Garān, Iran 84 C5 34 5N 46 2 E
Kasempa, Zambia 107 E2 13 30 S 25 44 E
Kasenga, Zaïre 107 E2 10 20 S 28 45 E
Kasese, Uganda 106 B3 0 13N 30 3 E
Kasewa, Zambia 107 E2 14 28 S 28 53 E
Kasganj, India 81 F8 27 48N 78 42 E
Kashabowie, Canada 128 C1 48 40N 90 26W
Kāshān, Iran 85 C6 34 5N 51 30 E
Kashi, China 64 C2 39 30N 76 2 E
Kashihara, Japan 63 C7 34 27N 135 46 E
Kashima, Ibaraki, Japan 63 B12 35 58N 140 38 E
Kashima, Saga, Japan 62 D2 33 7N 130 6 E
Kashima-Nada, Japan 63 B12 36 0N 140 45 E
Kashimbo, Zaïre 107 E2 11 12 S 26 19 E
Kashin, Russia 51 C10 57 20N 37 36 E
Kashipur, Orissa, India 82 E6 19 16N 83 3 E
Kashipur, Ut. P., India 81 E8 29 15N 79 0 E
Kashira, Russia 51 D11 54 45N 38 10 E
Kashiwa, Japan 63 B11 35 52N 139 59 E
Kashiwazaki, Japan 61 F9 37 22N 138 33 E
Kashk-e Kohneh, Afghan. 79 B1 34 55N 62 30 E
Kashkasu, Kirghizia 55 D6 39 54N 72 44 E
Kāshmar, Iran 85 C8 35 16N 58 26 E
Kashmir, Asia 81 C7 34 0N 76 0 E
Kashmor, Pakistan 79 C3 28 28N 69 32 E
Kashpirovka, Russia 51 E16 53 0N 48 30 E
Kashun Noerh = Gaxun Nur, China 64 B5 42 22N 100 30 E
Kasimov, Russia 51 D12 54 55N 41 20 E
Kasinge, Zaïre 106 D2 6 15 S 26 58 E
Kasiruta, Indonesia 72 B3 0 25 S 127 12 E
Kaskaskia →, U.S.A. 140 G7 37 58N 89 57W
Kaskattama →, Canada 131 B10 57 3N 90 4W
Kaskelen, Kazakhstan 55 B8 43 20N 76 35 E
Kaskinen, Finland 12 E16 62 22N 21 15 E
Kaskö, Finland 12 E16 62 22N 21 15 E
Kasli, Russia 54 D7 55 53N 60 46 E
Kaslo, Canada 130 D5 49 55N 116 55W
Kasmere L., Canada 131 B8 59 34N 101 10W
Kasongan, Indonesia 75 C4 2 0 S 113 23 E
Kasongo, Zaïre 106 C2 4 30 S 26 33 E
Kasongo Lunda, Zaïre 103 D3 6 35 S 16 49 E
Kásos, Greece 45 J8 35 20N 26 55 E
Kásos, Stenón, Greece 45 J8 35 30N 26 30 E
Kaspi, Georgia 53 F11 41 54N 44 17 E
Kaspichan, Bulgaria 43 D12 43 18N 27 11 E
Kaspiysk, Russia 53 E12 42 52N 47 40 E
Kaspiyskiy, Russia 53 D12 45 22N 47 23 E

Kinistino 217


Kewanna, *U.S.A.* **141 C10** 41 1N 86 25W
Kewaunee, *U.S.A.* **134 C2** 44 27N 87 31W
Keweenaw B., *U.S.A.* **134 B1** 47 0N 88 15W
Keweenaw Pen., *U.S.A.* **134 B2** 47 30N 88 0W
Keweenaw Pt., *U.S.A.* **134 B2** 47 25N 87 43W
Key Harbour, *Canada* **128 C3** 45 50N 80 45W
Key West, *U.S.A.* **133 F10** 24 33N 81 48W
Keyesport, *U.S.A.* **140 F7** 38 45N 89 17W
Keyser, *U.S.A.* **134 F6** 39 26N 78 59W
Keystone, *U.S.A.* **138 D3** 43 54N 103 25W
Keytesville, *U.S.A.* **140 E4** 39 26N 92 56W
Kez, *Russia* **54 C3** 57 55N 53 46 E
Kezhma, *Russia* **57 D11** 58 59N 101 9 E
Kežmarok, *Slovak Rep.* **31 B13** 49 10N 20 28 E
Khabarovo, *Russia* **56 C7** 69 30N 60 30 E
Khabarovsk, *Russia* **57 E14** 48 30N 135 5 E
Khabr, *Iran* **85 D8** 28 51N 56 22 E
Khābūr →, *Syria* **84 C4** 35 0N 40 30 E
Khachmas, *Azerbaijan* **53 F13** 41 31N 48 42 E
Khachrod, *India* **80 H6** 23 25N 75 20 E
Khadari, W. el →, *Sudan* **95 E2** 10 29N 27 15 E
Khadro, *Pakistan* **80 F3** 26 11N 68 50 E
Khadyzhensk, *Russia* **53 D8** 44 26N 39 32 E
Khadzhilyangar, *India* **81 B8** 35 45N 79 20 E
Khagaria, *India* **81 G12** 25 30N 86 32 E
Khaipur, *Bahawalpur, Pakistan* **80 E5** 29 34N 72 17 E
Khaipur, *Hyderabad, Pakistan* **80 F3** 27 32N 68 49 E
Khair, *India* **80 F7** 27 57N 77 46 E
Khairabad, *India* **81 F9** 27 33N 80 47 E
Khairagarh, *India* **81 J9** 21 27N 81 2 E
Khairpur, *Pakistan* **79 D3** 27 32N 68 49 E
Khāk Dow, *Afghan.* **79 B2** 34 57N 67 16 E
Khakhea, *Botswana* **104 C3** 24 48 S 23 22 E
Khalach, *Turkmenistan* **55 D2** 38 4N 64 52 E
Khalafābād, *Iran* **85 D6** 30 54N 49 24 E
Khalfallah, *Algeria* **99 B5** 34 20N 0 16 E
Khalfūt, *Yemen* **87 D6** 15 52N 52 10 E
Khalilabad, *India* **81 F10** 26 48N 83 5 E
Khalīlī, *Iran* **85 E7** 27 38N 53 17 E
Khalkhāl, *Iran* **85 B6** 37 37N 48 32 E
Khálki, *Greece* **44 E4** 39 36N 22 30 E
Khalkidhikí □, *Greece* **44 D5** 40 25N 23 20 E
Khalkís, *Greece* **45 F5** 38 27N 23 42 E
Khalmer-Sede = Tazovskiy, *Russia* **56 C8** 67 30N 78 44 E
Khalmer Yu, *Russia* **48 A12** 67 58N 65 1 E
Khalturin, *Russia* **51 B16** 58 40N 48 50 E
Khalūf, *Oman* **90 C6** 20 30N 58 13 E
Kham Keut, *Laos* **76 C5** 18 15N 104 43 E
Khamaria, *India* **82 C5** 23 10N 80 52 E
Khamas Country, *Botswana* **104 C4** 21 45 S 26 30 E
Khambat, G. of, *India* **80 J5** 20 45N 72 30 E
Khambhaliya, *India* **80 H3** 22 14N 69 41 E
Khambhat, *India* **80 H5** 22 23N 72 33 E
Khamgaon, *India* **82 D3** 20 42N 76 37 E
Khamilonísion, *Greece* **45 J8** 35 50N 26 15 E
Khamīr, *Iran* **85 E7** 26 57N 55 36 E
Khamir, *Yemen* **86 C3** 16 2N 44 0 E
Khamīs Mushayṭ, *Si. Arabia* **86 C3** 18 18N 42 44 E
Khammam, *India* **82 F5** 17 11N 80 6 E
Khamsa, *Egypt* **91 E1** 30 27N 32 23 E
Khān Abū Shāmat, *Syria* **91 B5** 33 39N 36 53 E
Khān Azād, *Iraq* **84 C5** 33 7N 44 22 E
Khān Mujiddah, *Iraq* **84 C4** 32 21N 43 48 E
Khān Shaykhūn, *Syria* **84 C3** 35 26N 36 38 E
Khān Yūnis, *Egypt* **91 D3** 31 21N 34 18 E
Khānābād, *Afghan.* **79 A3** 36 45N 69 5 E
Khanabad, *Uzbekistan* **55 C5** 40 59N 70 38 E
Khānaqīn, *Iraq* **84 C5** 34 23N 45 25 E
Khānbāghī, *Iran* **85 B7** 36 10N 55 25 E
Khandrá, *Greece* **45 J8** 35 3N 26 8 E
Khandwa, *India* **82 D3** 21 49N 76 22 E
Khandyga, *Russia* **57 C14** 62 42N 135 35 E
Khāneh, *Iran* **84 B5** 36 41N 45 8 E
Khanewal, *Pakistan* **79 C3** 30 20N 71 55 E
Khanh Duong, *Vietnam* **76 F7** 12 44N 108 44 E
Khaniá, *Greece* **32 D6** 35 30N 24 4 E
Khaniá □, *Greece* **32 D6** 35 30N 24 0 E
Khaníon, Kólpos, *Greece* **32 D5** 35 33N 23 55 E
Khanka, Ozero, *Asia* **57 E14** 45 0N 132 24 E
Khankendy, *Azerbaijan* **89 D12** 39 40N 46 25 E
Khanna, *India* **80 D7** 30 42N 76 16 E
Khanpur, *Pakistan* **79 C3** 28 42N 70 35 E
Khantau, *Kazakhstan* **55 A6** 44 13N 73 48 E
Khanty-Mansiysk, *Russia* **56 C7** 61 0N 69 0 E
Khapalu, *Pakistan* **81 B7** 35 10N 76 20 E
Khapcheranga, *Russia* **57 E12** 49 42N 112 24 E
Kharagpur, *India* **81 H12** 22 20N 87 25 E
Khárakas, *Greece* **32 D7** 35 1N 25 7 E
Kharan Kalat, *Pakistan* **79 C2** 28 34N 65 21 E
Kharānaq, *Iran* **85 C7** 32 20N 54 45 E
Kharda, *India* **82 E2** 18 40N 75 34 E
Khardung La, *India* **81 B7** 34 20N 77 43 E
Khârga, El Wâhât el, *Egypt* **94 B3** 25 10N 30 35 E
Khargon, *India* **82 D2** 21 45N 75 40 E
Kharit, Wadi el →, *Egypt* **94 C3** 24 26N 33 3 E
Khārk, Jazireh, *Iran* **85 D6** 29 15N 50 28 E
Kharkiv = Kharkov, *Ukraine* **52 B7** 49 58N 36 20 E
Kharkov, *Ukraine* **52 B7** 49 58N 36 20 E
Kharmanli, *Bulgaria* **43 F10** 41 55N 25 55 E
Kharovsk, *Russia* **51 B12** 59 56N 40 13 E
Khartoum = El Khartûm, *Sudan* **95 D3** 15 31N 32 35 E
Khasan, *Russia* **60 C5** 42 25N 130 40 E
Khasavyurt, *Russia* **53 E12** 43 16N 46 40 E
Khāsh, *Iran* **85 D9** 28 15N 61 15 E
Khashm el Girba, *Sudan* **95 E4** 14 59N 35 58 E
Khashuri, *Georgia* **53 F10** 42 3N 43 35 E
Khasi Hills, *India* **78 C3** 25 30N 91 30 E
Khaskovo, *Bulgaria* **43 F10** 41 56N 25 30 E
Khatanga, *Russia* **57 B11** 72 0N 102 20 E
Khatanga →, *Russia* **57 B11** 72 55N 106 0 E
Khatauli, *India* **80 E7** 29 17N 77 43 E
Khātūnābād, *Iran* **85 C6** 35 30N 51 40 E
Khatyrchi, *Uzbekistan* **55 C2** 40 2N 65 58 E
Khatyrka, *Russia* **57 C18** 62 3N 175 15 E
Khavast, *Uzbekistan* **55 C4** 40 10N 68 49 E
Khawlaf, Ra's, *Yemen* **87 D6** 12 40N 54 7 E
Khay', *Si. Arabia* **86 C3** 18 45N 41 24 E
Khaybar, Harrat, *Si. Arabia* **84 E4** 25 45N 40 0 E
Khaydarken, *Kirghizia* **55 D5** 39 57N 71 20 E
Khāzimiyah, *Iraq* **84 C4** 34 46N 43 37 E
Khazzân Jabal el Awliyâ, *Sudan* **95 D3** 15 24N 32 20 E
Khe Bo, *Vietnam* **76 C5** 19 8N 104 41 E
Khe Long, *Vietnam* **76 B5** 21 29N 104 46 E
Khed, *Maharashtra, India* **82 F1** 17 43N 73 27 E
Khed, *Maharashtra, India* **82 E1** 18 51N 73 56 E
Khekra, *India* **80 E7** 28 52N 77 20 E
Khemarak Phouminville, *Cambodia* **77 G4** 11 37N 102 59 E
Khemelnik, *Ukraine* **52 B2** 49 33N 27 58 E
Khemis Miliana, *Algeria* **99 A5** 36 11N 2 14 E
Khemissèt, *Morocco* **98 B3** 33 50N 6 1W
Khemmarat, *Thailand* **76 D5** 16 10N 105 15 E
Khenāmān, *Iran* **85 D8** 30 27N 56 29 E
Khenchela, *Algeria* **99 A6** 35 28N 7 11 E
Khenifra, *Morocco* **98 B3** 32 58N 5 46W
Kherrata, *Algeria* **99 A6** 36 27N 5 13 E
Khérson, *Greece* **44 C4** 41 5N 22 47 E
Kherson, *Ukraine* **52 C5** 46 35N 32 35 E
Khersónisos Akrotíri, *Greece* **32 D6** 35 30N 24 10 E
Kheta →, *Russia* **57 B11** 71 54N 102 6 E
Khiliomódhion, *Greece* **45 G4** 37 48N 22 51 E
Khilok, *Russia* **57 D12** 51 30N 110 45 E
Khimki, *Russia* **51 D10** 55 50N 37 20 E
Khíos, *Greece* **45 F8** 38 27N 26 9 E
Khirbat Qanāfār, *Lebanon* **91 B4** 33 39N 35 43 E
Khisar-Momina Banya, *Bulgaria* **43 E9** 42 30N 24 44 E
Khiuma = Hiiumaa, *Estonia* **50 B3** 58 50N 22 45 E
Khiva, *Uzbekistan* **56 E7** 41 30N 60 18 E
Khīyāv, *Iran* **84 B5** 38 30N 47 45 E
Khlebarovo, *Bulgaria* **43 D11** 43 37N 26 15 E
Khlong Khlung, *Thailand* **76 D2** 16 12N 99 43 E
Khmelnitskiy, *Ukraine* **50 G5** 49 23N 27 0 E
Khmelnytskyy = Khmelnitskiy, *Ukraine* **50 G5** 49 23N 27 0 E
Khmer Rep. = Cambodia ■, *Asia* **76 F5** 12 15N 105 0 E
Khoai, Hon, *Vietnam* **77 H5** 8 26N 104 50 E
Khodzent, *Tajikistan* **55 C4** 40 17N 69 37 E
Khojak P., *Afghan.* **79 C2** 30 55N 66 30 E
Khok Kloi, *Thailand* **77 H2** 8 17N 98 19 E
Khok Pho, *Thailand* **77 J3** 6 43N 101 6 E
Khokholskiy, *Russia* **51 F11** 51 35N 38 40 E
Kholm, *Afghan.* **79 A2** 36 45N 67 40 E
Kholm, *Russia* **50 C7** 57 10N 31 15 E
Kholmsk, *Russia* **57 E15** 47 40N 142 5 E
Khomas Hochland, *Namibia* **104 C2** 22 40 S 16 0 E
Khomayn, *Iran* **85 C6** 33 40N 50 7 E
Khon Kaen, *Thailand* **76 D4** 16 30N 102 47 E
Khong, *Laos* **76 E5** 14 7N 105 51 E
Khong Sedone, *Laos* **76 E5** 15 34N 105 49 E
Khonu, *Russia* **57 C15** 66 30N 143 12 E
Khoper →, *Russia* **51 G13** 49 30N 42 20 E
Khor el 'Atash, *Sudan* **95 E3** 13 20N 34 15 E
Khóra, *Greece* **45 G3** 37 3N 21 42 E
Khóra Sfakíon, *Greece* **32 D6** 35 15N 24 9 E
Khorāsān □, *Iran* **85 C8** 34 0N 58 0 E
Khorat = Nakhon Ratchasima, *Thailand* **76 E4** 14 59N 102 12 E
Khorat, Cao Nguyen, *Thailand* **76 E4** 15 30N 102 50 E
Khorb el Ethel, *Algeria* **98 C3** 28 30N 6 17W
Khorixas, *Namibia* **104 C1** 20 16 S 14 59 E
Khorog, *Tajikistan* **55 E5** 37 30N 71 36 E
Khorol, *Ukraine* **52 B5** 49 48N 33 15 E
Khorramābād, *Khorāsān, Iran* **85 C8** 35 6N 57 57 E
Khorramābād, *Lorestān, Iran* **85 C6** 33 30N 48 25 E
Khorrāmshahr, *Iran* **85 D6** 30 29N 48 15 E
Khosravī, *Iran* **85 D6** 30 48N 51 28 E
Khosrowābād, *Khuzestān, Iran* **85 D6** 30 10N 48 25 E
Khosrowābād, *Kordestān, Iran* **84 C5** 35 31N 47 38 E
Khosūyeh, *Iran* **85 D7** 28 32N 54 26 E
Khotin, *Ukraine* **52 B2** 48 31N 26 27 E
Khouribga, *Morocco* **98 B3** 32 58N 6 57W
Khoyniki, *Belorussia* **50 F6** 51 54N 29 55 E
Khrami →, *Azerbaijan* **53 F11** 41 25N 45 0 E
Khrenovoye, *Russia* **51 F12** 51 4N 40 16 E
Khristianá, *Greece* **45 H7** 36 14N 25 13 E
Khromtau, *Kazakhstan* **54 F6** 50 17N 58 27 E
Khrysokhou B., *Cyprus* **32 D11** 35 6N 32 25 E
Khtapodhiá, *Greece* **45 G7** 37 24N 25 34 E
Khu Khan, *Thailand* **76 E5** 14 42N 104 12 E
Khudrah, W. →, *Yemen* **87 C5** 18 10N 50 20 E
Khuff, *Si. Arabia* **84 E5** 24 55N 44 53 E
Khūgīānī, *Qandahar, Afghan.* **79 C2** 31 34N 66 32 E
Khūgīānī, *Qandahar, Afghan.* **79 C2** 31 28N 65 14 E
Khulayṣ, *Si. Arabia* **86 B2** 22 9N 39 19 E
Khulna, *Bangla.* **78 D2** 22 45N 89 34 E
Khulna □, *Bangla.* **78 D2** 22 25N 89 35 E
Khulo, *Georgia* **53 F10** 41 33N 42 19 E
Khumago, *Botswana* **104 C3** 20 26 S 24 32 E
Khumrah, *Si. Arabia* **86 B2** 21 22N 39 13 E
Khūnsorkh, *Iran* **85 E8** 27 9N 56 7 E
Khunzakh, *Russia* **53 E12** 42 35N 46 42 E
Khūr, *Iran* **85 C8** 32 55N 58 18 E
Khurai, *India* **80 G8** 24 3N 78 23 E
Khuraydah, *Yemen* **87 D5** 15 33N 48 18 E
Khurayṣ, *Si. Arabia* **85 E6** 25 6N 48 2 E
Khūrīyā Mūrīyā, Jazā 'ir, *Oman* **87 C6** 17 30N 55 58 E
Khurja, *India* **80 E7** 28 15N 77 58 E
Khūsf, *Iran* **85 C8** 32 46N 58 53 E
Khush, *Afghan.* **79 B4** 32 20N 72 20 E
Khuzdar, *Pakistan* **79 D2** 27 52N 66 30 E
Khūzestān □, *Iran* **85 D6** 31 0N 49 0 E
Khvājeh, *Iran* **84 B5** 38 9N 46 35 E
Khvājeh Moḥammad, Kūh-e, *Afghan.* **79 A3** 36 22N 70 17 E
Khvalynsk, *Russia* **51 E16** 52 30N 48 2 E
Khvānsār, *Iran* **85 D7** 29 56N 54 8 E
Khvatovka, *Russia* **51 E15** 52 24N 46 32 E
Khvor, *Iran* **85 C7** 33 45N 55 0 E
Khvorgū, *Iran* **85 E8** 27 34N 56 27 E
Khvormūj, *Iran* **85 D6** 28 40N 51 30 E
Khvoy, *Iran* **84 B5** 38 35N 45 0 E
Khvoynaya, *Russia* **50 B9** 58 58N 34 28 E
Khyber Pass, *Afghan.* **79 B3** 34 10N 71 8 E
Kia, *Solomon Is.* **121 L10** 7 32 S 158 26 E
Kiabukwa, *Zaïre* **103 D4** 8 40 S 24 48 E
Kiadho →, *India* **82 E3** 19 37N 77 40 E
Kiama, *Australia* **117 C9** 34 40 S 150 50 E
Kiamba, *Phil.* **71 H5** 6 2N 124 46 E
Kiambi, *Zaïre* **106 D2** 7 15 S 28 0 E
Kiambu, *Kenya* **106 C4** 1 8 S 36 50 E
Kiangsi = Jiangxi □, *China* **69 D10** 27 30N 116 0 E
Kiangsu = Jiangsu □, *China* **67 H10** 33 0N 120 0 E
Kiáton, *Greece* **45 F4** 38 2N 22 43 E
Kibæk, *Denmark* **15 H2** 56 2N 8 51 E
Kibanga Port, *Uganda* **106 B3** 0 10N 32 58 E
Kibangou, *Congo* **102 C2** 3 26 S 12 22 E
Kibara, *Tanzania* **106 C3** 2 8 S 33 30 E
Kibare, Mts., *Zaïre* **106 D2** 8 25 S 27 10 E
Kibawe, *Phil.* **71 H5** 7 34N 125 0 E
Kibombo, *Zaïre* **103 C5** 3 57 S 25 53 E
Kibondo, *Tanzania* **106 C3** 3 35 S 30 45 E
Kibondo □, *Tanzania* **106 C3** 4 0 S 30 55 E
Kibumbu, *Burundi* **106 C2** 3 32 S 29 45 E
Kibungu, *Rwanda* **106 C3** 2 10 S 30 32 E
Kibuye, *Burundi* **106 C2** 3 39 S 29 59 E
Kibuye, *Rwanda* **106 C2** 2 3 S 29 21 E
Kibwesa, *Tanzania* **106 D2** 6 30 S 29 58 E
Kibwezi, *Kenya* **106 C4** 2 27 S 37 57 E
Kičevo, *Macedonia* **42 F5** 41 34N 20 59 E
Kichiga, *Russia* **57 D17** 59 50N 163 5 E
Kicking Horse Pass, *Canada* **130 C5** 51 28N 116 16W
Kidal, *Mali* **101 B5** 18 26N 1 22 E
Kidapawan, *Phil.* **71 H5** 7 1N 125 3 E
Kidderminster, *U.K.* **17 E5** 52 24N 2 13W
Kidete, *Tanzania* **106 D4** 6 25 S 37 17 E
Kidira, *Senegal* **100 C2** 14 28N 12 13W
Kidnappers, C., *N.Z.* **118 F6** 39 38 S 177 5 E
Kidston, *Australia* **114 B3** 18 52 S 144 8 E
Kidugallo, *Tanzania* **106 D4** 6 49 S 38 15 E
Kidurong, Tanjong, *Malaysia* **75 B4** 3 16N 113 3 E
Kiel, *Germany* **26 A6** 54 16N 10 8 E
Kiel Kanal = Nord-Ostsee Kanal, *Germany* **26 A5** 54 15N 9 40 E
Kielce, *Poland* **47 E7** 50 52N 20 42 E
Kielce □, *Poland* **47 E7** 50 40N 20 40 E
Kieldrecht, *Belgium* **21 F4** 51 17N 4 11 E
Kieler Bucht, *Germany* **26 A6** 54 30N 10 30 E
Kien Binh, *Vietnam* **77 H5** 9 55N 105 19 E
Kien Tan, *Vietnam* **77 G5** 10 7N 105 17 E
Kienge, *Zaïre* **107 E2** 10 30 S 27 30 E
Kiessé, *Niger* **101 C5** 13 29N 4 1 E
Kieta, *Papua N. G.* **120 D8** 6 12 S 155 36 E
Kiev = Kiyev, *Ukraine* **50 F7** 50 30N 30 28 E
Kiffa, *Mauritania* **100 B2** 16 37N 11 24W
Kifisiá, *Greece* **45 F5** 38 4N 23 49 E
Kifissós →, *Greece* **45 F5** 38 35N 23 20 E
Kifrī, *Iraq* **84 C5** 34 45N 45 0 E
Kigali, *Rwanda* **106 C3** 1 59 S 30 4 E
Kigarama, *Tanzania* **106 C3** 1 1 S 31 50 E
Kigoma □, *Tanzania* **106 D2** 5 0 S 30 0 E
Kigoma-Ujiji, *Tanzania* **106 C2** 4 55 S 29 36 E
Kigomasha, Ras, *Tanzania* **106 C4** 4 58 S 38 58 E
Kihee, *Australia* **115 D3** 27 23 S 142 37 E
Kihikihi, *N.Z.* **118 E4** 38 2 S 175 22 E
Kii-Hantō, *Japan* **63 D7** 34 0N 135 45 E
Kii-Sanchi, *Japan* **63 C8** 34 20N 136 0 E
Kii-Suidō, *Japan* **62 D6** 33 40N 134 45 E
Kikaiga-Shima, *Japan* **61 K4** 28 19N 129 59 E
Kikinda, *Serbia* **42 B5** 45 50N 20 30 E
Kikládhes, *Greece* **45 G6** 37 20N 24 30 E
Kikládhes □, *Greece* **45 G6** 37 0N 25 0 E
Kikoira, *Australia* **117 B7** 33 39 S 146 40 E
Kikori, *Papua N. G.* **120 D3** 7 25 S 144 15 E
Kikori →, *Papua N. G.* **120 D3** 7 38 S 144 20 E
Kikuchi, *Japan* **62 E2** 32 59N 130 47 E
Kikwit, *Zaïre* **103 D3** 5 0 S 18 45 E
Kila' Drosh, *Pakistan* **79 B3** 35 33N 71 52 E
Kilakkarai, *India* **83 K4** 9 12N 78 47 E
Kílalki, *Greece* **45 H9** 36 15N 27 35 E
Kilauea Crater, *U.S.A.* **132 J17** 19 25N 155 17W
Kilchberg, *Switz.* **29 B7** 47 18N 8 33 E
Kilcoy, *Australia* **115 D5** 26 59 S 152 30 E
Kildare, *Ireland* **19 C5** 53 10N 6 50W
Kildare □, *Ireland* **19 C5** 53 10N 6 50W
Kilembe, *Zaïre* **103 D3** 5 42 S 19 55 E
Kilgore, *U.S.A.* **139 J7** 32 23N 94 53W
Kilifi, *Kenya* **106 C4** 3 40 S 39 48 E
Kilifi □, *Kenya* **106 C4** 3 30 S 39 40 E
Kilimanjaro, *Tanzania* **106 C4** 3 7 S 37 20 E
Kilimanjaro □, *Tanzania* **106 C4** 4 0 S 38 0 E
Kilinailau Is., *Papua N. G.* **120 C8** 4 45 S 155 20 E
Kilindini, *Kenya* **106 C4** 4 4 S 39 40 E
Kilis, *Turkey* **88 E7** 36 42N 37 6 E
Kiliya, *Ukraine* **52 D3** 45 28N 29 16 E
Kilju, *N. Korea* **67 D15** 40 57N 129 25 E
Kilkee, *Ireland* **19 D2** 52 41N 9 40W
Kilkenny, *Ireland* **19 D4** 52 40N 7 17W
Kilkenny □, *Ireland* **19 D4** 52 35N 7 15W
Kilkieran B., *Ireland* **19 C2** 53 18N 9 45W
Kilkís, *Greece* **44 D4** 40 58N 22 57 E
Kilkís □, *Greece* **44 C4** 41 5N 22 50 E
Killala, *Ireland* **19 B2** 54 13N 9 12W
Killala B., *Ireland* **19 B2** 54 20N 9 12W
Killaloe, *Ireland* **19 D3** 52 48N 8 28W
Killaloe Sta., *Canada* **136 A7** 45 33N 77 25W
Killam, *Canada* **130 C6** 52 47N 111 51W
Killarney, *Australia* **115 D5** 28 20 S 152 18 E
Killarney, *Canada* **128 C3** 45 55N 81 30W
Killarney, *Ireland* **19 D2** 52 2N 9 30W
Killarney, Lakes of, *Ireland* **19 E2** 52 0N 9 30W
Killary Harbour, *Ireland* **19 C2** 53 38N 9 52W
Killdeer, *Canada* **131 D7** 49 6N 106 22W
Killdeer, *U.S.A.* **138 B3** 47 26N 102 48W
Killeen, *U.S.A.* **139 K6** 31 7N 97 44W
Killiecrankie, Pass of, *U.K.* **18 E5** 56 44N 3 46W
Killin, *U.K.* **18 E4** 56 28N 4 20W
Killíni, *Ilía, Greece* **45 G3** 37 55N 21 8 E
Killíni, *Korinthía, Greece* **45 G4** 37 54N 22 25 E
Killybegs, *Ireland* **19 B3** 54 38N 8 26W
Kilmarnock, *U.K.* **18 F4** 55 36N 4 30W
Kilmez, *Russia* **54 C2** 56 58N 50 55 E
Kilmez →, *Russia* **54 C2** 56 58N 50 28 E
Kilmore, *Australia* **117 D6** 37 25 S 144 53 E
Kilondo, *Tanzania* **107 D3** 9 45 S 34 20 E
Kilosa, *Tanzania* **106 D4** 6 48 S 37 0 E
Kilosa □, *Tanzania* **106 D4** 6 48 S 37 0 E
Kilrush, *Ireland* **19 D2** 52 39N 9 30W
Kilwa □, *Tanzania* **107 D4** 9 0 S 39 0 E
Kilwa Kisiwani, *Tanzania* **107 D4** 8 58 S 39 32 E
Kilwa Kivinje, *Tanzania* **107 D4** 8 45 S 39 25 E
Kilwa Masoko, *Tanzania* **107 D4** 8 55 S 39 30 E
Kim, *U.S.A.* **139 G3** 37 15N 103 21W
Kimaam, *Indonesia* **73 C5** 7 58 S 138 53 E
Kimamba, *Tanzania* **106 D4** 6 45 S 37 10 E
Kimba, *Australia* **116 B2** 33 8 S 136 23 E
Kimball, *Nebr., U.S.A.* **138 E3** 41 14N 103 40W
Kimball, *S. Dak., U.S.A.* **138 D5** 43 45N 98 57W
Kimbe, *Papua N. G.* **120 C6** 5 33 S 150 11 E
Kimbe B., *Papua N. G.* **120 C6** 5 15 S 150 30 E
Kimberley, *Australia* **116 B4** 32 50 S 141 4 E
Kimberley, *Canada* **130 D5** 49 40N 115 59W
Kimberley, *S. Africa* **104 D3** 28 43 S 24 46 E
Kimberley Downs, *Australia* **112 C3** 17 24 S 124 22 E
Kimberley Plateau, *Australia* **110 D4** 16 20 S 127 0 E
Kimberly, *U.S.A.* **142 E6** 42 32N 114 22W
Kimchaek, *N. Korea* **67 D15** 40 40N 129 10 E
Kimchŏn, *S. Korea* **67 F15** 36 11N 128 4 E
Kími, *Greece* **45 F6** 38 38N 24 6 E
Kimje, *S. Korea* **67 G14** 35 48N 126 45 E
Kímolos, *Greece* **45 H6** 36 48N 24 37 E
Kimovsk, *Russia* **51 D11** 54 0N 38 29 E
Kimparana, *Mali* **100 C4** 12 48N 5 0W
Kimry, *Russia* **51 C10** 56 55N 37 15 E
Kimsquit, *Canada* **130 C3** 52 45N 126 57W
Kimstad, *Sweden* **15 F9** 58 35N 15 58 E
Kimvula, *Zaïre* **103 D3** 5 44 S 15 58 E
Kinabalu, Gunong, *Malaysia* **75 A5** 6 3N 116 14 E
Kínaros, *Greece* **45 H8** 36 59N 26 15 E
Kinaskan L., *Canada* **130 B2** 57 38N 130 8W
Kinbasket L., *Canada* **130 C5** 52 0N 118 10W
Kincaid, *Canada* **131 D7** 49 40N 107 0W
Kincaid, *U.S.A.* **140 E7** 39 35N 89 25W
Kincardine, *Canada* **128 D3** 44 10N 81 40W
Kinda, *Kasai Or., Zaïre* **103 D5** 9 18 S 25 4 E
Kinda, *Shaba, Zaïre* **103 C4** 4 47 S 21 48 E
Kinder Scout, *U.K.* **16 D6** 53 24N 1 53W
Kindersley, *Canada* **131 C7** 51 30N 109 10W
Kindia, *Guinea* **100 C2** 10 0N 12 52W
Kindu, *Zaïre* **102 C5** 2 55 S 25 50 E
Kinel, *Russia* **54 E2** 53 15N 50 40 E
Kineshma, *Russia* **51 C13** 57 30N 42 5 E
Kinesi, *Tanzania* **106 C3** 1 25 S 33 50 E
King, L., *Australia* **113 F2** 33 10 S 119 35 E
King, Mt., *Australia* **114 D4** 25 10 S 147 30 E
King City, *Calif., U.S.A.* **144 J5** 36 13N 121 8W
King City, *Mo., U.S.A.* **140 D2** 40 3N 94 31W
King Cr. →, *Australia* **114 C2** 24 35 S 139 30 E
King Edward →, *Australia* **112 B4** 14 14 S 126 35 E
King Frederick VI Land = Kong Frederik VI.s Kyst, *Greenland* **6 C5** 63 0N 43 0W
King George B., *Falk. Is.* **160 D4** 51 30 S 60 30W
King George I., *Antarctica* **7 C18** 60 0 S 60 0W
King George Is., *Canada* **127 C11** 57 20N 80 30W
King I., *Australia* **114 F3** 39 50 S 144 0 E
King I., *Canada* **130 C3** 52 10N 127 40W
King Leopold Ras., *Australia* **112 C4** 17 30 S 125 45 E
King Sd., *Australia* **112 C3** 16 50 S 123 20 E
King William I., *Canada* **126 B10** 69 10N 97 25W
King William's Town, *S. Africa* **104 E4** 32 51 S 27 22 E
Kingaroy, *Australia* **115 D5** 26 32 S 151 51 E
Kingfisher, *U.S.A.* **139 H6** 35 52N 97 56W
Kingirbān, *Iraq* **84 C5** 34 40N 44 54 E
Kingisepp = Kuressaare, *Estonia* **50 B3** 58 15N 22 30 E
Kingisepp, *Russia* **50 B6** 59 25N 28 40 E
Kingking, *Phil.* **71 H5** 7 9N 125 54 E
Kingman, *Ariz., U.S.A.* **145 K12** 35 12N 114 4W
Kingman, *Ind., U.S.A.* **141 E9** 39 58N 87 18W
Kingman, *Kans., U.S.A.* **139 G5** 37 39N 98 7W
Kingoonya, *Australia* **115 E2** 30 55 S 135 19 E
Kings →, *U.S.A.* **144 J7** 36 3N 119 50W
Kings Canyon National Park, *U.S.A.* **144 J8** 36 50N 118 40W
King's Lynn, *U.K.* **16 E8** 52 45N 0 25 E
Kings Mountain, *U.S.A.* **135 H5** 35 15N 81 20W
King's Peak, *U.S.A.* **142 F8** 40 46N 110 27W
Kingsbridge, *U.K.* **17 G4** 50 17N 3 46W
Kingsburg, *U.S.A.* **144 J7** 36 31N 119 33W
Kingsbury, *U.S.A.* **141 C10** 41 31N 86 42W
Kingscote, *Australia* **116 C2** 35 40 S 137 38 E
Kingscourt, *Ireland* **19 C5** 53 55N 6 48W
Kingsley, *U.S.A.* **138 D7** 42 35N 95 58W
Kingsport, *U.S.A.* **135 G4** 36 33N 82 33W
Kingston, *Canada* **128 D4** 44 14N 76 30W
Kingston, *Jamaica* **148 C4** 18 0N 76 50W
Kingston, *N.Z.* **119 F3** 45 20 S 168 43 E
Kingston, *Mo., U.S.A.* **140 E2** 39 39N 94 2W
Kingston, *N.Y., U.S.A.* **137 E10** 41 56N 73 59W
Kingston, *Pa., U.S.A.* **137 E9** 41 16N 75 54W
Kingston, *R.I., U.S.A.* **137 E13** 41 29N 71 30W
Kingston Pk., *U.S.A.* **145 K11** 35 45N 115 54W
Kingston South East, *Australia* **116 D3** 36 51 S 139 55 E
Kingston upon Hull, *U.K.* **16 D7** 53 45N 0 20W
Kingston-upon-Thames, *U.K.* **17 F7** 51 23N 0 20W
Kingstown, *Australia* **117 A9** 30 29 S 151 6 E
Kingstown, *St. Vincent* **149 D7** 13 10N 61 10W
Kingstree, *U.S.A.* **135 J6** 33 40N 79 50W
Kingsville, *Canada* **128 D3** 42 2N 82 45W
Kingsville, *U.S.A.* **139 M6** 27 31N 97 52W
Kingussie, *U.K.* **18 D4** 57 5N 4 2W
Kinistino, *Canada* **131 C7** 52 57N 105 2W

220 Kozáni


Kozáni, Greece 44 D3 40 19N 21 47 E
Kozáni □, Greece 44 D3 40 18N 21 45 E
Kozara, Bos.-H. 39 D14 45 0N 17 0 E
Kozarac, Bos.-H. 39 D13 44 58N 16 48 E
Kozelsk, Russia 50 D9 54 2N 35 48 E
Kozhikode = Calicut, India 83 J2 11 15N 75 43 E
Kozhva, Russia 48 A10 65 10N 57 0 E
Koziegłowy, Poland 47 E6 50 37N 19 8 E
Kozienice, Poland 47 D8 51 35N 21 34 E
Kozje, Slovenia 39 B12 46 5N 15 35 E
Kozle, Poland 47 E5 50 20N 18 8 E
Kozloduy, Bulgaria 43 D8 43 45N 23 42 E
Kozlovets, Bulgaria 43 D10 43 30N 25 20 E
Kozlu, Turkey 88 C4 41 26N 31 45 E
Kozluk, Turkey 89 D9 38 11N 41 31 E
Koźmin, Poland 47 D4 51 48N 17 27 E
Kozmodemyansk, Russia 51 C15 56 20N 46 36 E
Kōzu-Shima, Japan 63 C11 34 13N 139 10 E
Kozuchów, Poland 47 D2 51 45N 15 31 E
Kpabia, Ghana 101 D4 9 10N 0 20W
Kpalimé, Togo 101 D5 6 57N 0 44 E
Kpandae, Ghana 101 D4 8 30N 0 2W
Kpessi, Togo 101 D5 8 4N 1 16 E
Kra, Isthmus of = Kra, Kho Khot, Thailand 77 G2 10 15N 99 30 E
Kra, Kho Khot, Thailand 77 G2 10 15N 99 30 E
Kra Buri, Thailand 77 G2 10 22N 98 46 E
Krabbendijke, Neths. 21 F4 51 26N 4 7 E
Krabi, Thailand 77 H2 8 4N 98 55 E
Kragan, Indonesia 75 D4 6 43 S 111 38 E
Kragerø, Norway 14 F3 58 52N 9 25 E
Kragujevac, Serbia 42 C5 44 2N 20 56 E
Krajenka, Poland 47 B3 53 18N 16 59 E
Krajina, Bos.-H. 39 D13 44 45N 16 35 E
Krakatau = Rakata, Pulau, Indonesia 74 D3 6 10 S 105 20 E
Krakor, Cambodia 76 F5 12 32N 104 12 E
Kraków, Poland 31 A12 50 4N 19 57 E
Kraków □, Poland 31 A13 50 0N 20 0 E
Kraksaan, Indonesia 75 D4 7 43 S 113 23 E
Kråkstad, Norway 14 E4 59 39N 10 55 E
Kralanh, Cambodia 76 F4 13 35N 103 25 E
Králiky, Czech. 31 A9 50 6N 16 45 E
Kraljevo, Serbia 42 D5 43 44N 20 41 E
Kralovice, Czech. 30 B6 49 59N 13 29 E
Královský Chlmec, Slovak Rep. 31 C14 48 27N 22 0 E
Kralupy, Czech. 30 A7 50 13N 14 20 E
Kramatorsk, Ukraine 52 B7 48 50N 37 30 E
Kramfors, Sweden 14 B11 62 55N 17 48 E
Kramis, C., Algeria 99 A5 36 26N 0 45 E
Krångede, Sweden 14 A10 63 9N 16 10 E
Kraniá, Greece 44 E3 39 53N 21 18 E
Kranídhion, Greece 45 G5 37 20N 23 10 E
Kranj, Slovenia 39 B11 46 16N 14 22 E
Kranjska Gora, Slovenia 39 B10 46 29N 13 48 E
Krankskop, S. Africa 105 D5 28 0 S 30 47 E
Krapina, Croatia 39 B12 46 10N 15 52 E
Krapina →, Croatia 39 C12 45 50N 15 50 E
Krapivna, Russia 51 E10 53 58N 37 10 E
Krapkowice, Poland 47 E4 50 29N 17 56 E
Krasavino, Russia 48 B8 60 58N 46 29 E
Krashyy Klyuch, Russia 54 D5 55 23N 56 39 E
Kraskino, Russia 57 E14 42 44N 130 48 E
Kraslice, Czech. 30 A5 50 19N 12 31 E
Krasnaya Gorbatka, Russia 51 D12 55 52N 41 45 E
Krasnaya Polyana, Russia 53 E9 43 40N 40 13 E
Kraśnik, Poland 47 E9 50 55N 22 5 E
Kraśnik Fabryczny, Poland 47 E9 50 58N 22 11 E
Krasnoarmeisk, Ukraine 52 B7 48 18N 37 11 E
Krasnoarmeysk, Russia 51 F14 51 0N 45 42 E
Krasnoarmeysk, Russia 53 B11 48 30N 44 25 E
Krasnodar, Russia 53 D8 45 5N 39 0 E
Krasnodon, Ukraine 53 B8 48 17N 39 44 E
Krasnodonetskaya, Russia 53 B9 48 5N 40 50 E
Krasnogorskiy, Russia 51 C16 56 10N 48 28 E
Krasnograd, Ukraine 52 B6 49 27N 35 27 E
Krasnogvardeysk, Uzbekistan 55 D3 39 46N 67 16 E
Krasnogvardeyskoye, Russia 53 D9 45 52N 41 33 E
Krasnogvardyesk, Ukraine 52 D6 45 32N 34 16 E
Krasnokamsk, Russia 54 B4 58 4N 55 48 E
Krasnokutsk, Ukraine 50 F9 50 10N 34 50 E
Krasnoperekopsk, Ukraine 52 D5 46 0N 33 54 E
Krasnorechenskiy, Russia 60 B7 44 41N 135 14 E
Krasnoselkupsk, Russia 56 C9 65 20N 82 10 E
Krasnoslobodsk, Russia 51 D13 54 25N 43 45 E
Krasnoslobodsk, Russia 53 B11 48 42N 44 33 E
Krasnoturinsk, Russia 54 B7 59 46N 60 12 E
Krasnoufimsk, Russia 54 C5 56 57N 57 46 E
Krasnouralsk, Russia 54 B7 58 21N 60 3 E
Krasnousolskiy, Russia 54 E5 53 54N 56 27 E
Krasnovishersk, Russia 54 A5 60 23N 57 3 E
Krasnovodsk, Turkmenistan 49 F9 40 0N 52 52 E
Krasnoyarsk, Russia 57 D10 56 8N 93 0 E
Krasnoyarskiy, Russia 54 F6 51 58N 59 55 E
Krasnoye = Krasnyy, Russia 50 D7 54 25N 31 30 E
Krasnoye, Russia 51 B15 59 15N 47 40 E
Krasnoye, Russia 53 C11 46 16N 45 0 E
Krasnozavodsk, Russia 51 C11 56 27N 38 25 E
Krasny Liman, Ukraine 52 B7 48 58N 37 50 E
Krasny Sulin, Russia 53 C9 47 52N 40 8 E
Krasnystaw, Poland 47 E10 50 57N 23 5 E
Krasnyy, Russia 50 D7 54 25N 31 30 E
Krasnyy Kholm, Russia 51 B10 58 10N 37 10 E
Krasnyy Kholm, Russia 54 F4 51 35N 54 9 E
Krasnyy Kut, Russia 51 F15 50 50N 47 0 E
Krasnyy Luch, Ukraine 53 B8 48 13N 39 0 E
Krasnyy Profintern, Russia 51 C12 57 45N 40 27 E
Krasnyy Yar, Russia 51 F14 50 42N 44 45 E
Krasnyy Yar, Russia 53 C13 46 43N 48 23 E
Krasnyy Yar, Russia 54 E2 53 30N 50 22 E
Krasnyye Baki, Russia 51 C14 57 8N 45 10 E
Krasnyyoskolskoye Vdkhr., Ukraine 52 B7 49 30N 37 30 E
Kraszna →, Hungary 31 C15 48 4N 22 20 E
Kratie, Cambodia 76 F6 12 32N 106 10 E
Kratke Ra., Papua N. G. 120 D3 6 45 S 146 0 E
Kratovo, Macedonia 42 E7 42 6N 22 10 E
Krau, Indonesia 73 B6 3 19 S 140 5 E
Kravanh, Chuor Phnum, Cambodia 77 G4 12 0N 103 32 E
Krefeld, Germany 26 D2 51 20N 6 32 E
Krémaston, Límni, Greece 45 F3 38 52N 21 30 E
Kremenchug, Ukraine 52 B5 49 5N 33 25 E
Kremenchugskoye Vdkhr., Ukraine 52 B5 49 20N 32 30 E
Kremenchuk = Kremenchug, Ukraine 52 B5 49 5N 33 25 E
Kremenets, Ukraine 52 A1 50 8N 25 43 E
Kremenica, Macedonia 44 D3 40 55N 21 25 E
Kremennaya, Ukraine 52 B8 49 1N 38 10 E
Kremges = Svetlovodsk, Ukraine 50 G8 49 2N 33 13 E
Kremikovtsi, Bulgaria 43 E8 42 46N 23 28 E
Kremmen, Germany 26 C9 52 45N 13 1 E
Kremmling, U.S.A. 142 F10 40 4N 106 24W
Kremnica, Slovak Rep. 31 C11 48 45N 18 50 E
Krems, Austria 30 C8 48 25N 15 36 E
Kremsmünster, Austria 30 C7 48 3N 14 8 E
Kretinga, Lithuania 50 D2 55 53N 21 15 E
Krettamia, Algeria 98 C4 28 47N 3 27W
Krettsy, Russia 50 B8 58 15N 32 30 E
Kreuzberg, Germany 27 E5 50 22N 9 58 E
Kreuzlingen, Switz. 29 A8 47 38N 9 10 E
Kribi, Cameroon 101 E6 2 57N 9 56 E
Krichem, Bulgaria 43 E9 42 8N 24 28 E
Krichev, Belorussia 50 E7 53 45N 31 50 E
Krim, Slovenia 39 C11 45 53N 14 30 E
Krimpen, Neths. 20 E5 51 55N 4 34 E
Krionéri, Greece 45 F3 38 20N 21 35 E
Kriós, Ákra, Greece 32 D5 35 13N 23 34 E
Krishna →, India 83 G5 15 57N 80 59 E
Krishnagiri, India 83 H4 12 32N 78 16 E
Krishnanagar, India 81 H13 23 24N 88 33 E
Krishnaraja Sagara, India 83 H3 12 20N 76 30 E
Kristiansand, Norway 13 G10 58 9N 8 1 E
Kristianstad, Sweden 13 H13 56 2N 14 9 E
Kristianstads län □, Sweden 13 H13 56 15N 14 0 E
Kristiansund, Norway 14 A1 63 7N 7 45 E
Kristiinankaupunki, Finland 12 E16 62 16N 21 21 E
Kristinehamn, Sweden 13 G13 59 18N 14 13 E
Kristinestad, Finland 12 E16 62 16N 21 21 E
Kríti, Greece 32 D7 35 15N 25 0 E
Kritsá, Greece 32 D7 35 10N 25 41 E
Kriva →, Macedonia 42 E6 42 5N 21 47 E
Kriva Palanka, Macedonia 42 E7 42 11N 22 19 E
Krivaja →, Bos.-H. 42 C3 44 27N 18 9 E
Krivelj, Serbia 42 C7 44 10N 22 5 E
Krivoy Rog, Ukraine 52 C5 47 51N 33 20 E
Križevci, Croatia 39 B13 46 3N 16 32 E
Krk, Croatia 39 C11 45 8N 14 40 E
Krka →, Slovenia 39 C12 45 50N 15 30 E
Krkonoše, Czech. 30 A8 50 50N 15 35 E
Krnov, Czech. 31 A10 50 5N 17 40 E
Krobia, Poland 47 D3 51 47N 16 59 E
Kročehlavy, Czech. 30 A7 50 8N 14 9 E
Krokeaí, Greece 45 H4 36 53N 22 32 E
Krokodil →, Mozam. 105 D5 25 14 S 32 18 E
Krokom, Sweden 14 A8 63 20N 14 30 E
Krokowa, Poland 47 A5 54 47N 18 9 E
Krolevets, Ukraine 50 F8 51 35N 33 20 E
Kroměríz, Czech. 31 B10 49 18N 17 21 E
Krommenie, Neths. 20 D5 52 30N 4 46 E
Krompachy, Slovak Rep. 31 C13 48 54N 20 52 E
Kromy, Russia 50 E9 52 48N 35 48 E
Kronach, Germany 27 E7 50 14N 11 19 E
Kronobergs län □, Sweden 13 H13 56 45N 14 30 E
Kronprins Olav Kyst, Antarctica 7 C5 69 0 S 42 0 E
Kronshtadt, Russia 50 A6 60 5N 29 45 E
Kroonstad, S. Africa 104 D4 27 43 S 27 19 E
Kröpelin, Germany 26 A7 54 4N 11 48 E
Kropotkin, Russia 53 D9 45 28N 40 28 E
Kropotkin, Russia 57 D12 59 0N 115 30 E
Kropp, Germany 26 A5 54 24N 9 32 E
Krościenko, Poland 31 B13 49 29N 20 25 E
Krośniewice, Poland 47 C6 52 15N 19 11 E
Krosno, Poland 31 B14 49 42N 21 46 E
Krosno □, Poland 31 B14 49 35N 22 0 E
Krosno Odrzańskie, Poland 47 C2 52 3N 15 7 E
Krotoszyn, Poland 47 D4 51 42N 17 23 E
Krotovka, Russia 54 E2 53 18N 51 10 E
Kroussón, Greece 32 D6 35 13N 24 59 E
Krraba, Albania 44 C2 41 13N 20 0 E
Krško, Slovenia 39 C12 45 57N 15 30 E
Krstača, Serbia 42 E5 42 57N 20 8 E
Kruger Nat. Park, S. Africa 105 C5 23 30 S 31 40 E
Krugersdorp, S. Africa 105 D4 26 5 S 27 46 E
Kruiningen, Neths. 21 F4 51 27N 4 2 E
Kruisfontein, S. Africa 104 E3 33 59 S 24 43 E
Kruishoutem, Belgium 21 G3 50 54N 3 32 E
Kruisland, Neths. 21 E4 51 34N 4 25 E
Kruja, Albania 44 C1 41 32N 19 46 E
Krulevshchina, Belorussia 50 D5 55 5N 27 45 E
Kruma, Albania 44 B2 42 14N 20 28 E
Krumbach, Germany 27 G6 48 15N 10 22 E
Krumovgrad, Bulgaria 43 F10 41 29N 25 38 E
Krung Thep = Bangkok, Thailand 76 F3 13 45N 100 35 E
Krupanj, Serbia 42 C4 44 25N 19 22 E
Krupina, Slovak Rep. 31 C12 48 22N 19 5 E
Krupinica →, Slovak Rep. 31 C11 48 15N 18 52 E
Kruševac, Serbia 42 D6 43 35N 21 28 E
Kruševo, Macedonia 42 F6 41 23N 21 19 E
Kruszwica, Poland 47 C5 52 40N 18 20 E
Kruzof I., U.S.A. 130 B1 57 10N 135 40W
Krychaw = Krichev, Belorussia 50 E7 53 45N 31 50 E
Krymsk Abinsk, Russia 52 D8 44 50N 38 0 E
Krymskiy Poluostrov, Ukraine 52 D5 45 0N 34 0 E
Krynica, Poland 31 B13 49 25N 20 57 E
Krynica Morska, Poland 47 A6 54 23N 19 28 E
Krynki, Poland 47 B10 53 17N 23 43 E
Kryvyy Rih = Krivoy Rog, Ukraine 52 C5 47 51N 33 20 E
Krzepice, Poland 47 E5 50 58N 18 50 E
Krzeszów, Poland 47 E9 50 24N 22 21 E
Krzeszowice, Poland 31 A12 50 8N 19 37 E
Krzna →, Poland 47 D9 51 59N 22 47 E
Krzywiń, Poland 47 D3 51 58N 16 50 E
Krzyz, Poland 47 C3 52 52N 16 0 E
Ksabi, Morocco 98 B4 32 51N 4 13W
Ksar Chellala, Algeria 99 A5 35 13N 2 19 E
Ksar el Boukhari, Algeria 99 A5 35 51N 2 52 E
Ksar el Kebir, Morocco 98 B3 35 0N 6 0W
Ksar es Souk = Ar Rachidiya, Morocco 98 B4 31 58N 4 20W
Ksar Rhilane, Tunisia 96 B1 33 0N 9 39 E
Ksour, Mts. des, Algeria 99 B4 32 45N 0 30W
Kstovo, Russia 51 C14 56 12N 44 13 E
Kuala, Indonesia 74 B3 2 55N 105 47 E
Kuala Belait, Malaysia 75 B4 4 35N 114 11 E
Kuala Berang, Malaysia 77 K4 5 5N 103 1 E
Kuala Dungun, Malaysia 77 K4 4 45N 103 25 E
Kuala Kangsar, Malaysia 77 K3 4 46N 100 56 E
Kuala Kelawang, Malaysia 77 L4 2 56N 102 5 E
Kuala Kerai, Malaysia 77 K4 5 30N 102 12 E
Kuala Kubu Baharu, Malaysia 77 L3 3 34N 101 39 E
Kuala Lipis, Malaysia 77 K4 4 10N 102 3 E
Kuala Lumpur, Malaysia 77 L3 3 9N 101 41 E
Kuala Nerang, Malaysia 77 J3 6 16N 100 37 E
Kuala Pilah, Malaysia 77 L4 2 45N 102 15 E
Kuala Rompin, Malaysia 77 L4 2 49N 103 29 E
Kuala Selangor, Malaysia 77 L3 3 20N 101 15 E
Kuala Terengganu, Malaysia 77 K4 5 20N 103 8 E
Kualajelai, Indonesia 75 C4 2 58 S 110 46 E
Kualakapuas, Indonesia 75 C4 2 55 S 114 20 E
Kualakurun, Indonesia 75 C4 1 10 S 113 50 E
Kualapembuang, Indonesia 75 C4 3 14 S 112 38 E
Kualasimpang, Indonesia 74 B1 4 17N 98 3 E
Kuamat, Malaysia 75 A5 5 13N 117 30 E
Kuancheng, China 67 D10 40 37N 118 30 E
Kuandang, Indonesia 72 A2 0 56N 123 1 E
Kuandian, China 67 D13 40 45N 124 45 E
Kuangchou = Guangzhou, China 69 F9 23 5N 113 10 E
Kuantan, Malaysia 77 L4 3 49N 103 20 E
Kuba, Azerbaijan 53 F13 41 21N 48 32 E
Kuban →, Russia 52 D7 45 20N 37 30 E
Kubenskoye, Oz., Russia 51 B11 59 40N 39 25 E
Kuberle, Russia 53 C10 47 0N 42 20 E
Kubokawa, Japan 62 D5 33 12N 133 8 E
Kubor, Mt., Papua N. G. 120 D3 6 10 S 144 44 E
Kubrat, Bulgaria 43 D11 43 49N 26 31 E
Kučevo, Serbia 42 C6 44 30N 21 40 E
Kucha Gompa, India 81 B7 34 25N 76 56 E
Kuchaman, India 80 F6 27 13N 74 47 E
Kuchenspitze, Austria 30 D3 47 7N 10 12 E
Kuchino-eruba-Jima, Japan 61 J5 30 28N 130 12 E
Kuchino-Shima, Japan 61 K4 29 57N 129 55 E
Kuchinotsu, Japan 62 E2 32 36N 130 11 E
Kucing, Malaysia 75 B4 1 33N 110 25 E
Kuçove = Qytet Stalin, Albania 44 D1 40 47N 19 57 E
Kücük Kuyu, Turkey 44 E8 39 35N 26 27 E
Kud →, Pakistan 80 F2 26 5N 66 20 E
Kudalier →, India 82 E4 18 35N 79 48 E
Kudamatsu, Japan 62 D3 34 0N 131 52 E
Kudara, Tajikistan 55 D6 38 25N 72 39 E
Kudat, Malaysia 75 A5 6 55N 116 55 E
Kudayd, Si. Arabia 86 C3 19 21N 41 48 E
Kudremukh, India 83 H2 13 15N 75 20 E
Kudus, Indonesia 75 D4 6 48 S 110 51 E
Kudymkar, Russia 54 B4 59 1N 54 39 E
Kueiyang = Guiyang, China 68 D6 26 32N 106 40 E
Kufstein, Austria 30 D5 47 35N 12 11 E
Kugong I., Canada 128 A4 56 18N 79 50W
Kūh-e Dīnār, Iran 85 D6 30 40N 51 0 E
Kūh-e-Hazārām, Iran 85 D8 29 35N 57 20 E
Kūhak, Iran 79 D1 27 12N 63 10 E
Kūhbonān, Iran 85 D8 31 23N 56 19 E
Kūhestak, Iran 85 E8 26 47N 57 2 E
Kūhestān, Afghan. 79 B1 34 39N 61 12 E
Kūhīn, Iran 85 C6 35 13N 48 25 E
Kūhīrī, Iran 85 E9 26 55N 61 2 E
Kuhnsdorf, Austria 30 E7 46 37N 14 38 E
Kūhpāyeh, Eşfahan, Iran 85 C7 32 44N 52 20 E
Kūhpāyeh, Kermān, Iran 85 D8 30 35N 57 15 E
Kui Buri, Thailand 77 F2 12 3N 99 52 E
Kuinre, Neths. 20 C7 52 47N 5 51 E
Kuito, Angola 103 E3 12 22 S 16 55 E
Kujang, N. Korea 67 E14 39 57N 126 1 E
Kuji, Japan 60 D10 40 11N 141 46 E
Kujū-San, Japan 62 D3 33 5N 131 15 E
Kujukuri-Heiya, Japan 63 B12 35 45N 140 30 E
Kukavica, Serbia 42 E6 42 48N 21 57 E
Kukawa, Nigeria 101 C7 12 58N 13 27 E
Kukerin, Australia 113 F2 33 13 S 118 0 E
Kukësi, Albania 44 B2 42 5N 20 20 E
Kukësi □, Albania 44 B2 42 25N 20 15 E
Kukmor, Russia 54 C2 56 11N 50 54 E
Kukup, Malaysia 77 M4 1 20N 103 27 E
Kukvidze, Russia 51 F13 50 40N 43 0 E
Kula, Bulgaria 42 D7 43 52N 22 36 E
Kula, Serbia 42 B4 45 37N 19 32 E
Kula Gulf, Solomon Is. 121 M9 8 5 S 157 18 E
Kulai, Malaysia 77 M4 1 44N 103 35 E
Kulal, Mt., Kenya 106 B4 2 42N 36 57 E
Kulaly, Os., Kazakhstan 53 D14 45 0N 50 0 E
Kulanak, Kirghizia 55 C7 41 22N 75 30 E
Kulasekarappattinam, India 83 K4 8 20N 78 5 E
Kuldiga, Latvia 50 C2 56 58N 21 59 E
Kuldja = Yining, China 56 E9 43 58N 81 10 E
Kuldu, Sudan 95 E2 12 50N 28 30 E
Kulebaki, Russia 51 D13 55 22N 42 25 E
Kulen Vakuf, Bos.-H. 39 D13 44 35N 16 2 E
Kulgam, India 81 C6 33 36N 75 2 E
Kuli, Russia 53 E12 42 2N 47 12 E
Kulim, Malaysia 77 K3 5 22N 100 34 E
Kulin, Australia 113 F2 32 40 S 118 2 E
Kulja, Australia 113 F2 30 28 S 117 18 E
Küllük, Turkey 45 G9 37 12N 27 36 E
Kulm, U.S.A. 138 B5 46 18N 98 57W
Kulmbach, Germany 27 E7 50 6N 11 27 E
Kulp, Turkey 89 D9 38 29N 41 2 E
Kulsary, Kazakhstan 49 E9 46 59N 54 1 E
Kultay, Kazakhstan 53 D14 45 5N 51 40 E
Kulti, India 81 H12 23 43N 86 50 E
Kulu, Turkey 88 D5 39 5N 33 4 E
Kulumbura, Australia 112 B4 13 55 S 126 35 E
Kulunda, Russia 56 D8 52 35N 78 57 E
Kulungar, Afghan. 80 C3 34 0N 69 2 E
Kūlvand, Iran 85 D7 31 21N 54 35 E
Kulwin, Australia 116 C5 35 0 S 142 42 E
Kulyab, Tajikistan 55 E4 37 55N 69 50 E
Kum Tekei, Kazakhstan 56 E8 43 10N 79 30 E
Kuma, Japan 62 D4 33 39N 132 54 E
Kuma →, Russia 53 D12 44 55N 47 0 E
Kumaganum, Nigeria 101 C7 13 8N 10 38 E
Kumagaya, Japan 63 A11 36 9N 139 22 E
Kumai, Indonesia 75 C4 2 44 S 111 43 E
Kumak, Russia 54 F7 51 10N 60 8 E
Kumamba, Kepulauan, Indonesia 73 B5 1 36 S 138 45 E
Kumamoto, Japan 62 E2 32 45N 130 45 E
Kumamoto □, Japan 62 E2 32 55N 130 55 E
Kumano, Japan 63 D8 33 54N 136 5 E
Kumano-Nada, Japan 63 D8 33 47N 136 20 E
Kumanovo, Macedonia 42 E6 42 9N 21 42 E
Kumara, N.Z. 119 C6 42 37 S 171 12 E
Kumarkhali, Bangla. 78 D2 23 51N 89 15 E
Kumarl, Australia 113 F3 32 47 S 121 33 E
Kumasi, Ghana 100 D4 6 41N 1 38W
Kumayri, Armenia 53 F10 40 47N 43 50 E
Kumba, Cameroon 101 E6 4 36N 9 24 E
Kumbakonam, India 83 J4 10 58N 79 25 E
Kumbarilla, Australia 115 D5 27 15 S 150 55 E
Kumbo, Cameroon 101 D7 6 15N 10 36 E
Kumbukkan Oya →, Sri Lanka 83 L5 6 35N 81 40 E
Kŭmchŏn, N. Korea 67 E14 38 10N 126 29 E
Kumdah, Si. Arabia 86 B4 20 23N 45 5 E
Kumdok, India 81 C8 33 32N 78 10 E
Kume-Shima, Japan 61 L3 26 20N 126 47 E
Kumeny, Russia 54 B1 58 10N 49 47 E
Kumertau, Russia 54 E4 52 46N 55 47 E
Kŭmhwa, S. Korea 67 E14 38 17N 127 28 E
Kumi, Uganda 106 B3 1 30N 33 58 E
Kumkale, Turkey 44 E8 40 0N 26 13 E
Kumla, Sweden 13 G13 59 8N 15 10 E
Kumluca, Turkey 88 E4 36 11N 30 17 E
Kummerower See, Germany 26 B8 53 47N 12 52 E
Kumo, Nigeria 101 C7 10 1N 11 12 E
Kumon Bum, Burma 78 B6 26 30N 97 15 E
Kumotori-Yama, Japan 63 B10 35 51N 138 57 E
Kumta, India 83 G2 14 29N 74 25 E
Kumtorkala, Russia 53 E12 43 2N 46 50 E
Kumusi →, Papua N. G. 120 E5 8 16 S 148 13 E
Kumylzhenskaya, Russia 53 B10 49 51N 42 38 E
Kunágota, Hungary 31 E14 46 26N 21 3 E
Kunak, Malaysia 75 B5 4 41N 118 15 E
Kunama, Australia 117 C8 35 35 S 148 4 E
Kunashir, Ostrov, Russia 57 E15 44 0N 146 0 E
Kunda, Estonia 50 B5 59 30N 26 34 E
Kundiawa, Papua N. G. 120 D3 6 2 S 145 1 E
Kundla, India 80 J4 21 21N 71 25 E
Kundur, Indonesia 74 C3 3 8 S 107 48 E
Kungala, Australia 115 D5 29 58 S 153 7 E
Kungälv, Sweden 15 G5 57 53N 11 59 E
Kungey Alatau, Khrebet, Kirghizia 55 B8 42 50N 77 0 E
Kunghit I., Canada 130 C2 52 6N 131 3W
Kungrad, Uzbekistan 56 E6 43 6N 58 54 E
Kungsbacka, Sweden 15 G6 57 30N 12 5 E
Kungu, Zaïre 102 B3 2 47N 19 12 E
Kungur, Russia 54 C5 57 25N 56 57 E
Kungurri, Australia 114 C4 21 3 S 148 46 E
Kungyangon, Burma 78 G6 16 27N 96 20 E
Kunhar →, Pakistan 81 B5 34 20N 73 30 E
Kunhegyes, Hungary 31 D13 47 22N 20 36 E
Kunimi-Dake, Japan 62 E3 32 33N 131 1 E
Kuningan, Indonesia 75 D3 6 59 S 108 29 E
Kunisaki, Japan 62 D3 33 33N 131 45 E
Kunlara, Australia 116 C3 34 54 S 139 55 E
Kunlong, Burma 78 D7 23 20N 98 50 E
Kunlun Shan, Asia 64 C3 36 0N 86 30 E
Kunmadaras, Hungary 31 D13 47 28N 20 45 E
Kunming, China 68 E4 25 1N 102 41 E
Kunnamkulam, India 83 J3 10 38N 76 7 E
Kunrade, Neths. 21 G7 50 53N 5 57 E
Kunsan, S. Korea 67 G14 35 59N 126 45 E
Kunshan, China 69 B13 31 22N 120 58 E
Kunszentmárton, Hungary 31 E13 46 50N 20 20 E
Kununurra, Australia 112 C4 15 40 S 128 50 E
Kunwarara, Australia 114 C5 22 55 S 150 9 E
Kunya-Urgench, Turkmenistan 56 E6 42 19N 59 10 E
Künzelsau, Germany 27 F5 49 17N 9 41 E
Kuopio, Finland 12 E19 62 53N 27 35 E
Kuopion lääni □, Finland 12 E19 63 25N 27 10 E
Kupa →, Croatia 39 C13 45 28N 16 24 E
Kupang, Indonesia 72 D2 10 19 S 123 39 E
Kupiano, Papua N. G. 120 F5 10 4 S 148 14 E
Kupres, Bos.-H. 42 C2 44 1N 17 15 E
Kupyansk, Ukraine 52 B7 49 52N 37 35 E
Kupyansk-Uzlovoi, Ukraine 52 B7 49 45N 37 34 E
Kuqa, China 64 B3 41 35N 82 30 E
Kur →, Bhutan 78 B3 26 50N 91 0 E
Kura →, Azerbaijan 49 G8 39 50N 49 20 E
Kurahashi-Jima, Japan 62 C4 34 8N 132 31 E
Kuranda, Australia 114 B4 16 48 S 145 35 E
Kurashiki, Japan 62 C5 34 40N 133 50 E
Kurayoshi, Japan 62 B5 35 26N 133 50 E
Kurday, Kazakhstan 55 B7 43 21N 74 59 E
Kurdistan, Asia 89 E10 37 20N 43 30 E
Kurduvadi, India 82 E2 18 8N 75 29 E
Kŭrdzhali, Bulgaria 43 F10 41 38N 25 21 E
Kure, Japan 62 C4 34 14N 132 32 E
Küre, Turkey 88 C5 41 48N 33 43 E
Küre Dağları, Turkey 88 C6 41 50N 34 10 E
Kuressaare, Estonia 50 B3 58 15N 22 30 E
Kurgaldzhino, Kazakhstan 56 D8 50 35N 70 20 E
Kurgan, Russia 54 D9 55 26N 65 18 E
Kurgan-Tyube, Tajikistan 55 E4 37 50N 68 47 E
Kurganinsk, Russia 53 D9 44 54N 40 34 E
Kurgannaya = Kurganinsk, Russia 53 D9 44 54N 40 34 E
Kuria Maria Is. = Khūrīyā Mūrīyā, Jazā 'ir, Oman 87 C6 17 30N 55 58 E
Kuria Muria B., Oman 87 C6 17 40N 55 45 E
Kurichchi, India 83 J3 11 36N 77 35 E
Kuridala, Australia 114 C3 21 16 S 140 29 E

Kurigram, *Bangla.* 78 C2 25 49N 89 39 E
Kurihashi, *Japan* 63 A11 36 8N 139 42 E
Kuril Is. = Kurilskiye Ostrova, *Russia* 57 E15 45 0N 150 0 E
Kuril Trench, *Pac. Oc.* 122 C7 44 0N 153 0 E
Kurilsk, *Russia* 57 E15 45 14N 147 53 E
Kurilskiye Ostrova, *Russia* 57 E15 45 0N 150 0 E
Kuringen, *Belgium* 21 G6 50 56N 5 18 E
Kurino, *Japan* 62 F2 31 57N 130 43 E
Kurkur, *Egypt* 94 C3 23 50N 32 0 E
Kurkūrah, *Libya* 96 B4 31 30N 20 1 E
Kurla, *India* 82 E1 19 5N 72 52 E
Kurlovskiy, *Russia* 51 D12 55 25N 40 40 E
Kurmuk, *Sudan* 95 E3 10 33N 34 21 E
Kurnool, *India* 83 G4 15 45N 78 0 E
Kuro-Shima, *Kagoshima, Japan* 61 J4 30 50N 129 57 E
Kuro-Shima, *Okinawa, Japan* 61 M2 24 14N 124 1 E
Kurobe-Gawe →, *Japan* 63 A9 36 55N 137 25 E
Kurogi, *Japan* 62 D2 33 12N 130 40 E
Kurovskoye, *Russia* 51 D11 55 35N 38 55 E
Kurow, *N.Z.* 119 E5 44 44 S 170 29 E
Kurów, *Poland* 47 D9 51 23N 22 12 E
Kurrajong, *Australia* 117 B9 33 33 S 150 42 E
Kurram →, *Pakistan* 79 B3 32 36N 71 20 E
Kurri Kurri, *Australia* 117 B9 32 50 S 151 28 E
Kursavka, *Russia* 53 D10 44 29N 42 32 E
Kuršėnai, *Lithuania* 50 C3 56 1N 23 3 E
Kursk, *Russia* 51 F10 51 42N 36 11 E
Kuršumlija, *Serbia* 42 D6 43 9N 21 19 E
Kuršumlijska Banja, *Serbia* 42 D6 43 3N 21 11 E
Kurşunlu, *Turkey* 88 C5 40 51N 33 15 E
Kurtalan, *Turkey* 89 E9 37 56N 41 44 E
Kurtamysh, *Russia* 54 D9 54 55N 64 27 E
Kurty →, *Kazakhstan* 55 A8 44 16N 76 42 E
Kuru, Bahr el →, *Sudan* 95 F2 8 10N 26 50 E
Kurucaşile, *Turkey* 88 C5 41 49N 32 42 E
Kuruktag, *China* 64 B3 41 0N 89 0 E
Kuruman, *S. Africa* 104 D3 27 28 S 23 28 E
Kuruman →, *S. Africa* 104 D3 26 56 S 20 39 E
Kurume, *Japan* 62 D2 33 15N 130 30 E
Kurunegala, *Sri Lanka* 83 L5 7 30N 80 23 E
Kurupukari, *Guyana* 153 C6 4 43N 58 37W
Kurya, *Russia* 57 C11 61 15N 108 10 E
Kus Gölü, *Turkey* 88 C2 40 10N 27 55 E
Kusa, *Russia* 54 D6 55 20N 59 29 E
Kuşada Körfezı, *Turkey* 45 G9 37 56N 27 0 E
Kuşadası, *Turkey* 45 G9 37 52N 27 15 E
Kusatsu, *Gumma, Japan* 63 A10 36 37N 138 36 E
Kusatsu, *Shiga, Japan* 63 C7 34 58N 135 57 E
Kusawa L., *Canada* 130 A1 60 20N 136 13W
Kusel, *Germany* 27 F3 49 31N 7 25 E
Kushchevskaya, *Russia* 53 C8 46 33N 39 35 E
Kushikino, *Japan* 62 F2 31 44N 130 16 E
Kushima, *Japan* 62 F3 31 29N 131 14 E
Kushimoto, *Japan* 63 D7 33 28N 135 47 E
Kushiro, *Japan* 60 C12 43 0N 144 25 E
Kushiro →, *Japan* 60 C12 42 59N 144 23 E
Kūshk, *Iran* 85 D8 28 46N 56 51 E
Kushka, *Turkmenistan* 56 F7 35 20N 62 18 E
Kūshkī, *Īlām, Iran* 84 C5 33 31N 47 13 E
Kūshkī, *Khorāsān, Iran* 85 B8 37 2N 57 26 E
Kūshkū, *Iran* 85 E7 27 19N 53 28 E
Kushmurun, *Kazakhstan* 54 E9 52 27N 64 36 E
Kushmurun, Ozero, *Kazakhstan* 54 E9 52 40N 64 48 E
Kushnarenkovo, *Russia* 54 D4 55 6N 55 22 E
Kushol, *India* 81 C7 33 40N 76 36 E
Kushrabat, *Uzbekistan* 55 C3 40 18N 66 32 E
Kushtia, *Bangla.* 78 D2 23 55N 89 5 E
Kushum →, *Kazakhstan* 53 B14 49 0N 50 20 E
Kushva, *Russia* 54 B6 58 18N 59 45 E
Kuskokwim →, *U.S.A.* 126 B3 60 5N 162 25W
Kuskokwim B., *U.S.A.* 126 C3 59 45N 162 25W
Küsnacht, *Switz.* 29 B7 47 19N 8 35 E
Kussharo-Ko, *Japan* 60 C12 43 38N 144 21 E
Küssnacht, *Switz.* 29 B6 47 5N 8 26 E
Kustanay, *Kazakhstan* 54 E8 53 10N 63 35 E
Kusu, *Japan* 62 D3 33 16N 131 9 E
Kut, Ko, *Thailand* 77 G4 11 40N 102 35 E
Kutacane, *Indonesia* 74 B1 3 50N 97 50 E
Kütahya, *Turkey* 88 D4 39 30N 30 2 E
Kütahya □, *Turkey* 88 D3 39 10N 29 30 E
Kutaisi, *Georgia* 53 E10 42 19N 42 40 E
Kutaraja = Banda Aceh, *Indonesia* 74 A1 5 35N 95 20 E
Kutch, Gulf of = Kachchh, Gulf of, *India* 80 H3 22 50N 69 15 E
Kutch, Rann of = Kachchh, Rann of, *India* 80 G4 24 0N 70 0 E
Kutina, *Croatia* 39 C13 45 29N 16 48 E
Kutiyana, *India* 80 J4 21 36N 70 2 E
Kutjevo, *Croatia* 42 B2 45 23N 17 55 E
Kutkai, *Burma* 78 D6 23 27N 97 56 E
Kutkashen, *Azerbaijan* 53 F12 40 58N 47 47 E
Kutná Hora, *Czech.* 30 B8 49 57N 15 16 E
Kutno, *Poland* 47 C6 52 15N 19 23 E
Kuttabul, *Australia* 114 C4 21 5 S 148 48 E
Kutu, *Zaïre* 102 C3 2 40 S 18 11 E
Kutum, *Sudan* 95 E1 14 10N 24 40 E
Kúty, *Slovak Rep.* 31 C10 48 40N 17 3 E
Kuujjuaq, *Canada* 127 C13 58 6N 68 15W
Kuŭp-tong, *N. Korea* 67 D14 40 45N 126 1 E
Kuurne, *Belgium* 21 G2 50 51N 3 18 E
Kuvandyk, *Russia* 54 F5 51 28N 57 21 E
Kuvango, *Angola* 103 E3 14 28 S 16 20 E
Kuvasay, *Uzbekistan* 55 C5 40 18N 71 59 E
Kuvshinovo, *Russia* 50 C9 57 2N 34 11 E
Kuwait = Al Kuwayt, *Kuwait* 84 D5 29 30N 48 0 E
Kuwait ■, *Asia* 84 D5 29 30N 47 30 E
Kuwana, *Japan* 63 B8 35 5N 136 43 E
Kuybyshev = Samara, *Russia* 51 E17 53 8N 50 6 E
Kuybyshev, *Russia* 56 D8 55 27N 78 19 E
Kuybyshevo, *Ukraine* 52 C7 47 25N 36 40 E
Kuybyshevo, *Uzbekistan* 55 C5 40 20N 71 15 E
Kuybyshevskiy, *Tajikistan* 55 E4 37 52N 68 44 E
Kuybyshevskoye Vdkhr., *Russia* 51 D16 55 2N 49 30 E
Kuye He →, *China* 66 E6 38 23N 110 46 E
Kūyeh, *Iran* 84 B5 38 45N 47 57 E
Kuylyuk, *Uzbekistan* 55 C4 41 14N 69 17 E
Kūysanjaq, *Iraq* 84 B5 36 5N 44 38 E
Kuyto, Oz., *Russia* 48 B5 64 40N 31 0 E
Kuyumba, *Russia* 57 C10 60 58N 96 59 E
Kuzey Anadolu Dağları, *Turkey* 88 C6 41 30N 35 0 E
Kuzhitturai, *India* 83 K3 8 18N 77 11 E
Kuzino, *Russia* 54 C6 57 1N 59 27 E
Kuzmin, *Serbia* 42 B4 45 2N 19 25 E
Kuznetsk, *Russia* 51 E15 53 12N 46 40 E
Kuzomen, *Russia* 48 A6 66 22N 36 50 E
Kvænangen, *Norway* 12 A16 70 5N 21 15 E
Kvam, *Norway* 14 C3 61 40N 9 42 E
Kvareli, *Georgia* 53 F11 41 27N 45 47 E
Kvarner, *Croatia* 39 D11 44 50N 14 10 E
Kvarnerič, *Croatia* 39 D11 44 43N 14 37 E
Kviteseid, *Norway* 14 E2 59 24N 8 29 E
Kwabhaca, *S. Africa* 105 E4 30 51 S 29 0 E
Kwadacha →, *Canada* 130 B3 57 28N 125 38W
Kwakhanai, *Botswana* 104 C3 21 39 S 21 16 E
Kwakoegron, *Surinam* 153 B6 5 12N 55 25W
Kwale, *Kenya* 106 C4 4 15 S 39 31 E
Kwale, *Nigeria* 101 D6 5 46N 6 26 E
Kwale □, *Kenya* 106 C4 4 15 S 39 10 E
KwaMashu, *S. Africa* 105 D5 29 45 S 30 58 E
Kwamouth, *Zaïre* 102 C3 3 9S 16 12 E
Kwando →, *Africa* 103 F4 18 27 S 23 32 E
Kwangdaeri, *N. Korea* 67 D14 40 31N 127 32 E
Kwangju, *S. Korea* 67 G14 35 9N 126 54 E
Kwango →, *Zaïre* 102 C3 3 14 S 17 22 E
Kwangsi-Chuang = Guangxi Zhuangzu Zizhiqu □, *China* 68 E7 24 0N 109 0 E
Kwangtung = Guangdong □, *China* 69 F9 23 0N 113 0 E
Kwara □, *Nigeria* 101 D5 8 45N 4 30 E
Kwataboahegan →, *Canada* 128 B3 51 9N 80 50W
Kwatisore, *Indonesia* 73 B4 3 18 S 134 50 E
Kweichow = Guizhou □, *China* 68 D6 27 0N 107 0 E
Kwekwe, *Zimbabwe* 107 F2 18 58 S 29 48 E
Kwidzyn, *Poland* 47 B5 53 44N 18 55 E
Kwikila, *Papua N. G.* 120 E4 9 49 S 147 38 E
Kwimba □, *Tanzania* 106 C3 3 0S 33 0 E
Kwinana New Town, *Australia* 113 F2 32 15 S 115 47 E
Kwisa →, *Poland* 47 D2 51 34N 15 24 E
Kwoka, *Indonesia* 73 B4 0 31 S 132 27 E
Kya-in-Seikkyi, *Burma* 78 G7 16 2N 98 8 E
Kyabé, *Chad* 97 G3 9 30N 19 0 E
Kyabra Cr. →, *Australia* 115 D3 25 36 S 142 55 E
Kyabram, *Australia* 115 F4 36 19 S 145 4 E
Kyaiklat, *Burma* 78 G5 16 25N 95 40 E
Kyaikmaraw, *Burma* 78 G6 16 23N 97 44 E
Kyaikthin, *Burma* 78 D5 23 32N 95 40 E
Kyaikto, *Burma* 76 D1 17 20N 97 3 E
Kyakhta, *Russia* 57 D11 50 30N 106 25 E
Kyancutta, *Australia* 115 E2 33 8 S 135 33 E
Kyangin, *Burma* 78 F5 18 20N 95 20 E
Kyaukhnyat, *Burma* 78 F6 18 15N 97 31 E
Kyaukse, *Burma* 78 E6 21 36N 96 10 E
Kyauktaw, *Burma* 78 E4 20 51N 92 59 E
Kyawkku, *Burma* 78 E6 21 48N 96 56 E
Kyburz, *U.S.A.* 144 G6 38 47N 120 18W
Kybybolite, *Australia* 116 D4 36 53 S 140 55 E
Kycen, *Russia* 57 D11 51 45N 101 45 E
Kyeintali, *Burma* 78 G5 18 0N 94 29 E
Kyenjojo, *Uganda* 106 B3 0 40N 30 37 E
Kyidaunggan, *Burma* 78 F6 19 53N 96 12 E
Kyle Dam, *Zimbabwe* 107 G3 20 15 S 31 0 E
Kyle of Lochalsh, *U.K.* 18 D3 57 17N 5 43W
Kyll →, *Germany* 27 F2 49 48N 6 42 E
Kyllburg, *Germany* 27 E2 50 2N 6 35 E
Kyneton, *Australia* 116 D6 37 10 S 144 29 E
Kynuna, *Australia* 114 C3 21 37 S 141 55 E
Kyō-ga-Saki, *Japan* 63 B7 35 45N 135 15 E
Kyoga, L., *Uganda* 106 B3 1 35N 33 0 E
Kyogle, *Australia* 115 D5 28 40 S 153 0 E
Kyongju, *S. Korea* 67 G15 35 51N 129 14 E
Kyŏngsŏng, *N. Korea* 67 D15 41 35N 129 36 E
Kyōto, *Japan* 63 B7 35 0N 135 45 E
Kyōto □, *Japan* 63 B7 35 15N 135 45 E
Kyparissovouno, *Cyprus* 32 D12 35 19N 33 10 E
Kyperounda, *Cyprus* 32 E11 34 56N 32 58 E
Kyrenia, *Cyprus* 32 D12 35 20N 33 20 E
Kyrgystan = Kirghizia ■, *Asia* 55 C7 42 0N 75 0 E
Kyritz, *Germany* 26 C8 52 57N 12 25 E
Kyshtym, *Russia* 54 D7 55 42N 60 34 E
Kystatyam, *Russia* 57 C13 67 20N 123 10 E
Kytal Ktakh, *Russia* 57 C13 65 30N 123 40 E
Kythréa, *Cyprus* 32 D12 35 15N 33 29 E
Kytlym, *Russia* 54 B6 59 30N 59 12 E
Kyu-hkok, *Burma* 78 C7 24 4N 98 4 E
Kyulyunken, *Russia* 57 C14 64 10N 137 5 E
Kyunhla, *Burma* 78 D5 23 25N 95 15 E
Kyuquot, *Canada* 130 C3 50 3N 127 25W
Kyurdamir, *Azerbaijan* 53 F13 40 25N 48 3 E
Kyūshū, *Japan* 62 E3 33 0N 131 0 E
Kyūshū □, *Japan* 62 E3 33 0N 131 0 E
Kyūshū-Sanchi, *Japan* 62 E3 32 35N 131 17 E
Kyustendil, *Bulgaria* 42 E7 42 16N 22 41 E
Kyusyur, *Russia* 57 B13 70 19N 127 30 E
Kywong, *Australia* 117 C7 34 58 S 146 44 E
Kyyiv = Kiyev, *Ukraine* 50 F7 50 30N 30 28 E
Kyzyl, *Russia* 57 D10 51 50N 94 30 E
Kyzyl-Kiya, *Kirghizia* 55 C6 40 16N 72 8 E
Kyzylkum, Peski, *Uzbekistan* 55 B2 42 30N 65 0 E
Kyzylsu →, *Kirghizia* 55 D6 38 50N 70 0 E
Kzyl-Orda, *Kazakhstan* 55 A2 44 48N 65 28 E

L

La Albuera, *Spain* 37 G4 38 45N 6 49W
La Alcarria, *Spain* 34 E2 40 31N 2 45W
La Algaba, *Spain* 37 H4 37 27N 6 1W
La Almarcha, *Spain* 34 F2 39 41N 2 24W
La Almunia de Doña Godina, *Spain* 34 D3 41 29N 1 23W
La Asunción, *Venezuela* 153 A5 11 2N 63 53W
La Banda, *Argentina* 158 B3 27 45 S 64 10W
La Bañeza, *Spain* 36 C5 42 17N 5 54W
La Barca, *Mexico* 146 C4 20 20N 102 40W
La Barge, *U.S.A.* 142 E8 42 16N 110 12W
La Bassée, *France* 23 B9 50 31N 2 49 E
La Bastide-Puylaurent, *France* 24 D7 44 35N 3 55 E
La Baule, *France* 22 E4 47 17N 2 24W
La Belle, *Fla., U.S.A.* 135 M5 26 46N 81 26W
La Belle, *Mo., U.S.A.* 140 D5 40 7N 91 55W
La Biche →, *Canada* 130 B4 59 57N 123 50W
La Bisbal, *Spain* 34 D8 41 58N 3 2 E
La Blanquilla, *Venezuela* 153 A5 11 51N 64 37W
La Bomba, *Mexico* 146 A1 31 53N 115 2W
La Bresse, *France* 23 D13 48 2N 6 53 E
La Bureba, *Spain* 34 C1 42 36N 3 24W
La Cal →, *Bolivia* 157 D6 17 27 S 58 15W
La Calera, *Chile* 158 C1 32 50 S 71 10W
La Campiña, *Spain* 37 H6 37 45N 4 45W
La Canal, *Spain* 33 C7 38 51N 1 23 E
La Cañiza, *Spain* 36 C2 42 13N 8 16W
La Capelle, *France* 23 C10 49 59N 3 50 E
La Carlota, *Argentina* 158 C3 33 30 S 63 20W
La Carlota, *Phil.* 71 F4 10 25N 122 55 E
La Carolina, *Spain* 37 G7 38 17N 3 38W
La Castellana, *Phil.* 71 F4 10 20N 123 3 E
La Cavalerie, *France* 24 D7 44 1N 3 10 E
La Ceiba, *Honduras* 148 C2 15 40N 86 50W
La Chaise-Dieu, *France* 24 C7 45 18N 3 42 E
La Chaize-le-Vicomte, *France* 22 F5 46 40N 1 18W
La Chapelle d'Angillon, *France* 23 E9 47 21N 2 25 E
La Chapelle-Glain, *France* 22 E5 47 38N 1 11W
La Charité-sur-Loire, *France* 23 E10 47 10N 3 1 E
La Chartre-sur-le-Loir, *France* 22 E7 47 44N 0 34 E
La Châtaigneraie, *France* 24 B3 46 39N 0 44W
La Châtre, *France* 24 B5 46 35N 2 0 E
La Chaux de Fonds, *Switz.* 28 B3 47 7N 6 50 E
La Chorrera, *Colombia* 152 D3 0 44 S 73 1W
La Ciotat, *France* 25 E9 43 10N 5 37 E
La Clayette, *France* 25 B8 46 17N 4 19 E
La Cocha, *Argentina* 158 B2 27 50 S 65 40W
La Concepción = Ri-Aba, *Eq. Guin.* 101 E6 3 28N 8 40 E
La Concepción, *Venezuela* 152 A3 10 30N 71 50W
La Concordia, *Mexico* 147 D6 16 8N 92 38W
La Conner, *U.S.A.* 142 B2 48 23N 122 30W
La Coruña, *Spain* 36 B2 43 20N 8 25W
La Coruña □, *Spain* 36 B2 43 10N 8 30W
La Côte, *Switz.* 28 D2 46 25N 6 15 E
La Côte-St.-André, *France* 25 C9 45 24N 5 15 E
La Courtine-le-Trucq, *France* 24 C6 45 41N 2 15 E
La Crau, *France* 25 E8 43 32N 4 40 E
La Crete, *Canada* 130 B5 58 11N 116 24W
La Crosse, *Kans., U.S.A.* 138 F5 38 32N 99 18W
La Crosse, *Wis., U.S.A.* 138 D9 43 48N 91 15W
La Cruz, *Costa Rica* 148 D2 11 4N 85 39W
La Cruz, *Mexico* 146 C3 23 55N 106 54W
La Dorada, *Colombia* 152 B3 5 30N 74 40W
La Ensenada, *Chile* 160 B2 41 12 S 72 33W
La Escondida, *Mexico* 146 C5 24 6N 99 55W
La Esmeralda, *Paraguay* 158 A3 22 16 S 62 33W
La Esperanza, *Argentina* 160 B3 40 26 S 68 32W
La Esperanza, *Cuba* 148 B3 22 46N 83 44W
La Esperanza, *Honduras* 148 D2 14 15N 88 10W
La Estrada, *Spain* 36 C2 42 43N 8 27W
La Fayette, *U.S.A.* 135 H3 34 42N 85 17W
La Fé, *Cuba* 148 B3 22 2N 84 15W
La Fère, *France* 23 C10 49 39N 3 21 E
La Ferté-Bernard, *France* 22 D7 48 10N 0 40 E
La Ferté-Macé, *France* 22 D6 48 35N 0 22W
La Ferté-St.-Aubin, *France* 23 E8 47 42N 1 57 E
La Ferté-sous-Jouarre, *France* 23 D10 48 56N 3 8 E
La Ferté-Vidame, *France* 22 D7 48 37N 0 53 E
La Flèche, *France* 22 E6 47 42N 0 4W
La Foa, *N. Cal.* 121 U19 21 43 S 165 50 E
La Follette, *U.S.A.* 135 G3 36 23N 84 7W
La Fontaine, *U.S.A.* 141 D11 40 40N 85 43W
La Fregeneda, *Spain* 36 E4 40 58N 6 54W
La Fría, *Venezuela* 152 B3 8 13N 72 15W
La Fuente de San Esteban, *Spain* 36 E4 40 49N 6 15W
La Gineta, *Spain* 35 F2 39 8N 2 1W
La Gloria, *Colombia* 152 B3 8 37N 73 48W
La Gran Sabana, *Venezuela* 153 B5 5 30N 61 30W
La Grand-Combe, *France* 25 D8 44 13N 4 2 E
La Grande, *U.S.A.* 142 D4 45 20N 118 5W
La Grande-Motte, *France* 25 E8 43 23N 4 5 E
La Grange, *Calif., U.S.A.* 144 H6 37 42N 120 27W
La Grange, *Ga., U.S.A.* 135 J3 33 2N 85 2W
La Grange, *Ky., U.S.A.* 134 F3 38 25N 85 23W
La Grange, *Mo., U.S.A.* 140 D5 40 3N 91 35W
La Grange, *Tex., U.S.A.* 139 L6 29 54N 96 52W
La Grita, *Venezuela* 152 B3 8 8N 71 59W
La Guaira, *Venezuela* 152 A4 10 36N 66 56W
La Guardia, *Spain* 36 D2 41 56N 8 52W
La Gudiña, *Spain* 36 C3 42 4N 7 8W
La Güera, *Mauritania* 98 D1 20 51N 17 0W
La Guerche-de-Bretagne, *France* 22 E5 47 57N 1 16W
La Guerche-sur-l'Aubois, *France* 23 F9 46 58N 2 56 E
La Habana, *Cuba* 148 B3 23 8N 82 22W
La Harpe, *U.S.A.* 140 D6 40 35N 90 58W
La Haye-du-Puits, *France* 22 C5 49 17N 1 33W
La Horqueta, *Venezuela* 153 B5 7 55N 60 20W
La Horra, *Spain* 36 D7 41 44N 3 53W
La Independencia, *Mexico* 147 D6 16 31N 91 47W
La Isabela, *Dom. Rep.* 149 C5 19 58N 71 2W
La Jara, *U.S.A.* 143 H11 37 16N 105 58W
La Joya, *Peru* 156 D3 16 43 S 71 52W
La Junquera, *Spain* 34 C7 42 25N 2 53 E
La Junta, *U.S.A.* 139 F3 37 59N 103 33W
La Laguna, *Canary Is.* 33 F3 28 28N 16 18W
La Libertad, *Guatemala* 148 C1 16 47N 90 7W
La Libertad, *Mexico* 146 B2 29 55N 112 41W
La Libertad □, *Peru* 156 B2 8 0 S 78 30W
La Ligua, *Chile* 158 C1 32 30 S 71 16W
La Línea de la Concepción, *Spain* 37 J5 36 15N 5 23W
La Loche, *Canada* 131 B7 56 29N 109 26W
La Londe-les-Maures, *France* 25 E10 43 8N 6 14 E
La Lora, *Spain* 36 C7 42 45N 4 0W
La Loupe, *France* 22 D8 48 29N 1 1 E
La Louvière, *Belgium* 21 H4 50 27N 4 10 E
La Machine, *France* 23 F10 46 54N 3 27 E
La Maddalena, *Italy* 40 A2 41 13N 9 25 E
La Malbaie, *Canada* 129 C5 47 40N 70 10W
La Mancha, *Spain* 35 F2 39 10N 2 54W
La Mariña, *Spain* 36 B3 43 30N 7 40W
La Mesa, *Calif., U.S.A.* 145 N9 32 46N 117 3W
La Mesa, *N. Mex., U.S.A.* 143 K10 32 7N 106 42W
La Misión, *Mexico* 146 A1 32 5N 116 50W
La Moille, *U.S.A.* 140 C7 41 32N 89 17W
La Moine →, *U.S.A.* 140 E6 39 59N 90 31W
La Monte, *U.S.A.* 140 F3 38 46N 93 26W
La Mothe-Achard, *France* 22 F5 46 37N 1 40W
La Motte, *France* 25 D10 44 20N 6 3 E
La Motte-Chalançon, *France* 25 D9 44 30N 5 21 E
La Moure, *U.S.A.* 138 B5 46 21N 98 18W
La Muela, *Spain* 34 D3 41 36N 1 7W
La Mure, *France* 25 D9 44 55N 5 48 E
La Negra, *Chile* 158 A1 23 46 S 70 18W
La Neuveville, *Switz.* 28 B4 47 4N 7 6 E
La Oliva, *Canary Is.* 33 F6 28 36N 13 57W
La Oraya, *Peru* 156 C2 11 32 S 75 54W
La Orotava, *Canary Is.* 33 F3 28 22N 16 31W
La Pacaudière, *France* 24 B7 46 11N 3 52 E
La Palma, *Canary Is.* 33 F2 28 40N 17 50W
La Palma, *Panama* 148 E4 8 15N 78 0W
La Palma, *Spain* 37 H4 37 21N 6 38W
La Paloma, *Chile* 158 C1 30 35 S 71 0W
La Pampa □, *Argentina* 158 D2 36 50 S 66 0W
La Paragua, *Venezuela* 153 B5 6 50N 63 20W
La Paz, *Entre Ríos, Argentina* 158 C4 30 50 S 59 45W
La Paz, *San Luis, Argentina* 158 C2 33 30 S 67 20W
La Paz, *Bolivia* 156 D4 16 20 S 68 10W
La Paz, *Honduras* 148 D2 14 20N 87 47W
La Paz, *Mexico* 146 C2 24 10N 110 20W
La Paz, *Phil.* 70 D3 15 26N 120 45 E
La Paz □, *Bolivia* 156 D4 15 30 S 68 0W
La Paz Centro, *Nic.* 148 D2 12 20N 86 41W
La Pedrera, *Colombia* 152 D4 1 18 S 69 43W
La Perouse Str., *Asia* 60 B11 45 40N 142 0 E
La Pesca, *Mexico* 147 C5 23 46N 97 47W
La Piedad, *Mexico* 146 C4 20 20N 102 1W
La Pine, *U.S.A.* 142 E3 43 40N 121 30W
La Plant, *U.S.A.* 138 C4 45 9N 100 39W
La Plata, *Argentina* 158 D4 35 0 S 57 55W
La Plata, *Colombia* 152 C2 2 23N 75 53W
La Plata, *U.S.A.* 140 D4 40 2N 92 29W
La Plata, L., *Argentina* 160 B2 44 55 S 71 50W
La Pobla de Lillet, *Spain* 34 C6 42 16N 1 59 E
La Pola de Gordón, *Spain* 36 C5 42 51N 5 41W
La Porte, *U.S.A.* 141 C10 41 36N 86 43W
La Porte City, *U.S.A.* 140 B4 42 19N 92 12W
La Puebla, *Spain* 34 F8 39 46N 3 1 E
La Puebla de Cazalla, *Spain* 37 H5 37 10N 5 20W
La Puebla de los Infantes, *Spain* 37 H5 37 47N 5 24W
La Puebla de Montalbán, *Spain* 36 F6 39 52N 4 22W
La Puerta, *Spain* 35 G2 38 22N 2 45W
La Punt, *Switz.* 29 C9 46 35N 9 56 E
La Purísima, *Mexico* 146 B2 26 10N 112 4W
La Push, *U.S.A.* 144 C2 47 55N 124 38W
La Quiaca, *Argentina* 158 A2 22 5 S 65 35W
La Rambla, *Spain* 37 H6 37 37N 4 45W
La Reine, *Canada* 128 C4 48 50N 79 30W
La Réole, *France* 24 D3 44 35N 0 1W
La Restinga, *Canary Is.* 33 G2 27 38N 17 59W
La Rioja, *Argentina* 158 B2 29 20 S 67 0W
La Rioja □, *Argentina* 158 B2 29 30 S 67 0W
La Rioja □, *Spain* 34 C2 42 20N 2 20W
La Robla, *Spain* 36 C5 42 50N 5 41W
La Roche, *Switz.* 28 C4 46 42N 7 7 E
La Roche-Bernard, *France* 22 E4 47 31N 2 19W
La Roche-Canillac, *France* 24 C5 45 12N 1 57 E
La Roche-en-Ardenne, *Belgium* 21 H7 50 11N 5 35 E
La Roche-sur-Yon, *France* 22 F5 46 40N 1 25W
La Rochefoucauld, *France* 24 C4 45 44N 0 24 E
La Rochelle, *France* 24 B2 46 10N 1 9W
La Roda, *Albacete, Spain* 35 F2 39 13N 2 15W
La Roda, *Sevilla, Spain* 37 H6 37 12N 4 46W
La Romana, *Dom. Rep.* 149 C6 18 27N 68 57W
La Ronge, *Canada* 131 B7 55 5N 105 20W
La Rue, *U.S.A.* 141 D13 40 35N 83 23W
La Rumorosa, *Mexico* 145 N10 32 33N 116 4W
La Sabina, *Spain* 33 C7 38 44N 1 25 E
La Sagra, *Spain* 35 H2 37 57N 2 35W
La Salle, *U.S.A.* 140 C7 41 20N 89 6W
La Sanabria, *Spain* 36 C4 42 0N 6 30W
La Santa, *Canary Is.* 33 E6 29 5N 13 40W
La Sarraz, *Switz.* 28 C3 46 38N 6 32 E
La Sarre, *Canada* 128 C4 48 45N 79 15W
La Scie, *Canada* 129 C8 49 57N 55 36W
La Selva, *Spain* 34 D7 42 0N 2 45 E
La Selva Beach, *U.S.A.* 144 J5 36 56N 121 51W
La Serena, *Chile* 158 B1 29 55 S 71 10W
La Serena, *Spain* 37 G5 38 45N 5 40W
La Seyne, *France* 25 E9 43 7N 5 52 E
La Sila, *Italy* 41 C9 39 15N 16 35 E
La Solana, *Spain* 35 G1 38 59N 3 14W
La Souterraine, *France* 24 B5 46 15N 1 30 E
La Spézia, *Italy* 38 D6 44 8N 9 50 E
La Suze-sur-Sarthe, *France* 22 E7 47 53N 0 2 E
La Tagua, *Colombia* 152 C3 0 3N 74 40W
La Teste, *France* 24 D2 44 37N 1 8W
La Tortuga, *Venezuela* 149 D6 11 0N 65 22W
La Tour-du-Pin, *France* 25 C9 45 33N 5 27 E
La Tranche-sur-Mer, *France* 22 F5 46 20N 1 27W
La Tremblade, *France* 24 C2 45 46N 1 8W
La Trinidad, *Phil.* 70 C3 16 28N 120 35 E
La Tuque, *Canada* 128 C5 47 30N 72 50W
La Unión, *Chile* 160 B2 40 10 S 73 0W
La Unión, *Colombia* 152 C2 1 35N 77 5W
La Unión, *El Salv.* 148 D2 13 20N 87 50W
La Unión, *Mexico* 146 D4 17 58N 101 49W

Legrad 223


Långsele, *Sweden* **14 A11** 63 12N 17 4 E
Langtao, *Burma* **78 B6** 27 15N 97 34 E
Langting, *India* **78 C4** 25 31N 93 7 E
Langtry, *U.S.A.* **139 L4** 29 49N 101 34W
Langu, *Thailand* **77 J2** 6 53N 99 47 E
Languedoc, *France* **24 E7** 43 58N 3 55 E
Langwies, *Switz.* **29 C9** 46 50N 9 44 E
Langxi, *China* **69 B12** 31 10N 119 12 E
Langxiangzhen, *China* **66 E9** 39 43N 116 8 E
Langzhong, *China* **68 B5** 31 38N 105 58 E
Lanigan, *Canada* **131 C7** 51 51N 105 2W
Lankao, *China* **66 G8** 34 48N 114 50 E
Lannemezan, *France* **24 E4** 43 8N 0 23 E
Lannilis, *France* **22 D2** 48 35N 4 32W
Lannion, *France* **22 D3** 48 46N 3 29W
L'Annonciation, *Canada* **128 C5** 46 25N 74 55W
Lanouaille, *France* **24 C5** 45 24N 1 9 E
Lanping, *China* **68 D2** 26 28N 99 15 E
Lansdale, *U.S.A.* **137 F9** 40 14N 75 17W
Lansdowne, *Australia* **117 A10** 31 48 S 152 30 E
Lansdowne, *Canada* **137 B8** 44 24N 76 1W
Lansdowne House, *Canada* **128 B2** 52 14N 87 53W
L'Anse, *U.S.A.* **128 C2** 46 45N 88 27W
L'Anse au Loup, *Canada* **129 B8** 51 32N 56 50W
Lansford, *U.S.A.* **137 F9** 40 50N 75 53W
Lanshan, *China* **69 E9** 25 24N 112 10 E
Lansing, *U.S.A.* **141 B12** 42 44N 84 33W
Lanslebourg-Mont-Cenis, *France* **25 C10** 45 17N 6 52 E
Lanta Yai, Ko, *Thailand* **77 J2** 7 35N 99 3 E
Lantian, *China* **66 G5** 34 11N 109 20 E
Lanus, *Argentina* **158 C4** 34 44 S 58 27W
Lanusei, *Italy* **40 C2** 39 53N 9 31 E
Lanuza, *Phil.* **71 G6** 9 14N 126 4 E
Lanxi, *China* **69 C12** 29 13N 119 28 E
Lanzarote, *Canary Is.* **33 E6** 29 0N 13 40W
Lanzhou, *China* **66 F2** 36 1N 103 52 E
Lanzo Torinese, *Italy* **38 C4** 45 16N 7 29 E
Lao →, *Italy* **41 C8** 39 45N 15 45 E
Lao Bao, *Laos* **76 D6** 16 35N 106 30 E
Lao Cai, *Vietnam* **76 A4** 22 30N 103 57 E
Laoag, *Phil.* **70 B3** 18 7N 120 34 E
Laoang, *Phil.* **70 E5** 12 32N 125 8 E
Laoha He →, *China* **67 C11** 43 25N 120 35 E
Laois □, *Ireland* **19 D4** 53 0N 7 20W
Laon, *France* **23 C10** 49 33N 3 35 E
Laona, *U.S.A.* **134 C1** 45 34N 88 40W
Laos ■, *Asia* **76 D5** 17 45N 105 0 E
Lapa, *Brazil* **159 B6** 25 46 S 49 44W
Lapalisse, *France* **24 B7** 46 15N 3 38 E
Lapeer, *U.S.A.* **141 A13** 43 3N 83 19W
Lapi □ = Lapin lääni □, *Finland* **12 C19** 67 43N 25 30 E
Lapin lääni □, *Finland* **12 C19** 67 43N 25 30 E
Lapithos, *Cyprus* **32 D12** 35 21N 33 11 E
Lapland = Lappland, *Europe* **12 B18** 68 7N 24 0 E
Lapog, *Phil.* **70 C3** 17 45N 120 27 E
Laporte, *U.S.A.* **137 E8** 41 25N 76 30W
Lapovo, *Serbia* **42 C6** 44 10N 21 2 E
Lappland, *Europe* **12 B18** 68 7N 24 0 E
Laprida, *Argentina* **158 D3** 37 34 S 60 45W
Laptev Sea, *Russia* **57 B13** 76 0N 125 0 E
Lapuş, Munţii, *Romania* **46 B4** 47 20N 23 50 E
Lăpuşul →, *Romania* **46 B4** 47 25N 23 40 E
Łapy, *Poland* **47 C9** 52 59N 22 52 E
L'Aquila, *Italy* **39 F10** 42 21N 13 24 E
Lār, *Āzarbājān-e Sharqī, Iran* **84 B5** 38 30N 47 52 E
Lār, *Fārs, Iran* **85 E7** 27 40N 54 14 E
Lara, *Australia* **116 E6** 38 2 S 144 26 E
Lara, *Phil.* **71 G1** 8 48N 117 52 E
Lara □, *Venezuela* **152 A4** 10 10N 69 50W
Larabanga, *Ghana* **100 D4** 9 16N 1 56W
Laracha, *Spain* **36 B2** 43 15N 8 35W
Larache, *Morocco* **98 A3** 35 10N 6 5W
Laragne-Montéglin, *France* **25 D9** 44 18N 5 49 E
Laramie, *U.S.A.* **138 E2** 41 19N 105 35W
Laramie Mts., *U.S.A.* **138 E2** 42 0N 105 30W
Laranjeiras, *Brazil* **154 D4** 10 48 S 37 10W
Laranjeiras do Sul, *Brazil* **159 B5** 25 23 S 52 23W
Larantuka, *Indonesia* **72 C2** 8 21 S 122 55 E
Larap, *Phil.* **70 D4** 14 18N 122 39 E
Larat, *Indonesia* **73 C4** 7 0 S 132 0 E
L'Arbresle, *France* **25 C8** 45 50N 4 36 E
Larde, *Mozam.* **107 F4** 16 28 S 39 43 E
Larder Lake, *Canada* **128 C4** 48 5N 79 40W
Lardhos, Ákra, *Greece* **32 C10** 36 4N 28 10 E
Lardhos, Órmos, *Greece* **32 C10** 36 4N 28 2 E
Laredo, *Spain* **34 B1** 43 26N 3 28W
Laredo, *U.S.A.* **139 M5** 27 30N 99 30W
Laredo Sd., *Canada* **130 C3** 52 30N 128 53W
Laren, *Neths.* **20 D6** 52 16N 5 14 E
Larena, *Phil.* **71 G4** 9 15N 123 35 E
Largentière, *France* **25 D8** 44 34N 4 18 E
L'Argentière-la-Bessée, *France* **25 D10** 44 47N 6 33 E
Largs, *U.K.* **18 F4** 55 48N 4 51W
Lari, *Italy* **38 E7** 43 34N 10 35 E
Lariang, *Indonesia* **72 B1** 1 26 S 119 17 E
Larimore, *U.S.A.* **138 B6** 47 54N 97 38W
Lārīn, *Iran* **85 C7** 35 55N 52 19 E
Larino, *Italy* **41 A7** 41 48N 14 54 E
Lárisa, *Greece* **44 E4** 39 49N 22 28 E
Lárisa □, *Greece* **44 E4** 39 39N 22 24 E
Larkana, *Pakistan* **79 D3** 27 32N 68 18 E
Larnaca, *Cyprus* **32 E12** 34 55N 33 55 E
Larnaca Bay, *Cyprus* **32 E12** 34 53N 33 45 E
Larne, *U.K.* **19 B6** 54 52N 5 50W
Larned, *U.S.A.* **138 F5** 38 11N 99 6W
Larochette, *Belgium* **21 J8** 49 47N 6 13 E
Laroquebrou, *France* **24 D6** 44 58N 2 12 E
Larrimah, *Australia* **112 C5** 15 35 S 133 12 E
Larsen Ice Shelf, *Antarctica* **7 C17** 67 0 S 62 0W
Larvik, *Norway* **14 E4** 59 4N 10 4 E
Laryak, *Russia* **56 C8** 61 15N 80 0 E
Larzac, Causse du, *France* **24 E7** 43 50N 3 17 E
Las Alpujarras, *Spain* **35 J1** 36 55N 3 20W
Las Animas, *U.S.A.* **138 F3** 38 4N 103 13W
Las Anod, *Somali Rep.* **90 F4** 8 26N 47 19 E
Las Blancos, *Spain* **35 H4** 37 38N 0 49W
Las Brenãs, *Argentina* **158 B3** 27 5 S 61 7W
Las Cabezas de San Juan, *Spain* **37 J5** 37 0N 5 58W
Las Chimeneas, *Mexico* **145 N10** 32 8N 116 5W
Las Coloradas, *Argentina* **160 A2** 39 34 S 70 36W
Las Cruces, *U.S.A.* **143 K10** 32 19N 106 47W
Las Flores, *Argentina* **158 D4** 36 10 S 59 7W
Las Heras, *Argentina* **158 C2** 32 51 S 68 49W
Las Horquetas, *Argentina* **160 C2** 48 14 S 71 11W
Las Khoreh, *Somali Rep.* **90 E4** 11 10N 48 20 E
Las Lajas, *Argentina* **160 A2** 38 30 S 70 25W
Las Lomas, *Peru* **156 A1** 4 40 S 80 10W
Las Lomitas, *Argentina* **158 A3** 24 43 S 60 35W
Las Marismas, *Spain* **37 H4** 37 5N 6 20W
Las Mercedes, *Venezuela* **152 B4** 9 7N 66 24W
Las Navas de la Concepción, *Spain* **37 H5** 37 56N 5 30W
Las Navas de Tolosa, *Spain* **37 G7** 38 18N 3 38W
Las Navas del Marqués, *Spain* **36 E6** 40 36N 4 20W
Las Palmas, *Argentina* **158 B4** 27 8 S 58 45W
Las Palmas, *Canary Is.* **33 F4** 28 7N 15 26W
Las Palmas →, *Mexico* **145 N10** 32 26N 116 54W
Las Piedras, *Uruguay* **159 C4** 34 44 S 56 14W
Las Pipinas, *Argentina* **158 D4** 35 30 S 57 19W
Las Plumas, *Argentina* **160 B3** 43 40 S 67 15W
Las Rosas, *Argentina* **158 C3** 32 30 S 61 35W
Las Tablas, *Panama* **148 E3** 7 49N 80 14W
Las Termas, *Argentina* **158 B3** 27 29 S 64 52W
Las Truchas, *Mexico* **146 D4** 17 57N 102 13W
Las Varillas, *Argentina* **158 C3** 31 50 S 62 50W
Las Vegas, *N. Mex., U.S.A.* **143 J11** 35 36N 105 13W
Las Vegas, *Nev., U.S.A.* **145 J11** 36 10N 115 9W
Lascano, *Uruguay* **159 C5** 33 35 S 54 12W
Lashburn, *Canada* **131 C7** 53 10N 109 40W
Lashio, *Burma* **78 D6** 22 56N 97 45 E
Lashkar, *India* **80 F8** 26 10N 78 10 E
Lashkar Gāh, *Afghan.* **79 C2** 31 35N 64 21 E
Łasin, *Poland* **47 B6** 53 30N 19 2 E
Lasíthi, *Greece* **32 D7** 35 11N 25 31 E
Lasíthi □, *Greece* **32 D7** 35 5N 25 50 E
Lask, *Poland* **47 D6** 51 34N 19 8 E
Łaskarzew, *Poland* **47 D8** 51 48N 21 36 E
Laško, *Slovenia* **39 B12** 46 10N 15 16 E
Lassance, *Brazil* **155 E3** 17 54 S 44 34W
Lassay, *France* **22 D6** 48 27N 0 30W
Lassen Pk., *U.S.A.* **142 F3** 40 29N 121 31W
Last Mountain L., *Canada* **131 C7** 51 5N 105 14W
Lastchance Cr. →, *U.S.A.* **144 E5** 40 2N 121 15W
Lastoursville, *Gabon* **102 C2** 0 55 S 12 38 E
Lastovo, *Croatia* **39 F13** 42 46N 16 55 E
Lastovski Kanal, *Croatia* **39 F13** 42 50N 17 0 E
Lat Yao, *Thailand* **76 E2** 15 45N 99 48 E
Latacunga, *Ecuador* **152 D2** 0 50 S 78 35W
Latakia = Al Lādhiqīyah, *Syria* **84 C2** 35 30N 35 45 E
Latchford, *Canada* **128 C4** 47 20N 79 50W
Late, *Tonga* **121 P13** 18 48 S 174 39W
Laterza, *Italy* **41 B9** 40 38N 16 47 E
Latham, *Australia* **113 E2** 29 44 S 116 20 E
Lathen, *Germany* **26 C3** 52 51N 7 21 E
Lathrop, *U.S.A.* **140 E2** 39 33N 94 20W
Lathrop Wells, *U.S.A.* **145 J10** 36 39N 116 24W
Latiano, *Italy* **41 B10** 40 33N 17 43 E
Latina, *Italy* **40 A5** 41 26N 12 53 E
Latisana, *Italy* **39 C10** 45 47N 13 1 E
Latium = Lazio □, *Italy* **39 F9** 42 10N 12 30 E
Laton, *U.S.A.* **144 J7** 36 26N 119 41W
Latorica →, *Slovak Rep.* **31 C14** 48 28N 21 50 E
Latouche Treville, C., *Australia* **112 C3** 18 27 S 121 49 E
Latrobe, *Australia* **114 G4** 41 14 S 146 30 E
Latrobe, *U.S.A.* **136 F5** 40 19N 79 23W
Latrónico, *Italy* **41 B9** 40 5N 16 0 E
Latur, *India* **82 E3** 18 25N 76 40 E
Latvia ■, *Europe* **50 C3** 56 50N 24 0 E
Lau Group, *Fiji* **121 A3** 17 0 S 178 30W
Lauca →, *Bolivia* **156 D4** 19 9 S 68 10W
Lauchhammer, *Germany* **26 D9** 51 35N 13 48 E
Lauenburg, *Germany* **26 B6** 53 23N 10 33 E
Läufelfingen, *Switz.* **28 B5** 47 24N 7 52 E
Laufen, *Switz.* **28 B5** 47 25N 7 30 E
Lauffen, *Germany* **27 F5** 49 4N 9 9 E
Laugarbakki, *Iceland* **12 D3** 65 20N 20 55W
Laujar, *Spain* **35 J2** 37 0N 2 54W
Launceston, *Australia* **114 G4** 41 24 S 147 8 E
Launceston, *U.K.* **17 G3** 50 38N 4 21W
Laune →, *Ireland* **19 D2** 52 5N 9 40W
Laupheim, *Germany* **27 G5** 48 13N 9 53 E
Laur, *Phil.* **70 D3** 15 35N 121 11 E
Laura, *Queens., Australia* **114 B3** 15 32 S 144 32 E
Laura, *S. Austral., Australia* **116 B3** 33 10 S 138 18 E
Laureana di Borrello, *Italy* **41 D9** 38 28N 16 5 E
Laurel, *Ind., U.S.A.* **141 E11** 39 31N 85 11W
Laurel, *Miss., U.S.A.* **139 K10** 31 41N 89 8W
Laurel, *Mont., U.S.A.* **142 D9** 45 40N 108 46W
Laurencekirk, *U.K.* **18 E6** 56 50N 2 30W
Laurens, *U.S.A.* **135 H4** 34 30N 82 1W
Laurentian Plateau, *Canada* **129 B6** 52 0N 70 0W
Laurentides, Parc Prov. des, *Canada* **129 C5** 47 45N 71 15W
Lauria, *Italy* **41 B8** 40 3N 15 50 E
Laurie L., *Canada* **131 B8** 56 35N 101 57W
Laurinburg, *U.S.A.* **135 H6** 34 47N 79 28W
Laurium, *U.S.A.* **134 B1** 47 14N 88 27W
Lausanne, *Switz.* **28 C3** 46 32N 6 38 E
Laut, *Indonesia* **75 B3** 4 45N 108 0 E
Laut, Pulau, *Indonesia* **75 C5** 3 40 S 116 10 E
Laut Ketil, Kepulauan, *Indonesia* **75 C5** 4 45 S 115 40 E
Lautaro, *Chile* **160 A2** 38 31 S 72 27W
Lauterbach, *Germany* **26 E5** 50 39N 9 23 E
Lauterbrunnen, *Switz.* **28 C5** 46 36N 7 55 E
Lauterecken, *Germany* **27 F3** 49 38N 7 35 E
Lautoka, *Fiji* **121 A1** 17 37 S 177 27 E
Lauwe, *Belgium* **21 G2** 50 47N 3 12 E
Lauwers, *Neths.* **20 A8** 53 32N 6 23 E
Lauwers Zee, *Neths.* **20 B8** 53 21N 6 13 E
Lauzon, *Canada* **129 C5** 46 48N 71 10W
Lava Hot Springs, *U.S.A.* **142 E7** 42 37N 112 1W
Lavadores, *Spain* **36 C2** 42 14N 8 41W
Lavagna, *Italy* **38 D6** 44 18N 9 22 E
Laval, *France* **22 D6** 48 4N 0 48W
Lavalle, *Argentina* **158 B2** 28 15 S 65 15W
Lávara, *Greece* **44 C8** 41 19N 26 22 E
Lavardac, *France* **24 D4** 44 12N 0 20 E
Lavaur, *France* **24 E5** 43 40N 1 49 E
Lavaux, *Switz.* **28 D3** 46 30N 6 45 E
Lavelanet, *France* **24 F5** 42 57N 1 51 E
Lavello, *Italy* **41 A8** 41 4N 15 47 E
Laverne, *U.S.A.* **139 G5** 36 43N 99 54W
Lavers Hill, *Australia* **116 E5** 38 40 S 143 25 E
Laverton, *Australia* **113 E3** 28 44 S 122 29 E
Lávkos, *Greece* **45 E5** 39 9N 23 14 E
Lavos, *Portugal* **36 E2** 40 6N 8 49W
Lavras, *Brazil* **155 F3** 21 20 S 45 0W
Lavre, *Portugal* **37 G2** 38 46N 8 22W
Lavrentiya, *Russia* **57 C19** 65 35N 171 0W
Lávrion, *Greece* **45 G6** 37 40N 24 4 E
Lávris, *Greece* **32 D6** 35 25N 24 40 E
Lavumisa, *Swaziland* **105 D5** 27 20 S 31 55 E
Lawa, *Phil.* **71 H5** 6 12N 125 41 E
Lawa-an, *Phil.* **71 F5** 11 51N 125 5 E
Lawas, *Malaysia* **75 B5** 4 55N 115 25 E
Lawdar, *Yemen* **86 D4** 13 53N 45 52 E
Lawele, *Indonesia* **72 C2** 5 16 S 123 3 E
Lawksawk, *Burma* **78 E6** 21 15N 96 52 E
Lawn Hill, *Australia* **114 B2** 18 36 S 138 33 E
Lawqar, *Si. Arabia* **84 D4** 29 49N 42 45 E
Lawra, *Ghana* **100 C4** 10 39N 2 51W
Lawrence, *N.Z.* **119 F4** 45 55 S 169 41 E
Lawrence, *Ind., U.S.A.* **141 E10** 39 50N 86 2W
Lawrence, *Kans., U.S.A.* **138 F7** 38 58N 95 14W
Lawrence, *Mass., U.S.A.* **137 D13** 42 43N 71 10W
Lawrenceburg, *Ind., U.S.A.* **141 E12** 39 6N 84 52W
Lawrenceburg, *Ky., U.S.A.* **141 F12** 38 2N 84 54W
Lawrenceburg, *Tenn., U.S.A.* **135 H2** 35 14N 87 20W
Lawrenceville, *Ga., U.S.A.* **135 J4** 33 57N 83 59W
Lawrenceville, *Ill., U.S.A.* **141 F9** 38 44N 87 41W
Laws, *U.S.A.* **144 H8** 37 24N 118 20W
Lawson, *U.S.A.* **140 E2** 39 26N 94 12W
Lawton, *Mich., U.S.A.* **141 B11** 42 10N 85 50W
Lawton, *Okla., U.S.A.* **139 H5** 34 37N 98 25W
Lawu, *Indonesia* **75 D4** 7 40 S 111 13 E
Laxford, L., *U.K.* **18 C3** 58 25N 5 10W
Layht, Ra's, *Yemen* **87 D6** 12 38N 53 25 E
Laylá, *Si. Arabia* **86 B4** 22 10N 46 40 E
Laylān, *Iraq* **84 C5** 35 18N 44 31 E
Layon →, *France* **22 E6** 47 20N 0 45W
Laysan I., *Pac. Oc.* **123 E11** 25 30N 167 0W
Laytonville, *U.S.A.* **142 G2** 39 41N 123 29W
Laza, *Burma* **78 B6** 26 30N 97 38 E
Lazarevac, *Serbia* **42 C5** 44 23N 20 17 E
Lazi, *Phil.* **71 G4** 9 8N 123 38 E
Lazio □, *Italy* **39 F9** 42 10N 12 30 E
Lazo, *Russia* **60 C6** 43 25N 133 55 E
Łazy, *Poland* **47 E6** 50 27N 19 24 E
Le Barcarès, *France* **24 F7** 42 47N 3 2 E
Le Beausset, *France* **25 E9** 43 12N 5 48 E
Le Blanc, *France* **24 B5** 46 37N 1 3 E
Le Bleymard, *France* **24 D7** 44 30N 3 42 E
Le Bourgneuf-la-Fôret, *France* **22 D6** 48 10N 0 59W
Le Bouscat, *France* **24 D3** 44 53N 0 37W
Le Brassus, *Switz.* **28 C2** 46 35N 6 13 E
Le Bugue, *France* **24 D4** 44 55N 0 56 E
Le Canourgue, *France* **24 D7** 44 26N 3 13 E
Le Cateau, *France* **23 B10** 50 7N 3 32 E
Le Chambon-Feugerolles, *France* **25 C8** 45 24N 4 19 E
Le Château-d'Oléron, *France* **24 C2** 45 54N 1 12W
Le Châtelard, *Switz.* **28 D3** 46 4N 6 57 E
Le Châtelet, *France* **24 B6** 46 38N 2 16 E
Le Châtelet-en-Brie, *France* **23 D9** 48 31N 2 48 E
Le Chesne, *France* **23 C11** 49 30N 4 45 E
Le Cheylard, *France* **25 D8** 44 55N 4 25 E
Le Claire, *U.S.A.* **140 C6** 41 36N 90 21W
Le Conquet, *France* **22 D2** 48 21N 4 46W
Le Creusot, *France* **23 F11** 46 48N 4 24 E
Le Croisic, *France* **22 E4** 47 18N 2 30W
Le Donjon, *France* **24 B7** 46 22N 3 48 E
Le Dorat, *France* **24 B5** 46 14N 1 5 E
Le François, *Martinique* **149 D7** 14 38N 60 57W
Le Grand-Lucé, *France* **22 E7** 47 52N 0 28 E
Le Grand-Pressigny, *France* **22 F7** 46 55N 0 48 E
Le Havre, *France* **22 C7** 49 30N 0 5 E
Le Lavandou, *France* **25 E10** 43 8N 6 22 E
Le Lion-d'Angers, *France* **22 E6** 47 37N 0 43W
Le Locle, *Switz.* **28 B3** 47 3N 6 44 E
Le Louroux-Béconnais, *France* **22 E6** 47 30N 0 55W
Le Luc, *France* **25 E10** 43 23N 6 21 E
Le Madonie, *Italy* **40 E6** 37 50N 13 50 E
Le Maire, Est. de, *Argentina* **160 D4** 54 50 S 65 0W
Le Mans, *France* **22 E7** 48 0N 0 10 E
Le Marinel, *Zaïre* **103 E5** 10 25 S 25 17 E
Le Mars, *U.S.A.* **138 D6** 42 47N 96 10W
Le Mêle-sur-Sarthe, *France* **22 D7** 48 31N 0 22 E
Le Merlerault, *France* **22 D7** 48 41N 0 16 E
Le Monastier-sur-Gazeille, *France* **24 D7** 44 57N 3 59 E
Le Monêtier-les-Bains, *France* **25 D10** 44 58N 6 30 E
Le Mont d'Or, *France* **23 F13** 46 45N 6 18 E
Le Mont-Dore, *France* **24 C6** 45 35N 2 49 E
Le Mont-St.-Michel, *France* **22 D5** 48 40N 1 30W
Le Moule, *Guadeloupe* **149 C7** 16 20N 61 22W
Le Muy, *France* **25 E10** 43 28N 6 34 E
Le Palais, *France* **22 E3** 47 20N 3 10W
Le Perthus, *France* **24 F6** 42 30N 2 53 E
Le Pont, *Switz.* **28 C2** 46 41N 6 20 E
Le Pouldu, *France* **22 E3** 47 41N 3 36W
Le Puy, *France* **24 C7** 45 3N 3 52 E
Le Quesnoy, *France* **23 B10** 50 15N 3 38 E
Le Roy, *Ill., U.S.A.* **141 D8** 40 21N 88 46W
Le Roy, *Kans., U.S.A.* **139 F7** 38 5N 95 38W
Le Sentier, *Switz.* **28 C2** 46 37N 6 15 E
Le Sueur, *U.S.A.* **138 C8** 44 28N 93 55W
Le Teil, *France* **25 D8** 44 33N 4 40 E
Le Teilleul, *France* **22 D6** 48 32N 0 53W
Le Theil, *France* **22 D7** 48 16N 0 42 E
Le Thillot, *France* **23 E13** 47 53N 6 46 E
Le Thuy, *Vietnam* **76 D6** 17 14N 106 49 E
Le Touquet-Paris-Plage, *France* **23 B8** 50 30N 1 36 E
Le Tréport, *France* **22 B8** 50 3N 1 20 E
Le Val-d'Ajol, *France* **23 E13** 47 55N 6 30 E
Le Verdon-sur-Mer, *France* **24 C2** 45 33N 1 4W
Le Vigan, *France* **24 E7** 43 59N 3 36 E
Lea →, *U.K.* **17 F7** 51 30N 0 10W
Leach, *Cambodia* **77 F4** 12 21N 103 46 E
Lead, *U.S.A.* **138 C3** 44 21N 103 46W
Leader, *Canada* **131 C7** 50 50N 109 30W
Leadhills, *U.K.* **18 F5** 55 25N 3 47W
Leadville, *U.S.A.* **143 G10** 39 15N 106 18W
Leaf →, *U.S.A.* **139 K10** 30 59N 88 44W
Leakey, *U.S.A.* **139 L5** 29 44N 99 46W
Lealui, *Zambia* **103 F4** 15 10 S 23 2 E
Leamington, *Canada* **128 D3** 42 3N 82 36W
Leamington, *N.Z.* **118 D4** 37 55 S 175 30 E
Leamington, *U.S.A.* **142 G7** 39 32N 112 17W
Leamington Spa = Royal Leamington Spa, *U.K.* **17 E6** 52 18N 1 32W
Le'an, *China* **69 D10** 27 22N 115 48 E
Leandro Norte Alem, *Argentina* **159 B4** 27 34 S 55 15W
Learmonth, *Australia* **112 D1** 22 13 S 114 10 E
Leask, *Canada* **131 C7** 53 5N 106 45W
Leavenworth, *Ind., U.S.A.* **141 F10** 38 12N 86 21W
Leavenworth, *Kans., U.S.A.* **138 F7** 39 19N 94 55W
Leavenworth, *Wash., U.S.A.* **142 C3** 47 36N 120 40W
Leawood, *U.S.A.* **140 F2** 38 57N 94 37W
Łeba, *Poland* **47 A4** 54 45N 17 32 E
Łeba →, *Poland* **47 A4** 54 46N 17 33 E
Lebak, *Phil.* **71 H5** 6 32N 124 5 E
Lebam, *U.S.A.* **144 D3** 46 34N 123 33W
Lebane, *Serbia* **42 E6** 42 56N 21 44 E
Lebango, *Congo* **102 B2** 0 39N 14 21 E
Lebanon, *Ill., U.S.A.* **140 F7** 38 38N 89 49W
Lebanon, *Ind., U.S.A.* **141 D10** 40 3N 86 28W
Lebanon, *Kans., U.S.A.* **138 F5** 39 49N 98 33W
Lebanon, *Ky., U.S.A.* **134 G3** 37 34N 85 15W
Lebanon, *Mo., U.S.A.* **139 G8** 37 41N 92 40W
Lebanon, *Ohio, U.S.A.* **141 E12** 39 26N 84 13W
Lebanon, *Oreg., U.S.A.* **142 D2** 44 32N 122 55W
Lebanon, *Pa., U.S.A.* **137 F8** 40 20N 76 26W
Lebanon, *Tenn., U.S.A.* **135 G2** 36 12N 86 18W
Lebanon ■, *Asia* **91 B4** 34 0N 36 0 E
Lebanon Junction, *U.S.A.* **141 G11** 37 50N 85 44W
Lebbeke, *Belgium* **21 G4** 50 58N 4 8 E
Lebec, *U.S.A.* **145 L8** 34 50N 118 52W
Lebedin, *Ukraine* **50 F9** 50 35N 34 30 E
Lebedyan, *Russia* **51 E11** 53 0N 39 10 E
Lebomboberge, *S. Africa* **105 C5** 24 30 S 32 0 E
Lębork, *Poland* **47 A4** 54 33N 17 46 E
Lebrija, *Spain* **37 J4** 36 53N 6 5W
Łebsko, Jezioro, *Poland* **47 A4** 54 40N 17 25 E
Lebu, *Chile* **158 D1** 37 40 S 73 47W
Lecce, *Italy* **41 B11** 40 20N 18 10 E
Lecco, *Italy* **38 C6** 45 50N 9 27 E
Lecco, L. di, *Italy* **38 C6** 45 51N 9 22 E
Lécera, *Spain* **34 D4** 41 13N 0 43W
Lech, *Austria* **30 D3** 47 13N 10 9 E
Lech →, *Germany* **27 G6** 48 44N 10 56 E
Lechang, *China* **69 E9** 25 10N 113 20 E
Lechtaler Alpen, *Austria* **30 D3** 47 15N 10 30 E
Lectoure, *France* **24 E4** 43 56N 0 38 E
Łeczna, *Poland* **47 D9** 51 18N 22 53 E
Łęczyca, *Poland* **47 C6** 52 5N 19 15 E
Ledang, Gunong, *Malaysia* **74 B2** 2 22N 102 37 E
Ledbury, *U.K.* **17 E5** 52 3N 2 25W
Lede, *Belgium* **21 G3** 50 58N 3 59 E
Ledeberg, *Belgium* **21 F3** 51 2N 3 45 E
Ledeč, *Czech.* **30 B8** 49 41N 15 18 E
Ledesma, *Spain* **36 D5** 41 6N 5 59W
Ledong, *China* **76 C7** 18 41N 109 5 E
Leduc, *Canada* **130 C6** 53 15N 113 30W
Ledyczek, *Poland* **47 B3** 53 33N 16 59 E
Lee, *U.S.A.* **137 D11** 42 19N 73 15W
Lee →, *Ireland* **19 E3** 51 50N 8 30W
Lee Vining, *U.S.A.* **144 H7** 37 58N 119 7W
Leech L., *U.S.A.* **138 B7** 47 10N 94 24W
Leedey, *U.S.A.* **139 H5** 35 52N 99 21W
Leeds, *U.K.* **16 D6** 53 48N 1 34W
Leeds, *U.S.A.* **135 J2** 33 33N 86 33W
Leek, *Neths.* **20 B8** 53 10N 6 24 E
Leek, *U.K.* **16 D5** 53 7N 2 2W
Leende, *Neths.* **21 F7** 51 21N 5 33 E
Leer, *Germany* **26 B3** 53 13N 7 29 E
Leerdam, *Neths.* **20 E6** 51 54N 5 6 E
Leersum, *Neths.* **20 E6** 52 0N 5 26 E
Lee's Summit, *U.S.A.* **140 F2** 38 55N 94 23W
Leesburg, *Fla., U.S.A.* **135 L5** 28 49N 81 53W
Leesburg, *Ohio, U.S.A.* **141 E13** 39 21N 83 33W
Leeston, *N.Z.* **119 D7** 43 45 S 172 19 E
Leesville, *U.S.A.* **139 K8** 31 9N 93 16W
Leeton, *Australia* **117 C7** 34 33 S 146 23 E
Leetonia, *U.S.A.* **136 F4** 40 53N 80 45W
Leeu Gamka, *S. Africa* **104 E3** 32 47 S 21 59 E
Leeuwarden, *Neths.* **20 B7** 53 15N 5 48 E
Leeuwin, C., *Australia* **113 F2** 34 20 S 115 9 E
Leeward Is., *Atl. Oc.* **149 C7** 16 30N 63 30W
Léfini, *Congo* **102 C3** 2 55 S 15 39 E
Lefka, *Cyprus* **32 D11** 35 6N 32 51 E
Lefkoniko, *Cyprus* **32 D12** 35 18N 33 44 E
Lefors, *U.S.A.* **139 H4** 35 26N 100 48W
Lefroy, L., *Australia* **113 F3** 31 21 S 121 40 E
Łeg →, *Poland* **47 E8** 50 42N 21 50 E
Legal, *Canada* **130 C6** 53 55N 113 35W
Leganés, *Spain* **36 E7** 40 19N 3 45W
Legazpi, *Phil.* **70 E4** 13 10N 123 45 E
Legendre I., *Australia* **112 D2** 20 22 S 116 55 E
Leghorn = Livorno, *Italy* **38 E7** 43 32N 10 18 E
Legionowo, *Poland* **47 C7** 52 25N 20 50 E
Léglise, *Belgium* **21 J7** 49 48N 5 32 E
Legnago, *Italy* **39 C8** 45 10N 11 19 E
Legnano, *Italy* **38 C5** 45 35N 8 55 E
Legnica, *Poland* **47 D3** 51 12N 16 10 E
Legnica □, *Poland* **47 D3** 51 30N 16 0 E
Legrad, *Croatia* **39 B13** 46 17N 16 51 E

**Lochem 225**


Ligny-le-Châtel, *France* **23 E10** 47 54N 3 45 E
Ligoúrion, *Greece* **45 G5** 37 37N 23 2 E
Ligueil, *France* **22 E7** 47 2N 0 49 E
Liguria □, *Italy* **38 D6** 44 30N 9 0 E
Ligurian Sea, *Italy* **38 E5** 43 20N 9 0 E
Lihir Group, *Papua N. G.* **120 B7** 3 0 S 152 35 E
Lihou Reefs and Cays, *Australia* **114 B5** 17 25 S 151 40 E
Lihue, *U.S.A.* **132 H15** 21 59N 159 23W
Lijiang, *China* **68 D3** 26 55N 100 20 E
Likasi, *Zaïre* **107 E2** 10 55 S 26 48 E
Likati, *Zaïre* **102 B4** 3 20N 24 0 E
Likhoslavl, *Russia* **50 C9** 57 12N 35 30 E
Likhovski, *Russia* **53 B9** 48 10N 40 10 E
Likokou, *Gabon* **102 C2** 0 12 S 12 48 E
Likoma I., *Malawi* **107 E3** 12 3 S 34 45 E
Likumburu, *Tanzania* **107 D4** 9 43 S 35 8 E
L'Île-Bouchard, *France* **22 E7** 47 7N 0 26 E
L'Île-Rousse, *France* **25 F12** 42 38N 8 57 E
Liling, *China* **69 D9** 27 42N 113 29 E
Lille, *Belgium* **21 F5** 51 15N 4 50 E
Lille, *France* **23 B10** 50 38N 3 3 E
Lille Bælt, *Denmark* **15 J3** 55 20N 9 45 E
Lillebonne, *France* **22 C7** 49 30N 0 32 E
Lillehammer, *Norway* **14 C4** 61 8N 10 30 E
Lillers, *France* **23 B9** 50 35N 2 28 E
Lillesand, *Norway* **15 F2** 58 15N 8 23 E
Lilleshall, *U.K.* **17 E5** 52 45N 2 22W
Lillestrøm, *Norway* **14 E5** 59 58N 11 5 E
Lillian Point, Mt., *Australia* **113 E4** 27 40 S 126 6 E
Lillo, *Spain* **34 F1** 39 45N 3 20W
Lillooet →, *Canada* **130 D4** 49 15N 121 57W
Lilongwe, *Malawi* **107 E3** 14 0 S 33 48 E
Liloy, *Phil.* **71 G4** 8 4N 122 39 E
Lim →, *Bos.-H.* **42 D4** 43 45N 19 15 E
Lima, *Indonesia* **72 B3** 3 37 S 128 4 E
Lima, *Peru* **156 C2** 12 0 S 77 0W
Lima, *Mont., U.S.A.* **142 D7** 44 38N 112 36W
Lima, *Ohio, U.S.A.* **141 D12** 40 44N 84 6W
Lima □, *Peru* **156 C2** 12 3 S 77 3W
Lima →, *Portugal* **36 D2** 41 41N 8 50W
Limages, *Canada* **137 A9** 45 20N 75 16W
Liman, *Russia* **53 D12** 45 45N 47 12 E
Limanowa, *Poland* **31 B13** 49 42N 20 22 E
Limassol, *Cyprus* **32 E12** 34 42N 33 1 E
Limavady, *U.K.* **19 A5** 55 3N 6 58W
Limavady □, *U.K.* **19 B5** 55 0N 6 55W
Limay →, *Argentina* **160 A3** 39 0 S 68 0W
Limay Mahuida, *Argentina* **158 D2** 37 10 S 66 45W
Limbang, *Brunei* **75 B5** 4 42N 115 6 E
Limbara, Monti, *Italy* **40 B2** 40 50N 9 10 E
Limbdi, *India* **80 H4** 22 34N 71 51 E
Limbe, *Cameroon* **101 E6** 4 1N 9 10 E
Limbourg, *Belgium* **21 G7** 50 37N 5 56 E
Limbri, *Australia* **117 A9** 31 3 S 151 5 E
Limbueta, *Angola* **103 E3** 12 30 S 18 42 E
Limbunya, *Australia* **112 C4** 17 14 S 129 50 E
Limburg, *Germany* **27 E4** 50 22N 8 4 E
Limburg □, *Belgium* **21 F6** 51 2N 5 25 E
Limburg □, *Neths.* **21 F7** 51 20N 5 55 E
Limeira, *Brazil* **159 A6** 22 35 S 47 28W
Limenária, *Greece* **44 D6** 40 38N 24 32 E
Limerick, *Ireland* **19 D3** 52 40N 8 38W
Limerick □, *Ireland* **19 D3** 52 30N 8 50W
Limestone, *U.S.A.* **136 D6** 42 2N 78 38W
Limestone →, *Canada* **131 B10** 56 31N 94 7W
Limfjorden, *Denmark* **15 H3** 56 55N 9 0 E
Limia = Lima →, *Portugal* **36 D2** 41 41N 8 50W
Limmared, *Sweden* **15 G7** 57 34N 13 20 E
Limmat →, *Switz.* **29 B6** 47 26N 8 20 E
Limmen, *Neths.* **20 C5** 52 34N 4 42 E
Limmen Bight, *Australia* **114 A2** 14 40 S 135 35 E
Limmen Bight →, *Australia* **114 B2** 15 7 S 135 44 E
Límni, *Greece* **45 F5** 38 43N 23 18 E
Límnos, *Greece* **44 E7** 39 50N 25 5 E
Limoeiro, *Brazil* **154 C4** 7 52 S 35 27W
Limoeiro do Norte, *Brazil* **154 C4** 5 5 S 38 0W
Limoges, *France* **24 C5** 45 50N 1 15 E
Limón, *Costa Rica* **148 D3** 10 0N 83 2W
Limon, *U.S.A.* **138 F3** 39 16N 103 41W
Limone Piemonte, *Italy* **38 D4** 44 12N 7 32 E
Limousin, *France* **24 C5** 45 30N 1 30 E
Limousin, Plateaux du, *France* **24 C5** 45 45N 1 15 E
Limoux, *France* **24 E6** 43 4N 2 12 E
Limpopo →, *Africa* **105 D5** 25 5 S 33 30 E
Limuru, *Kenya* **106 C4** 1 2 S 36 35 E
Lin Xian, *China* **66 F6** 37 57N 110 58 E
Lin'an, *China* **69 B12** 30 15N 119 42 E
Linapacan, *Phil.* **71 F2** 11 30N 119 52 E
Linapacan I., *Phil.* **71 F2** 11 27N 119 49 E
Linapacan Str., *Phil.* **71 F2** 11 37N 119 56 E
Linares, *Chile* **158 D1** 35 50 S 71 40W
Linares, *Colombia* **152 C2** 1 23N 77 31W
Linares, *Mexico* **147 C5** 24 50N 99 40W
Linares, *Spain* **35 G1** 38 10N 3 40W
Linares □, *Chile* **158 D1** 36 0 S 71 0W
Línas Mte., *Italy* **40 C1** 39 25N 8 38 E
Lincang, *China* **68 F3** 23 58N 100 1 E
Lincheng, *China* **66 F8** 37 25N 114 30 E
Linchuan, *China* **69 D11** 27 57N 116 15 E
Lincoln, *Argentina* **158 C3** 34 55 S 61 30W
Lincoln, *N.Z.* **119 D7** 43 38 S 172 30 E
Lincoln, *U.K.* **16 D7** 53 14N 0 32W
Lincoln, *Calif., U.S.A.* **144 G5** 38 54N 121 17W
Lincoln, *Ill., U.S.A.* **140 D7** 40 9N 89 22W
Lincoln, *Kans., U.S.A.* **138 F5** 39 3N 98 9W
Lincoln, *Maine, U.S.A.* **129 C6** 45 22N 68 30W
Lincoln, *N.H., U.S.A.* **137 B13** 44 3N 71 40W
Lincoln, *N. Mex., U.S.A.* **143 K11** 33 30N 105 23W
Lincoln, *Nebr., U.S.A.* **138 E6** 40 49N 96 41W
Lincoln Hav = Lincoln Sea, *Arctic* **6 A5** 84 0N 55 0W
Lincoln Park, *U.S.A.* **141 B13** 42 15N 83 11W
Lincoln Sea, *Arctic* **6 A5** 84 0N 55 0W
Lincoln Wolds, *U.K.* **16 D7** 53 20N 0 5W
Lincolnshire □, *U.K.* **16 D7** 53 14N 0 32W
Lincolnton, *U.S.A.* **135 H5** 35 29N 81 16W
L'Incudine, *France* **25 G13** 41 50N 9 12 E
Lind, *U.S.A.* **142 C4** 46 58N 118 37W
Linda, *U.S.A.* **144 F5** 39 8N 121 34W
Lindau, *Germany* **27 H5** 47 33N 9 41 E
Linde →, *Neths.* **20 C7** 52 50N 5 57 E
Linden, *Guyana* **153 B6** 6 0N 58 10W
Linden, *Calif., U.S.A.* **144 G5** 38 1N 121 5W
Linden, *Ind., U.S.A.* **141 D10** 40 11N 86 54W
Linden, *Mich., U.S.A.* **141 B13** 42 49N 83 47W
Linden, *Tex., U.S.A.* **139 J7** 33 1N 94 22W
Lindenheuvel, *Neths.* **21 G7** 50 59N 5 48 E
Lindenhurst, *U.S.A.* **137 F11** 40 41N 73 23W
Linderöd, *Sweden* **15 J7** 55 56N 13 47 E
Linderödsåsen, *Sweden* **15 J7** 55 53N 13 53 E
Lindesnes, *Norway* **10 D7** 57 58N 7 3 E
Líndhos, *Greece* **32 C10** 36 6N 28 4 E
Lindi, *Tanzania* **107 D4** 9 58 S 39 38 E
Lindi □, *Tanzania* **107 D4** 9 40 S 38 30 E
Lindi →, *Zaïre* **106 B2** 0 33N 25 5 E
Lindoso, *Portugal* **36 D2** 41 52N 8 11W
Lindow, *Germany* **26 C8** 52 58N 12 58 E
Lindsay, *Canada* **128 D4** 44 22N 78 43W
Lindsay, *Calif., U.S.A.* **144 J7** 36 12N 119 5W
Lindsay, *Okla., U.S.A.* **139 H6** 34 50N 97 38W
Lindsborg, *U.S.A.* **138 F6** 38 35N 97 40W
Lineville, *U.S.A.* **140 D3** 40 35N 93 32W
Linfen, *China* **66 F6** 36 3N 111 30 E
Ling Xian, *Hunan, China* **69 D9** 26 29N 113 48 E
Ling Xian, *Shandong, China* **66 F9** 37 22N 116 30 E
Lingao, *China* **76 C7** 19 56N 109 42 E
Lingayen, *Phil.* **70 C3** 16 1N 120 14 E
Lingayen G., *Phil.* **70 C3** 16 10N 120 15 E
Lingbi, *China* **67 H9** 33 33N 117 33 E
Lingchuan, *Guangxi Zhuangzu, China* **69 E8** 25 26N 110 21 E
Lingchuan, *Shanxi, China* **66 G7** 35 45N 113 12 E
Lingen, *Germany* **26 C3** 52 32N 7 21 E
Lingga, *Indonesia* **74 C2** 0 12 S 104 37 E
Lingga, Kepulauan, *Indonesia* **74 C2** 0 10 S 104 30 E
Lingga Arch. = Lingga, Kepulauan, *Indonesia* **74 C2** 0 10 S 104 30 E
Lingle, *U.S.A.* **138 D2** 42 8N 104 21W
Lingling, *China* **69 D8** 26 17N 111 37 E
Lingqiu, *China* **66 E8** 39 28N 114 22 E
Lingshan, *China* **68 F7** 22 25N 109 18 E
Lingshi, *China* **66 F6** 36 48N 111 48 E
Lingshou, *China* **66 E8** 38 20N 114 20 E
Lingshui, *China* **76 C8** 18 27N 110 0 E
Lingtai, *China* **66 G4** 35 0N 107 40 E
Linguéré, *Senegal* **100 B1** 15 25N 15 5W
Linguisan, *Phil.* **71 H4** 7 30N 122 27 E
Lingwu, *China* **66 E4** 38 6N 106 20 E
Lingyuan, *China* **67 D10** 41 10N 119 15 E
Lingyun, *China* **68 E6** 25 2N 106 35 E
Linh Cam, *Vietnam* **76 C5** 18 31N 105 31 E
Linhai, *China* **69 C13** 28 50N 121 8 E
Linhares, *Brazil* **155 E3** 19 25 S 40 4W
Linhe, *China* **66 D4** 40 48N 107 20 E
Linjiang, *China* **67 D14** 41 50N 127 0 E
Linköping, *Sweden* **15 F9** 58 28N 15 36 E
Linkou, *China* **67 B16** 45 15N 130 18 E
Linli, *China* **69 C8** 29 27N 111 30 E
Linlithgow, *U.K.* **18 F5** 55 58N 3 38W
Linn, *U.S.A.* **140 F5** 38 29N 91 51W
Linneus, *U.S.A.* **140 E3** 39 53N 93 11W
Linnhe, L., *U.K.* **18 E3** 56 36N 5 25W
Linosa, I., *Medit. S.* **96 A2** 35 51N 12 50 E
Linqi, *China* **66 G7** 35 45N 113 52 E
Linqing, *China* **66 F8** 36 50N 115 42 E
Linqu, *China* **67 F10** 36 25N 118 30 E
Linru, *China* **66 G7** 34 11N 112 52 E
Lins, *Brazil* **159 A6** 21 40 S 49 44W
Linshui, *China* **68 B6** 30 21N 106 57 E
Lintao, *China* **66 G2** 35 18N 103 52 E
Linth →, *Switz.* **27 H5** 47 7N 9 7 E
Linthal, *Switz.* **29 C8** 46 54N 9 0 E
Lintlaw, *Canada* **131 C8** 52 4N 103 14W
Linton, *Canada* **129 C5** 47 15N 72 16W
Linton, *Ind., U.S.A.* **141 E9** 39 2N 87 10W
Linton, *N. Dak., U.S.A.* **138 B4** 46 16N 100 14W
Lintong, *China* **66 G5** 34 20N 109 10 E
Linville, *Australia* **115 D5** 26 50 S 152 11 E
Linwood, *Canada* **136 C4** 43 35N 80 43W
Linwu, *China* **69 E9** 25 19N 112 31 E
Linxi, *China* **67 C10** 43 36N 118 2 E
Linxia, *China* **64 C5** 35 36N 103 10 E
Linxiang, *China* **69 C9** 29 28N 113 23 E
Linyanti →, *Africa* **104 B4** 17 50 S 25 5 E
Linyi, *China* **67 G10** 35 5N 118 21 E
Linz, *Austria* **30 C7** 48 18N 14 18 E
Linz, *Germany* **26 E3** 50 33N 7 18 E
Linzhenzhen, *China* **66 F5** 36 30N 109 59 E
Linzi, *China* **67 F10** 36 50N 118 20 E
Lion, G. du, *France* **25 E8** 43 10N 4 0 E
Lionárisso, *Cyprus* **32 D13** 35 28N 34 8 E
Lioni, *Italy* **41 B8** 40 52N 15 10 E
Lions, G. of = Lion, G. du, *France* **25 E8** 43 10N 4 0 E
Lion's Den, *Zimbabwe* **107 F3** 17 15 S 30 5 E
Lion's Head, *Canada* **136 B3** 44 58N 81 15W
Liouesso, *Congo* **102 B3** 1 2N 15 43 E
Liozno, *Belorussia* **50 D7** 55 0N 30 50 E
Lipa, *Phil.* **70 E3** 13 57N 121 10 E
Lipali, *Mozam.* **107 F4** 15 50 S 35 50 E
Lípari, *Italy* **41 D7** 38 26N 14 58 E
Lípari, Is., *Italy* **41 D7** 38 30N 14 50 E
Lipetsk, *Russia* **51 E11** 52 37N 39 35 E
Lipiany, *Poland* **47 B1** 53 2N 14 58 E
Liping, *China* **68 D7** 26 15N 109 7 E
Lipkany, *Moldavia* **52 B2** 48 14N 26 48 E
Lipljan, *Serbia* **42 E6** 42 31N 21 7 E
Lipnik, *Czech.* **31 B10** 49 32N 17 36 E
Lipno, *Poland* **47 C6** 52 49N 19 15 E
Lipova, *Romania* **42 A6** 46 8N 21 42 E
Lipovcy Manzovka, *Russia* **60 B6** 44 12N 132 26 E
Lipovets, *Ukraine* **52 B3** 49 12N 29 1 E
Lippe →, *Germany* **26 D2** 51 39N 6 38 E
Lippstadt, *Germany* **26 D4** 51 40N 8 19 E
Lipscomb, *U.S.A.* **139 G4** 36 14N 100 16W
Lipsko, *Poland* **47 D8** 51 9N 21 40 E
Lipsói, *Greece* **45 G8** 37 19N 26 50 E
Liptovsky Svaty Milkulaš, *Slovak Rep.* **31 B12** 49 6N 19 35 E
Liptrap C., *Australia* **117 E6** 38 50 S 145 55 E
Lipu, *China* **69 E8** 24 30N 110 22 E
Lira, *Uganda* **106 B3** 2 17N 32 57 E
Liri →, *Italy* **40 A6** 41 25N 13 52 E
Liria, *Spain* **34 F4** 39 37N 0 35W
Lisala, *Zaïre* **102 B4** 2 12N 21 38 E
Lisboa, *Portugal* **37 G1** 38 42N 9 10W
Lisboa □, *Portugal* **37 G1** 39 0N 9 12W
Lisbon = Lisboa, *Portugal* **37 G1** 38 42N 9 10W
Lisbon, *N. Dak., U.S.A.* **138 B6** 46 27N 97 41W
Lisbon, *N.H., U.S.A.* **137 B13** 44 13N 71 55W
Lisbon, *Ohio, U.S.A.* **136 F4** 40 46N 80 46W
Lisburn, *U.K.* **19 B5** 54 30N 6 9W
Lisburne, C., *U.S.A.* **126 B3** 68 53N 166 13W
Liscannor, B., *Ireland* **19 D2** 52 57N 9 24W
Liscia →, *Italy* **40 A2** 41 11N 9 9 E
Lishe Jiang →, *China* **68 E3** 24 15N 101 35 E
Lishi, *China* **66 F6** 37 31N 111 8 E
Lishu, *China* **67 C13** 43 20N 124 18 E
Lishui, *Jiangsu, China* **69 B12** 31 38N 119 2 E
Lishui, *Zhejiang, China* **69 C12** 28 28N 119 54 E
Lisianski I., *Pac. Oc.* **122 E10** 26 2N 174 0W
Lisichansk, *Ukraine* **52 B8** 48 55N 38 30 E
Lisieux, *France* **22 C7** 49 10N 0 12 E
Liski, *Russia* **51 F11** 51 3N 39 30 E
L'Isle-Adam, *France* **23 C9** 49 6N 2 14 E
L'Isle-Jourdain, *Gers, France* **24 E5** 43 36N 1 5 E
L'Isle-Jourdain, *Vienne, France* **24 B4** 46 13N 0 31 E
L'Isle-sur-le-Doubs, *France* **23 E13** 47 26N 6 34 E
Lisle-sur-Tarn, *France* **24 E5** 43 52N 1 49 E
Lismore, *Australia* **115 D5** 28 44 S 153 21 E
Lismore, *Ireland* **19 D4** 52 8N 7 58W
Lisse, *Neths.* **20 D5** 52 16N 4 33 E
List, *Germany* **26 A4** 55 1N 8 26 E
Lista, *Norway* **13 G9** 58 7N 6 39 E
Lista, *Sweden* **13 G14** 59 19N 16 16 E
Lister, Mt., *Antarctica* **7 D11** 78 0 S 162 0 E
Liston, *Australia* **115 D5** 28 39 S 152 6 E
Listowel, *Canada* **128 D3** 43 44N 80 58W
Listowel, *Ireland* **19 D2** 52 27N 9 30W
Lit-et-Mixe, *France* **24 D2** 44 2N 1 15W
Litang, *Guangxi Zhuangzu, China* **68 F7** 23 12N 109 8 E
Litang, *Sichuan, China* **68 B3** 30 1N 100 17 E
Litang, *Malaysia* **75 A5** 5 27N 118 31 E
Litang Qu →, *China* **68 C3** 28 4N 101 32 E
Litani →, *Lebanon* **91 B4** 33 20N 35 15 E
Litchfield, *Australia* **116 D5** 36 18 S 142 52 E
Litchfield, *Calif., U.S.A.* **144 E6** 40 24N 120 23W
Litchfield, *Conn., U.S.A.* **137 E11** 41 45N 73 11W
Litchfield, *Ill., U.S.A.* **140 E7** 39 11N 89 39W
Litchfield, *Minn., U.S.A.* **138 C7** 45 8N 94 32W
Liteni, *Romania* **46 B7** 47 32N 26 32 E
Lithgow, *Australia* **117 B9** 33 25 S 150 8 E
Líthinon, Ákra, *Greece* **32 E6** 34 55N 24 44 E
Lithuania ■, *Europe* **50 D3** 55 30N 24 0 E
Litija, *Slovenia* **39 B11** 46 3N 14 50 E
Litókhoron, *Greece* **44 D4** 40 8N 22 34 E
Litoměřice, *Czech.* **30 A7** 50 33N 14 10 E
Litomysl, *Czech.* **31 B9** 49 52N 16 20 E
Litschau, *Austria* **30 C8** 48 58N 15 4 E
Little Abaco I., *Bahamas* **148 A4** 26 50N 77 30W
Little Aden, *Yemen* **86 D4** 12 45N 44 52 E
Little Barrier I., *N.Z.* **118 C4** 36 12 S 175 8 E
Little Belt Mts., *U.S.A.* **142 C8** 46 40N 110 45W
Little Blue →, *U.S.A.* **138 F6** 39 42N 96 41W
Little Bushman Land, *S. Africa* **104 D2** 29 10 S 18 10 E
Little Cadotte →, *Canada* **130 B5** 56 41N 117 6W
Little Cayman, I., *Cayman Is.* **148 C3** 19 41N 80 3W
Little Churchill →, *Canada* **131 B9** 57 30N 95 22W
Little Colorado →, *U.S.A.* **143 H8** 36 12N 111 48W
Little Current, *Canada* **128 C3** 45 55N 82 0W
Little Current →, *Canada* **128 B3** 50 57N 84 36W
Little Falls, *Minn., U.S.A.* **138 C7** 45 59N 94 22W
Little Falls, *N.Y., U.S.A.* **137 C10** 43 3N 74 51W
Little Fork →, *U.S.A.* **138 A8** 48 31N 93 35W
Little Grand Rapids, *Canada* **131 C9** 52 0N 95 29W
Little Humboldt →, *U.S.A.* **142 F5** 41 1N 117 43W
Little Inagua I., *Bahamas* **149 B5** 21 40N 73 50W
Little Karoo, *S. Africa* **104 E3** 33 45 S 21 0 E
Little Lake, *U.S.A.* **145 K9** 35 56N 117 55W
Little Laut Is. = Laut Ketil, Kepulauan, *Indonesia* **75 C5** 4 45 S 115 40 E
Little Minch, *U.K.* **18 D2** 57 35N 6 45W
Little Missouri →, *U.S.A.* **138 B3** 47 36N 102 25W
Little Namaqualand, *S. Africa* **104 D2** 29 0 S 17 9 E
Little Ouse →, *U.K.* **17 E8** 52 25N 0 50 E
Little Rann, *India* **80 H4** 23 25N 71 25 E
Little Red →, *U.S.A.* **139 H9** 35 11N 91 27W
Little River, *N.Z.* **119 D7** 43 45 S 172 49 E
Little Rock, *U.S.A.* **139 H8** 34 45N 92 17W
Little Ruaha →, *Tanzania* **106 D4** 7 57 S 37 53 E
Little Sable Pt., *U.S.A.* **134 D2** 43 38N 86 33W
Little Sioux →, *U.S.A.* **138 E6** 41 48N 96 4W
Little Smoky →, *Canada* **130 C5** 54 44N 117 11W
Little Snake →, *U.S.A.* **142 F9** 40 27N 108 26W
Little Valley, *U.S.A.* **136 D6** 42 15N 78 48W
Little Wabash →, *U.S.A.* **141 G8** 37 55N 88 5W
Little York, *U.S.A.* **140 C6** 41 1N 90 45W
Littlefield, *U.S.A.* **139 J3** 33 55N 102 20W
Littlefork, *U.S.A.* **138 A8** 48 24N 93 34W
Littlehampton, *U.K.* **17 G7** 50 48N 0 32W
Littleton, *U.S.A.* **137 B13** 44 18N 71 46W
Liu He →, *China* **67 D11** 40 55N 121 35 E
Liu Jiang →, *China* **68 F7** 23 55N 109 30 E
Liuba, *China* **66 H4** 33 38N 106 55 E
Liucheng, *China* **68 E7** 24 38N 109 14 E
Liugou, *China* **67 D10** 40 57N 118 15 E
Liuhe, *China* **67 C13** 42 17N 125 43 E
Liuheng Dao, *China* **69 C14** 29 40N 122 5 E
Liukang Tenggaja, *Indonesia* **72 C1** 6 45 S 118 50 E
Liuli, *Tanzania* **107 E3** 11 3 S 34 38 E
Liuwa Plain, *Zambia* **103 E4** 14 20 S 22 30 E
Liuyang, *China* **69 C9** 28 10N 113 37 E
Liuzhou, *China* **68 E7** 24 22N 109 22 E
Liuzhuang, *China* **67 H11** 33 12N 120 18 E
Livada, *Romania* **46 B4** 47 52N 23 5 E
Livadherón, *Greece* **44 D3** 40 2N 21 57 E
Livadhia, *Cyprus* **32 E12** 34 57N 33 38 E
Livanovka, *Kazakhstan* **54 E7** 52 6N 61 59 E
Livarot, *France* **22 D7** 48 58N 0 9 E
Live Oak, *Calif., U.S.A.* **144 F5** 39 17N 121 40W
Live Oak, *Fla., U.S.A.* **135 K4** 30 18N 82 59W
Liveras, *Cyprus* **32 D11** 35 23N 32 57 E
Liveringa, *Australia* **112 C3** 18 3 S 124 10 E
Livermore, *U.S.A.* **144 H5** 37 41N 121 47W
Livermore, Mt., *U.S.A.* **139 K2** 30 38N 104 11W
Liverpool, *Australia* **117 B9** 33 54 S 150 58 E
Liverpool, *Canada* **129 D7** 44 5N 64 41W
Liverpool, *U.K.* **16 D5** 53 25N 3 0W
Liverpool Plains, *Australia* **117 A9** 31 15 S 150 15 E
Liverpool Ra., *Australia* **117 A9** 31 50 S 150 30 E
Livingston, *Guatemala* **148 C2** 15 50N 88 50W
Livingston, *Calif., U.S.A.* **144 H6** 37 23N 120 43W
Livingston, *Mont., U.S.A.* **142 D8** 45 40N 110 34W
Livingston, *Tex., U.S.A.* **139 K7** 30 43N 94 56W
Livingston, *Wis., U.S.A.* **140 B6** 42 54N 90 26W
Livingstone, *Zambia* **107 F2** 17 46 S 25 52 E
Livingstone Mts., *N.Z.* **119 F3** 45 15 S 168 9 E
Livingstone Mts., *Tanzania* **107 D3** 9 40 S 34 20 E
Livingstonia, *Malawi* **107 E3** 10 38 S 34 5 E
Livno, *Bos.-H.* **42 D2** 43 50N 17 0 E
Livny, *Russia* **51 E10** 52 30N 37 30 E
Livonia, *U.S.A.* **141 B13** 42 23N 83 23W
Livorno, *Italy* **38 E7** 43 32N 10 18 E
Livramento, *Brazil* **159 C4** 30 55 S 55 30W
Livramento do Brumado, *Brazil* **155 D3** 13 39 S 41 50W
Livron-sur-Drôme, *France* **25 D8** 44 46N 4 51 E
Liwale, *Tanzania* **107 D4** 9 48 S 37 58 E
Liwale □, *Tanzania* **107 D4** 9 0 S 38 0 E
Liwiec →, *Poland* **47 C8** 52 36N 21 34 E
Lixi, *China* **68 D3** 26 23N 101 59 E
Lixoúrion, *Greece* **45 F2** 38 14N 20 24 E
Liyang, *China* **69 B12** 31 26N 119 28 E
Lizard I., *Australia* **114 A4** 14 42 S 145 30 E
Lizard Pt., *U.K.* **17 H2** 49 57N 5 11W
Lizarda, *Brazil* **154 C2** 9 36 S 46 41W
Lizzano, *Italy* **41 B10** 40 23N 17 25 E
Ljig, *Serbia* **42 C5** 44 13N 20 18 E
Ljubija, *Bos.-H.* **39 D13** 44 55N 16 35 E
Ljubinje, *Bos.-H.* **42 E3** 42 58N 18 5 E
Ljubljana, *Slovenia* **39 B11** 46 4N 14 33 E
Ljubno, *Slovenia* **39 B11** 46 25N 14 46 E
Ljubovija, *Serbia* **42 C4** 44 11N 19 22 E
Ljubuški, *Bos.-H.* **42 D2** 43 12N 17 34 E
Ljung, *Sweden* **15 F7** 58 1N 13 3 E
Ljungan →, *Sweden* **14 B11** 62 18N 17 23 E
Ljungaverk, *Sweden* **14 B10** 62 30N 16 5 E
Ljungby, *Sweden* **13 H12** 56 49N 13 55 E
Ljusdal, *Sweden* **14 C10** 61 46N 16 3 E
Ljusnan = Ljungan →, *Sweden* **14 B11** 62 18N 17 23 E
Ljusnan →, *Sweden* **13 F14** 61 12N 17 8 E
Ljusne, *Sweden* **13 F14** 61 13N 17 7 E
Ljutomer, *Slovenia* **39 B13** 46 31N 16 11 E
Llagostera, *Spain* **34 D7** 41 50N 2 54 E
Llamellín, *Peru* **156 B2** 9 0 S 76 54W
Llancanelo, Salina, *Argentina* **158 D2** 35 40 S 69 8W
Llandeilo, *U.K.* **17 F3** 51 53N 4 3W
Llandovery, *U.K.* **17 F4** 51 59N 3 49W
Llandrindod Wells, *U.K.* **17 E4** 52 15N 3 23W
Llandudno, *U.K.* **16 D4** 53 19N 3 51W
Llanelli, *U.K.* **17 F3** 51 41N 4 11W
Llanes, *Spain* **36 B6** 43 25N 4 50W
Llangollen, *U.K.* **16 E4** 52 58N 3 10W
Llanidloes, *U.K.* **17 E4** 52 28N 3 31W
Llano, *U.S.A.* **139 K5** 30 45N 98 41W
Llano →, *U.S.A.* **139 K5** 30 39N 98 26W
Llano Estacado, *U.S.A.* **139 J3** 33 30N 103 0W
Llanos, *S. Amer.* **150 B2** 5 0N 71 35W
Llanquihue □, *Chile* **160 B2** 41 30 S 73 0W
Llanquihue, L., *Chile* **160 B1** 41 10 S 75 50W
Llebetx, C., *Spain* **33 B9** 39 33N 2 18 E
Lleida = Lérida, *Spain* **34 D5** 41 37N 0 39 E
Llentrisca, C., *Spain* **33 C7** 38 52N 1 15 E
Llera, *Mexico* **147 C5** 23 19N 99 1W
Llerena, *Spain* **37 G4** 38 17N 6 0W
Llica, *Bolivia* **156 D4** 19 52 S 68 16W
Llico, *Chile* **158 C1** 34 46 S 72 5W
Llobregat →, *Spain* **34 D7** 41 19N 2 9 E
Llorente, *Phil.* **71 F5** 11 25N 125 33 E
Lloret de Mar, *Spain* **34 D7** 41 41N 2 53 E
Lloyd B., *Australia* **114 A3** 12 45 S 143 27 E
Lloyd L., *Canada* **131 B7** 57 22N 108 57W
Lloydminster, *Canada* **131 C6** 53 17N 110 0W
Lluchmayor, *Spain* **33 B9** 39 29N 2 53 E
Llullaillaco, Volcán, *S. Amer.* **158 A2** 24 43 S 68 30W
Lo, *Belgium* **21 G1** 50 59N 2 45 E
Lo →, *Vietnam* **76 B5** 21 18N 105 25 E
Loa, *U.S.A.* **143 G8** 38 24N 111 39W
Loa →, *Chile* **158 A1** 21 26 S 70 41W
Loano, *Italy* **38 D5** 44 8N 8 14 E
Loay, *Phil.* **71 G5** 9 36N 124 1 E
Lobatse, *Botswana* **104 D4** 25 12 S 25 40 E
Löbau, *Germany* **26 D10** 51 5N 14 42 E
Lobaye →, *C.A.R.* **102 B3** 3 41N 18 35 E
Lobbes, *Belgium* **21 H4** 50 21N 4 16 E
Lobenstein, *Germany* **26 E7** 50 25N 11 39 E
Lobería, *Argentina* **158 D4** 38 10 S 58 40W
Łobez, *Poland* **47 B2** 53 38N 15 39 E
Lobito, *Angola* **103 E2** 12 18 S 13 35 E
Lobo, *Phil.* **70 E3** 13 39N 121 13 E
Lobón, Canal de, *Spain* **37 G4** 38 50N 6 55W
Lobos, *Argentina* **158 D4** 35 10 S 59 0W
Lobos, I., *Mexico* **146 B2** 27 15N 110 30W
Lobos, I., *Peru* **150 C1** 6 57 S 80 45W
Lobos, I. de, *Canary Is.* **33 F6** 28 45N 13 50W
Lobos de Tierra, I., *Peru* **156 B1** 6 27 S 80 52W
Lobva, *Russia* **54 B7** 59 10N 60 30 E
Lobva →, *Russia* **54 B7** 59 8N 60 48 E
Loc Binh, *Vietnam* **76 B6** 21 46N 106 54 E
Loc Ninh, *Vietnam* **77 G6** 11 50N 106 34 E
Locarno, *Switz.* **29 D7** 46 10N 8 47 E
Lochaber, *U.K.* **18 E4** 56 55N 5 0W
Lochcarron, *U.K.* **18 D3** 57 25N 5 30W
Lochem, *Neths.* **20 D8** 52 9N 6 26 E

226 Loches


Loches, *France* **22 E8** 47 7N 1 0 E
Lochgelly, *U.K.* **18 E5** 56 7N 3 18W
Lochgilphead, *U.K.* **18 E3** 56 2N 5 37W
Lochinver, *U.K.* **18 C3** 58 9N 5 15W
Lochnagar, *Australia* **114 C4** 23 33 S 145 38 E
Lochnagar, *U.K.* **18 E5** 56 57N 3 14W
Łochów, *Poland* **47 C8** 52 33N 21 42 E
Lochy →, *U.K.* **18 E3** 56 52N 5 3W
Lock, *Australia* **115 E2** 33 34 S 135 46 E
Lock Haven, *U.S.A.* **136 E7** 41 8N 77 28W
Lockeford, *U.S.A.* **144 G5** 38 10N 121 9W
Lockeport, *Canada* **129 D6** 43 47N 65 4W
Lockerbie, *U.K.* **18 F5** 55 7N 3 21W
Lockhart, *Australia* **117 C7** 35 14 S 146 40 E
Lockhart, *U.S.A.* **139 L6** 29 53N 97 40W
Lockhart, L., *Australia* **113 F2** 33 15 S 119 3 E
Lockington, *Australia* **116 D6** 36 16 S 144 34 E
Lockney, *U.S.A.* **139 H4** 34 7N 101 27W
Lockport, *Ill., U.S.A.* **141 C8** 41 35N 88 3W
Lockport, *N.Y., U.S.A.* **136 C6** 43 10N 78 42W
Locminé, *France* **22 E4** 47 54N 2 51W
Locri, *Italy* **41 D9** 38 14N 16 14 E
Locronan, *France* **22 D2** 48 7N 4 15W
Loctudy, *France* **22 E2** 47 50N 4 12W
Locust Cr. →, *U.S.A.* **140 E3** 39 40N 93 17W
Lod, *Israel* **91 D3** 31 57N 34 54 E
Lodeinoye Pole, *Russia* **48 B5** 60 44N 33 33 E
Lodève, *France* **24 E7** 43 44N 3 19 E
Lodge Grass, *U.S.A.* **142 D10** 45 19N 107 22W
Lodgepole, *U.S.A.* **138 E3** 41 9N 102 38W
Lodgepole Cr. →, *U.S.A.* **138 E2** 41 20N 104 30W
Lodhran, *Pakistan* **80 E4** 29 32N 71 30 E
Lodi, *Italy* **38 C6** 45 19N 9 30 E
Lodi, *U.S.A.* **144 G5** 38 8N 121 16W
Lodja, *Zaïre* **102 C4** 3 30 S 23 23 E
Lodosa, *Spain* **34 C2** 42 25N 2 4W
Lödöse, *Sweden* **15 F6** 58 2N 12 9 E
Lodwar, *Kenya* **106 B4** 3 10N 35 40 E
Łódź, *Poland* **47 D6** 51 45N 19 27 E
Łódź □, *Poland* **47 D6** 51 45N 19 27 E
Loei, *Thailand* **76 D3** 17 29N 101 35 E
Loenen, *Neths.* **20 D8** 52 7N 6 1 E
Loengo, *Zaïre* **103 C5** 4 48 S 26 30 E
Loeriesfontein, *S. Africa* **104 E2** 31 0 S 19 26 E
Lofer, *Austria* **30 D5** 47 35N 12 41 E
Lofoten, *Norway* **12 B13** 68 30N 15 0 E
Lofsdalen, *Sweden* **14 B7** 62 10N 13 20 E
Lofsen →, *Sweden* **14 B7** 62 7N 13 57 E
Logan, *Kans., U.S.A.* **138 F5** 39 40N 99 34W
Logan, *Ohio, U.S.A.* **134 F4** 39 32N 82 25W
Logan, *Utah, U.S.A.* **142 F8** 41 44N 111 50W
Logan, *W. Va., U.S.A.* **134 G5** 37 51N 81 59W
Logan, Mt., *Canada* **126 B5** 60 31N 140 22W
Logan Pass, *U.S.A.* **130 D6** 48 41N 113 44W
Logandale, *U.S.A.* **145 J12** 36 36N 114 29W
Logansport, *Ind., U.S.A.* **141 D10** 40 45N 86 22W
Logansport, *La., U.S.A.* **139 K8** 31 58N 94 0W
Logo, *Sudan* **95 F3** 5 20N 30 18 E
Logone →, *Chad* **97 F3** 12 6N 15 2 E
Logroño, *Spain* **34 C2** 42 28N 2 27W
Logrosán, *Spain* **37 F5** 39 20N 5 32W
Løgstør, *Denmark* **15 H3** 56 58N 9 14 E
Loh, *Vanuatu* **121 C4** 13 21 S 166 38 E
Lohardaga, *India* **81 H11** 23 27N 84 45 E
Lohr, *Germany* **27 F5** 50 0N 9 35 E
Lohrville, *U.S.A.* **140 B2** 42 17N 94 33W
Loi-kaw, *Burma* **78 F6** 19 40N 97 17 E
Loimaa, *Finland* **13 F17** 60 50N 23 5 E
Loir →, *France* **22 E6** 47 33N 0 32W
Loir-et-Cher □, *France* **22 E8** 47 40N 1 20 E
Loire □, *France* **25 C8** 45 40N 4 5 E
Loire →, *France* **22 E4** 47 16N 2 10W
Loire-Atlantique □, *France* **22 E5** 47 25N 1 40W
Loiret □, *France* **23 E9** 47 55N 2 30 E
Loitz, *Germany* **26 B9** 53 58N 13 8 E
Loja, *Ecuador* **156 A2** 3 59 S 79 16W
Loja, *Spain* **37 H6** 37 10N 4 10W
Loja □, *Ecuador* **152 D2** 4 0 S 79 13W
Loji, *Indonesia* **72 B3** 1 38 S 127 28 E
Loka, *Sudan* **95 G3** 4 13N 31 0 E
Lokandu, *Zaïre* **102 C5** 2 30 S 25 45 E
Løken, *Norway* **14 E5** 59 48N 11 29 E
Lokeren, *Belgium* **21 F3** 51 6N 3 59 E
Lokhvitsa, *Ukraine* **50 F8** 50 25N 33 18 E
Lokichokio, *Kenya* **106 B3** 4 19N 34 13 E
Lokitaung, *Kenya* **106 B4** 4 12N 35 48 E
Lokka, *Finland* **12 C19** 67 55N 27 35 E
Løkken, *Denmark* **15 G3** 57 22N 9 41 E
Løkken Verk, *Norway* **14 A3** 63 7N 9 43 E
Loknya, *Russia* **50 C7** 56 49N 30 4 E
Lokoja, *Nigeria* **101 D6** 7 47N 6 45 E
Lokolama, *Zaïre* **102 C3** 2 35 S 19 50 E
Lokuru, *Solomon Is.* **121 M9** 8 20 S 157 0 E
Lol →, *Sudan* **95 F2** 9 13N 26 30 E
Lola, *Guinea* **100 D3** 7 52N 8 29W
Lola, Mt., *U.S.A.* **144 F6** 39 26N 120 22W
Lolibai, Gebel, *Sudan* **95 G3** 3 50N 33 0 E
Lolimi, *Sudan* **95 G3** 4 35N 34 0 E
Loliondo, *Tanzania* **106 C4** 2 2 S 35 39 E
Lolland, *Denmark* **15 K5** 54 45N 11 30 E
Lollar, *Germany* **26 E4** 50 39N 8 43 E
Lolo, *U.S.A.* **142 C6** 46 45N 114 5W
Lolodorf, *Cameroon* **101 E7** 3 16N 10 49 E
Lolowai, *Vanuatu* **121 E6** 15 18 S 168 0 E
Lom, *Bulgaria* **43 D8** 43 48N 23 12 E
Lom →, *Bulgaria* **42 D8** 43 45N 23 15 E
Lom Kao, *Thailand* **76 D3** 16 53N 101 14 E
Lom Sak, *Thailand* **76 D3** 16 47N 101 15 E
Loma, *U.S.A.* **142 C8** 47 56N 110 30W
Loma Linda, *U.S.A.* **145 L9** 34 3N 117 16W
Lomaloma, *Fiji* **121 A3** 17 17 S 178 59W
Lomami →, *Zaïre* **102 B4** 0 46N 24 16 E
Lomas de Zamóra, *Argentina* **158 C4** 34 45 S 58 25W
Lombadina, *Australia* **112 C3** 16 31 S 122 54 E
Lombard, *U.S.A.* **141 C8** 41 53N 88 1W
Lombardia □, *Italy* **38 C6** 45 35N 9 45 E
Lombardy = Lombardia □, *Italy* **38 C6** 45 35N 9 45 E
Lombe, *Angola* **103 D3** 9 27 S 16 13 E
Lombez, *France* **24 E4** 43 29N 0 55 E
Lomblen, *Indonesia* **72 C2** 8 30 S 123 32 E
Lombok, *Indonesia* **75 D5** 8 45 S 116 30 E
Lomé, *Togo* **101 D5** 6 9N 1 20 E
Lomela, *Zaïre* **102 C4** 2 19 S 23 15 E
Lomela →, *Zaïre* **102 C4** 0 15 S 20 40 E
Lomello, *Italy* **38 C5** 45 5N 8 46 E
Lometa, *U.S.A.* **139 K5** 31 13N 98 24W
Lomié, *Cameroon* **102 B2** 3 13N 13 38 E
Lomma, *Sweden* **15 J7** 55 43N 13 6 E
Lomme →, *Belgium* **21 H6** 50 8N 5 10 E
Lommel, *Belgium* **21 F6** 51 14N 5 19 E
Lomond, *Canada* **130 C6** 50 24N 112 36W
Lomond, L., *U.K.* **18 E4** 56 8N 4 38W
Lomonosov, *Russia* **50 B6** 59 57N 29 53 E
Lomphat, *Cambodia* **76 F6** 13 30N 106 59 E
Lompobatang, *Indonesia* **72 C1** 5 24 S 119 56 E
Lompoc, *U.S.A.* **145 L6** 34 38N 120 28W
Lomsegga, *Norway* **14 C2** 61 49N 8 21 E
Łomza, *Poland* **47 B9** 53 10N 22 2 E
Łomza □, *Poland* **47 B9** 53 0N 22 30 E
Lonavale, *India* **82 E1** 18 46N 73 29 E
Loncoche, *Chile* **160 A2** 39 20 S 72 50W
Loncopuè, *Argentina* **160 A2** 38 4 S 70 37W
Londa, *India* **83 G2** 15 30N 74 30 E
Londerzeel, *Belgium* **21 G4** 51 0N 4 19 E
Londiani, *Kenya* **106 C4** 0 10 S 35 33 E
Londinières, *France* **22 C8** 49 50N 1 25 E
London, *Canada* **128 D3** 42 59N 81 15W
London, *U.K.* **17 F7** 51 30N 0 5W
London, *Ky., U.S.A.* **134 G3** 37 8N 84 5W
London, *Ohio, U.S.A.* **141 E13** 39 53N 83 27W
London, Greater □, *U.K.* **17 F7** 51 30N 0 5W
London Mills, *U.S.A.* **140 D6** 40 43N 90 11W
Londonderry, *U.K.* **19 B4** 55 0N 7 23W
Londonderry □, *U.K.* **19 B4** 55 0N 7 20W
Londonderry, C., *Australia* **112 B4** 13 45 S 126 55 E
Londonderry, I., *Chile* **160 E2** 55 0 S 71 0W
Londrina, *Brazil* **159 A5** 23 18 S 51 10W
Londuimbale, *Angola* **103 E3** 12 15 S 15 19 E
Lone Pine, *U.S.A.* **144 J8** 36 36N 118 4W
Long Akah, *Malaysia* **75 B4** 3 19N 114 47 E
Long Beach, *Calif., U.S.A.* **145 M8** 33 47N 118 11W
Long Beach, *N.Y., U.S.A.* **137 F11** 40 35N 73 39W
Long Beach, *Wash., U.S.A.* **144 D2** 46 21N 124 3W
Long Branch, *U.S.A.* **137 F11** 40 18N 74 0W
Long Creek, *U.S.A.* **142 D4** 44 43N 119 6W
Long Eaton, *U.K.* **16 E6** 52 54N 1 16W
Long I., *Australia* **114 C4** 22 8 S 149 53 E
Long I., *Bahamas* **149 B4** 23 20N 75 10W
Long I., *Papua N. G.* **120 C4** 5 20 S 147 5 E
Long I., *U.S.A.* **137 F11** 40 45N 73 30W
Long Island Sd., *U.S.A.* **137 E12** 41 10N 73 0W
Long L., *Canada* **128 C2** 49 30N 86 50W
Long Lake, *U.S.A.* **137 C10** 43 58N 74 25W
Long Pine, *U.S.A.* **138 D5** 42 32N 99 42W
Long Pt., *Nfld., Canada* **129 C8** 48 47N 58 46W
Long Pt., *Ont., Canada* **136 D4** 42 35N 80 2W
Long Pt., *N.Z.* **119 G4** 46 34 S 169 36 E
Long Point B., *Canada* **136 D4** 42 40N 80 10W
Long Range Mts., *Canada* **129 C8** 49 30N 57 30W
Long Reef, *Australia* **112 B4** 14 1 S 125 48 E
Long Str. = Longa, Proliv, *Russia* **6 C16** 70 0N 175 0 E
Long Thanh, *Vietnam* **77 G6** 10 47N 106 57 E
Long Xian, *China* **66 G4** 34 55N 106 55 E
Long Xuyen, *Vietnam* **77 G5** 10 19N 105 28 E
Longa, *Angola* **103 E3** 14 42 S 18 32 E
Longá, *Greece* **45 H3** 36 53N 21 55 E
Longa, Proliv, *Russia* **6 C16** 70 0N 175 0 E
Long'an, *China* **68 F6** 23 10N 107 40 E
Longarone, *Italy* **39 B9** 46 15N 12 18 E
Longburn, *N.Z.* **118 G4** 40 23 S 175 35 E
Longchang, *China* **68 C5** 29 18N 105 15 E
Longchi, *China* **68 C4** 29 25N 103 24 E
Longchuan, *Guangdong, China* **69 E10** 24 5N 115 17 E
Longchuan, *Yunnan, China* **68 E1** 24 23N 97 58 E
Longde, *China* **66 G4** 35 30N 106 20 E
Longeau, *France* **23 E12** 47 47N 5 20 E
Longford, *Australia* **114 G4** 41 32 S 147 3 E
Longford, *Ireland* **19 C4** 53 43N 7 50W
Longford □, *Ireland* **19 C4** 53 42N 7 45W
Longguan, *China* **66 D8** 40 45N 115 30 E
Longhua, *China* **67 D9** 41 18N 117 45 E
Longhui, *China* **69 D8** 27 7N 111 2 E
Longido, *Tanzania* **106 C4** 2 43 S 36 42 E
Longiram, *Indonesia* **75 C5** 0 5 S 115 45 E
Longkou, *Jiangxi, China* **69 D10** 26 8N 115 10 E
Longkou, *Shandong, China* **67 F11** 37 40N 120 18 E
Longlac, *Canada* **128 C2** 49 45N 86 25W
Longli, *China* **68 D6** 26 25N 106 58 E
Longlier, *Belgium* **21 J6** 49 52N 5 27 E
Longlin, *China* **68 E5** 24 47N 105 20 E
Longling, *China* **68 E2** 24 37N 98 39 E
Longmen, *China* **69 F10** 23 40N 114 18 E
Longming, *China* **68 F6** 22 59N 107 7 E
Longmont, *U.S.A.* **138 E2** 40 10N 105 6W
Longnan, *China* **69 E10** 24 55N 114 47 E
Longnawan, *Indonesia* **75 B4** 1 51N 114 55 E
Longobucco, *Italy* **41 C9** 39 27N 16 37 E
Longquan, *China* **69 C12** 28 7N 119 10 E
Longreach, *Australia* **114 C3** 23 28 S 144 14 E
Longshan, *China* **68 C7** 29 29N 109 25 E
Longsheng, *China* **69 E8** 25 48N 110 0 E
Longton, *Australia* **114 C4** 20 58 S 145 55 E
Longtown, *U.K.* **17 F5** 51 58N 2 59W
Longué-Jumelles, *France* **22 E6** 47 22N 0 8W
Longueau, *France* **23 C9** 49 52N 2 21 E
Longueuil, *Canada* **137 A11** 45 32N 73 28W
Longuyon, *France* **23 C12** 49 27N 5 35 E
Longview, *Canada* **130 C6** 50 32N 114 10W
Longview, *Tex., U.S.A.* **139 J7** 32 30N 94 44W
Longview, *Wash., U.S.A.* **144 D4** 46 8N 122 57W
Longvilly, *Belgium* **21 H7** 50 2N 5 50 E
Longwy, *France* **23 C12** 49 30N 5 46 E
Longxi, *China* **66 G3** 34 53N 104 40 E
Longyou, *China* **69 C12** 29 1N 119 8 E
Longzhou, *China* **68 F6** 22 22N 106 50 E
Lonigo, *Italy* **39 C8** 45 23N 11 22 E
Löningen, *Germany* **26 C3** 52 43N 7 44 E
Lonja →, *Croatia* **39 C13** 45 22N 16 40 E
Lonkin, *Burma* **78 C6** 25 39N 96 22 E
Lonoke, *U.S.A.* **139 H9** 34 47N 91 54W
Lonquimay, *Chile* **160 A2** 38 26 S 71 14W
Lons-le-Saunier, *France* **23 F12** 46 40N 5 31 E
Lønstrup, *Denmark* **15 G3** 57 29N 9 47 E
Loogootee, *U.S.A.* **141 F10** 38 41N 86 55W
Lookout, C., *U.S.A.* **135 H7** 34 35N 76 32W
Lookout, C., *Canada* **128 A3** 55 18N 83 56W
Loolmalasin, *Tanzania* **106 C4** 3 0 S 35 53 E
Loon →, *Alta., Canada* **130 B5** 57 8N 115 3W
Loon →, *Man., Canada* **131 B8** 55 53N 101 59W
Loon Lake, *Canada* **131 C7** 54 2N 109 10W
Loon-op-Zand, *Neths.* **21 E6** 51 38N 5 5 E
Loongana, *Australia* **113 F4** 30 52 S 127 5 E
Loop Hd., *Ireland* **19 D2** 52 34N 9 55W
Loosduinen, *Neths.* **20 D4** 52 3N 4 14 E
Lop Buri, *Thailand* **76 E3** 14 48N 100 37 E
Lop Nor = Lop Nur, *China* **64 B4** 40 20N 90 10 E
Lop Nur, *China* **64 B4** 40 20N 90 10 E
Lopare, *Bos.-H.* **42 C3** 44 39N 18 46 E
Lopatin, *Russia* **53 E12** 43 50N 47 35 E
Lopatina, G., *Russia* **57 D15** 50 47N 143 10 E
Lopaye, *Sudan* **95 F3** 6 37N 33 40 E
Lopera, *Spain* **37 H6** 37 56N 4 14W
Lopevi, *Vanuatu* **121 F6** 16 30 S 168 21 E
Lopez, *Phil.* **70 E4** 13 53N 122 15 E
Lopez, C., *Gabon* **102 C1** 0 47 S 8 40 E
Lopez I., *Gabon* **102 C1** 0 50 S 8 47 E
Loppersum, *Neths.* **20 B9** 53 20N 6 44 E
Lopphavet, *Norway* **12 A16** 70 27N 21 15 E
Lora →, *Afghan.* **79 C2** 31 35N 65 50 E
Lora, Hamun-i-, *Pakistan* **79 C2** 29 38N 64 58 E
Lora Cr. →, *Australia* **115 D2** 28 10 S 135 22 E
Lora del Río, *Spain* **37 H5** 37 39N 5 33W
Lorain, *U.S.A.* **136 E2** 41 28N 82 11W
Loraine, *U.S.A.* **140 D5** 40 9N 91 13W
Loralai, *Pakistan* **79 C3** 30 20N 68 41 E
Lorca, *Spain* **35 H3** 37 41N 1 42W
Lord Howe I., *Pac. Oc.* **122 L7** 31 33 S 159 6 E
Lord Howe Ridge, *Pac. Oc.* **122 L8** 30 0 S 162 30 E
Lordsburg, *U.S.A.* **143 K9** 32 21N 108 43W
Lorengau, *Papua N. G.* **120 B4** 2 1 S 147 15 E
Loreto, *Bolivia* **157 D5** 15 13 S 64 40W
Loreto, *Brazil* **154 C2** 7 5 S 45 10W
Loreto, *Italy* **39 E10** 43 26N 13 36 E
Loreto, *Mexico* **146 B2** 26 1N 111 21W
Loreto □, *Peru* **152 D3** 5 0 S 75 0W
Loreto Aprutina, *Italy* **39 F10** 42 24N 13 59 E
Lorgues, *France* **25 E10** 43 28N 6 22 E
Lorica, *Colombia* **152 B2** 9 14N 75 49W
Lorient, *France* **22 E3** 47 45N 3 23W
Lorimor, *U.S.A.* **140 C2** 41 8N 94 3W
Lorn, *U.K.* **18 E3** 56 26N 5 10W
Lorn, Firth of, *U.K.* **18 E3** 56 20N 5 40W
Lorne, *Australia* **116 E5** 38 33 S 143 59 E
Lorovouno, *Cyprus* **32 D11** 35 8N 32 36 E
Lörrach, *Germany* **27 H3** 47 36N 7 38 E
Lorraine, *France* **23 D12** 48 53N 6 0 E
Lorrainville, *Canada* **128 C4** 47 21N 79 23W
Los, Îles de, *Guinea* **100 D2** 9 30N 13 50W
Los Alamos, *Calif., U.S.A.* **145 L6** 34 44N 120 17W
Los Alamos, *N. Mex., U.S.A.* **143 J10** 35 53N 106 19W
Los Altos, *U.S.A.* **144 H4** 37 23N 122 7W
Los Andes, *Chile* **158 C1** 32 50 S 70 40W
Los Angeles, *Chile* **158 D1** 37 28 S 72 23W
Los Angeles, *U.S.A.* **145 L8** 34 4N 118 15W
Los Angeles Aqueduct, *U.S.A.* **145 K9** 35 22N 118 5W
Los Antiguos, *Argentina* **160 C2** 46 35 S 71 40W
Los Banos, *U.S.A.* **144 H6** 37 4N 120 51W
Los Barrios, *Spain* **37 J5** 36 11N 5 30W
Los Blancos, *Argentina* **158 A3** 23 40 S 62 30W
Los Cristianos, *Canary Is.* **33 F3** 28 3N 16 42W
Los Gatos, *U.S.A.* **144 H5** 37 14N 121 59W
Los Hermanos, *Venezuela* **149 D7** 11 45N 64 25W
Los Islotes, *Canary Is.* **33 E6** 29 4N 13 44W
Los Lagos, *Chile* **160 A2** 39 51 S 72 50W
Los Llanos de Aridane, *Canary Is.* **33 F2** 28 38N 17 54W
Los Lomas, *Peru* **156 A1** 4 40 S 80 10W
Los Lunas, *U.S.A.* **143 J10** 34 48N 106 44W
Los Menucos, *Argentina* **160 B3** 40 50 S 68 10W
Los Mochis, *Mexico* **146 B3** 25 45N 109 5W
Los Monegros, *Spain* **34 D4** 41 29N 0 13W
Los Monos, *Argentina* **160 C3** 46 1 S 69 36W
Los Olivos, *U.S.A.* **145 L6** 34 40N 120 7W
Los Palacios, *Cuba* **148 B3** 22 35N 83 15W
Los Palacios y Villafranca, *Spain* **37 H5** 37 10N 5 55W
Los Reyes, *Mexico* **146 D4** 19 34N 102 30W
Los Ríos □, *Ecuador* **152 D2** 1 30 S 79 25W
Los Roques, *Venezuela* **152 A4** 11 50N 66 45W
Los Santos de Maimona, *Spain* **37 G4** 38 27N 6 22W
Los Teques, *Venezuela* **152 A4** 10 21N 67 2W
Los Testigos, *Venezuela* **153 A5** 11 23N 63 6W
Los Vilos, *Chile* **158 C1** 32 10 S 71 30W
Los Yébenes, *Spain* **37 F7** 39 36N 3 55W
Losada →, *Colombia* **152 C3** 2 12N 73 55W
Loshkalakh, *Russia* **57 C15** 62 45N 147 20 E
Łosice, *Poland* **47 C9** 52 13N 22 43 E
Lošinj, *Croatia* **39 D11** 44 30N 14 30 E
Losser, *Neths.* **20 D10** 52 16N 7 1 E
Lossiemouth, *U.K.* **18 D5** 57 43N 3 17W
Losuia, *Papua N. G.* **120 E6** 8 30 S 151 4 E
Lot □, *France* **24 D5** 44 39N 1 40 E
Lot →, *France* **24 D4** 44 18N 0 20 E
Lot-et-Garonne □, *France* **24 D4** 44 22N 0 30 E
Lota, *Chile* **158 D1** 37 5 S 73 10W
Løten, *Norway* **14 D5** 60 51N 11 21 E
Loţfābād, *Iran* **85 B8** 37 32N 59 20 E
Lothair, *S. Africa* **105 D5** 26 22 S 30 27 E
Lothian □, *U.K.* **18 F5** 55 50N 3 0W
Lothiers, *France* **23 F8** 46 42N 1 33 E
Lotofaga, *W. Samoa* **121 X24** 14 1 S 171 30W
Lötschbergtunnel, *Switz.* **28 D5** 46 26N 7 43 E
Lottefors, *Sweden* **14 C10** 61 25N 16 24 E
Lotzwil, *Switz.* **28 B5** 47 12N 7 48 E
Loubomo, *Congo* **102 C2** 4 9 S 12 47 E
Loudéac, *France* **22 D4** 48 11N 2 47W
Loudi, *China* **69 D8** 27 42N 111 59 E
Loudima, *Congo* **102 C2** 4 6 S 13 5 E
Loudon, *U.S.A.* **135 H3** 35 45N 84 20W
Loudonville, *U.S.A.* **136 F2** 40 38N 82 14W
Loudun, *France* **22 E7** 47 3N 0 5 E
Loué, *France* **22 E6** 47 59N 0 9W
Loue →, *France* **23 E12** 47 1N 5 28 E
Louga, *Senegal* **100 B1** 15 45N 16 5W
Loughborough, *U.K.* **16 E6** 52 46N 1 11W
Loughrea, *Ireland* **19 C3** 53 11N 8 33W
Loughros More B., *Ireland* **19 B3** 54 48N 8 30W
Louhans, *France* **25 B9** 46 38N 5 12 E
Louis Trichardt, *S. Africa* **105 C4** 23 1 S 29 43 E
Louis XIV, Pte., *Canada* **128 B4** 54 37N 79 45W
Louisa, *U.S.A.* **134 F4** 38 7N 82 36W
Louisbourg, *Canada* **129 C8** 45 55N 60 0W
Louisburg, *U.S.A.* **140 F2** 38 37N 94 41W
Louise I., *Canada* **130 C2** 52 55N 131 50W
Louiseville, *Canada* **128 C5** 46 20N 72 56W
Louisiade Arch., *Papua N. G.* **120 F7** 11 10 S 153 0 E
Louisiana, *U.S.A.* **140 E6** 39 27N 91 3W
Louisiana □, *U.S.A.* **139 K9** 30 50N 92 0W
Louisville, *Ky., U.S.A.* **141 F11** 38 15N 85 46W
Louisville, *Miss., U.S.A.* **139 J10** 33 7N 89 3W
Loukouo, *Congo* **102 C2** 3 38 S 14 39 E
Loulay, *France* **24 B3** 46 3N 0 30W
Loulé, *Portugal* **37 H2** 37 9N 8 0W
Louny, *Czech.* **30 A6** 50 20N 13 48 E
Loup City, *U.S.A.* **138 E5** 41 17N 98 58W
Lourdes, *France* **24 E3** 43 6N 0 3W
Lourdes-du-Blanc-Sablon, *Canada* **129 B8** 51 24N 57 12W
Lourenço, *Brazil* **153 C7** 2 30N 51 40W
Lourenço-Marques = Maputo, *Mozam.* **105 D5** 25 58 S 32 32 E
Loures, *Portugal* **37 G1** 38 50N 9 9W
Lourinhã, *Portugal* **37 F1** 39 14N 9 17W
Lousã, *Portugal* **36 E2** 40 7N 8 14W
Louth, *Australia* **117 A6** 30 30 S 145 8 E
Louth, *Ireland* **19 C5** 53 47N 6 33W
Louth, *U.K.* **16 D7** 53 23N 0 0 E
Louth □, *Ireland* **19 C5** 53 55N 6 30W
Loutrá Aidhipsoú, *Greece* **45 F5** 38 54N 23 2 E
Loutráki, *Greece* **45 G4** 37 58N 22 57 E
Louvain = Leuven, *Belgium* **21 G5** 50 52N 4 42 E
Louveigné, *Belgium* **21 G7** 50 32N 5 42 E
Louviers, *France* **22 C8** 49 12N 1 10 E
Louwsburg, *S. Africa* **105 D5** 27 37 S 31 7 E
Lovat →, *Russia* **50 B7** 58 14N 31 28 E
Lovćen, *Montenegro* **42 E3** 42 23N 18 51 E
Love, *Canada* **131 C8** 53 29N 104 10W
Lovech, *Bulgaria* **43 D9** 43 8N 24 42 E
Loveland, *Colo., U.S.A.* **138 E2** 40 24N 105 5W
Loveland, *Ohio, U.S.A.* **141 E12** 39 16N 84 16W
Lovell, *U.S.A.* **142 D9** 44 50N 108 24W
Lovelock, *U.S.A.* **142 F4** 40 11N 118 28W
Lóvere, *Italy* **38 C7** 45 50N 10 4 E
Loves Park, *U.S.A.* **140 B7** 42 19N 89 3W
Loviisa = Lovisa, *Finland* **13 F19** 60 28N 26 12 E
Lovilia, *U.S.A.* **140 C4** 41 8N 92 55W
Loving, *U.S.A.* **139 J2** 32 17N 104 6W
Lovington, *Ill., U.S.A.* **141 E8** 39 43N 88 38W
Lovington, *N. Mex., U.S.A.* **139 J3** 32 57N 103 21W
Lovios, *Spain* **36 D2** 41 55N 8 4W
Lovisa, *Finland* **13 F19** 60 28N 26 12 E
Lovosice, *Czech.* **30 A7** 50 30N 14 2 E
Lovran, *Croatia* **39 C11** 45 18N 14 15 E
Lovrin, *Romania* **46 D1** 45 58N 20 48 E
Low Pt., *Australia* **113 F4** 32 25 S 127 25 E
Low Tatra = Nizké Tatry, *Slovak Rep.* **31 C12** 48 55N 19 30 E
Lowa, *Zaïre* **106 C2** 1 25 S 25 47 E
Lowa →, *Zaïre* **106 C2** 1 24 S 25 51 E
Lowden, *U.S.A.* **140 C6** 41 52N 90 56W
Lowell, *Ind., U.S.A.* **141 C9** 41 18N 87 25W
Lowell, *Mass., U.S.A.* **137 D13** 42 38N 71 19W
Lower Arrow L., *Canada* **130 D5** 49 40N 118 5W
Lower Austria = Niederösterreich □, *Austria* **30 C8** 48 25N 15 40 E
Lower California = Baja California, *Mexico* **146 A1** 31 10N 115 12W
Lower California = California, Baja, *Mexico* **146 A1** 32 10N 115 12W
Lower Hutt, *N.Z.* **118 H3** 41 10 S 174 55 E
Lower L., *U.S.A.* **142 F3** 41 16N 120 2W
Lower Lake, *U.S.A.* **144 G4** 38 55N 122 37W
Lower Post, *Canada* **130 B3** 59 58N 128 30W
Lower Red L., *U.S.A.* **138 B7** 47 58N 95 0W
Lower Saxony = Niedersachsen □, *Germany* **26 C5** 52 45N 9 0 E
Lower Tunguska = Tunguska, Nizhnyaya →, *Russia* **57 C9** 65 48N 88 4 E
Lowestoft, *U.K.* **17 E9** 52 29N 1 44 E
Łowicz, *Poland* **47 C6** 52 6N 19 55 E
Lowry City, *U.S.A.* **140 F3** 38 8N 93 44W
Lowville, *U.S.A.* **137 C9** 43 47N 75 29W
Loxton, *Australia* **116 C4** 34 28 S 140 31 E
Loxton, *S. Africa* **104 E3** 31 30 S 22 22 E
Loyalton, *U.S.A.* **144 F6** 39 41N 120 14W
Loyalty Is. = Loyauté, Is., *N. Cal.* **121 K4** 20 50 S 166 30 E
Loyang = Luoyang, *China* **66 G7** 34 40N 112 26 E
Loyauté, Is., *N. Cal.* **121 K4** 20 50 S 166 30 E
Loyev, *Belorussia* **50 F7** 51 56N 30 46 E
Loyoro, *Uganda* **106 B3** 3 22N 34 14 E
Lož, *Slovenia* **39 C11** 45 43N 14 30 E
Lozère □, *France* **24 D7** 44 35N 3 30 E
Loznica, *Serbia* **42 C4** 44 32N 19 14 E
Lozovaya, *Ukraine* **52 B7** 49 0N 36 20 E
Lozva →, *Russia* **54 B8** 59 36N 62 20 E
Luachimo, *Angola* **103 D4** 7 23 S 20 48 E
Luacono, *Angola* **103 E4** 11 15 S 21 37 E
Lualaba →, *Zaïre* **102 B5** 0 26N 25 20 E
Luampa, *Zambia* **107 F1** 15 4 S 24 20 E
Lu'an, *China* **69 B11** 31 45N 116 29 E
Luan Chau, *Vietnam* **76 B4** 21 38N 103 24 E
Luan He →, *China* **67 E10** 39 20N 119 5 E
Luan Xian, *China* **67 E10** 39 40N 118 40 E
Luancheng, *Guangxi Zhuangzu, China* **68 F7** 22 48N 108 55 E
Luancheng, *Hebei, China* **66 F8** 37 53N 114 40 E

McCusker 227


Luanda, *Angola* **103 D2** 8 50S 13 15 E
Luanda □, *Angola* **103 D2** 9 0S 13 10 E
Luang Prabang, *Laos* **76 C4** 19 52N 102 10 E
Luang Thale, *Thailand* **77 J3** 7 30N 100 15 E
Luangwa, *Zambia* **107 F3** 15 35S 30 16 E
Luangwa →, *Zambia* **107 E3** 14 25S 30 25 E
Luangwa Valley, *Zambia* **107 E3** 13 30S 31 30 E
Luanne, *China* **67 D9** 40 55N 117 40 E
Luanping, *China* **67 D9** 40 53N 117 23 E
Luanshya, *Zambia* **107 E2** 13 3S 28 28 E
Luapula □, *Zambia* **107 E2** 11 0S 29 0 E
Luapula →, *Africa* **107 D2** 9 26S 28 33 E
Luarca, *Spain* **36 B4** 43 32N 6 32W
Luashi, *Zaïre* **103 E4** 10 50S 23 36 E
Luau, *Angola* **103 E4** 10 40S 22 10 E
Luba, *Phil.* **70 C3** 17 19N 120 42 E
Lubaczów, *Poland* **47 E10** 50 10N 23 8 E
Lubalo, *Angola* **103 D3** 9 10S 19 15 E
Luban, *Phil.* **71 H6** 6 26N 126 13 E
Lubań, *Poland* **47 D2** 51 5N 15 15 E
Lubana, Ozero, *Latvia* **50 C5** 56 45N 27 0 E
Lubang, *Phil.* **70 E3** 13 52N 120 7 E
Lubang Is., *Phil.* **70 E3** 13 50N 120 12 E
Lubango, *Angola* **103 E2** 14 55S 13 30 E
Lubao, *Phil.* **70 D3** 14 56N 120 36 E
Lubartów, *Poland* **47 D9** 51 28N 22 42 E
Lubawa, *Poland* **47 B6** 53 30N 19 48 E
Lubbeek, *Belgium* **21 G5** 50 54N 4 50 E
Lübben, *Germany* **26 D9** 51 56N 13 54 E
Lübbenau, *Germany* **26 D9** 51 49N 13 59 E
Lubbock, *U.S.A.* **139 J4** 33 35N 101 51W
Lübeck, *Germany* **26 B6** 53 52N 10 41 E
Lübecker Bucht, *Germany* **26 A7** 54 3N 11 0 E
Lubefu, *Zaïre* **103 C4** 4 47S 24 27 E
Lubefu →, *Zaïre* **103 C4** 4 10S 23 0 E
Lubero = Luofu, *Zaïre* **106 C2** 0 10S 29 15 E
Lubicon L., *Canada* **130 B5** 56 23N 115 56W
Lubień Kujawski, *Poland* **47 C6** 52 23N 19 9 E
Lubin, *Poland* **47 D3** 51 24N 16 11 E
Lublin, *Poland* **47 D9** 51 12N 22 38 E
Lublin □, *Poland* **47 D9** 51 5N 22 30 E
Lubliniec, *Poland* **47 E5** 50 43N 18 45 E
Lubnān, J., *Lebanon* **91 B4** 33 50N 35 45 E
Lubny, *Ukraine* **50 F8** 50 3N 32 58 E
Lubon, *Poland* **47 C3** 52 21N 16 51 E
Lubongola, *Zaïre* **106 C2** 2 35S 27 50 E
Lubotin, *Slovak Rep.* **31 B13** 49 17N 20 53 E
Lubraniec, *Poland* **47 C5** 52 33N 18 50 E
Lubsko, *Poland* **47 D1** 51 45N 14 57 E
Lübtheen, *Germany* **26 B7** 53 18N 11 4 E
Lubuagan, *Phil.* **70 C3** 17 21N 121 10 E
Lubudi →, *Zaïre* **103 D5** 9 0S 25 35 E
Lubuklinggau, *Indonesia* **74 C2** 3 15S 102 55 E
Lubuksikaping, *Indonesia* **74 B2** 0 10N 100 15 E
Lubumbashi, *Zaïre* **107 E2** 11 40S 27 28 E
Lubunda, *Zaïre* **103 D5** 5 12S 26 41 E
Lubungu, *Zambia* **107 E2** 14 35S 26 24 E
Lubutu, *Zaïre* **106 C2** 0 45S 26 30 E
Luc An Chau, *Vietnam* **76 A5** 22 6N 104 43 E
Luc-en-Diois, *France* **25 D9** 44 36N 5 28 E
Lucala, *Angola* **103 D3** 9 7S 15 58 E
Lucan, *Canada* **136 C3** 43 11N 81 24W
Lucban, *Phil.* **70 D3** 14 6N 121 33 E
Lucca, *Italy* **38 E7** 43 50N 10 30 E
Luce Bay, *U.K.* **18 G4** 54 45N 4 48W
Lucea, *Jamaica* **148 C4** 18 25N 78 10W
Lucedale, *U.S.A.* **135 K1** 30 56N 88 35W
Lucena, *Phil.* **70 E3** 13 56N 121 37 E
Lucena, *Spain* **37 H6** 37 27N 4 31W
Lucena del Cid, *Spain* **34 E4** 40 9N 0 17W
Lučenec, *Slovak Rep.* **31 C12** 48 18N 19 42 E
Lucens, *Switz.* **28 C3** 46 43N 6 51 E
Lucera, *Italy* **41 A8** 41 30N 15 20 E
Lucerne = Luzern, *Switz.* **29 B6** 47 3N 8 18 E
Lucerne, *U.S.A.* **144 F4** 39 6N 122 48W
Lucerne Valley, *U.S.A.* **145 L10** 34 27N 116 57W
Lucero, *Mexico* **146 A3** 30 49N 106 30W
Luchena →, *Spain* **35 H3** 37 44N 1 50W
Lucheng, *China* **66 F7** 36 20N 113 11 E
Lucheringo →, *Mozam.* **107 E4** 11 43S 36 17 E
Lüchow, *Germany* **26 C7** 52 58N 11 8 E
Luchuan, *China* **69 F8** 22 21N 110 12 E
Lucie →, *Surinam* **153 C6** 3 35N 57 38W
Lucira, *Angola* **103 E2** 14 0S 12 35 E
Luckau, *Germany* **26 D9** 51 50N 13 43 E
Luckenwalde, *Germany* **26 C9** 52 5N 13 11 E
Luckey, *U.S.A.* **141 C13** 41 27N 83 29W
Lucknow, *India* **81 F9** 26 50N 81 0 E
Luçon, *France* **24 B2** 46 28N 1 10W
Lucusse, *Angola* **103 E4** 12 32S 20 48 E
Lüda = Dalian, *China* **67 E11** 38 50N 121 40 E
Luda Kamchiya →, *Bulgaria* **43 D12** 43 3N 27 29 E
Ludbreg, *Croatia* **39 B13** 46 15N 16 38 E
Lüdenscheid, *Germany* **26 D3** 51 13N 7 37 E
Lüderitz, *Namibia* **104 D2** 26 41S 15 8 E
Ludewe □, *Tanzania* **107 D3** 10 0S 34 50 E
Ludhiana, *India* **80 D6** 30 57N 75 56 E
Ludian, *China* **68 D4** 27 10N 103 33 E
Luding Qiao, *China* **68 C4** 29 53N 102 12 E
Lüdinghausen, *Germany* **26 D3** 51 46N 7 28 E
Ludington, *U.S.A.* **134 D2** 43 57N 86 27W
Ludlow, *U.K.* **17 E5** 52 23N 2 42W
Ludlow, *Calif., U.S.A.* **145 L10** 34 43N 116 10W
Ludlow, *Vt., U.S.A.* **137 C12** 43 24N 72 42W
Ludus, *Romania* **46 C5** 46 29N 24 5 E
Ludvika, *Sweden* **13 F13** 60 8N 15 14 E
Ludwigsburg, *Germany* **27 G5** 48 53N 9 11 E
Ludwigshafen, *Germany* **27 F4** 49 27N 8 27 E
Ludwigslust, *Germany* **26 B7** 53 19N 11 28 E
Ludza, *Latvia* **50 C5** 56 32N 27 43 E
Lue, *Australia* **117 B8** 32 38S 149 50 E
Luebo, *Zaïre* **103 D4** 5 21S 21 23 E
Lueki, *Zaïre* **102 C5** 3 20S 25 48 E
Luena, *Angola* **103 E3** 12 13S 19 51 E
Luena, *Zaïre* **107 D2** 9 28S 25 43 E
Luena, *Zambia* **107 E3** 10 40S 30 25 E
Luepa, *Venezuela* **153 B5** 5 43N 61 31W
Lüeyang, *China* **66 H4** 33 22N 106 10 E
Lufeng, *Guangdong, China* **69 F10** 22 57N 115 38 E
Lufeng, *Yunnan, China* **68 E4** 25 0N 102 5 E
Lufico, *Angola* **103 D2** 6 24S 13 23 E
Lufira →, *Zaïre* **107 D2** 9 30S 27 0 E
Lufkin, *U.S.A.* **139 K7** 31 21N 94 44W
Lufupa, *Zaïre* **103 E4** 10 37S 24 56 E
Luga, *Russia* **50 B6** 58 40N 29 55 E
Luga →, *Russia* **50 B6** 59 40N 28 18 E
Lugang, *Taiwan* **69 E13** 24 4N 120 23 E
Lugano, *Switz.* **29 D7** 46 0N 8 57 E
Lugano, L. di, *Switz.* **29 E8** 46 0N 9 0 E
Lugansk, *Ukraine* **53 B8** 48 38N 39 15 E
Lugard's Falls, *Kenya* **106 C4** 3 6S 38 41 E
Lugela, *Mozam.* **107 F4** 16 25S 36 43 E
Lugenda →, *Mozam.* **107 E4** 11 25S 38 33 E
Lugh Ganana, *Somali Rep.* **90 G3** 3 48N 42 34 E
Lugnaquilla, *Ireland* **19 D5** 52 58N 6 28W
Lugnvik, *Sweden* **14 B11** 62 56N 17 55 E
Lugo, *Italy* **39 D8** 44 25N 11 53 E
Lugo, *Spain* **36 B3** 43 2N 7 35W
Lugo □, *Spain* **36 C3** 43 0N 7 30W
Lugoj, *Romania* **42 B6** 45 42N 21 57 E
Lugones, *Spain* **36 B5** 43 26N 5 50W
Lugovoye, *Kazakhstan* **55 B6** 42 55N 72 43 E
Luhansk = Lugansk, *Ukraine* **53 B8** 48 38N 39 15 E
Luhe, *China* **69 A12** 32 19N 118 50 E
Luhe →, *Germany* **26 B6** 53 18N 10 11 E
Luhuo, *China* **68 B3** 31 21N 100 48 E
Luiana, *Angola* **103 F4** 17 25S 22 59 E
Luino, *Italy* **38 C5** 45 58N 8 42 E
Luís Correia, *Brazil* **154 B3** 3 0S 41 35W
Luís Gonçalves, *Brazil* **154 C1** 5 37S 50 25W
Luitpold Coast, *Antarctica* **7 D1** 78 30S 32 0W
Luiza, *Zaïre* **103 D4** 7 40S 22 30 E
Luizi, *Zaïre* **106 D2** 6 0S 27 25 E
Luján, *Argentina* **158 C4** 34 45S 59 5W
Lujiang, *China* **69 B11** 31 20N 117 15 E
Lukala, *Zaïre* **103 D2** 5 31S 14 32 E
Lukanga Swamp, *Zambia* **107 E2** 14 30S 27 40 E
Lukenie →, *Zaïre* **102 C3** 3 0S 18 50 E
Lukhisaral, *India* **81 G12** 25 11N 86 5 E
Lŭki, *Bulgaria* **43 F9** 41 50N 24 43 E
Lukk, *Libya* **96 B4** 32 1N 24 46 E
Lukolela, *Equateur, Zaïre* **102 C3** 1 10S 17 12 E
Lukolela, *Kasai Or., Zaïre* **103 D4** 5 23S 24 32 E
Lukosi, *Zimbabwe* **107 F2** 18 30S 26 30 E
Lukovit, *Bulgaria* **43 D9** 43 13N 24 11 E
Łuków, *Poland* **47 D9** 51 55N 22 23 E
Lukoyanov, *Russia* **51 D14** 55 2N 44 29 E
Lule älv →, *Sweden* **12 D17** 65 35N 22 10 E
Luleå, *Sweden* **12 D17** 65 35N 22 10 E
Lüleburgaz, *Turkey* **43 F12** 41 23N 27 22 E
Luliang, *China* **68 E4** 25 0N 103 40 E
Luling, *U.S.A.* **139 L6** 29 41N 97 39W
Lulong, *China* **67 E10** 39 53N 118 51 E
Lulonga →, *Zaïre* **102 B3** 1 0N 18 10 E
Lulua →, *Zaïre* **103 C4** 4 30S 20 30 E
Luluabourg = Kananga, *Zaïre* **103 D4** 5 55S 22 18 E
Lumai, *Angola* **103 E4** 13 13S 21 25 E
Lumajang, *Indonesia* **75 D4** 8 8S 113 13 E
Lumaku, Gunong, *Malaysia* **75 B5** 4 52N 115 38 E
Lumbala Kaquengue, *Angola* **103 E4** 12 39S 22 34 E
Lumbala N'guimbo, *Angola* **103 E4** 14 18S 21 18 E
Lumberton, *Miss., U.S.A.* **139 K10** 31 0N 89 27W
Lumberton, *N.C., U.S.A.* **135 H6** 34 37N 79 0W
Lumberton, *N. Mex., U.S.A.* **143 H10** 36 56N 106 56W
Lumbres, *France* **23 B9** 50 40N 2 5 E
Lumbwa, *Kenya* **106 C4** 0 12S 35 28 E
Lumding, *India* **78 C4** 25 46N 93 10 E
Lumi, *Papua N. G.* **120 B2** 3 30S 142 2 E
Lummen, *Belgium* **21 G6** 50 59N 5 12 E
Lumsden, *N.Z.* **119 F3** 45 44S 168 27 E
Lumut, *Malaysia* **77 K3** 4 13N 100 37 E
Lumut, Tg., *Indonesia* **74 C3** 3 50S 105 58 E
Luna, *Luzon, Phil.* **70 B3** 18 18N 121 21 E
Luna, *Luzon, Phil.* **70 C3** 16 51N 120 23 E
Lunan, *China* **68 E4** 24 40N 103 18 E
Lunavada, *India* **80 H5** 23 8N 73 37 E
Lunca, *Romania* **46 B6** 47 22N 25 1 E
Lund, *Sweden* **15 J7** 55 44N 13 12 E
Lund, *U.S.A.* **142 G6** 38 52N 115 0W
Lunda Norte □, *Angola* **103 D3** 8 0S 20 0 E
Lunda Sul □, *Angola* **103 D4** 10 0S 20 0 E
Lundazi, *Zambia* **107 E3** 12 20S 33 7 E
Lunde, *Norway* **14 E3** 59 17N 9 5 E
Lunderskov, *Denmark* **15 J3** 55 29N 9 19 E
Lundi →, *Zimbabwe* **107 G3** 21 43S 32 34 E
Lundu, *Malaysia* **75 B3** 1 40N 109 50 E
Lundy, *U.K.* **17 F3** 51 10N 4 41W
Lune →, *U.K.* **16 C5** 54 0N 2 51W
Lüneburg, *Germany* **26 B6** 53 15N 10 23 E
Lüneburg Heath = Lüneburger Heide, *Germany* **26 C6** 53 0N 10 0 E
Lüneburger Heide, *Germany* **26 C6** 53 0N 10 0 E
Lunel, *France* **25 E8** 43 39N 4 9 E
Lünen, *Germany* **26 D3** 51 36N 7 31 E
Lunenburg, *Canada* **129 D7** 44 22N 64 18W
Lunéville, *France* **23 D13** 48 36N 6 30 E
Lunga →, *Zambia* **107 E2** 14 34S 26 25 E
Lungern, *Switz.* **28 C6** 46 48N 8 10 E
Lungi Airport, *S. Leone* **100 D2** 8 40N 13 17W
Lunglei, *India* **78 D4** 22 55N 92 45 E
Lungngo, *Burma* **78 E4** 21 57N 93 36 E
Luni, *India* **80 F5** 26 0N 73 6 E
Luni →, *India* **80 G4** 24 41N 71 14 E
Luninets, *Belorussia* **50 E5** 52 15N 26 50 E
Luning, *U.S.A.* **142 G4** 38 30N 118 11W
Lunino, *Russia* **51 E14** 53 35N 45 6 E
Luninyets = Luninets, *Belorussia* **50 E5** 52 15N 26 50 E
Lunner, *Norway* **14 D4** 60 19N 10 35 E
Lunsemfwa →, *Zambia* **107 E3** 14 54S 30 12 E
Lunsemfwa Falls, *Zambia* **107 E2** 14 30S 29 6 E
Lunteren, *Neths.* **20 D7** 52 5N 5 38 E
Luo He →, *China* **66 G6** 34 35N 110 20 E
Luocheng, *China* **68 E7** 24 48N 108 53 E
Luochuan, *China* **66 G5** 35 45N 109 26 E
Luoci, *China* **68 E4** 25 19N 102 18 E
Luodian, *China* **68 E6** 25 24N 106 43 E
Luoding, *China* **69 F8** 22 45N 111 40 E
Luodong, *Taiwan* **69 E13** 24 41N 121 46 E
Luofu, *Zaïre* **106 C2** 0 10S 29 15 E
Luohe, *China* **66 H8** 33 32N 114 2 E
Luojiang, *China* **68 B5** 31 18N 104 33 E
Luonan, *China* **66 G6** 34 5N 110 10 E
Luoning, *China* **66 G6** 34 35N 111 40 E
Luoshan, *China* **69 A10** 32 13N 114 30 E
Luotian, *China* **69 B10** 30 46N 115 22 E
Luoyang, *China* **66 G7** 34 40N 112 26 E
Luoyuan, *China* **69 D12** 26 28N 119 30 E
Luozi, *Zaïre* **103 C2** 4 54S 14 0 E
Luozigou, *China* **67 C16** 43 42N 130 18 E
Lupeni, *Romania* **46 D4** 45 21N 23 13 E
Lupilichi, *Mozam.* **107 E4** 11 47S 35 13 E
Lupire, *Angola* **103 E3** 14 36S 19 29 E
Łupków, *Poland* **31 B15** 49 15N 22 4 E
Lupoing, *China* **68 E5** 24 53N 104 21 E
Lupon, *Phil.* **71 H5** 6 54N 126 0 E
Luquan, *China* **68 E4** 25 35N 102 25 E
Luque, *Paraguay* **158 B4** 25 19S 57 25W
Luque, *Spain* **37 H6** 37 35N 4 16W
Luray, *U.S.A.* **134 F6** 38 40N 78 28W
Lure, *France* **23 E13** 47 40N 6 30 E
Luremo, *Angola* **103 D3** 8 30S 17 50 E
Lurgan, *U.K.* **19 B5** 54 28N 6 20W
Luribay, *Bolivia* **156 D4** 17 6S 67 39W
Lurin, *Peru* **156 C2** 12 17S 76 52W
Lusaka, *Zambia* **107 F2** 15 28S 28 16 E
Lusambo, *Zaïre* **103 C4** 4 58S 23 28 E
Lusangaye, *Zaïre* **103 C5** 4 54S 26 0 E
Luseland, *Canada* **131 C7** 52 5N 109 24W
Lushan, *Henan, China* **66 H7** 33 45N 112 55 E
Lushan, *Sichuan, China* **68 B4** 30 12N 102 52 E
Lushi, *China* **66 G6** 34 3N 111 3 E
Lushnja, *Albania* **44 D1** 40 55N 19 41 E
Lushoto, *Tanzania* **106 C4** 4 47S 38 20 E
Lushoto □, *Tanzania* **106 C4** 4 45S 38 20 E
Lushui, *China* **68 E2** 25 58N 98 44 E
Lüshun, *China* **67 E11** 38 45N 121 15 E
Lusignan, *France* **24 B4** 46 26N 0 8 E
Lusigny-sur-Barse, *France* **23 D11** 48 16N 4 15 E
Lusk, *U.S.A.* **138 D2** 42 46N 104 27W
Lussac-les-Châteaux, *France* **24 B4** 46 24N 0 43 E
Lussanvira, *Brazil* **155 F1** 20 42S 51 7W
Luta = Dalian, *China* **67 E11** 38 50N 121 40 E
Lutembo, *Angola* **103 E4** 13 26S 21 16 E
Luti, *Solomon Is.* **121 L9** 7 14S 157 0 E
Luton, *U.K.* **17 F7** 51 53N 0 24W
Lutong, *Malaysia* **75 B4** 4 28N 114 0 E
Lutry, *Switz.* **28 C3** 46 31N 6 42 E
Lutsk, *Ukraine* **50 F4** 50 50N 25 15 E
Lutuai, *Angola* **103 E4** 12 41S 20 7 E
Lützow Holmbukta, *Antarctica* **7 C4** 69 10S 37 30 E
Lutzputs, *S. Africa* **104 D3** 28 3S 20 40 E
Luverne, *U.S.A.* **138 D6** 43 39N 96 13W
Luvo, *Angola* **103 D2** 5 51S 14 5 E
Luvua, *Zaïre* **103 D5** 8 48S 25 17 E
Luvua →, *Zaïre* **106 D2** 6 50S 27 30 E
Luwegu →, *Tanzania* **107 D4** 8 31S 37 23 E
Luwuk, *Indonesia* **72 B2** 0 56S 122 47 E
Luxembourg, *Lux.* **21 J8** 49 37N 6 9 E
Luxembourg □, *Belgium* **21 J7** 49 58N 5 30 E
Luxembourg ■, *Europe* **21 J8** 49 45N 6 0 E
Luxeuil-les-Bains, *France* **23 E13** 47 49N 6 24 E
Luxi, *Hunan, China* **69 C8** 28 20N 110 7 E
Luxi, *Yunnan, China* **68 E4** 24 40N 103 55 E
Luxi, *Yunnan, China* **68 E2** 24 27N 98 36 E
Luxor = El Uqsur, *Egypt* **94 B3** 25 41N 32 38 E
Luy →, *France* **24 E2** 43 39N 1 9W
Luy-de-Béarn →, *France* **24 E3** 43 39N 0 48W
Luy-de-France →, *France* **24 E3** 43 39N 0 48W
Luyi, *China* **66 H8** 33 50N 115 35 E
Luyksgestel, *Neths.* **21 F6** 51 17N 5 20 E
Luz-St.-Sauveur, *France* **24 F4** 42 53N 0 0 E
Luza, *Russia* **48 B8** 60 39N 47 10 E
Luzern, *Switz.* **29 B6** 47 3N 8 18 E
Luzern □, *Switz.* **28 B5** 47 2N 7 55 E
Luzhai, *China* **68 E7** 24 29N 109 42 E
Luzhou, *China* **68 C5** 28 52N 105 20 E
Luziânia, *Brazil* **155 E2** 16 20S 48 0W
Luzilândia, *Brazil* **154 B3** 3 28S 42 22W
Luzon, *Phil.* **70 C3** 16 0N 121 0 E
Luzy, *France* **23 F10** 46 47N 3 58 E
Luzzi, *Italy* **41 C9** 39 28N 16 17 E
Lviv = Lvov, *Ukraine* **50 G4** 49 50N 24 0 E
Lvov, *Ukraine* **50 G4** 49 50N 24 0 E
Lwówek, *Poland* **47 C3** 52 28N 16 10 E
Lwówek Śląski, *Poland* **47 D2** 51 7N 15 38 E
Lyakhovichi, *Belorussia* **50 E5** 53 2N 26 32 E
Lyakhovskiye, Ostrova, *Russia* **57 B15** 73 40N 141 0 E
Lyaki, *Azerbaijan* **53 F12** 40 34N 47 22 E
Lyall Mt., *N.Z.* **119 F2** 45 16S 167 32 E
Lyallpur = Faisalabad, *Pakistan* **79 C4** 31 30N 73 5 E
Lyalya →, *Russia* **54 B7** 59 9N 61 29 E
Lyaskovets, *Bulgaria* **43 D10** 43 6N 25 44 E
Lycaonia, *Turkey* **88 D5** 38 0N 33 0 E
Lychen, *Germany* **26 B9** 53 13N 13 20 E
Lycia, *Turkey* **88 E3** 36 30N 29 30 E
Lycksele, *Sweden* **12 D15** 64 38N 18 40 E
Lycosura, *Greece* **45 G4** 37 20N 22 3 E
Lydda = Lod, *Israel* **91 D3** 31 57N 34 54 E
Lydenburg, *S. Africa* **105 D5** 25 10S 30 29 E
Lydia, *Turkey* **88 D3** 39 0N 28 0 E
Lyell, *N.Z.* **119 B7** 41 48S 172 4 E
Lyell I., *Canada* **130 C2** 52 40N 131 35W
Lygnern, *Sweden* **15 G6** 57 30N 12 15 E
Lyman, *U.S.A.* **142 F8** 41 20N 110 18W
Lyme Regis, *U.K.* **17 G5** 50 44N 2 57W
Lymington, *U.K.* **17 G6** 50 46N 1 32W
Łyńa →, *Poland* **47 A8** 54 37N 21 14 E
Lynchburg, *Ohio, U.S.A.* **141 E13** 39 15N 83 48W
Lynchburg, *Va., U.S.A.* **134 G6** 37 25N 79 9W
Lynd →, *Australia* **114 B3** 16 28S 143 18 E
Lynd Ra., *Australia* **115 D4** 25 30S 149 20 E
Lynden, *Canada* **136 C4** 43 14N 80 9W
Lynden, *U.S.A.* **144 B4** 48 57N 122 27W
Lyndhurst, *Queens., Australia* **114 B3** 19 12S 144 20 E
Lyndhurst, *S. Austral., Australia* **115 E2** 30 15S 138 18 E
Lyndon →, *Australia* **113 D1** 23 29S 114 6 E
Lyndonville, *N.Y., U.S.A.* **136 C6** 43 20N 78 23W
Lyndonville, *Vt., U.S.A.* **137 B12** 44 31N 72 1W
Lyngdal, *Norway* **14 E3** 59 54N 9 32 E
Lynher Reef, *Australia* **112 C3** 15 27S 121 55 E
Lynn, *Ind., U.S.A.* **141 D12** 40 3N 84 56W
Lynn, *Mass., U.S.A.* **137 D14** 42 28N 70 57W
Lynn Canal, *U.S.A.* **130 B1** 58 50N 135 15W
Lynn Lake, *Canada* **131 B8** 56 51N 101 3W
Lynnwood, *U.S.A.* **144 C4** 47 49N 122 19W
Lynton, *U.K.* **17 F4** 51 14N 3 50W
Lyntupy, *Belorussia* **50 D5** 55 4N 26 23 E
Lynx L., *Canada* **131 A7** 62 25N 106 15W
Lyø, *Denmark* **15 J4** 55 3N 10 9 E
Lyon, *France* **25 C8** 45 46N 4 50 E
Lyonnais, *France* **25 C8** 45 45N 4 15 E
Lyons = Lyon, *France* **25 C8** 45 46N 4 50 E
Lyons, *Colo., U.S.A.* **138 E2** 40 14N 105 16W
Lyons, *Ga., U.S.A.* **135 J4** 32 12N 82 19W
Lyons, *Kans., U.S.A.* **138 F5** 38 21N 98 12W
Lyons, *N.Y., U.S.A.* **136 C8** 43 5N 77 0W
Lyrestad, *Sweden* **15 F8** 58 48N 14 4 E
Lys = Leie →, *Belgium* **23 A10** 51 2N 3 45 E
Lysá, *Czech.* **30 A7** 50 11N 14 51 E
Lysekil, *Sweden* **15 F5** 58 17N 11 26 E
Lyskovo, *Russia* **51 D14** 56 0N 45 3 E
Lyss, *Switz.* **28 B4** 47 4N 7 19 E
Lysva, *Russia* **54 B5** 58 7N 57 49 E
Lytle, *U.S.A.* **139 L5** 29 14N 98 48W
Lyttelton, *N.Z.* **119 D7** 43 35S 172 44 E
Lytton, *Canada* **130 C4** 50 13N 121 31W
Lyuban, *Russia* **50 B7** 59 16N 31 18 E
Lyubcha, *Belorussia* **50 E5** 53 46N 26 1 E
Lyubertsy, *Russia* **51 D10** 55 39N 37 50 E
Lyubim, *Russia* **51 B12** 58 20N 40 39 E
Lyubimets, *Bulgaria* **43 F11** 41 50N 26 5 E
Lyuboml, *Ukraine* **50 F4** 51 11N 24 4 E
Lyubotin, *Ukraine* **52 B6** 50 0N 36 0 E
Lyubytino, *Russia* **50 B8** 58 50N 33 16 E
Lyudinovo, *Russia* **50 E9** 53 52N 34 28 E


# M


Ma →, *Vietnam* **76 C5** 19 47N 105 56 E
Ma'adaba, *Jordan* **91 E4** 30 43N 35 47 E
Maamba, *Zambia* **104 B4** 17 17S 26 28 E
Ma'ān, *Jordan* **91 E4** 30 12N 35 44 E
Ma'ān □, *Jordan* **91 F5** 30 0N 36 0 E
Ma'anshan, *China* **69 B12** 31 44N 118 29 E
Maarheeze, *Neths.* **21 F7** 51 19N 5 36 E
Maarianhamina, *Finland* **13 F15** 60 5N 19 55 E
Maarn, *Neths.* **20 D6** 52 3N 5 22 E
Ma'arrat an Nu'mān, *Syria* **84 C3** 35 43N 36 43 E
Maarssen, *Neths.* **20 D6** 52 9N 5 2 E
Maartensdijk, *Neths.* **20 D6** 52 9N 5 10 E
Maas →, *Neths.* **20 E5** 51 45N 4 32 E
Maasbracht, *Belgium* **21 F7** 51 9N 5 54 E
Maasbree, *Neths.* **21 F8** 51 22N 6 3 E
Maasdam, *Neths.* **20 E5** 51 48N 4 34 E
Maasdijk, *Neths.* **20 E4** 51 58N 4 13 E
Maaseik, *Belgium* **21 F7** 51 6N 5 45 E
Maasland, *Neths.* **20 E4** 51 57N 4 16 E
Maasniel, *Neths.* **21 F8** 51 12N 6 1 E
Maassluis, *Neths.* **20 E4** 51 56N 4 16 E
Maastricht, *Neths.* **21 G7** 50 50N 5 40 E
Maave, *Mozam.* **105 C5** 21 4S 34 47 E
Ma'bar, *Yemen* **86 D4** 14 48N 44 17 E
Mabaruma, *Guyana* **153 B6** 8 10N 59 50W
Mabein, *Burma* **78 D6** 23 29N 96 37 E
Mabel L., *Canada* **130 C5** 50 35N 118 43W
Mabenge, *Zaïre* **106 B1** 4 15N 24 12 E
Mabian, *China* **68 C4** 28 47N 103 37 E
Mablethorpe, *U.K.* **16 D8** 53 21N 0 14 E
Maboma, *Zaïre* **106 B2** 2 30N 28 10 E
Maboukou, *Congo* **102 C2** 3 39S 12 31 E
Mabrouk, *Mali* **101 B4** 19 29N 1 15W
Mabton, *U.S.A.* **142 C3** 46 13N 120 0W
Mabungo, *Somali Rep.* **108 D2** 0 49N 42 35 E
Mac Bac, *Vietnam* **77 H6** 9 46N 106 7 E
Macachín, *Argentina* **158 D3** 37 10S 63 43W
Macaé, *Brazil* **155 F3** 22 20S 41 43W
Macaíba, *Brazil* **154 C4** 5 51S 35 21W
Macajuba, *Brazil* **155 D3** 12 9S 40 22W
Macalelon, *Phil.* **70 E4** 13 45N 122 8 E
McAlester, *U.S.A.* **139 H7** 34 56N 95 46W
McAllen, *U.S.A.* **139 M5** 26 12N 98 14W
Macamic, *Canada* **128 C4** 48 45N 79 0W
Macao = Macau ■, *China* **69 F9** 22 16N 113 35 E
Macão, *Portugal* **37 F3** 39 35N 7 59W
Macapá, *Brazil* **153 C7** 0 5N 51 4W
Macará, *Ecuador* **152 D2** 4 23S 79 57W
Macarani, *Brazil* **155 E3** 15 33S 40 24W
Macarena, Serranía de la, *Colombia* **152 C3** 2 45N 73 55W
Macarthur, *Australia* **116 E5** 38 5S 142 0 E
McArthur →, *Australia* **114 B2** 15 54S 136 40 E
McArthur, Port, *Australia* **114 B2** 16 4S 136 23 E
McArthur River, *Australia* **114 B2** 16 27S 136 7 E
Macas, *Ecuador* **152 D2** 2 19S 78 7W
Macate, *Peru* **156 B2** 8 48S 78 7W
Macau, *Brazil* **154 C4** 5 15S 36 40W
Macau ■, *China* **69 F9** 22 16N 113 35 E
Macaúbas, *Brazil* **155 D3** 13 2S 42 42W
Macaya →, *Colombia* **152 C3** 0 59N 72 20W
McBride, *Canada* **130 C4** 53 20N 120 19W
McCall, *U.S.A.* **142 D5** 44 55N 116 6W
McCamey, *U.S.A.* **139 K3** 31 8N 102 14W
McCammon, *U.S.A.* **142 E7** 42 39N 112 12W
McCauley I., *Canada* **130 C2** 53 40N 130 15W
McCleary, *U.S.A.* **144 C3** 47 3N 123 16W
Macclesfield, *U.K.* **16 D5** 53 16N 2 9W
McClintock, *Canada* **131 B10** 57 50N 94 10W
McClintock Ra., *Australia* **112 C4** 18 44S 127 38 E
McCloud, *U.S.A.* **142 F2** 41 15N 122 8W
McCluer I., *Australia* **112 B5** 11 5S 133 0 E
McClure, *U.S.A.* **136 F7** 40 42N 77 19W
McClure, L., *U.S.A.* **144 H6** 37 35N 120 16W
M'Clure Str., *Canada* **6 B2** 75 0N 119 0W
McClusky, *U.S.A.* **138 B4** 47 29N 100 27W
McComb, *U.S.A.* **139 K9** 31 15N 90 27W
McConaughy, L., *U.S.A.* **138 E4** 41 14N 101 40W
McCook, *U.S.A.* **138 E4** 40 12N 100 38W
McCullough Mt., *U.S.A.* **145 K11** 35 35N 115 13W
McCusker →, *Canada* **131 B7** 55 32N 108 39W

Mangyshlakskiy Zaliv 229


Maiyema, *Nigeria* **101 C5** 12 5N 4 25 E
Maiyuan, *China* **69 E11** 25 34N 117 28 E
Maiz, Is. del, *Nic.* **148 D3** 12 15N 83 4W
Maizuru, *Japan* **63 B7** 35 25N 135 22 E
Majagual, *Colombia* **152 B3** 8 33N 74 38W
Majalengka, *Indonesia* **75 D3** 6 50 S 108 13 E
Majari →, *Brazil* **153 C5** 3 29N 60 58W
Majene, *Indonesia* **72 B1** 3 38 S 118 57 E
Majes →, *Peru* **156 D3** 16 40 S 72 44W
Majevica, *Bos.-H.* **42 C3** 44 45N 18 50 E
Maji, *Ethiopia* **95 F4** 6 12N 35 30 E
Majiang, *China* **68 D6** 26 28N 107 32 E
Major, *Canada* **131 C7** 51 52N 109 37W
Majorca = Mallorca, *Spain* **33 B10** 39 30N 3 0 E
Majors Creek, *Australia* **117 C8** 35 33 S 149 45 E
Majuriã, *Brazil* **157 B5** 7 30 S 64 55W
Maka, *Senegal* **100 C2** 13 40N 14 10W
Makak, *Cameroon* **101 E7** 3 36N 11 0 E
Makakou, *Gabon* **102 C2** 0 11 S 12 12 E
Makale, *Indonesia* **72 B1** 3 6 S 119 51 E
Makamba, *Burundi* **106 C2** 4 8 S 29 49 E
Makarewa, *N.Z.* **119 G3** 46 20 S 168 21 E
Makarikari = Makgadikgadi Salt Pans, *Botswana* **104 C4** 20 40 S 25 45 E
Makarovo, *Russia* **57 D11** 57 40N 107 45 E
Makarska, *Croatia* **42 D2** 43 20N 17 2 E
Makaryev, *Russia* **51 C13** 57 52N 43 50 E
Makasar = Ujung Pandang, *Indonesia* **72 C1** 5 10 S 119 20 E
Makasar, Selat, *Indonesia* **72 B1** 1 0 S 118 20 E
Makasar, Str. of = Makasar, Selat, *Indonesia* **72 B1** 1 0 S 118 20 E
Makat, *Kazakhstan* **49 E9** 47 39N 53 19 E
Makedhonía □, *Greece* **44 D3** 40 39N 22 0 E
Makedonija = Macedonia ■, *Europe* **42 F6** 41 53N 21 40 E
Makena, *U.S.A.* **132 H16** 20 39N 156 27W
Makeni, *S. Leone* **100 D2** 8 55N 12 5W
Makeyevka, *Ukraine* **52 B7** 48 0N 38 0 E
Makgadikgadi Salt Pans, *Botswana* **104 C4** 20 40 S 25 45 E
Makhachkala, *Russia* **53 E12** 43 0N 47 30 E
Makhambet, *Kazakhstan* **53 C14** 47 43N 51 40 E
Makharadze = Ozurgety, *Georgia* **53 F10** 41 55N 42 2 E
Makhmūr, *Iraq* **84 C4** 35 46N 43 35 E
Makhyah, W. →, *Yemen* **87 C5** 17 40N 49 1 E
Makian, *Indonesia* **72 A3** 0 20N 127 20 E
Makindu, *Kenya* **106 C4** 2 18 S 37 50 E
Makinsk, *Kazakhstan* **56 D8** 52 37N 70 26 E
Makiyivka = Makeyevka, *Ukraine* **52 B7** 48 0N 38 0 E
Makkah, *Si. Arabia* **86 B2** 21 30N 39 54 E
Makkovik, *Canada* **129 A8** 55 10N 59 10W
Makkum, *Neths.* **20 B6** 53 3N 5 25 E
Makó, *Hungary* **31 E13** 46 14N 20 33 E
Makok, *Gabon* **102 C1** 0 1 S 9 35 E
Makokou, *Gabon* **102 B2** 0 40N 12 50 E
Makongo, *Zaïre* **106 B2** 3 25N 26 17 E
Makoro, *Zaïre* **106 B2** 3 10N 29 59 E
Makoua, *Congo* **102 C3** 0 5 S 15 50 E
Maków Mazowiecki, *Poland* **47 C8** 52 52N 21 6 E
Maków Podhal, *Poland* **31 B12** 49 43N 19 45 E
Makrá, *Greece* **45 H7** 36 15N 25 54 E
Makran, *Asia* **79 D1** 26 13N 61 30 E
Makran Coast Range, *Pakistan* **79 D2** 25 40N 64 0 E
Makrana, *India* **80 F6** 27 2N 74 46 E
Mákri, *Greece* **44 D7** 40 52N 25 40 E
Makriyialos, *Greece* **32 D7** 35 2N 25 59 E
Maksimkin Yar, *Russia* **56 D9** 58 42N 86 50 E
Maktar, *Tunisia* **96 A1** 35 48N 9 12 E
Mākū, *Iran* **84 B5** 39 15N 44 31 E
Makum, *India* **78 B5** 27 30N 95 23 E
Makumbi, *Zaïre* **103 D4** 5 50 S 20 43 E
Makunda, *Botswana* **104 C3** 22 30 S 20 7 E
Makurazaki, *Japan* **62 F2** 31 15N 130 20 E
Makurdi, *Nigeria* **101 D6** 7 43N 8 35 E
Makūyeh, *Iran* **85 D7** 28 7N 53 9 E
Makwassie, *S. Africa* **104 D4** 27 17 S 26 0 E
Mal, *India* **78 B2** 26 51N 88 45 E
Mal B., *Ireland* **19 D2** 52 50N 9 30W
Mal i Gjalicës së Lumës, *Albania* **44 B2** 42 2N 20 25 E
Mal i Gribës, *Albania* **44 D1** 40 17N 19 45 E
Mal i Nemërçkës, *Albania* **44 D2** 40 15N 20 15 E
Mal i Tomorit, *Albania* **44 D2** 40 42N 20 11 E
Mala, *Peru* **156 C2** 12 40 S 76 38W
Mala, Pta., *Panama* **148 E3** 7 28N 80 2W
Mala Kapela, *Croatia* **39 D12** 44 45N 15 30 E
Malabang, *Phil.* **71 H5** 7 36N 124 3 E
Malabar Coast, *India* **83 J2** 11 0N 75 0 E
Malabo = Rey Malabo, *Eq. Guin.* **101 E6** 3 45N 8 50 E
Malabon, *Phil.* **70 D3** 14 21N 121 0 E
Malabrigo Pt., *Phil.* **70 E3** 13 36N 121 15 E
Malabungan, *Phil.* **71 G1** 9 3N 117 38 E
Malacca, Str. of, *Indonesia* **77 L3** 3 0N 101 0 E
Malacky, *Slovak Rep.* **31 C10** 48 27N 17 0 E
Malad City, *U.S.A.* **142 E7** 42 12N 112 15W
Maladzyechna = Molodechno, *Belorussia* **50 D5** 54 20N 26 50 E
Málaga, *Colombia* **152 B3** 6 42N 72 44W
Málaga, *Spain* **37 J6** 36 43N 4 23W
Malaga, *U.S.A.* **139 J2** 32 14N 104 4W
Málaga □, *Spain* **37 J6** 36 38N 4 58W
Malagarasi, *Tanzania* **106 D3** 5 5 S 30 50 E
Malagarasi →, *Tanzania* **106 D2** 5 12 S 29 47 E
Malagón, *Spain* **37 F7** 39 11N 3 52W
Malagón →, *Spain* **37 H3** 37 35N 7 29W
Malaimbandy, *Madag.* **105 C8** 20 20 S 45 36 E
Malaita, *Pac. Oc.* **121 M11** 9 0 S 161 0 E
Malakâl, *Sudan* **95 F3** 9 33N 31 40 E
Malakand, *Pakistan* **79 B3** 34 40N 71 55 E
Malakoff, *U.S.A.* **139 J7** 32 10N 96 1W
Malalag, *Phil.* **71 H5** 6 36N 125 24 E
Malam, *Chad* **97 F4** 11 27N 20 59 E
Malamyzh, *Russia* **57 E14** 49 50N 136 50 E
Malang, *Indonesia* **75 D4** 7 59 S 112 45 E
Malangas, *Phil.* **71 H4** 7 37N 123 1 E
Malange □, *Angola* **103 D3** 9 30 S 16 0 E
Malanje, *Angola* **103 D3** 9 36 S 16 17 E
Mälaren, *Sweden* **14 E11** 59 30N 17 10 E
Malargüe, *Argentina* **158 D2** 35 32 S 69 30W
Malartic, *Canada* **128 C4** 48 9N 78 9W
Malatya, *Turkey* **89 D8** 38 25N 38 20 E
Malatya □, *Turkey* **89 D8** 38 15N 38 0 E
Malawali, *Malaysia* **75 A5** 7 3N 117 18 E
Malawi ■, *Africa* **107 E3** 11 55 S 34 0 E
Malawi, L., *Africa* **107 E3** 12 30 S 34 30 E
Malay, *Phil.* **71 F3** 11 54N 121 55 E
Malay Pen., *Asia* **77 J3** 7 25N 100 0 E
Malaya Belozërka, *Ukraine* **52 C6** 47 12N 34 56 E
Malaya Vishera, *Russia* **50 B8** 58 55N 32 25 E
Malaya Viska, *Ukraine* **52 B4** 48 39N 31 36 E
Malaybalay, *Phil.* **71 G5** 8 5N 125 7 E
Malāyer, *Iran* **85 C6** 34 19N 48 51 E
Malaysia ■, *Asia* **74 B4** 5 0N 110 0 E
Malazgirt, *Turkey* **89 D10** 39 10N 42 33 E
Malbon, *Australia* **114 C3** 21 5 S 140 17 E
Malbooma, *Australia* **115 E1** 30 41 S 134 11 E
Malbork, *Poland* **47 A6** 54 3N 19 1 E
Malca Dube, *Ethiopia* **108 C2** 6 47N 42 4 E
Malcésine, *Italy* **38 C7** 45 46N 10 48 E
Malchin, *Germany* **26 B8** 53 43N 12 44 E
Malchow, *Germany* **26 B8** 53 29N 12 25 E
Malcolm, *Australia* **113 E3** 28 51 S 121 25 E
Malcolm, Pt., *Australia* **113 F3** 33 48 S 123 45 E
Malczyce, *Poland* **47 D3** 51 14N 16 29 E
Maldegem, *Belgium* **21 F2** 51 14N 3 26 E
Malden, *Mass., U.S.A.* **137 D13** 42 26N 71 4W
Malden, *Mo., U.S.A.* **139 G10** 36 34N 89 57W
Malden I., *Kiribati* **123 H12** 4 3 S 155 1W
Maldives ■, *Ind. Oc.* **59 J11** 5 0N 73 0 E
Maldon, *Australia* **116 D6** 37 0 S 144 6 E
Maldonado, *Uruguay* **159 C5** 34 59 S 55 0W
Maldonado, Punta, *Mexico* **147 D5** 16 19N 98 35W
Malé, *Italy* **38 B7** 46 20N 10 55 E
Malé Karpaty, *Slovak Rep.* **31 C10** 48 30N 17 20 E
Maléa, Ákra, *Greece* **45 H5** 36 28N 23 7 E
Malebo, Pool, *Africa* **103 C3** 4 17 S 15 20 E
Malegaon, *India* **82 D2** 20 30N 74 38 E
Malei, *Mozam.* **107 F4** 17 12 S 36 58 E
Malek Kandī, *Iran* **84 B5** 37 9N 46 6 E
Malekula, *Vanuatu* **121 F5** 16 15 S 167 30 E
Malela, *Bas Zaïre, Zaïre* **103 D2** 5 59 S 12 37 E
Malela, *Kivu, Zaïre* **103 C5** 4 22 S 26 8 E
Malema, *Mozam.* **107 E4** 14 57 S 37 20 E
Máleme, *Greece* **32 D5** 35 31N 23 49 E
Malerkotla, *India* **80 D6** 30 32N 75 58 E
Máles, *Greece* **32 D7** 35 6N 25 35 E
Malesherbes, *France* **23 D9** 48 15N 2 24 E
Maleshevska Planina, *Europe* **42 F8** 41 38N 23 7 E
Malestroit, *France* **22 E4** 47 49N 2 25W
Malfa, *Italy* **41 D7** 38 35N 14 50 E
Malgobek, *Russia* **53 E11** 43 30N 44 34 E
Malgomaj, *Sweden* **12 D14** 64 40N 16 30 E
Malgrat, *Spain* **34 D7** 41 39N 2 46 E
Malha, *Sudan* **95 D2** 15 8N 25 10 E
Malheur →, *U.S.A.* **142 D5** 44 4N 116 59W
Malheur L., *U.S.A.* **142 E4** 43 20N 118 48W
Mali, *Guinea* **100 C2** 12 10N 12 20W
Mali ■, *Africa* **100 B4** 17 0N 3 0W
Mali Hka →, *Burma* **78 C6** 25 42N 97 30 E
Mali Kanal, *Serbia* **42 B4** 45 36N 19 24 E
Malibu, *U.S.A.* **145 L8** 34 2N 118 41W
Maligaya, *Phil.* **70 E3** 12 59N 121 30 E
Malik, *Indonesia* **72 B2** 0 39 S 123 16 E
Malili, *Indonesia* **72 B2** 2 42 S 121 6 E
Malimba, Mts., *Zaïre* **106 D2** 7 30 S 29 30 E
Malin, *Ukraine* **50 F6** 50 46N 29 3 E
Malin Hd., *Ireland* **19 A4** 55 18N 7 24W
Malindang, Mt., *Phil.* **71 G4** 8 13N 123 38 E
Malindi, *Kenya* **106 C5** 3 12 S 40 5 E
Malines = Mechelen, *Belgium* **21 F4** 51 2N 4 29 E
Maling, *Indonesia* **72 A2** 1 0N 121 0 E
Malinyi, *Tanzania* **107 D4** 8 56 S 36 0 E
Malipo, *China* **68 F5** 23 7N 104 42 E
Maliqi, *Albania* **44 D2** 40 45N 20 48 E
Malita, *Phil.* **71 H5** 6 19N 125 39 E
Maljenik, *Serbia* **42 D6** 43 59N 21 55 E
Malkapur, *Maharashtra, India* **82 F3** 16 57N 76 17 E
Malkapur, *Maharashtra, India* **82 D1** 20 53N 73 58 E
Malkara, *Turkey* **88 C2** 40 53N 26 53 E
Małkinia Górna, *Poland* **47 C9** 52 42N 22 5 E
Malko Tŭrnovo, *Bulgaria* **43 F12** 41 59N 27 31 E
Mallacoota, *Australia* **117 D8** 37 40 S 149 40 E
Mallacoota Inlet, *Australia* **117 D8** 37 34 S 149 40 E
Mallaig, *U.K.* **18 E3** 57 0N 5 50W
Mallala, *Australia* **116 C3** 34 26 S 138 30 E
Mallard, *U.S.A.* **140 B2** 42 56N 94 41W
Mallawan, *India* **81 F9** 27 4N 80 12 E
Mallawi, *Egypt* **94 B3** 27 44N 30 44 E
Malleco □, *Chile* **160 A2** 38 10 S 72 20W
Mallemort, *France* **25 E9** 43 43N 5 11 E
Málles Venosta, *Italy* **38 B7** 46 42N 10 32 E
Mállia, *Greece* **32 D7** 35 17N 25 27 E
Mallicolo = Malekula, *Vanuatu* **121 F5** 16 15 S 167 30 E
Mallig, *Phil.* **70 C3** 17 8N 121 42 E
Mallión, Kólpos, *Greece* **32 D7** 35 19N 25 27 E
Mallorca, *Spain* **33 B10** 39 30N 3 0 E
Mallorytown, *Canada* **137 B9** 44 29N 75 53W
Mallow, *Ireland* **19 D3** 52 8N 8 40W
Malmberget, *Sweden* **12 C16** 67 11N 20 40 E
Malmédy, *Belgium* **21 H8** 50 25N 6 2 E
Malmesbury, *S. Africa* **104 E2** 33 28 S 18 41 E
Malmö, *Sweden* **15 J6** 55 36N 12 59 E
Malmöhus län □, *Sweden* **15 J7** 55 45N 13 30 E
Malmslätt, *Sweden* **15 F9** 58 27N 15 33 E
Malmyzh, *Russia* **54 C2** 56 31N 50 41 E
Malnaş, *Romania* **46 C6** 46 2N 25 49 E
Malo, *Vanuatu* **121 E5** 15 40 S 167 11 E
Malo Konare, *Bulgaria* **43 E9** 42 12N 24 24 E
Maloarkhangelsk, *Russia* **51 E10** 52 28N 36 30 E
Maloca, *Brazil* **153 C6** 0 43N 55 57W
Maloja, *Switz.* **29 D9** 46 25N 9 35 E
Maloja, P., *Switz.* **29 D9** 46 23N 9 42 E
Malolos, *Phil.* **70 D3** 14 50N 120 49 E
Malomalsk, *Russia* **54 B6** 58 45N 59 53 E
Malombe L., *Malawi* **107 E4** 14 40 S 35 15 E
Malomir, *Bulgaria* **43 E11** 42 16N 26 30 E
Malone, *U.S.A.* **137 B10** 44 51N 74 18W
Malong, *China* **68 E4** 25 24N 103 34 E
Malonga, *Zaïre* **103 E4** 10 24 S 23 10 E
Malorad, *Bulgaria* **43 D8** 43 28N 23 41 E
Malorita, *Belorussia* **50 F4** 51 50N 24 3 E
Maloyaroslovets, *Russia* **51 D10** 55 2N 36 20 E
Malozemelskaya Tundra, *Russia* **48 A9** 67 0N 50 0 E
Malpartida, *Spain* **37 F4** 39 26N 6 30W
Malpaso, *Canary Is.* **33 G1** 27 43N 18 3W
Malpica, *Spain* **36 B2** 43 19N 8 50W
Malprabha →, *India* **83 F3** 16 20N 76 5 E
Malta, *Brazil* **154 C4** 6 54 S 37 31W
Malta, *Idaho, U.S.A.* **142 E7** 42 18N 113 22W
Malta, *Mont., U.S.A.* **142 B10** 48 21N 107 52W
Malta ■, *Europe* **32 D1** 35 50N 14 30 E
Malta Channel, *Medit. S.* **40 F6** 36 40N 14 0 E
Maltahöhe, *Namibia* **104 C2** 24 55 S 17 0 E
Malters, *Switz.* **28 B6** 47 3N 8 11 E
Malton, *Canada* **136 C5** 43 42N 79 38W
Malton, *U.K.* **16 C7** 54 9N 0 48W
Malu'a, *Solomon Is.* **121 M11** 8 0 S 160 0 E
Maluku, *Indonesia* **72 B3** 1 0 S 127 0 E
Maluku □, *Indonesia* **72 B3** 3 0 S 128 0 E
Maluku Sea, *Indonesia* **72 A3** 2 0 S 124 0 E
Malumfashi, *Nigeria* **101 C6** 11 48N 7 39 E
Malungun, *Phil.* **71 H5** 6 16N 125 14 E
Maluso, *Phil.* **71 H3** 6 33N 121 53 E
Malvalli, *India* **83 H3** 12 28N 77 8 E
Malvan, *India* **83 F1** 16 2N 73 30 E
Malvern, *U.S.A.* **139 H8** 34 22N 92 49W
Malvern Hills, *U.K.* **17 E5** 52 0N 2 19W
Malvik, *Norway* **14 A4** 63 25N 10 40 E
Malvinas, Is. = Falkland Is. ■, *Atl. Oc.* **160 D5** 51 30 S 59 0W
Malya, *Tanzania* **106 C3** 3 5 S 33 38 E
Malybay, *Kazakhstan* **55 B9** 43 30N 78 25 E
Malyy Lyakhovskiy, Ostrov, *Russia* **57 B15** 74 7N 140 36 E
Mama, *Russia* **57 D12** 58 18N 112 54 E
Mamadysh, *Russia* **54 D2** 55 44N 51 23 E
Mamaia, *Romania* **46 E9** 44 18N 28 37 E
Mamaku, *N.Z.* **118 E5** 38 5 S 176 8 E
Mamanguape, *Brazil* **154 C4** 6 50 S 35 4W
Mamasa, *Indonesia* **72 B1** 2 55 S 119 20 E
Mambajao, *Phil.* **71 G5** 9 15N 124 43 E
Mambasa, *Zaïre* **106 B2** 1 22N 29 3 E
Mamberamo →, *Indonesia* **73 B5** 2 0 S 137 50 E
Mambilima Falls, *Zambia* **107 E2** 10 31 S 28 45 E
Mambirima, *Zaïre* **107 E2** 11 25 S 27 33 E
Mambo, *Tanzania* **106 C4** 4 52 S 38 22 E
Mambrui, *Kenya* **106 C5** 3 5 S 40 5 E
Mamburao, *Phil.* **70 E3** 13 13N 120 39 E
Mameigwess L., *Canada* **128 B2** 52 35N 87 50W
Mamer, *Lux.* **21 J8** 49 38N 6 2 E
Mamers, *France* **22 D7** 48 21N 0 22 E
Mamfe, *Cameroon* **101 D6** 5 50N 9 15 E
Māmī, Ra's, *Yemen* **87 D6** 12 32N 54 30 E
Mamiña, *Chile* **156 E4** 20 5 S 69 14W
Mámmola, *Italy* **41 D9** 38 23N 16 13 E
Mammoth, *U.S.A.* **143 K8** 32 43N 110 39W
Mamoré →, *Bolivia* **157 C4** 10 23 S 65 53W
Mamou, *Guinea* **100 C2** 10 15N 12 0W
Mamparang Mts., *Phil.* **70 C3** 16 21N 121 28 E
Mampatá, *Guinea-Biss.* **100 C2** 11 54N 14 53W
Mampong, *Ghana* **101 D4** 7 6N 1 26W
Mamry, Jezioro, *Poland* **47 A8** 54 5N 21 50 E
Mamuil Malal, Paso, *S. Amer.* **160 A2** 39 35 S 71 28W
Mamuju, *Indonesia* **72 B1** 2 41 S 118 50 E
Ma'mūl, *Oman* **87 C6** 18 8N 55 16 E
Man, *Ivory C.* **100 D3** 7 30N 7 40W
Man →, *India* **82 F2** 17 31N 75 32 E
Man, I. of, *U.K.* **16 C3** 54 15N 4 30W
Man Na, *Burma* **78 D6** 23 27N 97 19 E
Man Tun, *Burma* **78 D7** 23 22N 98 38 E
Mana, *Fr. Guiana* **153 B7** 5 45N 53 55W
Mana →, *Fr. Guiana* **153 B7** 5 45N 53 55W
Måna →, *Norway* **14 E2** 59 55N 8 50 E
Manaar, G. of = Mannar, G. of, *Asia* **83 K4** 8 30N 79 0 E
Manabí □, *Ecuador* **152 D1** 0 40 S 80 5W
Manacacías →, *Colombia* **152 C3** 4 23N 72 4W
Manacapuru, *Brazil* **153 D5** 3 16 S 60 37W
Manacapuru →, *Brazil* **153 D5** 3 18 S 60 37W
Manacor, *Spain* **33 B10** 39 34N 3 13 E
Manado, *Indonesia* **72 A2** 1 29N 124 51 E
Manage, *Belgium* **21 G4** 50 31N 4 15 E
Managua, *Nic.* **148 D2** 12 6N 86 20W
Managua, L., *Nic.* **148 D2** 12 20N 86 30W
Manaia, *N.Z.* **118 F3** 39 33 S 174 8 E
Manakara, *Madag.* **105 C8** 22 8 S 48 1 E
Manakau Mt., *N.Z.* **119 C8** 42 15 S 173 42 E
Manākhah, *Yemen* **86 D3** 15 5N 43 44 E
Manakino, *N.Z.* **118 E4** 38 22 S 175 47 E
Manam I., *Papua N. G.* **120 C3** 4 5 S 145 0 E
Manama = Al Manāmah, *Bahrain* **85 E6** 26 10N 50 30 E
Manambao →, *Madag.* **105 B7** 17 35 S 44 0 E
Manambato, *Madag.* **105 A8** 13 43 S 49 7 E
Manambolo →, *Madag.* **105 B7** 19 18 S 44 22 E
Manambolosy, *Madag.* **105 B8** 16 2 S 49 40 E
Mananara, *Madag.* **105 B8** 16 10 S 49 46 E
Mananara →, *Madag.* **105 C8** 23 21 S 47 42 E
Mananjary, *Madag.* **105 C8** 21 13 S 48 20 E
Manantenina, *Madag.* **105 C8** 24 17 S 47 19 E
Manaos = Manaus, *Brazil* **153 D6** 3 0 S 60 0W
Manapala, *Phil.* **71 F4** 10 58N 123 5 E
Manapire →, *Venezuela* **152 B4** 7 42N 66 7W
Manapouri, *N.Z.* **119 F2** 45 34 S 167 39 E
Manapouri, L., *N.Z.* **119 F2** 45 32 S 167 32 E
Manar →, *India* **82 E3** 18 50N 77 20 E
Manār, Jabal, *Yemen* **86 D4** 14 2N 44 17 E
Manas, *China* **64 B3** 44 17N 85 56 E
Manas, *Somali Rep.* **108 D2** 2 57N 43 28 E
Manas, Gora, *Kirghizia* **55 B5** 42 22N 71 2 E
Manaslu, *Nepal* **81 E11** 28 33N 84 33 E
Manasquan, *U.S.A.* **137 F10** 40 8N 74 3W
Manassa, *U.S.A.* **143 H11** 37 11N 105 56W
Manaung, *Burma* **78 F4** 18 45N 93 40 E
Manaus, *Brazil* **153 D6** 3 0 S 60 0W
Manavgat, *Turkey* **88 E4** 36 47N 31 26 E
Manawan L., *Canada* **131 B8** 55 24N 103 14W
Manawatu →, *N.Z.* **118 G4** 40 28 S 175 12 E
Manay, *Phil.* **71 H6** 7 17N 126 33 E
Manbij, *Syria* **84 B3** 36 31N 37 57 E
Mancelona, *U.S.A.* **134 C3** 44 54N 85 4W
Mancha Real, *Spain* **37 H7** 37 48N 3 39W
Manche □, *France* **22 C5** 49 10N 1 20W
Manchegorsk, *Russia* **48 A5** 67 40N 32 40 E
Manchester, *U.K.* **16 D5** 53 30N 2 15W
Manchester, *Calif., U.S.A.* **144 G3** 38 58N 123 41W
Manchester, *Conn., U.S.A.* **137 E12** 41 47N 72 31W
Manchester, *Ga., U.S.A.* **135 J3** 32 51N 84 37W
Manchester, *Iowa, U.S.A.* **140 B5** 42 29N 91 27W
Manchester, *Ky., U.S.A.* **134 G4** 37 9N 83 46W
Manchester, *Mich., U.S.A.* **141 B12** 42 9N 84 2W
Manchester, *N.H., U.S.A.* **137 D13** 42 59N 71 28W
Manchester, *N.Y., U.S.A.* **136 D7** 42 56N 77 16W
Manchester, *Vt., U.S.A.* **137 C11** 43 10N 73 5W
Manchester L., *Canada* **131 A7** 61 28N 107 29W
Manchuria = Dongbei, *China* **67 D13** 42 0N 125 0 E
Manciano, *Italy* **39 F8** 42 35N 11 30 E
Mancifa, *Ethiopia* **95 F5** 6 53N 41 50 E
Mancora, Pta., *Peru* **156 A1** 4 9 S 81 1W
Mand →, *Iran* **85 D7** 28 20N 52 30 E
Manda, *Chunya, Tanzania* **106 D3** 6 51 S 32 29 E
Manda, *Ludewe, Tanzania* **107 E3** 10 30 S 34 40 E
Mandabé, *Madag.* **105 C7** 21 0 S 44 55 E
Mandaguari, *Brazil* **159 A5** 23 32 S 51 42W
Mandah, *Mongolia* **66 B5** 44 27N 108 2 E
Mandal, *Norway* **13 G9** 58 2N 7 25 E
Mandalay, *Burma* **78 D6** 22 0N 96 4 E
Mandale = Mandalay, *Burma* **78 D6** 22 0N 96 4 E
Mandalgovi, *Mongolia* **66 B4** 45 45N 106 10 E
Mandalī, *Iraq* **84 C5** 33 43N 45 28 E
Mandalya Körfezi, *Turkey* **45 G9** 37 15N 27 20 E
Mandan, *U.S.A.* **138 B4** 46 50N 100 54W
Mandaon, *Phil.* **70 E4** 12 13N 123 17 E
Mandapeta, *India* **82 F5** 16 47N 81 56 E
Mandar, Teluk, *Indonesia* **72 B1** 3 35 S 119 15 E
Mandas, *Italy* **40 C2** 39 40N 9 8 E
Mandasor = Mandsaur, *India* **80 G6** 24 3N 75 8 E
Mandaue, *Phil.* **71 F4** 10 20N 123 56 E
Mandayar, *Phil.* **71 H6** 7 34N 126 14 E
Mandelieu-la-Napoule, *France* **25 E10** 43 34N 6 57 E
Mandera, *Kenya* **106 B5** 3 55N 41 53 E
Mandera □, *Kenya* **106 B5** 3 30N 41 0 E
Manderfeld, *Belgium* **21 H8** 50 20N 6 20 E
Mandi, *India* **80 D7** 31 39N 76 58 E
Mandimba, *Mozam.* **107 E4** 14 20 S 35 40 E
Mandioli, *Indonesia* **72 B3** 0 40 S 127 20 E
Mandioré, L., *S. Amer.* **157 D6** 18 8 S 57 33W
Mandji I. = Lopez I., *Gabon* **102 C1** 0 50 S 8 47 E
Mandla, *India* **81 H9** 22 39N 80 30 E
Mandø, *Denmark* **15 J2** 55 18N 8 33 E
Mandoto, *Madag.* **105 B8** 19 34 S 46 17 E
Mandoúdhion, *Greece* **45 F5** 38 48N 23 29 E
Mandra, *Pakistan* **80 C5** 33 23N 73 12 E
Mandráki, *Greece* **45 H9** 36 36N 27 11 E
Mandrare →, *Madag.* **105 D8** 25 10 S 46 30 E
Mandritsara, *Madag.* **105 B8** 15 50 S 48 49 E
Mandsaur, *India* **80 G6** 24 3N 75 8 E
Mandurah, *Australia* **113 F2** 32 36 S 115 48 E
Mandúria, *Italy* **41 B10** 40 25N 17 38 E
Mandvi, *India* **80 H3** 22 51N 69 22 E
Mandya, *India* **83 H3** 12 30N 77 0 E
Mandzai, *Pakistan* **80 D2** 30 55N 67 6 E
Mané, *Burkina Faso* **101 C4** 12 59N 1 21W
Maneh, *Iran* **85 B8** 37 39N 57 7 E
Manengouba, Mts., *Cameroon* **101 D6** 5 0N 9 50 E
Maner →, *India* **82 E4** 18 30N 79 40 E
Maneroo, *Australia* **114 C3** 23 22 S 143 53 E
Maneroo Cr. →, *Australia* **114 C3** 23 21 S 143 53 E
Manfalût, *Egypt* **94 B3** 27 20N 30 52 E
Manfred, *Australia* **116 B5** 33 19 S 143 45 E
Manfredónia, *Italy* **41 A8** 41 40N 15 55 E
Manfredónia, G. di, *Italy* **41 A9** 41 30N 16 10 E
Manga, *Brazil* **155 D3** 14 46 S 43 56W
Manga, *Burkina Faso* **101 C4** 11 40N 1 4W
Manga, *Niger* **97 F2** 15 0N 14 0 E
Mangabeiras, Chapada das, *Brazil* **154 D2** 10 0 S 46 30W
Mangal, *Phil.* **71 H3** 6 25N 121 58 E
Mangalagiri, *India* **83 F5** 16 26N 80 36 E
Mangaldai, *India* **78 B4** 26 26N 92 2 E
Mangalia, *Romania* **46 F9** 43 50N 28 35 E
Mangalore, *Australia* **117 D6** 36 56 S 145 10 E
Mangalore, *India* **83 H2** 12 55N 74 47 E
Manganeses, *Spain* **36 D5** 41 45N 5 43W
Mangaon, *India* **82 E1** 18 15N 73 20 E
Mangaweka, *N.Z.* **118 F4** 39 48 S 175 47 E
Mangaweka, Mt., *N.Z.* **118 F5** 39 49 S 176 5 E
Mange, *Zaïre* **102 B4** 0 54N 20 30 E
Manggar, *Indonesia* **75 C3** 2 50 S 108 10 E
Manggawitu, *Indonesia* **73 B4** 4 8 S 133 32 E
Mangin Range, *Burma* **78 C5** 24 15N 95 45 E
Mangkalihat, Tanjung, *Indonesia* **75 B5** 1 2N 118 59 E
Mangla Dam, *Pakistan* **81 C5** 33 9N 73 44 E
Manglares, C., *Colombia* **152 C2** 1 36N 79 2W
Manglaur, *India* **80 E7** 29 44N 77 49 E
Mangnai, *China* **64 C4** 37 52N 91 43 E
Mango, *Togo* **101 C5** 10 20N 0 30 E
Mangoche, *Malawi* **107 E4** 14 25 S 35 16 E
Mangoky →, *Madag.* **105 C7** 21 29 S 43 41 E
Mangole, *Indonesia* **72 B3** 1 50 S 125 55 E
Mangombe, *Zaïre* **106 C2** 1 20 S 26 48 E
Mangonui, *N.Z.* **118 B2** 35 1 S 173 32 E
Mangualde, *Portugal* **36 E3** 40 38N 7 48W
Mangueigne, *Chad* **97 F4** 10 30N 21 15 E
Mangueira, L. da, *Brazil* **159 C5** 33 0 S 52 50W
Manguéni, Hamada, *Niger* **96 D2** 22 35N 12 40 E
Mangum, *U.S.A.* **139 H5** 34 53N 99 30W
Mangyshlak Poluostrov, *Kazakhstan* **53 D15** 44 30N 52 30 E
Mangyshlakskiy Zaliv, *Kazakhstan* **53 D14** 44 40N 50 50 E

**Mawlaik 231**


Marla, *Australia* 115 D1 27 19 S 133 33 E
Marlboro, *U.S.A.* 137 D13 42 19N 71 33W
Marlborough, *Australia* 114 C4 22 46 S 149 52 E
Marlborough Downs, *U.K.* 17 F6 51 25N 1 55W
Marle, *France* 23 C10 49 43N 3 47 E
Marlin, *U.S.A.* 139 K6 31 18N 96 54W
Marlow, *Germany* 26 A8 54 8N 12 34 E
Marlow, *U.S.A.* 139 H6 34 39N 97 58W
Marly-le-Grand, *Switz.* 28 C4 46 47N 7 10 E
Marmagao, *India* 83 G1 15 25N 73 56 E
Marmande, *France* 24 D4 44 30N 0 10 E
Marmara, *Turkey* 52 F2 40 35N 27 38 E
Marmara, Sea of = Marmara Denizi, *Turkey* 88 C3 40 45N 28 15 E
Marmara Denizi, *Turkey* 88 C3 40 45N 28 15 E
Marmara Gölü, *Turkey* 88 D3 38 37N 28 0 E
Marmaris, *Turkey* 88 E3 36 50N 28 14 E
Marmarth, *U.S.A.* 138 B3 46 18N 103 54W
Marmelos →, *Brazil* 157 B5 6 6 S 61 46W
Marmion, Mt., *Australia* 113 E2 29 16 S 119 50 E
Marmion L., *Canada* 128 C1 48 55N 91 20W
Marmolada, Mte., *Italy* 39 B8 46 25N 11 55 E
Marmolejo, *Spain* 37 G6 38 3N 4 13W
Marmora, *Canada* 128 D4 44 28N 77 41W
Marnay, *France* 23 E12 47 16N 5 48 E
Marne, *Germany* 26 B5 53 57N 9 1 E
Marne □, *France* 23 D11 48 50N 4 10 E
Marne →, *France* 23 D9 48 48N 2 24 E
Marneuli, *Georgia* 53 F11 41 30N 44 48 E
Maro, *Chad* 97 G3 8 30N 19 0 E
Maroa, *Venezuela* 152 C4 2 43N 67 33W
Maroala, *Madag.* 105 B8 15 23 S 47 59 E
Maroantsetra, *Madag.* 105 B8 15 26 S 49 44 E
Maromandia, *Madag.* 105 A8 14 13 S 48 5 E
Marondera, *Zimbabwe* 107 F3 18 5 S 31 42 E
Maroni →, *Fr. Guiana* 153 B7 5 30N 54 0W
Marónia, *Greece* 44 D7 40 53N 25 24 E
Maronne →, *France* 24 C5 45 5N 1 56 E
Maroochydore, *Australia* 115 D5 26 29 S 153 5 E
Maroona, *Australia* 116 D5 37 27 S 142 54 E
Maros, *Indonesia* 72 C1 5 0 S 119 34 E
Maros →, *Hungary* 31 E13 46 15N 20 13 E
Marosakoa, *Madag.* 105 B8 15 26 S 46 38 E
Marostica, *Italy* 39 C8 45 44N 11 40 E
Maroua, *Cameroon* 101 C7 10 40N 14 20 E
Marovoay, *Madag.* 105 B8 16 6 S 46 39 E
Marowijne □, *Surinam* 153 C7 4 0N 55 0W
Marowijne →, *Surinam* 153 B7 5 45N 53 58W
Marquard, *S. Africa* 104 D4 28 40 S 27 28 E
Marqueira, *Portugal* 37 G1 38 41N 9 9W
Marquesas Is. = Marquises, Is., *Pac. Oc.* 123 H14 9 30 S 140 0W
Marquette, *U.S.A.* 134 B2 46 33N 87 24W
Marquise, *France* 23 B8 50 50N 1 40 E
Marquises, Is., *Pac. Oc.* 123 H14 9 30 S 140 0W
Marra, Gebel, *Sudan* 95 F2 7 20N 27 35 E
Marracuene, *Mozam.* 105 D5 25 45 S 32 35 E
Marradi, *Italy* 39 D8 44 5N 11 37 E
Marrakech, *Morocco* 98 B3 31 9N 8 0W
Marrawah, *Australia* 114 G3 40 55 S 144 42 E
Marrecas, Serra das, *Brazil* 154 C3 9 0 S 41 0W
Marree, *Australia* 115 D2 29 39 S 138 1 E
Marrilla, *Australia* 112 D1 22 31 S 114 25 E
Marrimane, *Mozam.* 105 C5 22 58 S 33 34 E
Marromeu, *Mozam.* 105 B6 18 15 S 36 25 E
Marroquí, Punta, *Spain* 37 K5 36 0N 5 37W
Marrowie Cr. →, *Australia* 117 B6 33 23 S 145 40 E
Marrubane, *Mozam.* 107 F4 18 0 S 37 0 E
Marrum, *Neths.* 20 B7 53 19N 5 48 E
Marrupa, *Mozam.* 107 E4 13 8 S 37 30 E
Marsa Brega, *Libya* 96 B3 30 24N 19 37 E
Marsá Matrûh, *Egypt* 94 A2 31 19N 27 9 E
Marsá Susah, *Libya* 96 B4 32 52N 21 59 E
Marsabit, *Kenya* 106 B4 2 18N 38 0 E
Marsabit □, *Kenya* 106 B4 2 45N 37 45 E
Marsala, *Italy* 40 E5 37 48N 12 25 E
Marsalforn, *Malta* 32 C1 36 4N 14 15 E
Marsberg, *Germany* 26 D4 51 28N 8 52 E
Marsciano, *Italy* 39 F9 42 54N 12 20 E
Marsden, *Australia* 117 B7 33 47 S 147 32 E
Marsdiep, *Neths.* 20 C5 52 58N 4 46 E
Marseillan, *France* 24 E7 43 23N 3 31 E
Marseille, *France* 25 E9 43 18N 5 23 E
Marseilles = Marseille, *France* 25 E9 43 18N 5 23 E
Marseilles, *U.S.A.* 141 C8 41 20N 88 43W
Marsh I., *U.S.A.* 139 L9 29 34N 91 53W
Marsh L., *U.S.A.* 138 C6 45 5N 96 0W
Marshall, *Liberia* 100 D2 6 8N 10 22W
Marshall, *Ark., U.S.A.* 139 H8 35 55N 92 38W
Marshall, *Ill., U.S.A.* 141 E9 39 23N 87 42W
Marshall, *Mich., U.S.A.* 141 B12 42 16N 84 58W
Marshall, *Minn., U.S.A.* 138 C7 44 25N 95 45W
Marshall, *Mo., U.S.A.* 140 E3 39 7N 93 12W
Marshall, *Tex., U.S.A.* 139 J7 32 33N 94 23W
Marshall →, *Australia* 114 C2 22 59 S 136 59 E
Marshall Is. ■, *Pac. Oc.* 122 G9 9 0N 171 0 E
Marshalltown, *U.S.A.* 140 B4 42 3N 92 55W
Marshfield, *Mo., U.S.A.* 139 G8 37 15N 92 54W
Marshfield, *Wis., U.S.A.* 138 C9 44 40N 90 10W
Marshūn, *Iran* 85 B6 36 19N 49 23 E
Mársico Nuovo, *Italy* 41 B8 40 26N 15 43 E
Märsta, *Sweden* 14 E11 59 37N 17 52 E
Marstal, *Denmark* 15 K4 54 51N 10 30 E
Marstrand, *Sweden* 15 G5 57 53N 11 35 E
Mart, *U.S.A.* 139 K6 31 33N 96 50W
Marta →, *Italy* 39 F8 42 14N 11 42 E
Martaban, *Burma* 78 G6 16 30N 97 35 E
Martaban, G. of, *Burma* 78 G6 16 5N 96 30 E
Martano, *Italy* 41 B11 40 14N 18 18 E
Martapura, *Kalimantan, Indonesia* 75 C4 3 22 S 114 47 E
Martapura, *Sumatera, Indonesia* 74 C2 4 19 S 104 22 E
Marte, *Nigeria* 101 C7 12 23N 13 46 E
Martel, *France* 24 D5 44 57N 1 37 E
Martelange, *Belgium* 21 J7 49 49N 5 43 E
Martensdale, *U.S.A.* 140 C3 41 23N 93 45W
Martés, Sierra, *Spain* 35 F4 39 20N 1 0W
Martha's Vineyard, *U.S.A.* 137 E14 41 25N 70 38W
Martigné-Ferchaud, *France* 22 E5 47 50N 1 20W
Martigny, *Switz.* 28 D4 46 6N 7 3 E
Martigues, *France* 25 E9 43 24N 5 4 E
Martil, *Morocco* 98 A3 35 36N 5 15W
Martin, *Slovak Rep.* 31 B11 49 6N 18 48 E
Martin, *S. Dak., U.S.A.* 138 D4 43 11N 101 44W
Martin, *Tenn., U.S.A.* 139 G10 36 21N 88 51W
Martín →, *Spain* 34 D4 41 18N 0 19W
Martin L., *U.S.A.* 135 J3 32 41N 85 55W
Martina, *Switz.* 29 C10 46 53N 10 28 E
Martina Franca, *Italy* 41 B10 40 42N 17 20 E
Martinborough, *N.Z.* 118 H4 41 14 S 175 29 E
Martinez, *U.S.A.* 144 G4 38 1N 122 8W
Martinho Campos, *Brazil* 155 E2 19 20 S 45 13W
Martinique ■, *W. Indies* 149 D7 14 40N 61 0W
Martinique Passage, *W. Indies* 149 C7 15 15N 61 0W
Martínon, *Greece* 45 F5 38 35N 23 15 E
Martinópolis, *Brazil* 159 A5 22 11 S 51 12W
Martins Ferry, *U.S.A.* 136 F4 40 6N 80 44W
Martinsberg, *Austria* 30 C8 48 22N 15 9 E
Martinsburg, *Pa., U.S.A.* 136 F6 40 19N 78 20W
Martinsburg, *W. Va., U.S.A.* 134 F7 39 27N 77 58W
Martinsville, *Ill., U.S.A.* 141 E9 39 20N 87 53W
Martinsville, *Ind., U.S.A.* 141 E10 39 26N 86 25W
Martinsville, *Va., U.S.A.* 135 G6 36 41N 79 52W
Marton, *N.Z.* 118 G4 40 4 S 175 23 E
Martorell, *Spain* 34 D6 41 28N 1 56 E
Martos, *Spain* 37 H7 37 44N 3 58W
Martūbah, *Libya* 96 B4 32 35N 22 46 E
Martuk, *Kazakhstan* 54 F5 50 46N 56 31 E
Martuni, *Armenia* 53 F11 40 9N 45 10 E
Maru, *Nigeria* 101 C6 12 22N 6 22 E
Marudi, *Malaysia* 75 B4 4 11N 114 19 E
Ma'ruf, *Afghan.* 79 C2 31 30N 67 6 E
Marugame, *Japan* 62 C5 34 15N 133 40 E
Marúggio, *Italy* 41 B10 40 20N 17 33 E
Marui, *Papua N. G.* 120 C2 4 4 S 143 2 E
Maruia →, *N.Z.* 119 B7 41 47 S 172 13 E
Maruim, *Brazil* 154 D4 10 45 S 37 5W
Marulan, *Australia* 117 C9 34 43 S 150 3 E
Marum, *Neths.* 20 B8 53 9N 6 16 E
Marum, Mt., *Vanuatu* 121 F6 16 15 S 168 7 E
Marunga, *Angola* 103 F4 17 28 S 20 2 E
Marungu, Mts., *Zaïre* 106 D2 7 30 S 30 0 E
Maruoka, *Japan* 63 A8 36 9N 136 16 E
Marvast, *Iran* 85 D7 30 30N 54 15 E
Marvejols, *France* 24 D7 44 33N 3 19 E
Marwar, *India* 80 G5 25 43N 73 45 E
Mary, *Turkmenistan* 56 F7 37 40N 61 50 E
Mary Frances L., *Canada* 131 A7 63 19N 106 13W
Mary Kathleen, *Australia* 114 C2 20 44 S 139 48 E
Maryborough = Port Laoise, *Ireland* 19 C4 53 2N 7 20W
Maryborough, *Queens., Australia* 115 D5 25 31 S 152 37 E
Maryborough, *Vic., Australia* 116 D5 37 0 S 143 44 E
Maryfield, *Canada* 131 D8 49 50N 101 35W
Maryland □, *U.S.A.* 134 F7 39 0N 76 30W
Maryland Junction, *Zimbabwe* 107 F3 17 45 S 30 31 E
Maryport, *U.K.* 16 C4 54 43N 3 30W
Mary's Harbour, *Canada* 129 B8 52 18N 55 51W
Marystown, *Canada* 129 C8 47 10N 55 10W
Marysvale, *U.S.A.* 143 G7 38 27N 112 14W
Marysville, *Canada* 130 D5 49 35N 116 0W
Marysville, *Calif., U.S.A.* 144 F5 39 9N 121 35W
Marysville, *Kans., U.S.A.* 138 F6 39 51N 96 39W
Marysville, *Mich., U.S.A.* 136 D2 42 54N 82 29W
Marysville, *Ohio, U.S.A.* 141 D13 40 14N 83 22W
Marysville, *Wash., U.S.A.* 144 B4 48 3N 122 11W
Maryvale, *Australia* 115 D5 28 4 S 152 12 E
Maryville, *Mo., U.S.A.* 140 D2 40 21N 94 52W
Maryville, *Tenn., U.S.A.* 135 H4 35 46N 83 58W
Marzo, Punta, *Colombia* 152 B2 6 50N 77 42W
Marzūq, *Libya* 96 C2 25 53N 13 57 E
Masahunga, *Tanzania* 106 C3 2 6 S 33 18 E
Masai, *Malaysia* 77 M4 1 29N 103 55 E
Masai Steppe, *Tanzania* 106 C4 4 30 S 36 30 E
Masaka, *Uganda* 106 C3 0 21 S 31 45 E
Masalembo, Kepulauan, *Indonesia* 75 D4 5 35 S 114 30 E
Masalima, Kepulauan, *Indonesia* 75 D5 5 4 S 117 5 E
Masamba, *Indonesia* 72 B2 2 30 S 120 15 E
Masan, *S. Korea* 67 G15 35 11N 128 32 E
Masanasa, *Spain* 35 F4 39 25N 0 25W
Masasi, *Tanzania* 107 E4 10 45 S 38 52 E
Masasi □, *Tanzania* 107 E4 10 45 S 38 50 E
Masaya, *Nic.* 148 D2 12 0N 86 7W
Masba, *Nigeria* 101 C7 10 35N 13 1 E
Masbate, *Phil.* 70 E4 12 21N 123 36 E
Masbate Pass, *Phil.* 70 E4 12 30N 123 35 E
Mascara, *Algeria* 99 A5 35 26N 0 6 E
Mascarene Is., *Ind. Oc.* 109 G4 22 0 S 55 0 E
Mascota, *Mexico* 146 C4 20 30N 104 50W
Mascoutah, *U.S.A.* 140 F7 38 29N 89 48W
Masela, *Indonesia* 73 C3 8 9 S 129 51 E
Maseru, *Lesotho* 104 D4 29 18 S 27 30 E
Mashaba, *Zimbabwe* 107 G3 20 2 S 30 29 E
Mashābih, *Si. Arabia* 84 E3 25 35N 36 30 E
Mashan, *China* 68 F7 23 40N 108 11 E
Masherbrum, *Pakistan* 81 B7 35 38N 76 18 E
Mashhad, *Iran* 85 B8 36 20N 59 35 E
Mashi, *Nigeria* 101 C6 13 0N 7 54 E
Mashiki, *Japan* 62 E2 32 51N 130 53 E
Mashīz, *Iran* 85 D8 29 56N 56 37 E
Mashkel, Hamun-i-, *Pakistan* 79 C1 28 30N 63 0 E
Mashki Chāh, *Pakistan* 79 C1 29 5N 62 30 E
Mashonaland Central □, *Zimbabwe* 105 B5 17 30 S 31 0 E
Mashonaland East □, *Zimbabwe* 105 B5 18 0 S 32 0 E
Mashonaland West □, *Zimbabwe* 105 B4 17 30 S 29 30 E
Mashtaga, *Azerbaijan* 53 F13 40 35N 49 57 E
Masi, *Norway* 12 B17 69 26N 23 40 E
Masi Manimba, *Zaïre* 103 C3 4 40 S 17 54 E
Masindi, *Uganda* 106 B3 1 40N 31 43 E
Masindi Port, *Uganda* 106 B3 1 43N 32 2 E
Masinloc, *Phil.* 70 D2 15 32N 119 57 E
Maşīrah, Khalīj, *Oman* 87 B7 20 10N 58 10 E
Maşīrah, Tur'at, *Oman* 87 B7 20 30N 58 40 E
Masisea, *Peru* 156 B3 8 35 S 74 22W
Masisi, *Zaïre* 106 C2 1 23 S 28 49 E
Masjed Soleyman, *Iran* 85 D6 31 55N 49 18 E
Mask, L., *Ireland* 19 C2 53 36N 9 24W
Maskelyne Is., *Vanuatu* 121 F5 16 32 S 167 49 E
Maski, *India* 83 G3 15 56N 76 46 E
Maslen Nos, *Bulgaria* 43 E12 42 18N 27 48 E
Maslinica, *Croatia* 39 E13 43 24N 16 13 E
Maşna'ah, *Yemen* 87 D5 14 27N 48 17 E
Masnou, *Spain* 34 D7 41 28N 2 20 E
Masoala, Tanjon' i, *Madag.* 105 B9 15 59 S 50 13 E
Masoarivo, *Madag.* 105 B7 19 3 S 44 19 E
Masohi, *Indonesia* 73 B3 3 20 S 128 55 E
Masomeloka, *Madag.* 105 C8 20 17 S 48 37 E
Mason, *Mich., U.S.A.* 141 B12 42 35N 84 27W
Mason, *Nev., U.S.A.* 144 G7 38 56N 119 8W
Mason, *Ohio, U.S.A.* 141 E12 39 22N 84 19W
Mason, *Tex., U.S.A.* 139 K5 30 45N 99 14W
Mason B., *N.Z.* 119 G2 46 55 S 167 45 E
Mason City, *Ill., U.S.A.* 140 D7 40 12N 89 42W
Mason City, *Iowa, U.S.A.* 140 A3 43 9N 93 12W
Maspalomas, *Canary Is.* 33 G4 27 46N 15 35W
Maspalomas, Pta., *Canary Is.* 33 G4 27 43N 15 36W
Masqat, *Oman* 87 B7 23 37N 58 36 E
Massa, *Congo* 102 C3 3 45 S 15 29 E
Massa, *Italy* 38 D7 44 2N 10 7 E
Massa, O. →, *Morocco* 98 B3 30 2N 9 40W
Massa Maríttima, *Italy* 38 E7 43 3N 10 52 E
Massachusetts □, *U.S.A.* 137 D12 42 30N 72 0W
Massachusetts B., *U.S.A.* 137 D14 42 20N 70 50W
Massafra, *Italy* 41 B10 40 35N 17 8 E
Massaguet, *Chad* 97 F3 12 28N 15 26 E
Massakory, *Chad* 97 F3 13 0N 15 49 E
Massanella, *Spain* 33 B9 39 48N 2 51 E
Massangena, *Mozam.* 105 C5 21 34 S 33 0 E
Massapê, *Brazil* 154 B3 3 31 S 40 19W
Massarosa, *Italy* 38 E7 43 53N 10 17 E
Massat, *France* 24 F5 42 53N 1 21 E
Massava, *Russia* 54 A8 60 40N 62 6 E
Massawa = Mitsiwa, *Eritrea* 95 D4 15 35N 39 25 E
Massena, *U.S.A.* 137 B10 44 56N 74 54W
Masséna, *Chad* 97 F3 11 21N 16 9 E
Masset, *Canada* 130 C2 54 2N 132 10W
Massiac, *France* 24 C7 45 15N 3 11 E
Massif Central, *France* 24 D7 44 55N 3 0 E
Massillon, *U.S.A.* 136 F3 40 48N 81 32W
Massinga, *Mozam.* 105 C6 23 15 S 35 22 E
Masson, *Canada* 137 A9 45 32N 75 25W
Masson I., *Antarctica* 7 C7 66 10 S 93 20 E
Mastābah, *Si. Arabia* 86 B2 20 49N 39 26 E
Mastanli = Momchilgrad, *Bulgaria* 43 F10 41 33N 25 23 E
Masterton, *N.Z.* 118 G4 40 56 S 175 39 E
Mástikho, Ákra, *Greece* 45 F8 38 10N 26 2 E
Mastuj, *Pakistan* 81 A5 36 20N 72 36 E
Mastung, *Pakistan* 79 C2 29 50N 66 56 E
Mastūrah, *Si. Arabia* 86 B2 23 7N 38 52 E
Masuda, *Japan* 62 C3 34 40N 131 51 E
Masuika, *Zaïre* 103 D4 7 37 S 22 32 E
Masvingo, *Zimbabwe* 107 G3 20 8 S 30 49 E
Masvingo □, *Zimbabwe* 107 G3 21 0 S 31 30 E
Maswa □, *Tanzania* 106 C3 3 30 S 34 0 E
Maşyāf, *Syria* 84 C3 35 4N 36 20 E
Mata de São João, *Brazil* 155 D4 12 31 S 38 17W
Mata Utu, *Wall. & F. Is.* 111 C15 13 17 S 176 8W
Matabeleland North □, *Zimbabwe* 107 F2 19 0 S 28 0 E
Matabeleland South □, *Zimbabwe* 107 G2 21 0 S 29 0 E
Mataboor, *Indonesia* 73 B5 1 41 S 138 3 E
Matachel →, *Spain* 37 G4 38 50N 6 17W
Matachewan, *Canada* 128 C3 47 56N 80 39W
Matacuni →, *Venezuela* 153 C4 3 2N 65 16W
Matadi, *Zaïre* 103 D2 5 52 S 13 31 E
Matagalpa, *Nic.* 148 D2 13 0N 85 58W
Matagami, *Canada* 128 C4 49 45N 77 34W
Matagami, L., *Canada* 128 C4 49 50N 77 40W
Matagorda, *U.S.A.* 139 L7 28 42N 95 58W
Matagorda B., *U.S.A.* 139 L6 28 40N 96 0W
Matagorda I., *U.S.A.* 139 L6 28 15N 96 30W
Mataguinao, *Phil.* 70 E5 12 5N 124 55 E
Matak, P., *Indonesia* 77 L6 3 18N 106 16 E
Matakana, *Australia* 117 B6 32 59 S 145 54 E
Matakana, *N.Z.* 118 C3 36 21 S 174 43 E
Matakana I., *N.Z.* 118 C3 36 21 S 174 43 E
Matala, *Angola* 103 E3 14 46 S 15 4 E
Mátala, *Greece* 32 E6 34 59N 24 45 E
Matalaque, *Peru* 156 D3 16 26 S 70 49W
Matale, *Sri Lanka* 83 L5 7 30N 80 37 E
Matam, *Phil.* 71 G4 8 25N 123 19 E
Matam, *Senegal* 100 B2 15 34N 13 17W
Matamata, *N.Z.* 118 D4 37 48 S 175 47 E
Matameye, *Niger* 97 F1 13 26N 8 28 E
Matamoros, *Campeche, Mexico* 147 D6 18 50N 90 50W
Matamoros, *Coahuila, Mexico* 146 B4 25 33N 103 15W
Matamoros, *Puebla, Mexico* 147 D5 18 2N 98 17W
Matamoros, *Tamaulipas, Mexico* 147 B5 25 50N 97 30W
Ma'ţan as Sarra, *Libya* 97 D4 21 45N 22 0 E
Matandu →, *Tanzania* 107 D3 8 45 S 34 19 E
Matane, *Canada* 129 C6 48 50N 67 33W
Matang, *China* 68 F5 23 30N 104 7 E
Matankari, *Niger* 101 C5 13 46N 4 1 E
Matanzas, *Cuba* 148 B3 23 0N 81 40W
Matapan, C. = Taínaron, Ákra, *Greece* 45 H4 36 22N 22 27 E
Matapédia, *Canada* 129 C6 48 0N 66 59W
Matara, *Sri Lanka* 83 M5 5 58N 80 30 E
Mataram, *Indonesia* 75 D5 8 41 S 116 10 E
Matarani, *Peru* 156 D3 17 0 S 72 10W
Mataranka, *Australia* 112 B5 14 55 S 133 4 E
Matarma, Râs, *Egypt* 91 E1 30 27N 32 44 E
Mataró, *Spain* 34 D7 41 32N 2 29 E
Matarraña →, *Spain* 34 D5 41 14N 0 22 E
Mataruška Banja, *Serbia* 42 D5 43 40N 20 45 E
Mataso, *Vanuatu* 121 G6 17 14 S 168 26 E
Matata, *N.Z.* 118 D5 37 54 S 176 48 E
Matatiele, *S. Africa* 105 E4 30 20 S 28 49 E
Mataura, *N.Z.* 119 G3 46 11 S 168 51 E
Mataura →, *N.Z.* 119 G3 46 34 S 168 44 E
Mategua, *Bolivia* 157 C5 13 1 S 62 48W
Matehuala, *Mexico* 146 C4 23 40N 100 40W
Mateira, *Brazil* 155 E1 18 54 S 50 30W
Mateke Hills, *Zimbabwe* 107 G3 21 48 S 31 0 E
Matélica, *Italy* 39 E10 43 15N 13 0 E
Matera, *Italy* 41 B9 40 40N 16 37 E
Mátészalka, *Hungary* 31 D15 47 58N 22 20 E
Matetsi, *Zimbabwe* 107 F2 18 12 S 26 0 E
Mateur, *Tunisia* 96 A1 37 0N 9 40 E
Matfors, *Sweden* 14 B11 62 21N 17 2 E
Matha, *France* 24 C3 45 52N 0 20W
Matheson Island, *Canada* 131 C9 51 45N 96 56W
Mathis, *U.S.A.* 139 L6 28 6N 97 50W
Mathoura, *Australia* 117 C6 35 50 S 144 55 E
Mathura, *India* 80 F7 27 30N 77 40 E
Mati, *Phil.* 71 H6 6 55N 126 15 E
Mati →, *Albania* 44 C1 41 40N 19 35 E
Matías Romero, *Mexico* 147 D5 16 53N 95 2W
Matibane, *Mozam.* 107 E5 14 49 S 40 45 E
Matican, *Phil.* 71 H3 6 39N 121 53 E
Matima, *Botswana* 104 C3 20 15 S 24 26 E
Matiri Ra., *N.Z.* 119 B7 41 38 S 172 20 E
Matlock, *U.K.* 16 D6 53 8N 1 32W
Matmata, *Tunisia* 96 B1 33 37N 9 59 E
Matna, *Sudan* 95 E4 13 49N 35 10 E
Matnog, *Phil.* 70 E5 12 35N 124 5 E
Mato →, *Venezuela* 153 B4 7 9N 65 7W
Mato, Serrania de, *Venezuela* 152 B4 6 25N 65 25W
Mato Grosso □, *Brazil* 157 C6 14 0 S 55 0W
Mato Grosso, Planalto do, *Brazil* 157 C7 15 0 S 55 0W
Mato Grosso do Sul □, *Brazil* 157 D7 18 0 S 55 0W
Matochkin Shar, *Russia* 56 B6 73 10N 56 40 E
Matong, *Papua N. G.* 120 C6 5 36 S 151 50 E
Matopo Hills, *Zimbabwe* 107 G2 20 36 S 28 20 E
Matopos, *Zimbabwe* 107 G2 20 20 S 28 29 E
Matosinhos, *Portugal* 36 D2 41 11N 8 42W
Matour, *France* 25 B8 46 19N 4 29 E
Matrah, *Oman* 87 B7 23 37N 58 30 E
Matsena, *Nigeria* 101 C7 13 5N 10 5 E
Matsesta, *Russia* 53 E8 43 34N 39 51 E
Matsubara, *Japan* 63 C7 34 33N 135 34 E
Matsudo, *Japan* 63 B11 35 47N 139 54 E
Matsue, *Japan* 62 B5 35 25N 133 10 E
Matsumae, *Japan* 60 D10 41 26N 140 7 E
Matsumoto, *Japan* 63 A9 36 15N 138 0 E
Matsusaka, *Japan* 63 C8 34 34N 136 32 E
Matsutō, *Japan* 63 A8 36 31N 136 34 E
Matsuura, *Japan* 62 D1 33 20N 129 49 E
Matsuyama, *Japan* 62 D4 33 45N 132 45 E
Matsuzaki, *Japan* 63 C10 34 43N 138 50 E
Mattagami →, *Canada* 128 B3 50 43N 81 29W
Mattancheri, *India* 83 K3 9 50N 76 15 E
Mattawa, *Canada* 128 C4 46 20N 78 45W
Mattawamkeag, *U.S.A.* 129 C6 45 32N 68 21W
Matterhorn, *Switz.* 28 E5 45 58N 7 39 E
Mattersburg, *Austria* 31 D9 47 44N 16 24 E
Matteson, *U.S.A.* 141 C9 41 30N 87 42W
Matthew Town, *Bahamas* 149 B5 20 57N 73 40W
Matthews, *U.S.A.* 141 D11 40 23N 85 30W
Matthew's Ridge, *Guyana* 153 B5 7 37N 60 10W
Mattice, *Canada* 128 C3 49 40N 83 20W
Mattituck, *U.S.A.* 137 F12 40 59N 72 32W
Mattmar, *Sweden* 14 A7 63 18N 13 45 E
Matuba, *Mozam.* 105 C5 24 28 S 32 49 E
Matucana, *Peru* 156 C2 11 55 S 76 25W
Matuku, *Fiji* 121 B2 19 10 S 179 44 E
Matun, *Afghan.* 80 C3 33 22N 69 58 E
Maturín, *Venezuela* 153 B5 9 45N 63 11W
Matutum, Mt., *Phil.* 71 H5 6 22N 125 5 E
Matveyev Kurgan, *Russia* 53 C8 47 35N 38 47 E
Mau, *India* 81 G10 25 56N 83 33 E
Mau Escarpment, *Kenya* 106 C4 0 40 S 36 0 E
Mau Ranipur, *India* 81 G8 25 16N 79 8 E
Mauban, *Phil.* 70 D3 14 12N 121 44 E
Maubeuge, *France* 23 B10 50 17N 3 57 E
Maubourguet, *France* 24 E4 43 29N 0 1 E
Maud, Pt., *Australia* 112 D1 23 6 S 113 45 E
Maude, *Australia* 116 C6 34 29 S 144 18 E
Maués, *Brazil* 153 D6 3 20 S 57 45W
Maui, *U.S.A.* 132 H16 20 48N 156 20W
Maulamyaing = Moulmein, *Burma* 78 G6 16 30N 97 40 E
Maule □, *Chile* 158 D1 36 5 S 72 30W
Mauléon-Licharre, *France* 24 E3 43 14N 0 54W
Maullín, *Chile* 160 B2 41 38 S 73 37W
Maulvibazar, *Bangla.* 78 C3 24 29N 91 42 E
Maumee, *U.S.A.* 141 C13 41 34N 83 39W
Maumee →, *U.S.A.* 141 C13 41 42N 83 28W
Maumere, *Indonesia* 72 C2 8 38 S 122 13 E
Maun, *Botswana* 104 B3 20 0 S 23 26 E
Mauna Kea, *U.S.A.* 132 J17 19 50N 155 28W
Mauna Loa, *U.S.A.* 132 J17 19 50N 155 35W
Maungaturoto, *N.Z.* 118 C3 36 6 S 174 23 E
Maungdow, *Burma* 78 E4 20 50N 92 40 E
Maupin, *U.S.A.* 142 D3 45 11N 121 5W
Maure-de-Bretagne, *France* 22 E5 47 53N 1 58W
Maurepas, L., *U.S.A.* 139 K9 30 15N 90 30W
Maures, *France* 25 E10 43 15N 6 15 E
Mauriac, *France* 24 C6 45 13N 2 19 E
Maurice, L., *Australia* 113 E5 29 30 S 131 0 E
Mauriceville, *N.Z.* 118 G4 40 45 S 175 42 E
Mauritania ■, *Africa* 98 D3 20 50N 10 0W
Mauritius ■, *Ind. Oc.* 93 J9 20 0 S 57 0 E
Mauron, *France* 22 D4 48 9N 2 18W
Maurs, *France* 24 D6 44 43N 2 12 E
Mauston, *U.S.A.* 138 D9 43 48N 90 5W
Mauterndorf, *Austria* 30 D6 47 9N 13 40 E
Mauvezin, *France* 24 E4 43 44N 0 53 E
Mauzé-sur-le-Mignon, *France* 24 B3 46 12N 0 41W
Mavaca →, *Venezuela* 153 C4 2 31N 65 11W
Mavelikara, *India* 83 K3 9 14N 76 32 E
Mavinga, *Angola* 103 F4 15 50 S 20 21 E
Mavli, *India* 80 G5 24 45N 73 55 E
Mavrova, *Albania* 44 D1 40 26N 19 32 E
Mavuradonha Mts., *Zimbabwe* 107 F3 16 30 S 31 30 E
Mawa, *Zaïre* 106 B2 2 45N 26 40 E
Mawana, *India* 80 E7 29 6N 77 58 E
Mawand, *Pakistan* 80 E3 29 33N 68 38 E
Mawk Mai, *Burma* 78 E6 20 14N 97 37 E
Mawlaik, *Burma* 78 D5 23 40N 94 26 E

232 Mawlawkho


Mawlawkho, *Burma* **78 G6** 17 50N 97 38 E
Mawquq, *Si. Arabia* **84 E4** 27 25N 41 8 E
Mawshij, *Yemen* **86 D3** 13 43N 43 17 E
Mawson Coast, *Antarctica* **7 C6** 68 30 S 63 0 E
Max, *U.S.A.* **138 B4** 47 49N 101 18W
Maxcanú, *Mexico* **147 C6** 20 40N 92 0W
Maxesibeni, *S. Africa* **105 E4** 30 49 S 29 23 E
Maxhamish L., *Canada* **130 B4** 59 50N 123 17W
Maxixe, *Mozam.* **105 C6** 23 54 S 35 17 E
Maxville, *Canada* **137 A10** 45 17N 74 51W
Maxwell, *N.Z.* **118 F3** 39 51 S 174 49 E
Maxwell, *U.S.A.* **144 F4** 39 17N 122 11W
Maxwelton, *Australia* **114 C3** 20 43 S 142 41 E
May Downs, *Australia* **114 C4** 22 38 S 148 55 E
May Pen, *Jamaica* **148 C4** 17 58N 77 15W
May River, *Papua N. G.* **120 C1** 4 19 S 141 58 E
Maya, *Indonesia* **75 C3** 1 10 S 109 35 E
Maya, *Spain* **34 B3** 43 12N 1 29W
Maya →, *Russia* **57 D14** 60 28N 134 28 E
Maya Mts., *Belize* **147 D7** 16 30N 89 0W
Mayaguana, *Bahamas* **149 B5** 22 30N 72 44W
Mayagüez, *Puerto Rico* **149 C6** 18 12N 67 9W
Mayahi, *Niger* **101 C6** 13 58N 7 40 E
Mayals, *Spain* **34 D5** 41 22N 0 30 E
Mayama, *Congo* **102 C2** 3 51 S 14 54 E
Mayāmey, *Iran* **85 B7** 36 24N 55 42 E
Mayang, *China* **68 D7** 27 53N 109 49 E
Mayarí, *Cuba* **149 B4** 20 40N 75 41W
Mayavaram = Mayuram, *India* **83 J4** 11 3N 79 42 E
Maybell, *U.S.A.* **142 F9** 40 31N 108 5W
Maychew, *Ethiopia* **95 E4** 12 50N 39 31 E
Maydān, *Iraq* **84 C5** 34 55N 45 37 E
Maydena, *Australia* **114 G4** 42 45 S 146 30 E
Maydī, *Yemen* **86 C3** 16 19N 42 48 E
Maydos, *Turkey* **44 D8** 40 13N 26 20 E
Mayen, *Germany* **27 E3** 50 18N 7 10 E
Mayenne, *France* **22 D6** 48 20N 0 38W
Mayenne □, *France* **22 D6** 48 10N 0 40W
Mayenne →, *France* **22 E6** 47 30N 0 32W
Mayer, *U.S.A.* **143 J7** 34 24N 112 14W
Mayerthorpe, *Canada* **130 C5** 53 57N 115 8W
Mayfield, *U.S.A.* **135 G1** 36 44N 88 38W
Mayhill, *U.S.A.* **143 K11** 32 53N 105 29W
Maykop, *Russia* **53 D9** 44 35N 40 10 E
Mayli-Say, *Kirghizia* **55 C6** 41 17N 72 24 E
Maymyo, *Burma* **76 A1** 22 2N 96 28 E
Maynard, *U.S.A.* **144 C4** 47 59N 122 55W
Maynard Hills, *Australia* **113 E2** 28 28 S 119 49 E
Mayne →, *Australia* **114 C3** 23 40 S 141 55 E
Maynooth, *Ireland* **19 C5** 53 22N 6 38W
Mayo, *Canada* **126 B6** 63 38N 135 57W
Mayo □, *Ireland* **19 C2** 53 47N 9 7W
Mayo →, *Argentina* **160 C3** 45 45 S 69 45W
Mayo →, *Peru* **156 B2** 6 38 S 76 15W
Mayo Bay, *Phil.* **71 H6** 6 56N 126 22 E
Mayo L., *Canada* **126 B6** 63 45N 135 0W
Mayoko, *Zaïre* **102 C2** 2 18 S 12 49 E
Mayon Volcano, *Phil.* **70 E4** 13 15N 123 41 E
Mayor I., *N.Z.* **118 D5** 37 16 S 176 17 E
Mayorga, *Spain* **36 C5** 42 10N 5 16W
Mayoyao, *Phil.* **70 C3** 16 59N 121 14 E
Mayraira Pt., *Phil.* **70 B3** 18 39N 120 51 E
Mayskiy, *Russia* **53 E11** 43 47N 44 2 E
Mayson L., *Canada* **131 B7** 57 55N 107 10W
Maysville, *Ky., U.S.A.* **141 F13** 38 39N 83 46W
Maysville, *Mo., U.S.A.* **140 E2** 39 53N 94 22W
Mayu, *Indonesia* **72 A3** 1 30N 126 30 E
Mayumba, *Gabon* **102 C2** 3 25 S 10 39 E
Mayuram, *India* **83 J4** 11 3N 79 42 E
Mayville, *N. Dak., U.S.A.* **138 B6** 47 30N 97 20W
Mayville, *N.Y., U.S.A.* **136 D5** 42 15N 79 30W
Mayya, *Russia* **57 C14** 61 44N 130 18 E
Mazabuka, *Zambia* **107 F2** 15 52 S 27 44 E
Mazagán = El Jadida, *Morocco* **98 B3** 33 11N 8 17W
Mazagão, *Brazil* **153 D7** 0 7 S 51 16W
Mazamet, *France* **24 E6** 43 30N 2 20 E
Mazán, *Peru* **152 D3** 3 30 S 73 0W
Māzandarān □, *Iran* **85 B7** 36 30N 52 0 E
Mazapil, *Mexico* **146 C4** 24 38N 101 34W
Mazar, O. →, *Algeria* **99 B5** 31 50N 1 36 E
Mazar-e Sharīf, *Afghan.* **79 A2** 36 41N 67 0 E
Mazara del Vallo, *Italy* **40 E5** 37 40N 12 34 E
Mazarredo, *Argentina* **160 C3** 47 10 S 66 50W
Mazarrón, *Spain* **35 H3** 37 38N 1 19W
Mazarrón, G. de, *Spain* **35 H3** 37 27N 1 19W
Mazaruni →, *Guyana* **153 B6** 6 25N 58 35W
Mazatán, *Mexico* **146 B2** 29 0N 110 8W
Mazatenango, *Guatemala* **148 D1** 14 35N 91 30W
Mazatlán, *Mexico* **146 C3** 23 10N 106 30W
Mažeikiai, *Lithuania* **50 C3** 56 20N 22 20 E
Māzhān, *Iran* **85 C8** 32 30N 59 0 E
Mazīnān, *Iran* **85 B8** 36 19N 56 56 E
Mazoe, *Mozam.* **107 F3** 16 42 S 33 7 E
Mazoe →, *Mozam.* **107 F3** 16 20 S 33 30 E
Mazomanie, *U.S.A.* **140 A7** 43 11N 89 48W
Mazon, *U.S.A.* **141 C8** 41 14N 88 25W
Mazowe, *Zimbabwe* **107 F3** 17 28 S 30 58 E
Mazrûb, *Sudan* **95 E2** 14 0N 29 20 E
Mazu Dao, *China* **69 D12** 26 10N 119 55 E
Mazurian Lakes = Mazurski, Pojezierze, *Poland* **47 B7** 53 50N 21 0 E
Mazurski, Pojezierze, *Poland* **47 B7** 53 50N 21 0 E
Mazzarino, *Italy* **41 E7** 37 19N 14 12 E
Mba, *Fiji* **121 A1** 17 33 S 177 41 E
Mbaba, *Senegal* **100 C1** 14 59N 16 44W
Mbabane, *Swaziland* **105 D5** 26 18 S 31 6 E
Mbagne, *Mauritania* **100 B2** 16 6N 14 47W
M'bahiakro, *Ivory C.* **100 D4** 7 33N 4 19W
Mbaïki, *C.A.R.* **102 B3** 3 53N 18 1 E
Mbakana, Mt. de, *Cameroon* **102 A3** 7 57N 15 6 E
Mbala, *Zambia* **107 D3** 8 46 S 31 24 E
Mbale, *Uganda* **106 B3** 1 8N 34 12 E
Mbalmayo, *Cameroon* **101 E7** 3 33N 11 33 E
Mbamba Bay, *Tanzania* **107 E3** 11 13 S 34 49 E
Mbandaka, *Zaïre* **102 B3** 0 1N 18 18 E
Mbanga, *Cameroon* **101 E6** 4 30N 9 33 E
Mbanza Congo, *Angola* **103 D2** 6 18 S 14 16 E
Mbanza Ngungu, *Zaïre* **103 D2** 5 12 S 14 53 E
Mbarara, *Uganda* **106 C3** 0 35 S 30 40 E
Mbashe →, *S. Africa* **105 E4** 32 15 S 28 54 E
Mbatto, *Ivory C.* **100 D4** 6 28N 4 22W
Mbengga, *Fiji* **121 B2** 18 23 S 178 8 E
Mbenkuru →, *Tanzania* **107 D4** 9 25 S 39 50 E
Mberengwa, *Zimbabwe* **107 G2** 20 29 S 29 57 E
Mberengwa, Mt., *Zimbabwe* **107 G2** 20 37 S 29 55 E
Mberubu, *Nigeria* **101 D6** 6 10N 7 38 E
Mbesuma, *Zambia* **107 D3** 10 0 S 32 2 E
Mbeya, *Tanzania* **107 D3** 8 54 S 33 29 E
Mbeya □, *Tanzania* **106 D3** 8 15 S 33 30 E
Mbigou, *Gabon* **102 C2** 1 53 S 11 56 E
Mbinga, *Tanzania* **107 E4** 10 50 S 35 0 E
Mbinga □, *Tanzania* **107 E3** 10 50 S 35 0 E
Mbini □, *Eq. Guin.* **102 B2** 1 30N 10 0 E
Mboki, *C.A.R.* **95 F2** 5 19N 25 58 E
Mboli, *Zaïre* **102 B4** 4 8N 23 9 E
Mboro, *Senegal* **100 B1** 15 9N 16 54W
Mboune, *Senegal* **100 C2** 14 42N 13 34W
Mbouoma, *Congo* **102 C3** 0 52 S 15 4 E
Mbour, *Senegal* **100 C1** 14 22N 16 54W
Mbout, *Mauritania* **100 B2** 16 1N 12 38W
Mbozi □, *Tanzania* **107 D3** 9 0 S 32 50 E
Mbrés, *C.A.R.* **102 A3** 6 40N 19 48 E
Mbuji-Mayi, *Zaïre* **103 D4** 6 9 S 23 40 E
Mbulu, *Tanzania* **106 C4** 3 45 S 35 30 E
Mbulu □, *Tanzania* **106 C4** 3 52 S 35 33 E
Mburucuyá, *Argentina* **158 B4** 28 1 S 58 14W
Mcherrah, *Algeria* **98 C4** 27 0N 4 30W
Mchinja, *Tanzania* **107 D4** 9 44 S 39 45 E
Mchinji, *Malawi* **107 E3** 13 47 S 32 58 E
Mdennah, *Mauritania* **98 D3** 24 37N 6 0W
Mead, L., *U.S.A.* **145 J12** 36 1N 114 44W
Meade, *U.S.A.* **139 G4** 37 17N 100 20W
Meadow, *Australia* **113 E1** 26 35 S 114 40 E
Meadow Lake, *Canada* **131 C7** 54 10N 108 26W
Meadow Lake Prov. Park, *Canada* **131 C7** 54 27N 109 0W
Meadow Valley Wash →, *U.S.A.* **145 J12** 36 40N 114 34W
Meadville, *Mo., U.S.A.* **140 E3** 39 47N 93 18W
Meadville, *Pa., U.S.A.* **136 E4** 41 39N 80 9W
Meaford, *Canada* **128 D3** 44 36N 80 35W
Mealhada, *Portugal* **36 E2** 40 22N 8 27W
Mealy Mts., *Canada* **129 B8** 53 10N 58 0W
Meander River, *Canada* **130 B5** 59 2N 117 42W
Meares, C., *U.S.A.* **142 D2** 45 37N 124 0W
Mearim →, *Brazil* **154 B3** 3 4 S 44 35W
Meath □, *Ireland* **19 C5** 53 32N 6 40W
Meath Park, *Canada* **131 C7** 53 27N 105 22W
Meatian, *Australia* **116 C5** 35 34 S 143 21 E
Meaulne, *France* **24 B6** 46 36N 2 36 E
Meaux, *France* **23 D9** 48 58N 2 50 E
Mebechi-Gawa →, *Japan* **60 D10** 40 31N 141 31 E
Mecanhelas, *Mozam.* **107 F4** 15 12 S 35 54 E
Mecaya →, *Colombia* **152 C2** 0 29N 75 11W
Mecca = Makkah, *Si. Arabia* **86 B2** 21 30N 39 54 E
Mecca, *U.S.A.* **145 M10** 33 34N 116 5W
Mechanicsburg, *U.S.A.* **136 F8** 40 13N 77 1W
Mechanicsville, *U.S.A.* **140 C5** 41 54N 91 16W
Mechanicville, *U.S.A.* **137 D11** 42 54N 73 41W
Mechara, *Ethiopia* **95 F5** 8 36N 40 20 E
Mechelen, *Antwerpen, Belgium* **21 F4** 51 2N 4 29 E
Mechelen, *Limburg, Belgium* **21 G7** 50 58N 5 41 E
Mecheria, *Algeria* **99 B4** 33 35N 0 18W
Mechernich, *Germany* **26 E2** 50 35N 6 39 E
Mechetinskaya, *Russia* **53 C9** 46 45N 40 32 E
Mechra Benâbbou, *Morocco* **98 B3** 32 39N 7 48W
Mecidiye, *Turkey* **44 D8** 40 38N 26 32 E
Mecitözü, *Turkey* **52 F6** 40 32N 35 17 E
Mecklenburg-Vorpommern □, *Germany* **26 B8** 53 50N 12 0 E
Mecklenburger Bucht, *Germany* **26 A7** 54 20N 11 40 E
Meconta, *Mozam.* **107 E4** 14 59 S 39 50 E
Meda, *Australia* **112 C3** 17 22 S 123 59 E
Meda, *Portugal* **36 E3** 40 57N 7 18W
Medak, *India* **82 E4** 18 1N 78 15 E
Medan, *Indonesia* **74 B1** 3 40N 98 38 E
Médanos, *Argentina* **160 A4** 38 50 S 62 42W
Medanosa, Pta., *Argentina* **160 C3** 48 8 S 66 0W
Medaryville, *U.S.A.* **141 C10** 41 5N 86 55W
Medawachchiya, *Sri Lanka* **83 K5** 8 30N 80 30 E
Medéa, *Algeria* **99 A5** 36 12N 2 50 E
Mededa, *Bos.-H.* **42 D4** 43 44N 19 15 E
Médégué, *Gabon* **102 B2** 0 37N 10 8 E
Medeiros Neto, *Brazil* **155 E3** 17 20 S 40 14W
Medel, Pic, *Switz.* **29 C7** 46 34N 8 55 E
Medellín, *Colombia* **152 B2** 6 15N 75 35W
Medemblik, *Neths.* **20 C6** 52 46N 5 8 E
Médenine, *Tunisia* **96 B2** 33 21N 10 30 E
Mederdra, *Mauritania* **100 B1** 17 0N 15 38W
Medford, *Mass., U.S.A.* **137 D13** 42 25N 71 7W
Medford, *Oreg., U.S.A.* **142 E2** 42 19N 122 52W
Medford, *Wis., U.S.A.* **138 C9** 45 9N 90 20W
Medgidia, *Romania* **46 E9** 44 15N 28 19 E
Medi, *Sudan* **95 F3** 5 4N 30 42 E
Media Agua, *Argentina* **158 C2** 31 58 S 68 25W
Media Luna, *Argentina* **158 C2** 34 45 S 66 44W
Mediapolis, *U.S.A.* **140 C5** 41 0N 91 10W
Mediaş, *Romania* **46 C5** 46 9N 24 22 E
Medical Lake, *U.S.A.* **142 C5** 47 34N 117 41W
Medicina, *Italy* **39 D8** 44 29N 11 38 E
Medicine Bow, *U.S.A.* **142 F10** 41 54N 106 12W
Medicine Bow Pk., *U.S.A.* **142 F10** 41 21N 106 19W
Medicine Bow Ra., *U.S.A.* **142 F10** 41 10N 106 25W
Medicine Hat, *Canada* **131 D6** 50 0N 110 45W
Medicine Lake, *U.S.A.* **138 A2** 48 30N 104 30W
Medicine Lodge, *U.S.A.* **139 G5** 37 17N 98 35W
Medina = Al Madīnah, *Si. Arabia* **84 E3** 24 35N 39 52 E
Medina, *Brazil* **155 E3** 16 15 S 41 29W
Medina, *Colombia* **152 C3** 4 30N 73 21W
Medina, *N. Dak., U.S.A.* **138 B5** 46 54N 99 18W
Medina, *N.Y., U.S.A.* **136 C6** 43 13N 78 23W
Medina, *Ohio, U.S.A.* **136 E3** 41 8N 81 52W
Medina →, *U.S.A.* **139 L5** 29 16N 98 29W
Medina de Ríoseco, *Spain* **36 D5** 41 53N 5 3W
Medina del Campo, *Spain* **36 D6** 41 18N 4 55W
Medina L., *U.S.A.* **139 L5** 29 32N 98 56W
Medina-Sidonia, *Spain* **37 J5** 36 28N 5 57W
Medinaceli, *Spain* **34 D2** 41 12N 2 30W
Medinipur, *India* **81 H12** 22 25N 87 21 E
Mediterranean Sea, *Europe* **92 C5** 35 0N 15 0 E
Medjerda, O. →, *Tunisia* **96 A2** 37 7N 10 13 E
Medley, *Canada* **131 C6** 54 25N 110 16W
Mednogorsk, *Russia* **54 F5** 51 24N 57 37 E
Médoc, *France* **24 C3** 45 10N 0 50W
Medora, *U.S.A.* **141 F10** 38 49N 86 10W
Médouneu, *Gabon* **102 B2** 0 57N 10 47 E
Medstead, *Canada* **131 C7** 53 19N 108 5W
Medulin, *Croatia* **39 D10** 44 49N 13 55 E
Medveda, *Serbia* **42 E6** 42 50N 21 32 E
Medveditsa →, *Russia* **51 G13** 49 35N 42 41 E
Medveditsa →, *Russia* **51 C10** 57 5N 37 30 E
Medvedok, *Russia* **54 C2** 57 20N 50 1 E
Medvezhi, Ostrava, *Russia* **57 B17** 71 0N 161 0 E
Medvezhyegorsk, *Russia* **48 B5** 63 0N 34 25 E
Medway →, *U.K.* **17 F8** 51 28N 0 45 E
Medyn, *Russia* **51 D9** 54 58N 35 52 E
Medzev, *Slovak Rep.* **31 C13** 48 43N 20 55 E
Medzilaborce, *Slovak Rep.* **31 B14** 49 17N 21 52 E
Meeberrie, *Australia* **113 E2** 26 57 S 115 51 E
Meekatharra, *Australia* **113 E2** 26 32 S 118 29 E
Meeker, *U.S.A.* **142 F10** 40 2N 107 55W
Meeniyan, *Australia* **117 E7** 38 35 S 146 0 E
Meer, *Belgium* **21 F5** 51 27N 4 45 E
Meerane, *Germany* **26 E8** 50 51N 12 30 E
Meerbeke, *Belgium* **21 G4** 50 50N 4 3 E
Meerhout, *Belgium* **21 F6** 51 7N 5 4 E
Meerle, *Belgium* **21 F5** 51 29N 4 48 E
Meersburg, *Germany* **27 H5** 47 42N 9 16 E
Meerssen, *Neths.* **21 G7** 50 53N 5 50 E
Meerut, *India* **80 E7** 29 1N 77 42 E
Meeteetse, *U.S.A.* **142 D9** 44 9N 108 52W
Meeuwen, *Belgium* **21 F7** 51 6N 5 31 E
Mega, *Ethiopia* **95 G4** 3 57N 38 19 E
Megálo Khorío, *Greece* **45 H9** 36 27N 27 24 E
Megálo Petalí, *Greece* **45 G6** 38 0N 24 15 E
Megalópolis, *Greece* **45 G4** 37 25N 22 7 E
Meganísi, *Greece* **45 F2** 38 39N 20 48 E
Mégara, *Greece* **45 G5** 37 58N 23 22 E
Megarine, *Algeria* **99 B6** 33 14N 6 2 E
Megdhova →, *Greece* **45 E3** 39 10N 21 45 E
Megève, *France* **25 C10** 45 51N 6 37 E
Meghalaya □, *India* **78 C3** 25 50N 91 0 E
Meghezez, *Ethiopia* **95 F4** 9 18N 39 26 E
Meghna →, *Bangla.* **78 D3** 22 50N 90 50 E
Mégiscane, L., *Canada* **128 C4** 48 35N 75 55W
Mehadia, *Romania* **46 E3** 44 56N 22 23 E
Mehaigne →, *Belgium* **21 G6** 50 32N 5 13 E
Mehaïguene, O. →, *Algeria* **99 B5** 32 15N 2 59 E
Mehedinţi □, *Romania* **46 E3** 44 40N 22 45 E
Meheisa, *Sudan* **94 D3** 19 38N 32 57 E
Mehndawal, *India* **81 F10** 26 58N 83 5 E
Mehr Jān, *Iran* **85 C7** 33 50N 55 6 E
Mehrābād, *Iran* **84 B5** 36 53N 47 55 E
Mehrān, *Iran* **84 C5** 33 7N 46 10 E
Mehrīz, *Iran* **85 D7** 31 35N 54 28 E
Mehun-sur-Yèvre, *France* **23 E9** 47 10N 2 13 E
Mei Jiang →, *China* **69 E11** 24 25N 116 35 E
Mei Xian, *Guangdong, China* **69 E11** 24 16N 116 6 E
Mei Xian, *Shaanxi, China* **66 G4** 34 18N 107 55 E
Meia Ponte →, *Brazil* **155 E2** 18 32 S 49 36W
Meicheng, *China* **69 C12** 29 29N 119 16 E
Meichengzhen, *China* **69 C8** 28 9N 111 40 E
Meichuan, *China* **69 B10** 30 8N 115 31 E
Meiganga, *Cameroon* **102 A2** 6 30N 14 25 E
Meijel, *Neths.* **21 F7** 51 21N 5 53 E
Meiktila, *Burma* **78 E5** 20 53N 95 54 E
Meilen, *Switz.* **29 B7** 47 16N 8 39 E
Meiningen, *Germany* **26 E6** 50 32N 10 25 E
Meio →, *Brazil* **155 D3** 13 36 S 44 7W
Meira, Sierra de, *Spain* **36 B3** 43 15N 7 15W
Meiringen, *Switz.* **28 C6** 46 43N 8 12 E
Meishan, *China* **68 B4** 30 3N 103 23 E
Meissen, *Germany* **26 D9** 51 10N 13 29 E
Meissner, *Germany* **26 D5** 51 13N 9 51 E
Meitan, *China* **68 D6** 27 45N 107 29 E
Mejillones, *Chile* **158 A1** 23 10 S 70 30W
Meka, *Australia* **113 E2** 27 25 S 116 48 E
Mékambo, *Gabon* **102 B2** 1 2N 13 50 E
Mekdela, *Ethiopia* **95 E4** 11 24N 39 10 E
Mekele, *Ethiopia* **95 E4** 13 33N 39 30 E
Mekhtar, *Pakistan* **79 C3** 30 30N 69 15 E
Meknès, *Morocco* **98 B3** 33 57N 5 33W
Meko, *Nigeria* **101 D5** 7 27N 2 52 E
Mekong →, *Asia* **77 H6** 9 30N 106 15 E
Mekongga, *Indonesia* **72 B2** 3 39 S 121 15 E
Melagiri Hills, *India* **83 H3** 12 20N 77 30 E
Melah, Sebkhet el, *Algeria* **99 C4** 29 20N 1 30W
Melaka, *Malaysia* **77 L4** 2 15N 102 15 E
Melaka □, *Malaysia* **74 B2** 2 15N 102 15 E
Mélambes, *Greece* **32 D6** 35 8N 24 40 E
Melanesia, *Pac. Oc.* **122 H7** 4 0 S 155 0 E
Melapalaiyam, *India* **83 K3** 8 39N 77 44 E
Melawi →, *Indonesia* **75 B4** 0 5N 111 29 E
Melbourne, *Australia* **117 D6** 37 50 S 145 0 E
Melbourne, *Fla., U.S.A.* **135 L5** 28 5N 80 37W
Melbourne, *Iowa, U.S.A.* **140 C3** 41 57N 93 6W
Melcher, *U.S.A.* **140 C3** 41 14N 93 15W
Melchor Múzquiz, *Mexico* **146 B4** 27 50N 101 30W
Melchor Ocampo, *Mexico* **146 C4** 24 52N 101 40W
Méldola, *Italy* **39 D9** 44 7N 12 3 E
Meldorf, *Germany* **26 A5** 54 5N 9 5 E
Meleden, *Somali Rep.* **108 B3** 10 25N 49 51 E
Melegnano, *Italy* **38 C6** 45 21N 9 20 E
Melenci, *Serbia* **42 B5** 45 32N 20 20 E
Melenki, *Russia* **51 D12** 55 20N 41 37 E
Meleuz, *Russia* **54 E4** 52 58N 55 55 E
Mélèzes →, *Canada* **127 C12** 57 30N 71 0W
Melfi, *Chad* **97 F3** 11 0N 17 59 E
Melfi, *Italy* **41 B8** 41 0N 15 33 E
Melfort, *Canada* **131 C8** 52 50N 104 37W
Melfort, *Zimbabwe* **107 F3** 18 0 S 31 25 E
Melgaço, *Madeira* **36 C2** 42 7N 8 15W
Melgar de Fernamental, *Spain* **36 C6** 42 27N 4 17W
Melhus, *Norway* **14 A4** 63 17N 10 18 E
Melick, *Neths.* **21 F8** 51 10N 6 1 E
Melide, *Switz.* **29 E7** 45 57N 8 57 E
Meligalá, *Greece* **45 G3** 37 15N 21 59 E
Melilla, *Morocco* **99 A4** 35 21N 2 57W
Melipilla, *Chile* **158 C1** 33 42 S 71 15W
Mélissa, Ákra, *Greece* **32 D6** 35 6N 24 33 E
Mélissa Óros, *Greece* **45 G8** 37 32N 26 4 E
Melita, *Canada* **131 D8** 49 15N 101 0W
Mélito di Porto Salvo, *Italy* **41 E8** 37 55N 15 47 E
Melitopol, *Ukraine* **52 C6** 46 50N 35 22 E
Melk, *Austria* **30 C8** 48 13N 15 20 E
Mellansel, *Sweden* **12 E15** 63 25N 18 17 E
Melle, *Belgium* **21 G3** 51 0N 3 49 E
Melle, *France* **24 B3** 46 14N 0 10W
Melle, *Germany* **26 C4** 52 12N 8 20 E
Mellégue, O. →, *Tunisia* **96 A1** 36 32N 8 51 E
Mellen, *U.S.A.* **138 B9** 46 20N 90 40W
Mellerud, *Sweden* **15 F6** 58 41N 12 28 E
Mellette, *U.S.A.* **138 C5** 45 9N 98 30W
Mellid, *Spain* **36 C2** 42 55N 8 1W
Mellieha, *Malta* **32 D1** 35 57N 14 21 E
Mellit, *Sudan* **95 E2** 14 7N 25 34 E
Mellizo Sur, Cerro, *Chile* **160 C2** 48 33 S 73 10W
Mellrichstadt, *Germany* **27 E6** 50 26N 10 19 E
Melnik, *Bulgaria* **43 F8** 41 30N 23 25 E
Mělník, *Czech.* **30 A7** 50 22N 14 23 E
Melo, *Uruguay* **159 C5** 32 20 S 54 10W
Melolo, *Indonesia* **72 C2** 9 53 S 120 40 E
Melouprey, *Cambodia* **76 F5** 13 48N 105 16 E
Melovoye, *Ukraine* **53 B9** 49 25N 40 5 E
Melrhir, Chott, *Algeria* **99 B6** 34 25N 6 24 E
Melrose, *N.S.W., Australia* **117 B7** 32 42 S 146 57 E
Melrose, *W. Austral., Australia* **113 E3** 27 50 S 121 15 E
Melrose, *U.K.* **18 F6** 55 35N 2 44W
Melrose, *Iowa, U.S.A.* **140 D3** 40 59N 93 3W
Melrose, *N. Mex., U.S.A.* **139 H3** 34 26N 103 38W
Mels, *Switz.* **29 B8** 47 3N 9 25 E
Melsele, *Belgium* **21 F4** 51 13N 4 17 E
Melstone, *U.S.A.* **142 C10** 46 36N 107 52W
Melsungen, *Germany* **26 D5** 51 8N 9 34 E
Melton Mowbray, *U.K.* **16 E7** 52 46N 0 52W
Melun, *France* **23 D9** 48 32N 2 39 E
Melur, *India* **83 J4** 10 2N 78 23 E
Melut, *Sudan* **95 E3** 10 30N 32 13 E
Melville, *Canada* **131 C8** 50 55N 102 50W
Melville, C., *Australia* **114 A3** 14 11 S 144 30 E
Melville, L., *Canada* **129 B8** 53 30N 60 0W
Melville B., *Australia* **114 A2** 12 0 S 136 45 E
Melville I., *Australia* **112 B5** 11 30 S 131 0 E
Melville I., *Canada* **124 B8** 75 30N 112 0W
Melville Pen., *Canada* **127 B11** 68 0N 84 0W
Melvin →, *Canada* **130 B5** 59 11N 117 31W
Mélykút, *Hungary* **31 E12** 46 11N 19 25 E
Memaliaj, *Albania* **44 D1** 40 25N 19 58 E
Memba, *Mozam.* **107 E5** 14 11 S 40 30 E
Memboro, *Indonesia* **72 C1** 9 30 S 119 30 E
Membrilla, *Spain* **35 G1** 38 59N 3 21W
Memel = Klaìpéda, *Lithuania* **50 D2** 55 43N 21 10 E
Memel, *S. Africa* **105 D4** 27 38 S 29 36 E
Memmingen, *Germany* **27 H6** 47 59N 10 12 E
Mempawah, *Indonesia* **75 B3** 0 30N 109 5 E
Memphis, *Mo., U.S.A.* **140 D4** 40 28N 92 10W
Memphis, *Tenn., U.S.A.* **139 H10** 35 8N 90 3W
Memphis, *Tex., U.S.A.* **139 H4** 34 44N 100 33W
Mena, *U.S.A.* **139 H7** 34 35N 94 15W
Mena →, *Ethiopia* **95 F5** 5 40N 40 50 E
Menai Strait, *U.K.* **16 D3** 53 14N 4 10W
Ménaka, *Mali* **101 B5** 15 59N 2 18 E
Menaldum, *Neths.* **20 B7** 53 13N 5 40 E
Menamurtee, *Australia* **116 A5** 31 25 S 143 11 E
Menan = Chao Phraya →, *Thailand* **76 F3** 13 32N 100 36 E
Menarandra →, *Madag.* **105 D7** 25 17 S 44 30 E
Menard, *U.S.A.* **139 K5** 30 55N 99 47W
Menasha, *U.S.A.* **134 C1** 44 13N 88 26W
Menate, *Indonesia* **75 C4** 0 12 S 113 3 E
Mendawai →, *Indonesia* **75 C4** 3 30 S 113 0 E
Mende, *France* **24 D7** 44 31N 3 30 E
Mendebo, *Ethiopia* **95 F4** 7 0N 39 22 E
Mendez, *Mexico* **147 B5** 25 7N 98 34W
Mendez Nunez, *Phil.* **70 D3** 14 8N 120 54 E
Mendhar, *India* **81 C6** 33 35N 74 10 E
Mendi, *Ethiopia* **95 F4** 9 47N 35 4 E
Mendi, *Papua N. G.* **120 D2** 6 11 S 143 39 E
Mendip Hills, *U.K.* **17 F5** 51 17N 2 40W
Mendocino, *U.S.A.* **142 G2** 39 19N 123 48W
Mendocino, C., *U.S.A.* **142 F1** 40 26N 124 25W
Mendon, *U.S.A.* **141 B11** 42 0N 85 27W
Mendota, *Calif., U.S.A.* **144 J6** 36 45N 120 23W
Mendota, *Ill., U.S.A.* **140 C7** 41 33N 89 7W
Mendoza, *Argentina* **158 C2** 32 50 S 68 52W
Mendoza □, *Argentina* **158 C2** 33 0 S 69 0W
Mendrisio, *Switz.* **29 E7** 45 52N 8 59 E
Mene Grande, *Venezuela* **152 B3** 9 49N 70 56W
Menemen, *Turkey* **88 D2** 38 34N 27 3 E
Menen, *Belgium* **21 G2** 50 47N 3 7 E
Menéndez, L., *Argentina* **160 B2** 42 40 S 71 51W
Menfi, *Italy* **40 E5** 37 36N 12 57 E
Mengcheng, *China* **69 A11** 33 18N 116 31 E
Mengdingjie, *China* **68 F2** 23 31N 98 58 E
Mengeš, *Slovenia* **39 B11** 46 10N 14 35 E
Menggala, *Indonesia* **74 C3** 4 30 S 105 15 E
Menghai, *China* **68 G3** 21 49N 100 55 E
Mengíbar, *Spain* **37 H7** 37 58N 3 48W
Mengjin, *China* **66 G7** 34 55N 112 45 E
Mengla, *China* **68 G3** 21 20N 101 25 E
Menglian, *China* **68 F2** 22 21N 99 27 E
Mengoub, *Algeria* **98 C3** 29 49N 5 26W
Mengshan, *China* **69 E8** 24 14N 110 55 E
Mengyin, *China* **67 G9** 35 40N 117 58 E
Mengzhe, *China* **68 F3** 22 2N 100 15 E
Mengzi, *China* **68 F4** 23 20N 103 22 E
Menihek L., *Canada* **129 B6** 54 0N 67 0W
Menin = Menen, *Belgium* **21 G2** 50 47N 3 7 E
Menindee, *Australia* **116 B5** 32 20 S 142 25 E
Menindee L., *Australia* **116 B5** 32 20 S 142 25 E
Meningie, *Australia* **116 C3** 35 50 S 139 18 E
Menlo Park, *U.S.A.* **144 H4** 37 27N 122 12W
Menominee, *U.S.A.* **134 C2** 45 6N 87 37W
Menominee →, *U.S.A.* **134 C2** 45 6N 87 36W
Menomonee Falls, *U.S.A.* **141 A8** 43 11N 88 7W
Menomonie, *U.S.A.* **138 C9** 44 53N 91 55W
Menongue, *Angola* **103 E3** 14 48 S 17 52 E
Menorca, *Spain* **33 B11** 40 0N 4 0 E

Mentakab, *Malaysia* **77 L4** 3 29N 102 21 E
Mentawai, Kepulauan, *Indonesia* **74 C1** 2 0S 99 0E
Menton, *France* **25 E11** 43 50N 7 29 E
Mentone, *U.S.A.* **141 C10** 41 10N 86 2W
Mentor, *U.S.A.* **136 E3** 41 40N 81 21W
Mentz Dam, *S. Africa* **104 E4** 33 10 S 25 9 E
Menyamya, *Papua N. G.* **120 D3** 7 10 S 145 59 E
Menzel-Bourguiba, *Tunisia* **96 A1** 37 9N 9 49 E
Menzel Chaker, *Tunisia* **96 B2** 35 0N 10 26 E
Menzel-Temime, *Tunisia* **96 A2** 36 46N 11 0 E
Menzelinsk, *Russia* **54 D3** 55 53N 53 1 E
Menzies, *Australia* **113 E3** 29 40 S 121 2 E
Me'ona, *Israel* **91 B4** 33 1N 35 15 E
Meoqui, *Mexico* **146 B3** 28 17N 105 29W
Mepaco, *Mozam.* **107 F3** 15 57 S 30 48 E
Meppel, *Neths.* **20 C8** 52 42N 6 12 E
Meppen, *Germany* **26 C3** 52 41N 7 20 E
Mequinenza, *Spain* **34 D5** 41 22N 0 17 E
Mequon, *U.S.A.* **141 A9** 43 14N 87 59W
Mer Rouge, *U.S.A.* **139 J9** 32 47N 91 48W
Mera Lava, *Vanuatu* **121 D6** 14 25 S 168 3 E
Merabéllou, Kólpos, *Greece* **32 D7** 35 10N 25 50 E
Merai, *Papua N. G.* **120 C7** 4 52 S 152 19 E
Meramangye, L., *Australia* **113 E5** 28 25 S 132 13 E
Meramec →, *U.S.A.* **140 F6** 38 24N 90 21W
Meran = Merano, *Italy* **39 B8** 46 40N 11 10 E
Merano, *Italy* **39 B8** 46 40N 11 10 E
Merate, *Italy* **38 C6** 45 42N 9 23 E
Merauke, *Indonesia* **73 C6** 8 29 S 140 24 E
Merbabu, *Indonesia* **75 D4** 7 30 S 110 40 E
Merbein, *Australia* **116 C5** 34 10 S 142 2 E
Merca, *Somali Rep.* **90 G3** 1 48N 44 50 E
Mercadal, *Spain* **33 B11** 39 59N 4 5 E
Mercato Saraceno, *Italy* **39 E9** 43 57N 12 11 E
Merced, *U.S.A.* **144 H6** 37 18N 120 29W
Merced Pk., *U.S.A.* **144 H7** 37 36N 119 24W
Mercedes, *Buenos Aires, Argentina* **158 C4** 34 40 S 59 30W
Mercedes, *Corrientes, Argentina* **158 B4** 29 10 S 58 5W
Mercedes, *San Luis, Argentina* **158 C2** 33 40 S 65 21W
Mercedes, *Camarines N., Phil.* **70 D4** 14 7N 123 1 E
Mercedes, *Leyte, Phil.* **71 F5** 10 41N 124 24 E
Mercedes, *Zamboanga del S., Phil.* **71 H4** 6 57N 122 9 E
Mercedes, *Uruguay* **158 C4** 33 12 S 58 0W
Merceditas, *Chile* **158 B1** 28 20 S 70 35W
Mercer, *N.Z.* **118 D4** 37 16 S 175 5 E
Mercer, *Mo., U.S.A.* **140 D3** 40 31N 93 32W
Mercer, *Pa., U.S.A.* **136 E4** 41 14N 80 15W
Merchtem, *Belgium* **21 G4** 50 58N 4 14 E
Mercier, *Bolivia* **156 C4** 10 42 S 68 5W
Mercury, *U.S.A.* **145 J11** 36 40N 115 58W
Mercury B., *N.Z.* **118 C4** 36 48 S 175 45 E
Mercury Is., *N.Z.* **118 C4** 36 37 S 175 52 E
Mercy C., *Canada* **127 B13** 65 0N 63 30W
Merdrignac, *France* **22 D4** 48 11N 2 27W
Mere, *Belgium* **21 G3** 50 55N 3 58 E
Meredith, C., *Falk. Is.* **160 D4** 52 15 S 60 40W
Meredith, L., *U.S.A.* **139 H4** 35 43N 101 33W
Meredosia, *U.S.A.* **140 E6** 39 50N 90 34W
Meregh, *Somali Rep.* **108 D3** 3 46N 47 18 E
Merei, *Romania* **46 D7** 45 7N 26 43 E
Merelbeke, *Belgium* **21 G3** 51 0N 3 45 E
Méréville, *France* **23 D9** 48 20N 2 5 E
Merga = Nukheila, *Sudan* **94 D2** 19 1N 26 21 E
Mergenevsky, *Kazakhstan* **53 B14** 49 59N 51 15 E
Mergui Arch. = Myeik Kyunzu, *Burma* **77 G1** 11 30N 97 30 E
Meribah, *Australia* **116 C4** 34 43 S 140 51 E
Mérida, *Mexico* **147 C7** 20 9N 89 40W
Merida, *Phil.* **71 F5** 10 55N 124 32 E
Mérida, *Spain* **37 G4** 38 55N 6 25W
Mérida, *Venezuela* **152 B3** 8 24N 71 8W
Mérida □, *Venezuela* **152 B3** 8 30N 71 10W
Mérida, Cord. de, *Venezuela* **152 B3** 9 0N 71 0W
Meriden, *U.S.A.* **137 E12** 41 32N 72 48W
Meridian, *Calif., U.S.A.* **144 F5** 39 9N 121 55W
Meridian, *Idaho, U.S.A.* **142 E5** 43 37N 116 24W
Meridian, *Miss., U.S.A.* **135 J1** 32 22N 88 42W
Meridian, *Tex., U.S.A.* **139 K6** 31 56N 97 39W
Mering, *Germany* **27 G7** 48 15N 11 0 E
Meriruma, *Brazil* **153 C7** 1 15N 54 50W
Merke, *Kazakhstan* **55 B6** 42 52N 73 11 E
Merkel, *U.S.A.* **139 J4** 32 28N 100 1W
Merksem, *Belgium* **21 F4** 51 16N 4 25 E
Merksplas, *Belgium* **21 F5** 51 22N 4 52 E
Mermaid Reef, *Australia* **112 C2** 17 6 S 119 36 E
Mern, *Denmark* **15 J6** 55 3N 12 3 E
Merowe, *Sudan* **94 D3** 18 29N 31 46 E
Merredin, *Australia* **113 F2** 31 28 S 118 18 E
Merrick, *U.K.* **18 F4** 55 8N 4 30W
Merrickville, *Canada* **137 B9** 44 55N 75 50W
Merrill, *Oreg., U.S.A.* **142 E3** 42 1N 121 36W
Merrill, *Wis., U.S.A.* **138 C10** 45 11N 89 41W
Merrillville, *U.S.A.* **141 C9** 41 29N 87 20W
Merriman, *U.S.A.* **138 D4** 42 55N 101 42W
Merritt, *Canada* **130 C4** 50 10N 120 45W
Merriwa, *Australia* **117 B9** 32 6 S 150 22 E
Merriwagga, *Australia* **117 B6** 33 47 S 145 43 E
Merry I., *Canada* **128 A4** 55 29N 77 31W
Merrygoen, *Australia* **117 A8** 31 51 S 149 12 E
Merryville, *U.S.A.* **139 K8** 30 45N 93 33W
Mersa Fatma, *Eritrea* **90 E3** 14 57N 40 17 E
Mersch, *Lux.* **21 J8** 49 44N 6 7 E
Merseburg, *Germany* **26 D7** 51 20N 12 0 E
Mersey →, *U.K.* **16 D5** 53 20N 2 56W
Merseyside □, *U.K.* **16 D5** 53 25N 2 55W
Mersin, *Turkey* **88 E6** 36 51N 34 36 E
Mersing, *Malaysia* **77 L4** 2 25N 103 50 E
Merta, *India* **80 F6** 26 39N 74 4 E
Mertert, *Lux.* **21 J8** 49 43N 6 29 E
Merthyr Tydfil, *U.K.* **17 F4** 51 45N 3 23W
Mértola, *Portugal* **37 H3** 37 40N 7 40W
Mertzig, *Lux.* **21 J8** 49 51N 6 1 E
Mertzon, *U.S.A.* **139 K4** 31 16N 100 49W
Méru, *France* **23 C9** 49 13N 2 8 E
Meru, *Kenya* **106 B4** 0 3N 37 40 E
Meru, *Tanzania* **106 C4** 3 15 S 36 46 E
Meru □, *Kenya* **106 B4** 0 3N 37 46 E
Merville, *France* **23 B9** 50 38N 2 38 E
Méry-sur-Seine, *France* **23 D10** 48 31N 3 54 E
Merzifon, *Turkey* **52 F6** 40 53N 35 32 E
Merzig, *Germany* **27 F2** 49 26N 6 37 E
Merzouga, Erg Tin, *Algeria* **99 D7** 24 0N 11 4 E
Mesa, *U.S.A.* **143 K8** 33 25N 111 50W
Mesach Mellet, *Libya* **96 D2** 24 30N 11 30 E
Mesagne, *Italy* **41 B10** 40 34N 17 48 E
Mesanagrós, *Greece* **32 C9** 36 1N 27 49 E
Mesaoría □, *Cyprus* **32 D12** 35 12N 33 14 E
Mesarás, Kólpos, *Greece* **32 D6** 35 6N 24 47 E
Meschede, *Germany* **26 D4** 51 20N 8 17 E
Mesfinto, *Ethiopia* **95 E4** 13 20N 37 22 E
Mesgouez, L., *Canada* **128 B4** 51 20N 75 0W
Meshchovsk, *Russia* **50 D9** 54 22N 35 17 E
Meshed = Mashhad, *Iran* **85 B8** 36 20N 59 35 E
Meshoppen, *U.S.A.* **137 E8** 41 36N 76 3W
Meshra er Req, *Sudan* **95 F2** 8 25N 29 18 E
Mesick, *U.S.A.* **134 C3** 44 24N 85 43W
Mesilinka →, *Canada* **130 B4** 56 6N 124 30W
Mesilla, *U.S.A.* **143 K10** 32 16N 106 48W
Meslay-du-Maine, *France* **22 E6** 47 58N 0 33W
Mesocco, *Switz.* **29 D8** 46 23N 9 12 E
Mesolóngion, *Greece* **45 F3** 38 21N 21 28 E
Mesopotamia = Al Jazirah, *Iraq* **84 C5** 33 30N 44 0 E
Mesoraca, *Italy* **41 C9** 39 5N 16 47 E
Mésou Volímais, *Greece* **45 G2** 37 53N 20 35 E
Mesquite, *U.S.A.* **143 H6** 36 47N 114 6W
Mess Cr. →, *Canada* **130 B2** 57 55N 131 14W
Messac, *France* **22 E5** 47 49N 1 50W
Messad, *Algeria* **99 B5** 34 8N 3 30 E
Messalo →, *Mozam.* **107 E4** 12 25 S 39 15 E
Méssaména, *Cameroon* **101 E7** 3 48N 12 49 E
Messancy, *Belgium* **21 J7** 49 36N 5 49 E
Messeue, *Greece* **45 G3** 37 12N 21 58 E
Messier, Canal, *Chile* **160 C2** 48 20 S 74 33W
Messina, *Italy* **41 D8** 38 10N 15 32 E
Messina, *S. Africa* **105 C5** 22 20 S 30 5 E
Messina, Str. di, *Italy* **41 D8** 38 5N 15 35 E
Messíni, *Greece* **45 G4** 37 4N 22 1 E
Messínía □, *Greece* **45 G3** 37 10N 22 0 E
Messiniakós Kólpos, *Greece* **45 H4** 36 45N 22 5 E
Messkirch, *Germany* **27 H5** 47 59N 9 7 E
Messonghi, *Greece* **32 B3** 39 29N 19 56 E
Mesta →, *Bulgaria* **43 F9** 41 30N 24 12 E
Mestà, Ákra, *Greece* **45 F7** 38 16N 25 53 E
Mestanza, *Spain* **37 G6** 38 35N 4 4W
Město Teplá, *Czech.* **30 B5** 49 59N 12 52 E
Mestre, *Italy* **39 C9** 45 30N 12 13 E
Mestre, Espigão, *Brazil* **155 D2** 12 30 S 46 10W
Městys Zelezná Ruda, *Czech.* **30 B6** 49 8N 13 15 E
Meta, *U.S.A.* **140 F4** 38 19N 92 10W
Meta □, *Colombia* **152 C3** 3 30N 73 0W
Meta →, *S. Amer.* **152 B4** 6 12N 67 28W
Metairie, *U.S.A.* **139 L9** 29 58N 90 10W
Metalici, Munţii, *Romania* **46 C3** 46 15N 22 50 E
Metaline Falls, *U.S.A.* **142 B5** 48 52N 117 22W
Metamora, *U.S.A.* **140 D7** 40 47N 89 22W
Metán, *Argentina* **158 B3** 25 30 S 65 0W
Metangula, *Mozam.* **107 E3** 12 40 S 34 50 E
Metauro →, *Italy* **39 E10** 43 50N 13 3 E
Metema, *Ethiopia* **95 E4** 12 56N 36 13 E
Metengobalame, *Mozam.* **107 E3** 14 49 S 34 30 E
Méthana, *Greece* **45 G5** 37 35N 23 23 E
Methóni, *Greece* **45 H3** 36 49N 21 42 E
Methven, *N.Z.* **119 D6** 43 38 S 171 40 E
Methy L., *Canada* **131 B7** 56 28N 109 30W
Metil, *Mozam.* **107 F4** 16 24 S 39 0 E
Metkovets, *Bulgaria* **43 D8** 43 37N 23 10 E
Metković, *Croatia* **42 D2** 43 6N 17 39 E
Metlakatla, *U.S.A.* **130 B2** 55 8N 131 35W
Metlaoui, *Tunisia* **96 B1** 34 24N 8 24 E
Metlika, *Slovenia* **39 C12** 45 40N 15 20 E
Metro, *Indonesia* **74 D3** 5 5 S 105 20 E
Metropolis, *U.S.A.* **139 G10** 37 9N 88 44W
Métsovon, *Greece* **44 E3** 39 48N 21 12 E
Mettet, *Belgium* **21 H5** 50 19N 4 41 E
Mettuppalaiyam, *India* **83 J3** 11 18N 76 59 E
Mettur, *India* **83 J3** 11 48N 77 47 E
Metz, *France* **23 C13** 49 8N 6 10 E
Meulaboh, *Indonesia* **74 B1** 4 11N 96 3 E
Meulan, *France* **23 C8** 49 3N 1 55 E
Meung-sur-Loire, *France* **23 E8** 47 50N 1 40 E
Meureudu, *Indonesia* **74 A1** 5 19N 96 10 E
Meurthe →, *France* **23 D13** 48 47N 6 9 E
Meurthe-et-Moselle □, *France* **23 D13** 48 52N 6 0 E
Meuse □, *France* **23 C12** 49 8N 5 25 E
Meuse →, *Europe* **21 G7** 50 45N 5 41 E
Meuselwitz, *Germany* **26 D8** 51 3N 12 18 E
Meutapok, Mt., *Malaysia* **75 A5** 5 40N 117 0 E
Mexborough, *U.K.* **16 D6** 53 29N 1 18W
Mexia, *U.S.A.* **139 K6** 31 41N 96 29W
Mexiana, I., *Brazil* **154 A2** 0 0 49 30W
Mexicali, *Mexico* **146 A1** 32 40N 115 30W
México, *Mexico* **147 D5** 19 20N 99 10W
Mexico, *Maine, U.S.A.* **137 B14** 44 34N 70 33W
Mexico, *Mo., U.S.A.* **140 E5** 39 10N 91 53W
México □, *Mexico* **146 D5** 19 20N 99 10W
Mexico ■, *Cent. Amer.* **146 C4** 25 0N 105 0W
Mexico, G. of, *Cent. Amer.* **147 C7** 25 0N 90 0W
Meyenburg, *Germany* **26 B8** 53 19N 12 15 E
Meymac, *France* **24 C6** 45 32N 2 10 E
Meymaneh, *Afghan.* **79 B2** 35 53N 64 38 E
Meyrargues, *France* **25 E9** 43 38N 5 32 E
Meyrueis, *France* **24 D7** 44 12N 3 27 E
Meyssac, *France* **24 C5** 45 3N 1 40 E
Mezdra, *Bulgaria* **43 D8** 43 12N 23 42 E
Mèze, *France* **24 E7** 43 27N 3 36 E
Mezen, *Russia* **48 A7** 65 50N 44 20 E
Mezen →, *Russia* **48 A7** 66 11N 43 59 E
Mézenc, Mt., *France* **25 D8** 44 54N 4 11 E
Mezeş, Munţii, *Romania* **46 B4** 47 5N 23 5 E
Mezha →, *Russia* **50 D7** 55 50N 31 45 E
Mezhdurechenskiy, *Russia* **54 B9** 59 36N 65 56 E
Mézidon, *France* **22 C6** 49 5N 0 1W
Mézilhac, *France* **25 D8** 44 49N 4 21 E
Mézin, *France* **24 D4** 44 4N 0 16 E
Mezőberény, *Hungary* **31 E14** 46 49N 21 3 E
Mezőfalva, *Hungary* **31 E11** 46 55N 18 49 E
Mezőhegyes, *Hungary* **31 E13** 46 19N 20 49 E
Mezőkövácsháza, *Hungary* **31 E13** 46 25N 20 57 E
Mezőkövesd, *Hungary* **31 D13** 47 49N 20 35 E
Mézos, *France* **24 D2** 44 5N 1 10W
Mezőtúr, *Hungary* **31 E13** 46 58N 20 41 E
Mezquital, *Mexico* **146 C4** 23 29N 104 23W
Mezzolombardo, *Italy* **38 B8** 46 13N 11 5 E
Mgeta, *Tanzania* **107 D4** 8 22 S 36 6 E
Mglin, *Russia* **50 E8** 53 2N 32 50 E
Mhlaba Hills, *Zimbabwe* **107 F3** 18 30 S 30 30 E
Mhow, *India* **80 H6** 22 33N 75 50 E
Mi-Shima, *Japan* **62 C3** 34 46N 131 9 E
Miahuatlán, *Mexico* **147 D5** 16 21N 96 36W
Miajadas, *Spain* **37 F5** 39 9N 5 54W
Miallo, *Australia* **114 B4** 16 28 S 145 22 E
Miami, *Ariz., U.S.A.* **143 K8** 33 24N 110 52W
Miami, *Fla., U.S.A.* **135 N5** 25 47N 80 11W
Miami, *Tex., U.S.A.* **139 H4** 35 42N 100 38W
Miami →, *U.S.A.* **134 F3** 39 20N 84 40W
Miami Beach, *U.S.A.* **135 N5** 25 47N 80 8W
Miamisburg, *U.S.A.* **141 E12** 39 38N 84 17W
Mian Xian, *China* **66 H4** 33 10N 106 32 E
Mianchi, *China* **66 G6** 34 48N 111 48 E
Mīāndowāb, *Iran* **84 B5** 37 0N 46 5 E
Miandrivazo, *Madag.* **105 B8** 19 31 S 45 29 E
Mīāneh, *Iran* **84 B5** 37 30N 47 40 E
Mianning, *China* **68 C4** 28 32N 102 9 E
Mianwali, *Pakistan* **79 B3** 32 38N 71 28 E
Mianyang, *Hubei, China* **69 B9** 30 25N 113 25 E
Mianyang, *Sichuan, China* **68 B5** 31 22N 104 47 E
Mianzhu, *China* **68 B5** 31 22N 104 7 E
Miaoli, *Taiwan* **69 E13** 24 37N 120 49 E
Miarinarivo, *Madag.* **105 B8** 18 57 S 46 55 E
Miass, *Russia* **54 D7** 54 59N 60 6 E
Miass →, *Russia* **54 C9** 56 6N 64 30 E
Miasteczko Kraj, *Poland* **47 B4** 53 7N 17 1 E
Miastko, *Poland* **47 B3** 54 0N 16 58 E
Micăsasa, *Romania* **46 C5** 46 7N 24 7 E
Michael, Mt., *Papua N. G.* **120 D3** 6 27 S 145 22 E
Michalovce, *Slovak Rep.* **31 C14** 48 47N 21 58 E
Michelstadt, *Germany* **27 F5** 49 40N 9 0 E
Michigan □, *U.S.A.* **134 C3** 44 0N 85 0W
Michigan, L., *U.S.A.* **134 C2** 44 0N 87 0W
Michigan Center, *U.S.A.* **141 B12** 42 14N 84 20W
Michigan City, *U.S.A.* **141 C10** 41 43N 86 54W
Michikamau L., *Canada* **129 B7** 54 20N 63 10W
Michipicoten, *Canada* **128 C3** 47 55N 84 55W
Michipicoten I., *Canada* **128 C2** 47 40N 85 40W
Michoacan □, *Mexico* **146 D4** 19 0N 102 0W
Michurin, *Bulgaria* **43 E12** 42 9N 27 51 E
Michurinsk, *Russia* **51 E12** 52 58N 40 27 E
Miclere, *Australia* **114 C4** 22 34 S 147 32 E
Mico, Pta., *Nic.* **148 D3** 12 0N 83 30W
Micronesia, Federated States of ■, *Pac. Oc.* **122 G7** 9 0N 150 0 E
Mid Glamorgan □, *U.K.* **17 F4** 51 40N 3 25W
Mid-Indian Ridge, *Ind. Oc.* **109 H6** 30 0 S 75 0 E
Midai, P., *Indonesia* **75 B3** 3 0N 107 47 E
Midale, *Canada* **131 D8** 49 25N 103 20W
Middagsfjället, *Sweden* **14 A6** 63 27N 12 19 E
Middelbeers, *Neths.* **21 F6** 51 28N 5 15 E
Middelburg, *Neths.* **21 F3** 51 30N 3 36 E
Middelburg, *C. Prov., S. Africa* **104 E3** 31 30 S 25 0 E
Middelburg, *Trans., S. Africa* **105 D4** 25 49 S 29 28 E
Middelfart, *Denmark* **15 J3** 55 30N 9 43 E
Middelharnis, *Neths.* **20 E4** 51 46N 4 10 E
Middelkerke, *Belgium* **21 F1** 51 11N 2 49 E
Middelrode, *Neths.* **21 E6** 51 41N 5 26 E
Middelwit, *S. Africa* **104 C4** 24 51 S 27 3 E
Middle →, *U.S.A.* **140 C3** 41 26N 93 30W
Middle Alkali L., *U.S.A.* **142 F3** 41 27N 120 5W
Middle Fork Feather →, *U.S.A.* **144 F5** 38 33N 121 30W
Middle I., *Australia* **113 F3** 34 6 S 123 11 E
Middle Loup →, *U.S.A.* **138 E5** 41 17N 98 24W
Middle Raccoon →, *U.S.A.* **140 C3** 41 35N 93 35W
Middleboro, *U.S.A.* **137 E14** 41 54N 70 55W
Middleburg, *N.Y., U.S.A.* **137 D10** 42 36N 74 20W
Middleburg, *Pa., U.S.A.* **136 F7** 40 47N 77 3W
Middlebury, *Ind., U.S.A.* **141 C11** 41 41N 85 42W
Middlebury, *Vt., U.S.A.* **137 B11** 44 1N 73 10W
Middlemarch, *N.Z.* **119 F5** 45 30 S 170 9 E
Middleport, *U.S.A.* **134 F4** 39 0N 82 3W
Middlesboro, *Ky., U.S.A.* **133 C10** 36 36N 83 43W
Middlesboro, *Ky., U.S.A.* **135 G4** 36 36N 83 43W
Middlesbrough, *U.K.* **16 C6** 54 35N 1 14W
Middlesex, *Belize* **148 C2** 17 2N 88 31W
Middlesex, *U.S.A.* **137 F10** 40 36N 74 30W
Middleton, *Australia* **114 C3** 22 22 S 141 32 E
Middleton, *Canada* **129 D6** 44 57N 65 4W
Middleton, *U.S.A.* **140 A7** 43 6N 89 30W
Middletown, *Calif., U.S.A.* **144 G4** 38 45N 122 37W
Middletown, *Conn., U.S.A.* **137 E12** 41 34N 72 39W
Middletown, *N.Y., U.S.A.* **137 E10** 41 27N 74 25W
Middletown, *Ohio, U.S.A.* **141 E12** 39 31N 84 24W
Middletown, *Pa., U.S.A.* **137 F8** 40 12N 76 44W
Middleville, *U.S.A.* **141 B11** 42 43N 85 28W
Midelt, *Morocco* **98 B4** 32 46N 4 44W
Midhirst, *N.Z.* **118 F3** 39 17 S 174 18 E
Midi, Canal du →, *France* **24 E5** 43 45N 1 21 E
Midi d'Ossau, Pic du, *France* **24 F3** 42 50N 0 26W
Midland, *Canada* **128 D4** 44 45N 79 50W
Midland, *Calif., U.S.A.* **145 M12** 33 52N 114 48W
Midland, *Mich., U.S.A.* **134 D3** 43 37N 84 14W
Midland, *Pa., U.S.A.* **136 F4** 40 39N 80 27W
Midland, *Tex., U.S.A.* **139 K3** 32 0N 102 3W
Midlands □, *Zimbabwe* **107 F2** 19 40 S 29 0 E
Midleton, *Ireland* **19 E3** 51 52N 8 12W
Midlothian, *U.S.A.* **139 J6** 32 30N 97 0W
Midongy, Tangorombohitr' i, *Madag.* **105 C8** 23 30 S 47 0 E
Midongy Atsimo, *Madag.* **105 C8** 23 35 S 47 1 E
Midou →, *France* **24 E3** 43 54N 0 30W
Midouze →, *France* **24 E3** 43 48N 0 51W
Midsayap, *Phil.* **71 H5** 7 12N 124 32 E
Midu, *China* **68 E3** 25 18N 100 30 E
Midway Is., *Pac. Oc.* **122 E10** 28 13N 177 22W
Midway Wells, *U.S.A.* **145 N11** 32 41N 115 7W
Midwest, *U.S.A.* **133 B9** 42 0N 90 0W
Midwest, *Wyo., U.S.A.* **142 E10** 43 25N 106 16W
Midwolda, *Neths.* **20 B9** 53 12N 6 52 E
Midyat, *Turkey* **89 E9** 37 25N 41 23 E
Midzur, *Bulgaria* **42 D7** 43 24N 22 40 E
Mie □, *Japan* **63 C8** 34 30N 136 10 E
Miechów, *Poland* **47 E7** 50 21N 20 5 E
Miedwie, Jezioro, *Poland* **47 B1** 53 17N 14 54 E
Międzybód, *Poland* **47 D4** 51 25N 17 34 E
Międzychód, *Poland* **47 C2** 52 35N 15 53 E
Międzylesie, *Poland* **47 E3** 50 8N 16 40 E
Międzyrzec Podlaski, *Poland* **47 D9** 51 58N 22 45 E
Międzyrzecz, *Poland* **47 C2** 52 26N 15 35 E
Międzyzdroje, *Poland* **47 B1** 53 56N 14 26 E
Miejska, *Poland* **47 D3** 51 39N 16 58 E
Miélan, *France* **24 E4** 43 27N 0 19 E
Mielec, *Poland* **47 E8** 50 15N 21 25 E
Mienga, *Angola* **103 F3** 17 12 S 19 48 E
Miercurea Ciuc, *Romania* **46 C6** 46 21N 25 48 E
Mieres, *Spain* **36 B5** 43 18N 5 48W
Mierlo, *Neths.* **21 F7** 51 27N 5 37 E
Mieroszów, *Poland* **47 E3** 50 40N 16 11 E
Mieso, *Ethiopia* **95 F5** 9 15N 40 43 E
Mieszkowice, *Poland* **47 C1** 52 47N 14 30 E
Mifflintown, *U.S.A.* **136 F7** 40 34N 77 24W
Mifraz Hefa, *Israel* **91 C4** 32 52N 35 0 E
Migdāl, *Israel* **91 C4** 32 51N 35 30 E
Migennes, *France* **23 E10** 47 58N 3 31 E
Migliarino, *Italy* **39 D8** 44 45N 11 56 E
Miguel Alemán, Presa, *Mexico* **147 D5** 18 15N 96 40W
Miguel Alves, *Brazil* **154 B3** 4 11 S 42 55W
Miguel Calmon, *Brazil* **154 D3** 11 26 S 40 36W
Mihaliççık, *Turkey* **88 D4** 39 53N 31 30 E
Mihara, *Japan* **62 C5** 34 24N 133 5 E
Mihara-Yama, *Japan* **63 C11** 34 43N 139 23 E
Mijares →, *Spain* **34 F4** 39 55N 0 1W
Mijas, *Spain* **37 J6** 36 36N 4 40W
Mikese, *Tanzania* **106 D4** 6 48 S 37 55 E
Mikha-Tskhakaya = Senaki, *Georgia* **53 E10** 42 15N 42 7 E
Mikhailovka, *Ukraine* **52 C6** 47 36N 35 16 E
Mikhaylovgrad, *Bulgaria* **43 D8** 43 27N 23 16 E
Mikhaylovka, *Azerbaijan* **53 F13** 41 31N 48 52 E
Mikhaylovka, *Russia* **51 D11** 54 14N 39 0 E
Mikhaylovka, *Russia* **51 F13** 50 3N 43 5 E
Mikhaylovski, *Russia* **54 C6** 56 27N 59 7 E
Mikhnevo, *Russia* **51 D10** 55 4N 37 59 E
Miki, *Hyōgo, Japan* **62 C6** 34 48N 134 59 E
Miki, *Kagawa, Japan* **62 C6** 34 12N 134 7 E
Mikínai, *Greece* **45 G4** 37 43N 22 46 E
Mikkeli, *Finland* **13 F19** 61 43N 27 15 E
Mikkeli □ = Mikkelin lääni □, *Finland* **12 F20** 61 56N 28 0 E
Mikkelin lääni □, *Finland* **12 F20** 61 56N 28 0 E
Mikkwa →, *Canada* **130 B6** 58 25N 114 46W
Mikniya, *Sudan* **95 D3** 17 0N 33 45 E
Mikołajki, *Poland* **47 B8** 53 49N 21 37 E
Mikołów, *Poland* **31 A11** 50 10N 18 50 E
Míkonos, *Greece* **45 G7** 37 30N 25 25 E
Mikrí Préspa, Límni, *Greece* **44 D3** 40 47N 21 3 E
Mikrón Dhérion, *Greece* **44 C8** 41 19N 26 6 E
Mikstat, *Poland* **47 D4** 51 32N 17 59 E
Mikulov, *Czech.* **31 C9** 48 48N 16 39 E
Mikumi, *Tanzania* **106 D4** 7 26 S 37 0 E
Mikun, *Russia* **48 B9** 62 20N 50 0 E
Mikuni, *Japan* **63 A8** 36 13N 136 9 E
Mikuni-Tōge, *Japan* **63 A10** 36 50N 138 50 E
Mikura-Jima, *Japan* **63 D11** 33 52N 139 36 E
Milaca, *U.S.A.* **138 C8** 45 45N 93 39W
Milagro, *Ecuador* **152 D2** 2 11 S 79 36W
Milagros, *Phil.* **70 E4** 12 13N 123 30 E
Milan = Milano, *Italy* **38 C6** 45 28N 9 10 E
Milan, *Ill., U.S.A.* **140 C6** 41 27N 90 34W
Milan, *Mich., U.S.A.* **141 B13** 42 5N 83 41W
Milan, *Mo., U.S.A.* **140 D3** 40 12N 93 7W
Milan, *Tenn., U.S.A.* **135 H1** 35 55N 88 46W
Milang, *S. Austral., Australia* **115 E2** 32 2 S 139 10 E
Milang, *S. Austral., Australia* **116 C3** 35 24 S 138 58 E
Milange, *Mozam.* **107 F4** 16 3 S 35 45 E
Milano, *Italy* **38 C6** 45 28N 9 10 E
Milâs, *Turkey* **88 E2** 37 20N 27 50 E
Milátos, *Greece* **32 D7** 35 18N 25 34 E
Milazzo, *Italy* **41 D8** 38 13N 15 13 E
Milbank, *U.S.A.* **138 C6** 45 13N 96 38W
Milden, *Canada* **131 C7** 51 29N 107 32W
Mildmay, *Canada* **136 B3** 44 3N 81 7W
Mildura, *Australia* **116 C5** 34 13 S 142 9 E
Mile, *China* **68 E4** 24 28N 103 20 E
Miléai, *Greece* **44 E5** 39 20N 23 9 E
Mileh Tharthār, *Iraq* **84 C4** 34 0N 43 15 E
Miles, *Australia* **115 D5** 26 40 S 150 9 E
Miles, *U.S.A.* **139 K4** 31 36N 100 11W
Miles City, *U.S.A.* **138 B2** 46 25N 105 51W
Milestone, *Canada* **131 D8** 49 59N 104 31W
Mileto, *Italy* **41 D9** 38 37N 16 3 E
Miletto, Mte., *Italy* **41 A7** 41 26N 14 23 E
Miletus, *Turkey* **45 G9** 37 30N 27 18 E
Mileura, *Australia* **113 E2** 26 22 S 117 20 E
Milevsko, *Czech.* **30 B7** 49 27N 14 21 E
Milford, *Calif., U.S.A.* **144 E6** 40 10N 120 22W
Milford, *Conn., U.S.A.* **137 E11** 41 14N 73 3W
Milford, *Del., U.S.A.* **134 F8** 38 55N 75 26W
Milford, *Ill., U.S.A.* **141 D9** 40 38N 87 42W
Milford, *Mass., U.S.A.* **137 D13** 42 8N 71 31W
Milford, *Mich., U.S.A.* **141 B13** 42 35N 83 36W
Milford, *Pa., U.S.A.* **137 E10** 41 19N 74 48W
Milford, *Utah, U.S.A.* **143 G7** 38 24N 113 1W
Milford Haven, *U.K.* **17 F2** 51 43N 5 2W
Milford Sd., *N.Z.* **119 E2** 44 41 S 167 47 E
Milgun, *Australia* **113 D2** 24 56 S 118 18 E
Milḥ, Baḥr al, *Iraq* **84 C4** 32 40N 43 35 E
Miliana, *Aïn Salah, Algeria* **99 C5** 27 20N 2 32 E
Miliana, *Médéa, Algeria* **99 A5** 36 20N 2 15 E
Milicz, *Poland* **47 D4** 51 31N 17 19 E
Milingimbi, *Australia* **113 F2** 30 30 S 116 17 E
Militello in Val di Catánia, *Italy* **41 E7** 37 16N 14 46 E
Milk →, *U.S.A.* **142 B10** 48 4N 106 19W

234 Milk, Wadi el


Milk, Wadi el →, *Sudan* **94 D3** 17 55N 30 20 E
Milk River, *Canada* **130 D6** 49 10N 112 5W
Mill, *Neths.* **21 E7** 51 41N 5 48 E
Mill City, *U.S.A.* **142 D2** 44 45N 122 29W
Mill I., *Antarctica* **7 C8** 66 0 S 101 30 E
Mill Shoals, *U.S.A.* **141 F8** 38 15N 88 21W
Mill Valley, *U.S.A.* **144 H4** 37 54N 122 32W
Millau, *France* **24 D7** 44 8N 3 4 E
Millbridge, *Canada* **136 B7** 44 41N 77 36W
Millbrook, *Canada* **136 B6** 44 10N 78 29W
Mille Lacs, L. des, *Canada* **128 C1** 48 45N 90 35W
Mille Lacs L., *U.S.A.* **138 B8** 46 15N 93 39W
Milledgeville, *Ga., U.S.A.* **135 J4** 33 5N 83 14W
Milledgeville, *Ill., U.S.A.* **140 C7** 41 58N 89 46W
Millen, *U.S.A.* **135 J5** 32 48N 81 57W
Miller, *U.S.A.* **138 C5** 44 31N 98 59W
Millerovo, *Russia* **53 B9** 48 57N 40 28 E
Miller's Flat, *N.Z.* **119 F4** 45 39 S 169 23 E
Millersburg, *Ind., U.S.A.* **141 C11** 41 32N 85 42W
Millersburg, *Ohio, U.S.A.* **136 F3** 40 33N 81 55W
Millersburg, *Pa., U.S.A.* **136 F8** 40 32N 76 58W
Millerton, *N.Z.* **119 B6** 41 39 S 171 54 E
Millerton, *U.S.A.* **137 E11** 41 57N 73 31W
Millerton L., *U.S.A.* **144 J7** 37 1N 119 41W
Millevaches, Plateau de, *France* **24 C6** 45 45N 2 0 E
Millicent, *Australia* **116 D4** 37 34 S 140 21 E
Millingen, *Neths.* **20 E8** 51 52N 6 2 E
Millinocket, *U.S.A.* **129 C6** 45 39N 68 43W
Millmerran, *Australia* **115 D5** 27 53 S 151 16 E
Mills L., *Canada* **130 A5** 61 30N 118 20W
Millsboro, *U.S.A.* **136 G4** 40 0N 80 0W
Milltown Malbay, *Ireland* **19 D2** 52 51N 9 25W
Millville, *U.S.A.* **134 F8** 39 24N 75 2W
Millwood L., *U.S.A.* **139 J8** 33 42N 93 58W
Milly-la-Forêt, *France* **23 D9** 48 24N 2 28 E
Milna, *Croatia* **39 E13** 43 20N 16 28 E
Milne →, *Australia* **114 C2** 21 10 S 137 33 E
Milne Inlet, *Canada* **127 A11** 72 30N 80 0W
Milnor, *U.S.A.* **138 B6** 46 16N 97 27W
Milo, *Canada* **130 C6** 50 34N 112 53W
Mílos, *Greece* **45 H6** 36 44N 24 25 E
Miloševo, *Serbia* **42 B5** 45 42N 20 20 E
Miłosław, *Poland* **47 C4** 52 12N 17 32 E
Milparinka P.O., *Australia* **115 D3** 29 46 S 141 57 E
Milroy, *U.S.A.* **141 E11** 39 30N 85 28W
Miltenberg, *Germany* **27 F5** 49 41N 9 13 E
Milton, *Canada* **136 C5** 43 31N 79 53W
Milton, *N.Z.* **119 G4** 46 7 S 169 59 E
Milton, *U.K.* **18 D4** 57 18N 4 32W
Milton, *Calif., U.S.A.* **144 G6** 38 3N 120 51W
Milton, *Fla., U.S.A.* **135 K2** 30 38N 87 3W
Milton, *Iowa, U.S.A.* **140 D4** 40 41N 92 10W
Milton, *Pa., U.S.A.* **136 F8** 41 1N 76 51W
Milton, *Wis., U.S.A.* **141 B8** 42 47N 88 56W
Milton-Freewater, *U.S.A.* **142 D4** 45 56N 118 23W
Milton Keynes, *U.K.* **17 E7** 52 3N 0 42W
Miltou, *Chad* **97 F3** 10 14N 17 26 E
Milverton, *Canada* **136 C4** 43 34N 80 55W
Milwaukee, *U.S.A.* **141 A9** 43 2N 87 55W
Milwaukee Deep, *Atl. Oc.* **8 G2** 19 50N 68 0W
Milwaukie, *U.S.A.* **144 E4** 45 27N 122 38W
Mim, *Ghana* **100 D4** 6 57N 2 33W
Mimizan, *France* **24 D2** 44 12N 1 13W
Mimon, *Czech.* **30 A7** 50 38N 14 43 E
Mimongo, *Gabon* **102 C2** 1 11 S 11 36 E
Mimoso, *Brazil* **155 E2** 15 10 S 48 5W
Min Chiang →, *China* **69 E12** 26 0N 119 35 E
Min Jiang →, *China* **68 C5** 28 45N 104 40 E
Min-Kush, *Kirghizia* **55 C7** 41 40N 74 28 E
Min Xian, *China* **66 G3** 34 25N 104 5 E
Mina, *U.S.A.* **143 G4** 38 24N 118 7W
Mina Pirquitas, *Argentina* **158 A2** 22 40 S 66 30W
Mīnā Su'ud, *Si. Arabia* **85 D6** 28 45N 48 28 E
Mīnā'al Aḥmadī, *Kuwait* **85 D6** 29 5N 48 10 E
Mīnāb, *Iran* **85 E8** 27 10N 57 1 E
Minago →, *Canada* **131 C9** 54 33N 98 59W
Minakami, *Japan* **63 A10** 36 49N 138 59 E
Minaki, *Canada* **131 D10** 49 59N 94 40W
Minakuchi, *Japan* **63 C8** 34 58N 136 10 E
Minamata, *Japan* **62 E2** 32 10N 130 30 E
Minami-Tori-Shima, *Pac. Oc.* **122 E7** 24 0N 153 45 E
Minas, *Uruguay* **159 C4** 34 20 S 55 10W
Minas, Sierra de las, *Guatemala* **148 C2** 15 9N 89 31W
Minas Basin, *Canada* **129 C7** 45 20N 64 12W
Minas de Rio Tinto, *Spain* **37 H4** 37 42N 6 35W
Minas de San Quintín, *Spain* **37 G6** 38 49N 4 23W
Minas Gerais □, *Brazil* **155 E2** 18 50 S 46 0W
Minas Novas, *Brazil* **155 E3** 17 15 S 42 36W
Minatitlán, *Mexico* **147 D6** 17 58N 94 35W
Minbu, *Burma* **78 E5** 20 10N 94 52 E
Minbya, *Burma* **78 E4** 20 22N 93 16 E
Mincio →, *Italy* **38 C7** 45 4N 10 59 E
Mindanao, *Phil.* **71 H5** 8 0N 125 0 E
Mindanao Sea = Bohol Sea, *Phil.* **71 G5** 9 0N 124 0 E
Mindanao Trench, *Pac. Oc.* **70 E5** 12 0N 126 6 E
Mindel →, *Germany* **27 G6** 48 31N 10 23 E
Mindelheim, *Germany* **27 G6** 48 4N 10 30 E
Minden, *Canada* **136 B6** 44 55N 78 43W
Minden, *Germany* **26 C4** 52 18N 8 45 E
Minden, *La., U.S.A.* **139 J8** 32 37N 93 17W
Minden, *Nev., U.S.A.* **144 G7** 38 57N 119 46W
Mindiptana, *Indonesia* **73 C6** 5 55 S 140 22 E
Mindon, *Burma* **78 F5** 19 21N 94 44 E
Mindoro, *Phil.* **70 E3** 13 0N 121 0 E
Mindoro Occidental □, *Phil.* **70 E3** 13 0N 120 55 E
Mindoro Oriental □, *Phil.* **70 E3** 13 0N 121 5 E
Mindoro Str., *Phil.* **70 E3** 12 30N 120 30 E
Mindouli, *Congo* **103 C2** 4 12 S 14 28 E
Mine, *Japan* **62 C3** 34 12N 131 7 E
Minehead, *U.K.* **17 F4** 51 12N 3 29W
Mineiros, *Brazil* **157 D7** 17 34 S 52 34W
Mineola, *U.S.A.* **139 J7** 32 40N 95 29W
Mineral King, *U.S.A.* **144 J8** 36 27N 118 36W
Mineral Point, *U.S.A.* **140 B6** 42 52N 90 11W
Mineral Wells, *U.S.A.* **139 J5** 32 48N 98 7W
Mineralnyye Vody, *Russia* **53 D10** 44 15N 43 8 E
Minersville, *Pa., U.S.A.* **137 F8** 40 41N 76 16W
Minersville, *Utah, U.S.A.* **143 G7** 38 13N 112 56W
Minerva, *U.S.A.* **136 F3** 40 44N 81 6W
Minervino Murge, *Italy* **41 A9** 41 6N 16 4 E
Minetto, *U.S.A.* **137 C8** 43 24N 76 28W
Mingan, *Canada* **129 B7** 50 20N 64 0W
Mingary, *Australia* **116 B4** 32 8 S 140 45 E
Mingechaur, *Azerbaijan* **53 F12** 40 45N 47 0 E
Mingechaurskoye Vdkhr., *Azerbaijan* **53 F12** 40 56N 47 20 E
Mingela, *Australia* **114 B4** 19 52 S 146 38 E
Mingenew, *Australia* **113 E2** 29 12 S 115 21 E
Mingera Cr. →, *Australia* **114 C2** 20 38 S 137 45 E
Minggang, *China* **69 A10** 32 24N 114 3 E
Mingin, *Burma* **78 D5** 22 50N 94 30 E
Minglanilla, *Spain* **34 F3** 39 34N 1 38W
Minglun, *China* **68 E7** 25 10N 108 21 E
Mingorria, *Spain* **36 E6** 40 45N 4 40W
Mingt'iehkaitafan = Mintaka Pass, *Pakistan* **81 A6** 37 0N 74 58 E
Mingxi, *China* **69 D11** 26 18N 117 12 E
Mingyuegue, *China* **67 C15** 43 2N 128 50 E
Minhou, *China* **69 E12** 26 0N 119 15 E
Minićevo, *Serbia* **42 D7** 43 42N 22 18 E
Minidoka, *U.S.A.* **142 E7** 42 45N 113 29W
Minier, *U.S.A.* **140 D7** 40 26N 89 19W
Minigwal, L., *Australia* **113 E3** 29 31 S 123 14 E
Minilya, *Australia* **113 D1** 23 55 S 114 0 E
Minilya →, *Australia* **113 D1** 23 45 S 114 0 E
Mininera, *Australia* **116 D5** 37 37 S 142 58 E
Minipi, L., *Canada* **129 B7** 52 25N 60 45W
Minj, *Papua N. G.* **120 C3** 5 54 S 144 37 E
Mink L., *Canada* **130 A5** 61 54N 117 40W
Minlaton, *Australia* **116 C2** 34 45 S 137 35 E
Minna, *Nigeria* **101 D6** 9 37N 6 30 E
Minneapolis, *Kans., U.S.A.* **138 F6** 39 8N 97 42W
Minneapolis, *Minn., U.S.A.* **138 C8** 44 59N 93 16W
Minnedosa, *Canada* **131 C9** 50 14N 99 50W
Minnesota □, *U.S.A.* **138 B7** 46 0N 94 15W
Minnesund, *Norway* **14 D5** 60 23N 11 14 E
Minnie Creek, *Australia* **113 D2** 24 3 S 115 42 E
Minnipa, *Australia* **115 E2** 32 51 S 135 9 E
Minnitaki L., *Canada* **128 C1** 49 57N 92 10W
Mino, *Japan* **63 B8** 35 32N 136 55 E
Miño →, *Spain* **36 D2** 41 52N 8 40W
Mino-Kamo, *Japan* **63 B9** 35 23N 137 2 E
Mino-Mikawa-Kōgen, *Japan* **63 B9** 35 10N 137 23 E
Minoa, *Greece* **45 J7** 35 6N 25 45 E
Minobu, *Japan* **63 B10** 35 22N 138 26 E
Minobu-Sanchi, *Japan* **63 B10** 35 14N 138 20 E
Minonk, *U.S.A.* **140 D7** 40 54N 89 2W
Minooka, *U.S.A.* **141 C8** 41 27N 88 16W
Minorca = Menorca, *Spain* **33 B11** 40 0N 4 0 E
Minore, *Australia* **117 B8** 32 14 S 148 27 E
Minot, *U.S.A.* **138 A4** 48 14N 101 18W
Minqin, *China* **66 E2** 38 38N 103 20 E
Minqing, *China* **69 D12** 26 15N 118 50 E
Minsen, *Germany* **26 B3** 53 43N 7 58 E
Minsk, *Belorussia* **50 E5** 53 52N 27 30 E
Mińsk Mazowiecki, *Poland* **47 C8** 52 10N 21 33 E
Minster, *U.S.A.* **141 D12** 40 24N 84 23W
Mintaka Pass, *Pakistan* **81 A6** 37 0N 74 58 E
Minthami, *Burma* **78 D5** 23 55N 94 16 E
Minto, *U.S.A.* **126 B5** 64 53N 149 11W
Minton, *Canada* **131 D8** 49 10N 104 35W
Mintoum, *Gabon* **102 B2** 0 27N 12 16 E
Minturn, *U.S.A.* **142 G10** 39 35N 106 26W
Minturno, *Italy* **40 A6** 41 15N 13 43 E
Minûf, *Egypt* **94 H7** 30 26N 30 52 E
Minusinsk, *Russia* **57 D10** 53 50N 91 20 E
Minutang, *India* **78 A6** 28 15N 96 30 E
Minvoul, *Gabon* **102 B2** 2 9N 12 8 E
Minwakh, *Yemen* **87 C5** 16 48N 48 6 E
Minya el Qamh, *Egypt* **94 H7** 30 31N 31 21 E
Minyar, *Russia* **54 D5** 55 4N 57 33 E
Minyip, *Australia* **116 D5** 36 29 S 142 36 E
Mionica, *Serbia* **42 C5** 44 14N 20 6 E
Mir, *Niger* **97 F2** 14 5N 11 59 E
Mir-Bashir, *Azerbaijan* **53 F12** 40 20N 46 58 E
Mīr Kūh, *Iran* **85 E8** 26 22N 58 55 E
Mīr Shahdād, *Iran* **85 E8** 26 15N 58 29 E
Mira, *Italy* **39 C9** 45 26N 12 9 E
Mira, *Portugal* **36 E2** 40 26N 8 44W
Mira →, *Colombia* **152 C2** 1 36N 79 1W
Mira →, *Portugal* **37 H2** 37 43N 8 47W
Mira por vos Cay, *Bahamas* **149 B5** 22 9N 74 30W
Mīrābād, *Afghan.* **79 C1** 30 25N 61 50 E
Mirabella Eclano, *Italy* **41 A7** 41 3N 14 59 E
Miracema do Norte, *Brazil* **154 C2** 9 33 S 48 24W
Mirador, *Brazil* **154 C3** 6 22 S 44 22W
Miraflores, *Colombia* **152 C3** 1 25N 72 13W
Miraj, *India* **82 F2** 16 50N 74 45 E
Miram Shah, *Pakistan* **79 B3** 33 0N 70 2 E
Miramar, *Argentina* **158 D4** 38 15 S 57 50W
Miramar, *Mozam.* **105 C6** 23 50 S 35 35 E
Miramas, *France* **25 E8** 43 33N 4 59 E
Mirambeau, *France* **24 C3** 45 23N 0 35W
Miramichi B., *Canada* **129 C7** 47 15N 65 0W
Miramont-de-Guyenne, *France* **24 D4** 44 37N 0 21 E
Miranda, *Brazil* **157 E6** 20 10 S 56 15W
Miranda □, *Venezuela* **152 A4** 10 15N 66 25W
Miranda →, *Brazil* **157 D6** 19 25 S 57 20W
Miranda de Ebro, *Spain* **34 C2** 42 41N 2 57W
Miranda do Corvo, *Spain* **36 E2** 40 6N 8 20W
Miranda do Douro, *Portugal* **36 D4** 41 30N 6 16W
Mirande, *France* **24 E4** 43 31N 0 25 E
Mirandela, *Portugal* **36 D3** 41 32N 7 10W
Mirando City, *U.S.A.* **139 M5** 27 26N 99 0W
Mirandola, *Italy* **38 D8** 44 53N 11 2 E
Mirandópolis, *Brazil* **159 A5** 21 9 S 51 6W
Mirango, *Malawi* **107 E3** 13 32 S 34 58 E
Mirani, *Australia* **114 C4** 21 9 S 148 53 E
Mirano, *Italy* **39 C9** 45 29N 12 6 E
Mirassol, *Brazil* **159 A6** 20 46 S 49 28W
Mirbāṭ, *Oman* **87 C6** 17 0N 54 45 E
Mirboo North, *Australia* **117 E7** 38 24 S 146 10 E
Mirear, *Egypt* **94 C4** 23 15N 35 41 E
Mirebeau, *Côte-d'Or, France* **23 E12** 47 25N 5 20 E
Mirebeau, *Vienne, France* **22 F7** 46 49N 0 10 E
Mirecourt, *France* **23 D13** 48 20N 6 10 E
Mirgorod, *Ukraine* **50 G8** 49 58N 33 37 E
Miri, *Malaysia* **75 B4** 4 23N 113 59 E
Miriam Vale, *Australia* **114 C5** 24 20 S 151 33 E
Mirim, L., *S. Amer.* **159 C5** 32 45 S 52 50W
Mirimire, *Venezuela* **152 A4** 11 10N 68 43W
Miriti, *Brazil* **157 B6** 6 15 S 59 0W
Mirnyy, *Russia* **57 C12** 62 33N 113 53 E
Miroč, *Serbia* **42 C7** 44 32N 22 16 E
Mirond L., *Canada* **131 B8** 55 6N 102 47W
Mirosławiec, *Poland* **47 B3** 53 20N 16 5 E
Mirpur, *Pakistan* **79 B4** 33 32N 73 56 E
Mirpur Bibiwari, *Pakistan* **80 E2** 28 33N 67 44 E
Mirpur Khas, *Pakistan* **79 D3** 25 30N 69 0 E
Mirpur Sakro, *Pakistan* **80 G2** 24 33N 67 41 E
Mirria, *Niger* **97 F1** 13 43N 9 7 E
Mirror, *Canada* **130 C6** 52 30N 113 7W
Mîrşani, *Romania* **46 E4** 44 1N 23 59 E
Mirsk, *Poland* **47 E2** 50 58N 15 23 E
Miryang, *S. Korea* **67 G15** 35 31N 128 44 E
Mirzaani, *Georgia* **53 F12** 41 24N 46 5 E
Mirzapur, *India* **81 G10** 25 10N 82 34 E
Mirzapur-cum-Vindhyachal = Mirzapur, *India* **81 G10** 25 10N 82 34 E
Misamis Occidental □, *Phil.* **71 G4** 8 20N 123 42 E
Misamis Oriental □, *Phil.* **71 G5** 8 45N 125 0 E
Misantla, *Mexico* **147 D5** 19 56N 96 50W
Misawa, *Japan* **60 D10** 40 41N 141 24 E
Miscou I., *Canada* **129 C7** 47 57N 64 31W
Mish'āb, Ra'as al, *Si. Arabia* **85 D6** 28 15N 48 43 E
Mishagua →, *Peru* **156 C3** 11 12 S 72 58W
Mishan, *China* **65 B8** 45 37N 131 48 E
Mishawaka, *U.S.A.* **141 C10** 41 40N 86 11W
Mishbih, Gebel, *Egypt* **94 C3** 22 38N 34 44 E
Mishima, *Japan* **63 B10** 35 10N 138 52 E
Mishkino, *Russia* **54 D8** 55 20N 63 55 E
Mishmi Hills, *India* **78 A5** 29 0N 96 0 E
Misilmeri, *Italy* **40 D6** 38 2N 13 25 E
Misima I., *Papua N. G.* **120 F7** 10 40 S 152 45 E
Misión, *Mexico* **145 N10** 32 6N 116 53W
Misión Fagnano, *Argentina* **160 D3** 54 32 S 67 17W
Misiones □, *Argentina* **159 B5** 27 0 S 55 0W
Misiones □, *Paraguay* **158 B4** 27 0 S 56 0W
Miskah, *Si. Arabia* **84 E4** 24 49N 42 56 E
Miskitos, Cayos, *Nic.* **148 D3** 14 26N 82 50W
Miskolc, *Hungary* **31 C13** 48 7N 20 50 E
Misoke, *Zaïre* **106 C2** 0 42 S 28 2 E
Misool, *Indonesia* **73 B4** 1 52 S 130 10 E
Misrātah, *Libya* **96 B3** 32 24N 15 3 E
Misrātah □, *Libya* **96 C3** 29 0N 16 0 E
Missanabie, *Canada* **128 C3** 48 20N 84 6W
Missão Velha, *Brazil* **154 C4** 7 15 S 39 10W
Missinaibi →, *Canada* **128 B3** 50 43N 81 29W
Missinaibi L., *Canada* **128 C3** 48 23N 83 40W
Mission, *S. Dak., U.S.A.* **138 D4** 43 18N 100 39W
Mission, *Tex., U.S.A.* **139 M5** 26 13N 98 20W
Mission City, *Canada* **130 D4** 49 10N 122 15W
Mission Viejo, *U.S.A.* **145 M9** 33 36N 117 40W
Missisa L., *Canada* **128 B2** 52 20N 85 7W
Mississagi →, *Canada* **128 C3** 46 15N 83 9W
Mississinewa Res., *U.S.A.* **141 D10** 40 46N 86 3W
Mississippi □, *U.S.A.* **139 J10** 33 0N 90 0W
Mississippi →, *U.S.A.* **139 L10** 29 9N 89 15W
Mississippi L., *Canada* **137 A8** 45 5N 76 10W
Mississippi River Delta, *U.S.A.* **139 L9** 29 10N 89 15W
Mississippi Sd., *U.S.A.* **139 K10** 30 20N 89 0W
Missoula, *U.S.A.* **142 C6** 46 52N 114 1W
Missour, *Morocco* **98 B4** 33 3N 4 0W
Missouri □, *U.S.A.* **138 F8** 38 25N 92 30W
Missouri →, *U.S.A.* **138 F9** 38 49N 90 7W
Missouri Valley, *U.S.A.* **138 E7** 41 34N 95 53W
Mist, *U.S.A.* **144 E3** 45 59N 123 15W
Mistake B., *Canada* **131 A10** 62 8N 93 0W
Mistassini →, *Canada* **129 C5** 48 42N 72 20W
Mistassini L., *Canada* **128 B5** 51 0N 73 30W
Mistastin L., *Canada* **129 A7** 55 57N 63 20W
Mistatim, *Canada* **131 C8** 52 52N 103 22W
Mistelbach, *Austria* **31 C9** 48 34N 16 34 E
Misterbianco, *Italy* **41 E8** 37 32N 15 2 E
Mistretta, *Italy* **41 E7** 37 56N 14 20 E
Misty L., *Canada* **131 B8** 58 53N 101 40W
Misugi, *Japan* **63 C8** 34 31N 136 16 E
Misumi, *Japan* **62 E2** 32 37N 130 27 E
Misurata = Misrātah, *Libya* **96 B3** 32 24N 15 3 E
Mît Ghamr, *Egypt* **94 H7** 30 42N 31 12 E
Mitaka, *Japan* **63 B11** 35 40N 139 33 E
Mitan, *Uzbekistan* **55 C3** 40 5N 66 35 E
Mitatib, *Sudan* **95 D4** 15 59N 36 12 E
Mitchell, *Australia* **115 D4** 26 29 S 147 58 E
Mitchell, *Canada* **136 C3** 43 28N 81 12W
Mitchell, *Ind., U.S.A.* **141 F10** 38 44N 86 28W
Mitchell, *Nebr., U.S.A.* **138 E3** 41 57N 103 49W
Mitchell, *Oreg., U.S.A.* **142 D3** 44 34N 120 9W
Mitchell, *S. Dak., U.S.A.* **138 D5** 43 43N 98 2W
Mitchell →, *Australia* **114 B3** 15 12 S 141 35 E
Mitchell, Mt., *U.S.A.* **135 H4** 35 46N 82 16W
Mitchell Ras., *Australia* **114 A2** 12 49 S 135 36 E
Mitchelstown, *Ireland* **19 D3** 52 16N 8 18W
Mitha Tiwana, *Pakistan* **80 C5** 32 13N 72 6 E
Míthimna, *Greece* **44 E8** 39 20N 26 12 E
Mitiamo, *Australia* **116 D6** 36 12 S 144 15 E
Mitilíni, *Greece* **45 E8** 39 6N 26 35 E
Mitilinoí, *Greece* **45 G8** 37 42N 26 56 E
Mito, *Japan* **63 A12** 36 20N 140 30 E
Mitre, Mt., *N.Z.* **118 G4** 40 50 S 175 30 E
Mitsinjo, *Madag.* **105 B8** 16 1 S 45 52 E
Mitsiwa, *Eritrea* **95 D4** 15 35N 39 25 E
Mitsiwa Channel, *Eritrea* **95 D5** 15 30N 40 0 E
Mitsukaidō, *Japan* **63 A11** 36 1N 139 59 E
Mittagong, *Australia* **117 C9** 34 28 S 150 29 E
Mittelland, *Switz.* **28 C4** 46 50N 7 23 E
Mittelland Kanal, *Germany* **26 C3** 52 23N 7 45 E
Mittenwalde, *Germany* **26 C9** 52 16N 13 33 E
Mitterteich, *Germany* **27 F8** 49 57N 12 15 E
Mittweida, *Germany* **26 E8** 50 59N 13 0 E
Mitú, *Colombia* **152 C3** 1 8N 70 3W
Mituas, *Colombia* **152 C4** 3 52N 68 49W
Mitumba, *Tanzania* **106 D3** 7 8 S 31 2 E
Mitumba, Chaîne des, *Zaïre* **106 D2** 7 0 S 27 30 E
Mitumba Mts. = Mitumba, Chaîne des, *Zaïre* **106 D2** 7 0 S 27 30 E
Mitwaba, *Zaïre* **107 D2** 8 2 S 27 17 E
Mityana, *Uganda* **106 B3** 0 23N 32 2 E
Mitzic, *Gabon* **102 B2** 0 45N 11 40 E
Miura, *Japan* **63 B11** 35 12N 139 40 E
Mixteco →, *Mexico* **147 D5** 18 11N 98 30W
Miyagi □, *Japan* **60 E10** 38 15N 140 45 E
Miyâh, W. el →, *Egypt* **94 B3** 25 0N 33 23 E
Miyah, W. el →, *Syria* **84 C3** 34 44N 39 57 E
Miyake-Jima, *Japan* **63 C11** 34 5N 139 30 E
Miyako, *Japan* **60 E10** 39 40N 141 59 E
Miyako-Jima, *Japan* **61 M2** 24 45N 125 20 E
Miyako-Rettō, *Japan* **61 M2** 24 24N 125 0 E
Miyakonojō, *Japan* **62 F3** 31 40N 131 5 E
Miyanojō, *Japan* **62 F2** 31 54N 130 27 E
Miyanoura-Dake, *Japan* **61 J5** 30 20N 130 31 E
Miyata, *Japan* **62 D2** 33 49N 130 42 E
Miyazaki, *Japan* **62 F3** 31 56N 131 30 E
Miyazaki □, *Japan* **62 E3** 32 30N 131 30 E
Miyazu, *Japan* **63 B7** 35 35N 135 10 E
Miyet, Bahr el = Dead Sea, *Asia* **91 D4** 31 30N 35 30 E
Miyi, *China* **68 D4** 26 47N 102 9 E
Miyoshi, *Japan* **62 C4** 34 48N 132 51 E
Miyun, *China* **66 D9** 40 28N 116 50 E
Miyun Shuiku, *China* **67 D9** 40 30N 117 0 E
Mizamis = Ozamiz, *Phil.* **71 G4** 8 15N 123 50 E
Mizdah, *Libya* **96 B2** 31 30N 13 0 E
Mizen Hd., *Cork, Ireland* **19 E2** 51 27N 9 50W
Mizen Hd., *Wick., Ireland* **19 D5** 52 52N 6 4W
Mizhi, *China* **66 F6** 37 47N 110 12 E
Mizil, *Romania* **46 E7** 44 59N 26 29 E
Mizoram □, *India* **78 D4** 23 30N 92 40 E
Mizpe Ramon, *Israel* **91 E3** 30 34N 34 49 E
Mizuho, *Japan* **63 B7** 35 6N 135 17 E
Mizunami, *Japan* **63 B9** 35 22N 137 15 E
Mizusawa, *Japan* **60 E10** 39 8N 141 8 E
Mjöbäck, *Sweden* **15 G6** 57 28N 12 53 E
Mjölby, *Sweden* **15 F9** 58 20N 15 10 E
Mjörn, *Sweden* **15 G6** 57 55N 12 25 E
Mjøsa, *Norway* **14 D5** 60 48N 11 0 E
Mkata, *Tanzania* **106 D4** 5 45 S 38 20 E
Mkokotoni, *Tanzania* **106 D4** 5 55 S 39 15 E
Mkomazi, *Tanzania* **106 C4** 4 40 S 38 7 E
Mkomazi →, *S. Africa* **105 E5** 30 12 S 30 50 E
Mkulwe, *Tanzania* **107 D3** 8 37 S 32 20 E
Mkumbi, Ras, *Tanzania* **106 D4** 7 38 S 39 55 E
Mkushi, *Zambia* **107 E2** 14 25 S 29 15 E
Mkushi River, *Zambia* **107 E2** 13 32 S 29 45 E
Mkuze, *S. Africa* **105 D5** 27 10 S 32 0 E
Mkuze →, *S. Africa* **105 D5** 27 45 S 32 30 E
Mladá Boleslav, *Czech.* **30 A7** 50 27N 14 53 E
Mladenovac, *Serbia* **42 C5** 44 28N 20 44 E
Mlala Hills, *Tanzania* **106 D3** 6 50 S 31 40 E
Mlange, *Malawi* **107 F4** 16 2 S 35 33 E
Mlava →, *Serbia* **42 C6** 44 45N 21 13 E
Mława, *Poland* **47 B7** 53 9N 20 25 E
Mliniśte, *Bos.-H.* **39 D13** 44 15N 16 50 E
Mljet, *Croatia* **42 E2** 42 43N 17 30 E
Mljetski Kanal, *Croatia* **42 E2** 42 48N 17 35 E
Młynary, *Poland* **47 A6** 54 12N 19 46 E
Mmabatho, *S. Africa* **104 D4** 25 49 S 25 30 E
Mme, *Cameroon* **101 D7** 6 18N 10 14 E
Mo i Rana, *Norway* **12 C13** 66 15N 14 7 E
Moa, *Indonesia* **72 C3** 8 0 S 128 0 E
Moa →, *S. Leone* **100 D2** 6 59N 11 36W
Moab, *U.S.A.* **143 G9** 38 35N 109 33W
Moabi, *Gabon* **102 C2** 2 24 S 10 59 E
Moaco →, *Brazil* **156 B4** 7 41 S 68 18W
Moala, *Fiji* **121 B2** 18 36 S 179 53 E
Moalie Park, *Australia* **115 D3** 29 42 S 143 3 E
Moaña, *Spain* **36 C2** 42 18N 8 43W
Moba, *Zaïre* **106 D2** 7 0 S 29 48 E
Mobara, *Japan* **63 B12** 35 25N 140 18 E
Mobārakābād, *Iran* **85 D7** 28 24N 53 20 E
Mobārakīyeh, *Iran* **85 C6** 35 5N 51 47 E
Mobaye, *C.A.R.* **102 B4** 4 25N 21 5 E
Mobayi, *Zaïre* **102 B4** 4 15N 21 8 E
Moberly, *U.S.A.* **140 E4** 39 25N 92 26W
Moberly →, *Canada* **130 B4** 56 12N 120 55W
Mobile, *U.S.A.* **135 K1** 30 41N 88 3W
Mobile B., *U.S.A.* **135 K2** 30 30N 88 0W
Mobridge, *U.S.A.* **138 C4** 45 32N 100 26W
Mobutu Sese Seko, L., *Africa* **106 B3** 1 30N 31 0 E
Moc Chau, *Vietnam* **76 B5** 20 50N 104 38 E
Moc Hoa, *Vietnam* **77 G5** 10 46N 105 56 E
Mocaba, Sa. de, *Angola* **103 D3** 7 12 S 15 0 E
Mocabe Kasari, *Zaïre* **107 D2** 9 58 S 26 12 E
Mocajuba, *Brazil* **154 B2** 2 35 S 49 30W
Moçambique, *Mozam.* **107 F5** 15 3 S 40 42 E
Moçâmedes = Namibe, *Angola* **103 F2** 15 7 S 12 11 E
Mocapra →, *Venezuela* **152 B4** 7 56N 66 46W
Mocha, I., *Chile* **160 A2** 38 22 S 73 56W
Mochudi, *Botswana* **104 C4** 24 27 S 26 7 E
Mocimboa da Praia, *Mozam.* **107 E5** 11 25 S 40 20 E
Mociu, *Romania* **46 C5** 46 46N 24 3 E
Moclips, *U.S.A.* **144 C2** 47 14N 124 13W
Mocoa, *Colombia* **152 C2** 1 7N 76 35W
Mococa, *Brazil* **159 A6** 21 28 S 47 0W
Mocorito, *Mexico* **146 B3** 25 30N 107 53W
Moctezuma, *Mexico* **146 B3** 29 50N 109 0W
Moctezuma →, *Mexico* **147 C5** 21 59N 98 34W
Mocuba, *Mozam.* **107 F4** 16 54 S 36 57 E
Mocúzari, Presa, *Mexico* **146 B3** 27 10N 109 10W
Moda, *Burma* **78 C6** 24 22N 96 29 E
Modane, *France* **25 C10** 45 12N 6 40 E
Modasa, *India* **80 H5** 23 30N 73 21 E
Modave, *Belgium* **21 H6** 50 27N 5 18 E
Modder →, *S. Africa* **104 D3** 29 2 S 24 37 E
Modderrivier, *S. Africa* **104 D3** 29 2 S 24 38 E
Módena, *Italy* **38 D7** 44 39N 10 55 E
Modena, *U.S.A.* **143 H7** 37 48N 113 56W
Modesto, *U.S.A.* **144 H6** 37 39N 121 0W
Módica, *Italy* **41 F7** 36 52N 14 45 E
Modigliana, *Italy* **39 D8** 44 9N 11 48 E
Modjamboli, *Zaïre* **102 B4** 2 28N 22 6 E
Modlin, *Poland* **47 C7** 52 24N 20 41 E
Mödling, *Austria* **31 C9** 48 5N 16 17 E
Modo, *Sudan* **95 F3** 5 31N 30 33 E
Modra, *Slovak Rep.* **31 C10** 48 19N 17 20 E

Montmirail 235


Modriča, *Bos.-H.* **42 C3** 44 57N 18 17 E
Moe, *Australia* **117 E7** 38 12 S 146 19 E
Moebase, *Mozam.* **107 F4** 17 3 S 38 41 E
Moëlan-sur-Mer, *France* **22 E3** 47 49N 3 38W
Moengo, *Surinam* **153 B7** 5 45N 54 20W
Moergestel, *Neths.* **21 E6** 51 33N 5 11 E
Moers, *Germany* **21 F9** 51 27N 6 38 E
Moësa →, *Switz.* **29 D8** 46 12N 9 10 E
Moffat, *U.K.* **18 F5** 55 20N 3 27W
Moga, *India* **80 D6** 30 48N 75 8 E
Mogadishu = Muqdisho, *Somali Rep.* **90 G4** 2 2N 45 25 E
Mogador = Essaouira, *Morocco* **98 B3** 31 32N 9 42W
Mogadouro, *Portugal* **36 D4** 41 22N 6 47W
Mogalakwena →, *S. Africa* **105 C4** 22 38 S 28 40 E
Mogami →, *Japan* **60 E10** 38 45N 140 0 E
Mogán, *Canary Is.* **33 G4** 27 53N 15 43W
Mogaung, *Burma* **78 C6** 25 20N 97 0 E
Møgeltønder, *Denmark* **15 K2** 54 57N 8 48 E
Mogente, *Spain* **35 G4** 38 52N 0 45W
Mogho, *Ethiopia* **95 G5** 4 54N 40 16 E
Mogi das Cruzes, *Brazil* **159 A6** 23 31 S 46 11W
Mogi-Guaçu →, *Brazil* **159 A6** 20 53 S 48 10W
Mogi-Mirim, *Brazil* **159 A6** 22 29 S 47 0W
Mogielnica, *Poland* **47 D7** 51 42N 20 41 E
Mogilev, *Belorussia* **50 E7** 53 55N 30 18 E
Mogilev-Podolskiy, *Moldavia* **52 B2** 48 20N 27 40 E
Mogilno, *Poland* **47 C4** 52 39N 17 55 E
Mogincual, *Mozam.* **107 F5** 15 35 S 40 25 E
Mogliano Véneto, *Italy* **39 C9** 45 33N 12 15 E
Mogocha, *Russia* **57 D12** 53 40N 119 50 E
Mogoi, *Indonesia* **73 B4** 1 55 S 133 10 E
Mogok, *Burma* **78 D6** 23 0N 96 40 E
Mogriguy, *Australia* **117 B8** 32 3 S 148 40 E
Moguer, *Spain* **37 H4** 37 15N 6 52W
Mogumber, *Australia* **113 F2** 31 2 S 116 3 E
Mohács, *Hungary* **31 F11** 45 58N 18 41 E
Mohaka →, *N.Z.* **118 F6** 39 7 S 177 12 E
Mohales Hoek, *Lesotho* **104 E4** 30 7 S 27 26 E
Mohall, *U.S.A.* **138 A4** 48 46N 101 31W
Moḩammadābād, *Iran* **85 B8** 37 52N 59 5 E
Mohammadia, *Algeria* **99 A5** 35 33N 0 3 E
Mohammedia, *Morocco* **98 B3** 33 44N 7 21W
Mohave, L., *U.S.A.* **145 K12** 35 12N 114 34W
Mohawk →, *U.S.A.* **137 D11** 42 47N 73 41W
Möhne →, *Germany* **26 D3** 51 29N 7 57 E
Mohnyin, *Burma* **78 C6** 24 47N 96 22 E
Moholm, *Sweden* **15 F8** 58 37N 14 5 E
Mohoro, *Tanzania* **106 D4** 8 6 S 39 8 E
Moia, *Sudan* **95 F2** 5 3N 28 2 E
Moidart, L., *U.K.* **18 E3** 56 47N 5 40W
Moinabad, *India* **82 F3** 17 44N 77 16 E
Moindou, *N. Cal.* **121 U19** 21 42 S 165 41 E
Moineşti, *Romania* **46 C7** 46 28N 26 31 E
Mointy, *Kazakhstan* **56 E8** 47 10N 73 18 E
Moirans, *France* **25 C9** 45 20N 5 33 E
Moirans-en-Montagne, *France* **25 B9** 46 26N 5 43 E
Moíres, *Greece* **32 D6** 35 4N 24 56 E
Moisaküla, *Estonia* **50 B4** 58 3N 25 12 E
Moisie, *Canada* **129 B6** 50 12N 66 1W
Moisie →, *Canada* **129 B6** 50 14N 66 5W
Moissac, *France* **24 D5** 44 7N 1 5 E
Moïssala, *Chad* **97 G3** 8 21N 17 46 E
Moita, *Portugal* **37 G2** 38 38N 8 58W
Mojácar, *Spain* **35 H3** 37 6N 1 55W
Mojados, *Spain* **36 D6** 41 26N 4 40W
Mojave, *U.S.A.* **145 K8** 35 3N 118 10W
Mojave Desert, *U.S.A.* **145 L10** 35 0N 116 30W
Mojiang, *China* **68 F3** 23 37N 101 35 E
Mojo, *Bolivia* **158 A2** 21 48 S 65 33W
Mojo, *Ethiopia* **95 F4** 8 35N 39 5 E
Mojokerto, *Indonesia* **75 D4** 7 28 S 112 26 E
Mojos, Llanos de, *Bolivia* **157 D5** 15 10 S 65 0W
Moju →, *Brazil* **154 B2** 1 40 S 48 25W
Mokai, *N.Z.* **118 E4** 38 32 S 175 56 E
Mokambo, *Zaïre* **107 E2** 12 25 S 28 20 E
Mokameh, *India* **81 G11** 25 24N 85 55 E
Mokane, *U.S.A.* **140 F5** 38 41N 91 53W
Mokau, *N.Z.* **118 E3** 38 42 S 174 39 E
Mokau →, *N.Z.* **118 E3** 38 35 S 174 35 E
Mokelumne →, *U.S.A.* **144 G5** 38 13N 121 28W
Mokelumne Hill, *U.S.A.* **144 G6** 38 18N 120 43W
Mokhós, *Greece* **32 D7** 35 16N 25 27 E
Mokhotlong, *Lesotho* **105 D4** 29 22 S 29 2 E
Mokihinui →, *N.Z.* **119 B6** 41 33 S 171 58 E
Moknine, *Tunisia* **96 A2** 35 35N 10 58 E
Mokpalin, *Burma* **78 G6** 17 26N 96 53 E
Mokra Gora, *Serbia* **42 E5** 42 50N 20 30 E
Mokronog, *Slovenia* **39 C12** 45 57N 15 9 E
Moksha →, *Russia* **51 D12** 54 45N 41 53 E
Mokshan, *Russia* **51 E14** 53 25N 44 35 E
Mol, *Belgium* **21 F6** 51 11N 5 5 E
Mola, C. de la, *Spain* **34 F9** 39 40N 4 20 E
Mola di Bari, *Italy* **41 A10** 41 3N 17 5 E
Moláoi, *Greece* **45 H4** 36 49N 22 56 E
Molat, *Croatia* **39 D11** 44 15N 14 50 E
Molave, *Phil.* **71 G4** 8 5N 123 30 E
Molchanovo, *Russia* **56 D9** 57 40N 83 50 E
Mold, *U.K.* **16 D4** 53 10N 3 10W
Moldava nad Bodvou, *Slovak Rep.* **31 C14** 48 38N 21 0 E
Moldavia = Moldova, *Romania* **46 C8** 46 30N 27 0 E
Moldavia ■, *Europe* **52 C3** 47 0N 28 0 E
Molde, *Norway* **12 E9** 62 45N 7 9 E
Moldotau, Khrebet, *Kirghizia* **55 C7** 41 35N 75 0 E
Moldova, *Romania* **46 C8** 46 30N 27 0 E
Moldova ■ = Moldavia ■, *Europe* **52 C3** 47 0N 28 0 E
Moldova Nouă, *Romania* **46 E2** 44 45N 21 41 E
Moldoveanu, *Romania* **46 D5** 45 36N 24 45 E
Molepolole, *Botswana* **104 C4** 24 28 S 25 28 E
Moléson, *Switz.* **28 C4** 46 33N 7 1 E
Molesworth, *N.Z.* **119 C8** 42 5 S 173 16 E
Molfetta, *Italy* **41 A9** 41 12N 16 35 E
Molina de Aragón, *Spain* **34 E3** 40 46N 1 52W
Moline, *U.S.A.* **140 C6** 41 30N 90 31W
Molinella, *Italy* **39 D8** 44 38N 11 40 E
Molinos, *Argentina* **158 B2** 25 28 S 66 15W
Moliro, *Zaïre* **106 D3** 8 12 S 30 30 E
Molise □, *Italy* **39 G11** 41 45N 14 30 E
Moliterno, *Italy* **41 B8** 40 14N 15 50 E
Mollahat, *Bangla.* **81 H13** 22 56N 89 48 E
Mölle, *Sweden* **15 H6** 56 17N 12 31 E
Molledo, *Spain* **36 B6** 43 8N 4 6W
Mollendo, *Peru* **156 D3** 17 0 S 72 0W
Mollerin, L., *Australia* **113 F2** 30 30 S 117 35 E
Mollerusa, *Spain* **34 D5** 41 37N 0 54 E
Mollina, *Spain* **37 H6** 37 8N 4 38W
Mölln, *Germany* **26 B6** 53 37N 10 41 E
Mölltorp, *Sweden* **15 F8** 58 30N 14 26 E
Mölndal, *Sweden* **15 G6** 57 40N 12 3 E
Molo, *Burma* **78 D6** 23 22N 96 53 E
Molochansk, *Ukraine* **52 C6** 47 15N 35 35 E
Molochnaya →, *Ukraine* **52 C6** 46 44N 35 15 E
Molodechno, *Belorussia* **50 D5** 54 20N 26 50 E
Molokai, *U.S.A.* **132 H16** 21 8N 157 0W
Moloma →, *Russia* **51 B16** 58 20N 48 15 E
Molong, *Australia* **117 B8** 33 5 S 148 54 E
Molopo →, *Africa* **104 D3** 27 30 S 20 13 E
Mólos, *Greece* **45 F4** 38 47N 22 37 E
Molotov = Perm, *Russia* **54 C5** 58 0N 56 10 E
Moloundou, *Cameroon* **102 B3** 2 8N 15 15 E
Molsheim, *France* **23 D14** 48 33N 7 29 E
Molson L., *Canada* **131 C9** 54 22N 96 40W
Molteno, *S. Africa* **104 E4** 31 22 S 26 22 E
Molu, *Indonesia* **73 C4** 6 45 S 131 40 E
Molucca Sea = Maluku Sea, *Indonesia* **72 A3** 2 0 S 124 0 E
Moluccas = Maluku, *Indonesia* **72 B3** 1 0 S 127 0 E
Molundo, *Phil.* **71 H5** 7 57N 124 23 E
Moma, *Mozam.* **107 F4** 16 47 S 39 4 E
Moma, *Zaïre* **102 C4** 1 35 S 23 52 E
Momba, *Australia* **116 A5** 30 58 S 143 30 E
Mombaça, *Brazil* **154 C4** 5 43 S 39 45W
Mombasa, *Kenya* **106 C4** 4 2 S 39 43 E
Mombetsu, *Japan* **60 B11** 44 21N 143 22 E
Mombil, *Burma* **78 B7** 27 46N 98 6 E
Mombuey, *Spain* **36 C4** 42 3N 6 20W
Momchilgrad, *Bulgaria* **43 F10** 41 33N 25 23 E
Momence, *U.S.A.* **141 C9** 41 10N 87 40W
Momi, *Zaïre* **106 C2** 1 42 S 27 0 E
Momignies, *Belgium* **21 H4** 50 2N 4 10 E
Mompog Pass, *Phil.* **70 E4** 13 34N 122 13 E
Mompós, *Colombia* **152 B3** 9 14N 74 26W
Møn, *Denmark* **15 K6** 54 57N 12 15 E
Mona, Canal de la, *W. Indies* **149 C6** 18 30N 67 45W
Mona, Isla, *Puerto Rico* **149 C6** 18 5N 67 54W
Mona, Pta., *Costa Rica* **148 E3** 9 37N 82 36W
Mona, Pta., *Spain* **37 J7** 36 43N 3 45W
Mona Quimbundo, *Angola* **103 D3** 9 55 S 19 58 E
Monach Is., *U.K.* **18 D1** 57 32N 7 40W
Monaco ■, *Europe* **25 E11** 43 46N 7 23 E
Monadhliath Mts., *U.K.* **18 D4** 57 10N 4 4W
Monagas □, *Venezuela* **153 B5** 9 20N 63 0W
Monaghan, *Ireland* **19 B5** 54 15N 6 58W
Monaghan □, *Ireland* **19 B5** 54 15N 7 0W
Monahans, *U.S.A.* **139 K3** 31 36N 102 54W
Monapo, *Mozam.* **107 E5** 14 56 S 40 19 E
Monarch Mt., *Canada* **130 C3** 51 55N 125 57W
Monastir = Bitola, *Macedonia* **42 F6** 41 5N 21 10 E
Monastir, *Tunisia* **96 A2** 35 50N 10 49 E
Monastyriska, *Ukraine* **50 G4** 49 8N 25 14 E
Moncada, *Phil.* **70 D3** 15 44N 120 34 E
Moncada, *Spain* **34 F4** 39 30N 0 24W
Moncalieri, *Italy* **38 D4** 45 0N 7 40 E
Moncalvo, *Italy* **38 C5** 45 3N 8 15 E
Moncão, *Portugal* **36 C2** 42 4N 8 27W
Moncarapacho, *Portugal* **37 H3** 37 5N 7 46W
Moncayo, Sierra del, *Spain* **34 D3** 41 48N 1 50W
Mönchengladbach, *Germany* **26 D2** 51 12N 6 23 E
Monchique, *Portugal* **37 H2** 37 19N 8 38W
Monclova, *Mexico* **146 B4** 26 50N 101 30W
Moncontour, *France* **22 D4** 48 22N 2 38W
Moncoutant, *France* **24 B3** 46 43N 0 35W
Moncton, *Canada* **129 C7** 46 7N 64 51W
Mondego →, *Portugal* **36 E2** 40 9N 8 52W
Mondego, C., *Portugal* **36 E2** 40 11N 8 54W
Mondeodo, *Indonesia* **72 B2** 3 34 S 122 9 E
Mondo, *Chad* **97 F3** 13 47N 15 32 E
Mondolfo, *Italy* **39 E10** 43 45N 13 8 E
Mondoñedo, *Spain* **36 B3** 43 25N 7 23W
Mondovì, *Italy* **38 D4** 44 23N 7 49 E
Mondovi, *U.S.A.* **138 C9** 44 34N 91 40W
Mondragon, *France* **25 D8** 44 13N 4 44 E
Mondragon, *Phil.* **70 E5** 12 31N 124 45 E
Mondragone, *Italy* **40 A6** 41 8N 13 52 E
Mondrain I., *Australia* **113 F3** 34 9 S 122 14 E
Monduli □, *Tanzania* **106 C4** 3 0 S 36 0 E
Monemvasía, *Greece* **45 H5** 36 41N 23 3 E
Monessen, *U.S.A.* **136 F5** 40 9N 79 54W
Monesterio, *Spain* **37 G4** 38 6N 6 15W
Monestier-de-Clermont, *France* **25 D9** 44 55N 5 38 E
Monett, *U.S.A.* **139 G8** 36 55N 93 55W
Monfalcone, *Italy* **39 C10** 45 49N 13 32 E
Monflanquin, *France* **24 D4** 44 32N 0 47 E
Monforte, *Portugal* **37 F3** 39 6N 7 25W
Monforte de Lemos, *Spain* **36 C3** 42 31N 7 33W
Mong Hta, *Burma* **78 F7** 19 50N 98 35 E
Mong Ket, *Burma* **78 D7** 23 8N 98 22 E
Mong Kung, *Burma* **78 E6** 21 35N 97 35 E
Mong Kyawt, *Burma* **78 F7** 19 56N 98 45 E
Mong Nai, *Burma* **78 E6** 20 32N 97 46 E
Mong Ping, *Burma* **78 E7** 21 22N 99 2 E
Mong Pu, *Burma* **78 E7** 20 55N 98 44 E
Mong Ton, *Burma* **78 E7** 20 17N 98 45 E
Mong Tung, *Burma* **78 D6** 22 2N 97 41 E
Mong Yai, *Burma* **78 D7** 22 21N 98 3 E
Monga, *Zaïre* **102 B4** 4 12N 22 49 E
Mongalla, *Sudan* **95 F3** 5 8N 31 42 E
Mongers, L., *Australia* **113 E2** 29 25 S 117 5 E
Monghyr = Munger, *India* **81 G12** 25 23N 86 30 E
Mongla, *Bangla.* **78 D2** 22 8N 89 35 E
Mongngaw, *Burma* **78 D6** 22 47N 96 59 E
Mongo, *Chad* **97 F3** 12 14N 18 43 E
Mongó, *Eq. Guin.* **102 B2** 1 52N 10 10 E
Mongolia ■, *Asia* **57 E10** 47 0N 103 0 E
Mongomo, *Eq. Guin.* **102 B2** 1 38N 11 19 E
Mongonu, *Nigeria* **101 C7** 12 40N 13 32 E
Mongororo, *Chad* **97 F4** 12 3N 22 26 E
Mongu, *Zambia* **103 F4** 15 16 S 23 12 E
Mônguа, *Angola* **103 F3** 16 43 S 15 20 E
Monistrol-d'Allier, *France* **24 D7** 44 58N 3 38 E
Monistrol-sur-Loire, *France* **25 C8** 45 17N 4 11 E
Monkayo, *Phil.* **71 H6** 7 50N 126 5 E
Monkey Bay, *Malawi* **107 E4** 14 7 S 35 1 E
Monkey River, *Belize* **147 D7** 16 22N 88 29W
Mońki, *Poland* **47 B9** 53 23N 22 48 E
Monkira, *Australia* **114 C3** 24 46 S 140 30 E
Monkoto, *Zaïre* **102 C4** 1 38 S 20 35 E
Monmouth, *U.K.* **17 F5** 51 48N 2 43W
Monmouth, *U.S.A.* **140 D6** 40 55N 90 39W
Mono, *Solomon Is.* **121 L8** 7 20 S 155 35 E
Mono L., *U.S.A.* **144 H7** 38 1N 119 1W
Monolith, *U.S.A.* **145 K8** 35 7N 118 22W
Monólithos, *Greece* **32 C9** 36 7N 27 45 E
Monon, *U.S.A.* **141 D10** 40 52N 86 53W
Monona, *Iowa, U.S.A.* **140 A5** 43 3N 91 23W
Monona, *Wis., U.S.A.* **140 A7** 43 4N 89 20W
Monongahela, *U.S.A.* **136 F5** 40 12N 79 56W
Monópoli, *Italy* **41 B10** 40 57N 17 18 E
Monor, *Hungary* **31 D12** 47 21N 19 27 E
Monóvar, *Spain* **35 G4** 38 28N 0 53W
Monowai, *N.Z.* **119 F2** 45 53 S 167 31 E
Monowai, L., *N.Z.* **119 F2** 45 53 S 167 25 E
Monqoumba, *C.A.R.* **102 B3** 3 33N 18 40 E
Monreal del Campo, *Spain* **34 E3** 40 47N 1 20W
Monreale, *Italy* **40 D6** 38 6N 13 16 E
Monroe, *Ga., U.S.A.* **135 J4** 33 47N 83 43W
Monroe, *Iowa, U.S.A.* **140 C3** 41 31N 93 6W
Monroe, *La., U.S.A.* **139 J8** 32 30N 92 7W
Monroe, *Mich., U.S.A.* **141 C13** 41 55N 83 24W
Monroe, *N.C., U.S.A.* **135 H5** 34 59N 80 33W
Monroe, *N.Y., U.S.A.* **137 E10** 41 20N 74 11W
Monroe, *Ohio, U.S.A.* **141 E12** 39 27N 84 22W
Monroe, *Utah, U.S.A.* **143 G7** 38 38N 112 7W
Monroe, *Wash., U.S.A.* **144 C5** 47 51N 121 58W
Monroe, *Wis., U.S.A.* **140 B7** 42 36N 89 38W
Monroe City, *U.S.A.* **140 E5** 39 39N 91 44W
Monroe Res., *U.S.A.* **141 E10** 39 1N 86 31W
Monroeville, *Ala., U.S.A.* **135 K2** 31 31N 87 20W
Monroeville, *Ind., U.S.A.* **141 D12** 40 59N 84 52W
Monroeville, *Pa., U.S.A.* **136 F5** 40 26N 79 45W
Monrovia, *Liberia* **100 D2** 6 18N 10 47W
Monrovia, *U.S.A.* **143 J4** 34 7N 118 1W
Mons, *Belgium* **21 H3** 50 27N 3 58 E
Monsaraz, *Portugal* **37 G3** 38 28N 7 22W
Monse, *Indonesia* **72 B2** 4 0 S 123 10 E
Monsefú, *Peru* **156 B2** 6 52 S 79 52W
Monségur, *France* **24 D4** 44 38N 0 4 E
Monsélice, *Italy* **39 C8** 45 16N 11 46 E
Monster, *Neths.* **20 D4** 52 1N 4 10 E
Mont Cenis, Col du, *France* **25 C10** 45 15N 6 55 E
Mont-de-Marsan, *France* **24 E3** 43 54N 0 31W
Mont-Joli, *Canada* **129 C6** 48 37N 68 10W
Mont-Laurier, *Canada* **128 C4** 46 35N 75 30W
Mont-St.-Michel, Le = Le Mont-St.-Michel, *France* **22 D5** 48 40N 1 30W
Mont-sous-Vaudrey, *France* **23 F12** 46 58N 5 36 E
Mont-sur-Marchienne, *Belgium* **21 H4** 50 23N 4 24 E
Mont Tremblant Prov. Park, *Canada* **128 C5** 46 30N 74 30W
Montabaur, *Germany* **26 E3** 50 26N 7 49 E
Montagnac, *France* **24 E7** 43 29N 3 28 E
Montagnana, *Italy* **39 C8** 45 13N 11 29 E
Montagu, *S. Africa* **104 E3** 33 45 S 20 8 E
Montagu I., *Antarctica* **7 B1** 58 25 S 26 20W
Montague, *Canada* **129 C7** 46 10N 62 39W
Montague, *U.S.A.* **142 F2** 41 44N 122 32W
Montague, I., *Mexico* **146 A2** 31 40N 114 56W
Montague Ra., *Australia* **113 E2** 27 15 S 119 30 E
Montague Sd., *Australia* **112 B4** 14 28 S 125 20 E
Montaigu, *France* **22 F5** 46 59N 1 18W
Montalbán, *Spain* **34 E4** 40 50N 0 45W
Montalbano di Elicona, *Italy* **41 D8** 38 1N 15 0 E
Montalbano Iónico, *Italy* **41 B9** 40 17N 16 33 E
Montalbo, *Spain* **34 F2** 39 53N 2 42W
Montalcino, *Italy* **39 E8** 43 4N 11 30 E
Montalegre, *Portugal* **36 D3** 41 49N 7 47W
Montalto di Castro, *Italy* **39 F8** 42 20N 11 36 E
Montalto Uffugo, *Italy* **41 C9** 39 25N 16 9 E
Montalvo, *U.S.A.* **145 L7** 34 15N 119 12W
Montamarta, *Spain* **36 D5** 41 39N 5 49W
Montaña, *Peru* **156 B3** 6 0 S 73 0W
Montana, *Switz.* **28 D4** 46 19N 7 29 E
Montana □, *U.S.A.* **142 C9** 47 0N 110 0W
Montaña Clara, I., *Canary Is.* **33 E6** 29 17N 13 33W
Montánchez, *Spain* **37 F4** 39 15N 6 8W
Montañita, *Colombia* **152 C2** 1 22N 75 28W
Montargis, *France* **23 E9** 47 59N 2 43 E
Montauban, *France* **24 D5** 44 2N 1 21 E
Montauk, *U.S.A.* **137 E13** 41 3N 71 57W
Montauk Pt., *U.S.A.* **137 E13** 41 4N 71 52W
Montbard, *France* **23 E11** 47 38N 4 20 E
Montbéliard, *France* **23 E13** 47 31N 6 48 E
Montblanch, *Spain* **34 D6** 41 23N 1 4 E
Montbrison, *France* **25 C8** 45 36N 4 3 E
Montcalm, Pic de, *France* **24 F5** 42 40N 1 25 E
Montceau-les-Mines, *France* **23 F11** 46 40N 4 23 E
Montchanin, *France* **25 B8** 46 47N 4 30 E
Montclair, *U.S.A.* **137 F10** 40 49N 74 13W
Montcornet, *France* **23 C11** 49 40N 4 1 E
Montcuq, *France* **24 D5** 44 21N 1 13 E
Montdidier, *France* **23 C9** 49 38N 2 35 E
Monte Albán, *Mexico* **147 D5** 17 2N 96 45W
Monte Alegre, *Brazil* **153 D7** 2 0 S 54 0W
Monte Alegre de Goiás, *Brazil* **155 D2** 13 14 S 47 10W
Monte Alegre de Minas, *Brazil* **155 E2** 18 52 S 48 52W
Monte Azul, *Brazil* **155 E3** 15 9 S 42 53W
Monte Bello Is., *Australia* **112 D2** 20 30 S 115 45 E
Monte-Carlo, *Monaco* **25 E11** 43 46N 7 23 E
Monte Carmelo, *Brazil* **155 E2** 18 43 S 47 29W
Monte Caseros, *Argentina* **158 C4** 30 10 S 57 50W
Monte Comán, *Argentina* **158 C2** 34 40 S 67 53W
Monte Cristi, *Dom. Rep.* **149 C5** 19 52N 71 39W
Monte Dinero, *Argentina* **160 D3** 52 18 S 68 33W
Monte Lindo →, *Paraguay* **158 A4** 23 56 S 57 12W
Monte Quemado, *Argentina* **158 B3** 25 53 S 62 41W
Monte Redondo, *Portugal* **36 F2** 39 53N 8 50W
Monte Rio, *U.S.A.* **144 G4** 38 28N 123 0W
Monte San Giovanni, *Italy* **40 A6** 41 39N 13 33 E
Monte San Savino, *Italy* **39 E8** 43 20N 11 42 E
Monte Sant' Ángelo, *Italy* **41 A8** 41 42N 15 59 E
Monte Santu, C. di, *Italy* **40 B2** 40 5N 9 42 E
Monte Vista, *U.S.A.* **143 H10** 37 35N 106 9W
Monteagudo, *Argentina* **159 B5** 27 14 S 54 8W
Monteagudo, *Bolivia* **157 D5** 19 49 S 63 59W
Montealegre, *Spain* **35 G3** 38 48N 1 17W
Montebello, *Canada* **128 C5** 45 40N 74 55W
Montebelluna, *Italy* **39 C9** 45 47N 12 3 E
Montebourg, *France* **22 C5** 49 30N 1 20W
Montecastrilli, *Italy* **39 F9** 42 40N 12 30 E
Montecatini Terme, *Italy* **38 E7** 43 55N 10 48 E
Montecito, *U.S.A.* **145 L7** 34 26N 119 40W
Montecristi, *Ecuador* **152 D1** 1 0 S 80 40W
Montecristo, *Italy* **38 F7** 42 20N 10 20 E
Montefalco, *Italy* **39 F9** 42 53N 12 38 E
Montefiascone, *Italy* **39 F9** 42 31N 12 2 E
Montefrío, *Spain* **37 H6** 37 20N 4 0W
Montegnée, *Belgium* **21 G7** 50 38N 5 31 E
Montego Bay, *Jamaica* **148 C4** 18 30N 78 0W
Montegranaro, *Italy* **39 E10** 43 13N 13 38 E
Monteiro, *Brazil* **154 C4** 7 48 S 37 2W
Monteith, *Australia* **116 C3** 35 11 S 139 23 E
Montejicar, *Spain* **35 H1** 37 33N 3 30W
Montejinnie, *Australia* **112 C5** 16 40 S 131 38 E
Montelíbano, *Colombia* **152 B2** 8 5N 75 29W
Montélimar, *France* **25 D8** 44 33N 4 45 E
Montella, *Italy* **41 B8** 40 50N 15 2 E
Montellano, *Spain* **37 J5** 36 59N 5 36W
Montello, *U.S.A.* **138 D10** 43 48N 89 20W
Montelupo Fiorentino, *Italy* **38 E8** 43 44N 11 2 E
Montemor-o-Novo, *Portugal* **37 G2** 38 40N 8 12W
Montemor-o-Velho, *Portugal* **36 E2** 40 11N 8 40W
Montemorelos, *Mexico* **147 B5** 25 11N 99 42W
Montendre, *France* **24 C3** 45 16N 0 26W
Montenegro, *Brazil* **159 B5** 29 39 S 51 29W
Montenegro □, *Montenegro* **42 E4** 42 40N 19 20 E
Montenero di Bisaccia, *Italy* **39 G11** 41 58N 14 47 E
Montepuez, *Mozam.* **107 E4** 13 8 S 38 59 E
Montepuez →, *Mozam.* **107 E5** 12 32 S 40 27 E
Montepulciano, *Italy* **39 E8** 43 5N 11 46 E
Montereale, *Italy* **39 F10** 42 31N 13 13 E
Montereau-Fault-Yonne, *France* **23 D9** 48 22N 2 57 E
Monterey, *Calif., U.S.A.* **144 J5** 36 37N 121 55W
Monterey, *Ind., U.S.A.* **141 C10** 41 11N 86 30W
Monterey B., *U.S.A.* **144 J5** 36 45N 122 0W
Montería, *Colombia* **152 B2** 8 46N 75 53W
Montero, *Bolivia* **157 D5** 17 20 S 63 15W
Monteros, *Argentina* **158 B2** 27 11 S 65 30W
Monterotondo, *Italy* **39 F9** 42 3N 12 36 E
Monterrey, *Mexico* **146 B4** 25 40N 100 30W
Montes Altos, *Brazil* **154 C2** 5 50 S 47 4W
Montes Claros, *Brazil* **155 E3** 16 30 S 43 50W
Montesano, *U.S.A.* **144 D3** 46 59N 123 36W
Montesárchio, *Italy* **41 A7** 41 5N 14 37 E
Montescaglioso, *Italy* **41 B9** 40 34N 16 40 E
Montesilvano, *Italy* **39 F11** 42 30N 14 8 E
Montevarchi, *Italy* **39 E8** 43 30N 11 32 E
Montevideo, *Uruguay* **159 C4** 34 50 S 56 11W
Montevideo, *U.S.A.* **138 C7** 44 57N 95 43W
Montezuma, *Ind., U.S.A.* **141 E9** 39 48N 87 22W
Montezuma, *Iowa, U.S.A.* **140 C4** 41 35N 92 32W
Montfaucon, *France* **23 C12** 49 16N 5 8 E
Montfaucon-en-Velay, *France* **25 C8** 45 11N 4 20 E
Montfort, *France* **22 D5** 48 9N 1 58W
Montfort, *Neths.* **21 F7** 51 7N 5 58 E
Montfort-l'Amaury, *France* **23 D8** 48 47N 1 49 E
Montgenèvre, *France* **25 D10** 44 56N 6 43 E
Montgomery = Sahiwal, *Pakistan* **79 C4** 30 45N 73 8 E
Montgomery, *U.K.* **17 E4** 52 34N 3 9W
Montgomery, *Ala., U.S.A.* **135 J2** 32 23N 86 19W
Montgomery, *Ill., U.S.A.* **141 C8** 41 44N 88 21W
Montgomery, *W. Va., U.S.A.* **134 F5** 38 11N 81 19W
Montgomery City, *U.S.A.* **140 F5** 38 59N 91 30W
Montguyon, *France* **24 C3** 45 12N 0 12W
Monthey, *Switz.* **28 D3** 46 15N 6 56 E
Monticelli d'Ongina, *Italy* **38 C6** 45 3N 9 56 E
Monticello, *Ark., U.S.A.* **139 J9** 33 38N 91 47W
Monticello, *Fla., U.S.A.* **135 K4** 30 33N 83 52W
Monticello, *Ill., U.S.A.* **141 D8** 40 1N 88 34W
Monticello, *Ind., U.S.A.* **141 D10** 40 45N 86 46W
Monticello, *Iowa, U.S.A.* **140 B5** 42 15N 91 12W
Monticello, *Ky., U.S.A.* **135 G3** 36 50N 84 51W
Monticello, *Minn., U.S.A.* **138 C8** 45 18N 93 48W
Monticello, *Miss., U.S.A.* **139 K9** 31 33N 90 7W
Monticello, *Mo., U.S.A.* **140 D5** 40 7N 91 43W
Monticello, *N.Y., U.S.A.* **137 E10** 41 39N 74 42W
Monticello, *Utah, U.S.A.* **143 H9** 37 52N 109 21W
Montichiari, *Italy* **38 C7** 45 28N 10 29 E
Montier-en-Der, *France* **23 D11** 48 30N 4 45 E
Montignac, *France* **24 C5** 45 4N 1 10 E
Montignies-sur-Sambre, *Belgium* **21 H4** 50 24N 4 29 E
Montigny, *France* **23 C13** 49 7N 6 10 E
Montigny-sur-Aube, *France* **23 E11** 47 57N 4 45 E
Montijo, *Spain* **37 G4** 38 52N 6 39W
Montijo, Presa de, *Spain* **37 G4** 38 55N 6 26W
Montilla, *Spain* **37 H6** 37 36N 4 40W
Montlhéry, *France* **23 D9** 48 39N 2 15 E
Montluçon, *France* **24 B6** 46 22N 2 36 E
Montmagny, *Canada* **129 C5** 46 58N 70 34W
Montmarault, *France* **24 B6** 46 19N 2 57 E
Montmartre, *Canada* **131 C8** 50 14N 103 27W
Montmédy, *France* **23 C12** 49 30N 5 20 E
Montmélian, *France* **25 C10** 45 30N 6 4 E
Montmirail, *France* **23 D10** 48 51N 3 30 E

Müritz See 237


Mount Molloy, *Australia* **114 B4** 16 42 S 145 20 E
Mount Monger, *Australia* **113 F3** 31 0 S 122 0 E
Mount Morgan, *Australia* **114 C5** 23 40 S 150 25 E
Mount Morris, *U.S.A.* **136 D7** 42 44N 77 52W
Mount Mulligan, *Australia* **114 B3** 16 45 S 144 47 E
Mount Narryer, *Australia* **113 E2** 26 30 S 115 55 E
Mount Olive, *U.S.A.* **140 E7** 39 4N 89 44W
Mount Olivet, *U.S.A.* **141 F12** 38 32N 84 2W
Mount Olympus = Uludağ, *Turkey* **88 C3** 40 4N 29 13 E
Mount Orab, *U.S.A.* **141 E13** 39 2N 83 55W
Mount Oxide Mine, *Australia* **114 B2** 19 30 S 139 29 E
Mount Pearl, *Canada* **129 C9** 47 31N 52 47W
Mount Perry, *Australia* **115 D5** 25 13 S 151 42 E
Mount Phillips, *Australia* **112 D2** 24 25 S 116 15 E
Mount Pleasant, *Iowa, U.S.A.* **140 D5** 40 58N 91 33W
Mount Pleasant, *Mich., U.S.A.* **134 D3** 43 36N 84 46W
Mount Pleasant, *Pa., U.S.A.* **136 F5** 40 9N 79 33W
Mount Pleasant, *S.C., U.S.A.* **135 J6** 32 47N 79 52W
Mount Pleasant, *Tenn., U.S.A.* **135 H2** 35 32N 87 12W
Mount Pleasant, *Tex., U.S.A.* **139 J7** 33 9N 94 58W
Mount Pleasant, *Utah, U.S.A.* **142 G8** 39 33N 111 27W
Mount Pocono, *U.S.A.* **137 E9** 41 7N 75 22W
Mount Pulaski, *U.S.A.* **140 D7** 40 1N 89 17W
Mount Rainier National Park, *U.S.A.* **144 D5** 46 55N 121 50W
Mount Revelstoke Nat. Park, *Canada* **130 C5** 51 5N 118 30W
Mount Robson Prov. Park, *Canada* **130 C5** 53 0N 119 0W
Mount Roskill, *N.Z.* **118 C3** 36 55 S 174 45 E
Mount Sandiman, *Australia* **113 D2** 24 25 S 115 30 E
Mount Shasta, *U.S.A.* **142 F2** 41 19N 122 19W
Mount Signal, *U.S.A.* **145 N11** 32 39N 115 37W
Mount Somers, *N.Z.* **119 D6** 43 45 S 171 27 E
Mount Sterling, *Ill., U.S.A.* **140 E6** 39 59N 90 45W
Mount Sterling, *Ky., U.S.A.* **141 F13** 38 4N 83 56W
Mount Sterling, *Ohio, U.S.A.* **141 E13** 39 43N 83 16W
Mount Surprise, *Australia* **114 B3** 18 10 S 144 17 E
Mount Union, *U.S.A.* **136 F7** 40 23N 77 53W
Mount Vernon, *Australia* **112 D2** 24 9 S 118 2 E
Mount Vernon, *Ind., U.S.A.* **138 F10** 38 17N 88 57W
Mount Vernon, *Ind., U.S.A.* **141 F8** 37 56N 87 54W
Mount Vernon, *Iowa, U.S.A.* **140 C5** 41 55N 91 23W
Mount Vernon, *N.Y., U.S.A.* **137 F11** 40 55N 73 50W
Mount Vernon, *Ohio, U.S.A.* **136 F2** 40 23N 82 29W
Mount Vernon, *Wash., U.S.A.* **144 B4** 48 25N 122 20W
Mount Victor, *Australia* **116 B3** 32 11 S 139 44 E
Mount Washington, *U.S.A.* **141 F11** 38 3N 85 33W
Mount Wellington, *N.Z.* **118 C3** 36 55 S 174 52 E
Mount Zion, *U.S.A.* **141 E8** 39 46N 88 53W
Mountain □, *Phil.* **70 C3** 17 20N 121 10 E
Mountain Center, *U.S.A.* **145 M10** 33 42N 116 44W
Mountain City, *Nev., U.S.A.* **142 F6** 41 50N 115 58W
Mountain City, *Tenn., U.S.A.* **135 G5** 36 29N 81 48W
Mountain Grove, *U.S.A.* **139 G8** 37 8N 92 16W
Mountain Home, *Ark., U.S.A.* **139 G8** 36 20N 92 23W
Mountain Home, *Idaho, U.S.A.* **142 E6** 43 8N 115 41W
Mountain Iron, *U.S.A.* **138 B8** 47 32N 92 37W
Mountain Park, *Canada* **130 C5** 52 50N 117 15W
Mountain Pass, *U.S.A.* **145 K11** 35 29N 115 35W
Mountain View, *Ark., U.S.A.* **139 H8** 35 52N 92 7W
Mountain View, *Calif., U.S.A.* **144 H4** 37 23N 122 5W
Mountainair, *U.S.A.* **143 J10** 34 31N 106 15W
Mountmellick, *Ireland* **19 C4** 53 7N 7 20W
Moura, *Australia* **114 C4** 24 35 S 149 58 E
Moura, *Brazil* **153 D5** 1 32 S 61 38W
Moura, *Portugal* **37 G3** 38 7N 7 30W
Mourão, *Portugal* **37 G3** 38 22N 7 22W
Mourdi, Dépression du, *Chad* **97 E4** 18 10N 23 0 E
Mourdiah, *Mali* **100 C3** 14 35N 7 25W
Mourenx-Ville-Nouvelle, *France* **24 E3** 43 22N 0 38W
Mouri, *Ghana* **101 D4** 5 6N 1 14W
Mourilyan, *Australia* **114 B4** 17 35 S 146 3 E
Mourmelon-le-Grand, *France* **23 C11** 49 8N 4 22 E
Mourne →, *U.K.* **19 B4** 54 45N 7 39W
Mourne Mts., *U.K.* **19 B5** 54 10N 6 0W
Mournies, *Greece* **32 D6** 35 29N 24 1 E
Mouscron, *Belgium* **21 G2** 50 45N 3 12 E
Moussoro, *Chad* **97 F3** 13 41N 16 35 E
Mouthe, *France* **23 F13** 46 44N 6 12 E
Moutier, *Switz.* **28 B4** 47 16N 7 21 E
Moûtiers, *France* **25 C10** 45 29N 6 32 E
Moutohara, *N.Z.* **118 E6** 38 27 S 177 32 E
Moutong, *Indonesia* **72 A2** 0 28N 121 13 E
Mouy, *France* **23 C9** 49 18N 2 20 E
Mouzáki, *Greece* **44 E3** 39 25N 21 37 E
Movas, *Mexico* **146 B3** 28 10N 109 25W
Moville, *Ireland* **19 A4** 55 11N 7 3W
Moweaqua, *U.S.A.* **140 E7** 39 38N 89 1W
Moxhe, *Belgium* **21 G6** 50 38N 5 5 E
Moxico □, *Angola* **103 E4** 12 0 S 20 30 E
Moxotó →, *Brazil* **154 C4** 9 19 S 38 14W
Moy →, *Ireland* **19 B3** 54 5N 8 50W
Moyale, *Kenya* **106 B4** 3 30N 39 0 E
Moyamba, *S. Leone* **100 D2** 8 4N 12 30W
Moyen Atlas, *Morocco* **98 B3** 33 0N 5 0W
Moyle □, *U.K.* **19 A5** 55 10N 6 15W
Moyo, *Indonesia* **72 C1** 8 10 S 117 40 E
Moyobamba, *Peru* **156 B2** 6 0 S 77 0W
Moyyero →, *Russia* **57 C11** 68 44N 103 42 E
Mozambique = Moçambique, *Mozam.* **107 F5** 15 3 S 40 42 E
Mozambique ■, *Africa* **107 F4** 19 0 S 35 0 E
Mozambique Chan., *Africa* **105 B7** 17 30 S 42 30 E
Mozdok, *Russia* **53 E11** 43 45N 44 48 E
Mozdūrān, *Iran* **85 B9** 36 9N 60 35 E
Mozhaysk, *Russia* **51 D10** 55 30N 36 2 E
Mozhga, *Russia* **54 C3** 56 26N 52 15 E
Mozhnābād, *Iran* **85 C9** 34 7N 60 6 E
Mozirje, *Slovenia* **39 B11** 46 22N 14 58 E
Mozyr, *Belorussia* **50 E6** 51 59N 29 15 E
Mpanda, *Tanzania* **106 D3** 6 23 S 31 1 E
Mpanda □, *Tanzania* **106 D3** 6 23 S 31 40 E
Mpésoba, *Mali* **100 C3** 12 31N 5 39W
Mpika, *Zambia* **107 E3** 11 51 S 31 25 E
Mpulungu, *Zambia* **107 D3** 8 51 S 31 5 E
Mpumalanga, *S. Africa* **105 D5** 29 50 S 30 33 E
Mpwapwa, *Tanzania* **106 D4** 6 23 S 36 30 E
Mpwapwa □, *Tanzania* **106 D4** 6 30 S 36 20 E
Mrągowo, *Poland* **47 B8** 53 52N 21 18 E
Mrakovo, *Russia* **54 E5** 52 43N 56 38 E
Mramor, *Serbia* **42 D6** 43 20N 21 45 E
Mrimina, *Morocco* **98 C3** 29 50N 7 9W
Mrkonjić Grad, *Bos.-H.* **42 C2** 44 26N 17 4 E
Mrkopalj, *Croatia* **39 C11** 45 21N 14 52 E
Mrocza, *Poland* **47 B4** 53 16N 17 35 E
Msab, Oued en →, *Algeria* **99 B6** 32 25N 5 20 E
Msaken, *Tunisia* **96 A2** 35 49N 10 33 E
Msambansovu, *Zimbabwe* **107 F3** 15 50 S 30 3 E
M'sila, *Algeria* **99 A5** 35 46N 4 30 E
Msoro, *Zambia* **107 E3** 13 35 S 31 50 E
Msta →, *Russia* **50 B7** 58 25N 31 20 E
Mstislavl, *Belorussia* **50 E7** 54 0N 31 50 E
Mszana Dolna, *Poland* **31 B13** 49 41N 20 5 E
Mszczonów, *Poland* **47 D7** 51 58N 20 33 E
Mtama, *Tanzania* **107 E4** 10 17 S 39 21 E
Mtilikwe →, *Zimbabwe* **107 G3** 21 9 S 31 30 E
Mtsensk, *Russia* **51 E10** 53 25N 36 30 E
Mtskheta, *Georgia* **53 F11** 41 52N 44 45 E
Mtubatuba, *S. Africa* **105 D5** 28 30 S 32 8 E
Mtwara-Mikindani, *Tanzania* **107 E5** 10 20 S 40 20 E
Mu →, *Burma* **78 E5** 21 56N 95 38 E
Mu Gia, Deo, *Vietnam* **76 D5** 17 40N 105 47 E
Mu Us Shamo, *China* **66 E5** 39 0N 109 0 E
Muacandalo, *Angola* **103 E3** 10 2 S 19 40 E
Muaná, *Brazil* **154 B2** 1 25 S 49 15W
Muanda, *Zaïre* **103 D2** 6 0 S 12 20 E
Muang Chiang Rai, *Thailand* **76 C2** 19 52N 99 50 E
Muang Lamphun, *Thailand* **76 C2** 18 40N 99 2 E
Muang Pak Beng, *Laos* **76 C3** 19 54N 101 8 E
Muar, *Malaysia* **77 L4** 2 3N 102 34 E
Muarabungo, *Indonesia* **74 C2** 1 28 S 102 52 E
Muaraenim, *Indonesia* **74 C2** 3 40 S 103 50 E
Muarajuloi, *Indonesia* **75 C4** 0 12 S 114 3 E
Muarakaman, *Indonesia* **75 C5** 0 2 S 116 45 E
Muaratebo, *Indonesia* **74 C2** 1 30 S 102 26 E
Muaratembesi, *Indonesia* **74 C2** 1 42 S 103 8 E
Muaratewe, *Indonesia* **75 C4** 0 58 S 114 52 E
Mubarakpur, *India* **81 F10** 26 6N 83 18 E
Mubarraz = Al Mubarraz, *Si. Arabia* **85 E6** 25 30N 49 40 E
Mubende, *Uganda* **106 B3** 0 33N 31 22 E
Mubi, *Nigeria* **101 C7** 10 18N 13 16 E
Mubur, P., *Indonesia* **77 L6** 3 20N 106 12 E
Mucajaí →, *Brazil* **153 C5** 2 25N 60 52W
Mucajaí, Serra do, *Brazil* **153 C5** 2 23N 61 10W
Mucari, *Angola* **103 D3** 9 30 S 16 54 E
Muchachos, Roque de los, *Canary Is.* **33 F2** 28 44N 17 52W
Mücheln, *Germany* **26 D7** 51 18N 11 49 E
Muchinga Mts., *Zambia* **107 E3** 11 30 S 31 30 E
Muchkapskiy, *Russia* **51 F13** 51 52N 42 28 E
Muck, *U.K.* **18 E2** 56 50N 6 15W
Muckadilla, *Australia* **115 D4** 26 35 S 148 23 E
Muco →, *Colombia* **152 C3** 4 15N 70 21W
Mucoma, *Angola* **103 F2** 15 18 S 13 39 E
Muconda, *Angola* **103 E4** 10 31 S 21 15 E
Mucuim →, *Brazil* **157 B5** 6 33 S 64 18W
Mucur, *Turkey* **88 D6** 39 3N 34 22 E
Mucura, *Brazil* **153 D5** 2 31 S 62 43W
Mucuri, *Brazil* **155 E4** 18 0 S 39 36W
Mucurici, *Brazil* **155 E3** 18 6 S 40 31W
Mucusso, *Angola* **103 F4** 18 1 S 21 25 E
Muda, *Canary Is.* **33 F6** 28 34N 13 57W
Mudan Jiang →, *China* **67 A15** 46 20N 129 30 E
Mudanjiang, *China* **67 B15** 44 38N 129 30 E
Mudanya, *Turkey* **52 F3** 40 25N 28 50 E
Muddy Cr. →, *U.S.A.* **143 H8** 38 24N 110 42W
Mudgee, *Australia* **117 B8** 32 32 S 149 31 E
Mudjatik →, *Canada* **131 B7** 56 1N 107 36W
Mudon, *Burma* **78 G6** 16 15N 97 44 E
Mudugh, *Somali Rep.* **108 C3** 7 0N 47 30 E
Mudurnu, *Turkey* **88 C4** 40 27N 31 12 E
Muecate, *Mozam.* **107 E4** 14 55 S 39 40 E
Muêda, *Mozam.* **107 E4** 11 36 S 39 28 E
Mueller Ra., *Australia* **112 C4** 18 18 S 126 46 E
Muende, *Mozam.* **107 E3** 14 28 S 33 0 E
Muerto, Mar, *Mexico* **147 D6** 16 10N 94 10W
Muertos, Punta de los, *Spain* **35 J3** 36 57N 1 54W
Mufindi □, *Tanzania* **107 D4** 8 30 S 35 20 E
Mufu Shan, *China* **69 C10** 29 20N 114 30 E
Mufulira, *Zambia* **107 E2** 12 32 S 28 15 E
Mufumbiro Range, *Africa* **106 C2** 1 25 S 29 30 E
Mugardos, *Spain* **36 B2** 43 27N 8 15W
Muge, *Portugal* **37 F2** 39 3N 8 40W
Muge →, *Portugal* **37 F2** 39 8N 8 44W
Múggia, *Italy* **39 C10** 45 36N 13 47 E
Mughayrā', *Si. Arabia* **84 D3** 29 17N 37 41 E
Mugi, *Japan* **62 D6** 33 40N 134 25 E
Mugia, *Spain* **36 B1** 43 3N 9 10W
Mugila, Mts., *Zaïre* **106 D2** 7 0 S 28 50 E
Muğla, *Turkey* **88 E3** 37 15N 28 22 E
Muğla □, *Turkey* **88 E3** 37 0N 28 0 E
Müglizh, *Bulgaria* **43 E10** 42 37N 25 32 E
Mugu, *Nepal* **81 E10** 29 45N 82 30 E
Muhammad, Râs, *Egypt* **94 B3** 27 44N 34 16 E
Muhammad Qol, *Sudan* **94 C4** 20 53N 37 9 E
Muhammadabad, *India* **81 F10** 26 4N 83 25 E
Muhayriqah, *Si. Arabia* **86 B4** 23 59N 45 4 E
Muhesi →, *Tanzania* **106 D4** 7 0 S 35 20 E
Muheza □, *Tanzania* **106 C4** 5 0 S 39 0 E
Mühldorf, *Germany* **27 G8** 48 14N 12 33 E
Mühlhausen, *Germany* **26 D6** 51 12N 10 29 E
Mühlig Hofmann fjella, *Antarctica* **7 D3** 72 30 S 5 0 E
Muhutwe, *Tanzania* **106 C3** 1 35 S 31 45 E
Muiden, *Neths.* **20 D6** 52 20N 5 4 E
Muikamachi, *Japan* **61 F9** 37 15N 138 50 E
Muine Bheag, *Ireland* **19 D5** 52 42N 6 57W
Muiños, *Spain* **36 D3** 41 58N 7 59W
Muir, L., *Australia* **113 F2** 34 30 S 116 40 E
Mukachevo, *Ukraine* **50 G3** 48 27N 22 45 E
Mukah, *Malaysia* **75 B4** 2 55N 112 5 E
Mukawwa, Geziret, *Egypt* **94 C4** 23 55N 35 53 E
Mukdahan, *Thailand* **76 D5** 16 32N 104 43 E
Mukden = Shenyang, *China* **67 D12** 41 48N 123 27 E
Mukhtolovo, *Russia* **51 D13** 55 29N 43 15 E
Mukhtuya = Lensk, *Russia* **57 C12** 60 48N 114 55 E
Mukinbudin, *Australia* **113 F2** 30 55 S 118 5 E
Mukishi, *Zaïre* **103 D4** 8 30 S 24 44 E
Mukomuko, *Indonesia* **74 C2** 2 30 S 101 10 E
Mukomwenze, *Zaïre* **106 D2** 6 49 S 27 15 E
Mukry, *Turkmenistan* **55 E2** 37 54N 65 12 E
Muktsar, *India* **80 D6** 30 30N 74 30 E
Mukur, *Afghan.* **80 C2** 32 50N 67 42 E
Mukutawa →, *Canada* **131 C9** 53 10N 97 24W
Mukwela, *Zambia* **107 F2** 17 0 S 26 40 E
Mukwonago, *U.S.A.* **141 B8** 42 52N 88 20W
Mula, *Spain* **35 G3** 38 3N 1 33W
Mula →, *India* **82 E2** 18 34N 74 21 E
Mulanay, *Phil.* **70 E4** 13 31N 122 24 E
Mulange, *Zaïre* **106 C2** 3 40 S 27 10 E
Mulberry Grove, *U.S.A.* **140 F7** 38 56N 89 16W
Mulchén, *Chile* **158 D1** 37 45 S 72 20W
Mulde →, *Germany* **26 D8** 51 50N 12 15 E
Muldraugh, *U.S.A.* **141 G11** 37 56N 85 59W
Mule Creek, *U.S.A.* **138 D2** 43 19N 104 8W
Muleba, *Tanzania* **106 C3** 1 50 S 31 37 E
Muleba □, *Tanzania* **106 C3** 2 0 S 31 30 E
Mulegns, *Switz.* **29 C9** 46 32N 9 38 E
Muleshoe, *U.S.A.* **139 H3** 34 13N 102 43W
Mulga Valley, *Australia* **116 A4** 31 8 S 141 3 E
Mulgathing, *Australia* **115 E1** 30 15 S 134 8 E
Mulgrave, *Canada* **129 C7** 45 38N 61 31W
Mulgrave I., *Papua N. G.* **120 F2** 10 5 S 142 10 E
Mulhacén, *Spain* **35 H1** 37 4N 3 20W
Mülheim, *Germany* **26 D2** 51 26N 6 53 E
Mulhouse, *France* **23 E14** 47 40N 7 20 E
Muli, *China* **68 D3** 27 52N 101 8 E
Mulifanua, *W. Samoa* **121 W24** 13 50 S 171 59W
Muling, *China* **67 B16** 44 35N 130 10 E
Mull, *U.K.* **18 E3** 56 27N 6 0W
Mullaittvu, *Sri Lanka* **83 K5** 9 15N 80 49 E
Mullen, *U.S.A.* **138 D4** 42 3N 101 1W
Mullengudgery, *Australia* **117 A7** 31 43 S 147 23 E
Mullens, *U.S.A.* **134 G5** 37 35N 81 23W
Muller, Pegunungan, *Indonesia* **75 B4** 0 30N 113 30 E
Mullet Pen., *Ireland* **19 B1** 54 10N 10 2W
Mullewa, *Australia* **113 E2** 28 29 S 115 30 E
Müllheim, *Germany* **27 H3** 47 48N 7 37 E
Mulligan →, *Australia* **114 C2** 25 0 S 139 0 E
Mullin, *U.S.A.* **139 K5** 31 33N 98 40W
Mullingar, *Ireland* **19 C4** 53 31N 7 20W
Mullins, *U.S.A.* **135 H6** 34 12N 79 15W
Mullumbimby, *Australia* **115 D5** 28 30 S 153 30 E
Mulobezi, *Zambia* **107 F2** 16 45 S 25 7 E
Mulshi L., *India* **82 E1** 18 30N 73 48 E
Multai, *India* **82 D4** 21 50N 78 21 E
Multan, *Pakistan* **79 C3** 30 15N 71 36 E
Multrå, *Sweden* **14 A11** 63 10N 17 24 E
Mulu, Gunong, *Malaysia* **75 B4** 4 3N 114 56 E
Mulumbe, Mts., *Zaïre* **107 D2** 8 40 S 27 30 E
Mulungushi Dam, *Zambia* **107 E2** 14 48 S 28 48 E
Mulvane, *U.S.A.* **139 G6** 37 29N 97 15W
Mulwad, *Sudan* **94 D3** 18 45N 30 39 E
Mulwala, *Australia* **117 C7** 35 59 S 146 0 E
Mumbondo, *Angola* **103 E2** 10 9 S 14 15 E
Mumbwa, *Zambia* **107 E2** 15 0 S 27 0 E
Mumeng, *Papua N. G.* **120 D4** 7 1 S 146 37 E
Mumra, *Russia* **53 D12** 45 45N 47 41 E
Mun →, *Thailand* **76 E5** 15 19N 105 30 E
Muna, *Indonesia* **72 B2** 5 0 S 122 30 E
Munamagi, *Estonia* **50 C5** 57 43N 27 4 E
Münchberg, *Germany* **27 E7** 50 11N 11 48 E
Müncheberg, *Germany* **26 C10** 52 30N 14 9 E
München, *Germany* **27 G7** 48 8N 11 33 E
Munchen-Gladbach = Mönchengladbach, *Germany* **26 D2** 51 12N 6 23 E
Muncho Lake, *Canada* **130 B3** 59 0N 125 50W
Munchŏn, *N. Korea* **67 E14** 39 14N 127 19 E
Münchwilen, *Switz.* **29 B7** 47 28N 8 59 E
Muncie, *U.S.A.* **141 D11** 40 12N 85 23W
Muncoonie, L., *Australia* **114 D2** 25 12 S 138 40 E
Munda, *Solomon Is.* **121 M9** 8 20 S 157 16 E
Mundakayam, *India* **83 K3** 9 30N 76 50 E
Mundala, *Indonesia* **73 B6** 4 30 S 141 0 E
Mundare, *Canada* **130 C6** 53 35N 112 20W
Munday, *U.S.A.* **139 J5** 33 27N 99 38W
Münden, *Germany* **26 D5** 51 25N 9 42 E
Mundiwindi, *Australia* **112 D3** 23 47 S 120 9 E
Mundo →, *Spain* **35 G2** 38 30N 2 15W
Mundo Novo, *Brazil* **155 D3** 11 50 S 40 29W
Mundra, *India* **80 H3** 22 54N 69 48 E
Mundrabilla, *Australia* **113 F4** 31 52 S 127 51 E
Munducurus, *Brazil* **153 D6** 4 47 S 58 16W
Munenga, *Angola* **103 E2** 10 2 S 14 41 E
Munera, *Spain* **35 F2** 39 2N 2 29W
Muneru →, *India* **83 F5** 16 45N 80 3 E
Mungallala, *Australia* **115 D4** 26 28 S 147 34 E
Mungallala Cr. →, *Australia* **115 D4** 28 53 S 147 5 E
Mungana, *Australia* **114 B3** 17 8 S 144 27 E
Mungaoli, *India* **80 G8** 24 24N 78 7 E
Mungari, *Mozam.* **107 F3** 17 12 S 33 30 E
Mungbere, *Zaïre* **106 B2** 2 36N 28 28 E
Munger, *India* **81 G12** 25 23N 86 30 E
Mungindi, *Australia* **115 D4** 28 58 S 149 1 E
Munhango, *Angola* **103 E3** 12 10 S 18 38 E
Munich = München, *Germany* **27 G7** 48 8N 11 33 E
Munising, *U.S.A.* **134 B2** 46 25N 86 40W
Munka-Ljungby, *Sweden* **15 H6** 56 16N 12 58 E
Munkedal, *Sweden* **15 F5** 58 28N 11 40 E
Munku-Sardyk, *Russia* **57 D11** 51 45N 100 20 E
Münnerstadt, *Germany* **27 E6** 50 15N 10 11 E
Munoz, *Phil.* **70 D3** 15 43N 120 54 E
Muñoz Gamero, Pen., *Chile* **160 D2** 52 30 S 73 5W
Munro, *Australia* **117 D7** 37 56 S 147 11 E
Munroe L., *Canada* **131 B9** 59 13N 98 35W
Munsan, *S. Korea* **67 F14** 37 51N 126 48 E
Munshiganj, *Bangla.* **78 D3** 23 33N 90 32 E
Münsingen, *Switz.* **28 C5** 46 52N 7 32 E
Munster, *France* **23 D14** 48 2N 7 8 E
Munster, *Niedersachsen, Germany* **26 C6** 52 59N 10 5 E
Münster, *Nordrhein-Westfalen, Germany* **26 D3** 51 58N 7 37 E
Münster, *Switz.* **29 D6** 46 29N 8 17 E
Munster □, *Ireland* **19 D3** 52 20N 8 40W
Muntadgin, *Australia* **113 F2** 31 45 S 118 33 E
Muntele Mare, *Romania* **46 C4** 46 30N 23 12 E
Muntok, *Indonesia* **74 C3** 2 5 S 105 10 E
Munyak, *Uzbekistan* **56 E6** 43 30N 59 15 E
Munyama, *Zambia* **107 F2** 16 5 S 28 31 E
Muong Beng, *Laos* **76 B3** 20 23N 101 46 E
Muong Boum, *Vietnam* **76 A4** 22 24N 102 49 E
Muong Et, *Laos* **76 B5** 20 49N 104 1 E
Muong Hai, *Laos* **76 B3** 21 3N 101 49 E
Muong Hiem, *Laos* **76 B4** 20 5N 103 22 E
Muong Houn, *Laos* **76 B3** 20 8N 101 23 E
Muong Hung, *Vietnam* **76 B4** 20 56N 103 53 E
Muong Kau, *Laos* **76 E5** 15 6N 105 47 E
Muong Khao, *Laos* **76 C4** 19 38N 103 32 E
Muong Khoua, *Laos* **76 B4** 21 5N 102 31 E
Muong Liep, *Laos* **76 C3** 18 29N 101 40 E
Muong May, *Laos* **76 E6** 14 49N 106 56 E
Muong Ngeun, *Laos* **76 B3** 20 36N 101 3 E
Muong Ngoi, *Laos* **76 B4** 20 43N 102 41 E
Muong Nhie, *Vietnam* **76 A4** 22 12N 102 28 E
Muong Nong, *Laos* **76 D6** 16 22N 106 30 E
Muong Ou Tay, *Laos* **76 A3** 22 7N 101 48 E
Muong Oua, *Laos* **76 C3** 18 18N 101 20 E
Muong Peun, *Laos* **76 B4** 20 13N 103 52 E
Muong Phalane, *Laos* **76 D5** 16 39N 105 34 E
Muong Phieng, *Laos* **76 C3** 19 6N 101 32 E
Muong Phine, *Laos* **76 D6** 16 32N 106 2 E
Muong Sai, *Laos* **76 B3** 20 42N 101 59 E
Muong Saiapoun, *Laos* **76 C3** 18 24N 101 31 E
Muong Sen, *Vietnam* **76 C5** 19 24N 104 8 E
Muong Sing, *Laos* **76 B3** 21 11N 101 9 E
Muong Son, *Laos* **76 B4** 20 27N 103 19 E
Muong Soui, *Laos* **76 C4** 19 33N 102 52 E
Muong Va, *Laos* **76 B4** 21 53N 102 19 E
Muong Xia, *Vietnam* **76 B5** 20 19N 104 50 E
Muonio, *Finland* **12 C17** 67 57N 23 40 E
Muotathal, *Switz.* **29 C7** 46 58N 8 46 E
Mupa, *Angola* **103 F3** 16 5 S 15 50 E
Muping, *China* **67 F11** 37 22N 121 36 E
Muqaddam, Wadi →, *Sudan* **94 D3** 18 4N 31 30 E
Muqdisho, *Somali Rep.* **90 G4** 2 2N 45 25 E
Muqshin, W. →, *Oman* **87 C6** 19 44N 55 14 E
Muquequete, *Angola* **103 E2** 14 50 S 14 16 E
Mur →, *Austria* **30 E9** 46 35N 16 3 E
Mur-de-Bretagne, *France* **22 D4** 48 12N 3 0W
Mura →, *Slovenia* **39 B13** 46 30N 16 33 E
Muradiye, *Turkey* **89 D10** 39 0N 43 44 E
Murakami, *Japan* **60 E9** 38 14N 139 29 E
Murallón, Cuerro, *Chile* **160 C2** 49 48 S 73 30W
Muralto, *Switz.* **29 D7** 46 11N 8 49 E
Muranda, *Rwanda* **106 C2** 1 52 S 29 20 E
Murang'a, *Kenya* **106 C4** 0 45 S 37 9 E
Murashi, *Russia* **51 B16** 59 30N 49 0 E
Murat, *France* **24 C6** 45 7N 2 53 E
Murat →, *Turkey* **89 D8** 38 39N 39 50 E
Muratlı, *Turkey* **88 C2** 41 10N 27 29 E
Murau, *Austria* **30 D7** 47 6N 14 10 E
Muravera, *Italy* **40 C2** 39 25N 9 35 E
Murayama, *Japan* **60 E10** 38 30N 140 25 E
Murban, *U.A.E.* **85 F7** 23 50N 53 45 E
Murça, *Portugal* **36 D3** 41 24N 7 28W
Murchison, *N.Z.* **119 B7** 41 49 S 172 21 E
Murchison →, *Australia* **113 E1** 27 45 S 114 0 E
Murchison, Mt., *Antarctica* **7 D11** 73 0 S 168 0 E
Murchison Falls = Kabarega Falls, *Uganda* **106 B3** 2 15N 31 30 E
Murchison House, *Australia* **113 E1** 27 39 S 114 14 E
Murchison Mt., *N.Z.* **119 D6** 43 0 S 171 22 E
Murchison Mts., *N.Z.* **119 F2** 45 13 S 167 23 E
Murchison Ra., *Australia* **114 C1** 20 0 S 134 10 E
Murchison Rapids, *Malawi* **107 F3** 15 55 S 34 35 E
Murcia, *Spain* **35 G3** 38 5N 1 10W
Murcia □, *Spain* **35 H3** 37 50N 1 30W
Murdo, *U.S.A.* **138 D4** 43 53N 100 43W
Murdoch Pt., *Australia* **114 A3** 14 37 S 144 55 E
Mureş □, *Romania* **46 C5** 46 45N 24 40 E
Mureş →, *Romania* **46 C1** 46 15N 20 13 E
Mureşul = Mureş →, *Romania* **46 C1** 46 15N 20 13 E
Muret, *France* **24 E5** 43 30N 1 20 E
Murfatlar, *Romania* **46 E9** 44 10N 28 26 E
Murfreesboro, *U.S.A.* **135 H2** 35 51N 86 24W
Murg, *Switz.* **29 B8** 47 6N 9 13 E
Murg →, *Germany* **27 G4** 48 55N 8 10 E
Murgab, *Tajikistan* **55 D7** 38 10N 74 2 E
Murgeni, *Romania* **46 C9** 46 12N 28 1 E
Murgenthal, *Switz.* **28 B5** 47 16N 7 50 E
Murgon, *Australia* **115 D5** 26 15 S 151 54 E
Murgoo, *Australia* **113 E2** 27 24 S 116 28 E
Muri, *Switz.* **29 B6** 47 17N 8 21 E
Muria, *Indonesia* **75 D4** 6 36 S 110 53 E
Muriaé, *Brazil* **155 F3** 21 8 S 42 23W
Murias de Paredes, *Spain* **36 C4** 42 52N 6 11W
Murici, *Brazil* **154 C4** 9 19 S 35 56W
Muriége, *Angola* **103 D4** 9 58 S 21 11 E
Muriel Mine, *Zimbabwe* **107 F3** 17 14 S 30 40 E
Murila, *Angola* **103 E4** 10 44 S 20 20 E
Müritz See, *Germany* **26 B8** 53 25N 12 40 E

238 Murka


Murka, Kenya 106 C4 3 27 S 38 0 E
Murmansk, Russia 48 A5 68 57N 33 10 E
Murmerwoude, Neths. 20 B8 53 18N 6 0 E
Murnau, Germany 27 H7 47 40N 11 11 E
Muro, France 25 F12 42 34N 8 54 E
Muro, Spain 33 B10 39 44N 3 3 E
Muro, C. de, France 25 G12 41 44N 8 37 E
Muro Lucano, Italy 41 B8 40 45N 15 30 E
Murom, Russia 51 D13 55 35N 42 3 E
Muroran, Japan 60 C10 42 25N 141 0 E
Muros, Spain 36 C1 42 45N 9 5W
Muros y de Noya, Ría de, Spain 36 C2 42 45N 9 0W
Muroto, Japan 62 D6 33 18N 134 9 E
Muroto-Misaki, Japan 62 D6 33 15N 134 10 E
Murowana Goślina, Poland 47 C4 52 35N 17 0 E
Murphy, U.S.A. 142 E5 43 13N 116 33W
Murphys, U.S.A. 144 G6 38 8N 120 28W
Murphysboro, U.S.A. 139 G10 37 46N 89 20W
Murrat, Sudan 94 D2 18 51N 29 33 E
Murray, Iowa, U.S.A. 140 C3 41 3N 93 57W
Murray, Ky., U.S.A. 135 G1 36 37N 88 19W
Murray, Utah, U.S.A. 142 F8 40 40N 111 53W
Murray →, Australia 116 C3 35 20 S 139 22 E
Murray →, Canada 130 B4 56 11N 120 45W
Murray, L., Papua N. G. 120 D1 7 0 S 141 35 E
Murray, L., U.S.A. 135 H5 34 3N 81 13W
Murray Bridge, Australia 116 C3 35 6 S 139 14 E
Murray Downs, Australia 114 C1 21 4 S 134 40 E
Murray Harbour, Canada 129 C7 46 0N 62 28W
Murraysburg, S. Africa 104 E3 31 58 S 23 47 E
Murrayville, U.S.A. 140 E6 39 35N 90 15W
Murree, Pakistan 80 C5 33 56N 73 28 E
Murrieta, U.S.A. 145 M9 33 33N 117 13W
Murrin Murrin, Australia 113 E3 28 58 S 121 33 E
Murrumbidgee →, Australia 116 C5 34 43 S 143 12 E
Murrumburrah, Australia 117 C8 34 32 S 148 22 E
Murrurundi, Australia 117 A9 31 42 S 150 51 E
Mursala, Indonesia 74 B1 1 41N 98 28 E
Murshid, Sudan 94 C3 21 40N 31 10 E
Murshidabad, India 81 G13 24 11N 88 19 E
Murska Sobota, Slovenia 39 B13 46 39N 16 12 E
Murtazapur, India 82 D3 20 40N 77 25 E
Murten, Switz. 28 C4 46 56N 7 4 E
Murtensee, Switz. 28 C4 46 56N 7 7 E
Murtle L., Canada 130 C5 52 8N 119 38W
Murtoa, Australia 116 D5 36 35 S 142 28 E
Murtosa, Portugal 36 E2 40 44N 8 40W
Muru →, Brazil 156 B3 8 9 S 70 45W
Murungu, Tanzania 106 C3 4 12 S 31 10 E
Murupara, N.Z. 118 E5 38 28 S 176 42 E
Murwara, India 81 H9 23 46N 80 28 E
Murwillumbah, Australia 115 D5 28 18 S 153 27 E
Mürz →, Austria 30 D8 47 30N 15 25 E
Mürzzuschlag, Austria 30 D8 47 36N 15 41 E
Muş, Turkey 89 D9 38 45N 41 30 E
Muş □, Turkey 89 D9 38 45N 41 30 E
Musa, Zaïre 102 B3 2 40N 19 18 E
Musa →, Papua N. G. 120 E5 9 3 S 148 55 E
Mûsa, G., Egypt 94 J8 28 33N 33 59 E
Musa Khel, Pakistan 79 C3 30 59N 69 52 E
Mūsá Qal'eh, Afghan. 79 B2 32 20N 64 50 E
Musala, Bulgaria 43 E8 42 13N 23 37 E
Musan, N. Korea 67 C15 42 12N 129 12 E
Musangu, Zaïre 103 E4 10 28 S 23 55 E
Musasa, Tanzania 106 C3 3 25 S 31 30 E
Musashino, Japan 63 B11 35 42N 139 34 E
Musay'īd, Qatar 85 E6 25 0N 51 33 E
Musaymīr, Yemen 86 D4 13 27N 44 37 E
Muscat = Masqat, Oman 87 B7 23 37N 58 36 E
Muscat & Oman = Oman ■, Asia 87 B7 23 0N 58 0 E
Muscatine, U.S.A. 140 C5 41 25N 91 3W
Muscoda, U.S.A. 140 A6 43 11N 90 27W
Musel, Spain 36 B5 43 34N 5 42W
Musgrave, Australia 114 A3 14 47 S 143 30 E
Musgrave Ras., Australia 113 E5 26 0 S 132 0 E
Mushie, Zaïre 102 C3 2 56 S 16 55 E
Mushin, Nigeria 101 D5 6 32N 3 21 E
Musi →, India 82 F4 16 41N 79 40 E
Musi →, Indonesia 74 C2 2 20 S 104 56 E
Muskeg →, Canada 130 A4 60 20N 123 20W
Muskegon, U.S.A. 141 A10 43 14N 86 16W
Muskegon →, U.S.A. 134 D2 43 14N 86 21W
Muskegon Heights, U.S.A. 141 A10 43 12N 86 16W
Muskogee, U.S.A. 139 H7 35 45N 95 22W
Muskwa →, Canada 130 B4 58 47N 122 48W
Muslīmiyah, Syria 84 B3 36 19N 37 12 E
Musmar, Sudan 94 D4 18 13N 35 40 E
Musofu, Zambia 107 E2 13 30 S 29 0 E
Musoma, Tanzania 106 C3 1 30 S 33 48 E
Musoma □, Tanzania 106 C3 1 50 S 34 30 E
Musquaro, L., Canada 129 B7 50 38N 61 5W
Musquodoboit Harbour, Canada 129 D7 44 50N 63 9W
Mussau I., Papua N. G. 120 A5 1 30 S 149 40 E
Musselburgh, U.K. 18 F5 55 57N 3 3W
Musselkanaal, Neths. 20 C10 52 57N 7 0 E
Musselshell →, U.S.A. 142 C10 47 21N 107 57W
Mussende, Angola 103 E3 10 32 S 16 5 E
Mussidan, France 24 C4 45 2N 0 22 E
Mussolo, Angola 103 D3 9 59 S 17 19 E
Mussomeli, Italy 40 E6 37 35N 13 43 E
Musson, Belgium 21 J7 49 33N 5 42 E
Mussoorie, India 80 D8 30 27N 78 6 E
Mussuco, Angola 103 F3 17 2 S 19 3 E
Mustafakemalpaşa, Turkey 88 C3 40 2N 28 24 E
Mustahil, Ethiopia 108 C2 5 16N 44 45 E
Mustang, Nepal 81 E10 29 10N 83 55 E
Musters, L., Argentina 160 C3 45 20 S 69 25W
Musudan, N. Korea 67 D15 40 50N 129 43 E
Muswellbrook, Australia 117 B9 32 16 S 150 56 E
Muszyna, Poland 31 B13 49 22N 20 55 E
Mût, Egypt 94 B2 25 28N 28 58 E
Mut, Turkey 88 E5 36 40N 33 28 E
Mutanda, Mozam. 105 C5 21 0 S 33 34 E
Mutanda, Zambia 107 E2 12 24 S 26 13 E
Mutaray, Russia 57 C11 60 56N 101 0 E
Mutare, Zimbabwe 107 F3 18 58 S 32 38 E
Mu'tariḑah, Al 'Urūq al, Si. Arabia 87 B6 21 15N 54 0 E
Muting, Indonesia 73 C6 7 23 S 140 20 E
Mutooroo, Australia 116 B4 32 26 S 140 55 E
Mutoto, Zaïre 103 D4 5 42 S 22 42 E
Mutshatsha, Zaïre 103 E4 10 35 S 24 20 E
Mutsu, Japan 60 D10 41 5N 140 55 E
Mutsu-Wan, Japan 60 D10 41 5N 140 55 E
Muttaburra, Australia 114 C3 22 38 S 144 29 E
Muttama, Australia 117 C8 34 46 S 148 8 E
Mutuáli, Mozam. 107 E4 14 55 S 37 0 E
Mutunópolis, Brazil 155 D2 13 40 S 49 15W
Muvatupusha, India 83 K3 9 53N 76 35 E
Muweilih, Egypt 91 E3 30 42N 34 19 E
Muxima, Angola 103 D2 9 33 S 13 58 E
Muy Muy, Nic. 148 D2 12 39N 85 36W
Muya, Russia 57 D12 56 27N 115 50 E
Muyinga, Burundi 106 C3 3 14 S 30 33 E
Muyunkum, Peski, Kazakhstan 55 A5 44 12N 71 0 E
Muzaffarabad, Pakistan 81 B5 34 25N 73 30 E
Muzaffargarh, Pakistan 79 C3 30 5N 71 14 E
Muzaffarnagar, India 80 E7 29 26N 77 40 E
Muzaffarpur, India 81 F11 26 7N 85 23 E
Muzeze, Angola 103 F3 15 3 S 17 43 E
Muzhi, Russia 56 C7 65 25N 64 40 E
Muzillac, France 22 E4 47 35N 2 30W
Muzkol, Khrebet, Tajikistan 55 D6 38 22N 73 20 E
Muzon, C., U.S.A. 130 C2 54 40N 132 42W
Mvadhi-Ousyé, Gabon 102 B2 1 13N 13 12 E
Mvam, Gabon 102 C1 0 13 S 9 39 E
Mvôlô, Sudan 95 F2 6 2N 29 53 E
Mvuma, Zimbabwe 107 F3 19 16 S 30 30 E
Mvurwi, Zimbabwe 107 F3 17 0 S 30 57 E
Mwadui, Tanzania 106 C3 3 26 S 33 32 E
Mwambo, Tanzania 107 E5 10 30 S 40 22 E
Mwandi, Zambia 107 F1 17 30 S 24 51 E
Mwanza, Tanzania 106 C3 2 30 S 32 58 E
Mwanza, Zaïre 103 D5 7 55 S 26 43 E
Mwanza, Zambia 107 F1 16 58 S 24 28 E
Mwanza □, Tanzania 106 C3 2 0 S 33 0 E
Mwaya, Tanzania 107 D3 9 32 S 33 55 E
Mweelrea, Ireland 19 C2 53 37N 9 48W
Mweka, Zaïre 103 C4 4 50 S 21 34 E
Mwendjila, Zaïre 103 D3 7 12 S 18 51 E
Mwene, Zaïre 103 D4 6 35 S 22 27 E
Mwenezi, Zimbabwe 107 G3 21 15 S 30 48 E
Mwenezi →, Mozam. 107 G3 22 40 S 31 50 E
Mwenga, Zaïre 106 C2 3 1 S 28 28 E
Mweru, L., Zambia 107 D2 9 0 S 28 40 E
Mweza Range, Zimbabwe 107 G3 21 0 S 30 0 E
Mwilambwe, Zaïre 103 D5 8 7 S 25 5 E
Mwimbi, Tanzania 107 D3 8 38 S 31 39 E
Mwinilunga, Zambia 107 E1 11 43 S 24 25 E
My Tho, Vietnam 77 G6 10 29N 106 23 E
Mya, O. →, Algeria 99 B5 30 46N 4 54 E
Myajlar, India 80 F4 26 15N 70 20 E
Myanaung, Burma 78 F5 18 18N 95 22 E
Myanmar = Burma ■, Asia 78 E6 21 0N 96 30 E
Myaungmya, Burma 78 G5 16 30N 94 40 E
Mycenae = Mikínai, Greece 45 G4 37 43N 22 46 E
Myeik Kyunzu, Burma 77 G1 11 30N 97 30 E
Myerstown, U.S.A. 137 F8 40 22N 76 19W
Myingyan, Burma 78 E5 21 30N 95 20 E
Myitkyina, Burma 78 C6 25 24N 97 26 E
Myittha →, Burma 78 D5 23 12N 94 17 E
Myjava, Slovak Rep. 31 C10 48 41N 17 37 E
Mykolayiv = Nikolayev, Ukraine 52 C4 46 58N 32 0 E
Mymensingh, Bangla. 78 C3 24 45N 90 24 E
Myndus, Turkey 45 G9 37 3N 27 14 E
Mynydd Du, U.K. 17 F4 51 45N 3 45W
Mynzhilgi, Gora, Kazakhstan 55 B4 43 48N 68 51 E
Mýrdalsjökull, Iceland 12 E4 63 40N 19 6W
Myroodah, Australia 112 C3 18 7 S 124 16 E
Myrtle Beach, U.S.A. 135 J6 33 42N 78 53W
Myrtle Creek, U.S.A. 142 E2 43 1N 123 17W
Myrtle Point, U.S.A. 142 E1 43 4N 124 8W
Myrtleford, Australia 117 D7 36 34 S 146 44 E
Myrtou, Cyprus 32 D12 35 18N 33 4 E
Mysen, Norway 14 E5 59 33N 11 20 E
Mysia, Turkey 88 D2 39 50N 27 0 E
Myslenice, Poland 31 B12 49 51N 19 57 E
Myślibórz, Poland 47 C1 52 55N 14 50 E
Mysłowice, Poland 31 A12 50 15N 19 12 E
Mysore = Karnataka □, India 83 H3 13 15N 77 0 E
Mysore, India 83 H3 12 17N 76 41 E
Mystic, Conn., U.S.A. 137 E13 41 21N 71 58W
Mystic, Iowa, U.S.A. 140 D4 40 47N 92 57W
Myszków, Poland 47 E6 50 45N 19 22 E
Myszyniec, Poland 47 B8 53 23N 21 21 E
Mythen, Switz. 29 B7 47 2N 8 42 E
Mytishchi, Russia 51 D10 55 50N 37 50 E
Myton, U.S.A. 142 F8 40 12N 110 4W
Mývatn, Iceland 12 D5 65 36N 17 0W
Mze →, Czech. 30 B6 49 46N 13 24 E
Mzimba, Malawi 107 E3 11 55 S 33 39 E
Mzimkulu →, S. Africa 105 E5 30 44 S 30 28 E
Mzimvubu →, S. Africa 105 E4 31 38 S 29 33 E
Mzuzu, Malawi 107 E3 11 30 S 33 55 E


## N


N' Dioum, Senegal 100 B2 16 31N 14 39W
Na-lang, Burma 78 D6 22 42N 97 33 E
Na Noi, Thailand 76 C3 18 19N 100 43 E
Na Phao, Laos 76 D5 17 35N 105 44 E
Na Sam, Vietnam 76 A6 22 3N 106 37 E
Na San, Vietnam 76 B5 21 12N 104 2 E
Naab →, Germany 27 F8 49 1N 12 2 E
Naaldwijk, Neths. 20 E4 51 59N 4 13 E
Na'am, Sudan 95 F2 6 42N 28 27 E
Naantali, Finland 13 F17 60 29N 22 2 E
Naarden, Neths. 20 D6 52 18N 5 9 E
Naas, Ireland 19 C5 53 12N 6 40W
Nababiep, S. Africa 104 D2 29 36 S 17 46 E
Nabadwip = Navadwip, India 81 H13 23 34N 88 20 E
Nabari, Japan 63 C8 34 37N 136 5 E
Nabawa, Australia 113 E1 28 30 S 114 48 E
Nabberu, L., Australia 113 E3 25 50 S 120 30 E
Nabburg, Germany 27 F8 49 27N 12 11 E
Naberezhnyye Chelny, Russia 54 D3 55 42N 52 19 E
Nabeul, Tunisia 96 A2 36 30N 10 44 E
Nabha, India 80 D7 30 26N 76 14 E
Nabīd, Iran 85 D8 29 40N 57 38 E
Nabire, Indonesia 73 B5 3 15 S 135 26 E
Nabisar, Pakistan 80 G3 25 8N 69 40 E
Nabisipi →, Canada 129 B7 50 14N 62 13W
Nabiswera, Uganda 106 B3 1 27N 32 15 E
Nablus = Nābulus, Jordan 91 C4 32 14N 35 15 E
Naboomspruit, S. Africa 105 C4 24 32 S 28 40 E
Nabua, Phil. 70 E4 13 24N 123 22 E
Nābulus, Jordan 91 C4 32 14N 35 15 E
Nābulus □, Jordan 91 C4 32 20N 35 20 E
Nabunturan, Phil. 71 H5 7 35N 125 58 E
Nacala, Mozam. 107 E5 14 31 S 40 34 E
Nacala-Velha, Mozam. 107 E5 14 32 S 40 34 E
Nacaome, Honduras 148 D2 13 31N 87 30W
Nacaroa, Mozam. 107 E4 14 22 S 39 56 E
Naches, U.S.A. 142 C3 46 44N 120 42W
Naches →, U.S.A. 144 D6 46 38N 120 31W
Nachikatsuura, Japan 63 D7 33 33N 135 58 E
Nachingwea, Tanzania 107 E4 10 23 S 38 49 E
Nachingwea □, Tanzania 107 E4 10 30 S 38 30 E
Nachna, India 80 F4 27 34N 71 41 E
Náchod, Czech. 31 A9 50 25N 16 8 E
Nacimiento Reservoir, U.S.A. 144 K6 35 46N 120 53W
Nacka, Sweden 14 E12 59 17N 18 12 E
Nackara, Australia 116 B3 32 48 S 139 12 E
Naco, Mexico 146 A3 31 20N 109 56W
Naco, U.S.A. 143 L9 31 20N 109 57W
Nacogdoches, U.S.A. 139 K7 31 36N 94 39W
Nácori Chico, Mexico 146 B3 29 39N 109 1W
Nacozari, Mexico 146 A3 30 24N 109 39W
Nadi, Sudan 94 D3 18 40N 33 41 E
Nadiad, India 80 H5 22 41N 72 56 E
Nădlac, Romania 46 C1 46 10N 20 50 E
Nador, Morocco 99 A4 35 14N 2 58W
Nadur, Malta 32 C1 36 2N 14 17 E
Nadūshan, Iran 85 C7 32 2N 53 35 E
Nadvoitsy, Russia 48 B5 63 52N 34 14 E
Nadvornaya, Ukraine 52 B1 48 37N 24 30 E
Nadym, Russia 56 C8 65 35N 72 42 E
Nadym →, Russia 56 C8 66 12N 72 0 E
Næstved, Denmark 15 J5 55 13N 11 44 E
Nafada, Nigeria 101 C7 11 8N 11 20 E
Näfels, Switz. 29 B8 47 6N 9 4 E
Naftshahr, Iran 84 C5 34 0N 45 30 E
Nafud Desert = An Nafūd, Si. Arabia 84 D4 28 15N 41 0 E
Nafūsah, Jabal, Libya 96 B2 32 12N 12 30 E
Nag Hammâdi, Egypt 94 B3 26 2N 32 18 E
Naga, Cebu, Phil. 71 F4 10 13N 123 45 E
Naga, Luzon, Phil. 70 E4 13 38N 123 15 E
Naga, Zamboanga del S., Phil. 71 H4 7 46N 122 45 E
Naga, Kreb en, Africa 98 D3 24 12N 6 0W
Naga-Shima, Kagoshima, Japan 62 E2 32 10N 130 9 E
Naga-Shima, Yamaguchi, Japan 62 D4 33 49N 132 5 E
Nagagami →, Canada 128 C3 49 40N 84 40W
Nagahama, Ehime, Japan 62 D4 33 36N 132 29 E
Nagahama, Shiga, Japan 63 B8 35 23N 136 16 E
Nagai, Japan 60 E10 38 6N 140 2 E
Nagaland □, India 78 B5 26 0N 94 30 E
Nagambie, Australia 117 D6 36 47 S 145 10 E
Nagano, Japan 63 A10 36 40N 138 10 E
Nagano □, Japan 63 A10 36 15N 138 0 E
Nagaoka, Japan 61 F9 37 27N 138 51 E
Nagappattinam, India 83 J4 10 46N 79 51 E
Nagar Parkar, Pakistan 80 G4 24 28N 70 46 E
Nagara →, Japan 63 B8 35 40N 136 43 E
Nagari Hills, India 83 H4 13 3N 79 45 E
Nagarjuna Sagar, India 83 F4 16 35N 79 17 E
Nagasaki, Japan 62 E1 32 47N 129 50 E
Nagasaki □, Japan 62 E1 32 50N 129 40 E
Nagato, Japan 62 C3 34 19N 131 5 E
Nagaur, India 80 F5 27 15N 73 45 E
Nagbhir, India 82 D4 20 34N 79 55 E
Nagercoil, India 83 K3 8 12N 77 26 E
Nagina, India 81 E8 29 30N 78 30 E
Nagīneh, Iran 85 C8 34 20N 57 15 E
Nagir, Pakistan 81 A6 36 12N 74 42 E
Nagold, Germany 27 G4 48 33N 8 43 E
Nagold →, Germany 27 G4 48 52N 8 42 E
Nagoorin, Australia 114 C5 24 17 S 151 15 E
Nagornyy, Russia 57 D13 55 58N 124 57 E
Nagorsk, Russia 54 B2 59 18N 50 48 E
Nagoya, Japan 63 B8 35 10N 136 50 E
Nagpur, India 82 D4 21 8N 79 10 E
Nagua, Dom. Rep. 149 C6 19 23N 69 50W
Nagyatád, Hungary 31 E10 46 14N 17 22 E
Nagyecsed, Hungary 31 D15 47 53N 22 24 E
Nagykanizsa, Hungary 31 E10 46 28N 17 0 E
Nagykörös, Hungary 31 D12 47 5N 19 48 E
Nagyléta, Hungary 31 D14 47 23N 21 55 E
Naha, Japan 61 L3 26 13N 127 42 E
Nahanni Butte, Canada 130 A4 61 2N 123 31W
Nahanni Nat. Park, Canada 130 A3 61 15N 125 0W
Nahariyya, Israel 91 C4 33 1N 35 5 E
Nahāvand, Iran 85 C6 34 10N 48 22 E
Nahe →, Germany 27 F3 49 58N 7 57 E
Nahīya, Wadi →, Egypt 94 J7 28 55N 31 0 E
Nahlin, Canada 130 B2 58 55N 131 38W
Nahuel Huapi, L., Argentina 160 B2 41 0 S 71 32W
Naicá, Mexico 146 B3 27 53N 105 31W
Naicam, Canada 131 C8 52 30N 104 30W
Nā'ifah, Si. Arabia 90 D5 19 59N 50 46 E
Naila, Germany 27 E7 50 19N 11 43 E
Nain, Canada 129 A7 56 34N 61 40W
Nā'īn, Iran 85 C7 32 54N 53 0 E
Naini Tal, India 81 E8 29 30N 79 30 E
Naintré, France 22 F7 46 46N 0 29 E
Naipu, Romania 46 E6 44 12N 25 47 E
Naira, Indonesia 73 B3 4 28 S 130 0 E
Nairn, U.K. 18 D5 57 35N 3 54W
Nairobi, Kenya 106 C4 1 17 S 36 48 E
Naivasha, Kenya 106 C4 0 40 S 36 30 E
Naivasha, L., Kenya 106 C4 0 48 S 36 20 E
Najac, France 24 D5 44 14N 1 58 E
Najafābād, Iran 85 C6 32 40N 51 15 E
Nájera, Spain 34 C2 42 26N 2 48W
Najerilla →, Spain 34 C2 42 32N 2 48W
Najibabad, India 80 E8 29 40N 78 20 E
Najin, N. Korea 67 C16 42 12N 130 15 E
Najmah, Si. Arabia 85 E6 26 42N 50 6 E
Naju, S. Korea 67 G14 35 3N 126 43 E
Naka →, Japan 63 A12 36 20N 140 36 E
Nakadōri-Shima, Japan 61 H4 32 57N 129 4 E
Nakalagba, Zaïre 106 B2 2 50N 27 58 E
Nakama, Japan 62 D2 33 56N 130 43 E
Nakaminato, Japan 63 A12 36 21N 140 36 E
Nakamura, Japan 62 E4 32 59N 132 56 E
Nakanai Mts., Papua N. G. 120 C6 5 40 S 151 0 E
Nakano, Japan 63 A10 36 45N 138 22 E
Nakano-Shima, Japan 61 K4 29 51N 129 52 E
Nakanojō, Japan 63 A10 36 35N 138 51 E
Nakashibetsu, Japan 60 C12 43 33N 144 59 E
Nakatsu, Japan 62 D3 33 34N 131 15 E
Nakatsugawa, Japan 63 B9 35 29N 137 30 E
Nakfa, Eritrea 95 D4 16 40N 38 32 E
Nakhichevan, Azerbaijan 89 D11 39 12N 45 15 E
Nakhichevan Republic □, Azerbaijan 49 G8 39 14N 45 30 E
Nakhl, Egypt 91 F2 29 55N 33 43 E
Nakhl-e Taqī, Iran 85 E7 27 28N 52 36 E
Nakhodka, Russia 57 E14 42 53N 132 54 E
Nakhon Nayok, Thailand 76 E3 14 12N 101 13 E
Nakhon Pathom, Thailand 76 F3 13 49N 100 3 E
Nakhon Phanom, Thailand 76 D5 17 23N 104 43 E
Nakhon Ratchasima, Thailand 76 E4 14 59N 102 12 E
Nakhon Sawan, Thailand 76 E3 15 35N 100 10 E
Nakhon Si Thammarat, Thailand 77 H3 8 29N 100 0 E
Nakhon Thai, Thailand 76 D3 17 5N 100 44 E
Nakina, B.C., Canada 130 B2 59 12N 132 52W
Nakina, Ont., Canada 128 B2 50 10N 86 40W
Nakło nad Notecią, Poland 47 B4 53 9N 17 38 E
Nakodar, India 80 D6 31 8N 75 31 E
Nakskov, Denmark 15 K5 54 50N 11 8 E
Näkten, Sweden 14 B8 62 48N 14 38 E
Naktong →, S. Korea 67 G15 35 7N 128 57 E
Nakuru, Kenya 106 C4 0 15 S 36 4 E
Nakuru □, Kenya 106 C4 0 15 S 35 5 E
Nakuru, L., Kenya 106 C4 0 23 S 36 5 E
Nakusp, Canada 130 C5 50 20N 117 45W
Nal →, Pakistan 79 D2 25 20N 65 30 E
Nalchik, Russia 53 E10 43 30N 43 33 E
Nälden, Sweden 14 A8 63 21N 14 14 E
Näldsjön, Sweden 14 A8 63 25N 14 15 E
Nalerigu, Ghana 101 C4 10 35N 0 25W
Nalgonda, India 82 F4 17 6N 79 15 E
Nalhati, India 81 G12 24 17N 87 52 E
Nalinnes, Belgium 21 H4 50 19N 4 27 E
Nallamalai Hills, India 83 G4 15 30N 78 50 E
Nallıhan, Turkey 88 C4 40 11N 31 20 E
Nalón →, Spain 36 B4 43 32N 6 4W
Nālūt, Libya 96 B2 31 54N 11 0 E
Nam Can, Vietnam 77 H5 8 46N 104 59 E
Nam Co, China 64 C4 30 30N 90 45 E
Nam Dinh, Vietnam 76 B6 20 25N 106 5 E
Nam Du, Hon, Vietnam 77 H5 9 41N 104 21 E
Nam Ngum Dam, Laos 76 C4 18 35N 102 34 E
Nam-Phan, Vietnam 77 G6 10 30N 106 0 E
Nam Phong, Thailand 76 D4 16 42N 102 52 E
Nam Tha, Laos 76 B3 20 58N 101 30 E
Nam Tok, Thailand 76 E2 14 21N 99 4 E
Namachire, Angola 103 E4 11 26 S 22 43 E
Namacunde, Angola 103 F3 17 18 S 15 50 E
Namacurra, Mozam. 105 B6 17 30 S 36 50 E
Namak, Daryācheh-ye, Iran 85 C7 34 30N 52 0 E
Namak, Kavir-e, Iran 85 C8 34 30N 57 30 E
Namakkal, India 83 J4 11 13N 78 13 E
Namaland, Namibia 104 C2 24 30 S 17 0 E
Namangan, Uzbekistan 55 C5 41 0N 71 40 E
Namapa, Mozam. 107 E4 13 43 S 39 50 E
Namaqualand, S. Africa 104 D2 30 0 S 17 25 E
Namasagali, Uganda 106 B3 1 2N 33 0 E
Namatanai, Papua N. G. 120 B7 3 40 S 152 29 E
Namber, Indonesia 73 B4 1 2 S 134 49 E
Nambour, Australia 115 D5 26 32 S 152 58 E
Nambouwalu, Fiji 121 A2 17 0 S 178 45 E
Nambucca Heads, Australia 117 A10 30 37 S 153 0 E
Namcha Barwa, China 64 D4 29 40N 95 10 E
Namche Bazar, Nepal 81 F12 27 51N 86 47 E
Namchonjŏm, N. Korea 67 E14 38 15N 126 26 E
Namêche, Belgium 21 H6 50 28N 5 0 E
Namecunda, Mozam. 107 E4 14 54 S 37 37 E
Nameh, Indonesia 75 B5 2 34N 116 21 E
Nameponda, Mozam. 107 F4 15 50 S 39 50 E
Nameraikawa, Japan 63 A9 36 46N 137 20 E
Náměšť nad Oslavou, Czech. 31 B9 49 12N 16 10 E
Námestovo, Slovak Rep. 31 B12 49 24N 19 25 E
Nametil, Mozam. 107 F4 15 40 S 39 21 E
Namew L., Canada 131 C8 54 14N 101 56W
Namhsan, Burma 78 D6 22 48N 97 2 E
Namib Desert = Namibwoestyn, Namibia 104 C2 22 30 S 15 0 E
Namibe, Angola 103 F2 15 7 S 12 11 E
Namibe □, Angola 103 F2 16 35 S 12 30 E
Namibia ■, Africa 104 C2 22 0 S 18 9 E
Namibwoestyn, Namibia 104 C2 22 30 S 15 0 E
Namkhan, Burma 78 D6 23 50N 97 41 E
Namlea, Indonesia 72 B3 3 18 S 127 5 E
Namoi →, Australia 117 A8 30 12 S 149 30 E
Namous, O. en →, Algeria 99 B4 31 0N 0 15W
Nampa, U.S.A. 142 E5 43 34N 116 34W
Nampō-Shotō, Japan 61 J10 32 0N 140 0 E
Nampula, Mozam. 107 F4 15 6 S 39 15 E
Namrole, Indonesia 72 B3 3 46 S 126 46 E
Namsen →, Norway 12 D11 64 27N 11 42 E
Namsos, Norway 12 D11 64 29N 11 30 E
Namtay, Russia 57 C13 62 43N 129 37 E
Namtu, Burma 78 D6 23 5N 97 28 E
Namtumbo, Tanzania 107 E4 10 30 S 36 4 E
Namu, Canada 130 C3 51 52N 127 50W
Namuac, Phil. 70 B3 18 37N 121 10 E
Namur, Belgium 21 H5 50 27N 4 52 E

North Bend 241


Nicholson, *Australia* **112 C4** 18 2 S 128 54 E
Nicholson, *U.S.A.* **137 E9** 41 37N 75 47W
Nicholson →, *Australia* **114 B2** 17 31 S 139 36 E
Nicholson Ra., *Australia* **113 E2** 27 15 S 116 45 E
Nickerie □, *Surinam* **153 C6** 4 0N 57 0W
Nickerie →, *Surinam* **153 B6** 5 58N 57 0W
Nicobar Is., *Ind. Oc.* **58 J13** 9 0N 93 0 E
Nicoclí, *Colombia* **152 B2** 8 26N 76 48W
Nicola, *Canada* **130 C4** 50 12N 120 40W
Nicolet, *Canada* **128 C5** 46 17N 72 35W
Nicolls Town, *Bahamas* **148 A4** 25 8N 78 0W
Nicopolis, *Greece* **45 E2** 39 2N 20 37 E
Nicosia, *Cyprus* **32 D12** 35 10N 33 25 E
Nicosia, *Italy* **41 E7** 37 45N 14 22 E
Nicótera, *Italy* **41 D8** 38 33N 15 57 E
Nicoya, *Costa Rica* **148 D2** 10 9N 85 27W
Nicoya, G. de, *Costa Rica* **148 E3** 10 0N 85 0W
Nicoya, Pen. de, *Costa Rica* **148 E2** 9 45N 85 40W
Nidau, *Switz.* **28 B4** 47 7N 7 15 E
Nidd →, *U.K.* **16 C6** 54 1N 1 32W
Nidda, *Germany* **26 E5** 50 24N 9 2 E
Nidda →, *Germany* **27 E4** 50 6N 8 34 E
Nidwalden □, *Switz.* **29 C6** 46 50N 8 25 E
Nidzica, *Poland* **47 B7** 53 25N 20 28 E
Niebüll, *Germany* **26 A4** 54 47N 8 49 E
Nied →, *Germany* **23 C13** 49 23N 6 40 E
Niederaula, *Germany* **26 E5** 50 48N 9 37 E
Niederbipp, *Switz.* **28 B5** 47 16N 7 42 E
Niederbronn-les-Bains, *France* **23 D14** 48 57N 7 39 E
Niedere Tauern, *Austria* **30 D7** 47 20N 14 0 E
Niederösterreich □, *Austria* **30 C8** 48 25N 15 40 E
Niedersachsen □, *Germany* **26 C5** 52 45N 9 0 E
Niefang, *Eq. Guin.* **102 B2** 1 50N 10 14 E
Niekerkshoop, *S. Africa* **104 D3** 29 19 S 22 51 E
Niel, *Belgium* **21 F4** 51 7N 4 20 E
Niellé, *Ivory C.* **100 C3** 10 5N 5 38W
Niem, *C.A.R.* **102 A3** 6 12N 15 14 E
Niemba, *Zaïre* **106 D2** 5 58 S 28 24 E
Niemcza, *Poland* **47 E3** 50 42N 16 47 E
Niemen = Neman →, *Lithuania* **50 D2** 55 25N 21 10 E
Niemodlin, *Poland* **47 E4** 50 38N 17 38 E
Niemur, *Australia* **116 C6** 35 17 S 144 9 E
Nienburg, *Germany* **26 C5** 52 38N 9 15 E
Niepołomice, *Poland* **31 A13** 50 3N 20 13 E
Niers →, *Germany* **26 D2** 51 35N 6 13 E
Niesen, *Switz.* **28 C5** 46 38N 7 39 E
Niesky, *Germany* **26 D10** 51 18N 14 48 E
Nieszawa, *Poland* **47 C5** 52 52N 18 50 E
Nieu Bethesda, *S. Africa* **104 E3** 31 51 S 24 34 E
Nieuw-Amsterdam, *Neths.* **20 C9** 52 43N 6 52 E
Nieuw Amsterdam, *Surinam* **153 B6** 5 53N 55 5W
Nieuw Beijerland, *Neths.* **20 E4** 51 49N 4 20 E
Nieuw-Dordrecht, *Neths.* **20 C9** 52 45N 6 59 E
Nieuw Loosdrecht, *Neths.* **20 D6** 52 12N 5 8 E
Nieuw Nickerie, *Surinam* **153 B6** 6 0N 56 59W
Nieuw-Schoonebeek, *Neths.* **20 C10** 52 39N 7 0 E
Nieuw-Vennep, *Neths.* **20 D5** 52 16N 4 38 E
Nieuw-Vossemeer, *Neths.* **21 E4** 51 34N 4 12 E
Nieuwe-Niedorp, *Neths.* **20 C5** 52 44N 4 54 E
Nieuwe-Pekela, *Neths.* **20 B9** 53 5N 6 58 E
Nieuwe-Schans, *Neths.* **20 B10** 53 11N 7 12 E
Nieuwendijk, *Neths.* **20 E5** 51 46N 4 55 E
Nieuwerkerken, *Belgium* **21 G6** 50 52N 5 12 E
Nieuwkoop, *Neths.* **20 D5** 52 9N 4 48 E
Nieuwleusen, *Neths.* **20 C8** 52 34N 6 17 E
Nieuwnamen, *Neths.* **21 F4** 51 18N 4 9 E
Nieuwolda, *Neths.* **20 B9** 53 15N 6 58 E
Nieuwoudtville, *S. Africa* **104 E2** 31 23 S 19 7 E
Nieuwpoort, *Belgium* **21 F1** 51 8N 2 45 E
Nieuwveen, *Neths.* **20 D5** 52 12N 4 46 E
Nieves, *Spain* **36 C2** 42 7N 8 26W
Nieves, Pico de las, *Canary Is.* **33 G4** 27 57N 15 35W
Nièvre □, *France* **23 E10** 47 10N 3 40 E
Nigata, *Japan* **62 C4** 34 13N 132 39 E
Niğde, *Turkey* **88 E6** 37 58N 34 40 E
Niğde □, *Turkey* **88 E6** 38 0N 34 30 E
Nigel, *S. Africa* **105 D4** 26 27 S 28 25 E
Niger □, *Nigeria* **101 C6** 10 0N 5 30 E
Niger ■, *W. Afr.* **97 E2** 17 30N 10 0 E
Niger →, *W. Afr.* **101 D6** 5 33N 6 33 E
Nigeria ■, *W. Afr.* **101 D6** 8 30N 8 0 E
Nightcaps, *N.Z.* **119 F3** 45 57 S 168 2 E
Nigríta, *Greece* **44 D5** 40 56N 23 29 E
Nihtaur, *India* **81 E8** 29 20N 78 23 E
Nii-Jima, *Japan* **63 C11** 34 20N 139 15 E
Niigata, *Japan* **60 F9** 37 58N 139 0 E
Niigata □, *Japan* **61 F9** 37 15N 138 45 E
Niihama, *Japan* **62 D5** 33 55N 133 16 E
Niihau, *U.S.A.* **132 H14** 21 54N 160 9W
Niimi, *Japan* **62 C5** 34 59N 133 28 E
Niitsu, *Japan* **60 F9** 37 48N 139 7 E
Níjar, *Spain* **35 J2** 36 53N 2 15W
Nijil, *Jordan* **91 E4** 30 32N 35 33 E
Nijkerk, *Neths.* **20 D7** 52 13N 5 30 E
Nijlen, *Belgium* **21 F5** 51 10N 4 40 E
Nijmegen, *Neths.* **20 E7** 51 50N 5 52 E
Nijverdal, *Neths.* **20 D8** 52 22N 6 28 E
Nīk Pey, *Iran* **85 B6** 36 50N 48 10 E
Nike, *Nigeria* **101 D6** 6 26N 7 29 E
Nikel, *Russia* **12 B21** 69 24N 30 12 E
Nikiniki, *Indonesia* **72 C2** 9 49 S 124 30 E
Nikítas, *Greece* **44 D5** 40 13N 23 34 E
Nikki, *Benin* **101 D5** 9 58N 3 12 E
Nikkō, *Japan* **63 A11** 36 45N 139 35 E
Nikolayev, *Ukraine* **52 C4** 46 58N 32 0 E
Nikolayevsk, *Russia* **51 G14** 50 0N 45 35 E
Nikolayevsk-na-Amur, *Russia* **57 D15** 53 8N 140 44 E
Nikolsk, *Russia* **51 B14** 59 30N 45 28 E
Nikolskoye, *Russia* **57 D17** 55 12N 166 0 E
Nikopol, *Bulgaria* **43 D9** 43 43N 24 54 E
Nikopol, *Ukraine* **52 C5** 47 35N 34 25 E
Niksar, *Turkey* **52 F7** 40 31N 37 2 E
Nīkshahr, *Iran* **85 E9** 26 15N 60 10 E
Nikšić, *Montenegro* **42 E3** 42 50N 18 57 E
Nîl, Nahr en →, *Africa* **94 H7** 30 10N 31 6 E
Nîl el Abyad →, *Sudan* **95 D3** 15 38N 32 31 E
Nîl el Azraq →, *Sudan* **95 D3** 15 38N 32 31 E
Niland, *U.S.A.* **145 M11** 33 14N 115 31W
Nile = Nîl, Nahr en →, *Africa* **94 H7** 30 10N 31 6 E
Nile □, *Uganda* **106 B3** 2 0N 31 30 E
Nile Delta, *Egypt* **94 H7** 31 40N 31 0 E
Niles, *U.S.A.* **136 E4** 41 11N 80 46W
Nilgiri Hills, *India* **83 J3** 11 30N 76 30 E
Nilo Peçanha, *Brazil* **155 D4** 13 37 S 39 6W
Nilpena, *Australia* **116 A3** 30 58 S 138 20 E
Nimach, *India* **80 G6** 24 30N 74 56 E
Nimbahera, *India* **80 G6** 24 37N 74 45 E
Nîmes, *France* **25 E8** 43 50N 4 23 E
Nimfaíon, Ákra-, *Greece* **44 D6** 40 5N 24 20 E
Nimmitabel, *Australia* **117 D8** 36 29 S 149 15 E
Nimneryskiy, *Russia* **57 D13** 57 50N 125 10 E
Nimule, *Sudan* **95 G3** 3 32N 32 3 E
Nin, *Croatia* **39 D12** 44 16N 15 12 E
Nīnawá, *Iraq* **84 B4** 36 25N 43 10 E
Ninda, *Angola* **103 E4** 14 47 S 21 24 E
Nindigully, *Australia* **115 D4** 28 21 S 148 50 E
Ninemile, *U.S.A.* **130 B2** 56 0N 130 7W
Ninety Mile Beach, *N.Z.* **118 A1** 34 48 S 173 0 E
Ninety Mile Beach, The, *Australia* **117 E7** 38 15 S 147 24 E
Nineveh = Nīnawá, *Iraq* **84 B4** 36 25N 43 10 E
Ning Xian, *China* **66 G4** 35 30N 107 58 E
Ningaloo, *Australia* **112 D1** 22 41 S 113 41 E
Ning'an, *China* **67 B15** 44 22N 129 20 E
Ningbo, *China* **69 C13** 29 51N 121 28 E
Ningcheng, *China* **67 D10** 41 32N 119 53 E
Ningde, *China* **69 D12** 26 38N 119 23 E
Ningdu, *China* **69 D10** 26 25N 115 59 E
Ninggang, *China* **69 D9** 26 42N 113 55 E
Ningguo, *China* **69 B12** 30 35N 119 0 E
Ninghai, *China* **69 C13** 29 15N 121 27 E
Ninghua, *China* **69 D11** 26 14N 116 45 E
Ningjin, *China* **66 F8** 37 35N 114 57 E
Ningjing Shan, *China* **68 B2** 30 0N 98 20 E
Ninglang, *China* **68 D3** 27 20N 100 55 E
Ningling, *China* **66 G8** 34 25N 115 22 E
Ningming, *China* **68 F6** 22 8N 107 4 E
Ningnan, *China* **68 D4** 27 5N 102 36 E
Ningpo = Ningbo, *China* **69 C13** 29 51N 121 28 E
Ningqiang, *China* **66 H4** 32 47N 106 15 E
Ningshan, *China* **66 H5** 33 21N 108 21 E
Ningsia Hui A.R. = Ningxia Huizu Zizhiqu □, *China* **66 E3** 38 0N 106 0 E
Ningwu, *China* **66 E7** 39 0N 112 18 E
Ningxia Huizu Zizhiqu □, *China* **66 E3** 38 0N 106 0 E
Ningxiang, *China* **69 C9** 28 15N 112 30 E
Ningyang, *China* **66 G9** 35 47N 116 45 E
Ningyuan, *China* **69 E8** 25 37N 111 57 E
Ninh Binh, *Vietnam* **76 B5** 20 15N 105 55 E
Ninh Giang, *Vietnam* **76 B6** 20 44N 106 24 E
Ninh Hoa, *Vietnam* **76 F7** 12 30N 109 7 E
Ninh Ma, *Vietnam* **76 F7** 12 48N 109 21 E
Ninove, *Belgium* **21 G4** 50 51N 4 2 E
Nioaque, *Brazil* **159 A4** 21 5 S 55 50W
Niobrara, *U.S.A.* **138 D6** 42 45N 98 2W
Niobrara →, *U.S.A.* **138 D6** 42 46N 98 3W
Nioki, *Zaïre* **102 C3** 2 47 S 17 40 E
Niono, *Mali* **100 C3** 14 15N 6 0W
Nioro du Rip, *Senegal* **100 C1** 13 40N 15 50W
Nioro du Sahel, *Mali* **100 B3** 15 15N 9 30W
Niort, *France* **24 B3** 46 19N 0 29W
Nipa, *Papua N. G.* **120 D2** 6 9 S 143 29 E
Nipani, *India* **83 F2** 16 20N 74 25 E
Nipawin, *Canada* **131 C8** 53 20N 104 0W
Nipawin Prov. Park, *Canada* **131 C8** 54 0N 104 37W
Nipigon, *Canada* **128 C2** 49 0N 88 17W
Nipigon, L., *Canada* **128 C2** 49 50N 88 30W
Nipin →, *Canada* **131 B7** 55 46N 108 35W
Nipishish L., *Canada* **129 B7** 54 12N 60 45W
Nipissing L., *Canada* **128 C4** 46 20N 80 0W
Nipomo, *U.S.A.* **145 K6** 35 3N 120 29W
Nipton, *U.S.A.* **145 K11** 35 28N 115 16W
Niquelândia, *Brazil* **155 D2** 14 33 S 48 23W
Nīr, *Iran* **84 B5** 38 2N 47 59 E
Nira →, *India* **82 F2** 17 58N 75 8 E
Nirasaki, *Japan* **63 B10** 35 42N 138 27 E
Nirmal, *India* **82 E4** 19 3N 78 20 E
Nirmali, *India* **81 F12** 26 20N 86 35 E
Niš, *Serbia* **42 D6** 43 19N 21 58 E
Nisa, *Portugal* **37 F3** 39 30N 7 41W
Nişāb, *Yemen* **86 D4** 14 25N 46 29 E
Nišava →, *Serbia* **42 D6** 43 20N 21 46 E
Niscemi, *Italy* **41 E7** 37 8N 14 21 E
Nishi-Sonogi-Hantō, *Japan* **62 E1** 32 55N 129 45 E
Nishinomiya, *Japan* **63 C7** 34 45N 135 20 E
Nishin'omote, *Japan* **61 J5** 30 43N 130 59 E
Nishio, *Japan* **63 C9** 34 52N 137 3 E
Nishiwaki, *Japan* **62 C6** 34 59N 134 58 E
Nísíros, *Greece* **45 H9** 36 35N 27 12 E
Niskibi →, *Canada* **128 A2** 56 29N 88 9W
Nisko, *Poland* **47 E9** 50 35N 22 7 E
Nispen, *Neths.* **21 F4** 51 29N 4 28 E
Nisporeny, *Moldavia* **46 B9** 47 4N 28 10 E
Nisqually →, *U.S.A.* **144 C4** 47 6N 122 42W
Nissáki, *Greece* **32 A3** 39 43N 19 52 E
Nissan →, *Sweden* **15 H6** 56 40N 12 51 E
Nissedal, *Norway* **14 E2** 59 10N 8 30 E
Nisser, *Norway* **14 E2** 59 7N 8 28 E
Nissum Fjord, *Denmark* **15 H2** 56 20N 8 11 E
Nistelrode, *Neths.* **21 E7** 51 42N 5 34 E
Nisutlin →, *Canada* **130 A2** 60 14N 132 34W
Nitchequon, *Canada* **129 B5** 53 10N 70 58W
Niterói, *Brazil* **155 F3** 22 52 S 43 0W
Nith →, *U.K.* **18 F5** 55 20N 3 5W
Nitra, *Slovak Rep.* **31 C11** 48 19N 18 4 E
Nitra →, *Slovak Rep.* **31 D11** 47 46N 18 10 E
Nitsa →, *Russia* **54 C9** 57 29N 64 33 E
Nittedal, *Norway* **14 D4** 60 1N 10 57 E
Nittendau, *Germany* **27 F8** 49 12N 12 16 E
Niuafo'ou, *Tonga* **111 D15** 15 30 S 175 58W
Niue, *Cook Is.* **123 J11** 19 2 S 169 54W
Niulan Jiang →, *China* **68 D4** 27 30N 103 5 E
Niut, *Indonesia* **75 B4** 0 55N 110 6 E
Niutou Shan, *China* **69 C13** 29 5N 121 59 E
Niuzhuang, *China* **67 D12** 40 58N 122 28 E
Nivelles, *Belgium* **21 G4** 50 35N 4 20 E
Nivernais, *France* **23 E10** 47 15N 3 30 E
Nixon, *U.S.A.* **139 L6** 29 16N 97 46W
Nizam Sagar, *India* **82 E3** 18 10N 77 58 E
Nizamabad, *India* **82 E4** 18 45N 78 7 E
Nizamghat, *India* **78 A5** 28 20N 95 45 E
Nizhiye Sergi, *Russia* **54 C6** 56 40N 59 18 E
Nizhne Kolymsk, *Russia* **57 C17** 68 34N 160 55 E
Nizhne-Vartovsk, *Russia* **56 C8** 60 56N 76 38 E
Nizhneangarsk, *Russia* **57 D11** 55 47N 109 30 E
Nizhnegorskiy, *Ukraine* **52 D6** 45 27N 34 38 E
Nizhnekamsk, *Russia* **54 D2** 55 38N 51 49 E
Nizhneudinsk, *Russia* **57 D10** 54 54N 99 3 E
Nizhneyansk, *Russia* **57 B14** 71 26N 136 4 E
Nizhniy Lomov, *Russia* **51 E13** 53 34N 43 38 E
Nizhniy Novgorod, *Russia* **51 C14** 56 20N 44 0 E
Nizhniy Pyandzh, *Tajikistan* **55 E4** 37 12N 68 35 E
Nizhniy Tagil, *Russia* **54 C6** 57 55N 59 57 E
Nizhny Salda, *Russia* **54 B7** 58 8N 60 42 E
Nizip, *Turkey* **89 E7** 37 5N 37 50 E
Nizké Tatry, *Slovak Rep.* **31 C12** 48 55N 19 30 E
Nizza Monferrato, *Italy* **38 D5** 44 46N 8 22 E
Njakwa, *Malawi* **107 E3** 11 1 S 33 56 E
Njanji, *Zambia* **107 E3** 14 25 S 31 46 E
Njinjo, *Tanzania* **107 D4** 8 48 S 38 54 E
Njombe, *Tanzania* **107 D3** 9 20 S 34 50 E
Njombe □, *Tanzania* **107 D3** 9 20 S 34 49 E
Njombe →, *Tanzania* **106 D4** 6 56 S 35 6 E
Nkambe, *Cameroon* **101 D7** 6 35N 10 40 E
Nkana, *Zambia* **107 E2** 12 50 S 28 8 E
Nkawkaw, *Ghana* **101 D4** 6 36N 0 49W
Nkayi, *Zimbabwe* **107 F2** 19 41 S 29 20 E
Nkhota Kota, *Malawi* **107 E3** 12 56 S 34 15 E
Nkolabona, *Gabon* **102 B2** 1 14N 11 43 E
Nkone, *Zaïre* **102 C4** 1 2 S 22 20 E
Nkongsamba, *Cameroon* **101 E6** 4 55N 9 55 E
Nkunga, *Zaïre* **103 C3** 4 41 S 18 34 E
Nkurenkuru, *Namibia* **104 B2** 17 42 S 18 32 E
Nkwanta, *Ghana* **100 D4** 6 10N 2 10W
Noakhali = Maijdi, *Bangla.* **78 D3** 22 48N 91 10 E
Noatak, *U.S.A.* **126 B3** 67 34N 162 58W
Nobel, *Canada* **136 A4** 45 25N 80 6W
Nobeoka, *Japan* **62 E3** 32 36N 131 41 E
Nōbi-Heiya, *Japan* **63 B8** 35 15N 136 45 E
Noble, *U.S.A.* **141 F8** 38 42N 88 14W
Noblejas, *Spain* **34 F1** 39 58N 3 26W
Noblesville, *U.S.A.* **141 D11** 40 3N 86 1W
Noce →, *Italy* **38 B8** 46 9N 11 4 E
Nocera Inferiore, *Italy* **41 B7** 40 45N 14 37 E
Nocera Terinese, *Italy* **41 C9** 39 2N 16 9 E
Nocera Umbra, *Italy* **39 E9** 43 8N 12 47 E
Noci, *Italy* **41 B10** 40 47N 17 7 E
Nockatunga, *Australia* **115 D3** 27 42 S 142 42 E
Nocona, *U.S.A.* **139 J6** 33 47N 97 44W
Nocrich, *Romania* **46 D5** 45 55N 24 26 E
Noda, *Japan* **63 B11** 35 56N 139 52 E
Noel, *U.S.A.* **139 G7** 36 33N 94 29W
Nogal Valley, *Somali Rep.* **108 C3** 8 35N 48 35 E
Nogales, *Mexico* **146 A2** 31 20N 110 56W
Nogales, *U.S.A.* **143 L8** 31 20N 110 56W
Nogat →, *Poland* **47 A6** 54 17N 19 17 E
Nōgata, *Japan* **62 D2** 33 48N 130 44 E
Nogent-en-Bassigny, *France* **23 D12** 48 1N 5 20 E
Nogent-le-Rotrou, *France* **22 D7** 48 20N 0 50 E
Nogent-sur-Seine, *France* **23 D10** 48 30N 3 30 E
Noggerup, *Australia* **113 F2** 33 32 S 116 5 E
Noginsk, *Russia* **51 D11** 55 50N 38 25 E
Noginsk, *Sib., Russia* **57 C10** 64 30N 90 50 E
Nogoa →, *Australia* **114 C4** 23 40 S 147 55 E
Nogoyá, *Argentina* **158 C4** 32 24 S 59 48W
Nógrád □, *Hungary* **31 D12** 48 0N 19 30 E
Nogueira de Ramuin, *Spain* **36 C3** 42 21N 7 43W
Noguera Pallaresa →, *Spain* **34 D5** 41 55N 0 55 E
Noguera Ribagorzana →, *Spain* **34 D5** 41 40N 0 43 E
Nohar, *India* **80 E6** 29 11N 74 49 E
Noing, *Phil.* **71 J5** 5 40N 125 28 E
Noire, Mt., *France* **22 D3** 48 11N 3 40W
Noirétable, *France* **24 C7** 45 48N 3 46 E
Noirmoutier, I. de, *France* **22 F4** 46 58N 2 10W
Noirmoutier-en-l'Ile, *France* **22 F4** 47 0N 2 14W
Nojane, *Botswana* **104 C3** 23 15 S 20 14 E
Nojima-Zaki, *Japan* **63 C11** 34 54N 139 53 E
Nok Kundi, *Pakistan* **79 C1** 28 50N 62 45 E
Nokaneng, *Botswana* **104 B3** 19 40 S 22 17 E
Nokhtuysk, *Russia* **57 C12** 60 0N 117 45 E
Nokomis, *Canada* **131 C8** 51 35N 105 0W
Nokomis, *U.S.A.* **140 E7** 39 18N 89 18W
Nokomis L., *Canada* **131 B8** 57 0N 103 0W
Nokou, *Chad* **97 F2** 14 35N 14 47 E
Nol, *Sweden* **15 G6** 57 56N 12 5 E
Nola, *C.A.R.* **102 B3** 3 35N 16 4 E
Nola, *Italy* **41 B7** 40 54N 14 29 E
Nolay, *France* **23 F11** 46 58N 4 35 E
Noli, C. di, *Italy* **38 D5** 44 12N 8 26 E
Nolinsk, *Russia* **54 C1** 57 28N 49 57 E
Noma Omuramba →, *Namibia* **104 B3** 18 52 S 20 53 E
Noma-Saki, *Japan* **62 F2** 31 25N 130 7 E
Nomad, *Papua N. G.* **120 D2** 6 19 S 142 13 E
Noman L., *Canada* **131 A7** 62 15N 108 55W
Nombre de Dios, *Panama* **148 E4** 9 34N 79 28W
Nome, *U.S.A.* **126 B3** 64 30N 165 25W
Nomo-Zaki, *Japan* **62 E1** 32 35N 129 44 E
Nomuka, *Tonga* **121 Q13** 20 17 S 174 48W
Nomuka Group, *Tonga* **121 Q13** 20 20 S 174 48W
Nonacho L., *Canada* **131 A7** 61 42N 109 40W
Nonancourt, *France* **22 D8** 48 47N 1 11 E
Nonant-le-Pin, *France* **22 D7** 48 42N 0 12 E
Nonda, *Australia* **114 C3** 20 40 S 142 28 E
Nong Chang, *Thailand* **76 E2** 15 23N 99 51 E
Nong Het, *Laos* **76 C4** 19 29N 103 59 E
Nong Khai, *Thailand* **76 D4** 17 50N 102 46 E
Nong'an, *China* **67 B13** 44 25N 125 5 E
Nongoma, *S. Africa* **105 D5** 27 58 S 31 35 E
Nonoava, *Mexico* **146 B3** 27 28N 106 44W
Nonoc I., *Phil.* **71 G5** 9 51N 125 37 E
Nonthaburi, *Thailand* **76 F3** 13 51N 100 34 E
Nontron, *France* **24 C4** 45 31N 0 40 E
Nonza, *France* **25 F13** 42 47N 9 21 E
Noonamah, *Australia* **112 B5** 12 40 S 131 4 E
Noonan, *U.S.A.* **138 A3** 48 54N 103 1W
Noondoo, *Australia* **115 D4** 28 35 S 148 30 E
Noonkanbah, *Australia* **112 C3** 18 30 S 124 50 E
Noord-Bergum, *Neths.* **20 B8** 53 14N 6 1 E
Noord Brabant □, *Neths.* **21 E6** 51 40N 5 0 E
Noord Holland □, *Neths.* **20 D5** 52 30N 4 45 E
Noordbeveland, *Neths.* **21 E3** 51 35N 3 50 E
Noordeloos, *Neths.* **20 E5** 51 55N 4 56 E
Noordhollandsch Kanaal, *Neths.* **20 C5** 52 55N 4 48 E
Noordhorn, *Neths.* **20 B8** 53 16N 6 24 E
Noordoostpolder, *Neths.* **20 C7** 52 45N 5 45 E
Noordwijk aan Zee, *Neths.* **20 D4** 52 14N 4 26 E
Noordwijk-Binnen, *Neths.* **20 D4** 52 14N 4 27 E
Noordwijkerhout, *Neths.* **20 D5** 52 16N 4 30 E
Noordzee Kanaal, *Neths.* **20 D5** 52 28N 4 35 E
Noorwolde, *Neths.* **20 C8** 52 54N 6 8 E
Nootka, *Canada* **130 D3** 49 38N 126 38W
Nootka I., *Canada* **130 D3** 49 32N 126 42W
Nóqui, *Angola* **103 D2** 5 55 S 13 30 E
Nora, *Eritrea* **95 D5** 16 6N 40 4 E
Nora Springs, *U.S.A.* **140 A4** 43 9N 93 1W
Noranda, *Canada* **128 C4** 48 20N 79 0W
Norborne, *U.S.A.* **140 E3** 39 18N 93 40W
Nórcia, *Italy* **39 F10** 42 50N 13 5 E
Norco, *U.S.A.* **145 M9** 33 56N 117 33W
Nord □, *France* **23 B10** 50 15N 3 30 E
Nord-Ostsee Kanal, *Germany* **26 A5** 54 15N 9 40 E
Nord-Trøndelag fylke □, *Norway* **12 D12** 64 20N 12 10 E
Nordagutu, *Norway* **14 E3** 59 25N 9 20 E
Nordaustlandet, *Svalbard* **6 B9** 79 14N 23 0 E
Nordborg, *Denmark* **15 J3** 55 5N 9 50 E
Nordby, *Århus, Denmark* **15 J4** 55 58N 10 32 E
Nordby, *Ribe, Denmark* **15 J2** 55 27N 8 24 E
Norddeich, *Germany* **26 B3** 53 37N 7 10 E
Nordegg, *Canada* **130 C5** 52 29N 116 5W
Norden, *Germany* **26 B3** 53 35N 7 12 E
Nordenham, *Germany* **26 B4** 53 29N 8 28 E
Norderhov, *Norway* **14 D4** 60 7N 10 17 E
Norderney, *Germany* **26 B3** 53 42N 7 15 E
Nordfriesische Inseln, *Germany* **26 A4** 54 40N 8 20 E
Nordhausen, *Germany* **26 D6** 51 29N 10 47 E
Nordhorn, *Germany* **26 C3** 52 27N 7 4 E
Nordjyllands Amtskommune □, *Denmark* **15 H4** 57 0N 10 0 E
Nordkapp, *Norway* **12 A18** 71 10N 25 44 E
Nordkapp, *Svalbard* **6 A9** 80 31N 20 0 E
Nordkinn = Kinnarodden, *Norway* **10 A11** 71 8N 27 40 E
Nordland fylke □, *Norway* **12 D12** 65 40N 13 0 E
Nördlingen, *Germany* **27 G6** 48 50N 10 30 E
Nordrhein-Westfalen □, *Germany* **26 D3** 51 45N 7 30 E
Nordstrand, *Germany* **26 A4** 54 27N 8 50 E
Nordvik, *Russia* **57 B12** 74 2N 111 32 E
Nore, *Norway* **14 D3** 60 10N 9 0 E
Norefjell, *Norway* **14 D3** 60 16N 9 29 E
Norembega, *Canada* **128 C3** 48 59N 80 43W
Noresund, *Norway* **14 D3** 60 11N 9 37 E
Norfolk, *Nebr., U.S.A.* **138 D6** 42 2N 97 25W
Norfolk, *Va., U.S.A.* **134 G7** 36 51N 76 17W
Norfolk □, *U.K.* **16 E9** 52 39N 1 0 E
Norfolk Broads, *U.K.* **16 E9** 52 30N 1 15 E
Norfolk I., *Pac. Oc.* **122 K8** 28 58 S 168 3 E
Norfork Res., *U.S.A.* **139 G8** 36 13N 92 15W
Norg, *Neths.* **20 B8** 53 4N 6 28 E
Norilsk, *Russia* **57 C9** 69 20N 88 6 E
Norley, *Australia* **115 D3** 27 45 S 143 48 E
Norma, Mt., *Australia* **114 C3** 20 55 S 140 42 E
Normal, *U.S.A.* **140 D8** 40 31N 88 59W
Norman, *U.S.A.* **139 H6** 35 13N 97 26W
Norman →, *Australia* **114 B3** 19 18 S 141 51 E
Norman Wells, *Canada* **126 B7** 65 17N 126 51W
Normanby, *N.Z.* **118 F3** 39 32 S 174 18 E
Normanby →, *Australia* **114 A3** 14 23 S 144 10 E
Normanby I., *Papua N. G.* **120 F6** 10 5 S 151 5 E
Normandie, *France* **22 D7** 48 45N 0 10 E
Normandie, Collines de, *France* **22 D6** 48 45N 0 45W
Normandin, *Canada* **128 C5** 48 49N 72 31W
Normandy = Normandie, *France* **22 D7** 48 45N 0 10 E
Normanhurst, Mt., *Australia* **113 E3** 25 4 S 122 30 E
Normanton, *Australia* **114 B3** 17 40 S 141 10 E
Normanville, *Australia* **116 C3** 35 27 S 138 18 E
Norquay, *Canada* **131 C8** 51 53N 102 5W
Norquinco, *Argentina* **160 B2** 41 51 S 70 55W
Norrbotten □, *Sweden* **12 C17** 66 30N 22 30 E
Norrby, *Sweden* **12 D15** 64 55N 18 15 E
Nørre Åby, *Denmark* **15 J3** 55 27N 9 52 E
Nørre Nebel, *Denmark* **15 J2** 55 47N 8 17 E
Nørresundby, *Denmark* **15 G3** 57 5N 9 52 E
Norris, *U.S.A.* **142 D8** 45 34N 111 41W
Norris City, *U.S.A.* **141 G8** 37 59N 88 20W
Norristown, *U.S.A.* **137 F9** 40 7N 75 21W
Norrköping, *Sweden* **15 F10** 58 37N 16 11 E
Norrland, *Sweden* **12 E13** 62 15N 15 45 E
Norrtälje, *Sweden* **14 E12** 59 46N 18 42 E
Norseman, *Australia* **113 F3** 32 8 S 121 43 E
Norsewood, *N.Z.* **118 G5** 40 3 S 176 13 E
Norsholm, *Sweden* **15 F9** 58 31N 15 59 E
Norsk, *Russia* **57 D14** 52 30N 130 5 E
Norsup, *Vanuatu* **121 F5** 16 3 S 167 24 E
Norte, Pta., *Argentina* **160 B4** 42 5 S 63 46W
Norte, Pta. del, *Canary Is.* **33 G2** 27 51N 17 57W
Norte de Santander □, *Colombia* **152 B3** 8 0N 73 0W
Nortelândia, *Brazil* **157 C6** 14 25 S 56 48W
North Adams, *U.S.A.* **137 D11** 42 42N 73 7W
North America **124 F10** 40 0N 100 0W
North Atlantic Ocean, *Atl. Oc.* **8 F4** 30 0N 50 0W
North Baltimore, *U.S.A.* **141 C13** 41 11N 83 41W
North Battleford, *Canada* **131 C7** 52 50N 108 17W
North Bay, *Canada* **128 C4** 46 20N 79 30W
North Belcher Is., *Canada* **128 A4** 56 50N 79 50W
North Bend, *Canada* **130 D4** 49 50N 121 27W
North Bend, *Oreg., U.S.A.* **142 E1** 43 24N 124 14W

Olascoaga 243


Nurzec →, Poland 47 C9 52 37N 22 25 E
Nusa Barung, Indonesia 75 D4 8 10 S 113 30 E
Nusa Kambangan, Indonesia 75 D3 7 40 S 108 10 E
Nusa Tenggara Barat □, Indonesia 75 D5 8 50 S 117 30 E
Nusa Tenggara Timur □, Indonesia 72 C2 9 30 S 122 0 E
Nusaybin, Turkey 49 G7 37 3N 41 10 E
Nushki, Pakistan 79 C2 29 35N 66 0 E
Nutak, Canada 127 C13 57 28N 61 59W
Nuth, Neths. 21 G7 50 55N 5 53 E
Nutwood Downs, Australia 114 B1 15 49 S 134 10 E
Nuuk = Godthåb, Greenland 127 B14 64 10N 51 35W
Nuwakot, Nepal 81 E10 28 10N 83 55 E
Nuwara Eliya, Sri Lanka 83 L5 6 58N 80 48 E
Nuweiba', Egypt 94 B3 28 59N 34 39 E
Nuweveldberge, S. Africa 104 E3 32 10 S 21 45 E
Nuyts, C., Australia 113 F5 32 2 S 132 21 E
Nuyts Arch., Australia 115 E1 32 35 S 133 20 E
Nuzvid, India 82 F5 16 47N 80 53 E
Nxau-Nxau, Botswana 104 B3 18 57 S 21 4 E
Nyaake, Liberia 100 E3 4 52N 7 37W
Nyack, U.S.A. 137 E11 41 5N 73 55W
Nyadal, Sweden 14 B11 62 48N 17 59 E
Nyah West, Australia 116 C5 35 16 S 143 21 E
Nyahanga, Tanzania 106 C3 2 20 S 33 37 E
Nyahua, Tanzania 106 D3 5 25 S 33 23 E
Nyahururu, Kenya 106 B4 0 2N 36 27 E
Nyainqentanglha Shan, China 64 D3 30 0N 90 0 E
Nyakanazi, Tanzania 106 C3 3 2 S 31 10 E
Nyakrom, Ghana 101 D4 5 40N 0 50W
Nyâlâ, Sudan 95 E1 12 2N 24 58 E
Nyamandhlovu, Zimbabwe 107 F2 19 55 S 28 16 E
Nyambiti, Tanzania 106 C3 2 48 S 33 27 E
Nyamwaga, Tanzania 106 C3 1 27 S 34 33 E
Nyandekwa, Tanzania 106 C3 3 57 S 32 32 E
Nyanding →, Sudan 95 F3 8 40N 32 41 E
Nyandoma, Russia 48 B7 61 40N 40 12 E
Nyanga →, Gabon 102 C2 2 58 S 10 15 E
Nyangana, Namibia 104 B3 18 0 S 20 40 E
Nyanguge, Tanzania 106 C3 2 30 S 33 12 E
Nyankpala, Ghana 101 D4 9 21N 0 58W
Nyanza, Burundi 106 C2 4 21 S 29 36 E
Nyanza, Rwanda 106 C2 2 20 S 29 42 E
Nyanza □, Kenya 106 C3 0 10 S 34 15 E
Nyarling →, Canada 130 A6 60 41N 113 23W
Nyasa, L. = Malawi, L., Africa 107 E3 12 30 S 34 30 E
Nyaunglebin, Burma 78 G6 17 52N 96 42 E
Nyazepetrovsk, Russia 54 C6 56 3N 59 36 E
Nyazura, Zimbabwe 107 F3 18 40 S 32 16 E
Nyazwidzi →, Zimbabwe 107 F3 20 0 S 31 17 E
Nyborg, Denmark 15 J4 55 18N 10 47 E
Nybro, Sweden 13 H13 56 44N 15 55 E
Nyda, Russia 56 C8 66 40N 72 58 E
Nyeri, Kenya 106 C4 0 23 S 36 56 E
Nyerol, Sudan 95 F3 8 41N 32 1 E
Nyhem, Sweden 14 B9 62 54N 15 37 E
Nyiel, Sudan 95 F3 6 9N 31 13 E
Nyinahin, Ghana 100 D4 6 43N 2 3W
Nyirbátor, Hungary 31 D15 47 49N 22 9 E
Nyíregyháza, Hungary 31 D14 47 58N 21 47 E
Nykarleby, Finland 12 E17 63 22N 22 31 E
Nykøbing, Sjælland, Denmark 15 J5 55 55N 11 40 E
Nykøbing, Storstrøm, Denmark 15 K5 54 56N 11 52 E
Nykøbing, Viborg, Denmark 15 H2 56 48N 8 51 E
Nyköping, Sweden 15 F11 58 45N 17 0 E
Nykvarn, Sweden 14 E11 59 11N 17 25 E
Nyland, Sweden 14 A11 63 1N 17 45 E
Nylstroom, S. Africa 105 C4 24 42 S 28 22 E
Nymagee, Australia 117 B7 32 7 S 146 20 E
Nymburk, Czech. 30 A8 50 10N 15 1 E
Nynäshamn, Sweden 14 F11 58 54N 17 57 E
Nyngan, Australia 115 E4 31 30 S 147 8 E
Nyon, Switz. 28 D2 46 23N 6 14 E
Nyong →, Cameroon 101 E6 3 17N 9 54 E
Nyons, France 25 D9 44 22N 5 10 E
Nyora, Australia 117 E6 38 20 S 145 41 E
Nyord, Denmark 15 J6 55 4N 12 13 E
Nyou, Burkina Faso 101 C4 12 42N 2 1W
Nysa, Poland 47 E4 50 30N 17 22 E
Nysa →, Europe 26 C10 52 4N 14 46 E
Nyssa, U.S.A. 142 E5 43 53N 117 0W
Nysted, Denmark 15 K5 54 40N 11 44 E
Nytva, Russia 54 C4 57 56N 55 20 E
Nyūgawa, Japan 62 D5 33 56N 133 5 E
Nyunzu, Zaïre 106 D2 5 57 S 27 58 E
Nyurba, Russia 57 C12 63 17N 118 28 E
Nzega, Tanzania 106 C3 4 10 S 33 12 E
Nzega □, Tanzania 106 C3 4 10 S 33 10 E
N'Zérékoré, Guinea 100 D3 7 49N 8 48W
Nzeto, Angola 103 D2 7 10 S 12 52 E
Nzilo, Chutes de, Zaïre 103 E5 10 18 S 25 27 E
Nzubuka, Tanzania 106 C3 4 45 S 32 50 E


# O


Ō-Shima, Fukuoka, Japan 62 D2 33 54N 130 25 E
Ō-Shima, Nagasaki, Japan 62 C1 34 29N 129 33 E
Ō-Shima, Shizuoka, Japan 63 C11 34 44N 139 24 E
Oacoma, U.S.A. 138 D5 43 48N 99 24W
Oahe, L., U.S.A. 138 C4 44 27N 100 24W
Oahe Dam, U.S.A. 138 C4 44 27N 100 24W
Oahu, U.S.A. 132 H16 21 28N 157 58W
Oak Creek, Colo., U.S.A. 142 F10 40 16N 106 57W
Oak Creek, Wis., U.S.A. 141 B9 42 52N 87 55W
Oak Harbor, U.S.A. 144 B4 48 18N 122 39W
Oak Hill, U.S.A. 134 G5 37 59N 81 9W
Oak Lawn, U.S.A. 141 C9 41 43N 87 44W
Oak Park, U.S.A. 141 C9 41 53N 87 47W
Oak Ridge, U.S.A. 135 G3 36 1N 84 16W
Oak View, U.S.A. 145 L7 34 24N 119 18W
Oakan-Dake, Japan 60 C12 43 27N 144 10 E
Oakbank, Australia 116 B4 33 4 S 140 33 E
Oakdale, Calif., U.S.A. 144 H6 37 46N 120 51W
Oakdale, La., U.S.A. 139 K8 30 49N 92 40W
Oakengates, U.K. 16 E5 52 42N 2 29W
Oakes, U.S.A. 138 B5 46 8N 98 6W
Oakesdale, U.S.A. 142 C5 47 8N 117 15W
Oakey, Australia 115 D5 27 25 S 151 43 E
Oakford, U.S.A. 140 D7 40 6N 89 58W
Oakham, U.K. 16 E7 52 40N 0 43W
Oakhurst, U.S.A. 144 H7 37 19N 119 40W
Oakland, Calif., U.S.A. 144 H4 37 49N 122 16W
Oakland, Ill., U.S.A. 141 E8 39 39N 88 2W
Oakland, Oreg., U.S.A. 142 E2 43 25N 123 18W
Oakland City, U.S.A. 141 F9 38 20N 87 21W
Oaklands, Australia 117 C7 35 34 S 146 10 E
Oakley, Idaho, U.S.A. 142 E7 42 15N 113 53W
Oakley, Kans., U.S.A. 138 F4 39 8N 100 51W
Oakley Creek, Australia 117 A8 31 37 S 149 46 E
Oakover →, Australia 112 D3 21 0 S 120 40 E
Oakridge, U.S.A. 142 E2 43 45N 122 28W
Oaktown, U.S.A. 141 F9 38 52N 87 27W
Oakville, U.S.A. 144 D3 46 51N 123 14W
Oakwood, U.S.A. 141 C12 41 6N 84 23W
Oamaru, N.Z. 119 F5 45 5 S 170 59 E
Ōamishirasato, Japan 63 B12 35 31N 140 18 E
Oarai, Japan 63 A12 36 21N 140 34 E
Oasis, Calif., U.S.A. 145 M10 33 28N 116 6W
Oasis, Nev., U.S.A. 144 H9 37 29N 117 55W
Oates Land, Antarctica 7 C11 69 0 S 160 0 E
Oatman, U.S.A. 145 K12 35 1N 114 19W
Oaxaca, Mexico 147 D5 17 2N 96 40W
Oaxaca □, Mexico 147 D5 17 0N 97 0W
Ob →, Russia 56 C7 66 45N 69 30 E
Oba, Canada 128 C3 49 4N 84 7W
Obala, Cameroon 101 E7 4 9N 11 32 E
Obama, Fukui, Japan 63 B7 35 30N 135 45 E
Obama, Nagasaki, Japan 62 E2 32 43N 130 13 E
Oban, U.K. 18 E3 56 25N 5 30W
Obbia, Somali Rep. 90 F4 5 25N 48 30 E
Obdam, Neths. 20 C5 52 41N 4 55 E
Obed, Canada 130 C5 53 30N 117 10W
Ober-Aagau, Switz. 28 B5 47 10N 7 45 E
Obera, Argentina 159 B4 27 21 S 55 2W
Oberalppass, Switz. 29 C7 46 39N 8 35 E
Oberalpstock, Switz. 29 C7 46 45N 8 47 E
Oberammergau, Germany 27 H7 47 35N 11 3 E
Oberdrauburg, Austria 30 E5 46 44N 12 58 E
Oberengadin, Switz. 29 C9 46 35N 9 55 E
Oberentfelden, Switz. 28 B6 47 21N 8 2 E
Oberhausen, Germany 26 D2 51 28N 6 50 E
Oberkirch, Germany 27 G4 48 31N 8 5 E
Oberland, Switz. 28 C5 46 35N 7 38 E
Oberlin, Kans., U.S.A. 138 F4 39 49N 100 32W
Oberlin, La., U.S.A. 139 K8 30 37N 92 46W
Oberlin, Ohio, U.S.A. 136 E2 41 18N 82 13W
Obernai, France 23 D14 48 28N 7 30 E
Oberndorf, Germany 27 G4 48 17N 8 35 E
Oberon, Australia 117 B8 33 45 S 149 52 E
Oberösterreich □, Austria 30 C6 48 10N 14 0 E
Oberpfälzer Wald, Germany 27 F8 49 30N 12 25 E
Obersiggenthal, Switz. 29 B6 47 29N 8 18 E
Oberstdorf, Germany 27 H6 47 25N 10 16 E
Oberting, Gabon 102 C1 0 22 S 9 46 E
Oberwil, Switz. 28 A5 47 32N 7 33 E
Obi, Kepulauan, Indonesia 72 B3 1 23 S 127 45 E
Obi Is. = Obi, Kepulauan, Indonesia 72 B3 1 23 S 127 45 E
Obiaruku, Nigeria 101 D6 5 51N 6 9 E
Óbidos, Brazil 153 D6 1 50 S 55 30W
Óbidos, Portugal 37 F1 39 19N 9 10W
Obihiro, Japan 60 C11 42 56N 143 12 E
Obilatu, Indonesia 72 B3 1 25 S 127 20 E
Obilnoye, Russia 53 C11 47 32N 44 30 E
Obing, Germany 27 H8 48 0N 12 25 E
Öbisfelde, Germany 26 C6 52 27N 10 57 E
Objat, France 24 C5 45 16N 1 24 E
Oblong, U.S.A. 141 E9 39 0N 87 55W
Obluchye, Russia 57 E14 49 1N 131 4 E
Obninsk, Russia 51 D10 55 8N 36 37 E
Obo, C.A.R. 102 A5 5 20N 26 32 E
Obo, Ethiopia 95 G4 3 46N 38 52 E
Oboa, Mt., Uganda 106 B3 1 45N 34 45 E
Obock, Djibouti 95 E5 12 0N 43 20 E
Oborniki, Poland 47 C3 52 39N 16 50 E
Oborniki Śląskie, Poland 47 D3 51 17N 16 53 E
Obouya, Congo 102 C3 0 56 S 15 43 E
Oboyan, Russia 51 F10 51 13N 36 37 E
Obozerskaya, Russia 56 C5 63 20N 40 15 E
Obrenovac, Serbia 42 C5 44 40N 20 11 E
Obrovac, Croatia 39 D12 44 11N 15 41 E
Obruk, Turkey 88 D5 38 18N 33 12 E
Observatory Inlet, Canada 130 B3 55 10N 129 54W
Obshchi Syrt, Kazakhstan 10 E16 52 0N 53 0 E
Obskaya Guba, Russia 56 C8 69 0N 73 0 E
Obuasi, Ghana 101 D4 6 17N 1 40W
Obubra, Nigeria 101 D6 6 8N 8 20 E
Obwalden □, Switz. 28 C6 46 55N 8 15 E
Obyachevo, Russia 54 A1 60 20N 49 37 E
Obzor, Bulgaria 43 E12 42 50N 27 52 E
Ocala, U.S.A. 135 L4 29 11N 82 8W
Ocamo →, Venezuela 153 C4 2 48N 65 14W
Ocampo, Mexico 146 B3 28 9N 108 24W
Ocaña, Colombia 152 B3 8 15N 73 20W
Ocaña, Spain 34 F1 39 55N 3 30W
Ocanomowoc, U.S.A. 138 D10 43 7N 88 30W
Ocate, U.S.A. 139 G2 36 11N 105 3W
Occidental, Cordillera, Colombia 152 C3 5 0N 76 0W
Occidental, Cordillera, Peru 156 C3 14 0 S 74 0W
Ocean City, N.J., U.S.A. 134 F8 39 17N 74 35W
Ocean City, Wash., U.S.A. 144 C2 47 4N 124 10W
Ocean I. = Banaba, Kiribati 122 H8 0 45 S 169 50 E
Ocean Park, U.S.A. 144 D2 46 30N 124 3W
Oceano, U.S.A. 145 K6 35 6N 120 37W
Oceanport, U.S.A. 137 F10 40 19N 74 3W
Oceanside, U.S.A. 145 M9 33 12N 117 23W
Ochagavia, Spain 34 C3 42 55N 1 5W
Ochamchire, Georgia 53 E9 42 46N 41 32 E
Ochamps, Belgium 21 J6 49 56N 5 16 E
Ocher, Russia 54 C4 57 53N 54 42 E
Ochiai, Japan 62 B5 35 1N 133 45 E
Ochil Hills, U.K. 18 E5 56 14N 3 40W
Ochre River, Canada 131 C9 51 4N 99 47W
Ochsenfurt, Germany 27 F6 49 38N 10 3 E
Ochsenhausen, Germany 27 G5 48 4N 9 57 E
Ocilla, U.S.A. 135 K4 31 36N 83 15W
Ocmulgee →, U.S.A. 135 K4 31 58N 82 33W
Ocna Mureş, Romania 46 C4 46 23N 23 55 E
Ocna Sibiului, Romania 46 D5 45 52N 24 2 E
Ocnele Mari, Romania 46 D5 45 8N 24 18 E
Ocoña, Peru 156 D3 16 26 S 73 8W
Ocoña →, Peru 156 D3 16 28 S 73 8W
Oconee →, U.S.A. 135 K4 31 58N 82 33W
Oconomowoc, U.S.A. 141 A8 43 7N 88 30W
Oconto, U.S.A. 134 C2 44 53N 87 52W
Oconto Falls, U.S.A. 134 C1 44 52N 88 9W
Ocosingo, Mexico 147 D6 17 10N 92 15W
Ocotal, Nic. 148 D2 13 41N 86 31W
Ocotlán, Mexico 146 C4 20 21N 102 42W
Ocquier, Belgium 21 H6 50 24N 5 24 E
Ocreza →, Portugal 37 F3 39 32N 7 50W
Ócsa, Hungary 31 D12 47 17N 19 15 E
Octave, U.S.A. 143 J7 34 10N 112 43W
Octeville, France 22 C5 49 38N 1 40W
Ocumare del Tuy, Venezuela 152 A4 10 7N 66 46W
Ocuri, Bolivia 157 D4 18 45 S 65 50W
Oda, Ghana 101 D4 5 50N 0 51W
Oda, Ehime, Japan 62 D4 33 36N 132 53 E
Ōda, Shimane, Japan 62 B4 35 11N 132 30 E
Oda, J., Sudan 94 C4 20 21N 36 39 E
Ódáðahraun, Iceland 12 D5 65 5N 17 0W
Ödåkra, Sweden 15 H6 56 7N 12 45 E
Odate, Japan 60 D10 40 16N 140 34 E
Odawara, Japan 63 B11 35 20N 139 6 E
Odda, Norway 13 F9 60 3N 6 35 E
Odder, Denmark 15 J4 55 58N 10 10 E
Oddur, Somali Rep. 90 G3 4 11N 43 52 E
Ödeborg, Sweden 15 F5 58 32N 11 58 E
Odei →, Canada 131 B9 56 6N 96 54W
Odell, U.S.A. 141 D8 41 0N 88 31W
Odemira, Portugal 37 H2 37 35N 8 40W
Ödemiş, Turkey 88 D3 38 15N 28 0 E
Odendaalsrus, S. Africa 104 D4 27 48 S 26 45 E
Odense, Denmark 15 J4 55 22N 10 23 E
Odenwald, Germany 27 F5 49 30N 9 0 E
Oder →, Germany 26 B10 53 33N 14 38 E
Oderzo, Italy 39 C9 45 47N 12 29 E
Odesa = Odessa, Ukraine 52 C4 46 30N 30 45 E
Odessa, Canada 137 B8 44 17N 76 43W
Odessa, Ukraine 52 C4 46 30N 30 45 E
Odessa, Mo., U.S.A. 140 F3 39 0N 93 57W
Odessa, Tex., U.S.A. 139 K3 31 52N 102 23W
Odessa, Wash., U.S.A. 142 C4 47 20N 118 41W
Odiakwe, Botswana 104 C4 20 12 S 25 17 E
Odiel →, Spain 37 H4 37 10N 6 55W
Odienné, Ivory C. 100 D3 9 30N 7 34W
Odintsovo, Russia 51 D10 55 39N 37 15 E
Odiongan, Phil. 70 E3 12 24N 121 59 E
Odobeşti, Romania 46 D8 45 43N 27 4 E
Odolanów, Poland 47 D4 51 34N 17 40 E
O'Donnell, Phil. 70 D3 15 21N 120 27 E
O'Donnell, U.S.A. 139 J4 32 58N 101 50W
Odoorn, Neths. 20 C9 52 51N 6 51 E
Odorheiu Secuiesc, Romania 46 C6 46 21N 25 21 E
Odoyevo, Russia 51 E10 53 56N 36 42 E
Odra →, Poland 47 B1 53 33N 14 38 E
Odra →, Spain 36 C6 42 14N 4 17W
Odweina, Somali Rep. 108 C3 9 25N 45 4 E
Odžaci, Serbia 42 B4 45 30N 19 17 E
Odžak, Bos.-H. 42 B3 45 3N 18 18 E
Odzi, Zimbabwe 105 B5 19 0 S 32 20 E
Oedelem, Belgium 21 F2 51 10N 3 21 E
Oegstgeest, Neths. 20 D4 52 11N 4 29 E
Oeiras, Brazil 154 C3 7 0 S 42 8W
Oeiras, Portugal 37 G1 38 41N 9 18W
Oelrichs, U.S.A. 138 D3 43 11N 103 14W
Oelsnitz, Germany 26 E8 50 24N 12 11 E
Oelwein, U.S.A. 138 D9 42 41N 91 55W
Oenpelli, Australia 112 B5 12 20 S 133 4 E
Of, Turkey 89 C9 40 59N 40 23 E
O'Fallon, U.S.A. 140 F6 38 49N 90 42W
Ofanto →, Italy 41 A9 41 22N 16 13 E
Offa, Nigeria 101 D5 8 13N 4 42 E
Offaly □, Ireland 19 C4 53 15N 7 30W
Offenbach, Germany 27 E4 50 6N 8 46 E
Offenburg, Germany 27 G3 48 29N 7 56 E
Offerdal, Sweden 14 A8 63 28N 14 0 E
Offida, Italy 39 F10 42 56N 13 40 E
Offranville, France 22 C8 49 52N 1 1 E
Ofidhousa, Greece 45 H8 36 33N 26 8 E
Ofotfjorden, Norway 12 B14 68 27N 16 40 E
Ofu, Amer. Samoa 121 X25 14 11 S 169 41W
Ōfunato, Japan 60 E10 39 4N 141 43 E
Oga, Japan 60 E9 39 55N 139 50 E
Oga-Hantō, Japan 60 E9 39 58N 139 47 E
Ogaden, Ethiopia 108 C3 7 30N 45 30 E
Ogahalla, Canada 128 B2 50 6N 85 51W
Ōgaki, Japan 63 B8 35 21N 136 37 E
Ogallala, U.S.A. 138 E4 41 8N 101 43W
Ogan →, Indonesia 74 C2 3 1 S 104 44 E
Ogasawara Gunto, Pac. Oc. 122 E6 27 0N 142 0 E
Ogbomosho, Nigeria 101 D5 8 1N 4 11 E
Ogden, Iowa, U.S.A. 140 B2 42 2N 94 2W
Ogden, Utah, U.S.A. 142 F7 41 13N 111 58W
Ogdensburg, U.S.A. 137 B9 44 42N 75 30W
Ogeechee →, U.S.A. 135 K5 31 50N 81 3W
Ogilby, U.S.A. 145 N12 32 49N 114 50W
Oglesby, U.S.A. 140 C7 41 18N 89 4W
Oglio →, Italy 38 C7 45 2N 10 39 E
Ogmore, Australia 114 C4 22 37 S 149 35 E
Ognon →, France 23 E12 47 16N 5 28 E
Ogo Mas, Indonesia 72 A2 0 50N 120 5 E
Ogoja, Nigeria 101 D6 6 38N 8 39 E
Ogoki →, Canada 128 B2 51 38N 85 57W
Ogoki L., Canada 128 B2 50 50N 87 10W
Ogoki Res., Canada 128 B2 50 45N 88 15W
Ogooué →, Gabon 102 C1 1 0 S 9 0 E
Ōgori, Japan 62 C3 34 6N 131 24 E
Ogosta →, Bulgaria 43 D8 43 48N 23 55 E
Ogowe = Ogooué →, Gabon 102 C1 1 0 S 9 0 E
Ogr = Sharafa, Sudan 95 E2 11 59N 27 7 E
Ograźden, Macedonia 42 F7 41 30N 22 50 E
Ogrein, Sudan 94 D3 17 55N 34 50 E
Ogulin, Croatia 39 C12 45 16N 15 16 E
Ogun □, Nigeria 101 D5 7 0N 3 0 E
Oguni, Japan 62 D3 33 11N 131 8 E
Oguta, Nigeria 101 D6 5 44N 6 44 E
Ogwashi-Uku, Nigeria 101 D6 6 15N 6 30 E
Ogwe, Nigeria 101 E6 5 0N 7 14 E
Ohai, N.Z. 119 F3 45 55 S 168 0 E
Ohakune, N.Z. 118 F4 39 24 S 175 24 E
Ohanet, Algeria 99 C6 28 44N 8 46 E
Ōhara, Japan 63 B12 35 15N 140 23 E
Ohata, Japan 60 D10 41 24N 141 10 E
Ohau, L., N.Z. 119 E4 44 15 S 169 53 E
Ohaupo, N.Z. 118 D4 37 56 S 175 20 E
Ohey, Belgium 21 H6 50 26N 5 8 E
Ohio □, U.S.A. 134 E3 40 15N 82 45W
Ohio →, U.S.A. 134 G1 36 59N 89 8W
Ohio City, U.S.A. 141 D12 40 46N 84 37W
Ohiwa Harbour, N.Z. 118 D6 37 59 S 177 10 E
Ohre →, Czech. 30 A7 50 30N 14 10 E
Ohre →, Germany 26 C7 52 18N 11 47 E
Ohrid, Macedonia 42 F5 41 8N 20 52 E
Ohridsko, Jezero, Macedonia 42 F5 41 8N 20 52 E
Ohrigstad, S. Africa 105 C5 24 39 S 30 36 E
Öhringen, Germany 27 F5 49 11N 9 31 E
Ohura, N.Z. 118 E3 38 51 S 174 59 E
Oiapoque →, Brazil 153 C7 4 8N 51 40W
Oikou, China 67 E9 38 35N 117 42 E
Oil City, U.S.A. 136 E5 41 26N 79 42W
Oildale, U.S.A. 145 K7 35 25N 119 1W
Oinousa, Greece 45 F8 38 33N 26 14 E
Oirschot, Neths. 21 E6 51 30N 5 18 E
Oise □, France 23 C9 49 28N 2 30 E
Oise →, France 23 D9 49 0N 2 4 E
Oisterwijk, Neths. 21 E6 51 35N 5 12 E
Ōita, Japan 62 D3 33 14N 131 36 E
Ōita □, Japan 62 D3 33 15N 131 30 E
Oiticica, Brazil 154 C3 5 3 S 41 5W
Ojai, U.S.A. 145 L7 34 27N 119 15W
Ojinaga, Mexico 146 B4 29 34N 104 25W
Ojiya, Japan 61 F9 37 18N 138 48 E
Ojos del Salado, Cerro, Argentina 158 B2 27 0 S 68 40W
Oka →, Russia 51 C13 56 20N 43 59 E
Okaba, Indonesia 73 C5 8 6 S 139 42 E
Okahandja, Namibia 104 C2 22 0 S 16 59 E
Okahukura, N.Z. 118 E4 38 48 S 175 14 E
Okaihau, N.Z. 118 B2 35 19 S 173 47 E
Okanagan L., Canada 130 C5 50 0N 119 30W
Okandja, Gabon 102 C2 0 35 S 13 45 E
Okanogan, U.S.A. 142 B4 48 22N 119 35W
Okanogan →, U.S.A. 142 B4 48 6N 119 44W
Okány, Hungary 31 E14 46 52N 21 21 E
Okapa, Papua N. G. 120 D3 6 38 S 145 39 E
Okaputa, Namibia 104 C2 20 5 S 17 0 E
Okara, Pakistan 79 C4 30 50N 73 31 E
Okarito, N.Z. 119 D5 43 15 S 170 9 E
Okato, N.Z. 118 F2 39 12 S 173 53 E
Okaukuejo, Namibia 104 B2 19 10 S 16 0 E
Okavango Swamps, Botswana 104 B3 18 45 S 22 45 E
Okawa, Japan 62 D2 33 9N 130 21 E
Okawville, U.S.A. 140 F7 38 26N 89 33W
Okaya, Japan 63 A10 36 5N 138 10 E
Okayama, Japan 62 C5 34 40N 133 54 E
Okayama □, Japan 62 C5 35 0N 133 50 E
Okazaki, Japan 63 C9 34 57N 137 10 E
Oke-Iho, Nigeria 101 D5 8 1N 3 18 E
Okeechobee, U.S.A. 135 M5 27 15N 80 50W
Okeechobee, L., U.S.A. 135 M5 27 0N 80 50W
Okefenokee Swamp, U.S.A. 135 K4 30 40N 82 20W
Okehampton, U.K. 17 G3 50 44N 4 1W
Okene, Nigeria 101 D6 7 32N 6 11 E
Oker →, Germany 26 C6 52 30N 10 22 E
Okha, Russia 57 D15 53 40N 143 0 E
Ókhi Óros, Greece 45 F6 38 5N 24 25 E
Okhotsk, Russia 57 D15 59 20N 143 10 E
Okhotsk, Sea of, Asia 57 D15 55 0N 145 0 E
Okhotskiy Perevoz, Russia 57 C14 61 52N 135 35 E
Okhotsko Kolymskoye, Russia 57 C16 63 0N 157 0 E
Oki-no-Shima, Japan 62 E4 32 44N 132 33 E
Oki-Shotō, Japan 62 A5 36 5N 133 15 E
Okiep, S. Africa 104 D2 29 39 S 17 53 E
Okigwi, Nigeria 101 D6 5 52N 7 20 E
Okija, Nigeria 101 D6 5 54N 6 55 E
Okinawa □, Japan 61 L3 26 40N 128 0 E
Okinawa-Guntō, Japan 61 L3 26 40N 128 0 E
Okinawa-Jima, Japan 61 L4 26 32N 128 0 E
Okino-erabu-Shima, Japan 61 L4 27 21N 128 33 E
Okitipupa, Nigeria 101 D5 6 31N 4 50 E
Oklahoma □, U.S.A. 139 H6 35 20N 97 30W
Oklahoma City, U.S.A. 139 H6 35 30N 97 30W
Okmulgee, U.S.A. 139 H7 35 37N 95 58W
Oknitsa, Ukraine 52 B2 48 25N 27 30 E
Okolo, Uganda 106 B3 2 37N 31 8 E
Okolona, Ky., U.S.A. 141 F11 38 8N 85 41W
Okolona, Miss., U.S.A. 139 H10 34 0N 88 45W
Okonek, Poland 47 B3 53 32N 16 51 E
Okrika, Nigeria 101 E6 4 40N 7 10 E
Oktabrsk, Kazakhstan 49 E10 49 28N 57 25 E
Oktyabr, Kazakhstan 55 B8 43 41N 77 12 E
Oktyabrsk, Russia 51 E16 53 11N 48 40 E
Oktyabrskiy, Belorussia 50 E6 52 38N 28 53 E
Oktyabrskiy, Russia 54 D3 54 28N 53 28 E
Oktyabrskoy Revolyutsii, Os., Russia 57 B10 79 30N 97 0 E
Oktyabrskoye = Zhovtnevoye, Ukraine 52 C5 46 54N 32 3 E
Oktyabrskoye, Russia 56 C7 62 28N 66 3 E
Ōkuchi, Japan 62 E2 32 4N 130 37 E
Okulovka, Russia 50 B8 58 25N 33 19 E
Okuru, N.Z. 119 D3 43 55 S 168 55 E
Okushiri-Tō, Japan 60 C9 42 15N 139 30 E
Okuta, Nigeria 101 D5 9 14N 3 12 E
Okwa →, Botswana 104 C3 22 30 S 23 0 E
Ola, U.S.A. 139 H8 35 2N 93 13W
Ólafsfjörður, Iceland 12 C4 66 4N 18 39W
Ólafsvík, Iceland 12 D2 64 53N 23 43W
Olancha, U.S.A. 145 J8 36 17N 118 1W
Olancha Pk., U.S.A. 145 J8 36 15N 118 7W
Olanchito, Honduras 148 C2 15 30N 86 30W
Öland, Sweden 13 H14 56 45N 16 38 E
Olargues, France 24 E6 43 34N 2 53 E
Olary, Australia 116 B4 32 18 S 140 19 E
Olascoaga, Argentina 158 D3 35 15 S 60 39W

244 Olathe


Olathe, *U.S.A.* **138 F7** 38 53N 94 49W
Olavarría, *Argentina* **158 D3** 36 55 S 60 20W
Oława, *Poland* **47 E4** 50 57N 17 20 E
Ólbia, *Italy* **40 B2** 40 55N 9 30 E
Ólbia, G. di, *Italy* **40 B2** 40 55N 9 35 E
Old Bahama Chan. = Bahama, Canal Viejo de, *W. Indies* **148 B4** 22 10N 77 30W
Old Baldy Pk. = San Antonio, Mt., *U.S.A.* **145 L9** 34 17N 117 38W
Old Castile = Castilla y Leon □, *Spain* **36 D6** 42 0N 5 0W
Old Castle, *Ireland* **19 C4** 53 46N 7 10W
Old Cork, *Australia* **114 C3** 22 57 S 141 52 E
Old Crow, *Canada* **126 B6** 67 30N 139 55W
Old Dale, *U.S.A.* **145 L11** 34 8N 115 47W
Old Dongola, *Sudan* **94 D3** 18 11N 30 44 E
Old Fletton, *U.K.* **17 E7** 52 34N 0 13W
Old Forge, *N.Y., U.S.A.* **137 C10** 43 43N 74 58W
Old Forge, *Pa., U.S.A.* **137 E9** 41 22N 75 45W
Old Fort →, *Canada* **131 B6** 58 36N 110 24W
Old Shinyanga, *Tanzania* **106 C3** 3 33 S 33 27 E
Old Speck Mt., *U.S.A.* **137 B14** 44 34N 70 57W
Old Town, *U.S.A.* **129 D6** 44 56N 68 39W
Old Wives L., *Canada* **131 C7** 50 5N 106 0W
Oldbury, *U.K.* **17 F5** 51 38N 2 30W
Oldeani, *Tanzania* **106 C4** 3 22 S 35 35 E
Oldenburg, *Niedersachsen, Germany* **26 B4** 53 10N 8 10 E
Oldenburg, *Schleswig-Holstein, Germany* **26 A6** 54 16N 10 53 E
Oldenzaal, *Neths.* **20 D9** 52 19N 6 53 E
Oldham, *U.K.* **16 D5** 53 33N 2 8W
Oldman →, *Canada* **130 D6** 49 57N 111 42W
Olds, *Canada* **130 C6** 51 50N 114 10W
Olean, *U.S.A.* **136 D6** 42 5N 78 26W
Olecko, *Poland* **47 A9** 54 2N 22 31 E
Oléggio, *Italy* **38 C5** 45 36N 8 38 E
Oleiros, *Portugal* **36 F3** 39 56N 7 56W
Olekma →, *Russia* **57 C13** 60 22N 120 42 E
Olekminsk, *Russia* **57 C13** 60 25N 120 30 E
Olema, *U.S.A.* **144 G4** 38 3N 122 47W
Olen, *Belgium* **21 F5** 51 9N 4 52 E
Olenegorsk, *Russia* **48 A5** 68 9N 33 18 E
Olenek, *Russia* **57 C12** 68 28N 112 18 E
Olenek →, *Russia* **57 B13** 73 0N 120 10 E
Olenino, *Russia* **50 C8** 56 15N 33 30 E
Oléron, I. d', *France* **24 C2** 45 55N 1 15W
Oleśnica, *Poland* **47 D4** 51 13N 17 22 E
Olesno, *Poland* **47 E5** 50 51N 18 26 E
Olevsk, *Ukraine* **50 F5** 51 12N 27 39 E
Olga, *Russia* **57 E14** 43 50N 135 14 E
Olga, L., *Canada* **128 C4** 49 47N 77 15W
Olga, Mt., *Australia* **113 E5** 25 20 S 130 50 E
Ølgod, *Denmark* **15 J2** 55 49N 8 36 E
Olhão, *Portugal* **37 H3** 37 3N 7 48W
Olib, *Croatia* **39 D11** 44 23N 14 44 E
Oliena, *Italy* **40 B2** 40 18N 9 22 E
Oliete, *Spain* **34 D4** 41 1N 0 41W
Olifants →, *Africa* **105 C5** 23 57 S 31 58 E
Olifantshoek, *S. Africa* **104 D3** 27 57 S 22 42 E
Ólimbos, *Greece* **45 J9** 35 44N 27 11 E
Ólimbos, Óros, *Greece* **44 D4** 40 6N 22 23 E
Olímpia, *Brazil* **159 A6** 20 44 S 48 54W
Olin, *U.S.A.* **140 B5** 42 0N 91 9W
Olinda, *Brazil* **154 C5** 8 1 S 34 51W
Olindiná, *Brazil* **154 D4** 11 22 S 38 21W
Olite, *Spain* **34 C3** 42 29N 1 40W
Oliva, *Argentina* **158 C3** 32 0 S 63 38W
Oliva, *Spain* **35 G4** 38 58N 0 9W
Oliva, Punta del, *Spain* **36 B5** 43 37N 5 28W
Oliva de la Frontera, *Spain* **37 G4** 38 17N 6 54W
Olivares, *Spain* **34 F2** 39 46N 2 20W
Olive Hill, *U.S.A.* **141 F13** 38 18N 83 13W
Olivehurst, *U.S.A.* **144 F5** 39 6N 121 34W
Oliveira, *Brazil* **155 F3** 20 39 S 44 50W
Oliveira de Azemeis, *Portugal* **36 E2** 40 49N 8 29W
Oliveira dos Brejinhos, *Brazil* **155 D3** 12 19 S 42 54W
Olivenza, *Spain* **37 G3** 38 41N 7 9W
Oliver, *Canada* **130 D5** 49 13N 119 37W
Oliver L., *Canada* **131 B8** 56 56N 103 22W
Olivine Ra., *N.Z.* **119 E3** 44 15 S 168 30 E
Olivone, *Switz.* **29 C7** 46 32N 8 57 E
Olkhovka, *Russia* **53 B11** 49 48N 44 32 E
Olkusz, *Poland* **47 E6** 50 18N 19 33 E
Ollagüe, *Chile* **158 A2** 21 15 S 68 10W
Olloy, *Belgium* **21 H5** 50 5N 4 36 E
Olmedo, *Spain* **36 D6** 41 20N 4 43W
Olmos, *Peru* **156 B2** 5 59 S 79 46W
Olney, *Ill., U.S.A.* **141 F8** 38 44N 88 5W
Olney, *Tex., U.S.A.* **139 J5** 33 22N 98 45W
Oloma, *Cameroon* **101 E7** 3 29N 11 19 E
Olomane →, *Canada* **129 B7** 50 14N 60 37W
Olombo, *Congo* **102 C3** 1 18 S 15 53 E
Olomouc, *Czech.* **31 B10** 49 38N 17 12 E
Olonets, *Russia* **48 B5** 61 10N 33 0 E
Olongapo, *Phil.* **70 D3** 14 50N 120 18 E
Oloron, Gave d' →, *France* **24 E2** 43 33N 1 5W
Oloron-Ste.-Marie, *France* **24 E3** 43 11N 0 38W
Olot, *Spain* **34 C7** 42 11N 2 30 E
Olovo, *Bos.-H.* **42 C3** 44 8N 18 35 E
Olovo, *Yugoslavia* **42 C3** 44 3N 19 0 E
Olovyannaya, *Russia* **57 D12** 50 58N 115 35 E
Oloy →, *Russia* **57 C16** 66 29N 159 29 E
Olpe, *Germany* **26 D3** 51 2N 7 50 E
Olshanka, *Ukraine* **52 B4** 48 16N 30 58 E
Olshany, *Ukraine* **52 A6** 50 3N 35 53 E
Olst, *Neths.* **20 D8** 52 20N 6 7 E
Olsztyn, *Poland* **47 B7** 53 48N 20 29 E
Olsztyn □, *Poland* **47 B7** 54 0N 21 0 E
Olsztynek, *Poland* **47 B7** 53 34N 20 19 E
Olt □, *Romania* **46 E5** 44 20N 24 30 E
Olt →, *Romania* **46 F5** 43 43N 24 51 E
Olten, *Switz.* **28 B5** 47 21N 7 53 E
Olteniţa, *Romania* **46 E7** 44 7N 26 42 E
Olton, *U.S.A.* **139 H3** 34 11N 102 8W
Oltu, *Turkey* **89 C9** 40 35N 41 58 E
Olur, *Turkey* **89 C10** 40 49N 42 8 E
Olutanga, *Phil.* **71 H4** 7 26N 122 54 E
Olutanga I., *Phil.* **71 H4** 7 22N 122 52 E
Olvega, *Spain* **34 D3** 41 47N 2 0W
Olvera, *Spain* **37 J5** 36 55N 5 18W
Olymbos, *Cyprus* **32 D12** 35 21N 33 45 E
Olympia, *Greece* **45 G3** 37 39N 21 39 E
Olympia, *U.S.A.* **144 D4** 47 3N 122 53W
Olympic Mts., *U.S.A.* **144 C3** 47 55N 123 45W
Olympic Nat. Park, *U.S.A.* **144 C3** 47 48N 123 30W
Olympus, *Cyprus* **32 E11** 34 56N 32 52 E
Olympus, Mt. = Ólimbos, Óros, *Greece* **44 D4** 40 6N 22 23 E
Olympus, Mt., *U.S.A.* **144 C3** 47 48N 123 43W
Olyphant, *U.S.A.* **137 E9** 41 27N 75 36W
Om →, *Russia* **56 D8** 54 59N 73 22 E
Om Hajer, *Eritrea* **95 E4** 14 20N 36 41 E
Om Koi, *Thailand* **76 D2** 17 48N 98 22 E
Ōma, *Japan* **60 D10** 41 45N 141 5 E
Ōmachi, *Japan* **63 A9** 36 30N 137 50 E
Omae-Zaki, *Japan* **63 C10** 34 36N 138 14 E
Ōmagari, *Japan* **60 E10** 39 27N 140 29 E
Omagh, *U.K.* **19 B4** 54 36N 7 20W
Omagh □, *U.K.* **19 B4** 54 35N 7 15W
Omaha, *U.S.A.* **138 E7** 41 17N 95 58W
Omak, *U.S.A.* **142 B4** 48 25N 119 31W
Omalos, *Greece* **32 D5** 35 19N 23 55 E
Oman ■, *Asia* **87 B7** 23 0N 58 0 E
Oman, G. of, *Asia* **85 E8** 24 30N 58 30 E
Omapere, *N.Z.* **118 B2** 35 37 S 173 25 E
Omar Combon, *Somali Rep.* **108 D3** 3 10N 45 47 E
Omaruru, *Namibia* **104 C2** 21 26 S 16 0 E
Omaruru →, *Namibia* **104 C1** 22 7 S 14 15 E
Omate, *Peru* **156 D3** 16 45 S 71 0W
Ombai, Selat, *Indonesia* **72 C2** 8 30 S 124 50 E
Omboué, *Gabon* **102 C1** 1 35 S 9 15 E
Ombrone →, *Italy* **38 F8** 42 39N 11 0 E
Omchi, *Chad* **97 D3** 21 22N 17 53 E
Omdurmân, *Sudan* **95 D3** 15 40N 32 28 E
Ōme, *Japan* **63 B11** 35 47N 139 15 E
Omegna, *Italy* **38 C5** 45 52N 8 23 E
Omeonga, *Zaïre* **102 C4** 3 40 S 24 22 E
Ometepe, I. de, *Nic.* **148 D2** 11 32N 85 35W
Ometepec, *Mexico* **147 D5** 16 39N 98 23W
Ōmi-Shima, *Ehime, Japan* **62 C5** 34 15N 133 0 E
Ōmi-Shima, *Yamaguchi, Japan* **62 C3** 34 25N 131 9 E
Omihachiman, *Japan* **63 B8** 35 7N 136 3 E
Ominato, *Japan* **60 D10** 41 17N 141 10 E
Omineca →, *Canada* **130 B4** 56 3N 124 16W
Omiš, *Croatia* **39 E13** 43 28N 16 40 E
Omišalj, *Croatia* **39 C11** 45 13N 14 32 E
Omitara, *Namibia* **104 C2** 22 16 S 18 2 E
Ōmiya, *Japan* **63 B11** 35 54N 139 38 E
Omme Å →, *Denmark* **15 J2** 55 56N 8 32 E
Ommen, *Neths.* **20 C8** 52 31N 6 26 E
Ömnögovĭ □, *Mongolia* **66 C3** 43 15N 104 0 E
Omo →, *Ethiopia* **95 F4** 6 25N 36 10 E
Omodhos, *Cyprus* **32 E11** 34 51N 32 48 E
Omolon →, *Russia* **57 C16** 68 42N 158 36 E
Omono-Gawa →, *Japan* **60 E10** 39 46N 140 3 E
Omsk, *Russia* **56 D8** 55 0N 73 12 E
Omsukchan, *Russia* **57 C16** 62 32N 155 48 E
Ōmu, *Japan* **60 B11** 44 34N 142 58 E
Omul, Vf., *Romania* **46 D6** 45 27N 25 29 E
Omulew →, *Poland* **47 B8** 53 5N 21 33 E
Ōmura, *Japan* **62 E1** 32 56N 129 57 E
Omura-Wan, *Japan* **62 E1** 32 57N 129 52 E
Omurtag, *Bulgaria* **43 D11** 43 8N 26 26 E
Ōmuta, *Japan* **62 D2** 33 5N 130 26 E
Omutninsk, *Russia* **54 B3** 58 45N 52 4 E
On, *Belgium* **21 H6** 50 11N 5 18 E
On-Take, *Japan* **62 F2** 31 35N 130 39 E
Oña, *Spain* **34 C1** 42 43N 3 25W
Onaga, *U.S.A.* **138 F6** 39 29N 96 10W
Onalaska, *U.S.A.* **138 D9** 43 53N 91 14W
Onamia, *U.S.A.* **138 B8** 46 4N 93 40W
Onancock, *U.S.A.* **134 G8** 37 43N 75 45W
Onang, *Indonesia* **72 B1** 3 2 S 118 49 E
Onaping L., *Canada* **128 C3** 47 3N 81 30W
Onarga, *U.S.A.* **141 D8** 40 43N 88 1W
Onarhā, *Afghan.* **79 B3** 35 30N 71 0 E
Oñate, *Spain* **34 B2** 43 3N 2 25W
Onavas, *Mexico* **146 B3** 28 28N 109 30W
Onawa, *U.S.A.* **138 D6** 42 2N 96 6W
Onaway, *U.S.A.* **134 C3** 45 21N 84 14W
Oncesti, *Romania* **46 F6** 43 56N 25 52 E
Oncócua, *Angola* **103 F2** 16 30 S 13 25 E
Onda, *Spain* **34 F4** 39 55N 0 17W
Ondaejin, *N. Korea* **67 D15** 41 34N 129 40 E
Ondangua, *Namibia* **104 B2** 17 57 S 16 4 E
Ondárroa, *Spain* **34 B2** 43 19N 2 25W
Ondas →, *Brazil* **155 D3** 12 8 S 44 55W
Ondava →, *Slovak Rep.* **31 C14** 48 27N 21 48 E
Onderdijk, *Neths.* **20 C6** 52 45N 5 8 E
Ondjiva, *Angola* **103 F3** 16 48 S 15 50 E
Ondo, *Japan* **62 C4** 34 11N 132 32 E
Ondo, *Nigeria* **101 D5** 7 4N 4 47 E
Ondo □, *Nigeria* **101 D6** 7 0N 5 0 E
Öndörshil, *Mongolia* **66 B5** 45 13N 108 5 E
Öndverðarnes, *Iceland* **12 D1** 64 52N 24 0W
Onega, *Russia* **48 B6** 64 0N 38 10 E
Onega →, *Russia* **48 B6** 63 58N 37 55 E
Onega, G. of = Onezhskaya Guba, *Russia* **48 B6** 64 30N 37 0 E
Onega, L. = Onezhskoye Ozero, *Russia* **48 B6** 62 0N 35 30 E
Onehunga, *N.Z.* **118 C3** 36 55 S 174 48 E
Oneida, *Ill., U.S.A.* **140 C6** 41 4N 90 13W
Oneida, *N.Y., U.S.A.* **137 C9** 43 6N 75 39W
Oneida L., *U.S.A.* **137 C9** 43 12N 75 54W
O'Neill, *U.S.A.* **138 D5** 42 27N 98 39W
Onekotan, Ostrov, *Russia* **57 E16** 49 25N 154 45 E
Onema, *Zaïre* **103 C4** 4 35 S 24 30 E
Oneonta, *Ala., U.S.A.* **135 J2** 33 57N 86 28W
Oneonta, *N.Y., U.S.A.* **137 D9** 42 27N 75 4W
Onerahi, *N.Z.* **118 B3** 35 45 S 174 22 E
Onezhskaya Guba, *Russia* **48 B6** 64 30N 37 0 E
Onezhskoye Ozero, *Russia* **48 B6** 62 0N 35 30 E
Ongarue, *N.Z.* **118 E4** 38 42 S 175 19 E
Ongea Levu, *Fiji* **121 B3** 19 8 S 178 24W
Ongerup, *Australia* **113 F2** 33 58 S 118 28 E
Ongjin, *N. Korea* **67 F13** 37 56N 125 21 E
Ongkharak, *Thailand* **76 E3** 14 8N 101 1 E
Ongniud Qi, *China* **67 C10** 43 0N 118 38 E
Ongoka, *Zaïre* **106 C2** 1 20 S 26 0 E
Ongole, *India* **83 G5** 15 33N 80 2 E
Ongon, *Mongolia* **66 B7** 45 41N 113 5 E
Onguren, *Russia* **57 D11** 53 38N 107 36 E
Onhaye, *Belgium* **21 H5** 50 15N 4 50 E
Oni, *Georgia* **53 E10** 42 33N 43 26 E
Onida, *U.S.A.* **138 C4** 44 42N 100 4W
Onilahy →, *Madag.* **105 C7** 23 34 S 43 45 E
Onitsha, *Nigeria* **101 D6** 6 6N 6 42 E
Onmaka, *Burma* **78 D6** 22 17N 96 41 E
Ono, *Fiji* **121 B2** 18 55 S 178 29 E
Ono, *Fukui, Japan* **63 B8** 35 59N 136 29 E
Ono, *Hyōgo, Japan* **62 C6** 34 51N 134 56 E
Onoda, *Japan* **62 C3** 34 2N 131 25 E
Onoke, L., *N.Z.* **118 H4** 41 22 S 175 8 E
Onomichi, *Japan* **62 C5** 34 25N 133 12 E
Onpyŏng-ni, *S. Korea* **67 H14** 33 25N 126 55 E
Ons, Is. d', *Spain* **36 C2** 42 23N 8 55W
Onsala, *Sweden* **15 G6** 57 26N 12 0 E
Onslow, *Australia* **112 D2** 21 40 S 115 12 E
Onslow B., *U.S.A.* **135 H7** 34 20N 77 15W
Onstwedde, *Neths.* **20 B10** 53 2N 7 4 E
Ontake-San, *Japan* **63 B9** 35 53N 137 29 E
Ontaneda, *Spain* **36 B7** 43 12N 3 57W
Ontario, *Calif., U.S.A.* **145 L9** 34 4N 117 39W
Ontario, *Oreg., U.S.A.* **142 D5** 44 2N 116 58W
Ontario □, *Canada* **128 B2** 48 0N 83 0W
Ontario, L., *U.S.A.* **128 D4** 43 20N 78 0W
Onteniente, *Spain* **35 G4** 38 50N 0 35W
Ontonagon, *U.S.A.* **138 B10** 46 52N 89 19W
Ontur, *Spain* **35 G3** 38 38N 1 29W
Onyx, *U.S.A.* **145 K8** 35 41N 118 14W
Oodnadatta, *Australia* **115 D2** 27 33 S 135 30 E
Ooldea, *Australia* **113 F5** 30 27 S 131 50 E
Ooltgensplaat, *Neths.* **21 E4** 51 41N 4 21 E
Oombulgurri, *Australia* **112 C4** 15 15 S 127 45 E
Oona River, *Canada* **130 C2** 53 57N 130 16W
Oordegem, *Belgium* **21 G3** 50 58N 3 54 E
Oorindi, *Australia* **114 C3** 20 40 S 141 1 E
Oost-Vlaanderen □, *Belgium* **21 F3** 51 5N 3 50 E
Oost-Vlieland, *Neths.* **20 B6** 53 18N 5 4 E
Oostakker, *Belgium* **21 F3** 51 6N 3 46 E
Oostburg, *Neths.* **21 F3** 51 19N 3 30 E
Oostduinkerke, *Belgium* **21 F1** 51 7N 2 41 E
Oostelijk-Flevoland, *Neths.* **20 C7** 52 31N 5 38 E
Oostende, *Belgium* **21 F1** 51 15N 2 54 E
Oosterbeek, *Neths.* **20 E7** 51 59N 5 51 E
Oosterdijk, *Neths.* **20 C6** 52 44N 5 14 E
Oosterend, *Friesland, Neths.* **20 B6** 53 24N 5 23 E
Oosterend, *Noord-Holland, Neths.* **20 B5** 53 5N 4 52 E
Oosterhout, *Noord-Brabant, Neths.* **21 E7** 51 53N 5 50 E
Oosterhout, *Noord-Brabant, Neths.* **21 E5** 51 39N 4 47 E
Oosterschelde, *Neths.* **21 E4** 51 33N 4 0 E
Oosterwolde, *Neths.* **20 B8** 53 0N 6 17 E
Oosterzele, *Belgium* **21 G3** 50 57N 3 48 E
Oostkamp, *Belgium* **21 F2** 51 9N 3 14 E
Oostmalle, *Belgium* **21 F5** 51 18N 4 44 E
Oostrozebekke, *Belgium* **21 G2** 50 55N 3 21 E
Oostvleteven, *Belgium* **21 G1** 50 56N 2 45 E
Oostvoorne, *Neths.* **20 E4** 51 55N 4 5 E
Oostzaan, *Neths.* **20 D5** 52 26N 4 52 E
Ootacamund, *India* **83 J3** 11 30N 76 44 E
Ootha, *Australia* **117 B7** 33 6 S 147 29 E
Ootmarsum, *Neths.* **20 D9** 52 24N 6 54 E
Ootsa L., *Canada* **130 C3** 53 50N 126 2W
Opaka, *Bulgaria* **43 D11** 43 28N 26 10 E
Opala, *Russia* **57 D16** 51 58N 156 30 E
Opala, *Zaïre* **102 C4** 0 40 S 24 20 E
Opalenica, *Poland* **47 C3** 52 18N 16 24 E
Opan, *Bulgaria* **43 E10** 42 13N 25 41 E
Opanake, *Sri Lanka* **83 L5** 6 35N 80 40 E
Opapa, *N.Z.* **118 F5** 39 47 S 176 42 E
Opasatika, *Canada* **128 C3** 49 30N 82 50W
Opasquia, *Canada* **131 C10** 53 16N 93 34W
Opatija, *Croatia* **39 C11** 45 21N 14 17 E
Opatów, *Poland* **47 E8** 50 50N 21 27 E
Opava, *Czech.* **31 B10** 49 57N 17 58 E
Opeinde, *Neths.* **20 B8** 53 8N 6 4 E
Opelousas, *U.S.A.* **139 K8** 30 32N 92 5W
Opémisca, L., *Canada* **128 C5** 49 56N 74 52W
Open Bay Is., *N.Z.* **119 D3** 43 51 S 168 51 E
Opglabbeek, *Belgium* **21 F7** 51 3N 5 35 E
Opheim, *U.S.A.* **142 B10** 48 51N 106 24W
Ophthalmia Ra., *Australia* **112 D2** 23 15 S 119 30 E
Opi, *Nigeria* **101 D6** 6 36N 7 28 E
Opinaca →, *Canada* **128 B4** 52 15N 78 2W
Opinaca L., *Canada* **128 B4** 52 39N 76 20W
Opiskotish, L., *Canada* **129 B6** 53 10N 67 50W
Oploo, *Neths.* **21 E7** 51 37N 5 52 E
Opmeer, *Neths.* **20 C5** 52 42N 4 57 E
Opobo, *Nigeria* **101 E6** 4 35N 7 34 E
Opochka, *Russia* **50 C6** 56 42N 28 45 E
Opoczno, *Poland* **47 D7** 51 22N 20 18 E
Opol, *Phil.* **71 G5** 8 31N 124 34 E
Opole, *Poland* **47 E4** 50 42N 17 58 E
Opole □, *Poland* **47 E4** 50 40N 17 56 E
Opon = Capu-Lapu, *Phil.* **71 F4** 10 20N 123 55 E
Oporto = Porto, *Portugal* **36 D2** 41 8N 8 40W
Opotiki, *N.Z.* **118 E6** 38 1 S 177 19 E
Opp, *U.S.A.* **135 K2** 31 17N 86 16W
Oppenheim, *Germany* **27 F4** 49 50N 8 22 E
Opperdoes, *Neths.* **20 C6** 52 45N 5 4 E
Óppido Mamertina, *Italy* **41 D8** 38 16N 15 59 E
Oppland fylke □, *Norway* **14 C3** 61 15N 9 40 E
Oppstad, *Norway* **14 D5** 60 17N 11 40 E
Oprtalj, *Croatia* **39 C10** 45 23N 13 50 E
Opua, *N.Z.* **118 B3** 35 19 S 174 9 E
Opunake, *N.Z.* **118 F2** 39 26 S 173 52 E
Opuzen, *Croatia* **42 D2** 43 1N 17 34 E
Oquawka, *U.S.A.* **140 D6** 40 56N 90 57W
Ora, *Cyprus* **32 E12** 34 51N 33 12 E
Ora, *Italy* **39 B8** 46 20N 11 19 E
Ora Banda, *Australia* **113 F3** 30 20 S 121 0 E
Oracle, *U.S.A.* **143 K8** 32 37N 110 46W
Oradea, *Romania* **46 B2** 47 2N 21 58 E
Öræfajökull, *Iceland* **12 D5** 64 2N 16 39W
Orahovac, *Serbia* **42 E5** 42 24N 20 40 E
Orahovica, *Croatia* **42 B2** 45 35N 17 52 E
Orai, *India* **81 G8** 25 58N 79 30 E
Oraison, *France* **25 E9** 43 55N 5 55 E
Oral = Ural →, *Kazakhstan* **53 C14** 47 0N 51 48 E
Oral = Uralsk, *Kazakhstan* **54 F2** 51 20N 51 20 E
Oran, *Algeria* **99 A4** 35 45N 0 39W
Oran, *Argentina* **158 A3** 23 10 S 64 20W
Orange = Oranje →, *S. Africa* **104 D2** 28 41 S 16 28 E
Orange, *Australia* **117 B8** 33 15 S 149 7 E
Orange, *France* **25 D8** 44 8N 4 47 E
Orange, *Calif., U.S.A.* **145 M9** 33 47N 117 51W
Orange, *Mass., U.S.A.* **137 D12** 42 35N 72 19W
Orange, *Tex., U.S.A.* **139 K8** 30 6N 93 44W
Orange, *Va., U.S.A.* **134 F6** 38 15N 78 7W
Orange, C., *Brazil* **153 C7** 4 20N 51 30W
Orange Cove, *U.S.A.* **144 J7** 36 38N 119 19W
Orange Free State □, *S. Africa* **104 D4** 28 30 S 27 0 E
Orange Grove, *U.S.A.* **139 M6** 27 58N 97 56W
Orange Walk, *Belize* **147 D7** 18 6N 88 33W
Orangeburg, *U.S.A.* **135 J5** 33 30N 80 52W
Orangeville, *Canada* **128 D3** 43 55N 80 5W
Orangeville, *U.S.A.* **140 B7** 42 28N 89 39W
Orani, *Phil.* **70 D3** 14 49N 120 32 E
Oranienburg, *Germany* **26 C9** 52 45N 13 15 E
Oranje →, *S. Africa* **104 D2** 28 41 S 16 28 E
Oranje Vrystaat = Orange Free State □, *S. Africa* **104 D4** 28 30 S 27 0 E
Oranjemund, *Namibia* **104 D2** 28 38 S 16 29 E
Oranjerivier, *S. Africa* **104 D3** 29 40 S 24 12 E
Oras, *Phil.* **70 E5** 12 9N 125 28 E
Orašje, *Bos.-H.* **42 B3** 45 1N 18 42 E
Orăştie, *Romania* **46 D4** 45 50N 23 10 E
Oraşul Stalin = Braşov, *Romania* **46 D6** 45 38N 25 35 E
Orava →, *Slovak Rep.* **31 B12** 49 24N 19 20 E
Oravita, *Romania* **42 B6** 45 2N 21 43 E
Orawia, *N.Z.* **119 G2** 46 1 S 167 50 E
Orb →, *France* **24 E7** 43 15N 3 18 E
Orba →, *Italy* **38 D5** 44 53N 8 37 E
Ørbæk, *Denmark* **15 J4** 55 17N 10 39 E
Orbe, *Switz.* **28 C3** 46 43N 6 32 E
Orbec, *France* **22 C7** 49 1N 0 23 E
Orbetello, *Italy* **39 F8** 42 26N 11 11 E
Órbigo →, *Spain* **36 C5** 42 5N 5 42W
Orbost, *Australia* **117 D8** 37 40 S 148 29 E
Orce, *Spain* **35 H2** 37 44N 2 28W
Orce →, *Spain* **35 H2** 37 44N 2 28W
Orchies, *France* **23 B10** 50 28N 3 14 E
Orchila, I., *Venezuela* **152 A4** 11 48N 66 10W
Orco →, *Italy* **38 C4** 45 10N 7 52 E
Orcopampa, *Peru* **156 D3** 15 20 S 72 23W
Orcutt, *U.S.A.* **145 L6** 34 52N 120 27W
Ord →, *Australia* **112 C4** 15 33 S 128 15 E
Ord, Mt., *Australia* **112 C4** 17 20 S 125 34 E
Ordenes, *Spain* **36 B2** 43 5N 8 29W
Orderville, *U.S.A.* **143 H7** 37 17N 112 38W
Ording, *Germany* **26 A4** 54 23N 8 32 E
Ordos = Mu Us Shamo, *China* **66 E5** 39 0N 109 0 E
Ordu, *Turkey* **89 C7** 40 55N 37 53 E
Ordu □, *Turkey* **89 C7** 41 0N 37 50 E
Orduña, *Álava, Spain* **34 C7** 42 58N 2 58 E
Orduña, *Granada, Spain* **35 H1** 37 20N 3 30W
Ordway, *U.S.A.* **138 F3** 38 13N 103 46W
Ordzhonikidze = Vladikavkaz, *Russia* **53 E11** 43 0N 44 35 E
Ordzhonikidze, *Ukraine* **52 C6** 47 39N 34 3 E
Ordzhonikidze, *Uzbekistan* **55 C4** 41 21N 69 22 E
Ordzhonikidzeabad, *Tajikistan* **55 D4** 38 34N 69 1 E
Ore, *Zaïre* **106 B2** 3 17N 29 30 E
Ore Mts. = Erzgebirge, *Germany* **26 E9** 50 25N 13 0 E
Orealla, *Guyana* **153 B6** 5 15N 57 23W
Orebić, *Croatia* **42 D2** 43 0N 17 11 E
Örebro, *Sweden* **13 G13** 59 20N 15 18 E
Örebro län □, *Sweden* **13 G13** 59 27N 15 0 E
Oregon, *Ill., U.S.A.* **140 B7** 42 1N 89 20W
Oregon, *Ohio, U.S.A.* **141 C13** 41 38N 83 25W
Oregon, *Wis., U.S.A.* **140 B7** 42 56N 89 23W
Oregon □, *U.S.A.* **142 E3** 44 0N 121 0W
Oregon City, *U.S.A.* **144 E4** 45 21N 122 36W
Orekhov, *Ukraine* **52 C6** 47 30N 35 48 E
Orekhovo-Zuyevo, *Russia* **51 D11** 55 50N 38 55 E
Orel, *Russia* **51 E10** 52 57N 36 3 E
Orel →, *Ukraine* **52 B6** 48 45N 34 20 E
Orellana, Canal de, *Spain* **37 F5** 39 2N 6 0W
Orellana, Pantano de, *Spain* **37 F5** 39 5N 5 10W
Orellana la Vieja, *Spain* **37 F5** 39 1N 5 32W
Orem, *U.S.A.* **142 F8** 40 19N 111 42W
Ören, *Turkey* **45 G9** 37 3N 27 57 E
Orenburg, *Russia* **54 F4** 51 45N 55 6 E
Orense, *Spain* **36 C3** 42 19N 7 55W
Orense □, *Spain* **36 C3** 42 15N 7 51W
Orepuki, *N.Z.* **119 G2** 46 19 S 167 46 E
Orestiás, *Greece* **44 C8** 41 30N 26 33 E
Øresund, *Europe* **15 J6** 55 45N 12 45 E
Oreti →, *N.Z.* **119 G3** 46 28 S 168 14 E
Orford Ness, *U.K.* **17 E9** 52 6N 1 31 E
Organà, *Spain* **34 C6** 42 13N 1 20 E
Organos, Pta. de los, *Canary Is.* **33 F2** 28 12N 17 17W
Orgaz, *Spain* **37 F7** 39 39N 3 53W
Orgeyev, *Moldavia* **52 C3** 47 24N 28 50 E
Orgon, *France* **25 E9** 43 47N 5 3 E
Orgūn, *Afghan.* **79 B3** 32 55N 69 12 E
Orhaneli, *Turkey* **88 D3** 39 54N 28 59 E
Orhangazi, *Turkey* **88 C3** 40 29N 29 18 E
Orhon Gol →, *Mongolia* **64 A5** 50 21N 106 0 E
Ória, *Italy* **41 B10** 40 30N 17 38 E
Orient, *Australia* **115 D3** 28 7 S 142 50 E
Orient, *U.S.A.* **140 C2** 41 12N 94 25W
Oriental, Cordillera, *Bolivia* **157 D4** 17 0 S 66 0W
Oriental, Cordillera, *Colombia* **152 B3** 6 0N 73 0W
Oriente, *Argentina* **158 D3** 38 44 S 60 37W
Origny-Ste.-Benoite, *France* **23 C10** 49 50N 3 30 E
Orihuela, *Spain* **35 G4** 38 7N 0 55W
Orihuela del Tremedal, *Spain* **34 E3** 40 33N 1 39W

Owensboro 245


Oriku, *Albania* **44 D1** 40 20N 19 30 E
Orinduik, *Guyana* **153 C5** 4 40N 60 3W
Orinoco →, *Venezuela* **153 B5** 9 15N 61 30W
Orion, *U.S.A.* **140 C6** 41 21N 90 23W
Orissa □, *India* **82 D6** 20 0N 84 0 E
Oristano, *Italy* **40 C1** 39 54N 8 35 E
Oristano, G. di, *Italy* **40 C1** 39 50N 8 22 E
Orituco →, *Venezuela* **152 B4** 8 45N 67 27W
Orizaba, *Mexico* **147 D5** 18 50N 97 10W
Orizare, *Bulgaria* **43 E12** 42 44N 27 39 E
Orizona, *Brazil* **155 E2** 17 3 S 48 18W
Orjen, *Bos.-H.* **42 E3** 42 35N 18 34 E
Orjiva, *Spain* **35 J1** 36 53N 3 24W
Orkanger, *Norway* **14 A3** 63 18N 9 52 E
Örkelljunga, *Sweden* **15 H7** 56 17N 13 17 E
Örkény, *Hungary* **31 D12** 47 9N 19 26 E
Orkla →, *Norway* **14 A3** 63 18N 9 51 E
Orkney, *S. Africa* **104 D4** 26 58 S 26 40 E
Orkney □, *U.K.* **18 C6** 59 0N 3 0W
Orkney Is., *U.K.* **18 C6** 59 0N 3 0W
Orla, *Poland* **47 C10** 52 42N 23 20 E
Orland, *Calif., U.S.A.* **144 F4** 39 45N 122 12W
Orland, *Ind., U.S.A.* **141 C11** 41 47N 85 12W
Orlando, *U.S.A.* **135 L5** 28 33N 81 23W
Orlando, C. d', *Italy* **41 D7** 38 10N 14 43 E
Orléanais, *France* **23 E9** 48 0N 2 0 E
Orléans, *France* **23 E8** 47 54N 1 52 E
Orleans, *U.S.A.* **137 B12** 44 49N 72 12W
Orléans, I. d', *Canada* **129 C5** 46 54N 70 58W
Orlice →, *Czech.* **30 A9** 50 5N 16 10 E
Orlické Hory, *Czech.* **31 A9** 50 15N 16 30 E
Orlov, *Slovak Rep.* **31 B13** 49 17N 20 51 E
Orlov Gay, *Russia* **51 F16** 50 56N 48 19 E
Orlovat, *Serbia* **42 B5** 45 14N 20 33 E
Ormara, *Pakistan* **79 D2** 25 16N 64 33 E
Ormea, *Italy* **38 D4** 44 9N 7 54 E
Ormília, *Greece* **44 D5** 40 16N 23 39 E
Ormoc, *Phil.* **71 F5** 11 0N 124 37 E
Ormond, *N.Z.* **118 E6** 38 33 S 177 56 E
Ormond Beach, *U.S.A.* **135 L5** 29 17N 81 3W
Ormondville, *N.Z.* **118 G5** 40 5 S 176 19 E
Ormož, *Slovenia* **39 B13** 46 25N 16 10 E
Ormstown, *Canada* **137 A11** 45 8N 74 0W
Ornans, *France* **23 E13** 47 7N 6 10 E
Orne □, *France* **22 D7** 48 40N 0 5 E
Orne →, *France* **22 C6** 49 18N 0 15W
Orneta, *Poland* **47 A7** 54 8N 20 9 E
Ørnhøj, *Denmark* **15 H2** 56 13N 8 34 E
Ornö, *Sweden* **14 E12** 59 4N 18 24 E
Örnsköldsvik, *Sweden* **14 A12** 63 17N 18 40 E
Oro, *N. Korea* **67 D14** 40 1N 127 27 E
Oro →, *Mexico* **146 B3** 25 35N 105 2W
Oro Grande, *U.S.A.* **145 L9** 34 36N 117 20W
Orobie, Alpi, *Italy* **38 B6** 46 7N 10 0 E
Orocué, *Colombia* **152 C3** 4 48N 71 20W
Orodo, *Nigeria* **101 D6** 5 34N 7 4 E
Orogrande, *U.S.A.* **143 K10** 32 24N 106 5W
Orol, *Spain* **36 B3** 43 34N 7 39W
Oromocto, *Canada* **129 C6** 45 54N 66 29W
Oron, *Nigeria* **101 E6** 4 48N 8 14 E
Oron, *Switz.* **28 C3** 46 34N 6 50 E
Orono, *Canada* **136 C6** 43 59N 78 37W
Oropesa, *Spain* **36 F5** 39 57N 5 10W
Oroqen Zizhiqi, *China* **65 A7** 50 34N 123 43 E
Oroquieta, *Phil.* **71 G4** 8 32N 123 44 E
Orós, *Brazil* **154 C4** 6 15 S 38 55W
Orosei, G. di, *Italy* **40 B2** 40 15N 9 40 E
Orosháza, *Hungary* **31 E13** 46 32N 20 42 E
Orote Pen., *Guam* **121 R15** 13 26N 144 38 E
Orotukan, *Russia* **57 C16** 62 16N 151 42 E
Oroville, *Calif., U.S.A.* **144 F5** 39 31N 121 33W
Oroville, *Wash., U.S.A.* **142 B4** 48 56N 119 26W
Oroville, L., *U.S.A.* **144 F5** 39 33N 121 29W
Orrick, *U.S.A.* **140 E2** 39 13N 94 7W
Orroroo, *Australia* **116 B3** 32 43 S 138 38 E
Orrville, *U.S.A.* **136 F3** 40 50N 81 46W
Orsara di Púglia, *Italy* **41 A8** 41 17N 15 16 E
Orsha, *Belorussia* **50 D7** 54 30N 30 25 E
Orsières, *Switz.* **28 D4** 46 2N 7 9 E
Orsk, *Russia* **54 F6** 51 12N 58 34 E
Ørslev, *Denmark* **15 J5** 55 3N 11 56 E
Orsogna, *Italy* **39 F11** 42 13N 14 17 E
Orşova, *Romania* **46 E3** 44 41N 22 25 E
Ørsted, *Denmark* **15 H4** 56 30N 10 20 E
Orta, L. d', *Italy* **38 C5** 45 48N 8 21 E
Orta Nova, *Italy* **41 A8** 41 20N 15 40 E
Ortaca, *Turkey* **88 E3** 36 49N 28 45 E
Ortaköy, *Çorum, Turkey* **88 C6** 40 16N 35 15 E
Ortaköy, *Niğde, Turkey* **88 D6** 38 44N 34 3 E
Orte, *Italy* **39 F9** 42 28N 12 23 E
Ortegal, C., *Spain* **36 B3** 43 43N 7 52W
Orteguaza →, *Colombia* **152 C2** 0 43N 75 16W
Orthez, *France* **24 E3** 43 29N 0 48W
Ortho, *Belgium* **21 H7** 50 8N 5 37 E
Ortigueira, *Spain* **36 B3** 43 40N 7 50W
Orting, *U.S.A.* **144 C4** 47 6N 122 12W
Ortles, *Italy* **38 B7** 46 31N 10 33 E
Orto, Tokay, *Kirghizia* **55 B8** 42 20N 76 1 E
Ortón →, *Bolivia* **156 C4** 10 50 S 67 0W
Ortona, *Italy* **39 F11** 42 21N 14 24 E
Orūmīyeh, *Iran* **84 B5** 37 40N 45 0 E
Orūmīyeh, Daryācheh-ye, *Iran* **84 B5** 37 50N 45 30 E
Orune, *Italy* **40 B2** 40 25N 9 20 E
Oruro, *Bolivia* **156 D4** 18 0 S 67 9W
Oruro□, *Bolivia* **156 D4** 18 40 S 67 30W
Orust, *Sweden* **15 F5** 58 10N 11 40 E
Oruzgān □, *Afghan.* **79 B2** 33 30N 66 0 E
Orvault, *France* **22 E5** 47 17N 1 38W
Orvieto, *Italy* **39 F9** 42 43N 12 8 E
Orwell, *U.S.A.* **136 E4** 41 32N 80 52W
Orwell →, *U.K.* **17 E9** 52 2N 1 12 E
Oryakhovo, *Bulgaria* **43 D8** 43 40N 23 57 E
Orzinuovi, *Italy* **38 C6** 45 24N 9 55 E
Orzyc →, *Poland* **47 C8** 52 46N 21 14 E
Orzysz, *Poland* **47 B8** 53 50N 21 58 E
Osa, *Russia* **54 C4** 57 17N 55 26 E
Osa →, *Poland* **47 B5** 53 33N 18 46 E
Osa, Pen. de, *Costa Rica* **148 E3** 8 0N 84 0W
Osage, *Iowa, U.S.A.* **138 D8** 43 17N 92 49W
Osage, *Wyo., U.S.A.* **138 D2** 43 59N 104 25W
Osage →, *U.S.A.* **140 F5** 38 35N 91 57W
Osage City, *U.S.A.* **138 F7** 38 38N 95 50W
Ōsaka, *Japan* **63 C7** 34 40N 135 30 E
Ōsaka □, *Japan* **63 C7** 34 30N 135 30 E
Ōsaka-Wan, *Japan* **63 C7** 34 30N 135 18 E
Osan, *S. Korea* **67 F14** 37 11N 127 4 E
Osawatomie, *U.S.A.* **138 F7** 38 31N 94 57W
Osborne, *U.S.A.* **138 F5** 39 26N 98 42W
Osceola, *Ark., U.S.A.* **139 H10** 35 42N 89 58W
Osceola, *Iowa, U.S.A.* **140 C3** 41 2N 93 46W
Osceola, *Mo., U.S.A.* **140 F3** 38 3N 93 42W
Oschatz, *Germany* **26 D9** 51 17N 13 8 E
Oschersleben, *Germany* **26 C7** 52 2N 11 13 E
Óschiri, *Italy* **40 B2** 40 43N 9 7 E
Oscoda, *U.S.A.* **136 B1** 44 26N 83 20W
Osečina, *Serbia* **42 C4** 44 23N 19 34 E
Ösel = Saaremaa, *Estonia* **50 B3** 58 30N 22 30 E
Osëry, *Russia* **51 D11** 54 52N 38 28 E
Osgood, *U.S.A.* **141 E11** 39 8N 85 18W
Osh, *Kirghizia* **55 C6** 40 37N 72 49 E
Oshawa, *Canada* **128 D4** 43 50N 78 50W
Oshima, *Japan* **62 D4** 33 55N 132 14 E
Oshkosh, *Nebr., U.S.A.* **138 E3** 41 24N 102 21W
Oshkosh, *Wis., U.S.A.* **138 C10** 44 1N 88 33W
Oshmyany, *Belorussia* **50 D4** 54 26N 25 52 E
Oshnovīyeh, *Iran* **84 B5** 37 2N 45 6 E
Oshogbo, *Nigeria* **101 D5** 7 48N 4 37 E
Oshtorīnān, *Iran* **85 C6** 34 1N 48 38 E
Oshwe, *Zaïre* **102 C3** 3 25 S 19 28 E
Osica de Jos, *Romania* **46 E5** 44 14N 24 20 E
Osieczna, *Poland* **47 D3** 51 55N 16 40 E
Osijek, *Croatia* **42 B3** 45 34N 18 41 E
Ósilo, *Italy* **40 B1** 40 45N 8 41 E
Osimo, *Italy* **39 E10** 43 28N 13 30 E
Osintorf, *Belorussia* **50 D7** 54 40N 30 39 E
Osipenko = Berdyansk, *Ukraine* **52 C7** 46 45N 36 50 E
Osipovichi, *Belorussia* **50 E6** 53 19N 28 33 E
Osizweni, *S. Africa* **105 D5** 27 49 S 30 7 E
Oskaloosa, *U.S.A.* **140 C4** 41 18N 92 39W
Oskarshamn, *Sweden* **13 H14** 57 15N 16 27 E
Oskélanéo, *Canada* **128 C4** 48 5N 75 15W
Öskemen = Ust-Kamenogorsk, *Kazakhstan* **56 E9** 50 0N 82 36 E
Oskol →, *Ukraine* **51 G10** 49 6N 37 25 E
Oslo, *Norway* **14 E4** 59 55N 10 45 E
Oslob, *Phil.* **71 G4** 9 31N 123 26 E
Oslofjorden, *Norway* **14 E4** 59 20N 10 35 E
Osmanabad, *India* **82 E3** 18 5N 76 10 E
Osmancık, *Turkey* **52 F6** 40 58N 34 47 E
Osmaniye, *Turkey* **88 E7** 37 5N 36 10 E
Ösmo, *Sweden* **14 F11** 58 58N 17 55 E
Osnabrück, *Germany* **26 C4** 52 16N 8 2 E
Ośno Lubuskie, *Poland* **47 C1** 52 28N 14 51 E
Osoblaha, *Czech.* **31 A10** 50 17N 17 44 E
Osogovska Planina, *Macedonia* **42 E7** 42 10N 22 30 E
Osor, *Italy* **39 D11** 44 42N 14 24 E
Osorio, *Brazil* **159 B5** 29 53 S 50 17W
Osorno, *Chile* **160 B2** 40 25 S 73 0W
Osorno, *Spain* **36 C6** 42 24N 4 22W
Osorno □, *Chile* **160 B2** 40 34 S 73 9W
Osorno, Vol., *Chile* **160 B2** 41 0 S 72 30W
Osoyoos, *Canada* **130 D5** 49 0N 119 30W
Ospika →, *Canada* **130 B4** 56 20N 124 0W
Osprey Reef, *Australia* **114 A4** 13 52 S 146 36 E
Oss, *Neths.* **20 E7** 51 46N 5 32 E
Ossa, Mt., *Australia* **114 G4** 41 52 S 146 3 E
Óssa, Oros, *Greece* **44 E4** 39 47N 22 42 E
Ossa de Montiel, *Spain* **35 G2** 38 58N 2 45W
Ossabaw I., *U.S.A.* **135 K5** 31 50N 81 5W
Osse →, *France* **24 D4** 44 7N 0 17 E
Ossendrecht, *Neths.* **21 F4** 51 24N 4 20 E
Ossining, *U.S.A.* **137 E11** 41 10N 73 55W
Ossipee, *U.S.A.* **137 C13** 43 41N 71 7W
Ossokmanuan L., *Canada* **129 B7** 53 25N 65 0W
Ossora, *Russia* **57 D17** 59 20N 163 13 E
Ostashkov, *Russia* **50 C8** 57 4N 33 2 E
Oste →, *Germany* **26 B5** 53 30N 9 12 E
Ostend = Oostende, *Belgium* **21 F1** 51 15N 2 54 E
Oster, *Ukraine* **50 F7** 50 57N 30 53 E
Osterburg, *Germany* **26 C7** 52 47N 11 44 E
Osterburken, *Germany* **27 F5** 49 26N 9 25 E
Österdalälven →, *Sweden* **13 F12** 61 30N 13 45 E
Östergötlands län □, *Sweden* **15 F9** 58 35N 15 45 E
Osterholz-Scharmbeck, *Germany* **26 B4** 53 14N 8 48 E
Østerild, *Denmark* **15 G2** 57 2N 8 51 E
Ostermundigen, *Switz.* **28 C4** 46 58N 7 27 E
Östersund, *Sweden* **14 A8** 63 10N 14 38 E
Østfold fylke □, *Norway* **14 E5** 59 25N 11 25 E
Ostfriesische Inseln, *Germany* **26 B3** 53 45N 7 15 E
Ostfriesland, *Germany* **26 B3** 53 20N 7 30 E
Óstia, Lido di, *Italy* **40 A5** 41 43N 12 17 E
Ostiglía, *Italy* **39 C8** 45 4N 11 9 E
Ostra, *Italy* **39 E10** 43 40N 13 5 E
Ostrava, *Czech.* **31 B11** 49 51N 18 18 E
Ostróda, *Poland* **47 B6** 53 42N 19 58 E
Ostrog, *Ukraine* **50 F5** 50 20N 26 30 E
Ostrogozhsk, *Russia* **51 F11** 50 55N 39 7 E
Ostrogróg Sźamotuły, *Poland* **47 C3** 52 37N 16 33 E
Ostrołęka, *Poland* **47 B8** 53 4N 21 32 E
Ostrołeka □, *Poland* **47 C8** 53 0N 21 30 E
Ostrov, *Bulgaria* **43 D9** 43 40N 24 9 E
Ostrov, *Romania* **46 E8** 44 6N 27 24 E
Ostrov, *Russia* **50 C6** 57 25N 28 20 E
Ostrów Lubelski, *Poland* **47 D9** 51 29N 22 51 E
Ostrów Mazowiecka, *Poland* **47 C8** 52 50N 21 51 E
Ostrów Wielkopolski, *Poland* **47 D4** 51 36N 17 44 E
Ostrowiec-Świętokrzyski, *Poland* **47 E8** 50 55N 21 22 E
Ostrozac, *Bos.-H.* **42 D2** 43 43N 17 49 E
Ostrzeszów, *Poland* **47 D4** 51 25N 17 52 E
Ostseebad-Kühlungsborn, *Germany* **26 A7** 54 10N 11 40 E
Osttirol □, *Austria* **27 J8** 46 50N 12 30 E
Ostuni, *Italy* **41 B10** 40 44N 17 34 E
Osum →, *Bulgaria* **43 D9** 43 40N 24 50 E
Osumi →, *Albania* **44 D2** 40 40N 20 10 E
Ōsumi-Hantō, *Japan* **62 F2** 31 20N 130 55 E
Ōsumi-Kaikyō, *Japan* **61 J5** 30 55N 131 0 E
Ōsumi-Shotō, *Japan* **61 J5** 30 30N 130 0 E
Osun □, *Nigeria* **101 D5** 7 30N 4 30 E
Osuna, *Spain* **37 H5** 37 14N 5 8W
Oswego, *U.S.A.* **137 C8** 43 27N 76 31W
Oswestry, *U.K.* **16 E4** 52 52N 3 3W
Oświecim, *Poland* **31 A12** 50 2N 19 11 E
Ōta, *Japan* **63 A11** 36 18N 139 22 E
Ota-Gawa →, *Japan* **62 C4** 34 21N 132 18 E
Otago □, *N.Z.* **119 E4** 45 15 S 170 0 E
Otago Harbour, *N.Z.* **119 F5** 45 47 S 170 42 E
Otago Pen., *N.Z.* **119 F5** 45 48 S 170 39 E
Otahuhu, *N.Z.* **118 C3** 36 56 S 174 51 E
Ōtake, *Japan* **62 C4** 34 12N 132 13 E
Ōtaki, *Japan* **63 B12** 35 17N 140 15 E
Otaki, *N.Z.* **118 G4** 40 45 S 175 10 E
Otane, *N.Z.* **118 F5** 39 54 S 176 39 E
Otar, *Kazakhstan* **55 B7** 43 32N 75 12 E
Otaru, *Japan* **60 C10** 43 10N 141 0 E
Otaru-Wan = Ishikari-Wan, *Japan* **60 C10** 43 25N 141 1 E
Otautau, *N.Z.* **119 G3** 46 9 S 168 1 E
Otava →, *Czech.* **30 B7** 49 26N 14 12 E
Otavalo, *Ecuador* **152 C2** 0 13N 78 20W
Otavi, *Namibia* **104 B2** 19 40 S 17 24 E
Otchinjau, *Angola* **103 F2** 16 30 S 13 56 E
Otelec, *Romania* **46 D1** 45 36N 20 50 E
Otero de Rey, *Spain* **36 B3** 43 6N 7 36W
Othello, *U.S.A.* **142 C4** 46 50N 119 10W
Othonoí, *Greece* **44 E1** 39 52N 19 22 E
Óthris, Óros, *Greece* **45 E4** 39 4N 22 42 E
Otira, *N.Z.* **119 C6** 42 49 S 171 35 E
Otira Gorge, *N.Z.* **119 C6** 42 53 S 171 33 E
Otis, *U.S.A.* **138 E3** 40 9N 102 58W
Otjiwarongo, *Namibia* **104 C2** 20 30 S 16 33 E
Otmuchów, *Poland* **47 E4** 50 28N 17 10 E
Oto Tolu Group, *Tonga* **121 Q13** 20 21 S 174 32W
Otočac, *Croatia* **39 D12** 44 53N 15 12 E
Otoineppu, *Japan* **60 B11** 44 44N 142 16 E
Oton, *Phil.* **71 F4** 10 42N 122 29 E
Otorohanga, *N.Z.* **118 E4** 38 12 S 175 14 E
Otoskwin →, *Canada* **128 B2** 52 13N 88 6W
Otosquen, *Canada* **131 C8** 53 17N 102 1W
Ōtoyo, *Japan* **62 D5** 33 43N 133 45 E
Otranto, *Italy* **41 B11** 40 9N 18 28 E
Otranto, C. d', *Italy* **41 B11** 40 7N 18 30 E
Otranto, Str. of, *Italy* **41 B11** 40 15N 18 40 E
Otse, *S. Africa* **104 D4** 25 2 S 25 45 E
Otsego, *U.S.A.* **141 B11** 42 27N 85 42W
Ōtsu, *Japan* **63 B7** 35 0N 135 50 E
Ōtsuki, *Japan* **63 B10** 35 36N 138 57 E
Otta, *Norway* **14 C3** 61 46N 9 32 E
Ottapalam, *India* **83 J3** 10 46N 76 23 E
Ottawa = Outaouais →, *Canada* **128 C5** 45 27N 74 8W
Ottawa, *Canada* **128 C4** 45 27N 75 42W
Ottawa, *Ill., U.S.A.* **138 E10** 41 21N 88 51W
Ottawa, *Kans., U.S.A.* **138 F7** 38 37N 95 16W
Ottawa, *Ohio, U.S.A.* **141 C12** 41 1N 84 3W
Ottawa Is., *Canada* **127 C11** 59 35N 80 10W
Ottélé, *Cameroon* **101 E7** 3 38N 11 19 E
Ottensheim, *Austria* **30 C7** 48 21N 14 12 E
Otter L., *Canada* **131 B8** 55 35N 104 39W
Otter Rapids, *Ont., Canada* **128 B3** 50 11N 81 39W
Otter Rapids, *Sask., Canada* **131 B8** 55 38N 104 44W
Otterbein, *U.S.A.* **141 D9** 40 29N 87 6W
Otterndorf, *Germany* **26 B4** 53 47N 8 52 E
Otterup, *Denmark* **15 J4** 55 30N 10 22 E
Otterville, *Canada* **136 D4** 42 55N 80 36W
Otterville, *U.S.A.* **140 F4** 38 42N 93 0W
Ottignies, *Belgium* **21 G5** 50 40N 4 33 E
Otto Beit Bridge, *Zimbabwe* **107 F2** 15 59 S 28 56 E
Ottosdal, *S. Africa* **104 D4** 26 46 S 25 59 E
Ottoshoop, *S. Africa* **104 D4** 25 45 S 25 58 E
Ottoville, *U.S.A.* **141 D12** 40 57N 84 22W
Ottsjön, *Sweden* **14 A7** 63 13N 13 2 E
Ottumwa, *U.S.A.* **140 C4** 41 1N 92 25W
Otu, *Nigeria* **101 D5** 8 14N 3 22 E
Otukpa, *Nigeria* **101 D6** 7 9N 7 41 E
Oturkpo, *Nigeria* **101 D6** 7 16N 8 8 E
Otway, B., *Chile* **160 D2** 53 30 S 74 0W
Otway, C., *Australia* **116 E5** 38 52 S 143 30 E
Otwock, *Poland* **47 C8** 52 5N 21 20 E
Ötz, *Austria* **30 D3** 47 13N 10 53 E
Ötz →, *Austria* **30 D3** 47 14N 10 50 E
Ötztaler Alpen, *Austria* **30 E4** 46 56N 11 0 E
Ou →, *Laos* **76 B4** 20 4N 102 13 E
Ou Neua, *Laos* **76 A3** 22 18N 101 48 E
Ou-Sammyaku, *Japan* **60 E10** 39 20N 140 35 E
Ouachita →, *U.S.A.* **139 K9** 31 38N 91 49W
Ouachita, L., *U.S.A.* **139 H8** 34 34N 93 12W
Ouachita Mts., *U.S.A.* **139 H7** 34 40N 94 25W
Ouaco, *N. Cal.* **121 T18** 20 50 S 164 29 E
Ouadâne, *Mauritania* **98 D2** 20 50N 11 40W
Ouadda, *C.A.R.* **102 A4** 8 15N 22 20 E
Ouagadougou, *Burkina Faso* **101 C4** 12 25N 1 30W
Ouagam, *Chad* **97 F2** 14 22N 14 42 E
Ouahigouya, *Burkina Faso* **100 C4** 13 31N 2 25W
Ouahila, *Algeria* **98 C3** 27 50N 5 0W
Ouahran = Oran, *Algeria* **99 A4** 35 45N 0 39W
Oualâta, *Mauritania* **100 B3** 17 20N 6 55W
Ouallene, *Algeria* **99 D5** 24 41N 1 11 E
Ouanda Djallé, *C.A.R.* **102 A4** 8 55N 22 53 E
Ouandago, *C.A.R.* **102 A3** 7 13N 18 50 E
Ouango, *C.A.R.* **102 B4** 4 19N 22 30 E
Ouarâne, *Mauritania* **98 D2** 21 0N 10 30W
Ouargla, *Algeria* **99 B6** 31 59N 5 16 E
Ouarkziz, Djebel, *Algeria* **98 C3** 28 50N 8 0W
Ouarzazate, *Morocco* **98 B3** 30 55N 6 50W
Ouatagouna, *Mali* **101 B5** 15 11N 0 43 E
Ouatere, *C.A.R.* **102 A3** 5 30N 19 8 E
Oubangi →, *Zaïre* **102 C3** 0 30 S 17 50 E
Oubarakai, O. →, *Algeria* **99 C6** 27 20N 9 0 E
Oubatche, *N. Cal.* **121 T18** 20 26 S 164 39 E
Ouche →, *France* **23 E12** 47 6N 5 16 E
Oud-Beijerland, *Neths.* **20 E4** 51 50N 4 25 E
Oud-Gastel, *Neths.* **21 E4** 51 35N 4 28 E
Oud Turnhout, *Belgium* **21 F6** 51 19N 5 0 E
Ouddorp, *Neths.* **20 E3** 51 50N 3 57 E
Oude-Pekela, *Neths.* **20 B10** 53 6N 7 0 E
Oude Rijn →, *Neths.* **20 D4** 52 12N 4 24 E
Oudega, *Neths.* **20 B8** 53 8N 6 0 E
Oudenaarde, *Belgium* **21 G3** 50 50N 3 37 E
Oudenbosch, *Neths.* **21 E5** 51 35N 4 32 E
Oudenburg, *Belgium* **21 F2** 51 11N 3 1 E
Ouderkerk, *Utrecht, Neths.* **20 D5** 52 18N 4 55 E
Ouderkerk, *Zuid-Holland, Neths.* **20 E5** 51 56N 4 38 E
Oudeschild, *Neths.* **20 B5** 53 2N 4 50 E
Oudewater, *Neths.* **20 D5** 52 2N 4 52 E
Oudkarspel, *Neths.* **20 C5** 52 43N 4 49 E
Oudon, *France* **22 E5** 47 22N 1 19W
Oudtshoorn, *S. Africa* **104 E3** 33 35 S 22 14 E
Oued Zem, *Morocco* **98 B3** 32 52N 6 34W
Ouégoa, *N. Cal.* **121 T18** 20 20 S 164 26 E
Ouellé, *Ivory C.* **100 D4** 7 26N 4 1W
Ouen, I., *N. Cal.* **121 V20** 22 26 S 166 49 E
Ouenza, *Algeria* **99 A6** 35 57N 8 4 E
Ouessa, *Burkina Faso* **100 C4** 11 4N 2 47W
Ouessant, I. d', *France* **22 D1** 48 28N 5 6W
Ouesso, *Congo* **102 B3** 1 37N 16 5 E
Ouest, Pte., *Canada* **129 C7** 49 52N 64 40W
Ouezzane, *Morocco* **98 B3** 34 51N 5 35W
Ouffet, *Belgium* **21 H6** 50 26N 5 28 E
Ouidah, *Benin* **101 D5** 6 25N 2 0 E
Ouistreham, *France* **22 C6** 49 17N 0 18W
Oujda, *Morocco* **99 B4** 34 41N 1 55W
Oujeft, *Mauritania* **98 D2** 20 2N 13 0W
Ould Yenjé, *Mauritania* **100 B2** 15 38N 12 16W
Ouled Djellal, *Algeria* **99 B6** 34 28N 5 2 E
Ouled Naïl, Mts. des, *Algeria* **99 B5** 34 30N 3 30 E
Oulmès, *Morocco* **98 B3** 33 17N 6 0W
Oulu, *Finland* **12 D18** 65 1N 25 29 E
Oulu □ = Oulun lääni □, *Finland* **12 D19** 64 36N 27 20 E
Oulujärvi, *Finland* **12 D19** 64 25N 27 15 E
Oulujoki →, *Finland* **12 D18** 65 1N 25 30 E
Oulun lääni □, *Finland* **12 D19** 64 36N 27 20 E
Oulx, *Italy* **38 C3** 45 2N 6 49 E
Oum Chalouba, *Chad* **97 E4** 15 48N 20 46 E
Oum-el-Bouaghi, *Algeria* **99 A6** 35 55N 7 6 E
Oum el Ksi, *Algeria* **98 C3** 29 4N 6 59W
Oum-er-Rbia, O. →, *Morocco* **98 B3** 33 19N 8 21W
Oumè, *Ivory C.* **100 D3** 6 21N 5 27W
Ounane, Dj., *Algeria* **99 C6** 25 4N 7 19 E
Ounguati, *Namibia* **104 C2** 22 0 S 15 46 E
Ounianga-Kébir, *Chad* **97 E4** 19 4N 20 29 E
Ounianga Sérir, *Chad* **97 E4** 18 54N 20 51 E
Our →, *Lux.* **21 J8** 49 55N 6 5 E
Ouray, *U.S.A.* **143 G10** 38 1N 107 40W
Ourcq →, *France* **23 C10** 49 1N 3 1 E
Oureg, Oued el →, *Algeria* **99 B5** 32 34N 2 10 E
Ourém, *Brazil* **154 B2** 1 33 S 47 6W
Ourense = Orense, *Spain* **36 C3** 42 19N 7 55W
Ouricuri, *Brazil* **154 C3** 7 53 S 40 5W
Ourinhos, *Brazil* **159 A6** 23 0 S 49 54W
Ourique, *Portugal* **37 H2** 37 38N 8 16W
Ouro Fino, *Brazil* **159 A6** 22 16 S 46 25W
Ouro Prêto, *Brazil* **155 F3** 20 20 S 43 30W
Ouro Sogui, *Senegal* **100 B2** 15 36N 13 19W
Oursi, *Burkina Faso* **101 C4** 14 41N 0 27W
Ourthe →, *Belgium* **21 H7** 50 29N 5 35 E
Ouse, *Australia* **114 G4** 42 38 S 146 42 E
Ouse →, *E. Susx., U.K.* **17 G8** 50 43N 0 3 E
Ouse →, *N. Yorks., U.K.* **16 C8** 54 3N 0 7 E
Oust, *France* **24 F5** 42 52N 1 13 E
Oust →, *France* **22 E4** 47 35N 2 6W
Outaouais →, *Canada* **128 C5** 45 27N 74 8W
Outardes →, *Canada* **129 C6** 49 24N 69 30W
Outat Oulad el Haj, *Morocco* **99 B4** 33 22N 3 42W
Outer Hebrides, *U.K.* **18 D1** 57 30N 7 40W
Outer I., *Canada* **129 B8** 51 10N 58 35W
Outes, *Spain* **36 C2** 42 52N 8 55W
Outjo, *Namibia* **104 C2** 20 5 S 16 7 E
Outlook, *Canada* **131 C7** 51 30N 107 0W
Outlook, *U.S.A.* **138 A2** 48 53N 104 47W
Outreau, *France* **23 B8** 50 40N 1 36 E
Ouvèze →, *France* **25 E8** 43 59N 4 51 E
Ouyen, *Australia* **116 C5** 35 1 S 142 22 E
Ouzouer-le-Marché, *France* **23 E8** 47 54N 1 32 E
Ovada, *Italy* **38 D5** 44 39N 8 40 E
Ovalau, *Fiji* **121 A2** 17 40 S 178 48 E
Ovalle, *Chile* **158 C1** 30 33 S 71 18W
Ovar, *Portugal* **36 E2** 40 51N 8 40W
Ovejas, *Colombia* **152 B2** 9 32N 75 14W
Ovens, *Australia* **117 D7** 36 35 S 146 46 E
Overdinkel, *Neths.* **20 D10** 52 14N 7 2 E
Overflakkee, *Neths.* **20 E4** 51 44N 4 10 E
Overijse, *Belgium* **21 G5** 50 47N 4 32 E
Overijssel □, *Neths.* **20 D9** 52 25N 6 35 E
Overijsselsch Kanaal →, *Neths.* **20 C8** 52 31N 6 6 E
Overland, *U.S.A.* **140 F6** 38 41N 90 22W
Overpelt, *Belgium* **21 F6** 51 12N 5 20 E
Overton, *U.S.A.* **145 J12** 36 33N 114 27W
Övertorneå, *Sweden* **12 C17** 66 23N 23 38 E
Ovid, *Colo., U.S.A.* **138 E3** 40 58N 102 23W
Ovid, *Mich., U.S.A.* **141 A12** 43 1N 84 22W
Ovidiopol, *Ukraine* **52 C4** 46 15N 30 30 E
Oviedo, *Spain* **36 B5** 43 25N 5 50W
Oviedo □, *Spain* **36 B5** 43 20N 6 0W
Oviken, *Sweden* **14 A8** 63 0N 14 23 E
Oviksfjällen, *Sweden* **14 B7** 63 0N 13 49 E
Övör Hangay □, *Mongolia* **66 B2** 45 0N 102 30 E
Ovoro, *Nigeria* **101 D6** 5 26N 7 16 E
Ovruch, *Ukraine* **50 F6** 51 25N 28 45 E
Owaka, *N.Z.* **119 G4** 46 27 S 169 40 E
Owando, *Congo* **102 C3** 0 29 S 15 55 E
Owase, *Japan* **63 C8** 34 7N 136 12 E
Owatonna, *U.S.A.* **138 C8** 44 5N 93 14W
Owbeh, *Afghan.* **79 B1** 34 28N 63 10 E
Owego, *U.S.A.* **137 D8** 42 6N 76 16W
Owen, *Australia* **116 C3** 34 15 S 138 32 E
Owen Falls, *Uganda* **106 B3** 0 30N 33 5 E
Owen Mt., *N.Z.* **119 B7** 41 35 S 172 33 E
Owen Sound, *Canada* **128 D3** 44 35N 80 55W
Owen Stanley Ra., *Papua N. G.* **120 E4** 8 30 S 147 0 E
Owendo, *Gabon* **102 B1** 0 17N 9 30 E
Owens →, *U.S.A.* **144 J9** 36 32N 117 59W
Owens L., *U.S.A.* **145 J9** 36 26N 117 57W
Owensboro, *U.S.A.* **141 G9** 37 46N 87 7W

246 Owensville


Owensville, *Ind., U.S.A.* 141 F9 38 16N 87 41W
Owensville, *Mo., U.S.A.* 140 F5 38 21N 91 30W
Owenton, *U.S.A.* 141 F12 38 32N 84 50W
Owerri, *Nigeria* 101 D6 5 29N 7 0E
Owhango, *N.Z.* 118 F4 39 0S 175 23E
Owingsville, *U.S.A.* 141 F13 38 9N 83 46W
Owl →, *Canada* 131 B10 57 51N 92 44W
Owo, *Nigeria* 101 D6 7 10N 5 39E
Owosso, *U.S.A.* 141 B12 43 0N 84 10W
Owyhee, *U.S.A.* 142 F5 41 57N 116 6W
Owyhee →, *U.S.A.* 142 E5 43 49N 117 2W
Owyhee, L., *U.S.A.* 142 E5 43 38N 117 14W
Ox Mts., *Ireland* 19 B3 54 6N 9 0W
Oxapampa, *Peru* 156 C2 10 33S 75 26W
Oxelösund, *Sweden* 15 F11 58 43N 17 15E
Oxford, *N.Z.* 119 D7 43 18S 172 11E
Oxford, *U.K.* 17 F6 51 45N 1 15W
Oxford, *Iowa, U.S.A.* 140 C5 41 43N 91 47W
Oxford, *Mich., U.S.A.* 141 B13 42 49N 83 16W
Oxford, *Miss., U.S.A.* 139 H10 34 22N 89 31W
Oxford, *N.C., U.S.A.* 135 G6 36 19N 78 35W
Oxford, *Ohio, U.S.A.* 141 E12 39 31N 84 45W
Oxford L., *Canada* 131 C9 54 51N 95 37W
Oxfordshire □, *U.K.* 17 F6 51 45N 1 15W
Oxía, *Greece* 45 F3 38 16N 21 5E
Oxílithos, *Greece* 45 F6 38 35N 24 7E
Oxley, *Australia* 116 C6 34 11S 144 6E
Oxnard, *U.S.A.* 145 L7 34 12N 119 11W
Oxus = Amudarya →, *Uzbekistan* 56 E6 43 40N 59 0E
Oya, *Malaysia* 75 B4 2 55N 111 55E
Oyabe, *Japan* 63 A8 36 47N 136 56E
Oyama, *Japan* 63 A11 36 18N 139 48E
Oyana, *Japan* 62 E2 32 32N 130 30E
Oyapock →, *Fr. Guiana* 153 C7 4 8N 51 40W
Oyem, *Gabon* 102 B2 1 34N 11 31E
Oyen, *Canada* 131 C6 51 22N 110 28W
Øyeren, *Norway* 14 E5 59 50N 11 15E
Oykel →, *U.K.* 18 D4 57 55N 4 26W
Oymyakon, *Russia* 57 C15 63 25N 142 44E
Oyo, *Nigeria* 101 D5 7 46N 3 56E
Oyo □, *Nigeria* 101 D5 8 15N 3 30E
Oyón, *Peru* 156 C2 10 37S 76 47W
Oyonnax, *France* 25 B9 46 16N 5 40E
Oyster Bay, *U.S.A.* 137 F11 40 52N 73 32W
Oytal, *Kazakhstan* 55 B6 42 54N 73 17E
Oyūbari, *Japan* 60 C11 43 1N 142 5E
Özalp, *Turkey* 89 D10 38 39N 43 59E
Ozamiz, *Phil.* 71 G4 8 15N 123 50E
Ozark, *Ala., U.S.A.* 135 K3 31 28N 85 39W
Ozark, *Ark., U.S.A.* 139 H8 35 29N 93 50W
Ozark, *Mo., U.S.A.* 139 G8 37 1N 93 12W
Ozark Plateau, *U.S.A.* 139 G9 37 20N 91 40W
Ozarks, L. of the, *U.S.A.* 140 F4 38 12N 92 38W
Ózd, *Hungary* 31 C13 48 14N 20 15E
Ozërnyy, *Russia* 54 F7 51 8N 60 50E
Ozette L., *U.S.A.* 144 B2 48 6N 124 38W
Ozieri, *Italy* 40 B2 40 35N 9 0E
Ozimek, *Poland* 47 E5 50 41N 18 11E
Ozona, *U.S.A.* 139 K4 30 43N 101 12W
Ozorków, *Poland* 47 D6 51 57N 19 16E
Ozren, *Bos.-H.* 42 D3 43 55N 18 29E
Ozu, *Ehime, Japan* 62 D4 33 30N 132 33E
Ozu, *Kumamoto, Japan* 62 E2 32 52N 130 52E
Ozuluama, *Mexico* 147 C5 21 40N 97 50W
Ozun, *Romania* 46 D6 45 47N 25 50E
Ozurgety, *Georgia* 53 F10 41 55N 42 2E

## P

P.K. le Roux Dam, *S. Africa* 104 E3 30 4S 24 40E
Pa, *Burkina Faso* 100 C4 11 33N 3 19W
Pa-an, *Burma* 78 G6 16 51N 97 40E
Pa Mong Dam, *Thailand* 76 D4 18 0N 102 22E
Paagoumène, *N. Cal.* 121 T18 20 29S 164 11E
Paal, *Belgium* 21 F6 51 2N 5 10E
Paama, *Vanuatu* 121 F6 16 28S 168 14E
Paamiut = Frederikshåb, *Greenland* 6 C5 62 0N 49 43W
Paar →, *Germany* 27 G6 48 13N 10 59E
Paarl, *S. Africa* 104 E2 33 45S 18 56E
Paatsi →, *Russia* 12 B20 68 55N 29 0E
Paauilo, *U.S.A.* 132 H17 20 2N 155 22W
Pab Hills, *Pakistan* 79 D2 26 30N 66 45E
Pabianice, *Poland* 47 D6 51 40N 19 20E
Pabna, *Bangla.* 78 C2 24 1N 89 18E
Pabo, *Uganda* 106 B3 3 1N 32 10E
Pacaás Novos, Serra dos, *Brazil* 157 C5 10 45S 64 15W
Pacaipampa, *Peru* 156 B2 5 35S 79 39W
Pacaja →, *Brazil* 154 B1 1 56S 50 50W
Pacajus, *Brazil* 154 B4 4 10S 38 31W
Pacaraima, Sierra, *Venezuela* 153 C5 4 0N 62 30W
Pacarán, *Peru* 156 C2 12 50S 76 3W
Pacaraos, *Peru* 156 C2 11 12S 76 42W
Pacasmayo, *Peru* 156 B2 7 20S 79 35W
Paceco, *Italy* 40 E5 37 59N 12 32E
Pachacamac, *Peru* 156 C2 12 14S 77 53W
Pachhar, *India* 80 G7 24 40N 77 42E
Pachino, *Italy* 41 F8 36 43N 15 4E
Pachitea →, *Peru* 156 B3 8 46S 74 33W
Pachiza, *Peru* 156 B2 7 16S 76 46W
Pacho, *Colombia* 152 B3 5 8N 74 10W
Pachora, *India* 82 D2 20 38N 75 29E
Pachuca, *Mexico* 147 C5 20 10N 98 40W
Pacific, *Canada* 130 C3 54 48N 128 28W
Pacific, *U.S.A.* 140 F6 38 29N 90 45W
Pacific-Antarctic Ridge, *Pac. Oc.* 123 M16 43 0S 115 0W
Pacific Grove, *U.S.A.* 144 J5 36 38N 121 56W
Pacific Ocean, *Pac. Oc.* 123 G14 10 0N 140 0W
Pacifica, *U.S.A.* 144 H4 37 36N 122 30W
Pacitan, *Indonesia* 75 D4 8 12S 111 7E
Packsaddle, *Australia* 116 A4 30 36S 141 58E
Packwood, *U.S.A.* 144 D5 46 36N 121 40W
Pacov, *Czech.* 30 B8 49 27N 15 0E
Pacsa, *Hungary* 31 E10 46 44N 17 2E
Pacuí →, *Brazil* 155 E2 16 46S 45 1W
Paczków, *Poland* 47 E4 50 28N 17 0E
Padaido, Kepulauan, *Indonesia* 73 B5 1 5S 138 0E
Padang, *Indonesia* 74 C2 1 0S 100 20E
Padang Endau, *Malaysia* 74 B2 2 40N 103 38E
Padangpanjang, *Indonesia* 74 C2 0 40S 100 20E
Padangsidempuan, *Indonesia* 74 B1 1 30N 99 15E
Padangtikar, *Indonesia* 75 C3 0 44S 109 15E
Padatchuang, *Burma* 78 F5 19 46N 94 48E
Padauari →, *Brazil* 153 D5 0 15S 64 5W
Padborg, *Denmark* 15 K3 54 49N 9 21E
Padcaya, *Bolivia* 157 E5 21 52S 64 48W
Paddockwood, *Canada* 131 C7 53 30N 105 30W
Paderborn, *Germany* 26 D4 51 42N 8 44E
Padeşul, *Romania* 46 D3 45 40N 22 22E
Padilla, *Bolivia* 157 D5 19 19S 64 20W
Padina, *Romania* 46 E8 44 50N 27 8E
Padloping Island, *Canada* 127 B13 67 0N 62 50W
Padma →, *Bangla.* 78 D3 23 22N 90 32E
Padmanabhapuram, *India* 83 K3 8 16N 77 17E
Pádova, *Italy* 39 C8 45 24N 11 52E
Padra, *India* 80 H5 22 15N 73 7E
Padrauna, *India* 81 F10 26 54N 83 59E
Padre Burgos, *Phil.* 71 F5 10 1N 125 0E
Padre I., *U.S.A.* 139 M6 27 10N 97 25W
Padro, Mte., *France* 25 F12 42 28N 8 59E
Padrón, *Spain* 36 C2 42 41N 8 39W
Padstow, *U.K.* 17 G3 50 33N 4 57W
Padua = Pádova, *Italy* 39 C8 45 24N 11 52E
Paducah, *Ky., U.S.A.* 134 G1 37 5N 88 37W
Paducah, *Tex., U.S.A.* 139 H4 34 1N 100 18W
Padul, *Spain* 37 H7 37 1N 3 38W
Padula, *Italy* 41 B8 40 20N 15 40E
Padwa, *India* 82 E6 18 27N 82 47E
Paekakariki, *N.Z.* 118 G3 40 59S 174 58E
Paengaroa, *N.Z.* 118 D5 37 49S 176 29E
Paengnyong-do, *S. Korea* 67 F13 37 57N 124 40E
Paeroa, *N.Z.* 118 D4 37 23S 175 41E
Paesana, *Italy* 38 D4 44 40N 7 18E
Paete, *Phil.* 70 D3 14 23N 121 29E
Pafúri, *Mozam.* 105 C5 22 28S 31 17E
Pag, *Croatia* 39 D11 44 30N 14 50E
Paga, *Ghana* 101 C4 11 1N 1 8W
Pagadian, *Phil.* 71 H4 7 55N 123 30E
Pagai Selatan, P., *Indonesia* 74 C2 3 0S 100 15E
Pagai Utara, *Indonesia* 74 C2 2 35S 100 0E
Pagalu = Annobón, *Atl. Oc.* 93 G4 1 25S 5 36E
Pagastikós Kólpos, *Greece* 44 E5 39 15N 23 0E
Pagatan, *Indonesia* 75 C5 3 33S 115 59E
Page, *Ariz., U.S.A.* 143 H8 36 57N 111 27W
Page, *N. Dak., U.S.A.* 138 B6 47 10N 97 34W
Paglieta, *Italy* 39 F11 42 10N 14 30E
Pagny-sur-Moselle, *France* 23 D13 48 59N 6 2E
Pago Pago, *Amer. Samoa* 121 X24 14 16S 170 43W
Pagosa Springs, *U.S.A.* 143 H10 37 16N 107 1W
Pagwa River, *Canada* 128 B2 50 2N 85 14W
Pahala, *U.S.A.* 132 J17 19 12N 155 29W
Pahang □, *Malaysia* 74 B2 3 30N 102 45E
Pahang →, *Malaysia* 77 L4 3 30N 103 9E
Pahia Pt., *N.Z.* 119 G2 46 20S 167 41E
Pahiatua, *N.Z.* 118 G4 40 27S 175 50E
Pahokee, *U.S.A.* 135 M5 26 50N 80 40W
Pahrump, *U.S.A.* 145 J11 36 12N 115 59W
Pahute Mesa, *U.S.A.* 144 H10 37 20N 116 45W
Pai, *Thailand* 76 C2 19 19N 98 27E
Paia, *U.S.A.* 132 H16 20 54N 156 22W
Paicines, *U.S.A.* 144 J5 36 44N 121 17W
Paide, *Estonia* 50 B4 58 57N 25 31E
Paignton, *U.K.* 17 G4 50 26N 3 33W
Paiján, *Peru* 156 B2 7 42S 79 20W
Päijänne, *Finland* 13 F18 61 30N 25 30E
Paimbœuf, *France* 22 E4 47 17N 2 3W
Paimpol, *France* 22 D3 48 48N 3 4W
Painan, *Indonesia* 74 C2 1 21S 100 34E
Painesville, *U.S.A.* 136 E3 41 43N 81 15W
Paint Hills = Nouveau Comptoir, *Canada* 128 B4 53 0N 78 49W
Paint L., *Canada* 131 B9 55 28N 97 57W
Paint Rock, *U.S.A.* 139 K5 31 31N 99 55W
Painted Desert, *U.S.A.* 143 J8 36 0N 111 0W
Paintsville, *U.S.A.* 134 G4 37 49N 82 48W
País Vasco □, *Spain* 34 C2 42 50N 2 45W
Paisley, *Canada* 136 B3 44 18N 81 16W
Paisley, *U.K.* 18 F4 55 51N 4 27W
Paisley, *U.S.A.* 142 E3 42 42N 120 32W
Paita, *N. Cal.* 121 V20 22 8S 166 22E
Paita, *Peru* 156 B1 5 11S 81 9W
Paiva →, *Portugal* 36 D2 41 4N 8 16W
Paizhou, *China* 69 B9 30 12N 113 55E
Pajares, *Spain* 36 B5 43 1N 5 46W
Pajares, Puerto de, *Spain* 36 C5 42 58N 5 46W
Pajeczno, *Poland* 47 D6 51 10N 19 0E
Pak Lay, *Laos* 76 C3 18 15N 101 27E
Pak Phanang, *Thailand* 77 H3 8 21N 100 12E
Pak Sane, *Laos* 76 C4 18 22N 103 39E
Pak Song, *Laos* 76 E6 15 11N 106 14E
Pak Suong, *Laos* 76 C4 19 58N 102 15E
Pakala, *India* 83 H4 13 29N 79 8E
Pakaraima Mts., *Guyana* 153 B5 6 0N 60 0W
Pakenham, *Australia* 117 E6 38 6S 145 30E
Pákhnes, *Greece* 32 D6 35 16N 24 4E
Pakhtakor, *Uzbekistan* 55 C2 40 2N 65 46E
Pakistan ■, *Asia* 79 C3 30 0N 70 0E
Pakistan, East = Bangladesh ■, *Asia* 78 C3 24 0N 90 0E
Pakkading, *Laos* 76 C4 18 19N 103 59E
Pakokku, *Burma* 78 E5 21 20N 95 0E
Pakosc, *Poland* 47 C5 52 48N 18 6E
Pakpattan, *Pakistan* 79 C4 30 25N 73 27E
Pakrac, *Croatia* 42 B2 45 27N 17 12E
Paks, *Hungary* 31 E11 46 38N 18 55E
Pakse, *Laos* 76 E5 15 5N 105 52E
Paktīā □, *Afghan.* 79 B3 33 0N 69 15E
Paktīkā □, *Afghan.* 79 B3 32 30N 69 0E
Pakwach, *Uganda* 106 B3 2 28N 31 27E
Pala, *Chad* 97 G3 9 25N 15 5E
Pala, *U.S.A.* 145 M9 33 22N 117 5W
Pala, *Zaïre* 106 D2 6 45S 29 30E
Palabek, *Uganda* 106 B3 3 22N 32 33E
Palacios, *U.S.A.* 139 L6 28 42N 96 13W
Palafrugell, *Spain* 34 D8 41 55N 3 10E
Palagiano, *Italy* 41 B10 40 35N 17 2E
Palagonía, *Italy* 41 E7 37 20N 14 43E
Palagruža, *Croatia* 39 F13 42 24N 16 15E
Palaiokastron, *Greece* 45 J8 35 12N 26 18E
Palaiókastron, *Kríti, Greece* 32 D8 35 12N 26 15E
Palaiokhóra, *Greece* 32 D5 35 16N 23 39E
Pálairos, *Greece* 45 F2 38 45N 20 51E
Palakol, *India* 83 F5 16 31N 81 46E
Palam, *India* 82 E3 19 0N 77 0E
Palamás, *Greece* 44 E4 39 26N 22 4E
Palamós, *Spain* 34 D8 41 50N 3 10E
Palampur, *India* 80 C7 32 10N 76 30E
Palana, *Australia* 114 F4 39 45S 147 55E
Palana, *Russia* 57 D16 59 10N 159 59E
Palanan, *Phil.* 70 C4 17 8N 122 29E
Palanan Bay, *Phil.* 70 C4 17 9N 122 27E
Palanan Pt., *Phil.* 70 C4 17 17N 122 30E
Palandri, *Pakistan* 81 C5 33 42N 73 40E
Palangkaraya, *Indonesia* 75 C4 2 16S 113 56E
Palani, *India* 83 J3 10 30N 77 30E
Palani Hills, *India* 83 J3 10 14N 77 33E
Palanpur, *India* 80 G5 24 10N 72 25E
Palapye, *Botswana* 104 C4 22 30S 27 7E
Palar →, *India* 83 H5 12 27N 80 13E
Palas, *Pakistan* 81 B5 35 4N 73 14E
Palatine, *U.S.A.* 141 B8 42 7N 88 3W
Palatka, *Russia* 57 C16 60 6N 150 54E
Palatka, *U.S.A.* 135 L5 29 39N 81 38W
Palau = Belau ■, *Pac. Oc.* 122 G5 7 30N 134 30E
Palawan, *Phil.* 71 G2 9 30N 118 30E
Palawan □, *Phil.* 71 G2 10 0N 119 0E
Palawan Passage, *Phil.* 71 G1 10 0N 118 0E
Palayankottai, *India* 83 K3 8 45N 77 45E
Palazzo, Pte., *France* 25 F12 42 28N 8 30E
Palazzo San Gervásio, *Italy* 41 B8 40 53N 15 58E
Palazzolo Acreide, *Italy* 41 E7 37 4N 14 54E
Palca, *Chile* 156 D4 19 7S 69 9W
Paldiski, *Estonia* 50 B4 59 23N 24 9E
Pale, *Bos.-H.* 42 D3 43 50N 18 38E
Palel, *India* 78 C5 24 27N 94 2E
Paleleh, *Indonesia* 72 A2 1 10N 121 50E
Palembang, *Indonesia* 74 C2 3 0S 104 50E
Palena →, *Chile* 160 B2 43 50S 73 50W
Palena, L., *Chile* 160 B2 43 55S 71 40W
Palencia, *Spain* 36 C6 42 1N 4 34W
Palencia □, *Spain* 36 C6 42 31N 4 33W
Paleokastrítsa, *Greece* 32 A3 39 40N 19 41E
Paleometokho, *Cyprus* 32 D12 35 7N 33 11E
Palermo, *Colombia* 152 C2 2 54N 75 26W
Palermo, *Italy* 40 D6 38 8N 13 20E
Palermo, *U.S.A.* 142 G3 39 26N 121 33W
Palestine, *Asia* 91 D4 32 0N 35 0E
Palestine, *U.S.A.* 139 K7 31 46N 95 38W
Palestrina, *Italy* 40 A5 41 50N 12 52E
Paletwa, *Burma* 78 E4 21 10N 92 50E
Palghat, *India* 83 J3 10 46N 76 42E
Palgrave, Mt., *Australia* 112 D2 23 22S 115 58E
Pali, *India* 80 G5 25 50N 73 20E
Palin, Mt., *Malaysia* 75 A5 6 10N 117 10E
Palinit, *Phil.* 70 E5 12 15N 124 20E
Palinuro, C., *Italy* 41 B8 40 1N 15 14E
Palisade, *U.S.A.* 138 E4 40 21N 101 7W
Paliseul, *Belgium* 21 J6 49 54N 5 8E
Palitana, *India* 80 J4 21 32N 71 49E
Palizada, *Mexico* 147 D6 18 18N 92 8W
Palizzi, *Italy* 41 E8 37 58N 15 59E
Palk Bay, *Asia* 83 K4 9 30N 79 15E
Palk Strait, *Asia* 83 K4 10 0N 79 45E
Palkānah, *Iraq* 84 C5 35 49N 44 26E
Palkonda, *India* 82 E6 18 36N 83 48E
Palkonda Ra., *India* 83 H4 13 50N 79 20E
Palla Road = Dinokwe, *Botswana* 104 C4 23 29S 26 37E
Pallanza = Verbánia, *Italy* 38 C5 45 56N 8 43E
Pallasovka, *Russia* 51 F15 50 4N 47 0E
Palleru →, *India* 82 F5 16 45N 80 2E
Pallisa, *Uganda* 106 B3 1 12N 33 43E
Palliser, C., *N.Z.* 118 H4 41 37S 175 14E
Palliser B., *N.Z.* 118 H4 41 26S 175 5E
Pallu, *India* 80 E6 28 59N 74 14E
Palm Beach, *U.S.A.* 135 M6 26 43N 80 2W
Palm Desert, *U.S.A.* 145 M10 33 43N 116 22W
Palm Is., *Australia* 114 B4 18 40S 146 35E
Palm Springs, *U.S.A.* 145 M10 33 50N 116 33W
Palma, *Mozam.* 107 E5 10 46S 40 29E
Palma →, *Brazil* 155 D2 12 33S 47 52W
Palma, B. de, *Spain* 33 B9 39 30N 2 39E
Palma de Mallorca, *Spain* 33 B9 39 35N 2 39E
Palma del Río, *Spain* 37 H5 37 43N 5 17W
Palma di Montechiaro, *Italy* 40 E6 37 12N 13 46E
Palma Soriano, *Cuba* 148 B4 20 15N 76 0W
Palmanova, *Italy* 39 C10 45 54N 13 18E
Palmares, *Brazil* 154 C4 8 41S 35 28W
Palmarito, *Venezuela* 152 B3 7 37N 70 10W
Palmarola, *Italy* 40 B5 40 57N 12 50E
Palmas, *Brazil* 159 B5 26 29S 52 0W
Palmas, C., *Liberia* 100 E3 4 27N 7 46W
Pálmas, G. di, *Italy* 40 C1 39 0N 8 30E
Palmas de Monte Alto, *Brazil* 155 D3 14 16S 43 10W
Palmdale, *U.S.A.* 145 L8 34 35N 118 7W
Palmeira, *Brazil* 155 G2 25 25S 50 0W
Palmeira dos Índios, *Brazil* 154 C4 9 25S 36 37W
Palmeirais, *Brazil* 154 C3 6 0S 43 0W
Palmeiras →, *Brazil* 155 D2 12 22S 47 8W
Palmeirinhas, Pta. das, *Angola* 103 D2 9 2S 12 57E
Palmela, *Portugal* 37 G2 38 32N 8 57W
Palmelo, *Brazil* 155 E2 17 20S 48 27W
Palmer, *U.S.A.* 126 B5 61 36N 149 7W
Palmer →, *Australia* 114 B3 16 0S 142 26E
Palmer Arch., *Antarctica* 7 C17 64 15S 65 0W
Palmer Lake, *U.S.A.* 138 F2 39 7N 104 55W
Palmer Land, *Antarctica* 7 D18 73 0S 63 0W
Palmerston, *Canada* 136 C4 43 50N 80 51W
Palmerston, *N.Z.* 119 F5 45 29S 170 43E
Palmerston North, *N.Z.* 118 G4 40 21S 175 39E
Palmerton, *U.S.A.* 137 F9 40 48N 75 37W
Palmetto, *U.S.A.* 135 M4 27 31N 82 34W
Palmi, *Italy* 41 D8 38 21N 15 51E
Palmira, *Argentina* 158 C2 32 59S 68 34W
Palmira, *Colombia* 152 C2 3 32N 76 16W
Palmyra = Tudmur, *Syria* 84 C3 34 36N 38 15E
Palmyra, *Ill., U.S.A.* 140 E6 39 26N 90 0W
Palmyra, *Mo., U.S.A.* 140 E5 39 48N 91 32W
Palmyra, *N.Y., U.S.A.* 136 C7 43 5N 77 18W
Palmyra, *Wis., U.S.A.* 141 B8 42 52N 88 36W
Palmyra Is., *Pac. Oc.* 123 G11 5 52N 162 5W
Palo, *Phil.* 71 F5 11 10N 124 59E
Palo Alto, *U.S.A.* 144 H4 37 27N 122 10W
Palo del Colle, *Italy* 41 A9 41 4N 16 43E
Palo Verde, *U.S.A.* 145 M12 33 26N 114 44W
Palombara Sabina, *Italy* 39 F9 42 4N 12 45E
Palompon, *Phil.* 71 F5 11 3N 124 23E
Palopo, *Indonesia* 72 B2 3 0S 120 16E
Palos, C. de, *Spain* 35 H4 37 38N 0 40W
Palos Verdes, *U.S.A.* 145 M8 33 48N 118 23W
Palos Verdes, Pt., *U.S.A.* 145 M8 33 43N 118 26W
Palouse, *U.S.A.* 142 C5 46 55N 117 4W
Palpa, *Peru* 156 C2 14 30S 75 15W
Palparara, *Australia* 114 C3 24 47S 141 28E
Pålsboda, *Sweden* 14 E9 59 3N 15 22E
Palu, *Indonesia* 72 B1 1 0S 119 52E
Palu, *Turkey* 49 G7 38 45N 40 0E
Paluan, *Phil.* 70 E3 13 26N 120 29E
Palwal, *India* 80 E7 28 8N 77 19E
Pama, *Burkina Faso* 101 C5 11 19N 0 44E
Pamanukan, *Indonesia* 75 D3 6 16S 107 49E
Pamban I., *India* 83 K4 9 15N 79 20E
Pambuhan, *Phil.* 70 E4 13 59N 123 5E
Pamekasan, *Indonesia* 75 D4 7 10S 113 28E
Pamiers, *France* 24 E5 43 7N 1 39E
Pamir →, *Tajikistan* 55 E6 37 1N 72 41E
Pamirs, *Tajikistan* 55 E6 37 40N 73 0E
Pamlico →, *U.S.A.* 135 H7 35 20N 76 28W
Pamlico Sd., *U.S.A.* 135 H8 35 20N 76 0W
Pampa, *U.S.A.* 139 H4 35 32N 100 58W
Pampa de Agma, *Argentina* 160 B3 43 45S 69 40W
Pampa de las Salinas, *Argentina* 158 C2 32 1S 66 58W
Pampa Grande, *Bolivia* 157 D5 18 5S 64 6W
Pampa Hermosa, *Peru* 156 B2 7 7S 75 4W
Pampanga □, *Phil.* 70 D3 15 4N 120 40E
Pampanua, *Indonesia* 72 B2 4 16S 120 8E
Pamparato, *Italy* 38 D4 44 16N 7 54E
Pampas, *Argentina* 158 D3 35 0S 63 0W
Pampas, *Peru* 156 C3 12 20S 74 50W
Pampas →, *Peru* 156 C3 13 24S 73 12W
Pamphylia, *Turkey* 88 E4 37 0N 31 20E
Pamplona, *Colombia* 152 B3 7 23N 72 39W
Pamplona, *Phil.* 70 B3 18 31N 121 20E
Pamplona, *Spain* 34 C3 42 48N 1 38W
Pampoenpoort, *S. Africa* 104 E3 31 3S 22 40E
Pamukkale, *Turkey* 88 E3 37 57N 28 50E
Pan Xian, *China* 68 E5 25 46N 104 38E
Pana, *U.S.A.* 140 E7 39 23N 89 5W
Panabo, *Phil.* 71 H5 7 19N 125 42E
Panaca, *U.S.A.* 143 H6 37 47N 114 23W
Panagyurishte, *Bulgaria* 43 E9 42 30N 24 15E
Panaitan, *Indonesia* 74 D3 6 36S 105 12E
Panaji, *India* 83 G1 15 25N 73 50E
Panamá, *Panama* 148 E4 9 0N 79 25W
Panama ■, *Cent. Amer.* 148 E4 8 48N 79 55W
Panamá, G. de, *Panama* 148 E4 8 4N 79 20W
Panama Canal, *Panama* 148 E4 9 10N 79 37W
Panama City, *U.S.A.* 135 K3 30 10N 85 40W
Panamint Range, *U.S.A.* 145 J9 36 20N 117 20W
Panamint Springs, *U.S.A.* 145 J9 36 20N 117 28W
Panão, *Peru* 156 B2 9 55S 75 55W
Panaon I., *Phil.* 71 F5 10 3N 125 13E
Panare, *Thailand* 77 J3 6 51N 101 30E
Panarea, *Italy* 41 D8 38 38N 15 3E
Panaro →, *Italy* 38 D8 44 55N 11 25E
Panarukan, *Indonesia* 75 D4 7 42S 113 56E
Panay, *Phil.* 71 F4 11 10N 122 30E
Panay, G., *Phil.* 71 F4 11 0N 122 30E
Pancake Range, *U.S.A.* 143 G6 38 30N 115 50W
Pančevo, *Serbia* 42 C5 44 52N 20 41E
Panciu, *Romania* 46 D8 45 54N 27 8E
Pancol, *Phil.* 71 F2 10 52N 119 25E
Pancorbo, Paso, *Spain* 34 C1 42 32N 3 5W
Pandan, *Antique, Phil.* 71 F4 11 45N 122 10E
Pandan, *Catanduanes, Phil.* 70 D5 14 3N 124 10E
Pandan Bay, *Phil.* 71 F4 11 43N 122 0E
Pandegelang, *Indonesia* 74 D3 6 25S 106 5E
Pandharpur, *India* 82 F2 17 41N 75 20E
Pandhurna, *India* 82 D4 21 36N 78 35E
Pandilla, *Spain* 34 D1 41 32N 3 43W
Pando, *Uruguay* 159 C4 34 44S 56 0W
Pando □, *Bolivia* 156 C4 11 20S 67 40W
Pando, L. = Hope, L., *Australia* 115 D2 28 24S 139 18E
Pandokrátor, *Greece* 32 A3 39 45N 19 50E
Pandora, *Costa Rica* 148 E3 9 43N 83 3W
Pandu, *Zaïre* 102 B3 4 59N 19 16E
Panevėžys, *Lithuania* 50 D4 55 42N 24 25E
Panfilov, *Kazakhstan* 56 E8 44 10N 80 0E
Panfilovo, *Russia* 51 F13 50 25N 42 46E
Panga, *Zaïre* 106 B2 1 52N 26 18E
Pangaíon Óros, *Greece* 44 D6 40 50N 24 0E
Pangala, *Congo* 102 C2 4 1S 13 52E
Pangalanes, Canal des, *Madag.* 105 C8 22 48S 47 50E
Pangani, *Tanzania* 106 D4 5 25S 38 58E
Pangani □, *Tanzania* 106 D4 5 25S 39 0E
Pangani →, *Tanzania* 106 D4 5 26S 38 58E
Panganiban, *Phil.* 70 E5 13 55N 124 18E
Panganuran, *Phil.* 71 G4 8 2N 122 22E
Pangasinan □, *Phil.* 70 D3 15 55N 120 20E
Pangfou = Bengbu, *China* 67 H9 32 58N 117 20E
Pangil, *Zaïre* 106 C2 3 10S 26 35E
Pangkah, Tanjung, *Indonesia* 75 D4 6 51S 112 33E
Pangkai, *Burma* 78 D7 22 40N 98 40E
Pangkajene, *Indonesia* 72 B1 4 46S 119 34E
Pangkalanbrandan, *Indonesia* 74 B1 4 1N 98 20E
Pangkalanbuun, *Indonesia* 75 C4 2 41S 111 37E
Pangkalansusu, *Indonesia* 74 B1 4 2N 98 13E
Pangkalpinang, *Indonesia* 74 C3 2 0S 106 0E
Pangkoh, *Indonesia* 75 C4 3 5S 114 8E
Panglao, *Phil.* 71 G4 9 35N 123 45E
Panglao I., *Phil.* 71 G4 9 35N 123 48E
Pangnirtung, *Canada* 127 B13 66 8N 65 54W
Pangrango, *Indonesia* 74 D3 6 46S 107 1E
Pangsau Pass, *Burma* 78 B6 27 15N 96 10E
Pangtara, *Burma* 78 E6 20 57N 96 40E

Piteşti 249


Petroşeni, *Romania* **46 D4** 45 28N 23 20 E
Petrova Gora, *Croatia* **39 C12** 45 15N 15 45 E
Petrovac, *Montenegro* **42 E3** 42 13N 18 57 E
Petrovac, *Serbia* **42 C6** 44 22N 21 26 E
Petrovaradin, *Serbia* **42 B4** 45 16N 19 55 E
Petrovsk, *Russia* **51 E14** 52 22N 45 19 E
Petrovsk-Zabaykalskiy, *Russia* **57 D11** 51 20N 108 55 E
Petrovskoye = Svetlograd, *Russia* **53 D10** 45 25N 42 58 E
Petrovskoye, *Russia* **54 E5** 53 37N 56 23 E
Petrozavodsk, *Russia* **48 B5** 61 41N 34 20 E
Petrus Steyn, *S. Africa* **105 D4** 27 38 S 28 8 E
Petrusburg, *S. Africa* **104 D4** 29 4 S 25 26 E
Pettitts, *Australia* **117 C8** 34 56 S 148 10 E
Petukhovka, *Belorussia* **50 E7** 53 42N 30 54 E
Peumo, *Chile* **158 C1** 34 21 S 71 12W
Peureulak, *Indonesia* **74 B1** 4 48N 97 45 E
Peusangan →, *Indonesia* **74 A1** 5 16N 96 51 E
Pevek, *Russia* **57 C18** 69 41N 171 19 E
Peveragno, *Italy* **38 D4** 44 20N 7 37 E
Peyrehorade, *France* **24 E2** 43 34N 1 7W
Peyruis, *France* **25 D9** 44 1N 5 56 E
Pézenas, *France* **24 E7** 43 28N 3 24 E
Pezinok, *Slovak Rep.* **31 C10** 48 17N 17 17 E
Pfaffenhofen, *Germany* **27 G7** 48 31N 11 31 E
Pfäffikon, *Switz.* **29 B7** 47 13N 8 46 E
Pfarrkirchen, *Germany* **27 G8** 48 25N 12 57 E
Pfeffenhausen, *Germany* **27 G7** 48 40N 11 58 E
Pforzheim, *Germany* **27 G4** 48 53N 8 43 E
Pfullendorf, *Germany* **27 H5** 47 55N 9 15 E
Pfungstadt, *Germany* **27 F4** 49 47N 8 36 E
Phaistós, *Greece* **32 D6** 35 2N 24 50 E
Phala, *Botswana* **104 C4** 23 45 S 26 50 E
Phalera = Phulera, *India* **80 F6** 26 52N 75 16 E
Phalodi, *India* **80 F5** 27 12N 72 24 E
Phalsbourg, *France* **23 D14** 48 46N 7 15 E
Phan, *Thailand* **76 C2** 19 28N 99 43 E
Phan Rang, *Vietnam* **77 G7** 11 34N 109 0 E
Phan Ri = Hoa Da, *Vietnam* **77 G7** 11 16N 108 40 E
Phan Thiet, *Vietnam* **77 G7** 11 1N 108 9 E
Phanae, *Greece* **45 F7** 38 8N 25 57 E
Phanat Nikhom, *Thailand* **76 F3** 13 27N 101 11 E
Phangan, Ko, *Thailand* **77 H3** 9 45N 100 0 E
Phangnga, *Thailand* **77 H2** 8 28N 98 30 E
Phanh Bho Ho Chi Minh, *Vietnam* **77 G6** 10 58N 106 40 E
Phanom Sarakham, *Thailand* **76 F3** 13 45N 101 21 E
Pharenda, *India* **81 F10** 27 5N 83 17 E
Phatthalung, *Thailand* **77 J3** 7 39N 100 6 E
Phayao, *Thailand* **76 C2** 19 11N 99 55 E
Phelps, *N.Y., U.S.A.* **136 D7** 42 58N 77 3W
Phelps, *Wis., U.S.A.* **138 B10** 46 4N 89 5W
Phelps L., *Canada* **131 B8** 59 15N 103 15W
Phenix City, *U.S.A.* **135 J3** 32 28N 85 0W
Phet Buri, *Thailand* **76 F2** 13 1N 99 55 E
Phetchabun, *Thailand* **76 D3** 16 25N 101 8 E
Phetchabun, Thiu Khao, *Thailand* **76 E3** 16 0N 101 20 E
Phetchaburi = Phet Buri, *Thailand* **76 F2** 13 1N 99 55 E
Phi Phi, Ko, *Thailand* **77 J2** 7 45N 98 46 E
Phiafay, *Laos* **76 E6** 14 48N 106 0 E
Phibun Mangsahan, *Thailand* **76 E5** 15 14N 105 14 E
Phichai, *Thailand* **76 D3** 17 22N 100 10 E
Phichit, *Thailand* **76 D3** 16 26N 100 22 E
Philadelphia, *Miss., U.S.A.* **139 J10** 32 46N 89 7W
Philadelphia, *N.Y., U.S.A.* **137 B9** 44 9N 75 43W
Philadelphia, *Pa., U.S.A.* **137 F9** 39 57N 75 10W
Philip, *U.S.A.* **138 C4** 44 2N 101 40W
Philippeville, *Belgium* **21 H5** 50 12N 4 33 E
Philippi, *Greece* **44 C6** 41 1N 24 16 E
Philippi L., *Australia* **114 C2** 24 20 S 138 55 E
Philippines ■, *Asia* **70 E4** 12 0N 123 0 E
Philippolis, *S. Africa* **104 E4** 30 15 S 25 16 E
Philippopolis = Plovdiv, *Bulgaria* **43 E9** 42 8N 24 44 E
Philipsburg, *Mont., U.S.A.* **142 C7** 46 20N 113 18W
Philipsburg, *Pa., U.S.A.* **136 F6** 40 54N 78 13W
Philipstown, *S. Africa* **104 E3** 30 28 S 24 30 E
Phillip I., *Australia* **117 E6** 38 30 S 145 12 E
Phillips, *Tex., U.S.A.* **139 H4** 35 42N 101 22W
Phillips, *Wis., U.S.A.* **138 C9** 45 42N 90 24W
Phillipsburg, *Kans., U.S.A.* **138 F5** 39 45N 99 19W
Phillipsburg, *N.J., U.S.A.* **137 F9** 40 42N 75 12W
Phillott, *Australia* **115 D4** 27 53 S 145 50 E
Philmont, *U.S.A.* **137 D11** 42 15N 73 39W
Philomath, *U.S.A.* **142 D2** 44 32N 123 22W
Phimai, *Thailand* **76 E4** 15 13N 102 30 E
Phitsanulok, *Thailand* **76 D3** 16 50N 100 12 E
Phnom Dangrek, *Thailand* **76 E5** 14 20N 104 0 E
Phnom Penh, *Cambodia* **77 G5** 11 33N 104 55 E
Phoenix, *Ariz., U.S.A.* **143 K7** 33 27N 112 4W
Phoenix, *N.Y., U.S.A.* **137 C8** 43 14N 76 18W
Phoenix Is., *Kiribati* **122 H10** 3 30 S 172 0W
Phoenixville, *U.S.A.* **137 F9** 40 8N 75 31W
Phon, *Thailand* **76 E4** 15 49N 102 36 E
Phon Tiou, *Laos* **76 D5** 17 53N 104 37 E
Phong →, *Thailand* **76 D4** 16 23N 102 56 E
Phong Saly, *Laos* **76 B4** 21 42N 102 9 E
Phong Tho, *Vietnam* **76 A4** 22 32N 103 21 E
Phonhong, *Laos* **76 C4** 18 30N 102 25 E
Phonum, *Thailand* **77 H2** 8 49N 98 48 E
Phosphate Hill, *Australia* **114 C2** 21 53 S 139 58 E
Photharam, *Thailand* **76 F2** 13 41N 99 51 E
Phra Chedi Sam Ong, *Thailand* **76 E2** 15 16N 98 23 E
Phra Nakhon Si Ayutthaya, *Thailand* **76 E3** 14 25N 100 30 E
Phra Thong, Ko, *Thailand* **77 H2** 9 5N 98 17 E
Phrae, *Thailand* **76 C3** 18 7N 100 9 E
Phrom Phiram, *Thailand* **76 D3** 17 2N 100 12 E
Phrygia, *Turkey* **88 D3** 38 40N 30 0 E
Phu Dien, *Vietnam* **76 C5** 18 58N 105 31 E
Phu Loi, *Laos* **76 B4** 20 14N 103 14 E
Phu Ly, *Vietnam* **76 B5** 20 35N 105 50 E
Phu Tho, *Vietnam* **76 B5** 21 24N 105 13 E
Phuc Yen, *Vietnam* **76 B5** 21 16N 105 45 E
Phuket, *Thailand* **77 J2** 7 52N 98 22 E
Phuket, Ko, *Thailand* **77 J2** 8 0N 98 22 E
Phulbari, *India* **78 C3** 25 55N 90 2 E
Phulera, *India* **80 F6** 26 52N 75 16 E
Phumiphon, Khuan, *Thailand* **76 D2** 17 15N 98 58 E
Phun Phin, *Thailand* **77 H2** 9 7N 99 12 E
Piacá, *Brazil* **154 C2** 7 42 S 47 18W
Piacenza, *Italy* **38 C6** 45 2N 9 42 E
Piaçubaçu, *Brazil* **154 D4** 10 24 S 36 25W
Piádena, *Italy* **38 C7** 45 8N 10 22 E
Piako →, *N.Z.* **118 D4** 37 12 S 175 30 E
Pialba, *Australia* **115 D5** 25 20 S 152 45 E
Pian Cr. →, *Australia* **115 E4** 30 2 S 148 12 E
Piana, *France* **25 F12** 42 15N 8 34 E
Pianella, *Italy* **39 F11** 42 24N 14 5 E
Piangil, *Australia* **116 C5** 35 5 S 143 20 E
Pianoro, *Italy* **39 D8** 44 20N 11 20 E
Pianosa, *Puglia, Italy* **39 F12** 42 12N 15 44 E
Pianosa, *Toscana, Italy* **38 F7** 42 36N 10 4 E
Piapot, *Canada* **131 D7** 49 59N 109 8W
Piare →, *Italy* **39 C9** 45 32N 12 44 E
Pias, *Portugal* **37 G3** 38 1N 7 29W
Piaseczno, *Poland* **47 C8** 52 5N 21 2 E
Piaski, *Poland* **47 D9** 51 8N 22 52 E
Piastów, *Poland* **47 C7** 52 12N 20 48 E
Piatã, *Brazil* **155 D3** 13 9 S 41 48W
Piatra, *Romania* **46 F6** 43 51N 25 9 E
Piatra Neamţ, *Romania* **46 C7** 46 56N 26 21 E
Piatra Olt, *Romania* **46 E5** 44 22N 24 16 E
Piauí □, *Brazil* **154 C3** 7 0 S 43 0W
Piaui →, *Brazil* **154 C3** 6 38 S 42 42W
Piave →, *Italy* **39 C9** 45 32N 12 44 E
Piazza Ármerina, *Italy* **41 E7** 37 21N 14 20 E
Pibor →, *Sudan* **95 F3** 7 35N 33 0 E
Pibor Post, *Sudan* **95 F3** 6 47N 33 3 E
Pica, *Chile* **156 E4** 20 35 S 69 25W
Picardie, *France* **23 C9** 49 50N 3 0 E
Picardie, Plaine de, *France* **23 C9** 50 0N 2 0 E
Picardy = Picardie, *France* **23 C9** 49 50N 3 0 E
Picayune, *U.S.A.* **139 K10** 30 32N 89 41W
Picerno, *Italy* **41 B8** 40 40N 15 37 E
Pichilemu, *Chile* **158 C1** 34 22 S 72 0W
Pichincha, □, *Ecuador* **152 D2** 0 10 S 78 40W
Pickerel L., *Canada* **128 C1** 48 40N 91 25W
Pickle Lake, *Canada* **128 B1** 51 30N 90 12W
Pico Truncado, *Argentina* **160 C3** 46 40 S 68 0W
Picos, *Brazil* **154 C3** 7 5 S 41 28W
Picos Ancares, Sierra de, *Spain* **36 C4** 42 51N 6 52W
Picota, *Peru* **156 B2** 6 54 S 76 24W
Picquigny, *France* **23 C9** 49 56N 2 10 E
Picton, *Australia* **117 C9** 34 12 S 150 34 E
Picton, *Canada* **128 D4** 44 1N 77 9W
Picton, *N.Z.* **119 B9** 41 18 S 174 3 E
Picton, I., *Chile* **160 E3** 55 2 S 66 57W
Pictou, *Canada* **129 C7** 45 41N 62 42W
Picture Butte, *Canada* **130 D6** 49 55N 112 45W
Picuí, *Brazil* **154 C4** 6 31 S 36 21W
Picún Leufú, *Argentina* **160 A3** 39 30 S 69 5W
Pidurutalagala, *Sri Lanka* **83 L5** 7 10N 80 50 E
Piedecuesta, *Colombia* **152 B3** 6 59N 73 3W
Piedicavallo, *Italy* **38 C4** 45 41N 7 57 E
Piedmont = Piemonte □, *Italy* **38 D4** 45 0N 7 30 E
Piedmont, *U.S.A.* **135 J3** 33 55N 85 37W
Piedmont Plateau, *U.S.A.* **135 J5** 34 0N 81 30W
Piedmonte d'Alife, *Italy* **41 A7** 41 22N 14 22 E
Piedra →, *Spain* **34 D3** 41 18N 1 47W
Piedra del Anguila, *Argentina* **160 B2** 40 2 S 70 4W
Piedra Lais, *Venezuela* **152 C4** 3 10N 65 50W
Piedrabuena, *Spain* **37 F6** 39 0N 4 10W
Piedrahita, *Spain* **36 E5** 40 28N 5 23W
Piedras, R. de las →, *Peru* **156 C4** 12 30 S 69 15W
Piedras Negras, *Mexico* **146 B4** 28 35N 100 35W
Piedras Pt., *Phil.* **71 F2** 10 11N 118 48 E
Piemonte □, *Italy* **38 D4** 45 0N 7 30 E
Piensk, *Poland* **47 D2** 51 16N 15 2 E
Pier Millan, *Australia* **116 C5** 35 14 S 142 40 E
Pierce, *U.S.A.* **142 C6** 46 30N 115 48W
Piercefield, *U.S.A.* **137 B10** 44 13N 74 35W
Piería □, *Greece* **44 D4** 40 13N 22 25 E
Pierre, *U.S.A.* **138 C4** 44 22N 100 21W
Pierre Bénite, Barrage de la, *France* **25 C8** 45 42N 4 49 E
Pierre-de-Bresse, *France* **25 B9** 46 54N 5 13 E
Pierrefeu-du-Var, *France* **25 E10** 43 13N 6 9 E
Pierrefonds, *France* **23 C9** 49 20N 2 58 E
Pierrefontaine-les-Varans, *France* **23 E13** 47 14N 6 32 E
Pierrefort, *France* **24 D6** 44 55N 2 50 E
Pierrelatte, *France* **25 D8** 44 23N 4 43 E
Piešťany, *Slovak Rep.* **31 C10** 48 38N 17 55 E
Piesting →, *Austria* **31 C9** 48 6N 16 40 E
Pieszyce, *Poland* **47 E3** 50 43N 16 33 E
Piet Retief, *S. Africa* **105 D5** 27 1 S 30 50 E
Pietarsaari = Jakobstad, *Finland* **12 E17** 63 40N 22 43 E
Pietermaritzburg, *S. Africa* **105 D5** 29 35 S 30 25 E
Pietersburg, *S. Africa* **105 C4** 23 54 S 29 25 E
Pietraperzia, *Italy* **41 E7** 37 26N 14 8 E
Pietrasanta, *Italy* **38 E7** 43 57N 10 12 E
Pietrosu, *Romania* **46 B6** 47 12N 25 8 E
Pietrosul, *Romania* **46 B5** 47 35N 24 43 E
Pieve di Cadore, *Italy* **39 B9** 46 25N 12 22 E
Pieve di Teco, *Italy* **38 D4** 44 3N 7 54 E
Pievepélago, *Italy* **38 D7** 44 12N 10 35 E
Pigádhia, *Greece* **45 J9** 35 30N 27 12 E
Pigadhítsa, *Greece* **44 E3** 39 59N 21 23 E
Pigeon, *U.S.A.* **134 D4** 43 50N 83 16W
Pigeon I., *India* **83 G2** 14 2N 74 20 E
Piggott, *U.S.A.* **139 G9** 36 23N 90 11W
Pigna, *Italy* **38 E4** 43 57N 7 40 E
Pigüe, *Argentina* **158 D3** 37 36 S 62 25W
Pihani, *India* **81 F9** 27 36N 80 15 E
Pijnacker, *Neths.* **20 D4** 52 1N 4 26 E
Pikalevo, *Russia* **50 B9** 59 37N 34 0 E
Pikes Peak, *U.S.A.* **138 F2** 38 50N 105 3W
Piketberg, *S. Africa* **104 E2** 32 55 S 18 40 E
Pikeville, *U.S.A.* **134 G4** 37 29N 82 31W
Pikou, *China* **67 E12** 39 18N 122 22 E
Pikwitonei, *Canada* **131 B9** 55 35N 97 9W
Piła, *Poland* **47 B3** 53 10N 16 48 E
Pila, *Spain* **35 G3** 38 16N 1 11W
Piła □, *Poland* **47 B3** 53 0N 17 0 E
Pilaía, *Greece* **44 D4** 40 32N 22 59 E
Pilani, *India* **80 E6** 28 22N 75 33 E
Pilar, *Brazil* **154 C4** 9 36 S 35 56W
Pilar, *Paraguay* **158 B4** 26 50 S 58 20W
Pilas Group, *Phil.* **71 H3** 6 45N 121 35 E
Pilawa, *Poland* **47 D8** 51 57N 21 32 E
Pilaya →, *Bolivia* **157 E5** 20 55 S 64 4W
Pilcomayo →, *Paraguay* **158 B4** 25 21 S 57 42W
Pili, *Greece* **45 H9** 36 50N 27 15 E
Pili, *Phil.* **70 E4** 13 33N 123 19 E
Pilibhit, *India* **81 E8** 28 40N 79 50 E
Pilica →, *Poland* **47 D8** 51 52N 21 17 E
Pilion, *Greece* **44 E5** 39 27N 23 7 E
Pilis, *Hungary* **31 D12** 47 17N 19 35 E
Pilisvörösvár, *Hungary* **31 D11** 47 38N 18 56 E
Pilkhawa, *India* **80 E7** 28 43N 77 42 E
Pillaro, *Ecuador* **152 D2** 1 10 S 78 32W
Pílos, *Greece* **45 H3** 36 55N 21 42 E
Pilot Grove, *U.S.A.* **140 F4** 38 53N 92 55W
Pilot Mound, *Canada* **131 D9** 49 15N 98 54W
Pilot Point, *U.S.A.* **139 J6** 33 24N 96 58W
Pilot Rock, *U.S.A.* **142 D4** 45 29N 118 50W
Pilsen = Plzeň, *Czech.* **30 B6** 49 45N 13 22 E
Pilštanj, *Slovenia* **39 B12** 46 8N 15 39 E
Pilzno, *Poland* **31 B14** 49 58N 21 16 E
Pima, *U.S.A.* **143 K9** 32 54N 109 50W
Pimba, *Australia* **116 A2** 31 18 S 136 46 E
Pimenta Bueno, *Brazil* **157 C5** 11 35 S 61 10W
Pimentel, *Peru* **156 B2** 6 45 S 79 55W
Pina, *Spain* **34 D4** 41 29N 0 33W
Pinamalayan, *Phil.* **70 E3** 13 2N 121 29 E
Pinang, *Malaysia* **77 K3** 5 25N 100 15 E
Pinang □, *Malaysia* **74 A2** 5 20N 100 20 E
Pinar, C. del, *Spain* **33 B10** 39 53N 3 12 E
Pinar del Río, *Cuba* **148 B3** 22 26N 83 40W
Pinarbaşi, *Turkey* **88 D7** 38 43N 36 23 E
Pincehely, *Hungary* **31 E11** 46 41N 18 27 E
Pinchang, *China* **68 B6** 31 36N 107 3 E
Pincher Creek, *Canada* **130 D6** 49 30N 113 57W
Pinchi L., *Canada* **130 C4** 54 38N 124 30W
Pinckneyville, *U.S.A.* **140 F7** 38 5N 89 23W
Pîncota, *Romania* **42 A6** 46 20N 21 45 E
Pińczów, *Poland* **47 E7** 50 32N 20 32 E
Pind Dadan Khan, *Pakistan* **80 C5** 32 36N 73 7 E
Pindar, *Australia* **113 E2** 28 30 S 115 47 E
Pindaré →, *Brazil* **154 B3** 3 17 S 44 47W
Pindaré Mirim, *Brazil* **154 B2** 3 37 S 45 21W
Pindi Gheb, *Pakistan* **80 C5** 33 14N 72 21 E
Pindiga, *Nigeria* **101 D7** 9 58N 10 53 E
Pindobal, *Brazil* **154 B2** 3 16 S 48 25W
Pindos Óros, *Greece* **44 E3** 40 0N 21 0 E
Pindus Mts. = Pindos Óros, *Greece* **44 E3** 40 0N 21 0 E
Pine, *U.S.A.* **143 J8** 34 23N 111 27W
Pine →, *Canada* **131 B7** 58 50N 105 38W
Pine, C., *Canada* **129 C9** 46 37N 53 32W
Pine Bluff, *U.S.A.* **139 H8** 34 13N 92 1W
Pine City, *U.S.A.* **138 C8** 45 50N 92 59W
Pine Falls, *Canada* **131 C9** 50 34N 96 11W
Pine Flat L., *U.S.A.* **144 J7** 36 50N 119 20W
Pine Pass, *Canada* **130 B4** 55 25N 122 42W
Pine Point, *Canada* **130 A6** 60 50N 114 28W
Pine Ridge, *Australia* **117 A9** 31 30 S 150 28 E
Pine Ridge, *U.S.A.* **138 D3** 43 2N 102 33W
Pine River, *Canada* **131 C8** 51 45N 100 30W
Pine River, *U.S.A.* **138 B7** 46 43N 94 24W
Pine Valley, *U.S.A.* **145 N10** 32 50N 116 32W
Pinecrest, *U.S.A.* **144 G6** 38 12N 120 1W
Pinedale, *U.S.A.* **144 J7** 36 50N 119 48W
Pinega →, *Russia* **48 B8** 64 8N 46 54 E
Pinehill, *Australia* **114 C4** 23 38 S 146 57 E
Pinerolo, *Italy* **38 D4** 44 47N 7 21 E
Pineto, *Italy* **39 F11** 42 36N 14 4 E
Pinetop, *U.S.A.* **143 J9** 34 8N 109 56W
Pinetown, *S. Africa* **105 D5** 29 48 S 30 54 E
Pinetree, *U.S.A.* **142 E11** 43 42N 105 52W
Pineville, *Ky., U.S.A.* **135 G4** 36 46N 83 42W
Pineville, *La., U.S.A.* **139 K8** 31 19N 92 26W
Piney, *France* **23 D11** 48 22N 4 21 E
Ping →, *Thailand* **76 E3** 15 42N 100 9 E
Pingaring, *Australia* **113 F2** 32 40 S 118 32 E
Pingba, *China* **68 D6** 26 23N 106 12 E
Pingchuan, *China* **68 D3** 27 35N 101 55 E
Pingding, *China* **66 F7** 37 47N 113 38 E
Pingdingshan, *China* **66 H7** 33 43N 113 27 E
Pingdong, *Taiwan* **69 F13** 22 39N 120 30 E
Pingdu, *China* **67 F10** 36 42N 119 59 E
Pingelly, *Australia* **113 F2** 32 32 S 117 5 E
Pingguo, *China* **68 F6** 23 19N 107 36 E
Pinghe, *China* **69 E11** 24 17N 117 21 E
Pinghu, *China* **69 B13** 30 40N 121 2 E
Pingjiang, *China* **69 C9** 28 45N 113 36 E
Pingle, *China* **69 E8** 24 40N 110 40 E
Pingli, *China* **68 A7** 32 27N 109 22 E
Pingliang, *China* **66 G4** 35 35N 106 31 E
Pinglu, *China* **66 E7** 39 31N 112 30 E
Pingluo, *China* **66 E4** 38 52N 106 30 E
Pingnan, *Fujian, China* **69 D12** 26 55N 119 0 E
Pingnan, *Guangxi Zhuangzu, China* **69 F8** 23 33N 110 22 E
Pingquan, *China* **67 D10** 41 1N 118 37 E
Pingrup, *Australia* **113 F2** 33 32 S 118 29 E
Pingtan, *China* **69 E12** 25 31N 119 47 E
Pingtang, *China* **68 E6** 25 49N 107 17 E
Pingwu, *China* **66 H3** 32 25N 104 30 E
Pingxiang, *Guangxi Zhuangzu, China* **68 F6** 22 6N 106 46 E
Pingxiang, *Jiangxi, China* **69 D9** 27 43N 113 48 E
Pingyao, *China* **66 F7** 37 12N 112 10 E
Pingyi, *China* **67 G9** 35 30N 117 35 E
Pingyin, *China* **66 F9** 36 20N 116 25 E
Pingyuan, *Guangdong, China* **69 E10** 24 37N 115 57 E
Pingyuan, *Shandong, China* **66 F9** 37 10N 116 22 E
Pingyuanjie, *China* **68 F4** 23 45N 103 48 E
Pinhal, *Brazil* **159 A6** 22 10 S 46 46W
Pinheiro, *Brazil* **154 B2** 2 31 S 45 5W
Pinhel, *Portugal* **36 E3** 40 50N 7 1W
Pinhuá →, *Brazil* **157 B4** 6 21 S 65 0W
Pini, *Indonesia* **74 B1** 0 10N 98 40 E
Piniós →, *Ilía, Greece* **45 G3** 37 48N 21 20 E
Piniós →, *Trikkala, Greece* **44 E4** 39 55N 22 10 E
Pinjarra, *Australia* **113 F2** 32 37 S 115 52 E
Pink →, *Canada* **131 B8** 56 50N 103 50W
Pinkafeld, *Austria* **31 D9** 47 22N 16 9 E
Pinlebu, *Burma* **78 C5** 24 5N 95 22 E
Pinnacles, *Australia* **113 E3** 28 12 S 120 26 E
Pinnacles, *U.S.A.* **144 J5** 36 33N 121 19W
Pinnaroo, *Australia* **116 C4** 35 17 S 140 53 E
Pinneberg, *Germany* **26 B5** 53 39N 9 48 E
Pino Hachado, Paso, *S. Amer.* **160 A2** 38 39 S 70 54W
Pinon Hills, *U.S.A.* **145 L9** 34 26N 117 39W
Pinos, *Mexico* **146 C4** 22 20N 101 40W
Pinos, Mt., *U.S.A.* **145 L7** 34 49N 119 8W
Pinos Pt., *U.S.A.* **143 H3** 36 38N 121 57W
Pinos Puente, *Spain* **37 H7** 37 15N 3 45W
Pinotepa Nacional, *Mexico* **147 D5** 16 19N 98 3W
Pinrang, *Indonesia* **72 B1** 3 46 S 119 41 E
Pins, I. des, *N. Cal.* **121 V21** 22 37 S 167 30 E
Pinsk, *Belorussia* **50 E5** 52 10N 26 1 E
Pintados, *Chile* **156 E4** 20 35 S 69 40W
Pintumba, *Australia* **113 F5** 31 30 S 132 12 E
Pintuyan, *Phil.* **71 G5** 9 57N 125 15 E
Pinukpuk, *Phil.* **70 C3** 17 35N 121 22 E
Pinyang, *China* **69 D13** 27 42N 120 31 E
Pinyug, *Russia* **48 B8** 60 5N 48 0 E
Pinzolo, *Italy* **38 B7** 46 9N 10 45 E
Pio V. Corpuz, *Phil.* **71 F5** 11 55N 124 2 E
Pio XII, *Brazil* **154 B2** 3 53 S 45 17W
Pioche, *U.S.A.* **143 H6** 37 56N 114 27W
Pioduran, *Phil.* **70 E4** 13 2N 123 25 E
Piombino, *Italy* **38 F7** 42 54N 10 30 E
Piombino, Canale di, *Italy* **38 F7** 42 50N 10 25 E
Pioner, Os., *Russia* **57 B10** 79 50N 92 0 E
Pionki, *Poland* **47 D8** 51 29N 21 28 E
Piorini →, *Brazil* **153 D5** 3 23 S 63 30W
Piorini, L., *Brazil* **153 D5** 3 15 S 62 35W
Piotrków Trybunalski, *Poland* **47 D6** 51 23N 19 43 E
Piotrków Trybunalski □, *Poland* **47 D6** 51 30N 19 45 E
Piove di Sacco, *Italy* **39 C9** 45 18N 12 1 E
Pīp, *Iran* **85 E9** 26 45N 60 10 E
Pipar, *India* **80 F5** 26 25N 73 31 E
Piparia, *India* **80 H8** 22 45N 78 23 E
Pipéri, *Greece* **44 E6** 39 20N 24 19 E
Pipestone, *U.S.A.* **138 D6** 44 0N 96 19W
Pipestone →, *Canada* **128 B2** 52 53N 89 23W
Pipestone Cr. →, *Canada* **131 D8** 49 38N 100 15W
Pipiriki, *N.Z.* **118 F4** 39 28 S 175 5 E
Pipmuacan, Rés., *Canada* **129 C5** 49 45N 70 30W
Pippingarra, *Australia* **112 D2** 20 27 S 118 42 E
Pipriac, *France* **22 E5** 47 49N 1 58W
Piqua, *U.S.A.* **141 D12** 40 9N 84 15W
Piquet Carneiro, *Brazil* **154 C4** 5 48 S 39 25W
Piquiri →, *Brazil* **159 A5** 24 3 S 54 14W
Pīr Sohrāb, *Iran* **85 E9** 25 44N 60 54 E
Piracanjuba, *Brazil* **155 E2** 17 18 S 49 1W
Piracicaba, *Brazil* **159 A6** 22 45 S 47 40W
Piracuruca, *Brazil* **154 B3** 3 50 S 41 50W
Piræus = Piraiévs, *Greece* **45 G5** 37 57N 23 42 E
Piraiévs, *Greece* **45 G5** 37 57N 23 42 E
Piraiévs □, *Greece* **45 G5** 37 0N 23 30 E
Piráino, *Italy* **41 D7** 38 10N 14 52 E
Pirajuí, *Brazil* **159 A6** 21 59 S 49 29W
Piran, *Slovenia* **39 C10** 45 31N 13 33 E
Pirané, *Argentina* **158 B4** 25 42 S 59 6W
Piranhas, *Brazil* **154 C4** 9 27 S 37 46W
Pirano = Piran, *Slovenia* **39 C10** 45 31N 13 33 E
Pirapemas, *Brazil* **154 B3** 3 43 S 44 14W
Pirapora, *Brazil* **155 E3** 17 20 S 44 56W
Piray →, *Bolivia* **157 D5** 16 32 S 63 45W
Pirdop, *Bulgaria* **43 E9** 42 40N 24 10 E
Pires do Rio, *Brazil* **155 E2** 17 18 S 48 17W
Pirganj, *Bangla.* **78 C2** 25 51N 88 24 E
Pírgos, *Ilía, Greece* **45 G3** 37 40N 21 27 E
Pírgos, *Messinia, Greece* **45 H4** 36 50N 22 16 E
Pirgovo, *Bulgaria* **43 D10** 43 44N 25 43 E
Piriac-sur-Mer, *France* **22 E4** 47 22N 2 33W
Piribebuy, *Paraguay* **158 B4** 25 26 S 57 2W
Pirin Planina, *Bulgaria* **43 F8** 41 40N 23 30 E
Pirineos, *Spain* **34 C6** 42 40N 1 0 E
Piripiri, *Brazil* **154 B3** 4 15 S 41 46W
Piritu, *Venezuela* **152 B4** 9 23N 69 12W
Pirmasens, *Germany* **27 F3** 49 12N 7 30 E
Pirna, *Germany* **26 E9** 50 57N 13 57 E
Pirojpur, *Bangla.* **78 D3** 22 35N 90 1 E
Pirot, *Serbia* **42 D7** 43 9N 22 39 E
Piru, *Indonesia* **72 B3** 3 4 S 128 12 E
Piru, *U.S.A.* **145 L8** 34 25N 118 48W
Piryatin, *Ukraine* **50 F8** 50 15N 32 25 E
Piryí, *Greece* **45 F7** 38 13N 25 59 E
Pisa, *Italy* **38 E7** 43 43N 10 23 E
Pisa →, *Poland* **47 B8** 53 14N 21 52 E
Pisa Ra., *N.Z.* **119 E4** 44 52 S 169 12 E
Pisac, *Peru* **156 C3** 13 25 S 71 50W
Pisagua, *Chile* **156 D3** 19 40 S 70 15W
Pisarovina, *Croatia* **39 C12** 45 35N 15 50 E
Pisau, Tanjong, *Malaysia* **75 A5** 6 4N 117 59 E
Pisciotta, *Italy* **41 B8** 40 7N 15 12 E
Pisco, *Peru* **156 C2** 13 50 S 76 12W
Piscu, *Romania* **46 D8** 45 30N 27 43 E
Písek, *Czech.* **30 B7** 49 19N 14 10 E
Pishan, *China* **64 C2** 37 30N 78 33 E
Pishin Lora →, *Pakistan* **80 E1** 29 9N 64 5 E
Pisidia, *Turkey* **88 E4** 37 30N 31 40 E
Pising, *Indonesia* **72 C2** 5 8 S 121 53 E
Pismo Beach, *U.S.A.* **145 K6** 35 9N 120 38W
Pissos, *France* **24 D3** 44 19N 0 49W
Pissouri, *Cyprus* **32 E11** 34 40N 32 42 E
Pisticci, *Italy* **41 B9** 40 24N 16 33 E
Pistóia, *Italy* **38 E7** 43 57N 10 53 E
Pistol B., *Canada* **131 A10** 62 25N 92 37W
Pisuerga →, *Spain* **36 D6** 41 33N 4 52W
Pisz, *Poland* **47 B8** 53 38N 21 49 E
Pitalito, *Colombia* **152 C2** 1 51N 76 2W
Pitanga, *Brazil* **155 F1** 24 46 S 51 44W
Pitangui, *Brazil* **155 E3** 19 40 S 44 54W
Pitarpunga, L., *Australia* **116 C5** 34 24 S 143 30 E
Pitcairn I., *Pac. Oc.* **123 K14** 25 5 S 130 5W
Pite älv →, *Sweden* **12 D16** 65 20N 21 25 E
Piteå, *Sweden* **12 D16** 65 20N 21 25 E
Piterka, *Russia* **51 F15** 50 41N 47 29 E
Piteşti, *Romania* **46 E5** 44 52N 24 54 E

250 Pithapuram


Pithapuram, *India* **82 F6** 17 10N 82 15 E
Pithara, *Australia* **113 F2** 30 20 S 116 35 E
Píthion, *Greece* **44 C8** 41 24N 26 40 E
Pithiviers, *France* **23 D9** 48 10N 2 13 E
Pitigliano, *Italy* **39 F8** 42 38N 11 40 E
Pitlochry, *U.K.* **18 E5** 56 43N 3 43W
Pitoco, *Phil.* **71 F5** 10 8N 124 33 E
Pitrufquén, *Chile* **160 A2** 38 59 S 72 39W
Pitsilia □, *Cyprus* **32 E12** 34 55N 33 0 E
Pitt I., *Canada* **130 C3** 53 30N 129 50W
Pittem, *Belgium* **21 F2** 51 1N 3 13 E
Pittsburg, *Kans., U.S.A.* **139 G7** 37 25N 94 42W
Pittsburg, *Tex., U.S.A.* **139 J7** 33 0N 94 59W
Pittsburgh, *U.S.A.* **136 F5** 40 26N 80 1W
Pittsfield, *Ill., U.S.A.* **140 E6** 39 36N 90 49W
Pittsfield, *Mass., U.S.A.* **137 D11** 42 27N 73 15W
Pittsfield, *N.H., U.S.A.* **137 C13** 43 18N 71 20W
Pittston, *U.S.A.* **137 E9** 41 19N 75 47W
Pittsworth, *Australia* **115 D5** 27 41 S 151 37 E
Pituri →, *Australia* **114 C2** 22 35 S 138 30 E
Piuí, *Brazil* **155 F2** 20 28 S 45 58W
Pium, *Brazil* **154 D2** 10 27 S 49 11W
Piura, *Peru* **156 B1** 5 15 S 80 38W
Piura □, *Peru* **156 A2** 5 10 S 80 0W
Piva →, *Montenegro* **42 D3** 43 20N 18 50 E
Pivijay, *Colombia* **152 A3** 10 28N 74 37W
Piwniczna, *Poland* **31 B13** 49 27N 20 42 E
Pixley, *U.S.A.* **144 K7** 35 58N 119 18W
Piyai, *Greece* **44 E3** 39 17N 21 25 E
Pizarro, *Colombia* **152 C2** 4 58N 77 22W
Pizol, *Switz.* **29 C8** 46 57N 9 23 E
Pizzo, *Italy* **41 D9** 38 44N 16 10 E
Placentia, *Canada* **129 C9** 47 20N 54 0W
Placentia B., *Canada* **129 C9** 47 0N 54 40W
Placer, *Phil.* **71 F4** 11 52N 123 55 E
Placerville, *U.S.A.* **144 G6** 38 44N 120 48W
Placetas, *Cuba* **148 B4** 22 15N 79 44W
Plačkovica, *Macedonia* **42 F7** 41 45N 22 30 E
Plaffeien, *Switz.* **28 C4** 46 45N 7 17 E
Plain Dealing, *U.S.A.* **139 J8** 32 54N 93 42W
Plainfield, *Ill., U.S.A.* **141 C8** 41 37N 88 12W
Plainfield, *N.J., U.S.A.* **137 F10** 40 37N 74 25W
Plains, *Kans., U.S.A.* **139 G4** 37 16N 100 35W
Plains, *Mont., U.S.A.* **142 C6** 47 28N 114 53W
Plains, *Tex., U.S.A.* **139 J3** 33 11N 102 50W
Plainview, *Nebr., U.S.A.* **138 D6** 42 21N 97 47W
Plainview, *Tex., U.S.A.* **139 H4** 34 11N 101 43W
Plainville, *U.S.A.* **138 F5** 39 14N 99 18W
Plainwell, *U.S.A.* **134 D3** 42 27N 85 38W
Plaisance, *France* **24 E4** 43 36N 0 3 E
Pláka, *Greece* **44 E7** 40 0N 25 24 E
Pláka, Ákra, *Greece* **32 D8** 35 11N 26 19 E
Plakenska Planina, *Macedonia* **42 F6** 41 14N 21 2 E
Plakhino, *Russia* **56 C9** 67 45N 86 5 E
Planá, *Czech.* **30 B5** 49 50N 12 44 E
Plana Cays, *Bahamas* **149 B5** 22 38N 73 30W
Planada, *U.S.A.* **144 H6** 37 16N 120 19W
Plancoët, *France* **22 D4** 48 32N 2 13W
Plandište, *Serbia* **42 B6** 45 16N 21 10 E
Planeta Rica, *Colombia* **152 B2** 8 25N 75 36W
Planina, *Slovenia* **39 B12** 46 10N 15 20 E
Planina, *Slovenia* **39 C11** 45 47N 14 19 E
Plankinton, *U.S.A.* **138 D5** 43 43N 98 29W
Plano, *U.S.A.* **139 J6** 33 1N 96 42W
Plant City, *U.S.A.* **135 L4** 28 1N 82 7W
Plaquemine, *U.S.A.* **139 K9** 30 17N 91 14W
Plaridel, *Phil.* **71 G4** 8 37N 123 43 E
Plasencia, *Spain* **36 E4** 40 3N 6 8W
Plaški, *Croatia* **39 C12** 45 4N 15 22 E
Plast, *Russia* **54 D7** 54 22N 60 50 E
Plaster City, *U.S.A.* **145 N11** 32 47N 115 51W
Plaster Rock, *Canada* **129 C6** 46 53N 67 22W
Plastun, *Russia* **60 B8** 44 45N 136 19 E
Plata, Río de la, *S. Amer.* **158 C4** 34 45 S 57 30W
Platani →, *Italy* **40 E6** 37 23N 13 16 E
Plátanos, *Greece* **32 D5** 35 28N 23 33 E
Plateau □, *Nigeria* **101 D6** 8 0N 8 30 E
Plateau du Coteau du Missouri, *U.S.A.* **138 B4** 47 9N 101 5W
Platí, Ákra, *Greece* **44 D5** 40 27N 24 0 E
Plato, *Colombia* **152 B3** 9 47N 74 47W
Platta, Piz, *Switz.* **29 D9** 46 28N 9 35 E
Platte, *U.S.A.* **138 D5** 43 23N 98 51W
Platte →, *U.S.A.* **140 E2** 39 16N 94 50W
Platte City, *U.S.A.* **140 E2** 39 22N 94 47W
Platteville, *Colo., U.S.A.* **138 E2** 40 13N 104 49W
Platteville, *Wis., U.S.A.* **140 B6** 42 44N 90 29W
Plattling, *Germany* **27 G8** 48 46N 12 53 E
Plattsburg, *U.S.A.* **140 E2** 39 34N 94 27W
Plattsburgh, *U.S.A.* **137 B11** 44 42N 73 28W
Plattsmouth, *U.S.A.* **138 E7** 41 1N 95 53W
Plau, *Germany* **26 B8** 53 27N 12 16 E
Plauen, *Germany* **26 E8** 50 29N 12 9 E
Plav, *Montenegro* **42 E4** 42 38N 19 57 E
Plavinas, *Latvia* **50 C4** 56 35N 25 46 E
Plavnica, *Montenegro* **42 E4** 42 20N 19 13 E
Plavsk, *Russia* **51 E10** 53 40N 37 18 E
Playa Blanca, *Canary Is.* **33 F6** 28 55N 13 37W
Playa Blanca Sur, *Canary Is.* **33 F6** 28 51N 13 50W
Playa de las Americas, *Canary Is.* **33 F3** 28 5N 16 43W
Playa de Mogán, *Canary Is.* **33 G4** 27 48N 15 47W
Playa del Inglés, *Canary Is.* **33 G4** 27 45N 15 33W
Playa Esmerelda, *Canary Is.* **33 F5** 28 8N 14 16W
Playgreen L., *Canada* **131 C9** 54 0N 98 15W
Pleasant Bay, *Canada* **129 C7** 46 51N 60 48W
Pleasant Hill, *Calif., U.S.A.* **144 H4** 37 57N 122 4W
Pleasant Hill, *Ill., U.S.A.* **140 E6** 39 27N 90 52W
Pleasant Hill, *Mo., U.S.A.* **140 F2** 38 47N 94 16W
Pleasant Hills, *Australia* **117 C7** 35 28 S 146 50 E
Pleasant Pt., *N.Z.* **119 E6** 44 16 S 171 9 E
Pleasanton, *U.S.A.* **139 L5** 28 58N 98 29W
Pleasantville, *Iowa, U.S.A.* **140 C3** 41 23N 93 18W
Pleasantville, *N.J., U.S.A.* **134 F8** 39 24N 74 32W
Pleasure Ridge Park, *U.S.A.* **141 F11** 38 9N 85 50W
Pléaux, *France* **24 C6** 45 8N 2 13 E
Pleiku, *Vietnam* **76 F7** 13 57N 108 0 E
Plélan-le-Grand, *France* **22 D4** 48 0N 2 7W
Plémet-la-Pierre, *France* **22 D4** 48 11N 2 36W
Pléneuf-Val-André, *France* **22 D4** 48 35N 2 32W
Pleniţa, *Romania* **46 E4** 44 14N 23 10 E
Plenty →, *Australia* **114 C2** 23 25 S 136 31 E
Plenty, B. of, *N.Z.* **118 D6** 37 45 S 177 0 E
Plentywood, *U.S.A.* **138 A2** 48 47N 104 34W
Plesetsk, *Russia* **48 B7** 62 40N 40 10 E
Plessisville, *Canada* **129 C5** 46 14N 71 47W
Plestin-les-Grèves, *France* **22 D3** 48 40N 3 39W
Pleszew, *Poland* **47 D4** 51 53N 17 47 E
Pleternica, *Croatia* **42 B2** 45 17N 17 48 E
Pletipi L., *Canada* **129 B5** 51 44N 70 6W
Pleven, *Bulgaria* **43 D9** 43 26N 24 37 E
Plevlja, *Montenegro* **42 D4** 43 21N 19 21 E
Ploče = Kardeljovo, *Croatia* **42 D2** 43 4N 17 26 E
Płock, *Poland* **47 C6** 52 32N 19 40 E
Płock □, *Poland* **47 C6** 52 30N 19 45 E
Plöcken Passo, *Italy* **39 B9** 46 37N 12 57 E
Ploegsteert, *Belgium* **21 G1** 50 44N 2 53 E
Ploemeur, *France* **22 E3** 47 44N 3 26W
Ploërmel, *France* **22 E4** 47 55N 2 26W
Ploieşti, *Romania* **46 E7** 44 57N 26 5 E
Plomárion, *Greece* **45 F8** 38 58N 26 24 E
Plombières-les-Bains, *France* **23 E13** 47 58N 6 27 E
Plomin, *Croatia* **39 C11** 45 8N 14 10 E
Plön, *Germany* **26 A6** 54 8N 10 22 E
Plöner See, *Germany* **26 A6** 54 10N 10 22 E
Plonge, Lac la, *Canada* **131 B7** 55 8N 107 20W
Płońsk, *Poland* **47 C7** 52 37N 20 21 E
Płoty, *Poland* **47 B2** 53 48N 15 18 E
Plouaret, *France* **22 D3** 48 37N 3 28W
Plouay, *France* **22 E3** 47 55N 3 21W
Ploučnice →, *Czech.* **30 A7** 50 46N 14 13 E
Ploudalmézeau, *France* **22 D2** 48 34N 4 41W
Plougasnou, *France* **22 D3** 48 42N 3 49W
Plouha, *France* **22 D4** 48 41N 2 57W
Plouhinec, *France* **22 E2** 48 0N 4 29W
Plovdiv, *Bulgaria* **43 E9** 42 8N 24 44 E
Plum, *U.S.A.* **136 F5** 40 29N 79 47W
Plum I., *U.S.A.* **137 E12** 41 11N 72 12W
Plumas, *U.S.A.* **144 F7** 39 45N 119 4W
Plummer, *U.S.A.* **142 C5** 47 20N 116 53W
Plumtree, *Zimbabwe* **107 G2** 20 27 S 27 55 E
Plunge, *Lithuania* **50 D2** 55 53N 21 59 E
Pluvigner, *France* **22 E3** 47 46N 3 1W
Plymouth, *U.K.* **17 G3** 50 23N 4 9W
Plymouth, *Calif., U.S.A.* **144 G6** 38 29N 120 51W
Plymouth, *Ill., U.S.A.* **140 D6** 40 18N 90 58W
Plymouth, *Ind., U.S.A.* **141 C10** 41 21N 86 19W
Plymouth, *Mass., U.S.A.* **137 E14** 41 57N 70 40W
Plymouth, *N.C., U.S.A.* **135 H7** 35 52N 76 43W
Plymouth, *N.H., U.S.A.* **137 C13** 43 46N 71 41W
Plymouth, *Pa., U.S.A.* **137 E9** 41 14N 75 57W
Plymouth, *Wis., U.S.A.* **134 D2** 43 45N 87 59W
Plynlimon = Pumlumon Fawr, *U.K.* **17 E4** 52 29N 3 47W
Plyussa, *Russia* **50 B6** 58 40N 29 20 E
Plyussa →, *Russia* **50 B6** 59 10N 29 10 E
Plzeň, *Czech.* **30 B6** 49 45N 13 22 E
Pniewy, *Poland* **47 C3** 52 31N 16 16 E
Pô, *Burkina Faso* **101 C4** 11 14N 1 5W
Po →, *Italy* **39 D9** 44 57N 12 4 E
Po, Foci del, *Italy* **39 D9** 44 55N 12 30 E
Po Hai = Bo Hai, *China* **67 E10** 39 0N 119 0 E
Pobé, *Benin* **101 D5** 7 0N 2 56 E
Pobeda, *Russia* **57 C15** 65 12N 146 12 E
Pobedino, *Russia* **57 E15** 49 51N 142 49 E
Pobedy Pik, *Kirghizia* **56 E8** 40 45N 79 58 E
Pobiedziska, *Poland* **47 C4** 52 29N 17 11 E
Pobla de Segur, *Spain* **34 C5** 42 15N 0 58 E
Pobladura de Valle, *Spain* **36 C5** 42 6N 5 44W
Pocahontas, *Ark., U.S.A.* **139 G9** 36 16N 90 58W
Pocahontas, *Ill., U.S.A.* **140 F7** 38 50N 89 33W
Pocahontas, *Iowa, U.S.A.* **140 B2** 42 44N 94 40W
Pocatello, *U.S.A.* **142 E7** 42 52N 112 27W
Počátky, *Czech.* **30 B8** 49 15N 15 14 E
Pochep, *Russia* **50 E8** 52 58N 33 29 E
Pochinki, *Russia* **51 D14** 54 41N 44 59 E
Pochinok, *Russia* **50 D8** 54 28N 32 29 E
Pöchlarn, *Austria* **30 C8** 48 12N 15 12 E
Pochutla, *Mexico* **147 D5** 15 50N 96 31W
Poci, *Venezuela* **153 B5** 5 57N 61 29W
Pocinhos, *Brazil* **154 C4** 7 4 S 36 3W
Pocito Casas, *Mexico* **146 B2** 28 32N 111 6W
Poções, *Brazil* **155 D3** 14 31 S 40 21W
Pocomoke City, *U.S.A.* **134 F8** 38 5N 75 34W
Poconé, *Brazil* **157 D6** 16 15 S 56 37W
Poços de Caldas, *Brazil* **159 A6** 21 50 S 46 33W
Poddebice, *Poland* **47 D5** 51 54N 18 58 E
Poděbrady, *Czech.* **30 A8** 50 9N 15 8 E
Podensac, *France* **24 D3** 44 40N 0 22W
Podgorač, *Croatia* **42 B3** 45 27N 18 13 E
Podgorica, *Montenegro* **42 E4** 42 30N 19 19 E
Podkamennaya Tunguska →, *Russia* **57 C10** 61 50N 90 13 E
Podlapac, *Croatia* **39 D12** 44 37N 15 47 E
Podmokly, *Czech.* **30 A7** 50 48N 14 10 E
Podoleni, *Romania* **46 C7** 46 46N 26 39 E
Podolínec, *Slovak Rep.* **31 B13** 49 16N 20 31 E
Podolsk, *Russia* **51 D10** 55 25N 37 30 E
Podor, *Senegal* **100 B1** 16 40N 15 2W
Podporozhy, *Russia* **48 B5** 60 55N 34 2 E
Podravska Slatina, *Croatia* **42 B2** 45 42N 17 45 E
Podu Turcului, *Romania* **46 C8** 46 11N 27 25 E
Podujevo, *Serbia* **42 E6** 42 54N 21 10 E
Poel, *Germany* **26 B7** 54 0N 11 25 E
Pofadder, *S. Africa* **104 D2** 29 10 S 19 22 E
Pogamasing, *Canada* **128 C3** 46 55N 81 50W
Poggiardo, *Italy* **41 B11** 40 3N 18 21 E
Poggibonsi, *Italy* **39 E8** 43 27N 11 8 E
Pogoanele, *Romania* **46 E8** 44 55N 27 0 E
Pogorzela, *Poland* **47 D4** 51 50N 17 12 E
Pogoso, *Zaïre* **103 D3** 6 46 S 17 12 E
Pogradeci, *Albania* **44 D2** 40 57N 20 37 E
Pogranitšnyi, *Russia* **60 B5** 44 25N 131 24 E
Poh, *Indonesia* **72 B2** 0 46 S 122 51 E
Pohang, *S. Korea* **67 F15** 36 1N 129 23 E
Pohnpei, *Pac. Oc.* **122 G7** 6 55N 158 10 E
Pohorelá, *Slovak Rep.* **31 C13** 48 50N 20 2 E
Pohořelice, *Czech.* **31 C9** 48 59N 16 31 E
Pohorje, *Slovenia* **39 B12** 46 30N 15 20 E
Poiana Mare, *Romania* **46 F4** 43 57N 23 5 E
Poiana Ruscăi, Munţii, *Romania* **46 D3** 45 45N 22 25 E
Poindimié, *N. Cal.* **121 T19** 20 56 S 165 20 E
Poinsett, C., *Antarctica* **7 C8** 65 42 S 113 18 E
Point Edward, *Canada* **128 D3** 43 0N 82 30W
Point Pass, *Australia* **116 C3** 34 5 S 139 5 E
Point Pedro, *Sri Lanka* **83 K5** 9 50N 80 15 E
Point Pleasant, *N.J., U.S.A.* **137 F10** 40 5N 74 4W
Point Pleasant, *W. Va., U.S.A.* **134 F4** 38 51N 82 8W
Pointe-à-la Hache, *U.S.A.* **139 L10** 29 35N 89 55W
Pointe-à-Pitre, *Guadeloupe* **149 C7** 16 10N 61 30W
Pointe Noire, *Congo* **103 C2** 4 48 S 11 53 E
Poirino, *Italy* **38 D4** 44 55N 7 50 E
Poisonbush Ra., *Australia* **112 D3** 22 30 S 121 30 E
Poissy, *France* **23 D9** 48 55N 2 2 E
Poitiers, *France* **22 F7** 46 35N 0 20 E
Poitou, *France* **24 B3** 46 40N 0 10W
Poitou, Seuil du, *France* **24 B4** 46 20N 0 10 E
Poix de Picardie, *France* **23 C8** 49 47N 1 58 E
Poix-Terron, *France* **23 C11** 49 38N 4 38 E
Pojoaque Valley, *U.S.A.* **143 J11** 35 54N 106 1W
Pokataroo, *Australia* **115 D4** 29 30 S 148 36 E
Poko, *Sudan* **95 F3** 5 41N 31 55 E
Poko, *Zaïre* **106 B2** 3 7N 26 52 E
Pokrov, *Russia* **51 D11** 55 55N 39 7 E
Pokrovka, *Kirghizia* **55 B9** 42 20N 78 0 E
Pokrovsk, *Russia* **51 F15** 51 28N 46 6 E
Pokrovsk, *Russia* **57 C13** 61 29N 129 0 E
Pokrovsk-Uralskiy, *Russia* **54 A6** 60 10N 59 49 E
Pol, *Spain* **36 B3** 43 9N 7 20W
Pola = Pula, *Croatia* **39 D10** 44 54N 13 57 E
Pola de Allande, *Spain* **36 B4** 43 16N 6 37W
Pola de Lena, *Spain* **36 B5** 43 10N 5 49W
Pola de Siero, *Spain* **36 B5** 43 24N 5 39W
Pola de Somiedo, *Spain* **36 B4** 43 5N 6 15W
Polacca, *U.S.A.* **143 J8** 35 50N 110 23W
Polan, *Iran* **85 E9** 25 30N 61 10 E
Poland ■, *Europe* **47 D7** 52 0N 20 0 E
Polanów, *Poland* **47 A3** 54 7N 16 41 E
Polatsk = Polotsk, *Belorussia* **50 D6** 55 30N 28 50 E
Polcura, *Chile* **158 D1** 37 17 S 71 43W
Połczyn Zdrój, *Poland* **47 B3** 53 47N 16 5 E
Polden Hills, *U.K.* **17 F5** 51 7N 2 50W
Polessk, *Russia* **50 D2** 54 50N 21 8 E
Polesye, *Belorussia* **50 E6** 52 10N 28 10 E
Polevskoy, *Russia* **54 C7** 56 26N 60 11 E
Polewali, *Indonesia* **72 B1** 3 21 S 119 23 E
Polgar, *Hungary* **31 D14** 47 54N 21 6 E
Pŏlgyo-ri, *S. Korea* **67 G14** 34 51N 127 21 E
Poli, *Cameroon* **102 A2** 8 34N 13 15 E
Políaigos, *Greece* **45 H6** 36 45N 24 38 E
Policastro, G. di, *Italy* **41 C8** 39 55N 15 35 E
Police, *Poland* **47 B1** 53 33N 14 33 E
Polička, *Czech.* **31 B9** 49 43N 16 15 E
Polignano a Mare, *Italy* **41 B10** 41 0N 17 12 E
Poligny, *France* **23 F12** 46 50N 5 42 E
Políkhnitas, *Greece* **45 E8** 39 4N 26 10 E
Polillo, *Phil.* **70 D3** 14 43N 121 56 E
Polillo Is., *Phil.* **70 D4** 14 56N 122 0 E
Polillo Strait, *Phil.* **70 D3** 14 44N 121 51 E
Polis, *Cyprus* **32 D11** 35 2N 32 26 E
Polístena, *Italy* **41 D9** 38 25N 16 4 E
Políyiros, *Greece* **44 D5** 40 23N 23 25 E
Polk, *U.S.A.* **136 E5** 41 22N 79 56W
Polkowice, *Poland* **47 D3** 51 29N 16 3 E
Polla, *Italy* **41 B8** 40 31N 15 27 E
Pollachi, *India* **83 J3** 10 35N 77 0 E
Pollensa, *Spain* **33 B10** 39 54N 3 1 E
Pollensa, B. de, *Spain* **33 B10** 39 53N 3 8 E
Póllica, *Italy* **41 B8** 40 13N 15 3 E
Pollino, Mte., *Italy* **41 C9** 39 54N 16 13 E
Pollock, *U.S.A.* **138 C4** 45 55N 100 17W
Polna, *Russia* **50 B6** 58 31N 28 5 E
Polnovat, *Russia* **56 C7** 63 50N 65 54 E
Polo, *Ill., U.S.A.* **140 C7** 41 59N 89 35W
Polo, *Mo., U.S.A.* **140 E2** 39 33N 94 3W
Pologi, *Ukraine* **52 C7** 47 29N 36 15 E
Polonnoye, *Ukraine* **50 F5** 50 6N 27 30 E
Polotsk, *Belorussia* **50 D6** 55 30N 28 50 E
Polski Trŭmbesh, *Bulgaria* **43 D10** 43 20N 25 38 E
Polsko Kosovo, *Bulgaria* **43 D10** 43 23N 25 38 E
Polson, *U.S.A.* **142 C6** 47 41N 114 9W
Poltava, *Ukraine* **52 B6** 49 35N 34 35 E
Polunochnoye, *Russia* **48 B11** 60 52N 60 25 E
Polur, *India* **83 H4** 12 32N 79 11 E
Polyanovgrad, *Bulgaria* **43 E11** 42 39N 26 59 E
Polyarny, *Russia* **48 A5** 69 8N 33 20 E
Polynesia, *Pac. Oc.* **123 H11** 10 0 S 162 0W
Polynésie française □ = French Polynesia ■, *Pac. Oc.* **123 J13** 20 0 S 145 0W
Pomarance, *Italy* **38 E7** 43 18N 10 51 E
Pomarico, *Italy* **41 B9** 40 31N 16 33 E
Pomaro, *Mexico* **146 D4** 18 20N 103 18W
Pombal, *Brazil* **154 C4** 6 45 S 37 50W
Pombal, *Portugal* **36 F2** 39 55N 8 40W
Pómbia, *Greece* **32 D6** 35 0N 24 51 E
Pomeroy, *Ohio, U.S.A.* **134 F4** 39 2N 82 2W
Pomeroy, *Wash., U.S.A.* **142 C5** 46 28N 117 36W
Pomio, *Papua N. G.* **120 C6** 5 32 S 151 33 E
Pomme de Terre L., *U.S.A.* **140 G3** 37 54N 93 19W
Pomona, *U.S.A.* **145 L9** 34 4N 117 45W
Pomorie, *Bulgaria* **43 E12** 42 32N 27 41 E
Pomos, *Cyprus* **32 D11** 35 9N 32 33 E
Pomos, C., *Cyprus* **32 D11** 35 10N 32 33 E
Pomoshnaya, *Ukraine* **52 B4** 48 13N 31 36 E
Pompano Beach, *U.S.A.* **135 M5** 26 14N 80 8W
Pompei, *Italy* **41 B7** 40 45N 14 30 E
Pompey, *France* **23 D13** 48 46N 6 6 E
Pompeys Pillar, *U.S.A.* **142 D10** 45 59N 107 57W
Ponape = Pohnpei, *Pac. Oc.* **122 G7** 6 55N 158 10 E
Ponask, L., *Canada* **128 B1** 54 0N 92 41W
Ponass L., *Canada* **131 C8** 52 16N 103 58W
Ponca, *U.S.A.* **138 D6** 42 34N 96 43W
Ponca City, *U.S.A.* **139 G6** 36 42N 97 5W
Ponce, *Puerto Rico* **149 C6** 18 1N 66 37W
Ponchatoula, *U.S.A.* **139 K9** 30 26N 90 26W
Poncheville, L., *Canada* **128 B4** 50 10N 76 55W
Poncin, *France* **25 B9** 46 6N 5 25 E
Pond, *U.S.A.* **145 K7** 35 43N 119 20W
Pond Inlet, *Canada* **127 A12** 72 40N 77 0W
Pondicherry, *India* **83 J4** 11 59N 79 50 E
Pondooma, *Australia* **116 B2** 33 29 S 136 59 E
Pondrôme, *Belgium* **21 H6** 50 6N 5 0 E
Ponds, I. of, *Canada* **129 B8** 53 27N 55 52W
Ponérihouen, *N. Cal.* **121 U19** 21 5 S 165 24 E
Ponferrada, *Spain* **36 C4** 42 32N 6 35W
Pongo, Wadi →, *Sudan* **95 F2** 8 42N 27 40 E
Poniatowa, *Poland* **47 D9** 51 11N 22 3 E
Poniec, *Poland* **47 D3** 51 48N 16 50 E
Ponikva, *Slovenia* **39 B12** 46 16N 15 26 E
Ponnaiyar →, *India* **83 J4** 11 50N 79 45 E
Ponnani, *India* **83 J2** 10 45N 75 59 E
Ponneri, *India* **83 H5** 13 20N 80 15 E
Ponnuru, *India* **83 F5** 16 5N 80 34 E
Ponoi, *Russia* **48 A7** 67 0N 41 0 E
Ponoi →, *Russia* **48 A7** 66 59N 41 17 E
Ponoka, *Canada* **130 C6** 52 42N 113 40W
Ponomarevka, *Russia* **54 E4** 53 19N 54 8 E
Ponorogo, *Indonesia* **75 D4** 7 52 S 111 27 E
Ponot, *Phil.* **71 G4** 8 25N 123 0 E
Pons, *France* **24 C3** 45 35N 0 34W
Pons, *Spain* **34 D6** 41 55N 1 12 E
Ponsul →, *Portugal* **37 F3** 39 40N 7 31W
Pont-à-Celles, *Belgium* **21 G4** 50 30N 4 22 E
Pont-à-Mousson, *France* **23 D13** 48 54N 6 1 E
Pont-Audemer, *France* **22 C7** 49 21N 0 30 E
Pont-Aven, *France* **22 E3** 47 51N 3 47W
Pont Canavese, *Italy* **38 C4** 45 24N 7 33 E
Pont-de-Roide, *France* **23 E13** 47 23N 6 45 E
Pont-de-Salars, *France* **24 D6** 44 18N 2 44 E
Pont-de-Vaux, *France* **23 F11** 46 26N 4 56 E
Pont-de-Veyle, *France* **25 B8** 46 17N 4 53 E
Pont-l'Abbé, *France* **22 E2** 47 52N 4 15W
Pont-l'Évêque, *France* **22 C7** 49 18N 0 11 E
Pont-St.-Esprit, *France* **25 D8** 44 16N 4 40 E
Pont-sur-Yonne, *France* **23 D10** 48 18N 3 10 E
Ponta de Pedras, *Brazil* **154 B2** 1 23 S 48 52W
Ponta do Sol, *Madeira* **33 D2** 32 42N 17 7W
Ponta Grossa, *Brazil* **159 B5** 25 7 S 50 10W
Ponta Pora, *Brazil* **159 A4** 22 20 S 55 35W
Pontacq, *France* **24 E3** 43 11N 0 8W
Pontailler-sur-Saône, *France* **23 E12** 47 13N 5 25 E
Pontal →, *Brazil* **154 C3** 9 8 S 40 12W
Pontalina, *Brazil* **155 E2** 17 31 S 49 27W
Pontarlier, *France* **23 F13** 46 54N 6 20 E
Pontassieve, *Italy* **39 E8** 43 47N 11 25 E
Pontaubault, *France* **22 D5** 48 40N 1 20W
Pontaumur, *France* **24 C6** 45 52N 2 40 E
Pontcharra, *France* **25 C10** 45 26N 6 1 E
Pontchartrain L., *U.S.A.* **139 K9** 30 5N 90 5W
Pontchâteau, *France* **22 E4** 47 25N 2 5W
Ponte Alta, Serra do, *Brazil* **155 E2** 19 42 S 47 40W
Ponte Alta do Norte, *Brazil* **154 D2** 10 45 S 47 34W
Ponte Branca, *Brazil* **157 D7** 16 27 S 52 40W
Ponte da Barca, *Portugal* **36 D2** 41 48N 8 25W
Ponte de Sor, *Portugal* **37 F3** 39 17N 7 57W
Ponte dell 'Olio, *Italy* **38 D6** 44 52N 9 39 E
Ponte di Legno, *Italy* **38 B7** 46 15N 10 30 E
Ponte do Lima, *Portugal* **36 D2** 41 46N 8 35W
Ponte do Pungué, *Mozam.* **107 F3** 19 30 S 34 33 E
Ponte-Leccia, *France* **25 F13** 42 28N 9 13 E
Ponte nell' Alpi, *Italy* **39 B9** 46 10N 12 18 E
Ponte Nova, *Brazil* **155 F3** 20 25 S 42 54W
Ponte San Martino, *Italy* **38 C4** 45 36N 7 47 E
Ponte San Pietro, *Italy* **38 C6** 45 42N 9 35 E
Pontebba, *Italy* **39 B10** 46 30N 13 17 E
Pontecorvo, *Italy* **40 A6** 41 28N 13 40 E
Pontedera, *Italy* **38 E7** 43 40N 10 37 E
Pontefract, *U.K.* **16 D6** 53 42N 1 19W
Ponteix, *Canada* **131 D7** 49 46N 107 29W
Pontelandolfo, *Italy* **41 A7** 41 17N 14 41 E
Pontevedra, *Negros, Phil.* **71 F4** 10 22N 122 52 E
Pontevedra, *Panay, Phil.* **71 F4** 11 29N 122 50 E
Pontevedra, *Spain* **36 C2** 42 26N 8 40W
Pontevedra □, *Spain* **36 C2** 42 25N 8 39W
Pontevedra, R. de →, *Spain* **36 C2** 42 22N 8 45W
Pontevico, *Italy* **38 C7** 45 16N 10 6 E
Pontiac, *Ill., U.S.A.* **138 E10** 40 53N 88 38W
Pontiac, *Mich., U.S.A.* **141 B13** 42 38N 83 18W
Pontian Kecil, *Malaysia* **77 M4** 1 29N 103 23 E
Pontianak, *Indonesia* **75 C3** 0 3 S 109 15 E
Pontic Mts. = Kuzey Anadolu Dağları, *Turkey* **88 C6** 41 30N 35 0 E
Pontine Is. = Ponziane, Isole, *Italy* **40 B5** 40 55N 13 0 E
Pontine Mts. = Kuzey Anadolu Dağları, *Turkey* **88 C6** 41 30N 35 0 E
Pontínia, *Italy* **40 A6** 41 25N 13 2 E
Pontivy, *France* **22 D4** 48 5N 2 58W
Pontoise, *France* **23 C9** 49 3N 2 5 E
Ponton →, *Canada* **130 B5** 58 27N 116 11W
Pontorson, *France* **22 D5** 48 34N 1 30W
Pontrémoli, *Italy* **38 D6** 44 22N 9 52 E
Pontresina, *Switz.* **29 D9** 46 29N 9 48 E
Pontrieux, *France* **22 D3** 48 42N 3 10W
Pontypool, *Canada* **136 B6** 44 6N 78 38W
Pontypool, *U.K.* **17 F4** 51 42N 3 1W
Pontypridd, *U.K.* **17 F4** 51 36N 3 21W
Ponza, *Italy* **40 B5** 40 55N 12 57 E
Ponziane, Isole, *Italy* **40 B5** 40 55N 13 0 E
Poochera, *Australia* **115 E1** 32 43 S 134 51 E
Poole, *U.K.* **17 G6** 50 42N 1 58W
Pooley I., *Canada* **130 C3** 52 45N 128 15W
Poona = Pune, *India* **82 E1** 18 29N 73 57 E
Poona Bayabao, *Phil.* **71 H5** 7 56N 124 17 E
Poonamallee, *India* **83 H5** 13 3N 80 10 E
Pooncarie, *Australia* **116 B5** 33 22 S 142 31 E
Poonindie, *Australia* **116 C1** 34 34 S 135 54 E
Poopelloe L., *Australia* **116 A6** 31 40 S 144 0 E
Poopó, *Bolivia* **156 D4** 18 23 S 66 59W
Poopó, L. de, *Bolivia* **156 D4** 18 30 S 67 35W
Poor Knights Is., *N.Z.* **118 B3** 35 29 S 174 43 E
Popanyinning, *Australia* **113 F2** 32 40 S 117 2 E
Popayán, *Colombia* **152 C2** 2 27N 76 36W
Poperinge, *Belgium* **21 G1** 50 51N 2 42 E
Popigay, *Russia* **57 B12** 72 1N 110 39 E
Popilta, L., *Australia* **116 B4** 33 10 S 141 42 E
Popina, *Bulgaria* **43 C11** 44 7N 26 57 E

Pravara 251


Popio L., *Australia* **116 B4** 33 10 S 141 52 E
Poplar, *U.S.A.* **138 A2** 48 7N 105 12W
Poplar →, *Man., Canada* **131 C9** 53 0N 97 19W
Poplar →, *N.W.T., Canada* **130 A4** 61 22N 121 52W
Poplar Bluff, *U.S.A.* **139 G9** 36 46N 90 24W
Poplarville, *U.S.A.* **139 K10** 30 51N 89 32W
Popocatepetl, *Mexico* **147 D5** 19 10N 98 40W
Popokabaka, *Zaïre* **103 D3** 5 41 S 16 40 E
Pópoli, *Italy* **39 F10** 42 12N 13 50 E
Popondetta, *Papua N. G.* **120 E5** 8 48 S 148 17 E
Popovača, *Croatia* **39 C13** 45 30N 16 41 E
Popovo, *Bulgaria* **43 D11** 43 21N 26 18 E
Poppel, *Belgium* **21 F6** 51 27N 5 2 E
Poprád, *Slovak Rep.* **31 B13** 49 3N 20 18 E
Poprád →, *Slovak Rep.* **31 B13** 49 38N 20 42 E
Poradaha, *Bangla.* **78 D2** 23 51N 89 1 E
Porali →, *Pakistan* **79 D2** 25 35N 66 26 E
Porangaba, *Brazil* **156 B3** 8 48 S 70 36W
Porangahau, *N.Z.* **118 G5** 40 17 S 176 37 E
Porangatu, *Brazil* **155 D2** 13 26 S 49 10W
Porbandar, *India* **80 J3** 21 44N 69 43 E
Porce →, *Colombia* **152 B3** 7 28N 74 53W
Porcher I., *Canada* **130 C2** 53 50N 130 30W
Porco, *Bolivia* **157 D4** 19 50 S 65 59W
Porcos →, *Brazil* **155 D2** 12 42 S 45 7W
Porcuna, *Spain* **37 H6** 37 52N 4 11W
Porcupine →, *Canada* **131 B8** 59 11N 104 46W
Porcupine →, *U.S.A.* **126 B5** 66 34N 145 19W
Pordenone, *Italy* **39 C9** 45 58N 12 40 E
Pordim, *Bulgaria* **43 D9** 43 23N 24 51 E
Poreč, *Croatia* **39 C10** 45 14N 13 36 E
Porecatu, *Brazil* **155 F1** 22 43 S 51 24W
Poretskoye, *Russia* **51 D15** 55 9N 46 21 E
Pori, *Finland* **13 F16** 61 29N 21 48 E
Porí, *Greece* **45 J5** 35 58N 23 13 E
Porjus, *Sweden* **12 C15** 66 57N 19 50 E
Porkhov, *Russia* **50 C6** 57 45N 29 38 E
Porkkala, *Finland* **13 G18** 59 59N 24 26 E
Porlamar, *Venezuela* **153 A5** 10 57N 63 51W
Porlezza, *Italy* **38 B6** 46 2N 9 8 E
Porma →, *Spain* **36 C5** 42 49N 5 28W
Pornic, *France* **22 E4** 47 7N 2 5W
Poronaysk, *Russia* **57 E15** 49 13N 143 0 E
Póros, *Greece* **45 G5** 37 30N 23 30 E
Poroshiri-Dake, *Japan* **60 C11** 42 41N 142 52 E
Poroszló, *Hungary* **31 D13** 47 39N 20 40 E
Poroto Mts., *Tanzania* **107 D3** 9 0 S 33 30 E
Porpoise B., *Antarctica* **7 C9** 66 0 S 127 0 E
Porquerolles, I. de, *France* **25 F10** 43 0N 6 13 E
Porrentruy, *Switz.* **28 B4** 47 25N 7 6 E
Porreras, *Spain* **33 B10** 39 31N 3 2 E
Porretta, Passo di, *Italy* **38 D7** 44 2N 10 56 E
Porsangen, *Norway* **12 A18** 70 40N 25 40 E
Porsgrunn, *Norway* **14 E3** 59 10N 9 40 E
Port Adelaide, *Australia* **116 C3** 34 46 S 138 30 E
Port Alberni, *Canada* **130 D4** 49 14N 124 50W
Port Albert, *Australia* **117 E7** 38 42 S 146 42 E
Port Alfred, *Canada* **129 C5** 48 18N 70 53W
Port Alfred, *S. Africa* **104 E4** 33 36 S 26 55 E
Port Alice, *Canada* **130 C3** 50 20N 127 25W
Port Allegany, *U.S.A.* **136 E6** 41 48N 78 17W
Port Allen, *U.S.A.* **139 K9** 30 27N 91 12W
Port Alma, *Australia* **114 C5** 23 38 S 150 53 E
Port Angeles, *U.S.A.* **144 B3** 48 7N 123 27W
Port Antonio, *Jamaica* **148 C4** 18 10N 76 30W
Port Aransas, *U.S.A.* **139 M6** 27 50N 97 4W
Port Arthur = Lüshun, *China* **67 E11** 38 45N 121 15 E
Port Arthur, *Australia* **114 G4** 43 7 S 147 50 E
Port Arthur, *U.S.A.* **139 L8** 29 54N 93 56W
Port au Port B., *Canada* **129 C8** 48 40N 58 50W
Port-au-Prince, *Haiti* **149 C5** 18 40N 72 20W
Port Augusta, *Australia* **116 B2** 32 30 S 137 50 E
Port Augusta West, *Australia* **116 B2** 32 29 S 137 29 E
Port Austin, *U.S.A.* **128 D3** 44 3N 83 1W
Port Bell, *Uganda* **106 B3** 0 18N 32 35 E
Port Bergé Vaovao, *Madag.* **105 B8** 15 33 S 47 40 E
Port Blandford, *Canada* **129 C9** 48 20N 54 10W
Port Bou, *Spain* **34 C8** 42 25N 3 9 E
Port Bouët, *Ivory C.* **100 D4** 5 16N 3 57W
Port Bradshaw, *Australia* **114 A2** 12 30 S 137 20 E
Port Broughton, *Australia* **116 B2** 33 37 S 137 56 E
Port Burwell, *Canada* **128 D3** 42 40N 80 48W
Port Campbell, *Australia* **116 E5** 38 37 S 143 1 E
Port Canning, *India* **81 H13** 22 23N 88 40 E
Port-Cartier, *Canada* **129 B6** 50 2N 66 50W
Port Chalmers, *N.Z.* **119 F5** 45 49 S 170 30 E
Port Charles, *N.Z.* **118 C4** 36 33 S 175 30 E
Port Chester, *U.S.A.* **137 F11** 41 0N 73 40W
Port Clements, *Canada* **130 C2** 53 40N 132 10W
Port Clinton, *U.S.A.* **141 C14** 41 31N 82 56W
Port Colborne, *Canada* **128 D4** 42 50N 79 10W
Port Coquitlam, *Canada* **130 D4** 49 15N 122 45W
Port Credit, *Canada* **136 C5** 43 33N 79 35W
Port Curtis, *Australia* **114 C5** 23 57 S 151 20 E
Port Dalhousie, *Canada* **136 C5** 43 13N 79 16W
Port Darwin, *Australia* **112 B5** 12 24 S 130 45 E
Port Darwin, *Falk. Is.* **160 D5** 51 50 S 59 0W
Port Davey, *Australia* **114 G4** 43 16 S 145 55 E
Port-de-Bouc, *France* **25 E8** 43 24N 4 59 E
Port-de-Paix, *Haiti* **149 C5** 19 50N 72 50W
Port Dickson, *Malaysia* **77 L3** 2 30N 101 49 E
Port Douglas, *Australia* **114 B4** 16 30 S 145 30 E
Port Dover, *Canada* **136 D4** 42 47N 80 12W
Port Edward, *Canada* **130 C2** 54 12N 130 10W
Port Elgin, *Canada* **128 D3** 44 25N 81 25W
Port Elizabeth, *S. Africa* **104 E4** 33 58 S 25 40 E
Port Ellen, *U.K.* **18 F2** 55 38N 6 10W
Port-en-Bessin, *France* **22 C6** 49 21N 0 45W
Port Erin, *I. of Man* **16 C3** 54 5N 4 45W
Port Essington, *Australia* **112 B5** 11 15 S 132 10 E
Port Etienne = Nouâdhibou, *Mauritania* **98 D1** 20 54N 17 0W
Port Fairy, *Australia* **116 E5** 38 22 S 142 12 E
Port Fitzroy, *N.Z.* **118 C4** 36 8 S 175 20 E
Port Fouâd = Bûr Fuad, *Egypt* **94 H8** 31 15N 32 20 E
Port Gamble, *U.S.A.* **144 C4** 47 51N 122 35W
Port-Gentil, *Gabon* **102 C1** 0 40 S 8 50 E
Port Gibson, *U.S.A.* **139 K9** 31 58N 90 59W
Port Glasgow, *U.K.* **18 F4** 55 57N 4 40W
Port Harcourt, *Nigeria* **101 E6** 4 40N 7 10 E
Port Hardy, *Canada* **130 C3** 50 41N 127 30W
Port Harrison = Inoucdjouac, *Canada* **127 C12** 58 25N 78 15W
Port Hawkesbury, *Canada* **129 C7** 45 36N 61 22W
Port Hedland, *Australia* **112 D2** 20 25 S 118 35 E
Port Henry, *U.S.A.* **137 B11** 44 3N 73 28W
Port Hood, *Canada* **129 C7** 46 0N 61 32W
Port Hope, *Canada* **128 D4** 43 56N 78 20W
Port Hueneme, *U.S.A.* **145 L7** 34 7N 119 12W
Port Huron, *U.S.A.* **134 D4** 42 58N 82 26W
Port Isabel, *U.S.A.* **139 M6** 26 5N 97 12W
Port Jefferson, *U.S.A.* **137 F11** 40 57N 73 3W
Port Jervis, *U.S.A.* **137 E10** 41 22N 74 41W
Port-Joinville, *France* **22 F4** 46 45N 2 23W
Port Katon, *Russia* **53 C8** 46 52N 38 46 E
Port Kelang = Pelabuhan Kelang, *Malaysia* **77 L3** 3 0N 101 23 E
Port Kembla, *Australia* **117 C9** 34 52 S 150 49 E
Port Kenny, *Australia* **115 E1** 33 10 S 134 41 E
Port-la-Nouvelle, *France* **24 E7** 43 1N 3 3 E
Port Laoise, *Ireland* **19 C4** 53 2N 7 20W
Port Lavaca, *U.S.A.* **139 L6** 28 37N 96 38W
Port-Leucate, *France* **24 F7** 42 53N 3 3 E
Port Lincoln, *Australia* **116 C1** 34 42 S 135 52 E
Port Loko, *S. Leone* **100 D2** 8 48N 12 46W
Port Louis, *France* **22 E3** 47 42N 3 22W
Port Louis, *Mauritius* **109 G4** 20 10 S 57 30 E
Port Lyautey = Kenitra, *Morocco* **98 B3** 34 15N 6 40W
Port MacDonnell, *Australia* **116 E4** 38 5 S 140 48 E
Port Macquarie, *Australia* **117 A10** 31 25 S 152 25 E
Port Maria, *Jamaica* **148 C4** 18 25N 76 55W
Port Mellon, *Canada* **130 D4** 49 32N 123 31W
Port-Menier, *Canada* **129 C7** 49 51N 64 15W
Port Morant, *Jamaica* **148 C4** 17 54N 76 19W
Port Moresby, *Papua N. G.* **120 E4** 9 24 S 147 8 E
Port Mourant, *Guyana* **153 B6** 6 15N 57 20W
Port Mouton, *Canada* **129 D7** 43 58N 64 50W
Port Musgrave, *Australia* **114 A3** 11 55 S 141 50 E
Port-Navalo, *France* **22 E4** 47 34N 2 54W
Port Nelson, *Canada* **131 B10** 57 3N 92 36W
Port Nicholson, *N.Z.* **118 H3** 41 20 S 174 52 E
Port Nolloth, *S. Africa* **104 D2** 29 17 S 16 52 E
Port Nouveau-Québec, *Canada* **127 C13** 58 30N 65 59W
Port O'Connor, *U.S.A.* **139 L6** 28 26N 96 24W
Port of Spain, *Trin. & Tob.* **149 D7** 10 40N 61 31W
Port Orchard, *U.S.A.* **144 C4** 47 32N 122 38W
Port Orford, *U.S.A.* **142 E1** 42 45N 124 30W
Port Pegasus, *N.Z.* **119 H2** 47 12 S 167 41 E
Port Perry, *Canada* **128 D4** 44 6N 78 56W
Port Phillip B., *Australia* **115 F3** 38 10 S 144 50 E
Port Pirie, *Australia* **116 B3** 33 10 S 138 1 E
Port Pólnocny, *Poland* **47 A5** 54 25N 18 42 E
Port Radium = Echo Bay, *Canada* **126 B8** 66 5N 117 55W
Port Renfrew, *Canada* **130 D4** 48 30N 124 20W
Port Roper, *Australia* **114 A2** 14 45 S 135 25 E
Port Rowan, *Canada* **128 D3** 42 40N 80 30W
Port Safaga = Bûr Safâga, *Egypt* **94 B3** 26 43N 33 57 E
Port Said = Bûr Sa'îd, *Egypt* **94 H8** 31 16N 32 18 E
Port St. Joe, *U.S.A.* **135 L3** 29 49N 85 18W
Port St. Johns, *S. Africa* **105 E4** 31 38 S 29 33 E
Port-St.-Louis-du-Rhône, *France* **25 E8** 43 23N 4 49 E
Port San Vicente, *Phil.* **70 B4** 18 30N 122 8 E
Port Sanilac, *U.S.A.* **128 D3** 43 26N 82 33W
Port Saunders, *Canada* **129 B8** 50 40N 57 18W
Port Severn, *Canada* **136 B5** 44 48N 79 43W
Port Shepstone, *S. Africa* **105 E5** 30 44 S 30 28 E
Port Simpson, *Canada* **130 C2** 54 30N 130 20W
Port Stanley = Stanley, *Falk. Is.* **160 D5** 51 40 S 59 51W
Port Stanley, *Canada* **128 D3** 42 40N 81 10W
Port Sudan = Bûr Sûdân, *Sudan* **94 D4** 19 32N 37 9 E
Port-sur-Saône, *France* **23 E13** 47 42N 6 2 E
Port Talbot, *U.K.* **17 F4** 51 35N 3 48W
Port Taufiq = Bûr Taufiq, *Egypt* **94 J8** 29 54N 32 32 E
Port Townsend, *U.S.A.* **144 B4** 48 7N 122 45W
Port-Vendres, *France* **24 F7** 42 32N 3 8 E
Port Victoria, *Australia* **116 C2** 34 30 S 137 29 E
Port Vila, *Pac. Oc.* **111 D12** 17 45 S 168 18 E
Port Vladimir, *Russia* **48 A5** 69 25N 33 6 E
Port Wakefield, *Australia* **116 C3** 34 12 S 138 10 E
Port Washington, *U.S.A.* **134 D2** 43 23N 87 53W
Port Weld, *Malaysia* **77 K3** 4 50N 100 38 E
Portachuelo, *Bolivia* **157 D5** 17 10 S 63 20W
Portadown, *U.K.* **19 B5** 54 27N 6 26W
Portage, *Mich., U.S.A.* **141 B11** 42 12N 85 35W
Portage, *Wis., U.S.A.* **138 D10** 43 33N 89 28W
Portage →, *U.S.A.* **141 C14** 41 31N 83 5W
Portage La Prairie, *Canada* **131 D9** 49 58N 98 18W
Portageville, *U.S.A.* **139 G10** 36 26N 89 42W
Portalegre, *Portugal* **37 F3** 39 19N 7 25W
Portalegre □, *Portugal* **37 F3** 39 20N 7 40W
Portales, *U.S.A.* **139 H3** 34 11N 103 20W
Portarlington, *Ireland* **19 C4** 53 10N 7 10W
Porteirinha, *Brazil* **155 E3** 15 44 S 43 2W
Portel, *Brazil* **154 B1** 1 57 S 50 49W
Portel, *Portugal* **37 G3** 38 19N 7 41W
Porter, *U.S.A.* **141 C9** 41 36N 87 4W
Porter L., *N.W.T., Canada* **131 A7** 61 41N 108 5W
Porter L., *Sask., Canada* **131 B7** 56 20N 107 20W
Porterville, *S. Africa* **104 E2** 33 0 S 19 0 E
Porterville, *U.S.A.* **144 J8** 36 4N 119 1W
Porthcawl, *U.K.* **17 F4** 51 28N 3 42W
Porthill, *U.S.A.* **142 B5** 48 59N 116 30W
Portile de Fier, *Europe* **46 E3** 44 42N 22 30 E
Portimão, *Portugal* **37 H2** 37 8N 8 32W
Portland, *N.S.W., Australia* **117 B8** 33 20 S 150 0 E
Portland, *Vic., Australia* **116 E4** 38 20 S 141 35 E
Portland, *Canada* **137 B8** 44 42N 76 12W
Portland, *Conn., U.S.A.* **137 E12** 41 34N 72 38W
Portland, *Ind., U.S.A.* **141 D12** 40 26N 84 59W
Portland, *Maine, U.S.A.* **129 D5** 43 39N 70 16W
Portland, *Mich., U.S.A.* **141 B12** 42 52N 84 54W
Portland, *Oreg., U.S.A.* **144 E4** 45 32N 122 37W
Portland, I. of, *U.K.* **17 G5** 50 32N 2 25W
Portland B., *Australia* **116 E4** 38 15 S 141 45 E
Portland Bill, *U.K.* **17 G5** 50 31N 2 27W
Portland I., *N.Z.* **118 F6** 39 20 S 177 51 E
Portland Prom., *Canada* **127 C12** 58 40N 78 33W
Portlands Roads, *Australia* **114 A3** 12 36 S 143 25 E
Portneuf, *Canada* **129 C5** 46 43N 71 55W
Pôrto, *Brazil* **154 B3** 3 54 S 42 42W
Porto, *France* **25 F12** 42 16N 8 42 E
Porto, *Portugal* **36 D2** 41 8N 8 40W
Porto □, *Portugal* **36 D2** 41 8N 8 20W
Porto, G. de, *France* **25 F12** 42 17N 8 34 E
Pôrto Acre, *Brazil* **156 B4** 9 34 S 67 31W
Pôrto Alegre, *Pará, Brazil* **153 D7** 4 22 S 52 44W
Pôrto Alegre, *Rio Grande do S., Brazil* **159 C5** 30 5 S 51 10W
Porto Amboim = Gunza, *Angola* **103 E2** 10 50 S 13 50 E
Porto Argentera, *Italy* **38 D4** 44 15N 7 27 E
Porto Azzurro, *Italy* **38 F7** 42 46N 10 24 E
Porto Botte, *Italy* **40 C1** 39 3N 8 33 E
Pôrto Cajueiro, *Brazil* **157 C6** 11 3 S 55 53W
Porto Civitanova, *Italy* **39 E10** 43 19N 13 44 E
Porto Cristo, *Spain* **33 B10** 39 33N 3 20 E
Pôrto da Fôlha, *Brazil* **154 C4** 9 55 S 37 17W
Pôrto de Móz, *Brazil* **153 D7** 1 41 S 52 13W
Pôrto de Pedras, *Brazil* **154 C4** 9 10 S 35 17W
Pôrto des Meinacos, *Brazil* **157 C7** 12 33 S 53 7W
Porto Empédocle, *Italy* **40 E6** 37 18N 13 30 E
Pôrto Esperança, *Brazil* **157 D6** 19 37 S 57 29W
Pôrto Esperidião, *Brazil* **157 D6** 15 51 S 58 28W
Pôrto Franco, *Brazil* **154 C2** 6 20 S 47 24W
Porto Garibaldi, *Italy* **39 D9** 44 41N 12 14 E
Pôrto Grande, *Brazil* **153 C7** 0 42N 51 24W
Pôrto Jofre, *Brazil* **157 D6** 17 20 S 56 48W
Pórto Lágo, *Greece* **44 D7** 40 58N 25 6 E
Porto Mendes, *Brazil* **159 A5** 24 30 S 54 15W
Porto Moniz, *Madeira* **33 D2** 32 52N 17 11W
Pôrto Murtinho, *Brazil* **157 E6** 21 45 S 57 55W
Pôrto Nacional, *Brazil* **154 D2** 10 40 S 48 30W
Porto Novo, *Benin* **101 D5** 6 23N 2 42 E
Porto Petro, *Spain* **33 B10** 39 22N 3 13 E
Porto Recanati, *Italy* **39 E10** 43 26N 13 40 E
Porto San Giórgio, *Italy* **39 E10** 43 11N 13 49 E
Pôrto Santana, *Brazil* **153 D7** 0 3 S 51 11W
Porto Santo Stefano, *Italy* **38 F8** 42 26N 11 7 E
Pôrto São José, *Brazil* **159 A5** 22 43 S 53 10W
Pôrto Seguro, *Brazil* **155 E4** 16 26 S 39 5W
Porto Tolle, *Italy* **39 D9** 44 57N 12 20 E
Porto Tórres, *Italy* **40 B1** 40 50N 8 23 E
Pôrto União, *Brazil* **159 B5** 26 10 S 51 10W
Pôrto Válter, *Brazil* **156 B3** 8 15 S 72 40W
Porto-Vecchio, *France* **25 G13** 41 35N 9 16 E
Pôrto Velho, *Brazil* **157 B5** 8 46 S 63 54W
Portobelo, *Panama* **148 E4** 9 35N 79 42W
Portoferráio, *Italy* **38 F7** 42 50N 10 20 E
Portogruaro, *Italy* **39 C9** 45 47N 12 50 E
Portola, *U.S.A.* **144 F6** 39 49N 120 28W
Portomaggiore, *Italy* **39 D8** 44 41N 11 47 E
Portoscuso, *Italy* **40 C1** 39 12N 8 22 E
Portovénere, *Italy* **38 D6** 44 2N 9 50 E
Portovíejo, *Ecuador* **152 D1** 1 7 S 80 28W
Portpatrick, *U.K.* **18 G3** 54 50N 5 7W
Portree, *U.K.* **18 D2** 57 25N 6 11W
Portrush, *U.K.* **19 A5** 55 13N 6 40W
Portsall, *France* **22 D2** 48 37N 4 45W
Portsmouth, *Domin.* **149 C7** 15 34N 61 27W
Portsmouth, *U.K.* **17 G6** 50 48N 1 6W
Portsmouth, *N.H., U.S.A.* **137 C14** 43 5N 70 45W
Portsmouth, *Ohio, U.S.A.* **134 F4** 38 44N 82 57W
Portsmouth, *R.I., U.S.A.* **137 E13** 41 36N 71 15W
Portsmouth, *Va., U.S.A.* **134 G7** 36 50N 76 18W
Portsoy, *U.K.* **18 D6** 57 41N 2 41W
Porttipahta, *Finland* **12 B19** 68 5N 26 40 E
Portugal ■, *Europe* **36 F3** 40 0N 8 0W
Portugalete, *Spain* **34 B1** 43 19N 3 4W
Portuguesa □, *Venezuela* **152 B4** 9 10N 69 15W
Portuguese-Guinea = Guinea-Bissau ■, *Africa* **100 C2** 12 0N 15 0W
Portumna, *Ireland* **19 C3** 53 5N 8 12W
Portville, *U.S.A.* **136 D6** 42 3N 78 20W
Porvenir, *Bolivia* **156 C4** 11 10 S 68 50W
Porvenir, *Chile* **160 D2** 53 10 S 70 16W
Porvoo = Borgå, *Finland* **13 F18** 60 24N 25 40 E
Porzuna, *Spain* **37 F6** 39 9N 4 9W
Posada →, *Italy* **40 B2** 40 40N 9 45 E
Posadas, *Argentina* **159 B4** 27 30 S 55 50W
Posadas, *Spain* **37 H5** 37 47N 5 11W
Poschiavo, *Switz.* **29 D10** 46 19N 10 4 E
Posets, *Spain* **34 C5** 42 39N 0 25 E
Poseyville, *U.S.A.* **141 F9** 38 10N 87 47W
Poshan = Boshan, *China* **67 F9** 36 28N 117 49 E
Posht-e-Badam, *Iran* **85 C7** 33 2N 55 23 E
Posídhion, Ákra, *Greece* **44 E5** 39 57N 23 30 E
Posidium, *Greece* **45 J9** 35 30N 27 10 E
Poso, *Indonesia* **72 B2** 1 20 S 120 55 E
Posoegroenoe, *Surinam* **153 C6** 4 23N 55 43W
Posong, *S. Korea* **67 G14** 34 46N 127 5 E
Posse, *Brazil* **155 D2** 14 4 S 46 18W
Possel, *C.A.R.* **102 A3** 5 5N 19 10 E
Possession I., *Antarctica* **7 D11** 72 4 S 172 0 E
Pössneck, *Germany* **26 E7** 50 42N 11 34 E
Post, *U.S.A.* **139 J4** 33 12N 101 23W
Post Falls, *U.S.A.* **142 C5** 47 43N 116 57W
Postavy, *Belorussia* **50 D5** 55 4N 26 50 E
Poste Maurice Cortier, *Algeria* **99 D5** 22 14N 1 2 E
Postmasburg, *S. Africa* **104 D3** 28 18 S 23 5 E
Postojna, *Slovenia* **39 C11** 45 46N 14 12 E
Poston, *U.S.A.* **145 M12** 34 0N 114 24W
Postville, *U.S.A.* **140 A5** 43 5N 91 34W
Potamós, *Andikíthira, Greece* **45 H4** 35 52N 23 15 E
Potamós, *Kíthira, Greece* **45 H4** 36 15N 22 58 E
Potchefstroom, *S. Africa* **104 D4** 26 41 S 27 7 E
Potcoava, *Romania* **46 E5** 44 30N 24 39 E
Poté, *Brazil* **155 E3** 17 49 S 41 49W
Poteau, *U.S.A.* **139 H7** 35 3N 94 37W
Poteet, *U.S.A.* **139 L5** 29 2N 98 35W
Potelu, Lacul, *Romania* **46 F5** 43 44N 24 20 E
Potenza, *Italy* **41 B8** 40 40N 15 50 E
Potenza →, *Italy* **39 E10** 43 27N 13 38 E
Potenza Picena, *Italy* **39 E10** 43 22N 13 37 E
Poteriteri, L., *N.Z.* **119 G2** 46 5 S 167 10 E
Potes, *Spain* **36 B6** 43 15N 4 42W
Potgietersrus, *S. Africa* **105 C4** 24 10 S 28 55 E
Poti, *Georgia* **53 E9** 42 10N 41 38 E
Potiraguá, *Brazil* **155 E4** 15 36 S 39 53W
Potiskum, *Nigeria* **101 C7** 11 39N 11 2 E
Potlogi, *Romania* **46 E6** 44 34N 25 34 E
Potomac →, *U.S.A.* **134 F7** 38 0N 76 23W
Potosí, *Bolivia* **157 D4** 19 38 S 65 50W
Potosi, *U.S.A.* **140 G6** 37 56N 90 47W
Potosí □, *Bolivia* **156 E4** 20 31 S 67 0W
Potosi Mt., *U.S.A.* **145 K11** 35 57N 115 29W
Pototan, *Phil.* **71 F4** 10 54N 122 38 E
Potrerillos, *Chile* **158 B2** 26 30 S 69 30W
Potsdam, *Germany* **26 C9** 52 23N 13 4 E
Potsdam, *U.S.A.* **137 B10** 44 40N 74 59W
Pottenstein, *Germany* **27 F7** 49 46N 11 25 E
Potter, *U.S.A.* **138 E3** 41 13N 103 19W
Pottery Hill = Abû Ballas, *Egypt* **94 C2** 24 26N 27 36 E
Pottstown, *U.S.A.* **137 F9** 40 15N 75 39W
Pottsville, *U.S.A.* **137 F8** 40 41N 76 12W
Pouancé, *France* **22 E5** 47 44N 1 10W
Pouce Coupé, *Canada* **130 B4** 55 40N 120 10W
Pouembout, *N. Cal.* **121 U18** 21 8 S 164 53 E
Poughkeepsie, *U.S.A.* **137 E11** 41 42N 73 56W
Pouilly-sur-Loire, *France* **23 E9** 47 17N 2 57 E
Poulaphouca Res., *Ireland* **19 C5** 53 8N 6 30W
Poulsbo, *U.S.A.* **144 C4** 47 44N 122 39W
Poum, *N. Cal.* **121 T18** 20 14 S 164 2 E
Poumadji, *C.A.R.* **102 A4** 5 56N 22 10 E
Pounga-Nganda, *Gabon* **102 C2** 2 58 S 10 51 E
Pourri, Mt., *France* **25 C10** 45 32N 6 52 E
Pouso Alegre, *Mato Grosso, Brazil* **157 C6** 11 46 S 57 16W
Pouso Alegre, *Minas Gerais, Brazil* **159 A6** 22 14 S 45 57W
Pouzauges, *France* **22 F6** 46 47N 0 50W
Povenets, *Russia* **48 B5** 62 50N 34 50 E
Poverty B., *N.Z.* **118 E7** 38 43 S 178 2 E
Povlen, *Serbia* **42 C4** 44 9N 19 44 E
Póvoa de Lanhosa, *Portugal* **36 D2** 41 33N 8 15W
Póvoa de Varzim, *Portugal* **36 D2** 41 25N 8 46W
Povorino, *Russia* **51 F13** 51 12N 42 5 E
Powassan, *Canada* **128 C4** 46 5N 79 25W
Poway, *U.S.A.* **145 N9** 32 58N 117 2W
Powder →, *U.S.A.* **138 B2** 46 45N 105 26W
Powder River, *U.S.A.* **142 E10** 43 2N 106 59W
Powell, *U.S.A.* **142 D9** 44 45N 108 46W
Powell L., *U.S.A.* **143 H8** 36 57N 111 29W
Powell River, *Canada* **130 D4** 49 50N 124 35W
Powers, *Mich., U.S.A.* **134 C2** 45 41N 87 32W
Powers, *Oreg., U.S.A.* **142 E1** 42 53N 124 4W
Powers Lake, *U.S.A.* **138 A3** 48 34N 102 39W
Powys □, *U.K.* **17 E4** 52 20N 3 20W
Poxoreu, *Brazil* **157 D7** 15 50 S 54 23W
Poya, *N. Cal.* **121 U19** 21 19 S 165 7 E
Poyang Hu, *China* **69 C11** 29 5N 116 20 E
Poyarkovo, *Russia* **57 E13** 49 36N 128 41 E
Poysdorf, *Austria* **31 C9** 48 40N 16 37 E
Poza de la Sal, *Spain* **34 C1** 42 35N 3 31W
Poza Rica, *Mexico* **147 C5** 20 33N 97 27W
Pozanti, *Turkey* **88 E6** 37 25N 34 50 E
Požarevac, *Serbia* **42 C6** 44 35N 21 18 E
Požega, *Serbia* **42 D5** 43 53N 20 2 E
Pozhva, *Russia* **54 B5** 59 5N 56 5 E
Pozi, *Taiwan* **69 F13** 23 30N 120 13 E
Poznań, *Poland* **47 C3** 52 25N 16 55 E
Poznań □, *Poland* **47 C4** 52 30N 17 0 E
Pozo, *U.S.A.* **145 K6** 35 20N 120 24W
Pozo Alcón, *Spain* **35 H2** 37 42N 2 56W
Pozo Almonte, *Chile* **156 E4** 20 10 S 69 50W
Pozo Colorado, *Paraguay* **158 A4** 23 30 S 58 45W
Pozo del Dátil, *Mexico* **146 B2** 30 0N 112 15W
Pozoblanco, *Spain* **37 G6** 38 23N 4 51W
Pozorrubio, *Phil.* **70 C3** 16 7N 120 33 E
Pozuzo, *Peru* **156 C2** 10 5 S 75 35W
Pozzallo, *Italy* **41 F7** 36 44N 14 52 E
Pozzuoli, *Italy* **41 B7** 40 46N 14 6 E
Pra →, *Ghana* **101 D4** 5 1N 1 37W
Prabuty, *Poland* **47 B6** 53 47N 19 15 E
Prača, *Bos.-H.* **42 D3** 43 47N 18 43 E
Prachatice, *Czech.* **30 B7** 49 1N 14 0 E
Prachin Buri, *Thailand* **76 E3** 14 0N 101 25 E
Prachuap Khiri Khan, *Thailand* **77 G2** 11 49N 99 48 E
Pradelles, *France* **24 D7** 44 46N 3 52 E
Pradera, *Colombia* **152 C2** 3 25N 76 15W
Prades, *France* **24 F6** 42 38N 2 23 E
Prado, *Brazil* **155 E4** 17 20 S 39 13W
Prado del Rey, *Spain* **37 J5** 36 48N 5 33W
Præstø, *Denmark* **15 J6** 55 8N 12 2 E
Pragersko, *Slovenia* **39 B12** 46 27N 15 42 E
Prague = Praha, *Czech.* **30 A7** 50 5N 14 22 E
Praha, *Czech.* **30 A7** 50 5N 14 22 E
Prahecq, *France* **24 B3** 46 19N 0 26W
Prahita →, *India* **82 E4** 19 0N 79 55 E
Prahova □, *Romania* **46 D6** 45 10N 26 0 E
Prahova →, *Romania* **46 E6** 44 50N 25 50 E
Prahovo, *Serbia* **42 C7** 44 18N 22 39 E
Praid, *Romania* **46 C6** 46 32N 25 10 E
Prainha, *Amazonas, Brazil* **157 B5** 7 10 S 60 30W
Prainha, *Pará, Brazil* **153 D7** 1 45 S 53 30W
Prairie, *Australia* **114 C3** 20 50 S 144 35 E
Prairie →, *U.S.A.* **139 H5** 34 30N 99 23W
Prairie City, *U.S.A.* **142 D4** 44 28N 118 43W
Prairie du Chien, *U.S.A.* **140 A5** 43 3N 91 9W
Prairie du Rocher, *U.S.A.* **140 F6** 38 5N 90 6W
Prairies, *Canada* **126 C9** 52 0N 108 0W
Pramánda, *Greece* **44 E3** 39 32N 21 8 E
Pran Buri, *Thailand* **76 F2** 12 23N 99 55 E
Prang, *Ghana* **101 D4** 8 1N 0 56W
Prasonísi, Ákra, *Greece* **32 D9** 35 42N 27 46 E
Praszka, *Poland* **47 D5** 51 5N 18 31 E
Prata, *Brazil* **155 E2** 19 25 S 48 54W
Pratapgarh, *India* **80 G6** 24 2N 74 40 E
Pratica di Mare, *Italy* **40 A5** 41 40N 12 26 E
Prättigau, *Switz.* **29 C9** 46 56N 9 44 E
Prato, *Italy* **38 E8** 43 53N 11 5 E
Prátola Peligna, *Italy* **39 F10** 42 7N 13 51 E
Pratovécchio, *Italy* **39 E8** 43 44N 11 43 E
Prats-de-Mollo-la-Preste, *France* **24 F6** 42 25N 2 27 E
Pratt, *U.S.A.* **139 G5** 37 39N 98 44W
Pratteln, *Switz.* **28 A5** 47 31N 7 41 E
Prattville, *U.S.A.* **135 J2** 32 28N 86 29W
Pravara →, *India* **82 E2** 19 35N 74 45 E

252 Pravdinsk


Pravdinsk, Russia 51 C13 56 29N 43 28 E
Pravia, Spain 36 B4 43 30N 6 12W
Praya, Indonesia 75 D5 8 39 S 116 17 E
Pré-en-Pail, France 22 D6 48 28N 0 12W
Pré St. Didier, Italy 38 C4 45 45N 7 0 E
Precordillera, Argentina 158 C2 30 0 S 69 1W
Predáppio, Italy 39 D8 44 7N 11 58 E
Predazzo, Italy 39 B8 46 19N 11 37 E
Predejane, Serbia 42 E7 42 51N 22 9 E
Preeceville, Canada 131 C8 51 57N 102 40W
Préfailles, France 22 E4 47 9N 2 11W
Pregonero, Venezuela 152 B3 8 1N 71 46W
Pregrada, Croatia 39 B12 46 11N 15 45 E
Preko, Croatia 39 D12 44 7N 15 14 E
Prelate, Canada 131 C7 50 51N 109 24W
Prelog, Croatia 39 B13 46 18N 16 32 E
Premier, Canada 130 B3 56 4N 129 56W
Premont, U.S.A. 139 M5 27 22N 98 7W
Premuda, Croatia 39 D11 44 20N 14 36 E
Prenj, Bos.-H. 42 D2 43 33N 17 53 E
Prenjasi, Albania 44 C2 41 6N 20 32 E
Prentice, U.S.A. 138 C9 45 33N 90 17W
Prenzlau, Germany 26 B9 53 19N 13 51 E
Preobrazheniye, Russia 60 C6 42 54N 133 54 E
Prepansko Jezero,
Macedonia 44 D3 40 55N 21 0 E
Přerov, Czech. 31 B10 49 28N 17 27 E
Presanella, Italy 38 B7 46 13N 10 40 E
Prescott, Canada 128 D4 44 45N 75 30W
Prescott, Ariz., U.S.A. 143 J7 34 33N 112 28W
Prescott, Ark., U.S.A. 139 J8 33 48N 93 23W
Preservation Inlet, N.Z. 119 G1 46 8 S 166 35 E
Preševo, Serbia 42 E6 42 19N 21 39 E
Presho, U.S.A. 138 D4 43 54N 100 3W
Presicce, Italy 41 C11 39 53N 18 13 E
Presidencia de la Plaza,
Argentina 158 B4 27 0 S 59 50W
Presidencia Roque Saenz
Peña, Argentina 158 B3 26 45 S 60 30W
Presidente Epitácio, Brazil 155 F1 21 56 S 52 6W
Presidente Hayes □,
Paraguay 158 A4 24 0 S 59 0W
Presidente Hermes, Brazil 157 C5 11 17 S 61 55W
Presidente Prudente,
Brazil 159 A5 22 5 S 51 25W
Presidente Roxas, Phil. 71 F4 11 26N 122 56 E
Presidio, Mexico 146 B4 29 29N 104 23W
Presidio, U.S.A. 139 L2 29 34N 104 22W
Preslav, Bulgaria 43 D11 43 10N 26 52 E
Preslavska Planina,
Bulgaria 43 D11 43 10N 26 45 E
Prešov, Slovak Rep. 31 C14 49 0N 21 15 E
Prespa, Bulgaria 43 F9 41 44N 24 55 E
Prespa, L. = Prepansko
Jezero, Macedonia 44 D3 40 55N 21 0 E
Presque Isle, U.S.A. 129 C6 46 41N 68 1W
Presseger See, Austria 30 E6 46 37N 13 26 E
Prestbury, U.K. 17 F5 51 54N 2 2W
Prestea, Ghana 100 D4 5 22N 2 7W
Presteigne, U.K. 17 E5 52 17N 3 0W
Přeštice, Czech. 30 B6 49 34N 13 20 E
Presto, Bolivia 157 D5 18 55 S 64 56W
Preston, Canada 136 C4 43 23N 80 21W
Preston, U.K. 16 D5 53 46N 2 42W
Preston, Idaho, U.S.A. 142 E8 42 6N 111 53W
Preston, Iowa, U.S.A. 140 B6 42 3N 90 24W
Preston, Minn., U.S.A. 138 D8 43 40N 92 5W
Preston, Nev., U.S.A. 142 G6 38 55N 115 4W
Preston, C., Australia 112 D2 20 51 S 116 12 E
Prestonpans, U.K. 18 F6 55 58N 2 58W
Prestwick, U.K. 18 F4 55 30N 4 38W
Prêto →, Amazonas,
Brazil 153 D5 0 8 S 64 6W
Prêto →, Bahia, Brazil 154 D3 11 21 S 43 52W
Prêto do Igapó-Açu →,
Brazil 153 D6 4 26 S 59 48W
Pretoria, S. Africa 105 D4 25 44 S 28 12 E
Preuilly-sur-Claise, France 22 F7 46 51N 0 56 E
Préveza, Greece 45 F2 38 57N 20 47 E
Préveza □, Greece 44 E2 39 20N 20 40 E
Priazovskoye, Ukraine 52 C6 46 44N 35 40 E
Pribilof Is., Bering S. 6 D17 56 0N 170 0W
Priboj, Serbia 42 D4 43 35N 19 32 E
Příbram, Czech. 30 B7 49 41N 14 2 E
Price, U.S.A. 142 G8 39 36N 110 49W
Price I., Canada 130 C3 52 23N 128 41W
Prichalnaya, Russia 53 B11 48 57N 44 33 E
Prichard, U.S.A. 135 K1 30 44N 88 5W
Priego, Spain 34 E2 40 26N 2 21W
Priego de Córdoba, Spain 37 H6 37 27N 4 12W
Priekule, Latvia 50 C2 57 27N 21 45 E
Prien, Germany 27 H8 47 52N 12 20 E
Prieska, S. Africa 104 D3 29 40 S 22 42 E
Priest →, U.S.A. 142 B5 48 12N 116 54W
Priest L., U.S.A. 142 B5 48 35N 116 52W
Priest Valley, U.S.A. 144 J6 36 10N 120 39W
Priestly, Canada 130 C3 54 8N 125 20W
Prieto Diaz, Phil. 70 E5 13 2N 124 12 E
Prievidza, Slovak Rep. 31 C11 48 46N 18 36 E
Prijedor, Bos.-H. 39 D13 44 58N 16 41 E
Prijepolje, Serbia 42 D4 43 27N 19 40 E
Prikaspiyskaya
Nizmennost, Asia 53 C13 47 0N 48 0 E
Prilep, Macedonia 42 F6 41 21N 21 37 E
Priluki, Ukraine 50 F8 50 30N 32 24 E
Prime Seal I., Australia 114 G4 40 3 S 147 43 E
Primeira Cruz, Brazil 154 B3 2 30 S 43 26W
Primorsko, Bulgaria 43 E12 42 15N 27 44 E
Primorsko-Akhtarsk,
Russia 52 C8 46 2N 38 10 E
Primorskoye, Ukraine 52 C7 46 48N 36 20 E
Primrose L., Canada 131 C7 54 55N 109 45W
Prince Albert, Canada 131 C7 53 15N 105 50W
Prince Albert, S. Africa 104 E3 33 12 S 22 2 E
Prince Albert Mts.,
Antarctica 7 D11 76 0 S 161 30 E
Prince Albert Nat. Park,
Canada 131 C7 54 0N 106 25W
Prince Albert Pen.,
Canada 126 A8 72 30N 116 0W
Prince Albert Sd., Canada 126 A8 70 25N 115 0W
Prince Alfred, C., Canada 6 B1 74 20N 124 40W
Prince Charles I., Canada 127 B12 67 47N 76 12W
Prince Charles Mts.,
Antarctica 7 D6 72 0 S 67 0 E
Prince Edward I. □,
Canada 129 C7 46 20N 63 20W
Prince Edward Is.,
Ind. Oc. 109 J2 46 35 S 38 0 E
Prince George, Canada 130 C4 53 55N 122 50W
Prince of Wales, C.,
U.S.A. 124 C3 65 36N 168 5W
Prince of Wales I.,
Australia 114 A3 10 40 S 142 10 E
Prince of Wales I., Canada 126 A10 73 0N 99 0W
Prince of Wales I., U.S.A. 130 B2 55 47N 132 50W
Prince Patrick I., Canada 6 B2 77 0N 120 0W
Prince Regent Inlet,
Canada 6 B3 73 0N 90 0W
Prince Rupert, Canada 130 C2 54 20N 130 20W
Princenhage, Neths. 21 F5 51 9N 4 45 E
Princesa Isabel, Brazil 154 C4 7 44 S 38 0W
Princess Charlotte B.,
Australia 114 A3 14 25 S 144 0 E
Princess May Ras.,
Australia 112 C4 15 30 S 125 30 E
Princess Royal I., Canada 130 C3 53 0N 128 40W
Princeton, Canada 130 D4 49 27N 120 30W
Princeton, Calif., U.S.A. 144 F4 39 24N 122 1W
Princeton, Ill., U.S.A. 140 C7 41 23N 89 28W
Princeton, Ind., U.S.A. 141 F9 38 21N 87 34W
Princeton, Ky., U.S.A. 134 G2 37 7N 87 53W
Princeton, Mo., U.S.A. 140 D3 40 24N 93 35W
Princeton, N.J., U.S.A. 137 F10 40 21N 74 39W
Princeton, W. Va., U.S.A. 134 G5 37 22N 81 6W
Princeville, U.S.A. 140 D7 40 56N 89 46W
Príncipe, I. de, Atl. Oc. 102 B1 1 37N 7 27 E
Principe Chan., Canada 130 C2 53 28N 130 0W
Principe da Beira, Brazil 157 C5 12 20 S 64 30W
Prineville, U.S.A. 142 D3 44 18N 120 51W
Prins Harald Kyst,
Antarctica 7 D4 70 0 S 35 1 E
Prinsesse Astrid Kyst,
Antarctica 7 D3 70 45 S 12 30 E
Prinsesse Ragnhild Kyst,
Antarctica 7 D4 70 15 S 27 30 E
Prinzapolca, Nic. 148 D3 13 20N 83 35W
Prior, C., Spain 36 B2 43 34N 8 17W
Priozersk, Russia 48 B5 61 2N 30 7 E
Pripet = Pripyat →,
Europe 50 F7 51 20N 30 15 E
Pripet Marshes = Polesye,
Belorussia 50 E6 52 10N 28 10 E
Pripyat →, Europe 50 F7 51 20N 30 15 E
Pripyat Marshes =
Polesye, Belorussia 50 E6 52 10N 28 10 E
Prislop, Pasul, Romania 46 B6 47 37N 25 15 E
Pristen, Russia 51 F10 51 15N 36 44 E
Priština, Serbia 42 E6 42 40N 21 13 E
Pritzwalk, Germany 26 B8 53 10N 12 11 E
Privas, France 25 D8 44 45N 4 37 E
Priverno, Italy 40 A6 41 29N 13 10 E
Privolzhsk, Russia 51 C12 57 23N 41 16 E
Privolzhskaya
Vozvyshennost, Russia 51 F15 51 0N 46 0 E
Privolzhskiy, Russia 51 F15 51 25N 46 3 E
Privolzhye, Russia 51 E16 52 52N 48 33 E
Priyutnoye, Russia 53 C10 46 12N 43 40 E
Prizren, Serbia 42 E5 42 13N 20 45 E
Prizzi, Italy 40 E6 37 44N 13 24 E
Prnjavor, Bos.-H. 42 C2 44 52N 17 43 E
Probolinggo, Indonesia 75 D4 7 46 S 113 13 E
Prochowice, Poland 47 D3 51 17N 16 20 E
Procida, Italy 41 B7 40 46N 14 2 E
Proddatur, India 83 G4 14 45N 78 30 E
Prodhromos, Cyprus 32 E11 34 57N 32 50 E
Proença-a-Nova, Portugal 37 F3 39 45N 7 54W
Prof. Van Blommestein
Meer, Surinam 153 C6 4 45N 55 5W
Profítis Ilías, Greece 32 C9 36 17N 27 56 E
Profondeville, Belgium 21 H5 50 23N 4 52 E
Progreso, Mexico 147 C7 21 20N 89 40W
Prokhladnyy, Russia 53 E11 43 50N 44 2 E
Prokletije, Albania 44 B1 42 30N 19 45 E
Prokopyevsk, Russia 56 D9 54 0N 86 45 E
Prokuplje, Serbia 42 D6 43 16N 21 36 E
Proletarskaya, Russia 53 C9 46 42N 41 50 E
Prome = Pyè, Burma 78 F5 18 49N 95 13 E
Prophet →, Canada 130 B4 58 48N 122 40W
Prophetstown, U.S.A. 140 C7 41 40N 89 56W
Propriá, Brazil 154 D4 10 13 S 36 51W
Propriano, France 25 G12 41 41N 8 52 E
Proserpine, Australia 114 C4 20 21 S 148 36 E
Prosna, Poland 47 D5 51 1N 18 30 E
Prosperidad, Phil. 71 G5 8 34N 125 52 E
Prosser, U.S.A. 142 C4 46 12N 119 46W
Prostějov, Czech. 31 B10 49 30N 17 9 E
Prostki, Poland 47 B9 53 42N 22 25 E
Proston, Australia 115 D5 26 8 S 151 32 E
Proszowice, Poland 31 A13 50 13N 20 16 E
Protection, U.S.A. 139 G5 37 12N 99 29W
Próti, Greece 45 G3 37 5N 21 32 E
Provadiya, Bulgaria 43 D12 43 12N 27 30 E
Proven, Belgium 21 G1 50 54N 2 40 E
Provence, France 25 E9 43 40N 5 46 E
Providence, Ky., U.S.A. 134 G2 37 24N 87 46W
Providence, R.I., U.S.A. 137 E13 41 49N 71 24W
Providence Bay, Canada 128 C3 45 41N 82 15W
Providence C., N.Z. 119 F1 45 59 S 166 29 E
Providence Mts., U.S.A. 143 J6 35 10N 115 15W
Providencia, Ecuador 152 D2 0 28 S 76 28W
Providencia, I. de,
Colombia 148 D3 13 25N 81 26W
Provideniya, Russia 57 C19 64 23N 173 18W
Provins, France 23 D10 48 33N 3 15 E
Provo, U.S.A. 142 F8 40 14N 111 39W
Provost, Canada 131 C6 52 25N 110 20W
Prozor, Bos.-H. 42 D2 43 50N 17 34 E
Prudentópolis, Brazil 155 G1 25 12 S 50 57W
Prud'homme, Canada 131 C7 52 20N 105 54W
Prudnik, Poland 47 E4 50 20N 17 38 E
Prüm, Germany 27 E2 50 14N 6 22 E
Pruszcz Gdański, Poland 47 A5 54 17N 18 40 E
Pruszków, Poland 47 C7 52 9N 20 49 E
Prut →, Romania 46 D9 45 28N 28 10 E
Pruzhany, Belorussia 50 E4 52 33N 24 28 E
Prvič, Croatia 39 D11 44 55N 14 47 E
Prydz B., Antarctica 7 C6 69 0 S 74 0 E
Pryluky = Priluki, Ukraine 50 F8 50 30N 32 24 E
Pryor, U.S.A. 139 G7 36 19N 95 19W
Przasnysz, Poland 47 B7 53 2N 20 45 E
Przedbórz, Poland 47 D6 51 6N 19 53 E
Przedecz, Poland 47 C5 52 20N 18 53 E
Przemysl, Poland 31 B15 49 50N 22 45 E
Przeworsk, Poland 31 A15 50 6N 22 32 E
Przewóz, Poland 47 D1 51 28N 14 57 E
Przhevalsk, Kirghizia 55 B9 42 30N 78 20 E
Przysuchla, Poland 47 D7 51 22N 20 38 E
Psakhná, Greece 45 F5 38 34N 23 35 E
Psará, Greece 45 F7 38 37N 25 38 E
Psathoúra, Greece 44 E6 39 30N 24 12 E
Psel →, Ukraine 52 B5 49 5N 33 20 E
Pserimos, Greece 45 H9 36 56N 27 12 E
Psíra, Greece 32 D7 35 12N 25 52 E
Pskem →, Uzbekistan 55 C5 41 38N 70 1 E
Pskemskiy Khrebet,
Uzbekistan 55 C5 42 0N 70 45 E
Pskent, Uzbekistan 55 C4 40 54N 69 20 E
Pskov, Russia 50 C6 57 50N 28 25 E
Psunj, Croatia 42 B2 45 25N 17 19 E
Pszczyna, Poland 31 B11 49 59N 18 58 E
Pteleón, Greece 45 E4 39 3N 22 57 E
Ptich →, Belorussia 50 E6 52 9N 28 52 E
Ptolemaís, Greece 44 D3 40 30N 21 43 E
Ptuj, Slovenia 39 B12 46 28N 15 50 E
Ptujska Gora, Slovenia 39 B12 46 23N 15 47 E
Pu Xian, China 66 F6 36 24N 111 6 E
Pua, Thailand 76 C3 19 11N 100 55 E
Puán, Argentina 158 D3 37 30 S 62 45W
Pu'an, China 68 E5 25 46N 104 57 E
Puan, S. Korea 67 G14 35 44N 126 44 E
Pu'apu'a, W. Samoa 121 W23 13 34 S 172 9W
Pubei, China 68 F7 22 16N 109 31 E
Pucacuro →, Peru 152 D3 3 20 S 74 58W
Pucallpa, Peru 156 B3 8 25 S 74 30W
Pucará, Bolivia 157 D5 18 43 S 64 11W
Pucará, Peru 156 D3 15 5 S 70 24W
Pucarani, Bolivia 156 D4 16 23 S 68 30W
Pucheng, China 69 D12 27 59N 118 31 E
Pucheni, Romania 46 D6 45 12N 25 17 E
Pucio Pt., Phil. 71 F3 11 46N 121 51 E
Pučišće, Croatia 39 E13 43 22N 16 43 E
Puck, Poland 47 A5 54 45N 18 23 E
Pucka, Zatoka, Poland 47 A5 54 30N 18 40 E
Puding, China 68 D5 26 18N 105 44 E
Pudozh, Russia 48 B6 61 48N 36 32 E
Pudtol, Phil. 70 B3 18 13N 121 22 E
Pudukkottai, India 83 J4 10 28N 78 47 E
Puebla, Mexico 147 D5 19 0N 98 10W
Puebla □, Mexico 147 D5 18 30N 98 0W
Puebla de Alcocer, Spain 37 G5 38 59N 5 14W
Puebla de Don Fadrique,
Spain 35 H2 37 58N 2 25W
Puebla de Don Rodrigo,
Spain 37 F6 39 5N 4 37W
Puebla de Guzmán, Spain 37 H3 37 37N 7 15W
Puebla de Sanabria, Spain 36 C4 42 4N 6 38W
Puebla de Trives, Spain 36 C3 42 20N 7 10W
Puebla del Caramiñal,
Spain 36 C2 42 37N 8 56W
Pueblo, U.S.A. 138 F2 38 16N 104 37W
Pueblo Hundido, Chile 158 B1 26 20 S 70 5W
Pueblo Nuevo, Venezuela 152 B3 8 26N 71 26W
Puelches, Argentina 158 D2 38 5 S 65 51W
Puelén, Argentina 158 D2 37 32 S 67 38W
Puente Alto, Chile 158 C1 33 32 S 70 35W
Puente del Arzobispo,
Spain 36 F5 39 48N 5 10W
Puente-Genil, Spain 37 H6 37 22N 4 47W
Puente la Reina, Spain 34 C3 42 40N 1 49W
Puenteareas, Spain 36 C2 42 10N 8 28W
Puentedeume, Spain 36 B2 43 24N 8 10W
Puentes de Garcia
Rodriguez, Spain 36 B3 43 27N 7 50W
Pu'er, China 68 F3 23 0N 101 15 E
Puerco →, U.S.A. 143 J10 34 22N 107 50W
Puerta Galera, Phil. 70 E3 13 30N 120 57 E
Puerto, Canary Is. 33 F2 28 5N 17 20W
Puerto Acosta, Bolivia 156 D4 15 32 S 69 15W
Puerto Aisén, Chile 160 C2 45 27 S 73 0W
Puerto Ángel, Mexico 147 D5 15 40N 96 29W
Puerto Arista, Mexico 147 D6 15 56N 93 48W
Puerto Armuelles, Panama 148 E3 8 20N 82 51W
Puerto Ayacucho,
Venezuela 152 B4 5 40N 67 35W
Puerto Barrios, Guatemala 148 C2 15 40N 88 32W
Puerto Bermejo, Argentina 158 B4 26 55 S 58 34W
Puerto Bermúdez, Peru 156 C3 10 20 S 74 58W
Puerto Bolívar, Ecuador 152 D2 3 19 S 79 55W
Puerto Cabello, Venezuela 152 A4 10 28N 68 1W
Puerto Cabezas, Nic. 148 D3 14 0N 83 30W
Puerto Cabo Gracias á
Dios, Nic. 148 D3 15 0N 83 10W
Puerto Capaz = Jebba,
Morocco 98 A4 35 11N 4 43W
Puerto Carreño, Colombia 152 B4 6 12N 67 22W
Puerto Castilla, Honduras 148 C2 16 0N 86 0W
Puerto Chicama, Peru 156 B2 7 45 S 79 20W
Puerto Coig, Argentina 160 D3 50 54 S 69 15W
Puerto Cortes, Costa Rica 148 E3 8 55N 84 0W
Puerto Cortés, Honduras 148 C2 15 51N 88 0W
Puerto Cumarebo,
Venezuela 152 A4 11 29N 69 30W
Puerto de Alcudia, Spain 33 B10 39 50N 3 7 E
Puerto de Andraitx, Spain 33 B9 39 32N 2 23 E
Puerto de Cabrera, Spain 33 B9 39 8N 2 56 E
Puerto de Gran Tarajal,
Canary Is. 33 F5 28 13N 14 1W
Puerto de la Cruz,
Canary Is. 33 F3 28 24N 16 32W
Puerto de Pozo Negro,
Canary Is. 33 F6 28 19N 13 55W
Puerto de Santa María,
Spain 37 J4 36 36N 6 13W
Puerto de Sóller, Spain 33 B9 39 48N 2 42 E
Pto. del Carmen,
Canary Is. 33 F6 28 55N 13 38W
Puerto del Rosario,
Canary Is. 33 F6 28 30N 13 52W
Puerto Deseado, Argentina 160 C3 47 55 S 66 0W
Puerto Guaraní, Paraguay 157 E6 21 18 S 57 55W
Puerto Heath, Bolivia 156 C4 12 34 S 68 39W
Puerto Huitoto, Colombia 152 C3 0 18N 74 3W
Puerto Inca, Peru 156 B3 9 22 S 74 54W
Puerto Juárez, Mexico 147 C7 21 11N 86 49W
Puerto La Cruz, Venezuela 153 A5 10 13N 64 38W
Puerto Leguízamo,
Colombia 152 D3 0 12 S 74 46W
Puerto Limón, Colombia 152 C3 3 23N 73 30W
Puerto Lobos, Argentina 160 B3 42 0 S 65 3W
Puerto López, Colombia 152 C3 4 5N 72 58W
Puerto Lumbreras, Spain 35 H3 37 34N 1 48W
Puerto Madryn, Argentina 160 B3 42 48 S 65 4W
Puerto Maldonado, Peru 156 C4 12 30 S 69 10W
Puerto Manotí, Cuba 148 B4 21 22N 76 50W
Puerto Mazarrón, Spain 35 H3 37 34N 1 15W
Puerto Mercedes,
Colombia 152 C3 1 11N 72 53W
Puerto Miraña, Colombia 152 D3 1 20 S 70 19W
Puerto Montt, Chile 160 B2 41 28 S 73 0W
Puerto Morelos, Mexico 147 C7 20 49N 86 52W
Puerto Nariño, Colombia 152 C4 4 56N 67 48W
Puerto Natales, Chile 160 D2 51 45 S 72 15W
Puerto Nuevo, Colombia 152 B4 5 53N 69 56W
Puerto Nutrias, Venezuela 152 B4 8 5N 69 18W
Puerto Ordaz, Venezuela 153 B5 8 16N 62 44W
Puerto Padre, Cuba 148 B4 21 13N 76 35W
Puerto Páez, Venezuela 152 B4 6 13N 67 28W
Puerto Peñasco, Mexico 146 A2 31 20N 113 33W
Puerto Pinasco, Paraguay 158 A4 22 36 S 57 50W
Puerto Pirámides,
Argentina 160 B4 42 35 S 64 20W
Puerto Plata, Dom. Rep. 149 C5 19 48N 70 45W
Puerto Pollensa, Spain 33 B10 39 54N 3 4 E
Puerto Portillo, Peru 156 B3 9 45 S 72 42W
Puerto Princesa, Phil. 71 G2 9 46N 118 45 E
Puerto Quellón, Chile 160 B2 43 7 S 73 37W
Puerto Quepos, Costa Rica 148 E3 9 29N 84 6W
Puerto Real, Spain 37 J4 36 33N 6 12W
Puerto Rico, Bolivia 156 C4 11 5 S 67 38W
Puerto Rico, Canary Is. 33 G4 27 47N 15 42W
Puerto Rico ■, W. Indies 149 C6 18 15N 66 45W
Puerto Rico Trench,
Atl. Oc. 149 C6 19 50N 66 0W
Puerto Saavedra, Chile 160 A2 38 47 S 73 24W
Puerto Sastre, Paraguay 158 A4 22 2 S 57 55W
Puerto Siles, Bolivia 157 C4 12 48 S 65 5W
Puerto Suárez, Bolivia 157 D6 18 58 S 57 52W
Puerto Tejada, Colombia 152 C2 3 14N 76 24W
Puerto Umbría, Colombia 152 C2 0 52N 76 33W
Puerto Vallarta, Mexico 146 C3 20 36N 105 15W
Puerto Varas, Chile 160 B2 41 19 S 72 59W
Puerto Villazón, Bolivia 157 C5 13 32 S 61 57W
Puerto Wilches, Colombia 152 B3 7 21N 73 54W
Puertollano, Spain 37 G6 38 43N 4 7W
Puertomarin, Spain 36 C3 42 48N 7 36W
Puesto Cunambo, Peru 152 D2 2 10 S 76 0W
Pueyrredón, L., Argentina 160 C2 47 20 S 72 0W
Pugachev, Kazakhstan 51 F16 52 0N 48 49 E
Puge, China 68 D4 27 20N 102 31 E
Puge, Tanzania 106 C3 4 45 S 33 11 E
Puget Sound, U.S.A. 142 C2 47 50N 122 30W
Puget-Théniers, France 25 E10 43 58N 6 53 E
Púglia □, Italy 41 B9 41 0N 16 30 E
Pugo, Phil. 70 C3 16 8N 121 31 E
Pugŏdong, N. Korea 67 C16 42 5N 130 0 E
Pugu, Tanzania 106 D4 6 55 S 39 4 E
Pūgūnzī, Iran 85 E8 25 49N 59 10 E
Puha, N.Z. 118 E6 38 30 S 177 50 E
Pui, Romania 46 D4 45 30N 23 4 E
Puica, Peru 156 C3 15 0 S 72 33W
Puieşti, Romania 46 C8 46 25N 27 33 E
Puig Mayor, Spain 33 B9 39 48N 2 47 E
Puigcerdá, Spain 34 C6 42 24N 1 50 E
Puigmal, Spain 34 C7 42 23N 2 7 E
Puigpuñent, Spain 33 B9 39 38N 2 32 E
Puisaye, Collines de la,
France 23 E10 47 37N 3 20 E
Puiseaux, France 23 D9 48 11N 2 30 E
Pujilí, Ecuador 152 D2 0 57 S 78 41W
Pujon-chosuji, N. Korea 67 D14 40 35N 127 35 E
Puka, Albania 44 B1 42 2N 19 53 E
Pukaki L., N.Z. 119 E5 44 4 S 170 1 E
Pukapuka, Cook Is. 123 J11 10 53 S 165 49W
Pukatawagan, Canada 131 B8 55 45N 101 20W
Pukchin, N. Korea 67 D13 40 12N 125 45 E
Pukchŏng, N. Korea 67 D15 40 14N 128 10 E
Pukearuhe, N.Z. 118 E3 38 55 S 174 31 E
Pukekohe, N.Z. 118 D3 37 12 S 174 55 E
Puketeraki Ra., N.Z. 119 C7 42 58 S 172 13 E
Puketoi Ra., N.Z. 118 G5 40 30 S 176 5 E
Pukeuri, N.Z. 119 F6 45 4 S 171 2 E
Pukou, China 69 A12 32 7N 118 38 E
Pula, Croatia 39 D10 44 54N 13 57 E
Pula, Italy 40 D2 39 0N 9 0 E
Pulacayo, Bolivia 156 E4 20 25 S 66 41W
Pulaski, N.Y., U.S.A. 137 C8 43 34N 76 8W
Pulaski, Tenn., U.S.A. 135 H2 35 12N 87 2W
Pulaski, Va., U.S.A. 134 G5 37 3N 80 47W
Puławy, Poland 47 D8 51 23N 21 59 E
Pulga, U.S.A. 144 F5 39 48N 121 29W
Pulgaon, India 82 D4 20 44N 78 21 E
Pulicat, L., India 83 H5 13 40N 80 15 E
Puliyangudi, India 83 K3 9 11N 77 24 E
Pullabooka, Australia 117 B7 33 44 S 147 46 E
Pullman, U.S.A. 142 C5 46 44N 117 10W
Pulog, Phil. 70 C3 16 40N 120 50 E
Púlpito do Sul, Angola 103 F2 15 46 S 12 0 E
Pułtusk, Poland 47 C8 52 43N 21 6 E
Pülümür, Turkey 89 D8 39 30N 39 51 E
Pulupandan, Phil. 71 F4 10 31N 122 48 E
Pumlumon Fawr, U.K. 17 E4 52 29N 3 47W
Puna, Bolivia 157 D4 19 45 S 65 28W
Puná, I., Ecuador 152 D1 2 55 S 80 5W
Punakha, Bhutan 78 B2 27 42N 89 52 E
Punalur, India 83 K3 9 0N 76 56 E
Punasar, India 80 F5 27 6N 73 6 E
Punata, Bolivia 157 D4 17 32 S 65 50W
Punch, India 81 C6 33 48N 74 4 E
Pune, India 82 E1 18 29N 73 57 E
Pungsan, N. Korea 67 D15 40 50N 128 9 E
Pungue, Ponte de,
Mozam. 107 F3 19 0 S 34 0 E
Puning, China 69 F11 23 20N 116 12 E
Punjab □, India 80 D6 31 0N 76 0 E
Punjab □, Pakistan 79 C4 32 0N 74 30 E
Puno, Peru 156 D3 15 55 S 70 3W
Punta Alta, Argentina 160 A4 38 53 S 62 4W
Punta Arenas, Chile 160 D2 53 10 S 71 0W
Punta Cardón, Venezuela 152 A3 11 38N 70 14W
Punta Coles, Peru 156 D3 17 43 S 71 23W
Punta de Bombón, Peru 156 D3 17 10 S 71 48W

254 Qurein


Qurein, *Sudan* 95 E3 13 30N 34 50 E
Qurnat as Sawdā', *Lebanon* 91 A5 34 18N 36 6 E
Qûs, *Egypt* 94 B3 25 55N 32 50 E
Qusaybah, *Iraq* 84 C4 34 24N 40 59 E
Quşay'ir, *Yemen* 87 D5 14 55N 50 20 E
Quseir, *Egypt* 94 B3 26 7N 34 16 E
Qūshchī, *Iran* 84 B5 37 59N 45 3 E
Quthing, *Lesotho* 105 E4 30 25 S 27 36 E
Qūţīābād, *Iran* 85 C6 35 47N 48 30 E
Quwo, *China* 66 G6 35 38N 111 25 E
Quyang, *China* 66 E8 38 35N 114 40 E
Quynh Nhai, *Vietnam* 76 B4 21 49N 103 33 E
Quzi, *China* 66 F4 36 20N 107 20 E
Qytet Stalin, *Albania* 44 D1 40 47N 19 57 E
Qyzylorda = Kzyl-Orda, *Kazakhstan* 55 A2 44 48N 65 28 E

# R

Ra, Ko, *Thailand* 77 H2 9 13N 98 16 E
Råå, *Sweden* 15 J6 56 0N 12 45 E
Raab, *Austria* 30 C6 48 21N 13 39 E
Raahe, *Finland* 12 D18 64 40N 24 28 E
Raalte, *Neths.* 20 D8 52 23N 6 16 E
Raamsdonksveer, *Neths.* 21 E5 51 43N 4 52 E
Raasay, *U.K.* 18 D2 57 25N 6 4W
Raasay, Sd. of, *U.K.* 18 D2 57 30N 6 8W
Rab, *Croatia* 39 D11 44 45N 14 45 E
Raba, *Indonesia* 72 C1 8 36 S 118 55 E
Rába →, *Hungary* 31 D10 47 38N 17 38 E
Raba →, *Poland* 31 A13 50 8N 20 30 E
Rabaçal →, *Portugal* 36 D3 41 30N 7 12W
Rabah, *Nigeria* 101 C6 13 5N 5 30 E
Rabai, *Kenya* 106 C4 3 50 S 39 31 E
Rabaraba, *Papua N. G.* 120 E5 9 58 S 149 49 E
Rabastens, *France* 24 E5 43 50N 1 43 E
Rabastens-de-Bigorre, *France* 24 E4 43 23N 0 9 E
Rabat, *Malta* 32 D1 35 53N 14 25 E
Rabat, *Morocco* 98 B3 34 2N 6 48W
Rabaul, *Papua N. G.* 120 C7 4 24 S 152 18 E
Rabbit →, *Canada* 130 B3 59 41N 127 12W
Rabbit Lake, *Canada* 131 C7 53 8N 107 46W
Rabbitskin →, *Canada* 130 A4 61 47N 120 42W
Rābigh, *Si. Arabia* 86 B2 22 50N 39 5 E
Rabka, *Poland* 31 B12 49 37N 19 59 E
Rābor, *Iran* 85 D8 29 17N 56 55 E
Rača, *Serbia* 42 C5 44 14N 21 0 E
Răcale, *Italy* 41 C11 39 57N 18 6 E
Racalmuto, *Italy* 40 E6 37 25N 13 41 E
Răcăşdia, *Romania* 42 C6 44 59N 21 36 E
Racconigi, *Italy* 38 D4 44 47N 7 41 E
Raccoon →, *U.S.A.* 140 C3 41 35N 93 37W
Raccoon Cr. →, *U.S.A.* 141 E9 39 47N 87 23W
Race, C., *Canada* 129 C9 46 40N 53 5W
Rach Gia, *Vietnam* 77 G5 10 5N 105 5 E
Raciąż, *Poland* 47 C7 52 46N 20 10 E
Racibórz, *Poland* 31 A11 50 7N 18 18 E
Racine, *U.S.A.* 141 B9 42 41N 87 51W
Rackerby, *U.S.A.* 144 F5 39 26N 121 22W
Radama, Nosy, *Madag.* 105 A8 14 0 S 47 47 E
Radama, Saikanosy, *Madag.* 105 A8 14 16 S 47 53 E
Radan, *Serbia* 42 E6 42 59N 21 29 E
Rădăuţi, *Romania* 46 B6 47 50N 25 59 E
Radbuza →, *Czech.* 30 B6 49 35N 13 5 E
Radcliff, *U.S.A.* 141 G11 37 51N 85 57W
Radeburg, *Germany* 26 D9 51 6N 13 55 E
Radeče, *Slovenia* 39 B12 46 5N 15 14 E
Radekhov, *Ukraine* 50 F4 50 25N 24 32 E
Radew →, *Poland* 47 A2 54 2N 15 52 E
Radford, *U.S.A.* 134 G5 37 8N 80 34W
Radhanpur, *India* 80 H4 23 50N 71 38 E
Radiska →, *Macedonia* 42 F5 41 38N 20 37 E
Radisson, *Canada* 131 C7 52 30N 107 20W
Radium Hot Springs, *Canada* 130 C5 50 35N 116 2W
Radków, *Poland* 47 E3 50 30N 16 24 E
Radlin, *Poland* 31 A11 50 3N 18 29 E
Radna, *Romania* 42 A6 46 7N 21 41 E
Radnevo, *Bulgaria* 43 E10 42 17N 25 58 E
Radnice, *Czech.* 30 B6 49 51N 13 35 E
Radnor Forest, *U.K.* 17 E4 52 17N 3 10W
Radolfzell, *Germany* 27 H4 47 44N 8 58 E
Radom, *Poland* 47 D8 51 23N 21 12 E
Radom □, *Poland* 47 D8 51 30N 21 0 E
Radomir, *Bulgaria* 42 E8 42 37N 23 4 E
Radomka →, *Poland* 47 D8 51 31N 21 11 E
Radomsko, *Poland* 47 D6 51 5N 19 28 E
Radomyshl, *Ukraine* 50 F6 50 30N 29 12 E
Radomysl Wielki, *Poland* 31 A14 50 14N 21 15 E
Radoszyce, *Poland* 47 D7 51 4N 20 15 E
Radoviš, *Macedonia* 42 F7 41 38N 22 28 E
Radovljica, *Slovenia* 39 B11 46 22N 14 12 E
Radstadt, *Austria* 30 D6 47 24N 13 28 E
Radstock, *U.K.* 17 F5 51 17N 2 25W
Radstock, C., *Australia* 115 E1 33 12 S 134 20 E
Răducăneni, *Romania* 46 C8 46 58N 27 54 E
Raduša, *Serbia* 42 E6 42 7N 21 15 E
Radviliškis, *Lithuania* 50 D3 55 49N 23 33 E
Radville, *Canada* 131 D8 49 30N 104 15W
Radymno, *Poland* 31 B15 49 59N 22 52 E
Radzanów, *Poland* 47 C7 52 56N 20 8 E
Radziejów, *Poland* 47 C5 52 40N 18 30 E
Radzymin, *Poland* 47 C8 52 25N 21 11 E
Radzyń Chełmiński, *Poland* 47 B5 53 23N 18 55 E
Radzyń Podlaski, *Poland* 47 D9 51 47N 22 37 E
Rae, *Canada* 130 A5 62 50N 116 3W
Rae Bareli, *India* 81 F9 26 18N 81 20 E
Rae Isthmus, *Canada* 127 B11 66 40N 87 30W
Raeren, *Belgium* 21 G8 50 41N 6 7 E
Raeside, L., *Australia* 113 E3 29 20 S 122 0 E
Raetihi, *N.Z.* 118 F4 39 25 S 175 17 E
Rafaela, *Argentina* 158 C3 31 10 S 61 30W
Rafah, *Egypt* 91 D3 31 18N 34 14 E
Rafai, *C.A.R.* 102 B4 4 59N 23 58 E
Raffadali, *Italy* 40 E6 37 23N 13 29 E
Rafḩā, *Si. Arabia* 84 D4 29 35N 43 35 E
Rafsanjān, *Iran* 85 D8 30 30N 56 5 E
Raft Pt., *Australia* 112 C3 16 4 S 124 26 E
Ragag, *Sudan* 95 E1 10 59N 24 40 E
Ragang, Mt., *Phil.* 71 H5 7 43N 124 32 E
Ragay, *Phil.* 70 E4 13 49N 122 47 E
Ragay G., *Phil.* 70 E4 13 30N 122 45 E
Ragged, Mt., *Australia* 113 F3 33 27 S 123 25 E
Raglan, *Australia* 114 C5 23 42 S 150 49 E
Raglan, *N.Z.* 118 D3 37 55 S 174 55 E
Raglan Harbour, *N.Z.* 118 D3 37 47 S 174 50 E
Ragunda, *Sweden* 14 A10 63 6N 16 23 E
Ragusa, *Italy* 41 F7 36 56N 14 42 E
Raha, *Indonesia* 72 B2 4 55 S 123 0 E
Rahad, Nahr ed →, *Sudan* 95 E3 14 28N 33 31 E
Rahad al Bardī, *Sudan* 97 F4 11 20N 23 40 E
Rahaeng = Tak, *Thailand* 76 D2 16 52N 99 8 E
Rahden, *Germany* 26 C4 52 26N 8 36 E
Raheita, *Eritrea* 95 E5 12 46N 43 4 E
Raḩīmah, *Si. Arabia* 85 E6 26 42N 50 4 E
Rahimyar Khan, *Pakistan* 79 C3 28 30N 70 25 E
Rāhjerd, *Iran* 85 C6 34 22N 50 22 E
Rahotu, *N.Z.* 118 F2 39 20 S 173 49 E
Raichur, *India* 83 F3 16 10N 77 20 E
Raiganj, *India* 81 G13 25 37N 88 10 E
Raigarh, *India* 82 D6 21 56N 83 25 E
Raighar, *India* 82 E6 19 51N 82 6 E
Raijua, *Indonesia* 72 D2 10 37 S 121 36 E
Railton, *Australia* 114 G4 41 25 S 146 28 E
Rainbow, *Australia* 116 C5 35 55 S 142 0 E
Rainbow Lake, *Canada* 130 B5 58 30N 119 23W
Rainier, *U.S.A.* 144 D4 46 53N 122 41W
Rainier, Mt., *U.S.A.* 144 D5 46 52N 121 46W
Rainy L., *Canada* 131 D10 48 42N 93 10W
Rainy River, *Canada* 131 D10 48 43N 94 29W
Raipur, *India* 82 D5 21 17N 81 45 E
Raj Nandgaon, *India* 82 D5 21 5N 81 5 E
Raja, Ujung, *Indonesia* 74 B1 3 40N 96 25 E
Raja Ampat, Kepulauan, *Indonesia* 73 B4 0 30 S 130 0 E
Rajahmundry, *India* 82 F5 17 1N 81 48 E
Rajajooseppi, *Finland* 12 B20 68 28N 28 29 E
Rajang →, *Malaysia* 75 B4 2 30N 112 0 E
Rajapalaiyam, *India* 83 K3 9 25N 77 35 E
Rajasthan □, *India* 80 F5 26 45N 73 30 E
Rajasthan Canal, *India* 80 E5 28 0N 72 0 E
Rajauri, *India* 81 C6 33 25N 74 21 E
Rajbari, *Bangla.* 78 D2 23 47N 89 41 E
Rajgarh, *Mad. P., India* 80 G7 24 2N 76 45 E
Rajgarh, *Raj., India* 80 E6 28 40N 75 25 E
Rajgród, *Poland* 47 B9 53 42N 22 42 E
Rajhenburg, *Slovenia* 39 B12 46 1N 15 29 E
Rajkot, *India* 80 H4 22 15N 70 56 E
Rajmahal Hills, *India* 81 G12 24 30N 87 30 E
Rajpipla, *India* 82 D1 21 50N 73 30 E
Rajpura, *India* 80 D7 30 25N 76 32 E
Rajshahi, *Bangla.* 78 C2 24 22N 88 39 E
Rajshahi □, *Bangla.* 81 G13 25 0N 89 0 E
Rakaia, *N.Z.* 119 D7 43 45 S 172 1 E
Rakaia →, *N.Z.* 119 D7 43 36 S 172 15 E
Rakan, Ra's, *Qatar* 85 E6 26 10N 51 20 E
Rakaposhi, *Pakistan* 81 A6 36 10N 74 25 E
Rakata, Pulau, *Indonesia* 74 D3 6 10 S 105 20 E
Rakhawt, W. →, *Yemen* 87 C5 18 16N 51 50 E
Rakhneh-ye Jamshīdī, *Afghan.* 79 B1 34 22N 62 19 E
Rakhni, *Pakistan* 80 D3 30 4N 69 56 E
Rakhyūt, *Oman* 87 C6 16 44N 53 20 E
Rakitnoye, *Russia* 60 B7 45 36N 134 17 E
Rakitovo, *Bulgaria* 43 F9 41 59N 24 5 E
Rakkestad, *Norway* 14 E5 59 25N 11 21 E
Rakoniewice, *Poland* 47 C3 52 10N 16 16 E
Rakops, *Botswana* 104 C3 21 1 S 24 28 E
Rákospalota, *Hungary* 31 D12 47 30N 19 5 E
Rakov, *Belorussia* 50 E5 53 58N 26 59 E
Rakovica, *Croatia* 39 D12 44 59N 15 38 E
Rakovník, *Czech.* 30 A6 50 6N 13 42 E
Rakovski, *Bulgaria* 43 E9 42 21N 24 57 E
Rakvere, *Estonia* 50 B5 59 20N 26 25 E
Raleigh, *U.S.A.* 135 H6 35 47N 78 39W
Raleigh B., *U.S.A.* 135 H7 34 50N 76 15W
Ralja, *Serbia* 42 C5 44 33N 20 34 E
Ralls, *U.S.A.* 139 J4 33 41N 101 24W
Ram →, *Canada* 130 A4 62 1N 123 41W
Rām Allāh, *Jordan* 91 D4 31 55N 35 10 E
Ram Hd., *Australia* 117 D8 37 47 S 149 30 E
Rama, *Nic.* 148 D3 12 9N 84 15W
Ramacca, *Italy* 41 E7 37 24N 14 40 E
Ramachandrapuram, *India* 82 F6 16 50N 82 4 E
Ramales de la Victoria, *Spain* 34 B1 43 15N 3 28W
Ramalho, Serra do, *Brazil* 155 D3 13 45 S 44 0W
Raman, *Thailand* 77 J3 6 29N 101 18 E
Ramanathapuram, *India* 83 K4 9 25N 78 55 E
Ramanetaka, B. de, *Madag.* 105 A8 14 13 S 47 52 E
Ramas C., *India* 83 G1 15 5N 73 55 E
Ramat Gan, *Israel* 91 C3 32 4N 34 48 E
Ramatlhabama, *S. Africa* 104 D4 25 37 S 25 33 E
Ramban, *India* 81 C6 33 14N 75 12 E
Rambervillers, *France* 23 D13 48 20N 6 38 E
Rambi, *Fiji* 121 A3 16 30 S 179 59W
Rambipuji, *Indonesia* 75 D4 8 12 S 113 37 E
Rambouillet, *France* 23 D8 48 39N 1 50 E
Ramdurg, *India* 83 G2 15 58N 75 22 E
Ramea, *Canada* 129 C8 47 31N 57 23W
Ramechhap, *Nepal* 81 F12 27 25N 86 10 E
Ramelau, *Indonesia* 72 C3 8 55 S 126 22 E
Ramenskoye, *Russia* 51 D11 55 32N 38 15 E
Ramgarh, *Bihar, India* 81 H11 23 40N 85 35 E
Ramgarh, *Raj., India* 80 F6 27 16N 75 14 E
Ramgarh, *Raj., India* 80 F4 27 30N 70 36 E
Rāmhormoz, *Iran* 85 D6 31 15N 49 35 E
Ramīān, *Iran* 85 B7 37 3N 55 16 E
Ramingining, *Australia* 114 A2 12 19 S 135 3 E
Ramla, *Israel* 91 D3 31 55N 34 52 E
Ramlat Zalţan, *Libya* 96 C3 28 30N 19 30 E
Ramlu, *Eritrea* 95 E5 13 32N 41 40 E
Ramme, *Denmark* 15 H2 56 30N 8 11 E
Ramnad = Ramanathapuram, *India* 83 K4 9 25N 78 55 E
Ramnagar, *India* 81 C6 32 47N 75 18 E
Ramnäs, *Sweden* 14 E10 59 46N 16 12 E
Ramon, *Russia* 51 F11 51 55N 39 21 E
Ramona, *U.S.A.* 145 M10 33 2N 116 52W
Ramore, *Canada* 128 C3 48 30N 80 25W
Ramotswa, *Botswana* 104 C4 24 50 S 25 52 E
Rampur, *H.P., India* 80 D7 31 26N 77 43 E
Rampur, *Mad. P., India* 80 H5 23 25N 73 53 E
Rampur, *Orissa, India* 82 D6 21 48N 83 58 E
Rampur, *Ut. P., India* 81 E8 28 50N 79 5 E
Rampur Hat, *India* 81 G12 24 10N 87 50 E
Rampura, *India* 80 G6 24 30N 75 27 E
Rāmsar, *Iran* 85 B6 36 53N 50 41 E
Ramsel, *Belgium* 21 F5 51 2N 4 50 E
Ramsey, *Canada* 128 C3 47 25N 82 20W
Ramsey, *U.K.* 16 C3 54 20N 4 21W
Ramsey, *U.S.A.* 140 E7 39 8N 89 7W
Ramsgate, *U.K.* 17 F9 51 20N 1 25 E
Ramshai, *India* 78 B2 26 44N 88 51 E
Ramsjö, *Sweden* 14 B9 62 11N 15 37 E
Ramtek, *India* 82 D4 21 20N 79 15 E
Ramu →, *Papua N. G.* 120 C3 4 0 S 144 41 E
Ramvik, *Sweden* 14 B11 62 49N 17 51 E
Ranaghat, *India* 81 H13 23 15N 88 35 E
Ranahu, *Pakistan* 80 G3 25 55N 69 45 E
Rancagua, *Chile* 158 C1 34 10 S 70 50W
Rance, *Belgium* 21 H4 50 9N 4 16 E
Rance →, *France* 22 D5 48 34N 1 59W
Rance, Barrage de la, *France* 22 D4 48 30N 2 3W
Rancharia, *Brazil* 155 F1 22 15 S 50 55W
Rancheria →, *Canada* 130 A3 60 13N 129 7W
Ranchester, *U.S.A.* 142 D10 44 54N 107 10W
Ranchi, *India* 81 H11 23 19N 85 27 E
Ranco, L., *Chile* 160 B2 40 15 S 72 25W
Rancu, *Romania* 46 E5 44 32N 24 15 E
Rand, *Australia* 117 C7 35 33 S 146 32 E
Randan, *France* 24 B7 46 2N 3 21 E
Randazzo, *Italy* 41 E7 37 53N 14 56 E
Randers, *Denmark* 15 H4 56 29N 10 1 E
Randers Fjord, *Denmark* 15 H4 56 37N 10 20 E
Randfontein, *S. Africa* 105 D4 26 8 S 27 45 E
Randle, *U.S.A.* 144 D5 46 32N 121 57W
Randolph, *Mass., U.S.A.* 137 D13 42 10N 71 2W
Randolph, *N.Y., U.S.A.* 136 D6 42 10N 78 59W
Randolph, *Utah, U.S.A.* 142 F8 41 40N 111 11W
Randolph, *Vt., U.S.A.* 137 C12 43 55N 72 40W
Randsfjord, *Norway* 14 D4 60 15N 10 25 E
Råne älv →, *Sweden* 12 D17 65 50N 22 20 E
Ranfurly, *N.Z.* 119 F5 45 7 S 170 6 E
Rangae, *Thailand* 77 J3 6 19N 101 44 E
Rangamati, *Bangla.* 78 D4 22 38N 92 12 E
Rangataua, *N.Z.* 118 F4 39 26 S 175 28 E
Rangaunu B., *N.Z.* 118 A2 34 51 S 173 15 E
Rångedala, *Sweden* 15 G7 57 47N 13 9 E
Rangeley, *U.S.A.* 137 B14 44 58N 70 39W
Rangely, *U.S.A.* 142 F9 40 5N 108 48W
Ranger, *U.S.A.* 139 J5 32 28N 98 41W
Rangia, *India* 78 B3 26 28N 91 38 E
Rangiora, *N.Z.* 119 D7 43 19 S 172 36 E
Rangitaiki, *N.Z.* 118 E5 38 52 S 176 24 E
Rangitaiki →, *N.Z.* 118 D5 37 54 S 176 49 E
Rangitata →, *N.Z.* 119 D6 43 45 S 171 15 E
Rangitikei →, *N.Z.* 118 G4 40 17 S 175 15 E
Rangitoto Ra., *N.Z.* 118 E4 38 25 S 175 35 E
Rangkasbitung, *Indonesia* 74 D3 6 21 S 106 15 E
Rangoon, *Burma* 78 G6 16 45N 96 20 E
Rangpur, *Bangla.* 78 C2 25 42N 89 22 E
Rangsang, *Indonesia* 74 B2 1 20N 103 5 E
Rangsit, *Thailand* 76 F3 13 59N 100 37 E
Ranibennur, *India* 83 G2 14 35N 75 30 E
Raniganj, *India* 81 H12 23 40N 87 5 E
Ranippettai, *India* 83 H4 12 56N 79 23 E
Rāniyah, *Iraq* 84 B5 36 15N 44 53 E
Ranken →, *Australia* 114 C2 20 31 S 137 36 E
Rankin, *Ill., U.S.A.* 141 D9 40 28N 87 54W
Rankin, *Tex., U.S.A.* 139 K4 31 13N 101 56W
Rankin Inlet, *Canada* 126 B10 62 30N 93 0W
Rankins Springs, *Australia* 117 B7 33 49 S 146 14 E
Rannoch, L., *U.K.* 18 E4 56 41N 4 20W
Rannoch Moor, *U.K.* 18 E4 56 38N 4 48W
Ranobe, Helodranon' i, *Madag.* 105 C7 23 3 S 43 33 E
Ranohira, *Madag.* 105 C8 22 29 S 45 24 E
Ranomafana, *Toamasina, Madag.* 105 B8 18 57 S 48 50 E
Ranomafana, *Toliara, Madag.* 105 C8 24 34 S 47 0 E
Ranong, *Thailand* 77 H2 9 56N 98 40 E
Rānsa, *Iran* 85 C6 33 39N 48 18 E
Ransiki, *Indonesia* 73 B4 1 30 S 134 10 E
Ransom, *U.S.A.* 141 C8 41 9N 88 39W
Rantau, *Indonesia* 75 C5 2 56 S 115 9 E
Rantauprapat, *Indonesia* 74 B1 2 15N 99 50 E
Rantekombola, *Indonesia* 72 B1 3 15 S 119 57 E
Rantoul, *U.S.A.* 141 D8 40 19N 88 9W
Ranum, *Denmark* 15 H3 56 54N 9 14 E
Ranyah, W. →, *Si. Arabia* 86 B3 21 18N 43 20 E
Raon l'Étape, *France* 23 D13 48 24N 6 50 E
Raoui, Erg er, *Algeria* 99 C4 29 0N 2 0W
Raoyang, *China* 66 E8 38 15N 115 45 E
Rapa, *Pac. Oc.* 123 K13 27 35 S 144 20W
Rapallo, *Italy* 38 D6 44 21N 9 12 E
Rāpch, *Iran* 85 E8 25 40N 59 15 E
Rapid →, *Canada* 130 B3 59 15N 129 5W
Rapid City, *U.S.A.* 138 D3 44 5N 103 14W
Rapid River, *U.S.A.* 134 C2 45 55N 86 58W
Rapides des Joachims, *Canada* 128 C4 46 13N 77 43W
Rapla, *Estonia* 50 B4 59 1N 24 52 E
Rapperswil, *Switz.* 29 B7 47 14N 8 45 E
Rapu Rapu I., *Phil.* 70 E5 13 12N 124 9 E
Rarotonga, *Cook Is.* 123 K12 21 30 S 160 0W
Ra's al' Ayn, *Syria* 84 B4 36 51N 40 4 E
Ra's al Khaymah, *U.A.E.* 85 E8 25 50N 56 5 E
Ra's al-Unuf, *Libya* 96 B3 30 25N 18 15 E
Ra's an Naqb, *Jordan* 91 F4 30 0N 35 29 E
Ras Bânâs, *Egypt* 94 C4 23 57N 35 59 E
Ras Dashen, *Ethiopia* 95 E4 13 8N 38 26 E
Ras el Ma, *Algeria* 99 B4 34 26N 0 50W
Ras Mallap, *Egypt* 94 J8 29 18N 32 50 E
Râs Timirist, *Mauritania* 100 B1 19 21N 16 30W
Rasa, Punta, *Argentina* 160 B4 40 50 S 62 15W
Rasca, Pta. de la, *Canary Is.* 33 G3 27 59N 16 41W
Raseiniai, *Lithuania* 50 D3 55 25N 23 5 E
Rashad, *Sudan* 95 E3 11 55N 31 0 E
Rashîd, *Egypt* 94 H7 31 21N 30 22 E
Rashîd, Masabb, *Egypt* 94 H7 31 22N 30 17 E
Rasht, *Iran* 85 B6 37 20N 49 40 E
Rasi Salai, *Thailand* 76 E5 15 20N 104 9 E
Rasipuram, *India* 83 J4 11 30N 78 15 E
Raška, *Serbia* 42 D5 43 19N 20 39 E
Rason L., *Australia* 113 E3 28 45 S 124 25 E
Raşova, *Romania* 46 E8 44 15N 27 55 E
Rasovo, *Bulgaria* 43 D8 43 42N 23 17 E
Rasra, *India* 81 G10 25 50N 83 50 E
Rass el Oued, *Algeria* 99 A6 35 57N 5 2 E
Rasskazovo, *Russia* 51 E12 52 35N 41 50 E
Rastatt, *Germany* 27 G4 48 50N 8 12 E
Rastu, *Romania* 46 F4 43 53N 23 16 E
Raszków, *Poland* 47 D4 51 43N 17 40 E
Rat Buri, *Thailand* 76 F2 13 30N 99 54 E
Rat Islands, *U.S.A.* 126 C1 52 0N 178 0 E
Rat River, *Canada* 130 A6 61 7N 112 36W
Ratangarh, *India* 80 E6 28 5N 74 35 E
Raţāwī, *Iraq* 84 D5 30 38N 47 13 E
Rath, *India* 81 G8 25 36N 79 37 E
Rath Luirc, *Ireland* 19 D3 52 21N 8 40W
Rathbun Res., *U.S.A.* 140 D4 40 49N 92 53W
Rathdrum, *Ireland* 19 D5 52 57N 6 13W
Rathedaung, *Burma* 78 E4 20 29N 92 45 E
Rathenow, *Germany* 26 C8 52 38N 12 23 E
Rathkeale, *Ireland* 19 D3 52 32N 8 57W
Rathlin, *U.K.* 19 A5 55 18N 6 14W
Rathlin O'Birne I., *Ireland* 19 B3 54 40N 8 50W
Ratibor = Racibórz, *Poland* 31 A11 50 7N 18 18 E
Rätikon, *Austria* 30 D2 47 0N 9 55 E
Ratlam, *India* 80 H6 23 20N 75 0 E
Ratnagiri, *India* 82 F1 16 57N 73 18 E
Ratnapura, *Sri Lanka* 83 L5 6 40N 80 20 E
Raton, *U.S.A.* 139 G2 36 54N 104 24W
Rattaphum, *Thailand* 77 J3 7 8N 100 16 E
Ratten, *Austria* 30 D8 47 28N 15 44 E
Rattray Hd., *U.K.* 18 D7 57 38N 1 50W
Ratz, Mt., *Canada* 130 B2 57 23N 132 12W
Ratzeburg, *Germany* 26 B6 53 41N 10 46 E
Raub, *Malaysia* 77 L3 3 47N 101 52 E
Rauch, *Argentina* 158 D4 36 45 S 59 5W
Raufarhöfn, *Iceland* 12 C6 66 27N 15 57W
Raufoss, *Norway* 14 D4 60 44N 10 37 E
Raukumara Ra., *N.Z.* 118 E6 38 5 S 177 55 E
Raul Soares, *Brazil* 155 F3 20 5 S 42 22W
Rauland, *Norway* 14 E2 59 43N 8 0 E
Rauma, *Finland* 13 F16 61 10N 21 30 E
Rauma →, *Norway* 14 B1 62 34N 7 43 E
Raurkela, *India* 81 H11 22 14N 84 50 E
Rausu-Dake, *Japan* 60 B12 44 4N 145 7 E
Rava Russkaya, *Ukraine* 50 F3 50 15N 23 42 E
Ravānsar, *Iran* 84 C5 34 43N 46 40 E
Ravanusa, *Italy* 40 E6 37 16N 13 58 E
Rāvar, *Iran* 85 D8 31 20N 56 51 E
Ravels, *Belgium* 21 F6 51 22N 5 0 E
Ravena, *U.S.A.* 137 D11 42 28N 73 49W
Ravenna, *Italy* 39 D9 44 28N 12 15 E
Ravenna, *Ky., U.S.A.* 141 G13 37 42N 83 55W
Ravenna, *Nebr., U.S.A.* 138 E5 41 1N 98 55W
Ravenna, *Ohio, U.S.A.* 136 E3 41 9N 81 15W
Ravensburg, *Germany* 27 H5 47 48N 9 38 E
Ravenshoe, *Australia* 114 B4 17 37 S 145 29 E
Ravenstein, *Neths.* 20 E7 51 47N 5 39 E
Ravensthorpe, *Australia* 113 F3 33 35 S 120 2 E
Ravenswood, *Australia* 114 C4 20 6 S 146 54 E
Ravenswood, *U.S.A.* 134 F5 38 57N 81 47W
Ravensworth, *Australia* 117 B9 32 26 S 151 4 E
Ravenwood, *U.S.A.* 140 D2 40 22N 94 41W
Ravi →, *Pakistan* 80 D4 30 35N 71 49 E
Ravna Gora, *Croatia* 39 C11 45 24N 14 50 E
Ravna Reka, *Serbia* 42 D6 43 59N 21 35 E
Rawa Mazowiecka, *Poland* 47 D7 51 46N 20 12 E
Rawalpindi, *Pakistan* 79 B4 33 38N 73 8 E
Rawāndūz, *Iraq* 84 B5 36 40N 44 30 E
Rawang, *Malaysia* 77 L3 3 20N 101 35 E
Rawdon, *Canada* 128 C5 46 3N 73 40W
Rawene, *N.Z.* 118 B2 35 25 S 173 32 E
Rawicz, *Poland* 47 D3 51 36N 16 52 E
Rawka →, *Poland* 47 C7 52 9N 20 8 E
Rawlinna, *Australia* 113 F4 30 58 S 125 28 E
Rawlins, *U.S.A.* 142 F10 41 47N 107 14W
Rawlinson Ra., *Australia* 113 D4 24 40 S 128 30 E
Rawson, *Argentina* 160 B3 43 15 S 65 5W
Ray, *U.S.A.* 138 A3 48 21N 103 10W
Ray, C., *Canada* 129 C8 47 33N 59 15W
Rayachoti, *India* 83 G4 14 4N 78 50 E
Rayadurg, *India* 83 G3 14 40N 76 50 E
Rayagada, *India* 82 E6 19 15N 83 20 E
Raychikhinsk, *Russia* 57 E13 49 46N 129 25 E
Rāyen, *Iran* 85 D8 29 34N 57 26 E
Rayevskiy, *Russia* 54 D4 54 4N 54 56 E
Raymond, *Canada* 130 D6 49 30N 112 35W
Raymond, *Calif., U.S.A.* 144 H7 37 13N 119 54W
Raymond, *Ill., U.S.A.* 140 E7 39 19N 89 34W
Raymond, *Wash., U.S.A.* 144 D3 46 41N 123 44W
Raymond Terrace, *Australia* 117 B9 32 45 S 151 44 E
Raymondville, *U.S.A.* 139 M6 26 29N 97 47W
Raymore, *Canada* 131 C8 51 25N 104 31W
Rayne, *U.S.A.* 139 K8 30 14N 92 16W
Rayón, *Mexico* 146 B2 29 43N 110 35W
Rayong, *Thailand* 76 F3 12 40N 101 20 E
Raytown, *U.S.A.* 140 E2 39 1N 94 28W
Rayville, *U.S.A.* 139 J9 32 29N 91 46W
Raz, Pte. du, *France* 22 D2 48 2N 4 47W
Razan, *Iran* 85 C6 35 23N 49 2 E
Ražana, *Serbia* 42 C4 44 6N 19 55 E
Ražanj, *Serbia* 42 D6 43 40N 21 31 E
Razdelna, *Bulgaria* 43 D12 43 13N 27 41 E
Razdel'naya, *Ukraine* 52 C4 46 50N 30 2 E
Razdolnoye, *Russia* 60 C5 43 30N 131 52 E
Razdolnoye, *Ukraine* 52 D5 45 46N 33 29 E
Razeh, *Iran* 85 C6 32 47N 48 9 E
Razelm, Lacul, *Romania* 46 E10 44 50N 29 0 E
Razgrad, *Bulgaria* 43 D11 43 33N 26 34 E
Razlog, *Bulgaria* 43 F8 41 53N 23 28 E
Razmak, *Pakistan* 79 B3 32 45N 69 50 E
Razole, *India* 83 F5 16 36N 81 48 E
Ré, I. de, *France* 24 B2 46 12N 1 30W
Reading, *U.K.* 17 F7 51 27N 0 57W
Reading, *Mich., U.S.A.* 141 C12 41 50N 84 45W
Reading, *Ohio, U.S.A.* 141 E12 39 13N 84 26W
Reading, *Pa., U.S.A.* 137 F9 40 20N 75 56W
Real, Cordillera, *Bolivia* 156 D4 17 0 S 67 10W
Realicó, *Argentina* 158 D3 35 0 S 64 15W
Réalmont, *France* 24 E6 43 48N 2 10 E

256 Rimrock


Rimrock, *U.S.A.* **144 D5** 46 38N 121 10W
Rinca, *Indonesia* **72 C1** 8 45 S 119 35 E
Rincón de Romos, *Mexico* **146 C4** 22 14N 102 18W
Rinconada, *Argentina* **158 A2** 22 26 S 66 10W
Ringarum, *Sweden* **15 F10** 58 21N 16 26 E
Ringe, *Denmark* **15 J4** 55 13N 10 28 E
Ringgold Is., *Fiji* **121 A3** 16 15 S 179 25W
Ringim, *Nigeria* **101 C6** 12 13N 9 10 E
Ringkøbing, *Denmark* **15 H2** 56 5N 8 15 E
Ringling, *U.S.A.* **142 C8** 46 16N 110 49W
Ringsaker, *Norway* **14 D4** 60 54N 10 45 E
Ringsted, *Denmark* **15 J5** 55 25N 11 46 E
Ringvassøy, *Norway* **12 B15** 69 56N 19 15 E
Rinía, *Greece* **45 G7** 37 23N 25 13 E
Rinjani, *Indonesia* **75 D5** 8 24 S 116 28 E
Rinteln, *Germany* **26 C5** 52 11N 9 3 E
Río, Punta del, *Spain* **35 J2** 36 49N 2 24W
Rio Branco, *Brazil* **156 B4** 9 58 S 67 49W
Río Branco, *Uruguay* **159 C5** 32 40 S 53 40W
Rio Brilhante, *Brazil* **159 A5** 21 48 S 54 33W
Río Bueno, *Chile* **160 B2** 40 19 S 72 58W
Río Chico, *Venezuela* **152 A4** 10 19N 65 59W
Rio Claro, *Brazil* **159 A6** 22 19 S 47 35W
Rio Claro, *Trin. & Tob.* **149 D7** 10 20N 61 25W
Río Colorado, *Argentina* **160 A4** 39 0 S 64 0W
Río Cuarto, *Argentina* **158 C3** 33 10 S 64 25W
Rio das Pedras, *Mozam.* **105 C6** 23 8 S 35 28 E
Rio de Contas, *Brazil* **155 D3** 13 36 S 41 48W
Rio de Janeiro, *Brazil* **155 F3** 23 0 S 43 12W
Rio de Janeiro □, *Brazil* **155 F3** 22 50 S 43 0W
Rio do Prado, *Brazil* **155 E3** 16 35 S 40 34W
Rio do Sul, *Brazil* **159 B6** 27 13 S 49 37W
Río Gallegos, *Argentina* **160 D3** 51 35 S 69 15W
Río Grande, *Argentina* **160 D3** 53 50 S 67 45W
Río Grande, *Bolivia* **156 E4** 20 51 S 67 17W
Rio Grande, *Brazil* **159 C5** 32 0 S 52 20W
Río Grande, *Mexico* **146 C4** 23 50N 103 2W
Río Grande, *Nic.* **148 D3** 12 54N 83 33W
Rio Grande →, *U.S.A.* **139 N6** 25 57N 97 9W
Rio Grande City, *U.S.A.* **139 M5** 26 23N 98 49W
Río Grande del Norte →, *N. Amer.* **133 E7** 26 0N 97 0W
Rio Grande do Norte □, *Brazil* **154 C4** 5 40 S 36 0W
Rio Grande do Sul □, *Brazil* **159 C5** 30 0 S 53 0W
Río Hato, *Panama* **148 E3** 8 22N 80 10W
Río Lagartos, *Mexico* **147 C7** 21 36N 88 10W
Rio Largo, *Brazil* **154 C4** 9 28 S 35 50W
Rio Maior, *Portugal* **37 F2** 39 19N 8 57W
Rio Marina, *Italy* **38 F7** 42 48N 10 25 E
Río Mayo, *Argentina* **160 C2** 45 40 S 70 15W
Río Mulatos, *Bolivia* **156 D4** 19 40 S 66 50W
Río Muni = Mbini □, *Eq. Guin.* **102 B2** 1 30N 10 0 E
Rio Negro, *Brazil* **159 B6** 26 0 S 49 55W
Río Negro, *Chile* **160 B2** 40 47 S 73 14W
Rio Negro, Pantanal do, *Brazil* **157 D6** 19 0 S 56 0W
Rio Pardo, *Brazil* **159 C5** 30 0 S 52 30W
Río Pico, *Argentina* **160 B2** 44 0 S 70 22W
Rio Real, *Brazil* **155 D4** 11 28 S 37 56W
Río Segundo, *Argentina* **158 C3** 31 40 S 63 59W
Río Tercero, *Argentina* **158 C3** 32 15 S 64 8W
Rio Tinto, *Brazil* **154 C4** 6 48 S 35 5W
Rio Tinto, *Portugal* **36 D2** 41 11N 8 34W
Rio Verde, *Brazil* **155 E1** 17 50 S 51 0W
Río Verde, *Mexico* **147 C5** 21 56N 99 59W
Rio Verde de Mato Grosso, *Brazil* **157 D7** 18 56 S 54 52W
Rio Vista, *U.S.A.* **144 G5** 38 10N 121 42W
Ríobamba, *Ecuador* **152 D2** 1 50 S 78 45W
Ríohacha, *Colombia* **152 A3** 11 33N 72 55W
Rioja, *Peru* **156 B2** 6 11 S 77 5W
Riom, *France* **24 C7** 45 54N 3 7 E
Riom-ès-Montagnes, *France* **24 C6** 45 17N 2 39 E
Rion-des-Landes, *France* **24 E3** 43 55N 0 56W
Rionegro, *Colombia* **152 B2** 6 9N 75 22W
Rionero in Vúlture, *Italy* **41 B8** 40 55N 15 40 E
Rioni →, *Georgia* **53 E9** 42 5N 41 50 E
Rios, *Spain* **36 D3** 41 58N 7 16W
Riosucio, Caldas, *Colombia* **152 B2** 5 30N 75 40W
Ríosucio, Choco, *Colombia* **152 B2** 7 27N 77 7W
Riou L., *Canada* **131 B7** 59 7N 106 25W
Rioz, *France* **23 E13** 47 26N 6 5 E
Riozinho →, *Brazil* **152 D4** 2 55 S 67 7W
Riparia, Dora →, *Italy* **38 C4** 45 7N 7 24 E
Ripatransone, *Italy* **39 F10** 43 0N 13 45 E
Ripley, *Canada* **136 B3** 44 4N 81 35W
Ripley, *Calif., U.S.A.* **145 M12** 33 32N 114 39W
Ripley, *N.Y., U.S.A.* **136 D5** 42 16N 79 43W
Ripley, *Ohio, U.S.A.* **141 F13** 38 45N 83 51W
Ripley, *Tenn., U.S.A.* **139 H10** 35 45N 89 32W
Ripoll, *Spain* **34 C7** 42 15N 2 13 E
Ripon, *U.K.* **16 C6** 54 8N 1 31W
Ripon, *Calif., U.S.A.* **144 H5** 37 44N 121 7W
Ripon, *Wis., U.S.A.* **134 D1** 43 51N 88 50W
Riposto, *Italy* **41 E8** 37 44N 15 12 E
Risalpur, *Pakistan* **80 B4** 34 3N 71 59 E
Risan, *Montenegro* **42 E3** 42 32N 18 42 E
Risaralda □, *Colombia* **152 B2** 5 0N 76 10W
Riscle, *France* **24 E3** 43 39N 0 5W
Rishā', W. ar →, *Si. Arabia* **84 E5** 25 33N 44 5 E
Rishiri-Tō, *Japan* **60 B10** 45 11N 141 15 E
Rishon le Ziyyon, *Israel* **91 D3** 31 58N 34 48 E
Rising Sun, *U.S.A.* **141 F12** 38 57N 84 51W
Risle →, *France* **22 C7** 49 26N 0 23 E
Rîsnov, *Romania* **46 D6** 45 35N 25 27 E
Rison, *U.S.A.* **139 J8** 33 58N 92 11W
Risør, *Norway* **15 F3** 58 43N 9 13 E
Rissani, *Morocco* **98 B4** 31 18N 4 12W
Riti, *Nigeria* **101 D6** 7 57N 9 41 E
Ritidian Pt., *Guam* **121 R15** 13 39N 144 51 E
Rittman, *U.S.A.* **136 F3** 40 58N 81 47W
Ritzville, *U.S.A.* **142 C4** 47 8N 118 23W
Riu, *India* **78 A5** 28 19N 95 3 E
Riva Bella, *France* **22 C6** 49 17N 0 18W
Riva del Garda, *Italy* **38 C7** 45 53N 10 50 E
Rivadavia, Buenos Aires, *Argentina* **158 D3** 35 29 S 62 59W
Rivadavia, Mendoza, *Argentina* **158 C2** 33 13 S 68 30W
Rivadavia, Salta, *Argentina* **158 A3** 24 5 S 62 54W
Rivadavia, *Chile* **158 B1** 29 57 S 70 35W
Rivarolo Canavese, *Italy* **38 C4** 45 20N 7 42 E
Rivas, *Nic.* **148 D2** 11 30N 85 50W
Rive-de-Gier, *France* **25 C8** 45 32N 4 37 E
River Cess, *Liberia* **100 D3** 5 30N 9 32W
Rivera, *Uruguay* **159 C4** 31 0 S 55 50W
Riverdale, *U.S.A.* **144 J7** 36 26N 119 52W
Riverhead, *U.S.A.* **137 F12** 40 55N 72 40W
Riverhurst, *Canada* **131 C7** 50 55N 106 50W
Riverina, *Australia* **113 E3** 29 45 S 120 40 E
Rivers, *Canada* **131 C8** 50 2N 100 14W
Rivers □, *Nigeria* **101 E6** 5 0N 6 30 E
Rivers, L. of the, *Canada* **131 D7** 49 49N 105 44W
Rivers Inlet, *Canada* **130 C3** 51 42N 127 15W
Riversdale, *N.Z.* **119 F3** 45 54 S 168 44 E
Riversdale, *S. Africa* **104 E3** 34 7 S 21 15 E
Riverside, *Calif., U.S.A.* **145 M9** 33 59N 117 22W
Riverside, *Wyo., U.S.A.* **142 F10** 41 13N 106 47W
Riversleigh, *Australia* **114 B2** 19 5 S 138 40 E
Riverton, *Australia* **116 C3** 34 10 S 138 46 E
Riverton, *Canada* **131 C9** 51 1N 97 0W
Riverton, *N.Z.* **119 G2** 46 21 S 168 0 E
Riverton, *Ill., U.S.A.* **140 E7** 39 51N 89 33W
Riverton, *Wyo., U.S.A.* **142 E9** 43 2N 108 23W
Riverton Heights, *U.S.A.* **144 C4** 47 28N 122 17W
Rives, *France* **25 C9** 45 21N 5 31 E
Rivesaltes, *France* **24 F6** 42 47N 2 50 E
Riviera, *Europe* **38 E5** 44 0N 8 30 E
Rivière-à-Pierre, *Canada* **129 C5** 46 59N 72 11W
Rivière-au-Renard, *Canada* **129 C7** 48 59N 64 23W
Rivière-du-Loup, *Canada* **129 C6** 47 50N 69 30W
Rivière-Pentecôte, *Canada* **129 C6** 49 57N 67 1W
Rivière-Pilote, *Martinique* **149 D7** 14 26N 60 53W
Rivne = Rovno, *Ukraine* **50 F5** 50 40N 26 10 E
Rívoli, *Italy* **38 C4** 45 3N 7 31 E
Rivoli B., *Australia* **116 D4** 37 32 S 140 3 E
Riwaka, *N.Z.* **119 B7** 41 5 S 172 59 E
Rixensart, *Belgium* **21 G5** 50 43N 4 32 E
Riyadh = Ar Riyāḑ, *Si. Arabia* **84 E5** 24 41N 46 42 E
Rizal, *Cagayan, Phil.* **70 C3** 17 51N 121 21 E
Rizal, *Nueva Ecija, Phil.* **70 D3** 15 43N 121 6 E
Rizal, *Zamboanga del N., Phil.* **71 G4** 8 35N 123 26 E
Rize, *Turkey* **89 C9** 41 0N 40 30 E
Rize □, *Turkey* **89 C9** 41 0N 40 30 E
Rizhao, *China* **67 G10** 35 25N 119 30 E
Rizokarpaso, *Cyprus* **32 D13** 35 36N 34 23 E
Rizzuto, C., *Italy* **41 D10** 38 54N 17 5 E
Rjukan, *Norway* **14 E2** 59 54N 8 33 E
Rô, *N. Cal.* **121 U21** 21 22 S 167 50 E
Roa, *Norway* **14 D4** 60 17N 10 37 E
Roa, *Spain* **36 D7** 41 41N 3 56W
Roachdale, *U.S.A.* **141 E10** 39 51N 86 48W
Road Town, *Virgin Is.* **149 C7** 18 27N 64 37W
Roag, L., *U.K.* **18 C2** 58 10N 6 55W
Roanne, *France* **25 B8** 46 3N 4 4 E
Roanoke, *Ala., U.S.A.* **135 J3** 33 9N 85 22W
Roanoke, *Ind., U.S.A.* **141 D11** 40 58N 85 22W
Roanoke, *Va., U.S.A.* **134 G6** 37 16N 79 56W
Roanoke →, *U.S.A.* **135 H7** 35 57N 76 42W
Roanoke I., *U.S.A.* **135 H8** 35 55N 75 40W
Roanoke Rapids, *U.S.A.* **135 G7** 36 28N 77 40W
Roatán, *Honduras* **148 C2** 16 18N 86 35W
Rob Roy, *Solomon Is.* **121 L9** 7 23 S 157 36 E
Robbins I., *Australia* **114 G4** 40 42 S 145 0 E
Robe →, *Australia* **112 D2** 21 42 S 116 15 E
Robe →, *Ireland* **19 C2** 53 38N 9 10W
Röbel, *Germany* **26 B8** 53 24N 12 37 E
Robert Lee, *U.S.A.* **139 K4** 31 54N 100 29W
Roberts, *Idaho, U.S.A.* **142 E7** 43 43N 112 8W
Roberts, *Ill., U.S.A.* **141 D8** 40 37N 88 11W
Robertsganj, *India* **81 G10** 24 44N 83 4 E
Robertson, *Australia* **117 C9** 34 37 S 150 36 E
Robertson, *S. Africa* **104 E2** 33 46 S 19 50 E
Robertson I., *Antarctica* **7 C18** 65 15 S 59 30W
Robertson Ra., *Australia* **112 D3** 23 15 S 121 0 E
Robertsport, *Liberia* **100 D2** 6 45N 11 26W
Robertstown, *Australia* **116 B3** 33 58 S 139 5 E
Roberval, *Canada* **129 C5** 48 32N 72 15W
Robeson Chan., *Greenland* **6 A4** 82 0N 61 30W
Robinson, *U.S.A.* **141 E9** 39 0N 87 44W
Robinson →, *Australia* **114 B2** 16 3 S 137 16 E
Robinson Ra., *Australia* **113 E2** 25 40 S 119 0 E
Robinson River, *Australia* **114 B2** 16 45 S 136 58 E
Robinvale, *Australia* **116 C5** 34 40 S 142 45 E
Roblin, *Canada* **131 C8** 51 14N 101 21W
Roboré, *Bolivia* **157 D6** 18 10 S 59 45W
Robson, Mt., *Canada* **130 C5** 53 10N 119 10W
Robstown, *U.S.A.* **139 M6** 27 47N 97 40W
Roca, C. da, *Portugal* **10 H4** 38 40N 9 31W
Roca Partida, I., *Mexico* **146 D2** 19 1N 112 2W
Rocas, I., *Brazil* **154 B5** 4 0 S 34 1W
Rocca d'Aspidé, *Italy* **41 B8** 40 27N 15 10 E
Rocca San Casciano, *Italy* **39 D8** 44 3N 11 45 E
Roccalbegna, *Italy* **39 F8** 42 47N 11 30 E
Roccastrada, *Italy* **39 F8** 43 0N 11 10 E
Roccella Iónica, *Italy* **41 D9** 38 20N 16 24 E
Rocha, *Uruguay* **159 C5** 34 30 S 54 25W
Rochdale, *U.K.* **16 D5** 53 36N 2 10W
Rochechouart, *France* **24 C4** 45 50N 0 49 E
Rochedo, *Brazil* **157 D7** 19 57 S 54 52W
Rochefort, *Belgium* **21 H6** 50 9N 5 12 E
Rochefort, *France* **24 C3** 45 56N 0 57W
Rochefort-en-Terre, *France* **22 E4** 47 42N 2 22W
Rochelle, *U.S.A.* **140 C7** 41 56N 89 4W
Rocher River, *Canada* **130 A6** 61 23N 112 44W
Rocherath, *Belgium* **21 H8** 50 26N 6 18 E
Rocheservière, *France* **22 F5** 46 57N 1 30W
Rochester, *Australia* **116 D6** 36 22 S 144 41 E
Rochester, *Canada* **130 C6** 54 22N 113 27W
Rochester, *U.K.* **17 F8** 51 22N 0 30 E
Rochester, *Ind., U.S.A.* **141 C10** 41 4N 86 13W
Rochester, *Mich., U.S.A.* **141 B13** 42 41N 83 8W
Rochester, *Minn., U.S.A.* **138 C8** 44 1N 92 28W
Rochester, *N.H., U.S.A.* **137 C14** 43 18N 70 59W
Rochester, *N.Y., U.S.A.* **136 C7** 43 10N 77 37W
Rociana, *Spain* **37 H4** 37 19N 6 35W
Rociu, *Romania* **46 E6** 44 43N 25 2 E
Rock →, *Canada* **130 A3** 60 7N 127 7W
Rock Falls, *U.S.A.* **140 C7** 41 47N 89 41W
Rock Flat, *Australia* **117 D8** 36 21 S 149 13 E
Rock Hill, *U.S.A.* **135 H5** 34 56N 81 1W
Rock Island, *U.S.A.* **140 C6** 41 30N 90 34W
Rock Rapids, *U.S.A.* **138 D6** 43 26N 96 10W
Rock River, *U.S.A.* **142 F11** 41 44N 105 58W
Rock Sound, *Bahamas* **148 B4** 24 54N 76 12W
Rock Springs, Mont., *U.S.A.* **142 C10** 46 49N 106 15W
Rock Springs, Wyo., *U.S.A.* **142 F9** 41 35N 109 14W
Rock Valley, *U.S.A.* **138 D6** 43 12N 96 18W
Rockall, *Atl. Oc.* **10 D3** 57 37N 13 42W
Rockanje, *Neths.* **20 E4** 51 52N 4 4 E
Rockdale, *Tex., U.S.A.* **139 K6** 30 39N 97 0W
Rockdale, *Wash., U.S.A.* **144 C5** 47 22N 121 28W
Rockefeller Plateau, *Antarctica* **7 E14** 80 0 S 140 0W
Rockford, *Ill., U.S.A.* **140 B7** 42 16N 89 6W
Rockford, *Iowa, U.S.A.* **140 A4** 43 3N 92 57W
Rockford, *Mich., U.S.A.* **141 A11** 43 7N 85 34W
Rockford, *Ohio, U.S.A.* **141 D12** 40 41N 84 39W
Rockglen, *Canada* **131 D7** 49 11N 105 57W
Rockhampton, *Australia* **114 C5** 23 22 S 150 32 E
Rockhampton Downs, *Australia* **114 B2** 18 57 S 135 10 E
Rockingham, *Australia* **113 F2** 32 15 S 115 38 E
Rockingham B., *Australia* **114 B4** 18 5 S 146 10 E
Rockingham Forest, *U.K.* **17 E7** 52 28N 0 42W
Rocklake, *U.S.A.* **138 A5** 48 47N 99 15W
Rockland, *Canada* **137 A9** 45 33N 75 17W
Rockland, *Idaho, U.S.A.* **142 E7** 42 34N 112 53W
Rockland, *Maine, U.S.A.* **129 D6** 44 6N 69 7W
Rockland, *Mich., U.S.A.* **138 B10** 46 44N 89 11W
Rocklin, *U.S.A.* **144 G5** 38 48N 121 14W
Rockmart, *U.S.A.* **135 H3** 34 0N 85 3W
Rockport, *Ind., U.S.A.* **141 G9** 37 53N 87 3W
Rockport, *Mo., U.S.A.* **138 E7** 40 25N 95 31W
Rockport, *Tex., U.S.A.* **139 L6** 28 2N 97 3W
Rocksprings, *U.S.A.* **139 K4** 30 1N 100 13W
Rockville, *Conn., U.S.A.* **137 E12** 41 52N 72 28W
Rockville, *Ind., U.S.A.* **141 E9** 39 46N 87 14W
Rockville, *Md., U.S.A.* **134 F7** 39 5N 77 9W
Rockwall, *U.S.A.* **139 J6** 32 56N 96 28W
Rockwell City, *U.S.A.* **140 B2** 42 24N 94 38W
Rockwood, *U.S.A.* **135 H3** 35 52N 84 41W
Rocky Ford, *U.S.A.* **138 F3** 38 3N 103 43W
Rocky Fork Lake, *U.S.A.* **141 E13** 39 12N 83 23W
Rocky Gully, *Australia* **113 F2** 34 30 S 116 57 E
Rocky Lane, *Canada* **130 B5** 58 31N 116 22W
Rocky Mount, *U.S.A.* **135 H7** 35 57N 77 48W
Rocky Mountain House, *Canada* **130 C6** 52 22N 114 55W
Rocky Mts., *N. Amer.* **130 C4** 55 0N 121 0W
Rockyford, *Canada* **130 C6** 51 14N 113 10W
Rocroi, *France* **23 C11** 49 55N 4 30 E
Rod, *Pakistan* **79 C1** 28 10N 63 5 E
Rødberg, *Norway* **14 D2** 60 17N 8 56 E
Rødby, *Denmark* **15 K5** 54 41N 11 23 E
Rødbyhavn, *Denmark* **15 K5** 54 39N 11 22 E
Roddickton, *Canada* **129 B8** 50 51N 56 8W
Rødding, *Denmark* **15 J3** 55 23N 9 3 E
Rødekro, *Denmark* **15 J3** 55 4N 9 20 E
Roden, *Neths.* **20 B8** 53 8N 6 26 E
Rødenes, *Norway* **14 E5** 59 35N 11 34 E
Rodenkirchen, *Germany* **26 B4** 53 24N 8 26 E
Roderick I., *Canada* **130 C3** 52 38N 128 22W
Rodez, *France* **24 D6** 44 21N 2 33 E
Rodholívas, *Greece* **44 D5** 40 55N 24 0 E
Rodhópi □, *Greece* **44 C7** 41 5N 25 30 E
Rodhopoú, *Greece* **32 D5** 35 34N 23 45 E
Ródhos, *Greece* **32 C10** 36 15N 28 10 E
Rodi Garganico, *Italy* **41 A8** 41 55N 15 53 E
Rodna, *Romania* **46 B5** 47 25N 24 50 E
Rodnei, Munţii, *Romania* **46 B5** 47 35N 24 35 E
Rodney, *Canada* **136 D3** 42 34N 81 41W
Rodney, C., *N.Z.* **118 C3** 36 17 S 174 50 E
Rodniki, *Russia* **51 C12** 57 7N 41 47 E
Rodriguez, *Ind. Oc.* **109 F5** 19 45 S 63 20 E
Roe →, *U.K.* **19 A5** 55 10N 6 59W
Roebling, *U.S.A.* **137 F10** 40 7N 74 47W
Roebourne, *Australia* **112 D2** 20 44 S 117 9 E
Roebuck B., *Australia* **112 C3** 18 5 S 122 20 E
Roebuck Plains, *Australia* **112 C3** 17 56 S 122 28 E
Roer →, *Neths.* **21 F7** 51 12N 5 59 E
Roermond, *Neths.* **21 F7** 51 12N 6 0 E
Roes Welcome Sd., *Canada* **127 B11** 65 0N 87 0W
Roeselare, *Belgium* **21 G2** 50 57N 3 7 E
Rœulx, *Belgium* **21 G4** 50 31N 4 7 E
Rogachev, *Belorussia* **50 E7** 53 8N 30 5 E
Rogaçica, *Serbia* **42 C4** 44 4N 19 40 E
Rogagua, L., *Bolivia* **156 C4** 13 43 S 66 50W
Rogaland fylke □, *Norway* **13 G9** 59 12N 6 20 E
Rogaška Slatina, *Slovenia* **39 B12** 46 15N 15 42 E
Rogatec, *Slovenia* **39 B12** 46 15N 15 46 E
Rogatica, *Bos.-H.* **42 D4** 43 47N 19 0 E
Rogatin, *Ukraine* **50 G4** 49 24N 24 36 E
Rogdhia, *Greece* **32 D7** 35 22N 25 1 E
Rogers, *U.S.A.* **139 G7** 36 20N 94 7W
Rogers City, *U.S.A.* **134 C4** 45 25N 83 49W
Rogerson, *U.S.A.* **142 E6** 42 13N 114 36W
Rogersville, *U.S.A.* **135 G4** 36 24N 83 1W
Roggan River, *Canada* **128 B4** 54 25N 79 32W
Roggel, *Neths.* **21 F7** 51 16N 5 56 E
Roggeveldberge, *S. Africa* **104 E3** 32 10 S 20 10 E
Roggiano Gravina, *Italy* **41 C9** 39 37N 16 9 E
Rogliano, *France* **25 F13** 42 57N 9 30 E
Rogliano, *Italy* **41 C9** 39 11N 16 20 E
Rogoaguado, L., *Bolivia* **157 C4** 13 0 S 65 30W
Rogowo, *Poland* **47 C4** 52 43N 17 38 E
Rogozno, *Poland* **47 C3** 52 45N 16 59 E
Rogue →, *U.S.A.* **142 E1** 42 26N 124 26W
Rohan, *France* **22 D4** 48 4N 2 45W
Róhda, *Greece* **32 A3** 39 48N 19 46 E
Rohnert Park, *U.S.A.* **144 G4** 38 16N 122 40W
Rohrbach-lès-Bitche, *France* **23 C14** 49 3N 7 15 E
Rohri, *Pakistan* **79 D3** 27 45N 68 51 E
Rohri Canal, *Pakistan* **80 F3** 26 15N 68 27 E
Rohtak, *India* **80 E7** 28 55N 76 43 E
Roi Et, *Thailand* **76 D4** 16 4N 103 40 E
Roisel, *France* **23 C10** 49 58N 3 6 E
Rojas, *Argentina* **158 C3** 34 10 S 60 45W
Rojo, C., *Mexico* **147 C5** 21 33N 97 20W
Rokan →, *Indonesia* **74 B2** 2 0N 100 50 E
Rokeby, *Australia* **114 A3** 13 39 S 142 40 E
Rokiškis, *Lithuania* **50 D4** 55 55N 25 35 E
Rokitno, *Russia* **50 F9** 50 57N 35 56 E
Rokycany, *Czech.* **30 B6** 49 43N 13 35 E
Rolândia, *Brazil* **159 A5** 23 18 S 51 23W
Rolde, *Neths.* **20 C9** 52 59N 6 39 E
Rolette, *U.S.A.* **138 A5** 48 40N 99 51W
Rolfe, *U.S.A.* **140 B2** 42 49N 94 31W
Rolla, *Kans., U.S.A.* **139 G4** 37 7N 101 38W
Rolla, *Mo., U.S.A.* **139 G9** 37 57N 91 46W
Rolla, *N. Dak., U.S.A.* **138 A5** 48 52N 99 37W
Rollag, *Norway* **14 D3** 60 2N 9 18 E
Rollands Plains, *Australia* **117 A10** 31 17 S 152 42 E
Rolle, *Switz.* **28 D2** 46 28N 6 20 E
Rolleston, *Australia* **114 C4** 24 28 S 148 35 E
Rolleston, *N.Z.* **119 D7** 43 35 S 172 24 E
Rolling Fork →, *U.S.A.* **141 G11** 37 55N 85 50W
Rollingstone, *Australia* **114 B4** 19 2 S 146 24 E
Rom, *Sudan* **95 F3** 9 54N 32 16 E
Roma, *Australia* **115 D4** 26 32 S 148 49 E
Roma, *Italy* **40 A5** 41 54N 12 30 E
Roma, *Sweden* **13 H15** 57 32N 18 26 E
Roman, *Bulgaria* **43 D8** 43 8N 23 54 E
Roman, *Romania* **46 C7** 46 57N 26 55 E
Roman, *Russia* **57 C12** 60 4N 112 14 E
Roman-Kosh, Gora, *Ukraine* **52 D6** 44 37N 34 15 E
Romanche →, *France* **25 C9** 45 5N 5 43 E
Romang, *Indonesia* **72 C3** 7 30 S 127 20 E
Români, *Egypt* **91 E1** 30 59N 32 38 E
Romania ■, *Europe* **46 C5** 46 0N 25 0 E
Romanija, *Bos.-H.* **42 D3** 43 50N 18 45 E
Romano, Cayo, *Cuba* **148 B4** 22 0N 77 30W
Romano di Lombardía, *Italy* **38 C6** 45 32N 9 45 E
Romanovka = Bessarabka, *Moldavia* **52 C3** 46 21N 28 58 E
Romans-sur-Isère, *France* **25 C9** 45 3N 5 3 E
Romanshorn, *Switz.* **29 A8** 47 33N 9 22 E
Romblon, *Phil.* **70 E4** 12 33N 122 17 E
Romblon □, *Phil.* **70 E4** 12 30N 122 15 E
Romblon Pass, *Phil.* **70 E4** 12 27N 122 12 E
Rombo □, *Tanzania* **106 C4** 3 10 S 37 30 E
Rome = Roma, *Italy* **40 A5** 41 54N 12 30 E
Rome, *Ga., U.S.A.* **135 H3** 34 15N 85 10W
Rome, *N.Y., U.S.A.* **137 C9** 43 13N 75 27W
Romeleåsen, *Sweden* **15 J7** 55 34N 13 33 E
Romenay, *France* **25 B9** 46 30N 5 1 E
Romerike, *Norway* **14 D5** 60 7N 11 10 E
Romilly-sur-Seine, *France* **23 D10** 48 31N 3 44 E
Romîni, *Romania* **46 E5** 44 59N 24 11 E
Rommani, *Morocco* **98 B3** 33 31N 6 40W
Romney, *U.S.A.* **134 F6** 39 21N 78 45W
Romney Marsh, *U.K.* **17 F8** 51 4N 0 58 E
Romny, *Ukraine* **50 F8** 50 48N 33 28 E
Rømø, *Denmark* **15 J2** 55 10N 8 30 E
Romodan, *Ukraine* **50 G8** 49 55N 33 15 E
Romodanovo, *Russia* **51 D14** 54 26N 45 23 E
Romont, *Switz.* **28 C3** 46 42N 6 54 E
Romorantin-Lanthenay, *France* **23 E8** 47 21N 1 45 E
Rompin →, *Malaysia* **74 B2** 2 49N 103 29 E
Romsdalen, *Norway* **14 B2** 62 25N 8 0 E
Ron, *Vietnam* **76 D6** 17 53N 106 27 E
Rona, *U.K.* **18 D3** 57 33N 5 57W
Ronan, *U.S.A.* **142 C6** 47 32N 114 6W
Roncador, Cayos, *Caribbean* **148 D3** 13 32N 80 4W
Roncador, Serra do, *Brazil* **155 D1** 12 30 S 52 30W
Roncesvalles, Paso, *Spain* **34 B3** 43 1N 1 19W
Ronceverte, *U.S.A.* **134 G5** 37 45N 80 28W
Ronciglione, *Italy* **39 F9** 42 18N 12 12 E
Ronco →, *Italy* **39 D9** 44 24N 12 12 E
Ronda, *Spain* **37 J5** 36 46N 5 12W
Ronda, Serranía de, *Spain* **37 J5** 36 44N 5 3W
Rondane, *Norway* **14 C3** 61 57N 9 50 E
Rondón, *Colombia* **152 B3** 6 17N 71 6W
Rondônia, *Brazil* **157 C5** 10 52 S 61 57W
Rondônia □, *Brazil* **157 C5** 11 0 S 63 0W
Rondonópolis, *Brazil* **157 D7** 16 28 S 54 38W
Rong Jiang →, *China* **68 E7** 24 35N 109 20 E
Rong Xian, Guangxi Zhuangzu, *China* **69 F8** 22 50N 110 31 E
Rong Xian, Sichuan, *China* **68 C5** 29 23N 104 22 E
Rong'an, *China* **68 E7** 25 14N 109 22 E
Rongchang, *China* **68 C5** 29 20N 105 32 E
Ronge, L. la, *Canada* **131 B7** 55 6N 105 17W
Rongjiang, *China* **68 E7** 25 57N 108 28 E
Rongotea, *N.Z.* **118 G4** 40 19 S 175 25 E
Rongshui, *China* **68 E7** 25 5N 109 12 E
Ronne Ice Shelf, *Antarctica* **7 D18** 78 0 S 60 0W
Ronsard, C., *Australia* **113 D1** 24 46 S 113 10 E
Ronse, *Belgium* **21 G3** 50 45N 3 35 E
Ronuro →, *Brazil* **157 C7** 11 56 S 53 33W
Roodepoort, *S. Africa* **105 D4** 26 11 S 27 54 E
Roodeschool, *Neths.* **20 B9** 53 25N 6 46 E
Roodhouse, *U.S.A.* **140 E6** 39 29N 90 24W
Roof Butte, *U.S.A.* **143 H9** 36 28N 109 5W
Roompot, *Neths.* **21 E3** 51 37N 3 44 E
Roorkee, *India* **80 E7** 29 52N 77 59 E
Roosendaal, *Neths.* **21 E4** 51 32N 4 29 E
Roosevelt, *Minn., U.S.A.* **138 A7** 48 48N 95 6W
Roosevelt, *Utah, U.S.A.* **142 F8** 40 18N 109 59W
Roosevelt →, *Brazil* **157 B5** 7 35 S 60 20W
Roosevelt, Mt., *Canada* **130 B3** 58 26N 125 20W
Roosevelt I., *Antarctica* **7 D12** 79 30 S 162 0W
Roosevelt Res., *U.S.A.* **143 K8** 33 46N 111 0W
Ropczyce, *Poland* **31 A14** 50 4N 21 38 E
Roper →, *Australia* **114 A2** 14 43 S 135 27 E
Ropesville, *U.S.A.* **139 J3** 33 26N 102 9W
Roque Pérez, *Argentina* **158 D4** 35 25 S 59 24W
Roquefort, *France* **24 D3** 44 2N 0 20W
Roquemaure, *France* **25 D8** 44 3N 4 48 E
Roquetas, *Spain* **34 E5** 40 50N 0 30 E
Roquevaire, *France* **25 E9** 43 20N 5 36 E
Roraima □, *Brazil* **153 C5** 2 0N 61 30W
Roraima, Mt., *Venezuela* **153 B5** 5 10N 60 40W
Rorketon, *Canada* **131 C9** 51 24N 99 35W
Røros, *Norway* **14 B5** 62 35N 11 23 E
Rorschach, *Switz.* **29 B8** 47 28N 9 28 E

Šabac 257


Rosa, Zambia 107 D3 9 33 S 31 15 E
Rosa, C., Algeria 99 A6 37 0N 8 16 E
Rosa, Monte, Europe 28 E5 45 57N 7 53 E
Rosal, Spain 36 D2 41 57N 8 51W
Rosal de la Frontera, Spain 37 H3 37 59N 7 13W
Rosales, Phil. 70 D3 15 54N 120 38 E
Rosalia, U.S.A. 142 C5 47 14N 117 22W
Rosamond, U.S.A. 145 L8 34 52N 118 10W
Rosans, France 25 D9 44 24N 5 29 E
Rosario, Argentina 158 C3 33 0 S 60 40W
Rosário, Brazil 154 B3 3 0 S 44 15W
Rosario, Baja Calif. N., Mexico 146 A1 30 0N 115 50W
Rosario, Sinaloa, Mexico 146 C3 23 0N 105 52W
Rosario, Paraguay 158 A4 24 30 S 57 35W
Rosario, Phil. 71 G5 8 24N 125 59 E
Rosario, Villa del, Venezuela 152 A3 10 19N 72 19W
Rosario de la Frontera, Argentina 158 B3 25 50 S 65 0W
Rosario de Lerma, Argentina 158 A2 24 59 S 65 35W
Rosario del Tala, Argentina 158 C4 32 20 S 59 10W
Rosário do Sul, Brazil 159 C5 30 15 S 54 55W
Rosário Oeste, Brazil 157 C6 14 50 S 56 25W
Rosarito, Mexico 145 N9 32 18N 117 4W
Rosarno, Italy 41 D8 38 29N 15 59 E
Rosas, Spain 34 C8 42 19N 3 10 E
Roscoe, Miss., U.S.A. 140 G3 37 58N 93 48W
Roscoe, S. Dak., U.S.A. 138 C5 45 27N 99 20W
Roscoff, France 22 D3 48 44N 3 58W
Roscommon, Ireland 19 C3 53 38N 8 11W
Roscommon, U.S.A. 134 C3 44 30N 84 35W
Roscommon □, Ireland 19 C3 53 40N 8 15W
Roscrea, Ireland 19 D4 52 58N 7 50W
Rose →, Australia 114 A2 14 16 S 135 45 E
Rose Blanche, Canada 129 C8 47 38N 58 45W
Rose Harbour, Canada 130 C2 52 15N 131 10W
Rose Pt., Canada 130 C2 54 11N 131 39W
Rose Valley, Canada 131 C8 52 19N 103 49W
Roseau, Domin. 149 C7 15 20N 61 24W
Roseau, U.S.A. 138 A7 48 51N 95 46W
Rosebery, Australia 114 G4 41 46 S 145 33 E
Rosebud, U.S.A. 139 K6 31 4N 96 59W
Roseburg, U.S.A. 142 E2 43 13N 123 20W
Rosedale, Australia 114 C5 24 38 S 151 53 E
Rosedale, U.S.A. 139 J9 33 51N 91 2W
Rosée, Belgium 21 H5 50 14N 4 41 E
Roseland, U.S.A. 144 G4 38 25N 122 43W
Rosemary, Canada 130 C6 50 46N 112 5W
Rosenberg, U.S.A. 139 L7 29 34N 95 49W
Rosendaël, France 23 A9 51 3N 2 24 E
Rosendale, U.S.A. 140 D2 40 4N 94 51W
Rosenheim, Germany 27 H8 47 51N 12 9 E
Roseto degli Abruzzi, Italy 39 F11 42 40N 14 2 E
Rosetown, Canada 131 C7 51 35N 107 59W
Rosetta = Rashîd, Egypt 94 H7 31 21N 30 22 E
Roseville, Calif., U.S.A. 144 G5 38 45N 121 17W
Roseville, Ill., U.S.A. 140 D6 40 44N 90 40W
Roseville, Mich., U.S.A. 141 B14 42 30N 82 56W
Rosewood, N.S.W., Australia 117 C7 35 38 S 147 52 E
Rosewood, N. Terr., Australia 112 C4 16 28 S 128 58 E
Rosewood, Queens., Australia 115 D5 27 38 S 152 36 E
Roshkhvār, Iran 85 C8 34 58N 59 37 E
Rosières-en-Santerre, France 23 C9 49 49N 2 42 E
Rosignano Marittimo, Italy 38 E7 43 23N 10 28 E
Rosignol, Guyana 153 B6 6 15N 57 30W
Roşiori de Vede, Romania 46 E6 44 9N 25 0 E
Rositsa, Bulgaria 43 D12 43 57N 27 57 E
Rositsa →, Bulgaria 43 D10 43 10N 25 30 E
Roskilde, Denmark 15 J6 55 38N 12 3 E
Roskilde Amtskommune □, Denmark 15 J6 55 35N 12 5 E
Roskilde Fjord, Denmark 15 J6 55 50N 12 2 E
Roslavl, Russia 50 E8 53 57N 32 55 E
Roslyn, Australia 117 C8 34 29 S 149 37 E
Rosmaninhal, Portugal 37 F3 39 44N 7 5W
Rosmead, S. Africa 104 E4 31 29 S 25 8 E
Røsnæs, Denmark 15 J4 55 44N 10 55 E
Rosolini, Italy 41 F7 36 49N 14 58 E
Rosporden, France 22 E3 47 57N 3 50W
Ross, Australia 114 G4 42 2 S 147 30 E
Ross, N.Z. 119 C5 42 53 S 170 49 E
Ross I., Antarctica 7 D11 77 30 S 168 0 E
Ross Ice Shelf, Antarctica 7 E12 80 0 S 180 0 E
Ross L., U.S.A. 142 B3 48 44N 121 4W
Ross-on-Wye, U.K. 17 F5 51 55N 2 34W
Ross Sea, Antarctica 7 D11 74 0 S 178 0 E
Rossa, Switz. 29 D8 46 23N 9 8 E
Rossan Pt., Ireland 19 B3 54 42N 8 47W
Rossano Cálabro, Italy 41 C9 39 36N 16 39 E
Rossburn, Canada 131 C8 50 40N 100 49W
Rosseau, Canada 136 A5 45 16N 79 39W
Rossel, C., Vanuatu 121 K4 20 23 S 166 36 E
Rossford, U.S.A. 141 C13 41 36N 83 34W
Rossignol, L., Canada 128 B5 52 43N 73 40W
Rossignol Res., Canada 129 D6 44 12N 65 10W
Rossland, Canada 130 D5 49 6N 117 50W
Rosslare, Ireland 19 D5 52 17N 6 23W
Rosslau, Germany 26 D8 51 52N 12 15 E
Rosso, Mauritania 100 B1 16 40N 15 45W
Rossosh, Russia 53 A8 50 15N 39 28 E
Rossport, Canada 128 C2 48 50N 87 30W
Rossum, Neths. 20 E6 51 48N 5 20 E
Røssvatnet, Norway 12 D13 65 45N 14 5 E
Rossville, Australia 114 B4 15 48 S 145 15 E
Rossville, U.S.A. 141 D10 40 25N 86 36W
Rostāq, Afghan. 79 A3 37 7N 69 49 E
Rosthern, Canada 131 C7 52 40N 106 20W
Rostock, Germany 26 A8 54 4N 12 9 E
Rostov, Russia 51 C11 57 14N 39 25 E
Rostov, Russia 53 C8 47 15N 39 45 E
Rostrenen, France 22 D3 48 14N 3 21W
Roswell, U.S.A. 139 J2 33 24N 104 32W
Rosyth, U.K. 18 E5 56 2N 3 26W
Rota, Spain 37 J4 36 37N 6 20W
Rotälven →, Sweden 14 C8 61 15N 14 3 E
Rotan, U.S.A. 139 J4 32 51N 100 28W
Rotem, Belgium 21 F7 51 3N 5 45 E
Rotenburg, Germany 26 B5 53 6N 9 24 E
Roth, Germany 27 F7 49 15N 11 6 E
Rothaargebirge, Germany 26 E4 51 0N 8 5 E
Rothenburg, Switz. 29 B6 47 6N 8 16 E
Rothenburg ob der Tauber, Germany 27 F6 49 21N 10 11 E
Rother →, U.K. 17 G8 50 59N 0 40 E
Rotherham, U.K. 16 D6 53 26N 1 21W
Rothes, U.K. 18 D5 57 31N 3 12W
Rothesay, Canada 129 C6 45 23N 66 0W
Rothesay, U.K. 18 F3 55 50N 5 3W
Rothrist, Switz. 28 B5 47 18N 7 54 E
Roti, Indonesia 72 D2 10 50 S 123 0 E
Roto, Australia 117 B6 33 0 S 145 30 E
Roto Aira L., N.Z. 118 F4 39 3 S 175 45 E
Rotoehu L., N.Z. 118 E5 38 1 S 176 32 E
Rotoiti, L., N.Z. 118 E5 38 2 S 176 26 E
Rotoiti L., N.Z. 119 B7 41 51 S 172 49 E
Rotoma L., N.Z. 118 E5 38 2 S 176 35 E
Rotondella, Italy 41 B9 40 10N 16 30 E
Rotoroa, L., N.Z. 119 B7 41 55 S 172 39 E
Rotorua, N.Z. 118 E5 38 9 S 176 16 E
Rotorua, L., N.Z. 118 E5 38 5 S 176 18 E
Rotselaar, Belgium 21 G5 50 57N 4 42 E
Rott →, Germany 27 G9 48 26N 13 26 E
Rotten →, Switz. 28 D5 46 18N 7 36 E
Rottenburg, Germany 27 G4 48 28N 8 56 E
Rottenmann, Austria 30 D7 47 31N 14 22 E
Rotterdam, Neths. 20 E5 51 55N 4 30 E
Rottnest I., Australia 113 F2 32 0 S 115 27 E
Rottumeroog, Neths. 20 A9 53 33N 6 34 E
Rottweil, Germany 27 G4 48 9N 8 38 E
Rotuma, Fiji 122 J9 12 25 S 177 5 E
Roubaix, France 23 B10 50 40N 3 10 E
Roudnice, Czech. 30 A7 50 25N 14 15 E
Rouen, France 22 C8 49 27N 1 4 E
Rough Ridge, N.Z. 119 F4 45 10 S 169 55 E
Rouillac, France 24 C3 45 47N 0 4W
Rouleau, Canada 131 C8 50 10N 104 56W
Round Mt., Australia 115 E5 30 26 S 152 16 E
Round Mountain, U.S.A. 142 G5 38 43N 117 4W
Roundup, U.S.A. 142 C9 46 27N 108 33W
Roura, Fr. Guiana 153 C7 4 44N 52 20W
Rousay, U.K. 18 B5 59 10N 3 2W
Rouses Point, U.S.A. 137 B11 44 59N 73 22W
Roussillon, Isère, France 25 C8 45 24N 4 49 E
Roussillon, Pyrénées-Or., France 24 F6 42 30N 2 35 E
Roussin, C., N. Cal. 121 U21 21 20 S 167 59 E
Rouveen, Neths. 20 C8 52 37N 6 11 E
Rouxville, S. Africa 104 E4 30 25 S 26 50 E
Rouyn, Canada 128 C4 48 20N 79 0W
Rovaniemi, Finland 12 C18 66 29N 25 41 E
Rovato, Italy 38 C7 45 34N 10 0 E
Rovenki, Ukraine 53 B8 48 5N 39 21 E
Rovereto, Italy 38 C8 45 53N 11 3 E
Rovigo, Italy 39 C8 45 4N 11 48 E
Rovinari, Romania 46 E4 44 56N 23 10 E
Rovinj, Croatia 39 C10 45 5N 13 40 E
Rovira, Colombia 152 C2 4 15N 75 20W
Rovno, Ukraine 50 F5 50 40N 26 10 E
Rovnoye, Russia 51 F15 50 52N 46 3 E
Rovuma →, Tanzania 107 E5 10 29 S 40 28 E
Row'ān, Iran 85 C6 35 8N 48 51 E
Rowena, Australia 115 D4 29 48 S 148 55 E
Rowes, Australia 117 D8 37 0 S 149 6 E
Rowley Shoals, Australia 112 C2 17 30 S 119 0 E
Roxa, Guinea-Biss. 100 C1 11 15N 15 45W
Roxas = Barbacan, Phil. 71 F2 10 20N 119 21 E
Roxas, Capiz, Phil. 71 F4 11 36N 122 49 E
Roxas, Isabela, Phil. 70 C3 17 8N 121 36 E
Roxas, Mindoro, Phil. 70 E3 12 35N 121 31 E
Roxboro, U.S.A. 135 G6 36 24N 78 59W
Roxborough Downs, Australia 114 C2 22 30 S 138 45 E
Roxburgh, N.Z. 119 F4 45 33 S 169 19 E
Roxen, Sweden 15 F9 58 30N 15 40 E
Roy, Mont., U.S.A. 142 C9 47 20N 108 58W
Roy, N. Mex., U.S.A. 139 H2 35 57N 104 12W
Roy Hill, Australia 112 D2 22 37 S 119 58 E
Roya, Peña, Spain 34 E4 40 25N 0 40W
Royal Center, U.S.A. 141 D10 40 52N 86 30W
Royal Leamington Spa, U.K. 17 E6 52 18N 1 32W
Royalla, Australia 117 C8 35 30 S 149 9 E
Royan, France 24 C2 45 37N 1 2W
Roye, France 23 C9 49 42N 2 48 E
Røyken, Norway 14 E4 59 45N 10 23 E
Rožaj, Montenegro 42 E5 42 50N 20 15 E
Rózan, Poland 47 C8 52 52N 21 25 E
Rozay-en-Brie, France 23 D9 48 41N 2 58 E
Rozhishche, Ukraine 50 F4 50 54N 25 15 E
Rožňava, Slovak Rep. 31 C13 48 37N 20 35 E
Rozogi, Poland 47 B8 53 48N 21 9 E
Rozoy-sur-Serre, France 23 C11 49 40N 4 8 E
Rozwadów, Poland 47 E9 50 37N 22 2 E
Rrësheni, Albania 44 C1 41 47N 19 49 E
Rrogozhino, Albania 44 C1 41 2N 19 50 E
Rtanj, Serbia 42 D6 43 45N 21 50 E
Rtishchevo, Russia 51 D13 55 16N 43 50 E
Rúa, Spain 36 C3 42 24N 7 6W
Ruacaná, Angola 103 F2 17 20 S 14 12 E
Ruahine Ra., N.Z. 118 F5 39 55 S 176 2 E
Ruamahanga →, N.Z. 118 H4 41 24 S 175 8 E
Ruapehu, N.Z. 118 F4 39 17 S 175 35 E
Ruapuke I., N.Z. 119 G3 46 46 S 168 31 E
Ruâq, W. →, Egypt 91 F2 30 0N 33 49 E
Ruatoria, N.Z. 118 D7 37 55 S 178 20 E
Ruaus, Wadi →, Libya 96 B3 30 26N 15 24 E
Ruawai, N.Z. 118 C2 36 8 S 173 59 E
Rub' al Khali, Si. Arabia 87 C5 18 0N 48 0 E
Rubeho Mts., Tanzania 106 D4 6 50 S 36 25 E
Rubezhnoye, Ukraine 52 B8 49 6N 38 25 E
Rubh a' Mhail, U.K. 18 F2 55 55N 6 10W
Rubha Hunish, U.K. 18 D2 57 42N 6 20W
Rubiataba, Brazil 155 E2 15 8 S 49 48W
Rubicon →, U.S.A. 144 G5 38 53N 121 4W
Rubicone →, Italy 39 D9 44 8N 12 28 E
Rubinéia, Brazil 155 F1 20 13 S 51 2W
Rubino, Ivory C. 100 D4 6 4N 4 18W
Rubio, Venezuela 152 B3 7 43N 72 22W
Rubizhne = Rubezhnoye, Ukraine 52 B8 49 6N 38 25 E
Rubtsovsk, Russia 56 D9 51 30N 81 10 E
Ruby L., U.S.A. 142 F6 40 10N 115 28W
Ruby Mts., U.S.A. 142 F6 40 30N 115 20W
Rucava, Latvia 50 C2 56 9N 21 12 E
Rucheng, China 69 E9 25 33N 113 38 E
Ruciane-Nida, Poland 47 B8 53 40N 21 32 E
Rud, Norway 14 D4 60 1N 10 1 E
Rūd Sar, Iran 85 B6 37 8N 50 18 E
Ruda Śląska, Poland 47 E5 50 16N 18 50 E
Rudall, Australia 116 B2 33 43 S 136 17 E
Rudall →, Australia 112 D3 22 34 S 122 13 E
Rūdbār, Afghan. 79 C1 30 9N 62 36 E
Ruden, Germany 26 A9 54 13N 13 47 E
Rüdersdorf, Germany 26 C9 52 28N 13 48 E
Rudewa, Tanzania 107 E3 10 7 S 34 40 E
Rudkøbing, Denmark 15 K4 54 56N 10 41 E
Rudna, Poland 47 D3 51 30N 16 17 E
Rudnichnyy, Russia 54 B3 59 38N 52 26 E
Rudnik, Bulgaria 43 E12 42 36N 27 30 E
Rudnik, Poland 47 E9 50 26N 22 15 E
Rudnik, Serbia 42 C5 44 7N 20 35 E
Rudnogorsk, Russia 57 D11 57 15N 103 42 E
Rudnya, Russia 50 D7 54 55N 31 7 E
Rudnyy, Kazakhstan 54 E8 52 57N 63 7 E
Rudo, Bos.-H. 42 D4 43 41N 19 23 E
Rudolf, Ostrov, Russia 56 A6 81 45N 58 30 E
Rudolstadt, Germany 26 E7 50 44N 11 20 E
Rudong, China 69 A13 32 20N 121 12 E
Rudozem, Bulgaria 43 F9 41 29N 24 51 E
Rudyard, U.S.A. 134 B3 46 14N 84 36W
Rue, France 23 B8 50 15N 1 40 E
Ruelle, France 24 C4 45 41N 0 14 E
Rufa'a, Sudan 95 E3 14 44N 33 22 E
Ruffec, France 24 B4 46 2N 0 12 E
Rufiji □, Tanzania 106 D4 8 0 S 38 30 E
Rufiji →, Tanzania 106 D4 7 50 S 39 15 E
Rufino, Argentina 158 C3 34 20 S 62 50W
Rufisque, Senegal 100 C1 14 40N 17 15W
Rufunsa, Zambia 107 F2 15 4 S 29 34 E
Rugao, China 69 A13 32 23N 120 31 E
Rugby, U.K. 17 E6 52 23N 1 16W
Rugby, U.S.A. 138 A5 48 22N 100 0W
Rügen, Germany 26 A9 54 22N 13 25 E
Rugles, France 22 D7 48 50N 0 40 E
Ruhea, Bangla. 78 B2 26 10N 88 25 E
Ruhengeri, Rwanda 106 C2 1 30 S 29 36 E
Ruhla, Germany 26 E6 50 53N 10 21 E
Ruhland, Germany 26 D9 51 27N 13 52 E
Ruhr →, Germany 26 D2 51 25N 6 44 E
Ruhuhu →, Tanzania 107 E3 10 31 S 34 34 E
Rui Barbosa, Brazil 155 D3 12 18 S 40 27W
Rui'an, China 69 D13 27 47N 120 40 E
Ruichang, China 69 C10 29 40N 115 39 E
Ruidosa, U.S.A. 139 L2 29 59N 104 41W
Ruidoso, U.S.A. 143 K11 33 20N 105 41W
Ruili, China 68 E1 24 1N 97 43 E
Ruinen, Neths. 20 C8 52 46N 6 21 E
Ruinerwold, Neths. 20 C8 52 44N 6 15 E
Ruiten A Kanaal →, Neths. 20 C10 52 54N 7 8 E
Ruivo, Pico, Madeira 33 D3 32 45N 16 56W
Ruj, Bulgaria 42 E7 42 52N 22 42 E
Rujen, Macedonia 42 E7 42 9N 22 30 E
Rujm Tal'at al Jamā'ah, Jordan 91 E4 30 24N 35 30 E
Ruk, Pakistan 80 F3 27 50N 68 42 E
Rukwa □, Tanzania 106 D3 7 0 S 31 30 E
Rukwa L., Tanzania 106 D3 8 0 S 32 20 E
Rulhieres, C., Australia 112 B4 13 56 S 127 22 E
Rulles, Belgium 21 J7 49 43N 5 32 E
Rum Cay, Bahamas 149 B5 23 40N 74 58W
Rum Jungle, Australia 112 B5 13 0 S 130 59 E
Ruma, Serbia 42 B4 45 0N 19 50 E
Rumādah, Yemen 86 D3 13 34N 43 52 E
Rumāḥ, Si. Arabia 84 E5 25 29N 47 10 E
Rumania = Romania ■, Europe 46 C5 46 0N 25 0 E
Rumaylah, Iraq 84 D5 30 47N 47 37 E
Rumaylah, 'Urūq ar, Si. Arabia 86 B4 21 0N 47 30 E
Rumbalara, Australia 114 D1 25 20 S 134 29 E
Rumbêk, Sudan 95 F2 6 54N 29 37 E
Rumbeke, Belgium 21 G2 50 56N 3 10 E
Rumburk, Czech. 30 A7 50 57N 14 32 E
Rumelange, Lux. 21 K8 49 27N 6 2 E
Rumford, U.S.A. 137 B14 44 33N 70 33W
Rumia, Poland 47 A5 54 37N 18 25 E
Rumilly, France 25 C9 45 53N 5 56 E
Rumoi, Japan 60 C10 43 56N 141 39 E
Rumonge, Burundi 106 C2 3 59 S 29 26 E
Rumsey, Canada 130 C6 51 51N 112 48W
Rumula, Australia 114 B4 16 35 S 145 20 E
Rumuruti, Kenya 106 B4 0 17N 36 32 E
Runan, China 66 H8 33 0N 114 30 E
Runanga, N.Z. 119 C6 42 25 S 171 15 E
Runaway, C., N.Z. 118 D6 37 32 S 177 59 E
Runcorn, U.K. 16 D5 53 20N 2 44W
Rungwa, Tanzania 106 D3 6 55 S 33 32 E
Rungwa →, Tanzania 106 D3 7 36 S 31 50 E
Rungwe, Tanzania 107 D3 9 11 S 33 32 E
Rungwe □, Tanzania 107 D3 9 25 S 33 32 E
Runka, Nigeria 101 C6 12 28N 7 20 E
Runton Ra., Australia 112 D3 23 31 S 123 6 E
Ruoqiang, China 64 C3 38 55N 88 10 E
Rupa, India 78 B4 27 15N 92 21 E
Rupar, India 80 D7 31 2N 76 38 E
Rupat, Indonesia 74 B2 1 45N 101 40 E
Rupea, Romania 46 C6 46 2N 25 13 E
Rupert →, Canada 128 B4 51 29N 78 45W
Rupert House = Fort Rupert, Canada 128 B4 51 30N 78 40W
Rupsa, Bangla. 78 E2 21 44N 89 30 E
Rupununi →, Guyana 153 C6 4 3N 58 35W
Rur →, Germany 26 E2 50 54N 6 24 E
Rurrenabaque, Bolivia 156 C4 14 30 S 67 32W
Rus →, Spain 35 F2 39 30N 2 30W
Rusambo, Zimbabwe 107 F3 16 30 S 32 4 E
Rusape, Zimbabwe 107 F3 18 35 S 32 8 E
Ruschuk = Ruse, Bulgaria 43 D10 43 48N 25 59 E
Ruse, Bulgaria 43 D10 43 48N 25 59 E
Ruşeţu, Romania 46 E8 44 57N 27 14 E
Rushan, China 67 F11 36 56N 121 30 E
Rushden, U.K. 17 E7 52 17N 0 37W
Rushford, U.S.A. 138 D9 43 49N 91 46W
Rushville, Ill., U.S.A. 140 D6 40 7N 90 34W
Rushville, Ind., U.S.A. 141 E11 39 37N 85 27W
Rushville, Nebr., U.S.A. 138 D3 42 43N 102 28W
Rushworth, Australia 117 D6 36 32 S 145 1 E
Russas, Brazil 154 B4 4 55 S 37 50W
Russell, Canada 131 C8 50 50N 101 20W
Russell, N.Z. 118 B3 35 16 S 174 10 E
Russell, U.S.A. 138 F5 38 54N 98 52W
Russell Is., Solomon Is. 121 M10 9 4 S 159 12 E
Russell L., Man., Canada 131 B8 56 15N 101 30W
Russell L., N.W.T., Canada 130 A5 63 5N 115 44W
Russellkonda, India 82 E7 19 57N 84 42 E
Russellville, Ala., U.S.A. 135 H2 34 30N 87 44W
Russellville, Ark., U.S.A. 139 H8 35 17N 93 8W
Russellville, Ky., U.S.A. 135 G2 36 51N 86 53W
Russi, Italy 39 D9 44 21N 12 1 E
Russia ■, Eurasia 57 C11 62 0N 105 0 E
Russian →, U.S.A. 144 G3 38 27N 123 8W
Russiaville, U.S.A. 141 D10 40 25N 86 16W
Russkaya Polyana, Kazakhstan 56 D8 53 47N 73 53 E
Russkoye Ustie, Russia 6 B15 71 0N 149 0 E
Rust, Austria 31 D9 47 49N 16 42 E
Rustam, Pakistan 80 B5 34 25N 72 13 E
Rustam Shahr, Pakistan 80 F2 26 58N 66 6 E
Rustavi, Georgia 53 F11 41 30N 45 0 E
Rustenburg, S. Africa 104 D4 25 41 S 27 14 E
Ruston, U.S.A. 139 J8 32 32N 92 38W
Ruswil, Switz. 28 B6 47 5N 8 8 E
Rutana, Burundi 106 C2 3 55 S 30 0 E
Rute, Spain 37 H6 37 19N 4 23W
Ruteng, Indonesia 72 C2 8 35 S 120 30 E
Ruth, Mich., U.S.A. 136 C2 43 42N 82 45W
Ruth, Nev., U.S.A. 142 G6 39 17N 114 59W
Rutherford, U.S.A. 144 G4 38 26N 122 24W
Rutherglen, Australia 117 D7 36 5 S 146 29 E
Rutherglen, U.K. 18 F4 55 50N 4 11W
Rüti, Switz. 29 B7 47 16N 8 51 E
Rutigliano, Italy 41 A10 41 1N 17 0 E
Rutland Plains, Australia 114 B3 15 38 S 141 43 E
Rutledge →, Canada 131 A6 61 4N 112 0W
Rutledge L., Canada 131 A6 61 33N 110 47W
Rutshuru, Zaïre 106 C2 1 13 S 29 25 E
Ruurlo, Neths. 20 D8 52 5N 6 24 E
Ruvo di Púglia, Italy 41 A9 41 7N 16 27 E
Ruvu, Tanzania 106 D4 6 49 S 38 43 E
Ruvu →, Tanzania 106 D4 6 23 S 38 52 E
Ruvuma □, Tanzania 107 E4 10 20 S 36 0 E
Ruwais, U.A.E. 85 E7 24 5N 52 50 E
Ruwenzori, Africa 106 B2 0 30N 29 55 E
Ruyigi, Burundi 106 C3 3 29 S 30 15 E
Ruyuan, China 69 E9 24 46N 113 16 E
Ruzayevka, Russia 51 D14 54 4N 45 0 E
Růzhevo Konare, Bulgaria 43 E9 42 23N 24 46 E
Ružomberok, Slovak Rep. 31 B12 49 3N 19 17 E
Rwanda ■, Africa 106 C3 2 0 S 30 0 E
Ry, Denmark 15 H3 56 5N 9 45 E
Ryakhovo, Bulgaria 43 D11 43 58N 26 18 E
Ryan, L., U.K. 18 G3 55 0N 5 2W
Ryazan, Russia 51 D11 54 40N 39 40 E
Ryazhsk, Russia 51 E12 53 45N 40 3 E
Rybache, Kazakhstan 56 E9 46 40N 81 20 E
Rybachiy Poluostrov, Russia 48 A5 69 43N 32 0 E
Rybachye = Issyk-Kul, Kirghizia 55 B8 42 26N 76 12 E
Rybinsk, Russia 51 B11 58 5N 38 50 E
Rybinskoye Vdkhr., Russia 51 B11 58 30N 38 25 E
Rybnik, Poland 31 A11 50 6N 18 32 E
Rybnitsa, Moldavia 52 C3 47 45N 29 0 E
Rybnoye, Russia 51 D11 54 45N 39 30 E
Rychwał, Poland 47 C5 52 4N 18 10 E
Ryde, U.K. 17 G6 50 44N 1 9W
Ryderwood, U.S.A. 144 D3 46 23N 123 3W
Rydöbruk, Sweden 15 H7 56 58N 13 7 E
Rydultowy, Poland 31 A11 50 4N 18 23 E
Rydzyna, Poland 47 D3 51 47N 16 39 E
Rye, U.K. 17 G8 50 57N 0 46 E
Rye →, U.K. 16 C7 54 12N 0 53W
Rye Patch Reservoir, U.S.A. 142 F4 40 28N 118 19W
Ryegate, U.S.A. 142 C9 46 18N 109 15W
Ryki, Poland 47 D8 51 38N 21 56 E
Rylsk, Russia 50 F9 51 36N 34 43 E
Rylstone, Australia 117 B8 32 46 S 149 58 E
Rymanów, Poland 31 B14 49 35N 21 51 E
Ryn, Poland 47 B8 53 57N 21 34 E
Ryōhaku-Sanchi, Japan 63 A8 36 9N 136 49 E
Ryōthu, Japan 60 E9 38 5N 138 26 E
Rypin, Poland 47 B6 53 3N 19 25 E
Ryūgasaki, Japan 63 B12 35 54N 140 11 E
Ryūkyū Is. = Ryūkyū-rettō, Japan 61 M2 26 0N 126 0 E
Ryūkyū-rettō, Japan 61 M2 26 0N 126 0 E
Rzepin, Poland 47 C1 52 20N 14 49 E
Rzeszów, Poland 31 A14 50 5N 21 58 E
Rzeszów □, Poland 31 B15 50 0N 22 0 E
Rzhev, Russia 50 C9 56 20N 34 20 E


# S


Sa, Thailand 76 C3 18 34N 100 45 E
Sa Dec, Vietnam 77 G5 10 20N 105 46 E
Sa-koi, Burma 78 F6 19 54N 97 3 E
Sa'ādatābād, Fārs, Iran 85 D7 30 10N 53 5 E
Sa'ādatābād, Kermān, Iran 85 D7 28 3N 55 53 E
Saale →, Germany 26 D7 51 57N 11 56 E
Saaler Bodden, Germany 26 A8 54 20N 12 25 E
Saalfeld, Germany 26 E7 50 39N 11 21 E
Saalfelden, Austria 30 D5 47 25N 12 51 E
Saane →, Switz. 28 B4 47 8N 7 10 E
Saar →, Europe 23 C13 49 41N 6 32 E
Saarbrücken, Germany 27 F2 49 15N 6 58 E
Saarburg, Germany 27 F2 49 36N 6 32 E
Saaremaa, Estonia 50 B3 58 30N 22 30 E
Saariselkä, Finland 12 B20 68 16N 28 15 E
Saarland □, Germany 23 C13 49 15N 7 0 E
Saarlouis, Germany 27 F2 49 19N 6 45 E
Saas Fee, Switz. 28 D5 46 7N 7 56 E
Sab 'Bi'ār, Syria 84 C3 33 46N 37 41 E
Saba, W. Indies 149 C7 17 42N 63 26W
Šabac, Serbia 42 C4 44 48N 19 42 E

Sambawizi 259


St. Lucia ■, *W. Indies* **149 D7** 14 0N 60 50W
St. Lucia, L., *S. Africa* **105 D5** 28 5 S 32 30 E
St. Lucia Channel, *W. Indies* **149 D7** 14 15N 61 0W
St. Lunaire-Griquet, *Canada* **129 B8** 51 31N 55 28W
St. Maarten, *W. Indies* **149 C7** 18 0N 63 5W
St.-Maixent-l'École, *France* **24 B3** 46 24N 0 12W
St.-Malo, *France* **22 D4** 48 39N 2 1W
St.-Malo, G. de, *France* **22 D4** 48 50N 2 30W
St.-Mandrier-sur-Mer, *France* **25 E9** 43 4N 5 57 E
St-Marc, *Haiti* **149 C5** 19 10N 72 41W
St.-Marcellin, *France* **25 C9** 45 9N 5 20 E
St.-Marcouf, Is., *France* **22 C5** 49 30N 1 10W
St. Maries, *U.S.A.* **142 C5** 47 19N 116 35W
St-Martin, *W. Indies* **149 C7** 18 0N 63 0W
St. Martin, L., *Canada* **131 C9** 51 40N 98 30W
St.-Martin-de-Ré, *France* **24 B2** 46 12N 1 21W
St.-Martin-Vésubie, *France* **25 D11** 44 4N 7 15 E
St. Martins, *Canada* **129 C6** 45 22N 65 34W
St. Martinville, *U.S.A.* **139 K9** 30 7N 91 50W
St.-Martory, *France* **24 E4** 43 9N 0 56 E
St. Mary, Mt., *Papua N. G.* **120 E4** 8 8 S 147 2 E
St. Mary Is., *India* **83 H2** 13 20N 74 35 E
St. Mary Pk., *Australia* **116 A3** 31 32 S 138 34 E
St. Marys, *Australia* **114 G4** 41 35 S 148 11 E
St. Marys, *Canada* **136 C3** 43 20N 81 10W
St. Mary's, *U.K.* **17 H1** 49 55N 6 18W
St. Marys, *Mo., U.S.A.* **140 G7** 37 53N 89 57W
St. Marys, *Pa., U.S.A.* **136 E6** 41 26N 78 34W
St. Mary's, C., *Canada* **129 C9** 46 50N 54 12W
St. Mary's B., *Canada* **129 C9** 46 50N 53 50W
St. Marys Bay, *Canada* **129 D6** 44 25N 66 10W
St.-Mathieu, Pte., *France* **22 D2** 48 20N 4 45W
St. Matthews, *U.S.A.* **141 F11** 38 15N 85 39W
St. Matthews, I. = Zadetkyi Kyun, *Burma* **77 H2** 10 0N 98 25 E
St. Matthias Group, *Papua N. G.* **120 A5** 1 30 S 150 0 E
St.-Maur-des-Fossés, *France* **23 D9** 48 48N 2 30 E
St. Maurice, *Switz.* **28 D4** 46 13N 7 0 E
St-Maurice →, *Canada* **128 C5** 46 21N 72 31W
St.-Médard-de-Guizières, *France* **24 C3** 45 1N 0 4W
St.-Méen-le-Grand, *France* **22 D4** 48 11N 2 12W
St. Meinrad, *U.S.A.* **141 F10** 38 10N 86 49W
St. Michael's Mount, *U.K.* **17 G2** 50 7N 5 30W
St.-Michel-de-Maurienne, *France* **25 C10** 45 12N 6 28 E
St.-Mihiel, *France* **23 D12** 48 54N 5 32 E
St.-Nazaire, *France* **22 E4** 47 17N 2 12W
St. Neots, *U.K.* **17 E7** 52 14N 0 16W
St.-Nicolas-de-Port, *France* **23 D13** 48 38N 6 18 E
St. Niklass = Sint Niklaas, *Belgium* **21 F4** 51 10N 4 9 E
St. Niklaus, *Switz.* **28 D5** 46 10N 7 49 E
St.-Omer, *France* **23 B9** 50 45N 2 15 E
St-Pacome, *Canada* **129 C6** 47 24N 69 58W
St.-Palais-sur-Mer, *France* **24 C2** 45 38N 1 5W
St-Pamphile, *Canada* **129 C6** 46 58N 69 48W
St.-Pardoux-la-Rivière, *France* **24 C4** 45 29N 0 45 E
St. Paris, *U.S.A.* **141 D13** 40 8N 83 58W
St. Pascal, *Canada* **129 C6** 47 32N 69 48W
St. Paul, *Canada* **130 C6** 54 0N 111 17W
St. Paul, *Ind., U.S.A.* **141 E11** 39 26N 85 38W
St. Paul, *Minn., U.S.A.* **138 C8** 44 57N 93 6W
St. Paul, *Nebr., U.S.A.* **138 E5** 41 13N 98 27W
St. Paul, I., *Ind. Oc.* **109 H6** 38 55 S 77 34 E
St.-Paul-de-Fenouillet, *France* **24 F6** 42 48N 2 30 E
St. Paul I., *Canada* **129 C7** 47 12N 60 9W
St.-Paul-lès-Dax, *France* **24 E2** 43 44N 1 3W
St.-Péray, *France* **25 D8** 44 57N 4 50 E
St.-Père-en-Retz, *France* **22 E4** 47 11N 2 2W
St. Peter, *U.S.A.* **138 C8** 44 20N 93 57W
St. Peter Port, *Chan. Is.* **17 H5** 49 27N 2 31W
St. Peters, *N.S., Canada* **129 C7** 45 40N 60 53W
St. Peters, *P.E.I., Canada* **129 C7** 46 25N 62 35W
St. Petersburg = Sankt-Peterburg, *Russia* **50 B7** 59 55N 30 20 E
St. Petersburg, *U.S.A.* **135 M4** 27 46N 82 39W
St.-Philbert-de-Grand-Lieu, *France* **22 E5** 47 2N 1 39W
St.-Pierre, *St- P. & M.* **129 C8** 46 46N 56 12W
St. Pierre, *Seychelles* **109 E3** 9 20 S 46 0 E
St-Pierre, L., *Canada* **128 C5** 46 12N 72 52W
St.-Pierre-d'Oléron, *France* **24 C2** 45 57N 1 19W
St.-Pierre-Église, *France* **22 C5** 49 40N 1 24W
St.-Pierre-en-Port, *France* **22 C7** 49 48N 0 30 E
St.-Pierre et Miquelon □, *St- P. & M.* **129 C8** 46 55N 56 10W
St.-Pierre-le-Moûtier, *France* **23 F10** 46 47N 3 7 E
St.-Pierre-sur-Dives, *France* **22 C6** 49 2N 0 1W
St.-Pieters Leew, *Belgium* **21 G4** 50 47N 4 16 E
St.-Pol-de-Léon, *France* **22 D2** 48 41N 4 0W
St.-Pol-sur-Mer, *France* **23 A9** 51 1N 2 20 E
St.-Pol-sur-Ternoise, *France* **23 B9** 50 23N 2 20 E
St.-Pons, *France* **24 E6** 43 30N 2 45 E
St.-Pourçain-sur-Sioule, *France* **24 B7** 46 18N 3 18 E
St.-Quay-Portrieux, *France* **22 D4** 48 39N 2 51W
St.-Quentin, *France* **23 C10** 49 50N 3 16 E
St.-Rambert-d'Albon, *France* **25 C8** 45 17N 4 49 E
St.-Raphaël, *France* **25 E10** 43 25N 6 46 E
St. Regis, *U.S.A.* **142 C6** 47 18N 115 6W
St.-Rémy-de-Provence, *France* **25 E8** 43 48N 4 50 E
St.-Renan, *France* **22 D2** 48 26N 4 37W
St.-Saëns, *France* **22 C8** 49 41N 1 16 E
St.-Sauveur-en-Puisaye, *France* **23 E10** 47 37N 3 12 E
St.-Sauveur-le-Vicomte, *France* **22 C5** 49 23N 1 32W
St.-Savin, *France* **24 B4** 46 34N 0 53 E
St.-Savinien, *France* **24 C3** 45 53N 0 42W
St. Sebastien, Tanjon' i, *Madag.* **105 A8** 12 26 S 48 44 E
St.-Seine-l'Abbaye, *France* **23 E11** 47 26N 4 47 E
St.-Sernin-sur-Rance, *France* **24 E6** 43 54N 2 35 E
St.-Servan-sur-Mer, *France* **22 D4** 48 38N 2 2W
St.-Sever, *France* **24 E3** 43 45N 0 35W
St.-Sever-Calvados, *France* **22 D5** 48 50N 1 3W
St-Siméon, *Canada* **129 C6** 47 51N 69 54W
St. Stephen, *Canada* **129 C6** 45 16N 67 17W
St.-Sulpice, *France* **24 E5** 43 46N 1 41 E
St.-Sulpice-Laurière, *France* **24 B5** 46 3N 1 29 E
St.-Syprien, *France* **24 F7** 42 37N 3 2 E
St.-Thégonnec, *France* **22 D3** 48 31N 3 57W
St. Thomas, *Canada* **128 D3** 42 45N 81 10W
St. Thomas I., *Virgin Is.* **149 C7** 18 20N 64 55W
St-Tite, *Canada* **128 C5** 46 45N 72 34W
St.-Tropez, *France* **25 E10** 43 17N 6 38 E
St. Troud = Sint Truiden, *Belgium* **21 G6** 50 48N 5 10 E
St.-Vaast-la-Hougue, *France* **22 C5** 49 35N 1 17W
St.-Valéry-en-Caux, *France* **22 C7** 49 52N 0 43 E
St.-Valéry-sur-Somme, *France* **23 B8** 50 11N 1 38 E
St.-Vallier, *France* **25 C8** 45 11N 4 50 E
St.-Vallier-de-Thiey, *France* **25 E10** 43 42N 6 51 E
St.-Varent, *France* **22 F6** 46 53N 0 13W
St. Vincent, *C. Verde Is.* **8 G6** 18 0N 26 1W
St. Vincent, *W. Indies* **149 D7** 13 10N 61 10W
St. Vincent, G., *Australia* **116 C3** 35 0 S 138 0 E
St. Vincent & the Grenadines ■, *W. Indies* **149 D7** 13 0N 61 10W
St.-Vincent-de-Tyrosse, *France* **24 E2** 43 39N 1 19W
St. Vincent Passage, *W. Indies* **149 D7** 13 30N 61 0W
St-Vith, *Belgium* **21 H8** 50 17N 6 9 E
St.-Yrieix-la-Perche, *France* **24 C5** 45 31N 1 12 E
Ste.-Adresse, *France* **22 C7** 49 31N 0 5 E
Ste-Agathe-des-Monts, *Canada* **128 C5** 46 3N 74 17W
Ste-Anne de Beaupré, *Canada* **129 C5** 47 2N 70 58W
Ste-Anne-des-Monts, *Canada* **129 C6** 49 8N 66 30W
Ste-Croix, *Switz.* **28 C3** 46 49N 6 34 E
Ste.-Enimie, *France* **24 D7** 44 22N 3 26 E
Ste.-Foy-la-Grande, *France* **24 D4** 44 50N 0 13 E
Ste. Genevieve, *U.S.A.* **140 G6** 37 59N 90 2W
Ste.-Hermine, *France* **24 B2** 46 32N 1 4W
Ste.-Livrade-sur-Lot, *France* **24 D4** 44 24N 0 36 E
Ste-Marguerite →, *Canada* **129 B6** 50 9N 66 36W
Ste.-Marie, *Martinique* **149 D7** 14 48N 61 1W
Ste.-Marie-aux-Mines, *France* **23 D14** 48 15N 7 12 E
Ste-Marie de la Madeleine, *Canada* **129 C5** 46 26N 71 0W
Ste.-Maure-de-Touraine, *France* **22 E7** 47 7N 0 37 E
Ste.-Maxime, *France* **25 E10** 43 19N 6 39 E
Ste.-Menehould, *France* **23 C11** 49 5N 4 54 E
Ste.-Mère-Église, *France* **22 C5** 49 24N 1 19W
Ste.-Rose, *Guadeloupe* **149 C7** 16 20N 61 45W
Ste. Rose du Lac, *Canada* **131 C9** 51 4N 99 30W
Saintes, *France* **24 C3** 45 45N 0 37W
Saintes, I. des, *Guadeloupe* **149 C7** 15 50N 61 35W
Stes.-Maries-de-la-Mer, *France* **25 E8** 43 26N 4 26 E
Saintonge, *France* **24 C3** 45 40N 0 50W
Saipan, *Pac. Oc.* **122 F6** 15 12N 145 45 E
Sairecábur, Cerro, *Bolivia* **158 A2** 22 43 S 67 54W
Saitama □, *Japan* **63 A11** 36 25N 139 30 E
Saito, *Japan* **62 E3** 32 3N 131 24 E
Sajama, *Bolivia* **156 D4** 18 7 S 69 0W
Sajan, *Serbia* **42 B5** 45 50N 20 20 E
Sajószentpéter, *Hungary* **31 C13** 48 12N 20 44 E
Sajum, *India* **81 C8** 33 20N 79 0 E
Sak →, *S. Africa* **104 E3** 30 52 S 20 25 E
Sakai, *Japan* **63 C7** 34 30N 135 30 E
Sakaide, *Japan* **62 C5** 34 15N 133 50 E
Sakaiminato, *Japan* **62 B5** 35 38N 133 11 E
Sakākah, *Si. Arabia* **84 D4** 30 0N 40 8 E
Sakakawea, L., *U.S.A.* **138 B3** 47 30N 101 25W
Sakami, L., *Canada* **128 B4** 53 15N 77 0W
Sâkâne, 'Erg i-n, *Mali* **98 D4** 20 30N 1 30W
Sakania, *Zaïre* **107 E2** 12 43 S 28 30 E
Sakarya = Adapazarı, *Turkey* **88 C4** 40 48N 30 25 E
Sakarya □, *Turkey* **88 C4** 40 45N 30 25 E
Sakarya →, *Turkey* **52 F4** 41 7N 30 39 E
Sakashima-Guntō, *Japan* **61 M2** 24 46N 124 0 E
Sakata, *Japan* **60 E9** 38 55N 139 50 E
Sakchu, *N. Korea* **67 D13** 40 23N 125 2 E
Sakeny →, *Madag.* **105 C8** 20 0 S 45 25 E
Sakété, *Benin* **101 D5** 6 40N 2 45 E
Sakha = Yakut Republic □, *Russia* **57 C13** 62 0N 130 0 E
Sakhalin, *Russia* **57 D15** 51 0N 143 0 E
Sakhalinskiy Zaliv, *Russia* **57 D15** 54 0N 141 0 E
Sakhi Gopal, *India* **82 E7** 19 58N 85 50 E
Saki, *Ukraine* **52 D5** 45 9N 33 34 E
Šakiai, *Lithuania* **50 D3** 54 59N 23 0 E
Sakmara, *Russia* **54 E4** 52 0N 55 20 E
Sakmara →, *Russia* **54 F4** 51 46N 55 1 E
Sakon Nakhon, *Thailand* **76 D5** 17 10N 104 9 E
Sakrand, *Pakistan* **80 F3** 26 10N 68 15 E
Sakri, *India* **82 D2** 21 2N 74 20 E
Sakrivier, *S. Africa* **104 E3** 30 54 S 20 28 E
Sakskøbing, *Denmark* **15 K5** 54 49N 11 39 E
Saku, *Japan* **63 A10** 36 17N 138 31 E
Sakuma, *Japan* **63 B9** 35 3N 137 49 E
Sakura, *Japan* **63 B12** 35 43N 140 14 E
Sakurai, *Japan* **63 C7** 34 30N 135 51 E
Sal →, *Russia* **53 C9** 47 31N 40 45 E
Šal'a, *Slovak Rep.* **31 C10** 48 10N 17 50 E
Sala, *Sweden* **13 G14** 59 58N 16 35 E
Sala Consilina, *Italy* **41 B8** 40 23N 15 35 E
Sala-y-Gómez, *Pac. Oc.* **123 K17** 26 28 S 105 28W
Salaberry-de-Valleyfield, *Canada* **128 C5** 45 15N 74 8W
Saladas, *Argentina* **158 B4** 28 15 S 58 40W
Saladillo, *Argentina* **158 D4** 35 40 S 59 55W
Salado →, *Buenos Aires, Argentina* **158 D4** 35 44 S 57 22W
Salado →, *La Pampa, Argentina* **160 A3** 37 30 S 67 0W
Salado →, *Río Negro, Argentina* **160 B3** 41 34 S 65 3W
Salado →, *Santa Fe, Argentina* **158 C3** 31 40 S 60 41W
Salado →, *Mexico* **146 B5** 26 52N 99 19W
Salaga, *Ghana* **101 D4** 8 31N 0 31W
Sālah, *Syria* **91 C5** 32 40N 36 45 E
Sălaj □, *Romania* **46 B4** 47 15N 23 0 E
Sálakhos, *Greece* **32 C9** 36 17N 27 57 E
Salala, *Liberia* **100 D2** 6 42N 10 7W
Salala, *Sudan* **94 C4** 21 17N 36 16 E
Salālah, *Oman* **87 C6** 16 56N 53 59 E
Salamanca, *Chile* **158 C1** 31 46 S 70 59W
Salamanca, *Spain* **36 E5** 40 58N 5 39W
Salamanca, *U.S.A.* **136 D6** 42 10N 78 43W
Salamanca □, *Spain* **36 E5** 40 57N 5 40W
Salāmatābād, *Iran* **84 C5** 35 39N 47 50 E
Salamina, *Colombia* **152 B2** 5 25N 75 29W
Salamis, *Cyprus* **32 D12** 35 11N 33 54 E
Salamis, *Greece* **45 G5** 37 56N 23 30 E
Salamonie L., *U.S.A.* **141 D11** 40 46N 85 37W
Salar de Atacama, *Chile* **158 A2** 23 30 S 68 25W
Salar de Uyuni, *Bolivia* **156 E4** 20 30 S 67 45W
Sălard, *Romania* **46 B3** 47 12N 22 3 E
Salas, *Spain* **36 B4** 43 25N 6 15W
Salas de los Infantes, *Spain* **34 C1** 42 2N 3 17W
Salatiga, *Indonesia* **75 D4** 7 19 S 110 30 E
Salavat, *Russia* **54 E4** 53 21N 55 55 E
Salaverry, *Peru* **156 B2** 8 15 S 79 0W
Salawati, *Indonesia* **73 B4** 1 7 S 130 52 E
Salay, *Phil.* **71 G5** 8 52N 124 47 E
Salayar, *Indonesia* **72 C2** 6 7 S 120 30 E
Salazar →, *Spain* **34 C3** 42 40N 1 20W
Salbris, *France* **23 E9** 47 25N 2 3 E
Salcia, *Romania* **46 F5** 43 56N 24 55 E
Salcombe, *U.K.* **17 G4** 50 14N 3 47W
Salda Gölü, *Turkey* **88 E3** 37 22N 29 41 E
Saldaña, *Spain* **36 C6** 42 32N 4 48W
Saldanha, *S. Africa* **104 E2** 33 0 S 17 58 E
Saldanha B., *S. Africa* **104 E2** 33 6 S 18 0 E
Saldus, *Latvia* **50 C3** 56 38N 22 30 E
Sale, *Australia* **117 E7** 38 6 S 147 6 E
Salé, *Morocco* **98 B3** 34 3N 6 48W
Sale, *U.K.* **16 D5** 53 26N 2 19W
Salekhard, *Russia* **48 A12** 66 30N 66 35 E
Salem, *India* **83 J4** 11 40N 78 11 E
Salem, *Ill., U.S.A.* **140 F8** 38 38N 88 57W
Salem, *Ind., U.S.A.* **141 F10** 38 36N 86 6W
Salem, *Mass., U.S.A.* **137 D14** 42 31N 70 53W
Salem, *Mo., U.S.A.* **139 G9** 37 39N 91 32W
Salem, *N.J., U.S.A.* **134 F8** 39 34N 75 28W
Salem, *Ohio, U.S.A.* **136 F4** 40 54N 80 52W
Salem, *Oreg., U.S.A.* **142 D2** 44 56N 123 2W
Salem, *S. Dak., U.S.A.* **138 D6** 43 44N 97 23W
Salem, *Va., U.S.A.* **134 G5** 37 18N 80 3W
Salemi, *Italy* **40 E5** 37 49N 12 47 E
Salernes, *France* **25 E10** 43 34N 6 15 E
Salerno, *Italy* **41 B7** 40 40N 14 44 E
Salerno, G. di, *Italy* **41 B7** 40 35N 14 45 E
Salford, *U.K.* **16 D5** 53 30N 2 17W
Salgir →, *Ukraine* **52 D6** 45 38N 35 1 E
Salgótarján, *Hungary* **31 C12** 48 5N 19 47 E
Salgueiro, *Brazil* **154 C4** 8 4 S 39 6W
Salida, *U.S.A.* **132 C5** 38 32N 106 0W
Salies-de-Béarn, *France* **24 E3** 43 28N 0 56W
Şalif, *Yemen* **86 D3** 15 18N 42 41 E
Salihli, *Turkey* **88 D3** 38 28N 28 8 E
Salin, *Burma* **78 E5** 20 35N 94 40 E
Salina, *Italy* **41 D7** 38 35N 14 50 E
Salina, *U.S.A.* **138 F6** 38 50N 97 37W
Salina Cruz, *Mexico* **147 D5** 16 10N 95 10W
Salinas, *Brazil* **155 E3** 16 10 S 42 10W
Salinas, *Chile* **158 A2** 23 31 S 69 29W
Salinas, *Ecuador* **152 D1** 2 10 S 80 58W
Salinas, *U.S.A.* **144 J5** 36 40N 121 39W
Salinas →, *Guatemala* **147 D6** 16 28N 90 31W
Salinas →, *U.S.A.* **144 J5** 36 45N 121 48W
Salinas, B. de, *Nic.* **148 D2** 11 4N 85 45W
Salinas, C. de, *Spain* **33 B10** 39 16N 3 4 E
Salinas, Pampa de las, *Argentina* **158 C2** 31 58 S 66 42W
Salinas Ambargasta, *Argentina* **158 B3** 29 0 S 65 0W
Salinas de Hidalgo, *Mexico* **146 C4** 22 30N 101 40W
Salinas Grandes, *Argentina* **158 B2** 30 0 S 65 0W
Saline →, *Ark., U.S.A.* **139 J8** 33 10N 92 8W
Saline →, *Kans., U.S.A.* **138 F6** 38 52N 97 30W
Salines, *Spain* **33 B10** 39 21N 3 3 E
Salinópolis, *Brazil* **154 B2** 0 40 S 47 20W
Salins-les-Bains, *France* **23 F12** 46 58N 5 52 E
Salir, *Portugal* **37 H2** 37 14N 8 2W
Salisbury = Harare, *Zimbabwe* **107 F3** 17 43 S 31 2 E
Salisbury, *Australia* **116 C3** 34 46 S 138 40 E
Salisbury, *U.K.* **17 F6** 51 4N 1 48W
Salisbury, *Md., U.S.A.* **134 F8** 38 22N 75 36W
Salisbury, *Mo., U.S.A.* **140 E4** 39 25N 92 48W
Salisbury, *N.C., U.S.A.* **135 H5** 35 40N 80 29W
Salisbury Plain, *U.K.* **17 F6** 51 13N 1 50W
Săliște, *Romania* **46 D4** 45 45N 23 56 E
Salitre →, *Brazil* **154 C3** 9 29 S 40 39W
Salka, *Nigeria* **101 C5** 10 20N 4 58 E
Salkhad, *Jordan* **91 C5** 32 30N 36 43 E
Sallent, *Spain* **34 D6** 41 49N 1 54 E
Salles-Curan, *France* **24 D6** 44 11N 2 48 E
Salling, *Denmark* **15 H2** 56 40N 8 55 E
Sallisaw, *U.S.A.* **139 H7** 35 28N 94 47W
Sallom Junction, *Sudan* **94 D4** 19 17N 37 6 E
Salmās, *Iran* **84 B5** 38 11N 44 47 E
Salmerón, *Spain* **34 E2** 40 33N 2 29W
Salmo, *Canada* **130 D5** 49 10N 117 20W
Salmon, *U.S.A.* **142 D7** 45 11N 113 54W
Salmon →, *Canada* **130 C4** 54 3N 122 40W
Salmon →, *U.S.A.* **142 D5** 45 51N 116 47W
Salmon Arm, *Canada* **130 C5** 50 40N 119 15W
Salmon Falls, *U.S.A.* **142 E6** 42 48N 114 59W
Salmon Gums, *Australia* **113 F3** 32 59 S 121 38 E
Salmon Res., *Canada* **129 C8** 48 5N 56 0W
Salmon River Mts., *U.S.A.* **142 D6** 45 0N 114 30W
Salo, *Finland* **13 F17** 60 22N 23 10 E
Salò, *Italy* **38 C7** 45 37N 10 32 E
Salobreña, *Spain* **37 J7** 36 44N 3 35W
Salome, *U.S.A.* **145 M13** 33 47N 113 37W
Salon-de-Provence, *France* **25 E9** 43 39N 5 6 E
Salonica = Thessaloníki, *Greece* **44 D4** 40 38N 22 58 E
Salonta, *Romania* **46 C2** 46 49N 21 42 E
Salor →, *Spain* **37 F3** 39 39N 7 3W
Salou, C., *Spain* **34 D6** 41 3N 1 10 E
Salsacate, *Argentina* **158 C2** 31 20 S 65 5W
Salses, *France* **24 F6** 42 50N 2 55 E
Salsette I., *India* **82 E1** 19 5N 72 50 E
Salsk, *Russia* **53 C9** 46 28N 41 30 E
Salso →, *Italy* **40 E6** 37 6N 13 55 E
Salsomaggiore, *Italy* **38 D6** 44 48N 9 59 E
Salt →, *Canada* **130 B6** 60 0N 112 25W
Salt →, *Ariz., U.S.A.* **143 K7** 33 23N 112 19W
Salt →, *Mo., U.S.A.* **140 E5** 39 28N 91 4W
Salt Creek, *Australia* **116 D3** 36 8 S 139 38 E
Salt Fork Arkansas →, *U.S.A.* **139 G6** 36 36N 97 3W
Salt Lake City, *U.S.A.* **142 F8** 40 45N 111 53W
Salt Range, *Pakistan* **80 C5** 32 30N 72 25 E
Salta, *Argentina* **158 A2** 24 57 S 65 25W
Salta □, *Argentina* **158 A2** 24 48 S 65 30W
Saltcoats, *U.K.* **18 F4** 55 38N 4 47W
Saltee Is., *Ireland* **19 D5** 52 7N 6 37W
Saltfjorden, *Norway* **12 C13** 67 15N 14 10 E
Saltholm, *Denmark* **15 J6** 55 38N 12 43 E
Salthólmavík, *Iceland* **12 D3** 65 24N 21 57W
Saltillo, *Mexico* **146 B4** 25 30N 100 57W
Salto, *Argentina* **158 C3** 34 20 S 60 15W
Salto, *Uruguay* **158 C4** 31 27 S 57 50W
Salto da Divisa, *Brazil* **155 E4** 16 0 S 39 57W
Salton City, *U.S.A.* **145 M11** 33 29N 115 51W
Salton Sea, *U.S.A.* **145 M11** 33 15N 115 45W
Saltpond, *Ghana* **101 D4** 5 15N 1 3W
Saltsjöbaden, *Sweden* **14 E12** 59 15N 18 20 E
Saltville, *U.S.A.* **134 G5** 36 53N 81 46W
Saluda →, *U.S.A.* **135 H5** 34 1N 81 4W
Salûm, *Egypt* **94 A2** 31 31N 25 7 E
Salûm, Khâlig el, *Egypt* **94 A2** 31 30N 25 9 E
Salur, *India* **82 E6** 18 27N 83 18 E
Salut, Is. du, *Fr. Guiana* **153 B7** 5 15N 52 35W
Saluzzo, *Italy* **38 D4** 44 39N 7 29 E
Salvacion, *Phil.* **71 G2** 9 56N 118 47 E
Salvación, B., *Chile* **160 D1** 50 50 S 75 10W
Salvador, *Brazil* **155 D4** 13 0 S 38 30W
Salvador, *Canada* **131 C7** 52 10N 109 32W
Salvador, L., *U.S.A.* **139 L9** 29 43N 90 15W
Salvaterra, *Brazil* **154 B2** 0 46 S 48 31W
Salvaterra de Magos, *Portugal* **37 F2** 39 1N 8 47W
Salvisa, *U.S.A.* **141 G12** 37 54N 84 51W
Sálvora, I., *Spain* **36 C2** 42 30N 8 58W
Salween →, *Burma* **78 G6** 16 31N 97 37 E
Salyany, *Azerbaijan* **89 D13** 39 10N 48 50 E
Salyersville, *U.S.A.* **134 G4** 37 45N 83 4W
Salza →, *Austria* **30 D7** 47 40N 14 43 E
Salzach →, *Austria* **30 C5** 48 12N 12 56 E
Salzburg, *Austria* **30 D6** 47 48N 13 2 E
Salzburg □, *Austria* **30 D6** 47 15N 13 0 E
Salzgitter, *Germany* **26 C6** 52 13N 10 22 E
Salzwedel, *Germany* **26 C7** 52 50N 11 11 E
Sam, *Gabon* **102 B2** 0 58N 11 16 E
Sam Neua, *Laos* **76 B5** 20 29N 104 5 E
Sam Ngao, *Thailand* **76 D2** 17 18N 99 0 E
Sam Rayburn Reservoir, *U.S.A.* **139 K7** 31 4N 94 5W
Sam Son, *Vietnam* **76 C5** 19 44N 105 54 E
Sam Teu, *Laos* **76 C5** 19 59N 104 38 E
Sama, *Russia* **54 A7** 60 12N 60 22 E
Sama de Langreo, *Spain* **36 B5** 43 18N 5 40W
Samacimbo, *Angola* **103 E3** 13 33 S 16 59 E
Samagaltai, *Russia* **57 D10** 50 36N 95 3 E
Samā'il, *Oman* **87 B7** 23 40N 57 50 E
Samaipata, *Bolivia* **157 D5** 18 9 S 63 52W
Samal, *Phil.* **71 H5** 7 5N 125 42 E
Samal I., *Phil.* **71 H5** 7 3N 125 44 E
Samales Group, *Phil.* **71 J3** 6 0N 122 0 E
Samalkot, *India* **82 F6** 17 3N 82 13 E
Samâlût, *Egypt* **94 J7** 28 20N 30 42 E
Samana, *India* **80 D7** 30 10N 76 13 E
Samana Cay, *Bahamas* **149 B5** 23 3N 73 45W
Samandağı, *Turkey* **88 E6** 36 5N 35 59 E
Samanga, *Tanzania* **107 D4** 8 20 S 39 13 E
Samangán □, *Afghan.* **79 A3** 36 15N 68 3 E
Samangwa, *Zaïre* **103 C4** 4 23 S 24 10 E
Samani, *Japan* **60 C11** 42 7N 142 56 E
Samar, *Phil.* **71 E5** 12 0N 125 0 E
Samar □, *Phil.* **71 F5** 11 50N 125 0 E
Samar Sea, *Phil.* **70 E5** 12 0N 124 15 E
Samara, *Russia* **51 E17** 53 8N 50 6 E
Samara →, *Russia* **54 E2** 53 10N 50 4 E
Samarai, *Papua N. G.* **120 F6** 10 39 S 150 41 E
Samaria = Shōmrōn, *Jordan* **91 C4** 32 15N 35 13 E
Samariá, *Greece* **32 D5** 35 17N 23 58 E
Samarinda, *Indonesia* **75 C5** 0 30 S 117 9 E
Samarkand, *Uzbekistan* **55 D3** 39 40N 66 55 E
Samarqand = Samarkand, *Uzbekistan* **55 D3** 39 40N 66 55 E
Sāmarrā, *Iraq* **84 C4** 34 12N 43 52 E
Samastipur, *India* **81 G11** 25 50N 85 50 E
Samatan, *France* **24 E4** 43 29N 0 55 E
Samaúma, *Brazil* **157 B5** 7 50 S 60 2W
Samba, *India* **81 C6** 32 32N 75 10 E
Samba, *Zaïre* **103 C5** 4 38 S 26 22 E
Samba Caju, *Angola* **103 D3** 8 46 S 15 24 E
Sambaíba, *Brazil* **154 C2** 7 8 S 45 21W
Sambalpur, *India* **82 D7** 21 28N 84 4 E
Sambar, Tanjung, *Indonesia* **75 C4** 2 59 S 110 19 E
Sambas, *Indonesia* **75 B3** 1 20N 109 20 E
Sambava, *Madag.* **105 A9** 14 16 S 50 10 E
Sambawizi, *Zimbabwe* **107 F2** 18 24 S 26 13 E

Santa Rosa de Osos 261


San Pedro, Jujuy, Argentina 158 A3 24 12 S 64 55W
San Pedro, Colombia 152 C3 4 56N 71 53W
San-Pédro, Ivory C. 100 E3 4 50N 6 33W
San Pedro, Mexico 146 C2 23 55N 110 17W
San Pedro, Peru 156 C3 14 49 S 74 5W
San Pedro □, Paraguay 158 A4 24 0 S 57 0W
San Pedro →, Chihuahua, Mexico 146 B3 28 20N 106 10W
San Pedro →, Michoacan, Mexico 146 D4 19 23N 103 51W
San Pedro →, Nayarit, Mexico 146 C3 21 45N 105 30W
San Pedro →, U.S.A. 143 K8 32 59N 110 47W
San Pedro, Pta., Chile 158 B1 25 30 S 70 38W
San Pedro, Sierra de, Spain 37 F4 39 18N 6 40W
San Pedro Channel, U.S.A. 145 M8 33 30N 118 25W
San Pedro de Arimena, Colombia 152 C3 4 37N 71 42W
San Pedro de Atacama, Chile 158 A2 22 55 S 68 15W
San Pedro de Jujuy, Argentina 158 A3 24 12 S 64 55W
San Pedro de las Colonias, Mexico 146 B4 25 50N 102 59W
San Pedro de Lloc, Peru 156 B2 7 15 S 79 28W
San Pedro de Macorís, Dom. Rep. 149 C6 18 30N 69 18W
San Pedro del Norte, Nic. 148 D3 13 4N 84 33W
San Pedro del Paraná, Paraguay 158 B4 26 43 S 56 13W
San Pedro del Pinatar, Spain 35 H4 37 50N 0 50W
San Pedro Mártir, Sierra, Mexico 146 A1 31 0N 115 30W
San Pedro Mixtepec, Mexico 147 D5 16 2N 97 7W
San Pedro Ocampo = Melchor Ocampo, Mexico 146 C4 24 52N 101 40W
San Pedro Sula, Honduras 148 C2 15 30N 88 0W
San Pietro, I., Italy 40 C1 39 9N 8 17 E
San Pietro Vernótico, Italy 41 B11 40 28N 18 0 E
San Quintín, Mexico 146 A1 30 29N 115 57W
San Rafael, Argentina 158 C2 34 40 S 68 21W
San Rafael, Calif., U.S.A. 144 H4 37 58N 122 32W
San Rafael, N. Mex., U.S.A. 143 J10 35 7N 107 53W
San Rafael, Venezuela 152 A3 10 58N 71 46W
San Rafael Mt., U.S.A. 145 L7 34 41N 119 52W
San Rafael Mts., U.S.A. 145 L7 34 40N 119 50W
San Ramón, Bolivia 157 C5 13 17 S 64 43W
San Ramón, Peru 156 C2 11 8 S 75 20W
San Ramón de la Nueva Orán, Argentina 158 A3 23 10 S 64 20W
San Remo, Italy 38 E4 43 48N 7 47 E
San Román, C., Venezuela 152 A3 12 12N 70 0W
San Roque, Argentina 158 B4 28 25 S 58 45W
San Roque, Phil. 70 E5 12 37N 124 52 E
San Roque, Spain 37 J5 36 17N 5 21W
San Rosendo, Chile 158 D1 37 16 S 72 43W
San Saba, U.S.A. 139 K5 31 12N 98 43W
San Salvador, Bahamas 149 B5 24 0N 74 40W
San Salvador, El Salv. 148 D2 13 40N 89 10W
San Salvador, Spain 33 B10 39 27N 3 11 E
San Salvador de Jujuy, Argentina 158 A3 24 10 S 64 48W
San Salvador I., Bahamas 149 B5 24 0N 74 32W
San Sebastián, Argentina 160 D3 53 10 S 68 30W
San Sebastián, Spain 34 B3 43 17N 1 58W
San Sebastián, Venezuela 152 B4 9 57N 67 11W
San Sebastian de la Gomera, Canary Is. 33 F2 28 5N 17 7W
San Serra, Spain 33 B10 39 43N 3 13 E
San Serverino Marche, Italy 39 E10 43 13N 13 10 E
San Simeon, U.S.A. 144 K5 35 39N 121 11W
San Simon, U.S.A. 143 K9 32 16N 109 14W
San Stéfano di Cadore, Italy 39 B9 46 34N 12 33 E
San Telmo, Mexico 146 A1 30 58N 116 6W
San Telmo, Spain 33 B9 39 35N 2 21 E
San Teodoro, Phil. 70 E3 13 26N 121 1 E
San Tiburcio, Mexico 146 C4 24 8N 101 32W
San Valentin, Mte., Chile 160 C2 46 30 S 73 30W
San Vicente de Alcántara, Spain 37 F3 39 22N 7 8W
San Vicente de la Barquera, Spain 36 B6 43 23N 4 29W
San Vicente del Caguán, Colombia 152 C3 2 7N 74 46W
San Vincenzo, Italy 38 E7 43 6N 10 29 E
San Vito, Italy 40 C2 39 26N 9 32 E
San Vito, C., Italy 40 D5 38 11N 12 41 E
San Vito al Tagliamento, Italy 39 C9 45 55N 12 50 E
San Vito Chietino, Italy 39 F11 42 19N 14 27 E
San Vito dei Normanni, Italy 41 B10 40 40N 17 40 E
San Yanaro, Colombia 152 C4 2 47N 69 42W
San Ygnacio, U.S.A. 139 M5 27 3N 99 26W
Saña, Peru 156 B2 6 54 S 79 36W
Sana', Yemen 86 D4 15 27N 44 12 E
Sana →, Bos.-H. 39 C13 45 3N 16 23 E
Sanaba, Burkina Faso 100 C4 12 25N 3 47W
Şanāfīr, Si. Arabia 94 B3 27 56N 34 42 E
Sanaga →, Cameroon 101 E6 3 35N 9 38 E
Sanaloa, Presa, Mexico 146 C3 24 50N 107 20W
Sanām, Si. Arabia 86 B4 23 40N 44 45 E
Sanana, Indonesia 72 B3 2 5 S 125 59 E
Sanana, Indonesia 72 B3 2 4 S 125 58 E
Sanand, India 80 H5 22 59N 72 25 E
Sanandaj, Iran 84 C5 35 18N 47 1 E
Sanandita, Bolivia 158 A3 21 40 S 63 45W
Sanary-sur-Mer, France 25 E9 43 7N 5 49 E
Sanāw, Yemen 87 C5 17 50N 51 5 E
Sanawad, India 80 H7 22 11N 76 5 E
Sanbe-San, Japan 62 B4 35 6N 132 38 E
Sancellas, Spain 33 B9 39 39N 2 54 E
Sancergues, France 23 E9 47 10N 2 54 E
Sancerre, France 23 E9 47 20N 2 50 E
Sancerrois, Collines du, France 23 E9 47 20N 2 40 E
Sancha He →, China 68 D6 26 48N 106 7 E
Sanchahe, China 67 B14 44 50N 126 2 E
Sánchez, Dom. Rep. 149 C6 19 15N 69 36W
Sanchor, India 80 G4 24 45N 71 55 E
Sanco Pt., Phil. 71 G6 8 15N 126 27 E
Sancoins, France 23 F9 46 47N 2 55 E
Sancti-Spíritus, Cuba 148 B4 21 52N 79 33W
Sancy, Puy de, France 24 C6 45 32N 2 50 E
Sand →, S. Africa 105 C5 22 25 S 30 5 E
Sand Cr. →, U.S.A. 141 E11 39 3N 85 51W
Sand Springs, U.S.A. 139 G6 36 9N 96 7W
Sanda, Japan 63 C7 34 53N 135 14 E
Sandakan, Malaysia 75 A5 5 53N 118 4 E
Sandalwood, Australia 116 C4 34 55 S 140 9 E
Sandan = Sambor, Cambodia 76 F6 12 46N 106 0 E
Sandanski, Bulgaria 43 F8 41 35N 23 16 E
Sandaré, Mali 100 C2 14 40N 10 15W
Sanday, U.K. 18 B6 59 15N 2 30W
Sandefjord, Norway 14 E4 59 10N 10 15 E
Sanders, Ariz., U.S.A. 143 J9 35 13N 109 20W
Sanders, Ky., U.S.A. 141 F12 38 40N 84 56W
Sanderson, U.S.A. 139 K3 30 9N 102 24W
Sanderston, Australia 116 C3 34 46 S 139 15 E
Sandfly L., Canada 131 B7 55 43N 106 6W
Sandgate, Australia 115 D5 27 18 S 153 3 E
Sandía, Peru 156 C4 14 10 S 69 30W
Sandıklı, Turkey 88 D4 38 30N 30 20 E
Sandnes, Norway 13 G8 58 50N 5 45 E
Sandness, U.K. 18 A7 60 18N 1 38W
Sandoa, Zaïre 103 D4 9 41 S 23 0 E
Sandomierz, Poland 47 E8 50 40N 21 43 E
Sandona, Colombia 152 C2 1 17N 77 28W
Sandongo, Angola 103 F4 15 30 S 21 28 E
Sandoval, U.S.A. 140 F7 38 37N 89 7W
Sandover →, Australia 114 C2 21 43 S 136 32 E
Sandpoint, U.S.A. 142 B5 48 17N 116 33W
Sandringham, U.K. 16 E8 52 50N 0 30 E
Sandslån, Sweden 14 A11 63 2N 17 49 E
Sandspit, Canada 130 C2 53 14N 131 49W
Sandstone, Australia 113 E2 27 59 S 119 16 E
Sandu, China 68 E6 26 0N 107 52 E
Sandusky, Mich., U.S.A. 128 D3 43 25N 82 50W
Sandusky, Ohio, U.S.A. 136 E2 41 27N 82 42W
Sandusky →, U.S.A. 141 C14 41 27N 83 0W
Sandvig, Sweden 15 J8 55 18N 14 47 E
Sandviken, Sweden 13 F14 60 38N 16 46 E
Sandwich, U.S.A. 141 C8 41 39N 88 37W
Sandwich, C., Australia 114 B4 18 14 S 146 18 E
Sandwich B., Canada 129 B8 53 40N 57 15W
Sandwich B., Namibia 104 C1 23 25 S 14 20 E
Sandy, Nev., U.S.A. 145 K11 35 49N 115 36W
Sandy, Oreg., U.S.A. 144 E4 45 24N 122 16W
Sandy Bight, Australia 113 F3 33 50 S 123 20 E
Sandy C., Queens., Australia 114 C5 24 42 S 153 15 E
Sandy C., Tas., Australia 114 G3 41 25 S 144 45 E
Sandy Cay, Bahamas 149 B4 23 13N 75 18W
Sandy Cr. →, U.S.A. 142 F9 41 51N 109 47W
Sandy L., Canada 128 B1 53 2N 93 0W
Sandy Lake, Canada 128 B1 53 0N 93 15W
Sandy Narrows, Canada 131 B8 55 5N 103 4W
Sanford, Fla., U.S.A. 135 L5 28 48N 81 16W
Sanford, Maine, U.S.A. 137 C14 43 27N 70 47W
Sanford, N.C., U.S.A. 135 H6 35 29N 79 10W
Sanford →, Australia 113 E2 27 22 S 115 53 E
Sanford, Mt., U.S.A. 126 B5 62 13N 144 8W
Sang-i-Masha, Afghan. 80 C2 33 8N 67 27 E
Sanga, Mozam. 107 E4 12 22 S 35 21 E
Sanga →, Congo 102 C3 1 5 S 17 0 E
Sanga-Tolon, Russia 57 C15 61 50N 149 40 E
Sangamner, India 82 E2 19 37N 74 15 E
Sangamon →, U.S.A. 140 D6 40 7N 90 20W
Sangar, Afghan. 80 C1 32 56N 65 30 E
Sangar, Russia 57 C13 64 2N 127 31 E
Sangar Sarai, Afghan. 80 B4 34 27N 70 35 E
Sangasangadalam, Indonesia 75 C5 0 36 S 117 13 E
Sangay, Ecuador 152 D2 2 0 S 78 20W
Sange, Zaïre 106 D2 6 58 S 28 21 E
Sangeang, Indonesia 72 C1 8 12 S 119 6 E
Sanger, U.S.A. 144 J7 36 42N 119 33W
Sangerhausen, Germany 26 D7 51 28N 11 18 E
Sanggan He →, China 66 E9 38 12N 117 15 E
Sanggau, Indonesia 75 B4 0 5N 110 30 E
Sangihe, Kepulauan, Indonesia 72 A3 3 0N 126 0 E
Sangihe, P., Indonesia 72 A3 3 45N 125 30 E
Sangju, S. Korea 67 F15 36 25N 128 10 E
Sangkapura, Indonesia 75 D4 5 52 S 112 40 E
Sangkhla, Thailand 76 E2 14 57N 98 28 E
Sangli, India 82 F2 16 55N 74 33 E
Sangmélina, Cameroon 101 E7 2 57N 12 1 E
Sangonera →, Spain 35 H3 37 59N 1 4W
Sangpang Bum, Burma 78 B5 26 30N 95 50 E
Sangre de Cristo Mts., U.S.A. 139 G2 37 0N 105 0W
Sangro →, Italy 39 F11 42 14N 14 32 E
Sangudo, Canada 130 C6 53 50N 114 54W
Sangue →, Brazil 157 C6 11 1 S 58 39W
Sangüesa, Spain 34 C3 42 37N 1 17W
Sanguinaires, Is., France 25 G12 41 51N 8 36 E
Sangzhi, China 69 C8 29 25N 110 12 E
Sanhala, Ivory C. 100 C3 10 3N 6 51W
Sāniyah, Iraq 84 C4 33 49N 42 43 E
Sanje, Uganda 106 C3 0 49 S 31 30 E
Sanjiang, China 68 E7 25 48N 109 37 E
Sanjo, Japan 60 F9 37 37N 138 57 E
Sankarankovil, India 83 K3 9 10N 77 35 E
Sankeshwar, India 83 F2 16 23N 74 32 E
Sankosh →, India 78 B2 26 24N 89 47 E
Sankt Andrä, Austria 30 E7 46 46N 14 50 E
Sankt Antönien, Switz. 29 C9 46 58N 9 48 E
Sankt Blasien, Germany 27 H4 47 47N 8 7 E
Sankt Gallen, Switz. 29 B8 47 26N 9 22 E
Sankt Gallen □, Switz. 29 B8 47 25N 9 22 E
Sankt Goar, Germany 27 E3 50 12N 7 43 E
Sankt Ingbert, Germany 27 F3 49 16N 7 6 E
Sankt Johann, Salzburg, Austria 30 D6 47 22N 13 12 E
Sankt Johann, Tirol, Austria 30 D5 47 30N 12 25 E
Sankt Margrethen, Switz. 29 B9 47 28N 9 37 E
Sankt Moritz, Switz. 29 D9 46 30N 9 50 E
Sankt-Peterburg, Russia 50 B7 59 55N 30 20 E
Sankt Pölten, Austria 30 C8 48 12N 15 38 E
Sankt Valentin, Austria 30 C7 48 11N 14 33 E
Sankt Veit, Austria 30 E7 46 54N 14 22 E
Sankt Wendel, Germany 27 F3 49 27N 7 9 E
Sankt Wolfgang, Austria 30 D6 47 43N 13 27 E
Sankuru →, Zaïre 103 C4 4 17 S 20 25 E
Sanlúcar de Barrameda, Spain 37 J4 36 46N 6 21W
Sanlúcar la Mayor, Spain 37 H4 37 26N 6 18W
Sanluri, Italy 40 C1 39 35N 8 55 E
Sanmenxia, China 66 G6 34 47N 111 12 E
Sanming, China 65 D6 26 13N 117 35 E
Sanming, Fujian, China 69 D11 26 15N 117 40 E
Sannan, Japan 63 B7 35 2N 135 1 E
Sannaspos, S. Africa 104 D4 29 6 S 26 34 E
Sannicandro Gargánico, Italy 41 A8 41 50N 15 34 E
Sannidal, Norway 14 F3 58 55N 9 15 E
Sannieshof, S. Africa 104 D4 26 30 S 25 47 E
Sannīn, J., Lebanon 91 B4 33 57N 35 52 E
Sano, Japan 63 A11 36 19N 139 35 E
Sanok, Poland 31 B15 49 35N 22 10 E
Sanquhar, U.K. 18 F5 55 21N 3 56W
Sansanding Dam, Mali 100 C3 13 48N 6 0W
Sansepolcro, Italy 39 E9 43 34N 12 8 E
Sansha, China 69 D13 26 58N 120 12 E
Sanshui, China 69 F9 23 10N 112 56 E
Sanski Most, Bos.-H. 39 D13 44 46N 16 40 E
Sansui, China 68 D7 26 58N 108 39 E
Santa, Peru 156 B2 8 59 S 78 40W
Sant' Ágata de Goti, Italy 41 A7 41 6N 14 30 E
Sant' Ágata di Militello, Italy 41 D7 38 2N 14 8 E
Santa Ana, Beni, Bolivia 157 C4 13 50 S 65 40W
Santa Ana, Santa Cruz, Bolivia 157 D6 18 43 S 58 44W
Santa Ana, Santa Cruz, Bolivia 157 D5 16 37 S 60 43W
Santa Ana, Ecuador 152 D1 1 16 S 80 20W
Santa Ana, El Salv. 148 D2 14 0N 89 31W
Santa Ana, Mexico 146 A2 30 31N 111 8W
Santa Ana, Phil. 70 B4 18 28N 122 20 E
Santa Ana, U.S.A. 145 M9 33 46N 117 52W
Santa Ana →, Venezuela 152 B3 9 30N 71 57W
Sant' Ángelo Lodigiano, Italy 38 C6 45 14N 9 25 E
Sant' Antíoco, Italy 40 C1 39 2N 8 30 E
Sant' Arcángelo di Romagna, Italy 39 D9 44 4N 12 26 E
Santa Bárbara, Colombia 152 B2 5 53N 75 35W
Santa Bárbara, Honduras 148 D2 14 53N 88 14W
Santa Bárbara, Mexico 146 B3 26 48N 105 50W
Santa Barbara, Phil. 71 F4 10 50N 122 32 E
Santa Bárbara, Spain 34 E5 40 42N 0 29 E
Santa Barbara, U.S.A. 145 L7 34 25N 119 42W
Santa Bárbara, Venezuela 152 B3 7 47N 71 10W
Santa Bárbara, Mt., Spain 35 H2 37 23N 2 50W
Santa Barbara Channel, U.S.A. 145 L7 34 15N 120 0W
Santa Barbara I., U.S.A. 145 M7 33 29N 119 2W
Santa Catalina, Colombia 152 A2 10 36N 75 17W
Santa Catalina, Mexico 146 B2 25 40N 110 50W
Santa Catalina, Gulf of, U.S.A. 145 N9 33 10N 117 50W
Santa Catalina I., U.S.A. 145 M8 33 23N 118 25W
Santa Catarina □, Brazil 159 B6 27 25 S 48 30W
Santa Catarina, I. de, Brazil 159 B6 27 30 S 48 40W
Santa Caterina Villarmosa, Italy 41 E7 37 37N 14 1 E
Santa Cecília, Brazil 159 B5 26 56 S 50 18W
Santa Clara, Cuba 148 B4 22 20N 80 0W
Santa Clara, Calif., U.S.A. 144 H5 37 21N 121 57W
Santa Clara, Utah, U.S.A. 143 H7 37 8N 113 39W
Santa Clara de Olimar, Uruguay 159 C5 32 50 S 54 54W
Santa Clotilde, Peru 152 D3 2 33 S 73 45W
Santa Coloma de Farners, Spain 34 D7 41 50N 2 39 E
Santa Coloma de Gramanet, Spain 34 D7 41 27N 2 13 E
Santa Comba, Spain 36 B2 43 2N 8 49W
Santa Croce Camerina, Italy 41 F7 36 50N 14 30 E
Santa Croce di Magliano, Italy 41 A7 41 43N 14 59 E
Santa Cruz, Argentina 160 D3 50 0 S 68 32W
Santa Cruz, Bolivia 157 D5 17 43 S 63 10W
Santa Cruz, Brazil 154 C4 6 13 S 36 1W
Santa Cruz, Chile 158 C1 34 38 S 71 27W
Santa Cruz, Costa Rica 148 D2 10 15N 85 35W
Santa Cruz, Madeira 33 D3 32 42N 16 46W
Santa Cruz, Peru 156 B2 5 40 S 75 56W
Santa Cruz, Davao del S., Phil. 71 H5 6 50N 125 25 E
Santa Cruz, Laguna, Phil. 70 D3 14 20N 121 24 E
Santa Cruz, Marinduque, Phil. 70 E4 13 28N 122 2 E
Santa Cruz, U.S.A. 144 J4 36 58N 122 1W
Santa Cruz, Venezuela 153 B5 8 3N 64 27W
Santa Cruz □, Argentina 160 C3 49 0 S 70 0W
Santa Cruz □, Bolivia 157 D5 17 43 S 63 10W
Santa Cruz →, Argentina 160 D3 50 10 S 68 20W
Santa Cruz Cabrália, Brazil 155 E4 16 17 S 39 2W
Santa Cruz de la Palma, Canary Is. 33 F2 28 41N 17 46W
Santa Cruz de Mudela, Spain 35 G1 38 39N 3 28W
Santa Cruz de Tenerife, Canary Is. 33 F3 28 28N 16 15W
Santa Cruz del Norte, Cuba 148 B3 23 9N 81 55W
Santa Cruz del Retamar, Spain 36 E6 40 8N 4 14W
Santa Cruz del Sur, Cuba 148 B4 20 44N 78 0W
Santa Cruz do Rio Pardo, Brazil 159 A6 22 54 S 49 37W
Santa Cruz do Sul, Brazil 159 B5 29 42 S 52 25W
Santa Cruz I., Solomon Is. 122 J8 10 30 S 166 0 E
Santa Cruz I., U.S.A. 145 M7 34 1N 119 43W
Santa Domingo, Cay, Bahamas 148 B4 21 25N 75 15W
Santa Elena, Argentina 158 C4 30 58 S 59 47W
Santa Elena, Ecuador 152 D1 2 16 S 80 52W
Santa Elena, C., Costa Rica 148 D2 10 54N 85 56W
Sant' Eufémia, G. di, Italy 41 D9 38 50N 16 10 E
Santa Eugenia, Pta., Mexico 146 B1 27 50N 115 5W
Santa Eulalia, Spain 33 C8 38 59N 1 32 E
Santa Fe, Argentina 158 C3 31 35 S 60 41W
Santa Fe, Nueva Viscaya, Phil. 70 C3 16 10N 120 57 E
Santa Fe, Tablas, Phil. 70 E4 12 10N 122 0 E
Santa Fe, Spain 37 H7 37 11N 3 43W
Santa Fe, U.S.A. 143 J11 35 41N 105 57W
Santa Fé □, Argentina 158 C3 31 50 S 60 55W
Santa Filomena, Brazil 154 C2 9 6 S 45 50W
Santa Galdana, Spain 33 B10 39 56N 3 58 E
Santa Gertrudis, Spain 33 B7 39 0N 1 26 E
Santa Helena, Brazil 154 B2 2 14 S 45 18W
Santa Helena de Goiás, Brazil 155 E1 17 53 S 50 35W
Santa Inês, Brazil 155 D4 13 17 S 39 48W
Santa Inés, Baleares, Spain 33 B7 39 3N 1 21 E
Santa Inés, Extremadura, Spain 37 G5 38 32N 5 37W
Santa Inés, I., Chile 160 D2 54 0 S 73 0W
Santa Isabel = Rey Malabo, Eq. Guin. 101 E6 3 45N 8 50 E
Santa Isabel, Argentina 158 D2 36 10 S 66 54W
Santa Isabel, Brazil 155 D1 11 45 S 51 30W
Santa Isabel, Solomon Is. 121 M10 8 0 S 159 0 E
Santa Isabel, Pico, Eq. Guin. 101 E6 3 36N 8 49 E
Santa Isabel do Araguaia, Brazil 154 C2 6 7 S 48 19W
Santa Isabel do Morro, Brazil 155 D1 11 34 S 50 40W
Santa Lucía, Corrientes, Argentina 158 B4 28 58 S 59 5W
Santa Lucía, San Juan, Argentina 158 C2 31 30 S 68 30W
Santa Lucia, Phil. 70 C3 17 7N 120 27 E
Santa Lucía, Spain 35 H4 37 35N 0 58W
Santa Lucía, Uruguay 158 C4 34 27 S 56 24W
Santa Lucia Range, U.S.A. 144 K5 36 0N 121 20W
Santa Magdalena, I., Mexico 146 C2 24 40N 112 15W
Santa Margarita, Argentina 158 D3 38 28 S 61 35W
Santa Margarita, Mexico 146 C2 24 30N 111 50W
Santa Margarita, Spain 33 B10 39 42N 3 6 E
Santa Margarita, U.S.A. 144 K6 35 23N 120 37W
Santa Margarita →, U.S.A. 145 M9 33 13N 117 23W
Santa Margherita, Italy 38 D6 44 20N 9 11 E
Santa María, Argentina 158 B2 26 40 S 66 0W
Santa Maria, Brazil 159 B5 29 40 S 53 48W
Santa Maria, Ilocos S., Phil. 70 C3 17 22N 120 29 E
Santa Maria, Isabela, Phil. 70 C3 17 28N 121 45 E
Santa Maria, Spain 33 B9 39 38N 2 47 E
Santa Maria, Switz. 29 C10 46 36N 10 25 E
Santa Maria, U.S.A. 145 L6 34 57N 120 26W
Santa María →, Mexico 146 A3 31 0N 107 14W
Santa María, B. de, Mexico 146 B3 25 10N 108 40W
Santa Maria, C. de, Portugal 37 J3 36 58N 7 53W
Santa Maria Capua Vetere, Italy 41 A7 41 3N 14 15 E
Santa Maria da Vitória, Brazil 155 D3 13 24 S 44 12W
Santa María de Ipire, Venezuela 153 B4 8 49N 65 19W
Santa Maria di Leuca, C., Italy 41 C11 39 48N 18 20 E
Santa Maria do Suaçuí, Brazil 155 E3 18 12 S 42 25W
Santa Maria dos Marmelos, Brazil 157 B5 6 7 S 61 51W
Santa María la Real de Nieva, Spain 36 D6 41 4N 4 24W
Santa Marta, Colombia 152 A3 11 15N 74 13W
Santa Marta, Spain 37 G4 38 37N 6 39W
Santa Marta, Ría de, Spain 36 B3 43 44N 7 45W
Santa Marta, Sierra Nevada de, Colombia 152 A3 10 55N 73 50W
Santa Marta Grande, C., Brazil 159 B6 28 43 S 48 50W
Santa Maura = Levkás, Greece 45 F2 38 40N 20 43 E
Santa Monica, U.S.A. 145 M8 34 1N 118 29W
Santa Olalla, Huelva, Spain 37 H4 37 54N 6 14W
Santa Olalla, Toledo, Spain 36 E6 40 2N 4 25W
Sant' Onofrio, Italy 41 D9 38 42N 16 10 E
Santa Pola, Spain 35 G4 38 13N 0 35W
Santa Ponsa, Spain 33 B9 39 30N 2 28 E
Santa Quitéria, Brazil 154 B3 4 20 S 40 10W
Santa Rita, U.S.A. 143 K10 32 48N 108 4W
Santa Rita, Guarico, Venezuela 152 B4 8 8N 66 16W
Santa Rita, Zulia, Venezuela 152 A3 10 32N 71 32W
Santa Rita do Araquaia, Brazil 157 D7 17 20 S 53 12W
Santa Rosa, La Pampa, Argentina 158 D3 36 40 S 64 17W
Santa Rosa, San Luis, Argentina 158 C2 32 21 S 65 10W
Santa Rosa, Bolivia 156 C4 10 36 S 67 20W
Santa Rosa, Brazil 159 B5 27 52 S 54 29W
Santa Rosa, Colombia 152 C4 3 32N 69 48W
Santa Rosa, Ecuador 152 D2 3 27 S 79 58W
Santa Rosa, Peru 156 C3 14 30 S 70 50W
Santa Rosa, Phil. 70 D3 15 25N 120 57 E
Santa Rosa, Calif., U.S.A. 144 G4 38 26N 122 43W
Santa Rosa, N. Mex., U.S.A. 139 H2 34 57N 104 41W
Santa Rosa, Venezuela 152 C4 1 29N 66 55W
Santa Rosa de Cabal, Colombia 152 C2 4 52N 75 38W
Santa Rosa de Copán, Honduras 148 D2 14 47N 88 46W
Santa Rosa de Osos, Colombia 152 B2 6 39N 75 28W

Sierra Blanca Peak 265


Shawano, *U.S.A.* **134 C1** 44 47N 88 36W
Shawinigan, *Canada* **128 C5** 46 35N 72 50W
Shawnee, *Kans., U.S.A.* **140 E2** 39 1N 94 43W
Shawnee, *Okla., U.S.A.* **139 H6** 35 20N 96 55W
Shaybārā, *Si. Arabia* **84 E3** 25 26N 36 47 E
Shayib el Banat, Gebel, *Egypt* **94 B3** 26 59N 33 29 E
Shaykh Sa'īd, *Iraq* **84 C5** 32 34N 46 17 E
Shaykh 'Uthmān, *Yemen* **86 D4** 12 52N 44 59 E
Shaymak, *Tajikistan* **55 E7** 37 33N 74 50 E
Shchekino, *Russia* **51 D10** 54 1N 37 34 E
Shcherbakov = Rybinsk, *Russia* **51 B11** 58 5N 38 50 E
Shchigri, *Russia* **51 F10** 51 55N 36 58 E
Shchors, *Ukraine* **50 F7** 51 48N 31 56 E
Shchuchiosk, *Kazakhstan* **56 D8** 52 56N 70 12 E
Shchuchye, *Russia* **54 D8** 55 12N 62 46 E
She Xian, *Anhui, China* **69 C12** 29 50N 118 25 E
She Xian, *Hebei, China* **66 F7** 36 30N 113 40 E
Shea, *Guyana* **153 C6** 2 48N 59 4W
Shebekino, *Russia* **51 F10** 50 28N 36 54 E
Shebele = Scebeli, Wabi →, *Somali Rep.* **90 G3** 2 0N 44 0 E
Sheboygan, *U.S.A.* **134 D2** 43 46N 87 45W
Shediac, *Canada* **129 C7** 46 14N 64 32W
Sheelin, L., *Ireland* **19 C4** 53 48N 7 20W
Sheep Haven, *Ireland* **19 A4** 55 12N 7 55W
Sheerness, *U.K.* **17 F8** 51 26N 0 47 E
Sheet Harbour, *Canada* **129 D7** 44 56N 62 31W
Sheffield, *N.Z.* **119 D7** 43 23 S 172 1 E
Sheffield, *U.K.* **16 D6** 53 23N 1 28W
Sheffield, *Ala., U.S.A.* **135 H2** 34 46N 87 41W
Sheffield, *Ill., U.S.A.* **140 C7** 41 21N 89 44W
Sheffield, *Iowa, U.S.A.* **140 A3** 42 54N 93 13W
Sheffield, *Mass., U.S.A.* **137 D11** 42 5N 73 21W
Sheffield, *Pa., U.S.A.* **136 E5** 41 42N 79 3W
Sheffield, *Tex., U.S.A.* **139 K4** 30 41N 101 49W
Shegaon, *India* **82 D3** 20 48N 76 47 E
Sheho, *Canada* **131 C8** 51 35N 103 13W
Shehojele, *Ethiopia* **95 E4** 10 40N 35 9 E
Shehong, *China* **68 B5** 30 54N 105 18 E
Shehuen →, *Argentina* **160 C3** 49 35 S 69 34W
Sheikhpura, *India* **81 G11** 25 9N 85 53 E
Shek Hasan, *Ethiopia* **95 E4** 12 5N 35 58 E
Shekhupura, *Pakistan* **79 C4** 31 42N 73 58 E
Sheki, *Azerbaijan* **53 F12** 41 10N 47 5 E
Sheksna →, *Russia* **51 B11** 59 0N 38 30 E
Shelbina, *U.S.A.* **140 E4** 39 47N 92 2W
Shelburn, *U.S.A.* **141 E9** 39 11N 87 24W
Shelburne, *N.S., Canada* **129 D6** 43 47N 65 20W
Shelburne, *Ont., Canada* **128 D3** 44 4N 80 15W
Shelburne, *U.S.A.* **137 B11** 44 23N 73 14W
Shelburne B., *Australia* **114 A3** 11 50 S 142 50 E
Shelburne Falls, *U.S.A.* **137 D12** 42 36N 72 45W
Shelby, *Mich., U.S.A.* **134 D2** 43 37N 86 22W
Shelby, *Mont., U.S.A.* **142 B8** 48 30N 111 51W
Shelby, *N.C., U.S.A.* **135 H5** 35 17N 81 32W
Shelby, *Ohio, U.S.A.* **136 F2** 40 53N 82 40W
Shelbyville, *Ill., U.S.A.* **138 F10** 39 24N 88 48W
Shelbyville, *Ind., U.S.A.* **141 E11** 39 31N 85 47W
Shelbyville, *Ky., U.S.A.* **141 F11** 38 13N 85 14W
Shelbyville, *Mo., U.S.A.* **140 E4** 39 48N 92 2W
Shelbyville, *Tenn., U.S.A.* **135 H2** 35 29N 86 28W
Shelbyville, L., *U.S.A.* **141 E8** 39 26N 88 46W
Sheldon, *Iowa, U.S.A.* **138 D7** 43 11N 95 51W
Sheldon, *Mo., U.S.A.* **140 G2** 37 40N 94 18W
Sheldrake, *Canada* **129 B7** 50 20N 64 51W
Shelikhova, Zaliv, *Russia* **57 D16** 59 30N 157 0 E
Shell Lake, *Canada* **131 C7** 53 19N 107 2W
Shell Lakes, *Australia* **113 E4** 29 20 S 127 30 E
Shellbrook, *Canada* **131 C7** 53 13N 106 24W
Shellharbour, *Australia* **117 C9** 34 31 S 150 51 E
Shelling Rocks, *Ireland* **19 E1** 51 45N 10 35W
Shellsburg, *U.S.A.* **140 B5** 42 6N 91 52W
Shelon →, *Russia* **50 B7** 58 10N 30 30 E
Shelton, *Conn., U.S.A.* **137 E11** 41 19N 73 5W
Shelton, *Wash., U.S.A.* **144 C3** 47 13N 123 6W
Shemakha, *Azerbaijan* **53 F13** 40 38N 48 37 E
Shen Xian, *China* **66 F8** 36 15N 115 40 E
Shenandoah, *Iowa, U.S.A.* **138 E7** 40 46N 95 22W
Shenandoah, *Pa., U.S.A.* **137 F8** 40 49N 76 12W
Shenandoah, *Va., U.S.A.* **134 F6** 38 29N 78 37W
Shenandoah →, *U.S.A.* **134 F7** 39 19N 77 44W
Shenchi, *China* **66 E7** 39 8N 112 10 E
Shencottah, *India* **83 K3** 8 59N 77 18 E
Shendam, *Nigeria* **101 D6** 8 49N 9 30 E
Shendî, *Sudan* **95 D3** 16 46N 33 22 E
Shendurni, *India* **82 D2** 20 39N 75 36 E
Sheng Xian, *China* **69 C13** 29 35N 120 50 E
Shengfang, *China* **66 E9** 39 3N 116 42 E
Shëngjergji, *Albania* **44 C2** 41 17N 20 10 E
Shëngjini, *Albania* **44 C1** 41 50N 19 35 E
Shenjingzi, *China* **67 B13** 44 40N 124 30 E
Shenmëria, *Albania* **44 B2** 42 7N 20 13 E
Shenmu, *China* **66 E6** 38 50N 110 29 E
Shennongjia, *China* **69 B8** 31 43N 110 44 E
Shenqiu, *China* **66 H8** 33 25N 115 5 E
Shenqiucheng, *China* **66 H8** 33 24N 115 2 E
Shensi = Shaanxi □, *China* **66 G5** 35 0N 109 0 E
Shenyang, *China* **67 D12** 41 48N 123 27 E
Shepetovka, *Ukraine* **50 F5** 50 10N 27 10 E
Shepherd Is., *Vanuatu* **121 F6** 16 55 S 168 36 E
Shepherdsville, *U.S.A.* **141 G11** 37 59N 85 43W
Shepparton, *Australia* **117 D6** 36 23 S 145 26 E
Sheqi, *China* **66 H7** 33 12N 112 57 E
Sher Qila, *Pakistan* **81 A6** 36 7N 74 2 E
Sherborne, *U.K.* **17 G5** 50 56N 2 31W
Sherbro I., *S. Leone* **100 D2** 7 30N 12 40W
Sherbrooke, *Canada* **129 C5** 45 28N 71 57W
Sherda, *Chad* **97 D3** 20 7N 16 46 E
Shereik, *Sudan* **94 D3** 18 44N 33 47 E
Sheridan, *Ark., U.S.A.* **139 H8** 34 19N 92 24W
Sheridan, *Ill., U.S.A.* **141 C8** 41 32N 88 41W
Sheridan, *Ind., U.S.A.* **141 D10** 40 8N 86 13W
Sheridan, *Mo., U.S.A.* **140 D2** 40 31N 94 37W
Sheridan, *Wyo., U.S.A.* **142 D10** 44 48N 106 58W
Sherkot, *India* **81 E8** 29 22N 78 35 E
Sherman, *U.S.A.* **139 J6** 33 40N 96 35W
Sherpur, *Afghan.* **79 B3** 34 32N 69 10 E
Sherpur, *Bangla.* **78 C3** 25 0N 90 0 E
Sherridon, *Canada* **131 B8** 55 8N 101 5W
Sherwood, *N. Dak., U.S.A.* **138 A4** 48 57N 101 38W
Sherwood, *Ohio, U.S.A.* **141 C12** 41 17N 84 33W
Sherwood, *Tex., U.S.A.* **139 K4** 31 18N 100 45W
Sherwood Forest, *U.K.* **16 D6** 53 5N 1 5W
Sheslay, *Canada* **130 B2** 58 17N 131 52W
Sheslay →, *Canada* **130 B2** 58 48N 132 5W
Shethanei L., *Canada* **131 B9** 58 48N 97 50W
Shetland □, *U.K.* **18 A7** 60 30N 1 30W
Shetland Is., *U.K.* **18 A7** 60 30N 1 30W
Shevaroy Hills, *India* **83 J4** 11 58N 78 12 E
Shewa □, *Ethiopia* **95 F4** 9 33N 38 10 E
Shewa Gimira, *Ethiopia* **95 F4** 7 4N 35 51 E
Sheyenne, *U.S.A.* **138 B5** 47 50N 99 7W
Sheyenne →, *U.S.A.* **138 B6** 47 2N 96 50W
Shibām, *Yemen* **87 D5** 16 0N 48 36 E
Shibata, *Japan* **60 F9** 37 57N 139 20 E
Shibecha, *Japan* **60 C12** 43 17N 144 36 E
Shibetsu, *Japan* **60 B11** 44 10N 142 23 E
Shibîn el Kôm, *Egypt* **94 H7** 30 31N 30 55 E
Shibîn el Qanâtir, *Egypt* **94 H7** 30 19N 31 19 E
Shibing, *China* **68 D7** 27 2N 108 7 E
Shibogama L., *Canada* **128 B2** 53 35N 88 15W
Shibukawa, *Japan* **63 A10** 36 29N 139 0 E
Shibushi, *Japan* **62 F3** 31 25N 131 8 E
Shibushi-Wan, *Japan* **62 F3** 31 24N 131 8 E
Shicheng, *China* **69 D11** 26 22N 116 20 E
Shickshock Mts. = Chic-Chocs, Mts., *Canada* **129 C6** 48 55N 66 0W
Shidād, *Si. Arabia* **86 B3** 21 19N 40 3 E
Shidao, *China* **67 F12** 36 50N 122 25 E
Shidian, *China* **68 E2** 24 40N 99 5 E
Shido, *Japan* **62 C6** 34 19N 134 10 E
Shiel, L., *U.K.* **18 E3** 56 48N 5 32W
Shield, C., *Australia* **114 A2** 13 20 S 136 20 E
Shiga □, *Japan* **63 B8** 35 20N 136 0 E
Shigaib, *Sudan* **97 E4** 15 5N 23 35 E
Shigaraki, *Japan* **63 C8** 34 57N 136 2 E
Shigu, *China* **68 D2** 26 51N 99 56 E
Shiguaigou, *China* **66 D6** 40 52N 110 15 E
Shihan, W. →, *Yemen* **87 C5** 17 24N 51 26 E
Shihchiachuangi = Shijiazhuang, *China* **66 E8** 38 2N 114 28 E
Shiiba, *Japan* **62 E3** 32 29N 131 4 E
Shijaku, *Albania* **44 C1** 41 21N 19 33 E
Shijiazhuang, *China* **66 E8** 38 2N 114 28 E
Shijiu Hu, *China* **69 B12** 31 25N 118 50 E
Shikarpur, *India* **80 E8** 28 17N 78 7 E
Shikarpur, *Pakistan* **79 D3** 27 57N 68 39 E
Shikine-Jima, *Japan* **63 C11** 34 19N 139 13 E
Shikoku, *Japan* **62 D5** 33 30N 133 30 E
Shikoku □, *Japan* **62 D5** 33 30N 133 30 E
Shikoku-Sanchi, *Japan* **62 D5** 33 30N 133 30 E
Shilabo, *Ethiopia* **90 F3** 6 22N 44 32 E
Shilda, *Russia* **54 F6** 51 49N 59 47 E
Shiliguri, *India* **78 B2** 26 45N 88 25 E
Shilka, *Russia* **57 D12** 52 0N 115 55 E
Shilka →, *Russia* **57 D13** 53 20N 121 26 E
Shillelagh, *Ireland* **19 D5** 52 46N 6 32W
Shillong, *India* **78 C3** 25 35N 91 53 E
Shilo, *Jordan* **91 C4** 32 4N 35 18 E
Shilong, *China* **69 F9** 23 5N 113 52 E
Shilou, *China* **66 F6** 37 0N 110 48 E
Shilovo, *Russia* **51 D12** 54 25N 40 57 E
Shima-Hantō, *Japan* **63 C8** 34 22N 136 45 E
Shimabara, *Japan* **62 E2** 32 48N 130 20 E
Shimada, *Japan* **63 C10** 34 49N 138 10 E
Shimane □, *Japan* **62 C4** 35 0N 132 30 E
Shimane-Hantō, *Japan* **62 B5** 35 30N 133 0 E
Shimanovsk, *Russia* **57 D13** 52 15N 127 30 E
Shimen, *China* **69 C8** 29 35N 111 20 E
Shimenjie, *China* **69 C11** 29 29N 116 48 E
Shimian, *China* **68 C4** 29 17N 102 23 E
Shimizu, *Japan* **63 C10** 35 0N 138 30 E
Shimo-Jima, *Japan* **62 E2** 32 15N 130 7 E
Shimo-Koshiki-Jima, *Japan* **62 F1** 31 40N 129 43 E
Shimoda, *Japan* **63 C10** 34 40N 138 57 E
Shimodate, *Japan* **63 A11** 36 20N 139 55 E
Shimoga, *India* **83 H2** 13 57N 75 32 E
Shimoni, *Kenya* **106 C4** 4 38 S 39 20 E
Shimonita, *Japan* **63 A10** 36 13N 138 47 E
Shimonoseki, *Japan* **62 D2** 33 58N 130 55 E
Shimotsuma, *Japan* **63 A11** 36 11N 139 58 E
Shimpuru Rapids, *Angola* **103 F3** 17 45 S 19 55 E
Shimsha →, *India* **83 H3** 13 15N 77 10 E
Shimsk, *Russia* **50 B7** 58 15N 30 50 E
Shin, L., *U.K.* **18 C4** 58 7N 4 30W
Shin-Tone →, *Japan* **63 B12** 35 44N 140 51 E
Shinan, *China* **68 F7** 22 44N 109 53 E
Shinano →, *Japan* **61 F9** 36 50N 138 30 E
Shīndand, *Afghan.* **79 B1** 33 12N 62 8 E
Shingbwiyang, *Burma* **78 B6** 26 41N 96 13 E
Shingleton, *U.S.A.* **128 C2** 46 21N 86 28W
Shingū, *Japan* **63 D7** 33 40N 135 55 E
Shinji, *Japan* **62 B4** 35 24N 132 54 E
Shinji Ko, *Japan* **62 B4** 35 26N 132 57 E
Shinjō, *Japan* **60 E10** 38 46N 140 18 E
Shinkafe, *Nigeria* **101 C6** 13 8N 6 29 E
Shīnkay, *Afghan.* **79 C2** 31 57N 67 26 E
Shinminato, *Japan* **63 A9** 36 47N 137 4 E
Shinonoi, *Japan* **63 A10** 36 35N 138 9 E
Shinshār, *Syria* **91 A5** 34 36N 36 43 E
Shinshiro, *Japan* **63 C9** 34 54N 137 30 E
Shinyanga, *Tanzania* **106 C3** 3 45 S 33 27 E
Shinyanga □, *Tanzania* **106 C3** 3 50 S 34 0 E
Shio-no-Misaki, *Japan* **63 D7** 33 25N 135 45 E
Shiogama, *Japan* **60 E10** 38 19N 141 1 E
Shiojiri, *Japan* **63 A9** 36 6N 137 58 E
Ship I., *U.S.A.* **139 K10** 30 13N 88 55W
Shipehenski Prokhod, *Bulgaria* **43 E10** 42 45N 25 15 E
Shiping, *China* **68 F4** 23 45N 102 23 E
Shippegan, *Canada* **129 C7** 47 45N 64 45W
Shippensburg, *U.S.A.* **136 F7** 40 3N 77 31W
Shiprock, *U.S.A.* **143 H9** 36 47N 108 41W
Shiqian, *China* **68 D7** 27 32N 108 13 E
Shiqma, N. →, *Israel* **91 D3** 31 37N 34 30 E
Shiquan, *China* **66 H5** 33 5N 108 15 E
Shīr Kūh, *Iran* **85 D7** 31 39N 54 3 E
Shirabad, *Uzbekistan* **55 E3** 37 40N 67 1 E
Shiragami-Misaki, *Japan* **60 D10** 41 24N 140 12 E
Shirahama, *Japan* **63 D7** 33 41N 135 20 E
Shirakawa, *Fukushima, Japan* **61 F10** 37 7N 140 13 E
Shirakawa, *Gifu, Japan* **63 A8** 36 17N 136 56 E
Shirane-San, *Gumma, Japan* **63 A11** 36 48N 139 22 E
Shirane-San, *Yamanashi, Japan* **63 B10** 35 42N 138 9 E
Shiraoi, *Japan* **60 C10** 42 33N 141 21 E
Shīrāz, *Iran* **85 D7** 29 42N 52 30 E
Shirbin, *Egypt* **94 H7** 31 11N 31 32 E
Shire →, *Africa* **107 F4** 17 42 S 35 19 E
Shiretoko-Misaki, *Japan* **60 B12** 44 21N 145 20 E
Shirinab →, *Pakistan* **80 D2** 30 15N 66 28 E
Shiringushi, *Russia* **51 E13** 53 51N 42 46 E
Shiriya-Zaki, *Japan* **60 D10** 41 25N 141 30 E
Shirley, *U.S.A.* **141 E11** 39 53N 85 35W
Shiroishi, *Japan* **60 E10** 38 0N 140 37 E
Shirol, *India* **82 F2** 16 47N 74 41 E
Shirpur, *India* **82 D2** 21 21N 74 57 E
Shīrvān, *Iran* **85 B8** 37 30N 57 50 E
Shirwa, L. = Chilwa, L., *Malawi* **107 F4** 15 15 S 35 40 E
Shishmanova, *Bulgaria* **43 E8** 42 58N 23 12 E
Shishou, *China* **69 C9** 29 38N 112 22 E
Shitai, *China* **69 B11** 30 12N 117 25 E
Shively, *U.S.A.* **141 F11** 38 12N 85 49W
Shivpuri, *India* **80 G7** 25 26N 77 42 E
Shixian, *China* **67 C15** 43 5N 129 50 E
Shixing, *China* **69 E10** 24 46N 114 5 E
Shiyan, *China* **69 A8** 32 35N 110 45 E
Shiyata, *Egypt* **94 B2** 29 25N 25 7 E
Shizhu, *China* **68 C7** 29 58N 108 7 E
Shizong, *China* **68 E5** 24 50N 104 0 E
Shizuishan, *China* **66 E4** 39 15N 106 50 E
Shizuoka, *Japan* **63 C10** 34 57N 138 24 E
Shizuoka □, *Japan* **63 B10** 35 15N 138 40 E
Shklov, *Belorussia* **50 D7** 54 16N 30 15 E
Shkoder = Shkodra, *Albania* **44 B1** 42 6N 19 20 E
Shkodra, *Albania* **44 B1** 42 6N 19 20 E
Shkodra □, *Albania* **44 B1** 42 25N 19 20 E
Shkumbini →, *Albania* **44 C1** 41 5N 19 50 E
Shmidta, O., *Russia* **57 A10** 81 0N 91 0 E
Shō-Gawa →, *Japan* **63 A9** 36 47N 137 4 E
Shoal Cr. →, *U.S.A.* **140 E3** 39 44N 93 32W
Shoal Lake, *Canada* **131 C8** 50 30N 100 35W
Shoals, *U.S.A.* **141 F10** 38 40N 86 47W
Shōbara, *Japan* **62 C5** 34 51N 133 1 E
Shōdo-Shima, *Japan* **62 C6** 34 30N 134 15 E
Shoeburyness, *U.K.* **17 F8** 51 31N 0 49 E
Shokpar, *Kazakhstan* **55 B7** 43 49N 74 21 E
Sholapur = Solapur, *India* **82 F2** 17 43N 75 56 E
Shologontsy, *Russia* **57 C12** 66 13N 114 0 E
Shōmrōn, *Jordan* **91 C4** 32 15N 35 13 E
Shoranur, *India* **83 J3** 10 46N 76 19 E
Shorapur, *India* **83 F3** 16 31N 76 48 E
Shortland I., *Solomon Is.* **121 L8** 7 0 S 155 45 E
Shoshone, *Calif., U.S.A.* **145 K10** 35 58N 116 16W
Shoshone, *Idaho, U.S.A.* **142 E6** 43 0N 114 25W
Shoshone L., *U.S.A.* **142 D8** 44 22N 110 43W
Shoshone Mts., *U.S.A.* **142 G5** 39 20N 117 25W
Shoshong, *Botswana* **104 C4** 22 56 S 26 31 E
Shoshoni, *U.S.A.* **142 E9** 43 14N 108 7W
Shostka, *Ukraine* **50 F8** 51 57N 33 32 E
Shou Xian, *China* **69 A11** 32 37N 116 42 E
Shouchang, *China* **69 C12** 29 18N 119 12 E
Shouguang, *China* **67 F10** 37 52N 118 45 E
Shouning, *China* **69 D12** 27 27N 119 31 E
Shouyang, *China* **66 F7** 37 54N 113 8 E
Show Low, *U.S.A.* **143 J9** 34 15N 110 2W
Shpola, *Ukraine* **52 B4** 49 1N 31 30 E
Shreveport, *U.S.A.* **139 J8** 32 31N 93 45W
Shrewsbury, *U.K.* **16 E5** 52 42N 2 45W
Shrirampur, *India* **81 H13** 22 44N 88 21 E
Shrirangapattana, *India* **83 H3** 12 26N 76 43 E
Shropshire □, *U.K.* **17 E5** 52 36N 2 45W
Shuangbai, *China* **68 E3** 24 42N 101 38 E
Shuangcheng, *China* **67 B14** 45 20N 126 15 E
Shuangfeng, *China* **69 D9** 27 29N 112 11 E
Shuanggou, *China* **67 G9** 34 2N 117 30 E
Shuangjiang, *China* **68 F2** 23 26N 99 58 E
Shuangliao, *China* **67 C12** 43 29N 123 30 E
Shuangshanzi, *China* **67 D10** 40 20N 119 8 E
Shuangyang, *China* **67 C13** 43 28N 125 40 E
Shuangyashan, *China* **65 B8** 46 28N 131 5 E
Shu'b, Ra's, *Yemen* **87 D6** 12 30N 53 25 E
Shucheng, *China* **69 B11** 31 28N 116 57 E
Shuguri Falls, *Tanzania* **107 D4** 8 33 S 37 22 E
Shuhayr, *Yemen* **87 D5** 14 41N 49 23 E
Shuicheng, *China* **68 D5** 26 38N 104 48 E
Shuiji, *China* **69 D12** 27 13N 118 20 E
Shuiye, *China* **66 F8** 36 7N 114 8 E
Shujalpur, *India* **80 H7** 23 18N 76 46 E
Shukpa Kunzang, *India* **81 B8** 34 22N 78 22 E
Shulan, *China* **67 B14** 44 28N 127 0 E
Shule, *China* **64 C2** 39 25N 76 3 E
Shullsburg, *U.S.A.* **140 B6** 42 35N 90 13W
Shumagin Is., *U.S.A.* **126 C4** 55 7N 159 45W
Shumerlya, *Russia* **51 D15** 55 30N 46 25 E
Shumikha, *Russia* **54 D8** 55 10N 63 15 E
Shunchang, *China* **69 D11** 26 54N 117 48 E
Shunde, *China* **69 F9** 22 42N 113 14 E
Shungay, *Kazakhstan* **53 B12** 48 30N 46 45 E
Shungnak, *U.S.A.* **126 B4** 66 52N 157 9W
Shuo Xian, *China* **66 E7** 39 20N 112 33 E
Shūr →, *Iran* **85 D7** 28 30N 55 0 E
Shūr Āb, *Iran* **85 C6** 34 23N 51 11 E
Shūr Gaz, *Iran* **85 D8** 29 10N 59 20 E
Shūrāb, *Iran* **85 C8** 33 43N 56 29 E
Shurab, *Tajikistan* **55 C5** 40 3N 70 33 E
Shurchi, *Uzbekistan* **55 E3** 37 59N 67 47 E
Shūrjestān, *Iran* **85 D7** 31 24N 52 25 E
Shurkhua, *Burma* **78 D4** 22 15N 93 38 E
Shurma, *Russia* **54 C2** 56 58N 50 21 E
Shurugwi, *Zimbabwe* **107 F3** 19 40 S 30 0 E
Shūsf, *Iran* **85 D9** 31 50N 60 5 E
Shūshtar, *Iran* **85 D6** 32 0N 48 50 E
Shuswap L., *Canada* **130 C5** 50 55N 119 3W
Shuya, *Russia* **51 C12** 56 50N 41 28 E
Shuyang, *China* **67 G10** 34 10N 118 42 E
Shuzenji, *Japan* **63 C10** 34 58N 138 56 E
Shūzū, *Iran* **85 D7** 29 52N 54 30 E
Shwebo, *Burma* **78 D5** 22 30N 95 45 E
Shwegu, *Burma* **78 C6** 24 15N 96 26 E
Shwegun, *Burma* **78 G6** 17 9N 97 39 E
Shwenyaung, *Burma* **78 E6** 20 46N 96 57 E
Shymkent = Chimkent, *Kazakhstan* **55 B4** 42 18N 69 36 E
Shyok, *India* **81 B8** 34 15N 78 12 E
Shyok →, *Pakistan* **81 B6** 35 13N 75 53 E
Si Chon, *Thailand* **77 H2** 9 0N 99 54 E
Si Kiang = Xi Jiang →, *China* **69 F9** 22 5N 113 20 E
Si-ngan = Xi'an, *China* **66 G5** 34 15N 109 0 E
Si Prachan, *Thailand* **76 E3** 14 37N 100 9 E
Si Racha, *Thailand* **76 F3** 13 10N 100 48 E
Si Xian, *China* **67 H9** 33 30N 117 50 E
Siahan Range, *Pakistan* **79 D2** 27 30N 64 40 E
Siak →, *Indonesia* **74 B2** 1 13N 102 9 E
Siaksrindrapura, *Indonesia* **74 B2** 0 51N 102 0 E
Sialkot, *Pakistan* **79 B4** 32 32N 74 30 E
Sialsuk, *India* **78 D4** 23 24N 92 45 E
Siam = Thailand ■, *Asia* **76 E4** 16 0N 102 0 E
Siam, *Australia* **116 B2** 32 35 S 136 41 E
Siantan, P., *Indonesia* **77 L6** 3 10N 106 15 E
Siàpo →, *Venezuela* **152 C4** 2 7N 66 28W
Sīāreh, *Iran* **85 D9** 28 5N 60 14 E
Siargao, *Phil.* **71 G6** 9 52N 126 3 E
Siari, *Pakistan* **81 B7** 34 55N 76 40 E
Siari, *Phil.* **71 G4** 8 19N 122 58 E
Siasi I., *Phil.* **71 J3** 5 33N 120 51 E
Siassi, *Papua N. G.* **120 C4** 5 40 S 147 51 E
Siátista, *Greece* **44 D3** 40 15N 21 33 E
Siaton, *Phil.* **71 G4** 9 4N 123 2 E
Siau, *Indonesia* **72 A3** 2 50N 125 25 E
Šiauliai, *Lithuania* **50 D3** 55 56N 23 15 E
Siaya □, *Kenya* **106 B3** 0 0 34 20 E
Siazan, *Azerbaijan* **53 F13** 41 3N 49 10 E
Sibâi, Gebel el, *Egypt* **94 B3** 25 45N 34 10 E
Sibang, *Gabon* **102 B1** 0 25N 9 31 E
Sibari, *Italy* **41 C9** 39 47N 16 27 E
Sibasa, *S. Africa* **105 C5** 22 53 S 30 33 E
Sibay, *Russia* **54 E6** 52 42N 58 39 E
Sibay I., *Phil.* **71 F3** 11 51N 121 29 E
Sibayi, L., *S. Africa* **105 D5** 27 20 S 32 45 E
Šibenik, *Croatia* **39 E12** 43 48N 15 54 E
Siberia, *Russia* **58 D14** 60 0N 100 0 E
Siberut, *Indonesia* **74 C1** 1 30 S 99 0 E
Sibi, *Pakistan* **79 C2** 29 30N 67 54 E
Sibil, *Indonesia* **73 B6** 4 59 S 140 35 E
Sibiti, *Congo* **102 C2** 3 38 S 13 19 E
Sibiu, *Romania* **46 D5** 45 45N 24 9 E
Sibiu □, *Romania* **46 D5** 45 50N 24 15 E
Sibley, *Ill., U.S.A.* **141 D8** 40 35N 88 23W
Sibley, *Iowa, U.S.A.* **138 D7** 43 24N 95 45W
Sibley, *La., U.S.A.* **139 J8** 32 33N 93 18W
Sibolga, *Indonesia* **74 B1** 1 42N 98 45 E
Sibret, *Belgium* **21 J7** 49 58N 5 38 E
Sibsagar, *India* **78 B5** 27 0N 94 36 E
Sibu, *Malaysia* **75 B4** 2 18N 111 49 E
Sibuco, *Phil.* **71 H4** 7 20N 122 10 E
Sibuguey B., *Phil.* **71 H4** 7 50N 122 45 E
Sibutu, *Phil.* **71 J2** 4 45N 119 30 E
Sibutu Group, *Phil.* **71 J2** 4 45N 119 20 E
Sibutu Passage, *E. Indies* **71 J2** 4 50N 120 0 E
Sibuyan, *Phil.* **70 E4** 12 25N 122 40 E
Sibuyan Sea, *Phil.* **70 E4** 12 30N 122 20 E
Sicamous, *Canada* **130 C5** 50 49N 119 0W
Sicapoo, Mt., *Phil.* **70 B3** 18 1N 120 56 E
Sichuan □, *China* **68 B5** 31 0N 104 0 E
Sicilia, *Italy* **41 E7** 37 30N 14 30 E
Sicilia □, *Italy* **41 E7** 37 30N 14 30 E
Sicilia, Canale di, *Italy* **40 E5** 37 25N 12 30 E
Sicilian Channel = Sicilia, Canale di, *Italy* **40 E5** 37 25N 12 30 E
Sicily = Sicilia, *Italy* **41 E7** 37 30N 14 30 E
Sicuani, *Peru* **156 C3** 14 21 S 71 10W
Siculiana, *Italy* **40 E6** 37 20N 13 23 E
Šid, *Serbia* **42 B4** 45 8N 19 14 E
Sidamo □, *Ethiopia* **95 G4** 5 0N 37 50 E
Sidaouet, *Niger* **97 E1** 18 34N 8 3 E
Sidári, *Greece* **32 A3** 39 47N 19 41 E
Siddeburen, *Neths.* **20 B9** 53 15N 6 52 E
Siddhapur, *India* **80 H5** 23 56N 72 25 E
Siddipet, *India* **82 E4** 18 5N 78 51 E
Side, *Turkey* **88 E4** 36 45N 31 23 E
Sidell, *U.S.A.* **141 E9** 39 55N 87 49W
Sidéradougou, *Burkina Faso* **100 C4** 10 42N 4 12W
Siderno Marina, *Italy* **41 D9** 38 16N 16 17 E
Sídheros, Ákra, *Greece* **32 D8** 35 19N 26 19 E
Sidhirókastron, *Greece* **44 C5** 41 13N 23 24 E
Sîdi Abd el Rahmân, *Egypt* **94 H6** 30 55N 29 44 E
Sîdi Barrâni, *Egypt* **94 A2** 31 38N 25 58 E
Sidi-bel-Abbès, *Algeria* **99 A4** 35 13N 0 39W
Sidi Bennour, *Morocco* **98 B3** 32 40N 8 25W
Sidi Haneish, *Egypt* **94 A2** 31 10N 27 35 E
Sidi Kacem, *Morocco* **98 B3** 34 11N 5 49W
Sidi Omar, *Egypt* **94 A1** 31 24N 24 57 E
Sidi Slimane, *Morocco* **98 B3** 34 16N 5 56W
Sidi Smaïl, *Morocco* **98 B3** 32 50N 8 31W
Sidi 'Uzayz, *Libya* **96 B4** 31 41N 24 55 E
Sidlaw Hills, *U.K.* **18 E5** 56 32N 3 10W
Sidley, Mt., *Antarctica* **7 D14** 77 2 S 126 2W
Sidmouth, *U.K.* **17 G4** 50 40N 3 13W
Sidmouth, C., *Australia* **114 A3** 13 25 S 143 36 E
Sidney, *Canada* **130 D4** 48 39N 123 24W
Sidney, *Mont., U.S.A.* **138 B2** 47 43N 104 9W
Sidney, *N.Y., U.S.A.* **137 D9** 42 19N 75 24W
Sidney, *Nebr., U.S.A.* **138 E3** 41 8N 102 59W
Sidney, *Ohio, U.S.A.* **141 D12** 40 17N 84 9W
Sidoarjo, *Indonesia* **75 D4** 7 27 S 112 43 E
Sidoktaya, *Burma* **78 E5** 20 27N 94 15 E
Sidon = Saydā, *Lebanon* **91 B4** 33 35N 35 25 E
Sidra, G. of = Surt, Khalīj, *Libya* **96 B3** 31 40N 18 30 E
Siedlce, *Poland* **47 C9** 52 10N 22 20 E
Siedlce □, *Poland* **47 C9** 52 0N 22 0 E
Sieg →, *Germany* **26 E3** 50 46N 7 7 E
Siegburg, *Germany* **26 E3** 50 48N 7 12 E
Siegen, *Germany* **26 E4** 50 52N 8 2 E
Siem Pang, *Cambodia* **76 E6** 14 7N 106 23 E
Siem Reap, *Cambodia* **76 F4** 13 20N 103 52 E
Siena, *Italy* **39 E8** 43 20N 11 20 E
Sieniawa, *Poland* **31 A15** 50 11N 22 38 E
Sieradź, *Poland* **47 D5** 51 37N 18 41 E
Sieraków, *Poland* **47 C3** 52 39N 16 2 E
Sierck-les-Bains, *France* **23 C13** 49 26N 6 20 E
Sierpc, *Poland* **47 C6** 52 55N 19 43 E
Sierpe, Bocas de la, *Venezuela* **153 B5** 10 0N 61 30W
Sierra Blanca, *U.S.A.* **143 L11** 31 11N 105 22W
Sierra Blanca Peak, *U.S.A.* **143 K11** 33 23N 105 49W

266 Sierra City


Sierra City, *U.S.A.* **144 F6** 39 34N 120 38W
Sierra Colorada, *Argentina* **160 B3** 40 35 S 67 50W
Sierra de Yeguas, *Spain* **37 H6** 37 7N 4 52W
Sierra Gorda, *Chile* **158 A2** 22 50 S 69 15W
Sierra Grande, *Argentina* **160 B3** 41 36 S 65 22W
Sierra Leone ■, *W. Afr.* **100 D2** 9 0N 12 0W
Sierra Madre, *Mexico* **147 D6** 16 0N 93 0W
Sierra Mojada, *Mexico* **146 B4** 27 19N 103 42W
Sierraville, *U.S.A.* **144 F6** 39 36N 120 22W
Sierre, *Switz.* **28 D5** 46 17N 7 31 E
Sif Fatima, *Algeria* **99 B6** 31 6N 8 41 E
Sífnos, *Greece* **45 H6** 37 0N 24 45 E
Sifton, *Canada* **131 C8** 51 21N 100 8W
Sifton Pass, *Canada* **130 B3** 57 52N 126 15W
Sig, *Algeria* **99 A4** 35 32N 0 12W
Sigaboy, *Phil.* **71 H6** 6 39N 126 5 E
Sigdal, *Norway* **14 D3** 60 4N 9 38 E
Sigean, *France* **24 E6** 43 2N 2 58 E
Sighetu-Marmatiei, *Romania* **46 B4** 47 57N 23 52 E
Sighişoara, *Romania* **46 C5** 46 12N 24 50 E
Sigira, *Yemen* **87 D6** 12 37N 54 20 E
Sigli, *Indonesia* **74 A1** 5 25N 96 0 E
Siglufjörður, *Iceland* **12 C4** 66 12N 18 55W
Sigmaringen, *Germany* **27 G5** 48 5N 9 13 E
Signakhi, *Georgia* **53 F11** 41 40N 45 57 E
Signal, *U.S.A.* **145 L13** 34 30N 113 38W
Signal Pk., *U.S.A.* **145 M12** 33 20N 114 2W
Signau, *Switz.* **28 C5** 46 56N 7 45 E
Signy-l'Abbaye, *France* **23 C11** 49 40N 4 25 E
Sigourney, *U.S.A.* **140 C4** 41 20N 92 12W
Sigsig, *Ecuador* **152 D2** 3 0 S 78 50W
Sigtuna, *Sweden* **14 E11** 59 36N 17 44 E
Sigüenza, *Spain* **34 D2** 41 3N 2 40W
Siguiri, *Guinea* **100 C3** 11 31N 9 10W
Sigulda, *Latvia* **50 C4** 57 10N 24 55 E
Sigurd, *U.S.A.* **143 G8** 38 50N 111 58W
Sihanoukville = Kompong Som, *Cambodia* **77 G4** 10 38N 103 30 E
Sihaus, *Peru* **156 B2** 8 40 S 77 40W
Sihui, *China* **69 F9** 23 20N 112 40 E
Siirt, *Turkey* **89 E9** 37 57N 41 55 E
Siirt □, *Turkey* **89 E9** 37 55N 41 55 E
Siit, *Phil.* **71 J5** 5 59N 124 13 E
Sijarira Ra., *Zimbabwe* **107 F2** 17 36 S 27 45 E
Sijungjung, *Indonesia* **74 C2** 0 42 S 100 58 E
Sikao, *Thailand* **77 J2** 7 34N 99 21 E
Sikar, *India* **80 F6** 27 33N 75 10 E
Sikasso, *Mali* **100 C3** 11 18N 5 35W
Sikeston, *U.S.A.* **139 G10** 36 53N 89 35W
Sikhote Alin, Khrebet, *Russia* **57 E14** 45 0N 136 0 E
Sikhote Alin Ra. = Sikhote Alin, Khrebet, *Russia* **57 E14** 45 0N 136 0 E
Sikiá., *Greece* **44 D5** 40 2N 23 56 E
Síkinos, *Greece* **45 H7** 36 40N 25 8 E
Sikkani Chief →, *Canada* **130 B4** 57 47N 122 15W
Sikkim □, *India* **78 B2** 27 50N 88 30 E
Siklós, *Hungary* **31 F11** 45 50N 18 19 E
Sikotu-Ko, *Japan* **60 C10** 42 45N 141 25 E
Sil →, *Spain* **36 C3** 42 27N 7 43W
Silacayoapan, *Mexico* **147 D5** 17 30N 98 9W
Silandro, *Italy* **38 B7** 46 38N 10 48 E
Silanga, *Phil.* **71 F2** 11 1N 119 34 E
Silay, *Phil.* **71 F4** 10 47N 123 14 E
Silba, *Croatia* **39 D11** 44 24N 14 41 E
Silchar, *India* **78 C4** 24 49N 92 48 E
Silcox, *Canada* **131 B10** 57 12N 94 10W
Şile, *Turkey* **88 C3** 41 10N 29 37 E
Silenrieux, *Belgium* **21 H4** 50 14N 4 27 E
Siler City, *U.S.A.* **135 H6** 35 44N 79 28W
Sileru →, *India* **82 F5** 17 49N 81 24 E
Silet, *Algeria* **99 D5** 22 44N 4 37 E
Silgarhi Doti, *Nepal* **81 E9** 29 15N 81 0 E
Silghat, *India* **78 B4** 26 35N 93 0 E
Silifke, *Turkey* **88 E5** 36 22N 33 58 E
Siliguri = Shiliguri, *India* **78 B2** 26 45N 88 25 E
Siling Co, *China* **64 C3** 31 50N 89 20 E
Silíqua, *Italy* **40 C1** 39 20N 8 49 E
Silistra, *Bulgaria* **43 C12** 44 6N 27 19 E
Silivri, *Turkey* **88 C3** 41 4N 28 14 E
Siljan, *Sweden* **13 F13** 60 55N 14 45 E
Silkeborg, *Denmark* **15 H3** 56 10N 9 32 E
Sillajhuay, Cordillera, *Chile* **156 D4** 19 46 S 68 40W
Sillé-le-Guillaume, *France* **22 D6** 48 10N 0 8W
Sillustani, *Peru* **156 D3** 15 50 S 70 7W
Siloam Springs, *U.S.A.* **139 G7** 36 11N 94 32W
Silopi, *Turkey* **89 E10** 37 15N 42 27 E
Silsbee, *U.S.A.* **139 K7** 30 21N 94 11W
Šilute, *Lithuania* **50 D2** 55 21N 21 33 E
Silva Porto = Kuito, *Angola* **103 E3** 12 22 S 16 55 E
Silvan, *Turkey* **89 D9** 38 7N 41 2 E
Silvaplana, *Switz.* **29 D9** 46 28N 9 48 E
Silver City, *N. Mex., U.S.A.* **143 K9** 32 46N 108 17W
Silver City, *Nev., U.S.A.* **142 G4** 39 15N 119 48W
Silver Cr. →, *U.S.A.* **142 E4** 43 16N 119 13W
Silver Creek, *U.S.A.* **136 D5** 42 33N 79 10W
Silver Grove, *U.S.A.* **141 E12** 39 2N 84 24W
Silver L., *Calif., U.S.A.* **144 G6** 38 39N 120 6W
Silver L., *Calif., U.S.A.* **145 K10** 35 21N 116 7W
Silver Lake, *Ind., U.S.A.* **141 C11** 41 4N 85 53W
Silver Lake, *Oreg., U.S.A.* **142 E3** 43 8N 121 3W
Silver Lake, *Wis., U.S.A.* **141 B8** 42 33N 88 13W
Silver Streams, *S. Africa* **104 D3** 28 20 S 23 33 E
Silverton, *Australia* **116 A4** 31 52 S 141 10 E
Silverton, *Colo., U.S.A.* **143 H10** 37 49N 107 40W
Silverton, *Tex., U.S.A.* **139 H4** 34 28N 101 19W
Silves, *Portugal* **37 H2** 37 11N 8 26W
Silvi, *Italy* **39 F11** 42 32N 14 5 E
Silvia, *Colombia* **152 C2** 2 37N 76 21W
Silvies →, *U.S.A.* **142 E4** 43 34N 119 2W
Silvolde, *Neths.* **20 E8** 51 55N 6 23 E
Silvretta-Gruppe, *Switz.* **29 C10** 46 50N 10 6 E
Silwa Bahari, *Egypt* **94 C3** 24 45N 32 55 E
Silz, *Austria* **30 D3** 47 16N 10 56 E
Sim, C., *Morocco* **98 B3** 31 26N 9 51W
Simanggang, *Malaysia* **75 B4** 1 15N 111 32 E
Simao, *China* **68 F3** 22 47N 101 5 E
Simão Dias, *Brazil* **154 D4** 10 44 S 37 49W
Simara I., *Phil.* **70 E4** 12 48N 122 3 E
Simard, L., *Canada* **128 C4** 47 40N 78 40W
Sîmărtin, *Romania* **46 C6** 46 19N 25 58 E
Simav, *Turkey* **88 D3** 39 4N 28 58 E
Simba, *Tanzania* **106 C4** 2 10 S 37 36 E
Simbach, *Germany* **27 G9** 48 16N 13 3 E
Simbirsk, *Russia* **51 D16** 54 20N 48 25 E
Simbo, *Tanzania* **106 C2** 4 51 S 29 41 E
Simcoe, *Canada* **128 D3** 42 50N 80 20W
Simcoe, L., *Canada* **128 D4** 44 25N 79 20W
Simenga, *Russia* **57 C11** 62 42N 108 25 E
Simeto →, *Italy* **41 E8** 37 25N 15 10 E
Simeulue, *Indonesia* **74 B1** 2 45N 95 45 E
Simferopol, *Ukraine* **52 D6** 44 55N 34 3 E
Sími, *Greece* **45 H9** 36 35N 27 50 E
Simi Valley, *U.S.A.* **145 L8** 34 16N 118 47W
Simikot, *Nepal* **81 E9** 30 0N 81 50 E
Simití, *Colombia* **152 B3** 7 58N 73 57W
Simitli, *Bulgaria* **42 F8** 41 52N 23 7 E
Simla, *India* **80 D7** 31 2N 77 9 E
Şimleu-Silvaniei, *Romania* **46 B3** 47 17N 22 50 E
Simme →, *Switz.* **28 C4** 46 38N 7 25 E
Simmern, *Germany* **27 F3** 49 59N 7 32 E
Simmie, *Canada* **131 D7** 49 56N 108 6W
Simmler, *U.S.A.* **145 K7** 35 21N 119 59W
Simões, *Brazil* **154 C3** 7 36 S 40 49W
Simojärvi, *Finland* **12 C19** 66 5N 27 3 E
Simojoki →, *Finland* **12 D18** 65 35N 25 1 E
Simojovel, *Mexico* **147 D6** 17 12N 92 38W
Simonette →, *Canada* **130 B5** 55 9N 118 15W
Simonstown, *S. Africa* **104 E2** 34 14 S 18 26 E
Simontornya, *Hungary* **31 E11** 46 45N 18 33 E
Simpangkiri →, *Indonesia* **74 B1** 2 50N 97 40 E
Simplício Mendes, *Brazil* **154 C3** 7 51 S 41 54W
Simplon, *Switz.* **28 D6** 46 12N 8 4 E
Simplon Pass = Simplonpass, *Switz.* **28 D6** 46 15N 8 3 E
Simplon Tunnel, *Switz.* **28 D6** 46 15N 8 7 E
Simplonpass, *Switz.* **28 D6** 46 15N 8 3 E
Simpson Desert, *Australia* **114 D2** 25 0 S 137 0 E
Simpungdong, *N. Korea* **67 D15** 40 56N 129 29 E
Simunjan, *Malaysia* **75 B4** 1 25N 110 45 E
Simushir, Ostrov, *Russia* **57 E16** 46 50N 152 30 E
Sina →, *India* **82 F2** 17 30N 75 55 E
Sinabang, *Indonesia* **74 B1** 2 30N 96 24 E
Sinadogo, *Somali Rep.* **90 F4** 5 50N 47 0 E
Sinai = Es Sînâ', *Egypt* **94 J8** 29 0N 34 0 E
Sinai, Mt. = Mûsa, G., *Egypt* **94 J8** 28 33N 33 59 E
Sinai Peninsula, *Egypt* **91 F2** 29 30N 34 0 E
Sinaia, *Romania* **46 D6** 45 21N 25 38 E
Sinait, *Phil.* **70 C3** 17 52N 120 27 E
Sinako, Mt., *Phil.* **71 H5** 7 30N 125 17 E
Sinaloa □, *Mexico* **146 C3** 25 0N 107 30W
Sinaloa de Levya, *Mexico* **146 B3** 25 50N 108 20W
Sinalunga, *Italy* **39 E8** 43 12N 11 43 E
Sinan, *China* **68 D7** 27 56N 108 13 E
Sînandrei, *Romania* **46 D2** 45 52N 21 13 E
Sinarádhes, *Greece* **32 A3** 39 34N 19 51 E
Sīnāwan, *Libya* **96 B2** 31 0N 10 37 E
Sinbaungwe, *Burma* **78 F5** 19 43N 95 10 E
Sinbo, *Burma* **78 C6** 24 46N 97 3 E
Sincé, *Colombia* **152 B2** 9 15N 75 9W
Sincelejo, *Colombia* **152 B2** 9 18N 75 24W
Sinchang, *N. Korea* **67 D15** 40 7N 128 28 E
Sinchang-ni, *N. Korea* **67 E14** 39 24N 126 8 E
Sinclair, *U.S.A.* **142 F10** 41 47N 107 7W
Sinclair Mills, *Canada* **130 C4** 54 5N 121 40W
Sincorá, Serra do, *Brazil* **155 D3** 13 30 S 41 0W
Sind, *Pakistan* **80 G3** 26 0N 68 30 E
Sind □, *Pakistan* **79 D3** 26 0N 69 0 E
Sind →, *India* **81 B6** 34 18N 74 45 E
Sind Sagar Doab, *Pakistan* **80 D4** 32 0N 71 30 E
Sindal, *Denmark* **15 G4** 57 28N 10 10 E
Sindangan, *Phil.* **71 G4** 8 10N 123 5 E
Sindangan Bay, *Phil.* **71 G4** 8 11N 122 50 E
Sindangbarang, *Indonesia* **75 D3** 7 27 S 107 1 E
Sinde, *Zambia* **107 F2** 17 28 S 25 51 E
Sinegorski, *Russia* **53 C9** 47 55N 40 52 E
Sinelnikovo, *Ukraine* **52 B6** 48 25N 35 30 E
Sines, *Portugal* **37 H2** 37 56N 8 51W
Sines, C. de, *Portugal* **37 H2** 37 58N 8 53W
Sineu, *Spain* **33 B10** 39 38N 3 1 E
Sinewit, Mt., *Papua N. G.* **120 C7** 4 44 S 152 2 E
Sinfra, *Ivory C.* **100 D3** 6 35N 5 56W
Sing Buri, *Thailand* **76 E3** 14 53N 100 25 E
Singa, *Sudan* **95 E3** 13 10N 33 57 E
Singanallur, *India* **83 J3** 11 2N 77 1 E
Singapore ■, *Asia* **77 M4** 1 17N 103 51 E
Singapore, Straits of, *Asia* **77 M5** 1 15N 104 0 E
Singaraja, *Indonesia* **75 D5** 8 6 S 115 10 E
Singen, *Germany* **27 H4** 47 45N 8 50 E
Singida, *Tanzania* **106 C3** 4 49 S 34 48 E
Singida □, *Tanzania* **106 D3** 6 0 S 34 30 E
Singitikós Kólpos, *Greece* **44 D5** 40 6N 24 0 E
Singkaling Hkamti, *Burma* **78 C5** 26 0N 95 39 E
Singkawang, *Indonesia* **75 B3** 1 0N 108 57 E
Singleton, *Australia* **117 B9** 32 33 S 151 0 E
Singleton, Mt., *N. Terr., Australia* **112 D5** 22 0 S 130 46 E
Singleton, Mt., *W. Austral., Australia* **113 E2** 29 27 S 117 15 E
Singoli, *India* **80 G6** 25 0N 75 22 E
Singora = Songkhla, *Thailand* **77 J3** 7 13N 100 37 E
Singosan, *N. Korea* **67 E14** 38 52N 127 25 E
Sinhung, *N. Korea* **67 D14** 40 11N 127 34 E
Sînî □, *Egypt* **91 F2** 30 0N 34 0 E
Siniátsikon, Óros, *Greece* **44 D3** 40 25N 21 35 E
Siniloan, *Phil.* **70 D3** 14 25N 121 27 E
Siniscóla, *Italy* **40 B2** 40 35N 9 40 E
Sinj, *Croatia* **39 E13** 43 42N 16 39 E
Sinjai, *Indonesia* **72 C2** 5 7 S 120 20 E
Sinjajevina, *Montenegro* **42 E4** 42 57N 19 22 E
Sinjār, *Iraq* **84 B4** 36 19N 41 52 E
Sinkat, *Sudan* **94 D4** 18 55N 36 49 E
Sinkiang Uighur = Xinjiang Uygur Zizhiqu □, *China* **64 B3** 42 0N 86 0 E
Sinmak, *N. Korea* **67 E14** 38 25N 126 14 E
Sinnai, *Italy* **40 C2** 39 18N 9 13 E
Sinnar, *India* **82 E2** 19 48N 74 0 E
Sinni →, *Italy* **41 B9** 40 9N 16 42 E
Sînnicolau Maré, *Romania* **42 A5** 46 5N 20 39 E
Sinnuris, *Egypt* **94 J7** 29 26N 30 31 E
Sinoe, L., *Romania* **46 E9** 44 35N 28 50 E
Sinop, *Turkey* **52 E6** 42 1N 35 11 E
Sinop □, *Turkey* **88 C6** 42 0N 35 0 E
Sinpo, *N. Korea* **67 E15** 40 0N 128 13 E
Sins, *Switz.* **29 B6** 47 12N 8 24 E
Sinskoye, *Russia* **57 C13** 61 8N 126 48 E
Sint-Amandsberg, *Belgium* **21 F3** 51 4N 3 45 E
Sint Annaland, *Neths.* **21 E4** 51 36N 4 6 E
Sint Annaparoch, *Neths.* **20 B7** 53 16N 5 40 E
Sint-Denijs, *Belgium* **21 G2** 50 45N 3 23 E
Sint Eustatius, I., *Neth. Ant.* **149 C7** 17 30N 62 59W
Sint-Genesius-Rode, *Belgium* **21 G4** 50 45N 4 22 E
Sint-Gillis-Waas, *Belgium* **21 F4** 51 13N 4 6 E
Sint-Huibrechts-Lille, *Belgium* **21 F6** 51 13N 5 29 E
Sint-Katelinje-Waver, *Belgium* **21 F5** 51 5N 4 32 E
Sint-Kruis, *Belgium* **21 F2** 51 13N 3 15 E
Sint-Laureins, *Belgium* **21 F3** 51 14N 3 32 E
Sint Maarten, I., *W. Indies* **149 C7** 18 4N 63 4W
Sint-Michiels, *Belgium* **21 F2** 51 11N 3 15 E
Sint Nicolaasga, *Neths.* **20 C7** 52 55N 5 45 E
Sint Niklaas, *Belgium* **21 F4** 51 10N 4 9 E
Sint Oedenrode, *Neths.* **21 E6** 51 35N 5 29 E
Sint Pancras, *Neths.* **20 C5** 52 40N 4 48 E
Sint Philipsland, *Neths.* **21 E4** 51 37N 4 10 E
Sint Truiden, *Belgium* **21 G6** 50 48N 5 10 E
Sint Willebrord, *Neths.* **21 E5** 51 33N 4 33 E
Sîntana, *Romania* **46 C2** 46 20N 21 30 E
Sintang, *Indonesia* **75 B4** 0 5N 111 35 E
Sintjohannesga, *Neths.* **20 C7** 52 55N 5 52 E
Sinton, *U.S.A.* **139 L6** 28 2N 97 31W
Sintra, *Portugal* **37 G1** 38 47N 9 25W
Sinugif, *Somali Rep.* **108 C3** 8 33N 48 59 E
Sinŭiju, *N. Korea* **67 D13** 40 5N 124 24 E
Sinyukha →, *Ukraine* **52 B4** 48 3N 30 51 E
Siocon, *Phil.* **71 H4** 7 40N 122 10 E
Siófok, *Hungary* **31 E11** 46 54N 18 3 E
Sioma, *Zambia* **104 B3** 16 25 S 23 28 E
Sion, *Switz.* **28 D4** 46 14N 7 20 E
Sioux City, *U.S.A.* **138 D6** 42 30N 96 24W
Sioux Falls, *U.S.A.* **138 D6** 43 33N 96 44W
Sioux Lookout, *Canada* **128 B1** 50 10N 91 50W
Sip Song Chau Thai, *Vietnam* **76 B4** 21 30N 103 30 E
Sipalay, *Phil.* **71 G4** 9 45N 122 24 E
Šipan, *Croatia* **42 E2** 42 45N 17 52 E
Sipang, Tanjong, *Malaysia* **75 B4** 1 48N 110 20 E
Siping, *China* **67 C13** 43 8N 124 21 E
Sipiwesk L., *Canada* **131 B9** 55 5N 97 35W
Sipocot, *Phil.* **70 E4** 13 46N 122 58 E
Sipora, *Indonesia* **74 C1** 2 18 S 99 40 E
Siquia →, *Nic.* **148 D3** 12 10N 84 20W
Siquijor, *Phil.* **71 G4** 9 12N 123 35 E
Siquijor □, *Phil.* **71 G4** 9 11N 123 35 E
Siquirres, *Costa Rica* **148 D3** 10 6N 83 30W
Siquisique, *Venezuela* **152 A4** 10 34N 69 42W
Sir Edward Pellew Group, *Australia* **114 B2** 15 40 S 137 10 E
Sir Graham Moore Is., *Australia* **112 B4** 13 53 S 126 34 E
Sira, *India* **83 H3** 13 41N 76 49 E
Siracusa, *Italy* **41 E8** 37 4N 15 17 E
Sirajganj, *Bangla.* **81 G13** 24 25N 89 47 E
Sirakoro, *Mali* **100 C3** 12 41N 9 14W
Şiran, *Turkey* **89 C8** 40 11N 39 7 E
Sirasso, *Ivory C.* **100 D3** 9 16N 6 6W
Siraway, *Phil.* **71 H4** 7 34N 122 8 E
Sīrdān, *Iran* **85 B6** 36 39N 49 12 E
Sirer, *Spain* **33 C7** 38 56N 1 22 E
Siret, *Romania* **46 B7** 47 55N 26 5 E
Siret →, *Romania* **46 D9** 45 24N 28 1 E
Şiria, *Romania* **46 C2** 46 16N 21 38 E
Sirik, Tanjong, *Malaysia* **75 B4** 2 47N 111 15 E
Sirino, Monte, *Italy* **41 B8** 40 7N 15 50 E
Sirkali = Sirkazhi, *India* **83 J4** 11 15N 79 41 E
Sirkazhi, *India* **83 J4** 11 15N 79 41 E
Sírna, *Greece* **45 H8** 36 22N 26 42 E
Sirnach, *Switz.* **29 B7** 47 28N 8 59 E
Şirnak, *Turkey* **89 E10** 37 32N 42 28 E
Sirohi, *India* **80 G5** 24 52N 72 53 E
Široki Brijeg, *Bos.-H.* **42 D2** 43 21N 17 36 E
Sironj, *India* **80 G7** 24 5N 77 39 E
Síros, *Greece* **45 G6** 37 28N 24 57 E
Sirrayn, *Si. Arabia* **86 C3** 19 38N 40 36 E
Sirretta Pk., *U.S.A.* **145 K8** 35 56N 118 19W
Sirsa, *India* **80 E6** 29 33N 75 4 E
Sirsi, *India* **83 G2** 14 40N 74 49 E
Siruela, *Spain* **37 G5** 38 58N 5 3W
Sisak, *Croatia* **39 C13** 45 30N 16 21 E
Sisaket, *Thailand* **76 E5** 15 8N 104 23 E
Sisante, *Spain* **35 F2** 39 25N 2 12W
Sisargas, Is., *Spain* **36 B2** 43 21N 8 50W
Sishen, *S. Africa* **104 D3** 27 47 S 22 59 E
Sishui, *Henan, China* **66 G7** 34 48N 113 15 E
Sishui, *Shandong, China* **67 G9** 35 42N 117 18 E
Sisipuk L., *Canada* **131 B8** 55 45N 101 50W
Sisophon, *Cambodia* **76 F4** 13 38N 102 59 E
Sissach, *Switz.* **28 B5** 47 27N 7 48 E
Sisseton, *U.S.A.* **138 C6** 45 40N 97 3W
Sissonne, *France* **23 C10** 49 34N 3 51 E
Sīstān va Balūchestān □, *Iran* **85 E9** 27 0N 62 0 E
Sisteron, *France* **25 D9** 44 12N 5 57 E
Sisters, *U.S.A.* **142 D3** 44 18N 121 33W
Sitamarhi, *India* **81 F11** 26 37N 85 30 E
Sitapur, *India* **81 F9** 27 38N 80 45 E
Siteki, *Swaziland* **105 D5** 26 32 S 31 58 E
Sitges, *Spain* **34 D6** 41 17N 1 47 E
Sithoniá, *Greece* **44 D5** 40 0N 23 45 E
Sitía, *Greece* **32 D8** 35 13N 26 6 E
Sítio da Abadia, *Brazil* **155 D2** 14 48 S 46 16W
Sitka, *U.S.A.* **126 C6** 57 3N 135 20W
Sitoti, *Botswana* **104 C3** 23 15 S 23 40 E
Sitra, *Egypt* **94 B2** 28 40N 26 53 E
Sittang Myit →, *Burma* **78 G6** 17 20N 96 45 E
Sittard, *Neths.* **21 G7** 51 0N 5 52 E
Sittaung, *Burma* **78 C5** 24 10N 94 35 E
Sittensen, *Germany* **26 B5** 53 17N 9 32 E
Sittona, *Eritrea* **95 E4** 14 25N 37 23 E
Sittwe, *Burma* **78 E4** 20 18N 92 45 E
Siuna, *Nic.* **148 D3** 13 37N 84 45W
Siuri, *India* **81 H12** 23 50N 87 34 E
Sivaganga, *India* **83 K4** 9 50N 78 28 E
Sivagiri, *India* **83 K3** 9 16N 77 26 E
Sivakasi, *India* **83 K3** 9 24N 77 47 E
Sivana, *India* **80 E8** 28 37N 78 6 E
Sīvand, *Iran* **85 D7** 30 5N 52 55 E
Sivas, *Turkey* **88 D7** 39 43N 36 58 E
Sivas □, *Turkey* **88 D7** 39 45N 37 0 E
Siverek, *Turkey* **89 E8** 37 50N 39 19 E
Sivomaskinskiy, *Russia* **48 A11** 66 40N 62 35 E
Sivrihisar, *Turkey* **88 D4** 39 30N 31 35 E
Sivry, *Belgium* **21 H4** 50 10N 4 12 E
Sîwa, *Egypt* **94 B2** 29 11N 25 31 E
Sîwa, El Wâhât es, *Egypt* **94 B2** 29 10N 25 30 E
Siwalik Range, *Nepal* **81 F10** 28 0N 83 0 E
Siwan, *India* **81 F11** 26 13N 84 21 E
Siyâl, Jazâ'ir, *Egypt* **94 C4** 22 49N 36 12 E
Sizewell, *U.K.* **17 E9** 52 13N 1 38 E
Siziwang Qi, *China* **66 D6** 41 25N 111 40 E
Sjælland, *Denmark* **15 J5** 55 30N 11 30 E
Sjællands Odde, *Denmark* **15 J5** 56 0N 11 15 E
Själevad, *Sweden* **14 A12** 63 18N 18 36 E
Sjarinska Banja, *Yugoslavia* **42 E6** 42 45N 21 38 E
Sjenica, *Serbia* **42 D4** 43 16N 20 0 E
Sjoa, *Norway* **14 C3** 61 41N 9 33 E
Sjöbo, *Sweden* **15 J7** 55 37N 13 45 E
Sjösa, *Sweden* **15 F11** 58 47N 17 4 E
Sjumen = Šumen, *Bulgaria* **43 D11** 43 18N 26 55 E
Skadarsko Jezero, *Montenegro* **42 E4** 42 10N 19 20 E
Skadovsk, *Ukraine* **52 C5** 46 17N 32 52 E
Skagafjörður, *Iceland* **12 D4** 65 54N 19 35W
Skagastølstindane, *Norway* **13 F9** 61 28N 7 52 E
Skagen, *Denmark* **15 G4** 57 43N 10 35 E
Skagerrak, *Denmark* **15 G3** 57 30N 9 0 E
Skagit →, *U.S.A.* **144 B4** 48 23N 122 22W
Skagway, *U.S.A.* **130 B1** 59 28N 135 19W
Skaidi, *Norway* **12 A18** 70 26N 24 30 E
Skala Podolskaya, *Ukraine* **52 B2** 48 50N 26 15 E
Skalat, *Ukraine* **50 G4** 49 23N 25 55 E
Skalbmierz, *Poland* **47 E7** 50 20N 20 25 E
Skalica, *Slovak Rep.* **31 C10** 48 50N 17 15 E
Skalni Dol = Kamenyak, *Bulgaria* **43 D11** 43 24N 26 57 E
Skals, *Denmark* **15 H3** 56 34N 9 24 E
Skanderborg, *Denmark* **15 H3** 56 2N 9 55 E
Skanör, *Sweden* **15 J6** 55 24N 12 50 E
Skantzoúra, *Greece* **45 E6** 39 5N 24 6 E
Skara, *Sweden* **13 G12** 58 25N 13 30 E
Skaraborgs län □, *Sweden* **13 G12** 58 20N 13 30 E
Skardu, *Pakistan* **81 B6** 35 20N 75 44 E
Skarrild, *Denmark* **15 J2** 55 58N 8 53 E
Skarszewy, *Poland* **47 A5** 54 4N 18 25 E
Skaryszew, *Poland* **47 D8** 51 19N 21 15 E
Skarzysko Kamienna, *Poland* **47 D7** 51 7N 20 52 E
Skebokvarn, *Sweden* **14 E10** 59 7N 16 45 E
Skeena →, *Canada* **130 C2** 54 9N 130 5W
Skeena Mts., *Canada* **130 B3** 56 40N 128 30W
Skegness, *U.K.* **16 D8** 53 9N 0 20 E
Skeldon, *Guyana* **153 B6** 5 55N 57 20W
Skellefte älv →, *Sweden* **12 D16** 64 45N 21 10 E
Skellefteå, *Sweden* **12 D16** 64 45N 20 50 E
Skelleftehamn, *Sweden* **12 D16** 64 40N 20 59 E
Skender Vakuf, *Bos.-H.* **42 C2** 44 29N 17 22 E
Skene, *Sweden* **15 G6** 57 30N 12 37 E
Skerries, The, *U.K.* **16 D3** 53 27N 4 40W
Skhíza, *Greece* **45 H3** 36 41N 21 40 E
Skhoinoúsa, *Greece* **45 H7** 36 53N 25 31 E
Ski, *Norway* **14 E4** 59 43N 10 52 E
Skíathos, *Greece* **45 E5** 39 12N 23 30 E
Skibbereen, *Ireland* **19 E2** 51 33N 9 16W
Skiddaw, *U.K.* **16 C4** 54 39N 3 9W
Skien, *Norway* **14 E3** 59 12N 9 35 E
Skierniewice, *Poland* **47 D7** 51 58N 20 10 E
Skierniewice □, *Poland* **47 D7** 52 0N 20 10 E
Skikda, *Algeria* **99 A6** 36 50N 6 58 E
Skillet →, *U.S.A.* **141 F8** 38 5N 88 5W
Skilloura, *Cyprus* **32 D12** 35 14N 33 10 E
Skinári, Ákra, *Greece* **45 G2** 37 56N 20 40 E
Skipton, *Australia* **116 D5** 37 39 S 143 40 E
Skipton, *U.K.* **16 D5** 53 57N 2 1W
Skirmish Pt., *Australia* **114 A1** 11 59 S 134 17 E
Skiropoúla, *Greece* **45 F6** 38 50N 24 21 E
Skíros, *Greece* **45 F6** 38 55N 24 34 E
Skivarp, *Sweden* **15 J7** 55 26N 13 34 E
Skive, *Denmark* **15 H3** 56 33N 9 2 E
Skjálfandafljót →, *Iceland* **12 D5** 65 59N 17 25W
Skjálfandi, *Iceland* **12 C5** 66 5N 17 30W
Skjeberg, *Norway* **14 E5** 59 12N 11 12 E
Skjern, *Denmark* **15 J2** 55 57N 8 30 E
Skoczów, *Poland* **31 B11** 49 49N 18 45 E
Škofja Loka, *Slovenia* **39 B11** 46 9N 14 19 E
Skoghall, *Sweden* **13 G12** 59 20N 13 30 E
Skoki, *Poland* **47 C4** 52 40N 17 11 E
Skokie, *U.S.A.* **141 B9** 42 3N 87 45W
Skole, *Ukraine* **50 G3** 49 3N 23 30 E
Skópelos, *Greece* **45 E5** 39 9N 23 47 E
Skopí, *Greece* **32 D8** 35 11N 26 2 E
Skopin, *Russia* **51 E11** 53 55N 39 32 E
Skopje, *Macedonia* **42 E6** 42 1N 21 32 E
Skórcz, *Poland* **47 B5** 53 47N 18 30 E
Skövde, *Sweden* **13 G12** 58 24N 13 50 E
Skovorodino, *Russia* **57 D13** 54 0N 124 0 E
Skowhegan, *U.S.A.* **129 D6** 44 46N 69 43W
Skownan, *Canada* **131 C9** 51 58N 99 35W
Skradin, *Croatia* **39 E12** 43 52N 15 53 E
Skreanäs, *Sweden* **15 H6** 56 52N 12 35 E
Skrwa →, *Poland* **47 C6** 52 35N 19 32 E
Skudeneshavn, *Norway* **13 G8** 59 10N 5 10 E
Skull, *Ireland* **19 E2** 51 32N 9 40W
Skultorp, *Sweden* **15 F7** 58 24N 13 51 E
Skunk →, *U.S.A.* **140 D5** 40 42N 91 7W
Skuodas, *Lithuania* **50 C2** 56 21N 21 45 E
Skurup, *Sweden* **15 J7** 55 28N 13 30 E
Skutskär, *Sweden* **14 D11** 60 37N 17 25 E
Skvira, *Ukraine* **52 B3** 49 44N 29 40 E
Skwierzyna, *Poland* **47 C2** 52 33N 15 30 E
Skye, *U.K.* **18 D2** 57 15N 6 10W
Skykomish, *U.S.A.* **142 C3** 47 42N 121 22W
Skyros = Skíros, *Greece* **45 F6** 38 55N 24 34 E
Slagelse, *Denmark* **15 J5** 55 23N 11 19 E
Slagharen, *Neths.* **20 C9** 52 37N 6 34 E
Slamannon, *Australia* **116 B5** 32 1 S 143 41 E
Slamet, *Indonesia* **75 D3** 7 16 S 109 8 E
Slaney →, *Ireland* **19 D5** 52 52N 6 45W

Sopron 267


Slangerup, *Denmark* **15 J6** 55 50N 12 11 E
Slănic, *Romania* **46 D6** 45 14N 25 58 E
Slankamen, *Serbia* **42 B5** 45 8N 20 15 E
Slano, *Croatia* **42 E2** 42 48N 17 53 E
Slantsy, *Russia* **50 B6** 59 7N 28 5 E
Slany, *Czech.* **30 A7** 50 13N 14 6 E
Slate Is., *Canada* **128 C2** 48 40N 87 0W
Slater, *U.S.A.* **140 E3** 39 13N 93 4W
Slatina, *Romania* **46 E5** 44 28N 24 22 E
Slaton, *U.S.A.* **139 J4** 33 26N 101 39W
Slave →, *Canada* **130 A6** 61 18N 113 39W
Slave Coast, *W. Afr.* **101 D5** 6 0N 2 30 E
Slave Lake, *Canada* **130 B6** 55 17N 114 43W
Slave Pt., *Canada* **130 A5** 61 11N 115 56W
Slavgorod, *Russia* **56 D8** 53 1N 78 37 E
Slavinja, *Serbia* **42 D7** 43 9N 22 50 E
Slavkov, *Czech.* **31 B9** 49 10N 16 52 E
Slavnoye, *Belorussia* **50 D6** 54 24N 29 15 E
Slavonska Požega, *Croatia* **42 B2** 45 20N 17 40 E
Slavonski Brod, *Croatia* **42 B3** 45 11N 18 0 E
Slavuta, *Ukraine* **50 F5** 50 15N 27 2 E
Slavyanka, *Russia* **60 C5** 42 53N 131 21 E
Slavyansk, *Ukraine* **52 B7** 48 55N 37 36 E
Slavyansk-na-Kubani, *Russia* **52 D8** 45 15N 38 11 E
Sława, *Poland* **47 D3** 51 52N 16 2 E
Sławno, *Poland* **47 A3** 54 20N 16 41 E
Sławoborze, *Poland* **47 B2** 53 55N 15 42 E
Sleaford, *U.K.* **16 E7** 53 0N 0 22W
Sleaford B., *Australia* **115 E2** 34 55 S 135 45 E
Sleat, Sd. of, *U.K.* **18 D3** 57 5N 5 47W
Sleeper Is., *Canada* **127 C11** 58 30N 81 0W
Sleepy Eye, *U.S.A.* **138 C7** 44 18N 94 43W
Sleidinge, *Belgium* **21 F3** 51 8N 3 41 E
Sleman, *Indonesia* **75 D4** 7 40 S 110 20 E
Slemon L., *Canada* **130 A5** 63 13N 116 4W
Ślesin, *Poland* **47 C5** 52 22N 18 14 E
Slidell, *U.S.A.* **139 K10** 30 17N 89 47W
Sliedrecht, *Neths.* **20 E5** 51 50N 4 45 E
Sliema, *Malta* **32 D2** 35 54N 14 30 E
Slieve Aughty, *Ireland* **19 C3** 53 4N 8 30W
Slieve Bloom, *Ireland* **19 C4** 53 4N 7 40W
Slieve Donard, *U.K.* **19 B6** 54 10N 5 57W
Slieve Gullion, *U.K.* **19 B5** 54 8N 6 26W
Slieve Mish, *Ireland* **19 D2** 52 12N 9 50W
Slievenamon, *Ireland* **19 D4** 52 25N 7 37W
Sligo, *Ireland* **19 B3** 54 17N 8 28W
Sligo □, *Ireland* **19 B3** 54 10N 8 35W
Sligo B., *Ireland* **19 B3** 54 20N 8 40W
Slijpe, *Belgium* **21 F1** 51 9N 2 51 E
Slikkerveer, *Neths.* **20 E5** 51 53N 4 36 E
Slite, *Sweden* **13 H15** 57 42N 18 48 E
Sliven, *Bulgaria* **43 E11** 42 42N 26 19 E
Slivnitsa, *Bulgaria* **42 E8** 42 50N 23 0 E
Sljeme, *Croatia* **39 C12** 45 57N 15 58 E
Sloan, *U.S.A.* **145 K11** 35 57N 115 13W
Sloansville, *U.S.A.* **137 D10** 42 45N 74 22W
Slobodskoy, *Russia* **54 B2** 58 40N 50 6 E
Slobozia, *Argeş, Romania* **46 E6** 44 30N 25 14 E
Slobozia, *Ialomiţa, Romania* **46 E8** 44 34N 27 23 E
Slocan, *Canada* **130 D5** 49 48N 117 28W
Slochteren, *Neths.* **20 B9** 53 12N 6 48 E
Slöinge, *Sweden* **15 H6** 56 51N 12 42 E
Słomniki, *Poland* **47 E7** 50 16N 20 4 E
Slonim, *Belorussia* **50 E4** 53 4N 25 19 E
Slotermeer, *Neths.* **20 C7** 52 55N 5 38 E
Slough, *U.K.* **17 F7** 51 30N 0 35W
Sloughhouse, *U.S.A.* **144 G5** 38 26N 121 12W
Slovak Rep. ■, *Europe* **31 C13** 48 30N 20 0 E
Slovakia = Slovak Rep. ■, *Europe* **31 C13** 48 30N 20 0 E
Slovakian Ore Mts. = Slovenské Rudohorie, *Slovak Rep.* **31 C12** 48 45N 20 0 E
Slovenia ■, *Europe* **39 C11** 45 58N 14 30 E
Slovenija = Slovenia ■, *Europe* **39 C11** 45 58N 14 30 E
Slovenj Gradec, *Slovenia* **39 B12** 46 31N 15 5 E
Slovenska Bistrica, *Slovenia* **39 B12** 46 24N 15 35 E
Slovenská Republika = Slovak Rep. ■, *Europe* **31 C13** 48 30N 20 0 E
Slovenské Rudohorie, *Slovak Rep.* **31 C12** 48 45N 20 0 E
Slovyansk = Slavyansk, *Ukraine* **52 B7** 48 55N 37 36 E
Słubice, *Poland* **47 C1** 52 22N 14 35 E
Sluch →, *Ukraine* **50 F5** 51 37N 26 38 E
Sluis, *Neths.* **21 F2** 51 18N 3 23 E
Slunchev Bryag, *Bulgaria* **43 E12** 42 40N 27 41 E
Slunj, *Croatia* **39 C12** 45 6N 15 33 E
Słupca, *Poland* **47 C4** 52 15N 17 52 E
Słupia →, *Poland* **47 A3** 54 35N 16 51 E
Słupsk, *Poland* **47 A4** 54 30N 17 3 E
Słupsk □, *Poland* **47 A4** 54 15N 17 30 E
Slurry, *S. Africa* **104 D4** 25 49 S 25 42 E
Slutsk, *Belorussia* **50 E5** 53 2N 27 31 E
Slyne Hd., *Ireland* **19 C1** 53 25N 10 10W
Slyudyanka, *Russia* **57 D11** 51 40N 103 40 E
Smålandsfarvandet, *Denmark* **15 J5** 55 10N 11 20 E
Smålandsstenar, *Sweden* **15 G7** 57 10N 13 25 E
Small Nggela, *Solomon Is.* **121 M11** 9 0 S 160 0 E
Smalltree L., *Canada* **131 A7** 61 0N 105 0W
Smarje, *Slovenia* **39 B12** 46 15N 15 34 E
Smartt Syndicate Dam, *S. Africa* **104 E3** 30 45 S 23 10 E
Smartville, *U.S.A.* **144 F5** 39 13N 121 18W
Smeaton, *Canada* **131 C8** 53 30N 104 49W
Smederevo, *Serbia* **42 C5** 44 40N 20 57 E
Smederevska Palanka, *Serbia* **42 C5** 44 22N 20 58 E
Smela, *Ukraine* **52 B4** 49 15N 31 58 E
Smethport, *U.S.A.* **136 E6** 41 49N 78 27W
Smidovich, *Russia* **57 E14** 48 36N 133 49 E
Smigiel, *Poland* **47 C3** 52 1N 16 32 E
Smilde, *Neths.* **20 C8** 52 58N 6 28 E
Smiley, *Canada* **131 C7** 51 38N 109 29W
Smilyan, *Bulgaria* **43 F9** 41 29N 24 46 E
Smith, *Canada* **130 B6** 55 10N 114 0W
Smith →, *Canada* **130 B3** 59 34N 126 30W
Smith Arm, *Canada* **126 B7** 66 15N 123 0W
Smith Center, *U.S.A.* **138 F5** 39 47N 98 47W
Smith Sund, *Greenland* **6 B4** 78 30N 74 0W
Smithburne →, *Australia* **114 B3** 17 3 S 140 57 E
Smithers, *Canada* **130 C3** 54 45N 127 10W
Smithfield, *S. Africa* **105 E4** 30 9 S 26 30 E
Smithfield, *N.C., U.S.A.* **135 H6** 35 31N 78 21W
Smithfield, *Utah, U.S.A.* **142 F8** 41 50N 111 50W
Smiths Falls, *Canada* **128 D4** 44 55N 76 0W
Smithton, *Australia* **114 G4** 40 53 S 145 6 E
Smithtown, *Australia* **117 A10** 30 58 S 152 48 E
Smithville, *Canada* **136 C5** 43 6N 79 33W
Smithville, *Mo., U.S.A.* **140 E2** 39 23N 94 35W
Smithville, *Tex., U.S.A.* **139 K6** 30 1N 97 10W
Smoky →, *Canada* **130 B5** 56 10N 117 21W
Smoky Bay, *Australia* **115 E1** 32 22 S 134 13 E
Smoky Falls, *Canada* **128 B3** 50 4N 82 10W
Smoky Hill →, *U.S.A.* **138 F6** 39 4N 96 48W
Smoky Lake, *Canada* **130 C6** 54 10N 112 30W
Smøla, *Norway* **14 A2** 63 23N 8 3 E
Smolensk, *Russia* **50 D8** 54 45N 32 5 E
Smolikas, Óros, *Greece* **44 D2** 40 9N 20 58 E
Smolník, *Slovak Rep.* **31 C13** 48 43N 20 44 E
Smolyan, *Bulgaria* **43 F9** 41 36N 24 38 E
Smooth Rock Falls, *Canada* **128 C3** 49 17N 81 37W
Smoothstone L., *Canada* **131 C7** 54 40N 106 50W
Smorgon, *Belorussia* **50 D5** 54 20N 26 24 E
Smulţi, *Romania* **46 D8** 45 57N 27 44 E
Smyadovo, *Bulgaria* **43 D12** 43 2N 27 1 E
Smyrna = İzmir, *Turkey* **88 D2** 38 25N 27 8 E
Snaefell, *U.K.* **16 C3** 54 18N 4 26W
Snæfellsjökull, *Iceland* **12 D2** 64 49N 23 46W
Snake →, *U.S.A.* **142 C4** 46 12N 119 2W
Snake I., *Australia* **117 E7** 38 47 S 146 33 E
Snake L., *Canada* **131 B7** 55 32N 106 35W
Snake Range, *U.S.A.* **142 G6** 39 0N 114 20W
Snake River Plain, *U.S.A.* **142 E7** 42 50N 114 0W
Snarum, *Norway* **14 D3** 60 1N 9 54 E
Snedsted, *Denmark* **15 H2** 56 55N 8 32 E
Sneek, *Neths.* **20 B7** 53 2N 5 40 E
Sneeker-meer, *Neths.* **20 B7** 53 2N 5 45 E
Sneeuberge, *S. Africa* **104 E3** 31 46 S 24 20 E
Snejbjerg, *Denmark* **15 H2** 56 8N 8 54 E
Snelling, *U.S.A.* **144 H6** 37 31N 120 26W
Snezhnoye, *Ukraine* **53 C8** 48 0N 38 58 E
Sněžka, *Europe* **30 A8** 50 41N 15 50 E
Snežnik, *Slovenia* **39 C11** 45 36N 14 35 E
Sniadowo, *Poland* **47 B8** 53 2N 22 0 E
Sniardwy, Jezioro, *Poland* **47 B8** 53 48N 21 50 E
Snigirevka, *Ukraine* **52 C5** 47 2N 32 49 E
Snina, *Slovak Rep.* **31 C15** 48 58N 22 9 E
Snizort, L., *U.K.* **18 D2** 57 33N 6 28W
Snøhetta, *Norway* **14 B3** 62 19N 9 16 E
Snohomish, *U.S.A.* **144 C4** 47 55N 122 6W
Snoul, *Cambodia* **77 F6** 12 4N 106 26 E
Snow Hill, *U.S.A.* **134 F8** 38 11N 75 24W
Snow Lake, *Canada* **131 C8** 54 52N 100 3W
Snow Mt., *U.S.A.* **144 F4** 39 23N 122 45W
Snowbird L., *Canada* **131 A8** 60 45N 103 0W
Snowdon, *U.K.* **16 D3** 53 4N 4 8W
Snowdrift, *Canada* **131 A6** 62 24N 110 44W
Snowdrift →, *Canada* **131 A6** 62 24N 110 44W
Snowflake, *U.S.A.* **143 J8** 34 30N 110 5W
Snowshoe Pk., *U.S.A.* **142 B6** 48 13N 115 41W
Snowtown, *Australia* **116 B3** 33 46 S 138 14 E
Snowville, *U.S.A.* **142 F7** 41 58N 112 43W
Snowy →, *Australia* **117 D8** 37 46 S 148 30 E
Snowy Mts., *Australia* **117 D8** 36 30 S 148 20 E
Snug Corner, *Bahamas* **149 B5** 22 33N 73 52W
Snyatyn, *Ukraine* **52 B1** 48 30N 25 50 E
Snyder, *Okla., U.S.A.* **139 H5** 34 40N 98 57W
Snyder, *Tex., U.S.A.* **139 J4** 32 44N 100 55W
Soacha, *Colombia* **152 C3** 4 35N 74 13W
Soahanina, *Madag.* **105 B7** 18 42 S 44 13 E
Soalala, *Madag.* **105 B8** 16 6 S 45 20 E
Soan →, *Pakistan* **80 C4** 33 1N 71 44 E
Soanierana-Ivongo, *Madag.* **105 B8** 16 55 S 49 35 E
Soap Lake, *U.S.A.* **142 C4** 47 23N 119 29W
Sobat, Nahr →, *Sudan* **95 F3** 9 22N 31 33 E
Soběslav, *Czech.* **30 B7** 49 16N 14 45 E
Sobhapur, *India* **80 H8** 22 47N 78 17 E
Sobinka, *Russia* **51 D12** 56 0N 40 0 E
Sobo-Yama, *Japan* **62 E3** 32 51N 131 22 E
Sobótka, *Poland* **47 E3** 50 54N 16 44 E
Sobrado, *Spain* **36 B2** 43 2N 8 2W
Sobral, *Brazil* **154 B3** 3 50 S 40 20W
Sobreira Formosa, *Portugal* **37 F3** 39 46N 7 51W
Soc Giang, *Vietnam* **76 A6** 22 54N 106 1 E
Soc Trang, *Vietnam* **77 H5** 9 37N 105 50 E
Soča →, *Europe* **39 B10** 46 20N 13 40 E
Sochaczew, *Poland* **47 C7** 52 15N 20 13 E
Soch'e = Shache, *China* **64 C2** 38 20N 77 10 E
Sochi, *Russia* **53 E8** 43 35N 39 40 E
Société, Is. de la, *Pac. Oc.* **123 J12** 17 0 S 151 0W
Society Is. = Société, Is. de la, *Pac. Oc.* **123 J12** 17 0 S 151 0W
Socompa, Portezuelo de, *Chile* **158 A2** 24 27 S 68 18W
Socorro, *Colombia* **152 B3** 6 29N 73 16W
Socorro, *Phil.* **71 G5** 9 37N 125 58 E
Socorro, *U.S.A.* **143 J10** 34 4N 106 54W
Socorro, I., *Mexico* **146 D2** 18 45N 110 58W
Socotra, *Ind. Oc.* **87 D6** 12 30N 54 0 E
Socúellmos, *Spain* **35 F2** 39 16N 2 47W
Soda L., *U.S.A.* **143 J5** 35 10N 116 4W
Soda Plains, *India* **81 B8** 35 30N 79 0 E
Soda Springs, *U.S.A.* **142 E8** 42 39N 111 36W
Söderhamn, *Sweden* **13 F14** 61 18N 17 10 E
Söderköping, *Sweden* **13 G14** 58 31N 16 20 E
Södermanlands län □, *Sweden* **14 E10** 59 10N 16 30 E
Södertälje, *Sweden* **14 E11** 59 12N 17 39 E
Sodiri, *Sudan* **95 E2** 14 27N 29 0 E
Sodo, *Ethiopia* **95 F4** 7 0N 37 41 E
Sodražica, *Slovenia* **39 C11** 45 45N 14 39 E
Sodus, *U.S.A.* **136 C7** 43 14N 77 4W
Soe, *Indonesia* **72 C2** 9 52 S 124 17 E
Soekmekaar, *S. Africa* **105 C4** 23 30 S 29 55 E
Soest, *Germany* **26 D4** 51 34N 8 7 E
Soest, *Neths.* **20 D6** 52 9N 5 19 E
Soestdijk, *Neths.* **20 D6** 52 11N 5 17 E
Sofádhes, *Greece* **44 E4** 39 20N 22 4 E
Sofara, *Mali* **100 C4** 13 59N 4 9W
Sofia = Sofiya, *Bulgaria* **43 E8** 42 45N 23 20 E
Sofia →, *Madag.* **105 B8** 15 27 S 47 23 E
Sofievka, *Ukraine* **52 B5** 48 6N 33 55 E
Sofiiski, *Russia* **57 D14** 52 15N 133 59 E
Sofikón, *Greece* **45 G5** 37 47N 23 3 E
Sofiya, *Bulgaria* **43 E8** 42 45N 23 20 E
Sōfu-Gan, *Japan* **61 K10** 29 49N 140 21 E
Sogakofe, *Ghana* **101 D5** 6 2N 0 39 E
Sogamoso, *Colombia* **152 B3** 5 43N 72 56W
Sogār, *Iran* **85 E8** 25 53N 58 6 E
Sögel, *Germany* **26 C3** 52 50N 7 32 E
Sogeri, *Papua N. G.* **120 E4** 9 26 S 147 35 E
Sogn og Fjordane fylke □, *Norway* **13 F9** 61 40N 6 0 E
Sogndalsfjøra, *Norway* **13 F9** 61 14N 7 5 E
Sognefjorden, *Norway* **13 F8** 61 10N 5 50 E
Söğüt, *Turkey* **88 C4** 40 2N 30 11 E
Söğüt Gölü, *Turkey* **88 E3** 37 3N 29 51 E
Sŏgwi-po, *S. Korea* **67 H14** 33 13N 126 34 E
Soh, *Iran* **85 C6** 33 26N 51 27 E
Sohâg, *Egypt* **94 B3** 26 33N 31 43 E
Sohano, *Papua N. G.* **120 C8** 5 22 S 154 37 E
Sŏhori, *N. Korea* **67 D15** 40 7N 128 23 E
Soignies, *Belgium* **21 G4** 50 35N 4 5 E
Soira, *Eritrea* **95 E4** 14 45N 39 30 E
Soissons, *France* **23 C10** 49 25N 3 19 E
Sōja, *Japan* **62 C5** 34 40N 133 45 E
Sojat, *India* **80 G5** 25 55N 73 45 E
Sok →, *Russia* **54 E2** 53 24N 50 8 E
Sokal, *Ukraine* **50 F4** 50 31N 24 15 E
Söke, *Turkey* **45 G9** 37 48N 27 28 E
Sokelo, *Zaïre* **103 D4** 9 55 S 24 36 E
Sokhós, *Greece* **44 D5** 40 48N 23 22 E
Sokhumi = Sukhumi, *Georgia* **53 E9** 43 0N 41 0 E
Sokki, Oued In →, *Algeria* **99 C5** 29 30N 3 42 E
Sokna, *Norway* **14 D3** 60 16N 9 50 E
Soknedal, *Norway* **14 B4** 62 57N 10 13 E
Soko Banja, *Serbia* **42 D6** 43 40N 21 51 E
Sokodé, *Togo* **101 D5** 9 0N 1 11 E
Sokol, *Russia* **51 B12** 59 30N 40 5 E
Sokolac, *Bos.-H.* **42 D3** 43 56N 18 48 E
Sokółka, *Poland* **47 B10** 53 25N 23 30 E
Sokolo, *Mali* **100 C3** 14 53N 6 8W
Sokolov, *Czech.* **30 A5** 50 12N 12 40 E
Sokołów Małpolski, *Poland* **31 A15** 50 12N 22 7 E
Sokołów Podlaski, *Poland* **47 C9** 52 25N 22 15 E
Sokoły, *Poland* **47 C9** 52 59N 22 42 E
Sokoto, *Nigeria* **101 C6** 13 2N 5 16 E
Sokoto □, *Nigeria* **101 C6** 12 30N 6 0 E
Sokoto →, *Nigeria* **101 C5** 11 20N 4 10 E
Sokuluk, *Kirghizia* **55 B7** 42 52N 74 18 E
Sol Iletsk, *Russia* **54 F4** 51 10N 55 0 E
Sola →, *Poland* **31 A12** 50 4N 19 15 E
Solai, *Kenya* **106 B4** 0 2N 36 12 E
Solana, *Phil.* **70 C3** 17 39N 121 41 E
Solander I., *N.Z.* **119 G1** 46 34 S 166 54 E
Solano, *Phil.* **70 C3** 16 31N 121 15 E
Solapur, *India* **82 F2** 17 43N 75 56 E
Solares, *Spain* **36 B7** 43 23N 3 43W
Solca, *Romania* **46 B6** 47 40N 25 50 E
Soléa □, *Cyprus* **32 D12** 35 5N 33 4 E
Solec Kujawski, *Poland* **47 B5** 53 5N 18 14 E
Soledad, *Colombia* **152 A3** 10 55N 74 46W
Soledad, *U.S.A.* **144 J5** 36 26N 121 20W
Soledad, *Venezuela* **153 B5** 8 10N 63 34W
Solent, The, *U.K.* **17 G6** 50 45N 1 25W
Solenzara, *France* **25 G13** 41 53N 9 23 E
Solesmes, *France* **23 B10** 50 10N 3 30 E
Solfonn, *Norway* **13 F9** 60 2N 6 57 E
Solhan, *Turkey* **89 D9** 38 57N 41 3 E
Soligalich, *Russia* **51 B13** 59 5N 42 10 E
Soligorsk, *Belorussia* **50 E5** 52 51N 27 27 E
Solikamsk, *Russia* **54 B5** 59 38N 56 50 E
Solila, *Madag.* **105 C8** 21 25 S 46 37 E
Solimões = Amazonas →, *S. Amer.* **153 D7** 0 5 S 50 0W
Solingen, *Germany* **21 F10** 51 10N 7 4 E
Sollebrunn, *Sweden* **15 F6** 58 8N 12 32 E
Sollefteå, *Sweden* **14 A11** 63 12N 17 20 E
Sollentuna, *Sweden* **14 E11** 59 26N 17 56 E
Sóller, *Spain* **33 B9** 39 46N 2 43 E
Solling, *Germany* **26 D5** 51 44N 9 36 E
Solna, *Sweden* **14 E12** 59 22N 18 1 E
Solnechnogorsk, *Russia* **51 C10** 56 10N 36 57 E
Sologne, *France* **23 E8** 47 40N 1 45 E
Solok, *Indonesia* **74 C2** 0 45 S 100 40 E
Sololá, *Guatemala* **148 D1** 14 49N 91 10W
Solomon, N. Fork →, *U.S.A.* **138 F5** 39 29N 98 26W
Solomon, S. Fork →, *U.S.A.* **138 F5** 39 25N 99 12W
Solomon Is. ■, *Pac. Oc.* **121 L8** 6 0 S 155 0 E
Solomon Sea, *Papua N. G.* **120 D6** 7 0 S 150 0 E
Solon, *China* **65 B7** 46 32N 121 10 E
Solon Springs, *U.S.A.* **138 B9** 46 22N 91 49W
Solonópole, *Brazil* **154 C4** 5 44 S 39 1W
Solor, *Indonesia* **72 C2** 8 27 S 123 0 E
Solotcha, *Russia* **51 D11** 54 48N 39 53 E
Solothurn, *Switz.* **28 B5** 47 13N 7 32 E
Solothurn □, *Switz.* **28 B5** 47 18N 7 40 E
Solotobe, *Kazakhstan* **55 A3** 44 37N 66 3 E
Solsona, *Spain* **34 D6** 42 0N 1 31 E
Solt, *Hungary* **31 E12** 46 45N 19 1 E
Solta, *Croatia* **39 E13** 43 24N 16 15 E
Solţānābād, *Khorāsān, Iran* **85 C8** 34 13N 59 58 E
Solţānābād, *Khorāsān, Iran* **85 B8** 36 29N 58 5 E
Solţānābād, *Markazī, Iran* **85 C6** 35 31N 51 10 E
Soltau, *Germany* **26 C5** 52 59N 9 50 E
Soltsy, *Russia* **50 B7** 58 10N 30 30 E
Solunska Glava, *Macedonia* **42 F6** 41 44N 21 31 E
Solvang, *U.S.A.* **145 L6** 34 36N 120 8W
Solvay, *U.S.A.* **137 C8** 43 3N 76 13W
Solvychegodsk, *Russia* **48 B8** 61 21N 46 56 E
Solway Firth, *U.K.* **16 C4** 54 45N 3 38W
Solwezi, *Zambia* **107 E2** 12 11 S 26 21 E
Sōma, *Japan* **60 F10** 37 40N 140 50 E
Soma, *Turkey* **88 D2** 39 10N 27 35 E
Somali Rep. ■, *Africa* **90 F4** 7 0N 47 0 E
Somalia ■ = Somali Rep. ■, *Africa* **90 F4** 7 0N 47 0 E
Sombe Dzong, *Bhutan* **78 B2** 27 13N 89 8 E
Sombernon, *France* **23 E11** 47 20N 4 40 E
Sombor, *Serbia* **42 B4** 45 46N 19 9 E
Sombra, *Canada* **136 D2** 42 43N 82 29W
Sombrerete, *Mexico* **146 C4** 23 40N 103 40W
Sombrero, *Anguilla* **149 C7** 18 37N 63 30W
Someren, *Neths.* **21 F7** 51 23N 5 42 E
Somers, *U.S.A.* **142 B6** 48 5N 114 13W
Somerset, *Canada* **131 D9** 49 25N 98 39W
Somerset, *Colo., U.S.A.* **143 G10** 38 56N 107 28W
Somerset, *Ky., U.S.A.* **134 G3** 37 5N 84 36W
Somerset, *Mass., U.S.A.* **137 E13** 41 47N 71 8W
Somerset, *Pa., U.S.A.* **136 F5** 40 1N 79 5W
Somerset □, *U.K.* **17 F5** 51 9N 3 0W
Somerset East, *S. Africa* **104 E4** 32 42 S 25 35 E
Somerset I., *Canada* **126 A10** 73 30N 93 0W
Somerset West, *S. Africa* **104 E2** 34 8 S 18 50 E
Somerton, *U.S.A.* **143 K6** 32 36N 114 43W
Somerville, *U.S.A.* **137 F10** 40 35N 74 38W
Someş →, *Romania* **46 B3** 47 49N 22 43 E
Someşul Mare →, *Romania* **46 B5** 47 18N 24 30 E
Somma Lombardo, *Italy* **38 C5** 45 41N 8 42 E
Somma Vesuviana, *Italy* **41 B7** 40 52N 14 23 E
Sommariva, *Australia* **115 D4** 26 24 S 146 36 E
Sommatino, *Italy* **40 E6** 37 20N 14 0 E
Somme □, *France* **23 C9** 49 57N 2 20 E
Somme →, *France* **23 B8** 50 11N 1 38 E
Somme, B. de la, *France* **22 B8** 50 14N 1 33 E
Sommelsdijk, *Neths.* **20 E4** 51 46N 4 9 E
Sommepy-Tahure, *France* **23 C11** 49 15N 4 31 E
Sömmerda, *Germany* **26 D7** 51 10N 11 8 E
Sommesous, *France* **23 D11** 48 44N 4 12 E
Sommières, *France* **25 E8** 43 47N 4 6 E
Somogy □, *Hungary* **31 E10** 46 19N 17 30 E
Somogyszob, *Hungary* **31 E10** 46 18N 17 20 E
Somosomo Str., *Fiji* **121 A3** 16 0 S 180 0 E
Somoto, *Nic.* **148 D2** 13 28N 86 37W
Sompolno, *Poland* **47 C5** 52 26N 18 30 E
Somport, Paso, *Spain* **34 C4** 42 48N 0 31W
Somport, Puerto de, *Spain* **34 C4** 42 48N 0 31W
Somuncurá, Meseta de, *Argentina* **160 B3** 41 30 S 67 0W
Son, *Neths.* **21 E6** 51 31N 5 30 E
Son, *Norway* **14 E4** 59 32N 10 42 E
Son, *Spain* **36 C2** 42 43N 8 58W
Son Ha, *Vietnam* **76 E7** 15 3N 108 34 E
Son Hoa, *Vietnam* **76 F7** 13 2N 108 58 E
Son La, *Vietnam* **76 B4** 21 20N 103 50 E
Son Tay, *Vietnam* **76 B5** 21 8N 105 30 E
Soná, *Panama* **148 E3** 8 0N 81 20W
Sonamarg, *India* **81 B6** 34 18N 75 21 E
Sonamukhi, *India* **81 H12** 23 18N 87 27 E
Sonamura, *India* **78 D3** 23 29N 91 15 E
Sŏnchŏn, *N. Korea* **67 E13** 39 48N 124 55 E
Soncino, *Italy* **38 C6** 45 24N 9 52 E
Sondags →, *S. Africa* **104 E4** 33 44 S 25 51 E
Sóndalo, *Italy* **38 B7** 46 20N 10 20 E
Sondar, *India* **81 C6** 33 28N 75 56 E
Sønder Omme, *Denmark* **15 J2** 55 50N 8 54 E
Sønder Tornby, *Denmark* **15 G3** 57 31N 9 58 E
Sønderborg, *Denmark* **15 K3** 54 55N 9 49 E
Sønderjyllands Amtskommune □, *Denmark* **15 J3** 55 10N 9 10 E
Sondershausen, *Germany* **26 D6** 51 22N 10 50 E
Søndre Strømfjord, *Greenland* **127 B14** 66 59N 50 40W
Sondrio, *Italy* **38 B6** 46 10N 9 53 E
Sone, *Mozam.* **107 F3** 17 23 S 34 55 E
Sonepur, *India* **82 D6** 20 55N 83 50 E
Song, *Thailand* **76 C3** 18 28N 100 11 E
Song Cau, *Vietnam* **76 F7** 13 27N 109 18 E
Song Xian, *China* **66 G7** 34 12N 112 8 E
Songchŏn, *N. Korea* **67 E14** 39 12N 126 15 E
Songea, *Tanzania* **107 E4** 10 40 S 35 40 E
Songea □, *Tanzania* **107 E4** 10 30 S 36 0 E
Songeons, *France* **23 C8** 49 32N 1 50 E
Songhua Hu, *China* **67 C14** 43 35N 126 50 E
Songhua Jiang →, *China* **65 B8** 47 45N 132 30 E
Songjiang, *China* **69 B13** 31 1N 121 12 E
Songjin, *N. Korea* **67 D15** 40 40N 129 10 E
Songjŏng-ni, *S. Korea* **67 G14** 35 8N 126 47 E
Songkan, *China* **68 C6** 28 35N 106 52 E
Songkhla, *Thailand* **77 J3** 7 13N 100 37 E
Songming, *China* **68 E4** 25 12N 103 2 E
Songnim, *N. Korea* **67 E13** 38 45N 125 39 E
Songo, *Angola* **103 D2** 7 22 S 14 51 E
Songololo, *Zaïre* **103 D2** 5 40 S 14 2 E
Songpan, *China* **68 A4** 32 40N 103 30 E
Songtao, *China* **68 C7** 28 11N 109 10 E
Songwe, *Zaïre* **106 C2** 3 20 S 26 16 E
Songwe →, *Africa* **107 D3** 9 44 S 33 58 E
Songxi, *China* **69 D12** 27 31N 118 44 E
Songzi, *China* **69 B8** 30 12N 111 45 E
Sonid Youqi, *China* **66 C7** 42 45N 112 48 E
Sonipat, *India* **80 E7** 29 0N 77 5 E
Sonkel, Ozero, *Kirghizia* **55 C7** 41 50N 75 12 E
Sonkovo, *Russia* **51 C10** 57 50N 37 5 E
Sonmiani, *Pakistan* **79 D2** 25 25N 66 40 E
Sonnino, *Italy* **40 A6** 41 25N 13 13 E
Sono →, *Goiás, Brazil* **154 C2** 9 58 S 48 11W
Sono →, *Minas Gerais, Brazil* **155 E2** 17 2 S 45 32W
Sonobe, *Japan* **63 B7** 35 6N 135 28 E
Sonogno, *Switz.* **29 D7** 46 22N 8 47 E
Sonora, *Calif., U.S.A.* **144 H6** 37 59N 120 23W
Sonora, *Tex., U.S.A.* **139 K4** 30 34N 100 39W
Sonora □, *Mexico* **146 B2** 29 0N 111 0W
Sonora →, *Mexico* **146 B2** 28 50N 111 33W
Sonora Desert, *U.S.A.* **145 M12** 33 40N 114 15W
Sonoyta, *Mexico* **146 A2** 31 51N 112 50W
Sŏnsan, *S. Korea* **67 F15** 36 14N 128 17 E
Sonsonate, *El Salv.* **148 D2** 13 43N 89 44W
Sonthofen, *Germany* **27 H6** 47 31N 10 16 E
Soochow = Suzhou, *China* **69 B13** 31 19N 120 38 E
Sop Hao, *Laos* **76 B5** 20 33N 104 27 E
Sop Prap, *Thailand* **76 D2** 17 53N 99 20 E
Sopachuy, *Bolivia* **157 D5** 19 29 S 64 31W
Sopi, *Indonesia* **72 A3** 2 34N 128 28 E
Sopo, Nahr →, *Sudan* **95 F2** 8 40N 26 30 E
Sopot, *Poland* **47 A5** 54 27N 18 31 E
Sopot, *Serbia* **42 C5** 44 29N 20 30 E
Sopotnica, *Macedonia* **42 F6** 41 23N 21 13 E
Sopron, *Hungary* **31 D9** 47 45N 16 32 E

**Sudeten Mts.** **269**


Stanislaus →, *U.S.A.* ... **144 H5** 37 40N 121 14W
Stanislav = Ivano-Frankovsk, *Ukraine* ... **50 G4** 48 40N 24 40 E
Stanisławów, *Poland* .... **47 C8** 52 18N 21 33 E
Stanke Dimitrov, *Bulgaria* **42 E8** 42 17N 23 9 E
Stanley, *Australia* ....... **114 G4** 40 46 S 145 19 E
Stanley, *N.B., Canada* ... **129 C6** 46 20N 66 44W
Stanley, *Sask., Canada* .. **131 B8** 55 24N 104 22W
Stanley, *Falk. Is.* ....... **160 D5** 51 40 S 59 51W
Stanley, *Idaho, U.S.A.* .. **142 D6** 44 13N 114 56W
Stanley, *N. Dak., U.S.A.* **138 A3** 48 19N 102 23W
Stanley, *N.Y., U.S.A.* ... **136 D7** 42 48N 77 6W
Stanley, *Wis., U.S.A.* ... **138 C9** 44 58N 90 56W
Stanley Res., *India* ...... **83 J3** 11 50N 77 40 E
Stanovoy Khrebet, *Russia* **57 D13** 55 0N 130 0 E
Stanovoy Ra. = Stanovoy Khrebet, *Russia* ...... **57 D13** 55 0N 130 0 E
Stans, *Switz.* ........... **29 C6** 46 58N 8 21 E
Stansmore Ra., *Australia* **112 D4** 21 23 S 128 33 E
Stanthorpe, *Australia* .... **115 D5** 28 36 S 151 59 E
Stanton, *U.S.A.* ........ **139 J4** 32 8N 101 48W
Stantsiya Karshi, *Uzbekistan* .......... **55 D2** 38 49N 65 47 E
Stanwood, *U.S.A.* ...... **144 B4** 48 15N 122 23W
Staphorst, *Neths.* ....... **20 C8** 52 39N 6 12 E
Staples, *U.S.A.* ......... **138 B7** 46 21N 94 48W
Stapleton, *U.S.A.* ....... **138 E4** 41 29N 100 31W
Staporków, *Poland* ...... **47 D7** 51 9N 20 31 E
Star City, *Canada* ....... **131 C8** 52 50N 104 20W
Stara-minskaya, *Russia* .. **53 C8** 46 33N 39 0 E
Stara Moravica, *Serbia* .. **42 B4** 45 50N 19 30 E
Stara Pazova, *Serbia* .... **42 C5** 44 58N 20 10 E
Stara Planina, *Bulgaria* .. **43 D8** 43 15N 23 0 E
Stara Zagora, *Bulgaria* .. **43 E10** 42 26N 25 39 E
Starachowice, *Poland* .... **47 D8** 51 3N 21 2 E
Starashcherbinovskaya, *Russia* .............. **53 C8** 46 40N 38 53 E
Staraya Russa, *Russia* ... **50 C7** 57 58N 31 23 E
Starbuck I., *Kiribati* ..... **123 H12** 5 37 S 155 55W
Stargard Szczeciński, *Poland* ............. **47 B2** 53 20N 15 0 E
Stari Bar, *Montenegro* ... **42 E4** 42 7N 19 13 E
Stari Trg, *Slovenia* ...... **39 C12** 45 29N 15 7 E
Staritsa, *Russia* ......... **50 C9** 56 33N 34 55 E
Starke, *U.S.A.* .......... **135 K4** 29 57N 82 7W
Starkville, *Colo., U.S.A.* . **139 G2** 37 8N 104 30W
Starkville, *Miss., U.S.A.* . **135 J1** 33 28N 88 49W
Starnberg, *Germany* ..... **27 G7** 48 0N 11 20 E
Starnberger See, *Germany* **27 H7** 47 55N 11 20 E
Starobelsk, *Ukraine* ..... **53 B8** 49 16N 39 0 E
Starodub, *Russia* ........ **50 E8** 52 30N 32 50 E
Starogard, *Poland* ....... **47 B5** 53 59N 18 30 E
Starokonstantinov, *Ukraine* ............. **52 B2** 49 48N 27 10 E
Starosielce, *Poland* ...... **47 B10** 53 8N 23 5 E
Start Pt., *U.K.* ......... **17 G4** 50 13N 3 38W
Stary Sącz, *Poland* ...... **31 B13** 49 33N 20 35 E
Staryy Biryuzyak, *Russia* . **53 D12** 44 46N 46 50 E
Staryy Chartoriysk, *Ukraine* ............. **50 F4** 51 15N 25 54 E
Staryy Kheydzhan, *Russia* **57 C15** 60 0N 144 50 E
Staryy Krym, *Ukraine* ... **52 D6** 45 3N 35 8 E
Staryy Oskol, *Russia* .... **51 F10** 51 19N 37 55 E
Stassfurt, *Germany* ...... **26 D7** 51 51N 11 34 E
Staszów, *Poland* ........ **47 E8** 50 33N 21 10 E
State Center, *U.S.A.* .... **140 B3** 42 1N 93 10W
State College, *U.S.A.* ... **136 F7** 40 48N 77 52W
Stateline, *U.S.A.* ....... **144 G7** 38 57N 119 56W
Staten, I. = Estados, I. de Los, *Argentina* ........ **160 D4** 54 40 S 64 30W
Staten I., *U.S.A.* ....... **137 F10** 40 35N 74 9W
Statesboro, *U.S.A.* ...... **135 J5** 32 27N 81 47W
Statesville, *U.S.A.* ...... **135 H5** 35 47N 80 53W
Stauffer, *U.S.A.* ........ **145 L7** 34 45N 119 3W
Staunton, *Ill., U.S.A.* .... **140 E7** 39 1N 89 47W
Staunton, *Va., U.S.A.* ... **134 F6** 38 9N 79 4W
Stavanger, *Norway* ...... **13 G8** 58 57N 5 40 E
Staveley, *N.Z.* .......... **119 D6** 43 40 S 171 32 E
Stavelot, *Belgium* ....... **21 H7** 50 23N 5 55 E
Stavenhagen, *Germany* .. **26 B8** 53 41N 12 54 E
Stavenisse, *Neths.* ...... **21 E4** 51 35N 4 1 E
Staveren, *Neths.* ........ **20 C6** 52 53N 5 22 E
Stavern, *Norway* ........ **14 F4** 59 0N 10 1 E
Stavre, *Sweden* ......... **14 B9** 62 51N 15 19 E
Stavropol, *Russia* ....... **53 D10** 45 5N 42 0 E
Stavros, *Cyprus* ......... **32 D11** 35 1N 32 38 E
Stavrós, *Greece* ......... **32 D6** 35 12N 24 45 E
Stavros, Ákra, *Greece* ... **32 D6** 35 26N 24 58 E
Stavroúpolis, *Greece* .... **44 C6** 41 12N 24 45 E
Stawell, *Australia* ....... **116 D5** 37 5 S 142 47 E
Stawell →, *Australia* .... **114 C3** 20 20 S 142 55 E
Stawiski, *Poland* ........ **47 B9** 53 22N 22 9 E
Stawiszyn, *Poland* ....... **47 D5** 51 56N 18 4 E
Stayner, *Canada* ........ **136 B4** 44 25N 80 5W
Steamboat Springs, *U.S.A.* **142 F10** 40 29N 106 50W
Stębark, *Poland* ........ **47 B7** 53 30N 20 10 E
Stebleva, *Albania* ....... **44 C2** 41 18N 20 33 E
Steckborn, *Switz.* ....... **29 A7** 47 44N 8 59 E
Steele, *U.S.A.* .......... **138 B5** 46 51N 99 55W
Steelton, *U.S.A.* ........ **136 F8** 40 14N 76 50W
Steelville, *U.S.A.* ....... **139 G9** 37 58N 91 22W
Steen River, *Canada* .... **130 B5** 59 40N 117 12W
Steenbergen, *Neths.* ..... **21 E4** 51 35N 4 19 E
Steenkool = Bintuni, *Indonesia* ........... **73 B4** 2 7 S 133 32 E
Steenvoorde, *France* .... **23 B9** 50 48N 2 33 E
Steenwijk, *Neths.* ....... **20 C8** 52 47N 6 7 E
Steep Pt., *Australia* ..... **113 E1** 26 8 S 113 8 E
Steep Rock, *Canada* .... **131 C9** 51 30N 98 48W
Ştefăneşti, *Romania* .... **46 B8** 47 44N 27 15 E
Stefanie L. = Chew Bahir, *Ethiopia* ............ **95 G4** 4 40N 36 50 E
Stefansson Bay, *Antarctica* **7 C5** 67 20 S 59 8 E
Steffisburg, *Switz.* ...... **28 C5** 46 47N 7 38 E
Stege, *Denmark* ........ **15 K6** 55 0N 12 18 E
Steiermark □, *Austria* ... **30 D8** 47 26N 15 0 E
Steigerwald, *Germany* ... **27 F6** 49 45N 10 30 E
Steilacoom, *U.S.A.* ..... **144 C4** 47 10N 122 36W
Stein, *Neths.* ........... **21 G7** 50 58N 5 45 E
Steinbach, *Canada* ...... **131 D9** 49 32N 96 40W
Steinfort, *Lux.* .......... **21 J7** 49 39N 5 55 E
Steinfurt, *Germany* ...... **26 C3** 52 9N 7 23 E
Steinheim, *Germany* ..... **26 D5** 51 50N 9 6 E
Steinhuder Meer, *Germany* ............ **26 C5** 52 48N 9 20 E
Steinkjer, *Norway* ....... **12 E11** 63 59N 11 31 E
Steinkopf, *S. Africa* ..... **104 D2** 29 18 S 17 43 E
Stekene, *Belgium* ....... **21 F4** 51 12N 4 2 E
Stellarton, *Canada* ...... **129 C7** 45 32N 62 30W
Stellenbosch, *S. Africa* .. **104 E2** 33 58 S 18 50 E
Stellendam, *Neths.* ...... **20 E4** 51 49N 4 1 E
Stelvio, Paso dello, *Italy* . **29 C10** 46 32N 10 27 E
Stemshaug, *Norway* ..... **14 A2** 63 19N 8 44 E
Stendal, *Germany* ....... **26 C7** 52 36N 11 50 E
Stene, *Belgium* ......... **21 F1** 51 12N 2 56 E
Stensele, *Sweden* ....... **12 D14** 65 3N 17 8 E
Stenstorp, *Sweden* ...... **15 F7** 58 17N 13 45 E
Stepanakert = Khankendy, *Azerbaijan* **89 D12** 39 40N 46 25 E
Stephen, *U.S.A.* ........ **138 A6** 48 27N 96 53W
Stephens, C., *N.Z.* ...... **119 A8** 40 42 S 173 58 E
Stephens Creek, *Australia* **116 A4** 31 50 S 141 30 E
Stephens I., *Canada* ..... **130 C2** 54 10N 130 45W
Stephens I., *N.Z.* ....... **119 A9** 40 40 S 174 1 E
Stephenville, *Canada* .... **129 C8** 48 31N 58 35W
Stephenville, *U.S.A.* .... **139 J5** 32 13N 98 12W
Stepnica, *Poland* ........ **47 B1** 53 38N 14 36 E
Stepnoi = Elista, *Russia* . **53 C11** 46 16N 44 14 E
Stepnoye, *Russia* ....... **54 D7** 54 4N 60 26 E
Stepnyak, *Kazakhstan* ... **56 D8** 52 50N 70 50 E
Steppe, *Asia* ........... **58 E9** 50 0N 50 0 E
Stereá Ellas □, *Greece* .. **45 F4** 38 50N 22 0 E
Sterkstroom, *S. Africa* ... **104 E4** 31 32 S 26 32 E
Sterling, *Colo., U.S.A.* ... **138 E3** 40 37N 103 13W
Sterling, *Ill., U.S.A.* .... **140 C7** 41 48N 89 42W
Sterling, *Kans., U.S.A.* .. **138 F5** 38 13N 98 12W
Sterling City, *U.S.A.* .... **139 K4** 31 51N 101 0W
Sterling Heights, *U.S.A.* . **141 B13** 42 35N 83 0W
Sterling Run, *U.S.A.* .... **136 E6** 41 25N 78 12W
Sterlitamak, *Russia* ..... **54 E4** 53 40N 56 0 E
Sternberg, *Germany* ..... **26 B7** 53 42N 11 48 E
Šternberk, *Czech.* ....... **31 B10** 49 45N 17 15 E
Stérnes, *Greece* ........ **32 D6** 35 30N 24 9 E
Stettin = Szczecin, *Poland* **47 B1** 53 27N 14 27 E
Stettiner Haff, *Germany* . **26 B10** 53 50N 14 25 E
Stettler, *Canada* ........ **130 C6** 52 19N 112 40W
Steubenville, *U.S.A.* .... **136 F4** 40 22N 80 37W
Stevens Point, *U.S.A.* ... **138 C10** 44 31N 89 34W
Stevenson, *U.S.A.* ...... **144 E5** 45 42N 121 53W
Stevenson L., *Canada* ... **131 C9** 53 55N 96 0W
Stevns Klint, *Denmark* ... **15 J6** 55 17N 12 28 E
Steward, *U.S.A.* ........ **140 C7** 41 51N 89 1W
Stewardson, *U.S.A.* ..... **141 E8** 39 16N 88 38W
Stewart, *B.C., Canada* ... **130 B3** 55 56N 129 57W
Stewart, *N.W.T., Canada* **126 B6** 63 19N 139 26W
Stewart, *U.S.A.* ........ **144 F7** 39 5N 119 46W
Stewart, C., *Australia* ... **114 A1** 11 57 S 134 56 E
Stewart, I., *Chile* ....... **160 D2** 54 50 S 71 15W
Stewart I., *N.Z.* ........ **119 G2** 46 58 S 167 54 E
Stewarts Point, *U.S.A.* .. **144 G3** 38 39N 123 24W
Stewartsville, *U.S.A.* .... **140 E2** 39 45N 94 30W
Stewiacke, *Canada* ...... **129 C7** 45 9N 63 22W
Steynsburg, *S. Africa* ... **104 E4** 31 15 S 25 49 E
Steyr, *Austria* .......... **30 C7** 48 3N 14 25 E
Steyr →, *Austria* ....... **30 C7** 48 17N 14 15 E
Steytlerville, *S. Africa* .. **104 E3** 33 17 S 24 19 E
Stia, *Italy* .............. **39 E8** 43 48N 11 41 E
Stiens, *Neths.* .......... **20 B7** 53 16N 5 46 E
Stigler, *U.S.A.* ......... **139 H7** 35 15N 95 8W
Stigliano, *Italy* ......... **41 B9** 40 24N 16 13 E
Stigsnæs, *Denmark* ..... **15 J5** 55 13N 11 18 E
Stigtomta, *Sweden* ...... **15 F10** 58 47N 16 48 E
Stikine →, *Canada* ..... **130 B2** 56 40N 132 30W
Stilfontein, *S. Africa* .... **104 D4** 26 51 S 26 50 E
Stilís, *Greece* ........... **45 F4** 38 55N 22 47 E
Stillwater, *N.Z.* ........ **119 C6** 42 27 S 171 20 E
Stillwater, *Minn., U.S.A.* **138 C8** 45 3N 92 49W
Stillwater, *N.Y., U.S.A.* . **137 D11** 42 55N 73 41W
Stillwater, *Okla., U.S.A.* . **139 G6** 36 7N 97 4W
Stillwater Range, *U.S.A.* **142 G4** 39 50N 118 5W
Stilwell, *U.S.A.* ......... **139 H7** 35 49N 94 38W
Stimfalías, L., *Greece* ... **45 G4** 37 51N 22 27 E
Štip, *Macedonia* ........ **42 F7** 41 42N 22 10 E
Stíra, *Greece* ........... **45 F6** 38 9N 24 14 E
Stirling, *Australia* ....... **114 B3** 17 12 S 141 35 E
Stirling, *Canada* ........ **130 D6** 49 30N 112 30W
Stirling, *N.Z.* ........... **119 G4** 46 14 S 169 49 E
Stirling, *U.K.* ........... **18 E5** 56 7N 3 57W
Stirling Ra., *Australia* ... **113 F2** 34 23 S 118 0 E
Stittsville, *Canada* ...... **137 A9** 45 15N 75 55W
Stockach, *Germany* ..... **27 H5** 47 51N 9 1 E
Stockbridge, *U.S.A.* .... **141 B12** 42 27N 84 11W
Stockerau, *Austria* ...... **31 C9** 48 24N 16 12 E
Stockett, *U.S.A.* ........ **142 C8** 47 21N 111 10W
Stockholm, *Sweden* ..... **14 E12** 59 20N 18 3 E
Stockholms län □, *Sweden* **14 E12** 59 30N 18 20 E
Stockhorn, *Switz.* ....... **28 C5** 46 42N 7 33 E
Stockport, *U.K.* ......... **16 D5** 53 25N 2 11W
Stockton, *Australia* ...... **117 B9** 32 50 S 151 47 E
Stockton, *Calif., U.S.A.* .. **144 H5** 37 58N 121 17W
Stockton, *Ill., U.S.A.* .... **140 B6** 42 21N 90 1W
Stockton, *Kans., U.S.A.* .. **138 F5** 39 26N 99 16W
Stockton, *Mo., U.S.A.* ... **139 G8** 37 42N 93 48W
Stockton-on-Tees, *U.K.* .. **16 C6** 54 34N 1 20W
Stockvik, *Sweden* ....... **14 B11** 62 17N 17 23 E
Stoczek Łukowski, *Poland* **47 D8** 51 58N 21 58 E
Stöde, *Sweden* ......... **14 B10** 62 28N 16 35 E
Stogovo, *Macedonia* .... **42 F5** 41 31N 20 38 E
Stoke, *N.Z.* ............ **119 B8** 41 19 S 173 14 E
Stoke on Trent, *U.K.* .... **16 D5** 53 1N 2 11W
Stokes Bay, *Canada* .... **128 C3** 45 0N 81 28W
Stokes Pt., *Australia* .... **114 G3** 40 10 S 143 56 E
Stokes Ra., *Australia* ... **112 C5** 15 50 S 130 50 E
Stokkseyri, *Iceland* ..... **12 E3** 63 50N 21 2W
Stokksnes, *Iceland* ..... **12 D6** 64 14N 14 58W
Stolac, *Bos.-H.* ......... **42 D2** 43 8N 17 59 E
Stolberg, *Germany* ...... **26 E2** 50 48N 6 13 E
Stolbovaya, *Russia* ...... **51 D10** 55 10N 37 32 E
Stolbovaya, *Russia* ...... **57 C16** 64 50N 153 50 E
Stolbovoy, Ostrov, *Russia* **57 D17** 74 44N 135 14 E
Stolbtsy, *Belorussia* ..... **50 E5** 53 30N 26 43 E
Stolin, *Belorussia* ....... **50 F5** 51 53N 26 50 E
Stolnici, *Romania* ....... **46 E5** 44 31N 24 48 E
Stolwijk, *Neths.* ......... **20 E5** 51 59N 4 47 E
Stomion, *Greece* ........ **32 D5** 35 21N 23 32 E
Ston, *Croatia* ........... **42 E2** 42 51N 17 43 E
Stonehaven, *U.K.* ....... **18 E6** 56 58N 2 11W
Stonehenge, *Australia* ... **114 C3** 24 22 S 143 17 E
Stonewall, *Canada* ...... **131 C9** 50 10N 97 19W
Stonington, *U.S.A.* ..... **140 E7** 39 44N 89 12W
Stony L., *Man., Canada* . **131 B9** 58 51N 98 40W
Stony L., *Ont., Canada* .. **136 B6** 44 30N 78 5W
Stony Rapids, *Canada* ... **131 B7** 59 16N 105 50W
Stony Tunguska = Podkamennaya Tunguska →, *Russia* .. **57 C10** 61 50N 90 13 E
Stonyford, *U.S.A.* ...... **144 F4** 39 23N 122 33W
Stopnica, *Poland* ........ **47 E7** 50 27N 20 57 E
Stora Lulevatten, *Sweden* **12 C15** 67 10N 19 30 E
Stora Sjöfallet, *Sweden* .. **12 C15** 67 29N 18 40 E
Storavan, *Sweden* ....... **12 D15** 65 45N 18 10 E
Store Bælt, *Denmark* ... **15 J5** 55 20N 11 0 E
Store Creek, *Australia* ... **117 B8** 32 54 S 149 6 E
Store Heddinge, *Denmark* **15 J6** 55 18N 12 23 E
Støren, *Norway* ......... **14 A4** 63 3N 10 18 E
Storlulea = Stora Lulevatten, *Sweden* ... **12 C15** 67 10N 19 30 E
Storm B., *Australia* ..... **114 G4** 43 10 S 147 30 E
Storm Lake, *U.S.A.* ..... **138 D7** 42 39N 95 13W
Stormberge, *S. Africa* ... **104 E4** 31 16 S 26 17 E
Stormsrivier, *S. Africa* .. **104 E3** 33 59 S 23 52 E
Stornoway, *U.K.* ........ **18 C2** 58 12N 6 23W
Storozhinets, *Ukraine* ... **52 B1** 48 14N 25 45 E
Storsjö, *Sweden* ........ **14 B7** 62 49N 13 5 E
Storsjøen, *Hedmark, Norway* .............. **14 D5** 60 20N 11 40 E
Storsjøen, *Hedmark, Norway* .............. **14 C5** 61 30N 11 14 E
Storsjön, *Sweden* ....... **14 B7** 62 50N 13 8 E
Storstrøms Amt. □, *Denmark* ............ **15 K5** 54 50N 11 45 E
Storuman, *Sweden* ...... **12 D14** 65 5N 17 10 E
Story City, *U.S.A.* ...... **140 B3** 42 11N 93 36W
Stoughton, *Canada* ...... **131 D8** 49 40N 103 0W
Stoughton, *U.S.A.* ...... **140 B8** 42 55N 89 13W
Stour →, *Dorset, U.K.* .. **17 G5** 50 48N 2 7W
Stour →, *Here. & Worcs., U.K.* . **17 E5** 52 25N 2 13W
Stour →, *Kent, U.K.* ... **17 F9** 51 15N 1 20 E
Stour →, *Suffolk, U.K.* . **17 F9** 51 55N 1 5 E
Stourbridge, *U.K.* ....... **17 E5** 52 28N 2 8W
Stout, L., *Canada* ....... **131 C10** 52 0N 94 40W
Stove Pipe Wells Village, *U.S.A.* .............. **145 J9** 36 35N 117 11W
Stowmarket, *U.K.* ....... **17 E9** 52 11N 1 0 E
Strabane, *U.K.* ......... **19 B4** 54 50N 7 28W
Strabane □, *U.K.* ....... **19 B4** 54 45N 7 25W
Stracin, *Macedonia* ..... **42 E7** 42 13N 22 2 E
Stradella, *Italy* ......... **38 C6** 45 4N 9 20 E
Strahan, *Australia* ...... **114 G4** 42 9 S 145 20 E
Strakonice, *Czech.* ...... **30 B6** 49 15N 13 53 E
Straldzha, *Bulgaria* ..... **43 E11** 42 35N 26 40 E
Stralsund, *Germany* ..... **26 A9** 54 17N 13 5 E
Strand, *S. Africa* ....... **104 E2** 34 9 S 18 48 E
Strangford L., *U.K.* ..... **19 B6** 54 30N 5 37W
Strängnäs, *Sweden* ...... **14 E11** 59 23N 17 2 E
Strangsville, *U.S.A.* ..... **136 E3** 41 19N 81 50W
Stranraer, *U.K.* ......... **18 G3** 54 54N 5 0W
Strasbourg, *Canada* ..... **131 C8** 51 4N 104 55W
Strasbourg, *France* ...... **23 D14** 48 35N 7 42 E
Strasburg, *Germany* ..... **26 B9** 53 30N 13 44 E
Strasburg, *U.S.A.* ....... **138 B4** 46 8N 100 10W
Strassen, *Lux.* .......... **21 J8** 49 37N 6 4 E
Stratford, *N.S.W., Australia* ............ **117 B9** 32 7 S 151 55 E
Stratford, *Vic., Australia* . **117 D7** 37 59 S 147 7 E
Stratford, *Canada* ....... **128 D3** 43 23N 81 0W
Stratford, *N.Z.* ......... **118 F3** 39 20 S 174 19 E
Stratford, *Calif., U.S.A.* . **144 J7** 36 11N 119 49W
Stratford, *Conn., U.S.A.* **137 E11** 41 12N 73 8W
Stratford, *Tex., U.S.A.* .. **139 G3** 36 20N 102 4W
Stratford-upon-Avon, *U.K.* ................ **17 E6** 52 12N 1 42W
Strath Spey, *U.K.* ....... **18 D5** 57 15N 3 40W
Strathalbyn, *Australia* ... **116 C3** 35 13 S 138 53 E
Strathclyde □, *U.K.* ..... **18 F4** 56 0N 4 50W
Strathcona Prov. Park, *Canada* .............. **130 D3** 49 38N 125 40W
Strathmore, *Australia* .... **114 B3** 17 50 S 142 35 E
Strathmore, *Canada* ..... **130 C6** 51 5N 113 18W
Strathmore, *U.K.* ....... **18 E5** 56 40N 3 4W
Strathmore, *U.S.A.* ..... **144 J7** 36 9N 119 4W
Strathnaver, *Canada* .... **130 C4** 53 20N 122 33W
Strathpeffer, *U.K.* ....... **18 D4** 57 35N 4 32W
Strathroy, *Canada* ....... **128 D3** 42 58N 81 38W
Strathy Pt., *U.K.* ........ **18 C4** 58 35N 4 3W
Stratton, *U.S.A.* ........ **138 F3** 39 19N 102 36W
Straubing, *Germany* ..... **27 G8** 48 53N 12 35 E
Straumnes, *Iceland* ...... **12 C2** 66 26N 23 8W
Strausberg, *Germany* .... **26 C9** 52 40N 13 52 E
Strawberry Point, *U.S.A.* **140 B5** 42 41N 91 32W
Strawberry Reservoir, *U.S.A.* ............... **142 F8** 40 8N 111 9W
Strawn, *U.S.A.* ......... **139 J5** 32 33N 98 30W
Strážnice, *Czech.* ....... **31 C10** 48 54N 17 19 E
Streaky B., *Australia* .... **115 E1** 32 48 S 134 13 E
Streaky Bay, *Australia* .. **115 E1** 32 51 S 134 18 E
Streator, *U.S.A.* ........ **138 E10** 41 8N 88 50W
Středočeský □, *Czech.* ... **30 B7** 49 55N 14 30 E
Středoslovenský □, *Slovak Rep.* ........... **31 C12** 48 30N 19 15 E
Streé, *Belgium* .......... **21 H4** 50 17N 4 18 E
Streeter, *U.S.A.* ........ **138 B5** 46 39N 99 21W
Streetsville, *Canada* ..... **136 C5** 43 35N 79 42W
Strehaia, *Romania* ...... **46 E4** 44 37N 23 10 E
Strelcha, *Bulgaria* ....... **43 E9** 42 25N 24 19 E
Strelka, *Russia* ......... **57 D10** 58 5N 93 3 E
Streng →, *Cambodia* .... **76 F4** 13 12N 103 37 E
Strésa, *Italy* ........... **38 C5** 45 52N 8 28 E
Strezhevoy, *Russia* ...... **56 C8** 60 42N 77 34 E
Stříbro, *Czech.* ......... **30 B6** 49 44N 13 2 E
Strickland →, *Papua N. G.* ........ **120 D1** 7 35 S 141 36 E
Strijen, *Neths.* ......... **20 E5** 51 45N 4 33 E
Strimón →, *Greece* ..... **44 D5** 40 46N 23 51 E
Strimonikós Kólpos, *Greece* ............... **44 D5** 40 33N 24 0 E
Stroeder, *Argentina* ..... **160 B4** 40 12 S 62 37W
Strofádhes, *Greece* ...... **45 G3** 37 15N 21 0 E
Strömbacka, *Sweden* .... **14 C10** 61 58N 16 44 E
Strómboli, *Italy* ......... **41 D8** 38 48N 15 12 E
Stromeferry, *U.K.* ....... **18 D3** 57 20N 5 33W
Stromness, *U.K.* ........ **18 C5** 58 58N 3 18W
Ströms vattudal, *Sweden* . **12 D13** 64 15N 14 55 E
Stromsburg, *U.S.A.* ..... **138 E6** 41 7N 97 36W
Strömstad, *Sweden* ...... **13 G11** 58 55N 11 15 E
Strömsund, *Sweden* ..... **12 E13** 63 51N 15 33 E
Stronghurst, *U.S.A.* ..... **140 D6** 40 45N 90 55W
Stróngoli, *Italy* ......... **41 C10** 39 16N 17 2 E
Stronsay, *U.K.* ......... **18 B6** 59 8N 2 38W
Stropkov, *Slovak Rep.* ... **31 B14** 49 13N 21 39 E
Stroud, *U.K.* ........... **17 F5** 51 44N 2 12W
Stroud Road, *Australia* .. **117 B9** 32 18 S 151 57 E
Stroudsburg, *U.S.A.* .... **137 F9** 40 59N 75 12W
Stroumbi, *Cyprus* ....... **32 E11** 34 53N 32 29 E
Struer, *Denmark* ........ **15 H2** 56 30N 8 35 E
Struga, *Macedonia* ...... **42 F5** 41 13N 20 44 E
Strugi Krasnyye, *Russia* .. **50 B6** 58 21N 29 1 E
Strumica, *Macedonia* .... **42 F7** 41 28N 22 41 E
Strumica →, *Europe* .... **42 F8** 41 20N 23 22 E
Struthers, *Canada* ...... **128 C2** 48 41N 85 51W
Struthers, *U.S.A.* ....... **136 E4** 41 4N 80 39W
Stryama, *Bulgaria* ....... **43 E9** 42 16N 24 54 E
Stryi, *Ukraine* .......... **50 G3** 49 16N 23 48 E
Stryker, *U.S.A.* ......... **142 B6** 48 41N 114 46W
Stryków, *Poland* ........ **47 D6** 51 55N 19 33 E
Strzegom, *Poland* ....... **47 E3** 50 58N 16 20 E
Strzelce Krajeńskie, *Poland* ............. **47 C2** 52 52N 15 33 E
Strzelce Opolskie, *Poland* **47 E5** 50 31N 18 18 E
Strzelecki Cr. →, *Australia* ............. **115 D2** 29 37 S 139 59 E
Strzelin, *Poland* ........ **47 E4** 50 46N 17 2 E
Strzelno, *Poland* ........ **47 C5** 52 35N 18 9 E
Strzybnica, *Poland* ...... **47 E5** 50 28N 18 48 E
Strzyzów, *Poland* ....... **31 B14** 49 52N 21 47 E
Stuart, *Fla., U.S.A.* ..... **135 M5** 27 12N 80 15W
Stuart, *Iowa, U.S.A.* .... **140 C2** 41 30N 94 19W
Stuart, *Nebr., U.S.A.* .... **138 D5** 42 36N 99 8W
Stuart →, *Canada* ...... **130 C4** 54 0N 123 35W
Stuart Bluff Ra., *Australia* **112 D5** 22 50 S 131 52 E
Stuart L., *Canada* ....... **130 C4** 54 30N 124 30W
Stuart Mts., *N.Z.* ....... **119 F2** 45 2 S 167 39 E
Stuart Ra., *Australia* .... **115 D1** 29 10 S 134 56 E
Stubbekøbing, *Denmark* . **15 K6** 54 53N 12 9 E
Stuben, *Austria* ......... **30 D3** 47 10N 10 8 E
Studen Kladenets, Yazovir, *Bulgaria* ...... **43 F10** 41 37N 25 30 E
Studholme, *N.Z.* ........ **119 E6** 44 42 S 171 9 E
Stugun, *Sweden* ......... **14 A9** 63 10N 15 40 E
Stull, L., *Canada* ....... **128 B1** 54 24N 92 34W
Stung Treng, *Cambodia* . **76 F5** 13 31N 105 58 E
Stupart →, *Canada* ..... **131 B10** 56 0N 93 25W
Stupino, *Russia* ......... **51 D11** 54 57N 38 2 E
Sturgeon B., *Canada* .... **131 C9** 52 0N 97 50W
Sturgeon Bay, *U.S.A.* ... **134 C2** 44 50N 87 23W
Sturgeon Falls, *Canada* .. **128 C4** 46 25N 79 57W
Sturgeon L., *Alta., Canada* ............. **130 B5** 55 6N 117 32W
Sturgeon L., *Ont., Canada* **128 B1** 50 0N 90 45W
Sturgeon L., *Ont., Canada* **136 B6** 44 28N 78 43W
Sturgis, *Mich., U.S.A.* ... **141 C11** 41 48N 85 25W
Sturgis, *S. Dak., U.S.A.* . **138 C3** 44 25N 103 31W
Štúrovo, *Slovak Rep.* .... **31 D11** 47 48N 18 41 E
Sturt Cr. →, *Australia* .. **112 C4** 19 8 S 127 50 E
Sturt Creek, *Australia* ... **112 C4** 19 12 S 128 8 E
Sturts Meadows, *Australia* **116 A4** 31 18 S 141 42 E
Stutterheim, *S. Africa* ... **104 E4** 32 33 S 27 28 E
Stuttgart, *Germany* ..... **27 G5** 48 46N 9 10 E
Stuttgart, *U.S.A.* ....... **139 H9** 34 30N 91 33W
Stuyvesant, *U.S.A.* ..... **137 D11** 42 23N 73 45W
Stykkishólmur, *Iceland* .. **12 D2** 65 2N 22 40W
Styr →, *Belorussia* ..... **50 E5** 52 7N 26 35 E
Styria = Steiermark □, *Austria* .............. **30 D8** 47 26N 15 0 E
Su-no-Saki, *Japan* ...... **63 C11** 34 58N 139 45 E
Su Xian, *China* ......... **66 H9** 33 41N 116 59 E
Suakin, *Sudan* .......... **94 D4** 19 8N 37 20 E
Sual, *Phil.* .............. **70 C3** 16 4N 120 5 E
Suan, *N. Korea* ......... **67 E14** 38 42N 126 22 E
Suapure →, *Venezuela* .. **152 B4** 6 48N 67 1W
Suaqui, *Mexico* ......... **146 B3** 29 12N 109 41W
Suatá →, *Venezuela* .... **153 B4** 7 52N 65 22W
Subang, *Indonesia* ...... **75 D3** 6 34 S 107 45 E
Subansiri →, *India* ..... **78 B4** 26 48N 93 50 E
Subayhah, *Si. Arabia* ... **84 D3** 30 2N 38 50 E
Subi, *Indonesia* ......... **75 B3** 2 58N 108 50 E
Subiaco, *Italy* .......... **39 G10** 41 56N 13 5 E
Subotica, *Serbia* ........ **42 A4** 46 6N 19 39 E
Success, *Canada* ........ **131 C7** 50 28N 108 6W
Suceava, *Romania* ...... **46 B7** 47 38N 26 16 E
Suceava □, *Romania* .... **46 B6** 47 37N 25 40 E
Suceava →, *Romania* ... **46 B7** 47 38N 26 16 E
Sucha-Beskidzka, *Poland* **31 B12** 49 44N 19 35 E
Suchan, *Poland* ......... **47 B2** 53 18N 15 18 E
Suchan, *Russia* ......... **60 C6** 43 8N 133 9 E
Suchedniów, *Poland* ..... **47 D7** 51 3N 20 49 E
Suchitoto, *El Salv.* ...... **148 D2** 13 56N 89 0W
Suchou = Suzhou, *China* **69 B13** 31 19N 120 38 E
Süchow = Xuzhou, *China* **67 G9** 34 18N 117 10 E
Suchowola, *Poland* ...... **47 B10** 53 33N 23 3 E
Sucio →, *Colombia* ..... **152 B2** 7 27N 77 7W
Suck →, *Ireland* ........ **19 C3** 53 17N 8 18W
Suckling, Mt., *Papua N. G.* ......... **120 E5** 9 49 S 148 53 E
Sucre, *Bolivia* .......... **157 D4** 19 0 S 65 15W
Sucre, *Colombia* ........ **152 B3** 8 49N 74 44W
Sucre □, *Colombia* ...... **152 B2** 8 50N 75 40W
Sucre □, *Venezuela* ..... **153 A5** 10 25N 63 30W
Sucuaro, *Colombia* ...... **152 C4** 4 34N 68 50W
Sućuraj, *Croatia* ........ **39 E14** 43 10N 17 8 E
Sucuriju, *Brazil* ......... **154 A2** 1 39N 49 57W
Sucuriú →, *Brazil* ...... **157 E7** 20 47 S 51 38W
Sud, Pte., *Canada* ...... **129 C7** 49 3N 62 14W
Sud-Ouest, Pte. du, *Canada* .............. **129 C7** 49 23N 63 36W
Suda →, *Russia* ........ **51 B10** 59 0N 37 40 E
Sudak, *Ukraine* ......... **52 D6** 44 51N 34 57 E
Sudan, *U.S.A.* .......... **139 H3** 34 4N 102 32W
Sudan ■, *Africa* ........ **95 E3** 15 0N 30 0 E
Suday, *Russia* .......... **51 B13** 59 0N 43 0 E
Sudbury, *Canada* ....... **128 C3** 46 30N 81 0W
Sudbury, *U.K.* .......... **17 E8** 52 2N 0 44 E
Sûdd, *Sudan* ........... **95 F2** 8 20N 30 0 E
Suddie, *Guyana* ......... **153 B6** 7 8N 58 29W
Süderbrarup, *Germany* ... **26 A5** 54 38N 9 47 E
Süderlügum, *Germany* ... **26 A4** 54 50N 8 55 E
Süderoog-Sand, *Germany* **26 A4** 54 27N 8 30 E
Sudeten Mts. = Sudety, *Europe* ............... **31 A9** 50 20N 16 45 E

Tamerza 271


Świnoujście, *Poland* 47 B1 53 54N 14 16 E
Switzerland ■, *Europe* 28 D6 46 30N 8 0 E
Swords, *Ireland* 19 C5 53 27N 6 15W
Syasstroy, *Russia* 50 A8 60 5N 32 15 E
Sychevka, *Russia* 50 D9 55 59N 34 16 E
Syców, *Poland* 47 D4 51 19N 17 40 E
Sydney, *Australia* 117 B9 33 53 S 151 10 E
Sydney, *Canada* 129 C7 46 7N 60 7W
Sydney Mines, *Canada* 129 C7 46 18N 60 15W
Sydprøven, *Greenland* 6 C5 60 30N 45 35W
Sydra G. of = Surt,
Khalīj, *Libya* 96 B3 31 40N 18 30 E
Syke, *Germany* 26 C4 52 55N 8 50 E
Syktyvkar, *Russia* 48 B9 61 45N 50 40 E
Sylacauga, *U.S.A.* 135 J2 33 10N 86 15W
Sylarna, *Sweden* 12 E12 63 2N 12 13 E
Sylhet, *Bangla.* 78 C3 24 54N 91 52 E
Sylt, *Germany* 26 A4 54 50N 8 20 E
Sylva →, *Russia* 54 B5 58 0N 56 54 E
Sylvan Lake, *Canada* 130 C6 52 20N 114 3W
Sylvania, *Ga., U.S.A.* 135 J5 32 45N 81 38W
Sylvania, *Ohio, U.S.A.* 141 C13 41 43N 83 42W
Sylvester, *U.S.A.* 135 K4 31 32N 83 50W
Sym, *Russia* 56 C9 60 20N 88 18 E
Symón, *Mexico* 146 C4 24 42N 102 35W
Synnott Ra., *Australia* 112 C4 16 30 S 125 20 E
Syracuse, *Ind., U.S.A.* 141 C11 41 26N 85 45W
Syracuse, *Kans., U.S.A.* 139 F4 37 59N 101 45W
Syracuse, *N.Y., U.S.A.* 137 C8 43 3N 76 9W
Syrdarya, *Uzbekistan* 55 C4 40 50N 68 40 E
Syrdarya →, *Kazakhstan* 56 E7 46 3N 61 0 E
Syria ■, *Asia* 84 C3 35 0N 38 0 E
Syriam, *Burma* 78 G6 16 44N 96 19 E
Sysert, *Russia* 54 C7 56 29N 60 49 E
Syul'dzhyukyor, *Russia* 57 C12 63 14N 113 32 E
Syutkya, *Bulgaria* 43 F9 41 50N 24 16 E
Syzran, *Russia* 51 E16 53 12N 48 30 E
Szabolcs-Szatmár □,
*Hungary* 31 C14 48 2N 21 45 E
Szamocin, *Poland* 47 B4 53 2N 17 7 E
Szamos →, *Hungary* 31 C15 48 7N 22 20 E
Szaraz →, *Hungary* 31 E13 46 28N 20 44 E
Szarvas, *Hungary* 31 E13 46 50N 20 38 E
Szazhalombatta, *Hungary* 31 D11 47 20N 18 58 E
Szczawnica, *Poland* 31 B13 49 26N 20 30 E
Szczebrzeszyn, *Poland* 47 E9 50 42N 22 59 E
Szczecin, *Poland* 47 B1 53 27N 14 27 E
Szczecin □, *Poland* 47 B1 53 25N 14 32 E
Szczecinek, *Poland* 47 B3 53 43N 16 41 E
Szczekocimy, *Poland* 47 E6 50 38N 19 48 E
Szczucin, *Poland* 47 E8 50 18N 21 4 E
Szczuczyn, *Poland* 47 B9 53 36N 22 19 E
Szczytno, *Poland* 47 B8 53 33N 21 0 E
Szechwan = Sichuan □,
*China* 68 B5 31 0N 104 0 E
Szécsény, *Hungary* 31 C12 48 7N 19 30 E
Szeged, *Hungary* 31 E13 46 16N 20 10 E
Szeghalom, *Hungary* 31 D14 47 1N 21 10 E
Székesfehérvár, *Hungary* 31 D11 47 15N 18 25 E
Szekszárd, *Hungary* 31 E11 46 22N 18 42 E
Szendrö, *Hungary* 31 C13 48 24N 20 41 E
Szentendre, *Hungary* 31 D12 47 39N 19 4 E
Szentes, *Hungary* 31 E13 46 39N 20 21 E
Szentgotthárd, *Hungary* 31 E9 46 58N 16 19 E
Szentlörinc, *Hungary* 31 E11 46 3N 18 1 E
Szerencs, *Hungary* 31 C14 48 10N 21 12 E
Szigetvár, *Hungary* 31 E10 46 3N 17 46 E
Szikszó, *Hungary* 31 C13 48 12N 20 56 E
Szkwa →, *Poland* 47 B8 53 11N 21 43 E
Szlichtyngowa, *Poland* 47 D3 51 42N 16 15 E
Szob, *Hungary* 31 D11 47 48N 18 53 E
Szolnok, *Hungary* 31 D13 47 10N 20 15 E
Szolnok □, *Hungary* 31 D13 47 15N 20 30 E
Szombathely, *Hungary* 31 D9 47 14N 16 38 E
Szprotawa, *Poland* 47 D2 51 33N 15 35 E
Sztum, *Poland* 47 B6 53 55N 19 1 E
Sztutowo, *Poland* 47 A6 54 20N 19 15 E
Szubin, *Poland* 47 B4 53 1N 17 45 E
Szydłowiec, *Poland* 47 D7 51 15N 20 51 E
Szypliszki, *Poland* 47 A10 54 17N 23 2 E


# T


't Harde, *Neths.* 20 D7 52 24N 5 54 E
't Zandt, *Neths.* 20 B9 53 22N 6 46 E
Ta Khli Khok, *Thailand* 76 E3 15 18N 100 20 E
Ta Lai, *Vietnam* 77 G6 11 24N 107 23 E
Tabacal, *Argentina* 158 A3 23 15 S 64 15W
Tabaco, *Phil.* 70 E4 13 22N 123 44 E
Tabagné, *Ivory C.* 100 D4 7 59N 3 4W
Ţābah, *Si. Arabia* 84 E4 26 55N 42 38 E
Tabajara, *Brazil* 157 B5 8 56 S 62 8W
Tabalos, *Peru* 156 B2 6 26 S 76 37W
Tabango, *Phil.* 71 F5 11 19N 124 22 E
Tabar Is., *Papua N. G.* 120 B7 2 50 S 152 0 E
Tabarca, I. de, *Spain* 35 G4 38 17N 0 30W
Tabarka, *Tunisia* 96 A1 36 56N 8 46 E
Ţabas, *Khorāsān, Iran* 85 C9 32 48N 60 12 E
Ţabas, *Khorāsān, Iran* 85 C8 33 35N 56 55 E
Tabasará, Serranía de,
*Panama* 148 E3 8 35N 81 40W
Tabasco □, *Mexico* 147 D6 17 45N 93 30W
Tabatinga, Serra da,
*Brazil* 154 D3 10 30 S 44 0W
Tabayin, *Burma* 78 D5 22 42N 95 20 E
Tabāzīn, *Iran* 85 D8 31 12N 57 54 E
Tabelbala, Kahal de,
*Algeria* 99 C4 28 47N 2 0W
Taber, *Canada* 130 D6 49 47N 112 8W
Tabernas, *Spain* 35 H2 37 4N 2 26W
Tabernes de Valldigna,
*Spain* 35 F4 39 5N 0 13W
Tabi, *Angola* 103 D2 8 10 S 13 18 E
Tabira, *Brazil* 154 C4 7 35 S 37 33W
Tablas, *Phil.* 70 E4 12 25N 122 2 E
Tablas Strait, *Phil.* 70 E3 12 40N 121 48 E
Table B. = Tafelbaai,
*S. Africa* 104 E2 33 35 S 18 25 E
Table B., *Canada* 129 B8 53 40N 56 25W
Table Grove, *U.S.A.* 140 D6 40 20N 90 27W
Table Mt., *S. Africa* 104 E2 34 0 S 18 22 E
Tableland, *Australia* 112 C4 17 16 S 126 51 E
Tabletop, Mt., *Australia* 114 C4 23 24 S 147 11 E
Tabogon, *Phil.* 71 F5 10 57N 124 2 E
Tábor, *Czech.* 30 B7 49 25N 14 39 E
Tabora, *Tanzania* 106 D3 5 2 S 32 50 E
Tabora □, *Tanzania* 106 D3 5 0 S 33 0 E
Tabory, *Russia* 54 B9 58 31N 64 33 E
Tabou, *Ivory C.* 100 E3 4 30N 7 20W
Tabrīz, *Iran* 84 B5 38 7N 46 20 E
Tabuaeran, *Pac. Oc.* 123 G12 3 51N 159 22W
Tabuelan, *Phil.* 71 F4 10 49N 123 52 E
Tabuenca, *Spain* 34 D3 41 42N 1 33W
Tabuk, *Phil.* 70 C3 17 24N 121 25 E
Tabūk, *Si. Arabia* 84 D3 28 23N 36 36 E
Tabwemasana, Mt.,
*Vanuatu* 121 E4 15 20 S 166 44 E
Tacámbaro de Codallos,
*Mexico* 146 D4 19 14N 101 28W
Tacheng, *China* 64 B3 46 40N 82 58 E
Tachibana-Wan, *Japan* 62 E2 32 45N 130 7 E
Tachikawa, *Japan* 63 B11 35 42N 139 25 E
Tach'ing Shan = Daqing
Shan, *China* 66 D6 40 40N 111 0 E
Táchira □, *Venezuela* 152 B3 8 7N 72 15W
Tachov, *Czech.* 30 B5 49 47N 12 39 E
Tácina →, *Italy* 41 D9 38 57N 16 55 E
Tacloban, *Phil.* 71 F5 11 15N 124 58 E
Tacna, *Peru* 156 D3 18 0 S 70 20W
Tacna □, *Peru* 156 D3 17 40 S 70 20W
Tacoma, *U.S.A.* 144 C4 47 14N 122 26W
Tacuarembó, *Uruguay* 159 C4 31 45 S 56 0W
Tacutu →, *Brazil* 153 C5 3 1N 60 29W
Tademaït, Plateau du,
*Algeria* 99 C5 28 30N 2 30 E
Tadent, O. →, *Algeria* 99 D6 22 25N 6 40 E
Tadjerdjeri, O. →,
*Algeria* 99 C6 26 0N 8 0 E
Tadjerouna, *Algeria* 99 B5 33 31N 2 3 E
Tadjettaret, O. →,
*Algeria* 99 D6 21 20N 7 22 E
Tadjmout, *Oasis, Algeria* 99 B5 33 52N 2 30 E
Tadjmout, *Saoura, Algeria* 99 C5 25 37N 3 48 E
Tadjoura, *Djibouti* 90 E3 11 50N 42 55 E
Tadjoura, Golfe de,
*Djibouti* 95 E5 11 50N 43 0 E
Tadmor, *N.Z.* 119 B7 41 27 S 172 45 E
Tadotsu, *Japan* 62 C5 34 16N 133 45 E
Tadoule, L., *Canada* 131 B9 58 36N 98 20W
Tadoussac, *Canada* 129 C6 48 11N 69 42W
Tadzhikistan =
Tajikistan ■, *Asia* 55 D5 38 30N 70 0 E
Taechŏn-ni, *S. Korea* 67 F14 36 21N 126 36 E
Taegu, *S. Korea* 67 G15 35 50N 128 37 E
Taegwan, *N. Korea* 67 D13 40 13N 125 12 E
Taejŏn, *S. Korea* 67 F14 36 20N 127 28 E
Tafalla, *Spain* 34 C3 42 30N 1 41W
Tafar, *Sudan* 95 F2 6 52N 28 15 E
Tafassasset, O. →,
*Algeria* 99 D6 22 0N 9 57 E
Tafelbaai, *S. Africa* 104 E2 33 35 S 18 25 E
Tafelney, C., *Morocco* 98 B3 31 3N 9 51W
Tafermaar, *Indonesia* 73 C4 6 47 S 134 10 E
Taffermit, *Morocco* 98 C3 29 37N 9 15W
Tafí Viejo, *Argentina* 158 B2 26 43 S 65 17W
Tafīhān, *Iran* 85 D7 29 25N 52 39 E
Tafiré, *Ivory C.* 100 D3 9 4N 5 4W
Tafnidilt, *Morocco* 98 C2 28 47N 10 58W
Tafraoute, *Morocco* 98 C3 29 50N 8 58W
Taft, *Iran* 85 D7 31 45N 54 14 E
Taft, *Phil.* 71 F5 11 57N 125 30 E
Taft, *Calif., U.S.A.* 145 K7 35 8N 119 28W
Taft, *Tex., U.S.A.* 139 M6 27 59N 97 24W
Taga, *W. Samoa* 121 W23 13 46 S 172 28W
Taga Dzong, *Bhutan* 78 B2 27 5N 89 55 E
Tagana-an, *Phil.* 71 G5 9 42N 125 35 E
Taganrog, *Russia* 53 C8 47 12N 38 50 E
Taganrogskiy Zaliv, *Russia* 52 C8 47 0N 38 30 E
Tagânt, *Mauritania* 100 B2 18 20N 11 0W
Tagap Ga, *Burma* 78 B6 26 56N 96 13 E
Tagapula I., *Phil.* 70 E5 12 4N 124 12 E
Tagatay, *Phil.* 70 D3 14 6N 120 56 E
Tagauayan I., *Phil.* 71 F3 10 58N 121 13 E
Tagbilaran, *Phil.* 71 G4 9 39N 123 51 E
Tage, *Papua N. G.* 120 D2 6 19 S 143 20 E
Tággia, *Italy* 38 E4 43 52N 7 50 E
Taghrīfat, *Libya* 96 C3 29 5N 17 26 E
Taghzout, *Morocco* 98 B4 33 30N 4 49W
Tagish, *Canada* 130 A2 60 19N 134 16W
Tagish L., *Canada* 130 A2 60 10N 134 20W
Tagkawayan, *Phil.* 70 E4 13 58N 122 32 E
Tagliacozzo, *Italy* 39 F10 42 4N 13 13 E
Tagliamento →, *Italy* 39 C10 45 38N 13 5 E
Táglio di Po, *Italy* 39 D9 45 0N 12 12 E
Tagna, *Colombia* 152 D3 2 24 S 70 37W
Tago, *Phil.* 71 G6 9 2N 126 13 E
Tago, Mt., *Phil.* 71 G5 8 23N 125 5 E
Tagomago, I. de, *Spain* 33 B8 39 2N 1 39 E
Taguatinga, *Brazil* 155 D3 12 16 S 42 26W
Tagudin, *Phil.* 70 C3 16 56N 120 27 E
Tagula, *Papua N. G.* 120 F7 11 22 S 153 15 E
Tagula I., *Papua N. G.* 120 F7 11 30 S 153 30 E
Tagum, *Phil.* 71 H5 7 33N 125 53 E
Tagus = Tejo →, *Europe* 37 G1 38 40N 9 24W
Tahakopa, *N.Z.* 119 G4 46 30 S 169 23 E
Tahala, *Morocco* 98 B4 34 0N 4 28W
Tahan, Gunong, *Malaysia* 77 K4 4 34N 102 17 E
Tahānah-ye sūr Gol,
*Afghan.* 79 C2 31 43N 67 53 E
Tahara, *Japan* 63 C9 34 40N 137 16 E
Tahat, *Algeria* 99 D6 23 18N 5 33 E
Tāherī, *Iran* 85 E7 27 43N 52 20 E
Tahiti, *Pac. Oc.* 123 J13 17 37 S 149 27W
Tahoe, L., *U.S.A.* 144 G6 39 6N 120 2W
Tahoe City, *U.S.A.* 144 F6 39 10N 120 9W
Taholah, *U.S.A.* 144 C2 47 21N 124 17W
Tahora, *N.Z.* 118 F3 39 2 S 174 49 E
Tahoua, *Niger* 101 C6 14 57N 5 16 E
Tahta, *Egypt* 94 B3 26 44N 31 32 E
Tahtali Dağları, *Turkey* 88 D6 38 20N 36 0 E
Tahuamanu →, *Bolivia* 156 C4 11 6 S 67 36W
Tahulandang, *Indonesia* 72 A3 2 27N 125 23 E
Tahuna, *Indonesia* 72 A3 3 38N 125 30 E
Taï, *Ivory C.* 100 D3 5 55N 7 30W
Tai Shan, *China* 67 F9 36 25N 117 20 E
Tai Xian, *China* 69 A13 32 30N 120 7 E
Tai'an, *China* 67 F9 36 12N 117 8 E
Taibei, *Taiwan* 69 E13 25 4N 121 29 E
Taibique, *Canary Is.* 33 G2 27 42N 17 58W
Taibus Qi, *China* 66 D8 41 54N 115 22 E
T'aichung = Taizhong,
*Taiwan* 69 E13 24 12N 120 35 E
Taidong, *Taiwan* 69 F13 22 43N 121 9 E
Taieri →, *N.Z.* 119 G5 46 3 S 170 12 E
Taiga Madema, *Libya* 96 D3 23 46N 15 25 E
Taigu, *China* 66 F7 37 28N 112 30 E
Taihang Shan, *China* 66 G7 36 0N 113 30 E
Taihape, *N.Z.* 118 F4 39 41 S 175 48 E
Taihe, *Anhui, China* 66 H8 33 20N 115 42 E
Taihe, *Jiangxi, China* 69 D10 26 47N 114 52 E
Taihu, *China* 69 B11 30 22N 116 20 E
Taijiang, *China* 68 D7 26 39N 108 21 E
Taikang, *China* 66 G8 34 5N 114 50 E
Taikkyi, *Burma* 78 G6 17 20N 96 0 E
Tailem Bend, *Australia* 116 C3 35 12 S 139 29 E
Tailfingen, *Germany* 27 G5 48 15N 9 1 E
Taimyr Peninsula =
Taymyr, Poluostrov,
*Russia* 57 B11 75 0N 100 0 E
Tain, *U.K.* 18 D4 57 49N 4 4W
Tainan, *Taiwan* 69 F13 23 17N 120 18 E
Taínaron, Ákra, *Greece* 45 H4 36 22N 22 27 E
Tainggyo, *Burma* 78 G5 17 49N 94 29 E
Taining, *China* 69 D11 26 54N 117 9 E
Taintignies, *Belgium* 21 G2 50 33N 3 22 E
Taiobeiras, *Brazil* 155 E3 15 49 S 42 14W
T'aipei = Taibei, *Taiwan* 69 E13 25 4N 121 29 E
T'aipei, *Taiwan* 65 D7 25 2N 121 30 E
Taiping, *China* 69 B12 30 15N 118 6 E
Taiping, *Malaysia* 77 K3 4 51N 100 44 E
Taipingzhen, *China* 66 H6 33 35N 111 42 E
Taipu, *Brazil* 154 C4 5 37 S 35 36W
Taisha, *Japan* 62 B4 35 24N 132 40 E
Taishan, *China* 69 F9 22 14N 112 41 E
Taishun, *China* 69 D12 27 30N 119 42 E
Taita □, *Kenya* 106 C4 4 0 S 38 30 E
Taita Hills, *Kenya* 106 C4 3 25 S 38 15 E
Taitao, C., *Chile* 160 C1 45 53 S 75 5W
Taitao, Pen. de, *Chile* 160 C2 46 30 S 75 0W
Taivalkoski, *Finland* 12 D20 65 33N 28 12 E
Taiwan ■, *Asia* 69 F13 23 30N 121 0 E
Taiwan Shan, *Taiwan* 69 F13 23 40N 121 20 E
Taixing, *China* 69 A13 32 11N 120 0 E
Taïyetos Óros, *Greece* 45 H4 37 0N 22 23 E
Taiyiba, *Israel* 91 C4 32 36N 35 27 E
Taiyuan, *China* 66 F7 37 52N 112 33 E
Taizhong, *Taiwan* 69 E13 24 12N 120 35 E
Taizhou, *China* 69 A12 32 28N 119 55 E
Taizhou Liedao, *China* 69 C13 28 30N 121 55 E
Ta'izz, *Yemen* 86 D4 13 35N 44 2 E
Tājābād, *Iran* 85 D7 30 2N 54 24 E
Tajapuru, Furo do, *Brazil* 154 B1 1 50 S 50 25W
Tajarḥī, *Libya* 96 D2 24 21N 14 28 E
Tajikistan ■, *Asia* 55 D5 38 30N 70 0 E
Tajima, *Japan* 61 F9 37 12N 139 46 E
Tajimi, *Japan* 63 B9 35 19N 137 8 E
Tajo = Tejo →, *Europe* 37 G1 38 40N 9 24W
Tajrīsh, *Iran* 85 C6 35 48N 51 25 E
Tājūrā, *Libya* 96 B2 32 51N 13 21 E
Tak, *Thailand* 76 D2 16 52N 99 8 E
Takāb, *Iran* 84 B5 36 24N 47 7 E
Takachiho, *Japan* 62 E3 32 42N 131 18 E
Takada, *Japan* 61 F9 37 7N 138 15 E
Takahagi, *Japan* 61 F10 36 43N 140 45 E
Takahashi, *Japan* 62 C5 34 51N 133 39 E
Takaka, *N.Z.* 119 A7 40 51 S 172 50 E
Takamatsu, *Japan* 62 C6 34 20N 134 5 E
Takanabe, *Japan* 62 E3 32 8N 131 30 E
Takaoka, *Japan* 63 A8 36 47N 137 0 E
Takapau, *N.Z.* 118 G5 40 2 S 176 21 E
Takapuna, *N.Z.* 118 C3 36 47 S 174 47 E
Takasago, *Japan* 62 C6 34 45N 134 48 E
Takasaki, *Japan* 63 A10 36 20N 139 0 E
Takase, *Japan* 62 C5 34 7N 133 48 E
Takatsuki, *Japan* 63 C7 34 51N 135 37 E
Takaungu, *Kenya* 106 C4 3 38 S 39 52 E
Takawa, *Japan* 62 D2 33 38N 130 51 E
Takayama, *Japan* 63 A9 36 18N 137 11 E
Takayama-Bonchi, *Japan* 63 B9 36 0N 137 18 E
Take-Shima, *Japan* 61 J5 30 49N 130 26 E
Takefu, *Japan* 63 B8 35 50N 136 10 E
Takehara, *Japan* 62 C4 34 21N 132 55 E
Takengon, *Indonesia* 74 B1 4 45N 96 50 E
Takeo, *Cambodia* 77 G5 10 59N 104 47 E
Takeo, *Japan* 62 D2 33 12N 130 1 E
Tåkern, *Sweden* 15 F8 58 22N 14 45 E
Tākestān, *Iran* 85 C6 36 0N 49 40 E
Taketa, *Japan* 62 E3 32 58N 131 24 E
Takh, *India* 81 C7 33 6N 77 32 E
Takhār □, *Afghan.* 79 A3 36 40N 70 0 E
Takhman, *Cambodia* 77 G5 11 29N 104 57 E
Taki, *Papua N. G.* 120 D8 6 29 S 155 52 E
Takikawa, *Japan* 60 C10 43 33N 141 54 E
Takla L., *Canada* 130 B3 55 15N 125 45W
Takla Landing, *Canada* 130 B3 55 30N 125 50W
Takla Makan =
Taklamakan Shamo,
*China* 58 F12 38 0N 83 0 E
Taklamakan Shamo, *China* 58 F12 38 0N 83 0 E
Taku, *Japan* 62 D2 33 18N 130 3 E
Taku →, *Canada* 130 B2 58 30N 133 50W
Takum, *Nigeria* 101 D6 7 18N 9 36 E
Takuma, *Japan* 62 C5 34 13N 133 40 E
Takundi, *Zaïre* 103 C3 4 45 S 16 34 E
Takuran, *Phil.* 71 H4 7 51N 123 34 E
Takutu →, *Guyana* 153 C5 3 1N 60 29W
Tal Halāl, *Iran* 85 D7 28 54N 55 1 E
Tala, *Uruguay* 159 C4 34 21 S 55 46W
Talacogan, *Phil.* 71 G5 8 32N 125 39 E
Talagante, *Chile* 158 C1 33 40 S 70 50W
Talaïnt, *Morocco* 98 C3 29 41N 9 40W
Talak, *Niger* 101 B6 18 0N 5 0 E
Talakag, *Phil.* 71 G5 8 16N 124 37 E
Talamanca, Cordillera de,
*Cent. Amer.* 148 E3 9 20N 83 20W
Talara, *Peru* 156 A1 4 38 S 81 18W
Talas, *Kirghizia* 55 B6 42 30N 72 13 E
Talas, *Turkey* 88 D6 38 41N 35 33 E
Talas →, *Kazakhstan* 55 B5 44 0N 70 20 E
Talasea, *Papua N. G.* 120 C6 5 20 S 150 2 E
Talasskiy Alatau, Khrebet,
*Kirghizia* 55 B6 42 15N 72 0 E
Talâta, *Egypt* 91 E1 30 36N 32 20 E
Talata Mafara, *Nigeria* 101 C6 12 38N 6 4 E
Talaud, Kepulauan,
*Indonesia* 72 A3 4 30N 127 10 E
Talaud Is. = Talaud,
Kepulauan, *Indonesia* 72 A3 4 30N 127 10 E
Talavera de la Reina,
*Spain* 36 F6 39 55N 4 46W
Talawana, *Australia* 112 D3 22 51 S 121 9 E
Talawgyi, *Burma* 78 C6 25 4N 97 19 E
Talayan, *Phil.* 71 H5 6 52N 124 24 E
Talbert, Sillon de, *France* 22 D3 48 53N 3 5W
Talbot, C., *Australia* 112 B4 13 48 S 126 43 E
Talbragar →, *Australia* 117 B8 32 12 S 148 37 E
Talca, *Chile* 158 D1 35 28 S 71 40W
Talca □, *Chile* 158 D1 35 20 S 71 46W
Talcahuano, *Chile* 158 D1 36 40 S 73 10W
Talcher, *India* 82 D7 21 0N 85 18 E
Talcho, *Niger* 101 C5 14 44N 3 28 E
Taldy Kurgan, *Kazakhstan* 56 E8 45 10N 78 45 E
Taldyqorghan = Taldy
Kurgan, *Kazakhstan* 56 E8 45 10N 78 45 E
Talesh, *Iran* 85 B6 37 58N 48 58 E
Ţalesh, Kūhhā-ye, *Iran* 85 B6 39 0N 48 30 E
Talgar, *Kazakhstan* 55 B8 43 19N 77 15 E
Talgar, Pik, *Kazakhstan* 55 B8 43 5N 77 20 E
Talguharai, *Sudan* 94 D4 18 19N 35 56 E
Tali Post, *Sudan* 95 F3 5 55N 30 44 E
Taliabu, *Indonesia* 72 B2 1 45 S 124 55 E
Talibon, *Phil.* 71 F5 10 9N 124 20 E
Talibong, Ko, *Thailand* 77 J2 7 15N 99 23 E
Talihina, *U.S.A.* 139 H7 34 45N 95 3W
Talikota, *India* 83 F3 16 29N 76 17 E
Talimardzhan,
*Turkmenistan* 55 D2 38 23N 65 37 E
Talisay, *Phil.* 71 F4 10 44N 122 58 E
Talisayan, *Phil.* 71 G5 9 0N 124 55 E
Talitsa, *Russia* 54 C8 57 0N 63 43 E
Taliwang, *Indonesia* 72 C1 8 50 S 116 55 E
Tall 'Asūr, *Jordan* 91 D4 31 59N 35 17 E
Tall Kalakh, *Syria* 91 A5 34 41N 36 15 E
Talla, *Egypt* 94 J7 28 5N 30 43 E
Talladega, *U.S.A.* 135 J2 33 26N 86 6W
Tallahassee, *U.S.A.* 135 K3 30 27N 84 17W
Tallangatta, *Australia* 117 D7 36 15 S 147 19 E
Tallarook, *Australia* 117 D6 37 5 S 145 6 E
Tallawang, *Australia* 117 B8 32 12 S 149 28 E
Tallering Pk., *Australia* 113 E2 28 6 S 115 37 E
Tallinn, *Estonia* 50 B4 59 22N 24 48 E
Tallulah, *U.S.A.* 139 J9 32 25N 91 11W
Tălmaciu, *Romania* 46 D5 45 38N 24 19 E
Talmest, *Morocco* 98 B3 31 48N 9 21W
Talmont, *France* 24 B2 46 27N 1 37W
Talnoye, *Ukraine* 52 B4 48 50N 30 44 E
Taloda, *India* 82 D2 21 34N 74 11 E
Talodi, *Sudan* 95 E3 10 35N 30 22 E
Talomo, *Phil.* 71 H5 7 3N 125 32 E
Talovaya, *Russia* 51 F12 51 6N 40 45 E
Talpa de Allende, *Mexico* 146 C4 20 23N 104 51W
Tālqān, *Afghan.* 79 A3 36 44N 69 33 E
Talsi, *Latvia* 50 C3 57 10N 22 30 E
Talsinnt, *Morocco* 99 B4 32 33N 3 27W
Taltal, *Chile* 158 B1 25 23 S 70 33W
Taltson →, *Canada* 130 A6 61 24N 112 46W
Talwood, *Australia* 115 D4 28 29 S 149 29 E
Talyawalka Cr. →,
*Australia* 116 B5 32 28 S 142 22 E
Tam Chau, *Vietnam* 77 G5 10 48N 105 12 E
Tam Ky, *Vietnam* 76 E7 15 34N 108 29 E
Tam Quan, *Vietnam* 76 E7 14 35N 109 3 E
Tama, *U.S.A.* 140 C4 41 58N 92 35W
Tamala, *Australia* 113 E1 26 42 S 113 47 E
Tamalameque, *Colombia* 152 B3 8 52N 73 49W
Tamale, *Ghana* 101 D4 9 22N 0 50W
Taman, *Russia* 52 D7 45 14N 36 41 E
Tamana, *Japan* 62 E2 32 58N 130 32 E
Tamanar, *Morocco* 98 B3 31 1N 9 46W
Tamano, *Japan* 62 C5 34 29N 133 59 E
Tamanrasset, *Algeria* 99 D6 22 50N 5 30 E
Tamanrasset, O. →,
*Algeria* 99 D5 22 0N 2 0 E
Tamanthi, *Burma* 78 C5 25 19N 95 17 E
Tamaqua, *U.S.A.* 137 F9 40 48N 75 58W
Tamar →, *U.K.* 17 G3 50 33N 4 15W
Támara, *Colombia* 152 B3 5 50N 72 10W
Tamarang, *Australia* 117 A9 31 27 S 150 5 E
Tamarinda, *Spain* 33 B10 39 55N 3 49 E
Tamarite de Litera, *Spain* 34 D5 41 52N 0 25 E
Tamaroa, *U.S.A.* 140 F7 38 8N 89 14W
Tamashima, *Japan* 62 C5 34 32N 133 40 E
Tamási, *Hungary* 31 E11 46 40N 18 18 E
Tamaské, *Niger* 101 C6 14 49N 5 43 E
Tamaulipas □, *Mexico* 147 C5 24 0N 99 0W
Tamaulipas, Sierra de,
*Mexico* 147 C5 23 30N 98 20W
Tamazula, *Mexico* 146 C3 24 55N 106 58W
Tamazunchale, *Mexico* 147 C5 21 16N 98 47W
Tamba-Dabatou, *Guinea* 100 C2 11 50N 10 40W
Tambacounda, *Senegal* 100 C2 13 45N 13 40W
Tambelan, Kepulauan,
*Indonesia* 74 B3 1 0N 107 30 E
Tambellup, *Australia* 113 F2 34 4 S 117 37 E
Tambo, *Australia* 114 C4 24 54 S 146 14 E
Tambo, *Peru* 156 C3 12 57 S 74 1W
Tambo →, *Peru* 156 C3 10 42 S 73 47W
Tambo de Mora, *Peru* 156 C2 13 30 S 76 8W
Tambobamba, *Peru* 156 C3 13 54 S 72 8W
Tambohorano, *Madag.* 105 B7 17 30 S 43 58 E
Tambopata →, *Peru* 156 C4 13 21 S 69 36W
Tambora, *Indonesia* 72 C1 8 12 S 118 5 E
Tamboritha, Mt., *Australia* 117 D7 37 31 S 146 40 E
Tambov, *Russia* 51 E12 52 45N 41 28 E
Tambre →, *Spain* 36 C2 42 49N 8 53W
Tambuku, *Indonesia* 75 D4 7 8 S 113 40 E
Tambun Sigumbal, *Phil.* 71 H3 6 5N 121 47 E
Tamburâ, *Sudan* 95 F2 5 40N 27 25 E
Tambuyukan, Gunong,
*Malaysia* 75 A5 6 13N 116 39 E
Tâmchekket, *Mauritania* 100 B2 17 25N 10 40W
Tamdybulak, *Uzbekistan* 55 C2 41 46N 64 36 E
Tame, *Colombia* 152 B3 6 28N 71 44W
Tamega →, *Portugal* 36 D2 41 5N 8 21W
Tamelelt, *Morocco* 98 B3 31 50N 7 32W
Tamenglong, *India* 78 C4 25 0N 93 35 E
Tamerlanovka,
*Kazakhstan* 55 B4 42 36N 69 17 E
Tamerza, *Tunisia* 96 B1 34 23N 7 58 E

272 Tamiahua, L. de


Tamiahua, L. de, *Mexico* **147 C5** 21 30N 97 30W
Tamil Nadu □, *India* **83 J3** 11 0N 77 0 E
Tamines, *Belgium* **21 H5** 50 26N 4 36 E
Tamis →, *Serbia* **46 E1** 44 51N 20 39 E
Tamluk, *India* **81 H12** 22 18N 87 58 E
Tammerfors = Tampere, *Finland* **13 F17** 61 30N 23 50 E
Tammisaari, *Finland* **13 F17** 60 0N 23 26 E
Tamo Abu, Pegunungan, *Malaysia* **75 B5** 3 10N 115 5 E
Tampa, *U.S.A.* **135 M4** 27 57N 82 27W
Tampa B., *U.S.A.* **135 M4** 27 50N 82 30W
Tampere, *Finland* **13 F17** 61 30N 23 50 E
Tampico, *Mexico* **147 C5** 22 20N 97 50W
Tampico, *U.S.A.* **140 C7** 41 38N 89 47W
Tampin, *Malaysia* **77 L4** 2 28N 102 13 E
Tamrah, *Si. Arabia* **86 B4** 20 24N 45 25 E
Tamri, *Morocco* **98 B3** 30 49N 9 50W
Tamrida = Qādib, *Yemen* **87 D6** 12 37N 53 57 E
Tamsalu, *Estonia* **50 B5** 59 11N 26 8 E
Tamsweg, *Austria* **30 D6** 47 7N 13 49 E
Tamuja →, *Spain* **37 F4** 39 38N 6 29W
Tamworth, *Australia* **117 A9** 31 7 S 150 58 E
Tamworth, *U.K.* **17 E6** 52 38N 1 41W
Tamyang, *S. Korea* **67 G14** 35 19N 126 59 E
Tan An, *Vietnam* **77 G6** 10 32N 106 25 E
Tan-tan, *Morocco* **98 C2** 28 29N 11 1W
Tana, *Norway* **12 A20** 70 26N 28 14 E
Tana →, *Kenya* **106 C5** 2 32 S 40 31 E
Tana →, *Norway* **12 A20** 70 30N 28 23 E
Tana, L., *Ethiopia* **95 E4** 13 5N 37 30 E
Tana River, *Kenya* **106 C4** 2 0 S 39 30 E
Tanabe, *Japan* **63 D7** 33 44N 135 22 E
Tanabi, *Brazil* **155 F2** 20 37 S 49 37W
Tanafjorden, *Norway* **12 A20** 70 45N 28 25 E
Tanaga, Pta., *Canary Is.* **33 G1** 27 42N 18 10W
Tanagro →, *Italy* **41 B8** 40 35N 15 25 E
Tanah Merah, *Malaysia* **74 A2** 5 48N 102 9 E
Tanahbala, *Indonesia* **74 C1** 0 30 S 98 30 E
Tanahgrogot, *Indonesia* **75 C5** 1 55 S 116 15 E
Tanahjampea, *Indonesia* **72 C2** 7 10 S 120 35 E
Tanahmasa, *Indonesia* **74 C1** 0 12 S 98 39 E
Tanahmerah, *Indonesia* **73 C6** 6 5 S 140 16 E
Tanakura, *Japan* **61 F10** 37 10N 140 20 E
Tanami, *Australia* **112 C4** 19 59 S 129 43 E
Tanami Desert, *Australia* **112 C5** 18 50 S 132 0 E
Tanana, *U.S.A.* **126 B4** 65 10N 152 4W
Tanana →, *U.S.A.* **126 B4** 65 10N 151 58W
Tananarive = Antananarivo, *Madag.* **105 B8** 18 55 S 47 31 E
Tanannt, *Morocco* **98 B3** 31 54N 6 56W
Tánaro →, *Italy* **38 C5** 45 1N 8 47 E
Tanauan, *Batangas, Phil.* **70 D3** 14 5N 121 10 E
Tanauan, *Leyte, Phil.* **71 F5** 11 7N 125 1 E
Tanaunella, *Italy* **40 B2** 40 42N 9 45 E
Tanay, *Phil.* **70 D3** 14 30N 121 17 E
Tanba-Sanchi, *Japan* **63 B7** 35 7N 135 48 E
Tanbar, *Australia* **114 D3** 25 51 S 141 55 E
Tancarville, *France* **22 C7** 49 29N 0 28 E
Tancheng, *China* **67 G10** 34 25N 118 20 E
Tanchŏn, *N. Korea* **67 D15** 40 27N 128 54 E
Tanda, *Ut. P., India* **81 F10** 26 33N 82 35 E
Tanda, *Ut. P., India* **81 E8** 28 57N 78 56 E
Tanda, *Ivory C.* **100 D4** 7 48N 3 10W
Tandag, *Phil.* **71 G6** 9 4N 126 9 E
Tandaia, *Tanzania* **107 D3** 9 25 S 34 15 E
Tăndărei, *Romania* **46 E8** 44 39N 27 40 E
Tandaué, *Angola* **103 F3** 16 58 S 18 5 E
Tandil, *Argentina* **158 D4** 37 15 S 59 6W
Tandil, Sa. del, *Argentina* **158 D4** 37 30 S 59 0W
Tandlianwala, *Pakistan* **80 D5** 31 3N 73 9 E
Tando Adam, *Pakistan* **79 D3** 25 45N 68 40 E
Tandou L., *Australia* **116 B5** 32 40 S 142 5 E
Tandsbyn, *Sweden* **14 A8** 63 3N 14 45 E
Tandur, *India* **82 E4** 19 11N 79 30 E
Tane-ga-Shima, *Japan* **61 J5** 30 30N 131 0 E
Taneatua, *N.Z.* **118 E6** 38 4 S 177 1 E
Tanen Tong Dan, *Burma* **76 D2** 16 30N 98 30 E
Tanew →, *Poland* **47 E9** 50 29N 22 16 E
Tanezrouft, *Algeria* **99 D5** 23 9N 0 11 E
Tang, Koh, *Cambodia* **77 G4** 10 16N 103 7 E
Tang Krasang, *Cambodia* **76 F5** 12 34N 105 3 E
Tanga, *Tanzania* **106 D4** 5 5 S 39 2 E
Tanga □, *Tanzania* **106 D4** 5 20 S 38 0 E
Tanga Is., *Papua N. G.* **120 B7** 3 20 S 153 15 E
Tangail, *Bangla.* **78 C2** 24 15N 89 55 E
Tanganyika, L., *Africa* **106 D2** 6 40 S 30 0 E
Tangawan, *Phil.* **71 H4** 7 30N 122 20 E
Tanger, *Morocco* **98 A3** 35 50N 5 49W
Tangerang, *Indonesia* **74 D3** 6 11 S 106 37 E
Tangerhütte, *Germany* **26 C7** 52 26N 11 50 E
Tangermünde, *Germany* **26 C7** 52 32N 11 57 E
Tanggu, *China* **67 E9** 39 2N 117 40 E
Tanggula Shan, *China* **64 C4** 32 40N 92 10 E
Tanghe, *China* **66 H7** 32 47N 112 50 E
Tangier = Tanger, *Morocco* **98 A3** 35 50N 5 49W
Tangkeleboke, *Indonesia* **72 B2** 3 10 S 121 30 E
Tangorin P.O., *Australia* **114 C3** 21 47 S 144 12 E
Tangshan, *China* **67 E10** 39 38N 118 10 E
Tangtou, *China* **67 G10** 35 28N 118 30 E
Tangub, *Phil.* **71 G4** 8 3N 123 44 E
Tanguiéta, *Benin* **101 C5** 10 35N 1 21 E
Tangxi, *China* **69 C12** 29 3N 119 25 E
Tangyan He →, *China* **68 C7** 28 54N 108 19 E
Tanimbar, Kepulauan, *Indonesia* **73 C4** 7 30 S 131 30 E
Tanimbar Is. = Tanimbar, Kepulauan, *Indonesia* **73 C4** 7 30 S 131 30 E
Taninges, *France* **25 B10** 46 7N 6 36 E
Taniyama, *Japan* **62 F2** 31 31N 130 31 E
Tanjay, *Phil.* **71 G4** 9 30N 123 5 E
Tanjong Malim, *Malaysia* **77 L3** 3 42N 101 31 E
Tanjore = Thanjavur, *India* **83 J4** 10 48N 79 12 E
Tanjung, *Indonesia* **75 C5** 2 10 S 115 25 E
Tanjungbalai, *Indonesia* **74 B1** 2 55N 99 44 E
Tanjungbatu, *Indonesia* **75 B5** 2 23N 118 3 E
Tanjungkarang Telukbetung, *Indonesia* **74 D3** 5 20 S 105 10 E
Tanjungpandan, *Indonesia* **75 C3** 2 43 S 107 38 E
Tanjungpinang, *Indonesia* **74 B2** 1 5N 104 30 E
Tanjungpriok, *Indonesia* **74 D3** 6 8 S 106 55 E
Tanjungredeb, *Indonesia* **75 B5** 2 9N 117 29 E
Tanjungselor, *Indonesia* **75 B5** 2 55N 117 25 E
Tank, *Pakistan* **79 B3** 32 14N 70 25 E
Tanna, *Vanuatu* **121 J7** 19 30 S 169 20 E
Tänndalen, *Sweden* **14 B6** 62 33N 12 18 E
Tannis Bugt, *Denmark* **15 G4** 57 40N 10 15 E
Tannu-Ola, *Russia* **57 D10** 51 0N 94 0 E
Tano →, *Ghana* **100 D4** 5 7N 2 56W
Tanon Str., *Phil.* **71 F4** 10 20N 123 30 E
Tanout, *Niger* **97 F1** 14 50N 8 55 E
Tanquinho, *Brazil* **155 D4** 11 58 S 39 6W
Tanta, *Egypt* **94 H7** 30 45N 30 57 E
Tantoyuca, *Mexico* **147 C5** 21 21N 98 10W
Tantung = Dandong, *China* **67 D13** 40 10N 124 20 E
Tanuku, *India* **82 F5** 16 45N 81 44 E
Tanumshede, *Sweden* **15 F5** 58 42N 11 20 E
Tanunda, *Australia* **116 C3** 34 30 S 139 0 E
Tanur, *India* **83 J2** 11 1N 75 52 E
Tanus, *France* **24 D6** 44 8N 2 19 E
Tanyeri, *Turkey* **89 D8** 39 36N 39 51 E
Tanza, *Phil.* **70 D3** 14 41N 120 56 E
Tanzania ■, *Africa* **106 D3** 6 0 S 34 0 E
Tanzawa-Sanchi, *Japan* **63 B11** 35 27N 139 0 E
Tanzilla →, *Canada* **130 B2** 58 8N 130 43W
Tao Ko, *Thailand* **77 G2** 10 5N 99 52 E
Tao'an, *China* **67 B12** 45 22N 122 40 E
Tao'er He →, *China* **67 B13** 45 45N 124 5 E
Taohua Dao, *China* **69 C14** 29 50N 122 20 E
Taolanaro, *Madag.* **105 D8** 25 2 S 47 0 E
Taole, *China* **66 E4** 38 48N 106 40 E
Taormina, *Italy* **41 E8** 37 52N 15 16 E
Taos, *U.S.A.* **143 H11** 36 24N 105 35W
Taoudenni, *Mali* **98 D4** 22 40N 3 55W
Taoudrart, Adrar, *Algeria* **99 D5** 24 25N 2 24 E
Taounate, *Morocco* **98 B4** 34 25N 4 41W
Taourirt, *Algeria* **99 C5** 26 37N 0 20 E
Taourirt, *Morocco* **99 B4** 34 25N 2 53W
Taouz, *Morocco* **98 B4** 30 53N 4 0W
Taoyuan, *China* **69 C8** 28 55N 111 16 E
Taoyuan, *Taiwan* **69 E13** 25 0N 121 13 E
Tapa, *Estonia* **50 B4** 59 15N 25 50 E
Tapa Shan = Daba Shan, *China* **68 B7** 32 0N 109 0 E
Tapachula, *Mexico* **147 E6** 14 54N 92 17W
Tapah, *Malaysia* **77 K3** 4 12N 101 15 E
Tapajós →, *Brazil* **153 D7** 2 24 S 54 41W
Tapaktuan, *Indonesia* **74 B1** 3 15N 97 10 E
Tapanahoni →, *Surinam* **153 C7** 4 20N 54 25W
Tapanui, *N.Z.* **119 F4** 45 56 S 169 18 E
Tapauá, *Brazil* **157 B5** 5 40 S 64 20W
Tapauá →, *Brazil* **157 B5** 5 40 S 64 21W
Tapaz, *Phil.* **71 F4** 11 16N 122 32 E
Tapeta, *Liberia* **100 D3** 6 29N 8 52W
Taphan Hin, *Thailand* **76 D3** 16 13N 100 26 E
Tapi →, *India* **82 D1** 21 8N 72 41 E
Tapia, *Spain* **36 B4** 43 34N 6 56W
Tapiantana Group, *Phil.* **71 H3** 6 20N 122 0 E
Tapilon, *Phil.* **71 F5** 11 17N 124 2 E
Tapini, *Papua N. G.* **120 E4** 8 19 S 147 0 E
Tápiószele, *Hungary* **31 D12** 47 25N 19 55 E
Tapiraí, *Brazil* **155 E2** 19 52 S 46 1W
Tapirapé →, *Brazil* **154 D1** 10 41 S 50 38W
Tapirapecó, Serra, *Venezuela* **153 C5** 1 10N 65 0W
Tapirapuã, *Brazil* **157 C6** 14 51 S 57 45W
Taplan, *Australia* **116 C4** 34 33 S 140 52 E
Tapoeripa, *Surinam* **153 B6** 5 22N 56 34W
Tapolca, *Hungary* **31 E10** 46 53N 17 29 E
Tappahannock, *U.S.A.* **134 G7** 37 56N 76 52W
Tapuaenuku, Mt., *N.Z.* **119 B8** 42 0 S 173 39 E
Tapul = Salvacion, *Phil.* **71 G2** 9 56N 118 47 E
Tapul Group, *Phil.* **71 J3** 5 35N 120 50 E
Tapun, *India* **78 B6** 27 35N 96 22 E
Tapurucuará, *Brazil* **153 D4** 0 24 S 65 2W
Taqīābād, *Iran* **85 C8** 35 33N 59 11 E
Ţaqţaq, *Iraq* **84 C5** 35 53N 44 35 E
Taquara, *Brazil* **159 B5** 29 36 S 50 46W
Taquari →, *Brazil* **157 D6** 19 15 S 57 17W
Taquaritinga, *Brazil* **155 F2** 21 24 S 48 30W
Tara, *Australia* **115 D5** 27 17 S 150 31 E
Tara, *Canada* **136 B3** 44 28N 81 9W
Tara, *Japan* **62 D2** 33 2N 130 11 E
Tara, *Russia* **56 D8** 56 55N 74 24 E
Tara, *Zambia* **107 F2** 16 58 S 26 45 E
Tara →, *Montenegro* **42 D3** 43 21N 18 51 E
Tara →, *Russia* **56 D8** 56 42N 74 36 E
Tara-Dake, *Japan* **62 E2** 32 58N 130 6 E
Taraba □, *Nigeria* **101 D7** 8 0N 10 30 E
Tarabagatay, Khrebet, *Kazakhstan* **56 E9** 48 0N 83 0 E
Tarabuco, *Bolivia* **157 D5** 19 10 S 64 57W
Tarābulus, *Lebanon* **91 A4** 34 31N 35 50 E
Tarābulus, *Libya* **96 B2** 32 49N 13 7 E
Taradale, *N.Z.* **118 F5** 39 33 S 176 53 E
Tarahouahout, *Algeria* **99 D6** 22 41N 5 59 E
Tarajalejo, *Canary Is.* **33 F5** 28 12N 14 7W
Tarakan, *Indonesia* **75 B5** 3 20N 117 35 E
Tarakit, Mt., *Kenya* **106 B4** 2 2N 35 10 E
Taralga, *Australia* **117 C8** 34 26 S 149 52 E
Tarama-Jima, *Japan* **61 M2** 24 39N 124 42 E
Taramakau →, *N.Z.* **119 C6** 42 34 S 171 8 E
Tarana, *Australia* **117 B8** 33 31 S 149 52 E
Taranagar, *India* **80 E6** 28 43N 74 50 E
Taranaki □, *N.Z.* **118 F3** 39 25 S 174 30 E
Tarancón, *Spain* **34 E1** 40 1N 3 1W
Taranga, *India* **80 H5** 23 56N 72 43 E
Taranga Hill, *India* **80 H5** 24 0N 72 40 E
Táranto, *Italy* **41 B10** 40 30N 17 11 E
Táranto, G. di, *Italy* **41 B10** 40 0N 17 15 E
Tarapacá, *Colombia* **152 D4** 2 56 S 69 46W
Tarapacá □, *Chile* **158 A2** 20 45 S 69 30W
Tarapoto, *Peru* **156 B2** 6 30 S 76 20W
Taraquá, *Brazil* **152 C4** 0 6N 68 28W
Tarare, *France* **25 C8** 45 54N 4 26 E
Tararua Ra., *N.Z.* **118 G4** 40 45 S 175 25 E
Tarascon, *France* **25 E8** 43 48N 4 39 E
Tarascon-sur-Ariège, *France* **24 F5** 42 50N 1 36 E
Tarashcha, *Ukraine* **52 B4** 49 30N 30 31 E
Tarata, *Peru* **156 D3** 17 27 S 70 2W
Tarauacá, *Brazil* **156 B3** 8 6 S 70 48W
Tarauacá →, *Brazil* **156 B4** 6 42 S 69 48W
Taravo →, *France* **25 G12** 41 42N 8 49 E
Tarawera, *N.Z.* **118 F5** 39 2 S 176 36 E
Tarawera L., *N.Z.* **118 E5** 38 13 S 176 27 E
Tarawera Mt., *N.Z.* **118 E5** 38 14 S 176 32 E
Tarazona, *Spain* **34 D3** 41 55N 1 43W
Tarazona de la Mancha, *Spain* **35 F3** 39 16N 1 55W
Tarbat Ness, *U.K.* **18 D5** 57 52N 3 48W
Tarbela Dam, *Pakistan* **80 B5** 34 8N 72 52 E
Tarbert, *Strath., U.K.* **18 F3** 55 55N 5 25W
Tarbert, *W. Isles, U.K.* **18 D2** 57 54N 6 49W
Tarbes, *France* **24 E4** 43 15N 0 3 E
Tarboro, *U.S.A.* **135 H7** 35 54N 77 32W
Tarbrax, *Australia* **114 C3** 21 7 S 142 26 E
Tarbū, *Libya* **96 C3** 26 0N 15 5 E
Tărcău, Munţii, *Romania* **46 C7** 46 39N 26 7 E
Tarcento, *Italy* **39 B10** 46 12N 13 12 E
Tarcoola, *Australia* **115 E1** 30 44 S 134 36 E
Tarcoon, *Australia* **115 E4** 30 15 S 146 43 E
Tardets-Sorholus, *France* **24 E3** 43 8N 0 52W
Tardoire →, *France* **24 C4** 45 52N 0 14 E
Taree, *Australia* **117 A10** 31 50 S 152 30 E
Tarentaise, *France* **25 C10** 45 30N 6 35 E
Tarf, Ras, *Morocco* **98 A3** 35 40N 5 11W
Ţarfā, Ra's aţ, *Si. Arabia* **86 C3** 17 2N 42 22 E
Tarfa, Wadi el →, *Egypt* **94 J7** 28 25N 30 50 E
Tarfaya, *Morocco* **98 C2** 27 55N 12 55W
Targon, *France* **24 D3** 44 44N 0 16W
Targuist, *Morocco* **98 B4** 34 59N 4 14W
Tărhăus, *Romania* **46 C7** 46 40N 26 8 E
Tarhbalt, *Morocco* **98 B3** 30 39N 5 20W
Tarhit, *Algeria* **99 B4** 30 58N 2 0W
Tarhūnah, *Libya* **96 B2** 32 27N 13 36 E
Tari, *Papua N. G.* **120 C2** 5 54 S 142 59 E
Táriba, *Venezuela* **152 B3** 7 49N 72 13W
Tarifa, *Spain* **37 J5** 36 1N 5 36W
Tarija, *Bolivia* **158 A3** 21 30 S 64 40W
Tarija □, *Bolivia* **158 A3** 21 30 S 63 30W
Tariku →, *Indonesia* **73 B5** 2 55 S 138 26 E
Tarīm, *Yemen* **87 C5** 16 3N 49 0 E
Tarim Basin = Tarim Pendi, *China* **64 B3** 40 0N 84 0 E
Tarim He →, *China* **64 C3** 39 30N 88 30 E
Tarim Pendi, *China* **64 B3** 40 0N 84 0 E
Tarime □, *Tanzania* **106 C3** 1 15 S 34 0 E
Taringo Downs, *Australia* **117 B6** 32 13 S 145 33 E
Taritatu →, *Indonesia* **73 B5** 2 54 S 138 27 E
Tarka →, *S. Africa* **104 E4** 32 10 S 26 0 E
Tarkastad, *S. Africa* **104 E4** 32 0 S 26 16 E
Tarkhankut, Mys, *Ukraine* **52 D5** 45 25N 32 30 E
Tarko Sale, *Russia* **56 C8** 64 55N 77 50 E
Tarkwa, *Ghana* **100 D4** 5 20N 2 0W
Tarlac, *Phil.* **70 D3** 15 29N 120 35 E
Tarlac □, *Phil.* **70 D3** 15 30N 120 30 E
Tarlton Downs, *Australia* **114 C2** 22 40 S 136 45 E
Tarm, *Denmark* **15 J2** 55 56N 8 31 E
Tarma, *Peru* **156 C2** 11 25 S 75 45W
Tarn □, *France* **24 E6** 43 49N 2 8 E
Tarn →, *France* **24 D5** 44 5N 1 6 E
Tarn-et-Garonne □, *France* **24 D5** 44 8N 1 20 E
Tarna →, *Hungary* **31 D12** 47 31N 19 59 E
Tårnby, *Denmark* **15 J6** 55 37N 12 36 E
Tarnica, *Poland* **31 B15** 49 4N 22 44 E
Tarnobrzeg, *Poland* **47 E8** 50 35N 21 41 E
Tarnobrzeg □, *Poland* **47 E8** 50 40N 22 0 E
Tarnogród, *Poland* **47 E9** 50 22N 22 45 E
Tarnów, *Poland* **31 A13** 50 3N 21 0 E
Tarnów □, *Poland* **31 B14** 50 0N 21 0 E
Tarnowskie Góry, *Poland* **47 E5** 50 27N 18 54 E
Táro →, *Italy* **38 D7** 44 56N 10 15 E
Taroom, *Australia* **115 D4** 25 36 S 149 48 E
Taroudannt, *Morocco* **98 B3** 30 30N 8 52W
Tarp, *Germany* **26 A5** 54 40N 9 25 E
Tarpon Springs, *U.S.A.* **135 L4** 28 9N 82 45W
Tarquínia, *Italy* **39 F8** 42 15N 11 45 E
Tarragona, *Spain* **34 D6** 41 5N 1 17 E
Tarragona □, *Spain* **34 D6** 41 5N 1 0 E
Tarrasa, *Spain* **34 D7** 41 34N 2 1 E
Tárrega, *Spain* **34 D6** 41 39N 1 9 E
Tarrytown, *U.S.A.* **137 E11** 41 4N 73 52W
Tarshiha = Me'ona, *Israel* **91 B4** 33 1N 35 15 E
Tarso Emissi, *Chad* **97 D3** 21 27N 18 36 E
Tarso Ourari, *Chad* **97 D3** 21 27N 17 27 E
Tarsus, *Turkey* **88 E6** 36 58N 34 55 E
Tartagal, *Argentina* **158 A3** 22 30 S 63 50W
Tartas, *France* **24 E3** 43 50N 0 49W
Tartu, *Estonia* **50 B5** 58 20N 26 44 E
Ţarţūs, *Syria* **84 C2** 34 55N 35 55 E
Tarumirim, *Brazil* **155 E3** 19 16 S 41 59W
Tarumizu, *Japan* **62 F2** 31 29N 130 42 E
Tarussa, *Russia* **51 D10** 54 44N 37 10 E
Tarutao, Ko, *Thailand* **77 J2** 6 33N 99 40 E
Tarutung, *Indonesia* **74 B1** 2 0N 98 54 E
Tarvisio, *Italy* **39 B10** 46 31N 13 35 E
Tarz Ulli, *Libya* **96 C2** 25 32N 10 8 E
Tas-Buget, *Kazakhstan* **55 A2** 44 46N 65 33 E
Tasahku, *Burma* **78 B6** 27 33N 97 52 E
Tasāwah, *Libya* **96 C2** 26 0N 13 30 E
Taschereau, *Canada* **128 C4** 48 40N 78 40W
Taseko →, *Canada* **130 C4** 52 8N 123 45W
Tasgaon, *India* **82 F2** 17 2N 74 39 E
Tash-Kumyr, *Kirghizia* **55 C6** 41 40N 72 10 E
Tashauz, *Turkmenistan* **56 E6** 41 49N 59 58 E
Tashi Chho Dzong = Thimphu, *Bhutan* **78 B2** 27 31N 89 45 E
Tashkent, *Uzbekistan* **55 C4** 41 20N 69 10 E
Tashtagol, *Russia* **56 D9** 52 47N 87 53 E
Tasikmalaya, *Indonesia* **75 D3** 7 18 S 108 12 E
Tåsjön, *Sweden* **12 D13** 64 15N 15 40 E
Taskan, *Russia* **57 C16** 62 59N 150 20 E
Taşköprü, *Turkey* **52 F6** 41 30N 34 15 E
Tasman →, *N.Z.* **119 D5** 43 48 S 170 8 E
Tasman, Mt., *N.Z.* **119 D5** 43 34 S 170 12 E
Tasman B., *N.Z.* **119 A8** 40 59 S 173 25 E
Tasman Mts., *N.Z.* **119 B7** 41 3 S 172 25 E
Tasman Pen., *Australia* **114 G4** 43 10 S 148 0 E
Tasman Sea, *Pac. Oc.* **122 L8** 36 0 S 160 0 E
Tasmania □, *Australia* **114 G4** 42 0 S 146 30 E
Tăşnad, *Romania* **46 B3** 47 30N 22 33 E
Tassil Tin-Rerhoh, *Algeria* **99 D5** 20 5N 3 55 E
Tassili n-Ajjer, *Algeria* **99 C6** 25 47N 8 1 E
Tassili-Oua-n-Ahaggar, *Algeria* **99 D6** 20 41N 5 30 E
Tasty, *Kazakhstan* **55 A4** 44 47N 69 7 E
Tasu Sd., *Canada* **130 C2** 52 47N 132 2W
Tata, *Hungary* **31 D11** 47 37N 18 19 E
Tata, *Morocco* **98 C3** 29 46N 7 56W
Tatabánya, *Hungary* **31 D11** 47 32N 18 25 E
Tatahouine, *Tunisia* **96 B2** 32 57N 10 29 E
Tatar Republic □, *Russia* **54 D2** 55 30N 51 30 E
Tatarbunary, *Ukraine* **52 D3** 45 50N 29 39 E
Tatarsk, *Russia* **56 D8** 55 14N 76 0 E
Tatau, *Malaysia* **75 B4** 2 53N 112 51 E
Tatebayashi, *Japan* **63 A11** 36 15N 139 32 E
Tateshina-Yama, *Japan* **63 A10** 36 8N 138 11 E
Tateyama, *Japan* **63 C11** 35 0N 139 50 E
Tathlina L., *Canada* **130 A5** 60 33N 117 39W
Tathlīth, *Si. Arabia* **86 C3** 19 32N 43 30 E
Tathlīth, W. →, *Si. Arabia* **86 B4** 20 35N 44 20 E
Tathra, *Australia* **117 D8** 36 44 S 149 59 E
Tatinnai L., *Canada* **131 A9** 60 55N 97 40W
Tatnam, C., *Canada* **131 B10** 57 16N 91 0W
Tatra = Tatry, *Slovak Rep.* **31 B12** 49 20N 20 0 E
Tatry, *Slovak Rep.* **31 B12** 49 20N 20 0 E
Tatsuno, *Japan* **62 C6** 34 52N 134 33 E
Tatta, *Pakistan* **79 D2** 24 42N 67 55 E
Tatuī, *Brazil* **159 A6** 23 25 S 47 53W
Tatum, *U.S.A.* **139 J3** 33 16N 103 19W
Tat'ung = Datong, *China* **66 D7** 40 6N 113 18 E
Tatura, *Australia* **117 D6** 36 29 S 145 16 E
Tatvan, *Turkey* **89 D10** 38 31N 42 15 E
Tau, *Amer. Samoa* **121 X25** 14 15 S 169 30W
Tauá, *Brazil* **154 C3** 6 1 S 40 26W
Taubaté, *Brazil* **159 A6** 23 0 S 45 36W
Tauberbischofsheim, *Germany* **27 F5** 49 37N 9 40 E
Taucha, *Germany* **26 D8** 51 22N 12 31 E
Tauern, *Austria* **30 D5** 47 15N 12 40 E
Tauern-tunnel, *Austria* **30 E6** 47 0N 13 12 E
Taufikia, *Sudan* **95 F3** 9 24N 31 37 E
Taumarunui, *N.Z.* **118 E4** 38 53 S 175 15 E
Taumaturgo, *Brazil* **156 B3** 8 54 S 72 51W
Taung, *S. Africa* **104 D3** 27 33 S 24 47 E
Taungdwingyi, *Burma* **78 E5** 20 1N 95 40 E
Taunggyi, *Burma* **78 E6** 20 50N 97 0 E
Taungtha, *Burma* **78 E5** 21 12N 95 25 E
Taungup, *Burma* **78 F5** 18 51N 94 14 E
Taungup Pass, *Burma* **78 F5** 18 40N 94 45 E
Taunsa Barrage, *Pakistan* **80 D4** 30 42N 70 50 E
Taunton, *U.K.* **17 F4** 51 1N 3 7W
Taunton, *U.S.A.* **137 E13** 41 54N 71 6W
Taunus, *Germany* **27 E4** 50 15N 8 20 E
Taupo, *N.Z.* **118 E5** 38 41 S 176 7 E
Taupo, L., *N.Z.* **118 E4** 38 46 S 175 55 E
Taurage, *Lithuania* **50 D3** 55 14N 22 16 E
Tauranga, *N.Z.* **118 D5** 37 42 S 176 11 E
Tauranga Harb., *N.Z.* **118 D5** 37 30 S 176 5 E
Tauri →, *Papua N. G.* **120 E4** 8 8 S 146 8 E
Taurianova, *Italy* **41 D9** 38 22N 16 1 E
Taurus Mts. = Toros Dağlari, *Turkey* **88 E5** 37 0N 32 30 E
Tauste, *Spain* **34 D3** 41 58N 1 18W
Tauz, *Azerbaijan* **53 F11** 41 0N 45 40 E
Tavaar, *Somali Rep.* **108 D3** 3 6N 46 1 E
Tavannes, *Switz.* **28 B4** 47 13N 7 12 E
Tavda, *Russia* **54 B9** 58 7N 65 8 E
Tavda →, *Russia* **54 B8** 59 20N 63 28 E
Taverny, *France* **23 C9** 49 2N 2 13 E
Taveta, *Tanzania* **106 C4** 3 23 S 37 37 E
Taveuni, *Fiji* **121 A3** 16 51 S 179 58W
Tavignano →, *France* **25 F13** 42 7N 9 33 E
Tavira, *Portugal* **37 H3** 37 8N 7 40W
Tavistock, *Canada* **136 C4** 43 19N 80 50W
Tavistock, *U.K.* **17 G3** 50 33N 4 9W
Tavolara, *Italy* **40 B2** 40 55N 9 40 E
Távora →, *Portugal* **36 D3** 41 8N 7 35W
Tavoy, *Burma* **76 E2** 14 2N 98 12 E
Tavşanlı, *Turkey* **88 D3** 39 32N 29 28 E
Taw →, *U.K.* **17 F3** 51 4N 4 11W
Tawas City, *U.S.A.* **134 C4** 44 16N 83 31W
Tawau, *Malaysia* **75 B5** 4 20N 117 55 E
Tawī Şulaym, *Oman* **87 B7** 22 33N 58 40 E
Tawitawi, *Phil.* **71 J2** 5 10N 120 0 E
Tawitawi □, *Phil.* **71 J3** 5 0N 120 0 E
Tawitawi Group, *Phil.* **71 J3** 5 10N 120 15 E
Tawngche, *Burma* **78 B5** 26 34N 95 38 E
Tāwurgha', *Libya* **96 B3** 32 1N 15 2 E
Taxila, *Pakistan* **80 C5** 33 42N 72 52 E
Tay →, *U.K.* **18 E5** 56 37N 3 38W
Tay, Firth of, *U.K.* **18 E5** 56 25N 3 8W
Tay, L., *Australia* **113 F3** 32 55 S 120 48 E
Tay, L., *U.K.* **18 E4** 56 30N 4 10W
Tay Ninh, *Vietnam* **77 G6** 11 20N 106 5 E
Tayabamba, *Peru* **156 B2** 8 15 S 77 16W
Tayabas, *Phil.* **70 D3** 14 1N 121 35 E
Tayabas Bay, *Phil.* **70 E3** 13 45N 121 45 E
Taylakovy, *Russia* **56 D8** 59 13N 74 0 E
Taylor, *Canada* **130 B4** 56 13N 120 40W
Taylor, *Mich., U.S.A.* **141 B13** 42 14N 83 16W
Taylor, *Nebr., U.S.A.* **138 E5** 41 46N 99 23W
Taylor, *Pa., U.S.A.* **137 E9** 41 23N 75 43W
Taylor, *Tex., U.S.A.* **139 K6** 30 34N 97 25W
Taylor, Mt., *N.Z.* **119 D6** 43 30 S 171 20 E
Taylor, Mt., *U.S.A.* **143 J10** 35 14N 107 37W
Taylorsville, *U.S.A.* **141 F11** 38 2N 85 21W
Taylorville, *U.S.A.* **140 E7** 39 33N 89 18W
Taymā, *Si. Arabia* **84 E3** 27 35N 38 45 E
Taymyr, Oz., *Russia* **57 B11** 74 20N 102 0 E
Taymyr, Poluostrov, *Russia* **57 B11** 75 0N 100 0 E
Tayog, *Phil.* **70 C3** 16 2N 120 45 E
Tayport, *U.K.* **18 E6** 56 27N 2 52W
Tayshet, *Russia* **57 D10** 55 58N 98 1 E
Tayside □, *U.K.* **18 E5** 56 25N 3 30W
Taytay, *Palawan, Phil.* **71 F2** 10 45N 119 30 E
Taytay, *Rizal, Phil.* **70 D3** 14 34N 121 8 E
Taytay Bay, *Phil.* **71 F2** 10 55N 119 35 E
Taz →, *Russia* **56 C8** 67 32N 78 40 E
Taza, *Morocco* **98 B4** 34 16N 4 6W
Tāzah Khurmātū, *Iraq* **84 C5** 35 18N 44 20 E
Tazawa-Ko, *Japan* **60 E10** 39 43N 140 40 E
Taze, *Burma* **78 D5** 22 57N 95 24 E
Tazenakht, *Morocco* **98 B3** 30 35N 7 12W
Tazerbo, *Libya* **96 C4** 25 45N 21 0 E
Tazin L., *Canada* **131 B7** 59 44N 108 42W
Tazoult, *Algeria* **99 A6** 35 29N 6 11 E
Tazovskiy, *Russia* **56 C8** 67 30N 78 44 E
Tbilisi, *Georgia* **53 F11** 41 43N 44 50 E
Tchad = Chad ■, *Africa* **97 F3** 15 0N 17 15 E
Tchad, L., *Chad* **97 F2** 13 30N 14 30 E
Tchaourou, *Benin* **101 D5** 8 58N 2 40 E
Tch'eng-tou = Chengdu, *China* **68 B5** 30 38N 104 2 E
Tchentlo L., *Canada* **130 B4** 55 15N 125 0W

**The Hamilton 273**


Tchibanga, *Gabon* **102 C2** 2 45S 11 0E
Tchien, *Liberia* **100 D3** 5 59N 8 15W
Tchikala-Tcholohanga, *Angola* **103 E3** 12 38S 16 3E
Tchin Tabaraden, *Niger* **101 B6** 15 58N 5 56E
Tchingou, Massif de, *N. Cal.* **121 T19** 20 54S 165 0E
Tcholliré, *Cameroon* **102 A2** 8 24N 14 10E
Tch'ong-k'ing = Chongqing, *China* **68 C6** 29 35N 106 25E
Tczew, *Poland* **47 A5** 54 8N 18 50E
Te Anau, *N.Z.* **119 F2** 45 25S 167 43E
Te Anau, L., *N.Z.* **119 F2** 45 15S 167 45E
Te Araroa, *N.Z.* **118 D7** 37 39S 178 25E
Te Aroha, *N.Z.* **118 D4** 37 32S 175 44E
Te Awamutu, *N.Z.* **118 E4** 38 1S 175 20E
Te Kaha, *N.Z.* **118 D6** 37 44S 177 52E
Te Karaka, *N.Z.* **118 E6** 38 26S 177 53E
Te Kauwhata, *N.Z.* **118 D4** 37 25S 175 9E
Te Kopuru, *N.Z.* **118 C2** 36 2S 173 56E
Te Kuiti, *N.Z.* **118 E4** 38 20S 175 11E
Te Puke, *N.Z.* **118 D5** 37 46S 176 22E
Te Teko, *N.Z.* **118 E5** 38 2S 176 48E
Te Waewae B., *N.Z.* **119 G2** 46 13S 167 33E
Tea →, *Brazil* **152 D4** 0 30S 65 9W
Tea Tree, *Australia* **114 C1** 22 5S 133 22E
Teaca, *Romania* **46 C5** 46 55N 24 30E
Teague, *U.S.A.* **139 K6** 31 38N 96 17W
Teano, *Italy* **41 A7** 41 15N 14 1E
Teapa, *Mexico* **147 D6** 18 35N 92 56W
Teba, *Spain* **37 J6** 36 59N 4 55W
Teberau, *Malaysia* **74 B2** 1 32N 103 45E
Teberda, *Russia* **53 E9** 43 30N 41 46E
Tébessa, *Algeria* **99 A6** 35 22N 8 8E
Tebicuary →, *Paraguay* **158 B4** 26 36S 58 16W
Tebingtinggi, *Indonesia* **74 B1** 3 20N 99 9E
Tebintinggi, *Indonesia* **74 B2** 1 0N 102 45E
Tébourba, *Tunisia* **96 A1** 36 49N 9 51E
Téboursouk, *Tunisia* **96 A1** 36 29N 9 10E
Tebulos, *Russia* **53 E11** 42 36N 45 17E
Tecate, *Mexico* **145 N10** 32 34N 116 38W
Tecer Dağı, *Turkey* **88 D7** 39 39N 37 15E
Tech →, *France* **24 F7** 42 36N 3 3E
Techa →, *Russia* **54 C8** 56 13N 62 58E
Techiman, *Ghana* **100 D4** 7 35N 1 58W
Techirghiol, *Romania* **46 E9** 43 4N 28 32E
Tecka, *Argentina* **160 B2** 43 29S 70 48W
Tecomán, *Mexico* **146 D4** 18 55N 103 53W
Tecopa, *U.S.A.* **145 K10** 35 51N 116 13W
Tecoripa, *Mexico* **146 B3** 28 37N 109 57W
Tecuala, *Mexico* **146 C3** 22 23N 105 27W
Tecuci, *Romania* **46 D8** 45 51N 27 27E
Tecumseh, *U.S.A.* **141 B13** 42 0N 83 57W
Ted, *Somali Rep.* **108 D2** 4 24N 43 55E
Tedzhen, *Turkmenistan* **56 F7** 37 23N 60 31E
Tees →, *U.K.* **16 C6** 54 36N 1 25W
Teesside, *U.K.* **16 C6** 54 37N 1 13W
Teeswater, *Canada* **136 C3** 43 59N 81 17W
Tefé, *Brazil* **153 D5** 3 25S 64 50W
Tefé →, *Brazil* **153 D5** 3 35S 64 47W
Tefenni, *Turkey* **88 E3** 37 18N 29 45E
Tegal, *Indonesia* **75 D3** 6 52S 109 8E
Tegelen, *Neths.* **21 F8** 51 20N 6 9E
Tegernsee, *Germany* **27 H7** 47 43N 11 46E
Teggiano, *Italy* **41 B8** 40 24N 15 32E
Teghra, *India* **81 G11** 25 30N 85 34E
Tegid, L. = Bala, L., *U.K.* **16 E4** 52 53N 3 38W
Tegina, *Nigeria* **101 C6** 10 5N 6 11E
Tegua, *Vanuatu* **121 C4** 13 15S 166 37E
Tegucigalpa, *Honduras* **148 D2** 14 5N 87 14W
Tehachapi, *U.S.A.* **145 K8** 35 8N 118 27W
Tehachapi Mts., *U.S.A.* **145 L8** 35 0N 118 30W
Tehamiyam, *Sudan* **94 D4** 18 20N 36 32E
Tehilla, *Sudan* **94 D4** 17 42N 36 6E
Téhini, *Ivory C.* **100 D4** 9 39N 3 40W
Tehrān, *Iran* **85 C6** 35 44N 51 30E
Tehuacán, *Mexico* **147 D5** 18 30N 97 30W
Tehuantepec, *Mexico* **147 D5** 16 21N 95 13W
Tehuantepec, G. de, *Mexico* **147 D5** 15 50N 95 12W
Tehuantepec, Istmo de, *Mexico* **147 D6** 17 0N 94 30W
Teide, *Canary Is.* **33 F3** 28 15N 16 38W
Teifi →, *U.K.* **17 E3** 52 4N 4 14W
Teign →, *U.K.* **17 G4** 50 41N 3 42W
Teignmouth, *U.K.* **17 G4** 50 33N 3 30W
Teiuş, *Romania* **46 C4** 46 12N 23 40E
Teixeira, *Brazil* **154 C4** 7 13S 37 15W
Teixeira Pinto, *Guinea-Biss.* **100 C1** 12 3N 16 0W
Tejo →, *Europe* **37 G1** 38 40N 9 24W
Tejon Pass, *U.S.A.* **145 L8** 34 49N 118 53W
Tekamah, *U.S.A.* **138 E6** 41 47N 96 13W
Tekapo →, *N.Z.* **119 E5** 44 13S 170 21E
Tekapo, L., *N.Z.* **119 D5** 43 53S 170 33E
Tekax, *Mexico* **147 C7** 20 11N 89 18W
Tekeli, *Kazakhstan* **55 A9** 44 50N 79 0E
Tekeze →, *Ethiopia* **95 E4** 14 20N 35 50E
Tekija, *Serbia* **42 C7** 44 42N 22 26E
Tekirdağ, *Turkey* **88 C2** 40 58N 27 30E
Tekirdağ □, *Turkey* **88 C2** 41 0N 27 0E
Tekkali, *India* **82 E7** 18 37N 84 15E
Tekke, *Turkey* **88 C7** 40 42N 36 12E
Tekman, *Turkey* **89 D9** 39 38N 41 29E
Tekoa, *U.S.A.* **142 C5** 47 14N 117 4W
Tekouiât, O. →, *Algeria* **99 D5** 22 25N 2 35E
Tel Aviv-Yafo, *Israel* **91 C3** 32 4N 34 48E
Tel Lakhish, *Israel* **91 D3** 31 34N 34 51E
Tel Megiddo, *Israel* **91 C4** 32 35N 35 11E
Tela, *Honduras* **148 C2** 15 40N 87 28W
Télagh, *Algeria* **99 B4** 34 51N 0 32W
Telanaipura = Jambi, *Indonesia* **74 C2** 1 38S 103 30E
Telavi, *Georgia* **53 F11** 42 0N 45 30E
Telciu, *Romania* **46 B5** 47 25N 24 24E
Telde, *Canary Is.* **33 G4** 27 59N 15 25W
Telefomin, *Papua N. G.* **120 C1** 5 10S 141 31E
Telegraph Creek, *Canada* **130 B2** 58 0N 131 10W
Telekhany, *Belorussia* **50 E4** 52 30N 25 46E
Telemark fylke □, *Norway* **14 E2** 59 25N 8 30E
Telén, *Argentina* **158 D2** 36 15S 65 31W
Telen →, *Indonesia* **75 C5** 0 10S 117 20E
Teleng, *Iran* **85 E9** 25 47N 61 3E
Teleño, *Spain* **36 C4** 42 23N 6 22W
Teleorman □, *Romania* **46 E6** 44 0N 25 0E
Teleorman →, *Romania* **46 E6** 44 15N 25 20E
Teles Pires →, *Brazil* **157 B6** 7 21S 58 3W
Telescope Pk., *U.S.A.* **145 J9** 36 10N 117 5W
Teletaye, *Mali* **101 B5** 16 31N 1 30E
Telford, *U.K.* **16 E5** 52 42N 2 31W
Telfs, *Austria* **30 D4** 47 19N 11 4E
Télimélé, *Guinea* **100 C2** 10 54N 13 2W
Telkwa, *Canada* **130 C3** 54 41N 127 5W
Tell City, *U.S.A.* **141 G10** 37 57N 86 46W
Tellicherry, *India* **83 J2** 11 45N 75 30E
Tellin, *Belgium* **21 H6** 50 5N 5 13E
Telluride, *U.S.A.* **143 H10** 37 56N 107 49W
Telok Datok, *Malaysia* **74 B2** 2 49N 101 31E
Teloloapán, *Mexico* **147 D5** 18 21N 99 51W
Telpos Iz, *Russia* **48 B10** 63 35N 57 30E
Telsen, *Argentina* **160 B3** 42 30S 66 50W
Telšiai, *Lithuania* **50 D3** 55 59N 22 14E
Teltow, *Germany* **26 C9** 52 24N 13 15E
Teluk Anson, *Malaysia* **77 K3** 4 3N 101 0E
Teluk Betung = Tanjungkarang Telukbetung, *Indonesia* **74 D3** 5 20S 105 10E
Teluk Intan = Teluk Anson, *Malaysia* **77 K3** 4 3N 101 0E
Telukbutun, *Indonesia* **75 B3** 4 13N 108 12E
Telukdalem, *Indonesia* **74 B1** 0 33N 97 50E
Tema, *Ghana* **101 D5** 5 41N 0 0E
Temanggung, *Indonesia* **75 D4** 7 18S 110 10E
Temapache, *Mexico* **147 C5** 21 4N 97 38W
Temax, *Mexico* **147 C7** 21 10N 88 50W
Temba, *S. Africa* **105 D4** 25 20S 28 17E
Tembe, *Zaïre* **106 C2** 0 16S 28 14E
Tembesi, *Indonesia* **74 C2** 1 43S 103 6E
Tembilahan, *Indonesia* **74 C2** 0 19S 103 9E
Temblador, *Venezuela* **153 B5** 8 59N 62 44W
Tembleque, *Spain* **34 F1** 39 41N 3 30W
Temblor Range, *U.S.A.* **145 K7** 35 20N 119 50W
Teme →, *U.K.* **17 E5** 52 23N 2 15W
Temecula, *U.S.A.* **145 M9** 33 30N 117 9W
Temerloh, *Malaysia* **77 L4** 3 27N 102 25E
Temir, *Kazakhstan* **56 E6** 49 21N 57 3E
Temirtau, *Kazakhstan* **56 D8** 50 5N 72 56E
Temirtau, *Russia* **56 D9** 53 10N 87 30E
Témiscaming, *Canada* **128 C4** 46 44N 79 5W
Temma, *Australia* **114 G3** 41 12S 144 48E
Temnikov, *Russia* **51 D13** 54 40N 43 11E
Temo →, *Italy* **40 B1** 40 20N 8 30E
Temora, *Australia* **117 C7** 34 30S 147 30E
Temosachic, *Mexico* **146 B3** 28 58N 107 50W
Tempe, *U.S.A.* **143 K8** 33 25N 111 56W
Tempe Downs, *Australia* **112 D5** 24 22S 132 24E
Témpio Pausania, *Italy* **40 B2** 40 53N 9 6E
Tempiute, *U.S.A.* **144 H11** 37 39N 115 38W
Temple, *U.S.A.* **139 K6** 31 6N 97 21W
Temple B., *Australia* **114 A3** 12 15S 143 3E
Templemore, *Ireland* **19 D4** 52 48N 7 50W
Templeton, *U.S.A.* **144 K6** 35 33N 120 42W
Templeton →, *Australia* **114 C2** 21 0S 138 40E
Templeuve, *Belgium* **21 G2** 50 39N 3 17E
Templin, *Germany* **26 B9** 53 8N 13 31E
Tempoal, *Mexico* **147 C5** 21 31N 98 23W
Temryuk, *Russia* **52 D7** 45 15N 37 24E
Temse, *Belgium* **21 F4** 51 7N 4 13E
Temska →, *Serbia* **42 D7** 43 17N 22 33E
Temuco, *Chile* **160 A2** 38 45S 72 40W
Temuka, *N.Z.* **119 E6** 44 14S 171 17E
Ten Boer, *Neths.* **20 B9** 53 16N 6 42E
Tena, *Ecuador* **152 D2** 0 59S 77 49W
Tenabo, *Mexico* **147 C6** 20 2N 90 12W
Tenaha, *U.S.A.* **139 K7** 31 57N 94 15W
Tenali, *India* **83 F5** 16 15N 80 35E
Tenancingo, *Mexico* **147 D5** 19 0N 99 33W
Tenango, *Mexico* **147 D5** 19 7N 99 33W
Tenasserim, *Burma* **77 F2** 12 6N 99 3E
Tenasserim □, *Burma* **76 F2** 14 0N 98 30E
Tenay, *France* **25 C9** 45 55N 5 31E
Tenby, *U.K.* **17 F3** 51 40N 4 42W
Tenda, Col di, *France* **25 D11** 44 7N 7 36E
Tendaho, *Ethiopia* **90 E3** 11 48N 40 54E
Tende, *France* **25 D11** 44 5N 7 35E
Tendelti, *Sudan* **95 E3** 13 1N 31 55E
Tendjedi, Adrar, *Algeria* **99 D6** 23 41N 7 32E
Tendrara, *Morocco* **99 B4** 33 3N 1 58W
Tendre, Mt., *Switz.* **28 C2** 46 35N 6 18E
Teneida, *Egypt* **94 B2** 25 30N 29 19E
Tenente Marques →, *Brazil* **157 C6** 11 10S 59 56W
Ténéré, *Niger* **97 E2** 19 0N 10 30E
Ténéré, Erg du, *Niger* **97 E2** 17 35N 10 55E
Tenerife, *Canary Is.* **33 F3** 28 15N 16 35W
Tenerife, Pico, *Canary Is.* **33 G1** 27 43N 18 1W
Ténès, *Algeria* **99 A5** 36 31N 1 14E
Teng Xian, *Guangxi Zhuangzu, China* **69 F8** 23 21N 110 56E
Teng Xian, *Shandong, China* **67 G9** 35 5N 117 10E
Tengah □, *Indonesia* **72 B2** 2 0S 122 0E
Tengah Kepulauan, *Indonesia* **75 D5** 7 5S 118 15E
Tengchong, *China* **68 E2** 25 0N 98 28E
Tengchowfu = Penglai, *China* **67 F11** 37 48N 120 42E
Tenggara □, *Indonesia* **72 B2** 3 0S 122 0E
Tenggarong, *Indonesia* **75 C5** 0 24S 116 58E
Tenggol, P., *Malaysia* **77 K4** 4 48N 103 41E
Tengiz, Ozero, *Kazakhstan* **56 D7** 50 30N 69 0E
Tenigerbad, *Switz.* **29 C7** 46 42N 8 57E
Tenino, *U.S.A.* **144 D4** 46 51N 122 51W
Tenkasi, *India* **83 K3** 8 55N 77 20E
Tenke, *Shaba, Zaïre* **107 E2** 11 22S 26 40E
Tenke, *Shaba, Zaïre* **107 E2** 10 32S 26 7E
Tenkodogo, *Burkina Faso* **101 C4** 11 54N 0 19W
Tenna →, *Italy* **39 E10** 43 12N 13 47E
Tennant Creek, *Australia* **114 B1** 19 30S 134 15E
Tennessee □, *U.S.A.* **135 H2** 36 0N 86 30W
Tennessee →, *U.S.A.* **134 G1** 37 4N 88 34W
Tenneville, *Belgium* **21 H7** 50 6N 5 32E
Tennille, *U.S.A.* **135 J4** 32 56N 82 48W
Tennsift, Oued →, *Morocco* **98 B3** 32 3N 9 28W
Tennyson, *U.S.A.* **141 F9** 38 5N 87 7W
Teno, Pta. de, *Canary Is.* **33 F3** 28 21N 16 55W
Tenom, *Malaysia* **75 A5** 5 4N 115 57E
Tenosique, *Mexico* **147 D6** 17 30N 91 24W
Tenri, *Japan* **63 C7** 34 39N 135 49E
Tenryū, *Japan* **63 C9** 34 52N 137 49E
Tenryū-Gawa →, *Japan* **63 B9** 35 39N 137 48E
Tent L., *Canada* **131 A7** 62 25N 107 54W
Tentelomatinan, *Indonesia* **72 A2** 0 56N 121 48E
Tenterfield, *Australia* **115 D5** 29 0S 152 0E
Teófilo Otoni, *Brazil* **155 E3** 17 50S 41 30W
Teotihuacán, *Mexico* **147 D5** 19 44N 98 50W
Tepa, *Indonesia* **73 C3** 7 52S 129 31E
Tepalcatepec →, *Mexico* **146 D4** 18 35N 101 59W
Tepehuanes, *Mexico* **146 B3** 25 21N 105 44W
Tepelena, *Albania* **44 D2** 40 17N 20 2E
Tepequem, Serra, *Brazil* **153 C5** 3 45N 61 45W
Tepetongo, *Mexico* **146 C4** 22 28N 103 9W
Tepic, *Mexico* **146 C4** 21 30N 104 54W
Teplice, *Czech.* **30 A6** 50 40N 13 48E
Teploklyuchenka, *Kirghizia* **55 B9** 42 30N 78 30E
Tepoca, C., *Mexico* **146 A2** 30 20N 112 25W
Tequila, *Mexico* **146 C4** 20 54N 103 47W
Ter →, *Spain* **34 C8** 42 2N 3 12E
Ter Apel, *Neths.* **20 C10** 52 53N 7 5E
Téra, *Niger* **101 C5** 14 0N 0 45E
Tera →, *Spain* **36 D5** 41 54N 5 44W
Teraina, *Kiribati* **123 G11** 4 43N 160 25W
Téramo, *Italy* **39 F10** 42 40N 13 40E
Terang, *Australia* **116 E5** 38 15S 142 55E
Terawhiti, C., *N.Z.* **118 H3** 41 16S 174 38E
Terazit, Massif de, *Niger* **97 D1** 20 2N 8 30E
Terborg, *Neths.* **20 E8** 51 56N 6 22E
Tercan, *Turkey* **89 D9** 39 47N 40 23E
Tercero →, *Argentina* **158 C3** 32 58S 61 47W
Terdal, *India* **82 F2** 16 33N 75 3E
Terebovlya, *Ukraine* **50 G4** 49 18N 25 44E
Teregova, *Romania* **46 D3** 45 10N 22 16E
Terek →, *Russia* **53 E12** 44 0N 47 30E
Terek-Say, *Kirghizia* **55 C5** 41 30N 71 11E
Terengganu □, *Malaysia* **74 B2** 4 55N 103 0E
Terenos, *Brazil* **157 E7** 20 26S 54 50W
Tereshka →, *Russia* **51 F15** 51 48N 46 26E
Teresina, *Brazil* **154 C3** 5 9S 42 45W
Teresinha, *Brazil* **153 C7** 0 58N 52 2W
Terespol, *Poland* **47 C10** 52 5N 23 37E
Terewah, L., *Australia* **115 D4** 29 52S 147 35E
Terges →, *Portugal* **37 H3** 37 49N 7 41W
Tergnier, *France* **23 C10** 49 40N 3 17E
Terhazza, *Mali* **98 D3** 23 38N 5 22W
Terheijden, *Neths.* **21 E5** 51 38N 4 45E
Teridgerie Cr. →, *Australia* **115 E4** 30 25S 148 50E
Terifa, *Yemen* **86 D3** 14 24N 43 48E
Terlizzi, *Italy* **41 A9** 41 8N 16 32E
Terme, *Turkey* **52 F7** 41 11N 37 0E
Termez, *Uzbekistan* **55 E3** 37 15N 67 15E
Términi Imerese, *Italy* **40 E6** 37 58N 13 42E
Términos, L. de, *Mexico* **147 D6** 18 35N 91 30W
Térmoli, *Italy* **39 F12** 42 0N 15 0E
Ternate, *Indonesia* **72 A3** 0 45N 127 25E
Terneuzen, *Neths.* **21 F3** 51 20N 3 50E
Terney, *Russia* **57 E14** 45 3N 136 37E
Terni, *Italy* **39 F9** 42 34N 12 38E
Ternitz, *Austria* **30 D9** 47 43N 16 2E
Ternopol, *Ukraine* **52 B1** 49 30N 25 40E
Terowie, *N.S.W., Australia* **115 E4** 32 27S 147 52E
Terowie, *S. Austral., Australia* **115 E2** 33 8S 138 55E
Terra Bella, *U.S.A.* **145 K7** 35 58N 119 3W
Terrace, *Canada* **130 C3** 54 30N 128 35W
Terrace Bay, *Canada* **128 C2** 48 47N 87 5W
Terracina, *Italy* **40 A6** 41 17N 13 12E
Terralba, *Italy* **40 C1** 39 42N 8 38E
Terranova = Ólbia, *Italy* **40 B2** 40 55N 9 30E
Terranuova Bracciolini, *Italy* **39 E8** 43 31N 11 35E
Terrasini Favarotta, *Italy* **40 D6** 38 10N 13 4E
Terrassa = Tarrasa, *Spain* **34 D7** 41 34N 2 1E
Terrasson-la-Villedieu, *France* **24 C5** 45 8N 1 18E
Terre Haute, *U.S.A.* **141 E9** 39 28N 87 25W
Terrebonne B., *U.S.A.* **139 L9** 29 5N 90 35W
Terrecht, *Mali* **99 D4** 20 10N 0 10W
Terrell, *U.S.A.* **139 J6** 32 44N 96 17W
Terrenceville, *Canada* **129 C9** 47 40N 54 44W
Terrick Terrick, *Australia* **114 C4** 24 44S 145 5E
Terry, *U.S.A.* **138 B2** 46 47N 105 19W
Terschelling, *Neths.* **20 B6** 53 25N 5 20E
Terskey Alatau, Khrebet, *Kirghizia* **55 C8** 41 50N 77 0E
Terter →, *Azerbaijan* **53 F12** 40 25N 47 10E
Teruel, *Spain* **34 E3** 40 22N 1 8W
Teruel □, *Spain* **34 E4** 40 48N 1 0W
Tervel, *Bulgaria* **43 D12** 43 45N 27 28E
Tervola, *Finland* **12 C18** 66 6N 24 49E
Teryaweyna L., *Australia* **116 B5** 32 18S 143 22E
Tešanj, *Bos.-H.* **42 C2** 44 38N 18 1E
Teseney, *Eritrea* **95 D4** 15 5N 36 42E
Tesha →, *Russia* **51 D13** 55 38N 42 9E
Teshio, *Japan* **60 B10** 44 53N 141 44E
Teshio-Gawa →, *Japan* **60 B10** 44 53N 141 45E
Tešica, *Serbia* **42 D6** 43 27N 21 45E
Tesiyn Gol →, *Mongolia* **64 A4** 50 40N 93 20E
Teslić, *Bos.-H.* **42 C2** 44 37N 17 54E
Teslin, *Canada* **130 A2** 60 10N 132 43W
Teslin →, *Canada* **130 A2** 61 34N 134 35W
Teslin L., *Canada* **130 A2** 60 15N 132 57W
Tesouro, *Brazil* **157 D7** 16 4S 53 34W
Tessalit, *Mali* **101 A5** 20 12N 1 0E
Tessaoua, *Niger* **97 F1** 13 47N 7 56E
Tessenderlo, *Belgium* **21 F6** 51 4N 5 5E
Tessin, *Germany* **26 A8** 54 2N 12 28E
Tessit, *Mali* **101 B5** 15 13N 0 18E
Test →, *U.K.* **17 F6** 51 7N 1 30W
Testa del Gargano, *Italy* **41 A9** 41 50N 16 10E
Tét, *Hungary* **31 D10** 47 30N 17 33E
Têt →, *France* **24 F7** 42 44N 3 2E
Tetachuck L., *Canada* **130 C3** 53 18N 125 55W
Tetas, Pta., *Chile* **158 A1** 23 31S 70 38W
Tete, *Mozam.* **107 F3** 16 13S 33 33E
Tete □, *Mozam.* **107 F3** 15 15S 32 40E
Teterev →, *Ukraine* **50 F7** 51 1N 30 5E
Teteringen, *Neths.* **21 E5** 51 37N 4 49E
Teterow, *Germany* **26 B8** 53 45N 12 34E
Teteven, *Bulgaria* **43 E9** 42 58N 24 17E
Tethul →, *Canada* **130 A6** 60 35N 112 12W
Tetiyev, *Ukraine* **52 B3** 49 22N 29 38E
Teton →, *U.S.A.* **142 C8** 47 56N 110 31W
Tétouan, *Morocco* **98 A3** 35 35N 5 21W
Tetovo, *Macedonia* **42 E6** 42 1N 21 2E
Tetuán = Tétouan, *Morocco* **98 A3** 35 35N 5 21W
Tetyukhe Pristan, *Russia* **60 B7** 44 22N 135 48E
Tetyushi, *Russia* **51 D16** 54 55N 48 49E
Teuco →, *Argentina* **158 B3** 25 35S 60 11W
Teufen, *Switz.* **29 B8** 47 24N 9 23E
Teulada, *Italy* **40 D1** 38 59N 8 47E
Teulon, *Canada* **131 C9** 50 23N 97 16W
Teun, *Indonesia* **73 C3** 6 59S 129 8E
Teutoburger Wald, *Germany* **26 C4** 52 5N 8 20E
Tevere →, *Italy* **39 G9** 41 44N 12 14E
Teverya, *Israel* **91 C4** 32 47N 35 32E
Teviot →, *U.K.* **18 F6** 55 21N 2 51W
Tewantin, *Australia* **115 D5** 26 27S 153 3E
Tewkesbury, *U.K.* **17 F5** 51 59N 2 8W
Texada I., *Canada* **130 D4** 49 40N 124 25W
Texarkana, *Ark., U.S.A.* **139 J8** 33 26N 94 2W
Texarkana, *Tex., U.S.A.* **139 J7** 33 26N 94 3W
Texas, *Australia* **115 D5** 28 49S 151 9E
Texas □, *U.S.A.* **139 K5** 31 40N 98 30W
Texas City, *U.S.A.* **139 L7** 29 24N 94 54W
Texel, *Neths.* **20 B5** 53 5N 4 50E
Texhoma, *U.S.A.* **139 G4** 36 30N 101 47W
Texline, *U.S.A.* **139 G3** 36 23N 103 2W
Texoma, L., *U.S.A.* **139 J6** 33 50N 96 34W
Teykovo, *Russia* **51 C12** 56 55N 40 30E
Teyvareh, *Afghan.* **79 B2** 33 30N 64 24E
Teza →, *Russia* **51 C12** 56 32N 41 53E
Tezin, *Afghan.* **80 B3** 34 24N 69 30E
Teziutlán, *Mexico* **147 D5** 19 50N 97 22W
Tezpur, *India* **78 B4** 26 40N 92 45E
Tezzeron L., *Canada* **130 C4** 54 43N 124 30W
Tha-anne →, *Canada* **131 A10** 60 31N 94 37W
Tha Deua, *Laos* **76 D4** 17 57N 102 53E
Tha Deua, *Laos* **76 C3** 19 26N 101 50E
Tha Pla, *Thailand* **76 D3** 17 48N 100 32E
Tha Rua, *Thailand* **76 E3** 14 34N 100 44E
Tha Sala, *Thailand* **77 H2** 8 40N 99 56E
Tha Song Yang, *Thailand* **76 D1** 17 34N 97 55E
Thaba Nchu, *S. Africa* **104 D4** 29 17S 26 52E
Thaba Putsoa, *Lesotho* **105 D4** 29 45S 28 0E
Thabana Ntlenyana, *Lesotho* **105 D4** 29 30S 29 16E
Thabazimbi, *S. Africa* **105 C4** 24 40S 27 21E
Thabeikkyin, *Burma* **78 D5** 22 53N 95 59E
Thai Binh, *Vietnam* **76 B6** 20 35N 106 1E
Thai Hoa, *Vietnam* **76 C5** 19 20N 105 20E
Thai Muang, *Thailand* **77 H2** 8 24N 98 16E
Thai Nguyen, *Vietnam* **76 B5** 21 35N 105 55E
Thailand ■, *Asia* **76 E4** 16 0N 102 0E
Thailand, G. of, *Asia* **77 G3** 11 30N 101 0E
Thakhek, *Laos* **76 D5** 17 25N 104 45E
Thakurgaon, *Bangla.* **78 B2** 26 2N 88 34E
Thal, *Pakistan* **79 B3** 33 28N 70 33E
Thal Desert, *Pakistan* **80 D4** 31 10N 71 30E
Thala, *Tunisia* **96 A1** 35 35N 8 40E
Thalabarivat, *Cambodia* **76 F5** 13 33N 105 57E
Thalkirch, *Switz.* **29 C8** 46 39N 9 17E
Thallon, *Australia* **115 D4** 28 39S 148 49E
Thalwil, *Switz.* **29 B7** 47 17N 8 35E
Thamarīt, *Oman* **87 C6** 17 39N 54 2E
Thame →, *U.K.* **17 F6** 51 35N 1 8W
Thames, *N.Z.* **118 D4** 37 7S 175 34E
Thames →, *Canada* **128 D3** 42 20N 82 25W
Thames →, *U.K.* **17 F8** 51 30N 0 35E
Thames →, *U.S.A.* **137 E12** 41 18N 72 5W
Thames, Firth of, *N.Z.* **118 D4** 37 0S 175 25E
Thamesford, *Canada* **136 C3** 43 4N 81 0W
Thamesville, *Canada* **136 D3** 42 33N 81 59W
Thāmit, W. →, *Libya* **96 B3** 30 51N 16 14E
Thamūd, *Yemen* **87 C5** 17 18N 49 55E
Than Uyen, *Vietnam* **76 B4** 22 0N 103 54E
Thanbyuzayat, *Burma* **78 G6** 15 58N 97 44E
Thane, *India* **82 E1** 19 12N 72 59E
Thanesar, *India* **80 D7** 30 1N 76 52E
Thanet, I. of, *U.K.* **17 F9** 51 21N 1 20E
Thangoo, *Australia* **112 C3** 18 10S 122 22E
Thangool, *Australia* **114 C5** 24 38S 150 42E
Thanh Hoa, *Vietnam* **76 C5** 19 48N 105 46E
Thanh Hung, *Vietnam* **77 H5** 9 55N 105 43E
Thanh Pho Ho Chi Minh = Phanh Bho Ho Chi Minh, *Vietnam* **77 G6** 10 58N 106 40E
Thanh Thuy, *Vietnam* **76 A5** 22 55N 104 51E
Thanjavur, *India* **83 J4** 10 48N 79 12E
Thann, *France* **23 E14** 47 48N 7 5E
Thaon-les-Vosges, *France* **23 D13** 48 15N 6 24E
Thap Sakae, *Thailand* **77 G2** 11 30N 99 37E
Thap Than, *Thailand* **76 E2** 15 27N 99 54E
Thar Desert, *India* **80 F4** 28 0N 72 0E
Tharad, *India* **80 G4** 24 30N 71 44E
Thargomindah, *Australia* **115 D3** 27 58S 143 46E
Tharrawaddy, *Burma* **78 G5** 17 38N 95 48E
Tharrawaw, *Burma* **78 G5** 17 41N 95 28E
Tharthar, W. →, *Iraq* **84 C4** 33 59N 43 12E
Thasopoúla, *Greece* **44 D6** 40 49N 24 45E
Thásos, *Greece* **44 D6** 40 40N 24 40E
That Khe, *Vietnam* **76 A6** 22 16N 106 28E
Thatcher, *Ariz., U.S.A.* **143 K9** 32 51N 109 46W
Thatcher, *Colo., U.S.A.* **139 G2** 37 33N 104 7W
Thaton, *Burma* **78 G6** 16 55N 97 22E
Thau, Bassin de, *France* **24 E7** 43 23N 3 36E
Thaungdut, *Burma* **78 C5** 24 30N 94 40E
Thayer, *U.S.A.* **139 G9** 36 31N 91 33W
Thayetmyo, *Burma* **78 F5** 19 20N 95 10E
Thayngen, *Switz.* **29 A7** 47 49N 8 43E
The Alberga →, *Australia* **115 D2** 27 6S 135 33E
The Bight, *Bahamas* **149 B4** 24 19N 75 24W
The Brothers, *Yemen* **87 D6** 12 8N 53 10E
The Coorong, *Australia* **116 C3** 35 50S 139 20E
The Dalles, *U.S.A.* **142 D3** 45 36N 121 10W
The English Company's Is., *Australia* **114 A2** 11 50S 136 32E
The Entrance, *Australia* **117 B9** 33 21S 151 30E
The Frome →, *Australia* **115 D2** 29 8S 137 54E
The Grampians, *Australia* **116 D5** 37 0S 142 20E
The Great Divide = Great Dividing Ra., *Australia* **114 C4** 23 0S 146 0E
The Hague = 's-Gravenhage, *Neths.* **20 D4** 52 7N 4 17E
The Hamilton →, *Australia* **115 D2** 26 40S 135 19E

274 The Hunter Hills


The Hunter Hills, *N.Z.* .. **119 E5** 44 26 S 170 46 E
The Macumba →, *Australia* .......... **115 D2** 27 52 S 137 12 E
The Neales →, *Australia* **115 D2** 28 8 S 136 47 E
The Oaks, *Australia* ..... **117 C9** 34 3 S 150 34 E
The Officer →, *Australia* **113 E5** 27 46 S 132 30 E
The Pas, *Canada* ....... **131 C8** 53 45N 101 15W
The Range, *Zimbabwe* .. **107 F3** 19 2 S 31 2 E
The Remarkables, *N.Z.* . **119 F3** 45 10 S 168 50 E
The Rock, *Australia* ..... **115 F4** 35 15 S 147 2 E
The Salt L., *Australia* ... **115 E3** 30 6 S 142 8 E
The Stevenson →, *Australia* .......... **115 D2** 27 6 S 135 33 E
The Warburton →, *Australia* .......... **115 D2** 28 4 S 137 28 E
Thebes = Thívai, *Greece* **45 F5** 38 19N 23 19 E
Thebes, *Egypt* ......... **94 B3** 25 40N 32 35 E
Thedford, *Canada* ...... **136 C3** 43 9N 81 51W
Thedford, *U.S.A.* ...... **138 E4** 41 59N 100 35W
Theebine, *Australia* ..... **115 D5** 25 57 S 152 34 E
Thekulthili L., *Canada* .. **131 A7** 61 3N 110 0W
Thelon →, *Canada* ..... **131 A8** 62 35N 104 3W
Thénezay, *France* ...... **22 F6** 46 44N 0 2W
Thenia, *Algeria* ........ **99 A5** 36 44N 3 33 E
Thenon, *France* ........ **24 C5** 45 9N 1 4 E
Theodore, *Australia* ..... **114 C5** 24 55 S 150 3 E
Thepha, *Thailand* ...... **77 J3** 6 52N 100 58 E
Thérain →, *France* ..... **23 C9** 49 15N 2 27 E
Theresa, *U.S.A.* ........ **137 B9** 44 13N 75 48W
Thermaïkos Kólpos, *Greece* .......... **44 D4** 40 15N 22 45 E
Thermopolis, *U.S.A.* .... **142 E9** 43 39N 108 13W
Thermopylae P., *Greece* . **45 F4** 38 48N 22 35 E
Thesprotía □, *Greece* ... **44 E2** 39 27N 20 22 E
Thessalía □, *Greece* .... **44 E3** 39 25N 21 50 E
Thessalon, *Canada* ..... **128 C3** 46 20N 83 30W
Thessaloníki, *Greece* .... **44 D4** 40 38N 22 58 E
Thessaloníki □, *Greece* .. **44 D5** 40 45N 23 0 E
Thessaloniki, Gulf of = Thermaïkos Kólpos, *Greece* .......... **44 D4** 40 15N 22 45 E
Thessaly = Thessalía □, *Greece* .......... **44 E3** 39 25N 21 50 E
Thetford, *U.K.* ........ **17 E8** 52 25N 0 44 E
Thetford Mines, *Canada* . **129 C5** 46 8N 71 18W
Theun →, *Laos* ....... **76 C5** 18 19N 104 0 E
Theunissen, *S. Africa* ... **104 D4** 28 26 S 26 43 E
Theux, *Belgium* ........ **21 G7** 50 32N 5 49 E
Thevenard, *Australia* .... **115 E1** 32 9 S 133 38 E
Thiámis →, *Greece* .... **44 E2** 39 15N 20 6 E
Thiberville, *France* ..... **22 C7** 49 8N 0 27 E
Thibodaux, *U.S.A.* ..... **139 L9** 29 48N 90 49W
Thicket Portage, *Canada* . **131 B9** 55 19N 97 42W
Thief River Falls, *U.S.A.* **138 A6** 48 7N 96 10W
Thiel Mts., *Antarctica* ... **7 E16** 85 15 S 91 0W
Thiene, *Italy* .......... **39 C8** 45 42N 11 29 E
Thiérache, *France* ...... **23 C10** 49 51N 3 45 E
Thiers, *France* ......... **24 C7** 45 52N 3 33 E
Thies, *Senegal* ......... **100 C1** 14 50N 16 51W
Thiet, *Sudan* .......... **95 F2** 7 37N 28 49 E
Thika, *Kenya* .......... **106 C4** 1 1 S 37 5 E
Thille-Boubacar, *Senegal* . **100 B1** 16 31N 15 5W
Thimphu, *Bhutan* ...... **78 B2** 27 31N 89 45 E
þingvallavatn, *Iceland* ... **12 D3** 64 11N 21 9W
Thio, *N. Cal.* .......... **121 U20** 21 37 S 166 14 E
Thionville, *France* ...... **23 C13** 49 20N 6 10 E
Thíra, *Greece* ......... **45 H7** 36 23N 25 27 E
Thirasía, *Greece* ....... **45 H7** 36 26N 25 21 E
Thirsk, *U.K.* .......... **16 C6** 54 15N 1 20W
Thiruvarur, *India* ...... **83 J4** 10 46N 79 38 E
Thisted, *Denmark* ...... **13 H10** 56 58N 8 40 E
Thistle I., *Australia* ..... **116 C2** 35 0 S 136 8 E
Thitgy, *Burma* ......... **78 F6** 18 15N 96 13 E
Thithia, *Fiji* .......... **121 A3** 17 45 S 179 18W
Thitpokpin, *Burma* ..... **78 F5** 19 24N 95 58 E
Thívai, *Greece* ......... **45 F5** 38 19N 23 19 E
Thiviers, *France* ....... **24 C4** 45 25N 0 54 E
Thizy, *France* ......... **25 B8** 46 2N 4 18 E
þjórsá →, *Iceland* ..... **12 E3** 63 47N 20 48W
Thlewiaza →, *Man., Canada* .......... **131 B8** 59 43N 100 5W
Thlewiaza →, *N.W.T., Canada* .......... **131 A10** 60 29N 94 40W
Thmar Puok, *Cambodia* . **76 F4** 13 57N 103 4 E
Tho Vinh, *Vietnam* ..... **76 C5** 19 16N 105 42 E
Thoa →, *Canada* ...... **131 A7** 60 31N 109 47W
Thoen, *Thailand* ....... **76 D2** 17 43N 99 12 E
Thoeng, *Thailand* ...... **76 C3** 19 41N 100 12 E
Thoissey, *France* ....... **25 B8** 46 12N 4 48 E
Tholdi, *Pakistan* ....... **81 B7** 35 5N 76 6 E
Tholen, *Neths.* ......... **21 E4** 51 32N 4 13 E
Thomas, *Okla., U.S.A.* .. **139 H5** 35 45N 98 45W
Thomas, *W. Va., U.S.A.* **134 F6** 39 9N 79 30W
Thomas, L., *Australia* ... **115 D2** 26 4 S 137 58 E
Thomas Hill Reservoir, *U.S.A.* .......... **140 E4** 39 34N 92 39W
Thomaston, *U.S.A.* ..... **135 J3** 32 53N 84 20W
Thomasville, *Ala., U.S.A.* **135 K2** 31 55N 87 44W
Thomasville, *Ga., U.S.A.* **135 K3** 30 50N 83 59W
Thomasville, *N.C., U.S.A.* **135 H5** 35 53N 80 5W
Thommen, *Belgium* ..... **21 H8** 50 14N 6 5 E
Thompson, *Canada* ..... **131 B9** 55 45N 97 52W
Thompson, *U.S.A.* ..... **143 G9** 38 58N 109 43W
Thompson →, *Canada* .. **130 C4** 50 15N 121 24W
Thompson →, *U.S.A.* .. **138 F8** 39 46N 93 37W
Thompson Falls, *U.S.A.* . **142 C6** 47 36N 115 21W
Thompson Landing, *Canada* .......... **131 A6** 62 56N 110 40W
Thompson Pk., *U.S.A.* .. **142 F2** 41 0N 123 0W
Thompson Sd., *N.Z.* .... **119 F1** 45 8 S 166 46 E
Thomson, *U.S.A.* ...... **140 C6** 41 58N 90 6W
Thomson's Falls = Nyahururu, *Kenya* .... **106 B4** 0 2N 36 27 E
Thon Buri, *Thailand* .... **77 F3** 13 43N 100 29 E
Thônes, *France* ........ **25 C10** 45 54N 6 18 E
Thongwa, *Burma* ...... **78 G6** 16 45N 96 33 E
Thonon-les-Bains, *France* **25 B10** 46 22N 6 29 E
Thonze, *Burma* ........ **78 G5** 17 38N 95 47 E
Thorez, *Ukraine* ....... **53 B8** 48 4N 38 34 E
þórisvatn, *Iceland* ..... **12 D4** 64 20N 18 55W
þorlákshöfn, *Iceland* .... **12 E3** 63 51N 21 22W
Thornaby on Tees, *U.K.* . **16 C6** 54 36N 1 19W
Thornbury, *Canada* ..... **136 B4** 44 34N 80 26W
Thornbury, *N.Z.* ....... **119 G3** 46 17 S 168 9 E
Thornton, *U.S.A.* ...... **140 B3** 42 57N 93 23W
Thornton-Beresfield, *Australia* .......... **117 B9** 32 50 S 151 40 E
Thorntown, *U.S.A.* .... **141 D10** 40 8N 86 36W
Thorold, *Canada* ....... **136 C5** 43 7N 79 12W
þórshöfn, *Iceland* ...... **12 C6** 66 12N 15 20W
Thouarcé, *France* ...... **22 E6** 47 17N 0 30W
Thouars, *France* ....... **22 F6** 46 58N 0 15W
Thouin, C., *Australia* ... **112 D2** 20 20 S 118 10 E
Thousand Oaks, *U.S.A.* . **145 L8** 34 10N 118 50W
Thrace = Thráki □, *Greece* .......... **44 C7** 41 9N 25 30 E
Thrace, *Turkey* ........ **88 C2** 41 0N 27 0 E
Thráki □, *Greece* ...... **44 C7** 41 9N 25 30 E
Thrakikón Pélagos, *Greece* **44 D6** 40 30N 25 0 E
Three Forks, *U.S.A.* .... **142 D8** 45 54N 111 33W
Three Hills, *Canada* .... **130 C6** 51 43N 113 15W
Three Hummock I., *Australia* .......... **114 G3** 40 25 S 144 55 E
Three Lakes, *U.S.A.* .... **138 C10** 45 48N 89 10W
Three Oaks, *U.S.A.* .... **141 C10** 41 48N 86 36W
Three Points, C., *Ghana* . **100 E4** 4 42N 2 6W
Three Rivers, *Australia* .. **113 E2** 25 10 S 119 5 E
Three Rivers, *Calif., U.S.A.* .......... **144 J8** 36 26N 118 54W
Three Rivers, *Mich., U.S.A.* .......... **141 C11** 41 57N 85 38W
Three Rivers, *Tex., U.S.A.* .......... **139 L5** 28 28N 98 11W
Three Sisters, *U.S.A.* .... **142 D3** 44 4N 121 51W
Three Sisters Is., *Solomon Is.* .......... **121 N11** 10 10 S 161 57 E
Throssell, L., *Australia* .. **113 E3** 27 33 S 124 10 E
Throssell Ra., *Australia* .. **112 D3** 22 3 S 121 43 E
Thuan Hoa, *Vietnam* .... **77 H5** 8 58N 105 30 E
Thubun Lakes, *Canada* .. **131 A6** 61 30N 112 0W
Thueyts, *France* ....... **25 D8** 44 41N 4 9 E
Thuillies, *Belgium* ...... **21 H4** 50 18N 4 20 E
Thuin, *Belgium* ........ **21 H4** 50 20N 4 17 E
Thuir, *France* ......... **24 F6** 42 38N 2 45 E
Thule, *Greenland* ...... **6 B4** 77 40N 69 0W
Thun, *Switz.* .......... **28 C5** 46 45N 7 38 E
Thundelarra, *Australia* ... **113 E2** 28 53 S 117 7 E
Thunder B., *U.S.A.* .... **136 B1** 45 0N 83 20W
Thunder Bay, *Canada* ... **128 C2** 48 20N 89 15W
Thunersee, *Switz.* ...... **28 C5** 46 43N 7 39 E
Thung Song, *Thailand* ... **77 H2** 8 10N 99 40 E
Thunkar, *Bhutan* ...... **78 B3** 27 55N 91 0 E
Thuong Tra, *Vietnam* .... **76 D6** 16 2N 107 42 E
Thur →, *Switz.* ....... **29 A8** 47 32N 9 10 E
Thurgau □, *Switz.* ..... **29 A8** 47 34N 9 10 E
Thüringen □, *Germany* .. **26 E7** 51 0N 11 0 E
Thüringer Wald, *Germany* **26 E7** 50 35N 11 0 E
Thurles, *Ireland* ....... **19 D4** 52 40N 7 53W
Thurloo Downs, *Australia* **115 D3** 29 15 S 143 30 E
Thurn P., *Austria* ...... **30 D5** 47 20N 12 25 E
Thursday I., *Australia* ... **114 A3** 10 30 S 142 3 E
Thurso, *Canada* ....... **128 C4** 45 36N 75 15W
Thurso, *U.K.* ......... **18 C5** 58 34N 3 31W
Thurston I., *Antarctica* .. **7 D16** 72 0 S 100 0W
Thury-Harcourt, *France* . **22 D6** 48 59N 0 30W
Thusis, *Switz.* ......... **29 C8** 46 42N 9 26 E
Thutade L., *Canada* .... **130 B3** 57 0N 126 55W
Thyborøn, *Denmark* .... **15 H2** 56 42N 8 12 E
Thylungra, *Australia* .... **115 D3** 26 4 S 143 28 E
Thyolo, *Malawi* ........ **107 F4** 16 7 S 35 5 E
Thysville = Mbanza Ngungu, *Zaïre* ....... **103 D2** 5 12 S 14 53 E
Ti-n-Barraouene, O. →, *Africa* .......... **101 B5** 18 40N 4 5 E
Ti-n-Medjerdam, O. →, *Algeria* .......... **99 C5** 25 45N 1 30 E
Ti-n-Tarabine, O. →, *Algeria* .......... **99 D6** 21 0N 7 25 E
Ti-n-Toumma, *Niger* ... **97 E2** 16 4N 12 40 E
Ti-n-Zaouaténe, *Algeria* . **99 E5** 19 55N 2 55 E
Tia, *Australia* ......... **117 A9** 31 10 S 151 50 E
Tiahuanacu, *Bolivia* .... **156 D4** 16 33 S 68 42W
Tian Shan, *China* ...... **64 B3** 43 0N 84 0 E
Tianchang, *China* ...... **69 A12** 32 40N 119 0 E
Tiandong, *China* ....... **68 F6** 23 36N 107 8 E
Tian'e, *China* ......... **68 E6** 25 1N 107 9 E
Tianguá, *Brazil* ....... **154 B3** 3 44 S 40 59W
Tianhe, *China* ......... **68 E7** 24 48N 108 40 E
Tianjin, *China* ......... **67 E9** 39 8N 117 10 E
Tiankoura, *Burkina Faso* **100 C4** 10 47N 3 17W
Tianlin, *China* ......... **68 E6** 24 21N 106 12 E
Tianmen, *China* ....... **69 B9** 30 39N 113 9 E
Tianquan, *China* ...... **68 B4** 30 7N 102 43 E
Tianshui, *China* ....... **66 G3** 34 32N 105 40 E
Tiantai, *China* ........ **69 C13** 29 10N 121 2 E
Tianyang, *China* ....... **68 F6** 23 42N 106 53 E
Tianzhen, *China* ....... **66 D8** 40 24N 114 5 E
Tianzhu, *China* ........ **68 D7** 26 54N 109 11 E
Tianzhuangtai, *China* ... **67 D12** 40 43N 122 5 E
Tiaret, *Algeria* ........ **99 A5** 35 20N 1 21 E
Tiarra, *Australia* ....... **117 B6** 32 46 S 145 1 E
Tiassalé, *Ivory C.* ...... **100 D4** 5 58N 4 57W
Ti'avea, *W. Samoa* .... **121 W24** 13 57 S 171 24W
Tibagi, *Brazil* ......... **159 A5** 24 30 S 50 24W
Tibagi →, *Brazil* ...... **159 A5** 22 47 S 51 1W
Tibati, *Cameroon* ...... **101 D7** 6 22N 12 30 E
Tiber = Tevere →, *Italy* **39 G9** 41 44N 12 14 E
Tiber Reservoir, *U.S.A.* . **142 B8** 48 19N 111 6W
Tiberias = Teverya, *Israel* **91 C4** 32 47N 35 32 E
Tiberias, L. = Yam Kinneret, *Israel* ...... **91 C4** 32 45N 35 35 E
Tibesti, *Chad* ......... **97 D3** 21 0N 17 30 E
Tibet = Xizang □, *China* **64 C3** 32 0N 88 0 E
Tibiao, *Phil.* .......... **71 F4** 11 17N 122 2 E
Tibiri, *Niger* .......... **101 C6** 13 34N 7 4 E
Ţibleş, *Romania* ....... **46 B5** 47 32N 24 15 E
Tibnī, *Syria* .......... **84 C3** 35 36N 39 50 E
Tibooburra, *Australia* ... **115 D3** 29 26 S 142 1 E
Tibro, *Sweden* ........ **15 F8** 58 28N 14 10 E
Tibugá, G. de, *Colombia* **152 B2** 5 45N 77 20W
Tiburón, *Mexico* ....... **146 B2** 29 0N 112 30W
Ticao I., *Phil.* ......... **70 E4** 12 31N 123 42 E
Tîchît, *Mauritania* ...... **100 B3** 18 21N 9 29W
Tichla, *Mauritania* ..... **98 D2** 21 36N 14 58W
Ticho, *Ethiopia* ........ **95 F4** 7 50N 39 32 E
Ticino □, *Switz.* ....... **29 D7** 46 20N 8 45 E
Ticino →, *Italy* ....... **38 C6** 45 9N 9 14 E
Ticonderoga, *U.S.A.* .... **137 C11** 43 51N 73 26W
Ticul, *Mexico* ......... **147 C7** 20 20N 89 31W
Tidaholm, *Sweden* ..... **15 F7** 58 12N 13 55 E
Tiddim, *Burma* ........ **78 D4** 23 28N 93 45 E
Tideridjaouine, Adrar, *Algeria* .......... **99 D5** 23 0N 2 15 E
Tidikelt, *Algeria* ....... **99 C5** 26 58N 1 30 E
Tidjikja, *Mauritania* .... **100 B2** 18 29N 11 35W
Tidore, *Indonesia* ...... **72 A3** 0 40N 127 25 E
Tiébissou, *Ivory C.* ..... **100 D3** 7 9N 5 10W
Tiéboro, *Chad* ......... **97 D3** 21 20N 17 7 E
Tiefencastel, *Switz.* .... **29 C9** 46 40N 9 33 E
Tiel, *Neths.* ........... **20 E6** 51 53N 5 26 E
Tiel, *Senegal* .......... **100 C1** 14 55N 15 5W
Tieling, *China* ......... **67 C12** 42 20N 123 55 E
Tielt, *Belgium* ......... **21 F2** 51 0N 3 20 E
Tien Shan, *Asia* ....... **55 C8** 42 0N 76 0 E
Tien-tsin = Tianjin, *China* **67 E9** 39 8N 117 10 E
Tien Yen, *Vietnam* ..... **76 B6** 21 20N 107 24 E
T'ienching = Tianjin, *China* .......... **67 E9** 39 8N 117 10 E
Tienen, *Belgium* ....... **21 G5** 50 48N 4 57 E
Tiénigbé, *Ivory C.* ..... **100 D3** 8 11N 5 43W
Tientsin = Tianjin, *China* **67 E9** 39 8N 117 10 E
Tierra Amarilla, *Chile* ... **158 B1** 27 28 S 70 18W
Tierra Amarilla, *U.S.A.* . **143 H10** 36 42N 106 33W
Tierra Colorada, *Mexico* . **147 D5** 17 10N 99 35W
Tierra de Barros, *Spain* .. **37 G4** 38 40N 6 30W
Tierra de Campos, *Spain* **36 C6** 42 10N 4 50W
Tierra del Fuego □, *Argentina* .......... **160 D3** 54 0 S 67 45W
Tierra del Fuego, I. Gr. de, *Argentina* ....... **160 D3** 54 0 S 69 0W
Tierralta, *Colombia* ..... **152 B2** 8 11N 76 4W
Tiétar →, *Spain* ....... **36 F4** 39 50N 6 1W
Tieté →, *Brazil* ....... **159 A5** 20 40 S 51 35W
Tieyon, *Australia* ...... **115 D1** 26 12 S 133 52 E
Tifarati, *W. Sahara* ..... **98 C2** 26 9N 10 33W
Tiffin, *U.S.A.* ......... **141 C13** 41 7N 83 11W
Tiffin →, *U.S.A.* ...... **141 C12** 41 20N 84 24W
Tiflèt, *Morocco* ........ **98 B3** 33 54N 6 20W
Tiflis = Tbilisi, *Georgia* . **53 F11** 41 43N 44 50 E
Tifton, *U.S.A.* ......... **135 K4** 31 27N 83 31W
Tifu, *Indonesia* ........ **72 B3** 3 39 S 126 24 E
Tiga, I., *N. Cal.* ....... **121 U21** 21 7 S 167 49 E
Tigaon, *Phil.* .......... **70 E4** 13 38N 123 30 E
Tigbauan, *Phil.* ........ **71 F4** 10 41N 122 27 E
Tigil, *Russia* .......... **57 D16** 57 49N 158 40 E
Tignish, *Canada* ....... **129 C7** 46 58N 64 2W
Tigray □, *Ethiopia* ..... **95 E4** 13 35N 39 15 E
Tigre →, *Peru* ........ **152 D3** 4 30 S 74 10W
Tigre →, *Venezuela* .... **153 B5** 9 20N 62 30W
Tigris = Dijlah, Nahr →, *Asia* .......... **84 D5** 31 0N 47 25 E
Tiguentourine, *Algeria* ... **99 C6** 27 52N 9 8 E
Tigveni, *Romania* ...... **46 D5** 45 10N 24 31 E
Tigyaing, *Burma* ....... **78 D6** 23 45N 96 10 E
Tigzerte, O. →, *Morocco* **98 C3** 28 10N 9 37W
Tîh, Gebel el, *Egypt* .... **94 J8** 29 32N 33 26 E
Tihodaine, Dunes de, *Algeria* .......... **99 C6** 25 15N 7 15 E
Tijesno, *Croatia* ....... **39 E12** 43 48N 15 39 E
Tījī, *Libya* ........... **96 B2** 32 0N 11 18 E
Tijuana, *Mexico* ....... **145 N9** 32 30N 117 10W
Tikal, *Guatemala* ...... **148 C2** 17 13N 89 24W
Tikamgarh, *India* ....... **81 G8** 24 44N 78 50 E
Tikhoretsk, *Russia* ..... **53 D9** 45 56N 40 5 E
Tikhvin, *Russia* ........ **50 B8** 59 35N 33 30 E
Tikkadouine, Adrar, *Algeria* .......... **99 D5** 24 28N 1 30 E
Tiko, *Cameroon* ....... **101 E6** 4 4N 9 20 E
Tikrīt, *Iraq* ........... **84 C4** 34 35N 43 37 E
Tiksi, *Russia* .......... **57 B13** 71 40N 128 45 E
Tilamuta, *Indonesia* .... **72 A2** 0 32N 122 23 E
Tilburg, *Neths.* ........ **21 E6** 51 31N 5 6 E
Tilbury, *Canada* ....... **128 D3** 42 17N 82 23W
Tilbury, *U.K.* ......... **17 F8** 51 27N 0 24 E
Tilcara, *Argentina* ...... **158 A2** 23 36 S 65 23W
Tilden, *Nebr., U.S.A.* ... **138 D6** 42 3N 97 50W
Tilden, *Tex., U.S.A.* .... **139 L5** 28 28N 98 33W
Tilemses, *Niger* ........ **101 B5** 15 37N 4 44 E
Tilemsi, Vallée du, *Mali* . **101 B5** 17 42N 0 15 E
Tilhar, *India* .......... **81 F8** 28 0N 79 45 E
Tilia, O. →, *Algeria* ... **99 C5** 27 32N 0 55 E
Tilichiki, *Russia* ....... **57 C17** 60 27N 166 5 E
Tiligul →, *Ukraine* ..... **52 C4** 47 4N 30 57 E
Tililane, *Algeria* ....... **99 C4** 27 49N 0 6W
Tilin, *Burma* ......... **78 E5** 21 41N 94 6 E
Tilissos, *Greece* ....... **32 D7** 35 20N 25 1 E
Till →, *U.K.* ......... **16 B5** 55 35N 2 3W
Tillabéri, *Niger* ........ **101 C5** 14 28N 1 28 E
Tillamook, *U.S.A.* ..... **142 D2** 45 27N 123 51W
Tillberga, *Sweden* ...... **14 E10** 59 52N 16 39 E
Tillia, *Niger* .......... **101 B5** 16 8N 4 47 E
Tillsonburg, *Canada* .... **128 D3** 42 53N 80 44W
Tillyeria □, *Cyprus* ..... **32 D11** 35 6N 32 40 E
Tílos, *Greece* ......... **45 H9** 36 27N 27 27 E
Tilpa, *Australia* ........ **115 E3** 30 57 S 144 24 E
Tilrhemt, *Algeria* ...... **99 B5** 33 9N 3 22 E
Tilsit = Sovetsk, *Russia* . **50 D2** 55 6N 21 50 E
Tilt →, *U.K.* ......... **18 E5** 56 50N 3 50W
Tilton, *U.S.A.* ........ **137 C13** 43 27N 71 36W
Timagami L., *Canada* ... **128 C3** 47 0N 80 10W
Timanskiy Kryazh, *Russia* **48 A9** 65 58N 50 5 E
Timareh, *Yemen* ....... **87 D6** 12 37N 54 17 E
Timaru, *N.Z.* .......... **119 E6** 44 23 S 171 14 E
Timashevo, *Russia* ..... **54 E2** 53 22N 51 9 E
Timashevsk, *Russia* .... **53 D8** 45 35N 39 0 E
Timau, *Italy* .......... **39 B10** 46 35N 13 0 E
Timau, *Kenya* ......... **106 B4** 0 4N 37 15 E
Timbákion, *Greece* ..... **32 D6** 35 4N 24 45 E
Timbaúba, *Brazil* ...... **154 C4** 7 31 S 35 19W
Timbedgha, *Mauritania* .. **100 B3** 16 17N 8 16W
Timber Lake, *U.S.A.* ... **138 C4** 45 26N 101 5W
Timber Mt., *U.S.A.* .... **144 H10** 37 6N 116 28W
Timbío, *Colombia* ...... **152 C2** 2 20N 76 40W
Timbiqui, *Colombia* ..... **152 C2** 2 46N 77 42W
Timboon, *Australia* ..... **116 E5** 38 30 S 142 58 E
Timbuktu = Tombouctou, *Mali* .......... **100 B4** 16 50N 3 0W
Timellouline, *Algeria* .... **99 C6** 29 22N 8 55 E
Timétrine Montagnes, *Mali* .......... **101 B4** 19 25N 1 0W
Timfi Óros, *Greece* ..... **44 E2** 39 59N 20 45 E
Timfristós, Óros, *Greece* . **45 F3** 38 57N 21 50 E
Timhadit, *Morocco* ..... **98 B3** 33 15N 5 4W
Timi, *Cyprus* .......... **32 E11** 34 44N 32 31 E
Tîmia, *Niger* .......... **97 E1** 18 4N 8 40 E
Timimoun, *Algeria* ..... **99 C5** 29 14N 0 16 E
Timiş = Tamis →, *Serbia* **46 E1** 44 51N 20 39 E
Timiş □, *Romania* ..... **46 D2** 45 40N 21 30 E
Timişoara, *Romania* .... **46 D2** 45 43N 21 15 E
Timmins, *Canada* ...... **128 C3** 48 28N 81 25W
Timok →, *Serbia* ...... **42 C7** 44 10N 22 40 E
Timon, *Brazil* ......... **154 C3** 5 8 S 42 52W
Timor, *Indonesia* ...... **72 C3** 9 0 S 125 0 E
Timor □, *Indonesia* .... **72 C3** 9 0 S 125 0 E
Timor Sea, *Ind. Oc.* .... **112 B4** 12 0 S 127 0 E
Tin Alkoum, *Algeria* .... **99 D7** 24 42N 10 17 E
Tin Gornai, *Mali* ...... **101 B4** 16 38N 0 38W
Tin Mt., *U.S.A.* ....... **144 J9** 36 50N 117 10W
Tîna, Khalîg el, *Egypt* ... **94 H8** 31 20N 32 42 E
Tinabog, *Phil.* ......... **70 E3** 12 1N 120 25 E
Tinaca Pt., *Phil.* ....... **71 J5** 5 30N 125 25 E
Tinaco, *Venezuela* ..... **152 B4** 9 42N 68 26W
Tinafak, O. →, *Algeria* . **99 C6** 27 10N 7 0 E
Tinajo, *Canary Is.* ...... **33 E6** 29 4N 13 42W
Tinaquillo, *Venezuela* ... **152 B4** 9 55N 68 18W
Tinca, *Romania* ........ **46 C2** 46 46N 21 58 E
Tinchebray, *France* ..... **22 D6** 48 47N 0 45W
Tindivanam, *India* ...... **83 H4** 12 15N 79 41 E
Tindouf, *Algeria* ....... **98 C3** 27 42N 8 10W
Tinée →, *France* ...... **25 E11** 43 55N 7 11 E
Tineg, *Phil.* ........... **70 C3** 17 48N 120 56 E
Tineo, *Spain* .......... **36 B4** 43 21N 6 27W
Tinerhir, *Morocco* ...... **98 B3** 31 29N 5 31W
Tinfouchi, *Algeria* ...... **98 C3** 28 52N 5 49W
Ting Jiang →, *China* ... **69 E11** 24 45N 116 35 E
Tinggi, Pulau, *Malaysia* .. **77 L5** 2 18N 104 7 E
Tingkawk Sakan, *Burma* . **78 B6** 26 4N 96 44 E
Tinglayan, *Phil.* ....... **70 C3** 17 15N 121 9 E
Tinglev, *Denmark* ...... **15 K3** 54 57N 9 13 E
Tingo Maria, *Peru* ...... **156 B2** 9 10 S 75 54W
Tinh Bien, *Vietnam* ..... **77 G5** 10 36N 104 57 E
Tinharé, I. de, *Brazil* ... **155 D4** 13 30 S 38 58W
Tiniguiban, *Phil.* ....... **71 F2** 11 22N 119 30 E
Tinjar →, *Malaysia* .... **75 B4** 4 4N 114 18 E
Tinkurrin, *Australia* ..... **113 F2** 32 59 S 117 46 E
Tinnevelly = Tirunelveli, *India* .......... **83 K3** 8 45N 77 45 E
Tinnoset, *Norway* ...... **14 E3** 59 55N 9 3 E
Tinnsjø, *Norway* ....... **14 E2** 59 55N 8 54 E
Tinogasta, *Argentina* ... **158 B2** 28 5 S 67 32W
Tínos, *Greece* ......... **45 G7** 37 33N 25 8 E
Tiñoso, C., *Spain* ...... **35 H3** 37 32N 1 6W
Tinsukia, *India* ........ **78 B5** 27 29N 95 20 E
Tinta, *Peru* ........... **156 C3** 14 3 S 71 20W
Tintigny, *Belgium* ...... **21 J7** 49 41N 5 31 E
Tintina, *Argentina* ..... **158 B3** 27 2 S 62 45W
Tintinara, *Australia* ..... **116 C4** 35 48 S 140 2 E
Tinto →, *Spain* ....... **37 H4** 37 12N 6 55W
Tinui, *N.Z.* ........... **118 G5** 40 52 S 176 5 E
Tinwald, *N.Z.* ......... **119 D6** 43 55 S 171 43 E
Tioga, *U.S.A.* ......... **136 E7** 41 55N 77 8W
Tioman, Pulau, *Malaysia* **77 L5** 2 50N 104 10 E
Tione di Trento, *Italy* ... **38 B7** 46 3N 10 44 E
Tionesta, *U.S.A.* ....... **136 E5** 41 30N 79 28W
Tior, *Sudan* .......... **95 F3** 6 26N 31 11 E
Tioulilin, *Algeria* ....... **99 C4** 27 1N 0 2W
Tipp City, *U.S.A.* ...... **141 E12** 39 58N 84 11W
Tippecanoe →, *U.S.A.* . **141 D10** 40 30N 86 45W
Tipperary, *Ireland* ...... **19 D3** 52 28N 8 10W
Tipperary □, *Ireland* .... **19 D4** 52 37N 7 55W
Tipton, *U.K.* .......... **17 E5** 52 32N 2 4W
Tipton, *Calif., U.S.A.* .. **144 J7** 36 4N 119 19W
Tipton, *Ind., U.S.A.* .... **141 D10** 40 17N 86 2W
Tipton, *Iowa, U.S.A.* ... **140 C5** 41 46N 91 8W
Tipton, *Mo., U.S.A.* .... **140 F4** 38 39N 92 47W
Tipton Mt., *U.S.A.* .... **145 K12** 35 32N 114 12W
Tiptonville, *U.S.A.* ..... **139 G10** 36 23N 89 29W
Tiptur, *India* .......... **83 H3** 13 15N 76 26 E
Tiquié →, *Brazil* ...... **152 C4** 0 5N 68 25W
Tiracambu, Serra do, *Brazil* .......... **154 B2** 3 15 S 46 30W
Tirān, *Iran* ........... **85 C6** 32 45N 51 8 E
Tirān, *Si. Arabia* ...... **94 B3** 27 57N 34 32 E
Tirana, *Albania* ........ **44 C1** 41 18N 19 49 E
Tirana-Durrësi □, *Albania* **44 C2** 41 35N 20 0 E
Tiranë = Tirana, *Albania* **44 C1** 41 18N 19 49 E
Tirano, *Italy* .......... **38 B7** 46 13N 10 11 E
Tiraspol, *Moldavia* ..... **52 C3** 46 55N 29 35 E
Tirat Karmel, *Israel* .... **91 C3** 32 46N 34 58 E
Tiratimine, *Algeria* ..... **99 C5** 25 56N 3 37 E
Tirau, *N.Z.* ........... **118 D4** 37 58 S 175 46 E
Tirdout, *Mali* ......... **101 B4** 16 7N 1 5W
Tire, *Turkey* .......... **88 D2** 38 5N 27 50 E
Tirebolu, *Turkey* ....... **89 C8** 40 58N 38 45 E
Tiree, *U.K.* ........... **18 E2** 56 31N 6 55W
Tîrgovişte, *Romania* .... **46 E6** 44 55N 25 27 E
Tîrgu Frumos, *Romania* .. **46 B8** 47 12N 27 2 E
Tîrgu-Jiu, *Romania* ..... **46 D4** 45 5N 23 19 E
Tîrgu Mureş, *Romania* .. **46 C5** 46 31N 24 38 E
Tîrgu Neamţ, *Romania* .. **46 B7** 47 12N 26 25 E
Tîrgu Ocna, *Romania* ... **46 C7** 46 16N 26 39 E
Tîrgu Secuiesc, *Romania* . **46 C7** 46 0N 26 10 E
Tirich Mir, *Pakistan* .... **79 A3** 36 15N 71 55 E
Tiriola, *Italy* .......... **41 D9** 38 57N 16 32 E
Tiririca, Serra da, *Brazil* . **155 E2** 17 6 S 47 6W
Tiris, *W. Sahara* ....... **98 D2** 23 10N 13 20W
Tirlyanskiy, *Russia* ..... **54 D6** 54 14N 58 35 E
Tîrna →, *India* ....... **82 E3** 18 4N 76 57 E
Tîrnava Mare →, *Romania* .......... **46 C5** 46 15N 24 30 E
Tîrnava Mică →, *Romania* .......... **46 C5** 46 17N 24 30 E
Tîrnăveni, *Romania* ..... **46 C5** 46 19N 24 13 E
Tírnavos, *Greece* ....... **44 E4** 39 45N 22 18 E
Tîrnova, *Romania* ...... **46 D3** 45 23N 22 1 E
Tirodi, *India* .......... **82 D4** 21 40N 79 44 E
Tirol □, *Austria* ....... **30 D3** 47 3N 10 43 E
Tiros, *Brazil* .......... **155 E2** 19 0 S 45 58W
Tirschenreuth, *Germany* . **27 F8** 49 51N 12 20 E
Tirso →, *Italy* ........ **40 C1** 39 52N 8 33 E
Tirso, L. del, *Italy* ..... **40 B1** 40 8N 8 56 E
Tirua, Pt., *N.Z.* ....... **118 E3** 38 25 S 174 40 E
Tiruchchendur, *India* .... **83 K4** 8 30N 78 11 E
Tiruchchirappalli, *India* .. **83 J4** 10 45N 78 45 E
Tiruchengodu, *India* .... **83 J3** 11 23N 77 56 E
Tirumangalam, *India* .... **83 K3** 9 49N 77 58 E
Tirunelveli, *India* ...... **83 K3** 8 45N 77 45 E
Tirupati, *India* ......... **83 H4** 13 39N 79 25 E
Tiruppattur, *India* ...... **83 H4** 12 30N 78 30 E
Tiruppur, *India* ........ **83 J3** 11 5N 77 22 E
Tirutturaippundi, *India* .. **83 J4** 10 32N 79 41 E
Tiruvadaimarudur, *India* . **83 J4** 11 2N 79 27 E
Tiruvallar, *India* ....... **83 H4** 13 9N 79 57 E

Tiruvannamalai, India ... 83 H4 12 15N 79 5 E
Tiruvettipuram, India ... 83 H4 12 39N 79 33 E
Tiruvottiyur, India ...... 83 H5 13 10N 80 22 E
Tisa →, Hungary ....... 31 E13 46 8N 20 2 E
Tisa →, Serbia ......... 42 B5 45 15N 20 17 E
Tisdale, Canada ........ 131 C8 52 50N 104 0W
Tishomingo, U.S.A. ..... 139 H6 34 14N 96 41W
Tisnaren, Sweden ....... 14 F9 58 58N 15 56 E
Tišnov, Czech. .......... 31 B9 49 21N 16 25 E
Tisovec, Slovak Rep. .... 31 C12 48 41N 19 56 E
Tissemsilt, Algeria ...... 99 A5 35 35N 1 50 E
Tissint, Morocco ........ 98 C3 29 57N 7 16W
Tissø, Denmark ......... 15 J5 55 35N 11 18 E
Tista →, India ......... 78 C2 25 23N 89 43 E
Tisza = Tisa →, Hungary 31 E13 46 8N 20 2 E
Tiszaföldvár, Hungary ... 31 E13 46 58N 20 14 E
Tiszafüred, Hungary ..... 31 D13 47 38N 20 50 E
Tiszalök, Hungary ...... 31 D14 48 0N 21 10 E
Tiszavasvári, Hungary ... 31 D14 47 58N 21 18 E
Tit, Ahaggar, Algeria .... 99 D6 23 0N 5 10 E
Tit, Tademait, Algeria ... 99 C5 27 0N 1 29 E
Tit-Ary, Russia ......... 57 B13 71 55N 127 2 E
Titaguas, Spain ......... 34 F3 39 53N 1 6W
Titahi Bay, N.Z. ........ 118 H3 41 6 S 174 50 E
Titel, Serbia ........... 42 B5 45 10N 20 18 E
Tithwal, Pakistan ....... 81 B5 34 21N 73 50 E
Titicaca, L., S. Amer. ... 156 D4 15 30 S 69 30W
Titiri Hd., N.Z. ........ 119 D4 43 36 S 169 25 E
Titiwa, Nigeria ......... 101 C7 12 14N 12 53 E
Titlagarh, India ........ 82 D6 20 15N 83 11 E
Titlis, Switz. ............ 29 C6 46 46N 8 27 E
Titograd = Podgorica, Montenegro .......... 42 E4 42 30N 19 19 E
Titov Veles, Macedonia .. 42 F6 41 46N 21 47 E
Titova Korenica, Croatia . 39 D12 44 45N 15 41 E
Titovo Užice, Serbia .... 42 D4 43 55N 19 50 E
Titule, Zaïre ........... 106 B2 3 15N 25 31 E
Titumate, Colombia ..... 152 B2 8 19N 77 5W
Titusville, Fla., U.S.A. ... 135 L5 28 37N 80 49W
Titusville, Pa., U.S.A. ... 136 E5 41 38N 79 41W
Tivaouane, Senegal ..... 100 C1 14 56N 16 45W
Tivat, Montenegro ...... 42 E3 42 28N 18 43 E
Tiveden, Sweden ........ 15 F8 58 50N 14 30 E
Tiverton, U.K. ......... 17 G4 50 54N 3 30W
Tívoli, Italy ............ 39 G9 41 58N 12 45 E
Tiwī, Oman ............ 87 B7 22 45N 59 12 E
Tiyo, Eritrea ........... 95 E5 14 41N 40 15 E
Tizga, Morocco ......... 98 B3 32 1N 5 9W
Ti'zi N'Isli, Morocco .... 98 B3 32 28N 5 47W
Tizi-Ouzou, Algeria ..... 99 A5 36 42N 4 3 E
Tizimín, Mexico ........ 147 C7 21 0N 88 1W
Tiznados →, Venezuela . 152 B4 8 16N 67 47W
Tiznit, Morocco ........ 98 C3 29 48N 9 45W
Tjeggelvas, Sweden ...... 12 C14 66 37N 17 45 E
Tjeukemeer, Neths. ..... 20 C7 52 53N 5 48 E
Tjirebon = Cirebon, Indonesia ............ 75 D3 6 45 S 108 32 E
Tjøme, Norway ......... 14 E4 59 8N 10 26 E
Tjonger Kanaal, Neths. .. 20 C7 52 52N 5 52 E
Tjörn, Sweden .......... 15 G5 58 0N 11 35 E
Tkibuli, Georgia ........ 53 E10 42 26N 43 0 E
Tkvarcheli, Georgia ..... 53 E9 42 47N 41 42 E
Tlacotalpan, Mexico ..... 147 D5 18 37N 95 40W
Tlahualilo, Mexico ...... 146 B4 26 20N 103 30W
Tlaquepaque, Mexico .... 146 C4 20 39N 103 19W
Tlaxcala, Mexico ........ 147 D5 19 20N 98 14W
Tlaxcala □, Mexico ..... 147 D5 19 30N 98 20W
Tlaxiaco, Mexico ........ 147 D5 17 18N 97 40W
Tlell, Canada ........... 130 C2 53 34N 131 56W
Tlemcen, Algeria ....... 99 B4 34 52N 1 21W
Tleta Sidi Bouguedra, Morocco ............ 98 B3 32 16N 9 59W
Tlumach, Ukraine ....... 52 B1 48 51N 25 0 E
Tłuszcz, Poland ........ 47 C8 52 25N 21 25 E
Tlyarata, Russia ........ 53 E12 42 9N 46 26 E
Tmassah, Libya ......... 96 C3 26 19N 15 51 E
Tnine d'Anglou, Morocco 98 C3 29 50N 9 50W
To Bong, Vietnam ....... 76 F7 12 45N 109 16 E
To-Shima, Japan ........ 63 C11 34 31N 139 17 E
Toad →, Canada ........ 130 B4 59 25N 124 57W
Toamasina, Madag. ...... 105 B8 18 10 S 49 25 E
Toamasina □, Madag. ... 105 B8 18 0 S 49 0 E
Toay, Argentina ........ 158 D3 36 43 S 64 38W
Toba, Japan ............ 63 C8 34 30N 136 51 E
Toba Kakar, Pakistan ... 79 C3 31 30N 69 0 E
Toba Tek Singh, Pakistan 80 D5 30 55N 72 25 E
Tobago, W. Indies ...... 149 D7 11 10N 60 30W
Tobarra, Spain ......... 35 G3 38 37N 1 44W
Tobelo, Indonesia ....... 72 A3 1 45N 127 56 E
Tobermorey, Australia ... 114 C2 22 12 S 138 0 E
Tobermory, Canada ..... 128 C3 45 12N 81 40W
Tobermory, U.K. ....... 18 E2 56 37N 6 4W
Tobin, U.S.A. .......... 144 F5 39 55N 121 19W
Tobin, L., Australia ..... 112 D4 21 45 S 125 49 E
Tobin L., Canada ....... 131 C8 53 35N 103 30W
Toboali, Indonesia ...... 74 C3 3 0 S 106 25 E
Tobol, Kazakhstan ...... 54 E8 52 40N 62 39 E
Tobol →, Russia ....... 56 D7 58 10N 68 12 E
Toboli, Indonesia ....... 72 B2 0 38 S 120 5 E
Tobolsk, Russia ......... 56 D7 58 15N 68 10 E
Toboso, Phil. ........... 71 F4 10 43N 123 31 E
Tobruk = Tubruq, Libya 96 B4 32 7N 23 55 E
Tobyhanna, U.S.A. ..... 137 E9 41 11N 75 25W
Tocache Nuevo, Peru ... 156 B2 8 9 S 76 26W
Tocantínia, Brazil ....... 154 C2 9 33 S 48 22W
Tocantinópolis, Brazil ... 154 C2 6 20 S 47 25W
Tocantins →, Brazil .... 154 B2 1 45 S 49 10W
Toccoa, U.S.A. ......... 135 H4 34 35N 83 19W
Toce →, Italy .......... 38 C5 45 56N 8 29 E
Tochigi, Japan .......... 63 A11 36 25N 139 45 E
Tochigi □, Japan ....... 63 A11 36 45N 139 45 E
Tocina, Spain ........... 37 H5 37 37N 5 44W
Tocopilla, Chile ......... 158 A1 22 5 S 70 10W
Tocumwal, Australia .... 117 C6 35 51 S 145 31 E
Tocuyo →, Venezuela .. 152 A4 11 3N 68 23W
Tocuyo de la Costa, Venezuela ........... 152 A4 11 2N 68 23W
Todd →, Australia ..... 114 C2 24 52 S 135 48 E
Todeli, Indonesia ....... 72 B2 1 38 S 124 34 E
Todenyang, Kenya ...... 106 B4 4 35N 35 56 E
Todi, Italy ............. 39 F9 42 47N 12 24 E
Tödi, Switz. ............ 29 C7 46 48N 8 55 E
Todos os Santos, B. de, Brazil .............. 155 D4 12 48 S 38 38W
Todos Santos, Mexico ... 146 C2 23 27N 110 13W
Todtnau, Germany ...... 27 H3 47 50N 7 56 E
Toecé, Burkina Faso .... 101 C4 11 50N 1 16W
Toetoes B., N.Z. ....... 119 G3 46 42 S 168 41 E
Tofield, Canada ........ 130 C6 53 25N 112 40W
Tofino, Canada ......... 130 D3 49 11N 125 55W
Töfsingdalens nationalpark, Sweden .. 14 B6 62 15N 12 44 E
Toftlund, Denmark ..... 15 J3 55 11N 9 2 E
Tofua, Tonga ........... 121 P13 19 45 S 175 5W
Toga, Vanuatu .......... 121 C4 13 26 S 166 42 E
Tōgane, Japan .......... 63 B12 35 33N 140 22 E
Togba, Mauritania ...... 100 B2 17 26N 10 12W
Togbo, C.A.R. ......... 102 A3 6 0N 17 27 E
Toggenburg, Switz. ..... 29 B8 47 16N 9 9 E
Togian, Kepulauan, Indonesia ............ 72 B2 0 20 S 121 50 E
Togliatti, Russia ........ 51 E16 53 32N 49 24 E
Togo ■, W. Afr. ........ 101 D5 8 30N 1 35 E
Togtoh, China .......... 66 D6 40 15N 111 10 E
Toguzak →, Kazakhstan 54 D8 54 3N 62 44 E
Tohma →, Turkey ..... 89 D8 38 29N 38 23 E
Tōhoku □, Japan ....... 60 E10 39 50N 141 45 E
Toi, Japan ............. 63 C10 34 54N 138 47 E
Toinya, Sudan .......... 95 F2 6 17N 29 46 E
Tojikiston = Tajikistan ■, Asia ................. 55 D5 38 30N 70 0 E
Tojo, Indonesia ......... 72 B2 1 20 S 121 15 E
Tōjō, Japan ............ 62 C5 34 53N 133 16 E
Tok →, Russia ......... 54 E3 52 46N 52 22 E
Toka, Guyana ........... 153 C6 3 58N 59 17W
Tokaanu, N.Z. ......... 118 E4 38 58 S 175 46 E
Tokachi-Dake, Japan .... 60 C11 43 17N 142 5 E
Tokachi-Gawa →, Japan 60 C11 42 44N 143 42 E
Tokai, Japan ........... 63 B8 35 2N 136 55 E
Tokaj, Hungary ......... 31 C14 48 8N 21 27 E
Tokala, Indonesia ....... 72 B2 1 30 S 121 40 E
Tōkamachi, Japan ...... 61 F9 37 8N 138 43 E
Tokanui, N.Z. .......... 119 G3 46 34 S 168 56 E
Tokar, Sudan ........... 94 D4 18 27N 37 56 E
Tokara-Rettō, Japan .... 61 K4 29 37N 129 43 E
Tokarahi, N.Z. ......... 119 E5 44 56 S 170 39 E
Tokashiki-Shima, Japan . 61 L3 26 11N 127 21 E
Tokat, Turkey .......... 88 C7 40 22N 36 35 E
Tokat □, Turkey ........ 88 C7 40 15N 36 30 E
Tŏkchŏn, N. Korea ..... 67 E14 39 45N 126 18 E
Tokeland, U.S.A. ....... 144 D3 46 42N 123 59W
Tokelau Is., Pac. Oc. ... 122 H10 9 0 S 171 45W
Toki, Japan ............ 63 B9 35 18N 137 8 E
Tokmak, Kirghizia ...... 55 B7 42 49N 75 15 E
Toko Ra., Australia ..... 114 C2 23 5 S 138 20 E
Tokomaru Bay, N.Z. .... 118 E7 38 8 S 178 22 E
Tokoname, Japan ....... 63 C8 34 53N 136 51 E
Tokoro-Gawa →, Japan 60 B12 44 7N 144 5 E
Tokoroa, N.Z. .......... 118 E4 38 13 S 175 50 E
Tokorozawa, Japan ..... 63 B11 35 47N 139 28 E
Toktogul, Kirghizia ..... 55 C6 41 50N 72 50 E
Toku, Tonga ............ 121 P13 18 10 S 174 11W
Tokuji, Japan ........... 62 C3 34 11N 131 42 E
Tokuno-Shima, Japan ... 61 L4 27 56N 128 55 E
Tokushima, Japan ...... 62 C6 34 4N 134 34 E
Tokushima □, Japan .... 62 D6 33 55N 134 0 E
Tokuyama, Japan ....... 62 C3 34 3N 131 50 E
Tōkyō, Japan .......... 63 B11 35 45N 139 45 E
Tōkyō □, Japan ........ 63 B11 35 40N 139 30 E
Tōkyō-Wan, Japan ...... 63 B11 35 25N 139 47 E
Tokzār, Afghan. ........ 79 B2 35 52N 66 26 E
Tolaga Bay, N.Z. ....... 118 E7 38 21 S 178 20 E
Tolbukhin, Bulgaria ..... 43 D12 43 37N 27 49 E
Toledo, Phil. ........... 71 F4 10 23N 123 38 E
Toledo, Spain .......... 36 F6 39 50N 4 2W
Toledo, Ill., U.S.A. ..... 141 E8 39 16N 88 15W
Toledo, Iowa, U.S.A. .... 140 B4 42 0N 92 35W
Toledo, Ohio, U.S.A. ... 141 C13 41 39N 83 33W
Toledo, Oreg., U.S.A. ... 142 D2 44 37N 123 56W
Toledo, Wash., U.S.A. .. 142 C2 46 26N 122 51W
Toledo, Montes de, Spain 37 F6 39 33N 4 20W
Tolentino, Italy ......... 39 E10 43 12N 13 17 E
Tolga, Algeria .......... 99 B6 34 40N 5 22 E
Tolga, Norway ......... 14 B5 62 26N 11 1 E
Toliara, Madag. ........ 105 C7 23 21 S 43 40 E
Toliara □, Madag. ..... 105 C8 21 0 S 45 0 E
Tolima, Colombia ....... 152 C2 4 40N 75 19W
Tolima □, Colombia .... 152 C2 3 45N 75 15W
Tolitoli, Indonesia ...... 72 A2 1 5N 120 50 E
Tolkamer, Neths. ....... 20 E8 51 52N 6 6 E
Tolkmicko, Poland ...... 47 A6 54 19N 19 31 E
Tolleson, U.S.A. ....... 143 K7 33 27N 112 16W
Tollhouse, U.S.A. ...... 144 H7 37 1N 119 24W
Tolmachevo, Russia ..... 50 B6 58 56N 29 51 E
Tolmezzo, Italy ......... 39 B10 46 23N 13 2 E
Tolmin, Slovenia ....... 39 B10 46 11N 13 45 E
Tolna, Hungary ........ 31 E11 46 25N 18 48 E
Tolna □, Hungary ...... 31 E11 46 30N 18 30 E
Tolo, Zaïre ............ 102 C3 2 55 S 18 34 E
Tolo, Teluk, Indonesia .. 72 B2 2 20 S 122 10 E
Tolochin, Belorussia .... 50 D6 54 25N 29 42 E
Tolong Bay, Phil. ....... 71 G4 9 20N 122 49 E
Tolono, U.S.A. ......... 141 E8 39 59N 88 16W
Tolosa, Spain .......... 34 B2 43 8N 2 5W
Tolox, Spain ........... 37 J6 36 41N 4 54W
Toltén, Chile ........... 160 A2 39 13 S 74 14W
Toluca, Mexico ......... 147 D5 19 20N 99 40W
Tom Burke, S. Africa ... 105 C4 23 5 S 28 0 E
Tom Price, Australia .... 112 D2 22 40 S 117 48 E
Tomah, U.S.A. ......... 138 D9 43 59N 90 30W
Tomahawk, U.S.A. ..... 138 C10 45 28N 89 44W
Tomakomai, Japan ..... 60 C10 42 38N 141 36 E
Tomales, U.S.A. ........ 144 G4 38 15N 122 53W
Tomales B., U.S.A. ..... 144 G3 38 15N 123 58W
Tomanlivi, Fiji ......... 121 A2 17 37 S 178 1 E
Tomar, Portugal ........ 37 F2 39 36N 8 25W
Tómaros Óros, Greece ... 44 E2 39 29N 20 48 E
Tomarza, Turkey ....... 88 D6 38 27N 35 48 E
Tomás Barrón, Bolivia .. 156 D4 17 35 S 67 31W
Tomaszów Mazowiecki, Poland .............. 47 D6 51 30N 19 57 E
Tomatlán, Mexico ....... 146 D3 19 56N 105 15W
Tombador, Serra do, Brazil ............... 157 C6 12 0 S 58 0W
Tombé, Sudan .......... 95 F3 5 53N 31 40 E
Tombigbee →, U.S.A. .. 135 K2 31 8N 87 57W
Tombôco, Angola ....... 103 D2 6 48 S 13 18 E
Tombouctou, Mali ...... 100 B4 16 50N 3 0W
Tombstone, U.S.A. ..... 143 L8 31 43N 110 4W
Tombua, Angola ........ 103 F2 15 55 S 11 55 E
Tomé, Chile ........... 158 D1 36 36 S 72 57W
Tomé-Açu, Brazil ....... 154 B2 2 25 S 48 9W
Tomelilla, Sweden ...... 15 J7 55 33N 13 58 E
Tomelloso, Spain ....... 35 F1 39 10N 3 2W
Tomingley, Australia ... 117 B8 32 26 S 148 16 E
Tomini, Indonesia ....... 72 A2 0 30N 120 30 E
Tomini, Teluk, Indonesia 72 B2 0 10 S 122 0 E
Tominian, Mali ......... 100 C4 13 17N 4 35W
Tomiño, Spain .......... 36 D2 41 59N 8 46W
Tomkinson Ras., Australia 113 E4 26 11 S 129 5 E
Tommot, Russia ........ 57 D13 59 4N 126 20 E
Tomnavoulin, U.K. ..... 18 D5 57 19N 3 18W
Tomnop Ta Suos, Cambodia ............ 77 G5 11 20N 104 15 E
Tomo, Colombia ........ 152 C4 2 38N 67 32W
Tomo, Japan ........... 62 C5 34 23N 133 23 E
Tomo →, Colombia ..... 152 B4 5 20N 67 48W
Tomobe, Japan ......... 63 A12 36 20N 140 20 E
Toms Place, U.S.A. ..... 144 H8 37 34N 118 41W
Toms River, U.S.A. ..... 137 G10 39 58N 74 12W
Tomsk, Russia .......... 56 D9 56 30N 85 5 E
Tonalá, Mexico ........ 147 D6 16 8N 93 41W
Tonale, Passo del, Italy .. 38 B7 46 15N 10 34 E
Tonalea, U.S.A. ........ 143 H8 36 19N 110 56W
Tonami, Japan ......... 63 A8 36 40N 136 58 E
Tonantins, Brazil ....... 152 D4 2 45 S 67 45W
Tonasket, U.S.A. ....... 142 B4 48 42N 119 26W
Tonate, Fr. Guiana ...... 153 C7 5 0N 52 28W
Tonawanda, U.S.A. ..... 136 D6 43 1N 78 53W
Tonbridge, U.K. ........ 17 F8 51 12N 0 18 E
Tondano, Indonesia ..... 72 A2 1 35N 124 54 E
Tondela, Portugal ...... 36 E2 40 31N 8 5W
Tønder, Denmark ....... 15 K2 54 58N 8 50 E
Tondi, India ............ 83 K4 9 45N 79 4 E
Tondi Kiwindi, Niger .... 101 C5 14 28N 2 2 E
Tondibi, Mali ........... 101 B4 16 39N 0 14W
Tonekābon, Iran ........ 85 B6 36 45N 51 12 E
Tong Xian, China ....... 66 E9 39 55N 116 35 E
Tonga ■, Pac. Oc. ...... 121 P13 19 50 S 174 30W
Tonga Trench, Pac. Oc. . 122 J10 18 0 S 173 0W
Tongaat, S. Africa ...... 105 D5 29 33 S 31 9 E
Tongala, Australia ...... 117 D6 36 14 S 144 56 E
Tong'an, China ......... 69 E12 24 37N 118 8 E
Tongareva, Cook Is. ..... 123 H12 9 0 S 158 0W
Tongatapu, Tonga ...... 121 Q14 21 10 S 174 0W
Tongatapu Group, Tonga 121 Q13 21 0 S 175 0W
Tongbai, China ......... 69 A9 32 20N 113 23 E
Tongcheng, Anhui, China 69 B11 31 4N 116 56 E
Tongcheng, Hubei, China 69 C9 29 15N 113 50 E
Tongchŏn-ni, N. Korea .. 67 E14 39 50N 127 25 E
Tongchuan, China ...... 66 G5 35 6N 109 3 E
Tongdao, China ........ 68 D7 26 10N 109 42 E
Tongeren, Belgium ...... 21 G6 50 47N 5 28 E
Tonggu, China ......... 69 C10 28 31N 114 20 E
Tongguan, China ....... 66 G6 34 40N 110 25 E
Tonghai, China ......... 68 E4 24 10N 102 53 E
Tonghua, China ........ 67 D13 41 42N 125 58 E
Tongjiang, China ....... 68 B6 31 58N 107 11 E
Tongjosŏn Man, N. Korea 67 E14 39 30N 128 0 E
Tongking, G. of = Tonkin, G. of, Asia ... 64 E5 20 0N 108 0 E
Tongliang, China ....... 68 C6 29 50N 106 3 E
Tongliao, China ........ 67 C12 43 38N 122 18 E
Tongling, China ........ 69 B11 30 55N 117 48 E
Tonglu, China ......... 69 C12 29 45N 119 37 E
Tongnae, S. Korea ..... 67 G15 35 12N 129 5 E
Tongnan, China ........ 68 B5 30 9N 105 50 E
Tongoa, Vanuatu ....... 121 F6 16 54 S 168 34 E
Tongobory, Madag. ..... 105 C7 23 32 S 44 20 E
Tongoy, Chile .......... 158 C1 30 16 S 71 31W
Tongren, China ........ 68 D7 27 43N 109 11 E
Tongres = Tongeren, Belgium ............. 21 G6 50 47N 5 28 E
Tongsa Dzong, Bhutan .. 78 B3 27 31N 90 31 E
Tongue, U.K. .......... 18 C4 58 29N 4 25W
Tongue →, U.S.A. ..... 138 B2 46 25N 105 52W
Tongwei, China ........ 66 G3 35 0N 105 5 E
Tongxin, China ........ 66 F3 36 59N 105 58 E
Tongyang, N. Korea .... 67 E14 39 9N 126 53 E
Tongyu, China ......... 67 B12 44 45N 123 4 E
Tongzi, China .......... 68 C6 28 9N 106 49 E
Tonica, U.S.A. ......... 140 C7 41 13N 89 4W
Tonj, Sudan ............ 95 F2 7 20N 28 44 E
Tonk, India ............ 80 F6 26 6N 75 54 E
Tonkawa, U.S.A. ....... 139 G6 36 41N 97 18W
Tonkin = Bac Phan, Vietnam ............ 76 B5 22 0N 105 0 E
Tonkin, G. of, Asia ..... 64 E5 20 0N 108 0 E
Tonlé Sap, Cambodia ... 76 F4 13 0N 104 0 E
Tonnay-Charente, France 24 C3 45 56N 0 55W
Tonneins, France ....... 24 D4 44 23N 0 19 E
Tonnerre, France ....... 23 E10 47 51N 3 59 E
Tönning, Germany ...... 26 A4 54 18N 8 57 E
Tono, Japan ........... 60 E10 39 19N 141 32 E
Tonopah, U.S.A. ....... 143 G5 38 4N 117 14W
Tonoshō, Japan ........ 62 C6 34 29N 134 11 E
Tonosí, Panama ........ 148 E3 7 20N 80 20W
Tønsberg, Norway ...... 14 E4 59 19N 10 25 E
Tonumea, Tonga ........ 121 Q13 20 30 S 174 30W
Tonzang, Burma ........ 78 D4 23 36N 93 42 E
Tonzi, Burma .......... 78 C5 24 39N 94 57 E
Tooele, U.S.A. ......... 142 F7 40 32N 112 18W
Toolondo, Australia ..... 116 D4 36 58 S 141 58 E
Toompine, Australia ..... 115 D3 27 15 S 144 19 E
Toongi, Australia ....... 117 B8 32 28 S 148 30 E
Toonpan, Australia ..... 114 B4 19 28 S 146 48 E
Toora, Australia ........ 117 E7 38 39 S 146 23 E
Toora-Khem, Russia .... 57 D10 52 28N 96 17 E
Toowoomba, Australia .. 115 D5 27 32 S 151 56 E
Top-ozero, Russia ...... 48 A5 65 35N 32 0 E
Topalu, Romania ....... 46 E9 44 31N 28 3 E
Topaz, U.S.A. ......... 144 G7 38 41N 119 30W
Topeka, U.S.A. ........ 138 F7 39 3N 95 40W
Topki, Russia .......... 56 D9 55 20N 85 35 E
Topl'a →, Slovak Rep. .. 31 C14 48 45N 21 45 E
Topley, Canada ........ 130 C3 54 49N 126 18W
Toplica →, Serbia ...... 42 D6 43 15N 21 49 E
Toplița, Romania ....... 46 C6 46 55N 25 20 E
Topocalma, Pta., Chile .. 158 C1 34 10 S 72 2W
Topock, U.S.A. ........ 145 L12 34 46N 114 29W
Topola, Serbia ......... 42 C5 44 17N 20 41 E
Topolčane, Macedonia ... 42 F6 41 14N 21 56 E
Topoľčany, Slovak Rep. . 31 C11 48 35N 18 12 E
Topoli, Kazakhstan ..... 53 C14 47 59N 51 38 E
Topolnitsa →, Bulgaria . 43 E9 42 11N 24 18 E
Topolobampo, Mexico ... 146 B3 25 40N 109 4W
Topolovgrad, Bulgaria ... 43 E11 42 5N 26 20 E
Topolvătu Mare, Romania 42 B6 45 46N 21 41 E
Toppenish, U.S.A. ...... 142 C3 46 23N 120 19W
Topusko, Croatia ....... 39 C12 45 18N 15 59 E
Toquepala, Peru ........ 156 D3 17 24 S 70 25W
Torá, Spain ............ 34 D6 41 49N 1 25 E
Tora Kit, Sudan ........ 95 E3 11 2N 32 36 E
Toraka Vestale, Madag. . 105 B7 16 20 S 43 58 E
Torata, Peru ........... 156 D3 17 23 S 70 1W
Torbalı, Turkey ........ 88 D2 38 10N 27 21 E
Torbay, Canada ........ 129 C9 47 40N 52 42W
Torbay, U.K. .......... 17 G4 50 26N 3 31W
Tørdal, Norway ........ 14 E2 59 10N 8 45 E
Tordesillas, Spain ...... 36 D6 41 30N 5 0W
Tordoya, Spain ........ 36 B2 43 6N 8 36W
Töreboda, Sweden ...... 15 F8 58 41N 14 7 E
Torfajökull, Iceland ..... 12 E4 63 54N 19 0W
Torgau, Germany ....... 26 D8 51 32N 13 0 E
Torgelow, Germany ..... 26 B9 53 40N 13 59 E
Torhout, Belgium ....... 21 F2 51 5N 3 7 E
Tori, Ethiopia .......... 95 F3 7 53N 33 35 E
Tori-Shima, Japan ...... 61 J10 30 29N 140 19 E
Torigni-sur-Vire, France . 22 C6 49 3N 0 58W
Torija, Spain ........... 34 E1 40 44N 3 2W
Torin, Mexico .......... 146 B2 27 33N 110 15W
Toriñana, C., Spain ..... 36 B1 43 3N 9 17W
Torino, Italy ........... 38 C4 45 4N 7 40 E
Torit, Sudan ........... 95 G3 4 27N 32 31 E
Torkovichi, Russia ...... 50 B7 58 51N 30 21 E
Tormac, Romania ....... 42 B6 45 30N 21 30 E
Tormes →, Spain ...... 36 D4 41 18N 6 29W
Tornado Mt., Canada ... 130 D6 49 55N 114 40W
Tornala, Slovak Rep. ... 31 C13 48 25N 20 20 E
Torne älv →, Sweden ... 12 D18 65 50N 24 12 E
Torneå = Tornio, Finland 12 D18 65 50N 24 12 E
Torneträsk, Sweden ..... 12 B15 68 24N 19 15 E
Tornio, Finland ........ 12 D18 65 50N 24 12 E
Tornionjoki →, Finland . 12 D18 65 50N 24 12 E
Tornquist, Argentina .... 158 D3 38 8 S 62 15W
Toro, Baleares, Spain ... 33 B11 39 59N 4 8 E
Toro, Zamora, Spain .... 36 D5 41 35N 5 24W
Torö, Sweden .......... 15 F11 58 48N 17 50 E
Toro, Cerro del, Chile ... 158 B2 29 10 S 69 50W
Toro Pk., U.S.A. ....... 145 M10 33 34N 116 24W
Törökszentmiklós, Hungary .............. 31 D13 47 11N 20 27 E
Toronîos Kólpos, Greece 44 D5 40 5N 23 30 E
Toronto, Australia ...... 117 B9 33 0 S 151 30 E
Toronto, Canada ....... 128 D4 43 39N 79 20W
Toronto, U.S.A. ........ 136 F4 40 28N 80 36W
Toropets, Russia ....... 50 C7 56 30N 31 40 E
Tororo, Uganda ........ 106 B3 0 45N 34 12 E
Toros Dağları, Turkey ... 88 E5 37 0N 32 30 E
Torotoro, Bolivia ....... 157 D4 18 7 S 65 46W
Torpshammar, Sweden .. 14 B10 62 29N 16 20 E
Torquay, Australia ...... 116 E6 38 20 S 144 19 E
Torquay, Canada ....... 131 D8 49 9N 103 30W
Torquay, U.K. ......... 17 G4 50 27N 3 31W
Torquemada, Spain ..... 36 C6 42 2N 4 19W
Torralba de Calatrava, Spain ................ 37 F7 39 1N 3 44W
Torrance, U.S.A. ....... 145 M8 33 50N 118 19W
Torrão, Portugal ....... 37 G2 38 16N 8 11W
Torre Annunziata, Italy . 41 B7 40 45N 14 26 E
Tôrre de Moncorvo, Portugal ............. 36 D3 41 12N 7 8W
Torre del Greco, Italy ... 41 B7 40 47N 14 22 E
Torre del Mar, Spain ... 37 J6 36 44N 4 6W
Torre-Pacheco, Spain ... 35 H4 37 44N 0 57W
Torre Pellice, Italy ..... 38 D4 44 49N 7 13 E
Torreblanca, Spain ..... 34 E5 40 14N 0 12 E
Torrecampo, Spain ..... 37 G6 38 29N 4 41W
Torrecilla en Cameros, Spain ............... 34 C2 42 15N 2 38W
Torredembarra, Spain ... 34 D6 41 9N 1 24 E
Torredonjimeno, Spain .. 37 H7 37 46N 3 57W
Torrejoncillo, Spain ..... 36 F4 39 54N 6 29W
Torrelaguna, Spain ..... 34 E1 40 50N 3 38W
Torrelavega, Spain ..... 36 B6 43 20N 4 5W
Torremaggiore, Italy .... 41 A8 41 42N 15 17 E
Torremolinos, Spain .... 37 J6 36 38N 4 30W
Torrens, L., Australia ... 116 A2 31 0 S 137 50 E
Torrens Cr. →, Australia 114 C4 22 23 S 145 9 E
Torrens Creek, Australia 114 C4 20 48 S 145 3 E
Torrente, Spain ........ 35 F4 39 27N 0 28W
Torrenueva, Spain ...... 35 G1 38 38N 3 22W
Torreón, Mexico ....... 146 B4 25 33N 103 25W
Torreperogil, Spain ..... 35 G1 38 2N 3 17W
Torres, Mexico ......... 146 B2 28 46N 110 47W
Torres, Is., Vanuatu ..... 121 C4 13 15 S 166 37 E
Torres Novas, Portugal .. 37 F2 39 27N 8 33W
Torres Strait, Australia .. 120 E2 9 50 S 142 20 E
Torres Vedras, Portugal . 37 F1 39 5N 9 15W
Torrevieja, Spain ....... 35 H4 37 59N 0 42W
Torrey, U.S.A. ......... 143 G8 38 18N 111 25W
Torridge →, U.K. ...... 17 G3 50 51N 4 10W
Torridon, L., U.K. ...... 18 D3 57 35N 5 50W
Torrijos, Phil. .......... 70 E4 13 19N 122 5 E
Torrijos, Spain ......... 36 F6 39 59N 4 18W
Torrington, Conn., U.S.A. 137 E11 41 48N 73 7W
Torrington, Wyo., U.S.A. 138 D2 42 4N 104 11W
Torroella de Montgri, Spain ................ 34 C8 42 2N 3 8 E
Torrox, Spain .......... 37 J7 36 46N 3 57W
Torsö, Sweden ......... 15 F7 58 48N 13 45 E
Tortola, Virgin Is. ...... 149 C7 18 19N 64 45W
Tórtoles de Esgueva, Spain ................ 36 D6 41 49N 4 2W
Tortona, Italy .......... 38 D5 44 53N 8 54 E
Tortoreto, Italy ........ 39 F10 42 50N 13 55 E
Tortorici, Italy ......... 41 D7 38 2N 14 48 E
Tortosa, Spain ......... 34 E5 40 49N 0 31 E
Tortosa, C., Spain ..... 34 E5 40 41N 0 52 E
Tortosendo, Portugal ... 36 E3 40 15N 7 31W
Tortue, I. de la, Haiti ... 149 B5 20 5N 72 57W
Tortum, Turkey ........ 89 C9 40 19N 41 35 E
Ţorūd, Iran ........... 85 C7 35 25N 55 5 E
Torugart, Pereval, Kirghizia ............. 55 C7 40 32N 75 24 E
Torul, Turkey .......... 89 C8 40 34N 39 18 E
Toruń, Poland ......... 47 B5 53 2N 18 39 E
Toruń □, Poland ....... 47 B6 53 20N 19 0 E
Torup, Denmark ....... 15 G3 57 5N 9 5 E
Torup, Sweden ......... 15 H7 56 57N 13 5 E
Tory I., Ireland ........ 19 A3 55 17N 8 12W
Torysa →, Slovak Rep. . 31 C14 48 39N 21 21 E
Torzhok, Russia ....... 50 C9 57 5N 34 55 E
Tosa, Japan ........... 62 D5 33 24N 133 23 E

276 Tosa-Shimizu


Tosa-Shimizu, Japan 62 E4 32 52N 132 58 E
Tosa-Wan, Japan 62 D5 33 15N 133 30 E
Tosa-yamada, Japan 62 D5 33 36N 133 38 E
Toscana, Italy 38 E8 43 30N 11 5 E
Toscano, Arcipelago, Italy 38 F7 42 30N 10 30 E
Toshkent = Tashkent, Uzbekistan 55 C4 41 20N 69 10 E
Tosno, Russia 50 B7 59 38N 30 46 E
Tossa, Spain 34 D7 41 43N 2 56 E
Tostado, Argentina 158 B3 29 15 S 61 50W
Tostedt, Germany 26 B5 53 17N 9 42 E
Tostón, Pta. de, Canary Is. 33 F5 28 42N 14 2W
Tosu, Japan 62 D2 33 22N 130 31 E
Tosya, Turkey 88 C6 41 1N 34 2 E
Toszek, Poland 47 E5 50 27N 18 32 E
Totana, Spain 35 H3 37 45N 1 30W
Toten, Norway 14 D4 60 37N 10 53 E
Toteng, Botswana 104 C3 20 22 S 22 58 E
Tôtes, France 22 C8 49 41N 1 3 E
Tótkomlós, Hungary 31 E13 46 24N 20 45 E
Totma, Russia 51 B13 60 0N 42 40 E
Totnes, U.K. 17 G4 50 26N 3 41W
Totness, Surinam 153 B6 5 53N 56 19W
Totonicapán, Guatemala 148 D1 14 58N 91 12W
Totora, Bolivia 157 D4 17 42 S 65 9W
Totoya, I., Fiji 121 B3 18 57 S 179 50W
Totskoye, Russia 54 E3 52 32N 52 45 E
Totten Glacier, Antarctica 7 C8 66 45 S 116 10 E
Tottenham, Australia 117 B7 32 14 S 147 21 E
Tottenham, Canada 136 B5 44 1N 79 49W
Tottori, Japan 62 B6 35 30N 134 15 E
Tottori □, Japan 62 B6 35 30N 134 12 E
Touat, Algeria 99 C5 27 27N 0 30 E
Touba, Ivory C. 100 D3 8 22N 7 40W
Toubkal, Djebel, Morocco 98 B3 31 0N 8 0W
Toucy, France 23 E10 47 44N 3 15 E
Tougan, Burkina Faso 100 C4 13 11N 2 58W
Touggourt, Algeria 99 B6 33 6N 6 4 E
Tougué, Guinea 100 C2 11 25N 11 50W
Touho, N. Cal. 121 T19 20 47 S 165 14 E
Toukmatine, Algeria 99 D6 24 49N 7 11 E
Toul, France 23 D12 48 40N 5 53 E
Toulepleu, Ivory C. 100 D3 6 32N 8 24W
Toulon, France 25 E9 43 10N 5 55 E
Toulon, U.S.A. 140 C7 41 6N 89 52W
Toulouse, France 24 E5 43 37N 1 27 E
Toummo, Niger 96 D2 22 45N 14 8 E
Toummo Dhoba, Niger 96 D2 22 30N 14 31 E
Toumodi, Ivory C. 100 D3 6 32N 5 4W
Tounassine, Hamada, Algeria 98 C3 28 48N 5 0W
Toungoo, Burma 78 F6 19 0N 96 30 E
Touques →, France 22 C7 49 22N 0 8 E
Touraine, France 22 E7 47 20N 0 30 E
Tourane = Da Nang, Vietnam 76 D7 16 4N 108 13 E
Tourcoing, France 23 B10 50 42N 3 10 E
Tourine, Mauritania 98 D2 22 23N 11 50W
Tournai, Belgium 21 G2 50 35N 3 25 E
Tournan-en-Brie, France 23 D9 48 44N 2 46 E
Tournay, France 24 E4 43 13N 0 13 E
Tournon, France 25 C8 45 4N 4 50 E
Tournon-St.-Martin, France 22 F7 46 45N 0 58 E
Tournus, France 25 B8 46 35N 4 54 E
Touros, Brazil 154 C4 5 12 S 35 28W
Tours, France 22 E7 47 22N 0 40 E
Touside, Pic, Chad 97 D3 21 1N 16 29 E
Touwsrivier, S. Africa 104 E3 33 20 S 20 2 E
Tovar, Venezuela 152 B3 8 20N 71 46W
Tovarkovskiy, Russia 51 E11 53 40N 38 14 E
Tovdal, Norway 15 F2 58 47N 8 10 E
Tovdalselva →, Norway 15 F2 58 15N 8 5 E
Towada, Japan 60 D10 40 37N 141 13 E
Towada-Ko, Japan 60 D10 40 28N 140 55 E
Towamba, Australia 117 D8 37 6 S 149 43 E
Towanda, Ill., U.S.A. 141 D8 40 36N 88 53W
Towanda, Pa., U.S.A. 137 E8 41 46N 76 27W
Tower, U.S.A. 138 B8 47 48N 92 17W
Towerhill Cr. →, Australia 114 C3 22 28 S 144 35 E
Towner, U.S.A. 138 A4 48 21N 100 25W
Townsend, U.S.A. 142 C8 46 19N 111 31W
Townshend I., Australia 114 C5 22 10 S 150 31 E
Townsville, Australia 114 B4 19 15 S 146 45 E
Towson, U.S.A. 134 F7 39 24N 76 36W
Toya-Ko, Japan 60 C10 42 35N 140 51 E
Toyah, U.S.A. 139 K3 31 19N 103 48W
Toyahvale, U.S.A. 139 K3 30 57N 103 47W
Toyama, Japan 63 A9 36 40N 137 15 E
Toyama □, Japan 63 A9 36 45N 137 30 E
Toyama-Wan, Japan 61 F8 37 0N 137 30 E
Tōyō, Japan 62 D6 33 26N 134 16 E
Toyohashi, Japan 63 C9 34 45N 137 25 E
Toyokawa, Japan 63 C9 34 48N 137 27 E
Toyonaka, Japan 63 C7 34 50N 135 28 E
Toyooka, Japan 62 B6 35 35N 134 48 E
Toyota, Japan 63 B9 35 3N 137 7 E
Toyoura, Japan 62 C2 34 6N 130 57 E
Toytepa, Uzbekistan 55 C4 41 3N 69 20 E
Tozeur, Tunisia 96 B1 33 56N 8 8 E
Tra On, Vietnam 77 H5 9 58N 105 55 E
Trabancos →, Spain 36 D5 41 36N 5 15W
Traben Trarbach, Germany 27 F3 49 57N 7 7 E
Trabzon, Turkey 52 F8 41 0N 39 45 E
Trabzon □, Turkey 89 C8 41 10N 39 45 E
Tracadie, Canada 129 C7 47 30N 64 55W
Tracy, Calif., U.S.A. 144 H5 37 44N 121 26W
Tracy, Minn., U.S.A. 138 C7 44 14N 95 37W
Tradate, Italy 38 C5 45 43N 8 54 E
Tradovoye, Russia 60 C6 43 17N 132 5 E
Traer, U.S.A. 140 B4 42 12N 92 28W
Trafalgar, Australia 117 E7 38 14 S 146 12 E
Trafalgar, C., Spain 37 J4 36 10N 6 2W
Trāghān, Libya 96 C2 26 0N 14 30 E
Tragowel, Australia 116 C5 35 50 S 144 0 E
Traian, Romania 46 D9 45 2N 28 15 E
Traiguén, Chile 160 A2 38 15 S 72 41W
Trail, Canada 130 D5 49 5N 117 40W
Trainor L., Canada 130 A4 60 24N 120 17W
Traíra →, Brazil 152 D4 1 4 S 69 26W
Trákhonas, Cyprus 32 D12 35 12N 33 21 E
Tralee, Ireland 19 D2 52 16N 9 42W
Tralee B., Ireland 19 D2 52 17N 9 55W
Tramelan, Switz. 28 B4 47 13N 7 7 E
Tramore, Ireland 19 D4 52 10N 7 10W
Tran Ninh, Cao Nguyen, Laos 76 C4 19 30N 103 10 E
Tranås, Sweden 13 G13 58 3N 14 59 E
Trancas, Argentina 158 B2 26 11 S 65 20W
Trancoso, Portugal 36 E3 40 49N 7 21W
Tranebjerg, Denmark 15 J4 55 51N 10 36 E
Tranemo, Sweden 15 G7 57 30N 13 20 E
Trang, Thailand 77 J2 7 33N 99 38 E
Trangahy, Madag. 105 B7 19 7 S 44 31 E
Trangan, Indonesia 73 C4 6 40 S 134 20 E
Trangie, Australia 117 B7 32 4 S 148 0 E
Trångsviken, Sweden 14 A8 63 19N 14 0 E
Trani, Italy 41 A9 41 17N 16 24 E
Tranoroa, Madag. 105 C8 24 42 S 45 4 E
Tranquebar, India 83 J4 11 1N 79 54 E
Tranqueras, Uruguay 159 C4 31 13 S 55 45W
Trans Nzoia □, Kenya 106 B3 1 0N 35 0 E
Transantarctic Mts., Antarctica 7 E12 85 0 S 170 0W
Transcaucasia = Zakavkazye, Asia 53 F11 42 0N 44 0 E
Transcona, Canada 131 D9 49 55N 97 0W
Transilvania, Romania 46 D6 45 19N 25 0 E
Transkei □, S. Africa 105 E4 32 15 S 28 15 E
Transvaal □, S. Africa 104 D4 25 0 S 29 0 E
Transylvania = Transilvania, Romania 46 D6 45 19N 25 0 E
Transylvanian Alps, Romania 46 D6 45 30N 25 0 E
Trápani, Italy 40 D5 38 1N 12 30 E
Trapper Pk., U.S.A. 142 D6 45 54N 114 18W
Traralgon, Australia 117 E7 38 12 S 146 34 E
Trarza, Mauritania 100 B2 17 30N 15 0W
Trás-os-Montes, Angola 103 E3 10 17 S 19 5 E
Trasacco, Italy 39 G10 41 58N 13 30 E
Trăscău, Munţii, Romania 46 C4 46 14N 23 14 E
Trasimeno, L., Italy 39 E9 43 10N 12 5 E
Trat, Thailand 77 F4 12 14N 102 33 E
Traun, Austria 30 C7 48 14N 14 15 E
Traunsee, Austria 30 D6 47 55N 13 50 E
Traunstein, Germany 27 H8 47 52N 12 40 E
Tråvad, Sweden 15 F7 58 15N 13 5 E
Traveller's L., Australia 116 B5 33 20 S 142 0 E
Travemünde, Germany 26 B6 53 58N 10 52 E
Travers, Mt., N.Z. 119 C7 42 1 S 172 45 E
Traverse City, U.S.A. 134 C3 44 46N 85 38W
Travnik, Bos.-H. 42 C2 44 17N 17 39 E
Trayning, Australia 113 F2 31 7 S 117 40 E
Trazo, Spain 36 B2 43 2N 8 30W
Trbovlje, Slovenia 39 B12 46 12N 15 5 E
Treasury Is., Solomon Is. 121 L8 7 22 S 155 37 E
Trébbia →, Italy 38 C6 45 4N 9 41 E
Trebel →, Germany 26 B9 53 55N 13 1 E
Třebíč, Czech. 30 B8 49 14N 15 55 E
Trebinje, Bos.-H. 42 E3 42 44N 18 22 E
Trebisacce, Italy 41 C9 39 52N 16 32 E
Trebišnica →, Bos.-H. 42 E3 42 47N 18 8 E
Trebišov, Slovak Rep. 31 C14 48 38N 21 41 E
Trebižat →, Bos.-H. 42 D2 43 15N 17 30 E
Trebnje, Slovenia 39 C12 45 54N 15 1 E
Třeboň, Czech. 30 C7 48 59N 14 48 E
Trebujena, Spain 37 J4 36 52N 6 11W
Trecate, Italy 38 C5 45 26N 8 42 E
Trece Martires, Phil. 70 D3 14 20N 120 50 E
Tredegar, U.K. 17 F4 51 47N 3 16W
Tregaron, U.K. 17 E4 52 14N 3 56W
Trégastel-Plage, France 22 D3 48 49N 3 31W
Tregnago, Italy 39 C8 45 31N 11 10 E
Tregrosse Is., Australia 114 B5 17 41 S 150 43 E
Tréguier, France 22 D3 48 47N 3 16W
Trégunc, France 22 E3 47 51N 3 51W
Treherne, Canada 131 D9 49 38N 98 42W
Tréia, Italy 39 E10 43 20N 13 20 E
Treignac, France 24 C5 45 32N 1 48 E
Treinta y Tres, Uruguay 159 C5 33 16 S 54 17W
Treis, Germany 27 E3 50 9N 7 19 E
Treklyano, Bulgaria 42 E7 42 33N 22 36 E
Trekveld, S. Africa 104 E2 30 35 S 19 45 E
Trelde Næs, Denmark 15 J3 55 38N 9 53 E
Trelew, Argentina 160 B3 43 10 S 65 20W
Trélissac, France 24 C4 45 11N 0 47 E
Trelleborg, Sweden 15 J7 55 20N 13 10 E
Trélon, France 23 B11 50 5N 4 6 E
Tremiti, Italy 39 F12 42 8N 15 30 E
Tremonton, U.S.A. 142 F7 41 43N 112 10W
Tremp, Spain 34 C5 42 10N 0 52 E
Trenche →, Canada 128 C5 47 46N 72 53W
Trenčín, Slovak Rep. 31 C11 48 52N 18 4 E
Trenggalek, Indonesia 75 D4 8 3 S 111 43 E
Trenque Lauquen, Argentina 158 D3 36 5 S 62 45W
Trent →, U.K. 16 D7 53 33N 0 44W
Trentino-Alto Adige □, Italy 38 B8 46 30N 11 0 E
Trento, Italy 38 B8 46 5N 11 8 E
Trenton, Canada 128 D4 44 10N 77 34W
Trenton, Mich., U.S.A. 141 B13 42 8N 83 11W
Trenton, Mo., U.S.A. 140 D3 40 5N 93 37W
Trenton, N.J., U.S.A. 137 F10 40 14N 74 46W
Trenton, Nebr., U.S.A. 138 E4 40 11N 101 1W
Trenton, Tenn., U.S.A. 139 H10 35 59N 88 56W
Trepassey, Canada 129 C9 46 43N 53 25W
Trepuzzi, Italy 41 B11 40 26N 18 4 E
Tres Arroyos, Argentina 158 D3 38 26 S 60 20W
Três Corações, Brazil 155 F2 21 44 S 45 15W
Três Lagoas, Brazil 155 F1 20 50 S 51 43W
Tres Lagos →, Argentina 160 C2 49 35 S 71 25W
Tres Marías, Mexico 146 C3 21 25N 106 28W
Três Marias, Represa, Brazil 155 E2 18 12 S 45 15W
Tres Montes, C., Chile 160 C1 46 50 S 75 30W
Tres Pinos, U.S.A. 144 J5 36 48N 121 19W
Três Pontas, Brazil 155 F2 21 23 S 45 29W
Tres Puentes, Chile 158 B1 27 50 S 70 15W
Tres Puntas, C., Argentina 160 C3 47 0 S 66 0W
Três Rios, Brazil 155 F3 22 6 S 43 15W
Tres Valles, Mexico 147 D5 18 15N 96 8W
Treska →, Macedonia 42 F6 42 0N 21 20 E
Treskavica, Bos.-H. 42 D3 43 40N 18 20 E
Trespaderne, Spain 34 C1 42 47N 3 24W
Trets, France 25 E9 43 27N 5 41 E
Treuchtlingen, Germany 27 G6 48 58N 10 55 E
Treuenbrietzen, Germany 26 C8 52 6N 12 51 E
Treungen, Norway 13 G10 59 1N 8 31 E
Trevíglio, Italy 38 C6 45 31N 9 35 E
Trevinca, Peña, Spain 36 C4 42 15N 6 46W
Treviso, Italy 39 C9 45 40N 12 15 E
Trévoux, France 25 C8 45 57N 4 47 E
Treysa, Germany 26 E5 50 55N 9 12 E
Trgovište, Serbia 42 E7 42 20N 22 10 E
Triabunna, Australia 114 G4 42 30 S 147 55 E
Triánda, Greece 32 C10 36 25N 28 10 E
Triang, Malaysia 77 L4 3 15N 102 26 E
Triaucourt-en-Argonne, France 23 D12 48 59N 5 2 E
Tribsees, Germany 26 A8 54 4N 12 46 E
Tribulation, C., Australia 114 B4 16 5 S 145 29 E
Tribune, U.S.A. 138 F4 38 28N 101 45W
Tricárico, Italy 41 B9 40 37N 16 9 E
Tricase, Italy 41 C11 39 56N 18 20 E
Trichinopoly = Tiruchchirappalli, India 83 J4 10 45N 78 45 E
Trichur, India 83 J3 10 30N 76 18 E
Trida, Australia 117 B6 33 1 S 145 1 E
Trier, Germany 27 F2 49 45N 6 37 E
Trieste, Italy 39 C10 45 39N 13 45 E
Trieste, G. di, Italy 39 C10 45 37N 13 40 E
Trieux →, France 22 D3 48 43N 3 9W
Triggiano, Italy 41 A9 41 4N 16 58 E
Triglav, Slovenia 39 B10 46 21N 13 50 E
Trigno →, Italy 39 F11 42 4N 14 48 E
Trigueros, Spain 37 H4 37 24N 6 50W
Tríkeri, Greece 45 E5 39 6N 23 5 E
Trikhonis, Límni, Greece 45 F3 38 34N 21 30 E
Tríkkala, Greece 44 E3 39 34N 21 47 E
Tríkkala □, Greece 44 E3 39 41N 21 30 E
Trikomo, Cyprus 32 D12 35 17N 33 52 E
Trikora, Puncak, Indonesia 73 B5 4 15 S 138 45 E
Trilj, Croatia 39 E13 43 38N 16 42 E
Trillo, Spain 34 E2 40 42N 2 35W
Trim, Ireland 19 C5 53 34N 6 48W
Trincomalee, Sri Lanka 83 K5 8 38N 81 15 E
Trindade, Brazil 155 E2 16 40 S 49 30W
Trindade, I., Atl. Oc. 9 L6 20 20 S 29 50W
Trinidad, Bolivia 157 C5 14 46 S 64 50W
Trinidad, Colombia 152 B3 5 25N 71 40W
Trinidad, Cuba 148 B3 21 48N 80 0W
Trinidad, Uruguay 158 C4 33 30 S 56 50W
Trinidad, U.S.A. 139 G2 37 10N 104 31W
Trinidad, W. Indies 149 D7 10 30N 61 15W
Trinidad →, Mexico 147 D5 17 49N 95 9W
Trinidad, G., Chile 160 C1 49 55 S 75 25W
Trinidad, I., Argentina 160 A4 39 10 S 62 0W
Trinidad & Tobago ■, W. Indies 149 D7 10 30N 61 20W
Trinitápoli, Italy 41 A9 41 22N 16 5 E
Trinity, Canada 129 C9 48 59N 53 55W
Trinity, U.S.A. 139 K7 30 57N 95 22W
Trinity →, Calif., U.S.A. 142 F2 41 11N 123 42W
Trinity →, Tex., U.S.A. 139 L7 29 45N 94 43W
Trinity B., Canada 129 C9 48 20N 53 10W
Trinity Range, U.S.A. 142 F4 40 15N 118 45W
Trinkitat, Sudan 94 D4 18 45N 37 51 E
Trino, Italy 38 C5 45 10N 8 18 E
Trion, U.S.A. 135 H3 34 33N 85 19W
Trionto, C., Italy 41 C9 39 38N 16 47 E
Triora, Italy 38 E4 43 58N 7 46 E
Tripoli = Tarābulus, Lebanon 91 A4 34 31N 35 50 E
Tripoli = Tarābulus, Libya 96 B2 32 49N 13 7 E
Tripoli, U.S.A. 140 B4 42 49N 92 16W
Trípolis, Greece 45 G4 37 31N 22 25 E
Tripp, U.S.A. 138 D6 43 13N 97 58W
Tripura □, India 78 D3 24 0N 92 0 E
Tripylos, Cyprus 32 E11 34 59N 32 41 E
Trischen, Germany 26 A4 54 3N 8 32 E
Tristan da Cunha, Atl. Oc. 9 M7 37 6 S 12 20W
Trivandrum, India 83 K3 8 41N 77 0 E
Trivento, Italy 41 A7 41 48N 14 31 E
Trnava, Slovak Rep. 31 C10 48 23N 17 35 E
Trobriand Is., Papua N. G. 120 E6 8 30 S 151 0 E
Trochu, Canada 130 C6 51 50N 113 13W
Trodely I., Canada 128 B4 52 15N 79 26W
Troezen, Greece 45 G5 37 25N 23 15 E
Trogir, Croatia 39 E13 43 32N 16 15 E
Troglav, Croatia 39 E13 43 56N 16 36 E
Trøgstad, Norway 14 E5 59 37N 11 16 E
Tróia, Italy 41 A8 41 22N 15 19 E
Troilus, L., Canada 128 B5 50 50N 74 35W
Troina, Italy 41 E7 37 47N 14 34 E
Trois Fourches, Cap des, Morocco 99 A4 35 26N 2 58W
Trois-Pistoles, Canada 129 C6 48 5N 69 10W
Trois-Rivières, Canada 128 C5 46 25N 72 34W
Troisvierges, Belgium 21 H8 50 8N 6 0 E
Troitsk, Russia 54 D7 54 10N 61 35 E
Troitsko Pechorsk, Russia 48 B10 62 40N 56 10 E
Trölladyngja, Iceland 12 D5 64 54N 17 16W
Trollhättan, Sweden 15 F6 58 17N 12 20 E
Trollheimen, Norway 14 B3 62 46N 9 1 E
Trombetas →, Brazil 153 D6 1 55 S 55 35W
Tromelin I., Ind. Oc. 109 F4 15 52 S 54 25 E
Troms fylke □, Norway 12 B15 68 56N 19 0 E
Tromsø, Norway 12 B15 69 40N 18 56 E
Trona, U.S.A. 145 K9 35 46N 117 23W
Tronador, Argentina 160 B2 41 10 S 71 50W
Trondheim, Norway 14 A4 63 36N 10 25 E
Trondheimsfjorden, Norway 12 E11 63 35N 10 30 E
Trönninge, Sweden 15 H6 56 37N 12 51 E
Trönö, Sweden 14 C10 61 22N 16 54 E
Tronto →, Italy 39 F10 42 54N 13 55 E
Troodos, Cyprus 32 E11 34 55N 32 52 E
Troon, U.K. 18 F4 55 33N 4 40W
Tropea, Italy 41 D8 38 40N 15 53 E
Tropic, U.S.A. 143 H7 37 37N 112 5W
Tropoja, Albania 44 B2 42 23N 20 10 E
Trossachs, The, U.K. 18 E4 56 14N 4 24W
Trostan, U.K. 19 A5 55 4N 6 10W
Trostberg, Germany 27 G8 48 2N 12 33 E
Trostyanets, Ukraine 50 F9 50 33N 34 59 E
Trotternish, U.K. 18 D2 57 32N 6 15W
Troup, U.S.A. 139 J7 32 9N 95 7W
Trout →, Canada 130 A5 61 19N 119 51W
Trout L., N.W.T., Canada 130 A4 60 40N 121 14W
Trout L., Ont., Canada 131 C10 51 20N 93 15W
Trout Lake, Mich., U.S.A. 128 C2 46 12N 85 1W
Trout Lake, Wash., U.S.A. 144 E5 46 0N 121 32W
Trout River, Canada 129 C8 49 29N 58 8W
Trouville-sur-Mer, France 22 C7 49 21N 0 5 E
Trowbridge, U.K. 17 F5 51 18N 2 12W
Troy, Turkey 44 E8 39 57N 26 12 E
Troy, Ala., U.S.A. 135 K3 31 48N 85 58W
Troy, Idaho, U.S.A. 142 C5 46 44N 116 46W
Troy, Ill., U.S.A. 140 F7 38 44N 89 54W
Troy, Ind., U.S.A. 141 F10 37 59N 86 55W
Troy, Kans., U.S.A. 138 F7 39 47N 95 5W
Troy, Mich., U.S.A. 141 B13 42 37N 83 9W
Troy, Mo., U.S.A. 140 F6 38 59N 90 59W
Troy, Mont., U.S.A. 142 B6 48 28N 115 53W
Troy, N.Y., U.S.A. 137 D11 42 44N 73 41W
Troy, Ohio, U.S.A. 141 D12 40 2N 84 12W
Troyan, Bulgaria 43 E9 42 57N 24 43 E
Troyes, France 23 D11 48 19N 4 3 E
Trpanj, Croatia 42 D2 43 1N 17 15 E
Trstena, Slovak Rep. 31 B12 49 21N 19 37 E
Trstenik, Serbia 42 D5 43 36N 21 0 E
Trubchevsk, Russia 50 E8 52 33N 33 47 E
Trucial States = United Arab Emirates ■, Asia 85 F7 23 50N 54 0 E
Truckee, U.S.A. 144 F6 39 20N 120 11W
Trujillo, Colombia 152 C2 4 10N 76 19W
Trujillo, Honduras 148 C2 16 0N 86 0W
Trujillo, Peru 156 B2 8 6 S 79 0W
Trujillo, Spain 37 F5 39 28N 5 55W
Trujillo, U.S.A. 139 H2 35 32N 104 42W
Trujillo, Venezuela 152 B3 9 22N 70 38W
Trujillo □, Venezuela 152 B3 9 25N 70 30W
Truk, Pac. Oc. 122 G7 7 25N 151 46 E
Trumann, U.S.A. 139 H9 35 41N 90 31W
Trumbull, Mt., U.S.A. 143 H7 36 25N 113 8W
Trŭn, Bulgaria 42 E7 42 51N 22 38 E
Trun, France 22 D7 48 50N 0 2 E
Trun, Switz. 29 C7 46 45N 8 59 E
Trundle, Australia 117 B7 32 53 S 147 35 E
Trung-Phan, Vietnam 76 E7 16 0N 108 0 E
Truro, Australia 116 C3 34 24 S 139 9 E
Truro, Canada 129 C7 45 21N 63 14W
Truro, U.K. 17 G2 50 17N 5 2W
Truslove, Australia 113 F3 33 20 S 121 45 E
Trustrup, Denmark 15 H4 56 20N 10 46 E
Truth or Consequences, U.S.A. 143 K10 33 8N 107 15W
Trutnov, Czech. 30 A8 50 37N 15 54 E
Truyère →, France 24 D6 44 38N 2 34 E
Tryavna, Bulgaria 43 E10 42 54N 25 25 E
Tryon, U.S.A. 135 H4 35 13N 82 14W
Tryonville, U.S.A. 136 E5 41 42N 79 48W
Trzcianka, Poland 47 B3 53 3N 16 25 E
Trzciel, Poland 47 C2 52 23N 15 50 E
Trzcińsko Zdrój, Poland 47 C1 52 58N 14 35 E
Trzebiatów, Poland 47 A2 54 3N 15 18 E
Trzebiez, Poland 47 B1 53 38N 14 31 E
Trzebinia-Siersza, Poland 31 A12 50 11N 19 18 E
Trzebnica, Poland 47 D4 51 20N 17 1 E
Trzemeszno, Poland 47 C4 52 33N 17 48 E
Tržič, Slovenia 39 B11 46 22N 14 18 E
Tsageri, Georgia 53 E10 42 39N 42 46 E
Tsamandás, Greece 44 E2 39 46N 20 21 E
Tsaratanana, Madag. 105 B8 16 47 S 47 39 E
Tsaratanana, Mt. de, Madag. 105 A8 14 0 S 49 0 E
Tsarevo = Michurin, Bulgaria 43 E12 42 9N 27 51 E
Tsarichanka, Ukraine 52 B6 48 55N 34 30 E
Tsaritsáni, Greece 44 E4 39 53N 22 14 E
Tsau, Botswana 104 C3 20 8 S 22 22 E
Tsebrikovo, Ukraine 52 C4 47 9N 30 10 E
Tselinograd, Kazakhstan 56 D8 51 10N 71 30 E
Tsetserleg, Mongolia 64 B5 47 36N 101 32 E
Tshabong, Botswana 104 D3 26 2 S 22 29 E
Tshane, Botswana 104 C3 24 5 S 21 54 E
Tshela, Zaïre 103 C2 4 57 S 13 4 E
Tshesebe, Botswana 105 C4 21 51 S 27 32 E
Tshibeke, Zaïre 106 C2 2 40 S 28 35 E
Tshibinda, Zaïre 106 C2 2 23 S 28 43 E
Tshikapa, Zaïre 103 D4 6 28 S 20 48 E
Tshilenge, Zaïre 103 D4 6 17 S 23 48 E
Tshinsenda, Zaïre 107 E2 12 20 S 28 0 E
Tshofa, Zaïre 103 D5 5 13 S 25 16 E
Tshwane, Botswana 104 C3 22 24 S 22 1 E
Tsigara, Botswana 104 C4 20 22 S 25 54 E
Tsihombe, Madag. 105 D8 25 10 S 45 41 E
Tsimlyansk, Russia 53 C10 47 40N 42 6 E
Tsimlyansk Res. = Tsimlyanskoye Vdkhr., Russia 53 B10 48 0N 43 0 E
Tsimlyanskoye Vdkhr., Russia 53 B10 48 0N 43 0 E
Tsinan = Jinan, China 66 F9 36 38N 117 1 E
Tsineng, S. Africa 104 D3 27 5 S 23 5 E
Tsínga, Greece 44 C6 41 23N 24 44 E
Tsinghai = Qinghai □, China 64 C4 36 0N 98 0 E
Tsingtao = Qingdao, China 67 F11 36 5N 120 20 E
Tsinjomitondraka, Madag. 105 B8 15 40 S 47 8 E
Tsiroanomandidy, Madag. 105 B8 18 46 S 46 2 E
Tsivilsk, Russia 51 D15 55 50N 47 25 E
Tsivory, Madag. 105 C8 24 4 S 46 5 E
Tskhinvali, Georgia 53 E11 42 14N 44 1 E
Tsna →, Russia 51 D12 54 55N 41 58 E
Tso Moriri, L., India 81 C8 32 50N 78 20 E
Tsodilo Hill, Botswana 104 B3 18 49 S 21 43 E
Tsogttsetsiy, Mongolia 66 C3 43 43N 105 35 E
Tsolo, S. Africa 105 E4 31 18 S 28 37 E
Tsomo, S. Africa 105 E4 32 0 S 27 42 E
Tsu, Japan 63 C8 34 45N 136 25 E
Tsu L., Canada 130 A6 60 40N 111 52W
Tsuchiura, Japan 63 A12 36 5N 140 15 E
Tsugaru-Kaikyō, Japan 60 D10 41 35N 141 0 E
Tsukumi, Japan 62 D3 33 4N 131 52 E
Tsukushi-Sanchi, Japan 62 D2 33 25N 130 30 E
Tsumeb, Namibia 104 B2 19 9 S 17 44 E
Tsumis, Namibia 104 C2 23 39 S 17 29 E
Tsuna, Japan 62 C6 34 28N 134 56 E
Tsuno-Shima, Japan 62 C2 34 21N 130 52 E
Tsuru, Japan 63 B10 35 31N 138 57 E
Tsuruga, Japan 63 B8 35 45N 136 2 E
Tsuruga-Wan, Japan 63 B8 35 50N 136 3 E
Tsurugi, Japan 63 A8 36 29N 136 37 E
Tsurugi-San, Japan 62 D6 33 51N 134 6 E

Uffenheim 277


Tsurumi-Saki, Japan 62 E4 32 56N 132 5 E
Tsuruoka, Japan 60 E9 38 44N 139 50 E
Tsurusaki, Japan 62 D3 33 14N 131 41 E
Tsushima, Gifu, Japan 63 B8 35 10N 136 43 E
Tsushima, Nagasaki, Japan 62 C1 34 20N 129 20 E
Tsvetkovo, Ukraine 52 B4 49 8N 31 33 E
Tu →, Burma 78 E6 21 50N 96 15 E
Tua →, Portugal 36 D3 41 13N 7 26W
Tuai, N.Z. 118 E6 38 47 S 177 10 E
Tuakau, N.Z. 118 D3 37 16 S 174 59 E
Tual, Indonesia 73 C4 5 38 S 132 44 E
Tuam, Ireland 19 C3 53 30N 8 50W
Tuamarina, N.Z. 119 B8 41 25 S 173 59 E
Tuamotu Arch. = Tuamotu Is., Pac. Oc. 123 J13 17 0 S 144 0W
Tuamotu Is., Pac. Oc. 123 J13 17 0 S 144 0W
Tuamotu Ridge, Pac. Oc. 123 K14 20 0 S 138 0W
Tuanfeng, China 69 B10 30 38N 114 52 E
Tuanxi, China 68 D6 27 28N 107 8 E
Tuao, Phil. 70 C3 17 55N 121 22 E
Tuapse, Russia 53 D8 44 5N 39 10 E
Tuas, Singapore 74 B2 1 19N 103 39 E
Tuatapere, N.Z. 119 G2 46 8 S 167 41 E
Tuba City, U.S.A. 143 H8 36 8N 111 14W
Tuban, Indonesia 75 D4 6 54 S 112 3 E
Tubarão, Brazil 159 B6 28 30 S 49 0W
Tūbās, Jordan 91 C4 32 20N 35 22 E
Tubau, Malaysia 75 B4 3 10N 113 40 E
Tubbergen, Neths. 20 D9 52 24N 6 48 E
Tübingen, Germany 27 G5 48 31N 9 4 E
Tubize, Belgium 21 G4 50 42N 4 13 E
Tubruq, Libya 96 B4 32 7N 23 55 E
Tubuai Is., Pac. Oc. 123 K12 25 0 S 150 0W
Tuburan, Phil. 71 H4 6 39N 122 16 E
Tuc Trung, Vietnam 77 G6 11 1N 107 12 E
Tucacas, Venezuela 152 A4 10 48N 68 19W
Tucano, Brazil 154 D4 10 58 S 38 48W
Tuchang, Taiwan 69 E13 24 59N 121 30 E
Tuchodi →, Canada 130 B4 58 17N 123 42W
Tuchola, Poland 47 B4 53 33N 17 52 E
Tuchów, Poland 31 B14 49 54N 21 1 E
Tucson, U.S.A. 143 K8 32 13N 110 58W
Tucumán □, Argentina 158 B2 26 48 S 66 2W
Tucumcari, U.S.A. 139 H3 35 10N 103 44W
Tucunaré, Brazil 157 B6 5 18 S 55 51W
Tucupido, Venezuela 152 B4 9 17N 65 47W
Tucupita, Venezuela 153 B5 9 2N 62 3W
Tucuruí, Brazil 154 B2 3 42 S 49 44W
Tuczno, Poland 47 B3 53 13N 16 10 E
Tudela, Spain 34 C3 42 4N 1 39W
Tudela de Duero, Spain 36 D6 41 37N 4 39W
Tudmur, Syria 84 C3 34 36N 38 15 E
Tudor, L., Canada 129 A6 55 50N 65 25W
Tudora, Romania 46 B7 47 31N 26 45 E
Tuella →, Portugal 36 D3 41 30N 7 12W
Tuen, Australia 115 D4 28 33 S 145 37 E
Tueré →, Brazil 154 B1 2 48 S 50 59W
Tufi, Papua N. G. 120 E5 9 8 S 149 19 E
Tugela →, S. Africa 105 D5 29 14 S 31 30 E
Tuguegarao, Phil. 70 C3 17 35N 121 42 E
Tugur, Russia 57 D14 53 44N 136 45 E
Tuineje, Canary Is. 33 F5 28 19N 14 3W
Tukangbesi, Kepulauan, Indonesia 72 C2 6 0 S 124 0 E
Tukarak I., Canada 128 A4 56 15N 78 45W
Tukayyid, Iraq 84 D5 29 47N 45 36 E
Tûkh, Egypt 94 H7 30 21N 31 12 E
Tukituki →, N.Z. 118 F5 39 36 S 176 56 E
Tukobo, Ghana 100 D4 5 1N 2 47W
Tūkrah, Libya 96 B4 32 30N 20 37 E
Tuktoyaktuk, Canada 126 B6 69 27N 133 2W
Tukums, Latvia 50 C3 57 2N 23 10 E
Tukuyu, Tanzania 107 D3 9 17 S 33 35 E
Tula, Hidalgo, Mexico 147 C5 20 5N 99 20W
Tula, Tamaulipas, Mexico 147 C5 23 0N 99 40W
Tula, Nigeria 101 D7 9 51N 11 27 E
Tula, Russia 51 D10 54 13N 37 38 E
Tulak, Afghan. 79 B1 33 55N 63 40 E
Tulancingo, Mexico 147 C5 20 5N 99 22W
Tulangbawang →, Indonesia 74 C3 4 24 S 105 52 E
Tulare, U.S.A. 144 J7 36 13N 119 21W
Tulare Lake Bed, U.S.A. 144 K7 36 0N 119 48W
Tularosa, U.S.A. 143 K10 33 5N 106 1W
Tulbagh, S. Africa 104 E2 33 16 S 19 6 E
Tulcán, Ecuador 152 C2 0 48N 77 43W
Tulcea, Romania 46 D9 45 13N 28 46 E
Tulcea □, Romania 46 D9 45 0N 28 30 E
Tulchin, Ukraine 52 B3 48 41N 28 49 E
Tūleh, Iran 85 C7 34 35N 52 33 E
Tulemalu L., Canada 131 A9 62 58N 99 25W
Tulgheş, Romania 46 C6 46 58N 25 45 E
Tuli, Indonesia 72 B2 1 24 S 122 26 E
Tuli, Zimbabwe 107 G2 21 58 S 29 13 E
Tulia, U.S.A. 139 H4 34 32N 101 46W
Ţulkarm, Jordan 91 C4 32 19N 35 2 E
Tullahoma, U.S.A. 135 H2 35 22N 86 13W
Tullamore, Australia 117 B7 32 39 S 147 36 E
Tullamore, Ireland 19 C4 53 17N 7 30W
Tulle, France 24 C5 45 16N 1 46 E
Tullibigeal, Australia 117 B7 33 25 S 146 44 E
Tullins, France 25 C9 45 18N 5 29 E
Tulln, Austria 30 C9 48 20N 16 4 E
Tullow, Ireland 19 D4 52 48N 6 45W
Tullus, Sudan 95 E1 11 7N 24 31 E
Tully, Australia 114 B4 17 56 S 145 55 E
Ţulmaythah, Libya 96 B4 32 40N 20 55 E
Tulmur, Australia 114 C3 22 40 S 142 20 E
Tulnici, Romania 46 D7 45 51N 26 38 E
Tulovo, Bulgaria 43 E10 42 33N 25 32 E
Tulsa, U.S.A. 139 G7 36 10N 95 55W
Tulsequah, Canada 130 B2 58 39N 133 35W
Tulu Milki, Ethiopia 95 F4 9 55N 38 20 E
Tulu Welel, Ethiopia 95 F3 8 56N 34 47 E
Tulua, Colombia 152 C2 4 6N 76 11W
Tulun, Russia 57 D11 54 32N 100 35 E
Tulungagung, Indonesia 75 D4 8 5 S 111 54 E
Tum, Indonesia 73 B4 3 36 S 130 21 E
Tuma, Russia 51 D12 55 10N 40 30 E
Tuma →, Nic. 148 D3 13 6N 84 35W
Tumaco, Colombia 152 C2 1 50N 78 45W
Tumaco, Ensenada, Colombia 152 C2 1 55N 78 45W
Tumatumari, Guyana 153 B6 5 20N 58 55W
Tumauini, Phil. 70 C3 17 17N 121 49 E
Tumba, Sweden 14 E11 59 12N 17 48 E
Tumba, L., Zaïre 102 C3 0 50 S 18 0 E
Tumbarumba, Australia 117 C8 35 44 S 148 0 E
Tumbaya, Argentina 158 A2 23 50 S 65 26W
Túmbes, Peru 156 A1 3 37 S 80 27W
Tumbes □, Peru 156 A1 3 50 S 80 30W
Tumbwe, Zaïre 107 E2 11 25 S 27 15 E
Tumby Bay, Australia 116 C2 34 21 S 136 8 E
Tumd Youqi, China 66 D6 40 30N 110 30 E
Tumen, China 67 C15 43 0N 129 50 E
Tumen Jiang →, China 67 C16 42 20N 130 35 E
Tumeremo, Venezuela 153 B5 7 18N 61 30W
Tumiritinga, Brazil 155 E3 18 58 S 41 38W
Tumkur, India 83 H3 13 18N 77 6 E
Tummel, L., U.K. 18 E5 56 43N 3 55W
Tump, Pakistan 79 D1 26 7N 62 16 E
Tumpat, Malaysia 77 J4 6 11N 102 10 E
Tumsar, India 82 D4 21 26N 79 45 E
Tumu, Ghana 100 C4 10 56N 1 56W
Tumucumaque, Serra, Brazil 153 C7 2 0N 55 0W
Tumupasa, Bolivia 156 C4 14 9 S 67 55W
Tumut, Australia 117 C8 35 16 S 148 13 E
Tumutuk, Russia 54 D3 55 1N 53 19 E
Tumwater, U.S.A. 142 C2 47 1N 122 54W
Tunas de Zaza, Cuba 148 B4 21 39N 79 34W
Tunbridge Wells, U.K. 17 F8 51 7N 0 16 E
Tunceli, Turkey 89 D8 39 6N 39 31 E
Tunceli □, Turkey 89 D8 39 5N 39 35 E
Tuncurry, Australia 117 B10 32 17 S 152 29 E
Tunduru, Tanzania 107 E4 11 8 S 37 25 E
Tunduru □, Tanzania 107 E4 11 5 S 37 22 E
Tundzha →, Bulgaria 43 F11 41 40N 26 35 E
Tunga →, India 83 G2 15 0N 75 50 E
Tunga Pass, India 78 A5 29 0N 94 14 E
Tungabhadra →, India 83 G4 15 57N 78 15 E
Tungabhadra Dam, India 83 G2 15 0N 75 50 E
Tungaru, Sudan 95 E3 10 9N 30 52 E
Tungi, Bangla. 78 D3 23 53N 90 24 E
Tungla, Nic. 148 D3 13 24N 84 21W
Tungnafellsjökull, Iceland 12 D5 64 45N 17 55W
Tungsten, Canada 130 A3 61 57N 128 16W
Tungurahua □, Ecuador 152 D2 1 15 S 78 35W
Tunguska, Nizhnyaya →, Russia 57 C9 65 48N 88 4 E
Tuni, India 82 F6 17 22N 82 36 E
Tunia, Colombia 152 C2 2 41N 76 31W
Tunica, U.S.A. 139 H9 34 41N 90 23W
Tunis, Tunisia 96 A2 36 50N 10 11 E
Tunis, Golfe de, Tunisia 96 A2 37 0N 10 30 E
Tunisia ■, Africa 96 B1 33 30N 9 10 E
Tunja, Colombia 152 B3 5 33N 73 25W
Tunkhannock, U.S.A. 137 E9 41 32N 75 57W
Tunliu, China 66 F7 36 13N 112 52 E
Tunnsjøen, Norway 12 D12 64 45N 13 25 E
Tunungayualok I., Canada 129 A7 56 0N 61 0W
Tunuyán, Argentina 158 C2 33 35 S 69 0W
Tunuyán →, Argentina 158 C2 33 33 S 67 30W
Tunxi, China 69 C12 29 42N 118 25 E
Tuo Jiang →, China 68 C5 28 50N 105 35 E
Tuolumne, U.S.A. 144 H6 37 58N 120 15W
Tuolumne →, U.S.A. 144 H5 37 36N 121 13W
Tuoy-Khaya, Russia 57 C12 62 32N 111 25 E
Tūp Āghāj, Iran 84 B5 36 3N 47 50 E
Tupã, Brazil 159 A5 21 57 S 50 28W
Tupaciguara, Brazil 155 E2 18 35 S 48 42W
Tupelo, U.S.A. 135 H1 34 16N 88 43W
Tupik, Russia 50 D8 55 42N 33 22 E
Tupik, Russia 57 D12 54 26N 119 57 E
Tupinambaranas, Brazil 153 D6 3 0 S 58 0W
Tupirama, Brazil 154 C2 8 58 S 48 12W
Tupiratins, Brazil 154 C2 8 23 S 48 8W
Tupiza, Bolivia 158 A2 21 30 S 65 40W
Tupižnica, Serbia 42 D7 43 43N 22 10 E
Tupman, U.S.A. 145 K7 35 18N 119 21W
Tupper, Canada 130 B4 55 32N 120 1W
Tupper Lake, U.S.A. 137 B10 44 14N 74 28W
Tupungato, Cerro, S. Amer. 158 C2 33 15 S 69 50W
Tuquan, China 67 B11 45 18N 121 38 E
Túquerres, Colombia 152 C2 1 5N 77 37W
Tura, India 78 C3 25 30N 90 16 E
Tura, Russia 57 C11 64 20N 100 17 E
Turabah, Si. Arabia 84 D4 28 20N 43 15 E
Turagua, Serranía, Venezuela 153 B5 7 20N 64 35W
Turaiyur, India 83 J4 11 9N 78 38 E
Turakina, N.Z. 118 G4 40 3 S 175 16 E
Turakina →, N.Z. 118 G4 40 5 S 175 8 E
Turakirae Hd., N.Z. 118 H3 41 26 S 174 56 E
Tūrān, Iran 85 C8 35 39N 56 42 E
Turan, Russia 57 D10 51 55N 95 0 E
Turayf, Si. Arabia 84 D3 31 41N 38 39 E
Turbacz, Poland 31 B13 49 30N 20 8 E
Turbe, Bos.-H. 42 C2 44 15N 17 35 E
Turbenthal, Switz. 29 B7 47 27N 8 51 E
Turda, Romania 46 C4 46 34N 23 47 E
Turégano, Spain 36 D6 41 9N 4 1W
Turek, Poland 47 C5 52 3N 18 30 E
Turen, Venezuela 152 B4 9 17N 69 6W
Turfan = Turpan, China 64 B3 43 58N 89 10 E
Turgay, Kazakhstan 54 G8 49 38N 63 30 E
Tŭrgovishte, Bulgaria 43 D11 43 17N 26 38 E
Turgutlu, Turkey 88 D2 38 30N 27 48 E
Turhal, Turkey 52 F7 40 24N 36 5 E
Turia →, Spain 35 F4 39 27N 0 19W
Turiaçu, Brazil 154 B2 1 40 S 45 19W
Turiaçu →, Brazil 154 B2 1 36 S 45 19W
Turiec →, Slovak Rep. 31 B11 49 7N 18 55 E
Turin = Torino, Italy 38 C4 45 4N 7 40 E
Turin, Canada 130 D6 49 58N 112 31W
Turinsk, Russia 54 B8 58 3N 63 42 E
Turka, Ukraine 50 G3 49 10N 23 2 E
Turkana □, Kenya 106 B4 3 0N 35 30 E
Turkana, L., Africa 106 B4 3 30N 36 5 E
Turkestan, Kazakhstan 55 B4 43 17N 68 16 E
Turkestanskiy, Khrebet, Tajikistan 55 D4 39 35N 69 0 E
Túrkeve, Hungary 31 D13 47 6N 20 44 E
Turkey ■, Eurasia 88 D7 39 0N 36 0 E
Turkey →, U.S.A. 140 B5 42 43N 91 2W
Turkey Creek, Australia 112 C4 17 2 S 128 12 E
Turki, Russia 51 F13 52 0N 43 15 E
Turkmenistan ■, Asia 56 F6 39 0N 59 0 E
Türkoğlu, Turkey 88 E7 37 23N 36 50 E
Turks & Caicos Is. ■, W. Indies 149 B5 21 20N 71 20W
Turks Island Passage, W. Indies 149 B5 21 30N 71 30W
Turku, Finland 13 F17 60 30N 22 19 E
Turkwe →, Kenya 106 B4 3 6N 36 6 E
Turlock, U.S.A. 144 H6 37 30N 120 51W
Turnagain →, Canada 130 B3 59 12N 127 35W
Turnagain, C., N.Z. 118 G5 40 28 S 176 38 E
Turneffe Is., Belize 147 D7 17 20N 87 50W
Turner, Australia 112 C4 17 52 S 128 16 E
Turner, U.S.A. 142 B9 48 51N 108 24W
Turner Pt., Australia 114 A1 11 47 S 133 32 E
Turner Valley, Canada 130 C6 50 40N 114 17W
Turners Falls, U.S.A. 137 D12 42 36N 72 33W
Turnhout, Belgium 21 F5 51 19N 4 57 E
Türnitz, Austria 30 D8 47 55N 15 29 E
Turnor L., Canada 131 B7 56 35N 108 35W
Turnov, Czech. 30 A8 50 34N 15 10 E
Tŭrnovo, Bulgaria 43 D10 43 5N 25 41 E
Turnu Măgurele, Romania 46 F5 43 46N 24 56 E
Turnu Rosu Pasul, Romania 46 D5 45 33N 24 17 E
Turobin, Poland 47 E9 50 50N 22 44 E
Turon, U.S.A. 139 G5 37 48N 98 26W
Tuross Head, Australia 117 D9 36 3 S 150 8 E
Turpan, China 64 B3 43 58N 89 10 E
Turrës, Kalaja e, Albania 44 C1 41 10N 19 28 E
Turriff, U.K. 18 D6 57 32N 2 28W
Tursāq, Iraq 84 C5 33 27N 45 47 E
Tursha, Russia 51 C15 56 55N 47 36 E
Tursi, Italy 41 B9 40 15N 16 28 E
Turtle Head I., Australia 114 A3 10 56 S 142 37 E
Turtle Is., Phil. 71 H2 6 7N 118 14 E
Turtle L., Canada 131 C7 53 36N 108 38W
Turtle Lake, N. Dak., U.S.A. 138 B4 47 31N 100 53W
Turtle Lake, Wis., U.S.A. 138 C8 45 24N 92 8W
Turtleford, Canada 131 C7 53 23N 108 57W
Turua, N.Z. 118 D4 37 14 S 175 35 E
Turukhansk, Russia 57 C9 65 21N 88 5 E
Turun ja Porin lääni □, Finland 13 F17 60 27N 22 15 E
Turzovka, Slovak Rep. 31 B11 49 25N 18 35 E
Tuscaloosa, U.S.A. 135 J2 33 12N 87 34W
Tuscánia, Italy 39 F8 42 25N 11 53 E
Tuscany = Toscana, Italy 38 E8 43 30N 11 5 E
Tuscola, Ill., U.S.A. 141 E8 39 48N 88 17W
Tuscola, Tex., U.S.A. 139 J5 32 12N 99 48W
Tuscumbia, Ala., U.S.A. 135 H2 34 44N 87 42W
Tuscumbia, Mo., U.S.A. 140 F4 38 14N 92 28W
Tuskar Rock, Ireland 19 D5 52 12N 6 10W
Tuskegee, U.S.A. 135 J3 32 25N 85 42W
Tustna, Norway 14 A2 63 10N 8 5 E
Tuszyn, Poland 47 D6 51 36N 19 33 E
Tutak, Turkey 89 D10 39 31N 42 46 E
Tutayev, Russia 51 C11 57 53N 39 32 E
Tuticorin, India 83 K4 8 50N 78 12 E
Tutin, Serbia 42 E5 42 58N 20 20 E
Tutóia, Brazil 154 B3 2 45 S 42 20W
Tutong, Brunei 75 B4 4 47N 114 40 E
Tutova →, Romania 46 C8 46 20N 27 30 E
Tutrakan, Bulgaria 43 C11 44 2N 26 40 E
Tutshi L., Canada 130 B2 59 56N 134 30W
Tuttle, U.S.A. 138 B5 47 9N 100 0W
Tuttlingen, Germany 27 H4 47 59N 8 50 E
Tutuala, Indonesia 72 C3 8 25 S 127 15 E
Tutuila, Amer. Samoa 121 X24 14 19 S 170 50W
Tutuko Mt., N.Z. 119 E3 44 35 S 168 1 E
Tututepec, Mexico 147 D5 16 9N 97 38W
Tutye, Australia 116 C4 35 12 S 141 29 E
Tuva Republic □, Russia 57 D10 51 30N 95 0 E
Tuvalu ■, Pac. Oc. 122 H9 8 0 S 178 0 E
Tūwal, Si. Arabia 86 B2 22 17N 39 6 E
Tuxpan, Mexico 147 C5 20 58N 97 23W
Tuxtla Gutiérrez, Mexico 147 D6 16 50N 93 10W
Tuy, Spain 36 C2 42 3N 8 39W
Tuy An, Vietnam 76 F7 13 17N 109 16 E
Tuy Duc, Vietnam 77 F6 12 15N 107 27 E
Tuy Hoa, Vietnam 76 F7 13 5N 109 10 E
Tuy Phong, Vietnam 77 G7 11 14N 108 43 E
Tuya L., Canada 130 B2 59 7N 130 35W
Tuyen Hoa, Vietnam 76 D6 17 50N 106 10 E
Tuyen Quang, Vietnam 76 B5 21 50N 105 10 E
Tuymazy, Russia 54 D3 54 36N 53 42 E
Tūysarkān, Iran 85 C6 34 33N 48 27 E
Tuz Gölü, Turkey 88 D5 38 45N 33 30 E
Ţūz Khurmātū, Iraq 84 C5 34 56N 44 38 E
Tuzkan, Ozero, Uzbekistan 55 C3 40 35N 67 28 E
Tuzla, Bos.-H. 42 C3 44 34N 18 41 E
Tuzla Gölü, Turkey 88 D6 39 1N 35 49 E
Tuzlov →, Russia 53 C8 47 10N 39 10 E
Tvååker, Sweden 15 G6 57 4N 12 25 E
Tvedestrand, Norway 15 F2 58 38N 8 58 E
Tver, Russia 51 C9 56 55N 35 55 E
Tvŭrditsa, Bulgaria 43 E10 42 42N 25 53 E
Twain, U.S.A. 144 E5 40 1N 121 3W
Twain Harte, U.S.A. 144 G6 38 2N 120 14W
Twardogóra, Poland 47 D4 51 23N 17 28 E
Tweed, Canada 136 B7 44 29N 77 19W
Tweed →, U.K. 18 F7 55 42N 1 59W
Tweed Heads, Australia 115 D5 28 10 S 153 31 E
Tweedsmuir Prov. Park, Canada 130 C3 53 0N 126 20W
Twello, Neths. 20 D8 52 14N 6 6 E
Twentynine Palms, U.S.A. 145 L10 34 8N 116 3W
Twillingate, Canada 129 C9 49 42N 54 45W
Twin Bridges, U.S.A. 142 D7 45 33N 112 20W
Twin Falls, U.S.A. 142 E6 42 34N 114 28W
Twin Valley, U.S.A. 138 B6 47 16N 96 16W
Twinnge, Burma 78 D6 23 10N 96 2 E
Twisp, U.S.A. 142 B3 48 22N 120 7W
Twistringen, Germany 26 C4 52 48N 8 38 E
Two Harbors, U.S.A. 138 B9 47 2N 91 40W
Two Hills, Canada 130 C6 53 43N 111 52W
Two Rivers, U.S.A. 134 C2 44 9N 87 34W
Two Thumbs Ra., N.Z. 119 D5 43 45 S 170 44 E
Twofold B., Australia 117 D8 37 8 S 149 59 E
Tychy, Poland 31 A11 50 9N 18 59 E
Tyczyn, Poland 31 B15 49 58N 22 2 E
Tykocin, Poland 47 B9 53 13N 22 46 E
Tyldal, Norway 14 B4 62 8N 10 48 E
Tyler, U.S.A. 133 D7 32 18N 95 18W
Tyler, Minn., U.S.A. 138 C6 44 18N 96 8W
Tyler, Tex., U.S.A. 139 J7 32 21N 95 18W
Týn nad Vltavou, Czech. 30 B7 49 13N 14 26 E
Tynda, Russia 57 D13 55 10N 124 43 E
Tyne →, U.K. 16 C6 54 58N 1 28W
Tyne & Wear □, U.K. 16 C6 54 55N 1 35W
Tynemouth, U.K. 16 B6 55 1N 1 27W
Tynset, Norway 14 B4 62 17N 10 47 E
Tyre = Sūr, Lebanon 91 B4 33 19N 35 16 E
Tyrifjorden, Norway 14 D4 60 2N 10 8 E
Tyringe, Sweden 15 H7 56 9N 13 35 E
Tyristrand, Norway 14 D4 60 5N 10 5 E
Tyrnyauz, Russia 53 E10 43 21N 42 45 E
Tyrol = Tirol □, Austria 30 D3 47 3N 10 43 E
Tyrone, U.S.A. 136 F6 40 40N 78 14W
Tyrrell →, Australia 116 C5 35 26 S 142 51 E
Tyrrell, L., Australia 116 C5 35 20 S 142 50 E
Tyrrell Arm, Canada 131 A9 62 27N 97 30W
Tyrrell L., Canada 131 A7 63 7N 105 27W
Tyrrhenian Sea, Europe 40 B5 40 0N 12 30 E
Tysfjorden, Norway 12 B14 68 7N 16 25 E
Tystberga, Sweden 15 F11 58 51N 17 15 E
Tyub Karagan, Mys, Kazakhstan 53 D14 44 40N 50 19 E
Tyuleniy, Russia 53 D12 44 28N 47 30 E
Tyulgan, Russia 54 E5 52 22N 56 12 E
Tyumen, Russia 54 C9 57 11N 65 29 E
Tyumen-Aryk, Kazakhstan 55 A3 44 2N 67 1 E
Tyup, Kirghizia 55 B9 42 45N 78 20 E
Tywi →, U.K. 17 F3 51 48N 4 20W
Tywyn, U.K. 17 E3 52 36N 4 5W
Tzaneen, S. Africa 105 C5 23 47 S 30 9 E
Tzermiádhes, Greece 32 D7 35 12N 25 29 E
Tzermiádhes Neápolis, Greece 45 J7 35 11N 25 29 E
Tzoumérka, Óros, Greece 44 E3 39 30N 21 26 E
Tzukong = Zigong, China 68 C5 29 15N 104 48 E
Tzummarum, Neths. 20 B7 53 14N 5 32 E


# U


U Taphao, Thailand 76 F3 12 35N 101 0 E
U.S.A. = United States of America ■, N. Amer. 132 C7 37 0N 96 0W
Uacalla Iero, Somali Rep. 108 D2 1 48N 42 38 E
Uachadi, Sierra, Venezuela 153 C4 4 54N 65 18W
Uainambi, Colombia 152 C4 1 43N 69 51W
Uanda, Australia 114 C3 21 37 S 144 55 E
Uanle Uen, Somali Rep. 108 D2 2 37N 44 54 E
Uarsciek, Somali Rep. 90 G4 2 28N 45 55 E
Uascen, Somali Rep. 108 D2 4 11N 43 13 E
Uasin □, Kenya 106 B4 0 30N 35 20 E
Uato-Udo, Indonesia 72 C3 9 7 S 125 36 E
Uatumã →, Brazil 153 D6 2 26 S 57 37W
Uauá, Brazil 154 C4 9 50 S 39 28W
Uaupés, Brazil 152 D4 0 8 S 67 5W
Uaupés →, Brazil 152 C4 0 2N 67 16W
Uaxactún, Guatemala 148 C2 17 25N 89 29W
Ub, Serbia 42 C5 44 28N 20 6 E
Ubá, Brazil 155 F3 21 8 S 43 0W
Ubaitaba, Brazil 155 D4 14 18 S 39 20W
Ubangi = Oubangi →, Zaïre 102 C3 0 30 S 17 50 E
Ubaté, Colombia 152 B3 5 19N 73 49W
Ubauro, Pakistan 80 E3 28 15N 69 45 E
Ubay, Phil. 71 F5 10 3N 124 28 E
'Ubaydīyah, Yemen 86 D3 13 7N 43 20 E
Ubaye →, France 25 D10 44 28N 6 18 E
Ube, Japan 62 D3 33 56N 131 15 E
Ubeda, Spain 35 G1 38 3N 3 23W
Uberaba, Brazil 155 E2 19 50 S 47 55W
Uberaba, L., Brazil 157 D6 17 30 S 57 50W
Uberlândia, Brazil 155 E2 19 0 S 48 20W
Überlingen, Germany 27 H5 47 46N 9 10 E
Ubiaja, Nigeria 101 D6 6 41N 6 22 E
Ubolratna Res., Thailand 76 D4 16 45N 102 30 E
Ubombo, S. Africa 105 D5 27 31 S 32 4 E
Ubon Ratchathani, Thailand 76 E5 15 15N 104 50 E
Ubondo, Zaïre 106 C2 0 55 S 25 42 E
Ubort →, Belorussia 50 E6 52 6N 28 30 E
Ubrique, Spain 37 J5 36 41N 5 27W
Ubundu, Zaïre 102 C5 0 22 S 25 30 E
Ucayali →, Peru 156 A3 4 30 S 73 30W
Uccle, Belgium 21 G4 50 48N 4 22 E
Uchaly, Russia 54 D6 54 19N 59 27 E
Uchi Lake, Canada 131 C10 51 5N 92 35W
Uchiko, Japan 62 D4 33 33N 132 39 E
Uchiura-Wan, Japan 60 C10 42 25N 140 40 E
Uchiza, Peru 156 B2 8 25 S 76 20W
Uchte, Germany 26 C4 52 29N 8 52 E
Uchur →, Russia 57 D14 58 48N 130 35 E
Ucluelet, Canada 130 D3 48 57N 125 32W
Ucurîş, Romania 46 C2 46 41N 21 58 E
Uda →, Russia 57 D14 54 42N 135 14 E
Udaipur, India 80 G5 24 36N 73 44 E
Udaipur Garhi, Nepal 81 F12 27 0N 86 35 E
Udbina, Croatia 39 D12 44 31N 15 47 E
Uddel, Neths. 20 D7 52 15N 5 48 E
Uddevalla, Sweden 15 F5 58 21N 11 55 E
Uddjaur, Sweden 12 D16 65 25N 21 15 E
Uden, Neths. 21 E7 51 40N 5 37 E
Udgir, India 82 E3 18 25N 77 5 E
Udhampur, India 81 C6 33 0N 75 5 E
Udi, Nigeria 101 D6 6 17N 7 21 E
Údine, Italy 39 B10 46 5N 13 10 E
Udmurt Republic □, Russia 54 C3 57 30N 52 30 E
Udon Thani, Thailand 76 D4 17 29N 102 46 E
Udumalaippettai, India 83 J3 10 35N 77 15 E
Udupi, India 83 H2 13 25N 74 42 E
Udvoy Balkan, Bulgaria 43 E11 42 50N 26 50 E
Udzungwa Range, Tanzania 107 D4 9 30 S 35 10 E
Ueckermünde, Germany 26 B10 53 45N 14 1 E
Ueda, Japan 63 A10 36 24N 138 16 E
Uedineniya, Os., Russia 6 B12 78 0N 85 0 E
Uel Scimbirro, Somali Rep. 108 D2 2 23N 44 14 E
Uele →, Zaïre 102 B4 3 45N 24 45 E
Uelen, Russia 57 C19 66 10N 170 0W
Uelzen, Germany 26 C6 53 0N 10 33 E
Ueno, Japan 63 C8 34 45N 136 8 E
Uetendorf, Switz. 28 C5 46 47N 7 34 E
Ufa, Russia 54 D4 54 45N 55 55 E
Ufa →, Russia 54 D5 54 40N 56 0 E
Uffenheim, Germany 27 F6 49 32N 10 15 E

Ugab →, Namibia **104 C1** 20 55 S 13 30 E
Ugalla →, Tanzania **106 D3** 5 8 S 30 42 E
Ugamskiy, Khrebet, Kazakhstan **55 B5** 42 20N 70 30 E
Uganda ■, Africa **106 B3** 2 0N 32 0 E
Ugchelen, Neths. **20 D7** 52 11N 5 56 E
Ugento, Italy **41 C11** 39 55N 18 10 E
Ugep, Nigeria **101 D6** 5 53N 8 2 E
Ugie, S. Africa **105 E4** 31 10 S 28 13 E
Ugijar, Spain **35 J1** 36 58N 3 7W
Ugine, France **25 C10** 45 45N 6 25 E
Uglegorsk, Russia **57 E15** 49 5N 142 2 E
Uglich, Russia **51 C11** 57 33N 38 20 E
Ugljane, Croatia **39 E13** 43 35N 16 46 E
Ugolyak, Russia **57 C13** 64 33N 120 30 E
Ugra →, Russia **51 D10** 54 30N 36 7 E
Ugûn Mûsa, Egypt **91 F1** 29 53N 32 40 E
Ugŭrchin, Bulgaria **43 D9** 43 6N 24 26 E
Uh →, Slovak Rep. **31 C14** 48 7N 21 25 E
Uherske Hradiště, Czech. **31 B10** 49 4N 17 30 E
Uhersky Brod, Czech. **31 B10** 49 1N 17 40 E
Úhlava →, Czech. **30 B6** 49 45N 13 24 E
Uhrichsville, U.S.A. **136 F3** 40 24N 81 21W
Uíge, Angola **103 D2** 7 30 S 14 40 E
Uige □, Angola **103 D3** 7 0 S 16 0 E
Uiha, Tonga **121 P13** 19 54 S 174 25W
Uijŏngbu, S. Korea **67 F14** 37 48N 127 0 E
Ŭiju, N. Korea **67 D13** 40 15N 124 35 E
Uinta Mts., U.S.A. **142 F8** 40 45N 110 30W
Uitenhage, S. Africa **104 E4** 33 40 S 25 28 E
Uitgeest, Neths. **20 C5** 52 32N 4 43 E
Uithoorn, Neths. **20 D5** 52 14N 4 50 E
Uithuizen, Neths. **20 B9** 53 24N 6 41 E
Uitkerke, Belgium **21 F2** 51 18N 3 9 E
Újfehértó, Hungary **31 D14** 47 49N 21 41 E
Ujhani, India **81 F8** 28 0N 79 6 E
Uji, Japan **63 C7** 34 53N 135 48 E
Uji-guntō, Japan **61 J4** 31 15N 129 25 E
Ujjain, India **80 H6** 23 9N 75 43 E
Újpest, Hungary **31 D12** 47 32N 19 6 E
Újszász, Hungary **31 D13** 47 19N 20 7 E
Ujung Pandang, Indonesia **72 C1** 5 10 S 119 20 E
Uka, Russia **57 D17** 57 50N 162 0 E
Ukara I., Tanzania **106 C3** 1 50 S 33 0 E
Uke-Shima, Japan **61 K4** 28 2N 129 14 E
Ukerewe □, Tanzania **106 C3** 2 0 S 32 30 E
Ukerewe I., Tanzania **106 C3** 2 0 S 33 0 E
Ukholovo, Russia **51 E12** 53 47N 40 30 E
Ukhrul, India **78 C5** 25 10N 94 25 E
Ukhta, Russia **48 B9** 63 55N 54 0 E
Ukiah, U.S.A. **144 F3** 39 9N 123 13W
Ukki Fort, India **81 C7** 33 28N 76 54 E
Ukmerge, Lithuania **50 D4** 55 15N 24 45 E
Ukraine ■, Europe **52 B4** 49 0N 32 0 E
Uksyanskoye, Russia **54 D8** 55 57N 63 1 E
Uku, Angola **103 E2** 11 24 S 14 22 E
Ukwi, Botswana **104 C3** 23 29 S 20 30 E
Ulaanbaatar, Mongolia **57 E11** 47 55N 106 53 E
Ulaangom, Mongolia **64 A4** 50 5N 92 10 E
Ulamambri, Australia **117 A8** 31 19 S 149 23 E
Ulamba, Zaïre **103 D4** 9 3 S 23 38 E
Ulan Bator = Ulaanbaatar, Mongolia **57 E11** 47 55N 106 53 E
Ulan Ude, Russia **57 D11** 51 45N 107 40 E
Ulanbel, Kazakhstan **55 A5** 44 50N 71 7 E
Ulanga □, Tanzania **107 D4** 8 40 S 36 50 E
Ulanów, Poland **47 E9** 50 30N 22 16 E
Ulaş, Turkey **88 D7** 39 26N 37 2 E
Ulawa, Solomon Is. **121 M11** 9 46 S 161 57 E
Ulaya, Morogoro, Tanzania **106 D4** 7 3 S 36 55 E
Ulaya, Tabora, Tanzania **106 C3** 4 25 S 33 30 E
Ulcinj, Montenegro **42 F4** 41 58N 19 10 E
Ulco, S. Africa **104 D3** 28 21 S 24 15 E
Ulëza, Albania **44 C1** 41 46N 19 57 E
Ulfborg, Denmark **15 H2** 56 16N 8 20 E
Ulft, Neths. **20 E8** 51 53N 6 23 E
Ulhasnagar, India **82 E1** 19 15N 73 10 E
Ulinda, Australia **117 A8** 31 35 S 149 30 E
Uljma, Serbia **42 B6** 45 2N 21 10 E
Ulla →, Spain **36 C2** 42 39N 8 44W
Ulladulla, Australia **117 C9** 35 21 S 150 29 E
Ullånger, Sweden **14 B12** 62 58N 18 10 E
Ullapool, U.K. **18 D3** 57 54N 5 10W
Ullared, Sweden **15 G6** 57 8N 12 42 E
Ulldecona, Spain **34 E5** 40 36N 0 20 E
Ullswater, U.K. **16 C5** 54 35N 2 52W
Ullung-do, S. Korea **67 F16** 37 30N 130 30 E
Ulm, Germany **27 G5** 48 23N 10 0 E
Ulmarra, Australia **115 D5** 29 37 S 153 4 E
Ulmeni, Romania **46 D7** 45 4N 26 40 E
Ulonguè, Mozam. **107 E3** 14 37 S 34 19 E
Ulricehamn, Sweden **13 H12** 57 46N 13 26 E
Ulrum, Neths. **20 B8** 53 22N 6 20 E
Ulsan, S. Korea **67 G15** 35 20N 129 15 E
Ulsberg, Norway **14 B3** 62 45N 9 59 E
Ulster □, U.K. **19 B5** 54 35N 6 30W
Ulstrem, Bulgaria **43 E11** 42 1N 26 27 E
Ultima, Australia **116 C5** 35 30 S 143 18 E
Ulubaria, India **81 H13** 22 31N 88 4 E
Ulubat Gölü, Turkey **88 C3** 40 10N 28 25 E
Ulubey, Turkey **88 D3** 38 25N 29 18 E
Uluborlu, Turkey **88 D4** 38 4N 30 28 E
Uludağ, Turkey **88 C3** 40 4N 29 13 E
Uludere, Turkey **89 E10** 37 28N 42 42 E
Uluguru Mts., Tanzania **106 D4** 7 15 S 37 40 E
Ulukışla, Turkey **88 E6** 37 33N 34 28 E
Ulungur He →, China **64 B3** 47 1N 87 24 E
Ulutau, Kazakhstan **56 E7** 48 39N 67 1 E
Ulvenhout, Neths. **21 E5** 51 33N 4 48 E
Ulverston, U.K. **16 C4** 54 13N 3 7W
Ulverstone, Australia **114 G4** 41 11 S 146 11 E
Ulya, Russia **57 D15** 59 10N 142 0 E
Ulyanovsk = Simbirsk, Russia **51 D16** 54 20N 48 25 E
Ulyasutay, Mongolia **64 B4** 47 56N 97 28 E
Ulysses, U.S.A. **139 G4** 37 35N 101 22W
Umag, Croatia **39 C10** 45 26N 13 31 E
Umala, Bolivia **156 D4** 17 25 S 68 5W
Uman, Ukraine **52 B4** 48 40N 30 12 E
Umarkhed, India **82 E3** 19 37N 77 46 E
Umatac, Guam **121 R15** 13 18N 144 39 E
Umatilla, U.S.A. **142 D4** 45 55N 119 21W
Umba, Russia **48 A5** 66 50N 34 20 E
Umbertide, Italy **39 E9** 43 18N 12 20 E
Umboi I., Papua N. G. **120 C4** 5 40 S 148 0 E
Umbrella Mts., N.Z. **119 F4** 45 35 S 169 5 E
Umbria □, Italy **39 F9** 42 53N 12 30 E
Ume älv →, Sweden **12 E16** 63 45N 20 20 E
Umeå, Sweden **12 E16** 63 45N 20 20 E
Umera, Indonesia **73 B3** 0 12 S 129 37 E
Umfuli →, Zimbabwe **107 F2** 17 30 S 29 23 E
Umgusa, Zimbabwe **107 F2** 19 29 S 27 52 E
Umi, Japan **62 D2** 33 34N 130 30 E
Umka, Serbia **42 C5** 44 40N 20 19 E
Umkomaas, S. Africa **105 E5** 30 13 S 30 48 E
Umm ad Daraj, J., Jordan **91 C4** 32 18N 35 48 E
Umm al Arānib, Libya **96 C2** 26 10N 14 43 E
Umm al Qaywayn, U.A.E. **85 E7** 25 30N 55 35 E
Umm al Qittayn, Jordan **91 C5** 32 18N 36 40 E
Umm Arda, Sudan **95 D3** 15 17N 32 31 E
Umm Bāb, Qatar **85 E6** 25 12N 50 48 E
Umm Bel, Sudan **95 E2** 13 35N 28 0 E
Umm Dubban, Sudan **95 D3** 15 23N 32 52 E
Umm el Fahm, Israel **91 C4** 32 31N 35 9 E
Umm Koweika, Sudan **95 E3** 13 10N 32 16 E
Umm Lajj, Si. Arabia **84 E3** 25 0N 37 23 E
Umm Merwa, Sudan **94 D3** 18 4N 32 30 E
Umm Ruwaba, Sudan **95 E3** 12 50N 31 20 E
Umm Sidr, Sudan **95 E2** 14 29N 25 10 E
Umm Thalwīwah, Si. Arabia **86 B3** 21 9N 40 48 E
Ummanz, Germany **26 A9** 54 29N 13 9 E
Umnak I., U.S.A. **126 C3** 53 15N 168 20W
Umniati →, Zimbabwe **107 F2** 16 49 S 28 45 E
Umpqua →, U.S.A. **142 E1** 43 40N 124 12W
Umpulo, Angola **103 E3** 12 38 S 17 42 E
Umred, India **82 D4** 20 51N 79 18 E
Umreth, India **80 H5** 22 41N 73 4 E
Umtata, S. Africa **105 E4** 31 36 S 28 49 E
Umuahia, Nigeria **101 D6** 5 33N 7 29 E
Umuarama, Brazil **159 A5** 23 45 S 53 20W
Umvukwe Ra., Zimbabwe **107 F3** 16 45 S 30 45 E
Umzimvubu = Port St. Johns, S. Africa **105 E4** 31 38 S 29 33 E
Umzingwane →, Zimbabwe **107 G2** 22 12 S 29 56 E
Umzinto, S. Africa **105 E5** 30 15 S 30 45 E
Una, India **80 J4** 20 46N 71 8 E
Una →, Bos.-H. **39 C13** 45 0N 16 20 E
Unac →, Bos.-H. **39 D13** 44 30N 16 9 E
Unadilla, U.S.A. **137 D9** 42 20N 75 19W
Unalaska, U.S.A. **126 C3** 53 53N 166 32W
Uncastillo, Spain **34 C3** 42 21N 1 8W
Uncía, Bolivia **156 D4** 18 25 S 66 40W
Uncompahgre Peak, U.S.A. **143 G10** 38 4N 107 28W
Unden, Sweden **15 F8** 58 45N 14 25 E
Underberg, S. Africa **105 D4** 29 50 S 29 22 E
Underbool, Australia **116 C4** 35 10 S 141 51 E
Undersaker, Sweden **14 A7** 63 19N 13 21 E
Undersvik, Sweden **14 C10** 61 36N 16 20 E
Unecha, Russia **50 E8** 52 50N 32 37 E
Uneiuxi →, Brazil **152 D4** 0 37 S 65 34W
Ungarie, Australia **117 B7** 33 38 S 146 56 E
Ungarra, Australia **116 C2** 34 12 S 136 2 E
Ungava B., Canada **127 C13** 59 30N 67 30W
Ungava Pen., Canada **124 D12** 60 0N 74 0W
Ungeny, Moldavia **52 C2** 47 11N 27 51 E
Unggi, N. Korea **67 C16** 42 16N 130 28 E
Ungwatiri, Sudan **95 D4** 16 52N 36 10 E
Uni, Russia **54 C2** 57 44N 51 47 E
União da Vitória, Brazil **159 B5** 26 13 S 51 5W
União dos Palmares, Brazil **154 C4** 9 10 S 36 2W
Uniejów, Poland **47 D5** 51 59N 18 46 E
Unije, Croatia **39 D11** 44 40N 14 15 E
Unimak I., U.S.A. **126 C3** 54 45N 164 0W
Unini →, Brazil **153 D5** 1 41 S 61 31W
Union, Miss., U.S.A. **139 J10** 32 34N 89 7W
Union, Mo., U.S.A. **140 F6** 38 27N 91 0W
Union, S.C., U.S.A. **135 H5** 34 43N 81 37W
Union, Mt., U.S.A. **143 J7** 34 34N 112 21W
Union City, Calif., U.S.A. **144 H4** 37 36N 122 1W
Union City, N.J., U.S.A. **137 F10** 40 45N 74 2W
Union City, Pa., U.S.A. **136 E5** 41 54N 79 51W
Union City, Tenn., U.S.A. **139 G10** 36 26N 89 3W
Union Gap, U.S.A. **142 C3** 46 33N 120 28W
Union Grove, U.S.A. **141 B8** 42 41N 88 3W
Union of Soviet Socialist Republics = Commonwealth of Independent States ■, Eurasia **57 D11** 60 0N 100 0 E
Union Springs, U.S.A. **135 J3** 32 9N 85 43W
Union Star, U.S.A. **140 E2** 39 59N 94 36W
Uniondale, S. Africa **104 E3** 33 39 S 23 7 E
Uniontown, Ky., U.S.A. **141 G9** 37 47N 87 56W
Uniontown, Pa., U.S.A. **134 F6** 39 54N 79 44W
Unionville, U.S.A. **140 D3** 40 29N 93 1W
Unirea, Romania **46 E8** 44 15N 27 35 E
United Arab Emirates ■, Asia **85 F7** 23 50N 54 0 E
United Kingdom ■, Europe **11 E5** 53 0N 2 0W
United States of America ■, N. Amer. **132 C7** 37 0N 96 0W
Unity, Canada **131 C7** 52 30N 109 5W
Universales, Mtes., Spain **34 E3** 40 18N 1 33W
University City, U.S.A. **140 F6** 38 40N 90 20W
Unjha, India **80 H5** 23 46N 72 24 E
Unnao, India **81 F9** 26 35N 80 30 E
Uno, Ilha, Guinea-Biss. **100 C1** 11 15N 16 13W
Unst, U.K. **18 A8** 60 50N 0 55W
Unstrut →, Germany **26 D7** 51 10N 11 48 E
Unter-engadin, Switz. **29 C10** 46 48N 10 20 E
Unterägeri, Switz. **29 B7** 47 8N 8 36 E
Unterkulm, Switz. **28 B6** 47 18N 8 7 E
Unterseen, Switz. **28 C5** 46 41N 7 50 E
Unterwaldner Alpen, Switz. **29 C6** 46 55N 8 15 E
Unuk →, Canada **130 B2** 56 5N 131 3W
Ünye, Turkey **52 F7** 41 5N 37 15 E
Unzen-Dake, Japan **62 E2** 32 45N 130 17 E
Unzha, Russia **51 B14** 58 0N 44 0 E
Unzha →, Russia **51 C13** 57 30N 43 40 E
Uors, Switz. **29 C8** 46 42N 9 12 E
Uozu, Japan **63 A9** 36 48N 137 24 E
Upa →, Czech. **31 A9** 50 35N 16 15 E
Upata, Venezuela **153 B5** 8 1N 62 24W
Upemba, L., Zaïre **107 D2** 8 30 S 26 20 E
Upernavik, Greenland **6 B5** 72 49N 56 20W
Upington, S. Africa **104 D3** 28 25 S 21 15 E
Upleta, India **80 J4** 21 46N 70 16 E
Upolu, W. Samoa **121 W24** 13 58 S 172 0W
Upper Alkali Lake, U.S.A. **142 F3** 41 47N 120 8W
Upper Arlington, U.S.A. **141 D13** 40 0N 83 4W
Upper Arrow L., Canada **130 C5** 50 30N 117 50W
Upper Austria = Oberösterreich □, Austria **30 C6** 48 10N 14 0 E
Upper Foster L., Canada **131 B7** 56 47N 105 20W
Upper Hutt, N.Z. **118 H4** 41 8 S 175 5 E
Upper Juba, Somali Rep. **108 D2** 3 0N 43 0 E
Upper Klamath L., U.S.A. **142 E3** 42 25N 121 55W
Upper Lake, U.S.A. **144 F4** 39 10N 122 54W
Upper Manilla, Australia **117 A9** 30 38 S 150 40 E
Upper Musquodoboit, Canada **129 C7** 45 10N 62 58W
Upper Red L., U.S.A. **138 A7** 48 8N 94 45W
Upper Sandusky, U.S.A. **141 D13** 40 50N 83 17W
Upper Sheikh, Somali Rep. **108 C3** 9 56N 45 13 E
Upper Volta = Burkina Faso ■, Africa **100 C4** 12 0N 1 0W
Upphärad, Sweden **15 F6** 58 9N 12 19 E
Uppsala, Sweden **14 E11** 59 53N 17 38 E
Uppsala län □, Sweden **13 G14** 60 0N 17 30 E
Upshi, India **81 C7** 33 48N 77 52 E
Upstart, C., Australia **114 B4** 19 41 S 147 45 E
Upton, U.S.A. **138 C2** 44 6N 104 38W
Ur, Iraq **84 D5** 30 55N 46 25 E
Ura-Tyube, Tajikistan **55 D4** 39 55N 69 1 E
Urabá, G. de, Colombia **152 B2** 8 25N 76 53W
Uracara, Brazil **153 D6** 2 20 S 57 50W
Urad Qianqi, China **66 D5** 40 40N 108 30 E
Uraga-Suidō, Japan **63 B11** 35 13N 139 45 E
Urakawa, Japan **60 C11** 42 9N 142 47 E
Ural, Australia **117 B7** 33 21 S 146 12 E
Ural →, Kazakhstan **53 C14** 47 0N 51 48 E
Ural Mts. = Uralskie Gory, Russia **48 C10** 60 0N 59 0 E
Uralla, Australia **117 A9** 30 37 S 151 29 E
Uralsk, Kazakhstan **54 F2** 51 20N 51 20 E
Uralskie Gory, Russia **48 C10** 60 0N 59 0 E
Urambo, Tanzania **106 D3** 5 4 S 32 0 E
Urambo □, Tanzania **106 D3** 5 0 S 32 0 E
Urana, Australia **117 C7** 35 15 S 146 21 E
Urandangi, Australia **114 C2** 21 32 S 138 14 E
Uranium City, Canada **131 B7** 59 34N 108 37W
Uranquinty, Australia **115 F4** 35 10 S 147 12 E
Uraricaá →, Brazil **153 C5** 3 20N 61 56W
Uraricuera →, Brazil **153 C5** 3 2N 60 30W
Uravakonda, India **83 G3** 14 57N 77 12 E
Urawa, Japan **63 B11** 35 50N 139 40 E
Uray, Russia **56 C7** 60 5N 65 15 E
'Uray'irah, Si. Arabia **85 E6** 25 57N 48 53 E
Urbana, Ill., U.S.A. **141 D8** 40 7N 88 12W
Urbana, Mo., U.S.A. **140 G3** 37 51N 93 10W
Urbana, Ohio, U.S.A. **141 D13** 40 7N 83 45W
Urbandale, U.S.A. **140 C3** 41 38N 93 43W
Urbánia, Italy **39 E9** 43 40N 12 31 E
Urbano Santos, Brazil **154 B3** 3 12 S 43 23W
Urbel →, Spain **34 C1** 42 21N 3 40W
Urbino, Italy **39 E9** 43 43N 12 38 E
Urbión, Picos de, Spain **34 C2** 42 1N 2 52W
Urcos, Peru **156 C3** 13 40 S 71 38W
Urda, Kazakhstan **53 B12** 48 52N 47 23 E
Urda, Spain **37 F7** 39 25N 3 43W
Urdaneta, Phil. **70 D3** 15 59N 120 34 E
Urdinarrain, Argentina **158 C4** 32 37 S 58 52W
Urdos, France **24 F3** 42 51N 0 35W
Urdzhar, Kazakhstan **56 E9** 47 5N 81 38 E
Ure →, U.K. **16 C6** 54 20N 1 25W
Uren, Russia **51 C14** 57 35N 45 55 E
Ureparapara, Vanuatu **121 C5** 13 32 S 167 20 E
Ures, Mexico **146 B2** 29 30N 110 30W
Ureshino, Japan **62 D1** 33 6N 129 59 E
Urfa, Turkey **89 E8** 37 12N 38 50 E
Urfa □, Turkey **89 E8** 37 0N 39 0 E
Urfahr, Austria **30 C7** 48 19N 14 17 E
Urganch = Urgench, Uzbekistan **56 E7** 41 40N 60 41 E
Urgench, Uzbekistan **56 E7** 41 40N 60 41 E
Urgut, Uzbekistan **55 D3** 39 23N 67 15 E
Uri, India **81 B6** 34 8N 74 2 E
Uri □, Switz. **29 C7** 46 43N 8 35 E
Uribante →, Venezuela **152 B3** 7 25N 71 50W
Uribe, Colombia **152 C3** 3 13N 74 24W
Uribia, Colombia **152 A3** 11 43N 72 16W
Uriondo, Bolivia **158 A3** 21 41 S 64 41W
Urique, Mexico **146 B3** 27 13N 107 55W
Urique →, Mexico **146 B3** 26 29N 107 58W
Urirotstock, Switz. **29 C7** 46 52N 8 32 E
Urk, Neths. **20 C7** 52 39N 5 36 E
Urla, Turkey **88 D2** 38 20N 26 47 E
Urlati, Romania **46 E7** 44 59N 26 15 E
Urmia = Orūmīyeh, Iran **84 B5** 37 40N 45 0 E
Urmia, L. = Orūmīyeh, Daryācheh-ye, Iran **84 B5** 37 50N 45 30 E
Urner Alpen, Switz. **29 C7** 46 45N 8 45 E
Uroševac, Serbia **42 E6** 42 23N 21 10 E
Urrao, Colombia **152 B2** 6 20N 76 11W
Ursus, Poland **47 C7** 52 12N 20 53 E
Uruaçu, Brazil **155 D2** 14 30 S 49 10W
Uruana, Brazil **155 E2** 15 30 S 49 41W
Uruapan, Mexico **146 D4** 19 30N 102 0W
Uruará →, Brazil **153 D7** 2 6 S 53 38W
Urubamba, Peru **156 C3** 13 20 S 72 10W
Urubamba →, Peru **156 C3** 10 43 S 73 48W
Urubaxi →, Brazil **153 D5** 0 31 S 64 50W
Urubu →, Brazil **153 D6** 2 55 S 58 25W
Uruçara, Brazil **153 D6** 2 32 S 57 45W
Uruçuí, Brazil **154 C3** 7 20 S 44 28W
Uruçuí, Serra do, Brazil **154 C3** 9 0 S 44 45W
Uruçuí Prêto →, Brazil **154 C3** 7 20 S 44 38W
Urucuia →, Brazil **155 E2** 16 8 S 45 5W
Urucurituba, Brazil **153 D6** 2 41 S 57 40W
Uruguai →, Brazil **159 B5** 26 0 S 53 30W
Uruguaiana, Brazil **158 B4** 29 50 S 57 0W
Uruguay ■, S. Amer. **158 C4** 32 30 S 56 30W
Uruguay →, S. Amer. **158 C4** 34 12 S 58 18W
Urumchi = Ürümqi, China **56 E9** 43 45N 87 45 E
Ürümqi, China **56 E9** 43 45N 87 45 E
Urup →, Russia **53 D9** 45 0N 41 10 E
Urup, Os., Russia **57 E16** 46 0N 151 0 E
Urutaí, Brazil **155 E2** 17 28 S 48 12W
Uryung-Khaya, Russia **57 B12** 72 48N 113 23 E
Uryupinsk, Russia **51 F12** 50 45N 41 58 E
Urzhum, Russia **54 C1** 57 10N 49 56 E
Urziceni, Romania **46 E7** 44 46N 26 42 E
Usa, Japan **62 D3** 33 31N 131 21 E
Usa →, Russia **48 A10** 65 57N 56 55 E
Uşak, Turkey **88 D3** 38 43N 29 28 E
Uşak □, Turkey **88 D3** 38 30N 29 0 E
Usakos, Namibia **104 C2** 21 54 S 15 31 E
Usborne, Mt., Falk. Is. **160 D5** 51 42 S 58 50W
Ušće, Serbia **42 D5** 43 30N 20 39 E
Usedom, Germany **26 B9** 53 50N 13 55 E
'Usfān, Si. Arabia **86 B2** 21 58N 39 27 E
Ush-Tobe, Kazakhstan **56 E8** 45 16N 78 0 E
Ushakova, Os., Russia **6 A12** 82 0N 80 0 E
Ushant = Ouessant, I. d', France **22 D1** 48 28N 5 6W
Ushashi, Tanzania **106 C3** 1 59 S 33 57 E
Ushat, Sudan **95 F2** 7 59N 29 28 E
Ushibuka, Japan **62 E2** 32 11N 130 1 E
Ushuaia, Argentina **160 D3** 54 50 S 68 23W
Ushumun, Russia **57 D13** 52 47N 126 32 E
Usk →, U.K. **17 F5** 51 37N 2 56W
Üsküdar, Turkey **49 F4** 41 0N 29 5 E
Uslar, Germany **26 D5** 51 39N 9 39 E
Usman, Russia **51 E11** 52 5N 39 48 E
Usoke, Tanzania **106 D3** 5 8 S 32 24 E
Usolye, Russia **54 B5** 59 28N 56 31 E
Usolye Sibirskoye, Russia **57 D11** 52 48N 103 40 E
Usoro, Nigeria **101 D6** 5 33N 6 11 E
Uspallata, P. de, Argentina **158 C2** 32 37 S 69 22W
Uspenskiy, Kazakhstan **56 E8** 48 41N 72 43 E
Usquert, Neths. **20 B9** 53 24N 6 36 E
Ussel, France **24 C6** 45 32N 2 18 E
Ussuri →, Asia **60 A7** 48 27N 135 0 E
Ussuriysk, Russia **57 E14** 43 48N 131 59 E
Ussurka, Russia **60 B6** 45 12N 133 31 E
Ust-Aldan = Batamay, Russia **57 C13** 63 30N 129 15 E
Ust Amginskoye = Khandyga, Russia **57 C14** 62 42N 135 35 E
Ust-Bolsheretsk, Russia **57 D16** 52 50N 156 15 E
Ust Buzulukskaya, Russia **51 F13** 50 8N 42 11 E
Ust Chaun, Russia **57 C18** 68 47N 170 30 E
Ust-Donetskiy, Russia **53 C9** 47 35N 40 55 E
Ust'-Ilga, Russia **57 D11** 55 5N 104 55 E
Ust Ilimpeya = Yukti, Russia **57 C11** 63 26N 105 42 E
Ust-Ilimsk, Russia **57 D11** 58 3N 102 39 E
Ust Ishim, Russia **56 D8** 57 45N 71 10 E
Ust-Kamchatsk, Russia **57 D17** 56 10N 162 28 E
Ust-Kamenogorsk, Kazakhstan **56 E9** 50 0N 82 36 E
Ust-Karenga, Russia **57 D12** 54 25N 116 30 E
Ust Khayryuzova, Russia **57 D16** 57 15N 156 45 E
Ust-Kut, Russia **57 D11** 56 50N 105 42 E
Ust Kuyga, Russia **57 B14** 70 1N 135 43 E
Ust-Labinsk, Russia **53 D8** 45 15N 39 41 E
Ust Luga, Russia **50 B6** 59 35N 28 20 E
Ust Maya, Russia **57 C14** 60 30N 134 28 E
Ust-Mil, Russia **57 D14** 59 40N 133 11 E
Ust-Nera, Russia **57 C15** 64 35N 143 15 E
Ust-Nyukzha, Russia **57 D13** 56 34N 121 37 E
Ust Olenek, Russia **57 B12** 73 0N 120 5 E
Ust-Omchug, Russia **57 C15** 61 9N 149 38 E
Ust Port, Russia **56 C9** 69 40N 84 26 E
Ust Tsilma, Russia **48 A9** 65 25N 52 0 E
Ust-Tungir, Russia **57 D13** 55 25N 120 36 E
Ust Urt = Ustyurt, Plato, Kazakhstan **56 E6** 44 0N 55 0 E
Ust Usa, Russia **48 A10** 66 0N 56 30 E
Ust-Uyskoye, Russia **54 D8** 54 16N 63 54 E
Ust Vorkuta, Russia **56 C7** 67 24N 64 0 E
Ustaoset, Norway **14 D2** 60 30N 8 2 E
Ustaritz, France **24 E2** 43 24N 1 27W
Uste, Russia **51 B11** 59 35N 39 40 E
Uster, Switz. **29 B7** 47 22N 8 43 E
Ústí nad Labem, Czech. **30 A7** 50 41N 14 3 E
Ústí nad Orlicí, Czech. **31 B9** 49 58N 16 24 E
Ustica, Italy **40 D6** 38 42N 13 10 E
Ustinov = Izhevsk, Russia **54 C3** 56 51N 53 14 E
Ustka, Poland **47 A3** 54 35N 16 55 E
Ustroń, Poland **31 B11** 49 43N 18 48 E
Ustrzyki Dolne, Poland **31 B15** 49 27N 22 40 E
Ustye, Russia **57 D10** 57 46N 94 37 E
Ustyurt, Plato, Kazakhstan **56 E6** 44 0N 55 0 E
Ustyuzhna, Russia **51 B10** 58 50N 36 32 E
Usu, China **64 B3** 44 27N 84 40 E
Usuki, Japan **62 D3** 33 8N 131 49 E
Usulután, El Salv. **148 D2** 13 25N 88 28W
Usumacinta →, Mexico **147 D6** 17 0N 91 0W
Usumbura = Bujumbura, Burundi **106 C2** 3 16 S 29 18 E
Usure, Tanzania **106 C3** 4 40 S 34 22 E
Usva, Russia **54 B5** 58 41N 57 37 E
Uta, Indonesia **73 B5** 4 33 S 136 0 E
'Uta Vava'u, Tonga **121 P14** 18 36 S 174 0W
Utah □, U.S.A. **142 G8** 39 20N 111 30W
Utah, L., U.S.A. **142 F8** 40 10N 111 58W
Ute Creek →, U.S.A. **139 H3** 35 21N 103 50W
Utena, Lithuania **50 D4** 55 27N 25 40 E
Ütersen, Germany **26 B5** 53 40N 9 40 E
Utete, Tanzania **106 D4** 8 0 S 38 45 E
Uthai Thani, Thailand **76 E3** 15 22N 100 3 E
Uthal, Pakistan **80 G2** 25 44N 66 40 E
Utiariti, Brazil **157 C6** 13 0 S 58 10W
Utica, N.Y., U.S.A. **137 C9** 43 6N 75 14W
Utica, Ohio, U.S.A. **136 F2** 40 14N 82 27W
Utiel, Spain **34 F3** 39 37N 1 11W
Utik L., Canada **131 B9** 55 15N 96 0W
Utikuma L., Canada **130 B5** 55 50N 115 30W
Utinga, Brazil **155 D3** 12 6 S 41 5W
Uto, Japan **62 E2** 32 41N 130 40 E
Utrecht, Neths. **20 D6** 52 5N 5 8 E
Utrecht, S. Africa **105 D5** 27 38 S 30 20 E
Utrecht □, Neths. **20 D6** 52 6N 5 7 E
Utrera, Spain **37 H5** 37 12N 5 48W
Utsjoki, Finland **12 B19** 69 51N 26 59 E
Utsunomiya, Japan **63 A11** 36 30N 139 50 E
Uttar Pradesh □, India **81 F9** 27 0N 80 0 E
Uttaradit, Thailand **76 D3** 17 36N 100 5 E
Uttoxeter, U.K. **16 E6** 52 53N 1 50W
Utva →, Kazakhstan **54 F3** 51 28N 52 40 E
Ütze, Germany **26 C6** 52 28N 10 11 E

Veliki Popović 279


Uudenmaan lääni □, Finland 13 F18 60 25N 25 0 E
Uusikaarlepyy, Finland 12 E17 63 32N 22 31 E
Uusikaupunki, Finland 13 F16 60 47N 21 25 E
Uva, Russia 54 C3 56 59N 52 13 E
Uvá →, Colombia 152 C3 3 41N 70 3W
Uvac →, Serbia 42 D4 43 35N 19 30 E
Uvalde, U.S.A. 139 L5 29 13N 99 47W
Uvarovo, Russia 51 F13 51 59N 42 14 E
Uvat, Russia 56 D7 59 5N 68 50 E
Uvéa, I., Vanuatu 111 E12 20 30 S 166 35 E
Uvelskiy, Russia 54 D7 54 26N 61 22 E
Uvinza, Tanzania 106 D3 5 5 S 30 24 E
Uvira, Zaïre 106 C2 3 22 S 29 3 E
Uvs Nuur, Mongolia 64 A4 50 20N 92 30 E
Uwa, Japan 62 D4 33 22N 132 31 E
Uwajima, Japan 62 D4 33 10N 132 35 E
'Uwayfi, Oman 87 B7 22 15N 56 59 E
Uweinat, Jebel, Sudan 94 C1 21 54N 24 58 E
Uxbridge, Canada 136 B5 44 6N 79 7W
Uxin Qi, China 66 E5 38 50N 109 5 E
Uxmal, Mexico 147 C7 20 22N 89 46W
Uyandi, Russia 57 C15 69 19N 141 0 E
Uyo, Nigeria 101 D6 5 1N 7 53 E
Uyu →, Burma 78 C5 24 51N 94 57 E
Uyuk, Kazakhstan 55 B5 43 36N 71 16 E
Uyuni, Bolivia 156 E4 20 28 S 66 47W
Uzbekistan ■, Asia 55 C2 41 30N 65 0 E
Uzen, Kazakhstan 49 F9 43 27N 53 10 E
Uzen, Bol. →, Kazakhstan 51 G16 49 0N 49 30 E
Uzen, Mal. →, Kazakhstan 51 G16 50 0N 48 30 E
Uzerche, France 24 C5 45 25N 1 34 E
Uzès, France 25 D8 44 1N 4 26 E
Uzgen, Kirghizia 55 C6 40 46N 73 18 E
Uzh →, Ukraine 50 F7 51 15N 30 12 E
Uzhgorod, Ukraine 50 G3 48 36N 22 18 E
Uzlovaya, Russia 51 E11 54 0N 38 5 E
Uzun-Agach, Kazakhstan 55 B8 43 35N 76 20 E
Uzunköprü, Turkey 43 F11 41 16N 26 43 E
Uzwil, Switz. 29 B8 47 26N 9 9 E


# V


Vaal →, S. Africa 104 D3 29 4 S 23 38 E
Vaal Dam, S. Africa 105 D4 27 0 S 28 14 E
Vaals, Neths. 21 G8 50 46N 6 1 E
Vaalwater, S. Africa 105 C4 24 15 S 28 8 E
Vaasa, Finland 12 E16 63 6N 21 38 E
Vaasan lääni □, Finland 12 E17 63 2N 22 50 E
Vaassen, Neths. 20 D7 52 17N 5 58 E
Vabre, France 24 E6 43 42N 2 24 E
Vác, Hungary 31 D12 47 49N 19 10 E
Vacaria, Brazil 159 B5 28 31 S 50 52W
Vacaville, U.S.A. 144 G5 38 21N 121 59W
Vaccarès, Étang de, France 25 E8 43 32N 4 34 E
Vach →, Russia 56 C8 60 45N 76 45 E
Vache, I.-à-, Haiti 149 C5 18 2N 73 35W
Vadnagar, India 80 H5 23 47N 72 40 E
Vado Lígure, Italy 38 D5 44 16N 8 26 E
Vadodara, India 80 H5 22 20N 73 10 E
Vadsø, Norway 12 A20 70 3N 29 50 E
Vadstena, Sweden 15 F8 58 28N 14 54 E
Vaduz, Liech. 29 B9 47 8N 9 31 E
Værøy, Norway 12 C12 67 40N 12 40 E
Vagnhärad, Sweden 14 F11 58 57N 17 33 E
Vagos, Portugal 36 E2 40 33N 8 42W
Váh →, Slovak Rep. 31 D11 47 43N 18 7 E
Vahsel B., Antarctica 7 D1 75 0 S 35 0W
Váï, Greece 32 D8 35 15N 26 18 E
Vaigach, Russia 56 B6 70 10N 59 0 E
Vaigai →, India 83 K4 9 15N 79 10 E
Vaiges, France 22 D6 48 2N 0 30W
Vaihingen, Germany 27 G4 48 55N 8 58 E
Vaijapur, India 82 E2 19 58N 74 45 E
Vaikam, India 83 K3 9 45N 76 25 E
Vailly-sur-Aisne, France 23 C10 49 24N 3 31 E
Vaippar →, India 83 K4 9 0N 78 25 E
Vaison-la-Romaine, France 25 D9 44 14N 5 4 E
Vajpur, India 82 D1 21 24N 73 17 E
Vakarel, Bulgaria 43 E8 42 35N 23 40 E
Vakfikebir, Turkey 89 C8 41 2N 39 17 E
Vakhsh →, Tajikistan 55 E4 37 6N 68 18 E
Vál, Hungary 31 D11 47 22N 18 40 E
Val-de-Marne □, France 23 D9 48 45N 2 28 E
Val-d'Oise □, France 23 C9 49 5N 2 10 E
Val d'Or, Canada 128 C4 48 7N 77 47W
Val Marie, Canada 131 D7 49 15N 107 45W
Valadares, Portugal 36 D2 41 5N 8 38W
Valahia, Romania 46 E5 44 35N 25 0 E
Valais □, Switz. 28 D5 46 12N 7 45 E
Valais, Alpes du, Switz. 28 D5 46 7N 7 35 E
Valandovo, Macedonia 42 F7 41 19N 22 34 E
Valašské Meziříčí, Czech. 31 B10 49 29N 17 59 E
Valáxa, Greece 45 F6 38 50N 24 29 E
Vălcani, Romania 42 A5 46 0N 20 26 E
Valcheta, Argentina 160 B3 40 40 S 66 8W
Valdagno, Italy 39 C8 45 38N 11 18 E
Valday, Russia 50 C8 57 58N 33 9 E
Valdayskaya Vozvyshennost, Russia 50 C8 57 0N 33 30 E
Valdeazogues →, Spain 37 G6 38 45N 4 55W
Valdemarsvik, Sweden 15 F10 58 14N 16 40 E
Valdepeñas, Ciudad Real, Spain 37 G7 38 43N 3 25W
Valdepeñas, Jaén, Spain 37 H7 37 33N 3 47W
Valderaduey →, Spain 36 D5 41 31N 5 42W
Valderrobres, Spain 34 E5 40 53N 0 9 E
Valdés, Pen., Argentina 160 B4 42 30 S 63 45W
Valdez, Ecuador 152 C2 1 15N 79 0W
Valdez, U.S.A. 126 B5 61 7N 146 16W
Valdivia, Chile 160 A2 39 50 S 73 14W
Valdivia, Colombia 152 B2 7 11N 75 27W
Valdivia □, Chile 160 B2 40 0 S 73 0W
Valdobbiádene, Italy 39 C9 45 53N 12 0 E
Valdosta, U.S.A. 135 K4 30 50N 83 17W
Valdoviño, Spain 36 B2 43 36N 8 8W
Valdres, Norway 14 D3 60 55N 9 28 E
Vale, Georgia 53 F10 41 30N 42 58 E
Vale, U.S.A. 142 E5 43 59N 117 15W
Valea lui Mihai, Romania 46 B3 47 32N 22 11 E
Valença, Brazil 155 D4 13 20 S 39 5W
Valença, Portugal 36 C2 42 1N 8 34W
Valença do Piauí, Brazil 154 C3 6 20 S 41 45W
Valençay, France 23 E8 47 9N 1 34 E
Valence, Drôme, France 25 D8 44 57N 4 54 E
Valence, Tarn-et-Garonne, France 24 D4 44 6N 0 53 E
Valencia, Phil. 71 H5 7 57N 125 3 E
Valencia, Spain 35 F4 39 27N 0 23W
Valencia, Venezuela 152 A4 10 11N 68 0W
Valencia □, Spain 35 F4 39 20N 0 40W
Valencia, Albufera de, Spain 35 F4 39 20N 0 27W
Valencia, G. de, Spain 35 F5 39 30N 0 20 E
Valencia de Alcántara, Spain 37 F3 39 25N 7 14W
Valencia de Don Juan, Spain 36 C5 42 17N 5 31W
Valencia del Ventoso, Spain 37 G4 38 15N 6 29W
Valenciennes, France 23 B10 50 20N 3 34 E
Văleni, Romania 46 E5 44 15N 24 45 E
Valensole, France 25 E9 43 50N 5 59 E
Valentia Harbour, Ireland 19 E1 51 56N 10 17W
Valentia I., Ireland 19 E1 51 54N 10 22W
Valentim, Sa. do, Brazil 154 C3 6 0 S 43 30W
Valentin, Russia 60 C7 43 8N 134 17 E
Valentine, Nebr., U.S.A. 138 D4 42 52N 100 33W
Valentine, Tex., U.S.A. 139 K2 30 35N 104 30W
Valenza, Italy 38 C5 45 2N 8 39 E
Valera, Venezuela 152 B3 9 19N 70 37W
Valguarnera Caropepe, Italy 41 E7 37 30N 14 22 E
Valier, U.S.A. 142 B7 48 18N 112 16W
Valinco, G. de, France 25 G12 41 40N 8 52 E
Valjevo, Serbia 42 C4 44 18N 19 53 E
Valka, Estonia 50 C5 57 44N 26 5 E
Valkeakoski, Finland 13 F18 61 16N 24 2 E
Valkenburg, Neths. 21 G7 50 52N 5 50 E
Valkenswaard, Neths. 21 F6 51 21N 5 29 E
Vall de Uxó, Spain 34 F4 39 49N 0 15W
Valla, Sweden 14 E10 59 2N 16 20 E
Valladolid, Mexico 147 C7 20 40N 88 11W
Valladolid, Spain 36 D6 41 38N 4 43W
Valladolid □, Spain 36 D6 41 38N 4 43W
Vallata, Italy 41 A8 41 3N 15 16 E
Valldemosa, Spain 33 B9 39 43N 2 37 E
Valle d'Aosta □, Italy 38 C4 45 45N 7 22 E
Valle de Arán, Spain 34 C5 42 50N 0 55 E
Valle de Cabuérniga, Spain 36 B6 43 14N 4 18W
Valle de la Pascua, Venezuela 152 B4 9 13N 66 0W
Valle de las Palmas, Mexico 145 N10 32 20N 116 43W
Valle de Santiago, Mexico 146 C4 20 25N 101 15W
Valle de Suchil, Mexico 146 C4 23 38N 103 55W
Valle de Zaragoza, Mexico 146 B3 27 28N 105 49W
Valle del Cauca □, Colombia 152 C2 3 45N 76 30W
Valle Fértil, Sierra del, Argentina 158 C2 30 20 S 68 0W
Valle Hermoso, Mexico 147 B5 25 35N 97 40W
Vallecas, Spain 36 E7 40 23N 3 41W
Valledupar, Colombia 152 A3 10 29N 73 15W
Vallehermoso, Canary Is. 33 F2 28 10N 17 15W
Vallejo, U.S.A. 144 G4 38 7N 122 14W
Vallenar, Chile 158 B1 28 30 S 70 50W
Valleraugue, France 24 D7 44 6N 3 39 E
Vallet, France 22 E5 47 10N 1 15W
Valletta, Malta 32 D2 35 54N 14 31 E
Valley Center, U.S.A. 145 M9 33 13N 117 2W
Valley City, U.S.A. 138 B6 46 55N 98 0W
Valley Falls, U.S.A. 142 E3 42 29N 120 17W
Valley Park, U.S.A. 140 F6 38 33N 90 29W
Valley Springs, U.S.A. 144 G6 38 12N 120 50W
Valley Station, U.S.A. 141 F11 38 6N 85 52W
Valley Wells, U.S.A. 145 K11 35 27N 115 46W
Valleyview, Canada 130 B5 55 5N 117 17W
Valli di Comàcchio, Italy 39 D9 44 40N 12 15 E
Vallimanca, Arroyo, Argentina 158 D4 35 40 S 59 10W
Vallo della Lucánia, Italy 41 B8 40 14N 15 16 E
Vallon-Pont-d'Arc, France 25 D8 44 24N 4 24 E
Vallorbe, Switz. 28 C2 46 42N 6 20 E
Valls, Spain 34 D6 41 18N 1 15 E
Vallsta, Sweden 14 C10 61 31N 16 22 E
Valmaseda, Spain 34 B1 43 11N 3 12W
Valmeyer, U.S.A. 140 F6 38 18N 90 19W
Valmiera, Latvia 50 C4 57 37N 25 29 E
Valmont, France 22 C7 49 45N 0 30 E
Valmontone, Italy 40 A5 41 48N 12 55 E
Valmy, France 23 C11 49 5N 4 45 E
Valnera, Mte., Spain 34 B1 43 9N 3 40W
Valognes, France 22 C5 49 30N 1 28W
Valona = Vlóra, Albania 44 D1 40 32N 19 28 E
Valongo, Portugal 36 D2 41 8N 8 30W
Valpaços, Portugal 36 D3 41 36N 7 17W
Valparaíso, Chile 158 C1 33 2 S 71 40W
Valparaíso, Mexico 146 C4 22 50N 103 32W
Valparaiso, U.S.A. 141 C9 41 28N 87 4W
Valparaíso □, Chile 158 C1 33 2 S 71 40W
Valpovo, Croatia 42 B3 45 39N 18 25 E
Valréas, France 25 D8 44 24N 5 0 E
Vals, Switz. 29 C8 46 39N 9 11 E
Vals →, S. Africa 104 D4 27 23 S 26 30 E
Vals, Tanjung, Indonesia 73 C5 8 26 S 137 25 E
Vals-les-Bains, France 25 D8 44 42N 4 24 E
Valsad, India 82 D1 20 40N 72 58 E
Valskog, Sweden 14 E9 59 27N 15 57 E
Válta, Greece 44 D5 40 3N 23 25 E
Valtellina, Italy 38 B6 46 9N 9 55 E
Valuyki, Russia 51 F11 50 10N 38 5 E
Valverde, Canary Is. 33 G2 27 48N 17 55W
Valverde del Camino, Spain 37 H4 37 35N 6 47W
Valverde del Fresno, Spain 36 E4 40 15N 6 51W
Vama, Romania 46 B6 47 34N 25 42 E
Vámos, Greece 32 D6 35 24N 24 13 E
Vamsadhara →, India 82 E7 18 21N 84 8 E
Van, Turkey 89 D10 38 30N 43 20 E
Van □, Turkey 89 D10 38 30N 43 20 E
Van, L. = Van Gölü, Turkey 89 D10 38 30N 43 0 E
Van Alstyne, U.S.A. 139 J6 33 25N 96 35W
Van Bruyssel, Canada 129 C5 47 56N 72 9W
Van Buren, Canada 129 C6 47 10N 67 55W
Van Buren, Ark., U.S.A. 139 H7 35 26N 94 21W
Van Buren, Maine, U.S.A. 135 B11 47 10N 67 58W
Van Buren, Mo., U.S.A. 139 G9 37 0N 91 1W
Van Canh, Vietnam 76 F7 13 37N 109 0 E
Van Diemen, C., N. Terr., Australia 112 B5 11 9 S 130 24 E
Van Diemen, C., Queens., Australia 114 B2 16 30 S 139 46 E
Van Diemen G., Australia 112 B5 11 45 S 132 0 E
Van Gölü, Turkey 89 D10 38 30N 43 0 E
Van Horn, U.S.A. 139 K2 31 3N 104 50W
Van Horne, U.S.A. 140 B4 42 1N 92 4W
Van Ninh, Vietnam 76 F7 12 42N 109 14 E
Van Reenen P., S. Africa 105 D4 28 22 S 29 27 E
Van Rees, Pegunungan, Indonesia 73 B5 2 35 S 138 15 E
Van Tassell, U.S.A. 138 D2 42 40N 104 5W
Van Tivu, India 83 K4 8 51N 78 15 E
Van Wert, U.S.A. 141 D12 40 52N 84 35W
Van Yen, Vietnam 76 B5 21 4N 104 42 E
Vanavara, Russia 57 C11 60 22N 102 16 E
Vanceburg, U.S.A. 141 F13 38 36N 83 19W
Vancouver, Canada 130 D4 49 15N 123 10W
Vancouver, U.S.A. 144 E4 45 38N 122 40W
Vancouver, C., Australia 113 G2 35 2 S 118 11 E
Vancouver I., Canada 130 D3 49 50N 126 0W
Vandalia, Ill., U.S.A. 140 F7 38 58N 89 6W
Vandalia, Mo., U.S.A. 140 E5 39 19N 91 29W
Vandalia, Ohio, U.S.A. 141 E12 39 54N 84 12W
Vandavasi, India 83 H4 12 30N 79 30 E
Vandeloos B., Sri Lanka 83 K5 8 0N 81 45 E
Vandenburg, U.S.A. 145 L6 34 35N 120 33W
Vanderbijlpark, S. Africa 105 D4 26 42 S 27 54 E
Vandergrift, U.S.A. 136 F5 40 36N 79 34W
Vanderhoof, Canada 130 C4 54 0N 124 0W
Vanderlin I., Australia 114 B2 15 44 S 137 2 E
Vandyke, Australia 114 C4 24 10 S 147 51 E
Vänern, Sweden 15 F7 58 47N 13 30 E
Vänersborg, Sweden 15 F6 58 26N 12 19 E
Vang Vieng, Laos 76 C4 18 58N 102 32 E
Vanga, Kenya 106 C4 4 35 S 39 12 E
Vangaindrano, Madag. 105 C8 23 21 S 47 36 E
Vanguard, Canada 131 D7 49 55N 107 20W
Vangunu, Solomon Is. 121 M10 8 40 S 158 5 E
Vanier, Canada 128 C4 45 27N 75 40W
Vanimo, Papua N. G. 120 B1 2 42 S 141 21 E
Vanivilasa Sagara, India 83 H3 13 45N 76 30 E
Vaniyambadi, India 83 H4 12 46N 78 44 E
Vankarem, Russia 57 C18 67 51N 175 50W
Vankleek Hill, Canada 128 C5 45 32N 74 40W
Vanna, Norway 12 A15 70 6N 19 50 E
Vännäs, Sweden 12 E15 63 58N 19 48 E
Vannes, France 22 E4 47 40N 2 47W
Vanoise, Massif de la, France 25 C10 45 25N 6 40 E
Vanrhynsdorp, S. Africa 104 E2 31 36 S 18 44 E
Vanrook, Australia 114 B3 16 57 S 141 57 E
Vansbro, Sweden 13 F13 60 32N 14 15 E
Vansittart B., Australia 112 B4 14 3 S 126 17 E
Vanthli, India 80 J4 21 28N 70 25 E
Vanua Levu, Fiji 121 A2 16 33 S 179 15 E
Vanuatu ■, Pac. Oc. 121 E6 15 0 S 168 0 E
Vanwyksvlei, S. Africa 104 E3 30 18 S 21 49 E
Vanzylsrus, S. Africa 104 D3 26 52 S 22 4 E
Vapnyarka, Ukraine 52 B3 48 32N 28 45 E
Var □, France 25 E10 43 27N 6 18 E
Var →, France 25 E11 43 39N 7 12 E
Vara, Sweden 15 F6 58 16N 12 55 E
Varada →, India 83 G2 15 0N 75 40 E
Varades, France 22 E5 47 25N 1 1W
Varaita →, Italy 38 D4 44 49N 7 36 E
Varallo, Italy 38 C5 45 50N 8 13 E
Varanasi, India 81 G10 25 22N 83 0 E
Varangerfjorden, Norway 12 A20 70 3N 29 25 E
Varaždin, Croatia 39 B13 46 20N 16 20 E
Varazze, Italy 38 D5 44 21N 8 36 E
Varberg, Sweden 15 G6 57 6N 12 20 E
Vardar = Axiós →, Greece 44 D4 40 57N 22 35 E
Vardar →, Macedonia 42 F7 41 15N 22 33 E
Varde, Denmark 15 J2 55 38N 8 29 E
Varde Å →, Denmark 15 J2 55 35N 8 19 E
Varel, Germany 26 B4 53 23N 8 9 E
Varella, Mui, Vietnam 76 F7 12 54N 109 26 E
Varena, Lithuania 50 D4 54 12N 24 30 E
Varennes-sur-Allier, France 24 B7 46 19N 3 24 E
Vareš, Bos.-H. 42 C3 44 12N 18 23 E
Varese, Italy 38 C5 45 49N 8 50 E
Varese Lígure, Italy 38 D6 44 22N 9 33 E
Vårgårda, Sweden 15 F6 58 2N 12 49 E
Vargem Bonita, Brazil 155 F2 20 20 S 46 22W
Vargem Grande, Brazil 154 B3 3 33 S 43 56W
Varginha, Brazil 159 A6 21 33 S 45 25W
Vargön, Sweden 15 F6 58 22N 12 20 E
Variadero, U.S.A. 139 H2 35 43N 104 17W
Varillas, Chile 158 A1 24 0 S 70 10W
Väring, Sweden 15 F8 58 30N 14 0 E
Värmlands län □, Sweden 13 G12 60 0N 13 20 E
Varna, Bulgaria 43 D12 43 13N 27 56 E
Varna, Russia 54 E7 53 24N 60 58 E
Varna, U.S.A. 140 C7 41 2N 89 14W
Varna →, India 82 F2 16 48N 74 32 E
Värnamo, Sweden 13 H13 57 10N 14 3 E
Varnsdorf, Czech. 30 A7 50 55N 14 35 E
Värö, Sweden 15 G6 57 16N 12 11 E
Vars, Canada 137 A9 45 21N 75 21W
Varsseveld, Neths. 20 E8 51 56N 6 29 E
Varto, Turkey 89 D9 39 10N 41 27 E
Varvarin, Serbia 42 D6 43 43N 21 20 E
Varzaneh, Iran 85 C7 32 25N 52 40 E
Várzea Alegre, Brazil 154 C4 6 47 S 39 17W
Várzea da Palma, Brazil 155 E3 17 36 S 44 44W
Várzea Grande, Brazil 157 D6 15 39 S 56 8W
Varzi, Italy 38 D6 44 50N 9 12 E
Varzo, Italy 38 B5 46 12N 8 15 E
Varzy, France 23 E10 47 22N 3 20 E
Vas □, Hungary 31 D9 47 10N 16 55 E
Vasa, Finland 12 E16 63 6N 21 38 E
Vasa Barris →, Brazil 154 D4 11 10 S 37 10W
Vásárosnamény, Hungary 31 C15 48 9N 22 19 E
Vascão →, Portugal 37 H3 37 31N 7 31W
Vaşcău, Romania 46 C3 46 28N 22 30 E
Vascongadas = País Vasco □, Spain 34 C2 42 50N 2 45W
Vāshīr, Afghan. 79 B1 32 16N 63 51 E
Vasht = Khāsh, Iran 85 D9 28 15N 61 15 E
Vasilevichi, Belorussia 50 E6 52 15N 29 50 E
Vasilikón, Greece 45 F5 38 25N 23 40 E
Vasilkov, Ukraine 50 F7 50 7N 30 15 E
Vaslui, Romania 46 C8 46 38N 27 42 E
Vaslui □, Romania 46 C8 46 30N 27 45 E
Vassar, Canada 131 D9 49 10N 95 55W
Vassar, U.S.A. 134 D4 43 22N 83 35W
Västerås, Sweden 14 E10 59 37N 16 38 E
Västerbottens län □, Sweden 12 D14 64 58N 18 0 E
Västernorrlands län □, Sweden 14 A11 63 30N 17 30 E
Västervik, Sweden 13 H14 57 43N 16 43 E
Västmanlands län □, Sweden 13 G14 59 45N 16 20 E
Vasto, Italy 39 F11 42 8N 14 40 E
Vasvár, Hungary 31 D9 47 3N 16 47 E
Vatan, France 23 E8 47 4N 1 50 E
Vaté = Efate, I., Vanuatu 121 G6 17 40 S 168 25 E
Vathí, Itháki, Greece 45 F2 38 18N 20 40 E
Vathí, Sámos, Greece 45 G9 37 46N 27 1 E
Váthia, Greece 45 H4 36 29N 22 29 E
Vatican City ■, Europe 39 G9 41 54N 12 27 E
Vaticano, C., Italy 41 D8 38 40N 15 48 E
Vatili, Cyprus 32 D12 35 6N 33 40 E
Vatin, Serbia 42 B6 45 12N 21 20 E
Vatnajökull, Iceland 12 D5 64 30N 16 48W
Vatnås, Norway 14 E3 59 58N 9 37 E
Vatneyri, Iceland 12 D2 65 35N 24 0W
Vatólakkos, Greece 32 D5 35 27N 23 53 E
Vatoloha, Madag. 105 B8 17 52 S 47 48 E
Vatomandry, Madag. 105 B8 19 20 S 48 59 E
Vatra-Dornei, Romania 46 B6 47 22N 25 22 E
Vättern, Sweden 15 F8 58 25N 14 30 E
Vättis, Switz. 29 C8 46 55N 9 27 E
Vatulele, Fiji 121 B1 18 33 S 177 37 E
Vaucluse □, France 25 E9 43 50N 5 20 E
Vaucouleurs, France 23 D12 48 37N 5 40 E
Vaud □, Switz. 28 C2 46 35N 6 30 E
Vaughn, Mont., U.S.A. 142 C8 47 33N 111 33W
Vaughn, N. Mex., U.S.A. 143 J11 34 36N 105 13W
Vaulruz, Switz. 28 C3 46 38N 6 58 E
Vaupés = Uaupés →, Brazil 152 C4 0 2N 67 16W
Vaupes □, Colombia 152 C3 1 0N 71 0W
Vauvert, France 25 E8 43 42N 4 17 E
Vauxhall, Canada 130 C6 50 5N 112 9W
Vava'u, Tonga 121 P14 18 36 S 174 0W
Vavoua, Ivory C. 100 D3 7 23N 6 29W
Vaxholm, Sweden 14 E12 59 25N 18 20 E
Växjö, Sweden 13 H13 56 52N 14 50 E
Vaygach, Ostrov, Russia 56 C6 70 0N 60 0 E
Váyia, Ákra, Greece 32 C10 36 15N 28 11 E
Vazovgrad, Bulgaria 43 E9 42 39N 24 45 E
Veadeiros, Brazil 155 D2 14 7 S 47 31W
Vechta, Germany 26 C4 52 47N 8 18 E
Vechte →, Neths. 20 C8 52 34N 6 6 E
Vecsés, Hungary 31 D12 47 26N 19 19 E
Vedaranniyam, India 83 J4 10 25N 79 50 E
Veddige, Sweden 15 G6 57 17N 12 20 E
Vedea →, Romania 46 F6 43 53N 25 59 E
Vedia, Argentina 158 C3 34 30 S 61 31W
Vedra, I. del, Spain 33 C7 38 52N 1 12 E
Vedrin, Belgium 21 G5 50 30N 4 52 E
Veendam, Neths. 20 B9 53 5N 6 52 E
Veenendaal, Neths. 20 D7 52 2N 5 34 E
Veerle, Belgium 21 F5 51 4N 4 59 E
Vefsna →, Norway 12 D12 65 48N 13 10 E
Vega, Norway 12 D11 65 40N 11 55 E
Vega, U.S.A. 139 H3 35 15N 102 26W
Vegadeo, Spain 36 B3 43 27N 7 4W
Vegafjorden, Norway 12 D12 65 37N 12 0 E
Veghel, Neths. 21 E7 51 37N 5 32 E
Vegorritis, Límni, Greece 44 D3 40 45N 21 45 E
Vegreville, Canada 130 C6 53 30N 112 5W
Vegusdal, Norway 15 F2 58 32N 8 10 E
Veii, Italy 39 F9 42 0N 12 24 E
Veitch, Australia 116 C4 34 39 S 140 31 E
Vejen, Denmark 15 J3 55 30N 9 9 E
Vejer de la Frontera, Spain 37 J5 36 15N 5 59W
Vejle, Denmark 15 J3 55 43N 9 30 E
Vejle Fjord, Denmark 15 J3 55 40N 9 50 E
Vela Luka, Croatia 39 F13 42 59N 16 44 E
Velanai I., Sri Lanka 83 K4 9 45N 79 45 E
Velas, C., Costa Rica 148 D2 10 21N 85 52W
Velasco, Sierra de, Argentina 158 B2 29 20 S 67 10W
Velay, Mts. du, France 24 D7 45 0N 3 40 E
Velddrif, S. Africa 104 E2 32 42 S 18 11 E
Veldegem, Belgium 21 F2 51 7N 3 10 E
Velden, Neths. 21 F8 51 25N 6 10 E
Veldhoven, Neths. 21 F6 51 24N 5 25 E
Velebit Planina, Croatia 39 D12 44 50N 15 20 E
Velebitski Kanal, Croatia 39 D11 44 45N 14 55 E
Veleka →, Bulgaria 43 E12 42 4N 27 58 E
Velenje, Slovenia 39 B12 46 23N 15 8 E
Velestínon, Greece 44 E4 39 23N 22 43 E
Velež, Bos.-H. 42 D3 43 19N 18 2 E
Vélez, Colombia 152 B3 6 1N 73 41W
Vélez Blanco, Spain 35 H2 37 41N 2 5W
Vélez Málaga, Spain 37 J6 36 48N 4 5W
Vélez Rubio, Spain 35 H2 37 41N 2 5W
Velhas →, Brazil 155 E3 17 13 S 44 49W
Velik Jastrebac, Serbia 42 D6 43 25N 21 30 E
Velika, Croatia 42 B2 45 27N 17 40 E
Velika Gorica, Croatia 39 C13 45 44N 16 5 E
Velika Gradište, Serbia 42 C6 44 46N 21 29 E
Velika Kapela, Croatia 39 C12 45 10N 15 5 E
Velika Kladuša, Bos.-H. 39 C12 45 11N 15 48 E
Velika Morava →, Serbia 42 C6 44 43N 21 3 E
Velika Plana, Serbia 42 C6 44 20N 21 1 E
Velikaya →, Russia 50 C6 57 48N 28 10 E
Velikaya Kema, Russia 60 B8 45 30N 137 12 E
Velikaya Lepetikha, Ukraine 52 C5 47 2N 33 58 E
Veliké Kapušany, Slovak Rep. 31 C15 48 34N 22 5 E
Velike Lašče, Slovenia 39 C11 45 49N 14 45 E
Veliki Backu Kanal, Serbia 42 B4 45 45N 19 15 E
Veliki Popović, Serbia 42 C6 44 8N 21 18 E

280 Veliki Ustyug


Veliki Ustyug, Russia 48 B8 60 47N 46 20 E
Velikiye Luki, Russia 50 C7 56 25N 30 32 E
Velikonda Range, India 83 G4 14 45N 79 10 E
Velikoye, Oz., Russia 51 D12 55 15N 40 10 E
Velingrad, Bulgaria 43 E8 42 4N 23 58 E
Velino, Mte., Italy 39 F10 42 10N 13 20 E
Velizh, Russia 50 D7 55 36N 31 11 E
Velké Karlovice, Czech. 31 B11 49 20N 18 17 E
Velke Meziřici, Czech. 30 B9 49 21N 16 1 E
Vel'ký Žitný ostrov, Slovak Rep. 31 C10 48 5N 17 20 E
Vella G., Solomon Is. 121 M9 8 0 S 156 50 E
Vella Lavella, Solomon Is. 121 L9 7 45 S 156 40 E
Vellar →, India 83 J4 11 30N 79 36 E
Velletri, Italy 40 A5 41 43N 12 43 E
Vellinge, Sweden 15 J7 55 29N 13 0 E
Vellore, India 83 H4 12 57N 79 10 E
Velp, Neths. 20 D7 52 0N 5 59 E
Velsen-Noord, Neths. 20 D5 52 27N 4 40 E
Velsk, Russia 48 B7 61 10N 42 5 E
Velten, Germany 26 C9 52 40N 13 11 E
Veluwe Meer, Neths. 20 D7 52 24N 5 44 E
Velva, U.S.A. 138 A4 48 4N 100 56W
Velvendós, Greece 44 D4 40 15N 22 6 E
Vembanad L., India 83 K3 9 36N 76 15 E
Veme, Norway 14 D4 60 14N 10 7 E
Ven, Sweden 15 J6 55 55N 12 45 E
Venaco, France 25 F13 42 14N 9 11 E
Venado Tuerto, Argentina 158 C3 33 50 S 62 0W
Venafro, Italy 41 A7 41 28N 14 3 E
Venarey-les-Laumes, France 23 E11 47 32N 4 26 E
Venaria, Italy 38 C4 45 6N 7 39 E
Venčane, Serbia 42 C5 44 24N 20 28 E
Vence, France 25 E11 43 43N 7 6 E
Venda □, S. Africa 105 C5 22 40 S 30 35 E
Vendas Novas, Portugal 37 G2 38 39N 8 27W
Vendée □, France 22 F5 46 50N 1 35W
Vendée →, France 22 F5 46 20N 1 10W
Vendéen, Bocage, France 24 B2 46 40N 1 20W
Vendeuvre-sur-Barse, France 23 D11 48 14N 4 28 E
Vendôme, France 22 E8 47 47N 1 3 E
Vendrell, Spain 34 D6 41 10N 1 30 E
Vendsyssel, Denmark 15 G4 57 22N 10 0 E
Véneta, L., Italy 39 C9 45 23N 12 25 E
Véneto □, Italy 39 C8 45 40N 12 0 E
Venev, Russia 51 D11 54 22N 38 17 E
Venézia, Italy 39 C9 45 27N 12 20 E
Venézia, G. di, Italy 39 C10 45 20N 13 0 E
Venezuela ■, S. Amer. 152 B4 8 0N 66 0W
Venezuela, G. de, Venezuela 152 A3 11 30N 71 0W
Vengurla, India 83 G1 15 53N 73 45 E
Vengurla Rocks, India 83 G1 15 55N 73 22 E
Venice = Venézia, Italy 39 C9 45 27N 12 20 E
Venkatagiri, India 83 G4 14 0N 79 35 E
Venkatapuram, India 82 E5 18 20N 80 30 E
Venlo, Neths. 21 F8 51 22N 6 11 E
Venraij, Neths. 21 E7 51 31N 6 0 E
Venta de Cardeña, Spain 37 G6 38 16N 4 20W
Venta de San Rafael, Spain 36 E6 40 42N 4 12W
Ventana, Punta de la, Mexico 146 C3 24 4N 109 48W
Ventana, Sa. de la, Argentina 158 D3 38 0 S 62 30W
Ventersburg, S. Africa 104 D4 28 7 S 27 9 E
Venterstad, S. Africa 104 E4 30 47 S 25 48 E
Ventimíglia, Italy 38 E4 43 50N 7 39 E
Ventnor, U.K. 17 G6 50 35N 1 12W
Ventotene, Italy 40 B6 40 48N 13 25 E
Ventoux, Mt., France 25 D9 44 10N 5 17 E
Ventspils, Latvia 13 H16 57 25N 21 32 E
Ventuarí →, Venezuela 152 C4 3 58N 67 2W
Ventucopa, U.S.A. 145 L7 34 50N 119 29W
Ventura, U.S.A. 145 L7 34 17N 119 18W
Venus B., Australia 117 E6 38 40 S 145 42 E
Vera, Argentina 158 B3 29 30 S 60 20W
Vera, Spain 35 H3 37 15N 1 51W
Veracruz, Mexico 147 D5 19 10N 96 10W
Veracruz □, Mexico 147 D5 19 0N 96 15W
Veraval, India 80 J4 20 53N 70 27 E
Verbánia, Italy 38 C5 45 56N 8 43 E
Verbicaro, Italy 41 C8 39 46N 15 54 E
Verbier, Switz. 28 D4 46 6N 7 13 E
Vercelli, Italy 38 C5 45 19N 8 25 E
Verchovchevo, Ukraine 52 B6 48 32N 34 10 E
Verdalsøra, Norway 12 E11 63 48N 11 30 E
Verde →, Argentina 160 B3 41 56 S 65 5W
Verde →, Goiás, Brazil 155 E1 19 11 S 50 44W
Verde →, Goiás, Brazil 155 E1 18 1 S 50 14W
Verde →, Mato Grosso, Brazil 157 E7 21 25 S 52 20W
Verde →, Mato Grosso, Brazil 157 C6 11 54 S 55 48W
Verde →, Chihuahua, Mexico 146 B3 26 29N 107 58W
Verde →, Oaxaca, Mexico 147 D5 15 59N 97 50W
Verde →, Veracruz, Mexico 146 C4 21 10N 102 50W
Verde →, Paraguay 158 A4 23 9 S 57 37W
Verde, Cay, Bahamas 148 B4 23 0N 75 5W
Verde Grande →, Brazil 155 E3 16 13 S 43 49W
Verde I., Phil. 70 E3 13 33N 121 5 E
Verde Island Pass, Phil. 70 E3 13 34N 120 51 E
Verde Pequeno →, Brazil 155 D3 14 48 S 43 31W
Verden, Germany 26 C5 52 58N 9 18 E
Verdhikoúsa, Greece 44 E3 39 47N 21 59 E
Verdi, U.S.A. 144 F7 39 31N 119 59W
Verdigre, U.S.A. 138 D5 42 36N 98 2W
Verdon →, France 25 E9 43 43N 5 46 E
Verdun, France 23 C12 49 9N 5 24 E
Verdun-sur-le-Doubs, France 23 F12 46 54N 5 2 E
Vereeniging, S. Africa 105 D4 26 38 S 27 57 E
Vérendrye, Parc Prov. de la, Canada 128 C4 47 20N 76 40W
Vereshchagino, Russia 54 B4 58 5N 54 40 E
Verga, C., Guinea 100 C2 10 30N 14 10W
Vergato, Italy 38 D8 44 18N 11 8 E
Vergemont, Australia 114 C3 23 33 S 143 1 E
Vergemont Cr. →, Australia 114 C3 24 16 S 143 16 E
Vergennes, U.S.A. 137 B11 44 10N 73 15W
Vergt, France 24 C4 45 2N 0 43 E
Verín, Spain 36 D3 41 57N 7 27W
Veriña, Spain 36 B5 43 32N 5 43W
Verkhnedvinsk, Belorussia 50 D5 55 45N 27 58 E
Verkhneuralsk, Russia 54 E6 53 53N 59 13 E
Verkhnevilyuysk, Russia 57 C13 63 27N 120 18 E
Verkhneye Kalinino, Russia 57 D11 59 54N 108 8 E
Verkhniy-Avzyan, Russia 54 E5 53 32N 57 33 E
Verkhniy Baskunchak, Russia 53 B12 48 14N 46 44 E
Verkhniy Tagil, Russia 54 C6 57 22N 59 56 E
Verkhniy Ufaley, Russia 54 C7 56 4N 60 14 E
Verkhniye Kigi, Russia 54 D6 55 25N 58 37 E
Verkhnyaya Salda, Russia 54 B7 58 2N 60 33 E
Verkhoturye, Russia 54 B7 58 52N 60 48 E
Verkhovye, Russia 51 E10 52 55N 37 15 E
Verkhoyansk, Russia 57 C14 67 35N 133 25 E
Verkhoyansk Ra. = Verkhoyanskiy Khrebet, Russia 57 C13 66 0N 129 0 E
Verkhoyanskiy Khrebet, Russia 57 C13 66 0N 129 0 E
Verlo, Canada 131 C7 50 19N 108 35W
Verma, Norway 14 B2 62 21N 8 3 E
Vermenton, France 23 E10 47 40N 3 42 E
Vermilion, Canada 131 C6 53 20N 110 50W
Vermilion →, Alta., Canada 131 C6 53 22N 110 51W
Vermilion →, Qué., Canada 128 C5 47 38N 72 56W
Vermilion →, Ill., U.S.A. 140 C7 41 19N 89 4W
Vermilion →, Ind., U.S.A. 141 E9 39 57N 87 27W
Vermilion, B., U.S.A. 139 L9 29 45N 91 55W
Vermilion Bay, Canada 131 D10 49 51N 93 34W
Vermilion Chutes, Canada 130 B6 58 22N 114 51W
Vermilion L., U.S.A. 138 B8 47 53N 92 26W
Vermillion, U.S.A. 138 D6 42 47N 96 56W
Vermont, U.S.A. 140 D6 40 18N 90 26W
Vermont □, U.S.A. 137 C12 44 0N 73 0W
Vernal, U.S.A. 142 F9 40 27N 109 32W
Vernalis, U.S.A. 144 H5 37 36N 121 17W
Vernayaz, Switz. 28 D4 46 8N 7 3 E
Verner, Canada 128 C3 46 25N 80 8W
Verneuil-sur-Avre, France 22 D7 48 45N 0 55 E
Verneukpan, S. Africa 104 D3 30 0 S 21 0 E
Vernier, Switz. 28 D2 46 13N 6 5 E
Vernon, Canada 130 C5 50 20N 119 15W
Vernon, France 22 C8 49 5N 1 30 E
Vernon, Ill., U.S.A. 140 F7 38 48N 89 5W
Vernon, Ind., U.S.A. 141 F11 38 59N 85 36W
Vernon, Tex., U.S.A. 139 H5 34 9N 99 17W
Vernonia, U.S.A. 144 E3 45 52N 123 11W
Vero Beach, U.S.A. 135 M5 27 38N 80 24W
Véroia, Greece 44 D4 40 34N 22 12 E
Verolanuova, Italy 38 C7 45 20N 10 5 E
Véroli, Italy 40 A6 41 43N 13 24 E
Verona, Italy 38 C8 45 27N 11 0 E
Verona, U.S.A. 140 B7 42 59N 89 32W
Veropol, Russia 57 C17 65 15N 168 40 E
Versailles, France 23 D9 48 48N 2 8 E
Versailles, Ill., U.S.A. 140 E6 39 53N 90 39W
Versailles, Ind., U.S.A. 141 E11 39 4N 85 15W
Versailles, Ky., U.S.A. 141 F12 38 3N 84 44W
Versailles, Mo., U.S.A. 140 F4 38 26N 92 51W
Versailles, Ohio, U.S.A. 141 D12 40 13N 84 29W
Versalles, Bolivia 157 C5 12 44 S 63 18W
Versoix, Switz. 28 D2 46 17N 6 10 E
Vert, C., Senegal 100 C1 14 45N 17 30W
Vertou, France 22 E5 47 10N 1 28W
Vertus, France 23 D11 48 54N 4 2 E
Verulam, S. Africa 105 D5 29 38 S 31 2 E
Verviers, Belgium 21 G7 50 37N 5 52 E
Vervins, France 23 C10 49 50N 3 53 E
Verzej, Slovenia 39 B13 46 34N 16 13 E
Vescavoto, France 25 F13 42 30N 9 27 E
Vesdre →, Belgium 21 G7 50 36N 5 34 E
Veselí nad Lužnicí, Czech. 30 B7 49 12N 14 43 E
Veseliye, Bulgaria 43 E12 42 18N 27 38 E
Veselovskoye Vdkhr., Russia 53 C9 47 0N 41 0 E
Veshenskaya, Russia 53 B9 49 35N 41 44 E
Vesle →, France 23 C10 49 23N 3 28 E
Veslyana →, Russia 54 A4 60 20N 54 0 E
Vesoul, France 23 E13 47 40N 6 11 E
Vessigebro, Sweden 15 H6 56 58N 12 40 E
Vest-Agder fylke □, Norway 13 G9 58 30N 7 15 E
Vesterålen, Norway 12 B13 68 45N 15 0 E
Vestersche Veld, Neths. 20 C8 52 52N 6 9 E
Vestfjorden, Norway 12 C13 67 55N 14 0 E
Vestfold fylke □, Norway 13 G11 59 15N 10 0 E
Vestmannaeyjar, Iceland 12 E3 63 27N 20 15W
Vestmarka, Norway 14 E5 59 56N 11 59 E
Vestone, Italy 38 C7 45 43N 10 25 E
Vestsjællands Amtskommune □, Denmark 15 J5 55 30N 11 20 E
Vestspitsbergen, Svalbard 6 B8 78 40N 17 0 E
Vestvågøy, Norway 12 B12 68 18N 13 50 E
Vesuvio, Italy 41 B7 40 50N 14 22 E
Vesuvius, Mt. = Vesuvio, Italy 41 B7 40 50N 14 22 E
Vesyegonsk, Russia 51 B10 58 40N 37 16 E
Veszprém, Hungary 31 D10 47 8N 17 57 E
Veszprém □, Hungary 31 D10 47 5N 17 55 E
Vésztő, Hungary 31 E14 46 55N 21 16 E
Vetapalem, India 83 G5 15 47N 80 18 E
Vetlanda, Sweden 13 H13 57 24N 15 3 E
Vetluga, Russia 51 C14 57 53N 45 45 E
Vetlugu →, Russia 51 C15 56 18N 46 24 E
Vetluzhskiy, Russia 51 C14 57 17N 45 12 E
Vetovo, Bulgaria 43 D11 43 42N 26 16 E
Vetralia, Italy 39 F9 42 20N 12 2 E
Vetren, Bulgaria 43 E9 42 15N 24 3 E
Vettore, Monte, Italy 39 F10 42 49N 13 16 E
Veurne, Belgium 21 F1 51 5N 2 40 E
Vevay, U.S.A. 141 F11 38 45N 85 4W
Vevey, Switz. 28 D3 46 28N 6 51 E
Vévi, Greece 44 D3 40 47N 21 38 E
Veynes, France 25 D9 44 32N 5 49 E
Veys, Iran 85 D6 31 30N 49 0 E
Vézelise, France 23 D13 48 30N 6 5 E
Vézère →, France 24 D4 44 53N 0 53 E
Vezhen, Bulgaria 43 E9 42 50N 24 20 E
Vezirköprü, Turkey 88 C6 41 8N 35 27 E
Vi Thanh, Vietnam 77 H5 9 42N 105 26 E
Viacha, Bolivia 156 D4 16 39 S 68 18W
Viadana, Italy 38 D7 44 55N 10 30 E
Viamão, Brazil 159 C5 30 5 S 51 0W
Viana, Brazil 154 B3 3 13 S 44 55W
Viana, Spain 34 C2 42 31N 2 22W
Viana del Bollo, Spain 36 C3 42 11N 7 6W
Viana do Alentejo, Portugal 37 G3 38 17N 7 59W
Viana do Castelo, Portugal 36 D2 41 42N 8 50W
Vianden, Belgium 21 J8 49 56N 6 12 E
Vianen, Neths. 20 E6 51 59N 5 5 E
Vianna do Castelo □, Portugal 36 D2 41 50N 8 30W
Vianópolis, Brazil 155 E2 16 40 S 48 35W
Viar →, Spain 37 H5 37 36N 5 50W
Viaréggio, Italy 38 E7 43 52N 10 13 E
Viaur →, France 24 D5 44 8N 1 58 E
Vibank, Canada 131 C8 50 20N 103 56W
Vibo Valéntia, Italy 41 D9 38 40N 16 5 E
Viborg, Denmark 15 H3 56 27N 9 23 E
Vibraye, France 22 D7 48 3N 0 44 E
Vic-en-Bigorre, France 24 E4 43 24N 0 3 E
Vic-Fézensac, France 24 E4 43 47N 0 19 E
Vic-sur-Cère, France 24 D6 44 59N 2 38 E
Vicenza, Italy 39 C8 45 32N 11 31 E
Vich, Spain 34 D7 41 58N 2 19 E
Vichada □, Colombia 152 C4 5 0N 69 30W
Vichada →, Colombia 152 C4 4 55N 67 50W
Vichuga, Russia 51 C12 57 12N 41 55 E
Vichy, France 24 B7 46 9N 3 26 E
Vicksburg, Ariz., U.S.A. 145 M13 33 45N 113 45W
Vicksburg, Mich., U.S.A. 141 B11 42 7N 85 32W
Vicksburg, Miss., U.S.A. 139 J9 32 21N 90 53W
Vico, L. di, Italy 39 F9 42 20N 12 10 E
Vico del Gargaro, Italy 41 A8 41 54N 15 57 E
Viçosa, Brazil 154 C4 9 28 S 36 14W
Viçosa do Ceará, Brazil 154 B3 3 34 S 41 5W
Vicosoprano, Switz. 29 D9 46 22N 9 38 E
Victor, India 80 J4 21 0N 71 30 E
Victor, Colo., U.S.A. 138 F2 38 43N 105 9W
Victor, N.Y., U.S.A. 136 D7 42 58N 77 24W
Victor Emanuel Ra., Papua N. G. 120 C2 5 20 S 142 15 E
Victor Harbor, Australia 115 F2 35 30 S 138 37 E
Victoria, Argentina 158 C3 32 40 S 60 10W
Victoria, Canada 130 D4 48 30N 123 25W
Victoria, Chile 160 A2 38 13 S 72 20W
Victoria, Guinea 100 C2 10 50N 14 32W
Victoria, Malaysia 75 A5 5 20N 115 14 E
Victoria, Malta 37 C1 36 2N 14 14 E
Victoria, Mindoro, Phil. 70 E3 13 12N 121 12 E
Victoria, Tarlac, Phil. 70 D3 15 35N 120 41 E
Victoria, Seychelles 109 E4 5 0 S 55 40 E
Victoria, Ill., U.S.A. 140 C6 41 2N 90 6W
Victoria, Kans., U.S.A. 138 F5 38 52N 99 9W
Victoria, Tex., U.S.A. 139 L6 28 48N 97 0W
Victoria □, Australia 116 D6 37 0 S 144 0 E
Victoria →, Australia 112 C4 15 10 S 129 40 E
Victoria, Grand L., Canada 128 C4 47 31N 77 30W
Victoria, L., Africa 106 C3 1 0 S 33 0 E
Victoria, L., Australia 116 B4 33 57 S 141 15 E
Victoria, Mt., Burma 78 E4 21 15N 93 55 E
Victoria, Mt., Papua N. G. 120 E4 8 55 S 147 32 E
Victoria Beach, Canada 131 C9 50 40N 96 35W
Victoria de Durango, Mexico 146 C4 24 3N 104 39W
Victoria de las Tunas, Cuba 148 B4 20 58N 76 59W
Victoria Falls, Zimbabwe 107 F2 17 58 S 25 52 E
Victoria Harbour, Canada 128 D4 44 45N 79 45W
Victoria I., Canada 126 A8 71 0N 111 0W
Victoria Ld., Antarctica 7 D11 75 0 S 160 0 E
Victoria Nile →, Uganda 106 B3 2 14N 31 26 E
Victoria Peaks, Phil. 71 G2 9 22N 118 20 E
Victoria Ra., N.Z. 119 C7 42 12 S 172 7 E
Victoria Res., Canada 129 C8 48 20N 57 27W
Victoria River Downs, Australia 112 C5 16 25 S 131 0 E
Victoria West, S. Africa 104 E3 31 25 S 23 4 E
Victorias, Phil. 71 F4 10 54N 123 5 E
Victoriaville, Canada 129 C5 46 4N 71 56W
Victorica, Argentina 158 D2 36 20 S 65 30W
Victorville, U.S.A. 145 L9 34 32N 117 18W
Vicuña, Chile 158 C1 30 0 S 70 50W
Vicuña Mackenna, Argentina 158 C3 33 53 S 64 25W
Vidal, U.S.A. 145 L12 34 7N 114 31W
Vidal Junction, U.S.A. 145 L12 34 11N 114 34W
Vidalia, U.S.A. 135 J4 32 13N 82 25W
Vidauban, France 25 E10 43 25N 6 27 E
Vídho, Greece 32 A3 39 38N 19 55 E
Vidigueira, Portugal 37 G3 38 12N 7 48W
Vidin, Bulgaria 42 D7 43 59N 22 50 E
Vidio, C., Spain 36 B4 43 35N 6 14W
Vidisha, India 80 H7 23 28N 77 53 E
Vidra, Romania 46 D7 45 56N 26 55 E
Viduša, Bos.-H. 42 E3 42 55N 18 21 E
Vidzy, Belorussia 50 D5 55 23N 26 37 E
Viechtach, Germany 27 F8 49 5N 12 53 E
Viedma, Argentina 160 B4 40 50 S 63 0W
Viedma, L., Argentina 160 C2 49 30 S 72 30W
Vieira, Portugal 36 D2 41 38N 8 8W
Viella, Spain 34 C5 42 43N 0 44 E
Vielsalm, Belgium 21 H7 50 17N 5 54 E
Vienenburg, Germany 26 D6 51 57N 10 35 E
Vieng Pou Kha, Laos 76 B3 20 41N 101 4 E
Vienna = Wien, Austria 31 C9 48 12N 16 22 E
Vienna, Ill., U.S.A. 139 G10 37 25N 88 54W
Vienna, Mo., U.S.A. 140 F5 38 11N 91 57W
Vienne, France 25 C8 45 31N 4 53 E
Vienne □, France 24 B4 46 30N 0 42 E
Vienne →, France 22 E7 47 13N 0 5 E
Vientiane, Laos 76 D4 17 58N 102 36 E
Vientos, Paso de los, Caribbean 149 C5 20 0N 74 0W
Vierlingsbeek, Neths. 21 E8 51 36N 6 1 E
Viersen, Germany 26 D2 51 15N 6 23 E
Vierwaldstättersee, Switz. 29 C7 47 0N 8 30 E
Vierzon, France 23 E9 47 13N 2 5 E
Vieste, Italy 41 A9 41 52N 16 14 E
Vietnam ■, Asia 76 C5 19 0N 106 0 E
Vieux-Boucau-les-Bains, France 24 E2 43 48N 1 23W
Vif, France 25 C9 45 5N 5 41 E
Vigan, Phil. 70 C3 17 35N 120 28 E
Vigévano, Italy 38 C5 45 18N 8 50 E
Vigia, Brazil 154 B2 0 50 S 48 5W
Vigía Chico, Mexico 147 D7 19 46N 87 35W
Víglas, Ákra, Greece 32 D9 35 54N 27 51 E
Vignemale, Pic du, France 24 F3 42 47N 0 10W
Vigneulles-lès-Hattonchâtel, France 23 D12 48 59N 5 43 E
Vignola, Italy 38 D8 44 29N 11 0 E
Vigo, Spain 36 C2 42 12N 8 41W
Vigo, Ría de, Spain 36 C2 42 15N 8 45W
Vihiers, France 22 E6 47 10N 0 30W
Vijayadurg, India 82 F1 16 30N 73 25 E
Vijayawada, India 83 F5 16 31N 80 39 E
Vijfhuizen, Neths. 20 D5 52 22N 4 41 E
Viken, Sweden 15 F8 58 39N 14 20 E
Viking, Canada 130 C6 53 7N 111 50W
Vikna, Norway 12 D11 64 55N 10 58 E
Vikramasingapuram, India 83 K3 8 40N 76 47 E
Viksjö, Sweden 14 B11 62 45N 17 26 E
Vikulovo, Russia 56 D8 56 50N 70 40 E
Vila da Maganja, Mozam. 107 F4 17 18 S 37 30 E
Vila de João Belo = Xai-Xai, Mozam. 105 D5 25 6 S 33 31 E
Vila de Rei, Portugal 37 F2 39 41N 8 9W
Vila do Bispo, Portugal 37 H2 37 5N 8 53W
Vila do Chibuto, Mozam. 105 C5 24 40 S 33 33 E
Vila do Conde, Portugal 36 D2 41 21N 8 45W
Vila Franca de Xira, Portugal 37 G2 38 57N 8 59W
Vila Gamito, Mozam. 107 E3 14 12 S 33 0 E
Vila Gomes da Costa, Mozam. 105 C5 24 20 S 33 37 E
Vila Machado, Mozam. 107 F3 19 15 S 34 14 E
Vila Mouzinho, Mozam. 107 E3 14 48 S 34 25 E
Vila Nova de Foscôa, Portugal 36 D3 41 5N 7 9W
Vila Nova de Ourém, Portugal 37 F2 39 40N 8 35W
Vila Novo de Gaia, Portugal 36 D2 41 4N 8 40W
Vila Pouca de Aguiar, Portugal 36 D3 41 30N 7 38W
Vila Real, Portugal 36 D3 41 17N 7 48W
Vila Real de Santo António, Portugal 37 H3 37 10N 7 28W
Vila Vasco da Gama, Mozam. 107 E3 14 54 S 32 14 E
Vila Velha, Amapá, Brazil 153 C7 3 13N 51 13W
Vila Velha, Espírito Santo, Brazil 155 F3 20 20 S 40 17W
Vila Viçosa, Portugal 37 G3 38 45N 7 27W
Vilaboa, Spain 36 C2 42 21N 8 39W
Vilaine →, France 22 E4 47 30N 2 27W
Vilanandro, Tanjona, Madag. 105 B7 16 11 S 44 27 E
Vilanculos, Mozam. 105 C6 22 1 S 35 17 E
Vilar Formosa, Portugal 36 E4 40 38N 6 45W
Vilareal □, Portugal 36 D3 41 36N 7 35W
Vilaseca-Salou, Spain 34 D6 41 7N 1 9 E
Vilcabamba, Cordillera, Peru 156 C3 13 0 S 73 0W
Vilcanchos, Peru 156 C3 13 40 S 74 25W
Vîlcea □, Romania 46 D5 45 0N 24 10 E
Vileyka, Belorussia 50 D5 54 30N 26 53 E
Vilhelmina, Sweden 12 D14 64 35N 16 39 E
Vilhena, Brazil 157 C5 12 40 S 60 5W
Viliga, Russia 57 C16 61 36N 156 56 E
Viliya →, Lithuania 50 D3 55 8N 24 16 E
Viljandi, Estonia 50 B4 58 28N 25 30 E
Vilkovo, Ukraine 52 D3 45 28N 29 32 E
Villa Abecia, Bolivia 158 A2 21 0 S 68 18W
Villa Ahumada, Mexico 146 A3 30 38N 106 30W
Villa Ana, Argentina 158 B4 28 28 S 59 40W
Villa Ángela, Argentina 158 B3 27 34 S 60 45W
Villa Bella, Bolivia 157 C4 10 25 S 65 22W
Villa Bens = Tarfaya, Morocco 98 C2 27 55N 12 55W
Villa Cañás, Argentina 158 C3 34 0 S 61 35W
Villa Carlos, Spain 33 B11 39 53N 4 17 E
Villa Cisneros = Dakhla, W. Sahara 98 D1 23 50N 15 53W
Villa Colón, Argentina 158 C2 31 38 S 68 20W
Villa Constitución, Argentina 158 C3 33 15 S 60 20W
Villa de Cura, Venezuela 152 A4 10 2N 67 29W
Villa de María, Argentina 158 B3 29 55 S 63 43W
Villa del Rosario, Venezuela 152 A3 10 19N 72 19W
Villa Dolores, Argentina 158 C2 31 58 S 65 15W
Villa Frontera, Mexico 146 B4 26 56N 101 27W
Villa Grove, U.S.A. 141 E8 39 52N 88 10W
Villa Guillermina, Argentina 158 B4 28 15 S 59 29W
Villa Hayes, Paraguay 158 B4 25 5 S 57 20W
Villa Iris, Argentina 158 D3 38 12 S 63 12W
Villa Juárez, Mexico 146 B4 27 37N 100 44W
Villa María, Argentina 158 C3 32 20 S 63 10W
Villa Mazán, Argentina 158 B2 28 40 S 66 30W
Villa Minozzo, Italy 38 D7 44 21N 10 30 E
Villa Montes, Bolivia 158 A3 21 10 S 63 30W
Villa Ocampo, Argentina 158 B4 28 30 S 59 20W
Villa Ocampo, Mexico 146 B3 26 29N 105 30W
Villa Ojo de Agua, Argentina 158 B3 29 30 S 63 44W
Villa San Giovanni, Italy 41 D8 38 13N 15 38 E
Villa San José, Argentina 158 C4 32 12 S 58 15W
Villa San Martín, Argentina 158 B3 28 15 S 64 9W
Villa Santina, Italy 39 B9 46 25N 12 55 E
Villa Unión, Mexico 146 C3 23 12N 106 14W
Villaba, Phil. 71 F5 11 13N 124 24 E
Villablino, Spain 36 C4 42 57N 6 19W
Villacañas, Spain 34 F1 39 38N 3 20W
Villacarriedo, Spain 34 B1 43 14N 3 48W
Villacarrillo, Spain 35 G1 38 7N 3 3W
Villacastín, Spain 36 E6 40 46N 4 25W
Villach, Austria 30 E6 46 37N 13 51 E
Villacidro, Italy 40 C1 39 27N 8 45 E
Villada, Spain 36 C6 42 15N 4 59W
Villadiego, Spain 36 C6 42 31N 4 1W
Villadóssola, Italy 38 B5 46 4N 8 16 E
Villafeliche, Spain 34 D3 41 10N 1 30W

Vrakhnéïka 281


Villafranca, *Spain* **34 C3** 42 17N 1 46W
Villafranca de los Barros, *Spain* **37 G4** 38 35N 6 18W
Villafranca de los Caballeros, *Spain* **33 B10** 39 34N 3 25 E
Villafranca de los Caballeros, *Spain* **35 F1** 39 26N 3 21W
Villafranca del Bierzo, *Spain* **36 C4** 42 38N 6 50W
Villafranca del Cid, *Spain* **34 E4** 40 26N 0 16W
Villafranca del Panadés, *Spain* **34 D6** 41 21N 1 40 E
Villafranca di Verona, *Italy* **38 C7** 45 20N 10 51 E
Villagarcía de Arosa, *Spain* **36 C2** 42 34N 8 46W
Villagrán, *Mexico* **147 C5** 24 29N 99 29W
Villaguay, *Argentina* **158 C4** 32 0S 59 0W
Villaharta, *Spain* **37 G6** 38 9N 4 54W
Villahermosa, *Mexico* **147 D6** 18 0N 92 50W
Villahermosa, *Spain* **35 G2** 38 46N 2 52W
Villaines-la-Juhel, *France* **22 D6** 48 21N 0 20W
Villajoyosa, *Spain* **35 G4** 38 30N 0 12W
Villalba, *Spain* **36 B3** 43 26N 7 40W
Villalba de Guardo, *Spain* **36 C6** 42 42N 4 49W
Villalcampo, Pantano de, *Spain* **36 D4** 41 31N 6 0W
Villalón de Campos, *Spain* **36 C5** 42 5N 5 4W
Villalpando, *Spain* **36 D5** 41 51N 5 25W
Villaluenga, *Spain* **36 E7** 40 2N 3 54W
Villamanán, *Spain* **36 C5** 42 19N 5 35W
Villamartín, *Spain* **37 J5** 36 52N 5 38W
Villamayor, *Spain* **34 F2** 39 50N 2 59W
Villamblard, *France* **24 C4** 45 2N 0 32 E
Villanova Monteleone, *Italy* **40 B1** 40 30N 8 28 E
Villanueva, *Colombia* **152 A3** 10 37N 72 59W
Villanueva, *U.S.A.* **143 J11** 35 16N 105 22W
Villanueva de Castellón, *Spain* **35 F4** 39 5N 0 31W
Villanueva de Córdoba, *Spain* **37 G6** 38 20N 4 38W
Villanueva de la Fuente, *Spain* **35 G2** 38 42N 2 42W
Villanueva de la Serena, *Spain* **37 G5** 38 59N 5 50W
Villanueva de la Sierra, *Spain* **36 E4** 40 12N 6 24W
Villanueva de los Castillejos, *Spain* **37 H3** 37 30N 7 15W
Villanueva del Arzobispo, *Spain* **35 G1** 38 10N 3 0W
Villanueva del Duque, *Spain* **37 G5** 38 20N 5 0W
Villanueva del Fresno, *Spain* **37 G3** 38 23N 7 10W
Villanueva y Geltrú, *Spain* **34 D6** 41 13N 1 40 E
Villaodrid, *Spain* **36 B3** 43 20N 7 11W
Villaputzu, *Italy* **40 C2** 39 28N 9 33 E
Villar del Arzobispo, *Spain* **34 F4** 39 44N 0 50W
Villar del Rey, *Spain* **37 F4** 39 7N 6 50W
Villarcayo, *Spain* **34 C1** 42 56N 3 34W
Villard-Bonnot, *France* **25 C9** 45 14N 5 53 E
Villard-de-Lans, *France* **25 C9** 45 3N 5 33 E
Villarino de los Aires, *Spain* **36 D4** 41 18N 6 23W
Villarosa, *Italy* **41 E7** 37 36N 14 9 E
Villarramiel, *Spain* **36 C6** 42 2N 4 55W
Villarreal, *Spain* **34 F4** 39 55N 0 3W
Villarrica, *Chile* **160 A2** 39 15 S 72 15W
Villarrica, *Paraguay* **158 B4** 25 40 S 56 30W
Villarrobledo, *Spain* **35 F2** 39 18N 2 36W
Villarroya de la Sierra, *Spain* **34 D3** 41 27N 1 46W
Villarrubia de los Ojos, *Spain* **35 F1** 39 14N 3 36W
Villars-les-Dombes, *France* **25 B9** 46 0N 5 3 E
Villarta de San Juan, *Spain* **35 F1** 39 15N 3 25W
Villasayas, *Spain* **34 D2** 41 24N 2 39W
Villaseca de los Gamitos, *Spain* **36 D4** 41 2N 6 7W
Villastar, *Spain* **34 E3** 40 17N 1 9W
Villatobas, *Spain* **34 F1** 39 54N 3 20W
Villavicencio, *Argentina* **158 C2** 32 28 S 69 0W
Villavicencio, *Colombia* **152 C3** 4 9N 73 37W
Villaviciosa, *Spain* **36 B5** 43 32N 5 27W
Villazón, *Bolivia* **158 A2** 22 0 S 65 35W
Ville-Marie, *Canada* **128 C4** 47 20N 79 30W
Ville Platte, *U.S.A.* **139 K8** 30 41N 92 17W
Villedieu-les-Poêlles, *France* **22 D5** 48 50N 1 13W
Villefort, *France* **24 D7** 44 28N 3 56 E
Villefranche-de-Lauragais, *France* **24 E5** 43 25N 1 44 E
Villefranche-de-Rouergue, *France* **24 D6** 44 21N 2 2 E
Villefranche-du-Périgord, *France* **24 D5** 44 38N 1 5 E
Villefranche-sur-Cher, *France* **23 E8** 47 18N 1 46 E
Villefranche-sur-Saône, *France* **25 C8** 45 59N 4 43 E
Villegrande, *Bolivia* **157 D5** 18 30 S 64 10W
Villel, *Spain* **34 E3** 40 14N 1 12W
Villemaur-sur-Vanne, *France* **23 D10** 48 15N 3 44 E
Villemur-sur-Tarn, *France* **24 E5** 43 51N 1 31 E
Villena, *Spain* **35 G4** 38 39N 0 52W
Villenauxe-la-Grande, *France* **23 D10** 48 35N 3 33 E
Villenave-d'Ornon, *France* **24 D3** 44 46N 0 33W
Villeneuve, *Italy* **38 C4** 45 40N 7 10 E
Villeneuve, *Switz.* **28 D3** 46 24N 6 56 E
Villeneuve-l'Archevêque, *France* **23 D10** 48 14N 3 32 E
Villeneuve-lès-Avignon, *France* **25 E8** 43 58N 4 49 E
Villeneuve-St.-Georges, *France* **23 D9** 48 44N 2 28 E
Villeneuve-sur-Allier, *France* **24 B7** 46 40N 3 13 E
Villeneuve-sur-Lot, *France* **24 D4** 44 24N 0 42 E
Villeréal, *France* **24 D4** 44 38N 0 45 E
Villers-Bocage, *France* **22 C6** 49 3N 0 40W
Villers-Bretonneux, *France* **23 C9** 49 50N 2 30 E
Villers-Cotterêts, *France* **23 C10** 49 15N 3 4 E
Villers-le-Bouillet, *Belgium* **21 G6** 50 34N 5 15 E
Villers-le-Gambon, *Belgium* **21 H5** 50 11N 4 37 E
Villers-sur-Mer, *France* **22 C6** 49 21N 0 2W
Villersexel, *France* **23 E13** 47 33N 6 26 E
Villerupt, *France* **23 C12** 49 28N 5 55 E
Villerville, *France* **22 C7** 49 26N 0 5 E
Villiers, *S. Africa* **105 D4** 27 2 S 28 36 E
Villingen, *Germany* **27 G4** 48 4N 8 28 E
Villisca, *U.S.A.* **140 D2** 40 56N 94 59W
Villupuram, *India* **83 J4** 11 59N 79 31 E
Vilna, *Canada* **130 C6** 54 7N 111 55W
Vilnius, *Lithuania* **50 D4** 54 38N 25 19 E
Vils →, *Germany* **27 G9** 48 38N 13 11 E
Vilsbiburg, *Germany* **27 G8** 48 27N 12 23 E
Vilshofen, *Germany* **27 G9** 48 38N 13 11 E
Vilskutskogo, Proliv, *Russia* **57 B11** 78 0N 103 0 E
Vilusi, *Montenegro* **42 E3** 42 44N 18 34 E
Vilvoorde, *Belgium* **21 G4** 50 56N 4 26 E
Vilyuy →, *Russia* **57 C13** 64 24N 126 26 E
Vilyuysk, *Russia* **57 C13** 63 40N 121 35 E
Vimercate, *Italy* **38 C6** 45 38N 9 25 E
Vimiosa, *Portugal* **36 D4** 41 35N 6 31W
Vimoutiers, *France* **22 D7** 48 57N 0 10 E
Vimperk, *Czech.* **30 B6** 49 3N 13 46 E
Viña del Mar, *Chile* **158 C1** 33 0 S 71 30W
Vinaroz, *Spain* **34 E5** 40 30N 0 27 E
Vincennes, *U.S.A.* **141 F9** 38 41N 87 32W
Vincent, *U.S.A.* **145 L8** 34 33N 118 11W
Vinces, *Ecuador* **152 D2** 1 32 S 79 45W
Vinchina, *Argentina* **158 B2** 28 45 S 68 15W
Vindel älven →, *Sweden* **12 E15** 63 55N 19 50 E
Vindeln, *Sweden* **12 D15** 64 12N 19 43 E
Vinderup, *Denmark* **15 H2** 56 29N 8 45 E
Vindhya Ra., *India* **80 H7** 22 50N 77 0 E
Vine Grove, *U.S.A.* **141 G11** 37 49N 85 59W
Vineland, *U.S.A.* **134 F8** 39 29N 75 2W
Vinga, *Romania* **46 C2** 46 0N 21 14 E
Vingnes, *Norway* **14 C4** 61 7N 10 26 E
Vinh, *Vietnam* **76 C5** 18 45N 105 38 E
Vinh Linh, *Vietnam* **76 D6** 17 4N 107 2 E
Vinh Long, *Vietnam* **77 G5** 10 16N 105 57 E
Vinh Yen, *Vietnam* **76 B5** 21 21N 105 35 E
Vinhais, *Portugal* **36 D3** 41 50N 7 5W
Vinica, *Croatia* **39 B13** 46 20N 16 9 E
Vinica, *Slovenia* **39 C12** 45 28N 15 16 E
Vinita, *U.S.A.* **139 G7** 36 39N 95 9W
Vinkeveen, *Neths.* **20 D5** 52 13N 4 56 E
Vinkovci, *Croatia* **42 B3** 45 19N 18 48 E
Vinnitsa, *Ukraine* **52 B3** 49 15N 28 30 E
Vinnytsya = Vinnitsa, *Ukraine* **52 B3** 49 15N 28 30 E
Vinstra, *Norway* **14 C3** 61 37N 9 44 E
Vintar, *Phil.* **70 B3** 18 14N 120 39 E
Vinton, *Calif., U.S.A.* **144 F6** 39 48N 120 10W
Vinton, *Iowa, U.S.A.* **140 B4** 42 10N 92 1W
Vinton, *La., U.S.A.* **139 K8** 30 11N 93 35W
Vinţu de Jos, *Romania* **46 D4** 46 0N 23 30 E
Viöl, *Germany* **26 A5** 54 32N 9 12 E
Viola, *U.S.A.* **140 C6** 41 12N 90 35W
Violet Town, *Australia* **117 D6** 36 38 S 145 42 E
Vipava, *Slovenia* **39 C10** 45 51N 13 58 E
Vipiteno, *Italy* **39 B8** 46 55N 11 25 E
Viqueque, *Indonesia* **72 C3** 8 52 S 126 23 E
Vir, *Croatia* **39 D12** 44 17N 15 3 E
Vir, *Tajikistan* **55 E6** 37 45N 72 5 E
Virac, *Phil.* **70 E5** 13 30N 124 20 E
Virachei, *Cambodia* **76 F6** 13 59N 106 49 E
Virago Sd., *Canada* **130 C2** 54 0N 132 30W
Virajpet = Virarajendrapet, *India* **83 H2** 12 10N 75 50 E
Viramgam, *India* **80 H5** 23 5N 72 0 E
Viranşehir, *Turkey* **89 E8** 37 13N 39 45 E
Virarajendrapet, *India* **83 H2** 12 10N 75 50 E
Viravanallur, *India* **83 K3** 8 40N 77 30 E
Virden, *Canada* **131 D8** 49 50N 100 56W
Virden, *U.S.A.* **140 E7** 39 30N 89 46W
Vire, *France* **22 D6** 48 50N 0 53W
Vire →, *France* **22 C5** 49 20N 1 7W
Virgem da Lapa, *Brazil* **155 E3** 16 49 S 42 21W
Vírgenes, C., *Argentina* **160 D3** 52 19 S 68 21W
Virgin →, *Canada* **131 B7** 57 2N 108 17W
Virgin →, *U.S.A.* **143 H6** 36 28N 114 21W
Virgin Gorda, *Virgin Is.* **149 C7** 18 30N 64 26W
Virgin Is. (British) ■, *W. Indies* **149 C7** 18 30N 64 30W
Virgin Is. (U.S.) ■, *W. Indies* **149 C7** 18 20N 65 0W
Virginia, *S. Africa* **104 D4** 28 8 S 26 55 E
Virginia, *Ill., U.S.A.* **140 E6** 39 57N 90 13W
Virginia, *Minn., U.S.A.* **138 B8** 47 31N 92 32W
Virginia □, *U.S.A.* **134 G7** 37 30N 78 45W
Virginia Beach, *U.S.A.* **134 G8** 36 51N 75 59W
Virginia City, *Mont., U.S.A.* **142 D8** 45 18N 111 56W
Virginia City, *Nev., U.S.A.* **144 F7** 39 19N 119 39W
Virginia Falls, *Canada* **130 A3** 61 38N 125 42W
Virginiatown, *Canada* **128 C4** 48 9N 79 36W
Virieu-le-Grand, *France* **25 C9** 45 51N 5 39 E
Virje, *Croatia* **42 A1** 46 4N 16 59 E
Viroqua, *U.S.A.* **138 D9** 43 34N 90 53W
Virovitica, *Croatia* **42 B2** 45 51N 17 21 E
Virpazar, *Montenegro* **42 E4** 42 14N 19 6 E
Virton, *Belgium* **21 J7** 49 35N 5 32 E
Virtsu, *Estonia* **50 B3** 58 32N 23 33 E
Virú, *Peru* **156 B2** 8 25 S 78 45W
Virudunagar, *India* **83 K3** 9 30N 77 58 E
Vis, *Croatia* **39 E13** 43 4N 16 10 E
Vis Kanal, *Croatia* **39 E13** 43 4N 16 5 E
Visalia, *U.S.A.* **144 J7** 36 20N 119 18W
Visayan Sea, *Phil.* **71 F4** 11 30N 123 30 E
Visby, *Sweden* **13 H15** 57 37N 18 18 E
Viscount Melville Sd., *Canada* **6 B2** 74 10N 108 0W
Visé, *Belgium* **21 G7** 50 44N 5 41 E
Višegrad, *Bos.-H.* **42 D4** 43 47N 19 17 E
Viseu, *Brazil* **154 B2** 1 10 S 46 5W
Viseu, *Portugal* **36 E3** 40 40N 7 55W
Viseu □, *Portugal* **36 E3** 40 40N 7 55W
Vişeu de Sus, *Romania* **46 B5** 47 45N 24 25 E
Vishakhapatnam, *India* **82 F6** 17 45N 83 20 E
Vishera →, *Russia* **54 B5** 59 55N 56 25 E
Viskafors, *Sweden* **15 G6** 57 37N 12 50 E
Visnagar, *India* **80 H5** 23 45N 72 32 E
Višnja Gora, *Slovenia* **39 C11** 45 58N 14 45 E
Viso, Mte., *Italy* **38 D4** 44 38N 7 5 E
Viso del Marqués, *Spain* **35 G1** 38 32N 3 34W
Visoko, *Bos.-H.* **42 D3** 43 58N 18 10 E
Visokoi I., *Antarctica* **7 B1** 56 43 S 27 15W
Visp, *Switz.* **28 D5** 46 17N 7 52 E
Vispa →, *Switz.* **28 D5** 46 9N 7 48 E
Visselhövede, *Germany* **26 C5** 52 59N 9 36 E
Vissoie, *Switz.* **28 D5** 46 13N 7 36 E
Vista, *U.S.A.* **145 M9** 33 12N 117 14W
Vistonikos, Ormos, *Greece* **44 D7** 41 0N 25 7 E
Vistula = Wisła →, *Poland* **47 A5** 54 22N 18 55 E
Vit →, *Bulgaria* **43 D9** 43 30N 24 30 E
Vitanje, *Slovenia* **39 B12** 46 25N 15 18 E
Vitebsk, *Belorussia* **50 D7** 55 10N 30 15 E
Viterbo, *Italy* **39 F9** 42 25N 12 8 E
Viti Levu, *Fiji* **121 A1** 17 30 S 177 30 E
Vitiaz Str., *Papua N. G.* **120 C4** 5 40 S 147 10 E
Vitigudino, *Spain* **36 D4** 41 1N 6 26W
Vitim, *Russia* **57 D12** 59 28N 112 35 E
Vitim →, *Russia* **57 D12** 59 26N 112 34 E
Vitina, *Bos.-H.* **42 D2** 43 17N 17 29 E
Vitína, *Greece* **45 G4** 37 40N 22 10 E
Vitória, *Brazil* **155 F3** 20 20 S 40 22W
Vitoria, *Spain* **34 C2** 42 50N 2 41W
Vitória da Conquista, *Brazil* **155 D3** 14 51 S 40 51W
Vitória de São Antão, *Brazil* **154 C4** 8 10 S 35 20W
Vitorino Friere, *Brazil* **154 B2** 4 4 S 45 10W
Vitré, *France* **22 D5** 48 8N 1 12W
Vitry-le-François, *France* **23 D11** 48 43N 4 33 E
Vitsi, Óros, *Greece* **44 D3** 40 40N 21 25 E
Vitsyebsk = Vitebsk, *Belorussia* **50 D7** 55 10N 30 15 E
Vitteaux, *France* **23 E11** 47 24N 4 30 E
Vittel, *France* **23 D12** 48 12N 5 57 E
Vittória, *Italy* **41 F7** 36 58N 14 30 E
Vittório Véneto, *Italy* **39 C9** 45 59N 12 18 E
Vitu Is., *Papua N. G.* **120 C5** 4 50 S 149 25 E
Vivario, *France* **25 F13** 42 10N 9 11 E
Vivegnis, *Belgium* **21 G7** 50 42N 5 39 E
Viver, *Spain* **34 F4** 39 55N 0 36W
Vivero, *Spain* **36 B3** 43 39N 7 38W
Viviers, *France* **25 D8** 44 30N 4 40 E
Vivonne, *Australia* **116 C2** 35 59 S 137 9 E
Vivonne, *France* **24 B4** 46 25N 0 15 E
Vivonne B., *Australia* **116 C2** 35 59 S 137 9 E
Vizcaíno, Desierto de, *Mexico* **146 B2** 27 40N 113 50W
Vizcaíno, Sierra, *Mexico* **146 B2** 27 30N 114 0W
Vizcaya □, *Spain* **34 B2** 43 15N 2 45W
Vize, *Turkey* **88 C2** 41 34N 27 45 E
Vizianagaram, *India* **82 E6** 18 6N 83 30 E
Vizille, *France* **25 C9** 45 5N 5 46 E
Viziñada, *Croatia* **39 C10** 45 20N 13 46 E
Viziru, *Romania* **46 D8** 45 0N 27 43 E
Vizovice, *Czech.* **31 B10** 49 12N 17 56 E
Vizzini, *Italy* **41 E7** 37 9N 14 43 E
Vjosa →, *Albania* **44 D1** 40 37N 19 42 E
Vlaardingen, *Neths.* **20 E4** 51 55N 4 21 E
Vlădeasa, *Romania* **46 C3** 46 47N 22 50 E
Vladicin Han, *Serbia* **42 E7** 42 42N 22 1 E
Vladikavkaz, *Russia* **53 E11** 43 0N 44 35 E
Vladimir, *Russia* **51 C12** 56 15N 40 30 E
Vladimir Volynskiy, *Ukraine* **50 F4** 50 50N 24 18 E
Vladimirci, *Serbia* **42 C4** 44 36N 19 45 E
Vladimirovac, *Serbia* **42 B5** 45 1N 20 53 E
Vladimirovka, *Russia* **53 B12** 48 27N 46 10 E
Vladimirovka, *Russia* **53 D11** 44 45N 44 41 E
Vladimirovo, *Bulgaria* **43 D8** 43 32N 23 22 E
Vladislavovka, *Ukraine* **52 D6** 45 15N 35 15 E
Vladivostok, *Russia* **57 E14** 43 10N 131 53 E
Vlamertinge, *Belgium* **21 G1** 50 51N 2 49 E
Vlasenica, *Bos.-H.* **42 C3** 44 11N 18 59 E
Vlašić, *Bos.-H.* **42 C2** 44 19N 17 37 E
Vlašim, *Czech.* **30 B7** 49 40N 14 53 E
Vlasinsko Jezero, *Serbia* **42 E7** 42 44N 22 22 E
Vlasotinci, *Serbia* **42 E7** 42 59N 22 7 E
Vleuten, *Neths.* **20 D6** 52 6N 5 1 E
Vlieland, *Neths.* **20 B5** 53 16N 4 55 E
Vliestroom, *Neths.* **20 B6** 53 19N 5 8 E
Vlijmen, *Neths.* **21 E6** 51 42N 5 14 E
Vlissingen, *Neths.* **21 F3** 51 26N 3 34 E
Vlóra, *Albania* **44 D1** 40 32N 19 28 E
Vlóra □, *Albania* **44 D2** 40 12N 20 0 E
Vlorës, Gjiri i, *Albania* **44 D1** 40 29N 19 27 E
Vltava →, *Czech.* **30 A7** 50 21N 14 30 E
Vo Dat, *Vietnam* **77 G6** 11 9N 107 31 E
Vobarno, *Italy* **38 C7** 45 38N 10 30 E
Voćin, *Croatia* **42 B2** 45 37N 17 33 E
Vöcklabruck, *Austria* **30 C6** 48 1N 13 39 E
Vodice, *Croatia* **39 E12** 43 47N 15 47 E
Vodňany, *Czech.* **30 B7** 49 9N 14 11 E
Vodnjan, *Croatia* **39 D10** 44 59N 13 52 E
Vogelkop = Doberai, Jazirah, *Indonesia* **73 B4** 1 25 S 133 0 E
Vogelsberg, *Germany* **26 E5** 50 37N 9 15 E
Voghera, *Italy* **38 D6** 44 59N 9 1 E
Voh, *N. Cal.* **121 T18** 20 58 S 164 42 E
Vohibinany, *Madag.* **105 B8** 18 49 S 49 4 E
Vohimarina, *Madag.* **105 A9** 13 25 S 50 0 E
Vohimena, Tanjon' i, *Madag.* **105 D8** 25 36 S 45 8 E
Vohipeno, *Madag.* **105 C8** 22 22 S 47 51 E
Voi, *Kenya* **106 C4** 3 25 S 38 32 E
Void, *France* **23 D12** 48 40N 5 36 E
Voineşti, *Iaşi, Romania* **46 B8** 47 5N 27 27 E
Voineşti, *Prahova, Romania* **46 D6** 45 5N 25 14 E
Voiotía □, *Greece* **45 F5** 38 20N 23 0 E
Voiron, *France* **25 C9** 45 22N 5 35 E
Voisey B., *Canada* **129 A7** 56 15N 61 50W
Voitsberg, *Austria* **30 D8** 47 3N 15 9 E
Voiviïs Límni, *Greece* **44 E4** 39 30N 22 45 E
Vojens, *Denmark* **15 J3** 55 16N 9 18 E
Vojmsjön, *Sweden* **12 D14** 64 55N 16 40 E
Vojnić, *Croatia* **39 C12** 45 19N 15 43 E
Vojnik, *Italy* **39 B12** 46 18N 15 19 E
Vojvodina □, *Serbia* **42 B4** 45 20N 20 0 E
Vokhma, *Russia* **51 B15** 59 0N 46 45 E
Vokhma →, *Russia* **51 C15** 56 20N 46 20 E
Vokhtoga, *Russia* **51 B12** 58 46N 41 8 E
Volary, *Czech.* **30 C6** 48 54N 13 52 E
Volborg, *U.S.A.* **138 C2** 45 51N 105 41W
Volcano Is. = Kazan-Rettō, *Pac. Oc.* **122 E6** 25 0N 141 0 E
Volchansk, *Ukraine* **52 A7** 50 17N 36 58 E
Volchayevka, *Russia* **57 E14** 48 40N 134 30 E
Volchya →, *Ukraine* **52 C7** 48 32N 36 0 E
Volda, *Norway* **12 E9** 62 9N 6 5 E
Volendam, *Neths.* **20 D6** 52 30N 5 4 E
Volga, *Russia* **51 C11** 57 58N 38 16 E
Volga →, *Russia* **53 C13** 46 0N 48 30 E
Volga Hts. = Privolzhskaya Vozvyshennost, *Russia* **51 F15** 51 0N 46 0 E
Volgodonsk, *Russia* **53 C10** 47 33N 42 5 E
Volgograd, *Russia* **53 B11** 48 40N 44 25 E
Volgogradskoye Vdkhr., *Russia* **51 F14** 50 0N 45 20 E
Volgorechensk, *Russia* **51 C12** 57 28N 41 14 E
Volissós, *Greece* **45 F7** 38 29N 25 54 E
Volkach, *Germany* **27 F6** 49 52N 10 14 E
Volkerak, *Neths.* **21 E4** 51 39N 4 18 E
Völkermarkt, *Austria* **30 E7** 46 39N 14 39 E
Volkhov, *Russia* **50 B8** 59 55N 32 15 E
Volkhov →, *Russia* **50 A8** 60 8N 32 20 E
Völklingen, *Germany* **27 F2** 49 15N 6 50 E
Volkovysk, *Belorussia* **50 E4** 53 9N 24 30 E
Volksrust, *S. Africa* **105 D4** 27 24 S 29 53 E
Vollenhove, *Neths.* **20 C7** 52 40N 5 58 E
Vol'n'ansk, *Ukraine* **52 C6** 48 2N 35 29 E
Volnovakha, *Ukraine* **52 C7** 47 35N 37 30 E
Volochanka, *Russia* **57 B10** 71 0N 94 28 E
Volodarsk, *Russia* **51 C13** 56 12N 43 15 E
Vologda, *Russia* **51 B11** 59 10N 39 45 E
Volokolamsk, *Russia* **51 C9** 56 5N 35 57 E
Volokonovka, *Russia* **51 F10** 50 33N 37 52 E
Vólos, *Greece* **44 E4** 39 24N 22 59 E
Volosovo, *Russia* **50 B6** 59 27N 29 32 E
Volozhin, *Belorussia* **50 D5** 54 3N 26 30 E
Volsk, *Russia* **51 E15** 52 5N 47 22 E
Volta →, *Ghana* **101 D5** 5 46N 0 41 E
Volta, L., *Ghana* **101 D5** 7 30N 0 15 E
Volta Blanche = White Volta →, *Ghana* **101 D4** 9 10N 1 15W
Volta Redonda, *Brazil* **155 F3** 22 31 S 44 5W
Voltaire, C., *Australia* **112 B4** 14 16 S 125 35 E
Volterra, *Italy* **38 E7** 43 24N 10 50 E
Voltri, *Italy* **38 D5** 44 25N 8 43 E
Volturara Áppula, *Italy* **41 A8** 41 30N 15 2 E
Volturno →, *Italy* **40 A6** 41 1N 13 55 E
Volubilis, *Morocco* **98 B3** 34 2N 5 33W
Volujak, *Bos.-H.* **42 D2** 43 53N 17 47 E
Vólvi, L., *Greece* **44 D5** 40 40N 23 34 E
Volvo, *Australia* **116 A5** 31 41 S 143 57 E
Volzhsk, *Russia* **51 D16** 55 57N 48 23 E
Volzhskiy, *Russia* **53 B11** 48 56N 44 46 E
Vondrozo, *Madag.* **105 C8** 22 49 S 47 20 E
Vónitsa, *Greece* **45 F2** 38 53N 20 58 E
Voorburg, *Neths.* **20 D4** 52 5N 4 24 E
Voorne Putten, *Neths.* **20 E4** 51 52N 4 10 E
Voorst, *Neths.* **20 D8** 52 10N 6 8 E
Voorthuizen, *Neths.* **20 D7** 52 11N 5 36 E
Vopnafjörður, *Iceland* **12 D6** 65 45N 14 40W
Vorarlberg □, *Austria* **30 D2** 47 20N 10 0 E
Vóras Óros, *Greece* **44 D3** 40 57N 21 45 E
Vorbasse, *Denmark* **15 J3** 55 39N 9 6 E
Vorden, *Neths.* **20 D8** 52 6N 6 19 E
Vorderrhein →, *Switz.* **29 C8** 46 49N 9 25 E
Vordingborg, *Denmark* **15 K5** 55 0N 11 54 E
Voreppe, *France* **25 C9** 45 18N 5 39 E
Voríai Sporádhes, *Greece* **45 E5** 39 15N 23 30 E
Vórios Evvoïkos Kólpos, *Greece* **45 F5** 38 45N 23 15 E
Vorkuta, *Russia* **48 A11** 67 48N 64 20 E
Vorma →, *Norway* **14 D5** 60 9N 11 27 E
Vorona →, *Russia* **51 F13** 51 22N 42 3 E
Voronezh, *Russia* **51 F11** 51 40N 39 10 E
Voronezh, *Ukraine* **50 F8** 51 47N 33 28 E
Voronezh →, *Russia* **51 F10** 51 32N 39 0 E
Vorontsovo-Aleksandrovskoye = Zelenokumsk, *Russia* **53 D10** 44 24N 44 0 E
Voroshilovgrad = Lugansk, *Ukraine* **53 B8** 48 38N 39 15 E
Voroshilovsk = Kommunarsk, *Ukraine* **53 B8** 48 30N 38 45 E
Vorovskoye, *Russia* **57 D16** 54 30N 155 50 E
Vorselaar, *Belgium* **21 F5** 51 12N 4 46 E
Vorskla →, *Ukraine* **52 B6** 48 50N 34 10 E
Võru, *Estonia* **50 C5** 57 48N 26 54 E
Vorukh, *Kirghizia* **55 D5** 39 52N 70 35 E
Vorupør, *Denmark* **15 H2** 56 58N 8 22 E
Vosges, *France* **23 D14** 48 20N 7 10 E
Vosges □, *France* **23 D13** 48 12N 6 20 E
Voskopoja, *Albania* **44 D2** 40 40N 20 33 E
Voskresensk, *Russia* **51 D11** 55 19N 38 43 E
Voskresenskoye, *Russia* **51 C14** 56 51N 45 30 E
Voss, *Norway* **13 F9** 60 38N 6 26 E
Vosselaar, *Belgium* **21 F5** 51 19N 4 52 E
Vostok I., *Kiribati* **123 J12** 10 5 S 152 23W
Votice, *Czech.* **30 B7** 49 38N 14 39 E
Votkinsk, *Russia* **54 C3** 57 0N 53 55 E
Votkinskoye Vdkhr., *Russia* **54 C4** 57 30N 55 0 E
Vouga →, *Portugal* **36 E2** 40 41N 8 40W
Vouillé, *France* **22 F7** 46 38N 0 10 E
Voulou, *C.A.R.* **102 A4** 8 33N 22 36 E
Vouvray, *France* **22 E7** 47 25N 0 48 E
Vouvry, *Switz.* **28 D3** 46 21N 6 51 E
Voúxa, Ákra, *Greece* **32 D5** 35 37N 23 32 E
Vouzela, *Portugal* **36 E2** 40 43N 8 7W
Vouziers, *France* **23 C11** 49 22N 4 40 E
Voves, *France* **23 D8** 48 15N 1 38 E
Voxna, *Sweden* **14 C9** 61 20N 15 40 E
Vozhe Oz., *Russia* **48 B6** 60 45N 39 0 E
Vozhgaly, *Russia* **51 B17** 58 9N 50 11 E
Voznesenka, *Russia* **57 D10** 56 40N 95 3 E
Voznesensk, *Ukraine* **52 C4** 47 35N 31 21 E
Voznesenye, *Russia* **48 B6** 61 0N 35 45 E
Vrâble, *Slovak Rep.* **31 C11** 48 15N 18 16 E
Vraćevšnica, *Serbia* **42 C5** 44 2N 20 34 E
Vrådal, *Norway* **14 E2** 59 20N 8 25 E
Vraka, *Albania* **44 B1** 42 8N 19 28 E
Vrakhnéïka, *Greece* **45 F3** 38 10N 21 40 E

282 Vrancea


Vrancea □, Romania 46 D7 45 50N 26 45 E
Vrancei, Munţii, Romania 46 D7 46 0N 26 30 E
Vrangelya, Ostrov, Russia 57 B19 71 0N 180 0 E
Vranica, Bos.-H. 42 D2 43 55N 17 50 E
Vranje, Serbia 42 E6 42 34N 21 54 E
Vranjska Banja, Serbia 42 E7 42 34N 22 1 E
Vranov, Slovak Rep. 31 C14 48 53N 21 40 E
Vransko, Slovenia 39 B11 46 17N 14 58 E
Vratsa, Bulgaria 43 D8 43 13N 23 30 E
Vrbas, Serbia 42 B4 45 40N 19 40 E
Vrbas →, Bos.-H. 42 B2 45 8N 17 29 E
Vrbnik, Croatia 39 C11 45 4N 14 40 E
Vrbovec, Croatia 39 C13 45 53N 16 28 E
Vrbovsko, Croatia 39 C12 45 24N 15 5 E
Vrchlabí, Czech. 30 A8 50 38N 15 37 E
Vrede, S. Africa 105 D4 27 24 S 29 6 E
Vredefort, S. Africa 104 D4 27 0 S 27 22 E
Vredenburg, S. Africa 104 E2 32 56 S 18 0 E
Vredendal, S. Africa 104 E2 31 41 S 18 35 E
Vreeswijk, Neths. 20 D6 52 1N 5 6 E
Vrena, Sweden 15 F10 58 54N 16 41 E
Vrgorac, Croatia 42 D2 43 12N 17 20 E
Vrhnika, Slovenia 39 C11 45 58N 14 15 E
Vriddhachalam, India 83 J4 11 30N 79 20 E
Vridi, Ivory C. 100 D4 5 15N 4 3W
Vries, Neths. 20 B9 53 5N 6 35 E
Vriezenveen, Neths. 20 D9 52 25N 6 38 E
Vrindavan, India 80 F7 27 37N 77 40 E
Vríses, Greece 32 D6 35 23N 24 13 E
Vrnograč, Bos.-H. 39 C12 45 10N 15 57 E
Vrondádhes, Greece 45 F8 38 25N 26 7 E
Vroomshoop, Neths. 20 D9 52 27N 6 34 E
Vrpolje, Croatia 42 B3 45 13N 18 24 E
Vršac, Serbia 42 B6 45 8N 21 18 E
Vrsacki Kanal, Serbia 42 B5 45 15N 21 0 E
Vryburg, S. Africa 104 D3 26 55 S 24 45 E
Vryheid, S. Africa 105 D5 27 45 S 30 47 E
Vsetín, Czech. 31 B11 49 20N 18 0 E
Vu Liet, Vietnam 76 C5 18 43N 105 23 E
Vucha →, Bulgaria 43 E9 42 10N 24 26 E
Vučitrn, Serbia 42 E5 42 49N 20 59 E
Vught, Neths. 21 E6 51 38N 5 20 E
Vukovar, Croatia 42 B3 45 21N 18 59 E
Vulcan, Canada 130 C6 50 25N 113 15W
Vulcan, Romania 46 D4 45 23N 23 17 E
Vulcan, U.S.A. 134 C2 45 47N 87 53W
Vulcano, Italy 41 D7 38 25N 14 58 E
Vŭlchedruma, Bulgaria 43 D8 43 42N 23 27 E
Vulci, Italy 39 F8 42 23N 11 37 E
Vulkaneshty, Moldavia 52 D3 45 35N 28 30 E
Vunduzi →, Mozam. 107 F3 18 56 S 34 1 E
Vung Tau, Vietnam 77 G6 10 21N 107 4 E
Vunisea, Fiji 121 B2 19 3 S 178 10 E
Vŭrbitsa, Bulgaria 43 E11 42 59N 26 40 E
Vurshets, Bulgaria 43 D8 43 15N 23 23 E
Vutcani, Romania 46 C8 46 26N 27 59 E
Vuyyuru, India 83 F5 16 28N 80 50 E
Vvedenka, Kazakhstan 54 D4 54 0N 63 53 E
Vyara, India 82 D1 21 8N 73 28 E
Vyasniki, Russia 51 C13 56 10N 42 10 E
Vyatka, Russia 54 B1 58 35N 49 40 E
Vyatka →, Russia 54 C2 55 30N 51 20 E
Vyatskiye Polyany, Russia 54 C2 56 5N 51 0 E
Vyazemskiy, Russia 57 E14 47 32N 134 45 E
Vyazma, Russia 50 D9 55 10N 34 15 E
Vyborg, Russia 48 B4 60 43N 28 47 E
Vychegda →, Russia 48 B8 61 18N 46 36 E
Vychodné Beskydy, Europe 31 B15 49 20N 22 0 E
Východočeský □, Czech. 30 A8 50 20N 15 45 E
Východoslovenský □, Slovak Rep. 31 C14 48 50N 21 0 E
Vyg-ozero, Russia 48 B5 63 30N 34 0 E
Vyksa, Russia 51 D13 55 19N 42 11 E
Vypin, India 83 J3 10 10N 76 15 E
Vyrnwy, L., U.K. 16 E4 52 48N 3 30W
Vyshniy Volochek, Russia 50 C9 57 30N 34 30 E
Vyshzha = imeni 26 Bakinskikh Komissarov, Turkmenistan 49 G9 39 22N 54 10 E
Vyškov, Czech. 31 B10 49 17N 17 0 E
Vysoké Mýto, Czech. 31 B9 49 58N 16 10 E
Vysokovsk, Russia 51 C10 56 22N 36 30 E
Vysotsk, Ukraine 50 F5 51 43N 26 32 E
Vyšší Brod, Czech. 30 C7 48 37N 14 19 E
Vytegra, Russia 48 B6 61 0N 36 27 E


## W


W.A.C. Bennett Dam, Canada 130 B4 56 2N 122 6W
Wa, Ghana 100 C4 10 7N 2 25W
Waal →, Neths. 20 E6 51 37N 5 0 E
Waalwijk, Neths. 21 E6 51 42N 5 4 E
Waarschoot, Belgium 21 F3 51 10N 3 36 E
Waasmunster, Belgium 21 F4 51 6N 4 5 E
Wabag, Papua N. G. 120 C2 5 32 S 143 40 E
Wabakimi L., Canada 128 B2 50 38N 89 45W
Wabana, Canada 129 C9 47 40N 53 0W
Wabao, C., N. Cal. 121 U21 21 35 S 167 53 E
Wabasca, Canada 130 B6 55 57N 113 56W
Wabash, U.S.A. 141 D11 40 48N 85 49W
Wabash →, U.S.A. 134 G1 37 48N 88 2W
Wabawng, Burma 78 B6 26 20N 97 25 E
Wabeno, U.S.A. 134 C1 45 26N 88 39W
Wabi →, Ethiopia 95 F5 7 45N 40 50 E
Wabigoon L., Canada 131 D10 49 44N 92 44W
Wabowden, Canada 131 C9 54 55N 98 38W
Wąbrzeźno, Poland 47 B5 53 16N 18 57 E
Wabu Hu, China 69 A11 32 20N 116 50 E
Wabuk Pt., Canada 128 A2 55 20N 85 5W
Wabush, Canada 129 B6 52 55N 66 52W
Wabuska, U.S.A. 142 G4 39 9N 119 11W
Wachtebeke, Belgium 21 F3 51 11N 3 52 E
Wächtersbach, Germany 27 E5 50 16N 9 18 E
Waco, U.S.A. 139 K6 31 33N 97 9W
Waconichi, L., Canada 128 B5 50 8N 74 0W
Wad Ban Naqa, Sudan 95 D3 16 32N 33 9 E
Wad Banda, Sudan 95 E2 13 10N 27 56 E
Wad el Haddad, Sudan 95 E3 13 50N 33 30 E
Wad en Nau, Sudan 95 E3 14 10N 33 34 E
Wad Hamid, Sudan 95 D3 16 30N 32 45 E
Wâd Medanî, Sudan 95 E3 14 28N 33 30 E
Wad Thana, Pakistan 79 D2 27 22N 66 23 E
Wadayama, Japan 62 B6 35 19N 134 52 E
Waddān, Libya 96 C3 29 9N 16 10 E
Waddān, Jabal, Libya 96 C3 29 0N 16 15 E
Waddeneilanden, Neths. 20 B6 53 25N 5 10 E
Waddenzee, Neths. 20 B6 53 6N 5 10 E
Wadderin Hill, Australia 113 F2 32 0 S 118 25 E
Waddington, U.S.A. 137 B9 44 52N 75 12W
Waddington, Mt., Canada 130 C3 51 23N 125 15W
Waddinxveen, Neths. 20 D5 52 2N 4 40 E
Waddy Pt., Australia 115 C5 24 58 S 153 21 E
Wadena, Canada 131 C8 51 57N 103 47W
Wadena, U.S.A. 138 B7 46 26N 95 8W
Wädenswil, Switz. 29 B7 47 14N 8 40 E
Wadesboro, U.S.A. 135 H5 34 58N 80 5W
Wadhams, Canada 130 C3 51 30N 127 30W
Wādī as Sīr, Jordan 91 D4 31 56N 35 49 E
Wādī ash Shāţi', Libya 96 C2 27 30N 15 0 E
Wādī Banī Walīd, Libya 96 B2 31 49N 14 0 E
Wadi Gemâl, Egypt 94 C4 24 35N 35 10 E
Wadi Halfa, Sudan 94 C3 21 53N 31 19 E
Wadian, China 69 A9 32 42N 112 29 E
Wadim, Oman 87 B7 22 40N 57 21 E
Wadlew, Poland 47 D6 51 31N 19 23 E
Wadowice, Poland 31 B12 49 52N 19 30 E
Wadsworth, U.S.A. 142 G4 39 38N 119 17W
Waegwan, S. Korea 67 G15 35 59N 128 23 E
Wafrah, Si. Arabia 84 D5 28 33N 47 56 E
Wagenberg, Neths. 21 E5 51 40N 4 46 E
Wageningen, Neths. 20 E7 51 58N 5 40 E
Wageningen, Surinam 153 B6 5 50N 56 50W
Wager B., Canada 127 B11 65 26N 88 40W
Wager Bay, Canada 127 B10 65 56N 90 49W
Wagga Wagga, Australia 117 C7 35 7 S 147 24 E
Waghete, Indonesia 73 B5 4 10 S 135 50 E
Wagin, Australia 113 F2 33 17 S 117 25 E
Wagon Mound, U.S.A. 139 G2 36 1N 104 42W
Wagoner, U.S.A. 139 G7 35 58N 95 22W
Wagrowiec, Poland 47 C4 52 48N 17 11 E
Wah, Pakistan 79 B4 33 45N 72 40 E
Wahai, Indonesia 73 B3 2 48 S 129 35 E
Waharoa, N.Z. 118 D4 37 46 S 175 45 E
Wahiawa, U.S.A. 132 H15 21 30N 158 2W
Wâḥid, Egypt 91 E1 30 48N 32 21 E
Wahnai, Afghan. 80 C1 32 40N 65 50 E
Wahoo, U.S.A. 138 E6 41 13N 96 37W
Wahpeton, U.S.A. 138 B6 46 16N 96 36W
Wahratta, Australia 116 A4 31 58 S 141 50 E
Wai, India 82 F1 17 56N 73 57 E
Wai, Koh, Cambodia 77 H4 9 55N 102 55 E
Waiai →, N.Z. 119 G2 46 12 S 167 38 E
Waiapu →, N.Z. 118 D7 37 47 S 178 29 E
Waiau, N.Z. 119 C8 42 39 S 173 5 E
Waiau →, N.Z. 119 C8 42 47 S 173 22 E
Waiawe Ganga →, Sri Lanka 83 L5 6 15N 81 0 E
Waibeem, Indonesia 73 B4 0 30 S 132 59 E
Waiblingen, Germany 27 G5 48 49N 9 20 E
Waidhofen, Niederösterreich, Austria 30 C8 48 49N 15 17 E
Waidhofen, Niederösterreich, Austria 30 D7 47 57N 14 46 E
Waigeo, Indonesia 73 B4 0 20 S 130 40 E
Waihao →, N.Z. 119 E6 44 52 S 171 11 E
Waihao Downs, N.Z. 119 E5 44 48 S 170 55 E
Waiheke I., N.Z. 118 C4 36 48 S 175 6 E
Waihi, N.Z. 118 D4 37 23 S 175 52 E
Waihola, N.Z. 119 G5 46 1 S 170 8 E
Waihola L., N.Z. 119 F5 45 59 S 170 8 E
Waihou →, N.Z. 118 D4 37 15 S 175 40 E
Waika, Zaïre 102 C5 2 22 S 25 42 E
Waikabubak, Indonesia 72 C1 9 45 S 119 25 E
Waikaia, N.Z. 119 F3 45 44 S 168 51 E
Waikaka, N.Z. 119 F4 45 55 S 169 1 E
Waikare, L., N.Z. 118 D4 37 26 S 175 13 E
Waikareiti, L., N.Z. 118 E6 38 43 S 177 10 E
Waikaremoana, N.Z. 118 E6 38 42 S 177 12 E
Waikaremoana L., N.Z. 118 E6 38 49 S 177 9 E
Waikari, N.Z. 119 C7 42 58 S 172 41 E
Waikato →, N.Z. 118 D3 37 23 S 174 43 E
Waikerie, Australia 116 C3 34 9 S 140 0 E
Waikiekie, N.Z. 118 B3 35 57 S 174 16 E
Waikokopu, N.Z. 118 F6 39 3 S 177 52 E
Waikouaiti, N.Z. 119 F5 45 36 S 170 41 E
Waikouaiti Downs, N.Z. 119 F5 45 30 S 170 30 E
Waimakariri →, N.Z. 119 D7 43 24 S 172 42 E
Waimangaroa, N.Z. 119 B6 41 43 S 171 46 E
Waimarie, N.Z. 119 B6 41 35 S 171 58 E
Waimate, N.Z. 119 E6 44 45 S 171 3 E
Waimea Plain, N.Z. 119 F3 45 55 S 168 35 E
Waimes, Belgium 21 H8 50 25N 6 7 E
Wainganga →, India 82 E4 18 50N 79 55 E
Waingapu, Indonesia 72 C2 9 35 S 120 11 E
Waingmaw, Burma 78 C6 25 21N 97 26 E
Waini →, Guyana 153 B6 8 20N 59 50W
Wainuiomata, N.Z. 118 H3 41 17 S 174 56 E
Wainwright, Canada 131 C6 52 50N 110 50W
Wainwright, U.S.A. 126 A3 70 38N 160 2W
Waiotapu, N.Z. 118 E5 38 21 S 176 25 E
Waiouru, N.Z. 118 F4 39 28 S 175 41 E
Waipa →, N.Z. 118 E4 38 16 S 175 21 E
Waipahi, N.Z. 119 G4 46 6 S 169 15 E
Waipapa Pt., N.Z. 119 G3 46 40 S 168 51 E
Waipara, N.Z. 119 D7 43 3 S 172 46 E
Waipawa, N.Z. 118 F5 39 56 S 176 38 E
Waipiro, N.Z. 118 E7 38 2 S 178 22 E
Waipu, N.Z. 118 B3 35 59 S 174 29 E
Waipukurau, N.Z. 118 G5 40 1 S 176 33 E
Wairakei, N.Z. 118 E5 38 37 S 176 6 E
Wairarapa, L., N.Z. 118 H4 41 14 S 175 15 E
Wairau →, N.Z. 119 B9 41 32 S 174 7 E
Wairio, N.Z. 119 F3 45 59 S 168 3 E
Wairoa, N.Z. 118 F6 39 3 S 177 25 E
Wairoa →, Hawke's Bay, N.Z. 118 F6 39 4 S 177 25 E
Wairoa →, Northland, N.Z. 118 C2 36 5 S 173 59 E
Waitaha, N.Z. 119 D5 43 0 S 170 45 E
Waitaki →, N.Z. 119 E6 44 56 S 171 7 E
Waitaki Plains, N.Z. 119 E5 44 22 S 170 0 E
Waitara, N.Z. 118 E3 38 59 S 174 15 E
Waitara →, N.Z. 118 E3 38 59 S 174 14 E
Waitchie, Australia 116 C5 35 22 S 143 8 E
Waitoa, N.Z. 118 D4 37 37 S 175 35 E
Waitotara, N.Z. 118 F3 39 49 S 174 44 E
Waitotara →, N.Z. 118 F3 39 51 S 174 41 E
Waitsburg, U.S.A. 142 C5 46 16N 118 9W
Waiuku, N.Z. 118 D3 37 15 S 174 45 E
Waiyevo, Fiji 121 A3 16 48 S 179 59W
Wajima, Japan 61 F8 37 30N 137 0 E
Wajir, Kenya 106 B5 1 42N 40 5 E
Wajir □, Kenya 106 B5 1 42N 40 20 E
Waka, Zaïre 102 B4 1 1N 20 13 E
Wakarusa, U.S.A. 141 C10 41 32N 86 1W
Wakasa, Japan 62 B6 35 20N 134 24 E
Wakasa-Wan, Japan 63 B7 35 40N 135 30 E
Wakatipu, L., N.Z. 119 F3 45 5 S 168 33 E
Wakaw, Canada 131 C7 52 39N 105 44W
Wakayama, Japan 63 C7 34 15N 135 15 E
Wakayama-ken □, Japan 63 D7 33 50N 135 30 E
Wake, Japan 62 C6 34 48N 134 8 E
Wake Forest, U.S.A. 135 H6 35 59N 78 30W
Wake I., Pac. Oc. 122 F8 19 18N 166 36 E
Wakefield, N.Z. 119 B8 41 24 S 173 5 E
Wakefield, U.K. 16 D6 53 41N 1 31W
Wakefield, Mass., U.S.A. 137 D13 42 30N 71 4W
Wakefield, Mich., U.S.A. 138 B10 46 29N 89 56W
Wakeham Bay = Maricourt, Canada 127 C12 56 34N 70 49W
Wakema, Burma 78 G5 16 30N 95 11 E
Wakkanai, Japan 60 B10 45 28N 141 35 E
Wakkerstroom, S. Africa 105 D5 27 24 S 30 10 E
Wakool, Australia 116 C6 35 28 S 144 23 E
Wakool →, Australia 116 C5 35 5 S 143 33 E
Wakre, Indonesia 73 B4 0 19 S 131 5 E
Waku, Papua N. G. 120 D5 6 5 S 149 9 E
Wakuach L., Canada 129 A6 55 34N 67 32W
Walamba, Zambia 107 E2 13 30 S 28 42 E
Wałbrzych, Poland 47 E3 50 45N 16 18 E
Walbury Hill, U.K. 17 F6 51 22N 1 28W
Walcha, Australia 117 A9 30 55 S 151 31 E
Walcha Road, Australia 117 A9 30 55 S 151 24 E
Walcheren, Neths. 21 E3 51 30N 3 35 E
Walcott, U.S.A. 142 F10 41 46N 106 51W
Wałcz, Poland 47 B3 53 17N 16 27 E
Wald, Switz. 29 B7 47 17N 8 56 E
Waldbröl, Germany 26 E3 50 52N 7 36 E
Waldburg Ra., Australia 112 D2 24 40 S 117 35 E
Waldeck, Germany 26 D5 51 12N 9 4 E
Walden, Colo., U.S.A. 142 F10 40 44N 106 17W
Walden, N.Y., U.S.A. 137 E10 41 34N 74 11W
Waldenburg, Switz. 28 B5 47 23N 7 45 E
Waldport, U.S.A. 142 D1 44 26N 124 4W
Waldron, U.S.A. 139 H7 34 54N 94 5W
Waldshut, Germany 27 H4 47 37N 8 12 E
Walembele, Ghana 100 C4 10 30N 1 58W
Walensee, Switz. 29 B8 47 7N 9 13 E
Walenstadt, Switz. 29 B8 47 8N 9 19 E
Wales □, U.K. 17 E4 52 30N 3 30W
Walewale, Ghana 101 C4 10 21N 0 50W
Walgett, Australia 115 E4 30 0 S 148 5 E
Walgreen Coast, Antarctica 7 D15 75 15 S 105 0W
Walhalla, Australia 117 D7 37 56 S 146 29 E
Walhalla, U.S.A. 131 D9 48 55N 97 55W
Walker, Minn., U.S.A. 138 B7 47 6N 94 35W
Walker, Mo., U.S.A. 140 G2 37 54N 94 14W
Walker L., Man., Canada 131 C9 54 42N 95 57W
Walker L., Qué., Canada 129 B6 50 20N 67 11W
Walker L., U.S.A. 142 G4 38 42N 118 43W
Walkerston, Australia 114 C4 21 11 S 149 8 E
Walkerton, Canada 136 B3 44 10N 81 10W
Walkerton, U.S.A. 141 C10 41 28N 86 29W
Wall, U.S.A. 138 C3 44 0N 102 8W
Walla Walla, Australia 117 C7 35 45 S 146 54 E
Walla Walla, U.S.A. 142 C4 46 4N 118 20W
Wallabadah, Australia 114 B3 17 57 S 142 15 E
Wallace, Idaho, U.S.A. 142 C6 47 28N 115 56W
Wallace, N.C., U.S.A. 135 H7 34 44N 77 59W
Wallace, Nebr., U.S.A. 138 E4 40 50N 101 10W
Wallaceburg, Canada 128 D3 42 34N 82 23W
Wallacetown, N.Z. 119 G3 46 21 S 168 19 E
Wallachia = Valahia, Romania 46 E5 44 35N 25 0 E
Wallal, Australia 115 D4 26 32 S 146 7 E
Wallal Downs, Australia 112 C3 19 47 S 120 40 E
Wallambin, L., Australia 113 F2 30 57 S 117 35 E
Wallaroo, Australia 116 B2 33 56 S 137 39 E
Wallasey, U.K. 16 D4 53 26N 3 2W
Walldürn, Germany 27 F5 49 34N 9 23 E
Wallerawang, Australia 117 B9 33 25 S 150 4 E
Wallhallow, Australia 114 B2 17 50 S 135 50 E
Wallingford, U.S.A. 137 E12 41 27N 72 50W
Wallis & Futuna, Is., Pac. Oc. 122 J10 13 18 S 176 10W
Wallisellen, Switz. 29 B7 47 25N 8 36 E
Wallowa, U.S.A. 142 D5 45 34N 117 32W
Wallowa Mts., U.S.A. 142 D5 45 20N 117 30W
Wallsend, Australia 117 B9 32 55 S 151 40 E
Wallsend, U.K. 16 C6 54 59N 1 30W
Wallula, U.S.A. 142 C4 46 5N 118 54W
Wallumbilla, Australia 115 D4 26 33 S 149 9 E
Walmsley, L., Canada 131 A7 63 25N 108 36W
Walney, I. of, U.K. 16 C4 54 5N 3 15W
Walnut, U.S.A. 140 C7 41 33N 89 36W
Walnut Creek, U.S.A. 144 H4 37 54N 122 4W
Walnut Ridge, U.S.A. 139 G9 36 4N 90 57W
Walpeup, Australia 116 C5 35 7 S 142 2 E
Walsall, U.K. 17 E6 52 36N 1 59W
Walsenburg, U.S.A. 139 G2 37 38N 104 47W
Walsh, U.S.A. 139 G3 37 23N 102 17W
Walsh →, Australia 114 B3 16 31 S 143 42 E
Walsh P.O., Australia 114 B3 16 40 S 144 0 E
Walshoutem, Belgium 21 G6 50 43N 5 4 E
Walsrode, Germany 26 C5 52 51N 9 37 E
Waltair, India 82 F6 17 44N 83 23 E
Walterboro, U.S.A. 135 J5 32 55N 80 40W
Walters, U.S.A. 139 H5 34 22N 98 19W
Waltershausen, Germany 26 E6 50 53N 10 33 E
Waltham, U.S.A. 137 D13 42 23N 71 14W
Waltham Station, Canada 128 C4 45 57N 76 57W
Waltman, U.S.A. 142 E10 43 4N 107 12W
Walton, Ky., U.S.A. 141 F12 38 52N 84 37W
Walton, N.Y., U.S.A. 137 D9 42 10N 75 8W
Waltonville, U.S.A. 140 F7 38 13N 89 2W
Walu, Burma 78 B7 26 28N 98 2 E
Walvisbaai, S. Africa 104 C1 23 0 S 14 28 E
Walwa, Australia 117 C7 35 59 S 147 44 E
Wamba, Kenya 106 B4 0 58N 37 19 E
Wamba, Zaïre 106 B2 2 10N 27 57 E
Wamego, U.S.A. 138 F6 39 12N 96 18W
Wamena, Indonesia 73 B5 4 4 S 138 57 E
Wamsasi, Indonesia 72 B3 3 27 S 126 7 E
Wan Hat, Burma 78 E6 20 14N 97 53 E
Wan Kinghao, Burma 78 E7 21 8N 98 17 E
Wan Lai-kam, Burma 78 E7 21 21N 98 22 E
Wan Tup, Burma 78 E7 21 13N 98 42 E
Wan Xian, China 66 E8 38 47N 115 7 E
Wana, Pakistan 79 B3 32 20N 69 32 E
Wanaaring, Australia 115 D3 29 38 S 144 9 E
Wanaka, N.Z. 119 E4 44 42 S 169 9 E
Wanaka L., N.Z. 119 E4 44 33 S 169 7 E
Wan'an, China 69 D10 26 26N 114 49 E
Wanapiri, Indonesia 73 B5 4 30 S 135 59 E
Wanapitei L., Canada 128 C3 46 45N 80 40W
Wanbi, Australia 116 C4 34 46 S 140 17 E
Wandaik, Guyana 153 C6 4 27N 59 35W
Wandandian, Australia 117 C9 35 6 S 150 30 E
Wandarrie, Australia 113 E2 27 50 S 117 52 E
Wanderer, Zimbabwe 107 F3 19 36 S 30 1 E
Wandoan, Australia 115 D4 26 5 S 149 55 E
Wandre, Belgium 21 G7 50 40N 5 39 E
Wanfercée-Baulet, Belgium 21 H5 50 28N 4 35 E
Wanfu, China 67 D12 40 8N 122 38 E
Wang →, Thailand 76 D2 17 8N 99 2 E
Wang Kai, Sudan 95 F2 9 3N 29 23 E
Wang Noi, Thailand 76 E3 14 13N 100 44 E
Wang Saphung, Thailand 76 D3 17 18N 101 46 E
Wang Thong, Thailand 76 D3 16 50N 100 26 E
Wanga, Zaïre 106 B2 2 58N 29 12 E
Wangal, Indonesia 73 C4 6 8 S 134 9 E
Wanganella, Australia 117 C6 35 6 S 144 49 E
Wanganui, N.Z. 118 F4 39 56 S 175 3 E
Wanganui →, W. Coast, N.Z. 119 D5 43 3 S 170 26 E
Wanganui →, Wanganui-Manawatu, N.Z. 118 F4 39 55 S 175 4 E
Wangaratta, Australia 117 D7 36 21 S 146 19 E
Wangary, Australia 115 E2 34 35 S 135 29 E
Wangcang, China 68 A6 32 18N 106 20 E
Wangdu, China 66 E8 38 40N 115 7 E
Wangdu Phodrang, Bhutan 78 B2 27 28N 89 54 E
Wangerooge, Germany 26 B3 53 47N 7 52 E
Wangi, Kenya 106 C5 1 58 S 40 58 E
Wangiwangi, Indonesia 72 C2 5 22 S 123 37 E
Wangjiang, China 69 B11 30 10N 116 42 E
Wangmo, China 68 E6 25 11N 106 5 E
Wangqing, China 67 C15 43 12N 129 42 E
Wankaner, India 80 H4 22 35N 71 0 E
Wanless, Canada 131 C8 54 11N 101 21W
Wannian, China 69 C11 28 42N 117 4 E
Wanon Niwat, Thailand 76 D4 17 38N 103 46 E
Wanquan, China 66 D8 40 50N 114 40 E
Wanrong, China 66 G6 35 25N 110 50 E
Wanshan, China 68 D7 27 30N 109 12 E
Wanshengchang, China 68 C6 28 57N 106 53 E
Wanssum, Neths. 21 E8 51 32N 6 5 E
Wanstead, N.Z. 118 G5 40 8 S 176 30 E
Wanxian, China 68 B7 30 42N 108 20 E
Wanyin, Burma 78 E6 20 23N 97 15 E
Wanyuan, China 68 A7 32 4N 108 3 E
Wanzai, China 69 C10 28 7N 114 30 E
Wanze, Belgium 21 G6 50 32N 5 13 E
Wapakoneta, U.S.A. 141 D12 40 34N 84 12W
Wapato, U.S.A. 142 C3 46 27N 120 25W
Wapawekka L., Canada 131 C8 54 55N 104 40W
Wapello, U.S.A. 140 C5 41 11N 91 11W
Wapikopa L., Canada 128 B2 52 56N 87 53W
Wappingers Falls, U.S.A. 137 E11 41 36N 73 55W
Wapsipinicon →, U.S.A. 140 C6 41 44N 90 19W
Warabi, Japan 63 B11 35 49N 139 41 E
Warangal, India 82 F4 17 58N 79 35 E
Waratah, Australia 114 G4 41 30 S 145 30 E
Waratah B., Australia 115 F4 38 54 S 146 5 E
Warburg, Germany 26 D5 51 29N 9 10 E
Warburton, Vic., Australia 117 D6 37 47 S 145 42 E
Warburton, W. Austral., Australia 113 E4 26 8 S 126 35 E
Warburton Ra., Australia 113 E4 25 55 S 126 28 E
Ward, N.Z. 119 B9 41 49 S 174 11 E
Ward →, Australia 115 D4 26 28 S 146 6 E
Ward Cove, U.S.A. 130 B2 55 25N 132 43W
Ward Hunt, C., Papua N. G. 120 E5 8 2 S 148 10 E
Ward Hunt Str., Papua N. G. 120 E6 9 30 S 150 0 E
Ward Mt., U.S.A. 144 H8 37 12N 118 54W
Warden, S. Africa 105 D4 27 50 S 29 0 E
Wardha, India 82 D4 20 45N 78 39 E
Wardlow, Canada 130 C6 50 56N 111 31W
Wards River, Australia 117 B9 32 11 S 151 56 E
Ware, Canada 130 B3 57 26N 125 41W
Ware, U.S.A. 137 D12 42 16N 72 14W
Waregem, Belgium 21 G2 50 53N 3 27 E
Wareham, U.S.A. 137 E14 41 46N 70 43W
Waremme, Belgium 21 G6 50 43N 5 15 E
Waren, Germany 26 B8 53 30N 12 41 E
Warendorf, Germany 26 D3 51 57N 7 57 E
Warialda, Australia 115 D5 29 29 S 150 33 E
Wariap, Indonesia 73 B4 1 30 S 134 5 E
Warin Chamrap, Thailand 76 E5 15 12N 104 53 E
Warka, Poland 47 D8 51 47N 21 12 E
Warkopi, Indonesia 73 B4 1 12 S 134 9 E
Warkworth, N.Z. 118 C3 36 24 S 174 41 E
Warley, U.K. 17 E6 52 30N 1 58W
Warm Springs, U.S.A. 143 G5 38 10N 116 20W
Warman, Canada 131 C7 52 19N 106 30W
Warmbad, Namibia 104 D2 28 25 S 18 42 E
Warmbad, S. Africa 105 C4 24 51 S 28 19 E
Warmenhuizen, Neths. 20 C5 52 43N 4 44 E
Warmeriville, France 23 C11 49 20N 4 13 E
Warmond, Neths. 20 D5 52 12N 4 30 E
Warnambool Downs, Australia 114 C3 22 48 S 142 52 E
Warnemünde, Germany 26 A8 54 9N 12 5 E
Warner, Canada 130 D6 49 17N 112 12W
Warner Mts., U.S.A. 142 F3 41 40N 120 15W
Warner Robins, U.S.A. 135 J4 32 37N 83 36W
Warnes, Bolivia 157 D5 17 30 S 63 10W
Warneton, Belgium 21 G1 50 45N 2 57 E
Warnow →, Germany 26 A8 54 6N 12 9 E
Warnsveld, Neths. 20 D8 52 8N 6 14 E
Waroona, Australia 113 F2 32 50 S 115 58 E

**West Point 283**


Warora, *India* **82 D4** 20 14N 79 1 E
Warracknabeal, *Australia* **116 D5** 36 9 S 142 26 E
Warragul, *Australia* **117 E6** 38 10 S 145 58 E
Warrawagine, *Australia* **112 D3** 20 51 S 120 42 E
Warrego →, *Australia* **115 E4** 30 24 S 145 21 E
Warrego Ra., *Australia* **114 C4** 24 58 S 146 0 E
Warren, *Australia* **117 A7** 31 42 S 147 51 E
Warren, *Ark., U.S.A.* **139 J8** 33 37N 92 4W
Warren, *Ill., U.S.A.* **140 B7** 42 29N 90 0W
Warren, *Mich., U.S.A.* **141 B13** 42 30N 83 0W
Warren, *Minn., U.S.A.* **138 A6** 48 12N 96 46W
Warren, *Ohio, U.S.A.* **136 E4** 41 14N 80 49W
Warren, *Pa., U.S.A.* **136 E5** 41 51N 79 9W
Warrenpoint, *U.K.* **19 B5** 54 7N 6 15W
Warrensburg, *Ill., U.S.A.* **140 E7** 39 56N 89 4W
Warrensburg, *Mo., U.S.A.* **138 F8** 38 46N 93 44W
Warrenton, *S. Africa* **104 D3** 28 9 S 24 47 E
Warrenton, *Mo., U.S.A.* **140 F5** 38 49N 91 9W
Warrenton, *Oreg., U.S.A.* **144 D3** 46 10N 123 56W
Warrenville, *Australia* **115 D4** 25 48 S 147 22 E
Warri, *Nigeria* **101 D6** 5 30N 5 41 E
Warrina, *Australia* **115 D2** 28 12 S 135 50 E
Warrington, *N.Z.* **119 F5** 45 43 S 170 35 E
Warrington, *U.K.* **16 D5** 53 25N 2 38W
Warrington, *U.S.A.* **135 K2** 30 23N 87 17W
Warrnambool, *Australia* **116 E5** 38 25 S 142 30 E
Warroad, *U.S.A.* **138 A7** 48 54N 95 19W
Warsa, *Indonesia* **73 B5** 0 47 S 135 55 E
Warsaw = Warszawa, *Poland* **47 C8** 52 13N 21 0 E
Warsaw, *Ill., U.S.A.* **140 D5** 40 22N 91 26W
Warsaw, *Ind., U.S.A.* **141 C11** 41 14N 85 51W
Warsaw, *Ky., U.S.A.* **141 F12** 38 47N 84 54W
Warsaw, *Mo., U.S.A.* **140 F3** 38 15N 93 23W
Warsaw, *N.Y., U.S.A.* **136 D6** 42 45N 78 8W
Warsaw, *Ohio, U.S.A.* **136 F2** 40 20N 82 0W
Warstein, *Germany* **26 D4** 51 26N 8 20 E
Warszawa, *Poland* **47 C8** 52 13N 21 0 E
Warszawa □, *Poland* **47 C7** 52 30N 21 0 E
Warta, *Poland* **47 D5** 51 43N 18 38 E
Warta →, *Poland* **47 C1** 52 35N 14 39 E
Warthe = Warta →, *Poland* **47 C1** 52 35N 14 39 E
Waru, *Indonesia* **73 B4** 3 30 S 130 36 E
Warud, *India* **82 D4** 21 30N 78 16 E
Warwick, *Australia* **115 D5** 28 10 S 152 1 E
Warwick, *U.K.* **17 E6** 52 17N 1 36W
Warwick, *U.S.A.* **137 E13** 41 42N 71 28W
Warwickshire □, *U.K.* **17 E6** 52 20N 1 30W
Wasaga Beach, *Canada* **136 B4** 44 31N 80 1W
Wasatch Ra., *U.S.A.* **142 F8** 40 30N 111 15W
Wasbank, *S. Africa* **105 D5** 28 15 S 30 9 E
Wasco, *Calif., U.S.A.* **145 K7** 35 36N 119 20W
Wasco, *Oreg., U.S.A.* **142 D3** 45 36N 120 42W
Waseca, *U.S.A.* **138 C8** 44 5N 93 30W
Wasekamio L., *Canada* **131 B7** 56 45N 108 45W
Wash, The, *U.K.* **16 E8** 52 58N 0 20 E
Washago, *Canada* **136 B5** 44 45N 79 20W
Washburn, *Ill., U.S.A.* **140 D7** 40 55N 89 17W
Washburn, *N. Dak., U.S.A.* **138 B4** 47 17N 101 2W
Washburn, *Wis., U.S.A.* **138 B9** 46 40N 90 54W
Washim, *India* **82 D3** 20 3N 77 0 E
Washington, *D.C., U.S.A.* **134 F7** 38 54N 77 2W
Washington, *Ga., U.S.A.* **135 J4** 33 44N 82 44W
Washington, *Ind., U.S.A.* **141 F9** 38 40N 87 10W
Washington, *Iowa, U.S.A.* **140 C5** 41 18N 91 42W
Washington, *Mo., U.S.A.* **140 F5** 38 33N 91 1W
Washington, *N.C., U.S.A.* **135 H7** 35 33N 77 3W
Washington, *N.J., U.S.A.* **137 F10** 40 46N 74 59W
Washington, *Pa., U.S.A.* **136 F4** 40 10N 80 15W
Washington, *Utah, U.S.A.* **143 H7** 37 8N 113 31W
Washington □, *U.S.A.* **142 C3** 47 30N 120 30W
Washington, Mt., *U.S.A.* **137 B13** 44 16N 71 18W
Washington Court House, *U.S.A.* **141 E13** 39 32N 83 26W
Washington I., *U.S.A.* **134 C2** 45 23N 86 54W
Washougal, *U.S.A.* **144 E4** 45 35N 122 21W
Washuk, *Pakistan* **79 D2** 27 42N 64 45 E
Wasian, *Indonesia* **73 B4** 1 47 S 133 19 E
Wasilków, *Poland* **47 B10** 53 12N 23 13 E
Wasior, *Indonesia* **73 B4** 2 43 S 134 30 E
Waskaiowaka, L., *Canada* **131 B9** 56 33N 96 23W
Waskesiu Lake, *Canada* **131 C7** 53 55N 106 5W
Wasmes, *Belgium* **21 H3** 50 25N 3 50 E
Waspik, *Neths.* **21 E5** 51 41N 4 57 E
Wassen, *Switz.* **29 C7** 46 42N 8 36 E
Wassenaar, *Neths.* **20 D4** 52 8N 4 24 E
Wasserburg, *Germany* **27 G8** 48 4N 12 15 E
Wasserkuppe, *Germany* **26 E5** 50 30N 9 56 E
Wassy, *France* **23 D11** 48 30N 4 58 E
Waswanipi, *Canada* **128 C4** 49 40N 76 29W
Waswanipi, L., *Canada* **128 C4** 49 35N 76 40W
Watangpone, *Indonesia* **72 B2** 4 29 S 120 25 E
Watansoppeng, *Indonesia* **72 B1** 4 10 S 119 56 E
Water Park Pt., *Australia* **114 C5** 22 56 S 150 47 E
Water Valley, *U.S.A.* **139 H10** 34 10N 89 38W
Waterberge, *S. Africa* **105 C4** 24 10 S 28 0 E
Waterbury, *Conn., U.S.A.* **137 E11** 41 33N 73 3W
Waterbury, *Vt., U.S.A.* **137 B12** 44 20N 72 46W
Waterbury L., *Canada* **131 B8** 58 10N 104 22W
Waterdown, *Canada* **136 C5** 43 20N 79 53W
Waterford, *Canada* **136 D4** 42 56N 80 17W
Waterford, *Ireland* **19 D4** 52 16N 7 8W
Waterford, *Calif., U.S.A.* **144 H6** 37 38N 120 46W
Waterford, *Wis., U.S.A.* **141 B8** 42 46N 88 13W
Waterford □, *Ireland* **19 D4** 52 10N 7 40W
Waterford Harbour, *Ireland* **19 D5** 52 10N 6 58W
Waterhen L., *Man., Canada* **131 C9** 52 10N 99 40W
Waterhen L., *Sask., Canada* **131 C7** 54 28N 108 25W
Wateringen, *Neths.* **20 D4** 52 2N 4 16 E
Waterloo, *Belgium* **21 G4** 50 43N 4 25 E
Waterloo, *Ont., Canada* **128 D3** 43 30N 80 32W
Waterloo, *Qué., Canada* **137 A12** 45 22N 72 32W
Waterloo, *S. Leone* **100 D2** 8 26N 13 8W
Waterloo, *Ill., U.S.A.* **140 F6** 38 20N 90 9W
Waterloo, *Ind., U.S.A.* **141 C11** 41 26N 85 1W
Waterloo, *Iowa, U.S.A.* **140 B4** 42 30N 92 21W
Waterloo, *N.Y., U.S.A.* **136 D8** 42 54N 76 52W
Waterloo, *Wis., U.S.A.* **140 A8** 43 11N 88 59W
Waterman, *U.S.A.* **141 C8** 41 46N 88 47W
Watermeal-Boitsford, *Belgium* **21 G4** 50 48N 4 25 E
Watersmeet, *U.S.A.* **138 B10** 46 16N 89 11W
Waterton-Glacier International Peace Park, *U.S.A.* **142 B7** 48 45N 115 0W
Watertown, *Conn., U.S.A.* **137 E11** 41 36N 73 7W
Watertown, *N.Y., U.S.A.* **137 C9** 43 59N 75 55W
Watertown, *S. Dak., U.S.A.* **138 C6** 44 54N 97 7W
Watertown, *Wis., U.S.A.* **138 D10** 43 12N 88 43W
Waterval-Boven, *S. Africa* **105 D5** 25 40 S 30 18 E
Waterville, *Canada* **137 A13** 45 16N 71 54W
Waterville, *Maine, U.S.A.* **129 D6** 44 33N 69 38W
Waterville, *N.Y., U.S.A.* **137 D9** 42 56N 75 23W
Waterville, *Pa., U.S.A.* **136 E7** 41 19N 77 21W
Waterville, *Wash., U.S.A.* **142 C3** 47 39N 120 4W
Watervliet, *Belgium* **21 F3** 51 17N 3 38 E
Watervliet, *Mich., U.S.A.* **141 B10** 42 11N 86 18W
Watervliet, *N.Y., U.S.A.* **137 D11** 42 44N 73 42W
Wates, *Indonesia* **75 D4** 7 51 S 110 10 E
Watford, *Canada* **136 D3** 42 57N 81 53W
Watford, *U.K.* **17 F7** 51 38N 0 23W
Watford City, *U.S.A.* **138 B3** 47 48N 103 17W
Wathaman →, *Canada* **131 B8** 57 16N 102 59W
Watheroo, *Australia* **113 F2** 30 15 S 116 0 E
Wating, *China* **66 G4** 35 40N 106 38 E
Watkins Glen, *U.S.A.* **136 D8** 42 23N 76 52W
Watling I. = San Salvador, *Bahamas* **149 B5** 24 0N 74 40W
Watonga, *U.S.A.* **139 H5** 35 51N 98 25W
Watou, *Belgium* **21 G1** 50 51N 2 38 E
Watrous, *Canada* **131 C7** 51 40N 105 25W
Watrous, *U.S.A.* **139 H2** 35 48N 104 59W
Watsa, *Zaïre* **106 B2** 3 4N 29 30 E
Watseka, *U.S.A.* **141 D9** 40 47N 87 44W
Watson, *Australia* **113 F5** 30 29 S 131 31 E
Watson, *Canada* **131 C8** 52 10N 104 30W
Watson Lake, *Canada* **130 A3** 60 6N 128 49W
Watsonville, *U.S.A.* **144 J5** 36 55N 121 45W
Wattenwil, *Switz.* **28 C5** 46 46N 7 30 E
Wattiwarriganna Cr. →, *Australia* **115 D2** 28 57 S 136 10 E
Wattwil, *Switz.* **29 B8** 47 18N 9 6 E
Watuata = Batuata, *Indonesia* **72 C2** 6 12 S 122 42 E
Watubela, Kepulauan, *Indonesia* **73 B4** 4 28 S 131 35 E
Watubela Is. = Watubela, Kepulauan, *Indonesia* **73 B4** 4 28 S 131 35 E
Wau, *Papua N. G.* **120 D4** 7 21 S 146 47 E
Waubach, *Neths.* **21 G8** 50 55N 6 3 E
Waubamik, *Canada* **136 A4** 45 27N 80 1W
Waubay, *U.S.A.* **138 C6** 45 20N 97 18W
Waubra, *Australia* **116 D5** 37 21 S 143 39 E
Wauchope, *Australia* **117 A10** 31 28 S 152 45 E
Wauchula, *U.S.A.* **135 M5** 27 33N 81 49W
Waugh, *Canada* **131 D9** 49 40N 95 11W
Waukarlycarly, L., *Australia* **112 D3** 21 18 S 121 56 E
Waukegan, *U.S.A.* **141 B9** 42 22N 87 50W
Waukesha, *U.S.A.* **141 B8** 43 1N 88 14W
Waukon, *U.S.A.* **138 D9** 43 16N 91 29W
Wauneta, *U.S.A.* **138 E4** 40 25N 101 23W
Waupaca, *U.S.A.* **138 C10** 44 21N 89 5W
Waupun, *U.S.A.* **138 D10** 43 38N 88 44W
Waurika, *U.S.A.* **139 H6** 34 10N 98 0W
Wausau, *U.S.A.* **138 C10** 44 58N 89 38W
Wauseon, *U.S.A.* **141 C12** 41 33N 84 8W
Wautoma, *U.S.A.* **138 C10** 44 4N 89 18W
Wauwatosa, *U.S.A.* **141 A9** 43 3N 88 0W
Wave Hill, *Australia* **112 C5** 17 32 S 131 0 E
Waveland, *U.S.A.* **141 E9** 39 53N 87 3W
Waveney →, *U.K.* **17 E9** 52 24N 1 20 E
Waverley, *N.Z.* **118 F3** 39 46 S 174 37 E
Waverly, *Ill., U.S.A.* **140 E7** 39 36N 89 57W
Waverly, *Iowa, U.S.A.* **140 B4** 42 44N 92 29W
Waverly, *Mo., U.S.A.* **140 E3** 39 13N 93 31W
Waverly, *N.Y., U.S.A.* **137 D8** 42 1N 76 32W
Wavre, *Belgium* **21 G5** 50 43N 4 38 E
Wavreille, *Belgium* **21 H6** 50 7N 5 15 E
Wâw, *Sudan* **95 F2** 7 45N 28 1 E
Wāw al Kabīr, *Libya* **96 C3** 25 20N 16 43 E
Wāw an Nāmūs, *Libya* **96 D3** 24 55N 17 46 E
Wawa, *Canada* **128 C3** 47 59N 84 47W
Wawa, *Nigeria* **101 D5** 9 54N 4 27 E
Wawa, *Sudan* **94 C3** 20 30N 30 22 E
Wawanesa, *Canada* **131 D9** 49 36N 99 40W
Wawasee, L., *U.S.A.* **141 C11** 41 24N 85 42W
Wawoi →, *Papua N. G.* **120 D2** 7 48 S 143 16 E
Wawona, *U.S.A.* **144 H7** 37 32N 119 39W
Waxahachie, *U.S.A.* **139 J6** 32 24N 96 51W
Way, L., *Australia* **113 E3** 26 45 S 120 16 E
Wayabula Rau, *Indonesia* **72 A3** 2 29N 128 17 E
Wayatinah, *Australia* **114 G4** 42 19 S 146 27 E
Waycross, *U.S.A.* **135 K4** 31 13N 82 21W
Wayi, *Sudan* **95 F3** 5 8N 30 10 E
Wayland, *U.S.A.* **141 B11** 42 40N 85 39W
Wayne, *Nebr., U.S.A.* **138 D6** 42 14N 97 1W
Wayne, *W. Va., U.S.A.* **134 F4** 38 13N 82 27W
Wayne City, *U.S.A.* **141 F8** 38 21N 88 35W
Waynesboro, *Ga., U.S.A.* **135 J4** 33 6N 82 1W
Waynesboro, *Miss., U.S.A.* **135 K1** 31 40N 88 39W
Waynesboro, *Pa., U.S.A.* **134 F7** 39 45N 77 35W
Waynesboro, *Va., U.S.A.* **134 F6** 38 4N 78 53W
Waynesburg, *U.S.A.* **134 F5** 39 54N 80 11W
Waynesville, *Mo., U.S.A.* **140 G4** 37 50N 92 12W
Waynesville, *N.C., U.S.A.* **135 H4** 35 28N 82 58W
Waynesville, *Ohio, U.S.A.* **141 E12** 39 32N 84 5W
Waynoka, *U.S.A.* **139 G5** 36 35N 98 53W
Wazay, *Afghan.* **79 B3** 33 22N 69 26 E
Wāzin, *Libya* **96 B2** 31 58N 10 40 E
Wazirabad, *Pakistan* **80 C6** 32 30N 74 8 E
Wda →, *Poland* **47 B5** 53 25N 18 29 E
We, *Indonesia* **74 A1** 5 51N 95 18 E
Weald, The, *U.K.* **17 F8** 51 7N 0 29 E
Wear →, *U.K.* **16 C6** 54 55N 1 22W
Weatherford, *Okla., U.S.A.* **139 H5** 35 32N 98 43W
Weatherford, *Tex., U.S.A.* **139 J6** 32 46N 97 48W
Weaubleau, *U.S.A.* **140 G3** 37 54N 93 32W
Weaverville, *U.S.A.* **142 F2** 40 44N 122 56W
Webb City, *U.S.A.* **139 G7** 37 9N 94 28W
Weber, *N.Z.* **118 G5** 40 24 S 176 20 E
Webo = Nyaake, *Liberia* **100 E3** 4 52N 7 37W
Webster, *Mass., U.S.A.* **137 D13** 42 3N 71 53W
Webster, *N.Y., U.S.A.* **136 C7** 43 13N 77 26W
Webster, *S. Dak., U.S.A.* **138 C6** 45 20N 97 31W
Webster, *Wis., U.S.A.* **138 C8** 45 53N 92 22W
Webster City, *U.S.A.* **140 B3** 42 28N 93 49W
Webster Green, *U.S.A.* **138 F9** 38 38N 90 20W
Webster Springs, *U.S.A.* **134 F5** 38 29N 80 25W
Weda, *Indonesia* **72 A3** 0 21N 127 50 E
Weda, Teluk, *Indonesia* **72 A3** 0 30N 127 50 E
Weddell I., *Falk. Is.* **160 D4** 51 50 S 61 0W
Weddell Sea, *Antarctica* **7 D1** 72 30 S 40 0W
Wedderburn, *Australia* **116 D5** 36 26 S 143 33 E
Wedgeport, *Canada* **129 D6** 43 44N 65 59W
Wedza, *Zimbabwe* **107 F3** 18 40 S 31 33 E
Wee Elwah, *Australia* **117 B6** 33 2 S 145 14 E
Wee Waa, *Australia* **115 E4** 30 11 S 149 26 E
Weed, *U.S.A.* **142 F2** 41 25N 122 23W
Weed Heights, *U.S.A.* **144 G7** 38 59N 119 13W
Weedsport, *U.S.A.* **137 C8** 43 3N 76 35W
Weedville, *U.S.A.* **136 E6** 41 17N 78 30W
Weemelah, *Australia* **115 D4** 29 2 S 149 15 E
Weenen, *S. Africa* **105 D5** 28 48 S 30 7 E
Weener, *Germany* **26 B3** 53 10N 7 23 E
Weert, *Neths.* **21 F7** 51 15N 5 43 E
Weesp, *Neths.* **20 D6** 52 18N 5 2 E
Weggis, *Switz.* **29 B6** 47 2N 8 26 E
Wegierska-Gorka, *Poland* **31 B12** 49 36N 19 7 E
Wegliniec, *Poland* **47 D2** 51 18N 15 10 E
Węgorzewo, *Poland* **47 A8** 54 13N 21 43 E
Węgrów, *Poland* **47 C9** 52 24N 22 0 E
Wehl, *Neths.* **20 E8** 51 58N 6 13 E
Wei He →, *Hebei, China* **66 F8** 36 10N 115 45 E
Wei He →, *Shaanxi, China* **66 G6** 34 38N 110 15 E
Weichang, *China* **67 D9** 41 58N 117 49 E
Weichuan, *China* **66 G7** 34 20N 113 59 E
Weida, *Germany* **26 E8** 50 47N 12 3 E
Weiden, *Germany* **27 F8** 49 40N 12 10 E
Weifang, *China* **65 C6** 36 47N 119 10 E
Weifang, *Shandong, China* **67 F10** 36 44N 119 7 E
Weihai, *China* **67 F12** 37 30N 122 6 E
Weilburg, *Germany* **26 E4** 50 28N 8 17 E
Weilheim, *Germany* **27 H7** 47 50N 11 9 E
Weimar, *Germany* **26 E7** 51 0N 11 20 E
Weinan, *China* **66 G5** 34 31N 109 29 E
Weinfelden, *Switz.* **29 A8** 47 34N 9 6 E
Weingarten, *Germany* **27 H5** 47 49N 9 39 E
Weinheim, *Germany* **27 F4** 49 33N 8 40 E
Weining, *China* **68 D5** 26 50N 104 17 E
Weipa, *Australia* **114 A3** 12 40 S 141 50 E
Weir →, *Australia* **115 D4** 28 20 S 149 50 E
Weir →, *Canada* **131 B10** 56 54N 93 21W
Weir River, *Canada* **131 B10** 56 49N 94 6W
Weirton, *U.S.A.* **136 F4** 40 24N 80 35W
Weisen, *Switz.* **29 C9** 46 42N 9 43 E
Weiser, *U.S.A.* **142 D5** 44 10N 117 0W
Weishan, *Shandong, China* **67 G9** 34 47N 117 5 E
Weishan, *Yunnan, China* **68 E3** 25 12N 100 20 E
Weissenburg, *Germany* **27 F6** 49 2N 10 58 E
Weissenfels, *Germany* **26 D8** 51 11N 12 0 E
Weisshorn, *Switz.* **28 D5** 46 7N 7 43 E
Weissmies, *Switz.* **28 D6** 46 8N 8 1 E
Weisstannen, *Switz.* **29 C8** 46 59N 9 22 E
Weisswasser, *Germany* **26 D10** 51 30N 14 36 E
Weiswampach, *Belgium* **21 H8** 50 8N 6 5 E
Wéitra, *Austria* **30 C7** 48 41N 14 54 E
Weixi, *China* **68 D2** 27 10N 99 10 E
Weixin, *China* **68 D5** 27 48N 105 3 E
Weiyuan, *China* **66 G3** 35 7N 104 10 E
Weiz, *Austria* **30 D8** 47 13N 15 39 E
Weizhou Dao, *China* **68 G7** 21 0N 109 5 E
Wejherowo, *Poland* **47 A5** 54 35N 18 12 E
Wekusko L., *Canada* **131 C9** 54 40N 99 50W
Welbourn Hill, *Australia* **115 D1** 27 21 S 134 6 E
Welch, *U.S.A.* **134 G5** 37 26N 81 35W
Weldya, *Ethiopia* **95 E4** 11 50N 39 34 E
Welega □, *Ethiopia* **95 F3** 9 25N 34 20 E
Welkenraedt, *Belgium* **21 G7** 50 39N 5 58 E
Welkite, *Ethiopia* **95 F4** 8 15N 37 42 E
Welkom, *S. Africa* **104 D4** 28 0 S 26 46 E
Welland, *Canada* **128 D4** 43 0N 79 15W
Welland →, *U.K.* **16 E7** 52 43N 0 10W
Wellen, *Belgium* **21 G6** 50 50N 5 21 E
Wellesley Is., *Australia* **114 B2** 16 42 S 139 30 E
Wellin, *Belgium* **21 H6** 50 5N 5 6 E
Wellingborough, *U.K.* **17 E7** 52 18N 0 41W
Wellington, *Australia* **117 B8** 32 35 S 148 59 E
Wellington, *Canada* **128 D4** 43 57N 77 20W
Wellington, *N.Z.* **118 H3** 41 19 S 174 46 E
Wellington, *S. Africa* **104 E2** 33 38 S 19 1 E
Wellington, *Shrops., U.K.* **16 E5** 52 42N 2 31W
Wellington, *Somst., U.K.* **17 G4** 50 58N 3 13W
Wellington, *Colo., U.S.A.* **138 E2** 40 42N 105 0W
Wellington, *Kans., U.S.A.* **139 G6** 37 16N 97 24W
Wellington, *Mo., U.S.A.* **140 E3** 39 8N 93 59W
Wellington, *Nev., U.S.A.* **144 G7** 38 45N 119 23W
Wellington, *Ohio, U.S.A.* **136 E2** 41 10N 82 13W
Wellington, *Tex., U.S.A.* **139 H4** 34 51N 100 13W
Wellington □, *N.Z.* **118 G4** 41 0 S 175 30 E
Wellington, I., *Chile* **160 C2** 49 30 S 75 0W
Wellington, L., *Australia* **117 E7** 38 6 S 147 20 E
Wells, *Norfolk, U.K.* **16 E8** 52 57N 0 51 E
Wells, *Somst., U.K.* **17 F5** 51 12N 2 39W
Wells, *Maine, U.S.A.* **137 C14** 43 20N 70 35W
Wells, *Minn., U.S.A.* **138 D8** 43 45N 93 44W
Wells, *Nev., U.S.A.* **142 F6** 41 7N 114 58W
Wells, L., *Australia* **113 E3** 26 44 S 123 15 E
Wells Gray Prov. Park, *Canada* **130 C4** 52 30N 120 15W
Wells River, *U.S.A.* **137 B12** 44 9N 72 4W
Wellsboro, *U.S.A.* **136 E7** 41 45N 77 18W
Wellsburg, *U.S.A.* **136 F4** 40 16N 80 37W
Wellsford, *N.Z.* **118 C3** 36 16 S 174 32 E
Wellsville, *Mo., U.S.A.* **140 E5** 39 4N 91 34W
Wellsville, *N.Y., U.S.A.* **136 D7** 42 7N 77 57W
Wellsville, *Ohio, U.S.A.* **136 F4** 40 36N 80 39W
Wellsville, *Utah, U.S.A.* **142 F8** 41 38N 111 56W
Wellton, *U.S.A.* **143 K6** 32 40N 114 8W
Welmel, Wabi →, *Ethiopia* **95 F5** 5 38N 40 47 E
Wełna →, *Poland* **47 C4** 52 46N 17 32 E
Welo, *Somali Rep.* **108 C3** 9 25N 48 55 E
Welo □, *Ethiopia* **95 E4** 11 50N 39 48 E
Wels, *Austria* **30 C7** 48 9N 14 1 E
Welshpool, *U.K.* **17 E4** 52 40N 3 9W
Wem, *U.K.* **16 E5** 52 52N 2 45W
Wembere →, *Tanzania* **106 C3** 4 10 S 34 15 E
Wemmel, *Belgium* **21 G4** 50 55N 4 18 E
Wen Xian, *Gansu, China* **66 H3** 32 43N 104 36 E
Wen Xian, *Henan, China* **66 G7** 34 55N 113 5 E
Wenatchee, *U.S.A.* **142 C3** 47 25N 120 19W
Wenchang, *China* **76 C8** 19 38N 110 42 E
Wencheng, *China* **69 D13** 27 46N 120 4 E
Wenchi, *Ghana* **100 D4** 7 46N 2 8W
Wenchow = Wenzhou, *China* **69 C13** 28 0N 120 38 E
Wenchuan, *China* **68 B4** 31 22N 103 35 E
Wendell, *U.S.A.* **142 E6** 42 47N 114 42W
Wenden, *U.S.A.* **145 M13** 33 49N 113 33W
Wendeng, *China* **67 F12** 37 15N 122 5 E
Wendesi, *Indonesia* **73 B4** 2 30 S 134 17 E
Wendo, *Ethiopia* **95 F4** 6 40N 38 27 E
Wendover, *U.S.A.* **142 F6** 40 44N 114 2W
Wenduine, *Belgium* **21 F2** 51 18N 3 5 E
Weng'an, *China* **68 D6** 27 5N 107 25 E
Wengcheng, *China* **69 E9** 24 22N 113 50 E
Wengen, *Switz.* **28 C5** 46 37N 7 55 E
Wengyuan, *China* **69 E10** 24 20N 114 9 E
Wenjiang, *China* **68 B4** 30 44N 103 55 E
Wenling, *China* **69 C13** 28 21N 121 20 E
Wenlock →, *Australia* **114 A3** 12 2 S 141 55 E
Wenona, *U.S.A.* **140 C7** 41 3N 89 3W
Wenshan, *China* **68 F5** 23 20N 104 18 E
Wenshang, *China* **66 G9** 35 45N 116 30 E
Wenshui, *Guizhou, China* **68 C6** 28 27N 106 28 E
Wenshui, *Shanxi, China* **66 F7** 37 26N 112 1 E
Wensu, *China* **64 B3** 41 15N 80 10 E
Wentworth, *Australia* **116 C4** 34 2 S 141 54 E
Wentzville, *U.S.A.* **140 F6** 38 49N 90 51W
Wenut, *Indonesia* **73 B4** 3 11 S 133 19 E
Wenxi, *China* **66 G6** 35 20N 111 10 E
Wenzhou, *China* **69 C13** 28 0N 120 38 E
Weott, *U.S.A.* **142 F2** 40 20N 123 55W
Wepener, *S. Africa* **104 D4** 29 42 S 27 3 E
Werbomont, *Belgium* **21 H7** 50 23N 5 41 E
Werda, *Botswana* **104 D3** 25 24 S 23 15 E
Werdau, *Germany* **26 E8** 50 45N 12 20 E
Werder, *Ethiopia* **90 F4** 6 58N 45 1 E
Werder, *Germany* **26 C8** 52 23N 12 56 E
Werdohl, *Germany* **26 D3** 51 15N 7 47 E
Wereilu, *Ethiopia* **95 E4** 10 40N 39 28 E
Weri, *Indonesia* **73 B4** 3 10 S 132 38 E
Werkendam, *Neths.* **20 E5** 51 50N 4 53 E
Werne, *Germany* **26 D3** 51 38N 7 38 E
Werneck, *Germany* **27 F6** 49 59N 10 6 E
Wernigerode, *Germany* **26 D6** 51 49N 10 45 E
Werra →, *Germany* **26 D5** 51 26N 9 39 E
Werribee, *Australia* **116 D6** 37 54 S 144 40 E
Werrimull, *Australia* **116 C4** 34 25 S 141 38 E
Werris Creek, *Australia* **117 A9** 31 18 S 150 38 E
Wersar, *Indonesia* **73 B4** 1 30 S 131 55 E
Wertach →, *Germany* **27 G6** 48 24N 10 53 E
Wertheim, *Germany* **27 F5** 49 44N 9 32 E
Wertingen, *Germany* **27 G6** 48 33N 10 41 E
Wervershoof, *Neths.* **20 C6** 52 44N 5 10 E
Wervik, *Belgium* **21 G2** 50 47N 3 3 E
Wesel, *Germany* **26 D2** 51 39N 6 34 E
Weser →, *Germany* **26 B4** 53 33N 8 30 E
Wesiri, *Indonesia* **72 C3** 7 30 S 126 30 E
Wesley Vale, *U.S.A.* **143 J10** 35 3N 106 2W
Wesleyville, *Canada* **129 C9** 49 8N 53 36W
Wesleyville, *U.S.A.* **136 D4** 42 9N 80 0W
Wessel, C., *Australia* **114 A2** 10 59 S 136 46 E
Wessel Is., *Australia* **114 A2** 11 10 S 136 45 E
Wesselburen, *Germany* **26 A4** 54 11N 8 53 E
Wessem, *Neths.* **21 F7** 51 11N 5 49 E
Wessington, *U.S.A.* **138 C5** 44 27N 98 42W
Wessington Springs, *U.S.A.* **138 C5** 44 5N 98 34W
West, *U.S.A.* **139 K6** 31 48N 97 6W
West Allis, *U.S.A.* **141 A10** 43 1N 88 0W
West B., *U.S.A.* **139 L10** 29 3N 89 22W
West Baines →, *Australia* **112 C4** 15 38 S 129 59 E
West Bend, *U.S.A.* **134 D1** 43 25N 88 11W
West Bengal □, *India* **81 H12** 23 0N 88 0 E
West Beskids = Západné Beskydy, *Europe* **31 B12** 49 30N 19 0 E
West Branch, *U.S.A.* **134 C3** 44 17N 84 14W
West Bromwich, *U.K.* **17 E5** 52 32N 2 1W
West Cape Howe, *Australia* **113 G2** 35 8 S 117 36 E
West Carrollton, *U.S.A.* **141 E12** 39 40N 84 17W
West Chazy, *U.S.A.* **137 B11** 44 49N 73 28W
West Chester, *U.S.A.* **134 F8** 39 58N 75 36W
West Chicago, *U.S.A.* **141 C8** 41 53N 88 12W
West Columbia, *U.S.A.* **139 L7** 29 9N 95 39W
West Covina, *U.S.A.* **145 L9** 34 4N 117 54W
West Des Moines, *U.S.A.* **140 C3** 41 35N 93 43W
West End, *Bahamas* **148 A4** 26 41N 78 58W
West Falkland, *Falk. Is.* **160 D4** 51 40 S 60 0W
West Fjord = Vestfjorden, *Norway* **12 C13** 67 55N 14 0 E
West Frankfort, *U.S.A.* **140 G8** 37 54N 88 55W
West Glamorgan □, *U.K.* **17 F4** 51 40N 3 55W
West Hartford, *U.S.A.* **137 E12** 41 45N 72 44W
West Haven, *U.S.A.* **137 E12** 41 17N 72 57W
West Helena, *U.S.A.* **139 H9** 34 33N 90 38W
West Ice Shelf, *Antarctica* **7 C7** 67 0 S 85 0 E
West Indies, *Cent. Amer.* **149 C7** 15 0N 65 0W
West Lafayette, *U.S.A.* **141 D10** 40 27N 86 55W
West Liberty, *Iowa, U.S.A.* **140 C5** 41 34N 91 16W
West Liberty, *Ky., U.S.A.* **141 G13** 37 55N 83 16W
West Liberty, *Ohio, U.S.A.* **141 D13** 40 15N 83 45W
West Lorne, *Canada* **136 D3** 42 36N 81 36W
West Lunga →, *Zambia* **107 E1** 13 6 S 24 39 E
West Manchester, *U.S.A.* **141 E12** 39 55N 84 38W
West Memphis, *U.S.A.* **139 H9** 35 9N 90 11W
West Midlands □, *U.K.* **17 E6** 52 30N 1 55W
West Mifflin, *U.S.A.* **136 F5** 40 22N 79 52W
West Milton, *U.S.A.* **141 E12** 39 58N 84 20W
West Monroe, *U.S.A.* **139 J8** 32 31N 92 9W
West Newton, *U.S.A.* **136 F5** 40 14N 79 46W
West Nicholson, *Zimbabwe* **107 G2** 21 2 S 29 20 E
West Palm Beach, *U.S.A.* **135 M5** 26 43N 80 3W
West Plains, *U.S.A.* **139 G9** 36 44N 91 51W
West Pt. = Ouest, Pte., *Canada* **129 C7** 49 52N 64 40W
West Pt., *Australia* **116 C1** 35 1 S 135 56 E
West Point, *Ga., U.S.A.* **135 J3** 32 53N 85 11W
West Point, *Ill., U.S.A.* **140 D5** 40 15N 91 11W
West Point, *Iowa, U.S.A.* **140 D5** 40 43N 91 27W

284 West Point


West Point, Ky., U.S.A. 141 G11 37 59N 85 57W
West Point, Miss., U.S.A. 135 J1 33 36N 88 39W
West Point, Nebr., U.S.A. 138 E6 41 51N 96 43W
West Point, Va., U.S.A. 134 G7 37 32N 76 48W
West Pokot □, Kenya 106 B4 1 30N 35 15 E
West Road →, Canada 130 C4 53 18N 122 53W
West Rutland, U.S.A. 137 C11 43 38N 73 5W
West Salem, U.S.A. 141 F8 38 31N 88 1W
West Schelde = Westerschelde →, Neths. 21 F2 51 25N 3 25 E
West Seneca, U.S.A. 136 D6 42 51N 78 48W
West Siberian Plain, Russia 58 C11 62 0N 75 0 E
West Sussex □, U.K. 17 G7 50 55N 0 30W
West Terre Haute, U.S.A. 141 E9 39 28N 87 27W
West-Terschelling, Neths. 20 B6 53 22N 5 13 E
West Union, Iowa, U.S.A. 140 B5 42 57N 91 49W
West Union, Ohio, U.S.A. 141 F13 38 48N 83 33W
West Unity, U.S.A. 141 C12 41 35N 84 26W
West Virginia □, U.S.A. 134 F5 38 45N 80 30W
West-Vlaanderen □, Belgium 21 G2 51 0N 3 0 E
West Walker →, U.S.A. 144 G7 38 54N 119 9W
West Wyalong, Australia 117 B7 33 56 S 147 10 E
West Yellowstone, U.S.A. 142 D8 44 40N 111 6W
West Yorkshire □, U.K. 16 D6 53 45N 1 40W
Westall Pt., Australia 115 E1 32 55 S 134 4 E
Westbrook, Maine, U.S.A. 135 D10 43 41N 70 22W
Westbrook, Tex., U.S.A. 139 J4 32 21N 101 1W
Westbury, Australia 114 G4 41 30 S 146 51 E
Westby, U.S.A. 138 A2 48 52N 104 3W
Westend, U.S.A. 145 K9 35 42N 117 24W
Westerbork, Neths. 20 C9 52 51N 6 37 E
Westerland, Germany 26 A4 54 51N 8 20 E
Western □, Kenya 106 B3 0 30N 34 30 E
Western □, Uganda 106 B3 1 45N 31 30 E
Western □, Zambia 107 F1 15 15 S 24 30 E
Western Australia □, Australia 113 E2 25 0 S 118 0 E
Western Ghats, India 83 H2 14 0N 75 0 E
Western Isles □, U.K. 18 D1 57 30N 7 10W
Western River, Australia 116 C2 35 42 S 136 56 E
Western Sahara ■, Africa 98 D2 25 0N 13 0W
Western Samoa ■, Pac. Oc. 121 X24 14 0 S 172 0W
Westernport, U.S.A. 134 F6 39 29N 79 3W
Westerschelde →, Neths. 21 F2 51 25N 3 25 E
Westerstede, Germany 26 B3 53 15N 7 55 E
Westervoort, Neths. 20 E7 51 58N 5 59 E
Westerwald, Germany 26 E4 50 39N 8 0 E
Westfield, Ill., U.S.A. 141 E8 39 27N 88 0W
Westfield, Ind., U.S.A. 141 D10 40 2N 86 8W
Westfield, Mass., U.S.A. 137 D12 42 7N 72 45W
Westfield, N.Y., U.S.A. 136 D5 42 20N 79 35W
Westfield, Pa., U.S.A. 136 E7 41 55N 77 32W
Westgat, Neths. 21 E3 51 39N 3 44 E
Westhope, U.S.A. 138 A4 48 55N 101 1W
Westkapelle, Belgium 21 F2 51 19N 3 19 E
Westkapelle, Neths. 21 E2 51 31N 3 28 E
Westland, U.S.A. 141 B13 42 15N 83 20W
Westland Bight, N.Z. 119 C5 42 55 S 170 5 E
Westlock, Canada 130 C6 54 9N 113 55W
Westmalle, Belgium 21 F5 51 18N 4 42 E
Westmeath □, Ireland 19 C4 53 30N 7 30W
Westminster, U.S.A. 134 F7 39 34N 76 59W
Westmorland, U.S.A. 143 K6 33 2N 115 37W
Weston, Malaysia 75 A5 5 10N 115 35 E
Weston, Ohio, U.S.A. 141 C13 41 21N 83 47W
Weston, Oreg., U.S.A. 142 D4 45 49N 118 26W
Weston, W. Va., U.S.A. 134 F5 39 2N 80 28W
Weston I., Canada 128 B4 52 33N 79 36W
Weston-super-Mare, U.K. 17 F5 51 20N 2 59W
Westphalia, U.S.A. 140 F5 38 26N 92 0W
Westport, Canada 137 B8 44 40N 76 25W
Westport, Ireland 19 C2 53 44N 9 31W
Westport, N.Z. 119 B6 41 46 S 171 37 E
Westport, Ind., U.S.A. 141 E11 39 11N 85 34W
Westport, Oreg., U.S.A. 144 D3 46 8N 123 23W
Westport, Wash., U.S.A. 142 C1 46 53N 124 6W
Westray, Canada 131 C8 53 36N 101 24W
Westray, U.K. 18 B6 59 18N 3 0W
Westree, Canada 128 C3 47 26N 81 34W
Westville, Calif., U.S.A. 144 F6 39 8N 120 42W
Westville, Ill., U.S.A. 141 D9 40 2N 87 38W
Westville, Ind., U.S.A. 141 C10 41 35N 86 55W
Westville, Okla., U.S.A. 139 G7 35 58N 94 40W
Westwood, U.S.A. 142 F3 40 18N 121 0W
Wetar, Indonesia 72 C3 7 30 S 126 30 E
Wetaskiwin, Canada 130 C6 52 55N 113 24W
Wethersfield, U.S.A. 137 E12 41 42N 72 40W
Wetlet, Burma 78 D5 22 20N 95 53 E
Wetteren, Belgium 21 G3 51 0N 3 52 E
Wettingen, Switz. 29 B6 47 28N 8 20 E
Wetzikon, Switz. 29 B7 47 19N 8 48 E
Wetzlar, Germany 26 E4 50 33N 8 30 E
Wevelgem, Belgium 21 G2 50 49N 3 12 E
Wewak, Papua N. G. 120 B2 3 38 S 143 41 E
Wewoka, U.S.A. 139 H6 35 9N 96 30W
Wexford, Ireland 19 D5 52 20N 6 28W
Wexford □, Ireland 19 D5 52 20N 6 25W
Wexford Harbour, Ireland 19 D5 52 20N 6 25W
Weyburn, Canada 131 D8 49 40N 103 50W
Weyburn L., Canada 130 A5 63 0N 117 59W
Weyer, Austria 30 D7 47 51N 14 40 E
Weyib →, Ethiopia 95 F5 7 15N 40 15 E
Weymouth, Canada 129 D6 44 30N 66 1W
Weymouth, U.K. 17 G5 50 36N 2 28W
Weymouth, U.S.A. 137 D14 42 13N 70 58W
Weymouth, C., Australia 114 A3 12 37 S 143 27 E
Wezemaal, Belgium 21 G5 50 57N 4 45 E
Wezep, Neths. 20 D7 52 28N 6 0 E
Whakamaru, N.Z. 118 E4 38 23 S 175 50 E
Whakatane, N.Z. 118 D6 37 57 S 177 1 E
Whakatane →, N.Z. 118 D6 37 57 S 177 1 E
Whale →, Canada 129 A6 58 15N 67 40W
Whale Cove, Canada 131 A10 62 11N 92 36W
Whales, B. of, Antarctica 7 D12 78 0 S 165 0W
Whalsay, U.K. 18 A7 60 22N 1 0W
Whangaehu →, N.Z. 118 G4 40 3 S 175 6 E
Whangamata, N.Z. 118 D4 37 12 S 175 53 E
Whangamomona, N.Z. 118 F3 39 8 S 174 44 E
Whangarei, N.Z. 118 B3 35 43 S 174 21 E
Whangarei Harb., N.Z. 118 B3 35 45 S 174 28 E
Whangaroa Harb., N.Z. 118 B2 35 4 S 173 46 E
Whangaruru Harb., N.Z. 118 B3 35 24 S 174 23 E
Wharanui, N.Z. 119 B9 41 55 S 174 6 E
Wharfe →, U.K. 16 D6 53 55N 1 30W
Wharfedale, U.K. 16 C5 54 7N 2 4W
Wharton, N.J., U.S.A. 137 F10 40 54N 74 35W
Wharton, Pa., U.S.A. 136 E6 41 31N 78 1W
Wharton, Tex., U.S.A. 139 L6 29 19N 96 6W
Whataroa, N.Z. 119 D5 43 18 S 170 24 E
Whataroa →, N.Z. 119 D5 43 7 S 170 16 E
Wheatfield, U.S.A. 141 C9 41 13N 87 4W
Wheatland, Calif., U.S.A. 144 F5 39 1N 121 25W
Wheatland, Ind., U.S.A. 141 F9 38 40N 87 19W
Wheatland, Wyo., U.S.A. 138 D2 42 3N 104 58W
Wheatley, Canada 136 D2 42 6N 82 27W
Wheaton, Ill., U.S.A. 141 C8 41 52N 88 6W
Wheaton, Minn., U.S.A. 138 C6 45 48N 96 30W
Wheelbarrow Pk., U.S.A. 144 H10 37 26N 116 5W
Wheeler, Oreg., U.S.A. 142 D2 45 41N 123 53W
Wheeler, Tex., U.S.A. 139 H4 35 27N 100 16W
Wheeler →, Canada 131 B7 57 25N 105 30W
Wheeler Pk., N. Mex., U.S.A. 143 H11 36 34N 105 25W
Wheeler Pk., Nev., U.S.A. 143 G6 38 57N 114 15W
Wheeler Ridge, U.S.A. 145 L8 35 0N 118 57W
Wheeling, U.S.A. 136 F4 40 4N 80 43W
Whernside, U.K. 16 C5 54 14N 2 24W
Whidbey I., U.S.A. 130 D4 48 12N 122 17W
Whiskey Gap, Canada 130 D6 49 0N 113 3W
Whiskey Jack L., Canada 131 B8 58 23N 101 55W
Whistleduck Cr. →, Australia 114 C2 20 15 S 135 18 E
Whitby, Canada 136 C6 43 52N 78 56W
Whitby, U.K. 16 C7 54 29N 0 37W
Whitcombe Pass, N.Z. 119 D5 43 13 S 170 55 E
White →, Ark., U.S.A. 139 J9 33 57N 91 5W
White →, Ind., U.S.A. 141 F9 38 25N 87 45W
White →, S. Dak., U.S.A. 138 D5 43 42N 99 27W
White →, Utah, U.S.A. 142 F9 40 4N 109 41W
White →, Wash., U.S.A. 144 C4 47 12N 122 15W
White, East Fork →, U.S.A. 141 F9 38 33N 87 14W
White, L., Australia 112 D4 21 9 S 128 56 E
White B., Canada 129 B8 50 0N 56 35W
White Bear Res., Canada 129 C8 48 10N 57 5W
White Bird, U.S.A. 142 D5 45 46N 116 18W
White Butte, U.S.A. 138 B3 46 23N 103 18W
White City, U.S.A. 138 F6 38 48N 96 44W
White Cliffs, Australia 116 A5 30 50 S 143 10 E
White Deer, U.S.A. 139 H4 35 26N 101 10W
White Hall, U.S.A. 140 E6 39 26N 90 24W
White Haven, U.S.A. 137 E9 41 4N 75 47W
White I., N.Z. 118 D6 37 30 S 177 13 E
White L., Canada 137 A8 45 18N 76 31W
White L., U.S.A. 139 L8 29 44N 92 30W
White Mts., Calif., U.S.A. 144 H8 37 30N 118 15W
White Mts., N.H., U.S.A. 137 B13 44 15N 71 15W
White Nile = Nîl el Abyad →, Sudan 95 D3 15 38N 32 31 E
White Nile Dam = Khazzân Jabal el Awliyâ, Sudan 95 D3 15 24N 32 20 E
White Otter L., Canada 128 C1 49 5N 91 55W
White Pass, Canada 130 B1 59 40N 135 3W
White Pass, U.S.A. 144 D5 46 38N 121 24W
White Pigeon, U.S.A. 141 C11 41 48N 85 39W
White Plains, U.S.A. 137 E11 41 2N 73 46W
White River, Canada 128 C2 48 35N 85 20W
White River, S. Africa 105 D5 25 20 S 31 0 E
White River, U.S.A. 138 D4 43 34N 100 45W
White Russia = Belorussia ■, Europe 50 E5 53 30N 27 0 E
White Sea = Beloye More, Russia 48 A6 66 30N 38 0 E
White Sulphur Springs, Mont., U.S.A. 142 C8 46 33N 110 54W
White Sulphur Springs, W. Va., U.S.A. 134 G5 37 48N 80 18W
White Swan, U.S.A. 144 D6 46 23N 120 44W
White Volta →, Ghana 101 D4 9 10N 1 15W
Whitecliffs, N.Z. 119 D6 43 26 S 171 55 E
Whitecourt, Canada 130 C5 54 10N 115 45W
Whiteface, U.S.A. 139 J3 33 36N 102 37W
Whitefield, U.S.A. 137 B13 44 23N 71 37W
Whitefish, U.S.A. 142 B6 48 25N 114 20W
Whitefish Bay, U.S.A. 141 A9 43 23N 87 54W
Whitefish L., Canada 131 A7 62 41N 106 48W
Whitefish Point, U.S.A. 134 B3 46 45N 84 59W
Whitegull, L., Canada 129 A7 55 27N 64 17W
Whitehall, Mich., U.S.A. 134 D2 43 24N 86 21W
Whitehall, Mont., U.S.A. 142 D7 45 52N 112 6W
Whitehall, N.Y., U.S.A. 137 C11 43 33N 73 24W
Whitehall, Wis., U.S.A. 138 C9 44 22N 91 19W
Whitehaven, U.K. 16 C4 54 33N 3 35W
Whitehorse, Canada 130 A1 60 43N 135 3W
Whitehorse, Vale of, U.K. 17 F6 51 37N 1 30W
Whiteman, U.S.A. 140 F3 38 45N 93 40W
Whiteman Ra., Papua N. G. 120 C5 5 55 S 150 0 E
Whitemark, Australia 114 G4 40 7 S 148 3 E
Whitemouth, Canada 131 D9 49 57N 95 58W
Whiteplains, Liberia 100 D2 6 28N 10 40W
Whitesboro, N.Y., U.S.A. 137 C9 43 7N 75 18W
Whitesboro, Tex., U.S.A. 139 J6 33 39N 96 54W
Whiteshell Prov. Park, Canada 131 C9 50 0N 95 40W
Whiteside, U.S.A. 140 E5 39 12N 91 2W
Whiteside, Canal, Chile 160 D2 53 55 S 70 15W
Whitetail, U.S.A. 138 A2 48 54N 105 10W
Whiteville, U.S.A. 135 H6 34 20N 78 42W
Whitewater, U.S.A. 141 B8 42 50N 88 44W
Whitewater Baldy, U.S.A. 143 K9 33 20N 108 39W
Whitewater L., Canada 128 B2 50 50N 89 10W
Whitewood, Australia 114 C3 21 28 S 143 30 E
Whitewood, Canada 131 C8 50 20N 102 20W
Whitfield, Australia 117 D7 36 42 S 146 24 E
Whithorn, U.K. 18 G4 54 44N 4 25W
Whitianga, N.Z. 118 C4 36 47 S 175 41 E
Whiting, U.S.A. 141 C9 41 41N 87 29W
Whitman, U.S.A. 137 D14 42 5N 70 56W
Whitmire, U.S.A. 135 H5 34 30N 81 37W
Whitney, Canada 128 C4 45 31N 78 14W
Whitney, Mt., U.S.A. 144 J8 36 35N 118 18W
Whitney Point, U.S.A. 137 D9 42 20N 75 58W
Whitstable, U.K. 17 F9 51 21N 1 2 E
Whitsunday I., Australia 114 C4 20 15 S 149 4 E
Whittemore, U.S.A. 140 A2 43 4N 94 26W
Whittier, U.S.A. 145 M8 33 58N 118 3W
Whittlesea, Australia 117 D6 37 27 S 145 9 E
Whitwell, U.S.A. 135 H3 35 12N 85 31W
Wholdaia L., Canada 131 A8 60 43N 104 20W
Whyalla, Australia 116 B2 33 2 S 137 30 E
Whyjonta, Australia 115 D3 29 41 S 142 28 E
Wiarton, Canada 128 D3 44 40N 81 10W
Wiawso, Ghana 100 D4 6 10N 2 25W
Wiazów, Poland 47 E4 50 50N 17 10 E
Wibaux, U.S.A. 138 B2 46 59N 104 11W
Wichabai, Guyana 153 C6 2 57N 59 35W
Wichian Buri, Thailand 76 E3 15 39N 101 7 E
Wichita, U.S.A. 139 G6 37 42N 97 20W
Wichita Falls, U.S.A. 139 J5 33 54N 98 30W
Wick, U.K. 18 C5 58 26N 3 5W
Wickenburg, U.S.A. 143 K7 33 58N 112 44W
Wickepin, Australia 113 F2 32 50 S 117 30 E
Wickham, C., Australia 114 F3 39 35 S 143 57 E
Wickliffe, U.S.A. 136 E3 41 36N 81 28W
Wicklow, Ireland 19 D5 53 0N 6 2W
Wicklow □, Ireland 19 D5 52 59N 6 25W
Wicklow Hd., Ireland 19 D5 52 59N 6 3W
Widawa, Poland 47 D5 51 27N 18 51 E
Widawka, Poland 47 D6 51 7N 19 36 E
Widgiemooltha, Australia 113 F3 31 30 S 121 34 E
Widnes, U.K. 16 D5 53 22N 2 44W
Więcbork, Poland 47 B4 53 21N 17 30 E
Wiedenbrück, Germany 26 D4 51 52N 8 15 E
Wiek, Germany 26 A9 54 37N 13 17 E
Wielbark, Poland 47 B7 53 24N 20 55 E
Wieleń, Poland 47 C3 52 53N 16 9 E
Wieliczka, Poland 31 B13 50 0N 20 5 E
Wieluń, Poland 47 D5 51 15N 18 34 E
Wien, Austria 31 C9 48 12N 16 22 E
Wiener Neustadt, Austria 31 D9 47 49N 16 16 E
Wieprz →, Koszalin, Poland 47 A3 54 26N 16 35 E
Wieprz →, Lublin, Poland 47 D8 51 34N 21 49 E
Wierden, Neths. 20 D9 52 22N 6 35 E
Wiers, Belgium 21 H3 50 30N 3 32 E
Wieruszów, Poland 47 D5 51 19N 18 9 E
Wiesbaden, Germany 27 E4 50 7N 8 17 E
Wiesental, Germany 27 F4 49 15N 8 30 E
Wigan, U.K. 16 D5 53 33N 2 38W
Wiggins, Colo., U.S.A. 138 E2 40 14N 104 4W
Wiggins, Miss., U.S.A. 139 K10 30 51N 89 8W
Wight, I. of □, U.K. 17 G6 50 40N 1 20W
Wigry, Jezioro, Poland 47 A10 54 2N 23 8 E
Wigtown, U.K. 18 G4 54 52N 4 27W
Wigtown B., U.K. 18 G4 54 46N 4 15W
Wijchen, Neths. 20 E7 51 48N 5 44 E
Wijhe, Neths. 20 D8 52 23N 6 8 E
Wijk bij Duurstede, Neths. 20 E6 51 59N 5 21 E
Wil, Switz. 29 B8 47 28N 9 3 E
Wilamowice, Poland 31 B12 49 55N 19 9 E
Wilangee, Australia 116 A4 31 28 S 141 20 E
Wilber, U.S.A. 138 E6 40 29N 96 58W
Wilberforce, Canada 136 A6 45 2N 78 13W
Wilberforce, C., Australia 114 A2 11 54 S 136 35 E
Wilburton, U.S.A. 139 H7 34 55N 95 19W
Wilcannia, Australia 116 A5 31 30 S 143 26 E
Wilcox, U.S.A. 136 E6 41 35N 78 41W
Wildbad, Germany 27 G4 48 44N 8 32 E
Wildcat →, U.S.A. 141 D10 40 28N 86 52W
Wildervank, Neths. 20 B9 53 5N 6 52 E
Wildeshausen, Germany 26 C4 52 54N 8 25 E
Wildhorn, Switz. 28 D4 46 22N 7 21 E
Wildon, Austria 30 E8 46 52N 15 31 E
Wildrose, Calif., U.S.A. 145 J9 36 14N 117 11W
Wildrose, N. Dak., U.S.A. 138 A3 48 38N 103 11W
Wildspitze, Austria 30 E3 46 53N 10 53 E
Wildstrubel, Switz. 28 D5 46 24N 7 32 E
Wildwood, U.S.A. 134 F8 38 59N 74 50W
Wilga →, Poland 47 D8 51 52N 21 18 E
Wilgaroon, Australia 117 A6 30 52 S 145 42 E
Wilge →, S. Africa 105 D4 27 3 S 28 20 E
Wilhelm, Mt., Papua N. G. 120 C3 5 50 S 145 1 E
Wilhelm II Coast, Antarctica 7 C7 68 0 S 90 0 E
Wilhelm-Pieck-Stadt Guben, Germany 26 D10 51 59N 14 48 E
Wilhelmina, Geb., Surinam 153 C6 3 50N 56 30W
Wilhelmina Kanaal, Neths. 21 E6 51 36N 5 6 E
Wilhelmsburg, Austria 30 C8 48 6N 15 36 E
Wilhelmshaven, Germany 26 B4 53 30N 8 9 E
Wilhelmstal, Namibia 104 C2 21 58 S 16 21 E
Wilkes-Barre, U.S.A. 137 E9 41 15N 75 53W
Wilkesboro, U.S.A. 135 G5 36 9N 81 10W
Wilkie, Canada 131 C7 52 27N 108 42W
Wilkinsburg, U.S.A. 136 F5 40 26N 79 53W
Wilkinson Lakes, Australia 113 E5 29 40 S 132 39 E
Willamina, U.S.A. 142 D2 45 5N 123 29W
Willamulka, Australia 116 B3 33 55 S 137 52 E
Willandra Billabong Creek →, Australia 116 B6 33 22 S 145 52 E
Willapa B., U.S.A. 142 C2 46 40N 124 0W
Willapa Hills, U.S.A. 144 D3 46 35N 123 25W
Willard, N. Mex., U.S.A. 143 J10 34 36N 106 2W
Willard, Utah, U.S.A. 142 F7 41 25N 112 2W
Willaura, Australia 116 D5 37 31 S 142 45 E
Willbriggie, Australia 117 C7 34 28 S 146 2 E
Willcox, U.S.A. 143 K9 32 15N 109 50W
Willebroek, Belgium 21 F4 51 4N 4 22 E
Willemstad, Neth. Ant. 149 D6 12 5N 69 0W
Willeroo, Australia 112 C5 15 14 S 131 37 E
William →, Canada 131 B7 59 8N 109 19W
William, Mt., Australia 116 D5 37 17 S 142 35 E
William Creek, Australia 115 D2 28 58 S 136 22 E
Williambury, Australia 113 D2 23 45 S 115 12 E
Williams, Australia 113 F2 33 2 S 116 52 E
Williams, Ariz., U.S.A. 143 J7 35 15N 112 11W
Williams, Calif., U.S.A. 144 F4 39 9N 122 9W
Williams Lake, Canada 130 C4 52 10N 122 10W
Williamsburg, Ky., U.S.A. 135 G3 36 44N 84 10W
Williamsburg, Pa., U.S.A. 136 F6 40 28N 78 12W
Williamsburg, Va., U.S.A. 134 G7 37 17N 76 44W
Williamsfield, U.S.A. 140 D6 40 55N 90 1W
Williamson, N.Y., U.S.A. 136 C7 43 14N 77 11W
Williamson, W. Va., U.S.A. 134 G4 37 41N 82 17W
Williamsport, Ind., U.S.A. 141 D9 40 17N 87 17W
Williamsport, Pa., U.S.A. 136 E7 41 15N 77 0W
Williamston, Mich., U.S.A. 141 B12 42 41N 84 17W
Williamston, N.C., U.S.A. 135 H7 35 51N 77 4W
Williamstown, Australia 117 D6 37 51 S 144 52 E
Williamstown, Ky., U.S.A. 141 F12 38 38N 84 34W
Williamstown, Mass., U.S.A. 137 D11 42 41N 73 12W
Williamstown, N.Y., U.S.A. 137 C9 43 26N 75 53W
Williamsville, Ill., U.S.A. 140 E7 39 57N 89 33W
Williamsville, Mo., U.S.A. 139 G9 36 58N 90 33W
Willimantic, U.S.A. 137 E12 41 43N 72 13W
Willis Group, Australia 114 B5 16 18 S 150 0 E
Willisau, Switz. 28 B6 47 7N 8 0 E
Willisburg, U.S.A. 141 G11 37 49N 85 8W
Williston, S. Africa 104 E3 31 20 S 20 53 E
Williston, Fla., U.S.A. 135 L4 29 23N 82 27W
Williston, N. Dak., U.S.A. 138 A3 48 9N 103 37W
Williston L., Canada 130 B4 56 0N 124 0W
Willits, U.S.A. 142 G2 39 25N 123 21W
Willmar, U.S.A. 138 C7 45 7N 95 3W
Willoughby, U.S.A. 136 E3 41 39N 81 24W
Willow Bunch, Canada 131 D7 49 20N 105 35W
Willow L., Canada 130 A5 62 10N 119 8W
Willow Lake, U.S.A. 138 C6 44 38N 97 38W
Willow Springs, U.S.A. 139 G8 37 0N 91 58W
Willow Tree, Australia 117 A9 31 40 S 150 45 E
Willow Wall, The, China 67 C12 42 10N 122 0 E
Willowlake →, Canada 130 A4 62 42N 123 8W
Willowmore, S. Africa 104 E3 33 15 S 23 30 E
Willows, Australia 114 C4 23 39 S 147 25 E
Willows, U.S.A. 144 F4 39 31N 122 12W
Willowvale = Gatyana, S. Africa 105 E4 32 16 S 28 31 E
Wills, L., Australia 112 D4 21 25 S 128 51 E
Wills Cr. →, Australia 114 C3 22 43 S 140 2 E
Wills Point, U.S.A. 139 J7 32 43N 96 1W
Willunga, Australia 116 C3 35 15 S 138 30 E
Wilmette, U.S.A. 134 D2 42 5N 87 42W
Wilmington, Australia 116 B3 32 39 S 138 7 E
Wilmington, Del., U.S.A. 134 F8 39 45N 75 33W
Wilmington, Ill., U.S.A. 141 C8 41 18N 88 9W
Wilmington, N.C., U.S.A. 135 H7 34 14N 77 55W
Wilmington, Ohio, U.S.A. 141 E13 39 27N 83 50W
Wilpena Cr. →, Australia 116 A3 31 25 S 139 29 E
Wilrijk, Belgium 21 F4 51 9N 4 22 E
Wilsall, U.S.A. 142 D8 45 59N 110 38W
Wilson, U.S.A. 135 H7 35 44N 77 55W
Wilson →, Queens., Australia 115 D3 27 38 S 141 24 E
Wilson →, W. Austral., Australia 112 C4 16 48 S 128 16 E
Wilson Bluff, Australia 113 F4 31 41 S 129 0 E
Wilson Str., Solomon Is. 121 M9 8 0 S 156 39 E
Wilsons Promontory, Australia 117 E7 38 55 S 146 25 E
Wilster, Germany 26 B5 53 55N 9 23 E
Wilton, U.K. 17 F6 51 5N 1 52W
Wilton, U.S.A. 138 B4 47 10N 100 47W
Wilton →, Australia 114 A1 14 45 S 134 33 E
Wiltshire □, U.K. 17 F6 51 20N 2 0W
Wiltz, Lux. 21 J7 49 57N 5 55 E
Wiluna, Australia 113 E3 26 36 S 120 14 E
Wimereux, France 23 B8 50 45N 1 37 E
Wimmera →, Australia 116 D4 36 8 S 141 56 E
Winam G., Kenya 106 C3 0 20 S 34 15 E
Winamac, U.S.A. 141 C10 41 3N 86 36W
Winburg, S. Africa 104 D4 28 30 S 27 2 E
Winchelsea, Australia 116 E6 38 10 S 144 1 E
Winchendon, U.S.A. 137 D12 42 41N 72 3W
Winchester, N.Z. 119 E6 44 11 S 171 17 E
Winchester, U.K. 17 F6 51 4N 1 19W
Winchester, Conn., U.S.A. 137 E11 41 53N 73 9W
Winchester, Idaho, U.S.A. 142 C5 46 14N 116 38W
Winchester, Ill., U.S.A. 140 E6 39 38N 90 27W
Winchester, Ind., U.S.A. 141 D12 40 10N 84 59W
Winchester, Ky., U.S.A. 141 G12 38 0N 84 11W
Winchester, N.H., U.S.A. 137 D12 42 46N 72 23W
Winchester, Nev., U.S.A. 145 J11 36 6N 115 10W
Winchester, Ohio, U.S.A. 141 F13 38 57N 83 40W
Winchester, Tenn., U.S.A. 135 H2 35 11N 86 7W
Winchester, Va., U.S.A. 134 F6 39 11N 78 10W
Wind →, U.S.A. 142 E9 43 12N 108 12W
Wind Point, U.S.A. 141 B9 42 47N 87 46W
Wind River Range, U.S.A. 142 E9 43 0N 109 30W
Windau = Ventspils, Latvia 13 H16 57 25N 21 32 E
Windber, U.S.A. 136 F6 40 14N 78 50W
Windermere, L., U.K. 16 C5 54 20N 2 57W
Windfall, Canada 130 C5 54 12N 116 13W
Windfall, U.S.A. 141 D11 40 22N 85 57W
Windflower L., Canada 130 A5 62 52N 118 30W
Windhoek, Namibia 104 C2 22 35 S 17 4 E
Windischgarsten, Austria 30 D7 47 42N 14 21 E
Windom, U.S.A. 138 D7 43 52N 95 7W
Windorah, Australia 114 D3 25 24 S 142 36 E
Window Rock, U.S.A. 143 J9 35 41N 109 3W
Windrush →, U.K. 17 F6 51 48N 1 35W
Windsor, Australia 117 B9 33 37 S 150 50 E
Windsor, N.S., Canada 129 D7 44 59N 64 5W
Windsor, Nfld., Canada 129 C8 48 57N 55 40W
Windsor, Ont., Canada 128 D3 42 18N 83 0W
Windsor, N.Z. 119 E5 44 59 S 170 49 E
Windsor, U.K. 17 F7 51 28N 0 36W
Windsor, Colo., U.S.A. 138 E2 40 29N 104 54W
Windsor, Conn., U.S.A. 137 E12 41 50N 72 39W
Windsor, Ill., U.S.A. 141 E8 39 26N 88 36W
Windsor, Mo., U.S.A. 140 F3 38 32N 93 31W
Windsor, N.Y., U.S.A. 137 D9 42 5N 75 37W
Windsor, Vt., U.S.A. 137 C12 43 29N 72 24W
Windsorton, S. Africa 104 D3 28 16 S 24 44 E
Windward Is., W. Indies 149 D7 13 0N 61 0W
Windward Passage = Vientos, Paso de los, Caribbean 149 C5 20 0N 74 0W
Windy L., Canada 131 A8 60 20N 100 2W
Winefred L., Canada 131 B6 55 30N 110 30W
Winejok, Sudan 95 F2 9 1N 27 30 E
Winfield, Iowa, U.S.A. 140 C5 41 7N 91 26W
Winfield, Kans., U.S.A. 139 G6 37 15N 96 59W
Winfield, Mo., U.S.A. 140 E6 39 0N 90 44W
Wingate Mts., Australia 112 B5 14 25 S 130 40 E
Wingen, Australia 117 A9 31 54 S 150 54 E
Wingene, Belgium 21 F2 51 3N 3 17 E

Zapadni Rodopi 287


Yhú, *Paraguay* 159 **B4** 25 0 S 56 0W
Yi →, *Uruguay* 158 **C4** 33 7 S 57 8W
Yi 'Allaq, G., *Egypt* 91 **E2** 30 22N 33 32 E
Yi He →, *China* 67 **G10** 34 10N 118 8 E
Yi Xian, *Anhui, China* 69 **C11** 29 55N 117 57 E
Yi Xian, *Hebei, China* 66 **E8** 39 20N 115 30 E
Yi Xian, *Liaoning, China* 67 **D11** 41 30N 121 22 E
Yialí, *Greece* 45 **H9** 36 41N 27 11 E
Yialiás →, *Cyprus* 32 **D12** 35 9N 33 44 E
Yi'allaq, G., *Egypt* 94 **H8** 30 21N 33 31 E
Yialousa, *Cyprus* 32 **D13** 35 32N 34 10 E
Yiáltra, *Greece* 45 **F4** 38 51N 22 59 E
Yianisádhes, *Greece* 32 **D8** 35 20N 26 10 E
Yiannitsa, *Greece* 44 **D4** 40 46N 22 24 E
Yibin, *China* 68 **C5** 28 45N 104 32 E
Yichang, *China* 69 **B8** 30 40N 111 20 E
Yicheng, *Henan, China* 69 **B9** 31 41N 112 12 E
Yicheng, *Shanxi, China* 66 **G6** 35 42N 111 40 E
Yichuan, *China* 66 **F6** 36 2N 110 10 E
Yichun, *Heilongjiang, China* 65 **B7** 47 44N 128 52 E
Yichun, *Jiangxi, China* 69 **D10** 27 48N 114 22 E
Yidhá, *Greece* 44 **D4** 40 35N 22 53 E
Yidu, *Hubei, China* 69 **B8** 30 25N 111 27 E
Yidu, *Shandong, China* 67 **F10** 36 43N 118 28 E
Yidun, *China* 68 **B2** 30 22N 99 21 E
Yihuang, *China* 69 **D11** 27 30N 116 12 E
Yijun, *China* 66 **G5** 35 28N 109 8 E
Yilan, *Taiwan* 69 **E13** 24 51N 121 44 E
Yıldızeli, *Turkey* 88 **D7** 39 51N 36 36 E
Yilehuli Shan, *China* 65 **A7** 51 20N 124 20 E
Yiliang, *Yunnan, China* 68 **D5** 27 38N 104 2 E
Yiliang, *Yunnan, China* 68 **E4** 24 56N 103 11 E
Yilong, *China* 68 **B6** 31 34N 106 23 E
Yimen, *China* 68 **E4** 24 40N 102 10 E
Yimianpo, *China* 67 **B15** 45 7N 128 2 E
Yinchuan, *China* 66 **E4** 38 30N 106 15 E
Yindarlgooda, L., *Australia* 113 **F3** 30 40 S 121 52 E
Ying He →, *China* 66 **H9** 32 30N 116 30 E
Ying Xian, *China* 66 **E7** 39 32N 113 10 E
Yingcheng, *China* 69 **B9** 30 56N 113 35 E
Yingde, *China* 69 **E9** 24 10N 113 25 E
Yingjiang, *China* 68 **E1** 24 41N 97 55 E
Yingjing, *China* 68 **C4** 29 41N 102 52 E
Yingkou, *China* 67 **D12** 40 37N 122 18 E
Yingshan, *Henan, China* 69 **B9** 31 35N 113 50 E
Yingshan, *Hubei, China* 69 **B10** 30 41N 115 32 E
Yingshan, *Sichuan, China* 68 **B6** 31 4N 106 35 E
Yingshang, *China* 69 **A11** 32 38N 116 12 E
Yining, *China* 56 **E9** 43 58N 81 10 E
Yinjiang, *China* 68 **C7** 28 1N 108 21 E
Yinnietharra, *Australia* 112 **D2** 24 39 S 116 12 E
Yiofiros →, *Greece* 32 **D7** 35 20N 25 6 E
Yioúra, *Notios Aiyaíon, Greece* 45 **G6** 37 32N 24 40 E
Yioúra, *Thessalía, Greece* 44 **E6** 39 23N 24 10 E
Yipinglang, *China* 68 **E3** 25 10N 101 52 E
Yirga Alem, *Ethiopia* 95 **F4** 6 48N 38 22 E
Yishan, *China* 68 **E7** 24 28N 108 38 E
Yishui, *China* 67 **G10** 35 47N 118 30 E
Yíthion, *Greece* 45 **H4** 36 46N 22 34 E
Yitiaoshan, *China* 66 **F3** 37 5N 104 2 E
Yitong, *China* 67 **C13** 43 13N 125 20 E
Yiwu, *China* 69 **C13** 29 20N 120 3 E
Yixing, *China* 69 **B12** 31 21N 119 48 E
Yiyang, *Henan, China* 66 **G7** 34 27N 112 10 E
Yiyang, *Hunan, China* 69 **C9** 28 35N 112 18 E
Yiyang, *Jiangxi, China* 69 **C11** 28 22N 117 20 E
Yizhang, *China* 69 **E9** 25 27N 112 57 E
Yizheng, *China* 69 **A12** 32 18N 119 10 E
Ylitornio, *Finland* 12 **C17** 66 19N 23 39 E
Ylivieska, *Finland* 12 **D18** 64 4N 24 28 E
Yngaren, *Sweden* 15 **F10** 58 50N 16 35 E
Ynykchanskiy, *Russia* 57 **C14** 60 15N 137 35 E
Yoakum, *U.S.A.* 139 **L6** 29 17N 97 9W
Yobe □, *Nigeria* 101 **C7** 12 0N 11 30 E
Yobuko, *Japan* 62 **D1** 33 32N 129 54 E
Yog Pt., *Phil.* 70 **D5** 14 6N 124 12 E
Yogan, *Togo* 101 **D5** 6 23N 1 30 E
Yogyakarta, *Indonesia* 75 **D4** 7 49 S 110 22 E
Yogyakarta □, *Indonesia* 75 **D4** 7 48 S 110 22 E
Yoho Nat. Park, *Canada* 130 **C5** 51 25N 116 30W
Yojoa, L. de, *Honduras* 148 **D2** 14 53N 88 0W
Yŏju, *S. Korea* 67 **F14** 37 20N 127 35 E
Yokadouma, *Cameroon* 102 **B2** 3 26N 14 55 E
Yŏkaichiba, *Japan* 63 **B12** 35 42N 140 33 E
Yokkaichi, *Japan* 63 **C8** 34 55N 136 38 E
Yoko, *Cameroon* 101 **D7** 5 32N 12 20 E
Yokohama, *Japan* 63 **B11** 35 27N 139 28 E
Yokosuka, *Japan* 63 **B11** 35 20N 139 40 E
Yokote, *Japan* 60 **E10** 39 20N 140 30 E
Yola, *Nigeria* 101 **D7** 9 10N 12 29 E
Yolaina, Cordillera de, *Nic.* 148 **D3** 11 30N 84 0W
Yolombo, *Zaïre* 102 **C4** 1 36 S 23 12 E
Yombi, *Gabon* 102 **C2** 1 26 S 10 37 E
Yonago, *Japan* 62 **B5** 35 25N 133 19 E
Yonaguni-Jima, *Japan* 61 **M1** 24 27N 123 0 E
Yŏnan, *N. Korea* 67 **F14** 37 55N 126 11 E
Yonezawa, *Japan* 60 **F10** 37 57N 140 4 E
Yong Peng, *Malaysia* 77 **L4** 2 0N 103 3 E
Yong Sata, *Thailand* 77 **J2** 7 8N 99 41 E
Yongampo, *N. Korea* 67 **E13** 39 56N 124 23 E
Yong'an, *China* 69 **E11** 25 59N 117 25 E
Yongcheng, *China* 66 **H9** 33 55N 116 20 E
Yŏngchŏn, *S. Korea* 67 **G15** 35 58N 128 56 E
Yongchuan, *China* 68 **C5** 29 17N 105 55 E
Yongchun, *China* 69 **E12** 25 16N 118 20 E
Yongdeng, *China* 66 **F2** 36 38N 103 25 E
Yongding, *China* 69 **E11** 24 43N 116 45 E
Yŏngdŏk, *S. Korea* 67 **F15** 36 24N 129 22 E
Yŏngdŭngpo, *S. Korea* 67 **F14** 37 31N 126 54 E
Yongfeng, *China* 69 **D10** 27 20N 115 22 E
Yongfu, *China* 68 **E7** 24 59N 109 59 E
Yonghe, *China* 66 **F6** 36 46N 110 38 E
Yŏnghŭng, *N. Korea* 67 **E14** 39 31N 127 18 E
Yongji, *China* 66 **G6** 34 52N 110 28 E
Yŏngju, *S. Korea* 67 **F15** 36 50N 128 40 E
Yongkang, *Yunnan, China* 68 **E2** 24 9N 99 20 E
Yongkang, *Zhejiang, China* 69 **C13** 28 55N 120 2 E
Yongnian, *China* 66 **F8** 36 47N 114 29 E
Yongning, *Guangxi Zhuangzu, China* 68 **F7** 22 44N 108 28 E
Yongning, *Ningxia Huizu, China* 66 **E4** 38 15N 106 14 E
Yongping, *China* 68 **E2** 25 27N 99 38 E
Yongqing, *China* 66 **E9** 39 25N 116 28 E
Yongren, *China* 68 **D3** 26 4N 101 40 E
Yongshan, *China* 68 **C4** 28 11N 103 35 E
Yongsheng, *China* 68 **D3** 26 38N 100 46 E
Yongshun, *China* 68 **C7** 29 2N 109 51 E
Yongtai, *China* 69 **E12** 25 49N 118 58 E
Yŏngwŏl, *S. Korea* 67 **F15** 37 11N 128 28 E
Yongxin, *China* 69 **D10** 26 58N 114 15 E
Yongxing, *China* 69 **D9** 26 9N 113 8 E
Yongxiu, *China* 69 **C10** 29 2N 115 42 E
Yonibana, *S. Leone* 100 **D2** 8 30N 12 19W
Yonkers, *U.S.A.* 137 **F11** 40 56N 73 54W
Yonne □, *France* 23 **E10** 47 50N 3 40 E
Yonne →, *France* 23 **D9** 48 23N 2 58 E
York, *Australia* 113 **F2** 31 52 S 116 47 E
York, *U.K.* 16 **D6** 53 58N 1 7W
York, *Ala., U.S.A.* 135 **J1** 32 29N 88 18W
York, *Nebr., U.S.A.* 138 **E6** 40 52N 97 36W
York, *Pa., U.S.A.* 134 **F7** 39 58N 76 44W
York, C., *Australia* 114 **A3** 10 42 S 142 31 E
York, Kap, *Greenland* 6 **B4** 75 55N 66 25W
York Sd., *Australia* 112 **B4** 15 0 S 125 5 E
Yorke Pen., *Australia* 116 **C2** 34 50 S 137 40 E
Yorkshire Wolds, *U.K.* 16 **D7** 54 0N 0 30W
Yorkton, *Canada* 131 **C8** 51 11N 102 28W
Yorktown, *U.S.A.* 139 **L6** 28 59N 97 30W
Yorkville, *Calif., U.S.A.* 144 **G3** 38 52N 123 13W
Yorkville, *Ill., U.S.A.* 141 **C8** 41 38N 88 27W
Yornup, *Australia* 113 **F2** 34 2 S 116 10 E
Yoro, *Honduras* 148 **C2** 15 9N 87 7W
Yoron-Jima, *Japan* 61 **L4** 27 2N 128 26 E
Yos Sudarso, Pulau, *Indonesia* 73 **C5** 8 0 S 138 30 E
Yosemite National Park, *U.S.A.* 144 **H7** 37 45N 119 40W
Yosemite Village, *U.S.A.* 144 **H7** 37 45N 119 35W
Yoshii, *Japan* 62 **D1** 33 16N 129 46 E
Yoshimatsu, *Japan* 62 **E2** 32 0N 130 47 E
Yoshkar Ola, *Russia* 51 **C15** 56 38N 47 55 E
Yŏsu, *S. Korea* 67 **G14** 34 47N 127 45 E
Yotala, *Bolivia* 157 **D4** 19 10 S 65 17W
Yotvata, *Israel* 91 **F4** 29 55N 35 2 E
You Xian, *China* 69 **D9** 27 1N 113 17 E
Youbou, *Canada* 130 **D4** 48 53N 124 13W
Youghal, *Ireland* 19 **E4** 51 58N 7 51W
Youghal B., *Ireland* 19 **E4** 51 55N 7 50W
Youkounkoun, *Guinea* 100 **C2** 12 35N 13 11W
Young, *Australia* 117 **C8** 34 19 S 148 18 E
Young, *Canada* 131 **C7** 51 47N 105 45W
Young, *Uruguay* 158 **C4** 32 44 S 57 36W
Young Ra., *N.Z.* 119 **E4** 44 10 S 169 30 E
Younghusband, L., *Australia* 116 **A2** 30 50 S 136 5 E
Younghusband Pen., *Australia* 116 **D3** 36 0 S 139 25 E
Youngstown, *Canada* 131 **C6** 51 35N 111 10W
Youngstown, *N.Y., U.S.A.* 136 **C5** 43 15N 79 3W
Youngstown, *Ohio, U.S.A.* 136 **E4** 41 6N 80 39W
Youngsville, *U.S.A.* 136 **E5** 41 51N 79 19W
Youssoufia, *Morocco* 98 **B3** 32 16N 8 31W
Youxi, *China* 69 **D12** 26 10N 118 13 E
Youyang, *China* 68 **C7** 28 47N 108 42 E
Youyu, *China* 66 **D7** 40 10N 112 20 E
Yoweragabbie, *Australia* 113 **E2** 28 14 S 117 39 E
Yowrie, *Australia* 117 **D8** 36 17 S 149 46 E
Yozgat, *Turkey* 88 **D6** 39 51N 34 47 E
Yozgat □, *Turkey* 88 **D6** 39 30N 35 0 E
Ypané →, *Paraguay* 158 **A4** 23 29 S 57 19W
Yport, *France* 22 **C7** 49 45N 0 15 E
Ypres = Ieper, *Belgium* 21 **G1** 50 51N 2 53 E
Ypsilanti, *U.S.A.* 141 **B13** 42 14N 83 37W
Yreka, *U.S.A.* 142 **F2** 41 44N 122 38W
Ysabel Chan., *Papua N. G.* 120 **B5** 2 0 S 150 0 E
Ysleta, *U.S.A.* 143 **L10** 31 45N 106 24W
Yssingeaux, *France* 25 **C8** 45 9N 4 8 E
Ystad, *Sweden* 15 **J7** 55 26N 13 50 E
Ysyk-Köl = Issyk-Kul, Ozero, *Kirghizia* 55 **B8** 42 25N 77 15 E
Ythan →, *U.K.* 18 **D7** 57 26N 2 0W
Ytterhogdal, *Sweden* 14 **B8** 62 12N 14 56 E
Ytyk-Kel, *Russia* 57 **C14** 62 30N 133 45 E
Yu Jiang →, *China* 65 **D6** 23 22N 110 3 E
Yu Shan, *Taiwan* 69 **F13** 23 30N 120 58 E
Yu Xian, *Hebei, China* 66 **E8** 39 50N 114 35 E
Yu Xian, *Henan, China* 66 **G7** 34 10N 113 28 E
Yu Xian, *Shanxi, China* 66 **E7** 38 5N 113 20 E
Yuan Jiang →, *Hunan, China* 69 **C8** 28 55N 111 50 E
Yuan Jiang →, *Yunnan, China* 68 **F4** 22 20N 103 59 E
Yuan'an, *China* 69 **B8** 31 3N 111 34 E
Yuanjiang, *Hunan, China* 69 **C9** 28 47N 112 21 E
Yuanjiang, *Yunnan, China* 68 **F4** 23 32N 102 0 E
Yuanli, *Taiwan* 69 **E13** 24 29N 120 39 E
Yuanlin, *Taiwan* 69 **F13** 23 58N 120 30 E
Yuanling, *China* 69 **C8** 28 29N 110 22 E
Yuanmou, *China* 68 **E3** 25 42N 101 53 E
Yuanqu, *China* 66 **G6** 35 18N 111 40 E
Yuanyang, *Henan, China* 66 **G7** 35 3N 113 58 E
Yuanyang, *Yunnan, China* 68 **F4** 23 10N 102 43 E
Yuat →, *Papua N. G.* 120 **C2** 4 10 S 143 52 E
Yuba →, *U.S.A.* 144 **F5** 39 8N 121 36W
Yuba City, *U.S.A.* 144 **F5** 39 8N 121 37W
Yūbari, *Japan* 60 **C10** 43 4N 141 59 E
Yūbetsu, *Japan* 60 **B11** 44 13N 143 50 E
Yucatán □, *Mexico* 147 **C7** 21 30N 86 30W
Yucatán, Canal de, *Caribbean* 148 **B2** 22 0N 86 30W
Yucatan Str. = Yucatán, Canal de, *Caribbean* 148 **B2** 22 0N 86 30W
Yucca, *U.S.A.* 145 **L12** 34 52N 114 9W
Yucca Valley, *U.S.A.* 145 **L10** 34 8N 116 27W
Yucheng, *China* 66 **F9** 36 55N 116 32 E
Yuci, *China* 66 **F7** 37 42N 112 46 E
Yudino, *Russia* 51 **D16** 55 51N 48 55 E
Yudino, *Russia* 56 **D7** 55 10N 67 55 E
Yudu, *China* 69 **E10** 25 59N 115 30 E
Yuendumu, *Australia* 112 **D5** 22 16 S 131 49 E
Yueqing, *China* 69 **C13** 28 9N 120 59 E
Yueqing Wan, *China* 69 **C13** 28 5N 121 20 E
Yuexi, *Anhui, China* 69 **B11** 30 50N 116 20 E
Yuexi, *Sichuan, China* 68 **C4** 28 37N 102 26 E
Yueyang, *China* 69 **C9** 29 21N 113 5 E
Yufu-Dake, *Japan* 62 **D3** 33 17N 131 33 E
Yugan, *China* 69 **C11** 28 43N 116 37 E
Yugoslavia ■, *Europe* 42 **D5** 44 0N 20 0 E
Yuhuan, *China* 69 **C13** 28 9N 121 12 E
Yujiang, *China* 69 **C11** 28 10N 116 43 E
Yukhnov, *Russia* 50 **D9** 54 44N 35 15 E
Yūki, *Japan* 63 **A11** 36 18N 139 53 E
Yukon →, *U.S.A.* 126 **B3** 62 32N 163 54W
Yukon Territory □, *Canada* 126 **B6** 63 0N 135 0W
Yüksekova, *Turkey* 89 **E11** 37 34N 44 16 E
Yukti, *Russia* 57 **C11** 63 26N 105 42 E
Yukuhashi, *Japan* 62 **D2** 33 44N 130 59 E
Yule →, *Australia* 112 **D2** 20 41 S 118 17 E
Yuli, *Nigeria* 101 **D7** 9 44N 10 12 E
Yulin, *Guangxi Zhuangzu, China* 69 **F8** 22 40N 110 8 E
Yulin, *Shaanxi, China* 66 **E5** 38 20N 109 30 E
Yuma, *Ariz., U.S.A.* 145 **N12** 32 43N 114 37W
Yuma, *Colo., U.S.A.* 138 **E3** 40 8N 102 43W
Yuma, B. de, *Dom. Rep.* 149 **C6** 18 20N 68 35W
Yumali, *Australia* 116 **C3** 35 32 S 139 45 E
Yumbe, *Uganda* 106 **B3** 3 28N 31 15 E
Yumbi, *Zaïre* 106 **C2** 1 12 S 26 15 E
Yumbo, *Colombia* 152 **C2** 3 35N 76 28W
Yumen, *China* 64 **C4** 39 50N 97 30 E
Yumurtalık, *Turkey* 88 **E6** 36 45N 35 43 E
Yun Ho →, *China* 67 **E9** 39 10N 117 10 E
Yun Xian, *Hubei, China* 69 **A8** 32 50N 110 46 E
Yun Xian, *Yunnan, China* 68 **E3** 24 27N 100 8 E
Yunak, *Turkey* 88 **D4** 38 49N 31 43 E
Yunan, *China* 69 **F8** 23 12N 111 30 E
Yuncheng, *Henan, China* 66 **G8** 35 36N 115 57 E
Yuncheng, *Shanxi, China* 66 **G6** 35 2N 111 0 E
Yundamindra, *Australia* 113 **E3** 29 15 S 122 6 E
Yunfu, *China* 69 **F9** 22 50N 112 5 E
Yungas, *Bolivia* 157 **D4** 17 0 S 66 0W
Yungay, *Chile* 158 **D1** 37 10 S 72 5W
Yungay, *Peru* 156 **B2** 9 2 S 77 45W
Yunhe, *China* 69 **C12** 28 8N 119 33 E
Yunlin, *Taiwan* 69 **F13** 23 42N 120 30 E
Yunling, *China* 68 **D2** 27 0N 99 20 E
Yunlong, *China* 68 **E2** 25 57N 99 13 E
Yunmeng, *China* 69 **B9** 31 2N 113 43 E
Yunnan □, *China* 68 **E4** 25 0N 102 0 E
Yunomae, *Japan* 62 **E2** 32 12N 131 0 E
Yunotso, *Japan* 62 **B4** 35 5N 132 21 E
Yunquera de Henares, *Spain* 34 **E1** 40 47N 3 11W
Yunta, *Australia* 116 **B3** 32 34 S 139 36 E
Yunxi, *China* 66 **H6** 33 0N 110 22 E
Yunxiao, *China* 69 **F11** 23 59N 117 18 E
Yunyang, *China* 68 **B7** 30 58N 108 54 E
Yuping, *China* 68 **D7** 27 13N 108 56 E
Yupukarri, *Guyana* 153 **C6** 3 45N 59 20W
Yupyongdong, *N. Korea* 67 **D15** 41 49N 128 53 E
Yuqing, *China* 68 **D6** 27 13N 107 53 E
Yur, *Russia* 57 **D14** 59 52N 137 41 E
Yurgao, *Russia* 56 **D9** 55 42N 84 51 E
Yuria, *Russia* 54 **B4** 59 22N 54 10 E
Yuribei, *Russia* 56 **B8** 71 8N 76 58 E
Yurimaguas, *Peru* 156 **B2** 5 55 S 76 7W
Yurya, *Russia* 51 **B16** 59 1N 49 13 E
Yuryev-Polskiy, *Russia* 51 **C11** 56 30N 39 40 E
Yuryevets, *Russia* 51 **C13** 57 25N 43 2 E
Yuryuzan, *Russia* 54 **D6** 54 57N 58 28 E
Yuscarán, *Honduras* 148 **D2** 13 58N 86 45W
Yushanzhen, *China* 68 **C7** 29 28N 108 22 E
Yushe, *China* 66 **F7** 37 4N 112 58 E
Yushu, *Jilin, China* 67 **B14** 44 43N 126 38 E
Yushu, *Qinghai, China* 64 **C4** 33 5N 96 55 E
Yutai, *China* 66 **G9** 35 0N 116 45 E
Yutian, *China* 67 **E9** 39 53N 117 45 E
Yuxi, *China* 68 **E4** 24 30N 102 35 E
Yuyao, *China* 69 **B13** 30 3N 121 10 E
Yuzawa, *Japan* 60 **E10** 39 10N 140 30 E
Yuzha, *Russia* 51 **C13** 56 34N 42 1 E
Yuzhno-Sakhalinsk, *Russia* 57 **E15** 46 58N 142 45 E
Yuzhno-Surkhanskoye Vdkhr., *Uzbekistan* 55 **E3** 37 53N 67 42 E
Yuzhno-Uralsk, *Russia* 54 **D7** 54 26N 61 15 E
Yuzhnyy Ural, *Russia* 54 **E6** 53 0N 58 0 E
Yvelines □, *France* 23 **D8** 48 40N 1 45 E
Yverdon, *Switz.* 28 **C3** 46 47N 6 39 E
Yvetot, *France* 22 **C7** 49 37N 0 44 E
Yvonand, *Switz.* 28 **C3** 46 48N 6 44 E


## Z


Zaalayskiy Khrebet, *Asia* 55 **D6** 39 20N 73 0 E
Zaamslag, *Neths.* 21 **F3** 51 19N 3 55 E
Zaan →, *Neths.* 20 **D5** 52 25N 4 52 E
Zaandam, *Neths.* 20 **D5** 52 26N 4 49 E
Zab, Monts du, *Algeria* 99 **B6** 34 55N 5 0 E
Žabalj, *Serbia* 42 **B5** 45 21N 20 5 E
Žabari, *Serbia* 42 **C6** 44 22N 21 15 E
Zabarjad, *Egypt* 94 **C4** 23 40N 36 12 E
Zabaykalskiy, *Russia* 57 **E12** 49 40N 117 25 E
Zabid, *Yemen* 86 **D3** 14 0N 43 10 E
Zabīd, W. →, *Yemen* 86 **D3** 14 7N 43 6 E
Ząbkowice Śląskie, *Poland* 47 **E3** 50 35N 16 50 E
Žabljak, *Montenegro* 42 **D4** 43 18N 19 7 E
Zabłudów, *Poland* 47 **B10** 53 0N 23 19 E
Żabno, *Poland* 31 **A13** 50 9N 20 53 E
Zābol, *Iran* 85 **D9** 31 0N 61 32 E
Zābol □, *Afghan.* 79 **B2** 32 0N 67 0 E
Zābolī, *Iran* 85 **E9** 27 10N 61 35 E
Zabré, *Burkina Faso* 101 **C4** 11 12N 0 36W
Zabrze, *Poland* 47 **E5** 50 18N 18 50 E
Zacapa, *Guatemala* 148 **D2** 14 59N 89 31W
Zacapu, *Mexico* 146 **D4** 19 50N 101 43W
Zacatecas, *Mexico* 146 **C4** 22 49N 102 34W
Zacatecas □, *Mexico* 146 **C4** 23 30N 103 0W
Zacatecoluca, *El Salv.* 148 **D2** 13 29N 88 51W
Zacoalco, *Mexico* 146 **C4** 20 14N 103 33W
Zacualtipán, *Mexico* 147 **C5** 20 39N 98 36W
Zadar, *Croatia* 39 **D12** 44 8N 15 14 E
Zadawa, *Nigeria* 101 **C7** 11 33N 10 19 E
Zadetkyi Kyun, *Burma* 77 **H2** 10 0N 98 25 E
Zadonsk, *Russia* 51 **E11** 52 25N 38 56 E
Zafarqand, *Iran* 85 **C7** 33 11N 52 29 E
Zafora, *Greece* 45 **H8** 36 5N 26 24 E
Zafra, *Spain* 37 **G4** 38 26N 6 30W
Żagań, *Poland* 47 **D2** 51 39N 15 22 E
Zagazig, *Egypt* 94 **H7** 30 40N 31 30 E
Zāgheh, *Iran* 85 **C6** 33 30N 48 42 E
Zaghouan, *Tunisia* 96 **A2** 36 23N 10 10 E
Zaglivérion, *Greece* 44 **D5** 40 36N 23 15 E
Zaglou, *Algeria* 99 **C4** 27 17N 0 3W
Zagnanado, *Benin* 101 **D5** 7 18N 2 28 E
Zagorá, *Greece* 44 **E5** 39 27N 23 6 E
Zagora, *Morocco* 98 **B3** 30 22N 5 51W
Zagórów, *Poland* 47 **C4** 52 10N 17 54 E
Zagorsk = Sergiyev Posad, *Russia* 51 **C11** 56 20N 38 10 E
Zagórz, *Poland* 31 **B15** 49 30N 22 14 E
Zagreb, *Croatia* 39 **C12** 45 50N 16 0 E
Zāgros, Kuhhā-ye, *Iran* 85 **C6** 33 45N 48 5 E
Zagros Mts. = Zāgros, Kuhhā-ye, *Iran* 85 **C6** 33 45N 48 5 E
Žagubica, *Serbia* 42 **C6** 44 15N 21 47 E
Zaguinaso, *Ivory C.* 100 **C3** 10 1N 6 14W
Zagyva →, *Hungary* 31 **D13** 47 5N 20 4 E
Zāhedān, *Fārs, Iran* 85 **D7** 28 46N 53 52 E
Zāhedān, *Sīstān va Balūchestān, Iran* 85 **D9** 29 30N 60 50 E
Zahirabad, *India* 82 **F3** 17 43N 77 37 E
Zahlah, *Lebanon* 91 **B4** 33 52N 35 50 E
Zahna, *Germany* 26 **D8** 51 54N 12 47 E
Zahrez Chergui, *Algeria* 99 **A5** 35 0N 3 30 E
Zahrez Rharbi, *Algeria* 99 **B5** 34 50N 2 55 E
Zailiyskiy Alatau, Khrebet, *Kazakhstan* 55 **B8** 43 5N 77 0 E
Zainsk, *Russia* 54 **D3** 55 18N 52 4 E
Zaïre □, *Angola* 103 **D2** 7 0 S 14 0 E
Zaïre ■, *Africa* 103 **C4** 3 0 S 23 0 E
Zaïre →, *Africa* 103 **D2** 6 4 S 12 24 E
Zaječar, *Serbia* 42 **D7** 43 53N 22 18 E
Zakamensk, *Russia* 57 **D11** 50 23N 103 17 E
Zakani, *Zaïre* 102 **B4** 2 33N 23 16 E
Zakataly, *Azerbaijan* 53 **F12** 41 38N 46 35 E
Zakavkazye, *Asia* 53 **F11** 42 0N 44 0 E
Zākhū, *Iraq* 84 **B4** 37 10N 42 50 E
Zákinthos, *Greece* 45 **G2** 37 47N 20 57 E
Zaklików, *Poland* 47 **E9** 50 46N 22 7 E
Zakopane, *Poland* 31 **B12** 49 18N 19 57 E
Zakroczym, *Poland* 47 **C7** 52 26N 20 38 E
Zákros, *Greece* 32 **D8** 35 6N 26 10 E
Zala, *Angola* 103 **D2** 7 52 S 13 42 E
Zala □, *Hungary* 31 **E9** 46 42N 16 50 E
Zala →, *Hungary* 31 **E10** 46 43N 17 16 E
Zalaegerszeg, *Hungary* 31 **E9** 46 53N 16 47 E
Zalakomár, *Hungary* 31 **E10** 46 33N 17 10 E
Zalalövö, *Hungary* 31 **E9** 46 51N 16 35 E
Zalamea de la Serena, *Spain* 37 **G5** 38 40N 5 38W
Zalamea la Real, *Spain* 37 **H4** 37 41N 6 38W
Zalău, *Romania* 46 **B4** 47 12N 23 3 E
Zalazna, *Russia* 54 **B3** 58 39N 52 31 E
Žalec, *Slovenia* 39 **B12** 46 16N 15 10 E
Zaleshchiki, *Ukraine* 52 **B1** 48 45N 25 45 E
Zalew Wislany, *Poland* 47 **A6** 54 20N 19 50 E
Zalewo, *Poland* 47 **B6** 53 50N 19 41 E
Zalīm, *Si. Arabia* 86 **B3** 22 43N 42 10 E
Zalingei, *Sudan* 97 **F4** 12 51N 23 29 E
Zaliv Vislinskil = Zalew Wislany, *Poland* 47 **A6** 54 20N 19 50 E
Zalţan, Jabal, *Libya* 96 **C3** 28 46N 19 45 E
Zaltbommel, *Neths.* 20 **E6** 51 48N 5 15 E
Zambales □, *Phil.* 70 **D3** 15 20N 120 10 E
Zambales Mts., *Phil.* 70 **D3** 15 45N 120 5 E
Zambeke, *Zaïre* 106 **B2** 2 8N 25 17 E
Zambeze →, *Africa* 107 **F4** 18 35 S 36 20 E
Zambezi = Zambeze →, *Africa* 107 **F4** 18 35 S 36 20 E
Zambezi, *Zambia* 103 **E4** 13 30 S 23 15 E
Zambezia □, *Mozam.* 107 **F4** 16 15 S 37 30 E
Zambia ■, *Africa* 107 **E2** 15 0 S 28 0 E
Zamboanga, *Phil.* 71 **H4** 6 59N 122 3 E
Zamboanga del Norte □, *Phil.* 71 **G4** 8 0N 123 0 E
Zamboanga del Sur □, *Phil.* 71 **H4** 7 40N 123 0 E
Zamboanguita, *Phil.* 71 **G4** 9 6N 123 12 E
Zambrano, *Colombia* 152 **B3** 9 45N 74 49W
Zambrów, *Poland* 47 **C9** 52 59N 22 14 E
Zametchino, *Russia* 51 **E13** 53 30N 42 30 E
Zamora, *Ecuador* 152 **D2** 4 4 S 78 58W
Zamora, *Mexico* 146 **C4** 20 0N 102 21W
Zamora, *Spain* 36 **D5** 41 30N 5 45W
Zamora □, *Spain* 36 **D5** 41 30N 5 46W
Zamora-Chinchipe □, *Ecuador* 152 **D2** 4 15 S 78 50W
Zamość, *Poland* 47 **E10** 50 43N 23 15 E
Zamość □, *Poland* 47 **E10** 50 40N 23 10 E
Zamuro, Sierra del, *Venezuela* 153 **C5** 4 0N 62 30W
Zamzam, W. →, *Libya* 96 **B2** 31 0N 14 30 E
Zan, *Ghana* 101 **D4** 9 26N 0 17W
Zanaga, *Congo* 102 **C2** 2 48 S 13 48 E
Záncara →, *Spain* 35 **F1** 39 18N 3 18W
Zandijk, *Neths.* 20 **D5** 52 28N 4 49 E
Zandvoort, *Neths.* 20 **D5** 52 22N 4 32 E
Zanesville, *U.S.A.* 136 **G2** 39 56N 82 1W
Zangābād, *Iran* 84 **B5** 38 26N 46 44 E
Zangue →, *Mozam.* 107 **F4** 17 50 S 35 21 E
Zanjan, *Iran* 85 **B6** 36 40N 48 35 E
Zanjān □, *Iran* 85 **B6** 37 20N 49 30 E
Zannone, *Italy* 40 **B6** 40 58N 13 2 E
Zante = Zákinthos, *Greece* 45 **G2** 37 47N 20 57 E
Zanthus, *Australia* 113 **F3** 31 2 S 123 34 E
Zanzibar, *Tanzania* 106 **D4** 6 12 S 39 12 E
Zanzūr, *Libya* 96 **B2** 32 55N 13 1 E
Zaouiet El-Kala = Bordj Omar Driss, *Algeria* 99 **C6** 28 10N 6 40 E
Zaouiet Reggane, *Algeria* 99 **C5** 26 32N 0 3 E
Zaoyang, *China* 69 **A9** 32 10N 112 45 E
Zaozhuang, *China* 67 **G9** 34 50N 117 35 E
Zapadna Morava →, *Serbia* 42 **D6** 43 38N 21 30 E
Zapadnaya Dvina, *Russia* 50 **C8** 56 15N 32 3 E
Zapadnaya Dvina →, *Belorussia* 50 **C4** 55 35N 28 10 E
Západné Beskydy, *Europe* 31 **B12** 49 30N 19 0 E
Zapadni Rodopi, *Bulgaria* 43 **F8** 41 50N 24 0 E

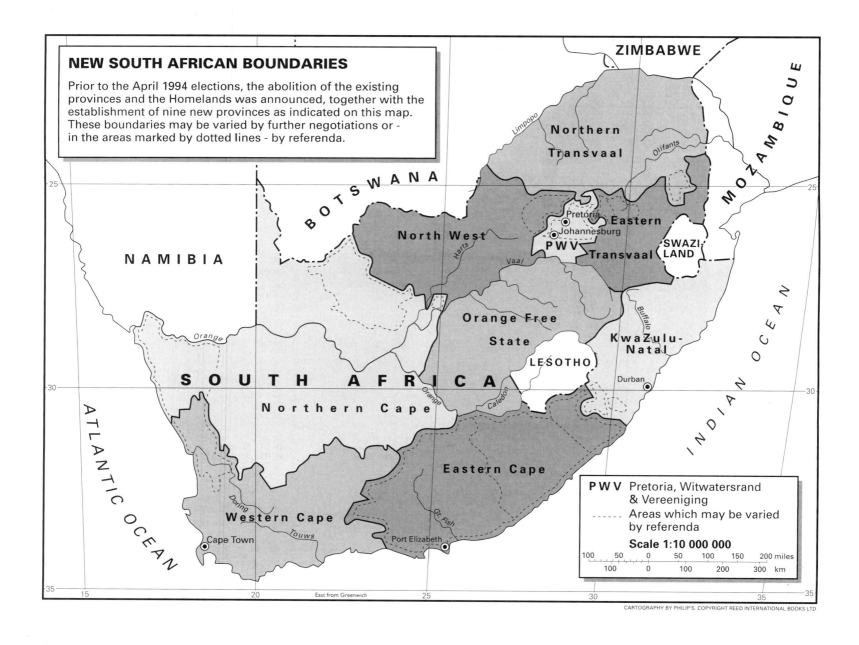

### NEW SOUTH AFRICAN BOUNDARIES

Prior to the April 1994 elections, the abolition of the existing provinces and the Homelands was announced, together with the establishment of nine new provinces as indicated on this map. These boundaries may be varied by further negotiations or - in the areas marked by dotted lines - by referenda.

ZIMBABWE

MOZAMBIQUE

BOTSWANA

NAMIBIA

Northern
Transvaal

North West

Pretoria
Johannesburg
PWV
Eastern
Transvaal

SWAZI-
LAND

Orange Free
State

KwaZulu-
Natal

LESOTHO

Durban

SOUTH AFRICA

Northern Cape

Eastern Cape

Western Cape

ATLANTIC OCEAN

INDIAN OCEAN

Cape Town

Port Elizabeth

Limpopo
Olifants
Harts
Vaal
Buffalo
Orange
Caledon
Gt. Fish
Doring
Touws

**PWV** Pretoria, Witwatersrand
& Vereeniging
------- Areas which may be varied
by referenda
**Scale 1:10 000 000**

| 100 | 50 | 0 | 50 | 100 | 150 | 200 miles |

| 100 | 0 | 100 | 200 | 300 | km |

East from Greenwich

# KEY TO WORLD MAP PAGES

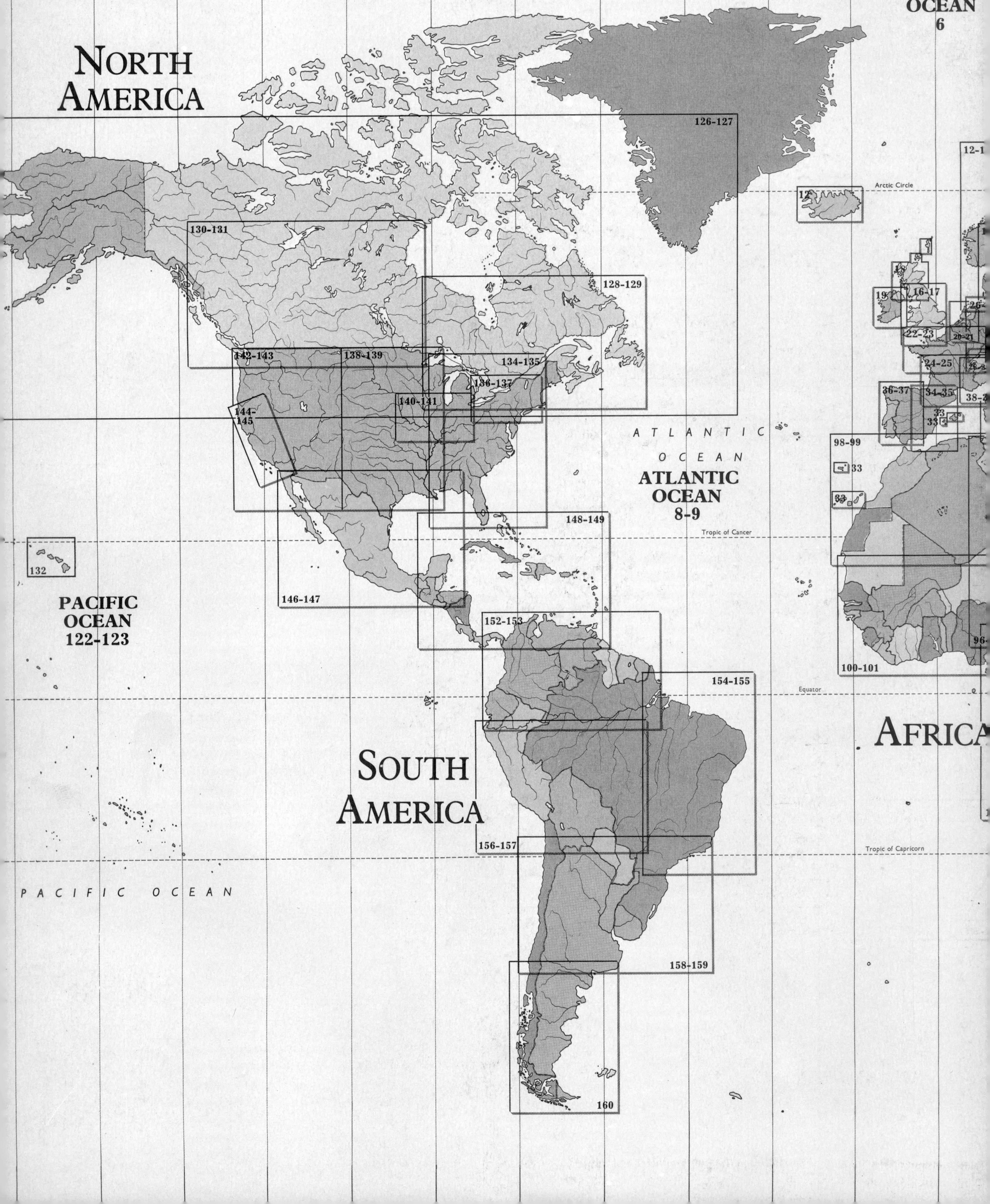

**ARCTIC OCEAN** 6

**NORTH AMERICA**

126-127

12-1

130-131

128-129

142-143   138-139   134-135

136-137

140-141

144-145

A T L A N T I C

O C E A N

**ATLANTIC OCEAN** 8-9

16-17

19

22-23   20-21

24-25

36-37   34-35   38-3

33   33

98-99

33

132

148-149

Tropic of Cancer

**PACIFIC OCEAN** 122-123

146-147

152-153

100-101   96

154-155

Equator

**SOUTH AMERICA**

**AFRICA**

156-157

Tropic of Capricorn

P A C I F I C   O C E A N

158-159

160